THE OFFICIAL®
OVERSTREET
Comic Book
PRICE GUIDE
1989-1990

19th Edition

BOOKS FROM 1900—PRESENT INCLUDED

CATALOGUE & EVALUATION GUIDE—ILLUSTRATED

By
Robert M. Overstreet

SPECIAL CONTRIBUTORS TO THIS EDITION

Tom Andrae, Bruce Hamilton, Tom Inge,
Bob Kane and Jerry Robinson

SPECIAL ADVISORS TO THIS EDITION

*Bruce Hamilton   *Hugh O'Kennon   *Ron Pussell   *Gary M. Carter
*Walter Wang   *John Snyder   *Terry Stroud   *Jon Warren
*Dan Malan   *Steve Geppi   *Gary Colabuono   *Jay Maybruck
*Joe Vereneault   *James Payette   *Harry Matetsky
*Stephen Fishler

THE HOUSE OF COLLECTIBLES
NEW YORK, NEW YORK 10022

Published by the House of Collectibles and distributed to the book trade by Ballantine Books, a division of Random House, Inc., New York and simultaneously in Canada by Random House of Canada Limited, Toronto.

Published and distributed to the collectors' market by Overstreet Publications, Inc., 780 Hunt Cliff Dr. N.W., Cleveland, TN 37311.

Manufactured in the United States of America

Cover Illustration by Jerry Robinson, rendered in the classic style of the Golden Age of comic books.

ISBN 0-876-37791-6
ISSN 0891-8872
10 9 8 7 6 5 4 3 2 1

19th Edition

TABLE OF CONTENTS

Preface A-8

Terminology A-9

Timely/Marvel/Atlas Publishers' Abbreviation Codes A-11

Advertising Information A-13

Grading Comic Books A-14

Storage of Comic Books A-16

1988 Market Report A-17

Investor's Data A-24

The Top 50 Titles A-25

The 50 Most Valuable Books A-26

The 30 Most Valuable Silver Age Titles A-28

The 30 Most Valuable Silver Age Books A-28

Hot Titles and Rate of Increase A-29

The First Wave of Comic Books 1933-1943 (Key Books Listed and Ranked) . A-29

Comics With Little If Any Value A-49

Collecting Foreign Comics and American Reprints A-49

Canadian Reprints, by J. B. Clifford and Ronald J. Ard A-49

How to Start Collecting A-50

Collecting Back Issues A-51

Proper Handling of Comic Books A-51

How to Sell Your Comics A-51

Where to Buy and Sell A-52

Comic Book Mail Order Services A-52

Comic Book Conventions A-53

Comic Book Conventions for 1989 . . . . A-53

Comic Book Clubs A-54

The History of Comics Fandom A-55

How to Select Fanzines A-55

Fan Publications of Interest A-56

Collecting Strips A-57

Collecting Original Art A-57

"A Chronology of the Development of the American Comic Book,"
   by M. Thomas Inge A-66

"Origins of The Dark Knight: A conversation with Batman artists
   Bob Kane and Jerry Robinson, " by Thomas Andrae A-71

Directory of Comic and Nostalgia Shops A-94

Directory of Advertisers in this edition A-107

"Explaining the Classics Series," by Dan Malan . . . . See Classic Comics

First Ad Section begins A-109

Second Ad Section begins 442

ACKNOWLEDGEMENTS

Larry Bigman (Frazetta-Williamson data); Glenn Bray (Kurtzman data); Dan Malan & Charles Heffelfinger (Classic Comics data); Gary Carter (DC data); J. B. Clifford Jr. (E. C. data); Gary Coddington (Superman data); Wilt Conine (Fawcett data); Dr. S. M. Davidson (Cupples & Leon data); Al Dellinges (Kubert data); Kevin Hancer (Tarzan data); Charles Heffelfinger and Jim Ivey (March of Comics listing); R. C. Holland and Ron Pussell (Seduction and Parade of Pleasure data); Grant Irwin (Quality data); Richard Kravitz (Kelly data); Phil Levine (giveaway data); Fred Nardelli (Frazetta data); Michelle Nolan (love comics); Mike Nolan (MLJ, Timely, Nedor data); George Olshevsky (Timely data); Don Rosa (Late 1940s to 1950s data); Richard Olson (LOA data); Scott Pell ('50s data); Greg Robertson (National data); Frank Scigliano (Little Lulu data); Gene Seger (Buck Rogers data); Rick Sloane (Archie data); David R. Smith, Archivist, Walt Disney Productions (Disney data); Don and Maggie Thompson (Four Color listing); Mike Tiefenbacher, Jerry Sinkovec, and Richard Yudkin (Atlas and National data); Raymond True (Classic Comics data); Jim Vadeboncoeur Jr. (Williamson and Atlas data); Kim Weston (Disney and Barks data); Cat Yronwode (Spirit data); Andrew Zerbe and Gary Behymer (M. E. data).

My appreciation must also be extended to Don Maris, John Snyder, Steve Geppi, Bruce Hamilton, Dan Malan and Jon Warren, who loaned material for photographing, and especially to Hugh and Louise O'Kennon for their support and help. Special acknowledgement is also given to Ron Pussell, Ken Mitchell, Michelle Nolan, Garth Wood, Terry Stroud, and especially to Quinton Clem for submitting an unusual amount of corrective data; to Dr. Richard Olson for rewriting grading definitions; to Larry Breed for his suggestions on re-organizing the introductory section; to Dan Malan for revamping the Classics section; to Terry Stroud, Hugh O'Kennon, Jon Warren, Dave Smith, Rod Dyke, Jay Maybruck, Joe Vereneault, James Payette, John Snyder, Gary Carter, Rick Sloane, Stephen Fishler, Jerry Weist, Walter Wang, Steve Geppi, Joe Mannarino, Gary Colabuono, Dave Anderson (Okla.) and Ron Pussell, (pricing); to Walter Wang for his editorial help on the market report; to Tom Inge for his "Chronology of the American Comic Book;" to Tom Andrae for his interview with Bob Kane and Jerry Robinson; to Jerry Robinson for his outstanding cover art; to Angelina Genduso and Joe Orlando for their help with this edition. to Landon Chesney and Dave Noah for their work on the key comic book list; to L. B. Cole, Steve Saffel, and Jerry DeFuccio for their counsel and help; to Bill Spicer and Zetta DeVoe (Western Publishing Co.) for their contribution of data; and especially to Bill for his kind permission to reprint portions of his and Jerry Bails' **America's Four Color Pastime**; and to Walter Presswood, Dave Noah, and Jeff Overstreet for their help in editing this volume.

I will always be indebted to Jerry Bails, Landon Chesney, Bruce Hamilton and Larry Bigman whose advice and concern have helped in making **The Comic Book Price Guide** a reality; to my wife Martha for her encouragement and help in putting this reference work together; and to everyone who placed ads in this edition.

Acknowledgement is also due to the following people who have so generously contributed much needed data for this edition:

David Anderson	Gerald S. Bluehdorn	Robert N. Cherry, Jr.
David Arsenault	Kent Boklan	Michael Clark
Stephen Baer	Jack W. Borges	L.B. Cole
Tim Barnes	David T. Breth	David H. Curtis
Steven Barrington	Phil Carpenter	Alexander M. Cutrone, Jr.
Robert Beerbohm	Bruce Cervon	Edward F. Fausel
John Binder, M.D.	Ted Chan	Stephen Fishler

Mike Freshwater
Danny Fuchs
Brett Sterling-Greene
Joseph Grissell
Jeff Hammons
Keith Handley
Ted Hanes
Steve Haynie
Anton Hermus
Lee M. Hester
Jef Hinds
Jno. B. Hosier
Randy James
Steven R. Johnson
Ray Leach
Phil Levine
Terry W. Malone
Joe Mannarino
Greg Z. Manos
Don Maris
Lt. Matthew Mason, USN
James P. McLoughlin
Jeff Melius

David McMenamin
David Miller
Harry W. Miller
Wayne R. Milewski
Ken Mitchell
Roger Morrison
Mathew Mutch
Robert E. Myers
Frank T. Nama
David Newton
Donald G. Norris
Emil Novack
Scott Pell
C.M. Peterson
Dennis Petilli
Brian Powell
Donald L. Puff
Wayne Richardson
Michael Sanchez
Joe Sarno
Mark Schnee
William Schoch
Herb Scott

Randall W. Scott
Michael Secula
James Shum
David R. Smith
Tony Starks
Bill Stevens
Ray Storch
Brad Tenan
Greg Theakston
Harry Thomas
Steve Thompson
Mike Tickal
William Tighe
John K. Vavra
Frank Verzyl
John Verzyl
Lawrence Watt-Evans
Bill Werle
Rollin M. Wilson
Garth Wood
Catherine Yronwode
Monty Zutz

PREFACE

Comic book values listed in this reference work were recorded from convention sales, dealers' lists, adzines, and by special contact with dealers and collectors from coast to coast. Prices paid for rare comics vary considerably from one locale to another. We have attempted to list a realistic average between the lowest and highest range observed. The reader should keep in mind that the prices listed only reflect the market just prior to publication. Any new trends that have developed since the preparation of this book would not be shown.

The values listed are reports, not estimates. Each new edition of the guide is actually an average report of sales that occurred during the year; not an estimate of what we feel the books will be bringing next year. Even though many prices listed will remain current throughout the year, the wise user of this book would keep abreast of current market trends to get the fullest potential out of his invested dollar.

By the same token, many of the scarcer books are seldom offered for sale in top condition. This makes it difficult to arrive at a realistic market value. Some of the issues in this category are: Action No. 1, All-American No. 16, Batman No. 1, Black and White No. 20, Captain America No. 1, Captain Marvel No. 1, Detective No. 27, Double Action No. 2, the No-Number Feature Books, Green Giant No. 1, March of Comics No. 4, Marvel No. 1, More Fun No. 52, Motion Picture Funnies Weekly No. 1, Famous Funnies No. 1, Superman No. 1, Tough Kid Squad No. 1, Whiz No. 2 (No. 1), Wonder No. 1, Amazing Man No. 5, and Wow No. 1.

Some rare comics were published in a complete black and white format; i.e., All-New No. 15, Blood Is the Harvest, Boy Explorers No. 2, Eerie No. 1, Flash Gordon No. 5, If the Devil Would Talk, Is This Tomorrow, and Stuntman No. 3. As we have learned in the case of Eerie No. 1, the collector or investor in these books would be well advised to give due consideration to the possibility of counterfeits before investing large sums of money.

This book is the most comprehensive listing of newsstand comic books ever attempted. Comic book titles, dates of first and last issues, publishing companies, origin and special issues are listed when known.

The Guide will be listing only American comic books due to space limitation. Some variations of the regular comic book format will be listed. These basically include those pre-1933 comic strip reprint books with varying size—usually with cardboard covers, but sometimes with hardback. As forerunners of the modern comic book format, they deserve to be listed despite their obvious differences in presentation. Other books that will be listed are key black and white comics of the 1980s, giveaway comics—but only those that contain known characters, work by known collectible artists, or those of special interest.

All titles are listed as if they were one word, ignoring spaces, hyphens and apostrophes. Page counts listed will always include covers.

IMPORTANT. Prices listed in this book are in U. S. currency and are for your reference only. This book is not a dealer's price list, although some dealers may base their prices on the values listed. The true value of any comic book is what you are willing to pay. Prices listed herein are an indication of what collectors (not dealers) would probably pay. For one reason or another, these collectors might want certain books badly, or else need specific issues to complete their runs and so are willing to pay more. Dealers are not in a position to pay the full prices listed, but work on a percentage depending largely on the amount of investment required and the quality of material offered. Usually they will pay from 20 to 70 percent of the list price depending on how long it will take them to sell the collection after making the investment; the higher the demand and better the condition, the more the percentage. Most dealers are faced with expenses such as advertising, travel, telephone and mailing, rent, employee salaries, plus convention costs. These costs all go in before the books are sold. The high demand books usually sell right away but there are many other titles that are difficult to sell due to low demand. Sometimes a dealer will have cost tied up in this type of material for several years before finally moving it. Remember, his position is that of handling, demand and overhead. Most dealers are victims of these economics.

Black and White comics of the 1980s: In recent years an explosion of new comic book titles has occurred in the direct market. Since many of these books are produced in an inexpensive black & white format, anyone today can become a publisher of comic books; the result has been dozens of new publishers and hundreds of new titles entering the market place. The quality of these publications vary from very poor to excellent. THE PRICE GUIDE'S POSITION: In the past, we have attempted to list all newsstand comic books that qualified for listing. Today, with the advent of the new formatted black and whites, consideration must be given for their inclusion, but obviously all cannot or should not be listed. Just because someone puts out a black and white comic out of their basement does not mean that we should acknowledge its existence in this book. However, there are many collectible and important titles that should and have been listed in this edition. The selection of titles to list was made by our panel of advisors who send in pricing information for the bi-monthly supplements. Of course a much better coverage of these books will be made in the Update next year.

TERMINOLOGY

Many of the following terms and abbreviations are used in the comic book market and are explained here:

a—Story art; **a(i)**—Story art inks; **a(p)**—Story art pencils; **a(r)**—Story art reprint.

B&W—Black and white art.

Bondage cover—Usually denotes a female in bondage.

c—Cover art; **c(i)**—Cover inks; **c(p)**—Cover pencils; **c(r)**—Cover reprint.

Cameo—When a character appears briefly in one or two panels.

Edgar Church collection—A large high grade comic book collection discovered by Mile High Comics in Colorado (over 22,000 books).

Colorist—Artist that applies color to the pen and ink art.

Con—A Convention or public gathering of fans.

Cosmic Aeroplane—Refers to a large collection discovered by Cosmic Aeroplane Books.

Debut—The first time that a character appears anywhere.

Drug propaganda story—Where comic makes an editorial stand about drug abuse.

Drug use story—Shows the actual use of drugs: shooting, taking a trip, harmful effects, etc.

Fanzine—An amateur fan publication.

File Copy—A high grade comic originating from the publisher's file.

First app.—Same as debut.

Flashback—When a previous story is being recalled.

G. A.—Golden Age (1930s—1950s).

Headlight—Protruding breasts.

i—Art inks.

Infinity cover—Shows a scene that repeats itself to infinity.

Inker—Artist that does the inking.

Intro—Same as debut.

JLA—Justice League of America.

JLI—Justice League International.

JSA—Justice Society of America.

Lamont Larson—Refers to a large high grade collection of comics. Many of the books have Lamont or Larson written on the cover.

Logo—The title of a strip or comic book as it appears on the cover or title page.

Mile High—Refers to a large NM-Mint collection of comics originating from Denver, Colorado (Edgar Church collection).

nd—No date.

nn—No number.

N. Y. Legis. Comm.—New York Legislative Committee to Study the Publication of Comics (1951).

Origin—When the story of the character's creation is given.

p—Art pencils.

Penciler—Artist that does the pencils.

POP—**Parade of Pleasure**, book about the censorship of comics.

Poughkeepsie—Refers to a large collection of Dell Comics' "file copies" believed to have originated from Poughkeepsie, N. Y.

R or r—Reprint.

Rare—10 to 20 copies estimated to exist.

Reprint comics—Comic books that contain newspaper strip reprints.

S. A.—Silver Age (1956—Present).

Scarce—20 to 100 copies estimated to exist.

Silver proof—A black & white actual size print on thick glossy paper given to the colorist to indicate colors to the engraver.

S&K—Simon and Kirby (artists).

SOTI—**Seduction of the Innocent**, book about the censorship of comics.

Splash panel—A large panel that usually appears at the front of a comic story.

Very rare—1 to 10 copies estimated to exist.

X-over—When one character crosses over into another's strip.

Zine—See Fanzine.

Marvel comic books are cover coded for the direct sales (comic shop), newsstand, and foreign markets. They are all first printings, with the special coding being the only difference. The comics sold to the comic shops have to be coded differently, as they are sold on a no-return basis while newsstand comics are not. The Price Guide has not detected any price difference between these versions.

Direct Sales
(Comic Shops)

Newsstand

Newsstand
Overseas

Marvel Reprints: In recent years Marvel has reprinted some of their comics. There has been confusion in identifying the reprints from the originals. However, in 99 percent of the cases, the reprints will list "reprint," or "2nd printing," etc. in the indicia, along with a later copyright date in some cases. The only known exceptions are a few of the movie books such as *Star Wars*, the *Marvel Treasury Editions*, and tie-in books such as *G. I. Joe*. These books were reprinted and not identified as reprints. The *Star Wars* reprints have a large diamond with no date and a blank UPC symbol on the cover. The other reprints will have some cover variation such as a date missing, different colors, etc.

Gold Key comics were sold with two different labels: Whitman and Gold Key.

There are collectors who prefer the Gold Key labels to Whitman, although the Price Guide does not differentiate in the price. Beginning in 1980, all comics produced by Western carried the Whitman label.

Many of the better artists are pointed out. When more than one artist worked on a story, their names are separated by a (/). The first name did the pencil drawings and the second did the inks. When two or more artists work on a story, only the most prominent will be noted in some cases. There has been some confusion in past editions as to which artists to list and which to leave out. We wish all good artists could be listed, but due to space limitation, only the most popular can. The following list of artists are considered to be either the most collected in the comic field or are historically significant and should be pointed out. Artists designated below with an (*) indicate that only their most noted work will be listed. The rest will eventually have all their work shown as the information becomes available. This list could change from year to year as new artists come into prominence.

Adams, Neal
*Aparo, Jim
*Austin, Terry
Baker, Matt
Barks, Carl
Beck, C. C.
Brunner, Frank
*Buscema, John
Byrne, John
*Check, Sid
Cole, Jack
Cole, L. B.
Craig, Johnny
Crandall, Reed
Davis, Jack
Disbrow, Jayson
*Ditko, Steve
Eisner, Will
*Elder, Bill
Evans, George
Everett, Bill

Feldstein, Al
Fine, Lou
Foster, Harold
Fox, Matt
Frazetta, Frank
Giffen, Keith
Golden, Michael
Gottfredson, Floyd
*Guardineer, Fred
Gustavson, Paul
*Heath, Russ
Howard, Wayne
Ingels, Graham
Jones, Jeff
Kamen, Jack
Kane, Bob
*Kane, Gil
Kelly, Walt
Kinstler, E. R.
Kirby, Jack
Krenkel, Roy

Krigstein, Bernie
*Kubert, Joe
Kurtzman, Harvey
Manning, Russ
*Meskin, Mort
Miller, Frank
Moreira, Ruben
*Morisi, Pete
*Nasser, Mike
*Newton, Don
Nostrand, Howard
Orlando, Joe
Pakula, Mac (Toth inspired)
*Palais, Rudy
*Perez, George
Powell, Bob
Raboy, Mac
Raymond, Alex
Ravielli, Louis
*Redondo, Nestor

Rogers, Marshall
Schomburg, Alex
Siegel & Shuster
Simon & Kirby (S&K)
*Simonson, Walt
Smith, Barry
Smith, Paul
Stanley, John
Starlin, Jim
Steranko, Jim
Torres, Angelo
Toth, Alex
Tuska, George
Ward, Bill
Williamson, Al
Woggon, Bill
Wolverton, Basil
Wood, Wallace
Wrightson, Bernie

The following abbreviations are used with the cover reproductions throughout the book for copyright credit purposes. The companies they represent are listed here:

ACE—Ace Periodicals
ACG—American Comics Group
AJAX—Ajax-Farrell
AP—Archie Publications
ATLAS—Atlas Comics (see below)
AVON—Avon Periodicals
BP—Better Publications
C & L—Cupples & Leon
CC—Charlton Comics
CEN—Centaur Publications
CCG—Columbia Comics Group
CG—Catechetical Guild
CHES—Harry 'A' Chesler
CLDS—Classic Det. Stories
CM—Comics Magazine
DC—DC Comics, Inc.
DELL—Dell Publishing Co.
DMP—David McKay Publishing
DS—D. S. Publishing Co.
EAS—Eastern Color Printing Co.
EC—E. C. Comics
ENWIL—Enwil Associates

EP—Elliott Publications
ERB—Edgar Rice Burroughs
FAW—Fawcett Publications
FF—Famous Funnies
FH—Fiction House Magazines
FOX—Fox Features Syndicate
GIL—Gilberton
GK—Gold Key
GP—Great Publications
HARV—Harvey Publications
HILL—Hillman Periodicals
HOKE—Holyoke Publishing Co.
KING—King Features Syndicate
LEV—Lev Gleason Publications
ME—Magazine Enterprises
MEG—Marvel Ent. Group
MLJ—MLJ Magazines
NOVP—Novelty Press
PG—Premier Group
PINE—Pines
PMI—Parents' Magazine Institute
PRIZE—Prize Publications

QUA—Quality Comics Group
REAL—Realistic Comics
RH—Rural Home
S & S—Street and Smith Publishers
SKY—Skywald Publications
STAR—Star Publications
STD—Standard Comics
STJ—St. John Publishing Co.
SUPR—Superior Comics
TC—Tower Comics
TM—Trojan Magazines
TOBY—Toby Press
UFS—United Features Syndicate
VITL—Vital Publications
WDC—The Walt Disney Company
WEST—Western Publishing Co.
WHIT—Whitman Publishing Co.
WHW—William H. Wise
WMG—William M. Gaines (E. C.)
WP—Warren Publishing Co.
YM—Youthful Magazines
Z-D—Ziff-Davis Publishing Co.

TIMELY/MARVEL/ATLAS COMICS. "A Marvel Magazine" and "Marvel Group" was the symbol used between December 1946 and May 1947 (not used on all titles/issues during period). The Timely Comics symbol was used between July 1942 and September 1942 (not used on all titles/issues during period). The round "Marvel Comic" symbol was used between February 1949 and June 1950. Early comics code symbol (star and bar) was used between April 1952 and February 1955. The Atlas globe symbol was used between December 1951 and September 1957. The M over C symbol (beginning of Marvel Comics) was used between July 1961 until the price increased to 12 cents on February 1962.

TIMELY/MARVEL/ATLAS Publishers' Abbreviation Codes:

ACI—Animirth Comics, Inc.	FCI—Fantasy Comics, Inc.	OMC—Official Magazine Corp.
AMI—Atlas Magazines, Inc.	FPI—Foto Parade, Inc.	OPI—Olympia Publications, Inc.
ANC—Atlas News Co., Inc.	GPI—Gem Publishing, Inc.	PPI—Postal Publications, Inc.
BPC—Bard Publishing Corp.	HPC—Hercules Publishing Corp.	PrPI—Prime Publications, Inc.
BFP—Broadcast Features Pubs.	IPS—Interstate Publishing Corp.	RCM—Red Circle Magazines, Inc.
CBS—Crime Bureau Stories	JPI—Jaygee Publications, Inc.	SAI—Sports Actions, Inc.
CIDS—Classic Detective Stories	LBI—Lion Books, Inc.	SePI—Select Publications, Inc.
CCC—Comic Combine Corp.	LCC—Leading Comic Corp.	SnPC—Snap Publishing Co.
CDS—Current Detective Stories	LMC—Leading Magazine Corp.	SPC—Select Publishing Co.
CFI—Crime Files, Inc.	MALE—Male Publishing Corp.	SPI—Sphere Publications, Inc.
CmPI—Comedy Publications, Inc.	MAP—Miss America Publishing Corp.	TCI—Timely Comics, Inc.
CmPS—Complete Photo Story	MCI—Marvel Comics, Inc.	TP—Timely Publications
CnPC—Cornell Publishing Corp.	MgPC—Margood Publishing Corp.	20 CC—20th Century Comics Corp.
CPC—Chipiden Publishing Corp.	MjMC—Marjean Magazine Corp.	USA—U.S.A. Publications, Inc.
CPI—Crime Publications, Inc.	MMC—Mutual Magazine Corp.	VPI—Vista Publications, Inc.
CPS—Canam Publishing Sales Corp.	MPC—Medalion Publishing Corp.	WFP—Western Fiction Publishing
CSI—Classics Syndicate, Inc.	MPI—Manvis Publications, Inc.	WPI—Warwick Publications, Inc.
DCI—Daring Comics, Inc.	NPI—Newsstand Publications, Inc.	YAI—Young Allies, Inc.
EPC—Euclid Publishing Co.	NPP—Non-Pareil Publishing Corp.	ZPC—Zenith Publishing Co., Inc.
EPI—Emgee Publications, Inc.	OCI—Official Comics, Inc.	

YOUR INFORMATION IS NEEDED: In order to make future Guides more accurate and complete, we are interested in any relevant information or facts that you might have. **Relevant and significant data includes:**

Works by the artists named elsewhere. **Caution:** Most artists did not sign their work and many were imitated by others. When submitting this data, advise whether the work was signed or not. In many cases, it takes an expert to identify certain artists— so extreme caution should be observed in submitting this data.

Issues mentioned by Wertham and others in **Seduction, Parade . . .**
Origin issues.
First and last appearances of strips or characters.
Title continuity information.
Beginning and ending numbers of runs.
Atomic bomb, Christmas, Flag and infinity covers.
Swipes.
Photo covers.

To record something in the Guide, **documented** facts are needed. Please send a photo copy of indicia or page in question if possible.
Non-relevent data—Most giveaway comics will not be listed. Literally thousands of titles came out, many of which have educational themes. We will only list significant collectible giveaways such as March of Comics, Disney items, communist books (but not civil defense educational comics), and books that contain illustrated stories by top artists or top collected characters.

Good Luck and Happy Hunting . . .

Robert M. Overstreet

Advertise in the Guide

This book reaches more serious comic collectors than any other publication and has proven ad results due to its world-wide circulation and use. Your ad will pull all year long until the new edition comes out.

Display Ad space is sold in full, half, fourth, and eighth page sizes. Shop listings are sold for the **State Directory**. Ad rates are set in the early fall prior to each edition's release. Write at that time for rates (Between Oct.—Dec.).

PRINTED SIZES

Full Page—8" long x 5" wide. **Half Page**—4" long x 5" wide.
Fourth Page—4" long x 2½" wide. **Eighth Page**—2" long x 2½" wide.

Classified Ads will be retyped and reduced about one-half. No artwork permitted. Rate is based on your 4" typed line. **Display Classified Ads:** The use of borders, bold face type, cuts or other decorations change your classified ad to display—rates same as regular display.

NOTE: Submit your ad on white paper in a proportionate version of the actual printed size. All Full to Quarter page advertisers will receive a complimentary copy of the Guide. The **New Guide** will be professionally done throughout . . . so to reflect a consistently high quality from cover to cover, we must ask that all ads be neatly and professionally done. **Full Payment** must be sent with all ads. All but classified ads will be run as is.

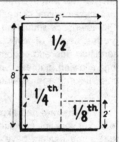

AD DEADLINE - COLOR—Dec. 15th
AD DEADLINE - Black & White—Jan. 15th

Overstreet Publications, Inc.
780 Hunt Cliff Dr. N.W.
Cleveland, Tennessee 37311

The **Price Guide** has become the **Standard Reference Work** in the field and is distributed to tens of thousands of comic collectors throughout the world. Don't miss this opportunity to advertise in the Guide.

NOTICE: All advertisements are accepted and placed in the Price Guide in good faith. However, we cannot be held responsible for any losses incurred in your dealings with the advertisers. If, after receiving legitimate complaints, and there is sufficient evidence to warrant such action, these advertisers will be dropped from future editions.

SPECIAL NOTICE

If copyrighted characters are planned for your ad, the following must be done: Send a copy of your ad layout (including characters) to the company(s) or copyright owner(s) involved requesting permission for their use. A copy of this permission must be sent to us with your ad. DC Comics and Marvel Comics have indicated that you will have no problem getting permission, so if you must use their characters . . . write for the permission. For DC, write: Public Relations, DC Comics, Inc. 666 Fifth Ave., New York, NY, 10103. For Marvel, write: Marvel Comics, 387 Park Ave. South, New York, NY 10016. Other companies such as Disney could be more of a problem. At any rate, we cannot accept any ads with copyrighted characters without a copy of the permission.

GRADING COMIC BOOKS

Before a comic book's true value can be assessed, its condition or state of preservation must be determined. In most comic books, especially in the rarer issues, the better the condition, the more desirable the book. The scarcer first and/or origin issues in PRISTINE MINT condition will bring several times the price of the same book in POOR condition. The grading of a comic book is done by simply looking at the book and describing its condition, which may range from absolutely perfect newsstand condition (PRISTINE MINT) to extremely worn, dirty, and torn (POOR). Numerous variables influence the evaluation of a comic's condition and **all** must be considered in the final evaluation. More important characteristics include tears, missing pieces, wrinkles, stains, yellowing, brittleness, tape repairs, water marks, spine roll, writing, and cover lustre. The significance of each of these will be described more fully in the grading scale definitions. As grading is the most subjective aspect of determining a comic's value, it is very important that the grader must be careful and not allow wishful thinking to influence what the eyes see. It is also very important to realize that older comics in above MINT condition are extremely scarce and are rarely advertised for sale; most of the nicer comics advertised range from VERY FINE to NEAR MINT. To the novice, grading will appear difficult at first, but as experience is gained, accuracy will improve. Whenever in doubt, consult with a reputable dealer or experienced collector in your area. The following grading guide is given to aid the panelologist.

GRADING DEFINITIONS

The hardest part of evaluating a comic is being honest and objective with yourself, and knowing what characteristics to look for in making your decision. The following characteristics should be checked in evaluating books, especially those in higher grades: degree of cover lustre, degree of color fading, staples, staple areas, spine condition, top and bottom of spine, edges of cover, centering, brittleness, browning/yellowing, flatness, tightness, interior damage, tape, tears, folds, water marks, color flaking, and general cleanliness.

WARNING ABOUT RESTORATION:

Many of the rare and expensive key books are being upgraded from lower grades to fine or very fine condition through restoration. It has been brought to our attention that some dealers have been selling these books to unsuspecting collectors/investors—not telling them of the restoration. In some cases these restored books are being priced the same as unrestored books. **Very Important:** Examine books very closely for repairing or restoration before purchase. The more expensive the book, the greater the likelihood of restoration. Major things to look for are: bleaching, whitening, trimming, interior spine and tear reinforcement, gluing, restapling, missing pieces replaced, wrinkles pressed out of covers, recoloring and reglossing covers. Dealers should state that a book has been restored and not expect to get as much as a book unrestored in that condition would bring. **Note:** Cleaning, stain removal, rolled spine removal, staple replacement, etc., if professionally done, would not be considered restoration as long as the printed condition of the comic has not been changed.

VERY IMPORTANT: A book must be graded in its entirety; not by just the cover alone. A book in any of the grades listed must be in its **ORIGINAL UNRESTORED** condition. **Restored books** must be graded as such; i.e., a restored book grading fine might only be worth the same as a Very Good or even a Good copy in its unrestored state. The value of an extensively restored book may improve a half-grade from its original unrestored state. After examining these characteristics a comic may be assigned to one of the following grades:

PRISTINE MINT (PM): Absolutely perfect in every way, regardless of age. The cover has full lustre, is crisp, and shows no imperfections of any sort. The cover and all pages are extra white and fresh; the spine is tight, flat, and clean; not even the slightest blemish can be detected around staples, along spine, at corners or edges. Arrival dates pencilled on the cover are acceptable. As comics must be truly perfect to be graded PM, they are obviously extremely scarce even on the newsstand. Books prior to 1960 in this grade bring 20 to 250 per cent more.

MINT (M): Like new or newsstand condition, as above, but with very slight loss of lustre, or a slight off-centered cover, or a minor printing error. Could have pencilled arrival dates, slight color fading, and white to extra white cover and pages. Any defects noticeable would be very minor and attributable to the cutting, folding and stapling process.

NEAR MINT (NM): Almost perfect; tight spine, flat and clean; just enough minor defects of wear noticeable with close inspection to keep it out of the MINT category; i.e., a small flake of color missing at a staple, corner or edge, or slight discoloration on inside cover or pages; near perfect cover gloss retained.

VERY FINE (VF): Slight wear beginning to show; possibly a small wrinkle or crease at staples or where cover has been opened a few times; still clean and flat with most of cover gloss retained. Slight yellowing acceptable.

FINE (FN): Tight cover with some wear, but still relatively flat, clean and shiny with no subscription crease, writing on cover, yellowed margins or tape repairs. Stress lines around staples and along spine beginning to show; minor color flaking possible at spine, staples, edges or corners. Slight yellowing acceptable.

VERY GOOD (vg): Obviously a read copy with original printing lustre and gloss almost gone; some discoloration, but not soiled; some signs of wear and minor markings, but none that deface the cover; usually needs slight repair around staples and along spine which could be rolled; cover could have a minor tear or crease where a corner was folded under or a loose centerfold; no chunks missing. Slight yellowing acceptable.

GOOD (g): An average used copy complete with both covers and no panels missing; slightly soiled or marked with possible creases, minor tears or splits, rolled spine and small color flaking, but perfectly sound and legible. A well-read copy, but perfectly acceptable with no chunks missing. **Minor** tape repairs usually occur and slight browning (no brittleness) acceptable, although tape repairs should be considered a defect and priced accordingly.

FAIR (f): Very heavily read and soiled, but complete with possibly a small chunk out of cover; tears needing repairs and multiple folds and wrinkles likely; damaged by the elements, but completely sound and legible, bringing 50-70% of good price.

POOR (p): Damaged; heavily weathered; soiled; or otherwise unsuited for collection purposes.

COVERLESS (c): Coverless comics turn up frequently, are usually hard to sell and in many cases are almost worthless. It takes ingenuity and luck to get a good price; e.g., color xerox covers will increase the salability. A cover of an expensive book is scarcer and worth more. However, certain "high demand" issues could bring up to 30 percent of the good price.

IMPORTANT: Comics in all grades with fresh extra white pages usually bring more. Books with defects such as pages or panels missing, coupons cut, torn or taped covers and pages, brown or brittle pages, restapled, taped spines, pages or covers, watermarked, printing defects, rusted staples, stained, holed, or other imperfections that distract from the original beauty, are worth less than if free of these defects.

Many of the early strip reprint comics were printed in hardback with dust jackets. Books with dust jackets are worth more. The value can increase from 20 to 50 percent depending on the rarity of book. Usually, the earlier the book, the greater the percentage. Unless noted, prices listed are without dust jackets. The condition of the dust jacket should be graded independently of the book itself.

STORAGE OF COMIC BOOKS

Acids left in comic book paper during manufacture are the primary cause of aging and yellowing. Improper storage can accelerate the aging process.

The importance of storage is proven when looking at the condition of books from large collections that have surfaced over the past few years. In some cases, an entire collection has brown or yellowed pages approaching brittleness. Collections of this type were probably stored in too much heat or moisture, or exposed to atmospheric pollution (sulfur dioxide) or light. On the other hand, other collections of considerable age (30 to 50 years) have emerged with snow white pages and little sign of aging. Thus we learn that proper storage is imperative to insure the long life of our comic book collections.

Store books in a dark, cool place with an ideal relative humidity of 50 percent and a temperature of 40 to 50 degrees or less. Air conditioning is recommended. Do not use regular cardboard boxes, since most contain harmful acids. Use acid-free boxes instead. Seal books in Mylar[1] or other suitable wrappings or bags and store them in the proper containers or cabinets, to protect them from heat, excessive dampness, ultraviolet light (use tungsten filament lights), polluted air, and dust.

Many collectors seal their books in plastic bags and store them in a cool dark room in cabinets or on shelving. Plastic bags should be changed every two to three years, since most contain harmful acids. Cedar chest storage is recommended, but the ideal method of storage is to stack your comics (preferably in Mylar[1] bags) vertically in acid-free boxes. The boxes can be arranged on shelving for easy access. Storage boxes, plastic bags, backing boards, Mylar[1] bags, archival supplies, etc. are available from dealers. (See ads in this edition.)

Some research has been done on deacidifying comic book paper, but no easy or inexpensive, clear-cut method is available to the average collector. The best and longest-lasting procedure involves soaking the paper in solutions or spraying each page with specially prepared solutions. These procedures should be left to experts. Covers of comics pose a special problem in deacidifying due to their varied composition of papers used.

Here is a list of persons who offer services in restoration or archival supplies:

—Bill Cole, P.O. Box 60, Randolph, MA 02368-0060. Archival supplies, storage protection, deacidification solutions.

—The Art Conservatory, Mark Wilson, P. O. Box 1609, Longview, WA 98632. Restoration

—Comic Conservation Lab, Jef Hinds, P.O. Box 5L, Bakersfield, CA 93385. PH: (805) 872-8428. Restoration & preservation supplies.

—Lee Tennant Enterprises, P. O. Box 296, Worth, IL 60482

[1]*Mylar is a registered trademark of the DuPont Company.*

by Bob Overstreet[1]

Propelled by continued economic stability, the comic marketplace posted further gains during the past year. Once again, increases in the market were, for the most part, of a more stable nature rather than the dramatic increases experienced in the early turbulent years of the market. Since we have seen increases of a more consistent nature for the past several years, one would expect less impact on the marketplace should an economic slowdown occur during the coming year. Should the economy proceed in its present slowly upward direction, then one would again anticipate similar gains in the comic marketplace.

Early 1988 saw an increased demand generated in the comic book market. The following factors may have contributed to this:

The stock market crash of October 1987 and subsequent modest returns available through investments such as certificates of deposit, treasury notes, and money markets sent investors seeking alternate avenues of investment. In general, the collectibles market became a prime target.

There was a lot of media exposure due to Superman's 50th anniversary, Mickey Mouse's 60th, and the upcoming Batman movie.

But certainly one of the biggest factors of influence was the increased circulation of *The Official Overstreet Comic Book Price Guide*. More newcomers than ever before were introduced to the comic book market, driving up demand for vintage material. This certainly also contributed to the discovery and assimilation of many new collections into the market.

The result of these and other factors created a huge demand for Golden Age and Silver Age books.

This edition has changed its highest grade listing from Mint to N-Mint. This was done to bring the Guide closer in balance with the real market. True mint condition books very seldom turn up, and when they do, always sell for over the listed mint price. This adjustment should bring the Guide more in line with the market, letting books in true mint seek their own price above the N-Mint value listed. The only exception would be the more recent 1970s to 1980s books which do exist in mint condition. There, the N-Mint listing should be interpreted as a Mint listing.

Batman and related comics *(Detective)* were again the hottest, most sought-after titles, even after substantial price increases last year.

Most key Golden and Silver Age books remained scarce last year. Books with a history or "pedigree" such as Edgar Church, Denver, Larson, San Francisco, etc., were selling at multiples of Guide.

All key Silver Age books and titles enjoyed high demand with dramatic price increases reflected in this edition.

Although many record sales occurred during the year, the most dramatic was a N-Mint *Detective* #27 for $35,000 and the Church copy of *Captain America* #1 for $22,500.

1988 saw an increased interest in good high-quality investment books such as those from the Edgar Church collection. The highest demand was for most DC and Centaur titles from this collection which sold to anxious buyers at 3 to 5 times Guide list. Most other Church books (Quality, Fox, Fiction House, Gleason, etc.) were selling for 2 to 3 times Guide list.

[1]*With helpful assistance from Steve Geppi, Hugh O'Kennon, Ron Pussell, Jay Maybruck, Joe Vereneault, Dan Malan, Rick Sloane, John Snyder, Terry Stroud, Gary Colabuono, Walter Wang, James Payette, Jon Warren, Stephen Fishler, Bruce Hamilton, Gary Carter, Mark Wilson and Joe Mannarino.*

1930s Titles—Supply was definitely unable to meet demand, which keeps forcing prices up. Dealers, fearful of not being able to replenish inventories, were asking (and in most cases getting) well over Guide list for most high grade books and key issues. Titles in the highest demand were pre-hero DCs followed by early Centaurs and other key number ones. Almost all pre-hero DCs were selling for 1.5 to 2 times Guide list. *New Fun, More Fun, New Comics, New Adventure, Adventure, Detective,* etc., continued to set sales records the entire year. The Church run of *More Fun*, which included #14, #16-19, #23-51, sold as a set for $41,000. Other sales of early DCs are: *Action* #1-11 (DC vs. Fox lawsuit copies), VG-FN sold for $25,000. *Action* #1, FN (restored)—$11,500; #3 VG (restored)—$1,050; #6 G + —$600; *Adventure* #25 M (Church)—$1,120; #33, 34 M (Church)—$920 each; #37 VF + —$375; *All-American* #1 VF + —$1,050; *Detective* #1 F-VF (restored)—$10,000; #27 FN—$11,500; #27 F-VF—$17,000; #27 NM—$35,000; *More Fun* #12 VG—$300; #14 FN + —$1,700; #51 VF + —$750; *New Adventure* #14 (Church)—$1,260; *New Comics* #1 G—$600; *New Fun* #2 FN—$2,800; #4 FN—$1,500; #6 VF—$3,800; *Superman* #1 VF (repaired)—$15,000.

A *Famous Funnies*, Series 1 in VF surfaced and sold for $3,000 cash and about $500 trade to a dealer. Other sales are as follows: *The Comics Magazine* #1 Fr-G—$1,850; *Crackajack Funnies* #1 VF—$500; *Famous Funnies* #1 F-VF—$2,250; #1 Fr—$800; *Famous Funnies, a Carnival of Comics* #1 FN—$725; *Funnies on Parade* VF + —$1,500; *Nickel* #1 ('38) VF + —$175; *Popular* #1 VF (repaired)—$1,000; #3 FN—$280; *Star Ranger* #1 NM (Church)—$1,650; *Super* #1 NM—$800; *Tip Top* #10 NM—$200; *Western Picture Stories* #3 Fr-G—$50. All titles from this period have remained scarce with demand continuing to increase. Expect excellent growth in these books in the years ahead.

1940s Titles—With the DC and Centaur titles showing highest demand, followed by Fiction House, Fox, Timely, MLJ, and others, most all books from this period in all grades enjoyed solid sales the entire year. Several collections surfaced, but not enough to supply the huge demand. Wholesale prices paid for collections are reported to be on the increase since many dealers are chasing the few good collections turning up. At the conventions, we saw DCs, Centaurs, and other key books priced at 1.5 to 3 times and more of Guide list. Dealers were not anxious to sell their best material too fast since it is becoming so difficult to replenish.

DC—Still the hottest and most collected company, even after strong price increases over the past several years. *Action Comics* #1 remained the most valuable comic book, but watch out for *Detective Comics* #27, which is really coming on strong. The popularity of Batman and the demand for his comic books seem to have no limits, and the movie due out in 1989 can only drive interest to even higher levels. A few examples of currently hot DC books to watch in the future are *Batman* #1, *Detective* #27, *Green Lantern* #1, *Flash* #1, and *All-American* #16. The following are reported sales: *Action* #56, 57 NM—$400 each; *All-American* #16 (SF)—$5,000 with coupon out of back cover; #25 VF + —$1,100; #61 F-VF—$475; #70 (Church)—$525; *All Flash* #1 NM + —$1,900; #2 VF + —$425; *All Star* #2 NM + (Church)—$5,300; #15 VF + (Church)—$1,900; #26 (Church)—$1,090; *Batman* #1 (Denver)—$17,500 (not confirmed); #1 G—$1,400; #1 G-VG (heavily restored)—$1,800; #1 VF + —$11,500; #13-15 (SF)—$1,120 each; #16 (SF)—$1,330; #23 NM—$600; #47 M—$600; *Big All-American* #1 VG + —$800; #1 VF—$1,100; *Detective* #27 FN + —$22,000; #30 NM + —$1,900; #44 NM + —$656; #48 NM + —$600; #70 NM—$300; #75 (Church)—$1,000; #113 NM—$450; Bound volumes of *Detective* #1-26 sold at $10,000 cash value in trade, which resold at a higher price. *Flash* #1 VF (restored)—$2,400; #70 NM—$300; #90 NM—$350; #95 NM—$500; #104 VF—$850; #104 (Church)—$4,200; *Leading* #1 VF—$650; #1 VF + (Denver)—$1,150; *More Fun* #52 FN (restored)—$3,000; #53 FN (restored)—$2,000; #54 FN + —$1,000; #101 VF (restored)—$1,000; *Real Screen* #1 NM—$350; *Sensation* #1 FN—$735; #1 FN + —$1,000; #2 VF—$600; #12 (SF)—$400;

Star Spangled #69 G-VG—$40; #92 G-VG—$32; *Superman* #1 VG (restored)—$9,000; #1 VG—$6,250 cash, $900 trade; #1 VG-F—$9,250; #2 VF (restored)—$1,750; #3 VF +—$1,800; #5 NM—$1,400; #6 VF—$600; #11 VF—$475; #30 NM—$800; #38 NM—$325; *Wonder Woman* #1 VF—$1,750; *World's Best* #1 F-VF—$1,300; #1 VG-F—$775; *World's Fair* 1940 VG +—$375.

CENTAUR—Enjoyed very strong demand with few copies entering the market. Above Guide list prices were observed on most copies offered for sale. Like DC, Centaur titles continue to be highly collected. A few sales are: *Amazing Mystery Funnies* #1 VF +—$1,200; *Funny Pages* V2/10 (Cosmic Aero.)—$543; #35 (Church)—$750; *Green Giant* #1 VF +—$2,400; *Keen Detective* V1/8 VF-NM—$485.

TIMELY—This company's books continued to be very popular in the market with most copies selling at and around Guide list. There seemed to be some price resistance when copies were offered at above Guide list, although a few books did sell at these prices. It was reported late in the year that Timelys sold very well at Creation Con in New York. They also sell very well in low grade.

Some of the titles most in demand were *Captain America, Marvel Mystery, Namora, Sun Girl,* and *Miss Fury*. The Church copy of *Captain America* #1 sold for $22,500; another NM + copy surfaced and sold for $8,000. Here are a few other documented sales: *All Select* #4 M—$500; *All Winners* #2 NM—$1,100; #6 VF +—$600; #8 (SF)—$700; *Captain America* #2 NM +—$3,500; #6 VF—$575; #19 (SF)—$900; *Human Torch* #1 VG-F—$1,100; #5 VF +—$980; #8 VF—$600; #12, 15 (SF)—$625 each; *Marvel Mystery* #1 VF—$20,000; #1 VF +—$20,750; #5 VF (restored)—$1,500; #7 F—$525; #8 VF +—$1,350; #10 VF—$740; #13 VF +—$720; #20 VF—$400; #23 NM +—$750; *Mystic* #2 NM +—$1,269; #3 NM +—$1,005; #5 VF—$575; *Namora* #2 VG—$125; *Sub-Mariner* #1 NM—$3,000; #5 VF—$475; #17 NM—$350; #27 NM—$300; *USA* #6 NM—$800.

FOX—A few high grade copies of early issues of *Fantastic, Wonderworld, Mystery Men, Wonder,* etc., turned up and sold quickly to anxious buyers, but most key runs and issues remained scarce. The late '40s titles showed continued steady demand with *Phantom Lady, Blue Beetle, Rulah, Zoot, All Top,* etc., the most popular. The Fox funny animal books such as *Cosmo Cat, Ribtickler,* etc., sold well, while the Fox Giants remained scarce. Sales include: *All-Top* #14 (Church)—$590; *Blue Beetle* #13 (Church)—$320; *Fantastic* #1 (Denver)—$1,150; *Flame* #2 (Church)—$530; *Mystery Men #2 (Church)—$960;* #2 NM +—$455; #7 VF +—$195; #9 NM +—$206; *Phantom Lady* #15 VF +—$325; *Rulah* #21 (Church)—$410; *Wonderworld* #3 NM +—$594; #4 NM +—$419; #6 NM +—$394; *Zoot* #11 (Church)—$400.

FAWCETT—Mixed reports on this company's titles. The early issues of *Master* were not available and sold very well when they did surface. *Captain Marvel* and *Whiz* sold at a slow to moderate pace, while *Bulletman, Captain Midnight, Spy Smasher,* and *Nickel* were in high demand. All Fawcett horror and science fiction titles sold very well. Sales included: *America's Greatest* #1 VG—$325; the Church run of *Bulletman* #2-7, 9-12, 14, 15 sold for $7,750; *Captain Marvel* #1 VG (restored)—$780; *Gift* #1 VF—$600; *Master* #1 VF—$650; #24 VF—$285; *Nickel* #2 NM +—$350; #3 NM +—$325; #6 NM +—$225; *Special Edition* #1 (Church)—$6,700; *Whiz* #3 NM—$2,200; #3 VG—$375.

GLEASON—*Daredevil* and *Silver Streak* remained scarce with solid demand. A *Daredevil* #1 NM + sold for $2,000, a #11 (Church) sold for $660; a *Silver Streak* #18 (Church) brought $550. The Gleason crime titles were in high demand.

DISNEY—Their new publisher Gladstone continued to produce high quality books which promoted the collectibility of all Disneys. Don Rosa, their new artist sensation, was at San Diego Con to sign autographs. Mickey's 60th birthday was media news throughout the year.

Demand for Disney books continued to pick up last year, fueled by the success of the animated TV show *Duck Tales* (rated the #1 animated TV show in the nation),

Mickey's 60th birthday, Snow White's 50th anniversary, and the subsequent re-release of the movie.

Demand for early vintage issues is on the increase, and they sold for over Guide list in high grade. Many of the early keys remained scarce, such as *Mickey Mouse* 4-Color 16, *Donald Duck* 4-Color 4 and 29, the early *Mickey Mouse Magazines*, *Mickey Mouse Book*, the early *Walt Disney C&Ss*, *March of Comics* #4, etc. *Uncle Scrooge* sold well, and also *Comics & Stories* (especially #1-100) and *Donald Duck*. A few sales are: *Four Color* #9 VF—$2,000; #16 F-VF—$1,500; #29 VG—$400; #62 NM—$1,200; #178 M—$650; #178 VF—$275; #386 M—$561; *Mickey Mouse Book* (1st printing, pg. missing) FN—$500; *Uncle Scrooge* #27 M—$42; *WDC&S* #1 G-VG—$550; #1 NM—$4,200.

FICTION HOUSE—All titles enjoyed good solid sales with *Planet* being very popular. The early issues of *Jumbo* were impossible to find. A *Jumbo* #1 VG + sold for $1,150.

QUALITY—The hottest titles this year were *Blackhawk*, *Military*, *Modern*, and *Lady Luck*, although the rest of the line, *National*, *Hit*, *Uncle Sam*, *Smash*, etc., enjoyed average good sales overall. *Buccaneers* was popular. Sales: *Blackhawk* #9 (Church)—$2,500; *Lady Luck* #87 VF—$130; *Military* #11 (Church)—$655; #20 (SF)—$303; #24 (SF)—$273; *National* #8 (Church) $695; #9 (Church)—$705; *Police* (Church) mid numbers sold at 2.4x Guide list.

MLJ—All 1940s superhero titles had moderate sales throughout the year. *Katy Keene* was in short supply, with other Archies showing average sales. *Blue Ribbon* #7 NM + —$155; *Pep* #8 NM + —$295; #12 NM + —$350; #16 (Church)—$850; *Shield-Wizard* #2 NM + —$425; #4 VF + —$225; *Top-Notch* #9 (Church)—$1,500; *Zip* #9 NM + —$212.

FUNNY ANIMAL—This is a large genre with most publishers producing dozens of titles in the '40s and '50s. *Looney Tunes* and *Bugs Bunny* showed renewed interest, with a *Looney Tunes* #1 (Denver) bringing $1,000 and another #1 VF selling for $750. This was due, in part, to the 1988 hit movie *Who Framed Roger Rabbit*, which had guest appearances of many of the best-known funny animal characters. A high grade set of later *Comic Cavalcade* sold at 1.5 times Guide; *Our Gang* #1—$650; *Terry-Toons* #38 NM—$275. *Mighty Mouse* is always a favorite. *Pogo Possum* enjoyed good sales, but the Kelly art books were slow. ACG's *Ha Ha*, *Giggle*, and other titles were hot. DC's *Real Screen*, *Fox & the Crow*, *Funny Stuff*, *Comic Cavalcade*, etc., and Fawcett's *Hoppy the Marvel Bunny* had solid sales. MLJ's *Super Duck*, as well as the many Marvel funny titles were in demand. There are many first issues in this genre valued at under $20 that could have good investment potential and collector appeal in the years ahead. All giant-size format books were in very high demand, as well as *Jingle Jangle*.

CLASSIC COMICS—This year saw continued strong growth in the Classics field. Many dealers have felt that Classics were a sleeper series for the last few years. There were many new discoveries of rare non-series items (giveaways, gift boxes, etc.) and foreign Classics. Early originals saw very strong growth, plus international trading drove up demand for any cheap copy of U. S. Nos. 8, 14, 20, 21, 33, 40, 43, 44, 53, 66, 73, 74, 84, 95, 110, and 169.

Classics #1 VF + —$1,750; another #1 VF + —$2,100; #1 FN + —$1,200. A FN copy of the Saks giveaway was auctioned at the end of the year, and it sold for $2,600.

MISCELLANEOUS—Many of the other companies' titles continued to show average demand. *Shadow* and *Doc Savage* comics were very strong. *Catman*, *Superworld*, *Rocket Comics*, *Crash Comics*, *Airboy*, *Air Fighters*, *Juke Box*, *Green Hornet*, etc., are some of the better titles. A few sales are: *All Your* (Church) (32 pg.)—$180; *Catman* #1 NM—$600; *Double Comics* (1941) VG + with Superman #12 inside—$300; *Exciting* #2 NM + —$135; *Four Color* #2 VG—$125; *Shadow* #3 NM—$350; *Speed* #1 NM + —$568.

1950s Titles—Several collections surfaced during the year, some in high grade, which sold rapidly to anxious collectors. TV-related, westerns, horror, science fiction, superhero, esoteric, good girl-art, sports, humor, 3-D, and many other types of comics were in high demand. Ditko, Wood, Matt Fox, and Kirby art books were in demand.

ATLAS—Showed very strong sales with pre-code issues of the horror titles being the most popular, as well as the science fiction titles such as *Marvel Tales, Spaceman,* and *Space Squadron.* The western titles such as *Black Rider, 2-Gun Kid, Rawhide Kid, Whip Wilson, Rex Hart,* etc., were hot. *Patsy Walker* and *Millie the Model* showed very strong demand. *Yellow Claw* was also a hot seller.

TV—The demand continues to increase for high grade copies. The Dell file copies sold very well at over Guide list prices despite significant increases last year. The hottest titles were those with photo covers, followed by Hanna-Barbera and Jay Ward books. *Avengers Starring Emma Peel* is very hot. Some of the other hottest titles are *I Love Lucy, Jackie Gleason, Space Ghost, Rawhide, Flintstones, Jetsons, Munsters, Dark Shadows, Maverick, Rocky & Bullwinkle, Three Stooges, Leave It to Beaver, Beatles Life Story, Bewitched, Beany and Cecil, The Monkees,* etc. A few sales are: *Aristocats* #1 M—$32; *Flintstones* #1 M—$100; *I Love Lucy* #3 M—$45; *The Jetsons* #11 M—$18; *Munsters* #1 M—$40; *Rocky & His Friends* #1 & 2 M set—$125; *Space Ghost* #1 M—$50; *Star Trek* #12 M—$25; *Supercar* #2 M—$30.

WESTERNS—*John Wayne* (his own book and Dell movie issues), *Sunset Carson,* and *Whip Wilson* were in the highest demand. The strongest Dell titles were *The Lone Ranger,* all the TV westerns with photo covers, and *Annie Oakley,* followed by *Gene Autry, Roy Rogers,* and *Red Ryder.* The Dell file copies, available on most titles, have, for the most part, been absorbed into collections. The Fawcett and Atlas westerns were scarce in high grade, and sold very well across the board. An *Andy Devine* #1 sold for $200; *Gene Autry* #1 (Faw) NM—$850; *Hopalong Cassidy* #1 (Denver)—$750; *Lash LaRue* #1 NM—$525; *Smiley Burnette* #1 VG +—$40. Most western titles continue to show strong demand and good steady growth.

DELL/GOLD KEY/OTHER GIANTS—Most Dell file copies disappeared in 1987 and 1988, selling to collectors at multiples of Guide. The *Bugs Bunny* giants showed increased demand, as well as all Jay Ward and Hanna-Barbera issues. All other companies' giants were in high demand as well. The market is waking up to the fact of the scarcity of these books in NM-M condition.

E.C.—Sales are slow to moderate at current Guide list prices. *Mads* (#1-23) showed some increased demand. There were reports of a couple of large, high-grade collections surfacing and selling to one or two buyers at 1.5 to 2 times Guide list.

ERB COMICS—Due to a large crossover market of Burroughs collectors, sales of *Tarzan Comics* (especially #1-100) were very strong.

GOOD GIRL-ART COMICS—All the Fox titles were in demand in 1988. *Rulah, Junior, Jo-Jo, Crimes By Women, Women Outlaws, All Top, Blue Beetle,* and *Phantom Lady* sold very well, including the I.W. Reprints. Other titles in high demand were *Seven Seas, Undercover Girl,* and *Slave Girl.*

HUMOR COMICS—*Barnyard, Goofy, Happy, Casper, Ha Ha, Giggle,* etc. were in high demand. *Abbott & Costello* issues sold well, along with *Peanuts.* The *Three Stooges* (St. John and Dell) issues were steady sellers. The DC humor titles had overall good sales, with *Ozzie & Harriet, Bob Hope, Jerry Lewis, Scribbly, Jackie Gleason,* and *Sugar & Spike* among the hottest titles.

HORROR AND CRIME COMICS—The pre-code issues were most in demand. There were a lot of sales in this area. Interestingly, many of the non-E.C. horror and crime comic prices have reached and surpassed the E.C.s, due to the heavy E.C. reprinting and the relative scarcity of the non-E.C. titles. *Adventures Into the Unknown, Forbidden Worlds,* and other ACG horror and crime titles were widely collected. *Dark Mysteries* was very strong, along with *The Thing* which has extreme violence in many issues. Books with spanking, torture, atomic blasts, etc. were in high demand. Most all Atlas horror, crime, and science fiction books were leaping off the shelves at over Guide list prices. The Harvey titles were available at current price levels.

ROMANCE COMICS—Sales overall were reported slow and at current listed price levels.

1960s-1970s TITLES—The demand for all early Silver Age DC and Marvel titles is very strong, with a low supply of high grade copies. The DC giants of titles such as *Action, Batman, Superman,* and *Adventure* were very hot. Many of the key issues like *Action* #242, *Green Lantern* #40, and *Flash* #123 sold for multiples of Guide list. *Adventure Legion* issues had high demand, as well as early *Jimmy Olsen, Challs. of Unknown, Green Lantern, Blackhawk, JLA, Brave & the Bold, Showcase* #1-50, etc. *Our Army at War* #81-110 (key Sgt. Rock issues) were very hot, as well as *Brother Power the Geek, Hawkman, Aquaman, Rip Hunter,* and *The Atom. Action* #242 VG-F sold for $100; *Adventure* #247 F-VF—$995; #300 NM—$170; #301 VF+—$42; *Flash* #105 F+—$200; *Green Lantern* #86 NM—$15; *Justice League* #1 VF—$475; *Showcase* #4 VG—$525; *Strange Adventures* #9 F-VF—$200.

Early issues (especially in fine or better) of *Amazing Spider-Man, Fantastic Four, X-Men, Tales of Suspense, Tales to Astonish,* etc. were showing very strong sales. All issues with the Punisher were in great demand, especially *Spider-Man* #129. *Sgt. Fury, Nick Fury Agent of Shield,* and *Silver Surfer* sold very well. In short, most 1960s and even early 1970s books are showing very strong demand. All rare key issues from this period in high grade are definitely on the move and should be watched closely in the months ahead. An *Amazing Fantasy* #15 NM+ brought $1,675; #15 NM+—$2,500; *Amazing Spider-Man* #1 M—$2,500; #1 NM+—$1,800; #1 F-VF—$650; #2 NM+—$425; #5 NM—$220; *Fantastic Four* #1 FN—$750; #1 VF—$900; *X-Men* #1 M—$800; #1 NM—$1,150; #1 NM—$900; #1 VF—$600.

1980s TITLES—1988 was an extension of the comic book marketplace of 1987. Both DC and Marvel continued to be the dominant publishers, competing with each other for market share at the expense of the smaller independent publishers. As a group, the small independent publishers continued to have their problems and several more ceased operation in 1988. CA Comics, Fish Wrap, Harrier, Onward, Pied Piper, Pyramid, Silverline, Victory, and Wee Bee, were among many smaller publishers who suspended operations during 1988. The continued decline in popularity of the small press black and white, as well as color, comics was due to many factors. Among them were increasing cover prices to compensate for smaller print runs, decreasing editorial quality due to the larger publishers luring the more talented people to work for them, decreasing speculative interest as collectors realized the resale value of many of these small press books was little to non-existant on the secondary market.

This trend was not universal, however, as several smaller publishers flourished in this narrowing market. Dark Horse Comics increased their sales with strong new titles, including *Aliens, The American, Dark Horse Presents,* and *Concrete.* Fans recognized the excellence of these products as Dark Horse won many awards in competitive voting by readers. Now Comics also made large strides forward as they garnered an increased market share with titles such as *Ghostbusters, Terminator, Astro Boy,* and *Speed Racer.* Mirage Studios continued their strong sales as *Teenage Mutant Ninja Turtles* took the country by storm with a syndicated cartoon series and a complete line of action figures and accessories with major national advertising and exposure. Archie grabbed a piece of the *Turtle* action with a successful mini-series of color comics with full newsstand as well as specialty shop distribution. The series sold extremely well in both markets. First Comics continued their successful ride on the backs of the Turtles with a fourth graphic novel, reprinting more of the original *TMNT* stories in color. These books expanded the visibility of the Turtles as they were available in many bookstores through the distribution arrangement with Berkley Books. Vortex produced the most controversial success of 1988 as they released several issues of *Black Kiss*. Each copy was produced in a sealed plastic bag with an **Adults Only** warning on the cover. The book contains sexual graphics, very strong language, as well as a great deal of violence. The book was inserted in *Hustler* magazine and sold out immediately. All issues were reprinted with first printings increasing in value in the collector market. Some retailers stayed away from *Black Kiss* and other adult comics as a major obscenity lawsuit was lost by a Midwest comic shop.

Another area of success among the independent publishers was a continuation of the Asian invasion begun in 1987 by First Comics' *Lone Wolf* and *Cub*, and Eclipse's *Mai, Area 88*, and *Kamui*. 1988, however, marked the first appearances of Asian comic books from Asian publishers directly. Jademan, a Hong Kong publisher, Viz, a Japanese publisher, and Eastern, a Korean publisher, were among the first to try to penetrate the American market themselves. Their early efforts left room for improvement as they attempted to overcome language, cultural, and scheduling problems while learning the American distribution system. They seem committed to make their programs work and eagerly and quickly adjust and adapt to their new market.

In an effort to streamline their administrative operations and secure the benefits of increased volume and marketshare, several mergers and distribution deals were worked out during 1988. Malibu and Eternity merged under the Eternity label, while Aircel worked out a distribution deal with Eternity. Comico, the fourth or fifth largest publisher in the direct market, worked out a distribution deal with DC Comics, the number two publisher in the direct market. These coalitions of publishers should strengthen the individual members both financially as well as editorially as greater efficiency is achieved. This should have a stabilizing effect on the surviving publishers in the direct sales market.

Marvel continued to reign as the number one publisher in the comic book marketplace. Several innovative projects came out of Marvel as they adjusted to the loss of their long time Editor-in-Chief, Jim Shooter. The *Marvel Masterworks* series, reprinting the first 10 issues of *Avengers, Fantastic Four, Spider-Man,* and *X-Men*, as well as the second 10 issues of *Fantastic Four, Spider-Man,* and *X-Men* offered readers a relatively inexpensive method of obtaining copies of these valuable and desirable issues and sparked interest among collectors of these titles. Marvel introduced the *Evolutionary War* storyline in their 1988 annuals, which became their most popular annuals in many years. Issues quickly sold out and increased interest in the monthly issues of these titles. The *Inferno* storyline crossovers in the *Marvel Universe* were another rousing success for Marvel as the tie-in issues sold significantly better than previous non-tie-in issues, and reader interest continued after the *Inferno* storyline was concluded. Marvel also successfully launched a bi-weekly anthology comic, *Marvel Comics Presents*, which featured several of Marvel's more popular characters including Wolverine. This bi-weekly schedule was used for three of Marvel's most popular titles during the best selling summer months. The titles included *Spider-Man, G.I. Joe,* and *X-Men*. Several new titles were well received by comic readers and included *Excalibur, X-Terminator*, and *Wolverine*. Marvel Comics was sold to a group of investors late in 1988. If the new owners are more interested in developing long term projects and characters than their predecessors, Marvel fans could be in for better times than they have had for the past few years.

The single biggest success in all of Comicdom in 1988 was the Batman *Death in the Family* series within a series. Issues #426-429 were all immediate sellouts with countless new readers seeking copies. The issues quickly became valuable collector issues, with reported sales as high as $45 for single issues. This unprecedented demand was created by a combination of forces. The death of Robin was the feature of the storyline. A very innovative 900 call-in number by which readers could vote for the death of either Robin or The Joker. The readers chose to let Robin die, and the wire services picked up the story which snowballed into an unanticipated avalanche of requests for the entire series. DC responded quickly to the demand by reprinting the entire series of four issues in a trade paperback priced at $3.95 which was released during the first week of December, making it a perfect stocking stuffer as well as being an inexpensive package for those interested in reading the story. Batman was hot all year long as the mini-series *The Cult* was highly touted and lived up to expectations. A long-awaited one shot also featured Batman and The Joker. "The Killing Joke," written by Alan Moore and illustrated by Brian Bolland was a huge success in the prestige format. First printings quickly commanded premium prices as it went into a second and third printing. DC continued all year to come up with new mini-series, new ongoing titles, and new one shots which were very well received by comic fandom. Among the hottest DC products were *Black Orchid, V For Vendetta, The Prisoner, Cosmic Odyssey, Invasion,* and *The Greatest Batman Stories Ever Told* hardcover.

INVESTOR'S DATA

The following table denotes the rate of appreciation of the top 50 most valuable Golden Age titles over the past year and the past five years (1984-1989). The retail value for a complete mint run of each title in 1989 is compared to its value in 1988 and 1984. The 1971 values are also included as an interesting point of reference. The rate of return for 1989 over 1988, and the yearly average rate of return for each year since 1984, is given.

For example, a complete mint run of *Detective Comics* retails at $148,016 in 1989, $118,121 in 1988, and $53,280 in 1984. The rate of increase of 1989 over 1988 can be easily calculated at 25.3%, while the average yearly increase or rate of return over the past five years is 35.6%. This means that the mint value of this title has increased an average of 35.6% each year over the past five years.

The place in rank is given for each title by year, with its corresponding mint value. This table can be very useful in forecasting trends in the market place. For instance, the investor might want to know which title is yielding the best dividend from one year to the next, or one might just be interested in seeing how the popularity of titles changes from year to year. For instance, *Famous Funnies* was in 8th place in 1971 and has dropped to 20th place in 1989. But this title could be on the move to reclaim its original position, as it has changed from 43rd place to 20th in the past five years and currently continues to show a strong price increase (1989 over 1988).

Batman overtook *Captain America* for the number 8 spot, and *More Fun Comics* overtook *Marvey Mystery Comics* for the number 3 spot this year. *The Shadow* entered the top 50 jumping from 57th to 50th spot. *Green Lantern* increased by 15.0% from 1988, but shows a yearly average increase of 24.1%. *World's Finest* was up 23.0% and *Planet Comics* up 11.1%.

The following tables are meant as a guide to the investor and it is hoped that they might aid him in choosing titles in which to invest. However, it should be pointed out that trends may change at anytime and that some titles can meet market resistance with a slowdown in price increases, while others can develop into real comers from a presently dormant state. In the long run, if the investor sticks to the titles that are appreciating steadily each year, he shouldn't go very far wrong.

The Silver Age titles continued to show movement, especially early issues of Marvel's and DC's in high grade. Golden & Silver Age titles are continuing to appreciate faster than economic inflationary values during the same period.

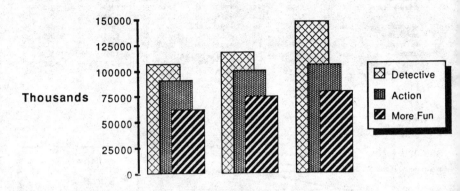

Top Three Titles

Thousands

Legend: Detective, Action, More Fun

TOP 50 TITLES
TOP 50 TITLES & RATE OF INCREASE OVER 1988 AND 1984 GUIDE VALUES

Title		1989 Guide Rank & Value	%Change From '88 Value	Avg.Yrly. Return '84-'89	1988 Guide Rank & Value		1984 Guide Rank & Value		1971 Guide Rank & Value	
Detective Comics	1	$148,016	+ 25.3	+ 35.6	1	$118,121	2	$53,280	4	$2,747
Action Comics	2	106,278	+ 6.0	+ 16.8	2	100,221	1	57,831	7	2,354
More Fun Comics	3	80,066	+ 6.2	+ 24.4	4	75,410	5	36,093	3	2,816
Marvel Mystery Comics	4	76,530	-0-	+ 9.2	3	76,530	3	52,445	5	2,584
Adventure Comics	5	73,210	+ 17.7	+ 23.8	6	62,226	7	33,422	2	3,066
Four Color	6	70,809	+ 8.8	+ 14.4	5	65,053	4	41,209	1	4,229
Superman	7	64,171	+ 7.7	+ 15.8	7	59,577	6	35,892	13	1,460
Batman	8	46,937	+ 17.5	+ 23.5	9	39,943	12	21,558	19	1,246
Captain America	9	44,547	+ 6.4	+ 13.4	8	41,875	8	26,650	17	1,303
All Star Comics	10	44,240	+ 13.2	+ 23.8	10	39,080	14	20,205	10	1,657
Whiz Comics	11	$39,861	+ 7.9	+ 10.5	11	$36,953	9	$26,156	14	$1,357
Flash Comics	12	39,300	+ 14.4	+ 23.0	12	34,350	15	18,260	15	1,344
All American Comics	13	38,540	+ 16.9	+ 24.7	13	32,965	16	17,230	24	1,189
Donald Duck	14	29,300	+ 3.0	+ 5.5	14	28,454	10	22,988	53	604
Walt Disney's C & S	15	27,194	+ 4.1	+ 4.9	15	26,111	11	21,802	12	1,487
Planet Comics	16	25,805	+ 11.1	+ 14.0	16	23,233	17	15,180	50	613
World's Best & Finest	17	25,496	+ 23.0	+ 16.5	20	20,725	20	13,962	33	841
Police Comics	18	22,890	+ 5.0	+ 10.2	17	21,793	18	15,169	30	903
Jumbo Comics	19	22,495	+ 7.6	+ 24.0	18	20,914	27	10,214	16	1,320
Famous Funnies	20	21,325	+ 25.8	+ 43.0	25	16,957	43	6,768	8	2,343
Mickey Mouse Magazine	21	$21,164	+ 13.1	+ 15.2	21	$18,717	22	$12,010	18	$1,252
Star Spangled Comics	22	20,020	+ 14.7	+ 20.2	24	17,454	28	9,970	35	830
Master Comics	23	19,451	+ 8.9	+ 13.4	23	17,866	23	11,657	28	1,021
Spirit	24	19,327	- 7.3	- 1.6	19	20,839	13	21,058	44	645
Captain Marvel Adventures	25	19,098	+ 6.2	+ 7.0	22	17,989	19	14,133	29	1,009
Dick Tracy	26	17,809	+ 8.2	+ 11.8	28	16,457	24	11,213	25	1,116
Green Lantern	27	17,280	+ 15.0	+ 24.1	31	15,025	33	7,830	87	390
Pep Comics	28	17,001	+ 3.0	+ 12.5	27	16,511	26	10,471	31	880
Sensation Comics	29	16,952	+ 7.8	+ 14.6	29	15,731	29	9,803	41	681
Human Torch	30	16,620	-0-	+ 7.0	26	16,620	21	12,315	46	632
Classic Comics	31	$15,919	+ 23.2	+ 27.1	36	$12,920	44	$6,763	189	$65
King Comics	32	15,315	+ 10.2	+ 28.9	33	13,903	51	6,270	6	2,490
Sub-Mariner	33	15,207	+ 0.7	+ 7.8	30	15,107	25	10,950	54	601
Feature Book	34	14,976	+ 4.6	+ 11.9	32	14,317	30	9,386	26	1,069
Tip Top Comics	35	14,570	+ 13.9	+ 22.4	37	12,793	41	6,876	9	2,088
Wonder Woman	36	14,184	+ 3.0	+ 11.1	34	13,775	31	9,132	64	537
Jungle Comics	37	13,374	+ 3.0	+ 18.3	35	12,983	39	6,980	32	861
Popular Comics	38	13,126	+ 18.5	+ 27.7	44	11,079	57	5,498	11	1,598
Amazing-Man Comics	39	13,035	+ 9.2	+ 25.4	39	11,935	56	5,745	108	314
Marge's Little Lulu	40	12,957	+ 5.3	+ 16.1	38	12,306	36	7,175	135	219

Title	1989 Guide Rank & Value		%Change From '88 Value	Avg.Yrly. Return '84-'89	1988 Guide Rank & Value		1984 Guide Rank & Value		1971 Guide Rank & Value	
Silver Streak Comics	41	$12,415	+ 5.8	+14.2	40	$11,729	35	$7,270	86	$394
Military Comics	42	12,406	+ 9.4	+17.9	43	11,343	46	6,555	68	520
Feature & Feature Funnies	43	12,198	+ 6.6	+19.9	41	11,448	54	6,109	22	1,214
Target Comics	44	12,008	+11.9	+16.0	45	10,730	45	6,680	38	746
Hit Comics	45	11,483	+ 0.6	+ 9.6	42	11,413	34	7,769	67	523
Large Feature Comic	46	10,997	+ 6.1	+ 5.6	47	10,360	32	8,599	27	1,058
Ace Comics	47	10,959	+ 8.7	+20.9	49	10,079	58	5,364	23	1,212
Superboy	48	10,815	+ 5.0	+10.7	48	10,298	38	7,044	94	360
Daredevil Comics	49	10,805	+ 7.4	+14.7	50	10,064	52	6,236	45	639
Shadow Comics	50	10,754	+16.2	+21.3	57	9,258	60	5,209	72	495

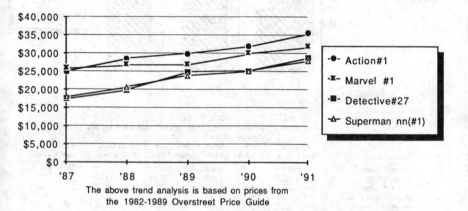

The above trend analysis is based on prices from the 1982-1989 Overstreet Price Guide

The following tables show the rate of return of the 50 most valuable Golden Age books, the 30 most valuable Silver Age titles and the 30 most valuable Silver Age books over the past year. It also shows the average yearly rate of return over the past five years (1989-1984). Comparisons can be made in the same way as in the previous table of the Top 50 titles. Ranking in many cases is relative since so many books have the same value. These books are listed alphabetically within the same value.

50 MOST VALUABLE GOLDEN AGE BOOKS AND RATE OF RETURN

Issue	1989Guide Rank & Value		%Change From '88 Value	Avg.Yrly. Return '84-'89	1988Guide Rank & Value		1984Guide Rank & Value	
Action Comics #1	1	$30,000	+ 4.7	+22.9	1	$28,650	2	$14,000
Marvel Comics #1	2	27,000	-0-	+10.9	2	27,000	1	17,500
Detective Comics #27	3	25,000	+25.0	+42.5	4	20,000	5	8,000
Superman #1	4	24,000	+15.4	+25.7	3	20,800	3	10,500
Whiz Comics #1	5	18,200	+12.0	+24.4	5	16,250	4	8,200
Detective Comics #1	6	10,000	+ 9.9	+70.9	6	9,100	24	2,200
Batman #1	7	9,800	+16.7	+14.4	8	8,400	6	5,700
More Fun Comics #52	8	9,000	+ 5.9	+17.5	7	8,500	11	4,800
All American Comics #16	9	7,700	+30.5	+31.3	12	5,900	16	3,000
Captain America #1	10	7,000	+11.1	+ 6.9	10	6,300	7	5,200
All Star Comics #3	11	$6,500	+13.2	+41.9	13	$5,740	25	$2,100
Double Action Comics #2	11	6,500	-0-	+ 6.0	9	6,500	8	5,000
Captain Marvel Advs. #1	13	6,300	+ 5.0	+ 5.2	11	6,000	8	5,000
More Fun Comics #53	14	5,800	+ 5.5	+16.3	14	5,500	15	3,200
New Fun Comics #1	15	5,600	+33.3	+77.4	21	4,200	72	1,150
Flash Comics #1	16	5,000	+13.6	+32.6	18	4,400	32	1,900

Issue	1989Guide Rank & Value		%Change From '88 Value	Avg.Yrly. Return '84'89	1988Guide Rank & Value		1984Guide Rank & Value	
Motion Pic. Funnies Wkly #1	16	5,000	-0-	-0-	15	5,000	8	5,000
Wow Comics #1	16	5,000	-0-	+ 5.6	15	5,000	12	3,900
Detective Comics #33	19	4,900	+16.7	+29.0	21	4,200	28	2,000
Detective Comics #38	19	4,900	+16.7	+36.0	21	4,200	40	1,750
Action Comics #2	21	$4,725	-0-	+ 7.8	17	$4,725	13	$3,400
Detective Comics #28	22	4,600	+ 4.5	+18.3	18	4,400	21	2,400
Marvel Mystery Comics #2	23	4,400	-0-	+ 5.9	18	4,400	13	3,400
New Fun Comics #2	24	4,200	+29.2	+115.5	27	3,250	-	620
Amazing-Man Comics #5	25	3,990	+14.0	+46.5	25	3,500	65	1,200
Action Comics #3	26	3,640	-0-	+ 9.1	24	3,640	19	2,500
All Star Comics #1	27	3,625	+ 9.8	+25.3	26	3,300	42	1,600
Walt Disney's C&S #1	28	3,500	+ 9.4	+ 5.0	28	3,200	17	2,800
Superman #2	29	3,220	+ 2.2	+ 8.0	31	3,150	23	2,300
Human Torch #1	30	3,200	-0-	+ 5.6	28	3,200	19	2,500
Marvel Mystery Comics #5	31	$3,185	-0-	+ 3.6	30	$3,185	18	$2,700
Red Raven Comics #1	32	3,010	+ 3.8	+10.1	35	2,900	28	2,000
Action Comics #5	33	3,000	-0-	+ 8.6	32	3,000	25	2,100
Big Book Of Fun Comics #1	33	3,000	+14.3	+80.0	43	2,625	-	600
Daring Mystery Comics #1	33	3,000	-0-	+13.3	32	3,000	35	1,800
Detective Comics #2	33	3,000	+ 8.5	+40.0	39	2,765	86	1,000
Detective Comics #29	33	3,000	+11.1	+22.9	40	2,700	57	1,400
Donald Duck March Of Comics #4	33	3,000	-0-	+ 5.0	32	3,000	21	2,400
Famous Funnies Series 1	33	3,000	+64.8	+76.0	75	1,820	-	625
Action Comics #7	40	2,975	+ 6.3	+13.1	36	2,800	35	1,800
Action Comics #10	40	$2,975	+ 6.3	+13.1	36	$2,800	35	$1,800
Detective Comics #31	42	2,940	+17.6	+29.0	46	2,500	65	1,200
Green Lantern #1	43	2,850	+14.0	+29.6	46	2,500	72	1,150
Batman #2	44	2,800	+12.0	+18.6	46	2,500	56	1,450
Dick Tracy Feature Book nn	44	2,800	-0-	+11.1	36	2,800	35	1,800
Captain America #2	46	2,765	+ 2.4	+ 7.7	40	2,700	28	2,000
Popeye Feature Book nn	47	2,700	-0-	+13.8	40	2,700	42	1,600
New Comics #1	48	2,625	+25.0	+35.6	57	2,100	98	945
Jumbo Comics #1	49	2,600	+14.3	+37.8	53	2,275	101	900
Sub-Mariner Comics #1	49	2,600	+ 4.0	+ 7.4	46	2,500	32	1,900

Top Ten Issues

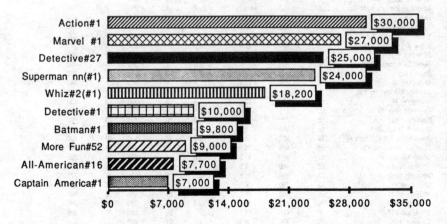

Action#1 $30,000
Marvel #1 $27,000
Detective#27 $25,000
Superman nn(#1) $24,000
Whiz#2(#1) $18,200
Detective#1 $10,000
Batman#1 $9,800
More Fun#52 $9,000
All-American#16 $7,700
Captain America#1 $7,000

$0 $7,000 $14,000 $21,000 $28,000 $35,000

30 MOST VALUABLE SILVER AGE TITLES AND RATE OF INCREASE

Issue	1989 Guide Rank & Value	%Change From '88 Value	Avg. Yrly. Return '84-'89	1988 Guide Rank & Value	1984 Guide Rank & Value
Showcase 1	$8,109	+ 10.9	+ 11.2	1	$7,311	1	$5,196
Amazing Spider-Man. 2	7,879	+ 35.3	+ 18.6	3	5,825	3	4,086
Fantastic Four. 3	6,953	+ 13.4	+ 9.7	2	6,132	2	4,676
The Flash. 4	5,891	+ 16.7	+ 15.8	4	5,048	4	3,288
X-Men 5	5,032	+ 21.9	+ 26.2	6	4,127	8	2,178
Brave And The Bold. 6	4,931	+ 11.8	+ 10.8	5	4,412	5	3,197
Justice League. 7	4,596	+ 29.8	+ 24.6	8	3,541	10	2,062
Tales To Astonish/Inc. Hulk. 8	4,404	+ 34.9	+ 13.2	9	3,265	7	2,652
Sugar & Spike 9	4,266	+ 9.8	+ 20.0	7	3,884	9	2,135
Green Lantern. 10	3,586	+ 19.0	+ 16.8	10	3,014	11	1,948
Avengers. 11	$2,963	+ 13.1	+ 12.7	12	$2,620	13	$1,813
Challengers Of The Unknown. . . . 12	2,892	+ 11.8	+ 14.1	13	2,587	14	1,695
Richie Rich. 13	2,736	+ 0.3	+ 0.5	11	2,728	6	2,668
Superman's Pal J. Olsen. 14	2,696	+ 9.5	+ 8.1	14	2,463	12	1,920
Journey Into Mystery/Thor. 15	2,475	+ 35.9	+ 11.3	18	1,748	16	1,579
Superman's Girl Friend L. Lane. . . 16	2,092	+ 9.5	+ 7.6	16	1,910	17	1,515
Tales Of Suspense/Capt. America. . 17	2,063	+ 49.7	+ 19.2	22	1,378	21	1,053
Mystery In Space. 18	2,056	+ 14.9	+ 14.2	17	1,790	20	1,204
Cerebus 19	2,053	-6.1	-0-	15	2,187	-	-0-
Harvey Hits. 20	1,736	+ 7.7	+ 3.0	19	1,612	18	1,508
Daredevil. 21	1,680	+ 7.2	+ 12.4	20	1,567	22	1,036
Tales Of The Unexpected. 22	1,642	+ 17.4	+ 18.0	21	1,399	24	865
Little Archie. 23	1,383	+ 2.7	+ 11.6	23	1,346	23	876
Advs. Of The Big Boy. 24	1,298	-0-	– 2.6	24	1,298	19	1,493
Strange Tales. 25	1,279	+ 27.4	+ 17.0	25	1,004	27	692
Doom Patrol. 26	949	+ 33.5	+ 116.5	28	711	48	139
G.I. Combat. 27	938	+ 25.1	+ 9.9	27	750	28	628
Playful Little Audrey. 28	897	+ 0.3	+ 2.9	26	894	25	783
Iron Man. 29	876	+ 39.0	+ 21.1	30	630	30	426
Atom 30	765	+ 53.9	+ 35.6	34	497	37	275

30 MOST VALUABLE SILVER AGE BOOKS AND RATE OF RETURN

Issue	1989 Guide Rank & Value	%Change From '88 Value	Avg. Yrly. Return '84-'89	1988 Guide Rank & Value	1984 Guide Rank & Value
Amazing Fantasy #15. 1	$1,800	+ 20.0	+ 12.7	1	$1,500	1	$1,100
Fantastic Four #1. 2	1,600	+ 15.9	+ 9.1	3	1,380	1	1,100
Showcase #4. 2	1,600	+ 10.3	+ 9.1	2	1,450	1	1,100
Amazing Spider-Man #1. 4	1,500	+ 50.0	+ 22.9	5	1,000	4	700
Adventure Comics #247. 5	1,400	+ 3.7	+ 26.7	4	1,350	5	600
Detective Comics #225. 6	750	+ 17.2	+ 16.6	7	640	12	410
Justice League #1. 6	750	+ 30.4	+ 30.0	9	575	23	300
X-Men #1. 6	750	+ 25.0	+ 25.5	8	600	19	330
Brave & The Bold #28. 9	700	+ 27.3	+ 25.9	10	550	22	305
Incredible Hulk #1. 9	700	+ 6.1	+ 4.1	6	660	6	580
Tales To Astonish #27. 9	700	+ 27.3	+ 15.0	10	550	13	400
Flash #105. 12	600	+ 9.1	+ 17.5	10	550	20	320
Showcase #8. 12	600	+ 17.6	+ 15.3	16	510	18	340
Journey Into Mystery #83. 14	580	+ 22.1	+ 7.6	19	475	10	420
Avengers #1. 15	575	+ 10.6	+ 12.9	15	520	15	350
Fantastic Four #2. 15	575	+ 4.5	+ 6.1	10	550	8	440
Showcase #22. 15	575	+ 16.2	+ 18.3	18	495	23	300
Brave & The Bold #1. 18	550	+ 1.9	+ 5.9	14	540	9	425
Superman's Pal J. Olsen #1. . . . 19	525	+ 5.0	+ 5.0	17	500	10	420
Tales Of Suspense #39. 19	525	+ 25.0	+ 15.0	25	420	23	300
Green Lantern #1. 21	490	+ 11.9	+ 23.6	24	438	32	225
Fantastic Four #3. 22	460	+ 4.5	+ 6.3	21	440	15	350
Amazing Spider-Man #2. 23	450	+ 18.4	+ 13.3	26	380	26	270
Showcase #1. 23	450	-0-	+ 5.7	20	450	15	350
Richie Rich #1. 25	440	-0-	-0-	21	440	8	440
Showcase #13. 26	425	+ 11.8	+ 12.7	26	380	27	260
Showcase #14. 26	425	+ 11.8	+ 12.7	26	380	27	260
Cerebus #1. 28	400	– 9.1	– 1.8	21	440	-	-
Showcase #6. 29	375	+ 7.1	+ 8.8	29	350	27	260
Fantastic Four #4. 30	355	+ 4.4	+ 7.3	30	340	27	260

The following table lists the really hot Silver Age titles over the past year. From one year to another, this list can change drastically.

HOT TITLES & RATE OF INCREASE 1989 GUIDE OVER 1988 GUIDE

Hawkman 160.8%	Tales Of Suspense 49.7%	Aquaman 35.4%
Metal Men 111.2%	X-Factor.....................45.7%	Amazing Spider-Man 35.3%
Sub-Mariner 68.7%	Sea Devils...................45.3%	Tales To Astonish 34.9%
Nam 67.8%	Iron Man 39.0%	Doom Patrol 33.5%
Captain America............66.3%	Sgt. Fury 41.2%	Flaming Carrot 27.6%
Nick Fury..................54.0%	Rip Hunter..................37.9%	Strange Tales 27.4%
Atom 53.9%	Journey Into Mystery 35.9%	Spec. Spider-Man...........26.8%

THE FIRST WAVE OF COMIC BOOKS 1933-1943 (Key books listed and ranked)

The first modern format comic book came out in 1933 and represents the beginning of comic books as we know them today. The impact of these early characters and ideas are today deeply engrained in American folklore and continue to feed and inspire this ever changing industry.

Over the years historians, collectors and bibliofiles have tried to make some sense out of this era. The question 'what are considered to be the most important books?' has been a topic of discussion and debate for many years. With certain criteria considered, how would the top key issues be ranked in order of importance? How would they relate to each other? In an attempt to answer some of these questions, the following list has been prepared. The books are grouped chronologically in the order they were published. The most important books are ranked into seven tiers, with the top six designated with stars. The more important the book is, the more stars it receives. The following criteria were used to determine the importance and placement of each book in each tier:

A. Durability of character(s)
b. Durability of title
c. Popularity of character(s)
d. First appearance anywhere of a major character
e. First issue of a title
f. Originality of character (first of a type)

g. First or most significant work of a major artist
h. Starts a trend
i. First of a genre
j. Historical significance
k. First of a publisher
l. First appearance in comic books of a character from another medium

This list was compiled by several people* and represents a collective opinion of all. The list is not perfect, not by any means. Adjustments will be made over time as more input is received. The final ranking of a book depends greatly on the overall importance and impact of that book on the comic book market. Obviously, the further you get away from the top key books, the more difficult it becomes for proper ranking. For this reason, books ranked in the lower numbered tiers could change drastically. The final rating given a book is not based entirely on the quantity of points it receives, but rather the overall weight of the points it does receive. For example, the first appearance of *The Fighting Yank* is not as important as the first appearance of *Superman* who was a trend setting character and long lasting.

In the comics market there are several comics that have become high demand, valuable books due primarily to rarity. A list of the top key books ranked due to value, demand and rarity would look entirely different than what we have here. As we have learned in coins, stamps and other hobbies, rarity is an important factor that affects value and it is not our intention to demean the collectibility of any particular book that is rare. Quite the contrary. There are many rare books that would enhance anyone's collection. Consideration of rarity, for the ranking of books in this list has been kept at a minimum.

The following list covers the period 1933 through 1943 and includes **every** key book of this period of which we are currently aware. Any omissions will be added in future lists. It should be noted that many other issues, although highly collectible, were not considered important for the purpose of this list: i.e., origin issues, early issues in a run, special cover and story themes, etc.

*Special thanks is due **Landon Chesney** who contributed considerable energy and thought to the individual write-ups; to **David Noah** who polished and edited, and to the following people who contributed their time and ideas to the compilation of this list: Hugh O'Kennon, Steve Geppi, Richard Halegua, John Snyder, Joe Tricarichi, Walter Wang, Jon Warren, Bruce Hamilton, Ray Belden and Chuck Wooley

NOTE: All **first issues** are included as well as books that introduce an important new character, or has key significance in some other way.

CHRONOLOGICAL LIST OF KEY COMIC
BOOKS FOR PERIOD 1933 - 1943
(All first issues listed)
GENRE CODES (Main theme)

An - Anthology (mixed)	**H** - Costumed/Superhero	**Mg** - Magic	**Sp** - Sport
Av - Aviation	**Hr** - Horror	**M** - Movie	**TA** - Teen-Age
Cr - Crime	**Hm** - Humor	**R** - Strip Reprints	**Tr** - True Fact
D - Detective	**J** - Jungle	**Re** - Religious	**W** - War
F - Funny Animal	**Lit** - Literature	**SF** - Science Fiction	**Ws** - Western

NOTE: The stars signify the ranking of books into seven different tiers of importance. The top (most important) books receive six stars (1st tier), dropping to no star (7th tier) as their significance diminishes. The following information is provided for each comic: 1. Ranking, 2. Title, 3. Issue number, 4. Date, 5. Publisher, 6. Genre code, 7. Description. 8. Criteria codes.

ANTEDILUVIAN PERIOD

1933 ■

★★★★ **FUNNIES ON PARADE** nn (1933, Eastern Color, R)-The very first comic book in the modern format reprinting popular strip characters. Given away to test the feasibility of demand for repackaged Sunday newspaper funnies. (An 8-page tabloid folded down to 32 pages). (a,c,d,e,h,i,j,k,l)

★★★★ **FAMOUS FUNNIES, A CARNIVAL OF COMICS** nn (1933, Eastern Color, R)-The second comic book. Given away to test reader demand. Its success set up another test to come in the following year to see if the public would actually pay 10 cents for this type of product (an 8-page tabloid folded down to 32 pages). The first of three first issues for this title.
(a,b,c,e,f,h,j)

★ **CENTURY OF COMICS** nn (1933, Eastern Color, R)-The third comic book. A 100-pager given away with three times the contents of the previous two books.
(e,j)

1934 ■

★ **SKIPPY'S OWN BOOK OF COMICS** nn (1934, Eastern Color, R)-The fourth comic book. The first to feature a single character-this wasn't tried again until **Superman** No. 1.
(e,j)

★★★★ **FAMOUS FUNNIES, SERIES I** (1934, Eastern Color, R)-The first comic book sold to the general public (through chain stores). The acid test, its unprecedented success set up the beginning of the first continuous series (anthology reprint) title in comics, and started the chain reaction.
(a,b,c,e,f,h,j)

★★★★★ **FAMOUS FUNNIES** No. 1 (7/34, Eastern Color, R)-Satisfied with the public response, this issue began the series and was the first comic book sold to the general public through newsstand distribution.
(a,b,c,e,f,h,j)

★ **FAMOUS FUNNIES** No. 3 (9/34, Eastern Color, R)-This issue ushered in the famous and very popular **Buck Rogers** strip reprints. Not trend setting, but important for the survival of the run which lasted 22 years.
(a,b,c,f,i,j,l)

1935 ■

★★★★ **NEW FUN COMICS** No. 1 (2/35, DC, An)-The first prototype of the modern comic in that it featured an anthology format of continuing characters and original rather than reprinted material. First of the DC line and the first tabloid-size book (albeit short-lived), surviving 13 years as **More Fun Comics**.
(b,e,h,i,j,k)

★ **MICKEY MOUSE MAGAZINE** No. 1 (Sum/35, K.K., F)-Magazine-size protocomic introducing the already legendary transfer characters to the fledgling comic book market. This title first appeared in 1933 as a black & white giveaway comic, and after going through format changes, eventually led to the ultimate "funny animal" comic, **Walt Disney's Comics & Stories**, to come five years later.
(a,b,c,e,g,j,k)

★ **NEW COMICS** No. 1 (12/35, DC, An)-DC felt enough confidence in the market to issue a second anthology title featuring original, continuing characters. It was second only to **New Fun** of its kind. Evolved into **Adventure Comics**, warhorse of the DC line. DC parlayed the second most perfect comic book title (the first is **Action**) into a forty plus year run.
(b,e,h,j)

1936 ■

MORE FUN COMICS No. 7 (1/36, DC, An)-DC cancelled the title **New Fun** due to the appearance of **New Comics** , continuing the series under this changed title.
(b,e,j)

★★★ **POPULAR COMICS** No. 1 (2/36, Dell, R)-The second anthology format title of continuing reprint strips. First of the Dell line, the third publisher to enter the field. Featuring the first comic book appearance of **Dick Tracy, Little Orphan Annie, Terry & the Pirates** and others, lasting 13 years.
(a , b , c , e , j , k , l)

BIG BOOK OF FUN COMICS (Spr/36, DC, An)-The first annual in comics (56 pages, large size; reprints from **New Fun** No. 1-5).
(e,h,i,j)

★★★ **KING COMICS** No. 1 (4/36, McKay, R)-Ties as the third continuous series reprint title. The first of a publisher (4th to enter the field). Showcase title of all the King Feature characters-the most popular and widely circulated in the

world, featuring Segar's *Popeye* and Raymond's *Flash Gordon* series as the mainstay, lasting 16 years.
(a,b,c,e,j,k,l)

★ ★ ★ **TIP TOP COMICS** No. 1 (4/36, UFS, R)-Ties as the third continuous series reprint anthology title. The first of a publisher (5th to enter the field). Featuring the *Tarzan* and *Li'l Abner* series and surviving 25 years.
(a,b,c,e,j,k,l)

★ **COMICS MAGAZINE, THE** (Funny Pages) No. 1 (5/36, Comics Mag., An)-The third anthology format title of original material. The first of a publisher (6th to enter the field). This book is unique in that its cover and entire contents were purchased from DC. This material created gaps in the story line continuity of DC's titles *More Fun* and *New Adventure* from which it came.
(e,j,k)

WOW COMICS No. 1 (7/36, McKay, An)-The fourth anthology title of original material. McKay's second series (first with original contents), lasting only 4 issues to 11/36. The Unpublished inventory formed the basis of the Eisner/Iger shop.
(e)

NEW BOOK OF COMICS No. 1 (6-8/36, DC, An)-The second annual in comics; 100 pages, reprinting popular strips from *More Fun* and *New Comics*. Second and last issue appeared in Spring of 1938.
(e)

FUNNIES, THE No. 1 (10/36, Dell, R)-Having published this title six years earlier as a tabloid, Dell brought it back as a regular comic book. Featuring more popular strip characters, this became Dell's second comic book title and ran for 6 years.
(b,e)

FUNNY PAGES No. 6 (11/36, Comics Mag., An)-Continued from *The Comics Magazine*; introduced The Clock(?), the first masked hero (detective type, transition hero) in a comic book.
(a,b,c,d,e,f,h,i,j)

FUNNY PICTURE STORIES No. 1 (11/36, Comics Mag., An)-Actually this company's second title, featuring their popular original character, *The Clock*, who appeared on the cover. Title continues for 3 years.
(e)

DETECTIVE PICTURE STORIES No. 1 (12/36, Comic Mag., D)-The first anthology comic title series devoted to a single theme and the first to focus on this subject. Popular in pulps, magazines and films of the time, lasted 7 issues.
(e,h,i,j)

1937 ■

NEW ADVENTURE COMICS No. 12 (1/37, DC, An)-Title change from *New Comics*, continues series.
(e)

STAR COMICS No. 1 (2/37, Chesler, An)-Ties as first of a publisher. Anthology format of continuing original material, but short lived (2½ years). Large-size format.
(e,k)

STAR RANGER No. 1 (2/37, Chesler, Ws)-Ties as first of a publisher, and as the first continuous series western anthology title (see *Western Picture Stories*). Large-size format of original material, lasting only 1 year.
(e,i,j,k)

WESTERN PICTURE STORIES No. 1 (2/37, Comics Mag, Ws)-Ties with *Star Ranger* as the first anthology comic title of original material to focus on this subject, the second of a single theme, not lasting out the year.
(e,i,j)

COMICS, THE No. 1 (3/37, Dell, R)-Dell's third anthology reprint title. The first comic book appearance of *Tom Mix*, lasting only one year.
(e,d)

★ ★ ★ **DETECTIVE COMICS** No. 1 (3/37, DC, D)-Inaugurated the longest run in comics. Initially a pulpy anthology of mystery men and private eyes, it emerged as the first important title on a single theme with the debut of the implacable *Batman* in '39 (Siegel and Shuster's *Slam Bradley* series is a flavorful example of title's '37-'38 period).
(a,b,c,e,f,h,i,j)

ACE COMICS No. 1 (4/37, McKay, R)-Due to the enormous success of McKay's first series, *King Comics*, this companion title was published featuring, among others, Raymond's *Jungle Jim*, lasting 12 years.
(a,b,c,e,j,l)

WESTERN ACTION THRILLERS No. 1 (4/37, Dell, Ws)-The third title devoted to westerns. A one-shot of 100 pages.
(e)

FEATURE BOOK nn (Popeye)(1937, McKay, R)-A new concept. The first series of comic books representing a divergence from the normal anthology format. Each issue in the run is actually a one-shot devoted to a single character. More than one issue in the run can be devoted to the same character. These books began in a B&W, magazine-size format. Improvements on this concept came a year later with UFS's *Single Series* (in color, comic book size), and still a year later with Dell's *Four Color* series, the only one to last.
(a,b,c,e,h,i,j)

FEATURE FUNNIES No. 1 (10/37, Chesler, R)-Another reprint title to add to the list, surviving 13 years as *Feature Comics*; carrying *Joe Palooka*, *Mickey Finn* and others.
(e)

100 PAGES OF COMICS No. 101 (1937, Dell, R)-Another 100-page reprint anthology book (Dell's 2nd) with a western cover. Only one issue.
(e)

1938 ■

ACE COMICS No. 11 (2/38, McKay, R)-First comic book appearance of *The Phantom*. Premiere mystery man and first costumed hero. The Ghost Who Walks never made the impact in comics that he enjoyed as a syndicated star.
(a,b,c,f,i,j,l)

FUNNY PAGES V2/6 (3/38, Centaur, An)-Ties with *Funny Picture Stories*, *Star Comics* and *Star Ranger* as first of a publisher. Series picked up from Chesler, ending two years later.
(k)

FUNNY PICTURE STORIES V2/6 (3/38, Centaur, An)-Ties with *Funny Pages*, *Star Comics*, and *Star Ranger* as first of a publisher. Series picked up from Comics Magazine, ending one year later.
(k)

STAR COMICS No. 10 (3/38, Centaur, An)-Ties with *Funny Pages*, *Funny Picture Stories*, and *Star Ranger* as first of

a publisher. Series picked up from Chesler, ending one year later.
(k)

STAR RANGER V2/10 (3/38, Centaur, Ws)-Ties with *Funny Picture Stories*, *Star Ranger*, and *Funny Pages* as first of a publisher. Series picked up from Chesler, lasting 2 more issues.
(k)

COMICS ON PARADE No. 1 (4/38, UFS, R)-The second title of this publisher, featuring much the same reprint strips as *Tip Top*, their first. This series survived 17 years.
(a,b,c,e,j)

MAMMOTH COMICS No. 1 (1938, Whitman, R)-First of a publisher, in the same format as the McKay *Feature Books*. Only one issue.
(e,k)

SUPER COMICS No. 1 (5/38, Dell, R)-A dynamic new title, Dell's fourth. Debuted with some of the heavy weights transferred from the already successful *Popular Comics*. This new line-up of *Dick Tracy, Terry & The Pirates,* etc. proved to be a sound marketing strategy, lasting 11 years.
(a,b,c,e,j)

GOLDEN AGE PERIOD

★ ★ ★ ★ ★ ★ **ACTION COMICS** No. 1 (6/38, DC, H)-The ultimate refinement of the anthology, continuing character title. The first appearance of *Superman*, the quintessential hero with extraordinary powers. Arguably the most imitated character in all of fiction. Standard bearer of the DC line. The most important comic book ever published, and in tandem with *Superman*, one of the most influential, prevailed beyond four decades.
(a,b,c,d,e,f,h,i,j)

CIRCUS COMICS No. 1 (6/38, Globe, An)-A unique short-lived title featuring a top artist line-up. Introduced Wolverton's *Spacehawks*, later to appear in *Target Comics* as *Spacehawk*. First of a publisher.
(d,e,f,j,k)

CRACKAJACK FUNNIES No. 1 (6/38, Dell, R)-A new Dell title, replacing the defunct *The Comics* with a similar but different mix of reprint strips. Lasted 4 years.
(e)

COWBOY COMICS No. 13 (7/38, Centaur, Ws)-Continued from *Star Ranger* and lasted only two issues. The fourth western anthology title.
(e)

KEEN DETECTIVE FUNNIES No. 8 (7/38, Centaur, An)-Continued from *Detective Picture Stories*, this title became one of Centaur's mainstays introducing the *Masked Marvel* one year later, lasting 2 years.
(e)

LITTLE GIANT COMICS No. 1 (7/38, Centaur, An)-Small-size diversion from the regular format and short-lived (4 issues).
(e)

AMAZING MYSTERY FUNNIES No. 1 (8/38, Centaur, An)-Standard bearer of the Centaur line. Top artist line-up due to its production by the Everett shop. Ran for two years.
(e,g)

LITTLE GIANT MOVIE FUNNIES No. 1 (8/38, Centaur, An)-

A miniature-sized format comic lasting two issues. A small cartoon panel appears on the right edge of each page giving the illusion of motion when riffled (a flip book) (the cover is set up to represent a movie theater).
(e,i)

★ **FUNNY PAGES** V2/10 (9/38, Centaur, H)-First appearance of *The Arrow* who is the very first costumed hero originating in the comic book (3 months after *Superman*). A primitive precursor of the more refined archers to come, *The Arrow* executed his adversaries with the medieval bluntness his uniform suggested.
(a,b,d,f,h,i,j)

★ ★ ★ **JUMBO COMICS** No. 1 (9/38, FH, J)-Publisher of the most perused, but least read, of Golden Age comics, Fiction House did not so much initiate a trend as continue the trusty formula that sustained their line of pulps, cheesecake cast against a variety of single theme adventurous backgrounds (aviation, s/f, jungle & war). *Jumbo* was the pilot model of the FH line and the first of the exploitation comics. The debut of *Sheena, Queen of the Jungle* heralded hordes of jungle goddesses to follow. The line overall is perhaps best remembered as a showcase for Matt Baker's patented 'calendar girl' art which, after Caniff and Raymond, was the most pervasive of Golden Age styles, enduring 15 years.
(a,b,c,e,f,h,i,j,k,l)

DETECTIVE COMICS No. 20 (10/38, DC, H)-First appearance of *The Crimson Avenger*, a *Shadow* look-a-like, who was the second comic book costumed hero (4 months after *Superman*).
(b,c,d,f,h,i,j)

LITTLE GIANT DETECTIVE FUNNIES No. 1 (10/38, Centaur, An)-Small-size format only lasting a few issues.
(e)

STAR RANGER FUNNIES No. 15 (10/38, Centaur, An)-Links to *Star Ranger* and *Cowboy Comics*, only lasting a few months. (Packaged by the Iger Shop.)
(e)

★ ★ ★ **DONALD DUCK** nn (1938, Whitman, F)-The first *Donald Duck*, as well as the first Walt Disney comic book; in the format of McKay's *Feature Book* (B&W with color cover), reprinting 1936 & 1937 Sunday comics. The first funny animal comic devoted to a single character. Precursor to great things to come for this character.
(a,b,c,e,f,i,j,l)

★ ★ **SINGLE SERIES** nn (Captain & The Kids) (1938, UFS, R)-UFS refined McKay's one-shot *Feature Book* format by adding color and adopting the standard comic book size, resulting in a more marketable package. Dell adopted this format for their *Four Color* series, which started a year later. This is UFS' third continuous series title.
(e,f,h,i,j)

COCOMALT BIG BOOK OF COMICS No. 1 (1938, Chesler, An)-A one-shot mixed anthology Charles Biro creation, packaged by the Chesler shop (top-notch art).
(e)

NICKEL COMICS No. 1 (1938, Dell, An)-A small-size divergent format one-shot, lasting only one issue.
(e)

1939 ∎

ALL-AMERICAN COMICS No. 1 (4/39, DC, R)-DC finally bends to the reprint anthology format, but includes some original material for flavor. *Scribbly* by Mayer begins; a ten-year run.
(a,b,c,d,e,j)

NEW YORK WORLD'S FAIR (3-5/39, DC, H)-The first newsstand comic with a commercial tie-in, capitalizing on the enormous publicity of a real life public event, featuring DC's top characters. The thick format, as well as the title segued into *World's Finest Comics* two years later.
(a,c,e,i,j)

★ **MOVIE COMICS** No. 1 (4/39, DC, M)-A unique but short-lived idea. The notion of adapting films to comics in fumetti form (the panels were half-tones of stills from the films) was a good one, but didn't work any better in '39 than it does today. (The first movie adaptation comic in standard comic book form and probably the first attempt at a fumetti continuity.)
(e,f,j,j)

★★★★★ **DETECTIVE COMICS** No. 27 (5/39, DC, H)-Reliable but predictable 'funny paper' cops 'n robbers anthology came into focus with the debut of *The Batman*. DC's second powerhouse set another standard for the industry to follow. The 'dynamic' hero—costumed athlete sans extraordinary powers—proved a viable alternative for the burgeoning competition to mimic, but Bob Kane broke the mold. The character's unique personna defied any but the most oblique imitation. *Detective* shared standard bearer honors with *Action* and provided the initials by which the company was known. One of the top four comics.
(a,b,c,d,f,h,j)

KEEN KOMICS V2/1 (5/39, Centaur, An)-A large size mixed anthology comic changing to regular size with number two. Packaged by the Everett shop and lasting only three issues.
(e)

★★ **WONDER COMICS** No. 1 (5/39, Fox, H)-Salutory effort of Fox (packaged by Eisner/Iger). First, and shortest-lived, of *Superman* imitations. Historically significant because the debut of Fox's *Wonder Man* prompted DC's first attempt to successfully defend their copyright on *Superman*. (A precedent that would prove decisive when the Man of Steel confronted a more formidable courtroom adversary a decade hence). Only one more issue followed.
(d,e,j,k)

★★★ **MOTION PICTURE FUNNIES WEEKLY** No.1 (5/39? Funnies, Inc., H)-Produced as a theatre giveaway, this title featured the first appearance of *Sub-Mariner*. His official newsstand debut occurred later in the year in *Marvel Comics* No. 1. Only seven known copies exist.
(a,c,d,e,f,g,h,i,j,k)

FEATURE COMICS No. 21 (6/39, Quality, An)-Continues from *Feature Funnies* of two years earlier. A discreet title change, indicating that original adventure comics were becoming a significant alternative to the formerly dominant reprints.
(b,e,k)

★★ **ADVENTURE COMICS** No. 40 (7/39, DC, H)-The *Sandman*, a transition crime fighter who stuck tenaciously to the trusty regalia of the pulp heroes. Finally, the pressure to adopt modern togs was brought to bear. The original mystery man vanished into oblivion, replaced by a swashbuckling Kirby hero.
(a,b,c,d,j)

AMAZING MYSTERY FUNNIES V2/7 (7/39, Centaur, H)-Debut of *The Fantom of the Fair*, mystery man, whose headquarters were under the World's Fair (An unexpected attraction for Fair goers). Destined for extinction with the 1940 wind-up of the Fair. Top artist line-up and exciting cover concepts.
(c,d,j)

COMIC PAGES V3/4 (7/39, Centaur, An)-A mixed anthology series continuing from *Funny Picture Stories* of three years earlier, lasting 3 issues.
(e)

KEEN DETECTIVE FUNNIES V2/7 (7/39, Centaur, H)-*The Masked Marvel*, super sleuth, and his three confederates began a terror campaign against lawless gangs. His big amphibian plane, secret laboratory and projected red shadow were devices used in the strip, lasting one year.
(d,j)

★★★ **MUTT AND JEFF** nn (Sum/39, DC, R)-This one shot represented a significant departure for DC. Formerly they had avoided the reprint title, preferring to develop their own original characters. This title was obviously a test to see if the market would support an entire book devoted to a single character (or in this case characters). This book has the honor of being the very first *newsstand* comic devoted to a single reprint strip. After a very slow start (four issues in four years), *Mutt And Jeff* was made a quarterly and soon became a popular run lasting 26 astounding years. It was the only successful reprint series of a single character to enjoy a respectable run. The syndicated *Mutt and Jeff* strip was, after *The Katzenjammer Kids*, the oldest continuously published newspaper strip.
(a,b,c,e,j)

★★★★★ **SUPERMAN** No. 1 (Sum/39, DC, H)-This landmark issue signaled a major turning point for the industry. Arguably, the second most important comic ever published (*Action* being the first), and possibly the most influential. *Superman* was the first original character promoted from headling an anthology title to starring in a book of his own. More importantly, this tandem exposure demonstrated to the industry that it could survive on its own original material, independent of the proven syndicated stars. As other publishers were attracted to the field in the months to come, they emulated not only *Superman*, but the tandem anthology/headline format that had contributed to his unprecedented success. A double trend setter. Contains reprint material from *Action* No. 1-4. Title has continued beyond four decades.
(a,b,c,e,h,i,j)

WONDERWORLD COMICS No. 3 (7/39, Fox, H)-After the *Wonder Man* debacle, Fox bounces back with a revised title and a new lead character (courtesy of the Iger shop). *The Flame* got off to a brilliant start, but was snuffed out when Iger and Fox parted company, lasting 3 years.
(a,c,d,e,j)

MAGIC COMICS No. 1 (8/39, McKay, R)-King Features' third reprint anthology (after *King* and *Ace Comics*) featured such popular syndicated stars as *Mandrake*, *Henry*, and *Blondie*. By 1940 *Blondie* had become the most widely syndicated newspaper strip in the world, and became the prime cover feature for the balance of the run, title enduring 10½ years.
(a,b,c,e,j)

★ **MYSTERYMEN COMICS** No. 1 (8/39, Fox, H)-Fox was on firm ground with a trio of potential contenders: *Wonder*

world's *The Flame* and, debuting in this title, *The Blue Beetle* and *The Green Mask*. These early products of the Eisner/Iger shop are worth a second look. Potential glows from every page. Soon, due to the E/I and Fox break up, the characters sunk into hack oblivion.
(a,c,d,e,j)

SMASH COMICS No. 1 (8/39, Quality, An)-This is the first title that Quality developed entirely on their own, (previous titles having been purchased from other publishers). The series lacked originality until the debut of Lou Fine's *Ray* which began in issue No. 14.
(b,e,j)

AMAZING MAN COMICS No. 5 (9/39, Centaur, H)-Everett's *A-Man* was launched here, the first Centaur character to headline his own title. The first costumed hero to shrink (*Minimidget*) begins. (This concept was better used later in Quality's *Doll Man*.) Top artist line-up in this series which ended in early 1942. The standard bearer of the Centaur line.
(e,j)

SPEED COMICS No. 1 (10/39, Harvey, H)-First of a publisher. *Shock Gibson* is the main hero. The characters in this series lacked the charisma of the competition's best; had a few bright moments when top artists entered the line-up, surviving as an average run for 7 years.
(a,b,e,k)

BEST COMICS No. 1 (11/39, BP, H)-First of a publisher. Debut of the Red Mask. An experimental large format book that read sideways; it failed to find an audience after four issues and folded.
(e,j,k)

BLUE RIBBON COMICS No. 1 (11/39, MLJ, An)-First of a publisher. Contents unremarkable (*Rang-A-Tang, The Wonder Dog*, for example). An MLJ anthology that failed to survive beyond 1942 despite the influx of super heroes.
(e,j,k)

★★★★★ **MARVEL COMICS** No. 1 (11/39, Timely, H)-Timely, the first publisher to hit with a smash twin bill in their inaugural title (courtesy of the Everett shop). From the onset, the formula of iconoclast as hero would prove to be Timely's most successful newsstand strategy. *The Human Torch* and *Sub-Mariner* won immediate reader approval, paving the way for more marvels to come from the pre-eminent Thrill Factory of comicdom. Possibly The most sought after of all Golden Age comics. Title lasted 10 years.
(a,b,c,d,e,f,g,h,i,j,k)

CHAMPION COMICS No. 2 (12/39, Harvey, An)-Early transitional anthology title with a sports theme, changing over to costumed heroes early on. None of the characters caught on enough to sustain the run for more than four years.
(e)

FANTASTIC COMICS No. 1 (12/39, Fox, H)-Biblical character *Samson* debuts. This series is more noted for the Lou Fine covers (Iger Shop). *Stardust* begins, one of the most bizarre super heroes in comics (Almost child-like, almost surrealistic art and plotting). He assassinated wrong doers regularly.
(e)

★★ **FEATURE COMICS** No. 27 (12/39, Quality, H)-Debut of the *Dollman* (Quality's first super hero), who was the second, but most significant, with the power to shrink (See *Amazing Man*). The stories were generally undistinguished but Quality's high standards of illustration (Eisner in this case) lent the strip a credibility that would have been lacking in lesser hands. This title lasted 11 years.
(a,b,c,d,j)

★ **SILVER STREAK COMICS** No. 1 (12/39, Lev, An)-First of a publisher. Debut of *The Claw*, one of the most bizarre villains in the annals of comics. Standing 100 feet tall with claws and fangs was the ultimate refinement of the 'yellow peril' theme from the pulps. Such a formidable figure had to have an adversary to match (See *Silver Streak* No. 7). The first comic book to display a metallic silver logo to insure prominence on the stands.
(a,c,d,e,f,k)

TOP-NOTCH COMICS No. 1 (12/39, MLJ, H)-*The Wizard*, one of MLJ's top characters debuted. Their second anthology title, lasting 4½ years.
(a,b,c,d,e,j)

LARGE FEATURE COMIC nn (1939, Dell, R)-Black and white, magazine size, one-shot series with color covers (identical to Mckay *Feature Books* of two years earlier), lasting four years.
(a,c,e)

CAPTAIN EASY nn (1939, Hawley, R)-First of a publisher. A one-shot reprint comic devoted to a single character, already proven successful by other publishers.
(a,c,e,k)

★★ **FOUR COLOR** No. 1 (Dick Tracy)(1939, Dell, R)-Exact format of UFS's *Single Series* of one year earlier. The most successful of the one-shot continuity titles, lasting 23 years. This series also provided a testing arena for new characters and concepts.
(a,b,c,e,j)

LONE RANGER COMICS, THE nn (1939, giveaway, Ws)-Fifth western title, first of a major character. This one-shot may have had newsstand distribution as price (10 cents) was stamped on cover.
(a,c,e)

1940 ■

★★ **BLUE BEETLE, THE** No. 1 (Wint/39-40, Fox, H)-The star of the second continuous series title devoted to a single character exemplified the pioneer 'crime fighter' of the early comics. His uniform was as simple and direct as the four-color medium itself– unadorned, form-fitting chain mail. Disdaining cloak, cape and the cover of night, *Blue Beetle* trounced crime where he found it, usually in the street and in broad daylight. Striking figure made an indelible impression on readers and, had Fox been more committed to long term development, would have doubtless gone the distance. The series eventually succumbed to tepid scripts and lacklustre art, but the character was of sufficient personal appeal to survive, in memory, not only the demise of his title but legions of better produced, longer tenured heroes.

★★★★★ **FLASH COMICS** No. 1 (1/40, DC, H)-DC reinforced its arsenal with two more dynamos: *The Flash* (first, and most significant hero with lightning speed), and *The Hawkman* (first and most significant winged hero). Both trend setters, with series lasting beyond 40 years.
(a,b,c,d,e,f,h,i,j)

★★ **FLASH COMICS** No. 1 (1/40, Faw, H)-An in-house b&w proof produced to secure pre-publication copyright. Important changes made before the book was officially released were, a title change from *Flash* to *Whiz* (DC had already gone to press with their *Flash Comics*), and the name of

the lead character was changed from *Captain Thunder* to *Captain Marvel*. (8 known copies exist.)
(e,f,g,j,k)

THRILL COMICS No. 1 (1/40, Faw, H)-Identical to *Flash Comics* listed above, only a different title. Only three known copies exist.
(e,f,g,j,k)

JUNGLE COMICS No. 1 (1/40, FH, J)-The second single theme anthology series of this subject (cloned from *Jumbo*). The title more perfectly suggested the 'jungle' theme with format selling rather than strong characters. Third series of a publisher, lasting as long as its parent (14½ years), with no competition until six years later.
(a,b,c,d,e,j)

★ ★ **PEP COMICS** No. 1 (1/40, MLJ, H)-Debut of *The Shield*, the first patriotic hero, later eclipsed by Simon & Kirby's *Captain America*, the bombshell of 1941. MLJ's third and longest lasting (over 40 years) anthology title. Archie eventually takes over the series.
(a,b,c,d,e,f,h,i,j)

★ ★ ★ ★ **PLANET COMICS** No. 1 (1/40, FH, SF)-The publisher's fourth anthology title of continuing characters. The first and by far the most successful science fiction run in comics. As with *Jumbo* and *Jungle*, this title had no competition for many years. Fiction House's style of action-packed covers and art made up for the routine plotting, lasting 14 years.
(a,b,c,e,f,h,i,j)

MIRACLE COMICS No. 1 (2/40, Hillman, H)-A mixed anthology series similar to *Rocket Comics* published a month later. First of a publisher. Covers have good eye-appeal, ending with the fourth issue.
(e,k)

★ ★ ★ **MORE FUN COMICS** No. 52,53 (2,3/40, DC, H)-DC modernizes its first anthology title, introducing the ominous *Spectre* in this two-part origin series. This frightening ethereal hero was too much a match for his adversaries, but gave DC an exciting alternative to their swelling ranks of wondermen. A trend setter, lasting 4 years in this title.
(a,b,c,d,f,h,i,j)

SCIENCE COMICS No. 1 (2/40, Fox, SF)-With qualifications, the second science fiction anthology title (very few of the stories dealt with outer space). Aside from the Lou Fine covers (No. 1 & 2), the artwork was not attractive and the series died after eight issues. First *Eagle* (the second winged hero).
(e)

TARGET COMICS No. 1 (2/40, Novelty, H)-First of a publisher. An early Everett shop super hero production. First *White Streak* by Burgos (the second android super hero). Top artist line-up featuring above average covers and stories, lasting 10 years.
(b,e,k)

THRILLING COMICS No. 1 (2/40, Better, H)-The first successful anthology title by this publisher (their second series). Debut of *Dr. Strange*. Logo carried over from the pulp. The Schomburg covers are the highlight of the run. The title lasted 11 years, switching to a jungle theme near the end.
(a,b,c,e,j)

★ ★ ★ ★ ★ **WHIZ COMICS** No. 2 (2/40, Faw, H)-After *Action*, the most significant of all hero/adventure anthologies was this late entry from Fawcett. Origin, first appearance

of *Captain Marvel*, humor hero par excellence. The most accessible of miracle men came from behind to eclipse the competition's best. He also founded the industry's first character dynasty (Marvel's *Junior*, *Mary* and even *Bunny*), a tactic that would prove as fundamental to comics' merchandising as DC's hero team concept. Landmark first issue also introduced such secondary stalwarts as *Sivana*, *Old Shazam*, *Spy Smasher* (the definitive aviator/mysteryman), and *Ibis the Invincible*, most memorable of comic book sorcerers. Flagship of the Fawcett line and a perennial favorite for 13 years.
(a,b,c,d,e,f,g,j,k)

ZIP COMICS No. 1 (2/40, MLJ, H)-MLJ's fourth anthology title (featuring *Steel Sterling*). Interesting stylized covers and art. Series lasted four years. With the exception of *Wilbur* (an Archie clone), none of the characters reached their own titles.
(a,b,c,d,j)

★ ★ **ADVENTURE COMICS** No. 48 (3/40, DC, H)-Debut of *The Hourman*. A substantial secondary feature that sold a few books for DC, but never received adequate creative support. Interesting premise came to dominate all the stories resulting in monotonous repetition.
(a,b,c,d,e,j)

COLOSSUS COMICS No. 1 (3/40, Sun, H)-An early esoteric book which ties to the esoteric *Green Giant* comic.
(e)

★ ★ ★ **DONALD DUCK FOUR COLOR** No. 4 (3/40?, Dell, F)-The first comic book devoted to this important transfer character. Still confined to one page gag strips. Full potential not yet reached.
(a,b,c,j)

MASTER COMICS No. 1 (3/40, Faw, H)-An experimental format at first (magazine size, priced at 15 cents and 52 pages). Debut of *Master Man*, an imitation of *Superman*, killed by DC after six issues; just in time for *Bulletman* to become the lead figure with issue no. 7, transferred from the defunct *Nickel Comics*.
(b,e,j,k)

MYSTIC COMICS No. 1 (3/40, Timely, H)-Unusual anthology title (their third) in that each issue featured a practically new line-up of costumed heroes. High impact covers and art, lasting only 10 issues.
(e)

PRIZE COMICS No. 1 (3/40, Prize, H)-High quality anthology series with the debut of *Power Nelson*. First of a publisher. Dick Briefer's unique *Frankenstein* was introduced in No. 7 as well as Simon & Kirby's *Black Owl*. The covers have tremendous eye-appeal.
(a,b,e,j,k)

ROCKET COMICS No. 1 (3/40, Hillman, H)-The title is misleading. This is actually a mixed anthology title with science fiction covers; short-lived with only three issues. Companion mag to *Miracle Comics*. The second Hillman title.
(e)

★ **SHADOW COMICS** No. 1 (3/40, S&S, H)-The venerable pulp hero tested the comic waters with a heavyweight who had dominated both the pulp and radio markets but never quite found his metier in a medium that relied on action over ethereal atmosphere. *Doc Savage*, another renowned pulp character, debuted in this issue. A respectable but

undistinguished run (9 years) probably sustained by popularity of radio program.
(a,b,c,e,f,i,j,k,l)

SLAM BANG COMICS No. 1 (3/40, Faw, An)-Fawcett's third title was an ill conceived adventure anthology starring civilian heroes. This formula had gone out two years before with the appearance of *Superman*. The title was retired after 8 issues.
(e)

SUN FUN KOMIKS No. 1 (3/40, Sun, Hm)-An esoteric one-shot printed in black and red. A satire on comic books. The first of its kind not to be fully developed until *Mad* of 12 years hence.
(e,i,j)

★ ★ ★ ★ **DETECTIVE COMICS** No. 38 (4/40, DC, H)-DC in-itiates yet another breakthrough concept—the apprentice costumed hero. Origin, first appearance of *Robin*, the first and most enduring juvenile aide. For the first time in popular literature, the youthful apprentice was accepted as an equal by his partner. Bob Kane set another standard for the industry to mimic. The foreboding and enigmatic *Batman* was never the same after this issue.
(a,b,c,d,f,h,i,j)

EXCITING COMICS No. 1 (4/40, Better, H)-A sister anthology title to *Thrilling*, becoming Better's second successful series. This title launched *The Black Terror* in No. 9, with Schomburg doing the covers early on (a poor man's Timely). Title lasted 9 years with jungle theme covers at the end.
(b,e,j)

★ ★ **NEW YORK WORLD'S FAIR** (3-5/40, DC, H)-The second comic book produced for a public event, ending the series. The first book to feature *Superman* and *Batman* together on a cover, as well as the first to showcase all of a company's stars, all in one book.
(a,c,j)

SUPERWORLD COMICS No. 1 (4/40, Gernsback, SF)-Following the success of *Planet*, this title takes the honors as the third continuous series science fiction anthology. But Gernsback soon learned that 'raw' science fiction without a unique art style or gimmick (cheesecake) wouldn't sell. Disappeared after only three issues.
(e,k)

WEIRD COMICS No. 1 (4/40, Fox, H)-Another mixed anthology title with costumed heroes. The first to capitalize on this title, which became more common a decade later. Early issues by the Iger shop. First *Birdman* (the third winged hero). First *Thor*, from Greek mythology. Title lasted 2 years.
(e)

BIG SHOT COMICS No. 1 (5/40, CCG, Av)-First *Skyman*, the second aviation hero (noted for his flying wing)(See *Whiz*). The first of a publisher. Mixed anthology series with original and reprint strips (*Joe Palooka*), lasting 9 years.
(a,b,c,d,e,j,k)

CRACK COMICS No. 1 (5/40, Quality, H)-Debut of Fine's *Black Condor* (the fourth winged hero). *Madame Fatal* begins, a bizarre hero who dresses as a woman to fight crime. A top quality series, lasting 9 years.
(a,b,c,d,e)

CRASH COMICS No. 1 (5/40, Tem/Holyoke, H)-The first Simon & Kirby art team-up, whose loose style of action reached maturity a year later with *Captain America*. Kirby was on his way to becoming one of the most influencial ar-

tists in comics. First of a publisher. A short lived mixed anthology series with costumed heroes, lasting 5 issues.
(e,g,k)

DOC SAVAGE COMICS No. 1 (5/40, S&S, H)-The legendary Man of Bronze headlined Street & Smith's second comic title. But it soon became evident that the original 'super man' was out of his depth. His prose adventures, which crackled with vitality in the pulps, seemed bland and derivative in the four-color medium. Outclassed by the characters he inspired, Doc and his title were retired after 3 years of so-so performance.
(c,e)

HYPER MYSTERY COMICS No. 1 (5/40, Hyper, H)-First of a publisher. A costumed hero anthology title which could not compete with the many heroes on the market at this time, lasting 2 issues.
(e,k)

★ **MORE FUN COMICS** No. 55 (5/40, DC, H)-First *Dr. Fate*, DC's second supernatural hero was given immediate cover exposure. Above average art and stories; colorful costume, lasting 3½ years and not achieving his own title.
(a,b,c,d,j)

★ ★ ★ **NICKEL COMICS** No. 1 (5/40, Faw, H)-Introduced *Bulletman*, Fawcett's third costumed hero. This book was experimental, selling for 5 cents, came out biweekly, and lasting only 8 issues. (After *Bulletman* was moved to *Master Comics*, he won his own title in 1941.)
(a,c,d,e,j)

WAR COMICS No. 1 (5/40, Dell, W)-The first single theme anthology series devoted to war. The combat genre did not find a significant market until the outbreak of the Korean conflict a decade later.
(e,i,j)

AMAZING ADVENTURE FUNNIES No. 1 (6/40, Centaur, H)-Outstanding collection of Centaur's best characters reprinted from earlier titles. Centaur was increasingly thrown back to all reprint books. Conjecture is that Timely's sudden success pre-empted all of the Everett shop's time.
(c,e)

★ ★ ★ ★ **BATMAN** No. 1 (Spr/40, DC, H)-Has arrival date of 4/25/40. DC's second strongest character achieved stardom and was given his own title. Assembled from *Detective Comics* inventory, containing the last solo appearance of *The Batman*. *The Joker* and *The Cat* debut. Title has run uninterrupted over four decades.
(a,b,c,e,j)

BLUE BOLT No. 1 (6/40, Novelty, H)-Second of a publisher. Costumed hero anthology title. Important early Simon & Kirby development began in No. 3. The heroes in this series could not be sustained, with *Dick Cole* eventually taking over, lasting 9 years.
(a,b,c,d,e,j)

CYCLONE COMICS No. 1 (6/40, Bilbara, An)-An anthology title with emphasis on subjects other than costumed hero. First of a publisher, expiring after 5 issues.
(e,j,k)

FUTURE COMICS No. 1 (6/40, McKay, R)-McKay's first new title in about a year. A reprint anthology with a science fiction theme (the fourth ever). This issue is noted for *The Phantom's* origin and science fiction cover. Went down for the count after 4 issues.
(e)

★ ★ ★ **SPIRIT, THE** No. 1 (6/2/40, Eisner, D)-A weekly comic book (the only in comics) featuring the blockbuster strip distributed through newspapers. Notably, one of the best written and illustrated strips ever. A trend setter. Ingenious themes; capital atmospheric art with movie-like continuity and humorous plotting. Focus on special effects, lighting and unusual angles, lasting 12 years and endlessly revived. (a,b,c,d,e,f,h,i,j)

STARTLING COMICS No. 1 (6/40, Better, H)-Better's third companion anthology series; *Wonder Man* and *Captain Future* begin. *The Fighting Yank* debuted in No. 10. Schomburg covers began early giving the books more impact. Cover theme changed to science fiction at the end. (a,b,c,e,j)

SURE-FIRE COMICS No. 1 (6/40, Ace, H)-First of a publisher. A super hero anthology title of average quality lasting 4 issues before a title change. (e,k)

WHIRLWIND COMICS No. 1 (6/40, Nita, H)-First of a publisher. A Three-issue run of mediocre quality with no sustaining characters. (e,k)

★ ★ ★ ★ **ALL-AMERICAN COMICS** No. 16 (7/40, DC, H)-DC scored with another winning variation on the mystery man/adventure theme. Origin and first appearance of most enduring of DC's magic oriented heroes. The ancient fable of the magic lamp was transformed into a modern and more accessible, more mysterious form. *The Green Lantern's* chant became a staple of school boy mythology and a great career was launched. Series ended in 1949, although the name continued beyond 4 decades. (a,b,c,d,j)

★ ★ ★ **ALL-STAR COMICS** No. 1 (Sum/40, DC, H)-The first continuous series showcase comic (see *New York World's Fair*, 1940) for giving more exposure to top characters, who all headlined anthology series but as yet were not strong enough to have titles of their own. (This abundance of popular characters was unique to DC, forcing them to come up with this new format.) (a,b,c,e)

FLAME, THE No. 1 (Sum/40, Fox, H)-One of Fox's top characters given prominence, reprinted from *Wonderworld*. Lou Fine art in this issue, but the quality dropped early on, with the title lasting only 1½ years. (c,e)

GREEN MASK, THE No. 1 (Sum/40, Fox, H)-Fox's emerald mystery man achieved stardom, but was squelched early on due to sub-standard art. An intriguing concept that was resurrected several times over the next 15 years, none of which were successful. (c,e)

★ **MARVEL MYSTERY COMICS** No. 9 (7/40, Timely, H)-Epic battle issue. The first time in comics that two super heroes appeared together in one story. *Sub-Mariner* and *The Human Torch* each give up their usual space and battle for 22 pages. A coming together of the ancient basic elements, Water and Fire. Ignited newsstands everywhere. (a,b,c,h,j)

HIT COMICS No. 1 (7/40, Quality, H)-Quality's fourth anthology title. Distinguished primarily by Iger shop graphics (Lou Fine). Non-memorable characters until *Kid Eternity* took over as main feature two years later. Series lasted 10 years. (a,b,e,j)

NATIONAL COMICS No. 1 (7/40, Quality, H)-Of equal quality to *Hit*, Lou Fine at his very best (covers and story art). Debut of *Uncle Sam*, Quality's top patriot. Legendary artist line-up with series lasting 9 years. (a,b,c,d,e,f,j)

OKAY COMICS No. 1 (7/40, UFS, R)-Not having published a new title since 1938 (*Single Series*), United decides to make a comeback. Three new titles are released simultaneously with a fourth the following month. This one-shot issue features *The Captain and the Kids* and *Hawkshaw the Detective*. (e)

OK COMICS No. 1 (7/40, UFS, H)-United tries their first super hero anthology title, but the characters were not strong enough to endure the stiff competition, lasting only two issues. Their second new title for the month. (e)

SHIELD-WIZARD COMICS No. 1 (Sum/40, MLJ, H)-MLJ gave their top two characters joint stardom. A unique concept, titling a book after more than one character to insure its survival—a first in comics. The series lasted 4 years (the dual title wasn't enough). (c,e)

SPARKLER COMICS No. 1 (7/40, UFS, R)-A two-issue reprint anthology series featuring *Jim Hardy* in No. 1 and *Frankie Doodle* in No. 2. United's third new title for the month. (c,e)

SUPER-MYSTERY COMICS No. 1 (7/40, Ace, H)-Ace's second title, featuring more prominent characters and art, becoming their mainstay run. The series lasted 9 years, sustained by colorful covers and top artists. (a,b,c,e)

FANTOMAN No. 2 (8/40, Centaur, H)-Centaur's second title reprinting their top characters and lasting three issues. Their second series of repackaged material. (e)

HEROIC COMICS No. 1 (8/40, Eastern Color, H)-Seven years after introducing *Famous Funnies*, Eastern came out with their second anthology title (their third ever). Original rather than reprinted material. *Hydroman*, a spin-off of the *Sub-Mariner* debuted. Eventually the format was changed to true stories of heroism, lasting 15 years. Top artists included throughout the run. (e)

RED RAVEN COMICS No. 1 (8/40, Timely, H)-A one-shot esoteric super hero book featuring Kirby art. Highly sought after due to its lineage and rarity. Timely's fourth title. (e)

★ ★ ★ ★ **SPECIAL EDITION COMICS** No. 1 (8/40, Fawcett, H)-Due to the enormous popularity of *Whiz's* explosive character, a single theme (Fawcett's first) anthology one-shot of *Captain Marvel* was published. A few months later, he began his own series. Beck cover and story art—high quality throughout. (a,c,e,j)

UNITED COMICS No. 1 (8/40, UFS, R)-The popular *Fritzi Ritz* strip was featured and sustained the run for 12½ years. United's fourth and only successful title in their recent comeback attempt beginning a month earlier. The first comic book series to focus on the career girl theme (proto-type of

Katy Keene).
(a,b,c,e)

CRASH COMICS No. 4(9/40, Holyoke, H)-*Catman* debuted for two issues then stayed dormant for six months before appearing in his own title.
(a,c,d,j)

MASKED MARVEL No. 1 (9/40, Centaur, H)-After exposure in *Keen Detective Funnies*, the crimson sleuth was given his own title, lasting only 3 issues.
(e)

★ **MICKEY MOUSE MAGAZINE** V5/12, (9/40, K.K. F)-This historically significant publication was one step removed from becoming the first official funny animal series. As a magazine, it had evolved through various sizes and formats to finally become a full-fledged comic book. The following month, a title change to *Walt Disney's Comics & Stories* completed the transition.
(a,c,h,j)

PRIZE COMICS No. 7 (9/40, Prize, H)-Debut of Dick Briefer's *Frankenstein* series, and *The Black Owl* by Simon & Kirby. Above average strips with eye-catching covers.
(a,b,c,d,j)

★ **RED RYDER COMICS** No. 1 (9/40, Hawley/Dell, Ws)-A one-shot devoted to the popular strip character by Fred Harman, not becoming a continuous series until Dell picked up the title a year later. Ties with *Tom Mix* as the second book devoted to a single western character, but the first to receive widespread newsstand distribution. Lasted 17 years due to popular movie series. The second title of a publisher.
(a,b,c,e,f,h,i,j,l)

★ ★ ★ **SILVER STREAK COMICS** No. 6 (9/40, Lev, H)-High impact cover of *The Claw* by Jack Cole. Debut of *Daredevil* with his unprecedented costume of dichromatic symmetry. *(See Silver Streak no. 7.)*
(a,b,c,d,f,j)

SKY BLAZERS No. 1 (9/40, Hawley, Av)-Ties with *Red Ryder* as 2nd of a publisher. Inspired by the radio show, not lasting beyond 2 issues.
(e)

★ ★ **TOM MIX** No. 1 (9/40, Ralston, Ws)-The first continuous series single theme western comic, but a giveaway by Ralston—not sold on the stands.
(a,b,c,e,j,k)

★ **WINGS COMICS** No. 1 (9/40, FH, Av)-The publisher's fifth single theme anthology title. The first to focus entirely on aviation (a subject of high appeal to boys of the era). With no competition, the series lasted 14 years.
(a,b,c,e,h,i,j)

ALL-AMERICAN COMICS No. 19 (10/40, DC, H)-Debut of *The Atom* (a hero for short people). Good filler material as a back-up to the main feature, who lasted 4½ years.
(a,b,c,d,f,h,j)

ARROW, THE No. 1 (10/40, Centaur, H)-The very first costume hero (pre-*Batman*) was given prominence after a two-year run in *Funny Pages*. Folded after 3 issues (Centaur phasing out).
(e)

BIG 3 No. 1 (Fall/40, Fox, H)-Fox's first showcase anthology title featuring their top characters together in one magazine. A good idea, but not surviving more than 7 issues.
(e)

BILL BARNES COMICS No. 1 (10/40, S&S, Av)-The celebrated pulp ace got his own comic title, but after three years failed to find an audience. Street & Smith's third title.
(c,e,l)

CHAMP COMICS No. 11 (10/40, Harvey, H)-Continued from *Champion*, now featuring super heroes in full swing. Later on the popular and saleable Simon & Kirby art style was copied as an attempt to sustain the run. The title ended in 1944.
(e)

★ ★ ★ **HUMAN TORCH, THE** No. 2(Fall/40, Timely, H)-From the pages of *Marvel Mystery*, the android flys into his own title. Inspired concept. High impact, eye-catching character, making appearances over the next 40 years.
(a,b,c,e,j)

REX DEXTER OF MARS No. 1 (Fall/40, Fox, SF)-A modest success in *Mysterymen*, but not important enough to carry a title of his own. Expired after one issue.
(e)

SAMSON No. 1 (Fall/40, Fox, H)-One of Fox's top characters from *Fantastic* achieves stardom. Lack-luster art leads to the early death of the run the following year.
(e)

SPORT COMICS No. 1 (10/40, S&S, Sp)-A good idea 'real life' comic series featuring notable sport figures and lasting (through a title change) for 9 years. The first comic series devoted entirely to this theme (see *Champion* and *Fight*).
(b,c,e,h,i,j)

SUPER SPY No. 1 (10/40, Centaur, H)-Late Centaur super hero anthology title, introducing *The Sparkler*. Interesting early vintage comic with only two issues published.
(e)

TOP-NOTCH COMICS No. 9 (10/40, MLJ, H)-Debut of *The Black Hood*, key MLJ hero. One of the few at MLJ to later star in his own title. The costume had eye-appeal which sustained the character, lasting 3 years.
(c,d,j)

★ ★ ★ ★ ★ **WALT DISNEY'S COMICS AND STORIES** No. 1 (10/40, Dell, F)-The first funny animal continuous series comic book title. Miscellaneous collection of proven Disney characters began to come into focus around consistently high quality strips by Taliaferro and Gottfredson, who consistently delivered the goods. The definitive funny animal anthology comic after which all others were modeled. A trend setter. Suspected to have achieved the highest circulation of any comic, lasting beyond 40 years.
(a,b,c,e,h,i,j)

WESTERN DESPERADO COMICS No. 8 (10/40, Fawcett, Ws)-Fawcett's first western theme anthology title, only one issue.
(e)

DETECTIVE EYE No. 1 (11/40, Centaur, H)-More exposure for characters from *Keen Detective Funnies*, lasting 2 issues.
(e)

HI-SPOT COMICS No. 2 (11/40, Hawley, An)-A one-shot book featuring an Edgar Rice Burroughs strip, *David Innes of Pellucidar*.
(e)

WHAM COMICS No. 1 (11/40, Centaur, H)-Another short-lived anthology title, similar to *Super Spy* (reprinting earlier

material).
(e)

★★ **GREEN HORNET COMICS** No. 1 (12/40, Harvey, H)-The respected radio and movie hero tried his wings in comics. Intriguing concept, with a few high points of good artists in the run. He never excelled in the medium, but did present a respectable run of 9 years—probably sustained by the popularity of the radio program.
(a,b,c,e,l)

LIGHTNING COMICS No. 4 (12/40, Ace, H)-Continued from *Sure-Fire*, becoming Ace's third title. Colorful covers (some exceptional) could not sustain the run beyond 18 months.
(e)

DOUBLE COMICS (1940, Elliot, H)-The first attempt at repackaging (and remarketing) remaindered comics. First of a publisher. Elliot produced these unique books for four years, taking advantage of the insatiable public demand for comics.
(e,h,j,k)

GREEN GIANT COMICS No. 1 (1940, Funnies, Inc.)-A very rare one-shot test comic. Conjecture is that its circulation was limited to the New York City area only.
(e,j)

1941 ■

★★★★★ **ALL-STAR COMICS** No. 3 (Wint/40-41, DC, H)-A breakthrough concept, second in importance only to the creation of the super hero. For the first time in comics, top characters come together in one book to form a crime fighting organization *The Justice Society*. A trend setter. Unprecedented in all of literature (the gods of Mt. Olympus weren't on speaking terms; the Knights of the Round Table didn't foregather to confront a common foe). Forerunner of *The Justice League*, and inspiration for many hero groups that followed.
(a,b,c,f,h,i,j)

BUCK ROGERS No. 1 (Wint/40-41, FF, R)-Due to the enormous popularity of the strip in *Famous Funnies*, he earned his own title, which is the first continuous title devoted to a reprint character. Unfortunately, like many other transfer characters, the series didn't last, running only 6 issues.
(a,c,e)

SILVER STREAK COMICS No. 7 (1/41, Lev, H)-Epic clash between *Daredevil* and *The Claw* began in this issue. (Rivaled only by the *Torch-Sub-Mariner* brouhaha). Early enthusiastic work by Jack Cole. *DD's* costume colors change to red and blue, giving him a sinister, demonic appearance (unforgettable). Smash hit series launched *DD* to stardom with own title.
(a,c,f,j)

WOW COMICS No. 1 (Wint/40-41, Faw, H)-Featuring the costumed hero *Mr. Scarlet* (imitation of *Batman*), drawn by Kirby. Included other features with small impact to the comic scene. The major feature of this title was *Mary Marvel*, a *Captain Marvel* clone, who dominated from No. 9 on. This particular issue is highly prized due to its rarity and early Kirby art.
(b,e)

★★★★ **CAPTAIN MARVEL ADVENTURES** nn (1-2/41?, Faw, H)-Following the wake of *Special Edition*, the celebrated character started his own series (this issue illustrated by Kirby), reaching a two-week publication frequen-

cy at one point, lasting 13 years.
(a,b,c,e,j)

BLUE RIBBON COMICS No. 9 (2/41, MLJ, H)-Inspired by DC's *The Spectre*, *Mr. Justice* began this issue and survived to the end of the run (1942).
(d)

★★★★★ **CAPTAIN AMERICA COMICS** No. 1 (3/41, Timely, H)-Simon & Kirby's most classic creation; a patriotic paragon (the second but foremost of patriotic heroes) that set the comics market reeling. A trend setter. One of the top ten most sought after books. With a few interruptions, the character has survived beyond 40 years.
(a,b,c,d,e,g,j)

JACKPOT COMICS No. 1 (Spr/41, MLJ, H)-MLJ's first showcase title to give more exposure to their top characters. The mediocre scripts and art could only keep the run alive for 2 years.
(c,e)

★★★ **SUB-MARINER COMICS** No. 1 (Spr/41, Timely, H)-The aquatic anti-hero is given prominence. The potential of the character was never fully realized. High impact covers, sustaining the run for 8 years.
(a,b,c,e,j)

★★★ **WORLD'S BEST COMICS** No. 1 (Spr/41, DC, H)-Using the successful format of *The World's Fair* books, DC created this title to feature their top two attractions, *Batman* and *Superman*. This was the first thick format continuous series comic (as *World's Finest*). Series lasted beyond 40 years without interruption.
(a,b,c,e,h,j)

★★★ **MICKEY MOUSE FOUR COLOR** No. 16 (4/41?, Dell, F)-The first comic devoted to this world renowned character. The subject of this landmark issue was Gottfredson's classic, *The Phantom Blot*.
(a,b,c,j)

★★ **ADVENTURE COMICS** No. 61 (4/41, DC, H)-*Starman* was introduced as DC continued to create new characters. Visually, an intriguing alternative with enough appeal to last 3½ years in this run, but not quite strong enough to appear in his own title.
(a,b,c,d,j)

TRUE COMICS No. 1 (4/41, PM, TR)-The second anthology series based on true stories (see *Sport Comics*). The first of a publisher, lasting 9 years.
(b,e,h,i,h,k)

AMERICA'S GREATEST COMICS No. 1 (5/41?, Faw, H)-Fawcett's first showcase anthology title (in thick format) featuring their top characters, lasting 8 issues.
(a,c,e)

ARMY AND NAVY No. 1 (5/41, S&S, W)-S&S's fifth anthology title, the second ever with a war theme, lasting 5 issues.
(e)

CATMAN COMICS No. 1 (5/41, Holyoke, H)-Continued from *Crash*, Catman got his own series. Second of a publisher. Adequate, but unexceptional covers and stories. Expired after 5 years.
(a,b,c,e)

EXCITING COMICS No. 9 (5/41, BP, H)-Debut of *The Black Terror*, nemesis of crime. Editors never adequately capitalized on the tremendous eye-appeal of the character. Indifferent scripts, lack-luster art disappointed more often than not. The

indomitable character endured despite lack of staff support. Logical yet striking appearance of costume sustained character.
(a,b,c,d,j)

STARS AND STRIPES COMICS No. 2 (5/41, Centaur, H)-After the failure of Centaur's last flurry of reprint books a year earlier, they tried to make a comeback. Following Timely's newsstand hit, Centaur picked up on the patriotic theme with the first of three books of this type, lasting only 5 issues.
(e)

SUPER MAGIC No. 1 (5/41, S&S, Mg)-A one-shot book featuring *Blackstone the Magician* and *Rex King*. The first title to focus on magicians. The title was modified to **Super Magician** and the series lasted 6 years.
(b,e,i,j)

LIBERTY SCOUTS No. 2 (6/41, Centaur, H)-Centaur's second patriotic theme series lasted only two issues.
(e)

★★★ **ALL FLASH COMICS** No. 1 (Sum/41, DC, H)-The hero of speed achieved stardom and was given his own title. Momentarily retired after 6 years.
(a,b,c,e)

★ **ALL WINNERS COMICS** No. 1 (Sum/41, Timely, H)-First Timely showcase title to give more exposure to their top characters. High impact covers and characters sustained run for 5 years.
(a,c,e)

★★ **BULLETMAN** No. 1 (7/41, Faw, H)-The hit of *Master Comics*, receives his own title, lasting 5 years. The Raboy cover and silver logo gets the series off to a good start.
(a,c,e)

CAPTAIN BATTLE COMICS No. 1 (Sum/41, Lev, H)-The third patriotic hero (see *Pep Comics* and **Captain America**) from *Silver Streak* is given his own title. Lacked necessary distinctiveness to compete, folding with the second issue.
(e)

★★ **DAREDEVIL COMICS** No. 1 (7/41, Lev, H)-High impact cover, inspired costume design and massive support from Biro's strong, complex plotting sustained momentum of ''The Greatest Name in Comics'' splash debut. Immediately stood out from the hordes of rival strongmen glutting the stands. Series prevailed for 15 years.
(a,b,c,e,j)

EAGLE, THE No. 1 (7/41, Fox, H)-Another publisher on the patriotic band wagon. *The Eagle* only flew for four issues.
(e)

FUNNIES, THE No. 57 (7/41, Dell, H)-Debut of *Captain Midnight*, a patriotic aviation hero who was an established attraction on radio. He was also featured in Dell's *Popular Comics* before being picked up by Fawcett as a regular series.
(a,c,d,j)

MINUTEMAN No. 1 (7/41, Faw, H)-Fawcett's answer to a patriotic hero who began in **Master Comics**. This less than distinguished hero only lasted three issues in his own title.
(e)

PEP COMICS No. 17 (7/41, MLJ, H)-Landmark issue. The first time in comics that a major character (*The Comet*) actually died, and a new character (*The Hangman*) was created in the same story.
(a,b,c,d,h)

SPARKLER COMICS No. 1 (7/41, UFS, R)-After three years of costumed heroes glutting the stands, UFS tries its second costumed hero series. Debut of *Sparkman*, a colorful character who eventually gave way to *Tarzan* and other reprint characters, title proved competitive through 14 years.
(a,b,c,e,j)

★ **YOUNG ALLIES** No. 1 (Sum/41, Timely, H)-The first sidekick team in comics. The *Red Skull* guest-starred to give the title a good send-off. Proto-type of the more successful *Teen Titans* of 25 years hence, it managed a respectable run of 5 years.
(e,f,h,i,j)

CAPTAIN FEARLESS No. 1 (8/41, Helnit, H)-Third of a publisher. An interesting mix of super patriots not lasting beyond the second issue.
(e)

★★★★ **MILITARY COMICS** No. 1 (8/41, Qua, Av)-Otherwise predictable war-theme anthology (the third of its kind) sparked by debut of aviation feature of geniune classic proportions. The crack *Blackhawk* team took command of the series and continued at the helm 9 years after a title change (to **Modern Comics**) indicated the public had grown jaded with war-themes generally. Ace concept (air-borne privateers meet the axis on its own terms) backed by sterling Iger graphics (the shop's piece de resistance) and top-drawer scripting propelled feature into its own title and a phenomenal 40 year run (with interruptions). The introduction of *Blackhawk*, and *Plastic Man* later the same month, lifted Quality into the first rank of comics publishers. A masterpiece of collaborative art.
(a,b,c,d,e,f,h,i,j)

OUR FLAG COMICS No. 1 (8/41, Ace, H)-Ace joined the other publishers with a host of patriotic strongmen debuting in this book. High impact patriotic cover. Series lasted 5 issues.
(e,j)

POCKET COMICS No. 1 (8/41, Harv, H)-An experimental pocket size comic book series featuring Harvey's top characters. Most divergent forms didn't last long and this was no exception, expiring after 4 issues.
(e)

★★★★ **POLICE COMICS** No. 1 (8/41, Quality, H)-Debut of one of the most ingenious super heroes in comics, *Plastic Man*. An original concept, fully exploited by Jack Cole in the ensuing years. Sheer entertainment with the incomparable *Cole* at the top of his form. Shares standard bearer honors with **Military**, lasting 12 years.
(a,b,c,d,e,f,i,j)

★ **RED RYDER COMICS** No. 3 (8/41, Hawley, Ws)-The first continuous series single theme western comic for newsstand sales. Ties back to a one-shot issue of a year earlier. Title lasted 16 years due to popular movie series.
(a,b,c,e,f,h,i,j)

SPITFIRE COMICS No. 1 (8/41, Harvey, Av)-An experimental aviation pocket size comic book, lasting 2 issues.
(e)

★ **UNCLE SAM QUARTERLY** No. 1 (8/41, Qua, H)-Eisner's version of a patriotic hero, the star of **National Comics**, is given his own book, lasting 8 issues. Usual Iger shop excellence.
(e)

USA COMICS No. 1 (8/41, Timely, H)-Timely, extending the

patriotic theme, created another showcase title for introducing new characters. After five issues, their trend setting *Captain America* was brought in to save the run and it endured 4 years.
(a,c,e)

VICTORY COMICS No. 1 (8/41, Hill, H)-Classic Everett Nazi war cover. Hillman tried their third title, this time with a patriotic costumed hero theme, again unsuccessfully. It lasted only 4 issues.
(e)

BANNER COMICS No. 3 (9/41, Ace, H)-Debut of *Captain Courageous*, a derivative patriotic hero—not prominent enough to survive more than 3 issues.
(e)

CALLING ALL GIRLS No. 1 (9/41, PMI, TR)-Second of a publisher. The true fact anthology, with biographies of famous persons and sketches of historic events (occassionally mixed with magazine-type photo features), was a comics format pioneered by Parent's Magazine Institute. Here the target audience was adolescent girls. Similar titles were cloned later on. Enjoyed a run of 7 years.
(b,e,f,h,i,j)

FOUR FAVORITES No. 1 (9/41, Ace, H)-Ace's first showcase title featuring their top characters together in one book, lasting 6 years.
(e)

REAL HEROES COMICS No. 1 (9/41, PMI, TR)-With the success of *True Comics*, the publisher attempted another title based on true stories. Their third series, lasting 5 years. *Heroic Comics* was later converted to this theme.
(e)

REAL LIFE COMICS No. 1 (9/41, BP, TR)-Inspired by the newsstand success of PMI's *True Comics*, this publisher came out with their version, lasting 11 years.
(b,e)

STARTLING COMICS No. 10 (9/41, BP, H)-Debut of *The Fighting Yank*, America's super patriot. Interesting variation on the patriotic theme in that he could call up heroes from the American revolution to assist in the modern fight against crime. Tremendous eye-appeal of character never fully realized due to low standard story art. High impact Schomburg covers sustained the run.
(a,b,c,d,j)

SUPER MAGICIAN COMICS No. 2 (9/41, S&S, Mg)-The first continuous series anthology title on the subject of magic, continuing from *Super Magic* and lasting 6 years.
(e,j)

YANKEE COMICS No. 1 (9/41, Chesler, H)-Chesler re-entered the comic market with this patriotic title. Debut of *Yankee Doodle Jones*. Sensational patriotic cover. Despite its visual appeal, it endured only 4 issues.
(e)

★ ★ ★ ★ **CLASSIC COMICS** No. 1 (10/41, Gil, Lit)-First and most enduring of 'educational' theme comics, Gilberton drew on works of great literature for their highly visible newsstand product. One of the few lines that could be endorsed without reservation by parents and educators, its marketing success was not tied to single-theme titles or continuing characters. Variable art quality somewhat diminished the overall impact of the line. The only comic publisher to place each issue into endless reprints while continuing to publish new titles on a monthly basis, lasting 30 years.

(a,b,c,e,f,h,i,j,k)

DOLL MAN No. 1 (Fall/41, Qua, H)-After a successful two-year run in *Feature*, the mighty mite leaped into his own title, lasting 12 years. The proto-type of the Silver Age Atom.
(a,b,c,e,j)

DYNAMIC COMICS No. 1 (10/41, Chesler, H)-Chesler's second patriotic super hero series. Debut of *Major Victory*. Suspended after three issues and brought back with a format change in 1944, lasting four more years.
(e)

★ ★ ★ **GREEN LANTERN** No. 1 (Fall/41, DC, H)-Having headlined *All-American* for one year, one of DC's foremost heroes achieved the distinction of his own title. It ran for 8 years and went on to become one of the key revival characters of the Silver Age.
(a,b,c,e)

★ ★ ★ ★ **LOONEY TUNES & MERRY MELODIES** No. 1 (Fall/41, Dell, F)-The companion title to the enormously successful *WDC&S*. Dell's second funny animal anthology featured *Bugs Bunny*, *Porky Pig* and *Elmer Fudd*. This was the first comic book appearance of Warner Brothers film characters. The series ran for 21 years.
(a,b,c,e,h,j,l)

RANGERS COMICS No. 1(10/41, FH, W)-The publisher's sixth single theme anthology title (war theme). Standard FH style of cheesecake art and covers, lasting 11 years.
(a,b,c,e)

SKYMAN No. 1 (Fall/41, CCG, Av)-After a year's successful run in *Big Shot*, he was given his own title. Second of a publisher, lasting only 4 issues. (He remained the main feature in *Big Shot* for 9 years.)
(a,c,e)

★ ★ **SPYSMASHER** No. 1 (Fall/41, Faw, Av)-Popular war hero graduating from *Whiz* into his own title, lasting 2 years. Maiden issue featured unusual logo printed in metallic silver.
(a,c,e)

STAR SPANGLED COMICS No. 1(10/41, DC, H)-DC's first patriotic theme title featuring the *Star Spangled Kid*. Due to the weak contents, the title had a dramatic format change with No. 7 when *The Guardian* and *The Newsboy Legion* were introduced.
(b,e)

WORLD FAMOUS HEROES MAGAZINE No. 1 (10/41, Comic Corp, TR)-Similar theme to PMI's *Real Heroes*, and Eastern's *Heroic*, with stories of famous people, lasting 4 issues.
(e)

AIRFIGHTERS COMICS No. 1 (11/41, Hill, Av)-An early attempt at an aviation theme comic (like *Wings*), lasting only one issue. A year later the title was revived more successfully with a new 'dynamic' character in *Airboy*.
(e)

GREAT COMICS No. 1 (11/41, Great, H)-First of a publisher, featuring super heroes. The third and last issue is a classic: *Futuro* takes *Hitler* to hell.
(e,k)

MAN OF WAR No. 1 (11/41, Centaur, H)-Centaur's third and last patriotic theme title, lasting 2 issues. Conjecture is that Centaur itself expired with this book.
(e)

SCOOP COMICS No. 1 (11/41, Chesler, H)-Chesler's third attempt at a comeback with this anthology of super heroes. Debut of *Rocketman* and *Rocketgirl*, lasting 8 issues.
(e)

U.S. JONES No. 1 (11/41, Fox, H)-Fox's second patriotic theme title, lasting 2 issues.
(e)

★ ★ ★ ★ **ALL-STAR COMICS** No. 8 (11-12/41, DC, H)-*Wonder Woman*, the first super-heroine, created by Charles Moulton and drawn by H.G. Peter, debuted in this issue as an 8 page add-on. Her origin continued in *Sensation* No. 1, where she becomes the lead feature. A trend setter.
(a,b,c,d,f,h,i,j)

BANG-UP COMICS No. 1 (12/41, Progressive, H)-A new publisher entered the field. This series was mediocre in its content only surviving 3 issues.
(e,k)

CAPTAIN AERO COMICS No. 7 (12/41, Hoke, Av)-Cashing in on the popularity of *Spy Smasher* and *Captain Midnight*, this publisher began with another aviation hero. With strong, colorful covers, the series lasted 5 years.
(e)

CHOICE COMICS No. 1 (12/41, Great, H)-The publisher's second title. A mixed anthology, lasting 3 issues.
(e)

MASTER COMICS No. 21 (12/41, Faw, H)-*Captain Marvel* and *Bulletman* team-up to fight *Captain Nazi*. A classic battle sequence, rare in comics at this time. High impact (classic) Raboy cover and story art.
(a,b,c)

PIONEER PICTURE STORIES No. 1 (12/41, S&S, TR)-An anthology of true stories about heroes (ala *Heroic Comics*), lasting 9 issues.
(e)

★ ★ ★ ★ **PEP COMICS** No. 22 (12/41, MLJ, TA)-The eternal sophomore and his friends began the first of over forty consecutive terms at Riverdale High. Never rose above pat formula, but survived vagaries of shifting market that did in a host of illustrious predecessors and glut of imitators (many of which originated at MLJ itself). Auxillary characters achieved stardom with their own titles. Trend setter, lasting beyond 40 years.
(a,b,c,d,f,h,i,j)

PUNCH COMICS No. 1 (12/41, Chesler, H)-Chesler's fourth attempt to get back into the market. A mixed anthology series with a successful format, lasting 6 years.
(e)

★ ★ ★ **WHIZ COMICS** No. 25 (12/12/41, Faw, H)-*Captain Marvel* was cloned for the second time (see *Lt. Marvels*) into a junior size as *Captain Marvel Jr*. Classic art by Mac Raboy gave the character a slick streamlined 'Raymond' look. He was given immediate headlining in *Master Comics*. This was the first significant character cloned.
(a,b,c,d,j)

X-MAS COMICS No. 1 (12/41, Faw, H)-A new concept. Earlier in the year, Fawcett began over-running certain selected comics with indicias, page numbers, etc. removed. These comics were then bound up into a thick book (324 pgs.) to be sold as a special comic for Christmas. This successful format evolved into several other titles and lasted for 11 years.

(a,b,c,e,f,h,j)

CAPTAIN MARVEL THRILL BOOK nn (1941, Faw, H)-A large-size black & white comic reprinting popular *Captain Marvel* stories, lasting one issue. (Half text, half illustration.)
(e)

DICKIE DARE No. 1 (1941, Eastern, R)-Another single theme anthology title of the popular strip, lasting 4 issues.
(e)

DOUBLE UP nn (1941, Elliott, H)-The same idea as *Double*, except this was a one-shot remarketing of remaindered digest-sized issues of *Speed*, *Spitfire* and *Pocket*. Probably a special deal to Elliott due to heavy returns?
(e)

FACE, THE No. 1 (1941, CCG, H)-The popular strip from *Big Shot* achieved brief stardom, lasting only two issues.
(e)

KEY RING COMICS (1941, Dell, An)-A special formated comic series of 16 pages each to put in a two-ring binder (sold as a set of five).
(e)

TRAIL BLAZERS No. 1 (1941, S&S, TR)-True fact anthology of heroic deeds, lasting 4 issues.
(e)

USA IS READY No. 1 (1941, Dell, W)-Dell's second war title lasting one issue.
(e)

★ ★ ★ **ANIMAL COMICS** No. 1 (12-1/41-42, Dell, F)-Debut of Walt Kelly's classic character, *Pogo*, which became syndicated in 1948. Dell's third funny animal single theme anthology title following the success of *WDC&S* and *Looney Tunes*. The first funny animal comic with original characters at Dell.
(a,c,d,e,j)

1942 ■

FOUR MOST No. 1 (Wint/41-42, Novelty, H)-A showcase title featuring Novelty's best characters from *Target* and *Blue Bolt*. Series taken over by *Dick Cole* with No. 3 on. Their third title.
(a,b,c,e)

★ **LEADING COMICS** No. 1 (Wint/41-42, DC, H)-Like *All-Star*, this title provided a showcase for DC's secondary heroes (a poor man's *All-Star*). Series ran 14 issues then changed to a funny animal format for the rest of its 7 year existance.
(e)

★ ★ ★ ★ ★ **SENSATION COMICS** No. 1 (1/42, DC, H)-*Wonder Woman's* origin continued from *All-Star* No. 8 (her first appearance). A very strong character from the onset, achieving stardom instantly as a headline feature of this series. She won her own title within a few months which has run uninterrupted for over 40 years. (One of the few characters to achieve this kind of exposure.)
(a,b,c,e,f,h,j)

SPECIAL COMICS No. 1 (Wint/41-42, MLJ, H)-A one-shot special featuring *The Hangman* from *Pep Comics*. A hit on the stands, the character was launched into his own series with No. 2.
(c,e)

V...- COMICS No. 1 (1/42, Fox, H)-another short-lived title

from Fox. His third patriotic theme comic. Introduced *V-Man*, lasted only two issues.
(e)

AMERICA'S BEST COMICS No. 1 (2/42, BP, H)-A showcase title to give more exposure to their top characters. The high impact covers (many by Schomburg) sustained the run, lasting 7 years.
(a,b,c,e)

CAMP COMICS No. 1 (2/42, Dell, Hm)-A mixed (humorous) anthology title with pretty girl photo covers. An unusual format slanted to the soldier boys at camp.
(e)

★ ★ **GENE AUTRY COMICS** No. 1 (2/42, Faw, Ws)-The second newsstand continuous series western title devoted to a single character. *Gene* ties with *Roy Rogers* as the most popular cowboy star of the sound era. Title survived 18 years.
(a,b,c,e,h,j,l)

JINGLE JANGLE COMICS No. 1 (2/42, Eastern Color, Hm)-A young children's comic, containing illustrations and script by George Carlson, a children's book heavyweight (*Uncle Wiggily*). Eastern's second anthology title of original material (see *Heroic*), lasting 7 years.
(a,b,e,j)

TRUE SPORT PICTURE STORIES No. 5 (2/42, S&S, Sp)-Continued from *Sport Comics*, lasting 7 years.
(e)

CAPTAIN COURAGEOUS COMICS No. 6 (3/42, Ace, H)-Introduced in *Banner*, the character was given his own title but lasted only one issue.
(e)

TOUGH KID SQUAD No. 1 (3/42, Timely, H)-Timely's second series devoted to sidekicks (see *Young Allies*). Highly prized due to its rarity.
(e)

★ ★ **BOY COMICS** No. 3 (4/42, Lev, H)-Gleason's second successful title, introducing *Crimebuster*. This series survived 14 years due to Biro's strong, complex plotting.
(a,b,c,d,e,j)

COMEDY COMICS No. 9 (4/42, Timely, H)-The title is misleading. A super hero anthology title changing to a humorous and funny animal format early on.
(e)

HANGMAN COMICS No. 2 (Spr/42, MLJ, H)-The smash hit of *Pep Comics* received his own series, but lasted only 7 issues.
(e)

★ **JOKER COMICS** No. 1 (4/42, Timely, Hm)-First *Powerhouse Pepper* by Wolverton. Wolverton, an original if there ever was one, stood totally aloof from the mainstream of comic art. His effect on later comics ranging from the original *Mad* to the sixties undergrounds, is incalculable. (He tried to fit in, but the effect of playing it straight made his work even more bizzarre.)
(a,b,c,d,e,f,g,j)

SHEENA, QUEEN OF THE JUNGLE No. 1 (Spr/42, FH, J)-After three years exposure in *Jumbo Comics*, *Sheena* finally graduated to her own title, lasting 18 issues spread over 11 years.
(a,b,c,e)

★ ★ **STAR SPANGLED COMICS** No. 7 (4/42, DC, H)-Debut

of *The Guardian* and *The Newsboy Legion* by Simon and Kirby (vintage). Title lasted 11 years.
(a,b,c,d,j)

WAMBI, JUNGLE BOY No. 1 (Spr/42, FH, J)-From *Jungle Comics*. Not strong enough to carry his own title which had erratic publishing (18 issues in 11 years).
(e)

★ ★ ★ ★ **CRIME DOES NOT PAY** No. 22 (6/42, Lev, C)-Aside from being the first crime comic, this title was the first of many to be deliberately targeted at the adult reader. Inspired by the widely read *True Detective* - style magazines of the time. Implicit and unsavory subject matter, in the context of what was popularly understood as publications for children, assured the attention and disapproval of Wertham and others. Established conventions of graphically depicted violence that would be exploited to the extreme in the horror comics of a decade later. Arguably the third most influential comic ever published (after *Action* and *Superman*), *CDNP* was a belated trend setter. Gleason had the field all to himself for six years. Then, in 1948 the industry suffered a severe slump in sales. In desperation, publishers turned en masse to the formerly untapped 'crime' market. This move was abetted in part by Gleason himself. In mid-1947 he had begun publishing circulation figures on the covers of *CDNP*, reporting sales of 5 million - 6 million copies (per issue?), an astounding record for a comics periodical and, an open invitation to imitation.
(a,b,c,e,f,h,i,j)

★ **DETECTIVE COMICS** No. 64 (6/42, DC, H)-Simon and Kirby introduce the *Boy Commandos*. A more timely version of the *Newsboy Legion*, this popular series found the Axis plagued with a platoon of wise-cracking juveniles. An immediate hit, the lads were rewarded with a quarterly of their own within a matter of months.
(a,c,d,j)

FAIRY TALE PARADE No. 1 (6-7/42, Dell, F)-Dell's second continuous series funny animal title with original characters. Its popularity was carried entirely by the imaginative illustrative genius of Walt Kelly.
(c,e)

BIG CHIEF WAHOO No. 1 (7/42, Eastern, R)-Popular transfer strip debuts in his own comic series, lasting 23 issues.
(c,e)

DIXIE DUGAN No. 1 (7/42, CCG, R)-Popular strip character given own title, lasting 7 years (13 issues).
(e)

KRAZY KOMICS No. 1 (7/42, Timely, F)-With four funny animal anthology titles on the stands (all by Dell), Timely entered this new developing field. This series had a humorous format with no strong characters, lasting 4 years. The second publisher in this genre.
(e)

NAPOLEON AND UNCLE ELBY No. 1 (7/42), Eastern Color, R)-A one-shot single theme anthology title of the popular transfer strip.
(e)

NEW FUNNIES No. 65 (7/42, Dell, F)-The funny animal fever was catching on as Dell gave stardom to their newly acquired characters, *Andy Panda* and *Woody Woodpecker*. Lantz created these characters who became an instant success for Dell's *The Funnies*. This was Dell's fifth funny animal series (with only six on the stands).

(a,b,c,e,j)

OAKY DOAKS No. 1 (7/42, Eastern Color, R)-A one-shot strip reprint book which couldn't compete on the stands.
(e)

STRICTLY PRIVATE No. 1 (7/42), Eastern Color, R)-A two-issue run of the famous strip, not surviving as a comic book.
(e)

WAR VICTORY ADVENTURES No. 1 (Sum/42, Harv, W)-A unique super hero title produced to promote purchase of war savings bonds, lasting 3 issues.
(e)

★ ★ ★ ★ **WONDER WOMAN** No. 1 (Sum/42, DC, H)-One of the few characters in comics to make her own title just months from her debut in **All-Star** No. 8. The only mythological character to flourish in the comics format, her only concession to the present was adopting a modern costume. The amazing Amazon was a trend setter whose popularity has lasted beyond 40 years.
(a,b,c,e,j)

WAR HEROES No. 1 (7-9/42, Dell, W)-Dell's third war title, lasting 11 issues.
(e)

★ **CAPTAIN MIDNIGHT** No. 1 (9/42, Faw, Av)-This book heralds one of the most changed transfer characters adapted successfully to the comic book format. Fawcett's version of the character is the most memorable (see **The Funnies** No. 57), lasting 6 years. Kept alive by the long lasting radio series and a movie serial. A spin-off of **Spy Smasher**.
(a,b,c,e)

FIGHTING YANK No. 1 (9/42, BP, H)-After a year's exposure in **Startling**, the colonial hero was given his own series. The outstanding Schomburg covers sustained the run, lasting 7 years.
(a,b,c,e,j)

OUR GANG COMICS No. 1 (9-10/42, Dell, F)-A strong early licensed group from MGM films who didn't quite come across as well in the comic medium due to necessary changes in the stereotyping of **Buckwheat** and others. The comic version is mainly collected due to the outstanding art by Walt Kelly and the back-up strips by Carl Barks.
(a,b,c,e,f,j,l)

★ **COO COO COMICS** No. 1 (10/42, BP, F)-Seeing the stands beginning to swell with Dell's funny animal titles (5), Better got on the band wagon. **Super Mouse** debuted, the first funny animal super hero (cloned from **Superman**). (7 funny animal titles now on the stands.)
(a,b,c,d,e,f,h,i,j)

★ ★ ★ ★ ★ **DONALD DUCK FOUR COLOR** No. 9 (10/42, Dell, F)-Debut of anonymous artist, who breathed life into the character and turned the strip into full-length adventure stories. Carl Barks' successful adaptation won him the position as **Donald Duck's** biographer for almost three decades beginning with **Walt Disney's Comics and Stories** No. 31.
(a,b,c,g,h,j)

★ **JUNGLE GIRL** No. 1 (Fall/42, Faw, J)-Inspired by the popular film serial, **Perils of Nyoka**, this one-shot introduced the jungle heroine to comics. The series was picked up again in 1945 (retitled **Nyoka**), lasting 8 years.
(a,b,c,e,f,j,l)

PICTURE STORIES FROM THE BIBLE No. 1 (Fall/42, DC, TR)-The pilot model of M. C. Gaines' projected 'educational comics' line was laudable in concept but squelched at the stands by abysmal art, pedantic scripting and the normal resistance of kids to anything even remotely preachy. Sustained primarily by lot sales to educators and church groups. Ironically, the first comic ever to bear the EC seal.
(a,c,e,i,j,l)

SUPERSNIPE COMICS No. 6 (10/42, S&S, H)-Probably the best, and certainly the most original comic book character of this pulp publisher. A super hero parody lasting 7 years.
(a,b,c,e,f,j)

★ **TERRY-TOONS COMICS** No. 1 (10/42, Timely, F)-20th Century Fox's characters enter the comic field with this book. Timely's second funny animal anthology series (8 titles are now on the stands). 20th Century Fox's **Mighty Mouse** appeared in films the following year and entered this run with No. 38.
(a,b,c,e,j,l)

★ **AIR FIGHTERS** No. 2 (11/42, Hill, Av)-First appearance of one of the top aviation features also marked Hillman's first successful title. Engaging origin featured air-minded monk who designed and built the premier imaginary aircraft in all of comics. At the controls of the unusual bat-winged orinthopter, dubbed **Birdie**, was the youth who would become known as **Airboy**. He managed to make the standard garb of the pilot—goggles, scarf, flight jacket, et al—look as if they were designed expressly for him. Thoughtful scripting and complimentary art (ala Caniff) propelled this feature through the war years and beyond. Duration 11 years. (**The Heap**, one of the most original characters in comics, began in the next issue.)
(a,b,c,d,j)

★ ★ **CAPTAIN MARVEL JR** No. 1 (11/42, Faw, H)-Fawcett's second most popular hero (from **Master**) was given his own series. Raboy classic covers/story art sustained the run, lasting 11 years.
(a,b,c,e)

MICKEY FINN No. 1 (11/42, Eastern Color, R)-The popular transfer character tried his wings in a title of his own. Like **Sparky Watts**, only 17 issues came out in a 10 year period.
(a,c,e)

SPARKY WATTS No. 1 (11/42, CCG, R)-Humorous, off-beat character (proven in **Big Shot**) is given own title, struggling through 10 issues in 7 years.
(a,c,e)

TOPIX No. 1 (11/42, CG, Re)-The first continuous series comic with a religious theme, lasting 10 years. First of a publisher.
(b,e,i,j,k)

★ **CAPTAIN MARVEL ADVENTURES** No. 18 (12/11/42, Faw, H)-Captain Marvel is cloned again. Debut of **Mary Marvel** and **The Marvel Family**. **Mary Marvel** was given instant stardom in **Wow**.
(a,b,c,d,j)

FAWCETT'S FUNNY ANIMAL COMICS No. 1 (12/42, Faw, F)-The first appearance of **Hoppy The Marvel Bunny**, (cloned from **Captain Marvel**), lasting 13 years. The second funny animal super hero (see **Coo Coo**). Fawcett joined Dell, Timely and Better entering the funny animal market (10 titles now on the stands). (**Captain Marvel** himself introduced **Hoppy** on the cover.)
(a,b,c,d,e,h,j)

FUNNY BOOK No. 1 (12/42, PMI, F)-Another publisher entered the funny animal market with this book. Weak con-

cepts overall, the title lasting 9 issues over 4 years (10 titles now on the stands).
(e)

GIFT COMICS No. 1 (12/42, Faw, H)-Fawcett's second thick-format title containing original comics to be released at Christmas with *Holiday* and *Xmas* for 50¢.
(a,c,e)

HIT COMICS No. 25 (12/42, Qua, H)-*Kid Eternity* debuts. Recurring war-era theme of life after life was given novel twist in this long running series. Youthful hero, dying ahead of his appointed time, was not only miraculously restored to life but granted the ability to call on all the great heroes of the past for assistance in solving crimes (see *The Fighting Yank*). Intriguing concept was given usual stellar Iger shop treatment.
(a,b,c,d,j)

HOLIDAY COMICS No. 1 (12/42, Faw, H)-Fawcett's third thick-format title of original comics to be released at Christmas with *Gift* and *Xmas* for 25¢.
(a,c,e)

SANTA CLAUS FUNNIES No. 1 (12/42, Dell, F)-A special Christmas book illustrated by Kelly. A successful concept that was repeated annually for 20 years.
(a,b,c,e)

AMERICA IN ACTION nn (1942, Dell, W)-A one-shot war anthology book.
(e)

FAMOUS STORIES No. 1 (1942, Dell, Lit)-An educational theme comic, similar to *Classic Comics*, not lasting beyond the 2nd issue.
(e)

JOE PALOOKA No. 1 (1942, CCG, R)-With proven success in *Big Shot* (not to mention syndication), the character became a star in his own title. Early issues boast "over 1,000,000 copies sold." The series lasted 19 years.
(a,b,c,e)

WAR STORIES No. 1 (1942, Dell, W)-Dell's fourth war theme anthology title, lasting 8 issues. *Night Devils*, a mysterious costumed war team debuted in No. 3.
(e)

1943 ■

ALL NEW COMICS No. 1 (1/43, Harv, H)-A super hero anthology title of mediocre quality, lasting 15 issues.
(e)

★ ★ ★ **ARCHIE COMICS** No. 1 (Wint/42-43, AP, TA)-Early stardom for a non-super hero theme. A successful formula with many spin-off characters, lasting beyond 40 years.
(a,b,c,d,e,h,i,j)

BLACK TERROR No. 1 (Wint/42-43, BP, H)-Fighting his way from *Exciting*, the character begins his own series. Sterling costume. High impact Schomburg covers mislead the buyer as to the quality of the contents. Lasted 7 years.
(a,b,c,e,j)

BOY COMMANDOS No. 1 (Wint/42-43, DC, W)-After *Captain America*, this was the second title that Simon and Kirby had all to themselves. Pat variation of favorite S&K theme: Kid group with adult mentor. Seldom rose above the expected, but S&K were at their loosest and the strip conveys the sense of fun they probably had doing it. Earlier covers, sans redundant blurbs and intrusive dialogue balloons, are

superb poster art.
(a,b,c,e,j)

CAPTAIN BATTLE No. 3 (Wint/42-43, Mag. Press, H)-After a year's delay, the character from *Silver Streak* was given another chance, only lasting 3 issues.
(e)

CLUE COMICS No. 1 (1/43, Hill, H)-Hillman's second most successful title. Unusual heroes and bizarre villains sustained run for four years.
(e)

COMIC CAVALCADE No. 1 (Wint/42-43, DC, H)-Following the success of *World's Finest*, DC launched this companion book in thick format featuring their next tier of top characters, *Wonder Woman*, *The Flash* and *Green Lantern*.
(a,b,c,e)

COMICS DIGEST No. 1 (Wint/42-43, PMI, TR)-A one-shot war theme reprint anthology (pocket size) from *True Comics*.
(e)

FLYING CADET No. 1 (1/43, Flying Cadet, Av)-A true theme World War II aviation anthology (with real photos), lasting 4 years.
(e)

GOLDEN ARROW No. 1 (Wint/42-43, Faw, Ws)-Fawcett's original western character from *Whiz* finally given own title, lasting 6 issues.
(a,e)

HELLO PAL COMICS No. 1 (1/43, Harv, An)-Unusual format featuring photographic covers of movie stars. *Rocketman* and *Rocketgirl* appear (see *Scoop*), lasting 3 issues.
(e)

MISS FURY COMICS No. 1 (Wint/42-43, Timely, H)-A strong transfer character by Tarpe Mills. Noteworthy and unique in that she rarely appeared in costume.
(a,c,e,f,j)

MAJOR HOOPLE COMICS No. 1 (1/43, BP, R)-A one-shot comic of the famous strip character, as Better tried to enter the reprint market.
(e)

REAL FUNNIES No. 1 (1/43, Nedor, F)-The publisher's second funny animal title (11 titles now on stands), only lasting 3 issues. First appearance of *The Black Terrier* (cloned from *The Black Terror*), the third funny animal super hero.
(e)

RED DRAGON COMICS No. 5 (1/43, S&S, An)-Pulpy anthology series not strong enough to last over 5 issues.
(e)

DON WINSLOW OF THE NAVY No. 1 (2/43, Faw, W)-His comic book career was launched here with an introduction by *Captain Marvel* himself. Successful adaptation of this popular transfer character, lasting 12 years.
(a,b,c,e,j,l)

HEADLINE COMICS No. 1 (2/43, Prize, TR)-Taking up the "True" theme of PMI's *True* and *Real Heroes* and Better's *Real Life*, Prize entered the field with this, their second title, which lasted 13 years.
(b,e)

HOPALONG CASSIDY No. 1 (2/43, Faw, Ws)-A one-shot issue continuing as a series three years later. The third continuous series newsstand western title, lasting 16 years. A transfer character kept alive by William Boyd's strong follow-

ing in the movies and on TV.
(a,b,c,e)

IBIS, THE INVINCIBLE No. 1 (2/43, Faw, Mg)-As a solid back-up feature in *Whiz*, he was invincible, but not invincible enough to support a title of his own. The title expired after 6 issues.
(e)

KID KOMICS No. 1 (2/43, Timely, H)-Timely's third series devoted to sidekicks. The Schomburg covers and guest appearances of secondary characters sustained the run through 10 issues.
(e)

ALL HERO COMICS No. 1 (3/43, Faw, H)-Fawcett's second title that showcased their top characters (see *America's Greatest*). A thick format one-shot.
(a,c,e)

CAPTAIN MARVEL ADVENTURES No. 22 (3/43, Faw, H)-Begins the 25-issue *Mr. Mind* serial which captured nationwide attention at the time. Tremendous and brilliant marketing strategy by Fawcett. An epic by any standard, unmatched before or since.
(c,d,f,h,i,j)

COMEDY COMICS No. 14 (3/43, Timely, F)-The first *Super Rabbit* (the fourth funny animal super hero) (the 12th title on the stands). Given his own title the following year. (An imitation of *Hoppy The Marvel Bunny*.)
(a,c,d,e,j)

FUNNY FUNNIES No. 1 (4/43, BP, F)-A one-shot funny animal title (their third) (13 titles now on the stands). No enduring characters.
(e)

★ ★ ★ ★ **WALT DISNEY'S COMICS AND STORIES** No. 31 (4/43, Dell, F)-Anonymous staffer who defined what funny animal continuity is all about began this issue (2nd Barks *DD* story; see *DD Four Color* No. 9). Cinched long-term success of Disney anthology. One of a half-dozen absolute masters of the form, Carl Barks' achievement on individual stories is exceeded only by remarkable consistency of the series over the length of its run (over 40 years).
(a,b,c,j)

GOOFY COMICS No. 1 (6/43, Nedor, F)-Nedor's fourth funny animal title and one of the most enduring, lasting 10 years. No memorable characters. (13 funny animal titles on the stands.)
(b,e)

JOLLY JINGLES No. 10 (Sum/43, MLJ, F)-A new publisher tried their hand at funny animals, introducing *Super Duck* (the fifth funny animal super hero). (A hybrid of *Superman* and *Donald Duck*.) (14 titles on the stands.)
(a,c,d,e,j)

★ ★ **PLASTIC MAN** No. 1 (Sum/43, Qua, H)-After a slow start, this title outlasts *Police Comics*, surviving 13 years. One of the top hero concepts carried by the exciting plotting/art of Jack Cole.
(a,b,c,e)

HAPPY COMICS No. 1 (8/43, Standard, F)-Their fifth funny animal title. No memorable characters, lasting 7 years (14 titles on the stands.)
(b,e)

ALL-SELECT COMICS No. 1 (Fall/43, Timely, H)-Timely's second showcase title featuring their top three characters

(see *All Winners*). Series carried by Schomburg covers (a proven sales feature), lasting 3 years.
(a,c,e)

ALL SURPRISE No. 1 (Fall/43, Timely, F)-Timely's fourth funny animal title, giving more exposure to their leading character, *Super Rabbit*, lasting 4 years. (15 titles on the stands.)
(e)

SUPER RABBIT No. 1 (Fall/43, Timely, F)-After his debut in *Comedy Comics*, *Super Rabbit* is given his own title, lasting 5 years. (15 titles on the stands.)
(e)

CAPTAIN BATTLE JR No. 1 (Fall/43, Comic House, H)-Clone of *Captain Battle*. The *Claw* vs. *The Ghost*, lasting 2 issues.
(e)

GIGGLE COMICS No. 1 (10/43, ACG, F)-Ties as first title of a new publisher, reinforcing the trend to funny animals. The quality and style of ACG's whole line was heavily influenced by the mastery of the teacher-artist of Ken Hultgren, the series' artist (beginning in 1944). This title lasted 12 years. (17 titles on the stands.)
(a,b,c,e,j,k)

HA HA COMICS No. 1 (10/43, ACG, F)-Ties as first title of a new publisher, reinforcing the trend to funny animals. A double impact-with sister title on the stands. Ingenious plotting and art by Ken Hultgren begins the following year. This series lasted 12 years. (17 titles on the stands.)
(a,b,c,e,j,k)

SUSPENSE COMICS No. 1 (12/43, Continental, D)-Debut of *The Grey Mask* (imitation of *The Spirit*). Atmospheric radio drama in a comic book form, lasting 3 years.
(e)

AVIATION CADETS nn (1943, S&S, Av)-A World War II aviation anthology one-shot. Navy pre-flight training involving sports.
(e)

COLUMBIA COMICS No. 1 (1943, Wise, R)-More exposure for Columbia's reprint characters, *Joe Palooka, Dixie Duggan*, etc.
(e)

POWERHOUSE PEPPER No. 1 (1943, Timely, Hm)-The protagonist of *Joker Comics* of a year earlier, Wolverton's humorous plotting made this character a memorable one. Popular enough to receive his own title.
(a,c,e,j)

TINY TOTS COMICS No. 1 (1943, Dell, F)-A one-shot anthology book of funny animals with Walt Kelly art.
(e)

TREASURE COMICS nn (1943, Prize, H)-Rebinding of coverless copies of *Prize* No. 7-11 from 1942. A very rare book with only one copy known to exist.
(e)

UNITED STATES MARINES nn (1943, Wise, W)-A documentary style war anthology series mixed with magazine-type photo features from the front, surviving one year. The title was resurrected for a brief period after the Korean conflict.
(e)

ALL FUNNY COMICS No. 1 (Wint/43-44, DC, Hm)-DC's first all funny anthology title. A popular series with the humorous plotting of *Genius Jones*, lasting 4½ years.

(e,j)

BLACK HOOD COMICS No. 9 (Wint/43-44, MLJ, H)-The Man of Mystery graduates from *Top-Notch* into his own title, lasting 11 issues.
(e)

CHRONOLOGICAL LIST OF COMIC BOOK TITLES BY PUBLISHER
FOR PERIOD 1933 - 1943
(The indented titles are key books other than No. 1's)

ACE MAGAZINES
Sure-Fire No. 1, 6/40
Super Mystery No. 1, 7/40
Lightning No. 4, 12/40
Our Flag No. 1, 8/41
Banner No. 3, 9/41
Four Favorites No. 1, 9/41
Captain Courageous No. 6, 3/42

AMERICAN COMICS GROUP
Giggle No. 1, 10/43
Ha Ha No. 1, 10/43

BETTER PUBL. (Standard)
Best No. 1, 11/39
Thrilling No. 2, 2/40
Exciting No. 1, 4/40
   Exciting No. 9, 5/41
Startling No. 1, 6/40
Real Life No. 1, 9/41
   Startling No. 10, 9/41
America's Best No. 1, 2/42
Fighting Yank No. 1, 9/42
Coo Coo No. 1, 10/42
Black Terror No. 1, Wint/42-43
Major Hoople No. 1, 1/43
Real Funnies No. 1, 1/43
Funny Funnies No. 1, 4/43
Goofy No. 1, 6/43
Happy No. 1, 8/43

BILBARA PUBLISHING CO.
Cyclone No. 1, 6/40

CENTAUR PUBLICATIONS
Funny Pages V2/6, 3/38
Funny Pic. Stories V2/6, 3/38
Star Comics No. 10, 3/38
Star Ranger No. 10, 3/38
Cowboy No. 13, 7/38
Keen Detective No. 8, 7/38
Little Giant No. 1, 7/38
Amazing Mystery Funnies No. 1, 8/38
Little Giant Movie No. 1, 8/38
   Funny Pages V2/10, 9/38
Star Ranger Funnies No. 15, 10/38
Little Giant Det. No. 1, 10/38
Keen Komics V2/1, 5/39
   Amazing Mystery Funnies V2/7, 7/39
Comic Pages V3/4, 7/39
   Keen Detective V2/7, 7/39
Amazing Man No. 5, 9/39
Amazing Adventure Funnies No. 1, 6/40
Fantoman No. 2, 8/40
Masked Marvel No. 9/40
Arrow, The No. 1, 10/40
Super Spy No. 1, 10/40
Detective Eye No. 1, 11/40
Wham No. 1, 11/40
Stars and Stripes No. 2, 5/41
Liberty Scouts No. 2, 6/41
World Famous Heroes No. 1, 10/41
Man Of War No. 1, 11/41

CATECHETICAL GUILD
Topix No. 1, 11/42

HARRY 'A' CHESLER
Star No. 1, 2/37
Star Ranger No. 1, 2/37
Feature Funnies No. 1, 10/37
Cocomalt Big Book No. 1, 1938
Yankee No. 1, 9/41
Dynamic No. 1, 10/41

Scoop No. 1, 11/41
Punch No. 1, 12/41

COLUMBIA COMICS GROUP
Big Shot No. 1, 5/40
Skyman No. 1, Fall/41
Face, The No. 1, 1941
Dixie Duggan No. 1, 7/42
Joe Palooka No. 1, 1942
Sparky Watts No. 1, 11/42

COMICS MAGAZINE
Comics Magazine No. 1, 5/36
Funny Pages No. 6, 11/36
Funny Picture Stories No. 1, 11/36
Detective Picture Stories No. 1, 12/36
Western Picture Stories No. 1, 2/37

DC COMICS
New Fun No. 1, 2/35
New Comics No. 1, 12/35
More Fun No. 7, 1/36
Big Book of Fun No. 1, Spr/36
New Book of Comics No. 1, 6-8/36
New Adventure No. 12, 1/37
Detective No. 1, 3/37
Action No. 1, 6/38
   Detective No. 20, 10/38
Adventure No. 32, 11/38
All-American No. 1, 4/39
New York World's Fair 3-5/39
Movie No. 1, 4/39
   Detective No. 27, 5/39
   Adventure No. 40, 7/39
Mutt and Jeff No. 1, Sum/39
Superman No. 1, Sum/39
Double Action No. 2, 1/40
Flash No. 1, 1/40
   More Fun 52,53, 2,3/40
   Adventure No. 48, 3/40
Batman No. 1, Spr/40
New York World's Fair 3-5/40
   More Fun No. 55, 5/40
   All-American No. 16, 7/40
All-Star No. 1, Sum/40
   All-American No. 19, 10/40
All-Star No. 3, Wint/40-41
   Adventure No. 61, 4/41
World's Best No. 1, Spr/41
All Flash No. 1, Sum/41
World's Finest No. 2, Sum/41
Green Lantern No. 1, Fall/41
Star Spangled No. 1, 10/41
   All-Star No. 8, 11-12/41
Leading No. 1, Wint/41-42
Sensation No. 1, 1/42
   Star Spangled No. 7, 4/42
   Detective No. 64, 6/42
Wonder Woman No. 1, Sum/42
Pic. Stories/Bible No. 1, Fall/42
Boy Commandos No. 1, Wint/42-43
Comic Cavalcade No. 1, Wint/42-43
All Funny No. 1, Wint/43-44

DELL PUBLISHING CO.
Popular No. 1, 2/36
Funnies No. 1, 10/36
Comics No. 1, 3/37
West. Action Thrillers No. 1, 4/37
100 Pages of Comics No. 1, 1937
Super No. 1, 5/38
Crackajack No. 1, 6/38
Nickel No. 1, 1938
Large Feature Comic No. 1, 1939
Four-Color No. 1, 1939

Donald Duck 4-Color No. 4, 3/40?
War No. 1, 5/40
W.D.'s Comics & Stories No. 1, 10/40
Mickey Mouse 4-Color No. 16, 4/41
   Funnies No. 57, 7/41
Red Ryder No. 3, 8/41
Looney Tunes No. 1, Fall/41
Key Ring No. 1, 1941
Large Feature No. 1, 1941
USA Is Ready No. 1, 1941
Animal No. 1, 12-1/41-42
Camp No. 1, 2/42
Fairy Tale Parade No. 1, 6-7/42
New Funnies No. 65, 7/42
War Heroes No. 1, 7-9/42
Our Gang No. 1, 9-10/42
Santa Claus Funnies No. 1, 12/42
America In Action No. 1, 1942
Donald Duck 4-Color No. 9, 1942
Famous Stories No. 1, 1942
War Stories No. 1, 1942
   W.D. Comics & Stories No. 31, 4/43
Tiny Tots No. 1, 1943

EASTERN COLOR
Funnies On Parade nn, 1933
F. F., A Carnival– nn, 1933
Century Of Comics nn, 1933
Skippy's Own Book nn, 1934
Famous Funnies Series 1, 1934
Famous Funnies No. 1, 7/34
Heroic No. 1, 8/40
Buck Rogers No. 1, Wint/40-41
Dickie Dare No. 1, 1941
Big Chief Wahoo No. 1, Wint/41-42
Jingle Jangle No. 1, 2/42
Oaky Doaks No. 1, 7/42
Mickey Finn No. 1, 11/42
Napoleon & Uncle Elby No. 1, 11/42
Strictly Private No. 1, 11/42
Tiny Tots No. 1, 1943

WILL EISNER
Spirit No. 1, 6/2/40

ELLIOT PUBLICATIONS
Double 1940
Double Up 1941

FAWCETT PUBLICATIONS
Flash No. 1, 1/40
Whiz No. 2, 2/40
Master No. 1, 3/40
Slam Bang No. 1, 3/40
Nickel No. 1, 5/40
Special Edition No. 1, 8/40
Western Desperado No. 8, 10/40
Wow No. 1, Wint/40-41
Captain Marvel No. 1, 1-2/41
America's Greatest No. 1, 5/41
Bulletman No. 1, 7/41
Minuteman No. 1, 7/41
Capt. Marvel Thrill Book 1941
Gene Autry No. 1, Fall/41
Spysmasher No. 1, Fall/41
   Master No. 21, Fall/41
   Whiz No. 25, 12/12/41
Xmas No. 1, 12/41
Captain Midnight No. 1, 9/42
Jungle Girl No. 1, Fall/42
Captain Marvel Jr. No. 1, 11/42
   Captain Marvel No. 18, 12/11/42
Fawcett's Funny Animals No. 1, 12/42
Gift No. 1, 12/42
Holiday No. 1, 12/42

Golden Arrow No. 1, Wint/42-43
Don Winslow No. 1, 2/43
Hopalong Cassidy No. 1, 2/43
Ibis No. 1, 2/43
All Hero No. 1, 3/43
  Captain Marvel No. 22, 3/43

FICTION HOUSE

Jumbo No. 1, 9/38
Fight No. 1, 1/40
Jungle No. 1, 1/40
Planet No. 1, l/40
Wings No. 1, 9/40
Rangers No. 1, 10/41
Sheena No. 1, Spr/42
Wambi No. 1, Spr/42

FLYING CADET

Flying Cadet No. 1, 1/43

FOX FEATURES SYNDICATE

Wonder No. 1, 5/39
Wonderworld No. 3, 7/39
Mysterymen No. 1, 8/39
Fantastic No. 1, 12/39
Blue Beetle No. 1, Wint/39-40
Science No. 1, 2/40
Weird No. 1, 4/40
Flame, The No. 1, Sum/40
Green Mask No. 1, Sum/40
Big 3 No. 1, Fall/40
Rex Dexter No. 1, Fall/40
Samson No. 1, Fall/40
Eagle, The No. 1, 7/41
U.S. Jones No. 1, 11/41
V-Comics No. 1, 1/42

FUNNIES, INC.

Motion Pic. Funn. Weekly No. 1, 5/39?
Green Giant No. 1, 1940

LEV GLEASON

Silver Streak No. 1, 12/39
  Silver Streak No. 6, 9/40
  Silver Streak No. 7, 1/41
Captain Battle No. 1, Sum/41
Daredevil No. 1, 7/41
Boy No. 3, 4/42
Crime Does Not Pay No. 22, 6/42
Captain Battle No. 3, Wint/42-43
Captain Battle Jr. No. 1, Fall/43

HUGO GERNSBACK

Superworld No. 1, 4/40

GILBERTON PUBLICATIONS

Classic No. 1, 10/41

GLOBE SYNDICATE

Circus No. 1, 6/38

GREAT PUBLICATIONS

Great No. 1, 11/41
Choice No. 1, 12/41

HARVEY PUBLICATIONS (Helnit)

Speed No. 1, 10/39
Champion No. 2, 12/39
Champ No. 11, 10/40
Green Hornet No. 1, 12/40
Pocket No. 1, 8/41
War Victory No. 1, Sum/42
All New No. 1, 1/43
Hello Pal No. 1, 1/43

HAWLEY PUBLICATIONS

Captain Easy nn, 1939

Red Ryder No. 1, 9/40
Sky Blazers No. 1, 9/40
Hi-Spot No. 2, 11/40

HILLMAN PERIODICALS

Miracle No. 1, 2/40
Rocket No. 1, 3/40
Victory No. 1, 8/41
Air Fighters No. 1, 11/41
  Air Fighters No. 2, 11/42
Clue No. 1, 1/43

HOLYOKE (Continental)

Crash No. 1, 5/40
  Crash No. 4, 9/40
Catman No. 1, 5/41
Captain Fearless No. 1, 8/41
Captain Aero No. 7, 12/41
Suspense No. 1, 12/43

HYPER PUBLICATIONS

Hyper Mystery No. 1, 5/40

K.K. PUBLICATIONS

Mickey Mouse Mag. No. 1, Sum/35
Mickey Mouse Mag. V5/12, 9/40

DAVID MCKAY PUBL.

King No. 1, 4/36
Wow No. 1, 5/36
Ace No. 1, 4/37
Feature Book nn, 1-4/37
Magic No. 1, 8/39
Future No. 1, 6/40

MLJ MAGAZINES

Blue Ribbon No. 1, 11/39
Top-Notch No. 1, 12/39
Pep No. 1, 1/40
Zip No. 1, 2/40
Shield-Wizard No. 1, Sum/40
  Top-Notch No. 9, 10/40
  Blue Ribbon No. 9, 2/41
Jackpot No. 1, Spr/41
  Pep No. 17, 7/41
  Pep No. 22, 12/41
Special No. 1, Wint/41-42
Hangman No. 2, Spr/42
Archie No. 1, Wint/42-43
Jolly Jingles No. 10, Sum/43
Black Hood No. 9, Wint/43-44

NITA PUBLICATIONS

Whirlwind No. 1, 6/40

NOVELTY PUBLICATIONS

Target No. 1, 2/40
Blue Bolt No. 1, 6/40
Four Most No. 1, Wint/41-42

PARENT'S MAGAZINE INST.

True No. 1, 4/41
Calling All Girls No. 1, 9/41
Real Heroes No. 1, 9/41
Funny Book No. 1, 12/42
Comics Digest No. 1, Wint/42-43

PRIZE PUBLICATIONS

Prize No. 1, 3/40
  Prize No. 7, 9/40
Headline No. 1, 2/43
Treasure nn, 1943

PROGRESSIVE PUBLISHERS

Bang-Up No. 1, 12/41

QUALITY COMICS GROUP

Feature No. 21, 6/39

Smash No. 1, 8/39
  Feature No. 27, 12/39
Crack No. 1, 5/40
Hit No. 1, 7/40
National No. 1, 7/40
Military No. 1, 8/41
Police No. 1, 8/41
Uncle Sam No. 1, 8/41
Doll Man No. 1, Fall/41
  Hit No. 25, 12/42
Plastic Man No. 1, Sum/43

RALSTON-PURINA CO.
Tom Mix No. 1, 9/40

STREET AND SMITH PUBL.

Shadow No. 1, 3/40
Doc Savage No. 1, 5/40
Bill Barnes No. 1, 10/40
Sport No. 1, 10/40
Army and Navy No. 1, 5/41
Super Magic No. 1, 5/41
Super Magician No. 2, 9/41
Pioneer Pic. Stories No. 1, 12/41
Trail Blazers No. 1, 1941
True Sport Pic. Stories No. 5, 2/42
Supersnipe No. 6, 10/42
Devil Dogs No. 1, 1942
Remember Pearl Harbor nn, 1942
Red Dragon No. 5, 1/43
Aviation Cadets No. 1, 1943

SUN PUBLICATIONS

Colossus No. 1, 3/40
Sun Fun No. 1, 3/40

TIMELY COMICS (Marvel)

Marvel No. 1, 11/39
Marvel Mystery No. 2, 12/39
Daring Mystery No. 1, 1/40
Mystic No. 1, 3/40
  Marvel Mystery No. 9, 7/40
Red Raven No. 1, 8/40
Human Torch No. 2, Fall/40
Captain America No. 1, 3/41
Sub-Mariner No. 1, Spr/41
All-Winners No. 1, Sum/41
Young Allies No. 1, Sum/41
USA No. 1, 8/41
Tough Kid Squad No. 1, 3/42
Comedy No. 9, 4/42
Joker No. 1, 4/42
Krazy No. 1, 7/42
Terry-Toons No. 1, 10/42
Miss Fury No. 1, Wint/42-43
Kid Komics No. 1, 2/43
  Comedy No. 14, 3/43
All-Select No. 1, Fall/43
All-Surprise No. 1, Fall/43
Super Rabbit No. 1, Fall/43
Powerhouse Pepper No. 1, 1943

UNITED FEATURES SYND.

Tip Top No. 1, 4/36
Comics On Parade No. 1, 4/38
Single Series No. 1, 1938
Okay No. 1, 7/40
O.K. No. 1, 7/40
Sparkler No. 1, 7/40
United No. 1, 8/40
Sparkler No. 1, 7/41

WHITMAN PUBLISHING CO.

Mammoth No. 1, 1937
Donald Duck nn, 1938

WILLIAM H. WISE

Columbia Comics No. 1, 1943
United States Marines No. 1, 1943

COMICS WITH LITTLE IF ANY VALUE

There exists in the comic book market, as in all other collector's markets, items, usually of recent origin, that have relatively little if any value. Why even mention it? We wouldn't, except for one thing—this is where you could probably take your worst beating, investment-wise. Since these books are listed by dealers in such profusion, at prices which will vary up to 500 percent from one dealer's price list to another, determining a realistic "market" value is almost impossible. And since the same books are listed repeatedly, list after list, month after month, it is difficult to determine whether or not these books are selling. In some cases, it is doubtful that they are even being collected. Most dealers must get a minimum price for their books; otherwise, it would not be profitable to handle. This will sometimes force a value on an otherwise valueless item. Most dealers who handle new comics get a minimum price of at least 75 cents to $2.00 per copy. This is the **available** price to obtain a **reading** copy. However, this is not what dealers will pay to restock. Since many of these books are not yet collector's items, their salvage value would be very low. You may not get more than 5 cents to 10 cents per copy selling them back to a dealer. This type of material, from an investment point of view, would be of maximum risk since the salvage value is so low. For this reason, recent comics should be bought for enjoyment as reading copies and if they go up in value, consider it a bonus.

COLLECTING FOREIGN COMICS AND AMERICAN REPRINTS

One extremely interesting source of comics of early vintage—one which does not necessarily have to be expensive—is the foreign market. Many American strips, from both newspapers and magazines, are reprinted abroad (both in English and in other languages) months and even years after they appear in the states. By working out trade agreements with foreign collectors, one can obtain, for practically the cover price, substantial runs of a number of newspaper strips and reprints of American comic books dating back five, ten, or occasionally even twenty or more years. These reprints are often in black and white, and sometimes the reproduction is poor, but this is not always the case. In any event, this is a source of material that every serious collector should look into.

Once the collector discovers comics published in foreign lands, he often becomes fascinated with the original strips produced in these countries. Many are excellent, and have a broader range of appeal than those of American comic books.

CANADIAN REPRINTS (E.C.s: by J. B. Clifford)

Several E.C. titles were published in Canada by Superior Comics from 1949 to at least 1953. Canadian editions of the following E.C. titles are known: (Pre-Trend) *Saddle Romances, Moon Girl, A Moon A Girl. . .Romance, Modern Love, Saddle Justice;* (New-Trend) *Crypt of Terror—Tales From the Crypt, Haunt of Fear, Vault of Horror, Weird Science, Weird Fantasy, Two-Fisted Tales, Frontline Combat,* and *Mad. Crime SuspenStories* was also published in Canada under the title *Weird SuspenStories* (Nos. 1-3 known). No reprints of *Shock SuspenStories* by Superior are known, nor have any "New Direction" reprints ever been reported. No reprints later than January 1954 are known. Canadian reprints sometimes exchanged cover and contents with adjacent numbers (e.g., a *Frontline Combat* 12 with a *Frontline Combat* No. 11 cover). They are distinguished both in cover and contents. As the interior pages are always reprinted poorly, these comics are of less value (about ½) than the U.S. editions; they were printed from asbestos plates made from the original plates. On some reprints, the Superior seal replaces the E.C. seal. Superior publishers took over Dynamic in 1947.

CANADIAN REPRINTS (Dells: by Ronald J. Ard)

Canadian editions of Dell comics, and presumably other lines, began in March-

April, 1948 and lasted until February-March, 1951. They were a response to the great Canadian dollar crisis of 1947. Intensive development of the post-war Canadian economy was financed almost entirely by American capital. This massive import or money reached such a level that Canada was in danger of having grossly disproportionate balance of payments which could drive it into technical bankruptcy in the midst of the biggest boom in its history. The Canadian government responded by banning a long list of imports. Almost 500 separate items were involved. Alas, the consumers of approximately 499 of them were politically more formidable than the consumers of comic books.

Dell responded by publishing its titles in Canada, through an arrangement with Wilson Publishing Company of Toronto. This company had not existed for a number of years and it is reasonable to assume that its sole business was the production and distribution of Dell titles in Canada. There is no doubt that they had a captive market. If you check the publication data on the U. S. editions of the period you will see the sentence "Not for sale in Canada." Canada was thus the only area of the Free World in those days technically beyond the reach of the American comic book industry.

We do not know whether French editions existed of the Dell titles put out by Wilson. The English editions were available nationwide. They were priced at 10 cents and were all 36 pages in length, at a time when their American parents were 52 pages. The covers were made of coarser paper, similar to that used in the Dell Four Color series in 1946 and 1947 and were abandoned as the more glossy cover paper became more economical. There was also a time lag of from six to eight weeks between, say, the date an American comic appeared and the date that the Canadian edition appeared.

Many Dell covers had seasonal themes and by the time the Canadian edition came out (two months later) the season was over. Wilson solved this problem by switching covers around so that the appropriate season would be reflected when the books hit the stands. Most Dell titles were published in Canada during this period including the popular Atom Bomb giveaway, *Walt Disney Comics and Stories* and the *Donald Duck* and *Mickey Mouse* Four Color one-shots. The quality of the Duck one-shots is equal to that of their American counterparts and generally bring about 30 percent less.

By 1951 the Korean War had so stimulated Canadian exports that the restrictions on comic book importation, which in any case were an offense against free trade principle, could be lifted without danger of economic collapse. Since this time Dell, as well as other companies, have been shipping direct into Canada.

CANADIAN REPRINTS (DCs: by Doug A. England)

Many DC comics were reprinted in Canada by National Comics Publications Limited and Simcoe Publishing and Distributing Co., both of Toronto, for years 1948-1950 at least. Like the Dells, these issues were 36 pages rather than the 52 pages offered in the U.S. editions, and the inscription "Published in Canada" would appear in place of "A 52 Page Magazine" or "52 Big Pages" appearing on U.S. editions. These issues contained no advertisements and some had no issue numbers.

HOW TO START COLLECTING

Most collectors of comic books begin by buying new issues in mint condition directly off the newsstand or from their local comic store. (Subscription copies are available from several mail-order services.) Each week new comics appear on the stands that are destined to become true collectors items. The trick is to locate a store that carries a complete line of comics. In several localities this may be difficult. Most panelologists frequent several magazine stands in order not to miss something they want. Even then, it pays to keep in close contact with collectors in other areas. Sooner or later, nearly every collector has to rely upon a friend in Fandom to obtain for him an item that is unavailable locally.

Before you buy any comic to add to your collection, you should carefully inspect its condition. Unlike stamps and coins, defective comics are generally not highly prized. The cover should be properly cut and printed. Remember that every blemish or sign of wear depreciates the beauty and value of your comics.

The serious panelologist usually purchases extra copies of popular titles. He may trade these multiples for items unavailable locally (for example, foreign comics), or he may store the multiples for resale at some future date. Such speculation is, of course, a gamble, but unless collecting trends change radically in the future, the value of certain comics in mint condition should appreciate greatly, as new generations of readers become interested in collecting.

COLLECTING BACK ISSUES

In addition to current issues, most panelologists want to locate back issues. Some energetic collectors have had great success in running down large hoards of rare comics in their home towns. Occasionally, rare items can be located through agencies that collect old papers and magazines, such as the Salvation Army. The lucky collector can often buy these items for much less than their current market value. Placing advertisements in trade journals, newspapers, etc., can also produce good results. However, don't be discouraged if you are neither energetic nor lucky. Most panelologists build their collections slowly but systematically by placing mail orders with dealers and other collectors.

Comics of early vintage are extremely expensive if they are purchased through a regular dealer or collector, and unless you have unlimited funds to invest in your hobby, you will find it necessary to restrict your collecting in certain ways. However you define your collection, you should be careful to set your goals well within your means.

PROPER HANDLING OF COMIC BOOKS

Before picking up an old rare comic book, caution should be exercised to handle it properly. Old comic books are very fragile and can be easily damaged. Because of this, many dealers hesitate to let customers personally handle their rare comics. They would prefer to remove the comic from its bag and show it to the customer themselves. In this way, if the book is damaged, it would be the dealer's responsibility—not the customer's. Remember, the slightest crease or chip could render an otherwise Mint book to Near Mint or even Very Fine. The following steps are provided to aid the novice in the proper handling of comic books: 1. Remove the comic from its protective sleeve or bag very carefully. 2. Gently lay the comic (unopened) in the palm of your hand so that it will stay relatively flat and secure. 3. You can now leaf through the book by carefully rolling or flipping the pages with the thumb and forefinger of your other hand. Caution: Be sure the book always remains relatively flat or slightly rolled. Avoid creating stress points on the covers with your fingers and be particularly cautious in bending covers back too far on Mint books. 4. After examining the book, carefully insert it back into the bag or protective sleeve. Watch corners and edges for folds or tears as you replace the book.

HOW TO SELL YOUR COMICS

If you have a collection of comics for sale, large or small, the following steps should be taken. (1) Make a detailed list of the books for sale, being careful to grade them accurately, showing any noticeable defects; i.e., torn or missing pages, centerfolds, etc. (2) Decide whether to sell or trade wholesale to a dealer all in one lump or to go through the long laborious process of advertising and selling piece by piece to collectors. Both have their advantages and disadvantages.

In selling to dealers, you will get the best price by letting everything go at once—the good with the bad—all for one price. Simply select names either from ads in this book or from some of the adzines mentioned below. Send them your list and ask for bids. The bids received will vary depending on the demand, rarity and condition of the books you have. The more in demand, and better the condition, the higher the bids will be.

On the other hand, you could become a "dealer" and sell the books yourself. Order a copy of one or more of the adzines. Take note how most dealers lay out their ads. Type up your ad copy, carefully pricing each book (using the Guide as a reference). Send finished ad copy with payment to adzine editor to be run. You will find that certain books will sell at once while others will not sell at all. The ad will probably have to be retyped, remaining books repriced, and run again. Price books according to how fast you want them to move. If you try to get top dollar, expect a much longer period of time. Otherwise, the better deal you give the collector, the faster they will move. Remember, in being your own dealer, you will have overhead expenses in postage, mailing supplies and advertising cost. Some books might even be returned for refund due to misgrading, etc.

In selling all at once to a dealer, you get instant cash, immediate profit, and eliminate the long process of running several ads to dispose of the books; but if you have patience, and a small amount of business sense, you could realize more profit selling them directly to collectors yourself.

WHERE TO BUY AND SELL

Throughout this book you will find the advertisements of many reputable dealers who sell back-issue comics magazines. If you are an inexperienced collector, be sure to compare prices before you buy. Never send large sums of cash through the mail. Send money orders or checks for your personal protection. Beware of bargains, as the items advertised sometimes do not exist, but are only a fraud to get your money.

The Price Guide is indebted to everyone who placed ads in this volume, whose support has helped in curbing printing costs. Your mentioning this book when dealing with the advertisers would be greatly appreciated.

THE BUYERS GUIDE, Krause Publications, 700 E. State St., Iola, WI 54990 PH:(715) 445-2214

The Price Guide highly recommends the above adzine, which is full of ads buying and selling comics, pulps, radio tapes, premiums, toys and other related items. You can also place ads to buy or sell your comics in the above publication.

COMIC BOOK MAIL ORDER SERVICES

The following offer a mail order service on new comic books. Write for rates and details:

COLLECTOR'S CHOICE, 3405 Keith St., Cleveland, TN 37311

THE COMIC SOURCE, Bruce B. Brittain, P.O. Box 863605, Plano, TX 75086-3605

COMICS TO ASTONISH, 4001-C Country Club Rd., Winston-Salem, NC 27104 (919) 765-0400

COMIX 4-U, INC., 1121 State St., 2nd Floor, Schenectady, NY 12304 (518) 372-6612

DOUG SULIPA'S COMIC WORLD, 374 Donald St., Winnipeg, Man., Canada R3B 2J2

FANTACO ENTERPRISES, INC., 21 Central Ave., Albany, NY 12210-1391. PH: (518) 463-1400.

FRIENDLY FRANK'S Distribution, Inc., 3990 Broadway, Gary IN 46408-2705 (219)884-5052 or 884-5053
    1025 North Vigo, Gary, IN 46403

GEPPI'S SUBSCRIPTION SERVICE, 1720 Belmont Ave., Bay-C, Baltimore, MD 21207

HEROES AREN'T HARD TO FIND, 1214 Thomas Ave., Charlotte, NC 28205

PRESIDENTIAL COMIC BOOK SERVICE, P. O. Box 41, Scarsdale, NY 10583

STYX COMIC SERVICE, 605 Roseberry St., Winnipeg, Manitoba Canada R3H 0T3

LEE TENNANT ENTERPRISES, P. O. Box 296, Worth, IL 60482-(312) 448-2937

THE WESTFIELD COMPANY, 8608 University Green, P.O. Box 470, Middleton, WI 53562 (608)836-1945

COMIC BOOK CONVENTIONS

As is the case with most other aspects of comic collecting, comic book conventions, or cons as they are referred to, were originally conceived as the comic-book counterpart to science-fiction fandom conventions. There were many attempts to form successful national cons prior to the time of the first one that materialized, but they were all stillborn. It is interesting that after only three relatively organized years of existence, the first comic con was held. Of course, its magnitude was nowhere near as large as most established cons held today.

What is a comic con? As might be expected, there are comic books to be found at these gatherings. Dealers, collectors, fans, whatever they call themselves can be found trading, selling, and buying the adventures of their favorite characters for hours on end. Additionally if at all possible, cons have guests of honor, usually professionals in the field of comic art, either writers, artists, or editors. The committees put together panels for the con attendees where the assembled pros talk about certain areas of comics, most of the time fielding questions from the assembled audience. At cons one can usually find displays of various and sundry things, usually original art. There might be radio listening rooms; there is most certainly a daily showing of different movies, usually science-fiction or horror type. Of course there is always the chance to get together with friends at cons and just talk about comics; one also has a good opportunity to make new friends who have similar interests and with whom one can correspond after the con.

It is difficult to describe accurately what goes on at a con. The best way to find out is to go to one or more if you can.

The addresses below are those currently available for conventions to be held in the upcoming year. Unfortunately, addresses for certain major conventions are unavailable as this list is being compiled. Once again, the best way to keep abreast of conventions is through the various adzines. Please remember when writing for convention information to include a self-addressed, stamped envelope for reply. Most conventions are non-profit, so they appreciate the help. Here is the list:

COMIC BOOK CONVENTIONS FOR 1989
(Note: All convention listings must be submitted to us by December 15th of each year)

ATLANTA FANTASY FAIR XV, June, 1989, Atlanta Hilton and Towers, Atlanta, GA. Info: Atlanta Fantasy Fair, 482 Gardner Rd., Stockbridge, GA 30281. PH: (404) 961-2347.

ATLANTA SPRING COMICS FAIR III, (Mar. 1989), Info: The Atlanta Spring Comics Fair, c/o The Atlanta Fantasy Fair, 482 Gardner Rd., Stockbridge, GA 30281. PH: (404) 961-2347.

CAROLINA CON VIII—Sponsored by The Carolina Pictorial Fiction Assn., Greenville, SC. Send SASE to S. Haynie, Rt. 6, Box 307, Easley, SC 29640

CHATTANOOGA COMIC CON, Collector's Choice, 3405 Keith St., Cleveland, TN 37311. Held in Spring and Fall each year.

CHICAGO COMICON—Larry Charet, 1219-A West Devon Ave., Chicago, IL 60660. Phone (312) 274-1832.

CHILDHOOD TREASURES SHOW AND CONVENTION, July, 1989, Dallas, TX. Write: Don Maris, Box 111266, Arlington, TX 76007. Phone (817)261-8745 before 10pm Central Time.

CREATION CON—249-04 Hillside Ave., Bellerose, N.Y. 11426. Phone (718) 343-0202. Holds major conventions in the following cities: Atlanta, Boston, Cincinnati, Cleveland, Detroit, London, Los Angeles, Philadelphia, Rochester, San Francisco, and Washington, D.C. Write or call for details.

DALLAS FANTASY FAIR, A Bulldog Prod. Convention. For info: Lary Lankford, P.O. Box 820488, Dallas, TX 75382, PH: (214) 349-3367.

DETROIT AREA COMIC BOOK/BASEBALL CARD SHOWS. Held every 2-3 weeks in Royal Oak and Livonia, Mich., write: Michael Goldman, Suite 231, 19827 W. 12 Mile Rd., Southfield, MI 48076. PH: (313) 350-2633.

EL PASO FANTASY FESTIVAL—c/o Rita's Fantasy Shop, No. 34 Sunrise Center, El Paso, TX 79904. PH: (915) 757-1143. Late July-Early August.

FANTACON 1989, Sept. 9,10, 1989, Empire State Plaza, between State and Madison, Albany, New York. For info: Tom Skulan, FantaCo Enterprises, FantaCo Building, Level 2, 21 Central Ave., Albany, NY 12210-1391. Please send SASE with inquiry or call (518) 463-1400.

ISLAND NOSTALGIA COMIC BOOK/BASEBALL CARD SHOWS, Hauppauge, N.Y.-Holiday Inn off L.I.E. exit 55, 1740 Express Drive South, Hauppauge, N.Y., For more info call Dennis (516) 724-7422.

KANSAS CITY MINI-CON—c/o Kansas City Comic Book Club, 136 East Longfellow, Kansas City, MO 64119. Three times a year.

LONG ISLAND COMIC BOOK & COLLECTOR'S MARKET CONVENTION—(Held monthly). Rockville Centre Holiday Inn, 173 Sunrise Hwy., Long Island, NY. For info: Cosmic Comics & Books of Rockville Centre, 139 N. Park Ave., Rockville Centre, NY 11570. (516) 763-1133.

LOS ANGELES COMIC BOOK & SCIENCE FICTION CONVENTION, First Sunday of every month. Bruce Schwartz, 1802 West Olive Ave., Burbank, CA 91506. PH: (818) 954-8432.

MOBI-CON, Days Inn Hotel, 3650 Airport Blvd., Mobile, AL. June 9-11, 1989. For information: Ron Hayes, P.O. Box 161257, Mobile, AL 36616. (205) 342-9073 or 661-4060.

MO-KAN COMIC FESTIVAL—c/o Kansas City Comic Book Club, 734 North 78th St., Kansas City, MO 66112. Twice a year.

ORLANDO CON, Sept. 23, 24, 1989, International Inn, Orlando, FL. Info: Jim Ivey, 4300 S. Semoran, Suite 109, Orlando, FL 32822-2453, PH: (407) 273-0141.

SAN DIEGO COMIC-CON—Box 17066, San Diego, CA 92117. July, 1987.

THE SAN FERNANDO VALLEY COMIC BOOK CONVENTION No. 19, Aug., 1989. Write for details: Original Valley Comic Book Con., 11684 Ventura, Bl. #335, Studio City, CA 91604.

Schenectady, New York, THE CAPITAL DISTRICT ANNUAL SHOW, S.A.S.E. with inquiry or call Jared Nathanson at 518-372-6612 or write: Comix 4-U, Inc., 1121 State St., 2nd Floor, Schenectady, NY 12304.

SEATTLE CENTER CON, Apr, July, Oct, 1989, Box 2043, Kirkland, Wash, 98033. Phone (206) 822-5709 or 827-5129.

SEATTLE QUEST NORTHWEST, Seattle, Wash. Write: Ron Church or Steve Sibra, P.O. Box 82676, Kenmore, WA 98028.

THE SUNDAY FUNNIES, Will Murray, 334 E. Squantum St., Quincy, MA 02171. Phone (617)328-5224.

COMIC BOOK CLUBS

ALABAMA—The Mobile Panelology Assoc. meets 1st Monday of each month at 2301 Airport Blvd. (Back Bldg. Mobile Recreation Dept.), Mobile, Ala.; 7:00 p.m. to 9:00 p.m. Club business address: 161 West Grant St., Chickasaw, AL 36611. (205) 456-4514. Founded 1973.

CALIFORNIA—The California Comic Book Collectors Club, c/o Matt Ornbaun, 23601 Hwy. 128, Yorkville, CA 95494. Send 50 cents and SASE for information and enrollment.

Alpha Omega—c/o Donald Ensign, 6011 Agnes Ave., Temple City, CA 91780. Puts out bi-monthly pub.

USC Comics Club, University of Southern California Intramural Recreation Dept., Heritage Hall 103, University Park, Los Angeles, CA 90089-0601. PH 213-743-5127.

GEORGIA—The Defenders of Dreams, Inc., c/o Will Rose, 3121 Shady Grove Rd., Carrollton, GA 30117. (Publishes its own clubzine *Excalibur* bi-monthly and a pulpzine *Real Pulp Adventures*.) Send business size SASE for details.

IDAHO—Mr. O's Comic Book Collectors Club, S. 1200 Agate Rd., Coeur D'Alene, Idaho 83814.

KANSAS—The Kansas City Comic Book Club meets the last Sunday of each month at 75th & Quivera (Sun Savings Bldg.), Shawnee, Kansas, 1:30-3:30 p.m. Write: 734 North 78th St., Kansas City, KS 66112. Holds two conventions a year. Annual dues: $6.00 or $7.50.

MASSACHUSETTS—The Gloo Club, c/o Ron Holmes, 140 Summit St., New Bedford, Mass. 02740. Write for details and send SASE. (This club is both national and international.)

MINNESOTA—The Pogo Fan Club. A mail club dedicated to Walt Kelly's career. Puts out a quarterly 'The Fort Mudge Most.'' Write: Steve Thompson, 6908 Wentworth Ave. So., Richfield, MN 55423.

MISSOURI—The Kansas City Comic Book Club meets the last Sunday of each month at 75th & Quivera (Sun Savings Building), Shawnee, Kansas; 1:30-3:30 p.m. Club business address: 136 East Longfellow, Kansas City, MO 64119. Puts on three conventions a year, publishes monthly newsletter, and gives away free comics to first 20 members that attend meetings. Annual dues $5.00.

NEW YORK—Comix 4-U Comic Club, meets 2nd Sunday every month. Write: 1121 State St., 2nd Floor, Schenectady, NY 12304.

OKLAHOMA—Fandom International. For information, write to: Dan DePalma, 5823 E. 22 St., Tulsa, OK 74114. Phone 834-8035.

TEXAS—The Gulf Coast Comic Collectors' Society (GCCCS). Write to GCCCS Headquarters, c/o Mike Mills, 4318 Iroquois St., Houston, TX 77504.

CANADA—The Collectors' Club. Write: T.M. Maple, Box 1272, Station B., Weston, Ontario M9L 2R9 Canada. Bimonthly newsletter.

THE HISTORY OF COMICS FANDOM

At this time it is possible to discern two distinct and largely unrelated movements in the history of Comics Fandom. The first of these movements began about 1953 as a response to the then-popular, trend-setting EC lines of comics. The first true comics fanzines of this movement were short-lived. Bhob Stewart's EC FAN BULLETIN was a hectographed newsletter that ran two issues about six months apart; and Jimmy Taurasi's FANTASY COMICS, a newsletter devoted to all science-fiction comics of the period, was a monthly that ran for about six months. These were followed by other newsletters, such as Mike May's EC FAN JOURNAL, and George Jennings' EC WORLD PRESS. EC fanzines of a wider and more critical scope appeared somewhat later. Two of the finest were POTRZEBIE, the product of a number of fans, and Ron Parker's HOOHAH. Gauging from the response that POTRZEBIE received from a plug in an EC letter column, Ted White estimated the average age of EC fans to lie in the range of 9 to 13, while many EC fans were in their mid-teens. This fact was taken as discouraging to many of the faneds, who had hoped to reach an older audience. Consequently, many of them gave up their efforts in behalf of Comics Fandom, especially with the demise of the EC groups, and turned their attention to science-fiction fandom with its longer tradition and older membership. While the flourish of fan activity in response to the EC comics was certainly noteworthy, it is fair to say that it never developed into a full-fledged, independent, and self-sustaining movement.

The second comics fan movement began in 1960. It was largely a response to (though it later became a stimulus for) the Second Heroic Age of Comics. Most fan historians date the Second Heroic Age from the appearance of the new FLASH comics magazine (numbered 105 and dated February 1959). The letter departments of Julius Schwartz (editor at National Periodicals), and later those of Stan Lee (Marvel Group) and Bill Harris (Gold Key) were most influential in bringing comics readers into Fandom. Beyond question, it was the reappearance of the costumed hero that sparked the comics fan movement of the sixties. Sparks were lit among some science-fiction fans first, when experienced fan writers, who were part of an established tradition, produced the first in a series of articles on the comics of the forties—ALL IN COLOR FOR A DIME. The series was introduced in XERO No. 1 (September 1960), a general fanzine for science-fiction fandom edited and published by Dick Lupoff.

Meanwhile, outside science-fiction fandom, Jerry Bails and Roy Thomas, two strictly comics fans of long-standing, conceived the first true comics fanzine in response to the Second Heroic Age. The fanzine, ALTER EGO, appeared in March 1961. The first several issues were widely circulated among comics fans, and were to influence profoundly the comics fan movement to follow. Unlike the earlier EC fan movement, this new movement attracted many fans in their twenties and thirties. A number of these older fans had been active collectors for years but had been largely unknown to each other. Joined by scores of new, younger fans, this group formed the nucleus of a new movement that is still growing and shows every indication of being self-sustaining. Although it has borrowed a few of the more appropriate terms coined by science-fiction fans, Comics Fandom of the Sixties was an independent if fledging movement, without, in most cases, the advantages and disadvantages of a longer tradition. What Comics Fandom did derive from science-fiction fandom it did so thanks largely to the fanzines produced by so-called double fans. The most notable of this type is COMIC ART, edited and published by Don and Maggie Thompson.

HOW TO SELECT FANZINES

In the early 1960s, only a few comic fanzines were being published. A fan could easily afford to subscribe to them all. Today, the situation has radically changed, and it has become something of a problem to decide which fanzines to order.

Fanzines are not all of equal quality or general interest. Even different issues of the same fanzine may vary significantly. To locate issues that will be of interest to you, learn to look for the names of outstanding amateur artists, writers, and editors, and consult fanzine review columns. Although you may not always agree with the judgements of the reviewers, you will find these reviews to be a valuable source of information about the content and quality of the current fanzines.

When ordering a fanzine, remember that print runs are small and the issue you may want may be out of print (OP). Ordinarily in this case, you will receive the next issue. Because of irregular publishing schedules that nearly all fanzines must, of necessity, observe, allow up to 90 days or more for your copy to reach you. It is common courtesy when addressing an inquiry to an ama-publisher to enclose a self-addressed, stamped envelope.

FAN PUBLICATIONS OF INTEREST

NOTE: We must be notified each year by December 1 for listing to be included, due to changes of address, etc. Please send sample copy.

AFTERMATH-Gulf Coast Comics, P.O. Box 310, Winnie, TX 77665. For science fiction fans. $2.50 postpaid. Back issues & reprints available.

ALPHA OMEGA, for Christian artists and fans, bi-mo. $4.50 for 3 bi-monthly issues. For info: Donald Ensign, 6011 Agnes Ave., Temple City, CA 91780.

AMAZING HEROES—4359 Cornell Rd., Agoura, CA 91301. Sample copy $2.50.

ANNIE PEOPLE, Jon Merrill, P.O. Box 431, Cedar Knolls, NJ 07927. Bi-monthly Little Orphan Annie newsletter.

BATMAN FANS: THE MIDNIGHT CONFERENCE, for Batman fans. Write: Martin R. Noreau, 3155 Pare #3, St-Hubert, Quebec, Canada J3Y 4R6.

THE CLASSICS JOURNAL—Mike Strauss, 26 Madera, San Carlos, CA 94070.

COLLECTORS' CLUB NEWSLETTER, a bi-monthly. Write: T.M. Maple, Box 1272, Station B., Weston, Ontario M9L 2R9 Canada.

COMICANA, 3, Boolimba Cres., Narrabundah, A.C.T., 2604 Australia. Covers all aspects of comic books; includes a special Australian section.

COMIC ART AND FANTASY—Stephen Barrington, 161 West Grant Street, Chickasaw, AL 36611. Published quarterly for comics, gaming & sf fans. $1.00 for two issues.

THE COMIC CORNER—Gulf Coast Comic Collectors' Society (GCCCS). For sample copy and subscription info, write: The Comic Corner, c/o Mike Mills, 4318 Iroquois St., Pasadena, TX 77504.

THE COMICS FORUM—Kansas City Comic Book Club, 136, East Longfellow, Kansas City, MO 64119. (News, reviews, interviews, and classifieds.)

COMICS INTERVIEW—c/o Fictioneer Books Ltd., #1 Screamer Mtn., Clayton, GA 30525.

THE COMICS JOURNAL—4359 Cornell Rd., Agoura, CA 91301. Sample copy $3.50.

COMIX EMPORIUM NEWSLETTER—P.O. Box 3742, Silver Spring, MD 20901. Pub. 8 times a year, w/Marvel, DC & major independents news. Sample free.

COMIX 4-U NEWSLETTER, free with stamp or S.A.S.E. Comix 4-U, Inc., 1121 State St., 2nd Floor, Schenectady, NY 12304.

THE COMPLETE EC LIBRARY—Russ Cochran, P. O. Box 437, West Plains, MO 65775. (A must for all EC collectors. Reprinting of the complete EC line is planned. Write for details.)

DITKOMANIA-A quarterly, digest size devoted to Steve Ditko's work. 98 cents per issue. Write: Bill Hall, 10 Farm Hill Rd., Middletown, CT 06457.

THE DUCKBURG TIMES—Irregular Barks/Disney fanzine. Sample copy $1.50. Dana Gabbard, 3010 Wilshire Blvd., #362, Los Angeles, CA 90010.

FANDOM JOURNAL—Kevin Collier, 18129 136th Ave. Apt. B, Nunica, MI 49448. (Monthly newspaper on small press comics and zines. 25 cents postpaid for sample.)

FANTACO'S CHRONICLES SERIES, FantaCo Enterprises Inc., 21 Central Ave., Albany, NY 12210-1391. Sample copy $3.50. Articles & indexes of popular comic series.

FANTASY ADVERTISER—Martin Skidmore, 25 Cornleaze, Withywood, Bristol, BS13 7SG, England.

FCA & ME TOO!—Teresa & William Harper, 301 E. Buena Vista Ave., North Augusta, SC 29841. Covers Golden Age Fawcett and Magazine Enterprises. Sample $1.00. 4 issue sub., $5.

THE GLOO CLUB NEWS—Ron Holmes, 140 Summit St., New Bedford, Mass. 02740. Pub. 6 times/year. Write for details.

HELLFIRE—c/o David & Paul Roach, 36 Lakeside Dr., Lakeside Cardiff, S-Glam Wales, U.K., CF2 6DF. Has articles on American, British, European comics.

KATY KEENE NEWSLETTER—QUARTERLY—Craig Leavitt, 1125 11th St., Modesto, CA 95354. ($6 yr. subscription)

NEMO: THE CLASSIC COMICS LIBRARY—4359 Cornell Rd., Agoura, CA 91301. Reprints classic strips with articles.

POW-WOW—The Harpers, 301 E. Buena Vista Ave., North Augusta, SC 29841. About Straight Arrow. Sample $1, 4 issue sub., $5.

THE STANLEY STEAMER, Jon Merrill, P.O. Box 431, Cedar Knolls, NJ 07927. Bi-monthly Little Lulu fanzine.

COLLECTING STRIPS

Collecting newspaper comic strips is somewhat different than collecting magazines, although it can be equally satisfying.

Obviously, most strip collectors begin by clipping strips from their local paper, but many soon branch out to strips carried in out-of-town papers. Naturally this can become more expensive and it is often frustrating, because it is easy to miss editions of out-of-town papers. Consequently, most strip collectors work out trade agreements with collectors in other cities in order to get an uninterrupted supply of the strips they want. This usually necessitates saving local strips to be used for trade purposes only.

Back issues of strips dating back several decades are also available from time to time from dealers. The prices per panel vary greatly depending on the age, condition, and demand for the strip. When the original strips are unavailable, it is sometimes possible to get photostatic copies from collectors, libraries, or newspaper morgues.

COLLECTING ORIGINAL ART

In addition to magazines and strips, some enthusiasts also collect the original art for the comics. These black and white, inked drawings are usually done on illustration paper at about 30 per cent up (i.e., 30 per cent larger than the original printed panels). Because original art is a one-of-a-kind article, it is highly prized and often difficult to obtain.

Interest in original comic art has increased tremendously in the past several years. Many companies now return the originals to the artists who have in turn offered them for sale, usually at cons but sometimes through agents and dealers. As with any other area of collecting, rarity and demand governs value. Although the masters' works bring fine art prices, most art is available at moderate prices. Comic strips are the most popular facet with collectors, followed by comic book art. Once scarce, current and older comic book art has surfaced within the last few years. In 1974 several original painted covers of vintage comic books and coloring books turned up from Dell, Gold Key, Whitman, and Classic Comics.

The following are sources for original art:

Artman, Bruce Bergstrom, 1620 Valley St., Fort Lee, NJ 07024
Cartoon Carnival, 408 Bickmore Dr., Wallingford, PA 19086, PH: 215-566-1292
The Cartoon Museum, Jim Ivey, 4300 S. Semoran, Suite 109, Orlando, FL 32822-2453 (407)273-0141
Russ Cochran, P.O. Box 437, West Plains, MO 65775.
Collectors Paradise Gallery, Harry Kleinman, P.O. Box 1540, Studio City, CA 91604
The Comic Character Shop, Old Firehouse Antiques, 110 Alaskan Way S., Seattle, WA 98104 206-283-0532
Tony Dispoto, Comic Art Showcase, P. O. Box 425, Lodi, NJ 07644
Scott Dunbier, P.O. Box 1446, Gracie Station, NY, NY, 10028
Graphic Collectibles, Mitch Itkowitz, P.O. Box 683, Staten Island, NY 10302, (718)273-3685
Richard Halegua, Comic Art & Graffix Gallery, 2033 Madison Rd., Cincinnati, OH 45208, (513) 321-4208
Steve Herrington, 30 W. 70th St., New York, NY 10023
Carsten Lagua, Dillgesstrasse 22, 1000 Berlin 46, Germany
Museum Graphics, Jerome K. Muller, Box 743, Costa Mesa, CA 92627
Original Artwork, Martin Hilland, AM Josefshaus 6, 4040 Neuss 21, West Germany
San Mateo Comic Books/Original art, 306 Baldwin Ave. San Mateo, CA 94401, (415)344-1536
TRH Gallery (Tom Horvitz), 1090 N. Palm Canyon Dr. #B, Palm Springs, CA 92262, PH: 1-619-320-9599

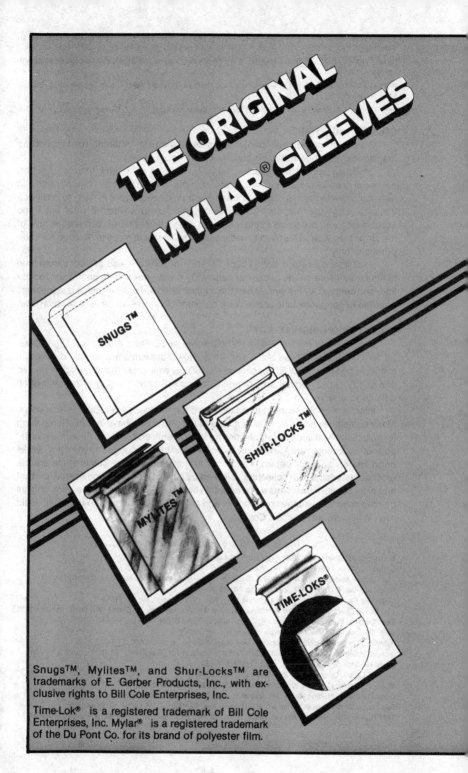

THE ORIGINAL MYLAR® SLEEVES

SNUGS™

SHUR-LOCKS™

MYLITES™

TIME-LOKS®

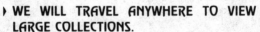

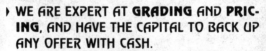

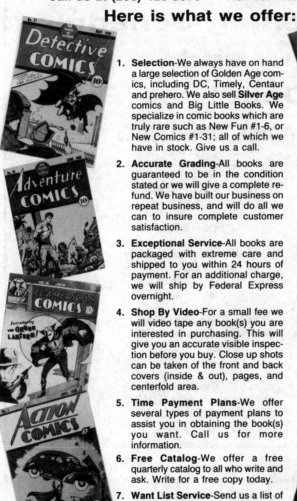

THE TWO GREATEST NAMES IN COMICS
GERRY ROSS PRESENT ROBERT CRESTOHL
RARE MARVELS AT SPECIAL DISCOUNT PRICES!

TERMS. Earliest issues have 3 prices listed. The first price is for gd/very good condition. The second (in brackets) is for vg/fine condition. The third is for vf/near mint condition. **Later Marvels (1966-75) have 2 prices listed.** vg/fine; and vf/near mint. **Nm/mint (scarce) or strict mint (rare)** are available in limited quantities To calculate, take vf/nm price: A) **For nm/mint** multiply vf/nm price by 1.33 B) **For strict mint** multiply vf/nm price x 2. Add prices carefully, minimum order **$10.00. 10% DISCOUNT WITH ALTERNATE CHOICES.** Prices subject to change. Payment MUST be in U.S. funds (cash, check (money order preferred)). Prices are per issue. (Canadian residents add 20% to Canadian funds) Comics shipped quickly! Our complete giant catalog is 25 cents (Free with order). **Postage: Add $3.00 to all orders.** Not responsible for typographical errors.

10% DISCOUNT WITH ALTERNATES

MAIL ALL ORDERS AND PAYMENT TO: Crestohl/Ross, 4732 Circle Rd. Dept.M, Montreal, Quebec, Canada. H3W 1Z1

10% DISCOUNT WITH ALTERNATES

AVENGERS
1 100.00 (160.00) 350.00
2,4 38.00 (58.00) 125.00
3 26.00 (37.50) 75.00
5 18.00 (25.00) 50.00
6-11 17.50 (35.00)
12-16 10.00 (18.00)
17-19 7.50 (13.50)
20-22 6.00 (9.50)
23-30 4.50 (6.75)
31-52, 54-56 3.00 (4.50)
53, 57, 58, 94-100 10.00 (15.00)
59-92 3.00 (4.50)
93 17.50 (26.00)
101-109, 112-115 2.50 (3.50)
119-163 2.00 (3.00)
164-166, 181-191 3.75
167-171, 200 3.00
172-180, 192-199 1.75
201 up 1.50

AMAZING SPIDERMAN
AAF 15 275.00 (440.00) 950.00
1 225.00 (360.00) 750.00
2 87.50 (137.50) 290.00
3 52.50 (80.00) 175.00
4 43.00 (65.00) 140.00
5,6 31.50 (48.00) 100.00
7-10, 14 26.00 (37.50) 75.00
11-13, 15 18.00 (25.00) 50.00
16-20 17.50 (35.00)
21-30, 100 12.00 (22.00)
31-38, 50 8.00 (12.00)
39, 40, 96-98 10.00 (14.00)
41-46, 101, 102 6.00 (8.50)
47-49, 51, 52 5.00 (7.00)
53-70, 90, 94 3.75 (5.25)
71-89, 91-93, 95, 99 2.75 (4.00)
103-120, 123, 124 2.50 (3.50)
121, 122, 129 20.00 (25.00)
125-128 130-133 136-150 2.25 (3.00)
134, 135, 161, 162 7.50 (10.00)
151-160, 163-173, 176-199 1.50
200, 203, 239-251, 253 2.50
204-237, 254 up 1.50
238, 252 6.00

CONAN
1 55.00 (70.00)
2, 3 25.00 (35.00)
4, 5 18.00 (27.00)

CONAN
6-10, 14, 15 12.00 (17.50)
11-13 9.00 (13.00)
16-24 7.00 (10.50)
25-30, 37 4.00 (5.00)
31-36, 38-40 3.00 (4.00)
41-58, 100 2.00 (3.00)
59-81, 115, 116 1.50 (2.00)
82-99 1.50
101-114, 117 up 1.25

DAREDEVIL
1 62.50 (100.00) 210.00
2 27.50 (44.00) 90.00
3, 158 18.00 (27.00) 55.00
4, 5 11.00 (15.00) 27.50
6-10, 16, 17 9.00 (20.00)
11-15, 131 6.00 (9.50)
18-20, 100 5.00 (7.00)
21-30, 50-53 3.00 (4.50)
31-49, 183 2.50 (4.50)
54-81 2.00 (3.25)
82-99, 101-105 1.75 (2.50)
106-130, 132-137 1.50 (2.00)
139-157, 184-225, 234 up 1.50

FANTASTIC FOUR
1 300.00 (480.00) 999.00
2 125.00 (200.00) 440.00
3 100.00 (160.00) 320.00
4, 5 75.00 (120.00) 240.00
6-12 33.00 (50.00) 110.00
13-15 23.00 (33.00) 70.00
16-20 18.00 (25.00) 50.00
21-28, 48 17.50 (35.00)
29-31, 100 12.00 (24.00)
32-40, 49, 50 9.00 (18.00)
41-47 6.00 (10.00)
51-60, 66, 67 5.00 (7.50)
61-65, 72-77, 112 4.00 (6.00)
68-71, 78-80, 116, 200 3.00 (4.50)
81-99, 121-123, 150 2.50 (3.50)
101-111, 113-115, 117-120 3.00
124-149 1.75 (2.50)
151-175 1.50 (2.00)
176-199, 201-208 1.25
209-259 2.00
260 up 1.25

INCREDIBLE HULK
1 175.00 (250.00) 500.00
2 70.00 (100.00) 200.00
3 47.50 (67.50) 135.00
4-6 35.00 (50.00) 100.00
102, 180, 182 10.00 (13.00)
103-105, 162, 172 3.00 (4.50)
106-110 2.50 (3.75)
111-120, 176-178, 272 2.00 (3.00)
121-161, 163-171 1.50 (2.00)
173-175, 183-200 1.25 (1.50)
181 30.00 (40.00)
201-271, 273-299 1.00

PETER PARKER (all nm/m)
1, 69, 70 6.00
2-10, 22, 23 3.00
11-21 2.50
24-26, 29-31 2.00
27, 28, 64 12.50
32-63, 65-68, 71-80 1.50
81-83 5.00
84 up 1.50

SILVER SURFER
1, 4 27.50 (49.50)
2, 3, 5 14.00 (20.00)
6, 7 9.00 (15.00)
8-18 7.00 (11.00)

TALES OF SUSPENSE
39 105.00 (150.00) 300.00
40 35.00 (50.00) 100.00
41 25.00 (35.00) 60.00
42-45 12.00 (16.00) 28.00
46-48 10.00 (18.00)
49-59 6.00 (9.00)
60-65 4.00 (6.00)
66-75, 99 2.50 (3.50)
76-98 2.00 (3.00)

TALES TO ASTONISH
27 112.50 (180.00) 360.00
35 42.50 (65.00) 130.00
36 20.00 (27.50) 55.00
37-40, 44 11.00 (15.00) 27.50
41-43, 49, 59 9.00 (16.00)
45-48, 50, 92, 93 6.00 (10.00)
51-58, 60, 100 5.00 (7.50)
61-65 4.00 (6.00)
66-75, 101 2.50 (3.50)
76-91, 94-99 2.00 (3.00)

THOR & JOURNEY INTO MYSTERY
83 112.50 (180.00) 360.00
84 35.00 (50.00) 100.00
85 24.00 (34.00) 68.00
86 17.50 (25.00) 50.00
87-89 15.00 (21.00) 40.00
90-100, 112 11.00 (15.00) 27.00
101-110, 115 7.50 (12.50)
113, 114 116-130, 193 5.00 (7.50)
165-166, 180-181 3.00 (4.50)
131-140 2.50 (3.50)
141-164, 167-179 1.75 (2.50)
182-192, 194-199 1.50 (2.00)
201-259, 261-263, 272-336 1.25
200, 264-271, 300, 338-340 2.00
260, 337 5.00
341 up 1.25

X-MEN
1 150.00 (250.00) 500.00
2 60.00 (90.00) 180.00
3, 4 33.00 (44.00) 88.00
5 25.00 (35.00) 60.00
6-10 25.00 (40.00)
11, 12 15.00 (25.00)
13-15, 56-65 12.00 (20.00)
16-20, 28, 50-55 10.00 (15.00)
21-27, 29, 30, 49 8.00 (12.00)
31-40 6.00 (8.50)
41-48, 67-72 5.00 (7.00)
73-93 4.50 (6.50)

For #s 94 up, two prices are listed: fine/very fine and nm/mint.
94 80.00 (120.00)
GS #1 70.00 (110.00)
95 26.00 (44.00)
96-99, 108, 109 18.00 (30.00)
120, 121 19.00 (32.00)
100, 101 21.00 (35.00)
102-107, 110, 111, 140 12.00 (20.00)
112-119, 10.00 (16.00)
122-130, 139 8.00 (13.00)
131-138 6.00 (9.00)
141-143, 171 4.00 (6.00)
144-150, 165, 166 3.50 (4.75)
151-164, 167-170 2.50 (3.00)
172 up 2.00 mint only

DORMAN·
AFTER
GIORDANO·

DC COMICS

COMMEMORATES

50 YEARS OF

BATMAN

Adventures Into The Unknown! #1, 1948.
© ACG

Airboy Comics Vol.3 #2, 1946. © HILL

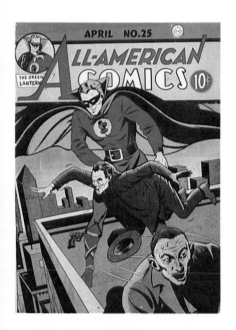

All-American Comics #25, 1941. © DC

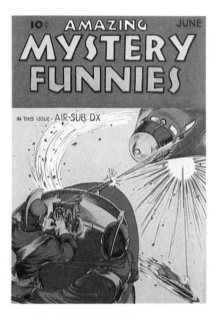

Amazing Mystery Funnies Vol. 2 #6, 1939.
© CEN

Army And Navy Comics #5, 1942. © S&S

The Arrow #2, 1940. © CEN

Astro Boy #1, 1965. © National Broadcasting Co.

Atoman #1, 1946. © Spark Publ. Jerry Robinson cover art.

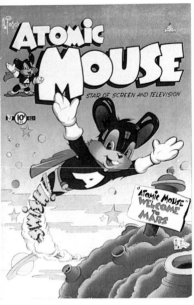

Atomic Mouse #1, 1953. © CC

Barney Google #1, 1923. © KING

Batman #44, 1947. © DC

Best Of The West #3, 1951. © ME

Black Knight #1, 1955. © MCG

The Black Terror #1, 1943. © STD

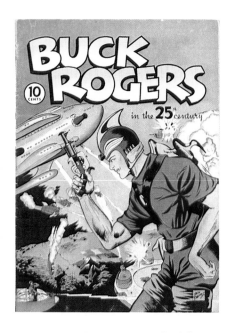

Buck Rogers #1, 1940. © KING

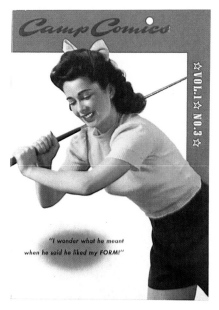

Camp Comics #3, 1942. © DELL

Captain America #15, 1942. © MCG

Captain Kangaroo #721, 1956. © Keeshan-Miller Ent.

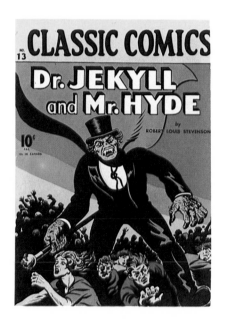

Classic Comics #13, 1943. © GIL

Cocomalt Big Book Of Comics #1, 1938. © CHES

Crash Comics #4, 1940. © TEM

Daredevil #5, 1941. © LEV

Dell Giant #39, 1960. © WDC

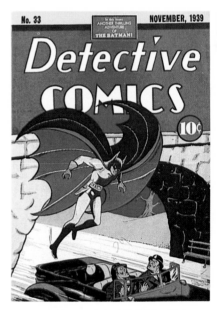

Detective Comics #33, 1939. Origin of Batman is told. © DC

Detective Comics #168, 1951. Origin the Joker is told. © DC

Dick Tracy, Four Color #6, 1940. © N.Y. News Synd.

Eerie Comics #1, 1947. © AVON

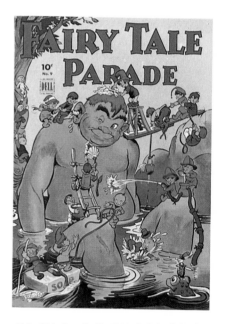

Fairy Tale Parade #9, 1944. © Oskar Lebeck

Famous Funnies #1, 1934. © EAS

Funny Picture Stories #1, 1936. © CEN

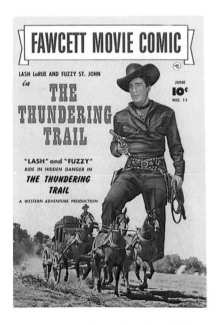

Fawcett Movie Comic #11, 1951. © FAW

Feature Funnies #1, 1937. © CHES

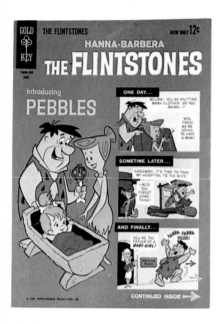

The Flintstones #11, 1963. © Hanna-Barbera

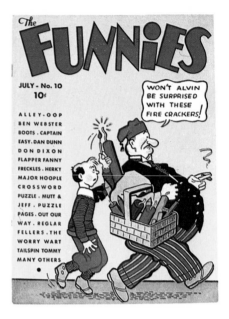

The Funnies #10, 1937. © DELL

Funny Stuff #1, 1944. © DC

Gene Autry #11, 1943. © Gene Autry

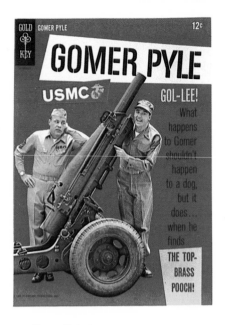

Gomer Pyle #1, 1966. © Ashland Prod.

Green Lama #1, 1944. © Spark

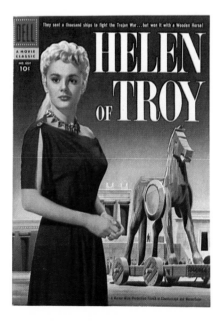

Helen Of Troy # 684, 1956. © Warner Bros.

Hot Rod Comics #1, 1951. © CC

7019 Security Blvd.
Baltimore, MD 21207
301-298-1758

1675 Crystal Square Arcade
Department 84
Arlington, VA 22202
703-521-4618

8317 Fenton Street
Silver Spring, MD 20910
301-588-2546

A Chronology of the Development of
THE AMERICAN COMIC BOOK

By
M. Thomas Inge

Precursors: The facsimile newspaper strip reprint collections constitute the earliest "comic books." The first of these was a collection of Richard Outcault's **Yellow Kid** from the Hearst **New York American** in March 1897. Commercial and promotional reprint collections, usually in cardboard covers, appeared through the 1920s and featured such newspaper strips as **Mutt and Jeff, Foxy Grandpa, Buster Brown,** and **Barney Google**. During 1922 a reprint magazine, **Comic Monthly**, appeared with each issue devoted to a separate strip, and from 1929 to 1930 George Delacorte published 36 issues of **The Funnies** in tabloid format with original comic pages in color, becoming the first four-color comic newsstand publication.

1933: The Ledger syndicate published a small broadside of their Sunday comics on 7" by 9" plates. Employees of Eastern Color Printing Company in New York, sales manager Harry I. Wildenberg and salesman Max C. Gaines, saw it and figured that two such plates would fit a tabloid page, which would produce a book about 7½" x 10" when folded. Thus 10,000 copies of **Funnies on Parade**, containing 32 pages of Sunday newspaper reprints, was published for Proctor and Gamble to be given away as premiums. Some of the strips included were: **Joe Palooka, Mutt and Jeff, Hairbreadth Harry,** and **Reg'lar Fellas**. M. C. Gaines was very impressed with this book and convinced Eastern Color that he could sell a lot of them to such big advertisers as Milk-O-Malt, Wheatena, Kinney Shoe Stores, and others to be used as premiums and radio give-aways. So, Eastern Color printed **Famous Funnies: A Carnival of Comics**, and then **Century of Comics**, both as before, containing Sunday newspaper reprints. Mr. Gaines sold these books in quantities of 100,000 to 250,000.

1934: The give-away comics were so successful that Mr. Gaines believed that youngsters would buy comic books for ten cents like the "Big Little Books" coming out at that time. So, early in 1934, Eastern Color ran off 35,000 copies of **Famous Funnies, Series 1**, 64 pages of reprints for Dell Publishing Company to be sold for ten cents in chain stores. Selling out promptly on the stands, Eastern Color, in May 1934, issued **Famous Funnies** No. 1 (dated July 1934) which became, with issue No. 2 in July, the first monthly comic magazine. The title continued for over 20 years through 218 issues, reaching a circulation peak of nearly one million copies. At the same time, Mr. Gaines went to the sponsors of Percy Crosby's **Skippy**, who was on the radio, and convinced them to put out a Skippy book, advertise it on the air, and give away a free copy to anyone who bought a tube of Phillip's toothpaste. Thus 500,000 copies of **Skippy's Own Book of Comics** was run off and distributed through drug stores everywhere. This was the first four-color comic book of reprints devoted to a single character.

1935: Major Malcolm Wheeler-Nicholson's National Periodical Publications issued in February a tabloid-sized comic publication called **New Fun**, which became **More Fun** after the sixth issue and converted to the normal comic-book size after issue eight. **More Fun** was the first comic book of a standard size to publish original material and continued publication until 1949. **Mickey Mouse Magazine** began in the summer, to become **Walt Disney's Comics and Stories** in 1940, and combined original material with reprinted newspaper strips in most issues.

1936: In the wake of the success of **Famous Funnies**, other publishers, in conjunction with the major newspaper strip syndicates, inaugurated more reprint comic books: **Popular Comics** (News-Tribune, February), **Tip Top Comics** (United Features, April), **King Comics** (King Features, April), and **The Funnies** (new series, NEA, October). Four issues of **Wow Comics**, from David McKay and Henle Publications, appeared, edited by S. M. Iger and including early art by Will Eisner, Bob Kane, and Alex Raymond. The first non-reprint comic book devoted to a single theme was **Detective Picture Stories** issued in December by The Comics Magazine Company.

1937: The second single-theme title, **Western Picture Stories**, came in February from The Comics Magazine Company, and the third was **Detective Comics**, an offshoot of **More Fun**, which began in March to be published to the present. The book's initials, "D.C.," have long served to refer to National Periodical Publications, which was purchased from Major Nicholson by Harry Donenfeld late this year.

1938: "DC" copped a lion's share of the comic book market with the publication of **Action Comics** No. 1 in June which contained the first appearance of Superman by writer Jerry Siegel and artist Joe Shuster, a discovery of Max C. Gaines. The "man of steel" inaugurated the "Golden Era" in comic book history. Fiction House, a pulp publisher, entered the comic book field in September with **Jumbo Comics**, featuring Sheena, Queen of the Jungle, and appearing in over-sized format for the first eight issues.

1939: The continued success of "DC" was assured in May with the publication of **Detective Comics** No. 27 containing the first episode of Batman by artist Bob Kane and writer Bill Finger. **Superman Comics** appeared in the summer. Also, during the summer, a black and white premium comic titled **Motion Picture Funnies Weekly** was published to be given away at motion picture theatres. The plan was to issue it weekly and to have continued stories so that the kids would come back week after week not to miss an episode. Four issues were planned but only one came out. This book contains the first appearance and origin of the Sub-Mariner by Bill Everett (8 pages) which was later reprinted in **Marvel Comics**. In November, the first issue of **Marvel Comics** came out, featuring the Human Torch by Carl Burgos and the Sub-Mariner reprint with color added.

1940: The April issue of **Detective Comics** No. 38 introduced Robin the Boy Wonder as a sidekick to Batman, thus establishing the "Dynamic Duo" and a major precedent for later costume heroes who would also have boy companions. **Batman Comics** began in the spring. Over 60 different comic book titles were being issued, including **Whiz Comics** begun in February by Fawcett Publications. A creation of writer Bill Parker and artist C. C. Beck, **Whiz's** Captain Marvel was the only superhero ever to surpass Superman in comic book sales. Drawing on their own popular pulp magazine heroes, Street and Smith Publications introduced **Shadow Comics** in March and **Doc Savage Comics** in May. A second trend was established with the summer appearance of the first issue of **All-Star Comics**, which brought several superheroes together in one story and in its third issue that winter would announce the establishment of the Justice Society of America.

1941: Wonder Woman was introduced in the spring issue of **All-Star Comics** No. 8, the creation of psychologist William Moulton Marston and artist Harry Peter. **Captain Marvel Adventures** began this year. By the end of 1941, over 160 titles were being published, including **Captain America** by Jack Kirby and Joe Simon, **Police Comics** with Jack Cole's Plastic Man and later Will Eisner's Spirit, **Military Comics** with Blackhawk by Eisner and Charles Cuidera, **Daredevil Comics** with the original character by Charles Biro, **Air Fighters** with Airboy also by Biro, and **Looney Tunes & Merrie Melodies** with Porky Pig, Bugs Bunny, and Elmer Fudd, reportedly created by Bob Clampett for the Leon Schlesinger Productions animated films and drawn for the comics by Chase Craig. Also, Albert Kanter's Gilberton Company initiated the **Classics Illustrated** series with **The Three Musketeers**.

1942: Crime Does Not Pay by editor Charles Biro and publisher Lev Gleason, devoted to factual accounts of criminals' lives, began a different trend in realistic crime stories. **Wonder Woman** appeared in the summer. John Goldwater's character Archie, drawn by Bob Montana, first published in **Pep Comics**, was given his own magazine **Archie Comics**, which has remained popular over 40 years. The first issue of **Animal Comics** contained Walt Kelly's "Albert Takes the Cake," featuring the new character of Pogo. In mid-1942, the undated Dell Four Color title, No. 9, **Donald Duck Finds Pirate Gold**, appeared with art by Carl Barks and Jack Hannah. Barks, also featured in **Walt Disney's Comics and Stories**, remained the most popular delineator of Donald Duck and later introduced his greatest creation, Uncle Scrooge, in **Christmas on Bear Mountain** (Dell Four Color No. 178). The fantasy work of George Carlson appeared in the first issue of **Jingle Jangle Comics**, one of the most imaginative titles for children ever to be published.

1945: The first issue of **Real Screen Comics** introduced the Fox and the Crow by James F. Davis, and John Stanley began drawing the **Little Lulu** comic book based on a popular feature in the **Saturday Evening Post** by Marjorie Henderson Buell from 1935 to 1944. Bill Woggon's Katy Keene appears in issue No. 5 of **Wilbur Comics** to be followed by appearances in **Laugh, Pep, Suzie** and her own comic book in 1950. The popularity of Dick Briefer's satiric version of the Frankenstein monster, originally drawn for **Prize Comics** in 1941, led to the publication of **Frankenstein** by Prize publications.

1950: The son of Max C. Gaines, William M. Gaines, who earlier had inherited his father's firm Educational Comics (later Entertaining Comics), began publication of a series of well-written and masterfully drawn titles which would establish a "New Trend" in comics magazines: **Crypt of Terror** (later **Tales from the Crypt**, April), **The Vault of Horror** (April), **The Haunt of Fear** (May), **Weird Science** (May), **Weird Fantasy** (May), **Crime SuspenStories** (October), and **Two-Fisted Tales** (November), the latter stunningly edited by Harvey Kurtzman.

1952: In October "E.C." published the first number of **Mad** under Kurtzman's creative editorship.

1953: All Fawcett titles featuring Captain Marvel were ceased after many years of litigation in the courts during which National Periodical Publications claimed that the super-hero was an infringement on the copyrighted Superman.

1954: The appearance of Fredric Wertham's book **Seduction of the Innocent** in the spring was the culmination of a continuing war against comic books fought by those who believed they corrupted youth and debased culture. The U. S. Senate Subcommittee on Juvenile Delinquency investigated comic books and in response the major publishers banded together in October to create the Comics Code Authority and adopted, in their own words, "the most stringent code in existence for any communications media." Before the Code took effect, more than 1,000,000,000 issues of comic books were being sold annually.

1955: In an effort to avoid the Code, "E.C." launched a "New Direction" series of titles, such as **Impact, Valor, Aces High, Extra, M.D.**, and **Psychoanalysis**, none of which lasted beyond the year. **Mad** was changed into a larger magazine format with issue No. 24 in July to escape the Comics Code entirely.

1956: Beginning with the Flash in **Showcase** No. 4, Julius Schwartz began a popular revival of "DC" superheroes which would lead to the "Silver Age" in comic book history.

1960: After several efforts at new satire magazines (**Trump** and **Humbug**), Harvey Kurtzman, no longer with Gaines, issued in August the first number of another abortive effort, **Help!**, where the early work of underground cartoonists Jay Lynch, Skip Williamson, Gilbert Shelton, and Robert Crumb appeared.

1961: Stan Lee edited in November the first **Fantastic Four**, featuring Mr. Fantastic, the Human Torch, the Thing, and the Invisible Girl, and inaugurated an enormously popular line of titles from Marvel Comics featuring a more contemporary style of superhero.

1962: Lee introduced **The Amazing Spider-Man** in August, with art by Steve Ditko, **The Hulk** in May and **Thor** in August, the last two produced by Dick Ayers and Jack Kirby.

1963: Marvel's **The X-Men**, with art by Jack Kirby, began a successful run in November, but the title would experience a revival and have an even more popular reception in the 1980s.

1965: James Warren issued **Creepy**, a larger black and white comic book, outside Comics Code's control, which emulated the "E.C." horror comic line. Warren's **Eerie** began in September and **Vampirella** in September 1969.

1967: Robert Crumb's **Zap** No. 1 appeared, the first popular underground comic book.

1970: Editor Roy Thomas at Marvel begins **Conan the Barbarian** based on fiction by Robert E. Howard with art by Barry Smith.

1972: The Swamp Thing by Berni Wrightson begins in November from "DC."

1973: In February, "DC" revived the original Captain Marvel with new art by C. C. Beck and reprints in the first issue of **Shazam** and in October **The Shadow** with scripts by Denny O'Neil and art by Mike Kaluta.

1974: "DC" began publication in the spring of a series of over-sized facsimile reprints of the most valued comic books of the past under the general title of "Famous First Editions," beginning with a reprint of **Action** No. 1 and including afterwards **Detective Comics** No. 27, **Sensation Comics** No. 1, **Whiz Comics** No. 2, **Batman** No. 1, **Wonder Woman** No. 1, **All-Star Comics** No. 3, and **Flash Comics** No. 1.

1975: In the first collaborative effort between the two major comic book publishers of the previous decade, Marvel and "DC" produced together an over-sized comic-book version of **MGM's Marvelous Wizard of Oz** in the fall, and then the following year in an unprecedented cross-over produced **Superman vs. the Amazing Spider-Man**, written by Gerry Conway, drawn by Ross Andru, and inked by Dick Giordano.

1976: Frank Brunner's Howard the Duck, who had appeared earlier in Marvel's **Fear** and **Man-Thing**, was given his own book in January, which because of distribution problems became an over-night collector's item. After decades of litigation, Jerry Siegel and Joe Shuster were given financial recompense and recognition by National Periodical Publications for their creation of Superman, after several friends of the team made a public issue of the case.

1977: Stan Lee's **Spider-Man** was given a second birth, fifteen years after his first, through a highly successful newspaper comic strip, which began syndication on January 3 with art by John Romita. This invasion of the comic strip by comic book characters continued with the appearance on June 6 of Marvel's **Howard the Duck**, with story by Steve Gerber and visuals by Gene Colan. In an unusually successful collaborative effort, Marvel began publication of the comic book adaption of the George Lucas film **Star Wars**, with script by Roy Thomas and art by Howard Chaykin, at least three months before the film was released nationally on May 25. The demand was so great that all six issues of **Star Wars** were reprinted at least seven times, and the installments were reprinted in two volumes of an over-sized Marvel Special Edition and a single paperback volume for the book trade.

1978: In an effort to halt declining sales, Warner Communications drastically cut back on the number of "DC" titles and overhauled its distribution process in June. The interest of the visual media in comic book characters reached a new high with the Hulk, Spider-Man, and Doctor Strange, the subjects of television shows; with various projects begun to produce film versions of Flash Gordon, Dick Tracy, Popeye, Conan, The Phantom, and Buck Rogers; and with the movement reaching an outlandish peak of publicity with the release of **Superman** in December. Two significant applications of the comic book format to traditional fiction appeared this year: **A Contract with God and Other Tenement Stories** by Will Eisner and **The Silver Surfer** by Stan Lee and Jack Kirby. Eclipse Enterprises published Paul Gulacy's **Sabre**, the first graphic album produced for the direct sales market, and initiated a policy of paying royalties and granting copyrights to comic book creators.

1979: **The Micronauts** with art by Michael Golden debuted from Marvel in January.

1980: Publication of the November premier issue of **The New Teen Titans**, with art by George Perez and story by Marv Wolfman, brought back to widespread popularity a title originally published by "DC" in 1966.

1981: The distributor Pacific Comics began publishing titles for direct sales through comic shops with the inaugural issue of Jack Kirby's **Captain Victory and the Galactic Rangers** and offered royalties to artists and writers on the basis of sales. "DC" would do the same for regular newsstand comics in November (with payments retroactive to July 1981), and Marvel followed suit by the end of the year.

1982: The first slick format comic book in regular size appeared, **Marvel Fanfare** No. 1, with a March date. The premier March issue of **Captain Carrot and His Amazing Zoo Crew**, with story by Roy Thomas and art by Scott Shaw, revived the concept of funny animal superheroes of the 1940s.

1983: This year saw more comic book publishers, aside from Marvel and DC, issuing more titles than has existed in the past 40 years, most small independent publishers relying on direct sales, such as Americomics, Capital, Eagle, Eclipse, First, Pacific, and Red Circle, and with Archie, Charlton, and Whitman publishing on a limited scale. Frank Miller's mini-series **Ronin** demonstrated a striking use of sword-play and martial arts typical of Japanese comic book art, and Howard Chaykin's stylish but controversial **American Flagg** appeared with an October date on its first issue.

1985: Ohio State University's Library of Communication and Graphic Arts hosted the first major exhibition devoted to the comic book May 19 through August 2. In what was billed as an irreversible decision, the silver age superheroine Supergirl was killed in the seventh (October) issue of **Crisis on Infinite Earths**, a limited series intended to reorganize and simplify the DC universe on the occasion of the publisher's 50th anniversary.

1986: In recognition of its twenty-fifth anniversary, Marvel began publication of several new ongoing titles comprising Marvel's "New Universe," a self-contained fictional world. DC attracted extensive publicity and media coverage with its revisions of the character of **Superman** by John Byrne and of **Batman** in the **Dark Knight** series by Frank Miller. **Watchmen**, a limited-series graphic novel by Alan Moore and artist Dave Gibbons, began publication with a September issue from DC and Marvel's **The 'Nam**, written by Vietnam veteran Doug Murray and penciled by Michael Golden, began with its December issue. DC issued guidelines in December for labelling their titles as either for mature readers or for readers of all ages; in response, many artists and writers publicly objected or threatened to resign.

1987: Art Spiegelman's **Maus: A Survivor's Tale** was nominated for the National Book Critics Circle Award in biography, the first comic book to be so honored. A celebration of Superman's fiftieth Birthday began with the opening of an exhibition on his history at the Smithsonian's Museum of American History in Washington, D.C., in June and a symposium on "The Superhero in America" in October.

1988: Superman's birthday celebration continued with a public party in New York and a CBS television special in February, a cover story in **Time** magazine in March (the first comic book character to appear on the cover), and an international exposition in Cleveland in June. With issue number 601 for May 24, **Action Comics** became the first modern weekly comic book. In August, DC initiated a new policy of allowing creators of new characters to retain ownership of them rather than rely solely on work-for-hire.

Detective Comics #27, May, 1939. The first appearance of *Batman*. Created by Bob Kane, *Batman* is celebrating his 50th anniversary this year. This book is highly prized and represents one of the most valuable comic books of all time. Batman is TM & © DC Comics, Inc.

ORIGINS OF THE DARK KNIGHT:
A Conversation With Batman Artists
Bob Kane and Jerry Robinson

By Thomas Andrae

From his first appearance in June, 1938, Superman captured the hearts and minds of America's youth. His success quickly established the superhero as the reigning monarch of comic books and catapulted the medium into a multi-million dollar business—or so most histories would tell us. But the truth is more complex. While Superman was certainly the catalyst for the rapid growth of the comics industry, there was, in actuality, no immediate boom in superheroes following his debut. As Ron Goulart observes, only one costumed hero appeared in the first four months following Superman's birth—The Crimson Avenger—and he was not a superhero. He wore civilian clothes except for a cloak and mask. Appearing in May, 1939, Will Eisner's Wonderman was the first to imitate Superman's costume and super powers, but he was a pale copy and folded after one appearance and a lawsuit from Superman's publisher.

It was only after the arrival of another masked avenger that the deluge in superheroes began. Appearing in **Detective Comics** No. 27 (in the same month as Wonderman) "The Bat-Man," as he was called then, was unlike anything seen before in comics. With long, prominent ears that looked disturbingly like Satanic horns, and enormous batwings for a cape, he was as menacing as any of the villains he faced. More significantly, he was the first comic book superhero without super powers. His precedent proved that superheroes need not be pallid imitations of Superman, nor even possess super strength. Before the year was out, The Sandman, The Flame, Blue Beetle, Amazing Man, The Human Torch, and Submariner had hit the newsstands. By 1940, The Flash, Green Lantern, and Captain

Marvel were added to the rolls, and scores would follow.

Batman was the creation of Bob Kane, a young cartoonist barely in his twenties. Kane began his career in 1936, drawing humorous strips like *Peter Pupp* and *Jest Laffs* for the Eisner/Iger Studio and later *Van Bragger* and *Side Streets of New York* for **Circus Comics**. He continued drawing humorous fillers for DC, as well as two features, *Rusty and His Pals*, inspired by Milt Caniff's *Terry and the Pirates*, and *Clip Carson*, about a globe-trotting soldier of fortune. Kane was still a novice at drawing adventure strips when he created Batman. Consequently, his art retained much of the cartoony quality of his humor strips, a style perfect for creating a surreal atmosphere of bizarre menace. "Batman's world took control of the reader," Jules Feiffer wrote. "Kane's was an authentic fantasy, a genuine vision, so that however one might nit-pick the components, the end product remained an imaginative whole." Using weird angle shots, Calgariesque landscapes, large moons in vacant nighttime skies, and brooding dark shadows, Kane expressively conveyed a mood of malice and derangement prefiguring the cinematic techniques of film noir detective films of the '40s and '50s.

Kane was aided by a Bronx croney, a former shoe salesman-turned-writer named Bill Finger. Finger had worked on *Rusty and His Pals* and *Clip Carson* and became chief scripter on the golden age Batman stories. Although he never received a byline while he was alive, his influence on the Batman mystique was so great that he must be considered a co-creator of the strip. Finger worked on Batman from the beginning, helping Kane to refine his first sketches of the Caped Crusader's costume and wrote the first story, "The Case of the

Chemical Syndicate." Finger also named Bruce Wayne and Dick Grayson and Batman's home port of Gotham City, and created the Batcave from a photograph he had seen in **Popular Science**, as well as many of the strip's cast of bizarre villains. It was Finger who made Batman a great detective, writing what are perhaps the most finely plotted stories in the superhero genre.

In September, 1939, Kane hired 17 year old artist Jerry Robinson as his assistant. Robinson soon took over inking Kane's pencils, and later drew and inked his own stories as well as many of the classic Batman covers of the 1941-1946 period. Tempering Kane's style with a more illustrative look, Robinson refined the cartoony elements in the strip. Robinson is also famous for creating what is unquestionably comic book's greatest villain—The Joker. The Crown Prince of Crime was the first in a series of nemeses which would become a permanent repertory of bizarre villains comparable only to those in Chester Gould's *Dick Tracy*.

In April, 1940, Kane created Robin, the Boy Wonder, adding him to the strip in order, in Robinson's words, "to humanize Batman." This dramatically altered the tone of the stories, transforming Batman from a grim, menacing loner to a paternal big brother to Robin, who had become his ward. The addition of Robin significantly lightened up the strip, The Boy Wonder's red and green costume offering a colorful counterpoint to Batman's sombre blue and gray uniform. The dialogue also became cheerier, filled with the puns and badinage between Batman and Robin and the criminals that became a trademark. The first boy wonder in comics, Robin was such a hit that it became *de rigeur* for every new superhero to have a young sidekick.

The addition of Robin and exotic villains like the Joker made Batman so popular that he began to rival Superman's success. For years the two would vie for the title of DC's most popular superhero, with Superman usually edging out his competitor. However, recent years have seen a reversal of this trend. With the appearance of a series of soft-covered, adult-oriented graphic novels, beginning with Frank Miller's Dark Knight books, Batman has become the most popular superhero in comics. The new live-action movie, with Michael Keaton as Batman and Jack Nicholson as the Joker, could well tip the scales, giving the Caped Crusader a prominence he has not enjoyed since the Batmania of the mid-'60s. Read now the story of Batman's origins from two members of the creative team that helped make him a super-star for 50 years—Bob Kane and Jerry Robinson.

A current photo of Bob Kane at his drawing board.

BOB KANE INTERVIEW

When did you become interested in Cartooning?

I was a confirmed doodler. When I was 13, I was doodling in all my school notebooks and all over the walls and sidewalks of New York, in the Bronx. I used to copy all the comics—my dad worked for **The Daily News** *in the printing department, so he brought home the Sun-*

day papers. And I found that I could copy the comics and make them look as good as the original. My dad used to know these famous cartoonists—the creators of Moon Mullins, Popeye, and Dick Tracy—and he'd ask them how much a week they made. And they said that if you're highly successful, you could make thousands a week. Well, that really appealed to a poor kid from the Bronx. So I set my sights on becoming a famous cartoonist.

How did you get involved in drawing comic books?

Being at the right place at the right time is extremely propitious in life, and I was fortunate to be in on the pioneering days of the comic book industry. In 1934, the first issue of **Famous Funnies** was published—it consisted entirely of reprints of newspaper comic strips. When some of the publishers got wind that it was selling well, they decided to publish original comic art instead of reprints. One of the early comic books was called **Wow Comics**, which started in 1936. It was produced by Jerry Iger and Will Eisner. Of course, Will Eisner later became famous for creating **The Spirit** comic book. He and I went to De Witt Clinton High School together. We were always vying to see who would be top cartoonist on our high school paper, The Clinton News.

After high school, I worked for Iger and Eisner doing a feature called "Peter Pupp"—it was my first good comic feature. "Peter Pupp" was drawn in a kind of Disney style. He was a puppy who had a little sidekick named Tagalong who was younger and shorter. They were kind of the basis of Batman and Robin who came along a few years later. In one story, they went to the moon in a little rocket ship, and the moon turned out to be made of green cheese. Then they stopped off at Saturn. It may be the first comic book story in which someone goes to the moon.

The style of Peter Pupp looks similar to that of Floyd Gottredson's Mickey Mouse comic strip. Did it influence you?

Yes. I used to copy Mickey Mouse all the time. It was one of my favorites as a kid. My dream at that time was to go to Hollywood and meet Walt Disney. But when I was 17, I got a job working for the Fleisher Studio in New York. I did fill-ins, inking and opaque painting on Betty Boop for seven to eight months. I made $25 a week, which wasn't bad and a lot better than the $5 a week I was making with Iger and Eisner. When the studio moved to Florida, I didn't want to make the move—I liked New York.

I started in the comic book industry again after that. I got a job at DC doing fill-in cartoons and some features like "Rusty and His Pals," which I did in a Caniff style, and "Clip Carson," who was a soldier of fortune and looked like me— tall, dark and lean. I also did some strips for **Circus Comics**—one was called "Van Bragger" and was a rich man's version of the Katzenjammer Kids. He had a sister with dimples who looked like Shirley Temple. I also drew "The Sidestreets of New York," which was a take-off on the Dead End Kids. I used the name Robert Kaye on that because the editor didn't want the same name on two features in one book.

How did you come to create Batman?

That was late in 1938 or early in January, 1939. We had an enterprising editor at DC called Vincent Sullivan. One day we had a drink and I showed him some Flash Gordon drawings I had done. I was a great copyist and he said, "You know, Bob, your stuff looks just like Alex Raymond's. You could switch to the superhero stuff." I had been doing slapstick comics and fill-ins for DC. Sullivan said, "There's a character called Superman by Siegel and Shuster, and they are making $800 a week a piece." I was only making $35-$50 a week at the time. I said, "My god, if I could make that kind of money!" Sullivan said, "We're looking for another superhero. Do you think you could come up with one?" This was Friday. I said, "I'll have one for you Monday."

So over the weekend I laid out a kind of naked superhero on the page, with a muscular figure that looked like Superman or Flash Gordon. He didn't have any costume. So I started to make sketches of a bird-man with bird wings. He looked like Hawkman with wings that were rounded out like a hawk's. Then I remembered Leonardo Da Vinci's flying machine. I had made sketches of it when I was 13 and stored them in an old trunk. So I dug them up.

I was always interested in the origins of things—how did it all begin? When I was 13, I saw this book of Da Vinci's inventions of 500 years ago—the flying machine, the parachute, the steam engine. What stuck in my mind was the flying machine. It was called an "orni" something, but it was the first airplane. It was actually a glider—a sled with bat wings attached to it with a man in the middle. He was supposed to fly by jumping off a mountain, and Leonardo actually sent men off mountains in the contraption. But in the beginning, even he made a mistake—he made wings that flapped so that, like an animated cartoon, a man would be suspended in mid-air, then sail down to the ground and crash. Then he noticed that seagulls would glide because their wings were stabilized. So, by stabilizing the wings of his glider, men were actually able to fly off the side of the mountain and glide to the bottom. Leonardo's sled looked like a bat-man to me. In fact, he even had a quote on the sketch—"And your bird shall have no other wings but that of a bat." So I changed the bird-man to a "Bat-Man," with a hyphen between the Bat and Man.

My second influence was from the movie **The Mark of Zorro** with Douglas Fairbanks Sr. It gave me the idea of the dual identity. By day he was this bored Spanish count, a foppish character called Don Diego, and at night he would come out as Zorro. He rode a black horse called Toronado and would enter the cave and exit from a grandfather clock in the living room. The Batcave may have been inspired by this cave in **Zorro**. He wore this kind of hankerchief mask with slits for eyes and would carve a "Z" on the foreheads of desperadoes when he duelled with them. So this was all engraved in my mind when I was creating Batman. In fact, at 13 I was imitating Fairbanks around my block. We had a clubhouse and called the club the Zorros; we wore black masks like Zorro.

The concept of Batman had to be different. I didn't want him to be a superhero with super powers. I wanted a superhero, but not to imitate Superman. I needed to be original—the company wouldn't take it if it was too close to Superman. And all my influences led me to create a "Bat-Man." Batman doesn't have any super powers. He's just an athlete. He has the athletic prowess of Douglas Fairbanks, who was my all-time favorite superhero in the movies. In films like **The Black Pirate**, in which he swung from one mast to another on his pirate ship, his daredevil acrobatics made him an "acro-Batman." I imitated all the acrobatics of Fairbanks in the early Batman books. He would do somersaults and bowl down 10 guys in a row and swing on a rope like Fairbanks.

I also saw a movie when I was a kid called **The Bat Whispers**. It was written

"Bob Kane gets that fog-laden Warner Brothers look."
© DC Comics, Inc.

by the mystery writer Mary Roberts Rhinehart. Chester Morris, who also played Boston Blackie, was in the dual role of "The Bat" and the detective. The story was about a lot of murders in an old mansion. I remember shadowy-like figures on the wall when he was about to kill somebody. They caught up with him in the attic—he wore a costume that looked a little like my early Batman's, with gloves, a mask, and scalloped wings. He looked like a bat—very ominous. [Note: A prototype of the Batsignal also appears in this film.]

I was a real movie buff as a kid. Jules Feiffer says, "Bob Kane gets that fog-laden Warner Brothers look" more than any other DC artist. Movies like Bela Lugosi in the first Dracula film—the fog swirling up around the moors, the evil old castle—left a real indelible impression upon me. The first year of Batman, he was a vigilante and we were more influenced by horror films and emulated a Dracula look. I loved mystery movies and serials; the Shadow on radio was also a big influence.

However, the plot thickens. I had a croney I went to De Witt Clinton with named Bill Finger. I didn't know him in high school—he was a couple years older than I was. I met him at a party. He was a shoe salesman then and deeply into pulps like **Doc Savage** and **The Shadow**. But he had aspirations of becoming a writer. I called Bill and said, "I have a new character called The Bat-Man and I've made some crude, elementary sketches I'd like you to look at." So he came over and I showed him the drawings. At that time I only had a small Halloween mask, like Robin's, on Batman's face. So he said, "Why not make him look more like a bat and put a hood on him, and take the eyeballs out and just put slits for eyes to make him look more mysterious." He wore a red union suit; the wings were black, the mask was black. I thought red and black would be a good combination. Bill said it was too bright—color it dark gray to make it look more ominous. So I followed his suggestions. The cape looked like two stiff bat wings attached to his arms. But this was cumbersome and would get in the way of his derring-do when he was fighting or swinging on a rope. So Bill suggested making it a cape that scalloped out like bat wings when Batman jumped through the air or swung down with a rope.

So Bill was a contributing force right from the beginning and wrote the first story, "The Case of the Chemical Syndicate." Bill wrote most of the great stories and was influential in setting the pace of the early stories and the genre the other writers emulated. He was like "the Cecil B. De Mille of the comic strips." He would write a script by getting a photograph of a giant prop—the Statue of Liberty, a giant typewriter or sewing machine—and that would generate the idea for a story and he would build the story around the giant prop. He was also a very good mystery writer, because of his interest in the pulps.

Bill was an unsung hero. He never realized his full potential, ever. He wrote a lot of comics for DC, created a lot of characters. But he never made much money and died broke. I never thought of giving him a by-line and he never asked for one. I often tell my wife if I could go back 13 or 14 years before he died, I would like to say, "I'll put your name on it now. You deserve it." I feel a slight sense of guilt that I didn't do it. I really loved the guy. Without Bill, Batman wouldn't be as great as he is today. Now they put everybody's name on a strip—the artist, writer, inker, letterer, colorist. My editor felt that only the creator's name should be on it. I think they were afraid writers would demand more of a piece of the action, so they tried to keep them down.

What was DC's reaction to Batman when you first showed it to them?

Vince Sullivan thought it was great; my boss, Jack Leibowitz, didn't understand it. But he thought Superman was doing well, so he said, "Let's try it." He asked me, "What is a Bat-Man?" I replied, "It's a man who wears a bat costume." He said, "It looks kind of mysterious and creepy. Do you think the public will like it?" I said, "Well, let's try it."

So they bought the first story. It was six pages long and I got $10 per page, or $60. They gave me a five year contract. I continued drawing "Clip Carson" and "Rusty and His Pals" for about a year. Then, when they expanded Batman, I stopped doing other comic features. Later, in 1940, my style really developed. I honed my drawing into a more professional illustrative style. Of course, what made Batman were the bizarre villains which were influenced by Dick Tracy's villains. He had marvelous villains—Prune Face, No Face, etc.

Tracy also had a square jaw like Batman's. Did this influence you?

Yes, Dick Tracy had an influence and I always thought the square jaw connoted strength. Movie heroes like Tom Mix always had virile, square jaws.

"Later in 1940, my style really developed." A recent drawing showing the vintage style that made Batman great. © DC Comics, Inc.

Batman's jaw was almost abstract in shape, giving him an archetypal, mythical quality.

Like it was carved out of stone. I also wanted my style a little cartoony—a cross between Dick Tracy and illustration. That's why the Penguin and the Joker are still kind of cartoony. I never wanted to get into full illustration—I wanted to retain the cartoon-comic quality that I admired early in my career.

How would you and Finger work?

A lot of stories I wrote with Bill or would give him an idea and he would go home and write it. He would come over to the house and we'd kick ideas around. We would kind of co-create an idea and then he would go and write it. Bill had one problem—he was a little tardy in getting things in on deadline. He wasn't a natural writer—he had to sweat over his stuff—it

didn't flow. But it came out good in the end. He was one hell of a writer.

Who came up with the idea of making Batman a master detective?

We both came up with the fact that he would be a crime fighter. I made him a superhero vigilante when I first created him. Bill made him into a scientific detective.

How did you come up with the idea of making Batman a vigilante?

I thought it was more exciting for him to work outside the law rather than inside it. I guess growing up as a rough kid in the Bronx, we used to be vigilantes to survive. Not that we'd steal anything, but we'd be tough. We were outsiders—outside the law. We'd break a few windows and a cop would chase us. We'd meet at our clubhouse and cook Mickeys from potatoes our mothers would throw out the window and charbroil them over the fire.

How did you create Bruce Wayne?

Bruce Wayne was a collaboration with Bill Finger. I suggested the dual identity from Zorro, and he saw Zorro also, so that influenced him, too. We draw ourselves or people we know into our strips. Bruce Wayne looked like me when I was young and handsome with acquiline features. Bruce Wayne was my image, Pat Ryan was Milt Caniff's when he was thinner, and Li'l Abner Al Capp's when he was younger. We emulate ourselves to a degree; the creation doesn't fall far from the creator's pen. The alliteration of the names—Bruce Wayne-Bob Kane—was probably one reason Bill came up with the name.

Did you encounter much censorship?

In the first Batman book, he originally had a gun. He had a machine gun on his plane and used it fighting monsters. The editorial policy was to bring him over to the side of the law and get away from the vigilante he originally was and not to carry a gun. They thought this was more in keeping with the social mores of the times, and making him a murderer would taint his character. The policy was to make him an honorary member of the police force who was outside the law but still working within it. The whole moral climate changed after 1940-1941—you couldn't kill or shoot villains. Bill Finger wrote one story in which Batman had a gun. It was his idea, not mine. It was inspired by The Shadow. We didn't think anything was wrong with it, because The Shadow used a gun. But I can't remember Batman ever killing anyone with a gun except the monsters in **Batman** No. 1.

When did you begin to use assistant artists?

In 1939, the first year, I pencilled, inked, and lettered the strip. In 1940, I had George Roussos come in. He did great backgrounds—I remember one of a train—he drew all the bolts in it. Then Jerry Robinson came along and did backgrounds and lettering. I always used to draw the main villains and Batman and Robin. It began to get away from me about the second year—I had Jerry Robinson do some of the secondary gangsters. I'd say the definitive Bob Kane art, art that's mostly by me, was in the first and part of the second year. I did 90 percent of the art in the first Batman book, Jerry did the lettering, and Roussos the backgrounds.

I feel that the ghost artist's job is to emulate the cartoonist he is imitating instead of changing the strip into his own style. That's always been a bone of contention with me. If I were to copy Dick Tracy, and in those days I did, it would look just like Dick Tracy; I wouldn't put Bob Kane into it. Dick Sprang came along and he was close to my style—very cartoony. I suppose you can't fault the ghost artists because your own style has to creep into the art no matter how closely you try to copy someone. Although when Chick Young died, his son took over Blondie and the style was exactly the same and did not change. After the first years, the style of Batman became more grotesque, more bizarre, and over-illustrated so that he looked like a Sloan's Liniment ad. They lost the simple, clean lines I had by throwing in another 15 or 20 lines—too many muscles, too much hay. The artists on Batman today are very fine artists, very illustrative, but any resemblance between what I drew and their drawings is strictly coincidental. I guess they call it progress.

Detective Comics #38. Origin & 1st app. Robin.
© DC Comics, Inc.

How did Robin originate?

I created Robin totally by myself; neither Bill Finger nor Jerry Robinson created him. The only boy wonder prior to Robin was Junior in Dick Tracy. I was the first to create a boy wonder in a costume. The idea evolved from my wish fulfillment fantasy of visualizing myself as a 12 or 13 year old fighting alongside some superhero like Doc Savage or the Shadow. I visualized that every kid would like to be a Robin. In their wish fulfillment dream-world, they wanted to fight alongside a superhero. Instead of waiting to grow up to become a superhero, they wanted to do it now. A laughing daredevil, free—no school, no homework, living in a mansion above the Batcave, riding in the Batmobile—appealed to the imagination of every kid in the world. I got the name and costume from Robin Hood. Robin wears a tunic and shoes like Robin Hood. Batman and Robin didn't rob the rich to give to the poor, but, like Robin Hood, they had empathy for the poor and the underdog.

Oddly enough, when I brought the idea to my publisher, Jack Leibowitz, he didn't want Robin in the book. He said Batman was doing well by himself. He thought mothers would object to a kid fighting gangsters. He had a point. I said,

"Why don't we try it for one issue. If you don't like it, we can take it out." But when the story appeared, it really hit. The comic book which introduced Robin [Detective No. 38, April, 1940] sold double what Batman sold as a single feature. I went to the office Monday and said, "Well, I guess we ought to take Robin out—right, Jack? You don't want a kid fighting with gangsters." "Well," he said sheepishly, "leave it in. It's okay—we'll let him go." [Kane laughs.] It was so successful that every new superhero had to have a boy wonder and a whole slew of them was created.

Which did you like best—Batman when he appeared solo or the Batman who teamed up with Robin?

I preferred the first year of Batman— the more sombre, mysterious character. They returned to this image about 10 years ago. Now they draw Batman without Robin. They have returned to the mysterioso roots I originally created for the character. Robin lightened up the strip by being a laughing young daredevil, and the lightness in the color of his costume was a counterpoint to Batman's sombre mood and costume. Children wanted a lighter hero and a lighter mood. So we appealed to two factions—the adults and older teenagers, and the younger children. So there was a nice balance there. I think they

are a great team. If Robin was in the strip today, if I were drawing it, I would have them pun somewhat and be lighthearted, but I would make Robin more serious. The punning got out of hand. In the early years, Robin was not the punster he later became—they made him into a buffoon.

How was the Joker created?

Jerry Robinson will insist to his dying day that he created the Joker. But it was actually Bill Finger. The only reason I make an issue out of it is that the Joker is the best villain ever created, outside of Moriarity in Sherlock Holmes. Some people even like him better than Batman.

We were looking for super-villains in the first year of Batman. Bill and I were kicking around ideas about a maniacal killer who would play perennial life-and-death jokes on Batman that would test his mettle and ingenuity to outwit him. Then, about a week later, Bill came in with a photograph of Conrad Veidt, a fine German actor, who had played in a movie I saw as a kid called The Man Who Laughs. It was based on a famous novel by Victor Hugo, about a young gypsy boy named Gynplaine who had his mouth cut into a ghastly grin by a rival gypsy gang out for revenge. And he grew up with a ghastly smile and funereal eyes. Bill showed me the photo and said, "Why don't we create

Batman #1. First appearance of the Joker and the Cat (Catwoman). © DC Comics, Inc.

"I literally drew the photograph of Conrad Veidt into the joker's face." © DC Comics, Inc.

a killer with the face of a ghastly white clown?'' So I literally drew the photograph of Conrad Veidt into the Joker's face in the first Batman comic book.

Jerry Robinson was my assistant then, just an 18 year old kid out of college. He came in with a drawing of a joker playing card, with a Joker that looked like a court jester. We used the card in a few stories as the Joker's playing card—he would drop it after he killed someone. So somehow Jerry got in there with the card. But this was after the fact; he did not create the original concept of the Joker. Now, I don't say that Jerry is doing this intentionally, but time has eroded his memory.

I drew the Joker straighter and more illustratively than my ghost artists. They made him grotesquely clown-like, longer and thinner, and so exaggerated he looked like a buffoon. I drew him ghastly and realistically from the photo of Conrad Veidt.

The Catwoman was another great foe of Batman's. How did she originate?

I think I came up with the Catwoman. My first girlfriend Gloria looked very feline. I always liked that type. But she was a redhead and looked like Vicki Vale and was more an inspiration for her. I had another girlfriend named Ann who had black hair and green cat eyes and was very sensual-looking. She was the inspiration for Catwoman. I made sketches of her prior to the creation of Catwoman. Then I asked her to pose as that character. In fact, she wore a costume of the Catwoman she had made. I usually didn't use live models—I drew mainly from my imagination.

Were there any other sources which inspired your creation of the Catwoman?

Yes, Jean Harlow had a great influence on me as a kid. I saw her in one of her first appearances in **Hell's Angels** with Ben Lyon and James Hall. At an impressionable young age, she seemed to personify feminine pulchritude at its most sensuous. Later on when I drew the Catwoman, I kind of had her in mind, although she was a blonde and Catwoman was a brunette. She was the first influence on the Catwoman; I wanted to draw

"I had another girlfriend named Ann who had black hair and green eyes...she was the inspiration for Catwoman." © DC Comics, Inc.

somebody in her image.

We knew we needed a female nemesis to give the strip sex appeal. So we came up with a kind of female Batman, except that she was a villainess and Batman was a hero. We figured there would be this cat and mouse, cat and bat, byplay between them—he would try to reform her and she was working outside the law. But she was never a murderer and not all evil like the Joker. We felt she would appeal to the female readers—I figured they would relate to her as much as to Batman, or, more likely, she would appeal to the male readers. So she was put in the strip for the boys and girls, as a female counterpoint to Batman.

How did you come up with the idea of associating her with cats?

It's kind of the antithesis of a bat—sort of a female version of Batman, only I made her a villain. I always felt women were feline. Men were like dogs—not that they looked like dogs, but had the personalities of dogs, faithful and friendly. Cats are cool and detached, unreliable. I feel much warmer with dogs around me—cats are hard to understand, they are erratic as women are. You feel more sure of yourself with a male friend than a woman. You always need to keep women at arm's length. We don't want anyone to take over our souls, and women generally have a habit of doing that. So there is a love-resentment thing with women. I guess women will feel I'm being chauvinistic for speaking this way, but I do feel that I've had better relationships with male friends than women. With women, when the romance is over, somehow they're never my friend after that.

Who created Vicki Vale, the photographer who was romantically involved with Bruce Wayne and Batman?

I created Vicki Vale. In 1948, I came to Hollywood when they were doing the second Batman serial. I went to a party after the serial was shot and met a beautiful blonde actress named Norma Jean. I talked with her and asked her to dance. "But the music isn't playing," she said. "That's okay," I replied, "That way I get a chance to hold you." We were just kidding around. She had this whispy voice. We danced together when the music played and I asked her for a date, but she said that she was married. She was only 17 or 18 years old. She had this little-girl-lost quality. I knew she would make it as an actress. I didn't see her again until 1958 when I came to Hollywood again, and she was on the Columbia lot. She was called Marilyn Monroe then and had become quite famous. She remembered me and I knew her for several months in Hollywood. Later, when I was in New York, she lived around the corner—she was married to Arthur Miller then. She'd wear bandanas over her head and dark glasses to camoflague herself, but she had that in-imitable wiggle. We became quite friendly until she died.

After I met Marilyn, I used her image to draw Vicki Vale, girl photographer. I did some sketches of Marilyn in Santa Monica in 1948. So when I went back to New York, I showed them the sketches and told them, "Remember to color her hair blonde," because it was Marilyn Monroe I was emulating, but the colorist inadvertantly gave her red hair. Oddly enough, a full cycle later, Vicki Vale is in the new Batman movie. She is Batman's chief love interest. We kept away from romance in the early Batman stories, because Batman was primarily a kid's vehicle and children think it's sissy stuff for a superhero to be involved with women.

Did Lois Lane also inspire you to create Vicki Vale?

Yes, she had an influence. She was kind of pushy—out for a scoop like Lois Lane.

What was the inspiration for Two-Face?

I created Two-Face. He was based on Dr. Jekyll and Mr. Hyde, who combined good and evil in one person. I saw the Frederic March movie when I was a kid. Two-Face was inspired by that—I hadn't read the book. I also came up with the idea of his flipping a coin to see whether he would be good or evil, in collaboration with Bill Finger.

"I came up with the visual design of the Penguin."
© DC Comics, Inc.

Who created the Penguin?

I did. I saw this cute little penguin on a Kool cigarette pack. To me, penguins always looked like little fat men in tuxedos. I also came up with the visual design of the character. Bill invented the Man of a Thousand Umbrellas idea and all the umbrella gimmicks he used. He was a more cartoony character—partly comedic because of his stature, but still evil and a killer.

What did you think of the Batman TV show?

The camp era of the '60s, when the TV show came into prominence, has come and gone. A lot of my died-in-the-wool fans didn't like the TV show. I thought it was a marvelous spoof and great for what it was. But it certainly wasn't the definitive Batman. I didn't have any influence over the show. I was in New York then. Hollywood is the kind of town that when you're out of sight, you're out of mind, and very often when you're in town it's out of sight, out of mind. But if you're in Hollywood, it's harder for them to deny your presence.

In 1965, they were planning to kill Batman off altogether, because sales were so terrible. I had terrible apprehensions because what else could I do—it was my life's vocation. Luckily, it was saved by the TV series and it became bigger than ever. There was a Batman hysteria in 1966. The TV show, with all its camp, caused more hysteria than any other TV show, ever. The reason it burned out so fast is that it was on twice a week with a cliffhanger on Tuesday which concluded on Thursday. If it had been on once a week, it would have lasted four or five years.

How did Batman become a TV show?

Hugh Heffner showed the old Batman serials from 1943 and 1949 in the Playboy mansion. His idea of fun was to string together 13 episodes and watch them in one long Saturday night popcorn session and, in a campy gesture, hiss the villains and applaud the heroes. Some ABC agent or executive was at the mansion that night when they showed the films, and the Bunnies and Hugh were so enthusiastic about these old serials that the agent went back to ABC and said, "You ought to see what's going on at the Playboy mansion every Saturday night. Why don't we try something like that?" And that's how the TV show started.

Batman is enjoying a great resurgence in popularity now, due primarily to Frank Miller's Dark Knight series. What do you think of it?

Batman: The Dark Knight #1 by Frank Miller. © DC Comics, Inc.

What we have here is a transition from television to comic books—an emulation of the TV mini-series. Frank Miller is a brilliant innovator. The drawings, although sometimes grotesque—sometimes Batman looks like Quasimodo—are extremely interesting. Miller's lines are sketchy, but his drawings are very beautiful—very avante garde. The color is beautiful. The story is also avant garde—bringing Bruce Wayne out of retirement to fight crime in the Gotham City of the year 2000. I can't knock success—it's an exciting new format for comic books, trying to capture the adult as well as the children's market. It's put Batman back into the limelight.

Frankly, I don't understand Miller's storyline as well as I'd like to. There are certain political associations that I'm not sure of. Why the Nazi Swastikas on women's breasts and buttocks? I don't know what place politics has in comic books, but in the '80s maybe it has. And why does Batman fight Superman? How can Superman be disintegrated into a skeleton and come back all of a sudden full blown? Why would Miller make Robin a girl? What happened to the real Robin? And Batman looks very old—he doesn't look like Bruce Wayne as I drew him. That's what bothers me. If I drew Bruce Wayne at 55, he would look like Bruce Wayne but with gray hair and a few wrinkles. But he looks nothing like Bruce Wayne. He's balding and has a pugalistic nose—where's the straight, aquiline nose and square chin? I picture an older Bruce Wayne like John Forsythe—still a handsome man. Miller's Bruce Wayne looks like a laborer or a fighter. But, all in all, it's a brilliant book. Miller is tapping into something the public understands as the tremendous sales of the book show.

What is your role in the new Batman movie?

I'm a creative consultant on the movie—I wrote the bible for it, to get it on the right track. We have a brilliant young director, Tim Burton, who directed **Pee Wee's Big Adventure** and **Beetlejuice**, and one of the best scripts I've ever read by a new writer named Sam Hamm, who will become a big name once the movie is out. The movie will be dramatic and definitely not a comedy. It will not be campy like the TV show. It will go back to Batman's roots—mysterioso, dark, and sombre. I designed a new Batplane which they will re-adapt, and a new Batcave. I also designed a cape which will look like a real wing and is mechanically riggged so that when Batman raises his arms, he's going to look like a real bat.

Jack Nicholson, one of the best actors in the world, will play the Joker. I've been opting for him to play the Joker for years. He will probably play it like black comedy, but not comedic. Nicholson wanted my input on the Joker, and we had lunch a few days ago. I told him that the Joker is very maniacal and psychotic, not the buffoon of Caesar Romaro. He agreed that's how he should be played. "He'll be based in reality," as he said. He won't caricature it.

Bruce Wayne will be a three dimensional character—complex, brooding. Someone with a handsome, pretty face wouldn't do. He suffers, has self-doubts. He's neurotic because he feels responsible

for the creation of the Joker, this wild killer, and the Joker feels he has to get revenge on Batman. So it's a dual thing—"therein lies my own image." The Joker sees the image of Batman within him and Batman sees the Joker in himself. It's frightening when you see some of your own warped, repressed ideas in the other person. Michael Keaton with arched eyebrows looks a little like the Joker, more than a handsome guy like Pierce Brosnan or Robert Wagner would. Keaton has a mobile, expressive, tortured face. You don't want a pretty face, because he has to reflect the Joker.

I critiqued the script—it has some of my input, also. There were flaws in the film that I showed them and were corrected. For example, they made Bruce Wayne a wimp in front of the Joker, groveling on the floor. I said Bruce Wayne wouldn't grovel to anyone, because he's really Batman. So that scene had to go. In another scene, a reporter suspects that Wayne is Batman and comes to confront him. And Bruce acquiesces and says you've caught me. Both the reporter and Bruce are in love with Vicki, so the reporter tells him to stop fooling around with his girl. But Bruce Wayne would never acquiesce—he would have a chess game with him, duel with him. So they agreed to take that out.

There is some controversy about Michael Keaton, who has been basically a comic actor, playing Batman. How do you feel about this?

Batman is going to be terrifying in the film. Put the costume on anyone and he'll look like Batman. The only problem is that Keaton doesn't have the strongest chin in the world—that's the problem. He looks okay with the mask full-face. The costume will look like chain mail, like the knights wore, and make him appear huskier, and they'll put lifts on his shoes so that he'll be about six feet tall. With the mechanical wings, the costume will make him look like a bat—he'll look awesome. I predict that once the movie is released, Batmania again will sweep the country like it did in 1966 with the TV show.

JERRY ROBINSON INTERVIEW

When did you first become interested in cartooning?

When I was a kid, I had no interest in becoming a cartoonist. However, I had always drawn from an early age. I would lie on the floor and sketch portaits of my family as they sat and talked. One of my favorite subjects was my grandfather, whom I greatly admired. I was fascinated by his mustache and the lines on his face. I never studied art in high school because you didn't get college credits for it. But I continued to draw and was usually the cartoonist for my school newspaper. I never thought of becoming a comic artist until I met Bob Kane and began working on Batman.

How did the two of you meet?

I met Bob the summer I graduated from high school. I was accepted at three universities—Columbia, Penn, and Syracuse, and decided to go to Syracuse to study Journalism. I was interested in becoming a writer and had been an editor

The current Jerry Robinson at his desk in New York.

jackets. I decorated mine with cartoons I had drawn for my school paper. Bob was at the courts watching the play, although I don't know what he was doing there, because I don't think he ever played. He struck up a conversation and asked me who did the cartoons on my jacket. I told him, "I did," and one thing led to another, and he introduced himself. Bob was about eight or ten years older than me, but still young enough to have rapport with someone my age. He told me he was drawing a comic book feature, which had just started, called Batman. To his chagrin, I had never heard of it. So we took a walk down to the village to see if we could find a copy at the candy store. We did find an issue, but I don't think I was overly impressed with it. I was an avid reader of the Sunday comics and had enjoyed the Cupples and Leon collections of comic strips, but this was the first comic book I'd seen.

One day Bob told me that he was going to need an assistant on Batman.

of my school newspaper. I sold ice cream in the summer to pay for the first year of college. They had carts on the back of bicycles—they weren't motorized. Being the latter applicant, I got the farthest franchise from the city, which meant having to pick the ice cream up and peddling five miles to the outskirts of the city to sell it. I was always thin as a rail, and at the end of the summer, after peddling all that ice cream back and forth, I could have made the 67 lb. track team. My mother didn't think I could survive the first year in college in that condition, so she persuaded me to take $25 of my hard-earned savings of the summer and go away for a week in the country to fatten up.

I went to a resort in the mountains where I could play tennis, which has always been a passion of mine. The first day I was there, I went to the courts and was wearing a white house-painter's jacket, with lots of pockets to put brushes and paraphanalia in. It was a fad at colleges to affect these jackets and to decorate them with slogans, fraternity insignia, and whatnot. High school kids are influenced by college fads, so a lot of us wore these

A 1941 shot of Jerry Robinson in his Tudor City studio drawing a Batman page.

When he learned that I was going to go to Syracuse, he said, "Well, that's too bad. If you were coming to New York, I could offer you a job." The pay was $25 a week. That seemed like all the money in the world to me and a lot more than the $17 a week I was making selling ice cream. It was enough I could live on. So I immediately switched to Columbia. I didn't even go home, but went straight to New York and rented a room near Bob. There was about a month before I was to go to work for Bob, so I decided I should know something about cartooning. So I enrolled in a school that offered cartooning courses. But they had me drawing plaster casts as an introduction—which was boring—and had no cartooning courses, so I stopped going before the month was out.

Detective Comics #29. Vintage Batman by Bob Kane.
© DC Comics, Inc.

What were your duties when you worked for Bob?

In the beginning, I just did the lettering, then I inked backgrounds and some of the secondary characters. I found it challenging, but at first I didn't think of it seriously as a career. I was interested in becoming a writer and thought of the job as a way to pay expenses. We had to turn out a lot of work, especially after the Batman quarterly appeared. Bob began to do very loose pencils—very rough—and this was good for me, because it forced me to learn to draw. So it was a great schooling. A couple of years later, we hired George Roussos to assist me with the inking. Within the first year I worked for Bob, I was inking complete stories.

I would work in my own apartment and then Bob, Bill, and I would get together to discuss the strip. We would talk about ideas to contribute to it and compare how well we were doing to other strips. It was very all-absorbing. We ate, breathed, and slept Batman. We felt we were doing something better than other strips—we had a better cast of characters, better plots, and a better initial concept. Superman's vulnerability, for example, made him a limited character. We felt we would always be able to inject more suspense into our stories, because Batman was human and could be harmed or killed. So we had the best stories. Bill Finger, in my opinion, was the best writer in the business.

Around late 1941 or early 1942, I began to pencil and ink my own stories, while I continued to ink some of Bob's, as well as draw and ink my own covers. That's when I was hired directly by DC rather than by Bob. Bill Finger and I were contemplating leaving. Batman was very popular and we had gotten a lot of offers. Other companies wanted anybody they imagined had something to do with Batman's success. Every other month, Busy Arnold wanted to take me out to dinner. He offered me several books I could write and draw by myself. But I had a sentimental attachment to Batman. I started on it and got my professional reputation from it, so I stayed. That's when DC hired me to work directly for them. They gave me a substantial raise and said I could do covers and my own stories if I continued to work for them. So I began working at the DC office. Bill also began to work directly for DC at this time.

I rarely saw Bob after this. The cohesion of the three of us working together had split up. Bill was working on his own; other writers came in. Everyone had their own approach. I would work on my own—Bob would work on his own. The strip came to have disparate people working on it, and Bob lost control of it. It would have been much better, in terms of the quality of the strip, if Bob had kept control over it and we continued to meet so there would be a guiding nucleus. But that didn't happen.

What was Bob Kane like?

Bob was something of a playboy at the time. He loved to go to nightclubs. This was fascinating to me as a kid from the country who, in effect, was his protege. He would recount his adventures to me in detail. He had a great memory for comic routines. Two weeks afterwards, he could retell every joke a comic had told at the Copa Cabana or some other nightclub. And he was a very attractive looking guy—fairly tall, slim, black hair.

What were Bill Finger's scripts like?

They were like film scripts—he wrote full scripts with not only the scene, location, mood, and dialogue, but even angle shots. He was a visual writer. He knew how the story would be visualized. If he plotted an action on shipboard where Batman was swinging down onto the deck, he would attach a photo or illustration of the deck and the construction of the ship. He would really do a lot of the research that artists normally do, but he would do it from a story standpoint as well, so everything worked and you didn't have to figure out what was going on.

It was an exciting time; we were experimenting with sequential narrative, inventing the "language of comics." Everything we tried was new—was an innovation.. We were among the first to start to break up the page into different patterns for a storytelling or visual effect. We began to do vertical panels, panels of different shapes, vignettes, and other visual effects. They seem simple now, but it was new then. We stretched a panel across the top of the page so that it was the equivalent of two panels. Then, we expanded it to maybe a third of a page until the opening shot encompassed the whole page. This was among the first splash panels. We had to fight for these innovations. The publisher's attitude was the more panels, the more they were getting for their money, and we had to battle to improve the art and storytelling.

We were all movie fans—Orson Welles, German films—and this was a major influence on us. We tried to emulate the atmosphere of German Expressionist

films and consciously tried to get the surreal quality of those films into the strip. And Bill would constantly be looking for things in those films that suggested story ideas. We liked Fritz Lang's **Metropolis** and **M**, and [Von Sternberg's] **The Blue Angel**. **The Cabinet of Dr. Caligari** especially impressed us.

With Orson Welles' **Citizen Kane** it was more the reverse. When we saw the film, it was a revelation, because he was doing things that we had already been doing in the comics. This was a re-affirmation that we were doing things right and were not so crazy after all. We felt, Gee, here not knowing anything, we were using the same techniques as Welles, and he was a genius. It was very exciting for us. We would go back and see it over and over. Once we made a bet on how many times we saw the film. I think Frederick Ray [one of the major Superman cover artists] won

"When we saw the film [Citizen Kane], it was a revelation, because he [Orson Welles] was doing things that we had already been doing in the comics." Citizen Kane movie lobby card © 1941 RKO Radio Pictures.

it. He saw the film 40 or 50 times; I was up in the 20s. We used to sit at our desks and recite whole sequences. We knew the dialogue by heart.

What kinds of techniques was Welles using that you also employed in Batman?

The way he manipulated the camera or manipulated time. For example, he would show an event by a reaction—like the scene in which the Marion Davies character, Kane's mistress, is singing in the opera house and the camera goes up and up to the backstage scaffolding to show a stagehand's reaction to her off-key singing. The scene is told through his reaction, and you just hear her voice. Welles also used extreme low angle shots like the sequence in which Kane first takes over the newspaper, which is shot from the ground looking up at him. Welles was the first to use full sets; sets didn't have ceilings before this. We had been doing that—shooting low angle shots to get the effects up on the ceiling. Welles also used a great depth of focus in some shots. We would use techniques like that—shooting past something you wanted to make a point of, to something else. We shot through key holes, through the floor, to give a sense of a vast room or to heighten a dramatic effect. We also began to experiment with creating illusions of time, like Welles was doing, like in the Rosebud sequence when he slowed down time to focus on the glass paper weight falling from Kane's hand as he dies.

Detective Comics #73. Early cover by Robinson.
© DC Comics, Inc.

In a way, it was fortunate that Bob and I didn't have any academic art training. Because it gave us a certain freedom in the design. It was more important how things looked than if an arm could actually twist a certain way or if the perspective was correct. The cartoony style was an advantage.

We were able to give the strip a surreal look and able to draw more abstractly. Very specifically, I remember we'd look at other stuff with disdain because it was too realistic and photographic. Some of it was directly copied. We thought that was not good cartooning. We didn't want to get too photographic. I admired Foster for his great virtuosity, but Caniff was more my favorite because he was more interpretive and an impeccable storyteller. I would study his work closely. He was a great influence on Bob, too. Bob liked Foster and once in awhile would adapt a pose of Tarzan or Prince Valiant. But most of the time he didn't do that—and he didn't do it deliberately.

How did you come to create the Joker?

I was still taking writing courses at Columbia at the time. I had to do a paper for a creative writing course, some original piece of writing. With going to school at night and working for Bob during the day, I didn't have much time. So I thought of doing a story that would do double duty— that I could write for Batman and that would serve as a piece of creative writing for the class. At that time we needed more stories. There was going to be a new Batman quarterly and we needed some stories for that issue. I think maybe we had two of them done and needed two more. So I told Bob I was going to work on a story, because Bill couldn't turn out that many at once.

That night I went to work on it in my little room. My first thought was to create a villain, a strong villain to oppose Batman. This was before I even tried to write any plot ideas. From my studies in literature and my own reading, I knew that all the great heroes had an anti-hero, and were stronger characters because they were pitted against strong antagonists. There was Moriarity in **Sherlock Holmes**, David and Goliath in the **Bible**, King Arthur and Modred. And in mythology there were strong villains. At the time, there were only minor hoods in Batman, but nothing of any super-dimensions, none that I would call exotic villains. We followed the pulps and popular crime fiction of the roaring '20s, basing our villains on gangsters like Dillinger, Pretty Boy Floyd, and Al Capone. They were bank robbers, high-jackers, hold-up men—the criminal stereotypes of the era. They would be disposed of and not really be worthy of a reprise.

There was a difference of opinion in those days, by the way. It seems obvious in retrospect, but at the time it was arguable. How strong to make the villain was discussed, and it was argued both ways. There was a concern that if you made your villain too strong, it would overpower and detract from your hero, so that he would not be a hero anymore. Anyway, I was not of this view. I thought the stronger the villain, the stronger the hero would be.

I knew I wanted a continuing nemesis in the vein of Moriarity or Dick Tracy—he had a marvelous cast of bizarre villains. I don't think at the time that I could have forseen that he would be continuing to this day, but I wanted a villain that would at least last for more than one story. I loved

writing satire and humor, so it was natural for me to want to create a villain with a sense of humor, someone who would taunt Batman and most of the time get away with it. All the stories I had written for my high school paper had been humorous. I loved De Maupassant's and O. Henry's short stories with the twist endings, and these were the kind of stories I was writing. I thought someone with an internal contradiction would be intriguing; you don't usually think of a villain who does mean and nasty things as having a sense of humor. And, I knew that I wanted someone who was bizarre and exotic—visually striking.

For some reason or other, I drew clowns in high school or grammar school—they were one of the few things I would draw. I liked to draw pirates, cowboys, and clowns. I enjoyed drawing pirates and clowns, because they had colorful costumes and an exotic, bizarre look. So, I think that also relates to my creation of the Joker. Clowns are sad—funny and sad. Contradictions like that are

Illustrated above are The Joker card designed by Jerry Robinson and a photograph of Conrad Veidt from the film *The Man Who Laughs*. The Joker, who first appeared in Batman #1 was modeled after this photograph. See Batman #1 and compare the drawings from the first Joker story with this photograph.

interesting. The pathos had an appeal for me as a kid. I loved the circus. Trenton had an annual fair—they had an old-fashioned midway with clowns and strongmen, etc. It was very exciting.

When I began to toss around ideas and to deliberately make associations, somehow I thought, well, he's got a sense of humor—he's a joker. I immediately made an association with the joker playing card with that marvelous grinning face. I was fascinated by the idea of a sinister clown. That was the contradiction I was looking for. Although I didn't know it then, the historic background of the joker on the playing card is a symbol that goes back for centuries. In all societies, they had jokers and jesters. So it had a built-in meaning.

This is now 12:00 or 1:00 a.m. in the morning, and I made a frantic search throughout my room for a deck of playing cards. I felt I couldn't continue with the script until I could actually see him and get his visual appearance set. Earlier in high school, I had played contract Bridge, so I found a deck and, low and behold, it was the one with the classic joker. I knew as soon as I saw it—that was it—that was how he should look. Everything crystallized then—his name was the Joker, he would give out the joker playing card as his calling card, and that would be how he looked. Then I made my first drawing of the Joker, a playing card with the Joker's face on it.

I can't tell you how excited I was. I couldn't wait to rush over to Bob's with the idea. The next morning I told him about the story I wanted to write. The idea seemed just right for Batman. The Joker served as a marvelous counterpoint to the sinister, shadowy figure of Batman. I always saw Batman as a surreal character, and the Joker fitted this mood. Bob loved the idea immediately. Bill came over shortly afterwards and also loved it. Then came the—would you call it—the denouement? Bob said it was so great an idea that they wanted to use it for the first Batman quarterly, which was then in production. This would have been my first story, and I anticipated taking my time and develop-

ing the character. I never expected a discussion about anyone else doing it. As they persuaded me, my heart was sinking by the minute. I can still feel it today, and I was only 17 or 18 then. This would have been my first story, and I was still going to school at the time, and it would have taken me weeks to write it. I was heartbroken, but, for the sake of the strip, I had to admit that Bill was far better equipped to write it. I never attempted to write another Batman story. I guess my experience with the Joker story turned me off.

Didn't Bill suggest modeling the Joker after a photo of Conrad Veidt from the film The Man Who Laughs ?

Yes. This was typical of what Bill would do. He thought visually, and my drawing of the Joker reminded him of Conrad Veidt. As I said before, he would often attach photos to his scripts. The Veidt photo reinforced the validity of the idea—so it helped flesh the concept out. That first story was a gem. Bill perfectly captured the bizarreness of the Joker using an idea many mystery writers were fond of—the closed room plot.

Why didn't the Joker have an origin? There was no explanation for his bizarre appearance.

We did that deliberately. Later on, long after I had left the strip, they gave him an origin and explained that he looked that way because of some chemical accident. Frankly, I don't think we would have written an origin for him. I would have prefered it if his origin had always remained unknown—it takes the mystery out of the character to explain it and makes him too ordinary. It would be better if characters in the story or the readers themselves speculated about it.

Why the white face and green hair?

The white face came from the fact that he appeared that way on the playing card. That was the idea—to give him a bizarre look and the face of a clown. The green hair was probably Bob's idea. No one else would have made a decision like that. After we invented a new character, we usually made suggestions about how to color him. The colorist would usually have made his hair dark blue to look like black hair. The idea of the Joker being very tall was also in Bob's first sketch, I believe.

Wasn't the Joker originally supposed to be killed off in the second story in Batman No. 1?

Yes. Bill killed the Joker off in the script he wrote, but our editor, Whitney Ellsworth, felt that he was such a great character that he had us redraw the last few panels to show that he hadn't really died. It was natural for Bill to decide to kill him off. For him to come back was a precedent. I can't think of any other villains in Batman that did continue before this. Batman usually disposed of them at the end.

Detective Comics #40. The first Joker cover.
© DC Comics, Inc.

You also helped create Robin, didn't you?

I had a hand in it. My contribution was limited to the name, not the idea of adding a boy. I remember the day specifically. I came in, and Bob and Bill were already discussing the idea of adding a kid. Everybody loved the idea. I also liked it because it gave another dimension to the strip. I always enjoyed stories like **Treasure Island** *which had a kid I could identify with. Kids relate to two things—a contemporary, a peer, or a hero figure they could look up to. This combined*

both—a father figure and a kid they could imagine themselves to be. It was the first boy wonder in comic books. So, we came up with a lot of firsts at this time—the first continuing villain in Batman and the idea of adding a boy wonder.

We had a big session about the name that day we were discussing adding a kid to the strip. When I came over, Bob had already started on some initial sketches of the new character. His original idea was for something along the lines of a super-costume. And Bob and Bill had a long list of names. Our practice was to put down every conceivable idea, even if it wasn't exactly the right one, because it might suggest something. We always felt that the names were very important. For some reason, their trend of thought was more towards a supernatural name—the one I remember specifically was Mercury. They were mostly mythological names. There wasn't any one I liked among them. I thought that it should not be anything of that kind—that would be a super-character, not an ordinary kid. This would be contrary to the concept of Batman. It inferred some super power that was in conflict with the concept of Batman being an ordinary human being. We always tried to keep Batman distinct from Superman, and I wanted to preserve that distinction. They were pretty settled on one name—something like Mercury. I kept saying, "No, no, I don't think that one is appropriate." I didn't know what to name him, but out of the depths, I came up with the name "Robin." I derived it from Robin Hood. In the beginning, I had to argue for "Robin," because their mindset was on something else.

After some discussion, it was agreed that the name Robin was best suited to the concept of the boy. Bob was at the drawing board and we were standing on both sides of him making suggestions. Once we agreed on the name, I suggested adapting the Robin Hood costume. So Bob started drawing a costume with imitation chain mail on the trunks and a jacket like a tunic a la Robin Hood. And he put little tails on the shoes to suggest medievil shoes and to give an illusion of speed when he was running. This also may have been a carry-over of the Mercury idea. *Then Bob drew the face and two spits of hair. I think that came from an earlier character of his—it was a trademark of his kids. I had designed this thing for the first letter of an opening caption—I would draw an elaborate letter like in an old manuscript in a little circle. So I suggested adding the "R" with a circle around it as a counterpart to Batman's insignia. Actually, it is an implied circle—there is no circle around it. It is black until it hits the circle. It worked well because the red of the jacket goes through the letter. I didn't know that much about lettering. It's probably one of the few kinds of lettering I knew. I didn't go to art school where you learn all kinds of type faces.*

Detective Comics #74. The first Tweedledee and Tweedledum by Robinson. Robinson cover art. © DC Comics, Inc.

Did you create any other characters for Batman?

I drew the first Tweedledee and Tweedledum story, and I think that I created them. Of course, they were based on Lewis Carroll's Alice in Wonderland.

You are also famous for drawing some of the best Batman covers of the '40s.

Outside of a few specific stories, I enjoyed drawing the covers most of all. I was very interested in doing symbolic covers which weren't typical in those days. Bob did a few which were kind of symbolic, which set a precedent—like the one which introduced Robin and showed him breaking through a circus hoop and the one of the two of them running. I was trying to do a completely symbolic cover of what the content was of the lead story, but without showing any scene from that story. Symbolic covers lent themselves to simple, strong visual images and meant I didn't have to worry about setting a natural scene and could use flat shapes like a poster. I went for the poster effect to make the book stand out visually on the newsstands. Comic books are relatively small and you would have to examine them carefully to see all the detail if you did a full scene. We would look at them on the stands, and I would be very pleased because you could spot our covers right away.*

Batman #13. Robinson parachute cover. © DC Comics, Inc.

Do you recall any specific covers that you did that you especially liked?

I especially liked the cover with Batman and Robin wearing parachutes and landing on spotlighted targets, and the cover for a Joker story, "Slay It With Flowers," in which the Joker was a florist. I liked to do covers where the Joker would be very large and Batman and Robin very small. The "Slay It With Flowers" cover was adapted from the splash panel and had a huge Joker coming out of a flower and spraying small figures of Batman and Robin with insecticide. Another favorite dealt with a story in which the Joker commits a crime a day and challenges Batman to stop him. It showed a huge figure of the Joker ripping out the pages of a calendar and diminutive figures of Batman and Robin being inundated by the pages. I would also color the covers I did or give color guides to the colorist.

What did you do after you left Batman?

I wanted to do more of my own stories and characters, and felt that I needed to do something new. I worked with Mort Meskin in the '40s. He created Johnny Quick and the Vigilante for DC. Then we got other accounts and did the Black Terror and the Fighting Yank for Standard and some other titles for Simon and Kirby. In 1950, I started teaching at what is now called the School for the Visual Arts in New York. I've had a number of students become successful artists; for example, Steve Ditko was one of my students. I also began to work for Stan Lee at Marvel in the '50s. In the mid-'50s, I collaborated on a science fiction comic strip set in the contemporary future called Jet Scott. We were syndicated in 75 papers and it lasted about two years. After that, I went into book illustration and have illustrated over

Detective Comics #70. Robinson cover art. © DC Comics, Inc.

30 books on various subjects. I started doing political cartoons in 1961 for my syndicated newspaper panel, "Still Life." It's still going, and is now titled "Life With Robinson." I have also started my own newspaper syndicate, the Cartoonist's and Writer's Syndicate, which represents cartoonists from 40 countries. Most recently, I have collaborated on a musical called "Astra," which combines science fiction and political satire, and am exploring the possibility of adapting it for films.

An example of Robinson's syndicated cartoon series. © 1978 Jerry Robinson, Cartoonist's & Writer's Syndicate.

DIRECTORY OF COMIC AND NOSTALGIA SHOPS

This is a current up-to-date list, but is not all-inclusive. We cannot assume any responsibility in your dealings with these shops. This list is provided for your information only. When planning your trips, it would be advisable to make appointments in advance. To get your shop included in the next edition, write for rates. Items stocked by these shops are listed just after the telephone numbers and are coded as follows:

(a) Golden Age comics
(b) Silver Age comics
(c) New comics, magazines
(d) Pulps
(e) Paperbacks
(f) Big Little Books
(g) Magazines (old)
(h) Books (old)

(i) Movie posters, lobby cards
(j) Original art
(k) Toys (old)
(l) Records (old)
(m) Gum trading cards
(n) Underground comics
(o) Old radio show tapes
(p) Premiums

(q) Comic related posters
(r) Comic supplies
(s) Role playing games
(t) Star Trek items
(u) Dr. Who items
(v) Japanese animation
    items

ALABAMA:

Camelot Books
500 South Quintard Avenue
Anniston, AL 36201
PH:205-236-3474 (a-v)

Discount Comic Book Shop
1301 Noble Street
Anniston, AL 36201
PH:205-238-8373 (a,b,e,q,r)

Books and Comics
2807-A Florence Blvd.
Mail: Rt. 8, Box 529-B
Florence, AL 35630
PH:205-767-3123 (a-c,e,h,i,l-o,r-u)

Sincere Comics
3738 Airport Blvd.
Mobile, AL 36608
PH:205-342-2603 (a-c,e,n,q-t)

ARIZONA:

AAA Best Comics, Etc.
9204 N. Seventh St., #12
Phoenix, AZ 85020
PH:602-997-4012 (a-c,e,g,q,r,s,v)

All About Books & Comics
529 E. Camelback
Phoenix, AZ 85012
PH:602-277-0757 (a-e,g-i,l-n,q-v)

All About Books & Comics West
4208 W. Dunlap
Phoenix, AZ 85051
PH:602-435-0410 (a-e,g-i,l-n,q-v)

CRC Collectibles
3033 North 24th Street
Phoenix, AZ 85016-7800
PH:602-957-8833 (b,c,g,l,m,q,r)

The ONE Book Shop
120-A East University Drive
Tempe, AZ 85281
PH:602-967-3551 (a-e,g,i,m-o,q-v)

The Comic Corner
P. O. Box 58779
Tucson, AZ 85702-8779
PH:602-326-2677 (b,c,e)

Fantasy Comics
6001 E. 22nd St.
Tucson, AZ 85711
PH:602-748-7483 (b,c,n,q,r)

Fantasy Comics
2745 N. Campbell
Tucson, AZ 85719
PH:602-325-9790 (b,c,n,q,r)

ARKANSAS:

Rock Bottom Used Book Shop
418 W. Dickson St.
Fayetteville, AR 72701
PH:501-521-2917 (a-c,e,g,h,n,q,r)

Paperbacks Plus
2207 Rogers Avenue
Fort Smith, AR 72901
PH:501-452-5446 (b,c,e,g-i,n,q,r)

Alternate Worlds Books & Comics
110 Bridge St., Suite #25
Hot Springs, AR 71901
PH:501-624-2040 (a-c,e,j,q-s)

Pie-Eyes
5211 W. 65th St.
Little Rock, AR 72209
PH:501-568-1414 (a-i,k-n,p-u)

Collector's Edition Comics
5310 MacArthur Drive
North Little Rock, AR 72118
PH:501-753-2586 (a-c,e,h,q-t)

TNT Collectors Hut
503 W. Hale Ave.
Osceola, AR 72370
PH:501-563-5760 (b,c,m,r)

CALIFORNIA:

Fantasy Kingdom
1802 W. Olive Ave.
Burbank, CA 91506
PH:818-954-8432 (a-c,i,m,n,q,r,t-v)

Graphitti Comics & Games
4325 Overland Ave.
Culver City, CA 90230
PH:213-559-2058 (b,c,g,i,l,q-s)

Comic Quest
24346 Muirlands
El Toro, CA 92630
PH:714-951-9668 (b,c,j,q-s)

Thrill Books
629 First Street
Encinitas, CA 92024
PH:619-753-4299 (b-g,m-o,q-v)

Comic Gallery
675 N. Broadway
Escondido, CA 92025
PH:619-745-5660 (a-c,j,m,n,q-t,v)

The Comic Castle
320 - 2nd St., Suite 2H
Eureka, CA 95501
PH:707-444-BOOK (b,c,n,q,r)

Adventureland Comics
106 N. Harbor Blvd.
Fullerton, CA 92632
PH:714-738-3698 (a-c,q,r,v)

Geoffrey's Comics
15530 Crenshaw Blvd.
Gardena, CA 90249
PH:213-538-3198 (a-c,g,m-o,q-s,v)

Fantasy Illustrated
12531 Harbor Blvd.
Garden Grove, CA 92640
PH:714-537-0087 (a-f,h,m)

Shooting Star Comics
700 E. Colorado Blvd.
Glendale, CA 91205
PH:818-502-1535 (a-c,k,m,o,q-s,v)

The American Comic Book Co.
2670 E. Florence
Huntington Park, CA 90255
PH:213-589-4500 (a-k,m,n,p)

The American Comic Book Co.
3972 Atlantic Ave.
Long Beach, CA 90807
PH:213-426-0393 (a-k,m,n,p)

Comet Books
5534 N. Figueroa St.
Los Angeles, CA 90042
PH:213-255-5490

Golden Apple Comics
7711 Melrose Ave.
Los Angeles, CA 90046
PH:213-658-6047 (a-c,f,g,j,m,n)

Golden Apple Comics #3
8934 West Pico Blvd.
Los Angeles, CA 90035
PH:213-274-2008 (a-c,f,g,j,m,n)

Graphitti Westwood—UCLA
960 Gayley Ave.
Los Angeles, CA 90024
PH:213-824-3656 (a-c,g,i,l-n,q-s)

Wonderworld Comics and Baseball Cards
1579 El Camino
Millbrae, CA 94030
(a-c,j,m,n,q-s)

Bonanza Books & Comics
Roseburg Square
813 W. Roseburg Avenue
Modesto, CA 95350-5058
PH:209-529-0415 (a-f,h,j,k,m,q-v)

Ninth Nebula:
The Comic Book Store
11517 Burbank Bl. in back
North Hollywood, CA 90000
PH:818-509-2901 (a-v)

Golden Apple Comics #2
8962 Reseda Blvd.
Northridge, CA 91324
PH:818-993-7804 (a-c,f,g,j,m,n)

Freedonia Funnyworks
350 S. Tustin Ave.
Orange, CA 92666
PH:714-639-5830
(a-c,f,j,k,m,n,p-r)

Desert Comics
174 N. Palm Canyon Dr.
Palm Springs, CA 92262
PH:619-325-5805

T•R•H Gallery
1090 N. Palm Canyon Dr. #B
Palm Springs, CA 92262-4420
PH:619-320-9599 (j)

Lee's Comics
3429 Alma St.
(In Alma Plaza)
Palo Alto, CA 94306
PH:415-493-3957 (a-c,e-g,l-o,q,r,t-v)

Galaxy Comics & Cards
1503 Aviation Blvd.
Redondo Beach, CA 90278
PH:213-374-7440 (a-m,o-v)

Rialto Coins
138 S. Riverside Ave.
Rialto, CA 92376
PH:714-874-3940 (a-i,k-n,p-r,t)

Virginia's Baseball Cards & Comics
402 E. Foothill Blvd., Suite F
Rialto, CA 92376
PH:714-820-1255 (a,c,e,m,q,r)

Markstu Discount Comics
3642 - 7th St.
Riverside, CA 92501
PH:714-684-8544 (a-c,q-s,u,v)

Comic Gallery
4224 Balboa Ave.
San Diego, CA 92117
PH:619-483-4853 (a-c,j,m,n,q-t,v)

San Francisco Card Exchange
1316 - 18th Ave.
San Francisco, CA 94122
PH:415-665-TEAM (a-c,g,m,r)

Gary's Corner Bookstore
1051 So. San Gabriel Blvd.
San Gabriel, CA 91776
PH:818-285-7575 (b,c,e,m,q-t,v)

Comic Collector Shop
73 E. San Fernando
San Jose, CA 95113
PH:408-287-2254 (a-h,l,n,q,r)

The Comic Shop
16390 E. 14th St.
San Leandro, CA 94578
PH:415-278-9545 (a-c,g,m,q,r,s)

The Sub
785 Marsh
San Luis Obispo, CA 93401
PH:805-541-3735 (b,c,i,n,q-v)

Lee's Comics Superstore
2222 S. El Camino Real
San Mateo, CA 94403
PH:415-571-1489
(a-c,e-g,l-o,q,r,t-v)

San Mateo Comics, Baseball Cards & Original Art
306 Baldwin Ave.
San Mateo, CA 94401
PH:415-344-1536 (a-c,j,m,n,q-s)

Brian's Books
3225 Cabrillo Ave.
Santa Clara, CA 95051
PH:408-985-7481 (a-c,g,m,q-s)

R & K Comics
3153 El Camino Real
Santa Clara, CA 95051
PH:408-554-6512 (a-c,f,n,o,q,r,v)

Atlantis Fantasyworld
707 Pacific Avenue
Santa Cruz, CA 95060
PH:408-426-0158 (a-c,e,n,q-t)

Markgraf's Comic Books
440 S. Broadway
Santa Maria, CA 93454
PH:805-925-7470 (a,c,g,i,m,q-t)

Hi De Ho Comics & Fantasy
525 Santa Monica Blvd.
Santa Monica, CA 90401
PH:213-394-2820
(a-d,f,g,i,j,m,n,q,r,t,u)

Outer Limits
14513 Ventura Blvd.
Sherman Oaks, CA 91403
PH:818-995-0151

Super Hero Universe
Sycamore Plaza
2955-A5 Cochran St.
Simi Valley, CA 93065
PH:805-583-3027 (b,c,e,g,n,p-s)

Cheap Comics
12123 Garfield Ave.
South Gate, CA 90280
PH:213-408-0900
(c-e,h,i,k,m-o,r-u)

The American Comic Book Co.
12206 Ventura Blvd.
Studio City, CA 91604
PH:818-980-4976 (a-k,m,n,p)

Roleplayers
5933 Adobe Rd.
29 Palms, CA 92277
PH:619-367-6282

Ralph's Comic Corner
2408 E. Main St.
Ventura, CA 93003
PH:805-653-2732 (a-c,m,n,q-s)

The Second Time Around Bookshop
391 E. Main St.
Ventura, CA 93001
PH:805-643-3154 (a,b,d-h,l)

Graphitti Comics & Records
Amfac Hotel (Rear) LAX
8639 Lincoln Blvd. #102
Westchester, L.A., CA 90045
PH:213-641-8661 (b,c,g,i,l,q-s)

COLORADO:

The Colorado Comic Book Co.
220 N. Tejon St.
Colorado Springs, CO 80903
PH:719-635-2516 (a-c,e,n,q-u)

Colorado Comic Book Co./ Heroes & Dragons
The Citadel #2158
Colorado Springs, CO 80909
PH:719-5509570 (b,c,e,q-t,v)

CONNECTICUT:

Outer Limits Comic Shop
Rt. 37 - 52½ Pembroke Rd.
Danbury, CT 06811
PH:203-746-1068 (a-c,f,k,m,q-s)

"The Bookie"
206 Burnside Ave.
East Hartford, CT 06108
PH:203-289-1208 (a-h,q,r,t)

F & S Comics & Fantasy Shop
54 Bank St.
New Milford, CT 06776
PH:203-355-3426 (a-k,m,o,q-v)

DISTRICT OF COLUMBIA:

Another World
1504 Wisconsin Ave.
Georgetown,
Washington, DC 20007
PH:202-333-8650 (a-c,k,q-s)

FLORIDA:

Dragon's Tale
28 Seminole Road
Atlantic Beach, FL 32233
PH:904-246-0163 (a-c,q-t,v)

The Funny Farm
422 26th St. W.
Bradenton, FL 34205
PH:813-747-7714 (a,b,f,k,m,p,r)

Comics Etc.
1271 Semoran Blvd., Suite 125
Lake Howell Square
Casselberry, FL 32707
PH:407-679-5665 (b,c,e,m,q-t)

Phil's Comic Shoppe
7778 Wiles Road
Coral Springs, FL 33065
PH:305-752-0580 (a-c,g,m,n,q,r)

Acevedo's Collectables
4761 S. University Drive
Davie, FL 33328
PH:305-434-0540 (b,c,g,i,k,m,r)

Cliff's Books
209 N. Woodland Blvd. (17-92)
De Land, FL 32720
PH:904-734-6963 (a-f,h,j,l-n,q-t)

Family Book Shop
1301 N. Woodland Blvd.
(near Daytona Beach & Orlando)
De Land, FL 32720
PH:904-736-6501
(b,c,e,g,h,m,n,r,s)

Charlie's Comics
1255 West 46th Street
Hialeah, FL 33014
PH:305-557-5994 (a-c,g,j,m-o,q-v)

Past—Present—Future Comics
6186 S. Congress Ave., Suite A4
Lantana, FL 33462
PH:407-433-3068 (b,c,q-s)

Geppi's Comic World
2200 East Bay Drive #203
Largo, FL 34601
PH:813-585-0325 (a-c,f)

Phil's Comic Shoppe
614 S. State Rd. 7
Margate, FL 33063
PH:305-977-6947 (a-c,g,m,n,q,r)

Stargate
277 N. Babcock Street
Melbourne, FL 32935
PH:407-259-2374
(a-c,e,g-j,m,n,p-v)

Frank's Comics & Baseball Card Store
2678 S.W. 87 Avenue
Miami, FL 33155
PH:305-226-5072
(a-c,g,i-k,m,p,r,t)

Comic Warehouse
1029 Airport Rd., #B-6
Naples, FL 33942
PH:813-643-1020
(b,c,e,g,j,m,n,q-u)

Comics & Fantasy
105 Bank St.
New Port Richey, FL 33552
PH:813-846-1261
(a-c,e,g,i-k,m,n,q-s)

Sea Level Comics & Collectibles
(Mail order) (phone for appointment)
P. O. Box 1665
New Port Richey, FL 34656
PH:813-845-6371 (a-c,i,m)

Tropic Comics South, Inc.
742 N.E. 167th St.
N. Miami Beach, FL 33162
PH:305-940-8700 (a-d,j,n,r)

Adventure Into Comics
841 Bennett Rd.
Orlando, FL 32803
PH:407-896-4047 (a-c,g,j,m,n,q,r)

The Cartoon Museum
4300 S. Semoran, Suite 109
Orlando, FL 32822-2453
PH:407-273-0141 (a-k,m,n,p-r)

Coliseum of Comics
4103 S. Orange Blossom Trail
Orlando, FL 32809
PH:407-422-5757 (b,c,g,q-s)

Enterprise 1701
2814 Corrine Drive
Orlando, FL 32803
PH:407-896-1701 (c,e,o,q-v)

Cloak and Dagger Comics
154 West Granada Blvd.
Ormond Beach, FL 32074
PH:904-677-6763 (a-c,e,i,j,m,q-v)

Past—Present—Future Comics North
4270 Northlake Blvd.
Palm Beach Gardens, FL 33410
PH:407-775-2141 (b,c,g,n,q-v)

Sincere Comics
Town & Country Plaza
3300 N. Pace Blvd.
Pensacola, FL 32505
PH:904-432-1352 (a-f,j,n,q-t)

Tropic Comics, Inc.
313 S. State Rd. 7
Plantation, FL 33317
PH:305-587-8878 (a-d,j,n,r)

Comics U.S.A.
3231 N. Federal Highway
Pompano Beach, FL 33064
PH:305-942-1455 (a-d,g,m,q-s)

Seminole Baseball Cards and Comics
9108 Seminole Blvd.
Seminole, FL 34642
PH:813-398-7180 (a-c,m,q-v)

Comic Exchange, Inc.
8432 W. Oakland Park Blvd.
Sunrise, FL 33351
PH:305-742-0777 (b-e,g,q-v)

Tropic Comics North, Inc.
1018 - 21st St. (U.S. 1)
Vero Beach, FL 32960
PH:407-562-8501 (a-c,j,n,r,s)

GEORGIA:

Titan Games & Comics, Inc.
5436 Riverdale Rd.
College Park, GA 30349
PH:404-996-9129 (a-d,i,n,q-v)

Art Moods Cards & Comics
1058 Mistletoe Rd.
Decatur, GA 30033
PH:404-321-1899
(a-c,f,g,m,n,p-s,v)

Titan Games & Comics IV
2131 Pleasant Hill Rd.
Duluth, GA 30136
PH:404-497-0202 (a-c,m-o,q-v)

Fischer's Book Store
6569 Riverdale Rd.
Riverdale, GA 30274
PH:404-997-7323
(b,c,e,g,h,l-n,q-u)

Titan Games & Comics III
2585 Spring Road
Smyrna, GA 30080
PH:404-433-8226 (a-c,n,q-v)

Titan Games & Comics II
3377 Lawrenceville Hwy.
Tucker, GA 30084
PH:404-491-8067 (a-c,e,h,n,o,q-v)

HAWAII:

Compleat Comics Company
1728 Kaahumanu Avenue
Wailuku, Maui, HI 96793
PH:808-242-5875 (a-c,m,n,q-s)

IDAHO:

King's Komix Kastle
1706 N. 18th St. (appointments)
Boise, ID 83702
PH:208-343-7142 (a-i,m,n,q,r)

King's Komix Kastle II
2560 Leadville (drop in)
Mail: 1706 N. 18th
Boise, ID 83706
PH:208-343-7055 (a-i,m,n,q,r)

**New Mythology Comics &
Science Fiction**
1725 Broadway
Boise, ID 83706
PH:208-344-6744 (a-e,n,q-s)

ILLINOIS:

Friendly Frank's Distribution
(Wholesale Only)
727 Factory Rd.
Addison, IL 60101

Friendly Frank's Comics
11941 S. Cicero
Alsip, IL 60658
PH:312-371-6760 (a-d,f,g,i,j,n,q,r)

Moondog's Comicland
1231 W. Dundee Rd.
Plaza Verde
Buffalo Grove, IL 60090
PH:312-259-6060 (b,c,m,q-s,u,v)

Comics for Heroes
1702 W. Foster (main store)
Chicago, IL 60640
PH:312-769-4745 (a-c,m,n,q-v)

Comics for Heroes
3937 W. Lawrence
Chicago, IL 60625
PH:312-478-8585 (a-c,m,n,q-v)

Larry Laws (by appointment only)
(Also Mail Order)
831 Cornelia
Chicago, IL 60657
PH:312-477-9247 (e,g,h)

Joe Sarno's Comic Kingdom
5941 W. Irving Park Rd.
Chicago, IL 60634
PH:312-545-2231 (a-d,j,r)

Yesterday
1143 W. Addison St.
Chicago, IL 60613
PH:312-248-8087 (a,b,d-g,i-n,r,t)

Moondog's Comicland
114 S. Waukegan Rd.
Deerbrook Mall
Deerfield, IL 60015
PH:312-272-6080 (b,c,m,q-s,u,v)

The Paper Escape
205 W. 1st Street
Dixon, IL 61021
PH:815-284-7567 (b,c,e,g,m,q-t)

Graham Crackers Comics
5228 South Main Street
Downers Grove, IL 60515
PH:312-852-1810 (a-d,f,n,q-s)

GEM Comics
156 N. York Rd.
Elmhurst, IL 60126
PH:312-833-8787 (a-c,q-s,u)

More Fun Comics
650 Roosevelt Rd., Suite #112
Glen Ellyn, IL 60137
PH:312-469-6141 (a-c,e,m,o,r-u)

Galaxy of Books
Rt. 137 & Sheridan Rd.
NCW Great Lakes Depot
Great Lakes, IL 60064
PH:312-473-1099 (a-g,q-t)

Moondog's Comicland
139 W. Prospect Ave.
Mt. Prospect, IL 60056
PH:312-398-6060 (a-c,m,q-s,u,v)

Moondog's Comicland
Randhurst Mall - Lower Level
Mt. Prospect, IL 60056
PH:312-577-8668 (c,m,q-s,u,v)

Graham Crackers Comics
5 East Chicago Ave.
Naperville, IL 60540
PH:312-355-4310 (a-d,f,n,q-s)

Tomorrow Is Yesterday
5600 N. Second St.
Rockford, IL 61111
PH:815-633-0330 (a-c,e-j,m-o,q-v)

Tomorrow Is Yesterday
1414 N. Main Street
Rockford, IL 61103
PH:815-961-0330 (a-c,e-j,m-o,q-v)

Moondog's Comicland
1455 W. Schaumburg Rd.
Schaumburg Plaza
Schaumburg, IL 60194
PH:312-529-6060 (b,c,m,q-s,u,v)

Unicorn Comics & Cards
216 S. Villa Avenue
Villa Park, IL 60181
PH:312-279-5777
(a-c,e,g,h,j,l-n,q-s)

Heroland Comics
6963 W. 111th St.
Worth, IL 60482
PH:312-448-2937 (a-c,g,k,n,q-v)
(area code 708 after Nov. 1, '89)

Galaxy of Books
1908 Sheridan Road
Zion, IL 60099
PH:312-872-3313 (a-h,l,q,r,t)

INDIANA:

25th Century Five & Dime
106 E. Kirkwood, P.O. Box 7
Bloomington, IN 47402
PH:812-332-0011 (b,c,e,g-i,n,q-s)

The Bookstack
112 W. Lexington Ave.
Elkhart, IN 46516
PH:219-293-3815 (a-c,e,h,r,s)

Spider's Web
51815 State Rd. 19 N.
Elkhart, IN 46514
PH:219-264-9178 (a-c,e,g,h,n,q,r)

The Book Broker
2127 S. Weinbach Ave.
Evansville, IN 47714
PH:812-479-5647 (a-h,l-o,q-t)

Books, Comics and Things
2212 Maplecrest Rd.
Fort Wayne, IN 46815
PH:219-749-4045 (a-c,e-h,m,q-u)

Books, Comics and Things
6105 West Jefferson Blvd.
Westland Mall
Fort Wayne, IN 46804
PH:219-436-0159 (a-c,e-h,m,q-u)

**Broadway Comic Book and
Baseball Card Shop**
2423 Broadway
Fort Wayne, IN 46807
PH:219-744-1456 (a-i,m,q-u)

Friendly Frank's Distr., Inc.
(Wholesale only)
3990 Broadway
Gary, IN 46408
PH:219-884-5052 (c,g,n,r,s)

Friendly Frank's Comics
220 Main Street
Hobart, IN 46342
PH:219-942-6020 (a-d,f,g,i,j,n,q,r)

**Comic Carnival & Nostalgia
Emporium**
6265 N. Carrollton Ave.
Indianapolis, IN 46220
PH:317-253-8882 (a-j,m-u)

**Comic Carnival & Nostalgia
Emporium**
5002 S. Madison Ave.
Indianapolis, IN 46227
PH:317-787-3773 (a-j,m-u)

**Comic Carnival & Nostalgia
Emporium**
982 N. Mitthoeffer Rd.
Indianapolis, IN 46229
PH:317-898-5010 (a-j,m-u)

**Comic Carnival & Nostalgia
Emporium**
3837 N. High School Rd.
Indianapolis, IN 46254
PH:317-293-4386 (a-j,m-u)

John's Comic Closet
4610 East 10th St.
Indianapolis, IN 46201
PH:317-357-6611
(b,c,e,g-j,m,n,q-u)

IOWA:

Oak Leaf Comics
5219 University Ave.
Cedar Falls, IA 50613
PH:319-277-1835 (a-c,n,q-v)

Comic World & Baseball Cards
1626 Central Ave.
Dubuque, IA 52001
PH:319-557-1897 (a-c,g,m,n,q-s,u)

Oak Leaf Comics
23 - 5th S.W.
Mason City, IA 50401
PH:515-424-0333 (a-c,e-v)

The Comiclogue
520 Elm St., P.O. Box 65304
West Des Moines, IA 50265
PH:515-279-9006 (a-c,m-r,t,u)

KANSAS:

Prairie Dog Comics East
Oxford Square Mall
6100 E. 21st St , Suite 190
Wichita, KS 67208
PH:316-688-5576 (a-n,p-s)

Prairie Dog Comics West
Central Heights Mall
7387 West Central
(New location in area pending)
Wichita, KS 67212
PH:316-722-6316 (a-n,p-s)

KENTUCKY:

Pac-Rat's, Inc.
428 E. Main Street
on Fountain Square
Bowling Green, KY 42101
PH:502-782-8092 (a-i,l,n,o,q-v)

The Paperback Place & Comic Shoppe
622 Maple Street
Campbellsville, KY 42718
PH:502-465-7710
(b,c,e,f,h,i,l-n,q-s)

Comic Book World
7130 Turfway Road
Florence, KY 41042
PH:606-371-9562 (a-c,e,m,q-v)

The Great Escape
2433 Bardstown Road
Louisville, KY 40205
PH:502-456-2216 (a-c,i,l-n,q-t,v)

LOUISIANA:

B.T. & W.D. Giles
P. O. Box 271
Keithville, LA 71047
PH:318-925-6654 (a,b,d-f,h)

BSI Comics
5039 Fairfield St.
Metairie, LA 70006
PH:504-889-2665 (a-c,g,q,r,t,v)

The Bookworm of N.O.E.
7011 Read Blvd.
New Orleans, LA 70127
PH:504-242-7608 (c,e,q-u)

MAINE:

Lippincott Books
624 Hammond St.
Bangor, ME 04401
PH:207-942-4398 (a,b,d-h,n,r,t,u)

Moonshadow Comics
10 Exchange St.
Portland, ME 04101
PH:207-772-3870 (a-c,n,q,r)

MARYLAND:

Universal Comics
5300 East Drive
Arbutus, MD 21227
PH:301-242-4578 (a-c,e,g,k,m,q,r,t)

Comic Book Kingdom, Inc.
4307 Harford Road
Baltimore, MD 21214
PH:301-426-4529 (a-i,k,m,q,r,t)

Geppi's Comic World
7019 Security Blvd.
Hechinger's Square
at Security Mall
Baltimore, MD 21207
PH:301-298-1758 (a-c,f)

Geppi's Comic World
Harbor Place
Upper Level, Light St. Pavilion
301 Light St.
Baltimore, MD 21202
PH:301-547-0910 (a-c,f)

Mindbridge, Ltd. I
1786 Merritt Boulevard
Merritt Park Shopping Center
Baltimore (Dundalk), MD 21222
PH:301-284-7880 (a-k,m-v)

Big Planet Comics
4865 Cordell Ave. (2nd Floor)
Bethesda, MD 20814
PH:301-654-6856 (c,j,n,q,r)

The Magic Page
7416 Laurel-Bowie Rd. (Rt. 197)
Bowie, MD 20715
PH:301-262-4735 (b,c,e,m,r,s,u,v)

Alternate Worlds
9924 York Road
Cockeysville, MD 21030
PH:301-667-0440 (b,c,n,q-v)

The Closet of Comics
7319 Baltimore Ave.
College Park, MD 20740
PH:301-699-0498 (a-c,g,n,r)

Collectors Choice
368 Armstrong Ave.
Laurel, MD 20707
PH:301-725-0887 (a-n,p-r,t,u)

Comic Classics
365 Main Street
Laurel, MD 20707
PH:301-792-4744, 490-9811
(a-c,e,m,n,q,r,t-v)

Mindbridge, Ltd. II
9847 Belair Road (Route 1)
Perry Hall, MD 21128
PH:301-256-7880 (a-c,e-v)

The Closet of Comics
Calvert Village Shopping Center
Prince Frederick, MD 20678
PH:301-535-4731 (a-c,e,g,n,r)

Geppi's Comic World
8317 Fenton St.
Silver Spring, MD 20910
PH:301-588-2546 (a-c,e,f)

The Barbarian Book Shop
11254 Triangle Lane
Wheaton, MD 20902
PH:301-946-4184 (a-c,e,f,h,n,r-v)

MASSACHUSETTS:

New England Comics
140A Harvard Ave.
Allston (Boston), MA 02134
PH:617-783-1848 (a-g,n,q-s)

New England Comics
139A Brighton Ave.
Allston (Boston), MA 02134
PH:617-783-3955 (a-g,n,q-s)

Comically Speaking
1322 Mass. Ave.
Arlington, MA 02174
PH:617-643-XMEN
(a-c,e-g,m,n,q-s)

Bargain Books and Collectibles
247 So. Main St.
Attleboro, MA 02703
PH:508-226-1668 (b,c,m,q,r)

Ayer Comics & Baseball Cards
28 Main St.
Ayer, MA 01432
PH:508-772-4994 (b,c,m,r,s)

Super Hero Universe
41 West St.
Boston, MA 02111
PH:617-423-6676 (a-c,e,g,m,p-s)

New England Comics
748 Crescent Street
East Crossing Plaza
Brockton, MA 02402
PH:617-559-5068 (a-g,n,q-s)

Super Hero Universe
1105 Massachusetts Ave.
Cambridge, MA 02138
PH:617-354-5344 & 800-338-0637
(b,c,e,g,n,p-r)

Michael Richards
P. O. Box 455
Dorchester, MA 02122
PH:617-436-7995

Bop City Comics
80 Worcester Road (Route 9)
Marshalls Mall
Framingham, MA 01701
PH:508-872-2317

New England Comics
12A Pleasant St.
Malden, MA 02148
PH:617-322-2404 (a-g,n,q-s)

New England Comics
714A Washington Street
Norwood, MA 02062
PH:617-769-4552 (a-g,n,q-s)

Imagine That Bookstore
58 Dalton Ave.
Pittsfield, MA 01201
PH:413-445-5934 (b-i,l,m,o,q-u)

New England Comics
11 Court Street
Plymouth, MA 02360
PH:508-746-8797 (a-g,n,q-s)

New England Comics
1350 Hancock Street
Quincy, MA 02169
PH:617-770-1848 (a-g,n,q-s)

Pages of Reading
25 Harnden Street
Reading, MA 01867
PH:617-944-9613 (b,c,e,h,l,q-u)

Blaine's Comics
1 Winter Street
(352 Bldg. Main St.)
Stoneham, MA 02180
PH:617-438-5813 (b,c,m,q-s,u)

The Outer Limits
457 Moody St.
Waltham, MA 02154
PH:617-891-0444 (a-k,m,n,q-v)

Golden Age Buyers
457-B Moody St.
Waltham, MA 02154
PH:617-891-0444 (a)

Mayo Beach Bookstore
Kendrick Ave.
Wellfleet, MA 02667
PH:617-349-3154 (a-i)

Bop City Comics
22 Front St.
Midtown Mall
Worcester, MA 01614
PH:508-797-4646

Fabulous Fiction Book Store
587 Park Avenue
Worcester, MA 01603
PH:508-754-8826 (a-e,g,o,q-s,u)

That's Entertainment
151 Chandler Street
Worcester, MA 01609
PH:508-755-4207 (a-h,j-o,q-v)

MICHIGAN:

Tom & Terry Comics
508 Lafayette Ave.
Bay City, MI 48708
PH:517-895-5525 (b,c,m,q,r)

The Reading Place
107 W. Lawrence Ave.
Charlotte, MI 48813
PH:517-543-7922 (b,c,e,m,r)

Taurus Comics
202 E. State St.
Cheboygan, MI 49721
PH:616-627-2820 (a-c,q-s)

Curious Book Shop
307 E. Grand River Ave.
East Lansing, MI 48823
PH:517-332-0112 (a-k,m-p)

The Amazing Book-Store, Inc.
3718 Richfield Rd.
Flint, MI 48506
PH:313-736-3025 (a-c,q,r)

Argos Book Shop
1405 Robinson Rd. S.E.
Grand Rapids, MI 49506
PH:616-454-0111 (a-h,m,n)

Capital City Comics & Books
2004 E. Michigan Ave.
Lansing, MI 48912
PH:517-485-0416 (a-k,n,p-v)

Taurus Comics
116 Spring St.
Marquette, MI 49855
PH:906-225-1499 (a-c,q-s)

Taurus Comics
609 Huron Ave.
Citadel Mall
Port Huron, MI 48060
PH:313-984-5556 (a-c,q-s)

Book Stop
1160 Chicago Drive S.W.
Wyoming, MI 49509-1004
PH:616-245-0090
(a-c,e,g,j,m-o,q,r,t)

MINNESOTA:

Collector's Connection
21 East Superior Street
Duluth, MN 55802-2088
PH:218-722-9551 (b,c,m,q-s)

College of Comic Book Knowledge
3151 Hennepin Ave. S.
Minneapolis, MN 55408
PH:612-822-2309
(a-c,e-i,k-n,p-r,t-v)

Midway Book & Comic
1579 University Ave.
St. Paul, MN 55104
PH:612-644-7605 (a-h,n,q-u)

MISSISSIPPI:

Gulf Coast Comics
Petit Bois Specialty Center
240 Eisenhower Drive, C/1
Biloxi, MS 39531
PH:601-388-2991 (a-c,e,q-u)

Star Store
4212 North State St.
Jackson, MS 39206
PH:601-362-8001 (a-v)

Spanish Trail Books
1006 Thorn Ave.
Ocean Springs, MS 39564
PH:601-875-1144
(a-c,e,f,h,m,q,r,t)

MISSOURI:

Parallel Worlds
2218 Main
Joplin, MO 64804
PH:417-781-5130 (c,m,n,r,s)

The Paperback Rack
126 E. 69 Highway
Kansas City, MO 64119
PH:816-452-7478 (b-e,n,r)

B & R Comix Center
4747 Morganford
St. Louis, MO 63116
PH:314-353-4013 (a-c,g,j,n,q,r,u)

Mo's Comics and Stories
4530 Gravois
St. Louis, MO 63116
PH:314-353-9500 (a-d,f,k,p-r)

The Book Rack
300 W. Olive
Springfield, MO 65806
PH:417-865-4945 (b,c,e,h,i,q,r,t)

MONTANA:

Marvel-Us Comics
Inside Antique Town
510 Central Avenue
Great Falls, MT 59401
PH:406-727-0209 (a-c,n,q,r)

The Book Exchange
Holiday Village Shopping Center
Missoula, MT 59801
PH:406-728-6342 (a-h,n,q-t)

NEBRASKA:

Star Realm
7305 South 85th St.
Omaha, NE 68128
PH:402-331-4844 (a-c,e,i,k,m,q-u)

NEVADA:

Fandom's Comicworld of Reno
2001 East Second St.
Reno, NV 89502
PH:702-786-6663 (a-c,g,o,q,r)

NEW HAMPSHIRE:

James F. Payette
P. O. Box 750
Bethlehem, NH 03574
PH:603-869-2097 (a,b,d-h)

Collectibles Unlimited
30A Warren St.
Concord, NH 03301
PH:603-228-3712 (a-c,m,n,r-u)

Collectibles Unlimited
20 Canal St.
Laconia, NH 03246
PH:603-528-5680 (a-c,m,n,r-u)

Comic Store
66 Lake Ave.
Manchester, NH 03101
PH:603-668-6705 (b,c,g,j,m,n,q-v)

Comic Store
300 Main St.
Simoneau Plaza
Nashua, NH 03060
PH:603-881-HULK
(b,c,g,j,m,n,q-v)

NEW JERSEY:

Dreamer's Comics
118 Rt. 206 N.
Andover, NJ 07821
PH:201-786-6640 (a-c,k,m,n,q,r,u)

The Comic Zone
71 Rte. 73 & Day Ave.
Berlin, NJ 08009
PH:609-768-8186 (b,c,g,j,n,r,s)

**Philip M. Levine, Alan Levine -
Rare Books**
292 Glenwood Avenue
Bloomfield, NJ 07003
PH:201-743-5288 (a,b,d-k,m,n,p-r)

Thunder Road Comics & Cards
424 High Street
Burlington, NJ 08016
(a-c,m,n,q,r)

Rainbow Collectables
Laurel Hill Plaza, Store #6
Clementon, NJ 08021
PH:609-627-1711 (a-c,f,g,m,q,r)

Comic Relief
24 Mill Run Plaza
Route 130
Delran, NJ 08075
PH:609-461-1770 (a-c,j,n,q,r,t-v)

Supreme Collectors Corner
2177 Woodbridge Ave. (Rt. 514)
Edison, NJ 08817
PH:201-985-9210
(a-c,e,g,k,m,n,p-s)

Collector's Center
729 Edgar Road
Elizabeth, NJ 07202
PH:201-355-7942 (a,b,m,r)

**Shore Video Comics & Baseball
Cards**
615 Lacey Road
Forked River, NJ 08731
PH:609-693-3831 (a-c,m,o,p,r)

Dreamer's II Comics & Cards
103 Church St.
Hackettstown, NJ 07840
PH:201-850-5255 (a-c,k,m,q,r,u)

Comic Relief
106 Clifton Avenue
Lakewood, NJ 08701
PH:201-363-3899 (a-c,j,n,q,r,t-v)

Comic Relief
156-A Mercer Mall
Route 1
Lawrenceville, NJ 08648
PH:609-452-7548 (a-c,j,n,q,r,t-v)

The Hobby Shop
Route 34
Strathmore Shopping Center
Matawan, NJ 07747
PH:201-583-0505 (a-c,m,q-v)

Comic Museum
58 High St.
Mount Holly, NJ 08060
PH:609-261-0996 (a-c,n,q-s,u,v)

A & S Comics
7113 Bergenline Ave.
North Bergen, NJ 07047
PH:201-869-0280 (b,c,m,q-s)

Comicrypt
521 White Horse Pike
Oaklyn, NJ 08107
PH:609-858-3877
(b,c,d,e,i,j,m,n,q-u)

Passaic Book Center
594 Main Ave.
Passaic, NJ 07055
PH:201-778-6646 (a-h,j,m,n,r,t,u)

Mr. Collector
311 Union Ave.
Paterson, NJ 07502
PH:201-595-0781 (a-c,g,h,m,r)

Sparkle City
(by appointment)
Sewell, NJ
PH:609-881-1174 (a,b,d,f)

**Philip M. Levine and Sons,
Rare & Esoteric Books**
P. O. Box 246 (appointment only)
Three Bridges, NJ 08887
PH:201-227-8800 (daytime; ask
for Philip Levine) (a,b,d-n,p)

Mr. Collector
327 Union Blvd.
Totowa Boro, NJ 07512
PH:201-595-0900 (a-c,g,h,m,r)

Thunder Road Comics & Cards
3694 Nottingham Way
Trenton, NJ 08690
PH:609-587-5353 (a-c,m,n,q,r)

Thunder Road Comics & Cards
Parkway Shopping Center
831 Parkway Ave.
Trenton, NJ 08618
PH:609-771-1055 (a-c,m,n,q,r)

TemDee
15 Whitman Square
Black Horse Pike
Turnersville, NJ 08012
PH:609-228-8645 (a-g,m,q-v)

Comic Book Emporium
643 Chestnut St.
Union, NJ 07083
PH:201-964-9673 (a-c,n,q-v)

Comic Relief
116-B Main Street
Off Route 35
Woodbridge, NJ 07095
PH:201-855-2922 (a-c,j,n,q,r,t-v)

1,000,000 Comix
875 Mantua Pike
Southwood Shopping Centre
Woodbury Heights, NJ 08096
PH:609-384-8844
(a-d,f-h,j,m,n,p-v)

NEW MEXICO:

**Over the Rainbow Comics and
Cards**
1560-F Juan Tabo, N.E.
Albuquerque, NM 87112
PH:505-292-1374 (a-g,j,k,m-v)

NEW YORK:

Earthworld Comics
327 Central Ave.
Albany, NY 12206
PH:518-465-5495 (b,c,j,k,m-o,q-u)

FantaCo Comic Shop
Level 1, The FantaCo Building
21 Central Avenue
Albany, NY 12210-1391
PH:518-463-1400 (c,e,g,i,n,q-v)

FantaCo Enterprises, Inc.
Level 2, The FantaCo Building
21 Central Avenue
Albany, NY 12210-1391
PH:518-463-3667 (e,g,m,n)

FantaCon Organization Offices
The FantaCo Building
21 Central Avenue
Albany, NY 12210-1391
PH:518-463-1400 (a-o,q-v)

FantaCo Publications
Level 2, The FantaCo Building
21 Central Avenue
Albany, NY 12210-1391
PH:518-463-1400 (c,e,m,n)

Collector's Comics
167 Deer Park Ave.
Babylon, NY 11702
PH:516-321-4347 (a-c,e,n,q-s)

Captain Comics
3104 E. Tremont Ave.
Bronx, NY 10461
PH:212-823-9532 (a-c,g,m,q-s)

Wow Comics
652 E. 233rd St.
Bronx, NY 10466
PH:212-231-0913 (a-c,m,n,q-s)

Wow Comics
642 Pelham Parkway S.
Bronx, NY 10462
PH:212-829-0461 (a-c,m,n,q-s)

Brain Damage Comics
1289 Prospect Avenue
Brooklyn, NY 11218
PH:718-438-1335
(a-c,e,g,h,m,n,q-s)

Fantasy Headquarters
2203 Bath Ave.
Brooklyn, NY 11214
PH:718-372-3695 (a-c,g,m,n,q-t)

Fantasy Headquarters II
511 - 85th St.
Brooklyn, NY 11214
PH:718-921-2827 (a-c,g,m,n,q-t)

Metro Comics
138 Montague St.
Brooklyn, NY 11201
PH:718-935-0911 (a-c,g,j,m-o,q-v)

Metropolis Comics
(by appointment)
P. O. Box 165
Brooklyn, NY 11214
PH:718-837-2538
(a,b,d,g,h,j,k,m,p)

Pinocchio Discounts
1814 McDonald Ave. near Ave. P
Brooklyn, NY 11223
PH:718-645-2573 (a,c,g,q,r)

The World of Fantasy
737 Long Island Ave.
Deer Park, NY 11729
PH:516-586-7314 (a-d,f,g,m,n,q,r)

The Book Stop
384 East Meadow Ave.
East Meadow, NY 11554
PH:516-794-9129 (a-c,e,g,h,n,r,t)

Comics for Collectors
211 West Water St.
Elmira, NY 14901
PH:607-732-2299 (a-c,m,n,q-v)

Video Ventures Comics & Video
777 Hempstead Turnpike
Franklin Square, NY 11010
PH:516-488-4105 (a-d,g,i,j,m-r)

Fantazia Record & Book Exchange
2 So. Central Ave.
Hartsdale, NY 10530
PH:914-946-3306 (a-j,l-n,q,r)

Comics for Collectors
148 The Commons
Ithaca, NY 14850
PH:607-272-3007 (a-c,m,n,q-v)

Long Beach Books, Inc.
17 E. Park Ave.
Long Beach, NY 11561
PH:516-432-2265 (a-h,n,r-u)

Comics & Hobbies
156 Mamaroneck Ave.
Mamaroneck, NY 10543
PH:914-698-9473 (a-d,j,m,n,r)

Port Comics and Cards
3120 Route 112
Medford, NY 11763
PH:516-732-9143 (a-c,g,m,o,q-v)

Action Comics
318 E. 84th St.
(Between 1st & 2nd Ave.)
New York, NY 10028
PH:212-249-7344 (a-c,j,k,m,n,q-s)

Big Apple Comics
2489 Broadway (92 - 93 St.)
New York, NY 10025
PH:212-724-0085 (a-d,j,m,n,r)

Funny Business
656 Amsterdam Ave.
(corner 92nd St.)
New York, NY 10025
PH:212-799-9477 (a-c,g,n,o,q,r)

Jerry Ohlinger's Movie Material Store, Inc.
242 West 14th St.
New York, NY 10011
PH:212-989-0869 (g,i,j,l)

St. Mark's Comics
11 St. Mark's Pl.
New York, NY 10003
PH:212-598-9439 or 212-353-3300
(a-c,g,j,m-o,q-v)

Fantastic Planet
Riverview Mall
14 Margaret St.
Plattsburgh, NY 12901
PH:518-563-2946 (b-e,g,m,q,r,t,u)

Iron Vic Comics
1 Raymond Ave.
Poughkeepsie, NY 12603
PH:914-473-8365 (a-d,g,j,m,n,r)

Ravenswood Too
Freedom Mall
Rome, NY 13440
PH:315-337-1651 (a-c,g,m,q-u)

Amazing Comics
12 Gillette Ave.
Sayville, NY 11782
PH:516-567-8069 (a-c,j,q-s)

Comix 4-U, Inc.
1121 State St., 2nd Floor
Schenectady, NY 12304
PH:518-372-6612
(a-c,e,g,h,n,q,r,v)

Electric City Comics
1704 Van Vranken Ave.
Schenectady, NY 12308
PH:518-377-1500 (a-c,g,j,n,q,r,u)

Jim Hanley's Universe
3842 Richmond Avenue
(at the Eltingville train station)
Staten Island, NY 10312
PH:718-948-6377 or 718-WIT-NESS (a-g,k,m,n,p-v)

Jim Hanley's Universe
2655 Richmond Avenue
Staten Island Mall - lower level
Staten Island, NY 10314
PH:718-983-5752 (a-g,k,m,n,p-v)

Comic Book Heaven
(formerly of Q.P. Market)
48-14 Skillman Avenue
Sunnyside, Queens, NY 11104
PH:718-899-4175 (b,c,e,g,m,q,r)

Dream Days Comic Book Shop
316 South Clinton St.
Syracuse, NY 13202
PH:315-475-3995 (a-h,n,r)

Michael Sagert
P. O. Box 456 - Downtown
Syracuse, NY 13201
PH:315-475-3995 (a,b,d,f,h)

Twilight Book & Game Emporium
1401 North Salina Street
Syracuse, NY 13208
PH:315-471-3139 (a-c,e,o,q-v)

Aquilonia Comics
459 Fulton St.
Troy, NY 12180
PH:518-271-1069 (a-c,g,j,q-u)

Ravenswood Inc.
1411 Oriskany St. W.
Utica, NY 13502
PH:315-735-3699
(a-c,g,i,k,m,q,r,t,u)

Collector's Comics
1971 Wantagh Ave.
Wantagh, NY 11793
PH:516-783-8700 (a-c,e,n,q-s)

The Dragon's Den
2614 Central Park Ave.
Yonkers, NY 10710
PH:914-793-3676 (a-e,g,m,q-t,v)

NORTH CAROLINA:

Super Giant Books
344 Merrimon Ave.
Asheville, NC 28801
PH:704-254-2103 (a-c,e,h,j)

Heroes Aren't Hard to Find
Corner Central Ave. & The Plaza
P. O. Box 9181
Charlotte, NC 28299
PH:704-375-7462
(a-c,g,j,k,m,n,q-t,v)

Heroes Aren't Hard to Find
Carmel Commons Shopping Ctr.
6648 Carmel Rd.
Charlotte, NC 28226
PH:704-542-8842
(a-c,g,j,k,m,n,q-t,v)

Heroes Aren't Hard to Find
Mail Order Subscription & Wholesale
P. O. Box 9181
Charlotte, NC 28299
PH:704-376-5766
(a-c,g,j,k,m,n,q-t,v)

Heroes Are Here
117 S. Center St.
Goldsboro, NC 27530
PH:919-734-3131 (a-c,e,m,q,r)

Crazy Dave's Comic Book Detective Agency
108 E. 5th St., P.O. Box 603
Greenville, NC 27835
(a-r) 11-7 daily & by appt.

The Nostalgia News Stand
919 Dickinson Ave.
Greenville, NC 27834
PH:919-758-6909 (b,c,e,n,q,r)

Tales Resold
3936 Atlantic Ave.
Raleigh, NC 27604
PH:919-878-8551 (a-c,e,h,j,q-t)

The Booktrader
121 Country Club Road
Rocky Mount, NC 27801
PH:919-443-3993 (b,c,e,r)

Comics to Astonish
4001-C Country Club Rd.
Winston-Salem, NC 27104
PH:919-765-0400 (b,c,g,q-t,v)

Heroes Aren't Hard to Find
1000 Brookstown Ave.
Winston-Salem, NC 27101
PH:919-724-6987
(a-c,g,j,k,m,n,q-t,v)

NORTH DAKOTA:

Collector's Corner
306 N. 4th St., P.O. Box 101
Grand Forks, ND 58201
PH:701-772-2518 (a-c,e-j,m,n,q-u)

Tom's Coin, Stamp, Gem, Comic & Baseball Shop
2 First St. S.W.
Minot, ND 58701
PH:701-852-4522
(a-c,e-g,i-k,m,n,q,r,v)

OHIO:

Book Exchange
112 W. Columbus, P.O. Box 55
Bellefontaine, OH 43311
PH:513-593-0381 (a-c,e,g-i)

Comics, Cards & Collectables
533 Market Ave. North
Canton, OH 44702
PH:216-456-8907 (a-c,g,k,m,q-s)

Comic Book World
5526 Colerain Ave.
Cincinnati, OH 45273
PH:513-541-8002 (a-c,e,m,q-v)

Collectors Warehouse Inc.
5437 Pearl Road
Cleveland, OH 44129
PH:216-842-2896 (a-g,i,m,n,q-t)

The Book Nook
Carriage House Plaza
1016 Tiffin Ave.
Findlay, OH 45840
PH:419-423-9738 (a-c,e,r)

Troll & Unicorn Comics
5460 Brandt Pike
Huber Heights, OH 45424
PH:513-233-6535 (a-e,k,m-o,q-v)

Comic Book City
2601 Hubbard Road
Madison, OH 44057
PH:216-428-4786 (a-c,m,n,q-u)

Toy Scouts, Inc. (Mail Order)
P. O. Box 268
Seville, OH 44273
PH:216-769-2523 (a,b,i,k,m,p,t)

Monarch Cards & Comics
2620 Airport Hwy.
Toledo, OH 43609
PH:419-382-1451 (b,c,m,q,r)

Funnie Farm Bookstore
328 N. Dixie Drive
Airline Shopping Center
Vandalia, OH 45377
PH:513-898-2794 (a-c,e,m,q-t)

Dark Star Books
231 Xenia Ave.
Yellow Springs, OH 45387
PH:513-767-9400 (a-c,e-h,m,n,q-v)

OKLAHOMA:

Books 4 Le$$
Bryant Sq., 324 S. Bryant
(in McCrory's)
Edmond, OK 73034
PH:405-348-6800 (a-e,g-i,l,n,q-u)

Books 4 Le$$
Heismen Sq. (in McCrory's)
1221 E. Alameda
Norman, OK 73071
PH:405-329-0104 (a-e,g-i,l,n,q-u)

Planet Comics & SF
918 W. Main
Norman, OK 73069
PH:405-329-9695 (a-i,n,q-v)

Mind Over Matter
1015 N.W. 43rd (at Western)
Oklahoma City, OK 73118
PH:405-524-7427 (a-k,m,n,p-r,t-v)

New World
6219 N. Meridian Avenue
Oklahoma City, OK 73112
PH:405-721-7634 (a-e,g-i,m,n,q-v)

New World
4420 S.E. 44th St.
Oklahoma City, OK 73135
PH:405-677-2559 (a-e,g-i,m,n,q-v)

Planet Comics & SF
2112 S.W. 74th
Oklahoma City, OK 73159
PH:405-682-9144 (a-i,n,q-v)

The Comic Empire of Tulsa
3122 S. Mingo Rd.
Tulsa, OK 74146
PH:918-664-5808 (a-c,f,n,q,r,t,u)

Want List Comics
Box 701932 (appointment only)
Tulsa, OK 74170-1932
PH:918-491-9191 (a-c,f,g,i-m,o-q)

OREGON:

More Fun
116 Lithia Way #3
Ashland, OR 97520
PH:503-488-1978 (c,e,m,r,s)

House of Fantasy
2005 E. Burnside
P. O. Box 472
Gresham, OR 97030
PH:503-661-1815 (a,c,m,q-s,u)

Nelscott Books
3412 S.E. Hwy. 101
Lincoln City, OR 97367
PH:503-994-3513 (a,b,d-f,h,r)

More Fun
413 E. Main
Medford, OR 97501
PH:503-776-1200 (b,c,e,m,r,s)

Future Dreams
1800 East Burnside
Portland, OR 97214-1599
PH:503-231-8311
(b,c,e,g,i,j,n,q,r,t-v)

Future Dreams
10506 N.E. Halsey
Portland, OR 97220
PH:503-255-5245
(b,c,e,g,i,j,q,r,t-v)

Future Dreams Comic Art Reading Library
10508 N.E. Halsey
Portland, OR 97220
PH:503-256-1885

PENNSYLVANIA:

Cap's Comic Cavalcade
1980 Catasauqua Rd.
Allentown, PA 18103
PH:215-264-5540 (a-e,g,j,m,n,q-v)

Dreamscape Comics
404 West Broad St.
Bethlehem, PA 18018
PH:215-867-1178 (a-c,e,m,n,q-s)

Dreamscape Comics
9 East Third St.
Bethlehem, PA 18015
PH:215-865-4636 (a-c,e,m,n,q-s)

Showcase Comics
824 W. Lancaster Ave.
#3 Bryn Mawr Theatre Arcade
Bryn Mawr, PA 19010
PH:215-527-6236 (a-c,g,o,q-s,v)

**Mr. Monster's Comic Crypt &
House of Horrors**
1636 Washington St.
Easton, PA 18042
PH:215-250-0659 (c,g,i,m,o,q,r)

Comic Universe
446 MacDade Blvd.
Folsom, PA 19033
PH:215-461-7960 (a-d,m,q-v)

Comic Universe
393-A Lancaster Avenue
Frazer, PA 19355
PH:215-889-3320 (a-d,m,q-v)

Golden Unicorn Comics
860 Alter St.
Hazleton, PA 18201
PH:717-455-4645 (b,c,m,q-s)

Ott's Trading Post
201 Allegheny Street
Hollidaysburg, PA 16648
PH:814-696-3494 (a-c,f,g,l,n,r)

Charlie's Collectors Corner
100-D West Second Street
Hummelstown, PA 17036
PH:717-566-7216 (b,c,m,r)

The Comic Store
The Golden Triangle
1264 Lititz Pike
Lancaster, PA 17601
PH:717-39-SUPER
(a-c,e,g,h,n,q-v)

Comic Relief
4153 Woerner Ave.
Off 5 Points
Levittown, PA 19057
PH:215-945-7954 (a-c,j,n,q,r,t-v)

**Chris Bass t/a
Japanimation Super Store**
3407 Kensington Ave.
Philadelphia, PA 19134
PH:215-634-5167 (c,e,g,i-l,q,v)

Comic Investments
Roosevelt Mall
Philadelphia, PA 19149
PH:215-333-3305 (c,g,m,n,q,r,u)

Fat Jack's Comicrypt I
2006 Sansom Street
Philadelphia, PA 19103
PH:215-963-0788 (a-c,g,n,q,r)

Fat Jack's Comicrypt II
7598 Haverford Ave. (rear)
Philadelphia, PA 19151
PH:215-473-6333 (b,c,g,n,q,r)

Fat Jack's Comicrypt III
5736 North 5th Street
Philadelphia, PA 19120
PH:215-924-8210 (b,c,g,q,r)

Sparkle City Comics
Philadelphia, PA
(Philly area by appointment)
PH:609-881-1174 (a,b,d,f)

Eide's Comics and Records
940 Penn Ave.
Pittsburgh, PA 15222-3706
PH:412-261-3666 (a-r,t-v)

Eide's Comics and Records
2713 Murray Avenue
Pittsburgh, PA 15217-2419
PH:412-422-4666 (a-r,t-v)

North American Video
3613 Brownsville Road
Pittsburgh, PA 15227
PH:412-884-1777 (a-c,i,o,r)

Book Swap
110 South Fraser St.
State College, PA 16801
PH:814-234-6005 (a-c,e,h,n,q-u)

The Comic Store - West
North Mall
351 Loucks Road
York, PA 17404
(a-c,e,g,h,n,q-v)

RHODE ISLAND:

Starship Excalibur
60 Washington St.
Providence, RI 02903-1731
PH:401-273-8390
(a-c,e,i,j,m-o,q-v)

Starship Excalibur
834 Hope St.
Providence, RI 02906-3744
PH:401-861-1177
(a-c,e,i,j,m-o,q-v)

Super Hero Universe
#56 Arcade Mall
65 Weybossett St.
Providence, RI 02903
PH:401-331-5637 (b,c,e,g,p-r)

Starship Excalibur
832 Post Rd., Warwick Plaza
Warwick, RI 02888
PH:401-941-8890
(a-c,e,i,j,m-o,q-v)

SOUTH CAROLINA:

Super Giant Comics & Records
Market Place/Cinema Center
3466 Clemson Blvd.
Anderson, SC 29621
PH:803-225-9024 (a-c,e,j,l,q,r)

Heroes Aren't Hard to Find
1415-A Laurens Rd.
Greenville, SC 29607
PH:803-235-3488 (a-c,g,j,k,m,n,q-t,v)

Haven for Heroes
1123 South Sea Village
Hwy. 544
Myrtle Beach, SC 29587
PH:803-238-9975 (a-c,e,m,q,r)

Super Giant Comics
Suite 24 - 660 Spartan Blvd.
Spartanburg, SC 29301
PH:803-576-4990 (a-c,j,q,r)

TENNESSEE:

Enterprise Comics
4154 N. Bonny Oaks Drive
Chattanooga, TN 37406
PH:615-629-6217 (a-e,g,i,l,m,q,r)

White Book Shop
Super Flea Market
4307 Rossville Blvd.
Chattanooga, TN 37407
PH:404-820-1449 (a-e,r)

Collector's Choice
3405 Keith St., Shoney's Plaza
Cleveland, TN 37311
PH:615-472-6649 (c,i,m,q-t)

Marnello's Comics & Cards
451 E. Elk Avenue
Elizabethton, TN 37643
PH:615-543-6564 (c,e,m,q,r,u,v)

Gotham City Comics
7869 Farmington Blvd.
Germantown, TN 38138
PH:901-757-9665
(b,c,e,g,h,k,m,n,q-s)

Mountain Empire Collectibles III
1210 N. Roan St.
Johnson City, TN 37602
PH:615-929-8245 (a-c,e,i,q-s)

Mountain Empire Collectibles II
1451 E. Center St.
Kingsport, TN 37664
PH:615-245-0364 (a-c,e,g,h,q-s)

Collector's Choice
2104 Cumberland Ave.
Knoxville, TN 37916
PH:615-546-2665 (c,i,m,q-t)

The Great Escape
139 North Gallatin Rd.
Madison, TN 37115
PH:615-865-8052 (a-i,l-o,q-v)

Memphis Comics & Records
665 S. Highland
Memphis, TN 38111
PH:901-452-1304 (a-v)

Book Rack
Rivergate Plaza
752 Two Mile Pike
Nashville, TN 37072
PH:615-859-9814 (b,c,e,q,r)

The Great Escape
1925 Broadway
Nashville, TN 37203
PH:615-327-0646 (a-i,l-o,q-v)

Walt's Paperback Books
2604 Franklin Rd.
Nashville, TN 37204
PH:615-298-2506 (a-c,e,o,r)

TEXAS:

Lone Star Comics Books & Games
511 East Abram Street
Arlington, TX 76010
PH:817-Metro 265-0491
(a-c,e,g,h,m,q-s)

Lone Star Comics Books & Games
5721 W. I-20 at Green Oaks Blvd.
Arlington, TX 76016
PH:817-478-5405 (b,c,e,g,h,m,q-s)

Dollar Video
813 Conrad Hilton Ave.
Cisco, TX 76437
PH:817-442-1998 (a,b,i,n,o,r)

Lone Star Comics Books & Games
7738 Forest Lane
Dallas, TX 75230
PH:214-373-0934 (a-c,e,h,m,n,q-s)

Remember When Comics & Movie Material
2431 Valwood Parkway
Dallas, TX 75234
PH:214-243-3439
(a-c,e,g,i,m,q,r,t,u)

Lone Star Comics Books & Games
3014 West 7th St.
Fort Worth, TX 76107
PH:817-654-0333 (a-c,e,g,h,m,q-s)

B & D Trophy Shop
4404 N. Shepherd
Houston, TX 77018
PH:713-694-8436 (a-c,i,r)

Lone Star Comics Books & Games
2550 N. Beltline Road
Irving, TX 75062
PH:214-659-0317 (a-c,e,g,h,m,q-s)

Alan's Comics, Cards, & Games
304 E. Tyler
P. O. Box 1301
Longview, TX 75606
PH:214-753-0493 (a-c,m,q-v)

Lone Star Comics Books & Games
3600 Gus Thomasson, Suite 107
Mesquite, TX 75150
PH:214-681-2040 (b,c,e,m,q-s)

The Book Cellar
2 S. Main St.
Temple, TX 76501
PH:817-773-7545 (a-c,e,h,q,r)

Excalibur Comics, Cards & Games
2811-A State Line Ave.
Texarkana, TX 75503
PH:214-792-5767 (a-f,i,k,m,n,q-u)

Lone Star Comics Books & Games
4032 Kemp Street
Wichita Falls, TX 76308
PH:817-691-3034
(a-c,e,g,h,m,q-s,u)

UTAH:

Comics Utah
1956 S. 1100 East
Salt Lake City, UT 84105
PH:801-487-5390 (b,c,e,n,q-s)

Comics Utah
2985 W. 3500 South
Salt Lake City, UT 84119
PH:801-966-8581 (b,c,e,n,q-s)

VERMONT:

Comics Outpost
27 Granite St.
Barre, VT 05641
PH:802-476-4553 (a-c,q-s,u)

Comics City, Inc.
6 No. Winooski Ave.
Burlington, VT 05401
PH:802-865-3828 (b,c,e,m,n,q-v)

VIRGINIA:

Capital Comics Center Storyland, U.S.A.
2008 Mt. Vernon Ave.
Alexandria, VA 22301 (D.C. area)
PH:703-548-3466 (a-c,e,f,m-o,q-u)

Geppi's Comic World Inc.
8330A Richmond Highway
Alexandria, VA 22309
PH:703-360-0120 (a-c,f)

Geppi's Crystal City Comics
1755 Jefferson Davis Hwy.
Crystal City Underground
Arlington, VA 22202
PH:703-521-4618 (a-c,f)

Mountain Empire Collectibles I
4 Piedmont Street
Bristol, VA 24201
PH:703-466-6337 (a-e,i,k-m,q-s)

Burke Centre Books
5741 Burke Centre Pkwy.
Burke, VA 22015
PH:703-250-5114 (b-h,m,q-v)

Fantasia Comics and Records
1419½ University Ave.
Charlottesville, VA 22903
PH:804-971-1029 (b,c,i,l,n,q-v)

Trilogy Shop #3
3580-F Forest Haven Ln.
Chesapeake, VA 23321
PH:804-483-4173 (b,c,e,m,q-v)

Zeno's Books
1112 Sparrow Road
Chesapeake, VA 23325
PH:804-420-2344 (a-j,m-o,q,r)

Hole in the Wall Books
905 West Broad St.
Falls Church, VA 22046
PH:703-536-2511 (b-e,g,h,l,q-s)

Marie's Books and Things
1701 Princess Anne St.
Fredericksburg, VA 22401
PH:703-373-5196 (a-c,e-h,l,r)

American Comics
6581 Commerce Court
Gainesville, VA 22065
PH:703-347-7081 (c,q-s)

Bender's
17 East Mellen St.
Hampton, VA 23663
PH:804-723-3741 (a-k,m,n,p-s)

Franklin Farm Books
13320-I Franklin Farm Rd.
Herndon, VA 22071
PH:703-437-9530 (b-h,m,q-v)

Sam's Comics & Collectibles
13262 Warwick Blvd.
Newport News, VA 23602
PH:804-874-5581
(a-c,f,g,m,n,q,r,t)

World's Best Comics & Collectibles
9825 Jefferson Ave.
Newport News, VA 23605
PH:804-595-9005 (a-c,e-i,q-s)

Trilogy Shop #2
340 E. Bayview Blvd.
Norfolk, VA 23503
PH:804-587-2540 (b,c,e,m,q-v)

Ward's Comics
3405 Clifford St.
Portsmouth, VA 23707
PH:804-397-7106 (b,c,q-s)

Dave's Comics
7019-E Three Chopt Rd.
Richmond, VA 23226
PH:804-282-1211 (b,c,m,q-u)

Nostalgia Plus
5610 Patterson Ave.
Richmond, VA 23226
PH:804-282-5532 (a-c,g,n,r)

B & D Comic Shop
3514 Williamson Rd. N.W.
Roanoke, VA 24012
PH:703-563-4161 (b,c,e,n,o,q-v)

Trilogy Shop #1
5773 Princess Anne Rd.
Virginia Beach, VA 23462
PH:804-490-2205 (b,c,e,m,q-v)

Trilogy Shop #4
867 S. Lynnhaven Rd.
Virginia Beach, VA 23452
PH:804-468-0412 (b,c,e,m,q-v)

Zeno's Books
338 Constitution Dr.
Virginia Beach, VA 23462
PH:804-490-1517 (a-j,m-o,q,r)

WASHINGTON:

Everett Comics & Cards
2934½ Colby Ave.
Everett, WA 98201
PH:206-252-8181 (a-c,k,m,n,q-u)

Tales of Kirkland
128 Park Lane
Kirkland, WA 98033
PH:206-822-7333 (a-e,h,j,m,n,q-s)

The Comic Character Shop
Old Firehouse Antique Mall
110 Alaskan Way South
Seattle, WA 98104
PH:206-283-0532 (a,b,f,h,j,k,q)

Corner Comics & Book Exchange
6521 N.E. 181st
Seattle (Kenmore), WA 98155
PH:206-486-XMEN (a-c,e,m)

Corner Comics II
5226 University Way N.E.
Seattle, WA 98105
PH:206-525-9394 (a-c,m)

Gemini Book Exchange
9614 - 16th Ave. S.W.
Seattle, WA 98106
PH:206-762-5543 (b,c,e,g,q-s)

Golden Age Collectables
1501 Pike Place Market
401 Lower Level
Seattle, WA 98101
PH:(206)622-9799 (a-d,f,i,j,n,o)

Psycho 5 Comics & Cards
12513 Lake City Way N.E.
Seattle, WA 98125
PH:206-367-1620 (a-c,m,q,r)

Rocket Comics & Collectibles
119 N. 85th
Seattle, WA 98103
PH:206-784-7300 (a-d,i,j,n,q,r)

Wonderworld Books
455 S.W. 152nd St.
Seattle, WA 98166
PH:206-433-0279
(b,c,e,g,i,j,m,n,q-v)

Zanadu Comics
"A Sense of Wonder" Bookstore
1923 3rd Ave.
Seattle, WA 98101
PH:206-443-1316
(a-c,e-h,j,m,n,q-v)

The Book Exchange
N. 6504 Division
Spokane, WA 99208
PH:509-489-2053 (a-h,n,q-t)

The Book Exchange
University City East
E. 10812 Sprague
Spokane, WA 99206
PH:509-928-4073 (a-h,n,q-t)

Collectors Nook
213 North "I" St.
Tacoma, WA 98403
PH:206-272-9828 (a,b,d,e,g,m)

Lady Jayne's Comics & Books
6611 S. 12th
Tacoma, WA 98465
PH:206-564-6168 (c,e,q-s)

Galaxy Comics
1720 - 5th St., Suite D
Wenatchee, WA 98801
PH:509-663-4330 (b,c,g,q-t)

WEST VIRGINIA:

Cheryl's Comics & Toys
5216½ MacCorkle Ave. S.E.
Charleston, WV 25304
PH:304-925-7269 (a-c,k,q-u)

Comic World
613 West Lee St.
Charleston, WV 25302
(a-c,g,q,r)

Comic World
1204 - 4th Avenue
Huntington, WV 25701
PH:304-522-3923 (a-c,g,q,r)

WISCONSIN:

River City Cards & Comics
115 South 6th Street
La Crosse, WI 54601
PH:608-782-5540 (a-c,i,m,q,r)

Capital City Comics
1910 Monroe St.
Madison, WI 53711
PH:608-251-8445 (a-c,f,n,q,r)

20th Century Books
108 King Street
Madison, WI 53703
PH:608-251-6226
(b-e,g,h,m,n,q-v)

Comics & Books
125 S. Central
Marshfield, WI 54449
PH:715-384-4941 (a-c,e,g,m,q-s)

Incredible Comics
4429 W. Lisbon Ave.
Milwaukee, WI 53208
PH:414-445-7006 (a-h,m-o,q,r)

Polaris Comics
4935 W. Center St.
Milwaukee, WI 53210
PH:414-442-0494 (a-c,n,q-t)

CANADA:

ALBERTA:

Another Dimension
324 - 10 Street N.W.
Calgary, Alberta, Can. T2N 1V8
PH:403-283-7078 (b,c,q-u)

Another Dimension
#1A - 3616 - 52 Ave. N.W.
Calgary, Alberta, Can. T2L 1V9
PH:403-282-7120 (b,c,q-u)

Another Dimension
2108B - 33 Ave. S.W.
Calgary, Alberta, Can. T2T 1Z6
PH:403-246-6768 (b,c,q-u)

Scorpio Memorabilia Search Service
10985 - 73rd Ave.
Edmonton, Alb., Can. T6G 0C3
(b,c,e,g,i,k,l,t,u)

BRITISH COLUMBIA:

L.A. Comics & Books
371 Victoria St.
Kamloops, B.C., Can. V2C 2A3
PH:604-828-1995 (a-c,e,l,m,q-s)

Page After Page
1763 Harvey Ave.
Kelowna, B.C., Can. V1Y 6G4
PH:604-860-6554 (a,c,e,h,q,r)

Ted's Paperback & Comics
269 Leon Ave.
Kelowna, B.C., Can. V1Y 6J1
PH:604-763-1258 (a-c,e,h,l)

Golden Age Collectables
830 Granville St.
Vancouver, B.C., Can. V3Z 1K3
PH:604-683-2819 (a-d,f,i,j,n,o)

Island Fantasy
#29 Market Square
560 Johnson St.
Victoria, B.C., Can. V8W 3C6
PH:604-381-1134 (a-c,f-h,j,n,q-v)

MANITOBA:

International Comic Book Co.
Calvin Slobodian
859 - 4th Avenue
Rivers, Man., Can. R0K 1X0
PH:204-328-7846 (a-d,f,g,j,r)

The Collector's Slave
156 Imperial Avenue
Winnipeg, Man., Can. R2M 0K8
PH:204-237-4428
(b,c,e-g,i,k,l-n,q,t,u)

Styx Comic Service
1858 Arlington St.
Winnipeg, Man., Can. R2X 1W6
PH:204-586-8547 (a-h,j,n,o,q-v)

Styx Comic Service
1711 Corydon Ave.
Winnipeg, Man., Can. R3N 0J9
PH:204-489-6666 (a-h,j,n,o,q-v)

Doug Sulipa's Comic World
374 Donald St.
Winnipeg, Man., Can. R3B 2J2
PH:204-943-3642

NEW BRUNSWICK:

1,000,000 Comix
345 Mountain Rd.
Moncton, N.B., Can. E1C 2M4
PH:506-855-0056
(a-d,f-h,j,m,n,p-v)

NOVA SCOTIA:

1,000,000 Comix
6251 Quinpool Rd.
Halifax, N.S., Can. B3L 1A4
PH:902-425-5594
(a-d,f-h,j,m,n,p-v)

ONTARIO:

1,000,000 Comix
2400 Guelph Line
Burlington, Ont., Can. L7P 4M7
PH:416-332-5600
(a-d,f-h,j,m,n,p-v)

Starlite Comics and Books
132 Westminster Drive South
Cambridge (Preston),
Ont., Can. N3H 1S8
PH:519-653-6571 (a-h,q,r,t,u)

Bid Time Return
225 Queens Ave.
London, Ont., Can. N6A 1J8
PH:519-679-0295
(a-c,e,g,i,m-o,q-v)

Comic Express
155 Main Street
Milton, Ont., Can. L9T 1N7
(a-c,m,q,r)

1,000,000 Comix
2150 Burnhamthorpe Rd.
South Common Mall
Mississauga, Ont., Can. L5L 3A2
PH:416-828-8208
(a-d,f-h,j,m,n,p-v)

Cosmic Comic Connection
159 Ross St.
St. Thomas, Ont., Can. N5R 3X9
PH:519-633-7948 (a-i,m,n,q-s)

Queen's Comics & Memorabilia
1009 Kingston Rd.
(at Victoria Pk.)
Toronto, Ont., Can. M4E 1T3
PH:416-698-8757 (a-c,m,q,r)

Ken Mitchell Comics & Collec-
tibles (by appointment only)
710 Conacher Drive
Willowdale, Ont., Can. M2M 3N6
PH:416-222-5808 (a-g)

QUEBEC:

1,000,000 Comix
1260 Dollard
Lasalle, Montreal, Que., Can.
H8N 2P2
PH:514-366-1233
(a-d,f-h,j,m,n,p-v)

Cosmix
11819 Laurentian Blvd.
Montreal, Que., Can. H4J 2M1
PH:514-337-6183
(a-c,e,g,n,o,q-t,v)

Komico
4210 Decarie St.
Montreal, Que., Can. H4A 3K3
PH:514-489-4009 (a-c,j,n,q,r)

Multinational Comic Distribution
5595 Place D'aiguillon
Montreal, Que., Can. H4J 1L8
PH:514-333-0883
(a-c,e,g,h,j,k,m,o,q-t)

Multinational Comics/Cards
8918 A Lajeunesse
Montreal, Que., Can. H2M 1R9
PH:514-385-6273
(a-c,e,g,h,j,k,m,o,q-t)

1,000,000 Comix
Corporate Headquarters
6290 Somerled
Montreal, Que., Can. H3X 2B6
PH:514-486-1175
(a-d,f-h,j,m,n,p-v)

1,000,000 Comix
1539 Van Horne
Outremont, Montreal, Que., Can.
PH:514-277-5788
(a-d,f-h,j,m,n,p-v)

Premiere Issue
54 St. Cyrille W.
Quebec City, Que., Can.
G1R 2A4
PH:418-648-8204 (a-c,e,g,i,q-v)

Comix Plus (a 1,000,000 Comix
affiliate)
1475 MacDonald St.
St. Laurent, Montreal, Que., Can.
PH:514-334-0732
(a-d,f-h,j,m,n,p-v)

Premiere Issue
27 Rue d'Auteuil
(Vieux Quebec), Quebec City,
Que., Can. G1R 4B9
PH:418-692-3985 (a-c,e,g,i,q-v)

LATE ADDITIONS:

OREGON:

Pegasus Books
4390 S.W. Lloyd
Beaverton, OR 97005
PH:503-643-4222
(a-c,e,f,i,j,m,o,q-v)

Pegasus Books
10902 S.E. Main St.
Milwaukie, OR 97222
PH:503-652-2752
(a-c,e,f,i,j,m,o,q-v)

The Comic Shop
(Mail Order Service)
P.O. Box 18178
Portland, OR 97218
(a-c,e,m,q-v)

Pegasus Books
5015 N.E. Sandy Blvd.
Portland, OR 97213
PH:503-284-4693 (a-c,e,i,m,q-v)

Pegasus Books
1401 S.E. Division
Portland, OR 97214
PH:503-233-0768 (a-c,e,i,m,o,q-v)

WASHINGTON:

Pegasus Books
813 Grand Blvd.
Vancouver, WA 98661
PH:206-693-1240 (a-c,e,i,m,q-v)

DIRECTORY OF ADVERTISERS (Cl = Classified, c = color)

A&S Comics 515
Abraxas Graphics (Mindbridge) A-155
Acme Rocket Co. (Visions) A-147,cl
Action Direct (Cavco) 519
Adventureland Comics 497
All Colour Productions 458
American Collectibles Exchange 472,473
American Comic Book Co. A-134,135
American Comics A-63
Andrae, Thomas 512,513
Andromeda Publ. Ltd 509
Another Rainbow Publ...................cover-4
Appelgren, Johan C. cl
Archie Comics..............................c
Artisan Systems 499

Ballantine Books 460-465
Barnes, Tim cl
BEA A-179,515
Bear Mountain (J. Nichols) A-136
Bid Time Return cl
Big Apple Comics 481,cover-2
Bookie, The...............................447
Brain Damage Comics A-152,154,452
Branyan Press cl
Bruegman, Bill (Toy Scouts) 482

Capital City Comics A-140
Cheap Comics.........................A-154
Christians, A cl
Christophers Comics & Books A-128
Classified Ads 516-518
Coddington, Gary 514,cl
Cole, Bill A-58,59
Collector Cards (Visions)................A-147
Collector's Choice A-178,468
Collectors' Classified cl
Collector's Comics 485
Collector's Paradise Gallery 484,cl
Collector's Slave, The.................A-146
Collector's Unlimited A-126
College of Comic Book Knowledge 485
Collins Publishing A-155,cl
Comet Books A-149
Comic Book Kingdom A-151
Comic Carnival A-162
Comic Connection A-124
Comic Conservation Lab (Hinds).......A-148,453
Comic Master Corp, The...A-64,A-122,182,486,487
Comic Store, The A-156
Comics & Hobbies 481
Comics And Stories.............A-120,121,c
Comics Buyers Guide.....................443
Comics For Heroes A-164
Comics To Astonish A-128
Comics Unlimited Ltd. A-118,141,446,493
Comix City 475
Comix 4-U Inc. (Comics) cl
CRC Collectibles cl
Crestohl, Robert A-64,122,182,486,487
Curious Book Shop A-149

Dark Horse Comics 455

Dark Star Books A-149
DC Comics, Inc. c
Diamond Comic Distr. A-116,451
Divider Index Systems 447
Dolgoff, Gary A-168-171,481,cover-2
Dragon's Den 470
Dunbier, Scott 514,cl

Edian 499
Eschenberg, Conrad 475
Excalibur Comics......................A-179

Fantasy Headquarters 467
Fantasy Illustrated......................499
Fantazia Record & Book Exchange 490,491
Farrell, D...........................475,cl
Fat Moose Comics & Games 454
First Team Press A-177
Fonograffiques cl
Forbidden Planet A-175,471
Frazer, Samuel 500
Friendly Frank's Comics A-132,133
Fuchs, Danny cl
Funny Business 495

Gallant Listing Service A-146,cl
Galaxy Comics........................A-151
Gaudino, Phil A-142
Gem Comics A-131
Geoffrey's Comics 496
Geppi's Comic World A-158,159,478,479,c
Gerber Products A-183,184
Golden Age Collectibles cover-3
Golden Age Comics A-162
Golden Apple A-155
Gooden, Roger cl
Goodfellow & Co............................cl
Graphitti A-176

Hake's Americana A-109
Halegua, Richard......................A-163
Hamilton, Bruce 501
Hawk, C.A.(Time Machine) cl
Hay, Marty A-142
Hero Land Comics (Lee Tennant) A-143,459
Heroes Aren't Hard To Find A-125
Heroes World Dist. Co. 466
Hi-De-Ho Comics.....................A-142
Hinds, Jef A-148,453
Hobby Shop, The A-146

Intergalactic Trading Co. A-144,469
International Comic Book Co. (Slobodian)....503,cl
Iron Vic Comics......................481

J&S Comics A-172,173
J.C. Video A-151,cl

Kalb, Ed A-160,161,504,505
Koch, Joseph 444,445
Koch, Peter A-144,470,484,cover-2
Kramer, Robert cl

DIRECTORY OF ADVERTISERS (continued)

Kubert School, Joe 515

L.A. Comics & Collectibles 497
La Tremouille, Robert J. cl
Levine, Phil 507
Levy, Bob 475
Levy, H.M. cl
Long Beach Books 499

M&M 494
Marvel Comics c
Metro Comics 506
Metropolis Comics A-114,115,165,447
Mitchell, Ken A-2,cl
Moondog's Comics A-117,153
More Fun Comics 514
Muchin, Richard (Tomorrow's Treas.) 488,489
Multi-Book & Periodical A-137
Multinational Comic Distr. cl

National Comic & Coin Coll. A-157,477
Nevada Bags (Restorations) 448
New England Comics 450
Nichols, John (Bear Mountain) A-136
Ninth Nebula A-139

Ohlinger, Jerry 497
O'Kennon, Hugh A-110,502
1,000,000 Comics 486,487
Outer Limits 510
Overstreet Publishing Schedule A-62

Passaic Book Center .A-154
Payette, James A-65,112,113,449
Penny Ranch A-127
Pierce Books, Ken A-155
Plant, Bud 520

Rann, Rick cl
Rauch, Glenn cl
Redbeard's Book Den c
Restoration Lab A-119
Restorations 448
Richards, Michael cl
Rogofsky, Howard A-1

Ross, Gerry A-64,122,182,486,487

St. Mark's Comics A-138
San Francisco Card Exchange cl
San Mateo Comics 476
Scorpio Memorabilia .A-142
Sea Level Comics A-147
Second Genesis A-130,480
Semowich, Rick cl
Sheridan, Thomas cl
Slobodian, Calvin 503,cl
Southeastern Front cl
Sparkle City Comics A-128,144,147,179,474,
 . . . . 497,518,cl
Starbase 21 . . . . .A-124
Styx A-150,457
Sulipa's Comic World, Doug A-166
Super Hero Universe 498
SWLS (Visions) A-147,cl
Szymanski, James cl

Tennant, Lee A-143,459
Time Machine (C.A. Hawk) cl
Titan Books A-174
Titan Distributors A-175
Tomorrow's Treasures (Muchin) 488,489
Toy Scouts 482
Troll & Unicorn cl
Tropic Comics 508
TV Guide Specialists cl

Verb, Hal 511
Visions A-147,cl

Want List Comics A-145,456
Westfield Company, The A-123,c
Westwind Distributors 492
Wonderland Comics & Science Fic. 518
Wong, E.K. cl
Wood, Peter (Golden Age Comics) A-162
World's Finest Comics . . A-60,61,129,180,181,483,c

Yaruss, David (DPY) cl
Yee, Harley A-111,167

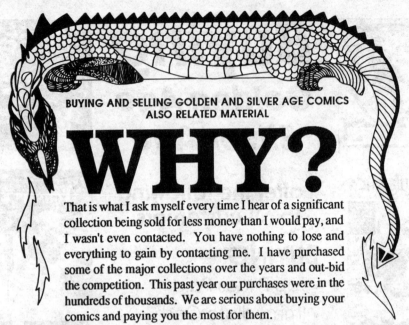

BUYING AND SELLING GOLDEN AND SILVER AGE COMICS
ALSO RELATED MATERIAL

WHY?

That is what I ask myself every time I hear of a significant collection being sold for less money than I would pay, and I wasn't even contacted. You have nothing to lose and everything to gain by contacting me. I have purchased some of the major collections over the years and out-bid the competition. This past year our purchases were in the hundreds of thousands. We are serious about buying your comics and paying you the most for them.

If you have comics or related items for sale please call or send a list for my quote. Or if you would like, just send me your comics and figure them by the percentages below. If your grading is by Overstreets standards you can expect the percentages paid by grade. Before I send any checks I will call to verify your satisfaction with the price. If we cannot reach a price we are both happy and I will ship your books back at my expense that day. Remember, no collection is too large or small, even if it's one hundred thousand or more.

These are some of the high prices I will pay for comics I need. Percentages stated will be paid for any grade unless otherwise stated. Percentages should be based on this guide.

— JAMES F. PAYETTE

Action (1-225)	70%	Detective (#27 Mint)	80%
Action (#1 Mint)	95%	Green Lantern (#1 Mint)	85%
Adventure (247)	75%	Jackie Gleason (1-12)	70%
All American (16 & 17)	75%	Keen Detective Funnies	70%
All Star (3 & 8)	70%	Ken Maynard	70%
Amazing Man	70%	More Fun (7-51)	70%
Amazing Mustery Funnies	70%	New Adventure (12-31)	70%
The Arrow	70%	New Comics (1-11)	70%
Batman (1-125)	70%	New Fun (1-6)	70%
Batman (#1 Mint)	85%	Sunset Carson	70%
Bob Steele	70%	Superman (#1 Mint)	95%
Captain Marvel (#1)	70%	Whip Wilson	70%
Detective (1-225)	70%		

We are paying 65% of guide for the following:

Andy Devine	Funny Picture Stories	Smiley Burnette
Congo Bill	Green Lantern (1st)	Start & Stripes
Detective Eye	Hangman	Tales of the Unexpected
Detec. Picture Stories	Hoot Gibson	Tim McCoy
Funny Pages	Jumbo (1-10)	Wonder Comics (Fox-1&2)

FIRST IN SERVICE...

DIAMOND IS NOW #1

Call us and find out why we have quietly grown to be the largest and finest comic distributor.

- **REORDERS**—We order plenty of extra copies to have important books on hand for your reorders. If sold out, we search all 17 Diamond warehouses and, if we can't fill your order, then we go directly to the publisher. It's important to us to fill your needs...promptly.

- **WIDEST PRODUCT SELECTION**— Our new comics and books selection is second to none. We also carry Donruss and other baseball cards, a full gaming line, plus T-shirts, posters, toys, videos, specialty magazines, and occasional exclusive items.

- **SUPPLIES**—We keep available your high profit steady sellers: Boxes, bags, mylar, dividers, backing boards, and baseball card supplies.

- **SEVENTEEN LOCATIONS**—From New York to

Los Angeles are ready to serve both U.S. and International Customers. Direct delivery by our trucks in many areas. Direct shipment via UPS and air freight from our Sparta, Illinois warehouse. Let us show you the best and fastest way to get your books.

- **QUALIFIED DIAMOND WAREHOUSE MANAGERS AND EMPLOYEES** who are fast, careful, and helpful. Just starting up? Ready to expand? We can help you with product selection, ordering tips, and far more.

- **INFORMATION**—We have the answers to your questions. We're here to serve you.

DIAMOND PREVIEWS describes and illustrates Coming Items each month, and the bi-monthly COMPLETE CATALOG describes and pictures all important specialty items still available for your reorders.

EXPERIENCED PEOPLE READY TO SERVE YOU.
DIAMOND COMIC DISTRIBUTORS

FOR INFORMATION Call (301) 298-2981 and ask for either of our account representatives, Bill Neuhaus or Mindy Moran.

1718-G Belmont Ave., Baltimore, MD 21207

The Restoration Lab

Comic Books, Original Comic Art, Baseball Cards

Susan Cicconi
Conservator of Ephemera

"In addition to my background as a professional art restorer in Belgium, France and New York, **I have worked on all of the most valuable Golden and Silver Age books-from Marvel #1 to F.F. #1.** I also restore original comic art and baseball cards."

My expertise includes:
Dry cleaning
Stain removal
Tape removal
Light bleaching
Invisible mending
Missing piece replacement
Spine rebuilding
Flattening wrinkles and creases
Reliable deacidification, and more.
My Specialties: color matching and touch-ups.

> **Restoration Services**
> **Starting at $40.00 per hour.** Please contact me by mail or phone before shipping any books. Items to be restored should be worth at least $150.00 in their present condition.
> **References**   **Insured**

Comments from satisfied customers

"**Unbelievable!** The work you did on our Marvel #1 and Adventure #247 was beyond what we could ever have imagined."

> - **Jim Pitts & Dan Fogel**
>   **Magic Lightning Comics & Collectibles**
>   **Menlo Park, California**

"Let me take this opportunity to express my appreciation and thanks for the excellent restoration you did on my Captain America #2, #74, and F.F. #3. Craig Dawson, proprietor of 'Comics and Robots,' remarked, "**This is the only person in the country qualified to do this kind of work.**" I agree, and thanks again."

> - **Hans Kosenkranius, Wilmington, Delaware**

P.O. BOX 632, NEW TOWN BRANCH
BOSTON, MA 02258
(617) 924 - 4297

	FAIR	FAIR/ GOOD	GOOD	GOOD/ VG	VERY GOOD	VG/ FINE	FINE	VERY FINE	NEAR MINT	MINT
AMAZING FANTASY 15	$55.00	$83.00	$110.00	$165.00	$220.00	$330.00	$440.00	$605.00	$770.00	$1600.00
AMAZING SPIDERMAN 1	45.00	65.00	90.00	120.00	175.00	230.00	320.00	400.00	600.00	1200.00
2	20.00	30.00	40.00	50.00	55.00	85.00	110.00	155.00	200.00	325.00
3	12.00	18.00	25.00	30.00	35.00	50.00	65.00	100.00	132.00	200.00
4	10.00	14.00	18.00	22.00	25.00	35.00	50.00	65.00	90.00	175.00
5, 6	8.00	12.00	16.00	18.00	20.00	30.00	40.00	50.00	65.00	135.00
7-10	6.00	9.00	11.00	12.00	15.00	22.00	27.00	40.00	50.00	100.00
11-15	4.00	6.00	7.00	8.00	9.00	14.00	17.00	25.00	35.00	65.00
16-20	3.00	4.00	5.00	5.50	6.00	9.00	11.00	16.00	20.00	35.00
21-30; 100, 129	1.50	2.00	3.00	3.30	3.50	4.00	6.00	7.00	12.00	25.00
AVENGERS 1	22.00	33.00	44.00	55.00	65.00	100.00	132.00	220.00	330.00	500.00
2, 4	8.00	12.00	17.00	20.00	22.00	33.00	44.00	65.00	110.00	145.00
3	6.00	9.00	11.00	15.00	16.00	25.00	33.00	44.00	65.00	100.00
5-10	3.00	4.00	6.00	6.50	7.00	10.00	14.00	22.00	33.00	45.00
DAREDEVIL 1	17.00	25.00	33.00	40.00	44.00	65.00	90.00	110.00	132.00	230.00
2	7.00	10.00	13.00	15.00	17.00	25.00	33.00	50.00	65.00	110.00
4, 5	3.00	4.00	5.00	5.50	6.00	9.00	11.00	15.00	20.00	40.00
FANTASTIC FOUR 1	55.00	82.00	110.00	165.00	220.00	330.00	440.00	610.00	770.00	1375.00
2	30.00	40.00	55.00	72.00	84.00	120.00	165.00	230.00	310.00	500.00
3	22.00	33.00	44.00	55.00	65.00	100.00	132.00	190.00	240.00	400.00
4	20.00	28.00	38.00	44.00	50.00	74.00	100.00	132.00	175.00	300.00
5	15.00	20.00	27.00	33.00	40.00	58.00	80.00	105.00	132.00	225.00
6-10	8.00	12.00	15.00	20.00	22.00	33.00	44.00	60.00	78.00	145.00
11, 12	6.00	8.00	11.00	14.00	17.00	25.00	33.00	44.00	55.00	100.00
13-15	5.00	7.00	9.00	11.00	14.00	20.00	27.00	35.00	44.00	66.00
16-20	3.00	4.00	6.00	7.00	8.00	9.00	17.00	22.00	27.00	50.00
21-30, 48	2.00	2.50	4.00	4.50	5.00	6.50	9.00	13.00	15.00	25.00
31-40	1.00	1.50	1.70	2.00	2.50	4.00	5.00	6.00	8.00	15.00
INCREDIBLE HULK 1	38.00	55.00	77.00	95.00	110.00	165.00	220.00	300.00	385.00	625.00
2	15.00	20.00	27.00	33.00	40.00	60.00	77.00	105.00	132.00	225.00
3	10.00	15.00	20.00	25.00	30.00	42.00	55.00	77.00	100.00	160.00
4, 5, 6	7.00	10.00	14.00	17.00	20.00	30.00	40.00	50.00	65.00	130.00
IRONMAN 1	—	—	7.00	9.00	10.00	15.00	20.00	25.00	30.00	60.00
TALES OF SUSPENSE 39	20.00	25.00	40.00	47.00	55.00	84.00	110.00	155.00	200.00	450.00
40	8.00	12.00	15.00	16.00	20.00	30.00	40.00	55.00	72.00	145.00
41	5.00	6.00	7.50	10.00	11.00	16.00	22.00	30.00	40.00	75.00
42-46	2.00	3.00	3.50	4.00	5.00	7.00	9.00	11.00	14.00	30.00
TALES TO ASTONISH 27	25.00	37.00	50.00	60.00	65.00	100.00	132.00	190.00	240.00	575.00
THOR 83	22.00	33.00	44.00	60.00	77.00	115.00	155.00	215.00	275.00	450.00
84	7.00	10.00	14.00	17.00	22.00	33.00	44.00	55.00	65.00	100.00
85	6.00	9.00	12.00	14.00	16.00	25.00	33.00	44.00	55.00	75.00
86	5.00	7.00	9.00	11.00	12.00	17.00	25.00	30.00	35.00	60.00
87-89	4.00	5.00	6.00	9.00	12.00	17.00	25.00	30.00	35.00	50.00
X-MEN 1	30.00	50.00	77.00	94.00	110.00	165.00	220.00	300.00	385.00	625.00
2	15.00	20.00	28.00	33.00	42.00	60.00	84.00	110.00	132.00	250.00
3, 4	6.00	9.00	11.00	14.00	17.00	25.00	33.00	44.00	55.00	110.00
5	4.50	5.50	7.50	10.00	12.00	18.00	24.00	32.00	38.00	75.00
6-10	2.50	3.50	4.50	5.50	6.50	10.00	13.00	20.00	24.00	55.00
11-20	—	2.50	3.50	5.50	6.50	10.00	12.00	14.00	20.00	25.00
21-44	—	—	2.50	3.50	4.50	5.50	8.00	10.00	11.00	15.00
56-63, 65	—	—	2.50	2.70	3.80	5.50	7.00	9.00	10.00	17.00
94	—	—	10.00	15.00	20.00	25.00	40.00	50.00	60.00	85.00
95	—	—	5.50	9.00	10.00	15.00	20.00	25.00	30.00	35.00
96-98, 100, 101, 108, 109, 120, 121	—	—	3.50	5.00	6.50	10.00	14.00	17.00	20.00	25.00
102-107, 110, 111	—	—	2.50	3.00	3.80	6.50	7.50	8.00	10.00	14.00
112-119	—	—	—	2.00	3.50	5.00	6.50	8.00	10.00	12.00
122-130, 137, 139, 140	—	—	—	1.50	3.00	3.50	4.50	5.50	7.50	10.00
131-136, 138	—	—	—	—	2.50	3.50	4.00	5.50	6.50	8.00
Giant Size 1	—	—	8.00	12.00	15.00	24.00	32.00	37.00	47.00	80.00

We pay similarly high prices for later issues of the same titles (50%-75% of guide).

SERIOUS?

Serious Business

No one takes comic book collecting more seriously than we do. If you're a hard-core comic book collector, subscribe to Westfield Comics Subscription Service.

Serious Savings

We provide the best in current comics and fan-related materials at 25% to 35% off cover price!

Serious Selection

Choose from comics galore! And buy just the titles and quantities you want on a monthly or biweekly basis.

- All Marvel and DC direct-only titles.
- All mainstream Marvel and DC annuals, limited series and graphic novels.
- An extensive line of the very best independent publishers' titles such as First, Eclipse, Comico and Gladstone.
- A top selection of small press black-and-white comic titles.
- The best specialty magazines and books.
- A growing line of trade paperback collections.

Serious Service

Westfield packs orders to perfection. So comics arrive crisp and clean with no bad scene.

Serious Info

To keep you up on the hottest comic news, we'll send you free promotional materials plus the notorious Westfield Newsletter with each order.

Serious Offer

If you're totally into comics, send us your name, address and a 25¢ stamp. We'll send you a price list and our order form. If you're a new customer, we'll throw in 25 bucks' worth of free comics, preselected, with your first order!

Get Serious

Subscribe to Westfield Comics Subscription Service today! It's the Collectors' Choice! Seriously.

What They're Saying:

"You are truly the best comics mail order company I have ever dealt with."
—*Salvatore J. Nardozzi, Jr., Dunmore, PA*

"Orders arrive like clockwork, with everything in perfect condition. All this . . . and great discounts . . . unbelievable! Thanks from a very satisfied customer."
—*Calvin B. Lee, San Francisco, CA*

"I really do enjoy collecting comics and with your excellent discounted prices it makes it not only affordable—but fun!"
—*Nigel Tickner, Missouri City, TX*

"The comics always come in great shape and you do one of the best newsletters in the industry! I know when I tell someone about Westfield, they'll get the best treatment there is."
—*Beau Smith, Sales Manager, Eclipse Comics*

THE WESTFIELD COMPANY OF WISCONSIN, INC.

8608 University Green • P.O. Box 470 • Middleton, WI 53562 • (608) 836-1945

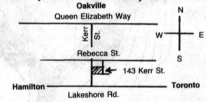

HEROES
Aren't Hard To Find ™
AMERICA'S COMIC SOURCE

- BEST SELECTION
- RELIABLE SERVICE
- FRIENDLY, KNOWLEDGEABLE PEOPLE

FIND **THE SOURCE**

HEROES AREN'T HARD TO FIND

Corner Of Central Avenue
& The Plaza
Charlotte NC
(704) 375 7462

•

Carmel Commons Shopping Center
Pineville/Matthews Road
(704) 542 8842

•

1000 Brookstown Avenue
Winston-Salem NC 27101
(919) 724 6987

•

1415-A Laurens Road
Greenville SC 29607
(803) 235 3488

•

FOR MAIL-ORDER SUBSCRIPTIONS,
WHOLESALE SUPPLIES & CONVENTION INFO:
PO BOX 9181
CHARLOTTE NC 28299

TM & © 1989 Marvel Entertainment Group, Inc.
All Rights Reserved.

eeck/BEATY

PLAN TO ATTEND
HEROES CONVENTION '89
JUNE 24 - 25, 1989
HOLIDAY INN - WOODLAWN
CHARLOTTE, NC

For The Latest Information About New Comics, Special Events, and Other Surprises,
Call The **HEROES HOTLINE!!!**
Dial **704 372 HERØ** Around The Clock In Charlotte, After-Hours At The Regular Numbers Everywhere Else!!

A-125

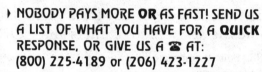
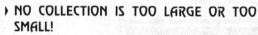
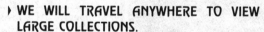

SECOND GENESIS
3 WEST COAST WAREHOUSES FOR RETAILER SERVICE

Complete line of comic book publishers: Marvel,DC, Gladstone, First, Eclipse, Comico, Dark Horse and all the independent publishers.

Specialty products: Trade Paperbacks, T-Shirts, Games, Calendars, Graphic Novels, and more.

Supplies: Long and short comic boxes, magazine boxes, dividers, 9 different sizes of polypropylene bags, baseball sheets, backing boards and mylar products.

Call one of our warehouses for our thick monthly catalog. **Providing wholesale services to retailers since 1976.**

NEW PUBLISHERS: Solicitation material or new product information should go to our Portland Warehouse.

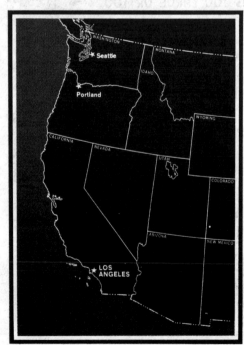

SEATTLE WAREHOUSE
Manager: Al Clover
223 1/2 Ninth Ave. North
Seattle, WA 98109
(206) 624-6210

PORTLAND WAREHOUSE
Main Office
Manager: Kathy Moullet
Catalog Editor: Tim Androes
Controller: Lance Casebeer
5860 NE Going Street
Portland, OR 97218
(503) 281-1821

LOS ANGELES WAREHOUSE
Manager: Glen Quasny
6223 Randolph Street
Commerce, CA 90040
(213) 888-0466

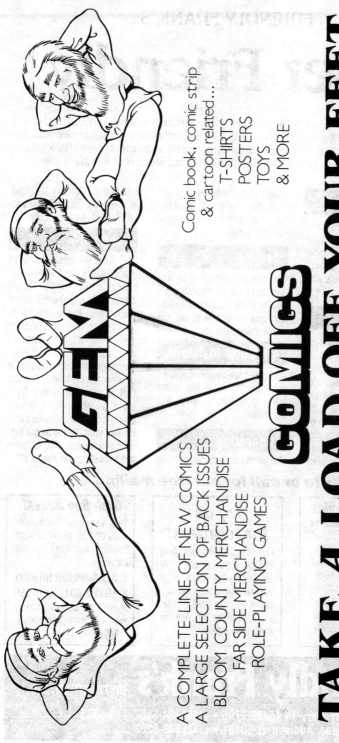
A-131

A-132

Multi-Book & Periodical Inc.

4380 South Service Road,
Unit #17,
Burlington, Ontario L7L 5Y6
TELEPHONE 416-632-5573
FAX. 416-632-3942

C A N A D A

THE DIRECT COMIC BOOK DISTRIBUTOR.

WE ARE STRICTLY WHOLESALE AND CURRENTLY DEALING WITH ALL COMIC
BOOK PUBLISHERS AND RELATED PUBLISHERS.

SO YOU THINK YOUR TOO SMALL TO DEAL WITH A DIRECT DISTRIBUTOR? TALK
TO US, WE HAVE SPECIAL START—UP PACKAGES TO HELP YOU TO BECOME
THAT MAJOR DEALER IN THE NEAR FUTURE. WE HAVE THANKFUL ACCOUNTS
THAT STARTED OUT THIS WAY.

FAST, DEPENDABLE SERVICE.
MULTI-BOOK CARRIES A HUGE SUPPLY OF EXTRA COMICS
EACH WEEK FOR YOUR RE-ORDERING CONVENIENCE. IF
YOU ARE CAUGHT SHORT, GIVE US A CALL.

WHEN YOU BECOME A WEEKLY SHIP OUT DEALER. YOU WILL ENJOY OUR
WEEKLY BACK ISSUE LIST ALONG WITH HIGHLY DISCOUNTED SPECIALS THAT
WE OFFER. OUR MONTHLY NEW COMIC BOOK CATALOGUE IS AVAILABLE ON
REQUEST. GO FOR IT!

WE ALSO CARRY A LARGE SELECTION OF FANTASY GAMES AND RELATED
PRODUCT. AS WELL AS COMIC BAGS, COMIC BOXES, DIVIDERS, MAGAZINE
BOXES, BACKING BOARDS AND MORE!

ALL DEALER ENQUIRIES ARE HELD IN THE STRICTEST CONFIDENCE.

Capital City Comics

1910 MONROE ST., MADISON, WIS. 53711
MON - FRI: 11-7   SAT: 10-5
PHONE (608) 251-8445

BRUCE AYRES, Owner
DAVID MACEY, Manager

A-143

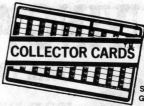

STYX COMIC SERVICE
<u>THE **ORIGINAL** RETURNS!</u>

Everything is NEW. We spent two years re-developing the original comics service, and it's operating with the BEST system available!

<u>Ordering and selection:</u>

We handle all major publishers and manufacturers, but in TWO ways:

1.) We have a standing order list of publishers who have proven themselves to be RELIABLE and ON TIME with their regular titles. You can make a standing order from this list and receive all your favorites shipped regularly!

2.)Every month we send out the COMPLETE DISTRIBUTION listing of new products, which includes not only everything from the standing order publishers, but ALSO everything from everyone else. You can order from this listing separately. This allows you to order special issues, double up on issues you want extras of without having to change your regular order, and get hundreds of items from specialty producers, including POSTERS, BUTTONS, T-SHIRTS, ROLE-PLAYING GAMES, MODELS, TOYS, and so forth!

This is the ULTIMATE in flexibility!

<u>Invoicing:</u>

Your invoices are beautiful, CLEAR, laser-printed invoices, and there's always a confirming copy in with your shipment!

<u>Packing:</u>

We developed the ULTIMATE in shipping containers, double-walled beauties that are unique to our service, and are practically INDESTRUCTIBLE, even after several trips back and forth. In addition, orders are wrapped in plastic, and padded inside the containers to ensure MINT arrival! Then the whole thing is specially sealed in a unique way that prevents any tampering, so your orders always get there intact!

<u>Postage and Shipping:</u>

We were the FIRST service to introduce FREE shipping. We pick up all costs within the US and CANADA. Where possible, we always ship via UPS to ensure efficient delivery, and our once-every-two weeks schedule makes deliveries consistent and convenient!

<u>Extras:</u>

We offer everything from the latest publisher fliers right on up to your own FREE OVERSTREET GUIDE every year!

<u>HOW TO JOIN:</u>

Send your name and address along with a S.A.S.E. (preferably larger size if possible to:
STYX COMIC SERVICE, 605 ROSEBERRY ST.,
WINNIPEG, MANITOBA, CANADA, R3H 0T3
Or call us at (204) 786-6165. Or even FAX us at (204) 786-2081.
We'll send you complete details **FREE!**

A-152

CHICAGO
CHICAGO
CHICAGO
CHICAGO
MOONDOG'S
MOONDOG'S
MOONDOG'S
MOONDOG'S

Since 1978, Moondog's has been the recognized leader in comics retailing in Chicagoland. We sell more new comics, more back issues, more rare high-grade Golden and Silver Age books, more games, baseball cards, toys, and supplies than any other store in Chicago.

Why?

It's simple. We've got the best service, selection and prices.

If you collect comics seriously or just read them, you owe it to yourself to make Moondog's your comic store. If you live too far away from one of our five conveniently located stores to be a regular weekly customer—no problem—we understand. But you've no excuse not to make it once a month!

Come see why Moondog's Comicland stores are the "Midwest's Finest Shops". We'll be expecting you.

Moondog's
COMICLAND
THE COLLECTOR'S PLACE

139 W. Prospect Ave.
Downtown Mt. Prospect
Mt. Prospect, IL 60056
(312) 398-6060

1231 W. Dundee Rd.
Plaza Verde
Buffalo Grove, IL 60090
(312) 259-6060

1403 W. Schaumburg Rd.
Schaumburg Plaza
Schaumburg, IL 60194
(312) 529-6060

114 S. Waukegan Rd.
Deerbrook Mall
Deerfield, IL 60015
(312) 272-6080

Randhurst Mall
Lower Level
Mt. Prospect, IL 60056
(312) 577-8668

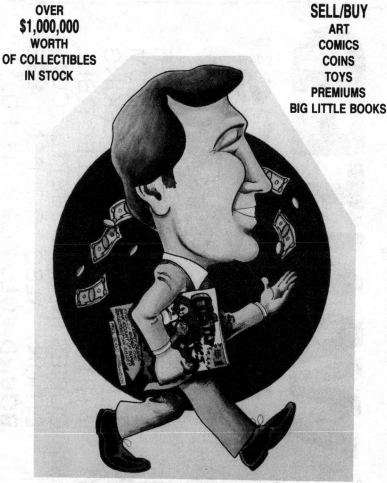

A-158

ED KALB

P.O. Box 4111, Mesa, AZ 85211-4111, 1-602-832-5176 (anytime 9-9 MST)

"SERVING COLLECTORS WORLDWIDE SINCE 1967"

QUALITY MATERIAL AND FAST DEPENDABLE SERVICE ARE GUARANTEED.
All items are returnable for refund or exchange, no explanation necessary.

CONDITION—Fine to Mint. 90% Near Mint to Mint. We send the best quality on hand - We're looking for **satisfied customers!**

ALTERNATE CHOICES—are greatly appreciated, but not a must. Your alternate selections are used **only** when your first choice is out of stock. Refunds are sent when an item is out of stock. Please note if you prefer credit vouchers.

POSTAGE—Please add $2.00 to all orders to help with postage. All orders are insured. Foreign customers are appreciated. Foreign lands please add extra postage and specify air or surface delivery. All unused postage (foreign) shall be reimbursed.

HOW TO ORDER—Simply list on any sheet of paper what you would like. Add $2.00

for postage. Print your name and address clearly. Payment with order please. All orders are securely packaged and sent out **promptly.**

All prices are per item.

All items are original first printings

10% DISCOUNT—To qualify for your 10% discount simply include a list of alternate choices that equal or exceed the value of your original order. All items qualify for discount except those with value of $15 or more. Deduct your 10% discount before adding postage (see postage).

This price list is good through March 1990.

The following is a sample listing of our inventory. For our complete catalog please send 50 cents. Catalog will be mailed free with any order.

ACTION COMICS	
330-350	4.00
351-380	3.00
381-413	2.50
414-443	2.00
444-650, up	1.00

ADVENTURE COMICS
381-424	2.50
425-466	2.00
467-490	1.00

ALL STAR
| 58-74 | 2.00 |

ALL STAR SQUADRON
1,25,26,50	4.00
2-24	2.00
27-49, 51-67	1.00
Annual 1-3	2.00

ALPHA FLIGHT
1	4.00
2-19	2.00
20-75, up	1.00

AMERICAN FLAGG!
| 1-4 | 4.00 |
| 5-60, up | 2.00 |

ANIMAL MAN
| 1 | 4.00 |
| 2-up | 1.50 |

AQUAMAN (1986)
| 1-4 | 2.50 |

AREA 88
| 3-40, up | 2.00 |

THE AVENGERS
31-52,54-56,60-65,68-	
70,72-82,84-91	4.00
53,57,58,94-96	12.00
59,66,67,71,83,92,97-	
99,110,111	6.00
93,100	20.00
101-109,112-119	4.00
120-140	3.00
141-163	2.50
164-166	4.00
167-180	2.00
181-191,200	2.50
192-199,201-250	1.50
251-310, up	1.00
Annual 1	12.00
2-7	4.00
8-17, up	2.50
Giant Size 1-5	4.00

BADGER
1,2	8.00
3,4	5.00
5-50, up	2.00

BATMAN
| 262-425 | 1.50 |

BATMAN & THE OUTSIDERS, 1 | 4.00 |
| 2-32, Annual 1,2 | 1.50 |

BIG LITTLE BOOKS
1930-'50, please write

BLACKHAWK
| 210-243 | 2.50 |

BLUE BEETLE
| 1 | 4.00 |
| 2-30, up | 1.00 |

BONANZA (TV)
| 4-37 | 4.50 |

BOOSTER GOLD
| 1 | 4.00 |
| 2-30, up | 1.00 |

BRAVE & THE BOLD
103-117	2.50
118-150,200	1.50
151-199	1.00

CAPTAIN AMERICA
100	25.00
101	6.00
102-108	4.50
109-111,113,117	8.00
112,114-116,118-140	
	3.00
141-160	2.50
161-171,176-181	2.00
172-175,200,241	1.50
182-199,201-240,242-	
331	1.50
332-340	2.50
341-360, up	1.25
Annual 1,2	4.00
3-8, up	2.00

CAPTAIN ATOM
| 1 | 4.00 |
| 2-30, up | 1.00 |

CAPTAIN MARVEL
1	12.00
2,26-34,36	4.00
3-24	3.00
25	8.00
35,37-62	1.50

CEREBUS
| 80-120, up | 2.00 |

CHAMPIONS
| 1,17 | 4.00 |
| 2-16 | 2.00 |

CHECKMATE
| 1 | 4.00 |
| 2-15, up | 2.00 |

CONAN THE BARBARIAN
1	60.00
2	20.00
3	25.00
4,5	15.00
6-11,14,15	10.00
12,13,16,23	8.00
17-22,24,25	7.50
26-29,37	4.00
30-36,38,39	3.00
40-60	2.50
61-100	2.00
101-150	1.50
151-220, up	1.00
King Size 1	7.50
Annual 2-12, up	2.50
Giant Size 1-5	3.00

CONTEST OF CHAMPIONS, 1-3 | 4.00 |

COSMIC ODYSSEY
| 1-4 | 3.00 |

CRISIS ON INFINITE EARTHS, 1-12 | 2.00 |

DANIEL BOONE (TV)
| 2-15 | 4.50 |

DAREDEVIL
6-10	12.00
11-20	8.00
21-40,50-53	4.00
41-49	2.50
54-99,101-120	2.00
100,131,138	4.00
121-130,132-137,139-	
157	1.50
158	30.00

159,168	12.00
160-167,169,170	6.50
162,171-184,196	4.00
185-195,197-200	1.50
201-225	1.50
226-233,248-250	1.25
234-247, 251-up	1.25
Annual 1	6.00
2-4	3.00

DAZZLER
| 1,2,38 | 4.00 |
| 3-37,39-42 | 1.50 |

DC COMICS PRESENTS
1,13	4.00
2-25,27-50	1.50
26	8.00
51-97	1.00
Annual 1-4	2.00

DEADMAN (1986)
| 1-4 | 2.00 |

DEFENDERS
1	15.00
2-10	4.00
11-54	2.00
55-151	1.25
Annual 1	3.00
Giant Size 1-5	3.00

DELL FOUR COLOR
Please write

DEMON (1972)
| 1-4 | 4.00 |
| 2-16 | 2.00 |

DETECTIVE COMICS
411-436	2.50
437-445	4.00
446-465,469,470,480	
	2.00
466-468,471-479,481-	
483,500	1.50
484-495,526	2.50
496-574,579-up	1.25

DOC SAVAGE PULPS
1935-'45, please write

DOCTOR SOLAR
| 11-31 | 2.50 |

DOCTOR STRANGE
169	7.50
170-183	3.00
1	6.50
2-5	2.50
6-50	1.50
51-95, up	1.00

DOOM PATROL (1987)
| 1 | 3.00 |
| 2-25, up | 1.00 |

ELEMENTALS
1,2	7.00
3-5	4.00
6-35, up	2.00

EXCALIBUR
| 1 | 5.00 |
| 2-10, up | 2.50 |

FALLEN ANGELS
| 1-8 | 1.50 |

FALCON
| 1-4 | 2.00 |

FAMOUS MONSTERS OF FILMLAND (Mag.)
please write

FANTASTIC FOUR
| 35-40,49,50 | 12.00 |

41-47	8.00
51-60	6.00
61-65,68-70	4.50
66,67,72,74-77,112	
	6.00
71,73,78-99	4.00
100	10.00
101-111,113-130	3.00
131-170	2.00
171-270	1.50
271-335, up	1.00
Annual 5-10	4.00
11-21, up	2.50
Vs X-Men 1-4	2.50

FIRESTAR
| 1-4 | 2.50 |

FLASH
234-250	2.00
251-299,301-305,314-	
349	1.00
300,306-313,350	2.00

FLASH (1987)
1	5.00
2,3	3.00
4-30, up	1.00

FLASH GORDON
Gold Key 19-37 | 2.00 |

FURY OF FIRESTORM
| 2-90, up | 1.00 |

GARRISONS GORILLAS
| 1-4 | 4.50 |

GHOST RIDER
1	10.00
2-20	2.50
21-81	1.50

G.I. JOE
1	22.00
2	40.00
3-12	10.00
13-27	8.00
28-40	4.00
41-50	3.00
51-90, up	2.00
Yearbook 1,2	5.00
3,4	2.50
Special Missions	
1-30, up	1.25

GREEN ARROW ('88)
| 1 | 4.00 |
| 2-20, up | 2.00 |

GREEN LANTERN
81-84,87,89	7.50
90-99,101-135	1.50
136,137,142,143	2.50
138-140,144-150	1.50
141	4.00
151-230, up	1.00

GRIM JACK
| 2-60, up | 2.00 |

GUNSMOKE
Gold Key 1-6 | 4.50 |

HAWKEYE
| 1-4 | 2.00 |

HERCULES Both
series, 1-4 | 2.00 |

HOWARD THE DUCK
1	10.00
2	4.00
3-33,Annual 1	2.00

ICEMAN
| 1-4 | 2.00 |

INCREDIBLE HULK
102	17.00
103-120	4.00
121-141	3.00
142-160,163-175,179	
	2.50
161,162,176-178,182,	
200	4.00
183-199	2.00
201-249	1.50
250,272,300,314	4.00
251-271,273-299,301-	
313,315-329	1.25
330-340	2.50
341-365, up	1.25
Annual 1	7.50
2-4,7,8	4.00
5,6,9-15, up	2.50

INFINITY INC.
| 2-60, up | 2.00 |

INVADERS
1	7.50
2-5	2.50
6-41	1.50
Annual 1, Giant 1	3.00

IRON FIST
1	8.00
2,14	6.00
3-13	2.50
15	15.00

IRON MAN
3-10	7.50
11-20	6.00
21-40	4.00
41-46,48-54,57-60	3.00
47,55,56	5.00
61-79	2.50
80-99,101-117,129-150	
	1.50
100,118	4.00
119-128	2.50
151-168,171-199	1.50
169,170,200	4.00
201-224,226-245, up	
	1.25
225	4.00
Annual 1	5.00
2,3	4.00
4-10, up	2.50

JIMMY OLSEN
| 67-90 | 2.50 |
| 91-163 | 2.00 |

JONAH HEX
| 1 | 4.00 |
| 2-92 | 2.00 |

JONNY QUEST
| 2-30, up | 2.00 |

JON SABLE. FREE-LANCE, 1-5 | 4.00 |
| 6-56 | 2.00 |

JUDGE DREDD, Quality, Eagle, all ish. | 2.00 |

JUSTICE LEAGUE
61-116	4.00
117-150	2.00
151-261	1.25
Annual 1-3	2.50

JUSTICE LEAGUE INTERNATIONAL (1987
1	8.00
2	6.00
3,4	4.00

A-160

5-30, up 1.50

JUSTICE MACHINE
1 . . . . 4.00
2-30, up 2.00

KITTY PRIDE & WOLVERINE
1,6 . . . . . . 4.00
2-5 . . . . . . 3.00

KORAK (Gold Key)
12-45 . . . . . 1.50

LEGION OF SUPER—HEROES
259,285-287 . . . . 4.00
260-284,288-300 . . 1.50
301-365, up . . . 1.00
Annual 1-5 . . . 2.00

LEGION OF SUPER HEROES
1,45 . . . . 4.00
2-44,46-65, up . . 2.00

LOIS LANE
60-137 . . . . . . 2.00

LONE RANGER
please write

LONGSHOT
1,6 . . . . . . 10.00
2-5 . . . . . . 8.00

LONGSHOT (1987)
1 . . . . 3.00
2-10, up 1.50

LONE WOLF & CUB
2-20, up 2.50

MAGIK
1-4 . . . . . . 3.00

MANHUNTER
1 . . . . 4.00
2-10, up 1.50

M.A.R.S. PATROL
4-10 . . . . . . 3.00

MARVEL CLASSICS
1-36 . . . . . . 1.50

MARVEL COMICS PRESENTS
1 . . . . 2.50
2-10, up 1.50

MARVEL FANFARE
1,2 . . . . . . 7.00
3,4 . . . . . . 4.00
5-55, up 2.00

MARVEL TALES
2 . . . . 12.00
3-10 . . . . . . 4.00
11-19 . . . . . . 3.00
20-33 . . . . . . 2.50
34-100 . . . . . 1.50

MARVEL TEAM UP
1 . . . . 15.00
2-4 . . . . . . 6.00
5-10 . . . . . . 4.00
11-20 . . . . . . 3.00
21-52,54-70,75,79 . 2.00
53 . . . . 8.00
71-74,76-78,80-88,90-99,101-116,119-149 . . . . . . 1.25
89,100,117,118,150 . . . . . . 4.00
Annual 1 . . . . 9.00
2-7 . . . . . . 2.50

MARVEL TWO IN ONE
1 . . . . 10.00
2-10,83,84,100 . . 2.50
11-82,85-99 . . 1.25
Annual 1,3-7 . . 2.50
4 . . . . 6.00

MARVEL UNIVERSE (1983), 1-15 . . 3.00

MARVEL UNIVERSE (1985), 1-25, up . 2.50

MASTER OF KUNG FU
15 . . . . 6.00
16-29 . . . . . . 2.50
30-50 . . . . . . 2.00
51-125 . . . . . 1.00

METAL MEN
40-56 . . . . . . 2.00

MICRONAUTS
1 . . . . 6.00
2-36,39-59 . . . 1.00
37,38 . . . . . . 4.00

MILLENIUM

1-8 . . . . 1.50

MOON KNIGHT
1 . . . . 5.00
2-38 . . . . . . 1.50

MS. MARVEL
1 . . . . 4.00
2-23 . . . . . . 2.00

THE NAM
1 . . . . 15.00
2 . . . . 7.00
3,4 . . . . . . 5.00
5-10 . . . . . . 2.50
11-30, up . . . 1.50

NEW MUTANTS
1 . . . . 5.00
2-10 . . . . . . 2.50
11-21 . . . . . . 2.00
22-80, up . . . 1.25
Annual 1-4 . . . 2.00

NEW TEEN TITANS
1 . . . . 15.00
2-4 . . . . . . 8.00
5-13 . . . . . . 4.00
14-50 . . . . . . 1.50
51-100, up . . . 1.00
Annual 1-4, up . . 2.00

NEW TEEN TITANS (1984), 1 . . 4.00
2-50, up 2.00

NEXUS (First)
7-60, up 2.00

NICK FURY (1968)
1 . . . . 15.00
2-5,12 . . . . . 5.00
6-11,13-18 . . . 3.00

NIGHTCRAWLER
1-4 . . . . . . 2.00

NOT BRAND ECHH
1,2,9-13 . . . . 4.00
3-8 . . . . . . 3.00

NOVA
1 . . . . 4.00
2-25 . . . . . . 1.50

NUKLA
1-4 . . . . . . 2.50

PETER PARKER/SPEC. SPIDER-MAN
1 . . . . 8.00
2 . . . . 4.00
3-10 . . . . . . 3.00
11-26 . . . . . . 2.50
27 . . . . 9.00
28,64 . . . . . . 8.00
29-63 . . . . . . 2.00
65-68,71-80,84-99,101-155, up . . 1.50
69,70,81-83,100 . . 4.00
Annual 1-8, up . . 2.50

PHANTOM STRANGER
1-10 . . . . . . 4.00
11-41 . . . . . . 1.50

PLANET OF THE VAMPIRES
1-3 . . . . . . 2.00

POWERMAN/IRON FIST (1972-1986)
1 . . . . 6.00
2-10 . . . . . . 2.50
11-30 . . . . . . 2.00
31-47,51-56,58-125 . . . . . . 1.00
48-50 . . . . . . 3.00
57 . . . . 6.00

POWER PACK
1 . . . . 5.00
2-50, up 1.25

PUNISHER (1987)
1 . . . . 4.00
2-10 . . . . . . 2.50
11-25, up . . . 1.25

PUNISHER WAR JOURNAL
1 . . . . 3.00
2-10, up 1.50

QUESTION, THE
1 . . . . 4.00
2-30, up 2.00

ROM
1,17,18 . . . . . 4.00
2-16,19-30 . . . 1.50
31-75 . . . . . . 1.00

ROY ROGERS
please write

SAVAGE SWORD OF CONAN, 1 . . 12.00
2-9 . . . . . . 6.00
10-20 . . . . . . 4.00
30-69 . . . . . . 3.00
70-155, up . . . 2.50

SCOUT
3-24 . . . . . . 2.50

SECRET ORIGINS (1973), 1-7 . 2.50

SECRET ORIGINS (1986), 1-45, up . 1.50

SECRET WARS I
1 . . . . 4.00
2-12 . . . . . . 2.00

SGT. FURY
14-30 . . . . . . 4.00
31-69 . . . . . . 2.00

SHADOW (1973)
2-12 . . . . . . 2.50

SHADOW (1987)
1 . . . . 4.00
2-25, up 2.00

SHADOW OF THE BATMAN
1-5 . . . . . . 3.00

SHAZAM (1973)
1,8,12-17 . . . . 3.00
2-7,9-11,18-35 . . 1.50

SHE HULK
1 . . . . 4.00
2-25 . . . . . . 1.50

SILVER SURFER ('87)
1 . . . . 4.00
2-25, up 1.50

SOLO AVENGERS
1-15, up 1.50

SPACE FAMILY ROBINSON, 20-59 . 2.50

SPECTRE (1987)
1 . . . . 4.00
2-30, up 2.00

SPIDER-MAN (Amaz)
51-60 . . . . . . 5.00
61-89,91-95,99 . . 4.00
90,96-98,101,102 . 8.00
100 . . . . 15.00
121,122 . . . . . 20.00
103-120,123-128,130-133 . . . . 3.00
134,135 . . . . . 4.00
136-160 . . . . . 2.00
161,162,174,175 . . 5.00
163-173,176-199 . 2.00
200-202,238,252 . . 4.00
203-237 . . . . . 1.50
239-251,253-320, up . 1.50
Giant 1-3,5,6 . . 3.00
Annual 4 . . . . 6.00
5-10,14,15 . . . 4.00
11-13,16-22, up . . 2.50

SPIDER-WOMAN
1,37,38,50 . . . 4.00
2-36,39-49 . . . 1.50

STAR TREK (DC)
1 . . . . 4.00
2-60, up 1.50

STAR WARS
1 . . . . 7.50
2-4 . . . . . . 4.00
5-10 . . . . . . 2.00
11-44 . . . . . . 2.00
45-107 . . . . . 1.50
Annual 1-3 . . . 2.00

STRANGE ADVENTURES
185-204,217-244 . 2.50
207-216 . . . . . 6.00

STRANGE TALES
140-168 . . . . . 3.00

SUB-MARINER
2-10 . . . . . . 4.00
11-20 . . . . . . 3.00
21-40 . . . . . . 2.50
41-72 . . . . . . 2.00
Special 1,2 . . . 3.00

SUICIDE SQUAD

1 . . . . 4.00
2-25, up 1.50

SUPERBOY
121-140 . . . . . 3.00
141-196 . . . . . 2.00
197-210 . . . . . 4.00
211-248 . . . . . 2.00
249-258 . . . . . 1.50

SUPER HEROES (Dell)
1-4 . . . . . . 3.00

SUPERMAN
201-253 . . . . . 2.00
Giants on above . 4.50
255-299 . . . . . 1.50
301-399,401-422,425-up 1.00

SUPERMAN (1987)
1 . . . . 3.00
2-35, up 1.50

SUPERMAN FAMILY
164-222 . . . . . 2.00

SWAMP THING ('72)
1 . . . . 8.50
2,3 . . . . . . 3.00
4-10 . . . . . . 2.50
11-24 . . . . . . 2.00

SWAMP THING ('82)
1,16-19 . . . . . 2.50
2-15 . . . . . . 1.50
20,21 . . . . . . 15.00
22-25 . . . . . . 6.00
26-30 . . . . . . 4.00
31-40 . . . . . . 2.00
41-90, up . . . 1.50

TALES OF SUSPENSE
71-79 . . . . . . 4.00
80-99 . . . . . . 2.50

TALES TO ASTONISH
71-80 . . . . . . 3.00
81-91,94-99,101 . . 2.50

TARZAN (Gold Key)
170-206 . . . . . 2.00

TARZAN (DC)
207-211,230-235 . 2.50
212-229,236-258 . 1.50

TEEN TITANS SPOTLIGHT, 1-25, up . 1.00

THE THING
1 . . . . 4.00
2-36 . . . . . . 1.00

THOR
120-125,127-130 . 5.00
131-133,136-140 . 4.00
141-169 . . . . . 3.00
170-179,182-192,194-199 . . . . . 2.50
201-336,339-350 . 1.50
337 . . . . 4.00
338 . . . . 2.00
351-372,375-400, up . 1.00
Specials/Annuals 3-14, up . . 2.50

THREE STOOGES
please write

TOKA, JUNGLE KING
1-10 . . . . . . 2.50

TOMAHAWK
87-140 . . . . . 2.00

TOMB OF DRACULA
1 . . . . 7.50
2-10 . . . . . . 2.50
11-70 . . . . . . 1.50

TRANSFORMERS
1 . . . . 5.00
2-4 . . . . . . 3.00
5-60, up 1.50

TV/MOVIE COMICS
please write

TWO FISTED TALES (EC), please write

UNCLE SCROOGE (Dell), please write
178-230, up . . . 2.00

V FOR VENDETTA
1-10, up 2.00

VIGILANTE
1 . . . . 4.00
2-50, Annual 1,2 . 2.00

VISION & THE SCARLET WITCH ('82 & '85)
all issues . . . 2.00

WALT DISNEY'S COMICS & STORIES
201-269 . . . . . 5.00

WARLOCK (1972)
1 . . . . 5.00
2-15 . . . . . . 2.50

WARLORD
1 . . . . 12.00
2-10 . . . . . . 4.00
11-30 . . . . . . 2.50
31-52 . . . . . . 1.50
53-135, up . . . 1.00
Annual 1-6, up . . 2.00

WATCHMEN
1 . . . . 4.00
2-12 . . . . . . 2.00

WEB OF SPIDER—MAN
1 . . . . 5.00
2,3 . . . . . . 3.00
4-13 . . . . . . 2.00
14-55, up . . . 1.50
Annual 1-4 . . . 2.50

WEIRD TALES (pulps)
-please write

WESTERNS (All publishers, please write

WEST COAST AVENGERS
1-4, mini series . 3.00
1 . . . . 5.00
2-19 . . . . . . 1.50
20-50, up . . . 1.00
Annual 1,2 . . . 2.00

WHAT IF?
1 . . . . 7.50
2-12 . . . . . . 2.50
13,27,28,31 . . . 4.50
14-26,29,30,32-47 . 2.00

WHISPER (First)
3-20, up 2.00

WHO'S WHO (DC)
1-26 . . . . . . 1.50

WOLVERINE (1982)
1 . . . . 7.50
2-4 . . . . . . 6.00

WOLVERINE (1987)
1 . . . . 2.50
2-10, up 1.50

WONDER WOMAN
171-200 . . . . . 2.50
201-250 . . . . . 1.50
251-328 . . . . . 1.00

WONDER WOMAN '87
1 . . . . 4.00
2-35, up 1.50

WORLDS FINEST
162-206 . . . . . 2.50
207-282 . . . . . 2.00
283-323 . . . . . 1.50

X-FACTOR
1 . . . . 5.00
2-4 . . . . . . 3.00
5-10 . . . . . . 2.50
11-45, up . . . 1.25
Annual 1-3 . . . 2.00

X-MEN
95 . . . . 40.00
96-99,108,109 . . 22.00
100,101 . . . . . 25.00
102-107 . . . . . 12.00
110,111 . . . . . 15.00
112-119,122-130 . 10.00
120,121 . . . . . 22.00
131-141 . . . . . 8.00
142,143 . . . . . 6.00
144-166,171 . . . 4.00
167-170,172-213 . 2.50
214-245, up . . . 1.50
Annual 3 . . . . 4.00
4,5,9,10 . . . . . 4.00
6-8,11-up 2.50
& Micronauts 1-4 . 2.50
& New Teen Titans 5.00
Vs Avengers 1-4 . 2.00

YOUNG ALL STARS
1-30, up 2.00

ALPHA FLIGHT			
1, 12, 13, 17	$5.00		
2-24 $2½ 25-78	1.25		
X-MEN & ALPHA			
1, 2, (sale)	1.25		

AVENGERS	
24-91, 101-129	$4.00
130-191, Ann 6-10	3.00
192-250, Ann 11-18	2.00
251-306 up	1.00
VS. X-MEN 1-4	3.00

BATMAN			
421-425, 430-440	$1.25		
CULT 1 $20	2	$15.00	
3, 4 $6 Year 1		9.95	
DARK KNIGHT	2*	5.00	
3, 4 $5 TRADE		12.95	
Death of Robin		3.95	
Greatest Joker		19.95	
Killing Joke 1*		3.50	

CAPT. AMERICA	
118-171, 300, 350	$2.50
176-362, Ann 3-7	1.00

CONAN		
1 $50 2, 3		$30.00
4, 5 $17 6-15		10.00
6-25, Ann 1		6.00
26-37, 50, 58, 100		3.00
38-57, Ann 2-13		1.50
59-199, 201-227		1.00
GS 1-5, 200		1.50

DAREDEVIL		
25-157 $2½ 100		$5.00
159-163 $12 162		5.00
164-167, 169		8.00
170-175 $5 176-181		3.00
182-184, 196, 200		5.00
185-199, 248, 249		2.50
201-225, 252		1.25
226, 227 $5 228		3.00
229-233 $2 234 up		1.00

DEFENDERS	
6-9, 100, 125	$3.00
11-20, 150, 152	1.50
21-149, 151	.75

ELEKTRA ASSASSIN	
1 $5 2 $4 3-8	$3.00

EXCALIBUR 1 SP		$8.00
1 $5 2-4 $3 5 up		1.50

FANTASTIC FOUR	
53-75, 200	$5.00
76-167, 236, 250	3.00
168-269, Ann 12-22	2.00
270-330 up	1.00
VS. X-MEN 1-4	3.00
F ANGELS 2-8	1.50

GI JOE	
1, 2G, 6-16, 24	$15.00
20-23 $10 25, 28	6.00
2, 26, 27, 29-38*	2.00
3-12, 14, 17-19, 23*	4.00
29-43	3.50
44-50 $2 51-95	1.00
SPECIAL MISSIONS	
1-30 up	1.00
UNIVERSE 1-4	2.00
VS TRANSF. 1-4	2.00
YB 1 $6 2 $4 3, 4	2.00

HULK 185-313	$1.00
314, 332-339	5.00
315-329 $1½ 330	8.00
331 $6 341-350	2.00
351-364 $1 Ann 9-15	1.50

IRONMAN	
57-117, 191, 192	$1.50
100, 118-128, 150	3.00
129-199, Ann 5-9	1.25
169-172, 200, 225	2.50
201-246 up	.80
JLI 1, 2 $15 3, 4	$5.00
5-10 $2½ 11-35	.80
EUROPE 1-5 up	1.00

MARVEL COMICS PRES	
1, 2 $3 3-28 up	1.25

MARVEL FANFARE	
1, 2 $9 3, 4	$6.00
5-12 $2½ 16-40 up	1.75

MARVEL TEAM-UP	
12-29 $2 30-79	$1.50
80-88, 90-149	1.00
53, 89, 100, 150	6.00

MARVEL UNIVERSE	
1-5 $5 6-15	$2.50
NEW 1-20	2.00
Trade 1-10	6.95

NAM 1 $12 1*		$2.00
2 $8 3-7 $4 11-41		1.50

NEW MUTANTS		
1 $7 SPECIAL 1		$4.50
2-10 $3½ 11-21, 50		2.50
22-84 $1 59, 71, 73		4.00

PETER PARKER	
1, 27, 28, 64	$10.00
2-10 $3½ 11-26	2.50
29-99 $1¼ 101-161	1.00
69, 70, 81-83	6.00
90-92, 100, 131, 132	3.00
Ann 1-9	1.75

PUNISHER 2-5		$10.00
NEW 1 $6 2-4, 10		5.00
5-9, 11 $3 12-27		1.25
WAR JOURNAL 1		5.00
2-12 $2 TRADE		8.00
Gr Novel $7 HB		17.00

SECRET WARS			
1-3 $3 4-11 $2	12	$1.00	
(II) 1-8 .75	9		1.25

SILVER SURFER		
NEW 1 $5 2-10		$2.00
11-34 $1 EPIC 1, 2		1.00
Hardback 1 $15 2		19.95

SPIDERMAN	
68-88 $4 105-118	$3.00
125-128, 138-160	3.00
163-248, 253-275	2.00
249, 251 $3 250	4.00
276-284 $1½ 285	4.00
286-297 $1¼ 289	3.00
298-303, 238, 252	5.00
304, 305 $3 306-312	2.50
313-328	1.00
Ann 10-12, 16-23	2.00
Trade 1 $12 2	6.00
Masterworks 1, 2	29.95

SUPERMAN 1-40	.80
M O STEEL 1-6	5.00

TURTLES 1-3*		$4.00
3 $15 4-6 $10	7	5.00
8-14 $4 15, 16 up		2.00
Adventures 1-3, 1 up		1.00
GR. NOVEL 1-4		9.95

TEEN TITANS, NEW	
1 $15 2-4 $8 5-10	$3.00
11-15 $2 16-24	1.25
25-91 .75 New 1	4.00
2-38 $1¼ 39-62	1.50

THOR 207-336	$1.00
337 $6 338, 400	3.00
339, 350, 373	2.25
340-365	1.25
366-399 $1 401 up	.80

TRANSFORMERS	
1 $4 2-4 $3 5-10	$1.00
11-49, 51 up $1 50	1.50

WEB OF SPIDERMAN	
1 $7 2, 3 $4 4-8	$3.00
9-13 $2½ 14-28, 30	1.50
29, 32, 33 $3½ 31	2.50
34-49, 51 up $1 50	1.50

WEST COAST AVEN	
OLD 1 $6 2-4	$4.00
NEW 1, 2 $4 3-10	2.00
11-30 $1¼ 31-49	1.00

WOLVERINE 3	7.00
NEW 1 $5 2-16	1.50
HAVOK & W. 1-4	3.50
KITTY & W. 1-6	3.00

X-MEN	
96-101, 108, 109	$30.00
102-104, 140, 141	18.00
105-107, 113-119	15.00
110 $20 111, 112	25.00
122, 129, 130	15.00
123-128, 139	12.00
131-138 $10 142	8.00
143, 146, 171	6.00
144-150, Ann 5, 10	5.00
151-174, Ann 9	4.00
163-166, 175	5.00
176-186, Ann 6-8	3.00
187-209	2.50
210-213	4.00
214-224, 228-243	1.50
225-227 $3 244-254	1.00
Ann 11-13, 250	2.00
CLASSIC X-MEN	
1 $4 2-4 $2½ 5-10	2.00
11-20 $1½ 21-44	1.25
HEROES F HOPE	1.00
MEPHISTO 1-4	3.00
NIGHT CRAWLER	
1-4	2.00
X TRADE 1 $10 2	14.95
X-FACTOR 1	6.00
2-5 $4 6-10	3.00
11-26, 38 $2 27-49	1.00
X-TERMINATORS	
1 $2 2 $1½ 3, 4	1.25

A-168

BUYING COMICS
Top Prices Paid!

If you have any of the comics listed on these 2 pages, we want to buy them and we'll pay very, very well to get them. We'll buy any quantity, from 1 book to 1 million books. Send us your list, with conditions, and we will make an offer promptly. Better still, just ship us any of the books listed on these 2 pages and we will send immediate payment for them. If you're not satisfied with our offer, just return our payment and we'll return your books, with our gradings, at our expense. We will reimburse your shipping expenses whether or not we buy your books. We will travel anywhere to buy valuable collections in person. We also buy many issues not listed here, and quantities of better recent books (X-Men, G.I. Joe, Alpha Flight, etc.)

TOP WANTS—For any books on this page, we will pay a **minimum** of 60% of this Price Guide value. Ship books for immediate payment or send your list.

Action 1-300	Flash Comics 1-104	Sgt. Bilko 1-18
Adventure 32-380	Flash 105-123	S.B.'s Pvt. Doberman 1-11
Advs. of Bob Hope 1-50	Fox & Crow 1-40	Showcase 1-43
Advs. of D. Martin &	Funny Pages 6-42	Star Spangled 1-130
J. Lewis 1-60	Funny Picture Stories (all)	Strange Adventures 1-120
All American 1-102	Green Lantern (1st) 1-38	Strange Tales 1-110
All Flash 1-32	Green Lantern (2nd) 1-20	Submariner Comics 1-42
All Select 1-11	Human Torch 1-38	Sugar & Spike 1-98
All Star 1-57	Hulk 1-6	Superboy 1-100
Amazing Fantasy 7-15	J. Gleason, Honeymooners	Superman 1-167
Amaz. Mystery Funnies (all)	(all)	SM's Girlfriend Lois Lane
Amazing Spider-Man 1-20	Journey into Mystery 1-100	1-10
Avengers 1-20	Justice League 1-22	SM's Pal Jimmy Olsen 1-40
Batman 1-150	Leading 1-14	Tales of Suspense 1-53
Blonde Phantom 12-22	Marvel Mystery 1-92	Tales to Astonish 1-50
Brave & the Bold 1-44	More Fun 7-127	Tomahawk 1-50
Captain America 1-78	My Greatest Adventure	U.S.A. 1-17
Congo Bill 1-7	1-30, 80-85	Wonder Woman 1-120
Daring Mystery 1-8	Mystery in Space 1-75	World's Finest 1-100
Detective 1-300	Phantom Stranger (1st) 1-6	X-Men 1-146
Fantastic Four 1-30	Planet 1-73	Young Allies 1-20
	Sensation 1-116	

J&S COMICS   P.O. Box 2057   Red Bank, NJ 07701
UPS Address - 98 Madison Avenue   Phone: (201) 747-7548 (No collect calls)

BUYING — J&S COMICS, P.O. BOX 2057, RED BANK, NJ 07701

WANTED—We will pay a **minimum** of 45% of this Price Guide value for any book on this page (50% for pre 1960 DC's). Ship for payment or send your list.

Air Fighters (all)
Advs. of Ozzie & Harriet 1-7
Advs. of Rex 1-46
All American Western 103-126
All Funny 1-23
All Hero 1
All Negro 1
All Star Western 58-117
All Top 8-18
All Winners 1-21
Amaz. Adventures (1950) 1-6
Amaz. Adventures (1961) 1-6
Amazing Man 5-27
America's Best 1-31
America's Greatest 1-8
Aquaman 1-10
Animal 1-30
Archie Group (all pre 1960)
Blackhawk 9-130
Boy Commandos 1-36
Blue Ribbon 1-22
Bulletman 1-16
Buster Crabbe 1-5
Buzzy 1-10
Capt. Marvel Advs. 1-150
Capt. Marvel Jr. 1-115
Capt. Midnight 1-67
Capt. Video 1-6
Challengers 1-10
Charlie Chan (DC) 1-6
Classics (originals) 1-50
Comic Cavalcade 1-63
Crack 1-30
Crime does not Pay 22-47
Crime Patrol 7-16
Crime Suspenstories 1-27
Crypt of Terror 17-19
Dale Evans (DC) 1-24
Danger Trail 1-5
Daredevil (Gleason) 1-31
Daredevil (Marvel) 1-10
Date with Judy 1-10
Dick Tracy 1-145
Doll Man 1-30
Donald Duck (Barks issues)
Durango Kid 1-17
Earthman on Venus
Eerie (Avon) 1-17
Famous Funnies 1-30, 209-216
Fantastic 1-23
Fawcett Movie Comics 1-20
Fight 1-86
Fighting Yank 1-29
Four Color (all worth over $2)
Frontier Fighters 1-8
Frontline Combat 1-15
Funny Stuff 1-20
Gang Busters 1-67
G.I. Combat 1-67
Green Hornet 1-47
Harvey Hits 1-30

Haunt of Fear 1-28
Hit 1-65
Hopalong Cassidy 1-135
House of Mystery 1-50-
House of Secrets 1-20
Jimmy Wakely 1-18
John Wayne 1-31
Jumbo 1-167
Jungle 1-163
Katy Keene (all)
Keen Detective Funnies 58-24
Kid 1-10
Little Dot 1-20
Little Lotta 1-10
Little Lulu FC 74-80
Lone Ranger 1-20
Mad 1-23
Mary Marvel 1-28
Master Comics 1-133
Military 1-43
Miss Fury 1-8
Modern 44-102
Moon Girl 1-12
Motion Picture Comics 101-114
Movie Comics (DC) 1-6
Mysterious Adventures 1-25
Mystery Men 1-31
Mystic Comics 1-10
Naitonal Comics 1-75
New Adventure 12-31
New Comics 1-11
New Fun 1-6
New York World's Fair 1,2
Nickel Comics
Nyoka 1-77
Our Army at War 1-91
Our Fighting Forces 1-45
Our Gang 1-36
Pep 1-100
Peter Panda 1-31
Phantom Lady 13-23, 1-4
Plastic Man (1st) 1-64
Pogo Possum 1-16
Police Comics 1-127
Popular 1-145
Prize Comics 1-119
Rangers 1-69
Real Fact 1-21
Real Screen 1-128
Red Raven 1
Red Ryder 1-40
Richie Rich 1-40
Roy Rogers 1-40
Saddle Justice (Romances) 3-11
Sheena 1-18
Shield Wizard 1-13
Shock Suspenstories 1-18
Silver Streak 1-24
Smash 1-85
Space Adventures 1-40

Sparkler Comics 1-70
Speed Comics 1-44
Spirit 1-22
Spy Smasher 1-11
Star Comics 1-23
Star Ranger (all)
Star Spangled War Stories 1-50
Startling Comics 1-53
Strange Fantasy 1-14
Strange Mysteries 1-21
Strange Stories of Suspense 1-14
Strange Suspense Stories 1-77
Strange Tales of the Unusual 1-11
Strange World of Your Dreams 1-4
Strange Worlds 1-22
Super Mystery (all)
Supersnipe (all)
Suspense Comics 1-25
Tales from the Crypt 20-46
Tales of Terror Annual 1-3
Tales of the Unexpected 1-40
Tarzan 1-20
Teen Age Romances 1-60
The Thing (Charlton) 1-17
This Magazine is Haunted 1-21
3-D Batman, Superman 1953
Three Mousketeers (1st) 1-26
Three Stooges (St. John) 1-7
Thrilling Comics 1-80
Thrilling Crime Cases 41-49
Tip Top Comics 1-61
Tomb of Terror 1-16
Tom Mix 1-40
Top Notch 1-45
Torchy 1-6
True Crime Comics 1-9
Tubby 1-20
Turok 1-10
Two Fisted Tales 1-41
Uncanny Tales 1-57
Uncle Sam 1-8
Uncle Scrooge 1-10
Vault of Horror 12-40
Venus 1-19
Voodoo 1-22
Walt Disney's Comics & Stories 1-170
War Against Crime 1-11
Web of Evil 1-21
Weird Comics 1-20
Weird Fantasy 1-22
Weird Science 1-22
Weird Science-Fantasy 23-29
Weird Tales of the Future 1-8
Western Comics (DC) 1-85
Whiz Comics 1-155
Wings Comics 1-124
Wonder Comics 1-20
World of Fantasy 1-19
Wow Comics 1-69
Yellow Claw 1-4
Zip Comics 1-47

THE LEADING PUBLISHER OF GRAPHIC NOVELS IN THE UK.

There is one publishing house that has risen to the peak of comics
publishing in both Britain and the US. There is one publishing house that has
generated an unprecedented interest in graphic novels and comics in the
UK. There is one publishing house that is making quality comics as
acceptable to read as they are in France, Italy and Spain.
Welcome to the future. Welcome to **TITAN BOOKS**.

TITAN BOOKS publishes a variety of ranges of graphic albums.
● The *2000 AD* series including *JUDGE DREDD, HALO JONES, D.R. &
QUINCH, NEMESIS, BAD COMPANY* and *ZENITH*.
● The Graphic Novel series including *WATCHMEN, DARK KNIGHT,
SWAMP THING, LOVE & ROCKETS, BROUGHT TO LIGHT, ELFQUEST*
and *LITTLE NEMO*.
● The European Graphic Novel series featuring the best of *MOEBIUS,
BILAL* and *HERMANN*.

TITAN BOOKS also publishes *JUDGE DREDD, BATMAN* and *GERRY
ANDERSON* paperbacks, mass market science fiction paperbacks including
the *STAR TREK & STAR TREK: THE NEXT GENERATION* novel series,
Film & TV Fantasy books & produces a full range of JUDGE DREDD,
MARVEL, GERRY ANDERSON and DC COMICS merchandise including
T- shirts and badges.

TITAN BOOKS LTD, 58 ST GILES HIGH STREET, LONDON WC2H 8LH.

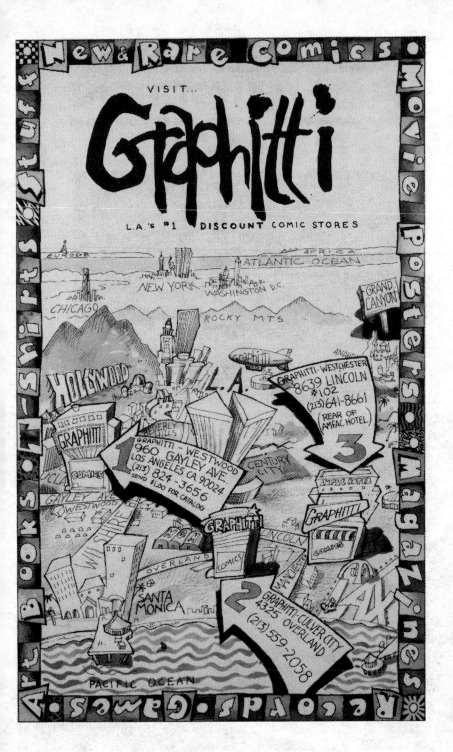

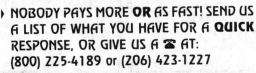
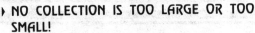

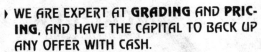

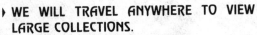

LOOKING FOR GOLD AND SILVERAGE COMIC BOOKS?

WORLD'S FINEST COMICS & COLLECTABLES
WANTS YOUR BUSINESS!

Call us at (206) 423-8673   Ask for Mark Wilson

Here is what we offer:

1. **Selection**-We always have on hand a large selection of Golden Age comics, including DC, Timely, Centaur and prehero. We also sell **Silver Age** comics and Big Little Books. We specialize in comic books which are truly rare such as New Fun #1-6, or New Comics #1-31; all of which we have in stock. Give us a call.

2. **Accurate Grading**-All books are guaranteed to be in the condition stated or we will give a complete refund. We have built our business on repeat business, and will do all we can to insure complete customer satisfaction.

3. **Exceptional Service**-All books are packaged with extreme care and shipped to you within 24 hours of payment. For an additional charge, we will ship by Federal Express overnight.

4. **Shop By Video**-For a small fee we will video tape any book(s) you are interested in purchasing. This will give you an accurate visible inspection before you buy. Close up shots can be taken of the front and back covers (inside & out), pages, and centerfold area.

5. **Time Payment Plans**-We offer several types of payment plans to assist you in obtaining the book(s) you want. Call us for more information.

6. **Free Catalog**-We offer a free quarterly catalog to all who write and ask. Write for a free copy today.

7. **Want List Service**-Send us a list of which book(s) you need and we will do our best to locate them for you. Give us a try.

WORLD'S FINEST COMICS & COLLECTABLES
P.O. Box 1609
Longview, WA 98632

(206) 423-8673   Ask for Mark Wilson

Action, Adventure, All-American, Detective comic covers above are © DC Comics, Inc. Jumbo Comics cover is © Fiction House.

A-183

A-184

Abbott And Costello #38, © STJ   Aces High #3, © WMG   Action Comics #1, © DC

The correct title listing for each comic book can be determined by consulting the indicia (publication data) on the beginning interior pages of the comic. The official title is determined by those words of the title in capital letters only, and not by what is on the cover.

Titles are listed in this book as if they were one word, ignoring spaces, hyphens, and apostrophes, to make finding titles easier.

A-1 (See A-One)

ABBIE AN' SLATS (. . .With Becky No. 1-4) (See Comics On Parade, Fight for Love, Giant Comics Edition 2, Sparkler Comics, Tip Topper, Treasury of Comics, & United Comics)
1940; March, 1948 - No. 4, Aug, 1948 (Reprints)
United Features Syndicate

	Good	Fine	N-Mint
Single Series 25 ('40)	17.00	51.00	120.00
Single Series 28	14.50	43.50	100.00
1 (1948)	8.00	24.00	56.00
2-4: 3 r-/Sparkler #68-72	4.00	12.00	28.00

ABBOTT AND COSTELLO (. . .Comics)(See Treasury of Comics)
Feb, 1948 - No. 40, Sept?, 1956 (Mort Drucker art in most issues)
St. John Publishing Co.

1	20.00	60.00	140.00
2	10.00	30.00	70.00
3-9 (#8, 8/49; #9, 2/50)	5.70	17.00	40.00
10-Son of Sinbad story by Kubert (new)	11.50	34.50	80.00
11,13-20 (#11, 10/50; #13, 8/51; #15, 12/52)	3.50	10.50	25.00
12-Movie issue	5.00	15.00	35.00
21-30: 28 r-#8. 30-Painted-c	2.65	8.00	18.00
31-40: #33, 38-r	2.15	6.50	15.00
3-D #1 (11/53)-Infinity-c	17.00	51.00	120.00

ABBOTT AND COSTELLO (TV)
Feb, 1968 - No. 22, Aug, 1971 (Hanna-Barbera)
Charlton Comics

1	1.70	5.00	12.00
2-10	1.00	3.00	6.00
11-22	.60	1.75	3.50

ABC (See America's Best TV Comics)

ABRAHAM LINCOLN LIFE STORY (See Dell Giants)

ABSENT-MINDED PROFESSOR, THE (See 4-Color Comics No. 1199)

ACE COMICS
April, 1937 - No. 151, Oct-Nov, 1949
David McKay Publications

1-Jungle Jim by Alex Raymond, Blondie, Ripley's Believe It Or Not, Krazy Kat begin	125.00	375.00	875.00
2	45.00	135.00	315.00
3-5	32.00	95.00	225.00
6-10	23.50	70.00	164.00
11-The Phantom begins(In brown costume, 2/38)	32.00	95.00	225.00
12-20	18.00	54.00	125.00
21-25,27-30	15.00	45.00	105.00
26-Origin Prince Valiant	44.00	132.00	310.00
31-40: 37-Krazy Kat ends	11.00	32.00	76.00
41-60	9.00	27.00	63.00
61-64,66-76-(7/43; last 68pgs.)	8.00	24.00	56.00
65-(8/42; Flag-c)	9.00	27.00	63.00
77-84 (3/44; all 60pgs.)	7.00	21.00	50.00
85-99 (52 pgs.)	6.00	18.00	42.00
100 (7/45; last 52 pgs.)	7.00	21.00	50.00
101-134: 128-11/47; Brick Bradford begins. 134-Last Prince Valiant (All 36 pgs.)	5.00	15.00	35.00
135-151: 135-6/48; Lone Ranger begins	4.00	12.00	28.00

ACE KELLY (See Tops Comics & Tops In Humor)

ACE KING (See Advs. of the Detective)

ACES
Apr, 1988 - Present ($2.95, B&W, Magazine)
Acme Press (Eclipse Comics)

	Good	Fine	N-Mint
1-3	.50	1.50	3.00

ACES HIGH
Mar-Apr, 1955 - No. 5, Nov-Dec, 1955
E.C. Comics

1-Not approved by code	7.00	21.00	50.00
2	6.00	18.00	42.00
3-5	5.00	15.00	35.00

NOTE: All have stories by *Davis, Evans, Krigstein,* and *Wood; Evans* c-1-5.

ACTION ADVENTURE (War) (Formerly Real Adventure)
June, 1955 - No. 4, Oct, 1955
Gillmor Magazines

V1#2-4	1.15	3.50	8.00

ACTION COMICS (See Special Edition; becomes Action Comics Weekly No. 601 on)
6/38 - No. 583, 9/86; No. 584, 1/87 - No. 600, 5/88
National Periodical Publ./Detective Comics/DC

1-Origin & 1st app. Superman by Siegel & Shuster, Marco Polo, Tex Thompson, Pep Morgan, Chuck Dawson & Scoop Scanlon; intro. Zatara & Lois Lane; Superman story missing 4 pgs. which were included when reprinted in Superman #1. Mentioned in **POP,** pg. 86

	Good	Fine	Vf-NM
	4600.00	13,800.00	30,000.00

(Only one known copy exists in Mint condition which has not sold)

1-Reprint, Oversize 13½''x10.'' **WARNING:** This comic is an exact reprint of the original except for its size. DC published it in 1974 with a second cover titling it as a **Famous First Edition.** There have been many reported cases of the outer cover being removed and the interior sold as the original edition. The reprint with the new outer cover removed is practically worthless.

	Good	Fine	N-Mint
1(1976,1983)-Giveaway; paper cover, 16pgs. in color; reprints complete Superman story from #1 ('38)	.70	2.00	4.00
1(1987 Nestle Quik giveaway; 1988, 50 cent-c)	.25		.50
2	675.00	2025.00	4725.00
3 (Scarce)	520.00	1560.00	3640.00
4	355.00	1065.00	2500.00
5 (Rare)	430.00	1290.00	3000.00
6-1st Jimmy Olsen (called office boy)	340.00	1020.00	2400.00
7,10-Superman covers	425.00	1275.00	2975.00
8,9	300.00	900.00	2100.00
11,12,14: 14-Clip Carson begins, ends #41	150.00	450.00	1050.00
13-Superman cover; last Scoop Scanlon	200.00	600.00	1400.00
15-Superman cover	215.00	615.00	1500.00
16	120.00	360.00	840.00
17-Superman cover; last Marco Polo	160.00	480.00	1120.00
18-Origin 3 Aces; 1st X-Ray Vision?	115.00	345.00	800.00
19-Superman covers begin	145.00	435.00	1000.00
20-'S' left off Superman's chest; Clark Kent works at 'Daily Star'	140.00	420.00	980.00
21,22,24,25: 24-Kent at Daily Planet. 25-Last app. Gargantua T. Potts, Tex Thompson's sidekick	85.00	255.00	600.00
23-1st app. Luthor & Black Pirate; Black Pirate by Moldoff	115.00	340.00	800.00
26-30	60.00	180.00	420.00
31,32	47.00	140.00	330.00
33-Origin Mr. America	54.00	160.00	380.00
34-40: 37-Origin Congo Bill. 40-Intro Star Spangled Kid & Stripesy	47.00	140.00	330.00
41	44.00	132.00	310.00
42-Origin Vigilante; Bob Daley becomes Fat Man; origin Mr. America's			

1

ACTION COMICS (continued) | Good | Fine | N-Mint

magic flying carpet; The Queen Bee & Luthor app; Black Pirate
ends; not in #41 — 62.00 185.00 435.00
43-50: 44-Fat Man's i.d. revealed to Mr. America. 45-Intro. Stuff — 44.00 132.00 310.00
51-1st app. The Prankster — 37.00 110.00 260.00
52-Fat Man & Mr. America become the Ameri-commandos; origin Vigilante retold — 44.00 132.00 310.00
53-60: 56-Last Fat Man. 59-Kubert Vigilante begins?, ends #70. 60-First app. Lois Lane as Superwoman — 33.00 100.00 230.00
61-63,65-70: 63-Last 3 Aces — 30.00 90.00 210.00
64-Intro Toyman — 33.00 100.00 230.00
71-79: 74-Last Mr. America — 26.00 78.00 182.00
80-2nd app. & 1st Mr. Mxyztplk-c (1/45) — 38.00 115.00 265.00
81-90: 83-Intro Hocus & Pocus — 26.00 78.00 182.00
91-99: 93-X-Mas-c. 99-1st small logo(7/46) — 23.00 70.00 160.00
100 — 42.00 125.00 295.00
101-Nuclear explosion-c — 27.00 81.00 190.00
102-120: 105,117-X-Mas-c — 24.00 70.00 160.00
121-126,128-140: 135,136,138-Zatara by Kubert — 21.00 63.00 148.00
127-Vigilante by Kubert; Tommy Tomorrow begins — 32.00 95.00 225.00
141-157,159-161: 156-Lois Lane as Super Woman. 160-1st 52 pgs. — 21.00 63.00 148.00
158-Origin Superman — 23.00 70.00 160.00
162-180: 168,176-Used in **POP**, pg. 90 — 14.50 44.00 100.00
181-201: 191-Intro. Janu in Congo Bill. 198-Last Vigilante. 201-Last pre-code ish — 14.00 42.00 100.00
202-220 — 11.50 34.00 80.00
221-240: 224-1st Golden Gorilla story — 8.50 25.50 60.00
241,243-251: 248-Congo Bill becomes Congorilla. 251-Last Tommy Tomorrow — 6.50 19.00 45.00
242-Origin & 1st app. Brainiac (7/58); 1st mention of Shrunken City of Kandor — 21.00 62.00 145.00
252-Origin & 1st app. Supergirl and Metallo (5/59) — 40.00 120.00 275.00
253-2nd app. Supergirl — 7.00 21.00 50.00
254-1st meeting of Bizarro & Superman — 6.50 19.00 45.00
255-1st Bizarro Lois & both Bizarros leave Earth to make Bizarro World — 6.85 21.00 48.00
256-260: 259-Red Kryptonite used — 5.50 10.50 24.00
261-1st X-Kryptonite which gave Streaky his powers; last Congorilla in Action; origin & 1st app. Streaky The Super Cat — 3.50 10.50 24.00
262-266,268-270: 263-Origin Bizarro World — 3.00 9.00 21.00
267(8/60)-3rd Legion app; 1st app. Chameleon Boy, Colossal Boy, & Invisible Kid — 25.00 75.00 175.00
271-275,277-282: 1st app. Legion 10 cent ish. — 2.65 8.00 18.00
276(5/61)-6th Legion app; 1st app. Brainiac 5, Phantom Girl, Triplicate Girl, Bouncing Boy, Sun Boy, & Shrinking Violet; Supergirl joins Legion — 8.50 25.50 60.00
283(12/61)-Legion of Super-Villains app. — 3.50 10.50 25.00
284(1/62)-Mon-el app. — 3.50 10.50 25.00
285(2/62)-12th Legion app; Brainiac 5 cameo; Supergirl's existance revealed to world — 3.50 10.50 25.00
286(3/62)-Legion of Super Villains app. — 2.00 6.00 14.00
287(4/62)-14th Legion app.(cameo) — 2.00 6.00 14.00
288-Mon-el app.; r-origin Supergirl — 2.00 6.00 14.00
289(6/62)-16th Legion app.(Adult); Lightning Man & Saturn Woman's marriage 1st revealed — 2.00 6.00 14.00
290(7/62)-17th Legion app; Phantom Girl app. — 2.00 6.00 14.00
291,292,294-299: 292-2nd app. Superhorse (see Adv. 293). 297-Mon-el app; 298-Legion app. — 1.00 3.00 7.00
293-Origin Comet(Superhorse) — 1.70 5.00 12.00
300 — 1.50 4.50 10.00
301-303,305-308,310-320: 306-Brainiac 5, Mon-el app. 307-Saturn Girl app. 314-r-origin Supergirl; J.L.A. x-over. 317-Death of Nor-

Good | Fine | N-Mint

Kan of Kandor. 319-Shrinking Violet app. — 1.00 3.00 6.00
304-Origin & 1st app. Black Flame — 1.00 3.00 6.00
309-Legion app. — 1.00 3.00 7.00
321-333,335-340: 336-Origin Akvar(Flamebird). 340-Origin, 1st app. Parasite — .70 2.10 4.20
334-Giant G-20; origin Supergirl; Legion-r — 1.15 3.50 8.00
341-346,348-359 — .60 1.75 3.50
347,360-Gnt. Supergirl G-33,G-45; 360-Legion-r; r-origin Supergirl — .90 2.75 5.50
361-372,374-380: 365-Legion app. 370-New facts about Superman's origin. 376-Last Supergirl in Action. 377-Legion begins — .35 1.00 2.00
373-Giant Supergirl G-57; Legion-r — .70 2.00 4.00
381-392: 392-Last Legion in Action. Saturn Girl gets new costume — .25 .75 1.50
393-402-All Superman issues — .25 .75 1.50
403-413: All 52pg. ish; 411-Origin Eclipso-(r). 413-Metamorpho begins; ends #418. — .25 .75 1.50
414-424: 419-Intro. Human Target. 421-Intro Capt. Strong; Green Arrow begins. 422/423-Origin Human Target. — .25 .75 1.50
425-Adams-a; Atom begins — .35 1.00 2.00
426-436,438,439,442,444-450 — .25 .75 1.50
437,443-100pg. giants — .35 1.00 2.00
440-1st Grell-a on Green Arrow — .70 2.00 4.00
441-Grell-a on Green Arrow — .40 1.25 2.50
451-499: 454-Last Atom. 458-Last Green Arrow. 487-488, 44pgs. 487-1st app. Microwave Man; origin Atom retold — .25 .75 1.50
500-Infinity-c; Superman life story; $1.00 size; 68 pgs.; shows Legion statues in museum — .60 1.20
501-520: 511-514-New Airwave. 513-The Atom begins. 517-Aquaman begins; ends #541 — .50 1.00
521-534,537-543,545: 521-Intro. & 1st app. The Vixen. 532-New Teen Titans cameo — .50 1.00
535,536-Omega Men app.; 536-New Teen Titans cameo. — .50 1.00
544: (Mando paper); 68pgs.; Origins New Luthor & Brainiac; Omega Men cameo — .50 1.00
546-J.L.A. & New Teen Titans guest — .50 1.00
547-565: 551-Starfire becomes Red-Star — .50 1.00
566-582 — .50 1.00
583-Alan Moore scripts — .85 2.50 5.00
584-Byrne-a begins; New Teen Titans app. — .25 .75 1.50
585-597,599: 586-Legends x-over. 596-Millenium x-over — .50 1.00
598-1st app. Checkmate — .50 1.50 3.00
600-($2.50, 84 pgs., 5/88) — .70 2.00 4.00
Annual 1 (10/87)-Art Adams c/a(p) — .40 1.25 2.50
Wheaties Giveaway (1947, 32 pgs., 6½x8¼", nn)-Vigilante story based on movie serial. NOTE: *All copies were taped to Wheaties boxes and never found in mint condition. The mint grade applies to slight tape residue on book.* — 25.00 75.00 175.00

NOTE: *Supergirl's* origin in 262, 280, 285, 291, 305, 309. **Adams**-c-356, 358, 359, 361-64, 366, 367, 370-74, 377-79, 398-400, 402, 404-06, 419(r), 466, 468, 473(, 485. **Bailey** a-24, 25. **Byrne** a-584-588p, 589(, 596, 597p, 598p, 599(, 600p; c-596-600. **Grell** a-440-442, 444-446, 450-452, 456-458; c-456. **Guardineer** a-24, 25; c-8, 11, 12, 14-16, 18, 25. **Bob Kane's** Clip Carson-14-41. **Gil Kane** a-493r, 539-541, 544-546, 551-554; c-535p, 540, 541, 544p, 545-49, 551-554. **Meskin** a-42-121(most); **Moldoff** a-23-25. **Perez** a-600i; c-529p. **Starlin** a-509. **Staton** a-525p, 526p, 531p, 535p, 536p; **Toth** a-406, 407, 413, 418, 419, 425, 431. **Tuska** a-486p, 550. **Williamson** a-568i.

ACTION COMICS WEEKLY
May 6, 1988 - No. 642, Dec 13, 1988 ($1.50, color, 48 pgs.)
DC Comics

601-642: 601-Re-intro Secret Six — .25 .75 1.50

ACTION FORCE (Also see G.I. Joe European Missions)
Mar, 1987 - No. 40?, 1988 (Magazine size, $1.00, color, weekly)
Marvel Comics Ltd. (British)

Action Comics #80, © DC

Action Comics #346, © DC

Action Comics #600, © DC

Adam-12 #9, © GK

Adventure Comics #40, © DC

Adventure Comics #72, © DC

	Good	Fine	N-Mint
ACTION FORCE (continued)			
1-British G.I. Joe series	.50	1.50	3.00
2	.25	.80	1.60
3-40: 3-w/poster insert		.50	1.00
ACTUAL CONFESSIONS (Formerly Love Adventures)			
No. 13, October, 1952 - No. 14, December, 1952			
Atlas Comics (MPI)			
13,14	1.15	3.50	8.00
ACTUAL ROMANCES			
October, 1949 - No. 2, Jan, 1950 (52 pgs.)			
Marvel Comics (IPS)			
1	2.50	7.50	17.50
2	1.25	3.75	8.75
ADAM AND EVE			
1975, 1978 (35-49 cents)			
Spire Christian Comics (Fleming H. Revell Co.)			
By Al Hartley		.25	.50
ADAM-12 (TV)			
Dec, 1973 - No. 10, Feb, 1976 (photo covers)			
Gold Key			
1	1.00	3.00	6.00
2-10	.70	2.00	4.00
ADDAMS FAMILY (TV)			
Oct, 1974 - No. 3, Apr, 1975 (Hanna-Barbera)			
Gold Key			
1	1.50	4.50	9.00
2,3	.85	2.50	5.00
ADLAI STEVENSON			
December, 1966			
Dell Publishing Co.			
12-007-612-Life story; photo-c	2.35	7.00	16.00
ADOLESCENT RADIOACTIVE BLACK BELT HAMSTERS (See Clint, Laffin Gas)			
1986 - No. 9, Jan, 1988 ($1.50, B&W)			
Comic Castle/Eclipse Comics			
1	.50	1.50	3.00
1-2nd print ($1.50)	.20	.70	1.40
2-9	.25	.80	1.60
3-D 1(7/86) - 4	.35	1.00	2.00
2-D 1(Limited edition)	.85	2.50	5.00
2-D 2-4 ($2.50)	.40	1.25	2.50
ADULT TALES OF TERROR ILL. (See Terror Ill.)			
ADVANCED DUNGEONS & DRAGONS			
Holiday, 1988-'89 - Present ($1.25, color)			
DC Comics			
1,2-Based on role playing game		.60	1.25
ADVENTURE BOUND (See 4-Color Comics No. 239)			
ADVENTURE COMICS (Formerly New Adventure)			
No. 32, 11/38 - No. 490, 2/82; No. 491, 9/82 - No. 503, 9/83			
National Periodical Publications/DC Comics			
32-Anchors Aweigh (ends #52), Barry O'Neil (ends #60, not in #33), Captain Desmo (ends #47), Dale Daring (ends #47), Federal Men (ends #70), The Golden Dragon (ends #36), Rusty & His Pals (ends #52) by Bob Kane, Todd Hunter (ends #38) and Tom Brent (ends #39) begin	65.00	195.00	455.00
33-38: 37-c-used on Double Action 2	40.00	120.00	280.00
39(1/39)-Jack Wood begins, ends #42: 1st mention of Marijuana in comics	42.00	125.00	295.00
40-Intro. & 1st app. The Sandman. Socko Strong begins, ends #54	265.00	795.00	1850.00

	Good	Fine	N-Mint
41	80.00	240.00	560.00
42-47: 47-Steve Conrad Adventurer begins, ends #76	55.00	165.00	385.00
48-Intro. & 1st app. The Hourman by Bernard Baily	260.00	780.00	1820.00
49,50: 50-Cotton Carver by Jack Lehti begins, ends #59?	55.00	165.00	385.00
51-60: 53-Intro Jimmy "Minuteman" Martin & the Minutemen of America in Hourman; ends #78. 58-Paul Kirk Manhunter begins, ends #72	50.00	150.00	350.00
61-Intro/1st app. Starman by Jack Burnley	200.00	600.00	1400.00
62-65,67,68: 67-Origin The Mist	48.00	145.00	335.00
66-Origin Shining Knight	65.00	195.00	455.00
69-Intro. Sandy the Golden Boy (Sandman's sidekick) by Bob Kane; Sandman dons new costume	60.00	180.00	420.00
70-Last Federal Men	50.00	150.00	350.00
71-Jimmy Martin becomes costume aide to the Hourman; intro Hourman's Miracle Ray machine	48.00	145.00	335.00
72-1st Simon & Kirby Sandman	175.00	525.00	1225.00
73-Origin Manhunter by Simon & Kirby; begin new series	228.00	685.00	1600.00
74-76: 74-Thorndyke replaces Jimmy, Hourman's assistant	72.00	215.00	505.00
77-Origin Genius Jones; Mist story	72.00	215.00	505.00
78-80-Last Simon & Kirby Manhunter & Burnley Starman	72.00	215.00	505.00
81-90: 83-Last Hourman. 84-Mike Gibbs begins, ends #102	44.00	132.00	310.00
91-Last Simon & Kirby Sandman	40.00	120.00	280.00
92-99,101,102-Last Starman, Sandman, & Genius Jones. Most-S&K-c. 92-Last Manhunter	30.00	90.00	210.00
100	45.00	135.00	315.00
103-Aquaman, Green Arrow, Johnny Quick, Superboy begin; 1st small logo (4/46)	80.00	240.00	560.00
104	37.00	110.00	260.00
105-110	32.00	95.00	225.00
111-120: 113-X-Mas-c	28.00	85.00	195.00
121-126,128-130: 128-1st meeting Superboy-Lois Lane	23.00	70.00	160.00
127-Brief origin Shining Knight retold	25.00	75.00	175.00
131-140: 132-Shining Knight 1st return to King Arthur time; origin aide Sir Butch	20.00	60.00	140.00
141,143-149	20.00	60.00	140.00
142-Origin Shining Knight & Johnny Quick retold	23.00	70.00	160.00
150,151,153,155,157,159,161,163-All have 6-pg. Shining Knight stories by Frank Frazetta. 159-Origin Johnny Quick	34.00	102.00	240.00
152,154,156,158,160,162,164-169: 166-Last Shining Knight. 168-Last 52 pgs.	17.00	51.00	120.00
170-180	16.00	48.00	110.00
181-199: 189-B&W and color illo in POP	14.50	44.00	100.00
200	18.00	54.00	125.00
201-209: 207-Last Johnny Quick (not in 205). 209-Last Pre-code ish; origin Speedy	15.00	45.00	105.00
210-1st app. Krypto	60.00	180.00	420.00
211-220	11.50	35.00	80.00
221-246: 237-1st Intergalactic Vigilante Squadron (Legion tryout)	11.00	32.00	75.00
247(4/58)-1st Legion of Super Heroes app.; 1st app. Cosmic Boy, Lightning Lad, & Saturn Girl (origin)	200.00	600.00	1400.00
248-255: All Kirby Green Arrow. 253-1st meeting Superboy-Robin. 255-Intro. Red Kryptonite in Superboy (used in #252 but with no effect)	6.50	19.00	45.00
256-Origin Green Arrow by Kirby	18.00	54.00	125.00
257-259	6.50	19.00	45.00

3

ADVENTURE COMICS (continued)	Good	Fine	N-Mint
260-Origin Aquaman retold	11.00	32.00	75.00
261-266,268,270: 262-Origin Speedy in Green Arrow. 270-Congorilla begins, ends #281,283	4.85	14.50	34.00
267(12/59)-2nd Legion of Super Heroes	43.00	128.00	300.00
269-Intro. Aqualad; last Green Arrow (not in #206)	7.00	21.00	50.00
271-Origin Luthor	5.15	15.50	36.00
272-280: 275-Origin Superman-Batman team retold (see World's Finest #94). 279-Intro White Kryptonite in Superboy. 280-1st meeting Superboy-Lori Lemaris	3.50	10.50	24.00
281,284,287-289: 281-Last Congorilla. 284-Last Aquaman in Adv. 287,288-Intro. Dev-Em, the Knave from Krypton. 287-1st Bizarro Perry White & J. Olsen. 289-Legion cameo (statues)	3.00	9.00	21.00
282(3/61)-5th Legion app; intro & origin Star Boy	8.50	25.50	60.00
283-Intro. The Phantom Zone	4.85	14.50	34.00
285-1st Bizarro World story (ends #299) in Adv. (See Action #255)	5.15	15.50	36.00
286-1st Bizarro Mxyzptlk	4.00	12.00	28.00
290(11/61)-8th Legion app; origin Sunboy in Legion (last 10 cent issue)	7.50	22.00	52.00
291,292,295-299: 292-1st Bizarro Lana Lang & Lucy Lane. 295-1st Bizarro Titano. 299-1st Gold Kryptonite (8/62)	2.65	8.00	18.00
293(2/62)-13th Legion app; Mon-el & Legion Super Pets (intro & origin) app. (1st Superhorse). 1st Bizarro Luthor & Kandor	5.50	16.50	38.00
294-1st Bizarro M. Monroe, Pres. Kennedy	3.15	9.50	22.00
300-Legion series begins; Mon-el leaves Phantom Zone (temporarily), joins Legion	25.00	75.00	175.00
301-Origin Bouncing Boy	8.00	24.00	55.00
302-305: 303-1st app. Matter Eater Lad. 304-Death of Lightning Lad in Legion	4.35	13.00	30.00
306-310: 306-Intro. Legion of Substitute Heroes. 307-Intro. Element Lad in Legion. 308-1st app. Lightning Lass in Legion	3.50	10.50	24.00
311-320: 312-Lightning Lad back in Legion. 315-Last new Superboy story; Colossal Boy app. 316-Origins & powers of Legion given. 317-Intro. Dream Girl in Legion; Lightning Lass becomes Light Lass; Hall of Fame series begins. 320-Dev-Em 2nd app.	2.65	8.00	18.00
321-Intro Time Trapper	2.00	6.00	14.00
322-326,328-330: 329-Intro Legion of Super Bizarros	1.70	5.00	12.00
327-Intro Timber Wolf in Legion	1.70	5.00	12.00
331-340: 337-Chlorophyll Kid & Night Girl app. 340-Intro Computo in Legion	1.60	4.80	11.00
341-Triplicate Girl becomes Duo Damsel	1.15	3.50	8.00
342-345,347,350: 345-Last Hall of Fame; returns in 356,371	1.00	3.00	7.00
346-1st app. Karate Kid, Princess Projectra, Ferro Lad, & Nemesis Kid	1.15	3.50	8.00
348-Origin Sunboy & intro Dr. Regulus in Legion	1.15	3.50	8.00
349-Intro Universo & Rond Vidar	1.15	3.50	8.00
351-1st app. White Witch	1.00	3.00	7.00
352,354-360: 355-Insect Queen joins Legion (4/67)	1.00	3.00	6.00
353-Death of Ferro Lad in Legion	1.50	4.50	10.00
361-364,366,368-370: 369-Intro Mordru in Legion	.75	2.25	4.50
365-Intro Shadow Lass; lists origins & powers of L.S.H.	.90	2.75	5.50
367-New Legion headquarters	.90	2.75	5.50
371-Intro. Chemical King	.90	2.75	5.50

	Good	Fine	N-Mint
372-Timber Wolf & Chemical King join	.90	2.75	5.50
373,374,376-380: Last Legion in Adv.	.75	2.25	4.50
375-Intro Quantum Queen & The Wanderers	.90	2.75	5.50
381-389,391-400: 381-Supergirl begins. 399-Unpubbed G.A. Black Canary story. 400-New costume for Supergirl	.60	1.20
390-Giant Supergirl G-69	.70	2.00	4.00
401,402,404-410: 409-52pg. issues begin; ends #420	.60	1.20
403-68pg. Giant G-81	.70	2.00	4.00
411-415: 412-Animal Man origin reprint/Str. Adv. #180. 413-Hawkman by Kubert; G.A. Robotman-r/Det. 178; Zatanna begins, ends #421	.40	.80
416-Giant DC-10. GA-r	.60	1.20
417-Morrow Vigilante; Frazetta Shining Knight r-/Adv. #161; origin The Enchantress	.60	1.20
418-424: Last Supergirl in Adv.	.40	.80
425-New look, content change to adventure; Toth-a, origin Capt. Fear	.25	.75	1.50
426-458: 427-Last Vigilante. 428-430-Black Orchid app. 431-440-Spectre app. 435-Mike Grell's 1st comic work ('74). 440-New Spectre origin. 441-452-Aquaman app. 445-447-The Creeper app. 449-451-Martian Manhunter app. 453-458-Superboy app; intro Mighty Girl No. 453. 457,458-Eclipso app.	.40	.80
459-466($1.00 size, 68pgs.): 459-Flash (ends 466), Deadman (ends 466), Wonder Woman (ends 464), Gr. Lantern (ends 460), New Gods begin (ends 460). 460-Aquaman begins; ends 478. 461-Justice Society begins; ends 466; death Earth II Batman (also No. 462)	.45	.90
467-490: 467-Starman, Plasticman begin, end 478. 469,470-Origin Starman. 479-Dial 'H' For Hero begins, ends 490.	.40	.80
491-499: 491-100pg. Digest size begins; r-Legion of Super Heroes/ Adv. 247 & 267; Spectre, Aquaman, Superboy, S&K Sandman, Bl. Canary-r & new Shazam by Newton begin. 493-Challengers of the Unknown begins by Tuska w/brief origin. 492,495,496,499-S&K Sandman-r/Adventure in all; 494-499-Spectre-r/Spectre 1-3, 5-7. 493-495,497-499-G.A. Captain Marvel-r. 498-Plastic Man-r begin; origin Bouncing Boy-r/#30	.60	1.20
500-All Legion-r (Digest size, 148 pgs.)	.25	.80	1.60
501-503-G.A.-r	.60	1.20

NOTE: Bizarro covers-285, 286, 288, 294, 295. Vigilante app-420, 426, 427. **Adams** a(r)-495-498; c-365-369, 371-373, 375-379, 381-383. **Austin** a-449l-451l. **Bernard Baily** c-50, 52-57, 59. **Ditko** a-467p-478p; c-467p. **Giffen** c-491p-494p, 500p. **Grell** a-435-437, 440. **Guardineer** c-34, 45. **Kaluta** c-425. **G. Kane** a-414r, 425; c-496-499, 537. **Kirby** a-250-256. **Kubert** a-413. **Meskin** a-81, 127. **Moldoff** a-494l; c-49. **Morrow** a-413-415, 417, 422, 502r, 503r. **Newton** a-459-461, 464-466, 491p, 492p. **Orlando** a-457p, 458p. **Perez** c-484-486, 490p. **Simon/Kirby** c-73-97, 101, 102. **Starlin** c-471. **Staton** a-445-447i, 456-458p, 459, 460, 461p-465p, 466, 467p-478p, 502p(r); c-458, 461(back). **Toth** a-418, 419, 425, 431, 495p-497p. **Tuska** a-494p.

ADVENTURE COMICS
No date (early 1940s) Paper cover, 32 pgs.
IGA
Two different issues; Super-Mystery reprints from 1941

	13.00	40.00	90.00

ADVENTURE IN DISNEYLAND (Giveaway)
May, 1955 (16 pgs., soft-c) (Dist. by Richfield Oil)
Walt Disney Productions

nn	3.00	9.00	21.00

ADVENTURE INTO FEAR
1951
Superior Publ. Ltd.

1	6.00	18.00	42.00

ADVENTURE INTO MYSTERY
May, 1956 - No. 8, July, 1957

Adventures In 3-D #1, © HARV

Adventures Into The Unknown #57, © ACG

Adventures Into Weird Worlds #6, © MEG

ADVENTURE INTO MYSTERY (continued)
Atlas Comics (BFP No. 1/OPI No. 2-8)

	Good	Fine	N-Mint
1-Everett-c	7.00	21.00	50.00
2-Flying Saucer story	3.50	10.50	25.00
3,6,8: 3,6-Everett-c	3.00	9.00	21.00
4-Williamson, 4 pgs; Powell-a	5.70	17.00	40.00
5-Everett-c/a, Orlando-a	3.00	9.00	21.00
7-Torres-a; Everett-c	3.50	10.50	24.00

ADVENTURE IS MY CAREER
1945 (44 pgs.)
U.S. Coast Guard Academy/Street & Smith

nn-Simon, Milt Gross-a	5.00	15.00	35.00

ADVENTURERS, THE
Aug., 1986 - Present ($1.50, B&W)
Aircel Comics/Adventure Publ.

1-Peter Hsu-a	1.50	4.50	9.00
1-Cover variant, limited ed.	4.35	13.00	26.00
1-2nd print (12/86); 1st app. Elf Warrior	.85	2.50	5.00
2,3	.60	1.75	3.50
0 (#4, 12/86)-Origin	.40	1.25	2.50
4-10	.35	1.00	2.00
Book II, regular ed. #1	.35	1.00	2.00
Book II, limited ed. #1	.35	1.00	2.00
Book II, #2-6	.35	1.00	2.00

ADVENTURES (No. 2 Spectacular. . . on cover)
11/49 - No. 2, 2/50 (No. 1 . . . in Romance on cover)
St. John Publishing Co. (Slightly large size)

1(Scarce); Bolle, Starr-a(2)	10.00	30.00	70.00
2(Scarce)-Slave Girl; China Bombshell app.; Bolle, L. Starr-a			
	16.00	48.00	110.00

ADVENTURES FOR BOYS
December, 1954
Bailey Enterprises

Comics, text, & photos	1.70	5.00	12.00

ADVENTURES IN PARADISE (See 4-Color No. 1301)

ADVENTURES IN ROMANCE (See Adventures)

ADVENTURES IN SCIENCE (See Classics Special)

ADVENTURES IN 3-D
Nov., 1953 - No. 2, Jan, 1954
Harvey Publications

1-Nostrand, Powell-a, 2-Powell-a	9.00	27.00	62.00

ADVENTURES INTO DARKNESS (See Seduction of/Innocent 3-D)
No. 5, Aug, 1952 - No. 14, 1954
Better-Standard Publications/Visual Editions

5-Katz c/a; Toth-a(p)	6.00	18.00	42.00
6-Tuska, Katz-a	4.50	13.50	32.00
7-Katz c/a	4.50	13.50	32.00
8,9-Toth-a(p)	5.70	17.00	40.00
10,11-Jack Katz-a	3.50	10.50	25.00
12-Toth-a?; lingerie panels	4.30	13.00	30.00
13-Toth-a(p); Cannibalism story cited by T. E. Murphy articles			
	5.00	15.00	35.00
14	3.15	9.50	22.00

NOTE: *Fawcette a-13. Moriera a-5. Sekowsky a-10, 11, 13(2).*

ADVENTURES INTO TERROR (Formerly Joker Comics)
No. 43, Nov, 1950 - No. 31, May, 1954
Marvel/Atlas Comics (CDS)

43	8.50	25.00	60.00
44(2/51)	6.50	20.00	45.00
3(4/51), 4	4.30	13.00	30.00

	Good	Fine	N-Mint
5-Wolverton-c panel/Mystic #6. Atom Bomb story			
	5.00	15.00	35.00
6,8: 8-Wolverton text illo r-/Marvel Tales 104	3.50	10.50	25.00
7-Wolverton-a ''Where Monsters Dwell'', 6 pgs.; Tuska-c			
	17.00	50.00	120.00
9,10,12-Krigstein-a. 9-Decapitation panels	5.00	15.00	35.00
11,13-20	3.00	9.00	21.00
21-24,26-31	2.30	7.00	16.00
25-Matt Fox-a	4.00	12.00	28.00

NOTE: *Ayers a-21. Colan a-3, 5, 14, 21, 24, 25, 28, 29; c-27. Everett c-13, 21, 25. Heath a-43, 44, 4-6, 22, 24, 26; c-43, 9, 11. Lazarus a-7. Maneely a-7, 10, 11, 21. Don Rico a-4, 5. Sekowsky a-43, 3, 4. Sinnott a-8, 9, 11. Tuska a-14.*

ADVENTURES INTO THE UNKNOWN
Fall, 1948 - No. 174, Aug, 1967 (No. 1-33, 52 pgs.)
American Comics Group

(1st continuous series horror comic; see Eerie #1)

1-Guardineer-a; adapt. of 'Castle of Otranto' by Horace Walpole			
	38.00	115.00	265.00
2	17.00	51.00	120.00
3-Feldstein-a, 9 pgs.	20.00	60.00	140.00
4,5	11.50	34.00	80.00
6-10	8.50	25.00	60.00
11-16,18-20	5.70	17.00	40.00
17-Story similar to movie 'The Thing'	8.50	25.00	60.00
21-26,28-30	5.00	15.00	35.00
27-Williamson/Krenkel-a, 8 pgs.	14.00	42.00	100.00
31-50	3.50	10.50	25.00
51(1/54) - 59 (3-D effect). 52-E.C. swipe/Haunt Of Fear 14			
	8.50	25.00	60.00
60-Woodesque-a by Landau	2.85	8.50	20.00
61-Last pre-code ish (1-2/55)	2.15	6.50	15.00
62-70	1.50	4.50	10.00
71-90	1.00	3.00	7.00
91,95,96(#95 on inside),107,116-All contain Williamson-a			
	2.65	8.00	18.00
92-94,97-99,101-106,108-115,117-127: 109-113,118-Whitney painted-c	.75	2.25	4.50
100	.85	2.50	5.00
128-Williamson/Krenkel/Torres-a(r)/Forbidden Worlds 63			
	.85	2.50	5.00
129-150	.35	1.10	2.20
151-153: 153-Magic Agent app.		.60	1.20
154-Nemesis series begins (origin), ends #170	.40	1.25	2.50
155-167,169-174: 157-Magic Agent app.	.30	.90	1.80
168-Ditko-a(p)	.40	1.25	2.50

NOTE: *''Spirit of Frankenstein'' series in 5, 6, 8-10, 12, 16. Buscema a-100, 106, 108-110, 158r, 165r. Craig a-152, 160. Goode a-45, 47, 60. Landau a-51, 59-63. Lazarus a-51, 79; c-51. Whitney c-most. Torres/Williamson a-116.*

ADVENTURES INTO WEIRD WORLDS
Jan, 1952 - No. 30, June, 1954
Marvel/Atlas Comics (ACI)

1-Atom bomb panels	10.00	30.00	70.00
2-sci/fic stories (2)	5.00	15.00	35.00
3-6,8,9	4.00	12.00	28.00
7-Tongue ripped out	5.00	15.00	35.00
10-Krigstein, Everett-a	4.30	13.00	30.00
11-20	3.00	9.00	21.00
21-Hitler in hell story	2.50	7.50	18.00
22,23,25,26	2.35	7.00	16.50
24-Man holding hypo and splitting in two	6.00	18.00	42.00
27-Matt Fox end of world story-a; severed head cover			
	7.00	21.00	50.00
28-Atom bomb story; decapitation panels	2.50	7.50	18.00
29,30	2.00	6.00	14.00

NOTE: *Everett a-4, 5; c-6, 8, 10-13, 18, 19, 22, 24, 25. Fass a-7. Forte a-21, 24.*

ADVENTURES INTO WEIRD WORLDS (continued)
Heath a-1, 4, 17, 22; c-7. Rico a-13. Maneely a-3, 11, 20, 22, 25; c-3, 25-27, 29. Reinman a-28. Robinson a-13. Sinnott a-25, 30. Tuska a-1, 12, 15. Wildey a-28. Bondage c-22.

ADVENTURES IN WONDERLAND
April, 1955 - No. 5, Feb, 1956 (Jr. Readers Guild)
Lev Gleason Publications

	Good	Fine	N-Mint
1-Maurer-a	3.00	9.00	21.00
2-4	1.70	5.00	12.00
5-Christmas issue	2.00	6.00	14.00

ADVENTURES OF ALAN LADD, THE
Oct-Nov, 1949 - No. 9, Feb-Mar, 1951 (All 52 pgs.)
National Periodical Publications

1-Photo-c	30.00	90.00	210.00
2-Photo-c	17.00	51.00	120.00
3-6: Last photo-c	14.50	44.00	100.00
7-9	12.00	36.00	84.00

NOTE: *Moreira a-3-7.*

ADVENTURES OF ALICE
1945 (Also see Alice in Wonderland & . . .at Monkey Island)
Civil Service Publ./Pentagon Publishing Co.

1	5.00	15.00	35.00
2-Through the Magic Looking Glass	4.00	12.00	28.00

ADVENTURES OF BOB HOPE, THE (Also see True Comics 59)
Feb-Mar, 1950 - No. 109, Feb-Mar, 1968 (#1-10, 52pgs.)
National Periodical Publications

1-Photo-c	40.00	120.00	280.00
2-Photo-c	20.00	60.00	140.00
3,4-Photo-c	13.00	40.00	90.00
5-10	10.00	30.00	70.00
11-20	5.70	17.00	40.00
21-30	4.00	12.00	28.00
31-40	3.00	9.00	21.00
41-50	2.00	6.00	14.00
51-70	1.15	3.50	8.00
71-93,95-105	.85	2.50	5.00
94-Aquaman cameo	1.00	3.00	6.00
106-109-Adams c/a	2.65	8.00	16.00

NOTE: *Kitty Karr of Hollywood in #17-20,28. Liz in #26. Miss Beverly Hills of Hollywood in #7, 10, 13, 14. Miss Melody Lane of Broadway in #15. Rusty in #23, 25. Tommy in #24. No 2nd feature in #2-4, 6, 8, 11, 12, 28-on.*

ADVENTURES OF CAPTAIN JACK, THE
June, 1986 - Present ($2.00, B&W, Adults)
Fantagraphics Books

1	.70	2.00	4.00
2	.50	1.50	3.00
3-11	.35	1.00	2.00

ADVENTURES OF DEAN MARTIN AND JERRY LEWIS, THE
(The Adventures of Jerry Lewis No. 41 on)
July-Aug, 1952 - No. 40, Oct, 1957
National Periodical Publications

1	30.00	90.00	210.00
2	14.50	44.00	100.00
3-10	8.00	24.00	56.00
11-19: Last precode (2/55)	4.35	13.00	30.00
20-30	3.00	9.00	21.00
31-40	2.30	7.00	16.00

ADVENTURES OF G. I. JOE
1969 (3¼''x7'') (20 & 16 pgs.)
Giveaways

First Series: 1-Danger of the Depths. 2-Perilous Rescue. 3-Secret Mission to Spy Island. 4-Mysterious Explosion. 5-Fantastic Free Fall. 6-Eight Ropes of Danger.

7-Mouth of Doom. 8-Hidden Missile Discovery. 9-Space Walk Mystery. 10-Fight for Survival. 11-The Shark's Surprise. **Second Series:** 2-Flying Space Adventure. 4-White Tiger Hunt. 7-Capture of the Pygmy Gorilla. 12-Secret of the Mummy's Tomb. **Third Series:** Reprinted surviving titles of First Series. **Fourth Series:** 13-Adventure Team Headquarters. 14-Search For the Stolen Idol.

	each....	.30	.60

ADVENTURES OF HAWKSHAW (See Hawkshaw The Detective)
1917 (9-3/4 x 13½'', 48 pgs., Color & two-tone)
The Saalfield Publishing Co.

	Good	Fine	N-Mint
By Gus Mager (only 24 pgs. of strips, reverse of each page is blank)	16.00	48.00	110.00

ADVENTURES OF HOMER COBB, THE
September, 1947 (Oversized)
Say/Bart Prod. (Canadian)

1-(Scarce)-Feldstein-a	17.00	50.00	120.00

ADVENTURES OF HOMER GHOST
June, 1957 - No. 2, August, 1957
Atlas Comics

V1#1, 2	1.30	4.00	9.00

ADVENTURES OF JERRY LEWIS, THE (Advs. of Dean Martin &
Jerry Lewis No. 1-40)(See Super DC Giant)
No. 41, Nov, 1957 - No. 124, May-June, 1971
National Periodical Publications

41-60	2.00	6.00	14.00
61-80: 68,74-Photo-c	1.50	4.50	9.00
81-91,93-96,98-100	1.00	3.00	6.00
92-Superman cameo	1.15	3.50	7.00
97-Batman/Robin x-over	1.15	3.50	7.00
101-104-Adams c/a; 102-Beatles app.	2.65	8.00	16.00
105-Superman x-over	1.00	3.00	6.00
106-111,113-116	.40	1.25	2.50
112-Flash x-over	.60	1.75	3.50
117-Wonder Woman x-over	.60	1.75	3.50
118-124	.20	.70	1.40

ADVENTURES OF LUTHER ARKWRIGHT, THE
Oct., 1987 - Present ($2.00, B&W)
Valkyrie Press

1	.50	1.50	3.00
2,3	.35	1.00	2.00

ADVENTURES OF MARGARET O'BRIEN, THE
1947 (20 pgs. in color; slick cover; regular size) (Premium)
Bambury Fashions (Clothes)

In ''The Big City''-movie adaptation (Scarce)	13.00	40.00	90.00

ADVENTURES OF MIGHTY MOUSE (Mighty Mouse Advs. No. 1)
No. 2, Jan, 1952 - No. 18, May, 1955
St. John Publishing Co.

2	7.00	21.00	50.00
3-5	4.30	13.00	30.00
6-18	2.65	8.00	18.00

ADVENTURES OF MIGHTY MOUSE (2nd Series)
(Two No. 144's; formerly Paul Terry's Comics; No. 129-137 have
nn's)(Becomes Mighty Mouse No. 161 on)
No. 126, Aug, 1955 - No. 160, Oct, 1963
St. John/Pines/Dell/Gold Key

126(8/55), 127(10/55), 128(11/55)-St. John	2.00	6.00	14.00
nn(129, 4/56)-144(8/59)-Pines	1.60	4.70	11.00
144(10-12/59)-155(7-9/62) Dell	1.20	3.60	8.50
156(10/62)-160(10/63) Gold Key	1.20	3.60	8.50

NOTE: *Early issues titled ''Paul Terry's Adventures of . . . .''*

ADVENTURES OF MIGHTY MOUSE (Formerly Mighty Mouse)
No. 166, Mar, 1979 - No. 172, Jan, 1980
Gold Key

Adventures In Wonderland #1, © LEV

The Adventures Of Bob Hope #2, © DC

The Adventures Of Captain Jack #1, © Fantagraphics

The Adventures Of Ozzie And Harriet #5, © DC

Adventures Of Superman #444, © DC

Adventures Of The Fly #5, © AP

	Good	Fine	N-Mint
ADVENTURES OF MIGHTY MOUSE (cont.)			
166-172	.50	1.50	3.00
ADVS. OF MR. FROG & MISS MOUSE (See Dell Jr. Treasury No. 4)			
ADVENTURES OF OZZIE AND HARRIET, THE (Radio)			
Oct-Nov, 1949 - No. 5, June-July, 1950			
National Periodical Publications			
1-Photo-c	25.00	75.00	175.00
2	18.00	54.00	125.00
3-5	15.00	45.00	105.00
ADVENTURES OF PATORUZU			
Aug, 1946 - Winter, 1946			
Green Publishing Co.			
nn's-Contains Animal Crackers reprints	1.50	4.50	10.00
ADVENTURES OF PINKY LEE, THE (TV)			
July, 1955 - No. 5, Dec, 1955			
Atlas Comics			
1	8.50	25.00	60.00
2-5	5.00	15.00	35.00
ADVENTURES OF PIPSQUEAK, THE (Formerly Pat the Brat)			
No. 34, Sept., 1959 - No. 39, July, 1960			
Archie Publications (Radio Comics)			
34	2.00	6.00	14.00
35-39	1.15	3.50	8.00
ADVENTURES OF QUAKE & QUISP, THE (See Quaker Oats ''Plenty of Glutton'')			
ADVENTURES OF REX THE WONDER DOG, THE (Rex . . No. 1)			
Jan-Feb, 1952 - No. 45, May-Jun, 1959; No. 46, Nov-Dec, 1959			
National Periodical Publications			
1-(Scarce)-Toth-a	45.00	135.00	315.00
2-(Scarce)-Toth-a	22.00	65.00	154.00
3-(Scarce)-Toth-a	18.00	54.00	125.00
4,5	13.00	40.00	90.00
6-10	8.50	25.00	60.00
11-Atom bomb c/story	5.70	17.00	40.00
12-19: Last precode, 1-2/55	4.50	13.50	31.50
20-46	2.85	8.50	20.00
NOTE: *Infantino, Gil Kane* art in most issues.			
ADVENTURES OF ROBIN HOOD, THE (Formerly Robin Hood)			
No. 7, 9/57 - No. 8, 11/57 (Based on Richard Greene TV Show)			
Magazine Enterprises (Sussex Publ. Co.)			
7,8-Richard Greene photo-c. 7-Powell-a	3.50	10.50	25.00
ADVENTURES OF ROBIN HOOD, THE			
March, 1974 - No. 7, Jan, 1975 (Disney Cartoon) (36 pgs.)			
Gold Key			
1(90291-403)-Part-r of $1.50 editions	.60	1.80	3.60
2-7: 1-7, part-r	.45	1.25	2.50
ADVENTURES OF SLIM AND SPUD, THE			
1924 (3¾''x9¾'')(104 pg. B&W strip reprints)			
Prairie Farmer Publ. Co.			
	8.00	24.00	56.00
ADVENTURES OF STUBBY, SANTA'S SMALLEST REINDEER, THE			
nd (early 1940s) 12 pgs.			
W. T. Grant Co. (Giveaway)			
nn	2.00	6.00	12.00
ADVENTURES OF SUPERMAN (Formerly Superman)			
No. 424, Jan, 1987 - Present			
DC Comics			
424	.50	1.50	3.00
425-435: 426-Legends x-over. 432-1st app. Jose Delgado who becomes Gangbuster in #434		.60	1.20

	Good	Fine	N-Mint
436-442: 436-Byrne scripts begin. 436,437-Millenium x-over. 438-New Brainiac app.		.60	1.20
Annual 1 (9/87)-Starlin-c	.25	.75	1.50
Annual 2 (1988)	.25	.75	1.50
ADVENTURES OF THE BIG BOY			
1956 - Present (Giveaway)(East & West editions of early issues)			
Timely Comics/Webs Adv. Corp./Illus. Features			
1-Everett-a	45.00	135.00	315.00
2-Everett-a	22.00	65.00	154.00
3-5	7.00	21.00	50.00
6-10: 6-Sci/fic ish.	4.50	13.50	30.00
11-20	2.35	7.00	15.00
21-30	1.35	4.00	8.00
31-50	.70	2.00	4.00
51-100	.35	1.00	2.00
101-150		.50	1.00
151-240		.20	.40
241-376: 266-Superman x-over			.10
1-50 ('76-'84,Paragon Prod.)		.10	.20
Summer, 1959 ish, large size	2.50	7.50	15.00
ADVENTURES OF THE DETECTIVE			
No date (1930's) 36 pgs.; 9½x12''; B&W (paper cover)			
Humor Publ. Co.			
Not reprints; Ace King by Martin Nadle	6.00	18.00	42.00
2nd version (printed in red & blue)	6.00	18.00	42.00
ADVENTURES OF THE DOVER BOYS			
September, 1950 - No. 2, 1950 (No month given)			
Archie Comics (Close-up)			
1,2	3.50	10.50	24.00
ADVENTURES OF THE FLY (The Fly, No. 2; Fly Man No. 32-39)			
Aug, 1959 - No. 30, Oct, 1964; No. 31, May, 1965			
Archie Publications/Radio Comics			
1-Shield app.; origin The Fly; S&K-c/a	22.00	65.00	154.00
2-Williamson, S&K, Powell-a	12.00	36.00	85.00
3-Origin retold; Davis, Powell-a	8.00	24.00	56.00
4-Adams-a(p)(1 panel); S&K-c; Powell-a; Shield x-over	5.50	16.50	38.00
5-10: 7-Black Hood app. 8,9-Shield x-over. 9-1st app. Cat Girl. 10-Black Hood app.	2.30	6.50	16.00
11-13,15-20: 20-Origin Flygirl retold	1.50	4.50	10.00
14-Intro. & origin Fly Girl	1.70	5.00	12.00
21-30: 23-Jaguar cameo. 29-Black Hood cameo. 30-Comet x-over in Fly Girl	1.00	3.00	6.00
31-Black Hood, Shield, Comet app.	1.00	3.00	6.00
NOTE: *Tuska* a-1. *Simon* c-2-4.			
ADVENTURES OF THE JAGUAR, THE (See Blue Ribbon Comics)			
Sept, 1961 - No. 15, Nov, 1963			
Archie Publications (Radio Comics)			
1-Origin Jaguar	7.00	21.00	50.00
2,3	3.00	9.00	21.00
4,5-Catgirl app.	1.70	5.00	12.00
6-10: 6-Catgirl app.	1.15	3.50	8.00
11-15: 13,14-Catgirl, Black Hood app. in both	.85	2.50	6.00
ADVENTURES OF THE OUTSIDERS, THE (Formerly Batman & The Outsiders)			
No. 33, May, 1986 - No. 46, June, 1987			
DC Comics			
33-46		.35	.70
ADVENTURES OF TINKER BELL (See 4-Color No. 982)			
ADVENTURES OF TOM SAWYER (See Dell Jr. Treasury No. 10)			

ADVENTURES OF WILLIE GREEN, THE
1915 (8½X16, 50 cents, B&W, soft-c)
Frank M. Acton Co.

	Good	Fine	N-Mint
Book 1-By Harris Brown; strip-r	10.00	30.00	70.00

ADVENTURES OF YOUNG DR. MASTERS, THE
Aug, 1964 - No. 2, Nov, 1964
Archie Comics (Radio Comics)

1,2	.70	2.00	4.00

ADVENTURES OF ZOT! IN DIMENSION 10 ½
Sept., 1987 (One shot, $2.00, B&W)
Eclipse Comics

14 ½	.35	1.00	2.00

ADVENTURES ON THE PLANET OF THE APES
Oct, 1975 - No. 11, Dec, 1976
Marvel Comics Group

1-Planet of the Apes-r in color; Starlin-c		.40	.80
2-11		.25	.50

NOTE: *Alcala a-10r, 11r. Buckler c-2p. Nasser c-7. Ploog a-1-9. Starlin c-6.*

ADVENTURES WITH SANTA CLAUS
No date (early 50's) (24 pgs.) (9¾x6¾''; paper cover) (Giveaway)
Promotional Publ. Co. (Murphy's Store)

Contains 8 pgs. ads	3.00	9.00	21.00
16 page version	3.00	9.00	21.00

AFRICA
1955
Magazine Enterprises

1(A-1 #137)-Cave Girl & Thun'da; Powell-c/a(4)	11.00	32.00	75.00

AFRICAN LION (See 4-Color No. 665)

AFTER DARK
May, 1955 - No. 8, Sept, 1955
Sterling Comics

6-8-Sekowsky-a in all	2.30	7.00	16.00

AGGIE MACK
Jan, 1948 - No. 8, Aug, 1949
Four Star Comics Corp./Superior Comics Ltd.

1-Feldstein-a, ''Johnny Prep''	9.00	27.00	63.00
2,3-Kamen-c	4.50	13.50	32.00
4-Feldstein ''Johnny Prep''; Kamen-c	6.00	18.00	42.00
5-8-Kamen c/a	4.30	13.00	30.00

AGGIE MACK (See 4-Color Comics No. 1335)

AIN'T IT A GRAND & GLORIOUS FEELING?
1922 (52 pgs.; 9x9¾''; stiff cardboard cover)
Whitman Publishing Co.

1921 daily strip-r; B&W, color-c; Briggs-a	10.00	30.00	70.00

AIR ACE (Bill Barnes No. 1-12)
V2#1, Jan, 1944 - V3/8(No. 20), Feb-Mar, 1947
Street & Smith Publications

V2#1	6.00	18.00	42.00
V2#2-12: 7-Powell-a	3.50	10.50	25.00
V3#1-6	2.15	6.50	15.00
V3#7-Powell bondage-c/a; all atomic ish.	5.50	16.50	38.00
V3#8 (V5#8 on-c)-Powell c/a	2.30	7.00	16.00

AIRBOY (Also see Airmaidens, Skywolf, Target: Airboy & Valkyrie)
July, 1986 - Present (#1-8, 20pgs., bi-weekly; #9-on, 36pgs, monthly
Eclipse Comics

1	.70	2.20	4.40
2-1st Marisa; Skywolf gets new costume	.35	1.10	2.20
3,4,6-8: 3-The Heap begins. 5-Valkyrie returns	.35	1.10	2.20

	Good	Fine	N-Mint
5-Dave Stevens-c	.50	1.50	3.00
9-20: 9-Skywolf begins. 11-Origin of G.A. Airboy & his plane Birdie	.30	.90	1.80
21-30	.25	.75	1.50
31-48: 41-r/1st app. Valkyrie from Air Fighters	.30	.90	1.80

NOTE: *Spiegle a-34, 35, 37. Ken Steacy painted-c 33.*

AIRBOY COMICS (Airfighters No. 1-22)
V2/11, Dec, 1945 - V10/4(May, 1953 (No V3/3)
Hillman Periodicals

V2#11	21.50	65.00	150.00
12-Valkyrie app.	15.00	45.00	105.00
V3#1,2(no #3)	12.00	36.00	84.00
4-The Heap app. in Skywolf	10.00	30.00	70.00
5-8: 6-Valkyrie app;	8.50	25.50	60.00
9-11: 9-Origin The Heap	8.50	25.50	60.00
12-Skywolf & Airboy x-over; Valkyrie app.	12.00	36.00	84.00
V4#1-Iron Lady app.	10.00	30.00	70.00
2-Rackman begins	6.00	18.00	42.00
3,12	6.00	18.00	42.00
4-Simon & Kirby-c	7.00	21.00	50.00
5-11-All S&K-a	8.50	25.50	60.00
V5#1-9: 4-Infantino Heap. 5-Skull-c	4.30	13.00	30.00
10,11: 10-Origin The Heap	4.30	13.00	30.00
12-Krigstein-a(p)	5.70	17.00	40.00
V6#1-3,5-12: 6,8-Origin The Heap	4.30	13.00	30.00
4-Origin retold	5.00	15.00	35.00
V7#1-12: 7,8,10-Origin The Heap	4.30	13.00	30.00
V8#1-3,6-12	3.60	10.00	25.00
4-Krigstein-a	5.70	17.00	40.00
5(#100)	4.30	13.00	30.00
V9#1-6,8-12: 2-Valkyrie app.	3.60	10.00	25.00
7-One pg. Frazetta ad	4.30	13.00	30.00
V10#1-4	3.60	10.00	25.00

NOTE: *Bolle a-V4#12. McWilliams a-V3#7. Powell a-V7#3, V8#1, 6. Starr a-V5#1, 12. Dick Wood a-V4#12. Bondage-c V5#8.*

AIRBOY MEETS THE PROWLER
Dec., 1987 (One shot, $1.95, color)
Eclipse Comics

1	.35	1.00	1.95

AIRBOY - MR. MONSTER SPECIAL
Aug, 1987 (One Shot) ($1.75, color)
Eclipse Comics

1	.30	.90	1.80

AIRBOY VERSUS THE AIR MAIDENS
July, 1988 ($1.95, color)
Eclipse Comics

1	.35	1.00	1.95

AIR FIGHTERS CLASSICS
Nov., 1987 - Present (68 pgs, $3.95, B&W)
Eclipse Comics

1-6: r/G.A. Air Fighters #2-5. 1-Origin Airboy	.70	2.00	3.95

AIR FIGHTERS COMICS (Airboy #23 (V2#11) on)
Nov, 1941; No. 2, Nov, 1942 - V2/10, Fall, 1945
Hillman Periodicals

V1#1-(Produced by Funnies, Inc.); Black Commander only app.	80.00	240.00	560.00
2(11/42)-(Produced by Quality artists & Biro for Hillman); Origin Airboy & Iron Ace; Black Angel, Flying Dutchman & Skywolf begin; Fuje-a; Biro c/a	120.00	360.00	840.00
3-Origin The Heap & Skywolf	65.00	195.00	455.00
4	48.00	145.00	335.00
5,6	35.00	105.00	245.00

Aggie Mack #2, © SUPR

Airboy Comics V9#9, © HILL

Airboy Meets The Prowler #1, © Eclipse

Air Fighters Comics V2#1, © HILL

Al Capp's Dogpatch #2, © TOBY

Alice #10, © Z-D

	Good	Fine	N-Mint
AIR FIGHTERS COMICS (continued)			
7-12	26.00	78.00	180.00
V2#1,3-9: 5-Flag-c; Fuje-a. 7-Valkyrie app.	24.00	72.00	170.00
2-Skywolf by Giunta; Flying Dutchman by Fuje; 1st meeting			
Valkyrie & Airboy (She worked for the Nazis in beginning).			
	27.00	81.00	190.00
10-Origin The Heap & Skywolf	27.00	81.00	190.00
AIRFIGHTERS MEET SGT. STRIKE SPECIAL, THE			
Jan, 1988 ($1.95, color, stiff-c)			
Eclipse Comics			
1-Airboy, Valkyrie, Skywolf app.	.35	1.00	2.00
AIR FORCES (See American Air Forces)			
AIRMAIDENS SPECIAL			
August, 1987 - Present ($1.75, color)(Baxter, One-shot)			
Eclipse Comics			
1-Marisa becomes La Lupina (origin)	.35	1.00	2.00
AIR POWER (CBS TV & the U.S. Air Force Presents)			
1956 (32pgs, 5¼x7¼", soft-c)			
Prudential Insurance Co. giveaway			
nn-Toth-a? Based on 'You Are There' TV program by Walter Cronkite			
	5.00	15.00	30.00
AIR RAIDERS			
Nov, 1987 - No. 5, Mar., 1988 ($1.00, color)			
Star Comics (Marvel)			
1-5		.50	1.00
AIR WAR STORIES			
Sept-Nov, 1964 - No. 8, Aug, 1966			
Dell Publishing Co.			
1-Painted-c; Glanzman c/a begins	1.00	3.00	6.00
2-8	.50	1.50	3.00
AKIRA			
Sept, 1988 - Present ($3.50, color, deluxe, 64pgs.)			
Epic Comics			
1-5	.60	1.75	3.50
ALADDIN (See Dell Jr. Treasury No. 2)			
ALAN LADD (See Adventures of . . .)			
ALARMING ADVENTURES			
Oct, 1962 - No. 3, Feb, 1963			
Harvey Publications			
1	2.50	7.50	17.50
2,3	1.65	5.00	11.50
NOTE: *Bailey* a-1,3. *Crandall* a-1, 2.*Powell* a-2(2). *Severin* c-1-3. *Torres* a-2? *Tuska* a-1. *Williamson* a-1i, 2i, 3.			
ALARMING TALES			
Sept, 1957 - No. 6, Nov, 1958			
Harvey Publications (Western Tales)			
1-Kirby c/a(4)	4.00	12.00	28.00
2-Kirby-a(4)	4.00	12.00	28.00
3,4-Kirby-a	3.00	9.00	21.00
5-Kirby/Williamson-a	3.50	10.50	24.50
6-Torres-a	3.00	9.00	21.00
ALBEDO			
April, 1985 - No. 5, 1986			
Thoughts And Images			
0-Yellow cover; 50 copies	32.00	95.00	190.00
0-White cover, 450 copies	28.00	85.00	170.00
0-Blue, 1st printing, 500 copies	15.00	45.00	90.00
0-Blue, 2nd printing, 1000 copies	12.00	35.00	70.00
0-3rd printing	.85	2.50	5.00
0-4th printing	.35	1.00	2.00

	Good	Fine	N-Mint
1-Dark red; 1st app. Usagi Yojimbo	15.00	45.00	90.00
1-Bright red	13.00	40.00	80.00
2	15.00	45.00	90.00
3	1.70	5.00	10.00
4	4.15	12.50	25.00
5	1.35	4.00	8.00
6	1.70	5.00	10.00
7-15	.40	1.25	2.50
(Prices vary widely on this series)			
ALBERTO (See The Crusaders)			
ALBERT THE ALLIGATOR & POGO POSSUM (See 4-Color Comics No. 105, 148)			
ALBUM OF CRIME (See Fox Giants)			
ALBUM OF LOVE (See Fox Giants)			
AL CAPP'S DOGPATCH (Also see Mammy Yokum)			
No. 71, June, 1949 - No. 4, Dec, 1949			
Toby Press			
71(#1)-R-/from Tip Top #112-114	11.50	34.00	80.00
2-4: 4-R-/from Li'l Abner #73	8.50	25.50	60.00
AL CAPP'S SHMOO (Also see Oxydol-Dreft)			
July, 1949 - No. 5, April, 1950 (None by Al Capp)			
Toby Press			
1	20.00	60.00	140.00
2-5: 3-Sci-fi trip to moon. 4-X-Mas-c; origin/1st app. Super-Shmoo			
	14.30	43.00	100.00
AL CAPP'S WOLF GAL			
1951 - No. 2, 1952			
Toby Press			
1,2-Edited-r from Li'l Abner No. 63,64	18.00	54.00	125.00
ALEXANDER THE GREAT (See 4-Color No. 688)			
ALF (TV) (See Star Comics Digest)			
Mar, 1988 - Present ($1.00, color)			
Marvel Comics			
1-Post-a; photo-c	1.50	4.50	9.00
2-Post-a	.85	2.50	5.00
3-5	.50	1.50	3.00
6-10: 6-Photo-c	.35	1.00	2.00
11-16		.50	1.00
Annual #1 ($1.75, 64 pgs.)-Revolutionary War x-over			
	.50	1.00	3.00
...Comics Digest #1(1988)-Reprints Alf #1,2	.25	.75	1.50
ALGIE			
Dec, 1953 - No. 3, 1954			
Timor Publ. Co.			
1-Teenage	1.50	4.50	10.00
2,3	.85	2.50	6.00
Accepted Reprint #2(nd)	.55	1.65	4.00
Super Reprint 15	.40	1.20	2.80
ALICE (New Advs. in Wonderland)			
No. 10, 7-8/51 - No. 2, 11-12/51			
Ziff-Davis Publ. Co.			
10-Painted-c (spanking scene); Berg-a	8.50	25.50	60.00
11-Dave Berg-a	4.30	13.00	30.00
2-Dave Berg-a	3.50	10.50	24.00
ALICE AT MONKEY ISLAND (See The Advs. of Alice)			
No. 3, 1946			
Pentagon Publ. Co. (Civil Service)			
3	3.50	10.50	24.00

ALICE IN BLUNDERLAND
1952 (Paper cover, 16 pages in color)
Industrial Services

	Good	Fine	N-Mint
nn-Facts about big government waste and inefficiency			
	12.00	36.00	84.00

ALICE IN WONDERLAND (See Advs. of Alice, 4-Color No. 331,341, Dell Jr. Treasury No. 1, Movie Comics, Single Series No. 24, Walt Disney Showcase No. 22, and World's Greatest Stories)

ALICE IN WONDERLAND
1965; 1982
Western Printing Company/Whitman Publ. Co.

	Good	Fine	N-Mint
...Meets Santa Claus(1950s), nd, 16pgs	2.75	8.00	16.00
Rexall Giveaway(1965, 16 pgs., 5x7¼") Western Printing (TV-Hanna-Barbera)	2.00	6.00	12.00
Wonder Bakery Giveaway(16 pgs, color, nn, nd) (Continental Baking Co. (1969)	2.00	6.00	12.00
1-(Whitman; 1982)-r/4-Color 331		.40	.80

ALICE IN WONDERLAND MEETS SANTA
nd (16 pgs., 6-5/8x9-11/16", paper cover)
No publisher (Giveaway)

	Good	Fine	N-Mint
	10.00	30.00	60.00

ALIEN ENCOUNTERS (Replaces Alien Worlds)
June, 1985 - No. 14, Aug, 1987 ($1.75) (Mature readers)
Eclipse Comics

	Good	Fine	N-Mint
1-14: Nudity, strong language	.35	1.00	2.00

ALIEN FIRE
1987 - No. 3 ($2.00, B&W)
Kitchen Sink Press

	Good	Fine	N-Mint
1-3	.40	1.25	2.50

ALIEN LEGION (See Marvel Graphic Novel #25)
April, 1984 - No. 20, Sept, 1987
Epic Comics (Marvel)

	Good	Fine	N-Mint
1-$2.00 cover, high quality paper	.60	1.75	3.50
2-5	.35	1.00	2.00
6-10	.30	.85	1.70
11-20	.25	.75	1.50

NOTE: Austin a-1i, 4i; c-3i-5i.

ALIEN LEGION (2nd series)
Aug, 1987 (indicia) (10/87 on-c) - Present ($1.25, color)
Epic Comics (Marvel)

	Good	Fine	N-Mint
V2#1	.35	1.00	2.00
V2#2-7	.25	.75	1.50

ALIEN NATION
Dec, 1988 ($2.50; 68 pgs.)
DC Comics

	Good	Fine	N-Mint
1-Adapts movie; painted-c	.40	1.25	2.50

ALIENS, THE (Captain Johner and...)(Also see Magnus Robot...
Sept-Dec, 1967; No. 2, May, 1982
Gold Key

	Good	Fine	N-Mint
1-Reprints from Magnus #1,3,4,6-10, all by Russ Manning	1.00	3.00	6.00
2-Magnus-r/#1 by Manning	.40	1.25	2.50

ALIENS
1988 - No. 6, 1989 ($1.95, B&W, mini-series)
Dark Horse Comics

	Good	Fine	N-Mint
1-Movie adaptation	1.00	3.00	6.00
2-4	.40	1.25	2.50

ALIEN TERROR (See 3-D Alien Terror)

ALIEN WORLDS
12/82; No. 2, 6/83 - No. 7, 4/84; No. 8, 11/84 - No. 9, 1/85
(Baxter paper, $1.50)
Pacific Comics No. 1-7/Eclipse No. 8, 9

	Good	Fine	N-Mint
1-Williamson, Redondo-a; nudity	.60	1.75	3.50
2-7: 4-Nudity scenes	.50	1.50	3.00
8-Williamson-a	.30	.85	1.70
9-($1.50 cover)	.35	1.00	2.00
3-D #1-Art Adams-a	.85	2.50	5.00

NOTE: Bolton c-5, 9. Brunner a-6p, 9; c-6. Conrad a-1. Corben a-7. J. Jones a-4p. Krenkel a-6. Morrow a-7. Perez a-7. Stevens a-2, 4i; c-2, 4. Williamson/Frazetta a-4r/Witzend No. 1.

ALIEN WORLDS
1988 - Present (Semi-annual, deluxe, color, $3.95)
Eclipse Books

	Good	Fine	N-Mint
1	.60	1.75	3.50

ALIEN WORLDS 3-D (See 3-Dimensional Alien Worlds)

ALL-AMERICAN COMICS (...Western #103-126, ...Men of War #127 on)
April, 1939 - No. 102, Oct, 1948
National Periodical Publications/All-American

	Good	Fine	N-Mint
1-Hop Harrigan, Scribbly, Toonerville Folks, Ben Webster, Spot Savage, Mutt & Jeff, Red White & Blue, Adv. in the Unknown, Tippie, Reg'lar Fellers, Skippy, Bobby Thatcher, Mystery Men of Mars, Daiseybelle, & Wiley of West Point begin	157.00	471.00	1100.00
2-Ripley's Believe It or Not begins, ends #24	65.00	195.00	455.00
3-5: 5-The American Way begins, ends #10	45.00	135.00	315.00
6,7: 6-Last Spot Savage; Popsicle Pete begins, ends #26, 28. 7-Last Bobby Thatcher	35.00	105.00	245.00
8-The Ultra Man begins	56.00	168.00	390.00
9,10: 10-X-Mas-c	40.00	120.00	280.00
11-15: 12-Last Toonerville Folks. 15-Last Tippie & Reg'lar Fellars	32.00	95.00	225.00
16-Origin & 1st app. Green Lantern (Rare), created by Martin Nodell. Inspired by Aladdin's Lamp; the suggested alter ego name Alan Ladd, was never capitalized on. It was changed to Alan Scott before Alan Ladd became a major film star (he was in two films before this issue)	1100.00	3300.00	7700.00
(Prices vary widely on this book)			
17-(Scarce)	250.00	750.00	1750.00
18	130.00	390.00	910.00
19-Origin & 1st app. The Atom; Last Ultra Man	195.00	585.00	1365.00
20-Atom dons costume; Hunkle becomes Red Tornado; Rescue on Mars begins, ends #25; 1 pg. origin Green Lantern	115.00	345.00	805.00
21-23: 21-Last Wiley of West Point & Skippy. 23-Last Daiseybelle; 3 Idiots begin, end #82	80.00	240.00	560.00
24-Sisty & Dinky become the Cyclone Kids; Ben Webster ends. Origin Dr. Mid-Nite & Sargon, The Sorcerer in text with app.	85.00	255.00	595.00
25-Origin & 1st story app. Dr. Mid-Nite by Stan Asch; Hop Harrigan becomes Guardian Angel; last Adventure in the Unknown	135.00	405.00	950.00
26-Origin & 1st story app. Sargon, the Sorcerer	95.00	285.00	665.00
27: #27-32 are misnumbered in indicia with correct No. appearing on cover. Intro. Doiby Dickles, Green Lantern's sidekick	95.00	285.00	665.00
28-Hop Harrigan gives up costumed i.d.	53.00	160.00	370.00
29,30	53.00	160.00	370.00

Alien Worlds #4, © Eclipse   All-American Comics #8, © DC   All-American Comics #17, © DC

All-American Western #113, © DC

All-Famous Crime #10, © STAR

All-Flash Quarterly #4, © DC

ALL-AMERICAN COMICS (continued)	Good	Fine	N-Mint
31-40: 35-Doiby learns Green Lantern's i.d.	40.00	120.00	280.00
41-50: 50-Sargon ends	35.00	105.00	245.00
51-60: 59-Scribbly & the Red Tornado ends	30.00	90.00	210.00
61-Origin Solomon Grundy	71.00	213.00	500.00
62-70: 70-Kubert Sargon; intro Sargon's helper, Maximillian O'Leary	30.00	90.00	210.00
71-Last Red White & Blue	23.50	70.00	165.00
72-Black Pirate begins (not in #74-82); last Atom	23.50	70.00	165.00
73-80: 73-Winky, Blinky & Noddy begins, ends #82	23.50	70.00	165.00
81-88,90: 90-Origin Icicle	23.50	70.00	165.00
89-Origin Harlequin	28.50	85.00	200.00
91-99-Last Hop Harrigan	23.50	70.00	165.00
100-1st app. Johnny Thunder by Alex Toth	43.00	130.00	300.00
101-Last Mutt & Jeff	30.00	90.00	210.00
102-Last Green Lantern, Black Pirate & Dr. Mid-Nite	30.00	90.00	210.00

NOTE: No Atom in 47,62-69. Kinstler Black Pirate-89. Stan Aschmeier a-25, 40, 55, 70; c-7. Moldoff c-16-23. Paul Reinman a-55, 70; c-55, 70, 75, 78, 80. Toth a-88, 92, 96, 98-102; c-92, 96-102.

ALL-AMERICAN MEN OF WAR (Previously All-American Western)
No. 127, Aug-Sept, 1952 - No. 117, Sept-Oct, 1966
National Periodical Publications

127 (1952)	19.00	58.00	135.00
128 (1952)	12.00	36.00	85.00
2(12-1/'52-53)-5	10.00	30.00	70.00
6-10	6.50	19.50	45.00
11-18: Last precode (2/55)	4.85	15.00	34.00
19-28	3.50	10.50	25.00
29,30,32-Wood-a	4.00	12.00	28.00
31,33-50	1.70	5.00	12.00
51-67: 67-1st Gunner & Sarge by Andru	1.30	4.00	9.00
68-80	.75	2.25	4.50
81-100: 82-Johnny Cloud begins, ends #111,114,115	.40	1.25	2.50
101-117: 112-Balloon Buster series begins, ends #114,116; 115-Johnny Cloud app.	.25	.75	1.50

NOTE: Colan a-112. Drucker a-47,65,74,77. Heath a-27, 32, 47, 95, 112; c-95, 100, 112. Krigstein a-128('52), 2, 3, 5. Kirby a-29. Kubert a-29, 36, 38, 41, 43, 47, 49, 50, 52, 53, 55, 56, 60, 63, 65, 69, 71-73, 103, 114; c-41, 77, 114. Tank Killer in 69, 71, 76 by Kubert. P. Reinman c-55, 57, 61, 62, 71, 72, 74-76, 80.

ALL-AMERICAN SPORTS
October, 1967
Charlton Comics

1		.60	1.20

ALL-AMERICAN WESTERN (Formerly All-American Comics; Becomes All-American Men of War)
No. 103, Nov, 1948 - No. 126, June-July, 1952 (52pgs, 103-121)
National Periodical Publications

103-Johnny Thunder & his horse Black Lightning continues by Toth, ends No. 126; Foley of The Fighting 5th, Minstrel Maverick, & Overland Coach begin; Captain Tootsie by Beck; mentioned in **Love and Death**	17.00	51.00	120.00
104-Kubert-a	12.00	36.00	84.00
105,107-Kubert-a	11.00	32.00	76.00
106,108-110,112: 112-Kurtzman "Pot-Shot Pete" 1pg.	8.00	24.00	56.00
111,114-116-Kubert-a	9.00	27.00	63.00
113-Intro. Swift Deer, J. Thunder's new sidekick; classic Toth-c; Kubert-a	10.00	30.00	70.00
117-120,122-125	7.00	21.00	50.00
121-Kubert-a	7.00	21.00	50.00
126-Last issue	7.00	21.00	50.00

NOTE: Kubert a-103-105, 107, 111, 112(1 pg.), 113-116, 121. Toth c/a 103-126.

ALL COMICS
1945
Chicago Nite Life News

	Good	Fine	N-Mint
1	5.00	15.00	35.00

ALLEY OOP (See The Comics, 4-Color No. 3, Red Ryder and Super Book No. 9)
ALLEY OOP
No. 10, 1947 - No. 18, Oct, 1949
Standard Comics

10	13.00	40.00	90.00
11-18: 17,18-Schomburg-c	10.00	30.00	70.00

ALLEY OOP
Nov, 1955 - No. 3, March, 1956 (Newspaper reprints)
Argo Publ.

1	10.00	30.00	70.00
2,3	7.00	21.00	50.00

ALLEY OOP
12-2/62-63 - No. 2, 9-11/63
Dell Publishing Co.

1,2	5.00	15.00	35.00

ALL-FAMOUS CRIME
1949 - No. 10, Nov, 1951
Star Publications

1	5.00	15.00	35.00
2	2.65	8.00	18.00
3-5	2.35	7.00	16.00
6-8,10	2.00	6.00	14.00
9-Used in SOTI, illo-"The wish to hurt or kill couples in lovers' lanes is not uncommon perversion;" L.B. Cole-c/a(r)/Law-Crime No. 3	9.00	27.00	62.00

NOTE: All have L.B. Cole covers.

ALL FAMOUS CRIME STORIES (See Fox Giants)

ALL-FAMOUS POLICE CASES
Oct, 1951 - No. 16, Sept, 1954
Star Publications

1	5.00	15.00	35.00
2	2.65	8.00	18.00
3-6,9,16	2.35	7.00	16.00
7-Kubert-a	3.00	9.00	21.00
8-Marijuana story	3.00	9.00	21.00

NOTE: L. B. Cole c-all; a-15, 1pg. Hollingsworth a-15.

ALL-FLASH (. . . Quarterly No. 1-5)
Summer, 1941 - No. 32, Dec-Jan, 1947-48
National Periodical Publications/All-American

1-Origin The Flash retold by E. Hibbard	230.00	690.00	1610.00
2-Origin recap	86.00	258.00	600.00
3,4	57.00	171.00	400.00
5-Winky, Blinky & Noddy begins, ends #32	46.00	138.00	320.00
6-10	40.00	120.00	280.00
11-13: 12-Origin The Thinker. 13-The King app.	32.00	95.00	225.00
14-Green Lantern cameo	35.00	105.00	245.00
15-20: 18-Mutt & Jeff begins, ends #22	28.00	85.00	195.00
21-31	25.00	75.00	175.00
32-Origin The Fiddler; 1st Star Sapphire	30.00	90.00	210.00

NOTE: Book length stories in 2-13,16. Bondage c-31, 32.

ALL FOR LOVE (Young Love V3/5-on)
Apr-May, 1957 - V3No.4, Dec-Jan, 1959-60
Prize Publications

V1#1	2.30	7.00	16.00

ALL FOR LOVE (continued)	Good	Fine	N-Mint
2-6: 5-Orlando-c	1.30	4.00	9.00
V2#1-5(1/59), 5(3/59)	.85	2.50	6.00
V3#1(5/59), 1(7/59)-4: 2-Powell-a	.70	2.00	4.00

ALL FUNNY COMICS
Winter, 1943-44 - No. 23, May-June, 1948
Tilsam Publ./National Periodical Publications (Detective)

	Good	Fine	N-Mint
1-Genius Jones, Buzzy (ends #4), Dover & Clover begin; Bailey-a	20.00	60.00	140.00
2	9.00	27.00	62.00
3-10	6.00	18.00	42.00
11-13,15,18,19-Genius Jones app.	5.00	15.00	35.00
14,17,20-23	3.50	10.50	25.00
16-DC Super Heroes app.	10.00	30.00	70.00

ALL GOOD COMICS (See Fox Giants)
Spring, 1946 (36 pgs.)
Fox Features Syndicate

	Good	Fine	N-Mint
1-Joy Family, Dick Transom, Rick Evans, One Round Hogan	6.50	19.50	45.00

ALL GOOD
Oct, 1949 (260 pages) (50 cents)
St. John Publishing Co.

	Good	Fine	N-Mint
(8 St. John comics bound together)	40.00	120.00	280.00

NOTE: *Also see Li'l Audrey Yearbook & Treasury of Comics.*

ALL GREAT (See Fox Giants)
1946 (36 pgs.)
Fox Features Syndicate

	Good	Fine	N-Mint
1-Crazy House, Bertie Benson Boy Detective, Gussie the Gob	5.00	15.00	35.00

ALL GREAT
nd (1945?) (132 pgs.)
William H. Wise & Co.

	Good	Fine	N-Mint
nn-Capt. Jack Terry, Joan Mason, Girl Reporter, Baron Doomsday; Torture scenes	15.00	45.00	105.00

ALL GREAT (Dagar, Desert Hawk No. 14 on)
No. 14, Oct. 1947 - No. 13, Dec, 1947
Fox Features Syndicate

	Good	Fine	N-Mint
14-Brenda Starr-r (Scarce)	15.00	45.00	105.00
13-Origin Dagar, Desert Hawk; Brenda Starr (all-r); Kamen-c	13.00	40.00	90.00

ALL-GREAT CONFESSIONS (See Fox Giants)

ALL GREAT CRIME STORIES (See Fox Giants)

ALL GREAT JUNGLE ADVENTURES (See Fox Giants)

ALL HERO COMICS
March, 1943 (100 pgs.) (Cardboard cover)
Fawcett Publications

	Good	Fine	N-Mint
1-Captain Marvel Jr., Capt. Midnight, Golden Arrow, Ibis the Invincible, Spy Smasher, & Lance O'Casey	65.00	195.00	455.00

ALL HUMOR COMICS
Spring, 1946 - No. 17, December, 1949
Quality Comics Group

	Good	Fine	N-Mint
1	5.70	17.00	40.00
2-Atomic Tot sty; Gustavson-a	2.85	8.50	20.00
3-9: 5-1st app. Hickory? 8-Gustavson-a	1.85	5.50	13.00
10-17	1.30	4.00	9.00

ALL LOVE (...Romances No. 26)(Formerly Ernie)
No. 26, May, 1949 - No. 32, May, 1950
Ace Periodicals (Current Books)

	Good	Fine	N-Mint
26(No. 1)-Ernie, Lily Belle app.	2.30	7.00	16.00
27-L. B. Cole-a	2.65	8.00	18.50

	Good	Fine	N-Mint
28-32	1.50	4.50	10.00

ALL-NEGRO COMICS
June, 1947 (15 cents)
All-Negro Comics

	Good	Fine	N-Mint
1 (Rare)	67.00	200.00	470.00

NOTE: *Seldom found in fine or mint condition; many copies have brown pages.*

ALL-NEW COLLECTORS' EDITION (Formerly Ltd. Collectors' Ed.)
Jan, 1978 - No. C-62, 1979 (No. 54-58: 76 pgs.)
DC Comics, Inc.

	Good	Fine	N-Mint
C-53-Rudolph the Red-Nosed Reindeer		.50	1.00
C-54-Superman Vs. Wonder Woman	.25	.75	1.50
C-55-Superboy & the Legion of Super-Heroes	.70	2.00	4.00
C-56-Superman Vs. Muhammad Ali: story & wraparound Adams-c	.35	1.00	2.00
C-58-Superman Vs. Shazam		.60	1.20
C-60-Rudolph's Summer Fun(8/78)		.60	1.20
C-62-Superman the Movie (68 pgs.; 1979)		.60	1.20

ALL-NEW COMICS (...Short Story Comics No. 1-3)
Jan, 1943 - No. 14, Nov. 1946; No. 15, Mar-Apr, 1947
Family Comics (Harvey Publications)

	Good	Fine	N-Mint
1-Steve Case, Crime Rover, Johnny Rebel, Kayo Kane, The Echo, Night Hawk, Ray O'Light, Detective Shane begin; Red Blazer on cover only; Sultan-a	50.00	150.00	350.00
2-Origin Scarlet Phantom by Kubert	25.00	75.00	175.00
3	20.00	60.00	140.00
4,5	17.00	51.00	120.00
6-The Boy Heroes & Red Blazer (text story) begin, end #12; Black Cat app.; intro. Sparky in Red Blazer	19.00	57.00	132.00
7-Kubert, Powell-a; Black Cat & Zebra app.	19.00	57.00	132.00
8-Shock Gibson app.; Kubert, Powell-a; Schomburg bondage-c	19.00	57.00	132.00
9-Black Cat app.; Kubert-a	19.00	57.00	132.00
10-The Zebra app.; Kubert-a(3)	17.00	51.00	120.00
11-Girl Commandos, Man In Black app.	17.00	51.00	120.00
12-Kubert-a	17.00	51.00	120.00
13-Stuntman by Simon & Kirby; Green Hornet, Joe Palooka, Flying Fool app.	19.00	57.00	132.00
14-The Green Hornet & The Man in Black Called Fate by Powell, Joe Palooka app.	17.00	51.00	120.00
15-(Rare)-Small size (5½x8½''; B&W; 32 pgs.). Distributed to mail subscribers only. Black Cat and Joe Palooka app.			

Estimated value....$200-250

NOTE: *Also see Boy Explorers No. 2, Flash Gordon No. 5, and Stuntman No. 3.*
Powell a-11. Schomburg c-7,8,10,11.

ALL-OUT WAR
Sept-Oct, 1979 - No. 6, Aug, 1980 ($1.00)
DC Comics, Inc.

	Good	Fine	N-Mint
1-The Viking Commando(origin), Force Three(origin), & Black Eagle Squadron begin		.25	.50
2-6		.25	.50

NOTE: *Evans a-1-6. Kubert c-1-6.*

ALL PICTURE ADVENTURE MAGAZINE
Oct, 1952 - No. 2, Nov, 1952 (100 pg. Giants)
St. John Publishing Co.

	Good	Fine	N-Mint
1-War comics	11.00	33.00	77.00
2-Horror-crime comics	15.00	45.00	105.00

NOTE: *Above books contain three St. John comics rebound; variations possible.*
Baker art known in both.

ALL PICTURE ALL TRUE LOVE STORY
October, 1952 (100 pages)
St. John Publishing Co.

	Good	Fine	N-Mint
1-Canteen Kate by Matt Baker	22.00	65.00	155.00

All Hero Comics #1, © FAW

All Love #27, © ACE

All-New Comics #7, © HARV

All-Select Comics #3, © MEG

All Star Comics #2, © DC

All-Star Squadron #41, © DC

ALL-PICTURE COMEDY CARNIVAL
October, 1952 (100 pages)
St. John Publishing Co.

	Good	Fine	N-Mint
1-(4 rebound comics)-Contents can vary; Baker-a	22.00	65.00	155.00

ALL REAL CONFESSION MAGAZINE (See Fox Giants)

ALL ROMANCES (Mr. Risk No. 7 on)
Aug, 1949 - No. 6, June, 1950
A. A. Wyn (Ace Periodicals)

	Good	Fine	N-Mint
1	3.00	9.00	21.00
2	1.50	4.50	10.00
3-6	1.15	3.50	8.00

ALL-SELECT COMICS (Blonde Phantom No. 12 on)
Fall, 1943 - No. 11, Fall, 1946
Timely Comics (Daring Comics)

	Good	Fine	N-Mint
1-Capt. America, Human Torch, Sub-Mariner begin; Black Widow app.	160.00	480.00	1120.00
2-Red Skull app.	70.00	210.00	490.00
3-The Whizzer begins	47.00	141.00	330.00
4,5-Last Sub-Mariner	39.00	117.00	272.00
6-The Destroyer app.	31.50	94.00	220.00
7-9: 8-No Whizzer	31.50	94.00	220.00
10-The Destroyer & Sub-Mariner app.; last Capt. America & Human Torch issue	31.50	94.00	220.00
11-1st app. Blonde Phantom; Miss America app.; all Blonde Phantom-c	52.00	155.00	365.00

NOTE: *Schomburg* c-2,4,9,10. No. 7 & 8 show 1944 in indicia, but should be 1945.

ALL SPORTS COMICS (Formerly Real Sports Comics; becomes All Time Sports Comics No. 4 on)
No. 2, Dec-Jan, 1948-49, No. 3, Feb-Mar, 1949
Hillman Periodicals

	Good	Fine	N-Mint
2-Krigstein-a(p), Powell, Starr-a	7.00	21.00	50.00
3-Mort Lawrence-a	5.70	17.00	40.00

ALL STAR COMICS (. . .Western No. 58 on)
Summer, 1940 - No. 57, Feb-Mar, 1951; No. 58, Jan-Feb, 1976 -
No. 74, Sept-Oct, 1978
National Periodical Publ./All-American/DC Comics

	Good	Fine	N-Mint
1-The Flash(No.1 by Harry Lampert), Hawkman(by Shelly), Hourman, The Sandman, The Spectre, Biff Bronson, Red White & Blue begin; Ultra Man's only app.	518.00	1555.00	3625.00
2-Green Lantern, Johnny Thunder begin	242.00	725.00	1695.00
3-Origin Justice Society of America; Dr. Fate & The Atom cameo, Red Tornado cameo; last Red White & Blue; reprinted in Famous First Edition	928.00	2785.00	6500.00
4	235.00	705.00	1650.00
5-Intro. & 1st app. Shiera Sanders as Hawkgirl	200.00	600.00	1400.00
6-Johnny Thunder joins JSA	200.00	600.00	1400.00
7-Batman, Superman, Flash cameo; last Hourman; Doiby Dickles app.	160.00	480.00	1120.00
8-Origin & 1st app. Wonder Woman (added as 8pgs. making book 76pgs.; origin cont'd in Sensation #1); Dr. Fate dons new helmet; Dr.Mid-Nite, Hop Harrigan text stories & Starman begin; Shiera app.; Hop Harrigan JSA guest	330.00	990.00	2300.00
9-Shiera app.	135.00	405.00	950.00
10-Flash, Green Lantern cameo, Sandman new costume	135.00	405.00	950.00
11-Wonder Woman begins; Spectre cameo; Shiera app.	130.00	390.00	910.00
12-Wonder Woman becomes JSA Secretary	130.00	390.00	910.00
13-15: Sandman w/Sandy in No. 14 & 15; 15-Origin Brain Wave; Shiera app.	117.00	350.00	820.00

	Good	Fine	N-Mint
16-19: 19-Sandman w/Sandy	90.00	270.00	630.00
20-Dr. Fate & Sandman cameo	90.00	270.00	630.00
21-Spectre & Atom cameo; Dr. Fate by Kubert; Dr. Fate, Sandman end	78.00	235.00	545.00
22,23: 22-Last Hop Harrigan; Flag-c. 23-Origin Psycho Pirate; last Spectre & Starman	78.00	235.00	545.00
24-Flash & Green Lantern cameo; Mr. Terrific only app.; Wildcat, JSA guest; Kubert Hawkman begins	78.00	235.00	545.00
25-27: 25-The Flash & Green Lantern start again. 27-Wildcat, JSA guest	72.00	215.00	505.00
28-32	62.00	185.00	435.00
33-Solomon Grundy, Hawkman, Doiby Dickles app.	117.00	350.00	820.00
34,35-Johnny Thunder cameo in both	56.00	168.00	390.00
36-Batman & Superman JSA guests	113.00	340.00	790.00
37-Johnny Thunder cameo; origin Injustice Society; last Kubert Hawkman	62.00	185.00	435.00
38-Black Canary begins; JSA Death issue	68.00	205.00	475.00
39,40: 39-Last Johnny Thunder	46.00	138.00	320.00
41-Black Canary joins JSA; Injustice Society app.	44.00	132.00	310.00
42-Atom & the Hawkman don new costume	44.00	132.00	310.00
43-49	44.00	132.00	310.00
50-Frazetta art, 3 pgs.	53.00	160.00	370.00
51-56: 55-Sci/fi story	44.00	132.00	310.00
57-Kubert-a, 6 pgs. (Scarce)	56.00	168.00	390.00
58('76)-Flash, Hawkman, Dr. Mid-Nite, Wildcat, Dr. Fate, Green Lantern, Star Spangled Kid & Robin app.; intro Power Girl		.25	.50
59-74: 69-1st app. Huntress		.25	.50

NOTE: *No Atom-27, 36; no Dr. Fate-13; no Flash-8, 9, 11-23; no Green Lantern-8, 9, 11-23; no Johnny Thunder-5, 36; no Wonder Woman-9, 10, 23. Book length stories in 4-9, 11-14, 18-22, 25, 26, 29, 30, 32-36, 42, 43. Johnny Peril in #42-46, 48, 49, 51, 52, 54-57. Baily a-1-10, 12, 13, 14; 15-20. Burnley Starman-8-13; c-12, 13. Grell c-58. Kubert Hawkman-24-30, 33-37. Moldoff Hawkman-3-23; c-11. Simon & Kirby Sandman -14-17, 19. Toth a-37(2), 38(2), 40, 41; c-38, 41. Wood a-58i-63i, 64, 65; c-63-65.*

ALL STAR INDEX, THE
Feb, 1987 ($2.00, Baxter)
Independent Comics Group (Eclipse)

	Good	Fine	N-Mint
1	.35	1.00	2.00

ALL-STAR SQUADRON
Sept, 1981 - No. 67, March, 1987
DC Comics

	Good	Fine	N-Mint
1-Original Atom, Hawkman, Dr. Mid-Nite, Robotman (origin), Plastic Man, Johnny Quick, Liberty Belle, Shining Knight begin	.25	.75	1.50
2	.50	1.00	
3-24: 5-Danette Reilly becomes new Firebrand. 12-Origin G.A. Hawkman retold. 23-Intro/origin The Amazing Man		.40	.80
25-1st Infinity, Inc.	.70	2.00	4.00
26-Origin Infinity, Inc.	.55	1.60	3.20
27-46,48,49: 31-Origin Freedom Fighters of Earth-X. 41-Origin Starman.		.40	.80
47-Origin Dr. Fate; McFarlane-a	.35	1.00	2.00
50-Double size; Crisis x-over	.25	.75	1.50
51-53-Crisis x-over		.50	1.00
54-67: 61-Origin Liberty Belle. 62-Origin The Shining Knight. 63-Origin Robotman. 65-Origin Johnny Quick. 66-Origin Tarantula		.40	.80
Annual 1(11/82)-Retells origin of G.A. Atom, Guardian & Wildcat		.50	1.00
Annual 2(11/83)-Infinity, Inc. app.		.50	1.00
Annual 3(9/84)		.65	1.30

NOTE: *Kubert c-2, 7-18.*

13

ALL-STAR STORY OF THE DODGERS, THE
April, 1979 (Full Color) ($1.00)
Stadium Communications

	Good	Fine	N-Mint
1		.50	1.00

ALL STAR WESTERN (All Star No. 1-57)
Apr-May, 1951 - No. 119, June-July, 1961
National Periodical Publications

	Good	Fine	N-Mint
58-Trigger Twins (end #116), Strong Bow, The Roving Ranger & Don Caballero begin	17.00	51.00	120.00
59,60: Last 52 pgs.	8.00	24.00	56.00
61-66: 61,64-Toth-a	7.00	21.00	50.00
67-Johnny Thunder begins; Gil Kane-a	8.00	24.00	56.00
68-81: Last precode, 2-3/55	4.00	12.00	28.00
82-98	3.00	9.00	21.00
99-Frazetta-a r-/Jimmy Wakely #4	5.50	16.00	38.00
100	4.00	12.00	28.00
101-107,109-116,118,119	2.30	7.00	16.00
108-Origin Johnny Thunder	5.00	15.00	35.00
117-Origin Super Chief	4.00	12.00	28.00

NOTE: *Infantino* art in most issues. Madame .44 app.-#117-119.

ALL-STAR WESTERN (Weird Western Tales No. 12 on)
Aug-Sept, 1970 - No. 11, Apr-May, 1972
National Periodical Publications

	Good	Fine	N-Mint
1-Pow-Wow Smith-r; Infantino-a	.50	1.50	3.00
2-Outlaw begins; El Diablo by Morrow begins; has cameos by Williamson, Torres, Gil Kane, Giordano & Phil Seuling	.35	1.00	2.00
3-8: 3-Origin El Diablo. 5-Last Outlaw ish. 6-Billy the Kid begins, ends #8	.35	1.00	2.00
9-Frazetta-a, 3pgs.(r)	.70	2.00	4.00
10-Jonah Hex begins (1st app.)	2.35	7.00	14.00
11	.70	2.00	4.00

NOTE: *Adams* c-1-5; *Aparo* a-5. *G. Kane* a-3, 4, 6, 8. *Kubert* a-4r, 7-9r. *Morrow* a-2-4, 10, 11. No. 7-11 have 52 pages.

ALL SURPRISE
Fall, 1943 - No. 12, Winter, 1946-47
Timely/Marvel (CPC)

	Good	Fine	N-Mint
1-Super Rabbit & Gandy & Sourpuss	10.00	30.00	70.00
2	4.30	13.00	30.00
3-10,12	3.00	9.00	21.00
11-Kurtzman "Pigtales" art	4.70	14.00	33.00

ALL TEEN (Formerly All Winners; Teen Comics No. 21 on)
No. 20, January, 1947
Marvel Comics (WFP)

	Good	Fine	N-Mint
20-Georgie, Mitzi, Patsy Walker, Willie app.	3.00	9.00	21.00

ALL THE FUNNY FOLKS
1926 (hardcover, 112 pgs., 11½x3½'') (Full color)
World Press Today, Inc.

	Good	Fine	N-Mint
nn-Barney Google, Spark Plug, Jiggs & Maggie, Tillie The Toiler, Happy Hooligan, Hans & Fritz, Toots & Casper, etc.	18.00	54.00	125.00

ALL-TIME SPORTS COMICS (Formerly All Sports Comics)
V2No. 4, Apr-May, 1949 - V2No. 7, Oct-Nov, 1949
Hillman Periodicals

	Good	Fine	N-Mint
V2#4	5.00	15.00	35.00
5-7: 5-Powell-a. 7-Krigstein-a(p)	3.50	10.50	25.00

ALL TOP
1944 (132 pages)
William H. Wise Co.

Capt. V, Merciless the Sorceress, Red Robbins, One Round Hogan,

	Good	Fine	N-Mint
Mike the M.P., Snooky, Pussy Katnip app.	12.00	36.00	84.00

ALL TOP COMICS (My Experience No. 19 on)
1945; No. 2, Sum, 1946 - No. 18, Mar, 1949; 1957 - 1959
Fox Features Synd./Green Publ./Norlen Mag.

	Good	Fine	N-Mint
1-Cosmo Cat & Flash Rabbit begin	9.00	27.00	62.00
2	4.50	13.50	32.00
3-7	3.50	10.50	25.00
8-Blue Beetle, Phantom Lady, & Rulah, Jungle Goddess begin (11/47); Kamen-c	55.00	165.00	385.00
9-Kamen-c	32.00	95.00	225.00
10-Kamen bondage-c	32.00	95.00	225.00
11-13,15-17: 15-No Blue Beetle	24.00	72.00	168.00
14-No Blue Beetle; used in **SOTI**, illo-''Corpses of colored people strung up by their wrists.''	32.00	95.00	225.00
18-Dagar, Jo-Jo app; no Phantom Lady or Blue Beetle	20.00	60.00	140.00
6(1957-Green Publ.)-Patoruzu the Indian; Cosmo Cat on cover only	1.50	4.50	10.00
6(1958-Literary Ent.)-Muggy Doo; Cosmo Cat on cover only	1.50	4.50	10.00
6(1959-Norlen)-Atomic Mouse; Cosmo Cat on cover only	1.50	4.50	10.00
6(1959)-Little Eva	1.50	4.50	10.00
6(Cornell)-Supermouse on-c	1.50	4.50	10.00

NOTE: *Jo-Jo by Kamen-12,18.*

ALL TRUE ALL PICTURE POLICE CASES
Oct., 1952 - No. 2, Nov, 1952 (100 pages)
St. John Publishing Co.

	Good	Fine	N-Mint
1-Three rebound St. John crime comics	20.00	60.00	140.00
2-Three comics rebound	17.00	51.00	120.00

NOTE: *Contents may vary.*

ALL-TRUE CRIME (. . .Cases No. 26-35; formerly Official True Crime Cases)
No. 26, Feb, 1948 - No. 52, Sept, 1952
Marvel/Atlas Comics(OFI No. 26,27/CFI No. 28,29/LCC No. 30-46/LMC No. 47-52)

	Good	Fine	N-Mint
26(No. 1)	4.50	14.00	32.00
27(4/48)-Electric chair-c	4.00	12.00	28.00
28-41,43-48,50-52: 36-Photo-c	1.50	4.50	10.00
42-Krigstein-a	2.85	8.50	20.00
49-Used in **POP**, Pg. 79; Krigstein-a	3.50	10.50	24.00

NOTE: *Robinson* a-47. *Tuska* a-48(3).

ALL-TRUE DETECTIVE CASES (Kit Carson No. 5 on)
Feb-Mar, 1954 - No. 4, Aug-Sept, 1954
Avon Periodicals

	Good	Fine	N-Mint
1	10.00	30.00	70.00
2-Wood-a	8.50	25.50	60.00
3-Kinstler-c	3.75	11.25	26.00
4-Wood(?), Kamen-a	7.00	21.00	50.00
nn(100 pgs.)-7 pg. Kubert-a, Kinstler back-c	20.00	60.00	140.00

ALL TRUE ROMANCE (. . .Illustrated No. 3)
3/51 - No. 20, 12/54; No. 22, 3/55 - No. 30?, 7/57; No. 3(#31), 9/57 - No. 4(#32), 11/57; No. 33?, 1/58 - No. 34, 3/58
Artful Publ. #1-3/Harwell(Comic Media) #4-20?/Ajax-Farrell(Excellent Publ.) No. 22 on/Four Star Comic Corp.

	Good	Fine	N-Mint
1 (3/51)	5.50	16.50	38.50
2 (10/51; 11/51 on-c)	3.50	10.50	24.00
3(12/51) - #5(5/52)	3.00	9.00	21.00
6-Wood-a, 9 pgs. (exceptional)	8.00	24.00	56.00
7-10	2.15	6.50	15.00
11-13,16-19 (2/54)	1.60	4.80	11.00
14-Marijuana story	2.50	7.50	17.00
20-22: Last precode (Ajax, 3/55)	1.50	4.50	10.00
23-27,29,30	1.20	3.60	8.40

All Star Western #62, © DC

All Top Comics #10, © FOX

All True Romance #3, © AJAX

All Winners Comics #3, © MEG

All Your Comics #1, © FOX

Amazing Adult Fantasy #7, © MEG

ALL TRUE ROMANCE (continued)	Good	Fine	N-Mint
28 (9/56)-L. B. Cole, Disbrow-a	2.50	7.50	17.00
3,4,33,34 (Farrell, '57-'58)	.60	1.80	4.00

ALL WESTERN WINNERS (Formerly All Winners; becomes Western Winners with No. 5; see Two-Gun Kid No. 5)
No. 2, Winter, 1948-49 - No. 4, April, 1949
Marvel Comics(CDS)

	Good	Fine	N-Mint
2-Black Rider (Origin & 1st app.) & his horse Satan, Kid Colt & his horse Steel, & Two-Gun Kid & his horse Cyclone begin	17.00	51.00	120.00
3-Anti-Wertham editorial	11.50	34.50	80.00
4-Black Rider i.d. revealed	11.50	34.50	80.00

ALL WINNERS COMICS (All Teen #20; #1 adv. as All Aces)
Summer, 1941 - No. 19, Fall, 1946; No. 21, Winter, 1946-47
(no No. 20) (No. 21 continued from Young Allies No. 20)
USA No. 1-7/WFP No. 10-19/YAI No. 21

1-The Angel & Black Marvel only app.; Capt. America by Simon & Kirby, Human Torch & Sub-Mariner begin	250.00	750.00	1750.00
2-The Destroyer & The Whizzer begin; Simon & Kirby Captain America	120.00	360.00	840.00
3,4	92.00	275.00	645.00
5,6: 6-The Black Avenger only app.; no Whizzer story	63.00	190.00	440.00
7-10	52.00	155.00	365.00
11-18: 12-Last Destroyer; no Whizzer story; no Human Torch No. 14-16	33.00	100.00	230.00
19-(Scarce)-1st app. & origin All Winners Squad	80.00	240.00	560.00
21-(Scarce)-All Winners Squad, Miss America app; bondage-c	75.00	235.00	525.00

NOTE: *Everett* Sub-Mariner-1, 3, 4; *Burgos* Torch-1, 3, 4. *Schomburg* c-12, 14, 15.

(2nd Series - August, 1948, Marvel Comics (CDS))
(Becomes All Western Winners with No. 2)

1-The Blonde Phantom, Capt. America, Human Torch, & Sub-Mariner app.	64.00	192.00	450.00

ALL YOUR COMICS (See Fox Giants)
Spring, 1946 (36 pages)
Fox Feature Syndicate (R. W. Voight)

1-Red Robbins, Merciless the Sorceress app.	6.00	18.00	42.00

ALMANAC OF CRIME (See Fox Giants)

AL OF FBI (See Little Al of the FBI)

ALONG THE FIRING LINE WITH ROGER BEAN
1916 (Hardcover, B&W) (6x17'') (66 pages)
Chas. B. Jackson

3-by Chic Jackson (1915 daily strips)	8.00	24.00	56.00

ALPHA AND OMEGA
1978 (49 cents)
Spire Christian Comics (Fleming H. Revell)

		.30	.60

ALPHA FLIGHT (See X-Men #120,121)
Aug, 1983 - Present (#52-on are direct sale only)
Marvel Comics Group

1-Byrne-a begins (52pgs.)-Wolverine & Nightcrawler cameo		.85	2.50	5.00
2-Vindicator becomes Guardian; origin Marrina & Alpha Flight	.60	1.75	3.50
3-5: 3-Concludes origin Alpha Flight	.50	1.50	3.00
6-11: 6-Origin Shaman. 7-Origin Snowbird. 10,11-Origin Sasquatch	.40	1.25	2.50

	Good	Fine	N-Mint
12-Double size; death of Guardian	.45	1.40	2.80
13-Wolverine app.	.60	1.75	3.50
14-16: 16-Wolverine app.	.25	.75	1.50
17-X-Men x-over; Wolverine cameo	.60	1.75	3.50
18-29: 20-New headquarters. 25-Return of Guardian. 29-Last Bryne issue	.25	.75	1.50
30-33,35-39: 33-X-Men app. 34-Origin Wolverine	.65	1.30	
34-Wolverine app.	.40	1.25	2.50
40-49,51		.65	1.30
50-Double size	.20	.70	1.40
52,53-Wolverine app.	.35	1.00	2.00
54-58		.65	1.30
60-68		.60	1.25
Annual 1 (9/86, $1.25)	.30	.90	1.80
Annual 2(12/87), $1.25)		.65	1.30

NOTE: *Austin* c-1i, 2i, 53i.

ALPHA TRACK
Feb, 1986 - Present (?) ($1.75 cover)
Fantasy General Comics

1,2	.25	.75	1.50

ALPHA WAVE
March, 1987 ($1.75, color, 36 pgs.)
Darkline Comics

1	.25	.75	1.50

ALPHONSE & GASTON & LEON
1903 (15x10'' Sunday strip reprints in color)
Hearst's New York American & Journal

by Fred Opper	27.00	81.00	190.00

ALTER EGO
May, 1986 - No. 4, Nov, 1986 (mini-series)
First Comics

1	.30	.90	1.80
2-4	.20	.70	1.40

ALVIN (TV) (See 4-Color Comics No. 1042)
Oct-Dec, 1962 - No. 28, Oct, 1973
Dell Publishing Co.

12-021-212	3.00	9.00	21.00
2	1.70	5.00	12.00
3-10	1.30	4.00	9.00
11-28	1.00	3.00	6.00
Alvin For President (10/64)	.85	2.50	5.00
...& His Pals in Merry Christmas with Clyde Crashcup & Leonardo 1(02-120-402)-12-2/64, reprinted in 1966 (12-023-604)			
	1.30	4.00	9.00

AMAZING ADULT FANTASY (Amazing Adventures #1-6; Amazing Fantasy #15)
No. 7, Dec, 1961 - No. 14, July, 1962
Marvel Comics Group (AMI)

7: Ditko-a No. 7-14; c-7-13	12.00	36.00	84.00
8-Last 10 cent issue	10.00	30.00	70.00
9-14: 12-1st app. Mailbag. 13-Anti-communist story	8.50	25.50	60.00

AMAZING ADVENTURE FUNNIES (Fantoman No. 2 on)
June, 1940 - No. 2, Sept. 1940
Centaur Publications

1-The Fantom of the Fair by Gustavson (r-/Amaz. Mystery Funnies V2/7, V2/8), The Arrow, Skyrocket Steele From the Year X by Everett (r-/AMF 2); Burgos-a	90.00	270.00	630.00
2-Reprints. Pub. after Fantoman #2	65.00	195.00	455.00

NOTE: *Burgos* a-1(2). *Everett* a-1(3). *Gustavson* a-1(5), 2(3). *Pinajian* a-2.

AMAZING ADVENTURES (Also see Science Comics)
1950 - No. 6, Fall, 1952 (Painted covers)
Ziff-Davis Publ. Co.

	Good	Fine	N-Mint
1950 (no month given) (8½x11'') (8 pgs.) Has the front & back cover plus Schomburg story used in Amazing Advs. #1 (Sent to subscribers of Z-D s/f magazines & ordered through mail for 10 cents. Used to test market) Estimated value....			180.00
1-Wood, Schomburg, Anderson, Whitney-a	28.00	84.00	185.00
2-5-Anderson-a. 3-Starr-a	10.00	30.00	70.00
6-Krigstein-a	14.00	43.00	100.00

AMAZING ADVENTURES (Amazing Adult Fantasy No. 7)
June, 1961 - No. 6, Nov, 1961
Atlas Comics (AMI)/Marvel Comics No. 3 on

1-Origin Dr. Droom (1st Marvel-Age Superhero) by Kirby; Ditko & Kirby-a in all; Kirby c-1-6	21.50	64.00	150.00
2	11.00	32.00	75.00
3-6: Last Dr. Droom	8.00	24.00	56.00

AMAZING ADVENTURES
Aug, 1970 - No. 39, Nov, 1976
Marvel Comics Group

1-Inhumans by Kirby(p) & Black Widow begin; Adams-a(p)	.35	1.50	3.00
2-4: Last Kirby Inhumans	.35	1.00	2.00
5-8-Adams-a; 8-Last Black Widow	.60	1.75	3.50
9,10: 10-Last Inhumans (origin-r by Kirby)	.25	.75	1.50
11-New Beast begins(Origin), ends #17; X-Men cameo	.70	2.00	4.00
12-17	.35	1.00	2.00
18-War of the Worlds begins; 1st app. Killraven; Adams-a(p)	.50	1.50	3.00
19-39: 35-Giffen's first story-art, along with Deadly Hands of Kung-Fu #22 (3/76)		.50	1.00

NOTE: *Adams c-6-8. Buscema a-1p, 2p. Colan a-3-5p, 26p. Ditko a-24r. Everett inks-5, 7-9. Giffen a-35i, 38p. G. Kane c-11, 25p, 29p. Ploog a-12i. Starlin a-17; c-15p, 16, 17, 27. Sutton a-11-15p.*

AMAZING ADVENTURES
December, 1979 - No. 14, January, 1981
Marvel Comics Group

V2#1: r-/X-Men-r. 1,38	.35	1.00	2.00
2-14: 2,4,6-X-Men-r. 7,8-Origin Iceman	.25	.75	1.50

NOTE: *Byrne c-6p, 9p. Kirby a-1-14r; c-7, 9. Steranko a-12r. Tuska a-7-9.*

AMAZING ADVENTURES OF CAPTAIN CARVEL AND HIS CARVEL CRUSADERS, THE (See Carvel Comics)

AMAZING CHAN & THE CHAN CLAN, THE (TV)
May, 1973 - No. 4, Feb, 1974 (Hanna-Barbera)
Gold Key

1	.70	2.00	4.00
2-4	.50	1.50	3.00

AMAZING COMICS (Complete No. 2)
Fall, 1944
Timely Comics (EPC)

1-The Destroyer, The Whizzer, The Young Allies, Sergeant Dix	65.00	195.00	455.00

AMAZING CYNICALMAN, THE
June, 1987 ($1.50, B&W)
Eclipse Comics

1	.25	.75	1.50

AMAZING DETECTIVE CASES (Formerly Suspense No. 2?)
No. 3, Nov, 1950 - No. 14, Sept, 1952
Marvel/Atlas Comics (CCC)

3	5.00	15.00	35.00

	Good	Fine	N-Mint
4-6	2.35	7.00	16.00
7-10	2.00	6.00	14.00
11,14: 11-(3/52)-change to horror	2.35	7.00	16.00
12-Krigstein-a	3.00	9.00	21.00
13-Everett-a; electrocution-c/story	3.50	10.50	25.00

NOTE: *Maneely c-13. Sekowsky a-12. Sinnott a-13. Tuska a-10.*

AMAZING FANTASY (. . .Adult Fantasy No. 7-14)
No. 15, Aug, 1962 (Sept, 1962 shown in indicia)
Marvel Comics Group (AMI)

15-Origin & 1st app. of Spider-Man by Ditko; Kirby/Ditko-c	180.00	720.00	1800.00

AMAZING GHOST STORIES (Formerly Nightmare)
No. 14, Oct, 1954 - No. 16, Feb, 1955
St. John Publishing Co.

14-Pit & the Pendulum story by Kinstler; Baker-c	10.00	30.00	70.00
15-Reprints Weird Thrillers #5; Baker-c, Powell-a	6.50	19.50	45.00
16-Kubert reprints of Weird Thrillers #4; Baker-c; Roussos, Tuska, Kinstler-a	7.00	21.00	50.00

AMAZING HIGH ADVENTURE
8/84; No. 2, 10/85; No. 3, 10/86 - No. 5, 1987 (Baxter No. 3,4)
Marvel Comics

1-5	.35	1.00	2.00

NOTE: *Bissette a-5. Bolton c/a-4, 5. Severin a-1, 3. P. Smith a-2. Williamson a-2i.*

AMAZING-MAN COMICS (Formerly Motion Pic. Funnies Wkly?)
(Also see Stars And Stripes Comics)
No. 5, Sept, 1939 - No. 27, Feb, 1942
Centaur Publications

5(No.1)(Rare)-Origin A-Man the Amazing Man by Bill Everett; The Cat-Man by Tarpe Mills (also No. 8), Mighty Man by Filchock, Minimidget & sidekick Ritty, & The Iron Skull by Burgos begins	570.00	1710.00	3990.00
6-Origin The Amazing Man retold; The Shark begins; Ivy Menace by Tarpe Mills app.	170.00	510.00	1190.00
7-Magician From Mars begins; ends #11	105.00	315.00	735.00
8-Cat-Man dresses as woman	77.00	230.00	540.00
9-Magician From Mars battles the 'Elemental Monster,' swiped into The Spectre in More Fun 54 & 55	75.00	225.00	525.00
10,11: 11-Zardi, the Eternal Man begins; ends #16; Amazing Man dons costume; last Everett issue	65.00	195.00	455.00
12,13	75.00	225.00	525.00
14-Reef Kinkaid, Rocke Wayburn (ends #20), & Dr. Hypno (ends #21) begin; no Zardi or Chuck Hardy	50.00	150.00	350.00
15,17-20: 15-Zardi returns; no Rocke Wayburn. 17-Dr. Hypno returns; no Zardi	35.00	105.00	245.00
16-Mighty Man's powers of super strength & ability to shrink & grow explained; Rocke Wayburn returns; no Dr. Hypno; Al Avison (a character) begins, ends #18 (a tribute to the famed artist)	38.00	115.00	265.00
21-Origin Dash Dartwell (drug-use story); origin & only app. T.N.T.	35.00	105.00	245.00
22-Dash Dartwell, the Human Meteor & The Voice app; last Iron Skull & The Shark; Silver Streak app.	35.00	105.00	245.00
23-Two Amazing Man stories; intro/origin Tommy the Amazing Kid; The Marksman only app.	38.00	115.00	265.00
24,27: 24-King of Darkness, Nightshade, & Blue Lady begin; end #26; 1st App. Super-Ann	35.00	105.00	245.00
25,26 (Scarce)-Meteor Martin by Wolverton in both; 26-Electric Ray app.	72.00	215.00	505.00

NOTE: *Everett a-5-11; c-5-11. Gilman a-14-20. Giunta/Mirando a-7-10. Sam Glanzman a-14-16, 18-21, 23. Louis Glanzman a-6, 9-11, 14-21; c-14-19, 21. Robert Golden a-9. Gustavson a-6; c-22, 23. Lubbers a-14-21. Simon a-10. Frank Thomas a-6, 9-11, 14,*

Amazing Adventures #3, © Z-D

Amazing Fantasy #15, © MEG

Amazing-Man Comics #6, © CEN

Amazing Mystery Comics #21, © CEN

The Amazing Spider-Man #18, © MEG

The Amazing Spider-Man #129, © MEG

AMAZING-MAN COMICS (continued)
15, 17-21.

AMAZING MYSTERIES (Formerly Sub-Mariner No. 31)
No. 32, May, 1949 - No. 35, Jan, 1950
Marvel Comics (CCC)

	Good	Fine	N-Mint
32-The Witness app; 1st Marvel horror comic			
	20.00	60.00	140.00
33-Horror format	6.00	18.00	42.00
34,35-Change to Crime	4.00	12.00	28.00

AMAZING MYSTERY FUNNIES
Aug, 1938 - No. 24, Sept, 1940 (All 52 pgs.)
Centaur Publications

	Good	Fine	N-Mint
V1#1-Everett-c(1st); Dick Kent Adv. story; Skyrocket Steele in the			
Year X on cover only	160.00	480.00	1120.00
2-Everett 1st-a (Skyrocket Steele)	77.00	230.00	540.00
3	46.00	137.00	320.00
3(#4, 12/38)-nn on cover, #3 on inside; bondage-c			
	38.00	115.00	265.00
V2#1-4,6: 2-Drug use story. 3-Air-Sub DX begins by Burgos. 4-Dan			
Hastings, Sand Hog begins (ends #5). 6-Last Skyrocket Steele			
	33.00	100.00	230.00
5-Classic Everett-c	38.00	115.00	265.00
7 (Scarce)-Intro. The Fantom of the Fair; Everett, Gustavson,			
Burgos-a	170.00	510.00	1190.00
8-Origin & 1st app. Speed Centaur	70.00	210.00	490.00
9-11: 11-Self portrait and biog. of Everett; Jon Linton begins			
	38.00	115.00	265.00
12 (Scarce)-Wolverton Space Patrol-a (12/39)			
	92.00	275.00	645.00
V3#1(#17, 1/40)-Intro. Bullet; Tippy Taylor serial begins, ends			
#24 (cont. in The Arrow 2)	38.00	115.00	265.00
18,20	33.00	100.00	230.00
19,21-24-All have Space Patrol by Wolverton			
	65.00	195.00	455.00

NOTE: *Burgos* a-V2#3-9. *Eisner* a-V1#2, 3(2). *Everett* a-V1#2-4, V2#1, 3-6; c-V1#1-4, V2#3, 5, 18. *Filchock* a-V2#9. *Guardineer* a-V1#4, V2#4-6; *Gustavson* a-V2#4, 5, 9-12, V3#1, 19, 20; c-V2#7, 9, 12, V3#1, 21, 22; *McWilliams* a-V2#9, 10. *Tarpe Mills* a-V2#2, 4-6, 9-12, V3#1. *Leo Morey*(Pulp artist) c-V2#10; text illo-V2#11. *Frank Thomas* c-V2/11. *Webster* a-V2#4.

AMAZING SAINTS
1974 (39 cents)
Logos International

True story of Phil Saint	.20	.40

AMAZING SPIDER-MAN, THE (See All Detergent Comics, Amazing Fantasy, America's Best TV Comics, Aurora, Giant Size Super-Heroes Feat. . . ., Marvel Coll. Item Classics, Marvel Fanfare, Marvel Graphic Novel, Marvel Spec. Ed., Marvel Tales, Marvel Team-Up, Marvel Treasury Ed., Official Marvel Index To. . ., Spectacular. . ., Spider-Man Digest, Spider-Man Vs. Wolverine, Spidey Super Stories, Superman Vs. . . ., & Web of Spiderman)

AMAZING SPIDER-MAN, THE
March, 1963 - Present
Marvel Comics Group

	Good	Fine	N-Mint
1-Retells origin by Steve Ditko; F.F. x-over; intro. John Jameson			
& The Chameleon; Kirby-c	150.00	540.00	1500.00
1-Reprint from the Golden Record Comic set	3.50	10.50	25.00
with record	7.00	21.00	50.00
2-Intro the Vulture & the Terrible Tinkerer	64.00	160.00	460.00
3-Human Torch cameo; intro. & 1st app. Doc Octopus			
	38.00	95.00	265.00
4-Origin & 1st app. The Sandman; Intro. Betty Brant & Liz Allen			
	33.00	82.00	230.00
5,6: 5-Dr. Doom app. 6-1st app. Lizard	25.00	63.00	175.00
7-10: 8-Fantastic 4 app. 9-1st app. Electro (origin). 10-1st app.			
Big Man & Enforcers	19.00	47.00	132.00
11-13,15: 11-1st app. Bennett Brant. 13-1st app. Mysterio. 15-Intro.			

	Good	Fine	N-Mint
Kraven the Hunter	12.00	30.00	85.00
14-Intro. Green Goblin; Hulk x-over	14.00	36.00	100.00
16-19: 18-Fant.-4 app; 19-Intro. Ned Leeds	8.00	20.00	55.00
20-Intro & origin The Scorpion	8.00	20.00	55.00
21-30: 22-1st app. Princess Python. 25-1st app. Spencer Smythe.			
26-1st app. Crime Master; dies in #27. 28-Origin/1st app. Molten			
Man	5.15	13.00	36.00
31-38: 31-Intro. Harry Osborn, Gwen Stacy & Prof. Warren. 36-1st			
app. Looter. 37-Intro. Norman Osborn. 38-Last Ditko issue			
	3.50	8.50	24.00
39,40-Green Goblin in both; origin #40	3.00	9.00	21.00
41,43-49: 41-1st app. Rhino. 46-Intro. Shocker	2.15	5.50	15.00
42-1st app. Mary Jane Watson	3.15	8.00	22.00
50-Intro. Kingpin	3.60	9.00	25.00
51-60: 52-Intro. Joe Robertson. 56-Intro. Capt. George Stacy. 57-58-			
Ka-Zar app. 59-Intro. Brainwasher (alias Kingpin)			
	1.15	3.50	8.00
61-80: 67-Intro. Randy Robertson. 73-Intro. Silvermane. 78-Intro.			
Prowler	1.10	3.25	6.50
81-89: 83-Intro. Schemer & Vanessa (Kingpin's wife)			
	1.00	3.00	6.00
90-Death of Capt. Stacey	1.15	3.50	8.00
91-93,95,99: 93-Intro. Arthur Stacy	1.00	3.00	6.00
94-Origin retold	1.30	4.00	9.00
96-98-Drug books not approved by CCA	2.00	5.00	14.00
100-Anniversary issue	2.85	7.00	20.00
101-Intro. Morbius	1.30	4.00	9.00
102-Origin Morbius (52 pgs.)	1.30	4.00	9.00
103-112,115-118: 108-Intro. Sha-Shan. 110-Intro. Gibbon			
	.75	2.25	4.50
113,114,119,120: 113-Intro. Hammerhead	.85	2.50	5.00
121-Death of Gwen Stacy (r-/in Marvel Tales #98)			
	3.50	10.50	24.00
122-Death of Green Goblin	3.50	10.50	24.00
123-128: 124-Intro. Man Wolf, origin-#125.	.70	2.00	4.00
129-1st app. The Punisher	11.00	32.00	75.00
130-133,136-140: 139-Intro. Grizzly. 140-Intro. Glory Grant			
	.60	1.75	3.50
134-Punisher cameo; intro Tarantula	1.20	3.60	8.50
135-Punisher app.	2.00	6.00	14.00
141-160: 143-Intro. Cyclone	.40	1.25	2.50
161-Nightcrawler app. from X-Men; Punisher cameo			
	1.50	4.50	10.00
162-Punisher, Nightcrawler app.	1.50	4.50	10.00
163-173,176-181: 167-1st app. Will O' The Wisp. 171-Nova app.			
177-180-Green Goblin app. 181-Origin retold; gives life history of			
Spider-Man	.35	1.00	2.00
174,175-Punisher app.	1.15	3.50	7.00
182-188	.35	1.00	2.00
189,190-Byrne-a(p)	.40	1.25	2.50
191-193,195-199,204,205,207-219: 196-Faked death of Aunt May.			
210-Intro. & 1st app. Madame Web. 212-Intro. Hydro Man			
	.35	1.00	2.00
194-1st Black Cat	.35	1.00	2.00
200-Giant origin issue	.50	1.50	3.00
201,202-Punisher app.	.85	2.50	5.00
203-2nd Dazzler app.	.35	1.00	2.00
206-Byrne-a(p)	.25	.75	1.50
220-237: 226,227-Black Cat returns. 236-Tarantula dies. 235-			
Origin Will-'O-The-Wisp	.25	.75	1.50
238-1st app. Hobgoblin	1.00	3.00	6.00
239	.50	1.50	3.00
240-251: 241-Origin The Vulture	.25	.75	1.50
252-Spider-Man dons new costume (5/84)	.85	2.50	5.00
253-1st app. The Rose	.50	1.50	3.00
254	.35	1.00	2.00

AMAZING SPIDER-MAN, THE (continued)

	Good	Fine	N-Mint
255-260: 259-Sp-M back to old costume. 261-Hobgoblin app.			
	.25	.75	1.50
261-274,276-283		.60	1.20
275-Origin-r($1.25)	.40	1.25	2.50
284-Punisher cameo app.	.35	1.00	2.00
285-Punisher app.	.70	2.00	4.00
286-288,290-292		.60	1.20
289-Double size, origin Hobgoblin	.60	1.75	3.50
293-Part 2 of Kraven sty. from Web of . . .	.50	1.50	3.00
294-297: 294-Part 5 of Kraven story	.35	1.00	2.00
298-Todd McFarlane-a begins	.70	2.00	4.00
299-McFarlane-a	.40	1.25	2.50
300 ($1.50, 52 pgs.; 25th Anniv.)-Last black costume			
	.60	1.75	3.50
301-305: 301 ($1.00 issues begin). 304-1st bi-weekly ish.			
	.30	.85	1.70
306-318: 306-Cover swipe from Action #1	.20	.70	1.40
Annual 1 (1964)-Origin S-M; Intro. Sinister Six	8.50	25.50	60.00
Annual 2	3.00	9.00	21.00
Special 3,4	1.50	4.50	10.00
Special 5-8 (12/71)	.85	2.50	5.00
King Size 9 ('73)-Green Goblin app.	.50	1.50	3.00
Giant-Size 1(7/74)-Kirby/Ditko-r	.70	2.00	4.00
Giant-Size 2(10/74)	.35	1.00	2.00
Giant-Size 3(1/75), 5(7/75), 6(9/75)	.35	1.00	2.00
Giant-Size 4(4/75)-Punisher app.	1.50	4.50	9.00
Annual 10(6/76)-Old Human Fly app.	.50	1.50	3.00
Annual 11(9/77), 12(8/78)	.50	1.50	3.00
Annual 13(11/79)-Byrne-a	.70	2.00	4.00
Annual 14(12/80)-Miller c/a(p), 40pgs.	.85	2.50	5.00
Annual 15(1981)-Miller c/a(p); Punisher app.	1.15	3.50	7.00
Annual 16(12/82)-Origin/1st app. new Capt. Marvel (female heroine)			
	.35	1.00	2.00
Annual 17(12/83), 18 ('84), 19(11/85)	.35	1.00	2.00
Annual 20(11/86)-Origin Iron Man of 2020	.35	1.00	2.00
Annual 21('87)-Special wedding issue	.60	1.75	3.50
Annual 21-Wedding issue, 2nd cover	.50	1.50	3.00
Annual 22('88, $1.75, 64 pgs.)-Intro/1st app. Speedball; Evolutionary War x-over			
	.50	1.50	3.00
Aim Toothpaste giveaway(36pgs., reg. size)-Green Goblin app.			
	.35	1.00	2.00
Aim Toothpaste giveaway (16pgs., reg. size)-Dr. Octopus app.			
	.50	1.00	
All Detergent Giveaway ('79, 36 pgs.), nn-Origin-r			
	.85	2.50	5.00
Giveaway-Acme & Dingo Children's Boots(1980)-Spider-Woman app.			
	.50	1.00	
. . .& Power Pack ('84, nn)(Nat'l Committee for Prevention of Child Abuse. (two versions, mail offer & store giveaway)-Mooney-a; Byrne-c			
	.30	.60	
. . .& The Hulk (Special Edition)(6/8/80; 20 pgs.; Chicago Tribune giveaway)	.70	2.00	4.00
. . .& The Incredible Hulk (1981, 1982; 36 pgs.), Sanger Harris, Dallas Times, Denver Post, Kansas City Star, The Jones Store-giveaway; 16 pgs. (1983)	1.00	3.00	6.00
. . ., Captain America, The Incredible Hulk, & Spider-Woman ('81) (7-11 Stores giveaway; 36 pgs.)	.30	.60	
Giveaway-Esquire & Eye Magazines(2/69)-Miniature-Still attached			
	4.15	12.50	25.00
. . ., Storm & Powerman ('82) (20 pgs.)(American Cancer Society)-giveaway	.30	.60	
. . .Vs. The Hulk (Special Edition; 1979)(Supplement to Columbus Dispatch)-Giveaway	.50	1.50	3.00
. . .vs. the Prodigy Giveaway, 16 pgs. in color ('76)-5x6½''-Sex education; (1 million printed;35-50 cents)	.25	.50	

NOTE: *Austin a-248i, Annual 13i; c-188i, 241i, 242i, 248i. J. Buscema a(p)-72, 73,*
76-81, 84, 85. *Byrne a-189p, 190p, 206p, Annual 3r, 6r, 7r, 13p, Gnt-Size 1r, 3-5r; c-189p, 268, 296, Annual 12. Ditko a-1-38, Annual 1, 2, Gnt-Size 4r; c-1-38. Gil Kane a(p)-89-105, 120-124, 150, Annual 10, 12i; c-90p, 96, 98, 99, 101-105p, 129p, 131p, 132p, 137-140p, 143p, 148p, 149p, 151p, 153p, 160p, 161p, Annual 10p. Kirby a-8. McFarlane a-298p, 299p, 300-303, 304p-311p; c-298-311. Mooney a-65i, 67-82i, 84-88i, 173i, 178i, 189i, 190i, 192i, 193i, 196-202i, 211-219i, 221i, 226i, 227i, 229-233i, Annual 11i, 17i. Nasser c-228p. Pollard a-193-195p, 197p; c-187, 190. Simonson c-222. Starlin a-187p.*

AMAZING WILLIE MAYS, THE
No date (Sept, 1954)
Famous Funnies Publ.

	Good	Fine	N-Mint
nn	27.00	81.00	190.00

AMAZING WORLD OF SUPERMAN (See Superman)

AMBUSH (See 4-Color Comics No. 314)

AMBUSH BUG (Also see Son of . . .)
June, 1985 - No. 4, Sept, 1985 (mini-series)
DC Comics

1-Giffen c/a begins		.50	1.00
2-4		.40	.80
. . .Stocking Stuffer (2/86, $1.25)-Giffen c/a		.65	1.30

AMERICA IN ACTION
1942; Winter, 1945 (36 pages)
Dell(Imp. Publ. Co.)/Mayflower House Publ.

1942-De!l-(68 pages)	8.00	24.00	56.00
1(1945)-Has 3 adaptations from American history; Kiefer, Schrotter & Webb-a	5.00	15.00	35.00

AMERICA MENACED!
1950 (Paper cover)
Vital Publications

Anti-communism.	estimated value. . . .		150.00

AMERICAN, THE
July, 1987 - Present ($1.75, B&W)
Dark Horse Comics

1	1.00	3.00	6.00
2	.70	2.00	4.00
3-7	.40	1.25	2.50

AMERICAN AIR FORCES, THE (See A-1 Comics)
Sept-Oct, 1944 - 1945; 1951 - 1954
William H. Wise(Flying Cadet Publ. Co./Hasan(No.1)/Life's Romances/Magazine Ent. No. 5 on)

1-Article by Zack Mosley, creator of Smilin' Jack			
	5.50	16.50	38.00
2-4	3.75	11.25	26.00

NOTE: *All part comic, part magazine. Art by Whitney, Chas. Quinlan, H. C. Kiefer, and Tony Dipreta.*

5(A-1 45)(Formerly Jet Powers), 6(A-1 54),7(A-1 58),8(A-1 65) 9(A-1 67),10(A-1 74),11(A-1 79),12(A-1 91)	2.00	6.00	14.00

NOTE: *Powell c/a-5-12.*

AMERICAN COMICS
1940's
Theatre Giveaways (Liberty Theatre, Grand Rapids, Mich. known)

Many possible combinations. "Golden Age" superhero comics with new cover added and given away at theaters. Following known: Superman #59, Capt. Marvel #20, Capt. Marvel Jr. #5, Action #33, Classics Comics #8, Whiz #39. Value would vary with book and should be 70-80 percent of the original.

AMERICAN FLAGG! (Also see First Comics Graphic Novel 3 & 9, and Howard Chaykin's . . .)
Oct, 1983 - No. 50, Mar, 1988
First Comics

1-Chaykin c/a begins	.70	2.00	4.00
2-12	.35	1.00	2.00
13-50: 21-27-Alan Moore scripts. 31-Origin Bob Violence			

The Amazing Spider-Man #298, © MEG

The Amazing Willie Mays, © FF

American Flagg! #1, © First

America's Best Comics #31, © STD

America's Biggest Comics Book #1, © WHW

America's Greatest Comics #8, © FAW

	Good	Fine	N-Mint
AMERICAN FLAGG! (continued)	.25	.75	1.50
Special 1 (11/86)	.35	1.00	2.00

AMERICAN GRAPHICS
No. 1, 1954; No. 2, 1957 (25 cents)
Henry Stewart

	Good	Fine	N-Mint
1-The Maid of the Mist, The Last of the Eries (Indian Legends of Niagara) (Sold at Niagara Falls)	3.50	10.50	24.00
2-Victory at Niagara & Laura Secord (Heroine of the War of 1812)	2.35	7.00	16.50

AMERICAN INDIAN, THE (See Picture Progress)

AMERICAN LIBRARY
1944 (68 pages) (15 cents, B&W, text & pictures)
David McKay Publications

	Good	Fine	N-Mint
3-6: 3-Look to the Mountain. 4-Case of the Crooked Candle (Perry Mason). 5-Duel in the Sun. 6-Wingate's Raiders	6.00	18.00	42.00

NOTE: *Also see Guadalcanal Diary & Thirty Seconds Over Tokyo (part of series?).*

AMERICA'S BEST COMICS
Feb, 1942 - No. 31, July, 1949
Nedor/Better/Standard Publications

	Good	Fine	N-Mint
1-The Woman in Red, Black Terror, Captain Future, Doc Strange, The Liberator, & Don Davis, Secret Ace begin	53.00	160.00	370.00
2-Origin The American Eagle; The Woman in Red ends	27.00	81.00	190.00
3-Pyroman begins	20.00	60.00	140.00
4	18.00	54.00	125.00
5-Last Captain Future-not in #4; Lone Eagle app.	16.00	48.00	110.00
6,7: 6-American Crusader app.	14.00	42.00	100.00
8-Last Liberator	11.00	32.00	76.00
9-The Fighting Yank begins; The Ghost app.	11.00	32.00	76.00
10-14: 10-Flag-c. 14-American Eagle ends	10.00	30.00	70.00
15-20	9.00	27.00	62.00
21-Infinity-c	8.00	24.00	56.00
22-Capt. Future app.	8.00	24.00	56.00
23-Miss Masque begins; last Doc Strange	10.00	30.00	70.00
24-Miss Masque bondage-c	9.00	27.00	62.00
25-Last Fighting Yank; Sea Eagle app.	8.00	24.00	56.00
26-The Phantom Detective & The Silver Knight app.; Frazetta text illo & some panels in Miss Masque	10.00	30.00	70.00
27-31: 27,28-Commando Cubs. 28-Doc Strange. 28-Tuska Bl. Terror.			
29-Last Pyroman	8.00	24.00	56.00

NOTE: *American Eagle not in 3, 8, 9, 13. Fighting Yank not in 10, 12. Liberator not in 2, 6, 7. Pyroman not in 9, 11, 14-16, 23, 25-27. Schomburg (Xela) c-5, 7-31. Bondage c-18, 24.*

AMERICA'S BEST TV COMICS (TV)
1967 (Produced by Marvel Comics) (68 pgs. 25 cents)
American Broadcasting Company

	Good	Fine	N-Mint
1-Spider-Man, Fantastic Four, Casper, King Kong, George of the Jungle, Journey to the Center of the Earth app. (Promotes new TV cartoon show)	1.50	4.50	10.00

AMERICA'S BIGGEST COMICS BOOK
1944 (196 pages) (One Shot)
William H. Wise

	Good	Fine	N-Mint
1-The Grim Reaper, The Silver Knight, Zudo, the Jungle Boy, Commando Cubs, Thunderhoof app.	20.00	60.00	140.00

AMERICA'S FUNNIEST COMICS
1944 (80 pages) (15 cents)
William H. Wise

	Good	Fine	N-Mint
nn(#1), 2	9.00	27.00	62.00

AMERICA'S GREATEST COMICS
5?/1941 - No. 8, Summer, 1943 (100 pgs.) (Soft cardboard covers)
Fawcett Publications

	Good	Fine	N-Mint
1-Bulletman, Spy Smasher, Capt. Marvel, Minute Man & Mr. Scarlet begin; Mac Raboy-c	115.00	345.00	800.00
2	57.00	170.00	400.00
3	38.00	115.00	265.00
4-Commando Yank begins; Golden Arrow, Ibis the Invincible & Spy Smasher cameo in Captain Marvel	32.00	95.00	225.00
5	32.00	95.00	225.00
6	25.00	75.00	175.00
7-Balbo the Boy Magician app.; Captain Marvel, Bulletman cameo in Mr. Scarlet	25.00	75.00	175.00
8-Capt. Marvel Jr. & Golden Arrow app.; Spy Smasher x-over in Capt. Midnight; no Minute Man or Commando Yank	25.00	75.00	175.00

AMERICA'S SWEETHEART SUNNY (See Sunny)

AMERICA VS. THE JUSTICE SOCIETY
Jan, 1985 - No. 4, Apr, 1985 (mini-series)
DC Comics

	Good	Fine	N-Mint
1-Double size; Alcala-a in all	.30	.90	1.80
2-4		.60	1.20

AMERICOMICS
April, 1983 - No. 6, Mar, 1984 (Baxter paper; color)
Americomics

	Good	Fine	N-Mint
1-Intro/origin The Shade; The Slayer, Captain Freedom and The Liberty Corps intro. Perez-c	.40	1.25	2.50
2-6: 2-Messenger, & Tara on Jungle Island app. 3-New & old Blue Beetle battle. 4-Origin Dragonfly & Shade. 6-Origin the Scarlet Scorpion.	.40	1.25	2.50
Special 1(8/83, $2.00)-Sentinels of Justice (Blue Beetle, Captain Atom, Nightshade, & the Question)	.40	1.25	2.50

AMETHYST
Jan, 1985 - No. 16, Aug, 1986
DC Comics

	Good	Fine	N-Mint
1-16: 8-Fire Jade's i.d. revealed		.50	1.00
Special 1 (10/86)		.65	1.30

AMETHYST
Nov, 1987 - No. 4, Feb, 1988 ($1.25, color, mini-series)
DC Comics

	Good	Fine	N-Mint
1-4	.25	.75	1.50

AMETHYST, PRINCESS OF GEMWORLD
May, 1983 - No. 12, May, 1984 (12 issue maxi-series)
DC Comics

	Good	Fine	N-Mint
1-60 cent cover	.25	.75	1.50
1-35 cent-tested in Austin & Kansas City	1.35	4.00	8.00
2-35 cent-tested in Austin & Kansas City	1.00	3.00	6.00
2-12: Perez-c(p) #6-11		.50	1.00
Annual 1(9/84)		.65	1.30

ANARCHO DICTATOR OF DEATH (See Comics Novel)

ANCHORS ANDREWS (The Saltwater Daffy)
Jan, 1953 - No. 4, July, 1953 (Anchors the Saltwater. . . No. 4)
St. John Publishing Co.

	Good	Fine	N-Mint
1-Canteen Kate by Matt Baker, 9 pgs.	7.00	21.00	50.00
2-4	2.00	6.00	14.00

ANDY & WOODY (See March of Comics No. 40,55,76)

ANDY BURNETT (See 4-Color Comics No. 865)

ANDY COMICS (Formerly Scream Comics; becomes Ernie Comics)
No. 20, June, 1948 - No. 21, Aug, 1948
Current Publications (Ace Magazines)

ANDY COMICS (continued)	Good	Fine	N-Mint
20,21-Archie-type comic	2.00	6.00	14.00

ANDY DEVINE WESTERN
Dec, 1950 - No. 10, 1952
Fawcett Publications

	Good	Fine	N-Mint
1	20.00	60.00	140.00
2	12.00	36.00	84.00

ANDY GRIFFITH SHOW, THE (See 4-Color No. 1252,1341)

ANDY HARDY COMICS (See Movie Comics No. 3, Fiction House)
April, 1952 - No. 6, Sept-Nov, 1954
Dell Publishing Co.

4-Color 389	1.70	5.00	12.00
4-Color 447,480,515,5,6	1.15	3.50	8.00
. . .& the New Automatic Gas Clothes Dryer ('52, 16 pgs., 5x7¼'') Bendix Giveaway (soft-c)	2.00	6.00	14.00

ANDY PANDA (Also see Crackajack Funnies #39, The Funnies, New Funnies & Walter Lantz . . .)
1943 - Nov-Jan, 1961-62 (Walter Lantz)
Dell Publishing Co.

4-Color 25('43)	23.50	70.00	165.00
4-Color 54('44)	14.00	42.00	98.00
4-Color 85('45)	9.00	27.00	62.00
4-Color 130('46),154,198	4.50	13.50	32.00
4-Color 216,240,258,280,297	2.65	8.00	18.00
4-Color 326,345,358	1.70	5.00	12.00
4-Color 383,409	1.15	3.50	8.00
16(11-1/52-53) - 30	.70	2.10	5.00
31-56	.55	1.80	4.00

(See March of Comics No. 5,22,79, & Super Book No. 4,15,27.)

ANGEL
Aug, 1954 - No. 16, Nov-Jan, 1958-59
Dell Publishing Co.

4-Color 576(8/54)	1.00	3.00	7.00
2(5-7/55) - 16	.55	1.80	4.00

ANGEL AND THE APE (Meet Angel No. 7) (See Limited Collector's Edition C-34 & Showcase No. 77)
Nov-Dec, 1968 - No. 6, Sept-Oct, 1969
National Periodical Publications

1-Not Wood-a	.70	2.00	4.00
2-6-Wood inks in all	.50	1.50	3.00

ANGELIC ANGELINA
1909 (11½x17''; 30 pgs.; 2 colors)
Cupples & Leon Company

By Munson Paddock	12.00	36.00	84.00

ANGEL LOVE
Aug, 1986 - No. 8, Mar, 1987 (mini-series)
DC Comics

1-8		.40	.80
Special 1		.60	1.20

ANGEL OF LIGHT, THE (See The Crusaders)

ANIMAL ADVENTURES
Dec, 1953 - No. 3, Apr?, 1954
Timor Publications/Accepted Publications (reprints)

1	1.50	4.50	10.00
2,3	.85	2.50	6.00
1-3 (reprints, nd)	.70	2.10	5.00

ANIMAL ANTICS (Movie Town . . . No. 24 on)
Mar-Apr, 1946 - No. 23, Nov-Dec, 1949
National Periodical Publications

1-Raccoon Kids begins by Otto Feur; some-c by Grossman

	Good	Fine	N-Mint
	20.00	60.00	140.00
2	9.00	27.00	62.00
3-10	6.00	18.00	42.00
11-23	3.70	11.00	26.00

NOTE: **Post** a-10,14,15,19; c-10.

ANIMAL COMICS
Dec-Jan, 1941-42 - No. 30, Dec-Jan, 1947-48
Dell Publishing Co.

1-1st Pogo app. by Walt Kelly (Dan Noonan art in most issues)

	83.00	250.00	580.00
2-Uncle Wiggily begins	34.00	100.00	235.00
3,5	23.00	70.00	160.00
4,6,7-No Pogo	13.00	40.00	90.00
8-10	16.00	48.00	110.00
11-15	10.00	30.00	70.00
16-20	6.50	20.00	45.00
21-30: 25-30-''Jigger'' by John Stanley	4.60	14.00	32.00

NOTE: **Dan Noonan** a-18-30. **Gollub** art in most later issues.

ANIMAL CRACKERS (Also see Advs. of Patoruzu)
1946; No. 31, July, 1950; 1959
Green Publ. Co./Norlen/Fox Feat.(Hero Books)

1-Super Cat begins	4.50	13.50	32.00
2	2.15	6.50	15.00
3-10 (Exist?)	1.15	3.50	8.00
31(Fox)-Formerly My Love Secret	2.30	7.00	16.00
9(1959-Norlen)	.70	2.00	5.00
nn, nd ('50s), no publ.; infinity-c	.70	2.00	5.00

ANIMAL FABLES
July-Aug, 1946 - No. 7, Nov-Dec, 1947
E. C. Comics(Fables Publ. Co.)

1-Freddy Firefly (clone of Human Torch), Korky Kangaroo, Petey Pig, Danny Demon begin	22.00	65.00	154.00
2-Aesop Fables begins	13.00	40.00	90.00
3-6	11.00	33.00	77.00
7-Origin Moon Girl	38.00	115.00	265.00

ANIMAL FAIR (Fawcett's . . .)
March, 1946 - No. 11, Feb, 1947
Fawcett Publications

1	7.00	21.00	50.00
2	3.50	10.50	25.00
3-6	2.65	8.00	18.00
7-11	2.00	6.00	14.00

ANIMAL FUN
1953
Premier Magazines

1-(3-D)	20.00	60.00	140.00

ANIMAL MAN
Sept., 1988 - Present ($1.25, color)
DC Comics

1-8: Bolland c-1-6		.60	1.25

ANIMAL WORLD, THE (See 4-Color Comics No. 713)

ANIMATED COMICS
No date given (Summer, 1947?)
E. C. Comics

1 (Rare)	55.00	165.00	385.00

ANIMATED FUNNY COMIC TUNES (See Funny Tunes)

ANIMATED MOVIE-TUNES (Movie Tunes No. 3)
Fall, 1945 - No. 2, Sum, 1946
Margood Publishing Corp. (Timely)

1,2-Super Rabbit, Ziggy Pig & Silly Seal	6.50	19.50	45.00

Animal Comics #16, © DELL

Animal Man #2, © DC

Animated Movie-Tunes #1, © MEG

20

Annie Oakley #1, © MEG

Anthro #1, © DC

A-1 Comics #22, © ME

ANIMAX
Dec, 1986 - No. 4, June, 1987
Star Comics (Marvel)

	Good	Fine	N-Mint
1-4: Based on toys		.40	.80

ANNETTE (See 4-Color Comics No. 905)

ANNETTE'S LIFE STORY (See 4-Color No. 1100)

ANNIE
Oct, 1982 - No. 2, Nov, 1982
Marvel Comics Group

1,2-Movie adaptation		.25	.50
Treasury Edition (Tabloid size)	.35	1.00	2.00

ANNIE OAKLEY (Also see Tessie The Typist #19, Two-Gun Kid & Wild Western)
Spring, 1948 - No. 4, 11/48; No. 5, 6/55 - No. 11, 6/56
Marvel/Atlas Comics(MPI No. 1-4/CDS No. 5 on)

	Good	Fine	N-Mint
1 (1st Series, '48)-Hedy Devine app.	13.50	40.00	95.00
2 (7/48, 52 pgs.)-Kurtzman-a, "Hey Look," 1pg; Intro. Lana; Hedy Devine app; Captain Tootsie by Beck	10.00	30.00	70.00
3,4	7.50	22.50	52.00
5 (2nd Series)(1955)	5.00	15.00	35.00
6-8: 8-Woodbridge-a	3.70	11.00	26.00
9-Williamson-a, 4 pgs.	4.00	12.00	28.00
10,11: 11-Severin-c	3.00	9.00	21.00

ANNIE OAKLEY AND TAGG (TV)
1953 - No. 18, Jan-Mar, 1959; July, 1965 (all photo-c)
Dell Publishing Co./Gold Key

4-Color 438	6.00	18.00	42.00
4-Color 481,575	4.50	13.50	32.00
4(7-9/55)-10	3.50	10.50	24.50
11-18(1-3/59)	3.00	9.00	21.00
1(7/65-Gold Key)-Photo-c	2.65	8.00	18.00

NOTE: *Manning* a-13. Photo back c-4, 9, 11.

ANOTHER WORLD (See Strange Stories From . . .)

ANTHRO (See Showcase)
July-Aug, 1968 - No. 6, July-Aug, 1969
National Periodical Publications

1-Howie Post-a in all	1.00	3.00	7.00
2-6: 6-Wood c/a inks	.70	2.00	4.00

ANTONY AND CLEOPATRA (See Ideal, a Classical Comic)

ANYTHING GOES
Oct, 1986 - No. 6, 1987 (mini-series)(Adults, $2.00)
Fantagraphics Books   (#1-4: color & B&W; #5,6: B&W)

1-Flaming Carrot app. (1st in color?)	.60	1.75	3.50
2-6: 2-Alan Moore scripts. 3-Capt. Jack, Cerebus app. 5-TMNT app.	.35	1.00	2.00

A-1 COMICS (A-1 appears on covers No. 1-17 only)(See individual title listings. 1st two issues not numbered.)
1944 - No. 139, Sept-Oct, 1955
Life's Romances Publ.-No. 1/Compix/Magazine Ent.

nn-Kerry Drake, Johnny Devildog, Rocky, Streamer Kelly (Slightly large size)	12.00	36.00	84.00
1-Dotty Dripple(1 pg.), Mr. Ex, Bush Berry, Rocky, Lew Loyal (20 pgs.)	4.35	13.00	30.00
2-8,10-Texas Slim & Dirty Dalton, The Corsair, Teddy Rich, Dotty Dripple, Inca Dinca, Tommy Tinker, Little Mexico & Tugboat Tim, The Masquerader & others	2.00	6.00	14.00
9-Texas Slim (all)	2.00	6.00	14.00
11-Teena	2.30	7.00	16.00
12,15-Teena	1.70	5.00	12.00
13-Guns of Fact & Fiction (1948). Used in **SOTI**, pg. 19; narcotics,			

	Good	Fine	N-Mint
junkie mentioned; Ingels & J. Craig-a	12.00	36.00	84.00
14-Tim Holt Western Adventures #1 (1948)	32.00	95.00	225.00
16-Vacation Comics	1.30	4.00	9.00
17-Tim Holt #2. Last issue to carry A-1 on cover (9-10/48)	20.00	60.00	140.00
18-Jimmy Durante-Photo-c	10.00	30.00	70.00
19-Tim Holt #3	13.50	40.00	95.00
20-Jimmy Durante-Photo-c	10.00	30.00	70.00
21-Joan of Arc(1949)-Movie adapt.; Ingrid Bergman photo-cvrs & interior photos; Whitney-a	11.00	32.00	75.00
22-Dick Powell(1949)	7.00	21.00	50.00
23-Cowboys 'N' Indians #6	2.70	7.00	16.00
24-Trail Colt #1-Frazetta, r-in Manhunt #13; Ingels-c; L. B. Cole-a	26.00	78.00	180.00
25-Fibber McGee & Molly(1949) (Radio)	3.50	10.50	24.00
26-Trail Colt #2-Ingels-c	20.00	60.00	140.00
27-Ghost Rider #1(1950)-Origin G.R.	33.00	100.00	230.00
28-Christmas-(Koko & Kola #6)(5/47)	1.30	4.00	9.00
29-Ghost Rider #2-Frazetta-c (1950)	35.00	105.00	245.00
30-Jet Powers #1-Powell-a	14.00	42.00	100.00
31-Ghost Rider #3-Frazetta-c & origin ('51)	35.00	105.00	245.00
32-Jet Powers #2	10.00	30.00	70.00
33-Muggsy Mouse #1('51)	2.00	6.00	14.00
34-Ghost Rider #4-Frazetta-c (1951)	35.00	105.00	245.00
35-Jet Powers #3-Williamson/Evans-a	19.00	57.00	132.00
36-Muggsy Mouse #2; Racist-c	4.00	12.00	28.00
37-Ghost Rider #5-Frazetta-c (1951)	35.00	105.00	245.00
38-Jet Powers #4-Williamson & Wood-a	19.00	57.00	132.00
39-Muggsy Mouse #3	1.00	3.00	7.00
40-Dogface Dooley #1('51)	2.00	6.00	14.00
41-Cowboys 'N' Indians #7	1.70	5.00	12.00
42-Best of the West #1-Powell-a	19.00	57.00	132.00
43-Dogface Dooley #2	1.30	4.00	9.00
44-Ghost Rider #6	11.00	32.00	75.00
45-American Air Forces #5-Powell-c/a	2.00	6.00	14.00
46-Best of the West #2	10.00	30.00	70.00
47-Thun'da, King of the Congo #1-Frazetta-c/a('52)	97.00	290.00	680.00
48-Cowboys 'N' Indians #8	1.70	5.00	12.00
49-Dogface Dooley #3	1.30	4.00	9.00
50-Danger Is Their Business #11 (1952)-Powell-a	4.30	13.00	30.00
51-Ghost Rider #7 ('52)	11.00	32.00	75.00
52-Best of the West #3	8.50	25.50	60.00
53-Dogface Dooley #4	1.30	4.00	9.00
54-American Air Forces #6(8/52)-Powell-a	2.00	6.00	14.00
55-U.S. Marines #5-Powell-a	2.35	7.00	16.00
56-Thun'da #2-Powell-c/a	12.00	36.00	84.00
57-Ghost Rider #8	9.50	28.50	65.00
58-American Air Forces #7-Powell-a	2.00	6.00	14.00
59-Best of the West #4	8.50	25.50	60.00
60-The U.S. Marines #6-Powell-a	2.35	7.00	16.00
61-Space Ace #5(1953)-Guardineer-a	15.00	45.00	105.00
62-Starr Flagg, Undercover Girl #5 (#1)	18.00	54.00	125.00
63-Manhunt #13-Frazetta reprinted from A-1 #24	17.00	51.00	120.00
64-Dogface Dooley #5	1.30	4.00	9.00
65-American Air Forces #8-Powell-a	2.00	6.00	14.00
66-Best of the West #5	8.50	25.50	60.00
67-American Air Forces #9-Powell-a	2.00	6.00	14.00
68-U.S. Marines #7-Powell-a	2.35	7.00	16.00
69-Ghost Rider #9(10/52)	9.50	28.50	65.00
70-Best of the West #4	6.00	18.00	42.00
71-Ghost Rider #10(12/52)	9.50	28.50	65.00
72-U.S. Marines #7-Powell-a(3)	2.35	7.00	16.00
73-Thun'da #3-Powell-c/a	9.00	27.00	62.00

	Good	Fine	N-Mint
74-American Air Forces #10-Powell-a	2.00	6.00	14.00
75-Ghost Rider #11(3/52)	7.00	21.00	50.00
76-Best of the West #7	6.00	18.00	42.00
77-Manhunt #14	11.00	32.00	75.00
78-Thun'da #4-Powell-c/a	9.00	27.00	62.00
79-American Air Forces #11-Powell-a	2.00	6.00	14.00
80-Ghost Rider #12(6/52)	7.00	21.00	50.00
81-Best of the West #8	6.00	18.00	42.00
82-Cave Girl #11(1953)-Powell-c/a; origin (#1)	20.00	60.00	140.00
83-Thun'da #5-Powell-c/a	8.00	24.00	56.00
84-Ghost Rider #13(8/53)	7.00	21.00	50.00
85-Best of the West #9	6.00	18.00	42.00
86-Thun'da #6-Powell-c/a	8.00	24.00	56.00
87-Best of the West #10	6.00	18.00	42.00
88-Bobby Benson's B-Bar-B Riders #20	3.50	10.50	24.00
89-Home Run #3-Powell-a; Stan Musial photo-c			
	6.00	18.00	42.00
90-Red Hawk #11(1953)-Powell-c/a	4.00	12.00	28.00
91-American Air Forces #12-Powell-a	2.00	6.00	14.00
92-Dream Book of Romance #5-photo-c; Guardineer-a			
	2.30	7.00	16.00
93-Great Western #8('54)-Origin The Ghost Rider; Powell-a			
	8.50	25.50	60.00
94-White Indian #11-Frazetta-a(r)	18.00	54.00	126.00
95-Muggsy Mouse #4	1.00	3.00	7.00
96-Cave Girl #12, with Thun'da; Powell-c/a	14.00	42.00	100.00
97-Best of the West #11	6.00	18.00	42.00
98-Undercover Girl #6-Powell-c	15.00	45.00	105.00
99-Muggsy Mouse #5	1.00	3.00	7.00
100-Badmen of the West #1-Meskin-a(?)	10.00	30.00	70.00
101-White Indian #12-Frazetta-a(r)	18.00	54.00	126.00
101-Dream Book of Romance #6 (4-6/54); Marlon Brando photo-c; Powell, Bolle, Guardineer-a	5.70	17.00	40.00
103-Best of the West #12-Powell-a	6.00	18.00	42.00
104-White Indian #13-Frazetta-a(r)('54)	18.00	54.00	126.00
105-Great Western #9-Ghost Rider app.; Powell-a, 6 pgs.; Bolle-c	4.30	13.00	30.00
106-Dream Book of Love #1 (6-7/54)-Powell, Bolle-a; Montgomery Clift, Donna Reed photo-c	3.50	10.50	24.00
107-Hot Dog #1	2.30	7.00	16.00
108-Red Fox #15 (1954)-L.B. Cole c/a; Powell-a			
	8.00	24.00	56.00
109-Dream Book of Romance #7 (7-8/54). Powell-a; photo-c			
	2.30	7.00	16.00
110-Dream Book of Romance #8 (10/54)	2.30	7.00	16.00
111-I'm a Cop #1 ('54); drug mention story; Powell-a			
	5.00	15.00	35.00
112-Ghost Rider #14 ('54)	7.00	21.00	50.00
113-Great Western #10; Powell-a	4.30	13.00	30.00
114-Dream Book of Love #2-Guardineer, Bolle-a; Peter Lorre, Victor Mature photo-c	2.30	7.00	16.00
115-Hot Dog #3	1.30	4.00	9.00
116-Cave Girl #13-Powell-c/a	14.00	42.00	100.00
117-White Indian #14	6.50	19.50	45.00
118-Undercover Girl #7-Powell-c	15.00	45.00	105.00
119-Straight Arrow's Fury #1 (origin)	5.00	15.00	35.00
120-Badmen of the West #2	6.00	18.00	42.00
121-Mysteries of Scotland Yard #1; r-from Manhunt			
	5.00	15.00	35.00
122-Black Phantom #1(11/54)	14.00	42.00	100.00
123-Dream Book of Love #3(10-11/54)	2.30	7.00	16.00
124-Dream Book of Romance #8(10-11/54)	2.30	7.00	16.00
125-Cave Girl #14-Powell-c	14.00	42.00	100.00
126-I'm a Cop #2-Powell-a	2.65	8.00	18.00
127-Great Western #11('54)-Powell-a	4.30	13.00	30.00
128-I'm a Cop #3-Powell-a	2.65	8.00	18.00

	Good	Fine	N-Mint
129-The Avenger #1('55)-Powell-c	14.00	42.00	100.00
130-Strongman #1-Powell-a	8.50	25.50	60.00
131-The Avenger #2('55)-Powell-c/a	7.00	21.00	50.00
132-Strongman #2	7.00	21.00	50.00
133-The Avenger #3-Powell-c/a	7.00	21.00	50.00
134-Strongman #3	7.00	21.00	50.00
135-White Indian #15	6.50	19.50	45.00
136-Hot Dog #4	1.30	4.00	9.00
137-Africa #1-Powell-c/a(4)	11.00	32.00	75.00
138-The Avenger #4-Powell-a	7.00	21.00	50.00
139-Strongman #4-Powell-a	7.00	21.00	50.00

NOTE: *Bolle* a-110. Photo-c-110.

APACHE
1951
Fiction House Magazines

	Good	Fine	N-Mint
1-Baker-c	7.00	21.00	50.00
I.W. Reprint No. 1	.70	2.00	4.00

APACHE HUNTER
1954 (18 pgs. in color) (promo copy) (saddle stitched)
Creative Pictorials

Severin, Heath stories	13.00	39.00	90.00

APACHE KID (Formerly Reno Browne; Western Gunfighters #20 on)
(Also see Two-Gun Western & Wild Western)
No. 53, 12/50 - No. 10, 1/52; No. 11, 12/54 - No. 19, 4/56
Marvel/Atlas Comics(MPC No. 53-10/CPS No. 11 on)

	Good	Fine	N-Mint
53(#1)-A. Kid & his horse Nightwind (origin), Red Hawkins by Syd Shores begins	7.00	21.00	50.00
2(2/51)	4.00	12.00	28.00
3-5	2.65	8.00	18.00
6-10 (1951-52)	2.00	6.00	14.00
11-19 (1954-56)	1.70	5.00	12.00

NOTE: *Heath* c-11, 13. *Maneely* a-53; c-53(#1), 12,14-16. *Powell* a-14. *Severin* c-17.

APACHE MASSACRE (See Chief Victorio's . . .)

APACHE TRAIL
Sept, 1957 - No. 4, June, 1958
Steinway/America's Best

1	3.00	9.00	21.00
2-4: 2-Tuska-a	1.50	4.50	10.00

APPLESEED
Sept, 1988 - Present (B&W, $2.50, 52pgs)
Eclipse Comics

1,2	.40	1.25	2.50

APPROVED COMICS
March, 1954 - No. 12, Aug, 1954 (All painted-c)
St. John Publishing Co. (Most have no c-price)

1-The Hawk No. 5-r	3.50	10.50	24.00
2-Invisible Boy-r(3/54)-Origin; Saunders-c	6.50	19.50	45.00
3-Wild Boy of the Congo #11-r(4/54)	3.50	10.50	24.00
4-Kid Cowboy-r	3.50	10.50	24.00
5-Fly Boy-r	3.50	10.50	24.00
6-Daring Adv.-r(5/54); Krigstein-a(2); Baker-c	5.00	15.00	35.00
7-The Hawk #6-r	3.50	10.50	24.00
8-Crime on the Run; Powell-a; Saunders-c	3.50	10.50	24.00
9-Western Bandit Trails #3-r, with new-c; Baker c/a	4.50	13.50	32.00
11-Fightin' Marines #3-r; Kanteen Kate app; Baker-c/a	5.00	15.00	35.00
12-North West Mounties #4-r(8/54); new Baker-c	5.00	15.00	35.00

AQUAMAN (See Showcase, Brave & the Bold, Super DC Giant, Adventure, DC Super-Stars No. 7, Detective, DC Comics Presents No. 5, DC Special Series No. 1, DC

A-1 Comics #119, © ME

Apache Kid #16, © MEG

Approved Comics #5, © STJ

Aquaman #2 (4/62), © DC

Archie And Me #5, © AP

Archie Comics #37, © AP

AQUAMAN (continued)
Special No. 28, and World's Finest)

AQUAMAN
Jan-Feb, 1962 - No. 56, Mar-Apr, 1971; No. 57, Aug-Sept,
1977 - No. 63, Aug-Sept, 1978
National Periodical Publications/DC Comics

	Good	Fine	N-Mint
1-Intro. Quisp	11.50	34.00	80.00
2	5.00	15.00	35.00
3-5	3.50	11.00	25.00
6-10	2.65	8.00	18.00
11-20: 11-Intro. Mera. 18-Aquaman weds Mera; JLA cameo			
	1.50	4.50	10.00
21-30: 23-Birth of Aquababy. 26-Huntress app.(3-4/66). 29-Intro.			
Ocean Master, Aquaman's step-brother	1.00	3.00	6.00
31,32,34-40	1.00	3.00	6.00
33-Intro. Aqua-Girl	1.15	3.50	7.00
41-47,49	.70	2.00	4.00
48-Origin reprinted	.70	2.00	4.00
50-52-Adams Deadman	1.30	4.00	9.00
53-56('71): 56-Intro Crusader	.40	1.25	2.50
57('77)-63: 58-Origin retold	.25	.75	1.50

NOTE: *Aparo* a-40-59; c-57-60, 63. *Newton* a-60-63.

AQUAMAN
Feb, 1986 - No. 4, May, 1986 (mini-series)
DC Comics

1-New costume	.85	2.50	5.00
2-4	.50	1.50	3.00
Special 1 ('88, $1.50, 52 pgs.)	.35	1.00	2.00

AQUANAUTS (See 4-Color No. 1197)

ARABIAN NIGHTS (See Cinema Comics Herald)

ARAK/SON OF THUNDER (See Warlord #48)
Sept, 1981 - No. 50, Nov, 1985
DC Comics

1-Origin; 1st app. Angelica, Princess of White Cathay			
		.50	1.00
2-50: 3-Intro Valda, The Iron Maiden. 12-Origin Valda. 20-Origin			
Angelica. 24-$1.00 size. 50-double size		.50	1.00
Annual 1(10/84)		.45	.90

ARCHIE AND BIG ETHEL
1982 (69 cents)
Spire Christian Comics (Fleming H. Revell Co.)

		.30	.60

ARCHIE AND ME (See Archie Gnt. Series Mag. 578)
Oct, 1964 - No. 162, 1987
Archie Publications

1	7.00	21.00	50.00
2	3.50	10.50	24.00
3-5	2.00	6.00	14.00
6-10	1.00	3.00	6.00
11-20	.40	1.20	2.40
21-42: 26-X-Mas-c		.60	1.20
43-63-(All Giants)		.60	1.20
64-162-(Regular size)		.30	.60

ARCHIE AND MR. WEATHERBEE
1980 (59–)
Spire Christian Comics (Fleming H. Revell Co.)

nn		.30	.60

ARCHIE...ARCHIE ANDREWS, WHERE ARE YOU? (...Comics
Digest No. 9, 10; ...Comics Digest Mag. No. 11 on)
Feb, 1977 - Present (Digest size, 160-128 pages)
Archie Publications

	Good	Fine	N-Mint
1	.30	.80	1.60
2,3,5,7-9-Adams-a; 8-r-/origin The Fly by S&K. 9-Steel Sterling-r			
	.35	1.00	2.00
4,6,10-60 ($1.00-$1.35): 17-Katy Keene sty		.50	1.00

ARCHIE AS PUREHEART THE POWERFUL
Sept, 1966 - No. 6, Nov, 1967
Archie Publications (Radio Comics)

1	3.50	10.50	24.00
2	2.00	6.00	14.00
3-6	1.15	3.50	8.00

NOTE: *Evilheart cameos in all. Title:* ...As Capt. Pureheart the Powerful-No. 4,6;
...As Capt. Pureheart-No. 5.

ARCHIE AT RIVERDALE HIGH (See Archie Gnt. Ser. Mag. 573,586)
Aug., 1972 - No. 114, 1987
Archie Publications

1	2.50	7.50	15.00
2	1.15	3.50	7.00
3-5	.50	1.50	3.00
6-10	.25	.75	1.50
11-30		.50	1.00
31-114: 96-Anti-smoking issue		.30	.60

ARCHIE COMICS (Archie No. 158 on)(See Christmas & Archie,
Everything's..., Jackpot, Oxydol-Dreft, and Pep)
(First Teen-age comic)(Radio show 1st aired 6/2/45, by NBC)
Winter, 1942-43 - No. 19, 3-4/46; No. 20, 5-6/46 - Present
MLJ Magazines No. 1-19/Archie Publ.No. 20 on

1 (Scarce)-Jughead, Veronica app.	265.00	795.00	1855.00
2	100.00	300.00	700.00
3 (60 pgs.)	72.00	215.00	505.00
4,5	50.00	150.00	350.00
6-10	35.00	105.00	245.00
11-20: 15,17,18-Dotty & Ditto by Woggon	22.00	65.00	154.00
21-30: 23-Betty & Veronica by Woggon	15.00	45.00	105.00
31-40	10.00	30.00	70.00
41-50	7.00	21.00	50.00
51-70 (1954): 65-70-Katy Keene app.	4.00	12.00	28.00
71-99: 72-74-Katy Keene app.	2.35	7.00	16.00
100	3.00	9.00	18.00
101-130 (1962)	1.15	3.50	8.00
131-160	.70	2.00	4.00
161-200	.35	1.00	2.00
201-240		.50	1.00
241-282		.30	.60
283-Cover/story plugs ''International Children's Appeal'' which was			
a fraudulent charity, according to TV's 20/20 news program			
broadcast July 20, 1979.		.60	1.25
284-364: 300-Anniversary issue		.25	.50
Annual 1('50)-116 pgs.(Scarce)	72.00	215.00	505.00
Annual 2('51)	38.00	115.00	265.00
Annual 3('52)	20.00	60.00	140.00
Annual 4,5(1953-54)	15.00	45.00	105.00
Annual 6-10(1955-59)	8.00	24.00	56.00
Annual 11-15(1960-65)	3.50	10.50	24.00
Annual 16-20(1966-70)	1.15	3.50	7.00
Annual 21-26(1971-75)	.45	1.25	2.50
Annual Digest 27('75)-53('83-'88)(...Magazine #35 on)			
		.50	1.00
...All-Star Specials(Winter '75)-$1.25; 6 remaindered Archie comics			
rebound in each; titles: ''The World of Giant Comics,'' ''Giant			
Grab Bag of Comics,'' ''Triple Giant Comics,'' and ''Giant Spec.			
Comics''	.50	1.50	3.00
Mini-Comics (1970-Fairmont Potato Chips Giveaway-Miniature)(8			
issues-nn's., 8 pgs. each)	1.00	3.00	6.00
Official Boy Scout Outfitter(1946)-9½x6½'', 16 pgs., B. R. Baker Co.			

ARCHIE COMICS (continued)	Good	Fine	N-Mint
(Scarce)	20.00	60.00	140.00
Shoe Store giveaway (1948, Feb?)	6.00	18.00	42.00

ARCHIE COMICS DIGEST (. . . Magazine No. 37 on)
Aug, 1973 - Present (Small size, 160-128 pages)
Archie Publications

1	2.50	7.50	15.00
2	1.35	4.00	8.00
3-5	.70	2.00	4.00
6-10	.25	.75	1.50
11-33: 32,33-The Fly-r by S&K		.50	1.00
34-95: 36-Katy Keene story		.30	.60

NOTE: *Adams* a-1,2,4,5,19-21,24,25,27,29,31,33.

ARCHIE GETS A JOB
1977
Spire Christian Comics (Fleming H. Revell Co.)

		.30	.60

ARCHIE GIANT SERIES MAGAZINE
1954 - Present (No No. 36-135, no No. 252-451)
Archie Publications

	Good	Fine	N-Mint
1-Archie's Christmas Stocking	45.00	135.00	315.00
2-Archie's Christmas Stocking('55)	22.00	65.00	154.00
3-5-Archie's Christmas Stocking('56-'58)	15.00	45.00	105.00
6-Archie's Christmas Stocking('59)	15.00	45.00	105.00
7-Katy Keene Holiday Fun(9/60)	12.00	36.00	84.00
8-Betty & Veronica Summer Fun (10/60)			
9-The World of Jughead (12/60)			
10-Archie's Christmas Stocking (1/61)			
each....	10.00	30.00	70.00
11-Betty & Veronica Spectacular (6/61)	7.00	21.00	50.00
12-Katy Keene Holiday Fun (9/61)	7.00	21.00	50.00
13-Betty & Veronica Summer Fun (10/61)			
14-The World of Jughead (12/61)			
15-Archie's Christmas Stocking (1/62)			
16-Betty & Veronica Spectacular (6/62)			
17-Archie's Jokes (9/62); Katy Keene app.			
18-Betty & Veronica Summer Fun (10/62)			
19-The World of Jughead (12/62)			
20-Archie's Christmas Stocking (1/63)			
each....	6.00	18.00	42.00
21-Betty & Veronica Spectacular (6/63)			
22-Archie's Jokes (9/63)			
23-Betty & Veronica Summer Fun (10/63)			
24-The World of Jughead (12/63)			
25-Archie's Christmas Stocking (1/64)			
26-Betty & Veronica Spectacular (6/64)			
27-Archie's Jokes (8/64)			
28-Betty & Veronica Summer Fun (9/64)			
29-Around the World with Archie (10/64)			
30-The World of Jughead (12/64)			
each....	4.00	12.00	24.00
31-Archie's Christmas Stocking (1/65)			
32-Betty & Veronica Spectacular (6/65)			
33-Archie's Jokes (8/65)			
34-Betty & Veronica Summer Fun (9/65)			
35-Around the World with Archie (10/65)			
136-The World of Jughead (12/65)			
137-Archie's Christmas Stocking (1/66)			
138-Betty & Veronica Spectacular (6/66)			
139-Archie's Jokes (6/66)			
140-Betty & Veronica Summer Fun (8/66)			
141-Around the World with Archie (9/66)			
each....	2.65	8.00	16.00
142-Archie's Super-Hero Special (10/66)-Origin Capt. Pureheart, Capt. Hero, and Evilheart	2.35	7.00	14.00

143-The World of Jughead (12/66)
144-Archie's Christmas Stocking (1/67)
145-Betty & Veronica Spectacular (6/67)
146-Archie's Jokes (6/67)
147-Betty & Veronica Summer Fun (8/67)
148-World of Archie (9/67)
149-World of Jughead (10/67)
150-Archie's Christmas Stocking (1/68)
151-World of Archie (2/68)
152-World of Jughead (2/68)
153-Betty & Veronica Spectacular (6/68)
154-Archie Jokes (6/68)
155-Betty & Veronica Summer Fun (8/68)
156-World of Archie (10/68)
157-World of Jughead (12/68)
158-Archie's Christmas Stocking (1/69)
159-Betty & Veronica Christmas Spect. (1/69)

160-World of Archie (2/69)	Good	Fine	N-Mint
each....	1.35	4.00	8.00

161-World of Archie (2/69)
162-Betty & Veronica Spectacular (6/69)
163-Archie's Jokes (8/69)
164-Betty & Veronica Summer Fun (9/69)
165-World of Archie (9/69)
166-World of Jughead (9/69)
167-Archie's Christmas Stocking (1/70)
168-Betty & Veronica Christmas Spect. (1/70)
169-Archie's Christmas Love-In (1/70)
170-Jughead's Eat-Out Comic Book Mag. (12/69)
171-World of Archie (2/70)
172-World of Jughead (2/70)
173-Betty & Veronica Spectacular (6/70)
174-Archie's Jokes (8/70)
175-Betty & Veronica Summer Fun (9/70)
176-Li'l Jinx Giant Laugh-Out (8/70)
177-World of Archie (9/70)
178-World of Jughead (9/70)
179-Archie's Christmas Stocking (1/71)
180-Betty & Veronica Christmas Spect. (1/71)
181-Archie's Christmas Love-In (1/71)
182-World of Archie (2/71)
183-World of Jughead (2/71)
184-Betty & Veronica Spectacular (6/71)
185-Li'l Jinx Giant Laugh-Out (6/71)
186-Archie's Jokes (8/71)
187-Betty & Veronica Summer Fun (9/71)
188-World of Archie (9/71)
189-World of Jughead (9/71)
190-Archie's Christmas Stocking (12/71)
191-Betty & Veronica Christmas Spect. (2/72)
192-Archie's Christmas Love-In (1/72)
193-World of Archie (3/72)
194-World of Jughead (4/72)
195-Li'l Jinx Christmas Bag (1/72)
196-Sabrina's Christmas Magic (1/72)
197-Betty & Veronica Spectacular (6/72)
198-Archie's Jokes (8/72)
199-Betty & Veronica Summer Fun (9/72)

200-World of Archie (10/72)			
each....	.50	1.50	3.00

201-World of Archie (10/72)
202-World of Jughead (11/72)
203-Archie's Christmas Stocking (12/72)
204-Betty & Veronica Christmas Spect. (2/73)
205-Archie's Christmas Love-In (1/73)
206-Li'l Jinx Christmas Bag (12/72)
207-Sabrina's Christmas Magic (12/72)

Archie Annual #5, © AP

Archie Giant Series Magazine #1, © AP

Archie Giant Series Magazine #19, © AP

ARCHIE GIANT SERIES (continued)
208-World of Archie (3/73)
209-World of Jughead (4/73)
210-Betty & Veronica Spectacular (6/73)
211-Archie's Jokes (8/73)
212-Betty & Veronica Summer Fun (9/73)
213-World of Archie (10/73)
214-Betty & Veronica Spectacular (10/73)
215-World of Jughead (11/73)
216-Archie's Christmas Stocking (12/73)
217-Betty & Veronica Christmas Spect. (2/74)
218-Archie's Christmas Love-In (1/74)
219-Li'l Jinx Christmas Bag (12/73)
220-Sabrina's Christmas Magic (12/73)
221-Betty & Veronica Spectacular (Advertised as World of Archie)
   (6/74)
222-Archie's Jokes (Advertised as World of Jughead)(8/74)
223-Li'l Jinx (8/74)
224-Betty & Veronica Summer Fun (9/74)
225-World of Archie (9/74)
226-Betty & Veronica Spectacular (10/74)
227-World of Jughead (10/74)
228-Archie's Christmas Stocking (12/74)
229-Betty & Veronica Christmas Spect. (12/74)
230-Archie's Christmas Love-In (1/75)
231-Sabrina's Christmas Magic (1/75)
232-World of Archie (3/75)
233-World of Jughead (4/75)
234-Betty & Veronica Spectacular (6/75)
235-Archie's Jokes (8/75)
236-Betty & Veronica Summer Fun (9/75)
237-World of Archie (9/75)
238-Betty & Veronica Spectacular (10/75)
239-World of Jughead (10/75)
240-Archie's Christmas Stocking (12/75)
241-Betty & Veronica Christmas Spectacular (12/75)
242-Archie's Christmas Love-In (1/76)
243-Sabrina's Christmas Magic (1/76)
244-World of Archie (3/76)
245-World of Jughead (4/76)
246-Betty & Veronica Spectacular (6/76)
247-Archie's Jokes (8/76)
248-Betty & Veronica Summer Fun (9/76)
249-World of Archie (9/76)
250-Betty & Veronica Spectacular (10/76)

		Good	Fine	N-Mint
251-World of Jughead (10/76)				
each....			.60	1.20

452-Archie's Christmas Stocking (12/76)
453-Betty & Veronica Christmas Spect. (12/76)
454-Archie's Christmas Love-In (1/77)
455-Sabrina's Christmas Magic (1/77)
456-World of Archie (3/77)
457-World of Jughead (4/77)
458-Betty & Veronica Spectacular (6/77)
459-Archie's Jokes (8/77)-Shows 8/76 in error
460-Betty & Veronica Summer Fun (9/77)
461-World of Archie (9/77)
462-Betty & Veronica Spectacular (10/77)
463-World of Jughead (10/77)
464-Archie's Christmas Stocking (12/77)
465-Betty & Veronica Christmas Spectacular (12/77)
466-Archie's Christmas Love-In (1/78)
467-Sabrina's Christmas Magic (1/78)
468-World of Archie (2/78)
469-World of Jughead (2/78)
470-Betty & Veronica Spectacular (6/78)
471-Archie's Jokes (8/78)
472-Betty & Veronica Summer Fun (9/78)
473-World of Archie (9/78)
474-Betty & Veronica Spectacular (10/78)
475-World of Jughead (10/78)
476-Archie's Christmas Stocking (12/78)
477-Betty & Veronica Christmas Spectacular (12/78)
478-Archie's Christmas Love-In (1/79)
479-Sabrina Christmas Magic (1/79)
480-The World of Archie (3/79)
481-World of Jughead (4/79)
482-Betty & Veronica Spectacular (6/79)
483-Archie's Jokes (8/79)
484-Betty & Veronica Summer Fun (9/79)
485-The World of Archie (9/79)
486-Betty & Veronica Spectacular (10/79)
487-The World of Jughead (10/79)
488-Archie's Christmas Stocking (12/79)
489-Betty & Veronica Christmas Spect. (1/80)
490-Archie's Christmas Love-in (1/80)
491-Sabrina's Christmas Magic (1/80)
492-The World of Archie (2/80)
493-The World of Jughead (4/80)
494-Betty & Veronica Spectacular (6/80)

495-Archie's Jokes (8/80)
496-Betty & Veronica Summer Fun (9/80)
497-The World of Archie (9/80)
498-Betty & Veronica Spectacular (10/80)
499-The World of Jughead (10/80)
500-Archie's Christmas Stocking (12/80)
501-Betty & Veronica Christmas Spect. (12/80)
502-Archie's Christmas Love-in (1/81)
503-Sabrina Christmas Magic (1/81)
504-The World of Archie (3/81)
505-The World of Jughead (4/81)
506-Betty & Veronica Spectacular (6/81)
507-Archie's Jokes (8/81)
508-Betty & Veronica Summer Fun (9/81)
509-The World of Archie (9/81)
510-Betty & Vernonica Spectacular (9/81)
511-The World of Jughead (10/81)
512-Archie's Christmas Stocking (12/81)
513-Betty & Veronica Christmas Spectacular (12/81)
514-Archie's Christmas Love-in (1/82)
515-Sabrina's Christmas Magic (1/82)
516-The World of Archie (3/82)
517-The World of Jughead (4/82)
518-Betty & Veronica Spectacular (6/82)
519-Archie's Jokes (8/82)
520-Betty & Veronica Summer Fun (9/82)
521-The World of Archie (9/82)
522-Betty & Veronica Spectacular (10/82)
523-The World of Jughead (10/82)
524-Archie's Christmas Stocking (1/83)
525-Betty and Veronica Christmas Spectacular (1/83)
526-Betty and Veronica Spectacular (5/83)
527-Little Archie (8/83)
528-Josie and the Pussycats (8/83)
529-Betty and Veronica Summer Fun (8/83)
530-Betty and Veronica Spectacular (9/83)
531-The World of Jughead (9/83)
532-The World of Archie (10/83)
533-Space Pirates by Frank Bolling (10/83)
534-Little Archie (1/84)
535-Archie's Christmas Stocking (1/84)
536-Betty and Veronica Christmas Spectacular (1/84)
537-Betty and Veronica Spectacular (6/84)
538-Little Archie (8/84)
539-Betty and Veronica Summer Fun 8/84)
540-Josie and the Pussycats (8/84)
541-Betty and Veronica Spectacular (9/84)
542-The World of Jughead (9/84)
543-The World of Archie (10/84)
544-Sabrina the Teen-Age Witch (10/84)
545-Little Archie (12/84)
546-Archie's Christmas Stocking (12/84)
547-Betty and Veronica Christmas Spectacular (12/84)
548-
549-Little Archie
550-Betty and Veronica Summer Fun
551-Josie and the Pussycats
552-Betty and Veronica Spectacular
553-The World of Jughead
554-The World of Archie
555-Betty's Diary
556-Little Archie (1/86)
557-Archie's Christmas Stocking (1/86)
558-Betty & Veronica Christmas Spectacular (1/86)
559-Betty & Veronica Spectacular
560-
561-Betty & Veronica Summer Fun
562-Josie and the Pussycats
563-Betty & Veronica Spectacular
564-World of Jughead
565-World of Archie
566-Little Archie
567-Archie's Christmas Stocking
568-Betty & Veronica Christmas Spectacular
569-Betty & Veronica Spring Spectacular
570-Little Archie
571-Josie & The Pussycats
572-Betty & Veronica Summer Fun
573-Archie At Riverdale High
574-World of Archie
575-Betty & Veronica Spectacular
576-Pep
577-World of Jughead
578-Archie And Me
579-Archie's Christmas Stocking
580-Betty and Veronica Christmas Spectacular
581-Little Archie Christmas Special
582-Betty & Veronica Spring Spectacular
583-Little Archie
584-Josie and The Pussycats

ARCHIE GIANT SERIES (continued)
585-Betty & Veronica Summer Fun
586-Archie At Riverdale High
587-The World of Archie (10/88)
588-Betty & Veronica Spectacular
589-Pep (10/88)
590-The World of Jughead
591-Archie & Me
592-Archie's Christmas Stocking

	Good	Fine	N-Mint
593-Betty & Veronica Christmas Spectacular each....		.40	.80

ARCHIE'S ACTIVITY COMICS DIGEST MAGAZINE
1985 (Annual, 128 pgs.; digest size)
Archie Enterprises

1-4		.50	1.00

ARCHIE'S CAR
1979 (49-)
Spire Christian Comics (Fleming H. Revell Co.)

nn		.30	.60

ARCHIE'S CHRISTMAS LOVE-IN (See Archie Giant Series Mag. No. 169, 181, 192, 205, 218, 230, 242, 454, 466, 478, 490, 502, 514)
ARCHIE'S CHRISTMAS STOCKING (See Archie Giant Series Mag. No. 1-6, 10, 15, 20, 25, 31, 137, 144, 150, 158, 167, 179, 190, 203, 216, 228, 240, 452, 464, 476, 488, 500, 512, 524, 535, 546, 557, 567)

ARCHIE'S CLEAN SLATE
1973 (35-49 cents)
Spire Christian Comics (Fleming H. Revell Co.)

1(Some issues have nn)	.35	1.00	2.00

ARCHIE'S DATE BOOK
1981
Spire Christian Comics (Fleming H. Revell Co.)

		.30	.60

ARCHIE'S DOUBLE DIGEST QUARTERLY MAGAZINE
1981 - Present ($1.95-$2.25, 256pgs.) (A.D.D. Magazine No. 10 on)
Archie Comics

1-40: 6-Katy Keene sty	.35	1.10	2.25

ARCHIE'S FAMILY ALBUM
1978 (36 pages) (39 cents)
Spire Christian Comics (Fleming H. Revell Co.)

		.30	.60

ARCHIE'S FESTIVAL
1980 (49 cents)
Spire Christian Comics (Fleming H. Revell Co.)

		.30	.60

ARCHIE'S GIRLS, BETTY AND VERONICA (Becomes Betty & Veronica)
1950 - No. 347, 1987
Archie Publications (Close-Up)

1	60.00	180.00	420.00
2	30.00	90.00	210.00
3-5	17.00	51.00	120.00
6-10: 10-2pg. Katy Keene app.	13.00	40.00	90.00
11-20: 11,13,14,17-19-Katy Keene app. 20-Debbie's Diary, 2pgs.	8.00	24.00	56.00
21-30: 27-Katy Keene app.	6.50	19.50	45.00
31-50	5.00	15.00	35.00
51-74	3.00	9.00	21.00
75-Betty & Veronica sell soul to devil	6.00	18.00	42.00
76-99	1.70	5.00	12.00
100	2.30	7.00	16.00
101-140: 118-Origin Superteen. 119-Last Superteen story	.85	2.50	5.00

	Good	Fine	N-Mint
141-180	.35	1.00	2.00
181-220		.50	1.00
221-347: 300-Anniversary issue		.30	.60
Annual 1 (1953)	35.00	105.00	245.00
Annual 2(1954)	16.00	48.00	110.00
Annual 3-5 ('55-'57)	12.00	36.00	84.00
Annual 6-8 ('58-'60)	8.00	24.00	56.00

ARCHIE SHOE-STORE GIVEAWAY
1944-49 (12-15 pgs. of games, puzzles, stories like Superman-Tim books, No nos. - came out monthly)
Archie Publications

(1944-47)-issues	9.00	27.00	62.00
2/48-Peggy Lee photo-c	6.00	18.00	42.00
3/48-Marylee Robb photo-c	6.00	18.00	42.00
4/48-Gloria De Haven photo-c	6.00	18.00	42.00
5/48,6/48,7/48	6.00	18.00	42.00
8/48-Story on Shirley Temple	6.00	18.00	42.00
10/48-Archie as Wolf on cover	6.00	18.00	42.00
5/49-Kathleen Hughes photo-c	4.50	13.50	32.00
7/49	4.50	13.50	32.00
8/49-Archie photo-c from radio show	6.00	18.00	42.00
10/49-Gloria Mann photo-c from radio show	5.50	16.50	38.00
11/49,12/49	4.50	13.50	32.00

ARCHIE'S JOKEBOOK COMICS DIGEST ANNUAL (See Jokebook...)
ARCHIE'S JOKE BOOK MAGAZINE (See Joke Book...)
1953 - No. 3, Sum, 1954; No. 15, Fall, 1954 - No. 288, 11/82
Archie Publications

1953-One Shot (#1)	40.00	120.00	280.00
2	22.00	65.00	154.00
3 (nn.4-14)	14.50	44.00	100.00
15-20: 15-17-Katy Keene app.	10.00	30.00	70.00
21-30	7.00	21.00	50.00
31-40,42,43	3.50	10.50	25.00
41-1st professional comic work by Neal Adams ('59), 1 pg.	11.50	34.00	80.00
44-47-Adams-a in all, 1-2 pgs.	6.00	18.00	42.00
48-Four pgs. Adams-a	6.00	18.00	42.00
49-60 (1962)	2.00	6.00	12.00
61-80	1.15	3.50	7.00
81-100	.60	1.75	3.50
101-140	.25	.75	1.50
141-200		.40	.80
201-288		.25	.50
Drug Store Giveaway (No. 39 w/new-c)	2.00	6.00	12.00

ARCHIE'S JOKES (See Archie Giant Series Mag. No. 17, 22, 27, 33, 139, 146, 154, 163, 174, 186, 198, 211, 222, 235, 247, 459, 471, 483, 495, 519)
ARCHIE'S LOVE SCENE
1973 (35-49 cents)
Spire Christian Comics (Fleming H. Revell Co.)

1(Some issues have nn)	.35	1.00	2.00

ARCHIE'S MADHOUSE (Madhouse Ma-ad No. 67 on)
Sept, 1959 - No. 66, Feb, 1969
Archie Publications

1-Archie begins	14.50	44.00	100.00
2	7.00	21.00	50.00
3-5	5.00	15.00	35.00
6-10	3.75	11.25	26.00
11-16 (Last w/regular characters)	2.65	8.00	18.00
17-21,23-30 (New format)	1.00	3.00	6.00
22-1st app. Sabrina, the Teen-age Witch (10/62)	3.50	10.50	24.00
31-40	.25	.75	1.50
41-66: 43-Mighty Crusaders cameo		.40	.80

Archie's Girls, Betty And Veronica Annual #2, © AP

Archie's Joke Book #24, © AP

Archie's Madhouse #22, © AP

Archie's Mechanics #1, © AP

Archie's Rival Reggie #6, © AP

Area 88 #1, © Eclipse

ARCHIE'S MADHOUSE (continued)	Good	Fine	N-Mint
Annual 1 (1962-63)	2.65	8.00	18.00
Annual 2 (1964)	1.20	3.50	7.00
Annual 3 (1965)-Origin Sabrina The Teen-Age Witch			
	.70	2.00	4.00
Annual 4-6('66-69)(Becomes Madhouse Ma-ad Annual No. 7 on)			
	.35	1.00	2.00

NOTE: *Cover title to 61-65 is "Madhouse" and to 66 is "Madhouse Ma-ad Jokes."*

ARCHIE'S MECHANICS
Sept, 1954 - 1955
Archie Publications

	Good	Fine	N-Mint
1-(15 cents; 52 pgs.)	57.00	170.00	400.00
2-(10 cents)	32.00	95.00	225.00
3-(10 cents)	28.00	85.00	195.00

ARCHIE'S ONE WAY
1972 (35 cents, 39 cents, 49 cents) (36 pages)
Spire Christian Comics (Fleming H. Revell Co.)

nn	.35	1.00	2.00

ARCHIE'S PAL, JUGHEAD (Jughead No. 122 on)
1949 - No. 126, Nov, 1965
Archie Publications

1	58.00	175.00	405.00
2	28.00	84.00	195.00
3-5	17.00	51.00	120.00
6-10: 7-Suzie app.	11.00	32.00	75.00
11-20	8.00	24.00	56.00
21-30: 23-25,28-30-Katy Keene app. 28-Debbie's Diary app.			
	5.00	15.00	35.00
31-50	3.00	9.00	21.00
51-70	2.35	7.00	16.00
71-100	1.35	4.00	8.00
101-126	.85	2.50	5.00
Annual 1 (1953)	25.00	75.00	175.00
Annual 2 (1954)	15.00	45.00	105.00
Annual 3-5 (1955-57)	10.00	30.00	70.00
Annual 6-8 (1958-60)	7.00	21.00	50.00

ARCHIE'S PALS 'N' GALS
1952-53 - No. 6, 1957-58; No. 7, 1958 - Present
Archie Publications

1-(116 pages)	32.00	95.00	225.00
2(Annual)('53-'54)	17.00	51.00	120.00
3-5(Annual, '54-57)	11.00	32.00	75.00
6-10('58-'60)	6.00	18.00	42.00
11-20	3.00	9.00	21.00
21-40: 29-Beatle satire	1.50	4.50	10.50
41-60	.75	2.25	4.50
61-80	.35	1.10	2.20
81-110		.60	1.20
111-205		.35	.70

ARCHIE'S PARABLES
1973, 1975 (36 pages, 39-49 cents)
Spire Christian Comics (Fleming H. Revell Co.)

By Al Hartley	.40	.80

ARCHIE'S RIVAL REGGIE (Reggie No. 15 on)
1950 - No. 14, Aug, 1954
Archie Publications

1	44.00	132.00	310.00
2	22.00	65.00	154.00
3-5	14.50	44.00	100.00
6-10	9.00	27.00	62.00
11-14: Katy Keene in No. 10-14, 1-2pgs.	7.00	21.00	50.00

ARCHIE'S ROLLER COASTER
1981 (69 cents)
Spire Christian Comics (Fleming H. Revell Co.)

	Good	Fine	N-Mint
nn		.40	.80

ARCHIE'S SOMETHING ELSE
1975 (36 pages, 39-49 cents)
Spire Christian Comics (Fleming H. Revell Co.)

nn		.40	.80

ARCHIE'S SONSHINE
1973, 1974 (36 pages, 39-49 cents)
Spire Christian Comics (Fleming H. Revell Co.)

nn	.35	1.00	2.00

ARCHIE'S SPORTS SCENE
1983
Spire Christian Comics (Fleming H. Revell Co.)

nn		.40	.80

ARCHIE'S STORY & GAME COMICS DIGEST MAGAZINE
Nov, 1986 - Present (Digest size, $1.25, $1.35, 128 pgs.)
Archie Enterprises

1-10		.70	1.35

ARCHIE'S SUPER HERO SPECIAL (See Archie Giant Series Magazine No. 142)

ARCHIE'S SUPER HERO SPECIAL (...Comics Digest Mag. 2)
Jan, 1979 - No. 2, Aug, 1979 (148 pages, 95 cents)
Archie Publications (Red Circle)

1-Simon & Kirby r-/Double Life of Pvt. Strong No. 1,2; Black Hood, The Fly, Jaguar, The Web app.	.40	.80
2-Contains contents to the never published Black Hood No. 1; origin Black Hood; Adams, Wood, McWilliams, Morrow, S&K(r)-a; Adams-c. The Shield, The Fly, Jaguar, Hangman, Steel Sterling, The Web, The Fox-r	.40	.80

ARCHIE'S TV LAUGH-OUT
Dec, 1969 - No. 106, 1986
Archie Publications

1	3.50	10.50	24.00
2	1.50	4.50	9.00
3-5	.70	2.00	4.00
6-10	.25	.75	1.50
11-20		.40	.80
21-106		.25	.50

ARCHIE'S WORLD
1973, 1976 (39-49 cents)
Spire Christian Comics (Fleming H. Revell Co.)

		.40	.80

AREA 88
May 26, 1987 - Present ($1.50-$1.75, B&W)
Eclipse Comics/VIZ Comics #37 on

1	.70	2.10	4.25
1-2nd print	.35	1.00	2.00
2-5	.40	1.25	2.50
2-2nd print	.25	.75	1.50
6-10	.30	1.00	2.00
11-37	.25	.75	1.50

ARION, LORD OF ATLANTIS (Also see Warlord #55)
Nov, 1982 - No. 36, Oct, 1985
DC Comics

1-36-Story cont'd from Warlord 62	.50	1.00
Special #1 (11/85)	.50	1.00

ARISTOCATS (See Movie Comics & Walt Disney Showcase No. 16)

ARISTOCRATIC X-TRATERRESTRIAL TIME-TRAVELING THIEVES
Aug., 1986 - Present ($1.75, B&W)
Fictioneer Books, Ltd.

	Good	Fine	N-Mint
1-One shot	.50	1.50	3.00
1-2nd print (12/86)	.30	.90	1.80
1-Begin new series (2/87)	.35	1.00	2.00
2-10	.30	.90	1.80

ARISTOKITTENS, THE (. . . Meet Jiminy Cricket No. 1)(Disney)
Oct, 1971 - No. 9, Oct, 1975 (No. 6: 52 pages)
Gold Key

1	1.00	3.00	6.00
2-9	.50	1.50	3.00

ARIZONA KID, THE (Also see The Comics & Wild Western)
March, 1951 - No. 6, Jan, 1952
Marvel/Atlas Comics(CSI)

1	6.00	18.00	42.00
2-4: 2-Heath-a(3)	3.50	10.50	24.00
5,6	3.00	9.00	21.00
NOTE: *Heath a-1-3; c-1-3. Maneely c-4-6. Morisi a-4-6.*

ARK, THE (See The Crusaders)

ARMAGEDDON FACTOR, THE
1987 - Present ($1.95, color)
AC Comics

1-3: Sentinels of Justice, Dragonfly	.35	1.00	2.00

ARMOR (AND THE SILVER STREAK; see Revengers Feat. . . .)
Sept, 1985 - Present ($2.00, color)
Continuity Comics

1-Intro. The Silver Streak; Adams c/a	.50	1.50	3.00
2-5	.35	1.00	2.00

ARMY AND NAVY COMICS (Supersnipe No. 6 on)
May, 1941 - No. 5, July, 1942
Street & Smith Publications

1-Cap Fury & Nick Carter	20.00	60.00	140.00
2-Cap Fury & Nick Carter	10.00	30.00	70.00
3,4	7.00	21.00	50.00
5-Supersnipe app.; see Shadow V2#3 for 1st app. Story of Douglas MacArthur	19.00	57.00	132.00

ARMY ATTACK
July, 1964 - No. 47, Feb, 1967
Charlton Comics

V1#1	.35	1.00	2.00
2-4(2/65)		.50	1.00
V2#38(7/65)-47 (formerly U.S. Air Force #1-37)		.50	1.00
NOTE: *Glanzman a-1-3. Montes/Bache a-44.*

ARMY AT WAR (Also see Our Army at War, Cancelled Comic Cavalcade)
Oct-Nov, 1978
DC Comics

1-Kubert-c		.30	.60

ARMY SURPLUS KOMIKZ FEATURING CUTEY BUNNY (Cutey Bunny No. 5 on)
1982 - No. 4 ($1.50, B&W)
Army Surplus Komikz/Eclipse Comics

1-Cutey Bunny begins	2.50	7.50	15.00
2-4	1.35	4.00	8.00

ARMY WAR HEROES (Also see Iron Corporal)
Dec, 1963 - No. 38, June, 1970
Charlton Comics

1	.50	1.50	3.00
2-20		.50	1.00

	Good	Fine	N-Mint
21-38: 22-Origin & 1st app. Iron Corporal series by Glanzman.			
24-Intro. Archer & Corp. Jack series		.40	.80
Modern Comics Reprint 36 ('78) | | .30 | .60 |
NOTE: *Montes/Bache a-1,16,17,21,23-25,27-30.*

AROUND THE BLOCK WITH DUNC & LOO (See Dunc and Loo)

AROUND THE WORLD IN 80 DAYS (See 4-Color Comics No. 784 and A Golden Picture Classic)

AROUND THE WORLD UNDER THE SEA (See Movie Classics)

AROUND THE WORLD WITH ARCHIE (See Archie Giant Series Mag. No. 29, 35, 141)

AROUND THE WORLD WITH HUCKLEBERRY & HIS FRIENDS (See Dell Giant No. 44)

ARRGH! (Satire)
Dec, 1974 - No. 5, Sept, 1975
Marvel Comics Group

1		.40	.80
2-5		.25	.50
NOTE: *Alcala a-2; c-3. Everett a-1r, 2r. Maneely a-4r. Sekowsky a-1p. Sutton a-1.*

ARROW, THE (See Funny Pages)
Oct, 1940 - No. 2, Nov, 1940; No. 3, Oct, 1941
Centaur Publications

1-The Arrow begins(r/Funny Pages)	85.00	255.00	600.00
2-Tippy Taylor serial cont's/Amaz. Myst. Funnies 24	50.00	150.00	350.00
3-Origin Dash Dartwell, the Human Meteor; origin The Rainbow-r; bondage-c	50.00	150.00	350.00
NOTE: *Gustavson a-1,2; c-3.*

ARROWHEAD (See Black Rider, Wild Western)
April, 1954 - No. 4, Nov, 1954
Atlas Comics (CPS)

1-Arrowhead & his horse Eagle begin	4.30	13.00	30.00
2-4	2.65	8.00	18.00
NOTE: *Forte a-4. Heath c-3. Jack Katz a-3. Maneely c-2. Pakula a-2. Sinnott a-1-4; c-1.*

ASSASSINS, INC.
1987 - No. 2, 1987 ($1.95, color)
Silverline comics

1,2	.30	.95	1.90

ASTONISHING (Marvel Boy No. 1,2)
No. 3, April, 1951 - No. 63, Aug, 1957
Marvel/Atlas Comics(20CC)

3-Marvel Boy cont'd.	25.00	75.00	175.00
4-6-Last Marvel Boy; 4-Stan Lee app.	20.00	60.00	140.00
7-10	5.00	15.00	35.00
11,12,15,17,20	4.00	12.00	28.00
13,14,16,19-Krigstein-a	4.30	13.00	30.00
18-Jack The Ripper story	4.50	13.50	32.00
21,22,24	3.50	10.50	24.00
23-E.C. swipe-'The Hole In The Wall' from VOH 16	4.30	13.00	30.00
25-Crandall-a	4.30	13.00	30.00
26-29	3.00	9.00	21.00
30-Tentacled eyeball story	5.00	15.00	35.00
31-37-Last pre-code issue	2.65	8.00	18.00
38-43,46,48-52,56,58,59,61	1.70	5.00	12.00
44-Crandall swipe/Weird Fantasy 22	3.00	9.00	21.00
45,47-Krigstein-a	3.00	9.00	21.00
53-Crandall, Ditko-a	2.30	7.00	16.00
54-Torres-a	2.30	7.00	16.00
55-Crandall, Torres-a	3.00	9.00	21.00
57-Williamson/Krenkel-a, 4 pgs.	4.50	13.50	32.00
60-Williamson/Mayo-a, 4 pgs.	4.50	13.50	32.00

Army And Navy #5, © S & S

The Arrow #1, © CEN

Astonishing #57, © MEG

Astonishing Tales #25, © MEG

The Atom #2, © DC

Atom-Age Combat #4, © STJ

	Good	Fine	N-Mint
ASTONISHING (continued)			
62-Torres, Powell -a	2.00	6.00	14.00
63-Last issue; Woodbridge-a	2.00	6.00	14.00

NOTE: *Berg a-36, 53, 56. Cameron a-50. Gene Colan a-12, 20, 29, 56. Ditko a-50, 53. Drucker a-41, 62. Everett a-3-5(3), 6, 10, 12, 37, 47, 48, 58, 61; c-3-5, 13, 15, 16, 18, 29, 47, 49, 51, 53-55, 57, 59-63. Fass a-11, 34. Forte a-53, 58. Fuje a-11. Heath c/a-8; c-9, 26. Kirby a-56. Lawrence a-28, 37, 38, 42. Maneely c-31, 33, 34, 56. Moldoff a-33. Morisi a-107 Morrow a-52, 61. Orlando a-47, 58, 61. Powell a-43, 44, 48. Ravielli a-28. Reinman a-34. Robinson a-20. J. Romita a-7, 18, 24, 43, 57, 61. Roussos a-55. Sale a-59. Sekowsky a-13. Severin c-46. Sinnott a-11, 30. Ed Win a-20.* Canadian reprints exist.

ASTONISHING TALES (See Ka-Zar)
Aug, 1970 - No. 36, July, 1976
Marvel Comics Group

1-Ka-Zar by Kirby(p) & Dr. Doom by Wood begin	.40	1.25	2.50
2-Kirby, Wood-a	.25	.75	1.50
3-6: Smith-a(p); Wood-a#3,4. 5-Red Skull app.	.50	1.50	3.00
7-9: 8-Last Dr. Doom. (52 pgs.)	.50	.75	1.50
10-Smith-a(p)	.40	1.25	2.50
11-Origin Ka-Zar & Zabu	.25	.75	1.50
12-Man-Thing by Adams	.40	1.25	2.50
13-24: 20-Last Ka-Zar. 21-It! the Living Colossus begins, ends #24	.50		1.00
25-Deathlok the Demolisher begins; Perez 1st work, 2pgs. (8/74)	.50	1.50	3.00
26-30: 29-Guardians of the Galaxy app.	.50		1.00
31-36: 31-Wrightson-c(i)	.50		1.00

NOTE: *Buckler a-13i, 16p, 25, 26p, 27p, 28, 29p-36p; c-13, 25p, 26-30, 32-35p, 36. John Buscema a-9, 12p-14p, 16p; c-4-6p, 12p. Colan a-7p, 8p. Ditko a-21r. Everett a-6i. G. Kane a-11p, 15p; c-10p, 11p, 14, 15p, 21p. McWilliams a-30i. Starlin a-19p; c-16p. Sutton & Trimpe a-8. Tuska a-5p, 6p, 8p. Wood a-1-4.*

ASTRO BOY (TV) (Also see March of Comics #285 & The Original . . .)
August, 1965
Gold Key

1(10151-508)	9.35	28.00	65.00

ASTRO COMICS
1969 - 1979 (Giveaway)
American Airlines (Harvey)

nn-Harvey's Casper, Spooky, Hot Stuff, Stumbo the Giant, Little Audrey, Little Lotta, & Richie Rich reprints	.70	2.00	4.00

ATARI FORCE
Jan, 1984 - No. 20, Aug, 1985 (Mando paper)
DC Comics

1-20: 1st app. Tempest, Packrat, Babe, Morphea, & Dart	.50		1.00
Special 1 (4/86)	.50		1.00

NOTE: *Byrne c-Special 1i. Giffen a-12p, 13i. Rogers a-18p, Special 1p.*

A-TEAM, THE (TV)
March, 1984 - No. 3, May, 1984
Marvel Comics Group

1-3		.30	.60

ATLANTIS, THE LOST CONTINENT (See 4-Color No. 1188)

ATLAS (See First Issue Special)

ATOM, THE (See Action, All-American, Brave & the Bold, D.C. Special Series #1, Detective, Flash Comics, Showcase, Power Of The Atom, Sword Of The Atom & World's Finest)

ATOM, THE (. . . & the Hawkman No. 39 on)
June-July, 1962 - No. 38, Aug-Sept, 1968
National Periodical Publications

1-Intro Plant-Master	18.00	54.00	125.00
2	7.00	21.00	50.00

	Good	Fine	N-Mint
3-1st Time Pool story; 1st app. Chronos (origin)	5.70	17.00	40.00
4,5: 4-Snapper Carr x-over	4.30	13.00	30.00
6-10: 7-Hawkman x-over. 8-Justice League, Dr. Light app.	3.00	9.00	21.00
11-15	2.15	6.50	15.00
16-20: 19-Zatanna x-over	1.30	4.00	9.00
21-30: 29-Golden Age Atom x-over	1.00	3.00	6.00
31-38: 31-Hawkman x-over. 36-G.A. Atom x-over. 37-Intro. Major Mynah; Hawkman cameo	.70	2.00	4.00

NOTE: *Anderson a-1-11i, 13i; c-inks-1-25, 31-35, 37. Sid Greene a-8i-38i. Gil Kane a-1p-38p; c-1p-28p, 29, 33p, 34. Pool stories also in 6, 9,12, 17, 21, 27, 35.*

ATOM AGE (See Classics Special)

ATOM-AGE COMBAT
June, 1952 - No. 5, April, 1953; Feb, 1958
St. John Publishing Co.

1	17.00	51.00	120.00
2	11.00	32.00	75.00
3,5: 3-Mayo-a, 6 pgs.	8.00	24.00	56.00
4 (Scarce)	10.00	30.00	70.00
1(2/58-St. John)	6.00	18.00	42.00

ATOM-AGE COMBAT
Nov, 1958 - No. 3, March, 1959
Fago Magazines

1	9.00	27.00	62.00
2,3	6.00	18.00	42.00

ATOMAN
Feb, 1946 - No. 2, April, 1946
Spark Publications

1-Origin Atoman; Robinson/Meskin-a; Kidcrusaders, Wild Bill Hickok, Marvin the Great app.	20.00	60.00	140.00
2: Robinson/Meskin-a	14.50	44.00	100.00

ATOM & HAWKMAN, THE (Formerly The Atom)
No. 39, Oct-Nov, 1968 - No. 45, Oct-Nov, 1969
National Periodical Publications

39-45: 43-1st app. Gentlemen Ghost, origin-44	.70	2.00	4.00

NOTE: *Sid Greene a-40i-45i. Kubert a-40p, 41p; c-39-45.*

ATOM ANT (TV)
January, 1966 (Hanna-Barbera)
Gold Key

1(10170-601)	3.65	11.00	25.00

ATOMIC ATTACK (Formerly Attack, first series)
No. 5, Jan, 1953 - No. 8, Oct, 1953
Youthful Magazines

5-Atomic bomb-c	12.00	36.00	84.00
6-8	6.00	18.00	42.00

ATOMIC BOMB
1945 (36 pgs.)
Jay Burtis Publications

1-Airmale & Stampy	6.50	19.50	45.00

ATOMIC BUNNY (Formerly Atomic Rabbit)
No. 12, Aug, 1958 - No. 19, Dec, 1959
Charlton Comics

12	4.00	12.00	28.00
13-19	2.00	6.00	14.00

ATOMIC COMICS
1946 (Reprints)
Daniels Publications (Canadian)

1-Rocketman, Yankee Boy, Master Key; bondage-c

ATOMIC COMICS (continued)	Good	Fine	N-Mint
	8.00	24.00	56.00
2-4	5.00	15.00	35.00

ATOMIC COMICS
Jan, 1946 - No. 4, July-Aug, 1946
Green Publishing Co.

	Good	Fine	N-Mint
1-Radio Squad by Siegel & Shuster; Barry O'Neal app.; Fang Gow cover-r/Det. Comics	20.00	60.00	140.00
2-Inspector Dayton; Kid Kane by Matt Baker; Lucky Wings, Congo King, Prop Powers (only app.) begin	16.00	48.00	110.00
3,4: 3-Zero Ghost Detective app.; Baker-a(2) each; 4-Baker-c	9.00	27.00	62.00

ATOMIC MOUSE (See Blue Bird, Giant & Wotalife Comics) (TV, Movies)
3/53 - No. 54, 6/63; No. 1, 12/84; V2/10, 9/85 - No. 13, ?/86
Capitol Stories/Charlton Comics

1-Origin; Al Fago c/a	8.00	24.00	56.00
2	4.00	12.00	28.00
3-10: 5-Timmy The Timid Ghost app.; see Zoo Funnies	3.00	9.00	21.00
11-13,16-25	1.70	5.00	12.00
14,15-Hoppy The Marvel Bunny app.	2.00	6.00	14.00
26-(68 pages)	3.50	10.50	25.00
27-40: 36,37-Atom The Cat app.	1.15	3.50	8.00
41-54	.45	1.35	3.00
1 (1984)		.40	.80
V2/10 (10/85) -13-Fago-r. #12(1/86)		.40	.75

ATOMIC RABBIT (Atomic Bunny No. 12 on; see Wotalife Comics)
August, 1955 - No. 11, March, 1958
Charlton Comics

1-Origin; Al Fago-a	7.00	21.00	50.00
2	3.50	10.50	25.00
3-10-Fago-a in most	2.30	7.00	16.00
11-(68 pages)	3.50	10.50	25.00

ATOMIC SPY CASES
Mar-Apr, 1950
Avon Periodicals

1-Painted-c; No Wood-a	12.00	36.00	84.00

ATOMIC THUNDERBOLT, THE
Feb, 1946 - No. 2, April, 1946
Regor Company

1,2: 1-Intro. Atomic Thunderbolt & Mr. Murdo	7.00	21.00	50.00

ATOMIC WAR!
Nov, 1952 - No. 4, April, 1953
Ace Periodicals (Junior Books)

1-Atomic bomb-c	34.00	100.00	235.00
2,3: 3-Atomic bomb-c	23.00	70.00	160.00
4-Used in POP, pg. 96 & illo.	24.00	72.00	168.00

ATOM THE CAT (Formerly Tom Cat)
No. 9, Oct, 1957 - No. 17, Aug, 1959
Charlton Comics

9	2.65	8.00	18.00
10,13-17	1.30	4.00	9.00
11-(64pgs)-Atomic Mouse app., 12(100pgs)	3.50	10.50	25.00

ATTACK
May, 1952 - No. 4, Nov, 1952; No. 5, Jan, 1953 - No. 5, Sept, 1953
Youthful Mag./Trojan No. 5 on

1-(1st series)-Extreme violence	5.00	15.00	35.00
2,3: 3-Harrison c/a	2.35	7.00	16.00
4-Krenkel-a, 7 pgs, Harrison-a. (Becomes Atomic Attack No. 5 on)			

	Good	Fine	N-Mint
	3.00	9.00	21.00
5-(No. 1, Trojan, 2nd series)	2.65	8.00	18.00
6-8 (No. 2-4), 5	1.75	5.25	12.00

ATTACK
No. 54, 1958 - No. 60, Nov, 1959
Charlton Comics

54(100 pages)	3.00	9.00	21.00
55-60	.45	1.35	3.00

ATTACK!
1962 - No. 15, 3/75; No. 16, 8/79 - No. 48, 10/84
Charlton Comics

nn(#1)-('62) Special Edition	.50	1.50	3.00
2('63), 3(Fall, '64)	.35	1.00	2.00
V4#3(10/66), 4(10/67)-(Formerly Special War Series #2; becomes Attack At Sea V4#5)		.50	1.00
1(9/71)		.60	1.20
2-15(3/75): 4-American Eagle app.		.50	1.00
16(8/79) - 47		.40	.80
48(10/84)-Wood-r; S&K-c		.50	1.00
Modern Comics 13('78)-r		.30	.60

ATTACK!
1975 (39, 49 cents) (36 pages)
Spire Christian Comics (Fleming H. Revell Co.)

nn		.40	.80

ATTACK AT SEA (Formerly Attack!, 1967)
October, 1968
Charlton Comics

V4#5		.30	.60

ATTACK ON PLANET MARS
1951
Avon Periodicals

nn-Infantino, Fawcette, Kubert & Wood-a; adaptation of Tarrano the Conqueror by Ray Cummings	43.00	130.00	300.00

AUDREY & MELVIN (Formerly Little. . .)
No. 62, September, 1974
Harvey Publications

62		.30	.60

AUGIE DOGGIE (TV) (See Spotlight #2 & Whitman Comic Books)
October, 1963 (Hanna-Barbera)
Gold Key

1	3.00	9.00	21.00

AURORA COMIC SCENES INSTRUCTION BOOKLET
1974 (Slick paper, 8 pgs.)(6¼x9¾")(in full color)
(Included with superhero model kits)
Aurora Plastics Co.

181-140-Tarzan; Adams-a	.35	1.00	2.00
182-140-Spider-Man; 183-140-Tonto(Gil Kane art); 184-140-Hulk; 185-140-Superman; 186-140-Superboy; 187-140-Batman; 188-140-The Lone Ranger(1974-by Gil Kane); 192-140-Captain America (1975); 193-140-Robin			
each. . . .		.50	1.00

AUTHENTIC POLICE CASES
Feb, 1948 - No. 38, Mar, 1955
St. John Publishing Co.

1-Hale the Magician by Tuska begins	11.50	34.00	80.00
2-Lady Satan, Johnny Rebel app.	7.00	21.00	50.00
3-Veiled Avenger app.; blood drainage story plus 2 Lucky Coyne stories; used in SOTI, illo. from Red Seal #16	21.50	64.00	150.00
4,5: 4-Masked Black Jack app. 5-Late 1930s Jack Cole-a(r); trans-			

Atomic Rabbit #1, © CC

Atomic Spy Cases #1, © AVON

Attack On Planet Mars #1, © AVON

Authentic Police Cases #14, © STJ

The Avenger #1, © ME

The Avengers #3, © MEG

	Good	Fine	N-Mint
AUTHENTIC POLICE CASES (continued)			
vestism story	6.50	20.00	45.00
6-Matt Baker-c; used in SOTI, illo-"An invitation to learning"; r-in Fugitives From Justice #3; Jack Cole-a; also used by the N.Y. Legis. Comm.	21.50	64.00	150.00
7,8,10-14: 7-Jack Cole-a; Matt Baker art begins #8; Vic Flint in #10-14	6.50	20.00	45.00
9-No Vic Flint	5.50	16.50	38.00
15-Drug c/story; Vic Flint app.; Baker-c	7.00	21.00	50.00
16,18,20,21,23	3.70	11.00	26.00
17,19,22-Baker-c	3.85	11.50	27.00
24-28 (All 100 pages): 26-Transvestism	11.00	32.00	75.00
29,30	2.30	7.00	16.00
31,32,37-Baker-c	2.65	8.00	18.50
33-Transvestism; Baker-c	3.50	10.50	24.00
34-Drug-c by Baker	3.50	10.50	24.00
35-Baker c/a(2)	3.35	10.00	23.00
36-Vic Flint strip-r; Baker-c	2.50	7.50	17.50
38-Baker c/a	3.35	10.00	23.00

NOTE: Matt Baker c-7-16, 22, 27, 36-38; a-13, 16. Bondage c-1, 3.

AVENGER, THE (See A-1 Comics)
1955 - No. 4, Aug-Sept, 1955
Magazine Enterprises

	Good	Fine	N-Mint
1(A-1 129)-Origin	14.00	42.00	100.00
2(A-1 131), 3(A-1 133), 4(A-1 138)	7.00	21.00	50.00
IW Reprint #9('64)-Reprints #1 (new cover)	1.35	4.00	8.00

NOTE: Powell a-2-4; c-1-4.

AVENGERS, THE (See Kree/Skrull War Starring.., Marvel Super Action, Marvel Super Heroes('66), Marvel Treas. Ed., Marvel Triple Action, & Tales Of Suspense)
Sept, 1963 - Present
Marvel Comics Group

	Good	Fine	N-Mint
1-Origin The Avengers (Thor, Iron Man, Hulk, Ant-Man, Wasp)	82.00	205.00	575.00
2	28.00	71.00	200.00
3	18.00	56.00	130.00
4-Revival of Captain America who joins the Avengers	31.00	78.00	220.00
4-Reprint from the Golden Record Comic set	1.70	5.00	12.00
With Record....	4.30	13.00	30.00
5-Hulk leaves	11.50	29.00	80.00
6-10: 6-Intro The Masters of Evil. 8-Intro Kang. 9-Intro Wonder Man who dies in same story	8.50	21.00	60.00
11-15: 15-Death of Zemo	4.70	14.00	40.00
16-19: 16-New Avengers line-up (Hawkeye, Quicksilver, Scarlet Witch join; Thor, Iron Man, Giant-Man & Wasp leave.) 19-Intro. Swordsman; origin Hawkeye	4.00	10.00	28.00
20-22: Wood inks	2.85	7.00	20.00
23-30: 28-Giant-Man becomes Goliath	1.70	5.00	12.00
31-40	1.30	4.00	9.00
41-50: 48-Intro/Origin new Black Knight	1.00	3.00	7.00
51,52,54-56: 52-Black Panther joins; Intro The Grim Reaper. 54-Intro new Masters of Evil	1.00	3.00	7.00
53-X-Men app.	1.30	4.00	9.00
57-Intro. The Vision	2.30	7.00	16.00
58-Origin The Vision	2.00	6.00	14.00
59-65: 59-Intro. Yellowjacket. 60-Wasp & Yellowjacket wed. 63-Goliath becomes Yellowjacket; Hawkeye becomes the new Goliath	1.15	3.50	7.00
66,67: Smith-a	1.50	4.50	9.00
68-70	1.00	3.00	6.00
71-1st Invaders; Black Knight joins	.90	2.75	5.50
72-80: 80-Intro. Red Wolf	.75	2.25	4.50
81,82,84-91: 87-Origin The Black Panther. 88-Written by Harlan Ellison	.75	2.25	4.50

	Good	Fine	N-Mint
83-Intro. The Liberators (Wasp, Valkyrie, Scarlet Witch, Medusa & the Black Widow)	.90	2.75	5.50
92-Adams-c	.90	2.75	5.50
93-(52 pgs.)-Adams c/a	4.30	13.00	26.00
94-96-Adams c/a	2.65	8.00	16.00
97-G.A. Capt. America, Sub-Mariner, Human Torch, Patriot, Vision, Blazing Skull, Fin, Angel, & New Capt. Marvel x-over;	1.15	3.50	7.00
98-Goliath becomes Hawkeye; Smith c/a(i)	1.85	5.50	11.00
99-Smith/Sutton-a	1.85	5.50	11.00
100-Smith c/a; featuring everyone who was an Avenger	3.35	10.00	20.00
101-106,108,109: 101-Harlan Ellison scripts	.75	2.25	4.50
107-Starlin-a(p)	.85	2.50	5.00
110,111-X-Men app.	1.10	3.25	6.50
112-1st app. Mantis	.75	2.25	4.50
113-120: 116-118-Defenders/Silver Surfer app.	.70	2.00	4.00
121-130: 123-Origin Mantis	.60	1.75	3.50
131-133,136-140	.50	1.50	3.00
134,135-True origin The Vision	.60	1.75	3.50
141-149: 144-Origin & 1st app. Hellcat	.40	1.25	2.50
150-Kirby-a(r); new line-up begins: Capt. America, Scarlet Witch, Iron Man, Wasp, Yellowjacket, Vision & The Beast	.40	1.25	2.50
151-163: 151-Wonderman returns with new costume	.35	1.15	2.30
164-166-Byrne-a	.75	2.25	4.50
167-180	.35	1.00	2.00
181-191-Byrne-a. 181-New line-up: Capt. America, Scarlet Witch, Iron Man, Wasp, Vision, The Beast & The Falcon. 183-Ms Marvel joins. 186-Origin Quicksilver & Scarlet Witch	.45	1.30	2.60
192-202: Perez-a. 195-1st Taskmaster. 200-Dbl. size; Ms. Marvel leaves	.35	1.00	2.00
203-220: 211-New line-up: Capt. America, Iron Man, Tigra, Thor, Wasp & Yellowjacket. 213-Yellowjacket leaves. 216-Tigra leaves	.60	1.20	
221-230: 221-Hawkeye & She-Hulk join. 227-Capt. Marvel (Female) joins; origins of Ant-Man, Wasp, Giant-Man, Goliath, Yellowjacket, & Avengers	.60	1.20	
231-250: 231-Ironman leaves. 232-Starfox (Eros) joins. 234-Origin Quicksilver, Scarlet Witch. 236-New logo. 238-Origin Blackout. 240-Spider-Woman revived	.60	1.20	
251-262,264-271,273	.60	1.20	
263-X-Factor tie-in	.35	1.00	2.00
272-Alpha Flight guest	.35	1.00	2.00
274-299: 291-$1.00 issues begin. 297-Black Knight, She-Hulk & Thor resign	.60	1.20	
300 (68 pgs., $1.75)-Thor joins	.30	.90	1.75
301,302		.50	1.00
Annual 7(11/77)-Starlin c/a; Warlock dies	1.15	3.50	7.00
Annual 8(10/78)	.50	1.50	3.00
Annual 9(10/79)-Newton-a	.35	1.00	2.00
Annual 10(10/81)-Golden-p; X-Men cameo	.85	2.50	5.00
Annual 11(12/82), 12(1/84), 13(11/84),	.25	.75	1.50
Annual 14(11/85), 15(10/86), 16(10/87)	.25	.75	1.50
Annual 17(11/88)	.40	1.25	2.50
Special 1(9/67)	2.65	8.00	18.00
Special 2(9/68)	1.15	3.50	7.00
Special 3(9/69)	1.15	3.50	7.00
Special 4(1/71), 5(1/72)	.85	2.50	5.00
Special 6(11/76)	.60	1.75	3.50
Giant Size 1(8/74)	.75	2.25	4.50
Giant Size 2(11/74)(death of the Swordsman), 3(2/75)	.60	1.75	3.50
Giant Size 4(6/75)(Vision marries Scarlet Witch), 5(12/75)			

THE AVENGERS (continued)

	Good	Fine	N-Mint
	.40	1.25	2.50

NOTE: *Austin c(i)-157, 167, 168, 170-77, 181, 183-88, 198-201, Annual 8. John Buscema a-41-44p, 46p, 47p, 49, 50, 51-62p, 68-71, 74-77, 79-85, 87-91, 97, 105p, 121p, 124p, 125p, 152, 153p, 255p-279p, 281p-300p; c-41-66, 68-71, 73-91, 97-99, 178, 256p-259p, 261p-279p, 281p-300p. Byrne a-164-66p, 181-191p, 233p, Annual 13, 14p; c-186-190p, 233p, 260. Colan c/a(p)-63-65, 111, 206-208, 210, 211. Guice a-Annual 12p. Kane c-37p, 159p. Kane/ Everett c-97. Kirby a-1-8p, Special 3, 4p; c-1-30, 148, 151-158; layouts-14-16. Miller c-193p. Mooney a-86i, 179p, 180p. Nebres a-178i; c-179i. Newton a-204p, Annual 9p. Perez a(p)-141, 143, 144, 148, 154p, 155p, 160p, 161, 162, 167, 168, 170, 171, 194, 195, 196p, 198-202, Annual 6(p), 8; c-160-162p, 164-166p, 170-74p, 181p, 183-85p, 191p, 192p, 194-201p, Annual 8. Starlin c-121, 135. Staton a-127-134i. Tuska a-47i, 48i, 51i, 53i, 54i, 106p, 107p, 135p, 137-140p, 163p.*

AVENGERS, THE (TV)
Nov, 1968 ("John Steed & Emma Peel" cover title) (15 cents)
Gold Key

	Good	Fine	N-Mint
1-Photo-c	10.00	30.00	70.00

A-V IN 3-D
Dec, 1984 (28 pgs., w/glasses)
Aardvark-Vanaheim

	Good	Fine	N-Mint
1-Cerebus, Flaming Carrot, Normalman, Ms. Tree	.75	2.25	4.50

AVIATION ADVENTURES AND MODEL BUILDING
Dec, 1946 - No. 17, Feb, 1947 (True Aviation Adv. . . No. 15)
Parents' Magazine Institute

	Good	Fine	N-Mint
16,17-Half comics and half pictures	3.00	9.00	21.00

AVIATION CADETS
1943
Street & Smith Publications

	Good	Fine	N-Mint
	5.00	15.00	35.00

AWFUL OSCAR (Formerly & becomes Oscar with No. 13)
No. 11, June, 1949 - No. 12, Aug, 1949
Marvel Comics

	Good	Fine	N-Mint
11,12	2.30	7.00	16.00

AXA
Apr, 1987 - No. 2, Aug, 1987 ($1.75, color)
Eclipse Comics

	Good	Fine	N-Mint
1,2	.25	.80	1.60

AXEL PRESSBUTTON (Pressbutton No. 5; see Laser Eraser & Pressbutton)
11/84 - No. 6, 7/85 ($1.50-$1.75)
Eclipse Comics

	Good	Fine	N-Mint
1-r/Warrior (British mag.); Bolland-c; origin Laser Eraser & Pressbutton; Baxter paper	.35	1.00	2.00
2-6	.35	1.00	2.00

AZTEC ACE
3/84 - No. 15, 9/85 (Baxter paper, 36 pgs. No. 2 on)
Eclipse Comics

	Good	Fine	N-Mint
1-$2.25 cover (52 pgs.)	.50	1.50	3.00
2,3-$1.50 cover	.35	1.00	2.00
4-15-$1.75-$1.50 cover	.35	1.00	2.00

NOTE: *N. Redondo a-1i-8i, 10i; c-6-8i.*

BABE (. . .Darling of the Hills, later issues)(Also see Big Shot, Sparky Watts)
June-July, 1948 - No. 11, Apr-May, 1950
Prize/Headline/Feature

	Good	Fine	N-Mint
1-Boody Rogers-a	7.00	21.00	50.00
2-Boody Rogers-a	5.00	15.00	35.00
3-11-All by Boody Rogers	3.70	11.00	26.00

BABE AMAZON OF OZARKS
No. 5, 1948
Standard Comics

	Good	Fine	N-Mint
5	3.50	10.50	24.00

BABE RUTH SPORTS COMICS
April, 1949 - No. 11, Feb, 1951
Harvey Publications

	Good	Fine	N-Mint
1-Powell-a	10.00	30.00	70.00
2-Powell-a	8.00	24.00	56.00
3-11: Powell-a in most	6.00	18.00	42.00

BABES IN TOYLAND (See 4-Color No. 1282 & Golden Pix Story Book ST-3)

BABY HUEY AND PAPA (See Paramount Animated. . .)
May, 1962 - No. 33, Jan, 1968 (Also see Casper The Friendly. .)
Harvey Publications

	Good	Fine	N-Mint
1	7.00	21.00	50.00
2	3.50	10.50	24.00
3-5	2.00	6.00	14.00
6-10	1.50	4.50	9.00
11-20	.75	2.25	4.50
21-33	.50	1.50	3.00

BABY HUEY DUCKLAND
Nov, 1962 - No. 15, Nov, 1966 (25 cent Giant) (all 68 pgs.)
Harvey Publications

	Good	Fine	N-Mint
1	4.30	13.00	30.00
2-5	1.85	5.50	12.00
6-15	1.00	3.00	6.00

BABY HUEY, THE BABY GIANT (Also see Casper, Harvey Hits #22, Harvey Comics Hits #60, & Paramount Animated Comics)
9/56 - No. 97, 10/71; No. 98, 10/72; No. 99, 10/80
Harvey Publications

	Good	Fine	N-Mint
1-Infinity-c	20.00	60.00	140.00
2	10.00	30.00	70.00
3-Baby Huey takes anti-pep pills	6.00	18.00	42.00
4,5	4.35	13.00	30.00
6-10	2.15	6.50	15.00
11-20	1.35	4.00	9.00
21-40	1.00	3.00	7.00
41-60	.70	2.00	4.00
61-79(12/67)	.35	1.00	2.00
80(12/68) - 95-All 68 pg. Giants	.50	1.50	3.00
96,97-Both 52 pg. Giants	.50	1.50	3.00
98,99-regular size		.50	1.00

BABY SNOOTS (Also see March of Comics No. 359,371,396,401, 419,431,443,450,462,474,485)
Aug, 1970 - No. 22, Nov, 1975
Gold Key

	Good	Fine	N-Mint
1	.50	1.50	3.00
2-22: 22-Titled Snoots, the Forgetful Elefink		.60	1.20

BACHELOR FATHER (TV)
No. 1332, 4-6/62 - No. 2, 1962
Dell Publishing Co.

	Good	Fine	N-Mint
4-Color 1332 (#1)	4.00	12.00	28.00
2-Written by Stanley	4.00	12.00	28.00

BACHELOR'S DIARY
1949
Avon Periodicals

	Good	Fine	N-Mint
1(Scarce)-King Features panel cartoons & text-r; pin-up, girl wrestling photos	17.00	51.00	120.00

BAD COMPANY
Aug, 1988 - Present ($1.50, color, high quality paper)
Quality Comics

	Good	Fine	N-Mint
1,2	.25	.75	1.50

Awful Oscar #12, © MEG

Babe, Darling Of The Hills #11, © PRIZE

Babe Ruth Sports Comics #7, © HARV

The Badger #1, © First Comics

The Ballad Of Halo Jones #1, © Quality Comics

Banner Comics #4, © ACE

BADGE OF JUSTICE
No. 22, 1/55 - No. 23, 3/55; 4/55 - No. 4, 10/55
Charlton Comics

	Good	Fine	N-Mint
22(1/55)	2.65	8.00	18.00
23(3/55), 1	1.70	5.00	12.00
2-4	1.15	3.50	8.00

BADGER, THE (Also see Coyote #14)
10/83 - No. 4, 4/84; No. 5, 5/85 - Present (Baxter paper)
Capital Comics/First Comics No. 5 on

1-Badger, Ham the Weather Wizard begin	1.00	3.00	6.00
2-4	.75	2.25	4.50
5(5/85)	.70	2.00	4.00
6	.60	1.75	3.50
7-10	.55	1.60	3.20
11-20	.45	1.30	2.60
21-30	.35	1.10	2.20
31-45	.30	1.00	2.00

BADMEN OF THE WEST
1951 (Giant - 132 pages)(Painted-c)
Avon Periodicals

1-Contains rebound copies of Jesse James, King of the Bad Men of Deadwood, Badmen of Tombstone; other combinations possible. Issues with Kubert-a....	16.00	48.00	110.00

BADMEN OF THE WEST! (See A-1 Comics)
1953 - No. 3, 1954
Magazine Enterprises

1(A-1 100)-Meskin-a?	10.00	30.00	70.00
2(A-1 120), 3: 2-Larsen-a	6.00	18.00	42.00

BADMEN OF TOMBSTONE
1950
Avon Periodicals

nn	6.00	18.00	42.00

BAFFLING MYSTERIES (Formerly Indian Braves No. 1-4; Heroes of the Wild Frontier No. 26-on)
No. 5, Nov, 1951 - No. 26, Oct, 1955
Periodical House (Ace Magazines)

5	8.00	24.00	56.00
6,7,9,10: 10-E.C. Crypt Keeper swipe on-c	4.65	14.00	32.00
8-Woodish-a by Cameron	5.00	15.00	35.00
11-24: 24-Last pre-code ish	4.65	14.00	32.00
25-Reprints; surrealistic-c	4.35	13.00	30.00
26-Reprints	2.70	8.25	19.00

NOTE: *Cameron* a-8,16-18,20-22. *Colan* a-5, 11, 25r/5. *Sekowsky* a-5, 6, 22. Bondage c-20. Reprints in 18(1), 19(1), 24(3).

BALBO (See Master Comics #33 & Mighty Midget Comics)

BALDER THE BRAVE
Nov, 1985 - No. 4, 1986 (mini-series)
Marvel Comics Group

1-4: Simonson c/a		.50	1.00

BALLAD OF HALO JONES, THE
Sept, 1987 - No. 12, Aug, 1988 ($1.25-$1.50, color)
Quality Comics

1-12: Alan Moore scripts in all	.25	.80	1.60

BALOO & LITTLE BRITCHES
April, 1968 (Walt Disney)
Gold Key

1-From the Jungle Book	1.70	5.00	10.00

BALTIMORE COLTS
1950 (Giveaway)
American Visuals Corp.

	Good	Fine	N-Mint
Eisner-c	24.00	72.00	170.00

BAMBI (See 4-Color No. 12,30,186, Movie Classics, Movie Comics, and Walt Disney Showcase No. 31)

BAMBI (Disney)
1941, 1942, 1984
K. K. Publications (Giveaways)/Whitman Publ. Co.

1941-Horlick's Malted Milk & various toy stores - text & pictures; most copies mailed out with store stickers on cover

	13.00	40.00	90.00
1942-Same as 4-Color No. 12, but no price (Same as '41 issue?) (Scarce)	20.00	60.00	140.00
1-(Whitman, 1984; 60 cents)-r/4-Color 186		.30	.60

BAMM BAMM & PEBBLES FLINTSTONE (TV)
Oct, 1964 (Hanna-Barbera)
Gold Key

1	2.00	6.00	12.00

BANANA OIL
1924 (52 pages)(Black & White)
MS Publ. Co.

Milt Gross-a; not reprints	10.00	30.00	70.00

BANANA SPLITS, THE (TV) (See March of Comics No. 364)
June, 1969 - No. 8, Oct, 1971 (Hanna-Barbera)
Gold Key

1	1.00	3.00	6.00
2-8	.50	1.50	3.00

BAND WAGON (See Hanna-Barbera . . .)

BANG-UP COMICS
Dec, 1941 - No. 3, June, 1942
Progressive Publishers

1-Cosmo Mann & Lady Fairplay begin; Buzz Balmer by Rick Yager in all (origin #1)	35.00	105.00	245.00
2,3	20.00	60.00	140.00

BANNER COMICS (Captain Courageous No. 6)
No. 3, Sept., 1941 - No. 5, Jan, 1942
Ace Magazines

3-Captain Courageous & Lone Warrior & Sidekick Dicky begin	45.00	135.00	315.00
4,5: 4-Flag-c	30.00	90.00	210.00

BARBARIANS, THE
June, 1975
Atlas Comics/Seaboard Periodicals

1-Origin, only app. Andrax; Iron Jaw app.		.50	1.00

BARBIE & KEN
May-July, 1962 - No. 5, Nov-Jan, 1963-64
Dell Publishing Co.

01-053-207(#1)	6.50	19.50	45.00
2-5	4.65	14.00	32.00

BARKER, THE (Also see National Comics #42)
Autumn, 1946 - No. 15, Dec, 1949
Quality Comics Group/Comic Magazine

1	6.00	18.00	42.00
2	3.00	9.00	21.00
3-10	2.00	6.00	14.00
11-14	1.50	4.50	10.00
15-Jack Cole-a(p)	2.00	6.00	14.00

NOTE: *Jack Cole* art in some issues.

BARNEY AND BETTY RUBBLE (TV) (Flintstones' Neighbors)
Jan, 1973 - No. 23, Dec, 1976 (Hanna-Barbera)
Charlton Comics

BARNEY AND BETTY RUBBLE (continued)	Good	Fine	N-Mint
1	1.15	3.50	7.00
2-10	.60	1.80	3.60
11-23	.40	1.20	2.40

BARNEY BAXTER (Also see Magic Comics)
1938 - 1956
David McKay/Dell Publishing Co./Argo

Feature Books 15(McKay-1938)	16.00	48.00	110.00
4-Color 20(1942)	14.50	44.00	100.00
4,5	7.00	21.00	50.00
1,2(1956-Argo)	2.85	8.50	20.00

BARNEY BEAR HOME PLATE
1979 (49 cents)
Spire Christian Comics (Fleming H. Revell Co.)

		.30	.60

BARNEY BEAR LOST AND FOUND
1979 (49 cents)
Spire Christian Comics (Fleming H. Revell Co.)

nn		.30	.60

BARNEY BEAR OUT OF THE WOODS
1980 (49 cents)
Spire Christian Comics (Fleming H. Revell Co.)

nn		.30	.60

BARNEY BEAR SUNDAY SCHOOL PICNIC
1981 (69 cents)
Spire Christian Comics (Fleming H. Revell Co.)

nn		.30	.60

BARNEY BEAR THE SWAMP GANG!
1980 (59 cents)
Spire Christian Comics (Fleming H. Revell Co.)

nn		.30	.60

BARNEY BEAR WAKES UP
1977 (39 cents)
Spire Christian Comics (Fleming H. Revell Co.)

nn		.30	.60

BARNEY GOOGLE AND SPARK PLUG (See Comic Monthly & Giant Comic Album)
1923 - 1928 (Daily strip reprints; B&W) (52 pages)
Cupples & Leon Co.

1-By Billy DeBeck	15.00	45.00	105.00
2-6	10.00	30.00	70.00

NOTE: *Started in 1918 as newspaper strip; Spark Plug began 1922, 1923.*

BARNEY GOOGLE & SNUFFY SMITH
1942 - April, 1964
Dell Publishing Co./Gold Key

4-Color 19('42)	22.00	65.00	154.00
4-Color 40('44)	12.00	36.00	84.00
Large Feature Comic 11(1943)	12.00	36.00	84.00
1(10113-404)-Gold Key (4/64)	1.70	5.00	10.00

BARNEY GOOGLE & SNUFFY SMITH
June, 1951 - No. 4, Feb, 1952 (Reprints)
Toby Press

1	5.00	15.00	35.00
2,3	3.00	9.00	21.00
4-Kurtzman-a "Pot Shot Pete," 5 pgs.; reprints/John Wayne #5	3.70	11.00	26.00

BARNEY GOOGLE AND SNUFFY SMITH
March, 1970 - No. 6, Jan, 1971
Charlton Comics

	Good	Fine	N-Mint
1	1.00	3.00	6.00
2-6	.70	2.00	4.00

BARNYARD COMICS (Dizzy Duck No. 32 on)
June, 1944 - No. 31, Sept, 1950; 1957
Nedor/Polo Mag./Standard(Animated Cartoons)

1(nn, 52 pgs.)	8.00	24.00	56.00
2 (52 pgs.)	4.00	12.00	28.00
3-5	2.65	8.00	18.00
6-12,16	1.85	5.50	13.00
13-15,17,21,23,26,27,29-All contain Frazetta text illos	3.00	9.00	21.00
18-20,22,24,25-All contain Frazetta-a & text illos	8.00	24.00	56.00
28,30,31	1.00	3.00	7.00
10(1957)(Exist?)	.50	1.50	4.00

BARRY M. GOLDWATER
March, 1965 (Complete life story)
Dell Publishing Co.

12-055-503: Photo-c	2.35	7.00	14.00

BASEBALL COMICS
Spring, 1949 (Reprinted later as a Spirit section)
Will Eisner Productions

1-Will Eisner c/a	32.00	95.00	225.00

BASEBALL HEROES
1952 (One Shot)
Fawcett Publications

nn (Scarce)	28.50	85.00	200.00

BASEBALL THRILLS
No. 10, Sum, 1951 - No. 3, Sum, 1952 (Saunders painted-c No.1,2)
Ziff-Davis Publ. Co.

10(No. 1)	14.50	44.00	100.00
2-Powell-a(2)(Late Sum, '51)	8.50	25.50	60.00
3-Kinstler c/a	8.50	25.50	60.00

BASICALLY STRANGE (Magazine)
December, 1982 (B&W, $1.95)
JC Comics (Archie Comics Group)

1-(21,000 printed; all but 1,000 destroyed—pages out of sequence)	.30	1.00	2.00
1-Wood, Toth-a; Corben-c. Reprints & new art	.30	1.00	2.00

BASIC HISTORY OF AMERICA ILLUSTRATED
1976 (B&W)
Pendulum Press

07-1999 America Becomes a World Power 1890-1920
07-2251 The Industrial Era 1865-1915
07-226x Before the Civil War 1830-1860
07-2278 Americans Move Westward 1800-1850
07-2286 The Civil War 1850-1876 - Redondo-a
07-2294 The Fight for Freedom 1750-1783
07-2308 The New World 1500-1750
07-2316 Problems of the New Nation 1800-1830
07-2324 Roaring Twenties and the Great Depression 1920-1940
07-2332 The United States Emerges 1783-1800
07-2340 America Today 1945-1976
07-2359 World War II 1940-1945

Softcover			1.50
Hardcover			4.50

BASIL (. . .the Royal Cat)
Jan, 1953 - No. 4, Sept, 1953
St. John Publishing Co.

1	2.00	6.00	14.00
2-4	1.00	3.00	7.00
I.W. Reprint 1		.60	1.20

Barney Google And Spark Plug #2, © C & L

Barnyard Comics #1, © STD

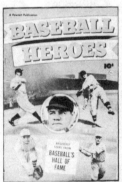

Baseball Heroes, © FAW

Batman #1, © DC

Batman #23, © DC

Batman #255, © DC

BASIL WOLVERTON'S GATEWAY TO HORROR
June, 1988 (One shot, $1.75, B&W)
Dark Horse Comics

	Good	Fine	N-Mint
1-Wolverton-r	.30	.90	1.75

BASIL WOLVERTON'S PLANET OF TERROR
Oct., 1987 ($1.75, B&W)
Dark Horse Comics

1-Wolverton-r	.30	.85	1.70

BATGIRL SPECIAL
1988 (One shot, color, $1.50, 52pgs)
DC Comics

1	.50	1.50	3.00

BAT LASH (See DC Spec. Series #16, Showcase #76 & Weird Western Tales)
Oct-Nov, 1968 - No. 7, Oct-Nov, 1969
National Periodical Publications

1	.25	.80	1.60
2-7		.50	1.00

BATMAN (See Aurora, The Best of DC #2, The Brave & the Bold, Detective, Dynamic Classics, 80-Page Giants, Heroes Against Hunger, Justice League Int., Limited Coll. Ed., DC 100-Page Super Spec., Real Fact #5, Saga of Ra's Al Ghul, Shadow of the..., Star Spangled, 3-D Batman, Untold Legends of.. & World's Finest)

BATMAN
Spring, 1940 - Present
National Periodical Publ./Detective Comics/DC Comics

	Good	Fine	N-Mint
1-Origin The Batman retold by Bob Kane; see Detective #33 for 1st origin; 1st app. Joker & The Cat (Catwoman); has Batman story without Robin originally planned for Detective #38. This book was created entirely from the inventory of Det. Comics	1400.00	4200.00	9800.00

(Prices vary widely on this book)

1-Reprint, oversize 13½"x10." **WARNING**: This comic is an exact duplicate reprint of the original except for its size. DC published it in 1974 with a second cover titling it as a **Famous First Edition**. There have been many reported cases of the outer cover being removed and the interior sold as the original edition. The reprint with the new outer cover removed is practically worthless.

	Good	Fine	N-Mint
2	400.00	1200.00	2800.00
3-1st Catwoman in costume; 1st Puppetmaster app.	255.00	765.00	1785.00
4	207.00	620.00	1450.00
5-1st app. of the Batmobile with its bat-head front	160.00	480.00	1120.00
6-10: 8-Infinity-c	117.00	350.00	820.00
11-Classic Joker-c	100.00	300.00	700.00
12-15: 13-Jerry Siegel, creator of Superman appears in a Batman story	95.00	285.00	665.00
16-Intro Alfred	110.00	330.00	770.00
17-20	60.00	180.00	420.00
21-26,28-30: 22-1st Alfred solo. 25-Only Joker/Penguin team-up	55.00	165.00	385.00
27-Christmas-c	58.00	175.00	405.00
31,32,34-40: 32-Origin Robin retold	35.00	105.00	245.00
33-Christmas-c	42.00	125.00	295.00
41-46: 45-Christmas-c	30.00	90.00	210.00
47-1st detailed origin The Batman	82.00	245.00	575.00
48-1000 Secrets of Bat Cave	32.00	95.00	225.00
49,50: 49-1st Vicki Vale & Mad Hatter. 50-Two-Face impostor app.	30.00	90.00	210.00
51-60: 57-Centerfold is a 1950 calendar	27.00	81.00	190.00
61-Origin Batman Plane II	27.00	81.00	190.00
62-Origin Catwoman	35.00	105.00	245.00
63-73: 68-Two-Face app. 72-Last 52 pgs.	22.00	65.00	155.00
74-Used in **POP**, pg. 90	23.00	70.00	160.00
75-77,79,80	22.00	65.00	155.00

	Good	Fine	N-Mint
78-(9/53)-Ron Kar, The Man Hunter from Mars story-the 1st lawman of Mars to come to Earth (green skinned)	26.50	79.00	185.00
81-89: 84-Two-Face app. 86-Intro Batmarine (Batman's submarine). 89-Last Pre-Code ish.	21.50	65.00	150.00
90-99: 92-1st app. Bat-Hound	13.50	40.50	95.00
100-Joker-c	43.00	128.00	300.00
101-110: 105-1st Batwoman in Batman	11.50	34.00	80.00
111-120: 113-1st app. Fatman	8.00	24.00	55.00
121-130: 127-Superman cameo. 129-Origin Robin retold; Bondage-c	6.50	19.50	45.00
131-143: Last 10 cent issue. 131-Intro 2nd Batman & Robin series. 133-1st Bat-Mite in Batman. 134-Origin The Dummy. 139-Intro old Bat-Girl	4.85	14.50	34.00
144-150	3.15	9.50	22.00
151-170: 164-New Batmobile; New look & Mystery Analysts series begins	2.65	8.00	18.00
171-Riddler app.(5/65), 1st since 12/48	4.30	13.00	30.00
172-175,177-180	1.85	5.50	11.00
176-80-Pg. Giant G-17	2.15	6.50	13.00
181,183,184,186,188-190: 181-Batman & Robin poster insert; Intro Poison Ivy	1.30	4.00	8.00
182,185,187-80 Pg. Gnt. G-24,G-27,G-30	1.50	4.50	9.00
191,192,194-197,199: 197-New Bat-Girl app.	1.00	3.00	6.00
193-80 Pg. Giant G-37; Batcave blueprints	1.15	3.50	7.00
198-80-Pg. Giant G-43; Origin-r	1.15	3.50	7.00
200-Retells origin of Batman & Robin	1.85	5.50	11.00
201-Joker story	.75	2.25	4.50
202,204-207,209,210	.60	1.75	3.50
203-80 Pg. Giant G-49	.85	2.50	5.00
208-80 Pg. Giant G-55; New origin Batman by Gil Kane	.85	2.50	5.00
211,212,214-217: 216-Alfred given a new last name-"Pennyworth." (see Det. 96)	.60	1.75	3.50
213-80-Pg. Giant G-61; origin Alfred; new origin Robin	.85	2.50	5.00
218-80-Pg. Giant G-67	.85	2.50	5.00
219-Adams-a	1.30	4.00	8.00
220,221,224-227,229-231	.60	1.75	3.50
222-Beatles take-off	1.15	3.50	7.00
223,228,233-80-Pg. Giant G-73,G-79,G-85	.85	2.50	5.00
232-Adams-a; Intro Ras Al Ghul	1.35	4.00	8.00
234,237: Adams-a. 234-52pg. ish begin, end #242. 237-GA Batman-r; Wrightson/Ellison plots	1.35	4.00	8.00
235,236,239-242: 241-r-Batman #5	.50	1.50	3.00
238-DC-8 100 pg. Super Spec.; unpubbed G.A. Atom, Sargon, Plastic Man stories; Doom Patrol origin-r; Batman, Legion, Aquaman-r; Adams-c	.60	1.75	3.50
243-245-Adams-a	1.00	3.00	6.00
246-250,252,253	.50	1.50	3.00
251-Adams-a; Joker app.	1.10	3.25	6.50
254-100pg. editions begin	.60	1.75	3.50
255-Adams-a; tells of Bruce Wayne's father who wore bat costume & fought crime	.90	2.75	5.50
256-261-Last 100pg. ish; part-r	.60	1.75	3.50
262-365,367,369,370: 262-68pgs. 266-Catwoman back to old costume. 311-Batgirl reteams w/Batman. 332-Catwoman's 1st solo. 345-New Dr. Death app.	.35	1.00	2.00
366-Jason Todd 1st in Robin costume	.90	2.75	5.50
368-1st new Robin in costume (Jason Todd)	1.00	3.00	6.00
371-399	.30	.90	1.75
400 ($1.50, 64pgs.)-Dark Knight special; intro by Steven King; Art Adams/Austin-a	1.10	3.25	6.50
401-403	.30	.90	1.75
404-Miller scripts begin (end 407); Year 1	.85	2.50	5.00
405-407: Year 1 cont.	.60	1.75	3.50
408-425: 408-410-New Origin Jason Todd (Robin)			

BATMAN (continued)	Good	Fine	N-Mint
	.25	.75	1.50
426,427 (52 pgs., $1.50)	1.35	4.00	8.00
428-Death of Robin (Jason Todd)	3.35	10.00	20.00
429	1.35	4.00	8.00
430-435		.50	1.00
Annual 1(8-10/61)-Swan-c	13.00	40.00	90.00
Annual 2	5.70	17.00	40.00
Annual 3(Summer, '62)	4.30	13.00	30.00
Annual 4,5	3.00	9.00	21.00
Annual 6,7(7/64)	2.30	7.00	16.00
Annual 8(10/82)	.50	1.50	3.00
Annual 9(7/85), 10(8/86), 12('88)	.35	1.00	2.00
Annual 11('87)-Alan Moore scripts	.50	1.50	3.00
Pizza Hut giveaway(12/77)-exact r-/of #122, 123		.50	1.00
Prell Shampoo giveaway('66)-16 pgs. "The Joker's Practical Jokes" (6-7/8"x3-3/8")	1.35	4.00	8.00
Special 1(4/84)-Golden c/a(p)	.40	1.25	2.50

NOTE: Art Adams a-400p. Neal Adams c-200, 203, 210, 217, 219, 220-22, 224-27, 229, 230, 232, 234, 236-41, 243-46, 251, 255. Burnley a-10, 12-18, 20, 25, 27; c-28. Byrne c-401, Annual 11i. Colan a-340p, 343p-45p, 348p-51p, 373p, 383p; c-343p, 345p, 350p. J. Cole a-238r. Golden a-295, 303r. Grell a-287, 288p, 289p, 290; c-287-90. Kaluta c-242, 248, 253. Bob Kane a-1, 2; c-1-5, 7. G. Kane a-(R)-254, 255, 259, 261, 353i. Kubert a-238r, 400; c-310,319p, 327, 328, 344. Lopez a-336p, 337p, 353p; c-272, 311, 313, 314, 318, 321, 353. Mooney a-255r. Newton a-305, 306, 328p, 331p, 332p, 337p, 338p, 346p, 352-57p, 360p-72p, 374p-378p; c-374p, 378p. Perez a-400. Robinson/Roussos a-12-17, 20, 22, 24, 25, 27, 28, 31, 33, 37. Robinson a-12, 14, 18, 22-32, 34, 36, 37, 255r, 260r, 261r; c-6, 8-10, 12-15, 18, 21, 24, 26, 27, 30, 37, 39. Simonson a-300p, 312p, 321p; c-300p, 312p, 366, 413i. P. Smith a-Annual 9. Starlin c/a-402. Staton a-334. Wrightson a-265i, 400; c-320r.

BATMAN (Kellogg's Poptarts comics)
1966 (set of 6) (16 pages)
National Periodical Publications

"The Man in the Iron Mask," "The Penguin's Fowl Play," "The Joker's Happy Victims," "The Catwoman's Catnapping Caper," "The Mad Hatter's Hat Crimes," "The Case of the Batman II" each 70 2.00 4.00
NOTE: All above were folded and placed in Poptarts boxes. Infantino art on Catwoman and Joker issues.

BATMAN AND THE OUTSIDERS (The Advs. of the Outsiders #33 on)(Also see The Outsiders & Brave & The Bold #200)
Aug, 1983 - No. 32, Apr, 1986 (Mando paper No. 5 on)
DC Comics

1-Batman, Halo, Geo-Force, Katana, Metamorpho & Black Lightning begin		.50	1.00
2-32: 9-Halo begins. 11,12-Origin Katana. 18-More facts about Metamorpho's origin. 28-31-Lookers origin		.50	1.00
Annual 1 (9/84)-Miller/Aparo-c; Aparo-i	.25	.75	1.50
Annual 2 (9/85)-Metamorpho & Sapphire Stagg wed; Aparo-c	.25	.75	1.50

NOTE: Aparo a-1-9, 11, 12p, 16-20; c-1-4, 5i, 6-21. B. Kane a-3r. Layton a-19i, 20i. Lopez a-3p. Perez c-5p. B. Willingham a-14p.

BATMAN FAMILY, THE
Sept-Oct, 1975 - No. 20, Oct-Nov, 1978 (No.1-4, 17-on: 68 pages)
(Combined with Detective Comics with No. 481)
National Periodical Publications/DC Comics

1-Origin Batgirl-Robin team-up (The Dynamite Duo); reprints plus one new story begins; Adams-a(r).	.60	1.75	3.50
2-5: 3-Batgirl & Robin learn each's i.d.	.35	1.00	2.00
6-10,14-16: 10-1st revival Batwoman	.35	1.00	2.00
11-13: Rogers-p. 11-New stories begin; Man-Bat begins		.50	1.50	3.00
17-($1.00 size)-Batman, Huntress begin	.35	1.00	2.00
18-20: Huntress by Staton in all. 20-Origin Ragman retold	.25	.75	1.50

NOTE: Aparo a-17; c-11-16. Austin a-12i. Chaykin a-14p. Michael Golden a-15-17, 18-20p. Grell a-1; c-1. Gil Kane a-2r. Kaluta c-17, 19. Newton a-13. Robinson a-1r, 3i(r), 9r. Russell a-18i, 19i. Starlin c-18, 20.

BATMAN MINIATURE (See Batman Kellogg's)

BATMAN RECORD COMIC
1966 (One Shot)
National Periodical Publications

	Good	Fine	N-Mint
1-With record	5.00	15.00	35.00
Comic only	1.35	4.00	8.00

BATMAN: SON OF THE DEMON
Sept, 1987 (80 pgs., hardcover, $14.95)
DC Comics

1	5.35	16.00	32.00
Softcover reprint; new-c ($8.95)	2.00	6.00	12.00

BATMAN SPECTACULAR (See DC Special Series No. 15)

BATMAN: THE CULT
1988 - No. 4, Nov, 1988 ($3.50, color, deluxe mini-series)
DC Comics

1-Wrightson-a/painted-c in all	1.15	3.50	7.00
2-4	.75	2.25	4.50

BATMAN: THE DARK KNIGHT RETURNS
March, 1986 - No. 4, 1986
DC Comics

1-Miller story & a(p); set in the future	5.35	16.00	32.00
1-2nd printing	1.30	4.00	8.00
1-3rd printing	.60	1.75	3.50
2-Carrie Kelly becomes Robin (female)	3.00	9.00	18.00
2-2nd printing	.85	2.50	5.00
2-3rd printing	.50	1.50	3.00
3-Death of Joker	1.35	4.00	8.00
3-2nd printing	.60	1.80	3.60
4-Death of Alfred	.85	2.50	5.00
Hardcover, signed & numbered edition ($40.00)(4000 copies)			
	43.00	130.00	260.00
Hardcover, trade edition	8.35	25.00	50.00
Softcover, trade edition	2.65	8.00	16.00

BATMAN: THE KILLING JOKE
1988 ($3.50, 52pgs. color, deluxe, adults)
DC Comics

1-Bolland-c/a; Alan Moore scripts	1.50	4.50	9.00
1-2nd print	.60	1.75	3.50

BATMAN VS. THE INCREDIBLE HULK (See DC Special Series No. 27)

BAT MASTERSON (TV)
Aug-Oct, 1959; Feb-Apr, 1960 - No. 9, Nov-Jan, 1961-62
Dell Publishing Co.

4-Color 1013 (8-10/59)	4.30	13.00	30.00
2-9: Gene Barry photo-c on all	2.85	8.50	20.00

BATS (See Tales Calculated to Drive You . . .)

BATTLE
March, 1951 - No. 70, June, 1960
Marvel/Atlas Comics(FPI No. 1-62/Male No. 63 on)

1	5.00	15.00	35.00
2	2.30	7.00	16.00
3-9: 4-1st Buck Pvt. O'Toole	1.70	5.00	12.00
10-Pakula-a	2.00	6.00	14.00
11-20: 11-Check-a	1.15	3.50	8.00
21,23-Krigstein-a	2.00	6.00	14.00
22,24-36: 36-Everett-a	1.00	3.00	7.00
37-Kubert-a (Last precode, 2/55)	1.35	4.00	9.00
38-40,42-48	.70	2.10	4.00
41-Kubert/Moskowitz-a	1.35	4.00	9.00
49-Davis-a	1.70	5.00	12.00
50-54,56-58	.60	2.00	4.00
55-Williamson-a, 5 pgs.	2.65	8.00	18.00

Batman #426, © DC

Batman: The Cult #2, © DC

Batman: The Killing Joke #1, © DC

Battle Action #3, © MEG

Battlefield #2, © MEG

Battlefront #5, © MEG

BATTLE (continued)	Good	Fine	N-Mint
59-Torres-a	1.20	3.50	8.00
60-62: Combat Kelly app.-#60,62; Combat Casey app.-#61			
	.50	1.50	3.00
63-65: 63-Ditko-a. 64,65-Kirby-a	1.20	3.50	8.00
66-Kirby, Davis-a	1.35	4.00	9.00
67-Williamson/Crandall-a, 4 pgs; Kirby, Davis-a			
	2.65	8.00	18.00
68-Kirby/Williamson-a, 4 pgs; Kirby/Ditko-a	2.65	8.00	18.00
69-Kirby-a	1.00	3.00	7.00
70-Kirby/Ditko-a	1.00	3.00	7.00

NOTE: Andru a-37. Berg a-8, 14, 60-62. Colan a-33. Everett a-36, 50, 70; c-56, 57. Heath a-6, 9, 13, 31, 69; c-6, 9, 26, 35, 37. Kirby c-64-69. Maneely a-4, 31; c-4, 61. Orlando a-47. Powell a-53, 55. Reinman a-26, 32. Robinson a-9. Romita a-26. Severin a-28, 32-34, 66-68; c-36. Sinnott a-33, 37. Tuska a-32. Woodbridge a-52, 55.

BATTLE ACTION
Feb, 1952 - No. 12, 5/53; No. 13, 11/54 - No. 30, 8/57
Atlas Comics (NPI)

	Good	Fine	N-Mint
1-Pakula-a	5.00	15.00	35.00
2	2.00	6.00	14.00
3,4,6,7,9,10: 6-Robinson c/a	1.50	4.50	10.00
5-Used in POP, pg. 93,94	1.70	5.00	12.00
8-Krigstein-a	2.00	6.00	14.00
11-15 (Last precode, 2/55)	1.15	3.50	8.00
16-26,28,29	.85	2.50	6.00
27,30-Torres-a	1.35	4.00	9.00

NOTE: Battle Brady app. 5,6,10-12. Check a-11. Everett c-13, 25. Heath a-8; c-3, 21. Maneely a-1. Reinman a-1. Woodbridge a-28,30.

BATTLE ATTACK
Oct, 1952 - No. 8, Dec, 1955
Stanmor Publications

1	2.50	7.50	18.00
2	1.30	3.85	9.00
3-8: 3-Hollingsworth-a	1.00	3.00	7.00

BATTLE BRADY (Men in Action No. 1-9)
No. 10, Jan, 1953 - No. 14, June, 1953
Atlas Comics (IPC)

10	2.30	7.00	16.00
11-Used in POP, pg. 95 plus B&W & color illos.			
	2.00	6.00	14.00
12-14	1.15	3.50	8.00

BATTLE CLASSICS (See Cancelled Comic Cavalcade)
Sept-Oct, 1978 (44 pages)
DC Comics

1-Kubert-r, new Kubert-c		.40	.80

BATTLE CRY
1952(May) - No. 20, Sept, 1955
Stanmor Publications

1	2.85	8.50	20.00
2	1.50	4.50	10.00
3,5-10: 8-Pvt. Ike begins, ends #13,17	1.00	3.00	7.00
4-Classic E.C. swipe	1.50	4.50	10.00
11-Opium-c	1.70	5.00	12.00
12-20	.70	2.00	5.00

NOTE: Hollingsworth a-9; c-20.

BATTLEFIELD (War Adventures on the...)
April, 1952 - No. 11, May, 1953
Atlas Comics (ACI)

1-Pakula, Reinman-a	4.00	12.00	28.00
2-5	1.70	5.00	12.00
6-11	.85	2.50	6.00

NOTE: Colan a-11. Everett c-8. Heath a-1, 5p; c-2, 9, 11. Ravielli a-11.

BATTLEFIELD ACTION (Formerly Foreign Intrigues)
No. 16, Nov, 1957 - No. 62, 2-3/66; No. 63, 7/80 - No. 89, 11/84
Charlton Comics

	Good	Fine	N-Mint
16	.85	2.50	6.00
17,18,20-30	.35	1.00	2.40
19-Check-a	.60	1.80	4.00
31-62(1966)		.50	2.00
63-89(1983-'84)		.30	.60

NOTE: Montes/Bache a-43,55,62. Glanzman a-87r.

BATTLE FIRE
April, 1955 -No. 7, 1955
Aragon Magazine/Stanmor Publications

1	1.50	4.50	10.00
2	.70	2.00	5.00
3-7	.60	1.80	4.00

BATTLE FOR A THREE DIMENSIONAL WORLD
May, 1983 (20 pgs., slick paper w/stiff covers, $3.00)
3D Cosmic Publications

nn-Kirby c/a in 3-D; shows history of 3-D	.50	1.50	3.00

BATTLEFORCE
Nov., 1987 ($1.75, color)
Blackthorne Publ.

1	.30	.90	1.75

BATTLEFRONT
June, 1952 - No. 48, Aug, 1957
Atlas Comics (PPI)

1-Heath-c	5.00	15.00	35.00
2	2.30	7.00	16.00
3-5-Robinson-a(4) in each	2.00	6.00	14.00
6-10: Combat Kelly in No. 6-10	1.70	5.00	12.00
11-22,24-28: Last precode (2/55). Battle Brady in #14,16			
	1.00	3.00	7.00
23-Check-a	1.20	3.50	8.00
29-39	.75	2.25	4.50
40,42-Williamson-a	2.65	8.00	18.00
41,44-47	.85	1.75	3.50
43-Check-a	1.00	3.00	7.00
48-Crandall-a	1.20	3.50	8.00

NOTE: Ayers a-19. Berg a-44. Colan a-21, 22, 33. Drucker a-28, 29. Everett a-44. Heath c-23, 26, 27, 29. Maneely c/a-22, c-35. Morisi a-42. Morrow a-41. Orlando a-47. Powell a-19, 21, 25, 29, 47. Robinson a-1, 2, 4, 5; c-4, 5. Robert Sale a-19. Severin c-40. Woodbridge a-45, 46.

BATTLEFRONT
No. 5, June, 1952
Standard Comics

5-Toth-a	4.00	12.00	28.00

BATTLE GROUND
Sept, 1954 - No. 20, Aug, 1957
Atlas Comics (OMC)

1	4.00	12.00	28.00
2-Jack Katz-a	2.00	6.00	14.00
3,4-Last precode (3/55)	1.50	4.50	10.00
5-8,10	1.15	3.50	8.00
9-Krigstein-a	2.00	6.00	14.00
11,13,18-Williamson-a in each	2.65	8.00	18.00
12,15-17,19,20	1.00	3.00	6.00
14-Kirby-a	1.15	3.50	8.00

NOTE: Colan a-11. Drucker a-7, 12, 13. Heath c-5. Orlando a-17. Pakula a-11. Severin a-5, 12, 19. Tuska a-11.

BATTLE HEROES
Sept, 1966 - No. 2, Nov, 1966 (25 cents)
Stanley Publications

	Good	Fine	N-Mint
BATTLE HEROES (continued)			
1,2	.30	.80	1.60
BATTLE OF THE BULGE (See Movie Classics)			
BATTLE OF THE PLANETS (TV)			
6/79 - No. 10, 12/80 (Based on syndicated cartoon by Sandy Frank)			
Gold Key/Whitman No. 6 on			
1		.40	.80
2-10: Mortimer a-1-4,7-10		.30	.60
BATTLE REPORT			
Aug, 1952 - No. 6, June, 1953			
Ajax/Farrell Publications			
1	1.70	5.00	12.00
2-6	.85	2.50	6.00
BATTLE SQUADRON			
April, 1955 - No. 5, Dec, 1955			
Stanmor Publications			
1	1.50	4.50	10.00
2-5: 3-Iwo Jima & flag-c	.70	2.00	5.00
BATTLESTAR GALACTICA (TV)(Also see Marvel Super Spec. #8)			
March, 1979 - No. 23, January, 1981			
Marvel Comics Group			
1		.35	.70
2-23: 1-3-Partial-r		.25	.50
NOTE: *Austin* c-9i, 10i. **Golden** c-18. **Simonson** a(p)-4, 5, 11-13, 15-20, 22, 23; c-4p, 5p, 11p-15p.			
BATTLE STORIES (See X-Mas Comics)			
Jan, 1952 - No. 11, Sept, 1953			
Fawcett Publications			
1-Evans-a	4.00	12.00	28.00
2	1.70	5.00	12.00
3-11	1.35	4.00	9.00
BATTLE STORIES			
1963 - 1964			
Super Comics			
Reprints #10-12,15-18; 15-r/Amer. Air Forces by Powell			
	.35	1.00	2.00
BATTLETECH			
Oct., 1987 - Present ($1.75, color)			
Blackthorne Publ.			
1-9	.30	.90	1.75
...In 3-D 1(4/88)	.40	1.25	2.50
BEACH BLANKET BINGO (See Movie Classics)			
BEAGLE BOYS, THE (Walt Disney)(See The Phantom Blot)			
11/64 - No. 2, 11/65; No. 3, 8/66 - No. 47, 2/79 (See WDC&S #134)			
Gold Key			
1	2.35	7.00	14.00
2-5	1.35	4.00	8.00
6-10	.85	2.50	5.00
11-20: 11,14,19-r	.50	1.50	3.00
21-47: 27-r	.25	.75	1.50
BEAGLE BOYS VERSUS UNCLE SCROOGE			
March, 1979 - No. 12, Feb, 1980			
Gold Key			
1	.25	.80	1.60
2-12: 9-r		.40	.80
BEANBAGS			
Winter, 1951 - No. 2, Spring, 1952			
Ziff-Davis Publ. Co. (Approved Comics)			
1,2	3.15	9.50	22.00

	Good	Fine	N-Mint
BEANIE THE MEANIE			
1958 - No. 3, May, 1959			
Fago Publications			
1-3	1.15	3.50	8.00
BEANY AND CECIL (TV) (Bob Clampett's...)			
Jan, 1952 - 1955; July-Sept, 1962 - No. 5, July-Sept, 1963			
Dell Publishing Co.			
4-Color 368	9.50	28.00	65.00
4-Color 414,448,477,530,570,635(1/55)	7.00	21.00	50.00
01-057-209	7.00	21.00	50.00
2-5	5.00	15.00	35.00
BEAR COUNTRY (Disney)(See 4-Color No. 758)			
BEATLES, THE (See Girls' Romances #109, Go-Go, Jimmy Olsen 79, Marvel Comics Super Special 4, My Little Margie 54, Not Brand Echh, Strange Tales 130, Summer Love, Teen Confessions 37, Tippy's Friends & Tippy Teen)			
BEATLES, LIFE STORY, THE			
Sept-Nov, 1964 (35 cents)			
Dell Publishing Co.			
1-(Scarce)-Stories with color photo pin-ups	30.00	90.00	210.00
BEATLES YELLOW SUBMARINE (See Movie Comics under Yellow...)			
BEAUTY AND THE BEAST, THE			
Jan, 1985 - No. 4, Apr, 1985 (Mini-series)			
Marvel Comics Group			
1-4: Dazzler & the Beast	.25	.70	1.40
BEAVER VALLEY (See 4-Color No. 625)			
BEDKNOBS AND BROOMSTICKS (See Walt Disney Showcase No. 6 & 50)			
BEDLAM!			
9/85 - No. 2, 9/85 (B&W-r in color)			
Eclipse Comics			
1,2-Bissette-a	.30	.90	1.75
BEDTIME STORY (See Cinema Comics Herald)			
BEEP BEEP, THE ROAD RUNNER (TV)(Also see Daffy)			
7/58 - No. 14, 8-10/62; 10/66 - No. 105, 1983			
Dell Publishing Co./Gold Key No. 1-88/Whitman No. 89 on			
4-Color 918	3.00	9.00	21.00
4-Color 1008,1046	1.70	5.00	12.00
4(2-4/60)-14(Dell)	1.15	3.50	8.00
1	1.30	4.00	9.00
2-5	.85	2.50	5.00
6-14	.50	1.50	3.00
15-18,20-40	.35	1.00	2.00
19-w/pull-out poster	1.35	4.00	8.00
41-60		.60	1.20
61-105		.40	.80
Kite Fun Book-Giveaway ('67,'71), 16pgs., soft-c, 5x7¼''			
	.70	2.00	4.00
NOTE: See March of Comics #351,353,375,387,397,416,430,442,455. #5,8-10,35,53,59-62, 68-r; 96-102, 104 ½-r.			
BEETLE BAILEY (Also see Comics Reading Library & Sarge Snorkel)			
No. 459, 5/53 - No. 38, 5-7/62; No. 39, 11/62 - No. 53, 5/66; No. 54, 8/66 - No. 65, 12/67; No. 67, 2/69 - No. 119, 11/76; No. 120, 4/78 - No. 132, 4/80			
Dell Publishing Co./Gold Key No. 39-53/King No. 54-66/Charlton No. 67-119/Gold Key No. 120-131/Whitman No. 132			
4-Color 469 (No. 1)-By Mort Walker	4.00	12.00	28.00
4-Color 521,552,622	2.30	7.00	16.00
5(2-4/56)-10(5-7/57)	1.70	5.00	12.00
11-20(4-5/59)	1.15	3.50	8.00
21-38(5-7/62)	.70	2.10	5.00

Battle Report #1, © AJAX

Bedlam! #2, © Eclipse

Beep Beep, The Road Runner #14, © Warner Bros.

Ben Bowie And His Mountain Men #16, © DELL   Berni Wrightson, Master Of The Macabre #1, © Eclipse   Best Love #36, © MEG

	Good	Fine	N-Mint
BEETLE BAILEY (continued)			
39-53(5/66)	.45	1.35	3.00
54-119 (No. 66 publ. overseas only?)	.25	.75	1.50
120-132		.50	1.00
Bold Detergent Giveaway('69)-same as regular ish (No. 67) minus			
price		.50	1.00
Cerebral Palsy Assn. Giveaway V2No.71('69)-V2No.73)(No. 1), 1/70,			
Charlton		.50	1.00
Giant Comic Album(1972, 59 cents, 11x14'') Color cover, B&W inter-			
ior, Modern Promotions (r)		.40	.80
Red Cross Giveaway, 16pp, 5x7'', 1969, paper-c		.40	.80
BEE 29, THE BOMBARDIER			
Feb, 1945			
Neal Publications			
1-(Funny animal)	4.65	14.00	32.00
BEHIND PRISON BARS			
1952			
Realistic Comics (Avon)			
1-Kinstler-c	13.00	40.00	90.00
BEHOLD THE HANDMAID			
1954 (Religious) (25 cents with a 20 cent sticker price)			
George Pflaum			
	4.00	12.00	28.00
BELIEVE IT OR NOT (See Ripley's . . .)			
BEN AND ME (See 4-Color No. 539)			
BEN BOWIE AND HIS MOUNTAIN MEN			
1952 - No. 17, Nov-Jan, 1958-59			
Dell Publishing Co.			
4-Color 443 (No. 1)	2.65	8.00	18.00
4-Color 513,557,599,626,657	1.70	5.00	12.00
7(5-7/56)-11: 11-Intro/origin Yellow Hair	1.30	4.00	9.00
12-17	1.00	3.00	7.00
BEN CASEY (TV)			
June-July, 1962 - No. 10, June-Aug, 1965 (Photo-c)			
Dell Publishing Co.			
12-063-207	2.00	6.00	14.00
2(10/62)-10	1.30	4.00	9.00
BEN CASEY FILM STORY (TV)			
November, 1962 (25 cents) (Photo-c)			
Gold Key			
30009-211-All photos	4.00	12.00	28.00
BENEATH THE PLANET OF THE APES (See Movie Comics)			
BEN FRANKLIN KITE FUN BOOK			
1975, 1977 (16 pages; 5-1/8''x6-5/8'')			
Southern Calif. Edison Co./PG&E('77)			
	.35	1.00	2.00
BEN HUR (See 4-Color No. 1052)			
BEN ISRAEL			
1974 (39 cents)			
Logos International			
		.50	1.00
BEOWULF (See First Comics Graphic Novel)			
April-May, 1975 - No. 6, Feb-Mar, 1976			
National Periodical Publications			
1		.45	.90
2-6		.25	.50
BERNI WRIGHTSON, MASTER OF THE MACABRE			
July, 1983 - No. 5, Nov, 1984 ($1.50; Baxter paper)			
Pacific Comics/Eclipse Comics No. 5			

	Good	Fine	N-Mint
1-Wrightson c/a-r begins	.40	1.25	2.50
2-5	.35	1.00	2.00
BERRYS, THE			
May, 1956			
Argo Publ.			
1-Reprints daily & Sunday strips & daily Animal Antics by Ed			
Nofziger	2.00	6.00	14.00
BEST COMICS			
Nov, 1939 - 1940 (large size, reads sideways)			
Better Publications			
1-(Scarce)-Red Mask begins	27.00	81.00	190.00
2-4: 4-Cannibalism sty	16.00	48.00	110.00
BEST FROM BOY'S LIFE, THE			
Oct, 1957 - No. 5, Oct, 1958 (35 cents)			
Gilberton Company			
1-Space Conquerors & Kam of the Ancient Ones app.; also No. 3			
	3.00	9.00	21.00
2,3,5	1.30	4.00	9.00
4-L.B. Cole-a	1.70	5.00	12.00
BEST LOVE (Formerly Sub-Mariner No. 32)			
No. 33, Aug, 1949 - No. 36, April, 1950 (Photo-c 33-36)			
Marvel Comics (MPI)			
33-Kubert-a	3.50	10.50	24.00
34	1.70	5.00	12.00
35,36-Everett-a	2.65	8.00	18.00
BEST OF BUGS BUNNY, THE			
Oct, 1966 - No. 2, Oct, 1968			
Gold Key			
1,2-Giants	1.75	5.25	14.00
BEST OF DC, THE (Blue Ribbon Digest) (See Limited Coll. Ed. C-52)			
9-10/79 - No. 71, 4/86 (100-148 pgs; all reprints)			
DC Comics			
1-17,19-34,36-71		.40	.80
18-The New Teen Titans	.25	.80	1.60
35-The Year's Best Comics Stories(148pgs.)		.60	1.20
NOTE: **Adams** a-26, 51. **Aparo** a-9, 14, 26, 30; c-9, 14, 26. **Austin** a-51i. **Buckler** a-40p; c-22. **Giffen** a-50, 52; c-33p. **Grell** a-33p. **Grossman** a-37. **Heath** a-26. **Kaluta** a-40. **G. Kane** c-40, 44. **Kubert** a-21, 26. **Layton** a-21. **S. Mayer** c-29, 37, 41, 43, 47; a-28, 29, 37, 41, 43, 47, 58, 65, 68. **Moldoff** c-64p. **Morrow** a-40; c-40. **W. Mortimer** a-39p. **Newton** a-5, 51. **Perez** a-24, 50p; c-18, 21, 23. **Rogers** a-14, 51p. **Spiegle** a-52. **Starlin** a-51. **Staton** a-5, 21. **Tuska** a-24. **Wolverton** a-60. **Wood** a-60; 63; c-60, 63. **Wrightson** a-60. New art in No. 14, 18, 24.			
BEST OF DENNIS THE MENACE, THE			
Summer, 1959 - No. 5, Spring, 1961 (100 pages)			
Hallden/Fawcett Publications			
1 (all reprints; Wiseman-a)	2.30	7.00	16.00
2-5	1.50	4.50	10.00
BEST OF DONALD DUCK, THE			
Nov, 1965 (36 pages)			
Gold Key			
1-Reprints 4-Color 223 by Barks	5.00	15.00	30.00
BEST OF DONALD DUCK & UNCLE SCROOGE, THE			
Nov, 1964 - No. 2, Sept, 1967 (25 cent giant)			
Gold Key			
1(30022-411)('64)-Reprints 4-Color 189 & 408 by Carl Barks			
No. 189-c redrawn by Barks	6.00	18.00	36.00
2(30022-709)('67)-Reprints 4-Color 256 & ''Seven Cities of Cibola''			
& U.S. 8 by Barks	5.00	15.00	30.00
BEST OF HORROR AND SCIENCE FICTION COMICS			
1987 ($2.00, color)			

BEST OF HORROR AND SCIENCE FICTION COMICS (continued)
Bruce Webster

	Good	Fine	N-Mint
1-Wolverton, Frazetta, Powell, Ditko-r	.35	1.00	2.00

BEST OF MARMADUKE, THE
1960 (a dog)
Charlton Comics

| 1-Brad Anderson's strip reprints | .70 | 2.10 | 5.00 |

BEST OF MS. TREE, THE
1987 - No. 4, 1988 ($2.00, mini-series)
Pyramid Comics

| 1-3 | .35 | 1.00 | 2.00 |

BEST OF THE BRAVE AND THE BOLD, THE (See Super DC Giant)
Oct., 1988 - No. 6, Jan, 1989 (mini-series, $2.50, color)
DC Comics

| 1-6: Adams-r in all | .40 | 1.25 | 2.50 |

BEST OF THE WEST (See A-1 Comics)
1951 - No. 12, April-June, 1954
Magazine Enterprises

1(A-1 42)-Ghost Rider, Durango Kid, Straight Arrow, Bobby Benson			
begin	19.00	57.00	132.00
2(A-1 46)	10.00	30.00	70.00
3(A-1 52), 4(A-1 59), 5(A-1 66)	8.50	25.50	60.00
6(A-1 70), 7(A-1 76), 8(A-1 81), 9(A-1 85), 10(A-1 87), 11(A-1 97),			
12(A-1 103)	6.00	18.00	42.00

NOTE: *Borth a-12. Guardineer a-5, 12. Powell a-1,12.*

BEST OF UNCLE SCROOGE & DONALD DUCK, THE
November, 1966 (25 cents)
Gold Key

| 1(30030-611)-Reprints part 4-Color 159 & 456 & Uncle | | | |
| Scrooge 6,7 by Carl Barks | 5.00 | 15.00 | 30.00 |

BEST OF WALT DISNEY COMICS, THE
1974 (In color; $1.50; 52 pages) (Walt Disney)
8½x11'' cardboard covers; 32,000 printed of each
Western Publishing Co.

96170-Reprints 1st two stories less 1 pg. each from 4-Color 62			
	1.00	3.00	7.00
96171-Reprints Mickey Mouse and the Bat Bandit of Inferno Gulch			
from 1934 (strips) by Gottfredson	1.00	3.00	7.00
96172-Reprints Uncle Scrooge 386 & two other stories			
	1.00	3.00	7.00
96173-Reprints ''Ghost of the Grotto'' (from 4-Color 159) &			
''Christmas on Bear Mtn.'' (from 4-Color 178)			
	1.00	3.00	7.00

BEST ROMANCE
No. 5, Feb-Mar, 1952 - No. 7, Aug, 1952
Standard Comics (Visual Editions)

| 5-Toth-a; photo-c | 4.65 | 14.00 | 32.00 |
| 6,7-Photo-c | 1.50 | 4.50 | 10.00 |

BEST SELLER COMICS (See Tailspin Tommy)

BEST WESTERN (Formerly Terry Toons?) (Western Outlaws & Sheriffs No. 60 on)
No. 58, June, 1949 - No. 59, Aug, 1949
Marvel Comics (IPC)

| 58,59-Black Rider, Kid Colt, Two-Gun Kid app. | | | |
| | 5.00 | 15.00 | 35.00 |

BETTY AND HER STEADY (Going Steady with Betty No. 1)
No. 2, Mar-Apr, 1950
Avon Periodicals

| 2 | 4.50 | 13.50 | 31.50 |

BETTY AND ME
Aug, 1965 - Present
Archie Publications

	Good	Fine	N-Mint
1	7.00	21.00	42.00
2	3.35	10.00	20.00
3-5: 3-Origin Superteen. Superteen in new costume #4-7; dons			
new helmet #5, ends #8	2.35	7.00	14.00
6-10	1.00	3.00	6.00
11-30	.40	1.20	2.40
31-55 (52 pages #36-55)		.60	1.20
56-175		.30	.60

BETTY AND VERONICA (Also see Archie's Girls . . .)
June, 1987 - Present
Archie Enterprises

| 1-18 | | .40 | .75 |

BETTY & VERONICA ANNUAL DIGEST (. . .Digest Mag. #2-4;
. . .Comics Digest Mag. #5 on)
November, 1980 - Present ($1.00 - 1.35)
Archie Publications

| 1, 2(11/81-Katy Keene sty), 3(8/82), 4-6(11/83), 7-35('88) | | | |
| | | .40 | .80 |

BETTY & VERONICA CHRISTMAS SPECTACULAR (See Archie Giant
Series Mag. #159, 168, 180, 191, 204, 217, 229, 241, 453, 465, 477, 489, 501, 513, 525,
536, 547, 558, 568)

BETTY & VERONICA DOUBLE DIGEST MAGAZINE
1987 - Present (Digest size, 256 pgs., $2.25)
Archie Enterprises

| 1-12: 5-Christmas-c | .35 | 1.10 | 2.25 |

BETTY & VERONICA SPECTACULAR (See Archie Giant Series Mag. #11,
16, 21, 26, 32, 138, 145, 153, 162, 173, 184, 197, 201, 210, 214, 221, 226, 234, 238, 246,
250, 458, 462, 470, 482, 486, 494, 498, 506, 510, 518, 522, 526, 530, 537, 552, 559,
563, 569, 575, 582, 588)

BETTY & VERONICA SUMMER FUN (See Archie Giant Series Mag. #8, 13,
18, 23, 28, 34, 140, 147, 155, 164, 175, 187, 199, 212, 224, 236, 248, 460, 484, 496, 508,
520, 529, 539, 550, 561, 585)

BETTY BOOP IN 3-D
Sept, 1986
Blackthorne Publ.

| 1 | .40 | 1.25 | 2.50 |

BETTY'S DIARY (See Archie Giant Series Mag. No. 555)
April, 1986 - Present
Archie Enterprises

| 1-24 | | .40 | .75 |

BEVERLY HILLBILLIES (TV)
4-6/63 - No. 18, 8/67; No. 19; No. 20, 10/70; No. 21, Oct, 1971
Dell Publishing Co.

1	5.00	15.00	35.00
2	2.65	8.00	18.00
3-10	2.00	6.00	14.00
11-21	1.50	4.50	10.00

NOTE: *#1-3,5,8-14,17-21 are photo covers. #19 reprints #1.*

BEWARE (Formerly Fantastic; Chilling Tales No. 13 on)
No. 10, June, 1952 - No. 12, Oct, 1952
Youthful Magazines

10-Pit & the Pendulum adaptation; Wildey, Harrison-a; atom bomb-c			
	10.00	30.00	70.00
11-Harrison-a; Ambrose Bierce adapt.	7.00	21.00	50.00
12-Used in SOTI, pg. 388; Harrison-a	8.00	24.00	56.00

BEWARE
No. 13, 1/53 - No. 13, 1/55; No. 14, 3/55, No. 15, 5/55
Trojan Magazines No. 13-16,5/13/Merit Publ. No. 14,15

The Best Of The Brave And The Bold #1, © DC

Best Romance #5, © STD

Beverly Hillbillies #18, © Filmways TV Prod.

Beware The Creeper #1, © DC   Bewitched #5, © Screen Gems   The Big All-American Comic Book #1, © DC

BEWARE (continued)	Good	Fine	N-Mint
13(#1)-Harrison-a	9.00	27.00	62.00
14(#2)	6.00	18.00	42.00
15,16(#3,4)-Harrison-a	5.00	15.00	35.00
5,9,12,13	5.00	15.00	35.00
6-Ill. in SOTI-"Children are first shocked and then desensitized by all this brutality." Corpse on cover swipe/V.O.H. #26; girl on cover swipe/Advs. Into Darkness #10	13.00	40.00	90.00
7,8-Check-a	7.00	21.00	50.00
10-Frazetta/Check-c; Disbrow, Check-a	27.00	81.00	190.00
11-Disbrow-a; heart torn out, blood drainage	7.00	21.00	50.00
14-Krenkel/Harrison-c; dismemberment, severed head panels	6.00	18.00	42.00
15-Harrison-a	5.00	15.00	35.00

NOTE: *Fass* a-5, 6; c-6, 11. *Hollingsworth* a-15(3), 16(4),9; c-16(4),8,9. *Kiefer* a-5,6,10.

BEWARE! (Tomb of Darkness No. 9 on)
March, 1973 - No. 8, May, 1974
Marvel Comics Group

1-Everett-c		.30	.60
2-8: 6-Tuska-a. 7-Torres r-/Mystical Tales #7		.20	.40

BEWARE TERROR TALES
May, 1952 - No. 8, July, 1953
Fawcett Publications

1-E.C. art swipe/Haunt of Fear 5 & Vault of Horror 26	8.00	24.00	56.00
2	5.00	15.00	35.00
3-8: 8-Tothish-a	4.00	12.00	28.00

NOTE: *Andru* a-2. *Bernard Bailey* a-1; c-1-5. *Powell* a-1, 2, 8. *Sekowsky* a-2.

BEWARE THE CREEPER (See Adventure, Brave & the Bold, First Issue Special, Showcase, and World's Finest)
May-June, 1968 - No. 6, March-April, 1969
National Periodical Publications

1	1.15	3.50	8.00
2-6	1.00	3.00	6.00

NOTE: *Ditko* a-1-4, 5p; c-1-5. *G. Kane* c-6. *Sparling* a-6p.

BEWITCHED (TV)
4-6/65 - No. 11, 10/67; No. 12 - No. 14, Oct, 1969
Dell Publishing Co.

1	5.00	15.00	35.00
2	3.00	9.00	21.00
3-14: Photo-c #3-13	2.00	6.00	14.00

BEYOND, THE
Nov, 1950 - No. 30, Jan, 1955
Ace Magazines

1-Bakerish-a(p)	12.00	36.00	84.00
2-Bakerish-a(p)	7.00	21.00	50.00
3-10: 10-Woodish-a by Cameron	5.00	15.00	35.00
11-17,19,20	3.50	10.50	24.00
18-Used in POP, pgs. 81,82	4.00	12.00	28.00
21-26,28-30	3.00	9.00	21.00
27-Used in SOTI, pg. 111	3.50	10.50	24.00

NOTE: *Cameron* a-10, 11p, 12p, 15, 20-27, 30; c-20. *Colan* a-6, 13, 17. *Sekowsky* a-2, 3, 5, 7, 11, 14, 27r. No. 1 was to appear as Challenge of the Unknown No. 7.

BEYOND THE GRAVE
7/75 - No. 6, 6/76; No. 7, 1/83 - No. 17, 10/84
Charlton Comics

1-Ditko-a	.30	.80	1.60
2-6-Ditko-a		.60	1.20
7-17: ('83-'84) Reprints		.30	.60
Modern Comics Reprint 2('78)		.20	.40

NOTE: *Ditko* c-2,3,6. *Sutton* c-15.

BIBLE TALES FOR YOUNG FOLK (...Young People No. 3-5)
Aug, 1953 - No. 5, Mar, 1954
Atlas Comics (OMC)

	Good	Fine	N-Mint
1	6.00	18.00	42.00
2-Everett, Krigstein-a	5.00	15.00	35.00
3-5: 4-Robinson-c	3.50	10.50	24.00

BIG ALL-AMERICAN COMIC BOOK, THE
1944 (One Shot) (132 pages)
All-American/National Publ.

1-Wonder Woman, Green Lantern, Flash, The Atom, Wildcat, Scribbly, The Whip, Ghost Patrol, Hawkman by Kubert (1st on Hawkman), Hop Harrigan, Johnny Thunder, Little Boy Blue, Mr. Terrific, Mutt & Jeff app.; Sargon on cover only	190.00	570.00	1330.00

BIG BOOK OF FUN COMICS (1st DC Annual)
Spring, 1936 (52 pages, large size) (1st comic book annual)
National Periodical Publications

1 (Very rare)-r-/New Fun No. 1-5	430.00	1290.00	3000.00

BIG BOOK ROMANCES
February, 1950(no date given) (148 pages)
Fawcett Publications

1-Contains remaindered Fawcett romance comics - several combinations possible	13.00	40.00	90.00

BIG BOY (See Adventures of the...)

BIG CHIEF WAHOO
July, 1942 - No. 23, 1945?
Eastern Color Printing/George Dougherty

1-Newspaper-r (on sale 6/15/42)	18.00	54.00	125.00
2-Steve Roper app.	9.00	27.00	62.00
3-5	6.00	18.00	42.00
6-10	4.50	13.50	32.00
11-23	3.30	10.00	23.00

NOTE: *Kerry Drake* in some issues.

BIG CIRCUS, THE (See 4-Color No. 1036)

BIG COUNTRY, THE (See 4-Color No. 946)

BIG DADDY ROTH
Oct-Nov, 1964 - No. 4, Apr-May, 1965 (Magazine; 35 cents)
Millar Publications

1-Toth-a	7.00	21.00	50.00
2-4-Toth-a	5.50	16.50	38.50

BIG HERO ADVENTURES (See Jigsaw)

BIG JIM'S P.A.C.K.
No date (16 pages)
Mattel, Inc. (Marvel Comics)

Giveaway with Big Jim doll		.15	.30

BIG JOHN AND SPARKIE (Formerly Sparkie, Radio Pixie)
1952
Ziff-Davis Publ. Co.

4	5.50	16.50	38.50

BIG LAND, THE (See 4-Color No. 812)

BIG RED (See Movie Comics)

BIG SHOT COMICS
May, 1940 - No. 104, Aug, 1949
Columbia Comics Group

1-Intro. Skyman; The Face (Tony Trent), The Cloak (Spy Master), Marvelo, Monarch of Magicians, Joe Palooka, Charlie Chan, Tom Kerry, Dixie Dugan, Rocky Ryan begin	60.00	180.00	420.00
2	26.00	78.00	182.00
3-The Cloak called Spy Chief; Skyman-c	22.00	65.00	154.00
4,5	20.00	60.00	140.00

BIG SHOT COMICS (continued)	Good	Fine	N-Mint
6-10	16.00	48.00	110.00
11-14: 14-Origin Sparky Watts	14.50	44.00	100.00
15-Origin The Cloak	16.00	48.00	110.00
16-20	9.00	27.00	62.00
21-30: 29-Intro. Capt. Yank; Bo (a dog) newspaper strip reprints			
by Frank Beck begins, ends #104	7.00	21.00	50.00
31-40: 32-Vic Jordan newspaper strip reprints begin, ends #52			
	6.00	18.00	42.00
41-50: 42-No Skyman. 50-Origin The Face retold			
	4.50	13.50	32.00
51-60	4.00	12.00	28.00
61-70: 63 on-Tony Trent, the Face	3.50	10.50	24.00
71-80: 73-The Face cameo. 74,80: The Face app. in Tony Trent.			
78-Last Charlie Chan strip reprints	3.00	9.00	21.00
81-90: 85-Tony Trent marries Babs Walsh	2.30	7.00	16.00
91-99,101-104: 69-94-Skyman in Outer Space. 96-Xmas-c			
	2.00	6.00	14.00
100	2.65	8.00	18.00

NOTE: **Mart Bailey** art on "The Face"-No. 1-104. **Guardineer** a-5. Sparky Watts by **Boody Rogers**-No. 14-42, 77-104, (by others No. 43-76). Others than Tony Trent wear "The Face" mask in No. 46-63, 93. Skyman by **Ogden Whitney**-No. 1, 2, 4, 12-37, 49, 70-101. Skyman covers-No. 1, 6, 10, 11, 14, 16, 20, 27, 89, 95, 100.

BIG TEX
June, 1953
Toby Press

1-Contains (3) John Wayne stories-r with name changed to Big Tex			
	3.50	10.50	24.00

BIG-3
Fall, 1940 - No. 7, Jan, 1942
Fox Features Syndicate

1-Blue Beetle, The Flame, & Samson begin	70.00	210.00	490.00
2	30.00	90.00	210.00
3-5	24.00	72.00	168.00
6-Last Samson; bondage-c	21.00	62.00	147.00
7-V-Man app.	21.00	62.00	147.00

BIG TOP COMICS, THE
1951 (no month)
Toby Press

1,2	2.35	7.00	16.00

BIG TOWN (Radio/TV)
Jan, 1951 - No. 50, Mar-Apr, 1958 (No. 1-9, 52pgs.)
National Periodical Publications

1-Dan Barry-a begins	20.00	60.00	140.00
2	10.00	30.00	70.00
3-10	5.70	17.00	40.00
11-20	3.50	10.50	24.00
21-31: Last pre-code (1-2/55)	2.35	7.00	16.00
32-50	1.70	5.00	12.00

BIG VALLEY, THE (TV)
6/66 - No. 5, 10/67; No. 6, 10/69
Dell Publishing Co.

1: Photo-c #1-5	2.65	8.00	18.00
2-6: 6 r-/#1	1.30	4.00	9.00

BILL BARNES COMICS (...America's Air Ace Comics No. 2 on)
(Air Ace V2No.1 on; also see Shadow Comics)
Oct, 1940(No. month given) - No. 12, Oct, 1943
Street & Smith Publications

1-23 pgs.-comics; Rocket Rooney begins	32.00	95.00	225.00
2-Barnes as The Phantom Flyer app.; Tuska-a			
	19.00	57.00	132.00
3-5	16.00	48.00	110.00
6-12	12.00	36.00	84.00

BILL BATTLE, THE ONE MAN ARMY (Also see Master No. 133)
Oct, 1952 - No. 4, Apr, 1953 (All photo-c)
Fawcett Publications

	Good	Fine	N-Mint
1	2.35	7.00	16.00
2	1.15	3.50	8.00
3,4	1.00	3.00	7.00

BILL BOYD WESTERN (Movie star; see Hopalong Cassidy & Western Hero)
Feb, 1950 - No. 23, June, 1952 (36pgs., 1-3,7,11,14-on)
Fawcett Publications

1-Bill Boyd & his horse Midnite begin; photo front/back-c			
	18.00	54.00	125.00
2-Painted-c	13.00	40.00	90.00
3-Photo-c begin, end #23; last photo back-c	11.50	34.50	80.00
4-6(52pgs.)	9.00	27.00	62.00
7,11(36pgs.)	7.00	21.00	50.00
8-10,12,13(52pgs.)	7.50	22.50	52.50
14-22	6.00	18.00	42.00
23-Last issue	6.50	19.50	46.00

BILL BUMLIN (See Treasury of Comics No. 3)

BILL ELLIOTT (See Wild Bill Elliott)

BILL STERN'S SPORTS BOOK
Spring-Summer, 1951 - V2No.2, Winter, 1952
Ziff-Davis Publ. Co.(Approved Comics)

V1#10(1951)	6.00	18.00	42.00
2(Sum'52-reg. size)	4.00	12.00	28.00
V2#2(1952,96 pgs.)-Krigstein, Kinstler-a	8.00	24.00	56.00

BILLY AND BUGGY BEAR
1958; 1964
I.W. Enterprises/Super

I.W. Reprint #1(early Timely funny animal), #7(1958)			
	.50	1.50	3.00
Super Reprint #10(1964)	.50	1.50	3.00

BILLY BUCKSKIN WESTERN (2-Gun Western No. 4)
Nov, 1955 - No. 3, March, 1956
Atlas Comics (IMC No. 1/MgPC No. 2,3)

1-Mort Drucker-a; Maneely-c/a	5.00	15.00	35.00
2-Mort Drucker-a	3.00	9.00	21.00
3-Williamson, Drucker-a	5.00	15.00	35.00

BILLY BUNNY (Black Cobra No. 6 on)
Feb-Mar, 1954 - No. 5, Oct-Nov, 1954
Excellent Publications

1	2.35	7.00	16.00
2	1.15	3.50	8.00
3-5	.85	2.50	6.00

BILLY BUNNY'S CHRISTMAS FROLICS
1952 (100 pages)
Farrell Publications

1	5.00	15.00	35.00

BILLY MAKE BELIEVE (See Single Series No. 14)

BILLY THE KID (Formerly Masked Raider; see Return of the Outlaw)
No. 9, Nov, 1957 - No. 121, Dec, 1976; No. 122, Sept, 1977 - No. 123, Oct, 1977; No. 124, Feb, 1978 - No. 153, Mar, 1983
Charlton Publ. Co.

9	3.00	9.00	21.00
10,12,14,17-19	1.85	6.00	13.00
11-(68 pgs., origin, 1st app. The Ghost Train)	2.35	7.00	16.00
13-Williamson/Torres-a	3.00	9.00	21.00
15-Origin; 2pgs. Williamson-a	3.00	9.00	21.00
16-Two pgs. Williamson	3.00	9.00	21.00

Big Shot Comics #3, © CCG

Bill Barnes Comics #1, © S & S

Billy Buckskin Western #3, © MEG

Billy The Kid Adventure Magazine #1, © TOBY

Bingo Comics #1, © Howard Publ.

Black Cat #29, © HARV

BILLY THE KID (continued)	Good	Fine	N-Mint
20-22,25-Severin-a(3-4)	3.00	9.00	21.00
23,24,26-30	1.00	3.00	7.00
31-40	.60	1.80	4.20
41-60	.50	1.50	3.00
61-80: 66-Bounty Hunter series begins. Not in No. 79,82,84-86			
	.40		.80
81-123: 87-Last Bounty Hunter. 111-Origin The Ghost Train; 117-Gun-smith & Co., The Cheyenne Kid app.		.30	.60
124(2/78)-129		.30	.60
130-153		.30	.60
Modern Comics 109 (1977 reprint)		.15	.30

NOTE: Severin a(r)-121-129,134. Sutton a-111.

BILLY THE KID ADVENTURE MAGAZINE
Oct, 1950 - No. 30, 1955
Toby Press

1-Williamson/Frazetta, 4 pgs; photo-c	13.00	40.00	90.00
2-Photo-c	3.50	10.50	24.00
3-Williamson/Frazetta "The Claws of Death," 4 pgs. plus William-son-a	16.00	48.00	110.00
4,5,7,8,10: 7-Photo-c	2.00	6.00	14.00
6-Frazetta story assist on 'Nightmare;' photo-c	6.00	18.00	42.00
9-Kurtzman Pot-Shot Pete; photo-c	5.00	15.00	35.00
11,12,15-20	1.85	5.50	13.00
13-Kurtzman r-/John Wayne 12 (Genius)	2.30	7.00	16.00
14-Williamson/Frazetta; r-of #1, 2 pgs.	5.00	15.00	35.00
21,23-30	1.30	4.00	9.00
22-Williamson/Frazetta r(1pg.)-/#1; photo-c	1.70	5.00	12.00

BILLY THE KID AND OSCAR
Winter, 1945 - No. 3, Summer, 1946 (funny animal)
Fawcett Publications

1	4.50	13.50	32.00
2,3	2.35	7.00	16.00

BILLY WEST (Bill West No. 9,10)
1949 - No. 9, Feb, 1951; No. 10, Feb, 1952
Standard Comics (Visual Editions)

1	4.50	13.50	32.00
2	2.35	7.00	16.00
3-10: 7,8-Schomburg-c	1.70	5.00	12.00

NOTE: Celardo a-1-6,9; c-1-3. Moreira a-3. Roussos a-2.

BING CROSBY (See Feature Films)

BINGO (. . . Comics) (H. C. Blackerby)
1945 (Reprints National material)
Howard Publ.

1-L. B. Cole opium-c	8.00	24.00	56.00

BINGO, THE MONKEY DOODLE BOY
Aug, 1951; Oct, 1953
St. John Publishing Co.

1(8/51)-by Eric Peters	2.65	8.00	18.00
1(10/53)	1.70	5.00	12.00

BINKY (Formerly Leave It to. . .)
No. 72, 4-5/70 - No. 81, 10-11/71; No. 82, Summer/77
National Periodical Publ./DC Comics

72-81		.50	1.00
82('77)-(One Shot)		.30	.60

BINKY'S BUDDIES
Jan-Feb, 1969 - No. 12, Nov-Dec, 1970
National Periodical Publications

1	.50	1.50	3.00
2-12	.35	1.00	2.00

BIONIC WOMAN, THE (TV)
October, 1977 - No. 5, June, 1978
Charlton Publications

	Good	Fine	N-Mint
1-5		.50	1.00

BIZARRE ADVENTURES (Formerly Marvel Preview)
No. 25, 3/81 - No. 34, 2/83 (Magazine-$1.50, 25-33)
Marvel Comics Group

25-Lethal Ladies. 26-King Kull		.60	1.20
27-Phoenix, Iceman & Nightcrawler app. 28-The Unlikely Heroes; Elektra by Miller; Adams-a	.25	.75	1.50
29-Horror. 30-Tomorrow. 31-After The Violence Stops; new Hang-man story; Miller-a. 32-Gods. 33-Horror		.60	1.20
34 ($2.00, Baxter paper, comic size)-Son of Santa; Christmas spec.; Howard the Duck by P. Smith	.25	.75	1.50

NOTE: Alcala a-27i. Austin a-25i, 28i. J. Buscema a-27p, 29, 30p; c-26. Byrne a-31(2pgs.). Golden a-25p, 28p. Perez a-27p. Reese a-31i. Rogers a-25p. Simonson a-29; c-29. Paul Smith a-34.

BIZARRE 3-D ZONE (Blackthorne 3-D Series No. 5)
July, 1986 (One shot)($2.25)
Blackthorne Publishing

1-D. Stevens-a	.40	1.25	2.50

BLACK AND WHITE (See Large Feature Comic, Series I)

BLACKBEARD'S GHOST (See Movie Comics)

BLACK BEAUTY (See 4-Color No. 440)

BLACK CAT COMICS (. .West. No. 16-19; . . Mystery No. 30 on)
(See All-New #7,9, The Original Black Cat, Pocket & Speed Comics)
June-July, 1946 - No. 29, June, 1951
Harvey Publications (Home Comics)

1-Kubert-a	25.00	75.00	175.00
2-Kubert-a	14.00	42.00	100.00
3	10.00	30.00	70.00
4-The Red Demons begin (The Demon #4 & 5)	10.00	30.00	70.00
5,6-The Scarlet Arrow app. in ea. by Powell; S&K-a in both.			
6-origin Red Demon	11.50	34.00	80.00
7-Vagabond Prince by S&K plus 1 more story	11.50	34.00	80.00
8-S&K-a; Kerry Drake begins, ends #13	10.00	30.00	70.00
9-Origin Stuntman (r-/Stuntman #1)	14.00	43.00	100.00
10-20: 14,15,17-Mary Worth app. plus Invisible Scarlet O'Neil-#15,20,24	8.00	24.00	56.00
21-26	6.50	19.50	46.00
27-Used in SOTI, pg. 193; X-Mas-c	8.00	24.00	56.00
28-Intro. Kit, Black Cat's new sidekick	8.00	24.00	56.00
29-Black Cat bondage-c; Black Cat stories	6.50	19.50	46.00

BLACK CAT MYSTERY (Formerly Black Cat; . . .Western Mystery #54; . . .Western #55,56; . . .Mystery #57; . . .Mystic #58-62; Black Cat #63-65)
No. 30, Aug, 1951 - No. 65, April, 1963
Harvey Publications

30-Black Cat on cover only	6.00	18.00	42.00
31,32,34,37,38,40	4.00	12.00	28.00
33-Used in POP, pg. 89; electrocution-c	4.50	13.50	32.00
35-Atomic disaster cover/story	5.00	15.00	35.00
36,39-Used in SOTI: #36-Pgs. 270,271; #39-Pgs. 386-388	8.50	25.50	60.00
41-43	4.00	12.00	28.00
44-Eyes, ears, tongue cut out; Nostrand-a	4.50	13.50	32.00
45-Classic "Colorama" by Powell; Nostrand-a	7.00	21.00	50.00
46-49,51-Nostrand-a in all	4.50	13.50	32.00
50-Check-a; Warren Kremer?-c showing a man's face burning away	7.00	21.00	50.00
52,53 (r-#34 & 35)	3.50	10.50	24.00

43

BLACK CAT MYSTERY (continued)		Good	Fine	N-Mint
54-Two Black Cat stories		4.50	13.50	32.00
55,56-Black Cat app.		3.00	9.00	21.00
57(7/56)-Simon?-c		2.65	8.00	18.00
58-60-Kirby-a(4)		4.00	12.00	28.00
61-Nostrand-a; "Colorama" r-/45		3.50	10.50	24.00
62(3/58)-E.C. story swipe		2.65	8.00	18.00
63-Giant(10/62); Reprints; Black Cat app.; origin Black Kitten		4.00	12.00	28.00
64-Giant(1/63); Reprints; Black Cat app.		4.00	12.00	28.00
65-Giant(4/63); Reprints; Black Cat app.		4.00	12.00	28.00

NOTE: Kremer a-37, 39, 43; c-36, 37, 47. Meskin a-51. Palais a-30, 31(2), 32(2), 33-35, 37-40. Powell a-32-35, 36(2), 40, 41, 43-53, 57. Simon c-63-65. Sparling a-44. Bondage-c No. 32, 34, 43.

BLACK COBRA
No. 1, 10-11/54; No. 6(No. 2), 12-1/54-55; No. 3, 2-3/55
Ajax/Farrell Publications
| | Good | Fine | N-Mint
---|---|---|---|---
1 | | 9.00 | 27.00 | 62.00
6(No. 2)-Formerly Billy Bunny | | 5.70 | 17.00 | 40.00
3-(pre-code)-Torpedoman app. | | 5.70 | 17.00 | 40.00

BLACK CROSS SPECIAL (See Dark Horse Presents)
Jan., 1988 ($1.75, B&W, One shot)
Dark Horse Comics
| | Good | Fine | N-Mint
---|---|---|---|---
1 | | .40 | 1.25 | 2.50

BLACK DIAMOND
May, 1983 - No. 5, 1984 (no month) ($2.00-$1.75)(Baxter paper)
Americomics
| | Good | Fine | N-Mint
---|---|---|---|---
1-Movie adaptation; Colt back up begins | | .40 | 1.25 | 2.50
2,3-Movie adaptation | | .40 | 1.25 | 2.50
4,5 | | .25 | .75 | 1.50
NOTE: Bill Black a-1i; c-1. Gulacy c-2-5. Photo back-c 1,2.

BLACK DIAMOND WESTERN (Desperado No. 1-8)
No. 9, Mar, 1949 - No. 60, Feb, 1956 (No. 9-28, 52 pgs.)
Lev Gleason Publications
| | Good | Fine | N-Mint
---|---|---|---|---
9-Origin | | 7.00 | 21.00 | 50.00
10 | | 4.00 | 12.00 | 28.00
11-15 | | 3.50 | 10.50 | 24.00
16-28-Wolverton's Bing Bang Buster | | 4.00 | 12.00 | 28.00
29,30,32-40 | | 1.70 | 5.00 | 12.00
31-One pg. Frazetta-a | | 2.15 | 6.50 | 15.00
41-50,53-59 | | 1.50 | 4.50 | 10.00
51-3-D effect c/story | | 4.30 | 13.00 | 30.00
52-3-D effect story | | 4.00 | 12.00 | 28.00
60-Last issue | | 1.70 | 5.00 | 12.00
NOTE: Biro c-9-24?. Fass a-58, c-54, 55, 56, 58. Guardineer a-18. Morisi a-55. Tuska a-48.

BLACK DRAGON, THE
5/85 - No. 6, 10/85 (Baxter paper; mini-series; adults only)
Epic Comics (Marvel)
| | Good | Fine | N-Mint
---|---|---|---|---
1: Bolton c/a in all | | .70 | 2.00 | 4.00
2-6 | | .35 | 1.00 | 2.00

BLACK FURY (Wild West No. 58) (See Blue Bird)
May, 1955 - No. 57, Mar-Apr, 1966 (Horse stories)
Charlton Comics Group
| | Good | Fine | N-Mint
---|---|---|---|---
1 | | 2.35 | 7.00 | 16.00
2 | | 1.15 | 3.50 | 8.00
3-15 | | .75 | 2.25 | 5.00
16-18-Ditko-a | | 2.35 | 7.00 | 16.00
19-30 | | .45 | 1.35 | 3.00
31-57 | | | .60 | 1.20

BLACK GOLD
1945? (8 pgs. in color)
Esso Service Station (Giveaway)

| | Good | Fine | N-Mint
---|---|---|---|---
Reprints from True Comics | | 3.00 | 9.00 | 21.00

BLACK GOLIATH
Feb, 1976 - No. 5, Nov, 1976
Marvel Comics Group
| | Good | Fine | N-Mint
---|---|---|---|---
1 | | | .40 | .80
2-5: 1-3-Tuska-a(p) | | | .30 | .60

BLACKHAWK (Formerly Uncle Sam No. 1-8)
No. 9, Winter, 1944 - No. 243, 10-11/68; No. 244, 1-2/76 - No.
250, 1-2/77; No. 251, 10/82 - No. 273, 11/84
Comic Magazines(Quality)No. 9-107(12/56); National Periodical Publ.
No. 108(1/57)-250; DC Comics No. 251 on
| | Good | Fine | N-Mint
---|---|---|---|---
9 (1944) | | 90.00 | 270.00 | 630.00
10 (1946) | | 42.00 | 125.00 | 295.00
11-15: 14-Ward-a; 13,14-Fear app. | | 30.00 | 90.00 | 210.00
16-20: 20-Ward Blackhawk | | 25.00 | 75.00 | 175.00
21-30 | | 19.00 | 57.00 | 132.00
31-40: 31-Chop Chop by Jack Cole | | 14.50 | 43.50 | 100.00
41-49,51-60 | | 10.00 | 30.00 | 70.00
50-1st Killer Shark; origin in text | | 12.00 | 36.00 | 84.00
61-Used in POP, pg. 91 | | 10.00 | 30.00 | 70.00
62-Used in POP, pg. 92 & color illo | | 10.00 | 30.00 | 70.00
63-65,67-70,72-80: 70-Return of Killer Shark. 75-Intro. Blackie the Hawk | | 8.50 | 25.50 | 60.00
66-B&W and color illos in POP | | 10.00 | 30.00 | 70.00
71-Origin retold; flying saucer-c; A-Bomb panels | | 8.50 | 25.50 | 60.00
81-86: Last precode, 3/55 | | 7.00 | 21.00 | 50.00
87-92,94-99,101-107 | | 5.00 | 15.00 | 35.00
93-Origin in text | | 6.50 | 19.50 | 45.00
100 | | 6.50 | 19.50 | 45.00
108-Re-intro. Blackie, the Hawk, their mascot; not in #115 | | 14.00 | 42.00 | 100.00
109-117 | | 3.65 | 11.00 | 25.00
118-Frazetta r-/Jimmy Wakely 4, 3 pgs. | | 6.50 | 19.50 | 45.00
119-130 | | 2.00 | 6.00 | 14.00
131-142,144-163,165,166: 133-Intro. Lady Blackhawk. 166-Last 10 cent issue | | 1.50 | 4.50 | 10.00
143-Kurtzman r-/Jimmy Wakely 4 | | 1.60 | 4.80 | 11.00
164-Origin retold | | 1.60 | 4.80 | 11.00
167-180 | | .85 | 2.50 | 5.00
181-190 | | .60 | 1.75 | 3.50
191-197,199-202,204-210: Combat Diary series begins. 197-New look for Blackhawks | | .45 | 1.30 | 2.60
198-Origin retold | | .60 | 1.75 | 3.50
203-Origin Chop Chop | | .50 | 1.50 | 3.00
211-243(1968): 228-Batman, Green Lantern, Superman, The Flash cameos. 230-Blackhawks become superheroes. 242-Return to old costumes | | .40 | 1.20 | 2.40
244 ('76) -250: 250-Chuck dies | | .25 | .75 | 1.50
251-Origin retold; Black Knights return | | | .50 | 1.00
252-264: 252-Intro Domino. 253-Part origin Hendrickson. 259-Part origin Chop-Chop | | | .50 | 1.00
265-273 (75 cent cover price) | | | .50 | 1.00

NOTE: Chaykin a-260; c-257-60, 262. Crandall a-10, 11, 13, 16, 18-20, 22-26, 30-33, 36(2), 37, 39-44, 46-50, 52-58, 60, 63, 64, 66, 67; c-18-20, 22-on(most). Evans a-244, 245, 246i; 248-250i. G. Kane a-263, 264. Kubert a-244, 245. Newton a-266p. Severin a-257. Spiegle a-261-67, 269-73; c-265-72. Toth a-260p. Ward a-16-27(Chop Chop, 8pgs. ea.); pencilled stories-No. 17-63(approx.). Wildey a-268.

BLACKHAWK
Mar, 1988 - No. 3, May, 1988 ($2.95 mini-series)
DC Comics
| | Good | Fine | N-Mint
---|---|---|---|---
1-3: Chaykin painted c/a | | .70 | 2.00 | 4.00

Black Diamond Western #16, © LEV

Blackhawk #32, © DC

Blackhawk #1, © DC

Black Hood Comics #14, © AP   The Black Knight #1, © TOBY   Black Magic #3, © PRIZE

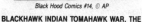

BLACKHAWK INDIAN TOMAHAWK WAR, THE
1951
Avon Periodicals

	Good	Fine	N-Mint
nn-Kinstler-c; Kit West story	6.50	19.50	45.00

BLACK HOLE (See Walt Disney Showcase #54)
March, 1980 - No. 4, September, 1980 (Disney movie)
Whitman Publ. Co.

11295-Photo-c; Spiegle-a		.50	1.00
2,3-Spiegle-a; 3-McWilliams-a; photo-c		.50	1.00
4-Spiegle-a		.40	.80

BLACK HOOD, THE (See Blue Ribbon Comics)
Jun, 1983 - No. 3, Oct, 1983 (Printed on Mandell paper)
Red Circle Comics (Archie)

1-Morrow, McWilliams, Wildey-a; Toth-c		.60	1.20
2,3: MLJ's The Fox by Toth, c/a		.50	1.00
(Also see Archie's Super-Hero Special Digest #2)			

BLACK HOOD COMICS (Formerly Hangman #2-8; Laugh Comics
#20 on; also see Black Swan, Roly Poly & Top-Notch #9)
No. 9, Winter, 1943-44 - No. 19, Summer, 1946 (on radio in 1943)
MLJ Magazines

9-The Hangman & The Boy Buddies cont'd	28.00	84.00	195.00
10-The Hangman & Dusty, the Boy Detective app.; Fuje-a			
	13.00	40.00	90.00
11-Dusty app.; no Hangman	11.00	32.00	75.00
12-18	11.00	32.00	75.00
19-I.D. exposed	11.50	35.00	80.00
NOTE: *Fuje a-9. Kinstler a-15, c-15, 16.*			

BLACK JACK (Rocky Lane's . . ., formerly Jim Bowie)
No. 20, Nov, 1957 - No. 30, Nov, 1959
Charlton Comics

20	2.35	7.00	16.00
21,27,29,30	1.15	3.50	8.00
22-(68 pages)	2.00	6.00	14.00
23-Williamson/Torres-a	3.50	10.50	24.00
24-26,28-Ditko-a	2.35	7.00	16.00

BLACK KISS
June, 1988 - Present ($1.25, B&W, 16 pgs., adult)
Vortex Comics

1-By Howard Chaykin	1.00	3.00	6.00
1-2nd print		.60	1.25
2	.70	2.00	4.00
3	.40	1.25	2.50
4-6	.35	1.00	2.00

BLACK KNIGHT, THE
May, 1953; 1963
Toby Press

1-Bondage-c	6.00	18.00	42.00
Super Reprint No. 11 (1963)	1.00	3.00	6.00

BLACK KNIGHT, THE (Also see Marvel Super Heroes & Tales To
Astonish)
May, 1955 - No. 5, April, 1956
Atlas Comics (MgPC)

1-Origin Crusader; Maneely c/a	35.00	105.00	245.00
2	24.00	72.00	168.00
3-5: 4-Maneely c/a	19.00	57.00	132.00

BLACK LIGHTNING (See Brave & The Bold, Canc. Comic Caval.,
DC Comics Presents #16, Detective and World's Finest)
April, 1977 - No. 11, Sept-Oct, 1978
National Periodical Publications/DC Comics

1		.40	.80
2-11: 4-Intro Cyclotronic Man		.25	.50

NOTE: *Buckler c-1-3p, 6-11p.*

BLACK MAGIC (. . .Magazine) (Becomes Cool Cat)
10-11/50 - V4/1, 6-7/53; V4/2, 9-10/53 - V5/3, 11-12/54; V6/1,
9-10/57 - V7/2, 11-12/58: V7/3, 7-8/60 - V8/5, 11-12/61
(V1/1-5, 52pgs.; V1/6-V3/3, 44pgs.)
Crestwood Publ. V1No.1-4,V6No.1-V7No.2/Headline V1No.5-
V5No.3,V7No.3-V8No.5

	Good	Fine	N-Mint
V1/1-S&K-a, 10 pgs.; Meskin-a(2)	13.50	40.50	95.00
2-S&K-a, 17 pgs.; Meskin-a	5.70	17.00	40.00
3-6(8-9/51)-S&K, Roussos, Meskin-a	4.35	13.00	30.00
V2/1(10-11/51),4,5,7(#13),9(#15),12(#18)-S&K-a	3.50	10.50	24.00
2,3,6,8,10,11(#17)	2.35	7.00	16.00
V3/1(#19, 12/52) - 6(#24, 5/53)-S&K-a	2.65	8.00	18.00
V4/1(#25, 6-7/53), 2(#26, 9-10/53)-S&K-a(3-4)	3.00	9.00	21.00
3(#27, 11-12/53)-S&K-a; Ditko-a(1st in comics)			
	8.50	25.50	60.00
4(#28)-Eyes ripped out/story-S&K, Ditko-a	7.00	21.00	50.00
5(#29, 3-4/54)-S&K, Ditko	6.00	18.00	42.00
6(#30, 5-6/54)-S&K, Powell?-a	2.65	8.00	18.00
V5/1(#31, 7-8/54) - 3(#33, 11-12/54)-S&K-a	2.65	8.00	18.00
V6/1(#34, 9-10/57), 2(#35, 11-12/57)	1.50	4.50	10.00
3(1-2/58) - 6(7-8/58)	1.50	4.50	10.00
V7/1(9-10/58) - 3(7-8/60)	1.15	3.50	8.00
4(9-10/60), 5(11-12/60)-Torres-a	1.60	4.70	11.00
6(1-2/61)-Powell-a(2)	1.15	3.50	8.00
V8/1(3-4/61)-Powell-c/a	1.15	3.50	8.00
2(5-6/61)-E.C. story swipe/W.F. #22; Ditko, Powell-a			
	1.70	5.00	12.00
3(7-8/61)-E.C. story swipe/W.F. #22; Powell-a(2)			
	1.50	4.50	10.00
4(9-10/61)-Powell-a(5)	1.15	3.50	8.00
5-E.C. story swipe/W.S.F. #28; Powell-a(3)			
	1.50	4.50	10.00

NOTE: *Bernard Baily a-V4#6?, V5#3(2). Grandenetti a-V2#3. Ti. Kirby c-V1#1-6,
V2#1-12, V3#1-6, V4#1, 2, 4-6, V5#1-3. McWilliams a-V3#2i. Meskin a-V1#1(2), 2, 3,
4(2), 5(2), 6, V2/1, 2, 3(2), 4(3), 5, 6(2), 7-9, 11, 12i, V3#1(2), 5, 6, V5#1(2), 2. Orlando
a-V6#1, 4, V7#2; c-V6/1-6. Powell a-V5#1?. Roussos a-V1#3-5, 6(2), V2#3(2), 4, 5(2), 6,
8, 9, 10(2), 11, 12p, V3#1(2), 2i, 5, V5#2. Simon a-V2#12, V3#2, V7#5? c-V4#3?,
V7#3?, 4, 5?, 6?, V8#1-5. Simon & Kirby a-V1#1, 2(2), 3-6, V2#1, 4, 5, 7, 9, 12, V3#1-6,
V4#1(3), 2(4), 3(2), 4(2), 5, 6-V2#1. Leonard Starr a-V1#1. Tuska a-V6#3, 4.
Woodbridge a-V7#4.*

BLACK MAGIC
Oct-Nov, 1973 - No. 9, Apr-May, 1975
National Periodical Publications

1-S&K reprints		.30	.60
2-9-S&K reprints		.20	.40

BLACKMAIL TERROR (See Harvey Comics Library)

BLACKMAN
No Date (1981)
Leader Comics Group

V1#1		.30	.60

BLACK ORCHID
Holiday, 1988-'89 - No. 3, 1989 ($3.50, mini-series, prestige format)
DC Comics

1-3	.60	1.75	3.50

BLACKOUTS (See Broadway Hollywood . . .)

BLACK PANTHER, THE (Also see Jungle Action)
1/77 - No. 15, 5/79
Marvel Comics Group

1		.40	.80
2-15		.25	.50
NOTE: *J. Buscema c-15p. Kirby c/a 1-12. Layton c-13i.*			

BLACK PANTHER
July, 1988 - No. 4, Oct., 1988 ($1.25, color)
Marvel Comics Group

	Good	Fine	N-Mint
1-4	.25	.75	1.50

BLACK PHANTOM (See Tim Holt)
Nov., 1954 - No. 2, Feb?, 1955 (Female outlaw)
Magazine Enterprises

	Good	Fine	N-Mint
1 (A-1 122)-The Ghost Rider app.; Headlight c/a	14.50	42.00	100.00
2 (Rare)	20.00	60.00	140.00

BLACK PHANTOM, RETURN OF THE (See Wisco)

BLACK RIDER (Formerly Western Winners; Western Tales of Black Rider #28-31; Gunsmoke Western #32 on)(Also see All Western Winners, Best Western, Kid Colt, Outlaw Kid, Rex Hart, Two-Gun Kid, Two-Gun Western, Western Gunfighters, Western Winners, Wild Western)
No. 8, 3/50 - No. 18, 1/52; No. 19, 11/53 - No. 27, 3/55
Marvel/Atlas Comics(CDS No. 8-17/CPS No. 19 on)

	Good	Fine	N-Mint
8 (#1)-Black Rider & his horse Satan begin; 36pgs; photo-c	14.50	44.00	100.00
9-52 pgs. begin, end #14	7.00	21.00	50.00
10-Origin Black Rider	9.50	28.00	65.00
11-14(Last 52pgs.)	5.00	15.00	35.00
15-19: 19-Two-Gun Kid app.	4.65	14.00	32.00
20-Classic-c; Two-Gun Kid app.	5.00	15.00	35.00
21-26: 21-23-Two-Gun Kid app. 24,25-Arrowhead app. 26-Kid Colt app.	3.50	10.50	24.00
27-Last issue; last precode. Kid Colt app. The Spider (a villain) burns to death	4.00	12.00	28.00

NOTE:*Ayers* c-22. *Jack Keller* a-15, 26, 27. *Maneely* a-14; c-16, 17, 25, 27. *Syd Shores* a-19, 21, 22, 23(3), 24(3), 25-27; c-19, 21, 23. *Sinnott* a-24, 25. *Tuska* a-12, 19-21.

BLACK RIDER RIDES AGAIN!, THE
September, 1957
Atlas Comics (CPS)

	Good	Fine	N-Mint
1-Kirby-a(3); Powell-a; Severin-c	5.50	16.50	38.00

BLACKSTONE (See Wisco Giveaways & Super Magician Comics)

BLACKSTONE, MASTER MAGICIAN COMICS
Mar-Apr, 1946 - No. 3, July-Aug, 1946
Vital Publications/Street & Smith Publ.

	Good	Fine	N-Mint
1	10.00	30.00	70.00
2,3	7.00	21.00	50.00

BLACKSTONE, THE MAGICIAN
No. 2, May, 1948 - No. 4, Sept, 1948 (no No.1)
Marvel Comics (CnPC)

	Good	Fine	N-Mint
2-The Blonde Phantom begins	20.00	60.00	140.00
3,4-(. . .Detective on cover only). 3,4-Bondage-c	15.00	45.00	105.00

BLACKSTONE, THE MAGICIAN DETECTIVE FIGHTS CRIME
Fall, 1947
E. C. Comics

	Good	Fine	N-Mint
1-1st app. Happy Houlihans	24.00	72.00	168.00

BLACK SWAN COMICS
1945
MLJ Magazines (Pershing Square Publ. Co.)

	Good	Fine	N-Mint
1-The Black Hood reprints from Black Hood No. 14; Bill Woggon-a; Suzie app.	7.00	21.00	50.00

BLACK TARANTULA (See Feature Presentations No. 5)

BLACK TERROR (See Exciting & America's Best)
Wint, 1942-43 - No. 27, June, 1949
Better Publications/Standard

	Good	Fine	N-Mint
1-Black Terror, Crime Crusader begin	55.00	165.00	385.00
2	27.00	81.00	190.00
3	20.00	60.00	140.00
4,5	15.00	45.00	105.00
6-10: 7-The Ghost app.	11.50	34.00	80.00
11-19	10.00	30.00	70.00
20-The Scarab app.	10.00	30.00	70.00
21-Miss Masque app.	11.00	32.00	76.00
22-Part Frazetta-a on one Black Terror story	11.50	34.00	80.00
23	10.00	30.00	70.00
24-¼ pg. Frazetta-a	11.00	32.00	76.00
25-27	10.00	30.00	70.00

NOTE: *Schomburg (Xela)* c-2-27; bondage c-2, 17, 24. *Meskin* a-27. *Moreira* a-27. *Robinson/Meskin* a-23, 24(3), 25, 26. *Roussos/Mayo* a-24. *Tuska* a-26, 27.

BLACK ZEPPELIN (See Gene Day's. . .)

BLADE OF SHURIKEN
1987 - Present ($1.95, B&W)
Eternity Comics

	Good	Fine	N-Mint
1-6	.35	1.00	2.00

BLADERUNNER
Oct., 1982 - No. 2, Nov, 1982
Marvel Comics Group

	Good	Fine	N-Mint
1-Movie adaptation; Williamson c/a		.30	.60
2-Movie adapt. concludes; Williamson a		.30	.60

BLAKE HARPER (See City Surgeon. . .)

BLAST (Satire Magazine)
Feb, 1971 - No. 2, May, 1971
G & D Publications

	Good	Fine	N-Mint
1-Wrightson & Kaluta-a	1.70	5.00	10.00
2-Kaluta-a	1.20	3.50	7.00

BLAST-OFF (Three Rocketeers)
October, 1965
Harvey Publications (Fun Day Funnies)

	Good	Fine	N-Mint
1-Kirby/Williamson-a(2); Williamson/Crandall-a; Williamson/Torres/Krenkel-a; Kirby/Simon-c	2.00	6.00	12.00

BLAZE CARSON (Rex Hart No. 6 on)
(See Kid Colt, Tex Taylor, Wild Western, Wisco)
Sept, 1948 - No. 5, June, 1949
Marvel Comics (USA)

	Good	Fine	N-Mint
1	7.00	21.00	50.00
2	5.00	15.00	35.00
3-Used by N.Y. State Legis. Comm.(Injury to eye splash); Tex Morgan app.	6.00	18.00	42.00
4,5: 4-Two-Gun Kid app. 5-Tex Taylor app.	4.50	13.50	32.00

BLAZE THE WONDER COLLIE
No. 2, Oct, 1949 - No. 3, Feb, 1950
Marvel Comics(SePI)

	Good	Fine	N-Mint
2(#1), 3-photo-c (Scarce)	8.50	26.00	60.00

BLAZING BATTLE TALES
July, 1975
Seaboard Periodicals (Atlas)

	Good	Fine	N-Mint
1-Intro. Sgt. Hawk & the Sky Demon; Severin; McWilliams, Sparling-a; Thorne-c		.30	.60

BLAZING COMBAT (Magazine) (35 cents)
Oct, 1965 - No. 4, July, 1966 (Black & White)
Warren Publishing Co.

	Good	Fine	N-Mint
1-Frazetta-c	6.75	20.00	40.00
2-Frazetta-c	2.50	7.50	15.00
3,4-Frazetta-c; 4-Frazetta ½ pg. ad	1.70	5.00	10.00
. . .Anthology (reprints from No. 1-4)	.70	2.00	4.00

Black Rider #27, © MEG

Blackstone, The Master Magician Fights Crime #1, © WMG

Black Terror #5, © STD

Blazing Western #1, © Timor Publ. Blonde Phantom #19, © MEG Blondie #127, © KING

BLAZING COMBAT (continued)
NOTE: *Above has art by Colan, Crandall, Evans, Morrow, Orlando, Severin, Torres, Toth, Williamson, and Wood.*

BLAZING COMICS
June, 1944 - #3, 9/44; #4, 2/45; #5, 1945; #5(V2#2), 3/55 - #6(V2#3), 1955?
Enwil Associates/Rural Home

	Good	Fine	N-Mint
1-The Green Turtle, Red Hawk, Black Buccaneer begin; origin Jun-Gal	18.00	54.00	125.00
2-5: 3-Briefer-a	11.50	34.00	80.00
5(3/55, V2#2-inside)-Black Buccaneer-c, 6(V2#3-inside, 1955)-Indian/Jap-c	2.85	8.50	20.00

NOTE: No. 5 & 6 contain remaindered comics rebound and the contents can vary. Cloak & Dagger, Will Rogers, Superman 64, Star Spangled 130, Kaanga known. Value would be half of contents.

BLAZING SIXGUNS
December, 1952
Avon Periodicals

1-Kinstler c/a; Larsen/Alascia-a(2), Tuska?-a; Jesse James, Kit Carson, Wild Bill Hickok app.	7.00	21.00	50.00

BLAZING SIXGUNS
1964
I.W./Super Comics

I.W. Reprint #1,8,9: 8-Kinstler-c; 9-Ditko-a	.60	1.25	3.50
Super Reprint #10,11,15,16(Buffalo Bill, Swift Deer),17(1964)	.50	1.50	3.00
12-Reprints Bullseye #3; S&K-a	2.00	6.00	12.00
18-Powell's Straight Arrow	.85	2.50	5.00

BLAZING SIX-GUNS (Also see Sundance Kid)
Feb, 1971 - No. 2, April, 1971 (52 pages)
Skywald Comics

1-The Red Mask, Sundance Kid begin, Avon's Geronimo reprint by Kinstler; Wyatt Earp app.		.50	1.00
2-Wild Bill Hickok, Jesse James, Kit Carson-r		.40	.80

BLAZING WEST
Fall, 1948 - No. 22, Mar-Apr, 1952
American Comics Group(B&I Publ./Michel Publ.)

1-Origin & 1st app. Injun Jones, Tenderfoot & Buffalo Belle; Texas Tim & Ranger begins, ends #13	6.50	19.00	45.00
2,3	3.30	10.00	23.00
4-Origin & 1st app. Little Lobo; Starr-a	2.50	7.50	17.00
5-10: 5-Starr-a	2.00	6.00	14.00
11-13	1.60	4.70	11.00
14-Origin & 1st app. The Hooded Horseman	3.50	10.50	24.00
15-22: 15,16,19-Starr-a	2.00	6.00	14.00

BLAZING WESTERN
Jan, 1954 - No. 5, Sept, 1954
Timor Publications

1-Ditko-a; Text story by Bruce Hamilton	4.65	14.00	32.00
2-4	2.00	6.00	14.00
5-Disbrow-a	2.30	7.00	16.00

BLESSED PIUS X
No date (32 pages; ½ text, ½ comics) (Paper cover)
Catechetical Guild (Giveaway)

	3.00	9.00	21.00

BLITZKRIEG
Jan-Feb, 1976 - No. 5, Sept-Oct, 1976
National Periodical Publications

1-Kubert-c on all		.25	.50
2-5		.20	.40

BLONDE PHANTOM (Formerly All-Select #1-11; Lovers #23 on)
(Also see Blackstone, Millie The Model #2 and Marvel Mystery)
No. 12, Winter, 1946-47 - No. 22, March, 1949
Marvel Comics (MPC)

	Good	Fine	N-Mint
12-Miss America begins, ends #14	42.00	125.00	295.00
13-Sub-Mariner begins	28.00	84.00	195.00
14,15; 14-Male Bondage-c; Namora app. 15-Kurtzman's 'Hey Look'	24.00	72.00	170.00
16-Captain America with Bucky app.; Kurtzman's "Hey Look"	24.00	72.00	170.00
17-22: 22-Anti Wertham editorial	23.00	70.00	160.00

BLONDIE (See Ace Comics, Dagwood, Daisy & Her Pups, Eat Right to Work..., Comics Reading Libraries, King & Magic Comics)
1942 - 1946
David McKay Publications

Feature Books 12 (Rare)	37.00	110.00	260.00
Feature Books 27-29,31,34(1940)	8.00	24.00	56.00
Feature Books 36,38,40,42,43,45,47	7.00	21.00	50.00
...1944, hard-c, 1938-'44 daily strip-r, B&W, 128 pgs.	9.00	27.00	62.00

BLONDIE & DAGWOOD FAMILY
Oct, 1963 - No. 4, Dec, 1965 (68 pages)
Harvey Publications (King Features Synd.)

1	1.50	4.50	10.00
2-4	1.00	3.00	6.00

BLONDIE COMICS (...Monthly No. 16-141)
Spring, 1947 - No. 163, Nov, 1965; No. 164, Aug, 1966 - No. 175, Dec, 1967; No. 177, Feb, 1969 - No. 222, Nov, 1976
David McKay No. 1-15/Harvey No. 16-163/King No. 164-175/
Charlton No. 177 on

1	8.50	25.50	60.00
2	4.30	13.00	30.00
3-5	3.50	10.50	24.00
6-10	2.50	7.50	17.50
11-15	1.85	5.50	13.00
16-(3/50; Harvey)	2.00	6.00	14.00
17-20	1.50	4.50	10.00
21-30	1.15	3.50	8.00
31-50	1.00	3.00	6.00
51-80	.85	2.50	5.00
81-100	.75	2.25	4.50
101-124,126-130	.70	2.00	4.00
125 (80 pgs.)	1.00	3.00	6.00
131-136,138,139	.50	1.50	3.00
137,140-(80 pages)	.85	2.50	5.00
141-166(#148,155,157-159,161-163 are 68 pgs.)	.85	2.50	5.00
167-One pg. Williamson ad	.35	1.00	2.00
168-175,177-222 (no #176)		.50	1.00
Blondie, Dagwood & Daisy 1(100 pgs., 1953)	7.00	21.00	50.00
1950 Giveaway	1.50	4.50	10.00
1962,1964 Giveaway	.40	1.20	2.40
N. Y. State Dept. of Mental Hygiene Giveaway-('50,'56,'61) Regular size (Diff. issues) 16 pages; no #	1.00	3.00	6.00

BLOOD
Feb, 1988 - No. 4, Apr, 1988 ($3.25, adults)
Epic Comics (Marvel)

1	.70	2.00	4.00
2-4	.55	1.65	3.30

BLOOD IS THE HARVEST
1950 (32 pages) (paper cover)
Catechetical Guild

(Scarce)-Anti-communism(13 known copies)	64.00	190.00	450.00

47

	Good	Fine	N-Mint
BLOOD IS THE HARVEST (continued)			

Black & white version (5 known copies), saddle stitched

	Good	Fine	N-Mint
	30.00	90.00	200.00

Untrimmed version (only one known copy); estimated value-$800

NOTE: *In 1979 nine copies of the color version surfaced from the old Guild's files plus the five black & white copies.*

BLOOD OF DRACULA
Nov., 1987 - Present ($1.75, B&W)
Apple Comics

1-6	.30	.85	1.70

BLOOD OF THE BEAST
Sum, 1986 - No. 4 (mini-series; $2.00, color)
Fantagraphics Books

1-4	.35	1.00	2.00

BLOOD OF THE INNOCENT (See Warp Graphics Annual)
1/7/86 - No. 4, 1/28/86 (Weekly mini-series; adults only)
WaRP Graphics

1-4	.50	1.50	3.00
Bound Volume	1.30	4.00	7.95

BLOOD RITES (See Americomics Graphic Novel)

BLOODSCENT
Oct, 1988 (One-shot, color, $2.00, Baxter paper)
Comico

1-Colan-p	.35	1.00	2.00

BLOOD SWORD, THE
Aug., 1988 - Present ($1.50, color)
Jademan Comics

1-3	.25	.75	1.50

BLUE BEETLE, THE (Also see All Top, Big-3, Mystery Men & Weekly Comic Mag.)
Winter, 1939-40 - No. 60, Aug, 1950
Fox Publ. No. 1-11, 31-60; Holyoke No. 12-30

1-Reprints from Mystery Men 1-5; Blue Beetle origin; Yarko the Great-r/from Wonder/Wonderworld 2-5 all by Eisner; Master Magician app.; (Blue Beetle in 4 different costumes)			
	110.00	330.00	770.00
2-K-51-r by Powell/Wonderworld 8,9	50.00	150.00	350.00
3-Simon-c	35.00	105.00	245.00
4-Marijuana drug mention story	26.00	78.00	182.00
5-Zanzibar The Magician by Tuska	22.00	65.00	154.00
6-Dynamite Thor begins; origin Blue Beetle	20.00	60.00	140.00
7,8-Dynamo app. in both. 8-Last Thor	18.00	54.00	125.00
9,10-The Blackbird & The Gorilla app. in both. 10-Bondage/hypo-c			
	16.00	48.00	110.00
11(2/42)-The Gladiator app.	16.00	48.00	110.00
12(6/42)-The Black Fury app.	16.00	48.00	110.00
13-V-Man begins, ends #18; Kubert-a	19.00	57.00	132.00
14,15-Kubert-a in both. 14-Intro. side-kick (c/text only), Sparky (called Spunky #17-19)	18.00	54.00	125.00
16-18	13.00	40.00	90.00
19-Kubert-a	16.00	48.00	110.00
20-Origin/1st app. Tiger Squadron; Arabian Nights begin	16.00	48.00	110.00
21-26: 24-Intro. & only app. The Halo. 26-General Patton sty & photo			
	11.00	32.00	75.00
27-Tamaa, Jungle Prince app.	8.50	25.50	60.00
28-30(2/44)	7.00	21.00	50.00
31(6/44)-40: 32-Hitler-c. ''The Threat from Saturn'' serial in #34-38			
	5.70	17.00	40.00
41-45	4.50	13.50	31.50
46-The Puppeteer app.	5.00	15.00	35.00
47-Kamen & Baker-a begin	30.00	90.00	210.00
48-50	25.00	75.00	175.00

	Good	Fine	N-Mint
51,53	23.00	70.00	160.00
52-Kamen bondage-c	30.00	90.00	210.00
54-Used in SOTI. Illo-''Children call these 'headlights' comics''			
	60.00	180.00	420.00
55,57(7/48)-Last Kamen issue	22.00	66.00	154.00
56-Used in SOTI, pg. 145	26.00	78.00	182.00
58(4/50)-60-No Kamen-a	4.30	13.00	30.00

NOTE: *Kamen a-47-51, 53, 55-57; c-47, 49-52. Powell a-4(2). Bondage-c 9-12, 46, 52.*

BLUE BEETLE (Formerly The Thing; becomes Mr. Muscles No. 22 on) (See Charlton Bullseye & Space Adventures)
No. 18, Feb, 1955 - No. 21, Aug, 1955
Charlton Comics

18,19-(Pre-1944-r). 19-Bouncer, Rocket Kelly-r	4.50	13.50	32.00
20-Joan Mason by Kamen	5.50	16.50	38.00
21-New material	4.00	12.00	28.00

BLUE BEETLE (Unusual Tales #1-49; Ghostly Tales #55 on)
V2No.1, 6/64 - V2No.5, 3-4/65; V3No.50, 7/65 - V3No.54,
2-3/66; No. 1, 6/67 - No. 5, 11/68
Charlton Comics

V2#1-Origin Dan Garrett-Blue Beetle	2.00	6.00	14.00
2-5, V3#50-54	1.50	4.50	10.00
1(1967)-Question series begins by Ditko	2.30	7.00	16.00
2-Origin Ted Kord-Blue Beetle; Dan Garrett x-over			
	1.50	4.50	10.00
3-5 (#1-5-Ditko-c/a)	1.00	3.00	7.00
1,3(Modern Comics-1977)-Reprints	.15		.30

NOTE: *#6 only appeared in the fanzine 'The Charlton Portfolio.'*

BLUE BEETLE
June, 1986 - No. 24, May, 1988
DC Comics

1-Origin retold; intro. Firefist	.25	.75	1.50
2-10: 2-Origin Firefist. 5-7-The Question app.		.50	1.00
11-17: 14-New Teen Titans x-over		.50	1.00
18-24 ($1.00)		.50	1.00

BLUE BIRD COMICS
Late 1940's - 1964 (Giveaway)
Various Shoe Stores/Charlton Comics

nn(1947-50)(36 pgs.)-Several issues; Human Torch, Sub-Mariner app. in some	3.35	10.00	20.00
1959-Li'l Genius, Timmy the Timid Ghost, Wild Bill Hickok (All #1)			
	.70	2.00	4.00
1959-(6 titles; all #2) Black Fury #1,4,5, Freddy #4, Li'l Genius, Timmy the Timid Ghost #4, Masked Raider #4, Wild Bill Hickok (Charlton)	.70	2.00	4.00
1959-(#5) Masked Raider #21	.70	2.00	4.00
1960-(6 titles)(All #4) Black Fury #8,9, Masked Raider, Freddy #8,9, Timmy the Timid Ghost #9, Li'l Genius #9 (Charlton)			
	.30	.80	1.60
1961,1962-(All #10's) Atomic Mouse #12,13,16, Black Fury #11,12, Freddy, Li'l Genius, Masked Raider, Six Gun Heroes, Texas Rangers in Action, Timmy the Ghost, Wild Bill Hickok, Wyatt Earp #3,11-13,16-18 (Charlton)	.50	1.00
1963-Texas Rangers #17 (Charlton)	.40	.80
1964-Mysteries of Unexplored Worlds #18, Teenage Hotrodders #18, War Heroes #18 (Charlton)	.30	.60
1965-War Heroes #18	.25	.50

NOTE: *More than one issue of each character could have been published each year. Numbering is sporatic.*

BLUE BIRD CHILDREN'S MAGAZINE, THE
1957 (16 pages; soft cover; regular size)
Graphic Information Service

V1#2-6: Pat, Pete & Blue Bird app.	.40	1.20	2.40

Blood Of The Innocent #1, © WaRP Graphics

The Blue Beetle #11, © FOX

Blue Beetle #1, © DC

Blue Bolt V1#3, © NOVP

Blue Ribbon Comics #5 (7/40), © AP

Blue Ribbon Comics #5 (8/49), STJ

BLUE BOLT	Good	Fine	N-Mint
June, 1940 - No. 101 (V10No.2), Sept-Oct, 1949			
Funnies, Inc. No. 1/Novelty Press/Premium Group of Comics			

V1#1-Origin Blue Bolt by Joe Simon, Sub-Zero, White Rider & Super
    Horse, Dick Cole, Wonder Boy & Sgt. Spook

	100.00	300.00	700.00
2-Simon-a	60.00	180.00	420.00
3-1 pg. Space Hawk by Wolverton; S&K-a	46.00	138.00	320.00
4,5-S&K-a in each; 5-Everett-a begins on Sub-Zero			
	38.00	115.00	265.00
6,8-10-S&K-a	35.00	105.00	245.00
7-S&K c/a	36.00	108.00	250.00
11,12	16.00	48.00	110.00

V2#1-Origin Dick Cole & The Twister; Twister x-over in Dick Cole,
    Sub-Zero, & Blue Bolt. Origin Simba Karno who battles Dick
    Cole through V2/5 & becomes main supporting character V2/6
    on; battle-c

	11.00	32.00	75.00
2-Origin The Twister retold in text	7.00	21.00	50.00
3-5- 5-Intro. Freezum	5.00	15.00	35.00
6-Origin Sgt. Spook retold	4.00	12.00	28.00
7-12- 7-Lois Blake becomes Blue Bolt's costume aide; last Twister	3.30	10.00	23.00
V3#1-3	2.50	7.50	17.50
4-12- 4-Blue Bolt abandons costume	2.20	6.50	15.50
V4#1-Hitler, Tojo, Mussolini-c	2.20	6.50	15.50
V4#2-12- 3-Shows V4#3 on-c, V4#4 inside (9-10/43). 8-Last Sub-Zero	1.70	5.00	12.00
V5#1-8, V6#1-3,5-10, V7#1-12	1.50	4.50	10.00
V6#4-Racist cover	1.65	4.75	11.00
V8#1-6,8-12, V9#1-5,7,8	1.30	4.00	9.00
V8#7,V9#6,9-L. B. Cole-c	1.85	5.50	13.00
V10#1(#100)	1.65	4.75	11.00
V10#2(#101)-Last Dick Cole, Blue Bolt	1.50	4.50	10.00

NOTE: Everett c-V1#4,11, V2#1,7. Gustavson a-V1#1-12, V2#1-7. Kiefer c-V3#1. Rico a-V6#10, V7#4. Blue Bolt not in V9#8.

BLUE BOLT (Becomes Ghostly Weird Stories #120 on; continuation
of Novelty Blue Bolt) (. .Weird Tales #112-119)
No. 102, Nov-Dec, 1949 - No. 119, May-June, 1953
Star Publications

102-The Chameleon, & Target app.	9.00	27.00	62.00
103,104-The Chameleon app.; last Target-#104	8.00	24.00	56.00
105-Origin Blue Bolt (from #1) retold by Simon; Chameleon & Target app.; opium den story	20.00	60.00	140.00
106-Blue Bolt by S&K begins; Spacehawk reprints from Target by Wolverton begins, ends #110; Sub-Zero begins; ends #109	16.00	48.00	110.00
107-110- 108-Last S&K Blue Bolt reprint. 109-Wolverton-c(r)/inside Spacehawk splash. 110-Target app.	16.00	48.00	110.00
111-Red Rocket & The Mask-r; last Blue Bolt; 1pg. L. B. Cole-a	17.00	51.00	120.00
112-Last Torpedo Man app.	15.00	45.00	105.00
113-Wolverton's Spacehawk r-/Target V3#7	15.00	45.00	105.00
114,116: 116-Jungle Jo-r	15.00	45.00	105.00
115-Sgt. Spook app.	17.00	51.00	120.00
117-Jo-Jo & Blue Bolt-r	15.00	45.00	105.00
118-"White Spirit" by Wood	17.00	51.00	120.00
119-Disbrow/Cole-c; Jungle Jo-r	15.00	45.00	105.00
Accepted Reprint #103(1957?, nd)	3.00	9.00	21.00

NOTE: L. B. Cole c-102-108, 110 on. Disbrow a-112(2), 113(3), 114(2), 115(2), 116-118. Hollingsworth a-117. Palais a-112r.

BLUE CIRCLE COMICS (Also see Roly Poly)
June, 1944 - No. 6, April, 1945
Enwil Associates/Rural Home

1-The Blue Circle begins; origin Steel Fist	9.00	27.00	62.00
2	4.50	13.50	32.00

	Good	Fine	N-Mint
3-5: Last Steel Fist	3.50	10.50	24.00
6-Colossal Features-r	3.50	10.50	24.00

BLUE DEVIL (See Fury of Firestorm #24)
June, 1984 - No. 31, Dec, 1986
DC Comics

1	.25	.75	1.50
2-31: 4-Origin Nebiros. 17-19: Crisis x-over. 27-Godfrey Goose app.			
31-Double size	.50		1.00
Annual 1 (11/85)-Team-ups with Black Orchid, The Creeper, Demon, Madame Xanadu, Man-Bat & Phantom Stranger	.25	.70	1.40

BLUE PHANTOM, THE
June-Aug, 1962
Dell Publishing Co.

1(01-066-208)-by Fred Fredericks	1.70	5.00	12.00

BLUE RIBBON COMICS (. . .Mystery Comics No. 9-18)
Nov, 1939 - No. 22, March, 1942 (1st MLJ series)
MLJ Magazines

1-Dan Hastings, Richy the Amazing Boy, Rang-A-Tang the Wonder
    Dog begin; Little Nemo app. (not by W. McCay); Jack Cole-a(3)

	110.00	330.00	770.00
2-Bob Phantom, Silver Fox (both in #3), Rang-A-Tang Club & Cpl. Collins begin; Jack Cole-a	45.00	135.00	315.00
3-J. Cole-a	30.00	90.00	210.00
4-Doc Strong, The Green Falcon, & Hercules begin; origin & 1st app. The Fox & Ty-Gor, Son of the Tiger	35.00	105.00	245.00
5-8: 8-Last Hercules; 6,7-Biro, Meskin-a. 7-Fox app. on-c	20.00	60.00	140.00
9-(Scarce)-Origin & 1st app. Mr. Justice	100.00	300.00	700.00
10-12: 12-Last Doc Strong	40.00	120.00	280.00
13-Inferno, the Flame Breather begins #19. Devil-c	40.00	120.00	280.00
14,15,17,18: 15-Last Green Falcon	35.00	105.00	245.00
16-Origin & 1st app. Captain Flag	67.00	200.00	470.00
19-22: 20-Last Ty-Gor. 22-Origin Mr. Justice retold	30.00	90.00	210.00

Note: Biro c-3-5.

BLUE RIBBON COMICS (Teen-Age Diary Secrets No. 6)
Feb, 1949 - No. 6, Aug, 1949 (See Heckle & Jeckle)
Blue Ribbon (St. John)

1,3-Heckle & Jeckle	3.50	10.50	24.00
2(4/49)-Diary Secrets; Baker-c	5.00	15.00	35.00
4(6/49)-Teen-Age Diary Secrets; Baker c/a(2)	6.00	18.00	42.00
5(8/49)-Teen-Age Diary Secrets; Oversize; photo-c; Baker-a(2)- Continues as Teen-Age Diary Secrets	6.00	18.00	42.00
6-Dinky Duck(8/49)	1.30	4.00	9.00

BLUE-RIBBON COMICS
Oct, 1983 - No. 14, Dec, 1984
Red Circle Prod./Archie Ent. No. 5 on

1-The Fly No. 1-r	.50		1.00
2-4: 3-Origin Steel Sterling	.50		1.00
5-14: 5-S&M Shield-r. 6,7-The Fox app. 8,11-Black Hood. 12-Thunder Agents. 13-Thunder Bunny. 14-Web & Jaguar	.50		1.00

NOTE: Adams a(r)-8. Buckler a-4i. Nino a-2i. McWilliams a-8. Morrow a-8.

BLUE STREAK (See Holyoke One-Shot No. 8)

BLYTHE (See 4-Color No. 1072)

B-MAN (See Double-Dare Adventures)

BO (Also see Big Shot No. 29; Tom Cat No. 4 on)
June, 1955 - No. 3, Oct, 1955 (a dog)
Charlton Comics Group

	Good	Fine	N-Mint
BO (continued)			
1-3-Newspaper reprints by Frank Beck	3.50	10.50	24.00
BOATNIKS, THE (See Walt Disney Showcase No. 1)			
BOB & BETTY & SANTA'S WISHING WELL			
1941 (12 pages) (Christmas giveaway)			
Sears Roebuck & Co.			
	6.00	18.00	42.00
BOBBY BENSON'S B-BAR-B RIDERS (Radio) (See Best of The			
West, & Model Fun)			
May-June, 1950 - No. 20, May-June, 1953			
Magazine Enterprises			
1-Powell-a	12.00	36.00	84.00
2	6.00	18.00	42.00
3-5: 4-Lemonade Kid-c	5.00	15.00	35.00
6-8,10	4.00	12.00	28.00
9,11,13-Frazetta-c; Ghost Rider in #13-15 (Ayers-a)			
	18.00	54.00	125.00
12,17-20(A-1 88)	3.50	10.50	24.00
14-Decapitation/Bondage-c & story	4.65	14.00	32.00
15-Ghost Rider-c	4.65	14.00	32.00
16-Photo-c	4.65	14.00	32.00
. . . in the Tunnel of Gold-(1936, 5¼x8''; 100 pgs.) Radio giveaway			
by Hecker-H.O. Company(H.O. Oats); contains 22 color pages of			
comics, rest in novel form	5.00	15.00	35.00
. . . And The Lost Herd-same as above	5.00	15.00	35.00
NOTE: *Ayers* a-13-15, 20. *Powell* a-1-12(4 ea.), 13(3), 14-16(Red Hawk only); c-1-8,10,12.			
Lemonade Kid in most 1-13.			
BOBBY COMICS			
May, 1946			
Universal Phoenix Features			
1-by S. M. Iger	4.00	12.00	28.00
BOBBY SHELBY COMICS			
1949			
Shelby Cycle Co./Harvey Publications			
	1.85	5.50	13.00
BOBBY SHERMAN (TV)			
Feb, 1972 - No. 7, Oct, 1972 (Photo-c, 4)			
Charlton Comics			
1-7-Based on TV show ''Getting Together''	1.20	3.50	7.00
BOBBY THATCHER & TREASURE CAVE			
1932 (86 pages; B&W; hardcover; 7x9'')			
Altemus Co.			
Reprints; Storm-a	5.50	16.50	38.00
BOBBY THATCHER'S ROMANCE			
1931			
The Bell Syndicate/Henry Altemus Co.			
nn-By Storm	5.50	16.50	38.00
BOB COLT (Movie star)(See X-Mas Comics)			
Nov, 1950 - No. 10, May, 1952			
Fawcett Publications			
1-Bob Colt, his horse Buckskin & sidekick Pablo begin; photo			
front/back-c begin	18.00	54.00	125.00
2	13.00	40.00	90.00
3-5	11.00	32.00	75.00
6-Flying Saucer story	9.30	28.00	65.00
7-10: 9-Last photo back-c	8.00	24.00	56.00
BOB HOPE (See Adventures of . . .)			
BOB SCULLY, TWO-FISTED HICK DETECTIVE			
No date (1930's) (36 pages; 9½x12''; B&W; paper cover)			
Humor Publ. Co.			

	Good	Fine	N-Mint
By Howard Dell; not reprints	5.00	15.00	35.00
BOB SON OF BATTLE (See 4-Color No. 729)			
BOB STEELE WESTERN (Movie star)			
Dec, 1950 - No. 10, June, 1952			
Fawcett Publications			
1-Bob Steele & his horse Bullet begin; photo front/back-c begin			
	18.00	54.00	125.00
2	13.00	40.00	90.00
3-5: 4-Last photo back-c	11.00	32.00	75.00
6-10: 10-Last photo-c	8.00	24.00	56.00
BOB SWIFT (Boy Sportsman)			
May, 1951 - No. 5, Jan, 1952			
Fawcett Publications			
1	2.50	7.50	17.50
2-5: Saunders painted-c #1-5	1.50	4.50	10.00
BOLD ADVENTURES			
Oct, 1983 - No. 3, June, 1984			
Pacific Comics			
1-Time Force, Spitfire, & The Weirdling begin	.30	.90	1.80
2,3	.25	.75	1.50
NOTE: *Kaluta* c-3. *Nebres* a-3. *Nino* a-2, 3. *Severin* a-3.			
BOLD STORIES (Also see Candid Tales, It Rhymes With Lust)			
Mar, 1950 - July, 1950 (Digest size; 144 pgs.; full color)			
Kirby Publishing Co.			
March issue (Very Rare) - Contains ''The Ogre of Paris'' by Wood			
	34.00	102.00	240.00
May issue (Very Rare) - Contains ''The Cobra's Kiss'' by Graham			
Ingels (21 pgs.)	25.00	75.00	175.00
July issue (Very Rare) - Contains ''The Ogre of Paris'' by Wood			
	27.00	81.00	190.00
BOMBARDIER (See Bee 29, the Bombardier & Cinema Comics Herald)			
BOMBA, THE JUNGLE BOY (TV)			
Sept-Oct, 1967 - No. 7, Sept-Oct, 1968			
National Periodical Publications			
1-Infantino/Anderson-c	.50	1.50	3.00
2-7	.25	.75	1.50
BOMBER COMICS			
March, 1944 - No. 4, Winter, 1944-45			
Elliot Publ. Co./Melverne Herald/Farrell/Sunrise Times			
1-Wonder Boy, & Kismet, Man of Fate begin	16.00	48.00	110.00
2-4: 2-4-Have Classics Comics ad to HRN 20			
	11.00	32.00	75.00
BONANZA (TV)			
June-Aug, 1960 - No. 37, Aug, 1970 (All Photo-c)			
Dell/Gold Key			
4-Color 1110	6.00	18.00	42.00
4-Color 1221,1283, also No. 01070-207, 01070-210			
	5.00	15.00	35.00
1(12/62-Gold Key)	5.00	15.00	35.00
2	3.00	9.00	21.00
3-10	2.30	7.00	16.00
11-20	1.70	5.00	12.00
21-37: 29-r	1.15	3.50	8.00
BONGO (See Story Hour Series)			
BONGO & LUMPJAW (See 4-Color #706,886, & Walt Disney Showcase #3)			
BON VOYAGE (See Movie Classics)			
BOOK OF ALL COMICS			
1945 (196 pages)			

Bobby Benson's B-Bar-B Riders #15, © ME

Bob Steele Western #8, © FAW

Bomber Comics #2, © EP

Boots And Her Buddies #5, © NEA Service

Boris The Bear #1, © Dark Horse

Boy Comics #5, © LEV

BOOK OF ALL COMICS (continued)
William H. Wise

	Good	Fine	N-Mint
Green Mask, Puppeteer	19.00	57.00	132.00

BOOK OF COMICS, THE
No date (1944) (132 pages) (25 cents)
William H. Wise

nn-Captain V app.	19.00	57.00	132.00

BOOK OF LOVE (See Fox Giants)

BOOK OF NIGHT, THE
July, 1987 - No. 3, 1987 ($1.75, B&W)
Dark Horse Comics

1-3	.30	.85	1.70

BOOSTER GOLD
Feb, 1986 - No. 25, Feb, 1988
DC Comics

1	.40	1.25	2.50
2-5	.25	.80	1.60
6-25: 6-Origin. 23-Byrne-c(i)		.50	1.00

NOTE: *Austin* c-22i.

BOOTS AND HER BUDDIES
No. 5, 9/48 - No. 9, 9/49; 12/55 - No. 3, 1956
Standard Comics/Visual Editions/Argo (NEA Service)

5-Strip-r	6.50	19.50	45.00
6,8	4.00	12.00	28.00
7-(Scarce)-Spanking panels(3)	14.50	44.00	100.00
9-(Scarce)-Frazetta-a, 2 pgs.	17.00	51.00	120.00
1-3(Argo-1955-56)-Reprints	1.70	5.00	12.00

BOOTS & SADDLES (See 4-Color No. 919,1029,1116)

BORDER PATROL
May-June, 1951 - No. 3, Sept-Oct, 1951
P. L. Publishing Co.

1	3.50	10.50	24.00
2,3	2.00	6.00	14.00

BORDER WORLDS (Also see Megaton Man)
July, 1986 - No. 7, 1987 ($1.95, B&W), adults
Kitchen Sink Press

1-7	.35	1.00	2.00

BORIS KARLOFF TALES OF MYSTERY (. . .Thriller No. 1,2)
No. 3, April, 1963 - No. 97, Feb, 1980 (TV)
Gold Key

3-8,10-(Two #5's, 10/63,11/63)	1.15	3.50	7.00
9-Wood-a	1.50	4.50	9.00
11-Williamson-a, Orlando-a, 8 pgs.	1.50	4.50	9.00
12-Torres, McWilliams-a; Orlando-a(2)	1.00	3.00	6.00
13,14,16-20	.70	2.00	4.00
15-Crandall,Evans-a	.85	2.50	5.00
21-Jones-a	.85	2.50	5.00
22-50: 23-Reprint; photo-c	.35	1.00	2.00
51-74: 74-Origin & 1st app. Taurus		.60	1.20
75-79,87-97: 78,81-86,88,90,92,95,97-Reprints		.40	.80
80-86-(52 pages)		.40	.80
Story Digest 1(7/70-Gold Key)-All text	.50	1.50	3.00

(See Mystery Comics Digest No. 2,5,8,11,14,17,20,23,26)

NOTE: *Bolle* a-51-54, 56, 58, 59. *McWilliams* a-12, 14, 18, 19, 80, 81, 93. *Orlando* a-11-15, 21.

BORIS KARLOFF THRILLER (TV) (Becomes Boris Karloff Tales of Mystery No. 3)
Oct, 1962 - No. 2, Jan, 1963 (80 pages)
Gold Key

1-Photo-c	2.35	6.75	18.00
2	2.00	6.00	16.00

BORIS THE BEAR
Aug., 1986 - Present ($1.50, B&W)
Dark Horse Comics/Nicotat Comics no. 13 on

	Good	Fine	N-Mint
1	1.25	3.75	7.50
1-2nd print	.40	1.25	2.50
2	.60	1.75	3.50
3	.50	1.50	3.00
4	.45	1.40	2.80
5,6	.40	1.25	2.50
7	.30	.95	1.90
8 (44 pgs.)	.40	1.20	2.40
9-22	.25	.70	1.40
Annual 1 ('88, $2.50)	.40	1.25	2.50

BORIS THE BEAR INSTANT COLOR CLASSICS
July, 1987 - No. 3?, 1987 ($1.75, $1.95, color)
Dark Horse Comics

1-3	.30	.90	1.80

BORN AGAIN
1978 (39 cents)
Spire Christian Comics (Fleming H. Revell Co.)

Watergate, Nixon, etc.		.50	1.00

BOUNCER, THE (Formerly Green Mask?)
1944 - No. 14, Jan, 1945
Fox Features Syndicate

nn(1944)-Same as #14	7.00	21.00	50.00
11(#1)(9/44)-Origin; Rocket Kelly, One Round Hogan app.			
	7.00	21.00	50.00
12-14	5.00	15.00	35.00

BOUNTY GUNS (See 4-Color No. 739)

BOY AND HIS BOT, A
Jan, 1987 ($1.95, color)
Now Comics

1	.35	1.00	2.00

BOY AND THE PIRATES, THE (See 4-Color No. 1117)

BOY COMICS (Captain Battle No. 1&2; Boy Illustories No. 43-108)
(Stories by Charles Biro)
No. 3, April, 1942 - No. 119, March, 1956
Lev Gleason Publications (Comic House)

3(No.1)-Origin Crimebuster, Bombshell & Young Robin Hood; Yankee Longago, Case 1001-1008, Swoop Storm, & Boy Movies begin; intro. Iron Jaw	90.00	270.00	630.00
4-Hitler, Tojo, Mussolini-c	38.00	115.00	265.00
5	33.00	100.00	230.00
6-Origin Iron Jaw; origin & death of Iron Jaw's son; Little Dynamite begins, ends #39	65.00	195.00	455.00
7,9: 7-Flag & Hitler, Tojo, Mussolini-c	27.00	81.00	190.00
8-Death of Iron Jaw	30.00	90.00	210.00
10-Return of Iron Jaw; classic Biro-c	38.00	115.00	265.00
11-14	19.00	57.00	132.00
15-Death of Iron Jaw	23.00	70.00	160.00
16,18-20	12.00	36.00	84.00
17-Flag-c	13.00	40.00	90.00
21-26	8.00	24.00	56.00
27-29-(68 pages). 28-Yankee Longago ends	9.00	27.50	62.00
30-Origin Crimebuster retold	10.00	30.00	70.00
31-40: 32(68pgs.)-Swoop Storm, Young Robin Hood ends. 34-Suicide c/story	4.00	12.00	28.00
41-50	2.65	8.00	18.00
51-59: 57-Dilly Duncan begins, ends #71	2.00	6.00	14.00
60-Iron Jaw returns	2.30	7.00	16.00
61-Origin Crimebuster & Iron Jaw retold	2.85	8.50	20.00
62-Death of Iron Jaw explained	3.30	10.00	23.00

BOY COMICS (continued)	Good	Fine	N-Mint
63-72	1.85	5.50	13.00
73-Frazetta 1-pg. ad	2.00	6.00	14.00
74-80: 80-1st app. Rocky X of the Rocketeers; becomes "Rocky X"			
#101; Iron Jaw, Sniffer & the Deadly Dozen begins, ends #118			
	1.60	4.80	11.00
81-88	1.60	4.80	11.00
89-92-The Claw serial app. in all	1.85	5.50	13.00
93-Claw cameo; Check-a(Rocky X)	2.65	8.00	18.00
94-97,99	1.60	4.80	11.00
98-Rocky X by Sid Check	2.85	8.50	20.00
100	2.30	7.00	16.00
101-107,109,111,119: 111-Crimebuster becomes Chuck Chandler.			
119-Last Crimebuster	1.60	4.80	11.00
108,110,112-118-Kubert-a	2.30	7.00	16.00
(See Giant Boy Book of Comics)			

NOTE: *Boy Movies in 3-5,40,41. Iron Jaw app.-3, 4, 6, 8, 10, 11, 13-15; returns-60-62, 68, 69, 72-79, 81-118. Biro c-all. Briefer a-18, 19. Fuje a-55, 18 pgs. Palais a-19.*

BOY COMMANDOS (See Detective & World's Finest Comics)
Winter, 1942-43 - No. 36, Nov-Dec, 1949
National Periodical Publications

	Good	Fine	N-Mint
1-Origin Liberty Belle; The Sandman & The Newsboy Legion x-over in Boy Commandos; S&K-a, 48 pgs.	120.00	360.00	840.00
2-Last Liberty Belle; S&K-a, 46 pgs.	60.00	180.00	420.00
3-S&K-a, 45 pgs.	42.00	125.00	295.00
4,5	24.00	72.00	168.00
6-8,10: 6-S&K-a	16.00	48.00	110.00
9-No S&K-a	11.00	32.00	75.00
11-Infinity-c	11.50	34.50	80.00
12-16,18-20	8.50	25.50	60.00
17-Sci/fi c/story	9.00	27.00	63.00
21,22,24,25: 22-Judy Canova x-over	5.50	16.50	38.00
23-S&K c/a(all)	6.50	19.50	45.00
26-Flying Saucer story (3-4/48)-4th of this theme			
	6.00	18.00	42.00
27,28,30	5.50	16.50	38.00
29-S&K story (1)	6.00	18.00	42.00
31-35: 32-Dale Evans app. on-c & story. 34-Intro. Wolf, their mascot			
	3.85	11.50	27.00
36-Intro The Atomobile c/sci-fi story	5.00	15.00	35.00

NOTE: *Most issues signed by Simon & Kirby are not by them. S&K c-1-9.*

BOY COMMANDOS
Sept-Oct, 1973 - No. 2, Nov-Dec, 1973
National Periodical Publications

	Good	Fine	N-Mint
1,2-G.A. S&K reprints		.30	.60

BOY DETECTIVE
May-June, 1951 - No. 4, May, 1952
Avon Periodicals

	Good	Fine	N-Mint
1	8.00	24.00	56.00
2,3: 3-Kinstler-c	5.00	15.00	35.00
4-Kinstler c/a	8.00	24.00	56.00

BOY EXPLORERS COMICS (Terry and The Pirates No. 3 on)
May-June, 1946 - No. 2, Sept-Oct, 1946
Family Comics (Harvey Publications)

	Good	Fine	N-Mint
1-Intro The Explorers, Duke of Broadway, Calamity Jane & Danny Dixon...Cadet; S&K-c/a, 24 pgs	35.00	105.00	245.00
2-(Scarce)-Small size (5½x8½"; B&W; 32 pgs.) Distributed to mail			
subscribers only; S&K-a. Estimated value			$250-$400

(Also see All New No. 15, Flash Gordon No. 5, and Stuntman No. 3)

BOY ILLUSTORIES (See Boy Comics)

BOY LOVES GIRL (Boy Meets Girl No. 1-24)
No. 25, July, 1952 - No. 57, June, 1956
Lev Gleason Publications

	Good	Fine	N-Mint
25(#1)	2.30	7.00	16.00
26,27,29-42: 30-33-Serial, 'Loves of My Life.' 39-Lingerie panels			
	1.50	4.50	10.00
28-Drug propaganda story	2.35	7.00	16.00
43-Toth-a	3.50	10.50	24.00
44-50: 50-Last pre-code (2/55)	1.15	3.50	8.00
51-57: 57-Ann Brewster-a	.70	2.00	6.00

BOY MEETS GIRL (Boy Loves Girl No. 25 on)
Feb, 1950 - No. 24, June, 1952 (No. 1-17, 52 pgs.)
Lev Gleason Publications

	Good	Fine	N-Mint
1-Guardineer-a	3.50	10.50	24.00
2	1.70	5.00	12.00
3-10	1.35	4.00	9.00
11-24	1.15	3.50	8.00

NOTE: *Briefer a-24. Fuje c-3,7. Painted-c 1-17. Photo-c 19-21,23.*

BOYS' AND GIRLS' MARCH OF COMICS (See March of Comics)

BOYS' RANCH (Also see Western Tales & Witches' Western Tales)
Oct, 1950 - No. 6, Aug, 1951 (No.1-3, 52 pgs.; No. 4-6, 36 pgs.)
Harvey Publications

	Good	Fine	N-Mint
1-S&K-a(3)	30.00	90.00	210.00
2-S&K-a(3)	24.00	72.00	168.00
3-S&K-a(2); Meskin-a	20.00	60.00	140.00
4-S&K-c/a	15.00	45.00	105.00
5,6-S&K splashes & centerspread only; Meskin-a			
	8.50	26.00	60.00
Shoe Store Giveaway #5,6 (Identical to regular issues except S&K centerfold replaced with ad)	7.00	21.00	50.00

NOTE: *Simon & Kirby c-1-6.*

BOZO THE CLOWN (TV) (Bozo No. 7 on)
July, 1950 - No. 4, Oct-Dec, 1963
Dell Publishing Co.

	Good	Fine	N-Mint
4-Color 285	6.00	18.00	42.00
2(7-9/51)-7(10-12/52)	3.50	10.50	24.00
4-Color 464,508,551,594(10/54)	3.50	10.50	24.00
1(nn, 5-7/62) - 4(1963)	1.70	5.00	12.00
Giveaway-1961, 16 pgs., 3½x7¼", Apsco Products			
	1.00	3.00	6.00

BOZO THE CLOWN 3-D
Fall, 1987 - Present ($2.50)
Blackthorne Publishing

	Good	Fine	N-Mint
1,2	.40	1.25	2.50

BOZZ CHRONICLES, THE
Dec, 1985 - No. 6, 1986 (Adults only)(Mini-series)
Epic Comics (Marvel)

	Good	Fine	N-Mint
1-6	.35	1.00	2.00

BRADY BUNCH, THE (TV)
Feb, 1970 - No. 2, May, 1970
Dell Publishing Co.

	Good	Fine	N-Mint
1,2	1.70	5.00	10.00
Kite Fun Book (PG&E, 1976)	1.00	3.00	6.00

BRAIN, THE
Sept, 1956 - 1958
Sussex Publ. Co./Magazine Enterprises

	Good	Fine	N-Mint
1	2.15	6.50	15.00
2,3	1.15	3.50	8.00
4-7	.75	2.25	5.00
I.W. Reprints #1,3,4,8,9,10('63),14	.35	1.00	2.00
I.W. Reprint #2-Reprints Sussex #2 with new cover added			
	.35	1.00	2.00
Super Reprint #17,18(nd)	.35	1.00	2.00

Boy Commandos #36, © DC

Boy Detective #1, © AVON

Boy's Ranch #1, © HARV

The Brave And The Bold #35, © DC

The Brave And The Bold #100, © DC

Brenda Starr #13 (#1), © SUPR

BRAIN BOY
April-June, 1962 - No. 6, Sept-Nov, 1963 (Painted c-5,6)
Dell Publishing Co.

	Good	Fine	N-Mint
4-Color 1330-Gil Kane-a; origin	3.50	10.50	24.00
2(7-9/62),3-6: 4-origin retold	2.00	6.00	14.00

BRAND ECHH (See Not Brand Echh)

BRAND OF EMPIRE (See 4-Color No. 771)

BRAVADOS, THE (See Wild Western Action)
August, 1971 (52 pages) (One-Shot)
Skywald Publ. Corp.

1-Red Mask, The Durango Kid, Billy Nevada-r		.30	.60

BRAVE AND THE BOLD, THE (See Best Of . . . & Super DC Giant)
Aug-Sept, 1955 - No. 200, July, 1983
National Periodical Publications/DC Comics

	Good	Fine	N-Mint
1-Kubert Viking Prince, Silent Knight, Golden Gladiator begin			
	78.00	235.00	550.00
2	33.00	100.00	230.00
3,4	18.00	54.00	125.00
5-Robin Hood begins	13.00	40.00	90.00
6-10: 6-Kubert Robin Hood; G. Gladiator last app.; Silent Knight;			
no V. Prince	13.50	41.00	90.00
11-22: 22-Last Silent Knight	11.00	32.00	75.00
23-Kubert Viking Prince origin	13.00	40.00	90.00
24-Last Kubert Viking Prince	13.00	40.00	90.00
25-27-Suicide Squad	3.65	11.00	25.00
28-Justice League intro.; origin Snapper Carr			
	100.00	300.00	700.00
29,30-Justice League	43.00	128.00	300.00
31-33-Cave Carson	3.65	11.00	25.00
34-Origin Hawkman & Byth by Kubert	11.50	34.00	80.00
35,36-Kubert Hawkman; origin Shadow Thief #36			
	5.70	17.00	40.00
37-39-Suicide Squad. 38-Last 10 cent ish.	2.65	8.00	18.00
40,41-Cave Carson Inside Earth; #40 has Kubert art			
	3.50	10.50	24.00
42,44-Kubert Hawkman	4.30	13.00	30.00
43-Origin Hawkman by Kubert	5.00	15.00	35.00
45-49-Infantino Strange Sports Stories	.75	2.25	4.50
50-The Green Arrow & Manhunter From Mars	2.00	6.00	14.00
51-Aquaman & Hawkman	.85	2.50	5.00
52-Kubert Sgt. Rock, Haunted Tank, Johnny Cloud, & Mlle. Marie			
	1.25	3.75	7.50
53-Toth Atom & The Flash	1.25	3.75	7.50
54-Kid Flash, Robin & Aqualad; 1st app./origin Teen Titans (6-7/64)			
	8.50	25.50	60.00
55-Metal Men & The Atom	.70	2.00	4.00
56-The Flash & Manhunter From Mars	.70	2.00	4.00
57-Intro & Origin Metamorpho	1.70	5.00	10.00
58-Metamorpho by Fradon	.70	2.00	4.00
59-Batman & Green Lantern	.70	2.00	4.00
60-Teen Titans	2.65	8.00	18.00
61,62-Origin Starman & Black Canary by Anderson. 62-Huntress app.			
	.90	2.75	5.50
63-Supergirl & Wonder Woman	.55	1.60	3.25
64-Batman Versus Eclipso	.55	1.60	3.25
65-Flash & Doom Patrol	.55	1.60	3.25
66-Metamorpho & Metal Men	.55	1.60	3.25
67-Infantino Batman & The Flash	.55	1.60	3.25
68-72	.55	1.60	3.25
73-78	.45	1.30	2.60
79-Batman-Deadman by Adams	1.85	5.50	11.00
80-Batman-Creeper; Adams-a	1.50	4.50	9.00
81-Batman-Flash; Adams-a	1.50	4.50	9.00
82-Batman-Aquaman; Adams-a; origin Ocean Master retold			

	Good	Fine	N-Mint
83-Batman-Teen Titans; Adams-a	1.50	4.50	9.00
	2.30	7.00	16.00
84-Batman(GA)-Sgt. Rock; Adams-a	1.50	4.50	9.00
85-Batman-Green Arrow; new costume for Green Arrow by Adams			
	1.50	4.50	9.00
86-Batman-Deadman; Adams-a	1.50	4.50	9.00
87-92	.35	1.10	2.20
93-Batman-House of Mystery; Adams-a	1.50	4.50	9.00
94-Batman-Teen Titans	.55	1.60	3.25
95-99: 97-Origin Deadman-r	.35	1.10	2.20
100-Batman-Gr. Lantern-Gr. Arrow-Black Canary-Robin; Deadman			
by Adams	1.15	3.50	7.00
101-Batman-Metamorpho; Kubert Viking Prince	.30	.90	1.70
102-Batman-Teen Titans; Adams-a(p)	.55	1.60	3.25
103-116		.50	1.00
117-150: 149-Batman-Teen Titans		.50	1.00
151-199: 196-Origin Ragman retold		.50	1.00
200-Double-sized (64 pgs.); printed on Mando paper; Earth One &			
Earth Two Batman team-up; Intro/1st app. Batman & The			
Outsiders	.40	1.25	2.50

NOTE: **Adams**-a-79-86, 93, 100r, 102; c-75, 76, 79-86, 88-90, 93, 95, 99, 100r. **Anderson**-a-115r; c-72l, 96i. **Aparo**-a-98, 100-02, 104-25, 126i, 127-36, 138-45, 147, 148i, 149-52, 154, 155, 157-62, 168-70, 173-78, 180-82, 184, 186i-89i, 191i-93i, 195, 196, 200; c-105-09, 111-36, 137i, 138-75, 177, 180-84, 186-200. **Austin**-a-166i. **Buckler**-a-185, 186p; c-137, 178p, 185p, 186p. **Giordano**-a-143, 144. **Infantino**-a-67p, 72p, 97r, 98r, 172p, 183p, 190p, 194p; c-45-49, 67p, 69p, 70p, 72p, 96p, 98r. **Kaluta**-c-176. **Kane**-a-115r. **Kubert &/or Heath** a-1-24; reprints-101, 113, 115, 117. **Kubert** c-22-24, 34-36, 40, 42-44, 52. **Mooney**-a-114r. **Newton**-a-153p, 156p, 165p. **Roussos**-a-114r. **Staton** 148p. 52 pgs.-97, 100; 64 pgs.-120; 100 pgs.-112-117.

BRAVE AND THE BOLD SPECIAL, THE (See DC Special Series No. 8)

BRAVE EAGLE (See 4-Color No. 705,770,816,879,929)

BRAVE ONE, THE (See 4-Color No. 773)

BRAVE STARR IN 3-D
1987 - No. 2, 1988 ($2.50, with glasses)
Blackthorne Publishing

1,2-Based on TV show	.40	1.25	2.50

BREEZE LAWSON, SKY SHERIFF (See Sky Sheriff)

BRENDA LEE STORY, THE
September, 1962
Dell Publishing Co.

01-078-209	4.65	14.00	32.00

BRENDA STARR (Also see All Great)
No. 13, 9/47; No. 14, 3/48; V2No.3, 6/48 - V2No.12, 12/49
Four Star Comics Corp./Superior Comics Ltd.

	Good	Fine	N-Mint
V1#13-By Dale Messick	28.00	84.00	195.00
14-Kamen bondage-c	28.00	84.00	195.00
V2#3-Baker-a?	23.00	70.00	160.00
4-Used in **SOTI**, pg. 21; Kamen bondage-c			
	25.00	75.00	175.00
5-10	19.00	57.00	132.00
11,12 (Scarce)	23.00	70.00	160.00

NOTE: Newspaper reprints plus original material through #6. All original #7 on.

BRENDA STARR (. . . Reporter)(Young Lovers No. 16 on?)
No. 13, June, 1955 - No. 15, Oct, 1955
Charlton Comics

13-15-Newspaper-r	13.00	40.00	90.00

BRENDA STARR REPORTER
October, 1963
Dell Publishing Co.

1	9.00	27.00	62.00

BRER RABBIT (See 4-Color No. 129,208,693, Walt Disney Showcase No. 28, and Wheaties)

	Good	Fine	N-Mint
BRER RABBIT IN "A KITE TAIL"			
1955 (16 pages, 5x7¼", soft-c) (Walt Disney) (Premium)			
Pacific Gas & Electric Co./Southern Calif. Edison			
(Rare)-Kite fun book	14.00	42.00	100.00
BRER RABBIT IN "ICE CREAM FOR THE PARTY"			
1955 (16 pages, 5x7¼", soft-c) (Walt Disney) (Premium)			
American Dairy Association			
(Rare)	8.00	24.00	56.00
BRIAN BOLLAND'S BLACK BOOK			
July, 1985 (One-shot)			
Eclipse Comics			
1-British B&W-r in color	.25	.75	1.50
BRICK BRADFORD (Also see King Comics)			
1948 - 1949 (Ritt & Grey reprints)			
King Features Syndicate/Standard			
5	8.00	24.00	56.00
6-8: 7-Schomburg-c	6.50	19.50	45.00
BRIDE'S DIARY			
No. 4, May, 1955 - No. 10, Aug, 1956			
Ajax/Farrell Publ.			
4 (#1)	2.30	7.00	16.00
5-8	1.60	4.70	11.00
9,10-Disbrow-a	2.50	7.50	17.50
BRIDES IN LOVE (Hollywood Romances & Summer Love No. 46 on)			
Aug, 1956 - No. 45, Feb, 1965			
Charlton Comics			
1	2.30	7.00	16.00
2	1.30	4.00	9.00
3-10	.85	2.50	6.00
11-20	.50	1.50	3.00
21-45	.30	.90	1.80
BRIDES ROMANCES			
Nov, 1953 - No. 23, Dec, 1956			
Quality Comics Group			
1	4.00	12.00	28.00
2	2.00	6.00	14.00
3-10: Last precode (3/55)	1.60	4.70	11.00
11-14,16,17,19-22	1.15	3.50	8.00
15-Baker-a(p); Colan-a	1.30	4.00	9.00
18-Baker-a	1.65	5.00	11.50
23-Baker c/a	2.50	7.50	17.00
BRIDE'S SECRETS			
Apr-May, 1954 - No. 19, May, 1958			
Ajax/Farrell(Excellent Publ.)/Four-Star Comic			
1	4.00	12.00	28.00
2	2.00	6.00	14.00
3-6: Last precode (3/55)	1.50	4.50	10.00
7-19: 12-Disbrow-a. 18-Hollingsworth-a	1.15	3.50	8.00
BRIDE-TO-BE ROMANCES (See True...)			
BRIGAND, THE (See Fawcett Movie Comics No. 18)			
BRINGING UP FATHER (See 4-Color #37 & Large Feature Comic #9)			
BRINGING UP FATHER			
1917 (16½x5½"; cardboard cover; 100 pages; B&W)			
Star Co. (King Features)			
(Rare) Daily strip reprints by George McManus (no price on cover)			
	27.00	81.00	190.00
BRINGING UP FATHER			
1919 - 1934 (by George McManus)			
(10x10"; stiff cardboard covers; B&W; daily strip reprints; 52 pgs.)			
(No. 22 is 9¼x9½")			

	Good	Fine	N-Mint
Cupples & Leon Co.			
1	22.00	65.00	154.00
2-10	11.00	32.00	75.00
11-26 (Scarcer)	17.00	51.00	120.00
The Big Book 1(1926)-Thick book (hardcover); 10¼x10¼", 142pgs.			
	27.00	81.00	190.00
The Big Book 2(1929)	22.00	65.00	154.00
NOTE: The Big Books contain 3 regular issues rebound and probably with dust jackets.			
BRINGING UP FATHER, THE TROUBLE OF			
1921 (9x15") (Sunday reprints in color)			
Embee Publ. Co.			
(Rare)	27.00	81.00	190.00
BROADWAY HOLLYWOOD BLACKOUTS			
Mar-Apr, 1954 - No. 3, July-Aug, 1954			
Stanhall			
1	4.65	14.00	32.00
2,3	2.85	8.50	20.00
BROADWAY ROMANCES			
January, 1950 - No. 5, Sept, 1950			
Quality Comics Group			
1-Ward c/a, 9pgs.; Gustavson-a	14.00	42.00	100.00
2-Ward-a, 9pgs., photo-c	8.50	25.50	60.00
3-5: 4,5-Photo-c	3.70	11.00	26.00
BROKEN ARROW (See 4-Color No. 855,947)			
BROKEN CROSS, THE (See The Crusaders)			
BRONCHO BILL (See Comics On Parade, Sparkler & Tip Top Comics)			
1939 - 1940; No. 5, 1?/48 - No. 16, 8?/50			
United Features Syndicate/Standard(Visual Editions) No. 5-on			
Single Series 2 ('39)	22.00	65.00	154.00
Single Series 19 ('40)(#2 on cvr)	18.00	54.00	125.00
5	4.30	13.00	30.00
6(4/48)-10(4/49)	2.65	8.00	18.00
11(6/49)-16	2.00	6.00	14.00
NOTE: **Schomburg** c-6,7,9-13,16.			
BROTHER POWER, THE GEEK			
Sept-Oct, 1968 - No. 2, Nov-Dec, 1968			
National Periodical Publications			
1-Origin; Simon-c(i?)	1.30	4.00	9.00
2	1.00	3.00	6.00
BROTHERS, HANG IN THERE, THE			
1979 (49 cents)			
Spire Christian Comics (Fleming H. Revell Co.)			
		.30	.60
BROTHERS OF THE SPEAR (Also see Tarzan)			
6/72 - No. 17, 2/76; No. 18, 5/82			
Gold Key/Whitman No. 18 on			
1	1.00	3.00	6.00
2	.70	2.00	4.00
3-10	.45	1.25	2.50
11-17		.50	1.00
18-Manning-r/No. 2; Leopard Girl-r		.40	.80
NOTE: Painted-c 2-17. Spiegle a-13-17.			
BROTHERS, THE CULT ESCAPE, THE			
1980 (49 Cents)			
Spire Christian Comics (Fleming H. Revell Co.)			
		.30	.60
BROWNIES (See 4-Color No. 192, 244, 293, 337, 365, 398, 436, 482, 522, 605 & New Funnies)			

Brick Bradford #5, © KING

Bride's Secrets #1, © AJAX

Brothers Of The Spear #1, © WEST

Bruce Gentry #7, © SUPR   Buck Rogers #4, © KING   Buffalo Bill Picture Stories #1, © S & S

	Good	Fine	N-Mint

BRUCE GENTRY
Jan., 1948 - No. 2, Nov., 1948; No. 3, Jan., 1949 - No. 8, July, 1949
Better/Standard/Four Star Publ./Superior No. 3

1-Ray Bailey strip reprints begin, end #3; E. C. emblem appears
as a monogram on stationery in story; negligee panels

	Good	Fine	N-Mint
	18.00	54.00	125.00
2,3	12.00	36.00	84.00
4-8	9.00	27.00	63.00

NOTE: *Kamenish a-2-7; c-1-8.*

BRUTE, THE
Feb, 1975 - No. 3, July, 1975
Seaboard Publ. (Atlas)

1-Origin & 1st app; Sekowsky-a		.40	.80
2,3: 2-Sekowsky-a		.25	.50

BUCCANEER
No date (1963)
I. W. Enterprises

I.W. Reprint #1(r-/Quality #20), #8(r-/#23): Crandall-a in each

	1.15	3.50	7.00
Super Reprint #12('64, r-/#21)-Crandall-a	1.15	3.50	7.00

BUCCANEERS (Formerly Kid Eternity)
No. 19, Jan., 1950 - No. 27, May, 1951 (No.24-27: 52 pages)
Quality Comics Group

19-Captain Daring, Black Roger, Eric Falcon & Spanish Main begin;

Crandall-a	20.00	60.00	140.00
20,23-Crandall-a	14.50	44.00	100.00
21-Crandall c/a	18.00	54.00	125.00
22-Bondage-c	10.00	30.00	70.00

24,26: 24-Adam Peril, U.S.N. begins; last Spanish Main

	9.00	27.00	62.00
25-Origin & 1st app. Corsair Queen	9.00	27.00	62.00
27-Crandall c/a	16.00	48.00	110.00

BUCCANEERS, THE (See 4-Color No. 800)

BUCKAROO BANZAI
Dec, 1984 - No. 2, Feb, 1985
Marvel Comics Group

1,2-r/Marvel Super Special		.40	.80

BUCK DUCK
June, 1953 - No. 4, Dec, 1953
Atlas Comics (ANC)

1-(funny animal)	2.65	8.00	18.00
2-4-(funny animal)	1.60	4.80	11.00

BUCK JONES (Also see Crackajack Funnies & Master Comics #7)
No. 299, Oct, 1950 - No. 850, Oct, 1957 (All Painted-c)
Dell Publishing Co.

4-Color 299(#1)-Buck Jones & his horse Silver-B begin; painted

back-c begins, ends #5	7.00	21.00	50.00
2(4-6/51)	4.00	12.00	28.00
3-8(10-12/52)	3.00	9.00	21.00
4-Color 460,500,546,589	3.00	9.00	21.00
4-Color 652,733,850	2.00	6.00	14.00

BUCK ROGERS (In the 25th Century)
1933 (36 pages in color) (6x8'')
Kelloggs Corn Flakes Giveaway

370A-By Phil Nowlan & Dick Calkins; 1st Buck Rogers radio

premium (tells origin)	25.00	75.00	175.00

BUCK ROGERS (Also see Famous Funnies, Pure Oil Comics, Saler-
no Carnival of Comics, 24 Pages of Comics, & Vicks Comics)
Winter, 1940-41 - No. 6, Sept, 1943
Famous Funnies

1-Sunday strip reprints by Rick Yager; begins with strip #190;

	Good	Fine	N-Mint
Calkins-c	110.00	330.00	770.00
2 (7/41)-Calkins-c	65.00	195.00	455.00
3 (12/41), 4 (7/42)	52.00	155.00	365.00

5-Story continues with Famous Funnies No. 80; ½ Buck Rogers,
½ Sky Roads

	47.00	140.00	330.00

6-Reprints of 1939 dailies; contains B.R. story ''Crater of Doom''
(2 pgs.) by Calkins not reprinted from Famous Funnies

	47.00	140.00	330.00

BUCK ROGERS
No. 100, Jan, 1951 - No. 9, May-June, 1951
Toby Press

100(7)	13.00	40.00	90.00
101(8), 9-All Anderson-a('47-'49-r/dailies)	11.00	32.00	75.00

BUCK ROGERS (. . .in the 25th Century No. 5 on) (TV)
10/64; No. 2, 7/79 - No. 16, 5/82 (no No. 10)
Gold Key/Whitman No. 7 on

1(10128-410)	2.65	8.00	16.00
2(8/79)-Movie adaptation	.35	1.00	2.00
3-9,11-16: 3,4-Movie adaptation; 5-new stories	.50	1.00

Giant Movie Edition 11296(64pp, Whitman, $1.50), reprints GK No.

2-4 minus cover	.35	1.00	2.00

Giant Movie Edition 02489(Western/Marvel, $1.50), reprints GK No.

2-4 minus cover	.35	1.00	2.00

NOTE: *Bolle a-2p-4p. McWilliams a-2i-4i, 5-11. Painted-c No. 1-13.*

BUCKSKIN (See 4-Color No. 1011,1107 (Movie))

BUDDIES IN THE U.S. ARMY
Nov, 1952 - No. 2, 1953
Avon Periodicals

1-Lawrence-c	6.00	18.00	42.00
2-Mort Lawrence c/a	4.60	14.00	32.00

BUDDY TUCKER & HIS FRIENDS
1906 (11x17'') (In color)
Cupples & Leon Co.

1905 Sunday strip reprints by R. F. Outcault	18.00	54.00	125.00

BUFFALO BEE (See 4-Color No. 957,1002,1061)

BUFFALO BILL (Also see Frontier Fighters, Super West. Comics &
Western Action Thrillers)
No. 2, Oct., 1950 - No. 9, Dec, 1951
Youthful Magazines

2	3.00	9.00	21.00
3-9: 3,4-Walter Johnson c/a	1.60	4.80	11.00

BUFFALO BILL CODY (See Cody of the Pony Express)

BUFFALO BILL, JR. (TV) (Also see Western Roundup)
Jan., 1956 - No. 13, Aug-Oct, 1959; 1965 (All photo-c)
Dell Publishing Co./Gold Key

4-Color 673 (#1)	3.50	10.50	24.00
4-Color 742,766,798,828,856(11/57)	2.30	7.00	16.00
7(2-4/58)-13	1.85	5.50	13.00
1(6/65-Gold Key)	1.35	4.00	8.00

BUFFALO BILL PICTURE STORIES
June-July, 1949 - No. 2, Aug-Sept, 1949
Street & Smith Publications

1,2-Wildey, Powell-a in each	4.30	13.00	30.00

BUFFALO BILL'S PICTURE STORIES
1909 (Soft cardboard cover)
Street & Smith Publications

	9.00	27.00	62.00

BUGALOOS (TV)
Sept, 1971 - No. 4, Feb, 1972

Charlton Comics	Good	Fine	N-Mint
1-4	.35	1.00	2.00

NOTE: No. 3(1/72) went on sale late in 1972 (after No. 4) with the 1/73 issues.

BUGHOUSE (Satire)
Mar-Apr, 1954 - No. 4, Sept-Oct, 1954
Ajax/Farrell (Excellent Publ.)

V1#1	5.50	16.50	38.00
2-4	3.50	10.50	24.00

BUGHOUSE FABLES
1921 (48 pgs.) (4x4½'') (10 cents)
Embee Distributing Co. (King Features)

1-Barney Google	7.00	21.00	50.00

BUG MOVIES
1931 (52 pages) (B&W)
Dell Publishing Co.

Not reprints; Stookie Allen-a	6.00	18.00	42.00

BUGS BUNNY (See Dell Giants for annuals)
1942 - No. 245, 1983
Dell Publishing Co./Gold Key No. 86-218/Whitman No. 219 on
Large Feature Comic 8(1942)-(Rarely found in fine-mint condition)

	Good	Fine	N-Mint
	53.00	160.00	370.00
4-Color 33 ('43)	30.00	90.00	210.00
4-Color 51	18.00	54.00	125.00
4-Color 88	11.00	32.00	75.00
4-Color 123('46),142,164	6.00	18.00	42.00
4-Color 187,200,217,233	5.00	15.00	35.00
4-Color 250-Used in **SOTI**, pg. 309	5.00	15.00	35.00
4-Color 266,274,281,289,298('50)	4.00	12.00	28.00
4-Color 307,317(#1),327(#2),338,347,355,366,376,393			
	3.00	9.00	21.00
4-Color 407,420,432	2.00	6.00	14.00
28(12-1/52-53)-30	1.30	4.00	9.00
31-50	.85	2.50	5.00
51-85(7-9/62)	.70	2.00	4.00
86(10/62)-88-Bugs Bunny's Showtime-(80 pgs.)(25 cents)			
	1.75	5.25	14.00
89-100	.60	1.75	3.50
101-120	.40	1.25	2.50
121-140	.35	1.00	2.00
141-170		.60	1.20
171-228,230-245		.30	.60
229-Swipe of Barks story/WDC&S 223		.35	.70

NOTE: Reprints-100, 102, 104, 123, 143, 144, 147, 167, 173, 175-77, 179-85, 187, 190.

...Comic-Go-Round 11196-(224 pgs.)($1.95)(Golden Press, 1979)			
	.40	1.20	2.40
Kite Fun Book ('60,'68)-Giveaway, 16 pgs., 5x7¼''			
	.70	2.00	4.00
Winter Fun 1(12/67-Gold Key)-Giant	1.25	3.75	10.00

BUGS BUNNY (See The Best of...; Camp Comics; Comic Album #2, 6, 10, 14; Dell Giant #28, 32, 46; Dynabrite; Golden Comics Digest #1, 3, 5, 6, 8, 10, 14, 15, 17, 21, 26, 30, 34, 39, 42, 47; Large Feature Comic 8; Looney Tunes...; March of Comics #44, 59, 75, 83, 97, 115, 132, 149, 160, 179, 188, 201, 220, 231, 245, 259, 273, 287, 301, 315, 329, 343, 363, 367, 380, 392, 403, 415, 428, 440, 452, 464, 476, 487; Puffed Wheat, Story Hour Series #802, Super Book #14, 26; and Whitman Comic Books)

BUGS BUNNY (Puffed Rice Giveaway)
1949 (32 pages each, 3-1/8x6-7/8'')
Quaker Cereals
A1-Traps the Counterfeiters, A2-Aboard Mystery Submarine, A3- Rocket to the Moon, A4-Lion Tamer, A5-Rescues the Beautiful Princess, B1-Buried Treasure, B2-Outwits the Smugglers, B3-Joins the Marines, B4-Meets the Dwarf Ghost, B5-Finds Aladdin's Lamp, C1-Lost in the Frozen North, C2-Secret Agent, C3-Captured by Cannibals, C4-Fights the Man from Mars, C5-And the Haunted Cave

each....	1.70	5.00	10.00

BUGS BUNNY (3-D)
1953 (Pocket size) (15 titles)

Cheerios Giveaway	Good	Fine	N-Mint
each....	5.00	15.00	35.00

BUGS BUNNY & PORKY PIG
Sept, 1965 (100 pages; paper cover; giant)
Gold Key

1(30025-509)	2.15	6.50	15.00

BUGS BUNNY'S ALBUM (See 4-Color No. 498,585,647,724)

BUGS BUNNY LIFE STORY ALBUM (See 4-Color No. 838)

BUGS BUNNY MERRY CHRISTMAS (See 4-Color No. 1064)

BULLETMAN (See Fawcett Miniatures, Master Comics, Mighty Midget Comics, Nickel Comics & X-Mas Comics)
Sum, 1941 - No. 12, 2/12/43; No. 14, Spr, 1946 - No. 16, Fall, 1946
(nn 13)
Fawcett Publications

1	110.00	330.00	770.00
2	70.00	210.00	490.00
3	45.00	135.00	315.00
4,5	38.00	115.00	265.00
6-10: 7-Ghost Stories as told by the night watchman of the cemetery begins; Eisnerish-a	33.00	100.00	230.00
11,12,14-16 (nn 13)	28.00	84.00	195.00
...Well Known Comics (1942)-Paper-c, glued binding; printed in red (Bestmaid/Samuel Lowe giveaway)	12.00	36.00	72.00

NOTE: *Mac Raboy c-1-3,5,10.*

BULLS-EYE (Cody of The Pony Express No. 8 on)
7-8/54 - No. 5, 3-4/55; No. 6, 6/55; No. 7, 8/55
Mainline No. 1-5/Charlton No. 6,7

1-S&K-c, 2 pages	21.50	64.00	150.00
2-S&K c/a	20.00	60.00	140.00
3-5-S&K c/a(2)	13.00	40.00	90.00
6-S&K c/a	10.00	30.00	70.00
7-S&K c/a(3)	13.00	40.00	90.00
Great Scott Shoe Store giveaway-Reprints #2 with new cover			
	8.00	24.00	56.00

BULLS-EYE COMICS
No. 11, 1944
Harry 'A' Chesler

11-Origin K-9, Green Knight's sidekick, Lance; The Green Knight, Lady Satan, Yankee Doodle Jones app.	12.00	36.00	84.00

BULLWHIP GRIFFIN (See Movie Comics)

BULLWINKLE (TV) (...and Rocky No. 20 on; See March of Comics No. 233, and Rocky & Bullwinkle)
3-5/62 - No. 11, 4/74; No. 12, 6/76 - No. 19, 3/78; No. 20, 4/79 - No. 25, 2/80 (Jay Ward)
Dell/Gold Key

4-Color 1270 (3-5/62)	5.00	15.00	35.00
01-090-209 (Dell, 7-9/62)	5.00	15.00	35.00
1(11/62, Gold Key)	4.00	12.00	28.00
2(2/63)	3.00	9.00	21.00
3(4/72)-11(4/74-Gold Key)	1.00	3.00	6.00
12(6/76)-reprints	.70	2.00	4.00
13(9/76), 14-new stories	.70	2.00	4.00
15-25	.70	2.00	4.00
Mother Moose Nursery Pomes 01-530-207 (5-7/62-Dell)			
	4.30	13.00	30.00

NOTE: Reprints-6,7,20-24.

BULLWINKLE (...& Rocky No. 2 on)(TV)
July, 1970 - No. 7, July, 1971
Charlton Comics

Bughouse #2, © AJAX

Bulletman #2, © FAW

Bulls-Eye #1, © PRIZE

Buster Brown's Amusing Capers (C & L), © Buster Brown *Buster Crabbe #10, © FF* *Butch Cassidy #1, © AVON*

BULLWINKLE (continued)	Good	Fine	N-Mint
1	1.30	4.00	8.00
2-7	.85	2.50	5.00

BULLWINKLE AND ROCKY
Nov, 1987 - No. 9, Mar, 1989
Star/Marvel Comics No. 3 on

1-9		.50	1.00

BULLWINKLE AND ROCKY 3-D
Mar, 1987 (Blackthorne 3-D Series #18, $2.50)
Blackthorne Publ.

1	.45	1.25	2.50

BUNNY (Also see Rock Happening)
Dec, 1966 - No. 20, Dec, 1971; No. 21, Nov, 1976
Harvey Publications

1: 68 pg. Giant	2.00	4.00	8.00
2-18: 68 pg. Giants	1.15	3.50	7.00
19-21: 52 pg. Giants	1.00	3.00	6.00

BURKE'S LAW (TV)
1-3/64; No. 2, 5-7/64; No. 3, 3-5/65 (Gene Barry photo-c, all)
Dell Publishing Co.

1-Photo-c	2.00	6.00	14.00
2,3-Photo-c	1.35	4.00	9.00

BURNING ROMANCES (See Fox Giants)

BUSTER BEAR
Dec, 1953 - No. 10, June, 1955
Quality Comics Group (Arnold Publ.)

1-Funny animal	2.35	7.00	16.00
2	1.15	3.50	8.00
3-10	.85	2.50	6.00
I.W. Reprint #9,10 (Super on inside)	.35	1.00	2.00

BUSTER BROWN
1903 - 1909 (11x17'' strip reprints in color)
Frederick A. Stokes Co.

	Good	Fine	VF
. . .& His Resolutions (1903) by R. F. Outcault	40.00	120.00	280.00
. . .Abroad (1904)-86 pgs.; hardback; 8x10¼''; B&W; by R. F. Out-cault(76pgs.)	32.00	95.00	225.00
. . .His Dog Tige & Their Troubles (1904)	32.00	95.00	225.00
. . .Pranks (1905)	32.00	95.00	225.00
. . .Antics (1906)-11x17'', 30 pages color strip reprints	32.00	95.00	225.00
. . .And Company (1906)-11x17'' in color	32.00	95.00	225.00
. . .Mary Jane & Tige (1906)	32.00	95.00	225.00
. . .My Resolutions (1906)-68 pgs.; B&W; hardcover; Sunday panel reprints	32.00	95.00	225.00
Collection of Buster Brown Comics (1908)	32.00	95.00	225.00
Buster Brown Up to Date (1910)	32.00	95.00	225.00
. . .The Fun Maker (1912)	32.00	95.00	225.00
. . .The Little Rogue (1916)(10x15¾,'' 62pp, in color)	23.00	70.00	160.00

NOTE: *Rarely found in fine or mint condition.*

BUSTER BROWN
1906 - 1917 (11x17'' strip reprints in color)
Cupples & Leon Co./N. Y. Herald Co.

	Good	Fine	VF
(By R. F. Outcault)			
. . .His Dog Tige & Their Jolly Times (1906)	30.00	90.00	210.00
. . .Latest Frolics (1906), 58 pgs.	26.00	78.00	182.00
. . .Amusing Capers (1908)	26.00	78.00	182.00
. . .And His Pets (1909)	26.00	78.00	182.00
. . .On His Travels (1910)	26.00	78.00	182.00
. . .Happy Days (1911)	26.00	78.00	182.00

	Good	Fine	VF
. . .In Foreign Lands (1912)	24.00	72.00	168.00
. . .And the Cat (1917)	23.00	70.00	160.00

NOTE: *Rarely found in fine or mint condition.*

BUSTER BROWN COMICS (Also see My Dog Tige)
1945 - 1959 (No. 5: paper cover)
Brown Shoe Co.

	Good	Fine	N-Mint
nn, nd (#1)	8.50	25.50	60.00
2	4.30	13.00	30.00
3-10	2.15	6.50	15.00
11-20	1.70	5.00	12.00
21-24,26-28	1.30	4.00	9.00
25,31,33-37,40-43-Crandall-a in all	3.65	11.00	25.00
29,30,32-''Interplanetary Police Vs. the Space Siren'' by Crandall	3.65	11.00	25.00
38,39	1.00	3.00	7.00
. . .Goes to Mars (2/58-Western Printing), slick-c, 20 pgs., reg. size	2.00	6.00	14.00
. . .In ''Buster Makes the Team!'' (1959-Custom Comics)	1.00	3.00	7.00
. . .In The Jet Age ('50s), slick-c, 20 pgs., 5x7¼''	1.70	5.00	12.00
. . .Of the Safety Patrol ('60-Custom Comics)	1.00	3.00	7.00
. . .Out of This World ('59-Custom Comics)	1.00	3.00	7.00
. . .Safety Coloring Book (1958)-Slick paper, 16 pages	1.00	3.00	7.00

BUSTER BUNNY
Nov, 1949 - No. 16, Oct, 1953
Standard Comics(Animated Cartoons)/Pines

1-Frazetta 1 pg. text illo.	3.00	9.00	21.00
2	1.50	4.50	10.00
3-16	1.00	3.00	7.00

BUSTER CRABBE (TV)
Nov, 1951 - No. 12, 1953
Famous Funnies

1-Frazetta drug pusher back-c	15.00	45.00	105.00
2-Williamson/Evans-c	18.00	54.00	125.00
3-Williamson/Evans c/a	20.00	60.00	140.00
4-Frazetta c/a, 1pg.; bondage-c	24.00	72.00	168.00
5-Frazetta-c; Williamson/Krenkel/Orlando-a, 11pgs. (per Mr. Williamson)	110.00	330.00	770.00
6,8,10-12	4.00	12.00	28.00
7,9-One pg. of Frazetta in each	4.30	13.00	30.00

BUSTER CRABBE (The Amazing Adventures of. .)
Dec, 1953 - No. 4, June, 1954
Lev Gleason Publications

1	6.00	18.00	42.00
2,3-Toth-a	8.50	25.50	60.00
4-Flash Gordon-c	6.00	17.00	42.00

BUTCH CASSIDY
June, 1971 - No. 3, Oct, 1971 (52 pages)
Skywald Comics

1-Red Mask reprint, retitled Maverick; Bolle-a		.40	.80
2-Whip Wilson reprint		.30	.60
3-Dead Canyon Days reprint/Crack Western No. 63; Sundance Kid app.; Crandall-a		.30	.60

BUTCH CASSIDY (. . .& the Wild Bunch)
1951
Avon Periodicals

1-Kinstler c/a	9.00	27.00	62.00

NOTE: ***Reinman*** *story; Issue No. on inside spine.*

BUTCH CASSIDY (See Fun-In No. 11 & Western Adventure Comics)

BUZ SAWYER
June, 1948 - 1949
Standard Comics

	Good	Fine	N-Mint
1-Roy Crane-a	8.00	24.00	56.00
2-Intro his pal Sweeney	5.00	15.00	35.00
3-5	4.00	12.00	28.00

BUZ SAWYER'S PAL, ROSCOE SWEENEY (See Sweeney)

BUZZY (See All Funny Comics)
Winter, 1944-45 - No. 75, 1-2/57; No. 76, 10/57; No. 77, 10/58
National Periodical Publications/Detective Comics

	Good	Fine	N-Mint
1 (52 pgs. begin)	13.00	40.00	90.00
2	6.00	18.00	42.00
3-5	4.35	13.00	30.00
6-10	2.80	8.60	20.00
11-20	2.15	6.50	15.00
21-30	1.70	5.00	12.00
31,35-38	1.30	4.00	9.00
32-34,39-Last 52 pgs. Scribbly by Mayer in all (These four stories were done for Scribbly #14 which was delayed for a year)			
	1.50	4.50	10.00
40-77: 62-Last precode (2/55)	1.00	3.00	7.00

BUZZY THE CROW (See Harvey Hits #18 & Paramount Animated Comics #1)

CADET GRAY OF WEST POINT (See Dell Giants)

CAIN'S HUNDRED (TV)
May-July, 1962 - No. 2, Sept-Nov, 1962
Dell Publishing Co.

	Good	Fine	N-Mint
nn(01-094-207)	1.50	4.50	10.00
2	1.00	3.00	7.00

CALIFORNIA GIRLS
June, 1987 - Present ($2.00, B&W, 40pgs)
Eclipse Comics

	Good	Fine	N-Mint
1-8: All contain color paper dolls	.35	1.00	2.00

CALIFORNIA RAISINS IN 3-D
1988 - Present ($2.50)
Blackthorne Publ.

	Good	Fine	N-Mint
1-4	.40	1.25	2.50

CALL FROM CHRIST
1952 (36 pages)
Catechetical Educational Society (Giveaway)

	Good	Fine	N-Mint
	2.30	7.00	16.00

CALLING ALL BOYS (Tex Granger No. 18 on)
Jan, 1946 - No. 17, May, 1948
Parents' Magazine Institute

	Good	Fine	N-Mint
1	3.50	10.50	24.00
2	1.70	5.00	12.00
3-9,11,14-17: 11-Rin Tin Tin photo-c. 14-J. Edgar Hoover photo-c			
	1.30	4.00	9.00
10-Gary Cooper photo-c	2.35	7.00	16.00
12-Bob Hope photo-c	2.00	6.00	14.00
13-Bing Crosby photo-c	2.00	6.00	14.00

CALLING ALL GIRLS
Sept, 1941 - No. 72, April, 1948 (Part magazine, part comic)
Parents' Magazine Institute

	Good	Fine	N-Mint
1	5.00	15.00	35.00
2	2.65	8.00	18.00
3-Shirley Temple photo-c	4.00	12.00	28.00
4-10: 9-Flag-c	1.70	5.00	12.00
11-20: 11-Photo-c	1.30	4.00	9.00
21-39,41-43(10-11/45)-Last issue with comics	.80	2.40	5.50
40-Liz Taylor photo-c	2.00	6.00	14.00
44-51(7/46)-Last comic book size issue	.60	1.80	3.50

	Good	Fine	N-Mint
52-72	.35	1.00	2.00

NOTE: *Jack Sparling* art in many issues.

CALLING ALL KIDS (Also see True Comics)
Dec-Jan, 1945-46 - No. 26, Aug, 1949
Parents' Magazine Institute

	Good	Fine	N-Mint
1-Funny animal	3.00	9.00	21.00
2	1.50	4.50	10.00
3-10	1.00	3.00	6.00
11-26	.55	1.65	4.00

CALVIN (See Li'l Kids)

CALVIN & THE COLONEL (TV)
No. 1354, 4-6/62 - No. 2, July-Sept, 1962
Dell Publishing Co.

	Good	Fine	N-Mint
4-Color 1354	3.50	10.50	24.00
2	2.30	7.00	16.00

CAMELOT 3000
12/82 - No. 11, 7/84; No. 12, 4/85 (Direct Sale; Mando paper)
DC Comics (Maxi-series)

	Good	Fine	N-Mint
1	.35	1.00	2.00
2-12: 5-Intro Knights of New Camelot	.25	.75	1.50

NOTE: *Austin* a-7i-12i.

CAMERA COMICS
July, 1944 - No. 9, Summer, 1946
U.S. Camera Publishing Corp./ME

	Good	Fine	N-Mint
nn (7/44)	9.00	27.00	62.00
nn (9/44)	6.50	19.50	46.00
1(10/44)-The Grey Comet	6.50	19.50	46.00
2	4.30	13.00	30.00
3-Nazi WW II-c; ½ photos	4.00	12.00	28.00
4-9: All ½ photos	3.00	9.00	21.00

CAMP COMICS
Feb, 1942 - No. 3, April, 1942 (All have photo-c)
Dell Publishing Co.

	Good	Fine	N-Mint
1-''Seaman Sy Wheeler'' by Kelly, 7 pgs.; Bugs Bunny app.			
	32.00	95.00	225.00
2-Kelly-a, 12 pgs.; Bugs Bunny app.	24.00	72.00	168.00
3-(Scarce)-Kelly-a	32.00	95.00	225.00

CAMP RUNAMUCK (TV)
April, 1966
Dell Publishing Co.

	Good	Fine	N-Mint
1-Photo-c	1.35	4.00	8.00

CAMPUS LOVES
Dec, 1949 - No. 5, Aug, 1950
Quality Comics Group (Comic Magazines)

	Good	Fine	N-Mint
1-Ward c/a, 9 pgs.	13.00	40.00	90.00
2-Ward c/a	10.00	30.00	70.00
3,4	4.60	14.00	32.00
5-Spanking panels (2)	6.00	18.00	42.00

NOTE: *Gustavson* a-1-5. Photo-c-3-5.

CAMPUS ROMANCE (. . . Romances on cover)
Sept-Oct, 1949 - No. 3, Feb-Mar, 1950
Avon Periodicals/Realistic

	Good	Fine	N-Mint
1-Walter Johnson-a; c-/Avon paperback 348	10.00	30.00	70.00
2-Grandenetti-a; c-/Avon paperback 151	8.50	25.50	60.00
3-c-/Avon paperback 201	8.50	25.50	60.00
Realistic reprint	3.50	10.50	24.00

CANADA DRY PREMIUMS (See Swamp Fox, The & Terry & The Pirates)

CANCELLED COMIC CAVALCADE
Summer, 1978 - No. 2, Fall, 1978 (8½x11''; B&W)

Buzzy #32, © DC

Calling All Girls #3, © PMI

Campus Romance #3, © AVON

Canteen Kate #2, © STJ   Captain America #100, © MEG   Captain America #241, © MEG

CANCELLED COMIC CAVALCADE (continued)
(Xeroxed pages on one side only w/blue cover and taped spine)
DC Comics, Inc.

	Good	Fine	N-Mint

1-(412 pages) Contains xeroxed copies of art for: Black Lightning #12, cover to #13; Claw #13,14; The Deserter #1; Doorway to Nightmare #6; Firestorm #6; The Green Team #2,3.

2-(532 pages) Contains xeroxed copies of art for: Kamandi #60 (including Omac); #61; Prez #5; Shade #9 (including The Odd Man); Showcase #105 (Deadman), 106 (The Creeper); The Vixen #1; and covers to Army at War #2, Battle Classics #3, Demand Classics #1 & 2, Dynamic Classics #3, Mr. Miracle #26, Ragman #6, Weird Mystery #25 & 26, & Western Classics #1 & 2. (Rare)
(One set sold in 1986 for $550.00)
NOTE: In June, 1978, DC cancelled several of their titles. For copyright purposes, the unpublished original art for these titles was xeroxed, bound in the above books, published and distributed. Only 35 copies were made.

CANDID TALES (Also see Bold Stories & It Rhymes With Lust)
April, 1950, June, 1950 (Digest size) (144 pages) (Full color)
Kirby Publishing Co.

(Scarce) Contains Wood female pirate story, 15 pgs., and 14
pgs. in June issue; Powell-a   35.00   105.00   245.00
NOTE: Another version exists with Dr. Kilmore by Wood; no female pirate story.

CANDY
Fall, 1944 - No. 3, Spring, 1945
William H. Wise & Co.

1-Two Scoop Scuttle stories by Wolverton	12.00	36.00	84.00
2,3-Scoop Scuttle by Wolverton, 2-4 pgs.	8.50	25.50	60.00

CANDY (Teen-age)
Autumn, 1947 - No. 64, July, 1956
Quality Comics Group (Comic Magazines)

1-Gustavson-a	6.00	18.00	42.00
2-Gustavson-a	3.00	9.00	21.00
3-10	2.00	6.00	14.00
11-30	1.50	4.50	10.00
31-63	1.15	3.50	8.00
64-Ward-c(p)?	1.65	5.00	11.50
Super Reprint No. 2,10,12,16,17,18('63-'64)	.50	1.50	3.00
NOTE: Jack Cole 1-2 pg. art in many issues.

CANNONBALL COMICS
Feb, 1945 - No. 2, Mar, 1945
Rural Home Publishing Co.

1-The Crash Kid, Thunderbrand, The Captive Prince & Crime Crusader begin	19.00	57.00	132.00
2	11.50	34.00	80.00

CANTEEN KATE (Also see All Picture All True Love Story & Fightin' Marines)
June, 1952 - No. 3, Nov, 1952
St. John Publishing Co.

1-Matt Baker c/a	23.00	70.00	160.00
2-Matt Baker c/a	20.00	60.00	140.00
3-(Rare)-Used in POP, pg. 75; Baker c/a; transvestism story			
	24.00	72.00	170.00

CAP'N CRUNCH COMICS (See Quaker Oats)
1963; 1965 (16 pgs.; miniature giveaways; 2½x6½'')
Quaker Oats Co.

(1963 titles)-"The Picture Pirates," "The Fountain of Youth," "I'm Dreaming of a Wide Isthmus." (1965 titles)-"Bewitched, Betwitched, & Betweaked," Seadog Meets the Witch Doctor"
| | .75 | 2.25 | 5.00 |

CAP'N QUICK & A FOOZLE
July, 1985 - No. 3, Nov, 1985 ($1.50; Baxter paper)
Eclipse Comics

1-3-Rogers c/a	.20	.70	1.40

CAPTAIN ACTION
Oct-Nov, 1968 - No. 5, June-July, 1969
National Periodical Publications

	Good	Fine	N-Mint
1-Origin; Wood-a	1.00	3.00	6.00
2-5; 2,3,5-Kane/Wood-a	.50	1.50	3.00
...& Action Boy('67)-Ideal Toy Co. giveaway	.40	1.25	2.50

CAPTAIN AERO COMICS (Samson No. 1-6; also see Veri Best Sure Fire & Veri Best Sure Shot Comics)
V1No.7(No.1), Dec, 1941 - V2No.4(No.10), Jan, 1943; V3No.9(No. 11), Sept, 1943 - V4No.3(No.17), Oct, 1944; No. 21, Dec, 1944 - No. 26, Aug, 1946 (no No. 18-20)
Holyoke Publishing Co.

V1#7(#1)-Flag-Man & Solar, Master of Magic, Captain Aero, Cap Stone, Adventurer begin	42.00	125.00	295.00
8(#2)-Pals of Freedom app.	25.00	75.00	175.00
9(#3)-Alias X begins; Pals of Freedom app.			
	25.00	75.00	175.00
10(#4)-Origin The Gargoyle; Kubert-a	25.00	75.00	175.00
11,12(#5,6)-Kubert-a; Miss Victory app. in #6			
	21.00	63.00	147.00
V2#1(#7)	12.00	36.00	84.00
2(#8)-Origin The Red Cross; Miss Victory app.			
	12.00	36.00	84.00
3(#9)-Miss Victory app.	9.00	27.00	62.00
4(#10)-Miss Victory app.	7.00	21.00	50.00
V3#9 - V3#13(#11-15): 11,15-Miss Victory app.	5.00	15.00	35.00
V4#2, V4#3(#16,17)	4.00	12.00	28.00
21-24,26-L. B. Cole-c	6.35	19.00	44.00
25-L. B. Cole S/F-c	8.00	24.00	56.00
NOTE: Hollingsworth a-23. Infantino a-23.

CAPTAIN AMERICA (See All-Select, All Winners, Aurora, The Invaders, Marvel Double Feature, Marvel Fanfare, Marvel Mystery, Marvel Super-Action, Marvel Super Heroes, Marvel Team-Up, Marvel Treasury Special, USA Comics, Young Allies & Young Men)

CAPTAIN AMERICA (Tales of Suspense #1-99; ...and the Falcon #134-223)
No. 100, April, 1968 - Present
Marvel Comics Group

100-Flashback on Cap's revival with Avengers & Sub-Mariner			
	2.60	8.00	18.00
101	1.50	4.50	9.00
102-108	1.15	3.50	7.00
109-Origin Capt. America	1.45	4.25	8.50
110,111,113-Steranko c/a. 110-Rick becomes Cap's partner. 111-Death of Steve Rogers. 113-Cap's funeral	2.00	6.00	14.00
112,114-116,118-120	.60	1.75	3.50
117-1st app. The Falcon	.60	1.75	3.50
121-130: 121-Retells origin	.60	1.75	3.50
131-139: 133-The Falcon becomes Cap's partner; origin Modok.			
137,138-Spider-Man x-over	.60	1.75	3.50
140-Origin Grey Gargoyle retold	.60	1.75	3.50
141-150: 143-(52 pgs.)	.40	1.25	2.50
151-171,176-179: 155-Origin; redrawn with Falcon added. 164-1st app. Nightshade. 176-End of Capt. America	.90	1.25	2.50
172-175-X-Men x-over	.90	2.70	5.50
180-199: 180-Intro & origin of Nomad. 181-Intro & origin of new Capt. America. 183-Death of New Cap; Nomad becomes Cap. 186-True origin The Falcon	.25	.75	1.50
200-Double size	.35	1.00	2.00
201-240,242-246		.60	1.20
241-Punisher app.	1.35	4.00	8.00
247-255-Byrne-a. 255-Origin	.40	1.25	2.50
256-331: 269-1st Team America. 281-1950s Bucky returns. 282-Bucky becomes Nomad. 284-Patriot (Jack Mace) app. 285-Death of Patriot. 298-Origin Red Skull	.60	1.20	

CAPTAIN AMERICA (continued)	Good	Fine	N-Mint
332-Old Cap resigns	1.50	3.50	7.00
333-Intro new Captain	.85	2.50	5.00
334	.55	1.70	3.50
335-340	.35	1.00	2.00
341-343,345-349		.50	1.00
344-Double size, $1.50	.25	.75	1.50
350 (64 pgs., $1.75)	.30	.90	1.75
. . .& The Campbell Kids (1980, 36pg. giveaway, Campbell's			
soup/U.S. Dept. of Energy)	.35	1.00	2.00
Giant Size 1(12/75)	.40	1.25	2.50
Special 1(1/71)	.60	1.75	3.50
Special 2(1/72)	.60	1.75	3.50
Annual 3(4/76), 4(8/77)-Kirby c/a, 5(1981), 6(11/82), 7('83),			
	.25	.75	1.50
Annual 8(9/86)-Wolverine feat.	.70	2.00	4.00

NOTE: *Austin* c-225i, 239i, 246i. *Buscema* a-115p, 217p; c-136p, 217. *Byrne* part c-223, 238, 239, 247p-54p, 290, 291, 313; a-247-254p, 255, 313p. *Colan* a(p)-116-137, 256, Annual 5; c(p)-116-123, 126, 129. *Everett* a-136i, 137i; c-126i. *Gil Kane* a-145p; c-147p, 149p, 150p, 170p, 172-174, 180, 181p, 183-190p, 215, 216, 220, 221. *Kirby* a(p)-100-109, 112, 193-214, 216, Giant Size 1, Special 1, 2(layouts), Annual 3,4; c-100-109, 112, 126p, 193-214. *Miller* c-241p, 244p, 245p, 255p, Annual No. 5. *Mooney* a-149i. *Morrow* a-144. *Perez* c-243p, 246p. *Roussos* a-140i, 168i. *Starlin/Sinnott* c-162. *Sutton* a-244i. *Tuska* a-112i, 215p, Special 2. *Williamson* a-313i. *Wood* a-127i.

CAPTAIN AMERICA COMICS

Mar, 1941 - No. 75, Jan, 1950; No. 76, 5/54 - No. 78, 9/54
(No. 74 & 75 titled Capt. America's Weird Tales)
Timely/Marvel Comics (TCI 1-20/CmPS 21-68/MjMC 69-75/Atlas Comics (PrPD 76-78)

	Good	Fine	N-Mint
1-Origin & 1st app. Captain America & Bucky by S&K; Hurricane,			
Tuk the Caveboy begin by S&K; Red Skull app.			
	1000.00	3000.00	7000.00
(Prices vary widely on this book)			
2-S&K Hurricane; Tuk by Avison (Kirby splash)			
	395.00	1185.00	2765.00
3-Red Skull app; Stan Lee's 1st text	280.00	840.00	1960.00
4	185.00	555.00	1295.00
5	170.00	510.00	1190.00
6-Origin Father Time; Tuk the Caveboy ends			
	145.00	435.00	1015.00
7-Red Skull app	145.00	435.00	1015.00
8-10-Last S&K issue, (S&K centerfold #6-10)			
	122.00	365.00	854.00
11-Last Hurricane, Headline Hunter; Al Avison Captain America be-			
gins, ends #20	90.00	270.00	630.00
12-The Imp begins, ends #16; Last Father Time			
	90.00	270.00	630.00
13-Origin The Secret Stamp; classic-c	95.00	285.00	665.00
14,15	90.00	270.00	630.00
16-Red Skull unmasks Cap	95.00	285.00	665.00
17-The Fighting Fool only app.	75.00	225.00	525.00
18,19-Human Torch begins #19	70.00	210.00	490.00
20-Sub-Mariner app.; no H. Torch	70.00	210.00	490.00
21-25-Cap drinks liquid opium	62.00	185.00	435.00
26-30: 27-Last Secret Stamp. 30-Last 68 pg. issue			
	56.00	168.00	390.00
31-36,38-40: 31-60 pg. issues begin	50.00	150.00	350.00
37-Red Skull app.	52.00	155.00	365.00
41-45,47: 41-Last Jap War-c. 47-Last German War-c			
	44.00	132.00	305.00
46-German Holocaust-c	44.00	132.00	305.00
48-58,60	40.00	120.00	280.00
59-Origin retold	55.00	165.00	385.00
61-Red Skull c/story	48.00	145.00	335.00
62,64,65: 65-"Hey Look" by Kurtzman	40.00	120.00	280.00
63-Intro/origin Asbestos Lady	44.00	132.00	305.00
66-Bucky is shot; Golden Girl teams up with Captain America &			

	Good	Fine	N-Mint
learns his i.d; origin Golden Girl	48.00	145.00	335.00
67-Captain America/Golden Girl team-up; Mxyztplk swipe; last Toro			
in Human Torch	40.00	120.00	280.00
68,70-Sub-Mariner/Namora, and Captain America/Golden Girl team-			
up in each. 70-Science fiction c/story	40.00	120.00	280.00
69-Human Torch/Sun Girl team-up	40.00	120.00	280.00
71-Anti Wertham editorial; The Witness, Bucky app.			
	32.00	95.00	225.00
72,73	32.00	95.00	225.00
74-(Scarce)(1949)-Titled "C.A.'s Weird Tales;" Red Skull app.			
	65.00	195.00	455.00
75(2/50)-Titled "C.A.'s Weird Tales;" no C.A. app.; horror cover/			
stories	47.00	140.00	330.00
76-78(1954); Human Torch/Toro app.	28.00	84.00	195.00
132-Pg. Issue (B&W-1942)(Canadian)	200.00	600.00	1400.00
Shoestore Giveaway No. 77	16.00	48.00	110.00

NOTE: Bondage c-3, 7, 15, 16, 34, 38. *Crandall* a-2i, 3i, 9i, 10i. *Romita* c-77, 78. *Schomburg* c-26-29, 31, 33, 37-39, 41-43, 45-54, 58. *Shores* c-20-25, 30, 32, 34-36, 40, 59, 61-63. *S&K* c-1, 2, 5-7, 9, 10.

CAPTAIN AMERICA SPECIAL EDITION

Feb, 1984 - No. 2, Mar, 1984 ($2.00) (Baxter paper)
Marvel Comics Group

	Good	Fine	N-Mint
1,2-Steranko-r, c/a	.40	1.25	2.50

CAPTAIN AND THE KIDS, THE (See Famous Comics Cartoon Books)

CAPTAIN AND THE KIDS, THE (See Comics on Parade, Okay Comics & Sparkler Comics)
1938 - 4-Color No. 881, Feb, 1958
United Features Syndicate/Dell Publ. Co.

	Good	Fine	N-Mint
Single Series 1('38)	35.00	105.00	245.00
Single Series 1(Reprint)(12/39-"Reprint" on cover)			
	20.00	60.00	140.00
1(Summer, 1947-UFS)	5.50	16.50	38.00
2	3.00	9.00	21.00
3-10	2.00	6.00	14.00
11-20	1.50	4.50	10.00
21-32(1955)	1.15	3.50	8.00
50th Anniversary issue('48)-Contains a 2 page history of the strip,			
including an account of the famous Supreme Court decision			
allowing both Pulitzer & Hearst to run the same strip under diff-			
erent names	3.00	9.00	21.00
Special Summer issue, Fall issue (1948)	2.35	7.00	16.00
4-Color 881 (Dell)	1.50	4.50	10.00

CAPTAIN ATOM

1950 - 1951 (5x7¼") (5 cents, 52 pgs.)
Nationwide Publishers

	Good	Fine	N-Mint
1-Sci/fic	2.65	8.00	18.00
2-7	1.85	5.50	13.00

CAPTAIN ATOM (Formerly Strange Suspense Stories No. 77)
No. 78, Dec, 1965 - No. 89, Dec, 1967 (Also see Space Advs.)
Charlton Comics

	Good	Fine	N-Mint
78-Origin retold	2.15	6.50	15.00
79-81	1.70	5.00	12.00
82-Intro. Nightshade	1.70	5.00	12.00
83-86: Ted Kord Blue Beetle in all	1.50	4.50	10.00
87-89-Nightshade by Aparo in all	1.50	4.50	10.00
83-85(Modern Comics-1977)-reprints		.15	.30

NOTE: *Aparo* a-87-89. *Ditko* c/a(p) 78-87; c-88, 89. #90 only published in fanzine 'The Charlton Bullseye' #1, 2.

CAPTAIN ATOM

March, 1987 - Present
DC Comics

1-44 pgs. ($1.00)-Origin/1st app. with new costume

Captain America #332, © MEG

Captain America Comics #14, © MEG

Captain America Comics #78, © MEG

Captain Battle #3, © CHES

Captain Canuck #1, © Comely Comics

Captain Easy #10, © NEA Service

	Good	Fine	N-Mint
CAPTAIN ATOM (continued)	.35	1.00	2.00
2-10: 5-Firestorm x-over. 6-Intro. new Dr. Spectro		.60	1.20
11-16: 14-Nightshade app. 16-Justice League app. 20-Blue Beetle x-over		.60	1.20
17-26: 17-$1.00 ish. begin; Justice League app.		.60	1.20
Annual 1 (3/88, $1.25)-Intro Major Force	.25	.75	1.50
Annual 2 (12/88, $1.50)	.25	.75	1.50

CAPTAIN BATTLE (Boy No. 3 on) (See Silver Streak)
Summer, 1941 - No. 2, Fall, 1941
New Friday Publ./Comic House

1-Origin Blackout by Rico; Captain Battle begins	45.00	135.00	315.00
2	28.00	84.00	195.00

CAPTAIN BATTLE (2nd Series)
Wint, 1942-43 - No. 5, Sum, 1943 (No.3: 52pgs., nd)(No.5: 68pgs.)
Magazine Press/Picture Scoop No. 5

3-Origin Silver Streak-r/SS#3; Origin Lance Hale-r/Silver Streak; Simon-a(r)	23.00	70.00	160.00
4	16.00	48.00	110.00
5-Origin Blackout retold	16.00	48.00	110.00

CAPTAIN BATTLE, JR.
Fall, 1943 - No. 2, Winter, 1943-44
Comic House (Lev Gleason)

1-The Claw vs. The Ghost	35.00	105.00	245.00
2-Wolverton's Scoop Scuttle; Don Rico-c/a; The Green Claw story	30.00	90.00	210.00

CAPTAIN BRITAIN (Also see Marvel Team-Up No. 65,66)
Oct. 13, 1976 - No. 39, July 6, 1977 (Weekly)
Marvel Comics International

1-Origin; with Capt. Britain's face mask inside	.85	2.50	5.00
2-Origin, conclusion; Britain's Boomerang inside		.60	1.80	3.60
3-Vs. Bank Robbers	.35	1.00	2.00
4-7-Vs. Hurricane	.35	1.00	2.00
8-Vs. Bank Robbers	.35	1.00	2.00
9-13-Vs. Dr. Synne	.30	.90	1.80
14,15-Vs. Mastermind	.30	.90	1.80
16-20-With Capt. America; 17 misprinted & color section reprinted in No. 18	.30	.90	1.80
21-23,25,26-With Capt. America	.30	.90	1.80
24-With C.B.'s Jet Plane inside	.60	1.80	3.60
27-Origin retold	.30	.90	1.80
28-32-Vs. Lord Hawk	.25	.75	1.50
33-35-More on origin	.30	.90	1.80
36-Star Sceptre	.25	.75	1.50
37-39-Vs. Highwayman & Munipulator	.25	.75	1.50
Annual(1978,Hardback,64pgs.)-Reprints No. 1-7 with pin-ups of Marvel characters	1.35	4.00	8.00
Summer Special (1980, 52pp)-Reprints	.35	1.00	2.00

NOTE: No. 1,2, & 24 are rarer in mint due to inserts. Distributed in Great Britain only. Nick Fury-r by Steranko in 1-20, 24-31, 35-37. Fantastic Four-r by J. Buscema in all. New Buscema-a in 24-30. Story from No. 39 continues in Super Spider-Man (British weekly) No. 231-247. Following cancellation of his series, new Captain Britain stories appeared in "Super Spider-Man" (British weekly) No. 231-247. Captain Britain stories which appear in Super-Spider-Man No. 248-253 are reprints of Marvel Team-Up No. 65&66. Capt. Britain strips also appeared in Hulk Comic (weekly) 1, 3-30, 42-55, 57-60, in Marvel Superheroes (monthly) 377-388, in Daredevils (monthly) 1-11, Mighty World of Marvel (monthly) 7-16 & Captain Britain (monthly) 1-present.

CAPTAIN CANUCK
7/75 - No. 4, 7/77; No. 4, 7-8/79 - No. 14, 3-4/81
Comely Comix (Canada) (All distr. in U. S.)

1-1st app. Bluefox	.40	1.25	2.50
2-1st app. Dr. Walker, Redcoat & Kebec	.30	.90	1.80

	Good	Fine	N-Mint
3(5-7/76)-1st app. Heather	.30	.90	1.80
4(1st printing-2/77)-10x14½''; (5.00); B&W; 300 copies serially numbered and signed with one certificate of authenticity	5.00	15.00	30.00
4(2nd printing-7/77)-11x17'', B&W; only 15 copies printed; signed by creator Richard Comely, serially #'d and two certificates of authenticity inserted; orange cardboard covers (Very Rare)	8.00	25.00	50.00
4(7-8/79)-1st app. Tom Evans & Mr. Gold; origin The Catman		.40	.80
5-Origin Capt. Canuck's powers; 1st app. Earth Patrol & Chaos Corps		.40	.80
6-14: 8-Jonn 'The Final Chapter'. 9-1st World Beyond. 11-1st 'Chariots of Fire' story		.40	.80
Summer Special 1(7-9/80, 95~, 64pgs.)		.50	1.00

NOTE: 30,000 copies of No. 2 were destroyed in Winnipeg.

CAPTAIN CARROT AND HIS AMAZING ZOO CREW
March, 1982 - No. 20, Nov. 1983 (Also see New Teen Titans)
DC Comics

1-Superman app.		.50	1.00
2-20: 3-Re-intro Dodo & The Frog. 9-Re-intro Three Mouseketeers, the Terrific Whatzit. 10,11- Pig Iron reverts back to Peter Porkchops. 20-The Changeling app.		.50	1.00

CAPTAIN CARVEL AND HIS CARVEL CRUSADERS (See Carvel Comics)

CAPTAIN CONFEDERACY
1986 - No. 12, Oct, 1988 ($1.50/$1.95, B&W)
SteelDragon Press

1	.70	2.00	4.00
2-12	.25	.75	1.50
Special 1(Sum/87)	.30	.90	1.75
Special 2(Aut/87), 3('88)	.25	.75	1.50

CAPTAIN COURAGEOUS COMICS (Banner No. 3-5)
March, 1942
Periodical House (Ace Magazines)

6-Origin & 1st app. The Sword; Lone Warrior, Capt. Courageous app.	33.00	100.00	230.00

CAPT'N CRUNCH COMICS (See Cap'n...)

CAPTAIN DAVY JONES (See 4-Color No. 598)

CAPTAIN EASY (See Red Ryder #3-32)
1939 - No. 17, Sept, 1949; April, 1956
Hawley/Dell Publ./Standard(Visual Editions)/Argo

Hawley(1939)-Contains reprints from The Funnies & 1938 Sunday strips by Roy Crane	28.00	84.00	195.00
4-Color 24 (1943)	19.00	57.00	132.00
4-Color 111(6/46)	8.00	24.00	56.00
10(Standard-10/47)	3.70	11.00	26.00
11-17: All contain 1930's & '40's strip-r	2.85	8.50	20.00
Argo 1(4/56)-(r)	2.30	7.00	16.00

NOTE: Schomburg c-13,16.

CAPTAIN EASY & WASH TUBBS (See Famous Comics Cartoon Books)

CAPTAIN ELECTRON
Aug, 1986 ($2.25, color)
Brick Computer Science Institute

1-Disbrow-a	.35	1.00	2.00

CAPTAIN EO 3-D (Disney)
July, 1987 (Eclipse 3-D Special #18, $3.50, Baxter)
Eclipse Comics

1-Adapts 3-D movie	.60	1.75	3.50
1-2-D limited edition	.85	2.50	5.00
1-Large size (11x17'', 8/87)-Sold only at Disney Theme parks ($6.95)	1.20	3.50	6.95

CAPTAIN FEARLESS COMICS (Also see Holyoke One-Shot #6 & Old Glory Comics)
August, 1941 - No. 2, Sept, 1941
Helnit Publishing Co. (Holyoke Publishing Co.)

	Good	Fine	N-Mint
1-Origin Mr. Miracle, Alias X, Captain Fearless, Citizen Smith Son of the Unknown Soldier; Miss Victory begins	28.00	84.00	195.00
2-Grit Grady, Captain Stone app.	16.00	48.00	110.00

CAPTAIN FLASH
Nov., 1954 - No. 4, July, 1955
Sterling Comics

	Good	Fine	N-Mint
1-Origin; Sekowsky-a; Tomboy (female super hero) begins Last pre-code ish	10.00	30.00	70.00
2-4	6.00	18.00	42.00

CAPTAIN FLEET
Fall, 1952
Ziff-Davis Publishing Co.

	Good	Fine	N-Mint
1-Painted-c	5.50	16.50	38.00

CAPTAIN FLIGHT COMICS
Mar, 1944 - No. 11, Feb-Mar, 1947
Four Star Publications

	Good	Fine	N-Mint
nn	9.00	27.00	62.00
2	5.00	15.00	35.00
3,4: 4-Rock Raymond begins, ends #7	4.00	12.00	28.00
5-Bondage, torture-c; Red Rocket begins; the Grenade app.	6.00	18.00	42.00
6,7	5.00	15.00	35.00
8-Yankee Girl, Black Cobra begin; intro. Cobra Kid	8.00	24.00	56.00
9-Torpedoman app.; last Yankee Girl; Kinstler-a	8.00	24.00	56.00
10-Deep Sea Dawson, Zoom of the Jungle, Rock Raymond, Red Rocket, & Black Cobra app; L. B. Cole bondage-c	8.00	24.00	56.00
11-Torpedoman, Blue Flame app.; last Black Cobra, Red Rocket; L. B. Cole-c	8.00	24.00	56.00

NOTE: *L. B. Cole c-7-11.*

CAPTAIN FORTUNE PRESENTS
1955 - 1959 (16 pages; 3¼x6-7/8'') (Giveaway)
Vital Publications

"Davy Crockett in Episodes of the Creek War," "Davy Crockett at the Alamo," "In Sherwood Forest Tells Strange Tales of Robin Hood" ('57), "Meets Bolivar the Liberator"('59), "Tells How Buffalo Bill Fights the Dog Soldiers"('57), "Young Davy Crockett"

	.85	2.50	5.00

CAPTAIN GALLANT (. . .of the Foreign Legion) (TV)
(Texas Rangers in Action No. 5 on?)
1955 - No. 4, Sept, 1956
Charlton Comics

	Good	Fine	N-Mint
1-Buster Crabbe	5.50	16.50	38.00
2-4	2.65	8.00	18.00
Heinz Foods Premium(1955; regular size)-U.S. Pictorial; contains Buster Crabbe photos; Don Heck-a	1.70	5.00	12.00
Non-Heinz version (same as above except pictures of show replaces ads)	1.70	5.00	12.00

CAPTAIN HERO (See Jughead as . . .)

CAPTAIN HERO COMICS DIGEST MAGAZINE
Sept, 1981
Archie Publications

1-Reprints of Jughead as Super-Guy		.30	.60

CAPTAIN HOBBY COMICS
Feb, 1948 (Canadian)
Export Publication Ent. Ltd. (Dist. in U.S. by Kable News Co.)

	Good	Fine	N-Mint
1	2.35	7.00	16.00

CAPTAIN HOOK & PETER PAN (See 4-Color No. 446 and Peter Pan)

CAPTAIN JET (Fantastic Fears No. 7 on)
May, 1952 - No. 5, Jan, 1953
Four Star Publ./Farrell/Comic Media

	Good	Fine	N-Mint
1-Bakerish-a	5.50	16.50	38.00
2	3.50	10.50	24.00
3-5,6(?)	2.65	8.00	18.00

CAPTAIN JUSTICE
March, 1988 - No. 2, April, 1988
Marvel Comics

1,2-Based on TV series, True Colors		.65	1.30

CAPTAIN KANGAROO (See 4-Color No. 721,780,872)

CAPTAIN KIDD (Formerly Dagar; My Secret Story #26 on)(Also see Fantastic Comics)
No. 24, June, 1949 - No. 25, Aug, 1949
Fox Feature Syndicate

	Good	Fine	N-Mint
24,25	6.00	18.00	42.00

CAPTAIN MARVEL (See All Hero, All-New Coll. Ed., America's Greatest, Fawcett Min., Gift, Limited Coll. Ed., Marvel Family, Master No. 21, Mighty Midget Comics, Shazam, Special Edition Comics, Whiz, Wisco, and X-Mas)

CAPTAIN MARVEL (. . .Presents the Terrible 5 No. 5)
April, 1966 - No. 4, Nov, 1966 (25 cents)
M. F. Enterprises

nn-(#1 on page 5)-Origin	.35	1.00	2.00
2,4		.60	1.20
3-(#3 on page 4)-Fights the Bat		.60	1.20

CAPTAIN MARVEL (See Life Of . . ., Marvel Spotlight, Marvel Graphic Novel & Marvel Super-Heroes 12)
May, 1968 - No. 19, Dec, 1969; No. 20, June, 1970 - No. 21, Aug, 1970; No. 22, Sept, 1972 - No. 62, May, 1979
Marvel Comics Group

	Good	Fine	N-Mint
1	2.15	6.50	15.00
2-5	.60	1.75	3.50
6-10	.40	1.25	2.50
11-Smith/Trimpe-c; Death of Una	.60	1.75	3.50
12-24: 17-New costume	.25	.75	1.50
25-Starlin c/a	1.35	4.00	8.00
26-Starlin c/a	1.00	3.00	6.00
27-34-Starlin c/a. 29-C.M. gains more powers	.75	2.25	4.50
35-62: 39-Origin Watcher. 41,43-Wrightson part inks; #43-c(i)			
		.50	1.00
Giant-Size 1 (12/75)	.50	1.50	3.00

NOTE: *Alcala a-35. Austin a-46i, 49-53i; c-52i. Buscema a-18p-21p. Colan a(p)-1-4; c(p)-1-4, 8, 9. Heck a-5p-10p, 16p. Gil Kane a-17p-21p, Gnt-Size 1p; c-17p-24p, 37p, 53. McWilliams a-40i.*

CAPTAIN MARVEL ADVENTURES (See Special Edition Comics for pre-No. 1)
1941 - No. 150, Nov, 1953
Fawcett Publications

	Good	Fine	VF-NM
nn(#1)-Captain Marvel & Sivana by Jack Kirby. The cover was printed on unstable paper stock and is rarely found in Fine or Mint condition; blank inside-c	900.00	2700.00	6300.00

(Prices vary widely on this book)

	Good	Fine	N-Mint
2-(Advertised as #3, which was counting Special Edition Comics as the real #1); Tuska-a	150.00	450.00	1050.00
3-Metallic silver-c	75.00	225.00	525.00
4-Three Lt. Marvels app.	55.00	165.00	385.00
5	47.00	140.00	330.00
6-10	35.00	105.00	245.00
11-15: 13-Two-pg. Capt. Marvel pin-up. 15-Comic cards on back-c			

Captain Flight #10, © Four Star

Captain Marvel #1, © MEG

Captain Marvel Adventures #4, © FAW

Captain Marvel Adventures #18, © FAW

Captain Marvel Adventures #98, © FAW

Captain Marvel, Jr. #9, © FAW

CAPTAIN MARVEL ADVS. (continued)	Good	Fine	N-Mint
begin, end #26	28.00	84.00	195.00
16,17: 17-Painted-c	25.00	75.00	175.00
18-Origin & 1st app. Mary Marvel & Marvel Family; painted-c (12/11/42)	38.00	115.00	265.00
19-Mary Marvel x-over; Christmas-c	23.00	70.00	160.00

20,21-Attached to the cover, each has a miniature comic just like the Mighty Midget Comics #11, except that each has a full color promo ad on the back cover. Most copies were circulated without the miniature comic. These issues with miniatures attached are very rare, and should not be mistaken for copies with the similar Mighty Midget comic glued in its place. The Mighty Midgets had blank back covers except for a small victory stamp seal. Only the Capt. Marvel and Captain Marvel Jr. No. 11 miniatures have been positively documented as having been affixed to these covers. Each miniature was only partially glued by its back cover to the Captain Marvel comic making it easy to see if it's the genuine miniature rather than a Mighty Midget.

	Good	Fine	N-Mint
with miniature attached....	55.00	165.00	385.00
20,21-Without miniature	20.00	60.00	140.00
22-Mr. Mind serial begins	35.00	105.00	245.00
23-25	19.00	57.00	132.00
26-30: 26-Flag-c	16.00	48.00	110.00
31-35: 35-Origin Radar	14.50	43.00	100.00
36-40: 37-Mary Marvel x-over	12.00	36.00	84.00
41-46: 42-Christmas-c. 43-Captain Marvel 1st meets Uncle Marvel; Mary Batson cameo. 46-Mr. Mind serial ends	11.00	32.00	75.00
47-50	9.30	28.00	65.00
51-53,55-60: 52-Origin & 1st app. Sivana Jr.; Capt. Marvel Jr. x-over	6.50	19.50	45.00
54-Special oversize 68-pg. issue	8.50	25.50	60.00
61-The Cult of the Curse serial begins	9.50	28.50	66.00
62-66-Serial ends; Mary Marvel x-over in #65. 66-Atomic War-c	6.50	19.50	45.00
67-77,79: 69-Billy Batson's Christmas; Uncle Marvel, Mary Marvel, Capt. Marvel Jr. x-over. 71-Three Lt. Marvels app. No. 79-Origin Mr. Tawny	6.00	18.00	42.00
78-Origin Mr. Atom	6.50	19.50	45.00
80-Origin Capt. Marvel retold	10.00	30.00	70.00
81-84,86-90: 81,90-Mr. Atom app. 82-Infinity-c. 86-Mr. Tawny app.	6.50	19.50	45.00
85-Freedom Train issue	8.00	24.00	56.00
91-99: 96-Mr. Tawny app.	5.00	15.00	35.00
100-Origin retold	11.00	32.00	75.00
101-120: 116-Flying Saucer ish (1/51)	5.00	15.00	35.00
121-Origin retold	6.00	18.00	42.00
122-141,143-149: 138-Flying Saucer issue (11/52). 141-Pre-code horror story "The Hideous Head-Hunter"	4.65	14.00	32.00
142-Used in POP, pgs. 92,96	5.00	15.00	35.00
150-(Low distribution)	11.00	32.00	75.00

Bond Bread Giveaways-(24 pgs.; pocket size-7¼x3½''; paper cover): ''...& the Stolen City ('48),'' ''The Boy Who Never Heard of C.M.,''''Meets the Weatherman''-(1950)(reprint)

each...	13.00	40.00	80.00

...Well Known Comics (1944; 12 pgs.; 8½x10½'')-printed in red & in blue; soft-c; glued binding)-Bestmaid/Samuel Lowe Co. giveaway 16.00 48.00 96.00

CAPTAIN MARVEL ADVENTURES
1945 (6x8'') (Full color, paper cover)
Fawcett Publications (Wheaties Giveaway)

''Captain Marvel & the Threads of Life'' plus 2 other stories (32pgs.)
16.00 48.00 110.00

NOTE: All copies were taped at each corner to a box of Wheaties and are never found in Fine or Mint condition.

CAPTAIN MARVEL AND THE GOOD HUMOR MAN
1950
Fawcett Publications

	Good	Fine	N-Mint
nn	17.00	51.00	120.00

CAPTAIN MARVEL AND THE LTS. OF SAFETY
1950 - 1951 (3 issues - no No.'s)
Ebasco Services/Fawcett Publications

''Danger Flies a Kite''('50),'' ''Danger Takes to Climbing''('50), ''Danger Smashes Street Lights''('51) 10.00 30.00 70.00

CAPTAIN MARVEL COMIC STORY PAINT BOOK (See Comic Story....)

CAPTAIN MARVEL, JR. (See Fawcett Miniatures, Marvel Family, Master Comics, Mighty Midget Comics, Shazam & Whiz Comics)

CAPTAIN MARVEL, JR.
Nov., 1942 - No. 119, June, 1953 (nn 34)
Fawcett Publications

1-Origin Capt. Marvel Jr. retold (Whiz No. 25); Capt. Nazi app.	105.00	315.00	735.00
2-Vs. Capt. Nazi; origin Capt. Nippon	52.00	155.00	365.00
3,4	38.00	115.00	265.00
5-Vs. Capt. Nazi	30.00	90.00	210.00
6-10: 8-Vs. Capt. Nazi. 9-Flag-c. 10-Hitler-c	23.00	70.00	160.00
11,12,15-Capt. Nazi app.	18.50	56.00	130.00
13,14,16-20: 16-Capt. Marvel & Sivana x-over. 19-Capt. Nazi & Capt. Nippon app.	13.00	40.00	90.00
21-30: 25-Flag-c	8.50	25.50	60.00
31-33,36-40: 37-Infinity-c	5.50	16.50	38.00
35-#34 on inside; cover shows origin of Sivana Jr. which is not on inside. Evidently the cover to #35 was printed out of sequence and bound with contents to #34	5.50	16.50	38.00
41-50	4.00	12.00	28.00
51-70: 53-Atomic Bomb story	3.50	10.50	24.00
71-99,101-103	3.00	9.00	21.00
100	3.50	10.50	24.00
104-Used in POP, pg. 89	3.50	10.50	24.00
105-114,116-119: 119-Electric chair-c	2.85	8.50	20.00
115-Injury to eye-c; Eyeball story w/ injury-to-eye panels	4.00	12.00	28.00

...Well Known Comics (1944; 12 pgs.; 8½x10½'')(Printed in blue; paper-c, glued binding)-Bestmaid/Samuel Lowe Co. giveaway 12.00 36.00 72.00

NOTE: Mac Raboy c-1-10,12-14,16,19,22,25,27,28,30-33,57 among others.

CAPTAIN MARVEL PRESENTS THE TERRIBLE FIVE
Aug., 1966; V2No.5, Sept., 1967 (no No.2-4) (25 cents)
M. F. Enterprises

1	.35	1.00	1.50
V2#5-(Formerly Capt. Marvel)	.30	.80	1.20

CAPTAIN MARVEL'S FUN BOOK
1944 (½'' thick) (cardboard covers)
Samuel Lowe Co.

Puzzles, games, magic, etc.; infinity-c 9.00 27.00 62.00

CAPTAIN MARVEL SPECIAL EDITION (See Special Edition)

CAPTAIN MARVEL STORY BOOK
Summer, 1946 - No. 4, Summer?, 1948
Fawcett Publications

1-½ text	25.00	75.00	175.00
2-4	17.00	51.00	120.00

CAPTAIN MARVEL THRILL BOOK (Large-Size)
1941 (Black & White; color cover)

Fawcett Publications	Good	Fine	VF-NM
1-Reprints from Whiz #8,10, & Special Edition #1 (Rare)	142.00	425.00	1000.00

CAPTAIN MARVEL THRILL BOOK (continued)
NOTE: *Rarely found in Fine or Mint condition.*

CAPTAIN MIDNIGHT (Radio, films, TV) (See The Funnies & Popular
Comics) (Becomes Sweethearts No. 68 on)
Sept, 1942 - No. 67, Fall, 1948
Fawcett Publications

	Good	Fine	N-Mint
1-Origin Captain Midnight; Captain Marvel cameo on cover			
	85.00	255.00	595.00
2	42.00	125.00	295.00
3-5	28.00	84.00	195.00
6-10: 9-Raboy-c. 10-Raboy Flag-c	20.00	60.00	140.00
11-20: 11,17-Raboy-c	13.00	40.00	90.00
21-30	10.00	30.00	70.00
31-40	7.50	22.00	52.00
41-59,61-67: 54-Sci/fi theme begins?	5.50	16.50	38.00
60-Flying Saucer ish (2/48)-3rd of this theme; see Shadow Comics			
V7#10 & Boy Commandos #26	9.00	27.00	62.00

CAPTAIN NICE (TV)
Nov, 1967 (One Shot)
Gold Key

1(10211-711)-Photo-c	2.35	7.00	14.00

CAPTAIN PARAGON (Also see Bill Black's Fun Comics)
Dec, 1983 - No. 4, 1985? (#3 is in color)
Americomics

1-4: 1-Ms. Victory begins (Intro/1st app.)	.35	1.00	2.00

CAPTAIN PARAGON AND THE SENTINELS OF JUSTICE
April, 1985 - Present? ($1.75; color)
AC Comics

1-Capt. Paragon, Commando D., Nightveil, Scarlet Scorpion,			
Stardust & Atoman begin	.35	1.00	2.00
2-5	.30	.90	1.80

CAPTAIN PUREHEART (See Archie as . . .)

CAPTAIN ROCKET
November, 1951
P. L. Publ. (Canada)

1	14.50	44.00	100.00

CAPTAIN SAVAGE AND HIS LEATHERNECK RAIDERS
Jan, 1968 - No. 19, Mar, 1970 (See Sgt. Fury No. 10)
Marvel Comics Group

1-Sgt. Fury & Howlers cameo		.40	.80
2-19: 2-Origin Hydra		.25	.50

CAPTAIN SCIENCE (Fantastic No. 8 on)
Nov, 1950 - No. 7, Dec, 1951
Youthful Magazines

1-Wood-a; origin	40.00	120.00	280.00
2	18.00	54.00	125.00
3,6,7; 3-Bondage c-swipe/Wings 94	14.00	42.00	97.00
4,5-Wood/Orlando-c/a(2) each	34.00	100.00	240.00

NOTE: *Fass a-4. Bondage c-3,6,7.*

CAPTAIN SILVER'S LOG OF SEA HOUND (See Sea Hound)

CAPTAIN SINDBAD (Movie Adaptation) (See Movie Comics)

CAPTAIN STEVE SAVAGE (. . .& His Jet Fighters, No. 2-13)
1950 - 1952? No. 5, 9-10/54 - No. 13, 5-6/56
Avon Periodicals

nn(1st series)-Wood art, 22 pgs. (titled ''. . .Over Korea'')			
	18.00	54.00	125.00
1(4/51)-Reprints nn ish (Canadian)	8.50	25.50	60.00
2-Kamen-a	4.35	13.00	30.00
3-11	2.65	8.00	18.00
12-Wood-a, 6pp	5.15	15.50	36.00

	Good	Fine	N-Mint
13-Check, Lawrence-a	3.50	10.50	24.00

NOTE: *Kinstler c-2-5, 7-9, 11. Lawrence a-8. Ravielli a-5, 9.*

5(9-10/54-2nd series)(Formerly Sensational Police Cases)			
	3.00	9.00	21.00
6-Reprints nn ish; Wood-a	5.00	15.00	35.00
7-13	1.50	4.50	10.00

CAPTAIN STONE (See Holyoke One-Shot No. 10)

CAPT. STORM
May-June, 1964 - No. 18, Mar-Apr, 1967
National Periodical Publications

1-Origin	.35	1.00	2.00
2-18: 3,6,13-Kubert-a. 12-Kubert-c		.60	1.20

CAPTAIN 3-D
December, 1953
Harvey Publications

1-Kirby/Ditko-a	4.00	12.00	24.00

CAPTAIN THUNDER AND BLUE BOLT
Sept, 1987 - Present ($1.95, color)
Hero Comics

1-Origin Blue Bolt	.35	1.05	2.10
2-12: 3-Origin Capt. Thunder	.35	1.00	1.95
Book 1 ($9.95, color)	1.70	5.00	9.95

CAPTAIN TOOTSIE & THE SECRET LEGION (Advs. of . .)(Also see
Monte Hale #30,39 & Real Western Hero)
Oct, 1950 - No. 2, Dec, 1950
Toby Press

1-Not Beck-a	10.00	30.00	70.00
2-Not Beck-a	6.00	18.00	42.00

CAPTAIN VENTURE & THE LAND BENEATH THE SEA
Oct, 1968 - No. 2, Oct, 1969
Gold Key (See Space Family Robinson)

1,2: 1-r/Space Family Robinson serial; Spiegle-a in both			
	2.35	7.00	14.00

CAPTAIN VICTORY AND THE GALACTIC RANGERS
Nov, 1981 - No. 13, Jan, 1984 ($1.00) (36-48 pgs.)
Pacific Comics (Sold only through comic shops)

1-1st app. Mr. Mind	.25	.75	1.50
2-13: 3-Adams-a	.25	.75	1.50
Special Issue #1(10/83)-Kirby c/a(p)		.50	1.00

NOTE: *Conrad a-10, 11. Ditko a-6. Kirby a-1-13p; c-1-13.*

CAPTAIN VIDEO (TV) (See X-Mas Comics)
Feb, 1951 - No. 6, Dec, 1951 (No. 1,5,6-36pgs.; 2-4, 52pgs.)
Fawcett Publications

1-George Evans-a(2)	28.50	86.00	200.00
2-Used in SOTI, pg. 382	22.00	65.00	154.00
3-6-All Evans-a	19.00	57.00	132.00

NOTE: *Minor Williamson assist on most issues. Photo c-1, 5, 6; painted c-2-4.*

CAPTAIN WILLIE SCHULTZ (Also see Fightin' Army)
No. 76, Oct, 1985 - No. 77, Jan, 1986
Charlton Comics

76,77		.40	.75

CAPTAIN WIZARD COMICS (Also see Meteor)
1946
Rural Home

1-Capt. Wizard dons new costume; Impossible Man, Race Wilkins			
app.	6.50	19.50	45.00

CARDINAL MINDSZENTY (The Truth Behind the Trial of . . .)
1949 (24 pages; paper cover, in color)

Captain Midnight #2, © FAW   Captain Steve Savage #6 (2nd series), © AVON   Captain Tootsie And The Secret Legion #1, © TOBY

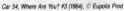

Car 54, Where Are You? #3 (1964), © Eupolis Prod.   Cases Of Sherlock Holmes #1, © Renegade Press   Casey-Crime Photographer #4, © MEG

CARDINAL MINDSZENTY (continued)
Catechetical Guild Education Society

	Good	Fine	N-Mint
nn-Anti-communism			50.00

Press Proof-(Very Rare)-(Full color, 7½x11¾", untrimmed)
  Only two known copies   150.00
Preview Copy (B&W, stapled), 18 pgs.; contains first 13 pgs. of
  Cardinal Mindszenty and was sent out as an advance promotion.
  Only one known copy $150.00 - $250.00
NOTE: Regular edition also printed in French.

CARE BEARS (TV, Movie)(See Star Comics Mag.)
Nov, 1985 - Present ($1.00 #11 on)
Star Comics/Marvel Comics No. 15 on

1-21: Post-a begins		.40	.80

CAREER GIRL ROMANCES (Formerly Three Nurses)
June, 1964 - No. 78, Dec, 1973
Charlton Comics

V4#24-31,33-78		.50	1.00
32-Presley, Hermans Hermits, Johnny Rivers line drawn-c	1.15	3.50	8.00

CAR 54, WHERE ARE YOU? (TV)
Mar-May, 1962 - No. 7, Sept-Nov, 1963; 1964 - 1965 (All photo-c)
Dell Publishing Co.

4-Color 1257(3-5/62)	2.65	8.00	18.00
2(6-8/62)-7	1.30	4.00	9.00
2,3(10-12/64), 4(1-3/65)-Reprints No. 2,3,&4 of 1st series			
	1.15	3.50	8.00

CARNATION MALTED MILK GIVEAWAYS (See Wisco)

CARNIVAL COMICS
1945
Harry 'A' Chesler/Pershing Square Publ. Co.

1	4.00	12.00	28.00

CARNIVAL OF COMICS
1954 (Giveaway)
Fleet-Air Shoes

nn-Contains a comic bound with new cover; several combinations

possible; Charlton's Eh! known	1.00	3.00	7.00

CAROLINE KENNEDY
1961 (One Shot)
Charlton Comics

	4.00	12.00	28.00

CAROUSEL COMICS
V1No.8, April, 1948
F. E. Howard, Toronto

V1#8	1.70	5.00	12.00

CARTOON KIDS
1957 (no month)
Atlas Comics (CPS)

1-Maneely c/a; Dexter The Demon, Willie The Wise-Guy, Little			
Zelda app.	1.70	5.00	12.00

CARVEL COMICS (Amazing Advs. of Capt. Carvel)
1975 (25 cents; No.4,5: 35 cents) (No.4,5: 3¼x5")
Carvel Corp. (Ice Cream)

1-3		.15	.30
4,5(1976)-Baseball theme	.85	2.50	5.00

CASE OF THE SHOPLIFTER'S SHOE (Perry Mason) (See Feature Book No. 50 McKay)

CASE OF THE WASTED WATER, THE
1972? (Giveaway)
Rheem Water Heating

	Good	Fine	N-Mint
Neal Adams-a	2.00	6.00	14.00

CASE OF THE WINKING BUDDHA, THE
1950 (132 pgs.; 25 cents; B&W; 5½x7-5½x8")
St. John Publ. Co.

Charles Raab-a; reprinted in Authentic Police Cases No. 25

	11.00	32.00	75.00

CASES OF SHERLOCK HOLMES
May, 1986 - Present (B&W)
Renegade Press

1-13	.35	1.00	2.00

CASEY-CRIME PHOTOGRAPHER (Two-Gun Western No. 5 on)
Aug, 1949 - No. 4, Feb, 1950 (Radio)
Marvel Comics (BFP)

1: Photo-c	5.50	16.50	38.00
2-4: Photo-c	3.70	11.00	26.00

CASEY JONES (See 4-Color No. 915)

CASPER AND...
1987 - Present (All reprints)
Harvey Comics

1-The Ghostly Trio		.40	.75
2-8 ($1.00): 2-Spooky, 3-Wendy, 4-Nightmare, 5-Ghostly Trio,			
6-Spooky, 7-Wendy		.50	1.00

CASPER AND NIGHTMARE (See Harvey Hits No. 37, 45, 52, 56, 59, 62, 65, 68, 71, 75)

CASPER AND NIGHTMARE (Nightmare & Casper No. 1-5) (25 cents)
No. 6, 11/64 - No. 44, 10/73; No. 45, 6/74 - No. 46, 8/74
Harvey Publications

6: 68 pg. Giants begin, ends #32	2.00	6.00	12.00
7-10	1.00	3.00	6.00
11-20	.50	1.50	3.00
21-32	.35	1.00	2.00
33-37: 52 pg. Giants	.35	1.00	2.00
38-46: regular size	.35	1.00	2.00

CASPER AND SPOOKY (See Harvey Hits No. 20)
Oct, 1972 - No. 7, Oct, 1973
Harvey Publications

1	.85	2.50	5.00
2-7	.35	1.00	2.00

CASPER AND THE GHOSTLY TRIO
Nov, 1972 - No. 7, Nov, 1973
Harvey Publications

1	.85	2.50	5.00
2-7	.35	1.00	2.00

CASPER AND WENDY
Sept, 1972 - No. 8, Nov, 1973
Harvey Publications

1: 52 pg. Giant	.85	2.50	5.00
2-8	.35	1.00	2.00

CASPER CAT (See Dopey Duck)
1958; 1963
I. W. Enterprises/Super

1,7-Reprint, Super No. 14('63)	.35	1.00	2.00

CASPER DIGEST (. . . Magazine #?; ...Halloween Digest #8)
Oct, 1986 - No. 7, Oct, 1987 ($1.25, digest-size)
Harvey Publications

1-7		.50	1.00

CASPER DIGEST STORIES
2/80 - No. 4, 11/80 (95 cents; 132 pgs.; digest size)

CASPER DIGEST STORIES (continued)
Harvey Publications

	Good	Fine	N-Mint
1	.50	1.50	3.00
2-4	.35	1.00	2.00

CASPER DIGEST WINNERS
April, 1980 - No. 3, Sept, 1980 (95 cents; 132 pgs.; digest size)
Harvey Publications

1	.35	1.00	2.00
2,3	.25	.75	1.50

CASPER HALLOWEEN DIGEST (Formerly Casper Digest)
Jan, 1989 - Present ($1.75)
Harvey Comics

8	.30	.90	1.75

CASPER HALLOWEEN TRICK OR TREAT
January, 1976 (52 pgs.)
Harvey Publications

1	.35	1.00	2.00

CASPER IN SPACE (Formerly Casper Spaceship)
No. 6, June, 1973 - No. 8, Oct, 1973
Harvey Publications

6-8	.35	1.00	2.00

CASPER'S GHOSTLAND
Winter, 1958-59 - No. 97, 12/77; No. 98, 12/79 (25 cents)
Harvey Publications

1: 68 pgs. begin, ends #61	6.50	19.50	45.00
2	3.35	10.00	23.00
3-10	2.75	8.00	18.00
11-20: 13-X-Mas-c	1.70	5.00	11.50
21-40	1.00	3.00	7.00
41-61: Last 68 pg. issue	.75	2.25	5.00
62-77: All 52 pgs.	.50	1.50	3.00
78-98: 94-X-Mas-c	.35	1.00	2.00

CASPER SPACESHIP (Casper in Space No. 6 on)
Aug, 1972 - No. 5, April, 1973
Harvey Publications

1: 52 pg. Giant	.85	2.50	5.00
2-5	.35	1.00	2.00

CASPER STRANGE GHOST STORIES
October, 1974 - No. 14, Jan, 1977 (All 52 pgs.)

1	.70	2.00	4.00
2-14	.35	1.00	2.00

CASPER, THE FRIENDLY GHOST (See America's Best TV Comics, Famous TV Funday Funnies, The Friendly Ghost..., Nightmare &..., Richie Rich, Tastee-Freez & Treasury of Comics)

CASPER, THE FRIENDLY GHOST (Becomes Harvey Comics Hits No. 61 (No. 6), and then continued with Harvey issue No. 7)
9/49 - No. 3, 8/50; 9/50 - No. 5, 5/51
St. John Publishing Co.

1(1949)-Origin & 1st app. Baby Huey	45.00	135.00	315.00
2,3	27.00	81.00	190.00
1(9/50)	33.00	100.00	230.00
2-5	22.00	65.00	155.00

CASPER, THE FRIENDLY GHOST (Paramount Picture Star...)
No. 7, Dec, 1952 - No 70, July, 1958
Harvey Publications (Family Comics)
Note: No. 6 is Harvey Comics Hits No. 61 (10/52)

7-Baby Huey begins, ends No. 17?	16.00	48.00	110.00
8-10: 8-Spooky begins(1st?), ends No. 70?	8.00	24.00	56.00
11-19: 19-1st app. Nightmare (4/54)	5.50	16.50	38.00

	Good	Fine	N-Mint
20-Wendy the Witch begins (1st app, 5/54)	6.00	18.00	42.00
21-30: 24-Infinity-c	4.30	13.00	30.00
31-40	3.75	11.25	26.00
41-50	3.00	9.00	21.00
51-70	2.30	7.00	16.00

American Dental Association (Giveaways):

...'s Dental Health Activity Book-1977	.30	.80	1.60
...Presents Space Age Dentistry-1972	.40	1.20	2.40
..., His Den, & Their Dentist Fight the Tooth Demons-1974			
	.40	1.20	2.40

CASPER T.V. SHOWTIME
Jan, 1980 - No. 5, Oct, 1980
Harvey Comics

1	.35	1.00	2.00
2-5		.50	1.00

CASSETTE BOOKS
(Classics Illustrated)
1984 (48 pgs, b&w comic with cassette tape)
Cassette Book Co./I.P.S. Publ.
Note: This series was illegal. The artwork was illegally obtained, and the Classics Illustrated copyright owner, Twin Circle Publ. sued to get an injunction to prevent the continued sale of this series. Many C.I. collectors obtained copies before the 1987 injunction, but now they are already scarce. Here again the market is just developing, but sealed mint copies of comic and tape should be worth at least $25.

1001(CI#1-A2)New-PC 1002(CI#3-A2)CI-PC 1003(CI#13-A2)CI-PC
1004(CI#25)CI-LDC 1005(CI#10-A2)New-PC 1006(CI#64)CI-LDC

CASTILIAN (See Movie Classics)

CAT, T.H.E. (TV) (See T.H.E. Cat)

CAT, THE (See Movie Classics)

CAT, THE
Nov, 1972 - No. 4, June, 1973
Marvel Comics Group

1-Origin The Cat; Wood, Mooney-a(i)	.40	1.25	2.50
2-Mooney-a(i), 3-Everett inks	.25	.80	1.60
4-Starlin/Weiss-a(p)	.30	.90	1.80

CAT FROM OUTER SPACE (See Walt Disney Showcase #46)

CATHOLIC COMICS (See Heroes All Catholic...)
June, 1946 - V3No.10, July, 1949
Catholic Publications

1	8.00	24.00	56.00
2	4.00	12.00	28.00
3-13(7/47)	2.50	7.50	17.50
V2#1-10	1.50	4.50	10.00
V3#1-10	1.15	3.50	8.00

CATHOLIC PICTORIAL
1947
Catholic Guild

1-Toth-a(2) (Rare)	14.00	40.00	90.00

CATMAN COMICS (Crash No. 1-5)
5/41 - No. 17, 1/43; No. 18, 7/43 - No. 22, 12/43; No. 23, 3/44 - No. 26, 11/44; No. 27, 4/45 - No. 30, 12/45; No. 31, 6/46 - No. 32, 8/46
Holyoke Publishing Co./Continental Magazines V2#12, 7/44 on

1(V1#6)-Origin The Deacon & Sidekick Mickey, Dr. Diamond & Rag-Man; The Black Widow app.; The Catman by Chas. Quinlan & Blaze Baylor begin	57.00	170.00	400.00
2(V1#7)	28.00	84.00	195.00
3(V1#8), 4(V1#9): 3-The Pied Piper begins	22.00	65.00	154.00
5(V2#10)-Origin Kitten; The Hood begins (c-redated),			

Casper, The Friendly Ghost #5, © Paramount

Catholic Comics V2#10, © Catholic Publ.

Catman Comics #1, © HOKE

66

Cave Girl #12, © ME

Century Of Comics, © EAS

Cerebus The Aardvark #7, © A-V

CATMAN COMICS (continued)	Good	Fine	N-Mint
6,7(V2#11,12)	17.00	51.00	120.00
8(V2#13,3/42)-Origin Little Leaders; Volton by Kubert begins (his			
1st comic book work)	24.00	72.00	168.00
9(V2#14)	13.50	40.00	95.00
10(V2#15)-Origin Blackout; Phantom Falcon begins			
	13.50	40.00	95.00
11(V3#1)-Kubert-a	13.50	40.00	95.00
12(V3#2) - 15, 17, 18(V3#8, 7/43)	11.50	34.00	80.00
16 (V3#5)-Hitler, Tojo, Mussolini, Stalin-c	11.50	34.00	80.00
19 (V2#6)-Hitler, Tojo, Mussolini-c	11.50	34.00	80.00
20(V2#7) - 23(V2#10, 3/44)	11.50	34.00	80.00
nn(V3#13, 5/44)-Rico-a; Schomburg bondage-c			
	9.00	27.00	62.00
nn(V2#12, 7/44)	9.00	27.00	62.00
nn(V3#1, 9/44)-Origin The Golden Archer; Leatherface app.;			
	7.00	21.00	50.00
nn(V3#2, 11/44)-L. B. Cole-c	14.00	42.00	100.00
27-Origin Kitten retold; L. B. Cole Flag-c	16.00	48.00	110.00
28-Catman learns Kitten's I.D.; Dr. Macabre, Deacon app.; L. B.			
Cole-c/a	17.00	51.00	120.00
29-32-L. B. Cole-c; bondage-#30	14.00	42.00	100.00

NOTE: *Fuje a-11, 29(3), 30. Palais a-11, 29(2), 30Rico a-11(2).*

CATWOMAN (Also see Batman)
Feb, 1989 - No. 4, May, 1989 ($1.50, mini-series, mature readers)
DC Comics

1-4	.25	.75	1.50

CAUGHT
Aug, 1956 - No. 5, April, 1957
Atlas Comics (VPI)

1	4.00	12.00	28.00
2,4: 4-Severin-c; Maneely-a	1.70	5.00	12.00
3-Torres-a	2.65	8.00	18.00
5-Crandall, Krigstein-a; Severin-c	3.50	10.50	24.00

CAVALIER COMICS
1945; 1952 (Early DC reprints)
A. W. Nugent Publ. Co.

2(1945)-Speed Saunders, Fang Gow	6.50	19.50	45.00
2(1952)	3.00	9.00	21.00

CAVE GIRL
1953 - 1954
Magazine Enterprises

11(A-1 82)-Origin	20.00	60.00	140.00
12(A-1 96), 13(A-1 116), 14(A-1 125)-Thunda by Powell			
	14.00	42.00	100.00

NOTE: *Powell c/a in all.*

CAVE KIDS (TV)
Feb, 1963 - No. 16, Mar, 1967 (Hanna-Barbera)
Gold Key

1	1.50	4.50	10.00
2-5	1.00	3.00	7.00
6-16: 7-Pebbles & Bamm Bamm app.	.70	2.00	5.00

CENTURION OF ANCIENT ROME, THE
1958 (no month listed) (36 pages) (B&W)
Zondervan Publishing House

(Rare) All by Jay Disbrow			
Estimated Value....			180.00

CENTURIONS
June, 1987 - No. 4, Sept,1987 (mini-series)
DC Comics

1-4		.45	.90

CENTURY OF COMICS
1933 (100 pages) (Probably the 3rd comic book)
Eastern Color Printing Co.
Bought by Wheatena, Milk-O-Malt, John Wanamaker, Kinney Shoe
Stores, & others to be used as premiums and radio giveaways.
No publisher listed.

	Good	Fine	N-Mint
nn-Mutt & Jeff, Joe Palooka, etc. reprints	300.00	900.00	2100.00

CEREBUS JAM
Apr, 1985
Aardvark-Vanaheim

1-Eisner, Austin-a	.85	2.50	5.00

CEREBUS THE AARDVARK (See A-V in 3-D & Nucleus)
Dec, 1977 - Present
Aardvark-Vanaheim

1-2000 print run; most copies poorly printed			
	70.00	200.00	400.00

Note: There is a counterfeit version known to exist. It can be
distinguished from the original in the following ways: inside cover is
glossy instead of flat, black background on the front cover is blotted
or spotty. These counterfeits sell for between $50.00 and $70.00.

2	32.00	95.00	190.00
3-Origin Red Sophia	23.00	70.00	140.00
4-Origin Elrod the Albino	15.00	45.00	90.00
5,6	13.00	40.00	80.00
7-10	9.00	28.00	55.00
11,12: 11-Origin Moon Roach	9.00	28.00	55.00
13-15: 14-Origin Lord Julius	5.50	16.00	32.00
16-20	3.50	10.50	21.00
21-Scarce	15.00	45.00	90.00
22	3.65	11.00	22.00
23-28	1.85	5.50	11.00
29-31	2.15	6.50	13.00
32-40	1.00	3.00	6.00
41-50,52	.85	2.50	5.00
51-Not reprinted	3.35	10.00	20.00
53-Intro. Wolveroach	1.15	3.50	7.00
54-Wolveroach 1st full story	2.00	6.00	12.00
55,56-Wolveroach	1.00	3.00	7.00
57-60	.60	1.75	3.50
61,62: Flaming Carrot app.	.85	2.50	5.00
63-68	.70	2.00	4.00
69-75	.55	1.60	3.20
76-79	.50	1.50	3.00
80-85	.45	1.25	2.50
86-118: 104-Flaming Carrot app.	.30	1.00	2.00

CHALLENGE OF THE UNKNOWN (Formerly Love Experiences)
No. 6, Sept, 1950 (See Web Of Mystery No. 19)
Ace Magazines

6-'Villa of the Vampire' used in N.Y. Joint Legislative Comm. Publ;			
Sekowsky-a	7.00	21.00	50.00

CHALLENGER, THE
1945 - No. 4, Oct-Dec, 1946
Interfaith Publications/T.C. Comics

nn; nd; 32 pgs.; Origin the Challenger Club; Anti-Fascist			
with funny animal filler	7.00	21.00	50.00
2-4-Kubert-a; 4-Fuje-a	10.00	30.00	70.00

CHALLENGERS OF THE UNKNOWN (See Showcase, Super DC
Giant, and Super Team Family)
4-5/58 - No.77, 12-1/70-71; No.78, 2/73 - No.80, 6-7/73;
No.81, 6-7/77 - No.87, 6-7/78
National Periodical Publications/DC Comics

1-Kirby/Stein-a(2)	50.00	150.00	350.00
2-Kirby/Stein-a(2)	24.00	72.00	170.00

	Good	Fine	N-Mint
CHALLENGERS OF THE UNK. (cont'd)			
3-Kirby/Stein-a(2)	20.00	60.00	140.00
4-8-Kirby/Wood-a plus c-#8	16.00	48.00	110.00
9,10	6.50	19.50	40.00
11-15: 14-Origin Multi-Man	5.00	15.00	35.00
16-22: 18-Intro. Cosmo, the Challs Spacepet. 22-Last 10 cent issue			
	3.50	10.50	24.00
23-30	1.70	5.00	12.00
31-40: 31-Retells origin of the Challengers	1.25	3.75	7.50
41-60: 43-New look begins. 48-Doom Patrol app. 49-Intro. Challenger Corps. 51-Sea Devils app. 55-Death of Red Ryan. 60-Red Ryan returns	.60	1.75	3.50
61-63,66-73: 69-Intro. Corinna	.35	1.10	2.20
64,65-Kirby origin-r, parts 1 & 2	.35	1.10	2.20
74-Deadman by Tuska/Adams	1.00	3.00	6.00
75-87: 82-Swamp Thing begins		.50	1.00

NOTE: *Adams c-67, 68, 70, 72, 74i, 81i. Buckler c-83-86p. Giffen a-83-87p. Kirby a-75-80r; c-75, 77, 78. Kubert c-64, 66, 69, 76, 79. Nasser c/a-81p, 82p. Tuska a-73. Wood r-76.*

CHALLENGE TO THE WORLD
1951 (36 pages) (10 cents)
Catechetical Guild

	Good	Fine	N-Mint
nn	5.00	14.00	28.00

CHAMBER OF CHILLS (. . .of Clues No. 27 on)
No. 21, June, 1951 - No. 26, Dec, 1954
Harvey Publications/Witches Tales

	Good	Fine	N-Mint
21	9.00	27.00	62.00
22,24	6.00	18.00	42.00
23-Excessive violence; eyes torn out	6.00	18.00	42.00
5(2/52)-Decapitation, acid in face scene	6.00	18.00	42.00
6-Woman melted alive	4.50	13.50	31.50
7-Used in **SOTI**, pg. 389; decapitation/severed head panels			
	4.50	13.50	31.50
8-10: 8-Decapitation panels	3.70	11.00	26.00
11,12,14	3.50	10.50	24.00
13,15-24-Nostrand-a in all; c-#20. 13,21-Decapitation panels. 18-Atom bomb panels	5.70	17.00	40.00
25,26	3.00	9.00	21.00

NOTE: *About half the issues contain bondage, torture, sadism, perversion, gore, cannabalism, eyes ripped out, acid in face, etc. Kremer a-12, 17. Palais a-21(1), 23. Nostrand/Powell a-13, 15, 16. Powell a-21, 23, 24('51), 5-8, 11, 13, 18-21, 23-25. Bondage-c-21, 24('51), 7. 25 r-No. 5; 26 r-No. 9.*

CHAMBER OF CHILLS
Nov, 1972 - No. 25, Nov, 1976
Marvel Comics Group

	Good	Fine	N-Mint
1-Harlan Ellison adapt.		.40	.80
2-25		.20	.40

NOTE: *Adkins a-1i, 2i. Brunner a-2-4; c-4. Ditko r-14, 16, 19, 23, 24. Everett a-3i, 11r, 21r. Heath a-1r. Gil Kane c-2p. Powell a-13r. Russell a-1p, 2p. Williamson/Mayo a-13r. Robert E. Howard horror story adaptation-2, 3.*

CHAMBER OF CLUES (Formerly Chamber of Chills)
Feb, 1955 - No. 28, April, 1955
Harvey Publications

	Good	Fine	N-Mint
27-Kerry Drake r-/No. 19; Powell-a	4.30	13.00	30.00
28-Kerry Drake	2.30	7.00	16.00

CHAMBER OF DARKNESS (Monsters on the Prowl #9 on)
Oct, 1969 - No. 8, Dec, 1970
Marvel Comics Group

	Good	Fine	N-Mint
1-Buscema-a(p)		.40	.80
2-Adams script		.40	.80
3-Smith, Buscema-a		.60	1.20
4-A Conanesque tryout by Smith; reprinted in Conan #16	1.25	3.75	7.50
5-8: 5-H.P. Lovecraft adapt.		.30	.60

	Good	Fine	N-Mint
7-Wrightson c/a, 7pgs. (his 1st work at Marvel); Wrightson draws himself in 1st & last panels	.35	1.00	2.00
1(1/72-25 cent Special)		.40	.80

NOTE: *Adkins/Everett a-8. Craig a-5. Ditko a-6-8r. Kirby a(p)-4, 5, 7. Kirby/Everett c-5. Severin/Everett a-6. Wrightson c-7, 8.*

CHAMP COMICS (Champion No. 1-10)
No. 11, Oct, 1940 - No. 29, March, 1944
Worth Publ. Co./Champ Publ./Family Comics(Harvey Publ.)

	Good	Fine	N-Mint
11-Human Meteor cont'd.	30.00	90.00	210.00
12-18: 14,15-Crandall-c	22.00	65.00	154.00
19-The Wasp app.	22.00	65.00	154.00
20-The Green Ghost app.	22.00	65.00	154.00
21-29: 22-The White Mask app. 23-Flag-c	19.00	57.00	132.00

CHAMPION (See Gene Autry's...)

CHAMPION COMICS (Champ No. 11 on)
No. 2, Dec, 1939 - No. 10, Aug, 1940 (no No.1)
Worth Publ. Co.(Harvey Publications)

	Good	Fine	N-Mint
2-The Champ, The Blazing Scarab, Neptina, Liberty Lads, Jungleman, Bill Handy, Swingtime Sweetie begin	40.00	120.00	280.00
3-7: 7-The Human Meteor begins?	22.00	65.00	154.00
8-10-Kirbyish-c; bondage #10	24.00	72.00	168.00

CHAMPIONS, THE
October, 1975 - No. 17, Jan, 1978
Marvel Comics Group

	Good	Fine	N-Mint
1-The Angel, Black Widow, Ghost Rider, Hercules, Ice Man (The Champions) begin; Kane/Adkins-c; Venus x-over	.50	1.50	3.00
2-10,16: 2,3-Venus x-over	.25	.75	1.50
11-15,17-Byrne-a	.50	1.50	3.00

NOTE: *Buckler/Adkins c-3. Kane/Layton c-11. Tuska a-3p, 4p, 6p.*

CHAMPIONS
June, 1986 - No. 6, Feb, 1987 (limited series)
Eclipse Comics

	Good	Fine	N-Mint
1-6: Based on role playing game	.25	.75	1.50

CHAMPIONS
Sept, 1987 - Present ($1.95, color)
Hero Comics

	Good	Fine	N-Mint
1-15	.35	1.00	2.00
Annual 1($2.75,'88)-Origin	.45	1.40	2.75

CHAMPION SPORTS
Oct-Nov, 1973 - No. 3, Feb-Mar, 1974
National Periodical Publications

	Good	Fine	N-Mint
1-3		.30	.60

CHAOS (See The Crusaders)

CHARLIE CHAN (See Columbia Comics, Feature Comics & The New Advs. of . . .)
CHARLIE CHAN (The Adventures of) (Zaza The Mystic No. 10 on)
6-7/48 - No.5, 2-3/49; No.6, 6/55 - No.9, 3/56
Crestwood(Prize) No.1-5; Charlton No.6(6/55) on

	Good	Fine	N-Mint
1-S&K-c, 2 pages; Infantino-a	19.00	57.00	132.00
2-S&K-c	11.00	32.00	75.00
3-5-All S&K-c	10.00	30.00	70.00
6(6/55-Charlton)-S&K-c	7.00	21.00	50.00
7-9	4.30	13.00	30.00

CHARLIE CHAN
Oct-Dec, 1965 - No. 2, Mar, 1966
Dell Publishing Co.

	Good	Fine	N-Mint
1-Springer-a	1.70	5.00	10.00
2	1.00	3.00	6.00

Challengers Of The Unknown #18, © DC

Chamber Of Chills #16, © HARV

Charlie Chan #1, © Crestwood

Charlie McCarthy #1, © Edgar Bergen

Charlton Bullseye #2, © CC

Checkmate #1, © DC

CHARLIE CHAPLIN
1917 (9x16"; large size; softcover; B&W)
Essanay/M. A. Donohue & Co.

	Good	Fine	N-Mint
Series 1, No. 315-Comic Capers (9¾x15¾")-18pp by Segar,			
Series 1, No. 316-In the Movies	40.00	120.00	280.00
Series 1, No. 317-Up in the Air. No. 318-In the Army			
	40.00	120.00	280.00
. . .Funny Stunts-(12½x16-3/8") in color	30.00	90.00	210.00

NOTE: *All contain Segar -a; pre-Thimble Theatre.*

CHARLIE McCARTHY (See Edgar Bergen Presents. . .)
No. 171, Nov, 1947 - No. 571, July, 1954 (See True Comics #14)
Dell Publishing Co.

4-Color 171	6.00	18.00	42.00
4-Color 196-Part photo-c; photo back-c	7.00	21.00	50.00
1(3-5/49)-Part photo-c; photo back-c	7.00	21.00	50.00
2-9(7/52; No. 5,6-52 pgs.)	2.65	8.00	18.00
4-Color 445,478,527,571	2.00	7.00	14.00

CHARLTON BULLSEYE
June, 1981 - No. 10, Dec, 1982; Nov, 1986
Charlton Publications

1-Blue Beetle, The Question		.40	.80
2-10: 2-1st app. Neil The Horse. 6-Origin & 1st app. Thunderbunny			
		.30	.60
Special 1(11/86)(½-in B&W)	.35	1.00	2.00
Special 2-Atomic Mouse app. ('87)	.25	.75	1.50

CHARLTON CLASSICS
April, 1980 - No. 9, Aug, 1981
Charlton Comics

1		.30	.60
2-9		.25	.50

CHARLTON CLASSICS LIBRARY (1776)
V10No.1, March, 1973 (One Shot)
Charlton Comics

1776 (title) - Adaptation of the film musical "1776"; given away at movie theatres	.35	1.00	2.00

CHARLTON PREMIERE (Formerly Marine War Heroes)
V1No.19, July, 1967; V2No.1, Sept, 1967 - No. 4, May, 1968
Charlton Comics

V1#19-Marine War Heroes, V2#1-Trio; intro. Shape, Tyro Team, & Spookman, 2-Children of Doom, 3-Sinistro Boy Fiend; Blue Beetle Peacemaker x-over, 4-Unlikely Tales; Ditko-a		.60	1.20

CHARLTON SPORT LIBRARY - PROFESSIONAL FOOTBALL
Winter, 1969-70 (Jan. on cover) (68 pages)
Charlton Comics

1	.50	1.50	3.00

CHASING THE BLUES
1912 (52 pages) (7½x10"; B&W; hardcover)
Doubleday Page

by Rube Goldberg	25.00	75.00	175.00

CHECKMATE (TV)
Oct, 1962 - No. 2, Dec, 1962
Gold Key

1,2-Photo-c	2.00	6.00	14.00

CHECKMATE (See Action #598)
April, 1988 - Present ($1.25)
DC Comics

1	.40	1.25	2.50
2-5	.30	.90	1.75
6-10	.25	.75	1.50
11,12		.60	1.25

NOTE: *Gil Kane c-2,4,7,8.*

CHEERIOS PREMIUMS (Disney)
1947 (32 pages) (Pocket size; 16 titles)
Walt Disney Productions

	Good	Fine	N-Mint
Set "W"-Donald Duck & the Pirates	3.35	10.00	20.00
Pluto Joins the F.B.I.	2.00	6.00	12.00
Bucky Bug & the Cannibal King	2.00	6.00	12.00
Mickey Mouse & the Haunted House	3.00	9.00	18.00
Set "X"-Donald Duck, Counter Spy	2.75	8.00	16.00
Goofy Lost in the Desert	2.00	6.00	12.00
Br'er Rabbit Outwits Br'er Fox	2.00	6.00	12.00
Mickey Mouse at the Rodeo	3.00	9.00	18.00
Set "Y"-Donald Duck's Atom Bomb by Carl Barks			
	57.00	170.00	380.00
Br'er Rabbit's Secret	2.00	6.00	12.00
Dumbo & the Circus Mystery	2.75	8.00	16.00
Mickey Mouse Meets the Wizard	3.00	9.00	18.00
Set "Z"-Donald Duck Pilots a Jet Plane (not by Barks)			
	2.75	8.00	16.00
Pluto Turns Sleuth Hound	2.00	6.00	12.00
The Seven Dwarfs & the Enchanted Mtn.			
	2.75	8.00	16.00
Mickey Mouse's Secret Room	3.00	9.00	18.00

CHEERIOS 3-D GIVEAWAYS (Disney)
1954 (Pocket size) (24 titles)
Walt Disney Productions

(Glasses were cut-outs on boxes)

Glasses only	4.00	12.00	28.00

(Set 1)
1-Donald Duck & Uncle Scrooge, the Firefighters
2-Mickey Mouse & Goofy, Pirate Plunder
3-Donald Duck's Nephews, the Fabulous Inventors
4-Mickey Mouse, Secret of the Ming Vase
5-Donald Duck with Huey, Dewey, & Louie; . . .the Seafarers (title on 2nd page)
6-Mickey Mouse, Moaning Mountain
7-Donald Duck, Apache Gold
8-Mickey Mouse, Flight to Nowhere

(per book). . . .	5.00	15.00	35.00

(Set 2)
1-Donald Duck, Treasure of Timbuktu
2-Mickey Mouse & Pluto, Operation China
3-Donald Duck in the Magic Cows
4-Mickey Mouse & Goofy, Kid Kokonut
5-Donald Duck, Mystery Ship
6-Mickey Mouse, Phantom Sheriff
7-Donald Duck, Circus Adventures
8-Mickey Mouse, Arctic Explorers

(per book). . . .	5.00	15.00	35.00

(Set 3)
1-Donald Duck & Witch Hazel
2-Mickey Mouse in Darkest Africa
3-Donald Duck & Uncle Scrooge, Timber Trouble
4-Mickey Mouse, Rajah's Rescue
5-Donald Duck in Robot Reporter
6-Mickey Mouse, Slumbering Sleuth
7-Donald Duck in the Foreign Legion
8-Mickey Mouse, Airwalking Wonder

(per book). . . .	5.00	15.00	35.00

CHESTY AND COPTIE
1946 (4 pages) (Giveaway) (Disney)
Los Angeles Community Chest

(Very Rare) by Floyd Gottfredson	14.00	42.00	100.00

CHESTY AND HIS HELPERS
1943 (12 pgs., Disney giveaway, 5½x7¼'')
Los Angeles War Chest

	Good	Fine	N-Mint
nn-Chesty & Coptie	17.00	51.00	120.00

CHEYENNE (TV)
No. 734, Oct., 1956 - No. 25, Dec-Jan, 1961-62
Dell Publishing Co.

4-Color 734(#1)-Ty Hardin photo-c begin	5.50	16.50	38.00
4-Color 772,803	4.00	12.00	28.00
4(8-10/57) - 12-Last Ty Hardin photo-c	3.50	10.50	24.00
13-25 (All Clint Walker photo-c)	3.00	9.00	21.00

CHEYENNE AUTUMN (See Movie Classics)
CHEYENNE KID (Wild Frontier No. 1-7)
No. 8, July, 1957 - No. 99, Nov, 1973
Charlton Comics

8 (No. 1)	2.35	7.00	16.00
9,15-17,19	1.15	3.50	8.00
10-Williamson/Torres-a(3); Ditko-c	5.50	16.50	38.00
11,12-Williamson/Torres-a(2) ea.; 11-(68 pgs.)	5.50	16.50	38.00
13-Williamson/Torres-a, 5 pgs.	3.50	10.50	24.00
14,18-Williamson-a, 5 pgs.?	3.50	10.50	24.00
20-22,25-Severin c/a(3) each	1.70	5.00	12.00
23,24,27-29	.75	2.25	5.00
26,30-Severin-a	.85	2.50	6.00
31-59	.35	1.00	2.00
60-99: 66-Wander by Aparo begins, ends #87. Apache Red begins			
#88, origin #89		.30	.60
Modern Comics Reprint 87,89('78)		.20	.40

CHICAGO MAIL ORDER (See C-M-O Comics)
CHIEF, THE (Indian Chief No. 3 on)
No. 290, Aug, 1950 - No. 2, Apr-June, 1951
Dell Publishing Co.

4-Color 290, 2	3.00	9.00	21.00

CHIEF CRAZY HORSE (See Wild Bill Hockok #21)
1950
Avon Periodicals

nn: Fawcette-c	10.00	30.00	70.00

CHIEF VICTORIO'S APACHE MASSACRE
1951
Avon Periodicals

nn-Williamson/Frazetta-a, 7 pgs.; Larsen; Kinstler-c			
	30.00	90.00	210.00

CHILDREN OF FIRE
Nov., 1987 - No. 3, 1988 (Color) (Mini-series, $2.00)
Fantagor Press

1-3: by Richard Corben	.35	1.00	2.00

CHILDREN'S BIG BOOK
1945 (68 pages; stiff covers) (25 cents)
Dorene Publ. Co.

Comics & fairy tales; David Icove-a	5.00	15.00	35.00

CHILI (Millie's Rival)
5/69 - No. 17, 9/70; No. 18, 8/72 - No. 26, 12/73
Marvel Comics Group

1	1.00	3.00	6.00
2-5	.50	1.50	3.00
6-17	.35	1.00	2.00
18-26		.50	1.00
Special 1(12/71)		.50	1.00

CHILLING ADVENTURES IN SORCERY (. . .as Told by Sabrina No.1, 2) (Red Circle Sorcery No. 6 on)

9/72 - No. 2, 10/72; No. 3, 10/73 - No. 5, 2/74
Archie Publications (Red Circle Prod.)

	Good	Fine	N-Mint
1,2-Sabrina cameo in both	.50	1.50	3.00
3-Morrow c/a, all	.35	1.00	2.00
4,5-Morrow c/a, 5,6 pgs.	.35	1.00	2.00

CHILLING TALES (Formerly Beware)
No. 13, Dec, 1952 - No. 17, Oct, 1953
Youthful Magazines

13(No.1)-Harrison-a; Matt Fox c/a	12.00	36.00	84.00
14-Harrison-a	7.00	21.00	50.00
15-Has No. 14 on-c; Matt Fox-c; Harrison-a	9.00	27.00	62.00
16-Poe adapt.-'Metzengerstein'; Rudyard Kipling adapt.-'Mark of the Beast,' by Kiefer; bondage-c	7.00	21.00	50.00
17-Matt Fox-c; Sir Walter Scott & Poe adapt.	9.00	27.00	62.00

CHILLING TALES OF HORROR (Magazine)
V1No.1, 6/69 - V1No.7, 12/70; V2No.2, 2/71 - V2No.5, 10/71
(52 pages; black & white) (50 cents)
Stanley Publications

V1No.1	.40	1.25	2.50
2-7: 7-Cameron-a	.30	.90	1.80
V2No.2-Spirit of Frankenstein r-/Adv. into Unknown No. 16;			
V2No.3,5	.30	.90	1.80
V2No.4-r-9 pg. Feldstein-a from Adv. into Unknown No. 3			
	.40	1.25	2.50

NOTE: Two issues of V2No.2 exist, Feb, 1971 and April, 1971.

CHILLY WILLY (See 4-Color No. 740,852,967,1017,1074,1122,1177,1212,1281)
CHINA BOY (See Wisco)
CHIP 'N' DALE (Walt Disney)(See WDC&S #204)
11/53 - No. 30, 6-8/62; 9/67 - No. 83, 1982
Dell Publishing Co./Gold Key/Whitman No. 65 on

4-Color 517	1.70	5.00	12.00
4-Color 581,636	1.30	4.00	9.00
4(12/55-2/56)-10	.75	2.25	5.00
11-30	.55	1.65	4.00
1(Gold Key reprints, 1967)	.70	2.00	4.00
2-10	.35	1.00	2.00
11-20		.60	1.20
21-83		.40	.80

NOTE: All Gold Key/Whitman issues have reprints except No. 32-35, 38-41, 45-47. No. 23-28, 30-42, 45-47, 49 have new covers.

CHITTY CHITTY BANG BANG (See Movie Comics)
CHOICE COMICS
Dec, 1941 - No. 3, Feb, 1942
Great Publications

1-Origin Secret Circle; Atlas the Mighty app.; Zomba, Jungle Fight, Kangaroo Man, & Fire Eater begin	42.00	125.00	295.00
2	27.00	81.00	190.00
3-Features movie 'The Lost City'' classic cover; continues in Great Comics #3	38.00	115.00	265.00

CHOO CHOO CHARLIE
Dec, 1969
Gold Key

1-John Stanley-a (scarce)	4.00	12.00	28.00

CHRISTIAN HEROES OF TODAY
1964 (36 pages)
David C. Cook

	.70	2.00	4.00

CHRISTMAS (See A-1 No. 28)
CHRISTMAS ADVENTURE, A (See Classics Comics Giveaway)
CHRISTMAS ADVENTURE, THE
1963 (16 pages)

Cheyenne #10, © Warner Bros.

Chief Crazy Horse #1, © AVON

Chilling Tales #17, © YM

Christmas Carnival, © Z-D

Christmas Coloring Fun, © H. Burnside

Christmas Parade #1, © WDC

	Good	Fine	N-Mint

THE CHRISTMAS ADVENTURE (continued)
S. Rose (H. L. Green Giveaway)

	.85	2.50	5.00

CHRISTMAS ALBUM (See March of Comics No. 312)

CHRISTMAS & ARCHIE ($1.00)
Jan, 1975 (68 pages) (10¼x13¼")
Archie Comics

1	1.70	5.00	10.00

CHRISTMAS AT THE ROTUNDA (Titled Ford Rotunda Christmas Bk. 1957 on) (Regular size)
Given away every Christmas at one location
1954 - 1961
Ford Motor Co. (Western Printing)

1954-56 issues (nn's)	1.75	5.25	12.00
1957-61 issues (nn's)	1.15	3.50	8.00

CHRISTMAS BELLS (See March of Comics No. 297)

CHRISTMAS CARNIVAL
1952 (100 pages) (One Shot)
Ziff-Davis Publ. Co./St. John Publ. Co. No. 2

nn	6.00	18.00	42.00
2-Reprints Ziff-Davis issue plus-c	4.35	13.00	30.00

CHRISTMAS CAROL, A (See March of Comics No. 33)

CHRISTMAS CAROL, A
No date (1942-43) (32 pgs.; 8¼x10¾"; paper cover)
Sears Roebuck & Co. (Giveaway)

nn-Comics & coloring book	5.00	15.00	30.00

CHRISTMAS CAROL, A
1940s ? (20 pgs.)
Sears Roebuck & Co. (Christmas giveaway)

Comic book & animated coloring book	4.00	12.00	24.00

CHRISTMAS CAROLS
1959 ? (16 pgs.)
Hot Shoppes Giveaway

	1.20	3.50	7.00

CHRISTMAS COLORING FUN
1964 (20 pgs.; slick cover; B&W inside)
H. Burnside

	.70	2.00	4.00

CHRISTMAS DREAM, A
1950 (16 pages) (Kinney Shoe Store Giveaway)
Promotional Publishing Co.

nn	1.35	4.00	8.00

CHRISTMAS DREAM, A
1952? (16 pgs.; paper cover)
J. J. Newberry Co. (Giveaway)

	1.35	4.00	8.00

CHRISTMAS DREAM, A
1952 (16 pgs.; paper cover)
Promotional Publ. Co. (Giveaway)

	1.35	4.00	8.00

CHRISTMAS EVE, A (See March of Comics No. 212)

CHRISTMAS FUN AROUND THE WORLD
No date (early 50's) (16 pages; paper cover)
No publisher

	2.00	6.00	12.00

CHRISTMAS IN DISNEYLAND (See Dell Giants)

CHRISTMAS JOURNEY THROUGH SPACE
1960
Promotional Publishing Co.

	Good	Fine	N-Mint

Reprints 1954 issue Jolly Christmas Book with new slick cover

	1.50	4.50	10.00

CHRISTMAS ON THE MOON
1958 (20 pgs.; slick cover)
W. T. Grant Co. (Giveaway)

	1.75	5.25	12.00

CHRISTMAS PARADE (See Dell Giant No. 26, Dell Giants, March of Comics No. 284, & Walt Disney's...)

CHRISTMAS PARADE (Walt Disney's)
1/63 (no month) - No. 9, 1/72 (No.1,5: 80pgs.; No.2-4,7-9: 36pgs.)
Gold Key/Gladstone Publ.

1 (30018-301)-Giant	3.75	11.00	26.00
2-Reprints 4-Color 367 by Barks	4.00	12.00	28.00
3-Reprints 4-Color 178 by Barks	4.00	12.00	28.00
4-Reprints 4-Color 203 by Barks	4.00	12.00	28.00
5-Reprints Christmas Parade 1(Dell) by Barks; giant			
	4.00	12.00	28.00
6-Reprints Christmas Parade 2(Dell) by Barks(64pp)-Giant			
	4.00	12.00	28.00
7,9: 7-Pull-out poster	2.00	6.00	14.00
8-Reprints 4-Color 367 by Barks; pull-out poster			
	4.00	12.00	28.00
1(2/89, $2.95, 100pgs, Gladstone): Barks-r/painted-c			
	.50	1.50	2.95

CHRISTMAS PARTY (See March of Comics No. 256)

CHRISTMAS PLAY BOOK
1946 (16 pgs.; paper cover)
Gould-Stoner Co. (Giveaway)

	2.75	8.00	16.00

CHRISTMAS ROUNDUP
1960
Promotional Publishing Co.

Marv Levy c/a	1.00	3.00	7.00

CHRISTMAS STORIES (See 4-Color 959,1062)

CHRISTMAS STORY (See March of Comics No. 326)

CHRISTMAS STORY BOOK (See Woolworth's Christmas Book)

CHRISTMAS STORY CUT-OUT BOOK, THE
1951 (36 pages) (15 cents)
Catechetical Guild

393-½ text, ½ comics	2.75	8.00	16.00

CHRISTMAS TREASURY, A (See Dell Giants & March of Comics No. 227)

CHRISTMAS USA (Through 300 Years) (Also see Uncle Sam's...)
1956
Promotional Publ. Co. (Giveaway)

Marv Levy c/a	1.00	3.00	6.00

CHRISTMAS WITH ARCHIE
1973, 1974 (52 pages) (49 cents)
Spire Christian Comics (Fleming H. Revell Co.)

nn		.60	1.20

CHRISTMAS WITH MOTHER GOOSE (See 4-Color No. 90,126,172,201,253)

CHRISTMAS WITH SANTA (See March of Comics No. 92)

CHRISTMAS WITH SNOW WHITE AND THE SEVEN DWARFS
1953 (16 pages, paper cover)
Kobackers Giftstore of Buffalo, N.Y.

	3.00	9.00	18.00

CHRISTMAS WITH THE SUPER-HEROES
Jan, 1989 ($2.95, 100pgs, all-r)
DC Comics

	Good	Fine	N-Mint
1-Miller, N. Adams-r; Byrne-c; Batman, Superman, JLA, LSH Christmas stories	.50	1.50	2.95

CHRISTOPHERS, THE
1951 (36 pages) (Some copies have 15 cent sticker)
Catechetical Guild (Giveaway)

nn-Hammer & sickle dripping blood-c; Stalin as Satan in Hell	25.00	75.00	175.00

CHROME
1986 - No. 3 ($1.50, color)
Hot Comics

1	.50	1.50	3.00
2,3	.35	1.00	2.00

CHRONICLES OF CORUM, THE (Also see Corum . . .)
Jan, 1987 - No. 12, Nov, 1988 ($1.75-$1.95, deluxe series)
First Comics

1-12: Adapt. M. Moorcock's novel	.35	1.00	2.00

CHRONICLES OF PANDA KHAN, THE (Becomes Panda Khan)
Feb., 1987 - No. 2, July, 1987 ($1.50, B&W)
Abacus Press

1,2-Character from A Distant Soil	.35	1.00	2.00

CHUCKLE, THE GIGGLY BOOK OF COMIC ANIMALS
1945 (132 pages) (One Shot)
R. B. Leffingwell Co.

1-Funny animal	8.00	24.00	56.00

CHUCK NORRIS (TV)
Jan, 1987 - No. 5, Sept, 1987
Star Comics (Marvel)

1-Ditko-a		.50	1.00
2-5		.40	.80

CHUCK WAGON (See Sheriff Bob Dixon's . . .)

CICERO'S CAT
July-Aug, 1959 - No. 2, Sept-Oct, 1959
Dell Publishing Co.

1,2	1.70	5.00	12.00

CIMARRON STRIP (TV)
January, 1968
Dell Publishing Co.

1	2.00	6.00	14.00

CINDER AND ASHE
May, 1988 - No. 4, Aug, 1988 ($1.75, mini-series)
DC Comics

1-4: Mature readers	.30	.90	1.75

CINDERELLA (See 4-Color No. 272,786, & Movie Comics)
CINDERELLA
April, 1982
Whitman Publishing Co.

nn-r-/4-Color 272		.30	.60

CINDERELLA IN "FAIREST OF THE FAIR"
1955 (16 pages, 5x7¼", soft-c) (Walt Disney)
American Dairy Association (Premium)

nn	5.00	15.00	30.00

CINDERELLA LOVE
No. 10, 1950; No. 11, 4/51 - No. 12, 9/51; No. 4, 10-11/51 -
No. 11, Fall, 1952; No. 12, 10/53 - No. 15, 8/54; No.25, 12/54 -No.29,
10/55 (no No.16-24)

Ziff-Davis/St. John Publ. Co. No. 12 on

	Good	Fine	N-Mint
10 (1st Series, 1950)	4.00	12.00	28.00
11(4/51), 12(9/51)	1.70	5.00	12.00
4-8: 4,7-Photo-c	1.50	4.50	10.00
9-Kinstler-a; photo-c	2.35	7.00	16.00
10-Whitney painted-c	2.00	6.00	14.00
11(Fall/'52)-Crandall-a; Saunders painted-c	3.00	9.00	21.00
12(St. John-10/53) - #14: 13-Painted-c	1.35	4.00	9.00
15 (8/54)-Matt Baker-c	2.65	8.00	18.00
25(2nd Series)(Formerly Romantic Marriage)	1.35	4.00	9.00
26-Baker-c; last precode (2/55)	3.00	9.00	21.00
27,28	1.00	3.00	7.00
29-Matt Baker-c	2.65	8.00	18.00

CINDY COMICS (. . .Smith No. 39,40; Crime Can't Win No. 41
on)(Formerly Krazy Komics)(See Teen Comics)
No. 27, Fall, 1947 - No. 40, July, 1950
Timely Comics

27-Kurtzman-a, 3 pgs: Margie, Oscar begin	6.00	18.00	42.00
28-31-Kurtzman-a	3.50	10.50	24.00
32-40: 33-Georgie sty; anti-Wertham edit.	2.30	7.00	16.00

NOTE: *Kurtzman's "Hey Look"-#27(3), 29(2), 30(2), 31; "Giggles 'N' Grins"- #28.*

CINEMA COMICS HERALD
1941 - 1943 (4-pg. movie "trailers," paper-c, 7½x10½")
Paramount Pictures/Universal/RKO/20th Century Fox/Republic
(Giveaway)

"Mr. Bug Goes to Town"-(1941)	3.35	10.00	20.00
"Bedtime Story"	3.35	10.00	20.00
"Lady For A Night," John Wayne, Joan Blondell (1942)	3.35	10.00	20.00
"Reap The Wild Wind"-(1942)	3.35	10.00	20.00
"Thunder Birds"-(1942)	3.35	10.00	20.00
"They All Kissed the Bride"	3.35	10.00	20.00
"Arabian Nights," nd	3.35	10.00	20.00
"Bombardier"-(1943)	3.35	10.00	20.00
"Crash Dive"-(1943)-Tyrone Power	3.35	10.00	20.00

NOTE: *The 1941-42 issues contain line art with color photos. The 1943 issues are line art.*

CIRCUS (. . .the Comic Riot)
June, 1938 - No. 3, Aug, 1938
Globe Syndicate

1-(Scarce)-Spacehawks (2 pgs.), & Disk Eyes by Wolverton (2 pgs.), Pewee Throttle by Cole (2nd comic book work; see Star Comics V1/11), Beau Gus, Ken Craig & The Lords of Crillon, Jack Hinton by Eisner, Van Bragger by Kane	180.00	540.00	1260.00
2,3-(Scarce)-Eisner, Cole, Wolverton, Bob Kane-a in each	90.00	270.00	630.00

CIRCUS BOY (See 4-Color No. 759,785,813)
CIRCUS COMICS
1945 - No. 2, June, 1945; Winter, 1948-49
Farm Women's Publishing Co./D. S. Publ.

1-Funny animal	4.00	12.00	28.00
2	2.50	7.50	17.50
1(1948)-D.S. Publ.; 2 pgs. Frazetta	13.50	41.00	95.00

CIRCUS OF FUN COMICS
1945 - 1947 (a book of games & puzzles)
A. W. Nugent Publishing Co.

1	4.00	12.00	28.00
2,3	2.50	7.50	17.50

CIRCUS WORLD (See Movie Classics)

CISCO KID, THE (TV)
July, 1950 - No. 41, Oct-Dec, 1958

Cinderella Love #25, © STJ

Cindy Comics #33, © MEG

Circus #1 (1938), © Globe Synd.

The Cisco Kid #14, © DELL

City Surgeon #1, © K.K. Publ.

Claire Voyant #2, © STD

THE CISCO KID (continued)
Dell Publishing Co.

	Good	Fine	N-Mint
4-Color 292(No.1)-Cisco Kid, his horse Diablo, & sidekick Pancho &			
his horse Loco begin; painted-c begin	8.00	24.00	56.00
2(1/51)-5	4.00	12.00	28.00
6-10	3.50	10.50	24.00
11-20	3.00	9.00	21.00
21-36-Last painted-c	2.65	8.00	18.00
37-41: All photo-c	5.00	15.00	35.00

NOTE: *Buscema* a-40. *Ernest Nordli* painted-c-5-16,20,35.

CISCO KID COMICS
Winter, 1944 - No. 3, 1945
Bernard Bailey/Swappers Quarterly

1-Illustrated Stories of the Operas: Faust; Funnyman by Giunta;			
Cisco Kid begins	20.00	60.00	140.00
2,3	14.00	42.00	100.00

CITIZEN SMITH (See Holyoke One-Shot No. 9)

CITY OF THE LIVING DEAD (See Fantastic Tales No. 1)
1952
Avon Periodicals

nn-Hollingsworth c/a	17.00	51.00	120.00

CITY SURGEON (Blake Harper. . .)
August, 1963
Gold Key

1(10075-308)-Painted-c	1.15	3.50	8.00

CIVIL WAR MUSKET, THE (Kadets of America Handbook)
1960 (36 pages) (Half-size; 25 cents)
Custom Comics, Inc.

nn	1.50	4.50	10.00

CLAIRE VOYANT (Also see Keen Teens)
1946 - 1947 (Sparling strip reprints)
Leader Publ./Standard/Pentagon Publ.

nn	26.00	78.00	180.00
2-Kamen-c	20.00	60.00	140.00
3-Kamen bridal-c; contents mentioned in **Love and Death**,			
a book by Gershom Legman('49) referenced by Dr. Wertham	32.00	95.00	225.00
4-Kamen bondage-c	20.00	60.00	140.00

CLANCY THE COP
1930 - 1931 (52 pages; B&W) (not reprints) (10''x10'')
Dell Publishing Co. (Soft cover)

1,2-Vep-a	6.00	18.00	42.00

CLASSIC COMICS/ILLUSTRATED - INTRODUCTION
by Dan Malan

Further revisions have been made to help in understanding the **Classics** section. **Classics** reprint editions prior to 1963 had either incorrect dates or no dates listed. Those reprint editions should be identified only by the highest number on the reorder list (HRN). Past price guides listed what were calculated to be approximately correct dates, but many people found it confusing for the price guide to list a date not listed in the comic itself.

We have also attempted to clear up confusion about edition variations, such as color, printer, etc. Such variations will be identified by letters. Editions will now be determined by three categories. Original edition variations will be Edition 1A, 1B, etc. All reprint editions prior to 1963 will be identified by HRN only. All reprint editions from 9/63 on will be identified by the correct date listed in the comic.

We have also included new information on four recent reprintings of **Classics** not previously listed. From 1968-1976 Twin Circle, the Catholic newspaper, serialized over 100 **Classics** titles. That list can be found under non-series items at the end of this section. In 1972 twelve **Classics** were reissued as **Now Age Books Illustrated**. They are listed under **Pendulum**

Illustrated Classics. In 1982, 20 Classics were reissued, adapted for teaching English as a second language. They are listed under **Regents Illustrated Classics**. Then in 1984, six Classics were reissued with cassette tapes. See the listing under **Cassette Books**.

UNDERSTANDING CLASSICS ILLUSTRATED
by Dan Malan

Since 1982, this book has been listing every **Classics** edition. That became possible because of Charles Heffelfinger's 1978 book, **The Classics Handbook**, detailing and illustrating every **Classics** edition. But there are still some areas of confusion, and this revised and expanded introduction will attempt to alleviate those problem areas.

THE HISTORY OF CLASSICS

The **Classics** series was the brainchild of Al Kanter, who sought for a way to introduce children to quality literature. In October 1941 his Gilberton Co. began the series **Classic Comics** with **The Three Musketeers**, with 64 pages of storyline. The early years saw irregular schedules and numerous printers, not to mention some second-class artwork and liberal story adaptations. With No. 13 the page total was dropped to 56 (except for No. 33, originally scheduled to be No. 9), and with No. 15 the next-issue ad on the outside back cover moved indoors. In 1945 the Iger shop began producing Classics, beginning with No. 23. In 1947 the search for a "classier" logo title produced **Classics Illustrated**, beginning with No. 35, **The Last Days Of Pompeii**. With No. 45 the story length dropped again to 48 pages, which was to become the standard.

What was probably the most important development for the success of the **Classics** series began in 1951 with the introduction of painted covers, instead of the old line drawn covers, beginning with No. 81, **The Odyssey**. That served as a good excuse to raise the cover price from 10 to 15 cents and did not hinder the growth of the series. From 1947 to 1953 **Classics** artwork was dominated by H.C. Kiefer and Alex Blum, together accounting for nearly 50 titles. Their distinctive styles gave real personality to the **Classics** series. **Classics** flourished during the fifties, and they diversified with **Juniors**, **Specials**, and **World Around Us** series.

But in the early sixties financial troubles set in. In 1962 the issuing of new titles ended with No. 167, **Faust**. In 1967 the company was sold to the Catholic publisher, Twin Circle. They issued two new titles in 1969 as part of an attempted revival, but succumbed to major distribution problems.

One of the major trademarks of the **Classics** series was the proliferation of reprint variations. Some titles had as many as 25 reprint editions. Reprinting began in 1943. Some of the **Classic Comic** (CC) reprints (r) had the logo format revised to the banner logo, and had the motto added under the banner. Then, reprints of all the CC titles were changed over to the new logo title, **Classics Illustrated** (CI), but still had line drawn covers (LDC). Nos. 13, 18, 29 and 41 received second covers (LDC2), replacing covers considered too violent. During 1948 and 1949, reprints of title Nos. 13 to 44 had pages reduced to 48 (except for No. 26, which had 48 pages to begin with).

Starting in the mid-fifties, 70 of the 80 LDC titles were reissued with new painted covers (PC). Thirty of them also received new interior artwork (A2). The new artwork was generally higher quality with larger art panels and more faithful but abbreviated storylines. There were also 29 second painted covers (PC2) issued, mostly by Twin Circle. The last reprints were issued in 1971. Altogether there were 199 interior artwork variations (169 (0)s plus 30 A2 editions) and 272 different covers (169 (0)s, four LDC2s, 70 new PCs of LDC (0) titles, and 29 PC2s). It is mildly astounding to realize that there were over 1,350 editions in the U.S. **Classics** series.

FOREIGN CLASSICS ILLUSTRATED

If U.S. **Classics** variations are mildly astounding, the veritable plethora of foreign **Classics** variations will boggle your imagination. While new information is still coming in, we definitely know about series in 22 languages, 25 countries of origin (some with two or three series), and

FOREIGN CLASSICS ILLUSTRATED (continued)
over 30 distribution countries. There were nearly 300 new **Classics** titles in foreign series and nearly 400 new foreign covers of U.S. titles. Altogether, there were over 4,000 foreign **Classics** editions.

The first foreign **Classics** series consisted of six Canadian **Classic Comic** reprints in 1946. By 1948 series had sprung up in Australia, Brazil, and the Netherlands. But the early series were isolated and often brief. In the mid-fifties, when the U.S. began developing its PCIA2 editions, that U.S. development was coordinated with multi-European country series utilizing the same editions in nine languages at once. This was the main thrust of foreign **Classics**. And when the U.S. stopped issuing new titles in the early sixties, the European series continued with 82 new European titles, which continued until 1976. There were also 88 new Greek History & Mythology titles, and 80 new Brazilian titles, almost all by Brazilian authors. Countries with large numbers of new covers of U.S. titles were Brazil, Mexico, Greece, and the early Australian series. All the rare U.S. titles which never had a painted cover can be found with a new cover in some foreign series.

Here is a chronological list of countries with **Classics** series:

Canada (1946)	Great Britain (1951)	Sweden (1956)
Australia (1947)	Argentina (1951)	Finland (1957)
Brazil (1948)	Mexico (1951)	France (1957)
Netherlands (1948)	W. Germany (1952)	Singapore (1962?)
Italy (1950)	Norway (1954)	India (1964)
Greece (1951)	New Zealand (1955)	Ireland (1971)
Japan (1951)	Iceland (1956)	Belgium (1971?)
Hong Kong (1951?)	Denmark (1956)	Philippines (1973?)

Other listed distribution countries included Austria, Switzerland, Luxemburg, Spain, Morocco, and South Africa.

REFERENCE WORKS ON CLASSICS

The Classics Handbook (3rd edition - 1986) by Charles Heffelfinger. This work identifies and illustrates all U.S. **Classics** editions. It also has illustrations of all **Juniors, Specials** & **World Around Us**, plus information on giveaways, artists, etc.

The Classics Index (1986) by Tom Fisher. This comprehensive subject index covers all **Classics** title stories and filler articles, plus all **Juniors, Specials** & **World Around Us**. *(These two items are available through Bob Levy, 2456 East 18 Street, Brooklyn, NY 11235. Write to him for further details.)*

The Foreign Classics Handbook (preliminary draft - 1986) by Dan Malan. This draft details over 30 series in 20 countries. It also includes a cross-reference index for all U.S. titles/artwork/covers, and a cross-reference comparison chart for all European country series.

All of these works are available through Bob Levy, 2456 East 18 Street, Brooklyn, NY 11235. Write to him for further details.

Worldwide Classics Newsletter (1987-89) Dan Malan, Editor. With subscribers from 18 countries, **WCN** is the nerve center for all new information about U.S. and foreign **Classics**, related series, and non-series collectible items. It also includes ads and market analysis of all **Classics**-related items. The above two items are available from Dan Malan, 7519 Lindberg Dr., St. Louis, MO 63117.

IDENTIFYING CLASSICS EDITIONS

HRN: This is the highest number on the reorder list. It is crucial to understanding the various **Classics** editions. It is shown in parentheses.

ORIGINALS (0): This is the all-important First Edition. There is one basic rule and two secondary rules (with exceptions) that apply here.

Rule No. 1: All (0s) and only (0s) have an ad for the next title (issue). **Exceptions:** No. 14(15) (reprint) has an ad on the last inside page of the text. No. 14(O) has an ad on the outside back cover and also says 10 cents on the front cover. Nos. 55(75) and 57(75) (reprints) have ads for the next issue. (Rules 2 and 3 apply here.) Nos. 168(O) and 169(O) do not have ads for the next issue. (No. 168 was never reprinted; No. 169(O) has HRN (166), No. 169(169) is the only reprint.)

Rule No. 2: All (0s) and only (0s) (Nos. 1-80) list 10 cents on the front cover. **Exceptions:** Nos. 39(71) and 46(62) (reprints) say 10 cents on the front cover. (Rules 1 and 3 apply here.)

Rule No. 3: All (0s) have HRN very close to the issue No. of that title. **Exceptions:** Many reprints also have HRN very close to the title number. Some CC(r)s, 58(62), 60(62), 149(149), 152(149), 153(149), (r)s of titles in 160's. (Rules 1 and 2 apply here.)

For information on variations of (O)s, see the next section (**TIPS. . .**).

DATES: As stated in the new Introduction, many reprints list either incorrect or no dates. **All Reprint Editions Which List Specific Dates Prior To 1963 Are Incorrect!** All HRNs of (167), (166), and (169) with listed dates of 9/63 or later are correct. Otherwise, ignore the listed date and go by the HRN. Trust me, this is like radar!

COVERS: A change from CC to LDC does not indicate a new cover, only a new logo title, while a change from LDC to PC does indicate a new cover. Keep in mind that there are only four new LDC covers—13, 18, 29 and 41. New PCs can be identified by the HRN, and PC2s should be identified by the HRN and the listed date. Remember that many little details can change on a cover and it will still be listed as the same cover.

NOTES: If a front cover states "15 cents in Canada," that does not necessarily mean that it is a Canadian edition. Check the return address to be certain. An HRN listed in the price guide with a "/" in it means that there are two different reorder lists in the front and back covers. Twin Circle editions have a back cover different from regular **Classics**.

TIPS ON LISTING CLASSICS FOR SALE

It may be easy to just list "Edition 17," but **Classics** collectors think of issues in terms of what the HRN is, and whether it is an (0) or an (r), and whether it is a CC, LDC, PC, A2, PC2, stiff cover, etc.

ORIGINALS: The best way to list Originals is to just say (0), unless there are variations of Originals, such as HRN (Nos. 95, 108, 160), printer (Nos. 18-22), color (Nos. 51, 61), etc.

REPRINTS: Just list HRN if it is 165 or below; above that, HRN and date. Also, please list type of logo/cover/art for the convenience of buyers. They will appreciate it.

CLASSIC COMICS (See America in Action, Stories by Famous Authors, Story of the Commandos, & The World Around Us)

CLASSIC COMICS (. . .'s Illustrated No. 35 on)
10/41 - No. 34, 2/47; No. 35, 3/47 - No. 169, Winter/71
(Painted Covers No. 81 on)
Gilberton Publications

Abbreviations:
A-Art; C or c—Cover; CC—Classic Comics; CI—Classics III.; Ed—Edition; LDC—Line Drawn Cover; PC—Painted Cover; r—Reprint

1. The Three Musketeers

Ed	HRN	Date	Details	A	C	Good	Fine	N-Mint
1	—	10/41	Date listed-1941; Elliot Pub; 68 pgs.	1	1	215.00	645.00	1500.00
2	10	—	10¢ price removed on all (r)s; Elliot Pub; CC-r	1	1	14.00	42.00	100.00
3	15	—	Long Isl. Ind. Ed.; CC-r	1	1	11.00	32.00	75.00
4	18/20	—	Sunrise Times Ed.; CC-r	1	1	9.00	27.00	62.00
5	21	—	Richmond Courier Ed.; CC-r	1	1	8.00	24.00	56.00
6	28	1946	CC-r	1	1	6.00	18.00	42.00
7	36	—	LDC-r	1	1	3.00	9.00	21.00
8	60	—	LDC-r	1	1	1.70	5.00	12.00
9	64	—	LDC-r	1	1	1.50	4.50	10.00
10	78	—	C-price 15¢; LDC-r	1	1	1.30	4.00	9.00
11	93	—	LDC-r	1	1	1.00	3.00	7.00
12	114	—	Last LDC-r	1	1	1.00	3.00	7.00
13	134	—	New-c; old-a; 64 pg. PC-r	1	2	1.50	5.00	10.00
14	143	—	Old-a; PC-r; 64 pg.	1	2	1.15	3.50	8.00
15	150	—	New-a; PC-r; Evans/Crandall-a	2	2	1.15	3.50	8.00
16	149	—	PC-r	2	2	.70	2.00	4.00
17	167	—	PC-r	2	2	.70	2.00	4.00
18	167	4/64	PC-r	2	2	.70	2.00	4.00
19	167	1/65	PC-r	2	2	.70	2.00	4.00
20	167	3/66	PC-r	2	2	.70	2.00	4.00
21	166	11/67	PC-r	2	2	.70	2.00	4.00
22	166	Spr/69	C-price 25¢; stiff-c; PC-r	2	2	.70	2.00	4.00
23	169	Spr/71	PC-r; stiff-c	2	2	.70	2.00	4.00

2. Ivanhoe

Ed	HRN	Date	Details	A	C	Good	Fine	N-Mint
1	(O)	12/41?	Date listed-1941; Elliot Pub; 68 pgs.	1	1	93.00	280.00	650.00
2	10	—	Price & 'Presents' removd; Elliot Pub; CC-r	1	1	12.00	36.00	84.00
3	15	—	Long Isl. Ind. ed.; CC-r	1	1	9.50	28.00	65.00
4	18/20	—	Sunrise Times ed.; CC-r	1	1	8.00	24.00	56.00
5	21	—	Richmond Courier ed.; CC-r	1	1	7.00	21.00	50.00
6	28	1946	Last 'Comics'-r	1	1	6.00	18.00	42.00
7	36	—	1st LDC-r	1	1	3.00	9.00	21.00
8	60	—	LDC-r	1	1	1.70	5.00	12.00
9	64	—	LDC-r	1	1	1.50	4.50	10.00
10	78	—	C-price 15¢; LDC-r	1	1	1.30	4.00	9.00
11	89	—	LDC-r	1	1	1.00	3.00	7.00
12	106	—	LDC-r	1	1	1.00	3.00	7.00
13	121	—	Last LDC-r	1	1	1.00	3.00	7.00
14	136	—	New-c&a; PC-r	2	2	1.70	5.00	12.00
15	142	—	PC-r	2	2	.70	2.00	4.00
16	153	—	PC-r	2	2	.70	2.00	4.00
17	149	—	PC-r	2	2	.70	2.00	4.00
18	167	—	PC-r	2	2	.70	2.00	4.00
19	167	5/64	PC-r	2	2	.70	2.00	4.00
20	167	1/65	PC-r	2	2	.70	2.00	4.00
21	167	3/66	PC-r	2	2	.70	2.00	4.00
22	166	9/67	PC-r	2	2	.70	2.00	4.00
23	166	R/1968	C-price 25¢; PC-r	2	2	.70	2.00	4.00
24	169	Win/69	Stiff-c	2	2	.70	2.00	4.00
25	169	Win/71	PC-r; stiff-c	2	2	.70	2.00	4.00

3. The Count of Monte Cristo

Classic Comics #1 (Orig.), © GIL

Classic Comics #3 (HRN 20), © GIL

Classics Illustrated #4 (HRN 167), © GIL

CLASSIC COMICS (continued)

Ed	HRN	Date	Details	A	C	Good	Fine	N-Mint
1	(O)	3/42	Elliot Pub; 68 pgs.	1	1	71.00	214.00	500.00
2	10	—	Conray Prods; CC-r	1	1	12.00	36.00	84.00
3	15	—	Long Isl. Ind. ed.; CC-r	1	1	9.00	27.00	62.00
4	18/20	—	Sunrise Times ed.; CC-r	1	1	8.00	24.00	56.00
5	20	—	Sunrise Times ed.; CC-r	1	1	8.00	24.00	56.00
6	21	—	Richmond Courier ed.; CC-r	1	1	7.00	21.00	50.00
7	28	1946	CC-r; new Banner logo	1	1	6.00	18.00	42.00
8	36	—	1st LDC-r	1	1	3.00	9.00	21.00
9	60	—	LDC-r	1	1	1.70	5.00	12.00
10	62	—	LDC-r	1	1	2.65	8.00	18.00
11	71	—	LDC-r	1	1	1.15	3.50	8.00
12	87	—	C-price 15 ¢; LDC-r	1	1	1.00	3.00	7.00
13	113	—	LDC-r	1	1	1.00	3.00	7.00
14	135	—	New-c&a; PC-r	2	2	1.50	4.50	10.00
15	143	—	PC-r	2	2	.70	2.00	4.00
16	153	—	PC-r	2	2	.70	2.00	4.00
17	161	—	PC-r	2	2	.70	2.00	4.00
18	167	—	PC-r	2	2	.70	2.00	4.00
19	167	7/64	PC-r	2	2	.70	2.00	4.00
20	167	7/65	PC-r	2	2	.70	2.00	4.00
21	167	7/66	PC-r	2	2	.70	2.00	4.00
22	166	R/1968	C-price 25¢;; PC-r	2	2	.70	2.00	4.00
23	169	Win/69	Stiff-c; PC-r	2	2	.70	2.00	4.00

4. The Last of the Mohicans

Ed	HRN	Date	Details	A	C	Good	Fine	N-Mint
1	(O)	8/42?	Date listed-1942; Gilberton #4(0) on; 68 pgs.	1	1	55.00	165.00	385.00
2	12	—	Elliot Pub; CC-r	1	1	11.00	32.00	76.00
3	15	—	Long Isl. Ind. ed.; CC-r	1	1	10.00	30.00	70.00
4	20	—	Long Isl. Ind. ed.; CC-r	1	1	9.00	27.00	62.00
5	21	—	Queens Home News ed.; CC-r	1	1	7.00	21.00	50.00
6	28	1946	Last CC-r; new banner logo	1	1	6.00	18.00	42.00
7	36	—	1st LDC-r	1	1	3.00	9.00	21.00
8	60	—	LDC-r	1	1	1.70	5.00	12.00
9	64	—	LDC-r	1	1	1.50	4.50	10.00
10	78	—	C-price 15¢; LDC-r	1	1	1.30	4.00	9.00
11	89	—	LDC-r	1	1	1.00	3.00	7.00
12	117	—	Last LDC-r	1	1	1.00	3.00	7.00
13	135	—	New-c; PC-r	1	2	1.50	4.50	10.00
14	141	—	PC-r	1	2	1.30	4.00	9.00
15	150	—	New-a; PC-r; Severin, L.B. Cole-a	2	2	1.50	4.50	10.00
16	161	—	PC-r	2	2	.85	2.50	5.00
17	167	—	PC-r	2	2	.70	2.00	4.00
18	167	6/64	PC-r	2	2	.70	2.00	4.00
19	167	8/65	PC-r	2	2	.70	2.00	4.00
20	167	8/66	PC-r	2	2	.70	2.00	4.00
21	166	R/1967	C-price 25¢; PC-r	2	2	.70	2.00	4.00
22	169	Spr/69	Stiff-c; PC-r	2	2	.70	2.00	4.00

5. Moby Dick

Ed	HRN	Date	Details	A	C	Good	Fine	N-Mint
1	(O)	9/42?	Date listed-1942; Gilberton; 68 pgs.	1	1	64.00	192.00	450.00
2	10	—	Conray Prods; Pg. 64 changed from 105 title list to letter from Editor; CC-r	1	1	12.00	36.00	84.00
3	15	—	Long Isl. Ind. ed.; Pg. 64 changed from Letter to the Editor to Ill. poem-Concord Hymn; CC-r	1	1	10.00	30.00	70.00
4	18/20	—	Sunrise Times ed.; CC-r	1	1	8.00	24.00	56.00
5	20	—	Sunrise Times ed.; CC-r	1	1	7.50	22.50	53.00
6	21	—	Sunrise Times ed.; CC-r	1	1	7.00	21.00	50.00
7	28	1946	CC-r; new banner logo	1	1	6.00	18.00	42.00
8	36	—	1st LDC-r	1	1	3.00	9.00	21.00
9	60	—	LDC-r	1	1	1.70	5.00	12.00
10	62	—	LDC-r	1	1	2.65	8.00	18.00
11	71	—	LDC-r	1	1	1.15	3.50	8.00
12	87	—	C-price 15¢; LDC-r	1	1	1.00	3.00	7.00
13	118	—	LDC-r	1	1	1.00	3.00	7.00
14	131	—	New c&a; PC-r	2	2	1.50	4.50	10.00
15	138	—	PC-r	2	2	.70	2.00	4.00
16	148	—	PC-r	2	2	.70	2.00	4.00
17	158	—	PC-r	2	2	.70	2.00	4.00
18	167	—	PC-r	2	2	.70	2.00	4.00
19	167	6/64	PC-r	2	2	.70	2.00	4.00
20	167	7/65	PC-r	2	2	.70	2.00	4.00
21	167	3/66	PC-r	2	2	.70	2.00	4.00
22	166	9/67	PC-r	2	2	.70	2.00	4.00
23	166	Win/69	New-c & c-price 25¢; Stiff-c; PC-r	2	3	1.50	4.50	10.00
24	169	Win/71	PC-r	2	3	1.50	4.50	10.00

6. A Tale of Two Cities

Ed	HRN	Date	Details	A	C	Good	Fine	N-Mint
1	(O)	10/42	Date listed-1942; 64 pgs. Zeckerberg c/a	1	1	55.00	165.00	385.00
2	14	—	Elliot Pub; CC-r	1	1	11.00	32.00	76.00
3	18	—	Long Isl. Ind. ed.; CC-r	1	1	9.50	28.00	65.00
4	20	—	Sunrise Times ed.; CC-r	1	1	8.00	24.00	56.00
5	28	1946	Last CC-r; new banner logo	1	1	6.00	18.00	42.00
6	51	—	1st LDC-r	1	1	2.65	8.00	18.00
7	64	—	LDC-r	1	1	1.50	4.50	10.00
8	78	—	C-price 15¢; LDC-r	1	1	1.00	3.00	7.00
9	89	—	LDC-r	1	1	1.00	3.00	7.00
10	117	—	LDC-r	1	1	1.00	3.00	7.00
11	132	—	New-c&a; PC-r; Joe Orlando-a	2	2	1.70	5.00	12.00
12	140	—	PC-r	2	2	.60	1.80	3.60
13	147	—	PC-r	2	2	.60	1.80	3.60
14	152	—	PC-r; very rare	2	2	7.00	21.00	50.00
15	153	—	PC-r	2	2	.60	1.80	3.60
16	149	—	PC-r	2	2	.60	1.80	3.60
17	167	—	PC-r	2	2	.60	1.80	3.60
18	167	6/64	PC-r	2	2	.60	1.80	3.60
19	167	8/65	PC-r	2	2	.60	1.80	3.60
20	166	5/67	PC-r	2	2	.60	1.80	3.60
21	166	Fall/68	New-c & 25¢-c; PC-r	2	3	1.50	4.50	10.00
22	169	Sum-70	Stiff-c; PC-r	2	3	1.50	4.50	10.00

7. Robin Hood

Ed	HRN	Date	Details	A	C	Good	Fine	N-Mint
1	(O)	12/42	Date listed-1942; first Gift Box ad-bc; 68 pgs.	1	1	46.00	138.00	320.00
2	12	—	Elliot Pub; CC-r	1	1	11.00	32.00	76.00
3	18	—	Long Isl. Ind. ed.; CC-r	1	1	9.00	27.00	62.00
4	20	—	Nassau Bulletin ed.; CC-r	1	1	8.00	24.00	56.00
5	22	—	Queens Cty. Times ed.; CC-r	1	1	7.00	21.00	50.00
6	28	—	CC-r	1		6.00	18.00	42.00
7	51	—	LDC-r	1	1	2.65	8.00	18.00
8	64	—	LDC-r	1	1	1.70	5.00	12.00
9	78	—	LDC-r	1	1	1.00	3.00	7.00
10	97	—	LDC-r	1	1	1.00	3.00	7.00
11	106	—	LDC-r	1	1	1.00	3.00	7.00
12	121	—	LDC-r	1	1	1.30	4.00	9.00
13	129	—	New-c; PC-r	1	2	1.50	4.50	10.00
14	136	—	New-a; PC-r	2	2	1.50	4.50	10.00
15	143	—	PC-r	2	2	.70	2.00	4.00
16	153	—	PC-r	2	2	.70	2.00	4.00
17	164	—	PC-r	2	2	.70	2.00	4.00
18	167	—	PC-r	2	2	.70	2.00	4.00
19	167	6/64	PC-r	2	2	1.00	3.00	6.00
20	167	5/65	PC-r	2	2	.70	2.00	4.00
21	167	7/66	PC-r	2	2	.70	2.00	4.00
22	166	12/67	PC-r	2	2	1.00	3.00	6.00
23	169	Sum-69	Stiff-c; c-price 25¢; PC-r	2	2	.70	2.00	4.00

8. Arabian Nights

Ed	HRN	Date	Details	A	C	Good	Fine	N-Mint
1	(O)	2/43	Original; 68 pgs. Lilian Chestney c/a	1	1	100.00	300.00	700.00
2	17	—	Long Isl. ed.; pg. 64 changed from Gift Box ad to Letter from British Medical Worker; CC-r	1	1	43.00	130.00	300.00
3	20	—	Nassau Bulletin; Pg. 64 changed from letter to article-Three Men Named Smith; CC-r	1	1	32.00	95.00	225.00
4	28	1946	CC-r; new banner logo	1	1	22.00	65.00	154.00
5	51	—	LDC-r	1	1	13.00	40.00	90.00
6	64	—	LDC-r	1	1	11.00	32.00	76.00
7	78	—	LDC-r	1	1	10.00	30.00	70.00
8	164	—	New-c&a; PC-r	2	2	9.00	27.00	62.00

9. Les Miserables

Ed	HRN	Date	Details	A	C	Good	Fine	N-Mint
1A	(O)	3/43	Original; slick paper cover; 68 pgs.	1	1	40.00	120.00	280.00
1B	(O)	3/43	Original; rough, pulp type-c; 68 pgs.	1	1	40.00	120.00	280.00
2	14	—	Elliot Pub; CC-r	1	1	12.00	36.00	84.00
3	18	3/44	Nassau Bul. Pg. 64 changed from Gift Box ad to Bill of Rights article; CC-r	1	1	10.00	30.00	70.00
4	20	—	Richmond Courier ed.; CC-r	1	1	8.50	26.00	60.00
5	28	1946	Gilberton; pgs. 60-64 rearranged/illos added; CC-r	1	1	6.50	19.50	46.00
6	51	—	LDC-r	1	1	3.50	10.50	24.00
7	71	—	LDC-r	1	1	2.65	8.00	18.00
8	87	—	C-price 15¢; LDC-r	1	1	2.15	6.50	15.00
9	161	—	New-c&a; PC-r	2	2	2.00	6.00	14.00
10	167	9/63	PC-r	2	2	1.50	4.50	10.00
11	167	12/65	PC-r	2	2	1.50	4.50	10.00
12	166	R/1968	New-c & price 25¢; PC-r	2	3	1.70	5.00	12.00

10. Robinson Crusoe (Used in SOTI, pg. 142)

Ed	HRN	Date	Details	A	C	Good	Fine	N-Mint
1A	(O)	4/43	Original; Violet-c; 68 pgs; Zeckerberg c/a	1	1	41.00	124.00	285.00
1B	(O)	4/43	Original; blue-grey -c, 68 pgs.	1	1	45.00	135.00	315.00
2A	14	—	Elliot Pub; violet-c; 68 pgs; CC-r	1	1	11.00	32.00	76.00
2B	14	—	Elliot Pub; blue-grey -c; CC-r	1	1	12.00	36.00	84.00
3	18	—	Nassau Bul. Pg. 64 changed from Gift Box ad to Bill of Rights article; CC-r	1	1	9.00	27.00	62.00
4	20	—	Queens Home News ed.; CC-r	1	1	8.00	24.00	56.00
5	28	1946	Gilberton; pg. 64 changes from Bill-Rights to WWII article-One Leg Shot Away; last CC-r	1	1	6.00	18.00	42.00
6	51	—	LDC-r	1	1	2.65	8.00	18.00
7	64	—	LDC-r	1	1	1.50	4.50	10.00
8	78	—	C-price 15¢; LDC-r	1	1	1.15	3.50	8.00
9	97	—	LDC-r	1	1	1.00	3.00	7.00
10	114	—	LDC-r	1	1	1.00	3.00	7.00
11	130	—	New-c; PC-r	1	2	1.50	4.50	10.00
12	140	—	New-a; PC-r	2	2	1.50	4.50	10.00
13	153	—	PC-r	2	2	.55	1.70	3.40
14	164	—	PC-r	2	2	.55	1.70	3.40
15	167	—	PC-r	2	2	.55	1.70	3.40
16	167	7/64	PC-r	2	2	.55	1.70	3.40
17	167	5/65	PC-r	2	2	1.30	4.00	9.00
18	167	6/66	PC-r	2	2	.55	1.70	3.40
19	166	Fall/68	C-price 25¢; PC-r	2	2	.55	1.70	3.40
20	166	R/68	(No Twin Circle ad)	2	2	1.00	3.00	6.00
21	169	Sm/70	Stiff-c; PC-r	2	2	.85	2.50	5.00

11. Don Quixote

Ed	HRN	Date	Details	A	C	Good	Fine	N-Mint
1	10	5/43	First (O) with HRN list; 68 pgs.	1	1	43.00	129.00	300.00
2	18	—	Nassau Bulletin ed.; CC-r	1	1	10.00	30.00	70.00
3	21	—	Queens Home News ed.; CC-r	1	1	8.50	25.50	60.00
4	28	—	CC-r	1	1	6.00	18.00	42.00
5	110	—	New-PC; PC-r	1	2	2.35	7.50	16.00
6	156	—	Pgs. reduced 68 to 52; PC-r	1	2	1.30	4.00	9.00
7	165	—	PC-r	1	2	1.00	3.00	6.00
8	167	1/64	PC-r	1	2	.70	2.00	4.00
9	167	11/65	PC-r	1	2	.70	2.00	4.00
10	166	R/1968	New-c & price 25¢;	1	3	1.70	5.00	12.00

Classic Comics #8 (HRN 20), © GIL

Classics Illustrated #9 (HRN 51), © GIL

Classic Comics #11 (Orig.), © GIL

Classics Illustrated #12 (HRN 167), © GIL

Classics Illustrated #15 (HRN 53), © GIL

Classic Comics #16 (Orig.), © GIL

CLASSIC COMICS (continued)

12. Rip Van Winkle and the Headless Horseman

Ed	HRN	Date	Details	A	C	Good	Fine	N-Mint
			PC-r					
1	11	6/43	Original; 68 pgs.	1	1	46.00	138.00	325.00
2	15	—	Long Isl. Ind. ed.; CC-r	1	1	12.00	36.00	84.00
3	20	—	Long Isl. Ind. ed.	1	1	9.00	27.00	62.00
4	22	—	Queens Cty. Times ed.; CC-r	1	1	8.00	24.00	56.00
5	28	—	CC-r	1	1	6.00	18.00	42.00
6	60	—	1st LDC-r	1	1	2.30	7.00	16.00
7	62	—	LDC-r	1	1	2.30	7.00	16.00
8	71	—	LDC-r	1	1	1.30	4.00	9.00
9	89	—	C-price 15¢; LDC-r	1	1	1.00	3.00	7.00
10	118	—	LDC-r	1	1	1.00	3.00	7.00
11	132	—	New-c; PC-r	1	2	1.50	4.50	10.00
12	150	—	New-a; PC-r	2	2	1.50	4.50	10.00
13	158	—	PC-r	2	2	.70	2.00	4.00
14	167	—	PC-r	2	2	.70	2.00	4.00
15	167	12/63	PC-r	2	2	.70	2.00	4.00
16	167	4/65	PC-r	2	2	1.00	3.00	6.00
17	167	4/66	PC-r	2	2	.70	2.00	4.00
18	166	R/1968	New-c&price 25¢; PC-r; stiff-c	2	3	1.50	4.50	10.00
19	169	Sm/70	PC-r; stiff-c	2	3	1.50	4.50	10.00

13. Dr. Jekyll and Mr. Hyde (Used in SOTI, pg. 143)

Ed	HRN	Date	Details	A	C	Good	Fine	N-Mint
1	12	8/43	Original 60 pgs.	1	1	49.00	147.00	340.00
2	15	—	Long Isl. Ind. ed.; CC-r	1	1	12.00	36.00	84.00
3	20	—	Long Isl. Ind. ed.; CC-r	1	1	9.00	27.00	62.00
4	28	—	No c-price; CC-r	1	1	7.00	21.00	50.00
5	60	—	New-c; Pgs. reduced from 60 to 52; H.C. Kiefer-c; LDC-r	1	2	2.15	6.50	15.00
6	62	—	LDC-r	1	2	2.15	6.50	15.00
7	71	—	LDC-r	1	2	1.30	4.00	9.00
8	87	—	Date returns (erroneous); LDC-r	1	2	1.30	4.00	9.00
9	112	—	New-c&a; PC-r	2	3	1.70	5.00	12.00
10	153	—	PC-r	2	3	.70	2.00	4.00
11	161	—	PC-r	2	3	.70	2.00	4.00
12	167	—	PC-r	2	3	.70	2.00	4.00
13	167	8/64	PC-r	2	3	.70	2.00	4.00
14	167	11/65	PC-r	2	3	.70	2.00	4.00
15	166	R/1968	C-price 25¢; PC-r	2	3	1.00	3.00	6.00
16	169	Wn/69	PC-r; stiff-c	2	3	.70	2.00	4.00

14. Westward Ho!

Ed	HRN	Date	Details	A	C	Good	Fine	N-Mint
1	13	9/43	Original; last outside bc coming-next ad; 60 pgs.			90.00	270.00	630.00
2	15	—	Long Isl. Ind. ed.; CC-r	1	1	46.00	138.00	320.00
3	21	—	Queens Home News; Pg. 56 changed from coming-next ad to Three Men Named Smith; CC-r	1	1	33.00	100.00	230.00
4	28	1946	Gilberton changed again to WWII article-	1	1	26.00	78.00	180.00

			Speaking for America; last CC-r			Good	Fine	N-Mint
5	53	—	Pgs. reduced from 60 to 52; LDC-r	1	1	20.00	60.00	140.00

15. Uncle Tom's Cabin (Used in SOTI, pgs. 102, 103)

Ed	HRN	Date	Details	A	C	Good	Fine	N-Mint
1	14	11/43	Original; Outside-bc ad: 2 Gift Boxes; 60 pgs.	1	1	36.00	108.00	250.00
2	15	—	Long Isl. Ind. listed-bottom inside-fc; also Gilberton listed bottom-pg. 1; CC-r	1	1	14.00	42.00	100.00
3	21	—	Nassau Bulletin ed.; CC-r	1	1	12.00	36.00	84.00
4	28	—	No c-price; CC-r	1	1	7.00	21.00	50.00
5	53	—	1st pgs. reduced 56 to 48; LDC-r	1	1	3.50	10.50	24.00
6	71	—	LDC-r	1	1	2.30	7.00	16.00
7	89	—	C-price 15¢; LDC-r	1	1	2.00	6.00	14.00
8	117	—	New-c/lettering changes; PC-r	1	2	1.50	4.50	10.00
9	128	—	'Picture Progress' promo; PC-r	1	2	1.20	3.50	8.00
10	137	—	PC-r	1	2	.70	2.00	4.00
11	146	—	PC-r	1	2	.70	2.00	4.00
12	154	—	PC-r	1	2	.70	2.00	4.00
13	161	—	PC-r	1	2	.70	2.00	4.00
14	167	—	PC-r	1	2	.70	2.00	4.00
15	167	6/64	PC-r	1	2	.70	2.00	4.00
16	167	5/65	PC-r	1	2	.70	2.00	4.00
17	166	5/67	PC-r	1	2	.70	2.00	4.00
18	166	Wn/69	New-stiff-c; PC-r	1	3	1.50	4.50	10.00
19	169	Sm/70	PC-r; stiff-c	1	3	1.50	4.50	10.00

16. Gullivers Travels

Ed	HRN	Date	Details	A	C	Good	Fine	N-Mint
1	15	12/43	Original-Lilian Chestney c/a; 60 pgs.	1	1	32.00	95.00	225.00
2	18/20	—	Price deleted; Queens Home News ed; CC-r	1	1	10.00	30.00	70.00
3	22	—	Queens Cty. Times ed.; CC-r	1	1	8.50	25.50	60.00
4	28	—	CC-r	1	1	6.00	18.00	42.00
5	60	—	Pgs. reduced to 48; LDC-r	1	1	2.00	6.00	14.00
6	62	—	LDC-r	1	1	1.70	5.00	12.00
7	78	—	C-price 15¢; LDC-r	1	1	1.30	4.00	9.00
8	89	—	LDC-r	1	1	1.00	3.00	7.00
9	155	—	New-c; PC-r	1	2	1.50	4.50	10.00
10	165	—	PC-r	1	2	.70	2.00	4.00
11	167	5/64	PC-r	1	2	.70	2.00	4.00
12	167	11/65	PC-r	1	2	.70	2.00	4.00
13	166	R/1968	C-price 25¢; PC-r	1	2	.70	2.00	4.00
14	169	Wn/69	PC-r; stiff-c	1	2	.70	2.00	4.00

17. The Deerslayer

Ed	HRN	Date	Details	A	C	Good	Fine	N-Mint
1	16	1/44	Original; Outside-bc ad: 3 Gift Boxes; 60 pgs.	1	1	30.00	90.00	210.00
2A	18	—	Queens Cty Times (inside-fc); CC-r	1	1	10.00	30.00	70.00
2B	18	—	Gilberton (bottom-pg. 1); CC-r; Scarce	1	1	13.00	40.00	90.00
3	22	—	Queens Cty. Times	1	1	8.00	24.00	56.00

CLASSIC COMICS (continued)

Ed	HRN	Date	Details	A	C	Good	Fine	N-Mint
			ed.;CC-r					
4	28	—	CC-r	1	1	6.00	18.00	42.00
5	60	—	Pgs.reduced to 52; LDC-r	1	1	2.00	6.00	14.00
6	64	—	LDC-r	1	1	1.50	4.50	10.00
7	85	—	C-price 15¢; LDC-r	1	1	.85	2.50	6.00
8	118	—	LDC-r	1	1	.85	2.50	6.00
9	132	—	LDC-r	1	1	.70	2.00	4.00
10	167	11/66	Last LDC-r	1	1	.70	2.00	4.00
11	166	R/1968	New-c & price 25¢; PC-r	1	2	1.50	4.50	10.00
12	169	Spr/71	Stiff-c; letters from parents & educators; PC-r	1	1	1.50	4.50	10.00

Ed	HRN	Date	Details	A	C	Good	Fine	N-Mint
9	117	—	LDC-r	1	1	1.00	3.00	7.00
10	131	—	New-c&a; PC-r	2	2	1.50	4.50	10.00
11	140	—	PC-r	2	2	.70	2.00	4.00
12	150	—	PC-r	2	2	.70	2.00	4.00
13	158	—	PC-r	2	2	.70	2.00	4.00
14	165	—	PC-r	2	2	.70	2.00	4.00
15	167	—	PC-r	2	2	.70	2.00	4.00
16	167	6/64	PC-r	2	2	.70	2.00	4.00
17	167	6/65	PC-r	2	2	.70	2.00	4.00
18	167	10/65	PC-r	2	2	.70	2.00	4.00
19	166	9/67	PC-r	2	2	.70	2.00	4.00
20	166	Win/69	C-price 25¢; PC-r; stiff-c	2	2	.70	2.00	4.00
21	169	Sm/70	PC-r; stiff-c	2	2	.70	2.00	4.00

18. The Hunchback of Notre Dame

Ed	HRN	Date	Details	A	C	Good	Fine	N-Mint
1A	17	3/44	Orig.; Gilberton ed.; 60 pgs.	1	1	40.00	120.00	280.00
1B	17	3/44	Orig.; Island Pub. Ed.; 60 pgs.	1	1	35.00	105.00	245.00
2	18/20	—	Queens Home News ed.; CC-r	1	1	10.00	30.00	70.00
3	22	—	Queens Cty. Times ed.; CC-r	1	1	8.00	24.00	56.00
4	28	—	CC-r	1	1	6.00	18.00	42.00
5	60	—	New-c; 8pgs. deleted; Kiefer-c; LDC-r	1	2	1.70	5.00	12.00
6	62	—	LDC-r	1	2	1.70	5.00	12.00
7	78	—	C-price 15¢; LDC-r	1	2	1.30	4.00	9.00
8A	89	—	H.C.Kiefer on bottom right-fc; LDC-r	1	2	1.00	3.00	7.00
8B	89	—	Name omitted; LDC-r	1	2	2.00	6.00	14.00
9	118	—	LDC-r	1	2	1.00	3.00	7.00
10	140	—	New-c; PC-r	1	3	2.65	8.00	18.00
11	146	—	PC-r	1	3	2.00	6.00	14.00
12	158	—	New-c&a; PC-r; Evans/Crandall-a	2	4	2.00	6.00	14.00
13	165	—	PC-r	2	4	1.00	3.00	6.00
14	167	9/63	PC-r	2	4	1.00	3.00	6.00
15	167	10/64	PC-r	2	4	1.00	3.00	6.00
16	167	4/66	PC-r	2	4	.50	1.50	3.00
17	166	R/1968	New price 25¢; PC-r	2	4	.50	1.50	3.00
18	169	Sm/70	Stiff-c; PC-r	2	4	.50	1.50	3.00

19. Huckleberry Finn

Ed	HRN	Date	Details	A	C	Good	Fine	N-Mint
1A	18	4/44	Orig.; Gilberton ed.; 60 pgs.	1	1	25.00	75.00	175.00
1B	18	4/44	Orig.; Island Pub.; 60 pgs.	1	1	30.00	90.00	210.00
2	18	—	Nassau Bulletin ed.; fc-price 15¢-Canada; no coming-next ad; CC-r	1	1	10.00	30.00	70.00
3	22	—	Queens Cty. Times ed.; CC-r	1	1	8.00	24.00	56.00
4	28	—	CC-r	1	1	6.00	18.00	42.00
5	60	—	Pgs. reduced to 48; LDC-r	1	1	2.00	6.00	14.00
6	62	—	LDC-r	1	1	1.70	5.00	12.00
7	78	—	LDC-r	1	1	1.00	3.00	7.00
8	89	—	LDC-r	1	1	1.00	3.00	7.00

20. The Corsican Brothers

Ed	HRN	Date	Details	A	C	Good	Fine	N-Mint
1A	20	6/44	Orig.; Gilberton ed.; bc-ad: 4 Gift Boxes; 60 pgs.	1	1	30.00	90.00	210.00
1B	20	6/44	Orig.; Courier ed.; 60 pgs.	1	1	28.00	84.00	195.00
1C	20	6/44	Orig.; Long Island Ind. ed.; 60 pgs.	1	1	28.00	84.00	195.00
1D	20	6/44	Orig.; Both Gilberton & Long Isl. Ind.; 60 pgs.	1	1	35.00	105.00	245.00
2	22	—	Queens Cty. Times ed.; white logo banner; CC-r	1	1	13.00	40.00	90.00
3	28	—	CC-r	1	1	11.00	32.00	76.00
4	60	—	CI logo; no price; 48 pgs.; LDC-r	1	1	9.00	27.00	62.00
5	62	—	LDC-r	1	1	8.00	24.00	56.00
6	78	—	C-price 15¢; LDC-r	1	1	7.00	21.00	50.00
7	97	—	LDC-r	1	1	6.50	19.50	45.00

21. 3 Famous Mysteries ("The Sign of the 4," "The Murders in the Rue Morgue," "The Flayed Hand")

Ed	HRN	Date	Details	A	C	Good	Fine	N-Mint
1A	21	7/44	Orig.; Gilberton ed.; 60 pgs.	1	1	46.00	140.00	320.00
1B	21	7/44	Orig. Island Pub. Co.; 60 pgs.	1	1	52.00	165.00	365.00
1C	21	7/44	Original; Courier Ed.; 60 pgs.	1	1	43.00	130.00	300.00
2	22	—	Nassau Bulletin ed.; CC-r	1	1	20.00	60.00	140.00
3	30	—	CC-r	1	1	17.00	51.00	120.00
4	62	—	LDC-r; 8 pgs. deleted; LDC-r	1	1	12.00	36.00	84.00
5	70	—	LDC-r	1	1	10.00	30.00	70.00
6	85	—	C-price 15¢; LDC-r	1	1	9.00	27.00	62.00
7	114	—	New-c; PC-r	1	2	9.00	27.00	62.00

22. The Pathfinder

Ed	HRN	Date	Details	A	C	Good	Fine	N-Mint
1A	22	10/44	Orig.; No printer listed; ownership statement inside fc lists Gilberton & date; 60 pgs.	1	1	22.00	65.00	155.00
1B	22	10/44	Orig.; Island Pub. ed.; 60 pgs.	1	1	20.00	60.00	140.00
1C	22	10/44	Orig.; Queens Cty Times ed. 60 pgs.	1	1	20.00	60.00	140.00
2	30	—	C-price removed;	1	1	8.00	24.00	56.00

Classics Illustrated #18 (HRN 60), © GIL

Classic Comics #19, © GIL

Classic Comics #21, © GIL

Classics Illustrated #23 (HRN 85?), © GIL

Classics Illustrated #25 (HRN 85?), © GIL

Classic Comics #28 (Orig?), © GIL

CLASSIC COMICS (continued)

Ed	HRN	Date	Details	A	C	Good	Fine	N-Mint
			CC-r					
						Good	Fine	N-Mint
3	60	—	Pgs. reduced to 52; LDC-r	1 1		2.00	6.00	14.00
4	70	—	LDC-r	1 1		1.30	4.00	9.00
5	85	—	C-price 15¢; LDC-r	1 1		.85	2.50	5.00
6	118	—	LDC-r	1 1		.85	2.50	5.00
7	132	—	LDC-r	1 1		.85	2.50	5.00
8	146	—	LDC-r	1 1		.85	2.50	5.00
9	167	11/63	New-c; PC-r	1 2		2.65	8.00	18.00
10	167	12/65	PC-r	1 2		2.00	6.00	14.00
11	166	8/67	PC-r	1 2		2.00	6.00	14.00

23. Oliver Twist (1st Classic produced by the Iger Shop)

Ed	HRN	Date	Details	A	C	Good	Fine	N-Mint
1	23	7/45	Original; 60 pgs.	1 1		18.50	56.00	130.00
2A	30	—	Printers Union logo on bottom left-fc—same as 23(Orig.) (very rare); CC-r	1 1		12.00	36.00	84.00
2B	30	—	Union logo omitted; CC-r	1 1		6.00	18.00	42.00
3	60	—	Pgs. reduced to 48; LDC-r	1 1		1.70	5.00	12.00
4	62	—	LDC-r	1 1		1.70	5.00	12.00
5	71	—	LDC-r	1 1		1.00	3.00	7.00
6	85	—	C-price 15¢; LDC-r	1 1		1.00	3.00	7.00
7	94	—	LDC-r	1 1		1.00	3.00	7.00
8	118	—	LDC-r	1 1		1.00	3.00	7.00
9	136	—	New-PC, old-a; PC-r	1 2		1.50	4.50	10.00
10	150	—	Old-a; PC-r	1 2		1.15	3.50	8.00
11	164	—	Old-a; PC-r	1 2		1.15	3.50	8.00
12	164	—	New-a; PC-r; Evans/Crandall-a	2 2		1.70	5.00	12.00
13	167	—	PC-r	2 2		1.30	4.00	9.00
14	167	8/64	PC-r	2 2		.70	2.00	5.00
15	167	12/65	PC-r	2 2		.70	2.00	5.00
16	166	R/1968	New 25¢-c; PC-r	2 2		.70	2.00	5.00
17	169	Win/69	Stiff-c; PC-r	2 2		.70	2.00	4.00

24. A Connecticut Yankee in King Arthur's Court

Ed	HRN	Date	Details	A	C	Good	Fine	N-Mint
1	—	9/45	Original	1 1		18.50	56.00	130.00
2	30	—	Price circle blank; CC-r	1 1		6.00	18.00	42.00
3	60	—	8 pgs. deleted; LDC-r	1 1		1.70	5.00	12.00
4	62	—	LDC-r	1 1		1.70	5.00	12.00
5	71	—	LDC-r	1 1		1.00	3.00	7.00
6	87	—	C-price 15¢; LDC-r	1 1		1.00	3.00	7.00
7	121	—	LDC-r	1 1		1.00	3.00	7.00
8	140	—	New-c&a; PC-r	2 2		1.30	4.00	9.00
9	153	—	PC-r	2 2		.50	1.50	3.00
10	164	—	PC-r	2 2		.50	1.50	3.00
11	167	—	PC-r	2 2		.50	1.50	3.00
12	167	7/64	PC-r	2 2		.50	1.50	3.00
13	167	6/66	PC-r	2 2		.50	1.50	3.00
14	166	R/1968	C-price 25¢; PC-r	2 2		.50	1.50	3.00
15	169	Spr/71	PC-r; stiff-c	2 2		.50	1.50	3.00

25. Two Years Before the Mast

Ed	HRN	Date	Details	A	C	Good	Fine	N-Mint
1	—	10/45	Original; Webb/ Heames-a&c	1 1		18.50	56.00	130.00
2	30	—	Price circle blank; CC-r	1 1		6.00	18.00	42.00
3	60	—	8 pgs. deleted;	1 1		1.70	5.00	12.00

(continued, right column)

Ed	HRN	Date	Details	A	C	Good	Fine	N-Mint
			LDC-r			Good	Fine	N-Mint
			LDC-r					
4	62	—	LDC-r	1 1		1.70	5.00	12.00
5	71	—	LDC-r	1 1		1.00	3.00	7.00
6	85	—	C-price 15¢; LDC-r	1 1		1.00	3.00	7.00
7	114	—	LDC-r	1 1		1.00	3.00	7.00
8	156	—	3 pgs. replaced by fillers; new-c; PC-r	1 2		1.00	3.00	7.00
9	167	12/63	PC-r	1 2		.50	1.50	3.00
10	167	12/65	PC-r	1 2		.50	1.50	3.00
11	166	9/67	PC-r	1 2		.50	1.50	3.00
12	169	Win/69	C-price 25¢; stiff-c	1 2		.50	1.50	3.00

26. Frankenstein

Ed	HRN	Date	Details	A	C	Good	Fine	N-Mint
1	26	12/45	Orig.; Webb/Brewster a&c; 52 pgs.	1 1		44.00	132.00	310.00
2	30	—	Price circle blank; CC-r	1 1		14.00	42.00	100.00
3	60	—	LDC-r	1 1		4.00	12.00	28.00
4	62	—	LDC-r	1 1		7.00	21.00	50.00
5	71	—	LDC-r	1 1		2.65	8.00	18.00
6	82	—	C-price 15¢; LDC-r	1 1		2.30	7.00	16.00
7	117	—	LDC-r	1 1		1.75	5.25	12.00
8	146	—	New Saunders-c PC-r	1 2		1.75	5.25	12.00
9	152	—	Scarce; PC-r	1 2		2.00	6.00	14.00
10	153	—	PC-r	1 2		.50	1.50	3.00
11	160	—	PC-r	1 2		.50	1.50	3.00
12	165	—	PC-r	1 2		.50	1.50	3.00
13	167	—	PC-r	1 2		.50	1.50	3.00
14	167	6/64	PC-r	1 2		.50	1.50	3.00
15	167	6/65	PC-r	1 2		.50	1.50	3.00
16	167	10/65	PC-r	1 2		.50	1.50	3.00
17	166	9/67	PC-r	1 2		.50	1.50	3.00
18	169	Fall/69	C-price 25¢; stiff-c	1 2		.50	1.50	3.00
19	169	Spr/71	PC-r; stiff-c	1 2		.50	1.50	3.00

27. The Adventures of Marco Polo

Ed	HRN	Date	Details	A	C	Good	Fine	N-Mint
1	—	4/46	Original	1 1		18.50	56.00	130.00
2	30	—	Last 'Comics' reprint; CC-r	1 1		6.00	18.00	42.00
3	70	—	8 pgs. deleted; no c-price; LDC-r	1 1		1.50	4.50	10.00
4	87	—	C-price 15¢; LDC-r	1 1		1.00	3.00	7.00
5	117	—	LDC-r	1 1		1.00	3.00	7.00
6	154	—	New-c; PC-r	1 2		1.15	3.50	8.00
7	165	—	PC-r	1 2		.50	1.50	3.00
8	167	4/64	PC-r	1 2		.50	1.50	3.00
9	167	6/66	PC-r	1 2		.50	1.50	3.00
10	169	Spr/69	New price 25¢; stiff-c; PC-r	1 2		.50	1.50	3.00

28. Michael Strogoff

Ed	HRN	Date	Details	A	C	Good	Fine	N-Mint
1	—	6/46	Original	1 1		18.50	56.00	130.00
2	51	—	8 pgs. cut; LDC-r	1 1		5.70	17.00	40.00
3	115	—	New-c; PC-r	1 2		1.70	5.00	12.00
4	155	—	PC-r	1 2		.70	2.00	5.00
5	167	11/63	PC-r	1 2		.70	2.00	5.00
6	167	7/66	PC-r	1 2		.70	2.00	5.00
7	169	Sm/69	C-price 25¢; stiff-c	1 3		1.50	4.50	10.00

29. The Prince and the Pauper

Ed	HRN	Date	Details	A	C

CLASSIC COMICS (continued)					Good	Fine	N-Mint
1	—	7/46	Orig.; ''Horror''-c	1 1	36.00	108.00	250.00
2	60	—	8 pgs. cut; new-c by Kiefer; LDC-r	1 2	1.70	5.00	12.00
3	62	—	LDC-r	1 2	1.70	5.00	12.00
4	71	—	LDC-r	1 2	1.30	4.00	9.00
5	93	—	LDC-r	1 2	1.00	3.00	7.00
6	114	—	LDC-r	1 2	1.00	3.00	7.00
7	128	—	New-c; PC-r	1 3	1.15	3.50	8.00
8	138	—	PC-r	1 3	.50	1.50	3.00
9	150	—	PC-r	1 3	.50	1.50	3.00
10	164	—	PC-r	1 3	.50	1.50	3.00
11	167	—	PC-r	1 3	.50	1.50	3.00
12	167	7/64	PC-r	1 3	.50	1.50	3.00
13	167	11/65	PC-r	1 3	.50	1.50	3.00
14	166	R/1968	C-price 25¢; PC-r	1 3	.50	1.50	3.00
15	169	Sm/70	PC-r; stiff-c	1 3	.50	1.50	3.00

30. The Moonstone

Ed	HRN	Date	Details	A C			
1	—	9/46	Original; Rico c/a	1 1	18.50	56.00	130.00
2	60	—	LDC-r; 8pgs. cut	1 1	3.00	9.00	21.00
3	70	—	LDC-r	1 1	2.00	6.00	14.00
4	155	—	New L.B. Cole-c; PC-r	1 2	5.00	15.00	35.00
5	165	—	PC-r; L.B. Cole-c	1 2	2.00	6.00	14.00
6	167	1/64	PC-r; L.B. Cole-c	1 2	1.35	4.00	8.00
7	167	9/65	PC-r; L.B. Cole-c	1 2	1.00	3.00	6.00
8	166	R/1968	C-price 25¢; PC-r	1 2	.70	2.00	4.00

31. The Black Arrow

Ed	HRN	Date	Details	A C			
1	—	10/46	Original	1 1	16.00	48.00	110.00
2	51	—	CI logo; LDC-r 8pgs. deleted	1 1	2.00	6.00	14.00
3	64	—	LDC-r	1 1	1.30	4.00	9.00
4	87	—	C-price 15¢; LDC-r	1 1	1.00	3.00	7.00
5	108	—	LDC-r	1 1	1.00	3.00	7.00
6	125	—	LDC-r	1 1	1.00	3.00	7.00
7	131	—	New-c; PC-r	1 2	.85	2.50	6.00
8	140	—	PC-r	1 2	.50	1.50	3.00
9	148	—	PC-r	1 2	.50	1.50	3.00
10	161	—	PC-r	1 2	.50	1.50	3.00
11	167	—	PC-r	1 2	.50	1.50	3.00
12	167	7/64	PC-r	1 2	.50	1.50	3.00
13	167	11/65	PC-r	1 2	.50	1.50	3.00
14	166	R/1968	C-price 25¢; PC-r	1 2	.50	1.50	3.00

32. Lorna Doone

Ed	HRN	Date	Details	A C			
1	—	12/46	Original; Matt Baker c/a	1 1	16.00	48.00	110.00
2	53/64	—	8 pgs. deleted; LDC-r	1 1	3.65	11.00	25.00
3	85	—	C-price 15¢; LDC-r; Baker c&a	1 1	3.00	9.00	21.00
4	118	—	LDC-r	1 1	2.00	6.00	14.00
5	138	—	New-c; old-c becomes new title pg.; PC-r	1 2	1.35	4.00	9.00
6	150	—	PC-r	1 2	.70	2.00	4.00
7	165	—	PC-r	1 2	.70	2.00	4.00
8	167	1/64	PC-r	1 2	.70	2.00	4.00
9	167	11/65	PC-r	1 2	.70	2.00	4.00
10	166	R/1968	New-c; PC-r	1 3	1.70	5.00	12.00

33. The Adventures of Sherlock Holmes

Ed	HRN	Date	Details	A C			
1	33	1/47	Original; Kiefer-c; contains Study in Scarlet & Hound of the Baskervilles; 68 pgs.	1 1	55.00	165.00	385.00
2	53	—	'A Study in Scarlet' (17 pgs.) deleted; LDC-r	1 1	25.00	75.00	175.00
3	71	—	LDC-r	1 1	20.00	60.00	140.00
4	89	—	C-price 15¢; LDC-r	1 1	18.00	54.00	125.00

34. Mysterious Island

Ed	HRN	Date	Details	A C			
1	—	2/47	Original; Last 'Classic Comic.' Webb/Heames c/a	1 1	18.00	54.00	125.00
2	60	—	8 pgs. deleted; LDC-r	1 1	2.00	6.00	14.00
3	62	—	LDC-r	1 1	2.00	6.00	14.00
4	71	—	LDC-r	1 1	3.00	9.00	21.00
5	78	—	C-price 15¢ in circle; LDC-r	1 1	1.00	3.00	7.00
6	92	—	LDC-r	1 1	1.00	3.00	7.00
7	117	—	LDC-r	1 1	1.00	3.00	7.00
8	140	—	New-c; PC-r	1 2	.85	2.50	6.00
9	156	—	PC-r	1 2	.70	2.00	4.00
10	167	10/63	PC-r	1 2	.70	2.00	4.00
11	167	5/64	PC-r	1 2	.70	2.00	4.00
12	167	6/66	PC-r	1 2	.70	2.00	4.00
13	166	R/1968	C-price 25¢; PC-r	1 2	.70	2.00	4.00

35. Last Days of Pompeii

Ed	HRN	Date	Details	A C			
1	—	3/47	Original; 1st 'Classics Illus.;'' LDC; Kiefer c/a	1 1	18.00	54.00	125.00
2	161	—	New c&a; 15¢; PC-r; Jack Kirby-a	2 2	2.30	7.00	16.00
3	167	1/64	PC-r	2 2	1.00	3.00	6.00
4	167	7/66	PC-r	2 2	1.00	3.00	6.00
5	169	Spr/70	New price 25¢; stiff-c; PC-r	2 2	1.15	3.50	8.00

36. Typee

Ed	HRN	Date	Details	A C			
1	—	4/47	Original	1 1	9.00	27.00	62.00
2	64	—	No c-price; 8 pg. ed.; LDC-r	1 1	2.65	8.00	18.00
3	155	—	New-c; PC-r	1 2	1.30	4.00	9.00
4	167	9/63	PC-r	1 2	1.20	3.50	7.00
5	167	7/65	PC-r	1 2	1.20	3.50	7.00
6	169	Sm/69	C-price 25¢; stiff-c PC-r	1 2	.85	2.50	6.00

37. The Pioneers

Ed	HRN	Date	Details	A C			
1	37	5/47	Original; Palais-c/a	1 1	9.00	27.00	62.00
2A	62	—	8 pgs. cut; LDC-r; price circle blank	1 1	2.65	8.00	18.00
2B	62	—	10 cent-c; LDC-r;	1 1	7.00	21.00	50.00
3	70	—	LDC-r	1 1	.70	2.00	5.00
4	92	—	15 cent-c; LDC-r	1 1	.50	1.50	3.50
5	118	—	LDC-r	1 1	.50	1.50	3.50
6	131	—	LDC-r	1 1	.50	1.50	3.50
7	132	—	LDC-r	1 1	.50	1.50	3.50
8	153	—	LDC-r	1 1	.50	1.50	3.50
9	167	5/64	LDC-r	1 1	.50	1.50	3.00

Classics Illustrated #30 (HRN 167), © GIL

Classic Comics #33 (Orig.), © GIL

Classics Illustrated #36 (Orig.), © GIL

Classics Illustrated #40 (Orig.), © GIL   Classics Illustrated #42 (Orig.?), © GIL   Classics Illustrated #45, © GIL

CLASSICS ILLUSTRATED (continued)

						Good	Fine	N-Mint
10	167	6/66	LDC-r	1 1		.50	1.50	3.00
11	166	R/1968	New-c; 15 cent-c; PC-r	1 2		1.70	5.00	12.00

38. Adventures of Cellini

Ed	HRN	Date	Details	A C		Good	Fine	N-Mint
1	—	6/47	Original; Froehlich c/a	1 1		16.50	50.00	115.00
2	164	—	New-c&a; PC-r	2 2		1.50	4.50	10.00
3	167	12/63	PC-r	2 2		1.00	3.00	6.00
4	167	7/66	PC-r	2 2		1.00	3.00	6.00
5	169	Spr/70	Stiff-c; new price 25¢; PC-r	2 2		1.35	4.00	8.00

39. Jane Eyre

Ed	HRN	Date	Details	A C		Good	Fine	N-Mint
1	—	7/47	Original	1 1		13.00	40.00	90.00
2	60	—	No c-price; 8 pgs. cut; LDC-r	1 1		3.00	9.00	21.00
3	62	—	LDC-r	1 1		2.65	8.00	18.00
4	71	—	LDC-r; c-price 10¢	1 1		2.65	8.00	18.00
5	92	—	C-price 15¢; LDC-r	1 1		1.70	5.00	12.00
6	118	—	LDC-r	1 1		1.70	5.00	12.00
7	142	—	New-a; old-a; PC-r	1 2		2.00	6.00	14.00
8	154	—	Old-a; PC-r	1 2		1.70	5.00	12.00
9	165	—	New-a; PC-r	2 2		2.00	6.00	14.00
10	167	12/63	PC-r	2 2		2.00	6.00	14.00
11	167	4/65	PC-r	2 2		1.70	5.00	12.00
12	167	8/66	PC-r	2 2		1.70	5.00	12.00
13	166	R/1968	New-c; PC-r	2 3		4.00	12.00	28.00

40. Mysteries ("The Pit and the Pendulum," "The Advs. of Hans Pfall," "The Fall of the House of Usher")

Ed	HRN	Date	Details	A C		Good	Fine	N-Mint
1	—	8/47	Original; Kiefer-c/a, Froehlich, Griffiths-a	1 1		43.00	130.00	300.00
2	62	—	LDC-r; 8pgs cut	1 1		14.00	42.00	100.00
3	75	—	LDC-r	1 1		11.00	32.00	76.00
4	92	—	C-price 15¢; LDC-r	1 1		9.00	27.00	62.00

41. Twenty Years After

Ed	HRN	Date	Details	A C		Good	Fine	N-Mint
1	—	9/47	Original; 'horror'-c	1 1		27.00	81.00	190.00
2	62	—	New-c; no c-price 8 pgs. cut; LDC-r; Kiefer-c	1 2		2.00	6.00	14.00
3	78	—	C-price 15¢; LDC-r	1 2		1.15	3.50	8.00
4	156	—	New-c; PC-r	1 3		1.00	3.00	7.00
5	167	12/63	PC-r	1 3		.70	2.00	4.00
6	167	11/66	PC-r	1 3		.70	2.00	4.00
7	169	Spr/70	New price 25¢; stiff-c; PC-r	1 3		.70	2.00	4.00

42. Swiss Family Robinson

Ed	HRN	Date	Details	A C		Good	Fine	N-Mint
1	42	10/47	Orig.; Kiefer a&c	1 1		8.00	24.00	56.00
2A	62	—	8 pgs. cut; outside-bc: Gift Box ad; LDC-r	1 1		2.00	6.00	14.00
2B	62	—	8 pgs. cut; outside-bc: Reorder list; scarce; LDC-r	1 1		4.00	12.00	28.00
3	75	—	LDC-r	1 1		1.30	4.00	9.00
4	93	—	LDC-r	1 1		1.00	3.00	7.00
5	117	—	LDC-r	1 1		1.00	3.00	7.00
6	131	—	New-c; old-a; PC-r	1 2		1.50	4.50	10.00

						Good	Fine	N-Mint
7	137	—	Old-a; PC-r	1 2		1.35	4.00	9.00
8	141	—	Old-a; PC-r	1 2		1.35	4.00	9.00
9	152	—	New-a; PC-r	2 2		.85	2.50	6.00
10	158	—	PC-r	2 2		.70	2.00	4.00
11	165	12/63	PC-r	2 2		1.30	4.00	9.00
12	167	12/63	PC-r	2 2		1.00	3.00	6.00
13	167	4/65	PC-r	2 2		1.00	3.00	6.00
14	167	5/66	PC-r	2 2		1.00	3.00	6.00
15	166	11/67	PC-r	2 2		.50	1.50	3.00
16	169	Spr/69	PC-r	2 2		.70	2.00	4.00

43. Great Expectations (Used in SOTI, pg. 311)

Ed	HRN	Date	Details	A C		Good	Fine	N-Mint
1	—	11/47	Original; Kiefer-a/c	1 1		47.00	140.00	330.00
2	62	—	No c-price; 8 pgs. cut; LDC-r	1 1		32.00	95.00	225.00

44. Mysteries of Paris (Used in SOTI, pg. 323)

Ed	HRN	Date	Details	A C		Good	Fine	N-Mint
1	44	12/47	Original; 56 pgs.; Kiefer-a/c	1 1		35.00	105.00	245.00
2A	62	—	8 pgs. cut; outside-bc: Gift Box ad; LDC-r	1 1		16.00	48.00	110.00
2B	62	—	8 pgs. cut; outside-bc: reorder list; LDC-r	1 1		16.00	48.00	110.00
3	78	—	C-price 15¢; LDC-r	1 1		12.00	36.00	84.00

45. Tom Brown's School Days

Ed	HRN	Date	Details	A C		Good	Fine	N-Mint
1	44	1/48	Original; 1st 48pg. issue	1 1		6.00	18.00	42.00
2	64	—	No c-price; LDC-r	1 1		2.35	7.00	16.00
3	161	—	New-c&a; PC-r	2 2		1.30	4.00	9.00
4	167	2/64	PC-r	2 2		1.00	3.00	7.00
5	167	8/66	PC-r	2 2		1.00	3.00	7.00
6	166	R/1968	C-price 25¢; PC-r	2 2		1.00	3.00	7.00

46. Kidnapped

Ed	HRN	Date	Details	A C		Good	Fine	N-Mint
1	47	4/48	Original; Webb-c/a	1 1		6.50	19.50	45.00
2A	62	—	Price circle blank; LDC-r	1 1		1.70	5.00	12.00
2B	62	—	C-price 10¢; rare; LDC-r	1 1		6.00	18.00	42.00
3	78	—	C-price 15¢; LDC-r	1 1		1.00	3.00	7.00
4	87	—	LDC-r	1 1		1.00	3.00	7.00
5	118	—	LDC-r	1 1		1.00	3.00	7.00
6	131	—	New-c; PC-r	1 2		1.00	3.00	7.00
7	140	—	PC-r	1 2		.60	1.80	4.20
8	150	—	PC-r	1 2		.60	1.80	4.20
9	164	—	Reduced pg.width; PC-r	1 2		.50	1.50	3.00
10	167	—	PC-r	1 2		.50	1.50	3.00
11	67	3/64	PC-r	1 2		.50	1.50	3.00
12	167	6/65	PC-r	1 2		.50	1.50	3.00
13	167	12/65	PC-r	1 2		.50	1.50	3.00
14	166	9/67	PC-r	1 2		.50	1.50	3.00
15	166	Win/69	New price 25¢; PC-r; stiff-c	1 2		.50	1.50	3.00
16	169	Sm/70	PC-r; stiff-c	1 2		.50	1.50	3.00

47. Twenty Thousand Leagues Under the Sea

Ed	HRN	Date	Details*	A C		Good	Fine	N-Mint
1	47	5/48	Orig.; Kiefer-a&c	1 1		8.00	24.00	56.00
2	64	—	No c-price; LDC-r	1 1		2.00	6.00	14.00

Ed	HRN	Date	Details	A C	Good	Fine	N-Mint
3	78	—	C-price 15¢; LDC-r	1 1	1.00	3.00	7.00
4	94	—	LDC-r	1 1	1.00	3.00	7.00
5	118	—	LDC-r	1 1	1.00	3.00	7.00
6	128	—	New-c; PC-r	1 2	1.30	4.00	9.00
7	133	—	PC-r	1 2	1.30	4.00	9.00
8	140	—	PC-r	1 2	.85	2.50	5.00
9	148	—	PC-r	1 2	.85	2.50	5.00
10	156	—	PC-r	1 2	.85	2.50	5.00
11	165	—	PC-r	1 2	.85	2.50	5.00
12	167	—	PC-r	1 2	.85	2.50	5.00
13	167	3/64	PC-r	1 2	.85	2.50	5.00
14	167	8/65	PC-r	1 2	.70	2.10	4.20
15	167	10/66	PC-r	1 2	.85	2.50	5.00
16	166	R/1968	C-price 25¢; new-c PC-r	1 3	1.50	4.50	10.00
17	169	Spr/70	Stiff-c; PC-r	1 3	1.50	4.50	10.00

48. David Copperfield

Ed	HRN	Date	Details	A C	Good	Fine	N-Mint
1	47	6/48	Original; Kiefer a/c	1 1	7.00	21.00	50.00
2	64	—	Price circle replaced by motif of boy reading; LDC-r	1 1	2.00	6.00	14.00
3	87	—	C-price 15¢; LDC-r	1 2	1.30	4.00	9.00
4	121	—	New-c; PC-r	1 2	1.30	4.00	9.00
5	130	—	PC-r	1 2	.80	2.30	5.60
6	140	—	PC-r	1 2	.80	2.30	5.60
7	148	—	PC-r	1 2	.80	2.30	5.60
8	156	—	PC-r	1 2	.80	2.30	5.60
9	167	—	PC-r	1 2	.60	1.80	3.60
10	167	4/64	PC-r	1 2	.60	1.80	3.60
11	167	6/65	PC-r	1 2	.60	1.80	3.60
12	166	5/67	PC-r	1 2	.60	1.80	3.60
13	166	R/67	PC-r	1 2	1.30	4.00	9.00
14	166	Spr/69	C-price 25¢; stiff-c PC-r	1 2	.50	1.50	3.00
15	169	Win/69	Stiff-c; PC-r	1 2	.50	1.50	3.00

49. Alice in Wonderland

Ed	HRN	Date	Details	A C	Good	Fine	N-Mint
1	47	7/48	Original; 1st Blum a & c	1 1	10.00	30.00	70.00
2	64	—	No c-price; LDC-r	1 1	2.65	8.00	18.00
3	85	—	C-price 15¢; LDC-r	1 1	2.00	6.00	14.00
4	155	—	New PC, similar to orig.; PC-r	1 2	2.00	6.00	14.00
5	165	—	PC-r	1 2	1.30	4.00	9.00
6	167	3/64	PC-r	1 2	1.30	4.00	9.00
7	167	6/66	PC-r	1 2	1.30	4.00	9.00
8A	166	Fall/68	New-c; soft-c; 25¢ c-price; PC-r	1 3	2.35	7.00	16.00
8B	166	Fall/68	New-c; stiff-c; 25¢ c-price; PC-r	1 3	5.00	15.00	35.00

50. Adventures of Tom Sawyer (Used in SOTI, pg. 37)

Ed	HRN	Date	Details	A C	Good	Fine	N-Mint
1A	51	8/48	Orig.; Aldo Rubano a&c	1 1	6.50	19.00	45.00
1B	51	9/48	Orig.; Rubano c&a	1 1	7.00	21.00	50.00
2	64	—	No c-price; LDC-r	1 1	2.00	6.00	14.00
3	78	—	C-price 15¢; LDC-r	1 1	1.30	4.00	9.00
4	94	—	LDC-r	1 1	1.00	3.00	7.00
5	117	—	LDC-r	1 1	1.00	3.00	7.00
6	132	—	LDC-r	1 1	.85	2.50	6.00
7	140	—	New-c; PC-r	1 2	1.30	4.00	9.00
8	150	—	PC-r	1 2	1.15	3.50	8.00
9	164	—	New-a; PC-r	2 2	.85	2.50	6.00
10	167	—	PC-r	2 2	.70	2.00	4.00
11	167	1/65	PC-r	2 2	.70	2.00	4.00
12	167	5/66	PC-r	2 2	.70	2.00	4.00
13	166	12/67	PC-r	2 2	.70	2.00	4.00
14	169	Fall/69	C-price 25¢; stiff-c PC-r	2 2	.50	1.50	3.00
15	169	Win/71	PC-r	2 2	.50	1.50	3.00

51. The Spy

Ed	HRN	Date	Details	A C	Good	Fine	N-Mint
1A	51	9/48	Original; inside-bc illo: Christmas Carol	1 1	6.50	19.00	45.00
1B	51	9/48	Original; inside-bc illo: Man in Iron Mask	1 1	7.00	21.00	50.00
1C	51	8/48	Original; outside-bc full color	1 1	7.00	21.00	50.00
1D	51	8/48	Original; outside-bc: blue & yellow only; scarce	1 1	10.00	30.00	70.00
2	89	—	C-price 15¢; LDC-r	1 1	1.00	3.00	7.00
3	121	—	LDC-r	1 1	1.00	3.00	7.00
4	139	—	New-c; PC-r	1 2	.85	2.50	6.00
5	156	—	PC-r	1 2	.70	2.00	4.00
6	167	11/63	PC-r	1 2	.70	2.00	4.00
7	167	7/66	PC-r	1 2	.70	2.00	4.00
8A	166	Win/69	C-price 25¢; soft-c; scarce; PC-r	1 2	1.30	4.00	9.00
8B	166	Win/69	C-price 25¢; stiff-c; PC-r	1 2	.70	2.00	4.00

52. The House of the Seven Gables

Ed	HRN	Date	Details	A C	Good	Fine	N-Mint
1	53	10/48	Orig.; Griffiths a&c	1 1	6.00	18.00	42.00
2	89	—	C-price 15¢; LDC-r	1 1	1.00	3.00	7.00
3	121	—	LDC-r	1 1	1.00	3.00	7.00
4	142	—	New-c&a; PC-r Woodbridge-a	2 2	1.00	3.00	7.00
5	156	—	PC-r	2 2	.70	2.00	4.00
6	165	—	PC-r	2 2	.70	2.00	4.00
7	167	5/64	PC-r	2 2	.70	2.00	4.00
8	167	3/66	PC-r	2 2	.70	2.00	4.00
9	166	R/1968	C-price 25¢; PC-r	2 2	.50	1.50	3.00
10	169	Spr/70	Stiff-c; PC-r	2 2	.50	1.50	3.00

53. A Christmas Carol

Ed	HRN	Date	Details	A C	Good	Fine	N-Mint
1	53	11/48	Original & only ed; Kiefer-a,c	1 1	9.00	27.00	62.00

54. Man in the Iron Mask

Ed	HRN	Date	Details	A C	Good	Fine	N-Mint
1	55	12/48	Original; Froehlich-a, Kiefer-c	1 1	6.00	18.00	42.00
2	93	—	C-price 15¢; LDC-r	1 1	1.00	3.00	7.00
3A	111	—	(O) logo lettering; scarce; LDC-r	1 1	3.00	9.00	21.00
3B	111	—	New logo as PC; LDC-r	1 1	1.30	4.00	9.00
4	142	—	New-c&a; PC-r	2 2	.85	2.50	6.00
5	154	—	PC-r	2 2	.50	1.50	3.00
6	165	—	PC-r	2 2	.50	1.50	3.00
7	167	5/64	PC-r	2 2	.50	1.50	3.00
8	167	4/66	PC-r	2 2	.50	1.50	3.00
9	166	Win/69	C-price 25¢; stiff-c PC-r	2 2	.50	1.50	3.00

55. Silas Marner (Used in SOTI, pgs. 311, 312)

Classics Illustrated #48 (Orig.), © GIL

Classics Illustrated #51 (Orig.), © GIL

Classics Illustrated #53 (Orig.), © GIL

Classics Illustrated #55 (Orig.), © GIL

Classics Illustrated #56 (Orig.), © GIL

Classics Illustrated #58, © GIL

CLASSICS ILLUSTRATED (continued)

Ed	HRN	Date	Details	A	C	Good	Fine	N-Mint
1	55	1/49	Original-Kiefer-c	1	1	6.85	21.00	48.00
2	75	—	Price circle blank; 'Coming Next' ad; LDC-r	1	1	2.00	6.00	14.00
3	97	—	LDC-r	1	1	1.00	3.00	7.00
4	121	—	New-c; PC-r	1	2	1.00	3.00	7.00
5	130	—	PC-r	1	2	.50	1.50	3.00
6	140	—	PC-r	1	2	.50	1.50	3.00
7	154	—	PC-r	1	2	.50	1.50	3.00
8	165	—	PC-r	1	2	.50	1.50	3.00
9	167	2/64	PC-r	1	2	.50	1.50	3.00
10	167	6/65	PC-r	1	2	.50	1.50	3.00
11	166	5/67	PC-r	1	2	.50	1.50	3.00
12A	166	Win/69	C-price 25¢; soft-c PC-r	1	2	2.00	6.00	14.00
12B	166	Win/69	C-price 25¢; stiff-c PC-r	1	2	.50	1.50	3.00

56. The Toilers of the Sea

Ed	HRN	Date	Details	A	C	Good	Fine	N-Mint
1	55	2/49	Original; A.M. Froehlich a,c	1	1	10.00	30.00	70.00
2	165	—	New-c&a; PC-r; Angelo Torres-a	2	2	2.65	8.00	18.00
3	167	3/64	PC-r	2	2	2.00	6.00	14.00
4	167	10/66	PC-r	2	2	2.00	6.00	14.00

57. The Song of Hiawatha

Ed	HRN	Date	Details	A	C	Good	Fine	N-Mint
1	55	3/49	Original; Alex Blum a&c	1	1	5.70	17.00	40.00
2	75	—	No c-price; 'Coming Next'ad; LDC-r	1	1	2.00	6.00	14.00
3	94	—	C-price 15¢; LDC-r	1	1	1.00	3.00	7.00
4	118	—	LDC-r	1	1	1.00	3.00	7.00
5	134	—	New-c; PC-r	1	2	1.00	3.00	7.00
6	139	—	PC-r	1	2	.50	1.50	3.00
7	154	—	PC-r	1	2	.50	1.50	3.00
8	167	—	Has orig.date; PC-r	1	2	.50	1.50	3.00
9	167	9/64	PC-r	1	2	.50	1.50	3.00
10	167	10/65	PC-r	1	2	.50	1.50	3.00
11	166	F/1968	C-price 25¢; PC-r	1	2	.50	1.50	3.00

58. The Prairie

Ed	HRN	Date	Details	A	C	Good	Fine	N-Mint
1	60	4/49	Original; Palais c/a	1	1	5.70	17.00	40.00
2	62	—	No c-price; no coming-next ad; LDC-r	1	1	3.50	10.50	24.00
3	78	—	C-price 15¢ in dbl circle; LDC-r	1	1	1.70	5.00	12.00
4	114	—	LDC-r	1	1	1.00	3.00	7.00
5	131	—	LDC-r	1	1	1.00	3.00	7.00
6	132	—	LDC-r	1	1	1.00	3.00	7.00
7	146	—	New-c; PC-r	1	2	.85	2.50	6.00
8	155	—	PC-r	1	2	.50	1.50	3.00
9	167	5/64	PC-r	1	2	.50	1.50	3.00
10	167	4/66	PC-r	1	2	.50	1.50	3.00
11	166	Sm/69	New price 25¢; stiff-c; PC-r	1	2	.50	1.50	3.00

59. Wuthering Heights

Ed	HRN	Date	Details	A	C	Good	Fine	N-Mint
1	60	5/49	Original; Kiefer a/c	1	1	7.00	21.00	50.00
2	85	—	C-price 15¢; LDC-r	1	1	2.30	7.00	16.00
3	156	—	New-c; PC-r	1	2	1.30	4.00	9.00

						Good	Fine	N-Mint
4	167	1/64	PC-r	1	2	.70	2.00	5.00
5	167	10/66	PC-r	1	2	.70	2.00	5.00
6	169	Sm/69	C-price 25¢; stiff-c; PC-r	1	2	.50	1.50	3.00

60. Black Beauty

Ed	HRN	Date	Details	A	C	Good	Fine	N-Mint
1	62	6/49	Original; Froehlich c/a	1	1	6.00	18.00	42.00
2	62	—	No c-price; no coming-next ad; LDC-r	1	1	7.00	21.00	50.00
3	85	—	C-price 15¢; LDC-r	1	1	2.20	6.50	15.00
4	158	—	New L.B. Cole -c&a; PC-r	2	2	2.65	8.00	18.00
5	167	2/64	PC-r	2	2	1.70	5.00	12.00
6	167	3/66	PC-r	2	2	1.70	5.00	12.00
7	167	3/66	'Open book'blank; (See Non-Series Items—Records)					
8	166	R/1968	New-c&price, 25¢; PC-r	2	3	5.00	15.00	35.00

61. The Woman in White

Ed	HRN	Date	Details	A	C	Good	Fine	N-Mint
1A	62	7/49	Original; Blum-c/a fc-purple; bc: top il-los light blue	1	1	6.00	18.00	42.00
1B	62	7/49	Original; Blum-c/a fc-pink; bc: top illos light violet	1	1	6.00	18.00	42.00
2	156	—	New-c; PC-r	1	2	1.70	5.00	12.00
3	167	1/64	PC-r	1	2	1.70	5.00	12.00
4	166	R/1968	C-price 25¢; PC-r	1	2	1.70	5.00	12.00

62. Western Stories ("The Luck of Roaring Camp" and "The Outcasts of Poker Flat")

Ed	HRN	Date	Details	A	C	Good	Fine	N-Mint
1	62	8/49	Original; Kiefer-a,c	1	1	5.70	17.00	40.00
2	89	—	C-price 15¢; LDC-r	1	1	1.30	4.00	9.00
3	121	—	LDC-r	1	1	1.00	3.00	7.00
4	137	—	New-c; PC-r	1	2	1.00	3.00	7.00
5	152	—	PC-r	1	2	.85	2.50	6.00
6	167	10/63	PC-r	1	2	.85	2.50	6.00
7	167	6/64	PC-r	1	2	.70	2.00	4.00
8	167	11/66	PC-r	1	2	.70	2.00	4.00
9	166	R/1968	New-c&price 25¢; PC-r	1	3	1.70	5.00	12.00

63. The Man Without a Country

Ed	HRN	Date	Details	A	C	Good	Fine	N-Mint
1	62	9/49	Original; Kiefer-a,c	1	1	6.00	18.00	42.00
2	78	—	C-price 15¢ in double circle; LDC-r	1	1	2.00	6.00	14.00
3	156	—	New-c, old-a; PC-r	1	2	2.35	7.00	16.00
4	165	—	New-a & text pgs.; PC-r; A. Torres-a	2	2	1.00	3.00	7.00
5	167	3/64	PC-r	2	2	.70	2.00	4.00
6	167	8/66	PC-r	2	2	.70	2.00	4.00
7	169	Sm/69	New price 25¢; stiff-c; PC-r	2	2	.70	2.00	4.00

64. Treasure Island

Ed	HRN	Date	Details	A	C	Good	Fine	N-Mint
1	62	10/49	Original; Blum-a,c	1	1	6.00	18.00	42.00
2	82	—	C-price 15¢; LDC-r	1	1	1.30	4.00	9.00
3	117	—	LDC-r	1	1	1.00	3.00	7.00

CLASSICS ILLUSTRATED (continued)

						Good	Fine	N-Mint
4	131	—	New-c; PC-r	1	2	1.00	3.00	7.00
5	138	—	PC-r	1	2	.50	1.50	3.00
6	146	—	PC-r	1	2	.50	1.50	3.00
7	158	—	PC-r	1	2	.50	1.50	3.00
8	165	—	PC-r	1	2	.50	1.50	3.00
9	167	—	PC-r	1	2	.50	1.50	3.00
10	167	6/64	PC-r	1	2	.50	1.50	3.00
11	167	12/65	PC-r	1	2	.50	1.50	3.00
12	166	10/67	PC-r	1	2	1.30	4.00	9.00
13	166	10/67	w/Grit ad stapled in book	1	2	7.00	21.00	50.00
14	169	Spr/69	New price 25¢; stiff-c; PC-r	1	2	.50	1.50	3.00

65. Benjamin Franklin

Ed	HRN	Date	Details	A	C			
1	64	11/49	Original; Kiefer-c Iger Shop-a	1	1	6.00	18.00	42.00
2	131	—	New-c; PC-r	1	2	1.00	3.00	7.00
3	167	—	PC-r	1	2	.70	2.00	5.00
4	167	2/64	PC-r	1	2	.70	2.00	5.00
5	167	4/66	PC-r	1	2	.70	2.00	5.00
6	169	Fall/69	New price 25¢; stiff-c; PC-r	1	2	.50	1.50	3.00

66. The Cloister and the Hearth

Ed	HRN	Date	Details	A	C			
1	67	12/49	Original & only ed; Kiefer-a & c	1	1	13.00	40.00	90.00

67. The Scottish Chiefs

Ed	HRN	Date	Details	A	C			
1	67	1/50	Original; Blum-a&c	1	1	5.00	15.00	35.00
2	85	—	C-price 15¢; LDC-r	1	1	1.30	4.00	9.00
3	118	—	LDC-r	1	1	1.00	3.00	7.00
4	136	—	New-c; PC-r	1	2	1.00	3.00	7.00
5	154	—	PC-r	1	2	.70	2.00	5.00
6	167	11/63	PC-r	1	2	.70	2.00	5.00
7	167	8/65	PC-r	1	2	.70	2.00	5.00

68. Julius Caesar (Used in **SOTI**, pgs. 36, 37)

Ed	HRN	Date	Details	A	C			
1	70	2/50	Original; Kiefer-a,c	1	1	5.70	17.00	40.00
2	85	—	C-price 15¢; LDC-r	1	1	1.30	4.00	9.00
3	108	—	LDC-r	1	1	1.00	3.00	7.00
4	156	—	New L.B. Cole-c; PC-r	1	2	2.00	6.00	14.00
5	165	—	New-a by Evans, Crandall; PC-r	2	2	2.00	6.00	14.00
6	167	2/64	PC-r	2	2	.70	2.00	4.00
7	167	10/65	Tarzan books inside cover; PC-r	2	2	.50	1.50	3.00
8	166	R/1967	PC-r	2	2	.50	1.50	3.00
9	169	Win/69	PC-r; stiff-c	2	2	.50	1.50	3.00

69. Around the World in 80 Days

Ed	HRN	Date	Details	A	C			
1	70	3/50	Original; Kiefer-a/c	1	1	5.70	17.00	40.00
2	89	—	C-price 15¢; LDC-r	1	1	1.30	4.00	9.00
3	125	—	LDC-r	1	1	1.00	3.00	7.00
4	136	—	New-c; PC-r	1	2	.85	2.50	6.00
5	146	—	PC-r	1	2	.70	2.00	4.00
6	152	—	PC-r	1	2	.70	2.00	4.00
7	164	—	PC-r	1	2	.70	2.00	4.00
8	167	—	PC-r	1	2	.70	2.00	4.00
9	167	7/64	PC-r	1	2	.70	2.00	4.00
10	167	11/65	PC-r	1	2	.70	2.00	4.00

						Good	Fine	N-Mint
11	166	7/67	PC-r	1	2	.50	1.50	3.00
12	169	Spr/69	C-price 25¢; stiff-c; PC-r	1	2	.50	1.50	3.00

70. The Pilot

Ed	HRN	Date	Details	A	C			
1	71	4/50	Original; Blum-a,c	1	1	4.30	13.00	30.00
2	92	—	C-price 15¢; LDC-r	1	1	1.30	4.00	9.00
3	125	—	LDC-r	1	1	1.00	3.00	7.00
4	156	—	New-c; PC-r	1	2	1.00	3.00	7.00
5	167	2/64	PC-r	1	2	.70	2.00	5.00
6	167	5/66	PC-r	1	2	.70	2.00	5.00

71. The Man Who Laughs

Ed	HRN	Date	Details	A	C			
1	71	5/50	Original; Blum-a,c	1	1	7.50	23.00	52.00
2	165	—	New-c&a; PC-r	2	2	5.70	17.00	40.00
3	167	4/64	PC-r	2	2	4.65	14.00	32.00

72. The Oregon Trail

Ed	HRN	Date	Details	A	C			
1	73	6/50	Original; Kiefer-a,c	1	1	4.30	13.00	30.00
2	89	—	C-price 15¢; LDC-r	1	1	1.30	4.00	9.00
3	121	—	LDC-r	1	1	1.00	3.00	7.00
4	131	—	New-c; PC-r	1	2	1.00	3.00	7.00
5	140	—	PC-r	1	2	.75	2.20	5.25
6	150	—	PC-r	1	2	.70	2.00	4.00
7	164	—	PC-r	1	2	.70	2.00	4.00
8	167	—	PC-r	1	2	.70	2.00	4.00
9	167	8/64	PC-r	1	2	.70	2.00	4.00
10	167	10/65	PC-r	1	2	.70	2.00	4.00
11	166	R/1968	C-price 25¢; PC-r	1	2	.50	1.50	3.00

73. The Black Tulip

Ed	HRN	Date	Details	A	C			
1	75	7/50	1st & only ed.; Alex Blum-a & c	1	1	15.00	45.00	105.00

74. Mr. Midshipman Easy

Ed	HRN	Date	Details	A	C			
1	75	8/50	1st & only edition	1	1	14.00	42.00	100.00

75. The Lady of the Lake

Ed	HRN	Date	Details	A	C			
1	75	9/50	Original; Kiefer-a/c	1	1	4.00	12.00	28.00
2	85	—	C-price 15¢; LDC-r	1	1	1.15	3.50	8.00
3	118	—	LDC-r	1	1	1.00	3.00	7.00
4	131	—	New-c; PC-r	1	2	1.00	3.00	7.00
5	154	—	PC-r	1	2	.50	1.50	3.00
6	165	—	PC-r	1	2	.50	1.50	3.00
7	167	4/64	PC-r	1	2	.50	1.50	3.00
8	167	5/66	PC-r	1	2	.50	1.50	3.00
9	169	Spr/69	New price 25¢; stiff-c; PC-r	1	2	.50	1.50	3.00

76. The Prisoner of Zenda

Ed	HRN	Date	Details	A	C			
1	75	10/50	Original; Kiefer-a,c	1	1	3.60	11.00	25.00
2	85	—	C-price 15¢; LDC-r	1	1	1.20	3.50	8.00
3	111	—	LDC-r	1	1	1.00	3.00	7.00
4	128	—	New-c; PC-r	1	2	1.00	3.00	7.00
5	152	—	PC-r	1	2	.50	1.50	3.00
6	165	—	PC-r	1	2	.50	1.50	3.00
7	167	4/64	PC-r	1	2	.50	1.50	3.00
8	167	9/66	PC-r	1	2	.50	1.50	3.00
9	169	Fall/69	New price 25¢; stiff-c; PC-r	1	2	.60	1.80	3.60

Classics Illustrated #72 (Orig.), © GIL

Classics Illustrated #74 (Orig.), © GIL

Classics Illustrated #76 (Orig.?), © GIL

Classics Illustrated #77 (Orig.), © GIL

Classics Illustrated #80, © GIL

Classics Illustrated #86, © GIL

CLASSICS ILLUSTRATED (continued)

77. The Iliad

Ed	HRN	Date	Details	A C	Good	Fine	N-Mint
1	78	11/50	Original; Blum-a,c	1 1	3.60	11.00	25.00
2	87	—	C-price 15¢; LDC-r	1 1	1.15	3.50	8.00
3	121	—	LDC-r	1 1	1.00	3.00	7.00
4	139	—	New-c; PC-r	1 2	1.00	3.00	7.00
5	150	—	PC-r	1 2	.50	1.50	3.00
6	165	—	PC-r	1 2	.50	1.50	3.00
7	167	10/63	PC-r	1 2	.50	1.50	3.00
8	167	7/64	PC-r	1 2	.50	1.50	3.00
9	167	5/66	PC-r	1 2	.50	1.50	3.00
10	166	R/1968	C-price 25¢; PC-r	1 2	.50	1.50	3.00

78. Joan of Arc

Ed	HRN	Date	Details	A C	Good	Fine	N-Mint
1	78	12/50	Original; Kiefer-a,c	1 1	3.60	11.00	25.00
2	87	—	C-price 15¢; LDC-r	1 1	1.15	3.50	8.00
3	113	—	LDC-r	1 1	1.00	3.00	7.00
4	128	—	New-c; PC-r	1 2	1.00	3.00	7.00
5	140	—	PC-r	1 2	.50	1.50	3.00
6	150	—	PC-r	1 2	.50	1.50	3.00
7	159	—	PC-r	1 2	.50	1.50	3.00
8	167	—	PC-r	1 2	.50	1.50	3.00
9	167	12/63	PC-r	1 2	.50	1.50	3.00
10	167	6/65	PC-r	1 2	.50	1.50	3.00
11	166	6/67	PC-r	1 2	.50	1.50	3.00
12	166	Win/69	New-c&price, 25¢; PC-r; stiff-c	1 3	1.70	5.00	12.00

79. Cyrano de Bergerac

Ed	HRN	Date	Details	A C	Good	Fine	N-Mint
1	78	1/51	Orig.; movie promo inside front-c; Blum-a & c	1 1	3.60	11.00	25.00
2	85	—	C-price 15¢; LDC-r	1 1	1.15	3.50	8.00
3	118	—	LDC-r	1 1	1.00	3.00	7.00
4	133	—	New-c; PC-r	1 2	1.50	4.50	10.00
5	156	—	PC-r	1 2	1.15	3.50	8.00
6	167	8/64	PC-r	1 2	1.15	3.50	8.00

80. White Fang (Last line drawn cover)

Ed	HRN	Date	Details	A C	Good	Fine	N-Mint
1	79	2/51	Orig.; Blum-a&c	1 1	3.60	11.00	25.00
2	87	—	C-price 15¢; LDC-r	1 1	1.00	3.00	7.00
3	125	—	LDC-r	1 1	1.00	3.00	7.00
4	132	—	New-c; PC-r	1 2	1.00	3.00	7.00
5	140	—	PC-r	1 2	.50	1.50	3.00
6	153	—	PC-r	1 2	.50	1.50	3.00
7	167	—	PC-r	1 2	.50	1.50	3.00
8	167	9/64	PC-r	1 2	.50	1.50	3.00
9	167	7/65	PC-r	1 2	.50	1.50	3.00
10	166	6/67	PC-r	1 2	.50	1.50	3.00
11	169	Fall/69	New price 25¢; PC-r; stiff	1 2	.50	1.50	3.00

81. The Odyssey (1st painted cover)

Ed	HRN	Date	Details	A C	Good	Fine	N-Mint
1	82	3/51	First 15¢ Original; Blum-c	1 1	2.65	8.00	18.00
2	167	8/64	PC-r	1 1	1.30	4.00	9.00
3	167	10/66	PC-r	1 1	1.30	4.00	9.00
4	169	Spr/69	New, stiff-c; PC-r	1 2	1.50	4.50	10.00

82. The Master of Ballantrae

Ed	HRN	Date	Details	A C	Good	Fine	N-Mint
1	82	4/51	Original; Blum-c	1 1	2.65	8.00	18.00
2	167	8/64	PC-r	1 1	1.30	4.00	9.00
3	166	Fall/68	New, stiff-c; PC-r	1 2	1.50	4.50	10.00

83. The Jungle Book

Ed	HRN	Date	Details	A C	Good	Fine	N-Mint
1	85	5/51	Original; Blum-c Bossert/Blum-a	1 1	2.30	7.00	16.00
2	110	—	PC-r	1 1	.70	2.00	4.00
3	125	—	PC-r	1 1	.50	1.50	3.00
4	134	—	PC-r	1 1	.50	1.50	3.00
5	142	—	PC-r	1 1	.50	1.50	3.00
6	150	—	PC-r	1 1	.50	1.50	3.00
7	159	—	PC-r	1 1	.50	1.50	3.00
8	167	—	PC-r	1 1	.70	2.00	5.00
9	167	3/65	PC-r	1 1	.70	2.00	5.00
10	167	11/65	PC-r	1 1	.70	2.00	5.00
11	167	5/66	PC-r	1 1	.70	2.00	5.00
12	166	R/1968	New c&a; stiff-c; PC-r	2 2	1.50	4.50	10.00

84. The Gold Bug and Other Stories ("The Gold Bug," "The Tell-Tale Heart," "The Cask of Amontillado")

Ed	HRN	Date	Details	A C	Good	Fine	N-Mint
1	85	6/51	Original; Blum-c/a Palais, Laverly-a	1 1	8.00	24.00	56.00
2	167	7/64	PC-r	1 1	5.00	15.00	35.00

85. The Sea Wolf

Ed	HRN	Date	Details	A C	Good	Fine	N-Mint
1	85	7/51	Original; Blum-a&c	1 1	2.30	7.00	16.00
2	121	—	PC-r	1 1	.50	1.50	3.00
3	132	—	PC-r	1 1	.50	1.50	3.00
4	141	—	PC-r	1 1	.50	1.50	3.00
5	161	—	PC-r	1 1	.50	1.50	3.00
6	167	2/64	PC-r	1 1	.50	1.50	3.00
7	167	11/65	PC-r	1 1	.50	1.50	3.00
8	169	Fall/69	New price 25¢; stiff-c; PC-r	1 1	.50	1.50	3.00

86. Under Two Flags

Ed	HRN	Date	Details	A C	Good	Fine	N-Mint
1	87	8/51	Original; first delBourgo-a	1 1	2.30	7.00	16.00
2	117	—	PC-r	1 1	.50	1.50	3.00
3	139	—	PC-r	1 1	.50	1.50	3.00
4	158	—	PC-r	1 1	.50	1.50	3.00
5	167	2/64	PC-r	1 1	.50	1.50	3.00
6	167	8/66	PC-r	1 1	.50	1.50	3.00
7	169	Sm/69	New price 25¢; stiff-c; PC-r	1 1	.50	1.50	3.00

87. A Midsummer Nights Dream

Ed	HRN	Date	Details	A C	Good	Fine	N-Mint
1	87	9/51	Original; Blum c/a	1 1	2.30	7.00	16.00
2	161	—	PC-r	1 1	.85	2.50	5.00
3	167	4/64	PC-r	1 1	.70	2.00	4.00
4	167	5/66	PC-r	1 1	.70	2.00	4.00
5	169	Sm/69	New price 25¢; stiff-c; PC-r	1 1	.50	1.50	3.00

88. Men of Iron

Ed	HRN	Date	Details	A C	Good	Fine	N-Mint
1	89	10/51	Original	1 1	2.30	7.00	16.00
2	154	—	PC-r	1 1	.70	2.00	4.00
3	167	1/64	PC-r	1 1	.70	2.00	4.00
4	166	R/1968	C-price 25¢; PC-r	1 1	.70	2.00	4.00

89. Crime and Punishment (Cover illo. in POP)

Ed	HRN	Date	Details	A C

CLASSICS ILLUSTRATED (continued)

Ed	HRN	Date	Details	A	C	Good	Fine	N-Mint
1	89	11/51	Original; Palais-a	1	1	2.65	8.00	18.00
2	152	—	PC-r	1	1	.50	1.50	3.00
3	167	4/64	PC-r	1	1	.50	1.50	3.00
4	167	5/66	PC-r	1	1	.50	1.50	3.00
5	169	Fall/69	New price 25¢ stiff-c; PC-r	1	1	.50	1.50	3.00

90. Green Mansions

Ed	HRN	Date	Details	A	C	Good	Fine	N-Mint
1	89	12/51	Original; Blum-a&c	1	2	2.65	8.00	18.00
2	148	—	New L.B. Cole -c; PC-r	1	2	1.35	4.00	8.00
3	165	—	PC-r	1	2	.50	1.50	3.00
4	167	4/64	PC-r	1	2	.50	1.50	3.00
5	167	9/66	PC-r	1	2	.50	1.50	3.00
6	169	Sm/69	New price 25¢; stiff-c; PC-r	1	2	.50	1.50	3.00

91. The Call of the Wild

Ed	HRN	Date	Details	A	C	Good	Fine	N-Mint
1	92	1/52	Orig.; delBourgo-a	1	1	2.30	7.00	16.00
2	112	—	PC-r	1	1	.50	1.50	3.00
3	125	—	'Picture Progress' on back-c; PC-r	1	1	.70	2.00	4.00
4	134	—	PC-r	1	1	.50	1.50	3.00
5	143	—	PC-r	1	1	.50	1.50	3.00
6	165	—	PC-r	1	1	.50	1.50	3.00
7	167	—	PC-r	1	1	.50	1.50	3.00
8	167	4/65	PC-r	1	1	.50	1.50	3.00
9	167	3/66	PC-r	1	1	.50	1.50	3.00
10	167	3/66	'Open Book' blank;	1	1			
			(See Non-Series Items-Records)					
11	166	11/67	PC-r	1	1	.50	1.50	3.00
12	169	Spr/70	New price 25¢; stiff-c; PC-r	1	1	.50	1.50	3.00

92. The Courtship of Miles Standish

Ed	HRN	Date	Details	A	C	Good	Fine	N-Mint
1	92	2/52	Original; Blum-a&c	1	1	2.30	7.00	16.00
2	165	—	PC-r	1	1	.50	1.50	3.00
3	167	3/64	PC-r	1	1	.50	1.50	3.00
4	166	5/67	PC-r	1	1	.50	1.50	3.00
5	169	Win/69	New price 25¢ stiff-c; PC-r	1	1	.50	1.50	3.00

93. Pudd'nhead Wilson

Ed	HRN	Date	Details	A	C	Good	Fine	N-Mint
1	94	3/52	Orig.; Kiefer-a&c	1	1	2.30	7.00	16.00
2	165	—	New-c; PC-r	1	2	.85	2.50	6.00
3	167	3/64	PC-r	1	2	.85	2.50	6.00
4	166	R/1968	New price 25¢; soft-c; PC-r	1	2	.85	2.50	6.00

94. David Balfour

Ed	HRN	Date	Details	A	C	Good	Fine	N-Mint
1	94	4/52	Original; Palais-a	1	1	2.30	7.00	16.00
2	167	5/64	PC-r	1	1	1.15	3.50	8.00
3	166	R/1968	C-price 25¢; PC-r	1	1	1.15	3.50	8.00

95. All Quiet on the Western Front

Ed	HRN	Date	Details	A	C	Good	Fine	N-Mint
1A	96	5/52	Orig.; del Bourgo-a	1	1	5.70	17.00	40.00
1B	99	5/52	Orig.; del Bourgo-a	1	1	5.00	15.00	35.00
2	167	10/64	PC-r	1	1	2.00	6.00	14.00
3	167	11/66	PC-r	1	1	2.00	6.00	14.00

96. Daniel Boone

Ed	HRN	Date	Details	A	C

Ed	HRN	Date	Details	A	C	Good	Fine	N-Mint
1	97	6/52	Original; Blum-a	1	1	2.30	7.00	16.00
2	117	—	PC-r	1	1	.50	1.50	3.00
3	128	—	PC-r	1	1	.50	1.50	3.00
4	132	—	PC-r	1	1	.50	1.50	3.00
5	134	—	'Story of Jesus' on back-c; PC-r	1	1	.50	1.50	3.00
6	158	—	PC-r	1	1	.50	1.50	3.00
7	167	1/64	PC-r	1	1	.50	1.50	3.00
8	167	5/65	PC-r	1	1	.50	1.50	3.00
9	167	11/66	PC-r	1	1	.50	1.50	3.00
10	166	Win/69	New-c; price 25¢; PC-r; stiff-c	1	2	1.50	4.50	10.00

97. King Solomon's Mines

Ed	HRN	Date	Details	A	C	Good	Fine	N-Mint
1	96	7/52	Orig.; Kiefer-a	1	1	2.30	7.00	16.00
2	118	—	PC-r	1	1	1.00	3.00	7.00
3	131	—	PC-r	1	1	.70	2.00	4.00
4	141	—	PC-r	1	1	.70	2.00	4.00
5	158	—	PC-r	1	1	.70	2.00	4.00
6	167	2/64	PC-r	1	1	.70	2.00	4.00
7	167	9/65	PC-r	1	1	.70	2.00	4.00
8	169	Sm/69	New price 25¢; stiff-c	1	1	.85	2.50	5.00

98. The Red Badge of Courage

Ed	HRN	Date	Details	A	C	Good	Fine	N-Mint
1	98	8/52	Original	1	1	2.30	7.00	16.00
2	118	—	PC-r	1	1	.50	1.50	3.00
3	132	—	PC-r	1	1	.50	1.50	3.00
4	142	—	PC-r	1	1	.50	1.50	3.00
5	152	—	PC-r	1	1	.50	1.50	3.00
6	167	—	PC-r	1	1	.50	1.50	3.00
7	167	—	Has orig.date; PC-r	1	1	.50	1.50	3.00
8	167	9/64	PC-r	1	1	.50	1.50	3.00
9	167	10/65	PC-r	1	1	.50	1.50	3.00
10	166	R/1968	New-c&price 25¢; PC-r; stiff-c	1	2	1.75	5.25	12.00

99. Hamlet (Used in POP, pg. 102)

Ed	HRN	Date	Details	A	C	Good	Fine	N-Mint
1	98	9/52	Original; Blum-a	1	1	2.65	8.00	18.00
2	121	—	PC-r	1	1	.70	2.00	4.00
3	141	—	PC-r	1	1	.70	2.00	4.00
4	158	—	PC-r	1	1	.70	2.00	4.00
5	167	—	Has orig.date; PC-r	1	1	.70	2.00	4.00
6	167	7/65	PC-r	1	1	.70	2.00	4.00
7	166	4/67	PC-r	1	1	.70	2.00	4.00
8	169	Spr/69	New-c&price 25¢; PC-r; stiff-c	1	2	1.50	4.50	10.00

100. Mutiny on the Bounty

Ed	HRN	Date	Details	A	C	Good	Fine	N-Mint
1	100	10/52	Original	1	1	2.00	6.00	14.00
2	117	—	PC-r	1	1	.50	1.50	3.00
3	132	—	PC-r	1	1	.50	1.50	3.00
4	142	—	PC-r	1	1	.50	1.50	3.00
5	155	—	PC-r	1	1	.50	1.50	3.00
6	167	—	Has orig. date; PC-r	1	1	.50	1.50	3.00
7	167	5/64	PC-r	1	1	.50	1.50	3.00
8	167	3/66	PC-r	1	1	.50	1.50	3.00
9	167	3/66	'Open Book' blank;					
			(See Non-Series Items-Records)					
10	169	Spr/70	PC-r; stiff-c	1	1	.50	1.50	3.00

101. William Tell

Ed	HRN	Date	Details	A	C

Classics Illustrated #90, © GIL

Classics Illustrated #94 (Orig.?), © GIL

Classics Illustrated #100 (Orig.), © GIL

Classics Illustrated #101 (Orig.), © GIL

Classics Illustrated #105 (HRN 167), © GIL

Classics Illustrated #109, © GIL

CLASSICS ILLUSTRATED (continued)

						Good	Fine	N-Mint
1	101	11/52	Original; Kiefer-c delBourgo-a	1	1	2.00	6.00	14.00
2	118	—	PC-r	1	1	.45	1.30	3.00
3	141	—	PC-r	1	1	.50	1.50	3.00
4	158	—	PC-r	1	1	.50	1.50	3.00
5	167	—	Has orig.date; PC-r	1	1	.50	1.50	3.00
6	167	11/64	PC-r	1	1	.50	1.50	3.00
7	166	4/67	PC-r	1	1	.50	1.50	3.00
8	169	Win/69	New price 25¢; stiff-c; PC-r	1	1	.50	1.50	3.00

102. The White Company
Ed	HRN	Date	Details	A	C			
1	101	12/52	Original; Blum-a	1	1	3.50	10.50	24.00
2	165	—	PC-r	1	1	1.70	5.00	12.00
3	167	4/64	PC-r	1	1	1.70	5.00	12.00

103. Men Against the Sea
Ed	HRN	Date	Details	A	C			
1	104	1/53	Original; Kiefer-c, Palais-a	1	1	2.30	7.00	16.00
2	114	—	PC-r	1	1	1.30	4.00	9.00
3	131	—	New-c; PC-r	1	1	1.30	4.00	9.00
4	158	—	PC-r	1	2	1.30	4.00	9.00
5	149	—	White reorder list; came after HRN-158; PC-r	1	2	1.30	4.00	9.00
6	167	3/64	PC-r	1	2	.70	2.00	4.00

104. Bring 'Em Back Alive
Ed	HRN	Date	Details	A	C			
1	105	2/53	Original; Kiefer c/a	1	1	2.00	6.00	14.00
2	118	—	PC-r	1	1	.50	1.50	3.00
3	133	—	PC-r	1	1	.50	1.50	3.00
4	150	—	PC-r	1	1	.50	1.50	3.00
5	158	—	PC-r	1	1	.50	1.50	3.00
6	167	10/63	PC-r	1	1	.50	1.50	3.00
7	167	9/65	PC-r	1	1	.50	1.50	3.00
8	169	Win/69	New price 25¢; stiff-c; PC-r	1	1	.50	1.50	3.00

105. From the Earth to the Moon
Ed	HRN	Date	Details	A	C			
1	106	3/53	Original; Blum-a	1	1	1.70	5.00	12.00
2	118	—	PC-r	1	1	.50	1.50	3.00
3	132	—	PC-r	1	1	.50	1.50	3.00
4	141	—	PC-r	1	1	.50	1.50	3.00
5	146	—	PC-r	1	1	.50	1.50	3.00
6	156	—	PC-r	1	1	.50	1.50	3.00
7	167	—	Has orig. date; PC-r	1	1	.50	1.50	3.00
8	167	5/64	PC-r	1	1	.50	1.50	3.00
9	167	5/65	PC-r	1	1	.50	1.50	3.00
10	166	10/67	PC-r	1	1	.50	1.50	3.00
11	169	Sm/69	New price 25¢; stiff-c; PC-r	1	1	.50	1.50	3.00
12	169	Spr/71	PC-r	1	1	.50	1.50	3.00

106. Buffalo Bill
Ed	HRN	Date	Details	A	C			
1	107	4/53	Orig.; delBourgo-a	1	1	1.70	5.00	12.00
2	118	—	PC-r	1	1	.50	1.50	3.00
3	132	—	PC-r	1	1	.50	1.50	3.00
4	142	—	PC-r	1	1	.50	1.50	3.00
5	161	—	PC-r	1	1	.50	1.50	3.00
6	167	3/64	PC-r	1	1	.50	1.50	3.00
7	166	7/67	PC-r	1	1	.50	1.50	3.00
8	169	Fall/69	PC-r; stiff-c	1	1	.50	1.50	3.00

107. King of the Khyber Rifles
Ed	HRN	Date	Details	A	C	Good	Fine	N-Mint
1	108	5/53	Original	1	1	2.00	6.00	14.00
2	118	—	PC-r	1	1	.70	2.00	4.00
3	146	—	PC-r	1	1	.70	2.00	4.00
4	158	—	PC-r	1	1	.70	2.00	4.00
5	167	—	Has orig.date; PC-r	1	1	.70	2.00	4.00
6	167	—	PC-r	1	1	.70	2.00	4.00
7	167	10/66	PC-r	1	1	.70	2.00	4.00

108. Knights of the Round Table
Ed	HRN	Date	Details	A	C			
1A	108	6/53	Original; Blum-a	1	1	2.30	7.00	16.00
1B	109	6/53	Original; scarce	1	1	3.70	11.00	26.00
2	117	—	PC-r	1	1	.50	1.50	3.00
3	165	—	PC-r	1	1	.50	1.50	3.00
4	167	4/64	PC-r	1	1	.50	1.50	3.00
5	166	4/67	PC-r	1	1	.50	1.50	3.00
6	169	Sm/69	New price 25¢; stiff-c; PC-r	1	1	.50	1.50	3.00

109. Pitcairn's Island
Ed	HRN	Date	Details	A	C			
1A	110	7/53	Original; Palais-a	1	1	2.65	8.00	18.00
1B	110	7/53	Original; bc missing red line 'Mail coupon…' above coupon (printing error); very rare; Palais-a	1	1	7.00	21.00	50.00
2	165	—	PC-r	1	1	1.00	3.00	7.00
3	167	3/64	PC-r	1	1	1.00	3.00	7.00
4	166	6/67	PC-r	1	1	1.00	3.00	7.00

110. A Study in Scarlet
Ed	HRN	Date	Details	A	C			
1	111	8/53	Original	1	1	7.00	21.00	50.00
2	165	—	PC-r	1	1	5.00	15.00	35.00

111. The Talisman
Ed	HRN	Date	Details	A	C			
1	112	9/53	Original; last H.C. Kiefer-a	1	1	4.00	12.00	28.00
2	165	—	PC-r	1	1	.50	1.50	3.00
3	167	5/64	PC-r	1	1	.50	1.50	3.00
4	166	Fall/68	C-price 25¢; PC-r	1	1	.50	1.50	3.00

112. Adventures of Kit Carson
Ed	HRN	Date	Details	A	C			
1	113	10/53	Original; Palais-a	1	1	4.00	12.00	28.00
2	129	—	PC-r	1	1	.50	1.50	3.00
3	141	—	PC-r	1	1	.50	1.50	3.00
4	152	—	PC-r	1	1	.50	1.50	3.00
5	161	—	PC-r	1	1	.50	1.50	3.00
6	167	—	PC-r	1	1	.50	1.50	3.00
7	167	2/65	PC-r	1	1	.50	1.50	3.00
8	167	5/66	PC-r	1	1	.50	1.50	3.00
9	166	Win/69	New-c&price 25¢; PC-r; stiff-c	1	2	1.50	4.50	10.00

113. The Forty-Five Guardsmen
Ed	HRN	Date	Details	A	C			
1	114	11/53	Orig.; delBourgo-a	1	1	4.00	12.00	28.00
2	166	7/67	PC-r	1	1	2.30	7.00	16.00

114. The Red Rover
Ed	HRN	Date	Details	A	C			
1	115	12/53	Original	1	1	4.00	12.00	28.00

CLASSICS ILLUSTRATED (continued)				A	C	Good	Fine	N-Mint
2	166	7/67	PC-r	1	1	2.30	7.00	16.00

115. How I Found Livingstone

Ed	HRN	Date	Details	A	C			
1	116	1/54	Original	1	1	4.00	12.00	28.00
2	167	1/67	PC-r	1	1	2.30	7.00	16.00

116. The Bottle Imp

Ed	HRN	Date	Details	A	C			
1	117	2/54	Orig.; Cameron-a	1	1	5.00	15.00	35.00
2	167	1/67	PC-r	1	1	2.30	7.00	16.00

117. Captains Courageous

Ed	HRN	Date	Details	A	C			
1	118	3/54	Orig.; Costanza-a	1	1	3.50	10.50	24.00
2	167	2/67	PC-r	1	1	1.00	3.00	7.00
3	169	Fall/69	New price 25¢; stiff-c; PC-r	1	1	1.00	3.00	7.00

118. Rob Roy

Ed	HRN	Date	Details	A	C			
1	119	4/54	Original; Rudy & Walter Palais-a	1	1	4.00	12.00	28.00
2	167	2/67	PC-r	1	1	2.30	7.00	16.00

119. Soldiers of Fortune

Ed	HRN	Date	Details	A	C			
1	120	5/54	Original Shaffenberger-a	1	1	4.00	12.00	28.00
2	166	3/67	PC-r	1	1	1.00	3.00	7.00
3	169	Spr/70	New price 25¢; stiff-c; PC-r	1	1	1.00	3.00	7.00

120. The Hurricane

Ed	HRN	Date	Details	A	C			
1	121	6/54	Orig.; Cameron-a	1	1	4.00	12.00	28.00
2	166	3/67	PC-r	1	1	2.65	8.00	18.00

121. Wild Bill Hickok

Ed	HRN	Date	Details	A	C			
1	122	7/54	Original	1	1	2.00	6.00	14.00
2	132	—	PC-r	1	1	.50	1.50	3.00
3	141	—	PC-r	1	1	.50	1.50	3.00
4	154	—	PC-r	1	1	.50	1.50	3.00
5	167	—	PC-r	1	1	.50	1.50	3.00
6	167	8/64	PC-r	1	1	.50	1.50	3.00
7	166	4/67	PC-r	1	1	.50	1.50	3.00
8	169	Win/69	PC-r; stiff-c	1	1	.50	1.50	3.00

122. The Mutineers

Ed	HRN	Date	Details	A	C			
1	123	9/54	Original	1	1	2.00	6.00	14.00
2	136	—	PC-r	1	1	.50	1.50	3.00
3	146	—	PC-r	1	1	.50	1.50	3.00
4	158	—	PC-r	1	1	.50	1.50	3.00
5	167	11/63	PC-r	1	1	.50	1.50	3.00
6	167	3/65	PC-r	1	1	.50	1.50	3.00
7	166	8/67	PC-r	1	1	.50	1.50	3.00

123. Fang and Claw

Ed	HRN	Date	Details	A	C			
1	124	11/54	Original	1	1	2.00	6.00	14.00
2	133	—	PC-r	1	1	.50	1.50	3.00
3	143	—	PC-r	1	1	.50	1.50	3.00
4	154	—	PC-r	1	1	.50	1.50	3.00
5	167	—	Has orig.date; PC-r	1	1	.50	1.50	3.00
6	167	9/65	PC-r	1	1	.50	1.50	3.00

124. The War of the Worlds

Ed	HRN	Date	Details	A	C	Good	Fine	N-Mint
1	125	1/55	Orig.; Cameron c/a	1	1	2.00	6.00	14.00
2	131	—	PC-r	1	1	.50	1.50	3.00
3	141	—	PC-r	1	1	.50	1.50	3.00
4	148	—	PC-r	1	1	.50	1.50	3.00
5	156	—	PC-r	1	1	.50	1.50	3.00
6	165	—	PC-r	1	1	.50	1.50	3.00
7	167	—	PC-r	1	1	.50	1.50	3.00
8	167	11/64	PC-r	1	1	.50	1.50	3.00
9	167	11/65	PC-r	1	1	.50	1.50	3.00
10	166	R/1968	C-price 25¢; PC-r	1	1	.50	1.50	3.00
11	169	Sm/70	PC-r; stiff-c	1	1	.50	1.50	3.00

125. The Ox Bow Incident

Ed	HRN	Date	Details	A	C			
1	—	3/55	Original; Picture Progress replaces reorder list	1	1	2.00	6.00	14.00
2	143	—	PC-r	1	1	.50	1.50	3.00
3	152	—	PC-r	1	1	.50	1.50	3.00
4	149	—	PC-r	1	1	.50	1.50	3.00
5	167	—	PC-r	1	1	.50	1.50	3.00
6	167	11/64	PC-r	1	1	.50	1.50	3.00
7	166	4/67	PC-r	1	1	.50	1.50	3.00
8	169	Win/69	New price 25¢; stiff-c; PC-r	1	1	.50	1.50	3.00

126. The Downfall

Ed	HRN	Date	Details	A	C			
1	—	5/55	Orig.; 'Picture Progress' replaces reorder list; Cameron c/a	1	1	2.00	6.00	14.00
2	167	8/64	PC-r	1	1	.70	2.00	4.00
3	166	R/1968	C-price 25¢; PC-r	1	1	.70	2.00	4.00

127. The King of the Mountains

Ed	HRN	Date	Details	A	C			
1	128	7/55	Original	1	1	2.00	6.00	14.00
2	167	6/64	PC-r	1	1	.70	2.00	5.00
3	166	F/1968	C-price 25¢; PC-r	1	1	.70	2.00	5.00

128. Macbeth (Used in **POP**, pg. 102)

Ed	HRN	Date	Details	A	C			
1	128	9/55	Orig.; last Blum-a	1	1	2.65	8.00	18.00
2	143	—	PC-r	1	1	.50	1.50	3.00
3	158	—	PC-r	1	1	.50	1.50	3.00
4	167	—	PC-r	1	1	.50	1.50	3.00
5	167	6/64	PC-r	1	1	.50	1.50	3.00
6	166	4/67	PC-r	1	1	.50	1.50	3.00
7	166	R/1968	C-Price 25¢; PC-r	1	1	.50	1.50	3.00
8	169	Spr/70	Stiff-c; PC-r	1	1	.50	1.50	3.00

129. Davy Crockett

Ed	HRN	Date	Details	A	C			
1	129	11/55	Orig.; Cameron-a	1	1	5.00	15.00	35.00
2	167	9/66	PC-r	1	1	3.00	9.00	21.00

130. Caesar's Conquests

Ed	HRN	Date	Details	A	C			
1	130	1/56	Original; Orlando-a	1	1	2.00	6.00	14.00
2	142	—	PC-r	1	1	.50	1.50	3.00
3	152	—	PC-r	1	1	.50	1.50	3.00
4	149	—	PC-r	1	1	.50	1.50	3.00
5	167	—	PC-r	1	1	.50	1.50	3.00
6	167	10/64	PC-r	1	1	.50	1.50	3.00
7	167	4/66	PC-r	1	1	.50	1.50	3.00

Classics Illustrated #115 (Orig.), © GIL

Classics Illustrated #124 (HRN 167), © GIL

Classics Illustrated #130 (HRN 167), © GIL

Classics Illustrated #133 (HRN 167), © GIL   Classics Illustrated #138, © GIL   Classics Illustrated #140 (HRN 160), © GIL

CLASSICS ILLUSTRATED (continued)

131. The Covered Wagon

Ed	HRN	Date	Details	A C	Good	Fine	N-Mint
1	131	3/56	Original	1 1	2.00	6.00	14.00
2	143	—	PC-r	1 1	.50	1.50	3.00
3	152	—	PC-r	1 1	.50	1.50	3.00
4	158	—	PC-r	1 1	.50	1.50	3.00
5	167	—	PC-r	1 1	.50	1.50	3.00
6	167	11/64	PC-r	1 1	.50	1.50	3.00
7	167	4/66	PC-r	1 1	.50	1.50	3.00
8	169	Win/69	New price 25 cents; stiff-c; PC-r	1 1	.50	1.50	3.00

132. The Dark Frigate

Ed	HRN	Date	Details	A C	Good	Fine	N-Mint
1	132	5/56	Original	1 1	2.00	6.00	14.00
2	150	—	PC-r	1 1	1.00	3.00	6.00
3	167	1/64	PC-r	1 1	1.00	3.00	6.00
4	166	5/67	PC-r	1 1	1.00	3.00	6.00

133. The Time Machine

Ed	HRN	Date	Details	A C	Good	Fine	N-Mint
1	132	7/56	Orig.; Cameron-a	1 1	2.65	8.00	18.00
2	142	—	PC-r	1 1	.60	1.80	4.20
3	152	—	PC-r	1 1	.60	1.80	4.20
4	158	—	PC-r	1 1	.60	1.80	4.20
5	167	—	PC-r	1 1	.60	1.80	4.20
6	167	6/64	PC-r	1 1	.60	1.80	4.20
7	167	3/66	PC-r	1 1	.60	1.80	4.20
8	167	3/66	'Open Book' blank				
			(See Non-Series Items—Records)				
9	166	12/67	PC-r	1 1	.60	1.80	4.20
10	169	Win/71	New price 25 cents; stiff-c; PC-r	1 1	.85	2.50	6.00

134. Romeo and Juliet

Ed	HRN	Date	Details	A C	Good	Fine	N-Mint
1	134	9/56	Original; Evans-a	1 1	2.00	6.00	14.00
2	161	—	PC-r	1 1	.50	1.50	3.00
3	167	9/63	PC-r	1 1	.50	1.50	3.00
4	167	5/65	PC-r	1 1	.50	1.50	3.00
5	166	6/67	PC-r	1 1	.50	1.50	3.00
6	166	Win/69	New c&price 25¢; stiff-c; PC-r	1 2	2.65	8.00	18.00

135. Waterloo

Ed	HRN	Date	Details	A C	Good	Fine	N-Mint
1	135	11/56	Orig.; G. Ingels-a	1 1	2.00	6.00	14.00
2	153	—	PC-r	1 1	.50	1.50	3.00
3	167	—	PC-r	1 1	.50	1.50	3.00
4	167	9/64	PC-r	1 1	.50	1.50	3.00
5	166	R/1968	C-price 25 cents;				
			PC-r	1 1	.50	1.50	3.00

136. Lord Jim

Ed	HRN	Date	Details	A C	Good	Fine	N-Mint
1	136	1/57	Original; Evans-a	1 1	2.00	6.00	14.00
2	165	—	PC-r	1 1	.50	1.50	3.00
3	167	3/64	PC-r	1 1	.50	1.50	3.00
4	167	9/66	PC-r	1 1	.50	1.50	3.00
5	169	Sm/69	New price 25 cents; stiff-c; PC-r	1 1	.50	1.50	3.00

137. The Little Savage

Ed	HRN	Date	Details	A C	Good	Fine	N-Mint
1	136	3/57	Original; Evans-a	1 1	2.00	6.00	14.00
2	148	—	PC-r	1 1	.50	1.50	3.00
3	156	—	PC-r	1 1	.50	1.50	3.00

					Good	Fine	N-Mint
4	167	—	PC-r	1 1	.50	1.50	3.00
5	167	10/64	PC-r	1 1	.50	1.50	3.00
6	166	8/67	PC-r	1 1	.50	1.50	3.00
7	169	Spr/70	New price 25 cents; stiff-c; PC-r	1 1	.50	1.50	3.00

138. A Journey to the Center of the Earth

Ed	HRN	Date	Details	A C	Good	Fine	N-Mint
1	136	5/57	Original	1 1	2.65	8.00	18.00
2	146	—	PC-r	1 1	.50	1.50	3.00
3	156	—	PC-r	1 1	.50	1.50	3.00
4	158	—	PC-r	1 1	.50	1.50	3.00
5	167	—	PC-r	1 1	.50	1.50	3.00
6	167	6/64	PC-r	1 1	.50	1.50	3.00
7	167	4/66	PC-r	1 1	.50	1.50	3.00
8	166	R/1968	C-price 25 cents; PC-r	1 1	.50	1.50	3.00

139. In the Reign of Terror

Ed	HRN	Date	Details	A C	Good	Fine	N-Mint
1	139	7/57	Original; Evans-a	1 1	2.00	6.00	14.00
2	154	—	PC-r	1 1	.50	1.50	3.00
3	167	—	Has orig.date; PC-r	1 1	.50	1.50	3.00
4	167	7/64	PC-r	1 1	.50	1.50	3.00
5	166	R/1968	C-price 25 cents; PC-r	1 1	.50	1.50	3.00

140. On Jungle Trails

Ed	HRN	Date	Details	A C	Good	Fine	N-Mint
1	140	9/57	Original	1 1	2.00	6.00	14.00
2	150	—	PC-r	1 1	.50	1.50	3.00
3	160	—	PC-r	1 1	.50	1.50	3.00
4	167	9/63	PC-r	1 1	.50	1.50	3.00
5	167	9/65	PC-r	1 1	.50	1.50	3.00

141. Castle Dangerous

Ed	HRN	Date	Details	A C	Good	Fine	N-Mint
1	141	11/57	Original	1 1	2.00	6.00	14.00
2	152	—	PC-r	1 1	.50	1.50	3.00
3	167	—	PC-r	1 1	.50	1.50	3.00
4	166	7/67	PC-r	1 1	.50	1.50	3.00

142. Abraham Lincoln

Ed	HRN	Date	Details	A C	Good	Fine	N-Mint
1	142	1/58	Original	1 1	2.00	6.00	14.00
2	154	—	PC-r	1 1	.50	1.50	3.00
3	158	—	PC-r	1 1	.50	1.50	3.00
4	167	10/63	PC-r	1 1	.50	1.50	3.00
5	167	7/65	PC-r	1 1	.50	1.50	3.00
6	166	11/67	PC-r	1 1	.50	1.50	3.00
7	169	Fall/69	New price 25 cents; stiff-c; PC-r	1 1	.50	1.50	3.00

143. Kim

Ed	HRN	Date	Details	A C	Good	Fine	N-Mint
1	143	3/58	Original; Orlando-a	1 1	2.00	6.00	14.00
2	165	—	PC-r	1 1	.50	1.50	3.00
3	167	11/63	PC-r	1 1	.50	1.50	3.00
4	167	8/65	PC-r	1 1	.50	1.50	3.00
5	169	Win/69	New price 25 cents; stiff-c; PC-r	1 1	.50	1.50	3.00

144. The First Men in the Moon

Ed	HRN	Date	Details	A C	Good	Fine	N-Mint
1	143	5/58	Original; Woodbridge/Williamson/Torres-a	1 1	2.65	8.00	18.00

CLASSICS ILLUSTRATED (continued)

						Good	Fine	N-Mint
2	153	—	PC-r	1	1	.50	1.50	3.00
3	161	—	PC-r	1	1	.50	1.50	3.00
4	167	—	PC-r	1	1	.50	1.50	3.00
5	167	12/65	PC-r	1	1	.50	1.50	3.00
6	166	Fall/68	New-c&price 25¢; PC-r; stiff-c	1	2	.85	2.50	6.00
7	169	Win/69	Stiff-c; PC-r	1	2	.85	2.50	6.00

145. The Crisis

Ed	HRN	Date	Details	A	C	Good	Fine	N-Mint
1	143	7/58	Original; Evans-a	1	1	2.00	6.00	14.00
2	156	—	PC-r	1	1	.50	1.50	3.00
3	167	10/63	PC-r	1	1	.50	1.50	3.00
4	167	3/65	PC-r	1	1	.50	1.50	3.00
5	166	R/1968	C-price 25¢; PC-r	1	1	.50	1.50	3.00

146. With Fire and Sword

Ed	HRN	Date	Details	A	C	Good	Fine	N-Mint
1	143	9/58	Original; Wood-bridge-a	1	1	2.00	6.00	14.00
2	156	—	PC-r	1	1	1.00	3.00	6.00
3	167	11/63	PC-r	1	1	1.00	3.00	6.00
4	167	3/65	PC-r	1	1	1.00	3.00	6.00

147. Ben-Hur

Ed	HRN	Date	Details	A	C	Good	Fine	N-Mint
1	147	11/58	Original; Orlando-a	1	1	2.00	6.00	14.00
2	152	—	Scarce; PC-r	1	1	2.00	6.00	14.00
3	153	—	PC-r	1	1	.50	1.50	3.00
4	158	—	PC-r	1	1	.50	1.50	3.00
5	167	—	Orig.date; but PC-r	1	1	.50	1.50	3.00
6	167	2/65	PC-r	1	1	.50	1.50	3.00
7	167	9/66	PC-r	1	1	.50	1.50	3.00
8A	166	Fall/68	New-c&price 25¢; PC-r; soft-c	1	2	1.70	5.00	12.00
8B	166	Fall/68	New-c&price 25¢; PCpr; stiff-c; scarce	1	2	3.50	10.50	24.00

148. The Buccaneer

Ed	HRN	Date	Details	A	C	Good	Fine	N-Mint
1	148	1/59	Orig.; Evans/Jenny-a; Saunders-c	1	1	2.00	6.00	14.00
2	568	—	Juniors list only PC-r	1	1	.85	2.50	6.00
3	167	—	PC-r	1	1	.50	1.50	3.00
4	167	9/65	PC-r	1	1	.50	1.50	3.00
5	169	Sm/69	New price 25¢; PC-r; stiff-c	1	1	.50	1.50	3.00

149. Off on a Comet

Ed	HRN	Date	Details	A	C	Good	Fine	N-Mint
1	149	3/59	Orig.; G.McCann-a; blue reorder list	1	1	2.00	6.00	14.00
2	155	—	PC-r	1	1	.50	1.50	3.00
3	149	—	PC-r; white reorder list; no coming-next ad	1	1	.50	1.50	3.00
4	167	12/63	PC-r	1	1	.50	1.50	3.00
5	167	2/65	PC-r	1	1	.50	1.50	3.00
6	167	10/66	PC-r	1	1	.50	1.50	3.00
7	166	Fall/68	New-c&price 25¢; PC-r	1	2	1.70	5.00	12.00

150. The Virginian

Ed	HRN	Date	Details	A	C	Good	Fine	N-Mint
1	150	5/59	Original	1	1	2.65	8.00	18.00
2	164	—	PC-r	1	1	1.30	4.00	9.00
3	167	10/63	PC-r	1	1	1.30	4.00	9.00
4	167	12/65	PC-r	1	1	1.30	4.00	9.00

151. Won By the Sword

Ed	HRN	Date	Details	A	C	Good	Fine	N-Mint
1	150	7/59	Original	1	1	2.30	7.00	16.00
2	164	—	PC-r	1	1	.70	2.00	4.00
3	167	10/63	PC-r	1	1	.70	2.00	4.00
4	166	7/67	PC-r	1	1	.70	2.00	4.00

152. Wild Animals I Have Known

Ed	HRN	Date	Details	A	C	Good	Fine	N-Mint
1	152	9/59	Orig.; L.B. Cole c/a	1	1	2.30	7.00	16.00
2	149	—	PC-r; white reorder list; no coming-next ad	1	1	.70	2.00	4.00
3	167	9/63	PC-r	1	1	.50	1.50	3.00
4	167	8/65	PC-r	1	1	.50	1.50	3.00
5	169	Fall/69	New price 25¢; stiff-c; PC-r	1	1	.50	1.50	3.00

153. The Invisible Man

Ed	HRN	Date	Details	A	C	Good	Fine	N-Mint
1	153	11/59	Original	1	1	2.30	7.00	16.00
2	149	—	PC-r; white reorder list; no coming-next ad	1	1	.50	1.50	3.00
3	167	—	PC-r	1	1	.50	1.50	3.00
4	167	2/65	PC-r	1	1	.50	1.50	3.00
5	167	9/66	PC-r	1	1	.50	1.50	3.00
6	166	Win/69	New price 25¢; PC-r; stiff-c	1	1	.50	1.50	3.00
7	169	Spr/71	Stiff-c; letters spelling 'Invisible Man' are 'solid' not'invisible;' PC-r	1	1	.50	1.50	3.00

154. The Conspiracy of Pontiac

Ed	HRN	Date	Details	A	C	Good	Fine	N-Mint
1	154	1/60	Original	1	1	2.30	7.00	16.00
2	167	11/63	PC-r	1	1	1.70	5.00	12.00
3	167	7/64	PC-r	1	1	1.70	5.00	12.00
4	166	12/67	PC-r	1	1	1.70	5.00	12.00

155. The Lion of the North

Ed	HRN	Date	Details	A	C	Good	Fine	N-Mint
1	154	3/60	Original	1	1	2.00	6.00	14.00
2	167	1/64	PC-r	1	1	1.00	3.00	7.00
3	166	R/1967	C-price 25¢; PC-r	1	1	1.00	3.00	7.00

156. The Conquest of Mexico

Ed	HRN	Date	Details	A	C	Good	Fine	N-Mint
1	156	5/60	Orig.; Bruno Premiani-a&c	1	1	2.00	6.00	14.00
2	167	1/64	PC-r	1	1	.70	2.00	5.00
3	166	8/67	PC-r	1	1	.70	2.00	5.00
4	169	Spr/70	New price 25¢; stiff-c; PC-r	1	1	.70	2.00	5.00

157. Lives of the Hunted

Ed	HRN	Date	Details	A	C	Good	Fine	N-Mint
1	156	7/60	Orig.; L.B. Cole-c	1	1	2.30	7.00	16.00
2	167	2/64	PC-r	1	1	1.70	5.00	12.00
3	166	10/67	PC-r	1	1	1.70	5.00	12.00

158. The Conspirators

Ed	HRN	Date	Details	A	C	Good	Fine	N-Mint
1	156	9/60	Original	1	1	2.30	7.00	16.00

Classics Illustrated #148 (Orig.?), © GIL

Classics Illustrated #149 (Orig.?), © GIL

Classics Illustrated #160 (HRN 160), © GIL

Classics Illustrated #161 (HRN 167), © GIL   Classics Illustrated #162 (HRN 167), © GIL   Classics Illustrated #169 (Orig.), © GIL

CLASSICS ILLUSTRATED (continued)

				A C	Good	Fine	N-Mint
2	167	7/64	PC-r	1 1	1.70	5.00	12.00
3	166	10/67	PC-r	1 1	1.70	5.00	12.00

159. The Octopus

Ed	HRN	Date	Details	A C			
1	159	11/60	Orig.; Gray Morrow & Evans-a; L.B. Cole-c	1 1	2.30	7.00	16.00
2	167	2/64	PC-r	1 1	1.30	4.00	9.00
3	166	R/1967	C-price 25¢; PC-r	1 1	1.30	4.00	9.00

160. The Food of the Gods

Ed	HRN	Date	Details	A C			
1A	159	1/61	Original	1 1	2.30	7.00	16.00
1B	160	1/61	Original; same, except for HRN	1 1	2.00	6.00	14.00
2	167	1/64	PC-r	1 1	1.30	4.00	9.00
3	166	6/67	PC-r	1 1	1.30	4.00	9.00

161. Cleopatra

Ed	HRN	Date	Details	A C			
1	161	3/61	Original	1 1	3.00	9.00	21.00
2	167	1/64	PC-r	1 1	1.70	5.00	12.00
3	166	8/67	PC-r	1 1	1.70	5.00	12.00

162. Robur the Conqueror

Ed	HRN	Date	Details	A C			
1	162	5/61	Original	1 1	2.30	7.00	16.00
2	167	7/64	PC-r	1 1	1.30	4.00	9.00
3	166	8/67	PC-r	1 1	1.30	4.00	9.00

163. Master of the World

Ed	HRN	Date	Details	A C			
1	163	7/61	Original; Gray Morrow-a	1 1	2.30	7.00	16.00
2	167	1/65	PC-r	1 1	1.30	4.00	9.00
3	166	R/1968	C-price 25¢; PC-r	1 1	1.30	4.00	9.00

164. The Cossack Chief

Ed	HRN	Date	Details	A C			
1	164	(1961)	Original; nd (10/61?)	1 1	2.65	8.00	18.00
2	167	4/65	PC-r	1 1	1.30	4.00	9.00
3	166	Fall/68	C-price 25¢; PC-r	1 1	1.30	4.00	9.00

165. The Queen's Necklace

Ed	HRN	Date	Details	A C			
1	164	1/62	Original; Morrow-a	1 1	2.65	8.00	18.00
2	167	4/65	PC-r	1 1	1.30	4.00	9.00
3	166	Fall/68	C-price 25¢; PC-r	1 1	1.30	4.00	9.00

166. Tigers and Traitors

Ed	HRN	Date	Details	A C			
1	165	5/62	Original	1 1	3.70	11.00	26.00
2	167	2/64	PC-r	1 1	2.00	6.00	14.00
3	167	11/66	PC-r	1 1	2.00	6.00	14.00

167. Faust

Ed	HRN	Date	Details	A C			
1	167	8/62	Original	1 1	6.50	19.50	45.00
2	167	2/64	PC-r	1 1	3.70	11.00	26.00
3	166	6/67	PC-r	1 1	3.70	11.00	26.00

168. In Freedom's Cause

Ed	HRN	Date	Details	A C			
1	169	Win/69	Original; Evans/ Crandall-a; stiff-c; 25¢; no coming-next ad; probably issued in '62 & was issued	1 1	6.00	18.00	42.00

in European Classics series in 1963

169. Negro Americans—The Early Years

Ed	HRN	Date	Details	A C	Good	Fine	N-Mint
1	166	Spr/69	Orig. & last issue; 25¢; Stiff-c; no coming-next ad; pub. 5/69.	1 1	5.70	17.00	40.00
2	169	Spr/69	Stiff-c	1 1	4.30	13.00	30.00

NOTE: Many other titles were prepared or planned but were only issued in British/European series.

CLASSICS NON-SERIES ITEMS
by Dan Malan

In this section we are attempting to organize the wide variety of Classics items which were not really part of the regular series. These include **Giveaways, Newspaper Editions, Gift Boxes, Giants,** and **Records.** All of these either are or contain comic books. There are many other non-comic book Classics collectibles not listed here, including posters, racks, binders, original letters from Gilberton/Twin Circle personnel, and publications containing ads for Classics, such as the teachers' magazine *The Instructor*.

The rarity of almost all of these items must be emphasized. Except for the Twin Circle editions and the 1969 Christmas giveaway, all items listed here vary from scarce to very rare. Some of these items have not been offered for sale in the last five years or so, and there are some items of which only one copy is known to exist. It is therefore very difficult to arrive at an accurate market value. Through the Worldwide Classics Newsletter we have attempted to determine what collectors would pay for these items if they were offered for sale. All dealers are encouraged to seek out these rare items. Three items have been reproduced (Shelter/Westinghouse/Daynor) with color photocopy outsides and black and white photocopy interiors. They state "W.C.N. Reprint" on the front cover.

NEWSPAPER CLASSICS—These are similar to the Spirit Sections, and were issued for one year, from 3/30/47 to 3/21/48. They were printed in the Sunday Funnies sections of various newspapers. At this point the known newspapers are the *New York Post, Queens Home News, Newark Star-Ledger, Chicago Sun, Milwaukee Journal, Indianapolis Star,* and *St. Louis Post-Dispatch.* Each section contains 16 reduced comic book pages. They are very significant because they predate the original comic book editions by as much as three years, and contain 64 pages of text of Classics titles that were issued with 48 pages. The last five newspaper titles were converted from a comic book page format to a comic strip format. Some newspapers did not complete the 14-title series. All of these editions are very rare, and only one copy is known to exist of the newspaper edition of No. 92, Miles Standish. *Indianapolis Star* editions are in black and white, and would be worth slightly less, and *St. Louis Post-Dispatch* editions are in strip format throughout, and would be worth slightly more.

The above newspaper editions must be distinguished from the Twin Circle newspaper editions issued from 1967-1976 of over 100 Classics titles, included with the Catholic newspaper. A list of Twin Circle Newspaper Classics immediately follows this list of the 1947-48 Sunday funnies Classics Newspaper Editons.

Cl#	Section	Date	Good	Fine	Mint
#46. Kidnapped					
	1 of 4	3/30/47	7.00	21.00	50.00
	2 of 4	4/06/47	7.00	21.00	50.00
	3 of 4	4/13/47	7.00	21.00	50.00
	4 of 4	4/20/47	7.00	21.00	50.00
#47. 20,000 Leagues Below the Sea					
	1 of 4	4/27/47	7.00	21.00	50.00
	2 of 4	5/04/47	7.00	21.00	50.00
	3 of 4	5/11/47	7.00	21.00	50.00
	4 of 4	5/18/47	7.00	21.00	50.00
#48. David Copperfield					

NEWSPAPER CLASSICS (continued)		Good	Fine	N-Mint
1 of 4	5/25/47	7.00	21.00	50.00
2 of 4	6/01/47	7.00	21.00	50.00
3 of 4	6/08/47	7.00	21.00	50.00
4 of 4	6/15/47	7.00	21.00	50.00
#49. Alice in Wonderland				
1 of 4	6/22/47	7.00	21.00	50.00
2 of 4	6/29/47	7.00	21.00	50.00
3 of 4	7/06/47	7.00	21.00	50.00
4 of 4	7/13/47	7.00	21.00	50.00
#51. The Spy				
1 of 4	7/20/47	7.00	21.00	50.00
2 of 4	7/27/47	7.00	21.00	50.00
3 of 4	8/03/47	7.00	21.00	50.00
4 of 4	8/10/47	7.00	21.00	50.00
#50. Tom Sawyer				
1 of 4	8/17/47	7.00	21.00	50.00
2 of 4	8/24/47	7.00	21.00	50.00
3 of 4	8/31/47	7.00	21.00	50.00
4 of 4	9/07/47	7.00	21.00	50.00
#52. House of the Seven Gables				
1 of 4	9/14/47	7.00	21.00	50.00
2 of 4	9/21/47	7.00	21.00	50.00
3 of 4	9/28/47	7.00	21.00	50.00
4 of 4	10/05/47	7.00	21.00	50.00
#68. Julius Caesar				
1 of 4	10/12/47	9.00	27.00	62.00
2 of 4	10/19/47	9.00	27.00	62.00
3 of 4	10/26/47	9.00	27.00	62.00
4 of 4	11/02/47	9.00	27.00	62.00
#55. Silas Marner				
1 of 4	11/09/47	9.00	27.00	62.00
2 of 4	11/16/47	9.00	27.00	62.00
3 of 4	11/23/47	9.00	27.00	62.00
4 of 4	11/30/47	9.00	27.00	62.00
#53. A Christmas Carol				
1 of 3	12/07/47	10.00	30.00	70.00
2 of 3	12/14/47	10.00	30.00	70.00
3 of 3	12/21/47	10.00	30.00	70.00
#75. Lady of the Lake				
1 of 4	12/28/47	9.00	27.00	62.00
2 of 4	1/04/48	9.00	27.00	62.00
3 of 4	1/11/48	9.00	27.00	62.00
4 of 4	1/18/48	9.00	27.00	62.00
#54. Man in the Iron Mask				
1 of 4	1/25/48	9.00	27.00	62.00
2 of 4	2/01/48	9.00	27.00	62.00
3 of 4	2/08/48	9.00	27.00	62.00
4 of 4	2/15/48	9.00	27.00	62.00
#56. Toilers of the Sea				
1 of 4	2/22/48	10.00	30.00	70.00
2 of 4	2/29/48	10.00	30.00	70.00
3 of 4	3/07/48	10.00	30.00	70.00
4 of 4	3/14/48	10.00	30.00	70.00
#92. The Courtship of Miles Standish				
1 of 1	3/21/48	40.00	120.00	280.00

* Listing researched and contributed by Dan Malan.

TWIN CIRCLE NEWSPAPER EDITIONS. From 1968-1976 the Catholic newspaper Twin Circle serialized over 100 Classics titles. Originally, they gave away full comic-books as inserts (see list under giveaways), but they ran afoul of postal regulations, and had to resort to serializing the stories. Early stories were in three sections, with later stories in six sections. Full information can be found in the reference book **The Classics Handbook.** This is a market that is just developing, but current market value is probably about $5 per high-grade section. These do not have extra pages not in the comic ver-

sions, and they are easily identified by date and 'Twin Circle.' Here is a brief listing of the Classics titles serialized, in chronological order: 57,60,512,117,32,30,80,63,137,42,64,35,55,98,45,62,69,142,99,134,75,143, 89,153,65,105,96,76,29,58,47,129,92,91,37,101,160,67,114,112,158,93,28,70, 85,150,113,162,146,2,4,16,5,10,68,128,48,19,25,46,72,52,27,34,135,124,127, 141,97,77,152,149,78,121,155,159,13,11,26,39,147,88,164,83-A1,156,100,111, 119,138,87,104,94,12,126,165,78,49,136,134,3,29,63,106,75,65.

CLASSICS GIFT BOXES (Very Rare)

Classic Comics Library Gift Boxes (& Classics Illustrated . . .) Note: **Prices listed** are for the box ONLY! The value of any contents should be determined independently. It now appears that these boxes only existed as **Classic Comics**. . . . Even though ads ran from 1947-50 listing **Classics Illustrated** boxes, no such copies have ever been found. There are two versions: two-piece boxes and one-piece boxes with flaps. There is also another early version of Box A with ornate lettering, later changed to standard lettering. Each variation is **rare or very rare.**

Box A containing #1-5 first appeared 12/42 as advertised on #7 (0). When first offered, it would have contained originals, but later would have contained reprints. The initial box-face illustration showed stories 1-6, but actually only contained 1-5.
Box B containing #6-10 first appeared 11/43 as advertised on #15 (0). When first offered, it would have contained either originals or the first reprint edition, but later would contain current reprints.
Box C containing #11-15 also first appeared 11/43 as per #15 (0), with same edition content variations as Box B.
Box D containing #16-20 first appeared 6/44 as advertised on #20 (0). When first offered, it would have contained partly originals and first reprint editions, but later would contain current reprints.

	Good	Fine	N-Mint
Box A (early version with ornate lettering)	70.00	210.00	500.00
Box A/B/C/D (two-piece version-standard lettering)	60.00	180.00	420.00
Box A/B/C/D (one-piece version with flaps)	53.00	160.00	370.00

Christmas Gift Boxes (Very Rare)

Series 4V (1950?) contained early LDC reprints of 17, 24, 47, 50.
Series 4W contained 64, 76 (first LDC reprints), & 82, 98 (originals).
Series 4X contained 52, 69, 80 (first LDC reprints) & 97 (original).
Series 4Y contained 19, 67, 79 (early LDC reprints) & 91 (original).
Series 4Z contained 63 (first LDC reprint) & 86, 90, 95 (originals).

NOTE: Series 4W, 4X, 4Y, 4Z probably all came out Christmas 1952.

	Good	Fine	N-Mint
Series 4V/4W/4X/4Y/4Z each	60.00	180.00	420.00

CLASSICS GIVEAWAYS (Arranged in chronological order)

1942—Double Comics containing CC#1 (orig.) (diff. cover) (not actually a giveaway) (very rare) (see also Double Comics); only one known copy) 110.00 330.00 770.00
12/42—Saks 34th St. Giveaway containing CC#7 (orig.) (diff. cover) (very rare; only 6 known copies) 200.00 600.00 1400.00
2/43—American Comics containing CC#8 (orig.) (Liberty Theatre Giveaway) (diff. cover) (only one known copy) (see American Comics) 63.00 190.00 440.00
12/44—Robin Hood Flour Co. Giveaway - #7-CC(R) (diff. cover) (rare) (edition probably 5 [22]) 70.00 210.00 500.00

NOTE: How are above editions determined without CC covers? 1942 is dated 1942, and CC#1-first reprint did not come out until 5/43. 12/42 and 2/43 are determined by blue note at bottom of first text page only in original edition. 12/44 is estimate from page width—each reprint edition had progressively slightly smaller page width.

1951—Shelter Thru the Ages (C.I. Educational Series) (actually Giveaway by the Ruberoid Co.) (16 pgs.) (contains original artwork by H. C. Kiefer) (there are back cover ad variations) (scarce) 43.00 130.00 300.00

Classics Gift Boxes, Box A, © GIL

Christmas Gift Boxes, Series 4W, © GIL

Classics Giveaways, 12/42 Saks 34th St., © GIL

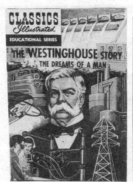

Classics Giveaways, 1952 George Daynor, © GIL   Classics Giveaways, 1953 Westinghouse, © GIL   Classics Illustrated Records, Space Stories..., © GIL

	Good	Fine	N-Mint
CLASSICS GIVEAWAYS (continued)			
1952—George Daynor Biography Giveaway (CC logo) (partly comic book/pictures/newspaper articles) (story of man who built Palace Depression out of junkyard swamp in NJ) (64 pgs.) (very rare; only 2 known copies, one missing-bc)	100.00	300.00	700.00
1953—Westinghouse/Dreams of a Man (C.I. Educational Series) (Westinghouse bio./Westinghouse Co. giveaway) (contains original artwork by H. C. Kiefer) (16 pgs.) (also French/Spanish/Italian versions) (scarce)	43.00	130.00	300.00
NOTE: *Reproductions of 1951, 1952, and 1953 exist — color photocopy covers and black & white photocopy interior ("W.C.N. Reprint")*	1.00	3.00	7.00
51-53—Coward Shoe Giveaways (all editions very rare) (two variations of back cover Coward Shoe ads) 5 (87), 12 (89), 49 (85), 69 (87), 72 (no HRN), 96 (0), 98 (0), 100 (0), 101 (0), 103 (0), 104 (0), 105 (0), 108 (0), 110 (0), 112 (0). (some above editions recently discovered—some only one copy currently known to exist)	30.00	90.00	210.00
1956—Ben Franklin 5-10 Store Giveaway (#65-PC with back cover ad) (scarce)	16.00	48.00	110.00
1956—Ben Franklin Insurance Co. Giveaway (#65-PC with diff. back cover ad) (very rare)	35.00	105.00	245.00
11/56—Sealtest Co. Edition - #4 (135) (identical to regular edition except for Sealtest logo printed, not stamped, on front cover) (only one copy known to exist)	18.00	54.00	125.00
1958—Get-Well Giveaway containing #15-CI (new cartoon-type cover) (Pressman Pharmacy) (only one copy known to exist)	17.00	50.00	120.00
67-68—Twin Circle Giveaway Editions - all HRN 166, with back cover ad for National Catholic Press.			
2(R68), 4(R67), 10(R68), 48(R67)	2.00	6.00	14.00
13(R68), 128(R68)	3.00	9.00	21.00
16(R68), 68(R67), 535(576-R68)	4.00	12.00	28.00
12/69—Christmas Giveaway ("A Christmas Adventure") (reprints Picture Parade #4-1953, new cover) (4 ad variations)			
Stacy's Dept. Store	1.65	5.00	12.00
Anne & Hope Store	5.00	15.00	35.00
Gibson's Dept. Store (rare)	5.00	15.00	35.00
"Merry Christmas" & blank ad space	2.00	6.00	14.00

CLASSICS ILLUSTRATED RECORDS

	Good	Fine	N-Mint
1958—Science Fiction Record: C.I. #105, 124, 133, 144 (narration of Classics Illustrated stories) (very rare)	23.00	70.00	160.00
1958—C. I. Juniors Record: C.I. Juniors #502, 504, 505, 507, 509, 512, 513, 514, 520, 525, 531, 535 (Robert Q. Lewis narration of Juniors stories) (advertised on some Juniors editions) (very rare)	20.00	60.00	140.00
1958-Space Stories and Sounds; Bill Stern narration of C.I. #124, 133, 138, 144. (Lion Records #L70087) (very rare)	14.00	42.00	98.00
1958—Wonder World of Fairy Tales; Robert Q. Lewis narration of C.I. Juniors #502,504,505,507,509,512,513,514,520,525,531,535 (Lion Records #L70080) (very rare)	14.00	42.00	98.00
1966—Golden Records Great Literature Series (SLP-189: Black Beauty, SLP-190: Mutiny on the Bounty, SLP-191: The Time Machine, SLP-192: The Call of the Wild) ($2.49 retail for comic and record) (scarce)			
Comic only	2.00	6.00	14.00
Comic & Record	12.00	36.00	84.00

CLASSICS ILLUSTRATED GIANTS
October, 1949 (One-Shots - "OS")
Gilberton Publications

These Giant Editions, all with new Kiefer front and back covers, were advertised from 10/49 to 2/52. They were 50 cents on the newsstand and 60 cents by mail. They are actually four classics in one volume. All the stories are reprints of the Classics Illustrated Series. NOTE: *There were also British hardback Adventure & Indian Giants in 1952, with the same covers but different contents: Adventure - 2, 7, 10; Indian - 17, 22, 37, 58. They are also rare.*

	Good	Fine	N-Mint
"An Illustrated Library of Great Adventure Stories" - reprints of No. 6,7,8,10 (Rare); Kiefer-c	67.00	200.00	470.00
"An Illustrated Library of Exciting Mystery Stories" - reprints of No. 30,21,40,13 (Rare)	70.00	210.00	500.00
"An Illustrated Library of Great Indian Stories" - reprints of No. 4,17, 22,37 (Rare)	63.00	190.00	440.00

INTRODUCTION TO CLASSICS ILLUSTRATED JUNIOR

This year we have done a major overhaul of the pricing for Juniors. Collectors of Juniors can be put into one of two categories — those who want any copy of each title, and those who want all the originals. Those seeking every original and reprint edition are a limited group, primarily because Juniors have no changes in art or covers to spark interest, and because reprints are so low in value it is difficult to get dealers to look for specific reprint editions. Anyone interested in information about the full scope of Junior editions should write to **Jim McLoughlin, 28 Mercury Ave., East Patchogue, NY 11772.** He has been doing research in this area for several years.

In recent years it has become apparent that most serious Classics collectors seek Junior originals. Those seeking reprints seek them for low cost. This has made the previous note about the comparative market value of reprints inadequate. Most dealers report difficulty in moving reprints for more than $2-$4 for mint copies. Some may be worth $5-$7, just because of the popularity of the title, such as Snow White, Sleeping Beauty, and Wizard of Oz. Others may be worth $5-$7, because of the scarcity of particular title nos., such as 514, 560, 562, 575 & 576. Three particular reprint editions are worth even more. For the 535-Twin Circle edition, see Giveaways. There are also reprint editions of 501 and 503 which have a full-page bc ad for the very rare Junior record. Those may sell as high as $10-$15 in mint. Original editions of 557 and 558 also have that ad.

There are no reprint editions of 577. The only edition, from 1969, is a 25 cent stiff-cover edition with no ad for the next issue. All other original editions have coming-next ad. But 577, like C.I. #168, was prepared in 1962 but not issued. Copies of 577 can be found in 1963 British/European series, which then continued with dozens of additional new Junior titles. One last note about the market value of originals: Many years ago when Junior prices were much lower, collectors would pay more for certain titles. In recent years that trend has been reversing itself. In this year's guide we have attempted to correct some of the wild divergence in pricing of originals.

PRICES LISTED BELOW ARE FOR ORIGINAL EDITIONS, WHICH HAVE AN AD FOR THE NEXT ISSUE.

CLASSICS ILLUSTRATED JUNIOR
Oct, 1953 - Spring, 1971
Famous Authors Ltd. (Gilberton Publications)

	Good	Fine	N-Mint
501-Snow White & the Seven Dwarfs; Alex Blum-a	8.00	24.00	56.00
502-The Ugly Duckling	5.00	15.00	35.00
503-Cinderella	3.00	9.00	21.00
504-The Pied Piper	2.00	6.00	14.00
505-The Sleeping Beauty	2.00	6.00	14.00
506-The Three Little Pigs	2.00	6.00	14.00
507-Jack & the Beanstalk	2.00	6.00	14.00
508-Goldilocks & the Three Bears	2.00	6.00	14.00
509-Beauty and the Beast	2.00	6.00	14.00
510-Little Red Riding Hood	2.00	6.00	14.00
511-Puss-N-Boots	2.00	6.00	14.00
512-Rumpel Stiltskin	2.00	6.00	14.00
513-Pinocchio	3.00	9.00	21.00
514-The Steadfast Tin Soldier	4.00	12.00	28.00
515-Johnny Appleseed	2.00	6.00	14.00
516-Aladdin and His Lamp	3.00	9.00	21.00
517-The Emperor's New Clothes	2.00	6.00	14.00

CLASSICS ILLUSTRATED JR. (continued)	Good	Fine	N-Mint
518-The Golden Goose	2.00	6.00	14.00
519-Paul Bunyan	2.00	6.00	14.00
520-Thumbelina	3.00	9.00	21.00
521-King of the Golden River	2.00	6.00	14.00
522-The Nightingale	1.30	4.00	9.00
523-The Gallant Tailor	1.30	4.00	9.00
524-The Wild Swans	1.30	4.00	9.00
525-The Little Mermaid	1.30	4.00	9.00
526-The Frog Prince	1.30	4.00	9.00
527-The Golden-Haired Giant	1.30	4.00	9.00
528-The Penny Prince	1.30	4.00	9.00
529-The Magic Servants	1.30	4.00	9.00
530-The Golden Bird	1.30	4.00	9.00
531-Rapunzel	2.00	6.00	14.00
532-The Dancing Princesses	1.30	4.00	9.00
533-The Magic Fountain	1.30	4.00	9.00
534-The Golden Touch	1.30	4.00	9.00
535-The Wizard of Oz	4.00	12.00	28.00
536-The Chimney Sweep	1.30	4.00	9.00
537-The Three Fairies	1.30	4.00	9.00
538-Silly Hans	1.30	4.00	9.00
539-The Enchanted Fish	3.00	9.00	21.00
540-The Tinder-Box	3.00	9.00	21.00
541-Snow White & Rose Red	2.00	6.00	14.00
542-The Donkey's Tale	2.00	6.00	14.00
543-The House in the Woods	1.30	4.00	9.00
544-The Golden Fleece	4.00	12.00	28.00
545-The Glass Mountain	2.00	6.00	14.00
546-The Elves & the Shoemaker	2.00	6.00	14.00
547-The Wishing Table	1.30	4.00	9.00
548-The Magic Pitcher	1.30	4.00	9.00
549-Simple Kate	1.30	4.00	9.00
550-The Singing Donkey	1.30	4.00	9.00
551-The Queen Bee	1.30	4.00	9.00
552-The Three Little Dwarfs	2.00	6.00	14.00
553-King Thrushbeard	1.30	4.00	9.00
554-The Enchanted Deer	1.30	4.00	9.00
555-The Three Golden Apples	1.30	4.00	9.00
556-The Elf Mound	1.30	4.00	9.00
557-Silly Willy	3.00	9.00	21.00
558-The Magic Dish; L.B. Cole-c; soft and stiff-c exist on (O)			
	3.00	9.00	21.00
559-The Japanese Lantern; 1 pg. Ingels-a; L.B. Cole-c			
	3.00	9.00	21.00
560-The Doll Princess; L.B. Cole-c	3.00	9.00	21.00
561-Hans Humdrum; L.B. Cole-c	1.30	4.00	9.00
562-The Enchanted Pony; L.B. Cole-c	3.00	9.00	21.00
563-The Wishing Well; L.B. Cole-c	1.30	4.00	9.00
564-The Salt Mountain; L.B. Cole-c	1.30	4.00	9.00
565-The Silly Princess; L.B. Cole-c	1.30	4.00	9.00
566-Clumsy Hans; L.B. Cole-c	1.30	4.00	9.00
567-The Bearskin Soldier; L.B. Cole-c	1.30	4.00	9.00
568-The Happy Hedgehog; L.B. Cole-c	1.30	4.00	9.00
569-The Three Giants	1.30	4.00	9.00
570-The Pearl Princess	.85	2.50	6.00
571-How Fire Came to the Indians	1.15	3.50	8.00
572-The Drummer Boy	1.70	5.00	12.00
573-The Crystal Ball	1.70	5.00	12.00
574-Brightboots	1.70	5.00	12.00
575-The Fearless Prince	2.00	6.00	14.00
576-The Princess Who Saw Everything	3.00	9.00	21.00
577-The Runaway Dumpling	4.00	12.00	28.00

NOTE: *Last reprint - Spring, 1971.* **Costanza & Shaffenberger** *art in many issues.*

CLASSICS ILLUSTRATED SPECIAL ISSUE
Dec, 1955 - July, 1962 (100 pages) (35 cents)

Gilberton Co. (Came out semi-annually)	Good	Fine	N-Mint
129-The Story of Jesus (titled ...Special Edition) "Jesus on			
Mountain" cover	3.00	9.00	21.00
"Three Camels" cover(12/58)	5.00	15.00	35.00
"Mountain" cover (1968 re-issue; has black 50 cent circle)			
	1.70	5.00	12.00
132A-The Story of America (6/56)	2.65	8.00	18.00
135A-The Ten Commandments(12/56)	3.70	11.00	26.00
138A-Adventures in Science(6/57)	3.00	9.00	21.00
141A-The Rough Rider (Teddy Roosevelt)(12/57); Evans-a			
	2.00	6.00	14.00
144A-Blazing the Trails West(6/58)- 73 pages of Crandall/Evans plus			
Severin-a	2.00	6.00	14.00
147A-Crossing the Rockies(12/58)-Crandall/Evans-a			
	4.00	12.00	28.00
150A-Royal Canadian Police(6/59)-Ingels, Sid Check-a			
	4.00	12.00	28.00
153A-Men, Guns & Cattle(12/59)-Evans-a, 26 pgs.; Kinstler-a			
	3.70	11.00	26.00
156A-The Atomic Age(6/60)-Crandall/Evans, Torres-a			
	2.65	8.00	18.00
159A-Rockets, Jets and Missiles(12/60)-Evans, Morrow-a			
	2.65	8.00	18.00
162A-War Between the States(6/61)-Kirby & Crandall/Evans-a;			
Ingels-a	5.00	15.00	35.00
165A-To the Stars(12/61)-Torres, Crandall/Evans, Kirby-a			
	3.00	9.00	21.00
166A-World War II('62)-Torres, Crandall/Evans, Kirby-a			
	3.50	10.50	24.00
167A-Prehistoric World(7/62)-Torres & Crandall/Evans-a			
	4.00	12.00	28.00
nn Special Issue-The United Nations (1964; 50 cents; scarce); This			
is actually part of the European Special Series, which continued			
on after the U.S. series stopped issuing new titles in 1962. This			
English edition was prepared specifically for sale at the U.N. It			
was printed in Norway.	18.00	54.00	125.00

NOTE: *158A appeared as DC's Showcase No. 43, "Dr. No" and was only published in Great Britain as 158A with different cover. There was another U.S. Special Issue prepared in 1962 with artwork by Kirby, Crandall & Evans, entitled* **World War I**. *Unfortunately, it was never issued in any English-language edition. It was issued in 1964 in West Germany, The Netherlands, and other Scandanavian countries, with another edition in 1974 with a new cover.*

CLASSICS LIBRARY (See King Classics)

CLASSIC X-MEN
Sept, 1986 - Present
Marvel Comics Group

1-Begins-r of New X-Men	.85	2.50	5.00
2-4	.50	1.50	3.00
5-10	.40	1.25	2.50
11-15	.35	1.00	2.00
16,18-20	.30	.90	1.75
17-Wolverine-c	.50	1.50	3.00
21-30: 26-r/X-Men #120. 27-r/X-Men #121.	.25	.75	1.50

NOTE: *Art Adams c(p)-1-10, 12-16, 18, 19, 25. Austin c-19i. Williamson c-12i, 13i.*

CLAW THE UNCONQUERED (See Cancelled Comic Cavalcade)
5-6/75 - No. 9, 9/10/76; No. 10, 4-5/78 - No. 12, 8-9/78
National Periodical Publications/DC Comics

1		.50	1.00
2,3: 3-Nudity panel		.40	.80
4-12: 9-Origin		.25	.50

NOTE: *Giffen a-8-12p. Kubert c-10-12. Layton a-9i, 12i.*

CLAY CODY, GUNSLINGER
Fall, 1957
Pines Comics

1-Painted-c	1.50	4.50	10.00

Classics Illustrated Junior #558, © GIL

Classics Illustrated Junior #565, © GIL

Classics Illustrated Special Issue #132A, © GIL

Cloak And Dagger #1, © Z-D   Clue Comics #9, © HILL   Clyde Beatty's African Jungle Book, © Richfield Oil

CLEAN FUN, STARRING "SHOOGAFOOTS JONES"
1944 (24 pgs.; B&W; oversized covers) (10 cents)
Specialty Book Co.

	Good	Fine	N-Mint
Humorous situations involving Negroes in the Deep South			
White cover issue....	2.75	8.00	16.00
Dark grey cover issue....	3.00	9.00	18.00

CLEMENTINA THE FLYING PIG (See Dell Jr. Treasury)

CLEOPATRA (See Ideal, a Classical Comic No. 1)

CLIFF MERRITT SETS THE RECORD STRAIGHT
Giveaway (2 different issues)
Brotherhood of Railroad Trainsmen

...and the Very Candid Candidate by Al Williamson	.40	1.20	2.40
...Sets the Record Straight by Al Williamson (2 diff.-c: one by Williamson, the other by McWilliams)	.40	1.20	2.40

CLIFFORD MCBRIDE'S IMMORTAL NAPOLEON & UNCLE ELBY
1932 (12x17"; softcover cartoon book)
The Castle Press

Intro. by Don Herod	6.50	19.50	45.00

CLIMAX!
July, 1955 - No. 2, Sept, 1955
Gillmor Magazines

1,2 (Mystery)	4.65	14.00	32.00

CLINT (Also see Adolescent Radioactive...)
Sept., 1986 - No. 2, Jan., 1987 ($1.50, B&W)
Eclipse Comics

1,2	.25	.75	1.50

CLINT & MAC (See 4-Color No. 889)

CLOAK AND DAGGER
Fall, 1952
Ziff-Davis Publishing Co.

1-Saunders painted-c	11.00	32.00	75.00

CLOAK AND DAGGER (Also see Marvel Fanfare)
Oct, 1983 - No. 4, Jan, 1984 (Mini-series)
Marvel Comics Group

1-Austin c/a(i) in all	.25	.75	1.50
2-4: 4-Origin	.25	.75	1.50

CLOAK AND DAGGER (Also see Strange Tales, 2nd series & Mutant Misadventures Of...)
July, 1985 - No. 11, Jan, 1987
Marvel Comics Group

1	.25	.75	1.50
2-8,10,11		.50	1.00
9-Art Adams-p	.50	1.50	3.00

CLOSE SHAVES OF PAULINE PERIL, THE (TV?)
June, 1970 - No. 4, March, 1971 (Jay Ward?)
Gold Key

1	1.00	3.00	6.00
2-4	.70	2.00	4.00

CLOWN COMICS (No. 1 titled Clown Comic Book)
1945 - No. 3, Wint, 1946
Clown Comics/Home Comics/Harvey Publ.

nn	3.70	11.00	26.00
2,3	2.15	6.50	15.00

CLUBHOUSE RASCALS (#1 titled ...Presents?)
June, 1956 - No. 2, Oct, 1956 (Also see Three Rascals)
Sussex Publ. Co. (Magazine Enterprises)

1,2: The Brain app.	1.70	5.00	12.00

CLUB "16"
June, 1948 - No. 4, Dec, 1948
Famous Funnies

	Good	Fine	N-Mint
1	4.65	14.00	32.00
2-4	2.15	6.50	15.00

CLUE COMICS (Real Clue Crime V2No.4 on)
Jan, 1943 - No. 15(V2No.3), May, 1947
Hillman Periodicals

1-Origin The Boy King, Nightmare, Micro-Face, Twilight, & Zippo	38.00	115.00	265.00
2	20.00	60.00	140.00
3	15.00	45.00	105.00
4	12.00	36.00	84.00
5	11.00	32.00	75.00
6,8,9	8.00	24.00	56.00
7-Classic torture-c	11.00	32.00	75.00
10-Origin The Gun Master	8.00	24.00	56.00
11	5.50	16.50	38.00
12-Origin Rackman	8.00	24.00	56.00
V2#1-Nightro new origin; Iron Lady app.; Simon & Kirby-a	10.00	30.00	70.00
V2#2-S&K-a(2)-Bondage/torture-c; man attacks & kills people with electric iron. Infantino-a	11.00	32.00	75.00
V2#3-S&K-a(3)	11.00	32.00	75.00

CLUTCHING HAND, THE
July-Aug, 1954
American Comics Group

1	8.00	24.00	56.00

CLYDE BEATTY COMICS (Also see Crackajack Funnies)
October, 1953 (84 pages)
Commodore Productions & Artists, Inc.

1-Photo front/back-c; includes movie scenes and comics	11.00	32.00	75.00
...African Jungle Book('56)-Richfield Oil Co. 16 pg. giveaway, soft-c	5.00	15.00	35.00

CLYDE CRASHCUP (TV)
Aug-Oct, 1963 - No. 5, Sept-Nov, 1964
Dell Publishing Co.

1-All written by John Stanley	3.50	10.50	24.00
2-5	2.30	7.00	16.00

C-M-O COMICS
1942 (68 pages, full color)
Chicago Mail Order Co.(Centaur)

1-Invisible Terror, Super Ann, & Plymo the Rubber Man app. (All Centaur costume heroes)	32.00	95.00	225.00
2-Invisible Terror, Super Ann app.	22.00	65.00	154.00

COCOMALT BIG BOOK OF COMICS
1938 (Regular size; full color; 52 pgs.)
Harry 'A' Chesler (Cocomalt Premium)

1-(Scarce)-Biro-c/a; Little Nemo by Winsor McCay Jr., Dan Hastings; Guardineer, Jack Cole, Gustavson, Bob Wood-a	52.00	155.00	365.00

CODE NAME: ASSASSIN (See First Issue Special)

CODENAME: DANGER
Aug, 1985 - No. 4, May, 1986 ($1.50 cover)
Lodestone Publ.

1-4	.25	.75	1.50

CODENAME SPITFIRE (Formerly Spitfire And The Troubleshooters)
No. 10, July, 1987 - No. 13, Oct, 1987
Marvel Comics Group

	Good	Fine	N-Mint
CODENAME SPITFIRE (continued)			
10-13: 10-Rogers c/a		.50	1.00

CODY OF THE PONY EXPRESS (See Colossal Features Magazine)
Sept, 1950 - No. 3, Jan, 1951 (See Women Outlaws)
Fox Features Syndicate

	Good	Fine	N-Mint
1-3 (actually #3-5). 1-Painted-c	4.65	14.00	32.00

CODY OF THE PONY EXPRESS (Buffalo Bill. . .) (Outlaws of the
West #11 on; Formerly Bullseye)
No. 8, Oct, 1955; No. 9, Jan, 1956; No. 10, June, 1956
Charlton Comics

8-Bullseye on splash pg; not S&K-a	2.65	8.00	18.00
9,10: 10-Buffalo Bill app.	1.70	5.00	12.00

CO-ED ROMANCES
November, 1951
P. L. Publishing Co.

1	2.30	7.00	16.00

COLLECTORS ITEM CLASSICS (See Marvel Collectors Item Classics)

COLOSSAL FEATURES MAGAZINE (Formerly I Loved) (See Cody of
the Pony Express)
No. 33, May, 1950 - No. 34, July, 1950; No. 3, Sept, 1950
Fox Features Syndicate

33,34-Cody of the Pony Express begins (based on Columbia serial).			
33-Painted-c; 34-Photo-c	5.00	15.00	35.00
3-Authentic criminal cases	4.30	13.00	30.00

COLOSSAL SHOW, THE (TV)
October, 1969
Gold Key

1	2.00	6.00	14.00

COLOSSUS COMICS (See Green Giant & Motion Pic. Fun. Wkly)
March, 1940
Sun Publications (Funnies, Inc.?)

1-(Scarce)-Tulpa of Tsang (hero); Colossus app.			
	80.00	240.00	560.00

NOTE: Cover by artist that drew Colossus in Green Giant Comics.

COLT .45 (TV)
No. 924, 8/58 - No. 1058, 11-1/59-60; No. 4, 2-4/60 - No. 9, 5-7/61
Dell Publishing Co.

4-Color 924-Wayde Preston photo-c on all	4.65	14.00	32.00
4-Color 1004,1058; #4,5,7-9	3.50	10.50	24.00
6-Toth-a	4.65	14.00	32.00

COLUMBIA COMICS
1943
William H. Wise Co.

1-Joe Palooka, Charlie Chan, Capt. Yank, Sparky Watts, Dixie Dugan	12.00	36.00	84.00

COMANCHE (See 4-Color No. 1350)

COMANCHEROS, THE (See 4-Color No. 1300)

COMBAT
June, 1952 - No. 11, April, 1953
Atlas Comics (ANC)

1	3.50	10.50	24.00
2	1.70	5.00	12.00
3,5-9,11	1.30	4.00	9.00
4-Krigstein-a	2.00	6.00	14.00
10-B&W and color illos. in **POP**	2.00	6.00	14.00

NOTE: Combat Casey in 7,8,10,11. Heath c-1. Maneely a-1. Pakula a-1. Reinman a-1.

COMBAT
Oct-Nov, 1961 - No. 40, Oct, 1973 (no No.9)
Dell Publishing Co.

	Good	Fine	N-Mint
1	1.50	4.50	10.00
2-5: 4-J. Kennedy c/story	.85	2.50	6.00
6,7,8(4-6/63), 8(7-9/63)	.50	1.50	3.00
10-27	.35	1.00	2.00
28-40(reprints #1-14)		.50	1.00

NOTE: Glanzman c/a-1.27.

COMBAT CASEY (Formerly War Combat)
No. 6, Jan, 1953 - No. 34, July, 1957
Atlas Comics (SAI)

6 (Indicia shows 1/52 in error)	3.00	9.00	21.00
7-Spanking panel	3.50	10.50	24.00
8-Used in **POP**, pg. 94	2.00	6.00	14.00
9	1.15	3.50	8.00
10,13-19-Violent art by R. Q. Sale; Battle Brady x-over #10			
	2.00	6.00	14.00
11,12,20-Last Precode (2/55)	.85	2.50	6.00
21-34	.70	2.00	5.00

NOTE: Everett a-6. Heath c-10, 17, 19, 30. Powell a-29(5); 30(5); 34. Severin c-26, 33.

COMBAT KELLY
Nov, 1951 - No. 44, Aug, 1957
Atlas Comics (SPI)

1-Heath-a	5.70	17.00	40.00
2	2.85	8.50	20.00
3-10	1.70	5.00	12.00
11-Used in **POP**, pages 94,95 plus color illo.	2.30	7.00	16.00
12-Color illo. in **POP**	2.30	7.00	16.00
13-16	.85	2.50	6.00
17-Violent art by R. Q. Sale; Combat Casey app.			
	2.30	7.00	16.00
18-20,22-44: 18-Battle Brady app. 28-Last precode (1/55). 38-Green Berets story(8/56)	.85	2.50	6.00
21-Transvestism-c	1.70	5.00	12.00

NOTE: Berg a-8, 12-14, 16, 17, 19-23, 25, 26, 28, 31-36, 42-44. Colan a-42. Heath c-31. Maneely a-6, 8; c-8, 25. Severin c-41, 42. Whitney a-5.

COMBAT KELLY (and the Deadly Dozen)
June, 1972 - No. 9, Oct, 1973
Marvel Comics Group

1-Intro. Combat Kelly; Mooney-a; Severin-c	.40	.80
2-9	.30	.60

COMBINED OPERATIONS (See The Story of the Commandos)

COMEDY CARNIVAL
no date (1950's) (100 pages)
St. John Publishing Co.

nn-Contains rebound St. John comics	11.00	32.00	75.00

COMEDY COMICS (1st Series) (Daring Mystery No. 1-8)
(Margie No. 35 on)
No. 9, April, 1942 - No. 34, Fall, 1946
Timely Comics (TCI 9,10)

9-(Scarce)-The Fin by Everett, Capt. Dash, Citizen V, & The Silver Scorpion app.; Wolverton-a; 1st app. Comedy Kid; satire on Hitler & Stalin	75.00	225.00	525.00
10-(Scarce)-Origin The Fourth Musketeer, Victory Boys; Monstro, the Mighty app.	55.00	165.00	385.00
11-Vagabond, Stuporman app.	18.00	54.00	125.00
12,13	5.00	15.00	35.00
14-Origin & 1st app. Super Rabbit	20.00	60.00	140.00
15-20	4.35	13.00	30.00
21-32	3.15	9.50	22.00
33-Kurtzman-a, 5 pgs.	4.35	13.00	30.00
34-Wolverton-a, 5 pgs.	6.00	18.00	42.00

COMEDY COMICS (2nd Series)
May, 1948 - No. 10, Jan, 1950

Colossal Features Magazine #33, © FOX

Combat Kelly #2 (1/52), © MEG

Comedy Comics #18 (1st series), © MEG

Comic Album #1, © WDC

Comic Cavalcade #2, © DC

Comic Cavalcade #63, © DC

COMEDY COMICS (continued)
Marvel Comics (ACI)

	Good	Fine	N-Mint
1-Hedy, Tessie, Millie begin; Kurtzman's "Hey Look" (he draws himself)	11.00	32.00	75.00
2	4.30	13.00	30.00
3,4-Kurtzman's "Hey Look"(?&3)	6.00	18.00	42.00
5-10	2.15	6.50	15.00

COMET, THE
Oct, 1983 - No. 2, Dec, 1983
Red Circle Comics

1-Origin The Comet; The American Shield begins		
	.50	1.00
2-Origin continues	.50	1.00

COMET MAN, THE
Feb, 1987 - No. 6, July, 1987 (mini-series)
Marvel Comics Group

1-6	.50	1.00

COMIC ALBUM
Mar-May, 1958 - No. 18, June-Aug, 1962
Dell Publishing Co.

	Good	Fine	N-Mint
1-Donald Duck	3.50	10.50	24.00
2-Bugs Bunny	1.50	4.50	10.00
3-Donald Duck	2.85	8.50	20.00
4-Tom & Jerry	1.30	4.00	9.00
5-Woody Woodpecker	1.30	4.00	9.00
6-Bugs Bunny	1.30	4.00	9.00
7-Popeye (9-11/59)	2.30	7.00	16.00
8-Tom & Jerry	1.30	4.00	9.00
9-Woody Woodpecker	1.30	4.00	9.00
10-Bugs Bunny	1.30	4.00	9.00
11-Popeye (9-11/60)	2.30	7.00	16.00
12-Tom & Jerry	1.30	4.00	9.00
13-Woody Woodpecker	1.30	4.00	9.00
14-Bugs Bunny	1.30	4.00	9.00
15-Popeye	2.30	7.00	16.00
16-Flintstones (12-2/61-62)-3rd app.	2.30	7.00	16.00
17-Space Mouse-3rd app.	1.30	4.00	9.00
18-Three Stooges; photo-c	4.00	12.00	28.00

COMIC BOOK (Also see Comics From Weatherbird)
1954 (Giveaway)
American Juniors Shoe

Contains a comic rebound with new cover. Several combinations possible. Contents determines price.

COMIC BOOK MAGAZINE
1940 - 1943 (Similar to Spirit Sections)
(7¾x10¾''; full color; 16-24 pages each)
Chicago Tribune & other newspapers

1940 issues	5.00	15.00	35.00
1941, 1942 issues	4.00	12.00	28.00
1943 issues	3.35	10.00	23.00

NOTE: Published weekly. Texas Slim, Kit Carson, Spooky, Josie, Nuts & Jolts, Lew Loyal, Brenda Starr, Daniel Boone, Captain Storm, Rocky, Smokey Stover, Tiny Tim, Little Joe, Fu Manchu appear among others. Early issues had photo stories with pictures from the movies; later issues had comic art.

COMIC BOOKS (Series 1)
1950 (16 pgs.; 5¼x8½''; full color; bound at top; paper cover)
Metropolitan Printing Co. (Giveaway)

1-Boots and Saddles; intro. The Masked Marshal			
	3.35	10.00	23.00
1-The Green Jet; Green Lama by Raboy	20.00	60.00	140.00
1-My Pal Dizzy (Teen-age)	1.70	5.00	12.00
1-New World; origin Atomaster (costumed hero)			
	5.00	15.00	35.00

	Good	Fine	N-Mint
1-Talullah (Teen-age)	1.70	5.00	12.00

COMIC CAPERS
Fall, 1944 - No. 6, Summer, 1946
Red Circle Mag./Marvel Comics

1-Super Rabbit, The Creeper, Silly Seal, Ziggy Pig, Sharpy Fox begin	8.00	24.00	56.00
2	4.65	14.00	32.00
3-6	3.00	9.00	21.00

COMIC CAVALCADE
Winter, 1942-43 - No. 63, June-July, 1954
(Contents change with No. 30, Dec-Jan, 1948-49 on)
All-American/National Periodical Publications

1-The Flash, Green Lantern, Wonder Woman, Wildcat, The Black Pirate by Moldoff (also #2), Ghost Patrol, and Red White & Blue begin; Scribbly app.; Minute Movies	155.00	465.00	1085.00
2-Mutt & Jeff begin; last Ghost Patrol & Black Pirate; Minute Movies	77.00	230.00	540.00
3-Hop Harrigan & Sargon, the Sorcerer begin; The King app.	57.00	170.00	400.00
4-The Gay Ghost, The King, Scribbly, & Red Tornado app.	47.00	140.00	330.00
5-Christmas-c	40.00	120.00	280.00
6-10: 7-Red Tornado & Black Pirate app.; last Scribbly. 9-X-mas-c	35.00	105.00	245.00
11,12,14-20: 12-Last Red White & Blue. 15-Johnny Peril begins, ends #29. 13-Christmas-c	30.00	90.00	210.00
13-Solomon Grundy app.	52.00	155.00	365.00
21-23	30.00	90.00	210.00
24-Solomon Grundy x-over in Gr. Lantern	35.00	105.00	245.00
25-29: 25-Black Canary app.; X-mas-c. 26-28-Johnny Peril app. 28-Last Mutt & Jeff. 29-Last Flash, Wonder Woman, Green Lantern & Johnny Peril	23.00	70.00	160.00
30-The Fox & the Crow, Dodo & the Frog & Nutsy Squirrel begin	17.00	51.00	120.00
31-35	8.00	24.00	56.00
36-49	6.00	18.00	42.00
50-62(Scarce)	8.00	24.00	56.00
63(Rare)	13.50	40.00	95.00
Giveaway (1945, 16 pages, paper-c, in color)-Movie "Tomorrow The World" (Nazi theme)	28.00	84.00	195.00
Giveaway (c. 1944-45; 8 pgs, paper-c, in color)-The Twain Shall Meet-r/C. Cavalcade	17.00	51.00	120.00

NOTE: Grossman a-30-63. Sheldon Mayer a(2-3)-40-63. Post a-31, 36. Reinman a-15, 20. Toth a-26(28)(Green Lantern); c-23, 27. Atom app.-22, 23.

COMIC COMICS
April, 1946 - No. 10, Feb, 1947
Fawcett Publications

1-Captain Kidd	5.00	15.00	35.00
2-10-Wolverton-a, 4 pgs. each. 5-Captain Kidd app.			
	5.50	16.50	38.00

COMIC CUTS (Also see The Funnies)
5/19/34 - 7/28/34 (5 cents; 24 pages) (Tabloid size in full color)
(Not reprints; published weekly; created for newsstand sale)
H. L. Baker Co., Inc.

V1#1 - V1#7(6/30/34), V1#8(7/14/34), V1#9(7/28/34)-Idle Jack strips			
	7.00	21.00	50.00

COMIC LAND
March, 1946
Fact and Fiction

1-Sandusky & the Senator, Sam Stuper, Marvin the Great, Sir Passer, Phineas Gruff app.; Irv Tirman & Perry Williams art			
	3.50	10.50	24.00

COMIC MONTHLY
Jan, 1922 - No. 12, Dec, 1922 (32 pgs.)(8½x9'')(10 cents)
(1st monthly newsstand comic publication) (Reprints 1921 B&W dailies)
Embee Dist. Co.

	Good	Fine	N-Mint
1-Polly & Her Pals	33.00	100.00	230.00
2-Mike & Ike	6.50	19.50	45.00
3-S'Matter, Pop?	6.50	19.50	45.00
4-Barney Google	13.00	40.00	90.00
5-Tillie the Toiler	9.30	28.00	65.00
6-Indoor Sports	5.00	15.00	35.00
7-Little Jimmy	5.00	15.00	35.00
8-Toots and Casper	5.00	15.00	35.00
9,10-Foolish Questions	5.00	15.00	35.00
11-Barney Google & Spark Plug in the Abadaba Handicap			
	5.00	15.00	35.00
12-Polly & Her Pals	5.00	15.00	35.00

COMICO CHRISTMAS SPECIAL
Dec, 1988 ($2.50, 44pgs, color)
Comico

1-Rude, Williamson-a; Stevens-c	.40	1.25	2.50

COMICO PRIMER (See Primer)

COMIC PAGES (Formerly Funny Picture Stories)
V3No.4, July, 1939 - V3No.6, Dec, 1939
Centaur Publications

V3#4-Bob Wood-a	23.00	70.00	160.00
5,6	16.00	48.00	110.00

COMIC PAINTING AND CRAYONING BOOK
1917 (32 pages)(10x13½'')(No price on cover)
Saalfield Publ. Co.

Tidy Teddy by F. M. Follett, Clarence the Cop, Mr. & Mrs. Butt-In.			
Regular comic stories to read or color	7.00	21.00	50.00

COMICS (See All Good)

COMICS, THE
March, 1937 - No. 11, 1938 (Newspaper strip reprints)
Dell Publishing Co.

1-1st Tom Mix in comics; Wash Tubbs, Tom Beatty, Myra North,			
Arizona Kid, Erik Noble & International Spy w/Doctor Doom begin			
	55.00	165.00	385.00
2	30.00	90.00	210.00
3-11: 3-Alley Oop begins	25.00	75.00	175.00

COMICS AND STORIES (See Walt Disney's. . .)

COMICS CALENDAR, THE (The 1946. . .)
1946 (116 pgs.; 25 cents)(Stapled at top)
True Comics Press (ordered through the mail)

(Rare) Has a "strip" story for every day of the year in color			
	17.00	51.00	120.00

COMICS DIGEST (Pocket size)
Winter, 1942-43 (100 pages) (Black & White)
Parents' Magazine Institute

1-Reprints from True Comics (non-fiction World War II stories)			
	5.00	15.00	35.00

COMIC SELECTIONS (Shoe store giveaway)
1944-46 (Reprints from Calling All Girls, True Comics, True Aviation, & Real Heroes)
Parents' Magazine Press

1	1.70	5.00	12.00
2-5	1.30	4.00	9.00

COMICS FOR KIDS
1945 (no month); No. 2, Sum, 1945 (Funny animal)

London Publishing Co./Timely

	Good	Fine	N-Mint
1,2-Puffy Pig, Sharpy Fox	5.00	15.00	35.00

COMICS FROM WEATHER BIRD (Also see Comic Book, Free Comics to You, Weather Bird & Edward's Shoes)
1954 - 1957 (Giveaway)
Weather Bird Shoes

Contains a comic bound with new cover. Many combinations possible. Contents would determine price. Some issues do not contain complete comics, but only parts of comics. Value equals 40 to 60 percent of contents.

COMICS HITS (See Harvey Comics Hits)

COMICS MAGAZINE, THE (. . .Funny Pages #3)(Funny Pages #6 on)
May, 1936 - No. 5, Sept, 1936 (Paper covers)
Comics Magazine Co.

1: Dr. Mystic, The Occult Detective by Siegel & Shuster (1st			
episode continues in More Fun #14); 1pg. Kelly-a; Sheldon			
Mayer-a	125.00	375.00	875.00
2: Federal Agent by Siegel & Shuster; 1pg. Kelly-a			
	75.00	225.00	525.00
3-5	60.00	180.00	420.00

COMICS NOVEL (Anarcho, Dictator of Death)
1947
Fawcett Publications

1-All Radar	17.00	51.00	120.00

COMICS ON PARADE (No. 30 on, continuation of Single Series)
April, 1938 - No. 104, Feb, 1955
United Features Syndicate

1-Tarzan by Foster; Captain & the Kids, Little Mary Mixup, Abbie &			
Slats, Ella Cinders, Broncho Bill, Li'l Abner begin			
	105.00	315.00	735.00
2	52.00	155.00	365.00
3	40.00	120.00	280.00
4,5	30.00	90.00	210.00
6-10	22.00	65.00	154.00
11-20	18.00	54.00	125.00
21-29: 22-Son of Tarzan begins. 29-Last Tarzan issue			
	15.00	45.00	105.00
30-Li'l Abner	11.00	32.00	75.00
31-The Captain & the Kids	8.00	24.00	56.00
32-Nancy & Fritzi Ritz	6.50	19.50	45.00
33-Li'l Abner	9.30	28.00	65.00
34-The Captain & the Kids (10/41)	7.00	21.00	50.00
35-Nancy & Fritzi Ritz	6.50	19.50	45.00
36-Li'l Abner	9.30	28.00	65.00
37-The Captain & the Kids (6/42)	7.00	21.00	50.00
38-Nancy & Fritzi Ritz; infinity-c	6.50	19.50	45.00
39-Li'l Abner	9.30	28.00	65.00
40-The Captain & the Kids (3/43)	7.00	21.00	50.00
41-Nancy & Fritzi Ritz	5.00	15.00	35.00
42-Li'l Abner	9.00	27.00	62.00
43-The Captain & the Kids	7.00	21.00	50.00
44-Nancy & Fritzi Ritz (3/44)	5.00	15.00	35.00
45-Li'l Abner	7.50	22.50	52.00
46-The Captain & the Kids	6.50	19.50	45.00
47-Nancy & Fritzi Ritz	5.00	15.00	35.00
48-Li'l Abner (3/45)	7.50	22.50	52.00
49-The Captain & the Kids	6.50	19.50	45.00
50-Nancy & Fritzi Ritz	5.00	15.00	35.00
51-Li'l Abner	6.50	19.50	45.00
52-The Captain & the Kids (3/46)	4.30	13.00	30.00
53-Nancy & Fritzi Ritz	4.30	13.00	30.00
54-Li'l Abner	6.50	19.50	45.00
55-Nancy & Fritzi Ritz	4.30	13.00	30.00
56-The Captain & the Kids (r-/Sparkler)	4.30	13.00	30.00
57-Nancy & Fritzi Ritz	4.30	13.00	30.00

Comic Pages V3#6, © CEN

The Comics Magazine #3, © CM

Comics On Parade #35, © UFS

Comic Story Paint Book #1055, © FAW   Commander Battle And The Atomic Sub #1, © ACG   Complete Book Of Comics And Funnies #1, © WHW

COMICS ON PARADE (continued)	Good	Fine	N-Mint
58-Li'l Abner	6.50	19.50	45.00
59-The Captain & the Kids	3.70	11.00	26.00
60-70-Nancy & Fritzi Ritz	3.70	11.00	26.00
71-76-Nancy only	2.65	8.00	18.00
77-99,101-104-Nancy & Sluggo	2.65	8.00	18.00
100-Nancy & Sluggo	3.50	10.50	24.00
Special Issue, 7/46; Summer, 1948 - The Capt. & the Kids app.			
	2.65	8.00	18.00

NOTE: Bound Volume (Very Rare) includes No. 1-12; bound by publisher in pictorial comic boards & distributed at the 1939 World's Fair and through mail order from ads in comicbooks (Also see Tip Top)   150.00 450.00 1050.00

NOTE: Li'l Abner reprinted from Tip Top.

COMICS READING LIBRARIES (Educational Series)
1973, 1977, 1979 (36 pages in color) (Giveaways)
King Features (Charlton Publ.)

R-01-Tiger, Quincy		.15	.30
R-02-Beetle Bailey, Blondie & Popeye		.15	.30
R-03-Blondie, Beetle Bailey		.30	.60
R-04-Tim Tyler's Luck, Felix the Cat	1.00	3.00	6.00
R-05-Quincy, Henry		.15	.30
R-06-The Phantom, Mandrake	2.00	6.00	12.00
1977 reprint(R-04)	.85	2.50	5.00
R-07-Popeye, Little King	.85	2.50	5.00
R-08-Prince Valiant(Foster), Flash Gordon	4.00	12.00	24.00
1977 reprint	1.35	4.00	8.00
R-09-Hagar the Horrible, Boner's Ark		.15	.30
R-10-Redeye, Tiger		.15	.30
R-11-Blondie, Hi & Lois		.25	.50
R-12-Popeye-Swee'pea, Brutus	.85	2.50	5.00
R-13-Beetle Bailey, Little King		.15	.30
R-14-Quincy-Hamlet		.15	.30
R-15-The Phantom, The Genius	2.00	6.00	12.00
R-16-Flash Gordon, Mandrake	4.00	12.00	24.00
1977 reprint	1.35	4.00	8.00
Other 1977 editions. . . .		.15	.30
1979 editions(68pgs.)		.20	.40

NOTE: Above giveaways available with purchase of $45.00 in merchandise. Used as a reading skills aid for small children.

COMICS REVUE
June, 1947 - No. 5, Jan, 1948
St. John Publ. Co. (United Features Synd.)

1-Ella Cinders & Blackie	5.00	15.00	35.00
2-Hap Hopper (7/47)	3.00	9.00	21.00
3-Iron Vic (8/47)	2.65	8.00	18.00
4-Ella Cinders (9/47)	3.00	9.00	21.00
5-Gordo No. 1 (1/48)	2.65	8.00	18.00

COMIC STORY PAINT BOOK
1943 (68 pages) (Large size)
Samuel Lowe Co.

1055-Captain Marvel & a Captain Marvel Jr. story to read & color; 3 panels in color per page (reprints)	30.00	90.00	210.00

COMIX BOOK (B&W Magazine - $1.00)
Oct, 1974 - No. 5, 1976
Marvel Comics Group/Krupp Comics Works No. 4

1-Underground comic artists; 2 pg. Wolverton-a			
	.70	2.00	4.00
2-Wolverton-a (1 pg.)	.40	1.20	2.40
3-Low distribution (3/75)	.50	1.50	3.00
4(2/76), 4(5/76), 5	.40	1.20	2.40

NOTE: Print run No. 1-3: 200-250M; No. 4&5: 10M each.

COMIX INTERNATIONAL
July, 1974 - No. 5, Spring, 1977 (Full color)
Warren Magazines

	Good	Fine	N-Mint
1-Low distribution; all Corben remainders from Warren			
	4.00	12.00	24.00
2-Wood, Wrightson-r	1.20	3.50	7.00
3-5: 4-Crandall-a	.70	2.00	4.00

NOTE: No. 4 had two printings with extra Corben story in one.

COMMANDER BATTLE AND THE ATOMIC SUB
July-Aug, 1954 - No. 7, July-Aug, 1955
American Comics Group (Titan Publ. Co.)

1 (3-D effect)	16.00	48.00	110.00
2	6.00	18.00	42.00
3-H-Bomb-c; Atomic Sub becomes Atomic Spaceship			
	8.00	24.00	56.00
4-7: 6,7-Landau-a	6.00	18.00	42.00

COMMANDMENTS OF GOD
1954, 1958
Catechetical Guild

300-Same contents in both editions; different-c			
	2.75	8.00	16.00

COMMANDO ADVENTURES
June, 1957 - No. 2, Aug, 1957
Atlas Comics (MMC)

1,2-Severin-c; 2-Drucker-a	1.50	4.50	10.00

COMMANDO YANK (See Mighty Midget & Wow Comics)

COMPLETE BOOK OF COMICS AND FUNNIES
1944 (196 pages) (One Shot) (25 cents)
William H. Wise & Co.

1-Origin Brad Spencer, Wonderman; The Magnet, The Silver Knight by Kinstler, & Zudo the Jungle Boy app.	19.00	57.00	132.00

COMPLETE BOOK OF TRUE CRIME COMICS
No date (Mid 1940's) (132 pages) (25 cents)
William H. Wise & Co.

nn-Contains Crime Does Not Pay rebound (includes #22)			
	45.00	135.00	315.00

COMPLETE COMICS (Formerly Amazing No. 1)
Winter, 1944-45
Timely Comics (EPC)

2-The Destroyer, The Whizzer, The Young Allies & Sergeant Dix			
	45.00	135.00	315.00

COMPLETE LOVE MAGAZINE (Formerly a pulp with same title)
V26/2, May-June, 1951 - V32/4(No.191), Sept, 1956
Ace Periodicals (Periodical House)

V26/2-Painted-c (52 pgs.)	2.30	7.00	16.00
V26/3-6(2/52), V27/1(4/52)-6(1/53)	1.50	4.50	10.00
V28/1(3/53), V28/2(5/53), V29/3(7/53)-6(12/53)	1.30	4.00	9.00
V30/1(2/54), V30/1(No. 176, 4/54)-6(No.181, 1/55)			
	1.15	3.50	8.00
V31/1(No.182, 3/55)-Last precode	1.00	3.00	7.00
V31/2(5/55)-6(No.187, 1/56)	.85	2.50	6.00
V32/1(No.188, 3/56)-4(No.191, 9/56)	.80	2.40	5.50

NOTE: (34 total issues). Photo-c V27/5-on. Painted-c V26/3.

COMPLETE MYSTERY (True Complete Mystery No. 5 on)
Aug, 1948 - No. 4, Feb, 1949 (Full length stories)
Marvel Comics (PrPI)

1-Seven Dead Men	13.00	40.00	90.00
2-Jigsaw of Doom!	8.00	24.00	56.00
3-Fear in the Night; Burgos-a	8.00	24.00	56.00
4-A Squealer Dies Fast	8.00	24.00	56.00

COMPLETE ROMANCE
1949
Avon Periodicals

	Good	Fine	N-Mint
COMPLETE ROMANCE (continued)			
1-(Scarce)-Reprinted as Women to Love	22.00	65.00	154.00
COMPLIMENTARY COMICS			
No date (1950's)			
Sales Promotion Publ. (Giveaway)			
1-Strongman by Powell, 3 stories	3.35	10.00	20.00
CONAN (See Chamber of Darkness #4, Handbook of . . ., King Conan, Marvel Treasury Ed., Robert E. Howard's . ., Savage Sword of Conan, and Savage Tales)			
CONAN SAGA, THE			
June, 1987 - Present (B&W magazine, $2.00)			
Marvel Comics			
1-Barry Smith-r begin	.35	1.00	2.00
2-23: 13,15-Boris-c	.35	1.00	2.00
CONAN, THE BARBARIAN			
Oct, 1970 - Present			
Marvel Comics Group			
1-Origin Conan by Barry Smith; Kull app.	11.00	32.50	65.00
2	4.15	12.50	25.00
3-(low distribution in some areas)	7.50	22.50	45.00
4,5	3.35	10.00	20.00
6-10: 8-Hidden panel message, pg. 14. 10-52 pgs.; Black Knight-r; Kull story by Severin	2.50	7.50	15.00
11-13: 11-52 pgs. 12-Wrightson c(i)	2.00	6.00	12.00
14,15-Elric app.	3.00	9.00	18.00
16,19,20: 16-Conan-r/Savage Tales #1	1.70	5.00	10.00
17,18-No Smith-a	1.00	3.00	6.00
21,22: 22-has r-from #1	1.35	4.00	8.00
23-1st app. Red Sonja	1.70	5.00	10.00
24-1st full story Red Sonja; last Smith-a	1.70	5.00	10.00
25-Buscema begins	1.00	3.00	6.00
26-30	.60	1.75	3.50
31-36,38-40	.40	1.20	2.40
37-Adams c/a	.85	2.50	5.00
41-43,46-49	.25	.75	1.50
44,45-Adams inks, c-45;	.35	1.00	2.00
50-57,60	.25	.80	1.60
58-2nd Belit app.(see Gnt-Size 1)	.50	1.50	3.00
59-Origin Belit	.25	.75	1.50
61-99		.50	1.00
100-(52 pg. Giant)-Death of Belit	.40	1.25	2.50
101-114,116-193		.50	1.00
115-double size		.60	1.20
194-199: $1.00 cover		.50	1.00
200-double size	.25	.75	1.50
201-218		.50	1.00

NOTE: **Adams** a-116r(i); c-49i. **Austin** a-125, 126; c-125i, 126i. **Brunner** c-17i. c-40. **Buscema** a-25-36p, 38, 39, 41-56p, 58-63p, 65-67p, 68, 70-78p, 84-86p, 88-91p, 93-126p, 136p, 140, 141-44p, 146-58p, 159, 161, 162, 163p, 165p-185p, 187p-190p, Annual 2-5p, 7p; c(p)-26, 34, 44, 46, 52, 56, 58, 59, 64, 65, 72, 78-80, 83-91, 93-103, 105-26, 136-51, 155-159, 161, 162, 168, 169, 171, 172, 174, 175, 178-185, 188, 189. **Golden** c-152. **Kaluta** c-167. **Gil Kane** a-12p, 17p, 18p, 127-30, 131-134p, Gnt-Size 1p-4p; c-12p, 17p, 18p, 23, 25, 27-32, 34, 35, 38, 39, 41-43, 45-51, 53-55, 57, 60-63, 65-71, 73p, 76p, 127-34, Gnt-Size 1, 3, 4. **Russell** a-21. **Simonson** c-135. **Smith** a-1p-11p, 12, 13p-15p, 16, 19-21, 23, 24; c-1-11, 13-16, 19-24p. **Sutton** inks-Gnt-Size 1-3. **Wood** a-47: Issues No. 3-5, 7-9, 11, 16-18, 21, 23, 25, 27-30, 35, 37, 38, 42, 45, 52, 57, 58, 65, 69-71, 73, 79-83, 99, 100, 104, 114, Annual 2 have original Robert E. Howard stories adapted. Issues #32-34 adapted from Norvell Page's novel **Flame Winds**.

	Good	Fine	N-Mint
Giant Size 1(9/74)-Smith r-/#3; start adaptation of Howard's "Hour of the Dragon." 1st app. Belit	.70	2.00	4.00
Giant Size 2(12/74)-Smith r-/#5; Sutton-a; Buscema-c	.70	2.00	4.00
Giant Size 3(4/75-Smith r-/#6; Sutton-a), Giant Size 4(6/75; Smith r-/#7), Giant Size 5('75; Smith r-/#14,15; Kirby-c)	.30	.90	1.80
King Size 1(9/73-35 cents)-Smith r-/#2,4; Smith-c	1.00	3.00	6.00

	Good	Fine	N-Mint
Annual 2(6/76)-50 cents; new stories	.40	1.20	2.40
Annual 3(2/78)-reprints	.30	.80	1.60
Annual 4(10/78), 5(12/79)-Buscema-a/part-c	.25	.70	1.40
Annual 6(10/81)-Kane c/a	.25	.70	1.40
Annual 7(11/82), 8(2/84)		.60	1.20
Annual 9(12/84), 10(2/87), 11(2/88)		.60	1.20
Special Edition 1(Red Nails)	.50	1.50	3.00
CONAN THE BARBARIAN MOVIE SPECIAL			
Oct, 1982 - No. 2, Nov, 1982			
Marvel Comics Group			
1,2-Movie adapt.; Buscema-a	.25		.50
CONAN THE DESTROYER			
Jan, 1985 - No. 2, Mar, 1985 (Movie adaptation)			
Marvel Comics Group			
1,2-r/Marvel Super Special	.40		.80
CONAN THE KING (Formerly King Conan)			
No. 20, Jan, 1984 - Present			
Marvel Comics Group			
20-52		.60	1.20

NOTE: **Kaluta** c-20-23, 24i, 26, 27. **Williamson** a-37i; c-37i, 38i.

	Good	Fine	N-Mint
CONCRETE (Also see Dark Horse Presents)			
March, 1987 - Present ($1.50, B&W)			
Dark Horse Comics			
1	1.50	4.50	9.00
1-2nd print	.40	1.25	2.50
2	.70	2.00	4.00
3-Origin	.50	1.50	3.00
4	.40	1.25	2.50
5-10	.35	1.00	2.00
11,12	.25	.75	1.50
Color Special #1	.50	1.50	2.95
CONDORMAN (Walt Disney)			
Oct, 1981 - No. 3, Jan, 1982			
Whitman Publ.			
1-3: 1,2-Movie adaptation; photo-c		.30	.60
CONFESSIONS ILLUSTRATED (Magazine)			
Jan-Feb, 1956 - No. 2, Spring, 1956			
E. C. Comics			
1-Craig, Kamen, Wood, Orlando-a	5.50	16.50	38.00
2-Craig, Crandall, Kamen, Orlando-a	6.50	19.50	45.00
CONFESSIONS OF LOVE			
4/50 - No. 2, 7/50 (25 cents; 132 pgs. in color)(7¼x5¼")			
Artful Publ.			
1-Bakerish-a	17.00	51.00	120.00
2-Art & text; Bakerish-a	8.50	25.50	60.00
CONFESSIONS OF LOVE (Confessions of Romance No. 7)			
No. 11, July, 1952 - No. 6, Aug, 1953			
Star Publications			
11	3.50	10.50	24.00
12,13-Disbrow-a	3.50	10.50	24.00
14, 6	2.00	6.00	14.00
4-Disbrow-a	2.75	8.00	18.00
5-Wood/?-a	4.00	12.00	28.00

NOTE: All have **L. B. Cole** covers.

	Good	Fine	N-Mint
CONFESSIONS OF ROMANCE (Formerly Confessions of Love)			
No. 7, Nov, 1953 - No. 11, Nov, 1954			
Star Publications			
7	3.50	10.50	24.00
8	2.35	7.00	16.00

Conan, The Barbarian #1, © MEG

Conan, The Barbarian #44, © MEG

Confessions Of Love #14, © STAR

Congo Bill #1, © DC

"Cookie" #1, © ACG

Corum: The Bull And The Spear #1, © First

CONFESSIONS OF ROMANCE (continued)	Good	Fine	N-Mint
9-Wood-a	6.00	18.00	42.00
10,11-Disbrow-a	3.00	9.00	21.00

NOTE: *L. B. Cole covers on all.*

CONFESSIONS OF THE LOVELORN (Formerly Lovelorn)
No. 52, Aug, 1954 - No. 114, June-July, 1960
American Comics Group (Regis Publ./Best Synd. Features)

	Good	Fine	N-Mint
52 (3-D effect)	9.00	27.00	62.00
53,55	1.50	4.50	10.00
54 (3-D effect)	8.00	24.00	56.00
56-Communist propaganda sty, 10pgs; last pre-code (2/55)			
	2.00	6.00	14.00
57-90	1.00	3.00	7.00
91-Williamson-a	4.00	12.00	28.00
92-99,101-114	.85	2.50	6.00
100	1.00	3.00	7.00

NOTE: *Whitney a-most issues. 106,107-painted-c.*

CONFIDENTIAL DIARY (Formerly High School Confidential Diary;
Three Nurses No. 18 on)
No. 12, May, 1962 - No. 17, March, 1963
Charlton Comics

12-17	.35	1.00	2.00

CONGO BILL (See Action Comics)
Aug-Sept, 1954 - No. 7, Aug-Sept, 1955
National Periodical Publications

	Good	Fine	VF-NM
1-(Scarce)	25.00	75.00	175.00
2-(Scarce)	23.00	70.00	160.00
3-7 (Scarce), 4-Last precode	19.00	57.00	132.00

NOTE: *(Rarely found in fine or mint condition.)*

CONNECTICUT YANKEE, A (See King Classics)

CONQUEROR, THE (See 4-Color No. 690)

CONQUEROR COMICS
Winter, 1945
Albrecht Publishing Co.

	Good	Fine	N-Mint
nn	5.50	16.50	38.00

CONQUEROR OF THE BARREN EARTH
Feb, 1985 - No. 4, May, 1985 (Mini-series)
DC Comics

1-Back-up series from Warlord		.60	1.20
2-4		.50	1.00

CONQUEST
1953 (6 cents)
Store Comics

1-Richard the Lion Hearted, Beowulf, Swamp Fox			
	1.70	5.00	12.00

CONQUEST
Spring, 1955
Famous Funnies

1-Crandall-a, 1 pg.; contains contents of 1953 issue			
	2.15	6.50	15.00

CONTACT COMICS
July, 1944 - No. 12, May, 1946
Aviation Press

nn-Black Venus, Flamingo, Golden Eagle, Tommy Tomahawk begin			
	12.00	36.00	84.00
2-5: 3-Last Flamingo. 3,4-Black Venus by L. B. Cole. 5-The Phantom Flyer app.	8.50	25.50	60.00
6,11-Kurtzman's Black Venus; 11-Last Golden Eagle, last Tommy Tomahawk; Feldstein-a	11.50	34.00	80.00
7-10,12: 12-Sky Rangers, Air Kids, Ace Diamond app.			
	7.00	21.00	50.00

NOTE: *L. B. Cole a-9; c-1-12. Giunta a-3. Hollingsworth a-5, 7, 10. Palais a-11,12.*

CONTEMPORARY MOTIVATORS
1977 - 1978 (5-3/8x8")(31 pgs., B&W, $1.45)
Pendelum Press

	Good	Fine	N-Mint

14-3002 The Caine Mutiny; 14-3010 Banner in the Sky; 14-3029 God Is My Co-Pilot; 14-3037 Guadalcanal Diary; 14-3045 Hiroshima; 14-3053 Hot Rod; 14-3061 Just Dial a Number; 14-307x Star Wars; 14-3088 The Diary of Anne Frank; 14-3096 Lost Horizon

			1.50

NOTE: *Also see Now Age III. Above may have been dist. the same.*

CONTEST OF CHAMPIONS (See Marvel Superhero. . .)

COO COO COMICS (. . . the Bird Brain No. 57 on)
Oct, 1942 - No. 62, April, 1952
Nedor Publ. Co./Standard (Animated Cartoons)

1-1st app./origin Super Mouse (cloned from Superman)-The first funny animal super hero	8.50	25.50	60.00
2	4.30	13.00	30.00
3-10 (3/44)	2.65	8.00	18.00
11-33: 33-1pg. Ingels-a	1.70	5.00	12.00
34-40,43-46,48-50-Text illos by Frazetta in all	3.00	9.00	21.00
41-Frazetta-a(2)	8.50	25.50	60.00
42,47-Frazetta-a & text illos.	6.00	18.00	42.00
51-62	1.50	4.50	10.00

"COOKIE" (Also see Topsy-Turvy)
April, 1946 - No. 55, Aug-Sept, 1955
Michel Publ./American Comics Group(Regis Publ.)

1	7.00	21.00	50.00
2	3.65	11.00	25.00
3-10	2.30	7.00	16.00
11-20	1.70	5.00	12.00
21-30	1.50	4.50	10.00
31-34,36-55	1.00	3.00	7.00
35-Starlett O'Hara story	1.30	4.00	9.00

COOL CAT (Formerly Black Magic)
V8/6, Mar-Apr, 1962 - V9/2, July-Aug, 1962
Prize Publications

V8#6, nn(V9#1), V9#2	1.15	3.50	8.00

COPPER CANYON (See Fawcett Movie Comics)

COPS (TV)
Aug., 1988 - Present ($1.50-$1.00, color)
DC Comics

1 ($1.50) Based on Hasbro Toys	.25	.75	1.50
2-7 ($1.00)		.50	1.00

CORBEN SPECIAL, A
May, 1984 (One-shot)
Pacific Comics

1-Corben c/a; E.A. Poe Adaptation	.35	1.00	2.00

CORKY & WHITE SHADOW (See 4-Color No. 707)

CORLISS ARCHER (See Meet . . .)

CORPORAL RUSTY DUGAN (See Holyoke One-Shot #2)

CORPSES OF DR. SACOTTI, THE (See Ideal a Classical Comic)

CORSAIR, THE (See A-1 Comics No. 5,7,10)

CORUM: THE BULL AND THE SPEAR (See Chronicles Of Corum)
Jan, 1989 - No. 4, July, 1989 ($1.95, limited series, color)
First Comics

1-4: Adapts Michael Moorcock's novel	.35	1.00	1.95

COSMIC BOOK, THE
Dec, 1986 - Present ($1.95, color)
Ace Comics

1-Wood, Toth-a	.35	1.00	2.00

THE COSMIC BOOK (continued)	Good	Fine	N-Mint
2-B&W	.25	.80	1.60

COSMIC BOY
Dec, 1986 - No. 4, Mar, 1987 (mini-series)
DC Comics

1-Legends tie-in, all issues	.25	.75	1.50
2-4		.50	1.00

COSMIC ODYSSEY
Nov, 1988 - No. 4, Holiday, 1988-'89 (Squarebound, $3.50, color)
DC Comics

1-Superman, Batman, Green Lantern app.	.75	2.25	4.50
2-4	.60	1.75	3.50

COSMO CAT (Also see Wotalife Comics)
July-Aug, 1946 - No. 10, Oct, 1947; 1957; 1959
Fox Publications/Green Publ. Co./Norlen Mag.

1	6.50	19.50	45.00
2	3.50	10.50	24.00
3-Origin	3.50	10.50	24.00
4-10	2.30	7.00	16.00
2-4(1957-Green Publ. Co.)	.85	2.50	6.00
2-4(1959-Norlen Mag.)	.75	2.25	5.00
I.W. Reprint #1	.35	1.00	2.00

COSMO THE MERRY MARTIAN
Sept, 1958 - No. 6, Oct, 1959
Archie Publications (Radio Comics)

1-Bob White-a in all	5.50	16.50	38.00
2-6	3.50	10.50	24.00

COTTON WOODS (See 4-Color No. 837)

COUGAR, THE (Cougar No. 2)
April, 1975 - No. 2, July, 1975
Seaboard Periodicals (Atlas)

1-Adkins-a(p)		.40	.80
2-Origin		.25	.50

COUNTDOWN (See Movie Classics)

COUNT DUCKULA (TV)
Nov., 1988 - Present ($1.00, color)
Marvel Comics

1,2; 2-Dangermouse app.		.50	1.00

COUNT OF MONTE CRISTO, THE (See 4-Color No. 794)

COURAGE COMICS
1945
J. Edward Slavin

1,2,77	3.50	10.50	24.00

COURTSHIP OF EDDIE'S FATHER (TV)
Jan, 1970 - No. 2, May, 1970
Dell Publishing Co.

1,2-Bill Bixby photo-c	1.50	4.50	10.00

COVERED WAGONS, HO (See 4-Color No. 814)

COWBOY ACTION (Western Thrillers No. 1-4; Quick Trigger Western No. 12 on)
No. 5, March, 1955 - No. 11, March, 1956
Atlas Comics (ACI)

5	3.50	10.50	24.00
6-10	2.00	6.00	14.00
11-Williamson-a, 4 pgs., Baker-a	4.00	12.00	28.00

NOTE: *Ayers a-8. Drucker a-6. Heath c-6-8. Maneely c/a-5, 6. Severin c-10. Shores a-7.*

COWBOY COMICS (...Stories No. 14, formerly Star Ranger)
(Star Ranger Funnies No. 15 on)

No. 13, July, 1938 - No. 14, Aug, 1938			
Centaur Publishing Co.	Good	Fine	N-Mint
13-(Rare)-Ace and Deuce, Lyin Lou, Air Patrol, Aces High, Lee Trent, Trouble Hunters begin	44.00	132.00	310.00
14	30.00	90.00	210.00

NOTE: *Gardineer a-13, 14. Gustavson a-13, 14.*

COWBOY IN AFRICA (TV)
March, 1968
Gold Key

1(10219-803)-Chuck Connors photo-c	1.70	5.00	12.00

COWBOY LOVE (Becomes Range Busters?)
7/49 - V2/10, 6/50; No. 11, 1951; No. 28, 2/55 - No. 31, 8/55
Fawcett Publications/Charlton Comics No. 28 on

V1#1-Rocky Lane photo back-c	4.35	13.00	30.00
2	1.70	5.00	12.00
V1#3,4,6 (12/49)	1.50	4.50	10.00
5-Bill Boyd photo back-c (11/49)	2.65	8.00	18.00
V2#7-Williamson/Evans-a	4.00	12.00	28.00
V2#8-11	1.15	3.50	8.00
V1#28 (Charlton)-Last precode (2/55) (Formerly Romantic Story?)	.85	2.50	6.00
V1#29-31 (Charlton; becomes Sweetheart Diary #32 on)	.85	2.50	6.00

NOTE: *Powell a-10. Photo c-1-11 No. 1-3,5-7,9,10, 52 pgs.*

COWBOY ROMANCES (Young Men No. 4 on)
Oct, 1949 - No. 3, Mar, 1950
Marvel Comics (IPC)

1-Photo-c	6.50	19.50	45.00
2-William Holden, Mona Freeman 'Streets of Laredo' photo-c	4.60	14.00	32.00
3	3.70	11.00	26.00

COWBOYS 'N' INJUNS (...'N' Indians No. 6 on)
1946 - No. 5, 1947; No. 6, 1949 - No. 8, 1952
Compix No. 1-5/Magazine Enterprises No. 6 on

1	3.00	9.00	21.00
2-5-All funny animal western	1.70	5.00	12.00
6(A-1 23)-half violent, half funny	2.30	7.00	16.00
7(A-1 41, 1950), 8(A-1 48)-All funny	1.70	5.00	12.00
I.W. Reprint No. 1,7 (reprinted in Canada by Superior, No. 7)	.50	1.50	3.00
Super Reprint #10 (1963)	.50	1.50	3.00

COWBOY WESTERN COMICS (Formerly Jack In The Box; Becomes Space Western No. 40-45 & Wild Bill Hickok & Jingles No. 68 on; title: . . .Heroes No. 47 & 48; Cowboy Western No. 49 on (TV))
No. 17, 7/48 - No. 39, 8/52; No. 46, 10/53; No. 47, 12/53; No. 48 Spr, '54; No. 49, 5-6/54 - No. 67, 3/58 (nn 40-45)
Charlton(Capitol Stories)

17-Jesse James, Annie Oakley, Wild Bill Hickok & Texas Rangers app.	5.00	15.00	35.00
18,19-Orlando c/a	3.50	10.50	24.00
20-25	2.00	6.00	14.00
26-George Montgomery photo-c	3.65	11.00	25.00
27,30-Sunset Carson photo-c	25.00	75.00	175.00
28,29-Sunset Carson app.	8.50	25.50	60.00
31-39,47-50 (no #40-45)	1.50	4.50	10.00
46-(Formerly Space Western)-Space western story	5.00	15.00	35.00
51-57,59-66	1.15	3.50	8.00
58 (68 pgs.)-Wild Bill Hickok & Jingles	1.70	5.00	10.00
67-Williamson/Torres-a, 5 pgs.	5.00	15.00	35.00

NOTE: *Many issues trimmed 1" shorter.*

COWGIRL ROMANCES (Formerly Jeanie)
No. 28, Jan, 1950 (52 pgs.)

Cosmic Odyssey #1, © DC

Cowboys 'n' Injuns #5, © ME

Cowboy Western Comics #27, © CC

Cow Puncher #1, © AVON   Crackajack Funnies #4, © DELL   Crack Comics #9, © QUA

COWGIRL ROMANCES (continued)			
Marvel Comics (CCC)	Good	Fine	N-Mint
28(#1)-Photo-c	7.00	21.00	50.00

COWGIRL ROMANCES
1950 - No. 12, Winter, 1952-53 (No. 1-3, 52 pgs.)
Fiction House Magazines

1-Kamen-a	12.00	36.00	84.00
2	6.00	18.00	42.00
3-5	5.00	15.00	35.00
6-9,11,12	4.00	12.00	28.00
10-Frazetta?/Williamson-a; Kamen/Baker-a	16.00	48.00	110.00

COW PUNCHER (...Comics)
Jan, 1947; No. 2, Sept, 1947 - No. 7, 1949
Avon Periodicals

1-Clint Cortland, Texas Ranger, Kit West, Pioneer Queen begin; Kubert-a; Alabam stories begin	17.00	51.00	120.00
2-Kubert, Kamen/Feldstein-a; Kamen bondage-c			
	14.00	42.00	100.00
3-5,7: 3-Kiefer story	9.00	27.00	63.00
6-Opium drug mention story; bondage, headlight-c; Reinman-a			
	11.00	33.00	76.00

COWPUNCHER
1953 (nn) (Reprints Avon's No. 2)
Realistic Publications

Kubert-a	5.00	15.00	35.00

COWSILLS, THE (See Harvey Pop Comics)

COYOTE
June, 1983 - No. 16, Mar, 1986 (Adults only) ($1.50)
Epic Comics (Marvel)

1-Origin	.25	.75	1.50
2-10,15,16: 2-Origin concludes. 7,9-Ditko-p	.25	.75	1.50
11-14-1st Todd McFarlane-a	.50	1.50	3.00

CRACKAJACK FUNNIES (Giveaway)
1937 (32 pgs.; full size; soft cover; full color)(Before No. 1?)
Malto-Meal

Features Dan Dunn, G-Man, Speed Bolton, Freckles, Buck Jones, Clyde Beatty, The Nebbs, Major Hoople, Wash Tubbs

	40.00	120.00	280.00

CRACKAJACK FUNNIES
June, 1938 - No. 43, Jan, 1942
Dell Publishing Co.

1-Dan Dunn, Freckles, Myra North, Wash Tubbs, Apple Mary, The Nebbs, Don Winslow, Tom Mix, Buck Jones, Major Hoople, Clyde Beatty, Boots begin	71.00	215.00	500.00
2	35.00	105.00	245.00
3	25.00	75.00	175.00
4,5	20.00	60.00	140.00
6-8,10	16.00	48.00	110.00
9-(3/39)-Red Ryder strip-r begin by Harman; 1st app. in comics & 1st cover	22.00	65.00	154.00
11-14	13.50	41.00	95.00
15-Tarzan text feature begins by Burroughs (9/39); not in #26,35			
	15.00	45.00	105.00
16-24	11.00	32.00	75.00
25-The Owl begins; in new costume #26 by Frank Thomas			
	25.00	75.00	175.00
26-30: 28-Owl-c. 29-Ellery Queen begins	19.00	57.00	132.00
31-Owl covers begin	17.00	51.00	120.00
32-Origin Owl Girl	19.00	57.00	132.00
33-38: 36-Last Tarzan ish	13.00	40.00	90.00
39-Andy Panda begins (intro/1st app.)	14.25	43.00	100.00
40-43: 42-Last Owl cover	12.00	36.00	84.00

NOTE: **McWilliams** art in most issues.

CRACK COMICS (...Western No. 63 on)
May, 1940 - No. 62, Sept, 1949
Quality Comics Group

	Good	Fine	N-Mint
1-Origin The Black Condor by Lou Fine, Madame Fatal, Red Torpedo, Rock Bradden & The Space Legion; The Clock, Alias the Spider, Wizard Wells, & Ned Brant begin; Powell-a; Note: Madame Fatal is a man dressed up as a woman	165.00	495.00	1155.00
2	83.00	250.00	585.00
3	60.00	180.00	420.00
4	52.00	156.00	364.00
5-10: 5-Molly The Model begins. 10-Tor, the Magic Master begins	40.00	120.00	280.00
11-20: 18-1st app. Spitfire?	35.00	105.00	245.00
21-24-Last Fine Black Condor	27.00	81.00	190.00
25,26	18.00	54.00	125.00
27-Intro & origin Captain Triumph by Alfred Andriola (Kerry Drake artist)	35.00	105.00	245.00
28-30	15.00	45.00	105.00
31-39: 31-Last Black Condor	9.00	27.00	62.00
40-46	6.00	18.00	42.00
47-57,59,60-Capt. Triumph by Crandall	7.00	21.00	50.00
58,61,62-Last Captain Triumph	5.00	15.00	35.00

NOTE: Black Condor by Fine: No. 1, 2, 4-6, 8, 10-24; by Sultan: No. 3, 7; by Fugitani: No. 9. Crandall c-55, 59, 60. Guardineer a-17. Gustavson a-17. McWilliams art-No. 15-21, 23-27.

CRACKED (Magazine) (Satire)
Feb-Mar, 1958 - Present
Major Magazines

1-One pg. Williamson	5.00	15.00	35.00
2-1st Shut-Ups & Bonus Cut-Outs	2.50	7.50	17.50
3-6	1.15	3.50	8.00
7-10: 7-R/1st 6 covers on-c	.85	2.50	6.00
11-12, 13(nn,3/60), 14-17, 18(nn,2/61), 19,20	.75	2.25	4.50
21-27(11/62), 27(No.28, 2/63; misnumbered), 29(5/63)			
	.45	1.25	2.50
31-60		.60	1.20
61-100: 99-Alfred E. Neuman on-c		.50	1.00
101-245: 234-Don Martin-a		.50	1.00
Biggest...(Winter, 1977)		1.50	3.00
Biggest, Greatest...nn('65)	1.00	3.00	6.00
Biggest, Greatest...2('66) - #12('76)	.25	.75	1.50
...Blockbuster 1,2('88)	.45	1.40	2.75
...Digest 1(Fall, '86, 148p) - #5	.35	1.00	2.00
...Collectors' Edition ('73; formerly ...Special)			
4	.50	1.50	3.00
5-70		.60	1.25
71-80	.45	1.40	2.75
...Party Pack 1,2('88)	.45	1.40	2.75
...Shut-Ups (2/72-'72; Cracked Special #3) 1,2			
	.50	1.50	3.00
...Special 3('73; formerly Cracked Shut-Ups; ...Collectors' Edition #4 on)	.50	1.50	3.00
Extra Special...1('76), 2('76)		.60	1.20
Giant...nn('65)	.85	2.50	5.00
Giant...2('66)-12('76), nn(9/77)-48('87)	.45	1.40	2.75
King Sized...1('67)	1.00	3.00	6.00
King Sized...2('68)-11('77)	.70	2.00	4.00
King Sized...12-22 (Sum/'86)	.35	1.00	2.00
Super...1('68)	1.00	3.00	6.00
Super...2('69)-24('88): 2-Spoof on Beatles movie by Severin			
	.50	1.50	3.00
Super...1('87, 100p)-Severin & Elder-a	.45	1.40	2.75

NOTE: Burgos a-1-10. Davis a-5, 11-17, 24, 40, 80; c-12-14, 16. Elder a-5, 6, 10-13; c-10. Everett a-1-10, 23-25, 61; c-1. Heath a-1-3, 6, 13, 14, 17, 110; c-6. Jaffee a-5, 6. Morrow a-8-10. Reinman a-1-4. Severin a-in most all issues. Shores a-3-7. Torres a-7-10. Ward

103

CRACKED (continued)

a-22-24, 143, 144, 149, 150, 152, 153, 156. *Williamson a-1 (1 pg.). Wolverton a-10 (2 pgs.), Giant a-27, 35, 40.*

CRACK WESTERN (Formerly Crack; Jonesy No. 85 on)
No. 63, Nov, 1949 - No. 84, May, 1953 (36pgs., 63-68,74-on)
Quality Comics Group

	Good	Fine	N-Mint
63(#1)-Two-Gun Lil (origin & 1st app.)(ends #84), Arizona Ames, his horse Thunder (sidekick Spurs & his horse Calico), Frontier Marshal (ends #70), & Dead Canyon Days (ends #69) begin; Crandall-a	8.00	24.00	56.00
64,65-Crandall-a	5.50	16.50	38.00
66,68-Photo-c. 66-Arizona Ames becomes A. Raines (ends #84)	5.50	16.50	38.00
67-Randolph Scott photo-c; Crandall-a	6.50	19.50	45.00
69(52pgs.)-Crandall-a	5.50	16.50	38.00
70(52pgs.)-The Whip (origin & 1st app.) & his horse Diablo begin (ends #84); Crandall-a	5.50	16.50	38.00
71(52pgs.)-Frontier Marshal becomes Bob Allen F. Marshal (ends #84); Crandall-c/a	6.50	19.50	45.00
72(52pgs.)-Tim Holt photo-c	5.50	16.50	38.00
73(52pgs.)-Photo-c	4.00	12.00	28.00
74,77,79,80,82	3.00	9.00	21.00
75,76,78,81,83-Crandall-c	4.00	12.00	28.00
84-Crandall c/a	5.50	16.50	38.00

CRASH COMICS (Catman No. 6 on)
May, 1940 - No. 5, Nov, 1940
Tem Publishing Co.

	Good	Fine	N-Mint
1-The Blue Streak, Strongman (origin), The Perfect Human, Shangra begin; Kirby-a	80.00	240.00	560.00
2-Simon & Kirby-a	40.00	120.00	280.00
3-Simon & Kirby-a	32.00	95.00	225.00
4-Origin & 1st app. The Catman; S&K-a	50.00	150.00	350.00
5-S&K-a	32.00	95.00	225.00

NOTE: *Solar Legion by Kirby No. 1-5 (5 pgs. each).*

CRASH DIVE (See Cinema Comics Herald)

CRASH RYAN
Oct, 1984 - No. 4, Jan, 1985 (Baxter paper, limited series)
Epic Comics (Marvel)

1-4	.25	.75	1.50

CRAZY
Dec, 1953 - No. 7, July, 1954
Atlas Comics (CSI)

1-Everett c/a	6.00	18.00	42.00
2	4.50	13.50	32.00
3-7: 4-I Love Lucy satire. 5-Satire on censorship			
	3.70	11.00	26.00

NOTE: *Ayers a-5. Berg a-1, 2. Burgos c-5, 6. Drucker a-6. Everett a-1-4. Heath a-3, 7; c-7. Maneely a-1-7; c-3, 4. Post a-3-6.*

CRAZY (People Who Buy This Magazine Is. . .) (Formerly This Magazine Is. . .)
V3No.3, Nov, 1957 - V4No.8, Feb, 1959 (Magazine) (Satire)
Charlton Publications

V3#3 - V4#7	.50	1.50	3.00
V4#8-Davis-a, 8 pgs.	1.00	3.00	6.00

CRAZY (Satire)
Feb, 1973 - No. 3, June, 1973
Marvel Comics Group

1-3-Not Brand Echh-r		.30	.60

CRAZY (Magazine) (Satire)
Oct, 1973 - No. 94, Mar, 1983 (40 cents) (Black & White)
Marvel Comics Group

1-Wolverton(1pg.), Ploog, Bode-a; 3 pg. photo story of Adams

	Good	Fine	N-Mint
& Giordano	.35	1.00	2.00
2-Adams-a; Kurtzman's "Hey Look" reprint, 2 pgs.; Buscema-a		.60	1.20
3,5,6,8: 3-Drucker-a		.40	.80
4,7-Ploog-a		.40	.80
9-16-Eisner-a		.40	.80
17-81,83-94: 43-E.C. swipe from Mad 131. 76-Best of. .Super Special		.30	.60
82-Super Special ish; X-Men on-c	.30	.60	1.20
Super Special 1(Summer,'75, 100pgs.)-Ploog, Adams-r			
	.30	.80	1.60

NOTE: *Austin a-82i. Buscema a-82. Byrne c-82p. Cardy c-7,8. Freas c-1,2,4,6; a-7. Rogers a-82.*

CRAZY, MAN, CRAZY (Magazine) (Satire)
June, 1956
Humor Magazines

V2#2-Wolverton-a, 3pgs.	3.50	10.50	24.00

CREATURE, THE (See Movie Classics)

CREATURES ON THE LOOSE (Tower of Shadows No. 1-9)
No. 10, March, 1971 - No. 37, Sept, 1975
Marvel Comics Group

10-First King Kull story; Wrightson-a	1.15	3.50	7.00
11-15: 13-Crandall-a		.50	1.00
16-Origin Warrior of Mars		.50	1.00
17-37: 21,22: Steranko-c; Thongor begins #22, ends #29. 30-Manwolf begins		.50	1.00

NOTE: *Ditko r-15, 17, 18, 20, 22, 24, 27, 28. Everett a-16i(r). Gil Kane a-16p(r); c-16, 20, 25, 29, 33p, 35p, 36p. Morrow a-20. 21. Perez a-33-37; c-34p. Tuska a-32p.*

CREEPER, THE (See Beware. . . & First Issue Special)

CREEPY (Magazine)(See Warren Presents)
1964 - No. 145, Feb, 1983; No. 146, 1985 (B&W)
Warren Publishing Co./Harris Publ. #146

1-Frazetta-a; Jack Davis-c	.85	2.50	5.00
2	.50	1.50	3.00
3-13: 7,10-Frazetta-a	.35	1.00	2.00
14-Adams 1st Warren work	.60	1.75	3.50
15-25	.35	1.00	2.00
26-40: 32-Harlan Ellison story	.25	.75	1.50
41-47,49-54,56-61: 61-Wertham parody		.60	1.20
48,55-(1973, 1974 Annuals)	.35	1.00	2.00
62-64,66-145		.50	1.00
65-(1975 Annual)	.25	.75	1.50
146 ($2.95)			
Year Book 1968, 1969	.50	1.50	3.00
Year Book 1970-Adams, Ditko-a(r)	.50	1.50	3.00
Annual 1971,1972	.35	1.00	2.00

NOTE: *Above books contain many good artists works: Adams, Brunner, Corben, Craig (Taycee), Crandall, Ditko, Evans, Frazetta, Heath, Jeff Jones, Krenkel, McWilliams, Morrow, Nino, Orlando, Ploog, Severin, Torres, Toth, Williamson, Wood, & Wrightson; covers by Crandall, Davis, Frazetta, Morrow, SanJulian, Todd/Bode; Otto Binder's "Adam Link" stories in No. 2, 4, 6, 8, 9, 12, 13, 15 with Orlando art.*

CREEPY THINGS
July, 1975 - No. 6, June, 1976
Charlton Comics

1		.50	1.00
2-6		.40	.80
Modern Comics Reprint 2-6('77)		.25	.50

NOTE: *Ditko a-3,5. Sutton c-3,4.*

CRIME AND JUSTICE (Rookie Cop? No. 27 on)
March, 1951 - No. 26, Sept, 1955
Capitol Stories/Charlton Comics

1-Spanking panel	10.00	30.00	70.00

Crash Comics #1, © HOKE

Crazy #1 (12/53), © MEG

Crack Western #65, © QUA

104

Crime And Justice #20, © CC   Crime Cases #26, © MEG   Crime Does Not Pay #26, © LEV

	Good	Fine	N-Mint
CRIME AND JUSTICE (continued)			
2	2.65	8.00	18.00
3-8,10,13: 6-Negligee panels	2.35	7.00	16.00
9-Classic story "Comics Vs. Crime"	5.50	16.50	38.00
11-Narcotics story	4.00	12.00	28.00
12-Bondage-c	3.50	10.50	24.00
14-Color illos in **POP**; gory story of man who beheads women			
	6.00	18.00	42.00
15-17,19-26	1.70	5.00	12.00
18-Ditko-a	10.00	30.00	70.00

NOTE:*Alascia* c-20. *Ayers* a-17. *Shuster* a-19-21; c-19. Bondage c-11.

CRIME AND PUNISHMENT (Title inspired by 1935 film)
April, 1948 - No. 74, Aug, 1955
Lev Gleason Publications

	Good	Fine	N-Mint
1-Mr. Crime app. on-c	8.00	24.00	56.00
2	3.70	11.00	26.00
3-Used in **SOTI**, pg. 112; injury-to-eye panel; Fuje-a			
	6.00	18.00	42.00
4,5	3.00	9.00	21.00
6-10	2.35	7.00	16.00
11-20	2.00	6.00	14.00
21-30	1.70	5.00	12.00
31-38,40-44	1.50	4.50	10.00
39-Drug mention story "The 5 Dopes"	3.50	10.50	24.00
45-"Hophead Killer" drug story	3.25	9.75	22.00
46-One page Frazetta	2.00	6.00	14.00
47-57,60-65,70-74	1.30	4.00	9.00
58-Used in **POP**, pg. 79	2.85	8.50	20.00
59-Used in **SOTI**, illo-"What comic-book America stands for"			
	11.00	32.00	75.00
66-Toth c/a(4); 3-D effect ish(3/54)	13.00	40.00	90.00
67-"Monkey on His Back"-heroin story; 3-D effect ish.			
	10.00	30.00	70.00
68-3-D effect ish; Toth-c (7/54)	9.00	27.00	62.00
69-"The Hot Rod Gang"-dope crazy kids	4.35	13.00	30.00

NOTE: *Biro* c-most. *Everett* a-31. *Fuje* a-3, 12, 13, 17, 18, 26, 27. *Guardineer* a-2, 3, 10, 14, 17, 18, 26-28, 32, 40-44. *Kinstler* c-69. *McWilliams* a-41, 48, 49. *Tuska* a-28, 30.

CRIME CAN'T WIN (Formerly Cindy Smith)
No. 41, 9/50 - No. 43, 2/51; No. 4, 4/51 - No. 12, 9/53
Marvel/Atlas Comics (TCI 41/CCC 42,43,4-12)

41	5.70	17.00	40.00
42	3.00	9.00	21.00
43-Horror story	3.00	9.00	21.00
4(4/51), 5-9,11,12	2.65	8.00	18.00
10-Possible use in **SOTI**, pg. 161	3.00	9.00	21.00

NOTE: *Robinson* a-9-11. *Tuska* a-43.

CRIME CASES COMICS (Formerly Willie Comics)
No. 24, 8/50 - No. 27, 3/51; No. 5, 5/51 - No. 12, 7/52
Marvel/Atlas Comics(CnPC No.24-8/MJMC No.9-12)

24 (52 pgs.)	3.50	10.50	24.00
25,26	2.30	7.00	16.00
27-Morisi-a	2.30	7.00	16.00
5-12: 11-Robinson-a, 12-Tuska-a	2.00	6.00	14.00

CRIME CLINIC
No. 10, July-Aug, 1951 - No. 5, Summer, 1952
Ziff-Davis Publishing Co.

10-Painted-c; origin Dr. Tom Rogers	8.00	24.00	56.00
11,4,5-Painted-c	5.00	15.00	35.00
3-Used in **SOTI**, pg. 18	6.50	19.50	45.00

NOTE: Painted covers by *Saunders*. *Starr* a-10.

CRIME DETECTIVE COMICS
Mar-Apr, 1948 - V3/8, May-June, 1953
Hillman Periodicals

	Good	Fine	N-Mint
V1#1-The Invisible 6, costumed villains app; Fuje-c			
	5.70	17.00	40.00
2	2.65	8.00	18.00
3,4,7,10-12	2.00	6.00	14.00
5-Krigstein-a	3.00	9.00	21.00
6-McWilliams-a	2.00	6.00	14.00
8-Kirbyish-a by McCann	2.65	8.00	18.00
9-Used in **SOTI**, pg. 16 & "Caricature of the author in a position comic book publishers wish he were in permanently" illo.			
	18.00	54.00	125.00
V2#1,4,7-Krigstein-a	2.65	8.00	18.00
2,3,5,6,8-12 (1-2/52)	1.50	4.50	10.00
V3#1-Drug use-c	2.00	6.00	14.00
2-8	1.30	4.00	9.00

NOTE: *Briefer* a-V3#1. *Kinstlerish* -a by McCann-V2#7, V3#2. *Powell* a-11.

CRIME DETECTOR
Jan, 1954 - No. 5, Sept, 1954
Timor Publications

1	4.50	13.50	32.00
2	2.30	7.00	16.00
3,4	2.00	6.00	14.00
5-Disbrow-a (classic)	6.00	18.00	42.00

CRIME DOES NOT PAY (Formerly Silver Streak No. 1-21)
No. 22, June, 1942 - No. 147, July, 1955 (1st crime comic)
Comic House/Lev Gleason/Golfing (Title inspired by film)

22(23 on cover, 22 on indicia)-Origin The War Eagle & only app.; Chip Gardner begins; No. 22 rebound in True Crime, Complete Book of (Scarce)	75.00	225.00	525.00
23 (Scarce)	42.00	125.00	295.00
24-Intro. & 1st app. Mr. Crime (Scarce)	35.00	105.00	245.00
25-30	19.00	57.00	132.00
31-40	11.50	34.00	80.00
41-Origin & 1st app. Officer Common Sense	7.00	21.00	50.00
42-Electrocution-c	8.00	24.00	56.00
43-46,48-50: 44,45-68 pgs.	5.70	17.00	40.00
47-Electric chair-c	8.00	24.00	56.00
51-62,65-70	3.00	9.00	21.00
63,64-Possible use in **SOTI**, pg. 306. #63-Contains Biro-Gleason's self censorship code of 12 listed restrictions (5/48)			
	3.00	9.00	21.00
71-99: 87-Chip Gardner begins, ends #99	2.00	6.00	14.00
100	2.30	7.00	16.00
101-104,107-110: 102-Chip Gardner app.	1.50	4.50	10.00
105-Used in **POP**, pg. 84	2.65	8.00	18.00
106,114-Frazetta, 1 pg.	2.00	6.00	14.00
111-Used in **POP**, pgs. 80,81 & injury-to-eye story illo			
	2.65	8.00	18.00
112,113,115-130	1.15	3.50	8.00
131-140	1.00	3.00	7.00
141,142-Last pre-code ish; Kubert-a(1)	2.30	7.00	16.00
143,147-Kubert-a, one each	2.30	7.00	16.00
144-146	1.00	3.00	7.00
1(Golfing-1945)	1.30	4.00	9.00
The Best of. . .(1944)-128 pgs.; Series contains 4 rebound issues			
	27.00	81.00	190.00
. . .1945 issue	22.00	65.00	154.00
. . .1946-48 issues	19.00	57.00	132.00
. . .1949-50 issues	13.50	41.00	95.00
. . .1951-53 issues	11.50	34.00	80.00

NOTE: Many issues contain violent covers and stories. Whodunnit by *Guardineer*-39-105, 108-110; Chip Gardner by *Bob Fujitani* (*Fuje*)-88-103; c-103 *Alderman* a-41-43. *Biro* c-1-76, 122, 142. *Fuje* c-89, 91-94, 96, 98, 99, 102. *Kubert* c-143 *Landau* a-118. *Maurer* a-41, 42. *McWilliams* a-91, 93, 95, 100-103. *Palais* a-41-43. *Powell* a-146, 147. *Tuska* a-51, 52, 56, 61, 63, 64, 66, 67. Painted c-87-102. Bondage c-62, 98.

CRIME EXPOSED
June, 1948; Dec, 1950 - No. 14, June, 1952
Marvel Comics (PPI)/Marvel Atlas Comics (PrPI)

	Good	Fine	N-Mint
1(6/48)	7.00	21.00	50.00
1(12/50)	4.30	13.00	30.00
2	2.30	7.00	16.00
3-9,11,14	1.70	5.00	12.00
10-Used in POP, pg. 81	2.00	6.00	14.00
12-Krigstein & Robinson-a	2.00	6.00	14.00
13-Used in POP, pg. 81; Krigstein-a	2.65	8.00	18.00

NOTE: *Maneely c-8. Robinson a-11,12. Tuska a-3, 4.*

CRIMEFIGHTERS
April, 1948 - No. 10, Nov, 1949
Marvel Comics (CmPS 1-3/CCC 4-10)

1-Some copies are undated & could be reprints			
	5.70	17.00	40.00
2	2.30	7.00	16.00
3-Morphine addict story	3.00	9.00	21.00
4-10: 6-Anti-Wertham editorial. 9,10-Photo-c	2.00	6.00	14.00

CRIME FIGHTERS (. . . Always Win)
No. 11, Sept, 1954 - No. 13, Jan, 1955
Atlas Comics (CnPC)

	Good	Fine	N-Mint
11,12: 11-Maneely-a	2.00	6.00	14.00
13-Pakula, Reinman, Severin-a	2.30	7.00	16.00

CRIME FIGHTING DETECTIVE (Shock Detective Cases No. 20 on; formerly Criminals on the Run?)
No. 11, Apr-May, 1950 - No. 19, June, 1952
Star Publications

11-L. B. Cole c/a, 2pgs.	3.00	9.00	21.00
12,13,15-19: 17-Young King Cole & Dr. Doom app.; L. B. Cole-c on all	2.35	7.00	16.00
14-L. B. Cole-c/a, r-Law-Crime No. 2	3.00	9.00	21.00

CRIME FILES
No. 5, Sept, 1952 - No. 6, Nov, 1952
Standard Comics

5-Alex Toth-a; used in SOTI, pg. 4 (text)	8.50	25.50	60.00
6-Sekowsky-a	3.50	10.50	24.00

CRIME ILLUSTRATED (Magazine)
Nov-Dec, 1955 - No. 2, Spring, 1956
E. C. Comics

1-Ingels & Crandall-a	7.00	21.00	50.00
2-Ingels & Crandall-a	5.70	17.00	40.00

NOTE: *Craig a-2. Crandall a-1; c-2. Evans a-1. Davis a-2. Ingels a-1, 2. Krigstein/Crandall a-1. Orlando a-1, c-1.*

CRIME INCORPORATED (Formerly Crimes Incorporated)
No. 2, Aug, 1950; No. 3, Aug, 1951
Fox Features Syndicate

2	6.00	18.00	42.00
3(1951)-Hollingsworth-a	4.00	12.00	28.00

CRIME MACHINE (Magazine)
Feb, 1971 - No. 2, May, 1971 (B&W)
Skywald Publications

1-Kubert-a(2)(r)(Avon)	1.00	3.00	7.00
2-Torres, Wildey-a; violent c/a	.70	2.00	5.00

CRIME MUST LOSE! (Formerly Sports Action?)
No. 4, Oct, 1950 - No. 12, April, 1952
Sports Action (Atlas Comics)

4-Ann Brewster-a in all; c-used in N.Y. Legis. Comm. documents			
	4.00	12.00	28.00
5-10,12	2.00	6.00	14.00
11-Used in POP, pg. 89	2.30	7.00	16.00

NOTE: *Robinson a-9.*

CRIME MUST PAY THE PENALTY (Formerly Four Favorites; Penalty No. 47,48)
No. 33, 2/48; No. 2, 6/48 - No. 48, 1/56
Ace Magazines (Current Books)

	Good	Fine	N-Mint
33(2/48)-Becomes Four Teeners #34?	8.00	24.00	56.00
2(6/48)-Extreme violence; Palais-a?	5.00	15.00	35.00
3-'Frisco Mary' story used in Senate Investigation report, pg. 7			
	2.65	8.00	18.00
4,8-Transvestism story	4.65	14.00	32.00
5-7,9,10	2.00	6.00	14.00
11-20	1.50	4.50	10.00
21-32,34-40,42-48	1.30	4.00	9.00
33(7/53)-"Dell Fabry-Junk King"-drug story; mentioned in Love and Death	3.00	9.00	21.00
41-Drug story-"Dealers in White Death"	3.00	9.00	21.00

NOTE: *Cameron a-30-32,34,39-41. Colan a-20, 31. Kremer a-3, 37r. Palais a-2?, 5?, 37.*

CRIME MUST STOP
October, 1952 (52 pgs.)
Hillman Periodicals

V1#1(Scarce)-Similar to Monster Crime; Mort Lawrence-a			
	25.00	75.00	175.00

CRIME MYSTERIES (Secret Mysteries No. 16 on; combined with Crime Smashers No. 7 on)
May, 1952 - No. 15, Sept, 1954
Ribage Publishing Corp. (Trojan Magazines)

1-Transvestism story	18.00	54.00	125.00
2-Marijuana story (7/52)	13.00	40.00	90.00
3-One pg. Frazetta	8.00	24.00	56.00
4-Cover shows girl in bondage having her blood drained; 1 pg. Frazetta	18.00	54.00	125.00
5-10	7.00	21.00	50.00
11,12,14	5.70	17.00	40.00
13-Angelo Torres 1st comic work; Check-a	8.00	24.00	56.00
15-Acid in face-c	11.50	34.00	80.00

NOTE: *Fass c-4. Hollingsworth a-10-12, 15; c-12, 15. Kiefer a-4. Woodbridge a-13. Bondage-c-1, 8, 12.*

CRIME ON THE RUN (See Approved Comics)
1949
St. John Publishing Co.

8 (Exist?)	3.00	9.00	21.00

CRIME ON THE WATERFRONT (Formerly Famous Gangsters)
No. 4, May, 1952 (Painted cover)
Realistic Publications

4	11.00	33.00	76.00

CRIME PATROL (International #1-5; International Crime Patrol #6, becomes Crypt of Terror #17 on)
No. 7, Summer, 1948 - No. 16, Feb-Mar, 1950
E. C. Comics

7-Intro. Captain Crime	28.00	84.00	195.00
8-14: 12-Ingels-a	25.00	75.00	175.00
15-Intro. of Crypt Keeper & Crypt of Terror; used by N.Y. Legis. Comm.-last pg. Feldstein-a	57.00	170.00	400.00
16-2nd Crypt Keeper app.	47.00	140.00	330.00

NOTE: *Craig c/a in most.*

CRIME PHOTOGRAPHER (See Casey. . .)

CRIME REPORTER
Aug, 1948 - No. 3, Dec, 1948 (Shows Oct.)
St. John Publ. Co.

1-Drug club story	16.00	48.00	110.00
2-Used in SOTI: illo-"Children told me what the man was going to			

Crime Smashers #7, © TM

Crime SuspenStories #6, © WMG

Criminals On The Run V4#7, © NOVP

	Good	Fine	N-Mint
CRIME REPORTER (continued)			
do with the red-hot poker;'' r-/Dynamic #17 with editing;			
Baker-c; Tuska-a	32.00	95.00	225.00
3-Baker-c; Tuska-a	11.50	34.00	80.00

CRIMES BY WOMEN
June, 1948 - No. 15, Aug, 1951; 1954
Fox Features Syndicate

1	38.00	115.00	265.00
2	20.00	60.00	140.00
3-Used in **SOTI**, pg. 234	23.00	70.00	160.00
4,5,7,9,11-15	18.00	54.00	125.00
6-Classic girl fight-c; acid-in-face panel	20.00	60.00	140.00
8-Used in **POP**	19.00	57.00	132.00
10-Used in **SOTI**, pg. 72	19.00	57.00	132.00
54(M.S. Publ.-'54)-Reprint; (formerly My Love Secret)	9.00	27.00	62.00

CRIMES INCORPORATED (Formerly My Past)
No. 12, June, 1950 (Crime Incorporated No. 2 on)
Fox Features Syndicate

12	4.00	12.00	28.00

CRIMES INCORPORATED (See Fox Giants)

CRIME SMASHER
Summer, 1948 (One Shot)
Fawcett Publications

1 (Spy Smasher)	13.00	40.00	90.00

CRIME SMASHERS (Secret Mysteries No. 16 on)
Oct, 1950 - No. 15, Mar, 1953
Ribage Publishing Corp.(Trojan Magazines)

1-Used in **SOTI**, pg. 19,20, & illo-''A girl raped and murdered;''			
Sally the Sleuth begins	27.00	81.00	190.00
2-Kubert-c	13.00	40.00	90.00
3,4	10.00	30.00	70.00
5-Wood-a	16.00	48.00	110.00
6,8-11	8.00	24.00	56.00
7-Female heroin junkie sty	8.50	25.50	60.00
12-Injury to eye panel; 1pg. Frazetta	10.00	30.00	70.00
13-Used in **POP**, pgs. 79,80; 1pg. Frazetta	9.00	27.00	62.00
14,15	7.00	21.00	50.00

NOTE: *Hollingsworth a-14. Kiefer a-15. Bondage c-7,9.*

CRIME SUSPENSTORIES (Formerly Vault of Horror No. 12-14)
No. 15, Oct-Nov, 1950 - No. 27, Feb-Mar, 1955
E. C. Comics

15-Identical to #1 in content; #1 printed on outside front cover. #15 (formerly ''The Vault of Horror'') printed and blackened out on inside front cover with Vol. 1, No. 1 printed over it. Evidently, several of No. 15 were printed before a decision was made not to drop the Vault of Horror and Haunt of Fear series. The print run was stopped on No. 15 and continued on No. 1. All of No. 15 were changed as described above.

	60.00	180.00	420.00
1	50.00	150.00	350.00
2	30.00	90.00	210.00
3-5	21.00	63.00	145.00
6-10	16.00	48.00	110.00
11,12,14,15	11.00	33.00	75.00
13,16-Williamson-a	15.00	45.00	105.00
17-Williamson/Frazetta-a, 6 pgs.	17.00	52.00	120.00
18	8.00	24.00	55.00
19-Used in **SOTI**, pg. 235	10.00	30.00	70.00
20-Cover used in **SOTI**, illo-''Cover of a children's comic book''			
	13.00	90.00	90.00
21,25-27	6.50	19.50	45.00
22,23-Used in Senate investigation on juvenile delinquency. 22-Ax			
decapitation-c	11.00	33.00	76.00
24-'Food For Thought' similar to 'Cave In' in Amaz. Det. #13 ('52)			
	6.50	19.50	45.00

NOTE: *Craig a-1-21; c-1-18,20-22. Crandall a-18-26. Davis a-4, 5, 7, 9-12, 20. Elder a-17, 18. Evans a-15, 19, 21, 23, 25, 27; c-23, 24. Feldstein c-19. Ingels a-1-12, 14, 15, 27. Kamen a-2, 4-18, 20-27; c-25-27. Krigstein a-22, 24, 25, 27. Kurtzman a-1, 3. Orlando a-16, 22, 24, 26. Wood a-1, 3. Issues No. 11-15 have E. C. "quickie" stories. No. 25 contains the famous "Are You a Red Dupe?" editorial.*

CRIMINALS ON THE RUN (Formerly Young King Cole)
(Crime Fighting Detective No. 11 on?)
Aug-Sept, 1947 - No. 10, Dec-Jan, 1949-50
Premium Group (Novelty Press)

	Good	Fine	N-Mint
V4#1-Young King Cole begins	6.50	19.50	45.00
2-6: 6-Dr. Doom app.	5.00	15.00	35.00
7-Classic ''Fish in the Face'' cover by L. B. Cole			
	12.00	36.00	84.00
V5#1,2	5.00	15.00	35.00
10-L. B. Cole-c	5.00	15.00	35.00

NOTE: *Most issues have L. B. Cole covers. McWilliams a-V4#6,7, V5#2; c-V4#5.*

CRIMSON AVENGER, THE (See Detective Comics #20 for 1st app.)
June, 1988 - No. 4, Sept., 1988 ($1.00, color, limited series)
DC Comics

1-4		.50	1.00

CRISIS ON INFINITE EARTHS (See Official . . . Index)
Apr, 1985 - No. 12, Mar, 1986 (12 issue maxi-series)
DC Comics

1-1st DC app. Blue Beetle & Detective Karp from Charlton; Perez-c			
on all	.70	2.00	4.00
2	.50	1.50	3.00
3	.40	1.25	2.50
4-6: 6-Intro Charlton's Capt. Atom, Nightshade, Question, Judomaster, Peacemaker & Thunderbolt	.35	1.00	2.00
7-Double size; death of Supergirl	.40	1.25	2.50
8-Death of Flash	.40	1.25	2.50
9-11: 9-Intro. Charlton's Ghost. 10-Intro. Charlton's Banshee, Dr. Spectro, Image, Punch & Jewellee	.35	1.00	2.00
12-Double size; deaths of Dove, Kole, Lori Lemaris, Sunburst, G.A. Robin & Huntress; Kid Flash becomes new Flash			
	.50	1.50	3.00

CRITTERS (Also see Usagi Yojimbo Summer Special)
1986 - Present ($1.70/$2.00, B&W)
Fantagraphics Books

1-Cutey Bunny, Usagi Yojimbo app.	1.50	4.50	9.00
2	.85	2.50	5.00
3-Usagi Yojimbo app.	.70	2.00	4.00
4-10	.40	1.25	2.50
11-68 pgs. Christmas special	.35	1.00	2.00
12-22,24-33	.35	1.00	2.00
23-With Flexi-disc	.70	2.00	4.00
Special 1 (1/88, $2.00)	.35	1.00	2.00

CROSLEY'S HOUSE OF FUN (Also see Tee and Vee Crosley . . .)
1950 (32 pgs.; full color; paper cover)
Crosley Div. AVCO Mfg. Corp. (Giveaway)

Strips revolve around Crosley appliances	1.70	5.00	10.00

CROSS AND THE SWITCHBLADE, THE
1972 (35-49 cents)
Spire Christian Comics/Fleming H. Revell Co.

1(Some issues have nn)		.40	.80

CROSSFIRE
1973 (39,49cents)
Spire Christian Comics (Fleming H. Revell Co.)

nn		.40	.80

CROSSFIRE
5/84 - No. 17, 3/86; No. 18, 1/87 - No. 26, 2/88 (Baxter paper)
Eclipse Comics

CROSSFIRE (continued)	Good	Fine	N-Mint
1-DNAgents x-over; Spiegle c/a begins	.30	.90	1.80
2-17: 12,13-Death of Marilyn Monroe; 12-Stevens-c	.25	.75	1.50
18-26 (B&W)	.30	.90	1.80

CROSSFIRE AND RAINBOW
June, 1986 - No. 4, Sept, 1986 (mini-series)
Eclipse Comics

	Good	Fine	N-Mint
1-3: Spiegle-a	.65		1.30
4-Dave Stevens-c	.35	1.00	2.00

CROSSING THE ROCKIES (See Classics Special)

CROSSROADS
July, 1988 - No. 5, Nov., 1988 ($3.25, color, deluxe)
First Comics

1-5	.55	1.60	3.25

CROWN COMICS
Winter, 1944-45 - No. 19, July, 1949
Golfing/McCombs Publ.

1-"The Oblong Box"-Poe adaptation	14.30	43.00	100.00
2,3-Baker-a	9.00	27.00	62.00
4-6-Baker c/a; Voodah app. #4,5	9.00	27.00	62.00
7-Feldstein, Baker, Kamen-a; Baker-c	7.00	21.00	50.00
8-Baker-a; Voodah app.	7.00	21.00	50.00
9-11,13-19: Voodah in #10-19	4.00	12.00	28.00
12-Feldstein?, Starr-a	5.00	15.00	35.00

NOTE: *Bolle* a-11, 13-16, 18, 19; c-11p, 15. *Powell* a-19. *Starr* a-11-13; c-11i

CRUSADER FROM MARS (See Tops in Adventure)
Jan-Mar, 1952 - No. 2, Fall, 1952
Ziff-Davis Publ. Co.

1	27.00	81.00	190.00
2-Bondage-c	22.00	65.00	154.00

CRUSADER RABBIT (See 4-Color No. 735,805)

CRUSADERS, THE
1974 - Vol. 16, 1985 (36 pg.) (39-69 cents) (Religious)
Chick Publications

Vol. 1-Operation Bucharest('74). Vol. 2-The Broken Cross('74). Vol.
3-Scarface('74). Vol. 4-Exorcists('75). Vol. 5-Chaos('75).

each. . . .		.40	.80

Vol. 6-Primal Man?('76)-(Disputes evolution theory). Vol. 7-The Ark-(Claims proof of existence, destroyed by Bolsheviks). Vol. 8-The Gift-(Life story of Christ). Vol. 9-Angel of Light-(Story of the Devil). Vol. 10-Spellbound?-(Tells how rock music is Satanical & produced by witches). 11-Sabotage?. 12-Alberto. 13-Double-Cross 14-The Godfathers. (No. 6-14 low in distribution; Loaded in religious propaganda.). 15-The Force. 16-The Four Horsemen

		.40	.80

CRUSADERS (Southern Knights No. 2 on)
1982 (Magazine size, B&W)
Guild Publs.

1-1st app. Southern Knights	3.65	11.00	25.00

CRYIN' LION, THE
Fall, 1944 - No. 3, Spring, 1945
William H. Wise Co.

1-Funny animal	5.00	15.00	35.00
2,3	3.00	9.00	21.00

CRYPT OF SHADOWS
Jan, 1973 - No. 21, Nov, 1975
Marvel Comics Group

1-Wolverton-a r-/Advs. Into Terror No. 7		.30	.60
2-21		.25	.50

NOTE: *Briefer* a-2r. *Ditko* a-13r; 18-20r. *Everett* a-6, 14r; c-2i. *Heath* a-1r. *Mort*

Lawrence a-1r. *Maneely* a-2r. *Moldoff* a-8. *Powell* a-12r; 14r.

CRYPT OF TERROR (Tales From the Crypt No. 20 on; formerly
Crime Patrol)
No. 17, Apr-May, 1950 - No. 19, Aug-Sept, 1950
E. C. Comics

	Good	Fine	N-Mint
17	70.00	210.00	490.00
18,19	52.00	156.00	365.00

NOTE: *Craig* c/a-17-19. *Feldstein* a-17-19. *Ingels* a-19. *Kurtzman* a-18. *Wood* a-18.
Canadian reprints known; see Table of Contents.

CUPID
Jan, 1950 - No. 2, Mar, 1950
Marvel Comics (U.S.A.)

1-Photo-c	4.00	12.00	28.00
2-Betty Page photo-c (see My Love #4, Miss Amer. #4)			

CURIO
1930's(?) (Tabloid size, 16-20 pages)
Harry 'A' Chesler

	6.00	18.00	42.00
	5.50	16.50	38.00

CURLY KAYOE COMICS
1946 - 1948; 1948 - 1950; Jan, 1958
United Features Syndicate/Dell Publ. Co.

1 (1946)	5.70	17.00	40.00
2	2.85	8.50	20.00
3-8	2.00	6.00	14.00
United Presents. . .(Fall, 1948)	2.00	6.00	14.00
4-Color 871 (Dell, 1/58)	1.70	5.00	12.00

CUSTER'S LAST FIGHT
1950
Avon Periodicals

nn-Partial reprint of Cowpuncher #1	8.50	25.50	60.00

CUTEY BUNNY (See Army Surplus)
1984? - Present (B&W)
Eclipse Comics

5	.50	1.50	3.00
6,7	.40	1.25	2.50

CUTIE PIE
May, 1955 - No. 5, Aug, 1956
Junior Reader's Guild (Lev Gleason)

1	2.00	6.00	14.00
2-5	1.15	3.50	8.00

CYCLONE COMICS
June, 1940 - No. 5, Nov, 1940
Bilbara Publishing Co.

1-Origin Tornado Tom; Volton begins, Mister Q app.	40.00	120.00	280.00
2	20.00	60.00	140.00
3-5: 4,5-Mr. Q app.	16.00	48.00	110.00

CYNTHIA DOYLE, NURSE IN LOVE (Formerly Sweetheart Diary)
No. 66, Oct, 1962 - No. 74, Feb, 1964
Charlton Publications

66-74 (#74, exist?)	.35	1.00	2.00

DAFFY (. . .Duck No. 18 on)(See Looney Tunes)
No. 457, 3/53 - No. 30, 7-9/62; No. 31, 10-12/62 - No. 145, 1983
(no No. 132,133)
Dell Publishing Co./Gold Key No. 31-127/Whitman No. 128 on

4-Color 457-Elmer Fudd x-overs begin	1.70	5.00	12.00
4-Color 536,615('55)	1.30	4.00	9.00
4(1-3/56)-11('57)	1.00	3.00	7.00
12-19(1958-59)	.85	2.50	6.00
20-40(1960-64)	.70	2.00	4.00

Crusaders #1, © Comics Interview

Custer's Last Fight, © AVON

Daffy #16, © Warner Bros.

Dagar, Desert Hawk #23, © FOX

Daisy Comics, © EAS

Daktari #3, © Ivan Tors Films

	Good	Fine	N-Mint
DAFFY (continued)			
41-60(1964-68)	.35	1.00	2.00
61-90(1969-73)-Road Runner in most	.60		1.20
91-131,134-145(1974-83)	.40		.80
Mini-Comic 1 (1976; 3¼x6½'')	.25		.50

NOTE: Reprint issues-No.41-46, 48, 50, 53-55, 58, 59, 65, 67, 69, 73, 81, 96, 103-08; 136-142, 144, 145(½-⅔-r). (See March of Comics No. 277, 288, 313, 331, 347, 357, 375, 387, 397, 402, 413, 425, 437, 460).

DAFFYDILS
1911 (52 pgs.; 6x8''; B&W; hardcover)
Cupples & Leon Co.

by Tad	8.00	24.00	56.00

DAFFY TUNES COMICS
June, 1947 - No. 2, Aug, 1947
Four Star Publications

nn	3.00	9.00	21.00
2-Al Fago c/a	2.65	8.00	18.00

DAGAR, DESERT HAWK (Capt. Kidd No. 24-on; formerly All Great)
No. 14, Feb, 1948 - No. 23, Apr, 1949 (No No.17,18)
Fox Features Syndicate

14-Tangi & Safari Cary begin; Edmond Good bondage-c/a			
	24.00	72.00	168.00
15,16-E. Good-a; 15-Bondage-c	14.00	42.00	100.00
19,20,22	12.00	36.00	84.00
21-'Bombs & Bums Away' panel in 'Flood of Death' story used in			
SOTI	15.00	45.00	105.00
23-Bondage-c	14.00	42.00	100.00

NOTE: Tangi by Kamen-14-16,19; c-21.

DAGAR THE INVINCIBLE (Tales of Sword & Sorcery. . .) (Also see
Dan Curtis & Gold Key Spotlight)
10/72 - No. 18, 12/76; No. 19, 4/82
Gold Key

1-Origin; intro. Villains Olstellon & Scorpio	1.00	3.00	6.00
2-5: 3-Intro. Graylin, Dagar's woman; Jarn x-over			
	.50	1.50	3.00
6-1st Dark Gods story	.35	1.00	2.00
7-10: 9-Intro. Torgus. 10-1st Three Witches story			
	.35	1.00	2.00
11-18: 13-Durak & Torgus x-over; story continues in Dr. Spektor			
No. 15. 14-Dagar's origin retold. 18-Origin retold	.60		1.20
19-Origin-r/#18	.40		.80

NOTE: Durak app.-7,12,13. Tragg app.-5,11.

DAGWOOD (Chic Young's) (Also see Blondie)
Sept, 1950 - No. 140, Nov, 1965
Harvey Publications

1	7.00	21.00	50.00
2	3.50	10.50	25.00
3-10	3.00	9.00	21.00
11-30	1.70	5.00	12.00
31-70	1.00	3.00	6.00
71-100	.85	2.50	5.00
101-128,130,135	.70	2.00	4.00
129,131-134,136-140-All are 68-pg. issues	1.00	3.00	6.00

NOTE: Popeye and other one page strips appeared in early issues.

DAGWOOD SPLITS THE ATOM (Also see Topix V8No.4)
1949 (Science comic with King Features characters) (Giveaway)
King Features Syndicate

nn-½ comic, ½ text; Popeye, Olive Oyl, Henry, Mandrake, Little			
King, Katzenjammer Kids app.	3.00	9.00	21.00

DAI KAMIKAZE!
June, 1987 - Present ($1.75, color)
Now Comics

	Good	Fine	N-Mint
1-1st app. Speed Racer	.50	1.50	3.00
1-2nd print	.25	.70	1.40
2-12	.25	.75	1.50

DAISY AND DONALD (See Walt Disney Showcase No. 8)
May, 1973 - No. 59, 1984 (no No. 48)
Gold Key/Whitman No. 42 on

1-Barks r-/WDC&S 280,308	.50	1.50	3.00
2-5: 4-Barks r-/WDC&S 224	.35	1.00	2.00
6-10	.25	.75	1.50
11-20		.50	1.00
21-47,49,50: 32-r/WDC&S 308. 50-r/No. 3		.40	.80
51-Barks r-/4-Color 1150		.50	1.00
52-59: 52-r/No. 2. 55-r/No. 5		.35	.70

DAISY & HER PUPS (Blondie's Dogs)
No. 21, 7/51 - No. 27, 7/52; No. 8, 9/52 - No. 25, 7/55
Harvey Publications

21-27: 26,27 have No. 6 & 7 on cover but No. 26 & 27 on inside			
	1.00	3.00	6.00
8-25: 19-25-Exist?	.85	2.50	5.00

DAISY COMICS
Dec, 1936 (Small size: 5¼x7½'')
Eastern Color Printing Co.

Joe Palooka, Buck Rogers (2 pgs. from Famous Funnies No. 18),			
Napoleon Flying to Fame, Butty & Fally	16.00	48.00	110.00

DAISY DUCK & UNCLE SCROOGE PICNIC TIME (See Dell Giant No.33)

DAISY DUCK & UNCLE SCROOGE SHOW BOAT (See Dell Giant No.55)

DAISY DUCK'S DIARY (See 4-Color No. 600,659,743,858,948,1055,1150,1247 & WDC&S (#298))

DAISY HANDBOOK
1946 - 1948 (132 pgs.)(10 cents)(Pocket-size)
Daisy Manufacturing Co.

1-Buck Rogers, Red Ryder	14.00	42.00	100.00
2-Captain Marvel & Ibis the Invincible, Red Ryder, Boy Comman-			
dos & Robotman; 2 pgs. Wolverton-a; contains 8pg. color catalog			
	14.00	42.00	100.00

DAISY LOW OF THE GIRL SCOUTS
1954, 1965 (16 pgs.; paper cover)
Girl Scouts of America

1954-Story of Juliette Gordon Low	2.15	6.50	15.00
1965	.70	2.00	4.00

DAISY MAE (See Oxydol-Dreft)

DAISY'S RED RYDER GUN BOOK
1955 (132 pages)(25 cents)(Pocket-size)
Daisy Manufacturing Co.

Boy Commandos, Red Ryder, 1 pg. Wolverton-a			
	10.00	30.00	70.00

DAKOTA LIL (See Fawcett Movie Comics)

DAKOTA NORTH
1986 - No. 5, Feb, 1987
Marvel Comics Group

1-5		.40	.80

DAKTARI (Ivan Tors) (TV)
7/67 - No. 3, 10/68; No. 4, 9/69 (Photo-c)
Dell Publishing Co.

1	1.50	4.50	10.00
2-4	1.00	3.00	7.00

DALE EVANS COMICS (Also see Queen of the West. . .)
Sept-Oct, 1948 - No. 24, July-Aug, 1952 (No. 1-19, 52 pgs.)

DALE EVANS COMICS (continued)
National Periodical Publications

	Good	Fine	N-Mint
1-Dale Evans & her horse Buttermilk begin; Sierra Smith begins by Alex Toth	20.00	60.00	140.00
2-Alex Toth-a	13.00	40.00	90.00
3-11-Alex Toth-a	11.00	32.00	75.00
12-24	5.50	16.50	38.00

NOTE: Photo-c-1, 2, 4-14.

DALGODA
Aug, 1984 - No. 8, Feb, 1986
Fantagraphics Books

1-Full color, high quality paper ($2.25 cover price). Fujitake a/c	.60	1.75	3.50
2-8-($1.50 cover price). 2,3-Debut Grimwood's Daughter	.35	1.00	2.00

DALTON BOYS, THE
1951
Avon Periodicals

1-(No. on spine)-Kinstler-c	8.50	25.50	60.00

DAN CURTIS GIVEAWAYS
1974 (24 pages) (3x6'') (in color, all reprints)
Western Publishing Co.

1-Dark Shadows, 2-Star Trek, 3-The Twilight Zone, 4-Ripley's Believe It or Not!, 5-Turok, Son of Stone, 6-Star Trek, 7-The Occult Files of Dr. Spektor, 8-Dagar the Invincible, 9-Grimm's Ghost Stories

Set...	.50	1.50	3.00

DANDEE
1947
Four Star Publications

	2.65	8.00	18.00

DAN DUNN (See Crackajack Funnies, Detective Dan & Red Ryder)

DANDY COMICS (Also see Happy Jack Howard)
Spring, 1947 - No. 7, Spring, 1948
E. C. Comics

1-Vince Fago-a in all	15.00	45.00	105.00
2	11.00	33.00	76.00
3-7	9.00	27.00	62.00

DANGER
January, 1953 - No. 11, Aug, 1954
Comic Media/Allen Hardy Assoc.

1-Heck-c/a	4.30	13.00	30.00
2,3,5-7,9-11	1.85	5.50	13.00
4-Marijuana cover/story	5.00	15.00	35.00
8-Bondage/torture/headlights panels	5.50	16.50	38.00

NOTE: Morisi a-2,5,8(3); c-2. Contains some-r from Danger & Dynamite.

DANGER (Jim Bowie No. 15 on; formerly Comic Media title)
No. 12, June, 1955 - No. 14, Oct, 1955
Charlton Comics Group

12(#1)	3.50	10.50	24.00
13,14: 14 r-/#12	1.85	5.50	13.00

DANGER
1964
Super Comics

Super Reprint #10-12 (Black Dwarf; #11-r/from Johnny Danger), #15,16 (Yankee Girl & Johnny Rebel), #17 (Capt. Courage & Enchanted Dagger), #18(nd) (Gun-Master, Annie Oakley, The Chameleon; L.B. Cole-a)

	.70	2.00	4.00

DANGER AND ADVENTURE (Formerly This Magazine Is Haunted; Robin Hood and His Merry Men No. 28 on)
No. 22, Feb, 1955 - No. 27, Feb, 1956
Charlton Comics

22-Ibis the Invincible, Nyoka app.	3.50	10.50	24.00

	Good	Fine	N-Mint
23-Nyoka, Lance O'Casey app.	3.50	10.50	24.00
24-27: 24-Mike Danger & Johnny Adventure begin	2.30	7.00	16.00

DANGER IS OUR BUSINESS!
1953(Dec.) - No. 10, June, 1955
Toby Press

1-Captain Comet by Williamson/Frazetta-a, 6 pgs. (Science Fiction)	25.00	75.00	175.00
2	3.15	9.50	22.00
3-10	2.65	8.00	18.00
I.W. Reprint #9('64)-Williamson/Frazetta-a r-/#1; Kinstler-c	7.00	21.00	40.00

DANGER IS THEIR BUSINESS (See A-1 Comics No. 50)

DANGER MAN (See 4-Color No. 1231)

DANGER TRAIL
July-Aug, 1950 - No. 5, Mar-Apr, 1951 (52 pgs.)
National Periodical Publications

1-King Farrady begins, ends #4; Toth-a	30.00	90.00	210.00
2-Toth-a	25.00	75.00	175.00
3-5-Toth-a in all; Johnny Peril app. #5	22.00	65.00	154.00

DANIEL BOONE (See The Exploits of..., 4-Color No. 1163, The Legends of..., Frontier Scout..., Fighting..., & March of Comics No. 306)

DAN'L BOONE
Sept, 1955 - No. 8, Sept, 1957
Magazine Enterprises/Sussex Publ. Co. No. 2 on

1	3.50	10.50	24.00
2	2.00	6.00	14.00
3-8	1.50	4.50	10.00

DANIEL BOONE (TV) (See March of Comics No. 306)
Jan, 1965 - No. 15, Apr, 1969
Gold Key

1	1.50	4.50	10.00
2-5	.85	2.50	5.00
6-15: 6-Photo-c	.70	2.00	4.00

DANNY BLAZE (Nature Boy No. 3 on)
Aug, 1955 - No. 2, Oct, 1955
Charlton Comics

1,2	2.65	8.00	18.00

DANNY DINGLE (See Single Series #17 & Sparkler Comics)

DANNY KAYE'S BAND FUN BOOK
1959
H & A Selmer (Giveaway)

	2.00	6.00	14.00

DANNY THOMAS SHOW, THE (See 4-Color No. 1180,1249)

DARBY O'GILL & THE LITTLE PEOPLE (See 4-Color No. 1024 & Movie Comics)

DAREDEVIL (...& the Black Widow #92-107; see Marvel Advs., Marvel Super Heroes, '66 & Spider-Man)
April, 1964 - Present
Marvel Comics Group

1-Origin Daredevil; r-/in Marvel Super Heroes #1, 1966. Death of Battling Murdock; intro Foggy Nelson & Karen Page	50.00	125.00	350.00
2-Fantastic Four cameo	21.00	54.00	150.00
3-Origin, 1st app. The Owl	13.00	32.00	90.00
4,5: 5-Wood-a begins	8.00	20.00	55.00
6,7,9,10: 7-dons new costume	5.70	14.00	40.00
8-Origin & 1st app. Stilt-Man	5.70	14.00	40.00
11-15: 12-Romita's 1st work at Marvel. 13-Facts about Ka-Zar's			

Dandy Comics #1, © WMG

Danger Trail #1, © DC

Daredevil #1, © MEG

Daredevil #196, © MEG   Daredevil Battles Hitler #1, © LEV   Daredevil Comics #31, © LEV

DAREDEVIL (continued)	Good	Fine	N-Mint
origin; Kirby-a	3.65	11.00	25.00
16-20: 16,17-Spider-Man x-over. 18-Origin & 1st app. Gladiator			
	2.15	6.50	15.00
21-30	1.70	5.00	12.00
31-40	1.50	4.50	10.00
41-49: 41-Death Mike Murdock. 43-vs. Capt. America			
	1.15	3.50	7.00
50-52-Smith-a	1.35	4.00	8.00
53-Origin retold	1.15	3.50	7.00
54-56,58-60	.70	2.00	4.00
57-Reveals i.d. to Karen Page	.85	2.50	5.00
61-99: 62-1st app. Nighthawk. 81-Oversize issue; Black Widow			
begins	.50	1.50	3.00
100-Origin retold	1.35	4.00	8.00
101-106,108,115,115-120	.35	1.00	2.00
107-Starlin-c	.40	1.25	2.50
114-1st app. Deathstalker	.40	1.25	2.50
121-130,132-137: 124-1st app. Copperhead; Black Widow leaves.			
126-1st New Torpedo	.25	.75	1.50
131-Origin & 1st app. Bullseye	1.00	3.00	6.00
138-Byrne-a	.50	1.50	3.00
139-150: 142-Nova cameo. 148-30 & 35 cent issues exist. 150-1st app.			
Paladin	.25	.75	1.50
151-Reveals i.d. to Heather Glenn	.25	.75	1.50
152-157	.25	.75	1.50
158-Frank Miller art begins (5/79); origin & death of Deathstalker			
	5.50	16.50	33.00
159	2.00	6.00	12.00
160,161	1.50	4.50	9.00
162	.35	1.00	2.00
163,164: 163-Hulk cameo. 164-Origin	1.35	4.00	8.00
165-167,170	1.00	3.00	6.00
168-Intro/origin Elektra	2.65	8.00	16.00
169-Elektra app.	1.35	4.00	8.00
171-175: 174,175-Elektra app.	.70	2.00	4.00
176-180-Elektra app. 179-Anti-smoking issue mentioned in the			
Congressional Record	.50	1.50	3.00
181-Double size; death of Elektra	.60	1.75	3.50
182-184-Punisher app. by Miller	1.00	3.00	6.00
185-189: 187-New Black Widow. 189-Death of Stick			
	.25	.75	1.50
190-Double size; Elektra returns, part origin	.25	.75	1.50
191-Last Miller Daredevil	.25	.75	1.50
192-195,197-210: 208-Harlan Ellison scripts	.60	1.20	
196-Wolverine app.	.85	2.50	5.00
211-225	.50	1.00	
226-Frank Miller plots begin	.25	.75	1.50
227-Miller scripts begin	.70	2.00	4.00
228-233-Last Miller script	.35	1.00	2.00
234-248,250,251,253-256,258	.50	1.00	
249-Wolverine app.	.40	1.25	2.50
252-Double size, 52 pgs.	.40	1.25	2.50
257-Punisher app.	.50	1.50	3.00
259-Double size	.35	1.00	2.00
260-265	.50	1.00	
Giant Size 1 ('75)	.50	1.50	3.00
Special 1(9/67)-new art	.70	2.00	4.00
Special 2(2/71)(Wood-r), 3(1/72)-r	.50	1.50	3.00
Annual 4(10/76)	.50	1.50	3.00

NOTE: Art Adams c-238p, 239. Austin a-191i; c-151i, 200i. John Buscema a-136, 137p, 234p, 235p; c-86p, 136i, 137p, 142, 219. Byrne c-200p, 201, 203, 223. Colan a(p)c-20-49, 53-82, 84-98, 100, 110, 112, 124, 153, 154, 156, 157, Spec. 1c; c(p)-20-42, 44-49, 63-60, 71, 92, 98, 138, 153, 154, 156, 157, Annual 1. Craig a-50i, 52i. Ditko a-162, 234p, 235p; c-162. Everett a/c-1; inks-21, 83. Gil Kane a-141p, 146-48p, 151p; c(p)-85, 90, 91, 93, 94, 115, 116, 119, 120, 125-28, 133, 139, 147, 152. Kirby c-2-4, 5p, 12p, 13p, 136p. Layton a-202. Miller script-168-182, 183(part), 184-191; a-158-161p, 163-184p, 191p; c-158-161p, 163-184p, 185-189, 190p, 191. Orlando a-2-4p. Powell a-9p,

11p, Special 1r, 2r. B. Smith a-83p, 236p. Smith c-51p, 52p. Simonson c-199. Starlin a-105p. Steranko c-44i. Tuska a-39i, 145p. Williamson a-237i, 239i, 240i, 243i, 248-257i, 259i-262i; c-237i, 243i, 244i, 248-257i, 259-262i. Wood a-5-9i, 10, 11i, Spec. 2i; c-5i, 6-11, 164i.

DAREDEVIL COMICS (See Silver Streak)	Good	Fine	N-Mint
July, 1941 - No. 134, Sept, 1956 (Charles Biro stories)			
Lev Gleason Publications (Funnies, Inc. No. 1)			

(No. 1 titled "Daredevil Battles Hitler")

	Good	Fine	N-Mint
1-The Silver Streak, Lance Hale, Cloud Curtis, Dickey Dean, Pirate Prince team up with Daredevil and battle Hitler; Daredevil battles the Claw; Origin of Hitler feature story. Hitler photo app. on-c			
	230.00	690.00	1610.00
2-London, Pat Patriot, Nightro, Real American No. 1, Dickie Dean, Pirate Prince, & Times Square begin; intro. & only app. The Pioneer, Champion of America	130.00	390.00	910.00
3-Origin of 13	73.00	220.00	510.00
4	60.00	180.00	420.00
5-Intro. Sniffer & Jinx; Ghost vs. Claw begins by Bob Wood, ends #20	55.00	165.00	385.00
6-(#7 on indicia)	45.00	125.00	315.00
7-10: 8-Nightro ends	40.00	120.00	280.00
11-London, Pat Patriot end; bondage/torture-c			
	35.00	105.00	245.00
12-Origin of The Claw; Scoop Scuttle by Wolverton begins (2-4 pgs.), ends #22, not in #21	50.00	150.00	350.00
13-Intro. of Little Wise Guys	50.00	150.00	350.00
14	26.00	78.00	180.00
15-Death of Meatball	40.00	120.00	280.00
16,17	24.00	72.00	168.00
18-New origin of Daredevil-Not same as Silver Streak #6			
	50.00	150.00	350.00
19,20	22.00	65.00	154.00
21-Reprints cover of Silver Streak #6(on inside) plus intro. of The Claw from Silver Streak #1	30.00	90.00	210.00
22-30	13.00	40.00	90.00
31-Death of The Claw	20.00	60.00	140.00
32-37: 34-Two Daredevil stories begin, end #68			
	8.50	25.50	60.00
38-Origin Daredevil retold from #18	17.00	51.00	120.00
39,40	8.50	25.50	60.00
41-50: 42-Intro. Kilroy in Daredevil	5.50	16.50	38.00
51-69-Last Daredevil ish.	3.70	11.00	26.00
70-Little Wise Guys take over book; McWilliams-a; Hot Rock Flanagan begins, ends #80	2.65	8.00	18.00
71-79,81: 79-Daredevil returns	2.00	6.00	14.00
80-Daredevil x-over	2.00	6.00	14.00
82,90-One page Frazetta ad in both	2.30	7.00	16.00
83-89,91-99,101-134	1.70	5.00	12.00
100	2.65	8.00	18.00

NOTE: Wolverton's Scoop Scuttle-12-20, 22. Biro c/a-all?. Bolle a-125. Maurer a-75. McWilliams a-73, 75, 79, 80.

DARING ADVENTURES (Also see Approved Comics)			
Nov, 1953 (3-D)			
St. John Publishing Co.			
1 (3-D)-Reprints lead story/Son of Sinbad #1 by Kubert			
	18.00	54.00	125.00

DARING ADVENTURES			
1963 - 1964			
I.W. Enterprises/Super Comics			
I.W. Reprint #9-Disbrow-a(3)	2.00	6.00	14.00
Super Reprint #10,11('63)-r/Dynamic #24,16; 11-Marijuana story; Yankee Boy app.	1.00	3.00	7.00
Super Reprint #12('64)-Phantom Lady from Fox(r/#14,15)			
	7.00	21.00	50.00
Super Reprint #15('64)-Hooded Menace	5.00	15.00	35.00

111

DARING ADVENTURES (continued)	Good	Fine	N-Mint
Super Reprint #16('64)-r/Dynamic #12	1.00	3.00	6.00
Super Reprint #17('64)-Green Lama by Raboy from Green Lama			
#3	2.00	6.00	14.00
Super Reprint #18-Origin Atlas	1.00	3.00	6.00

DARING COMICS (Formerly Daring Mystery) (Jeanie No. 13 on)
No. 9, Fall, 1944 - No. 12, Fall, 1945
Timely Comics (HPC)

9-Human Torch & Sub-Mariner begin	32.00	95.00	225.00
10-The Angel only app.	29.00	85.00	200.00
11,12-The Destroyer app.	29.00	85.00	200.00

DARING CONFESSIONS (Formerly Youthful Hearts)
No. 4, 11/52 - No. 7, 5/53; No. 8, 10/53
Youthful Magazines

4-Doug Wildey-a	3.70	11.00	26.00
5-8: 6,8-Wildey-a	2.65	8.00	18.00

DARING LOVE (Radiant Love No. 2 on)
Sept-Oct, 1953
Gillmor Magazines

1	3.00	9.00	21.00

DARING LOVE (Formerly Youthful Romances)
No. 15, 12/52 - No. 16, 2/53-c, 4/53-Indicia; No. 17-4/53-c & indicia
Ribage/Pix

15	3.00	9.00	21.00
16,17: 17-Photo-c	2.30	7.00	16.00

NOTE: *Colletta a-15. Wildey a-17.*

DARING LOVE STORIES (See Fox Giants)

DARING MYSTERY COMICS (Comedy No. 9 on; title changed to
Daring with No. 9)
Jan, 1940 - No. 8, Jan, 1942
Timely Comics (TPI 1-6/TCI 7,8)

1-Origin The Fiery Mask by Joe Simon; Monako, Prince of Magic, John Steele, Soldier of Fortune, Doc Doyle begin; Flash Foster & Barney Mullen, Sea Rover only app; bondage-c			
	428.00	1285.00	3000.00
2-(Rare)-Origin The Phantom Bullet & only app.; The Laughing Mask & Mr. E only app.; Trojak the Tiger Man begins, ends #6; Zephyr Jones & K-4 & His Sky Devils app., also #4			
	205.00	615.00	1435.00
3-The Phantom Reporter, Dale of FBI, Breeze Barton, Captain Strong & Marvex the Super-Robot only app.; The Purple Mask begins	147.00	440.00	1030.00
4-Last Purple Mask; Whirlwind Carter begins; Dan Gorman, G-Man app.	105.00	315.00	735.00
5-The Falcon begins; The Fiery Mask, Little Hercules app. by Sagendorf in the Segar style; bondage-c	100.00	300.00	700.00
6-Origin & only app. Marvel Boy by S&K; Flying Flame, Dynaman, & Stuporman only app.; The Fiery Mask by S&K; S&K-c	125.00	375.00	875.00
7-Origin The Blue Diamond, Captain Daring by S&K, The Fin by Everett, The Challenger, The Silver Scorpion & The Thunderer by Burgos; Mr. Millions app.	125.00	375.00	875.00
8-Origin Citizen V; Last Fin, Silver Scorpion, Capt. Daring by Borth, Blue Diamond & The Thunderer; S&K-c; Rudy the Robot only app.	95.00	285.00	665.00

NOTE: *Schomburg c-1-4. Simon a-2,3,5.*

DARING NEW ADVENTURES OF SUPERGIRL, THE
Nov, 1982 - No. 13, Nov, 1983 (Supergirl No. 14-on)
DC Comics

1-Origin retold		.40	.80
2-13: 13-New costume; flag-c		.25	.50

NOTE: *Buckler c-1p, 2p. Giffen c-3p, 4p. Gil Kane c-6, 8, 9, 11-13.*

DARK CRYSTAL, THE
April, 1983 - No. 2, May, 1983
Marvel Comics Group

	Good	Fine	N-Mint
1,2-Movie adaptation, part 1&2		.25	.50

DARKEWOOD
1987 - No. 5, 1988 ($2.00, color, 28 pgs., mini-series)
Aircel Publishing

1-5	.35	1.00	2.00

DARK HORSE PRESENTS
July, 1986 - Present ($1.50, B&W)
Dark Horse Comics

1-1st app. Concrete	2.00	6.00	12.00
1-2nd print	.25	.75	1.50
2-Concrete app.	1.50	4.50	9.00
3-Concrete app.	1.00	3.00	6.00
4,5-Concrete app.	.85	2.50	5.00
6,7,9	.40	1.25	2.50
8,10-Concrete app.	.60	1.75	3.50
11-19,21-26: 12,24-Concrete app.	.35	1.00	2.00
20-Double size ($2.95)-Flaming Carrot app.	.60	1.75	3.50

DARK KNIGHT (See Batman: The Dark Knight Returns)

DARKLON THE MYSTIC
Oct, 1983 (One shot)
Pacific Comics

1-Starlin c/a(r)	.35	1.00	2.00

DARK MANSION OF FORBIDDEN LOVE, THE (Becomes Forbidden
Tales of Dark Mansion No. 5 on)
Sept-Oct, 1971 - No. 4, Mar-Apr, 1972
National Periodical Publications

1-4: 2-Adams-c. 3-Jeff Jones-c		.40	.80

DARK MYSTERIES
June-July, 1951 - No. 25, 1955
"Master"-"Merit" Publications

1-Wood c/a, 8 pgs.	25.00	75.00	175.00
2-Wood/Harrison c/a, 8 pgs.	20.00	60.00	140.00
3-9: 7-Dismemberment, hypo blood drainage stories			
	6.00	18.00	42.00
10-Cannibalism story	7.00	21.00	50.00
11-13,15-18: 11-Severed head panels. 13-Dismemberment-c/story			
	5.50	16.50	38.00
14-Several E.C. Craig swipes	6.00	18.00	42.00
19-Injury to eye panel	7.00	21.00	50.00
20-Female bondage, blood drainage story	6.00	18.00	42.00
21,22-Last pre-code ish, mis-dated 3/54 instead of 3/55			
	4.50	13.50	32.00
23-25	3.50	10.50	24.00

NOTE: *Cameron a-1, 2. Myron Fass c/a-21. Harrison a-3, 7; c-3. Hollingsworth
a-7-17, 20, 21, 23. Wildey a-5. Woodish art by Fleishman-9; c-10. Bondage-c, 10, 18,
19.*

DARK SHADOWS
October, 1957 - 1958
Steinway Comic Publications (Ajax)(America's Best)

1	3.70	11.00	26.00
2,3	2.30	7.00	16.00

DARK SHADOWS (TV) (See Dan Curtis)
March, 1969 - No. 35, Feb, 1976 (Photo-c, 2-7)
Gold Key

1(30039-903)-with pull-out poster	5.70	17.00	40.00
2	2.65	8.50	20.00
3-with pull-out poster	3.50	10.50	24.00
4-7: Last photo-c	2.30	7.00	16.00
8-10	1.70	5.00	12.00

Daring Love #1, © Gillmor Magazines

Daring Mystery Comics #8, © MEG

Dark Shadows #1, © AJAX

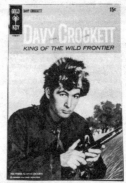

Darling Love #1, © AP · A Date With Millie #1 (10/56), © MEG · Davy Crockett King Of The Wild Frontier #2 (G.K.), © WDC

	Good	Fine	N-Mint
DARK SHADOWS (continued)			
11-20	1.50	4.50	10.00
21-35: 30-last painted-c	1.00	3.00	7.00
Story Digest 1 (6/70)	.85	2.50	6.00
DARK WOLF			
Jan., 1988 - Present ($1.95, B&W)			
Eternity Comics			
1-8	.25	.75	1.50
DARLING LOVE			
Oct-Nov, 1949 - No. 11, 1952 (no month) (52 pgs.)			
Close Up/Archie Publ. (A Darling Magazine)			
1-Photo-c	4.60	14.00	32.00
2	2.35	7.00	16.00
3-8,10,11: 5,6-photo-c	2.00	6.00	14.00
9-Krigstein-a	3.35	10.00	23.00
DARLING ROMANCE			
Sept-Oct, 1949 - No. 7, 1951			
Close Up (MLJ Publications)			
1-Photo-c	4.60	14.00	32.00
2	2.35	7.00	16.00
3-7	2.00	6.00	14.00

DASTARDLY & MUTTLEY IN THEIR FLYING MACHINES (See Fun-In No. 1-4,6)

DASTARDLY & MUTTLEY KITE FUN BOOK (Giveaway)
1969 (16 pages) (5x7'', soft-c) (Hanna-Barbera's)
Florida Power & Light Co./Sou. Calif. Edison/Pacific Gas & Electric

		.75	2.25	5.00
DATE WITH DANGER				
No. 5, Dec, 1952 - No. 6, Feb, 1953				
Standard Comics				
5,6		2.85	8.50	20.00
DATE WITH DEBBI				
1-2/69 - No. 17, 9-10/71; No. 18, 10-11/72				
National Periodical Publications				
1		.85	2.50	5.00
2-18		.50	1.50	3.00
DATE WITH JUDY, A (Radio/TV)				
Oct-Nov, 1947 - No. 79, Oct-Nov, 1960 (No. 1-25, 52 pgs.)				
National Periodical Publications				
1		11.00	32.00	75.00
2		5.50	16.50	38.00
3-10		3.70	11.00	26.00
11-20		2.35	7.00	16.00
21-40		1.70	5.00	12.00
41-45: 45-Last pre-code (2-3/55)		1.50	4.50	10.00
46-79: 79-Drucker c/a		1.15	3.50	8.00

DATE WITH MILLIE, A (Life With Millie No. 8 on)
Oct, 1956 - No. 7, Aug, 1957; Oct, 1959 - No. 7, Oct, 1960
Atlas/Marvel Comics (MPC)

1(10/56)-(1st Series)	6.00	18.00	42.00
2	3.00	9.00	21.00
3-7	2.30	7.00	16.00
1(10/59)-(2nd Series)	3.50	10.50	24.00
2-7	1.70	5.00	12.00

DATE WITH PATSY, A (Also see Patsy Walker)
September, 1957
Atlas Comics

1	3.00	9.00	21.00

DAVID AND GOLIATH (See 4-Color No. 1205)

DAVID CASSIDY (TV?)(See Swing With Scooter #33)
Feb, 1972 - No. 14, Sept, 1973
Charlton Comics

	Good	Fine	N-Mint
1	1.00	3.00	6.00
2-14: 7,9-Photo-c	.70	2.00	4.00

DAVID LADD'S LIFE STORY (See Movie Classics)

DAVY CROCKETT (See Dell Giants, Fightin. . ., Frontier Fighters, It's Game Time, Western Tales & Wild Frontier)

DAVY CROCKETT
1951
Avon Periodicals

nn-Tuska?, Reinman-a; Fawcette-c	8.00	24.00	56.00

DAVY CROCKETT (. . .King of the Wild Frontier No. 1,2)(TV)
5/55 - No. 671, 12/55; No. 1, 12/63; No. 2, 11/69 (Walt Disney)
Dell Publishing Co./Gold Key

4-Color 631-Fess Parker photo-c	3.00	9.00	21.00
4-Color 639-Fess Parker photo-c	3.00	9.00	21.00
4-Color 664,671(Marsh-a)-Photo-c	3.50	10.50	24.00
1(12/63-Gold Key)-r; Fess Parker photo-c	1.50	4.50	10.00
2(11/69)-r; Fess Parker photo-c	1.00	3.00	6.00
. .Christmas Book (no date, 16pgs, paper-c) Sears giveaway	1.70	5.00	12.00
. .In the Raid at Piney Creek (1955, 16pgs, 5x7¼'')American Motors giveaway; slick, photo-c	3.50	10.50	24.00
. .Safety Trails (1955, 16pgs, 3¼x7'') Cities Service giveaway	3.00	9.00	21.00

DAVY CROCKETT (. . .Frontier Fighter #1,2; Kid Montana #9 on)
Aug, 1955 - No. 8, Jan, 1957
Charlton Comics

1	3.00	9.00	21.00
2	1.50	4.50	10.00
3-8	1.00	3.00	7.00
Hunting With. . .('55, 16 pgs.)-Ben Franklin Store giveaway (Publ.- S. Rose)	1.15	3.50	8.00

DAYS OF THE MOB (See In the Days of the Mob)

DAZEY'S DIARY
June-Aug, 1962
Dell Publishing Co.

01-174-208: Bill Woggon-c/a	2.00	6.00	14.00

DAZZLER, THE (Also see Marvel Graphic Novel & X-Men #130)
March, 1981 - No. 42, Mar, 1986
Marvel Comics Group

1-X-Men app; Alcala art		.50	1.00
2-X-Men app.		.50	1.00
3-42: 21-Double size; photo-c		.50	1.00

NOTE: 1 distributed only through comic shops. Alcala a-1i, 2i. Guice a-42.

DC CHALLENGE
11/85 - No. 12, 10/86 ($1.25-$2.00; 12 issue maxi-series)
DC Comics

1-Colan-a	.25	.75	1.50
2-11: 4-G. Kane-c/a	.25	.75	1.50
12($2.00)-Perez/Austin-c	.25	.75	1.50

DC COMICS PRESENTS
July-Aug, 1978 - No. 97, Sept, 1986
DC Comics

(Superman team-ups with No. 1-on)

1-12,14-25,27-97	.25	.75	1.50
13-Legion of Super Heroes	.40	1.25	2.50
26-(10/80)-Green Lantern; intro Cyborg, Starfire, Raven, New Teen Titans; Starlin-c/a; Sargon the Sorcerer back-up; 16 pgs. preview			

113

DC COMICS PRESENTS (continued)	Good	Fine	N-Mint
of the New Teen Titans	1.50	4.50	9.00
Annual 1(9/82)-G.A. Superman	.60		1.20
Annual 2(7/83)-Intro/origin Superwoman	.60		1.20
Annual 3(9/84)-Shazam; intro Capt. Thunder	.60		1.20
Annual 4(10/85)-Superwoman	.60		1.20

NOTE: *Adkins a-2, 54; c-2. Gil Kane a-28, 35, Annual 3; c-48p, 56, 58, 60, 62, 64, 68, Annual 2, 3. Kirby c/a-84. Kubert c/a-66. Morrow c/a-65. Newton a/c-54p. Orlando c-53i. Perez a-26p, 61p; c-38, 61, 94. Starlin a-26-29p, 36p, 37p; c-26-29, 36, 37, 93. Toth a-84. Williamson i-79, 85, 87.*

DC GRAPHIC NOVEL (Also see DC Science Fiction...)
Nov, 1983 - No. 7, 1986 ($5.95, 68 pgs.)
DC Comics

	Good	Fine	N-Mint
1-Star Raiders	1.00	3.00	6.00
2-Warlords; not from the regular Warlord series	1.00	3.00	6.00
3-The Medusa Chain; Ernie Colon story/a	1.00	3.00	6.00
4-The Hunger Dogs; Kirby-c/a	1.00	3.00	6.00
5-Me And Joe Priest	1.00	3.00	6.00
6-Metalzoic	1.20	3.50	7.00
7-Space Clusters	1.00	3.00	6.00

DC 100 PAGE SUPER SPECTACULAR (50 cents)
(Title is 100 Page... No. 14 on)(Square bound) (Reprints)
1971 - No. 13, 6/72; No. 14, 2/73 - No. 22, 11/73 (No No.1-3)
National Periodical Publications

	Good	Fine	N-Mint
4-Weird Mystery Tales-Johnny Peril & Phantom Stranger; cover & splashes by Wrightson; origin Jungle Boy of Jupiter	.35	1.00	2.00
5-Love stories; Wood Inks, 7pgs.	.35	1.00	2.00
6-"World's Greatest Super-Heroes"-JLA, JSA, Spectre, Johnny Quick, Vigilante, Wildcat & Hawkman; Adams wrap-around-c	.40	1.25	2.50
7-(See Superman #245),8-(See Batman #238)			
9-(See Our Army at War #242),10-(See Adventure #416)			
11-(See Flash #214),12-(See Superboy #185)			
13-(See Superman #252)			
14-22: 21-r/Showcase 54. 22-r/All Flash 13	.50		1.00

NOTE: *Anderson a-11, 14, 18i, 22. B. Baily a-18r, 20r. Burnley a-18r, 20r. Crandall a-14p(r), 20r. Drucker a-4r. Infantino a-17, 20, 22. G. Kane a-18. Kubert a-6, 7, 16, 17; c-16,19. Meskin a-4, 22. Mooney a-15r, 21r. Toth a-17, 20.*

DC SCIENCE FICTION GRAPHIC NOVEL
1985 - No. 7, 1986? ($5.95)
DC Comics

SF1-Hell on Earth by Robert Bloch, SF2-Nightwings by Robert Silverberg, SF3-Frost & Fire by Bradbury	1.00	3.00	5.95
SF4-Merchants of Venus	1.00	3.00	5.95
SF5-Demon With A Glass Hand by Ellison; M. Rogers-a. SF6-The Magic Goes Away by Niven, SF7-Sandkings by George R.R. Martin	1.00	3.00	5.95

DC SPECIAL (Also see Super DC...)
10-12/68 - No. 15, 11-12/71; No. 16, Spr/75 - No. 29, 8/9/77
National Periodical Publications

1-All Infantino ish; Flash, Batman, Adam Strange-r (68 pgs.) begin	.35	1.00	2.00
2-4,6-11,13,14	.60		1.20
5-All Kubert ish. Viking Prince, Sgt. Rock-r	.60		1.20
12-Viking Prince; Kubert-c/a	.60		1.20
15-G.A. Plastic Man origin r/Police #1; origin Woozy by Cole Last 68 pg. ish	.60		1.20
16-27: 16-Super Heroes Battle Super Gorillas	.60		1.20
28-Earth Shattering Disaster Stories; Legion of Super-Heroes story	.60		1.20
29-Secret Origin of the Justice Society	.60		1.20

NOTE: *Adams c-3, 4, 6, 11, 29. Heath a-12r. G. Kane a-6p, 13r, 17r, 19-21r. Kubert a-6r, 12r, 22. Meskin a-10. Moreira a-10. Staton a-29p. Toth a-13, 20r.*

DC SPECIAL BLUE-RIBBON DIGEST
Mar-Apr, 1980 - No. 24, Aug, 1982
DC Comics

	Good	Fine	N-Mint
1-24		.50	1.00

NOTE: *Adams a-16(6)r, 17r, 23r; c-16. Aparo a-6r, 24r; c-23. Grell a-8, 10; c-10. Heath a-14. Kaluta a-17r. Gil Kane a-22r. Kirby a-23r. Kubert a-3, 18r, 21r; c-7, 12, 14, 17, 18, 21, 24. Morrow a-24r. Orlando a-17r, 22r; c-1, 20. Perez c-19p. Toth a-21r, 24r. Wood a-3, 17r, 24r. Wrightson a-16r, 17r, 24r.*

DC SPECIAL SERIES
9/77 - No. 16, Fall, 1978; No. 17, 8/79 - No. 27, Fall, 1981
(No. 23 & 24 - digest size; No. 25-27 - over-sized)
National Periodical Publications/DC Comics

1-Five-Star Super-Hero Spectacular; Atom, Flash, Green Lantern, Aquaman, Batman, Kobra app.; Adams-c; Staton, Nasser-a	.35	1.00	2.00
2(#1)-Original Swamp Thing Saga, The(9-10/77)-reprints Swamp Thing No. 1&2 by Wrightson; Wrightson wrap-around-c	.25	.75	1.50
3-20,22-24: 10-Origin Dr. Fate, Lightray & Black Canary	.50	1.00	2.00
21-Miller-a (1st on Batman)	.70	2.00	4.00
25-Superman II The Adventure Continues (Sum '81); photos from movie($2.95) (Same as All-New Coll. Ed. C-64?)	.35	1.00	2.00
26-Superman and His Incredible Fortress of Solitude (Sum '81) ($2.50) (Same as All-New Co.. Ed. C-63?)	.35	1.00	2.00
27-Batman vs. The Incredible Hulk($2.50)	.35	1.00	2.00

NOTE: *Golden a-15. Heath a-12i, 16. Kubert c-13. Rogers c/a-15. Starlin c-12.*

DC SPOTLIGHT
1985 (50th anniversary special)
DC Comics (giveaway)

1		.40	.80

DC SUPER-STARS
March, 1976 - No. 18, Winter, 1978 (No.3-18: 52 pgs.)
National Periodical Publications/DC Comics

1-Teen Titans (68 pgs.)	.25	.75	1.50
2-16,18		.50	1.00
17-Secret Origins of Super-Heroes(1st app./origin of The Huntress); Origin Green Arrow by Grell; Legion app.	.60		1.20

NOTE: *Aparo c-7, 14, 17, 18. Austin a-11i. Buckler a-14p; c-10. Grell a-17. G. Kane a-1r, 10r. Kubert c-15. Layton c/a-16i, 17i. Mooney a-4r; 6r. Morrow c/a-11r. Nasser a-11. Newton c/a-16p. Staton a-17; c-17. No. 10, 12-18 contain all new material; the rest are reprints.*

D-DAY (Also see Special War Series)
Sum/63; No. 2, Fall/64; No. 4, 9/66; No. 5, 10/67; No. 6, 11/68
Charlton Comics (no No. 3)

1(1963)-Montes/Bache-c	.70	2.00	4.00
2(Fall,'64)-Wood-a(3)	1.00	3.00	7.00
4-6('66-'68)-Montes/Bache-a #5	.50	1.50	3.00

DEAD END CRIME STORIES
April, 1949 (52 pages)
Kirby Publishing Co.

nn-(Scarce)-Powell, Roussos-a	20.00	60.00	140.00

DEAD-EYE WESTERN COMICS
Nov-Dec, 1948 - V3No.1, Apr-May, 1953
Hillman Periodicals

V1#1(52 pgs.)-Krigstein, Roussos-a	5.70	17.00	40.00
V1#2,3(52 pgs.)	2.85	8.50	20.00
V1#4-12	1.70	5.00	12.00
V2#1,2,5-8,10-12: 6,7-52 pgs.	1.30	4.00	9.00
3,4-Krigstein-a (52 pgs.)	2.65	8.00	18.00
9-One pg. Frazetta ad	1.70	5.00	12.00
V3#1	1.15	3.50	8.00

DC Graphic Novel #1, © DC

DC Super Stars #16, © DC

Dead-Eye Western Comics #1, © HILL

Deadshot #1, © DC

The Dead Who Walk, © REAL

Dear Beatrice Fairfax #9, © KING

DEAD-EYE WESTERN COMICS (continued)
NOTE: *Briefer a-V1No.8. Kinstleresque stories by McCann-12, V2No.1,2, V3No.1.*

DEADLIEST HEROES OF KUNG FU
Summer, 1975 (Magazine)
Marvel Comics Group

	Good	Fine	N-Mint
1	.30	.90	1.80

DEADLY HANDS OF KUNG FU, THE
April, 1974 - No. 33, Feb, 1977 (75 cents) (B&W - Magazine)
Marvel Comics Group

1(V1#4 listed in error)-Origin Sons of the Tiger; Shang-Chi, Master of Kung Fu begins; Bruce Lee photo pin-up	.40	1.25	2.50
2,3,5	.30	.90	1.80
4-Bruce Lee painted-c by Adams; 8 pg. biog of B. Lee	.40	1.25	2.50
6-14	.30	.90	1.80
15-(Annual 1, Summer '75)	.30	.90	1.80
16-19,21-27,29-33: 17-1st Giffen-a (1 pg.; 11/75). 19-1st White Tiger. 22-1st Giffen sty-a		.60	1.20
20-Origin The White Tiger; Perez-a	.30	.90	1.80
28-Origin Jack of Hearts; Bruce Lee life story	.40	1.25	2.50
Special Album Edition 1(Summer, '74)-Adams-i	.30	.90	1.80

NOTE: *Adams c-1, 2-4, 11, 12, 14, 17. Giffen a-22p, 24p. G. Kane a-23p. Kirby 3-5r. Perez a(p)-6-14, 16, 17, 19, 21. Rogers a-32, 33. Starlin a-1, 2r, 15r. Staton a-28p, 31, 32. Sons of the Tiger in 1, 3, 4, 6-14, 16-19.*

DEADMAN
May, 1985 - No. 7, Nov, 1985
DC Comics

1-Deadman-r by Infantino, Adams	.35	1.00	2.00
2-7	.30	.90	1.80

DEADMAN
Mar, 1986 - No. 4, June, 1986 (mini-series)
DC Comics

1-4-Lopez-c/a; 4-Byrne-c(p)		.45	.90

DEAD OF NIGHT
Dec, 1973 - No. 11, Aug, 1975
Marvel Comics Group

1-Reprints		.30	.60
2-11: 11-Kane/Wrightson-c		.25	.50

NOTE: *Ditko a-7r, 10r. Everett c-2.*

DEADSHOT
Nov., 1988 - No. 4, Feb, 1988 ($1.00, color, mini-series)
DC Comics

1-4		.50	1.00

DEAD WHO WALK, THE (Also see Strange Myst., Super-r #15,16)
1952 (One Shot)
Realistic Comics

nn	20.00	60.00	140.00

DEADWOOD GULCH
1931 (52 pages) (B&W)
Dell Publishing Co.

By Gordon Rogers	6.00	18.00	42.00

DEAN MARTIN & JERRY LEWIS (See Adventures of . . .)

DEAR BEATRICE FAIRFAX
No. 5, Nov, 1950 - No. 9, Sept, 1951 (Vern Greene art)
Best/Standard Comics(King Features)

5	3.00	9.00	21.00
6-9	1.85	5.50	13.00

NOTE: *Schomburg air brush-c-5-9.*

DEAR HEART (Formerly Lonely Heart)
No. 15, July, 1956 - No. 16, Sept, 1956

	Good	Fine	N-Mint
Ajax 15,16	1.70	5.00	12.00

DEAR LONELY HEART (. . . Illustrated No. 1-6)
Mar, 1951; No. 3, Dec, 1951 - No. 8, Oct, 1952
Artful Publications

1	8.00	24.00	56.00
2 (10/51)	3.70	11.00	26.00
3-Matt Baker Jungle Girl story	8.00	24.00	56.00
4-8	3.35	10.00	23.00

DEAR LONELY HEARTS (Lonely Heart #9 on)
Aug, 1953 - No. 8, Oct, 1954
Harwell Publ./Mystery Publ. Co. (Comic Media)

1	3.00	9.00	21.00
2-8	1.65	5.00	11.00

DEARLY BELOVED
Fall, 1952
Ziff-Davis Publishing Co.

1-Photo-c	6.00	18.00	42.00

DEAR NANCY PARKER
June, 1963 - No. 2, Sept, 1963
Gold Key

1,2-Painted-c	1.50	4.50	10.00

DEATH HAWK
1988 - Present ($1.95, B&W)
Adventure Publ.

1-4	.35	1.00	2.00

DEATH OF CAPTAIN MARVEL (See Marvel Graphic Novel #1)

DEATH RATTLE (Formerly an Underground)
V2/1, 10/85 - No. 18, 1988 ($1.95, Baxter)(Mature readers)
Kitchen Sink Press

V2/1-Corben-c	.35	1.00	2.00
2-5: 2-Unpubbed Spirit sty by Eisner. 5-Robot Woman by Wolverton-r	.35	1.00	2.00
6-18: 6-B&W issues begin. 16-Wolverton Spacehawk-r	.35	1.00	2.00

DEATH VALLEY
Oct, 1953 - No. 6, Aug, 1954?
Comic Media

1-Old Scout	3.70	11.00	26.00
2	2.15	6.50	15.00
3-6	1.50	4.50	10.00

NOTE: *Discount a-5. Morisi a-1, 3, 5.*

DEATH VALLEY (Becomes Frontier Scout, Daniel Boone No.10-13)
No. 7, 6/55 - No. 9, 10/55 (Cont. from Comic Media series)
Charlton Comics

7-9	1.50	4.50	10.00

DEBBIE DEAN, CAREER GIRL
April, 1945 - No. 2, 1945
Civil Service Publ.

1,2-Newspaper reprints by Bert Whitman	6.50	19.50	45.00

DEBBI'S DATES
Apr-May, 1969 - No. 11, Dec-Jan, 1970-71
National Periodical Publications

1	.50	1.50	3.00
2-11: 4-Adams text illo.	.25	.75	1.50

DEEP, THE (Movie)
November, 1977
Marvel Comics Group

1-Infantino c/a		.40	.80

DEFENDERS, THE (TV)
Sept-Nov, 1962 - No. 2, Feb-Apr, 1963
Dell Publishing Co.

	Good	Fine	N-Mint
12-176-211(#1), 304(#2)	1.30	4.00	9.00

DEFENDERS, THE (Also see Marvel Feature & Marvel Treas. Ed.;
The New. . .#140-on)
Aug, 1972 - No. 152, Feb, 1986
Marvel Comics Group

	Good	Fine	N-Mint
1-The Hulk, Doc Strange, & Sub-Mariner begin	1.35	4.00	8.00
2-5: 4-Valkyrie joins	.50	1.50	3.00
6-10: 9,10-Avengers app. 10-Thor-Hulk battle	.50	1.50	3.00
11-151: 31,32-Origin Nighthawk. 35-Intro. New Red Guardian. 44-Hellcat joins. 45-Dr. Strange leaves. 55-Origin Red Guardian. 77-Origin Omega. 100-Double size. 106-Death of Nighthawk. 125-(Dbl size; 1st app. Mad Dog; intro. new Defenders. 150-Dbl size; origin Cloud		.50	1.00
152-Double size; ties in with X-Factor & Secret Wars II	.30	.90	1.75

NOTE: *Art Adams c-142p. Austin a-53i; c-65i, 119i, 145i. Frank Bolle a-7i, 10i, 11i. Buckler c(p)-34, 38, 76, 77, 79-86, 90, 91. J. Buscema c-66. Ditko a-Gnt-Size 1-4r. Everett r-Gnt-Size 1-4. Giffen a-42-49p, 50, 51p, 52p, 53p, 54p. Golden a-53p, 54p; c-94, 96. Guice c-129. G. Kane c(p)-13, 16, 18, 19, 21-26, 31-33, 35-37, 40, 41, 52, 55, Gnt-Size 2, 4. Kirby c-42-45. Mooney a-3i, 31-34i, 62i, 63i, 85i. Nasser c-88p. Perez c(p)-51, 53, 54. Rogers c-98. Starlin c-110. Tuska a-57p. Silver Surfer in No. 2, 3, 6, 8-11, 92, 98-101, 107, 112-115, 122-125.*

	Good	Fine	N-Mint
Annual 1(11/76)	.35	1.00	2.00
Giant Size 1(7/74)-Silver Surfer app.; Starlin-a; Everett, Ditko, & Kirby-r	.50	1.50	3.00
Giant Size 2(10/74)-G. Kane-a; Everett, Ditko-r		.50	1.00
Giant Size 3(1/75)-Starlin, Newton, Everett-a		.50	1.00
Giant Size 4(4/75), 5(7/75)-Guardians app.		.50	1.00

DEFENDERS OF THE EARTH (TV)
Jan, 1987 - No. 5, Sept, 1987
Star Comics (Marvel)

	Good	Fine	N-Mint
1-5: The Phantom, Mandrake The Magician, Flash Gordon begin		.45	.90

THE DEFINITIVE DIRECTORY OF THE DC UNIVERSE (See Who's Who. . .)

DELECTA OF THE PLANETS (See Fawcett Miniatures & Don Fortune)

DELLA VISION (Patty Powers #4 on)
April, 1955 - No. 3, Aug, 1955
Atlas Comics

	Good	Fine	N-Mint
1	6.00	18.00	42.00
2,3	4.00	12.00	28.00

DELL GIANT COMICS
No. 21, Sept, 1959 - No. 55, Sept, 1961 (Most 84 pages, 25 cents)
Dell Publishing Co.

	Good	Fine	N-Mint
21-M.G.M.'s Tom & Jerry Picnic Time (84pp, stapled binding)	3.50	10.50	28.00
22-Huey, Dewey & Louie Back to School(10/59, 84pp, square binding begins)	3.50	14.00	35.00
23-Marge's Little Lulu & Tubby Halloween Fun (10/59)-Tripp-a	6.50	26.00	65.00
24-Woody Woodpecker's Family Fun (11/59)	2.50	10.00	25.00
25-Tarzan's Jungle World(11/59)-Marsh-a	4.00	16.00	40.00
26-Christmas Parade-Barks-a, 16pgs.(Disney. (12/59)-Barks draws himself on wanted poster pg. 13	8.00	32.00	80.00
27-Man in Space r-/4-Color 716,866, & 954 (100 pages, 35 cents) (Disney)(TV)	3.50	14.00	35.00
28-Bugs Bunny's Winter Fun (2/60)	3.00	12.00	30.00
29-Marge's Little Lulu & Tubby in Hawaii (4/60)-Tripp-a	6.50	26.00	65.00
30-Disneyland USA(6/60)-Reprinted in Vacation in Disneyland			

	Good	Fine	N-Mint
	4.50	18.00	45.00
31-Huckleberry Hound Summer Fun (7/60)(TV)	7.50	24.00	70.00
32-Bugs Bunny Beach Party	2.50	10.00	25.00
33-Daisy Duck & Uncle Scrooge Picnic Time (9/60)	4.00	16.00	40.00
34-Nancy & Sluggo Summer Camp (8/60)	3.00	12.00	30.00
35-Huey, Dewey & Louie Back to School (10/60)	3.50	14.00	35.00
36-Marge's Little Lulu & Witch Hazel Halloween Fun(10/60)-Tripp-a	6.50	26.00	65.00
37-Tarzan, King of the Jungle(11/60)-Marsh-a	3.50	14.00	35.00
38-Uncle Donald & His Nephews Family Fun (11/60)	3.50	14.00	35.00
39-Walt Disney's Merry Christmas(12/60)	3.50	14.00	35.00
40-Woody Woodpecker Christmas Parade(12/60)	2.50	10.00	25.00
41-Yogi Bear's Winter Sports (12/60)(TV)	5.50	22.00	55.00
42-Marge's Little Lulu & Tubby in Australia (4/61)	6.50	26.00	65.00
43-Mighty Mouse in Outer Space (7/61)	8.00	32.00	80.00
44-Around the World with Huckleberry & His Friends (7/61)(TV)	6.00	24.00	60.00
45-Nancy & Sluggo Summer Camp (8/61)	3.00	12.00	30.00
46-Bugs Bunny Beach Party (8/61)	2.50	10.00	25.00
47-Mickey & Donald in Vacationland (8/61)	3.50	14.00	35.00
48-The Flintstones (No. 1)(Bedrock Bedlam)(7/61)(TV)	7.00	28.00	70.00
49-Huey, Dewey & Louie Back to School (9/61)	3.50	14.00	35.00
50-Marge's Little Lulu & Witch Hazel Trick 'N' Treat (10/61)	6.50	26.00	65.00
51-Tarzan, King of the Jungle by Jesse Marsh (11/61)	3.50	14.00	35.00
52-Uncle Donald & His Nephews Dude Ranch (11/61)	3.50	14.00	35.00
53-Donald Duck Merry Christmas(12/61)-Not by Barks	3.50	14.00	35.00
54-Woody Woodpecker Christmas Party(12/61)-issued after No. 55	2.50	10.00	25.00
55-Daisy Duck & Uncle Scrooge Showboat (9/61)-1st app. Daisy Duck's nieces, April, May & June	5.00	20.00	50.00

NOTE: *All issues printed with & without ad on back cover.*

(OTHER DELL GIANT EDITIONS)

	Good	Fine	N-Mint
Abraham Lincoln Life Story 1(3/58, 100p)	3.00	12.00	30.00
Bugs Bunny Christmas Funnies 1(11/50, 116p)	7.00	28.00	70.00
. . .Christmas Funnies 2(11/51, 116p)	5.00	20.00	50.00
. . .Christmas Funnies 3-5(11/52-11/54, 100p)-Becomes Christmas Party No. 6	3.50	14.00	35.00
. . .Christmas Funnies 7-9(12/56-12/58, 100p)	3.00	12.00	30.00
. . .Christmas Party 6(11/55, 100p)-Formerly B.B. Christmas Funnies #5	3.50	14.00	35.00
. . .County Fair 1(9/57, 100p)	3.50	14.00	35.00
. . .Halloween Parade 1(10/53, 100p)	6.00	24.00	60.00
. . .Halloween Parade 2(10/54, 100p)-Trick 'N' Treat Halloween Fun No. 3-on	4.00	16.00	40.00
. . .Trick 'N' Treat Halloween Fun 3,4(10/55-10/56, 100p)-Formerly Halloween Parade 2	3.50	14.00	35.00
. . .Vacation Funnies 1(7/51, 112p)	7.00	28.00	70.00
. . .Vacation Funnies 2('52, 100p)	5.00	20.00	50.00
. . .Vacation Funnies 3-5('53-'55, 100p)	3.50	14.00	35.00
. . .Vacation Funnies 6-9('54-6/59, 100p)	3.00	12.00	30.00
Cadet Gray of West Point 1(4/58, 100p)-Williamson-a, 10pgs.			

The Defenders #3, © MEG Dell Giant Comics #43, © M.G.M. Bugs Bunny's Trick 'N' Treat. . . Fun #4, © Warner Bros.

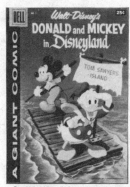

Donald And Mickey In Disneyland #1, © WDC   The Lone Ranger Movie Story, © Lone Ranger   Raggedy Ann And Andy #1, © DELL

	Good	Fine	N-Mint
DELL GIANTS (continued)			
Buscema-a, photo-c	4.00	16.00	40.00
Christmas In Disneyland 1(12/57, 100p)-Barks-a, 18pgs.			
	8.00	32.00	80.00
Christmas Parade 1(11/49)-Barks-a, 25pgs.; r-in G.K. Christmas			
Parade 5	33.00	130.00	325.00
Christmas Parade 2('50)-Barks-a, 25pgs.; r-in G.K. Christmas			
Parade 6	19.00	76.00	190.00
Christmas Parade 3-7('51-'55, 116-100p)	4.00	16.00	40.00
Christmas Parade 8(12/56, 100p)-Barks-a, 8pgs.			
	8.00	32.00	80.00
Christmas Parade 9(12/58, 100p)-Barks-a, 20pgs.			
	10.00	40.00	100.00
Christmas Treasury, A 1(11/54, 100p)	5.00	20.00	50.00
Davy Crockett, King Of The Wild Frontier 1(9/55, 100p)-Photo-c;			
Marsh-a	8.50	34.00	85.00
Disneyland Birthday Party 1(10/58, 100p)-Barks-a, 16pgs.			
	7.00	28.00	70.00
Donald and Mickey In Disneyland 1(5/58, 100p)			
	3.50	14.00	35.00
Donald Duck Beach Party 1(7/54, 100p)	6.00	24.00	60.00
...**Beach Party** 2('55, 100p)	4.00	16.00	40.00
...**Beach Party** 3-5('56-'58, 100p)	3.50	14.00	35.00
...**Beach Party** 6(8/59, 84p)-Stapled	2.50	10.00	25.00
Donald Duck Fun Book 1,2('53-10/54, 100p)-Games, puzzles,			
comics & cut-outs (Rare)	14.00	56.00	140.00
Donald Duck In Disneyland 1(9/55, 100p)	3.50	14.00	35.00
Golden West Rodeo Treasury 1(10/57, 100p)	4.00	16.00	40.00
Huey, Dewey and Louie Back To School 1(9/58, 100p)			
	4.00	16.00	40.00
Lady and The Tramp 1(6/55, 100p)	4.00	16.00	40.00
Life Stories of American Presidents 1(11/57, 100p)-Buscema-a			
	3.00	12.00	30.00
Lone Ranger Golden West 3(8/55, 100p)-Formerly West. Treasury			
	6.00	24.00	60.00
Lone Ranger Movie Story nn(3/56, 100p)-Origin Lone Ranger in			
text; Clayton Moore photo-c	15.00	60.00	150.00
...**Western Treasury** 1(9/53, 100p)-Origin L. Ranger, Silver,			
& Tonto	11.00	44.00	110.00
...**Western Treasury** 2(8/54, 100p)-Becomes Golden West No. 3			
	5.50	22.00	55.00
Marge's Little Lulu & Alvin Story Telling Time 1(3/59)-r/No.2,5,3,			
11,30,10,21,17,8,14,16; Stanley-a	7.50	30.00	75.00
...**& Her Friends** 4(3/56, 100p)-Tripp-a	6.50	26.00	65.00
...**& Her Special Friends** 3(3/55, 100p)-Tripp-a			
	6.50	26.00	65.00
...**& Tubby At Summer Camp** 5(10/57, 100p)-Tripp-a			
	6.50	26.00	65.00
...**& Tubby At Summer Camp** 2(10/58, 100p)-Tripp-a			
	6.50	26.00	65.00
...**& Tubby Halloween Fun** 6(10/57, 100p)-Tripp-a			
	6.50	26.00	65.00
...**& Tubby Halloween Fun** 2(10/58, 100p)-Tripp-a			
	6.50	26.00	65.00
...**& Tubby In Alaska** 1(7/59, 100p)-Tripp-a			
	6.50	26.00	65.00
...**On Vacation** 1(7/54, 100p)-r/4C-110,14,4C-146,5,4C-97,4,			
4C-158,3,1; Stanley-a	10.00	40.00	100.00
...**& Tubby Annual** 1(3/53, 100p)-r/4C-165,4C-74,4C-146,4C-97,			
4C-158,4C-139,4C-131; Stanley-a	15.00	60.00	150.00
...**& Tubby Annual** 2('54, 100p)-r/4C-139,6,4C-115,4C-74,5,			
4C-97,3,4C-146,18; Stanley-a	14.00	56.00	140.00
Marge's Tubby & His Clubhouse Pals 1(10/56, 100p)-1st app.			
Gran'pa Feeb, written by Stanley; 1st app. Janie; Tripp-a			
	9.00	36.00	90.00
Mickey Mouse Almanac 1(12/57, 100p)-Barks-a, 8pgs.			
	9.00	36.00	90.00

	Good	Fine	N-Mint
...**Birthday Party** 1(9/53, 100p)-r-/entire 48pgs. of Gottfredson's			
''M.M. in Love Trouble'' from WDC&S 36-39. Quality equal to			
original. Also reprints one story each from 4-Color 27, 29, &			
181 plus 6 panels of highlights in the career of Mickey Mouse			
	14.00	56.00	140.00
...**Club Parade** 1(12/55, 100p)-R/4-Color 16 with some art redrawn			
by Paul Murry & recolored with night scenes turned into day;			
quality much poorer than original	11.00	44.00	110.00
...**In Fantasy Land** 1(5/57, 100p)	5.00	20.00	50.00
...**In Frontier Land** 1(5/56, 100p)-M.M. Club issue			
	5.00	20.00	50.00
...**Summer Fun** 1(8/58, 100p)-Mobile cut-outs on back-c; becomes			
Summer Fun No. 2	5.00	20.00	50.00
Moses & The Ten Commandments 1(8/57, 100p)-Not based on			
movie; Dell's adapt; Sekowsky-a	3.00	12.00	30.00
Nancy & Sluggo Travel Time 1(9/58, 100p)	3.50	14.00	35.00
Peter Pan Treasure Chest 1(1/53, 212p)-Disney; contains movie			
adapt. plus other stories	25.00	100.00	250.00
Picnic Party 6,7(7/55-56/56, 100p)(Formerly Vacation Parade)-Uncle			
Scrooge, Mickey & Donald	3.50	14.00	35.00
Picnic Party 8(7/57, 100p)-Barks-a, 6pgs.	6.00	24.00	60.00
Pogo Parade 1(9/53, 100p)-Kelly-a(r-/Pogo from Animal Comics in			
this order: No. 11,13,21,14,27,16,23,9,18,15,17)			
	20.00	80.00	200.00
Raggedy Ann & Andy 1(2/55, 100p)	5.50	22.00	55.00
Santa Claus Funnies 1(11/52, 100p)-Dan Noonan -**A** Christmas			
Carol adaptation	5.00	20.00	50.00
Silly Symphonies 1(9/52, 100p)-r/Chicken Little, M. Mouse			
''The Brave Little Tailor,'' Mother Pluto, Three Little Pigs,			
Lady, Bucky Bug, Wise Little Hen, Little Hiawatha, Pedro, The			
Grasshopper & The Ants	9.00	36.00	90.00
Silly Symphonies 2(9/53, 100p)-r/M. Mouse-''The Sorcerer's			
Apprentice,'' Little Hiawatha, Peculiar Penguins, Lambert The			
Sheepish Lion, Pluto, Spotty Pig, The Golden Touch, Elmer			
Elephant, The Pelican & The Snipe	7.00	28.00	70.00
Silly Symphonies 3(2/54, 100p)-r/Mickey & The Beanstalk			
(4-Color 157), Little Minnehaha, Pablo, The Flying Gauchito,			
Pluto, & Bongo	6.50	26.00	65.00
Silly Symphonies 4(8/54, 100p)-r/Dumbo (4-Color 234), Morris			
The Midget Moose, The Country Cousin, Bongo, & Clara Cluck			
	5.00	20.00	50.00
Silly Symphonies 5(2/55, 100p)-r/Cinderella (4-Color 272), Bucky			
Bug, Pluto, Little Hiawatha, The 7 Dwarfs & Dumbo, Pinocchio			
	5.00	20.00	50.00
Silly Symphonies 6(8/55, 100p)-r/Pinocchio(WDC&S 63), The 7			
Dwarfs & Thumper (WDC&S 45), M. Mouse-''Adventures With			
Robin Hood,'' Johnny Appleseed, Pluto & Peter Pan, & Bucky			
Bug; Cut-out on back-c	5.00	20.00	50.00
Silly Symphonies 7(2/57, 100p)-r/Reluctant Dragon (4-Color 13),			
Ugly Duckling, M. Mouse & Peter Pan, Jiminy Cricket, Peter &			
The Wolf, Brer Rabbit, Bucky Bug; Cut-out on back-c			
	6.00	24.00	60.00
Silly Symphonies 8(2/58, 100p)-r/Thumper Meets The 7 Dwarfs			
(4-Color 19), Jiminy Cricket, Niok, Brer Rabbit; Cut-out on back-c			
	5.00	20.00	50.00
Silly Symphonies 9(2/59, 100p)-r/Paul Bunyan, Humphrey Bear,			
Jiminy Cricket, The Social Lion, Goliath II; Cut-out on back-c			
	5.00	20.00	50.00
Sleeping Beauty 1(4/59, 100p)	8.00	32.00	80.00
Summer Fun 2(8/59, 100p)(Formerly M. Mouse. . .)-Barks-a(2),			
24 pgs.	6.00	24.00	60.00
Tales From The Tomb (See Tales From The Tomb)			
Tarzan's Jungle Annual 1(8/52, 100p)	5.00	20.00	50.00
...**Annual** 2(8/53, 100p)	4.00	16.00	40.00
...**Annual** 3-7('54-9/58, 100p)(two No. 5s)-Manning-a-No. 3,5-7;			
Marsh-a in No. 1-7	3.00	12.00	30.00

DELL GIANTS (continued)

	Good	Fine	N-Mint
Tom And Jerry Back To School 1(9/56, 100p)	3.50	14.00	35.00
...Picnic Time 1(7/58, 100p)	3.00	12.00	30.00
...Summer Fun 1(7/54, 100p)-Droopy written by Barks			
	6.00	24.00	60.00
...Summer Fun 2-4(7/55-7/57, 100p)	3.00	12.00	30.00
...Toy Fair 1(6/58, 100p)	3.50	14.00	35.00
...Winter Carnival 1(12/52, 100p)-Droopy written by Barks			
	8.00	32.00	80.00
...Winter Carnival 2(12/53, 100p)-Droopy written by Barks			
	5.00	20.00	50.00
...Winter Fun 3(12/54, 100p)	3.50	14.00	35.00
...Winter Fun 4-7(12/55-11/58, 100p)	3.00	12.00	30.00
Treasury of Dogs, A 1(10/56, 100p)	2.50	10.00	25.00
Treasury of Horses, A 1(9/55, 100p)	2.50	10.00	25.00
Uncle Scrooge Goes To Disneyland 1(8/57, 100p)-Barks-a, 20pgs.			
	8.00	32.00	80.00

Universal Presents-Dracula-The Mummy & Other Stories
02-530-311 (9-11/63, 84p)-R-/Dracula 12-231-212, The Mummy

	Good	Fine	N-Mint
12-437-211 & part of Ghost Stories No. 1	3.00	12.00	30.00
Vacation In Disneyland 1(8/58, 100p)	4.00	16.00	40.00
Vacation Parade 1(7/50, 130p)-Donald Duck & M. Mouse; Barks-a,			
55 pgs.	50.00	200.00	500.00
Vacation Parade 2(7/51, 100p)	8.00	32.00	80.00
Vacation Parade 3-5(7/52-7/54, 100p)-Picnic Party No. 6 on			
	4.00	16.00	40.00
Western Roundup 1(6/52, 100p)-Photo-c; Gene Autry, Roy Rogers,			
Johnny Mack Brown, Rex Allen, & Bill Elliott begin; photo back-c			
begin, end No. 14,16,18	8.00	32.00	80.00
Western Roundup 2(2/53, 100p)-Photo-c	5.00	20.00	50.00
Western Roundup 3-5(7-9/53 - 1-3/54)-Photo-c			
	4.50	18.00	45.00
Western Roundup 6-10(4-6/54 - 4-6/55)-Photo-c			
	4.00	16.00	40.00
Western Roundup 11-13,16,17(100p)-Photo-c; Manning-a. 11-Flying			
A's Range Rider, Dale Evans begin	3.50	14.00	35.00
Western Roundup 14,15,25(1-3/59; 100p)-Photo-c			
	3.50	14.00	35.00
Western Roundup 18(100p)-Toth-a; last photo-c; Gene Autry ends			
	4.00	16.00	40.00
Western Roundup 19-24(100p)-Manning-a; 19-Buffalo Bill Jr. begins.			
21-Rex Allen, Johnny Mack Brown end. 22-Jace Pearson's. .			
Texas Rangers, Rin Tin Tin, Tales of Wells Fargo & Wagon			
Train begin	3.00	12.00	30.00
Woody Woodpecker Back To School 1(10/52, 100p)			
	3.00	12.00	30.00
...Back To School 2-4,6('53-10/57, 100p)-County Fair No. 5			
	2.50	10.00	25.00
...County Fair 5(9/56, 100p)-Formerly Back To School			
	2.50	10.00	25.00
...County Fair 2(11/58, 100p)	2.50	10.00	25.00

DELL JUNIOR TREASURY (15 cents)
June, 1955 - No. 10, Oct, 1957 (All painted-c)
Dell Publishing Co.

	Good	Fine	N-Mint
1-Alice in Wonderland-Reprints 4-Color 331 (52 pgs.)			
	5.50	17.00	40.00
2-Aladdin & the Wonderful Lamp	4.65	14.00	32.00
3-Gulliver's Travels(1/56)	3.50	10.50	24.00
4-Advs. of Mr. Frog & Miss Mouse	4.30	13.00	30.00
5-The Wizard of Oz(7/56)	4.65	14.00	32.00
6-Heidi (10/56)	3.50	10.50	24.00
7-Santa and the Angel	3.50	10.50	24.00
8-Raggedy Ann and the Camel with the Wrinkled Knees			
	3.50	10.50	24.00
9-Clementina the Flying Pig	3.70	11.00	26.00
10-Adventures of Tom Sawyer	4.30	13.00	30.00

DEMON, THE (See Detective No. 482-485)
8-9/72 - No. 16, 1/74; 1/87 - No. 4, 4/87
National Periodical Publications

	Good	Fine	N-Mint
1-Origin; Kirby-c/a in 1-16	.25	.75	1.50
2-16		.50	1.00
1-4('87)-Mini series		.50	1.00

DEMON DREAMS
Feb, 1984 - No. 2, May, 1984
Pacific Comics

	Good	Fine	N-Mint
1,2-Mostly r-/Heavy Metal	.25	.75	1.50

DEMON-HUNTER
September, 1975
Seaboard Periodicals (Atlas)

	Good	Fine	N-Mint
1-Origin; Buckler c/a		.30	.60

DEN
1988 - No. 5, 1989 ($2.00, color, mini-series)
Fantagor Press

	Good	Fine	N-Mint
1-3: Corben-a	.35	1.00	2.00

DENNIS THE MENACE (Becomes ...Fun Fest Series; See The Best
of... & The Very Best of...)
8/53 - No. 14, 1/56; No. 15, 3/56 - No. 31, 11/58; No. 32, 1/59
- No. 166, 11/79
Standard Comics/Pines No.15-31/Hallden (Fawcett) No.32 on

	Good	Fine	N-Mint
1-1st app. Mr. & Mrs. Wilson, Ruff & Dennis' mom & dad; Wise-man-a, written by Fred Toole-most issues	19.00	57.00	132.00
2	10.00	30.00	70.00
3-10	5.00	15.00	35.00
11-20	3.00	9.00	21.00
21-30: 22-1st app. Margaret w/blonde hair	1.50	4.50	10.00
31-40: 31-1st Joey app.	1.00	3.00	7.00
41-60	.75	2.25	5.00
61-90	.50	1.50	3.00
91-166	.30	.80	1.60
...& Dirt('59,'68)-Soil Conservation giveaway; r-No. 36; Wiseman c/a	.25	.70	1.40
...Away We Go('70)-Caladayl giveaway	.25	.70	1.40
...Coping with Family Stress-giveaway		.30	.60
...Takes a Poke at Poison('61)-Food & Drug Assn. giveaway; Wiseman c/a	.35	1.00	2.00
...Takes a Poke at Poison-Revised 1/66, 11/70, 1972, 1974, 1977, 1981		.30	.60

NOTE: Wiseman c/a-1-46,53,68,69.

DENNIS THE MENACE (Giants) (No. 1 titled Giant Vacation Special;
becomes D.T.M. Bonus Magazine No. 76 on)
(No. 1-8,18,23,25,30,38: 100 pgs.; rest to No. 41: 84 pgs.; No. 42-
75: 68 pgs.)
Summer, 1955 - No. 75, Dec, 1969
Standard/Pines/Hallden(Fawcett)

	Good	Fine	N-Mint
nn-Giant Vacation Special(Summer '55-Standard)			
	4.50	13.50	36.00
nn-Christmas issue (Winter '55)	3.50	10.50	28.00
2-Giant Vacation Special (Summer '56-Pines)			
3-Giant Christmas issue (Winter '56-Pines)			
4-Giant Vacation Special (Summer '57-Pines)			
5-Giant Christmas issue (Winter '57-Pines)			
6-In Hawaii (Giant Vacation Special)(Summer '58-Pines)-Reprinted			
Summer '59 plus 3 more times			
6-Giant Christmas issue (Winter '58)			
each....	3.00	9.00	24.00
7-In Hollywood (Winter '59-Hallden)			
8-In Mexico (Winter '60, 100 pgs.-Hallden/Fawcett)			
8-In Mexico (Summer '62, 2nd printing)			
9-Goes to Camp (Summer '61, 84 pgs., 2nd printing-Summer '62)-			

Uncle Scrooge Goes To Disneyland #1, © WDC

Woody Woodpecker's Back To School #2, © W. Lantz

Dell Junior Treasury #6, © DELL

Dennis The Menace Giant #14, © FAW

Deputy Dawg Presents... #1, © Terrytoons

Design For Survival, © American Security Council

	Good	Fine	N-Mint
DENNIS THE MENACE (continued)			
1st CCA approved ish.			
10-X-Mas issue (Winter '61)			
11-Giant Christmas issue (Winter '62)			
12-Triple Feature (Winter '62)			
each....	2.50	7.50	20.00
13-Best of Dennis the Menace (Spring '63)-Reprints			
14-And His Dog Ruff (Summer '63)			
15-In Washington, D.C. (Summer '63)			
16-Goes to Camp (Summer '63)-Reprints No. 9			
17-& His Pal Joey (Winter '63)			
18-In Hawaii (Reprints No. 6)			
19-Giant Christmas issue (Winter '63)			
20-Spring Special (Spring '64)			
each....	1.50	4.50	12.00
21-40	1.00	3.00	7.00
41-75	.70	2.00	4.00

NOTE: *Wiseman c/a-1-8,12,14,15,17,20,22,27,28,31,35,36,41,49.*

DENNIS THE MENACE
Nov., 1981 - No. 13, Nov, 1982
Marvel Comics Group

1,2-New art		.25	.50
3-13: 3-Part-r. 4,5-r		.25	.50

NOTE: *Hank Ketcham c-most; a-3,12. Wiseman a-4,5.*

DENNIS THE MENACE AND HIS DOG RUFF
Summer, 1961
Hallden/Fawcett

1-Wiseman c/a	2.25	6.75	18.00

DENNIS THE MENACE AND HIS FRIENDS
1969; No. 5, Jan, 1970 - No. 46, April, 1980 (All reprints)
Fawcett Publications

Dennis T.M. & Joey No. 2 (7/69)	1.35	4.00	8.00
Dennis T.M. & Ruff No. 2 (9/69)	1.00	3.00	6.00
Dennis T.M. & Mr. Wilson No. 1 (10/69)	1.00	3.00	6.00
Dennis & Margaret No. 1 (Winter '69)	.50	1.50	3.00
5-10: No. 5-Dennis T.M. & Margaret. No. 6-& Joey. No. 7-& Ruff.			
No. 8-& Mr. Wilson	.25	.70	1.40
11-20	.25	.70	1.40
21-37		.60	1.20
38(begin digest size, 148 pgs., 4/78, 95 cents) - 46			
		.60	1.20

NOTE: *Titles rotate every four issues, beginning with No. 5.*

DENNIS THE MENACE AND HIS PAL JOEY
Summer, 1961 (10 cents) (See Dennis the Menace Giants No. 45)
Fawcett Publications

1-Wiseman c/a	2.30	7.00	16.00

DENNIS THE MENACE AND THE BIBLE KIDS
1977 (36 pages)
Word Books

1-Jesus. 2-Joseph. 3-David. 4-The Bible Girls. 5-Moses. 6-More			
About Jesus. 7-The Lord's Prayer. 8-Stories Jesus told. 9-Paul,			
God's Traveller. 10-In the Beginning each....		.25	.50

NOTE: *Ketcham c/a in all.*

DENNIS THE MENACE BIG BONUS SERIES
No. 10, 1980 - No. 11, 1980
Fawcett Publications

10,11		.50	1.00

DENNIS THE MENACE BONUS MAGAZINE (Formerly Dennis the
Menace Giants Nos. 1-75)
No. 76, 1/70 - No. 194, 10/79; (No. 76-124: 68 pgs.; No. 125-163:
52 pgs.; No. 164 on: 36 pgs.)
Fawcett Publications

	Good	Fine	N-Mint
76-90	.30	.90	1.80
91-110		.60	1.20
111-140		.40	.80
141-194		.30	.60

DENNIS THE MENACE COMICS DIGEST
April, 1982 - No. 3, Aug, 1982 (Digest Size, $1.25)
Marvel Comics Group

1-3-Reprints	.20	.60	1.25

NOTE: *Hank Ketcham c-all. Wiseman a-all. A few thousand No. 1's were published
with a DC emblem on cover.*

DENNIS THE MENACE FUN BOOK
1960 (100 pages)
Fawcett Publications/Standard Comics

1-Part Wiseman-a	2.25	6.75	18.00

DENNIS THE MENACE FUN FEST SERIES (Formerly Dennis The
Menace #166)
No. 16, Jan, 1980 - No. 17, Mar, 1980 (40 cents)
Hallden (Fawcett)

16,17-By Hank Ketcham		.20	.40

DENNIS THE MENACE POCKET FULL OF FUN!
Spring, 1969 - No. 50, March, 1980 (196 pages) (Digest size)
Fawcett Publications (Hallden)

1-Reprints in all issues	.70	2.00	4.00
2-10	.35	1.00	2.00
11-28		.50	1.00
29-50: 35,40,46-Sunday strip-r		.40	.80

NOTE: *No. 1-28 are 196 pgs.; No. 29-36: 164 pgs.; No. 37: 148 pgs.; No. 38 on: 132
pgs. No. 8, 11, 15, 21, 25, 29 all contain strip reprints.*

DENNIS THE MENACE TELEVISION SPECIAL
Summer, 1961 - No. 2, Spring, 1962 (Giant)
Fawcett Publications (Hallden Div.)

1	2.00	6.00	16.00
2	1.25	3.75	10.00

DENNIS THE MENACE TRIPLE FEATURE
Winter, 1961 (Giant)
Fawcett Publications

1-Wiseman c/a	1.75	5.25	14.00

DEPUTY, THE (See 4-Color No. 1077,1130,1225)

DEPUTY DAWG (TV) (Also see New Terrytoons)
Oct-Dec, 1961 - No. 1, Aug, 1965
Dell Publishing Co./Gold Key

4-Color 1238,1299	4.00	12.00	28.00
1(10164-508)	3.65	11.00	25.00

DEPUTY DAWG PRESENTS DINKY DUCK AND HASHIMOTO-SAN
August, 1965 (TV)
Gold Key

1(10159-508)	3.65	11.00	25.00

DESIGN FOR SURVIVAL (Gen. Thomas S. Power's...)
1968 (36 pages in color) (25 cents)
American Security Council Press

nn-Propaganda against the Threat of Communism-Aircraft cover			
	3.00	9.00	18.00
Twin Circle edition-cover shows panels from inside			
	1.70	5.00	10.00

DESPERADO (Black Diamond Western No. 9 on)
June, 1948 - No. 8, Feb, 1949
Lev Gleason Publications

1-Biro-c	5.00	15.00	35.00
2	2.65	8.00	18.00

DESPERADO (continued)	Good	Fine	N-Mint
3-Story with over 20 killings	2.30	7.00	16.00
4-8	2.00	6.00	14.00

NOTE: *Barry a-2. Kida a-3-7. Fuje a-4, 8. Guardineer a-6, 7. Ed Moore a-4, 6.*

DESTINATION MOON (See Fawcett Movie Comics, Space Adventures #20, 23, & Strange Adventures #1)

DESTROY!!
1986 (One shot, B&W, Magazine size, $4.95)
Eclipse Comics

1	.70	2.00	4.00
3-D Special 1-r-/#1 ($2.50)	.40	1.25	2.50

DESTROYER DUCK
1982 (no month) - No. 7, 5/84 (2-7: Baxter paper) ($1.50)
Eclipse Comics

1-Origin D. Duck; 1st app., origin Groo	1.50	4.50	9.00
2-7: 2-Starling back-up begins	.25	.75	1.50

NOTE: *Adams c-1i. Kirby a-1-5p; c-1-5p. Miller c-7.*

DESTRUCTOR, THE
February, 1975 - No. 4, Aug, 1975
Atlas/Seaboard

1-Origin; Ditko/Wood-a; Wood-c(i)		.60	1.20
2-4: 2-Ditko/Wood-a. 3,4-Ditko-a(p)		.40	.80

DETECTIVE COMICS (See Special Edition)
March, 1937 - Present
National Periodical Publications/DC Comics

	Good	Fine	Vf-NM
1-(Scarce)-Slam Bradley & Spy by Siegel & Shuster, Speed Saunders by Guardineer, Flat Foot Flannigan by Gustavson, Cosmo, the Phantom of Disguise, Buck Marshall, Bruce Nelson begin; Chin Lung-c from 'Claws of the Red Dragon' serial; Flessel-c (1st?)	1550.00	4650.00	10,000.00

(No copy is known to exist beyond VF condition)

	Good	Fine	N-Mint
2 (Rare)	462.00	1390.00	3000.00
3 (Rare)	385.00	1155.00	2500.00
	Good	Fine	N-Mint
4,5: 5-Larry Steele begins	200.00	600.00	1400.00
6,7,9,10	135.00	405.00	945.00
8-Mister Chang-c	170.00	510.00	1190.00
11-17,19: 17-1st app. Fu Manchu in Det.	115.00	345.00	800.00
18-Fu Manchu-c	150.00	450.00	1050.00
20-The Crimson Avenger begins (intro. & 1st app.)	155.00	465.00	1085.00
21,23-25	80.00	240.00	560.00
22-1st Crimson Avenger-c (12/38)	110.00	330.00	770.00
26	85.00	255.00	595.00
	Good	Fine	Vf-NM
27-1st app. The Batman & Commissioner Gordon by Bob Kane	3850.00	11,550.00	25,000.00

(Only one copy known to exist beyond VF-NM condition which sold in 1988 for $35,000. Prices vary widely on this book)

27-Reprint, Oversize 13½''x10.'' **WARNING:** This comic is an exact duplicate reprint of the original except for its size. DC published it in 1974 with a second cover titling it as Famous First Edition. There have been many reported cases of the outer cover being removed and the interior sold as the original edition. The reprint with the new outer cover removed is practically worthless.

	Good	Fine	N-Mint
27(1984)-Oreo Cookies giveaway (32 pgs., paper-c, r-/Det. 27, 38 & Batman No. 1 (1st Joker)	1.00	3.00	6.00
28	660.00	1980.00	4600.00
29-Batman-c; Doctor Death app.	430.00	1290.00	3000.00
30,32: 30-Dr. Death app. 32-Batman uses gun	240.00	720.00	1680.00
31-Classic Batman-c; 1st Julie Madison, Bat Plane (Bat-Gyro) & Batarang	420.00	1260.00	2940.00

	Good	Fine	N-Mint
33-Origin The Batman; Batman gunholster-c	700.00	2100.00	4900.00
34-Steve Malone begins; 2nd Crimson Avenger-c	195.00	585.00	1360.00
35-37: Batman-c. 35-Hypo-c. 36-Origin Hugo Strange. 37-Cliff Crosby begins	210.00	630.00	1470.00
38-Origin/1st app. Robin the Boy Wonder	700.00	2100.00	4900.00
39	180.00	540.00	1260.00
40-Origin & 1st app. Clay Face; 1st Joker cover app.	145.00	435.00	1015.00
41-Robin's 1st solo	125.00	375.00	875.00
42-45: 44-Crimson Avenger dons new costume. 45-1st Joker story in Det. (3rd app.)	86.00	260.00	600.00
46-50: 48-1st time car called Batmobile; Gotham City 1st mention. 49-Last Clay Face	80.00	240.00	560.00
51-57,59: 59-Last Steve Malone; 2nd Penguin; Wing becomes Crimson Avenger's aide	65.00	195.00	455.00
58-1st Penguin app.; last Speed Saunders	100.00	300.00	700.00
60-Intro. Air Wave	65.00	195.00	455.00
61-63: 63-Last Cliff Crosby; 1st app. Mr. Baffle	60.00	180.00	420.00
64-Origin & 1st app. Boy Commandos by Simon & Kirby	150.00	450.00	1050.00
65-Boy Commandos-c	80.00	240.00	560.00
66-Origin & 1st app. Two-Face	85.00	255.00	595.00
67,69,70	50.00	150.00	350.00
68-Two-Face app.	55.00	165.00	385.00
71-75: 74-1st Tweedledum & Tweedledee; S&K-a	45.00	135.00	315.00
76-Newsboy Legion & The Sandman x-over in Boy Commandos; S&K-a	55.00	165.00	385.00
77-79: All S&K-a	45.00	135.00	315.00
80-Two-Face app.; S&K-a	47.00	140.00	330.00
81,82,84-90: 81-1st Cavalier app. 85-Last Spy. 89-Last Crimson Avenger	40.00	120.00	280.00
83-1st "Skinny" Alfred; last S&K Boy Commandos? Note: most issues No. 84 on signed S&K are not by them	45.00	135.00	315.00
91-99: 96-Alfred's last name 'Beagle' revealed, later changed to 'Pennyworth'-Batman 214	37.00	110.00	260.00
100	53.00	160.00	370.00
101-120: 114-1st small logo(7/46)	35.00	105.00	245.00
121-130: 126-Electrocution-c	32.00	95.00	225.00
131-137,139: 137-Last Air Wave	28.00	84.00	195.00
138-Origin Robotman (See Star Spangled No. 7, 1st app.); series ends No. 202	48.00	145.00	335.00
140-1st app. The Riddler	65.00	195.00	455.00
141,143-150: 150-Last Boy Commandos	29.00	87.00	200.00
142-2nd Riddler app.	34.00	100.00	238.00
151-Origin & 1st app. Pow Wow Smith	30.00	90.00	210.00
152,154,155,157-160: 152-Last Slam Bradley	29.00	87.00	200.00
153-1st Roy Raymond app.; origin The Human Fly	30.00	90.00	210.00
156(2/50)-The new classic Batmobile	30.00	90.00	210.00
161-167,169-176: Last 52 pgs.	30.00	90.00	210.00
168-Origin the Joker	65.00	195.00	455.00
177-189,191-199,201-204,206-212,214-216: 187-Two-Face app. 202-Last Robotman & Pow Wow Smith. 216-Last precode (2/55)	20.00	60.00	140.00
190-Origin Batman retold	25.00	75.00	175.00
200	28.00	84.00	195.00
205-Origin Batcave	29.00	87.00	205.00
213-Origin Mirror Man	27.00	81.00	190.00
217-224	18.00	54.00	125.00
225-(11/55)-Intro. & 1st app. Martian Manhunter-John Jones, later changed to J'onn J'onzz (1st National Silver Age hero); also see			

Detective Comics #27, © DC

Detective Comics #38, © DC

Detective Comics #109, © DC

Detective Comics #526, © DC

Detective Comics #576, © DC

Detective Picture Stories #1, © CM

DETECTIVE COMICS (continued)	Good	Fine	N-Mint
Batman 78	107.00	321.00	750.00
226	29.00	87.00	200.00
227-229	18.00	54.00	125.00
230-Mad Hatter app.	21.00	65.00	150.00
231-Origin Martian Manhunter retold	13.50	41.00	95.00
232,234-240	11.50	34.00	80.00
233-Origin & 1st app. Batwoman	25.00	75.00	175.00
241-260: 246-Intro. Diane Meade, J. Jones' girl. 257-Intro. & 1st app. Whirly Bats	9.00	28.00	65.00
261-264,266,268-270: 261-1st app. Dr. Double X. 262-Origin Jackal	5.70	17.00	40.00
265-Batman's origin retold	8.50	25.50	60.00
267-Origin & 1st app. Bat-Mite	6.50	19.50	45.00
271-280: 276-2nd Bat-Mite	5.00	15.00	35.00
281-297: 287-Origin J'onn J'onzz retold. 292-Last Roy Raymond. 293-Aquaman begins, ends #300. 297-Last 10 cent issue (11/61)	3.60	11.00	25.00
298-1st modern Clayface	4.00	12.00	28.00
299-327,329,330: 311-Intro. Zook in John Jones; 1st app. Catman. 322-Batgirl's 1st app. in Det. 326-Last J'onn J'onzz; intro. Idol-Head of Diabolu. 327-Elongated Man begins; new Batman costume	2.00	6.00	14.00
328-Death of Alfred	2.85	9.00	20.00
331-358,360-368,370: 345-Intro The Block Buster. 351-Elongated Man new costume. 355-Zatanna x-over in Elongated Man. 356-Alfred brought back in Batman.	1.15	3.50	8.00
359-Intro/origin new Batgirl	1.70	5.00	12.00
369-Adams-a	1.85	5.50	13.00
371-390: 383-Elongated Man series ends. 387-r/1st Batman story from #27	1.00	3.00	6.00
391-394,396,398,399,401,403,405,406,409: 392-1st app. Jason Bard. 400,401-1st Batgirl/Robin team-up	.75	2.25	4.50
395,397,400,402,404,407,408,410-Adams-a. 400-Origin & 1st app. Man-Bat	1.20	3.60	8.00
411-420: 414-52 pgs. begin, end #424. 418-Creeper x-over	.75	2.25	4.50
421-436: 424-Last Batgirl; 1st Sne-Bat. 426-Elongated Man begins, ends #436. 428,434-Hawkman begins, ends #467	.60	1.75	3.50
437-New Manhunter begins by Simonson, ends #443	.60	1.75	3.50
438,439(100 pgs.): 439-Origin Manhunter	.75	2.25	4.50
440(100 pgs.)-G.A. Manhunter, Hawkman, Dollman, Gr. Lantern; Toth-a	.75	2.25	4.50
441(100 pgs.)-G.A. Plastic Man, Batman, Ibis-r	.75	2.25	4.50
442(100 pgs.)-G.A. Newsboy Legion, Bl. Canary, Elongated Man, Dr. Fate-r	.75	2.25	4.50
443(100 pgs.)-Origin The Creeper-r; death of Manhunter; G.A. Gr. Lantern, Spectre-r	.75	2.25	4.50
444,445(100 pgs.): 444-G.A. Kid Eternity-r. 445-G.A. Dr. Midnite-r	.50	1.50	3.00
446-460: 457-Origin retold & updated	.50	1.50	3.00
461-465,469,470,480	.50	1.50	3.00
466-468,471-476,479-Rogers-a	1.00	3.00	6.00
477-Adams-a(r); Rogers-a, 3pgs.	.85	2.50	5.00
481-(Combined with Batman Family, 12/78-1/79)(Begin $1.00 issues)	.85	2.50	5.00
482-Starlin/Russell, Golden-a; origin Demon-r	.50	1.50	3.00
483-40th Anniversary ish.; origin retold; Newton Batman begins	.40	1.25	2.50
484-495: 485-Death of Batwoman. 487-The Odd Man by Ditko. 490-Black Lightning begins. 491(492 on inside)	.40	1.25	2.50
496-499,501-520: 519-Last Batgirl	.40	1.25	2.50
500-($1.50)-Batman/Deadman team-up	.70	2.00	4.00
501-525: 519-Last Batgirl. 521-Green Arrow series begins	.35	1.00	2.00

	Good	Fine	N-Mint
526-Batman's 500th app. in Det. Comics (68 pgs., $1.50)	.75	2.25	4.50
527-571: 535-Intro. new Robin (Jason Todd). 554-1st new Bl. Canary. 567-H. Ellison scripts	.25	.75	1.50
572 (60 pgs., $1.25)-50th Anniversary	.40	1.25	2.50
573,574: 574-Origin Batman & Jason Todd retold. 579-New logo		.60	1.20
575-Year 2 begins	.70	2.00	4.00
576-578: McFarlane-a	.50	1.50	3.00
579-598		.50	1.00
Annual 1(9/88, $1.50)	.35	1.00	2.00

NOTE: **Adams** c-369, 370, 372, 383, 385, 389, 391, 392, 394-422, 439. **Aparo** a-437, 438, 444-46, 500; c-430, 437, 440-46, 448, 468-70, 480, 484(back), 492-9, 500-02, 508, 509, 515, 518-22. **Austin** a-450i, 451i, 463i-68i, 471i-76i, c-474-76i, 478i. **Baily** a-443r. **Buckler** a-434, 446p, 479p; c-467p, 482p, 505p, 506p, 511p, 513-16p, 518p. **Colan** a(p)-510, 512, 517, 523, 528-38, 540-46, 555-64, 567; c(p)-510, 512, 528, 530-35, 537, 538, 540, 541, 543-45, 556-58, 560-64. **J. Craig** a-488. **Ditko** a-443r, 483-85, 487. **Golden** a-482p. **Grell** a-445, 455, 463p, 464p; c-455. **Gustavson** a-441r. **Kaluta** c-423, 424, 426-28, 431, 434, 438, 484, 486, 572. **Bob Kane** a-Most early ish. #27 on, 297r, 438-40r, 442r, 443r. **Gil Kane** a(p)-368, 370-74, 384, 385, 388-407, 438r, 439r, 520. **Kubert** a-438r, 439r, 500; c-348-500. **McFarlane** c/a(p) 576-578. **Meskin** a-420r. **Mooney** a-444r. **Moreira** a-153-300, 419r, 444r, 445r. **Newton** a(p)-480, 481, 483-99, 501-09r, 511, 513-16, 518-20, 524, 526, 539; c-526p. **Robinson** a-part: 66, 68, 71-73; all: 74-76, 79, 80; c-62, 64, 66, 68-74, 76, 79, 82, 86, 88, 442r, 443r. **Rogers** a-467, 478p, 479p, 481p; c-471p, 472p, 473, 474-479p. **Roussos** Airwave-76-105(most). **Russell** a-481i, 482i. **Simon/Kirby** a-440r, 442r. **Simonson** a-437-43, 450, 469, 470, 500. **Starlin** a-481p, 482p; c-503, 504, 567p. **Starr** a-444r. **Toth** a-414r, 416r, 418r, 424r, 440-44r. **Tuska** a-486p, 490p. **Wrightson** c-425.

DETECTIVE DAN, SECRET OP. 48
1933 (36 pgs.; 9½x12'') (B&W; Softcover)
Humor Publ. Co.

	Good	Fine	N-Mint
By Norman Marsh; forerunner of Dan Dunn	6.50	19.50	45.00

DETECTIVE EYE (See Keen Detective Funnies)
Nov, 1940 - No. 2, Dec, 1940
Centaur Publications

	Good	Fine	N-Mint
1-Air Man & The Eye Sees begins; The Masked Marvel app.	80.00	240.00	560.00
2-Origin Don Rance and the Mysticape; Binder-a; Frank Thomas-c	60.00	180.00	420.00

DETECTIVE PICTURE STORIES (Keen Det. Funnies No. 8 on?)
Dec, 1936 - No. 7, 1937 (1st comic of a single theme)
Comics Magazine Company

	Good	Fine	N-Mint
1	105.00	315.00	735.00
2-The Clock app.	50.00	150.00	350.00
3,4: 4-Eisner-a	45.00	135.00	315.00
5-7: 5-Kane-a	40.00	120.00	280.00

DETECTIVES, THE (See 4-Color No. 1168,1219,1240)

DETECTIVES, INC. (See Eclipse Graphic Album Series)
April, 1985 - No. 2, April, 1985 (Both have April dates)
Eclipse Comics

	Good	Fine	N-Mint
1,2: 2-Nudity	.35	1.00	2.00

DETECTIVES, INC.: A TERROR OF DYING DREAMS
June, 1987 - No. 3, Dec, 1987 ($1.75, duo-tone, mini-series)
Eclipse Comics

	Good	Fine	N-Mint
1-3: adapts movie; Colan-c/a	.30	.90	1.70

DEVIL DINOSAUR
April, 1978 - No. 9, Dec, 1978
Marvel Comics Group

	Good	Fine	N-Mint
1-9		.25	.50

NOTE: **Byrne** a(i)-4-8. All **Kirby** c/a. **Kirby/Byrne** c-9.

DEVIL-DOG DUGAN (Tales of the Marines No. 4 on)
July, 1956 - No. 3, Nov, 1956
Atlas Comics (OPI)

	Good	Fine	N-Mint
1-Severin-c	3.00	9.00	21.00

DEVIL-DOG DUGAN (continued)	Good	Fine	N-Mint
2-Iron Mike McGraw x-over; Severin-c	1.70	5.00	12.00
3	1.50	4.50	10.00

DEVIL DOGS
1942
Street & Smith Publishers

	Good	Fine	N-Mint
1-Boy Rangers, U.S. Marines	8.50	26.00	60.00

DEVILINA
Feb, 1975 - No. 2, May, 1975 (Magazine) (B&W)
Atlas/Seaboard

1,2: 1-Reese-a	.50	1.50	3.00

DEVIL KIDS STARRING HOT STUFF
July, 1962 - No. 107, Oct, 1981 (Giant-Size #41-55)
Harvey Publications (Illustrated Humor)

1	6.75	20.00	45.00
2	3.35	10.00	21.00
3-10 (1/64)	2.35	7.00	14.00
11-20	1.35	4.00	8.00
21-30	1.00	3.00	6.00
31-40 ('71)	.70	2.00	4.00
41-50: All 68 pg. Giants	.85	2.50	5.00
51-55: All 52 pg. Giants	.70	2.00	4.00
56-70	.40	1.20	2.40
71-90	.30	.80	1.60
91-107		.30	.60

DEXTER COMICS
Summer, 1948 - No. 5, July, 1949
Dearfield Publ.

1	3.00	9.00	21.00
2	1.70	5.00	12.00
3-5	1.30	4.00	9.00

DEXTER THE DEMON (Formerly Melvin The Monster)
No. 7, Sept, 1957 (Also see Cartoon Kids)
Atlas Comics (HPC)

7	1.15	3.50	8.00

DIARY CONFESSIONS (Formerly Ideal Romance)
No. 9, May, 1955 - No. 10, July, 1955
Stanmor/Key Publ.

9	2.30	7.00	16.00
10	1.50	4.50	10.00

DIARY LOVES (Formerly Love Diary #1; G. I. Sweethearts #32 on)
No. 2, Nov, 1944 - No. 31, April, 1953
Quality Comics Group

2-Ward c/a, 9 pgs.	8.50	25.00	60.00
3 (1/50)	3.00	9.00	21.00
4-Crandall-a	4.85	14.50	34.00
5-7,10	2.15	6.50	15.00
8,9-Ward-a 6,8 pgs. plus Gustavson-#8	5.70	17.00	40.00
11,13,14,17-20	1.70	5.00	12.00
12,15,16-Ward-a 9,7,8 pgs.	4.85	14.50	34.00
21-Ward-a, 7 pgs.	4.00	12.00	28.00
22-31: 31-Whitney-a	1.30	4.00	9.00
NOTE: Photo c-3-5,8,12-27.			

DIARY OF HORROR
December, 1952
Avon Periodicals

1-Hollingsworth c/a; bondage-c	14.00	42.00	100.00

DIARY SECRETS (Formerly Teen-Age Diary Secrets)
No. 10, Feb, 1952 - No. 30, Sept, 1955
St. John Publishing Co.

10	6.50	19.50	45.00

	Good	Fine	N-Mint
11-Spanking panel	8.50	25.50	60.00
12-16,18,19	4.85	14.50	34.00
17,20-Kubert-a	5.70	17.00	40.00
21-30: 28-Last precode (3/55)	3.00	9.00	21.00
(See Giant Comics Ed. for Annual)			
NOTE: *Baker c/a most issues.*			

DICK COLE (Sport Thrills No. 11 on)
Dec-Jan, 1948-49 - No. 10, June-July, 1950
Curtis Publ./Star Publications

1-Sgt. Spook; L. B. Cole-c; McWilliams-a; Curt Swan's 1st work	6.00	18.00	42.00
2	4.00	12.00	28.00
3-10	3.50	10.50	24.00
Accepted Reprint #7(V1#6 on-c)(1950's)-Reprints #7			
L.B. Cole-c	2.00	6.00	14.00
Accepted Reprint #9(nd)-(Reprints #9 & #8-c)	2.00	6.00	14.00
NOTE: *L. B. Cole a-all; c 1,3,4,6-10. Dick Cole in 1-9.*			

DICKIE DARE
1941 - No. 4, 1942 (#3 on sale 6/15/42)
Eastern Color Printing Co.

1-Caniff-a; Everett-c	17.00	51.00	120.00
2	10.00	30.00	70.00
3,4-Half Scorchy Smith by Noel Sickles who was very influential in Milton Caniff's development	11.00	32.00	75.00

DICK POWELL (See A-1 Comics No. 22)

DICK QUICK, ACE REPORTER (See Picture News #10)

DICK'S ADVENTURES IN DREAMLAND (See 4-Color No. 245)

DICK TRACY (See Merry Christmas, Popular Comics, Super Comics, Tastee-Freez, Limited Coll. Ed., Harvey Comics Library, & Super Book No. 1, 7, 13, 25)

DICK TRACY
May, 1937 - Jan, 1938
David McKay Publications

Feature Books nn - 100 pgs., part reprinted as 4-Color No. 1 (appeared before Large Feat. Comics, 1st Dick Tracy comic book) (Very Rare-three known copies)			
Estimated Value....	400.00	1200.00	2800.00
Feature Books 4 - Reprints nn issue but with new cover added	72.00	215.00	500.00
Feature Books 6,9	60.00	180.00	420.00

DICK TRACY
1939 - No. 24, Dec, 1949
Dell Publishing Co.

Large Feat. Comic 1(1939)	80.00	240.00	560.00
Large Feat. Comic 4	45.00	135.00	315.00
Large Feat. Comic 8,11,13,15	40.00	120.00	280.00
4-Color 1(1939)('35-r)	115.00	345.00	800.00
4-Color 6(1940)('37-r)-(Scarce)	70.00	210.00	490.00
4-Color 8(1940)('38-'39-r)	45.00	135.00	315.00
Large Feature Comics 3(1941)	38.00	115.00	265.00
4-Color 21('41)('38-r)	40.00	120.00	280.00
4-Color 34('43)('39-'40-r)	30.00	90.00	210.00
4-Color 56('44)('40-r)	22.00	65.00	154.00
4-Color 96('46)('40-r)	17.00	51.00	120.00
4-Color 133('47)('40-'41-r)	14.00	42.00	100.00
4-Color 163('47)('41-r)	11.00	32.00	75.00
4-Color 215('48)-Titled "Sparkle Plenty," Tracy-r	7.00	21.00	50.00
Buster Brown Shoes giveaway-36 pgs. in color (1938,'39-r)-by Gould	24.00	72.00	168.00

Gillmore Giveaway-(See Super Book)
...Hatful of Fun(no date, 1950-52)-32 pgs.; 8½x10''-Dick Tracy hat promotion; D. Tracy games, magic tricks. Miller Bros. prem-

Diary Loves #3, © QUA

Diary Of Horror #1, © AVON

Dick Cole #1, © STAR

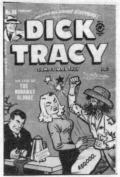

	Good	Fine	N-Mint
DICK TRACY (continued)			
ium	6.00	18.00	42.00

Motorola Giveaway('53)-Reprints Harvey Comics Library No. 2

	3.00	9.00	21.00

Popped Wheat Giveaway('47)-'40-r; 16 pgs. in color; Sig
Feuchtwanger publ.; Gould-a

	.85	2.50	5.00

. . .Presents the Family Fun Book-Tip Top Bread Giveaway, no date,
number (1940); 16 pgs. in color; Spy Smasher, Ibis, Lance
O'Casey app. Fawcett Publ.

	25.00	75.00	175.00

Same as above but without app. of heroes & Dick Tracy on cover
only

	7.50	22.50	45.00

Service Station giveaway(1958)-16 pgs. in color, regular size;
Harvey Info. Press(slick cover)

	1.70	5.00	12.00
Shoe Store Giveaway (1939, 16p)-Gould-a	10.00	30.00	70.00
1(1/48)('34-r)	32.00	95.00	225.00
2,3	17.00	51.00	120.00
4-10	15.00	45.00	105.00
11-18: 13-Bondage-c	10.00	30.00	70.00

19-1st app. Sparkle Plenty, B.O. Plenty & Gravel Gertie in a 3-pg.
strip not by Gould

	7.00	21.00	50.00
20-1st app. Sam Catchem c/a not by Gould	6.00	18.00	42.00
21-24-Only 2 pg. Gould-a in each	6.00	18.00	42.00

NOTE: No. 19-24 have a 2 pg. biography of a famous villain illustrated by Gould:
19-Little Face; 20-Flattop; 21-Breathless Mahoney; 22-Measles; 23-Itchy; 24-The Brow.

DICK TRACY (Cont'd. from Dell series)
No. 25, Mar, 1950 - No. 145, April, 1961
Harvey Publications

25	14.00	42.00	100.00
26-28,30: 28-Bondage-c	11.50	34.00	80.00
29-1st app. Gravel Gertie in a Gould-r	14.00	42.00	100.00
31,32,34,35,37-40	10.00	30.00	70.00
33-''Measles the Teen-Age Dope Pusher''	11.50	34.00	80.00
36-1st app. B.O. Plenty in a Gould-r	11.50	34.00	80.00
41-50	8.50	25.50	60.00
51-56,58-80: 51-2pgs Powell-a	8.00	24.00	56.00
57-1st app. Sam Catchem, Gould-r	10.00	30.00	70.00
81-99,101-140	6.00	18.00	42.00
100	6.50	19.50	45.00
141-145 (25 cents)	5.70	17.00	40.00

NOTE: Powell a(1-2pgs.)-43,44,104,145. No. 110-120, 141-145 are all reprints from
earlier issues.

**DICK TRACY & DICK TRACY JR. CAUGHT THE RACKETEERS,
HOW**
1933 (88 pages) (7x8½'') (Hardcover)
Cupples & Leon Co.

2-(numbered on pg. 84)-Continuation of Stooge Viller book (daily
strip reprints from 8/3/33 thru 11/8/33)

(Rarer than No. 1)	38.00	115.00	265.00
with dust jacket. . . .	60.00	180.00	420.00

Book 2 (32 pgs.; soft-c; has strips 9/18/33-11/8/33)

	19.00	57.00	132.00

**DICK TRACY & DICK TRACY JR. AND HOW THEY CAPTURED
''STOOGE'' VILLER** (See Treasure Box of Famous Comics)
1933 (7x8½'') (Hard cover; One Shot; 100 pgs.)
Reprints 1932 & 1933 Dick Tracy daily strips
Cupples & Leon Co.

nn(No.1)-1st app. of ''Stooge'' Viller	27.00	81.00	190.00
with dust jacket. . . .	42.00	125.00	295.00

DICK TRACY, EXPLOITS OF
1946 (Strip reprints) (Hardcover) ($1.00)
Rosdon Books, Inc.

1-Reprints the complete case of ''The Brow'' from early 1940s

	19.00	57.00	132.00
with dust jacket. . . .	32.00	95.00	225.00

	Good	Fine	N-Mint
DICK TRACY MONTHLY/WEEKLY			

May, 1986 - Present ($2.00, B&W) (becomes Weekly #26 on)
Blackthorne Publ.

1-60: Gould-r. 30,31-Mr. Crime app.	.35	1.00	2.00
3-D Special 1('86)('58-r)	.60	1.75	3.50

DICK TRACY SHEDS LIGHT ON THE MOLE
1949 (16 pgs.) (Ray-O-Vac Flashlights giveaway)
Western Printing Co.

Not by Gould	5.00	15.00	35.00

DICK TRACY UNPRINTED STORIES
Sept., 1987 - No. 4? ($2.95, B&W)
Blackthorne Publ.

1-4	.50	1.50	3.00

DICK TURPIN (See Legend of Young. . .)

DICK WINGATE OF THE U.S. NAVY
1951; 1953 (no month)
Superior Publ./Toby Press

nn-U.S. Navy giveaway	1.30	4.00	9.00
1(1953, Toby)	1.85	5.50	13.00

DIE, MONSTER, DIE (See Movie Classics)

DIG 'EM
1973 (16 pgs.) (2-3/8x6'')
Kellogg's Sugar Smacks Giveaway

4 different		.50	1.00

DILLY (Dilly Duncan from Daredevil Comics)
May, 1953 - No. 3, Sept, 1953
Lev Gleason Publications

1-Biro-c	2.00	6.00	14.00
2,3-Biro-c	1.15	3.50	8.00

DIME COMICS
1945; 1951
Newsbook Publ. Corp.

1-Silver Streak app.; L. B. Cole-c	13.00	40.00	90.00
1(1951), 5	1.70	5.00	12.00

DINGBATS (See First Issue Special)

DING DONG
Summer?, 1946 - No. 5, 1947 (52 pgs.)
Compix/Magazine Enterprises

1-Funny animal	3.00	9.00	21.00
2 (11/46)	1.50	4.50	10.00
3 (Wint '46-'47) - 5	1.00	3.00	7.00

DINKY DUCK (Paul Terry's. . .) (See Blue Ribbon & New Terrytoons)
11/51 - No. 16, 9/55; No. 16, Fall/'56; No. 17, 5/57 - No. 19,
Summer/'58
St. John Publishing Co./Pines No. 16 on

1	3.00	9.00	21.00
2	1.50	4.50	10.00
3-10	1.00	3.00	7.00
11-16(9/55)	.75	2.25	5.00
16(Fall,'56) - 19	.55	1.65	4.00

DINKY DUCK & HASHIMOTO-SAN (See Deputy Dawg Presents. . .)

DINO (TV)(The Flintstones)
Aug, 1973 - No. 20, Jan, 1977
Charlton Publications

1	.50	1.50	3.00
2-20		.50	1.00

DINO RIDERS
Feb, 1989 - Present ($1.00, color)

DINO RIDERS (continued)
Marvel Comics

	Good	Fine	N-Mint
1-Based on toys		.50	1.00

DINOSAUR REX
Sum, 1986 - No. 3, 1986 (mini-series; $2.00)
Upshot Graphics (Fantagraphics Books)

1-3	.30	.90	1.80

DINOSAURS FOR HIRE
Mar., 1988 - Present ($1.95, B&W)
Eternity Comics

1-4	.35	1.00	1.95

DINOSAURUS (See 4-Color No. 1120)

DIPPY DUCK
October, 1957
Atlas Comics (OPI)

1-Maneely-a	2.00	6.00	14.00

DIRECTORY TO A NONEXISTENT UNIVERSE
Dec., 1987 ($2.00, B&W)
Eclipse Comics

1	.35	1.00	2.00

DIRTY DOZEN (See Movie Classics)

DISHMAN
Sept., 1988 - Present ($2.50, B&W, 52pgs)
Eclipse Comics

1	.40	1.25	2.50

DISNEYLAND BIRTHDAY PARTY (Also see Dell Giants)
Aug, 1985 ($2.50)
Gladstone Publishing Co.

1-R-/Dell Giant with new-photo-c	.40	1.25	2.50
...Comics Digest #1-(Digest)		.60	1.25

DISNEYLAND, USA (See Dell Giant No. 30)

DISNEY'S DUCKTALES (TV)
Oct., 1988 - Present (1,2: $1.50; 3-on: 95 cents, color)
Gladstone Publishing

1-Barks-r	.40	1.25	2.50
2,3: 2-Barks-r	.25	.80	1.60
4,5: 4-Barks-r	.25	.75	1.50

DISTANT SOIL, A
Dec., 1983 - Present ($1.50, B&W)
WaRP Graphics

1-Panda Khan app.	.50	1.50	3.00
2-5	.35	1.00	2.00
6-10	.25	.75	1.50
Graphic Novel ($6.95)	1.20	3.50	7.00

DIVER DAN (TV)
Feb-Apr, 1962 - No. 2, June-Aug, 1962
Dell Publishing Co.

4-Color 1254, 2	2.65	8.00	18.00

DIXIE DUGAN (Also see Columbia Comics & Feature Funnies)
July, 1942 - No. 13, 1949
McNaught Syndicate/Columbia/Publication Ent.

1-Joe Palooka x-over by Ham Fisher	11.50	34.00	80.00
2	6.00	18.00	42.00
3	4.60	14.00	32.00
4,5(1945-46)	2.85	8.50	20.00
6-13(1948-49)	2.15	6.50	15.00

DIXIE DUGAN
Nov, 1951 - V4/4, Feb, 1954

Prize Publications (Headline)

	Good	Fine	N-Mint
V3No.1	3.00	9.00	21.00
2-4	2.00	6.00	14.00
V4No.1-4(No.5-8)	1.50	4.50	10.00

DIZZY DAMES
Sept-Oct, 1952 - No. 6, July-Aug, 1953
American Comics Group (B&M Distr. Co.)

1	3.70	11.00	26.00
2	2.30	7.00	16.00
3-6	1.50	4.50	10.00

DIZZY DON COMICS
1942 - No. 22, Oct, 1946 (B&W)
F. E. Howard Publications/Dizzy Don Ent. Ltd (Canada)

1	2.35	7.00	16.00
2	1.15	3.50	8.00
3-21	1.00	3.00	7.00
22-Full color, 52pgs.	1.70	5.00	12.00

DIZZY DUCK (Formerly Barnyard Comics)
No. 32, Nov, 1950 - No. 39, Mar, 1952
Standard Comics

32	3.00	9.00	21.00
33-39	1.50	4.50	10.00

DNAGENTS (The New DNAgents V2/1 on)(Also see Surge)
March, 1983 - No. 24, July, 1985 ($1.50, Baxter paper)
Eclipse Comics

1-Origin	.55	1.65	3.30
2-10: 4-Amber app.	.45	1.40	2.80
11-24: 18-Infinity-c	.35	1.00	2.00

NOTE: *Spiegle a-9. Dave Stevens c-24.*

DOBERMAN (See Sgt. Bilko's Private. . .)

DOBIE GILLIS (See The Many Loves of. . .)

DOC CARTER VD COMICS
1949 (16 pages in color) (Paper cover)
Health Publications Institute, Raleigh, N. C. (Giveaway)

	17.00	51.00	120.00

DOC SAVAGE
November, 1966
Gold Key

1-Adaptation of the Thousand-Headed Man; James Bama-c r-/'64			
Doc Savage paperback	2.00	6.00	14.00

DOC SAVAGE
Oct, 1972 - No. 8, Jan, 1974
Marvel Comics Group

1		.40	.80
2-8: 2,3-Steranko-c		.25	.50
Giant-Size 1(1975)-Reprints No. 1 & 2		.30	.60

NOTE: *Mooney a-1i, Gnt-Size fr. No. 1,2 adapts pulp story "The Man of Bronze," No. 3,4 adapts "Death in Silver," No. 5,6 adapts "The Monsters," No. 7,8 adapts "The Brand of The Werewolf."*

DOC SAVAGE (Magazine)
Aug, 1975 - No. 8, Spr, 1977 (Black & White)
Marvel Comics Group

1-Cover from movie poster	.25	.75	1.50
2-8		.50	1.00

NOTE: *John Buscema a-1,3.*

DOC SAVAGE
Nov, 1987 - No. 4, Feb, 1988 ($1.75, mini-series)
DC Comics

1-Adam & Andy Kubert c/a	.35	1.00	2.00
2-4	.35	1.00	2.00

Disney's Duck Tales #1, © WDC

Dixie Dugan #1 (7/42), © CCG

Dizzy Duck #33, © STD

Doc Savage #1 (11/88), © Conde Nast Publ./DC   *Doc Savage Comics #5, © S & S*   *Doctor Strange #169, © MEG*

DOC SAVAGE
Nov., 1988 - Present ($1.75, color)
DC Comics

	Good	Fine	N-Mint
1	.35	1.00	2.00
2-4	.30	.90	1.75

DOC SAVAGE COMICS (Also see Shadow Comics)
May, 1940 - No. 20, Oct, 1943 (1st app. in D. Savage pulp, 3/33)
Street & Smith Publications

1-Doc Savage, Cap Fury, Danny Garrett, Mark Mallory, The Whisperer, Captain Death, Billy the Kid, Sheriff Pete & Treasure Island begin; Norgil, the Magician app. — 100.00 300.00 700.00
2-Origin & 1st app. Ajax, the Sun Man; Danny Garrett, The Whisperer end — 50.00 150.00 350.00
3 — 40.00 120.00 280.00
4-Treasure Island ends; Tuska-a — 30.00 90.00 210.00
5-Origin & 1st app. Astron, the Crocodile Queen, not in No. 9 & 11; Norgil the Magician app. — 25.00 75.00 175.00
6-9: 6-Cap Fury ends; origin & only app. Red Falcon in Astron story. 8-Mark Mallory ends. 9-Supersnipe app.
— 20.00 60.00 140.00
10-Origin & only app. The Thunderbolt — 20.00 60.00 140.00
11,12 — 16.00 48.00 110.00
V2#1-8(#13-20): 16-The Pulp Hero, The Avenger app. 17-Sun Man ends; Nick Carter begins — 16.00 48.00 110.00

DR. ANTHONY KING, HOLLYWOOD LOVE DOCTOR
1952(Jan.) - No. 3, May, 1953; No. 4, May, 1954
Minoan Publishing Corp./Harvey Publications No. 4

1	4.50	13.50	32.00
2-4: 4-Powell-a	3.00	9.00	21.00

DR. ANTHONY'S LOVE CLINIC (See Mr. Anthony's . . .)

DR. BOBBS (See 4-Color No. 212)

DOCTOR BOOGIE
1987 ($1.75, color)
Media Arts Publ.

1	.30	.90	1.75

DR. FATE (See First Issue Special, The Immortal . . ., Justice League, More Fun, & Showcase)

DOCTOR FATE
July, 1987 - No. 4, Oct, 1987 (mini-series, $1.50, Baxter)
DC Comics

1-Giffen c/a begins	.35	1.00	2.00
2-4	.30	.90	1.80

DR. FATE
Winter, 1988-'89 - Present ($1.25, color)
DC Comics

1		.60	1.25

DR. FU MANCHU (See The Mask of . . .)
1964
I.W. Enterprises

1-Reprints Avon's "Mask of Dr. Fu Manchu;" Wood-a
6.75 20.00 45.00

DOCTOR GRAVES (Formerly The Many Ghosts of . . .)
No. 73, Sept, 1985 - No. 75, Jan, 1986
Charlton Comics

73-75		.40	.75

DR. JEKYLL AND MR. HYDE (See A Star Presentation)

DR. KILDARE (TV)
No. 1337, 4-6/62 - No. 9, 4-6/65 (All photo-c)
Dell Publishing Co.

4-Color 1337('62)	3.00	9.00	21.00

	Good	Fine	N-Mint
2-9	2.00	6.00	14.00

DR. MASTERS (See The Adventures of Young . . .)

DOCTOR SOLAR, MAN OF THE ATOM
10/62 - No. 27, 4/69; No. 28, 4/81 - No. 31, 3/82
Gold Key/Whitman No. 28 on (Painted-c No. 1-27)

1-Origin Dr. Solar (1st Gold Key comic-No. 10000-210)
3.50 10.50 24.00
2-Prof. Harbinger begins 1.70 5.00 12.00
3-5: 5-Intro. Man of the Atom in costume 1.30 4.00 9.00
6-10 1.00 3.00 7.00
11-14,16-20 .70 2.00 5.00
15-Origin retold .85 2.50 6.00
21-27 .60 1.80 4.00
28-31: 29-Magnus Robot Fighter begins. 31-The Sentinel app.
.40 .80

NOTE: **Frank Bolle** a-6-19, 29-31; c-29i, 30i. **Bob Fugitani** a-1-5. **Spiegle** a-29-31. **Al McWilliams** a-20-23.

DOCTOR SPEKTOR (See The Occult Files of . . .)

DOCTOR STRANGE (Strange Tales No. 1-168) (Also see The Defenders, Marvel Fanfare, Marvel Graphic Novel, Marvel Premiere, Marvel Treas. Ed. and Strange Tales, 2nd Series)
No. 169 - No. 183, 11/69; 6/74 - No. 81, 2/87
Marvel Comics Group

169(#1)-Origin; panel swipe/M.D. #1-c 1.15 3.50 8.00
170-183: 177-New costume .85 2.50 5.00
1(6/74)-Brunner c/a 1.15 3.50 7.00
2-5 .50 1.50 3.00
6-26: 21-Origin/Str. Tales 169 .30 .90 1.80
27-81: 56-Origin retold .60 1.20

NOTE: **Adkins** a-169, 170, 171i; c-169-71, 172i, 173. **Adams** a-4i. **Austin** a-48-60i, 66i, 68i, 70i; c-38i, 47-53i, 55i, 58-60i, 70i. **Brunner** a-1-5p; c-1-6, 22, 28-30, 33. **Colan** a(p)-172-78, 180-83, 6-18, 36-45, 47; c(p)-172, 174-83, 11-21, 23, 27, 35, 36, 47. **Ditko** a-179i; **Dr. Everett** c-183i. **Golden** a-46p, 55p; c-42-44, 46, 55p. **G. Kane** c(p)-8-10. **Miller** c-46p. **Nebres** a-20, 22, 23, 24i, 26i, 32i; c-32i, 34. **Rogers** a-48-53p; c-47p-53p. **Russell** a-34i, 46i, Annual 1. **B. Smith** c-179. **Paul Smith** a-54p, 56p, 65, 66p, 68p, 69, 71-73; c-56, 65, 66, 68, 71. **Starlin** a-23p, 26; c-25, 26. **Sutton** a-27-29p, 34p.

Annual 1(1976)-Russell-a .35 1.00 2.00
Giant Size 1(11/75)-Str. Tales-r .35 1.00 2.00
. . ./Silver Dagger (Special Edition)(3/83)($2.50, Baxter paper)-r-/ Dr. Strange 1,2,4,5 & Strange Tales 127; Wrightson-c
.35 1.00 2.00

DOCTOR STRANGE CLASSICS
Mar, 1984 - No. 4, June, 1984 ($1.50 cover price; Baxter paper)
Marvel Comics Group

1-4: Ditko reprints	.25	.75	1.50

DOCTOR STRANGE, SORCERER SUPREME
Nov., 1988 - Present (Color, Mando paper, direct sales only)
Marvel Comics

1 ($1.25) .60 1.25
2,3 ($1.50): 3-New Defenders app. .25 .75 1.50

DR. TOM BRENT, YOUNG INTERN
Feb, 1963 - No. 5, Oct, 1963
Charlton Publications

1	.50	1.50	3.00
2-5	.35	1.00	2.00

DR. VOLTZ (See Mighty Midget Comics)

DOCTOR WHO (Also see Marvel Premiere #57-60)
Oct, 1984 - No. 23, Aug, 1986 (Direct sales, Baxter paper, $1.50)
Marvel Comics Group

1-($1.50 cover)-British-r .40 1.25 2.50
2-23 .35 1.00 2.00

DR. WHO & THE DALEKS (See Movie Classics)

DOCTOR ZERO
April, 1988 - Present ($1.25/$1.00, color)
Epic Comics (Marvel)

	Good	Fine	N-Mint
1-4	.25	.75	1.50

DO-DO
1950 - 1951 (5x7¼'' Miniature) (5 cents)
Nation Wide Publishers

1 (52 pgs.); funny animal	1.15	3.50	8.00
2-7	.85	2.50	6.00

DODO & THE FROG, THE (Formerly Funny Stuff)
9-10/54 - No. 88, 1-2/56; No. 89, 8-9/56; No. 90, 10-11/56; No. 91, 9/57; No. 92, 11/57 (See Comic Cavalcade)
National Periodical Publications

80-Doodles Duck by Sheldon Mayer	4.30	13.00	30.00
81-91: Doodles Duck by Sheldon Mayer in No. 81,83-90			
	2.65	8.00	18.00
92-(Scarce)-Doodles Duck by S. Mayer	4.30	13.00	30.00

DOGFACE DOOLEY
1951 - 1953
Magazine Enterprises

1(A-1 40)	2.00	6.00	14.00
2(A-1 43), 3(A-1 49), 4(A-1 53), 5(A-1 64)	1.30	4.00	9.00
I.W. Reprint #1('64), Super Reprint #17	.70	2.00	4.00

DOG OF FLANDERS, A (See 4-Color No. 1088)

DOGPATCH (See Al Capp's . . . & Mammy Yokum)

DOINGS OF THE DOO DADS, THE
1922 (34 pgs.; 7¾x7¾''; B&W) (50 cents)
(Red & White cover; square binding)
Detroit News (Universal Feat. & Specialty Co.)

Reprints 1921 newspaper strip ''Text & Pictures'' given away as prize in the Detroit News Doo Dads contest; by Arch Dale

	7.00	21.00	50.00

DOLLFACE & HER GANG (See 4-Color No. 309)

DOLL MAN (Also see Feature Comics #27 for 1st app.)
Fall, 1941 - No. 7, Fall, '43; No. 8, Spring, '46 - No. 47, Oct, 1953
Quality Comics Group

1-Dollman (by Cassone) & Justin Wright begin			
	95.00	285.00	665.00
2-The Dragon begins; Crandall-a(5)	52.00	155.00	365.00
3	35.00	105.00	245.00
4	26.00	78.00	182.00
5-Crandall-a	23.00	70.00	160.00
6,7(1943)	18.00	54.00	125.00
8(1946)-1st app. Torchy by Bill Ward	20.00	60.00	140.00
9	15.00	45.00	105.00
10-20	12.00	36.00	84.00
21-30	11.00	32.00	75.00
31-36,38,40: Jeb Rivers app. #32-34	9.00	27.00	62.00
37-Origin Dollgirl; Dollgirl bondage-c	11.00	32.00	75.00
39-''Narcotics...the Death Drug''-c-/story	8.00	24.00	56.00
41-47	6.50	19.50	45.00
Super Reprint #11('64, r-#20),15(r-#23),17(r-#28): Torchy app.-#15,17			
	1.35	4.00	8.00

NOTE: **Ward** Torchy in 8, 9, 11, 12, 14-24, 27; by **Fox**-#30, 35-47. **Crandall** a-2,5,10,13 & Super #11,17,18. **Guardineer** a-3. Bondage-c #27,37,38,39.

DOLLY
1951 (Funny animal)
Ziff-Davis Publ. Co.

10	1.50	4.50	10.00

DOLLY DILL
1945
Marvel Comics/Newsstand Publ.

	Good	Fine	N-Mint
1	6.00	18.00	42.00

DOLLY DIMPLES & BOBBY BOONCE'
1933
Cupples & Leon Co.

	6.00	18.00	42.00

DOMINO CHANCE
May, 1984 - No. 9, May, 1985
Chance Ent.

1	2.50	7.50	15.00
1-Reprint, May 1985	.50	1.50	3.00
2-6,9		.50	1.00
7-1st app. Gizmo, 2 pgs.	1.35	4.00	8.00
8-1st full Gizmo story	2.00	6.00	12.00

DONALD AND MICKEY IN DISNEYLAND (See Dell Giants)

DONALD AND MICKEY MERRY CHRISTMAS (Formerly Famous Gang)
1943 - 1949 (20 pgs.)(Giveaway) Put out each Christmas; 1943 issue titled ''Firestone Presents Comics'' (Disney)
K. K. Publ./Firestone Tire & Rubber Co.

1943-Donald Duck reprint from WDC&S #32 by Carl Barks			
	53.00	160.00	370.00
1944-Donald Duck reprint from WDC&S #35 by Barks			
	50.00	150.00	350.00
1945-''Donald Duck's Best Christmas,'' 8 pgs. Carl Barks; intro. & 1st app. Grandma Duck in comic books	64.00	190.00	450.00
1946-Donald Duck in ''Santa's Stormy Visit,'' 8 pgs. Carl Barks			
	47.00	140.00	330.00
1947-Donald Duck in ''Three Good Little Ducks,'' 8 pgs. Carl Barks			
	40.00	120.00	280.00
1948-Donald Duck in ''Toyland,'' 8 pgs. Carl Barks			
	37.00	110.00	260.00
1949-Donald Duck in ''New Toys,'' 8 pgs. Carl Barks			
	46.00	138.00	320.00

DONALD AND THE WHEEL (See 4-Color No. 1190)

DONALD DUCK (See Cheerios, Gladstone Comic Album, Mickey Mouse Mag., Story Hour Series, Uncle Scrooge, Walt Disney's C&S, Wheaties & Whitman Comic Books)

DONALD DUCK
1935, 1936 (Linen-like text & color pictures; 1st book ever devoted to Donald Duck; see The Wise Little Hen for earlier app.) (9½x13'')
Whitman Publishing Co./Grosset & Dunlap/K.K.

978(1935)-16 pgs.; story book	50.00	150.00	350.00
nn(1936)-36 pgs.; reprints '35 edition with expanded ill. & text			
	40.00	120.00	280.00
with dust jacket....	50.00	150.00	350.00

DONALD DUCK (Walt Disney's) (10 cents)
1938 (B&W) (8½x11½'') (Cardboard covers)
Whitman/K.K. Publications

(Has Donald Duck with bubble pipe on front cover)

	Good	Fine	VF-NM
nn-The first Donald Duck & Walt Disney comic book; 1936 & 1937 Sunday strip-r(in B&W); same format as the Feature Books; 1st strips with Huey, Dewey & Louie from 10/17/37			
	95.00	285.00	665.00

(Prices vary widely on this book)

DONALD DUCK (Walt Disney's...#262 on; see 4-Color listings for titles & 4-Color No. 1109 for origin story)
1940 - No. 84, 9-11/62; No. 85, 12/62 - No. 245, 1984; No. 246, 10/86 - Present

Dogface Dooley #1, © ME   *Doll Man #29, © QUA*   *Donald And Mickey Merry Christmas 1944, © WDC*

Donald Duck 4-Color #9, © WDC   Donald Duck 4-Color #159, © WDC   Donald Duck 4-Color #275, © WDC

DONALD DUCK (continued)
Dell Publishing Co./Gold Key No. 85-216/Whitman No. 217-245/
Gladstone No. 246 on

	Good	Fine	N-Mint
4-Color 4(1940)-Daily 1939 strip-r by Al Taliaferro	300.00	900.00	2100.00
Large Feat. Comic 16(1/41?)-1940 Sunday strips-r in B&W	145.00	435.00	1015.00
Large Feat. Comic 20('41)-Comic Paint Book, r-single panels from Large Feat. 16 at top of each page to color; daily strip-r across bottom of each page	205.00	615.00	1435.00
4-Color 9('42)-"Finds Pirate Gold;"-64 pgs. by Carl Barks & Jack Hannah (pgs. 1,2,5,12-40 are by Barks, his 1st comic book work; © 8/17/42)	357.00	1070.00	2500.00
4-Color 29(9/43)-"Mummy's Ring" by Carl Barks; reprinted in Uncle Scrooge & Donald Duck No. 1('65) & W.D. Comics Digest #44('73)	225.00	675.00	1575.00

(Prices vary widely on all above books)

	Good	Fine	N-Mint
4-Color 62(1/45)-"Frozen Gold;" 52 pgs. by Carl Barks, reprinted in The Best of W.D. Comics & D.D. Advs. #4	120.00	360.00	840.00
4-Color 108(1946)-"Terror of the River;" 52 pgs. by Carl Barks	90.00	270.00	630.00
4-Color 147(5/47)-in "Volcano Valley" by Carl Barks	60.00	180.00	420.00
4-Color 159(8/47)-in "The Ghost of the Grotto;" 52 pgs. by Carl Barks-reprinted in Best of Uncle Scrooge & Donald Duck #1 ('66) & The Best of W.D. Comics & D.D. Advs. #9; two Barks stories	52.00	156.00	364.00
4-Color 178(12/47)-1st Uncle Scrooge by Carl Barks; reprinted in Gold Key Christmas Parade No. 3 & The Best of W.D. Comics	60.00	180.00	420.00
4-Color 189(6/48)-by Carl Barks; reprinted in Best of Donald Duck & Uncle Scrooge #1('64)	52.00	156.00	364.00
4-Color 199(10/48)-by Carl Barks; mentioned in Love and Death;r/in Gladstone Comic Album #5	52.00	156.00	364.00
4-Color 203(12/48)-by Barks; reprinted as Gold Key Christmas Parade #4	36.00	108.00	250.00
4-Color 223(4/49)-by Barks; reprinted as Best of Donald Duck #1 & D.D. Advs. #3	50.00	150.00	350.00
4-Color 238(8/49), 256(12/49)-by Barks; No. 256-reprinted in Best of Donald Duck & Uncle Scrooge #2('67) & W.D. Comics Digest #44('73)	27.00	81.00	190.00
4-Color 263(2/50)-Two Barks stories	27.00	81.00	190.00
4-Color 275(5/50), 282(7/50), 291(9/50), 300(11/50)-All by Carl Barks; #275,282 reprinted in W.D. Comics Digest #44('73). #275 r/in Gladstone Comic Album #10	25.00	75.00	175.00
4-Color 308(1/51), 318(3/51)-by Barks; #318-reprinted in W.D. Comics Digest #34 & D.D. Advs. #2	21.00	63.00	147.00
4-Color 328(5/51)-by Carl Barks (drug issue)	23.00	70.00	160.00
4-Color 339(7-8/51), 379-not by Barks	4.35	13.00	30.00
4-Color 348(9-10/51), 356,394-Barks-c only	6.00	18.00	42.00
4-Color 367(1-2/52) by Barks; reprinted as Gold Key Christmas Parade #2 & #8	20.00	60.00	140.00
4-Color 408(7-8/52), 422(9-10/52)-All by Carl Barks. #408-R/in Best of Donald Duck & Uncle Scrooge #1('64)	20.00	60.00	140.00
26(11-12/52)-In "Trick or Treat"(Barks-a, 36pgs.) 1st story r-/Walt Disney Digest #16	22.00	65.00	154.00
27-30-Barks-c only	4.30	13.00	30.00
31-40	2.65	8.00	18.00
41-44,47-50	2.00	6.00	14.00
45-Barks-a, 6 pgs.	7.00	21.00	50.00
46-"Secret of Hondorica" by Barks, 24 pgs.; reprinted in Donald Duck #98 & 154	8.00	24.00	56.00
51-Barks, ½ pg.	1.70	5.00	12.00
52-"Lost Peg-Leg Mine" by Barks, 10 pgs.	6.50	19.50	45.00
53,55-59	1.60	4.80	11.00
54-"Forbidden Valley" by Barks, 26 pgs.	7.50	22.00	52.00
60-"D.D. & the Titanic Ants" by Barks, 20 pgs. plus 6 more pgs.	6.50	19.50	45.00
61-67,69,70	1.30	4.00	9.00
68-Barks-a, 5 pgs.	3.75	11.25	26.00
71-Barks-r, ½ pg.	1.50	4.50	10.00
72-78,80,82-97,99,100: 96-Donald Duck Album	1.15	3.50	8.00
79,81-Barks-a, 1pg.	1.50	4.50	10.00
98-Reprints #46 (Barks)	2.15	6.50	15.00
101-133: 112-1st Moby Duck	.85	2.50	6.00
134-Barks-r/#52 & WDC&S 194	1.00	3.00	7.00
135-Barks-r/WDC&S 198, 19 pgs.	.70	2.00	5.00
136-153,155,156,158	.50	1.50	3.00
154-Barks-r/(#46)	.70	2.00	5.00
157-Barks-r/(#45)	.40	1.25	2.50
159-Reprints/WDC&S #192	.40	1.25	2.50
160-Barks-r/(#26)	.40	1.25	2.50
161-163,165-170	.25	.75	1.50
164-Barks-r/(#79)	.40	1.25	2.50
171-173,175-187,189-191		.60	1.20
174-Reprints 4-Color 394	.35	1.00	2.00
188-Barks-r/#68	.35	1.00	2.00
192-Barks-r(40 pgs.) from Donald Duck #60 & WDC&S #226,234 (52 pgs.)	.40	1.25	2.50
193-200,202-207,209-211,213-218: 217 has 216 on-c		.50	1.00
201-Barks-r/Christ. Parade 26, 16pgs.	.35	1.00	2.00
208-Barks-r/#60	.35	1.00	2.00
212-Barks-r/WDC&S 130	.35	1.00	2.00
219-Barks-r/WDC&S 106,107, 10 pgs. ea.		.60	1.20
220-227,231-245		.35	.70
228-Barks-r/F.C. 275	.25	.75	1.50
229-Barks-r/F.C. 282	.25	.75	1.50
230-Barks-r/#52 & WDC&S 194	.25	.75	1.50
246-(1st Gladstone)-Barks-r/FC 422	.85	2.50	5.00
247-249: 248-Barks-r/DD 54. 249-Barks-r/DD DD 26	.40	1.25	2.50
250-Barks-r/4-Color 9, 64 pgs.	.60	1.75	3.50
251-256: 251-Barks-r/'45 Firestone. 254-Barks-r/FC 328. 256-Barks-r/FC 147	.35	1.00	2.00
257-Barks-r/Vac. Parade #1 (52 pgs.)	.35	1.00	2.00
258-260	.25	.75	1.50
261-275: 261-Barks-r/FC 300		.50	1.00
Mini-Comic #1(1976)-(3¼x6½"); R/D.D. #150			.10

NOTE: Carl Barks wrote all issues he illustrated, but #117, 126, 138 contain his script only. Issues 4-Color #189, 199, 203, 223, 238, 256, 263, 275, 282, 308, 348, 356, 367, 394, 408, 422, 26-30, 35, 44, 46, 52, 55, 57, 60, 65, 70-73, 77-80, 83, 101, 103, 105, 106, 111, 126, 246r, 266r, 268r all have Barks covers. Barks a-263r-267r,269r. #96 titled "Comic Album," #99-"Christmas Album." New art issues (not reprints)-106-46, 148-63, 167, 169, 170, 172, 173, 175, 178, 179, 196, 209, 223, 225, 236.

DONALD DUCK
1944 (16 pg. Christmas giveaway)(paper cover)(2 versions)
K. K. Publications

	Good	Fine	N-Mint
Kelly cover reprint	37.00	110.00	260.00

DONALD DUCK ADVENTURES (Walt Disney's. . .#4 on)
Nov., 1987 - Present
Gladstone Publishing

	Good	Fine	N-Mint
1	.50	1.50	3.00
2-r/F.C. 308	.35	1.00	2.00
3-5: 3-r/F.C. 223. 4-r/F.C. 62	.25	.75	1.50
6-11: 5,8-Don Rosa-a. 9-r/F.C. 159		.50	1.00
12($1.50, 52pgs.)-Rosa-c/a w/poster insert	.25	.75	1.50

NOTE: Barks a-1-12r; c-10r.

DONALD DUCK ALBUM (See Duck Album & Comic Album No. 1,3)
May-July, 1959 - Oct, 1963

DONALD DUCK ALBUM (continued)
Dell Publishing Co./Gold Key

	Good	Fine	N-Mint
4-Color 995,1182, 01204-207 (1962-Dell)	2.00	6.00	14.00
4-Color 1099,1140,1239-Barks-c	2.30	7.00	16.00
1(8/63-Gold Key)-Barks-c	2.00	6.00	14.00
2(10/63)	1.00	3.00	7.00

DONALD DUCK AND THE BOYS (Also see Story Hour Series)
1948 (Hardcover book; 5¼x5½'') 100pgs., ½art, ½text
Whitman Publishing Co.

845-Partial r-/WDC&S No. 74 by Barks	17.00	51.00	120.00

(Prices vary widely on this book)

DONALD DUCK AND THE RED FEATHER
1948 (4 pages) (8½x11'') (Black & White)
Red Feather Giveaway

	4.60	14.00	32.00

DONALD DUCK BEACH PARTY (See Dell Giants)
Sept, 1965 (25 cents)
Gold Key

1(#10158-509)-Barks-r/WDC&S #45	3.00	9.00	21.00

DONALD DUCK BOOK (See Story Hour Series)

DONALD DUCK COMIC PAINT BOOK (See Large Feat. Comic No. 20)

DONALD DUCK COMICS DIGEST
1986 - No. 5, 1987? ($1.25-$1.50, 96 pgs.)
Gladstone Publishing

1-3: 1-Barks c/a-r		.60	1.25
4,5	.25	.75	1.50

DONALD DUCK FUN BOOK (See Dell Giants)

DONALD DUCK IN DISNEYLAND (See Dell Giants)

DONALD DUCK IN ''THE LITTERBUG''
1963 (16 pgs., 5x7¼'', soft-c) (Disney giveaway)
Keep America Beautiful

	2.00	6.00	14.00

DONALD DUCK MARCH OF COMICS
1947 - 1951 (Giveaway) (Disney)
K. K. Publications

nn(No.4)-''Maharajah Donald;'' 30 pgs. by Carl Barks-(1947)	428.00	1285.00	3000.00
20-''Darkest Africa'' by Carl Barks-(1948); 22 pgs.	257.00	770.00	1800.00
41-''Race to South Seas'' by Carl Barks-(1949); 22 pgs.(On Disney's band list)	200.00	600.00	1400.00
56-(1950)-Barks-a on back-c	22.00	65.00	140.00
69-(1951)-Not Barks	19.00	57.00	125.00
263	6.00	18.00	36.00

DONALD DUCK MERRY XMAS (See Dell Giant No. 53)

DONALD DUCK PICNIC PARTY (See Picnic Party under Dell Giant)

DONALD DUCK ''PLOTTING PICNICKERS''
1962 (16 pgs., 3¼x7'', soft-c) (Disney)(Also see Ludwig Von Drake &
Mickey Mouse)
Fritos Giveaway

	2.30	7.00	16.00

DONALD DUCK'S SURPRISE PARTY
1948 (16 pgs.) (Giveaway for Icy Frost Twins Ice Cream Bars)
Walt Disney Productions

(Rare)-Kelly c/a	100.00	300.00	700.00

DONALD DUCK TELLS ABOUT KITES
11/54 (Giveaway) (8 pgs. - no cover) (Disney)
Southern California Edison Co./Pacific Gas & Electric Co./Florida
Power & Light Co.

	Good	Fine	N-Mint
Fla. Power, S.C.E. & version with blank label issues-Barks pencils-8 pgs.; inks-7 pgs. (Rare)	285.00	850.00	1800.00
P.G.&E. issue-7th page redrawn changing middle 3 panels to show P.G.&E. in story line; (All Barks; last page Barks pencils only) (Scarce)	250.00	750.00	1600.00

(Prices vary widely on above books)

NOTE: *These books appeared one month apart in the fall and were distributed on the West and East Coasts.*

DONALD DUCK, THIS IS YOUR LIFE (See 4-Color No. 1109)

DONALD DUCK XMAS ALBUM (See regular Donald Duck No. 99)

DONALD IN MATHMAGIC LAND (See 4-Color No. 1051, 1198)

DONATELLO, TEENAGE MUTANT NINJA TURTLE
Aug, 1986 (One-shot, $1.50, B&W, 44 pgs.)
Mirage Studios

1	.90	2.75	5.50

DONDI (See 4-Color No. 1176,1276)

DON FORTUNE MAGAZINE
Aug, 1946 - No. 6, Feb, 1947
Don Fortune Publishing Co.

1-Delecta of the Planets by C. C. Beck in all	7.00	21.00	50.00
2	4.65	14.00	32.00
3-6: 3-Bondage-c	3.50	10.50	24.00

DON NEWCOMBE
1950 (Baseball)
Fawcett Publications

nn	14.00	42.00	100.00

DON'T GIVE UP THE SHIP (See 4-Color #1049)

DON WINSLOW OF THE NAVY (See Crackajack Funnies, 4-Color #2,22,
Popular Comics & Super Book #5,6)

DON WINSLOW OF THE NAVY (See TV Teens; Movie, Radio, TV)
Feb, 1943 - No. 73, Sept, 1955 (Fightin' Navy No. 74 on)
Fawcett Publications/Charlton No. 70 on

1-(68 pgs.)-Captain Marvel on cover	38.00	115.00	265.00
2	19.00	57.00	132.00
3	13.00	40.00	90.00
4,5	10.00	30.00	70.00
6-Flag-c	8.00	24.00	56.00
7-10: 8-Last 68pg. issue?	6.00	18.00	42.00
11-20	4.30	13.00	30.00
21-40	3.00	9.00	21.00
41-63	2.30	7.00	16.00
64(12/48)-Matt Baker-a	2.85	8.50	20.00
65(1/51) - 69(9/51): All photo-c. 65-Flying Saucer attack	3.50	10.50	24.00
70(3/55)-73: 70-73 r-/#26,58 & 59	2.00	6.00	14.00

DOOM PATROL, THE (My Greatest Adv. No. 1-85; see DC Spec. Bl.
Ribbon Digest 19, Official . . . Index & Showcase No. 94-96)
3/64 - No. 121, 9-10/68; 2/73 - No. 124, 6-7/73
National Periodical Publications

86-1pg. origin	5.50	16.00	38.00
87-99: 88-Origin The Chief. 91-Intro. Mento. 99-Intro. Beast Boy who later became the Changeling in the New Teen Titans	4.00	12.00	28.00
100-Origin Beast Boy; Robot-Maniac series begins	4.85	14.50	34.00
101-110: 102-Challengers/Unknown app. 105-Robot-Maniac series ends. 106-Negative Man begins (origin)	2.15	6.50	15.00
111-120	1.70	5.00	12.00
121-Death of Doom Patrol; Orlando-c	5.50	16.00	38.00
122-124(reprints)	.35	1.00	2.00

Donald Duck Adventures #1, © WDC

Donatello, Teenage Mutant Ninja Turtle #1, © Mirage

Don Fortune Magazine #1, © Don Fortune

The Doom Patrol #93, © DC   Dorothy Lamour #3, © FOX   The Double Life Of Private Strong #1, © AP

DOOM PATROL
Oct, 1987 - Present
DC Comics

	Good	Fine	N-Mint
1	.40	1.25	2.50
2-9: 3-1st app. Lodestone. 4-1st app. Karma		.50	1.00
10-18 ($1.00): 15,16-Art Adams-c(i)		.50	1.00
. . .And Suicide Squad Special 1(3/88)	.35	1.00	2.00
Annual 1 ('88, $1.50)	.25	.75	1.50

DOOMSDAY + 1
7/75 - No. 6, 6/76; No. 7, 6/68 - No. 12, 5/79
Charlton Comics

1	1.00	3.00	6.00
2	.75	2.25	4.50
3-6: 4-Intro Lor	.70	2.00	4.00
V3#7-12 (reprints #1-6)	.30	.80	1.60
5 (Modern Comics reprint, 1977)		.20	.40

NOTE: *Byrne c/a-1-12; Painted covers-2-7.*

DOOMSDAY SQUAD, THE
Aug, 1986 - No. 7, Feb, 1987 ($2.00)
Fantagraphics Books

1,2: 1-Byrne-a	.35	1.00	2.00
3-Usagi Yojimbo app. (1st in color)	.85	2.50	5.00
4-7	.35	1.00	2.00

DOORWAY TO NIGHTMARE (See Cancelled Comic Cavalcade)
Jan-Feb, 1978 - No. 5, Sept-Oct, 1978
DC Comics

1-5-Madame Xanadu in all. 4-Craig-a	.30		.60

NOTE: *Kaluta covers on all. Merged into The Unexpected with No. 190.*

DOPEY DUCK COMICS (Wacky Duck No. 3) (See Super Funnies)
Fall, 1945 - No. 2, April, 1946
Timely Comics (NPP)

1,2-Casper Cat, Krazy Krow	7.00	21.00	50.00

DOROTHY LAMOUR (Formerly Jungle Lil)(Stage, screen, radio)
No. 2, June, 1950 - No. 3, Aug, 1950
Fox Features Syndicate

2,3-Wood-a(3) each, photo-c	9.00	27.00	62.00

DOT AND DASH AND THE LUCKY JINGLE PIGGIE
1942 (12 pages)
Sears Roebuck Christmas giveaway

Contains a war stamp album and a punch out Jingle Piggie bank

	3.50	10.50	24.00

DOT DOTLAND (Formerly Little Dot. . .)
No. 62, Sept, 1974 - No. 63, November, 1974
Harvey Publications

62,63		.60	1.20

DOTTY (. . .& Her Boy Friends) (Formerly Four Teeners; Glamorous
Romances No. 41 on)
No. 35, July, 1948 - No. 40, May, 1949
Ace Magazines (A. A. Wyn)

35	3.70	11.00	26.00
36,38-40	2.00	6.00	14.00
37-Transvestism story	2.30	7.00	16.00

DOTTY DRIPPLE (Horace & Dotty Dripple No. 25 on)
1946 - No. 24, June, 1952 (See A-1 No. 1-8, 10)
Magazine Ent.(Life's Romances)/Harvey No. 3 on

nn (nd) (10 cent)	3.00	9.00	21.00
2	1.50	4.50	10.00
3-10: 3,4-Powell-a	1.00	3.00	7.00
11-24	.75	2.25	5.00

DOTTY DRIPPLE AND TAFFY
No. 646, Sept, 1955 - No. 903, May, 1958
Dell Publishing Co.

	Good	Fine	N-Mint
4-Color 646	1.70	5.00	12.00
4-Color 691,718,746,801,903	1.30	4.00	9.00

DOUBLE ACTION COMICS
No. 2, Jan, 1940 (Regular size; 68 pgs.; B&W, color cover)
National Periodical Publications

2-Contains original stories(?); pre-hero DC contents; same cover as
Adventure No. 37. (Five known copies) (not an ashcan)
Estimated value. . . .   6500.00

NOTE: *The cover to this book was probably reprinted from Adventure #37. #1 exists as an ash can copy with B&W cover; contains a coverless comic on inside with 1st & last page missing.*

DOUBLE COMICS
1940 - 1944 (132 pages)
Elliot Publications

1940 issues	90.00	270.00	630.00
1941 issues	60.00	180.00	430.00
1942 issues	50.00	150.00	350.00
1943,44 issues	40.00	120.00	280.00

NOTE: *Double Comics consisted of an almost endless combination of pairs of remaindered, unsold issues of comics representing most publishers and usually mixed publishers in the same book; e.g., a Captain America with a Silver Streak, or a Feature with a Detective, etc., could appear inside the same cover. The actual contents would have to determine its price. Prices listed are for average contents. Any containing rare origin or first issues are worth much more. Covers also vary in same year. Value would be approximately 50 percent of contents.*

DOUBLE-CROSS (See The Crusaders)

DOUBLE-DARE ADVENTURES
Dec, 1966 - No. 2, March, 1967 (35-25 cents, 68 pgs.)
Harvey Publications

1-Origin Bee-Man, Glowing Gladiator, & Magic-Master; Simon/Kirby-a	.85	2.50	6.00
2-Williamson/Crandall-a; r-/Alarming Adv. #3('63)	1.15	3.50	8.00

NOTE: *Powell a-1. Simon/Sparling c-1,2.*

DOUBLE LIFE OF PRIVATE STRONG, THE
June, 1959 - No. 2, Aug, 1959
Archie Publications/Radio Comics

1-Origin The Shield; Simon & Kirby c/a; The Fly app.	16.00	48.00	110.00
2-S&K c/a; Tuska-a; The Fly app.	10.00	30.00	70.00

DOUBLE TALK (Also see Two-Faces)
No date (1962?) (32 pgs.; full color; slick cover)
Christian Anti-Communism Crusade (Giveaway)
Feature Publications

	15.00	45.00	90.00

DOUBLE TROUBLE
Nov, 1957 - No. 2, Jan-Feb, 1958
St. John Publishing Co.

1,2	1.50	4.50	10.00

DOUBLE TROUBLE WITH GOOBER
No. 417, Aug, 1952 - No. 556, May, 1954
Dell Publishing Co.

4-Color 417	1.50	4.50	10.00
4-Color 471,516,556	1.00	3.00	7.00

DOUBLE UP
1941 (200 pages) (Pocket size)
Elliot Publications

1-Contains rebound copies of digest sized issues of Pocket Comics, Speed Comics, & Spitfire Comics	40.00	120.00	280.00

DOVER BOYS (See Adventures of the...)

DOVER THE BIRD
Spring, 1955
Famous Funnies Publishing Co.

	Good	Fine	N-Mint
1	1.50	4.50	10.00

DOWN WITH CRIME
Nov, 1952 - No. 7, Nov, 1953
Fawcett Publications

1	8.00	24.00	56.00
2,4-Powell-a each	4.65	14.00	32.00
3-Used in **POP**, pg. 106; heroin drug cover/story			
	7.00	21.00	50.00
5-Bondage-c	4.65	14.00	32.00
6-Used in **POP**, pg. 80	3.50	10.50	24.00
7	3.00	9.00	21.00

DO YOU BELIEVE IN NIGHTMARES?
Nov, 1957 - No. 2, Jan, 1958
St. John Publishing Co.

1-Ditko c/a(most)	10.00	30.00	70.00
2-Ayers-a	5.00	15.00	35.00

D.P. 7
Nov, 1986 - No. 32, Feb., 1989
Marvel Comics Group

1	.35	1.00	2.00
2-32		.60	1.25
Annual #1 (11/87)-Intro. The Witness		.65	1.30

NOTE: *Williamson a-9i, 11i; c-9i.*

DRACULA (See Tomb of..., Marvel Graphic Novel & Movie Classics under Universal Presents as well as Dracula)

DRACULA (See Movie Classics for No. 1)
11/66 - No. 4, 3/67; No. 6, 7/72 - No. 8, 7/73 (No No.5)
Dell Publishing Co.

2-Origin Dracula (11/66)	.70	2.00	4.00
3,4-Intro. Fleeta #4('67)	.50	1.50	3.00
6-('72)-r-/#2 w/origin	.35	1.00	2.00
7,8: 7 r-/#3, 8-r/#4		.50	1.00

DRACULA (Magazine)
1979 (120 pages) (full color)
Warren Publishing Co.

Book 1-Maroto art; Spanish material translated into English

	1.00	3.00	6.00

DRACULA LIVES! (Magazine)
1973(no month) - No. 13, July, 1975 (B&W) (75 cents)
Marvel Comics Group

1-3: 2-Origin	.50	1.50	3.00
4-Ploog-a	.45	1.25	2.50
5(V2#1)-13: 5-Dracula series begins	.35	1.00	2.00
Annual 1('75)	.35	1.00	2.00

NOTE: *Adams a-2, 3i, 10i, Annual 1r; 2, 3i. Alcala a-9. Buscema a-3p, 6p. Colan a(p)-1, 2, 5, 6, 8. Evans a-7. Heath a-1r, 13. Pakula a-6r. Starlin a-2.*

DRAFT, THE
1988 (One shot, $3.50, color, squarebound)
Marvel Comics

1	.70	2.00	4.00

DRAG 'N' WHEELS (Formerly Top Eliminator)
No. 30, Sept, 1968 - No. 59, May, 1973
Charlton Comics

30-50-Scot Jackson feat.	.25	.75	1.50
51-59-Scot Jackson		.50	1.00
Modern Comics Reprint 58('78)		.30	.60

DRAGONFLY
Sum, 1985 - Present ($1.75, $195)(#1&3, color)
Americomics

	Good	Fine	N-Mint
1-7	.40	1.25	2.50

DRAGONFORCE
1988 - Present ($2.00, color)
Aircel

1	.40	1.25	2.50
2-6	.35	1.00	2.00

DRAGONLANCE
Dec., 1988 - Present ($1.25, color, Mando paper)
DC Comics

1-3: Based on TSR game		.60	1.25

DRAGONRING
1986 - No. 15, 1988 ($1.70, B&W)
Aircel Publ.

1	.60	1.75	3.50
2-6: 6-Last B&W ish.	.35	1.10	2.20
V2#1 ($2.00, color)	.35	1.00	2.00
2-15	.30	.90	1.80

DRAGON'S CLAWS
July, 1988 - Present ($1.25, color, British)
Marvel Comics Ltd.

1-5		.60	1.25

DRAGONSLAYER
October, 1981 - No. 2, Nov, 1981
Marvel Comics Group

1,2-Paramount Disney movie adaptation		.25	.50

DRAGOON WELLS MASSACRE (See 4-Color No. 815)

DRAGSTRIP HOTRODDERS (World of Wheels No. 17 on)
Sum, 1963; No. 2, Jan, 1965 - No. 16, Aug, 1967
Charlton Comics

1	.85	2.50	5.00
2-5	.50	1.50	3.00
6-16	.35	1.00	2.00

DRAMA OF AMERICA, THE
1973 (224 pages) ($1.95)
Action Text

1-"Students' Supplement to History"	.50	1.50	3.00

DREADSTAR ($1.50) (Also see Marvel Graphic Novel & Epic III.)
Nov, 1982 - Present (Direct sale, Baxter paper)
Epic Comics (Marvel)/First Comics No. 27 on

1	.85	2.50	5.00
2	.60	1.70	3.50
3-5	.50	1.50	3.00
6-10	.40	1.25	2.50
11-26: 12-New costume. 16-New powers	.35	1.10	2.20
27-First Comics; new look	.35	1.10	2.20
28-38: New look	.35	1.00	2.00
39-43 ($1.95)	.35	1.00	2.00
Annual 1 (12/83)-Reprints The Price	.40	1.25	2.50

NOTE: *Starlin a-1-23, 25-32; c-1-32, Annual 1. Wrightson a-6, 7.*

DREADSTAR AND COMPANY
July, 1985 - No. 6, Dec, 1985
Epic Comics (Marvel)

1-6: Reprints of Dreadstar series		.50	1.00

DREAM BOOK OF LOVE (See A-1 Comics No. 106,114,123)

DREAM BOOK OF ROMANCE (See A-1 No. 92,101,109,110,124)

Down With Crime #6, © FAW

Dragonforce #1, © Aircel Publ.

Dreadstar #3, © First Comics

Dumbo (1941, 52pg.), © WDC

Dumbo Weekly #1, © WDC

The Durango Kid #9, © ME

DREAMERY, THE
Dec., 1986 - Present ($2.00, B&W)
Eclipse Comics

	Good	Fine	N-Mint
1-12	.35	1.00	2.00

DREAM OF LOVE
1958 (Reprints)
I. W. Enterprises

1,2,8: 1-Powell-a. 8-Kinstler-c	.50	1.50	3.00
9-Kinstler-c; 1pg. John Wayne interview	.50	1.50	3.00

DREAMS OF THE RAREBIT FIEND
1905
Doffield & Co.?

By Winsor McCay (Very Rare) (Three copies known to exist)
Estimated value.... $500.00—$900.00

DRIFT MARLO
May-July, 1962 - No. 2, Oct-Dec, 1962
Dell Publishing Co.

01-232-207, 2(12-232-212)	1.15	3.50	8.00

DRISCOLL'S BOOK OF PIRATES
1934 (124 pgs.) (B&W; hardcover; 7x9'')
David McKay Publ. (Not reprints)

By Montford Amory	6.50	19.50	45.00

DROIDS
April, 1986 - No. 8, June, 1987 (Based on Sat. morning cartoon)
Star Comics (Marvel)

1-R2D2, C3PO from Star Wars		.40	.80
2-8: 3-Romita/Williamson-a		.40	.80

NOTE: **Williamson** a-2i, 3i, 5i, 7i, 8i.

DRUM BEAT (See 4-Color No. 610)

DRUNKEN FIST
Aug., 1988 - Present ($1.50, color)
Jademan Comics

1-3	.25	.75	1.50

DUCK ALBUM (See Donald Duck Album)
Oct, 1951 - Sept, 1957
Dell Publishing Co.

4-Color 353-Barks-c	3.00	9.00	21.00
4-Color 450-Barks-c	2.65	8.00	18.00
4-Color 492,531,560,586,611,649,686	2.00	6.00	14.00
4-Color 726,782,840	1.70	5.00	12.00

DUCKTALES (See Disney's Ducktales)

DUDLEY (Teen-age)
Nov-Dec, 1949 - No. 3, Mar-Apr, 1950
Feature/Prize Publications

1-By Boody Rogers	5.50	16.50	38.00
2,3	2.85	8.50	20.00

DUDLEY DO-RIGHT (TV)
Aug, 1970 - No. 7, Aug, 1971 (Jay Ward)
Charlton Comics

1	2.00	6.00	14.00
2-7	1.30	4.00	9.00

DUKE OF THE K-9 PATROL
April, 1963
Gold Key

1 (10052-304)	1.75	5.25	12.00

DUMBO (See 4-Color #17,234,668, Movie Comics, & Walt Disney Showcase #12)

DUMBO (Walt Disney's. . .)
1941 (K.K. Publ. Giveaway)

Weatherbird Shoes/Ernest Kern Co.(Detroit)

	Good	Fine	N-Mint
16 pgs., 9x10'' (Rare)	22.00	65.00	154.00
52 pgs., 5½x8½'', slick cover in color; B&W interior; half text, half reprints/4-Color No. 17	13.00	40.00	90.00

DUMBO COMIC PAINT BOOK (See Large Feat. Comic No. 19)

DUMBO WEEKLY
1942 (Premium supplied by Diamond D-X Gas Stations)
Walt Disney Productions

1	10.00	30.00	60.00
2-16	5.00	15.00	30.00

NOTE: A cover and binder came separate at gas stations. Came with membership card.

DUNC AND LOO (1-3 titled ''Around the Block with Dunc and Loo'')
Oct-Dec, 1961 - No. 8, Oct-Dec, 1963
Dell Publishing Co.

1	5.00	15.00	35.00
2	3.50	10.50	24.00
3-8	2.30	7.00	16.00

NOTE: Written by **John Stanley**; **Bill Williams** art.

DUNE
April, 1985 - No. 3, June, 1985
Marvel Comics

1-3-r/Marvel Super Special; movie adaptation		.40	.80

DUNGEONEERS, THE
1987 - No. 5? ($1.50, B&W)
Silverwolf Comics

1-5	.25	.80	1.60

DURANGO KID, THE (Also see Best of the West, White Indian, & Great Western) (Charles Starrett starred in Columbia's Durango Kid movies)
Oct-Nov, 1949 - No. 41, Oct-Nov, 1955 (All 36pgs.)
Magazine Enterprises

1-Charles Starrett photo-c; Durango Kid & his horse Raider begin; Dan Brand & Tipi (origin) begin by Frazetta & continue through #16	35.00	105.00	245.00
2(Starrett photo-c)	23.00	70.00	160.00
3-5(All-Starrett photo-c)	20.00	60.00	140.00
6-10	14.00	42.00	100.00
11-16-Last Frazetta ish.	13.00	40.00	90.00
17-Origin Durango Kid	10.00	30.00	70.00
18-Fred Meagher-a on Dan Brand begins	5.00	15.00	35.00
19-30: 19-Guardineer c/a(3) begin, end #41. 23-Intro. The Red Scorpion	5.00	15.00	35.00
31-Red Scorpion returns	4.30	13.00	30.00
32-41-Bolle/Frazetta-a (Dan Brand)	5.50	16.50	38.00

NOTE: #6,8,14,15 contain **Frazetta** art not reprinted in White Indian. **Ayers** c-18. **Guardineer** a(3)-19-41; c-19-41. **Fred Meagher** a-18-29 at least.

DWIGHT D. EISENHOWER
December, 1969
Dell Publishing Co.

01-237-912 - Life story	2.00	6.00	12.00

DYNABRITE COMICS
1978 - 1979 (69 cents; 48 pgs.)(10x7-1/8''; cardboard covers) (Blank inside covers)
Whitman Publishing Co.

11350 - Walt Disney's Mickey Mouse & the Beanstalk (4-C 157)
11350-1 - Mickey Mouse Album (4-C 1057,1151,1246)
11351 - Mickey Mouse & His Sky Adventure (4-C 214,343)
11352 - Donald Duck (4-C 408, Donald Duck 45,52)-Barks
11352-1 - Donald Duck (4-C 318, 10 pg. Barks/WDC&S 125,128)-Barks-c(r)
11353 - Daisy Ducks Diary (4-C 1055,1150) - Barks-a
11354 - Goofy: A Gaggle of Giggles
11354-1 - Super Goof Meets Super Thief

DYNABRITE COMICS (continued)

	Good	Fine	N-Mint
11355 - Uncle Scrooge (Barks-a/U.S. 12,33)			
11355-1 - Uncle Scrooge (Barks-a/U.S. 13,16) - Barks-c(r)			
11356 - Bugs Bunny(?)			
11357 - Star Trek (r-Star Trek 33 & 41)			
11358 - Star Trek (r-Star Trek 34,36)			
11359 - Bugs Bunny-r			
11360 - Winnie the Pooh Fun and Fantasy (Disney-r)			
11361 - Gyro Gearloose & the Disney Ducks (4-C 1047,1184)-Barks-c(r)			
each		.50	1.00

DYNAMIC ADVENTURES
No. 8,9, 1964
I. W. Enterprises

	Good	Fine	N-Mint
8-Kayo Kirby by Baker?	1.20	3.50	7.00
9-Reprints Avon's "Escape From Devil's Island"-Kinstler-c			
	1.35	4.00	8.00
nn(no date)-Reprints Risks Unlimited with Rip Carson, Senorita Rio			
	1.20	3.50	7.00

DYNAMIC CLASSICS (See Cancelled Comic Cavalcade)
Sept-Oct, 1978 (44 pgs.)
DC Comics

	Good	Fine	N-Mint
1-Adams Batman, Simonson Manhunter-r		.30	.60

DYNAMIC COMICS (No No.7)
Oct, 1941 - No. 3, Feb, 1942; No. 8, 1944 - No. 25, May, 1948
Harry 'A' Chesler

	Good	Fine	N-Mint
1-Origin Major Victory by Charles Sultan (reprinted in Major Victory #1), Dynamic Man & Hale the Magician; The Black Cobra only app.	55.00	165.00	385.00
2-Origin Dynamic Boy & Lady Satan; intro. The Green Knight & sidekick Lance Cooper	27.00	81.00	190.00
3	22.00	65.00	154.00
8-Dan Hastings, The Echo, The Master Key, Yankee Boy begin; Yankee Doodle Jones app.; hypo story	22.00	65.00	154.00
9-Mr. E begins; Mac Raboy-c	23.00	70.00	160.00
10	19.00	57.00	132.00
11-15: 15-The Sky Chief app.	13.00	40.00	90.00
16-Marijuana story	14.00	42.00	100.00
17(1/46)-Illustrated in SOTI, "The children told me what the man was going to do with the hot poker," but Wertham saw this in Crime Reporter #2	20.00	60.00	140.00
18,19,21,22,24,25	9.00	27.00	62.00
20-Bare-breasted woman-c	12.00	36.00	84.00
23-Yankee Girl app.	9.00	27.00	62.00
I.W. Reprint #1,8('64): 1-r/#23	.70	2.00	4.00

NOTE: *Kinstler* c-IW #1. *Tuska* art in many issues, #3, 9, 11, 12, 16, 19. Bondage c-16.

DYNAMITE (Johnny Dynamite No. 10 on)
May, 1953 - No. 9, Sept, 1954
Comic Media/Allen Hardy Publ.

	Good	Fine	N-Mint
1-Pete Morisi-a; r-as Danger No. 6	6.00	18.00	42.00
2	3.50	10.50	24.00
3-Marijuana story; Johnny Dynamite begins by Pete Morisi			
	4.65	14.00	32.00
4-Injury-to-eye, prostitution; Morisi-a	5.50	16.50	38.00
5-9-Morisi-a in all. 6-Morisi-c	3.00	9.00	21.00

DYNAMO (Also see Thunder Agents)
Aug, 1966 - No. 4, June, 1967 (25 cents)
Tower Comics

	Good	Fine	N-Mint
1-Crandall/Wood, Ditko/Wood-a; Weed series begins; NoMan & Lightning cameos; Wood c/a	2.00	6.00	14.00
2-4: Wood c/a in all	1.50	4.50	10.00

NOTE: *Adkins/Wood* a-2. *Ditko* a-4. *Tuska* a-2,3.

DYNAMO JOE (Also see Mars & First Advs.)
May, 1986 - Present
First Comics

	Good	Fine	N-Mint
1	.50	1.50	3.00
2-11: 4-Cargonauts begin	.25	.75	1.50
12-16 ($1.75)	.30	.90	1.75
Special 1(1/87)-Mostly-r/Mars	.25	.75	1.50

DYNOMUTT (TV)(See Scooby-Doo, 3rd series)
Nov, 1977 - No. 6, Sept, 1978
Marvel Comics Group

	Good	Fine	N-Mint
1-6		.50	1.00

EAGLE, THE (1st Series) (Also see Science Comics)
July, 1941 - No. 4, Jan, 1942
Fox Features Syndicate

	Good	Fine	N-Mint
1-The Eagle begins; Rex Dexter of Mars app. by Briefer	55.00	165.00	385.00
2-The Spider Queen begins (origin)	28.00	84.00	195.00
3,4: 3-Joe Spook begins (origin)	22.00	65.00	154.00

EAGLE (2nd Series)
Feb-Mar, 1945 - No. 2, Apr-May, 1945
Rural Home Publ.

	Good	Fine	N-Mint
1-Aviation stories	7.00	21.00	50.00
2-Lucky Aces	6.00	18.00	42.00

NOTE: *L. B. Cole* c/a.

EAGLE
Sept., 1986 - Present ($1.50/1.95, B&W)
Crystal Comics/Apple Comics #17 on

	Good	Fine	N-Mint
1	.85	2.50	5.00
1-Signed and limited	1.00	3.00	6.00
2-11,13-21	.35	1.10	2.20
12-Origin issue ($2.50)	.45	1.40	2.80

EARTH MAN ON VENUS (An . . .) (Also see Strange Planets)
1951
Avon Periodicals

	Good	Fine	N-Mint
nn-Wood-a, 26 pgs.; Fawcette-c	71.00	215.00	500.00

EASTER BONNET SHOP (See March of Comics No. 29)

EASTER WITH MOTHER GOOSE (See 4-Color No. 103,140,185,220)

EAT RIGHT TO WORK AND WIN
1942 (16 pages) (Giveaway)
Swift & Company

Blondie, Henry, Flash Gordon by Alex Raymond, Toots & Casper, Thimble Threatre (Popeye), Tillie the Toiler, The Phantom, The Little Viking, & Bringing Up Father - original strips just for this book - (in daily strip form which shows what foods we should eat and why)

	Good	Fine	N-Mint
	18.00	54.00	125.00

EB'NN THE RAVEN
Oct., 1985 - Present (B&W)
Crowquill Comics/Now Comics #3 on

	Good	Fine	N-Mint
1	.85	2.50	5.00
2	.60	1.80	3.60
3	.35	1.10	2.20
4,5	.35	1.00	2.00
6-9	.30	.90	1.80
10-($1.50, color)	.25	.80	1.60

E. C. CLASSIC REPRINTS
May, 1973 - No. 12, 1976 (E. C. Comics reprinted in full color minus ads)
East Coast Comix Co.

	Good	Fine	N-Mint
1-The Crypt of Terror #1 (Tales From the Crypt #46)			
	.70	2.00	4.00
2-Weird Science #15('52)	.50	1.50	3.00
3-Shock SuspenStories #12	.35	1.00	2.00
4-12: 4-Haunt of Fear #12. 5-Weird Fantasy #13('52). 6-Crime SuspenStories #25. 7-Vault of Horror #26. 8-Shock SuspenStories #6			

Dynamic Comics #3, © CHES

Eagle #1 (limited ed.), © Apple Comics

An Earth Man On Venus, © AVON

Eclipse Graphic Album Series #14, © Eclipse   Eddie Stanky, © FAW   Eerie #4, © AVON

	Good	Fine	N-Mint
E. C. CLASSIC REPRINTS (continued)			
9-Two-Fisted Tales #34. 10-Haunt of Fear #23. 11-Weird Science			
#12(#1). 12-Shock SuspenStories #2	.35	1.00	2.00

EC CLASSICS
1985 - Present (High quality paper; r-/8 stories in color)
Russ Cochran

	Good	Fine	N-Mint
(All #1)-Shock Suspenstories, Two-Fisted Tales, Vault of Horror,			
Weird Fantasy	.85	2.50	4.95

ECHO OF FUTUREPAST
May, 1984 - Present? (52 pgs., $2.95)
Pacific Comics/Continuity Comics

1-Adams c/a begins	.60	1.80	3.50
2-11	.50	1.50	3.00

NOTE: *Adams* a-1-6; c-1-3, 5p, 8. *Golden* a-1-6; c-6. *Toth* a-6, 7.

ECLIPSE GRAPHIC ALBUM SERIES
Oct, 1978 - Present (8½x11") (B&W #1-5)
Eclipse Comics

1-Sabre (10/78, B&W, 1st print.)	1.35	4.00	7.95
1-Sabre (2nd print, 1/79)	1.35	4.00	7.95
1-Sabre (3rd print.)	1.00	3.00	5.95
2-Night Music (11/79, B&W)-Russell-a	1.35	4.00	7.95
3-Detectives, Inc. (5/80, B&W)-Rogers-a	1.35	4.00	7.95
4-Stewart The Rat ('80, B&W)-G. Colan-a	1.35	4.00	7.95
5-The Price (10/81, B&W)-Starlin-a	1.35	4.00	7.95
6-I Am Coyote (11/84, color)-Rogers c/a	1.35	4.00	7.95
7-The Rocketeer (9/85, color)-Stevens-a	1.35	4.00	7.95
7-The Rocketeer (2nd print.)	1.35	4.00	7.95
7-The Rocketeer (hardcover)	3.15	9.50	18.95
8-Zorro In Old California ('86, color)	1.15	3.50	6.95
8-Soft cover	1.15	3.50	6.95
8-Hard cover	2.00	6.00	11.95
9-Sacred And The Profane ('86)-Steacy-a	2.50	7.50	14.95
9-Hard cover	4.00	12.50	24.95
10-Somerset Holmes ('86, color)-Adults, soft-c	2.50	7.50	14.95
10-Hard cover	4.00	12.50	24.95
11-Floyd Farland, Citizen of the Future ('87, B&W)			
	.50	1.50	2.95
12-Silverheels ('87, color)	1.35	4.00	7.95
12-Hard cover	2.50	7.50	14.95
12-Hard cover, signed & #'d	4.00	12.50	24.95
13-The Sisterhood of Steel ('87, color)	1.15	4.50	8.95
14-Samurai, Son of Death ('87, B&W)	.70	2.00	3.95
14-Samurai, Son of Death (2nd print.)	.70	2.00	3.95
15-Twisted Tales (11/87, color)-Stevens-c	.70	2.00	3.95
16-See Airfighters Classics #1			
17-Valkyrie, Prisoner of the Past ('88, color)-soft-c			
	1.15	3.50	6.95
18-See Airfighters Classics #2			
19-Scout: The Four Monsters ('88, color)-r/Scouts #1-7; soft-c			
	2.50	7.50	14.95
20-See Airfighters Classics #3			
21-XYR-Multiple ending comic ('88, B&W)	.70	2.00	3.95

ECLIPSE MONTHLY
8/83 - No. 10, 7/84 (Baxter paper; 1-3: 52 pgs., $2.00)
Eclipse Comics

1-3: ($2.00)-Cap'n Quick and a Foozle by Rogers, Static by Ditko,			
Dope by Trina Robbins, Rio by Doug Wildey, The Masked Man			
by Boyer begin. 3-Ragamuffins begins	.30	.90	1.80
4-8 ($1.50 cover)	.30	.90	1.80
9,10-($1.75 cover)	.30	.90	1.80

NOTE: *Boyer* c-6. *Ditko* a-1-3. *Rogers* a-1-4; c-2, 4. *Wildey* a-1, 2, 5, 9, 10; c-5, 10.

E. C. 3-D CLASSICS (See Three Dimensional . . .)

EDDIE STANKY (Baseball Hero)
1951 (New York Giants)
Fawcett Publications

	Good	Fine	N-Mint
nn-Photo-c	6.50	19.50	45.00

EDGAR BERGEN PRESENTS CHARLIE McCARTHY
1938 (36 pgs.; 15x10½''; in color)
Whitman Publishing Co. (Charlie McCarthy Co.)

764 (Scarce)	38.00	115.00	265.00

EDGE OF CHAOS
July, 1983 - No. 3, Jan, 1984
Pacific Comics

1-3-Morrow c/a; all contain nudity	.35	1.00	2.00

EDWARD'S SHOES GIVEAWAY
1954 (Has clown on cover)
Edward's Shoe Store

Contains comic with new cover. Many combinations possible. Contents determines price, 50-60 percent of original. (Similar to Comics From Weatherbird & Free Comics to You)

ED WHEELAN'S JOKE BOOK STARRING FAT & SLAT (See Fat & Slat)

EERIE (Strange Worlds No. 18 on)
No. 1, Jan, 1947; No. 1, May-June, 1951 - No. 17, Aug-Sept, 1954
Avon Periodicals

1(1947)-1st horror comic; Kubert, Fugitani-a; bondage-c			
	35.00	105.00	245.00
1(1951)-Reprints story/'47 No. 1	20.00	60.00	140.00
2-Wood c/a; bondage-c	22.00	65.00	154.00
3-Wood-c, Kubert, Wood/Orlando-a	22.00	65.00	154.00
4,5-Wood-c	20.00	60.00	140.00
6,13,14	7.00	21.00	50.00
7-Wood/Orlando-c; Kubert-a	13.00	40.00	90.00
8-Kinstler-a; bondage-c; Phantom Witch Doctor story			
	7.00	21.00	50.00
9-Kubert-a; Check-c	8.50	25.50	60.00
10,11-Kinstler-a	7.00	21.00	50.00
12-25-pg. Dracula story from novel	10.00	30.00	70.00
15-Reprints No. 1('51)minus-c(bondage)	4.60	14.00	32.00
16-Wood-a r-/No. 2	6.00	18.00	42.00
17-Wood/Orlando & Kubert-a; reprints #3 minus inside &			
outside Wood-c	8.50	25.50	60.00

NOTE: *Hollingsworth* a-9-11; c-10,11.

EERIE
1964
I. W. Enterprises

I.W. Reprint #1(1964)-Wood-c(r)	1.20	3.50	7.00
I.W. Reprint #2,6,8: 8-Dr. Drew by Grandenetti from Ghost #9			
	.85	2.50	5.00
I.W. Reprint #9-From Eerie #2(Avon); Wood-c	1.35	4.00	8.00

EERIE (Magazine)(See Warren Presents)
No. 1, Sept, 1965; No. 2, Mar, 1966 - No. 139, Feb, 1983
Warren Publishing Co.

1-24 pgs., black & white, small size (5¼x7¼''), low distribution; cover from inside back cover of Creepy No. 2; stories reprinted from Creepy No. 7, 8. At least three different versions exist.

First Printing - B&W, 5¼'' wide x 7¼'' high, evenly trimmed. On page 18, panel 5, in the upper left-hand corner, the large rear view of a bald headed man blends into solid black and is unrecognizable. Overall printing quality is poor.

	13.00	40.00	90.00

Second Printing - B&W, 5¼x7¼'', with uneven, untrimmed edges (if one of these were trimmed evenly, the size would be less than as indicated). The figure of the bald headed man on page 18, panel 5 is clear and discernible. The staples have a ¼'' blue stripe.

	7.00	20.00	40.00

Other unauthorized reproductions for comparison's sake would be practically worthless.

EERIE (continued)

One known version was probably shot off a first printing copy with some loss of detail; the finer lines tend to disappear in this version which can be determined by looking at the lower right-hand corner of page one, first story. The roof of the house is shaded with straight lines. These lines are sharp and distinct on original, but broken on this version.

	Good	Fine	N-Mint
	1.35	4.00	8.00

NOTE: *The Official Overstreet Comic Book Price Guide* recommends that, before buying, you consult an expert.

	Good	Fine	N-Mint
2-Frazetta-c	1.00	3.00	6.00
3-Frazetta-c, 1 pg.	.70	2.00	4.00
4-10: 4-Frazetta ½ page	.50	1.50	3.00
11-25	.45	1.25	2.50
26-41,43-45	.35	1.00	2.00
42-(1973 Annual)	.50	1.50	3.00
46-50,52,53,56-78: 78-The Mummy-r		.75	1.50
51-(1974 Annual)	.50	1.50	3.00
54,55-Color Spirit story by Eisner, 12/21/47 & 6/16/46	.35	1.00	2.00
79,80-Origin Darklon the Mystic by Starlin		.75	1.50
81-139		.60	1.20
Year Book 1970-Reprints	.85	2.50	5.00
Year Book 1971-Reprints	.85	2.50	5.00
Year Book 1972-Reprints	.70	2.00	4.00

NOTE: *The above books contain art by many good artists: Adams, Brunner, Corben, Craig (Taycee), Crandall, Ditko, Eisner, Evans, Jeff Jones, Kinstler, Krenkel, McWilliams, Morrow, Orlando, Ploog, Severin, Starlin, Torres, Toth, Williamson, Wood, and Wrightson; covers by Bode', Corben, Davis, Frazetta, Morrow, and Orlando. Annuals from 1973-on are included in regular numbering. 1970-74 Annuals are complete reprints. Annuals from 1975-on are in the format of the regular issues.*

EERIE ADVENTURES (Also see Weird Adventures)
Winter, 1951
Ziff-Davis Publ. Co.

	Good	Fine	N-Mint
1-Powell-a(2), Kinstler-a; used in SOTI; bondage-c; Krigstein back-c	8.00	24.00	56.00

NOTE: *Title dropped due to similarity to Avon's Eerie & legal action.*

EERIE TALES (Magazine)
1959 (Black & White)
Hastings Associates

	Good	Fine	N-Mint
1-Williamson, Torres, Tuska-a, Powell(2), & Morrow(2)-a	4.00	12.00	28.00

EERIE TALES
1964
Super Comics

Super Reprint No. 10,11,12,18: Purple Claw in No. 11,12; No. 12

	Good	Fine	N-Mint
r-Avon Eerie No. 1('51)	.70	2.00	4.00
15-Wolverton-a, Spacehawk-r/Blue Bolt Weird Tales No. 113; Disbrow-a	2.00	6.00	12.00

EGBERT
Spring, 1946 - No. 20, 1950
Arnold Publications/Quality Comics Group

	Good	Fine	N-Mint
1-Funny animal; intro Egbert & The Count	8.00	24.00	56.00
2	4.00	12.00	28.00
3-10	2.30	7.00	16.00
11-20	1.50	4.50	10.00

EH! (. . .Dig This Crazy Comic) (From Here to Insanity No. 8 on)
Dec, 1953 - No. 7, Nov-Dec, 1954 (Satire)
Charlton Comics

	Good	Fine	N-Mint
1-Davisish-c/a by Ayers, Woodish-a by Giordano; Atomic Mouse app.	8.00	24.00	56.00
2-Ayers-c	5.00	15.00	35.00
3-7: 4,6-Sexual innuendo-c	4.65	14.00	32.00

80 PAGE GIANT (. . .Magazine No. 1-15) (25 cents)
8/64 - No. 15, 10/65; No. 16, 11/65 - No. 89, 7/71 (All-r)
National Periodical Publications (No.57-89: 68 pages)

	Good	Fine	N-Mint
1-Superman	6.00	18.00	50.00
2-Jimmy Olsen	2.50	7.50	20.00
3-Lois Lane	1.50	4.50	12.00
4-Flash-G.A.-r; Infantino-a	1.50	4.50	12.00
5-Batman; has Sunday newspaper strip	1.50	4.50	12.00
6-Batman	1.50	4.50	12.00
7-Sgt. Rock's Prize Battle Tales; Kubert c/a	1.50	4.50	12.00
8-More Secret Origins-origins of JLA, Aquaman, Robin, Atom, & Superman; Infantino-a	4.75	14.00	38.00
9-Flash(reprints Flash #123)-Infantino-a	1.50	4.50	12.00
10-Superboy	1.50	4.50	12.00
11-Superman-All Luthor issue	1.25	3.75	10.00
12-Batman; has Sunday newspaper strip	1.25	3.75	10.00
13-Jimmy Olsen	1.25	3.75	10.00
14-Lois Lane	1.25	3.75	10.00
15-Superman and Batman	1.25	3.75	10.00

Continued as part of regular series under each title in which that particular book came out, a Giant being published instead of the regular size. Issues No. 16 to No. 89 are listed for your information. See individual titles for prices.

16-JLA #39 (11/65)	17-Batman #176
18-Superman #183	19-Our Army at War #164
20-Action #334	21-Flash #160
22-Superboy #129	23-Superman #187
24-Batman #182	25-Jimmy Olsen #95
26-Lois Lane #68	27-Batman #185
28-World's Finest #161	29-JLA #48
30-Batman #187	31-Superman #193
32-Our Army at War #177	33-Action #347
34-Flash #169	35-Superboy #138
36-Superman #197	37-Batman #193
38-Jimmy Olsen #104	39-Lois Lane #77
40-World's Finest #170	41-JLA #58
42-Superman #202	43-Batman #198
44-Our Army at War #190	45-Action #360
46-Flash #178	47-Superboy #147
48-Superman #207	49-Batman #203
50-Jimmy Olsen #113	51-Lois Lane #86
52-World's Finest #179	53-JLA #67
54-Superman #212	55-Batman #208
56-Our Army at War #203	57-Action #373
58-Flash #187	59-Superboy #156
60-Superman #217	61-Batman #213
62-Jimmy Olsen #122	63-Lois Lane #95
64-World's Finest #188	65-JLA #76
66-Superman #222	67-Batman #218
68-Our Army at War #216	69-Adventure #390
70-Flash #196	71-Superboy #165
72-Superman #227	73-Batman #223
74-Jimmy Olsen #131	75-Lois Lane #104
76-World's Finest #197	77-JLA #85
78-Superman #232	79-Batman #228
80-Our Army at War #229	81-Adventure #403
82-Flash #205	83-Superboy #174
84-Superman #239	85-Batman #233
86-Jimmy Olsen #140	87-Lois Lane #113
88-World's Finest #206	89-JLA #93

87TH PRECINCT (TV)
Apr-June, 1962 - No. 2, July-Sept, 1962
Dell Publishing Co.

	Good	Fine	N-Mint
4-Color 1309; Krigstein-a	5.00	15.00	35.00
2	4.00	12.00	28.00

EINHERIAR: THE CHOSEN
1987 (color, $1.50)
Vanguard Graphics (Canadian)

Egbert #1, © QUA

Eh! #2, © CC

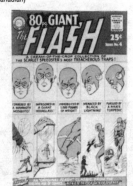

80 Page Giant #4, © DC

Elflord #20, © Aircel Publ.

Elfquest: Siege At Blue Mountain #3, © Apple Comics

Ellery Queen #2, © SUPR

	Good	Fine	N-Mint
EINHERIAR: THE CHOSEN (continued)			
1	.25	.75	1.50
EL BOMBO COMICS			
1946			
Standard Comics/Frances M. McQueeny			
nn(1946)	4.65	14.00	32.00
1(no date)	4.65	14.00	32.00
EL CID (See 4-Color No. 1259)			
EL DORADO (See Movie Classics)			
ELECTRIC WARRIOR			
May, 1986 - No. 18, Oct, 1987 (Baxter paper)			
DC Comics			
1	.50	1.50	3.00
2-18	.35	1.00	2.00
ELEKTRA: ASSASSIN			
Aug, 1986 - No. 8, Mar, 1987 (limited series)(Adults)			
Epic Comics (Marvel)			
1-Miller scripts in all	.85	2.50	5.00
2	.70	2.00	4.00
3-8	.50	1.50	3.00
ELEKTRA SAGA, THE			
Feb, 1984 - No. 4, June, 1984 ($2.00 cover; Baxter paper)			
Marvel Comics Group			
1-4-r/Daredevil 168-190; Miller a/c	1.00	3.00	6.00
ELEMENTALS, THE (Also see The Justice Machine)			
June, 1984 - Present ($1.50; Baxter paper)			
Comico The Comic Co.			
1-Willingham c/a, 1-8	1.70	5.00	10.00
2	.85	2.50	5.00
3	.60	1.75	3.50
4-7	.50	1.50	3.00
8-10: 9-Bissette-a(p)	.35	1.00	2.00
11-29	.30	.90	1.80
Special 1 (3/86)-Willingham-a(p)	.35	1.00	2.00
ELFLORD			
1986 - Present ($1.70/$2.00, B&W and color)			
Aircel Publishing			
1	1.15	3.50	7.00
1-2nd print	.30	.85	1.70
2	.60	1.75	3.50
2-2nd print	.30	.85	1.70
3	.50	1.50	3.00
4-6: Last B&W ish.	.30	.90	1.80
V2#1-(color begins)	.50	1.50	3.00
2-20	.30	.90	1.80
21-Double size, $4.95	.85	2.50	4.95
22-25: 22-New cast; 25-Begin B&W, $1.95-c	.35	1.00	2.00
ELFQUEST (Also see Fantasy Quarterly & Warp Graphics Annual)			
No. 2, Aug, 1978 - No. 21, Feb, 1985			
No. 1, April, 1979			
WaRP Graphics, Inc.			

NOTE: *Elfquest was originally published as one of the stories in Fantasy Quarterly #1. When the publisher went out of business, the creative team, Wendy and Richard Pini, formed WaRP Graphics and continued the series, beginning with Elfquest #2. Elfquest #1, which reprinted the story from Fantasy Quarterly, was published about the same time Elfquest #4 was released. Thereafter, most issues were reprinted as demand warranted, until Marvel announced it would reprint the entire series under its Epic imprint (Aug., 1985).*

	Good	Fine	N-Mint
1(4/79)-Reprints Elfquest story from Fantasy Quarterly No. 1			
1st printing ($1.00 cover)	4.15	12.50	25.00
2nd printing ($1.25 cover)	1.70	5.00	10.00
3rd printing ($1.50 cover)	.85	2.50	5.00
2(8/78)-5: 1st printing ($1.00 cover)	2.50	7.50	15.00
2nd printing ($1.25 cover)	.85	2.50	5.00
3rd printing ($1.50 cover)	.50	1.50	3.00
6-9: 1st printing ($1.25 cover)	1.35	4.00	8.00
2nd printing ($1.50 cover)	.70	2.00	4.00
10-21: ($1.50 cover); 16-8pg. preview of A Distant Soil			
	1.00	3.00	6.00
ELFQUEST			
Aug, 1985 - No. 32, Mar, 1988			
Epic Comics (Marvel)			
1-Reprints in color the Elfquest epic by WaRP Graphics			
	.85	2.50	5.00
2-5	.50	1.50	3.00
6-10	.35	1.10	2.20
11-20	.30	.90	1.80
21-32	.25	.75	1.50
ELFQUEST: SIEGE AT BLUE MOUNTAIN			
3/87 - No. 8, 12/88 (mini-series)($1.75/$1.95, B&W)			
WaRP Graphics/Apple Comics			
1-Staton-a(i) in all	1.10	3.25	6.50
2	.70	2.00	4.00
2-2nd printing	.30	.90	1.80
3-8	.40	1.25	2.50
ELF WARRIOR (See Adventurers)			
1987 - Present ($1.95, B&W)			
Adventure Publ.			
1	.50	1.50	3.00
2-4	.35	1.00	2.00
ELLA CINDERS (See Comics On Parade, Comics Revue #1,4, Famous Comics Cartoon Book, Sparkler Comics, Tip Top & Treasury of Comics)			
ELLA CINDERS			
1938 - 1940			
United Features Syndicate			
Single Series 3(1938)	20.00	60.00	140.00
Single Series 21(#2 on-c, #21 on inside), 28('40)			
	16.00	48.00	110.00
ELLA CINDERS			
March, 1948 - No. 5, 1949			
United Features Syndicate			
1	7.00	21.00	50.00
2	3.50	10.50	24.00
3-5	2.30	7.00	16.00
ELLERY QUEEN			
May, 1949 - No. 4, Nov, 1949			
Superior Comics Ltd.			
1-Kamen c; L.B. Cole-a	18.00	54.00	125.00
2,4	11.00	32.00	75.00
3-Drug use stories(2)	11.50	34.00	80.00
NOTE: *Iger shop art-all issues.*			
ELLERY QUEEN (TV)			
1-3/52 - No. 2, Summer/52 (Saunders painted covers)			
Ziff-Davis Publishing Co.			
1-Saunders-c	15.00	45.00	105.00
2-Saunders bondage, torture-c	15.00	45.00	105.00
ELLERY QUEEN (See 4-Color No. 1165,1243,1289)			
ELMER FUDD (Also see Camp Comics & Daffy)			
May, 1953 - No. 1293, Mar-May, 1962			
Dell Publishing Co.			
4-Color 470,558,628,689('56)	1.15	3.50	8.00

	Good	Fine	N-Mint
ELMER FUDD (continued)			
4-Color 725,783,841,888,938,977,1032,1081,1131,1171,1222,			
1293('61)	.85	2.50	6.00
(See Super Book #10,22)			

ELMO COMICS
January, 1948 (Daily strip-r)
St. John Publishing Co.

	Good	Fine	N-Mint
1-By Cecil Jensen	4.65	14.00	32.00

ELRIC OF MELNIBONE (See First Comics Graphic Novel)
Apr, 1983 - No. 6, Apr, 1984 ($1.50, Baxter paper)
Pacific Comics

1-Russell c/a(i) in all	.35	1.10	2.20
2-6	.35	1.00	2.00

ELRIC: SAILOR ON THE SEAS OF FATE
June, 1985 - No. 7, June, 1986 (Limited series; $1.75 cover)
First Comics

1-Adapts M. Moorcock's novel	.40	1.25	2.50
2-7	.30	.90	1.80

ELRIC: THE BANE OF THE BLACK SWORD
Aug., 1988 - No. 6, July, 1989 ($1.75-$1.95, color, limited series)
First Comics

1-4: Adapts Michael Moorcock's novel	.30	.90	1.80

ELRIC: THE VANISHING TOWER
Aug, 1987 - No. 6, June, 1988 ($1.75, color)
First Comics

1-6: Adapts Michael Moorcock's novel	.35	1.00	2.00

ELRIC: WEIRD OF THE WHITE WOLF
Oct, 1986 - No. 5, June, 1987 (limited series)
First Comics

1-5: Adapts M. Moorcock's novel	.35	1.00	2.00

ELSIE THE COW
Oct-Nov, 1949 - No. 3, July-Aug, 1950
D. S. Publishing Co.

1-(36 pages)	9.50	28.50	66.00
2,3	6.50	19.50	45.00
Borden Milk Giveaway-(16 pgs., nn) (3 issues, 1957)			
	3.00	9.00	21.00
Elsie's Fun Book(1950; Borden Milk)	4.50	13.50	31.00
Everyday Birthday Fun With...(1957; 20 pgs.)(100th Anniversary);			
Kubert-a	3.50	10.50	24.00

ELVIRA'S HOUSE OF MYSTERY
Jan, 1986 - No. 11, Jan, 1987
DC Comics

1 ($1.50, 68pgs.)-Photo back-c	.40	1.25	2.50
2-10: 6-Reads sideways. 7-Sci/fic ish. 9-Photo-c			
		.50	1.00
11-Double-size Halloween ish		.50	1.00
Special #1 (3/87, $1.25)-Haunted Holidays		.60	1.25
NOTE: Ayers/DeZuniga a-5. Bolland c-1. Spiegel a-1. Stevens c-11.

ELVIRA'S MISTRESS OF THE DARK
Oct., 1988 ($2.00, B&W, magazine size)
Marvel Comics

1	.35	1.00	2.00

ELVIS PRESLEY (See Career Girl Rom. 32, Humbug #8, I Love You 60 & Young Lovers 18)

E-MAN
Oct, 1973 - No. 10, Sept, 1975 (Painted-c No. 7-10)
Charlton Comics

1-Origin E-Man; Staton c/a in all	1.20	3.50	7.00
2-Ditko-a	.70	2.00	4.00

	Good	Fine	N-Mint
3,4: 3-Howard-a. 4-Ditko-a	.70	2.00	4.00
5-Miss Liberty Belle app. by Ditko	.50	1.50	3.00
6,7,9,10-Byrne-a in all	.70	2.00	4.00
8-Full-length story; Nova begins as E-Man's partner			
	.85	2.50	5.00
1-4,9,10(Modern Comics reprints, '77)		.15	.30
NOTE: Killjoy app.-No. 2,4. Liberty Belle app.-No. 5. Rog 2000 app.-No. 6, 7, 9, 10. Travis app.-No. 3. Tom Sutton a-1.

E-MAN (Also see The Original... & Michael Mauser)
Apr, 1983 - No. 25, Aug, 1985 (Direct Sale only, $1.00-$1.25)
First Comics

1		.50	1.00
2-25: 2-X-Men satire. 3-X-Men/Phoenix satire. 6-Origin retold.			
10-Origin Nova Kane		.50	1.00
NOTE: Staton a-1-5, 6-25p; c-1-25.

EMERGENCY (Magazine)
June, 1976 - No. 4, Jan, 1977 (B&W)
Charlton Comics

1-Adams c/a, Heath, Austin-a	.50	1.50	3.00
2-Adams-c	.30	.80	1.60
3-Adams-a	.35	1.00	2.00
4-Alcala-a	.30	.80	1.60

EMERGENCY (TV)
June, 1976 - No. 4, Dec, 1976
Charlton Comics

1-Staton-c, Byrne-a	.50	1.50	3.00
2-4: 2-Staton-c	.25	.75	1.50

EMERGENCY DOCTOR
Summer, 1963 (One Shot)
Charlton Comics

1	.50	1.50	3.00

EMIL & THE DETECTIVES (See Movie Comics)

EMMA PEEL & JOHN STEED (See The Avengers)

EMPIRE LANES
Dec., 1986 - No. 4, 1987 ($1.75, B&W)
Northern Lights Publ.

1	.50	1.50	3.00
2-4	.30	.90	1.80

EMPIRE STRIKES BACK, THE (See Marvel Comics Super Special 16)

ENCHANTED APPLES OF OZ, THE (See First Comics Graphic Novel)

ENCHANTING LOVE
Oct, 1949 - No. 6, July, 1950 (#1,2-52 pgs.)
Kirby Publishing Co.

1-Photo-c	4.35	13.00	30.00
2-Photo-c; Powell-a	2.35	7.00	16.00
3,4,6	2.00	6.00	14.00
5-Ingels-a, 9 pgs.; photo-c	8.00	24.00	56.00

ENCHANTMENT VISUALETTES (Magazine)
Dec, 1949 - No. 5, April, 1950
World Editions

1-Contains two romance comic strips each; painted-c			
	7.00	21.00	50.00
2	6.00	18.00	42.00
3-5	5.00	15.00	35.00

ENEMY ACE (See Star-Spangled War Stories)

ENSIGN O'TOOLE (TV)
Aug-Oct, 1963 - No. 2, 1964
Dell Publishing Co.

1,2	1.15	3.50	8.00

Elric: The Bane Of The Black Sword #1, © First Comics

Elvira's House Of Mystery #2, © DC

E-Man #1 (10/73), © CC

Epsilon Wave #1, © Elite Comics   Etta Kett #13, © KING   Everything Happens To Harvey #2, © DC

ENSIGN PULVER (See Movie Classics)

EPIC ILLUSTRATED (Magazine)
Spring, 1980 - No. 34, Mar, 1986 (B&W/Color) ($2.00-$2.50)
Marvel Comics Group

	Good	Fine	N-Mint
1	.35	1.00	2.00
2-10	.25	.75	1.50
11,13-15: 14-Revenge of the Jedi preview. 15-Vallejo-c & interview; ties into Dreadstar No. 1	.25	.75	1.50
12-Wolverton Spacehawk-r edited & recolored with article on him	.25	.75	1.50
16-B. Smith c/a(2)	.25	.75	1.50
17-26: 26-Galactus series begins, ends No. 34; Cerebus the Aardvark story by Dave Sim	.25	.75	1.50
27-34: ($2.50): 28-Cerebus app.	.40	1.25	2.50

NOTE: **Adams** a-7; c-6. **Austin** a-15-20i. **Bode** a-19, 23, 27r. **Bolton** a-7, 10-12, 15, 18, 22-25; c-10, 18, 22, 23. **Boris** c/a-15. **Brunner** c-12. **Buscema** a-1p, 9p, 11p-13p. **Byrne/Austin** a-26-34. **Chaykin** a-2; c-8. **Conrad** a-2-5, 7-9, 25-34. **Corben** a-15; c-2. **Frazetta** c-1. **Golden** a-3. **Gulacy** c/a-3. **Jeff Jones** c-25. **Kaluta** a-17r, 21, 24r, 26; c-4, 28. **Nebres** a-1. **Reese** a-12. **Russell** a-2-4, 9, 14, 33. **Smith** a-7, 16; c-7, 16. **Starlin** a-1-9, 14, 15, 34. **Steranko** c-19. **Williamson** a-27, 34. **Wrightson** a-13p, 22, 25, 27, 34; c-30.

EPSILON WAVE
Oct, 1985 - V2#2, 1987
Independent Comics/Elite Comics No. 5 on

1-Seadragon app.	.50	1.50	3.00
2-4: 2,3-Seadragon app.	.25	.75	1.50
5-10: 6-Seadragon app.	.25	.75	1.50
V2/1,2 (B&W)	.30	.80	1.60

ERNIE COMICS (Formerly Andy Comics No. 21; All Love Romances No. 26 on)
Sept, 1948 - No. 25, Mar, 1949
Current Books/Ace Periodicals

nn(9/48,11/48; No. 22,23)	2.85	8.50	20.00
24,25	1.60	4.80	11.00

ESCAPADE IN FLORENCE (See Movie Comics)

ESCAPE FROM DEVIL'S ISLAND
1952
Avon Periodicals

1-Kinstler-c; r/as Dynamic Adv. No. 9	14.00	42.00	100.00

ESCAPE FROM FEAR
1956, 1962, 1969 (8 pages full color) (On birth control)
Planned Parenthood of America (Giveaway)

1956 edition	13.00	40.00	80.00
1962 edition	10.00	30.00	60.00
1969 edition	5.00	15.00	30.00

ESCAPE TO WITCH MOUNTAIN (See Walt Disney Showcase No. 29)

ESPERS
July, 1986 - No. 5, April, 1987 (Mando paper)
Eclipse Comics

1-5	.35	1.00	2.00

ESPIONAGE (TV)
May-July, 1964 - No. 2, Aug-Oct, 1964
Dell Publishing Co.

1,2	1.30	4.00	9.00

ETERNAL BIBLE, THE
1946 (Large size) (16 pages in color)
Authentic Publications

1	5.00	15.00	35.00

ETERNALS, THE
July, 1976 - No. 19, Jan. 1978
Marvel Comics Group

	Good	Fine	N-Mint
1-Origin	.40	.80	
2-19: 2-1st app. Ajak & The Celestials	.40	.80	
Annual 1(10/77)	.25	.50	

NOTE: **Kirby** c/a(p) in all. Price changed from 25 cents to 30 cents during run of #1.

ETERNALS, THE
10/85 - No. 12, 9/86 (12 issue maxi-series, mando paper)
Marvel Comics Group

1 ($1.25 cover)		.50	1.00
2-11 (75 cents cover)		.50	1.00
12-Double size ($1.25)-Williamson-a(i)		.50	1.00

ETERNITY SMITH
Sept, 1986 - No. 5, May, 1987 (Color, 36 pgs.)
Renegade Press

1 ($1.25)		.65	1.30
2-5 ($1.50)		.65	1.30

ETERNITY SMITH
Sept, 1987 - Present ($1.95, color)
Hero Comics

V2#1-10: 8-Indigo begins	.30	.95	1.90
Book 1 ($7.95)	1.35	4.00	8.00

ETTA KETT
No. 11, Dec, 1948 - No. 14, Sept, 1949
King Features Syndicate/Standard

11	4.30	13.00	30.00
12-14	2.65	8.00	18.00

EVANGELINE (Also see Primer)
2/84 - No. 2, 6/84; V2#1, 5/87 - Present (Color; Baxter)
Comico/First Comics V2/1 on/Lodestone

1	1.00	3.00	6.00
2	.50	1.50	3.00
V2#1 (5/87) - 12	.35	1.00	2.00
Special #1 ('86, $2.00, color)-Lodestone	.35	1.00	2.00

EVA THE IMP
1957 - No. 2, Nov, 1957
Red Top Comic/Decker

1,2	1.15	3.50	8.00

EVEL KNIEVEL
1974 (20 pages) (Giveaway)
Marvel Comics Group (Ideal Toy Corp.)

nn		.40	.80

EVERYBODY'S COMICS (See Fox Giants)

EVERYTHING HAPPENS TO HARVEY
Sept-Oct, 1953 - No. 7, Sept-Oct, 1954
National Periodical Publications

1	9.00	27.00	62.00
2	5.00	15.00	35.00
3-7	4.00	12.00	28.00

EVERYTHING'S ARCHIE
May, 1969 - Present (Giant issues No. 1-20)
Archie Publications

1	4.65	14.00	32.00
2	2.30	7.00	16.00
3-5	1.30	4.00	9.00
6-10	.85	2.50	5.00
11-20	.35	1.00	2.00
21-40		.50	1.00
41-142		.30	.60

EVERYTHING'S DUCKY (See 4-Color No. 1251)

EWOKS (TV) (See Star Comics Mag.)
June, 1985 - No. 15, Sept, 1987
Star Comics (Marvel)

	Good	Fine	N-Mint
1-13: 10-Williamson-a		.35	.70
14,15($1.00)		.45	.90

EXCALIBER
Apr, 1988 - Present ($1.50, Baxter)
Marvel Comics

1 ($3.25, One shot)-X-Men spin-off	1.15	3.50	7.00
1-2nd print ($3.50, 10/88)	.60	1.75	3.50
1($1.50)-Monthly series begins	.50	1.50	3.00
2-4	.30	.90	1.80

EXCITING COMICS
April, 1940 - No. 69, Sept, 1949
Nedor/Better Publications/Standard Comics

1-Origin The Mask, Jim Hatfield, Sgt. Bill King, Dan Williams begin			
	60.00	180.00	420.00
2-The Sphinx begins; The Masked Rider app.			
	26.00	78.00	180.00
3	22.00	65.00	154.00
4	18.00	54.00	125.00
5	13.50	41.00	95.00
6-8	11.00	32.00	75.00
9-Origin/1st app. of The Black Terror & sidekick Tim, begin series			
	60.00	180.00	420.00
10-13	25.00	75.00	175.00
14-Last Sphinx, Dan Williams	16.00	48.00	110.00
15-The Liberator begins (origin)	20.00	60.00	140.00
16-20: 20-The Mask ends	11.00	32.00	75.00
21,23-30: 28-Crime Crusader begins, ends #58			
	11.00	32.00	75.00
22-Origin The Eaglet; The American Eagle begins			
	11.00	32.00	75.00
31-38: 35-Liberator ends, not in 31-33	10.00	30.00	70.00
39-Origin Kara, Jungle Princess	14.00	42.00	100.00
40-50: 42-The Scarab begins. 49-Last Kara, Jungle Princess. 50-Last American Eagle			
	12.00	36.00	84.00
51-Miss Masque begins	16.00	48.00	110.00
52-54: Miss Masque ends	12.00	36.00	84.00
55-Judy of the Jungle begins(origin), ends #69; 1 pg. Ingels-a			
	16.00	48.00	110.00
56-58: All airbrush-c	14.00	42.00	100.00
59-Frazetta art in Caniff style; signed Frank Frazeta (one t), 9 pgs.			
	20.00	60.00	140.00
60-65: 60-Rick Howard, the Mystery Rider begins			
	12.00	36.00	84.00
66-Robinson/Meskin-a	12.00	36.00	84.00
67-69	7.00	21.00	50.00

NOTE: *Schomburg (Xela) c-28-68; airbrush c-57-66. Black Terror by R. Moreira-#65. Roussos a-62. Bondage-c 9, 12, 13, 20, 23, 25, 30, 59.*

EXCITING ROMANCES
1949 (nd); No. 2, Spring, 1950 - No. 5, 10/50; No. 6 (1951, nd), No. 7, 9/51 - No. 14, 1/53
Fawcett Publications

1(1949)-Photo-c	3.50	10.50	24.00
2-5-(1950): 4-Photo-c	2.50	7.50	18.00
6-14	1.50	4.50	10.00

NOTE: *Powell a-8-10. Photo-c, 1,4-7,11,12.*

EXCITING ROMANCE STORIES (See Fox Giants)

EXCITING WAR (Korean war)
No. 5, Sept, 1952 - No. 8, May, 1953; No. 9, Nov, 1953
Standard Comics (Better Publ.)

5	2.35	7.00	16.00

	Good	Fine	N-Mint
6,7,9	1.35	4.00	9.00
8-Toth-a	3.00	9.00	21.00

EX-MUTANTS
Aug., 1986 - No. 7? ($1.80, B&W)
Eternity Comics/Amazing Comics

1	.50	1.50	3.00
2	.35	1.00	2.00
3-7	.30	.90	1.80
Special 1	.30	.90	1.80
Graphic Novel 1	1.00	3.00	5.95
Graphic Novel 1-2nd print w/new text	1.15	3.50	6.95
Graphic Novel 2 ('88, $7.95)	1.35	4.00	7.95
Pin-Up Book ($1.95, color)	.35	1.00	1.95

EX-MUTANTS: THE SHATTERED EARTH CHRONICLES
Apr., 1988 - Present ($1.95, B&W)
Eternity Comics

1-5	.35	1.00	1.95

EXORCISTS (See The Crusaders)

EXOTIC ROMANCES (Formerly True War Romances)
No. 22, Oct, 1955 - No. 31, Nov, 1956
Quality Comics Group (Comic Magazines)

22	3.50	10.50	24.00
23-26,29	1.70	5.00	12.00
27,31-Baker c/a	3.85	11.50	27.00
28,30-Baker-a	3.50	10.50	24.00

EXPLOITS OF DANIEL BOONE
Nov., 1955 - No. 6, Sept, 1956
Quality Comics Group

1	6.00	18.00	42.00
2	3.00	9.00	21.00
3-6	2.65	8.00	18.00

EXPLOITS OF DICK TRACY (See Dick Tracy)

EXPLORER JOE
Winter, 1951 - No. 2, Oct-Nov, 1952
Ziff-Davis Comic Group (Approved Comics)

1-Saunders painted-c	5.00	15.00	35.00
2-Krigstein-a	6.00	18.00	42.00

EXPOSED (...True Crime Cases)
Mar-Apr, 1948 - No. 9, July-Aug, 1949
D. S. Publishing Co.

1	6.00	18.00	42.00
2-Giggling killer story with excessive blood; two eye injury panels			
	7.00	21.00	50.00
3,8,9	3.50	10.50	24.00
4-Orlando-a	3.70	11.00	26.00
5-Breeze Lawson, Sky Sheriff by E. Good	3.00	9.00	21.00
6-Ingels-a; used in SOTI, illo-''How to prepare an alibi.''			
	15.00	45.00	105.00
7-Illo. in SOTI, ''Diagram for housebreakers''; used by N.Y. Legis. Comm.			
	14.00	42.00	100.00

EXTRA
1948
Magazine Enterprises

1-Giant; consisting of rebound ME comics. Two versions known: (1)-Funny Man by Siegel & Shuster, Space Ace, Undercover Girl, & (2)-All Funnyman			
	22.00	65.00	154.00

EXTRA!
Mar-Apr, 1955 - No. 5, Nov-Dec, 1955
E. C. Comics

Exciting Comics #32, © STD

Ex-Mutants #1, © Eternity Comics

Exposed #1, © DS

138

Fairy Tale Parade #3, © DELL   Faithful #2, © MEG   Famous Crimes #10, © FOX

	Good	Fine	N-Mint
EXTRA! (continued)			
1	6.00	18.00	42.00
2-5	4.00	12.00	28.00

NOTE: *Craig, Crandall, Severin* art in all.

FACE, THE (Tony Trent, the Face No. 3 on)
1941 (See Big Shot Comics)
Columbia Comics Group

1-The Face; Mart Bailey-c	28.00	84.00	195.00
2-Bailey-c	19.00	57.00	132.00

FAIRY TALE PARADE (See Famous Fairy Tales)
June-July, 1942 - No. 121, Oct, 1946 (Most all by Walt Kelly)
Dell Publishing Co.

1-Kelly-a begins	78.00	234.00	545.00
2(8-9/42)	44.00	132.00	305.00
3-5 (10-11/42 - 2-4/43)	28.00	84.00	195.00
6-9 (5-7/43 - 11-1/43-44)	22.00	65.00	155.00
4-Color 50('44)	21.00	63.00	145.00
4-Color 69('45)	18.00	54.00	125.00
4-Color 104,114('46)-Last Kelly ish.	16.00	48.00	110.00
4-Color 87('45)	12.00	36.00	84.00
4-Color 121('46)-Not Kelly	8.00	24.00	56.00

NOTE: #1-9, 4-Color #50,69 have **Kelly** c/a; 4-Color #87, 104, 114-**Kelly** art only. #9 has a redrawn version of The Reluctant Dragon. This series contains all the classic fairy tales from Jack In The Beanstalk to Cinderella.

FAIRY TALES
No. 10, 1951 - No. 11, June-July, 1951
Ziff-Davis Publ. Co. (Approved Comics)

10,11-Painted-c	5.00	15.00	35.00

FAITHFUL
November, 1949 - No. 2, Feb, 1950 (52 pgs.)
Marvel Comics/Lovers' Magazine

1,2-Photo-c	2.65	8.00	18.00

FALCON (Also see Captain America #117 & 133)
Nov, 1983 - No. 4, Feb, 1984 (mini-series)
Marvel Comics Group

1-Paul Smith c/a(p)		.50	1.00
2-4: 2-Smith-c		.50	1.00

FALLEN ANGELS
April, 1987 - No. 8, Nov, 1987 (mini-series)
Marvel Comics Group

1		.50	1.50	3.00
2,3		.35	1.00	2.00
4-8		.25	.70	1.40

FALLING IN LOVE
Sept-Oct, 1955 - No. 143, Oct-Nov, 1973
Arleigh Publ. Co./National Periodical Publications

1	11.00	32.00	75.00
2	5.00	15.00	35.00
3-10	3.00	9.00	21.00
11-20	1.70	5.00	12.00
21-40	1.30	4.00	9.00
41-46: 46-Last 10 cent ish.	.85	2.50	6.00
47-100	.50	1.50	3.00
101-107,109-143	.35	1.00	2.00
108-Wood-a, 4pgs. (7/69)	.50	1.50	3.00

NOTE: **Colan** c/a-75, 81. 52 pgs.-#125-133.

FALL OF THE HOUSE OF USHER, THE (See Corben Special, A)

FALL OF THE ROMAN EMPIRE (See Movie Comics)

FAMILY AFFAIR (TV)
Feb, 1970 - No. 4, Oct, 1970 (25 cents)
Gold Key

	Good	Fine	N-Mint
1-Pull-out poster; photo-c	2.00	6.00	14.00
2-4: 3,4-Photo-c	1.15	3.50	8.00

FAMILY FUNNIES
No. 9, Aug-Sept, 1946
Parents' Magazine Institute

9	2.30	7.00	16.00

FAMILY FUNNIES (Tiny Tot Funnies No. 9 on)
Sept, 1950 - No. 8, April?, 1951
Harvey Publications

1-Mandrake	3.50	10.50	24.00
2-Flash Gordon, 1 pg.	2.35	7.00	16.00
3-8: 4,5,7-Flash Gordon, 1 pg.	2.00	6.00	14.00
1(black & white)	1.20	3.50	8.00

FAMOUS AUTHORS ILL. (See Stories by . . .)

FAMOUS COMICS (Also see Favorite Comics)
No date; Mid 1930's (24 pages) (paper cover)
Zain-Eppy/United Features Syndicate

Reprinted from 1934 newspaper strips in color; Joe Palooka, Hairbreadth Harry, Napoleon, The Nebbs, etc. 17.00 51.00 120.00

FAMOUS COMICS
1934 (100 pgs., daily newspaper reprints)
(3½x8½''; paper cover) (came in a box)
King Features Syndicate (Whitman Publ. Co.)

684(#1)-Little Jimmy, Katzenjammer Kids & Barney Google			
	14.00	42.00	100.00
684(#2)-Polly, Little Jimmy, Katzenjammer Kids			
	14.00	42.00	100.00
684(#3)-Little Annie Rooney, Polly, Katzenjammer Kids			
	14.00	42.00	100.00
. . . .Box price. . . .	5.00	20.00	50.00

FAMOUS COMICS CARTOON BOOKS
1934 (72 pgs.; 8x7¼''; daily strip reprints)
Whitman Publishing Co. (B&W; hardbacks)

1200-The Captain & the Kids; Dirks reprints credited to Bernard Dibble	10.00	30.00	70.00
1202-Captain Easy & Wash Tubbs by Roy Crane			
	14.00	42.00	100.00
1203-Ella Cinders	10.00	30.00	70.00
1204-Freckles & His Friends	8.00	24.00	56.00

NOTE: Called Famous Funnies Cartoon Books inside.

FAMOUS CRIMES
June, 1948 - No. 19, Sept, 1950; No. 20, Aug, 1951
Fox Features Syndicate/M.S. Dist. No. 51,52

1-Blue Beetle app. & crime story r-/Phantom Lady #16. Hollingsworth-a	13.00	40.00	90.00
2-Shows woman dissolved in acid; lingerie-c/panels			
	10.00	30.00	70.00
3-Injury-to-eye story used in **SOTI**, pg. 112; has two electrocution stories	13.00	40.00	90.00
4-6	5.00	15.00	35.00
7-''Tarzan, the Wyoming Killer'' used in **SOTI**, pg. 44; drug trial/ possession story	11.00	32.00	75.00
8-20: 17-Morisi-a	3.70	11.00	26.00
51(nd, 1953)	4.35	13.00	30.00
52	2.65	8.00	18.00

FAMOUS FAIRY TALES
1943 (32 pgs.); 1944 (16 pgs.) (Soft covers)
K. K. Publ. Co. (Giveaway)

1943-Reprints from Fairy Tale Parade No. 2,3; Kelly inside art			
	40.00	120.00	260.00
1944-Kelly inside art	28.00	85.00	180.00

FAMOUS FEATURE STORIES
1938 (68 pgs., 7½x11")
Dell Publishing Co.

	Good	Fine	N-Mint
1-Tarzan, Terry & the Pirates, King of the Royal Mtd., Buck Jones, Dick Tracy, Smilin' Jack, Dan Dunn, Don Winslow, G-Man, Tailspin Tommy, Mutt & Jeff, & Little Orphan Annie reprints - all illustrated text	38.00	115.00	265.00

FAMOUS FIRST EDITION (See Limited Collectors Edition)
($1.00; 10x13½")-Giant Size(72pgs.; No.6-8, 68 pgs.)
1974 - No. 8, Aug-Sept, 1975; C-61, Sept, 1978
National Periodical Publications/DC Comics

	Good	Fine	N-Mint
C-26-Action No. 1	1.00	3.00	7.00
C-28-Detective No. 27	1.00	3.00	7.00
C-30-Sensation No. 1(1974)	1.00	3.00	7.00
F-4-Whiz No. 2(No.1)(10-11/74)-Cover not identical to original	1.00	3.00	7.00
F-5-Batman No. 1(F-6 on inside)	1.00	3.00	7.00
F-6-Wonder Woman No. 1	.85	2.50	6.00
F-7-All-Star Comics No. 3	1.00	3.00	7.00
F-8-Flash No. 1(8-9/75)	.85	2.50	6.00
C-61-Superman No. 1(9/78)	1.00	3.00	7.00
Hardbound editions w/dust jackets ($5.00) (Lyle Stuart, Inc.) C-26,C-28,C-30,F-4,F-6 known	1.75	5.25	12.00

Warning: The above books are almost **exact** reprints of the originals that they represent except for the Giant-Size format. None of the originals are Giant-Size. The first five issues and C-61 were printed with two covers. Reprint information can be found on the outside cover, but not on the inside cover which was reprinted exactly like the original (inside and out).

FAMOUS FUNNIES
1933 - No. 218, July, 1955
Eastern Color

	Good	Fine	Vf-NM
A Carnival of Comics (probably the second comic book), 36 pgs., no date given, no publisher, no number; contains strip reprints of The Bungle Family, Dixie Dugan, Hairbreadth Harry, Joe Palooka, Keeping Up With the Jones, Mutt & Jeff, Reg'lar Fellers, S'Matter Pop, Strange As It Seems, and others. This book was sold by M. C. Gaines to Wheatena, Milk-O-Malt, John Wanamaker, Kinney Shoe Stores, & others to be given away as premiums and radio giveaways (1933).	225.00	675.00	1575.00
Series 1-(Very rare)(nd-early 1934)(68 pgs.) No publisher given (Eastern Color Printing Co.); sold in chain stores for 10 cents. 35,000 print run. Contains Sunday strip reprints of Mutt & Jeff, Reg'lar Fellers, Nipper, Hairbreadth Harry, Strange As It Seems, Joe Palooka, Dixie Dugan, The Nebbs, Keeping Up With the Jones, and others. Inside front and back covers and pages 1-16 of Famous Funnies Series 1, #s 49-64 reprinted from Famous Funnies, A Carnival of Comics, and most of pages 17-48 reprinted from Funnies on Parade. This was the first comic book sold.	428.00	1285.00	3000.00
No. 1 (Rare)(7/34-on stands 5/34) - Eastern Color Printing Co. First monthly newsstand comic book. Contains Sunday strip reprints of Toonerville Folks, Mutt & Jeff, Hairbreadth Harry, S'Matter Pop, Nipper, Dixie Dugan, The Bungle Family, Connie, Ben Webster, Tailspin Tommy, The Nebbs, Joe Palooka, & others.	300.00	900.00	2100.00
2 (Rare)	100.00	300.00	700.00
3-Buck Rogers Sunday strip reprints by Rick Yager begins, ends #218; not in No. 191-208; the number of the 1st strip reprinted is pg. 190, Series No. 1	140.00	420.00	980.00

	Good	Fine	N-Mint
4	65.00	195.00	455.00
5	50.00	150.00	350.00
6-10	40.00	120.00	280.00
11,12,18-Four pgs. of Buck Rogers in each issue, completes stories in Buck Rogers No. 1 which lacks these pages; No. 18-Two pgs. of Buck Rogers reprinted in Daisy Comics No. 1	35.00	105.00	245.00
13-17,19,20: 14-Has two Buck Rogers panels missing. 17-1st Christmas-c on a newsstand comic	26.00	78.00	180.00
21,23-30: 27-War on Crime begins	18.00	54.00	125.00
22-Four pgs. of Buck Rogers needed to complete stories in Buck Rogers No. 1	20.00	60.00	140.00

	Good	Fine	N-Mint
31,32,34,36,37,39,40	14.00	42.00	100.00
33-Careers of Baby Face Nelson & John Dillinger traced	14.00	42.00	100.00
35-Two pgs. Buck Rogers omitted in Buck Rogers No. 2	16.00	48.00	110.00
38-Full color portrait of Buck Rogers	14.00	42.00	100.00
41-60: 55-Last bottom panel, pg. 4 in Buck Rogers redrawn in Buck Rogers No. 3	10.00	30.00	70.00
61-64,66,67,69,70	8.50	25.50	60.00
65,68-Two pgs. Kirby-a-"Lightnin & the Lone Rider"	9.30	28.00	65.00
71,73,77-80: 80-Buck Rogers story continues from B. R. No. 5	6.50	19.50	45.00
72-Speed Spaulding begins by Marvin Bradley (artist), ends No. 88. This series was written by Edwin Balmer & Philip Wylie and later appeared as film & book "When Worlds Collide".	8.50	25.50	60.00
74-76-Two pgs. Kirby-a in all	6.50	19.50	45.00
81-Origin Invisible Scarlet O'Neil; strip begins No. 82, ends No. 167	5.50	16.50	38.00
82-Buck Rogers-c	6.50	19.50	45.00
83-87,90: 87 has last Buck Rogers full page-r. 90-Bondage-c	5.50	16.50	38.00
88-Buck Rogers in "Moon's End" by Calkins, 2 pgs.(not reprints). Beginning with No. 88, all Buck Rogers pages have rearranged panels	6.00	18.00	42.00
89-Origin Fearless Flint, the Flint Man	6.00	18.00	42.00
91-93,95,96,98-99,101-110: 105-Series 2 begins (Strip Page No. 1)	4.35	13.00	30.00
94-Buck Rogers in "Solar Holocaust" by Calkins, 3 pgs.(not reprints)	5.00	15.00	35.00
97-War Bond promotion, Buck Rogers by Calkins, 2 pgs.(not reprints)	5.00	15.00	35.00
100	5.00	15.00	35.00
111-130	3.50	10.50	24.00
131-150: 137-Strip page No. 110½ omitted	2.30	7.00	16.00
151-162,164-168	2.00	6.00	14.00
163-St. Valentine's Day-c	2.65	8.00	18.00
169,170-Two text illos. by Williamson, his 1st comic book work	5.00	15.00	35.00
171-180: 171-Strip pgs. 227,229,230, Series 2 omitted. 172-Strip Pg. 232 omitted	2.00	6.00	14.00
181-190: Buck Rogers ends with start of strip pg. 302, Series 2	1.70	5.00	12.00
191-197,199,201,203,206-208: No Buck Rogers	1.50	4.50	10.00
198,202,205-One pg. Frazetta ads; no Buck Rogers	1.85	5.50	13.00
200-Frazetta 1 pg. ad	2.00	6.00	14.00
204-Used in POP, pgs. 79,99	2.15	6.50	15.00
209-Buck Rogers begins with strip pg. 480, Series 2; Frazetta-c	24.00	73.00	170.00
210-216: Frazetta-c. 211-Buck Rogers ads by Anderson begins, ends #217. #215-Contains B. Rogers strip pg. 515-518, series 2 followed by pgs. 179-181, Series 3	24.00	73.00	170.00
217,218-Buck Rogers ends with pg. 199, Series 3	2.00	6.00	14.00

NOTE: *Rick Yager* did the Buck Rogers Sunday strips reprinted in Famous Funnies. The Sundays were formerly done by Russ Keaton and Lt. Dick Calkins did the dailies, but would sometimes assist Yager on a panel or two from time to time. Strip No. 169 is Yager's first full Buck Rogers page. Yager did the strip until 1958 when *Murphy Anderson* took over. *Tuska* art from 4/26/59 - 1965. Virtually every panel was rewritten for Famous Funnies. Not identical to the original Sunday page. The Buck Rogers reprints ran continuously through Famous Funnies issue No. 190 (Strip No. 302) with no break in story line. The story line has no continuity after No. 190. The Buck Rogers newspaper strips came out in four series: Series 1, 3/30/30 - 9/21/41 (No. 1 - 600); Series 2, 9/28/41 -10/21/51 (No. 1 -525)(Strip No.110½ (½ pg.) published in only a few newspapers); Series 3, 10/28/51 -2/9/58 (No. 100-428)(No No. 1-99); Series 4, 2/16/58 -

Famous Funnies Series 1, © EAS

Famous Funnies #100, © EAS

Famous Funnies #216, © EAS

Fantasci #1, © Apple Comics

Fantastic #10, © AJAX

Fantastic Comics #7, © FOX

FAMOUS FUNNIES (continued)
6/13/65 (No numbers, dates only). *Everett c-86. Moulton a-100.*

FAMOUS FUNNIES
1964
Super Comics

	Good	Fine	N-Mint
Reprint No. 15-18	.50	1.50	3.00

FAMOUS GANG BOOK OF COMICS (Donald & Mickey Merry Christmas 1943 on)
Dec, 1942 (32 pgs.; paper cover) (Christmas giveaway)
Firestone Tire & Rubber Co.

(Rare)-Porky Pig, Bugs Bunny, Sniffles; r-/Looney Tunes	67.00	200.00	500.00

FAMOUS GANGSTERS (Crime on the Waterfront No. 4)
April, 1951 - No. 3, Feb, 1952
Avon Periodicals/Realistic

1-Narcotics mentioned; Capone, Dillinger; c-/Avon paperback No. 329	14.00	42.00	100.00
2-Wood-c/a (1 pg.); r-/Saint No. 7 & retitled "Mike Strong"	15.00	45.00	105.00
3-Lucky Luciano & Murder, Inc; c-/Avon paperback 66	15.00	45.00	105.00

FAMOUS INDIAN TRIBES
July-Sept, 1962; July, 1972
Dell Publishing Co.

12-264-209 (The Sioux)	1.00	3.00	7.00
2(7/72)-Reprints above	.25	.75	1.50

FAMOUS STARS
Nov-Dec, 1950 - No. 6, Spring, 1952 (All photo covers)
Ziff-Davis Publ. Co.

1-Shelley Winters, Susan Peters, Ava Gardner, Shirley Temple	12.00	36.00	84.00
2-Betty Hutton, Bing Crosby, Colleen Townsend, Gloria Swanson; Everett-a(2)	8.50	25.50	60.00
3-Farley Granger, Judy Garland's ordeal, Alan Ladd	8.00	24.00	56.00
4-Al Jolson, Bob Mitchum, Ella Raines, Richard Conte, Vic Damone; Crandall-a, 6pgs.	7.00	21.00	50.00
5-Liz Taylor, Betty Grable, Esther Williams, George Brent; Krigstein-a	10.00	30.00	70.00
6-Gene Kelly, Hedy Lamarr, June Allyson, William Boyd, Janet Leigh, Gary Cooper	7.00	21.00	50.00

NOTE: *Whitney a-1,3.*

FAMOUS STORIES (. . . Book No. 2)
1942
Dell Publishing Co.

1-Treasure Island	13.00	40.00	90.00
2-Tom Sawyer	13.00	40.00	90.00

FAMOUS TV FUNDAY FUNNIES
Sept, 1961
Harvey Publications

1-Casper the Ghost	3.00	9.00	21.00

FAMOUS WESTERN BADMEN (Formerly Redskin)
No. 13, Dec, 1952 - No. 15, 1953
Youthful Magazines

13	4.00	12.00	28.00
14,15	2.30	7.00	16.00

FANTASTIC (Formerly Capt. Science; Beware No. 10 on)
No. 8, Feb, 1952 - No. 9, April, 1952
Youthful Magazines

8-Capt. Science by Harrison; decapitation, shrunken head panels	11.00	32.00	75.00

	Good	Fine	N-Mint
9-Harrison-a	6.50	19.50	45.00

FANTASTIC (Fantastic Fears No. 1-9)
No. 10, Nov-Dec, 1954 - No. 11, Jan-Feb, 1955
Ajax/Farrell Publ.

10,11	3.70	11.00	26.00

FANTASTIC ADVENTURES
1963 - 1964 (Reprints)
Super Comics

9,10,12,15,16,18: 16-Briefer-a. 18-r/Superior Stories #1	1.15	3.50	8.00
11-Wood-a; r/Blue Bolt #118	1.70	5.00	12.00
17-Baker-a(2) . r-/Seven Seas #6	1.50	4.50	10.00

FANTASTIC COMICS
Dec, 1939 - No. 23, Nov, 1941
Fox Features Syndicate

1-Intro/Origin Samson; Stardust, The Super Wizard, Space Smith, Sub Saunders (by Kiefer), Capt. Kidd begin	110.00	330.00	770.00
2-Powell text illos	55.00	165.00	385.00
3-5: 3-Powell text illos	45.00	135.00	315.00
6-9: 6,7-Simon-c	36.00	110.00	250.00
10-Intro/origin David, Samson's aide	27.00	81.00	190.00
11-17: 16-Stardust ends	21.00	62.00	148.00
18-Intro. Black Fury & sidekick Chuck; ends #23	24.00	72.00	168.00
19,20	21.00	62.00	148.00
21-The Banshee begins(origin); ends #23. Hitler-c	24.00	72.00	168.00
22	21.00	62.00	148.00
23-Origin The Gladiator	24.00	72.00	168.00

NOTE: *Lou Fine c-1-5. Tuska a-3-5, 8. Bondage c-6, 8, 9.*

FANTASTIC FEARS (Formerly Captain Jet) (Fantastic No. 10 on)
No. 7, May, 1953 - No. 9, Sept-Oct, 1954
Ajax/Farrell Publ.

7(5/53)	8.50	25.50	60.00
8(7/53)	5.70	17.00	40.00
3,4	4.30	13.00	30.00
5-1st Ditko story is written by Bruce Hamilton reprinted in Weird V2#8	22.00	65.00	154.00
6-Decapitation of girl's head with paper cutter (classic)	11.50	34.00	80.00
7(5-6/54), 9(9-10/54)	4.00	12.00	28.00
8(7-8/54)-Contains story intended for Jo-Jo; name changed to Kaza; decapitation story	5.70	17.00	40.00

FANTASTIC FOUR (See America's Best TV . . . , Giant Size Super-Stars, Marvel Coll. Item Classics, Marvel's Greatest, Marvel Treas. Ed, Marvel Triple Action & Official Marvel Index to . . .)
Nov, 1961 - Present
Marvel Comics Group

1-Origin & 1st app. The Fantastic Four (Reed Richards: Mr. Fantastic, Johnny Storm: The Human Torch, Sue Storm: The Invisible Girl, & Ben Grimm: The Thing); origin The Mole Man	160.00	640.00	1600.00
1-Golden Record Comic Set-r	2.50	7.50	15.00
with record	5.70	17.00	40.00
2-Vs. The Skrulls (last 10 cent issue)	82.00	205.00	575.00
3-Fantastic Four don costumes & establish Headquarters; brief 1pg. origin. intro The Fantasticar. H. Torch drawn w/two left hands on-c	65.00	165.00	460.00
4-1st Silver Age Sub-Mariner app.	51.00	127.00	355.00
5-Origin & 1st app. Doctor Doom	40.00	100.00	280.00
6-10: 6-Sub-Mariner, Dr. Doom team up. 7-1st app. Kurrgo. 8-1st			

	Good	Fine	N-Mint
FANTASTIC FOUR (continued)			
app. Puppet-Master & Alicia Masters	26.00	64.00	180.00
11-Origin The Impossible Man	19.00	48.00	135.00
12-Fantastic Four Vs. The Hulk	17.00	43.00	120.00
13-Intro. The Watcher; 1st app. The Red Ghost			
	14.00	35.00	100.00
14-19: 18-Origin The Super Skrull. 19-Intro. Rama-Tut			
	11.00	27.00	75.00
20-Origin The Molecule Man	10.00	25.00	70.00
21-24,27: 21-Intro. The Hate Monger	5.70	14.00	40.00
25,26-The Thing vs. The Hulk	9.00	23.00	65.00
28-X-Men app.	6.50	16.00	45.00
29,30: 30-Intro. Diablo	4.00	10.00	28.00
31-40: 31-Avengers x-over. 33-1st app. Attuma. 35-Intro/1st app. Dragon Man. 36-Intro/1st app. Madam Medusa & the Frightful Four (Sandman, Wizard, Paste Pot Pete). 39-Wood inks on Daredevil	3.00	7.00	21.00
41-47: 41-43-Frightful Four app. 44-Intro. Gorgan. 45-Intro. The Inhumans	2.15	6.50	15.00
48-Intro/1st app. The Silver Surfer, & Galactus (3/66)			
	6.50	19.50	48.00
49,50-Silver Surfer x-over	3.00	9.00	21.00
51-60: 52-Intro. The Black Panther; origin-#53. Silver Surfer x-over in #55-60,61(cameo). 54,59,60-Inhumans cameo			
	1.85	5.50	11.00
61-65,68-70	1.35	4.00	8.00
66,67-1st app. & origin Him (Warlock)	1.50	4.50	9.00
71,73,78-80	.85	2.50	5.00
72,74-77: Silver Surfer app.	1.50	4.50	9.00
81-90: 81-Crystal joins & dons costume. 82,83-Inhumans app. 84-87-Dr. Doom app.	.75	2.25	4.50
91-99,101,102: 94-Intro. Agatha Harkness. Last Kirby issue #102,108	.75	2.25	4.50
100	2.50	7.50	15.00
103-111	.50	1.50	3.00
112-Hulk Vs. Thing	.85	2.50	5.00
113-120: 116-(52 pgs.)	.50	1.50	3.00
121-123-Silver Surfer x-over	.75	2.25	4.50
124-127,129-140: 126-Origin F.F. retold. 129-Intro. Thundra. 130-Sue leaves F.F. 132-Medusa joins. 133-Thundra Vs. Thing	.40	1.25	2.50
128-Four pg. insert of F.F. Friends & Fiends	.60	1.75	3.50
141-149,151-154,158-160: 142-Kirbyish art by Buckler begins. 151-Origin Thundra. 159-Medusa leaves, Sue rejoins	.40	1.25	2.50
150-Crystal & Quicksilver's wedding	.50	1.50	3.00
155-157: Silver Surfer in all	.40	1.25	2.50
161-180: 164-The Crusader (old Marvel Boy) revived; origin #165. 176-Re-intro Impossible Man; Marvel artists app.	.35	1.00	2.00
181-199: 190-191-F.F. breaks up	.25	.80	1.60
200-Giant size-FF re-united	.60	1.75	3.50
201-208,219		.60	1.25
209-216,218,220,221-Byrne-a. 209-1st Herbie the Robot. 220-Brief origin	.25	.80	1.60
217-Dazzler app. by Byrne	.45	1.30	2.60
222-231		.60	1.25
232-Byrne-a begins	.50	1.50	3.00
233-235,237-249: Byrne-a. 238-Origin Frankie Ray	.40	1.20	2.40
236-20th Anniversary issue(11/81, 64pgs., $1.00)-Brief origin F.F.	.50	1.50	3.00
250-Double size; Byrne-a; Skrulls impersonate New X-Men	.50	1.50	3.00
251-259: Byrne c/a. 252-Reads sideways; Annihilus app.	.35	1.10	2.20
260-Alpha Flight app.	.50	1.50	3.00

	Good	Fine	N-Mint
261-285: 261-Silver Surfer. 262-Origin Galactus	.35	1.00	2.00
286-Ties in w/X-Factor	.60	1.75	3.50
287-295		.50	1.00
296-Barry Smith c/a; Thing rejoins	.35	1.00	2.00
297-305,307-318, 320-325: 312-X-Factor x-over		.50	1.00
306-New team begins	.25	.75	1.50
319-Double size	.30	.90	1.80
Giant-Size 2(8/74) - 4: Formerly Giant-Size Super-Stars			
	.70	2.00	4.00
Giant-Size 5(5/75), 6(8/75)	.35	1.00	2.00
Annual 1('63)-Origin F.F.; Ditko-i	11.50	29.00	80.00
Annual 2('64)-Dr. Doom origin & x-over	5.70	14.00	40.00
Annual 3('65)-Reed & Sue wed	2.85	7.00	20.00
Special 4(11/66)-G.A. Torch x-over & origin retold			
	1.15	3.50	7.00
Special 5(11/67)-New art; Intro. Psycho-Man; Silver Surfer, Black Panther, Inhumans app.	.85	2.50	5.00
Special 6(11/68)-Intro. Annihilus; no reprints; birth of Franklin Richards	.85	2.50	5.00
Special 7(11/69), 8(12/70), 9(12/71), 10('73)	.50	1.50	3.00
Annual 11(6/76), 12(2/78)	.35	1.00	2.00
Annual 13(10/78), 14(1/80)	.35	1.00	2.00
Annual 15(10/80), 16(10/81), 17(9/83)	.35	1.00	2.00
Annual 18(11/84), 19(11/85), 20(9/87)	.35	1.00	2.00
Annual 21(9/88)-Evolutionary War x-over	.50	1.50	3.00
Special Edition 1 (5/84)-r/Annual #1; Byrne c/a	.35	1.00	2.00
Giveaway (nn, 1981, 32pgs., Young Model Builders Club)			
	.25	.80	1.60

NOTE: **Austin** c(i)-232-236, 238, 240-42, 250i, 286i. **John Buscema** a(p)-107, 108(w/Kirby & Romita),109-130, 132, 134-141, 160, 173-175, 202, 296p-309p, Annual 11, 13, Gnt-Size 1-4; c(p)-107-122, 124-129, 133-139, 202, Annual 12p, Special 10. **Byrne** a-209-218p, 220p, 221p, 232-65, 266i, 267-73, 274-93p, Annual 17; c-211-14p, 220p, 232-236p, 237, 238p, 239, 240-42p, 243-49, 250p, 251-67, 268-77p, 278p-81p, 283p, 284, 285, 286p, 288-293, Annual., 17. Ditko a-13i, Gnt Size 2r, Annual 16. **G. Kane** c-150p, 160p. **Kirby** a-1-102p, 108, 189r, 236p(r), Special 1-10, Giant-Size 5, 6r; c-1-101, 164, 167, 171-177, 180, 181, 190, 200, Annual 11, Giant-Size 5, Special 1-7, 9. **Marcos** a-Annual 14i. **Mooney** a-118i, 152i. **Perez** a-164-167, 170-172, 176-178, 184-188, 191p, 192p. Annual 14p, 15p; c(p)-183-88, 191, 192, 194-197. **Simonson** a-212. **Steranko** c-130-132p.

FANTASTIC FOUR INDEX (See Official...)

FANTASTIC FOUR ROAST
May, 1982 (One Shot, Direct Sale)
Marvel Comics Group

	Good	Fine	N-Mint
1-Celebrates 20th anniversary of Fantastic Four No. 1; Golden, Miller, Buscema, Rogers, Byrne, Anderson, Austin-a, c(i)			
	.60	1.75	3.50

FANTASTIC FOUR VS. X-MEN
Feb, 1987 - No. 4, Jun, 1987 (mini-series)
Marvel Comics

	Good	Fine	N-Mint
1	.60	1.75	3.50
2-4: 4-Austin-a(i)	.40	1.25	2.50

FANTASTIC GIANTS (Konga No. 1-23)
September, 1966 (25 cents, 68 pgs.)
Charlton Comics

	Good	Fine	N-Mint
V2#24-Origin Konga & Gorgo reprinted; two new Ditko stories			
	2.00	6.00	14.00

FANTASTIC TALES
1958 (no date) (Reprint)
I. W. Enterprises

	Good	Fine	N-Mint
1-Reprints Avon's "City of the Living Dead"	1.35	4.00	8.00

FANTASTIC VOYAGE (See Movie Comics)
Aug, 1969 - No. 2, Dec, 1969
Gold Key

	Good	Fine	N-Mint
1,2 (TV)	1.70	5.00	12.00

Fantastic Four #13, © MEG

Fantastic Four #49, © MEG

Fantastic Four #100, © MEG

FANTASTIC VOYAGES OF SINDBAD, THE
Oct, 1965 - No. 2, June, 1967
Gold Key

	Good	Fine	N-Mint
1,2-Painted-c	2.15	6.50	15.00

FANTASTIC WORLDS
No. 5, Sept, 1952 - No. 7, Jan, 1953
Standard Comics

5-Toth, Anderson-a	11.50	34.00	80.00
6-Toth story	10.00	30.00	70.00
7	5.70	17.00	40.00

FANTASY FEATURES
1987 - No. 2, 1987 ($1.75, color)
Americomics

1,2	.30	.90	1.80

FANTASY MASTERPIECES (Marvel Super Heroes No. 12 on)
Feb, 1966 - No. 11, Oct, 1967; Dec, 1979 - No. 14, Jan, 1981
Marvel Comics Group

1-Photo of Stan Lee	1.35	4.00	8.00
2	.50	1.50	3.00
3-G.A. Captain America-r begin; 1st Giant	.50	1.50	3.00
4-6-Capt. America-r	.50	1.50	3.00
7-Begin G.A. Sub-Mariner, Torch-r	.50	1.50	3.00
8-Torch battles the Sub-Mariner r-/Marvel Mystery #9	.50	1.50	3.00
9-Origin Human Torch r-/Marvel Comics #1	.70	2.00	4.00
10-All Winners-r	.50	1.50	3.00
11-Reprint of origin Toro & Black Knight	.50	1.50	3.00
V2#1(12/79)-52 pgs.; 75 cents r-/origin Silver Surfer from S. Surfer #1 with editing; J. Buscema-a	.30	.90	1.80
2-4-Silver Surfer-r		.60	1.20
5-14-Silver Surfer-r		.60	1.20

NOTE: *Buscema c-v2No.7-9(in part). Ditko a-1-3r, 7r, 9r. Everett a-9r. Matt Fox a-9i(r). Kirby a-2-4r, 8r, 11r. Starlin a-8-13r. Some direct sale V2No14's had a 50 cent cover price.*

FANTASY QUARTERLY (Also see Elfquest)
Spring, 1978 (B&W)
Independent Publishers Syndicate

1-1st app. Elfquest (2nd printing exist?)	12.00	35.00	70.00

FANTOMAN (Formerly Amazing Adv. Funnies)
No. 2, Aug, 1940 - No. 4, Dec, 1940
Centaur Publications

2-The Fantom of the Fair, The Arrow, Little Dynamite-r begin; origin The Ermine by Filchock; Burgos, J. Cole, Ernst, Gustavson-a	63.00	190.00	440.00
3,4: Gustavson-a(r). 4-Bondage-c	45.00	135.00	315.00

FARGO KID (Formerly Justice Traps the Guilty)
V11No.3(No.1), June-July, 1958 - V11No.5, Oct-Nov, 1958
Prize Publications

V11#3(#1)-Origin Fargo Kid; Severin-c/a; Williamson-a(2)	7.00	21.00	50.00
V11#4,5-Severin c/a	4.30	13.00	30.00

FARMER'S DAUGHTER, THE
2-3/54 - No. 3, 6-7/54; No. 4, 10/54
Stanhall Publ./Trojan Magazines

1-Lingerie, nudity panel	7.00	21.00	50.00
2-4(Stanhall)	3.70	11.00	26.00

FASHION IN ACTION
Aug, 1986 - Present ($1.75, color, Baxter)
Eclipse Comics

Summer Special 1	.30	.85	1.70
Winter Special 1(2/87, $2.00)	.30	.90	1.80

FASTEST GUN ALIVE, THE (See 4-Color No. 741)

FAST FICTION (...Action) (Stories by Fam. Authors III. #6 on)
Oct, 1949 - No. 5, Mar, 1950 (All have Kiefer-c)(48 pgs.)
Seaboard Publ./Famous Authors III.

	Good	Fine	N-Mint
1-Scarlet Pimpernel; Jim Lavery-a	19.00	57.00	132.00
2-Captain Blood; H. C. Kiefer-a	17.00	51.00	120.00
3-She, by Rider Haggard; Vincent Napoli-a	22.00	65.00	154.00
4-(52pgs, 1/50)-The 39 Steps; Lavery-a	13.00	40.00	90.00
5-Beau Geste; Kiefer-a	13.00	40.00	90.00

NOTE: *Kiefer a-2, 5; c-2, 3, 5. Lavery a-1, 4; c-1, 4. Napoli a-3.*

FAST WILLIE JACKSON
October, 1976 - No. 7, 1977
Fitzgerald Periodicals, Inc.

1		.50	1.00
2-7		.40	.80

FAT ALBERT (...& the Cosby Kids) (TV)
March, 1974 - No. 29, Feb, 1979
Gold Key

1	.35	1.00	2.00
2-29		.40	.80

FAT AND SLAT (Ed Wheelan) (Gunfighter No. 5 on)
Summer, 1947 - No. 4, Spring, 1948
E. C. Comics

1-Intro/origin Voltage, Man of Lightning	14.00	42.00	100.00
2,4	11.00	33.00	76.00
3	9.50	28.50	66.00

FAT AND SLAT JOKE BOOK
Summer, 1944 (One Shot, 52 pages)
All-American Comics (William H. Wise)

by Ed Wheelan	11.00	33.00	75.00

FATE (See Hand of Fate, & Thrill-O-Rama)

FATHER OF CHARITY
No date (32 pgs.; paper cover)
Catechetical Guild Giveaway

	2.00	6.00	12.00

FATHOM
May, 1987 - No. 3, July, 1987 ($1.50, mini-series, color)
Comico

1-3	.25	.75	1.50

FATIMA...CHALLENGE TO THE WORLD
1951, 36 pgs. (15 cent cover)
Catechetical Guild

nn (not same as 'Challenge to the World')	3.00	9.00	18.00

FATMAN, THE HUMAN FLYING SAUCER
April, 1967 - No. 3, Aug-Sept, 1967 (68 pgs.)
Lightning Comics(Milson Publ. Co.) (Written by Otto Binder)

1-Origin Fatman & Tinman by C. C. Beck	2.30	7.00	16.00
2-Beck-a	1.85	5.60	13.00
3-(Scarce)-Beck-a	3.70	11.00	26.00

FAUNTLEROY COMICS (Superduck Presents...)
1950 - No. 3, 1952
Close-Up/Archie Publications

1	3.70	11.00	26.00
2,3	2.00	6.00	14.00

FAVORITE COMICS (Also see Famous Comics)
1934 (36 pgs.)
Grocery Store Giveaway (Dif Corp.) (detergent)

Book #1-The Nebbs, Strange As It Seems, Napoleon, Dixie Dugan, Joe Palooka, S'Matter Pop, Hairbreadth Harry, etc.

FAVORITE COMICS (continued)

	Good	Fine	N-Mint
reprints	16.00	48.00	110.00
Book #2,3	13.00	40.00	90.00

FAWCETT MINIATURES (See Mighty Midget)
1946 (12-24 pgs.; 3¾x5") (Wheaties giveaways)
Fawcett Publications

Captain Marvel-"And the Horn of Plenty;" Bulletman story

	2.35	7.00	16.00

Captain Marvel-"& the Raiders From Space;" Golden Arrow story

	2.35	7.00	16.00

Captain Marvel Jr.-"The Case of the Poison Press!" Bulletman story

	2.35	7.00	16.00

Delecta of the Planets-C. C. Beck art; B&W inside; 12 pgs.; 3 printing variations (coloring) exist.

	8.00	24.00	56.00

FAWCETT MOTION PICTURE COMICS (See Motion Picture Comics)

FAWCETT MOVIE COMIC
1949 - No. 20, Dec, 1952 (All photo-c)
Fawcett Publications

	Good	Fine	N-Mint
nn-"Dakota Lil"-George Montgomery & Rod Cameron('49)	21.50	64.00	150.00
nn-"Copper Canyon"-Ray Milland & Hedy Lamarr('50)	16.00	48.00	110.00
nn-"Destination Moon"-(1950)	47.00	140.00	330.00
nn-"Montana"-Errol Flynn & Alexis Smith('50)	16.00	48.00	110.00
nn-"Pioneer Marshal"-Monte Hale(1950)	16.00	48.00	110.00
nn-"Powder River Rustlers"-Rocky Lane(1950)	17.00	51.00	120.00
nn-"Singing Guns"-Vaughn Monroe & Ella Raines(1950)	14.00	42.00	100.00
7-"Gunmen of Abilene"-Rocky Lane; Bob Powell-a(1950)	17.00	51.00	120.00
8-"King of the Bullwhip"-Lash LaRue; Bob Powell-a(1950)	22.00	65.00	154.00
9-"The Old Frontier"-Monte Hale; Bob Powell-a(2/51); mis-dated 2/50)	16.00	48.00	110.00
10-"The Missourians"-Monte Hale(4/51)	16.00	48.00	110.00
11-"The Thundering Trail"-Lash LaRue(6/51)	22.00	65.00	154.00
12-"Rustlers on Horseback"-Rocky Lane(8/51)	17.00	51.00	120.00
13-"Warpath"-Edmond O'Brien & Forrest Tucker(10/51)	13.00	40.00	90.00
14-"Last Outpost"-Ronald Reagan(12/51)	35.00	105.00	245.00
15-(Scarce)-"The Man From Planet X"-Robert Clark; Shaffenberger -a (2/52)	150.00	450.00	1050.00
16-"10 Tall Men"-Burt Lancaster	10.00	30.00	70.00
17-"Rose of Cimarron"-Jack Buetel & Mala Powers	6.50	19.50	45.00
18-"The Brigand"-Anthony Dexter; Shaffenberger-a	7.00	21.00	50.00
19-"Carbine Williams"-James Stewart; Costanza-a	9.00	27.00	62.00
20-"Ivanhoe"-Liz Taylor	13.00	40.00	90.00

FAWCETT'S FUNNY ANIMALS (No. 1-26, 80-on titled "Funny Animals;" Li'l Tomboy No. 92 on?)
12/42 - No. 79, 4/53; No. 80, 6/53 - No. 83, 12?/53; No. 84, 4/54 - No. 91, Feb, 1956
Fawcett Publications/Charlton Comics No. 84 on

	Good	Fine	N-Mint
1-Capt. Marvel on cover; intro. Hoppy The Captain Marvel Bunny, cloned from Capt. Marvel	23.50	70.00	165.00
2-Xmas-c	11.50	34.00	80.00
3-5	8.00	24.00	56.00
6,7,9,10	5.50	16.50	38.00
8-Flag-c	6.00	18.00	42.00

	Good	Fine	N-Mint
11-20	3.50	10.50	24.00
21-40: 25-Xmas-c. 26-St. Valentines Day-c	2.15	6.50	15.00
41-88,90,91	1.50	4.50	10.00
89-Merry Mailman ish	1.85	5.50	13.00

NOTE: *Marvel Bunny in all issues to at least No. 68 (not in 49-54).*

FAZE ONE FAZERS
1986 - No. 4, Sept, 1986 (mini-series)
Americomics (AC Comics)

1-4	.50	1.50	3.00

F.B.I., THE
April-June, 1965
Dell Publishing Co.

1-Sinnott-a	1.00	3.00	7.00

F.B.I. STORY, THE (See 4-Color No. 1069)

FEAR (Adventure into. . .)
Nov, 1970 - No. 31, Dec, 1975 (No.1-6 - Giant Size)
Marvel Comics Group

	Good	Fine	N-Mint
1-Reprints Fantasy & Sci-Fi stories	.25	.75	1.50
2-9,13-18		.50	1.00
10-Man-Thing begins; Morrow c/a(p)	.70	2.00	4.00
11-Adams-c	.25	.75	1.50
12-Starlin/Buckler-a	.25	.75	1.50
19-Intro. Howard the Duck; Val Mayerick-a	1.70	5.00	10.00
20-31: 20-Morbius, the Living Vampire begins, ends #31; Gulacy-a(p)		.50	1.00

NOTE: *Bolle a-13i. Brunner c-15-17. Colan a-23r. Craig a-10p. Ditko a-5. Evans a-30. Everett a-9, 10i, 21r. Gil Kane a-21p; c(p)-20, 21, 23-28, 31. Kirby a-8r, 9r. Maneely a-24r. Mooney a-11i, 26r. Paul Reinman a-14r. Russell a-23p, 24p. Severin c-8. Starlin c-12p.*

FEARBOOK
April, 1986 (One shot) ($1.75, adults)
Eclipse Comics

1-Scholastic Mag.-r; Bissette-a	.30	.90	1.80

FEAR IN THE NIGHT (See Complete Mystery No. 3)

FEARLESS FAGAN (See 4-Color No. 441)

FEATURE BOOK (Dell) (See Large Feature Comic)

FEATURE BOOKS (Newspaper-r, early issues)
May, 1937 - No. 57, 1948
David McKay Publications

nn-Popeye & the Jeep (#1, 100 pgs.); reprinted as Feature Books #3 (Very Rare; only 3 known copies, 1-vf, 2-in low grade)

	Estimated value....	385.00	1155.00	2700.00

nn-Dick Tracy (#1)-Reprinted as Feature Book #4 (100 pgs.) & in part as 4-Color #1 (Rare, less than 10 known copies)

	Estimated value....	400.00	1200.00	2800.00

NOTE: *Above books were advertised together with different covers from Feature Books No. 3 & 4.*

	Good	Fine	N-Mint
1-King of the Royal Mtd. (#1)	38.00	115.00	265.00
2-Popeye(6/37) by Segar	50.00	150.00	350.00
3-Popeye (7/37) by Segar; same as nn issue but a new cover added	42.00	125.00	295.00
4-Dick Tracy(8/37)-Same as nn issue but a new cover added	72.00	215.00	500.00
5-Popeye(9/37) by Segar	34.00	100.00	237.00
6-Dick Tracy(10/37)	60.00	180.00	420.00
7-Little Orphan Annie (#1) (Rare)	75.00	225.00	525.00
8-Secret Agent X-9-Not by Raymond	22.00	65.00	154.00
9-Dick Tracy(1/38)	60.00	180.00	420.00
10-Popeye(2/38)	34.00	100.00	237.00
11-Little Annie Rooney (#1)	17.00	51.00	120.00
12-Blondie (#1) (4/38) (Rare)	37.00	110.00	260.00

Fawcett Movie Comic #15, © FAW

Fawcett's Funny Animals #2, © FAW

Feature Books #4, © N.Y. News Syndicate

Feature Comics #78, © QUA

Feature Funnies #12, © CHES

Federal Men Comics #2, © Gerard Publ.

FEATURE BOOKS (continued)	Good	Fine	N-Mint
13-Inspector Wade	11.00	32.00	75.00
14-Popeye(6/38) by Segar (Scarce)	48.00	145.00	335.00
15-Barney Baxter (#1) (7/38)	16.00	48.00	110.00
16-Red Eagle	10.00	30.00	70.00
17-Gangbusters (#1)	22.00	65.00	154.00
18,19-Mandrake	22.00	65.00	154.00
20-Phantom (#1)	40.00	120.00	280.00
21-Lone Ranger	40.00	120.00	280.00
22-Phantom	34.00	100.00	237.00
23-Mandrake	22.00	65.00	154.00
24-Lone Ranger(1941)	40.00	120.00	280.00
25-Flash Gordon (#1)-Reprints not by Raymond			
	52.00	155.00	365.00
26-Prince Valiant(1941)-Harold Foster-a; newspaper strips reprinted,			
pgs. 1-28,30-63	70.00	210.00	490.00
27-29,31,34-Blondie	8.00	24.00	56.00
30-Katzenjammer Kids (#1)	8.50	25.50	60.00
32,35,41,44-Katzenjammer Kids	6.50	19.50	45.00
33(nn)-Romance of Flying-World War II photos			
	6.50	19.50	45.00
36('43),38,40('44),42,43,45,47-Blondie	7.00	21.00	50.00
37-Katzenjammer Kids; has photo & biog of Harold H. Knerr(1883-			
1949) who took over strip from Rudolph Dirks in 1914			
	8.00	24.00	56.00
39-Phantom	24.00	72.00	168.00
46-Mandrake in the Fire World-(58 pgs.)	18.00	54.00	125.00
48-Maltese Falcon('46)	38.00	115.00	265.00
49,50-Perry Mason	11.50	34.00	80.00
51,54-Rip Kirby c/a by Raymond; origin-#51	18.00	54.00	125.00
52,55-Mandrake	16.00	48.00	110.00
53,56,57-Phantom	19.00	57.00	132.00

NOTE: All Feature Books through #25 are over-sized 8½x11-3/8'' comics with color covers and black and white interiors. The covers are rough, heavy stock. The page counts, including covers, are as follows: nn, #3,4-100 pgs.; #1,2-52 pgs.; #5-25 are all 76 pgs. #33 was found in bound set from publisher.

FEATURE COMICS (Formerly Feature Funnies)
No. 21, June, 1939 - No. 144, May, 1950
Quality Comics Group

21-Strips cont. from Feature Funnies	20.00	60.00	140.00
22-26: 23-Charlie Chan begins	15.00	45.00	105.00
26-(nn, nd)-c-in one color, (10 cents, 36pgs.; issue No. blanked out.			
2 variations exist, each contain half of the regular #26)			
	5.00	15.00	35.00
27-Origin & 1st app. of Dollman by Eisner	135.00	405.00	945.00
28-1st Fine Dollman	60.00	180.00	420.00
29,30	36.00	108.00	250.00
31-Last Clock & Charlie Chan issue	30.00	90.00	210.00
32-37: 32-Rusty Ryan & Samar begin. 34-Captain Fortune app. 37-			
Last Fine Dollman	23.00	70.00	160.00
38-41: 38-Origin the Ace of Space. 39-Origin The Destroying			
Demon, ends #40. 40-Bruce Blackburn in costume			
	16.50	50.00	115.00
42-USA, the Spirit of Old Glory begins	11.00	32.00	75.00
43,45-50: 46-Intro. Boyville Brigadiers in Rusty Ryan. 48-USA ends			
	11.00	32.00	75.00
44-Dollman by Crandall begins, ends #63; Crandall-a(2)			
	16.00	48.00	110.00
51-55	9.00	27.00	62.00
56-Marijuana story in ''Swing Session''	9.50	28.00	65.00
57-Spider Widow begins	9.00	27.00	62.00
58-60: 60-Raven begins, ends #71	9.00	27.00	62.00
61-68 (5/43)	8.50	25.50	60.00
69,70-Phantom Lady x-over in Spider Widow	9.00	27.00	62.00
71-80: 71-Phantom Lady x-over. 72-Spider Widow ends			
	6.00	18.00	42.00

	Good	Fine	N-Mint
81-99	5.00	15.00	35.00
100	6.00	18.00	42.00
101-144: 139-Last Dollman. 140-Intro. Stuntman Stetson			
	4.35	13.00	30.00

NOTE: Celardo a-37-43. Crandall a-44-60, 62, 63-on(most). Gustavson a-(Rusty Ryan)-32-134. Powell a-34, 64-73.

FEATURE FILMS
Mar-Apr, 1950 - No. 4, Sept-Oct, 1950 (Photo-c 2,3)
National Periodical Publications

1-''Captain China'' with John Payne, Gail Russell, Lon Chaney			
& Edgar Bergen	26.00	80.00	185.00
2-''Riding High'' with Bing Crosby	22.00	65.00	154.00
3-''The Eagle & the Hawk'' with John Payne, Rhonda Fleming &			
D. O'Keefe	22.00	65.00	154.00
4-''Fancy Pants''-Bob Hope & Lucille Ball	24.00	72.00	170.00

FEATURE FUNNIES (Feature Comics No. 21 on)
Oct, 1937 - No. 20, May, 1939
Harry 'A' Chesler

1(V9/1-indicia)-Joe Palooka, Mickey Finn, The Bungles, Jane			
Arden, Dixie Dugan, Big Top, Ned Brant, Strange As It Seems,			
& Off the Record strip reprints begin	100.00	300.00	700.00
2-The Hawk app. (11/37); Goldberg-c	50.00	150.00	350.00
3-Hawks of Seas begins by Eisner, ends #12; The Clock begins;			
Christmas-c	35.00	105.00	245.00
4,5	25.00	75.00	175.00
6-12: 11-Archie O'Toole by Bud Thomas begins, ends #22			
	20.00	60.00	140.00
13-Espionage, Starring Black X begins by Eisner, ends #20			
	22.00	65.00	154.00
14-20	17.00	51.00	120.00

FEATURE PRESENTATION, A (Feature Presentations Mag. #6)
(Formerly Women in Love) (Also see Startling Terror Tales #11)
No. 5, April, 1950
Fox Features Syndicate

5-Black Tarantula	14.00	42.00	100.00

FEATURE PRESENTATIONS MAGAZINE (Formerly A Feature
Presentation #5; becomes Feature Stories Mag. #3 on)
No. 6, July, 1950
Fox Features Syndicate

6-Moby Dick; Wood-c	12.00	36.00	84.00

FEATURE STORIES MAGAZINE (Formerly Feat. Present. Mag. #6)
No. 3, Aug, 1950 - No. 4, Oct, 1950
Fox Features Syndicate

3-Jungle Lil, Zegra stories; bondage-c	11.00	32.00	75.00
4	8.00	24.00	56.00

FEDERAL MEN COMICS (See The Comics Magazine, New Adv.
Comics, New Book of Comics & New Comics)
1945 (DC reprints from 1930's)
Gerard Publ. Co.

2-Siegel & Shuster-a; cover redrawn from Detective #9; spanking			
panel	10.00	30.00	70.00

FELIX'S NEPHEWS INKY & DINKY
Sept, 1957 - No. 7, Oct, 1958
Harvey Publications

1-Cover shows Inky's left eye with 2 pupils	4.00	12.00	28.00
2-7	1.75	5.25	12.00

NOTE: Contains no Messmer art.

FELIX THE CAT
1927 - 1931 (24 pgs.; 8x10¼'')(1926,'27 color strip reprints)
McLoughlin Bros.

FELIX THE CAT (continued)	Good	Fine	N-Mint
260-(Rare)-by Otto Messmer	60.00	180.00	420.00

FELIX THE CAT (See The Funnies, March of Comics #24,36,51, New Funnies & Popular Comics)
1943 - No. 118, 11/61; 9-11/62 - No. 12, 7-9/65
Dell Publ. No.1-19/Toby No.20-61/Harvey No.62-118/Dell

	Good	Fine	N-Mint
4-Color 15	38.00	115.00	265.00
4-Color 46('44)	26.00	78.00	180.00
4-Color 77('45)	22.00	65.00	154.00
4-Color 135('46)	16.00	48.00	110.00
4-Color 162(9/47)	13.00	40.00	90.00
1(2-3/48)(Dell)	13.00	40.00	90.00
2	6.50	19.50	45.00
3-5	5.00	15.00	35.00
6-19(2-3/51-Dell)	4.00	12.00	28.00
20-30(Toby): 28-2/52 some copies have #29 on cover, #28 on inside			
	3.50	10.50	24.00
31,34,35-No Messmer-a	1.70	5.00	12.00
32,33,36-61(6/55-Toby)-Last Messmer ish.	2.30	7.00	16.00
62(8/55)-100 (Harvey)	1.00	3.00	7.00
101-118(11/61)	.85	2.50	6.00
12-269-211(9-11/62)(Dell)	1.50	4.50	10.00
2-12(7-9/65)(Dell, TV)	.75	2.25	5.00
. . .& His Friends 1(12/53-Toby)	3.50	10.50	24.00
. . .& His Friends 2-4	2.30	7.00	16.00
3-D Comic Book 1(1953-One Shot)	19.00	57.00	132.00
Summer Annual 2('52)-Early 1930s Sunday strip-r (Exist?)			
	17.00	51.00	120.00
Summer Annual nn('53, 100 pgs., Toby)-1930s daily & Sunday-r			
	14.00	42.00	100.00
Winter Annual 2('54, 100 pgs., Toby)-1930s daily & Sunday-r			
	10.00	30.00	70.00
Summer Annual 3('55) (Exist?)	8.50	25.50	60.00

NOTE: 4-Color No. 15, 46, 77 and the Toby Annuals are all daily or Sunday newspaper reprints from the 1930's drawn by Otto Messmer, who created Felix in 1915 for the Sullivan animation studio. He drew Felix from the beginning under contract to Pat Sullivan. In 1946 he went to work for Dell and wrote and pencilled most of the stories and inked some of them through the Toby Press issues. No. 107 reprints No. 71 interior. No. 110 reprints No. 56 interior.

FEMFORCE
Apr, 1985 - Present ($1.75, $1.95; in color)
Americomics

1: Black-a; Nightveil, Ms. Victory begin	.85	2.50	5.00
2	.50	1.50	3.00
3-16	.35	1.00	2.00
Special 1 (Fall, '84)(B&W, 52pgs.)	.35	1.00	2.00

FERDINAND THE BULL (See Mickey Mouse Mag. V4/3)
1938 (10 cents)(Large size; some color, rest B&W)
Dell Publishing Co.

nn	7.00	21.00	50.00

FIBBER McGEE & MOLLY (See A-1 Comics No. 25)

55 DAYS AT PEKING (See Movie Comics)

FIGHT AGAINST CRIME (Fight Against the Guilty #22,23)
May, 1951 - No. 21, Sept, 1954
Story Comics

1	8.00	24.00	56.00
2	3.50	10.50	24.00
3	3.00	9.00	21.00
4-Drug story-"Hopped Up Killers"	5.70	17.00	40.00
5-Frazetta, 1 pg.	3.00	9.00	21.00
6-Used in POP, pgs. 83,84	4.00	12.00	28.00
7	4.00	12.00	28.00
8-Last crime format issue	3.00	9.00	21.00

NOTE: No. 9-21 contain violent, gruesome stories with blood, dismemberment, decapitation, E.C. style plot twists and several E.C. swipes.

	Good	Fine	N-Mint
9-11,13	6.50	19.50	45.00
12-Morphine drug story-"The Big Dope"	8.50	25.50	60.00
14-Tothish art by Ross Andru; electrocution-c	6.50	19.50	45.00
15-B&W & color illos in POP	8.00	24.00	56.00
16-E.C. story swipe/Haunt of Fear No. 19; Tothish-a by Ross Andru; bondage-c	8.00	24.00	56.00
17-Wildey E.C. swipe/Shock SuspenStories No. 9; knife through neck-c (1/54)	8.00	24.00	56.00
18,19	5.70	17.00	40.00
20-Decapitation cover; contains hanging, ax murder, blood & violence	16.00	48.00	110.00
21-E.C. swipe	7.00	21.00	50.00

NOTE: Bondage covers, Lingerie, headlights panels are common. Tiger Girl by Baker-#36-60,62-65; Kayo Kirby by Baker-#52-64, 67. Eisner c-1-3, 5, 10, 11. Kamen a-547, 577. Tuska a-1, 5, 8, 10, 21, 29.

NOTE: Cameron a-5. Hollingsworth a-3, 9, 10, 13. Wildey a-15, 16.

FIGHT AGAINST THE GUILTY (Formerly Fight Against Crime)
No. 22, Dec, 1954 - No. 23, Mar, 1955
Story Comics

22-Tothish-a by Ross Andru; Ditko-a; E.C. story swipe; electrocution-c	6.50	19.50	45.00
23-Hollingsworth-a	4.30	13.00	30.00

FIGHT COMICS
Jan, 1940 - No. 86, Summer, 1953
Fiction House Magazines

1-Origin Spy Fighter, Starring Saber; Fine/Eisner-c; Eisner-a	80.00	240.00	560.00
2-Joe Louis life story	36.00	110.00	250.00
3-Rip Regan, the Power Man begins	32.00	95.00	225.00
4,5: 4-Fine-c	23.50	70.00	165.00
6-10	20.00	60.00	140.00
11-14: Rip Regan ends	18.00	54.00	125.00
15-1st Super American	23.50	70.00	165.00
16-Captain Fight begins; Spy Fighter ends	23.50	70.00	165.00
17,18: Super American ends	21.00	62.00	146.00
19-Captain Fight ends; Senorita Rio begins (origin & 1st app.); Rip Carson, Chute Trooper begins	21.00	62.00	146.00
20	15.00	45.00	105.00
21-30	10.00	30.00	70.00
31,33-35: 31-Decapitation-c	9.50	28.50	66.00
32-Tiger Girl begins	10.00	30.00	70.00
36-47,49,50: 44-Capt. Fight returns	9.00	27.00	62.00
48-Used in Love and Death by Legman	10.00	30.00	70.00
51-Origin Tiger Girl; Patsy Pin-Up app.	14.00	42.00	100.00
52-60	7.00	21.00	50.00
61-Origin Tiger Girl retold	9.00	27.00	62.00
62-65-Last Baker issue	7.00	21.00	50.00
66-77	6.00	18.00	42.00
78-Used in POP, pg. 99	6.00	18.00	42.00
79-The Space Rangers app.	6.00	18.00	42.00
80-85	5.00	15.00	35.00
86-Two Tigerman stories by Evans; Moreira-a	6.00	18.00	42.00

FIGHT FOR FREEDOM
1949, 1951 (16 pgs.) (Giveaway)
National Association of Mfgrs./General Comics

Dan Barry-c/a; used in POP, pg. 102	5.00	15.00	30.00

FIGHT FOR LOVE
1952 (no month)
United Features Syndicate

nn-Abbie & Slats newspaper-r	6.50	19.50	45.00

FIGHTING AIR FORCE (See United States Fighting Air Force)

Felix The Cat #16, © KING

Fight Against Crime #12, © Story Comics

Fight Comics #38, © FH

Fightin' Air Force #11, © CC

Fighting Leathernecks #1, © TOBY

The Fighting Man #7, © AJAX

FIGHTIN' AIR FORCE (Formerly Sherlock Holmes?; Never Again?
War and Attack #54 on)
No. 3, Feb, 1956 - No. 53, Feb-Mar, 1966
Charlton Comics

	Good	Fine	N-Mint
V1#3	1.15	3.50	8.00
4-10	.60	1.80	4.20
11(68 pgs.)(3/58)	.85	2.50	6.00
12 (100 pgs.)	1.15	3.50	8.00
13-30	.30	.90	2.00
31-50: 50-American Eagle begins		.60	1.20
51-53		.50	1.00

NOTE: *Glanzman* a-13,24; c-24.

FIGHTING AMERICAN
Apr-May, 1954 - No. 7, Apr-May, 1955
Headline Publications/Prize

1-Origin Fighting American & Speedboy; S&K c/a(3)	70.00	210.00	490.00
2-S&K-a(3)	35.00	105.00	245.00
3,4-S&K-a(3)	30.00	90.00	210.00
5-S&K-a(2), Kirby/?-a	30.00	90.00	210.00
6-Four pg. reprint of origin, plus 2 pgs. by S&K	27.00	81.00	190.00
7-Kirby-a	25.00	75.00	175.00

NOTE: *Simon & Kirby* covers on all.

FIGHTING AMERICAN
October, 1966 (25 cents)
Harvey Publications

1-Origin Fighting American & Speedboy by S&K-r; S&K-c/a(3); 1 pg. Adams ad	1.50	4.50	10.00

FIGHTIN' ARMY (Formerly Soldier and Marine Comics; see Capt. Willy Schultz)
No. 16, 1/56 - No. 127, 12/76; No. 128, 9/77 - No. 172, 11/84
Charlton Comics

16	.75	2.25	5.00
17-19,21-23,25-30	.35	1.00	2.50
20-Ditko-a	.85	2.50	6.00
24 (68 pgs.), 3/58)	.85	2.50	6.00
31-45	.25	.75	1.50
46-60		.40	.80
61-80: 75-The Lonely War of Willy Schultz begins, ends #92		.30	.60
81-172: 89,90,92-Ditko-a; Devil Brigade in #79,82,83		.30	.60
108(Modern Comics-1977)-Reprint		.15	.30

NOTE: *Aparo* c-154. *Montes/Bache* a-48,49,51,69,75,76, 170r.

FIGHTING DANIEL BOONE
1953
Avon Periodicals

nn-Kinstler c/a, 22 pgs.	8.00	24.00	56.00
I.W. Reprint #1-Kinstler c/a; Lawrence/Alascia-a	1.00	3.00	6.00

FIGHTING DAVY CROCKETT (Formerly Kit Carson)
No. 9, Oct-Nov, 1955
Avon Periodicals

9-Kinstler-c	3.50	10.50	24.00

FIGHTIN' 5, THE (Formerly Space War; also see The Peacemaker)
7/64 - No. 41, 1/67; No. 42, 10/81 - No. 49, 12/82
Charlton Comics

V2No.28-Origin Fightin' Five	.50	1.50	3.00
29-39,41	.35	1.00	2.00
40-Peacemaker begins	.40	1.25	2.50
42-49: Reprints		.30	.60

FIGHTING FRONTS!
Aug, 1952 - No. 5, Jan, 1953
Harvey Publications

	Good	Fine	N-Mint
1	1.70	5.00	12.00
2-Extreme violence; Nostrand/Powell-a	2.30	7.00	16.00
3-5: 3-Powell-a	1.20	3.50	8.00

FIGHTING INDIAN STORIES (See Midget Comics)

FIGHTING INDIANS OF THE WILD WEST!
Mar, 1952 - No. 2, Nov, 1952
Avon Periodicals

1-Kinstler, Larsen-a	7.00	21.00	50.00
2-Kinstler-a	4.60	14.00	32.00
100 Pg. Annual(1952, 25 cents)-Contains three comics rebound	15.00	45.00	105.00

FIGHTING LEATHERNECKS
Feb, 1952 - No. 6, Dec, 1952
Toby Press

1-"Duke's Diary"-full pg. pin-ups by Sparling	5.00	15.00	35.00
2-"Duke's Diary"	3.50	10.50	24.00
3-5-"Gil's Gals"-full pg. pin-ups	3.50	10.50	24.00
6-(Same as No. 3-5?)	2.30	7.00	16.00

FIGHTING MAN, THE (War)
May, 1952 - No. 8, July, 1953
Ajax/Farrell Publications(Excellent Publ.)

1	2.00	6.00	14.00
2	1.00	3.00	7.00
3-8	.85	2.50	6.00
Annual 1 (100 pgs, 1952)	11.50	34.00	80.00

FIGHTIN' MARINES (Formerly The Texan; see Approved Comics)
No. 15, 8/51 - No. 10, 12/52; No. 14, 5/55 - No. 132, 11/76;
No. 133, 10/77 - No. 176, 9/84 (no No. 11-13)
St. John(Approved Comics)/Charlton Comics No. 14 on

15(No.1)-Matt Baker c/a "Leatherneck Jack;" slightly large size; Fightin' Texan No. 16 & 17?	8.50	25.50	60.00
2-1st Canteen Kate by Baker; slightly large size	11.50	34.00	80.00
3-9-Canteen Kate by Matt Baker; Baker c-No. 2,3,5-9	6.00	18.00	42.00
10 (12/52; last St. John issue; see Approved Comics)-Baker-c	1.50	4.50	10.00
14 (5/55; 1st Charlton issue; formerly?)-Canteen Kate by Baker	4.60	14.00	32.00
15-Baker-c	1.50	4.50	10.00
16,18-20-Not Baker-c	.85	2.50	6.00
17-Canteen Kate by Baker	4.60	14.00	32.00
21-24	.50	1.50	3.50
25-(68 pgs.)(3/58)-Check-a?	1.30	4.00	9.00
26-(100 pgs.)(8/58)-Check-a(5)	2.30	7.00	16.00
27-50	.35	1.00	2.00
51-81,83-100: 78-Shotgun Harker & the Chicken series begin		.60	1.20
82-(100 pgs.)	.50	1.50	3.00
101-122: 122-Pilot issue for "War" title (Fightin' Marines Presents War)		.40	.80
123-176		.30	.60
120(Modern Comics reprint, 1977)		.20	.40

NOTE: *No. 14 & 16 (CC) reprints St. John issue; No. 16 reprints St. John insignia on cover. Colan a-3, 7. Glanzman c/a-92, 94. Montes/Bache a-48, 53, 55, 64, 65, 72-74, 77-83, 176r.*

FIGHTING MARSHAL OF THE WILD WEST (See The Hawk)

FIGHTIN' NAVY (Formerly Don Winslow)
No. 74, 1/56 - No. 125, 4-5/66; No. 126, 8/83 - No. 133, 10/84

147

FIGHTIN' NAVY (continued)
Charlton Comics

	Good	Fine	N-Mint
74	1.00	3.00	7.00
75-81	.70	2.00	4.00
82-Sam Glanzman-a	.50	1.50	3.00
83-99,101-105,106-125('66)	.35	1.00	2.00
100	.40	1.25	2.50
126-133('84)		.30	.60

NOTE: *Montes/Bache a-109. Glanzman a-131r.*

FIGHTING PRINCE OF DONEGAL, THE (See Movie Comics)

FIGHTIN' TEXAN (Formerly The Texan & Fightin' Marines No. 15?)
No. 16, Oct, 1952 - No. 17, Dec, 1952
St. John Publishing Co.

	Good	Fine	N-Mint
16,17-Tuska-a each. 17-Cameron-c/a	2.65	8.00	18.00

FIGHTING UNDERSEA COMMANDOS
1952 - No. 5, April, 1953
Avon Periodicals

1	4.00	12.00	28.00
2	2.65	8.00	18.00
3-5: 3-Ravielli-c. 4-Kinstler-c	2.35	7.00	16.00

FIGHTING WAR STORIES
Aug, 1952 - 1953
Men's Publications/Story Comics

1	1.75	5.25	12.00
2	1.00	3.00	7.00
3-5	.85	2.50	5.00

FIGHTING YANK (See Startling & America's Best)
Sept, 1942 - No. 29, Aug, 1949
Nedor/Better Publ./Standard

1-The Fighting Yank begins; Mystico, the Wonder Man app; bondage-c	55.00	165.00	385.00
2	26.00	78.00	180.00
3	18.00	54.00	125.00
4	13.00	40.00	90.00
5-10: 7-The Grim Reaper app.	11.50	34.00	80.00
11-The Oracle app.	10.00	30.00	70.00
12-17: 12-Hirohito bondage-c	10.00	30.00	70.00
18-The American Eagle app.	8.00	24.00	56.00
19,20	8.00	24.00	56.00
21,23,24: 21-Kara, Jungle Princess app. 24-Miss Masque app.	11.50	34.00	80.00
22-Miss Masque-c/story	13.00	40.00	90.00
25-Robinson/Meskin-a; strangulation, lingerie panel; The Cavalier app.	13.00	40.00	90.00
26-29: All-Robinson/Meskin-a. 28-One pg. Williamson-a	11.00	33.00	76.00

NOTE: *Schomburg (Xela) c-4-29; airbrush-c 28, 29. Bondage c-4, 8, 11, 15, 17.*

FIGHT THE ENEMY
Aug, 1966 - No. 3, Mar, 1967 (25 cents)
Tower Comics

1-Lucky 7 & Mike Manly begin	.70	2.00	4.00
2-Boris Vallejo, McWilliams-a	1.00	3.00	7.00
3-Wood-a ½pg; McWilliams, Bolle-a	.50	1.50	3.00

FILM FUNNIES
Nov, 1949 - No. 2, Feb, 1950 (52 pgs.)
Marvel Comics (CPC)

1-Krazy Krow	6.00	18.00	42.00
2	4.00	12.00	28.00

FILM STARS ROMANCES
Jan-Feb, 1950 - No. 3, May-June, 1950
Star Publications

	Good	Fine	N-Mint
1-Rudy Valentino story; L. B. Cole-c; lingerie panels	13.00	40.00	90.00
2-Liz Taylor/Robert Taylor photo-c	14.00	42.00	100.00
3-Photo-c	11.00	33.00	76.00

FINAL CYCLE, THE
July, 1987 - No. 4, 1988 (mini-series, color)
Dragon's Teeth Productions

1-4	.35	1.00	2.00

FIRE AND BLAST
1952 (16 pgs.; paper cover) (Giveaway)
National Fire Protection Assoc.

Mart Baily A-Bomb cover; about fire prevention	12.00	35.00	70.00

FIRE BALL XL5 (See Steve Zodiac)

FIRE CHIEF AND THE SAFE OL' FIREFLY, THE
1952 (16 pgs.) (Safety brochure given away at schools)
National Board of Fire Underwriters (produced by American Visuals Corp.) (Eisner)

(Rare) Eisner c/a	27.00	81.00	190.00

FIREHAIR COMICS (Pioneer West Romances #3-6; also see Rangers Comics)
Winter/48-49 - No. 2, Spr/49; No. 7, Spr/51 - No. 11, Spr/52
Fiction House Magazines (Flying Stories)

1	18.00	54.00	125.00
2	8.00	24.00	56.00
7-11	6.50	19.50	45.00
I.W. Reprint 8-Kinstler-c; reprints Rangers #57; Dr. Drew story by Grandenetti (nd)	.85	2.50	5.00

FIRESTAR
March, 1986 - No. 4, June, 1986 (From TV Spider-Man series)
Marvel Comics Group

1-X-Men & New Mutants app.	.35	1.00	2.00
2-4: 3-Art Adams c(p)	.25	.75	1.50

FIRESTONE (See Donald & Mickey)

FIRESTORM (See Cancelled Comic Cavalcade, DC Comics Presents & Flash #289)
March, 1978 - No. 5, Oct-Nov, 1978 (See The Fury of...)
DC Comics

1-Origin & 1st app.	.50	1.50	3.00
2-5: 2-Origin Multiplex. 3-Origin Killer Frost. 4-1st app. Hyena	.35	1.00	2.00

FIRESTORM, THE NUCLEAR MAN (Formerly Fury of Firestorm)
No. 65, Nov, 1987 - Present
DC Comics

65-82: 66-1st app. Zuggernaut. 71-Death of Capt. X		.50	1.00
Annual 5 (10/87)-1st app. new Firestorm		.65	1.30

FIRST ADVENTURES
Dec, 1985 - No. 5, Apr, 1986
First Comics

1-5: 1-Blaze Barlow, Whisper & Dynamo Joe begin		.65	1.30

FIRST AMERICANS, THE (See 4-Color No. 843)

FIRST CHRISTMAS, THE (3-D)
1953 (25 cents) (Oversized - 8¼x10¼'')
Fiction House Magazines (Real Adv. Publ. Co.)

nn-(Scarce)-Kelly Freas-c	26.00	78.00	180.00

Fighting Yank #14, © STD

Fight The Enemy #2, © TC

Film Stars Romances #2, © STAR

First Love Illustrated #1, © HARV

The Fish Police V2#5, © Steve Moncuse

Flaming Carrot #1 (5/84), © Bob Burden

FIRST COMICS GRAPHIC NOVEL
Jan, 1984 - Present (52-176 pgs, high quality paper)
First Comics

	Good	Fine	N-Mint
1-Beowulf ($5.95)	1.00	3.00	6.00
1-2nd printing	1.15	3.50	7.00
2-Time Beavers ($5.95)	1.00	3.00	6.00
3($11.95, 100 pgs.)-American Flagg! Hard Times. (2 printings)	2.00	6.00	11.95
4-Nexus ($6.95)-r/B&W 1-3	1.30	4.00	8.00
5-The Enchanted Apples of Oz ($7.95, 52pp)-Intro by Harlan Ellison (1986)	1.35	4.00	7.95
6-Elric of Melnibone ($14.95, 176pp)-r with new color	2.50	7.50	14.95
7-The Secret Island Of Oz ($7.95)	1.35	4.00	7.95
8-Teenage Mutant Ninja Turtles Book I(132 pgs., r-/TMNT #1-3 in color w/12 pgs. new-a ($9.95)-Origin	1.70	5.00	9.95
9-Time 2: The Epiphany by Chaykin, 52 pgs. ($7.95)	1.35	4.00	7.95
10-Teenage Mutant Ninja Turtles Book II	1.70	5.00	9.95
11-Sailor On The Sea of Fate	2.50	7.50	14.95
12-American Flagg! Southern Comfort	2.00	6.00	11.95
13-The Ice King Of Oz	1.35	4.00	7.95
14-Teenage Mutant Ninja Turtles Book III	1.70	5.00	9.95
15-Hex Breaker: Badger, 64 pgs.	1.35	4.00	7.95
16-The Forgotten Forest of Oz	1.50	4.50	8.95
17-Mazinger; 64pgs.	1.50	4.50	8.95
18-Teenage Mutant Ninja Turtles Book IV	1.70	5.00	9.95
19-The Original Nexus Graphic Novel ($7.95, 104pgs)-Reprints First Comics Graphic Novel #4	1.35	4.00	7.95

FIRST ISSUE SPECIAL
April, 1975 - No. 13, April, 1976
National Periodical Publications

		Good	Fine	N-Mint
1-Intro. Atlas; Kirby c/a			.50	1.00
2-7: 2-Green Team (See Cancelled Comic Cavalcade). 3-Metamorpho. 4-Lady Cop. 5-Manhunter; Kirby c/a. 6-Dingbats; Kirby c/a. 7-The Creeper			.50	1.00
8-The Warlord (origin); Grell c/a		1.70	5.00	10.00
9-Dr. Fate; Kubert-c; Simonson-a			.50	1.00
10-13: 10-The Outsiders. 11-Code Name: Assassin; Redondo-a. 12-Origin/1st app. new Starman. 13-Return of the New Gods			.50	1.00

FIRST KISS
Dec, 1957 - No. 40, Jan, 1965
Charlton Comics

		Good	Fine	N-Mint
V1#1		1.00	3.00	7.00
V1#2-10		.50	1.50	3.00
11-40			.60	1.20

FIRST LOVE ILLUSTRATED
2/49 - No. 9, 6/50; No. 10, 1/51 - No. 86, 3/58; No. 87, 9/58 - No. 88, 11/58; No. 89, 11/62, No. 90, 2/63
Harvey Publications(Home Comics)(True Love)

		Good	Fine	N-Mint
1-Powell-a(2)		3.50	10.50	24.00
2-Powell-a		2.00	6.00	14.00
3-''Was I Too Fat To Be Loved'' story		2.50	7.50	17.00
4-10		1.70	5.00	12.00
11-30: 30-Lingerie panel		1.00	3.00	7.00
31-34,37,39-49: 49-Last pre-code (2/55)		.85	2.50	6.00
35-Used in **SOTI**, illo-''The title of this comic book is First Love,''		8.00	24.00	56.00
36-Communism story, ''Love Slaves''		1.15	3.50	8.00
38-Nostrand-a		2.00	6.00	14.00
50-90		.50	1.50	3.50

NOTE: **Disbrow** a-13. **Orlando** c-87. **Powell** a-1, 3-5, 7, 10, 11, 13-17, 19-24, 26-29, 33, 35-41, 43, 45, 46, 50, 54, 55, 57, 58, 61-63, 65, 71-73, 76, 79r, 82, 84, 88.

FIRST MEN IN THE MOON (See Movie Comics)
FIRST ROMANCE MAGAZINE
8/49 - #6, 6/50; #7, 6/51 - #50, 2/58; #51, 9/58 - #52, 11/58
Home Comics(Harvey Publ.)/True Love

	Good	Fine	N-Mint
1	3.50	10.50	24.00
2	2.00	6.00	14.00
3-5	1.70	5.00	12.00
6-10	1.35	4.00	9.00
11-20	1.00	3.00	7.00
21-27,29-32: 32-Last pre-code (2/55)	.70	2.00	5.00
28-Nostrand-a(Powell swipe)	1.70	5.00	12.00
33-52	.50	1.50	3.50

NOTE: **Powell** a-1-5,8-10,14,18,20-22,24,25,28,36,46,48,51.

FIRST TRIP TO THE MOON (See Space Advs. No. 20)
FISH POLICE
Dec., 1985 - Present ($1.50-$1.75, B&W and color)
Fishwrap Productions/Comico V2#5 on

	Good	Fine	N-Mint
1	1.50	4.50	9.00
1-2nd print (5/86)	.35	1.00	2.00
2	.70	2.00	4.00
2-2nd print	.25	.75	1.50
3,4	.35	1.00	2.00
5-11	.25	.75	1.50
V2#5-13($1.75, color): V2#5-11-r/V1#5-11	.30	.90	1.75
Special 1 ($2.50, 7/87, Comico)	.40	1.25	2.50
Graphic Novel: The Hairball Saga (r/1-4, color)	1.35	4.00	8.00

5-STAR SUPER-HERO SPEC. (See DC Special Series No. 1)
FLAME, THE (See Big 3 & Wonderworld Comics)
Summer, 1940 - No. 8, Jan, 1942 (#1,2, 68 pgs; #3-8, 44 pgs.)
Fox Features Syndicate

	Good	Fine	N-Mint
1-Flame stories from Wonderworld #5-9; origin The Flame; Lou Fine-a, 36 pgs., r-/Wonderworld 3,10	110.00	330.00	770.00
2-Fine-a(2). Wing Turner by Tuska	55.00	165.00	385.00
3-8: 3-Powell-a	27.00	81.00	190.00

FLAME, THE (Formerly Lone Eagle)
No. 5, Dec-Jan, 1954-55 - No. 4, June-July, 1955
Ajax/Farrell Publications (Excellent Publ.)

	Good	Fine	N-Mint
5(#1)	10.00	30.00	70.00
2-4	7.00	21.00	50.00

FLAMING CARROT
Summer-Fall, 1981 (One Shot) (Large size, 8½x11'')
Kilian Barracks Press

	Good	Fine	N-Mint
1-By Bob Burden	13.50	41.00	95.00

FLAMING CARROT (Also see Anything Goes)
5/84 - No. 5, 1/85; No. 6, 3/85 - Present (B&W)
Aardvark-Vanaheim/Renegade Press No. 6 on

	Good	Fine	N-Mint
1-Bob Burden story/a	7.00	21.00	50.00
2	4.30	13.00	30.00
3	3.70	11.00	22.00
4-6	2.50	7.50	15.00
7-9	1.50	4.50	9.00
10-21	.50	1.50	3.00

FLAMING LOVE
Dec, 1949 - No. 6, Oct, 1950 (Photo covers No. 2-6)
Quality Comics Group (Comic Magazines)

	Good	Fine	N-Mint
1-Ward-c, 9 pgs.	15.00	45.00	105.00
2	6.50	19.50	45.00
3-Ward-c, 9 pgs.; Crandall-a	10.00	30.00	70.00
4-6: 4-Gustavson-a	5.00	15.00	35.00

FLAMING WESTERN ROMANCES
Nov-Dec, 1949 - No. 3, Mar-Apr, 1950

FLAMING WESTERN ROMANCES (continued)
Star Publications

	Good	Fine	N-Mint
1-L. B. Cole-c	11.00	33.00	75.00
2-L. B. Cole-c	7.00	21.00	50.00
3-Robert Taylor, Arlene Dahl photo-c with biographies inside; L. B. Cole-c; spanking panel	17.00	51.00	120.00

FLARE (Also see Champions for 1st app.)
Nov., 1988 - Present ($2.75, color, 52pgs)
Hero Comics

1	.45	1.40	2.75

FLASH, THE (Formerly Flash Comics)(See Adventure, The Brave & the Bold, DC Comics Presents, DC Special Series, DC Super-Stars, Green Lantern, Showcase, Super Team Family, & World's Finest)
No. 105, Feb-Mar, 1959 - No. 350, Oct, 1985
National Periodical Publications/DC Comics

	Good	Fine	N-Mint
105-Origin Flash(retold), & Mirror Master	86.00	215.00	600.00
106-Origin Grodd & Pied Piper	36.00	90.00	250.00
107-109	14.00	35.00	100.00
110-Intro/origin Kid Flash & The Weather Wizard	18.00	45.00	125.00
111,115	8.00	20.00	55.00
112-Intro & origin Elongated Man	8.50	21.00	60.00
113-Origin Trickster	7.00	18.00	50.00
114-Origin Captain Cold	7.00	18.00	50.00
116-120: 117-Origin Capt. Boomerang. 119-Elongated Man marries Sue Dearborn	5.70	14.00	40.00
121,122: 122-Origin & 1st app. The Top	4.30	11.00	30.00
123-Re-intro. Golden Age Flash; origins of both Flashes; 1st mention of an Earth II where DC Golden Age heroes live	28.00	71.00	200.00
124-Last 10 cent issue	3.60	9.00	25.00
125-128,130: 128-Origin Abra Kadabra	2.15	6.50	15.00
129-G.A. Flash x-over; J.S.A. cameo (1st since 2-3/51)	7.00	18.00	50.00
131-136,138-140: 136-1st Dexter Miles. 139-Origin Prof. Zoom. 140-Origin & 1st app. Heat Wave	2.15	6.50	15.00
137-G.A. Flash x-over; J.S.A. cameo; 1st Silver Age app. Vandall Savage	2.00	6.00	14.00
141-150	1.15	3.50	7.00
151-159: 151-G.A. Flash x-over	.85	2.50	5.00
160-80-Pg. Giant G-21-G.A.-r Flash & Johnny Quick	1.15	3.50	7.00
161-168,170: 165-Silver Age Flash weds Iris West. 167-New facts about Flash's origin. 170-Dr. Mid-Nite, Dr. Fate, G.A. Flash x-over	.70	2.00	4.00
169-80-Pg. Giant G-34	1.15	3.50	7.00
171-177,179,180: 171-JLA, Green Lantern, Atom flashbacks. 173-G.A. Flash story. 174-Barry Allen reveals I.D. to wife. 175-2nd Superman/Flash race; JLA cameo	.70	2.00	4.00
178-80-Pg. Giant G-46	.85	2.50	5.00
181-186,188-190: 186-Re-intro. Sargon	.40	1.25	2.50
187-68-Pg. Giant G-58	.70	2.00	4.00
191-195,197-200	.40	1.25	2.50
196-68-Pg. Giant G-70	.70	2.00	4.00
201-204,206-210: 201-New G.A. Flash story. 208-52 pg. begin, end #213,215,216. 206-Elongated Man begins	.35	1.00	2.00
205-68-Pg. Giant G-82	.70	2.00	4.00
211-213,216,220: 211-G.A. Flash origin (#104). 213-All-r.	.35	1.00	2.00
214-Giant DC-11; origin Metal Men-r; 1st pubbed G.A. Flash story	.50	1.50	3.00
215 (52 pgs.)-Flash-r/Showcase 4; G.A. Flash x-over, r-in #216	.35	1.00	2.00
217-219: Adams-a in all. 217-Green Lantern/Green Arrow series begins. 219-Last Green Arrow	1.00	3.00	6.00

	Good	Fine	N-Mint
221-225,227,228,230,231	.25	.75	1.50
226-Adams-a	.60	1.75	3.50
229,232,233-(100 pgs. each)	.40	1.25	2.50
234-270: 243-Death of The Top. 246-Last Green Lantern. 256-Death of The Top retold. 267-Origin of Flash's uniform. 270-Intro The Clown		.60	1.20
271-274,277-288,290: 286-Intro/origin Rainbow Raider		.60	1.20
275,276-Iris West Allen dies	.35	1.00	2.00
289-Perez 1st DC art; new Firestorm series begins, ends #304	.35	1.00	2.00
291-299,301-305: 291-Intro/origin Colonel Computron. 298-Intro/ origin Shade. 301-Atomic Bomb-c. 303-The Top returns. 305-G.A. Flash x-over		.50	1.00
300-52pgs.; origin Flash retold	.35	1.00	2.00
306-Dr. Fate by Giffen begins, ends #313	.35	1.00	2.00
307-313-Giffen-a. 309-Origin Flash retold	.25	.75	1.50
314-330: 324-Death of Reverse Flash (Prof. Zoom). 328-Iris West Allen's death retold		.50	1.00
331-349: 344-Origin Kid Flash		.50	1.00
350-Double size ($1.25)	.55	1.60	3.20
Annual 1(10-12/63, 84pgs.)-Origin Elongated Man & Kid Flash-r; origin Grodd, G.A. Flash-r	8.50	21.00	60.00

NOTE: **Adams** c-194, 195, 203, 204, 206-208, 211, 213, 215, 246. **Austin** a-233i, 234i, 246i. **Buckler** a-271p, 272p; c(p)-247-50, 252, 253p, 255, 256p, 258, 262, 265-67, 269-71. **Giffen** a-306p-313p; c-310p, 315. **Sid Greene** a-167-74i, 229i(r). **Grell** a-237p, 238p, 240-43p; c-236. **G. Kane** a-195p, 197-99p, 229r, 232r; c-197-99, 312p. **Kubert** a-108p, 215i(r); c-189-191. **Lopez** c-272. **Meskin** a-229r, 232r. **Perez** a-289-293p; c-293. **Starlin** a-294-296p. **Staton** c-263p, 264p. Green Lantern x-over-131, 143, 168, 171, 191.

FLASH
June, 1987 - Present
DC Comics

	Good	Fine	N-Mint
1-Guice c/a begins; New Teen Titans app.	1.35	4.00	8.00
2	.90	2.75	5.50
3-Intro. Kilgore	.60	1.75	3.50
4-6: 5-Intro. Speed McGee	.40	1.20	2.40
7-10: 7-1st app. Blue Trinity. 9-1st app. The Chunk. 12-extra 16pg. Dr. Light sty	.30	.85	1.70
11-20		.60	1.20
21-23		.50	1.00
Annual #1 (9/87)	.35	1.00	2.00
Annual #2 (10/88)	.35	1.00	2.00

NOTE: **Guice** a-1-9p, 11p, Annual 1p; c-1-9p, Annual 1p.

FLASH COMICS (Whiz Comics No. 2 on)
Jan, 1940 (12 pgs., B&W, regular size)
(Not distributed to newsstands; printed for in-house use)
Fawcett Publications
NOTE: **Whiz Comics** #2 was preceded by two books, **Flash Comics** and **Thrill Comics**, both dated Jan, 1940, (12 pgs., B&W, regular size) and were not distributed. These two books are identical except for the title. It is believed that the complete 68 page issue of Fawcett's **Flash** and **Thrill Comics** #1 was finished and ready for publication with the January date. Since D.C. Comics was also about to publish a book with the same date and title, Fawcett hurriedly printed up the black and white version of **Flash Comics** to secure copyright before D.C. The inside covers are blank, with the covers and inside pages printed on a high quality uncoated paper stock. The eight page origin story of Captain Thunder is composed of pages 1-7 and 13 of the Captain Marvel story. The balloon dialogue on page thirteen was relettered to tie the story into the end of page seven in **Flash** and **Thrill Comics** to produce a shorter version of the origin story for copyright purposes. Obviously, D.C. acquired the copyright and Fawcett dropped **Flash** as well as **Thrill** and came out with **Whiz Comics** a month later. Fawcett never used the cover to **Flash** and **Thrill** #1, designing a new cover for **Whiz Comics**. Fawcett also must have discovered that Captain Thunder had already been used by another publisher. All references to Captain Thunder were relettered to Captain Marvel before appearing in **Whiz**.

1 (nn on-c, #1 on inside)-Origin & 1st app. Captain Thunder.
Eight copies of **Flash** and three copies of **Thrill** exist. All 3 copies of Thrill sold in 1986 for between $4,000-$10,000 each. A NM copy of Thrill sold in 1987 for $12,000. A vg copy of Thrill sold in 1987 for

The Flash #105, © DC

The Flash Annual #1 (1963), © DC

Flash #2 (7/87), © DC

Flash Comics #8, © DC   Flash Comics #42, © DC   Flash Gordon #1 (DC), © KING

FLASH COMICS (continued)
$9000 cash; another copy sold in 1987 for $2000 cash, $10,000 trade.

FLASH COMICS (The Flash No. 105 on) (Also see All-Flash)
Jan, 1940 - No. 104, Feb, 1949
National Periodical Publications/All-American

	Good	Fine	N-Mint
1-Origin The Flash by Harry Lampert, Hawkman by Gardner Fox, The Whip, & Johnny Thunder by Stan Asch; Cliff Cornwall by Moldoff, Minute Movies begin; Moldoff (Shelly) cover; 1st app. Shiera Sanders who later becomes Hawkgirl; #24; reprinted in Famous First Edition	715.00	2145.00	5000.00
2-Rod Rian begins, ends #11	220.00	660.00	1540.00
3-The King begins, ends #41	170.00	510.00	1190.00
4-Moldoff (Shelly) Hawkman begins	145.00	435.00	1015.00
5	125.00	375.00	875.00
6,7	100.00	300.00	700.00
8-10	80.00	240.00	560.00
11-20: 12-Les Watts begins; ''Sparks'' #16 on. 17-Last Cliff Cornwall	60.00	180.00	420.00
21-23	50.00	150.00	350.00
24-Shiera becomes Hawkgirl	60.00	180.00	420.00
25-30: 28-Last Les Sparks. 29-Ghost Patrol begins(origin, 1st app.), ends #104	43.00	130.00	300.00
31-40: 35-Origin Shade	35.00	105.00	245.00
41-50	30.00	90.00	210.00
51-61: 59-Last Minute Movies. 61-Last Moldoff Hawkman	25.00	75.00	175.00
62-Hawkman by Kubert begins	35.00	105.00	245.00
63-70: 66-68-Hop Harrigan in all	28.00	84.00	195.00
71-80: 80-Atom dons new costume	28.00	84.00	195.00
81-85	28.00	84.00	195.00
86-Intro. The Black Canary in Johnny Thunder; rare in Mint due to black ink smearing on white cover	73.00	220.00	510.00
87-90: 88-Origin Ghost. 89-Intro villain Thorn	36.00	108.00	250.00
91,93-99: 98-Atom dons new costume	46.00	140.00	320.00
92-1st solo Black Canary	73.00	220.00	510.00
100,103(Scarce)	80.00	240.00	560.00
101,102(Scarce)	65.00	195.00	455.00
104-Origin The Flash retold (Scarce)	160.00	480.00	1120.00
Wheaties Giveaway (1946, 32 pgs., 6½x8¼'')-Johnny Thunder, Ghost Patrol, The Flash & Kubert Hawkman app. NOTE: All known copies were taped to Wheaties boxes and are never found in mint condition. Copies with light tape residue bring the listed prices in all grades	28.00	84.00	195.00

NOTE: *Infantino* a-86p, 90, 93-95, 99-104. *Kinstler* a-87, 89(Hawkman). *Chet Kozlak* c-77, 79, 81. *Krigstein* a-94. *Kubert* a-62-76, 83, 85, 86, 88-104; c-63, 65, 67, 70, 71, 73, 75, 83, 85, 86, 88, 89, 91, 94, 96, 98, 100, 104. *Moldoff* a-3; c-3, 7, 9, 17, 21, 23, 25, 27, 29, 31, 33, 37, 43, 55, 57. #8-Male bondage-c.

FLASH DIGEST, THE (See DC Spec. Series 24)

FLASH GORDON (See Defenders Of The Earth, Eat Right to Work..., Feature Book #25 (McKay), King Classics, King Comics, March of Comics #118, 133, 142, Street Comix & Wow Comics, 1st series)

FLASH GORDON
No. 10, 1943 - No. 512, Nov, 1953
Dell Publishing Co.

	Good	Fine	N-Mint
4-Color 10(1943)-by Alex Raymond; reprints/''The Ice Kingdom''	55.00	165.00	385.00
4-Color 84(1945)-by Alex Raymond; reprints/''The Fiery Desert''	33.00	100.00	230.00
4-Color 173,190: 190-Bondage-c	11.50	34.00	80.00
4-Color 204,247	9.00	27.00	62.00
4-Color 424	6.50	19.50	45.00
2(5-7/53-Dell)-Evans-a	3.50	10.50	24.00
4-Color 512	3.50	10.50	24.00
Macy's Giveaway(1943)-(Rare)-20 pgs.; not by Raymond	60.00	160.00	320.00

FLASH GORDON (See Tiny Tot Funnies)
Oct, 1950 - No. 4, April, 1951
Harvey Publications

	Good	Fine	N-Mint
1-Alex Raymond-a; bondage-c	17.00	51.00	120.00
2-Alex Raymond-a	13.00	40.00	90.00
3,4-Alex Raymond-a	12.00	36.00	80.00
5-(Rare)-Small size-5½x8½''; B&W; 32 pgs.; Distributed to some mail subscribers only Estimated value....		$200.00—$300.00	

(Also see All-New No. 15, Boy Explorers No. 2, and Stuntman No. 3)

FLASH GORDON
1951 (Paper cover; 16 pgs. in color; regular size)
Harvey Comics (Gordon Bread giveaway)

	Good	Fine	N-Mint
1 (1938), 2(1941?)-Reprints by Raymond each....	10.00	30.00	60.00

NOTE: *Most copies have brittle edges.*

FLASH GORDON
June, 1965
Gold Key

	Good	Fine	N-Mint
1 (1947 reprint)-Painted-c	1.75	5.25	12.00

FLASH GORDON (Also see Comics Reading Libraries)
9/66 - No. 1, 1/70; No. 19, 10-11/78 - No. 37, 3/82
(Painted covers No. 19-30,34)
King, No.1-11(12/67)/Charlton, No.12(2/69)-18/Gold Key, No.19-27/Whitman No. 28 on

	Good	Fine	N-Mint
1-Army giveaway(1968)(''Complimentary'' on cover)(Same as regular #1 minus Mandrake story & back-c)	1.20	3.50	8.00
1-Williamson c/a(2); E.C. swipe/Incred. S.F. 32. Mandrake sty	1.50	4.50	10.00
2-Bolle, Gil Kane-c/a; Mandrake sty	1.15	3.50	8.00
3-Williamson-c	1.30	4.00	9.00
4-Secret Agent X-9 begins, Williamson-c/a(3)	1.30	4.00	9.00
5-Williamson c/a(2)	1.30	4.00	9.00
6,8-Crandall-a. 8-Secret Agent X-9-r	1.50	4.50	12.00
7-Raboy-a	1.00	3.00	7.00
9,10-Raymond-r. 10-Buckler's 1st pro work (11/67)	1.30	4.00	9.00
11-Crandall-a	.85	2.50	6.00
12-Crandall c/a	1.00	3.00	7.00
13-Jeff Jones-a	1.00	3.00	7.00
14-17: 17-Brick Bradford sty	.50	1.50	3.00
18-Kaluta-a (1st pro work?)	.70	2.00	4.00
19(9/78, G.K.), 20-30(10/80)	.35	1.00	2.00
30 (7/81; re-issue)		.30	.60
31-33: Movie adapt; Williamson-a		.50	1.00
34-37: Movie adapt		.40	.80

NOTE: *Aparo* a-8. *Bolle* a-21, 22. *Buckler* a-10. *Crandall* c-6. *Estrada* a-3. *Gene Fawcette* a-29, 30, 34, 37. *McWilliams* a-31-33, 36.

FLASH GORDON
June, 1988 - No. 9, Holiday, 1988-'89 ($1.25, color, mini-series)
DC Comics

	Good	Fine	N-Mint
1-Painted-c	.35	1.00	2.00
2-9: 5-Painted-c	.25	.75	1.50

FLASH GORDON GIANT COMIC ALBUM
1972 (11x14''; cardboard covers; 48 pgs.; B&W; 59 cents)
Modern Promotions, N. Y.

	Good	Fine	N-Mint
Reprints 1968, 1969 dailies by Dan Barry	.25	.70	1.40

FLASH GORDON THE MOVIE
1980 ($1.95, color, 68pgs)
Western Publishing Co.

	Good	Fine	N-Mint
11294-Williamson-c/a; adapts movie	.35	1.00	2.00

FLASH SPECTACULAR, THE (See DC Special Series No. 11)

FLAT-TOP
11/53 - No. 3, 5/54; No. 4, 3/55 - No. 6, 7/55 **Good Fine N-Mint**
Mazie Comics/Harvey Publ.(Magazine Publ.) No. 4 on

	Good	Fine	N-Mint
1-Teenage	1.50	4.50	10.00
2,3	.85	2.50	6.00
4-6	.70	2.00	4.00

FLESH AND BONES
June, 1986 - No. 4, Dec, 1986 (mini-series)
Upshot Graphics (Fantagraphics Books)

1: Dalgoda by Fujitake-r; Alan Moore scripts	.40	1.25	2.50
2-4	.35	1.00	2.00

FLINTSTONE KIDS, THE (TV; See Star Comics Digest)
Aug, 1987 - Present
Star Comics/Marvel Comics #5 on

1-10		.50	1.00

FLINTSTONES, THE (TV)(See Dell Giant No.48 for No. 1)
No. 2, Nov-Dec, 1961 - No. 60, Sept, 1970 (Hanna-Barbera)
Dell Publ. Co./Gold Key No. 7 (10/62) on

2	3.50	10.50	24.00
3-6(7-8/62)	2.30	7.00	16.00
7 (10/62; 1st GK)	2.30	7.00	16.00
8-10: Mr. & Mrs. J. Evil Scientist begin?	2.00	6.00	14.00
11-1st app. Pebbles (6/63)	2.65	8.00	18.00
12-15,17-20	1.70	5.00	12.00
16-1st app. Bamm-Bamm (1/64)	2.00	6.00	14.00
21-30: 24-1st app. The Grusomes app.	1.50	4.50	8.00
31-33,35-40: 31-Xmas-c. 33-Meet Frankenstein & Dracula.			
39-Reprints	1.30	4.00	9.00
34-1st app. The Great Gazoo	1.70	5.00	12.00
41-60	1.15	3.50	8.00
At N. Y. World's Fair('64)-J.W. Books(25 cents)-1st printing; no			
date on-c	2.15	6.50	15.00
At N. Y. World's Fair (1965 on-c; re-issue). NOTE: Warehouse			
find in 1984	.50	1.50	3.00
Bigger & Boulder 1(30013-211)G.K. Giant(25 cents)			
	3.50	10.50	24.00
Bigger & Boulder 2-(25 cents)(1966)-reprints B&B No. 1			
	2.85	8.50	20.00
...With Pebbles & Bamm Bamm(100 pgs., G.K.)-30028-511 (paper-			
c, 25 cents)(11/65)	2.85	8.50	20.00

NOTE: (See Comic Album #16, Bamm-Bamm & Pebbles Flintstone, Dell Giant 48, March of Comics #229, 243, 271, 289, 299, 317, 327, 341, Pebbles Flintstone, and Whitman Comic Books.)

FLINTSTONES, THE (TV)(... & Pebbles)
Nov, 1970 - No. 50, Feb, 1977 (Hanna-Barbera)
Charlton Comics

1	1.50	4.50	10.00
2	.85	2.50	5.00
3-7,9,10	.70	2.00	4.00
8-"Flintstones Summer Vacation," 52 pgs. (Summer, 1971)			
	.85	2.50	5.00
11-20	.50	1.50	3.00
21-50: 42-Byrne-a, 2pgs.	.35	1.00	2.00

(Also see Barney & Betty Rubble, Dino, The Great Gazoo, & Pebbles & Bamm-Bamm)

FLINTSTONES, THE (TV)(See Yogi Bear, 3rd series)
October, 1977 - No. 9, Feb, 1979 (Hanna-Barbera)
Marvel Comics Group

1-9: Yogi Bear app. 4-The Jetsons app.		.50	1.00

FLINTSTONES CHRISTMAS PARTY, THE (See The Funtastic World of Hanna-Barbera No. 1)

FLINTSTONES 3-D
Apr, 1987 - No. 4, 1988 ($2.50)
Blackthorne Publ.

FLIP
April, 1954 - No. 2, June, 1954 (Satire)
Harvey Publications

	Good	Fine	N-Mint
1,2-Nostrand-a each. 2-Powell-a	7.00	21.00	50.00

FLIPPER (TV)
April, 1966 - No. 3, Nov, 1967 (Photo-c)
Gold Key

1	2.00	6.00	14.00
2,3	1.50	4.50	10.00

FLIPPITY & FLOP
12-1/51-52 - No. 46, 8-10/59; No. 47, 9-11/60
National Periodical Publ. (Signal Publ. Co.)

1	10.00	30.00	70.00
2	5.00	15.00	35.00
3-5	4.00	12.00	28.00
6-10	3.50	10.50	24.00
11-20: 20-Last precode (3/55)	2.30	7.00	16.00
21-47	1.50	4.50	10.00

FLOYD FARLAND (See Eclipse Graphic Album #11)

FLY, THE (Also see Blue Ribbon Comics)
May, 1983 - No. 9, Oct, 1984 (See The Advs. of...)
Archie Enterprises, Inc.

1-Mr. Justice app; origin Shield		.50	1.00
2-9: 2-Flygirl app.		.40	.80

NOTE: **Buckler** a-1, 2. **Ditko** a-2-9; c-4p-8p. **Nebres** c-4, 5i, 6, 7i. **Steranko** c-1-3.

FLY BOY (Also see Approved Comics)
Spring, 1952 - No. 4, 1953
Ziff-Davis Publ. Co. (Approved)

1-Saunders painted-c	5.00	15.00	35.00
2-Saunders painted-c	3.50	10.50	24.00
3,4-Saunders painted-c	2.35	7.00	16.00

FLYING ACES
July, 1955 - No. 5, March, 1956
Key Publications

1	1.70	5.00	12.00
2-5: 2-Trapani-a	1.00	3.00	7.00

FLYING A'S RANGE RIDER, THE (TV) (See 4-Color #404 for No. 1)
(See Western Roundup)
No. 2, June-Aug, 1953 - No. 24, Aug, 1959 (All photo-c)
Dell Publishing Co.

2	4.00	12.00	28.00
3-10	3.50	10.50	24.00
11-16,18-24	3.00	9.00	21.00
17-Toth-a	3.70	11.00	26.00

FLYING CADET (WW II Plane Photos)
Jan, 1943 - 1947 (½ photos, ½ comics)
Flying Cadet Publishing Co.

V1#1	5.00	15.00	35.00
2	2.65	8.00	18.00
3-9 (Two #6's, Sept. & Oct.)	2.00	6.00	14.00
V2#1-7(#10-16)	1.50	4.50	10.00
8(#17)-Bare-breasted woman-c	5.00	15.00	35.00

FLYIN' JENNY
1946 - 1947 (1945 strip reprints)
Pentagon Publ. Co.

nn	5.00	15.00	35.00
2-Baker-c	6.00	18.00	42.00

At top right:
	Good	Fine	N-Mint
1-4	.40	1.25	2.50

The Flintstones Bigger & Boulder #1, © Hanna-Barbera

Flying Aces #1, © Key Publ.

The Flying A's Range Rider #11, © Tie-Ups

Fly Man #36, © AP

Forbidden Love #1, © QUA

Forbidden Worlds #116, © ACG

FLYING MODELS
May, 1954 (16 pgs.) (5 cents)
H-K Publ. (Health-Knowledge Publs.)

	Good	Fine	N-Mint
V61#3 (Rare)	3.50	10.50	24.00

FLYING NUN (TV)
Feb, 1968 - No. 4, Nov, 1968
Dell Publishing Co.

1	1.50	4.50	10.00
2-4: 2-Sally Fields photo-c	1.00	3.00	7.00

FLYING NURSES (See Sue & Sally Smith . . .)

FLYING SAUCERS
1950 - 1953
Avon Periodicals/Realistic

1(1950)-Wood-a, 21 pgs.; Fawcette-c	35.00	105.00	245.00
nn(1952)-Cover altered plus 2 pgs. of Wood-a not in original	32.00	95.00	225.00
nn(1953)-Reprints above	18.00	54.00	125.00

FLYING SAUCERS (Comics)
April, 1967 - No. 4, Nov, 1967; No. 5, Oct, 1969
Dell Publishing Co.

1	1.00	3.00	6.00
2-5	.50	1.50	3.00

FLY MAN (Formerly Adv. of The Fly; Mighty Comics . . . No. 40 on)
No. 32, July, 1965 - No. 39, Sept, 1966
Mighty Comics Group (Radio Comics) (Archie)

32,33-Comet, Shield, Black Hood, The Fly & Flygirl x-over; re-intro. Wizard, Hangman #33	1.00	3.00	6.00
34-Shield begins	1.00	3.00	6.00
35-Origin Black Hood	1.00	3.00	6.00
36-Hangman x-over in Shield; re-intro. & origin of Web	1.00	3.00	6.00
37-Hangman, Wizard x-over in Flyman; last Shield issue	1.00	3.00	6.00
38-Web story	1.00	3.00	6.00
39-Steel Sterling story	1.00	3.00	6.00

FOLLOW THE SUN (TV)
May-July, 1962 - No. 2, Sept-Nov, 1962 (Photo-c)
Dell Publishing Co.

01-280-207(No.1), 12-280-211(No.?)	2.00	6.00	14.00

FOODINI (TV)(The Great . . ; see Pinhead & . . , & Jingle Dingle)
March, 1950 - No. 5, 1950
Continental Publications (Holyoke)

1 (52 pgs.)	5.00	15.00	35.00
2	2.65	8.00	18.00
3-5	1.70	5.00	12.00

FOOEY (Magazine) (Satire)
Feb, 1961 - No. 4, May, 1961
Scoff Publishing Co.

1	1.20	3.50	8.00
2-4	.85	2.50	5.00

FOOFUR (TV)
Aug, 1987 - No. 6, June, 1988
Star Comics/Marvel Comics No. 5 on

1-6		.50	1.00

FOOTBALL THRILLS (See Tops In Adventure)
Fall-Winter, 1951-52 - No. 2, 1952
Ziff-Davis Publ. Co.

1-Powell a(2); Saunders painted-c. Red Grange, Jim Thorpe app.	8.50	25.50	60.00
2-Saunders painted-c	5.70	17.00	40.00

FOR A NIGHT OF LOVE
1951
Avon Periodicals

	Good	Fine	N-Mint
nn-Two stories adapted from the works of Emile Zola; Astarita, Ravielli-a; Kinstler-c	16.00	48.00	110.00

FORBIDDEN LOVE
Mar, 1950 - No. 4, Sept, 1950
Quality Comics Group

1-(Scarce)Classic photo-c; Crandall-a	50.00	150.00	350.00
2,3(Scarce)-Photo-c	22.00	65.00	150.00
4-(Scarce)Ward/Cuidera-a; photo-c	24.00	72.00	170.00

FORBIDDEN LOVE (See Dark Mansion of . . .)

FORBIDDEN TALES OF DARK MANSION (Dark Mansion of Forbidden Love #1-4)
No. 5, May-June, 1972 - No. 15, Feb-Mar, 1974
National Periodical Publications

5-15: 13-Kane/Howard-a		.25	.50

NOTE: **Adams** c-9. **Alcala** a-9-11, 13. **Chaykin** a-7,15. **Evans** a-14. **Kaluta** c-7-11, 13. **G. Kane** a-13. **Kirby** a-6. **Nino** a-8, 12, 15. **Redondo** a-14.

FORBIDDEN WORLDS
7-8/51 - No. 34, 10-11/54; No. 35, 8/55 - No. 145, 8/67
(No.1-5: 52 pgs.; No.6-8: 44 pgs.)
American Comics Group

1-Williamson/Frazetta-a, 10pgs.	50.00	150.00	350.00
2	19.00	57.00	132.00
3-Williamson/Wood/Orlando-a, 7pgs.	23.00	70.00	160.00
4	10.00	30.00	70.00
5-Williamson/Krenkel-a, 8pgs.	19.00	57.00	132.00
6-Harrison/Williamson-a, 8pgs.	17.00	51.00	120.00
7,8,10	7.00	21.00	50.00
9-A-Bomb explosion story	8.00	24.00	56.00
11-20	5.00	15.00	35.00
21-33: 24-E.C. swipe by Landau	3.50	10.50	24.00
34(10-11/54)(Becomes Young Heroes #35 on)-Last pre-code ish; A-Bomb explosion story	3.50	10.50	24.00
35(8/55)-62	1.70	5.00	12.00
63,69,76,78-Williamson-a in all; w/Krenkel #69	3.00	9.00	21.00
64-68,70-72,74,75,77,79-90	1.15	3.50	8.00
65-"There's a New Moon Tonight" listed in #114 as holding 1st record fan mail response	1.50	4.50	10.00
73-Intro., 1st app. Herbie by Whitney	13.00	40.00	90.00
91-93,95,97-100	.85	2.50	5.00
94-Herbie app.	4.00	12.00	24.00
96-Williamson-a	2.35	7.00	14.00
101-109,111-113,115,117-120	.70	2.00	4.00
110,114,116-Herbie app. 114 contains list of editor's top 20 ACG stories	2.00	6.00	12.00
121-124: 124-Magic Agent app.	.50	1.50	3.00
125-Magic Agent app.; intro. & origin Magicman series, ends #141	.60	1.75	3.50
126-130	.50	1.50	3.00
131,132,134-141: 136-Nemesis x-over in Magicman. 140-Mark Midnight app. by Ditko	.40	1.25	2.50
133-Origin & 1st app. Dragonia in Magicman (1-2/66); returns #138	.40	1.25	2.50
142-145	.35	1.00	2.00

NOTE: **Buscema** a-75, 79, 81, 82, 140r. **Disbrow** a-10. **Ditko** a-137p, 138, 140. **Landau** a-24, 28, 29, 31-34, 48, 86r, 96, 143-45. **Lazarus** a-23. **Moldoff** a-31, 139r. **Whitney** a-115, 116, 137, c-40, 46, 57, 60, 68, 78, 79, 90, 93, 94, 100, 102, 103, 106-108, 114, 129.

FORCE, THE (See The Crusaders)

FORCE OF BUDDHA'S PALM THE
Aug., 1988 - Present ($1.50, color)
Jademan Comics

FORCE OF BUDDHA'S PALM (continued)	Good	Fine	N-Mint
1-3	.25	.75	1.50

FORD ROTUNDA CHRISTMAS BOOK (See Christmas at the Rotunda)

FOREIGN INTRIGUES (Formerly Johnny Dynamite;
Battlefield Action No. 16 on)
No. 13, 1956 - No. 15, Aug, 1956
Charlton Comics

| 13-15-Johnny Dynamite continues | 2.00 | 6.00 | 14.00 |

FOREMOST BOYS (See Four Most)

FOREST FIRE (Also see Smokey The Bear)
1949 (dated-1950) (16 pgs., paper-c)
American Forestry Assn.(Commerical Comics)

| nn-Intro/1st app. Smokey The Forest Fire Preventing Bear; created by Rudy Wendelein; Wendelein/Sparling-a; 'Carter Oil Co.' on back-c of original | 10.00 | 30.00 | 70.00 |

FOREVER, DARLING (See 4-Color No. 681)

FOREVER PEOPLE
Feb-Mar, 1971 - No. 11, Oct-Nov, 1972
National Periodical Publications

| 1-Superman x-over; Kirby-c/a begins | .70 | 2.00 | 4.00 |
| 2-11: 4-G.A.-r begin, end No. 9 | .35 | 1.00 | 2.00 |

NOTE: Kirby c/a(p)-1-11; #4-9 contain Sandman reprints from Adventure #85, 84, 75, 80, 77, 74 in that order. #1-3, 10-11 are 36pgs; #4-9 are 52pgs.

FOREVER PEOPLE
Feb, 1988 - No. 6, July, 1988 ($1.25, mini-series)
DC Comics

| 1-6 | .25 | .75 | 1.50 |

FOR GIRLS ONLY
Nov, 1953 (Digest size, 100 pgs.)
Bernard Bailey Enterprises

| 1-½ comic book, ½ magazine | 6.00 | 18.00 | 42.00 |

FORGOTTEN FOREST OF OZ, THE (See First Comics Graphic Novel)

FORGOTTEN STORY BEHIND NORTH BEACH, THE
No date (8 pgs.; paper cover)
Catechetical Guild

| | 3.00 | 9.00 | 18.00 |

FOR LOVERS ONLY (Formerly Hollywood Romances)
No. 60, Aug, 1971 - No. 87, Nov, 1976
Charlton Comics

| 60-87 | | .25 | .50 |

40 BIG PAGES OF MICKEY MOUSE
1936 (44 pgs.; 10¼x12½''; cardboard cover)
Whitman Publishing Co.

| 945-Reprints Mickey Mouse Magazine #1, but with a different cover. Ads were eliminated and some illustrated stories had expanded text. The book is ¾'' shorter than Mickey Mouse Mag. #1, but the reprints are the same size. (Rare) | 45.00 | 135.00 | 315.00 |

48 FAMOUS AMERICANS
1947 (Giveaway) (Half-size in color)
J. C. Penney Co. (Cpr. Edwin H. Stroh)

| Simon & Kirby-a | 6.75 | 20.00 | 40.00 |

FOR YOUR EYES ONLY (See James Bond)

FOUR COLOR
Sept?, 1939 - No. 1354, Apr-June, 1962
Dell Publishing Co.
NOTE: Four Color only appears on issues #19-25, 1-99,101. Dell Publishing Co. filed these as Series I, #1-25, and Series II, #1-1354. Issues beginning with #710? were printed with and without ads on back cover. Issues without ads are worth more.

SERIES I:

	Good	Fine	N-Mint
1(nn)-Dick Tracy	115.00	345.00	800.00
2(nn)-Don Winslow of the Navy (#1) (Rare) (11/39?)	65.00	195.00	455.00
3(nn)-Myra North (1/40?)	25.00	75.00	175.00
4-Donald Duck by Al Taliaferro('40)(Disney) (3/40?)	300.00	900.00	2100.00
(Prices vary widely on this book)			
5-Smilin' Jack (#1) (5/40?)	38.00	115.00	265.00
6-Dick Tracy (Scarce)	70.00	210.00	490.00
7-Gang Busters	19.00	57.00	132.00
8-Dick Tracy	45.00	135.00	315.00
9-Terry and the Pirates-r/Super 9-29	40.00	120.00	280.00
10-Smilin' Jack	35.00	105.00	245.00
11-Smitty (#1)	21.50	65.00	150.00
12-Little Orphan Annie	30.00	90.00	210.00
13-Walt Disney's Reluctant Dragon('41)-Contains 2 pages of photos from film; 2 pg. foreword to Fantasia by Leopold Stokowski; Donald Duck, Goofy, Baby Weems & Mickey Mouse (as the Sorcerer's Apprentice) app. (Disney)	75.00	225.00	525.00
14-Moon Mullins (#1)	19.00	57.00	132.00
15-Tillie the Toiler (#1)	19.00	57.00	132.00
	Good	Fine	VF-NM
16-Mickey Mouse (#1) (Disney) by Gottfredson	270.00	810.00	1890.00
(Prices vary widely on this book)			
	Good	Fine	N-Mint
17-Walt Disney's Dumbo, the Flying Elephant (#1)(1941)-Mickey Mouse, Donald Duck, & Pluto app. (Disney)	75.00	225.00	525.00
18-Jiggs and Maggie (#1)(1936-'38-r)	19.00	57.00	132.00
19-Barney Google and Snuffy Smith (#1)-(1st issue with Four Color on the cover)	22.00	65.00	154.00
20-Tiny Tim	19.00	57.00	132.00
21-Dick Tracy	40.00	120.00	280.00
22-Don Winslow	15.00	45.00	105.00
23-Gang Busters	14.00	42.00	100.00
24-Captain Easy	19.00	57.00	132.00
25-Popeye	37.00	110.00	260.00

SERIES II:

1-Little Joe	25.00	75.00	175.00
2-Harold Teen	15.00	45.00	105.00
3-Alley Oop (#1)	32.00	95.00	225.00
4-Smilin' Jack	28.00	84.00	195.00
5-Raggedy Ann and Andy (#1)	30.00	90.00	210.00
6-Smitty	12.00	36.00	84.00
7-Smokey Stover (#1)	20.00	60.00	140.00
8-Tillie the Toiler	11.50	34.00	80.00
9-Donald Duck Finds Pirate Gold, by Carl Barks & Jack Hannah (Disney) (c. 8/17/42)	357.00	1070.00	2500.00
(Prices vary widely on this book)			
10-Flash Gordon by Alex Raymond; r-/from "The Ice Kingdom"	55.00	165.00	385.00
11-Wash Tubbs	17.00	51.00	120.00
12-Walt Disney's Bambi (#1)	32.00	95.00	225.00
13-Mr. District Attorney (#1)-See The Funnies #35 for 1st app.	14.00	42.00	100.00
14-Smilin' Jack	23.00	70.00	160.00
15-Felix the Cat (#1)	38.00	115.00	265.00
16-Porky Pig (#1)(1942)-"Secret of the Haunted House"	35.00	105.00	245.00
17-Popeye	30.00	90.00	210.00
18-Little Orphan Annie's Junior Commandos; Flag-c	23.00	70.00	160.00
19-Walt Disney's Thumper Meets the Seven Dwarfs (Disney); r-in Silly Symphonies	35.00	105.00	245.00

Forever People #1 (2/88), © DC   *40 Big Pages Of Mickey Mouse #945, © WDC*   *Four Color #16 (Series II), © Warner Bros.*

Four Color #41, © DELL

Four Color #75, © Gene Autry

Four Color #105, © Walt Kelly

FOUR COLOR (continued)

	Good	Fine	N-Mint
20-Barney Baxter	14.50	44.00	100.00
21-Oswald the Rabbit (#1)(1943)	20.00	60.00	140.00
22-Tillie the Toiler	9.50	28.50	65.00
23-Raggedy Ann and Andy	22.00	65.00	154.00
24-Gang Busters	14.00	42.00	100.00
25-Andy Panda (#1) (Walter Lantz)	23.50	70.00	165.00
26-Popeye	28.00	84.00	195.00
27-Walt Disney's Mickey Mouse and the Seven Colored Terror			
	48.00	145.00	335.00
28-Wash Tubbs	13.00	40.00	90.00
29-Donald Duck and the Mummy's Ring, by Carl Barks (Disney)			
(9/43)	225.00	675.00	1575.00
(Prices vary widely on this book)			
30-Bambi's Children(1943)-Disney	30.00	90.00	210.00
31-Moon Mullins	11.50	34.00	80.00
32-Smitty	10.00	30.00	70.00
33-Bugs Bunny "Public Nuisance #1"	30.00	90.00	210.00
34-Dick Tracy	30.00	90.00	210.00
35-Smokey Stover	11.00	32.00	75.00
36-Smilin' Jack	13.00	40.00	90.00
37-Bringing Up Father	11.50	34.00	80.00
38-Roy Rogers (#1, c. 4/44)-1st western comic with photo-c			
	45.00	135.00	315.00
39-Oswald the Rabbit('44)	14.00	42.00	100.00
40-Barney Google and Snuffy Smith	12.00	36.00	84.00
41-Mother Goose and Nursery Rhyme Comics (#1)-All by Kelly			
	18.00	54.00	125.00
42-Tiny Tim (1934-r)	11.00	32.00	75.00
43-Popeye (1938-'42-r)	19.00	57.00	132.00
44-Terry and the Pirates ('38-r)	24.00	72.00	170.00
45-Raggedy Ann	17.00	51.00	120.00
46-Felix the Cat and the Haunted Castle	26.00	78.00	180.00
47-Gene Autry (© 6/16/44)	32.00	95.00	225.00
48-Porky Pig of the Mounties by Carl Barks (7/44)			
	70.00	210.00	490.00
49-Snow White and the Seven Dwarfs (Disney)			
	26.00	78.00	182.00
50-Fairy Tale Parade-Walt Kelly art (1944)	21.00	63.00	145.00
51-Bugs Bunny Finds the Lost Treasure	18.00	54.00	125.00
52-Little Orphan Annie	17.00	50.00	120.00
53-Wash Tubbs	9.50	28.50	65.00
54-Andy Panda	14.00	42.00	98.00
55-Tillie the Toiler	7.00	21.00	50.00
56-Dick Tracy	22.00	65.00	154.00
57-Gene Autry	26.00	78.00	180.00
58-Smilin' Jack	13.00	40.00	90.00
59-Mother Goose and Nursery Rhyme Comics-Kelly c/a			
	16.00	48.00	110.00
60-Tiny Folks Funnies	10.00	30.00	70.00
61-Santa Claus Funnies(11/44)-Kelly art	20.00	60.00	140.00
62-Donald Duck in Frozen Gold, by Carl Barks (Disney) (1/45)			
	120.00	360.00	840.00
63-Roy Rogers-Photo-c	30.00	90.00	210.00
64-Smokey Stover	8.00	24.00	56.00
65-Smitty	8.00	24.00	56.00
66-Gene Autry	26.00	78.00	180.00
67-Oswald the Rabbit	10.00	30.00	70.00
68-Mother Goose and Nursery Rhyme Comics, by Walt Kelly			
	16.00	48.00	110.00
69-Fairy Tale Parade, by Walt Kelly	18.00	54.00	125.00
70-Popeye and Wimpy	20.00	60.00	140.00
71-Walt Disney's Three Caballeros, by Walt Kelly(c. 4/45)-(Disney)			
	60.00	180.00	420.00
72-Raggedy Ann	15.00	45.00	105.00
73-The Gumps (No.1)	6.50	19.50	45.00
74-Marge's Little Lulu (No.1)	90.00	270.00	630.00

	Good	Fine	N-Mint
75-Gene Autry and the Wildcat	22.00	65.00	154.00
76-Little Orphan Annie	15.00	45.00	105.00
77-Felix the Cat	22.00	65.00	154.00
78-Porky Pig and the Bandit Twins	13.00	40.00	90.00
79-Walt Disney's Mickey Mouse in The Riddle of the Red Hat by Carl			
Barks(8/45)	60.00	180.00	420.00
80-Smilin' Jack	11.00	32.00	76.00
81-Moon Mullins	6.00	18.00	42.00
82-Lone Ranger	27.00	81.00	190.00
83-Gene Autry in Outlaw Trail	22.00	65.00	154.00
84-Flash Gordon by Alex Raymond-Reprints from "The Fiery			
Desert"	33.00	100.00	230.00
85-Andy Panda and the Mad Dog Mystery	9.00	27.00	62.00
86-Roy Rogers-Photo-c	23.00	70.00	160.00
87-Fairy Tale Parade by Walt Kelly; Dan Noonan cover			
	16.00	48.00	110.00
88-Bugs Bunny's Great Adventure	11.00	32.00	75.00
89-Tillie the Toiler	6.00	18.00	42.00
90-Christmas with Mother Goose by Walt Kelly (11/45)			
	15.00	45.00	105.00
91-Santa Claus Funnies by Walt Kelly (11/45)	14.00	42.00	100.00
92-Walt Disney's The Wonderful Adventures Of Pinocchio(1945);			
Donald Duck by Kelly, 16 pgs. (Disney)	25.00	75.00	175.00
93-Gene Autry in The Bandit of Black Rock	18.00	54.00	125.00
94-Winnie Winkle (1945)	8.00	24.00	56.00
95-Roy Rogers Comics-Photo-c	23.00	70.00	160.00
96-Dick Tracy	17.00	51.00	120.00
97-Marge's Little Lulu (1946)	47.00	140.00	330.00
98-Lone Ranger, The	22.00	65.00	154.00
99-Smitty	6.50	19.50	45.00
100-Gene Autry Comics-Photo-c	18.00	54.00	125.00
101-Terry and the Pirates	16.00	48.00	110.00

NOTE: No. 101 is last issue to carry "Four Color" logo on cover; all issues beginning with No. 100 are marked ".. . O.S." (One Shot) which can be found in the bottom left-hand panel on the first page; the numbers following "O.S." relate to the year/month issued.

102-Oswald the Rabbit-Walt Kelly art, 1 pg.	9.50	28.50	65.00
103-Easter with Mother Goose by Walt Kelly	14.00	42.00	100.00
104-Fairy Tale Parade by Walt Kelly	14.00	42.00	100.00
105-Albert the Alligator and Pogo Possum (No.1) by Kelly (4/46)			
	57.00	171.00	400.00
106-Tillie the Toiler	5.00	15.00	35.00
107-Little Orphan Annie	12.00	36.00	84.00
108-Donald Duck in The Terror of the River, by Carl Barks (Disney)			
(c. 4/16/46)	90.00	270.00	630.00
109-Roy Rogers Comics	18.00	54.00	125.00
110-Marge's Little Lulu	33.00	100.00	230.00
111-Captain Easy	8.00	24.00	56.00
112-Porky Pig's Adventure in Gopher Gulch	8.00	24.00	56.00
113-Popeye	8.50	25.50	60.00
114-Fairy Tale Parade by Walt Kelly	14.00	42.00	100.00
115-Marge's Little Lulu	33.00	100.00	230.00
116-Mickey Mouse and the House of Many Mysteries (Disney)			
	16.00	48.00	110.00
117-Roy Rogers Comics-Photo-c	13.00	40.00	90.00
118-Lone Ranger, The	22.00	65.00	154.00
119-Felix the Cat	16.00	48.00	110.00
120-Marge's Little Lulu	30.00	90.00	210.00
121-Fairy Tale Parade-(not Kelly)	8.00	24.00	56.00
122-Henry (No.1)(10/46)	5.00	15.00	35.00
123-Bugs Bunny's Dangerous Venture	6.00	18.00	42.00
124-Roy Rogers Comics-Photo-c	13.00	40.00	90.00
125-Lone Ranger, The	16.00	48.00	110.00
126-Christmas with Mother Goose by Walt Kelly (1946)			
	12.00	36.00	84.00
127-Popeye	8.50	25.50	60.00

FOUR COLOR (continued)	Good	Fine	N-Mint
128-Santa Claus Funnies-"Santa & the Angel" by Gollub; "A Mouse in the House" by Kelly	12.00	36.00	84.00
129-Walt Disney's Uncle Remus and His Tales of Brer Rabbit (No.1) (1946)	12.00	36.00	84.00
130-Andy Panda (Walter Lantz)	4.50	13.50	32.00
131-Marge's Little Lulu	30.00	90.00	210.00
132-Tillie the Toiler('47)	5.00	15.00	35.00
133-Dick Tracy	14.00	42.00	100.00
134-Tarzan and the Devil Ogre	34.00	105.00	240.00
135-Felix the Cat	13.00	40.00	90.00
136-Lone Ranger, The	16.00	48.00	110.00
137-Roy Rogers Comics-Photo-c	13.00	40.00	90.00
138-Smitty	5.70	17.00	40.00
139-Marge's Little Lulu (1947)	27.00	81.00	190.00
140-Easter with Mother Goose by Walt Kelly	12.00	36.00	84.00
141-Mickey Mouse and the Submarine Pirates (Disney)	14.00	42.00	100.00
142-Bugs Bunny and the Haunted Mountain	6.00	18.00	42.00
143-Oswald the Rabbit & the Prehistoric Egg	3.70	11.00	26.00
144-Roy Rogers Comics ('47)-Photo-c	13.00	40.00	90.00
145-Popeye	8.50	25.50	60.00
146-Marge's Little Lulu	27.00	81.00	190.00
147-Donald Duck in Volcano Valley, by Carl Barks (Disney)(5/47)	60.00	180.00	420.00
148-Albert the Alligator and Pogo Possum by Walt Kelly (5/47)	47.00	141.00	330.00
149-Smilin' Jack	8.00	24.00	56.00
150-Tillie the Toiler (6/47)	3.70	11.00	26.00
151-Lone Ranger, The	13.00	40.00	90.00
152-Little Orphan Annie	9.00	27.00	62.00
153-Roy Rogers Comics-Photo-c	10.00	30.00	70.00
154-Walter Lantz Andy Panda	4.50	13.50	32.00
155-Henry (7/47)	4.00	12.00	28.00
156-Porky Pig and the Phantom	5.70	17.00	40.00
157-Mickey Mouse & the Beanstalk (Disney)	14.00	42.00	100.00
158-Marge's Little Lulu	27.00	81.00	190.00
159-Donald Duck in the Ghost of the Grotto, by Carl Barks (Disney) (8/47)	52.00	156.00	364.00
160-Roy Rogers Comics-Photo-c	10.00	30.00	70.00
161-Tarzan and the Fires Of Tohr	30.00	90.00	210.00
162-Felix the Cat (9/47)	10.00	30.00	70.00
163-Dick Tracy	11.00	32.00	75.00
164-Bugs Bunny Finds the Frozen Kingdom	6.00	18.00	42.00
165-Marge's Little Lulu	27.00	81.00	190.00
166-Roy Rogers Comics-52 pgs.,Photo-c	10.00	30.00	70.00
167-Lone Ranger, The	13.00	40.00	90.00
168-Popeye (10/47)	8.50	25.50	60.00
169-Woody Woodpecker (No.1)-"Manhunter in the North"; drug use story	7.00	21.00	50.00
170-Mickey Mouse on Spook's Island (11/47)(Disney)-Reprinted in M. M. No. 103	12.00	36.00	84.00
171-Charlie McCarthy (No.1) and the Twenty Thieves	6.00	18.00	42.00
172-Christmas with Mother Goose by Walt Kelly (11/47)	12.00	36.00	84.00
173-Flash Gordon	11.50	34.00	80.00
174-Winnie Winkle	4.65	14.00	32.00
175-Santa Claus Funnies by Walt Kelly ('47)	12.00	36.00	84.00
176-Tillie the Toiler (12/47)	3.70	11.00	26.00
177-Roy Rogers Comics-36 pgs, Photo-c	10.00	30.00	70.00
178-Donald Duck "Christmas on Bear Mountain" by Carl Barks; 1st app. Uncle Scrooge (Disney)(12/47)	60.00	180.00	420.00
179-Uncle Wiggily (No.1)-Walt Kelly-c	9.00	27.00	62.00
180-Ozark Ike (No.1)	6.00	18.00	42.00
181-Walt Disney's Mickey Mouse in Jungle Magic	12.00	36.00	84.00

	Good	Fine	N-Mint
182-Porky Pig in Never-Never Land (2/48)	5.70	17.00	40.00
183-Oswald the Rabbit (Lantz)	3.70	11.00	26.00
184-Tillie the Toiler	3.70	11.00	26.00
185-Easter with Mother Goose by Walt Kelly (1948)	11.50	34.00	80.00
186-Walt Disney's Bambi (4/48)-Reprinted as Movie Classic Bambi #3('56)	8.00	24.00	56.00
187-Bugs Bunny and the Dreadful Dragon	5.00	15.00	35.00
188-Woody Woodpecker (Lantz, 5/48)	5.00	15.00	35.00
189-Donald Duck in The Old Castle's Secret, by Carl Barks (Disney) (6/48)	52.00	156.00	364.00
190-Flash Gordon ('48)	11.50	34.00	80.00
191-Porky Pig to the Rescue	5.70	17.00	40.00
192-The Brownies (No.1)-by Walt Kelly (7/48)	11.50	34.00	80.00
193-M.G.M. Presents Tom and Jerry (No.1)(1948)	7.00	21.00	50.00
194-Mickey Mouse in The World Under the Sea (Disney)-Reprinted in M.M. No. 101	12.00	36.00	84.00
195-Tillie the Toiler	3.50	10.50	24.00
196-Charlie McCarthy in The Haunted Hide-Out	7.00	21.00	50.00
197-Spirit of the Border (No.1) (Zane Grey) (1948)	6.00	18.00	42.00
198-Andy Panda	4.50	13.50	32.00
199-Donald Duck in Sheriff of Bullet Valley, by Carl Barks; Barks draws himself on wanted poster, last page; used in Love & Death (Disney) (10/48)	52.00	156.00	364.00
200-Bugs Bunny, Super Sleuth (10/48)	5.00	15.00	35.00
201-Christmas with Mother Goose by Walt Kelly	11.00	32.00	76.00
202-Woody Woodpecker	3.00	9.00	21.00
203-Donald Duck in the Golden Christmas Tree, by Carl Barks (Disney) (12/48)	36.00	108.00	250.00
204-Flash Gordon (12/48)	9.00	27.00	62.00
205-Santa Claus Funnies by Walt Kelly	11.00	32.00	76.00
206-Little Orphan Annie	5.70	17.00	40.00
207-King of the Royal Mounted	11.50	34.00	80.00
208-Brer Rabbit Does It Again (Disney)(1/49)	7.00	21.00	50.00
209-Harold Teen	2.30	7.00	16.00
210-Tippie and Cap Stubbs	2.30	7.00	16.00
211-Little Beaver (No.1)	3.00	9.00	21.00
212-Dr. Bobbs	2.30	7.00	16.00
213-Tillie the Toiler	3.50	10.50	24.00
214-Mickey Mouse and His Sky Adventure (2/49)(Disney)-Reprinted in M.M. No. 105	9.50	28.50	65.00
215-Sparkle Plenty (Dick Tracy reprints by Gould)	7.00	21.00	50.00
216-Andy Panda and the Police Pup (Lantz)	2.65	8.00	18.00
217-Bugs Bunny in Court Jester	5.00	15.00	35.00
218-3 Little Pigs and the Wonderful Magic Lamp (Disney)(3/49)	6.50	19.50	45.00
219-Swee'pea	6.50	19.50	45.00
220-Easter with Mother Goose by Walt Kelly	11.00	32.00	76.00
221-Uncle Wiggily-Walt Kelly cover in part	7.00	21.00	50.00
222-West of the Pecos (Zane Grey)	4.65	14.00	32.00
223-Donald Duck "Lost in the Andes" by Carl Barks (Disney-4/49) (square egg story)	50.00	150.00	350.00
224-Little Iodine (No.1), by Hatlo (4/49)	3.75	11.25	26.00
225-Oswald the Rabbit (Lantz)	2.30	7.00	16.00
226-Porky Pig and Spoofy, the Spook	4.00	12.00	28.00
227-Seven Dwarfs (Disney)	6.50	19.50	45.00
228-Mark of Zorro, The (No.1) ('49)	14.00	42.00	100.00
229-Smokey Stover	2.65	8.00	18.00
230-Sunset Pass (Zane Grey)	4.65	14.00	32.00
231-Mickey Mouse and the Rajah's Treasure (Disney)	9.50	28.50	65.00

Four Color #129, © WDC.

Four Color #165, © WEST.

Four Color #226, © Warner Bros.

Four Color #238, © WDC

Four Color #278, © DELL

Four Color #302, © DELL

FOUR COLOR (continued)	Good	Fine	N-Mint
232-Woody Woodpecker (Lantz, 6/49)	3.00	9.00	21.00
233-Bugs Bunny, Sleepwalking Sleuth	5.00	15.00	35.00
234-Dumbo in Sky Voyage (Disney)	5.70	17.00	40.00
235-Tiny Tim	3.50	10.50	24.00
236-Heritage of the Desert (Zane Grey)('49)	4.65	14.00	32.00
237-Tillie the Toiler	3.50	10.50	24.00
238-Donald Duck in Voodoo Hoodoo, by Carl Barks (Disney) (8/49)			
	27.00	81.00	190.00
239-Adventure Bound (8/49)	2.30	7.00	16.00
240-Andy Panda (Lantz)	2.65	8.00	18.00
241-Porky Pig, Mighty Hunter	4.00	12.00	28.00
242-Tippie and Cap Stubbs	1.70	5.00	12.00
243-Thumper Follows His Nose (Disney)	5.70	17.00	40.00
244-The Brownies by Walt Kelly	10.00	30.00	70.00
245-Dick's Adventures in Dreamland (9/49)	3.00	9.00	21.00
246-Thunder Mountain (Zane Grey)	3.50	10.50	24.00
247-Flash Gordon	9.00	27.00	62.00
248-Mickey Mouse and the Black Sorcerer (Disney)			
	9.50	28.50	65.00
249-Woody Woodpecker in the Globetrotter (10/49)			
	3.00	9.00	21.00
250-Bugs Bunny in Diamond Daze-Used in SOTI, pg. 309			
	5.00	15.00	35.00
251-Hubert at Camp Moonbeam	2.30	7.00	16.00
252-Pinocchio(Disney)-not Kelly; origin	6.50	19.50	45.00
253-Christmas with Mother Goose by Walt Kelly			
	9.50	28.50	65.00
254-Santa Claus Funnies by Walt Kelly; Pogo & Albert story by Kelly (11/49)	11.00	32.00	76.00
255-The Ranger (Zane Grey) (1949)	3.50	10.50	24.00
256-Donald Duck in "Luck of the North" by Carl Barks (Disney) (12/49)-Shows No. 257 on inside	27.00	81.00	190.00
257-Little Iodine	2.85	8.50	20.00
258-Andy Panda and the Balloon Race (Lantz)	2.65	8.00	18.00
259-Santa and the Angel (Gollub art-condensed from No. 128) & Santa at the Zoo (12/49)-two books in one	3.50	10.50	24.00
260-Porky Pig, Hero of the Wild West(12/49)	4.00	12.00	28.00
261-Mickey Mouse and the Missing Key (Disney)			
	9.50	28.50	65.00
262-Raggedy Ann and Andy	3.50	10.50	24.00
263-Donald Duck in "Land of the Totem Poles" by Carl Barks (Disney)(2/50)-has two Barks stories	27.00	81.00	190.00
264-Woody Woodpecker in the Magic Lantern (Lantz)			
	3.00	9.00	21.00
265-King of the Royal Mounted (Zane Grey)	7.00	21.00	50.00
266-Bugs Bunny on the Isle of Hercules"(2/50)-Reprinted in Best of B.B. No. 1	4.00	12.00	28.00
267-Little Beaver-Harmon c/a	2.00	6.00	14.00
268-Mickey Mouse's Surprise Visitor (1950) (Disney)			
	9.50	28.50	65.00
269-Johnny Mack Brown (No.1)-Photo-c	10.00	30.00	70.00
270-Drift Fence (Zane Grey) (3/50)	3.50	10.50	24.00
271-Porky Pig in Phantom of the Plains	4.00	12.00	28.00
272-Cinderella (Disney)(4/50)	4.65	14.00	32.00
273-Oswald the Rabbit (Lantz)	2.30	7.00	16.00
274-Bugs Bunny, Hare-brained Reporter	4.00	12.00	28.00
275-Donald Duck in "Ancient Persia" by Carl Barks (Disney) (5/50)			
	25.00	75.00	175.00
276-Uncle Wiggily	4.00	12.00	28.00
277-Porky Pig in Desert Adventure (5/50)	4.00	12.00	28.00
278-Bill Elliott Comics (No.1)-Photo-c	8.50	25.50	60.00
279-Mickey Mouse and Pluto Battle the Giant Ants (Disney); r-/in M.M. No. 102	8.00	24.00	56.00
280-Andy Panda in The Isle Of Mechanical Men (Lantz)			
	2.65	8.00	18.00
281-Bugs Bunny in The Great Circus Mystery	4.00	12.00	28.00

	Good	Fine	N-Mint
282-Donald Duck and the Pixilated Parrot by Carl Barks (Disney) (c. 5/23/50)	25.00	75.00	175.00
283-King of the Royal Mounted (7/50)	7.00	21.00	50.00
284-Porky Pig in the Kingdom of Nowhere	4.00	12.00	28.00
285-Bozo the Clown and His Minikin Circus (No.1)(TV)			
	6.00	18.00	42.00
286-Mickey Mouse in The Uninvited Guest (Disney)			
	8.00	24.00	56.00
287-Gene Autry's Champion in The Ghost Of Black Mountain (No.1)-Photo-c	5.00	15.00	35.00
288-Woody Woodpecker in Klondike Gold (Lantz)			
	3.00	9.00	21.00
289-Bugs Bunny in "Indian Trouble"	4.00	12.00	28.00
290-The Chief	3.00	9.00	21.00
291-Donald Duck in "The Magic Hourglass" by Carl Barks (Disney) (9/50)	25.00	75.00	175.00
292-The Cisco Kid Comics (No.1)	8.00	24.00	56.00
293-The Brownies-Kelly c/a	9.50	28.50	65.00
294-Little Beaver	2.00	6.00	14.00
295-Porky Pig in President Porky (9/50)	4.00	12.00	28.00
296-Mickey Mouse in Private Eye for Hire (Disney)			
	8.00	24.00	56.00
297-Andy Panda in The Haunted Inn (Lantz, 10/50)			
	2.65	8.00	18.00
298-Bugs Bunny in Sheik for a Day	4.00	12.00	28.00
299-Buck Jones & the Iron Horse Trail (No.1)	7.00	21.00	50.00
300-Donald Duck in "Big-Top Bedlam" by Carl Barks (Disney) (11/50)	25.00	75.00	175.00
301-The Mysterious Rider (Zane Grey)	3.50	10.50	24.00
302-Santa Claus Funnies (11/50)	2.30	7.00	16.00
303-Porky Pig in The Land of the Monstrous Flies			
	2.65	8.00	18.00
304-Mickey Mouse in Tom-Tom Island (Disney) (12/50)			
	5.70	17.00	40.00
305-Woody Woodpecker (Lantz)	2.00	6.00	14.00
306-Raggedy Ann	3.00	9.00	21.00
307-Bugs Bunny in Lumber Jack Rabbit	3.00	9.00	21.00
308-Donald Duck in "Dangerous Disguise" by Carl Barks (Disney) (1/51)	21.00	63.00	147.00
309-Betty Betz' Dollface and Her Gang ('51)	2.30	7.00	16.00
310-King of the Royal Mounted (1/51)	4.60	14.00	32.00
311-Porky Pig in Midget Horses of Hidden Valley			
	2.65	8.00	18.00
312-Tonto (No.1)	7.00	21.00	50.00
313-Mickey Mouse in The Mystery of the Double-Cross Ranch (No. 1)(Disney) (2/51)	5.70	17.00	40.00
314-Ambush (Zane Grey)	3.50	10.50	24.00
315-Oswald the Rabbit (Lantz)	1.50	4.50	10.00
316-Rex Allen (No.1)-Photo-c; Marsh-a	11.00	32.00	75.00
317-Bugs Bunny in Hair Today Gone Tomorrow (No.1)			
	3.00	9.00	21.00
318-Donald Duck in "No Such Varmint" by Carl Barks (No. 1) Indicia shows #317 (Disney, c. 1/23/51)	21.00	63.00	147.00
319-Gene Autry's Champion	3.00	9.00	21.00
320-Uncle Wiggily (No. 1)	3.00	9.00	21.00
321-Little Scouts (No.1)	1.70	4.00	9.00
322-Porky Pig in Roaring Rockets (No.1)	2.65	8.00	18.00
323-Susie Q. Smith (3/51)	1.50	4.50	10.00
324-I Met a Handsome Cowboy (3/51)	4.35	13.00	30.00
325-Mickey Mouse in The Haunted Castle (No. 2)(Disney)(4/51)	5.70	17.00	40.00
326-Andy Panda (No. 1, Lantz)	1.70	5.00	12.00
327-Bugs Bunny and the Rajah's Treasure (No. 2)			
	3.00	9.00	21.00
328-Donald Duck in Old California (No.2) by Carl Barks-Peyote drug use issue (Disney) (5/51)	23.00	70.00	160.00

FOUR COLOR (continued)	Good	Fine	N-Mint
329-Roy Roger's Trigger (No.1)(5/51)-Photo-c	5.70	17.00	40.00
330-Porky Pig Meets the Bristled Bruiser (No.2)	2.65	8.00	18.00
331-Alice in Wonderland (Disney) (1951)	5.70	17.00	40.00
332-Little Beaver	2.00	6.00	14.00
333-Wilderness Trek (Zane Grey) (5/51)	3.50	10.50	24.00
334-Mickey Mouse and Yukon Gold (Disney) (6/51)	5.70	17.00	40.00
335-Francis the Famous Talking Mule (No.1)	1.70	5.00	12.00
336-Woody Woodpecker (Lantz)	2.00	6.00	14.00
337-The Brownies-not by Walt Kelly	2.65	8.00	18.00
338-Bugs Bunny and the Rocking Horse Thieves	3.00	9.00	21.00
339-Donald Duck and the Magic Fountain-not by Carl Barks (Disney) (7-8/51)	4.35	13.00	30.00
340-King of the Royal Mounted (7/51)	4.60	14.00	32.00
341-Unbirthday Party with Alice in Wonderland (Disney) (7/51)	5.70	17.00	40.00
342-Porky Pig the Lucky Peppermint Mine	2.00	6.00	14.00
343-Mickey Mouse in The Ruby Eye of Homar-Guy-Am (Disney)-Reprinted in M.M. No. 104	4.30	13.00	30.00
344-Sergeant Preston from Challenge of The Yukon (No.1)(TV)	5.00	15.00	35.00
345-Andy Panda in Scotland Yard (8-10/51)(Lantz)	1.70	5.00	12.00
346-Hideout (Zane Grey)	3.50	10.50	24.00
347-Bugs Bunny the Frigid Hare (8-9/51)	3.00	9.00	21.00
348-Donald Duck "The Crocodile Collector"-Barks-c only (Disney) (9-10/51)	5.00	15.00	35.00
349-Uncle Wiggily	3.00	9.00	21.00
350-Woody Woodpecker (Lantz)	2.00	6.00	14.00
351-Porky Pig and the Grand Canyon Giant (9-10/51)	2.00	6.00	14.00
352-Mickey Mouse in The Mystery of Painted Valley (Disney)	4.30	13.00	30.00
353-Duck Album (No.1)-Barks-c (Disney)	3.00	9.00	21.00
354-Raggedy Ann & Andy	3.00	9.00	21.00
355-Bugs Bunny Hot-Rod Hare	3.00	9.00	21.00
356-Donald Duck in "Rags to Riches"-Barks-c only (Disney)	5.00	15.00	35.00
357-Comeback (Zane Grey)	2.65	8.00	18.00
358-Andy Panda (Lantz)(11-1/52)	1.70	5.00	12.00
359-Frosty the Snowman (No.1)	2.65	8.00	18.00
360-Porky Pig in Tree of Fortune (11-12/51)	2.00	6.00	14.00
361-Santa Claus Funnies	2.30	7.00	16.00
362-Mickey Mouse and the Smuggled Diamonds (Disney)	4.30	13.00	30.00
363-King of the Royal Mounted	4.00	12.00	28.00
364-Woody Woodpecker (Lantz)	1.70	5.00	12.00
365-The Brownies-not by Kelly	2.65	8.00	18.00
366-Bugs Bunny Uncle Buckskin Comes to Town (12-1/52)	3.00	9.00	21.00
367-Donald Duck in "A Christmas for Shacktown" by Carl Barks (Disney) (1-2/52)	20.00	60.00	140.00
368-Bob Clampett's Beany and Cecil (No.1)	9.50	28.00	65.00
369-The Lone Ranger's Famous Horse Hi-Yo Silver (No.1); Silver's origin	5.00	15.00	35.00
370-Porky Pig in Trouble in the Big Trees	2.00	6.00	14.00
371-Mickey Mouse in The Inca Idol Case ('52) (Disney)	4.30	13.00	30.00
372-Riders of the Purple Sage (Zane Grey)	2.65	8.00	18.00
373-Sergeant Preston (TV)	3.50	10.50	24.00
374-Woody Woodpecker (Lantz)	1.70	5.00	12.00
375-John Carter of Mars (E. R. Burroughs)-Jesse Marsh-a; origin	9.50	28.50	65.00
376-Bugs Bunny, "The Magic Sneeze"	3.00	9.00	21.00

	Good	Fine	N-Mint
377-Susie Q. Smith	1.50	4.50	10.00
378-Tom Corbett, Space Cadet (No.1)(TV)-McWilliams-a	6.00	18.00	42.00
379-Donald Duck in "Southern Hospitality"-not by Barks (Disney)	4.35	13.00	30.00
380-Raggedy Ann & Andy	3.00	9.00	21.00
381-Marge's Tubby (No.1)	11.00	36.00	84.00
382-Snow White and the Seven Dwarfs (Disney)-origin; partial reprint of 4-Color No. 49 (Movie)	5.00	15.00	35.00
383-Andy Panda (Lantz)	1.15	3.50	8.00
384-King of the Royal Mounted (3/52)(Zane Grey)	4.00	12.00	28.00
385-Porky Pig in The Isle of Missing Ships (3-4/52)	2.00	6.00	14.00
386-Uncle Scrooge No. 1 by Carl Barks (Disney) in "Only a Poor Old Man" (3/52)	58.00	175.00	405.00
387-Mickey Mouse in High Tibet (Disney) (4-5/52)	4.30	13.00	30.00
388-Oswald the Rabbit (Lantz)	1.50	4.50	10.00
389-Andy Hardy Comics (No.1)	1.70	5.00	12.00
390-Woody Woodpecker (Lantz)	1.70	5.00	12.00
391-Uncle Wiggily	2.65	8.00	18.00
392-Hi-Yo Silver	2.65	8.00	18.00
393-Bugs Bunny	3.00	9.00	21.00
394-Donald Duck in Malayalaya-Barks-c only (Disney)	5.00	15.00	35.00
395-Forlorn River (Zane Grey) (1952)-First Nevada (5/52)	2.65	8.00	18.00
396-Tales of the Texas Rangers (No.1)(TV)-Photo-c	5.00	15.00	35.00
397-Sergeant Preston of the Yukon (TV)(5/52)	3.50	10.50	24.00
398-The Brownies-not by Kelly	2.65	8.00	18.00
399-Porky Pig in The Lost Gold Mine	2.00	6.00	14.00
400-Tom Corbett, Space Cadet (TV)-McWilliams c/a	5.00	15.00	35.00
401-Mickey Mouse and Goofy's Mechanical Wizard (Disney) (6-7/52)	3.50	10.50	24.00
402-Mary Jane and Sniffles	6.00	18.00	42.00
403-Li'l Bad Wolf (Disney) (6/52)	2.00	6.00	14.00
404-The Range Rider (No.1)(TV)-Photo-c	5.50	16.50	38.00
405-Woody Woodpecker (Lantz)	1.70	5.00	12.00
406-Tweety and Sylvester (No.1)	1.70	5.00	12.00
407-Bugs Bunny, Foreign-Legion Hare	2.00	6.00	14.00
408-Donald Duck and the Golden Helmet by Carl Barks (Disney) (7-8/52)	20.00	60.00	140.00
409-Andy Panda (7-9/52)	1.15	3.50	8.00
410-Porky Pig in The Water Wizard (7/52)	2.00	6.00	14.00
411-Mickey Mouse and the Old Sea Dog (Disney) (8-9/52)	3.50	10.50	24.00
412-Nevada (Zane Grey)	2.65	8.00	18.00
413-Robin Hood (Disney-Movie) (8/52)-Photo-c	2.65	8.00	18.00
414-Bob Clampett's Beany and Cecil (TV)	7.00	21.00	50.00
415-Rootie Kazootie (No.1)(TV)	3.50	10.50	24.00
416-Woody Woodpecker (Lantz)	1.70	5.00	12.00
417-Double Trouble with Goober (No.1; 8/52)	1.50	4.50	10.00
418-Rusty Riley, a Boy, a Horse, and a Dog (No.1)-Frank Godwin-a (strip reprints) (8/52)	2.00	6.00	14.00
419-Sergeant Preston (TV)	3.50	10.50	24.00
420-Bugs Bunny in The Mysterious Buckaroo (8-9/52)	2.00	6.00	14.00
421-Tom Corbett, Space Cadet (TV)-McWilliams-a	5.00	15.00	35.00
422-Donald Duck and the Gilded Man, by Carl Barks (Disney) (9-10/52) (No.423 on inside)	20.00	60.00	140.00
423-Rhubarb, Owner of the Brooklyn Ball Club (The Millionaire Cat) (No.1)	1.15	3.50	8.00

Four Color #354, © DELL

Four Color #369, © Lone Ranger

Four Color #412, © DELL

Four Color #448, © Bob Clampett   Four Color #464, © Capitol Records   Four Color #523, © Screen Gems

FOUR COLOR (continued)	Good	Fine	N-Mint
424-Flash Gordon-Test Flight in Space (9/52)	6.50	19.50	45.00
425-Zorro, the Return of	7.00	21.00	50.00
426-Porky Pig in The Scalawag Leprechaun	2.00	6.00	14.00
427-Mickey Mouse and the Wonderful Whizzix (Disney) (10-11/52)-			
reprinted in M.M. No. 100	3.50	10.50	24.00
428-Uncle Wiggily	2.30	7.00	16.00
429-Pluto in ''Why Dogs Leave Home'' (Disney)(10/52)			
	2.65	8.00	18.00
430-Marge's Tubby, the Shadow of a Man-Eater			
	7.00	21.00	50.00
431-Woody Woodpecker (10/52)(Lantz)	1.70	5.00	12.00
432-Bugs Bunny and the Rabbit Olympics	2.00	6.00	14.00
433-Wildfire (Zane Grey)	2.65	8.00	18.00
434-Rin Tin Tin-''In Dark Danger'' (No.1)(TV)(11/52)-Photo-c			
	4.65	14.00	32.00
435-Frosty the Snowman	2.00	6.00	14.00
436-The Brownies-not by Kelly (11/52)	2.30	7.00	16.00
437-John Carter of Mars (E. R. Burroughs)-Marsh-a			
	8.00	24.00	56.00
438-Annie Oakley (No.1) (TV)	6.00	18.00	42.00
439-Little Hiawatha (Disney) (12/52)	2.00	6.00	14.00
440-Black Beauty (12/52)	1.70	5.00	12.00
441-Fearless Fagan	1.15	3.50	8.00
442-Peter Pan (Disney) (Movie)	5.00	15.00	35.00
443-Ben Bowie and His Mountain Men (No.1)	2.65	8.00	18.00
444-Marge's Tubby	7.00	21.00	50.00
445-Charlie McCarthy	2.00	6.00	14.00
446-Captain Hook and Peter Pan (Disney) (Movie) (1/53)			
	5.00	15.00	35.00
447-Andy Hardy Comics	1.15	3.50	8.00
448-Bob Clampett's Beany and Cecil (TV)	7.00	21.00	50.00
449-Tappan's Burro (Zane Grey) (2-4/53)	2.65	8.00	18.00
450-Duck Album-Barks-c (Disney)	2.65	8.00	18.00
451-Rusty Riley-Frank Godwin-a (strip reprints) (2/53)			
	1.70	5.00	12.00
452-Raggedy Ann & Andy ('53)	3.00	9.00	21.00
453-Susie Q. Smith (2/53)	1.30	4.00	9.00
454-Krazy Kat Comics-not by Herriman	2.30	7.00	16.00
455-Johnny Mack Brown Comics(3/53)-Photo-c			
	3.50	10.50	24.00
456-Uncle Scrooge Back to the Klondike (No.2) by Barks (3/53)			
(Disney)	27.00	81.00	190.00
457-Daffy (No.1)	1.70	5.00	12.00
458-Oswald the Rabbit (Lantz)	1.00	3.00	7.00
459-Rootie Kazootie (TV)	3.00	9.00	21.00
460-Buck Jones (4/53)	3.00	9.00	21.00
461-Marge's Tubby	6.50	19.50	45.00
462-Little Scouts	.85	2.50	6.00
463-Petunia (4/53)	1.30	4.00	9.00
464-Bozo (4/53)	3.50	10.50	24.00
465-Francis the Famous Talking Mule	1.00	3.00	7.00
466-Rhubarb, the Millionaire Cat	.85	2.50	6.00
467-Desert Gold (Zane Grey) (5-7/53)	2.65	8.00	18.00
468-Goofy (No.1) (Disney)	3.00	9.00	21.00
469-Beetle Bailey (No.1)(5/53)	4.00	12.00	28.00
470-Elmer Fudd	1.15	3.50	8.00
471-Double Trouble with Goober	1.00	3.00	7.00
472-Wild Bill Elliott (6/53)-Photo-c	3.70	11.00	26.00
473-Li'l Bad Wolf (Disney)(6/53)	2.00	6.00	14.00
474-Mary Jane and Sniffles	5.50	16.50	38.00
475-M.G.M.'s The Two Mouseketeers (No.1)	1.50	4.50	10.00
476-Rin Tin Tin (TV)-Photo-c	3.50	10.50	24.00
477-Bob Clampett's Beany and Cecil (TV)	7.00	21.00	50.00
478-Charlie McCarthy	2.00	6.00	14.00
479-Queen of the West Dale Evans (No.1)	7.00	21.00	50.00
480-Andy Hardy Comics	1.15	3.50	8.00

	Good	Fine	N-Mint
481-Annie Oakley And Tagg (TV)	4.50	13.50	32.00
482-Brownies-not by Kelly	2.30	7.00	16.00
483-Little Beaver (7/53)	1.70	5.00	12.00
484-River Feud (Zane Grey) (8-10/53)	2.65	8.00	18.00
485-The Little People-Walt Scott (No.1)	2.00	6.00	14.00
486-Rusty Riley-Frank Godwin strip-r	1.70	5.00	12.00
487-Mowgli, the Jungle Book (Rudyard Kipling's)			
	2.65	8.00	18.00
488-John Carter of Mars (Burroughs)-Marsh-a	7.00	21.00	50.00
489-Tweety and Sylvester	1.00	3.00	7.00
490-Jungle Jim (No.1)	2.65	8.00	18.00
491-Silvertip (No.1) (Max Brand)-Kinstler-a			
(8/53)	4.00	12.00	24.00
492-Duck Album (Disney)	2.00	6.00	14.00
493-Johnny Mack Brown-Photo-c	3.50	10.50	24.00
494-The Little King (No.1)	3.00	9.00	21.00
495-Uncle Scrooge (No.3)(Disney)-by Carl Barks (9/53)			
	24.00	72.00	170.00
496-The Green Hornet	8.00	24.00	56.00
497-Zorro (Sword of. . .)	7.00	21.00	50.00
498-Bugs Bunny's Album (9/53)	1.70	5.00	12.00
499-M.G.M.'s Spike and Tyke (No.1)(9/53)	1.30	4.00	9.00
500-Buck Jones	3.00	9.00	21.00
501-Francis the Famous Talking Mule	1.00	3.00	7.00
502-Rootie Kazootie (TV)	3.00	9.00	21.00
503-Uncle Wiggily (10/53)	2.30	7.00	16.00
504-Krazy Kat-not by Herriman	2.30	7.00	16.00
505-The Sword and the Rose (Disney) (10/53) (TV)-Photo-c			
	3.00	9.00	21.00
506-The Little Scouts	.85	2.50	6.00
507-Oswald the Rabbit (Lantz)	1.00	3.00	7.00
508-Bozo (10/53)	3.50	10.50	24.00
509-Pluto (Disney) (10/53)	2.65	8.00	18.00
510-Son of Black Beauty	1.70	5.00	12.00
511-Outlaw Trail (Zane Grey)-Kinstler-a	3.00	9.00	21.00
512-Flash Gordon (11/53)	3.50	10.50	24.00
513-Ben Bowie and His Mountain Men	1.70	5.00	12.00
514-Frosty the Snowman (11/53)	1.70	5.00	12.00
515-Andy Hardy	1.15	3.50	8.00
516-Double Trouble With Goober	1.00	3.00	7.00
517-Chip 'N' Dale (No.1)(Disney)	1.70	5.00	12.00
518-Rivets (11/53)	1.15	3.50	8.00
519-Steve Canyon (No.1)-not by Milton Caniff	4.00	12.00	28.00
520-Wild Bill Elliott-Photo-c	3.70	11.00	26.00
521-Beetle Bailey (12/53)	2.30	7.00	16.00
522-The Brownies	2.30	7.00	16.00
523-Rin Tin Tin (TV)-Photo-c (12/53)	3.50	10.50	24.00
524-Tweety and Sylvester	1.00	3.00	7.00
525-Santa Claus Funnies	1.15	3.50	8.00
526-Napoleon	1.15	3.50	8.00
527-Charlie McCarthy	2.00	6.00	14.00
528-Queen of the West Dale Evans-Photo-c	5.00	15.00	35.00
529-Little Beaver	1.70	5.00	12.00
530-Bob Clampett's Beany and Cecil (TV) (1/54)			
	7.00	21.00	50.00
531-Duck Album (Disney)	2.00	6.00	14.00
532-The Rustlers (Zane Grey) (2-4/54)	2.65	8.00	18.00
533-Raggedy Ann and Andy	3.00	9.00	21.00
534-Western Marshal (Ernest Haycox's)-Kinstler-a			
	3.00	9.00	21.00
535-I Love Lucy (No. 1)(TV) (2/54)-photo-c	10.00	30.00	70.00
536-Daffy (3/54)	1.30	4.00	9.00
537-Stormy, the Thoroughbred. . . (Disney-Movie) on top ⅔ of each			
page; Pluto story on bottom ⅓ of each page (2/54)			
	2.00	6.00	14.00
538-The Mask of Zorro-Kinstler-a	8.00	24.00	56.00

	Good	Fine	N-Mint
539-Ben and Me (Disney) (3/54)	1.50	4.50	10.00
540-Knights of the Round Table (3/54) (Movie)-Photo-c			
	3.50	10.50	24.00
541-Johnny Mack Brown-Photo-c	3.50	10.50	24.00
542-Super Circus Featuring Mary Hartline (TV) (3/54)			
	2.65	8.00	18.00
543-Uncle Wiggily (3/54)	2.30	7.00	16.00
544-Rob Roy (Disney-Movie)-Manning-a; photo-c			
	4.00	12.00	28.00
545-The Wonderful Adventures of Pinocchio-Partial reprint of 4-Color 92 (Disney-Movie)	3.00	9.00	21.00
546-Buck Jones	3.00	9.00	21.00
547-Francis the Famous Talking Mule	1.00	3.00	7.00
548-Krazy Kat-not by Herriman (4/54)	2.00	6.00	14.00
549-Oswald the Rabbit (Lantz)	1.00	3.00	7.00
550-The Little Scouts	.85	2.50	6.00
551-Bozo (4/54)	3.50	10.50	24.00
552-Beetle Bailey	2.30	7.00	16.00
553-Susie Q. Smith	1.30	4.00	9.00
554-Rusty Riley (Frank Godwin strip-r)	1.75	5.25	12.00
555-Range War (Zane Grey)	2.65	8.00	18.00
556-Double Trouble With Goober (5/54)	1.00	3.00	7.00
557-Ben Bowie and His Mountain Men	1.70	5.00	12.00
558-Elmer Fudd (5/54)	1.15	3.50	8.00
559-I Love Lucy (No. 2)(TV)-Photo-c	7.00	21.00	50.00
560-Duck Album (Disney)(5/54)	2.00	6.00	14.00
561-Mr. Magoo (5/54)	5.00	15.00	35.00
562-Goofy (Disney)	2.30	7.00	16.00
563-Rhubarb, the Millionaire Cat (6/54)	.85	2.50	6.00
564-Li'l Bad Wolf (Disney)	1.70	5.00	12.00
565-Jungle Jim	2.00	6.00	14.00
566-Son of Black Beauty	1.75	5.25	12.00
567-Prince Valiant (No.1)-by Bob Fuje (Movie)-Photo-c			
	5.70	17.00	40.00
568-Gypsy Colt (Movie)	2.30	7.00	16.00
569-Priscilla's Pop	1.30	4.00	9.00
570-Bob Clampett's Beany and Cecil (TV)	7.00	21.00	50.00
571-Charlie McCarthy	2.00	6.00	14.00
572-Silvertip (Max Brand)(7/54); Kinstler-a	3.00	9.00	21.00
573-The Little People by Walt Scott	1.50	4.50	10.00
574-The Hand of Zorro	7.00	21.00	50.00
575-Annie Oakley and Tagg(TV)-Photo-c	4.50	13.50	32.00
576-Angel (No.1) (8/54)	1.00	3.00	7.00
577-M.G.M.'s Spike and Tyke	1.00	3.00	7.00
578-Steve Canyon (8/54)	3.50	10.50	24.00
579-Francis the Famous Talking Mule	1.00	3.00	7.00
580-Six Gun Ranch (Luke Short-8/54)	2.30	7.00	16.00
581-Chip 'N' Dale (Disney)	1.30	4.00	9.00
582-Mowgli Jungle Book (Kipling)(8/54)	2.30	7.00	16.00
583-The Lost Wagon Train (Zane Grey)	2.65	8.00	18.00
584-Johnny Mack Brown-Photo-c	3.50	10.50	24.00
585-Bugs Bunny's Album	1.70	5.00	12.00
586-Duck Album (Disney)	2.00	6.00	14.00
587-The Little Scouts	.85	2.50	6.00
588-King Richard and the Crusaders (Movie) (10/54) Matt Baker-a; photo-c	8.00	24.00	56.00
589-Buck Jones	3.00	9.00	21.00
590-Hansel and Gretel	3.00	9.00	21.00
591-Western Marshal (Ernest Haycox's)-Kinstler-a			
	3.00	9.00	21.00
592-Super Circus (TV)	2.65	8.00	18.00
593-Oswald the Rabbit (Lantz)	1.00	3.00	7.00
594-Bozo (10/54)	3.50	10.50	24.00
595-Pluto (Disney)	2.00	6.00	14.00
596-Turok, Son of Stone (No.1)	21.50	65.00	150.00
597-The Little King	2.30	7.00	16.00

	Good	Fine	N-Mint
598-Captain Davy Jones	1.50	4.50	10.00
599-Ben Bowie and His Mountain Men	1.70	5.00	12.00
600-Daisy Duck's Diary (No.1)(Disney)(11/54)	2.00	6.00	14.00
601-Frosty the Snowman	1.70	5.00	12.00
602-Mr. Magoo and Gerald McBoing-Boing	5.00	15.00	35.00
603-M.G.M.'s The Two Mouseketeers	1.00	3.00	7.00
604-Shadow on the Trail (Zane Grey)	2.65	8.00	18.00
605-The Brownies-not by Kelly (12/54)	2.30	7.00	16.00
606-Sir Lancelot (not TV)	6.00	18.00	42.00
607-Santa Claus Funnies	1.70	5.00	12.00
608-Silvertip-"Valley of Vanishing Men" (Max Brand)-Kinstler-a			
	3.00	9.00	21.00
609-The Littlest Outlaw (Disney-Movie) (1/55)-Photo-c			
	2.65	8.00	18.00
610-Drum Beat (Movie); Alan Ladd photo-c	6.00	18.00	42.00
611-Duck Album (Disney)	2.00	6.00	14.00
612-Little Beaver (1/55)	1.30	4.00	9.00
613-Western Marshal (Ernest Haycox's) (2/55)-Kinstler-a			
	3.00	9.00	21.00
614-20,000 Leagues Under the Sea (Disney) (Movie) (2/55)			
	2.65	8.00	18.00
615-Daffy	1.30	4.00	9.00
616-To the Last Man (Zane Grey)	2.65	8.00	18.00
617-The Quest of Zorro	7.00	21.00	50.00
618-Johnny Mack Brown-Photo-c	3.50	10.50	24.00
619-Krazy Kat-not by Herriman	2.00	6.00	14.00
620-Mowgli Jungle Book (Kipling)	2.30	7.00	16.00
621-Francis the Famous Talking Mule	1.00	3.00	7.00
622-Beetle Bailey	2.30	7.00	16.00
623-Oswald the Rabbit (Lantz)	.85	2.50	6.00
624-Treasure Island (Disney-Movie) (4/55)-Photo-c			
	2.30	7.00	16.00
625-Beaver Valley (Disney-Movie)	1.50	4.50	10.00
626-Ben Bowie and His Mountain Men	1.70	5.00	12.00
627-Goofy (Disney) (5/55)	2.30	7.00	16.00
628-Elmer Fudd	1.15	3.50	8.00
629-Lady and the Tramp with Jock (Disney)	2.00	6.00	14.00
630-Priscilla's Pop	1.15	3.50	8.00
631-Davy Crockett, Indian Fighter (No.1)(5/55)(TV)-Fess Parker photo-c	3.00	9.00	21.00
632-Fighting Caravans (Zane Grey)	2.65	8.00	18.00
633-The Little People by Walt Scott (6/55)	1.50	4.50	10.00
634-Lady and the Tramp Album (Disney) (6/55)			
	1.70	5.00	12.00
635-Bob Clampett's Beany and Cecil (TV)	7.00	21.00	50.00
636-Chip 'N' Dale (Disney)	1.30	4.00	9.00
637-Silvertip (Max Brand)-Kinstler-a	3.00	9.00	21.00
638-M.G.M.'s Spike and Tyke (8/55)	1.00	3.00	7.00
639-Davy Crockett at the Alamo (Disney) (7/55)(TV)-Fess Parker photo-c	3.00	9.00	21.00
640-Western Marshal (Ernest Haycox's)-Kinstler-a			
	3.00	9.00	21.00
641-Steve Canyon ('55)-by Caniff	3.50	10.50	24.00
642-M.G.M.'s The Two Mouseketeers	1.00	3.00	7.00
643-Wild Bill Elliott-Photo-c	3.50	10.50	24.00
644-Sir Walter Raleigh (5/55)-Based on movie "The Virgin Queen"-Photo-c	3.50	10.50	24.00
645-Johnny Mack Brown-Photo-c	3.50	10.50	24.00
646-Dotty Dripple and Taffy (No.1)	1.70	5.00	12.00
647-Bugs Bunny's Album (9/55)	1.70	5.00	12.00
648-Jace Pearson of the Texas Rangers (TV)-Photo-c			
	3.50	10.50	24.00
649-Duck Album (Disney)	2.00	6.00	14.00
650-Prince Valiant - by Bob Fuje	3.50	10.50	24.00
651-King Colt (Luke Short)(9/55)-Kinstler-a	3.00	9.00	21.00
652-Buck Jones	2.00	6.00	14.00

Four Color #546, © DELL

Four Color #578, © Milton Caniff

Four Color #631, © WDC

Four Color #653, © DELL   Four Color #687, © United Artists   Four Color #751, © DELL

FOUR COLOR (continued)	Good	Fine	N-Mint
653-Smokey the Bear (No.1) (10/55)	2.65	8.00	18.00
654-Pluto (Disney)	2.00	6.00	14.00
655-Francis the Famous Talking Mule	1.00	3.00	7.00
656-Turok, Son of Stone (No.2) (10/55)	15.00	45.00	105.00
657-Ben Bowie and His Mountain Men	1.70	5.00	12.00
658-Goofy (Disney)	2.30	7.00	16.00
659-Daisy Duck's Diary (Disney)	1.70	5.00	12.00
660-Little Beaver	1.30	4.00	9.00
661-Frosty the Snowman	1.70	5.00	12.00
662-Zoo Parade (TV)-Marlin Perkins (11/55)	2.00	6.00	14.00
663-Winky Dink (TV)	3.50	10.50	24.00
664-Davy Crockett in the Great Keelboat Race (TV) (Disney)(11/55)-			
Fess Parker photo-c	3.50	10.50	24.00
665-The African Lion (Disney-Movie) (11/55)	2.00	6.00	14.00
666-Santa Claus Funnies	1.70	5.00	12.00
667-Silvertip and the Stolen Stallion (Max Brand) (12/55)-Kinstler-a			
	3.00	9.00	21.00
668-Dumbo (Disney) (12/55)	3.50	10.50	24.00
668-Dumbo (Disney) (1/58) different cover, same contents			
	3.50	10.50	24.00
669-Robin Hood (Disney-Movie) (12/55)-reprint of No. 413-Photo-c			
	2.00	6.00	14.00
670-M.G.M's Mouse Musketeers (No.1)(1/56)-Formerly the Two			
Mouseketeers	1.00	3.00	7.00
671-Davy Crockett and the River Pirates (TV) (Disney) (12/55)-Jesse			
Marsh-a; Fess Parker photo-c	3.50	10.50	24.00
672-Quentin Durward (1/56)(Movie)-Photo-c	3.00	9.00	21.00
673-Buffalo Bill, Jr. (No.1)(TV)-Photo-c	3.50	10.50	24.00
674-The Little Rascals (No.1) (TV)	2.00	6.00	14.00
675-Steve Donovan, Western Marshal (No.1)(TV)-Kinstler-a; photo-c			
	4.00	12.00	28.00
676-Will-Yum!	1.15	3.50	8.00
677-Little King	2.00	6.00	14.00
678-The Last Hunt (Movie)-Photo-c	3.00	9.00	21.00
679-Gunsmoke (No.1) (TV)	5.50	16.50	38.00
680-Out Our Way with the Worry Wart (2/56)	1.30	4.00	9.00
681-Forever, Darling (Movie) with Lucille Ball & Desi Arnaz (2/56)-			
Photo-c	5.00	15.00	35.00
682-When Knighthood Was in Flower (Disney-Movie)-Reprint of No.			
505-Photo-c	2.65	8.00	18.00
683-Hi and Lois (3/56)	1.00	3.00	7.00
684-Helen of Troy (Movie)-Buscema-a; photo-c	6.50	19.50	45.00
685-Johnny Mack Brown-Photo-c	3.50	10.50	24.00
686-Duck Album (Disney)	2.00	6.00	14.00
687-The Indian Fighter (Movie)-Kirk Douglas Photo-c			
	2.65	8.00	18.00
688-Alexander the Great (Movie) (5/56) Buscema-a; photo-c			
	3.50	10.50	24.00
689-Elmer Fudd (3/56)	1.15	3.50	8.00
690-The Conqueror (Movie) - John Wayne-Photo-c			
	9.00	27.00	62.00
691-Dotty Dripple and Taffy	1.30	4.00	9.00
692-The Little People-Walt Scott	1.50	4.50	10.00
693-Song of the South (Disney)(1956)-Partial reprint of No. 129			
	2.00	6.00	14.00
694-Super Circus (TV)-Photo-c	2.65	8.00	18.00
695-Little Beaver	1.30	4.00	9.00
696-Krazy Kat-not by Herriman (4/56)	2.00	6.00	14.00
697-Oswald the Rabbit (Lantz)	.85	2.50	6.00
698-Francis the Famous Talking Mule (4/56)	1.00	3.00	7.00
699-Prince Valiant-by Bob Fuje	3.50	10.50	24.00
700-Water Birds and the Olympic Elk (Disney-Movie)(4/56)			
	2.35	7.00	16.00
701-Jiminy Cricket (No.1)(Disney)(5/56)	2.35	7.00	16.00
702-The Goofy Success Story (Disney)	2.00	6.00	14.00
703-Scamp (No.1) (Disney)	1.70	5.00	12.00

	Good	Fine	N-Mint
704-Priscilla's Pop (5/56)	1.15	3.50	8.00
705-Brave Eagle (No.1) (TV)-Photo-c	2.00	6.00	14.00
706-Bongo and Lumpjaw (Disney)(6/56)	1.50	4.50	10.00
707-Corky and White Shadow (Disney)(5/56)-Mickey Mouse Club			
(TV)-Photo-c	2.30	7.00	16.00
708-Smokey the Bear	2.00	6.00	14.00
709-The Searchers (Movie) - John Wayne photo-c			
	13.00	40.00	90.00
710-Francis the Famous Talking Mule	1.00	3.00	7.00
711-M.G.M's Mouse Musketeers	.85	2.50	6.00
712-The Great Locomotive Chase (Disney-Movie) (9/56)-Photo-c			
	2.65	8.00	18.00
713-The Animal World (Movie) (8/56)	2.30	7.00	16.00
714-Spin and Marty (No.1)(TV)(Disney)-Mickey Mouse Club (6/56)-			
Photo-c	3.70	11.00	26.00
715-Timmy (8/56)	1.50	4.50	10.00
716-Man in Space (Disney-Movie)	2.00	6.00	14.00
717-Moby Dick (Movie)-Photo-c	4.60	14.00	32.00
718-Dotty Dripple and Taffy	1.30	4.00	9.00
719-Prince Valiant - by Bob Fuje (8/56)	3.50	10.50	24.00
720-Gunsmoke (TV)-Photo-c	3.70	11.00	26.00
721-Captain Kangaroo (TV)-Photo-c	7.00	21.00	50.00
722-Johnny Mack Brown-Photo-c	3.50	10.50	24.00
723-Santiago (Movie)-Kinstler-a(9/56); Alan Ladd photo-c			
	6.00	18.00	42.00
724-Bugs Bunny's Album	1.70	5.00	12.00
725-Elmer Fudd (9/56)	.85	2.50	6.00
726-Duck Album (Disney)	1.70	5.00	12.00
727-The Nature of Things (TV) (Disney)-Jesse Marsh-a			
	2.00	6.00	14.00
728-M.G.M's Mouse Musketeers	.85	2.50	6.00
729-Bob Son of Battle (11/56)	1.70	5.00	12.00
730-Smokey Stover	1.70	5.00	12.00
731-Silvertip and The Fighting Four (Max Brand)-Kinstler-a			
	3.00	9.00	21.00
732-Zorro, the Challenge of (10/56)	7.00	21.00	50.00
733-Buck Jones	2.00	6.00	14.00
734-Cheyenne (No.1)(TV)(10/56)-Photo-c	5.50	16.50	38.00
735-Crusader Rabbit (No. 1) (TV)	6.00	18.00	42.00
736-Pluto (Disney)	1.50	4.50	10.00
737-Steve Canyon-Caniff-a	3.50	10.50	24.00
738-Westward Ho, the Wagons (Disney-Movie)-Fess Parker photo-c			
	2.00	6.00	14.00
739-Bounty Guns (Luke Short)-Drucker-a	2.30	7.00	16.00
740-Chilly Willy (No.1)(Walter Lantz)	1.15	3.50	8.00
741-The Fastest Gun Alive (Movie) (9/56)-Photo-c			
	3.00	9.00	21.00
742-Buffalo Bill, Jr. (TV)-Photo-c	2.30	7.00	16.00
743-Daisy Duck's Diary (Disney) (11/56)	1.70	5.00	12.00
744-Little Beaver	1.30	4.00	9.00
745-Francis the Famous Talking Mule	1.00	3.00	7.00
746-Dotty Dripple and Taffy	1.30	4.00	9.00
747-Goofy (Disney)	2.30	7.00	16.00
748-Goofy Success Story (11/56)	1.50	4.50	10.00
749-Secrets of Life (Disney-Movie)-Photo-c	2.00	6.00	14.00
750-The Great Cat Family (Disney-Movie)	2.30	7.00	16.00
751-Our Miss Brooks (TV)-Photo-c	3.50	10.50	24.00
752-Mandrake, the Magician	3.70	11.00	26.00
753-Walt Scott's Little People (11/56)	1.50	4.50	10.00
754-Smokey the Bear	2.00	6.00	14.00
755-The Littlest Snowman (12/56)	2.15	6.50	16.00
756-Santa Claus Funnies	1.70	5.00	12.00
757-The True Story of Jesse James (Movie)-Photo-c			
	4.65	14.00	32.00
758-Bear Country (Disney-Movie)	2.00	6.00	14.00
759-Circus Boy (TV)-The Monkees' Mickey Dolenz photo-c (12/56)			

FOUR COLOR (continued)

	Good	Fine	N-Mint
	6.00	18.00	42.00
760-The Hardy Boys (No. 1) (TV) (Disney)-Mickey Mouse Club-Photo-c	4.00	12.00	28.00
761-Howdy Doody (TV) (1/57)	3.50	10.50	24.00
762-The Sharkfighters (Movie)(1/57)(Scarce); Buscema-a; photo-c	7.00	21.00	50.00
763-Grandma Duck's Farm Friends (No. 1) (Disney)	2.30	7.00	16.00
764-M.G.M's Mouse Musketeers	.85	2.50	6.00
765-Will-Yum!	1.00	3.00	7.00
766-Buffalo Bill, Jr. (TV)-Photo-c	2.30	7.00	16.00
767-Spin and Marty (TV)(Disney)-Mickey Mouse Club (2/57)	3.50	10.50	24.00
768-Steve Donovan, Western Marshal (TV)-Kinstler-a; photo-c	3.50	10.50	24.00
769-Gunsmoke (TV)	3.70	11.00	26.00
770-Brave Eagle (TV)-Photo-c	1.50	4.50	10.00
771-Brand of Empire (Luke Short)(3/57)-Drucker-a	2.30	7.00	16.00
772-Cheyenne (TV)-Photo-c	4.00	12.00	28.00
773-The Brave One (Movie)-Photo-c	2.00	6.00	14.00
774-Hi and Lois (3/57)	1.00	3.00	7.00
775-Sir Lancelot and Brian (TV)-Buscema-a; photo-c	5.50	16.50	38.00
776-Johnny Mack Brown-Photo-c	3.50	10.50	24.00
777-Scamp (Disney)(3/57)	1.15	3.50	8.00
778-The Little Rascals (TV)	1.70	5.00	12.00
779-Lee Hunter, Indian Fighter (3/57)	2.35	7.00	16.00
780-Captain Kangaroo (TV)-Photo-c	6.50	19.50	45.00
781-Fury (No.1)(TV)(3/57)-Photo-c	5.00	15.00	35.00
782-Duck Album (Disney)	1.70	5.00	12.00
783-Elmer Fudd	.85	2.50	6.00
784-Around the World in 80 Days (Movie) (2/57)-Photo-c	3.00	9.00	21.00
785-Circus Boy (TV) (4/57)-The Monkees' Mickey Dolenz photo-c	6.00	18.00	42.00
786-Cinderella (Disney) (3/57)-Partial reprint of No. 272	2.00	6.00	14.00
787-Little Hiawatha (Disney) (4/57)	1.50	4.50	10.00
788-Prince Valiant - by Bob Fuje	3.50	10.50	24.00
789-Silvertip-Valley Thieves (Max Brand) (4/57)-Kinstler-a	3.00	9.00	21.00
790-The Wings of Eagles (Movie) (John Wayne)-Toth-a; John Wayne photo-c; 10 & 15 cent editions exist	10.00	30.00	70.00
791-The 77th Bengal Lancers (TV)-Photo-c	3.50	10.50	24.00
792-Oswald the Rabbit (Lantz)	.85	2.50	6.00
793-Morty Meekle	1.50	4.50	10.00
794-The Count of Monte Cristo (5/ʳ7) (Movie)-Buscema-a	5.00	15.00	35.00
795-Jiminy Cricket (Disney)	2.00	6.00	14.00
796-Ludwig Bemelman's Madeleine and Genevieve	2.00	6.00	14.00
797-Gunsmoke (TV)-Photo-c	3.70	11.00	26.00
798-Buffalo Bill, Jr. (TV)-Photo-c	2.30	7.00	16.00
799-Priscilla's Pop	1.15	3.50	8.00
800-The Buccaneers (TV)-Photo-c	4.00	12.00	28.00
801-Dotty Dripple and Taffy	1.30	4.00	9.00
802-Goofy (Disney) (5/57)	2.30	7.00	16.00
803-Cheyenne (TV)-Photo-c	4.00	12.00	28.00
804-Steve Canyon-Caniff-a (1957)	3.50	10.50	24.00
805-Crusader Rabbit (TV)	5.00	15.00	35.00
806-Scamp (Disney) (6/57)	1.15	3.50	8.00
807-Savage Range (Luke Short)-Drucker-a	2.30	7.00	16.00
808-Spin and Marty (TV)(Disney)-Mickey Mouse Club-Photo-c	3.50	10.50	24.00
809-The Little People-Walt Scott	1.50	4.50	10.00

	Good	Fine	N-Mint
810-Francis the Famous Talking Mule	1.00	3.00	7.00
811-Howdy Doody (TV) (7/57)	3.50	10.50	24.00
812-The Big Land(Movie); Alan Ladd photo-c	6.00	18.00	42.00
813-Circus Boy (TV)-The Monkees' Mickey Dolenz photo-c	6.00	18.00	42.00
814-Covered Wagons, Ho! (Disney)-Donald Duck (TV)(6/57); Mickey Mouse app.	2.00	6.00	14.00
815-Dragoon Wells Massacre (Movie)-photo-c	4.00	12.00	28.00
816-Brave Eagle (TV)-photo-c	1.50	4.50	10.00
817-Little Beaver	1.30	4.00	9.00
818-Smokey the Bear (6/57)	2.00	6.00	14.00
819-Mickey Mouse in Magicland (Disney) (7/57)	2.00	6.00	14.00
820-The Oklahoman (Movie)-Photo-c	4.65	14.00	32.00
821-Wringle Wrangle (Disney)-Based on movie ''Westward Ho, the Wagons''-Marsh-a; Fess Parker photo-c	3.00	9.00	21.00
822-Paul Revere's Ride with Johnny Tremain (TV)(Disney)-Toth-a	5.70	17.00	40.00
823-Timmy	1.15	3.50	8.00
824-The Pride and the Passion (Movie)(8/57)-Frank Sinatra & Cary Grant photo-c	3.50	10.50	24.00
825-The Little Rascals (TV)	1.70	5.00	12.00
826-Spin and Marty and Annette (TV)(Disney)-Mickey Mouse Club-Annette photo-c	7.00	21.00	50.00
827-Smokey Stover (8/57)	1.70	5.00	12.00
828-Buffalo Bill, Jr. (TV)-Photo-c	2.30	7.00	16.00
829-Tales of the Pony Express (TV) (8/57)-Painted-c	2.00	6.00	14.00
830-The Hardy Boys (TV)(Disney)-Mickey Mouse Club (8/57)-Photo-c	3.50	10.50	24.00
831-No Sleep 'Til Dawn (Movie)-Carl Malden photo-c	3.00	9.00	21.00
832-Lolly and Pepper (No.1)	1.70	5.00	12.00
833-Scamp (Disney) (9/57)	1.15	3.50	8.00
834-Johnny Mack Brown-Photo-c	3.50	10.50	24.00
835-Silvertip-The Fake Rider (Max Brand)	2.30	7.00	16.00
836-Man in Flight (Disney) (TV)(9/57)	2.00	6.00	14.00
837-All-American Athlete Cotton Woods	2.00	6.00	14.00
838-Bugs Bunny's Life Story Album (9/57)	2.00	6.00	14.00
839-The Vigilantes (Movie)	3.50	10.50	24.00
840-Duck Album (Disney)	1.70	5.00	12.00
841-Elmer Fudd	.85	2.50	6.00
842-The Nature of Things (Disney-Movie)('57)-Jesse Marsh-a (TV series)	2.30	7.00	16.00
843-The First Americans (Disney)(TV)-Marsh-a	2.30	7.00	16.00
844-Gunsmoke (TV)-Photo-c	3.70	11.00	26.00
845-The Land Unknown (Movie)-Alex Toth-a	9.50	28.50	65.00
846-Gun Glory (Movie)-by Alex Toth-photo-c	8.00	24.00	56.00
847-Perri (squirrels) (Disney-Movie)-Two different covers published	1.50	4.50	10.00
848-Marauder's Moon	3.00	9.00	21.00
849-Prince Valiant-by Bob Fuje	3.50	10.50	24.00
850-Buck Jones	2.00	6.00	14.00
851-The Story of Mankind (Movie) (1/58)-Hedy Lamarr & Vincent Price photo-c	3.00	9.00	21.00
852-Chilly Willy (2/58)(Lantz)	.85	2.50	6.00
853-Pluto (Disney) (10/57)	1.50	4.50	10.00
854-The Hunchback of Notre Dame (Movie)-Photo-c	7.00	21.00	50.00
855-Broken Arrow (TV)-Photo-c	2.65	8.00	18.00
856-Buffalo Bill, Jr. (TV)-Photo-c	2.30	7.00	16.00
857-The Goofy Adventure Story (Disney) (11/57)	2.00	6.00	14.00
858-Daisy Duck's Diary (Disney) (11/57)	1.70	5.00	12.00
859-Topper and Neil (TV)(11/57)	1.30	4.00	9.00

Four Color #760, © WDC

Four Color #788, © DELL

Four Color #841, © Warner Bros.

Four Color #882, © WDC   Four Color #907, © DELL   Four Color #931, © DELL

FOUR COLOR (continued)	Good	Fine	N-Mint
860-Wyatt Earp (No.1)(TV)-Manning-a; photo-c	6.00	18.00	42.00
861-Frosty the Snowman	1.50	4.50	10.00
862-The Truth About Mother Goose (Disney-Movie) (11/57)			
	3.50	10.50	24.00
863-Francis the Famous Talking Mule	1.00	3.00	7.00
864-The Littlest Snowman	2.15	6.50	16.00
865-Andy Burnett (TV) (Disney) (12/57)-Photo-c			
	3.50	10.50	24.00
866-Mars and Beyond (Disney-Movie)	2.00	6.00	14.00
867-Santa Claus Funnies	1.70	5.00	12.00
868-The Little People (12/57)	1.50	4.50	10.00
869-Old Yeller (Disney-Movie)-Photo-c	2.65	8.00	18.00
870-Little Beaver (1/58)	1.30	4.00	9.00
871-Curly Kayoe	1.70	5.00	12.00
872-Captain Kangaroo (TV)-Photo-c	6.50	19.50	45.00
873-Grandma Duck's Farm Friends (Disney)	2.00	6.00	14.00
874-Old Ironsides (Disney-Movie with Johnny Tremain) (1/58)			
	2.30	7.00	16.00
875-Trumpets West (Luke Short) (2/58)	2.30	7.00	16.00
876-Tales of Wells Fargo (No.1) (TV) (2/58)-Photo-c			
	4.00	12.00	28.00
877-Frontier Doctor with Rex Allen (TV)-Alex Toth-a; photo-c			
	6.00	18.00	42.00
878-Peanuts (No.1)-Schulz-c only (2/58)	5.00	15.00	35.00
879-Brave Eagle (TV)(2/58)-Photo-c	1.50	4.50	10.00
880-Steve Donovan, Western Marshal-Drucker-a (TV)-Photo-c			
	2.30	7.00	16.00
881-The Captain and the Kids (2/58)	1.50	4.50	10.00
882-Zorro (Disney)-1st Disney issue by Alex Toth (TV) (2/58)-			
Photo-c	5.70	17.00	40.00
883-The Little Rascals (TV)	1.70	5.00	12.00
884-Hawkeye and the Last of the Mohicans (TV)-Photo-c (3/58)			
	3.00	9.00	21.00
885-Fury (TV) (3/58)-Photo-c	3.70	11.00	26.00
886-Bongo and Lumpjaw (Disney, 3/58)	1.30	4.00	9.00
887-The Hardy Boys (Disney)(TV)-Mickey Mouse Club (1/58)-			
Photo-c	3.50	10.50	24.00
888-Elmer Fudd (3/58)	.85	2.50	6.00
889-Clint and Mac (Disney)(TV)-Alex Toth-a (3/58)-Photo-c			
	5.70	17.00	40.00
890-Wyatt Earp (TV)-by Russ Manning; photo-c			
	3.70	11.00	26.00
891-Light in the Forest (Disney-Movie) (3/58)-Fess Parker photo-c			
	2.30	7.00	16.00
892-Maverick (No.1) (TV) (4/58)	5.70	17.00	40.00
893-Jim Bowie (TV)-Photo-c	2.65	8.00	18.00
894-Oswald the Rabbit (Lantz)	.85	2.50	6.00
895-Wagon Train (No.1)(TV)(3/58)-Photo-c	5.00	15.00	35.00
896-The Adventures of Tinker Bell (Disney)	3.00	9.00	21.00
897-Jiminy Cricket (Disney)	2.00	6.00	14.00
898-Silvertip (Max Brand)-Kinstler-a (5/58)	3.00	9.00	21.00
899-Goofy (Disney)(5/58)	2.00	6.00	14.00
900-Prince Valiant-by Bob Fuje	3.50	10.50	24.00
901-Little Hiawatha (Disney)	1.50	4.50	10.00
902-Will-Yum!	1.00	3.00	7.00
903-Dotty Dripple and Taffy	1.30	4.00	9.00
904-Lee Hunter, Indian Fighter	2.00	6.00	14.00
905-Annette (Disney,TV, 5/58)-Mickey Mouse Club-Photo-c			
	11.00	32.00	75.00
906-Francis the Famous Talking Mule	1.00	3.00	7.00
907-Sugarfoot (No.1)(TV)(5/58)Toth-a; photo-c	8.50	25.50	60.00
908-The Little People and the Giant-Walt Scott (5/58)			
	1.50	4.50	10.00
909-Smitty	1.50	4.50	10.00
910-The Vikings (Movie)-Buscema-a; Kirk Douglas photo-c			
	5.00	15.00	35.00

	Good	Fine	N-Mint
911-The Gray Ghost (TV)(Movie)-Photo-c	4.00	12.00	28.00
912-Leave It to Beaver (No.1)(TV)-Photo-c	10.00	30.00	70.00
913-The Left-Handed Gun (Movie) (7/58); Paul Newman photo-c			
	6.00	18.00	42.00
914-No Time for Sergeants (Movie)-Photo-c; Toth-a			
	6.00	18.00	42.00
915-Casey Jones (TV)-Photo-c	3.00	9.00	21.00
916-Red Ryder Ranch Comics	1.60	4.70	11.00
917-The Life of Riley (TV)-Photo-c	6.50	19.50	45.00
918-Beep Beep, the Roadrunner (No.1)(7/58)-Two different back			
covers published	3.00	9.00	21.00
919-Boots and Saddles (No.1)(TV)-Photo-c	4.00	12.00	28.00
920-Zorro (Disney-TV)(6/58)Toth-a; photo-c	5.70	17.00	40.00
921-Wyatt Earp (TV)-Manning-a; photo-c	3.70	11.00	26.00
922-Johnny Mack Brown by Russ Manning-Photo-c			
	4.00	12.00	28.00
923-Timmy	1.15	3.50	8.00
924-Colt .45 (No.1)(TV)(8/58)-Photo-c	4.65	14.00	32.00
925-Last of the Fast Guns (Movie) (8/58)-Photo-c			
	3.50	10.50	24.00
926-Peter Pan (Disney)-Reprint of No. 442	2.00	6.00	14.00
927-Top Gun (Luke Short) Buscema-a	2.30	7.00	16.00
928-Sea Hunt (No.1) (TV)-Lloyd Bridges photo-c			
	5.00	15.00	35.00
929-Brave Eagle (TV)-Photo-c	1.50	4.50	10.00
930-Maverick (TV) (7/58)-James Garner photo-c			
	5.00	15.00	35.00
931-Have Gun, Will Travel (No.1) (TV)-Photo-c	5.00	15.00	35.00
932-Smokey the Bear (His Life Story)	2.00	6.00	14.00
933-Zorro (Disney)-by Alex Toth (TV)(9/58)	5.70	17.00	40.00
934-Restless Gun (No.1)(TV)-Photo-c	5.00	15.00	35.00
935-King of the Royal Mounted	3.00	9.00	21.00
936-The Little Rascals (TV)	1.70	5.00	12.00
937-Ruff and Reddy (No.1)(TV)(Hanna-Barbera)			
	3.00	9.00	21.00
938-Elmer Fudd (9/58)	.85	2.50	6.00
939-Steve Canyon - not by Caniff	3.00	9.00	21.00
940-Lolly and Pepper (9/58)	1.30	4.00	9.00
941-Pluto (Disney) (10/58)	1.50	4.50	10.00
942-Pony Express (TV)	2.00	6.00	14.00
943-White Wilderness (Disney-Movie) (10/58	2.30	7.00	16.00
944-The 7th Voyage of Sindbad (Movie) (9/58)-Buscema-a			
	9.00	27.00	62.00
945-Maverick (TV)-James Garner photo-c	5.00	15.00	35.00
946-The Big Country (Movie)-Photo-c	3.00	9.00	21.00
947-Broken Arrow (TV)-Photo-c (11/58)	2.65	8.00	18.00
948-Daisy Duck's Diary (Disney) (11/58)	1.70	5.00	12.00
949-High Adventure (Lowell Thomas')(TV)-Photo-c			
	2.35	7.00	16.00
950-Frosty the Snowman	1.50	4.50	10.00
951-The Lennon Sisters Life Story (TV)-Toth-a, 32pgs.-Photo-c			
	8.00	24.00	56.00
952-Goofy (Disney) (11/58)	2.00	6.00	14.00
953-Francis the Famous Talking Mule	1.00	3.00	7.00
954-Man in Space-Satellites (Disney-Movie)	2.00	6.00	14.00
955-Hi and Lois (11/58)	1.00	3.00	7.00
956-Ricky Nelson (No.1)(TV)-Photo-c	10.00	30.00	70.00
957-Buffalo Bee (No.1)(TV)	3.50	10.50	24.00
958-Santa Claus Funnies	1.50	4.50	10.00
959-Christmas Stories-(Walt Scott's Little People)(1951-56 strip re-			
prints)	1.50	4.50	10.00
960-Zorro (Disney)(TV)(12/58)-Toth art	5.70	17.00	40.00
961-Jace Pearson's Tales of the Texas Rangers (TV)-Spiegle-a;			
photo-c	3.50	10.50	24.00
962-Maverick (TV) (1/59)-James Garner photo-c			
	5.00	15.00	35.00

FOUR COLOR (continued)	Good	Fine	N-Mint
963-Johnny Mack Brown-Photo-c	3.50	10.50	24.00
964-The Hardy Boys (TV)(Disney)-Mickey Mouse Club (1/59)-Photo-c			
	3.50	10.50	24.00
965-Grandma Duck's Farm Friends (Disney) (1/59)			
	2.00	6.00	14.00
966-Tonka (starring Sal Mineo; Disney-Movie)-Photo-c			
	3.00	9.00	21.00
967-Chilly Willy (2/59)(Lantz)	.85	2.50	6.00
968-Tales of Wells Fargo (TV)-Photo-c	3.50	10.50	24.00
969-Peanuts (2/59)	4.00	12.00	28.00
970-Lawman (No.1)(TV)-Photo-c	5.70	17.00	40.00
971-Wagon Train (TV)-Photo-c	3.50	10.50	24.00
972-Tom Thumb (Movie)-George Pal (1/59)	6.00	18.00	42.00
973-Sleeping Beauty and the Prince (Disney) (5/59)			
	4.00	12.00	28.00
974-The Little Rascals (TV)(3/59)	1.70	5.00	12.00
975-Fury (TV)-Photo-c	3.70	11.00	26.00
976-Zorro (Disney)(TV)-Toth-a; photo-c	5.70	17.00	40.00
977-Elmer Fudd (3/59)	.85	2.50	6.00
978-Lolly and Pepper	1.30	4.00	9.00
979-Oswald the Rabbit (Lantz)	.85	2.50	6.00
980-Maverick (TV) (4-6/59)-James Garner & Jack Kelly photo-c			
	5.00	15.00	35.00
981-Ruff and Reddy (TV)(Hanna-Barbera)	2.00	6.00	14.00
982-The New Adventures of Tinker Bell (TV-Disney)			
	3.00	9.00	21.00
983-Have Gun, Will Travel (TV) (4-6/59)-Photo-c			
	3.70	11.00	26.00
984-Sleeping Beauty's Fairy Godmothers (Disney)			
	4.00	12.00	28.00
985-Shaggy Dog (Disney-Movie)-Photo-c	2.30	7.00	16.00
986-Restless Gun (TV)-Photo-c	4.00	12.00	28.00
987-Goofy (Disney) (7/59)	2.00	6.00	14.00
988-Little Hiawatha (Disney)	1.50	4.50	10.00
989-Jiminy Cricket (Disney) (5-7/59)	2.00	6.00	14.00
990-Huckleberry Hound (No.1)(TV)(Hanna-Barbera)			
	2.65	8.00	18.00
991-Francis the Famous Talking Mule	1.00	3.00	7.00
992-Sugarfoot (TV)-Toth-a; photo-c	8.50	25.50	60.00
993-Jim Bowie (TV)-Photo-c	2.65	8.00	18.00
994-Sea Hunt (TV)-Lloyd Bridges photo-c	4.00	12.00	28.00
995-Donald Duck Album (Disney) (5-7/59)	2.00	6.00	14.00
996-Nevada (Zane Grey)	2.30	7.00	16.00
997-Walt Disney Presents-Tales of Texas John Slaughter (TV-Disney)-			
Photo-c	3.00	9.00	21.00
998-Ricky Nelson (TV)-Photo-c	10.00	30.00	70.00
999-Leave It to Beaver (TV)-Photo-c	8.50	25.50	60.00
1000-The Gray Ghost (Movie) (6-8/59)-Photo-c			
	4.00	12.00	28.00
1001-Lowell Thomas' High Adventure (TV) (8-10/59)-Photo-c			
	2.35	7.00	16.00
1002-Buffalo Bee (TV)	2.65	8.00	18.00
1003-Zorro (TV) (Disney)-Photo-c	4.65	14.00	32.00
1004-Colt .45 (TV) (6-8/59)-Photo-c	3.50	10.50	24.00
1005-Maverick (TV)-James Garner photo-c	5.00	15.00	35.00
1006-Hercules (Movie)-Buscema-a	6.50	19.50	45.00
1007-John Paul Jones (Movie)-Robert Stack photo-c			
	2.30	7.00	16.00
1008-Beep Beep, the Road Runner (7-9/59)	1.70	5.00	12.00
1009-The Rifleman (No.1) (TV)-Photo-c	7.00	21.00	50.00
1010-Grandma Duck's Farm Friends (Disney)-by Carl Barks			
	6.00	18.00	42.00
1011-Buckskin (No.1)(TV)-Photo-c	4.00	12.00	28.00
1012-Last Train from Gun Hill (Movie) (7/59)-Photo-c			
	4.00	12.00	28.00
1013-Bat Masterson (No.1) (TV) (8/59)-Gene Barry photo-c			

	Good	Fine	N-Mint
	4.30	13.00	30.00
1014-The Lennon Sisters (TV)-Toth-a; photo-c	7.00	21.00	50.00
1015-Peanuts-Schulz-c	4.00	12.00	28.00
1016-Smokey the Bear Nature Stories	1.30	4.50	10.00
1017-Chilly Willy (Lantz)	.85	2.50	6.00
1018-Rio Bravo (Movie)(6/59)-John Wayne; Toth-a; John Wayne, Dean Martin & Ricky Nelson photo-c	13.00	40.00	90.00
1019-Wagon Train (TV)-Photo-c	3.50	10.50	24.00
1020-Jungle Jim-McWilliams-a	1.70	5.00	12.00
1021-Jace Pearson's Tales of the Texas Rangers (TV)-Photo-c			
	3.00	9.00	21.00
1022-Timmy	1.15	3.50	8.00
1023-Tales of Wells Fargo (TV)-Photo-c	3.50	10.50	24.00
1024-Darby O'Gill and the Little People (Disney-Movie)-Toth-a; Photo-c	6.00	18.00	42.00
1025-Vacation in Disneyland (8-10/59)-Carl Barks-a (Disney)			
	6.00	18.00	42.00
1026-Spin and Marty (TV)(Disney)-Mickey Mouse Club (9-11/59)-Photo-c	3.00	9.00	21.00
1027-The Texan (TV)-Photo-c	3.50	10.50	24.00
1028-Rawhide (No.1)(TV)-Clint Eastwood photo-c			
	10.00	30.00	70.00
1029-Boots and Saddles (9/59, TV)-Photo-c	3.00	9.00	21.00
1030-Spanky and Alfalfa, the Little Rascals (TV)			
	1.50	4.50	10.00
1031-Fury (TV)-Photo-c	3.70	11.00	26.00
1032-Elmer Fudd	.85	2.50	6.00
1033-Steve Canyon-not by Caniff; photo-c	3.00	9.00	21.00
1034-Nancy and Sluggo Summer Camp (9-11/59)			
	1.70	5.00	12.00
1035-Lawman (TV)-Photo-c	4.00	12.00	28.00
1036-The Big Circus (Movie)-Photo-c	2.35	7.00	16.00
1037-Zorro (Disney)(TV)-Tufts-a; Annette Funicello photo-c			
	7.00	21.00	50.00
1038-Ruff and Reddy (TV)(Hanna-Barbera)('59)			
	2.00	6.00	14.00
1039-Pluto (Disney) (11-1/60)	1.50	4.50	10.00
1040-Quick Draw McGraw (No.1)(TV)(Hanna-Barbera)(12-2/60)			
	3.70	11.00	26.00
1041-Sea Hunt (TV)-Toth-a; Lloyd Bridges photo-c			
	5.70	17.00	40.00
1042-The Three Chipmunks (Alvin, Simon & Theodore) (No.1)(TV) (10-12/59)	.85	2.50	6.00
1043-The Three Stooges (No.1)-Photo-c	6.00	18.00	42.00
1044-Have Gun, Will Travel (TV)-Photo-c	3.70	11.00	26.00
1045-Restless Gun (TV)-Photo-c	4.00	12.00	28.00
1046-Beep Beep, the Road Runner (11-1/60)	1.70	5.00	12.00
1047-Gyro Gearloose (No.1)(Disney)-Barks c/a	6.00	18.00	42.00
1048-The Horse Soldiers (Movie) (John Wayne)-Sekowsky-a			
	11.50	34.00	80.00
1049-Don't Give Up the Ship (Movie) (8/59)-Jerry Lewis photo-c			
	3.50	10.50	24.00
1050-Huckleberry Hound (TV)(Hanna-Barbera)(10-12/59)			
	2.00	6.00	14.00
1051-Donald in Mathmagic Land (Disney-Movie)			
	3.50	10.50	24.00
1052-Ben-Hur (Movie) (11/59)-Manning-a	5.00	15.00	35.00
1053-Goofy (Disney) (11-1/60)	2.00	6.00	14.00
1054-Huckleberry Hound Winter Fun TV(Hanna-Barbera)(12/59)			
	2.00	6.00	14.00
1055-Daisy Duck's Diary (Disney)-by Carl Barks (11-1/60)			
	5.00	15.00	35.00
1056-Yellowstone Kelly (Movie)-Clint Walker photo-c			
	2.30	7.00	16.00
1057-Mickey Mouse Album (Disney)	1.70	5.00	12.00
1058-Colt .45 (TV)-Photo-c	3.50	10.50	24.00

Four Color #969, © C. Schulz

Four Color #1014, © DELL

Four Color #1047, © WDC

Four Color #1069, © Warner Bros. Four Color #1103, © Gomalco Prod. Four Color #1152, © Jay Ward

FOUR COLOR (continued)	Good	Fine	N-Mint
1059-Sugarfoot (TV)-Photo-c	5.00	15.00	35.00
1060-Journey to the Center of the Earth (Movie)-Photo-c			
	7.00	21.00	50.00
1061-Buffalo Bee (TV)	2.65	8.00	18.00
1062-Christmas Stories-(Walt Scott's Little People strip-r)			
	1.50	4.50	10.00
1063-Santa Claus Funnies	1.50	4.50	10.00
1064-Bugs Bunny's Merry Christmas (12/59)	1.70	5.00	12.00
1065-Frosty the Snowman	1.50	4.50	10.00
1066-77 Sunset Strip (No.1)(TV)-Toth-a (1-3/60)-Photo-c			
	5.70	17.00	40.00
1067-Yogi Bear (No.1)(TV)(Hanna-Barbera)	3.50	10.50	24.00
1068-Francis the Famous Talking Mule	1.00	3.00	7.00
1069-The FBI Story (Movie)-Toth-a; James Stewart photo-c			
	6.50	19.50	45.00
1070-Solomon and Sheba (Movie)-Sekowsky-a; photo-c			
	5.00	15.00	35.00
1071-The Real McCoys (No.1)(TV)-Toth-a; photo-c			
	6.00	18.00	42.00
1072-Blythe (Marge's)	2.00	6.00	14.00
1073-Grandma Duck's Farm Friends-Barks c/a (Disney)			
	6.00	18.00	42.00
1074-Chilly Willy (Lantz)	.85	2.50	6.00
1075-Tales of Wells Fargo (TV)-Photo-c	3.50	10.50	24.00
1076-The Rebel (No.1)(TV)-Sekowsky-a; photo-c			
	6.00	18.00	42.00
1077-The Deputy (No.1)(TV)-Buscema-a; Henry Fonda photo-c			
	6.00	18.00	42.00
1078-The Three Stooges (2-4/60)-Photo-c	4.30	13.00	30.00
1079-The Little Rascals (TV)(Spanky & Alfalfa)	1.50	4.50	10.00
1080-Fury (TV) (2-4/60)-Photo-c	3.70	11.00	26.00
1081-Elmer Fudd	.85	2.50	6.00
1082-Spin and Marty (Disney)(TV)-Photo-c	3.00	9.00	21.00
1083-Men into Space (TV)-Anderson-a; photo-c			
	2.65	8.00	18.00
1084-Speedy Gonzales	1.30	4.00	9.00
1085-The Time Machine (H.G. Wells) (Movie) (3/60)-Alex Toth-a			
	7.00	21.00	50.00
1086-Lolly and Pepper	1.30	4.00	9.00
1087-Peter Gunn (TV)-Photo-c	4.00	12.00	28.00
1088-A Dog of Flanders (Movie)-Photo-c	2.00	6.00	14.00
1089-Restless Gun (TV)-Photo-c	4.00	12.00	28.00
1090-Francis the Famous Talking Mule	1.00	3.00	7.00
1091-Jacky's Diary (4-6/60)	2.30	7.00	16.00
1092-Toby Tyler (Disney-Movie)-Photo-c	2.00	6.00	14.00
1093-MacKenzie's Raiders (Movie)-Photo-c	3.50	10.50	24.00
1094-Goofy (Disney)	2.00	6.00	14.00
1095-Gyro Gearloose (Disney)-Barks-c/a	5.00	15.00	35.00
1096-The Texan (TV)-Rory Calhoun photo-c	3.50	10.50	24.00
1097-Rawhide (TV)-Manning-a; Clint Eastwood photo-c			
	8.00	24.00	56.00
1098-Sugarfoot (TV)-Photo-c	5.00	15.00	35.00
1099-Donald Duck Album (Disney) (5-7/60) - Barks-c			
	2.30	7.00	16.00
1100-Annette's Life Story (Disney-Movie)(5/60)-Photo-c			
	11.50	34.00	80.00
1101-Robert Louis Stevenson's Kidnapped (Disney-Movie) (5/60); photo-c			
	3.00	9.00	21.00
1102-Wanted: Dead or Alive (No.1)(TV) (5-7/60); Steve McQueen			
	6.00	18.00	42.00
1103-Leave It to Beaver (TV)-Photo-c	8.50	25.50	60.00
1104-Yogi Bear Goes to College (TV)(Hanna-Barbera)(6-8/60)			
	2.65	8.00	18.00
1105-Gale Storm (Oh! Susanna) (TV)-Toth-a; photo-c			
	7.00	21.00	50.00
1106-77 Sunset Strip (TV)(6-8/60)-Toth-a; photo-c			

	Good	Fine	N-Mint
	5.00	15.00	35.00
1107-Buckskin (TV)-Photo-c	3.50	10.50	24.00
1108-The Troubleshooters (TV)-Keenan Wynn photo-c			
	3.00	9.00	21.00
1109-This Is Your Life, Donald Duck (Disney)(TV)(8-10/60)-Gyro flash-back to WDC&S 141. Origin Donald Duck (1st told)			
	7.00	21.00	50.00
1110-Bonanza (No.1) (TV) (6-8/60)-Photo-c	6.00	18.00	42.00
1111-Shotgun Slade (TV)	3.50	10.50	24.00
1112-Pixie and Dixie and Mr. Jinks (No.1)(TV)(Hanna-Barbera) (7-9/60)			
	3.00	9.00	21.00
1113-Tales of Wells Fargo (TV)-Photo-c	3.50	10.50	24.00
1114-Huckleberry Finn (Movie) (7/60)-Photo-c	2.30	7.00	16.00
1115-Ricky Nelson (TV)-Manning-a; photo-c	10.00	30.00	70.00
1116-Boots and Saddles (TV)(8/60)-Photo-c	3.00	9.00	21.00
1117-Boy and the Pirates (Movie)-Photo-c	3.50	10.50	24.00
1118-The Sword and the Dragon (Movie) (6/60)-Photo-c			
	4.00	12.00	28.00
1119-Smokey the Bear Nature Stories	1.50	4.50	10.00
1120-Dinosaurus (Movie)-Painted-c	2.65	8.00	18.00
1121-Hercules Unchained (Movie)(8/60)-Crandall/Evans-a			
	5.00	15.00	35.00
1122-Chilly Willy (Lantz)	.85	2.50	6.00
1123-Tombstone Territory (TV)-Photo-c	4.00	12.00	28.00
1124-Whirlybirds (No.1) (TV)-Photo-c	4.00	12.00	28.00
1125-Laramie (No.1)(TV)-Photo-c	5.00	15.00	35.00
1126-Sundance (TV) (8-10/60)-Earl Holliman photo-c			
	5.00	15.00	35.00
1127-The Three Stooges-Photo-c	4.30	13.00	30.00
1128-Rocky and His Friends (No.1)(TV) (Jay Ward) (8-10/60)			
	7.00	21.00	50.00
1129-Pollyanna (Disney-Movie)-Photo-c	6.00	18.00	42.00
1130-The Deputy (TV)-Buscema-a; Henry Fonda photo-c			
	5.00	15.00	35.00
1131-Elmer Fudd (9-11/60)	.85	2.50	6.00
1132-Space Mouse (Lantz)(8-10/60)	1.15	3.50	8.00
1133-Fury (TV)-Photo-c	3.70	11.00	26.00
1134-Real McCoys (TV)-Toth-a; photo-c	6.00	18.00	42.00
1135-M.G.M.'s Mouse Musketeers	.85	2.50	6.00
1136-Jungle Cat (Disney-Movie) (9-11/60)-Photo-c			
	3.00	9.00	21.00
1137-The Little Rascals (TV)	1.50	4.50	10.00
1138-The Rebel (TV)-Photo-c	5.00	15.00	35.00
1139-Spartacus (Movie) (11/60)-Buscema-a; photo-c			
	6.00	18.00	42.00
1140-Donald Duck Album (Disney)	2.30	7.00	16.00
1141-Huckleberry Hound for President (TV)(Hanna-Barbera)10/60)			
	2.00	6.00	14.00
1142-Johnny Ringo (TV)-Photo-c	4.00	12.00	28.00
1143-Pluto (Disney) (11-1/61)	1.50	4.50	10.00
1144-The Story of Ruth (Movie)-Photo-c	6.00	18.00	42.00
1145-The Lost World (Movie)-Gil Kane-a; photo-c			
	6.00	18.00	42.00
1146-Restless Gun (TV)-Photo-c; Wildey-a	4.00	12.00	28.00
1147-Sugarfoot (TV)-Photo-c	5.00	15.00	35.00
1148-I Aim at the Stars-the Wernher Von Braun Story (Movie) (11-1/61)-Photo-c	2.65	8.00	18.00
1149-Goofy (Disney) (11-1/61)	2.00	6.00	14.00
1150-Daisy Duck's Diary (Disney) (12-1/61) by Carl Barks			
	5.00	15.00	35.00
1151-Mickey Mouse Album (Disney) (11-1/61)	1.70	5.00	12.00
1152-Rocky and His Friends (Jay Ward) (TV) (12-2/61)			
	6.00	18.00	42.00
1153-Frosty the Snowman	1.30	4.00	9.00
1154-Santa Claus Funnies	1.50	4.50	10.00
1155-North to Alaska (Movie) - J. Wayne-Photo-c			

FOUR COLOR (continued)

	Good	Fine	N-Mint
	10.00	30.00	70.00
1156-Walt Disney Swiss Family Robinson (Movie) (12/60)-Photo-c			
	3.00	9.00	21.00
1157-Master of the World (Movie) (7/61)	3.00	9.00	21.00
1158-Three Worlds of Gulliver (2 issues with different covers)			
(Movie)-Photo-c	3.00	9.00	21.00
1159-77 Sunset Strip (TV)-Toth-a; photo-c	5.00	15.00	35.00
1160-Rawhide (TV)-Clint Eastwood photo-c	8.00	24.00	56.00
1161-Grandma Duck's Farm Friends (Disney) by Carl Barks (2-4/61)			
	6.00	18.00	42.00
1162-Yogi Bear Joins the Marines (TV)(Hanna-Barbera)(5-7/61)			
	2.65	8.00	18.00
1163-Daniel Boone (3-5/61); Marsh-a	2.65	8.00	18.00
1164-Wanted: Dead or Alive (TV); Steve McQueen photo-c			
	5.00	15.00	35.00
1165-Ellery Queen (No.1)(3-5/61)	5.00	15.00	35.00
1166-Rocky and His Friends (Jay Ward) (TV)	6.00	18.00	42.00
1167-Tales of Wells Fargo (TV)-Photo-c	3.50	10.50	24.00
1168-The Detectives (TV)-Robert Taylor photo-c			
	4.00	12.00	28.00
1169-New Adventures of Sherlock Holmes	10.00	30.00	70.00
1170-The Three Stooges-Photo-c	4.30	13.00	30.00
1171-Elmer Fudd	.85	2.50	6.00
1172-Fury (TV)-Photo-c	3.70	11.00	26.00
1173-The Twilight Zone (No.1)-Crandall/Evans-c/a (TV) (5/61)			
	5.00	15.00	35.00
1174-The Little Rascals (TV)	1.50	4.50	10.00
1175-M.G.M.'s Mouse Musketeers (3-5/61)	.85	2.50	6.00
1176-Dondi (Movie)-Origin; photo-c	1.70	5.00	12.00
1177-Chilly Willy (Lantz)(4-6/61)	.85	2.50	6.00
1178-Ten Who Dared (Disney-Movie) (12/60)	2.30	7.00	16.00
1179-The Swamp Fox (TV)(Disney)-Leslie Nielson photo-c			
	3.00	9.00	21.00
1180-The Danny Thomas Show (TV)-Toth-a; photo-c			
	8.00	24.00	56.00
1181-Texas John Slaughter (TV)(Disney)(4-6/61)-Photo-c			
	2.00	6.00	14.00
1182-Donald Duck Album (Disney) (5-7/61)	2.00	6.00	14.00
1183-101 Dalmatians (Disney-Movie) (3/61)	2.65	8.00	18.00
1184-Gyro Gearloose; Barks c/a (Disney) (5-7/61) Two variations			
exist	5.00	15.00	35.00
1185-Sweetie Pie	1.50	4.50	10.00
1186-Yak Yak (No.1) by Jack Davis (2 versions - one minus 3-pg.			
Davis-c/a)	4.00	12.00	28.00
1187-The Three Stooges (6-8/61)-Photo-c	4.30	13.00	30.00
1188-Atlantis, the Lost Continent (Movie) (5/61)-Photo-c			
	6.00	18.00	42.00
1189-Greyfriars Bobby (Disney-Movie, 11/61)-Photo-c			
	2.65	8.00	18.00
1190-Donald and the Wheel (Disney-Movie) (11/61); Barks-c			
	3.00	9.00	21.00
1191-Leave It to Beaver (TV)-Photo-c	8.50	25.50	60.00
1192-Ricky Nelson (TV)-Manning-a; photo-c	10.00	30.00	70.00
1193-The Real McCoys (TV)(6-8/61)-Photo-c	5.00	15.00	35.00
1194-Pepe (Movie) (4/61)-Photo-c	1.70	5.00	12.00
1195-National Velvet (No.1)(TV)-Photo-c	2.30	7.00	16.00
1196-Pixie and Dixie and Mr. Jinks (TV)(Hanna-Barbera)(7-9/61)			
	2.30	7.00	16.00
1197-The Aquanauts (TV)(5-7/61)-Photo-c	3.00	9.00	21.00
1198-Donald in Mathmagic Land - reprint of No. 1051 (Disney-Movie)			
	3.50	10.50	24.00
1199-The Absent-Minded Professor (Disney-Movie) (4/61)-Photo-c			
	3.00	9.00	21.00
1200-Hennessey (TV) (8-10/61)-Gil Kane-a; photo-c			
	3.50	10.50	24.00
1201-Goofy (Disney) (8-10/61)	2.00	6.00	14.00

	Good	Fine	N-Mint
1202-Rawhide (TV)-Clint Eastwood photo-c	8.00	24.00	56.00
1203-Pinocchio (Disney) (3/62)	2.00	6.00	14.00
1204-Scamp (Disney)	.85	2.50	6.00
1205-David and Goliath (Movie) (7/61)-Photo-c	3.00	9.00	21.00
1206-Lolly and Pepper (9-11/61)	1.30	4.00	9.00
1207-The Rebel (TV)-Sekowsky-a; photo-c	5.00	15.00	35.00
1208-Rocky and His Friends (Jay Ward) (TV)	5.70	17.00	40.00
1209-Sugarfoot (TV)-Photo-c	5.00	15.00	35.00
1210-The Parent Trap (Disney-Movie)(8/61)(Haley Mills photo-c)			
	6.50	19.50	45.00
1211-77 Sunset Strip (TV)-Manning-a; photo-c	4.00	12.00	28.00
1212-Chilly Willy (Lantz)(7-9/61)	.85	2.50	6.00
1213-Mysterious Island (Movie)-Photo-c	4.00	12.00	28.00
1214-Smokey the Bear	1.50	4.50	10.00
1215-Tales of Wells Fargo (TV) (10-12/61)-Photo-c			
	3.50	10.50	24.00
1216-Whirlybirds (TV)-Photo-c	3.50	10.50	24.00
1218-Fury (TV)-Photo-c	3.70	11.00	26.00
1219-The Detectives (TV)-Robert Taylor & Adam West photo-c			
	3.00	9.00	21.00
1220-Gunslinger (TV)-Photo-c	3.50	10.50	24.00
1221-Bonanza (TV) (9-11/61)-Photo-c	5.00	15.00	35.00
1222-Elmer Fudd (9-11/61)	.85	2.50	6.00
1223-Laramie (TV)-Gil Kane-a; photo-c	4.00	12.00	28.00
1224-The Little Rascals (TV)(10-12/61)	1.50	4.50	10.00
1225-The Deputy (TV)-Henry Fonda photo-c	5.00	15.00	35.00
1226-Nikki, Wild Dog of the North (Disney-Movie) (9/61)-Photo-c			
	2.00	6.00	14.00
1227-Morgan the Pirate (Movie)-Photo-c	5.50	16.50	38.00
1229-Thief of Baghdad (Movie)-Evans-a; photo-c			
	6.50	19.50	45.00
1230-Voyage to the Bottom of the Sea (#1)(Movie)-Photo insert on-c			
	3.50	10.50	24.00
1231-Danger Man (TV)(9-11/61); Patrick McGoohan photo-c			
	3.50	10.50	24.00
1232-On the Double (Movie)	2.00	6.00	14.00
1233-Tammy Tell Me True (Movie) (1961)	3.50	10.50	24.00
1234-The Phantom Planet (Movie) (1961)	3.00	9.00	21.00
1235-Mister Magoo (12-2/62)	4.00	12.00	28.00
1235-Mister Magoo (3-5/65) 2nd printing - reprints of '61 issue			
	2.35	7.00	16.00
1236-King of Kings (Movie)-Photo-c	4.00	12.00	28.00
1237-The Untouchables (No.1)(TV)-not by Toth; photo-c			
	4.00	12.00	28.00
1238-Deputy Dawg (TV)	4.00	12.00	28.00
1239-Donald Duck Album (Disney) (10-12/61)-Barks-c			
	2.30	7.00	16.00
1240-The Detectives (TV)-Tufts-a; Robert Taylor photo-c			
	3.00	9.00	21.00
1241-Sweetie Pie	1.50	4.50	10.00
1242-King Leonardo and His Short Subjects (No.1)(TV)(11-1/62)			
	4.00	12.00	28.00
1243-Ellery Queen	4.00	12.00	28.00
1244-Space Mouse (Lantz)(11-1/62)	1.15	3.50	8.00
1245-New Adventures of Sherlock Holmes	10.00	30.00	70.00
1246-Mickey Mouse Album (Disney)	1.70	5.00	12.00
1247-Daisy Duck's Diary (Disney) (12-2/62)	1.70	5.00	12.00
1248-Pluto (Disney)	1.50	4.50	10.00
1249-The Danny Thomas Show (TV)-Manning-a; photo-c			
	7.00	21.00	50.00
1250-The Four Horsemen of the Apocalypse (Movie)-Photo-c			
	3.50	10.50	24.00
1251-Everything's Ducky (Movie) (1961)	2.30	7.00	16.00
1252-The Andy Griffith Show (TV)-Photo-c; 1st show aired 10/3/60			
	7.00	21.00	50.00
1253-Space Man (No.1) (1-3/62)	3.00	9.00	21.00

Four Color #1170, © Norman Maurer Prod.

Four Color #1193, © Brennan-Westgate

Four Color #1230, © Cambridge Prod./20th Century-Fox

Four Color #1270, © Jay Ward   Four Favorites #9, © ACE   Four Most #1, © NOVP

FOUR COLOR (continued)

	Good	Fine	N-Mint
1254-"Diver Dan" (TV) (2-4/62)-Photo-c	2.65	8.00	18.00
1255-The Wonders of Aladdin (Movie) (1961)	3.00	9.00	21.00
1256-Kona, Monarch of Monster Isle (No.1)(2-4/62)-Glanzman-a	2.65	8.00	18.00
1257-Car 54, Where Are You? (No.1) (TV) (3-5/62)-Photo-c	2.65	8.00	18.00
1258-The Frogmen (No.1)-Evans-a	3.00	9.00	21.00
1259-El Cid (Movie) (1961)-Photo-c	3.00	9.00	21.00
1260-The Horsemasters (TV, Movie - Disney) (12-2/62)-Annette Funicello photo-c	4.00	12.00	28.00
1261-Rawhide (TV)-Clint Eastwood photo-c	8.00	24.00	56.00
1262-The Rebel (TV)-Photo-c	5.00	15.00	35.00
1263-77 Sunset Strip (TV) (12-2/62)-Manning-a; photo-c	4.00	12.00	28.00
1264-Pixie and Dixie and Mr. Jinks (TV)(Hanna-Barbera)	2.30	7.00	16.00
1265-The Real McCoys (TV)-Photo-c	5.00	15.00	35.00
1266-M.G.M.'s Spike and Tyke (12-2/62)	.85	2.50	6.00
1267-Gyro Gearloose; Barks c/a, 4 pgs. (Disney) (12-2/62)	3.70	11.00	26.00
1268-Oswald the Rabbit (Lantz)	.85	2.50	6.00
1269-Rawhide (TV)-Clint Eastwood photo-c	8.00	24.00	56.00
1270-Bullwinkle and Rocky (No.1)(Jay Ward)(TV)(3-5/62)	5.00	15.00	35.00
1271-Yogi Bear Birthday Party (TV)(Hanna-Barbera)(11/61)	2.00	6.00	14.00
1272-Frosty the Snowman	1.30	4.00	9.00
1273-Hans Brinker (Disney-Movie)-Photo-c	2.65	8.00	18.00
1274-Santa Claus Funnies	1.50	4.50	10.00
1275-Rocky and His Friends (Jay Ward) (TV)	5.70	17.00	40.00
1276-Dondi	1.50	4.50	10.00
1278-King Leonardo and His Short Subjects (TV)	4.00	12.00	28.00
1279-Grandma Duck's Farm Friends (Disney)	2.00	6.00	14.00
1280-Hennessey (TV)-Photo-c	3.00	9.00	21.00
1281-Chilly Willy (Lantz)(4-6/62)	.85	2.50	6.00
1282-Babes in Toyland (Disney-Movie) (1/62); Annette Funicello photo-c	5.00	15.00	35.00
1283-Bonanza (TV) (2-4/62)-Photo-c	5.00	15.00	35.00
1284-Laramie (TV)-Heath-a; photo-c	4.00	12.00	28.00
1285-Leave It to Beaver (TV)-Photo-c	8.50	25.50	60.00
1286-The Untouchables (TV)-Photo-c	4.00	12.00	28.00
1287-Man from Wells Fargo (TV)-Photo-c	3.50	10.50	24.00
1288-The Twilight Zone (TV) (4/62)-Crandall/Evans c/a	4.00	12.00	28.00
1289-Ellery Queen	4.00	12.00	28.00
1290-M.G.M.'s Mouse Musketeers	.85	2.50	6.00
1291-77 Sunset Strip (TV)-Manning-a; photo-c	4.00	12.00	28.00
1293-Elmer Fudd (3-5/62)	.85	2.50	6.00
1294-Ripcord (TV)	3.00	9.00	21.00
1295-Mister Ed, the Talking Horse (No.1)(TV)(3-5/62)-Photo-c	4.00	12.00	28.00
1296-Fury (TV) (3-5/62)-Photo-c	3.70	11.00	26.00
1297-Spanky, Alfalfa and the Little Rascals (TV)	1.50	4.50	10.00
1298-The Hathaways (TV)-Photo-c	2.30	7.00	16.00
1299-Deputy Dawg (TV)	4.00	12.00	28.00
1300-The Comancheros (Movie) (1961)-John Wayne	11.00	32.00	75.00
1301-Adventures in Paradise (TV) (2-4/62)	2.00	6.00	14.00
1302-Johnny Jason, Teen Reporter (2-4/62)	1.15	3.50	8.00
1303-Lad: A Dog (Movie)-Photo-c	2.65	8.00	18.00
1304-Nellie the Nurse (3-5/62)-Stanley-a	5.00	15.00	35.00
1305-Mister Magoo (3-5/62)	4.00	12.00	28.00
1306-Target: the Corrupters (TV) (3-5/62)	2.30	7.00	16.00
1307-Margie (TV) (3-5/62)	2.30	7.00	16.00

	Good	Fine	N-Mint
1308-Tales of the Wizard of Oz (TV) (3-5/62)	6.00	18.00	42.00
1309-87th Precinct (TV) (4-6/62)-Krigstein-a; photo-c	5.00	15.00	35.00
1310-Huck and Yogi Winter Sports (TV)(Hanna-Barbera)(3/62)	2.00	6.00	14.00
1311-Rocky and His Friends (Jay Ward) (TV)	5.70	17.00	40.00
1312-National Velvet (TV)-Photo-c	2.00	6.00	14.00
1313-Moon Pilot (Disney-Movie)-Photo-c	2.30	7.00	16.00
1328-The Underwater City (Movie)-Evans-a (1961)-Photo-c	3.50	10.50	24.00
1330-Brain Boy (No.1)-Gil Kane-a	3.50	10.50	24.00
1332-Bachelor Father (TV)	4.00	12.00	28.00
1333-Short Ribs (4-6/62)	2.30	7.00	16.00
1335-Aggie Mack (4-6/62)	1.70	5.00	12.00
1336-On Stage - not by Leonard Starr	2.30	7.00	16.00
1337-Dr. Kildare (No.1) (TV)-Photo-c	3.00	9.00	21.00
1341-The Andy Griffith Show (TV) (4-6/62)-Photo-c	7.00	21.00	50.00
1348-Yak Yak (No.2)-Jack Davis c/a	3.50	10.50	24.00
1349-Yogi Bear Visits the U.N. (TV)(Hanna-Barbera)(1/62)-Photo-c	2.00	6.00	14.00
1350-Comanche (Disney-Movie)(1962)-Reprints 4-Color 966 (title change from "Tonka" to "Comanche")(4-6/62)- Sal Mineo photo-c	2.00	6.00	14.00
1354-Calvin & the Colonel (4-6/62)	3.50	10.50	24.00

NOTE: *Missing numbers probably do not exist.*

FOUR FAVORITES (Crime Must Pay the Penalty No. 33 on)
Sept, 1941 - No. 32, Dec, 1947
Ace Magazines

	Good	Fine	N-Mint
1-Vulcan, Lash Lightning, Magno the Magnetic Man & The Raven begin; Flag-c	40.00	120.00	280.00
2-The Black Ace only app.	20.00	60.00	140.00
3-Last Vulcan	17.00	51.00	120.00
4,5: 4-The Raven & Vulcan end; Unknown Soldier begins, ends #28. 5-Captain Courageous begins, ends #28; not in #6	16.00	48.00	110.00
6-8: 6-The Flag app.; Mr. Risk begins	13.00	40.00	90.00
9,11-Kurtzman-a; 11-L.B. Cole-a	17.00	51.00	120.00
10-Classic Kurtzman c/a	19.00	57.00	132.00
12-L.B. Cole-a	10.00	30.00	70.00
13-20: 18,20-Palais c/a	8.00	24.00	56.00
21-No Unknown Soldier; The Unknown app.	6.00	18.00	42.00
22-Captain Courageous drops costume	6.00	18.00	42.00
23-26: 23-Unknown Soldier drops costume. 26-Last Magno	6.00	18.00	42.00
27-32: 29-Hap Hazard app.	5.00	15.00	35.00

NOTE: *Jim Mooney c-3. Palais c-18, 20, 24, 25.*

FOUR HORSEMEN, THE (See The Crusaders)

FOUR HORSEMEN OF THE APOCALYPSE, THE (See 4-Color No. 1250)

FOUR MOST (. . . Boys No. 32-41)
Winter, 1941-42 - V8No.5(No. 36), 9-10/49; No. 37, 11-12/49 -
No. 41, 6-7/50
Novelty Publications/Star Publications No. 37-on

	Good	Fine	N-Mint
V1#1-The Target by Sid Greene, The Cadet & Dick Cole begin w/origins retold; produced by Funnies Inc.	40.00	120.00	280.00
2-Last Target	20.00	60.00	140.00
3-Flag-c	17.00	51.00	120.00
4-1pg. Dr. Seuss(signed)	13.00	40.00	90.00
V2#1-4, V3#1-4	3.00	9.00	21.00
V4#1-4	2.30	7.00	16.00
V5#1-The Target & Targeteers app.	2.00	6.00	14.00
2-5	2.00	6.00	14.00
V6#1-White Rider & Super Horse begins	2.00	6.00	14.00

167

FOUR MOST (continued)	Good	Fine	N-Mint
2-4,6	2.00	6.00	14.00
5-L. B. Cole-c	3.50	10.50	24.00
V7#1,3,5, V8#1	2.00	6.00	14.00
2,4,6-L. B. Cole-c. 6-Last Dick Cole	3.50	10.50	24.00
V8#2,3,5-L. B. Cole c/a	4.60	14.00	32.00
4-L. B. Cole-a	2.65	8.00	18.00
37-41: 38,39-L.B. Cole-c. 38-J. Weismuller life story			
	2.65	8.00	18.00
Accepted Reprint 38-40 (nd); L.B. Cole-c	1.70	5.00	12.00

FOUR-STAR BATTLE TALES
Feb-Mar, 1973 - No. 5, Nov-Dec, 1973
National Periodical Publications

	Good	Fine	N-Mint
1-All reprints		.30	.60
2-5: 5-Krigstein-a(r)		.25	.50

NOTE: Drucker a-1,3-5r. Heath a-2r, 5r; c-1. Kubert a-4r; c-2.

FOUR STAR SPECTACULAR
Mar-Apr, 1976 - No. 6, Jan-Feb, 1977
National Periodical Publications

	Good	Fine	N-Mint
1-Superboy, Wonder Woman reprints begin		.30	.60
2-6: 2-Infinity cover		.25	.50

NOTE: All contain DC Superhero reprints. No. 1 has 68 pages; No. 2-6, 52 pages. No. 1,4-Hawkman app.; No. 2-Flash app.; No. 3-Green Lantern app; No. 4-Wonder Woman, Superboy app; No. 5-Gr. Arrow, Vigilante app; No. 6-Blackhawk G.A.-r.

FOUR TEENERS (Formerly Crime Must Pay The Penalty?; Dotty No. 35 on)
April, 1948 (Teen-age comic)
A. A. Wyn

	Good	Fine	N-Mint
34	2.00	6.00	14.00

FOX AND THE CROW (Stanley & His Monster No. 109 on)
(See Comic Cavalcade & Real Screen Comics)
Dec-Jan, 1951-52 - No. 108, Feb-Mar, 1968
National Periodical Publications

	Good	Fine	N-Mint
1	45.00	135.00	315.00
2(Scarce)	22.00	65.00	154.00
3-5	13.00	40.00	90.00
6-10	9.00	27.00	63.00
11-20	5.70	17.00	40.00
21-40: 22-Last precode (2/55)	3.50	10.50	24.00
41-60	2.15	6.50	15.00
61-80	1.50	4.50	10.00
81-94	1.00	3.00	7.00
95-Stanley & His Monster begins(origin)	1.50	4.50	10.00
96-99,101-108	.85	2.50	6.00
100	1.15	3.50	8.00

NOTE: Many covers by Mort Drucker.

FOX AND THE HOUND, THE (Disney)
Aug, 1981 - No. 3, Oct, 1981
Whitman Publishing Co.

	Good	Fine	N-Mint
11292 ('81)-Based on animated movie		.30	.60
2,3		.30	.60

FOX GIANTS
1944 - 1950 (132 - 196 pgs.)
Fox Features Syndicate

	Good	Fine	N-Mint
Album of Crime nn(1949, 132p)	24.00	72.00	168.00
Album of Love nn(1949, 132p)	18.00	54.00	125.00
All Famous Crime Stories nn('49, 132p)	24.00	72.00	168.00
All Good Comics 1(1944, 132p)(R.W. Voigt)-The Bouncer, Purple Tigress, Puppeteer, Green Mask; Infinity-c 18.00		54.00	125.00
All Great nn(1944, 132p)-Capt. Jack Terry, Rick Evans, Jaguar Man			
	18.00	54.00	125.00
All Great nn(Chicago Nite Life News)(1945, 132p)-Green Mask, Bouncer, Puppeteer, Rick Evans, Rocket Kelly 22.00		65.00	154.00

	Good	Fine	N-Mint
All-Great Confessions nn(1949, 132p)	18.00	54.00	125.00
All Great Crime Stories nn('49, 132p)	24.00	72.00	168.00
All Great Jungle Adventures nn('49, 132p)	24.00	72.00	168.00
All Real Confession Mag. 3 (3/49, 132p)	18.00	54.00	125.00
All Real Confession Mag. 4 (4/49, 132p)	18.00	54.00	125.00
All Your Comics 1(1944, 132p)-The Puppeteer, Red Robbins, & Merciless the Sorcerer	18.00	54.00	125.00
Almanac Of Crime nn(1948, 148p)	24.00	72.00	168.00
Almanac Of Crime 1(1950, 132p)	24.00	72.00	168.00
Book Of Love nn(1950, 132p)	18.00	54.00	125.00
Burning Romances 1(1949, 132p)	22.00	65.00	154.00
Crimes Incorporated nn(1950, 132p)	22.00	65.00	154.00
Daring Love Stories nn(1950, 132p)	18.00	54.00	125.00
Everybody's Comics 1(1944, 196p)-The Green Mask, The Bouncer; (50 cents)	21.50	64.00	150.00
Everybody's Comics 1(1946, 196p)-Green Lama, The Puppeteer	18.00	54.00	125.00
Everybody's Comics 1(1946, 196p)-Same as '45 Ribtickler	14.00	42.00	100.00
Everybody's Comics nn(1947, 132p)-Jo-Jo, Purple Tigress, Cosmo Cat, Bronze Man	18.00	54.00	125.00
Exciting Romance Stories nn('49, 132p)	18.00	54.00	125.00
Intimate Confessions nn(1950, 132p)	18.00	54.00	125.00
Journal Of Crime nn(1949, 132p)	22.00	66.00	154.00
Love Problems nn(1949, 132p)	18.00	54.00	125.00
Love Thrills nn(1950, 132p)	18.00	54.00	125.00
March of Crime nn('48, 132p)-female w/rifle-c 22.00		65.00	154.00
March of Crime nn('49, 132p)-cop w/pistol-c 22.00		65.00	154.00
March of Crime nn(1949, 132p)-coffin & man w/machine-gun-c			
	22.00	65.00	154.00
Revealing Love Stories nn(1950, 132p)	18.00	54.00	125.00
Ribtickler nn(1945, 196p, 50-)-Chicago Nite Life News; Marvel Mutt, Cosmo Cat, Flash Rabbit, The Nebbs app.			
	18.00	54.00	125.00
Romantic Thrills nn(1950, 132p)	18.00	54.00	125.00
Secret Love nn(1949, 132p)	18.00	54.00	125.00
Secret Love Stories nn(1949, 132p)	18.00	54.00	125.00
Strange Love nn(1950, 132p)-Photo-c	22.00	65.00	154.00
Sweetheart Scandals nn(1950, 132p)	18.00	54.00	125.00
Teen-Age Love nn(1950, 132p)	18.00	54.00	125.00
Throbbing Love nn(1950, 132p)-Photo-c	22.00	65.00	154.00
Truth About Crime nn(1949, 132p)	22.00	65.00	154.00
Variety Comics 1(1946, 132p)-Blue Beetle, Jungle Jo			
	18.00	54.00	125.00
Variety Comics nn(1950, 132p)	18.00	54.00	125.00
Western Roundup nn(1950, 132p)-Hoot Gibson			
	18.00	54.00	125.00

Note: Each of the above usually contain four remaindered Fox books minus covers. Since these missing covers often had the first page of the first story, most Giants therefore are incomplete. Approximate values are listed. Books with appearances of Phantom Lady, Rulah, Jo-Jo, etc. could bring more.

FOXHOLE (Becomes Never Again #8?)
9-10/54 - No. 4, 3-4/55; No. 5, 7/55 - No. 7, 3/56
Mainline/Charlton Comics No. 5 on

	Good	Fine	N-Mint
1-Kirby-c	5.00	15.00	35.00
2-Kirby c/a(2)	5.00	15.00	35.00
3,5-Kirby-c only	2.00	6.00	14.00
4,7	.85	2.50	6.00
6-Kirby c/a(2)	4.30	13.00	30.00
Super Reprints #10-12,15-18	.30	.80	1.60

NOTE: Kirby a(r)-Super #11,12. Powell a(r)-Super #15,16.

FOXY FAGAN COMICS
Dec, 1946 - No. 7, Summer, 1948
Dearfield Publishing Co.

Fox Giants (Journal of Crime), © FOX

Fox Giants (March Of Crime, 1948), © FOX

Foxhole #4, © PRIZE

Foxy Fagan #7, © Dearfield Publ.

Frankenstein Comics #15, © PRIZE

Frankie Comics #9, © MEG

FOXY FAGAN (continued)

	Good	Fine	N-Mint
1-Foxy Fagan & Little Buck begin	5.00	15.00	35.00
2	2.30	7.00	16.00
3-7	1.70	5.00	12.00

FOXY GRANDPA
1901 - 1916 (Hardcover; strip reprints)
N. Y. Herald/Frederick A. Stokes Co./M. A. Donahue & Co./Bunny Publ.(L. R. Hammersly Co.)

	Good	Fine	VF-NM
1901-9x15'' in color-N. Y. Herald	27.00	81.00	190.00
1902-''Latest Larks of . . .,'' 32 pgs. in color, 9½x15½''	27.00	81.00	190.00
1902-''The Many Advs. of . . .,'' 9x15'', 148pgs. in color (Hammersly)	35.00	105.00	245.00
1903-''Latest Advs.,'' 9x15'', 24 pgs. in color, Hammersly Co.	27.00	81.00	190.00
1903-''. . .'s New Advs.,'' 10x15, 32 pgs. in color, Stokes	27.00	81.00	190.00
1904-''Up to Date,'' 10x15'', 28 pgs. in color, Stokes	27.00	81.00	190.00
1905-''& Flip Flaps,'' 9½x15½'', 52 pgs., in color	27.00	81.00	190.00
1905-''The Latest Advs. of,'' 9x15'', 28 pgs., in color, M.A. Donohue Co.; re-issue of 1902 ish	17.00	51.00	120.00
1905-''Merry Pranks of,'' 9½x15½'', 52 pgs. in color, Donahue	17.00	51.00	120.00
1905-''Latest Larks of,'' 9½x15½'', 52 pgs. in color, Donahue; re-issue of 1902 ish	17.00	51.00	120.00
1906-''Frolics,'' 10x15'', 30 pgs. in color, Stokes	17.00	51.00	120.00
1907	15.00	45.00	105.00
1908?-''Triumphs,'' 10x15''	15.00	45.00	105.00
1908?-''& Little Brother,'' 10x15''	15.00	45.00	105.00
1911-''Latest Tricks,'' r-1910,1911 Sundays in color-Stokes Co.	16.00	48.00	110.00
1914-9½x15½'', 24 pgs., 6 color cartoons/page, Bunny Publ.	12.00	36.00	84.00
1916-''Merry Book,'' 10x15'', 30 pgs. in color, Stokes	12.00	36.00	84.00

FOXY GRANDPA SPARKLETS SERIES
1908 (6½x7¾''; 24 pgs. in color)
M. A. Donahue & Co.

'' . . Rides the Goat,'' '' . . & His Boys,'' '' . . Playing Ball,''
'' . . .Fun on the Farm,'' '' . . .Fancy Shooting,'' '' . . .Show the Boys Up Sports,'' '' . . .Plays Santa Claus''

	Good	Fine	N-Mint
each. . . .	17.00	51.00	120.00
900-. . .Playing Ball; Bunny illos; 8 pgs., linen like pgs., no date	10.00	30.00	70.00

FRACTURED FAIRY TALES (TV)
October, 1962 (Jay Ward)
Gold Key

	Good	Fine	N-Mint
1 (10022-210)	4.00	12.00	28.00

FRAGGLE ROCK (TV)
4/85 - No. 8, 9/86; V2#1, 4/88 - No. 6, 9/88
Star Comics (Marvel)/Marvel V2#1 on

1-8		.40	.80
V2#1-6($1.00): Reprints 1st series		.50	1.00

FRANCIS, BROTHER OF THE UNIVERSE
1980 (75 cents) (52 pgs.) (One Shot)
Marvel Comics Group

Buscema/Marie Severin-a; story of Francis Bernadone celebrating
his 800th birthday in 1982   .30   .60

FRANCIS THE FAMOUS TALKING MULE (All based on movie) (See 4-Color No. 335, 465, 501, 547, 579, 621, 655, 698, 710, 745, 810, 863, 906, 953, 991,

1068, 1090)

FRANK BUCK (Formerly My True Love)
No. 70, May, 1950 - No. 3, Sept, 1950
Fox Features Syndicate

	Good	Fine	N-Mint
70-Wood a(p)(3)-Photo-c	8.50	25.50	60.00
71-Wood a? (9 pgs.), 3-Painted-c	5.00	15.00	35.00

FRANKENSTEIN (See Movie Classics)
Aug-Oct, 1964; No. 2, Sept, 1966 - No. 4, Mar, 1967
Dell Publishing Co.

1(12-283-410)(1964)	.85	2.50	6.00
2-Intro. & origin super-hero character (9/66)	.50	1.50	3.00
3,4	.25	.75	1.50

FRANKENSTEIN (The Monster of . . .)
Jan, 1973 - No. 18, Sept, 1975
Marvel Comics Group

1-Ploog-a begins		.30	.60
2-18: 8,9-Dracula app.		.25	.50
Power Record giveaway-(12¼x12¼''; 16 pgs.); Adams, Ploog-a		.60	1.20

NOTE: **Adkins** c-17i. **Buscema** a-7-10p. **Ditko** a-12r. **G. Kane** c-15p. **Orlando** a-8r.
Ploog a-1-3, 4p, 5p, 6; c-1-6. **Wrightson** c-18i.

FRANKENSTEIN COMICS (Also See Prize Comics)
Sum, 1945 - V5/5(No.33), Oct-Nov, 1954
Prize Publications (Crestwood/Feature)

	Good	Fine	N-Mint
1-Frankenstein begins by Dick Briefer (origin); Frank Sinatra parody	28.00	84.00	195.00
2	13.00	40.00	90.00
3-5	11.00	32.00	75.00
6-10: 7-S&K a(r)/Headline Comics. 8(7-8/47)-Superman satire	10.00	30.00	70.00
11-17(1-2/49)-11-Boris Karloff parody c/story. 17-Last humor issue	7.00	21.00	50.00
18(3/52)-New origin, horror series begins	10.00	30.00	70.00
19,20(V3No.4, 8-9/52)	6.00	18.00	42.00
21(V3/5), 22(V3/6)	6.00	18.00	42.00
23(V4/1) - #28(V4/6)	5.00	15.00	35.00
29(V5/1) - #33(V5/5)	5.00	15.00	35.00

NOTE: **Briefer** c/a-all. **Meskin** a-21, 29.

FRANKENSTEIN, JR. (. . .& the Impossibles) (TV)
January, 1967 (Hanna-Barbera)
Gold Key

1	1.35	4.00	8.00

FRANK FRAZETTA'S THUNDA TALES
1987 (One shot, color, $2.00)
Fantagraphics Books

1	.35	1.00	2.00

FRANKIE COMICS (. . .& Lana No. 13-15) (Formerly Movie Tunes; becomes Frankie Fuddle No. 16 on)
No. 4, Wint, 1946-47 - No. 15, June, 1949
Marvel Comics (MgPC)

4-Mitzi, Margie, Daisy app.	4.65	14.00	32.00
5-8	2.30	7.00	16.00
9-Transvestism story	2.65	8.00	18.00
10-15: 13-Anti-Wertham editorial	1.70	5.00	12.00

FRANKIE DOODLE (See Single Series #7 and Sparkler, both series)

FRANKIE FUDDLE (Formerly Frankie & Lana)
No. 16, Aug, 1949 - No. 17, Nov, 1949
Marvel Comics

16,17	2.00	6.00	14.00

FRANK LUTHER'S SILLY PILLY COMICS (See Jingle Dingle . . .)
1950 (10 cents)

FRANK LUTHER'S SILLY PILLY COMICS (continued)

Children's Comics	Good	Fine	N-Mint
1-Characters from radio, records, & TV	2.30	7.00	16.00

FRANK MERRIWELL AT YALE (Speed Demons No. 5 on?)
June, 1955 - No. 4, Jan, 1956 (Also see Shadow Comics)
Charlton Comics

1	2.00	6.00	14.00
2-4	1.15	3.50	8.00

FRANTIC (Magazine) (See Zany & Ratfink)
Oct, 1958 - V2No.2, April, 1959 (Satire)
Pierce Publishing Co.

V1#1,2	.85	2.50	5.00
V2#1,2: 1-Burgos-a, Severin-c/a	.50	1.50	3.00

FRECKLES AND HIS FRIENDS (See Crackajack Funnies, Famous Comics
Cartoon Book, Honeybee Birdwhistle. .. & Red Ryder)

FRECKLES AND HIS FRIENDS
No. 5, 11/47 - No. 12, 8/49; 11/55 - No. 4, 6/56
Standard Comics/Argo

5-Reprints	4.00	12.00	28.00
6-12-Reprints; 11-Lingerie panels	2.00	6.00	14.00

NOTE: *Some copies of No. 8 & 9 contain a printing oddity. The negatives were
elongated in the engraving process, probably to conform to page dimensions on the
filler pages. Those pages only look normal when viewed at a 45 degree angle.*

1(Argo,'55)-Reprints (NEA Service)	2.30	7.00	16.00
2-4	1.30	4.00	9.00

FREDDY (Formerly My Little Margie's Boy Friends)
June, 1958 - No. 47, Feb, 1965 (Also see Blue Bird)
Charlton Comics

V2No.12	.85	2.50	6.00
13-15	.50	1.50	3.00
16-47	.35	1.00	2.00
Schiff's Shoes Presents. . . No. 1(1959)-Giveaway	.35	1.00	2.00

FREDDY
May-July, 1963 - No. 3, Oct-Dec, 1964
Dell Publishing Co.

1-3	.55	1.65	4.00

FREE COMICS TO YOU FROM. . . (name of shoe store) (Has
clown on cover & another with a rabbit) (Like comics from Weather
Bird & Edward's Shoes)
Circa 1956, 1960-61
Shoe Store Giveaway

Contains a comic bound with new cover - several combinations
possible; Some Harvey titles known. contents determines price.

FREEDOM AGENT (Also see John Steele)
April, 1963
Gold Key

1 (10054-304)-Painted-c	1.00	3.00	7.00

FREEDOM FIGHTERS (See Justice League No. 107,108)
Mar-Apr, 1976 - No. 15, July-Aug, 1978
National Periodical Publications/DC Comics

1-Uncle Sam, The Ray, Black Condor, Doll Man, Human Bomb, & Phantom Lady begin		.35	.70
2-15: 7-1st app. Crusaders. 10-Origin Doll Man. 11-Origin The Ray. 12-Origin Firebrand. 13-Origin Black Condor. 15-Origin Phantom Lady		.25	.50

NOTE: *Buckler c-5-11p, 13p, 14p.*

FREEDOM TRAIN
1948 (Giveaway)
Street & Smith Publ.

	Good	Fine	N-Mint
Powell-c	1.70	5.00	10.00

FRENZY (Magazine) (Satire)
April, 1958 - No. 6, March, 1959
Picture Magazine

1	.75	2.25	4.50
2-6	.40	1.25	2.50

FRIDAY FOSTER
October, 1972
Dell Publishing Co.

1	1.00	3.00	6.00

FRIENDLY GHOST, CASPER, THE (See Casper. . .)
8/58 - No. 224, 10/82; No. 225, 10/86 - Present
Harvey Publications

1-Infinity-c	14.00	42.00	100.00
2	7.00	21.00	50.00
3-10: 6-X-Mas-c	4.00	12.00	28.00
11-20: 18-X-Mas-c	2.65	8.00	18.00
21-30	1.20	3.50	8.00
31-50	.70	2.00	5.00
51-100: 54-X-Mas-c	.55	1.60	3.20
101-159		.60	1.20
160-163: All 52 pg. Giants	.25	.75	1.50
164-238: 173,179,185-Cub Scout Specials. 238-on $1.00 issues		.35	.70
239-245 ($1.00)		.50	1.00
American Dental Assoc. giveaway-Small size (1967, 16 pgs.)	.50	1.50	3.00

FRIGHT
June, 1975 (August on inside)
Atlas/Seaboard Periodicals

1-Origin The Son of Dracula; Frank Thorne c/a		.40	.80

FRIGHT NIGHT
Oct., 1988 - Present ($1.75, color)
Now Comics

1-4: 1-3-adapts movie	.30	.90	1.75

FRISKY ANIMALS (Formerly Frisky Fables)
No. 44, Jan, 1951 - No. 58, 1954
Star Publications

44-Super Cat	5.00	15.00	35.00
45-Classic L. B. Cole-c	8.00	24.00	56.00
46-51,53-58-Super Cat	4.35	13.00	30.00
52-L. B. Cole c/a, 3pgs.	5.00	15.00	35.00

NOTE: *All have L. B. Cole-c. No. 47-No Super Cat. Disbrow a-49,52. Fago a-51.*

FRISKY ANIMALS ON PARADE (Formerly Parade; becomes Super-
spook)
Sept, 1957 - No. 3, Dec/Jan, 1957-1958
Ajax-Farrell Publ. (Four Star Comic Corp.)

1-L. B. Cole-c	3.75	11.25	26.00
2-No L. B. Cole-c	1.85	5.50	13.00
3-L. B. Cole-c	2.65	8.00	18.00

FRISKY FABLES (Frisky Animals No. 44 on)
Spring, 1945 - No. 44, Oct-Nov, 1949
Premium Group/Novelty Publ.

V1/1-Al Fago c/a	5.00	15.00	35.00
2,3(1945)	2.65	8.00	18.00
4-7(1946)	1.70	5.00	12.00
V2/1-9,11,12(1947)	1.15	3.50	8.00
10-Christmas-c	1.30	4.00	9.00
V3/1-12(1948): 4-Flag-c. 9-Infinity-c	1.00	3.00	7.00

Freddy #16, © CC

The Friendly Ghost, Casper #4, © HARV

Frisky Animals #56, © STAR

Frogman Comics #7, © HILL

Frontier Fighters #2, © DC

Frontier Western #4, © MEG

FRISKY FABLES (continued)	Good	Fine	N-Mint
V4/1-7	1.00	3.00	7.00
36-44(V4/8-12, V5/1-4)-L. B. Cole-c; 40-X-mas-c			
	4.65	14.00	32.00
Accepted Reprint No. 43 (nd); L.B. Cole-c	1.70	5.00	12.00

FRITZI RITZ (See Comics On Parade, Single Series #5,1(reprint), Tip Top & United Comics)

FRITZI RITZ
Fall/48 - No. 42, 1/55; No. 43, 1955 - No. 55, 9-11/57; No. 56,
12-2/57-58 - No. 59, 9-11/58
United Features Synd./St. John No. 41-55/Dell No. 56 on

nn(1948)-Special Fall ish.	5.50	16.50	38.00
2	2.65	8.00	18.00
3-5	2.00	6.00	14.00
6-10: 6-Abbie & Slats app. 7-Lingerie panel	1.70	5.00	12.00
11-19,21-28	1.30	4.00	9.00
20-Strange As It Seems; Russell Patterson Cheesecake-a; negligee panel	1.70	5.00	12.00
29-Five pg. Abbie & Slats; 1 pg. Mamie by Russell Patterson	1.30	4.00	9.00
30-59: 36-1 pg. Mamie by Patterson. 43-Peanuts by Schulz	1.00	3.00	7.00

NOTE: Abbie & Slats in No. 7, 8, 11, 18, 20, 27, 29. Li'l Abner in No. 35, 36.

FROGMAN COMICS
Jan-Feb, 1952 - No. 11, May, 1953
Hillman Periodicals

1	3.70	11.00	26.00
2	2.00	6.00	14.00
3,4,6-11: 4-Meskin-a	1.50	4.50	10.00
5-Krigstein, Torres-a	3.00	9.00	21.00

FROGMEN, THE
No. 1258, 2-4/62 - No. 11, 11-1/1964-65 (Painted-c)
Dell Publishing Co.

4-Color 1258-Evans-a	3.00	9.00	21.00
2,3-Evans-a; part Frazetta inks in #2,3	3.70	11.00	26.00
4,6-11	1.15	3.50	8.00
5-Toth-a	2.00	6.00	14.00

FROM BEYOND THE UNKNOWN
10-11/69 - No.25, 11-12/73 (No.7-11: 64 pgs.; No.12-17: 52 pgs.)
National Periodical Publications

1		.30	.60
2-10: 7-Intro. Col. Glenn Merrit		.25	.50
11-25: Star Rovers-r begin #18,19. Space Museum in #23-25		.25	.50

NOTE: Adams c-3, 6, 8, 9. Anderson c-2, 4, 5, 10, 11i, 15-17, 22; reprints-3, 4, 6-8, 10, 11, 13-16, 24, 25. Infantino reprints-1-5, 7-19, 23-25; c-11p. Kaluta c-18,19. Kubert c-1,7, 12-14. Toth a-2r. Wood a-13i. Photo-c 22.

FROM HERE TO INSANITY (Satire) (See Frantic & Frenzy)
(See Frantic & Frenzy)
No. 8, Feb, 1955 - V3No.1, 1956
Charlton Comics

8	3.50	10.50	24.00
9	2.35	7.00	16.00
10-Ditko-c/a, 3 pgs.	5.50	16.50	38.00
11,12-All Kirby except 4 pgs.	6.50	19.50	45.00
V3#1(1956)-Ward-c/a(2)(signed McCartney); 5 pgs. Wolverton; 3 pgs. Ditko; magazine format	13.50	40.50	95.00

FRONTIER DAYS
1956 (Giveaway)
Robin Hood Shoe Store (Brown Shoe)

1	1.35	4.00	8.00

FRONTIER DOCTOR (See 4-Color No. 877)

FRONTIER FIGHTERS
Sept-Oct, 1955 - No. 8, Nov-Dec, 1956
National Periodical Publications

	Good	Fine	N-Mint
1-Davy Crockett, Buffalo Bill by Kubert, Kit Carson begin (Scarce)	20.00	60.00	140.00
2 (Scarce)	13.00	40.00	90.00
3-8	10.00	30.00	70.00

NOTE: Buffalo Bill by Kubert in all.

FRONTIER ROMANCES
Nov-Dec, 1949 - No. 2, Feb-Mar, 1950 (Painted-c)
Avon Periodicals/I. W.

1-Used in SOTI, pg. 180(General reference) & illo. "Erotic spanking in a western comic book"	33.00	100.00	230.00
2 (Scarce)	16.00	48.00	110.00
1-I.W.(reprints Avon's #1)	2.75	8.00	16.00
I.W. Reprint #9	1.35	4.00	8.00

FRONTIER SCOUT: DAN'L BOONE (Formerly Death Valley; The Masked Raider No. 14 on)
No. 10, Jan, 1956 - No. 13, Aug, 1956; No. 14, March, 1965
Charlton Comics

10	2.35	7.00	16.00
11-13(1956)	1.30	4.00	9.00
V2No.14(3/65)	.50	1.50	3.00

FRONTIER TRAIL (The Rider No. 1-5)
No. 6, May, 1958
Ajax/Farrell Publ.

6	1.30	4.00	9.00

FRONTIER WESTERN
Feb, 1956 - No. 10, Aug, 1957
Atlas Comics (PrPI)

1	5.00	15.00	35.00
2,3,6-Williamson-a, 4 pgs. each	4.65	14.00	32.00
4,7,9,10: 10-Check-a	1.70	5.00	12.00
5-Crandall, Baker, Wildey, Davis-a; Williamson text illos	3.50	10.50	24.00
8-Crandall, Morrow, & Wildey-a	2.00	6.00	14.00

NOTE: Drucker a-3,4. Heath c-5. Severin c-6,8,10. Ringo Kid in No. 4.

FRONTLINE COMBAT
July-Aug, 1951 - No. 15, Jan, 1954
E. C. Comics

1	34.00	102.00	240.00
2	23.00	70.00	160.00
3	17.00	51.00	120.00
4-Used in SOTI, pg. 257; contains "Airburst" by Kurtzman which is his personal all-time favorite story	14.00	42.00	100.00
5	12.00	36.00	84.00
6-10	10.00	30.00	70.00
11-15	8.00	24.00	56.00

NOTE: Davis a-in all; c-11,12. Evans a-10-15. Heath a-1. Kubert a-14. Kurtzman a-1-5; c-1-9. Severin a-5-7, 9, 13, 15. Severin/Elder a-2-11; c-10. Toth a-8, 12. Wood a-1-4, 6-10, 12-15; c-13-15. Special issues: No. 7 (Iwo Jima), No. 9 (Civil War), No. 12 (Air Force). (Canadian reprints known; see Table of Contents.)

FRONT PAGE COMIC BOOK
1945
Front Page Comics (Harvey)

1-Kubert-a; intro. & 1st app. Man in Black by Powell; Fuje-c	14.00	42.00	100.00

FROST AND FIRE (See DC Science Fic. Graphic Novel)

FROSTY THE SNOWMAN
No. 359, Nov, 1951 - No. 1272, Dec-Feb?/1961-62
Dell Publishing Co.

4-Color 359	2.65	8.00	18.00

FROSTY THE SNOWMAN (continued)	Good	Fine	N-Mint
4-Color 435	2.00	6.00	14.00
4-Color 514,601,661	1.70	5.00	12.00
4-Color 748,861,950,1065	1.50	4.50	10.00
4-Color 1153,1272	1.30	4.00	9.00

FRUITMAN SPECIAL
Dec, 1969 (68 pages)
Harvey Publications

1-Funny super hero	1.00	3.00	6.00

F-TROOP (TV)
Aug, 1966 - No. 7, Aug, 1967 (All have photo-c)
Dell Publishing Co.

1	2.65	8.00	18.00
2-7	1.50	4.50	10.00

FUGITIVES FROM JUSTICE
Feb, 1952 - No. 5, Oct, 1952
St. John Publishing Co.

1	5.70	17.00	40.00
2-Matt Baker-a; Vic Flint strip reprints begin, end No. 5	5.50	16.50	38.00
3-Reprints panel from Authentic Police Cases that was used in SOTI with changes; Tuska-a	8.00	24.00	56.00
4	2.65	8.00	18.00
5-Bondage-c	3.50	10.50	24.00

FUGITOID
Jan., 1986 (One shot, B&W)
Mirage Studios

1-Ties into TMNT #5	.75	2.25	4.50

FULL COLOR COMICS
1946
Fox Features Syndicate

nn	5.00	15.00	35.00

FULL OF FUN
Aug, 1957 - No. 2, Nov, 1957; 1964
Red Top (Decker Publ.)(Farrell)/I. W. Enterprises

1(1957)-Dave Berg-a	1.70	5.00	12.00
2-Reprints Bingo, the Monkey Doodle Boy	1.15	3.50	8.00
8-I.W. Reprint('64)	.35	1.00	2.00

FUN AT CHRISTMAS (See March of Comics No. 138)

FUN CLUB COMICS (See Interstate Theatres...)

FUN COMICS (Mighty Bear No. 13 on)
Jan, 1953 - No. 12, Oct, 1953
Star Publications

9(Giant)-L. B. Cole-c	5.50	16.50	38.00
10-12-L. B. Cole-c	3.50	10.50	24.00

FUNDAY FUNNIES (See Famous TV..., and Harvey Hits No. 35,40)

FUN-IN (TV)(Hanna-Barbera)
Feb, 1970 - No. 10, Jan, 1972; No. 11, 4/74 - No. 15, 12/74
Gold Key

1-Dastardly & Muttley in Their Flying Machines; Perils of Penelope Pitstop in 1-4; It's the Wolf in all	.85	2.50	5.00
2-4,6-Cattanooga Cats in 2-4	.50	1.50	3.00
5,7-Motormouse & Autocat, Dastardly & Muttley in both; It's the Wolf in No. 7	.40	1.20	2.40
8,10-The Harlem Globetrotters, Dastardly & Muttley in No. 10	.40	1.20	2.40
9-Where's Huddles?, Dastardly & Muttley, Motormouse & Autocat app.	.40	1.20	2.40
11-15: 11-Butch Cassidy. 12,15-Speed Buggy. 13-Hair Bear Bunch. 14-Inch High Private Eye	.25	.75	1.50

FUNKY PHANTOM, THE (TV)
Mar, 1972 - No. 13, Mar, 1975 (Hanna-Barbera)
Gold Key

	Good	Fine	N-Mint
1	1.00	3.00	7.00
2-5	.70	2.00	4.00
6-13	.50	1.50	3.00

FUNLAND
No date (25 cents)
Ziff-Davis (Approved Comics)

Contains games, puzzles, etc.	5.00	15.00	35.00

FUNLAND COMICS
1945
Croyden Publishers

1	3.70	11.00	26.00

FUNNIES, THE (Also see Comic Cuts)
1929 - No. 36, 10/18/30 (10 cents; 5 cents No.22 on) (16 pgs.)
Full tabloid size in color; not reprints; published every Saturday
Dell Publishing Co.

1-My Big Brudder, Johnathan, Jazzbo & Jim, Foxy Grandpa, Sniffy, Jimmy Jams & other strips begin; first four-color comic newsstand publication; also contains magic, puzzles & stories	25.00	75.00	175.00
2-21 (1930, 30 cents)	9.00	27.00	63.00
22(nn-7/12/30-5 cents)	6.50	19.50	45.00
23(nn-7/19/30-5 cents), 24(nn-7/26/30-5 cents), 25(nn-8/2/30), 26(nn-8/9/30), 27(nn-8/16/30), 28(nn-8/23/30), 29(nn-8/30/30), 30(nn-9/6/30), 31(nn-9/13/30), 32(nn-9/20/30), 33(nn-9/27/30), 34(nn-10/4/30), 35(nn-10/11/30), 36(nn, no date-10/18/30) each....	6.50	19.50	45.00

FUNNIES, THE (New Funnies No. 65 on)
Oct, 1936 - No. 64, May, 1942
Dell Publishing Co.

1-Tailspin Tommy, Mutt & Jeff, Alley Oop, Capt. Easy, Don Dixon begin	70.00	210.00	490.00
2-Scribbly by Mayer begins	35.00	105.00	245.00
3	30.00	90.00	210.00
4,5: 4-Christmas-c	25.00	75.00	175.00
6-10	20.00	60.00	140.00
11-20: 16-Christmas-c	17.00	51.00	120.00
21-29	14.00	42.00	100.00
30-John Carter of Mars (origin) begins by Edgar Rice Burroughs	45.00	135.00	315.00
31-44: 33-John Coleman Burroughs art begins on John Carter. 35-(9/39)-Mr. District Attorney begins-based on radio show	25.00	75.00	175.00
45-Origin Phantasmo, the Master of the World & intro. his sidekick Whizzer McGee	20.00	60.00	140.00
46-50: 46-The Black Knight begins, ends No. 62	17.00	51.00	120.00
51-56-Last ERB John Carter of Mars	17.00	51.00	120.00
57-Intro. & origin Captain Midnight	42.00	125.00	295.00
58-60	18.00	54.00	125.00
61-Andy Panda begins by Walter Lantz	19.00	57.00	132.00
62,63-Last Captain Midnight cover	17.00	51.00	120.00
64-Format change; Oswald the Rabbit, Felix the Cat, Li'l Eight Ball app.; origin & 1st app. Woody Woodpecker in Oswald; last Capt. Midnight	35.00	105.00	245.00

NOTE: *Mayer* c-26, 48. *McWilliams* art in many issues on "Rex King of the Deep."

FUNNIES ANNUAL, THE
1959 ($1.00)(B&W; tabloid-size, approx. 7x10")
Avon Periodicals

1-(Rare)-Features the best newspaper comic strips of the year: Archie, Snuffy Smith, Beetle Bailey, Henry, Blondie, Steve Canyon, Buz Sawyer, The Little King, Hi & Lois, Popeye,

Fugitives From Justice #2, © STJ

The Funnies #2 (11/36), © DELL

The Funnies #35, © DELL

172

Funny Folks #26, © DC

Funnyman nn (12/47), © ME

Funny Picture Stories V3#2, © CEN

	Good	Fine	N-Mint
THE FUNNIES ANNUAL (continued)			

& others. Also has a chronological history of the comics from 2000 B.C. to 1959.

	23.00	70.00	160.00

FUNNIES ON PARADE (Premium)
1933 (Probably the 1st comic book) (36 pgs.; slick cover)
No date or publisher listed
Eastern Color Printing Co.

nn-Contains Sunday page reprints of Mutt & Jeff, Joe Palooka, Hairbreadth Harry, Reg'lar Fellers, Skippy, & others (10,000 print run). This book was printed for Proctor & Gamble to be given away & came out before Famous Funnies or Century of Comics.

	215.00	645.00	1505.00

FUNNY ANIMALS (See Fawcett's Funny Animals)
Sept, 1984 - No. 2, Nov, 1984
Charlton Comics

	Good	Fine	N-Mint
1,2-Atomic Mouse-r		.30	.60

FUNNYBONE
1944 (132 pages)
La Salle Publishing Co.

	8.00	24.00	56.00

FUNNY BOOK (. . . Magazine) (Hocus Pocus No. 9)
Dec, 1942 - No. 9, Aug-Sept, 1946
Parents' Magazine Press

1-Funny animal; Alice In Wonderland app.	6.00	18.00	42.00
2	3.00	9.00	21.00
3-9	2.00	6.00	14.00

FUNNY COMICS (7 cents)
1955 (36 pgs.; 5x7''; in color)
Modern Store Publ.

1-Funny animal	.70	2.00	4.00

FUNNY COMIC TUNES (See Funny Tunes)

FUNNY FABLES
Aug, 1957 - V2No. 2, Nov, 1957
Decker Publications (Red Top Comics)

V1No.1	1.50	4.50	10.00
V2No.1,2	.85	2.50	6.00

FUNNY FILMS
Sept-Oct, 1949 - No. 29, May-June, 1954 (No. 1-4, 52 pgs.)
American Comics Group(Michel Publ./Titan Publ.)

1-Puss An' Boots, Blunderbunny begin	6.00	18.00	42.00
2	3.00	9.00	21.00
3-10	2.00	6.00	14.00
11-20	1.50	4.50	10.00
21-29	1.15	3.50	8.00

FUNNY FOLKS (Hollywood . . . on cover only No. 16-26; becomes Hollywood Funny Folks No. 27 on)
April-May, 1946 - No. 26, June-July, 1950 (52 pgs., #16 on)
National Periodical Publications

1-1st app. Nutsy Squirrel by Rube Grossman	16.00	48.00	110.00
2	8.00	24.00	56.00
3-5	6.00	18.00	42.00
6-10	4.00	12.00	28.00
11-26	2.85	8.50	20.00

NOTE: **Sheldon Mayer** a-in some issues.

FUNNY FROLICS
Summer, 1945 - No. 5, Dec, 1946
Timely/Marvel Comics (SPI)

1-Sharpy Fox, Puffy Pig, Krazy Krow	7.00	21.00	50.00
2	4.00	12.00	28.00
3,4	3.00	9.00	21.00
5-Kurtzman-a	4.00	12.00	28.00

FUNNY FUNNIES
April, 1943 (68 pages)
Nedor Publishing Co.

	Good	Fine	N-Mint
1 (Funny animals)	9.00	27.00	62.00

FUNNYMAN
Dec, 1947; No. 1, Jan, 1948 - No. 6, Aug, 1948
Magazine Enterprises

nn(12/47)-Prepublication B&W undistributed copy by Siegel & Shuster-(5¾x8''), 16 pgs.; Sold in San Francisco in 1976 for $300.00

1-Siegel & Shuster in all	13.00	40.00	90.00
2	10.00	30.00	70.00
3-6	8.00	24.00	56.00

FUNNY MOVIES (See 3-D Funny Movies)

FUNNY PAGES (Formerly The Comics Magazine)
No. 6, Nov, 1936 - No. 42, Oct, 1940
Comics Magazine Co./Ultem Publ.(Chesler)/Centaur Publications

V1#6 (nn, nd)-The Clock begins (2 pgs.), ends #11 (1st app.)			
	40.00	120.00	280.00
7-11	26.00	78.00	180.00
V2#1 (9/37)(V2#2 on-c; V2#1 in indicia)	20.00	60.00	140.00
V2#2 (10/37)(V2#3 on-c; V2#2 in indicia)	20.00	60.00	140.00
3(11/37)-5	20.00	60.00	140.00
6(1st Centaur, 3/38)	32.00	95.00	225.00
7-9	23.00	65.00	160.00
10(Scarce)-1st app. of The Arrow by Gustavson (Blue costume)			
	90.00	270.00	630.00
11,12	45.00	135.00	315.00
V3#1-6	45.00	135.00	315.00
7-1st Arrow-c; 9/39	55.00	165.00	385.00
8	45.00	135.00	315.00
9-Tarpe Mills jungle-c	45.00	135.00	315.00
10-2nd Arrow-c	50.00	150.00	350.00
V4#1(1/40, Arrow-c)-(Rare)-The Owl & The Phantom Rider app.;			

origin Mantoka, Maker of Magic by Jack Cole. Mad Ming begins, ends #42. Tarpe Mills-a

	55.00	165.00	385.00
35-Arrow-c	40.00	120.00	280.00
36-38-Mad Ming-c	40.00	120.00	280.00
39-42-Arrow-c. 42-Last Arrow	40.00	120.00	280.00

NOTE: **Burgos** c-V3#10. **Jack Cole** a-V2#3, 7, 8, 10, 11, V3#2, 6, 9, 10, V4#1, 37. **Eisner** a-V1#7, 8, 10. **Ken Ernest** a-#7. **Everett** a-V2#11 (illos). **Gill Fox** a-V2#11. **Sid Greene** a-39. **Guardineer** a-V2#2, 3, 5. **Gustavson** a-V2#5, 11, 12, V3#1-10, 35, 38-42; c-V3#7, 35, 39-42. **Bob Kane** a-V3#1. **McWilliams** a-V2#12, V3#1, 3-6. **Tarpe Mills** a-V3#8-10, V4#1; c-V3#9. **Ed Moore Jr.** a-V2#12. **Bob Wood** a-V2#2, 3, 8, 11, V3#6, 9, 10; c-V2#6, 7.

FUNNY PICTURE STORIES (Comic Pages V3#4 on)
Nov, 1936 - V3/3, May, 1939
Comics Magazine Co./Centaur Publications

V1#1-The Clock begins (c-feature)(See Funny Pages for 1st app.)			
	78.00	235.00	550.00
2	36.00	108.00	252.00
3-9: 4-Eisner-a; Christmas-c	26.00	78.00	180.00
V2#1 (9/37; V1#10 on-c; V2#1 in indicia)-Jack Strand begins			
	21.00	62.00	145.00
2 (10/37; V1#11 on-c; V2#2 in indicia)	21.00	62.00	145.00
3-5: 4-Xmas-c	18.00	54.00	125.00
6-(1st Centaur, 3/38)	30.00	90.00	210.00
7-11	20.00	60.00	140.00
V3#1-3	17.00	51.00	120.00

NOTE: **Biro** c-V2#1. **Guardineer** a-V1#11. **Bob Wood** a/c-V1#11, V2#2.

FUNNY STUFF (Becomes The Dodo & the Frog No. 80)
Summer, 1944 - No. 79, July-Aug, 1954
All-American/National Periodical Publications No. 7 on

1-The Three Mouseketeers & The ''Terrific Whatzit'' begin-Sheldon

FUNNY STUFF (continued)	Good	Fine	N-Mint
Mayer-a	40.00	120.00	280.00
2-Sheldon Mayer-a	20.00	60.00	140.00
3-5	11.50	34.00	80.00
6-10 (6/46)	8.50	25.50	60.00
11-20: 18-Dodo & the Frog begin?	5.70	17.00	40.00
21,23-30: 24-Infinity-c	4.00	12.00	28.00
22-Superman cameo	13.00	40.00	90.00
31-79: 75-Bo Bunny by Mayer	2.50	7.50	17.50
Wheaties Giveaway(1946, 6½x8¼'') (Scarce)	8.50	25.50	60.00

NOTE: *Mayer* a-1-8, 55, .57, 58, 61, 62, 64, 65, 68, 70, 72, 74-79; c-5, 6, 8.

FUNNY STUFF STOCKING STUFFER
March, 1985 (52 pgs.)
DC Comics

	Good	Fine	N-Mint
1-Almost every DC funny animal		.60	1.25

FUNNY 3-D
December, 1953
Harvey Publications

1	7.00	21.00	50.00

FUNNY TUNES (Animated Funny Comic Tunes No. 16-22; Funny Comic Tunes No. 23, on covers only; formerly Human Torch; Oscar No. 24 on)
No. 16, Summer, 1944 - No. 23, Fall, 1946
U.S.A. Comics Magazine Corp. (Timely)

16-Silly, Ziggy, Krazy Krow begin	5.00	15.00	35.00
17 (Fall/'44)-Becomes Gay Comics #18 on?	3.50	10.50	24.00
18-22: 21-Super Rabbit app.	3.00	9.00	21.00
23-Kurtzman-a	4.00	12.00	28.00

FUNNY TUNES
July, 1953 - No. 3, Dec-Jan, 1953-54
Avon Periodicals

1-Space Mouse begins	3.00	9.00	21.00
2,3	1.70	5.00	12.00

FUNNY WORLD
1947 - 1948
Marbak Press

1-The Berrys, The Toodles & other strip reprints begin	4.00	12.00	28.00
2,3	2.65	8.00	18.00

FUNTASTIC WORLD OF HANNA-BARBERA, THE (TV)
Dec, 1977 - No. 3, June, 1978 ($1.25) (Oversized)
Marvel Comics Group

1-The Flintstones Christmas Party(12/77); 2-Yogi Bear's Easter Parade(3/78); 3-Laff-a-lympics(6/78)			
each....	.35	1.00	2.00

FUN TIME
1953; No. 2, Spr, 1953; No. 3(nn), Sum, 1953; No. 4, Wint, 1953-54
Ace Periodicals

1	1.70	5.00	12.00
2-4 (100 pgs. each)	4.50	13.50	32.00

FUN WITH SANTA CLAUS (See March of Comics No. 11,108,325)

FURTHER ADVENTURES OF INDIANA JONES, THE
Jan, 1983 - No. 34, Mar, 1986
Marvel Comics Group

1-Byrne/Austin-a		.50	1.00
2-34: 2-Byrne/Austin-c/a		.50	1.00

NOTE: *Austin* a-6i, 9i; c-1i, 2i, 6i, 9i. *Chaykin* a-6p; c-6p, 8p-10p. *Ditko* a-21p, 25, 26, 34. *Simonson* c-9.

FURY (Straight Arrow's Horse. . .) (See A-1 No. 119)

FURY (TV) (See March Of Comics #200)
No. 781, Mar, 1957 - Nov, 1962 (All photo-c)
Dell Publishing Co./Gold Key

	Good	Fine	N-Mint
4-Color 781	5.00	15.00	35.00
4-Color 885,975	3.70	11.00	26.00
4-Color 1031,1080,1133,1172,1218,1296, 01292-208(#1-'62)			
	3.70	11.00	26.00
10020-211(11/62-G.K.)-Crandall-a	3.70	11.00	26.00

FURY OF FIRESTORM, THE (Becomes Firestorm The Nuclear Man #65 on; also see Firestorm)
June, 1982 - No. 64, Oct, 1987 (#19-on: 75 cents)
DC Comics

1-Intro The Black Bison; brief origin	.40	1.25	2.50
2	.25	.80	1.60
3-18: 17-1st app. Firehawk		.65	1.30
19-40: 21-Death of Killer Frost. 22-Origin. 23-Intro. Byte. 24-1st app. Blue Devil & Bug (origin); origin Byte. 34-1st app./origin Killer Frost II. 39-Weasel's i.d. revealed		.50	1.00
41,42-Crisis x-over		.60	1.20
43-61: 48-Intro. Moonbow. 53-Origin/1st app. Silver Shade. 55,56-Legends x-over. 58-1st app./origin Parasite		.45	.90
61-Test cover	5.00	15.00	30.00
62-64		.45	.90
Annual 1(11/83), 2(11/84), 3(11/85)		.65	1.30
Annual 4(10/86), 5(10/87)		.65	1.30

NOTE: *Colan* a-19p, Annual 4p. *Giffen* a-Annual 4p. *Gil Kane* c-30. *Nino* a-37. *Tuska* a-17p, 18p, 32p, 45p.

FUSION
Jan, 1987 - Present ($2.00, B&W, Baxter paper)
Eclipse Comics

1	.40	1.25	2.50
2-11	.35	1.00	2.00

FUTURE COMICS
June, 1940 - No. 4, Sept, 1940
David McKay Publications

1-Origin The Phantom; The Lone Ranger, & Saturn Against the Earth begin	105.00	315.00	735.00
2	55.00	165.00	385.00
3,4	45.00	135.00	315.00

FUTURE WORLD COMICS
Summer, 1946 - No. 2, Fall, 1946
George W. Dougherty

1,2	9.00	27.00	62.00

FUTURE WORLD COMIX (Warren Presents. . . on cover)
September, 1978
Warren Publications

1		.50	1.00

FUTURIANS, THE (See Marvel Graphic Novel #9)
Sept, 1985 - No. 3, 1985 ($1.50, color)
Lodestone Publ.

1	.50	1.50	3.00
2	.35	1.00	2.00
3	.25	.75	1.50
Graphic Novel 1 ($9.95)	1.70	5.00	9.95

G-8 (See G-Eight)

GABBY (Formerly Ken Shannon) (Teen humor)
No. 11, July, 1953; No. 2, Sept, 1953 - No. 9, Sept, 1954
Quality Comics Group

11(No.1)(7/53)	2.65	8.00	18.00
2	1.30	4.00	9.00
3-9	1.00	3.00	7.00

Funny 3-D #1, © HARV

The Fury Of Firestorm #1, © DC

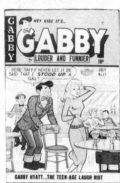
Gabby #11 (#1), © QUA

Gabby Hayes Western #12, © FAW

Gangsters Can't Win #1, © DS

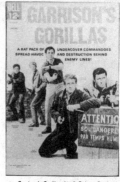

Garrison's Gorillas #1, © Belmur Prod.

GABBY GOB (See Harvey Hits No. 85,90,94,97,100,103,106,109)

GABBY HAYES WESTERN (Movie star) (See Monte Hale, Real Western Hero & Western Hero)
Nov., 1948 - No. 50, Jan, 1953; Dec, 1954 - No. 59, Jan, 1957
Fawcett/Toby Press/Charlton Comics No. 51 on

	Good	Fine	N-Mint
1-Gabby & his horse Corker begin; Photo front/back-c begin	22.00	65.00	154.00
2	11.00	32.00	75.00
3-5	8.00	24.00	56.00
6-10	6.50	19.50	45.00
11-20: 19-Last photo back-c?	5.00	15.00	35.00
21-49	3.50	10.50	24.00
50-(1/53)-Last Fawcett issue; last photo-c?	3.70	11.00	26.00
51-(12/54)-1st Charlton issue; photo-c	3.70	11.00	26.00
52-59(Charlton '54-57): 53,55-Photo-c	2.00	6.00	14.00
1 (. . .Adv. Comics; Toby; 12/53)-Photo-c	6.00	18.00	42.00
Quaker Oats Giveaway nn(#1-5, 1951) (Dell?)	2.50	7.50	17.00

GAGS
July, 1937 - V3No.10, Oct, 1944 (13¾x10¾'')
United Features Synd./Triangle Publ. No. 9 on

	Good	Fine	N-Mint
1(7/37)-52 pgs.; 20 pgs. Grin & Bear It, Fellow Citizen	3.50	10.50	24.00
V1#9 (36 pgs.) (7/42)	2.15	6.50	15.00
V3#10	1.50	4.50	10.00

GALACTIC WAR COMIX (Warren Presents. . . on cover)
December, 1978
Warren Publications

nn-Wood, Williamson-r		.50	1.00

GALLANT MEN, THE (TV)
October, 1963 (Photo-c)
Gold Key

1(10085-310)-Manning-a	1.15	3.50	8.00

GALLEGHER, BOY REPORTER (TV)
May, 1965 (Disney) (Photo-c)
Gold Key

1(10149-505)	1.15	3.50	8.00

GAMMARAUDERS
Jan, 1989 - Present ($1.25, color)
DC Comics

1,2-Based on TSR game		.60	1.25

GANDY GOOSE (See Paul Terry's & Terry-Toons Comics)
Mar, 1953 - No. 5, Nov, 1953; No. 5, Fall, 1956 - No. 6, Sum/58
St. John Publ. Co./Pines No. 5,6

	Good	Fine	N-Mint
1	2.65	8.00	18.00
2	1.30	4.00	9.00
3-5(1953)(St. John)	1.00	3.00	7.00
5,6(1956-58)(Pines)	.85	2.50	6.00

GANG BUSTERS (See Popular Comics #43)
1938 - 1943
David McKay/Dell Publishing Co.

	Good	Fine	N-Mint
Feature Books 17(McKay)('38)	22.00	65.00	154.00
Large Feat. Comic 10('39)-(Scarce)	27.00	81.00	190.00
Large Feat. Comic 17('41)	18.00	54.00	125.00
4-Color 7(1940)	19.00	57.00	132.00
4-Color 23,24('42-43)	14.00	42.00	100.00

GANG BUSTERS (Radio/TV)
Dec-Jan, 1947-48 - No. 67, Dec-Jan, 1958-59 (No. 1-23, 52 pgs.)
National Periodical Publications

	Good	Fine	N-Mint
1	26.00	78.00	180.00
2	12.00	36.00	84.00
3-8	7.00	21.00	50.00

	Good	Fine	N-Mint
9,10-Photo-c	8.00	24.00	56.00
11-13-Photo-c	6.00	18.00	42.00
14,17-Frazetta-a, 8 pgs. each. 14-Photo-c	18.00	54.00	125.00
15,16,18-20	4.65	14.00	32.00
21-30	3.50	10.50	24.00
31-44: 44-Last Pre-code (2-3/55)	2.65	8.00	18.00
45-67	1.70	5.00	12.00

NOTE: *Barry* a-6, 8, 10. *Drucker* a-51. *Moreira* a-48, 50, 59. *Roussos* a-8.

GANGSTERS AND GUN MOLLS
Sept, 1951 - No. 4, June, 1952 (Painted-c)
Avon Periodical/Realistic Comics

	Good	Fine	N-Mint
1-Wood-a, 1 pg; c-/Avon paperback 292	18.00	54.00	125.00
2-Check-a, 8 pgs.; Kamen-a	13.00	40.00	90.00
3-Marijuana mention story; used in POP, pg. 84-85	13.00	40.00	90.00
4	10.00	30.00	70.00

GANGSTERS CAN'T WIN
Feb-Mar, 1948 - No. 9, June-July, 1949
D. S. Publishing Co.

	Good	Fine	N-Mint
1	10.00	30.00	70.00
2	5.00	15.00	35.00
3	6.00	18.00	42.00
4-Acid in face story	6.00	18.00	42.00
5,6-Ingels-a. 5-McWilliams-a. 6-Reinman-c	6.00	18.00	42.00
7-McWilliams-a	3.00	9.00	21.00
8-9	3.00	9.00	21.00

GANG WORLD
No. 5, Nov, 1952 - No. 6, Jan, 1953
Standard Comics

	Good	Fine	N-Mint
5-Bondage-c	6.50	19.50	45.00
6-Opium story	4.30	13.00	30.00

GARGOYLE
June, 1985 - No. 4, Sept, 1985 (Limited series)
Marvel Comics Group

	Good	Fine	N-Mint
1-Character from The Defenders; Wrightson-c	.25	.75	1.50
2-4		.50	1.00

GARRISON'S GORILLAS (TV)
Jan, 1968 - No. 4, Oct, 1968; No. 5, Oct, 1969 (Photo-c)
Dell Publishing Co.

	Good	Fine	N-Mint
1	1.50	4.50	10.00
2-5: 5-Reprints #1	1.00	3.00	7.00

GASOLINE ALLEY (Also see Popular & Super Comics)
1929 (B&W daily strip reprints)(7x8¾''; hardcover)
Reilly & Lee Publishers

	Good	Fine	N-Mint
By King (96 pgs.)	9.00	27.00	62.00

GASOLINE ALLEY
Sept-Oct, 1950 - No. 2, 1950 (Newspaper reprints)
Star Publications

1-Contains 1 pg. intro. history of the strip (The Life of Skeezix); reprints 15 scenes of highlights from 1921-1935, plus an adventure from 1935 and 1936 strips; a 2-pg. filler is included on the life of the creator Frank King, with photo of the cartoonist.

	Good	Fine	N-Mint
	9.00	27.00	62.00
2-(1936-37 reprints)-L. B. Cole-c	9.50	28.50	66.00
(See Super Book No. 21)			

GASP!
March, 1967 - No. 4, Aug, 1967
American Comics Group

	Good	Fine	N-Mint
1-L.S.D. drug mention	1.00	3.00	7.00
2-4	.70	2.00	5.00

GAY COMICS (Honeymoon No. 41)   **Good**   **Fine**   **N-Mint**
Mar, 1944 (no month); No. 18, Fall, 1944 - No. 40, Oct, 1949
Timely Comics/USA Comic Mag. Co. No. 18-24

	Good	Fine	N-Mint
1-Wolverton's Powerhouse Pepper; Tessie the Typist begins; Millie The Model & Willie app. (One Shot)	18.00	54.00	125.00
18-(Formerly Funny Tunes #17?)-Wolverton-a	9.00	27.00	65.00
19-29-Wolverton-a in all. 24,29-Kurtzman-a	7.00	21.00	50.00
30,33,36,37-Kurtzman's ''Hey Look''	2.30	7.00	16.00
31-Kurtzman's ''Hey Look''(1), Giggles 'N' Grins (1½)	2.30	7.00	16.00
32,35,38-40: 35-Nellie The Nurse begins?	1.70	5.00	12.00
34-Three Kurtzman's ''Hey Look''	3.00	9.00	21.00

GAY COMICS (Also see Tickle, Smile, & Whee Comics)
1955 (52 pgs.; 5x7¼''; 7 cents)
Modern Store Publ.

1	.50	1.50	3.00

GAY PURR-EE (See Movie Comics)

GEEK, THE (See Brother Power. . .)

G-8 AND HIS BATTLE ACES
October, 1966
Gold Key

1 (10184-610)-Painted-c	1.75	5.25	12.00

GEM COMICS
April, 1945 (52 pgs.) (Bondage-c)
Spotlight Publishers

1-Little Mohee, Steve Strong app.	7.00	21.00	50.00

GENE AUTRY (See March of Comics No. 25,28,39,54,78,90,104,120,135,150, & Western Roundup)

GENE AUTRY COMICS (Movie, Radio star; singing cowboy)
(Dell takes over with No. 11)
1941 (On sale 12/31/41) - No. 10, 1943 (68 pgs.)
Fawcett Publications

1 (Rare)-Gene Autry & his horse Champion begin	107.00	320.00	750.00
2	44.00	132.00	310.00
3-5	34.00	102.00	240.00
6-10	29.00	87.00	205.00

GENE AUTRY COMICS (. . .& Champion No. 102 on)
No. 11, 1943 - No. 121, Jan-Mar, 1959 (TV)-later issues
Dell Publishing Co.

11,12(1943-2/44)-Continuation of Fawcett series (60pgs. each); #11-photo back-c	32.00	95.00	225.00
4-Color 47(1944, 60 pgs.)	32.00	95.00	225.00
4-Color 57(11/44),66('45)(52 pgs. each)	26.00	78.00	180.00
4-Color 75,83('45, 36 pgs. each)	22.00	65.00	154.00
4-Color 93,100('45-46, 36 pgs. each)	18.00	54.00	125.00
1(5-6/46, 52 pgs.)	32.00	95.00	225.00
2(7-8/46)-Photo-c begin, end #111	16.00	48.00	110.00
3-5: 4-Intro Flapjack Hobbs	12.00	36.00	84.00
6-10	8.50	25.50	60.00
11-20: 20-Panhandle Pete begins. 12-Line drawn-c	5.70	17.00	40.00
21-29(36pgs.)	4.30	13.00	30.00
30-40(52pgs.)	4.30	13.00	30.00
41-56(52pgs.)	3.50	10.50	24.00
57-66(36pgs.): 58-X-mas-c	2.35	7.00	16.00
67-80(52pgs.)	2.65	8.00	18.00
81-90(52pgs.): 82-X-mas-c. 87-Blank inside-c	2.00	6.00	14.00
91-99(36pgs. No. 91-on). 94-X-mas-c	1.60	4.80	11.00
100	2.35	7.00	16.00
101-111-Last Gene Autry photo-c	1.70	5.00	12.00
112-121-All Champion painted-c	1.15	3.50	8.00

	Good	Fine	N-Mint
. . .Adventure Comics And Play-Fun Book ('40s)-36 pgs., 8x6½''; games, comics, magic	11.00	32.00	75.00
Pillsbury Premium('47)-36 pgs., 6½x7½''; games, comics, puzzles	11.00	32.00	75.00
Quaker Oats Giveaway(1950)-2½x6¾''; 5 different versions; ''Death Card Gang, Phantom of the Cave, Riddle of Laughing Mtn., Secret of Lost Valley, Bond of Broken Arrow'' (came in wrapper). each. . .	5.00	15.00	35.00
3-D Giveaway(1953)-Pocket-size; 5 different	5.00	15.00	35.00

NOTE: Photo back-c, 4-18,20-45,48-65. **Manning** a-118. **Jesse Marsh** art: 4-Color No. 66, 75, 93, 100, No. 1-25, 27-37, 39, 40.

GENE AUTRY'S CHAMPION (TV)
No. 287, 8/50; No. 319, 2/51; No. 3, 8-10/51 - No. 19, 8-10/55
Dell Publishing Co.

4-Color 287('50, 52pgs.)-Photo-c	5.00	15.00	35.00
4-Color 319('51), 3-(Painted-c begin)	3.00	9.00	21.00
4-19: 19-Last painted-c	1.30	4.00	9.00

GENE AUTRY TIM (Formerly Tim) (Becomes Tim in Space)
1950 (Half-size) (Black & White Giveaway)
Tim Stores

Several issues (All Scarce)	5.00	15.00	35.00

GENE DAY'S BLACK ZEPPELIN
April, 1985 - No. 5, Oct., 1986 ($1.70, B&W)
Renegade Press

1	.35	1.00	2.00
2-5	.30	.90	1.80

GENERAL DOUGLAS MACARTHUR
1951
Fox Features Syndicate

nn	10.00	30.00	70.00

GENERIC COMIC, THE
April, 1984 (One-shot)
Marvel Comics Group

1		.30	.60

GENTLE BEN (TV)
Feb, 1968 - No. 5, Oct, 1969 (All photo-c)
Dell Publishing Co.

1	1.15	3.50	8.00
2-5: 5-Reprints #1	.75	2.25	5.00

GEORGE OF THE JUNGLE (TV)(See America's Best TV Comics)
Feb, 1969 - No. 2, Oct, 1969 (Jay Ward)
Gold Key

1,2	2.00	6.00	14.00

GEORGE PAL'S PUPPETOONS
Dec, 1945 - No. 18, Dec, 1947; No. 19, 1950
Fawcett Publications

1-Captain Marvel on cover	18.00	54.00	125.00
2	8.50	25.50	60.00
3-10	6.00	18.00	42.00
11-19	4.00	12.00	28.00

GEORGIE COMICS (. . .& Judy Comics #20-35?; see All Teen & Teen Comics)
Spring, 1945 - No. 39, Oct, 1952
Timely Comics/GPI No. 1-34

1-Dave Berg-a	7.00	21.00	50.00
2	3.70	11.00	26.00
3-5,7,8	2.30	7.00	16.00
6-Georgie visits Timely Comics	2.85	8.50	20.00
9,10-Kurtzman's ''Hey Look'' (1 & ?); Margie app.	3.50	10.50	24.00

Gay Comics #18, © MEG

Gene Autry Comics #2 (Fawcett). © Gene Autry

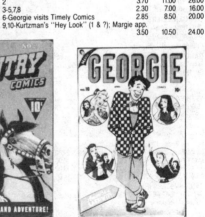

Georgie Comics #10, © MEG

Gerald McBoing-Boing And The Nearsighted... #5, © UPA

Geronimo #3, © AVON

Ghostly Weird Stories #121, © STAR

	Good	Fine	N-Mint
GEORGIE COMICS (continued)			
11,12: 11-Margie, Millie app.	2.00	6.00	14.00
13-Kurtzman's ''Hey Look,'' 3 pgs.	3.00	9.00	21.00
14-Wolverton art, 1 pg. & Kurtzman's ''Hey Look''	3.50	10.50	24.00
15,16,18-20	1.50	4.50	10.00
17,29-Kurtzman's ''Hey Look'' 1 pg.	2.30	7.00	16.00
21-24,27,28,30-39: 21-Anti-Wertham editorial	1.15	3.50	8.00
25-Painted cover by classic pin-up artist Peter Driben	3.00	9.00	21.00
26-Logo design swipe from Archie Comics	1.15	3.50	8.00

GERALD McBOING-BOING AND THE NEARSIGHTED MR. MAGOO
(TV)(Mr. Magoo No. 6)
Aug-Oct, 1952 - No. 5, Aug-Oct, 1953
Dell Publishing Co.

	Good	Fine	N-Mint
1	5.00	15.00	35.00
2-5	4.00	12.00	28.00

GERONIMO
1950 - No. 4, Feb, 1952
Avon Periodicals

	Good	Fine	N-Mint
1-Indian Fighter; Maneely-a; Texas Rangers r-/Cowpuncher No. 1; Fawcette-c	9.00	27.00	62.00
2-On the Warpath; Kit West app.; Kinstler c/a	5.50	16.50	38.00
3-And His Apache Murderers; Kinstler c/a(2); Kit West, drug story r-Cowpuncher No. 6	5.50	16.50	38.00
4-Savage Raids of; Kinstler c/a(3)	4.30	13.00	30.00

GERONIMO JONES
Sept, 1971 - No. 9, Jan, 1973
Charlton Comics

	Good	Fine	N-Mint
1		.50	1.00
2-9		.30	.60
Modern Comics Reprint #7('78)		.20	.40

GETALONG GANG, THE
May, 1985 - No. 6, March, 1986
Star Comics (Marvel)

	Good	Fine	N-Mint
1-6: Saturday morning TV stars		.35	.70

GET LOST
Feb-Mar, 1954 - No. 3, June-July, 1954 (Satire)
Mikeross Publications

	Good	Fine	N-Mint
1	6.50	19.50	45.00
2-Has 4 pg. E.C. parody featuring ''the Sewer Keeper''	4.65	14.00	32.00
3-John Wayne 'Hondo' parody	3.50	10.50	24.00

GET SMART (TV)
June, 1966 - No. 8, Sept, 1967 (All have photo-c)
Dell Publishing Co.

	Good	Fine	N-Mint
1	3.00	9.00	21.00
2-Ditko-a	3.00	9.00	21.00
3-8: 3-Ditko-a(p)	2.15	6.50	15.00

GHOST (...Comics #9)
1951(Winter) - No. 11, Summer, 1954
Fiction House Magazines

	Good	Fine	N-Mint
1	25.00	75.00	175.00
2	13.00	40.00	90.00
3-9: 3,6,7,9-Bondage-c	10.00	30.00	70.00
10,11-Dr. Drew by Grandenetti in each, reprinted from Rangers; Evans-a-No. 11	11.50	34.00	80.00

GHOST BREAKERS (Also see (CC) Sherlock Holmes Comics,
Racket Squad in Action & Red Dragon)
Sept, 1948 - No. 2, Dec, 1948 (52 pages)
Street & Smith Publications

	Good	Fine	N-Mint
1-Powell-c/a(3); Dr. Neff (magician) app.	13.00	40.00	90.00
2-Powell-c/a(2); Maneely-a	10.00	30.00	70.00

GHOSTBUSTERS (TV)(Also see Real...)
Feb, 1987 - No. 6, Aug, 1987
First Comics

	Good	Fine	N-Mint
1-Based on new animated TV series	.25	.75	1.50
2-6		.65	1.30

GHOST CASTLE (See Tales of...)

GHOSTLY HAUNTS (Formerly Ghost Manor)
No. 20, 9/71 - No. 53, 12/76; No. 54, 9/77 - No. 55, 10/77;
No. 56, 7/78 - No. 58, 4/78
Charlton Comics

	Good	Fine	N-Mint
20,21		.40	.80
22-41,43-58: 27-Dr. Graves x-over. 39-Origin & 1st app. Destiny Fox		.40	.80
42-Newton c/a		.40	.80
40,41(Modern Comics-r, 1977, 1978)		.15	.30

NOTE: *Ditko* a-22-28, 31-34, 36-41, 43-48, 50, 52, 54, 56r; c-22-27, 30, 33-37, 47, 54, 56. *Glanzman* a-20. *Howard* a-27, 30, 35, 42. *Staton* a-35; c-46. *Sutton* c-33, 39.

GHOSTLY TALES (Blue Beetle No. 50-54)
No. 55, 4-5/66 - No. 124, 12/76; No. 125, 9/77 - No. 169, 10/84
Charlton Comics

	Good	Fine	N-Mint
55-Intro. & origin Dr. Graves	.35	1.00	2.00
56-70-Dr. Graves ends		.50	1.00
71-106,108-113,115-169		.40	.80
107-Sutton, Wood-a		.50	1.00
114-Newton-a		.50	1.00

NOTE: *Ditko* a-55, 57, 58, 60, 61, 67, 69-73, 75-90, 92-99, 118, 120-122, 125r, 126r, 131-33r, 136-41r, 143r, 144r, 152, 155, 161, 163; c-67, 69, 73, 77, 78, 83, 84, 86-90, 92-97, 99, 102, 109, 111, 118, 120-22, 125, 131-33, 163. *Glanzman* a-167. *Howard* a-95, 98, 99, 117; c-98, 107, 120, 121, 161. *Newton* c-115. *Staton* a-161; c-117. *Sutton* a-112-114.

GHOSTLY WEIRD STORIES (Formerly Blue Bolt Weird)
No. 120, Sept, 1953 - No. 124, Sept, 1954
Star Publications

	Good	Fine	N-Mint
120-Jo-Jo-r	10.00	30.00	70.00
121-Jo-Jo-r	7.00	21.00	50.00
122-The Mask-r/Capt. Flight 5; Rulah-r; has 1pg. story 'Death and the Devil Pills'-r/Western Outlaws 17	7.00	21.00	50.00
123-Jo-Jo; Disbrow-a(2)	7.00	21.00	50.00
124-Torpedo Man	7.00	21.00	50.00

NOTE: *Disbrow* a-120-124. *L. B. Cole* covers-all issues.

GHOST MANOR (Ghostly Haunts No. 20 on)
July, 1968 - No. 19, July, 1971
Charlton Comics

	Good	Fine	N-Mint
1		.60	1.20
2-12,17		.50	1.00
13-16,18,19-Ditko-a; c-15,18,19		.60	1.20

GHOST MANOR (2nd Series)
Oct, 1971 - No. 32, Dec, 1976; No. 33, Sept, 1977 - No. 77, 11/84
Charlton Comics

	Good	Fine	N-Mint
1		.50	1.00
2-7,9,10		.40	.80
8-Wood-a	.35	1.00	2.00
11-17,19		.30	.60
18,20-22: 18,20-Newton-a. 22-Newton c/a. 21-E-Man, Blue Beetle, Capt. Atom cameos		.30	.60
23-39,41-56,58-77: 28-Nudity panels		.30	.60
40-Torture & drug use		.30	.60
57-Wood, Ditko, Howard-a		.40	.80
19(Modern Comics reprint, 1977)		.20	.40

NOTE: *Ditko* a-4, 8, 10, 11(2), 13, 14, 18, 20-22, 24-26, 28, 29, 31, 37r, 38r, 40r, 42-44r; 46r,47, 51r, 52r, 57, 60, 62(4), 64r, 71; c-2-7, 9-11, 14-16, 28, 31, 37, 38, 42, 43, 46, 47, 51, 52, 60, 62, 64. *Howard* a-4-4, 18, 19-21, 57. *Newton* a-64. *Sutton* a-19; c-8.

177

GHOST RIDER (See A-1 Comics, Best of the West, Black Phantom, Bobby Benson, Great Western, Red Mask & Tim Holt)
1950 - No. 14, 1954
Magazine Enterprises
NOTE: The character was inspired by Vaughn Monroe's "Ghost Riders in the Sky," and Disney's movie "The Headless Horseman."

	Good	Fine	N-Mint
1(A-1 27)-Origin Ghost Rider	33.00	100.00	230.00
2(A-1 29), 3(A-1 31), 4(A-1 34), 5(A-1 37)-All Frazetta-c only	35.00	105.00	245.00
6(A-1 44), 7(A-1 51)	11.00	32.00	75.00
8(A-1 57)-Drug use story, 9(A-1 69)-L.S.D. story	9.50	28.00	65.00
10(A-1 71)-vs. Frankenstein	9.50	28.00	65.00
11(A-1 75), 12(A-1 80, bondage-c), 13(A-1 84), 14(A-1 112)	7.00	21.00	50.00

NOTE: *Dick Ayers art in all; c-1, 6-14.*

GHOST RIDER, THE (See Night Rider & Western Gunfighters)
Feb, 1967 - No. 7, Nov, 1967
Marvel Comics Group

1-Origin Ghost Rider; Kid Colt-r begin	.35	1.00	2.00
2-7: 6-Last Kid Colt-r	.50	1.00	

GHOST RIDER (See Marvel Spotlight)
Sept, 1973 - No. 81, June, 1983 (Super-hero)
Marvel Comics Group

1	.85	2.50	5.00
2-19: 10-Ploog-a; origin-r/M. Spotlight 5	.35	1.00	2.00
20-Byrne-a	.70	2.00	4.00
21-81: 50-Double size. 68-Origin	.50		1.00

NOTE: *Anderson c-64p. Infantino a(p)-43, 44, 51. G. Kane a-25; c(p)-1, 2, 4, 5, 8, 9, 11-13, 19, 20, 24, 25. Kirby c-21-23. Mooney a-2-9p, 30i. Nebres c-26i. Newton a-23i. Perez c-26p. J. Sparling a-62p, 64p, 65p. Starlin a(p)-35. Sutton a-1p, 44i, 64i, 65i, 66, 67i. Tuska a-13p, 14p, 16p.*

GHOSTS (Ghost No. 1)
Sept-Oct, 1971 - No. 112, May, 1982 (No. 1-5: 52 pgs.)
National Periodical Publications/DC Comics

1,2		.40	.80
3-112: 97-99-The Spectre app. 100-Infinity-c		.25	.50

NOTE: *B. Baily a-77. J. Craig a-108. Ditko a-77, 111. Giffen a-104p, 106p, 111p. Golden a-88. Kaluta c-7, 93, 101. Kubert a-89, 105-08, 111. Sheldon Mayer a-111. McWilliams a-99. Win Mortimer a-89, 91, 94. Newton a-92p, 94p. Nino a-35, 37, 57. Orlando a-74i; c-80. Redondo a-8, 13, 45. Sparling a-90p, 93p, 94p. Spiegle a-103, 105.*

GHOSTS SPECIAL (See DC Special Series No. 7)

GHOST STORIES (See Amazing Ghost Stories)

GHOST STORIES
Sept-Nov, 1962; No. 2, Apr-June, 1963 - No. 37, Oct, 1973
Dell Publishing Co.

1 2-295-211-Written by John Stanley	2.00	6.00	14.00
2	1.00	3.00	7.00
3-10: Two No. 6's exist with diff. c/a(12-295-406,12-295-503)	.60	1.75	3.50
11-20	.35	1.00	2.00
21-37	.60		1.20

NOTE: *#21-34,36,37 all reprint earlier issues.*

GHOUL TALES (Magazine)
Nov, 1970 - No. 5, July, 1971 (52 pages) (B&W)
Stanley Publications

1-Aragon pre-code reprints; Mr. Mystery as host; bondage-c	.70	2.00	4.00
2-(1/71)Reprint/Climax #1	.35	1.00	2.00
3-(3/71)	.35	1.00	2.00
4-(5/71)Reprints story "The Way to a Man's Heart" used in SOTI	1.15	3.50	8.00
5-ACG reprints	.35	1.00	2.00

NOTE: *No. 1-4 contain pre-code Aragon reprints.*

GIANT BOY BOOK OF COMICS (See Boy)
1945 (Hardcover) (240 pages)
Newsbook Publications (Gleason)

	Good	Fine	N-Mint
1-Crimebuster & Young Robin Hood	45.00	135.00	315.00

GIANT COMIC ALBUM
1972 (52 pgs.; 11x14''; B&W; 59 cents)
King Features Syndicate
Newspaper reprints: Little Iodine, Katzenjammer Kids, Henry, Mandrake the Magician ('59 Falk), Popeye, Beetle Bailey, Barney Google, Blondie, Flash Gordon ('68-69 Dan Barry), & Snuffy Smith

each	1.00	3.00	6.00

GIANT COMICS
Summer, 1957 - No. 3, Winter, 1957 (100 pgs.) (25 cents)
Charlton Comics

1-Atomic Mouse, Hoppy app.	7.00	21.00	50.00
2,3-Atomic Mouse, Rabbit, Christmas Book, Romance stories known	5.00	15.00	35.00

NOTE: *The above may be rebound comics; contents could vary.*

GIANT COMICS (See Wham-O Giant Comics)

GIANT COMICS EDITION (See Terry-Toons)
1947 - No. 17, 1950 (All 100-164 pgs.) (25 cents)
St. John Publishing Co.

1-Mighty Mouse	19.00	57.00	132.00
2-Abbie & Slats	9.00	27.00	62.00
3-Terry-Toons Album; 100 pgs.	13.00	40.00	90.00
4-Crime comics; contains Red Seal No. 16, used & illo. in SOTI	22.00	65.00	154.00
5-Police Case Book(4/49)-Contents varies; contains remaindered St. John books - some volumes contain 5 copies rather than 4, with 160 pages; Matt Baker-c	20.00	60.00	140.00
5A-Terry-Toons Album, 132 pgs.	13.00	40.00	90.00
6-Western Picture Stories; Baker-c/a(3); The Sky Chief, Blue Monk, Ventrilo app.; Tuska-a	19.00	57.00	132.00
7-Contains a teen-age romance plus 3 Mopsy comics	13.00	40.00	90.00
8-The Advs. of Mighty Mouse (10/49)	13.00	40.00	90.00
9-Romance and Confession Stories; Kubert-a(4); Baker-a; photo-c	19.00	57.00	132.00
10-Terry-Toons	13.00	40.00	90.00
11-Western Picture Stories-Baker c/a(4); The Sky Chief, Desperado, & Blue Monk app.; another version with Son of Sinbad by Kubert	18.00	54.00	125.00
12-Diary Secrets; Baker prostitute-c; 4 St. John romance comics; Baker-a	40.00	120.00	280.00
13-Romances; Baker, Kubert-a	19.00	57.00	132.00
14-Mighty Mouse Album	13.00	40.00	90.00
15-Romances (4 love comics)-Baker-c	19.00	57.00	132.00
16-Little Audrey, Abbott & Costello, Casper	13.00	40.00	90.00
17(nn)-Mighty Mouse Album (nn, no date, but did follow No. 16); 100 pgs. on cover but has 148 pgs.	13.00	40.00	90.00

NOTE: *The above books contain remaindered comics and contents could vary with each issue. No. 11,12 have part photo mag. insides.*

GIANT COMICS EDITIONS
1940's (132 pages)
United Features Syndicate

1-Abbie & Slats, Abbott & Costello, Jim Hardy, Ella Cinders, Iron Vic	18.00	54.00	125.00
2-Jim Hardy & Gordo	13.00	40.00	90.00

NOTE: *Above books contain rebound copies; contents can vary.*

GIANT GRAB BAG OF COMICS (See Archie All-Star Specials under Archie Comics)

GIANTS (See Thrilling True Stories of . . .)

Ghost Rider #1, © ME

Ghost Rider #1 (2/67), © MEG

Giant Comics Edition #9, © STJ

G. I. Combat #23 (Quality), © DC

Giggle Comics #1, © ACG

G-I In Battle #1 (8/52), © AJAX

GIANT-SIZE (Avengers, Captain America, Captain Marvel, Conan, Daredevil, Defenders, Fantastic Four, Hulk, Invaders, Iron Man, Kid Colt, Man-Thing, Master of Kung Fu, Power Man, Spider-Man, Super-Villain Team-Up, Thor, Werewolf, and X-Men are listed under their own titles.)

GIANT-SIZE CHILLERS (Giant-Size Dracula No. 2)
June, 1974; Feb, 1975 - No. 3, Aug, 1975 (35 cents)
Marvel Comics Group

	Good	Fine	N-Mint
1-(6/74)-Curse of Dracula (52 pgs.); Origin & 1st app. Lilith, Dracula's daughter; Heath-a(r)	.50		1.00
1-(2/75)(50 cents)(68 pgs.)-Alcala-a	.40		.80
2-(5/75)-All-r	.30		.60
3-(8/75)-Wrightson c/a; Smith-a(r)	.50		1.00

NOTE: *Everett* reprint-No. 2/Advs. Into Weird Worlds No. 10.

GIANT SIZE CREATURES (Giant-Size Werewolf No. 2)
July, 1974 (52 pgs.) (35 cents)
Marvel Comics Group

1-Werewolf, Tigra app.; Crandall-a(r)	.30		.60

GIANT-SIZE DRACULA (Formerly Giant-Size Chillers)
No. 2, Sept, 1974 - No. 5, June, 1975 (50 cents)
Marvel Comics Group

2		.50	1.00
3-Fox-a/Uncanny Tales #6		.40	.80
4-Ditko-a(2)(r)		.30	.60
5-1st Byrne-a at Marvel	.70	2.00	4.00

GIANT-SIZE SUPER-HEROES FEATURING SPIDER-MAN
June, 1974 (35 cents) (52 pgs.)
Marvel Comics Group

1-Spider-Man vs. Man-Wolf; Morbius, The Living Vampire app. Ditko-a(r); G. Kane-a(p)	.50	1.50	3.00

GIANT-SIZE SUPER-STARS (Giant-Size Fantastic Four No. 2)
May, 1974 (35 cents) (52 pgs.)
Marvel Comics Group

1-Fantastic Four, Thing, Hulk by Buckler (p); Kirbyish-a		.50	1.00

GIANT SPECTACULAR COMICS (See Archie All-Star Special under Archie Comics)

GIANT SUMMER FUN BOOK (See Terry-Toons...)

G. I. COMBAT
Oct., 1952 - No. 43, Dec, 1956
Quality Comics Group

1-Crandall-c	11.50	34.00	80.00
2	5.00	15.00	35.00
3-5,10-Crandall c/a	5.00	15.00	35.00
6-Crandall-a	4.30	13.00	30.00
7-9	3.50	10.50	24.00
11-20	2.00	6.00	14.00
21-31,33,35-43	1.70	5.00	12.00
32-Nuclear attack-c	3.50	10.50	24.00
34-Crandall-a	3.35	10.00	23.00

G. I. COMBAT
No. 44, Jan, 1957 - No. 288, Mar, 1987
National Periodical Publications/DC Comics

44	11.50	34.00	80.00
45	5.70	17.00	40.00
46-50	3.40	11.00	24.00
51-60	2.00	6.00	14.00
61-66,68-80	1.50	4.50	10.00
67-1st Tank Killer	3.00	9.00	21.00
81,82,84-86	1.15	3.50	7.00
83-1st Big Al, Little Al, & Charlie Cigar	1.50	4.50	10.00
87-1st Haunted Tank	3.00	9.00	21.00
88-90: Last 10 cent issue	.75	2.25	4.50

	Good	Fine	N-Mint
91-113,115-120	.40	1.25	2.50
114-Origin Haunted Tank	1.15	3.50	7.00
121-137,139,140	.25	.75	1.50
138-Intro. The Losers (Capt. Storm, Gunner/Sarge, Johnny Cloud) in Haunted Tank	.35	1.00	2.00
141-150,152,154		.50	1.00
151,153-Medal of Honor series by Maurer		.50	1.00
155-200,207,208		.50	1.00
201-206,209-245,247-259 ($1.00 size). 232-Origin Kana the Ninja. 244-Death of Slim Stryker; 1st app. The Mercenaries. 257-Intro. Stuart's Raiders		.50	1.00
246-(72 pgs.)30th Anniversary issue		.50	1.00
260-281 ($1.25 size). 264-Intro Sgt. Bullet and the Bravos of Vietnam; origin Kana		.70	1.40
282-288 (75 pgs.)		.70	1.40

NOTE: *Adams* c-168, 201, 202. *Check* a-168, 173. *Drucker* a-48, 61, 63, 66, 71, 72, 76, 134, 140, 141, 144, 147, 148, 153. *Evans* a-135, 138, 158, 164, 166, 201, 202, 204, 205, 215, 256. *Giffen* a-267. *Glanzman* a-most issues. *Kubert/Heath* a-most issues; Kubert covers most issues. *Morrow* a-159-161(2 pgs.). *Redondo* a-189, 240i, 243i. *Sekowsky* a-162p. *Severin* a-147, 152. *Simonson* c-169. *Thorne* a-152, 156. *Wildey* a-153. Johnny Cloud app.-No. 112, 115, 120. Mlle. Marie app.-No. 123, 132, 200. Sgt. Rock app.-#111-113, 115, 120, 125, 141, 146, 147, 149, 200. USS Stevens by Glanzman-#115, 150-153, 157.

G. I. COMICS (Also see Jeep & Overseas Comics)
1945 (distributed to U. S. armed forces)
Giveaways

1-49-Contains Prince Valiant by Foster, Blondie, Smilin' Jack, Mickey Finn, Terry & the Pirates, Donald Duck, Alley Oop, Moon Mullins & Capt. Easy strip reprints	4.00	12.00	28.00

GIDGET (TV)
April, 1966 - No. 2, Dec, 1966
Dell Publishing Co.

1,2: 1-Sally Field photo-c	2.65	8.00	18.00

GIFT (See The Crusaders)

GIFT COMICS (50 cents)
1942 - No. 4, 1949 (No.1-3: 324 pgs.; No. 4: 152 pgs.)
Fawcett Publications

1-Captain Marvel, Bulletman, Golden Arrow, Ibis the Invincible, Mr. Scarlet, & Spy Smasher app. Not rebound, remaindered comics, printed at same time as originals	120.00	360.00	840.00
2	85.00	255.00	595.00
3	60.00	180.00	420.00
4-The Marvel Family, Captain Marvel, etc.; each issue can vary in contents	40.00	120.00	280.00

GIFTS FROM SANTA (See March of Comics No. 137)

GIGGLE COMICS (Spencer Spook No. 100) (Also see Ha Ha)
Oct, 1943 - No. 99, Jan-Feb, 1955
Creston No.1-63/American Comics Group No. 64 on

1	13.00	40.00	90.00
2	6.00	18.00	42.00
3-5: Ken Hultgren-a begins?	4.30	13.00	30.00
6-10: 9-1st Superkatt	3.50	10.50	24.00
11-20	2.15	6.50	15.00
21-40	1.70	5.00	12.00
41-54,56-59,61-99: 95-Spencer Spook app.	1.30	4.00	9.00
55,60-Milt Gross-a	1.70	5.00	12.00

G-I IN BATTLE (G-I No. 1 only)
Aug, 1952 - No. 9, July, 1953; Mar, 1957 - No. 6, May, 1958
Ajax-Farrell Publ./Four Star

1	2.35	7.00	16.00
2	1.15	3.50	8.00
3-9	.85	2.50	6.00
Annual 1(1952, 100 pgs.)	11.50	34.00	80.00

G-I IN BATTLE (continued)	Good	Fine	N-Mint
1(1957-Ajax)	1.50	4.50	10.00
2-6	.70	2.00	5.00

G. I. JANE
May, 1953 - No. 11, Mar, 1955 (Misdated 3/54)
Stanhall/Merit No. 11

	Good	Fine	N-Mint
1	4.00	12.00	28.00
2-7(5/54)	2.00	6.00	14.00
8-10(12/54, Stanhall)	1.70	5.00	12.00
11 (3/55, Merit)	1.50	4.50	10.00

G. I. JOE (Also see Advs. of. . ., Showcase #53,54 & The Yardbirds)
No. 10, 1950; No. 11,-4-5/51 - No. 51, 6/57 (52pgs., 10-14,6-17?)
Ziff-Davis Publ. Co. (Korean War)

	Good	Fine	N-Mint
10(#1, 1950)-Saunders painted-c begin	4.00	12.00	28.00
11-14(10/51)	2.30	7.50	16.00
V2#6(12/51)-17-(Last 52pgs.?)	2.00	6.00	14.00
18-(100 pg. Giant-'52)	7.00	21.00	50.00
19-30: 21-The Yardbirds app.	1.70	5.00	12.00
31-47,49-51	1.50	4.50	10.00
48-Atom bomb story	1.70	5.00	12.00

NOTE: *Powell* a-V2#7, 8, 11. *Norman Saunders* painted c-10-14, V2#6-14, 26, 30, 31, 35, 38, 39. *Bondage* c-29,35,38. *Tuska* a-7.

G. I. JOE (America's Movable Fighting Man)
1967 (36 pages) (5-1/8''x8-3/8'')
Custom Comics

	Good	Fine	N-Mint
Schaffenberger-a		.40	.80

G. I. JOE AND THE TRANSFORMERS
Jan, 1987 - No. 4, Apr, 1987 (mini-series)
Marvel Comics Group

	Good	Fine	N-Mint
1	.40	1.25	2.50
2-4	.30	.90	1.80

G. I. JOE, A REAL AMERICAN HERO (See Official Handbook. . .)
June, 1982 - Present
Marvel Comics Group

	Good	Fine	N-Mint
1-Printed on Baxter paper	3.35	10.00	20.00
2-Printed on reg. paper	5.00	15.00	30.00
2 (2nd printing)	.80	2.40	4.75
3-5	2.00	6.00	12.00
3-5 (2nd printing)	.70	2.00	4.00
6,8	2.15	6.50	13.00
6,8 (2nd printing)	.70	2.00	4.00
7,9,10	1.85	5.50	11.00
7,9,10 (2nd printing)	.70	2.00	4.00
11-Intro Airborne	1.35	4.00	8.00
12	2.00	6.00	12.00
13-15	1.70	5.00	10.00
14 (2nd printing)	.50	1.50	3.00
16	1.50	4.50	9.00
17-20	1.00	3.00	6.00
17-19 (2nd printing)	.35	1.00	2.00
21,22	1.25	3.75	7.50
23-25	.70	2.00	4.00
21,23,25 (2nd printing)	.35	1.00	2.00
26-Origin Snake-Eyes; ends #27	1.00	3.00	6.00
27	1.15	3.50	7.00
26,27 (2nd printing)	.25	.75	1.50
28-30	.70	2.00	4.00
29,30 (2nd printing)	.25	.75	1.50
31-35: 33-New headquarters	.55	1.70	3.40
36-40	.45	1.40	2.80
34,35,36,37 (2nd printing)		.60	1.20
41-49	.35	1.05	2.10
50-Double size; intro Special Missions	.65	1.90	3.80

	Good	Fine	N-Mint
51-60: 60-Todd McFarlane-a	.30	.85	1.70
51 (2nd printing)		.40	.80
61-85		.50	1.00
Special Treasury Edition (1982)-r/#1	1.30	4.00	8.00
. . .Yearbook 1 ('84)-r/#1	1.15	3.50	7.00
. . .Yearbook 2 ('85)	.70	2.00	4.00
. . .Yearbook 3 ('86, 68 pgs.)	.50	1.50	3.00
. . .Yearbook 4 (2/88)	.30	.90	1.80

NOTE: *Golden* c-23. *Heath* a-24. *Rogers* a-75p, 77-84p. 2nd printings exist.

G. I. JOE COMICS MAGAZINE
Dec, 1986 - No. 13, 1988 ($1.50, digest-size)
Marvel Comics Group

	Good	Fine	N-Mint
1-G.I. Joe-r	.35	1.00	2.00
2-13	.25	.75	1.50

G.I. JOE EUROPEAN MISSIONS (Action Force in indicia)
June, 1988 - Present ($1.50/$1.75, color)
Marvel Comics Ltd. (British)

	Good	Fine	N-Mint
1-5: Reprints Action Force	.25	.75	1.50

G.I. JOE IN 3-D
July, 1987 - Present ($2.50) (with glasses)
Blackthorne Publishing

	Good	Fine	N-Mint
1-5	.40	1.25	2.50
Annual 1 ('88)	.40	1.25	2.50

G. I. JOE ORDER OF BATTLE, THE
Dec, 1986 - No. 4, Mar, 1987 (mini-series)
Marvel Comics Group

	Good	Fine	N-Mint
1	.60	1.75	3.50
2-4	.35	1.00	2.00

G. I. JOE SPECIAL MISSIONS
Oct, 1986 - Present
Marvel Comics Group

	Good	Fine	N-Mint
1	.60	1.75	3.50
2	.35	1.00	2.00
3-10	.25	.75	1.50
11-18		.50	1.00

G. I. JUNIORS (See Harvey Hits No. 86, 91, 95, 98, 101, 104, 107, 110, 112, 114, 116, 118, 120, 122)

GIL THORP
May-July, 1963
Dell Publishing Co.

	Good	Fine	N-Mint
1-Caniffish-a	1.75	5.25	12.00

GINGER (Li'l Jinx No. 11 on?)
1951 - No. 10, Summer, 1954
Archie Publications

	Good	Fine	N-Mint
1	6.00	18.00	42.00
2	3.50	10.50	24.00
3-6	2.35	7.00	16.00
7-10-Katy Keene app.	3.70	11.00	26.00

GINGER FOX
Sept, 1988 - No. 4, Dec, 1988 ($1.75, color, mini-series)
Comico

	Good	Fine	N-Mint
1-4: 1,2-photo-c	.30	.90	1.75

G.I. RAMBOT
April, 1987 - No. 2? ($1.95, color)
Wonder Color Comics/Pied Piper #2

	Good	Fine	N-Mint
1,2	.25	.75	1.50

GIRL COMICS (Girl Confessions No. 13 on)
Nov, 1949 - No. 12, Jan, 1952 (Photo-c 1-4)
Marvel/Atlas Comics(CnPC)

G. I. Joe V1#12, © Z-D

G. I. Joe, A Real American Hero #12, © MEG

Ginger #2, © AP

180

Girl Confessions #24, © MEG

Girls' Romances #1, © DC

G. I. War Brides #1, © SUPR

	Good	Fine	N-Mint
GIRL COMICS (continued)			
1 (52 pgs.)	6.50	19.50	45.00
2-Kubert-a	3.50	10.50	24.00
3-Everett-a; Liz Taylor photo-c	4.30	13.00	30.00
4-11	1.70	5.00	12.00
12-Krigstein-a	3.15	9.50	22.00
GIRL CONFESSIONS (Formerly Girl Comics)			
No. 13, Mar, 1952 - No. 35, Aug, 1954			
Atlas Comics (CnPC/ZPC)			
13-Everett-a	3.50	10.50	24.00
14,15,19,20	1.70	5.00	12.00
16-18-Everett-a	2.30	7.00	16.00
21-35	1.30	4.00	9.00
GIRL FROM U.N.C.L.E., THE (TV)			
Jan, 1967 - No. 5, Oct, 1967			
Gold Key			
1-McWilliams-a; photo-c	2.65	8.00	18.00
2-5-Leonard Swift-Courier No. 5	1.70	5.00	12.00
GIRLS' FUN & FASHION MAGAZINE (Formerly Polly Pigtails)			
V5No.44, Jan, 1950 - V5No.47, July, 1950			
Parents' Magazine Institute			
V5#44	2.00	6.00	14.00
45-47	1.00	3.00	7.00
GIRLS IN LOVE			
May, 1950 - No. 2, July, 1950			
Fawcett Publications			
1,2-Photo-c	4.35	13.00	30.00
GIRLS IN LOVE (Formerly G. I. Sweethearts No. 45)			
No. 46, Sept, 1955 - No. 57, Dec, 1956			
Quality Comics Group			
46	2.65	8.00	18.00
47-56: 54-'Commie' story	1.30	4.00	9.00
57-Matt Baker c/a	3.35	10.00	23.00
GIRLS IN WHITE (See Harvey Comics Hits No. 58)			
GIRLS' LIFE			
Jan, 1954 - No. 6, Nov, 1954			
Atlas Comics (BFP)			
1-Patsy Walker	3.50	10.50	24.00
2	1.70	5.00	12.00
3-6	1.15	3.50	8.00
GIRLS' LOVE STORIES			
Aug-Sept, 1949 - No. 180, Nov-Dec, 1973 (No. 1-13, 52 pgs.)			
National Comics(Signal Publ. No.9-65/Arleigh No.83-117)			
1-Toth, Kinstler-a, 8 pgs. each; photo-c	17.00	51.00	120.00
2-Kinstler-a?	8.50	25.50	60.00
3-10: 1-9-Photo-c	5.00	15.00	35.00
11-20	3.15	9.50	22.00
21-33: 21-Kinstler-a. 33-Last pre-code (1-2/55)	2.00	6.00	14.00
34-50	1.60	4.70	11.00
51-99: 83-Last 10 cent ish.	.85	2.50	6.00
100	1.00	3.00	7.00
101-146: 113-117-April O'Day app.	.50	1.50	3.00
147-151-''Confessions'' serial	.35	1.00	2.00
152-180: 161-170, 52 pgs.	.25	.75	1.50
GIRLS' ROMANCES			
Feb-Mar, 1950 - No. 160, Oct, 1971 (No. 1-11, 52 pgs.)			
National Per. Publ.(Signal Publ. No.7-79/Arleigh No.84)			
1-Photo-c	17.00	51.00	120.00
2-Photo-c; Toth-a	8.50	25.50	60.00
3-10: 3-6-Photo-c	5.00	15.00	35.00
11,12,14-20	3.15	9.50	22.00

	Good	Fine	N-Mint
13-Toth-c	3.50	10.50	24.00
21-31: 31-Last pre-code (2-3/55)	2.00	6.00	14.00
32-50	1.50	4.50	10.00
51-99: 80-Last 10 cent ish.	.85	2.50	6.00
100	1.00	3.00	7.00
101-108,110-133,135-160: 159,160-52 pgs.	.45	1.35	3.00
109-Beatles c/story	2.00	6.00	14.00
134-Adams-c	.55	1.65	4.00
G. I. SWEETHEARTS (Formerly Diary Loves; Girls In Love #46 on)			
No. 32, June, 1953 - No. 45, May, 1955			
Quality Comics Group			
32	2.30	7.00	16.00
33-45: 44-Last pre-code (3/55)	1.30	4.00	9.00
G. I. TALES (Sgt. Barney Barker No. 1-3)			
No. 4, Feb, 1957 - No. 6, July, 1957			
Atlas Comics (MCI)			
4-Severin-a(4)	1.70	5.00	12.00
5	.85	2.50	6.00
6-Orlando, Powell, & Woodbridge-a	1.35	4.00	9.00
G. I. WAR BRIDES			
April, 1954 - No. 8, June, 1955			
Superior Publishers Ltd.			
1	2.30	7.00	16.00
2	1.20	3.50	8.00
3-8: 4-Kamenesque-a; lingerie panels	1.00	3.00	7.00
G. I. WAR TALES			
Mar-Apr, 1973 - No. 4, Oct-Nov, 1973			
National Periodical Publications			
1,3-Reprints		.15	.30
2-Adams-a(r), 4-Krigstein-a(r)		.15	.30
NOTE: Drucker a-3r,4r. Heath a-4r. Kubert a-2,3; c-4r.			
GLADSTONE COMIC ALBUM			
1987 - Present (8½x11'')($5.95)			
Gladstone Publishing			
1-Uncle Scrooge, Barks-r; Beck-c	1.00	3.00	5.95
2-Donald Duck, Barks-r, F.C. #108	1.00	3.00	5.95
3-Mickey Mouse-r by Gottfredson	1.00	3.00	5.95
4-Uncle Scrooge-r by Barks, F.C. #456	1.00	3.00	5.95
5-D. Duck Advs. r/F.C. #199	1.00	3.00	5.95
6-Uncle Scrooge-r by Barks	1.00	3.00	5.95
7-D. Duck-r by Barks	1.00	3.00	5.95
8-Mickey Mouse-r	1.00	3.00	5.95
9-Bambi, r/F.C. #12	1.00	3.00	5.95
10-Donald Duck Advs., r/F.C. #275	1.00	3.00	5.95
11-Uncle Scrooge, r/U.S. #4	1.00	3.00	5.95
12-Donald And Daisy, r/F.C. #1055, WDC&S	1.00	3.00	5.95
13-Donald Duck Advs., r/F.C. #408	1.00	3.00	5.96
14-Uncle Scrooge, Barks-r	1.00	3.00	5.95
15-Donald And Gladstone, Barks-r	1.00	3.00	5.96
16-Donald Duck Advs., r/F.C. #238	1.00	3.00	5.95
GLAMOROUS ROMANCES (Formerly Dotty)			
No. 41, Sept, 1949 - No. 90, Oct, 1956 (Photo-c 68-90)			
Ace Magazines (A. A. Wyn)			
41-Dotty app.	2.30	7.00	16.00
42-72,74-80: 50-61-Painted-c. 80-Last pre-code (2/55)			
	1.15	3.50	8.00
73-L.B. Cole-a(r)-/All Love #27	1.65	5.00	11.50
81-90	1.00	3.00	7.00
GLOBAL FORCE			
1987 - Present ($1.95, color)			
Silverline Comics			

	Good	Fine	N-Mint
GLOBAL FORCE (continued)			
1,2	.30	.90	1.80
GNOME MOBILE, THE (See Movie Comics)			
GOBBLEDYGOOK			
1984 - No. 2, 1984 (B&W)			
Mirage Studios			
1,2-24 pgs., early TMNT	33.00	100.00	200.00
GOBBLEDYGOOK			
Dec., 1986 (One shot, $3.50, B&W)			
Mirage Studios			
1-New 10 pg. TMNT story	.85	2.50	5.00
GOBLIN, THE			
June, 1982 - No. 4, Dec, 1982 (Magazine, $2.25)			
Warren Publishing Co.			
1-The Gremlin app; Golden-a(p)	.35	1.10	2.25
2-4: 1st Hobgoblin	.35	1.10	2.25
GODFATHERS, THE (See The Crusaders)			
GOD IS			
1973, 1975 (35-49 Cents)			
Spire Christian Comics (Fleming H. Revell Co.)			
By Al Hartley		.40	.80
GODS FOR HIRE			
Dec., 1986 - No. 3? ($1.50, color)			
Hot Comics			
1-3	.25	.75	1.50
GOD'S HEROES IN AMERICA			
1956 (nn) (68 pgs.) (25-35 cents)			
Catechetical Guild Educational Society			
307	1.70	5.00	10.00
GOD'S SMUGGLER (Religious)			
1972 (39 & 49 cents)			
Spire Christian Comics/Fleming H. Revell Co.			
1-Two variations exist		.40	.80
GODZILLA			
August, 1977 - No. 24, July, 1979			
Marvel Comics Group			
1-Mooney-i	.25	.75	1.50
2-24: 3-Champions x-over; 4,5-Sutton-a	.25	.75	1.50
GODZILLA			
May, 1988 - No. 6, 1988 ($1.95, B&W)			
Dark Horse Comics			
1	.40	1.25	2.50
2-6	.35	1.00	2.00
King Of The Monsters Special (8/87)	.35	1.00	2.00
GO-GO			
June, 1966 - No. 9, Oct, 1967			
Charlton Comics			
1-Miss Bikini Luv begins; Rolling Stones, Beatles, Elvis, Sonny & Cher, Sinatra, Bob Dylan parody; Herman's Hermits pin-ups	2.30	7.00	16.00
2-Ringo Starr, David McCallum, Beatles photo cover; Beatles story and photos	2.30	7.00	16.00
3-Blooperman begins, ends No. 6	.85	2.50	6.00
4	.85	2.50	6.00
5-Super Hero & TV satire by J. Aparo & Grass Green begin	1.20	3.50	8.00
6-9: 6-8-Aparo-a. 6-Petulia Clark photo-c	.85	2.50	6.00
GO-GO AND ANIMAL (See Tippy's Friends...)			
GOING STEADY (Formerly Teen-Age Temptations)			

No. 10, 1954 - No. 13, June, 1955; No. 14, Oct, 1955
St. John Publishing Co.

	Good	Fine	N-Mint
10(1954)-Matt Baker c/a	6.50	19.50	45.00
11(2/55, last precode), 12(4/55)-Baker-c	3.15	9.50	22.00
13(6/55)-Baker c/a	4.35	13.00	30.00
14(10/55)-Matt Baker-c/a, 25 pgs.	4.65	14.00	33.00
GOING STEADY (Formerly Personal Love)			
V3No.3, Feb., 1960 - V3No.6, Aug, 1960; V4No.1, Sept-Oct, 1960			
Prize Publications/Headline			
V3#3-6, V4#1	.60	1.75	3.50
GOING STEADY WITH BETTY (Betty & Her Steady No. 2)			
Nov-Dec, 1949			
Avon Periodicals			
1	6.00	18.00	42.00
GOLDEN ARROW (See Fawcett Miniatures, Mighty Midget & Whiz Comics)			
GOLDEN ARROW (...Western No. 6)			
Wint, 1942-43 - No. 6, Spring, 1947			
Fawcett Publications			
1-Golden Arrow begins	13.00	40.00	90.00
2	6.50	19.50	45.00
3-5	4.00	12.00	28.00
6-Krigstein-a	4.65	14.00	32.00
...Well Known Comics (1944; 12 pgs.; 8½x10½''; paper-c; glued binding)-Bestmaid/Samuel Lowe giveaway; printed in green	6.00	18.00	42.00
GOLDEN COMICS DIGEST			
May, 1969 - No. 48, Jan, 1976			
Gold Key			
1-Tom & Jerry, Woody Woodpecker, Bugs Bunny	1.15	3.50	8.00
2-Hanna-Barbera TV Fun Favorites; Space Ghost app.	.85	2.50	5.00
3-Tom & Jerry, Woody Woodpecker	.50	1.50	3.00
4-Tarzan; Manning & Marsh-a	1.70	5.00	12.00
5,8-Tom & Jerry, W. Woodpecker, Bugs Bunny	.35	1.00	2.00
6-Bugs Bunny	.35	1.00	2.00
7-Hanna-Barbera TV Fun Favorites	.70	2.00	4.00
9-Tarzan	1.50	4.50	10.00
10-Bugs Bunny	.50	1.50	3.00
11-Hanna-Barbera TV Fun Favorites	.50	1.50	3.00
12-Tom & Jerry, Bugs Bunny, W. Woodpecker Journey to the Sun	.50	1.50	3.00
13-Tom & Jerry	.50	1.50	3.00
14-Bugs Bunny Fun Packed Funnies	.50	1.50	3.00
15-Tom & Jerry, W. Woodpecker, Bugs Bunny	.50	1.50	3.00
16-Woody Woodpecker Cartoon Special	.50	1.50	3.00
17-Bugs Bunny	.50	1.50	3.00
18-Tom & Jerry; Barney Bear-r by Barks	.70	2.00	4.00
19-Little Lulu	1.70	5.00	12.00
20-Woody Woodpecker Falltime Funtime	.50	1.50	3.00
21-Bugs Bunny Showtime	.50	1.50	3.00
22-Tom & Jerry Winter Wingding	.50	1.50	3.00
23-Little Lulu & Tubby Fun Fling	1.70	5.00	12.00
24-Woody Woodpecker Fun Festival	.50	1.50	3.00
25,28-Tom & Jerry	.50	1.50	3.00
26-Bugs Bunny Halloween Hulla-Boo-Loo; Dr. Spektor article, also #25	.50	1.50	3.00
27-Little Lulu & Tubby in Hawaii	1.50	4.50	10.00
29-Little Lulu & Tubby	1.50	4.50	10.00
30-Bugs Bunny Vacation Funnies	.50	1.50	3.00
31-Turok, Son of Stone; reprints 4-Color #596,656	1.15	3.50	8.00

Going Steady #14, © STJ

Golden Arrow #4, © FAW

Golden Comics Digest #2, © Hanna-Barbera

Golden Lad #1, © Spark Publ.

Golden West Love #1, © Kirby Publ.

Gold Medal Comics #1, © Cambridge House

	Good	Fine	N-Mint
GOLDEN COMICS DIGEST (continued)			
32-Woody Woodpecker Summer Fun	.50	1.50	3.00
33-Little Lulu & Tubby Halloween Fun; Dr. Spektor app.			
	1.70	5.00	12.00
34-Bugs Bunny Winter Funnies	.50	1.50	3.00
35-Tom & Jerry Snowtime Funtime	.50	1.50	3.00
36-Little Lulu & Her Friends	1.70	5.00	12.00
37-Woody Woodpecker County Fair	.50	1.50	3.00
38-The Pink Panther	.50	1.50	3.00
39-Bugs Bunny Summer Fun	.50	1.50	3.00
40-Little Lulu & Tubby Trick or Treat; all by Stanley			
	1.70	5.00	12.00
41-Tom & Jerry Winter Carnival	.35	1.00	2.00
42-Bugs Bunny	.35	1.00	2.00
43-Little Lulu in Paris	1.70	5.00	12.00
44-Woody Woodpecker Family Fun Festival	.35	1.00	2.00
45-The Pink Panther	.35	1.00	2.00
46-Little Lulu & Tubby	1.50	4.50	10.00
47-Bugs Bunny	.35	1.00	2.00
48-The Lone Ranger	.70	2.00	4.00

NOTE: #1-30, 164 pages; #31 on, 132 pages.

GOLDEN LAD
July, 1945 - No. 5, June, 1946
Spark Publications

1-Origin Golden Lad & Swift Arrow	25.00	75.00	175.00
2-Mort Meskin-c/a	12.00	36.00	84.00
3,4: 3-Mort Meskin-a	11.00	33.00	76.00
5-Origin Golden Girl; Shaman & Flame app.	12.00	36.00	84.00

NOTE: All **Robinson, Meskin,** and **Roussos** art.

GOLDEN LEGACY
1966 - 1972 (Black History) (25 cents)
Fitzgerald Publishing Co.

1-Toussaint L'Ouverture (1966), 2-Harriet Tubman (1967), 3-Crispus Attucks & the Minutemen (1967), 4-Benjamin Banneker (1968), 5-Matthew Henson (1969), 6-Alexander Dumas & Family (1969), 7-Frederick Douglass, Part 1 (1969), 8-Frederick Douglass, Part 2 (1970), 9-Robert Smalls (1970), 10-J. Cinque & the Amistad Mutiny (1970), 11-Men in Action: White, Marshall J. Wilkins (1970), 12-Black Cowboys (1972), 13-The Life of Martin Luther King, Jr. (1972), 14-The Life of Alexander Pushkin (1971), 15-Ancient African Kingdoms (1972), 16-Black Inventors (1972)

each....	.25	.75	1.50
1-10,12,13,15,16(1976)-Reprints		.25	.50

GOLDEN LOVE STORIES (Formerly Golden West Love)
No. 4, April, 1950
Kirby Publishing Co.

4-Powell-a; Glenn Ford & Janet Leigh photo-c			
	6.50	19.50	45.00

GOLDEN PICTURE CLASSIC, A
1956-1957 (Text stories w/illustrations in color; 100 pgs. each)
Western Printing Co. (Simon & Shuster)

CL-401: Treasure Island	6.00	18.00	42.00
CL-402: Tom Sawyer	6.00	18.00	42.00
CL-403: Black Beauty	6.00	18.00	42.00
CL-404: Little Women	6.00	18.00	42.00
CL-405: Heidi	6.00	18.00	42.00
CL-406: Ben Hur	4.00	12.00	28.00
CL-407: Around the World in 80 Days	4.00	12.00	28.00
CL-408: Sherlock Holmes	5.00	15.00	35.00
CL-409: The Three Musketeers	4.00	12.00	28.00
CL-410: The Merry Advs. of Robin Hood	4.00	12.00	28.00
CL-411: Hans Brinker	5.00	15.00	35.00
CL-412: The Count of Monte Cristo	5.00	15.00	35.00

(Both soft & hardcover editions are valued the same)

NOTE: Recent research has uncovered new information. Apparently #s 1-6 were issued in 1956 and #7-12 in 1957. But they can be found in five different series listings: CL-1 to CL-12 (softbound); CL-401 to CL-412 (also softbound); CL-101 to CL-112 (hardbound); plus two new series discoveries: A GOLDEN READING ADVEN-TURE, publ. by Golden Press; edited down to 60 pages and reduced in size to

6''x9''; only #s discovered so far are #381 (CL-4), #382 (CL-6) & #387 (CL-3). They have no reorder list and some have covers different from GPC. There have also been discovered British editions of GPC with red hardbound covers, no reorder lists, no price, no cover illustrations, and unnumbered. Copies of all five listed series vary from scarce to very rare. Some editions of some series have not yet been found at all.

GOLDEN PICTURE STORY BOOK
Dec, 1961 (52 pgs.; 50 cents; large size)
Racine Press (Western)

	Good	Fine	N-Mint
ST-1-Huckleberry Hound (TV)	4.00	12.00	28.00
ST-2-Yogi Bear (TV)	4.00	12.00	28.00
ST-3-Babes in Toyland (Walt Disney's. . .)-Annette Funicello photo-c			
	4.00	12.00	28.00
ST-4-(. . .of Disney Ducks)-Walt Disney's Wonderful World of Ducks (Donald Duck, Uncle Scrooge, Donald's Nephews, Grandma Duck, Ludwig Von Drake, & Gyro Gearloose stories)			
	4.00	12.00	28.00

GOLDEN RECORD COMIC (See Amaz. Spider-Man #1, Avengers #1, Fantastic Four #1, Journey Into Mystery #83.

GOLDEN WEST LOVE (Golden Love Stories No. 4)
Sept-Oct, 1949 - No. 3, Feb, 1950 (All 52 pgs.)
Kirby Publishing Co.

1-Powell-a in all; Roussos-a	6.50	19.50	45.00
2,3: 3-Photo-c	5.00	15.00	35.00

GOLDEN WEST RODEO TREASURY (See Dell Giants)

GOLDILOCKS (See March of Comics No. 1)

GOLDILOCKS & THE THREE BEARS
1943 (Giveaway)
K. K. Publications

	6.75	20.00	40.00

GOLD KEY CHAMPION
Mar, 1978 - No. 2, May, 1978 (52 pages) (50 cents)
Gold Key

1-Space Family Robinson; ½-r		.40	.80
2-Mighty Samson; ½-r		.40	.80

GOLD KEY SPOTLIGHT
May, 1976 - No. 11, Feb, 1978
Gold Key

1-Tom, Dick & Harriet		.60	1.20
2-Wacky Advs. of Cracky		.50	1.00
3-Wacky Witch		.50	1.00
4-Tom, Dick & Harriet		.50	1.00
5-Wacky Advs. of Cracky		.50	1.00
6-Dagar the Invincible; Santos-a; origin Demonomicon			
	.50	1.50	3.00
7-Wacky Witch & Greta Ghost		.50	1.00
8-The Occult Files of Dr. Spektor, Simbar, Lu-sai; Santos-a			
	.50	1.50	3.00
9-Tragg		.50	1.50	3.00
10-O. G. Whiz		.50	1.00
11-Tom, Dick & Harriet		.50	1.00

GOLD MEDAL COMICS
1945 (132 pages)
Cambridge House

nn-Captain Truth by Fugitani, Crime Detector, The Witch of Salem, Luckyman, others app.	9.00	27.00	62.00
2	5.70	17.00	40.00
3-5	4.65	14.00	32.00

GOLDYN IN 3-D (Blackthorne 3-D Series No. 4)
June, 1986 ($2.25)
Blackthorne Publishing, Inc.

1		.35	1.15	2.30

GOMER PYLE (TV)
July, 1966 - No. 3, Jan, 1967
Gold Key

	Good	Fine	N-Mint
1-Photo front/back-c	3.00	9.00	21.00
2,3	2.65	8.00	18.00

GOODBYE, MR. CHIPS (See Movie Comics)

GOOFY (Disney)(See Mickey Mouse Mag. V4/7, Walt Disney
Showcase #35 & Wheaties)
No. 468, May, 1953 - Sept-Nov, 1962
Dell Publishing Co.

4-Color 468	3.00	9.00	21.00
4-Color 562,627,658,747,802	2.30	7.00	16.00
4-Color 899,952,987,1053,1094,1149,1201	2.00	6.00	14.00
12-308-211(Dell, 9-11/62)	2.00	6.00	14.00

GOOFY ADVENTURE STORY (See 4-Color No. 857)

GOOFY COMICS (Companion to Happy Comics)
June, 1943 - No. 48, 1953
Nedor Publ. Co. No. 1-14/Standard No. 14-48(Animated Cartoons)

1	10.00	30.00	70.00
2	5.00	15.00	35.00
3-10	3.50	10.50	24.00
11-19	2.65	8.00	18.00
20-35-Frazetta text illos in all	4.00	12.00	28.00
36-48	1.70	5.00	12.00

GOOFY SUCCESS STORY (See 4-Color No. 702)

GOOSE (Humor magazine)
Sept, 1976 - No. 3, 1976 (52 pgs.) (75 cents)
Cousins Publ. (Fawcett)

1-3		.50	1.00

GORDO (See Comics Revue No. 5)

GORGO (Based on movie) (See Return of...)
May, 1961 - No. 23, Sept, 1965
Charlton Comics

1-Ditko-a, 22 pgs.	11.00	32.00	75.00
2,3-Ditko c/a	5.50	16.50	38.00
4-10: 4-Ditko-c	3.70	11.00	26.00
11,13-16-Ditko-a	2.65	8.00	18.00
12,17-23: 12-Reptisaurus x-over; Montes/Bache-a-No. 17-23. 20-			
Giordano-c	1.00	3.00	7.00
Gorgo's Revenge('62)-Becomes Return of Gorgo			
	2.00	6.00	14.00

GOSPEL BLIMP, THE
1973, 1974 (36 pgs.) (35, 39 cents)
Spire Christian Comics (Fleming H. Revell Co.)

nn		.50	1.00

GOTHIC ROMANCES
January, 1975 (B&W Magazine) (75 cents)
Atlas/Seaboard Publ.

1-Adams-a	.30	.90	1.80

GOVERNOR & J. J., THE (TV)
Feb, 1970 - No. 3, Aug, 1970 (Photo-c)
Gold Key

1	2.00	6.00	14.00
2,3	1.50	4.50	10.00

GRANDMA DUCK'S FARM FRIENDS (See 4-Color #763, 873, 965, 1010,
1073, 1161, 1279 & Wheaties)

GRAND PRIX (Formerly Hot Rod Racers)
No. 16, Sept, 1967 - No. 31, May, 1970
Charlton Comics

16-31: Features Rick Roberts	.25	.75	1.50

GRAY GHOST, THE (See 4-Color No. 911,1000)

GREAT ACTION COMICS
1958 (Reprints)
I. W. Enterprises

	Good	Fine	N-Mint
1-Captain Truth	1.00	3.00	6.00
8,9-Phantom Lady No. 15 & 23	6.00	18.00	42.00

GREAT AMERICAN COMICS PRESENTS - THE SECRET VOICE
1945 (10 cents)
Peter George 4-Star Publ./American Features Syndicate

1-All anti-Nazi	6.50	19.50	45.00

GREAT AMERICAN WESTERN, THE
1987 - Present? ($1.75, color)
Americomics

1,2	.35	1.00	2.00

GREAT CAT FAMILY, THE (See 4-Color No. 750)

GREAT COMICS
Nov, 1941 - No. 3, Jan, 1942
Great Comics Publications

1-Origin The Great Zarro; Madame Strange begins			
	40.00	120.00	280.00
2	23.00	70.00	160.00
3-Futuro Takes Hitler to Hell; movie story cont'd./Choice No. 3			
	42.00	125.00	295.00

GREAT COMICS
1945
Novack Publishing Co./Jubilee Comics

1-The Defenders, Capt. Power app.; L. B. Cole-c			
	6.50	19.50	45.00
1-Same cover; Boogey Man, Satanas, & The Sorcerer & His			
Apprentice	4.00	12.00	28.00

GREAT DOGPATCH MYSTERY (See Mammy Yokum & the...)

GREAT EXPLOITS
October, 1957
Decker Publ./Red Top

1-Krigstein-a(2) (re-issue on cover); reprints/Daring Advs. No. 6			
	3.50	10.50	24.00

GREAT FOODINI, THE (See Foodini)

GREAT GAZOO, THE (The Flintstones)(TV)
Aug, 1973 - No. 20, Jan, 1977 (Hanna-Barbera)
Charlton Comics

1	.50	1.50	3.00
2-20		.50	1.00

GREAT GRAPE APE, THE (TV)(See TV Stars #1)
Sept, 1976 - No. 2, Nov, 1976 (Hanna-Barbera)
Charlton Comics

1,2	.35	1.00	2.00

GREAT LOCOMOTIVE CHASE, THE (See 4-Color No. 712)

GREAT LOVER ROMANCES (Young Lover Romances #4,5?)
3/51; No. 2, 1951(nd), No. 3, 1952 (nd) - No. 22, May, 1955 (Photo-c
#1-3,13,17)
Toby Press

1-Jon Juan-r/J.J. #1 by Schomburg; Dr. Anthony King app.			
	5.00	15.00	35.00
2-Jon Juan, Dr. Anthony King app.	2.30	7.00	16.00
3,7,9-14,16-22 (no #4,5)	1.15	3.50	8.00
6-Kurtzman-a (10/52)	2.65	8.00	18.00
8-Five pgs. of ''Pin-Up Pete'' by Sparling	3.50	10.50	24.00
15-Liz Taylor photo-c	2.30	7.00	16.00

The Governor & J. J. #3, © CBS

Great Comics #1 (1945), © Novack Publ.

Great Lover Romances #3, © TOBY

Green Arrow: The Long Bow Hunters #1 (1st print), © DC   Green Hornet Comics #1, © HARV   Green Lantern #2 (Winter)'41-42), © DC

GREAT PEOPLE OF GENESIS, THE
No date (64 pgs.) (Religious giveaway)
David C. Cook Publ. Co.

	Good	Fine	N-Mint
Reprint/Sunday Pix Weekly	1.50	4.50	10.00

GREAT RACE, THE (See Movie Classics)

GREAT SACRAMENT, THE
1953 (36 pages)
Catechetical Guild giveaway

	2.00	6.00	14.00

GREAT SCOTT SHOE STORE (See Bulls-Eye)

GREAT WEST (Magazine)
1969 (52 pages) (Black & White)
M. F. Enterprises

V1#1		.40	.80

GREAT WESTERN
Jan-Mar, 1954 - No. 11, Oct-Dec, 1954
Magazine Enterprises

8(A-1 93)-Trail Colt by Guardineer; Powell Red Hawk-r/Straight Arrow begins, ends #11	8.50	25.50	60.00
9(A-1 105), 11(A-1 127)-Ghost Rider, Durango Kid app.	4.30	13.00	30.00
10(A-1 113)-The Calico Kid by Guardineer-r/Tim Holt #8; Straight Arrow, Durango Kid app.	4.30	13.00	30.00
I.W. Reprint #1,2 9: Straight Arrow in #1,2	.85	2.50	5.00
I.W. Reprint #8-Origin Ghost Rider(Tim Holt #11); Tim Holt app.; Bolle-a	1.20	3.50	8.00

NOTE: *Guardineer* c-8. *Powell* a(r)-8-11 (from Straight Arrow).

GREEN ARROW (See Adventure, Action #440, Brave & the Bold, DC Super Stars #17, Flash, Green Lantern, Leading, More Fun, and World's Finest)

GREEN ARROW
May, 1983 - No. 4, Aug, 1983 (Mini-series)
DC Comics

1-Origin; Speedy cameo	.40	1.25	2.50
2-4	.30	.90	1.75

GREEN ARROW
Feb, 1988 - Present ($1.00)(Painted-c #1-3)
DC Comics

1-Mature readers	.70	2.00	4.00
2	.40	1.25	2.50
3	.35	1.00	2.00
4,5	.25	.75	1.50
6-13		.50	1.00
Annual 1 ('88)	.35	1.00	2.00

NOTE: *Grell* c-1-4, 10p.

GREEN ARROW: THE LONG BOW HUNTERS
Aug, 1987 - No. 3, Oct, 1987 ($2.95, color)
DC Comics

1-Grell c/a	2.00	6.00	14.00
1-2nd printing	.50	1.50	3.00
2	1.35	4.00	8.00
2-2nd printing	.50	1.50	3.00
3	.85	2.50	5.00

GREEN BERET, THE (See Tales of. . .)

GREEN GIANT COMICS (Also see Colossus Comics)
1940 (no price on cover)
Pelican Publications (Funnies, Inc.)

1-Dr. Nerod, Green Giant, Black Arrow, Mundoo & Master Mystic app; origin Colossus. (Rare, currently only 5 copies known)	330.00	990.00	2300.00

NOTE: The idea for this book came about by a stroll through a grocery store. Printed by Moreau Publ. of Orange, N.J. as an experiment to see if they could profitably use the idle time of their 40-page Hoe color press. The experiment failed due to the difficulty of obtaining good quality color registration and Mr. Moreau believes the book never reached the stands. The book has no price or date which lends credence to it. Contains five pages reprinted from Motion Picture Funnies Weekly.

GREENHAVEN
1988 - No. 3, 1988 ($2.00, color, 28pgs, mini-series)
Aircel Publishing

	Good	Fine	N-Mint
1-3	.35	1.00	2.00

GREEN HORNET, THE (TV)(See Four Color 496)
Feb, 1967 - No. 3, Aug, 1967 (All have photo-c)
Gold Key

1-Bruce Lee photo-c	4.65	14.00	32.00
2,3	3.50	10.50	24.00

GREEN HORNET COMICS (. . .Racket Buster #44) (Radio, movies)
Dec, 1940 - No. 47, Sept, 1949 (See All New #13,14)
Helnit Publ. Co.(Holyoke) No. 1-6/Family Comics No. 7-on(Harvey)

1-Green Hornet begins; painted-c	110.00	330.00	775.00
2	50.00	150.00	350.00
3	40.00	120.00	280.00
4-6 (8/41)	30.00	90.00	210.00
7 (6/42)-Origin The Zebra; Robin Hood & Spirit of 76 begin	28.00	84.00	195.00
8-10	22.00	65.00	154.00
11,12-Mr. Q in both	19.00	57.00	132.00
13-20	17.00	51.00	120.00
21-30: 24-Sci-Fi-c	15.00	45.00	105.00
31-The Man in Black Called Fate begins	16.00	48.00	110.00
32-36: 36-Spanking panel	13.00	40.00	90.00
37-Shock Gibson app. by Powell; S&K Kid Adonis reprinted from Stuntman No. 3	14.00	42.00	100.00
38-Shock Gibson, Kid Adonis app.	13.00	40.00	90.00
39-Stuntman story by S&K	17.00	51.00	120.00
40,41	10.00	30.00	70.00
42-45,47-Kerry Drake in all. 45-Boy Explorers on cover only	10.00	30.00	70.00
46-''Case of the Marijuana Racket'' cover/story; Kerry Drake app.	10.00	30.00	70.00

NOTE: *Fuje* a-23, 24, 26. *Kubert* a-20, 30. *Powell* a-7-10, 12, 14, 16-21, 30, 31(2), 32(3), 33, 34(3), 35, 36, 37(2). *Robinson* a-27. *Schomburg* c-15, 17-23. Kirbyish c-7, 9, 15. Bondage c-8, 14, 18, 26, 36.

GREEN JET COMICS, THE (See Comic Books, Series 1)

GREEN LAMA (Also see Comic Books, Series 1 & Prize Comics)
Dec, 1944 - No. 8, March, 1946 (Formerly a pulp hero who began in 1940)
Spark Publications/Prize No. 7 on

1-Intro. The Green Lama, Lt. Hercules & The Boy Champions; Mac Raboy-c/a #1-8	50.00	150.00	350.00
2-Lt. Hercules borrows the Human Torch's powers for one panel	35.00	105.00	245.00
3,6-8: 7-Christmas-c	25.00	75.00	175.00
4-Dick Tracy take-off in Lt. Hercules story by H. L. Gold (sci-fiction writer)	25.00	75.00	175.00
5-Lt. Hercules story; Little Orphan Annie, Smilin' Jack & Snuffy Smith take-off	25.00	75.00	175.00

NOTE: *Robinson* a-3-5.

GREEN LANTERN (1st Series) (See All-American, All Flash Quarterly, All Star Comics, The Big All-American & Comic Cavalcade)
Fall, 1941 - No. 38, May-June, 1949
National Periodical Publications/All-American

1-Origin retold	407.00	1220.00	2850.00
2-1st book-length story	180.00	540.00	1260.00
3	140.00	420.00	980.00
4	100.00	300.00	700.00
5	80.00	240.00	560.00

GREEN LANTERN (continued)	Good	Fine	N-Mint
6-8: 8-Hop Harrigan begins	70.00	210.00	490.00
9,10: 10-Origin Vandal Savage	60.00	180.00	420.00
11-17,19,20: 12-Origin Gambler	50.00	150.00	350.00
18-Christmas-c	55.00	165.00	385.00
21-29: 27-Origin Sky Pirate	42.00	125.00	295.00
30-Origin/1st app. Streak the Wonder Dog by Toth	42.00	125.00	295.00
31-35	36.00	108.00	250.00
36-38: 37-Sargon the Sorcerer app.	42.00	125.00	295.00

NOTE: *Book-length stories #2-8. Paul Reinman* c-11, 12, 15, 16, 18, 19, 22. *Toth* a-28, 30, 31, 34-38; c-28, 30, 34, 36-38.

GREEN LANTERN (2nd Series) (See Adventure, DC Spec., DC Spec. Series, Flash, Showcase & Tales of The . . .Corps; Gr. Lant. Corps #206 on)
7-8/60 - No. 89, 4-5/72; No. 90, 8-9/76 - No. 205, 10/86
National Periodical Publications/DC Comics

	Good	Fine	N-Mint
1-Origin retold; Gil Kane-a begins	70.00	175.00	490.00
2-1st Pieface	28.00	71.00	200.00
3	16.50	41.00	115.00
4,5: 5-Origin & 1st app. Hector Hammond; 1st 5700 A.D. story	13.00	32.00	90.00
6-10: 6-Intro Tomar-re the alien G.L. 7-Origin Sinestro. 9-1st Jordan Brothers; last 10 cent issue	7.00	18.00	50.00
11-15: 13-Flash x-over. 14-Origin Sonar	5.70	14.00	40.00
16-20: 16-Origin Star Sapphire. 20-Flash x-over	4.30	11.00	30.00
21-30: 21-Origin Dr. Polaris. 23-1st Tattooed Man. 24-Origin Shark. 29-JLA cameo; 1st Blackhand	3.00	7.00	21.00
31-39	2.00	6.00	14.00
40-1st app. Crisis; 1st G.A. Green Lantern in Silver Age; origin The Guardians	16.00	40.00	110.00
41-50: 42-Zatanna x-over. 43-Flash x-over. 45-G.A. Green Lantern x-over	1.35	4.00	8.00
51-58: 52-G.A. Gr. Lantern x-over	1.00	3.00	6.00
59-1st Guy Gardner	2.85	8.50	20.00
60-75: 61-G.A. Green Lantern x-over. 69-Wood inks	.85	2.50	5.00
76-Begin Green Lantern/Green Arrow series by Neal Adams	6.50	19.50	45.00
77	2.65	8.00	18.00
78-80	2.00	6.00	14.00
81-84: 82-One pg. Wrightson inks. 83-G.L. reveals i.d. to Carol Ferris. 84-Adams/Wrightson-a, 22p	1.50	4.50	10.00
85,86(52 pgs.)-Drug propaganda books. 86-G.A. Gr. Lant.-r; Toth-a	2.15	6.50	15.00
87,89(52 pgs.): 89-G.A. Green Lantern-r	1.00	3.00	6.00
88(52 pgs.,'72)-Unpubbed G.A. Gr. Lantern story; Gr. Lant.-r/Showcase 23. Adams-a(1 pg.)	.35	1.00	2.00
90('76)-99	.35	1.00	2.00
100-(Giant)-1st app. new Air Wave	.40	1.25	2.50
101-119: 108-110 (44pgs)-G.A. Gr. Lant. 111-Origin retold; G.A. Green Lant. app. 112-G.A. Gr. Lant. origin retold	.25	.75	1.50
120-135,138-140,144-149: 131,132-Tales of the G.L. Corps. 132-Adam Strange begins new series, ends 147. 148-Tales of the G.L. Corps begins, ends #173	.60		1.20
136,137-1st app. Citadel	.35	1.00	2.00
141-Ist app. Omega Men	.50	1.50	3.00
142,143-The Omega Men app.; Perez-c	.35	1.00	2.00
150-Anniversary ish., 52 pgs.	.25	.75	1.50
151-159,162-170: 159-Origin Evil Star		.50	1.00
160,161-Omega Men app.		.50	1.00
171-193,196,197: (75-cent cover). 174-Book-length stories begin		.50	1.00
194,195-Crisis x-over. 195-Guy Gardner becomes Gr. Lantern		.50	1.00

	Good	Fine	N-Mint
198,200 ($1.25): 198-Crisis x-over	.35	1.00	2.00
199,201-205		.50	1.00
Annual 1 (See Tales Of The . . .)			
Special 1($1.50, 52pgs., '88)	.25	.75	1.50

NOTE: *Adams* a-76, 77p-87p, 89; c-63, 76-89. *Austin* a-93i, 94i, 171i, Annual 3i. *Greene* a-39-49i, 58-63i; c-54-58i. *Grell* a-90, 91, 92-100p, 106p, 108-110p; c-90, 93-100, 101p, 102-106, 108-112. *Gil Kane* a-1-49p, 50-57, 58-61p, 68-75p, 85p(r), 87p(r), 88p(r), 156, 177, 184p; c-1-52, 54-61p, 67-75, 123, 154, 156, 165-71, 177, 184. *Newton* a-148p, 149p, 181. *Perez* c-132p, 141-144. *Sekowsky* a-65p, 170p. *Sparling* a-63p. *Starlin* c-129, 133. *Staton* a-117p, 123-127p, 128, 129-31p, 132-39, 140p, 141-46, 147p, 148-50, 151-55p; c-107p, 117p, 135(i), 138p, 145p, 146, 147, 148-152p, 155p. *Toth* a-86r, 171p. *Tuska* a-166-68p, 170p.

GREEN LANTERN CORPS (Formerly Green Lantern)
No. 206, Nov. 1986 - No. 224, May, 1988
DC Comics

		Fine	N-Mint
206-223		.50	1.00
224-Double size	.25	.75	1.50
. .Corps Annual 2 (12/86)-Moore scripts		.65	1.30
. .Corps Annual 3 (8/87)-Moore scripts; Byrne-a		.65	1.30

NOTE: *Gil Kane* a-223, 224p; c-223, 224. *Staton* a-207p-213p, 217p, 221p, 222p, Annual #3, c-207p-213p, 217p, 221p, 222p. *Willingham* a-213p, 219p, 220p, 218p, 219p, Annual 2, 3p; c-218p, 219p.

GREEN LANTERN/GREEN ARROW
Oct, 1983 - No. 7, April, 1984
DC Comics

	Good	Fine	N-Mint
1-Reprints begin	.45	1.25	2.50
2-7 (52-60 pgs.)	.45	1.25	2.50

NOTE: *Adams* a-1-7; c-1-4. *Wrightson* a-4, 5.

GREEN MASK, THE (The Bouncer No. 11 on? See Mystery Men)
Summer, 1940 - No. 9, 2/42; No. 10, 8/44 - No. 11, 11/44;
V2/1, Spr, 1945 - No. 6, 10-11/46
Fox Features Syndicate

	Good	Fine	N-Mint
V1/1-Origin The Green Mask & Domino; reprints/Mystery Men No. 1-3,5-7; Lou Fine-c	85.00	255.00	595.00
2-Zanzibar The Magician by Tuska	40.00	120.00	280.00
3-Powell-a; Marijuana story	25.00	75.00	175.00
4-Navy Jones begins, ends No. 6	20.00	60.00	140.00
5	17.00	51.00	120.00
6-The Nightbird begins, ends No. 9; bondage/torture-c	15.00	45.00	105.00
7-9	12.00	36.00	84.00
10,11: 10-Origin One Round Hogan & Rocket Kelly	11.00	32.00	75.00
V2/1	8.00	24.00	56.00
2-6	6.00	18.00	42.00

GREEN PLANET, THE
1962 (One Shot)
Charlton Comics

	Good	Fine	N-Mint
nn	2.00	6.00	14.00

GREEN TEAM (See Cancelled Comic Cavalcade & First Issue Special)

GREETINGS FROM SANTA (See March of Comics No. 48)

GRENDEL (Also see Primer No. 2 and Mage)
Mar, 1983 - No. 3, Feb, 1984 (B&W)
Comico

	Good	Fine	N-Mint
1-Origin Hunter Rose	7.50	22.50	45.00
2-Origin Argent	6.00	17.50	35.00
3	6.00	17.50	35.00

GRENDEL
Oct, 1986 - Present ($1.50, color) (Mature readers)
Comico

	Good	Fine	N-Mint
1	.80	2.35	4.70
1-2nd printing	.25	.75	1.50

Green Lantern #1 (1960). © DC

Green Lantern #78. © DC

The Green Mask #5. © FOX

Grendel #2 (color), © Comico

Groo The Wanderer #2 (Pacific), © S. Aragones

Gumby's Summer Fun Special #1, © Comico

GRENDEL (continued)	Good	Fine	N-Mint
2	.45	1.30	2.60
2-2nd printing	.25	.75	1.50
3-5	.35	1.10	2.20
6-10	.35	1.00	2.00
11-15,20-24: 13-15-Ken Steacy-c	.30	.90	1.80
16	.60	1.75	3.50
17-19	.45	1.40	2.75
Graphic Novel (10/86, $5.95)	1.15	3.50	7.00

GREYFRIARS BOBBY (See 4-Color No. 1189)

GREYLORE
12/85 - No. 5, 1986 ($1.50-$1.75, full color, high quality paper)
Sirius Comics

1-5	.25	.75	1.50

GRIM GHOST, THE
Jan, 1975 - No. 3, July, 1975
Atlas/Seaboard Publ.

1-Origin		.40	.80
2,3-Heath-c		.30	.60

GRIMJACK (Also see Starslayer)
Aug, 1984 - Present
First Comics

1	.40	1.20	2.40
2-5	.35	1.00	2.00
6-10	.25	.80	1.60
11-25: 20-Sutton c/a begins		.70	1.40
26-2nd color Teenage Mutant Ninja Turtles	.75	2.25	4.50
27-38: 30-Dynamo Joe x-over; 31-Mandrake c/a begins		.65	1.30
39-55	.35	1.00	1.95

GRIMM'S GHOST STORIES (See Dan Curtis)
Jan, 1972 - No. 60, June, 1982 (Painted-c No. 1-56)
Gold Key/Whitman No. 55 on

1	.50	1.50	3.00
2-4,6,7,9,10	.25	.75	1.50
5,8-Williamson-a	.40	1.25	2.50
11-16,18-20		.50	1.00
17-Crandall-a	.35	1.00	2.00
21-35: No. 32,34-reprints		.50	1.00
36-55,57-60: 43,44-(52 pgs.)		.40	.80
56-Williamson-a		.50	1.00
Mini-Comic No. 1 (3¼x6½'', 1976)		.30	.60

NOTE: Reprints-#32?, 34?, 39, 43, 44, 47?, 53; 56-60(⅓). *Bolle* a-23-25, 27, 29(2), 33, 35, 43r, 45(2), 48(2), 50, 52. *Lopez* a-24, 25. *McWilliams* a-33, 44r, 48, 58. *Win Mortimer* a-31, 33, 49, 51, 55, 56, 58(2), 59, 60. *Roussos* a-25, 30. *Sparling* a-23, 24, 28, 30, 31, 33, 43r, 45, 51(2), 52, 56, 58, 59(2), 60.

GRIN (The American Funny Book) (Magazine)
Nov, 1972 - No. 3, April, 1973 (52 pgs.) (Satire)
APAG House Pubs

1		.60	1.20
2,3		.40	.80

GRIN & BEAR IT (See Large Feature Comic No. 28)

GRIPS (Extreme violence)
Sept., 1986 - No. 4 ($1.50, B&W)
Silverwolf Comics

1	1.35	4.00	8.00
2	.50	1.50	3.00
3	.35	1.00	2.00
4-Extreme violence	.25	.75	1.50

GRIT GRADY (See Holyoke One-Shot No. 1)

GROO SPECIAL
Oct, 1984 (52 pgs.; $2.00; Baxter paper)

Eclipse Comics	Good	Fine	N-Mint
1	3.15	10.00	22.00

GROO THE WANDERER (See Destroyer Duck & Starslayer)
Dec, 1982 - No. 8, March, 1984
Pacific Comics

1-Aragones c/a(p) in all	2.65	8.00	18.00
2	2.00	6.00	12.00
3-7	1.70	5.00	10.00
8	2.00	6.00	12.00

GROO THE WANDERER (Sergio Aragones'. . .) (See Marvel Graphic
Novel #27 & Starslayer)
March, 1985 - Present
Epic Comics (Marvel)

1-Aragones-c/a	2.00	6.00	12.00
2	1.50	4.50	9.00
3-5	1.00	3.00	6.00
6-10	.75	2.25	4.50
11-20	.50	1.50	3.00
21-26	.35	1.00	2.00
27-35 ($1.00)	.35	1.00	2.00
36-50	.25	.75	1.50
Graphic Novel	1.35	4.00	8.00

GROOVY (Cartoon Comics - not CCA approved)
March, 1968 - No. 3, July, 1968
Marvel Comics Group

1-3: 1-Monkees, Ringo Starr photos	.85	2.50	6.00

GUADALCANAL DIARY (Also see American Library)
1945 (One Shot) (See Thirty Seconds Over Tokyo)
David McKay Publishing Co.

nn-B&W text & pictures; painted-c	12.00	36.00	84.00

GUERRILLA WAR (Formerly Jungle War Stories)
No. 12, July-Sept, 1965 - No. 14, Mar, 1966
Dell Publishing Co.

12-14	.70	2.00	4.00

GUILTY (See Justice Traps the Guilty)

GULF FUNNY WEEKLY (Gulf Comic Weekly No. 1-4)
1933 - No. 422, 5/23/41 (in full color; 4 pgs.; tabloid size to
2/3/39; 2/10/39 on, regular comic book size)(early issues undated)
Gulf Oil Company (Giveaway)

1	10.00	30.00	60.00
2-30	4.00	12.00	24.00
31-100	3.00	9.00	18.00
101-196	2.00	6.00	12.00
197-Wings Winfair begins(1/29/37); by Fred Meagher beginning in			
1938	15.00	45.00	90.00
198-300 (Last tabloid size)	7.00	20.00	40.00
301-350 (Regular size)	3.00	10.00	20.00
351-422	2.35	7.00	14.00

GULLIVER'S TRAVELS (See Dell Jr. Treasury No. 3)
Sept-Nov, 1965 - No. 3, May, 1966
Dell Publishing Co.

1	1.70	5.00	12.00
2,3	1.15	3.50	8.00

GUMBY'S SUMMER FUN SPECIAL
July, 1987 ($2.50, color)
Comico

1-Art Adams-c/a, B. Burden story	.75	2.25	4.50

GUMBY'S WINTER FUN SPECIAL
Dec., 1988 ($2.50, 44pgs.)
Comico

	Good	Fine	N-Mint
1-Art Adams-a	40	1.25	2.50

GUMBY 3-D
Oct, 1986 - Present ($2.50)
Blackthorne Publishing

1-9	.40	1.25	2.50

GUMPS, THE
1918 - No. 8, 1931 (10x10'')(52 pgs.; black & white)
Landfield-Kupfer/Cupples & Leon No. 2

	Good	Fine	N-Mint
Book No.2(1918)-(Rare); 5¼x13½''; paper cover; 36 pgs. daily strip reprints by Sidney Smith	16.00	48.00	110.00
nn(1924)-by Sidney Smith	10.00	30.00	70.00
2,3	8.50	25.50	60.00
4-7	8.00	24.00	56.00
8-(10x14''); 36 pgs.; B&W; National Arts Co.	8.00	24.00	56.00

GUMPS, THE (See Merry Christmas..., Popular & Super Comics)
1945 - No. 5, Nov-Dec, 1947
Dell Publ. Co./Bridgeport Herald Corp.

4-Color 73 (Dell)(1945)	6.50	19.50	45.00
1 (3-4/47)	6.50	19.50	45.00
2-5	4.00	12.00	28.00

GUNFIGHTER (Fat & Slat #1-4) (Becomes Haunt of Fear #15 on)
No. 5, Summer, 1948 - No. 14, Mar-Apr, 1950
E. C. Comics (Fables Publ. Co.)

5,6-Moon Girl in each	30.00	90.00	210.00
7-14: 14-Bondage-c	20.00	60.00	140.00

NOTE: Craig & H. C. Kiefer art in most issues. Craig c-5, 6, 13, 14. Feldstein/Craig a-10. Feldstein a-7-11. Harrison/Wood a-13, 14. Ingels a-5-14; c-7-12.

GUNFIGHTERS, THE
1963 - 1964
Super Comics (Reprints)

10,11(Billy the Kid), 12(Swift Arrow), 15(Straight Arrow-Powell-a), 16,18-All reprints	.50	1.50	3.00

GUNFIGHTERS, THE (Formerly Kid Montana)
No. 51, 10/66 - No. 52, 10/67; No. 53, 6/79 - No. 85, 7/84
Charlton Comics

51,52	.35	1.00	2.00
53,54-Williamson a(r)/Wild Bill Hickok		.40	.80
55,57-85		.30	.60
56-Williamson/Severin-c/a; r-Sheriff of Tombstone		.40	.80
85-S&K-r/1955 Bullseye		.40	.80

GUN GLORY (See 4-Color No. 846)

GUNHAWK, THE (Formerly Whip Wilson)(See Wild Western)
No. 12, Nov, 1950 - No. 18, Dec, 1951
Marvel Comics/Atlas (MCI)

12	5.00	15.00	35.00
13-18: 13-Tuska-a. 18-Maneely-c	4.00	12.00	28.00

GUNHAWKS (Gunhawk No. 7)
October, 1972 - No. 7, October, 1973
Marvel Comics Group

1-Reno Jones, Kid Cassidy	.25	.75	1.50
2-7: 6-Kid Cassidy dies. 7-Reno Jones solo		.50	1.00

GUNMASTER (Judo Master No. 89 on; formerly Six-Gun Heroes)
9/64 - No. 4, 1965; No. 84, 7/65 - No. 88, 3-4/66; No. 89, 10/67
Charlton Comics

V1#1	.70	2.00	4.00
2-4,V5#84-86: 4-Blank inside-c	.50	1.50	3.00
V5#87-89	.35	1.00	2.00

NOTE: Vol. 5 was originally cancelled with #88 (3-4/66). #89 on, became Judo Master, then later in 1967, Charlton issued #89 as a Gunmaster one-shot.

GUNS AGAINST GANGSTERS
Sept-Oct, 1948 - V2No.2, 1949
Curtis Publications/Novelty Press

	Good	Fine	N-Mint
1-Toni Gayle begins by Schomburg	9.00	27.00	62.00
2	6.00	18.00	42.00
3-6, V2#1,2: 6-Toni Gayle-c	5.50	16.50	38.00

NOTE: L. B. Cole c-1-6, V2#1, 2; a-1,2,3(2),4-6.

GUNSLINGER (See 4-Color No. 1220)

GUNSLINGER (Formerly Tex Dawson...)
No. 2, April, 1973 - No. 3, June, 1973
Marvel Comics Group

2,3		.30	.60

GUNSMOKE
Apr-May, 1949 - No. 16, Jan, 1952
Youthful Magazines

1-Gunsmoke & Masked Marvel begin by Ingels; Ingels bondage-c	17.00	51.00	120.00
2-Ingels c/a(2)	8.50	25.50	60.00
3-Ingels bondage-c/a	7.00	21.00	50.00
4-6: Ingels-c	5.00	15.00	35.00
7-10	3.50	10.50	24.00
11-16	2.30	7.00	16.00

GUNSMOKE (TV)
No. 679, 2/56 - No. 27, 6-7/61; 2/69 - No. 6, 2/70
Dell Publishing Co./Gold Key (All have James Arness photo-c)

4-Color 679(No. 1)	5.50	16.50	38.00
4-Color 720,769,797,844	3.70	11.00	26.00
6(11-1/57-58), 7	3.70	11.00	26.00
8,9,11,12-Williamson-a in all, 4 pgs. each	4.65	14.00	32.00
10-Williamson/Crandall-a, 4 pgs.	4.65	14.00	32.00
13-27	3.50	10.50	24.00
Gunsmoke Film Story (11/62-G.K. Giant) No. 30008-211	3.70	11.00	26.00
1 (G.K.)	2.00	6.00	14.00
2-6('69-70)	1.00	3.00	7.00

GUNSMOKE TRAIL
June, 1957 - No. 4, Dec, 1957
Ajax-Farrell Publ./Four Star Comic Corp.

1	3.00	9.00	21.00
2-4	1.70	5.00	12.00

GUNSMOKE WESTERN (Formerly Western Tales of Black Rider)
Dec, 1955 - No. 77, July, 1963
Atlas Comics No. 32-35(CPS/NPI); Marvel No. 36 on

32	4.30	13.00	30.00
33,35,36-Williamson-a in each: 5,6 & 4 pgs. plus Drucker No. 33	4.50	13.50	32.00
34-Baker-a, 3pgs.	2.00	6.00	14.00
37-Davis-a(2); Williamson text illo	2.30	7.00	16.00
38,39	1.50	4.50	10.00
40-Williamson/Mayo-a, 4 pgs.	4.00	12.00	28.00
41,42,45-49,51-55,57-60: 49,52-Kid From Texas story. 57-1st Two Gun Kid by Severin. 60-Sam Hawk app. in Kid Colt	1.00	3.00	7.00
43,44-Torres-a	1.50	4.50	10.00
50,61-Crandall-a	1.50	4.50	10.00
56-Matt Baker-a	1.50	4.50	10.00
62-77: 72-Origin Kid Colt	.85	2.50	6.00

NOTE: Colan a-36, 37, 72, 76. Davis a-37, 52, 54, 55; c-50, 54. Ditko a-56, 66. Jack Keller a-40, 60, 72; c-72. Kirby a-47, 50, 51, 59, 62(3), 63-67, 69, 71, 73, 77; c-56(w/Ditko),57, 58, 60, 61(w/Ayers), 62, 63, 66, 68, 69, 71-77. Severin a-60, 61; c-42, 43. Wildey a-10, 37, 42, 57. Kid Colt in all. Two-Gun Kid in No. 57; 59, 60-63. Wyatt Earp in No. 45, 48, 49, 52, 54, 55, 58.

GUNS OF FACT & FICTION (See A-1 Comics No. 13)

Gunfighter #5, © WMG

Gunsmoke #1, © YM

Gunsmoke Western #68, © MEG

Hand Of Fate #1, © Eclipse Comics   Hangman Comics #6, © AP   Hanna-Barbera Band Wagon #3, © Hanna-Barbera

	Good	Fine	N-Mint

GUN THAT WON THE WEST, THE
1956 (24 pgs.; regular size) (Giveaway)
Winchester-Western Division & Olin Mathieson Chemical Corp.

	Good	Fine	N-Mint
nn-Painted-c	2.30	7.00	16.00

GYPSY COLT (See 4-Color No. 568)

GYRO GEARLOOSE (See Walt Disney's C&S #140 & Walt Disney Showcase #18)
No. 1047, Nov-Jan/1959-60 - May-July, 1962 (Disney)
Dell Publishing Co.

4-Color 1047 (No. 1)-Barks c/a	6.00	18.00	42.00
4-Color 1095,1184-All by Carl Barks	5.00	15.00	35.00
4-Color 1267-Barks c/a, 4 pgs.	3.70	11.00	26.00
No. 01-329-207 (5-7/62)-Barks-c only	2.35	7.00	16.00

HAGAR THE HORRIBLE (See Comics Reading Libraries)

HA HA COMICS (Teepee Tim No. 100 on) (Also see Giggle)
Oct, 1943 - No. 99, Jan, 1955
Scope Mag.(Creston Publ.) No. 1-80/American Comics Group

1	13.00	40.00	90.00
2	6.00	18.00	42.00
3-5: Ken Hultgren-a begins?	4.30	13.00	30.00
6-10	3.50	10.50	24.00
11-20: 14-Infinity-c	2.15	6.50	15.00
21-40	1.70	5.00	12.00
41-94,96-99	1.30	4.00	9.00
95-3-D effect-c	5.00	15.00	35.00

HAIR BEAR BUNCH, THE (TV) (See Fun-In No. 13)
Feb, 1972 - No. 9, Feb, 1974 (Hanna-Barbera)
Gold Key

1	.85	2.50	5.00
2-9	.50	1.50	3.00

HALLELUJAH TRAIL, THE (See Movie Classics)

HALL OF FAME FEATURING THE T.H.U.N.D.E.R. AGENTS
May, 1983 - No. 3, Dec, 1983
JC Productions(Archie Comics Group)

1-3: T.H.U.N.D.E.R. Agents-r		.45	.90

HALLOWEEN HORROR
Oct, 1987 (Seduction of the Innocent #7)($1.75, color)
Eclipse Comics

1-Pre-code horror-r	.30	.90	1.80

HALO JONES (See The Ballad of...)

HANDBOOK OF THE CONAN UNIVERSE, THE
June, 1985 (One Shot)
Marvel Comics Group

1		.65	1.30

HAND OF FATE (Formerly Men Against Crime)
No. 8, Dec, 1951 - No. 26, March, 1955
Ace Magazines

8: Surrealistic text story	10.00	30.00	70.00
9,10	5.70	17.00	40.00
11-18,20,22,23	4.00	12.00	28.00
19-Bondage, hypo needle scenes	5.00	15.00	35.00
21-Necronomicon story; drug belladonna used	6.00	18.00	42.00
24-Electric chair-c	7.00	21.00	50.00
25(11/54), 25(12/54)	4.35	13.00	30.00
26-Nostrand-a	5.00	15.00	35.00

NOTE: Cameron art-No. 9, 10, 18-25; c-13. Sekowsky a-8, 9, 13, 14.

HAND OF FATE
Feb, 1988 - No. 3, Apr, 1988 ($1.75, color, Baxter)
Eclipse Comics

1,2 (color, $1.75)	.30	.90	1.75

	Good	Fine	N-Mint
3 (B&W, $2.00)	.30	.90	1.75

HANDS OF THE DRAGON
June, 1975
Seaboard Periodicals (Atlas)

1-Origin; Mooney inks		.50	1.00

HANGMAN COMICS (Special No. 1; Black Hood No. 9 on)
No. 2, Spring, 1942 - No. 8, Fall, 1943 (See Pep Comics)
MLJ Magazines

2-The Hangman, Boy Buddies begin	65.00	195.00	455.00
3-8	33.00	100.00	230.00

NOTE: Fuje a-7(3), 8(3); c-3. Reinman c-3. Bondage c-3.

HANK
1946
Pentagon Publications

nn-Coulton Waugh's newspaper reprint	3.70	11.00	26.00

HANNA-BARBERA (See Golden Comics Digest No. 2,7,11)

HANNA-BARBERA BAND WAGON (TV)
Oct, 1962 - No. 3, April, 1963
Gold Key

1,2-Giants, 84 pgs.	3.00	9.00	25.00
3-Regular size	1.70	5.00	12.00

HANNA-BARBERA HI-ADVENTURE HEROES (See Hi-Adventure...)

HANNA-BARBERA PARADE (TV)
Sept, 1971 - No. 10, Dec, 1972
Charlton Comics

1	1.30	4.00	9.00
2-6,8-10	.85	2.50	5.00
7-"Summer Picnic"-52 pgs.	.85	2.50	5.00

NOTE: No. 4 (1/72) went on sale late in 1972 with the January 1973 issues.

HANNA-BARBERA SPOTLIGHT (See Spotlight)

HANNA-BARBERA SUPER TV HEROES (TV)
April, 1968 - No. 7, Oct, 1969 (Hanna-Barbera)
Gold Key

1-The Birdman, The Herculoids(ends #2), Moby Dick, Young Samson & Goliath(ends #2,4), and The Mighty Mightor begin; Spiegle-a in all	3.50	11.00	25.00
2-The Galaxy Trio app.; Shazzan begins	2.65	8.00	18.00
3-7: The Space Ghost app. in all	2.15	6.50	15.00

HANNA-BARBERA (TV STARS) (See TV Stars)

HANS BRINKER (See 4-Color No. 1273)

HANS CHRISTIAN ANDERSEN
1953 (100 pgs. - Special Issue)
Ziff-Davis Publ. Co.

nn-Danny Kaye (movie)-Photo-c	8.50	25.50	60.00

HANSEL & GRETEL (See 4-Color No. 590)

HANSI, THE GIRL WHO LOVED THE SWASTIKA
1973, 1976 (39-49 cents)
Spire Christian Comics (Fleming H. Revell Co.)

	.35	1.00	2.00

HANS UND FRITZ
1917 (10x13½''; 1916 strip-r in B&W); 1929 (28 pgs.; 10x13½''
The Saalfield Publishing Co.

nn-by R. Dirks	27.00	81.00	190.00
193-(Very Rare)-By R. Dirks; contains B&W Sunday strip reprints of Katzenjammer Kids & Hawkshaw the Detective from 1916	27.00	81.00	190.00
...The Funny Larks of 2(1929)	27.00	81.00	190.00

HAP HAZARD COMICS (Real Love No. 25 on)
1944 - No. 24, Feb, 1949
Ace Magazines (Readers' Research)

	Good	Fine	N-Mint
1	5.00	15.00	35.00
2	2.65	8.00	18.00
3-10	1.70	5.00	12.00
11-13,15-24	1.15	3.50	8.00
14-Feldstein-c (4/47)	3.50	10.50	24.00

HAP HOPPER (See Comics Revue No. 2)

HAPPIEST MILLIONAIRE, THE (See Movie Comics)

HAPPINESS AND HEALING FOR YOU (Also see Oral Roberts'...)
1955 (36 pgs.; slick cover) (Oral Roberts Giveaway)
Commercial Comics

	7.00	20.00	40.00

NOTE: The success of this book prompted Oral Roberts to go into the publishing business himself to produce his own material.

HAPPI TIM (See March of Comics No. 182)

HAPPY COMICS (Happy Rabbit No. 41 on)
Aug, 1943 - No. 40, Dec, 1950 (Companion to Goofy Comics)
Nedor Publ./Standard Comics (Animated Cartoons)

1	10.00	30.00	70.00
2	5.00	15.00	35.00
3-10	3.50	10.50	24.00
11-19	2.00	6.00	14.00
20-31,34-37-Frazetta text illos in all; 2 in #34&35, 3 in #27,28,30	3.50	10.50	24.00
32-Frazetta-a, 7 pgs. plus two text illos; Roussos-a	10.00	30.00	70.00
33-Frazetta a(2), 6 pgs. each (Scarce)	17.00	51.00	120.00
38-40	1.50	4.50	10.00

NOTE: Al Fago a-27.

HAPPY DAYS (TV)
March, 1979 - No. 6, Feb, 1980
Gold Key

1	.35	1.00	2.00
2-6		.50	1.00
...With the Fonz Kite Fun Book(6¾x5¼''78)-PG&E	.35	1.00	2.00

HAPPY HOLIDAY (See March of Comics No. 181)

HAPPY HOOLIGAN (See Alphonse...)
1903 (18 pgs.) (Sunday strip reprints in color)
Hearst's New York American-Journal

Book 1-by Fred Opper	27.00	81.00	190.00
50 Pg. Edition(1903)-10x15'' in color	32.00	95.00	225.00

HAPPY HOOLIGAN (Handy...) (See The Travels of...)
1908 (32 pgs. in color) (10x15''; cardboard covers)
Frederick A. Stokes Co.

	22.00	65.00	154.00

HAPPY HOOLIGAN (Story of...)
1932 (16 pgs.; 9½x12''; softcover)
McLoughlin Bros.

281-Three-color text, pictures on heavy paper	7.00	21.00	50.00

HAPPY HOULIHANS (Saddle Justice No. 3 on; see Blackstone, The Magician Detective)
Fall, 1947 - No. 2, Winter, 1947-48
E. C. Comics

1-Origin Moon Girl	23.00	70.00	160.00
2	11.00	32.00	76.00

HAPPY JACK
August, 1957 - No. 2, Nov, 1957

Red Top (Decker)

	Good	Fine	N-Mint
V1#1,2	1.50	4.50	10.00

HAPPY JACK HOWARD
1957
Red Top (Farrell)/Decker

nn-Reprints Handy Andy story from E. C. Dandy Comics No. 5, renamed ''Happy Jack''	1.70	5.00	12.00

HAPPY RABBIT (Formerly Happy Comics)
No. 41, Feb, 1951 - No. 48, April, 1952
Standard Comics (Animated Cartoons)

41	2.65	8.00	18.00
42-48	1.30	4.00	9.00

HARDY BOYS, THE (See 4-Color No. 760,830,887,964-Disney)

HARDY BOYS, THE (TV)
April, 1970 - No. 4, Jan, 1971
Gold Key

1	.85	2.50	5.00
2-4	.40	1.25	2.50

HARLEM GLOBETROTTERS (TV) (See Fun-In No. 8,10)
April, 1972 - No. 12, Jan, 1975 (Hanna-Barbera)
Gold Key

1	.50	1.50	3.00
2-12	.25	.75	1.50

NOTE: #4, 8, and 12 contain 16 extra pages of advertising.

HAROLD TEEN (See 4-Color #2, 209, Popular Comics, Super Comics & Treasure Box of Famous Comics)

HAROLD TEEN (Adv. of...)
1929-31. (36-52 pgs.) (Paper covers)
Cupples & Leon Co.

B&W daily strip reprints by Carl Ed	8.50	25.50	60.00

HARVEY
Oct, 1970; No. 2, 12/70; No. 3, 6/72 - No. 6, 12/72
Marvel Comics Group

1	.50	1.50	3.00
2-6	.25	.75	1.50

HARVEY COLLECTORS COMICS (Richie Rich Collectors Comics #10 on, cover title only)
9/75 - No. 15, 1/78; No. 16, 10/79 (52 pgs.)
Harvey Publications

1-Reprints Richie Rich #1,2	.70	2.00	4.00
2-10	.40	1.20	2.40
11-16: 16-Sad Sack-r		.50	1.00

NOTE: All reprints: Casper-#2, 7, Richie Rich-#1, 3, 5, 6, 8-15, Wendy-#4. #6 titled 'Richie Rich...' on inside.

HARVEY COMICS HITS
No. 51, Oct, 1951 - No. 62, Dec, 1952
Harvey Publications

51-The Phantom	10.00	30.00	70.00
52-Steve Canyon	6.35	19.00	44.00
53-Mandrake the Magician	10.00	30.00	70.00
54-Tim Tyler's Tales of Jungle Terror	6.50	19.50	45.00
55-Mary Worth	3.35	10.00	23.00
56-The Phantom; bondage-c	8.50	25.50	60.00
57-Rip Kirby-''Kidnap Racket;'' entire book by Alex Raymond	9.25	28.00	65.00
58-Girls in White	3.00	9.00	21.00
59-Tales of the Invisible Scarlet O'Neil	6.50	20.00	45.00
60-Paramount Animated Comics No.1(2nd app. Baby Huey); 1st Harvey app. Baby Huey	17.00	51.00	120.00
61-Casper the Friendly Ghost; 1st Harvey Casper	17.00	51.00	120.00

Happy Comics #2, © STD

Happy Houlihans #1, © WMG

Harvey Comics Hits #52, © Milton Caniff

Harvey Hits #1, © KING   Harvey Hits #7, © HARV   Harvey Hits #98, © HARV

HARVEY COMICS HITS (continued)	Good	Fine	N-Mint
62-Paramount Animated Comics	7.00	21.00	50.00

HARVEY COMICS LIBRARY
April, 1952 - No. 2, 1952
Harvey Publications

	Good	Fine	N-Mint
1-Teen-Age Dope Slaves as exposed by Rex Morgan, M.D.; drug propaganda story; used in **SOTI**, pg. 27	57.00	171.00	400.00
(Prices vary widely on this book)			
2-Sparkle Plenty (Dick Tracy in "Blackmail Terror")	11.50	34.50	80.00

HARVEY COMICS SPOTLIGHT
Sept., 1987 - Present (#1-3, 75 cents, #4-on, $1.00)
Harvey Comics

		Fine	N-Mint
1-3: 1-Sad Sack, 2-Baby Huey, 3-Little Dot		.40	.75
4-Little Audrey		.50	1.00

HARVEY HITS
Sept., 1957 - No. 122, Nov., 1967
Harvey Publications

	Good	Fine	N-Mint
1-The Phantom	12.00	36.00	84.00
2-Rags Rabbit(10/57)	1.35	4.00	8.00
3-Richie Rich(11/57)-r/Little Dot; 1st book devoted to Richie Rich; see Little Dot for 1st app.	54.00	160.00	340.00
4-Little Dot's Uncles	8.00	24.00	48.00
5-Stevie Mazie's Boy Friend	1.35	4.00	8.00
6-The Phantom; Kirby-c; 2pg. Powell-a	5.70	17.00	40.00
7-Wendy the Witch	8.00	24.00	48.00
8-Sad Sack's Army Life	2.75	8.00	16.00
9-Richie Rich's Golden Deeds-r (2nd book devoted to Richie Rich)	26.00	78.00	180.00
10-Little Lotta	5.70	17.00	40.00
11-Little Audrey Summer Fun (7/58)	4.00	12.00	28.00
12-The Phantom; Kirby-c; 2pg. Powell-a	4.30	13.00	30.00
13-Little Dot's Uncles (9/58); Richie Rich 1pg.	5.50	16.50	38.00
14-Herman & Katnip (10/58)	1.35	4.00	8.00
15-The Phantom (1958)-1 pg. origin	4.00	12.00	28.00
16-Wendy the Witch (1/59)	4.00	12.00	24.00
17-Sad Sack's Army Life (2/59)	1.35	4.00	8.00
18-Buzzy & the Crow	1.35	4.00	8.00
19-Little Audrey (4/59)	2.75	8.00	16.00
20-Casper & Spooky	4.00	12.00	24.00
21-Wendy the Witch	3.00	9.00	18.00
22-Sad Sack's Army Life	1.00	3.00	6.00
23-Wendy the Witch (8/59)	3.00	9.00	18.00
24-Little Dot's Uncles (9/59); Richie Rich 1pg.	4.00	12.00	24.00
25-Herman & Katnip (10/59)	1.00	3.00	6.00
26-The Phantom (11/59)	4.00	12.00	28.00
27-Wendy the Good Little Witch	3.00	9.00	18.00
28-Sad Sack's Army Life	.50	1.50	3.00
29-Harvey-Toon (No.1)('60); Casper, Buzzy	2.00	6.00	12.00
30-Wendy the Witch (3/60)	2.75	8.00	16.00
31-Herman & Katnip (4/60)	.70	2.00	4.00
32-Sad Sack's Army Life (5/60)	.50	1.50	3.00
33-Wendy the Witch (6/60)	2.75	8.00	16.00
34-Harvey-Toon (7/60)	1.00	3.00	6.00
35-Funday Funnies (8/60)	.70	2.00	4.00
36-The Phantom (1960)	2.00	6.00	14.00
37-Casper & Nightmare	2.00	6.00	12.00
38-Harvey-Toon	1.35	4.00	8.00
39-Sad Sack's Army Life (12/60)	.50	1.50	3.00
40-Funday Funnies	.50	1.50	3.00
41-Herman & Katnip	.50	1.50	3.00
42-Harvey-Toon (3/61)	.80	2.30	4.60
43-Sad Sack's Army Life (4/61)	.50	1.50	3.00
44-The Phantom (5/61)	2.30	7.00	16.00
45-Casper & Nightmare	2.00	5.00	10.00

	Good	Fine	N-Mint
46-Harvey-Toon	.80	2.30	4.60
47-Sad Sack's Army Life (8/61)	.50	1.50	3.00
48-The Phantom (1961)	2.30	7.00	16.00
49-Stumbo the Giant (See Hot Stuff for 1st app.)	5.00	15.00	35.00
50-Harvey-Toon (11/61)	.80	2.30	4.60
51-Sad Sack's Army Life (12/61)	.50	1.50	3.00
52-Casper & Nightmare	1.70	5.00	10.00
53-Harvey-Toons (2/62)	.70	2.00	4.00
54-Stumbo the Giant	2.65	8.00	18.00
55-Sad Sack's Army Life (4/62)	.50	1.50	3.00
56-Casper & Nightmare	1.70	5.00	10.00
57-Stumbo the Giant	2.65	8.00	18.00
58-Sad Sack's Army Life	.50	1.50	3.00
59-Casper & Nightmare (7/62)	1.70	5.00	10.00
60-Stumbo the Giant (9/62)	2.65	8.00	18.00
61-Sad Sack's Army Life	.50	1.50	3.00
62-Casper & Nightmare	1.35	4.00	8.00
63-Stumbo the Giant	2.65	8.00	18.00
64-Sad Sack's Army Life (1/63)	.50	1.50	3.00
65-Casper & Nightmare	1.35	4.00	8.00
66-Stumbo The Giant	2.65	8.00	18.00
67-Sad Sack's Army Life (4/63)	.50	1.50	3.00
68-Casper & Nightmare	1.35	4.00	8.00
69-Stumbo the Giant (6/63)	2.65	8.00	18.00
70-Sad Sack's Army Life (7/63)	.50	1.50	3.00
71-Casper & Nightmare (8/63)	.40	1.20	2.40
72-Stumbo the Giant	2.65	8.00	18.00
73-Little Sad Sack (10/63)	.50	1.50	3.00
74-Sad Sack's Muttsy... (11/63)	.50	1.50	3.00
75-Casper & Nightmare	1.00	3.00	6.00
76-Little Sad Sack	.50	1.50	3.00
77-Sad Sack's Muttsy...	.50	1.50	3.00
78-Stumbo the Giant	2.65	8.00	18.00
79-Little Sad Sack (4/64)	.50	1.50	3.00
80-Sad Sack's Muttsy... (5/64)	.50	1.50	3.00
81-Little Sad Sack	.50	1.50	3.00
82-Sad Sack's Muttsy...	.50	1.50	3.00
83-Little Sad Sack (8/64)	.50	1.50	3.00
84-Sad Sack's Muttsy...	.50	1.50	3.00
85-Gabby Gob (No.1)(10/64)	.50	1.50	3.00
86-G. I. Juniors (No.1)	.50	1.50	3.00
87-Sad Sack's Muttsy... (12/64)	.50	1.50	3.00
88-Stumbo the Giant (1/65)	2.65	8.00	18.00
89-Sad Sack's Muttsy...	.50	1.50	3.00
90-Gabby Gob	.50	1.50	3.00
91-G. I. Juniors	.50	1.50	3.00
92-Sad Sack's Muttsy... (5/65)	.50	1.50	3.00
93-Sadie Sack (6/65)	.50	1.50	3.00
94-Gabby Gob	.50	1.50	3.00
95-G. I. Juniors	.50	1.50	3.00
96-Sad Sack's Muttsy... (9/65)	.50	1.50	3.00
97-Gabby Gob	.50	1.50	3.00
98-G. I. Juniors (11/65)	.50	1.50	3.00
99-Sad Sack's Muttsy... (12/65)	.50	1.50	3.00
100-Gabby Gob	.50	1.50	3.00
101-G. I. Juniors (2/66)	.50	1.50	3.00
102-Sad Sack's Muttsy... (3/66)	.50	1.50	3.00
103-Gabby Gob	.50	1.50	3.00
104-G. I. Juniors	.50	1.50	3.00
105-Sad Sack's Muttsy...	.50	1.50	3.00
106-Gabby Gob (7/66)	.50	1.50	3.00
107-G. I. Juniors (8/66)	.50	1.50	3.00
108-Sad Sack's Muttsy...	.50	1.50	3.00
109-Gabby Gob	.50	1.50	3.00
110-G. I. Juniors (11/66)	.50	1.50	3.00

HARVEY HITS (continued)	Good	Fine	N-Mint
111-Sad Sack's Muttsy... (12/66)	.50	1.50	3.00
112-G. I. Juniors	.50	1.50	3.00
113-Sad Sack's Muttsy...	.50	1.50	3.00
114-G. I. Juniors	.50	1.50	3.00
115-Sad Sack's Muttsy...	.50	1.50	3.00
116-G. I. Juniors	.50	1.50	3.00
117-Sad Sack's Muttsy...	.50	1.50	3.00
118-G. I. Juniors	.50	1.50	3.00
119-Sad Sack's Muttsy... (8/67)	.50	1.50	3.00
120-G. I. Juniors (9/67)	.50	1.50	3.00
121-Sad Sack's Muttsy... (10/67)	.50	1.50	3.00
122-G. I. Juniors	.50	1.50	3.00

HARVEY HITS COMICS
Nov, 1986 - No. 6, Oct, 1987
Harvey Publications

	Good	Fine	N-Mint
1-6: Little Lotta, Little Dot, Wendy, & Baby Huey app.		.40	.75

HARVEY POP COMICS (Teen Humor)
Oct, 1968 - No. 2, Nov, 1969 (Both are 68 pg. Giants)
Harvey Publications

	Good	Fine	N-Mint
1,2-The Cowsills	1.00	3.00	7.00

HARVEY 3-D HITS (See Sad Sack)

HARVEY-TOON (...S) (See Harvey Hits No. 29,34,38,42,46,50,53)

HARVEY WISEGUYS
Nov, 1987 - Present (98 pgs., digest-size, $1.25-$1.75)
Harvey Comics

	Good	Fine	N-Mint
1-Hot Stuff, Spooky, etc.		.60	1.25
2 (11/88, 68 pgs.)		.60	1.25
3 (4/89, $1.75)	.30	.90	1.75

HATARI (See Movie Classics)

HATHAWAYS, THE (See 4-Color No. 1298)

HAUNTED (See This Magazine Is Haunted)

HAUNTED
9/71 - No. 30, 11/76; No. 31, 9/77 - No. 75, 9/84
Charlton Comics

	Good	Fine	N-Mint
1		.60	1.20
2-5		.50	1.00
6-21		.40	.80
22-75: 64,75-r		.30	.60

NOTE: *Aparo* a-c45. *Ditko* a-1-8, 11-16, 18, 23, 24, 28, 30, 34r, 36r, 39-42r; 47r, 49-51r, 57, 60. c-1-7, 11, 13, 14, 16, 30, 41, 47, 49-51. *Howard* a-18, 22, 32. *Morisi* a-13. *Newton* a-17, 21, 59r; c-21,22(painted). *Staton* a-18, 21, 22, 30, 33; c-18, 33. *Sutton* a-21, 22, 38; c-17, 64r. #51 reprints #1; #49 reprints Tales/Myst. Traveler #4.

HAUNTED LOVE
April, 1973 - No. 11, Sept, 1975
Charlton Comics

	Good	Fine	N-Mint
1-Tom Sutton-a, 16 pgs.		.50	1.00
2,3,6-11		.30	.60
4,5-Ditko-a		.40	.80
Modern Comics #1(1978)		.20	.40

NOTE: *Howard* a-8i. *Newton* c-8,9. *Staton* a-5.

HAUNTED THRILLS
June, 1952 - No. 18, Nov-Dec, 1954
Ajax/Farrell Publications

	Good	Fine	N-Mint
1: r-/Ellery Queen 1	10.00	30.00	70.00
2-L. B. Cole-a r-/Ellery Queen 1	7.00	21.00	50.00
3-5: 3-Drug use story	5.00	15.00	35.00
6-12: 12-Webb-a	4.00	12.00	28.00
13,16,17	3.00	9.00	21.00
14-Jesus Christ apps. in story by Webb	3.00	9.00	21.00

	Good	Fine	N-Mint
15-Jo-Jo-r	4.00	12.00	28.00
18-Lingerie panels	3.00	9.00	21.00

NOTE: *Kamenish art in most issues.*

HAUNT OF FEAR (Formerly Gunfighter)
No. 15, May-June, 1950 - No. 28, Nov-Dec, 1954
E. C. Comics

	Good	Fine	N-Mint
15(#1, 1950)	100.00	300.00	700.00
16	52.00	156.00	365.00
17-Origin of Crypt of Terror, Vault of Horror, & Haunt of Fear; used in SOTI, pg. 43; last pg. Ingels-a used by N.Y. Legis. Comm.			
	52.00	156.00	365.00
4	40.00	120.00	280.00
5-Injury-to-eye panel, pg. 4	30.00	90.00	210.00
6-10	21.00	62.00	145.00
11-13,15-18	14.00	42.00	100.00
14-Origin Old Witch by Ingels	21.00	62.00	145.00
19-Used in SOTI, ill.-"A comic book baseball game" & Senate investigation on juvenile delinq. bondage/decapitation-c			
	21.00	62.00	150.00
20-Feldstein r-/Vault of Horror #12	13.00	40.00	90.00
21,22,25,27	8.50	25.50	60.00
23-Used in SOTI, pg. 241	11.00	32.00	75.00
24-Used in Senate Investigative Report, pg. 8			
	9.35	30.00	65.00
26-Contains anti-censorship editorial, 'Are you a Red Dupe?'			
	9.35	30.00	65.00
28-Low distribution	9.35	30.00	65.00

NOTE: *(Canadian reprints known; see Table of Contents.) Craig* a-15-17, 5, 7, 10, 12, 13; c-15-17, 5-7. *Crandall* a-20, 21, 26, 27. *Davis* a-4-26, 28. *Evans* a-15-19, 22-25, 27. *Feldstein* a-15-17, 20; c-4, 8-10. *Ingels* a-16, 17, 4-28; c-11-28. *Kamen* a-16, 4, 6, 7, 9-11, 13-19, 21-28. *Krigstein* a-28. *Kurtzman* a-15/1, 17/3. *Orlando* a-9, 12. *Wood* a-15, 16, 4-6.

HAUNT OF HORROR, THE (Magazine)
5/74 - No. 5, 1/75 (75 cents) (B&W)
Cadence Comics Publ. (Marvel)

	Good	Fine	N-Mint
1	.85	2.50	5.00
2-Origin & 1st app. Gabriel the Devil Hunter; Satana begins			
	.70	2.00	4.00
3	.50	1.50	3.00
4-Adams-a	.70	2.00	4.00
5-Evans-a(2)	.50	1.50	3.00

NOTE: *Alcala* a-2. *Colan* a-2p. *Heath* r-1. *Krigstein* r-3. *Reese* a-1. *Simonson* a-1.

HAVE GUN, WILL TRAVEL (TV)
No. 931, 8/58 - No. 14, 7-9/62 (All Richard Boone photo-c)
Dell Publishing Co.

	Good	Fine	N-Mint
4-Color 931 (#1)	5.00	15.00	35.00
4-Color 983,1044	3.70	11.00	26.00
4 (1-3/60) - 14	3.50	10.50	24.00

HAVOK AND WOLVERINE: MELTDOWN
Mar, 1989 - No. 4, 1989 ($3.50, mini-series, squarebound, adults)
Epic Comics (Marvel)

	Good	Fine	N-Mint
1-violent	.60	1.75	3.50

HAWAIIAN EYE (TV)
July, 1963 (Troy Donahue, Connie Stevens photo-c)
Gold Key

	Good	Fine	N-Mint
1 (10073-307)	2.00	6.00	14.00

HAWAIIAN ILLUSTRATED LEGENDS SERIES
1975 (B&W)(Cover printed w/blue, yellow, and green)
Hogarth Press

	Good	Fine	N-Mint
1-Kalelealuaka, the Mysterious Warrior		.60	1.20
2,3(Exist?)		.40	.80

Haunted Thrills #9, © AJAX

Haunt Of Fear #16 (#2), © WMG

Have Gun, Will Travel #5, © DELL

The Hawk #8, © STJ   The Hawk And The Dove #1 (1968), © DC   Headline Comics #22, © PRIZE

HAWK, THE (Also see Approved Comics & Tops In Adv.)
Wint/51 - No. 3, 11-12/52; No. 4, 1953 - No. 12, 5/55
Ziff-Davis/St. John Publ. Co. No. 4 on

	Good	Fine	N-Mint
1-Anderson-a	8.00	24.00	56.00
2-Kubert, Infantino-a; painted-c	4.65	14.00	32.00
3-8,10-11: 8-Reprints #3 with diff.-c. 10-Reprints one story/#2.			
11-Buckskin Belle & The Texan app.	3.50	10.50	24.00
9-Baker c/a; Kubert-a(r)/#2	3.70	11.00	26.00
12-Baker c/a; Buckskin Belle app.	3.70	11.00	26.00
3-D 1(11/53)-Baker-c	17.00	51.00	120.00

NOTE: *Baker c-8,9,11. Tuska a-9. 12. Painted c-1, 7.*

HAWK AND DOVE
Oct., 1988 - No. 5, Feb., 1989 ($1.00, color, mini-series)
DC Comics

1	.70	2.00	4.00
2	.50	1.50	3.00
3-5	.35	1.00	2.00

HAWK AND THE DOVE, THE (See Showcase)
Aug-Sept, 1968 - No. 6, June-July, 1969
National Periodical Publications

1-Ditko c/a	1.00	3.00	6.00
2-6: 5-Teen Titans cameo	.70	2.00	4.00

NOTE: *Ditko c/a-2. Gil Kane a-3p, 4p, 5, 6p; c-3-6.*

HAWKEYE (See The Avengers & Tales Of Suspense #57)
Sept, 1983 - No. 4, Dec, 1983 (Mini-series)
Marvel Comics Group

1-Origin	.35	1.00	2.00
2-4: 3-Origin Mockingbird	.35	1.00	2.00

HAWKEYE & THE LAST OF THE MOHICANS (See 4-Color No. 884)

HAWKMAN (See Atom & Hawkman, The Brave & the Bold, DC Comics Presents, Detective, Flash Comics, Mystery in Space, Shadow War Of..., Showcase, & World's Finest)
Apr-May, 1964 - No. 27, Aug-Sept, 1968
National Periodical Publications

1	8.00	24.00	55.00
2	4.30	13.00	30.00
3-5: 4-Zatanna x-over(origin-1st app.)	2.65	8.00	18.00
6-10: 9-Atom cameo; Hawkman & Atom learn each other's I.D.; 2nd app. Shadow Thief	1.20	3.60	8.50
11-15	1.15	3.50	7.00
16-27: Adam Strange x-over #18, cameo #19. 25-G.A. Hawkman-r	.85	2.50	5.00

NOTE: *Anderson a-1-21; c-1-21. Kubert c-27. Moldoff a-25r.*

HAWKMAN
Aug, 1986 - No. 15, Oct, 1987
DC Comics

1	.25	.75	1.50
2-15: 10-Byrne-c		.50	1.00
Special #1 ('86, $1.25)	.25	.75	1.50

HAWKMOON: COUNT BRASS
Feb, 1989 - No. 4, Aug, 1989 ($1.95, limited series, color)
First Comics

1-4: Adapts novel by Michael Moorcock	.35	1.00	2.00

HAWKMOON: THE JEWEL IN THE SKULL
May, 1986 - No. 4, Nov, 1986 (Limited series, Baxter)
First Comics

1-4: Adapts novel by Michael Moorcock	.35	1.00	2.00

HAWKMOON: THE MAD GOD'S AMULET
Jan, 1987 - No. 4, July, 1987 (Limited series, Baxter)
First Comics

1-4: Adapts novel by Michael Moorcock	.30	.90	1.80

HAWKMOON: THE RUNESTAFF
June, 1988 - No. 4, Dec., 1988 (Color, limited series)
First Comics

	Good	Fine	N-Mint
1-4: Adapts novel by Michael Moorcock	.35	1.00	1.95

HAWKMOON: THE SWORD OF DAWN
Sept, 1987 - No. 4, Mar, 1988 (Limited series, Baxter)
First Comics

1-4: Adapts novel by Michael Moorcock	.30	.90	1.80

HAWKSHAW THE DETECTIVE (See Advs. of..., Hans & Fritz & Okay)
1917 (24 pgs.; B&W; 10½x13½'') (Sunday strip reprints)
The Saalfield Publishing Co.

By Gus Mager	8.00	24.00	56.00

HAWTHORN-MELODY FARMS DAIRY COMICS
No date (1950's) (Giveaway)
Everybody's Publishing Co.

Cheerie Chick, Tuffy Turtle, Robin Koo Koo, Donald & Longhorn Legends	.70	2.50	5.00

HAYWIRE
Oct., 1988 - Present ($1.25, color)
DC Comics

1	.30	.90	1.80
2-5	.25	.75	1.50

HEADLINE COMICS (...Crime No. 32-39)
Feb, 1943 - No. 22, Nov-Dec, 1946; 1947 - No. 77, Oct, 1956
Prize Publications

1-Yank & Doodle x-over in Junior Rangers	16.00	48.00	110.00
2	6.50	19.50	45.00
3-Used in POP, pg. 84	6.50	19.50	45.00
4-7,9,10: 4,10-Hitler story	4.35	13.00	30.00
8-Classic Hitler-c	7.00	21.00	50.00
11,12	3.00	9.00	21.00
13-15-Blue Streak in all	3.50	10.50	24.00
16-Origin Atomic Man	7.00	21.00	50.00
17,18,20,21: 21-Atomic Man ends	4.00	12.00	28.00
19-S&K-a	10.00	30.00	70.00
22-Kiefer-c	2.00	6.00	14.00
23-(All S&K-a)	10.00	30.00	70.00
24-(All S&K-a); dope-crazy killer story	10.00	30.00	70.00
25-35-S&K c/a. 25-Powell-a	6.00	18.00	42.00
36-S&K-a	4.30	13.00	30.00
37-One pg. S&K, Severin-a	2.65	8.00	18.00
38,40-Meskin-a	1.70	5.00	12.00
39,41-43,45-48,50-55: 51-Kirby-a. 45-Kirby-a	1.00	3.00	7.00
44-S&K-c; Severin/Elder, Meskin-a	3.15	9.50	22.00
49-Meskin-a	1.30	4.00	9.00
56-S&K-a	2.65	8.00	18.00
57-77: 72-Meskin c/a(i)	1.00	3.00	7.00

HEAP, THE
Sept, 1971 (52 pages)
Skywald Publications

1-Kinstler-a, r-/Strange Worlds No. 8	.50	1.50	3.00

HEART AND SOUL
April-May, 1954 - No. 2, June-July, 1954
Mikeross Publications

1,2	2.30	7.00	16.00

HEART THROBS (Love Stories No. 147 on)
8/49 - No. 8, 10/50; No. 9, 3/52 - No. 146, Oct, 1972
Quality/National No. 47(4-5/57) on (Arleigh No. 48-101)

1-Classic Ward-c, Gustavson-a, 9pgs.	17.00	51.00	120.00
2-Ward c/a, 9 pgs; Gustavson-a	10.00	30.00	70.00

HEART THROBS (continued)	Good	Fine	N-Mint
3-Gustavson-a	4.00	12.00	28.00
4,6,8-Ward-a, 8-9 pgs.	6.50	19.50	45.00
5,7	2.15	6.50	15.00
9-Robert Mitchum, Jane Russell photo-c	2.50	7.50	17.50
10,15-Ward-a	4.65	14.00	32.00
11-14,16-20: 12 (7/52)	1.50	4.50	10.00
21-Ward-c	3.65	11.00	25.00
22,23-Ward-a(p)	2.65	8.00	18.00
24-33: 33-Last pre-code (3/55)	1.15	3.50	8.00
34-39,41-46 (12/56; last Quality)	1.00	3.00	7.00
40-Ward-a; r-7 pgs./#21	2.00	6.00	14.00
47-(4-5/57; 1st DC)	3.50	10.50	24.00
48-60	1.50	4.50	10.00
61-70	1.00	3.00	7.00
71-100: 74-Last 10 cent ish.	.70	2.00	4.00
101-The Beatles app. on-c	1.70	5.00	12.00
102-119,121-146: 102-123-(Serial)-Three Girls, Their Lives, Their Loves. #133-142, 52 pgs.	.35	1.00	2.00
120-Adams-c	.40	1.25	2.50

NOTE: Gustavson a-8. Photo-c 8-10, 15, 17. Tuska a-128.

HEATHCLIFF (See Star Comics Mag.)
Apr, 1985 - Present
Star Comics/Marvel Comics No. 23 on

		Fine	N-Mint
1-15: Post-a most issues		.45	.90
16-30 ($1.00)		.45	.90
Annual 1 ('87)		.60	1.20

HEATHCLIFF'S FUNHOUSE
May, 1987 - No. 10, 1988
Star Comics/Marvel Comics No. 6 on

		Fine	N-Mint
1-10		.50	1.00

HECKLE AND JECKLE (See Blue Ribbon, Paul Terry's & Terry-Toons Comics)
10/51 - No. 24, 10/55; No. 25, Fall/56 - No. 34, 6/59
St. John Publ. Co. No. 1-24/Pines No. 25 on

	Good	Fine	N-Mint
1	14.00	42.00	100.00
2	7.00	21.00	50.00
3-5	5.00	15.00	35.00
6-10	4.00	12.00	28.00
11-20	2.65	8.00	18.00
21-34	1.50	4.50	10.00

HECKLE AND JECKLE (TV) (See New Terrytoons)
11/62 - No. 4, 8/63; 5/66; No. 2, 10/66 - No. 3, 8/67
Gold Key/Dell Publishing Co.

	Good	Fine	N-Mint
1 (11/62; Gold Key)	1.70	5.00	12.00
2-4	1.00	3.00	7.00
1 (5/66; Dell)	1.30	4.00	9.00
2,3	.85	2.50	6.00

(See March of Comics No. 379,472,484)

HECKLE AND JECKLE 3-D
1987 - No. 2? ($2.50; color)
Spotlight Comics

	Good	Fine	N-Mint
1,2	.40	1.25	2.50

HECTOR COMICS
Nov, 1953 - 1954
Key Publications

	Good	Fine	N-Mint
1	2.35	7.00	16.00
2,3	1.30	4.00	9.00

HECTOR HEATHCOTE (TV)
March, 1964
Gold Key

	Good	Fine	N-Mint
1 (10111-403)	2.35	7.00	16.00

HEDY DEVINE COMICS (Formerly All Winners #21?; Hedy of Hollywood #36 on; also see Annie Oakley, Comedy & Venus)
No. 22, Aug, 1947 - No. 50, Sept, 1952
Marvel Comics (RCM)/Atlas #50

	Good	Fine	N-Mint
22	3.70	11.00	26.00
23,24,27-30: 23-Wolverton-a, 1 pg; Kurtzman's "Hey Look," 2 pgs. 24,27-30-"Hey Look" by Kurtzman, 1-3 pgs.	5.00	15.00	35.00
25-Classic "Hey Look" by Kurtzman-"Optical Illusion"	5.70	17.00	40.00
26-"Giggles & Grins" by Kurtzman	3.50	10.50	24.00
31-34,36-50: 32-Anti-Wertham editorial	1.70	5.00	12.00
35-Four pgs. "Rusty" by Kurtzman	3.50	10.50	24.00

HEDY-MILLIE-TESSIE COMEDY (See Comedy)

HEDY WOLFE
August, 1957
Atlas Publishing Co. (Emgee)

	Good	Fine	N-Mint
1	2.35	6.00	16.00

HEE HAW (TV)
July, 1970 - No. 7, Aug, 1971
Charlton Press

	Good	Fine	N-Mint
1	.70	2.00	4.00
2-7	.50	1.50	3.00

HEIDI (See Dell Jr. Treasury No. 6)

HELEN OF TROY (See 4-Color No. 684)

HELLBLAZER
Jan, 1988 - Present ($1.25, Adults)
DC Comics

	Good	Fine	N-Mint
1	.25	.75	1.50
2-14		.65	1.30

HELLO, I'M JOHNNY CASH
1976 (39-49 cents)
Spire Christian Comics (Fleming H. Revell Co.)

		Fine	N-Mint
nn		.40	.80

HELL ON EARTH (See DC Science Fic. Graphic Novel)

HELLO PAL COMICS (Short Story Comics)
Jan, 1943 - No. 3, May, 1943 (Photo-c)
Harvey Publications

	Good	Fine	N-Mint
1-Rocketman & Rocketgirl begin; Yankee Doodle Jones app.; Mickey Rooney cover	25.00	75.00	175.00
2-Charlie McCarthy cover	17.00	51.00	120.00
3-Bob Hope cover	18.00	54.00	125.00

HELL-RIDER (Magazine)
Aug, 1971 - No. 2, Oct, 1971 (B&W)
Skywald Publications

	Good	Fine	N-Mint
1-Origin & 1st app.; Butterfly & Wildbunch begins	.80	2.40	3.60
2	.70	2.00	3.00

NOTE: #3 advertised in Psycho #5 but did not come out. Buckler a-1,2. Morrow c-3.

HE-MAN (See Masters Of The Universe)

HE-MAN (Also see Tops In Adventure)
Fall, 1952
Ziff-Davis Publ. Co. (Approved Comics)

	Good	Fine	N-Mint
1-Kinstler-c; Powell-a	5.50	16.50	38.00

HE-MAN
May, 1954 - No. 2, July, 1954 (Painted-c)
Toby Press

	Good	Fine	N-Mint
1	5.00	15.00	35.00
2	3.50	10.50	24.00

Heart Throbs #9, © DC

Hedy Devine Comics #25, © MEG

He-Man #2, © TOBY

194

Henry Aldrich Comics #1, © DELL

Herbie #5, © ACG

Here's Howie Comics #8, © DC

HENNESSEY (See 4-Color No. 1200,1280)

HENRY
1935 (52 pages) (Daily B&W strip reprints)
David McKay Publications

	Good	Fine	N-Mint
1-by Carl Anderson	6.50	19.50	45.00

HENRY (See Magic Comics)
No. 122, Oct, 1946 - No. 65, Apr-June, 1961
Dell Publishing Co.

4-Color 122	5.00	15.00	35.00
4-Color 155 (7/47)	4.00	12.00	28.00
1 (1-3/48)	4.00	12.00	28.00
2	2.00	6.00	14.00
3-10	1.50	4.50	10.00
11-20: 20-Infinity-c	1.15	3.50	8.00
21-30	.85	2.50	6.00
31-40	.55	1.65	4.00
41-65	.40	1.25	3.00

HENRY (See March of Comics No. 43, 58, 84, 101, 112, 129, 147, 162, 178, 189 and Giant Comic Album)

HENRY ALDRICH COMICS (TV)
Aug-Sept, 1950 - No. 22, Sept-Nov, 1954
Dell Publishing Co.

1-Part series written by John Stanley; Bill Williams-a	4.00	12.00	28.00
2	2.30	7.00	16.00
3-5	2.00	6.00	14.00
6-10	1.70	5.00	12.00
11-22	1.30	4.00	9.00
Giveaway (16p, soft-c, 1951)-Capehart radio	2.00	6.00	14.00

HENRY BREWSTER
Feb, 1966 - V2No.7, Sept, 1967 (All Giants)
Country Wide (M.F. Ent.)

1-6(12/66)-Powell-a in most	.25	.75	1.50
V2#7		.60	1.20

HERBIE (See Forbidden Worlds)
April-May, 1964 - No. 23, Feb, 1967
American Comics Group

1	7.00	21.00	50.00
2-4	3.50	11.00	25.00
5-Beatles, Dean Martin, F. Sinatra app.	4.65	14.00	32.00
6,7,9,10	2.30	7.00	16.00
8-Origin The Fat Fury	3.50	10.50	24.00
11-22: 14-Nemesis & MagicMan app. 17-R-1st Herbie/F.W. #73	1.50	4.50	10.00
23-R-2nd Herbie/F.W. #94	1.50	4.50	10.00

NOTE: *Most have Whitney c/a.*

HERBIE GOES TO MONTE CARLO, HERBIE RIDES AGAIN (See Walt Disney Showcase No. 24, 41)

HERCULES
Oct, 1967 - No. 13, Sept, 1969; Dec, 1968
Charlton Comics

1-Thane of Bagarth series begins; Glanzman-a	.85	2.50	5.00
2-13: 10-Aparo-a	.50	1.50	3.00
8-(Low distribution)(12/68)-35 cents; magazine format; B&W-r	2.50	7.50	17.50
Modern Comics reprint 10('77), 11('78)		.20	.40

HERCULES (See Journey Into Mystery & The Mighty. . .)

HERCULES, PRINCE OF POWER
9/82 - No. 4, 12/82; 3/84 - No. 4, 6/84
Marvel Comics Group

1	.25	.75	1.50

	Good	Fine	N-Mint
2-4	.25	.75	1.50
V2#1 (Mini-series)	.25	.75	1.50
2-4		.50	1.00

NOTE: *Layton a-1, 2, 3p, 4p, V2#1-4; c-1-4, V2#1-4.*

HERCULES UNBOUND
Oct-Nov, 1975 - No. 12, Aug-Sept, 1977
National Periodical Publications

1-Wood inks begin		.40	.80
2-5		.30	.60
6-12: 10-Atomic Knights x-over		.25	.50

NOTE: *Buckler c-7p. Layton inks-No. 9, 10. Simonson a-7-10p, 11, 12; c- 8p, 9-12. Wood inks-1-8; c-7i, 8i.*

HERCULES UNCHAINED (See 4-Color No. 1006,1121)

HERE COMES SANTA (See March of Comics No. 30,213,340)

HERE IS SANTA CLAUS
1930s (16 pgs., 8 in color) (stiff paper covers)
Goldsmith Publishing Co. (Kann's in Washington, D.C.)

nn	3.50	10.50	24.00

HERE'S HOW AMERICA'S CARTOONISTS HELP TO SELL U.S. SAVINGS BONDS
1950? (16 pgs.; paper cover)
Harvey Comics giveaway
Contains: Joe Palooka, Donald Duck, Archie, Kerry Drake, Red
Ryder,Blondie & Steve Canyon 12.00 35.00 80.00

HERE'S HOWIE COMICS
Jan-Feb, 1952 - No. 18, Nov-Dec, 1954
National Periodical Publications

1	10.00	30.00	70.00
2	4.35	13.00	30.00
3-5	3.70	11.00	26.00
6-10	2.85	8.50	20.00
11-18	2.15	6.50	15.00

HERMAN & KATNIP (See Harvey Hits #14,25,31,41 & Paramount Animated Comics #1)

HERO ALLIANCE, THE
Dec, 1985 - No. 2, Sept, 1986 (No. 2, $1.50)
Sirius Comics

1,2		.65	1.30
The Special Edition 1 (7/86)-Full color	.25	.75	1.50

HERO ALLIANCE
May, 1987 - Present ($1.95, color)
Wonder Color Comics

1	.30	.95	1.90

HEROES AGAINST HUNGER
1986 (One shot) ($1.50) (For famine relief)
DC Comics

1-Superman, Batman app.; Adams-c(p); includes many artists work	.40	1.20	2.50

HEROES ALL CATHOLIC ACTION ILLUSTRATED
1943 - V6No.5, March 10, 1948 (paper covers)
Heroes All Co.

V1#1,2-(16 pgs., 8x11'')	4.00	12.00	28.00
V2#1(1/44)-3(3/44)-(16 pgs., 8x11'')	2.50	7.50	17.50
V3#1(1/45)-10(10/45)-(16 pgs., 8x11'')	2.00	6.00	14.00
V4#1-35 (12/20/46)-(16 pgs.)	1.50	4.50	10.00
V5#1(1/10/47)-8(2/28/47)-(16 pgs)	1.15	3.50	8.00
V5#9(3/7/47)-20(11/28/47)-(32 pgs.)	1.15	3.50	8.00
V6#1(1/10/48)-5(3/10/48)-(32 pgs.)	1.15	3.50	8.00

HEROES FOR HOPE STARRING THE X-MEN
Dec, 1985 ($1.50, One Shot, 52 pgs.)

HEROES FOR HOPE STARRING THE X-MEN (continued)
Markvel Comics Group

	Good	Fine	N-Mint
1-Proceeds donated to famine relief; scripts by Harlan Ellison, Stephen King; Wrightson, Corben-a	.60	1.75	3.50

HEROES, INC. PRESENTS CANNON
1969 - No. 2, 1976 (Sold at Army PX's)
Wally Wood/CPL/Gang Publ. No. 2

	Good	Fine	N-Mint
nn-Wood/Ditko-a	1.35	4.00	8.00
2-Wood-c; Ditko, Byrne, Wood-a; 8½x10½''; B&W $2.00	.70	2.00	4.00

NOTE: First issue not distributed by publisher; 1,800 copies were stored and 900 copies were stolen from warehouse. Many copies have surfaced in recent years.

HEROES OF THE WILD FRONTIER (Formerly Baffling Mysteries)
No. 26, 3/55; No. 27, 1/56 - No. 2, 4/56
Ace Periodicals

	Good	Fine	N-Mint
26(No.1)	2.35	7.00	16.00
27,28,2	1.30	4.00	9.00

HERO FOR HIRE (Power Man No. 17 on)
June, 1972 - No. 16, Dec, 1973
Marvel Comics Group

	Good	Fine	N-Mint
1-Origin Luke Cage retold; Tuska-a(p)	.60	1.80	3.50
2-10: 3-1st app. Mace. 4-1st app. Phil Fox of the Bugle; 2,3-Tuska-a(p)	.25	.75	1.50
11-16: 14-Origin retold. 15-Everett Subby-r('53). 16-Origin Stilletto; death of Rackham	.50	1.00	

HEROIC ADVENTURES (See Adventures)

HEROIC COMICS (Reg'lar Fellers...#1-15; New Heroic #41 on)
Aug, 1940 - No. 97, June, 1955
Eastern Color Printing Co./Famous Funnies(Funnies, Inc. No. 1)

	Good	Fine	N-Mint
1-Hydroman(origin) by Bill Everett, The Purple Zombie(origin) & Mann of India by Tarpe Mills begins	45.00	135.00	315.00
2	22.00	65.00	154.00
3,4	18.00	54.00	125.00
5,6	13.00	40.00	90.00
7-Origin Man O'Metal, 1 pg.	16.00	48.00	110.00
8-10: 10-Lingerie panels	9.00	27.00	62.00
11,13: 13-Crandall/Fine-a	8.00	24.00	56.00
12-Music Master(origin) begins by Everett, ends No. 31; last Purple Zombie & Mann of India	9.50	28.00	65.00
14-Hydroman x-over in Rainbow Boy; also in No. 15; origin Rainbow Boy	9.50	28.00	65.00
15-Intro. Downbeat	9.00	27.00	62.00
16-20: 17-Rainbow Boy x-over in Hydroman. 19-Rainbow Boy x-over in Hydroman & vice versa	6.00	18.00	42.00
21-30:25-Rainbow Boy x-over in Hydroman. 28-Last Man O'Metal. 29-Last Hydroman	4.00	12.00	28.00
31,34,38	1.50	4.50	10.00
32,36,37-Toth-a, 3-4 pgs.	2.65	8.00	18.00
33,35-Toth-a, 8 & 9 pgs.	3.00	9.00	21.00
39-42-Toth, Ingels-a	3.00	9.00	21.00
43,46,47,49-Toth-a, 2-4 pgs. 47-Ingels-a	2.00	6.00	14.00
44,45,50-Toth-a, 6-9 pgs.	2.35	7.00	16.00
48,52-54	1.00	3.00	7.00
51-Williamson-a	3.50	10.50	24.00
55-Toth c/a	2.00	6.00	14.00
56-60-Toth-c. 60-Everett-a	1.70	5.00	12.00
61-Everett-a	1.15	3.50	8.00
62,64-Everett-c/a	1.30	4.00	9.00
63-Everett-c	.85	2.50	6.00
65-Williamson/Frazetta-a; Evans-a, 2 pgs.	4.60	14.00	32.00
66,75,94-Frazetta-a, 2 pgs. each	1.70	5.00	12.00
67,73-Frazetta-a, 4 pgs. each	2.65	8.00	18.00
68,74,76-80,84,85,88-93,95-97	.70	2.00	5.00
69,72-Frazetta-a (6 & 8 pgs. each)	4.60	14.00	32.00

	Good	Fine	N-Mint
70,71,86,87-Frazetta, 3-4 pgs. each; 1 pg. drug mention by Frazetta in #70	2.65	8.00	18.00
81,82-One pg. Frazetta art	1.15	3.50	8.00
83-Frazetta-a, ½ pg.	1.15	3.50	8.00

NOTE: Evans a-64, 65. Everett a-(Hydroman-c/a-No. 1-9), 44, 60-64; c-1-9, 62-64. Sid Greene a-38-43, 46. Guardineer a-42(3), 43, 44, 45(2), 49(3), 50, 60, 61(2), 65, 67(2), 70-72. Ingels c-41. Kiefer a-46, 48; c-19-22, 24, 44, 46, 48, 51-53, 65, 67-69, 71-74, 76, 77, 79, 80, 82, 85, 88, 89. Mort Lawrence a-45. Tarpe Mills a-2(2), 3(2), 10. Ed Moore a-49, 52-54, 55-63, 65-69, 72-74, 76, 77. H.G. Peter a-58-74, 76, 77, 87. Paul Reinman a-49. Rico a-31. Captain Tootsie by Beck-31, 32. Painted-c #16 on.

HERO SANDWICH
Feb., 1987 - Present ($1.50, B&W)
Slave Labor Graphics

	Good	Fine	N-Mint
1-4	.35	1.00	2.00

HEX (Replaces Jonah Hex)
Sept, 1985 - No. 18, Feb, 1987
DC Comics

	Good	Fine	N-Mint
1-Hex in post-atomic war world; origin	.25	.75	1.50
2-18: 6-Origin Stilletta. 13-Intro The Dogs of War (Origin #15)		.50	1.00

HEY THERE, IT'S YOGI BEAR (See Movie Comics)

HI-ADVENTURE HEROES (Hanna-Barbera)(TV)
May, 1969 - No. 2, Aug, 1969
Gold Key

	Good	Fine	N-Mint
1-Three Musketeers, Gulliver, Arabian Knights stories	1.00	3.00	6.00
2-Three Musketeers, Micro-Venture, Arabian Knights	.70	2.00	4.00

HI AND LOIS (See 4-Color No. 683,774,955)

HI AND LOIS
Nov, 1969 - No. 11, July, 1971
Charlton Comics

	Good	Fine	N-Mint
1	.70	2.00	4.00
2-11	.50	1.50	3.00

HICKORY (See All Humor Comics)
Oct, 1949 - No. 6, Aug, 1950
Quality Comics Group

	Good	Fine	N-Mint
1-Sahl c/a in all; Feldstein?-a	5.70	17.00	40.00
2	3.00	9.00	21.00
3-6	2.35	7.00	16.00

HIDDEN CREW, THE (See The United States A. F.)

HIDE-OUT (See 4-Color No. 346)

HIDING PLACE, THE
1973 (35-49 cents)
Spire Christian Comics/Fleming H. Revell Co.

	Good	Fine	N-Mint
nn		.40	.80

HIGH ADVENTURE
October, 1957
Red Top(Decker) Comics (Farrell)

	Good	Fine	N-Mint
1-Krigstein-r from Explorer Joe (re-issue on cover)	2.00	6.00	14.00

HIGH ADVENTURE (See 4-Color No. 949,1001)

HIGH CHAPPARAL (TV)
August, 1968 (Photo-c)
Gold Key

	Good	Fine	N-Mint
1 (10226-808)-Tufts-a	2.65	8.00	18.00

HIGH SCHOOL CONFIDENTIAL DIARY (Confidential Diary #12 on)
June, 1960 - No. 11, March, 1962
Charlton Comics

Heroes, Inc. Presents Cannon #2, © Gang Publ.

Heroic Comics #14, © EAS

Hickory #6, © QUA

Hi-Spot Comics #2, © Hawley Publ.

Hit Comics #10, © QUA

Hogan's Heroes #9, © Bing Crosby

HIGH SCHOOL CONFIDENTIAL DIARY (continued)

	Good	Fine	N-Mint
1	1.00	3.00	6.00
2-11	.50	1.50	3.00

HI-HO COMICS
nd (2/46?) - No. 3, 1946
Four Star Publications

	Good	Fine	N-Mint
1-Funny Animal; L. B. Cole-c	6.00	18.00	42.00
2,3; 2-L. B. Cole-c	3.50	10.50	24.00

HI-JINX (See Teen-age Animal Funnies)
July-Aug, 1947 - No. 7, July-Aug, 1948
B&I Publ. Co.(American Comics Group)/Creston/LaSalle Publ. Co.

1-Teen-age, funny animal	5.70	17.00	40.00
2,3	3.00	9.00	21.00
4-7-Milt Gross	4.00	12.00	28.00
132 Pg. issue, nn, nd ('40s)(LaSalle)	7.00	21.00	50.00

HI-LITE COMICS
Fall, 1945
E. R. Ross Publishing Co.

1-Miss Shady	5.50	16.50	38.00

HILLBILLY COMICS
Aug, 1955 - No. 4, July, 1956 (Satire)
Charlton Comics

1	3.00	9.00	21.00
2-4	1.50	4.50	10.00

HIP-ITTY HOP (See March of Comics No. 15)

HI-SCHOOL ROMANCE (. . .Romances No. 41 on)
Oct, 1949 - No. 5, June, 1950; No. 6, Dec, 1950 - No. 73, Mar, 1958; No. 74, Sept, 1958 - No. 75, Nov, 1958
Harvey Publications/True Love(Home Comics)

1-Photo-c	3.50	10.50	24.00
2	2.00	6.00	14.00
3-9: 5-Photo-c	1.50	5.00	10.00
10-Rape story	2.00	6.00	14.00
11-20	1.15	3.50	8.00
21-31	1.00	3.00	7.00
32-''Unholy passion'' story	1.50	4.50	10.00
33-36: 36-Last pre-code (2/55)	.85	2.50	6.00
37-75	.70	2.00	5.00

NOTE: Powell a-1-3, 5, 8, 12-14, 16, 18, 21-23, 25-27, 30-34, 36, 37, 39, 45-48, 50-52, 57, 58, 60, 64, 65, 67, 69.

HI-SCHOOL ROMANCE DATE BOOK
Nov, 1962 - No. 3, Mar, 1963 (25 cent Giant)
Harvey Publications

1-Powell, Baker-a	2.35	7.00	14.00
2,3	1.00	3.00	6.00

HIS NAME IS SAVAGE (Magazine format)
No. 1, June, 1968 (One Shot)
Adventure House Press

1-Gil Kane-a	2.00	6.00	14.00

HI-SPOT COMICS (Red Ryder No. 1 & No. 3 on)
No. 2, Nov, 1940
Hawley Publications

2-David Innes of Pellucidar; art by J. C. Burroughs; written by			
Edgar R. Burroughs	55.00	165.00	385.00

HISTORY OF THE DC UNIVERSE
Sept, 1986 - No. 2, Nov, 1986 ($2.95)
DC Comics

1-Perez c/a	.85	2.50	5.00
2	.75	2.25	4.50
Limited Edition hardcover	7.50	22.50	45.00

HIT COMICS
July, 1940 - No. 65, July, 1950
Quality Comics Group

	Good	Fine	N-Mint
1-Origin Neon, the Unknown & Hercules; intro. The Red Bee; Bob & Swab, Blaze Barton, the Strange Twins, X-5 Super Agent, Casey Jones & Jack & Jill (ends #7) begin	175.00	525.00	1225.00
2-The Old Witch begins, ends #14	80.00	240.00	560.00
3-Casey Jones ends; transvestism story-'Jack & Jill'	65.00	195.00	455.00
4-Super Agent (ends #17), & Betty Bates (ends #65) begin; X-5 ends	54.00	160.00	380.00
5-Classic cover	80.00	240.00	560.00
6-10: 10-Old Witch by Crandall, 4 pgs.-1st work in comics	45.00	135.00	315.00
11-17: 13-Blaze Barton ends. 17-Last Neon; Crandall Hercules in all	42.00	125.00	295.00
18-Origin Stormy Foster, the Great Defender; The Ghost of Flanders begins; Crandall-c	45.00	135.00	315.00
19,20	42.00	125.00	295.00
21-24: 21-Last Hercules. 24-Last Red Bee & Strange Twins	36.00	108.00	252.00
25-Origin Kid Eternity by Moldoff	45.00	135.00	315.00
26-Blackhawk x-over in Kid Eternity	32.00	95.00	225.00
27-29	20.00	60.00	140.00
30,31-''Bill the Magnificent'' by Kurtzman, 11 pgs. in each	17.00	51.00	120.00
32-40: 32-Plastic Man x-over. 34-Last Stormy Foster	9.00	27.00	62.00
41-50	6.00	18.00	42.00
51-60-Last Kid Eternity	5.50	16.50	38.00
61,63-Crandall c/a; Jeb Rivers begins #61	6.00	18.00	42.00
62	4.60	14.00	32.00
64,65-Crandall-a	5.50	16.50	38.00

NOTE: Crandall a-11-17(Hercules), 23, 24(Stormy Foster); c-18-20, 23, 24. Fine c-1-14, 16, 17(most). Ward c-33. Bondage c-7, 64.

HI-YO SILVER (See Lone Ranger's Famous Horse. . . , March of Comics No. 215, and The Lone Ranger)

HOCUS POCUS (Formerly Funny Book)
No. 9, Aug-Sept, 1946
Parents' Magazine Press

9	2.35	7.00	16.00

HOGAN'S HEROES (TV) (No. 1-7 have photo-c)
June, 1966 - No. 8, Sept, 1967; No. 9, Oct, 1969
Dell Publishing Co.

1	3.00	9.00	21.00
2,3-Ditko-a(p)	2.00	6.00	14.00
4-9: 9-Reprints #1	1.50	4.50	10.00

HOLIDAY COMICS
1942 (196 pages) (25 cents)
Fawcett Publications

1-Contains three Fawcett comics; Capt. Marvel, Nyoka #1, & Whiz. Not rebound, remaindered comics—printed at the same time as originals	70.00	210.00	490.00

HOLIDAY COMICS
January, 1951 - No. 8, Oct, 1952
Star Publications

1-Funny animal contents (Frisky Fables) in all; L. B. Cole-c	8.50	25.50	60.00
2-Classic L. B. Cole-c	9.00	27.00	62.00
3-8: 5,8-X-Mas-c; all L.B. Cole-c	6.50	19.50	45.00
Accepted Reprint 4 (nd)-L.B. Cole-c	3.00	9.00	21.00

HOLIDAY DIGEST
1988 - Present ($1.25, digest-size)

HOLIDAY DIGEST (continued)
Harvey Comics

	Good	Fine	N-Mint
1		.60	1.25

HOLI-DAY SURPRISE (Formerly Summer Fun)
No. 55, Mar, 1967 (25 cents)
Charlton Comics

	Good	Fine	N-Mint
V2#55-Giant	.35	1.00	2.00

HOLLYWOOD COMICS
Winter, 1944 (52 pgs.)
New Age Publishers

	Good	Fine	N-Mint
1-Funny animals	5.50	16.50	38.00

HOLLYWOOD CONFESSIONS
Oct., 1949 - No. 2, Dec, 1949
St. John Publishing Co.

	Good	Fine	N-Mint
1-Kubert c/a-entire book	11.50	34.00	80.00
2-Kubert c/a(2) (Scarce)	17.00	51.00	120.00

HOLLYWOOD DIARY
Dec, 1949 - No. 5, July-Aug, 1950
Quality Comics Group

	Good	Fine	N-Mint
1	7.00	21.00	50.00
2-Photo-c	4.60	14.00	32.00
3-5: 3,5-Photo-c	4.00	12.00	28.00

HOLLYWOOD FILM STORIES
April, 1950 - No. 4, Oct, 1950
Feature Publications/Prize

	Good	Fine	N-Mint
1	8.00	24.00	56.00
2,4	5.00	15.00	35.00
3-A movie magazine; no comics	5.00	15.00	35.00

HOLLYWOOD FUNNY FOLKS (Formerly Funny Folks; Nutsy Squirrel #61 on)
No. 27, Aug-Sept, 1950 - No. 60, July-Aug, 1954
National Periodical Publications

	Good	Fine	N-Mint
27	4.00	12.00	28.00
28-40	2.30	7.00	16.00
41-60	1.70	5.00	12.00

NOTE: **Sheldon Mayer** a-27-35, 37-40, 43-46, 48-51, 53, 56, 57, 60.

HOLLYWOOD LOVE DOCTOR (See Doctor Anthony King...)

HOLLYWOOD PICTORIAL (...Romances on cover)
No. 3, January, 1950
St. John Publishing Co.

	Good	Fine	N-Mint
3-Matt Baker-a; photo-c	8.50	25.50	60.00

(Becomes a movie magazine - Hollywood Pictorial West. with No. 4.)

HOLLYWOOD ROMANCES (Formerly Brides In Love)
No. 46, 11/66; No. 47, 10/67; No. 48, 11/68; No. 49, 11/69 -
No. 59, 6/71 (Becomes For Lovers Only No. 60-on)
Charlton Comics

	Good	Fine	N-Mint
V2#46-Rolling Stones c/story	1.00	3.00	6.00
V2#47-59: 56-"Born to Heart Break" begins	.35	1.00	2.00

HOLLYWOOD SECRETS
Nov, 1949 - No. 6, Sept, 1950
Quality Comics Group

	Good	Fine	N-Mint
1-Ward-c/a, 9pgs.	17.00	51.00	120.00
2-Crandall-a, Ward c/a, 9 pgs.	10.00	30.00	70.00
3-6: All photo-c; 5-Lex Barker (Tarzan)-c	4.35	13.00	30.00
...of Romance, I.W. Reprint #9; Kinstler-c; Ward, Crandall-a	.85	2.50	5.00

HOLYOKE ONE-SHOT
1944 - 1945 (All reprints)
Holyoke Publishing Co. (Tem Publ.)

	Good	Fine	N-Mint
1-Grit Grady (on cover only), Miss Victory, Alias X (origin)-All reprints from Captain Fearless	5.50	16.50	38.00
2-Rusty Dugan (Corporal); Capt. Fearless (origin), Mr. Miracle (origin), app.	5.50	16.50	38.00
3-Miss Victory-Crash #4-r; Cat Man (origin), Solar Legion by Kirby app.; Miss Victory on cover only (1945)	12.00	36.00	84.00
4-Mr. Miracle-The Blue Streak app.	5.00	15.00	35.00
5-U.S. Border Patrol Comics (Sgt. Dick Carter of the...), Miss Victory (story matches cover #3), Citizen Smith, & Mr. Miracle app.	5.70	17.00	40.00
6-Capt. Fearless, Alias X, Capt. Stone (splash used as cover-#10); Diamond Jim & Rusty Dugan (splash from cover-#2)	5.00	15.00	35.00
7-Z-2, Strong Man, Blue Streak (story matches cover-#8)-Reprints from Crash #4	6.00	18.00	42.00
8-Blue Streak, Strong Man (story matches cover-#7)-Crash reprints-	5.00	15.00	35.00
9-Citizen Smith, The Blue Streak, Solar Legion by Kirby & Strongman, the Perfect Human app.; reprints from Crash #4 & 5; Citizen Smith on cover only-from story in #5(1944-before #3)	8.00	24.00	56.00
10-Captain Stone (Crash reprints); Solar Legion by S&K	8.00	24.00	56.00

HOMER COBB (See Adventures of...)

HOMER HOOPER
July, 1953 - No. 4, Dec., 1953
Atlas Comics

	Good	Fine	N-Mint
1	2.65	8.00	18.00
2-4	1.70	5.00	12.00

HOMER, THE HAPPY GHOST (See Adventures of...)
3/55 - No. 22, 11/58; V2No.1, 11/69 - V2No.5, 7/70
Atlas(ACI/PPI/WPI)/Marvel Comics

	Good	Fine	N-Mint
V1#1	3.50	10.50	24.00
2	1.70	5.00	12.00
3-10	1.30	4.00	9.00
11-22	1.00	3.00	7.00
V2#1 - V2#5 (1969-70)	.50	1.50	3.00

HOME RUN (See A-1 Comics No. 89)

HOME, SWEET HOME
1925 (10¼x x k10'')
M.S. Publishing Co.

	Good	Fine	N-Mint
nn-By Tuthill	9.00	27.00	62.00

HONEYBEE BIRDWHISTLE AND HER PET PEPI (Introducing)
1969 (24 pgs.; B&W; slick cover)
Newspaper Enterprise Association (Giveaway)

	Good	Fine	N-Mint
nn-Contains Freckles newspaper strips with a short biography of Henry Fornhals (artist) & Fred Fox (writer) of the strip	2.75	8.00	18.00

HONEYMOON (Formerly Gay Comics)
No. 41, January, 1950
A Lover's Magazine(USA) (Marvel)

	Good	Fine	N-Mint
41	2.65	8.00	18.00

HONEYMOONERS, THE
Oct, 1986 ($1.50; in color)
Lodestone Publishing

	Good	Fine	N-Mint
1-Photo-c	.50	1.50	3.00

HONEYMOONERS, THE
Sept, 1987 - No. 24 ($2.00, color)
Triad Publications

	Good	Fine	N-Mint
1	.50	1.50	3.00

Hollywood Confessions #2, © STJ

Homer, The Happy Ghost #16, © MEG

The Honeymooners #1, Lodestone Publ.

Hopalong Cassidy #86, © DC

Hoppy The Marvel Bunny #1, © FAW

Horrific #8, © Comic Media

	Good	Fine	N-Mint
THE HONEYMOONERS (continued)			
2,3,5-8,10	.35	1.00	2.00
4 ($3.50, X-Mas Special)	.60	1.75	3.50
9 ($3.95)-Jack Davis-c	.70	2.00	3.95

HONEYMOON ROMANCE
April, 1950 - No. 2, July, 1950 (25 cents) (digest size)
Artful Publications(Canadian)

	Good	Fine	N-Mint
1,2-(Rare)	17.00	51.00	120.00

HONEY WEST (TV)
September, 1966 (Photo-c)
Gold Key

	Good	Fine	N-Mint
1 (10186-609)	5.70	17.00	40.00

HONG KONG PHOOEY (Hanna-Barbera)(TV)
June, 1975 - No. 9, Nov, 1976
Charlton Comics

	Good	Fine	N-Mint
1-9		.40	.80

HOODED HORSEMAN, THE
No.21, 1-2/52 - No.27, 1-2/53; No.18, 12-1/54-55 - No.27, 6-7/56
American Comics Group (Michel Publ.)

	Good	Fine	N-Mint
21(1-2/52)-Hooded Horseman, Injun Jones continues			
	6.00	18.00	42.00
22	3.50	10.50	24.00
23-25,27(1-2/53)	2.65	8.00	18.00
26-Origin/1st app. Cowboy Sahib	3.50	10.50	24.00
18(12-1/54-55)(Formerly Out of the Night)	2.65	8.00	18.00
19-3-D effect-c; last precode, 1-2/55	5.70	17.00	40.00
20-Origin Johnny Injun	2.65	8.00	18.00
21-24,26,27(6-7/56)	2.30	7.00	16.00
25-Cowboy Sahib on cover only; Hooded Horseman i.d. revealed			
	2.65	8.00	18.00

NOTE: Whitney c/a-21('52), 20-22.

HOODED MENACE, THE (Also see Daring Advs.)
1951 (One Shot)
Realistic/Avon Periodicals

	Good	Fine	N-Mint
nn-Based on a band of hooded outlaws in the Pacific Northwest, 1900-1906; r-/in Daring Advs. #15	32.00	95.00	225.00

HOODS UP
1953 (16 pgs.; 15 cents) (Eisner c/a in all)
Fram Corp. (Dist. to service station owners)

	Good	Fine	N-Mint
1-(Very Rare; only 2 known)	33.00	100.00	230.00
2-6(Very Rare; only 1 known of each)	33.00	100.00	230.00

NOTE: Convertible Connie gives tips for service stations, selling Fram oil filters.

HOOT GIBSON'S WESTERN ROUNDUP (See Western Roundup under Fox Giants)

HOOT GIBSON WESTERN (Formerly My Love Story)
No. 5, May, 1950 - No. 3, Sept, 1950
Fox Features Syndicate

	Good	Fine	N-Mint
5,6(#1,2): 5-Photo-c	9.50	28.00	65.00
3-Wood-a	12.00	36.00	84.00

HOPALONG CASSIDY (Also see Bill Boyd Western, Master Comics, Real Western Hero, Six Gun Heroes & Bill Boyd star-red as H. Cassidy in the movies; H. Cassidy in movies, radio & TV)
Feb, 1943; No. 2, Summer, 1946 - No. 85, Jan, 1954
Fawcett Publications

	Good	Fine	N-Mint
1 (1943, 68pgs.)-H. Cassidy & his horse Topper begin (On sale 1/8/43)-Captain Marvel on-c	95.00	285.00	665.00
2-(Sum, '46)	35.00	105.00	245.00
3,4: 3-(Fall, '46, 52pgs. begin)	18.00	54.00	125.00
5-"Mad Barber" story mentioned in SOTI, pgs. 308,309			
	18.00	54.00	125.00
6-10	13.00	40.00	90.00

	Good	Fine	N-Mint
11-19: 11,13-19-Photo-c	10.00	30.00	70.00
20-29 (52pgs.)-Painted/photo-c	8.00	24.00	56.00
30,31,33,34,37-39,41 (52pgs.)-Painted-c	5.00	15.00	35.00
32,40 (36pgs.)-Painted-c	4.35	13.00	30.00
35,42,43,45 (52pgs.)-Photo-c	5.00	15.00	35.00
36,44,48 (36pgs.)-Photo-c	4.35	13.00	30.00
46,47,49-51,53,54,56 (52pgs.)-Photo-c	4.60	14.00	32.00
52,55,57-70 (36pgs.)-Photo-c	3.50	10.50	24.00
71-84-Photo-c	2.65	8.00	18.00
85-Last Fawcett issue; photo-c	3.00	9.00	21.00

NOTE: Line-drawn c-1-10, 12

	Good	Fine	N-Mint
Grape Nuts Flakes giveaway(1950,9x6'')	7.00	21.00	50.00
...& the Mad Barber(1951 Bond Bread giveaway)-7x5''; used in SOTI, pgs. 308,309	17.00	51.00	120.00
...in the Strange Legacy	6.00	18.00	42.00
...Meets the Brend Brothers Bandits	6.00	18.00	42.00
White Tower Giveaway (1946, 16pgs., paper-c)	6.00	18.00	42.00

HOPALONG CASSIDY (TV)
No. 86, Feb, 1954 - No. 135, May-June, 1959 (All-36pgs.)
National Periodical Publications

	Good	Fine	N-Mint
86-Photo-c continues	11.00	32.00	75.00
87	5.70	17.00	40.00
88-90	4.00	12.00	28.00
91-99 (98 has #93 on-c & is last precode ish, 2/55)			
	3.50	10.50	24.00
100	4.65	14.00	32.00
101-108-Last photo-c	3.00	9.00	21.00
109-135: 124-Painted-c	3.00	9.00	21.00

NOTE: Gil Kane art-1956 up. Kubert a-123.

HOPE SHIP
June-Aug, 1963
Dell Publishing Co.

	Good	Fine	N-Mint
1	1.35	4.00	8.00

HOPPY THE MARVEL BUNNY (See Fawcett's Funny Animals)
Dec, 1945 - No. 15, Sept, 1947
Fawcett Publications

	Good	Fine	N-Mint
1	11.00	32.00	75.00
2	5.00	15.00	35.00
3-15: 7-Xmas-c	4.00	12.00	28.00
...Well Known Comics (1944,8½x10½'',paper-c) Bestmaid/Samuel Lowe (Printed in red or blue)	6.75	20.00	40.00

HORACE & DOTTY DRIPPLE (Dotty Dripple No. 1-24)
No. 25, Aug, 1952 - No. 43, Oct, 1955
Harvey Publications

	Good	Fine	N-Mint
25-43	.70	2.00	5.00

HORIZONTAL LIEUTENANT, THE (See Movie Classics)

HORRIFIC (Terrific No. 14 on)
Sept, 1952 - No. 13, Sept, 1954
Artful/Comic Media/Harwell/Mystery

	Good	Fine	N-Mint
1	9.30	28.00	65.00
2	4.65	14.00	32.00
3-Bullet in head-c	7.00	21.00	50.00
4,5,7,9,10	3.00	9.00	21.00
6-Jack The Ripper story	3.50	10.50	24.00
8-Origin & 1st app. The Teller(E.C. parody)	4.65	14.00	32.00
11-Swipe/Witches Tales #6,27	2.65	8.00	18.00
12,13	2.65	8.00	18.00

NOTE: Don Heck a-8; c-3-13. Hollingsworth a-4. Morisi a-8. Palais a-5, 8, 11.

HORROR FROM THE TOMB (Mysterious Stories No. 2)
Sept, 1954
Premier Magazine Co.

HORROR FROM THE TOMB (continued)	Good	Fine	N-Mint
1-Woodbridge/Torres, Check-a	8.00	24.00	56.00

HORRORS, THE
No. 11, Jan, 1953 - No. 15, Apr, 1954
Star Publications

	Good	Fine	N-Mint
11-Horrors of War; Disbrow-a(2)	6.00	18.00	42.00
12-Horrors of War; color illo in **POP**	6.00	18.00	42.00
13-Horrors of Mystery; crime stories	5.50	16.50	38.00
14,15-Horrors of the Underworld	5.50	16.50	38.00

NOTE: All have **L. B. Cole** covers. **Hollingsworth** a-13. **Palais** a-13r.

HORROR TALES (Magazine)
V1No.7, 6/69 - V6No.6, 12/74; V7No.1, 2/75; V7No.2, 5/76 -
V8No.5, 1977; (V1-V6, 52 pgs.; V7, V8No.2, 112 pgs.; V8No.4 on,
68 pgs.) (No V5No.3, V8No.1,3)
Eerie Publications

	Good	Fine	N-Mint
V1#7	.50	1.50	3.00
V1#8,9	.35	1.00	2.00
V2#1-6('70), V3#1-6('71)	.35	1.00	2.00
V4#1-3,5-7('72)	.25	.75	1.50
V4#4-LSD story reprint/Weird V3#5	.85	2.50	5.00
V5#1,2,4,5(6/73),5(10/73),6(12/73)	.25	.75	1.50
V6#1-6('74),V7#1,2,4('76)	.25	.75	1.50
V7#3('76)-Giant issue	.25	.75	1.50
V8#2,4,5('77)	.25	.75	1.50

NOTE: Bondage-c-V6#1,3, V7#2.

HORSE FEATHERS COMICS
Nov, 1945 - No. 4, 1946 (52 pgs.)
Lev Gleason Publications

	Good	Fine	N-Mint
1-Wolverton's Scoop Scuttle, 2 pgs.	8.50	25.50	60.00
2	3.00	9.00	21.00
3,4	2.30	7.00	16.00

HORSEMASTERS, THE (See 4-Color No. 1260)

HORSE SOLDIERS, THE (See 4-Color No. 1048)

HORSE WITHOUT A HEAD, THE (See Movie Comics)

HOT DOG
June-July, 1954 - No. 4, Dec-Jan, 1954-55
Magazine Enterprises

	Good	Fine	N-Mint
1(A-1 107)	2.30	7.00	16.00
2,3(A-1 115),4(A-1 136)	1.30	4.00	9.00

HOTEL DEPAREE - SUNDANCE (See 4-Color No. 1126)

HOT ROD AND SPEEDWAY COMICS
Feb-Mar, 1952 - No. 5, Apr-May, 1953
Hillman Periodicals

	Good	Fine	N-Mint
1	6.00	18.00	42.00
2-Krigstein-a	4.65	14.00	32.00
3-5	1.70	5.00	12.00

HOT ROD COMICS (See X-Mas Comics)
Nov, 1951 (no month given) - V2No.7, Feb, 1953
Fawcett Publications

	Good	Fine	N-Mint
nn (V1#1)-Powell-c/a in all	8.00	24.00	56.00
2 (4/52)	4.00	12.00	28.00
3-6, V2#7	2.65	8.00	18.00

HOT ROD KING
Fall, 1952
Ziff-Davis Publ. Co.

	Good	Fine	N-Mint
1-Giacoia-a; painted-c	7.00	21.00	50.00

HOT ROD RACERS (Grand Prix No. 16 on)
Dec, 1964 - No. 15, July, 1967
Charlton Comics

	Good	Fine	N-Mint
1	1.00	3.00	6.00

	Good	Fine	N-Mint
2-5	.50	1.50	3.00
6-15	.35	1.00	2.00

HOT RODS AND RACING CARS
Nov, 1951 - No. 120, June, 1973
Charlton Comics (Motor Mag. No. 1)

	Good	Fine	N-Mint
1	5.00	15.00	35.00
2	2.30	7.00	16.00
3-10	1.50	4.50	10.00
11-20	1.15	3.50	8.00
21-34,36-40	.70	2.00	5.00
35 (68 pgs., 6/58)	1.15	3.50	8.00
41-60	.50	1.50	3.00
61-80	.25	.75	1.50
81-120		.50	1.00

HOT SHOT CHARLIE
1947 (Lee Elias)
Hillman Periodicals

	Good	Fine	N-Mint
1	2.65	8.00	18.00

HOTSPUR
June, 1987 - No. 3, Oct., 1987 ($1.75, color, Baxter)
Eclipse Comics

	Good	Fine	N-Mint
1-3	.30	.85	1.70

HOT STUFF CREEPY CAVES
Nov, 1974 - No. 7, Nov, 1975
Harvey Publications

	Good	Fine	N-Mint
1	.55	1.60	3.20
2-5	.30	.80	1.60
6,7		.40	.80

HOT STUFF SIZZLERS
July, 1960 - No. 59, March, 1974
Harvey Publications

	Good	Fine	N-Mint
1: 68 pgs. begin	5.00	15.00	35.00
2-5	1.70	5.00	12.00
6-10	1.15	3.50	8.00
11-20	.85	2.50	5.00
21-45: Last 68 pgs.	.50	1.50	3.00
46-52: All 52 pgs.	.40	1.20	2.40
53-59	.35	1.00	2.00

HOT STUFF, THE LITTLE DEVIL (Also see Harvey Hits & Devil Kids)
10/57 - No. 141, 7/77; No. 142, 2/78 - No. 164, 8/82; No. 165,
10/86 - No. 171, 11/87; No. 172, 11/88 - Present
Harvey Publications (Illustrated Humor)

	Good	Fine	N-Mint
1	13.00	40.00	90.00
2-1st app. Stumbo the Giant	8.00	24.00	56.00
3-5	6.00	18.00	42.00
6-10	3.00	9.00	21.00
11-20	1.50	4.50	10.00
21-40	.70	2.00	5.00
41-60	.55	1.60	3.20
61-105	.30	.80	1.60
106-112: All 52 pg. Giants	.35	1.00	2.00
113-172		.40	.80
Shoestore Giveaway('63)	.50	1.50	3.00

HOT WHEELS (TV)
Mar-Apr, 1970 - No. 6, Jan-Feb, 1971
National Periodical Publications

	Good	Fine	N-Mint
1	1.70	5.00	12.00
2,4,5	1.00	3.00	6.00
3-Adams-c	2.00	6.00	12.00
6-Adams c/a	2.50	7.50	15.00

NOTE: **Toth** a-1p, 2-5; c-1p, 4, 5.

The Horrors #13, © STAR

Hot Rod Comics #7, © FAW

Hotspur #1, © Eclipse Comics

The House Of Mystery #32, © DC   The House Of Mystery #186, © DC   House Of Secrets #66, © DC

HOUSE OF MYSTERY (See Limited Collectors' Edition & Super DC Giant)
HOUSE OF MYSTERY, THE (Also see Elvira's. . .)
Dec-Jan, 1951-52 - No. 321, Oct, 1983 (No. 199-203: 52 pgs.)
National Periodical Publications/DC Comics

	Good	Fine	N-Mint
1	40.00	120.00	280.00
2	16.00	48.00	110.00
3	13.00	40.00	90.00
4,5	11.50	34.00	80.00
6-10	9.50	28.50	65.00
11-15	7.50	22.50	52.00
16(7/53)-35(2/55)-Last pre-code ish; #30-Woodish-a			
	4.65	14.00	32.00
36-49	2.30	7.00	16.00
50-Text story of Orson Welles' War of the Worlds broadcast			
	1.35	4.00	9.00
51-60	1.15	3.50	8.00
61,63,65,66,70,72-Kirby-a	1.15	3.50	8.00
62,64,67-69,71,73-75	.85	2.50	6.00
76,84,85-Kirby-a	1.15	3.50	8.00
77-83,86-99	.85	2.50	6.00
100	1.00	3.00	7.00
101-108,110-116: Last 10 cent ish.	.75	2.25	5.00
109,120-Toth-a; Kubert #109	.75	2.25	5.00
117-119,121-130	.50	1.50	3.00
131-142,144-150: 149-Toth-a	.25	.75	1.50
143-J'onn J'onzz, Manhunter begins, ends #173 (6/64); story cont./			
Detective #326	.35	1.00	2.00
151-155,157-177: 158-Origin/last app. Diabolu Idol-Head in J'onn			
J'onzz. 160-Intro Marco Xavier (Martian Manhunter) & Vulture			
Crime Organization; ends #173. 169-Origin/1st app. Gem Girl.			
174-Mystery format begins	.75	1.50	
156-Robby Reed begins (Origin), ends #173	.35	1.00	2.00
178-Adams-a	.60	1.75	3.50
179-Adams/Orlando, Wrightson-a (1st pro work, 3 pgs.)			
	1.00	3.00	6.00
180,181,183: Wrightson-a(3, 10, & 3 pgs.). 180,183-Wood-a			
	.40	1.25	2.50
182-Toth-a(r)	.25	.75	1.50
184-Kane/Wood, Toth-a	.35	1.00	2.00
185-Williamson/Kaluta-a; 3 pgs. Wood-a	.60	1.75	3.50
186-Adams-a; Wrightson-a, 10 pgs.	.60	1.75	3.50
187	.25	.75	1.50
188-Wrightson-a, 8 pgs.	.60	1.75	3.50
189-Wood-a	.35	1.00	2.00
190,196-Toth-a(r)	.25	.75	1.50
191,195-Wrightson-a, 3 & 10 pgs.	.60	1.75	3.50
192,193,197,198	.25	.75	1.50
194-Toth, Kirby-a; 48pg. ish. begin, end #198	.25	.75	1.50
199-Wood, Kirby-a; 52pgs. begin, end 203	.40	1.25	2.50
200-203,205,206,208-220	.25	.75	1.50
204-Wrightson-a, 9 pgs.	.40	1.25	2.50
207-Wrightson, Starlin-a	.35	1.00	2.00
221-Wrightson/Kaluta-a, 8 pgs.	.35	1.00	2.00
222,223,225	.25	.75	1.50
224-Adams/Wrightson-a(r); begin 100 pg. issues; Phantom			
Stranger-r	.50	1.50	3.00
226-Wrightson-r; Phantom Stranger-r	.25	.75	1.50
227,230-250: 230-68 pgs.	.25	.75	1.50
228-Adams inks; Wrightson-r	.40	1.25	2.50
229-Wrightson-a(r); Toth-r; last 100 pg. issue	.25	.75	1.50
251-($1.00, 84 pgs.)-Wood-a, 8 pgs.	.25	.75	1.50
252,253,255,256,258	.25	.75	1.50
254,274,277-Rogers-a	.25	.75	1.50
257,259-Golden-a; last $1.00 size	.25	.75	1.50
260-273,275,276,278-282	.25	.75	1.50
283-321: 290-l, Vampire begins, ends #319	.25	.75	1.50

NOTE: **Adams** a-236i; c-175-192, 197, 199, 251-254. **Aragones** a-186, 251. **Baily** a-279p. **Colan** a-202r. **Craig** a-263, 275, 295, 300. **Ditko** a-236, 247, 254, 258, 276; c-277. **Drucker** a-37. **Evans** a-218. **Giunta** a-199. **Heath** a-194r; c-203. **Howard** a-182, 187, 196, 229r, 247r, 254, 279i. **Kaluta** a-195, 200, 250r; c-200-202, 210, 212, 233, 260, 261, 263, 265, 267, 268, 273, 276, 284, 287, 288, 293-295, 300, 302, 304, 305, 309-319, 321. **Bob Kane** a-84. **Gil Kane** a-196p, 253p, 300p. **Kirby** a-194r; 199r; c-65, 76, 78, 79, 85. **Kubert** c-282, 283, 285, 286, 289-292, 297-99, 301, 303, 306-308. **Mayer** a-317p. **Meskin** a-52-144 (most), 224r, 229r; c-63, 66, 124, 127. **Mooney** a-160. **Moreira** a-3, 20-50, 58, 59, 62, 68, 77, 79, 90, 123, 201r, 228; c-44, 47, 50, 54, 59, 62, 64, 68, 70, 73. **Morrow** a-192, 196, 255, 320i. **Mortimer** a-204. **Nasser** a-276. **Newton** a-259, 272. **Nino** a-204, 212, 213, 220, 224, 225, 245, 250, 252-256, 283. **Orlando** a-175(2 pgs.); 178; c-240, 258p, 262, 264p, 270p, 271, 272, 274, 275, 278, 296i. **Redondo** a-194, 195, 197, 202, 203, 207, 211, 214, 217, 219, 226, 227, 229, 235, 241, 287(layout), 302p, 303i, 308; c-229. **Reese** a-195, 200, 205i. **Roussos** a-65, 84, 224i. **Sekowsky** a-282p. **Sparling** a-203. **Starlin** a-207(2 pgs.), 282p; c-281. **Leonard Starr** a-9. **Staton** a-300p. **Sutton** a-271, 290, 291, 293, 295, 297-99, 302, 303, 306-09, 310-13i, 314. **Tuska** a-293p, 294p, 316p. **Wrightson** c-193-195, 204, 207, 209, 211, 213, 214, 217, 221, 231, 236, 255, 256.

HOUSE OF SECRETS
11-12/56 - No. 80, 9-10/66; No. 81, 8-9/69 - No. 140, 2-3/76;
No. 141, 8-9/76 - No. 154, 10-11/78
National Periodical Publications/DC Comics

	Good	Fine	N-Mint
1-Drucker-a; Moreira-c	23.00	70.00	160.00
2-Moreira-a	12.00	36.00	84.00
3-Kirby c/a	10.00	30.00	70.00
4,8-Kirby-a	5.00	15.00	35.00
5-7,9-11	3.60	11.00	25.00
12-Kirby c/a	4.30	13.00	30.00
13-15	2.65	8.00	18.00
16-20	2.15	6.50	15.00
21,22,24-30	1.60	4.70	11.00
23-Origin Mark Merlin	1.70	5.00	12.00
31-47,49,50: Last 10 cent ish.	1.15	3.50	8.00
48-Toth-a	1.35	4.00	10.00
51-60,62: 58-Origin Mark Merlin retold	.60	1.75	3.50
61-First Eclipso	.75	2.25	4.50
63-67-Toth-a	.75	2.25	4.50
68-80: 73-Mark Merlin ends, Prince Ra-Man begins. 80-Eclipso,			
Prince Ra-Man end	.25	.75	1.50
81,84,86,88,89: 81-Mystery format begins	.25	.75	1.50
82-Adams-c(i)	.60	1.75	3.50
83-Toth-a	.50	1.50	3.00
85-Adams-a(i)	.60	1.75	3.50
87-Wrightson & Kaluta-a	.60	1.75	3.50
90-Buckler/Adams-a	.60	1.75	3.50
91-Wood-i	.50	1.50	3.00
92-Intro. Swamp Thing; Wrightson-a (6-7/71); J. Jones part inks			
	3.65	11.00	25.00
93,96,98-Toth-a(r). 96-Wood-a	.25	.75	1.50
94-Wrightson inks; Toth-a(r)	.60	1.75	3.50
95,97,99,100	.25	.75	1.50
101-154: 140-Origin The Patchworkman		.50	1.00

NOTE: **Adams** c-81, 82, 84-88, 90, 91. **Colan** a-63. **Ditko** a-139p, 148. **Evans** a-118. **Finlay** a-7. **Glanzman** a-91. **Golden** a-151. **Kaluta** a-87, 98, 99; c-98, 99, 101, 102, 151, 154. **Bob Kane** a-18, 21. **G. Kane** a-85p. **Kirby** c-11. **Mayer** a-39. **Meskin** a-2-68 (most); c-55-60. **Moreira** a-7, 8, 102-104, 106, 108, 113, 116, 118, 121, 123, 127; c-2, 7-9. **Morrow** a-86, 89, 90; c-89, 146-148. **Nino** a-101, 103, 106, 109, 115, 117, 126, 128, 131, 147, 153. **Redondo** a-95, 99, 102, 104p, 113, 116, 134, 139, 140. **Reese** a-85. **Starlin** c-150. **Sutton** a-154. **Toth** a-63-67, 123. **Tuska** a-90, 104. **Wrightson** c-92-94, 96, 100, 103, 106, 107, 135, 139.

HOUSE OF TERROR (3-D)
October, 1953 (1st 3D horror comic)
St. John Publishing Co.

	Good	Fine	N-Mint
1-Kubert, Baker-a	14.00	42.00	100.00

HOUSE OF YANG, THE (See Yang)
July, 1975 - No. 6, June, 1976; 1978
Charlton Comics

1-Opium propaganda story		.40	.80

THE HOUSE OF YANG (continued)	Good	Fine	N-Mint
2-6		.30	.60
Modern Comics #1,2(1978)		.30	.60

HOUSE II: THE SECOND STORY
1987
Marvel Comics

1-Adapts movie	.35	1.00	2.00

HOWARD CHAYKIN'S AMERICAN FLAGG! (Formerly Amer. Flagg!)
May, 1988 - Present ($1.75-$1.95, Baxter)
First Comics

V2#1-8: Chaykin-c(p); 10-Elvis Presley photo-c .30		.90	1.80

HOWARD THE DUCK (See Bizarre Adventures #34, Fear, Man-Thing, & Marvel Treas. Ed.)
1/76 - No. 31, 5/79; No. 32, 1/86; No. 33, 9/86
Marvel Comics Group

	Good	Fine	N-Mint
1-Brunner c/a; Spider-Man x-over (low distribution)			
	1.15	3.50	7.00
2-Brunner c/a (low distr.)	.25	.75	1.50
3-Buscema-a	.25	.75	1.50
4-11	.25	.75	1.50
12-1st app. Kiss	.50	1.50	3.00
13-Kiss app.	.70	2.00	4.00
14-33: 16-Album issue; 3pgs. comics		.40	.80
Annual 1(9/77)		.40	.80

NOTE: Austin c-29i. Bolland c-33. Brunner a-1p, 2p; c-1, 2. Buckler c-3p. Buscema a-3p. Colan a(p)-4-15, 17-20, 24-27, 30, 31; c(p)-4-31, Annual 1. Leialoha a-1-13i; c(i)-3-5, 8-11. Mayerik a-22, 23, 33. P. Smith a-30p.

HOWARD THE DUCK MAGAZINE
October, 1979 - No. 9, March, 1981 (B&W)
Marvel Comics Group

1		.50	1.00
2,3,5-9: 7-Has poster by Byrne		.30	.60
4-Beatles, John Lennon, Elvis, Kiss & Devo cameos; Hitler app.			
		.40	.80

NOTE: Buscema a-4. Colan a-1-5p, 7-9p. Davis c-3. Golden a-1, 5p, 6p(51pgs.). Rogers a-7, 8. Simonson a-7.

HOWARD THE DUCK: THE MOVIE
Dec, 1986 - No. 3, Feb, 1987 (mini-series)
Marvel Comics Group

1-3: Movie adaptation		.40	.80

HOW BOYS AND GIRLS CAN HELP WIN THE WAR
1942 (One Shot) (10 cents)
The Parents' Magazine Institute

1-All proceeds used to buy war bonds	10.00	30.00	70.00

HOWDY DOODY (TV)(See Poll Parrot)
1/50 - No. 38, 7-9/56; No. 761, 1/57; No. 811, 7/57
Dell Publishing Co.

1-Photo-c; 1st TV comic?	14.00	42.00	100.00
2-Photo-c	7.00	21.00	50.00
3-5: All photo-c	5.00	15.00	35.00
6-Used in SOTI, pg. 309; painted-c begin	5.00	15.00	35.00
7-10	4.00	12.00	28.00
11-20	3.00	9.00	21.00
21-38	2.00	6.00	14.00
4-Color 761,811	3.50	10.50	24.00

HOW IT BEGAN (See Single Series No. 15)

HOW SANTA GOT HIS RED SUIT (See March of Comics No. 2)

HOW STALIN HOPES WE WILL DESTROY AMERICA
1951 (16 pgs.) (Giveaway)
Joe Lowe Co. (Pictorial News)

	Good	Fine	N-Mint
nn	47.00	140.00	280.00

(Prices vary widely on this book)

HOW THE WEST WAS WON (See Movie Comics)

HOW TO DRAW FOR THE COMICS
No date (1942?) (64 pgs.; B&W & color) (10 Cents) (No ads)
Street and Smith

nn-Art by Winsor McCay, George Marcoux(Supersnipe artist), Vernon Greene(The Shadow artist), Jack Binder(with biog), Thorton Fisher, Jon Small, & Jack Farr. Has biographies of each artist

	11.50	34.00	80.00

H. R. PUFNSTUF (TV) (See March of Comics 360)
Oct, 1970 - No. 8, July, 1972
Gold Key

1	.85	2.50	5.00
2-8	.35	1.00	2.00

HUBERT (See 4-Color No. 251)

HUCK & YOGI JAMBOREE (TV)
March, 1961 (116 pgs.; $1.00) (B&W original material)
(6¼x9''; cardboard cover; high quality paper)
Dell Publishing Co.

	2.15	6.50	15.00

HUCK & YOGI WINTER SPORTS (See 4-Color No. 1310)

HUCK FINN (See New Advs. of . . .)

HUCKLEBERRY FINN (See 4-Color No. 1114)

HUCKLEBERRY HOUND (See Dell Giant No. 31,44, Spotlight No. 1, March of Comics No. 199,214,235, Whitman Comic Books & Golden Picture Story Book)

HUCKLEBERRY HOUND (TV)
No. 990, 5-7/59 - No. 43, 10/70 (Hanna-Barbera)
Dell/Gold Key No. 18 (10/62) on

4-Color 990	2.65	8.00	18.00
4-Color 1050,1054 (12/59)	2.00	6.00	14.00
3(1-2/60) - 7 (9-10/60)	2.00	6.00	14.00
4-Color 1141 (10/60)	2.00	6.00	14.00
8-10	1.70	5.00	12.00
11-17 (6-8/62)	1.15	3.50	8.00
18,19 (84pgs.): 18-20 titled . . .Chuckleberry Tales)			
	3.00	9.00	24.00
20-30: 20-Titled Chuckleberry Tales	1.00	3.00	6.00
31-43: 37-reprints	.85	2.50	5.00
. . . Kite Fun Book('61)-16 pgs.; 5x7¼'', soft-c 1.70		5.00	12.00

HUCKLEBERRY HOUND (TV)
Nov, 1970 - No. 8, Jan, 1972 (Hanna-Barbera)
Charlton Comics

1	.70	2.00	4.00
2-8	.35	1.00	2.00

HUEY, DEWEY, & LOUIE (See Donald Duck, 1938 for 1st app)

HUEY, DEWEY, & LOUIE BACK TO SCHOOL (See Dell Giant #22,35,49 & Dell Giants)

HUEY, DEWEY AND LOUIE JUNIOR WOODCHUCKS (Disney)
Aug, 1966 - No. 81, 1984 (See Walt Disney's C&S #125)
Gold Key No. 1-61/Whitman No. 62 on

1	2.65	8.00	18.00
2,3(12/68)	1.70	5.00	12.00
4,5(4/70)-Barks-r	1.70	5.00	12.00
6-17-Written by Barks	1.15	3.50	8.00
18,27-30	.70	2.00	4.00
19-23,25-Written by Barks. 22,23,25-Barks-r	.85	2.50	5.00
24,26-Barks-r	.85	2.50	5.00
31-57,60-81: 41,70,80-Reprints	.25	.75	1.50

Howard Chaykin's American Flagg! #1, © First Comics

Howdy Doody #19, © Kagran Corp.

Huckleberry Hound #9, © Hanna-Barbera

The Human Torch #23, © MEG

Humbug #1, © Harvey Kurtzman

Humdinger #1, © NOVP

HUEY, DEWEY, & LOUIE JUNIOR WOODCHUCKS (continued)

	Good	Fine	N-Mint
58,59-Barks-r	.35	1.00	2.00

NOTE: *Barks* story reprints-No. 22-26,35,42,45,51.

HUGGA BUNCH (TV)
Oct, 1986 - No. 6, Aug, 1987
Star Comics (Marvel)

1-6		.45	.90

HULK, THE (See The Incredible Hulk)

HULK, THE (Formerly The Rampaging Hulk)
No. 10, 8/78 - No. 27, June, 1981 (Magazine)($1.50)(in color)
Marvel Comics Group

10-12: 11-Moon Knight begins by Colan		.60	1.20
13-27: 13-Color issues begin. 23-Anti-Gay issue			
		.60	1.20

NOTE: *Alcala* a(i)-15, 17-20, 22, 24-27. *Buscema* a-23; c-26. *Chaykin* a-21-25. *Colan* a(p)-11, 17, 19, 24-27. *Golden* a-20. *Nebres* a-16. *Simonson* a-27; c-23.

HUMAN FLY
1963 - 1964 (Reprints)
I.W. Enterprises/Super

I.W. Reprint No. 1-Reprints Blue Beetle No. 44('46)

	.70	2.00	4.00

Super Reprint No. 10-Reprints Blue Beetle No. 46('47)

	.70	2.00	4.00

HUMAN FLY, THE
Sept, 1977 - No. 19, Mar, 1979
Marvel Comics Group

1-Origin; Spider-Man x-over		.40	.80
2-19: 9-Daredevil x-over; Byrne/Austin-c		.25	.50

NOTE: *Austin* c-4i. *Elias* a-1, 3p, 4p, 7p, 10-12p, 15p, 18p, 19p. *Layton* c-19.

HUMAN TORCH, THE (Red Raven #1)(See All-Select, All Winners,
Marvel Mystery, Men's Advs., Sub-Mariner, USA & Young Men)
No. 2, Fall, 1940 - No. 15, Spring, 1944 (becomes Funny Tunes);
No. 16, Fall, 1944 - No. 35, Mar, 1949 (becomes Love Tales);
No. 36, April, 1954 - No. 38, Aug, 1954
Timely/Marvel Comics (TP 2,3/TCI 4-9/SePI 10/SnPC 11-25/CnPC
26-35/Atlas Comics (CPC 36-38))

	Good	Fine	N-Mint
2(#1)-Intro & Origin Toro; The Falcon, The Fiery Mask, Mantor the Magician, & Microman only app.; Human Torch by Burgos, Sub-Mariner by Everett begin (origin of each in text)			
	457.00	1370.00	3200.00
(Prices vary widely on this book)			
3(#2)-40pg. H.T. story; H.T & S.M. battle over who is best artist in text-Everett or Burgos	185.00	555.00	1300.00
4(#3)-Origin The Patriot in text; last Everett Sub-Mariner; Sid Greene-a	140.00	420.00	980.00
5(#4)-The Patriot app.; Angel x-over in Sub-Mariner. (Summer, 1941)	100.00	300.00	700.00
5-Human Torch battles Sub-Mariner (Fall,'41)			
	160.00	480.00	1120.00
6,7,9	65.00	195.00	455.00
8-Human Torch battles Sub-Mariner; Wolverton-a, 1 pg.			
	100.00	300.00	700.00
10-Human Torch battles Sub-Mariner; Wolverton-a, 1 pg.			
	80.00	240.00	560.00
11-15	50.00	150.00	350.00
16-20: 20-Last War issue	40.00	120.00	280.00
21-30	32.00	95.00	225.00
31-Namora x-over in Sub-Mariner (also #30); last Toro			
	25.00	75.00	175.00
32-Sungirl, Namora app.; Sungirl-c	25.00	75.00	175.00
33-Capt. America x-over	25.00	75.00	175.00
34-Sungirl solo	25.00	75.00	175.00

	Good	Fine	N-Mint
35-Captain America & Sungirl app. (1949)	25.00	75.00	175.00
36-38(1954)-Sub-Mariner in all	20.00	60.00	140.00

NOTE: *Burgos* c-36. *Everett* a-1-3, 27, 28, 30, 37, 38. *Powell* a-36. *Schomburg* c-5, 7, 12, 14-16, 19. *Mickey Spillane* text 4-6. *Bondage-c* #2, 12, 19. Since there is a six month delay between #15 & 16, it is believed that Funny Tunes #16 continued after Human Torch #15.

HUMAN TORCH, THE (Also see Fantastic Four, The Invaders &
Strange Tales #101)
Sept, 1974 - No. 8, Nov, 1975
Marvel Comics Group

1		.40	.80
2-8		.25	.50

NOTE: *Golden age Torch-r No. 1-8. Kirby/Ayers a-1-5,8r.*

HUMBUG (Satire by Harvey Kurtzman)
8/57 - No. 9, 5/58; No. 10, 6/58; No. 11, 10/58
Humbug Publications

1	7.00	21.00	50.00
2	3.50	10.50	24.00
3-9: 8-Elvis in Jailbreak Rock	2.65	8.00	18.00
10,11-Magazine format. 10-Photo-c	2.65	8.00	18.00
Bound Volume(#1-6)-Sold by publisher	17.00	51.00	120.00
Bound Volume(#1-9)	22.00	65.00	154.00

NOTE: *Davis* a-1-11. *Elder* a-2-4, 6-9, 11. *Heath* a-2, 4-8, 10. *Jaffee* a-2, 4-9. *Kurtzman* a-11. *Wood* a-1.

HUMDINGER
May-June, 1946 - V2/2, July-Aug, 1947
Novelty Press/Premium Group

1-Jerkwater Line, Mickey Starlight by Don Rico, Dink begin

	3.70	11.00	26.00
2	2.15	6.50	15.00
3-6,V2#1,2	1.50	4.50	10.00

HUMOR (See All Humor Comics)

HUMPHREY COMICS (Also see Joe Palooka)
October, 1948 - No. 22, April, 1952
Harvey Publications

1-Joe Palooka's pal (r); Powell-a	5.70	17.00	40.00
2,3: Powell-a	2.65	8.00	18.00
4-Boy Heroes app.; Powell-a	3.50	10.50	24.00
5-8,10: 5,6-Powell-a. 7-Little Dot app.	2.00	6.00	14.00
9-Origin Humphrey	2.65	8.00	18.00
11-22	1.60	4.70	11.00

HUNCHBACK OF NOTRE DAME, THE (See 4-Color No. 854)

HUNK
August, 1961 - No. 11, 1963
Charlton Comics

1	.70	2.00	4.00
2-11	.35	1.00	2.00

HUNTED (Formerly My Love Memoirs)
No. 13, July, 1950 - No. 2, Sept, 1950
Fox Features Syndicate

13(#1)-Used in SOTI, pg. 42 & illo.-''Treating police contemptuous-ly'' (lower left); Hollingsworth bondage-c	17.00	51.00	120.00
2	5.70	17.00	40.00

HURRICANE COMICS
1945 (52 pgs.)
Cambridge House

1-(Humor, funny animal)	3.50	10.50	24.00

HYPER MYSTERY COMICS
May, 1940 - No. 2, June, 1940 (68 pgs.)
Hyper Publications

	Good	Fine	N-Mint
HYPER MYSTERY COMICS (continued)			
1-Hyper, the Phenomenal begins	45.00	135.00	315.00
2	33.00	100.00	230.00

I AIM AT THE STARS (See 4-Color No. 1148)

I AM COYOTE (See Eclipse Graphic Album Series)

IBIS, THE INVINCIBLE (See Fawcett Min., Mighty Midget & Whiz)
1943 (Feb) - No. 2, 1943; No. 3, Wint, 1945 - No. 6, Spring, 1948
Fawcett Publications

	Good	Fine	N-Mint
1-Origin Ibis; Raboy-c; on sale 1/2/43	70.00	210.00	490.00
2-Bondage-c	35.00	105.00	245.00
3-Wolverton-a #3-6 (4 pgs. each)	28.00	84.00	195.00
4-6: 5-Bondage-c. 6-Beck-c	22.00	65.00	154.00

ICEMAN (See X-Men)
Dec, 1984 - No. 4, June, 1985 (Limited series)
Marvel Comics Group

1	.35	1.00	2.00
2-4	.25	.75	1.50

IDAHO
June-Aug, 1963 - No. 8, July-Sept, 1965
Dell Publishing Co.

1	1.15	3.50	8.00
2-8: 5-Painted-c	.75	2.25	5.00

IDEAL (. . . a Classical Comic) (2nd Series) (Love Romances No. 6?)
July, 1948 - No. 5, March, 1949 (Feature length stories)
Timely Comics

1-Antony & Cleopatra	13.00	40.00	90.00
2-The Corpses of Dr. Sacotti	11.50	34.00	80.00
3-Joan of Arc; used in **SOTI**, pg. 308-'Boer War'	10.00	30.00	70.00
4-Richard the Lion-hearted; titled ''. . .the World's Greatest Comics;'' The Witness app.	12.00	36.00	84.00
5-Ideal Love & Romance; photo-c	6.00	18.00	42.00

IDEAL COMICS (1st Series) (Willie No. 5 on)
Fall, 1944 - No. 4, Spring, 1946
Timely Comics (MgPC)

1-Super Rabbit in all	6.50	19.50	45.00
2	4.30	13.00	30.00
3,4	3.50	10.50	24.00

IDEAL LOVE & ROMANCE (See Ideal, A Classical Comic)

IDEAL ROMANCE (Formerly Tender Romance)
April, 1954 - No. 8, Feb, 1955 (Diary Confessions No. 9 on)
Key Publications

3	3.00	9.00	21.00
4-8	1.50	4.50	10.00

IDEAL ROMANCES
1950
Stanmor

6	1.70	5.00	12.00

I DREAM OF JEANNIE (TV)
April, 1965 - No. 2, Dec, 1966 (Photo-c)
Dell Publishing Co.

1,2	3.00	9.00	21.00

IF THE DEVIL WOULD TALK
1950; 1958 (32 pgs.; paper cover; in full color)
Roman Catholic Catechetical Guild/Impact Publ.

nn-(Scarce)-About secularism (20-30 copies known to exist); very low distribution	50.00	150.00	350.00
1958 Edition-(Rare)-(Impact Publ.); art & script changed to meet church criticism of earlier edition; only 6 known copies exist	50.00	150.00	350.00

	Good	Fine	N-Mint
Black & White version of nn edition; small size; only 4 known copies exist	30.00	90.00	200.00

NOTE: *The original edition of this book was printed and killed by the Guild's board of directors. It is believed that a very limited number of copies were distributed. The 1958 version was a complete bomb with very limited, if any, circulation. In 1979, 11 original, 4 1958 reprints, and 4 B&W's surfaced from the Guild's old files in St. Paul, Minnesota.*

ILLUSTRATED GAGS (See Single Series No. 16)

ILLUSTRATED LIBRARY OF. . . , AN (See Classics Illustrated Giants)

ILLUSTRATED STORIES OF THE OPERAS
1943 (16 pgs.; B&W) (25 cents) (cover-B&W & red)
Baily (Bernard) Publ. Co.

	Good	Fine	N-Mint
nn-(Rare)-Faust (part-r in Cisco Kid #1)	30.00	90.00	210.00
nn-(Rare)-Aida	30.00	90.00	210.00
nn-(Rare)-Carmen; Baily-a	30.00	90.00	210.00
nn-(Rare)-Rigoleito	30.00	90.00	210.00

ILLUSTRATED STORY OF ROBIN HOOD & HIS MERRY MEN, THE (See Classics Giveaways, 12/44)

ILLUSTRATED TARZAN BOOK, THE (See Tarzan Book)

I LOVED (Formerly Rulah; Colossal Feature Mag. No. 33 on)
No. 28, July, 1949 - No. 32, Mar, 1950
Fox Features Syndicate

28	4.00	12.00	28.00
29-32	2.65	8.00	18.00

I LOVE LUCY COMICS (TV) (Also see The Lucy Show)
No. 535, Feb, 1954 - No. 35, Apr-June, 1962 (All photo-c)
Dell Publishing Co.

4-Color 535(#1)	10.00	30.00	70.00
4-Color 559 (5/54)(#2)	7.00	21.00	50.00
3 (8-10/54) - 5	6.00	18.00	42.00
6-10	5.00	15.00	35.00
11-20	4.65	14.00	32.00
21-35	4.00	12.00	28.00

I LOVE YOU
June, 1950 (One shot)
Fawcett Publications

1-Photo-c	5.50	16.50	38.00

I LOVE YOU (Formerly In Love)
No. 7, 9/55 - No. 121, 12/76; No. 122, 3/79 - No. 130, 5/80
Charlton Comics

7-Kirby-c, Powell-a	3.70	11.00	26.00
8-10	1.15	3.50	8.00
11-16,18-20	1.00	3.00	7.00
17-68 pg. Giant	1.30	4.00	9.00
21-25,27-50	.55	1.65	4.00
26-Torres-a	1.00	3.00	7.00
51-59	.35	1.00	2.00
60(1/66)-Elvis Presley drawn c/story	5.00	15.00	35.00
61-95		.50	1.00
96-130		.40	.80

I'M A COP
1954
Magazine Enterprises

1(A-1 111)	5.00	15.00	35.00
2(A-1 126), 3(A-1 128)	2.65	8.00	18.00

NOTE: **Powell** c/a-1-3.

I'M DICKENS - HE'S FENSTER (TV)
May-July, 1963 - No. 2, Aug-Oct, 1963 (Photo-c)
Dell Publishing Co.

1,2	1.70	5.00	12.00

Ibis, The Invincible #5, © FAW

Ideal Comics #4 (Spring/46), © MEG

I Love Lucy #35, © Lucille Ball & Desi Arnaz

The Incredible Hulk #3, © MEG

The Incredible Hulk #340, © MEG

Incredible Science Fiction #31, © WMG

I MET A HANDSOME COWBOY (See 4-Color No. 324)

IMMORTAL DOCTOR FATE, THE
Jan, 1985 - No. 3, Mar, 1985 (Mini-series)
DC Comics

	Good	Fine	N-Mint
1-Simonson c/a	.35	1.00	2.00
2,3: 2-Giffen c/a(p)	.35	1.00	2.00

IMPACT
Mar-Apr, 1955 - No. 5, Nov-Dec, 1955
E. C. Comics

1	7.00	21.00	50.00
2	5.00	15.00	35.00
3-5: 4-Crandall-a	4.50	13.50	32.00

NOTE: **Crandall** a-1-4. **Davis** a-2-4; c-1-5. **Evans** a-1, 4, 5. **Ingels** a-in all. **Kamen** a-3. **Krigstein** a-1, 5. **Orlando** a-2, 5.

INCREDIBLE HULK, THE (See Aurora, The Defenders, Marvel Coll. Item Classics, Marvel Fanfare, Marvel Treas. Ed. & Rampaging Hulk)
May, 1962 - No. 6, Mar, 1963; No. 102, Apr, 1968 - Present
Marvel Comics Group

	Good	Fine	N-Mint
1-Origin	100.00	260.00	700.00
2	39.00	105.00	275.00
3-Origin retold	29.00	75.00	200.00
4-6: 4-Brief origin retold. 6-Intro. Teen Brigade	23.00	60.00	160.00
102-(Formerly Tales to Astonish)-Origin retold	3.60	11.00	25.00
103-110: 105-1st Missing Link	1.35	4.00	8.00
111-117 (Last 12 cent ish.)	.85	2.50	5.00
118-125	.70	2.00	4.00
126-139: 126-1st Barbara Norriss (Valkyrie). 131-1st Jim Wilson, Hulk's new sidekick. 136-1st Xeron, The Star-Slayer	.40	1.25	2.50
140-Written by Harlan Ellison; 1st Jarella, Hulk's love	.40	1.25	2.50
141-1st app. Doc Samson	.50	1.50	3.00
142-160: 145-52 pgs. 149-1st The Inheritor. 155-1st app. Shaper	.35	1.00	2.00
161,163-175,179: 161-The Mimic dies. 163-1st app. The Gremlin. 164-1st app. Capt. Omen & Colonel John D. Armbruster. 166-1st Zzzax. 168-1st The Harpy. 169-1st Bi-Beast. 172-X-Men cameo; origin Juggernaut retold	.25	.75	1.50
162-1st app. The Wendigo	.60	1.75	3.50
176-178-Warlock app.	.60	1.75	3.50
180-1st app. Wolverine(cameo)	2.85	8.50	20.00
181-Wolverine app.	11.00	32.00	75.00
182-Wolverine cameo; 1st Crackajack Jackson	2.85	8.50	20.00
183-199: 185-Death of Col. Armbruster	.40	1.25	2.50
200-Silver Surfer app.	.70	2.00	4.00
201-240: 212-1st The Constrictor	.25	.75	1.50
241-249,251-271: 271-Rocket Raccoon app.	.60	1.20	
250-Giant size; Silver Surfer app.	.25	.75	1.50
272-Alpha Flight app.	.40	1.25	2.50
273-299,301-313: 279-X-Men & Alpha Flight cameos	.60	1.20	
300-Double size	.25	.75	1.50
314-Byrne-c/a begins, ends #319	.85	2.50	5.00
315-319	.35	1.00	2.00
320-323,325-329	.60	1.20	
324-1st app. Grey Hulk	.50	1.50	3.00
330-1st McFarlane ish.	1.15	3.50	7.00
331-Grey Hulk series begins	.85	2.50	5.00
332-339	.60	1.75	3.50
340-Wolverine app.	.85	2.50	5.00
341-344	.40	1.25	2.50
345 ($1.50, 52 pgs.)	.35	1.00	2.00
346-Last McFarlane ish.	.25	.75	1.50
347-354		.50	1.00

	Good	Fine	N-Mint
Giant-Size 1 ('75)	.50	1.50	3.00
Special 1 (10/68)-New material; Steranko-c	1.35	4.00	8.00
Special 2 (10/69)-Origin retold	.85	2.50	5.00
Special 3(1/71)	.70	2.00	4.00
Annual 4 (1/72),5(10/76)	.35	1.00	2.00
Annual 6 (11/77)	.25	.75	1.50
Annual 7(8/78)-Byrne/Layton-c/a; Iceman & Angel app.	.50	1.50	3.00
Annual 8(11/79), 9(9/80), 10('81)	.25	.75	1.50
Annual 11(10/82)-Miller, Buckler-a(p)	.25	.75	1.50
Annual 12(8/83), 13(11/84)	.25	.75	1.50
Annual 14(12/85), 15(10/86)	.25	.75	1.50
Special 1(. . .Versus Quasimodo,3/83)-Based on Sat. morning cartoon		.50	1.00

NOTE: **Adkins** a-111-16i. **Austin** a-350i; c-302i, 350i. **J. Buscema** c-202p. **Byrne** a-314p-319p; c-314-316, 319. **Ditko** a-2, 6, 249, Annual 2r(3), 3r, 9p; c-2i, 6, 235, 249. **Everett** c-133i. **Golden** c-248, 251. **Kane** c(p)-193, 194, 196, 198. **Kirby** a-1-5, Special 2, 3p, Annual 5p; c-1-5, Annual 5. **McFarlane** a-330p-334p, 336p-339p, 340-343, 344p-346p; c-330p, 340p, 341-343, 344p, 345, 346p. **Miller** c-258p, 261, 264, 268. **Mooney** a-230p, 287i, 288i. **Powell** a-Special 3r(2). **Severin** a(i)-108-110, 131-33, 141-51, 153-55; c(i)-109, 110, 132, 142, 144-55. **Simonson** c-283. **Starlin** a-222p; c-217. **Staton** a(i)-187-89, 191-209. **Tuska** a-102i, 105i, 106i, 218p. **Williamson** a-310i; c-310i, 311i. **Wrightson** c-197.

INCREDIBLE HULK AND WOLVERINE, THE
Oct, 1986 (One shot, $2.50, color)
Marvel Comics Group

1-r-/1st app. Wolverine & Incr. Hulk	.85	2.50	5.00

INCREDIBLE MR. LIMPET, THE (See Movie Classics)

INCREDIBLE SCIENCE FICTION (Formerly Weird Science-Fantasy)
July-Aug, 1955 - No. 33, Jan-Feb, 1956
E. C. Comics

30,33: 33-Story-r/W.F. No. 18	18.00	54.00	125.00
31-Williamson/Krenkel-a, Wood-a(2)	22.00	65.00	154.00
32-Williamson/Krenkel-a	22.00	65.00	154.00

NOTE: **Davis** a-30, 32, 33; c-30-32. **Krigstein** a-in all. **Orlando** a-30, 32, 33("Judgement Day" reprint). **Wood** a-30, 31, 33; c-33.

INDIANA JONES (See Further Adventures of. . .)

INDIANA JONES AND THE TEMPLE OF DOOM
Sept, 1984 - No. 3, Nov, 1984
Marvel Comics Group

1-3-r/Marvel Super Special; movie adaptation by Guice		.50	1.00

INDIAN BRAVES (Baffling Mysteries No. 5 on)
March, 1951 - No. 4, Sept, 1951
Ace Magazines

1	3.50	10.50	24.00
2	1.70	5.00	12.00
3,4	1.30	4.00	9.00
I.W. Reprint #1 (nd)	.50	1.50	3.00

INDIAN CHIEF (White Eagle. . .) (Formerly The Chief)
No. 3, July-Sept, 1951 - No. 33, Jan-Mar, 1959 (All painted-c)
Dell Publishing Co.

3	1.70	5.00	12.00
4-11: 6-White Eagle app.	1.15	3.50	8.00
12-1st White Eagle(10-12/53)-Not same as earlier character	1.70	5.00	12.00
13-29	1.00	3.00	7.00
30-33-Buscema-a	1.15	3.50	8.00

INDIAN CHIEF (See March of Comics No. 94,110,127,140,159,170,187)

INDIAN FIGHTER, THE (See 4-Color No. 687)

INDIAN FIGHTER
May, 1950 - No. 11, Jan, 1952

205

INDIAN FIGHTER (continued)
Youthful Magazines

	Good	Fine	N-Mint
1	3.50	10.50	24.00
2-Wildey-a/c(bondage)	1.70	5.00	12.00
3-11: 3,4-Wildey-a	1.30	4.00	9.00

NOTE: *Walter Johnson c-1, 3, 4, 6. Wildey a-2-4; c-2, 5.*

INDIAN LEGENDS OF THE NIAGARA (See American Graphics)

INDIANS
Spring, 1950 - No. 17, Spring, 1953
Fiction House Magazines (Wings Publ. Co.)

	Good	Fine	N-Mint
1-Manzar The White Indian, Long Bow & Orphan of the Storm begin	8.00	24.00	56.00
2-Starlight begins	4.00	12.00	28.00
3-5	3.50	10.50	24.00
6-10	2.30	7.00	16.00
11-17	2.00	6.00	14.00

INDIANS OF THE WILD WEST
Circa 1958? (no date) (Reprints)
I. W. Enterprises

	Good	Fine	N-Mint
9-Kinstler-c; Whitman-a	.50	1.50	3.00

INDIANS ON THE WARPATH
No date (Late 40s, early 50s) (132 pages)
St. John Publishing Co.

	Good	Fine	N-Mint
nn-Matt Baker-c; contains St. John comics rebound. Many combinations possible	14.00	42.00	100.00

INDIAN TRIBES (See Famous Indian Tribes)

INDIAN WARRIORS (Formerly White Rider...)
No. 7, June, 1951 - No. 11, 1952
Star Publications

	Good	Fine	N-Mint
7-White Rider & Superhorse begin; L. B. Cole-c	3.50	10.50	24.00
8-11: 11-L. B. Cole-c	2.35	7.00	16.00
3-D 1(12/53)-L. B. Cole-c	16.00	48.00	110.00
Accepted Reprint(nn)(inside cover shows White Rider & Superhorse #11)-R-/cover/#7; origin White Rider &... L. B. Cole-c	1.70	5.00	12.00
Accepted Reprint #8 (nd); L.B. Cole-c	1.70	5.00	12.00

INDOORS-OUTDOORS (See Wisco)

INDOOR SPORTS
nd (64 pgs.; 6x9''; B&W reprints; hardcover)
National Specials Co.

	Good	Fine	N-Mint
By Tad	3.50	10.50	24.00

INFERIOR FIVE, THE (...5 No. 11,12) (See Showcase)
3-4/67 - No. 10, 9-10/68; No. 11, 8-9/72 - No. 12, 10-11/72
National Periodical Publications

	Good	Fine	N-Mint
1-Sekowsky-a(p)	1.00	3.00	6.00
2-Plastic Man app.; Sekowsky-a(p)	.70	2.00	4.00
3-10: 10-Superman x-over	.50	1.50	3.00
11,12-Orlando c/a; both r-/Showcase #62,63	.50	1.50	3.00

INFINITY, INC. (See All-Star Squadron #25)
3/84 - No. 53, 8/88 ($1.25; Baxter paper; 36 pgs.)
DC Comics

	Good	Fine	N-Mint
1-Brainwave, Jr., Fury, The Huntress, Jade, Northwind, Nuklon, Obsidian, Power Girl, Silver Scarab & Star Spangled Kid begin	.60	1.75	3.50
2-5: 2-Dr. Midnite, G.A. Flash, W. Woman, Dr. Fate, Hourman, Gr. Lantern, Wildcat app. 5-Nudity panels	.35	1.10	2.20
6-10	.30	.95	1.90
11-13,38-49,51-53	.25	.80	1.60
14-Todd McFarlane-a, (5/85)	.70	2.00	4.00
15-37-McFarlane-a; 18-22-Crisis x-over. 21-Intro new Hourman & Dr.			

	Good	Fine	N-Mint
Midnight. 26-New Wildcat app. 31-Star-Spangled Kid becomes Skyman. 32-Green Fury becomes Green Flame. 33-Origin Obsidian	.25	.70	1.40
50 ($2.50, 52 pgs.)	.40	1.25	2.50
Annual 1 (12/85)-Crisis x-over	.35	1.00	2.00
Special 1 ('87, $1.50)	.25	.75	1.50
Annual 2 ('88, $2.00)	.35	1.00	2.00

NOTE: *Kubert r-4. Newton a-12p, 13p(last work 4/85). Tuska a-11p. JSA app. 3-10.*

INFORMER, THE
April, 1954 - No. 5, Dec, 1954
Feature Television Productions

	Good	Fine	N-Mint
1-Sekowsky-a begins	3.70	11.00	26.00
2	2.65	8.00	18.00
3-5	2.00	6.00	14.00

IN HIS STEPS
1973, 1977 (39, 49 cents)
Spire Christian Comics (Fleming H. Revell Co.)

	Good	Fine	N-Mint
nn		.40	.80

INHUMANOIDS, THE (TV)
Jan, 1987 - No. 4, July, 1987
Star Comics (Marvel)

	Good	Fine	N-Mint
1-4: Based on Hasbro toys		.50	1.00

INHUMANS, THE (See Amazing Advs. & Thor #146)
Oct, 1975 - No. 12, Aug, 1977
Marvel Comics Group

	Good	Fine	N-Mint
1-12: 9-Reprints		.60	1.20

NOTE: *Buckler c-2p-4p, 5. Gil Kane a-5-7p; c-1p, 7p, 8p. Kirby a-9r. Mooney a-11i. Perez a-1-4p, 8p.*

INKY & DINKY (See Felix's Nephews...)

IN LOVE (I Love You No. 7 on)
Aug-Sept, 1954 - No. 6, July, 1955 ('Adult Reading' on-c)
Mainline/Charlton No. 5 (5/55)-on

	Good	Fine	N-Mint
1-Simon & Kirby-a	7.00	21.00	50.00
2-S&K-a	3.50	10.50	24.00
3,4-S&K-a	2.65	8.00	18.00
5-S&K-c only	1.65	5.00	11.50
6-No S&K-a	1.15	3.50	8.00

IN LOVE WITH JESUS
1952 (36 pages) (Giveaway)
Catechetical Educational Society

	Good	Fine	N-Mint
	4.00	12.00	28.00

INSANE
Feb., 1988 - Present? ($1.75, B&W)
Dark Horse Comics

	Good	Fine	N-Mint
1,2	.30	.90	1.80

IN SEARCH OF THE CASTAWAYS (See Movie Comics)

INSIDE CRIME (Formerly My Intimate Affair)
No. 3, July, 1950 - No. 2, Sept, 1950
Fox Features Syndicate (Hero Books)

	Good	Fine	N-Mint
3-Wood-a, 10 pgs.; L. B. Cole-c	11.00	32.00	75.00
2(9/50)-Used in SOTI, pg. 182-3; Lingerie panel; r-/Spook #24	10.00	30.00	70.00
nn(no publ. listed, nd)	3.50	10.50	24.00

INSPECTOR, THE (Also see The Pink Panther)
July, 1974 - No. 19, Feb, 1978
Gold Key

	Good	Fine	N-Mint
1	.60	1.75	3.50
2-5	.30	.90	1.80
6-19: 11-Reprints		.50	1.00

Indian Fighter #1, © YM

The Inferior Five #1, © DC

The Informer #3, © Feature TV Prod.

Intimate Confessions #4, © REAL   Intimate Secrets Of Romance #1, © STAR   Invisible Scarlet O'Neil #3, © HARV

INSPECTOR WADE (See Feature Books No. 13, McKay)

INTERNATIONAL COMICS (. . . Crime Patrol No. 6)
Spring, 1947 - No. 5, Nov-Dec, 1947
E. C. Comics

	Good	Fine	N-Mint
1	30.00	90.00	210.00
2	23.00	70.00	160.00
3-5	20.00	60.00	140.00

INTERNATIONAL CRIME PATROL (Formerly International Comics
No. 1-5; becomes Crime Patrol No. 7 on)
Spring, 1948
E. C. Comics

6-Moon Girl app.	30.00	90.00	210.00

INTERSTATE THEATRES' FUN CLUB COMICS
Mid 1940's (10 cents on cover) (B&W cover) (Premium)
Interstate Theatres

Cover features MLJ characters looking at a copy of Top-Notch Comics, but contains
an early Detective Comic on inside; many combinations possible

	5.35	16.00	24.00

IN THE DAYS OF THE MOB (Magazine)
Fall, 1971 (Black & White)
Hampshire Dist. Ltd. (National)

1-Kirby-a; has John Dillinger wanted poster inside

	.70	2.00	4.00

IN THE PRESENCE OF MINE ENEMIES
1973 (35-49 cents)
Spire Christian Comics/Fleming H. Revell Co.

		.50	1.00

INTIMATE (Teen-Age Love No. 4 on?)
December, 1957 - No. 3, May, 1958
Charlton Comics

1-3	1.00	3.00	7.00

INTIMATE CONFESSIONS (See Fox Giants)

INTIMATE CONFESSIONS
July-Aug, 1951 - No. 7, Aug, 1952; No. 8, Mar, 1953 (All painted-c)
Realistic Comics

1-Kinstler-c/a; c/Avon paperback 222	50.00	150.00	350.00
2	9.00	27.00	60.00
3-c/Avon paperback 250; Kinstler-c/a	12.00	36.00	80.00
4-c/Avon paperback 304; Kinstler-c	9.00	27.00	60.00
5	9.00	27.00	60.00
6-c/Avon paperback 120	9.00	27.00	60.00
7-Spanking panel	10.00	30.00	70.00
8-c/Avon paperback 375; Kinstler-a	9.00	27.00	60.00

INTIMATE CONFESSIONS
1964
I. W. Enterprises/Super Comics

I.W. Reprint #9,10	.70	2.00	4.00
Super Reprint #12,18	.70	2.00	4.00

INTIMATE LOVE
1950 - No. 28, Aug, 1954
Standard Comics

5	2.30	7.00	16.00
6-8-Severin/Elder-a	3.00	9.00	21.00
9	1.15	3.50	8.00
10-Jane Russell, Robert Mitchum photo-c	2.65	8.00	18.00
11-18,20,23,25,27,28	1.00	3.00	7.00
19,21,22,24,26-Toth-a	3.50	10.50	24.00

NOTE: Celardo a-8, 10. Colletta a-23. Moreira a-13(2). Photo-c-6, 7, 10, 12, 14, 15,
18-20, 24, 26, 27.

INTIMATE SECRETS OF ROMANCE
Sept, 1953 - No. 2, April, 1954
Star Publications

	Good	Fine	N-Mint
1,2-L. B. Cole-c	4.35	13.00	30.00

INTRIGUE
January, 1955
Quality Comics Group

1-Horror; Jack Cole reprt/Web of Evil	8.00	24.00	56.00

INVADERS, THE (TV)
Oct, 1967 - No. 4, Oct, 1968 (All have photo-c)
Gold Key

1-Spiegle-a in all	3.00	9.00	21.00
2-4	2.00	6.00	14.00

INVADERS, THE (Also see Avengers No. 71)
August, 1975 - No. 41, Sept, 1979
Marvel Comics Group

1-Captain America, Sub-Mariner & Human Torch begin	.40	1.20	2.40
2-1st app. Mailbag & Brain-Drain		.60	1.20
3-5: 3-Intro U-Man		.35	.70
6-Liberty Legion app; intro/1st app. Union Jack. Two cover prices, 25 & 30 cents		.35	.70
7-10: 7-Intro Baron Blood; Human Torch origin retold. 9-Origin Baron Blood. 10-G.A. C. Amer.-r		.35	.70
11-Origin Spitfire; intro The Blue Bullet		.25	.50
12-19: 14-1st app. The Crusaders. 16-Re-intro The Destroyer. 17-Intro Warrior Woman. 18-Re-intro The Destroyer w/new origin.		.25	.50
20-Reprints Sub-Mariner story/Motion Picture Funnies Weekly with color added & brief write-up about MPFW		.25	.50
21-r/Marvel Mystery #10		.25	.50
22-30: 22-New origin Toro. 24-r/Marvel Mystery #17. 28-Intro new Human Top & Golden Girl. 29-Intro Teutonic Knight		.25	.50
31-40(5/79): 34-Mighty Destroyer joins		.25	.50
41-Double size		.25	.50
Giant Size . . . 1(6/75)-50 cents; origin; GA Sub-Mariner r/Sub-Mariner 1; intro Master-Man		.50	1.00
Annual 1(9/77)-Schomburg, Rico stories; Schomburg-c; Avengers app; re-intro The Shark & The Hyena		.35	.70

NOTE: Buckler a-5. Everett a-21r(1940), 24r, Annual 1r. Gil Kane c(p)-13, 17, 18, 20-27.
Kirby c(p)-3-12, 14-16, 32, 33. Mooney a-5, 16, 22.

INVASION
Holiday, 1988-'89 - No 3, Jan, 1989 ($2.95, 84pgs, mini-series)
DC Comics

1-3: 1,2-McFarlane/Russell-a; 3-Russell-i	.50	1.50	2.95

INVINCIBLE FOUR OF KUNGFU & NINJA
April, 1988 - Present? ($2.75, color)
Leung Publ.

1	.45	1.40	2.75

INVISIBLE BOY (See Approved Comics)

INVISIBLE MAN, THE (See Superior Stories No. 1)

INVISIBLE SCARLET O'NEIL (Also see Famous Funnies #81 &
Harvey Comics Hits 59)
Dec, 1950 - No. 3, April, 1951
Famous Funnies (Harvey)

1	9.50	28.00	65.00
2,3	6.50	19.50	45.00

IRON CORPORAL, THE (See Army War Heroes)
No. 23, Oct, 1985 - No. 25, Feb, 1986
Charlton Comics

THE IRON CORPORAL (continued)	Good	Fine	N-Mint
23-25: Glanzman-a(r)		.40	.75

IRON FIST (Also see Marvel Premiere & Powerman & Iron Fist)
Nov, 1975 - No. 15, Sept, 1977
Marvel Comics Group

	Good	Fine	N-Mint
1-McWilliams-a(i); Iron Man app.	1.85	5.50	11.00
2	1.00	3.00	6.00
3-5	.75	2.25	4.50
6-10: 8-Origin retold	.60	1.80	3.60
11-13: 12-Capt. America app.	.45	1.40	2.80
14-1st app. Saber Tooth	1.70	5.00	10.00
15-New X-Men app., Byrne-a	3.35	10.00	20.00
15 (35 cent edition)	4.15	12.50	25.00

NOTE: Adkins a-8p, 13i; c-8i. Byrne a-1-15p; c-8p, 15p. G. Kane c-4-6p.

IRON HORSE (TV)
March, 1967 - No. 2, June, 1967
Dell Publishing Co.

	Good	Fine	N-Mint
1,2	1.15	3.50	8.00

IRON JAW (Also see The Barbarians)
Jan, 1975 - No. 4, July, 1975
Atlas/Seaboard Publ.

	Good	Fine	N-Mint
1-Adams-c; Sekowsky-a(p)	.25	.75	1.50
2-Adams-c		.50	1.00
3,4: 4-Origin		.30	.60

IRON MAN (Also see Marvel Coll. Item Classics, Marvel Double
Feat., Marvel Fanfare, & Tales of Suspense)
May, 1968 - Present
Marvel Comics Group

	Good	Fine	N-Mint
1-Origin	12.00	36.00	85.00
2	5.70	17.00	40.00
3-5	3.00	9.00	21.00
6-10	2.15	6.50	15.00
11-15 (Last 12 cent ish)	1.50	4.50	10.00
16-20	1.00	3.00	6.00
21-40: 22-Death of Janice Cord. 27-Intro Fire Brand. 33-Intro Spymaster	.85	2.50	5.00
41-46,48-50: 43-Intro The Guardsman. 46-The Guardsman dies. 50-Princess Python app.	.70	2.00	4.00
47-Origin retold; Smith-a(p)	1.15	3.50	7.00
51-54	.70	2.00	4.00
55,56-Starlin-a; 55-Starlin-c	1.00	3.00	6.00
57-67,69,70: 65-Origin Dr. Spectrum	.60	1.75	3.50
68-Starlin-c; origin retold	.70	2.00	4.00
71-85: 76 r-/#9	.50	1.50	3.00
86-1st app. Blizzard	.50	1.50	3.00
87-Origin Blizzard	.50	1.50	3.00
88-99	.50	1.50	3.00
100-Starlin-c	.85	2.50	5.00
101-117: 101-Intro DreadKnight. 109-1st app. new Crimson Dynamo. 110-Origin Jack of Hearts retold	.35	1.00	2.00
118-Byrne-a(p)	.70	2.00	4.00
119,120,123-128-Tony Stark recovers from alcohol problem	.45	1.25	2.50
121,122,129-149: 122-Origin	.25	.75	1.50
150-Double size	.30	.85	1.70
151-158,160: 152-New armor		.60	1.20
159-Paul Smith-c/a(p)		.60	1.20
161-Moon Knight app.		.60	1.20
162-168: 167-Tony Stark alcohol problem starts again		.60	1.20
169-New Iron Man (Jim Rhodes replaces Tony Stark)	.70	2.00	4.00
170	.40	1.25	2.50
171	.25	.75	1.50

	Good	Fine	N-Mint
172-199: 186-Intro Vibro. 191-Tony Stark new armor		.60	1.20
200-Double size ($1.25)	.35	1.00	2.00
201-224: 213-Intro new Dominic Fortune		.50	1.00
225-Double size	.40	1.25	2.50
226-240: 231-New armor. 233-Ant-Man app; intro new Iron Man		.50	1.00
Giant Size 1('75)-Ditko-a(r)	.50	1.50	3.00
Special 1(8/70)-Everett-c	.85	2.50	5.00
Special 2(11/71)	.50	1.50	3.00
Annual 3(6/76)-Man-Thing app.	.35	1.00	2.00
Annual 5(12/82), 6(11/83), 7(10/84)	.25	.75	1.50
Annual 8(10/86)-X-Factor app.	.25	.75	1.50
Annual 9(12/87)	.25	.75	1.50
King Size 4(8/77)-Newton-a(i)	.30	.90	1.80

NOTE: Austin c-105i, 109-11i, 151. Byrne a-118p; c-109p. Colan a-Special 1p(3). Craig a-1i, 2-4, 5-13i, 14, 15-19i, 24p, 25p, 26-28i; c-2-4. Ditko a-160p. Guice a-233p-241p. G. Kane c(p)-52-54, 63, 67, 72-75, 77, 78, 88, 98. Kirby a-Special 1p; c-80p, 90, 92-95. Mooney a-40i, 47i. Perez c-103p. Simonson c-Annual 8. B. Smith a-229, 232p; c-229, 232. Starlin a-53p, 55p, 56p; c-55p, 160, 163. Tuska a-5-13p, 15-23p, 24i, 32p, 38-46p, 48-54p, 57-61p, 63-69p, 70-72p, 78p, 86-92p, 95-106p, Annual 4p. Wood a-Special 1i.

IRON MAN & SUB-MARINER
April, 1968 (One Shot)
Marvel Comics Group

	Good	Fine	N-Mint
1-Colan/Craig-a-Iron Man; Colan-c	2.30	7.00	16.00

IRON VIC (See Comics Revue No. 3)
1940; Aug, 1947 - No. 3, 1947
United Features Syndicate/St. John Publ. Co.

	Good	Fine	N-Mint
Single Series 22	13.00	40.00	90.00
2,3(St. John)	2.30	7.00	16.00

IRONWOLF (See Weird Worlds #8)
1986 ($2.00, one shot)
DC Comics

	Good	Fine	N-Mint
1	.35	1.00	2.00

ISIS (TV) (Also see Shazam)
Oct-Nov, 1976 - No. 8, Dec-Jan, 1977-78
National Periodical Publications/DC Comics

	Good	Fine	N-Mint
1-Wood inks		.40	.80
2-8: 5-Isis new look. 7-Origin		.25	.50

ISLAND AT THE TOP OF THE WORLD (See Walt Disney Showcase 27)

ISLAND OF DR. MOREAU, THE (Movie)
October, 1977 (52 pgs.)
Marvel Comics Group

	Good	Fine	N-Mint
1-Gil Kane-c		.50	1.00

I SPY (TV)
Aug, 1966 - No. 6, Sept, 1968 (Photo-c)
Gold Key

	Good	Fine	N-Mint
1-Bill Cosby, Robert Culp photo covers	4.00	12.00	28.00
2-6: 3,4-McWilliams-a	2.30	7.00	16.00

IS THIS TOMORROW?
1947 (One Shot) (3 editions) (52 pages)
Catechetical Guild

	Good	Fine	N-Mint
1-Theme of communists taking over the USA; (no price on cover) Used in POP, pg. 102	12.00	36.00	80.00
1-(10 cents on cover)	17.00	51.00	120.00
1-Has blank circle with no price on cover	17.00	51.00	120.00
Black & White advance copy titled "Confidential"-(52 pgs.)-Contains script and art edited out of the color edition, including one page of extreme violence showing mob nailing a Cardinal to a door; (only two known copies)	50.00	150.00	320.00

NOTE: The original color version first sold for 10 cents. Since sales were good, it was later printed as a giveaway. Approximately four million in total were printed. The two

Iron Man #1, © MEG

Iron Man #232, © MEG

Iron Man & Sub-Mariner #1, © MEG

It's A Ducks Life #4, © MEG

Jack Armstrong #1, © PMI

Jackie Gleason And The Honeymooners #3, © DC

IS THIS TOMORROW? (continued)
black and white copies listed plus two other versions as well as a full color untrimmed version surfaced in 1979 from the Guild's old files in St. Paul, Minnesota.

IT! (See Supernatural Thrillers No.1 & Astonishing Tales No.21-24)

IT HAPPENS IN THE BEST FAMILIES
1920 (52 pages) (B&W Sundays)
Powers Photo Engraving Co.

	Good	Fine	N-Mint
By Briggs	7.00	21.00	50.00
Special Railroad Edition(30 cents)-r-/strips from 1914-1920	6.00	18.00	42.00

IT REALLY HAPPENED
1944 - No. 11, Oct, 1947
William H. Wise No. 1,2/Standard (Visual Editions)

1-Kit Carson story	6.00	18.00	42.00
2	3.50	10.50	24.00
3,4,6,9	2.65	8.00	18.00
5-Lou Gehrig story	3.00	9.00	21.00
7-Teddy Roosevelt story	2.65	8.00	18.00
8-Story of Roy Rogers	5.00	15.00	35.00
10-Honus Wagner story	3.15	9.50	22.00
11-Baker-a	4.35	13.00	30.00

NOTE: *Guardineer* a-7(2), 8(2), 11. Schomburg c-1-7, 9-11.

IT RHYMES WITH LUST (Also see Bold Stories, Candid Tales)
1950 (Digest size) (128 pages)
St. John Publishing Co.

(Rare)-Matt Baker & Ray Osrin-a	27.00	81.00	190.00

IT'S ABOUT TIME (TV)
January, 1967
Gold Key

1 (10195-701)-Photo-c	2.65	8.00	18.00

IT'S A DUCK'S LIFE
Feb, 1950 - No. 11, Feb, 1952
Marvel Comics/Atlas(MMC)

1-Buck Duck, Super Rabbit begin	5.00	15.00	35.00
2	2.65	8.00	18.00
3-11	1.50	4.50	10.00

IT'S FUN TO STAY ALIVE (Giveaway)
1948 (16 pgs.) (heavy stock paper)
National Automobile Dealers Association

Featuring: Bugs Bunny, The Berrys, Dixie Dugan, Elmer, Henry, Tim Tyler, Bruce Gentry, Abbie & Slats, Joe Jinks, The Toodles, & Cokey; all art copyright 1946-48 drawn especially for this book.

	11.50	34.00	80.00

IT'S GAMETIME
Sept-Oct, 1955 - No. 4, Mar-Apr, 1956
National Periodical Publications

1-(Scarce)-Infinity-c; Davy Crockett app. in puzzle	22.00	65.00	154.00
2-4(Scarce): 2-Dodo & The Frog	19.00	57.00	132.00

IT'S LOVE, LOVE, LOVE
November, 1957 - No. 2, Jan, 1958 (10 cents)
St. John Publishing Co.

1,2	2.15	6.50	15.00

IVANHOE (See Fawcett Movie Comics No. 20)

IVANHOE
July-Sept, 1963
Dell Publishing Co.

1 (12-373-309)	2.65	8.00	18.00

IWO JIMA (See Spectacular Features Magazine)

JACE PEARSON OF THE TEXAS RANGERS (Tales of the Texas
Rangers 4-Color 396; . . .'s Tales of . . . #11-on)(See Western

Roundup)
No. 396, 5/52 - No. 1021, 8-10/59 (No #10) (All-Photo-c)
Dell Publishing Co.

	Good	Fine	N-Mint
4-Color 396 (#1)	5.00	15.00	35.00
2(5-7/53)	3.50	10.50	24.00
3-9(2-4/55)	3.50	10.50	24.00
4-Color 648(9/55)	3.50	10.50	24.00
11(11-2/55/56) - 14,17-20(6-8/58)	3.00	9.00	21.00
15,16-Toth-a	4.00	12.00	28.00
4-Color 961-Spiegle-a	3.50	10.50	24.00
4-Color 1021	3.00	9.00	21.00

JACK & JILL VISIT TOYTOWN WITH ELMER THE ELF
1949 (16 pgs.) (paper cover)
Butler Brothers (Toytown Stores Giveaway)

	1.70	5.00	10.00

JACK ARMSTRONG (Radio)(See True Comics)
11/47 - No. 9, 9/48; No. 10, 3/49 - No. 13, Sept, 1949
Parents' Institute

1	10.00	30.00	70.00
2	5.00	15.00	35.00
3-5	4.00	12.00	28.00
6-13	3.00	9.00	21.00
12-Premium version(distr. in Chicago only); Free printed on upper right-c; no price (Rare)	10.00	30.00	70.00

JACK HUNTER
July, 1987 - Present? ($1.25, color)
Blackthorne Publishing

1-4		.60	1.20

JACKIE GLEASON (Also see The Honeymooners)
1948; Sept, 1955 - No. 5, Dec, 1955
St. John Publishing Co.

1(1948)	30.00	90.00	210.00
2(1948)	19.00	57.00	132.00
1(1955)(TV)-Photo-c	20.00	60.00	140.00
2-5	14.00	42.00	100.00

JACKIE GLEASON AND THE HONEYMOONERS (TV)
June-July, 1956 - No. 12, Apr-May, 1958
National Periodical Publications

1	37.00	110.00	260.00
2	23.00	70.00	160.00
3-11	17.00	51.00	120.00
12 (Scarce)	21.00	64.00	150.00

JACKIE JOKERS (Also see Richie Rich & . . .)
March, 1973 - No. 4, Sept, 1973
Harvey Publications

1-4; 2-President Nixon app.		.20	.40

JACKIE ROBINSON (Famous Plays of . . .)
May, 1950 - No. 6, 1952 (Baseball hero) (All photo-c)
Fawcett Publications

nn	25.00	75.00	175.00
2	17.00	51.00	120.00
3-6	14.00	42.00	100.00

JACK IN THE BOX (Formerly Yellowjacket No. 1-10)
(Cowboy Western Comics No. 17 on)
Feb, 1946; No. 11, Oct, 1946 - No. 16, Nov-Dec, 1947
Frank Comunale/Charlton Comics No. 11 on

1-Stitches, Marty Mouse & Nutsy McKrow	4.65	14.00	32.00
11-Yellowjacket	5.00	15.00	35.00
12,14-16	2.00	6.00	14.00
13-Wolverton-a	9.00	27.00	62.00

JACK OF HEARTS
Jan, 1984 - No. 4, April, 1984 (Mini-series)

Marvel Comics Group	Good	Fine	N-Mint
1-4		.50	1.00

JACKPOT COMICS (Jolly Jingles No. 10 on)
Spring, 1941 - No. 9, Spring, 1943
MLJ Magazines

	Good	Fine	N-Mint
1-The Black Hood, Mr. Justice, Steel Sterling & Sgt. Boyle begin; Biro-c	95.00	285.00	665.00
2	45.00	135.00	315.00
3	36.00	108.00	250.00
4-Archie begins (on sale 12/41)-(Also see Pep Comics No. 22); Montana-c	110.00	330.00	770.00
5-Hitler-c	45.00	135.00	315.00
6-9; 6,7-Bondage-c	40.00	120.00	280.00

JACK Q FROST (See Unearthly Spectaculars)

JACK THE GIANT KILLER (See Movie Classics)

JACK THE GIANT KILLER (New Advs. of . . .)
Aug-Sept, 1953
Bimfort & Co.

	Good	Fine	N-Mint
V1#1-H. C. Kiefer-c/a	8.00	24.00	56.00

JACKY'S DIARY (See 4-Color No. 1091)

JADEMAN KUNG FU SPECIAL
1988 ($1.50, color, 64pgs.)
Jademan Comics

	Good	Fine	N-Mint
1	.25	.75	1.50

JAGUAR, THE (See The Advs. of . . .)

JAKE THRASH
1988 - No. 3, 1988 ($2.00, color)
Aircel

	Good	Fine	N-Mint
1-3	.35	1.00	2.00

JAMBOREE
Feb, 1946(no mo. given) - No. 3, April, 1946
Round Publishing Co.

	Good	Fine	N-Mint
1-Funny animal	4.00	12.00	28.00
2,3	2.00	6.00	14.00

JAMES BOND FOR YOUR EYES ONLY
Oct., 1981 - No. 2, Nov., 1981
Marvel Comics Group

	Good	Fine	N-Mint
1,2-Movie adaptation r-/Marvel Super Spec.		.30	.60

JAM: SUPER COOL COLOR INJECTED TURBO ADVENTURE #1 FROM HELL!, THE
May, 1988 ($2.50, 44pgs)
Comico

	Good	Fine	N-Mint
1	.40	1.25	2.50

JANE ARDEN (See Feature Funnies & Pageant of Comics)
March, 1948 - No. 2, June, 1948
St. John (United Features Syndicate)

	Good	Fine	N-Mint
1-Newspaper reprints	8.50	25.50	60.00
2	5.00	15.00	35.00

JANN OF THE JUNGLE (Jungle Tales No. 1-7)
No. 8, Nov, 1955 - No. 17, June, 1957
Atlas Comics (CSI)

	Good	Fine	N-Mint
8(#1)	8.00	24.00	56.00
9,11-15	4.65	14.00	32.00
10-Williamson/Colleta-c	5.50	16.50	38.00
16,17-Williamson/Mayo-a(3), 5 pgs. each	8.50	25.50	60.00

NOTE: *Everett c-15-17.* **Heck** *a-8, 15, 17.* **Shores** *a-8.*

JASON & THE ARGONAUTS (See Movie Classics)

JAWS 2 (See Marvel Super Special, A)

JCP FEATURES
Feb, 1982-c; Dec, 1981-indicia ($2.00, One-shot, B&W)

J.C. Productions (Archie)	Good	Fine	N-Mint
1-T.H.U.N.D.E.R. Agents; Black Hood by Morrow & Adams	.35	1.00	2.00

JEANIE COMICS (Cowgirl Romances No. 28) (Formerly Daring)
No. 13, April, 1947 - No. 27, Oct, 1949
Marvel Comics/Atlas(CPC)

	Good	Fine	N-Mint
13-Mitzi, Willie begin	6.00	18.00	42.00
14,15	3.70	11.00	26.00
16-Used in Love and Death by Legman; Kurtzman's ''Hey Look''	5.70	17.00	40.00
17-19,22-Kurtzman's ''Hey Look,'' 1-3 pgs. each	3.70	11.00	26.00
20,21,23-27	2.35	7.00	16.00

JEEP COMICS (Also see G.I. and Overseas Comics)
Winter, 1944 - No. 3, Mar-Apr, 1948
R. B. Leffingwell & Co.

	Good	Fine	N-Mint
1-Capt. Power, Criss Cross & Jeep & Peep (costumed) begin	8.00	24.00	56.00
2	5.00	15.00	35.00
3-L. B. Cole-c	5.70	17.00	40.00
1-29(Giveaway)-Strip reprints in all; Tarzan, Flash Gordon, Blondie, The Nebbs, Little Iodine, Red Ryder, Don Winslow, The Phantom, Johnny Hazard, Katzenjammer Kids; distr. to U.S. Armed Forces in mid 1940's	3.35	10.00	20.00

NOTE: *L. B. Cole c-3.*

JEFF JORDAN, U.S. AGENT
Dec, 1947 - Jan, 1948
D. S. Publishing Co.

	Good	Fine	N-Mint
1	4.65	14.00	32.00

JEMM, SON OF SATURN
9/84 - No. 12, 8/85 (12 part maxi-series; mando paper)
DC Comics

	Good	Fine	N-Mint
1-Colan p-all; c-1-5p,7-12p		.50	1.00
2-12: 3-Origin		.50	1.00

JERRY DRUMMER (Formerly Soldier & Marine V2No.9)
No. 10, Apr, 1957 - No. 12, Oct, 1957
Charlton Comics

	Good	Fine	N-Mint
V2#10, V3#11,12	1.30	4.00	9.00

JERRY IGER'S CLASSIC SHEENA (Also see Sheena 3-D Special)
April, 1985 (One-shot)
Blackthorne Publishing

	Good	Fine	N-Mint
1	.25	.75	1.50

JERRY IGER'S FAMOUS FEATURES
July, 1984 (One-shot)
Pacific Comics

	Good	Fine	N-Mint
1-Unpub. Flamingo & Wonder Boy by Baker	.25	.75	1.50

JERRY IGER'S GOLDEN FEATURES
1986 - Present ($2.00, B&W)
Blackthrone Pub.

	Good	Fine	N-Mint
1-7	.30	.90	1.80

JERRY LEWIS (See Adventures of . . .)

JESSE JAMES (See 4-Color No. 757 & The Legend of . . .)

JESSE JAMES (See Badmen of the West & Blazing Sixguns)
Aug, 1950 - No. 29, Aug-Sept, 1956
Avon Periodicals

Jackpot Comics #4, © AP *Jann Of The Jungle #10, © MEG* *Jeff Jordan, U. S. Agent #1, © DS*

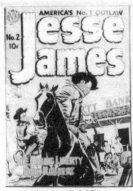

Jesse James #2, © AVON

Jet Powers #2, © ME

The Jetsons #5, © Hanna-Barbera

JESSE JAMES (continued)	Good	Fine	N-Mint
1-Kubert Alabam r-/Cowpuncher #1	11.00	33.00	76.00
2-Kubert-a(3)	8.50	25.50	60.00
3-Kubert Alabam r-/Cowpuncher #2	7.00	21.00	50.00
4-No Kubert	2.85	8.50	20.00
5,6-Kubert Jesse James-a(3); one pg. Wood-a, #5			
	7.00	21.00	50.00
7-Kubert Jesse James-a(2)	6.00	18.00	42.00
8-Kinstler-a(3)	4.00	12.00	28.00
9,10-No Kubert	2.85	8.50	20.00
11-14 (Exist?)	2.15	6.50	15.00
15-Kinstler r-/#3	2.15	6.50	15.00
16-Kinstler r-/#3 & Sheriff Bob Dixon's Chuck Wagon #1 with name changed to Sheriff Tom Wilson	2.65	8.00	18.00
17-Jesse James r-/#4; Kinstler-c idea from Kubert splash in #6			
	1.70	5.00	12.00
18-Kubert Jesse James r-/#5	1.70	5.00	12.00
19-Kubert Jesse James-r	1.70	5.00	12.00
20-Williamson/Frazetta-a; r-Chief Vic. Apache Massacre; Kubert Jesse James r-/#6	8.50	25.50	60.00
21-Two Jesse James r-/#4, Kinstler r-/#4	1.70	5.00	12.00
22,23-No Kubert	1.60	4.70	11.00
24-New McCarty strip by Kinstler plus Kinstler r-/#9			
	1.60	4.70	11.00
25-New McCarty Jesse James strip by Kinstler; Kinstler J. James r-/#7,9	1.60	4.70	11.00
26,27-New McCarty J. James strip plus a Kinstler/McCann Jesse James-r	1.60	4.70	11.00
28-Reprints most of Red Mountain, Featuring Quantrells Raiders			
	1.60	4.70	11.00
29	1.60	4.70	11.00
Annual(nn; 1952; 25 cents)-''...Brings Six-Gun Justice to the West''(100 pgs.)-3 earlier issues rebound; Kubert, Kinstler-a(3)			
	17.00	51.00	120.00

NOTE: Mostly reprints #10 on. Fawcette c-1, 2. Kinstler a-3, 4, 7-9, 15r, 16(2), 21-27; c-3, 4, 9, 17, 18, 20-27. Painted c-5, 6.

JESSE JAMES
July, 1953
Realistic Publications

	Good	Fine	N-Mint
nn-Reprints Avon's #1, same cover, colors different	4.35	13.00	30.00

JEST (Kayo No. 12) (Formerly Snap)
1944
Harry 'A' Chesler

	Good	Fine	N-Mint
10-Johnny Rebel & Yankee Boy app. in text	4.60	14.00	32.00
11-Little Nemo in Adventure Land	5.00	15.00	35.00

JESTER
1945
Harry 'A' Chesler

	Good	Fine	N-Mint
10	3.70	11.00	26.00

JESUS
1979 (49 cents)
Spire Christian Comics (Fleming H. Revell Co.)

		.40	.80

JET (See Jet Powers)

JET ACES
1952 - 1953
Fiction House Magazines

	Good	Fine	N-Mint
1	4.60	14.00	32.00
2	3.15	9.50	22.00
3,4	2.50	7.50	17.00

JET DREAM (...& Her Stuntgirl Counterspies)
June, 1968

Gold Key	Good	Fine	N-Mint
1	1.70	5.00	12.00

JET FIGHTERS (Korean War)
No. 5, Nov, 1952 - No. 7, Mar, 1953
Standard Magazines

	Good	Fine	N-Mint
5,7-Toth-a	5.00	15.00	35.00
6-Celardo-a	1.85	5.50	13.00

JET POWERS (American Air Forces No. 5 on)
1950 - 1951
Magazine Enterprises

	Good	Fine	N-Mint
1(A-1 30)-Powell-c/a begins	14.00	42.00	100.00
2(A-1 32)	10.00	30.00	70.00
3(A-1 35)-Williamson/Evans-a	19.00	57.00	132.00
4(A-1 38)-Williamson/Wood-a; ''The Rain of Sleep'' drug story	19.00	57.00	132.00
I.W. Reprint 1,2(1963)-r-/#1,2	1.50	4.50	10.00

JET PUP (See 3-D Features)

JETSONS, THE (TV)(See March of Comics 276,330,348, Spotlight 3)
Jan, 1963 - No. 36, Oct, 1970 (Hanna-Barbera)
Gold Key

	Good	Fine	N-Mint
1	7.00	21.00	50.00
2	4.30	13.00	30.00
3-10	2.85	8.50	20.00
11-20	2.30	7.00	16.00
21-36	2.00	6.00	14.00

JETSONS, THE (TV) (Hanna-Barbera)
Nov, 1970 - No. 20, Dec, 1973
Charlton Comics

	Good	Fine	N-Mint
1	3.50	10.50	24.00
2	2.00	6.00	14.00
3-10	1.50	4.50	10.00
11-20	1.15	3.50	8.00

JETTA OF THE 21ST CENTURY
No. 5, 1952 - No. 7, Mar, 1953 (Teen-age Archie type)
Standard Comics

	Good	Fine	N-Mint
5	6.00	18.00	42.00
6,7	3.50	10.50	24.00

JEZEBEL JADE (Hanna-Barbara)
Oct, 1988 - No. 3, Dec, 1988 ($2.00, color, mini-series)
Comico

1-3: Jonny Quest spin-off	.35	1.00	2.00

JIGGS & MAGGIE (See 4-Color No. 18)

JIGGS & MAGGIE
No. 11, 1949(Aug.) - No. 21, 2/53; No. 22, 4/53 - No. 27, 2-3/54
Standard Comics/Harvey Publications No. 22 on

	Good	Fine	N-Mint
11	6.50	19.50	45.00
12-15,17-21	3.50	10.50	24.00
16-Wood text illos.	4.30	13.00	30.00
22-25,27: 22-24-Little Dot app.	2.30	7.00	16.00
26-Four pgs. partially in 3-D	9.50	28.00	65.00

NOTE: Sunday page reprints by McManus loosely blended into story continuity. Based on Bringing Up Father strip. Advertised on covers as ''All New.''

JIGSAW (Big Hero Adventures)
Sept, 1966 - No. 2, Dec, 1966 (36 pgs.)
Harvey Publications (Funday Funnies)

	Good	Fine	N-Mint
1-Origin; Crandall-a, 5pgs.	.85	2.50	5.00
2-Man From S.R.A.M.	.50	1.50	3.00

JIGSAW OF DOOM (See Complete Mystery No. 2)

JIM BOWIE (Formerly Danger; Black Jack No. 20 on)
No. 15, 1955? - No. 19, April, 1957

JIM BOWIE (continued)
Charlton Comics

	Good	Fine	N-Mint
15	2.30	7.00	16.00
16-19	1.30	4.00	9.00

JIM BOWIE (See 4-Color No. 893,993, & Western Tales)

JIM DANDY
May, 1956 - No. 3, Sept, 1956 (Charles Biro)
Dandy Magazine (Lev Gleason)

1	2.65	8.00	18.00
2,3	1.30	4.00	9.00

JIM HARDY (Also see Treasury of Comics No. 2&5 & Sparkler)
1939; 1942; 1947
United Features Syndicate/Spotlight Publ.

Single Series 6 ('39)	18.00	54.00	125.00
Single Series 27('42)	13.00	40.00	90.00
1('47)-Spotlight Publ.	5.00	15.00	35.00
2	2.65	8.00	18.00

JIM HARDY
1944 (132 pages, 25 cents) (Tip Top, Sparkler-r)
Spotlight/United Features Syndicate

(1944)-Origin Mirror Man; Triple Terror app.	17.00	51.00	120.00

JIMINY CRICKET (See 4-Color No. 701,795,897,989, Mickey Mouse Mag. V5/3 & Walt Disney Showcase #37)

JIMMY (James Swinnerton)
1905 (10x15") (40 pages in color)
N. Y. American & Journal

	17.00	51.00	120.00

JIMMY DURANTE (See A-1 Comics No. 18,20)

JIMMY OLSEN (See Superman's Pal. . .)

JIMMY WAKELY (Cowboy movie star)
Sept-Oct, 1949 - No. 18, July-Aug, 1952 (52pgs., 1-13)
National Periodical Publications

1-Photo-c, 52pgs. begin; Alex Toth-a; Kit Colby Girl Sheriff begins	29.00	87.00	200.00
2-Toth-a	20.00	60.00	140.00
3,6,7-Frazetta-a in all, 3 pgs. each; Toth-a in all. 7-Last photo-c?	22.00	65.00	154.00
4-Frazetta-a, 3pgs.; Kurtzman "Pot-Shot Pete," 1pg; Toth-a	22.00	65.00	154.00
5,8-15,18-Toth-a; 12,14-Kubert-a, 3 & 2 pgs.	15.00	45.00	105.00
16,17	11.00	32.00	75.00

JIM RAY'S AVIATION SKETCH BOOK
Feb, 1946 - No. 2, May-June, 1946
Vital Publishers

1,2-Picture stories about planes and pilots	11.00	34.00	80.00

JIM SOLAR (See Wisco/Klarer)

JINGLE BELLS (See March of Comics No. 65)

JINGLE BELLS CHRISTMAS BOOK
1971 (20 pgs.; B&W inside; slick cover)
Montgomery Ward (Giveaway)

		.40	.80

JINGLE DINGLE CHRISTMAS STOCKING COMICS
V2No.1, 1951 (no date listed) (100 pgs.; giant-size)(25 cents)
Stanhall Publications (Publ.-annually)

V2#1-Foodini & Pinhead, Silly Pilly plus games & puzzles	7.00	18.00	42.00

JINGLE JANGLE COMICS (Also see Puzzle Fun)
Feb, 1942 - No. 42, Dec, 1949
Eastern Color Printing Co.

1-Pie-Face Prince of Old Pretzleburg, & Jingle Jangle Tales by
George Carlson, Hortense, & Benny Bear begin

	Good	Fine	N-Mint
	20.00	60.00	140.00
2,3-No Pie-Face Prince	9.00	27.00	62.00
4-Pie-Face Prince cover	9.00	27.00	62.00
5	8.00	24.00	56.00
6-10: 8-No Pie-Face Prince	7.00	21.00	50.00
11-15	4.65	14.00	32.00
16-30: 17,18-No Pie-Face Prince	3.50	10.50	24.00
31-42: 42-Xmas-c	2.30	7.00	16.00

NOTE: *George Carlson a-(2) in all except No. 2, 3, 8, 17, 18; c-1-6. Carlson 1 pg. puzzles in 9, 10, 12-15, 18, 20. Carlson illustrated a series of Uncle Wiggily books in 1930's.*

JING PALS
Feb, 1946 - No. 4, Aug?, 1946 (Funny animal)
Victory Publishing Corporation

1-Wishing Willie, Puggy Panda & Johnny Rabbit begin	4.65	14.00	32.00
2-4	2.65	8.00	18.00

JINKS, PIXIE, AND DIXIE (See Whitman Comic. . .)
1965 (Giveaway) (Hanna-Barbera)
Florida Power & Light

	.50	1.50	3.00

JOAN OF ARC (See A-1 Comics No. 21 & Ideal a Classical Comic)

JOAN OF ARC
No date (28 pages)
Catechetical Guild (Topix) (Giveaway)

	7.00	21.00	50.00

NOTE: *Unpublished version exists which came from the Guild's files.*

JOE COLLEGE
Fall, 1949 - No. 2, Winter, 1950
Hillman Periodicals

1,2-Powell-a; 1-Briefer-a	3.00	9.00	21.00

JOE JINKS (See Single Series No. 12)

JOE LOUIS (Also see True Comics #5)
Sept, 1950 - No. 2, Nov, 1950 (Photo-c) (Boxing champ)
Fawcett Publications

1-Photo-c; life story	20.00	60.00	140.00
2	16.00	48.00	110.00

JOE PALOOKA
1933 (B&W daily strip reprints) (52 pages)
Cupples & Leon Co.

nn-(Scarce)-by Fisher	45.00	135.00	315.00

JOE PALOOKA (1st Series)(Also see Big Shot, Columbia Comics & Feature Funnies)
1942 - 1944
Columbia Comic Corp. (Publication Enterprises)

1-1st to portray American president; gov't permission required	27.00	81.00	190.00
2 (1943)-Hitler-c	14.00	42.00	100.00
3,4	11.00	32.00	75.00

JOE PALOOKA (2nd Series) (Battle Adv. #68-74; . . .Advs. #75,77-81,83-85,87; Champ of the Comics #76,82,86,89-93) (See All-New)
Nov, 1945 - No. 118, Mar, 1961
Harvey Publications

1	20.00	60.00	140.00
2	10.00	30.00	70.00
3,4,6	6.50	19.50	45.00
5-Boy Explorers by S&K (7-8/46)	9.50	28.00	65.00
7-1st Powell Flyin' Fool, ends #25	5.70	17.00	40.00

Jimmy Wakely #11, © DC

Jingle Jangle Comics #4, © EAS

Joe Palooka #1 (1942), © CCG

Joe Yank #8, © STD   Johnny Dynamite #11, © CC   Johnny Hazard #6, © KING

	Good	Fine	N-Mint
JOE PALOOKA (continued)			
8-10	5.00	15.00	35.00
11-14,16-20: 19-Freedom Train-c	4.00	12.00	28.00
15-Origin Humphrey; Super heroine Atoma app. by Powell			
	5.00	15.00	35.00
21-30: 30-Nude female painting	3.00	9.00	21.00
31-61: 35-1st app. Little Max? 44-Joe Palooka marries Ann Howe			
	2.30	7.00	16.00
62-S&K Boy Explorers-r	3.00	9.00	21.00
63-80: 66,67-'commie' torture story	1.70	5.00	12.00
81-99,101-115	1.50	4.50	10.00
100	1.75	5.25	12.00
116-S&K Boy Explorers (r) (Giant, '60)	2.85	8.50	20.00
117,118-Giants	2.65	8.00	18.00
. . .Body Building Instruction Book (1958 Sports Toy giveaway, 16 pgs., 5¼x7'')-Origin	5.00	15.00	35.00
. . .Fights His Way Back (1945 Giveaway, 24 pgs.) Family Comics			
	14.00	42.00	100.00
. . .in Hi There! (1949 Red Cross giveaway, 12 pgs., 4¾x6'')			
	5.00	15.00	35.00
. . .in It's All in the Family (1945 Red Cross giveaway, regular size)	6.50	19.50	45.00
. . .Visits the Lost City (1945)(One Shot)(nn)(50 cents)-164 page continuous story strip reprint. Has biography & photo of Ham Fisher; possibly the single longest comic book story published (159 pgs.?)	50.00	150.00	350.00

NOTE: *Nostrand/Powell a-73. Powell a-7, 8, 10, 12, 14, 17, 19, 26-45, 47-53, 70, 73 at least. Black Cat text stories #8, 12, 13, 19. Bondage c-50.*

	Good	Fine	N-Mint
JOE YANK			
March, 1952 - 1954			
Standard Comics (Visual Editions)			
5-Celardo, Tuska-a	2.15	6.50	15.00
6-Toth, Severin/Elder-a	4.00	12.00	28.00
7	1.30	4.00	9.00
8-Toth-c	2.65	8.00	18.00
9-16: 12-Andru-a	1.00	3.00	7.00
JOHN BOLTON'S HALLS OF HORROR			
June, 1985 - No. 2, June, 1985 ($1.75 cover, color)			
Eclipse Comics			
1,2-British-r; Bolton c/a	.30	.90	1.80
JOHN CARTER OF MARS (See 4-Color No. 375,437,488, The Funnies & Weird Worlds)			
JOHN CARTER OF MARS			
April, 1964 - No. 3, Oct, 1964			
Gold Key			
1(10104-404)-Reprints 4-Color 375; Jesse Marsh-a			
	2.85	8.50	20.00
2(407), 3(410)-Reprints 4-Color 437 & 488; Marsh-a			
	2.30	7.00	16.00
JOHN CARTER OF MARS			
1970 (72 pgs.; paper cover; 10½x16½''; B&W)			
House of Greystoke			
1941-42 Sunday strip reprints; John Coleman Burroughs-a			
	2.65	8.00	18.00
JOHN CARTER, WARLORD OF MARS			
June, 1977 - No. 28, Oct, 1979			
Marvel Comics Group			
1-Origin by Gil Kane		.50	1.00
2-10-Last Kane issue		.30	.60
11-17,19-28: 11-Origin Dejah Thoris		.25	.50
18-Miller-a(p)	.35	1.00	2.00
Annual 1(10/77), 2(9/78), 3(10/79)		.40	.80

NOTE: *Austin c-24i. Gil Kane a-1-10p; c-1p, 2p, 3, 4-9p, 10, 15p, Annual 1p. Layton*

a-17i. Miller c-25, 26p. Nebres a-2-4i, 8-16i; c(i)-6-9, 11-22, 25, Annual 1. Perez c-24p. Simonson a-15p. Sutton a-7i.

	Good	Fine	N-Mint
JOHN F. KENNEDY, CHAMPION OF FREEDOM			
1964 (no month) (25 cents)			
Worden & Childs			
nn-Photo-c	2.65	8.00	18.00
JOHN F. KENNEDY LIFE STORY			
Aug-Oct, 1964; Nov, 1965; June, 1966 (12 cents)			
Dell Publishing Co.			
12-378-410	2.00	6.00	14.00
12-378-511 (reprint)	1.35	4.00	9.00
12-378-606 (reprint)	1.00	3.00	7.00
JOHN FORCE (See Magic Agent)			
JOHN HIX SCRAP BOOK, THE			
Late 1930's (no date) (68 pgs.; reg. size; 10 cents)			
Eastern Color Printing Co. (McNaught Synd.)			
1-Strange As It Seems (resembles Single Series books)			
	10.00	30.00	70.00
2-Strange As It Seems	8.50	25.50	60.00
JOHN LAW DETECTIVE (See Smash Comics #3)			
April, 1983 ($1.50, color, Baxter)			
Eclipse Comics			
1-Three Eisner stories originally drawn in 1948 for the never published John Law No. 1; original cover pencilled in 1948 & inked in 1982 by Eisner	.35	1.00	2.00
JOHNNY APPLESEED (See Story Hour Series)			
JOHNNY CASH (See Hello, I'm . . .)			
JOHNNY DANGER			
1950			
Toby Press			
1	6.00	18.00	42.00
JOHNNY DANGER PRIVATE DETECTIVE			
1954 (Reprinted in Danger No. 11 (Super))			
Toby Press			
1-Opium den story	5.00	15.00	35.00
JOHNNY DYNAMITE (Formerly Dynamite No. 1-9)			
No. 10, 6/55 - No. 12, 10/55 (Foreign Intrigues No. 13 on)			
Charlton Comics			
10-12	2.30	7.00	16.00
JOHNNY HAZARD			
No. 5, Aug, 1948 - No. 8, May, 1949			
Best Books (Standard Comics)			
5-Strip reprints by Frank Robbins	8.00	24.00	56.00
6,8-Strip reprints by Frank Robbins	5.50	16.50	38.00
7-New art, not Robbins	4.00	12.00	28.00
35	4.00	12.00	28.00
JOHNNY JASON (. . .Teen Reporter)			
Feb-Apr, 1962 - No. 2, June-Aug, 1962			
Dell Publishing Co.			
4-Color 1302, 2(01380-208)	1.15	3.50	8.00
JOHNNY JINGLE'S LUCKY DAY			
1956 (16 pgs.; 7¼x5-1/8'') (Giveaway) (Disney)			
American Dairy Association			
	2.35	7.00	14.00
JOHNNY LAW, SKY RANGER			
Apr, 1955 - No. 3, Aug, 1955; No. 4, Nov, 1955			
Good Comics (Lev Gleason)			
1-Edmond Good-c/a	3.50	10.50	24.00

JOHNNY LAW, SKY RANGER (continued)	Good	Fine	N-Mint
2-4	2.00	6.00	14.00

JOHNNY MACK BROWN (TV western star; see Western Roundup)
No. 269, Mar, 1950 - No. 963, Feb, 1959 (All Photo-c)
Dell Publishing Co.

4-Color 269(3/50, 52pgs.)-J. Mack Brown & his horse Rebel begin;
    photo front/back-c begin; Marsh-a begins, ends #9

	Good	Fine	N-Mint
	10.00	30.00	70.00
2(10-12/50, 52pgs.)	6.00	18.00	42.00
3(1-3/51, 52pgs.)	4.30	13.00	30.00
4-10 (9-11/52)(36pgs.)	3.50	10.50	24.00
4-Color 455,493,541,584,618	3.50	10.50	24.00
4-Color 645,685,722,776,834,963	3.50	10.50	24.00
4-Color 922-Manning-a	4.00	12.00	28.00

JOHNNY NEMO
Sept, 1985 - No. 3, Feb, 1986 (Mini-series)
Eclipse Comics

	Good	Fine	N-Mint
1,2 ($1.75 cover)	.30	.90	1.75
3 ($2.00 cover)	.35	1.00	2.00

JOHNNY RINGO (See 4-Color No. 1142)

JOHNNY STARBOARD (See Wisco)

JOHNNY THUNDER
Feb-Mar, 1973 - No. 3, July-Aug, 1973
National Periodical Publications

1-Johnny Thunder & Nighthawk-r begin	.25	.75	1.50
2,3: 2-Trigger Twins app.		.50	1.00

NOTE: *Drucker a-2r, 3r. G. Kane a-2r, 3r. Toth a-1r, 3r; c-1r, 3r. Also see All-American, All-Star Western, Flash Comics, Western Comics, World's Best & World's Finest.*

JOHN PAUL JONES (See Four Color No. 1007)

JOHN STEED & EMMA PEEL (See The Avengers)

JOHN STEELE SECRET AGENT (Also see Freedom Agent)
December, 1964 (Freedom Agent)
Gold Key

1	1.50	4.50	10.00

JOHN WAYNE ADVENTURE COMICS (Movie star; See Big Tex,
Oxydol-Dreft, Tim McCoy & With The Marines . . .#1)
Winter, 1949 - No. 31, May, 1955 (Photo-c, 1-12,17,25-on)
Toby Press

	Good	Fine	N-Mint
1 (36pgs.)-Photo-c begin	37.00	110.00	260.00
2 (36pgs.)-Williamson/Frazetta-a(2) (one r-/Billy the Kid #1), 6 & 2 pgs; photo back-c	38.00	115.00	265.00
3 (36pgs.)-Williamson/Frazetta-a(2), 16 pgs. total; photo back-c	38.00	115.00	265.00
4 (52pgs.)-Williamson/Frazetta-a(2), 16 pgs total	38.00	115.00	265.00
5 (52pgs.)-Kurtzman-a-(Alfred "L" Newman in Potshot Pete)	26.00	78.00	180.00
6 (52pgs.)-Williamson/Frazetta-a, 10 pgs; Kurtzman a-'Pot-Shot Pete, 5pgs.; & "Genius Jones," 1 pg.	36.00	108.00	250.00
7 (52pgs.)-Williamson/Frazetta-a, 10 pgs.	30.00	90.00	210.00
8 (36pgs.)-Williamson/Frazetta-a(2), 12 & 9 pgs.	36.00	108.00	250.00
9-11: Photo western-c	17.00	51.00	120.00
12-Photo war-c; Kurtzman-a, 2pgs. "Genius"	19.00	57.00	132.00
13-15: 13-Line-drawn-c begin, end #24	14.00	42.00	100.00
16-Williamson/Frazetta r-from Billy the Kid #1	20.00	60.00	140.00
17-Photo-c	17.00	51.00	120.00
18-Williamson/Frazetta-a r-/#4 & 8, 19 pgs.	25.00	75.00	175.00
19-24: 23-Evans-a?	13.00	40.00	90.00
25-Photo-c return; end #31; Williamson/Frazetta-a r-/Billy the Kid #3	25.00	75.00	175.00

	Good	Fine	N-Mint
26-28,30-Photo-c	16.00	48.00	110.00
29-Williamson/Frazetta-a r-/#4	23.00	70.00	160.00
31-Williamson/Frazetta-a r-/#2	23.00	70.00	160.00

NOTE: *Williamsonish art in later issues by Gerald McCann.*

JO-JO COMICS (. . .Congo King #7-29; My Desire #30 on)
(Also see Fantastic Fears and Jungle Jo)
1945 - No. 29, July, 1949 (two No.7's; no No. 13)
Fox Feature Syndicate

	Good	Fine	N-Mint
nn(1945)-Funny animal, humor	5.00	15.00	35.00
2(Sum,'46)-6: Funny animal; 2-Ten pg. Electro story	2.65	8.00	18.00
7(7/47)-Jo-Jo, Congo King begins	25.00	75.00	175.00
7(No.8) (9/47)	19.00	57.00	132.00
8-10(No.9-11): 8-Tanee begins	15.00	45.00	105.00
11,12(No.12,13),14,16	13.00	40.00	90.00
15-Cited by Dr. Wertham in 5/47 Saturday Review of Literature	14.00	42.00	100.00
17-Kamen bondage-c	14.00	42.00	100.00
18-20	13.00	40.00	90.00
21-29	11.50	34.00	80.00

NOTE: *Many bondage-c/a by Baker/Kamen/Feldstein/Good. No. 7's have Princesses Gwenna, Geesa, Yolda, & Safra before settling down on Tanee.*

JO-JOY (Adventures of . . .)
1945 - 1953 (Christmas gift comic)
W. T. Grant Dept. Stores

1945-53 issues	2.00	6.00	14.00

JOKEBOOK COMICS DIGEST ANNUAL (. . .Mag. No. 5 on)
10/77 - No. 13, 10/83 (Digest Size)
Archie Publications

1(10/77)-Reprints; Adams-a		.60	1.20
2(4/78)-13		.60	1.20

JOKER, THE (See Batman, Brave & the Bold, Detective & Justice League Int.)
May, 1975 - No. 9, Sept-Oct, 1976
National Periodical Publications

1-Two-Face app.	.35	1.00	2.00
2-4, V2/5-9	.25	.75	1.50

JOKER COMICS (Adventures Into Terror No. 43 on)
April, 1942 - No. 42, August, 1950
Timely/Marvel Comics No. 36 on (TCI/CDS)

1-(Rare)-1st app. Powerhouse Pepper by Wolverton; Stuporman app. from Daring	75.00	225.00	525.00
2-Wolverton-a continued; 1st app. Tessie the Typist	31.00	93.00	220.00
3-5-Wolverton-a	22.00	65.00	154.00
6-10-Wolverton-a	15.00	45.00	105.00
11-20-Wolverton-a	12.00	36.00	84.00
21,22,24-27,29,30-Wolverton cont'd. & Kurtzman's "Hey Look" in #24-27	9.50	28.50	65.00
23-1st "Hey Look" by Kurtzman; Wolverton-a	11.00	32.00	76.00
28,32,34,37-41	1.70	5.00	12.00
31-Last Powerhouse Pepper; not in #28	7.00	21.00	50.00
33,35,36-Kurtzman's "Hey Look"	3.00	9.00	21.00
42-Only app. 'Patty Pinup,' a clone of Millie the Model	2.00	6.00	14.00

JOLLY CHRISTMAS, A (See March of Comics No. 269)

JOLLY CHRISTMAS BOOK (See Christmas Journey Through Space)
1951; 1954; 1955 (36 pgs.; 24 pgs.)
Promotional Publ. Co.

1951-(Woolworth giveaway)-slightly oversized; no slick cover; Marv

John Wayne Adventure Comics #1, © TOBY

Jo-Jo Congo King #7 (7/47), © FOX

The Joker #1, © DC

Jolly Jingles #10, © AP

Jon Juan #1, © TOBY

Jonny Quest Classics #1, © Hanna-Barbera

	Good	Fine	N-Mint
JOLLY CHRISTMAS BOOK (continued)			
Levy c/a	2.00	6.00	14.00
1954-(Hot Shoppes giveaway)-regular size-reprints 1951 issue; slick			
cover added; 24 pgs.; no ads	2.00	6.00	14.00
1955-(J. M. McDonald Co. giveaway)-regular size			
	1.50	4.50	10.00

JOLLY COMICS
1947
Four Star Publishing Co.

1	3.00	9.00	21.00

JOLLY JINGLES (Formerly Jackpot)
No. 10, Sum, 1943 - No. 16, Wint, 1944/45
MLJ Magazines

10-Super Duck begins (origin & 1st app.). Woody The Woodpecker			
begins. (not same as Lantz character)	16.00	48.00	110.00
11 (Fall, '43)	7.00	21.00	50.00
12-16: 12-Hitler-c	3.70	11.00	26.00

JONAH HEX (See All-Star Western, Hex and Weird Western Tales)
Mar-Apr, 1977 - No. 92, Aug, 1985
National Periodical Publications/DC Comics

1	.50	1.50	3.00
2-6,8-10: 9-Wrightson-c		.50	1.00
7-Explains Hex's face disfigurement	.25	.75	1.50
11-20: 12-Starlin-c		.40	.80
21-92: 31,32-Origin retold		.25	.50

NOTE: *Aparo* c-76p. *Ayers* a(p)-35-37, 41,44-53, 56, 58-82. *Kubert* c-43-46. *Morrow* a-90-92; c-10. *Spiegle*(*Tothish*) a-34, 38, 40, 49, 52.

JONAH HEX AND OTHER WESTERN TALES (Blue Ribbon Digest)
Sept-Oct, 1979 - No. 3, Jan-Feb, 1980 (100 pgs.)
DC Comics

1-3: 1-Origin Scalphunter-r; painted-c. 2-Weird Western Tales-r;			
Adams, Toth, Aragones, Gil Kane-a	.40		.80

JONAH HEX SPECTACULAR (See DC Special Series No. 16)

JONESY (Formerly Crack Western)
No. 85, Aug, 1953; No. 2, Oct, 1953 - No. 8, Oct, 1954
Comic Favorite/Quality Comics Group

85(#1)-Teen-age humor	2.85	8.50	20.00
2	1.50	4.50	10.00
3-8	1.00	3.00	7.00

JON JUAN (Also see Great Lover Romances)
Spring, 1950
Toby Press

1-All Schomburg-a (signed Al Reid on-c); written by Siegel; used in			
SOTI, pg. 38	11.50	34.00	80.00

JONNI THUNDER
Feb, 1985 - No. 4, Aug, 1985 (Mini-series)
DC Comics

1-Origin		.50	1.00
2-4		.45	.90

JONNY QUEST (TV)
December, 1964 (Hanna-Barbera)
Gold Key

1 (10139-412)	5.70	17.00	40.00

JONNY QUEST (TV)
June, 1986 - No. 31, Dec, 1988 (Hanna-Barbera)
Comico

1	.85	2.50	5.00
2	.60	1.80	3.60
3	.50	1.50	3.00
4-10	.35	1.00	2.00

	Good	Fine	N-Mint
11-31: #15 on, $1.75	.25	.75	1.50
Special 1(9/88, $1.75), 2(10/88, $1.75)	.30	.90	1.75

NOTE: *Pini* a-2. *Rude* a-1. *Sienkiewicz* c-11. *Spiegle* a-12; c-21. *Staton* a-11. *Stevens* a-4i; c-3, 5. *Wildey* a-1, c-1, 7, 12. *Williamson* a-4i; c-4i.

JONNY QUEST CLASSICS (TV)
May, 1987 - Present ($2.00, color) (Hanna-Barbera)
Comico

1-3-Wildey c/a	.35	1.00	2.00

JON SABLE, FREELANCE (Also see Sable)
6/83 - No. 56, 2/88 (#1-17, $1; #18-33, $1.25; #34-on, $1.75)
First Comics

1-Created, story/a&c by Mike Grell	.75	2.25	4.50
2-5: 3-5-Origin, parts 1-3	.45	1.40	2.80
6-10: 6-Origin, part 4	.40	1.25	2.50
11-20: 14-Mando paper begins	.35	1.10	2.20
21-33: 25-30-Shatter app.	.30	.90	1.80
34-56: 34-Deluxe format begins ($1.75)	.30	.95	1.90

NOTE: *Aragones* a-33. *Grell* a-1-43; c-1-52, 53p, 54-56.

JOSEPH & HIS BRETHREN (See The Living Bible)

JOSIE (She's . . . #1-16) (. . .& the Pussycats #45 on) (See Archie
Giant Series 528,540,551,562,571,584)
2/63 - No. 106, 10/82
Archie Publications/Radio Comics

1	9.00	27.00	62.00
2	4.30	13.00	30.00
3-5	2.65	8.00	18.00
6-10	1.70	5.00	12.00
11-20	1.15	3.50	8.00
21,23-30	.75	2.25	5.00
22-Mighty Man & Mighty (Josie Girl) app.	.75	2.25	5.00
31-54	.45	1.35	3.00
55-74(52pg. ish.)		.50	1.00
75-106		.35	.70

JOURNAL OF CRIME (See Fox Giants)

JOURNEY
1983 - No. 14, 9/84; No. 15, 4/85 - No. 27, 7/86 (B&W)
Aardvark-Vanaheim #1-14/Fantagraphics Books #15-on

1	2.65	8.00	16.00
2	1.15	3.50	7.00
3	.70	2.00	4.00
4-27	.35	1.00	2.00

JOURNEY INTO FEAR
May, 1951 - No. 21, Sept, 1954
Superior-Dynamic Publications

1-Baker-a(2)-r	14.00	42.00	100.00
2	9.00	27.00	62.00
3,4	7.00	21.00	50.00
5-10	5.70	17.00	40.00
11-14,16-21	5.00	15.00	35.00
15-Used in **SOTI**, pg. 389	8.50	25.50	60.00

NOTE: *Kamensh*, 'headlight'-a most issues. *Robinson* a-10.

JOURNEY INTO MYSTERY (1st Series) (Thor No. 126 on)
6/52 - No. 48, 8/57; No. 49, 11/58 - No. 125, 2/66
Atlas(CPS No.1-48/AMI No.49-68/Marvel No.69(6/61) on)

1	45.00	135.00	315.00
2	23.00	70.00	160.00
3,4	18.00	54.00	125.00
5-11	11.50	34.00	80.00
12-20,22: 22-Davisesque-a; last pre-code issue (2/55)			
	8.50	25.50	60.00
21-Kubert-a; Tothish-a by Andru	9.00	27.00	65.00

JOURNEY INTO MYSTERY (continued)	Good	Fine	N-Mint
23-32,35-38,40: 24-Torres?-a	4.65	14.00	32.00
33-Williamson-a	7.00	21.00	50.00
34-Krigstein-a	6.50	19.50	45.00
39-Wood-a	6.50	19.50	45.00
41-Crandall-a; Frazettaesque-a by Morrow	4.00	12.00	28.00
42,48-Torres-a	4.00	12.00	28.00
43,44-Williamson/Mayo-a in both	4.00	12.00	28.00
45,47,52,53	3.00	9.00	21.00
46-Torres & Krigstein-a	4.00	12.00	28.00
49-Matt Fox, Check-a	4.00	12.00	28.00
50-Davis-a	2.85	8.50	20.00
51-Kirby/Wood-a	3.00	9.00	21.00
54-Williamson-a	2.85	8.50	20.00
55-61,63-73: 66-Return of Xemnu	2.65	8.00	18.00
62-1st app. Xemnu (Titan) called ''The Hulk''	4.65	14.00	32.00
74-82-Fantasy content #74 on. 75-Last 10 cent issue. 80-Anti-communist propaganda story by Ditko	2.00	6.00	14.00
83-R-/from the Golden Record Comic Set with the record....	2.15	6.50	15.00
	5.00	15.00	35.00
83-Origin & 1st app. The Mighty Thor by Kirby (8/62)			
	83.00	210.00	580.00
84	18.50	47.00	130.00
85-1st app. Loki & Heimdall	13.50	34.00	95.00
86-1st app. Odin	10.00	25.00	70.00
87,88	8.50	21.00	60.00
89-Origin Thor reprint/#83	8.50	21.00	60.00
90-No Kirby-a; Aunt May proto-type	5.70	14.00	40.00
91,92,94-96-Sinnott-a	4.30	11.00	30.00
93,97-Kirby-a; Tales of Asgard series begins #97(Origin which concludes #99)	5.70	14.00	40.00
98-100-Kirby/Heck-a. 98-Origin/1st app. The Human Cobra. 99-1st app. Surtur & Mr. Hyde	4.30	11.00	30.00
101-104,110: 102-Intro Sif	2.65	8.00	18.00
105-109-Ten extra pages Kirby-a. 107-1st app. Grey Gargoyle			
	2.65	8.00	18.00
111,113,114,116-125: 119-Intro Hogun, Fandrall, Volstagg			
	1.70	5.00	12.00
112-Thor Vs. Hulk; origin Loki begins; ends #113			
	2.65	8.00	18.00
115-Detailed origin Loki	2.65	8.00	18.00
Annual 1('65)-1st app. Hercules; Kirby c/a	3.60	11.00	25.00

NOTE: Ayers a-14, 39. Bailey a-43. Briefer a-5, 12. Check a-17. Colan a-23, 81. Ditko a-33, 38, 50-96; c-71, 88i. Ditko/Kirby a-50-83. Everett a-20, 48; c-4-7, 9, 37, 39, 40-42, 44, 45, 47. Forte a-19, 40. Heath a-4, 5, 11, 14; c-1, 11, 15, 51. Kirby a(p)-60, 66, 76, 80, 83-89, 93, 97, 98, 100(w/Heck), 101-125; c-50-62(w/Ditko), 83-152p. Leiber/Fox a-93, 98-102. Maneely c-21, 22. Morrow a-41, 42. Orlando a-30, 45, 57. Mac Pakula (Tothish) a-9. Powell a-20, 27, 34. Reinman a-39, 87, 92, 96i. Robinson a-9. Roussos a-39. Robert Sale a-14. Severin a-27. Sinnott c-50. Tuska a-11. Wildey a-16.

JOURNEY INTO MYSTERY (2nd Series)
Oct., 1972 - No. 19, Oct, 1975
Marvel Comics Group

1-Robert Howard adaptation; Starlin/Ploog-a	.40	.80
2,3,5-Bloch adaptation; 5-Last new story	.30	.60
4-H. P. Lovecraft adaptation	.30	.60
6-19	.30	.60

NOTE: Adams a-2i. Ditko a(r)-7, 10, 12, 14, 15, 19; c-10. Everett a-9r, 14r. G. Kane a-1p, 2p; c-1-3p. Kirby a-7r, 13r, 18r, 19r; c-7. Mort Lawrence a-2r. Maneely a-3r. Orlando a-16r. Reese a-1, 2i. Starlin a-3p. Torres a-16r. Wildey a-9r, 14r.

JOURNEY INTO UNKNOWN WORLDS (Formerly Teen)
No. 36, 9/50 - No. 38, 2/51; No. 4, 4/51 - No. 59, 8/57
Atlas Comics (WFP)

36(#1)-Science fiction/weird; 'End Of The Earth' c/story			
	30.00	90.00	210.00
37(#2)-Science fiction; 'When Worlds Collide' c/story; Everett-c/a			
	23.00	70.00	160.00
38(#3)-Science fiction	19.00	57.00	132.00

	Good	Fine	N-Mint
4-6,8,10-Science fiction/weird	12.00	36.00	84.00
7-Wolverton-a-''Planet of Terror,'' 6 pgs; electric chair c-inset/story			
	22.00	65.00	154.00
9-Giant eyeball story	12.00	36.00	84.00
11,12-Krigstein-a	9.50	28.50	65.00
13,16,17,20	5.70	17.00	40.00
14-Wolverton-a-''One of Our Graveyards Is Missing,'' 4 pgs; Tuska-a	19.50	58.00	136.00
15-Wolverton-a-''They Crawl By Night,'' 5 pgs.			
	19.50	58.00	136.00
18,19-Matt Fox-a	7.00	21.00	50.00
21-26,28-33-Last pre-code (2/55). 21-Decapitation-c. 24-Sci/fic story. 26-Atom bomb panel	3.00	9.00	21.00
27-Sid Check-a	3.50	10.50	24.00
34-Kubert, Torres-a	3.65	11.00	25.00
35-Torres-a	3.00	9.00	21.00
36-42	2.30	7.00	16.00
43-Krigstein-a	3.35	10.00	23.00
44-Davis-a	3.35	10.00	23.00
45,55,59-Williamson-a in all; with Mayo #55,59. Crandall-a #55,59			
	5.00	15.00	35.00
46,47,49,52,56-58	2.00	6.00	14.00
48,53-Crandall-a; Check-a, #48	4.45	13.00	30.00
50-Davis, Crandall-a	4.00	12.00	28.00
51-Ditko, Wood-a	3.65	11.00	25.00
54-Torres-a	2.85	8.50	20.00

NOTE: Ayers a-24, 43. Berg a-38(#3), 43. Lou Cameron a-33. Colan a-37(#2); 6, 17, 20, 39. Ditko a-45, 51. Evans a-20. Everett a-37(#2), 11, 14, 41, 55, 56; c-11, 13, 14, 17, 22, 47, 48, 50, 53-55, 59. Forte a-49. Fox a-21. Heath a-36(#1), 4, 6-8, 17, 20, 22, 36i. Mort Lawrence a-38, 39. Maneely a-7, 8, 15, 16, 22, 49; c-25, 52. Morrow a-48. Orlando a-44, 57. Powell a-42, 53, 54. Reinman a-8. Rico a-21. Robert Sale a-24, 49. Sekowsky a-4, 5, 9. Severin a-38, 51; c-38, 48i, 56. Sinnott a-9, 21. Tuska a-38(#3). Wildey a-25, 44.

JOURNEY OF DISCOVERY WITH MARK STEEL (See Mark Steel)

JOURNEY TO THE CENTER OF THE EARTH (See 4-Color No. 1060)

JOURNEY: WARDRUMS
Aug., 1987 ($1.75, B&W)
Fantagraphics Books

1	.30	.90	1.75

JUDE, THE FORGOTTEN SAINT
1954 (16 pgs.; 8x11''; full color; paper cover)
Catechetical Guild Education Society

nn	2.00	6.00	14.00

JUDGE COLT
Oct., 1969 - No. 4, Sept, 1970
Gold Key

1	.85	2.50	6.00
2-4	.70	2.00	4.00

JUDGE DREDD
Nov., 1983 - No. 35, 1986; Oct., 1986 - Present
Eagle Comics/IPC Magazines Ltd./Quality Comics No. 34 on

1-Bolland c/a begins	1.00	3.00	6.00
2,3	.60	1.80	3.60
4-10	.50	1.50	3.00
11-20	.40	1.20	2.40
21-35	.35	1.00	2.00
V2#1-('86)-New look begins	.35	1.00	2.00
V2#2-6	.25	.75	1.50
V2#7-19: 14-Bolland-a		.65	1.30
V2#20, 21/22, 23: 20-begin $1.50-c	.25	.75	1.50
Special 1		.70	1.40

JUDGE DREDD'S CRIME FILE
Aug, 1985 - No. 6, Feb, 1986 (Mini-series)

Journey Into Mystery #83, © MEG

Journey Into Unknown Worlds #36 (#1), © MEG

Judge Dredd V2#10, © Quality Comics

Judy Canova #24 (#2), © FOX

Juke Box Comics #1, © FF

Jumbo Comics #1, © FH

JUDGE DREDD'S CRIME FILE (continued)
Eagle Comics

	Good	Fine	N-Mint
1-6: 1-Byrne-a	.35	1.10	2.20

JUDGE DREDD: THE EARLY CASES
Feb, 1986 - No. 6, July, 1986 (Mega-series, Mando paper)
Eagle Comics

1-6: 2000 A.D.-r	.35	1.10	2.20

JUDGE DREDD: THE JUDGE CHILD QUEST
Aug, 1984 - No. 5, Oct, 1984 (Limited series, Baxter paper)
Eagle Comics

1-5: 2000 A.D.-r; Bolland c/a	.35	1.10	2.20

JUDGE PARKER
Feb, 1956
Argo

1	2.65	8.00	18.00
2	1.50	4.50	10.00

JUDO JOE
Aug, 1953 - No. 3, Dec, 1953
Jay-Jay Corp.

1-Drug ring story	3.50	10.50	24.00
2,3: 3-Hypo needle story	2.00	6.00	14.00

JUDOMASTER (Gun Master No. 84-89) (See Special War Series)
No. 89, May-June, 1966 - No. 98, Dec, 1967 (two No. 89's)
Charlton Comics

89-98: 91-Sarge Steel begins. 93-Intro. Tiger	.70	2.00	4.00
93,94,96,98(Modern Comics reprint, 1977)		.15	.30

NOTE: *Morisi Thunderbolt No. 90.*

JUDY CANOVA (Formerly My Experience) (Stage, screen, radio)
May, 1950 - No. 3, Sept, 1950
Fox Features Syndicate

23(#1)-Wood-c,a(p)?	8.50	25.50	60.00
24-Wood-a(p)	8.50	25.50	60.00
3-Wood-c; Wood/Orlando-a	10.00	30.00	70.00

JUDY GARLAND (See Famous Stars)

JUDY JOINS THE WAVES
1951 (For U.S. Navy)
Toby Press

nn	2.30	7.00	16.00

JUGHEAD (Formerly Archie's Pal . . .)
No. 127, Dec, 1965 - No. 352, 1987
Archie Publications

127-130	1.00	3.00	6.00
131,133,135-160	.70	2.00	4.00
132-Shield-c; The Fly & Black Hood app.; Shield cameo	.70	2.00	4.00
134-Shield-c	.70	2.00	4.00
161-200	.40	1.25	2.50
201-240		.60	1.20
241-352: 300-Anniversary issue		.30	.60

JUGHEAD
Aug, 1987 - Present
Archie Enterprises

1-10: 4-X-Mas issue		.40	.75

JUGHEAD AS CAPTAIN HERO
Oct, 1966 - No. 7, Nov, 1967
Archie Publications

1	2.50	7.50	17.50
2	1.35	4.00	9.00
3-7	.85	2.50	6.00

JUGHEAD JONES COMICS DIGEST, THE (. . . Magazine No. 10-on)
June, 1977 - Present (Digest-size)
Archie Publications

	Good	Fine	N-Mint
1-Adams-a; Capt. Hero-r	.70	2.00	4.00
2(9/77)-Adams-a	.35	1.00	2.00
3-55: 7-Origin Jaguar-r; Adams-a. 13-r-/1957 Jughead's Folly		.60	1.20

JUGHEAD'S EAT-OUT COMIC BOOK MAGAZINE (See Archie Giant
Series Mag. No. 170)

JUGHEAD'S FANTASY
Aug, 1960 - No. 3, Dec, 1960
Archie Publications

1	11.00	32.00	75.00
2	8.00	24.00	56.00
3	6.00	18.00	42.00

JUGHEAD'S FOLLY
1957
Archie Publications (Close-Up)

1-Jughead a la Elvis (Rare)	25.00	75.00	175.00

JUGHEAD'S JOKES
Aug, 1967 - No. 78, Sept, 1982
(No. 1-8, 38 on: reg. size; No. 9-23: 68 pgs.; No. 24-37: 52 pgs.)
Archie Publications

1	3.50	10.50	24.00
2	1.70	5.00	12.00
3-5	1.00	3.00	6.00
6-10	.70	2.00	4.00
11-30	.25	.75	1.50
31-50		.45	.90
51-78		.30	.60

JUGHEAD'S SOUL FOOD
1979 (49 cents)
Spire Christian Comics (Fleming H. Revell Co.)

		.30	.60

JUGHEAD WITH ARCHIE DIGEST (. . . Plus Betty Veronica & Reg-
gie Too No. 1,2; . . . Magazine No. 33 on)
March, 1974 - Present (Digest Size; $1.00-$1.25-$1.35)
Archie Publications

1	1.15	3.50	7.00
2	.50	1.50	3.00
3-10	.25	.75	1.50
11-20: Capt. Hero r-in #14-16; Pureheart the Powerful #18,21,22; Capt. Pureheart #17,19		.50	1.00
21-91: 29-The Shield-r. 30-The Fly-r		.50	1.00

JUKE BOX COMICS
March, 1948 - No. 6, Jan, 1949
Famous Funnies

1-Toth c/a; Hollingsworth-a	20.00	60.00	140.00
2-Transvestism story	10.00	30.00	70.00
3-6	8.50	25.50	60.00

JUMBO COMICS (Created by S.M. Iger)
Sept, 1938 - No. 167, Apr, 1953 (No.1-3: 68 pgs.; No.4-8: 52 pgs.)
(No. 1-8 oversized-10½x14½''; black & white)
Fiction House Magazines (Real Adv. Publ. Co.)

1-(Rare)-Sheena Queen of the Jungle by Meskin, The Hawk by
   Eisner, The Hunchback by Dick Briefer(ends #8) begin; 1st
   comic art by Jack Kirby (Count of Monte Cristo & Wilton of the
   West); Mickey Mouse appears (1 panel) with brief biography of
   Walt Disney. **Note:** Sheena was created by Iger for publication in
   England as a newspaper strip. The early issues of Jumbo contain
   Sheena strip-r

	370.00	1110.00	2600.00

2-(Rare)-Origin Sheena. Diary of Dr. Hayward by Kirby (also #3)

217

JUMBO COMICS (continued)

	Good	Fine	N-Mint
plus 2 other stories; contains strip from Universal Film featuring			
Edgar Bergen & Charlie McCarthy	190.00	570.00	1330.00
3-Last Kirby issue	145.00	435.00	1015.00
4-(Scarce)-Origin The Hawk by Eisner; Wilton of the West by Fine			
(ends #14)(1st comic work); Count of Monte Cristo by Fine			
(ends #15); The Diary of Dr. Hayward by Fine (cont'd. #8,9)			
	150.00	450.00	1050.00
5	95.00	285.00	665.00
6-8-Last B&W issue. #8 was a N. Y. World's Fair Special Edition			
	80.00	240.00	560.00
9-Stuart Taylor begins by Fine; Fine-c; 1st color issue(8-9/39)-			
8¼x10¼''(oversized in width only)	85.00	255.00	595.00
10-13: 10-Regular size 68 pg. issues begin; Sheena dons new			
costume #10	43.00	130.00	300.00
14-Lightning begins (Intro.)	38.00	115.00	265.00
15-20	25.00	75.00	175.00
21-30: 22-1st Tom, Dick & Harry; origin The Hawk retold			
	22.00	65.00	154.00
31-40: 35 shows V2#11 (correct number does not appear)			
	20.00	60.00	140.00
41-50	16.50	50.00	115.00
51-60: 52-Last Tom, Dick & Harry	14.00	42.00	100.00
61-70: 68-Sky Girl begins, ends #130; not in #79			
	11.00	32.00	76.00
71-80	9.50	28.00	65.00
81-93,95-99: 89-ZX5 becomes a private eye	9.50	28.00	65.00
94-Used in **Love and Death** by Legman	10.00	30.00	70.00
100	11.00	32.00	76.00
101-110: 103-Lingerie panel	8.00	24.00	56.00
111-140	6.50	19.50	45.00
141-149-Two Sheena stories. 141-Long Bow, Indian Boy begins, ends			
#160	8.00	24.00	56.00
150-154,156-158	6.50	19.50	45.00
155-Used in **POP**, pg. 98	7.00	21.00	50.00
159-163: Space Scouts serial in all; 163-Suicide Smith app.			
	6.50	19.50	45.00
164-The Star Pirate begins, ends #165	6.50	19.50	45.00
165-167: 165,167-Space Rangers app.	6.50	19.50	45.00

NOTE: Bondage covers, negligee panels, torture, etc. are common in this series. Hawks of the Seas, Inspector Dayton, Spies in Action, Sports Shorts, & Uncle Otto by **Eisner**, #1-7. Hawk by **Eisner**-#10-15, 114r?; **Eisner** c-1, 3-6, 12, 13, 15. 1pg. Patsy pin-ups in 92-97, 99-101. Sheena by **Meskin**-#1, 4; by **Powell**-#2, 3, 5-28. Sky Girl by **Matt Baker**-#69-78, 80-124. **Bailey** a-3-8. **Briefer** a-1-8, 10. **Fine** c-8-11. **Kamen** a-101, 105, 123, 132; c-105. **Bob Kane** a-1-8.

JUMPING JACKS PRESENTS THE WHIZ KIDS
1978 (In 3-D) with glasses (4 pages)
Jumping Jacks Stores giveaway

	Good	Fine	N-Mint
nn		.40	.80

JUNGLE ACTION
Oct., 1954 - No. 6, Aug, 1955
Atlas Comics (IPC)

1-Leopard Girl begins; Maneely c/a-all	9.50	28.50	65.00
2-(3-D effect cover)	11.00	32.00	75.00
3-6: 3-Last precode (2/55)	6.00	18.00	42.00

JUNGLE ACTION (. . .& Black Panther #18-21?)
Oct, 1972 - No. 24, Nov, 1976
Marvel Comics Group

1-Lorna, Jann-r		.40	.80
2-5: 5-Black Panther begins (new-a)		.30	.60
6-18-All new stories. 8-Origin Black Panther		.30	.60
19-23-KKK x-over. 23-r/#22		.30	.60
24-1st Wind Eagle		.30	.60

NOTE: **Buckler** a-6-9p, 22; c-8p, 12p. **Buscema** a-5p; c-22. **Byrne** c-23. **Gil Kane** c-2, 4, 10p, 11p, 13-17, 19, 24. **G. Kane** a-8p. **Kirby** c-18. **Maneely** r-1. **Russell** a-13i. **Starlin** c-3p.

JUNGLE ADVENTURES
1963 - 1964 (Reprints)
Super Comics

	Good	Fine	N-Mint
10,12(Rulah), 15(Kaanga/Jungle #152)	1.35	4.00	9.00
17(Jo-Jo)	1.35	4.00	9.00
18-Reprints/White Princess of the Jungle #1; no Kinstler-a; origin			
of both White Princess & Cap'n Courage	1.75	5.25	12.00

JUNGLE ADVENTURES
March, 1971 - No. 3, June, 1971
Skywald Comics

1-Zangar origin; reprints of Jo-Jo, Blue Gorilla(origin)/White Princ-			
ess #3, Kinstler-a/White Princess #2	.50	1.50	3.00
2-Zangar, Sheena/Sheena #17 & Jumbo #162, Jo-Jo, origin			
Slave Girl Princess-r	.50	1.50	3.00
3-Zangar, Jo-Jo, White Princess-r	.50	1.50	3.00

JUNGLE BOOK, THE (See Movie Comics & Walt Disney Showcase #45)

JUNGLE CAT (See 4-Color No. 1136)

JUNGLE COMICS
Jan, 1940 - No. 163, Summer, 1954
Fiction House Magazines

1-Origin The White Panther, Kaanga, Lord of the Jungle, Tabu,			
Wizard of the Jungle; Wambi, the Jungle Boy, Camilla & Capt.			
Terry Thunder begin	115.00	345.00	800.00
2-Fantomah, Mystery Woman of the Jungle begins			
	55.00	165.00	385.00
3,4	45.00	135.00	315.00
5	35.00	105.00	245.00
6-10	30.00	90.00	210.00
11-20	21.50	64.00	150.00
21-30: 25 shows V2#1 (correct number does not appear). #27-New			
origin Fantomah, Daughter of the Pharoahs; Camilla dons new			
costume	17.00	51.00	120.00
31-40	15.00	45.00	105.00
41,43-50	11.50	34.00	80.00
42-Kaanga by Crandall, 12 pgs.	14.00	42.00	100.00
51-60	10.00	30.00	70.00
61-70	8.50	25.50	60.00
71-80: 79-New origin Tabu	8.00	24.00	56.00
81-97,99,101-110	6.50	19.50	45.00
98-Used in SOTI, pg. 185 & illo-''In ordinary comic books, there are			
pictures within pictures for children who know how to look''; used			
by N.Y. Legis. Comm.	14.00	42.00	100.00
100	8.00	24.00	56.00
111-142,144,146-150: 118-Clyde Beatty app. 135-Desert Panther			
begins in Terry Thunder (origin), not in #137; ends (dies) #138			
	6.50	19.50	45.00
143,145-Used in POP, pg. 99	7.00	21.00	50.00
151-157,159-163: 152-Tiger Girl begins	6.50	19.50	45.00
158-Sheena app.	8.00	24.00	56.00
I.W. Reprint #1,9: 9-r-/#151	1.00	3.00	6.00

NOTE: Bondage covers, negligee panels, torture, etc. are common to this series. Camilla by **Fran Hopper**-#73, 78, 80-90; by **Baker**-#101, 103, 106, 107, 109, 111-13. Kaanga by **John Celardo**-#80-110; by **Maurice Whitman**-#124-163. Tabu by **Whitman**-#93-110. **Astarita** c-46. **Celardo** a-78; c-98-100, 103, 106, 109, 112. **Eisner** c-2, 5, 6. **Fine** c-1. **Larsen** a-65, 66, 72, 74, 75, 79, 83, 84, 87-90. **Morisi** a-51.

JUNGLE COMICS
May, 1988 - Present ($2.00, color)
Blackthorne Publishing

1-Dave Stevens-c	.40	1.25	2.50
2,3	.35	1.00	2.00

JUNGLE GIRL (See Lorna, . . .)

JUNGLE GIRL (Nyoka, Jungle Girl No. 2 on)
Fall, 1942 (No month listed) (Based on film character)

Jumbo Comics #166, © FH

Jungle Adventures #10 (Super reprint), © FOX

Jungle Comics #98, © FH

Jungle Jo #1, © FOX   Jungle Tales #1, © MEG   Junior Miss #1, © MEG

JUNGLE GIRL (continued)
Fawcett Publications

	Good	Fine	N-Mint
1-Bondage-c; photo of Kay Aldridge who played Nyoka in movie serial app. on-c	47.00	141.00	330.00

JUNGLE JIM (Also see Ace Comics)
Jan, 1949 - No. 20, Apr, 1951
Standard Comics (Best Books)

	Good	Fine	N-Mint
11	3.70	11.00	26.00
12-20	2.15	6.50	15.00

JUNGLE JIM
No. 490, 8/53 - No. 1020, 8-10/59 (Painted-c)
Dell Publishing Co.

4-Color 490	2.65	8.00	18.00
4-Color 565(6/54)	2.00	6.00	14.00
3(10-12/54)-5	1.70	5.00	12.00
6-19(1-3/59)	1.50	4.50	10.00
4-Color 1020(#20)	1.70	5.00	12.00

JUNGLE JIM
December, 1967
King Features Syndicate

5-Reprints Jungle Jim #5; Wood-c	.85	2.55	6.00

JUNGLE JIM (Continued from Dell)
No. 22, Feb, 1969 - No. 28, Feb, 1970 (No. 21 was an overseas edition only)
Charlton Comics

22-Dan Flagg begins; Ditko/Wood-a	1.50	4.50	9.00
23-28: 23-Last Dan Flagg; Howard-c. 24-Jungle People begin. 27-Ditko/Howard-a. 28-Ditko-a	1.00	3.00	7.00

JUNGLE JO
Mar, 1950 - No. 6, Mar, 1951
Fox Feature Syndicate (Hero Books)

nn-Jo-Jo blanked out, leaving Congo King; came out after Jo-Jo #29 (intended as Jo-Jo #30?)	11.50	34.00	80.00
1-Tangi begins; part Wood-a	13.00	40.00	90.00
2	10.00	30.00	70.00
3-6	9.00	27.00	62.00

JUNGLE LIL (Dorothy Lamour #2 on; Also see Feat. Stories Mag.)
April, 1950
Fox Feature Syndicate (Hero Books)

1	11.50	34.00	80.00

JUNGLE TALES (Jann of the Jungle No. 8 on)
Sept, 1954 - No. 7, Sept, 1955
Atlas Comics (CSI)

1-Jann of the Jungle	8.50	25.50	60.00
2-7: 3-Last precode (1/55)	6.00	18.00	42.00

NOTE: Heath c-5. Heck a-6, 7. Maneely a-2; c-1, 3. Shores a-5-7. Tuska a-2.

JUNGLE TALES OF TARZAN
Dec, 1964 - No. 4, July, 1965
Charlton Comics

1	1.70	5.00	12.00
2-4	1.30	4.00	9.00

NOTE: Giordano c-3p. Glanzman a-1-3. Montes/Bache a-4.

JUNGLE TERROR (See Comics Hits No. 54)

JUNGLE THRILLS (Terrors of the Jungle No. 17)
No. 16, February, 1952
Star Publications

16-Phantom Lady & Rulah story-reprint/All Top No. 15; used in POP, pg. 98,99; L. B. Cole-c	16.00	48.00	110.00
3-D 1(12/53)-Jungle Lil & Jungle Jo appear; L. B. Cole-c	20.00	60.00	140.00

JUNGLE TWINS, THE (Tono & Kono)
4/72 - No. 17, 11/75; No. 18, 5/82
Gold Key/Whitman No. 18 on

	Good	Fine	N-Mint
7-Titled 'Picture Scope Jungle Adventures;'(1954, 36 pgs, 15 cents)- 3-D effect c/stories; story & coloring book; Disbrow-a/script; L.B. Cole-c	13.00	40.00	90.00

1	.30	.90	1.80
2-5		.60	1.20
6-18: 18-r		.40	.80

NOTE: UFO c/story No. 13. Painted-c No. 1-17. Spiegle c-18.

JUNGLE WAR STORIES (Guerrilla War No. 12 on)
July-Sept, 1962 - No. 11, Apr-June, 1965 (Painted-c)
Dell Publishing Co.

01-384-209	.85	2.50	5.00
2-11	.70	2.00	4.00

JUNIE PROM
Winter, 1947-48 - No. 7, Aug, 1949
Dearfield Publishing Co.

1-Teen-age	4.65	14.00	32.00
2	2.30	7.00	16.00
3-7	1.50	4.50	10.00

JUNIOR COMICS
No. 9, Sept, 1947 - No. 16, July, 1948
Fox Feature Syndicate

9-Feldstein c/a; headlights-c	35.00	105.00	245.00
10-16-Feldstein c/a; headlights-c	30.00	90.00	210.00

JUNIOR FUNNIES (Formerly Tiny Tot Funnies No. 9)
No. 10, Aug, 1951 - No. 13, Feb, 1952
Harvey Publications (King Features Synd.)

10-Partial reprints in all-Blondie, Dagwood, Daisy, Henry, Popeye, Felix, Katzenjammer Kids	1.50	4.50	10.00
11-13	1.20	3.50	8.00

JUNIOR HOPP COMICS
Feb, 1952 - No. 3, July, 1952
Stanmor Publ.

1	3.70	11.00	26.00
2,3: 3-Dave Berg-a	2.00	6.00	14.00

JUNIOR MEDICS OF AMERICA, THE
1957 (15 cents)
E. R. Squire & Sons

1359	1.30	4.00	9.00

JUNIOR MISS
Winter, 1944; No. 24, April, 1947 - No. 39, Aug, 1950
Timely/Marvel Comics (CnPC)

1-Frank Sinatra & June Allyson life story	7.00	21.00	50.00
24	3.50	10.50	24.00
25-38	1.85	5.50	13.00
39-Kurtzman-a	2.30	7.00	16.00

NOTE: Painted-c 35-37. 37-all romance. 35,36,38-mostly teen humor.

JUNIOR PARTNERS (Formerly Oral Roberts' True Stories)
No. 120, Aug, 1959 - V3No.12, Dec, 1961
Oral Roberts Evangelistic Assn.

120(#1)	1.70	5.00	12.00
2(9/59)	1.15	3.50	8.00
3-12(7/60)	.60	1.80	4.00
V2#1(8/60)-5(12/60)	.50	1.50	3.00
V3#1(1/61)-12	.35	1.00	2.00

JUNIOR TREASURY (See Dell Junior...)

JUNIOR WOODCHUCKS (See Huey, Dewey & Louie...)

JUSTICE
Nov, 1986 - Present
Marvel Comics Group

	Good	Fine	N-Mint
1-19		.50	1.00
20-32		.60	1.25

JUSTICE COMICS (Tales of Justice #53 on; formerly Wacky Duck)
No. 7, Fall/47 - No. 9, 6/48; No. 4, 8/48 - No. 52, 3/55
Marvel/Atlas comics (NPP 7-9,4-19/CnPC 20-23/MjMC 24-38/Male 39-52

	Good	Fine	N-Mint
7('47)	5.70	17.00	40.00
8-Kurtzman-a-"Giggles 'N' Grins," (3)	4.30	13.00	30.00
9('48)	3.70	11.00	26.00
4	3.00	9.00	21.00
5-9: 8-Anti-Wertham editorial	2.00	6.00	14.00
10-15-Photo-c	2.00	6.00	14.00
16-30	1.70	5.00	12.00
31-40,42-47,49-52-Last precode	1.50	4.50	10.00
41-Electrocution-c	4.30	13.00	30.00
48-Pakula & Tuska-a	1.50	4.50	10.00

NOTE: Maneely c-44. Pakula a-43, 45. Louis Ravielli a-39. Robinson a-22, 25, 41. Wildey a-52.

JUSTICE, INC. (The Avenger)
May-June, 1975 - No. 4, Nov-Dec, 1975
National Periodical Publications

1-McWilliams-a; origin		.40	.80
2-4		.25	.50

NOTE: Kirby c-2, 3p; a-2-4p. Kubert c-1, 4.

JUSTICE LEAGUE (. . .International #7 on)
May, 1987 - Present
DC Comics

	Good	Fine	N-Mint
1-Batman, Gr. Lantern, Blue Beetle, others begin	2.00	6.00	12.00
2	1.15	3.50	7.00
3-Regular cover	.85	2.50	5.00
3-Limited cover	8.50	25.50	60.00
4	.70	2.00	4.00
5,6: 4-Booster Gold joins. 5-Origin Gray Man	.40	1.25	2.50
7-Double size ($1.25); Capt. Marvel & Dr. Fate resign; Capt. Atom, Rocket Red join	.50	1.50	3.00
8-10: 9,10-Millenium x-over	.35	1.00	2.00
11-24: 24-Intro/1st app. Justice League Europe		.60	1.20
Annual 1 (9/87)	.50	1.50	3.00
Annual 2 ('88)-Joker c/sty	.25	.75	1.50

NOTE: Austin c/a-1(i)Giffen a-8-10. Willingham a-Annual 2.

JUSTICE LEAGUE OF AMERICA (See Brave & the Bold)
(See Official. . .Index)
10-11/60 - No. 261, 4/87 (52pgs.-91-99,139-157)
National Periodical Publications/DC Comics

	Good	Fine	N-Mint
1-Origin Despero	107.00	270.00	750.00
2	37.00	93.00	260.00
3-Origin/1st app. Kanjar Ro	25.00	63.00	175.00
4-Green Arrow joins JLA	20.00	50.00	140.00
5-Origin Dr. Destiny	14.00	36.00	100.00
6-8,10: 6-Origin Prof. Amos Fortune. 7-Last 10 cent issue. 10-Origin Felix Faust; 1st app. Time Lord	11.50	29.00	80.00
9-Origin J.L.A.	17.00	43.00	120.00
11-15: 12-Origin & 1st app. Dr. Light. 13-Speedy app. 14-Atom joins JLA	6.50	16.00	45.00
16-20: 17-Adam Strange flashback	5.00	15.00	35.00
21,22: 21-Re-intro. of JSA. 22-JSA x-over	10.00	25.00	70.00
23-28: 24-Adam Strange app. 28-Robin app.	3.15	10.00	22.00
29,30-JSA x-over	3.15	10.00	22.00
31-Hawkman joins JLA, Hawkgirl cameo	1.85	5.50	11.00
32-Intro & Origin Brain Storm	1.85	5.50	11.00

	Good	Fine	N-Mint
33-36,40	1.50	4.50	9.00
37,38-JSA x-over	2.00	6.00	12.00
39-Giant G-16	2.15	6.50	15.00
41-Intro & Origin The Key	1.50	4.50	9.00
42-45: 42-Metamorpho app. 43-Intro. Royal Flush Gang	1.15	3.50	7.00
46,47-JSA x-over	1.40	4.25	8.50
48-Giant G-29	1.40	4.25	8.50
49-57,59,60: 55-Intro. Earth 2 Robin	1.00	3.00	6.00
58-Giant G-41	1.25	3.75	7.50
61-66,68-70: 64-Intro/origin Red Tornado. 69-Wonder Woman quits	.75	2.25	4.50
67-Giant G-53	.90	2.75	5.50
71-75,77-80: 71-Manhunter leaves JLA. 74-Black Canary joins. 78-Re-intro Vigilante	.60	1.75	3.50
76-Giant G-65	.75	2.25	4.50
81-84,86-92: 83-Death of Spectre	.60	1.75	3.50
85,93-(Giant G-77,G-89; 68 pgs.)	.75	2.25	4.50
94-Origin Sandman (Adv. #40) & Starman (Adv. #61); Deadman x-over; Adams-a	1.85	5.50	11.00
95-Origin Dr. Fate & Dr. Midnight reprint (More Fun #67, All-American #25)	.60	1.75	3.50
96-Origin Hourman (Adv. #48); Wildcat-r	.60	1.75	3.50
97-Origin JLA retold; Sargon, Starman-r	.70	2.00	4.00
98,99: 98-G.A. Sargon, Starman-r. 99-G.A. Sandman, Starman, Atom-r	.50	1.50	3.00
100	.85	2.50	5.00
101,102: 102-Red Tornado dies	.85	2.50	5.00
103-106: 103-Phantom Stranger joins. 105-Elongated Man joins. 106-New Red Tornado joins	.50	1.50	3.00
107,108-G.A. Uncle Sam, Black Condor, The Ray, Dollman, Phantom Lady, & The Human Bomb x-over	.85	2.50	5.00
109-Hawkman resigns	.40	1.25	2.50
110-116: All 100 pg. issues; 111-Shining Knight, Green Arrow-r. 112-Crimson Avenger, Vigilante, origin Starman-r	.40	1.25	2.50
117-190: 117-Hawkman rejoins. 128-Wonder Woman rejoins. 129-Death of Red Tornado. 135-37-G.A. Bulletman, Bulletgirl, Spy Smasher, Mr. Scarlet, Pinky & Ibis x-over. 137-Superman battles G.A. Capt. Marvel. 144-Origin retold; origin J'onn J'onnz. 145-Red Tornado resurrected. 161-Zatanna joins & new costume. 171-Mr. Terrific murdered. 179-Firestorm joins. 181-Gr. Arrow leaves	.35	1.00	2.00
191,194-199	.25	.75	1.50
192-Real origin Red Tornado, ends #193	.25	.75	1.50
193-1st app. All-Star Squadron as 16 pg. insert	.35	1.00	2.00
200-Anniversary ish. (76pgs., $1.50); origin retold; Green Arrow rejoins	.50	1.50	3.00
201-220: 203-Intro/origin new Royal Flush Gang. 208-All-Star Squadron app. 219,220-Origin Black Canary	.25	.75	1.50
221-249 (75 cents): 228-Re-intro Martian Manhunter. 233-New J.L.A. begins. 243-Aquaman leaves. 244,245-Crisis x-over. 253-Origin Despero. 258-Death of Vibe. 260-Death of Steel	.25	.75	1.50
250-Batman rejoins	.25	.75	1.50
251-260		.50	1.00
261-Last issue	.50	1.50	3.00
Annual 1(7/83)	.40	1.25	2.50
Annual 2(10/84)-Intro new J.L.A.	.25	.75	1.50
Annual 3(11/85)-Crisis x-over	.25	.75	1.50

NOTE: Adams c-63, 66, 67, 70, 74, 79, 81, 82, 86-89, 91, 92, 94, 96-98, 138, 139. Aparo a-200. Austin a-200i. Baily a-96r. Burnley a-94r, 98l; 99r. Greene a-46-61i, 64-73i, 110i(r). Grell c-117, 122. Kaluta c-154p. Gil Kane a-200. Krigstein a-96(r-Sensation #84.) Kubert c-200; c-72, 73. Nino a-228i, 230i. Orlando c-151i. Perez a-184-86p, 192-97p, 200p; c-184p, 186, 192-195, 196p, 197p, 199, 200, 201p, 202, 203-05p, 207-09, 212-15, 217, 219, 220. Reinman a-97i. Roussos a-62i. Sekowsky a-44-63p, 110-12p(r); c-46-48p, 51p. Smith c-185i. Starlin c-178-80, 183, 185p Staton

Justice Comics #11, © MEG

Justice League International Annual #2, © DC

Justice League Of America #9, © DC

JUSTICE LEAGUE OF AMERICA (continued)

a-244p; c-157p, 244p. *Toth* a-110r. **Tuska** a-153, 228p, 241-243p. JSA x-over-55, 56, 64, 65, 73, 74, 82, 83, 91, 92, 101, 102, 107, 108, 110, 113, 115, 123, 124, 135-37, 147, 148, 159, 160, 171, 172, 183-85, 195-97, 207, 208, 209, 219, 220, 231, 232.

JUSTICE MACHINE, THE
June, 1981 - No. 5, Nov, 1983 ($2.00, No. 1-3, Magazine size)
Noble Comics

	Good	Fine	N-Mint
1-Byrne-c(p)	4.20	12.50	25.00
2-Austin-c(i)	2.00	6.00	12.00
3	1.70	5.00	10.00
4,5	1.00	3.00	6.00
Annual 1 (1/84, 68 pgs.)(published by Texas Comics); 1st app. The Elementals; Golden-c(p)	2.50	7.50	15.00

JUSTICE MACHINE
Jan, 1987 - Present ($1.50, color)
Comico

1-23	.35	1.00	2.00

JUSTICE MACHINE FEATURING THE ELEMENTALS
May, 1986 - No. 4, Aug, 1986 (mini-series)
Comico

1	.50	1.50	3.00
2-4	.35	1.00	2.00

JUSTICE TRAPS THE GUILTY (Fargo Kid V11No.3 on)
Oct-Nov, 1947 - V11No.2(No.92), Apr-May, 1958
Prize/Headline Publications

V2#1-S&K c/a; electrocution-c	13.00	40.00	90.00
2-S&K c/a	7.00	21.00	50.00
3-5-S&K c/a	5.70	17.00	40.00
6-S&K c/a; Feldstein-a	6.50	19.50	45.00
7,9-S&K c/a	4.65	14.00	32.00
8,10-Krigstein-a; S&K-c. 10-S&K-a	5.70	17.00	40.00
11,19-S&K-c	2.65	8.00	18.00
12,14-17,20-No S&K	1.70	5.00	12.00
13-Used in SOTI, pg. 110-111	4.65	14.00	32.00
18-S&K-c, Elder-a	2.00	6.00	14.00
21-S&K c/a	2.00	6.00	14.00
22,23,27-S&K-c	1.70	5.00	12.00
24-26,28-50	1.15	3.50	8.00
51-57,59-70	1.00	3.00	7.00
58-Illo. in SOTI, "Treating police contemptuously"(top left); text on heroin	10.00	30.00	70.00
71-75,77-92	1.00	3.00	7.00
76-Orlando-a	1.15	3.50	8.00

NOTE: *Bailey* a-12, 13. *Elder* a-8. *Kirby* a-19p. *Meskin* a-22, 27, 63, 64; c-45, 46. *Robinson/Meskin* a-5, 19. *Severin* a-8, 11p. Photo-c #12, 15, 16.

JUST KIDS
1932 (16 pages; 9½x12''; paper cover)
McLoughlin Bros.

283-Three-color text, pictures on heavy paper	6.00	18.00	42.00

JUST MARRIED
January, 1958 - No. 114, Dec, 1976
Charlton Comics

1	1.50	4.50	10.00
2	.75	2.25	5.00
3-10	.45	1.35	3.00
11-30	.25	.75	1.50
31-50		.30	.60
51-114		.20	.40

KA'A'NGA COMICS (. . .Jungle King)(See Jungle Comics)
Spring, 1949 - No. 20, Summer, 1954
Fiction House Magazines (Glen-Kel Publ. Co.)

1-Ka'a'nga, Lord of the Jungle begins	22.00	65.00	154.00

	Good	Fine	N-Mint
2 (Wint., '49-'50)	11.50	34.00	80.00
3,4	8.50	25.50	60.00
5-Camilla app.	6.00	18.00	42.00
6-9: 7-Tuska-a. 9-Tabu, Wizard of the Jungle app.	4.35	13.00	30.00
10-Used in POP, pg. 99	4.60	14.00	34.00
11-15	3.50	10.50	24.00
16-Sheena app.	3.70	11.00	26.00
17-20	3.00	9.00	21.00
I.W. Reprint #1 (r-/#18) Kinstler-c	.70	2.00	4.00
I.W. Reprint #8 (reprints #10)	.70	2.00	4.00

KAMANDI, THE LAST BOY ON EARTH (Also see Cancelled Comic Cavalcade and Brave & the Bold No. 120)
Oct-Nov, 1972 - No. 59, Sept-Oct, 1978
National Periodical Publications/DC Comics

1-Origin	.50	1.50	3.00
2-10: 4-Intro. Prince Tuftan of the Tigers	.25	.75	1.50
11-59: 29-Superman x-over. 31-Intro Pyra. 32-68 pgs.; origin from #1	.25	.75	1.50

NOTE: *Ayers* a(p)-48-59 (most). *Kirby* a-1-40p; c-1-33. *Kubert* c-34-41. *Nasser* a-45p, 46p. *Starlin* a-59p; c-57, 59p.

KAMUI (Legend Of. . .#2 on)
May 12, 1987 - Present ($1.50, B&W, Bi-weekly)
Eclipse Comics/VIZ Comics #38 on

1	.70	2.00	4.00
1-2nd print	.25	.75	1.50
2	.35	1.10	2.20
2-2nd print	.25	.75	1.50
3	.30	.90	1.80
3-2nd print	.25	.75	1.50
4-10	.25	.80	1.60
11-38	.25	.75	1.50

KARATE KID (See Action, Adventure, Legion of Super-Heroes, & Superboy)
Mar-Apr, 1976 - No. 15, July-Aug, 1978
National Periodical Publications/DC Comics

1-Meets Iris Jacobs; Estrada/Staton-a		.40	.80
2-15: 2-Major Disaster app. 15-Continued into Kamandi #58		.30	.60

NOTE: *Grell* c-1-4, 5p, 6p, 7, 8. *Staton* a-1-9i. Legion x-over-No. 1, 2, 4, 6, 10, 12, 13. Princess Projectra x-over-#8, 9

KASCO KOMICS
1945; 1949 (regular size; paper cover)
Kasko Grainfeed (Giveaway)

1(1945)-Similar to Katy Keene; Bill Woggon-a; 28 pgs.; 6-7/8''x9-7/8''	9.35	28.00	65.00
2(1949)-Woggon-a	8.00	24.00	55.00

KATHY
September, 1949 - 1953
Standard Comics

1	3.50	10.50	24.00
2-Schomburg-c	1.70	5.00	12.00
3-5	1.30	4.00	9.00
6-16	.85	2.50	6.00

KATHY
Oct, 1959 - No. 27, Feb, 1964
Atlas Comics/Marvel (ZPC)

1-Teen-age	2.30	7.00	16.00
2	1.15	3.50	8.00
3-15	.75	2.25	5.00
16-27	.45	1.25	2.50

KAT KARSON
No date (Reprint)
I. W. Enterprises

	Good	Fine	N-Mint
1-Funny animals	.50	1.50	3.00

KATY AND KEN VISIT SANTA WITH MISTER WISH
1948 (16 pgs.; paper cover)
S. S. Kresge Co. (Giveaway)

	2.35	7.00	14.00

KATY KEENE (Also see Kasco Komics, Laugh, Pep, Suzie, & Wilbur)
1949 - No. 4, 1951; No. 5, 3/52 - No. 62, Oct, 1961
Archie Publ./Close-Up/Radio Comics

	Good	Fine	N-Mint
1-Bill Woggon-a begins	65.00	195.00	455.00
2	32.00	95.00	225.00
3-5	27.00	81.00	190.00
6-10	22.00	65.00	154.00
11,13-20	19.00	57.00	132.00
12-(Scarce)	21.00	62.00	146.00
21-40	13.00	40.00	90.00
41-62	9.00	27.00	62.00
Annual 1('54)	34.00	100.00	238.00
Annual 2-6('55-59)	17.00	51.00	120.00
3-D 1(1953-Large size)	28.00	84.00	195.00
Charm 1(9/58)	16.00	48.00	110.00
Glamour 1(1957)	16.00	48.00	110.00
Spectacular 1('56)	16.00	48.00	110.00

KATY KEENE COMICS DIGEST MAGAZINE
1987 - Present ($1.25-$1.35, digest size, annual)
Close-Up, Inc. (Archie Ent.)

1-4		.70	1.35

KATY KEENE FASHION BOOK MAGAZINE
1955 - No. 13, Sum, '56 - N. 23, Wint, '58-59 (nn 3-10)
Radio Comics/Archie Publications

1	32.00	95.00	225.00
2	18.00	54.00	125.00
11-18: 18-Photo Bill Woggon	14.00	42.00	100.00
19-23	11.00	32.00	75.00

KATY KEENE HOLIDAY FUN (See Archie Giant Series Mag. No. 7,12)

KATY KEENE PINUP PARADE
1955 - No. 15, Summer, 1961 (25 cents)
Radio Comics/Archie Publications

1	32.00	95.00	225.00
2	18.00	54.00	125.00
3-5	15.00	45.00	105.00
6-10,12-14: 8-Mad parody. 10-Photo Bill Woggon			
	12.00	36.00	84.00
11-Story of how comics get CCA approved, narrated by Katy			
	15.00	45.00	105.00
15(Rare)-Photo artist & family	32.00	95.00	225.00

KATY KEENE SPECIAL (Katy Keene No. 7 on)
Sept, 1983 - Present
Archie Enterprises

1-Woggon-r; new Woggon-c		.50	1.00
2-30: 3-Woggon-r		.30	.60

KATZENJAMMER KIDS, THE (Also see Hans Und Fritz)
1903 (50 pgs.; 10x15¼''; in color)
New York American & Journal

(by Rudolph Dirks, strip 1st appeared in 1898)

1903 (Rare)	27.00	81.00	190.00
1905-Tricks of . . .(10x15)	20.00	60.00	140.00
1906-Stokes-10x16'', 32 pgs. in color	20.00	60.00	140.00
1910-The Komical . . .(10x15)	20.00	60.00	140.00

	Good	Fine	N-Mint
1921-Embee Dist. Co., 10x16'', 20 pgs. in color			
	17.00	51.00	120.00

KATZENJAMMER KIDS, THE (See Giant Comic Album)
1945-1946; Summer, 1947 - No. 27, Feb-Mar, 1954
David McKay Publ./Standard No.12-21(Spring/'50 - 53)/Harvey No. 22, 4/53 on

Feature Books 30	8.50	25.50	60.00
Feature Books 32,35('45),41,44('46)	6.50	19.50	45.00
Feature Book 37-Has photos & biog. of Harold Knerr			
	8.00	24.00	56.00
1(1947)	8.00	24.00	56.00
2	4.00	12.00	28.00
3-11	3.00	9.00	21.00
12-14(Standard)	2.15	6.50	15.00
15-21(Standard)	1.50	4.50	10.00
22-25,27(Harvey): 22-24-Henry app.	1.15	3.50	8.00
26-½ in 3-D	11.00	33.00	76.00

KAYO (Formerly Jest?)
March, 1945
Harry 'A' Chesler

12-Green Knight, Capt. Glory, Little Nemo (not by McCay)			
	5.00	15.00	35.00

KA-ZAR (Also see Savage Tales & X-Men #10)
Aug, 1970 - No. 3, Mar, 1971 (Giant-Size, 68 pgs.)
Marvel Comics Group

1-Reprints earlier Ka-Zar stories; Avengers x-over in Hercules; Daredevil, X-Men app; hidden profanity-c	.35	1.00	2.00
2,3-Daredevil app., Ka-Zar origin #2	.35	1.00	2.00
NOTE: Kirby c/a-all. Colan a-1p(r).			

KA-ZAR (See Savage Tales #6)
Jan, 1974 - No. 20, Feb, 1977 (Regular Size)
Marvel Comics Group

1-20		.50	1.00
NOTE: Alcala a-6i, 8i. Brunner c-4. J. Buscema a-6-10p; c-1, 5, 7. Heath a-12. Gil Kane c(p)-3, 5, 8-11, 15, 20. Kirby c-12p. Reinman a-1p.			

KA-ZAR THE SAVAGE (See Marvel Fanfare)
4/81 - No. 34, 10/84 (Regular size) (Mando paper No. 10 on)
Marvel Comics Group

1-34: 11-Origin Zabu. 12-Two versions: With & without panel missing (1600 printed with panel). 29-Double size; Ka-Zar & Shanna wed			
		.50	1.00
NOTE: B. Anderson a-1p-15p, 18, 19; c-1-17, 18p, 20(back-c). Gil Kane a-11, 12, 14. Photo-c #26.			

KEEN DETECTIVE FUNNIES (Formerly Det. Picture Stories?)
No. 8, July, 1938 - No. 24, Sept, 1940
Centaur Publications

V1#8-The Clock continues-r/Funny Pic. Stories 1			
	63.00	190.00	440.00
9-Tex Martin by Eisner	40.00	120.00	280.00
10,11	35.00	105.00	245.00
V2#1,2-The Eye Sees by Frank Thomas begins; ends #23(Not in V2#3&5). 2-Jack Cole-a	30.00	90.00	210.00
3-TNT Todd begins	30.00	90.00	210.00
4,5: 4-Gabby Flynn begins. 5-Dean Denton begins			
	30.00	90.00	210.00
6,9-11	30.00	90.00	210.00
7-The Masked Marvel by Ben Thompson begins			
	60.00	180.00	420.00
8-Nudist ranch panel w/four girls	35.00	105.00	245.00
12(12/39)-Origin The Eye Sees by Frank Thomas; death of Masked Marvel's sidekick ZL	40.00	120.00	280.00
V3#1,2	35.00	105.00	245.00

Katy Keene 3-D #1, © AP   The Katzenjammer Kids #16, © KING   Keen Detective Funnies V2#11, © CEN

Ken Shannon #8, © QUA   Kent Blake Of The Secret Service #3, © MEG   Kewpies #1, © Will Eisner

	Good	Fine	N-Mint
KEEN DETECTIVE FUNNIES (continued)			
18,19,21,22: 18-Bondage/torture-c	35.00	105.00	245.00
20-Classic Eye Sees-c by Thomas	40.00	120.00	280.00
23-Air Man begins (intro)	40.00	120.00	280.00
24-Air Man-c	40.00	120.00	280.00

NOTE: *Burgos a-V2#2. Jack Cole a-V2#2. Eisner a-V2#6r. Ken Ernst a-V2#4-7, 9, 10, 19, 21. Everett a-V2#6, 7, 9, 11, 12, 20. Guardineer a-V2#5, 66. Gustavson a-V2#4-6. Simon c-V3#1.*

KEEN KOMICS
V2No.1, May, 1939 - V2No.3, Nov, 1939
Centaur Publications

V2#1(Large size)-Dan Hastings (s/f), The Big Top, Bob Phantom the Magician, The Mad Goddess app.	40.00	120.00	280.00
V2#2(Reg. size)-The Forbidden Idol of Machu Picchu; Cut Carson by Burgos begins	25.00	75.00	175.00
V2#3-Saddle Sniffl by Jack Cole, Circus Pays, Kings Revenge app.	25.00	75.00	175.00

NOTE: *Binder a-V2/2. Burgos a-V2/2,3. Ken Ernst a-V2/3. Gustavson a-V2/2. Jack Cole a-V2/3.*

KEEN TEENS
1945 - No. 6, Sept, 1947
Life's Romances Publ./Leader/Magazine Enterprises

nn-14 pgs. Claire Voyant (cont'd. in other nn issue) movie photos, Dotty Dripple, Gertie O'Grady & Sissy; Van Johnson, Frank Sinatra photo-c	9.50	28.50	65.00
nn-16 pgs. Claire Voyant & 16 pgs. movie photos	9.50	28.50	65.00
3-6: 4-Glenn Ford-c. 5-Perry Como-c	3.00	9.00	21.00

KEEPING UP WITH THE JONESES
1920 - No. 2, 1921 (52 pgs.; 9¼x9¼''; B&W daily strip reprints)
Cupples & Leon Co.

1,2-By Pop Momand	8.00	24.00	56.00

KELLYS, THE (Formerly Rusty; Spy Cases No. 26 on)
No. 23, Jan, 1950 - No. 25, June, 1950
Marvel Comics (HPC)

23	4.65	14.00	32.00
24,25: 24-Margie app.	2.65	8.00	18.00

KELVIN MACE
1986 - No. 2, 1986 ($2.00, B&W)
Vortex Publs.

1	.85	2.50	5.00
1-2nd print ($1.75)	.30	.85	1.70
2-color	.70	2.00	4.00

KEN MAYNARD WESTERN (Movie star)(See Wow Comics, '36)
Sept, 1950 - No. 8, Feb, 1952 (All 36pgs; photo front/back-c)
Fawcett Publications

1-K. Maynard & his horse Tarzan begin	23.00	70.00	170.00
2	16.00	48.00	110.00
3-8	13.00	40.00	90.00

KEN SHANNON (Gabby #11) (Also see Police Comics #103)
Oct, 1951 - No. 15, 1953 (a private eye)
Quality Comics Group

1-Crandall-a	11.00	32.00	75.00
2-Crandall c/a(2); text on narcotics	9.50	28.50	65.00
3-5-Crandall-a	5.70	17.00	40.00
6	3.50	10.50	24.00
7,9,10-Crandall-a	5.00	15.00	35.00
8-Opium den drug use story	5.00	15.00	35.00
11-15 (Exist?)	2.30	7.00	16.00

NOTE: *Jack Cole a-1-9. No. 11-15 published after title change to Gabby.*

KEN STUART
Jan, 1949 (Sea Adventures)

	Good	Fine	N-Mint
Publication Enterprises			
1-Frank Borth-c/a	3.50	10.50	24.00

KENT BLAKE OF THE SECRET SERVICE (Spy)
May, 1951 - No. 14, July, 1953
Marvel/Atlas Comics(20CC)

1-Injury to eye, bondage, torture	5.70	17.00	40.00
2-Drug use w/hypo scenes	3.00	9.00	21.00
3-14	1.70	5.00	12.00

NOTE: *Heath c-5, 7. Infantino c-12. Maneely c-3. Sinnott a-2(3).*

KERRY DRAKE (Also see Green Hornet)
Jan, 1956 - No. 2, March, 1956
Argo

1,2-Newspaper-r	2.65	8.00	18.00

KERRY DRAKE DETECTIVE CASES (. . . Racket Buster No. 32,33)
(Also see Chamber of Clues)
1944; No. 6, Jan, 1948 - No. 33, Aug, 1952
Life's Romances/Compix/Magazine Ent. No.1-5/Harvey No.6 on

nn(1944)(A-1 Comics)(slightly over-size)	12.00	36.00	84.00
2	8.00	24.00	56.00
3-5(1944)	6.00	18.00	42.00
6,8(1948); 8-Bondage-c	3.50	10.50	24.00
7-Kubert-a; biog of Andriola	4.00	12.00	28.00
9,10-Two-part marijuana story; Kerry smokes marijuana-No. 10	6.75	20.00	47.00
11-15	3.00	9.00	21.00
16-33	2.35	7.00	16.00
. . . in the Case of the Sleeping City-(1951-Publishers Synd.)-16 pg. giveaway for armed forces; paper cover	2.35	7.00	16.00

NOTE: *Berg a-5. Powell a-10-23, 28, 29.*

KEWPIES
Spring, 1949
Will Eisner Publications

1-Feiffer-a; used in **SOTI** in a non-seductive context, pg. 35	19.00	57.00	132.00

KEY COMICS
Jan, 1944 - No. 5, Aug, 1946
Consolidated Magazines

1-The Key, Will-O-The-Wisp begin	8.00	24.00	56.00
2	4.30	13.00	30.00
3-5	3.00	9.00	21.00

KEY COMICS
1951 - 1956 (32 pages) (Giveaway)
Key Clothing Co./Peterson Clothing

Contains a comic from different publishers bound with new cover. Cover changed each year. Many combinations possible. Distributed in Nebraska, Iowa, & Kansas. Contents would determine price, 40-60 percent of original.

KEY RING COMICS
1941 (16 pgs., two colors) (sold 5 for 10 cents)
Dell Publishing Co.

1-Sky Hawk	2.00	6.00	12.00
1-Viking Carter	2.00	6.00	12.00
1-Features Sleepy Samson	2.00	6.00	12.00
1-Origin Greg Gilday r-/War Comics No. 2	2.35	7.00	14.00
1-Radior(Super hero)	2.35	7.00	14.00

NOTE: *Each book has two holes in spine to put in binder.*

KICKERS, INC.
Nov, 1986 - No. 12, Oct, 1987
Marvel Comics Group

1		.50	1.00
2-12		.40	.80

KID CARROTS
September, 1953
St. John Publishing Co.

	Good	Fine	N-Mint
1-Funny animal	1.50	4.50	10.00

KID COLT OUTLAW (Kid Colt #1-4; . . .Outlaw #5-on)(Also see
All Western Winners, Best Western, Black Rider, Two-Gun Kid, Two-
Gun Western, Western Winners, Wild Western, & Wisco)
8/48 - No. 139, 3/68; No. 140, 11/69 - No. 229, 4/79
Marvel Comics(LCC) 1-16; Atlas(LMC) 17-102; Marvel 103-on

	Good	Fine	N-Mint
1-Kid Colt & his horse Steel begin; Two-Gun Kid app.			
	27.00	81.00	190.00
2	13.00	40.00	90.00
3-5: 4-Anti-Wertham editorial; Tex Taylor app. 5-Blaze Carson app.			
	8.00	24.00	56.00
6-8: 6-Tex Taylor app; 7-Nimo the Lion begins, ends #10			
	5.70	17.00	40.00
9,10 (52pgs.)	6.00	18.00	42.00
11-Origin	6.50	19.50	45.00
12-20	4.00	12.00	28.00
21-32	3.00	9.00	21.00
33-45: Black Rider in all	2.30	7.00	16.00
46,47,49,50	2.00	6.00	14.00
48-Kubert-a	2.65	8.00	18.00
51-53,55,56	1.50	4.50	10.00
54-Williamson/Maneely-c	2.50	7.50	17.00
57-60,66: 4-pg. Williamson-a in all. 59-Reprint Rawhide Kid #79			
	3.65	11.00	25.00
61-63,67-78,80-85	1.00	3.00	7.00
64,65-Crandall-a	1.30	4.00	9.00
79-Origin retold	1.30	4.00	9.00
86-Kirby-a(r)	1.00	3.00	7.00
87-Davis-a(r)	1.30	4.00	9.00
88,89-Williamson-a in both (4 pgs.). 89-Redrawn Matt Slade #2			
	2.15	6.50	15.00
90-99,101-Last 10 cent ish.	.45	1.25	3.00
100	.55	1.65	4.00
101-120	.35	1.00	2.00
121-140: 121-Rawhide Kid x-over. 125-Two-Gun Kid x-over. 130-132			
-68pg. issues with one new story each; 130-Origin. 140-			
Reprints begin		.50	1.00
141-160: 156-Giant; reprints		.40	.80
161-229: 170-Origin retold		.25	.50
. . .Album (no date; 1950's; Atlas Comics)-132 pgs.; random bind-			
ing, cardboard cover, B&W stories; contents can vary			
	12.00	36.00	84.00
Giant Size 1(1/75), 2(4/75), 3(7/75)		.50	1.00

NOTE: *Ayers* a-many. *Colan* a-52, 53; c(p)-223, 228, 229. *Crandall* a-140r, 167r.
Everett a-137l, 225i(r). *Heath* c-34, 35, 39, 44, 46, 48, 49, 57. *Jack Keller* a-25(2),
26-68(3-4), 78, 94p, 98, 99, 108, 110, 133. *Kirby* a-86r; 93, 96, 119, 176(part); c-87,
92-95, 97, 99-112, 114-117, 121-123, 197r. *Maneely* a-12, 68, 81; c-17, 19, 40-43, 47, 52,
53, 62, 65, 68, 78, 81. *Morrow* a-173r, 216r. *Rico* a-13, 18. *Severin* c-58. *Shores* a-39,
41-43; c-24. *Sutton* a-137p, 225p(r). *Wildey* a-82. *Williamson* a-147r, 170r, 172r, 216r.
Woodbridge a-64, 81. Black Rider in #33-45, 74, 86. Iron Mask in #110, 114, 121, 127.
Sam Hawk in #84, 101, 111, 121, 146, 174, 181, 188.

KID COWBOY (Also see Approved Comics #4)
1950 - 1954 (painted covers)
Ziff-Davis Publ./St. John (Approved Comics)

	Good	Fine	N-Mint
1-Lucy Belle & Red Feather begin	4.65	14.00	32.00
2	2.30	7.00	16.00
3-14: 11-Bondage-c	1.70	5.00	12.00

NOTE: *Berg* a-5. *Maneely* c-2.

KIDDIE KAPERS
1945?(nd); Oct, 1957; 1963 - 1964
Decker Publ. (Red Top-Farrell)

	Good	Fine	N-Mint
1(nd, 1945-46?)-Infinity-c	2.65	8.00	18.00

	Good	Fine	N-Mint
1(10/57)(Decker)-Little Bit reprints from Kiddie Karnival			
	1.15	3.50	8.00
Super Reprint #7, 10('63), 12, 14('63), 15,17('64), 18('64)			
	.35	1.00	2.00

KIDDIE KARNIVAL
1952 (100 pgs.) (One Shot)
Ziff-Davis Publ. Co. (Approved Comics)

	Good	Fine	N-Mint
nn-Rebound Little Bit #1,2	5.70	17.00	40.00

KID ETERNITY (Becomes Buccaneers) (See Hit)
Spring, 1946 - No. 18, Nov, 1949
Quality Comics Group

	Good	Fine	N-Mint
1	30.00	90.00	210.00
2	14.00	42.00	100.00
3-Mac Raboy-a	15.00	45.00	105.00
4-10	8.50	25.50	60.00
11-18	5.50	16.50	38.00

KID FROM DODGE CITY, THE
July, 1957 - No. 2, Sept, 1957
Atlas Comics (MMC)

	Good	Fine	N-Mint
1	2.65	8.00	18.00
2-Everett-c	1.30	4.00	9.00

KID FROM TEXAS, THE (A Texas Ranger)
June, 1957 - No. 2, Aug, 1957
Atlas Comics (CSI)

	Good	Fine	N-Mint
1-Powell-a; Severin-c	3.00	9.00	21.00
2	1.50	4.50	10.00

KID KOKO
1958
I. W. Enterprises

	Good	Fine	N-Mint
Reprint #1,2-(r/M.E.'s Koko & Kola #4, 1947)	.50	1.50	3.00

KID KOMICS (. . .Movie Komics No. 11)
Feb, 1943 - No. 10, Spring, 1946
Timely Comics (USA 1,2/FCI 3-10)

	Good	Fine	N-Mint
1-Origin Captain Wonder & sidekick Tim Mullrooney, & Subbie;			
intro the Sea-Going Lad, Pinto Pete, & Trixie Trouble; Knuckles &			
White-wash Jones only app.; Wolverton art, 7 pgs.			
	105.00	315.00	735.00
2-The Young Allies, Red Hawk, & Tommy Tyme begin; last Captain			
Wonder & Subbie	60.00	180.00	420.00
3-The Vision & Daredevils app.	40.00	120.00	280.00
4-The Destroyer begins; Sub-Mariner app.; Red Hawk & Tommy			
Tyme end	34.00	100.00	240.00
5,6	25.00	75.00	175.00
7-10: The Whizzer app. 7; Destroyer not in #7,8; 10-Last			
Destroyer, Young Allies & Whizzer	21.50	64.00	150.00

KID MONTANA (Formerly Davy Crockett Frontier Fighter; The Gun-
fighters No. 51 on)
V2No.9, Nov, 1957 - No. 50, Mar, 1965
Charlton Comics

	Good	Fine	N-Mint
V2#9	2.30	7.00	16.00
10	1.15	3.50	8.00
11,12,14-20	.70	2.00	5.00
13-Williamson-a	1.70	5.00	12.00
21-35	.45	1.35	3.00
36-50		.50	1.00

NOTE: *Title change to Montana Kid on cover only on No. 44; remained Kid Montana
on inside.*

KID MOVIE KOMICS (Formerly Kid Komics; Rusty No. 12 on)
No. 11, Summer, 1946
Timely Comics

Kid Carrots #1, © STJ

Kid Colt Outlaw #6, © MEG

Kid Komics #6, © MEG

The Killers #2, © ME | King Leonardo & His... #1, © Leonardo TV Prod. | King Of The Bad Men Of Deadwood, © AVON

	Good	Fine	N-Mint
KID MOVIE COMICS (continued)			
11-Silly Seal & Ziggy Pig; 2 pgs. Kurtzman "Hey Look" plus 6 pg.			
"Pigtales" story	9.00	27.00	62.00
KIDNAPPED (See 4-Color No. 1101 & Movie Comics)			
KIDNAP RACKET (See Comics Hits No. 57)			
KID SLADE GUNFIGHTER (Formerly Matt Slade...)			
No. 5, Jan, 1957 - No. 8, July, 1957			
Atlas Comics (SPI)			
5-Severin-a; Maneely-c	3.00	9.00	21.00
6,8: 8-Severin-c	1.50	4.50	10.00
7-Williamson/Mayo-a, 4 pgs.	3.70	11.00	26.00
KID ZOO COMICS			
July, 1948 (52 pgs.)			
Street & Smith Publications			
1-Funny Animal	3.70	11.00	26.00
KILLER			
March, 1985 (One-shot, color, Baxter)			
Eclipse Comics			
1-Timothy Truman c/a	.30	.90	1.80
KILLERS, THE			
1947 - 1948 (No month)			
Magazine Enterprises			
1-Mr. Zin, the Hatchet Killer; mentioned in SOTI, pgs. 179,180;			
Used by N.Y. Legis. Comm. L. B. Cole-c	45.00	135.00	315.00
2-(Scarce)-Hashish smoking story; "Dying, Dying, Dead" drug stry;			
Whitney, Ingels-a; Whitney hanging-c	45.00	135.00	315.00
KILROYS, THE			
June-July, 1947 - No. 54, June-July, 1955			
B&I Publ. Co. No. 1-19/American Comics Group			
1	8.00	24.00	56.00
2	4.30	13.00	30.00
3-5: 5-Gross-a	3.00	9.00	21.00
6-10: 8-Milt Gross's Moronica	2.30	7.00	16.00
11-20: 14-Gross-a	2.00	6.00	14.00
21-30	1.50	4.50	10.00
31-47,50-54	1.00	3.00	7.00
48,49-(3-D effect)	8.00	24.00	56.00
KING CLASSICS			
1977 (85 cents each) (36 pages, cardboard covers)			
King Features (Printed in Spain for U.S. distr.)			

1-Connecticut Yankee, 2-Last of the Mohicans, 3-Moby Dick, 4-Robin Hood, 5-Swiss Family Robinson, 6-Robinson Crusoe, 7-Treasure Island, 8-20,000 Leagues, 9-Christmas Carol, 10-Huck Finn, 11-Around the World in 80 Days, 12-Davy Crockett, 13-Don Quixote, 14-Gold Bug, 15-Ivanhoe, 16-Three Musketeers, 17-Baron Munchausen, 18-Alice in Wonderland, 19-Black Arrow, 20-Five Weeks in a Balloon, 21-Great Expectations, 22-Gulliver's Travels, 23-Prince & Pauper, 24-Lawrence of Arabia

	Good	Fine	N-Mint
(Originals, 1977-78) each....	1.00	3.00	7.00
Reprints, 1979; HRN-24	.85	2.50	5.00

NOTE: The first eight issues were not numbered. Issues No. 25-32 were advertised but not published. The 1977 originals have HRN 32a; the 1978 originals have HRN 32b.

KING COLT (See 4-Color No. 651)

KING COMICS (Strip reprints)
Apr, 1936 - No. 159, Feb, 1952 (Winter on cover)
David McKay Publications/Standard No. 156-on

	Good	Fine	N-Mint
1-Flash Gordon by Alex Raymond; Brick Bradford, Mandrake the			
Magician & Popeye begin	265.00	795.00	1855.00
2	117.00	350.00	820.00
3	85.00	255.00	595.00
4	60.00	180.00	420.00
5	45.00	135.00	315.00

	Good	Fine	N-Mint
6-10: 9-X-Mas-c	30.00	90.00	210.00
11-20	23.00	70.00	160.00
21-30	19.00	57.00	132.00
31-40: 33-Last Segar Popeye	17.00	51.00	120.00
41-50: 46-Little Lulu, Alvin & Tubby app. as text illos by Marge Buell			
50-The Lone Ranger begins	15.00	45.00	105.00
51-60: 52-Barney Baxter begins?	11.50	34.00	80.00
61-The Phantom begins	10.00	30.00	70.00
62-80: 76-Flag-c	8.50	25.50	60.00
81-99: 82-Blondie begins?	7.00	21.00	50.00
100	9.50	28.00	65.00
101-115-Last Raymond issue	6.50	19.50	45.00
116-145: 117-Phantom origin retold	5.00	15.00	35.00
146,147-Prince Valiant in both	3.70	11.00	26.00
148-155-Flash Gordon ends	3.70	11.00	26.00
156-159	2.85	8.50	20.00

NOTE: Marge Buell text illos in No. 24-46 at least.

KING CONAN (Conan The King No. 20 on)
March, 1980 - No. 19, Nov, 1983 (52 pgs.)
Marvel Comics Group

	Good	Fine	N-Mint
1	.50	1.50	3.00
2-6: 4-Death of Thoth Amon	.35	1.00	2.00
7-1st Paul Smith-a, 2 pgs. (9/81)	.35	1.00	2.00
8-19	.35	1.00	2.00

NOTE: Buscema a-1p-9p, 17p; c(p)-1-5, 7-9, 14, 17. Kaluta c-19. Nebres a-17i, 18, 19i. Severin c-18. Simonson c-6.

KING KONG (See Movie Comics)

KING LEONARDO & HIS SHORT SUBJECTS (TV)
Nov-Jan, 1961-62 - No. 4, Sept, 1963
Dell Publishing Co./Gold Key

	Good	Fine	N-Mint
4-Color 1242,1278	4.00	12.00	28.00
01390-207(5-7/62)(Dell)	3.50	10.50	24.00
1 (10/62)	3.50	10.50	24.00
2-4	2.00	6.00	14.00

KING LOUIE & MOWGLI
May, 1968 (Disney)
Gold Key

	Good	Fine	N-Mint
1 (10223-805). Characters from Jungle Book	1.50	4.50	10.00

KING OF DIAMONDS (TV)
July-Sept, 1962
Dell Publishing Co.

	Good	Fine	N-Mint
01-391-209-Photo-c	2.00	6.00	14.00

KING OF KINGS (See 4-Color No. 1236)

KING OF THE BAD MEN OF DEADWOOD
1950 (See Wild Bill Hickok #16)
Avon Periodicals

	Good	Fine	N-Mint
nn-Kinstler-c; Kamen/Feldstein-a r-/Cowpuncher 2			
	9.50	28.00	65.00

KING OF THE ROYAL MOUNTED (See Large Feat. Comic #9, Feature Books #1 (McKay), Red Ryder & Super Book #2,6)

KING OF THE ROYAL MOUNTED (Zane Grey's)
No. 207, Dec, 1948 - No. 935, Sept-Nov, 1958
Dell Publishing Co.

	Good	Fine	N-Mint
4-Color 207('48)	11.50	34.00	80.00
4-Color 265,283	7.00	2.00	50.00
4-Color 310,340	4.60	.4.00	32.00
4-Color 363,384	4.00	12.00	28.00
8(6-8/52)-10	4.00	12.00	28.00
11-20	3.50	10.50	24.00
21-28(3-5/58)	3.00	9.00	21.00
4-Color 935(9-11/58)	3.00	9.00	21.00

KING OF THE ROYAL MOUNTED (continued)
NOTE: *4-Color No. 207,265,283,310,340,363,384 are all newspaper reprints with Jim Gary art. No. 8 on are all Dell originals. Painted c-No. 9-on.*

KING RICHARD & THE CRUSADERS (See 4-Color No. 588)

KING SOLOMON'S MINES
1951 (Movie)
Avon Periodicals

	Good	Fine	N-Mint
nn#1 on 1st page)	20.00	60.00	140.00

KISS (See Marvel Comics Super Special & Howard the Duck #12, 13)

KIT CARSON (See Frontier Fighters)

KIT CARSON (Formerly All True Detective Cases No. 4; Fighting Davy Crockett No. 9; see Blazing Sixguns)
1950; No. 2, 8/51 - No. 3, 12/51; No. 5, 11-12/54 - No. 8, 9/55
Avon Periodicals

nn(#1) (1950)	6.50	19.50	45.00
2(8/51)	3.70	11.00	26.00
3(12/51)	3.00	9.00	21.00
5-6,8('54-'55)	2.65	8.00	18.00
7-Kinstler-a(2)	3.00	9.00	21.00
I.W. Reprint #10('63)-Severin-c	.85	2.50	5.00
NOTE: *Kinstler c-1-3,5-8.*

KIT CARSON & THE BLACKFEET WARRIORS
1953
Realistic

nn-Reprint; Kinstler-c	4.60	14.00	32.00

KIT KARTER
May-July, 1962
Dell Publishing Co.

1	1.15	3.50	8.00

KITTY
October, 1948
St. John Publishing Co.

1-Lily Renee-a	3.00	9.00	21.00

KITTY PRYDE AND WOLVERINE
Nov, 1984 - No. 6, April, 1985 (6 issue mini-series)
Marvel Comics Group

1 (From X-Men)	.60	1.75	3.50
2-6	.50	1.50	3.00

KLARER GIVEAWAYS (See Wisco)

KNIGHTS OF THE ROUND TABLE (See 4-Color No. 540)

KNIGHTS OF THE ROUND TABLE
No. 10, April, 1957
Pines Comics

10	1.50	4.50	10.00

KNIGHTS OF THE ROUND TABLE
Nov-Jan, 1963/64 (Painted-c)
Dell Publishing Co.

1 (12-397-401)	2.00	6.00	14.00

KNOCK KNOCK (...Who's There?)
1936 (52 pages) (8x9", B&W)
Whitman Publ./Gerona Publications

801-Joke book; Bob Dunn-a	5.00	15.00	35.00

KNOCKOUT ADVENTURES
Winter, 1953-54
Fiction House Magazines

1-Reprints/Fight Comics #53	4.65	14.00	32.00

KNOW YOUR MASS
1958 (100 Pg. Giant) (35 cents) (square binding)

Catechetical Guild

	Good	Fine	N-Mint
303-In color	4.00	12.00	28.00

KOBRA (See DC Special Series No. 1)
Feb-Mar, 1976 - No. 7, Mar-Apr, 1977
National Periodical Publications

1-Art plotted by Kirby		.40	.80
2-7: 3-Giffen-a		.25	.50
NOTE: *Austin a-3i. Buckler a-5p; c-5p. Kubert c-4. Nasser a-6p, 7; c-7.*

KOKEY KOALA
May, 1952
Toby Press

1	2.00	6.00	14.00

KOKO AND KOLA (Also see Tick Tock Tales)
Fall, 1946 - No. 5, May, 1947; No. 6, 1950
Compix/Magazine Enterprises

1-Funny animal	3.50	10.50	24.00
2	1.70	5.00	12.00
3-5,6(A-1 28)	1.30	4.00	9.00

KO KOMICS
October, 1945
Gerona Publications

1-The Duke of Darkness & The Menace (hero)	7.00	21.00	50.00

KOMIC KARTOONS
Fall, 1945 - No. 2, Winter, 1945
Timely Comics (EPC)

1,2-Andy Wolf, Bertie Mouse	5.70	17.00	40.00

KOMIK PAGES
April, 1945 (All-r)
Harry 'A' Chesler, Jr. (Our Army, Inc.)

10(#1 on inside)-Land O' Nod by Rick Yager (2 pgs.), Animal Crackers, Foxy GrandPa, Tom, Dick & Mary, Cheerio Minstrels, Red Starr plus other 1-2 pg. strips; Cole-a	7.00	21.00	50.00

KONA (...Monarch of Monster Isle)
Feb-Apr, 1962 - No. 21, Jan-Mar, 1967 (Painted-c)
Dell Publishing Co.

4-Color 1256	2.65	8.00	18.00
2-10: 4-Anak begins	1.15	3.50	8.00
11-21	.75	2.25	4.50
NOTE: *Glanzman a-all issues.*

KONGA (Fantastic Giants No. 24) (See Return of...)
1960; No. 2, Aug, 1961 - No. 23, Nov, 1965
Charlton Comics

1(1960)-Based on movie	13.00	40.00	90.00
2	6.50	19.50	45.00
3-5	5.00	15.00	35.00
6-15	3.50	10.50	24.00
16-23	2.00	6.00	14.00
NOTE: *Ditko a-1, 3-15; c-4, 6-9. Glanzman a-12. Montes & Bache a-16-23.*

KONGA'S REVENGE (Formerly Return of...)
No. 2, Summer, 1963 - No. 3, Fall, 1964; Dec, 1968
Charlton Comics

2,3: 2-Ditko c/a	2.30	7.00	16.00
1('68)-Reprints Konga's Revenge No. 3	1.15	3.50	8.00

KONG THE UNTAMED
June-July, 1975 - No. 5, Feb-Mar, 1976
National Periodical Publications

1		.40	.80
2-5		.25	.50
NOTE: *Alcala a-1-3. Wrightson c-1,2.*

Kit Carson #7, © AVON

Kokey Koala #1, © TOBY

Konga #1, © CC

Korak, Son Of Tarzan #6, © ERB

Krazy Komics #1 (7/42), © MEG

Krypton Chronicles #1, © DC

KOOKIE
Feb-Apr, 1962 - No. 2, May-July, 1962
Dell Publishing Co.

	Good	Fine	N-Mint
1,2-Written by John Stanley; Bill Williams-a	5.00	15.00	35.00

K. O. PUNCH, THE (Also see Lucky Fights It Through)
1948 (Educational giveaway)
E. C. Comics

Feldstein-splash; Kamen-a	117.00	340.00	700.00

KORAK, SON OF TARZAN (Edgar Rice Burroughs)
Jan, 1964 - No. 45, Jan, 1972 (Painted-c No. 1-?)
Gold Key

1-Russ Manning-a	3.00	9.00	21.00
2-11-Russ Manning-a	1.50	4.50	10.00
12-21: 14-Jon of the Kalahari ends. 15-Mabu, Jungle Boy begins; Manning-a #21	.85	2.50	6.00
22-30	.60	1.80	4.00
31-45	.50	1.50	3.00

NOTE: *Warren Tufts a-12, 13.*

KORAK, SON OF TARZAN (Tarzan Family No. 60 on)
No. 46, May-June, 1972 - No. 56, Feb-Mar, 1974; No. 57, May-June, 1975 - No. 59, Sept-Oct, 1975 (Edgar Rice Burroughs)
National Periodical Publications

46-(52 pgs.)-Carson of Venus begins (origin); Pellucidar feature		.50	1.00
47-50: 49-Origin Korak retold		.35	.70
51-59: 56-Last Carson of Venus		.25	.50

NOTE: *Kaluta a-46-56. All have covers by Joe Kubert. Manning strip reprints-No. 57-59. Frank Thorn a-46-51.*

KOREA MY HOME (Also see Yalta to Korea)
nd (1950s)
Johnstone and Cushing

nn-Anti-communist; Korean War	15.00	45.00	105.00

KORG: 70,000 B. C. (TV)
May, 1975 - No. 9, Nov, 1976 (Hanna-Barbera)
Charlton Publications

1	.25	.75	1.50
2-9		.50	1.00

KORNER KID COMICS
1947
Four Star Publications

1	3.50	10.50	24.00

KRAZY KAT
1946 (Hardcover)
Holt

Reprints daily & Sunday strips by Herriman	26.00	78.00	180.00
with dust jacket (Rare)....	54.00	162.00	380.00

KRAZY KAT (See Ace Comics & March of Comics No. 72,87)

KRAZY KAT COMICS (...& Ignatz the Mouse early issues)
May-June, 1951 - Jan, 1964 (None by Herriman)
Dell Publishing Co./Gold Key

1(1951)	4.30	13.00	30.00
2-5 (#5, 8-10/52)	3.00	9.00	21.00
4-Color 454,504	2.30	7.00	16.00
4-Color 548,619,696 (4/56)	2.00	6.00	14.00
1(10098-401)(1/64-Gold Key)(TV)	2.00	6.00	14.00

KRAZY KOMICS (1st Series) (Cindy No. 27 on)
July, 1942 - No. 26, Spr, 1947 (Also see Ziggy Pig)
Timely Comics (USA No. 1-21/JPC No. 22-26)

1-Ziggy Pig & Silly Seal begins	16.00	48.00	110.00
2	8.00	24.00	56.00

	Good	Fine	N-Mint
3-10	4.60	14.00	32.00
11,13,14	3.50	10.50	24.00
12-Timely's entire art staff drew themselves into a Creeper story	5.00	15.00	35.00
15-Has "Super Soldier" by Pfc. Stan Lee	3.50	10.50	24.00
16-24,26	2.30	7.00	16.00
25-Kurtzman-a, 6 pgs.	4.00	12.00	28.00

KRAZY KOMICS (2nd Series)
Aug, 1948 - No. 2, Nov, 1948
Timely/Marvel Comics

1-Wolverton (10 pgs.) & Kurtzman (8 pgs.)-a; Eustice Hayseed begins, Li'l Abner swipe	17.00	51.00	120.00
2-Wolverton-a, 10 pgs.; Powerhouse Pepper cameo	10.00	30.00	70.00

KRAZY KROW (Also see Dopey Duck, Film Funnies, Funny Frolics & Movie Tunes)
Summer, 1945 - No. 3, Wint, 1945/46
Marvel Comics (ZPC)

1	5.00	15.00	35.00
2,3	2.65	8.00	18.00
I.W. Reprint #1('57), 2('58), 7	.30	.80	1.60

KRAZYLIFE
1945 (no month)
Fox Feature Syndicate

1-Funny animal	5.00	15.00	35.00

KREE/SKRULL WAR STARRING THE AVENGERS, THE
Sept, 1983 - No. 2, Oct, 1983 ($2.50, 68 pgs.; Baxter paper)
Marvel Comics Group

1,2	.40	1.25	2.50

NOTE: *Adams p-1r, 2. Buscema a-1r, 2r. Simonson c(p)/a(p)-1.*

KRIM-KO COMICS
1936 - 1939 (4 pg. giveaway) (weekly)
Krim-ko Chocolate Drink

Lola, Secret Agent; 184 issues - all original stories each....	1.35	4.00	8.00

KROFFT SUPERSHOW (TV)
April, 1978 - No. 6, Jan, 1979
Gold Key

1		.60	1.20
2-6		.35	.70

KRULL
Nov, 1983 - No. 2, Dec, 1983
Marvel Comics Group

1,2-Film adapt. r/Marvel Super Spec.		.25	.50

KRYPTON CHRONICLES
Sept, 1981 - No. 3, Nov, 1981
DC Comics

1-Buckler-c(p)		.40	.80
2,3		.30	.60

KULL & THE BARBARIANS (Magazine)
May, 1975 - No. 3, Sept, 1975 (B&W) ($1.00)
Marvel Comics Group

1-Andru/Wood-r/Kull #1; 2 pgs. Adams; Gil Kane, Severin-a	.40	1.25	2.50
2-Red Sonja by Chaykin begins; Adams-i; Gil Kane-a	.30	.90	1.80
3-Origin Red Sonja by Chaykin; Adams-a; Solomon Kane app.	.30	.90	1.80

KULL THE CONQUEROR (...the Destroyer #11 on; see Marvel Preview)
June, 1971 - No. 2, Sept, 1971; No. 3, July, 1972 - No. 15, Aug, 1974; No. 16, Aug, 1976 - No. 29, Oct, 1978
Marvel Comics Group

	Good	Fine	N-Mint
1-Andru/Wood-a; origin Kull	.50	1.50	3.00
2-29: 11-15-Ploog-a	.50	1.00	

NOTE: No. 1,2,7-9,11 are based on Robert E. Howard stories. Alcala a-17p, 18-20i; c-24. Ditko a-12r, 15r. Gil Kane c-15p, 21. Nebres a-22i-27i; c-25i, 27i. Ploog c-11, 12p, 13. Severin a-2-9i; c-2-10i, 19. Starlin c-14.

KULL THE CONQUEROR
Dec, 1982 - No. 2, Mar, 1983 (52 pgs., printed on Baxter paper)
Marvel Comics Group

1,2: 1-Buscema-a(p)	.35	1.00	2.00

KULL THE CONQUEROR (No. 9,10 titled 'Kull')
5/83 - No. 10, 6/85 (52 pgs.; $1.25-60 cents; Mando paper)
Marvel Comics Group

V3#1-10	.50	1.00	

KUNG FU (See Deadly Hands of..., & Master of...)

KUNG FU FIGHTER (See Richard Dragon...)

LABOR IS A PARTNER
1949 (32 pgs. in color; paper cover)
Catechetical Guild Educational Society

nn-Anti-communism	30.00	80.00	160.00

Confidential Preview-(B&W, 8½x11''), saddle stitched)-only one known copy; text varies from color version, advertises next book on secularism (If the Devil Would Talk) 35.00 100.00 200.00

LABYRINTH
Nov, 1986 - No. 3, Jan, 1987 (mini-series)
Marvel Comics Group

1-3: R-/Marv. Super Spec. #40		.40	.80

LAD: A DOG
1961 - No. 2, July-Sept, 1962
Dell Publishing Co.

4-Color 1303 (movie), 2	2.65	8.00	18.00

LADY AND THE TRAMP (See Dell Giants, 4-Color No. 629,634, & Movie Comics)

LADY AND THE TRAMP IN ''BUTTER LATE THAN NEVER''
1955 (16 pgs., 5x7¼'', soft-c) (Walt Disney)
American Dairy Association (Premium)

	3.00	9.00	21.00

LADY BOUNTIFUL
1917 (10¼x13½''; 24 pgs.; B&W; cardboard cover)
Saalfield Publ. Co./Press Publ. Co.

by Gene Carr; 2 panels per page	7.00	21.00	50.00

LADY COP (See First Issue Special)

LADY FOR A NIGHT (See Cinema Comics Herald)

LADY LUCK (Formerly Smash #1-85) (Also see Spirit Sections)
Dec, 1949 - No. 90, Aug, 1950
Quality Comics Group

86(#1)	33.00	100.00	230.00
87-90	25.00	75.00	175.00

LAFF-A-LYMPICS (TV)(See The Funtastic World of Hanna-Barbera)
Mar, 1978 - No. 13, Mar, 1979
Marvel Comics Group

1		.30	.60
2-13		.25	.50

LAFFIN' GAS (See Adolescent Radioactive...)
June, 1986 - Present ($2.00, B&W)

Blackthorne Publ.

	Good	Fine	N-Mint
1	.40	1.20	2.40
2-4	.35	1.00	2.00
5-Boris The Bear	.40	1.25	2.50
6 (3-D ish., $2.50)	.40	1.25	2.50
7-13	.30	.90	1.80

LAFFY-DAFFY COMICS
Feb, 1945 - No. 2, March, 1945
Rural Home Publ. Co.

1,2	2.65	8.00	18.00

LANA (Little Lana No. 8 on)
Aug, 1948 - No. 7, Aug, 1949 (Also see Annie Oakley)
Marvel Comics (MjMC)

1-Rusty, Millie begin	4.65	14.00	32.00
2-Kurtzman's ''Hey Look'' (1); last Rusty	3.50	10.50	24.00
3-7: 3-Nellie begins	1.70	5.00	12.00

LANCELOT & GUINEVERE (See Movie Classics)

LANCELOT LINK, SECRET CHIMP (TV)
April, 1971 - No. 8, Feb, 1973
Gold Key

1-Photo-c	1.35	4.00	8.00
2-8: 2-Photo-c	.85	2.50	5.00

LANCELOT STRONG (See The Shield)

LANCE O'CASEY (See Mighty Midget & Whiz Comics)
Spring, 1946 - No. 3, Fall, 1946; No. 4, Summer, 1948
Fawcett Publications

1-Captain Marvel app. on-c	9.00	27.00	62.00
2	5.00	15.00	35.00
3,4	4.00	12.00	28.00

LANCER (TV)(Western)
Feb, 1969 - No. 3, Sept, 1969 (All photo-c)
Gold Key

1	2.30	7.00	16.00
2,3	1.70	5.00	12.00

LAND OF THE GIANTS (TV)
Nov, 1968 - No. 5, Sept, 1969
Gold Key

1-Photo-c	1.70	5.00	12.00
2-5: 4,5-Photo-c	1.15	3.50	8.00

LAND OF THE LOST COMICS (Radio)
July-Aug, 1946 - No. 9, Spring, 1948
E. C. Comics

1	16.00	48.00	110.00
2	11.00	32.00	76.00
3-9	9.50	28.00	65.00

LAND UNKNOWN, THE (See 4-Color No. 845)

LARAMIE (TV)
Aug, 1960 - July, 1962 (All photo-c)
Dell Publishing Co.

4-Color 1125	5.00	15.00	35.00
4-Color 1223,1284	4.00	12.00	28.00
01-418-207	4.00	12.00	28.00

LAREDO (TV)
June, 1966
Gold Key

1 (10179-606)-Photo-c	2.00	6.00	14.00

LARGE FEATURE COMIC (Formerly called Black & White)
1939 - No. 13, 1943
Dell Publishing Co.

Lady Luck #89, © QUA   Lance O'Casey #4, © FAW   Land Of The Lost Comics #3, © WMG

Large Feature Comic #1 (Series I), © N.Y. News Synd.   Lars Of Mars #10, © Z-D   Lash LaRue Western #6, © FAW

LARGE FEATURE COMIC (continued)	Good	Fine	N-Mint
1 (Series I)-Dick Tracy Meets the Blank	80.00	240.00	560.00
2-Terry & the Pirates (#1)	40.00	120.00	280.00
3-Heigh-Yo Silver! The Lone Ranger (text & ill.)(76 pgs.). Also			
exists as a Whitman #710	40.00	120.00	280.00
4-Dick Tracy Gets His Man	45.00	135.00	315.00
5-Tarzan (#1) by Harold Foster (origin); reprints 1st dailies from '29			
	80.00	240.00	560.00
6-Terry & the Pirates & The Dragon Lady; reprints dailies from 1936			
	38.00	115.00	265.00
7-(Scarce)-52 pgs.; The Lone Ranger-Hi-Yo Silver the Lone Ranger			
to the Rescue. Also exists as a Whitman #715			
	50.00	150.00	350.00
8-Dick Tracy Racket Buster	40.00	120.00	280.00
9-King of the Royal Mounted	18.00	54.00	125.00
10-(Scarce)-Gang Busters (No. appears on inside front cover); first			
slick cover	27.00	81.00	190.00
11-Dick Tracy Foils the Mad Doc Hump	40.00	120.00	280.00
12-Smilin' Jack	25.00	75.00	175.00
13-Dick Tracy & Scotty	40.00	120.00	280.00
14-Smilin' Jack	25.00	75.00	175.00
15-Dick Tracy & the Kidnapped Princes	40.00	120.00	280.00
16-Donald Duck-1st app. Daisy Duck on back cover (6/41-Disney)			
	145.00	435.00	1015.00
(Prices vary widely on this book)			
17-Gang Busters (1941)	18.00	54.00	125.00
18-Phantasmo	15.00	45.00	105.00
19-Dumbo Comic Paint Book (Disney); partial-r 4-Color 17			
	105.00	315.00	735.00
20-Donald Duck Comic Paint Book (Rarer than #16) (Disney)			
	205.00	615.00	1435.00
(Prices vary widely on this book)			
21-Private Buck	7.00	21.00	50.00
22-Nuts & Jolts	7.00	21.00	50.00
23-The Nebbs	8.00	24.00	56.00
24-Popeye (Thimble Theatre) ½ by Segar	34.00	100.00	237.00
25-Smilin' Jack-1st issue to show title on cover			
	25.00	75.00	175.00
26-Smitty	14.00	42.00	100.00
27-Terry & the Pirates; Caniff-c/a	27.00	81.00	190.00
28-Grin & Bear It	6.50	19.50	45.00
29-Moon Mullins	13.00	40.00	90.00
30-Tillie the Toiler	11.50	34.00	80.00
1 (Series II)-Peter Rabbit by Cady; arrival date-3/27/42			
	28.00	84.00	195.00
2-Winnie Winkle (#1)	10.00	30.00	70.00
3-Dick Tracy	38.00	115.00	265.00
4-Tiny Tim (#1)	18.00	54.00	125.00
5-Toots & Casper	6.50	19.50	45.00
6-Terry & the Pirates; Caniff-a	27.00	81.00	190.00
7-Pluto Saves the Ship (#1)(Disney) written by Carl Barks, Jack			
Hannah, & Nick George. (Barks' 1st comic book work)			
	60.00	180.00	420.00
8-Bugs Bunny (#1)('42)	53.00	160.00	370.00
9-Bringing Up Father	8.50	25.50	60.00
10-Popeye (Thimble Theatre)	28.00	84.00	195.00
11-Barney Google & Snuffy Smith	12.00	36.00	84.00
12-Private Buck	6.50	19.50	45.00
13-(nn)-1001 Hours Of Fun; puzzles & games; by A. W. Nugent. This			
book was bound as #13 with Large Feat. Comics in Publishers			
files	7.00	21.00	50.00

NOTE: The Black & White Feature Books are oversized 8½x11-3/8" comics with color covers and black and white interiors. The first nine issues all have rough, heavy stock covers and, except for #7, all have 76 pages, including covers. #7 and #10-on all have 52 pages. Beginning with #10 the covers are slick and thin and, because of their size, are difficult to handle without damaging. For this reason, they are seldom found in fine to mint condition. The paper stock, unlike Wow #1 and Capt. Marvel #1, is itself not unstable . . . just thin.

LARRY DOBY, BASEBALL HERO
1950 (Cleveland Indians)
Fawcett Publications

	Good	Fine	N-Mint
nn-Bill Ward-a; photo-c	25.00	75.00	175.00

LARHY HARMON'S LAUREL AND HARDY (. . . Comics)
July-Aug, 1972 (Regular size)
National Periodical Publications

1	.45	1.25	2.50

LARS OF MARS
Apr-May, 1951 - No. 11, July-Aug, 1951 (Painted-c)
Ziff-Davis Publishing Co.

10-Origin; Anderson-a(3) in each	26.00	78.00	180.00
11-Gene Colan-a	23.00	70.00	160.00

LARS OF MARS 3-D
Apr, 1987 ($2.50)
Eclipse Comics

1-r-/Lars of Mars #10,11 in 3-D + new story	.40	1.25	2.50
2-D limited edition	.85	2.50	5.00

LASER ERASER & PRESSBUTTON (See Axel Pressbutton & Miracleman 9)
11/85 - No. 6, 1987 (6 issue series)
Eclipse Comics

1-4		.40	.80
5,6 (.95 cents)		.50	1.00
. . . In 3-D 1 (8/86, $2.50)	.40	1.25	2.50
2-D 1 (B&W, limited to 100 copies signed & numbered)			
	.40	1.25	1.50

LASH LARUE WESTERN (Movie star; king of the bullwhip)(See Six-Gun Heroes)
Sum, 1949 - No. 46, Jan, 1954 (36pgs., 1-7,9,13,16-on)
Fawcett Publications

1-Lash & his horse Black Diamond begin; photo front/back-c begin			
	45.00	135.00	315.00
2(11/49)	25.00	75.00	175.00
3-5	21.50	64.00	150.00
6,7,9: 6-Last photo back-c; intro. Frontier Phantom (Lash's twin			
brother)	15.00	45.00	105.00
8,10 (52pgs.)	16.00	48.00	110.00
11,12,14,15 (52pgs.)	10.00	30.00	70.00
13,16-20 (36pgs.)	9.50	28.50	65.00
21-30: 21-The Frontier Phantom app.	8.00	24.00	56.00
31-45	6.50	19.50	45.00
46-Last Fawcett issue & photo-c	7.00	21.00	50.00

LASH LARUE WESTERN (Continues from Fawcett)
No. 47, Mar-Apr, 1954 - No. 84, June, 1961
Charlton Comics

47-Photo-c	6.00	18.00	42.00
48	4.30	13.00	30.00
49-60	3.50	10.50	24.00
61-66,69,70: 52-r/#8; 53-r/#22	3.00	9.00	21.00
67,68-(68 pgs.) 68-Check-a	3.50	10.50	24.00
71-83	2.00	6.00	14.00
84-Last issue	2.65	8.00	18.00

LASSIE (TV)(M-G-M's . . . No. 1-36)
Oct-Dec, 1950 - No. 70, July, 1969
Dell Publishing Co./Gold Key No. 59 (10/62) on

1-Photo-c	4.00	12.00	28.00
2-Painted-c begin	2.30	7.00	16.00
3-10	1.70	5.00	12.00
11-19: 12-Rocky Langford (Lassie's master) marries Gerry Law-			
rence. 15-1st app. Timbu	1.50	4.50	10.00
20-22-Matt Baker-a	2.00	6.00	14.00

LASSIE (continued)

	Good	Fine	N-Mint
23-40: 33-Robinson-a. 39-1st app. Timmy as Lassie picks up her TV family	.85	2.50	6.00
41-70: 63-Last Timmy. 64-r-/#19. 65-Forest Ranger Corey Stuart begins, ends #69. 70-Forest Rangers Bob Ericson & Scott Turner app. (Lassie's new masters)	.55	1.65	4.00
11193(1978-Golden Press)-224 pgs.; $1.95; Baker-a(r), 92 pgs.	.55	1.65	4.00

The Adventures of. . .(Red Heart Dog Food giveaway, 1949)-16 pgs,
| soft-c | 3.50 | 10.50 | 24.00 |
| Kite Fun Book('73)-(16 pgs.; 5x7'') | 2.00 | 6.00 | 14.00 |

NOTE: Photo c-57. (See March of Comics #210, 217, 230, 254, 266, 278, 296, 308, 324, 334, 346, 358, 370, 381, 394, 411, 432)

LAST DAYS OF THE JUSTICE SOCIETY SPECIAL
1986 (One shot, 68 pgs.)
DC Comics

1	.50	1.50	3.00

LAST GENERATION, THE
1986 - No. 3 ($1.95, B&W)
Black Tie Studios

1	1.15	3.50	7.00
2	.70	2.00	4.00
3	.50	1.50	3.00

LAST HUNT, THE (See 4-Color No. 678)

LAST OF THE COMANCHES (See Wild Bill Hickok #28)
1953 (Movie)
Avon Periodicals

nn-Kinstler c/a, 21pgs.; Ravielli-a	8.50	25.50	60.00

LAST OF THE ERIES, THE (See American Graphics)

LAST OF THE FAST GUNS, THE (See 4-Color No. 925)

LAST OF THE MOHICANS (See King Classics)

LAST OF THE VIKING HEROES, THE
Mar, 1987 - Present ($1.50, color)
Genesis West Comics

1-4: 4-Intro The Phantom Force	.40	1.25	2.50
5A-Kirby/Stevens-c	.40	1.25	2.50
5B	.35	1.00	2.00
6-9	.40	1.25	2.50
Summer Special 1 (1988)-Frazetta-c	.50	1.50	3.00

NOTE: Art Adams c-7. Byrne c-3. Kirby c-1, 5p. Perez c-2i. Stevens c-5i, 9.

LAST STARFIGHTER, THE
Oct, 1984 - No. 3, Dec, 1984
Marvel Comics Group

1-3: Movie adaptation-r/Marvel Super Special; Guice-c		.30	.60

LAST TRAIN FROM GUN HILL (See 4-Color No. 1012)

LATEST ADVENTURES OF FOXY GRANDPA (See Foxy. . .)

LATEST COMICS (Super Duper No. 3?)
March, 1945
Spotlight Publ./Palace Promotions (Jubilee)

1-Super Duper	3.70	11.00	26.00
2-Bee-29 (nd)	2.65	8.00	18.00

LAUGH
June, 1987 - Present
Archie Enterprises

V2#1-12: 5-X-Mas ish.		.40	.75

LAUGH COMICS (Formerly Black Hood #1-19) (Laugh #226 on)
No. 20, Fall, 1946 - No. 400, 1987
Archie Publications (Close-Up)
20-Archie begins; Katy Keene & Taffy begin by Woggon

	Good	Fine	N-Mint
	38.00	115.00	265.00
21-23,25	18.00	54.00	125.00
24-"Pipsy" by Kirby, 6 pgs.	18.00	55.00	125.00
26-30	10.00	30.00	70.00
31-40	8.00	24.00	50.00
41-60: 41,54-Debbi by Woggon. 57-Spanking panel	4.50	13.50	30.00
61-80: 67-Debbi by Woggon	2.85	8.50	20.00
81-99	2.00	6.00	14.00
100	3.00	9.00	21.00
101-126: 125-Debbi app.	1.35	4.00	9.00
127,130,131,133,135,140-142,144-Jaguar app.	1.35	4.00	9.00
128,129,132,134,138,139-Fly app.	1.35	4.00	9.00
136,143-Flygirl app.	1.35	4.00	9.00
137-Flyman & Flygirl app.	1.35	4.00	9.00
145-160: 157-Josie app.	.75	2.25	4.50
161-165,167-200	.50	1.50	3.00
166-Beatles-c	.85	2.50	5.00
201-240	.25	.75	1.50
241-280		.40	.80
281-400: 381-384-Katy Keene app.; by Woggon-381,382		.30	.60

NOTE: Josie app.-#145, 160, 164. Katy Keene app.-#20-125, 129, 130, 133. Many issues contain paper dolls.

LAUGH COMICS DIGEST (. . .Mag. No. 23 on)
8/74; No. 2, 9/75; No. 3, 3/76 - Present (Digest-size)
Archie Publications (Close-Up No. 1, 3 on)

1-Adams-a	.70	2.00	4.00
2,7,8,19-Adams-a	.35	1.00	2.00
3-6,9,10		.50	1.00
11-18,20-81		.50	1.00

NOTE: Katy Keene in 23, 25, 27, 32-38, 40, 45-48, 50. The Fly-r in 19, 20. The Jaguar-r in 25, 27. Mr. Justice-r in 21. The Web-r in 23.

LAUGH COMIX (Formerly Top Notch Laugh; Suzie No. 49 on)
No. 46, Summer, 1944 - No. 48, Winter, 1944-45
MLJ Magazines

46-Wilbur & Suzie in all	8.00	24.00	56.00
47,48	5.70	17.00	40.00

LAUGH-IN MAGAZINE (Magazine)
Oct, 1968 - No. 12, Oct, 1969 (50 cents) (Satire)
Laufer Publ. Co.

V1#1	1.00	3.00	7.00
2-12	.70	2.00	4.00

LAUREL & HARDY (See Larry Harmon's. . . & March of Comics No. 302,314)

LAUREL AND HARDY (. . .Comics)
March, 1949 - No. 28, March, 1956
St. John Publishing Co.

1	27.00	81.00	190.00
2	14.00	42.00	100.00
3,4	11.50	34.00	80.00
5-10	9.50	28.00	65.00
11-28; 26,28-r	7.00	21.00	50.00

LAUREL AND HARDY (TV)
Oct, 1962 - No. 4, Sept-Nov, 1963
Dell Publishing Co.

12-423-210 (8-10/62)	2.00	6.00	14.00
2-4 (Dell)	1.70	5.00	12.00

LAUREL AND HARDY
Jan, 1967 - No. 2, Oct, 1967 (Larry Harmon's)
Gold Key

1,2: 1-Photo back-c	1.50	4.50	10.00

Last Of The Comanches, © AVON

Laugh Comics #21, © AP

Laurel And Hardy #1, © STJ

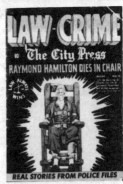
Law Against Crime #1, © Essenkay Publ.

Leading Comics #13, © DC

Legends #3, © DC

LAUREL AND HARDY IN 3-D
Fall, 1987 - Present ($1.75, B&W)
Blackthorne Publishing

	Good	Fine	N-Mint
1,2	.40	1.25	2.50

LAW AGAINST CRIME (Law-Crime on cover)
April, 1948 - No. 3, Aug, 1948
Essenkay Publishing Co.

1-(#1-3: ½ funny animal, ½ crime)-L. B. Cole electrocution-c/a			
	24.00	72.00	170.00
2-L. B. Cole c/a	17.00	51.00	120.00
3-L. B. Cole c/a; used in **SOTI**, pg. 180,181 & illo-"The wish to hurt or kill couples in lovers' lanes;" reprinted in All-Famous Crime #9			
	25.00	75.00	175.00

LAWBREAKERS (. . .Suspense Stories No. 10 on)
Mar, 1951 - No. 9, Oct-Nov, 1952
Law and Order Magazines (Charlton Comics)

1	7.00	21.00	50.00
2	3.50	10.50	24.00
3,5,6,8,9	2.65	8.00	18.00
4-"White Death" junkie story	5.00	15.00	35.00
7-"The Deadly Dopesters" drug story	4.30	13.00	30.00

LAWBREAKERS ALWAYS LOSE!
Spring, 1948 - No. 10, Oct, 1949
Marvel Comics (CBS)

1-2pg. Kurtzman-a, 'Giggles 'n Grins'	8.50	25.50	60.00
2	4.30	13.00	30.00
3-5: 4-Vampire story	3.00	9.00	21.00
6(2/49)-Has editorial defense against charges of Dr. Wertham			
	4.30	13.00	30.00
7-Used in **SOTI**, illo-"Comic-book philosophy;"			
	11.00	32.00	75.00
8-10: 9,10-Photo-c	2.00	6.00	14.00

LAWBREAKERS SUSPENSE STORIES (Formerly Lawbreakers; Strange Suspense Stories No. 16 on)
No. 10, Jan, 1953 - No. 15, Nov, 1953
Capitol Stories/Charlton Comics

10	4.65	14.00	32.00
11 (3/53)-Severed tongues c/story & woman negligee scene			
	22.00	65.00	154.00
12-14	3.00	9.00	21.00
15-Acid-in-face c/story; hands dissolved in acid story			
	10.00	30.00	70.00

LAW-CRIME (See Law Against Crime)

LAWMAN (TV)
No. 970, Feb, 1959 - No. 11, Apr-June, 1962 (All photo-c)
Dell Publishing Co.

4-Color 970(#1)	5.70	17.00	40.00
4-Color 1035('60)	4.00	12.00	28.00
3(2-4/60)-Toth-a	5.00	15.00	35.00
4-11	3.50	10.50	24.00

LAWRENCE (See Movie Classics)

LEADING COMICS (. . .Screen Comics No. 42 on)
Winter, 1941-42 - No. 41, Feb-Mar, 1950
National Periodical Publications

1-Origin The Seven Soldiers of Victory; Crimson Avenger, Green Arrow & Speedy, Shining Knight, The Vigilante, Star Spangled Kid & Stripesy begin. The Dummy (Vigilante villain) app.			
	135.00	405.00	945.00
2-Meskin-a	60.00	180.00	420.00
3	47.00	141.00	330.00
4,5	40.00	120.00	280.00
6-10	34.00	102.00	240.00

	Good	Fine	N-Mint
11-14(Spring, 1945)	24.00	72.00	165.00
15-(Sum,'45)-Content change to funny animal	9.50	28.50	65.00
16-22,24-30	4.00	12.00	28.00
23-1st app. Peter Porkchops by Otto Feur	10.00	30.00	70.00
31,32,34-41	3.00	9.00	21.00
33-(Scarce)	5.50	16.50	38.00

NOTE: *Rube Grossman-a(Peter Porkchops)-most #15-on; c-15-41. Post a-23-37, 39, 41.*

LEADING SCREEN COMICS (Formerly Leading Comics)
No. 42, Apr-May, 1950 - No. 77, Aug-Sept, 1955
National Periodical Publications

42	4.00	12.00	28.00
43-77	2.65	8.00	18.00

NOTE: *Grossman a-most. Mayer a-45-48, 50, 54-57, 60, 62-74, 75(3), 76, 77.*

LEATHERNECK THE MARINE (See Mighty Midget Comics)

LEAVE IT TO BEAVER (TV)
No. 912, June, 1958 - May-July, 1962 (All photo-c)
Dell Publishing Co.

4-Color 912	10.00	30.00	70.00
4-Color 999,1103,1191,1285, 01-428-207	8.50	25.50	60.00

LEAVE IT TO BINKY (Binky No. 72 on) (See Super DC Giant and Showcase) (No. 1-22, 52 pgs.)
2-3/48 - No. 60, 10/58; No. 61, 6-7/68 - No. 71, 2-3/70
National Periodical Publications

1	13.00	40.00	90.00
2	6.50	19.50	45.00
3-5	5.00	15.00	35.00
6-10	4.00	12.00	28.00
11-20	3.00	9.00	21.00
21-28,30-45: 45-Last pre-code (2/55)	1.70	5.00	12.00
29-Used in **POP**, pg. 78	2.35	7.00	16.00
46-60	1.00	3.00	7.00
61-71	.70	2.00	4.00

NOTE: *Drucker a-28. Mayer a-1, 2, 15.*

LEE HUNTER, INDIAN FIGHTER (See 4-Color No. 779,904)

LEFT-HANDED GUN, THE (See 4-Color No. 913)

LEGEND OF CUSTER, THE (TV)
January, 1968
Dell Publishing Co.

1	1.15	3.50	8.00

LEGEND OF JESSE JAMES, THE (TV)
February, 1966
Gold Key

10172-602-Photo-c	1.75	5.25	12.00

LEGEND OF KAMUI, THE (See Kamui)

LEGEND OF LOBO, THE (See Movie Comics)

LEGEND OF WONDER WOMAN, THE
May, 1986 - No. 4, Aug, 1986 (mini-series)
DC Comics

1-4		.60	1.20

LEGEND OF YOUNG DICK TURPIN, THE (TV)
May, 1966 (Disney TV episode)
Gold Key

1 (10176-605)-Photo/painted-c	1.15	3.50	8.00

LEGENDS
Nov, 1986 - No. 6, Apr, 1987 (mini-series)
DC Comics

1-Byrne c/a(p) begins. 1st new Capt. Marvel	.35	1.00	2.00
2	.25	.80	1.60
3-5: 3-Intro new Suicide Squad	.25	.70	1.40

LEGENDS (continued)	Good	Fine	N-Mint
6-Intro/1st app. New Justice League	1.00	3.00	6.00

LEGENDS OF DANIEL BOONE, THE
Oct-Nov, 1955 - No. 8, Dec-Jan, 1956-57
National Periodical Publications

	Good	Fine	N-Mint
1 (Scarce)	19.50	58.00	135.00
2 (Scarce)	13.00	40.00	90.00
3-8 (Scarce)	11.50	34.00	80.00

LEGIONNAIRES THREE
Jan, 1986 - No. 4, May, 1986 (Mini-series)
DC comics

1-4		.50	1.00

LEGION OF MONSTERS (Magazine)(Also see Marvel Premiere #28 & Marvel Preview #8)
September, 1975 (black & white)
Marvel Comics Group

1-Origin & 1st app. Legion of Monsters; Adams-c; Morrow-a; origin & only app. The Manphibian	.35	1.00	2.00

LEGION OF SUBSTITUTE HEROES SPECIAL
July, 1985 (One Shot)
DC Comics

1-Giffen c/a(p)	.25	.75	1.50

LEGION OF SUPER-HEROES (See Action, Adventure, All New Collectors Ed., Limited Collectors Ed., Superboy, & Superman)
Feb, 1973 - No. 4, July-Aug, 1973
National Periodical Publications

1-Legion & Tommy Tomorrow reprints begin	.75	2.25	4.50
2-4: 3-r/Adv. 340, Action 240. 4-r/Adv. 341, Action 233	.40	1.25	2.50

LEGION OF SUPER-HEROES (Formerly Superboy; Tales of The Legion No. 314 on)(See Secrets of . . .)
No. 259, Jan, 1980 - No. 313, July, 1984
DC Comics

259(#1)-Superboy leaves Legion	.60	1.75	3.50
260-264,266-270	.35	1.00	2.00
265-Contains 28pg. insert 'Superman & the TR5-80 Computer;' origin Tyroc; Tyroc leaves Legion	.35	1.00	2.00
271-284: 272-Blok joins; origin; 20pg. insert-Dial 'H' For Hero. 277-Intro Reflecto. 280-Superboy re-joins legion. 282-Origin Reflecto	.25	.75	1.50
285,286-Giffen back up story	.50	1.50	3.00
287-Giffen-a on Legion begins	.70	2.00	4.00
288-290: 290-Great Darkness saga begins, ends #294	.40	1.25	2.50
291-293	.25	.75	1.50
294-Double size (52 pgs.); Giffen-a(p)	.30	.90	1.80
295-299: 297-Origin retold	.60	1.20	
300-Double size, 64 pgs., Mando paper; c/a by almost everyone at D.C.	.40	1.25	2.50
301-305: 304-Karate Kid & Princess Projectra resign	.60	1.20	
306-313 (75 cent-c): 306-Brief origin Star Boy	.45	.90	
Annual 1(1982)-Giffen c/a; 1st app./origin new Invisible Kid who joins Legion	.35	1.00	2.00
Annual 2(10/83)-Giffen-c; Karate Kid & Princess Projectra wed	.25	.75	1.50
Annual 3('84)	.25	.75	1.50

NOTE: *Aparo* c-282, 283. *Austin* c-268i. *Buckler* c-273p, 274p, 276p. *Colan* a-311p. *Ditko* a(p)-267, 268, 272, 274, 276, 281. *Giffen* a-285p-313p, Annual 1p; c-287p, 288p, 289, 290p, 291p, 292, 293, 294-299p, 300, 301p-313p, Annual 1p, 2p. *Perez* c-268p, 277-80, 281p. *Starlin* a-265. *Staton* a-259p, 260p, 280. *Tuska* a-308p.

LEGION OF SUPER-HEROES
Aug, 1984 - Present ($1.25-$1.75, deluxe format)

DC Comics	Good	Fine	N-Mint
1	.50	1.50	3.00
2-5: 4-Death of Karate Kid. 5-Death of Nemesis Kid	.40	1.25	2.50
6-10	.35	1.00	2.00
11-14: 12-Cosmic Boy, Lightning Lad, & Saturn Girl resign. 14-Intro new members: Tellus, Sensor Girl, Quislet	.25	.75	1.50
15-18-Crisis x-over	.35	1.00	2.00
19-25: 25-Sensor Girl i.d. revealed as Princess Projectra	.25	.75	1.50
26-36,39-44: 35-Saturn Girl rejoins	.25	.70	1.40
37,38-Death of Superboy	.75	2.25	4.50
45 ($2.95, 68 pgs.)	.50	1.50	3.00
46-49,51-55	.25	.70	1.40
50-Double size, $2.50	.40	1.25	2.50
Annual 1 (10/85)-Crisis x-over	.35	1.10	2.20
Annual 2 (10/86), 3 (10/87)	.35	1.00	2.00
Annual 4(11/88, $2.50)	.40	1.25	2.50

NOTE: *Byrne* c-36p. *Giffen* a(p)-1, 2, 50-52, Annual 1p, 2; c-1-5p, Annual 1. *Orlando* a-6p. *Steacy* c-45-50, Annual 3.

LENNON SISTERS LIFE STORY, THE (See 4-Color No. 951,1014)

LEONARDO (Also see Teenage Mutant Ninja Turtles)
Dec., 1986 ($1.50, B&W, One shot)
Mirage Studios

1	.70	2.00	4.00

LEO THE LION
No date (10 cents)
I. W. Enterprises

1-Reprint	.50	1.50	3.00

LEROY (Teen-age)
Nov, 1949 - No. 6, Nov, 1950
Standard Comics

1	2.65	8.00	18.00
2-Frazetta text illo.	2.85	8.50	20.00
3-6: 3-Lubbers-a	1.50	4.50	10.00

LET'S PRETEND (CBS radio)
May-June, 1950 - No. 3, Sept-Oct, 1950
D. S. Publishing Co.

1	6.00	18.00	42.00
2,3	3.50	10.50	24.00

LET'S READ THE NEWSPAPER
1974
Charlton Press

Features Quincy by Ted Sheares		.30	.60

LET'S TAKE A TRIP (TV) (CBS TV Presents)
Spring, 1958
Pines

1-Marv Levy c/a	1.30	4.00	9.00

LETTERS TO SANTA (See March of Comics No. 228)

LIBBY ELLIS
7/87 - No. 4, 1987 ($1.95, B&W); 6/88 - Present
Malibu Graphics/Eternity Comics

1-4	.35	1.00	1.95
1-4 (2nd series)	.35	1.00	1.95
Graphic Novel ($7.95; B&W)	1.35	4.00	7.95

LIBERTY COMICS (Miss Liberty No. 1)
1945 - 1946 (MLJ & other reprints)
Green Publishing Co.

4	8.00	24.00	56.00
5 (5/46)-The Prankster app.; Starr-a	5.50	16.50	38.00
10-Hangman & Boy Buddies app.; Suzie & Wilbur begin; reprint of			

The Legends Of Daniel Boone #1, © DC

Legion Of Super-Heroes #37, © DC

Let's Pretend #2, © DS

Liberty Comics #12, © Green Publ.   *The Liberty Project #1, © Eclipse Comics*   *Life Story #45, © FAW*

	Good	Fine	N-Mint
LIBERTY COMICS (continued)			
Hangman #8	7.00	21.00	50.00
11(V2/2, 1/46)-Wilbur in women's clothes	9.50	28.00	65.00
12-Black Hood & Suzie app.	6.00	18.00	42.00
14,15-Patty of Airliner; Starr-a in both	3.50	10.50	24.00

LIBERTY GUARDS
No date (1946?)
Chicago Mail Order

	Good	Fine	N-Mint
nn-Reprints Man of War #1 with cover of Liberty Scouts #1; Gustavson-c	18.00	54.00	125.00

LIBERTY PROJECT, THE
June, 1987 - No. 8, May, 1988 ($1.75, color, Baxter)
Eclipse Comics

1	.35	1.00	2.00
2-8	.30	.85	1.70

LIBERTY SCOUTS (See Man of War & Liberty Guards)
June, 1941 - No. 3, Aug, 1941
Centaur Publications

	Good	Fine	N-Mint
2(#1)-Origin The Fire-Man, Man of War; Vapo-Man & Liberty Scouts begin; Gustavson-c/a	70.00	210.00	490.00
3(#2)-Origin & 1st app. The Sentinel; Gustavson-c/a	50.00	150.00	350.00

LIDSVILLE (TV)
Oct, 1972 - No. 5, Oct, 1973
Gold Key

1	1.15	3.50	7.00
2-5	.70	2.00	4.00

LIEUTENANT, THE (TV)
April-June, 1964
Dell Publishing Co.

1-Photo-c	1.15	3.50	8.00

LT. ROBIN CRUSOE, U.S.N. (See Movie Comics and Walt Disney Showcase 26)

LIFE OF CAPTAIN MARVEL, THE
Aug, 1985 - No. 5, Dec, 1985 ($2.00 cover; Baxter paper)
Marvel Comics Group

1-5: r-/Starlin issues of Capt. Marvel	.35	1.00	2.00

LIFE OF CHRIST, THE
1949 (100 pages) (35 cents)
Catechetical Guild Educational Society

301-Reprints from Topix(1949)-V5#11,12	4.00	12.00	28.00

LIFE OF CHRIST VISUALIZED
1942 - 1943
Standard Publishers

1-3: All came in cardboard case	2.75	8.00	16.00

LIFE OF CHRIST VISUALIZED
1946? (48 pgs. in color)
The Standard Publ. Co.

	1.00	3.00	6.00

LIFE OF ESTHER VISUALIZED
1947 (48 pgs. in color)
The Standard Publ. Co.

2062	1.00	3.00	6.00

LIFE OF JOSEPH VISUALIZED
1946 (48 pgs. in color)
The Standard Publ. Co.

1054	1.00	3.00	6.00

LIFE OF PAUL (See The Living Bible)

LIFE OF POPE JOHN PAUL II, THE
Jan, 1983
Marvel Comics Group

	Good	Fine	N-Mint
1	.25	.75	1.50

LIFE OF RILEY, THE (See 4-Color No. 917)

LIFE OF THE BLESSED VIRGIN
1950 (68 pages) (square binding)
Catechetical Guild (Giveaway)

nn-Contains "The Woman of the Promise" & "Mother of Us All" rebound	4.00	12.00	24.00

LIFE'S LIKE THAT
1945 (68 pgs.; B&W; 25 cents)
Croyden Publ. Co.

nn-Newspaper Sunday strip-r by Neher	2.35	7.00	16.00

LIFE'S LITTLE JOKES
No date (1924) (52 pgs.; B&W)
M.S. Publ. Co.

By Rube Goldberg	13.00	40.00	90.00

LIFE STORIES OF AMERICAN PRESIDENTS (See Dell Giants)

LIFE STORY
4/49 - V8/46, 1/53; V8/47, 4/53 (All have photo-c?)
Fawcett Publications

V1#1	4.00	12.00	28.00
2	1.85	5.50	13.00
3-6	1.60	4.70	11.00
V2#7-12	1.50	4.50	10.00
V3#13-Wood-a	6.50	19.50	45.00
V3#14-18, V4#19-21,23,24	1.30	4.00	9.00
V4#22-Drug use story	1.50	4.50	10.00
V5#25-30, V6#31-36	1.15	3.50	8.00
V7#37,40-42, V8#44,45	1.00	3.00	7.00
V7#38, V8#43-Evans-a	1.85	5.50	13.00
V7#39-Drug Smuggling & Junkie sty	1.30	4.00	9.00
V8#46,47 (Scarce)	1.15	3.50	8.00

NOTE: *Powell* a-13,23,24,26,28,30,32,39.

LIFE WITH ARCHIE
Sept, 1958 - Present
Archie Publications

1	20.00	60.00	140.00
2	10.00	30.00	70.00
3-5	7.00	20.00	50.00
6-10	3.50	10.50	24.00
11-20	1.70	5.00	12.00
21-30	1.30	4.00	9.00
31-41	.85	2.50	6.00
42-45: 42-Pureheart begins	.70	2.00	4.00
46-Origin Pureheart	.85	2.50	5.00
47-50: 50-United Three begin; Superteen, Capt. Hero app.	.50	1.50	3.00
51-59-Pureheart ends	.50	1.50	3.00
60-100: 60-Archie band begins	.35	1.00	2.00
101-150		.50	1.00
151-272		.30	.60

LIFE WITH MILLIE (Formerly A Date With Millie) (Modeling With Millie No. 21 on)
No. 8, Dec, 1960 - No. 20, Dec, 1962
Atlas/Marvel Comics Group

8	2.35	7.00	16.00
9-11	1.50	4.50	10.00
12-20	.85	2.50	6.00

	Good	Fine	N-Mint

LIFE WITH SNARKY PARKER (TV)
August, 1950
Fox Feature Syndicate

	Good	Fine	N-Mint
1	8.50	25.50	60.00

LIGHT AND DARKNESS WAR, THE
Oct., 1988 - No. 6 ($1.95, color, limited series)
Epic Comics (Marvel)

1-4	.35	1.00	1.95

LIGHT IN THE FOREST (See 4-Color No. 891)

LIGHTNING COMICS (Formerly Sure-Fire No. 1-3)
No. 4, Dec, 1940 - No. 13(V3No.1), June, 1942
Ace Magazines

4	32.00	95.00	225.00
5,6: 6-Dr. Nemesis begins	22.00	65.00	154.00
V2#1-6: 2-''Flash Lightning'' becomes ''Lash...''			
	20.00	60.00	140.00
V3#1-Intro. Lightning Girl & The Sword	20.00	60.00	140.00

NOTE: *Anderson a-V2#6. Bondage-c V2#6. Mooney c-V1#6, V2#2.*

LI'L (See Little)

LILY OF THE ALLEY IN THE FUNNIES
No date (1920's?) (10¼x15½'') (28 pgs. in color)
Whitman Publishers

W936 - by T. Burke	7.00	21.00	50.00

LIMITED COLLECTORS' EDITION (See Famous 1st Edition & Rudolph the Red Nosed Reindeer; becomes All-New Collectors' Edition) (#21-34,51-59: 84 pgs.; #35-41: 68 pgs.; #42-50: 60 pgs.)
C-21, Summer, 1973 - No. C-59, 1978 ($1.00) (10x13½'')
National Periodical Publications/DC Comics

nn(C-20)-Rudolph	.70	2.00	4.00
C-21: Shazam (TV); Captain Marvel Jr. reprint by Raboy			
	.50	1.50	3.00
C-22: Tarzan; complete origin reprinted from #207-210; all Kubert			
	.50	1.50	3.00
C-23: House of Mystery; Wrightson, Adams, Wood, Toth, Orlando-a			
	.35	1.00	2.00
C-24: Rudolph The Red-nosed Reindeer	.35	1.00	2.00
C-25: Batman; Adams-c/a	.50	1.50	3.00
C-27: Shazam (TV)	.35	1.00	2.00
C-29: Tarzan; reprints ''Return of Tarzan'' from #219-223 by Kubert	.50	1.50	3.00
C-31: Superman; origin-r; Adams-a	.50	1.50	3.00
C-32: Ghosts (new-a)	.35	1.00	2.00
C-33: Rudolph The Red-nosed Reindeer(new-a)	.35	1.00	2.00
C-34: Xmas with the Super-Heroes; unpublished Angel & Ape story by Oksner & Wood	.50	1.50	3.00
C-35: Shazam; cover features TV's Captain Marvel, Jackson Bostwick	.35	1.00	2.00
C-36: The Bible; all new adaptation beginning with Genesis by Kubert, Redondo & Mayer	.50	1.50	3.00
C-37: Batman; r-1946 Sundays	.35	1.00	2.00
C-38: Superman; 1 pg. Adams	.35	1.00	2.00
C-39: Secret Origins/Super Villains; Adams-a(r)			
	.35	1.00	2.00
C-40: Dick Tracy by Gould featuring Flattop; newspaper-r from 12/21/43 - 5/17/44	.50	1.50	3.00
C-41: Super Friends; Toth-c/a	.35	1.00	2.00
C-42: Rudolph	.35	1.00	2.00
C-43: Christmas with the Super-Heroes; Wrightson, S&K, Adams-a			
	.50	1.50	3.00
C-44: Batman; Adams-r; painted-c	.35	1.00	2.00
C-45: Secret Origins/Super Villains; Flash-r/105			
	.35	1.00	2.00
C-46: Justice League of America; 3 pg. Toth-a	.50	1.50	3.00

	Good	Fine	N-Mint
C-47: Superman Salutes the Bicentennial (Tomahawk interior); 2 pgs. new-a	.25	.75	1.50
C-48: The Superman-Flash Race; 6 pgs. Adams-a			
	.35	1.00	2.00
C-49: Superboy & the Legion of Super-Heroes	.35	1.00	2.00
C-50: Rudolph The Red-nosed Reindeer	.25	.75	1.50
C-51: Batman; Adams-c/a	.50	1.50	3.00
C-52: The Best of DC; Adams-c/a; Toth, Kubert-a			
	.35	1.00	2.00
C-57: Welcome Back, Kotter-r(TV)(5/78)	.25	.75	1.50
C-59: Batman's Strangest Cases; Adams, Wrightson-r; Adams/Wrightson-c	.35	1.00	2.00

NOTE: *All-r with exception of some special features and covers. Aparo a-52; c-37. Giordano a-39, 45. Grell c-49. Infantino a-25, 39, 44, 45, 52.*

LINDA (Phantom Lady No. 5 on)
Apr-May, 1954 - No. 4, Oct-Nov, 1954
Ajax-Farrell Publ. Co.

1-Kamenish-a	7.00	21.00	50.00
2-Lingerie panel	4.65	14.00	32.00
3,4	4.30	13.00	30.00

LINDA CARTER, STUDENT NURSE
Sept, 1961 - No. 9, Jan, 1963
Atlas Comics (AMI)

1-Al Hartley-c	1.70	5.00	12.00
2-9	1.00	3.00	7.00

LINDA LARK
Oct-Dec, 1961 - No. 8, Aug-Oct, 1963
Dell Publishing Co.

1	1.00	3.00	7.00
2-8	.55	1.65	4.00

LINUS, THE LIONHEARTED (TV)
September, 1965
Gold Key

1 (10155-509)	2.65	8.00	18.00

LION, THE (See Movie Comics)

LION OF SPARTA (See Movie Classics)

LIPPY THE LION AND HARDY HAR HAR (TV)
March, 1963 (Hanna-Barbera)
Gold Key

1 (10049-303)	2.65	8.00	18.00

LI'L ABNER (See Comics on Parade, Sparkle, Sparkler Comics, Tip Top Comics & Tip Topper)
1939 - 1940
United Features Syndicate

Single Series 4 ('39)	32.00	95.00	225.00
Single Series 18 ('40) (#18 on inside, #2 on cover)			
	25.00	75.00	175.00

LI'L ABNER (Al Capp's) (See Oxydol-Dreft)
No. 61, Dec, 1947 - No. 97, Jan, 1955
Harvey Publ. No. 61-69 (2/49)/Toby Press No. 70 on

61(#1)-Wolverton-a	13.50	40.00	95.00
62-65	10.00	30.00	70.00
66,67,69,70	8.00	24.00	56.00
68-Full length Fearless Fosdick story	9.00	27.00	62.00
71-74,76,80	6.00	18.00	42.00
75,77-79,86,91-All with Kurtzman art; 91 reprints #77			
	7.00	21.00	50.00
81-85,87-90,92-94,96,97: 93-reprints #71	5.00	15.00	35.00
95-Full length Fearless Fosdick story	6.50	19.50	45.00
...& the Creatures from Drop-Outer Space-nn (Job Corps giveaway;			

Lightning Comics #4, © ACE

Linda Carter, Student Nurse #5, © MEG

Li'l Abner #75, © UFS

Little Al Of The Secret Service #3, © Z-D   Little Ambrose #1, © AP   Little Audrey #25, © HARV

	Good	Fine	N-Mint
LI'L ABNER (continued)			
36pgs., in color	5.50	16.50	38.00
...Joins the Navy (1950) (Toby Press Premium)			
	5.50	16.50	38.00
...by Al Capp Giveaway (Circa 1955, nd)	5.50	16.50	38.00
NOTE: *Powell a-61, 65.*			

LI'L ABNER
1951
Toby Press

1	8.00	24.00	56.00

LI'L ABNER'S DOGPATCH (See Al Capp's...)

LITTLE AL OF THE F.B.I.
No. 10, 1950 (no month) - No. 11, Apr-May, 1951
Ziff-Davis Publications (Saunders painted-c)

10(1950)	5.00	15.00	35.00
11(1951)	3.70	11.00	26.00

LITTLE AL OF THE SECRET SERVICE
No. 10, 7-8/51; No. 2, 9-10/51; No. 3, Wint., 1951
Ziff-Davis Publications (Saunders painted-c)

10(#1)-Spanking panel	7.00	21.00	50.00
2,3	3.70	11.00	26.00

LITTLE AMBROSE
September, 1958
Archie Publications

1-Bob Bolling-c	8.00	24.00	56.00

LITTLE ANGEL
No. 5, Sept, 1954; No. 6, Sept, 1955 - No. 16, Sept, 1959
Standard (Visual Editions)/Pines

5	2.65	8.00	18.00
6-16	1.30	4.00	9.00

LITTLE ANNIE ROONEY
1935 (48 pgs.; B&W dailies) (25 cents)
David McKay Publications

Book 1-Daily strip-r by Darrell McClure	9.00	27.00	62.00

LITTLE ANNIE ROONEY (See Treasury of Comics)
1938; Aug, 1948 - No. 3, Oct, 1948
David McKay/St. John/Standard

Feature Books 11 (McKay, 1938)	17.00	51.00	120.00
1 (St. John)	6.00	18.00	42.00
2,3	3.50	10.50	24.00

LITTLE ARCHIE (The Adventures of... #13-on) (Also see Archie Giant Series #527,534,538,545,549,556,566,570,583)
1956 - No. 180, 2/83 (Giants No. 3-84)
Archie Publications

1-(Scarce)	25.00	75.00	175.00
2	12.00	36.00	84.00
3-5	8.00	24.00	56.00
6-10	5.00	15.00	35.00
11-20	3.35	10.00	23.00
21-30	2.00	6.00	14.00
31-40: Little Pureheart begins #40, ends #42,44			
	1.00	3.00	7.00
41-60: 42-Intro. The Little Archies. 59-Little Sabrina begins			
	.50	1.50	3.00
61-80	.35	1.00	2.00
81-100		.50	1.00
101-180		.40	.80
...In Animal Land 1('57)	9.20	27.50	64.00
...In Animal Land 17(Winter, 1957-58)-19(Summer,'58)-Formerly Li'l Jinx	4.50	13.50	31.00

LITTLE ARCHIE COMICS DIGEST ANNUAL (...Mag. #5 on)
Oct., 1977 - Present (Digest-size)
Archie Publications

	Good	Fine	N-Mint
1(10/77)-Reprints	.35	1.00	2.00
2(4/78)-Adams-a		.60	1.20
3(11/78)-The Fly-r by S&K; Adams-a		.60	1.20
4(4/79) - 35('89): 28-Christmas-c, ½ Little Jinx		.60	1.20

LITTLE ARCHIE MYSTERY
Aug., 1963 - No. 2, Oct, 1963
Archie Publications

1	7.50	22.50	45.00
2	3.35	10.00	20.00

LITTLE ASPIRIN (See Wisco)
July, 1949 - No. 3, Dec, 1949 (52 pages)
Marvel Comics (CnPC)

1-Kurtzman-a, 4 pgs.	5.70	17.00	40.00
2-Kurtzman-a, 4 pgs.	3.00	9.00	21.00
3-No Kurtzman	1.50	4.50	10.00

LITTLE AUDREY (Also see Playful...)
April, 1948 - No. 24, May, 1952
St. John Publ.

1-1st app. Little Audrey	17.00	51.00	120.00
2	9.00	27.00	62.00
3-5	7.00	21.00	50.00
6-10	4.00	12.00	28.00
11-20	2.00	6.00	14.00
21-24	1.30	4.00	9.00

LITTLE AUDREY (See Harvey Hits #11,19)
No. 25, Aug, 1952 - No. 53, April, 1957
Harvey Publications

25 (Paramount Pictures Famous Star)	4.35	13.00	30.00
26-30: 26-28-Casper app.	2.00	6.00	14.00
31-40: 32-35-Casper app.	1.50	4.50	10.00
41-53	1.00	3.00	7.00
...Clubhouse 1 (9/61, 68 pg. Giant) w/reprints	3.00	9.00	18.00

LITTLE AUDREY (...Yearbook)
1950 (260 pages) (50 cents)
St. John Publishing Co.

Contains 8 complete 1949 comics rebound; Casper, Alice in Wonderland, Little Audrey, Abbott & Costello, Pinocchio, Moon Mullins, Three Stooges (from Jubilee), Little Annie Rooney app. (Rare)

	45.00	135.00	315.00

(Also see All Good & Treasury of Comics)
NOTE: *This book was remaindered St. John comics; many variations possible.*

LITTLE AUDREY & MELVIN (Audrey & ... No. 62)
May, 1962 - No. 61, Dec, 1973
Harvey Publications

1	5.35	16.00	32.00
2-5	2.75	8.00	16.00
6-10	1.70	5.00	10.00
11-20	1.00	3.00	6.00
21-40	.70	2.00	4.00
41-50,54-61	.50	1.50	3.00
51-53: All 52 pg. Giants	.70	2.00	4.00

LITTLE AUDREY TV FUNTIME
Sept, 1962 - No. 33, Oct, 1971 (#1-31: 68 pgs.; #32,33: 52 pgs.)
Harvey Publications

1-Richie Rich app.	3.35	10.00	20.00
2,3: Richie Rich app.	2.00	6.00	12.00
4,5: 5-25 & 35 cent-c exists	1.70	5.00	10.00
6-10	.85	2.50	5.00
11-20	.70	2.00	4.00
21-33	.50	1.50	3.00

LITTLE BAD WOLF (See 4-Color #403,473,564, Walt Disney's C&S #52, Walt Disney Showcase #21 & Wheaties)

LITTLE BEAVER
No. 211, Jan, 1949 - No. 870, Jan, 1958 (All painted-c)
Dell Publishing Co.

	Good	Fine	N-Mint
4-Color 211('49)-All Harman-a	3.00	9.00	21.00
4-Color 267,294,332(5/51)	2.00	6.00	14.00
3(10-12/51)-8(1-3/53)	1.70	5.00	12.00
4-Color 483(8-10/53),529	1.70	5.00	12.00
4-Color 612,660,695,744,817,870	1.30	4.00	9.00

LITTLE BIT
March, 1949 - No. 2, 1949
Jubilee/St. John Publishing Co.

	Good	Fine	N-Mint
1,2	1.50	4.50	10.00

LITTLE DOT (See Tastee-Freez Comics, Li'l Max, Humphrey, and Sad Sack)
Sept, 1953 - No. 164, April, 1976
Harvey Publications

	Good	Fine	N-Mint
1-Intro./1st app. Richie Rich & Little Lotta	45.00	135.00	320.00
2	21.00	64.00	150.00
3	15.00	45.00	105.00
4	11.00	32.50	75.00
5-Origin dots on Little Dot's Dress	12.50	37.50	85.00
6-Richie Rich, Little Lotta, & Little Dot all on cover; 1st Richie Rich cover featured	12.50	37.50	85.00
7-10	5.00	15.00	35.00
11-20	4.00	12.00	28.00
21-40	2.00	6.00	14.00
41-60	1.00	3.00	7.00
61-80	.70	2.00	4.00
81-100	.50	1.50	3.00
101-141	.35	1.00	2.00
142-145: All 52 pg. Giants	.40	1.20	2.40
146-164		.50	1.00
Shoe store giveaway 2	4.00	12.00	28.00

NOTE: Richie Rich & Little Lotta in all.

LITTLE DOT DOTLAND (Dot Dotland No. 62,63)
July, 1962 - No. 61, Dec, 1973
Harvey Publications

	Good	Fine	N-Mint
1-Richie Rich begins	4.00	12.00	28.00
2,3	2.00	6.00	14.00
4,5	1.50	4.50	10.00
6-10	1.15	3.50	8.00
11-20	.85	2.50	6.00
21-30	.50	1.50	3.00
31-50,55-61	.35	1.00	2.00
51-54: All 52 pg. Giants	.40	1.20	2.40

LITTLE DOT'S UNCLES & AUNTS (See Harvey Hits No. 4,13,24)
Oct, 1961; No. 2, Aug, 1962 - No. 52, April, 1974
Harvey Enterprises

	Good	Fine	N-Mint
1-Richie Rich begins; 68 pgs. begin	4.00	12.00	28.00
2,3	2.00	6.00	14.00
4,5	1.50	4.50	10.00
6-10	1.15	3.50	8.00
11-20	.85	2.50	6.00
21-37: Last 68 pg. issue	.50	1.50	3.00
38-52: All 52 pg. Giants	.35	1.00	2.00

LITTLE EVA
May, 1952 - No. 31, Nov, 1956
St. John Publishing Co.

	Good	Fine	N-Mint
1	5.70	17.00	40.00
2	2.65	8.00	18.00
3-5	2.00	6.00	14.00

	Good	Fine	N-Mint
6-10	1.30	4.00	9.00
11-31	1.15	3.50	8.00
3-D 1,2(10/53-11/53); 1-Infinity-c	12.00	36.00	84.00
I.W. Reprint #1-3,6-8	.30	.90	1.80
Super Reprint #10,12('63),14,16,18('64)	.30	.90	1.80

LITTLE FIR TREE, THE
1942 (8½x11'') (12 pgs. with cover)
W. T. Grant Co. (Christmas giveaway)
8 pg. Kelly-a reprint/Santa Claus Funnies not signed.
(One copy in M sold for $1750.00 in 1986)

LI'L GENIUS (Summer Fun No. 54) (See Blue Bird)
1954 - No. 52, 1/65; No. 53, 10/65; No. 54, 10/85 - No. 55, 1/86
Charlton Comics

	Good	Fine	N-Mint
1	2.65	8.00	18.00
2	1.30	4.00	9.00
3-15,19,20	1.00	3.00	7.00
16,17-(68 pgs.)	1.30	4.00	9.00
18-(100 pgs., 10/58)	2.00	6.00	14.00
21-35	.75	2.25	5.00
36-53	.50	1.50	3.00
54,55	.25	.75	1.50

LI'L GHOST
Feb, 1958 - No. 3, Mar, 1959
St. John Publishing Co./Fago No. 1 on

	Good	Fine	N-Mint
1(St. John)	2.30	7.00	16.00
1(Fago)	1.75	5.25	12.00
2,3	1.00	3.00	7.00

LITTLE GIANT COMICS
7/38 - No. 3, 10/38; No. 4, 2/39 (132 pgs.) (6¾x4½'')
Centaur Publications

	Good	Fine	N-Mint
1-B&W with color-c	23.00	70.00	160.00
2,3-B&W with color-c	19.00	57.00	132.00
4 (6-5/8x9-3/8'')(68 pgs., B&W inside)	20.00	60.00	140.00

NOTE: Gustavson a-1. Pinajian a-4. Bob Wood a-1

LITTLE GIANT DETECTIVE FUNNIES
Oct, 1938 - No. 4, Jan, 1939 (132 pgs., B&W) (6¾x4½'')
Centaur Publications

	Good	Fine	N-Mint
1-B&W with color-c	23.00	70.00	160.00
2,3	19.00	57.00	132.00
4(1/39)-B&W; color-c; 68 pgs., 6½x9½''; Eisner-r	20.00	60.00	140.00

LITTLE GIANT MOVIE FUNNIES
Aug, 1938 - No. 2, Oct, 1938 (132 pgs., B&W) (6¾x4½'')
Centaur Publications

	Good	Fine	N-Mint
1-Ed Wheelan's ''Minute Movies''-r	23.00	70.00	160.00
2-Ed Wheelan's ''Minute Movies''-r	18.00	54.00	125.00

LITTLE GROUCHO (...Grouchy No. 2) (See Tippy Terry)
Feb-Mar, 1955 - No. 2, June-July, 1955
Reston Publ. Co.

	Good	Fine	N-Mint
16, 1 (2-3/55)	2.00	6.00	14.00
2(6-7/55)	1.15	3.50	8.00

LITTLE HIAWATHA (See 4-Color #439,787,901,988 & Walt Disney's C&S #143)

LITTLE IKE
April, 1953 - No. 4, Oct, 1953
St. John Publishing Co.

	Good	Fine	N-Mint
1	3.00	9.00	21.00
2	1.50	4.50	10.00
3,4	1.15	3.50	8.00

LITTLE IODINE (See Giant Comic Album)
April, 1949 - No. 56, Apr-June, 1962 (52pgs., 1-4)

Little Dot #15, © HARV

Little Eva 3-D #1, © STJ

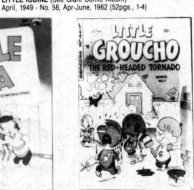

Little Groucho #1, © Reston Publ.

Little Iodine #3, © DELL

Little Lotta #1, © HARV

Little Max Comics #1, © HARV

	Good	Fine	N-Mint
LITTLE IODINE (continued)			
Dell Publishing Co.			
4-Color 224-By Jimmy Hatlo	3.75	11.25	26.00
4-Color 257	2.85	8.50	20.00
1(3-5/50)	2.85	8.50	20.00
2-5	1.75	5.25	12.00
6-10	1.15	3.50	8.00
11-20	1.00	3.00	7.00
21-30: 27-Xmas-c	.85	2.50	6.00
31-40	.55	1.65	4.00
41-56	.45	1.35	3.00

LITTLE JACK FROST
1951
Avon Periodicals

	Good	Fine	N-Mint
1	3.50	10.50	24.00

LI'L JINX (Formerly Ginger?) (Little Archie in Animal Land #17)
(Also see Pep Comics #62)
No. 1(#11), Nov, 1956 - No. 16, Sept, 1957
Archie Publications

11 (#1)	5.00	15.00	35.00
12-16	3.50	10.50	24.00

LI'L JINX (See Archie Giant Series Magazine No. 223)

LI'L JINX CHRISTMAS BAG (See Archie Giant Series Mag. No. 195,206,219)

LI'L JINX GIANT LAUGH-OUT
No. 33, Sept, 1971 - No. 43, Nov, 1973 (52 pgs.)
Archie Publications

33-43	.35	1.00	2.00

(See Archie Giant Series Mag. No. 176,185)

LITTLE JOE (See 4-Color #1, Popular & Super Comics)

LITTLE JOE
April, 1953
St. John Publishing Co.

1	1.30	4.00	9.00

LITTLE JOHNNY & THE TEDDY BEARS
1907 (10x14'') (32 pgs. in color)
Reilly & Britton Co.

By J. R. Bray	17.00	51.00	120.00

LI'L KIDS
8/70 - No. 2, 10/70; No. 3, 11/71 - No. 12, 6/73
Marvel Comics Group

1	.50	1.50	3.00
2-12: 10,11-Calvin app.	.25	.75	1.50

LITTLE KING (See 4-Color No. 494,597,677)

LITTLE KLINKER
Nov, 1960 (20 pgs.) (slick cover)
Little Klinker Ventures (Montgomery Ward Giveaway)

	.50	1.50	3.00

LITTLE LANA (Formerly Lana)
No. 8, Nov, 1949 - No. 9, Mar, 1950
Marvel Comics (MjMC)

8,9	1.70	5.00	12.00

LITTLE LENNY
June, 1949 - No. 3, Nov, 1949
Marvel Comics (CDS)

1	3.00	9.00	21.00
2,3	1.50	4.50	10.00

LITTLE LIZZIE
6/49 - No. 5, 4/50; 9/53 - No. 3, Jan, 1954
Marvel Comics (PrPl)/Atlas (OMC)

	Good	Fine	N-Mfnt
1	3.00	9.00	21.00
2-5	1.50	4.50	10.00
1 (1953)	2.30	7.00	16.00
2,3	1.15	3.50	8.00

LITTLE LOTTA (See Harvey Hits No. 10)
11/55 - No. 110, 11/73; No. 111, 9/74 - No. 121, 5/76
Harvey Publications

1-Richie Rich & Little Dot begin	17.00	51.00	120.00
2,3	8.00	24.00	56.00
4,5	4.35	13.00	30.00
6-10	3.00	9.00	21.00
11-20	1.70	5.00	12.00
21-40	1.15	3.50	8.00
41-60	.85	2.50	6.00
61-80	.50	1.50	3.00
81-99	.35	1.00	2.00
100-103: All 52 pg. Giants	.40	1.20	2.40
104-121	.25	.75	1.50

LITTLE LOTTA FOODLAND
9/63 - No. 14, 10/67; No. 15, 10/68 - No. 29, Oct, 1972
Harvey Publications

1: 68 pgs. begin, end #26	5.00	15.00	35.00
2,3	2.30	7.00	16.00
4,5	1.70	5.00	12.00
6-10	1.30	4.00	9.00
11-20	1.00	3.00	6.00
21-26	.85	2.50	5.00
27,28: Both 52 pgs.	.70	2.00	4.00
29: 36 pgs.	.50	1.50	3.00

LITTLE LULU (Formerly Marge's . . .)
No. 207, Sept., 1972 - No. 268, April, 1984
Gold Key 207-257/Whitman 258 on

207,209,220-Stanley-r. 207-1st app. Henrietta	.60	1.75	3.50
208,210-219: 208-1st app. Snobbly, Wilbur's brother			
	.49	1.25	2.50
221-240,242-249, 250(r/166), 251-254(r/206)	.25	.80	1.60
241,263,268-Stanley-r	.25	.80	1.60
255-262,264-267: 256 r/212		.50	1.00

LITTLE MARY MIXUP (See Comics On Parade & Single Series #10,26)

LITTLE MAX COMICS (Joe Palooka's Pal; see Joe Palooka)
Oct, 1949 - No. 73, Nov, 1961
Harvey Publications

1-Infinity-c; Little Dot begins	7.00	21.00	50.00
2-Little Dot app.	3.50	10.50	24.00
3-Little Dot app.	2.75	8.00	19.00
4-10: 5-Little Dot app., 1pg.	1.50	4.50	10.00
11-20	1.00	3.00	7.00
21-68,70-72: 23-Little Dot app. 38-r/20	.75	2.25	5.00
69,73-Richie Rich app.	.85	2.50	6.00

LI'L MENACE
Dec, 1958 - No. 3, May, 1959
Fago Magazine Co.

1-Peter Rabbit app.	2.00	6.00	14.00
2-Peter Rabbit (Vincent Fago's)	1.30	4.00	9.00
3	1.00	3.00	7.00

LITTLE MISS MUFFET
Dec, 1948 - No. 13, March, 1949
Best Books (Standard Comics)/King Features Synd.

11-Strip reprints; Fanny Cory-a	3.70	11.00	26.00
12,13-Strip reprints; Fanny Cory-a	2.00	6.00	14.00

LITTLE MISS SUNBEAM COMICS
June-July, 1950 - No. 4, Dec-Jan, 1950-51
Magazine Enterprises/Quality Bakers of America

	Good	Fine	N-Mint
1	5.00	15.00	35.00
2	2.65	8.00	18.00
3,4	2.35	7.00	16.00
. . .Advs. In Space ('55)	1.50	4.50	10.00
Bread Giveaway 1-4(Quality Bakers, 1949-50)-14 pgs. each			
	1.50	4.50	10.00
Bread Giveaway (1957,61; 16pgs, reg. size)	1.15	3.50	8.00

LITTLE MONSTERS, THE (See March of Comics No. 423 & Three Stooges No. 17)
Nov, 1964 - No. 44, Feb, 1978
Gold Key

	Good	Fine	N-Mint
1	1.50	4.50	10.00
2	.85	2.50	5.00
3-10	.70	2.00	4.00
11-20	.35	1.00	2.00
21-44: 20,34-39,43-reprints		.40	.80

LITTLE NEMO (See Cocomalt, Future Comics, Help, Jest, Kayo, Punch, Red Seal, & Superworld; most by Winsor McCay Jr., son of famous artist) (Other McCay books: see Little Sammy Sneeze & Dreams of the Rarebit Fiend)

LITTLE NEMO (. . . in Slumberland)
1906, 1909 (Sunday strip reprints in color) (cardboard covers)
Doffield & Co.(1906)/Cupples & Leon Co.(1909)

	Good	Fine	N-Mint
1906-11x16½'' in color by Winsor McCay; 30 pgs. (Very Rare)	120.00	360.00	850.00
1909-10x14'' in color by Winsor McCay (Very Rare)	100.00	300.00	700.00

LITTLE NEMO (. . . in Slumberland)
1945 (28 pgs.; 11x7¼''; B&W)
McCay Features/Nostalgia Press('69)

	Good	Fine	N-Mint
1905 & 1911 reprints by Winsor McCay	4.00	12.00	28.00
1969-70 (exact reprint)	1.50	4.00	8.00

LITTLE NEMO IN SLUMBERLAND 3-D
Jan, 1987 ($2.50)
Blackthorne Publishing

	Good	Fine	N-Mint
1-Winsor McCay-r in 3-D	.40	1.25	2.50

LITTLE ORPHAN ANNIE (See Annie, Feature Books #7, Marvel Super Special, Merry Christmas. . . ., Popular Comics, Super Book #7, 11, 23 & Super Comics)

LITTLE ORPHAN ANNIE (See Treasury Box of . . .)
1926 - 1934 (Daily strip reprints) (7x8¾'') (B&W)
Cupples & Leon Co.

(Hardcover Editions, 100 pages)

	Good	Fine	N-Mint
1(1926)-Little Orphan Annie	15.00	45.00	105.00
2('27)-In the Circus	11.50	34.00	80.00
3('28)-The Haunted House	11.50	34.00	80.00
4('29)-Bucking the World	11.50	34.00	80.00
5('30)-Never Say Die	11.50	34.00	80.00
6('31)-Shipwrecked	11.50	34.00	80.00
7('32)-A Willing Helper	8.50	25.50	60.00
8('33)-In Cosmic City	8.50	25.50	60.00
9('34)-Uncle Dan	11.50	34.00	80.00

NOTE: Hardcovers with dust jackets are worth 20-50 percent more; the earlier the book, the higher the percentage. Each book reprints dailies from the previous year.

LITTLE ORPHAN ANNIE
No. 7, 1937 - No. 3, Sept-Nov, 1948
David McKay Publ./Dell Publishing Co.

	Good	Fine	N-Mint
Feature Books(McKay) 7-('37) (Rare)	75.00	225.00	525.00
4-Color 12(1941)	30.00	90.00	210.00
4-Color 18('43)-Flag-c	23.00	70.00	160.00
4-Color 52('44)	17.00	50.00	120.00

	Good	Fine	N-Mint
4-Color 76('45)	15.00	45.00	105.00
4-Color 107('46)	12.00	36.00	84.00
4-Color 152('47)	9.00	27.00	62.00
4-Color 206(12/48)	5.70	17.00	40.00
1(3-5/48)	12.00	36.00	84.00
2,3	7.00	21.00	50.00
Junior Commandos Giveaway(same cover as 4-Color #18, K.K. Publ.) (Big Shoe Store); same back cover as '47 Popped Wheat giveaway; 16 pgs; flag-c	14.50	43.50	100.00
Popped Wheat Giveaway('47)-16 pgs. full color; '40 reprints	.85	2.50	6.00
Quaker Sparkies Giveaway(1940)	6.50	19.50	45.00
Quaker Sparkies Giveaway(1941, Full color-20 pgs.); ''LOA and the Rescue,'' ''LOA and the Kidnappers,''	5.70	17.00	40.00
Quaker Sparkies Giveaway(1942, Full color-20 pgs..); ''LOA and Mr. Grudge'' and ''LOA and the Great Am''	4.30	13.00	30.00

LI'L PALS
Sept, 1972 - No. 5, May, 1973
Marvel Comics Group

	Good	Fine	N-Mint
1-5		.40	.80

LI'L PAN
No. 6, Dec-Jan, 1947 - No. 8, Apr-May, 1947
Fox Features Syndicate

	Good	Fine	N-Mint
6	2.65	8.00	18.00
7,8	1.70	5.00	12.00

LITTLE PEOPLE (See 4-Color #485, 573, 633, 692, 753, 809, 868, 908, 959, 1024, 1062)

LITTLE RASCALS (See 4-Color #674, 778, 825, 883, 936, 974, 1030, 1079, 1137, 1174, 1224, 1297)

LI'L RASCAL TWINS (Formerly Nature Boy)
1957 - No. 18, Jan, 1960
Charlton Comics

	Good	Fine	N-Mint
6-Li'l Genius & Tomboy in all	1.70	5.00	12.00
7-18	.85	2.50	6.00

LITTLE ROQUEFORT COMICS
June, 1952 - No. 9, Oct, 1953; No. 10, Summer, 1958
St. John Publishing Co./Pines No. 10

	Good	Fine	N-Mint
1	3.00	9.00	21.00
2	1.50	4.50	10.00
3-10	1.15	3.50	8.00

LITTLE SAD SACK (See Harvey Hits No. 73,76,79,81,83)
Oct, 1964 - No. 19, Nov, 1967
Harvey Publications

	Good	Fine	N-Mint
1-Richie Rich app. cover only	1.35	4.00	9.00
2-19	.35	1.00	2.00

LITTLE SAMMY SNEEZE
1905 (28 pgs. in color; 11x16½'')
New York Herald Co.

	Good	Fine	N-Mint
By Winsor McCay (Rare)	150.00	450.00	950.00

NOTE: Rarely found in fine to mint condition.

LITTLE SCOUTS
No. 321, Mar, 1951 - No. 587, Oct, 1954
Dell Publishing Co.

	Good	Fine	N-Mint
4-Color #321 ('51)	1.30	4.00	9.00
2(10-12/51) - 6(10-12/52)	.85	2.50	6.00
4-Color #462,506,550,587	.85	2.50	6.00

LITTLE SHOP OF HORRORS SPECIAL
Feb, 1987 ($2.00, 68 pgs.) (Movie adaptation)
DC Comics

	Good	Fine	N-Mint
1-Colan-a	.35	1.00	2.00

Little Nemo In Slumberland 3-D #1, © Winsor McCay

Little Orphan Annie #2 (1948), © News Synd.

Little Scouts #4, © DELL

Lone Eagle #1, © AJAX — The Lone Ranger (1939 Ice Cream), © Lone Ranger — The Lone Ranger #5, © Lone Ranger

LITTLE SPUNKY
No date (1963?) (10 cents)
I. W. Enterprises

	Good	Fine	N-Mint
1-Reprint	.30	.80	1.60

LITTLE STOOGES, THE (The Three Stooges' Sons)
Sept, 1972 - No. 7, Mar, 1974
Gold Key

1-Norman Maurer cover/stories in all	.70	2.00	4.00
2-7	.35	1.00	2.00

LITTLEST OUTLAW (See 4-Color #609)

LITTLEST SNOWMAN, THE
No. 755, 12/56; No. 864, 12/57; 12-2/1963-64
Dell Publishing Co.

4-Color #755,864, 1(1964)	2.15	7.00	16.00

LI'L TOMBOY (Formerly Fawcett's Funny Animals)
V14No.92, 10/56; No. 93, 3/57 - No. 107, 2/60
Charlton Comics

V14#92	1.75	5.25	12.00
93-107: 97-Atomic Bunny app.	1.00	3.00	7.00

LI'L WILLIE COMICS (Formerly & becomes Willie Comics #22 on)
July, 1949 - No. 21, Sept, 1949
Marvel Comics (MgPC)

20,21: 20-Little Aspirin app.	1.60	4.80	11.00

LIVE IT UP
1973, 1976 (39-49 cents)
Spire Christian Comics (Fleming H. Revell Co.)

nn		.40	.80

LIVING BIBLE, THE
Fall, 1945 - No. 3, Spring, 1946
Living Bible Corp.

1-Life of Paul	8.00	24.00	56.00
2-Joseph & His Brethren	5.00	15.00	35.00
3-Chaplains At War (classic-c)	11.00	33.00	75.00

NOTE: All have L. B. Cole -c.

LOBO
Dec, 1965 - No. 2, Oct, 1966
Dell Publishing Co.

1,2	.85	2.50	6.00

LOCKE!
1987 - No. 3? ($1.25, color)
Blackthorne Publishing

1-3		.60	1.25

LOCO (Magazine) (Satire)
Aug, 1958 - V1No.3, Jan, 1959
Satire Publications

V1#1-Chic Stone-a	1.15	3.50	8.00
V1#2,3-Severin-a, 2 pgs. Davis; 3-Heath-a	.85	2.50	5.00

LOGAN'S RUN
Jan, 1977 - No. 7, July, 1977
Marvel Comics Group

1		.40	.80
2-7		.25	.50

NOTE: *Austin* a-6i. *Gulacy* c-6. *Kane* c-7p. *Perez* a-1-5p; c-1-5p. *Sutton* a-6p, 7p.

LOIS LANE (Also see Superman's Girlfriend . . .)
Aug, 1986 - No. 2, Sept, 1986 (52 pgs.)
DC Comics

1,2-Morrow c/a	.25	.75	1.50

LOLLY AND PEPPER
No. 832, Sept, 1957 - July, 1962
Dell Publishing Co.

	Good	Fine	N-Mint
4-Color 832	1.70	5.00	12.00
4-Color 940,978,1086,1206	1.30	4.00	9.00
01-459-207	1.30	4.00	9.00

LOMAX (See Police Action)

LONE EAGLE (The Flame No. 5 on)
Apr-May, 1954 - No. 4, Oct-Nov, 1954
Ajax/Farrell Publications

1	3.70	11.00	26.00
2-4	2.15	6.50	15.00

LONELY HEART (Formerly Dear Lonely Hearts; Dear Heart #15 on)
No. 9, March, 1955 - No. 14, Feb, 1956
Ajax/Farrell Publ. (Excellent Publ.)

9-Kamenesque-a; (Last precode)	3.00	9.00	21.00
10-14	1.50	4.50	10.00

LONE RANGER, THE (See Aurora, Dell Giants, Feature Books #21, 24(McKay), Future Comics, King Comics, Magic Comics & March of Comics #165, 174, 193, 208, 225, 238, 310, 322, 338, 350)

LONE RANGER, THE
No. 3, 1939 - No. 167, Feb, 1947
Dell Publishing Co.

Large Feat. Comic 3('39)-Heigh-Yo Silver; text with ill. by Robert Weisman	40.00	120.00	280.00
Large Feat. Comic 7('39)-Ill. by Henry Valleley; Hi-Yo Silver the Lone Ranger to the Rescue	50.00	150.00	350.00
4-Color 82('45)	27.00	81.00	190.00
4-Color 98('45),118('46)	22.00	65.00	154.00
4-Color 125('46),136('47)	16.00	48.00	110.00
4-Color 151,167('47)	13.00	40.00	90.00

LONE RANGER COMICS, THE (10 cents)
1939(inside) (shows 1938 on-c) (68 pgs. in color; regular size)
Lone Ranger, Inc. (Ice cream mail order)

(Scarce)-not by Valleley	50.00	150.00	350.00

LONE RANGER, THE (Movie, radio & TV; Clayton Moore starred as L. Ranger in the movies; No. 1-37: strip reprints)(See Dell Giants)
Jan-Feb, 1948 - No. 145, May-July, 1962
Dell Publishing Co.

1 (36pgs.)-The L. Ranger, his horse Silver, companion Tonto & his horse Scout begin	45.00	135.00	315.00
2 (52pgs. begin, end #41)	22.00	65.00	154.00
3-5	19.00	57.00	132.00
6,7,9,10	16.00	48.00	110.00
8-Origin retold; Indian back-c begin, end #35	20.00	60.00	140.00
11-20: 11-''Young Hawk'' Indian boy serial begins, ends #145	11.00	32.00	75.00
21,22,24-31: 51-Reprint. 31-1st Mask logo	8.50	25.55	60.00
23-Origin retold	11.50	34.00	80.00
32-37: 32-Painted-c begin. 36-Animal photo back-c begin, end #49. 37-Last newspaper-r issue; new outfit	6.50	19.50	45.00
38-41 (All 52pgs.)	4.65	14.00	32.00
42-50 (36pgs.)	3.50	10.50	24.00
51-74 (52pgs.): 71-Blank inside-c	3.50	10.50	24.00
75-99: 76-Flag-c. 79-X-mas-c	2.65	8.00	18.00
100	4.00	12.00	28.00
101-111: Last painted-c	2.30	7.00	16.00
112-Clayton Moore photo-c begin, end #145	11.50	34.00	80.00
113-117	6.50	19.50	45.00
118-Origin Lone Ranger, Tonto, & Silver retold; Special anniversary issue	11.00	32.00	75.00

	Good	Fine	N-Mint
THE LONE RANGER (continued)			
119-145: 139-Last issue by Fran Striker	5.00	15.00	35.00
Cheerios Giveaways (1954, 16 pgs., 2½x7'', soft-c) #1-"The Lone Ranger, His Mask & How He Met Tonto." #2-"The Lone Ranger & the Story of Silver" each....	5.00	15.00	35.00
Doll Giveaways (Gabriel Ind.)(1973, 3¼x5'')-"The Story of The L.R." & The Carson City Bank Robbery."	1.00	3.00	7.00
How the L. R. Captured Silver Book(1936)-Silvercup Bread giveaway	30.00	90.00	210.00
...In Milk for Big Mike(1955, Dairy Association giveaway), soft-c 5x7¼'', 16 pgs.	8.50	25.50	60.00
Merita Bread giveaway('54; 16 pgs.; 5x7¼'')-"How to Be a L. R. Health & Safety Scout"	8.50	25.50	60.00

NOTE: **Hank Hartman** painted c(signed)-65, 66, 70, 75, 82; unsigned-64?, 67-69?, 71, 72, 73?, 74?, 76-78, 80, 81, 83-91, 92?, 93-111. **Ernest Nordli** painted c(signed)-42, 50, 52, 53, 56, 59, 60; unsigned-39-41, 44-49, 51, 54, 55, 57, 58, 61-63?

LONE RANGER, THE
9/64 - No. 16, 12/69; No. 17, 11/72; No. 18, 9/74 - No. 28, 3/77
Gold Key (Reprints #13-20)

	Good	Fine	N-Mint
1-Retells origin	2.45	7.30	17.00
2	1.50	4.50	10.00
3-10: Small Bear-r in #6-10	1.00	3.00	7.00
11-17: Small Bear-r in #11,12	.85	2.50	6.00
18-28	.55	1.65	4.00
Golden West 1(30029-610)-Giant, 10/66-r/most Golden West #3-including Clayton Moore photo front/back-c	4.35	13.00	30.00

LONE RANGER'S COMPANION TONTO, THE (TV)
No. 312, Jan, 1951 - No. 33, Nov-Jan/58-59 (All painted-c)
Dell Publishing Co.

	Good	Fine	N-Mint
4-Color 312(1951)	7.00	21.00	50.00
2(8-10/51),3: (#2 titled 'Tonto')	3.50	10.50	24.00
4-10	2.00	6.00	14.00
11-20	1.75	5.25	12.00
21-33	1.30	4.00	9.00

NOTE: **Ernest Nordli** painted c(signed)-2, 7; unsigned-3-6, 8-11, 12?, 13, 14, 18?, 22-24? See Aurora Comic Booklets.

LONE RANGER'S FAMOUS HORSE HI-YO SILVER, THE (TV)
No. 369, Jan, 1952 - No. 36, Oct-Dec, 1960 (All painted-c)
Dell Publishing Co.

	Good	Fine	N-Mint
4-Color 369-Silver's origin as told by The L.R.	5.00	15.00	35.00
4-Color 392(4/52)	2.65	8.00	18.00
3(7-9/52)-10(4-6/52)	1.50	4.50	10.00
11-36	1.15	3.50	8.00

LONE RIDER (Also see The Rider)
April, 1951 - No. 26, July, 1955 (36pgs., 3-on)
Superior Comics(Farrell Publications)

	Good	Fine	N-Mint
1 (52pgs.)-The Lone Rider & his horse Lightnin' begin; Kamensh-a begins	6.50	19.50	45.00
2 (52pgs.)-The Golden Arrow begins (origin)	3.70	11.00	26.00
3-6: 6-Last Golden Arrow	2.85	8.50	20.00
7-G. Arrow becomes Swift Arrow; origin of his shield	3.50	10.50	24.00
8-Origin Swift Arrow	4.30	13.00	30.00
9,10	2.15	6.50	15.00
11-14	1.70	5.00	12.00
15-Golden Arrow origin-r from #2, changing name to Swift Arrow	2.15	6.50	15.00
16-20,22-26: 23-Apache Kid app.	1.50	4.50	10.00
21-3-D effect-c	5.50	16.50	38.00

LONE WOLF AND CUB
May, 1987 - Present ($1.95-$2.50, B&W, deluxe size)
First Comics

	Good	Fine	N-Mint
1	1.85	5.50	11.00
1-2nd print, 3rd print	.35	1.00	2.00

	Good	Fine	N-Mint
2	1.10	3.25	6.50
2-2nd print	.35	1.00	2.00
3	.70	2.00	4.00
4-12: 6-72 pg. origin issue	.45	1.30	2.60
13-18	.40	1.25	2.50
Deluxe Edition ($19.95; B&W)	3.35	10.00	19.95

NOTE: **Miller** c-1-12; intro-1-12.

LONG BOW (...Indian Boy)(See Indians & Jumbo Comics #141)
1951 - No. 9, Wint, 1952/53
Fiction House Magazines (Real Adventures Publ.)

	Good	Fine	N-Mint
1	6.00	18.00	42.00
2	3.50	10.50	24.00
3-9	2.30	7.00	16.00

LONG JOHN SILVER & THE PIRATES (Formerly Terry & the Pirates)
No. 30, Aug, 1956 - No. 32, March, 1957 (TV)
Charlton Comics

	Good	Fine	N-Mint
30-32: Whitman-c	2.65	8.00	18.00

LONGSHOT
Sept, 1985 - No. 6, Feb, 1986 (Limited-series)
Marvel Comics Group

	Good	Fine	N-Mint
1-Arthur Adams-c/a in all	2.15	6.50	13.00
2	1.50	4.50	9.00
3-5	1.25	3.75	7.50
6-Double size	1.70	5.00	10.00

LOONEY TUNES (2nd Series)
April, 1975 - No. 47, July, 1984
Gold Key/Whitman

	Good	Fine	N-Mint
1		.50	1.00
2-47: Reprints #1-4,16; 38-46(⅓r)		.30	.60

LOONEY TUNES AND MERRIE MELODIES COMICS ("Looney Tunes" #166 (8/55) on)
1941 - No. 246, July-Sept, 1962
Dell Publishing Co.

	Good	Fine	N-Mint
1-Porky Pig, Bugs Bunny, Daffy Duck, Elmer Fudd, Mary Jane & Sniffles, Pat, Patsy and Pete begin (1st comic book app.). Bugs Bunny story by Win Smith (early Mickey Mouse artist)	110.00	330.00	750.00
2 (11/41)	50.00	150.00	350.00
3-Kandi the Cave Kid begins by Walt Kelly; also in #4-6,8,11,15	45.00	135.00	315.00
4-Kelly-a	40.00	120.00	280.00
5-Bugs Bunny The Super Rabbit app. (1st funny animal super hero?); Kelly-a	70.00	210.00	490.00
6,8-Kelly-a	22.00	65.00	154.00
7,9,10: 9-Painted-c. 10-Flag-c	17.00	51.00	120.00
11,15-Kelly-a; 15-X-Mas-c	17.00	51.00	120.00
12-14,16-19	14.00	42.00	100.00
20-25: Pat, Patsy & Pete by Kelly in all	14.00	42.00	100.00
26-30	10.00	30.00	70.00
31-40	7.00	21.00	50.00
41-50	5.00	15.00	35.00
51-60	3.50	10.50	24.00
61-80	2.15	7.00	16.00
81-99: 87-X-Mas-c	2.00	6.00	14.00
100	2.15	7.00	16.00
101-120	1.60	4.80	11.00
121-150	1.30	4.00	9.00
151-200	1.00	3.00	7.00
201-246	.70	2.00	5.00

LOONY SPORTS (Magazine)
Spring, 1975 (68 pages)
3-Strikes Publishing Co.

Lone Rider #7, © SUPR

Lone Wolf And Cub #1 (1st print), © First Comics

Looney Tunes #3 (1st series), © L. Schlesinger

Lorna The Jungle Girl #8, © MEG

Lost Worlds #6, © STD

Love Confessions #1, © QUA

LOONY SPORTS (continued)	Good	Fine	N-Mint
1-Sports satire	.30	.80	1.60

LOOY DOT DOPE (See Single Series No. 13)

LORD JIM (See Movie Comics)

LORDS OF THE ULTRA-REALM
June, 1986 - No. 6, Nov, 1986 (mini-series)
DC Comics

1	.50	1.50	3.00
2-6	.30	.85	1.70
Special 1(12/87, $2.25)	.40	1.15	2.30

LORNA THE JUNGLE GIRL (. . .Jungle Queen #1-5)
July, 1953 - No. 26, Aug, 1957
Atlas Comics (NPI 1/OMC 2-11/NPI 12-26)

1-Origin	10.00	30.00	70.00
2-Intro. & 1st app. Greg Knight	5.50	16.50	38.00
3-5	4.65	14.00	32.00
6-11: 11-Last pre-code (1/55)	3.50	10.50	24.00
12-17,19-26	2.65	8.00	18.00
18-Williamson/Colleta-c	4.00	12.00	28.00

NOTE: *Everett* c-21, 23-26. *Heath* c-6, 7. *Maneely* c-12, 15. *Romita* a-20, 22. *Shores* a-16; c-13, 16. *Tuska* a-6.

LOSERS SPECIAL (Also see G.I.Combat #138)
Sept, 1985 ($1.25 cover) (One Shot)(See Our Fighting Forces #123)
DC Comics

1-Capt. Storm, Gunner & Sarge; Crisis x-over			
		.65	1.30

LOST IN SPACE (Space Family Robinson . . ., on Space Station One)(Formerly Space Family Robinson, see Gold Key Champion)
No. 37, 10/73 - No. 54, 11/78; No. 55, 3/81 - No. 59, 5/82
Gold Key

37-48	.35	1.00	2.00
49-59: Reprints-#49,50,55-59		.50	1.00

NOTE: *Spiegle* a-37-59. All have painted-c.

LOST PLANET
May, 1987 - No. 5, Mar, 1988 (mini-series, $1.75-$2.00, color)
Eclipse Comics

1-5: Bo Hampton c/a	.30	.85	1.70

LOST WORLD, THE (See 4-Color #1145)

LOST WORLDS
No. 5, Oct, 1952 - No. 6, Dec, 1952
Standard Comics

5-"Alice in Terrorland" by Toth; J. Katz-a	13.00	40.00	90.00
6-Toth-a	9.50	28.50	65.00

LOTS 'O' FUN COMICS
1940's? (5 cents) (heavy stock; blue covers)
Robert Allen Co.

nn-Contents can vary; Felix, Planet Comics known; contents would determine value. Similar to Up-To-Date Comics. Remainders - re-packaged.

LOU GEHRIG (See The Pride of the Yankees)

LOVE ADVENTURES (Actual Confessions #13)
10/49; No. 2, 1/50; No. 3, 2/51 - No. 12, 8/52
Marvel (IPS)/Atlas Comics (MPI)

1-Photo-c	3.00	9.00	21.00
2-Powell-a; Tyrone Power, Gene Tierney photo-c			
	3.00	9.00	21.00
3-8,10-12: 8-Robinson-a	1.50	4.50	10.00
9-Everett-a	2.00	6.00	14.00

LOVE AND MARRIAGE
March, 1952 - No. 16, Sept, 1954
Superior Comics Ltd.

	Good	Fine	N-Mint
1	4.00	12.00	28.00
2	2.00	6.00	14.00
3-10	1.50	4.50	10.00
11-16	1.15	3.50	8.00
I.W. Reprint #1,2,8,11,14	.30	.80	1.60
Super Reprint #10('63),15,17('64)	.30	.80	1.60

NOTE: All issues have Kamenish art.

LOVE AND ROCKETS
July, 1982 - Present (Adults only)
Fantagraphics Books

1-B&W-c ($2.95; small size, publ. by Hernandez Bros.)(800 printed)			
	25.00	75.00	150.00
1 (Fall, '82; 2nd printing; color-c)	14.00	42.50	85.00
1-2nd printing	.50	1.50	3.00
2	4.15	12.50	25.00
3-5	2.50	7.50	15.00
6-10	1.15	3.50	7.00
11-15	.50	1.50	3.00
16-26	.35	1.00	2.00

LOVE AND ROMANCE
Sept, 1971 - No. 24, Sept, 1975
Charlton Comics

1		.30	.60
2-24		.15	.30

LOVE AT FIRST SIGHT
Oct, 1949 - No. 42, Aug, 1956 (Photo-c 21-42)
Ace Magazines (RAR Publ. Co./Periodical House)

1-Painted-c	4.00	12.00	28.00
2-Painted-c	2.00	6.00	14.00
3-10: 4-Painted-c	1.50	4.50	10.00
11-20	1.15	3.50	8.00
21-33: 33-Last pre-code	1.00	3.00	7.00
34-42	.85	2.50	6.00

LOVE BUG, THE (See Movie Comics)

LOVE CLASSICS
Nov, 1949 - No. 2, Feb, 1950 (Photo-c)
A Lover's Magazine/Marvel Comics

1,2: 2-Virginia Mayo photo-c; 30 pg. story 'I Was a Small Town Flirt'	4.00	12.00	28.00

LOVE CONFESSIONS
Oct, 1949 - No. 54, Dec, 1956 (Photo-c 6,11-18,21)
Quality Comics Group

1-Ward c/a, 9 pgs; Gustavson-a	14.00	42.00	100.00
2-Gustavson-a	5.00	15.00	35.00
3	3.50	10.50	24.00
4-Crandall-a	4.65	14.00	32.00
5-Ward-a, 7 pgs.	5.50	16.50	38.00
6,7,9	1.70	5.00	12.00
8-Ward-a	4.65	14.00	32.00
10-Ward-a(2)	4.65	14.00	32.00
11-13,15,16,18	1.70	5.00	12.00
14,17,19,22-Ward-a; 17-Faith Domergue photo-c			
	3.85	11.50	27.00
20-Baker-a, Ward-a(2)	4.65	14.00	32.00
21,23-28,30-38,40-42: Last precode, 4/55	1.15	3.50	8.00
29-Ward-a	3.65	11.00	25.00
39-Matt Baker-a	1.70	5.00	12.00
43,44,46-48,50-54: 47-Ward-c?	1.00	3.00	7.00
45-Ward-a	2.15	6.50	15.00
49-Baker c/a	2.65	8.00	18.00

LOVE DIARY
July, 1949 - No. 48, Oct, 1955 (Photo-c 1-24,27,29) (52 pgs. #1-11?)

LOVE DIARY (continued)
Our Publishing Co./Toytown/Patches

	Good	Fine	N-Mint
1-Krigstein-a	6.00	18.00	42.00
2,3-Krigstein & Mort Leav-a in each	4.00	12.00	28.00
4-8	1.70	5.00	12.00
9,10-Everett-a	2.00	6.00	14.00
11-20	1.30	4.00	9.00
21-30,32-48: 47-Last precode (12/54)	1.00	3.00	7.00
31-J. Buscema headlights-c	1.15	3.50	8.00

LOVE DIARY (Diary Loves #2 on)
September, 1949
Quality Comics Group

	Good	Fine	N-Mint
1-Ward-c, 9 pgs.	11.50	34.50	80.00

LOVE DIARY
July, 1958 - No. 102, Dec, 1976
Charlton Comics

	Good	Fine	N-Mint
1	2.00	6.00	14.00
2	1.00	3.00	7.00
3-5,7-10	.55	1.65	4.00
6-Torres-a	1.15	3.50	8.00
11-20: 16,20-Leav-a	.35	1.00	2.50
21-40		.50	1.00
41-102: 45-Leav-a		.20	.40
NOTE: Photo c-10, 20.

LOVE DOCTOR (See Dr. Anthony King...)

LOVE DRAMAS (True Secrets No. 3 on?)
Oct, 1949 - No. 2, Jan, 1950
Marvel Comics (IPS)

	Good	Fine	N-Mint
1-Jack Kamen-a; photo-c	5.50	16.50	38.00
2	3.00	9.00	21.00

LOVE EXPERIENCES (Challenge of the Unknown No. 6)
10/49 - No. 5, 6/50; No. 6, 4/51 - No. 38, 6/56
Ace Periodicals (A.A. Wyn/Periodical House)

	Good	Fine	N-Mint
1-Painted-c	3.50	10.50	24.00
2	1.70	5.00	12.00
3-5: 5-Painted-c	1.30	4.00	9.00
6-10	1.00	3.00	7.00
11-30: 30-Last pre-code (2/55)	.85	2.50	6.00
31-38: 38-Indicia date-6/56; c-date-8/56	.75	2.25	5.00
NOTE: Anne Brewster a-15. Photo c-4,15-35,38.

LOVE JOURNAL
No. 10, Oct, 1951 - No. 25, July, 1954
Our Publishing Co.

	Good	Fine	N-Mint
10	2.65	8.00	18.00
11-25	1.30	4.00	9.00

LOVELAND
Nov, 1949 - No. 2, Feb, 1950
Mutual Mag./Eye Publ. (Marvel)

	Good	Fine	N-Mint
1,2-Photo-c	2.65	8.00	18.00

LOVE LESSONS
Oct, 1949 - No. 5, June, 1950
Harvey Comics/Key Publ. No. 5

	Good	Fine	N-Mint
1-Metallic silver-c printed over the cancelled covers of Love Letters #1; indicia title is 'Love Letters'	3.50	10.50	24.00
2-Powell-a	1.50	4.50	10.00
3-5: 3-Photo-c	1.15	3.50	8.00

LOVE LETTERS (10/49, Harvey; advertised but never published; covers were printed before cancellation and were used as the cover to Love Lessions #1)

LOVE LETTERS (Love Secrets No. 32 on)
11/49 - No. 6, 9/50; No. 7, 3/51 - No. 31, 6/53; No. 32, 2/54 - No. 51, Dec, 1956

Quality Comics Group

	Good	Fine	N-Mint
1-Ward-c, Gustavson-a	9.00	27.00	62.00
2-Ward-c, Gustavson-a	8.50	25.50	60.00
3-Gustavson-a	5.00	15.00	35.00
4-Ward-a, 9 pgs.	8.50	25.50	60.00
5-8,10	1.70	5.00	12.00
9-One pg. Ward-''Be Popular with the Opposite Sex''; Robert Mitchum photo-c	3.50	10.50	24.00
11-Ward-r/Broadway Romances #2 & retitled	3.50	10.50	24.00
12-15,18-20	1.30	4.00	9.00
16,17-Ward-a; 16-Anthony Quinn photo-c. 17-Jane Russell photo-c	4.60	14.00	32.00
21-29	1.15	3.50	8.00
30,31(6/53)-Ward-a	2.65	8.00	18.00
32(2/54) - 39: Last precode, 4/55	1.00	3.00	7.00
40-48	.70	2.00	5.00
49,50-Baker-a	2.65	8.00	18.00
51-Baker-c	2.15	6.50	15.00
NOTE: Photo-c on most 3-28.

LOVE LIFE
Nov, 1951
P. L. Publishing Co.

	Good	Fine	N-Mint
1	2.65	8.00	18.00

LOVELORN (Confessions of the Lovelorn #52 on)
Aug-Sept, 1949 - No. 51, July, 1954 (No. 1-26, 52 pgs.)
American Comics Group (Michel Publ./Regis Publ.)

	Good	Fine	N-Mint
1	3.00	9.00	21.00
2	1.50	4.50	10.00
3-10	1.30	4.00	9.00
11-20,22-48: 18-Drucker-a, 2pgs.	.85	2.50	6.00
21-Prostitution story	1.65	5.00	11.50
49-51-Has 3-D effect	6.00	18.00	42.00

LOVE MEMORIES
1949 (no month) - No. 4, July, 1950 (Photo-c all)
Fawcett Publications

	Good	Fine	N-Mint
1	3.50	10.50	24.00
2-4	1.70	5.00	12.00

LOVE MYSTERY
June, 1950 - No. 3, Oct, 1950 (All photo-c)
Fawcett Publications

	Good	Fine	N-Mint
1-George Evans-a	8.00	24.00	56.00
2,3-Evans-a. 3-Powell-a	5.50	16.50	38.00

LOVE PROBLEMS (See Fox Giants)

LOVE PROBLEMS AND ADVICE ILLUSTRATED (Becomes Romance Stories of True Love No. 45 on)
June, 1949 - No. 6, Apr, 1950; No. 7, Jan, 1951 - No. 44, Mar, 1957
McCombs/Harvey Publ./Home Comics

	Good	Fine	N-Mint
V1#1	3.00	9.00	21.00
2	1.50	4.50	10.00
3-10	1.15	3.50	8.00
11-13,15-23,25-31: 31-Last pre-code (1/55)	.70	2.00	5.00
14,24-Rape scene	.85	2.50	6.00
32-37,39-44	.60	1.80	4.00
38-S&K-c	1.35	4.00	9.00
NOTE: Powell a-1,2,7-14,17-25,28,29,33,40,41. #3 has True Love.. on inside.

LOVE ROMANCES (Formerly Ideal #5?)
No. 6, May, 1949 - No. 106, July, 1963
Timely/Marvel/Atlas(TCI No. 7-71/Male No. 72-106)

	Good	Fine	N-Mint
6-Photo-c	3.00	9.00	21.00
7-Kamen-a	2.00	6.00	14.00
8-Kubert-a; photo-c	3.15	9.50	22.00
9-20: 9-12-Photo-c	1.30	4.00	9.00

Love Diary #11, © Our Publ.

Love Dramas #1, © MEG

Love Letters #17, © QUA

Lovers' Lane #1, © LEV

Love Scandals #5, © QUA

Lucky Comics #2, © Consolidated Mag.

LOVE ROMANCES (continued)	Good	Fine	N-Mint
21,24-Krigstein-a	2.50	7.50	17.00
22,23,25-35,37,39,40	1.00	3.00	7.00
36,38-Krigstein-a	2.00	6.00	14.00
41-44,46,47: Last precode (2/55)	1.00	3.00	7.00
45,57-Matt Baker-a	1.65	5.00	11.50
48,50-52,54-56,58-74	.85	2.50	6.00
49,53-Toth-a, 6 & ? pgs.	2.00	6.00	14.00
75,77,82-Matt Baker-a	1.65	5.00	11.50
76,78-81,84,86-95: Last 10 cent ish.?	.55	1.65	4.00
83-Kirby-c, Severin-a	1.30	4.00	9.00
85,96-Kirby c/a	1.30	4.00	9.00
97,100-104	.35	1.00	2.40
98-Kirby-a(4)	2.35	7.00	16.00
99,105,106-Kirby-a	1.00	3.00	7.00

NOTE: *Anne Brewster a-67, 72. Colletta a-37, 40, 42, 44, 67(2); c-42, 44, 49, 80. Everett c-70. Kirby c-80, 85, 88. Robinson a-29.*

LOVERS (Formerly Blonde Phantom)
No. 23, May, 1949 - No. 86, Aug?, 1957
Marvel Comics No. 23,24/Atlas No. 25 on (ANC)

23-Photo-c	3.00	9.00	21.00
24-Tothish plus Robinson-a; photo-c	1.60	4.70	11.00
25,30-Kubert-a; 7, 10 pgs.	2.65	8.00	18.00
26-29,31-36,39,40: 26,27-photo-c	1.15	3.50	8.00
37,38-Krigstein-a	2.65	8.00	18.00
41-Everett-a(2)	1.85	5.50	13.00
42,44-65: 65-Last pre-code (1/55)	.85	2.50	6.00
43-1pg. Frazetta ad	1.30	4.00	9.00
66,68-86	.75	2.25	5.00
67-Toth-a	2.30	7.00	16.00

NOTE: *Anne Brewster a-86. Colletta a-54, 59, 62, 64, 69; c-64, 75. Powell a-27, 30. Robinson a-54, 56.*

LOVERS' LANE
Oct., 1949 - No. 41, June, 1954 (No. 1-18, 52 pgs.)
Lev Gleason Publications

1-Biro-c	3.00	9.00	21.00
2	1.50	4.50	10.00
3-10	1.15	3.50	8.00
11-19	.85	2.50	6.00
20-Frazetta 1 pg. ad	1.30	4.00	9.00
21-38,40,41	.85	2.50	6.00
39-Story narrated by Frank Sinatra	1.85	5.50	13.00

NOTE: *Briefer a-6, 21. Fuje a-4, 16; c-many. Guardineer a-1. Kinstler c-41. Tuska a-6. Painted-c 2-18. Photo-c 19-22, 26-28.*

LOVE SCANDALS
Feb, 1950 - No. 5, Oct, 1950 (Photo-c #2-5) (All 52 pgs.)
Quality Comics Group

1-Ward c/a, 9 pgs.	11.50	34.00	80.00
2,3: 2-Gustavson-a	3.65	11.00	25.00
4-Ward c/a, 18 pgs; Gil Fox-a	10.00	30.00	70.00
5-C. Cuidera-a; tomboy story 'I Hated Being a Woman'	3.65	11.00	25.00

LOVE SECRETS (Formerly Love Letters #31)
No. 32, Aug, 1953 - No. 56, Dec, 1956
Quality Comics Group

32	2.65	8.00	18.00
33,35-39	1.30	4.00	9.00
34-Ward-a	3.75	11.25	26.00
40-Matt Baker-c	2.50	7.50	17.00
41-43: 43-Last precode (3/55)	1.15	3.50	8.00
44,47-50,53,54	.85	2.50	6.00
45,46-Ward-a. 46-Baker-a	2.85	8.50	20.00
51,52-Ward(r). 52-r/Love Confessions #17	1.65	5.00	11.50
55,56-Baker-a; cover-#56	1.65	5.00	11.50

LOVE SECRETS
Oct., 1949 - No. 2, Jan, 1950 (52 pgs., photo-c)
Marvel Comics(IPC)

	Good	Fine	N-Mint
1	3.00	9.00	21.00
2	2.65	8.00	18.00

LOVE STORIES
No. 6, 1950 - No. 18, Aug, 1954
Fox Feature Syndicate/Star Publ. No. 13 on

6,8-Wood-a	8.00	24.00	56.00
7,9-12	2.85	8.50	20.00
13-18-L. B. Cole-a	3.35	10.00	23.00

LOVE STORIES (Formerly Heart Throbs)
No. 147, Nov, 1972 - No. 152, Oct-Nov, 1973
National Periodical Publications

147-152		.20	.40

LOVE STORIES OF MARY WORTH (See Harvey Comics Hits #55 & Mary Worth)
Sept, 1949 - No. 5, May, 1950
Harvey Publications

1-1940's newspaper reprints-#1-4	3.50	10.50	24.00
2	2.50	7.50	17.00
3-5: 3-Kamen/Baker-a?	2.35	7.00	16.00

LOVE TALES (Formerly The Human Torch #35)
No. 36, 5/49 - No. 58, 8/52; No. 59, date? - No. 75, Sept, 1957
Marvel/Atlas Comics (ZPC No. 36-50/MMC No. 67-75)

36-Photo-c	3.00	9.00	21.00
37	1.50	4.50	10.00
38-44,46-50: 40,41-Photo-c	1.00	3.00	7.00
45-Powell-a	1.20	3.50	8.00
51,69-Everett-a	1.65	5.00	11.50
52-Krigstein-a	2.15	6.50	15.00
53-60: 60-Last pre-code (2/55)	.85	2.50	6.00
61-68,70-75	.55	1.65	4.00

LOVE THRILLS (See Fox Giants)

LOVE TRAILS
Dec, 1949 - No. 2, Mar, 1950 (52 pgs.)
A Lover's Magazine (CDS)(Marvel)

1,2: 1-Photo-c	3.00	9.00	21.00

LOWELL THOMAS' HIGH ADVENTURE (See 4-Color #949,1001)

LT. (See Lieutenant)

LUCKY COMICS
Jan, 1944; No. 2, Summer, 1945 - No. 5, Summer, 1946
Consolidated Magazines

1-Lucky Starr, Bobbie	4.65	14.00	32.00
2-5	2.15	6.50	15.00

LUCKY DUCK
No. 5, Jan, 1953 - No. 8, Sept, 1953
Standard Comics (Literary Ent.)

5-Irving Spector-a	3.00	9.00	21.00
6-8-Irving Spector-a	2.00	6.00	14.00

LUCKY FIGHTS IT THROUGH (Also see The K. O. Punch)
1949 (16 pgs. in color; paper cover) (Giveaway)
Educational Comics

(Very Rare)-1st Kurtzman work for E. C.; V.D. prevention	142.00	425.00	1000.00

(Prices vary widely on this book)

NOTE: *Subtitled "The Story of That Ignorant, Ignorant Cowboy." Prepared for Communications Materials Center, Columbia University.*

LUCKY "7" COMICS
1944 (No date listed)

LUCKY "7" COMICS (continued)
Howard Publishers Ltd.

	Good	Fine	N-Mint
1-Congo Raider, Punch Powers; bondage-c	11.00	32.00	76.00

LUCKY STAR (Western)
1950 - No. 7, 1951; No. 8, 1953 - No. 14, 1955 (5x7¼''; full color)
Nation Wide Publ. Co.

1-Jack Davis-a; 52 pgs., 5 cents	4.60	14.00	32.00
2,3-(52 pgs.)-Davis-a	3.00	9.00	21.00
4-7-(52 pgs.)-Davis-a	2.65	8.00	18.00
8-14-(36 pgs.)	1.70	5.00	12.00
Given away with Lucky Star Western Wear by the Juvenile Mfg. Co.			
	1.70	5.00	12.00

LUCY SHOW, THE (TV) (Also see I Love Lucy)
June, 1963 - No. 5, June, 1964 (Photo-c, 1,2)
Gold Key

1	5.00	15.00	35.00
2	3.50	10.50	24.00
3-5: Photo back-c,1,2,4,5	2.85	8.50	20.00

LUCY, THE REAL GONE GAL (Meet Miss Pepper #5 on)
June, 1953 - No. 4, Dec, 1953
St. John Publishing Co.

1-Negligee panels	3.50	10.50	24.00
2	1.70	5.00	12.00
3,4: 3-Drucker-a	1.50	4.50	10.00

LUDWIG BEMELMAN'S MADELEINE & GENEVIEVE (See 4-Color #796)

LUDWIG VON DRAKE (TV)(Disney)(See Walt Disney's C&S #256)
Nov-Dec, 1961 - No. 4, June-Aug, 1962
Dell Publishing Co.

1	2.00	6.00	14.00
2-4	1.30	4.00	9.00
. . .Fish Stampede (1962, Fritos giveaway)-16 pgs., 3¼x7'', soft-c; also see D. Duck & M. Mouse	2.00	6.00	14.00

LUGER
Oct, 1986 - No. 3, Feb, 1987 (mini-series, $1.75, color)
Eclipse Comics

1-3	.30	.90	1.80

LUKE CAGE (See Hero for Hire)

LUKE SHORT'S WESTERN STORIES
No. 580, Aug, 1954 - No. 927, Aug, 1958
Dell Publishing Co.

4-Color 580(8/54)	2.30	7.00	16.00
4-Color 651(9/55)-Kinstler-a	3.00	9.00	21.00
4-Color 739,771,807,875,927	2.30	7.00	16.00
4-Color 848	3.00	9.00	21.00

LUNATICKLE (Magazine) (Satire)
Feb, 1956 - No. 2, Apr, 1956
Whitstone Publ.

1,2-Kubert-a	1.50	4.50	9.00

LYNDON B. JOHNSON
March, 1965
Dell Publishing Co.

12-445-503-Photo-c	1.50	4.50	10.00

MACHINE MAN (Also see 2001...)
4/78 - No. 9, 12/78; No. 10, 8/79 - No.19, 2/81
Marvel Comics Group

1	.35	1.00	2.00
2-17,19: 19-Intro Jack O'Lantern		.50	1.00
18-Wendigo, Alpha Flight-ties into X-Men #140			
	.85	2.50	6.00

NOTE: **Austin** c-7i, 19i. **Buckler** c-17p, 18p. **Byrne** c-14p. **Ditko** a-10-19; c-10-13, 14i,

15, 16. **Kirby** a-1-9p; c-1-5, 7-9p. **Layton** c-7i. **Miller** c-19p. **Simonson** c-6.

MACHINE MAN
Oct, 1984 - No. 4, Jan, 1985 (Limited-series)
Marvel Comics Group

	Good	Fine	N-Mint
1-Barry Smith-c/a(i) in all	.25	.75	1.50
2-4		.60	1.20

MACKENZIE'S RAIDERS (See 4-Color #1093)

MACO TOYS COMIC
1959 (36 pages; full color) (Giveaway)
Maco Toys/Charlton Comics

1-All military stories featuring Maco Toys	1.00	3.00	6.00

MACROSS (Robotech: The Macross Saga #2 on)
Dec, 1984 ($1.50)
Comico

1	2.50	7.50	15.00

MAD
Oct-Nov, 1952 - Present (No. 24 on, magazine format)
(Kurtzman editor No. 1-28, Feldstein No. 29 on)
E. C. Comics

1-Wood, Davis, Elder start as regulars	85.00	255.00	595.00
2-Davis-c	40.00	120.00	280.00
3	25.00	75.00	175.00
4-Reefer mention story "Flob Was a Slob" by Davis			
	25.00	75.00	175.00
5-Low distribution; Elder-c	52.00	155.00	365.00
6-10	18.00	54.00	125.00
11-Wolverton-a	18.00	54.00	125.00
12-15	16.00	48.00	110.00
16-23(5/55): 21-1st app. Alfred E. Neuman on-c in fake ad. 22-all by Elder. 23-Special cancel announcement	12.00	36.00	84.00
24(7/55)-1st magazine issue (25 cents); Kurtzman logo & border on-c			
	23.00	70.00	160.00
25-Jaffee starts as regular writer	13.00	40.00	90.00
26	8.50	25.50	60.00
27-Davis-c; Jaffee starts as story artist; new logo			
	8.50	25.50	60.00
28-Elder-c; Heath back-c; last issue edited by Kurtzman; (three cover variations exist with different wording on contents banner on lower right of cover; value of each the same)			
	7.00	21.00	50.00
29-Wood-c; Kamen-a; Don Martin starts as regular; Feldstein editing begins	7.00	21.00	50.00
30-1st A. E. Neuman cover by Mingo; Crandall inside-c; last Elder art; Bob Clarke starts as regular; Disneyland spoof			
	8.50	25.50	60.00
31-Freas starts as regular; last Davis art until #99			
	6.00	18.00	42.00
32-Orlando, Drucker, Woodbridge start as regulars; Wood back-c			
	5.70	17.00	40.00
33-Orlando back-c	5.70	17.00	40.00
34-Berg starts as regular	5.00	15.00	35.00
35-Mingo wraparound-c; Crandall-a	5.00	15.00	35.00
36-40	3.50	10.50	24.00
41-50	2.65	8.00	18.00
51-60: 60-Two Clarke-c; Prohias starts as regular			
	1.50	4.50	10.00
61-70: 64-Rickard starts as regular. 68-Martin-c			
	1.30	4.00	9.00
71-80: 76-Aragones starts as regular	1.15	3.50	8.00
81-90: 86-1st Fold-in. 89-One strip by Walt Kelly. 90-Frazetta back-c	1.00	3.00	7.00
91-100: 91-Jaffee starts as story artist. 99-Davis-a resumes			
	.85	2.50	5.00
101-120: 101-Infinity-c. 105-Batman TV show take-off. 106-Frazetta			

Lucky "7" Comics #1, © Howard Publ.

The Lucy Show #4, © Desilu

Mad #6, © WMG

The Mad Hatter #1, © O. W. Comics Corp.

Madhouse #4 (1954), © AJAX

Mage #10, © Comico

	Good	Fine	N-Mint
MAD (continued)			
back-c	.50	1.50	3.00
121-140: 122-Drucker & Mingo-c. 128-Last Orlando. 130-Torres begins			
as regular. 135,139-Davis-c	.40	1.25	2.50
141-170: 165-Martin-c. 169-Drucker-c	.25	.75	1.50
171-200: 173,178-Davis-c. 176-Drucker-c. 182-Bob Jones starts as			
regular. 186-Star Trek take-off. 187-Harry North starts as			
regular. 196-Star Wars take-off	.25	.75	1.50
201-285: 203-Star Wars take-off. 204-Hulk TV show take-off. 208-			
Superman movie take-off	.50		1.00

NOTE: *Jules Feiffer* a(r)-42. *Freas*-most-c and back covers-40-74. *Heath* a-14, 27. *Kamen* a-29. *Krigstein* a-12, 17, 24, 26. *Kurtzman* c-1, 3, 4, 6-10, 13, 14, 16, 18. *Mingo* c-30-37, 75-111. *John Severin* a-1-6, 9, 10. *Wolverton* c-11; a-11, 17, 29, 31, 36, 40, 82, 137. *Wood* a-24-45, 59; c-26, 29. *Woodbridge* a-43.

MAD (See ...Follies, ...Special, More Trash from..., and The Worst from...)

MAD ABOUT MILLIE
April, 1969 - No. 17, Dec, 1970
Marvel Comics Group

	Good	Fine	N-Mint
1-Giant issue	.85	2.50	5.00
2-17: 16,17-r	.50	1.50	3.00
Annual 1(11/71)	.25	.75	1.50

MADAME XANADU
July, 1981 (No ads; $1.00; 32 pgs.)
DC Comics

	Good	Fine	N-Mint
1-Marshall Rogers-a(25 pgs.); Kaluta-c/a(2 pgs.); pin-up of			
Madame Xanadu	.50		1.00

MADBALLS
9/86 - No. 3, 11/86; No. 4, 6/87 - No. 10, June, 1988
Star Comics/Marvel Comics #9 on

	Good	Fine	N-Mint
1-10: Based on toys. 9-Post-a	.50		1.00

MAD FOLLIES (Special)
1963 - No. 7, 1969
E. C. Comics

	Good	Fine	N-Mint
nn(1963)-Paperback book covers	7.00	21.00	50.00
2(1964)-Calendar	4.65	14.00	32.00
3(1965)-Mischief Stickers	3.50	10.50	24.00
4(1966)-Mobile; reprints Frazetta back-c/Mad #90			
	4.00	12.00	28.00
5(1967)-Stencils	3.00	9.00	21.00
6(1968)-Mischief Stickers	1.85	5.50	13.00
7(1969)-Nasty Cards	1.85	5.50	13.00

NOTE: *Clarke* c-4. *Mingo* c-1-3. *Orlando* a-5.

MAD HATTER, THE (Costume Hero)
Jan-Feb, 1946 - No. 2, Sept-Oct, 1946
O. W. Comics Corp.

	Good	Fine	N-Mint
1-Freddy the Firefly begins; Giunta-c/a	18.00	54.00	125.00
2-Has ad for E.C.'s Animal Fables #1	12.00	36.00	84.00

MADHOUSE
3-4/54 - No. 4, 9-10/54; 6/57 - No. 4, Dec?, 1957
Ajax/Farrell Publ. (Excellent Publ./4-Star)

	Good	Fine	N-Mint
1(1954)	8.00	24.00	56.00
2,3	4.00	12.00	28.00
4-Surrealistic-c	6.50	19.50	45.00
1(1957)	3.50	10.50	24.00
2-4	2.00	6.00	14.00

MADHOUSE (Formerly Madhouse Glads; ...Comics #104? on)
No. 95, 9/74 - No. 97, 1/75; No. 98, 8/75 - No. 130, 10/82
Red Circle Productions/Archie Publications

	Good	Fine	N-Mint
95-Horror stories through #97	.60		1.20
96	.60		1.20
97-Intro. Henry Hobson; Morrow, Thorne-a	.40		.80
98-130-Satire/humor stories	.30		.60

	Good	Fine	N-Mint
Annual 8(1970-71)- 12(1974-75)-Formerly Madhouse Ma-ad Annual.			
11-Wood-a(r)	.40		.80
...Comics Digest 1(1975-76)- 8(8/82)(...Mag. #5 on)			
	.50		1.00

NOTE: *B. Jones* a-96. *McWilliams* a-97. *Morrow* a-96; c-95-97. *Wildey* a-95, 96. See *Archie Comics Digest #1, 13.*

MADHOUSE GLADS (Formerly ...Ma-ad; Madhouse #95 on)
No. 73, May, 1970 - No. 94, Aug, 1974 (No. 78-92: 52 pgs.)
Archie Publications

	Good	Fine	N-Mint
73	.50		1.00
74-94	.30		.60

MADHOUSE MA-AD (...Jokes #67-70; ...Freak-Out #71-74)
(Formerly Archie's Madhouse) (Becomes Madhouse Glads #75 on)
No. 67, April, 1969 - No. 72, Jan, 1970
Archie Publications

	Good	Fine	N-Mint
67-72	.50		1.00
...Annual 7(1969-70)-Formerly Madhouse Annual; be-			
comes Madhouse Annual	.50		1.00

MAD MONSTER PARTY (See Movie Classics)

MAD SPECIAL (...Super Special)
Fall, 1970 - Present (84 - 116 pages)
E. C. Publications, Inc.

	Good	Fine	N-Mint
Fall 1970(#1)-Bonus-Voodoo Doll; contains 17 pgs. new material			
	3.00	9.00	21.00
Spring 1971(#2)-Wall Nuts; 17 pgs. new material			
	2.00	6.00	14.00
3-Protest Stickers	2.00	6.00	14.00
4-8: 4-Mini Posters. 5-Mad Flag. 7-Presidential candidate posters,			
Wild Shocking Message posters. 8-TV Guise			
	1.50	4.50	10.00
9(1972)-Contains Nostalgic Mad #1 (28pp)	1.30	4.00	9.00
10,11,13: 10-Nonsense Stickers (Don Martin). 11-33⅓ RPM record.			
13-Sickie Stickers; 3 pgs. new Wolverton	1.30	4.00	9.00
12-Contains Nostalgic Mad #2 (36 pgs.); Davis, Wolverton-a			
	1.30	4.00	9.00
14-Vital Message posters & Art Depreciation paintings			
	1.00	3.00	7.00
15-Contains Nostalgic Mad #3 (28 pgs.)	1.30	4.00	9.00
16,17,19,20: 16-Mad-hesive Stickers. 17-Don Martin posters.			
20-Martin Stickers	.85	2.50	6.00
18-Contains Nostalgic Mad #4 (36 pgs.)	1.00	3.00	7.00
21,24-Contains Nostalgic Mad #5 (28 pgs.) & #6 (28 pgs.)			
	1.00	3.00	7.00
22,23,25-27,29,30: 22-Diplomas. 23-Martin Stickers. 25-Martin Posters			
26-33⅓ RPM record. 27-Mad Shock-Sticks. 29-Mad Collectable-			
Correctables Posters. 30-The Movies	.55	1.65	4.00
28-Contains Nostalgic Mad #7 (36 pgs.)	.75	2.25	5.00
31,33-58	.55	1.65	4.00
32-Contains Nostalgic Mad #8	.85	2.50	6.00

NOTE: *#28-30: no number on cover. Mingo c-9, 11, 15, 19, 23.*

MAGE (The Hero Discovered...)
2/84 (no month) - No. 15, 12/86 ($1.50; 36 pgs; Mando paper)
Comico

	Good	Fine	N-Mint
1-Violence; Comico's 1st color comic	2.15	6.50	13.00
2	1.70	5.00	10.00
3-5: 3-Intro Edsel	1.00	3.00	6.00
6-Grendel begins (1st in color)	3.00	9.00	18.00
7-1st new Grendel story	1.35	4.00	8.00
8-14: 13-Grendel dies. 14-Grendel ends	.70	2.00	4.00
15-Dbl. size, photo-c	.85	2.50	5.00

MAGIC AGENT (See Unknown Worlds)
Jan-Feb, 1962 - No. 3, May-June, 1962

MAGIC AGENT (continued)
American Comics Group

	Good	Fine	N-Mint
1-Origin & 1st app. John Force	.70	2.00	4.00
2,3	.50	1.50	3.00

MAGIC COMICS
Aug, 1939 - No. 123, Nov-Dec, 1949
David McKay Publications

1-Mandrake the Magician, Henry, Popeye (not by Segar), Blondie, Barney Baxter, Secret Agent X-9 (not by Raymond), Bunky by Billy DeBeck & Thornton Burgess text stories illustrated by Harrison Cady begin	82.00	245.00	575.00
2	40.00	120.00	280.00
3	30.00	90.00	210.00
4	25.00	75.00	175.00
5	20.00	60.00	140.00
6-10	16.00	48.00	110.00
11-16,18-20	13.00	40.00	90.00
17-The Lone Ranger begins	14.00	42.00	100.00
21-30	9.50	28.50	65.00
31-40	7.00	21.00	50.00
41-50	6.00	18.00	42.00
51-60	5.00	15.00	35.00
61-70	3.70	11.00	26.00
71-99	3.00	9.00	21.00
100	3.70	11.00	26.00
101-106,109-123	2.30	7.00	16.00
107,108-Flash Gordon app; not by Raymond	3.75	11.25	26.00

MAGICA DE SPELL (See Walt Disney Showcase #30)

MAGIC OF CHRISTMAS AT NEWBERRYS, THE
1967 (20 pgs.; slick cover; B&W inside)
E. S. London (Giveaway)

		.60	1.20

MAGIC SWORD, THE (See Movie Classics)

MAGIK
Dec, 1983 - No. 4, Mar, 1984 (mini-series)
Marvel Comics Group

1-Illyana & Storm series from X-Men	.40	1.25	2.50
2-4	.35	1.00	2.00

NOTE: **Buscema** a-1p,2p; c-1p.

MAGILLA GORILLA (TV) (Hanna-Barbera)
May, 1964 - No. 10, Dec, 1968
Gold Key

1	2.65	8.00	18.00
2-10: 3-Vs. Yogi Bear for President	1.30	4.00	9.00
Kite Fun Book ('64, 16 pgs., 5x7¼'', soft-c)	2.00	6.00	14.00

MAGILLA GORILLA (TV) (See Spotlight #4)
Nov, 1970 - No. 5, July, 1971 (Hanna-Barbera)
Charlton Comics

1-5	.85	2.50	5.00

MAGNUS, ROBOT FIGHTER (. . .4000 A.D.) (See Doctor Solar)
Feb, 1963 - No. 46, Jan, 1977 (Painted-covers)
Gold Key

1-Origin Magnus; Aliens series begins	7.00	21.00	50.00
2,3	3.50	10.50	24.00
4-10	2.15	6.50	15.00
11-20	1.70	5.00	12.00
21,22,24-28: 22-Origin-r/#1. 28-Aliens ends	1.00	3.00	7.00
23-Exists with two different prices, 12 cents and 15 cents			
	1.00	3.00	7.00
29-46-Reprints	.70	2.00	4.00

NOTE: **Manning** a-1-22, 29-43(r). **Spiegle** a-23, 44r.

MAID OF THE MIST (See American Graphics)

MAI, THE PSYCHIC GIRL
May 19, 1987 - No. 28 (Bi-weekly, $1.50, B&W, 44pgs)
Eclipse Comics

	Good	Fine	N-Mint
1	.50	1.50	3.00
1-2nd print	.25	.75	1.50
2-5	.35	1.00	2.00
2-2nd print	.25	.75	1.50
6-10	.30	.85	1.70
11-20	.25	.80	1.70
21-28	.25	.75	1.50

MAJOR HOOPLE COMICS (See Crackajack Funnies)
nd (Jan, 1943)
Nedor Publications

1-Mary Worth, Phantom Soldier by Moldoff app.	16.00	48.00	110.00

MAJOR INAPAK THE SPACE ACE
1951 (20 pages) (Giveaway)
Magazine Enterprises (Inapac Foods)

1-Bob Powell-c/a	.30	.80	1.60

NOTE: Many warehouse copies surfaced in 1973.

MAJOR VICTORY COMICS
1944 - No. 3, Summer, 1945
H. Clay Glover/Service Publ./Harry 'A' Chesler

1-Origin Major Victory by C. Sultan (reprint from Dynamic #1); Spider Woman 1st app.	24.00	72.00	170.00
2-Dynamic Boy app.	15.00	45.00	105.00
3-Rocket Boy app.	12.00	36.00	84.00

MALTESE FALCON (See Feature Books No. 48 (McKay))

MALU IN THE LAND OF ADVENTURE
1964 (See White Princess of Jungle #2)
I. W. Enterprises

1-Reprints Avon's Slave Girl Comics #1; Severin-c	4.75	14.00	28.00

MAMMOTH COMICS
1938 (84 pages) (Black & White, 8½x11½'')
Whitman Publishing Co.(K. K. Publications)

1-Alley Oop, Terry & the Pirates, Dick Tracy, Little Orphan Annie, Wash Tubbs, Moon Mullins, Smilin' Jack, Tailspin Tommy & other reprints	52.00	155.00	365.00

MAMMY YOKUM & THE GREAT DOGPATCH MYSTERY
1951 (Giveaway)
Toby Press

Li'l Abner	11.50	34.00	80.00

MAN-BAT (Also see Detective #400, Brave & the Bold, and Batman Family)
Dec-Jan, 1975-76 - No. 2, Feb-Mar, 1976; Dec, 1984
National Periodical Publications/DC Comics

1-Ditko-a(p); Aparo-c; She-Bat app.		.30	.60
2-Aparo-c		.30	.60
. . .Vs. Batman 1 (12/84)-Adams-a(r)	.45	1.25	2.50

MAN COMICS
Dec, 1949 - No. 28, Sept, 1953 (52 pgs., #1-6)
Marvel/Atlas Comics (NPI)

1-Tuska-a	4.30	13.00	30.00
2-Tuska-a	2.15	6.50	15.00
3-5	1.70	5.00	12.00
6-8	1.50	4.50	10.00
9-13,15: 9-Format changes to war	1.00	3.00	7.00
14-Krenkel (3pgs.), Pakula-a	2.00	6.00	14.00

Magic Comics #3, © KING

Magnus, Robot Fighter #13, © GK

Mammoth Comics #1, © WHIT

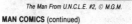
The Man From U.N.C.L.E. #2, © M.G.M.   *Manhunt! #1, © ME*   *Man Of War #2, © Eclipse Comics*

MAN COMICS (continued)	Good	Fine	N-Mint
16-21,23-28: 28-Crime ish.	.85	2.50	6.00
22-Krigstein-a, 5 pgs.	3.00	9.00	21.00

NOTE: *Berg* a-14, 15. *Colan* a-21. *Everett* a-8, 22; c-22, 25. *Heath* a-11, 17. *Kubertish* a-by *Bob Brown*-3. *Maneely* c-10, 11. *Robinson* a-10, 14.

MANDRAKE THE MAGICIAN (See Defenders Of The Earth, Feature Books #18,19,23,46,52,55, King Comics, Magic Comics, Tiny Tot Funnies & Wow Comics ('36)

MANDRAKE THE MAGICIAN (See Harvey Comics Hits #53)
No. 752, Nov, 1956; Sept, 1966 - No. 10, Nov, 1967
Dell Publishing Co./King Comics

4-Color 752('56)	3.70	11.00	26.00
1(King)-Begin S.O.S. Phantom, ends #3	1.00	3.00	7.00
2-5: 4-Girl Phantom app. 5-Brick Bradford app., also #6	.85	2.50	6.00
6,7,9: 7-Origin Lothar. 9-Brick Bradford app.	.70	2.00	5.00
8-Jeff Jones-a	1.15	3.50	8.00
10-Rip Kirby app.; Raymond-a (14 pgs.)	1.70	5.00	12.00

MANDRAKE THE MAGICIAN GIANT COMIC ALBUM
1972 (48 pgs.; 11x14''; B&W; cardboard covers)
Modern Promotions

nn-Strip reprints by Lee Falk	1.70	5.00	12.00

MAN FROM ATLANTIS (TV)
Feb, 1978 - No. 7, Aug, 1978
Marvel Comics Group

1-(84 pgs.; $1.00)-Sutton-a(p), Buscema-c; origin		.30	.60
2-7		.25	.50

MAN FROM PLANET X, THE
1987 (no price, color, probably unlicensed)
Planet X Productions

1-Reprints Fawcett Movie Comic	.50	1.50	3.00

MAN FROM U.N.C.L.E., THE (TV)
Feb, 1965 - No. 22, April, 1969 (All photo covers)
Gold Key

1	5.00	15.00	35.00
2-Photo back c-2-8	2.85	8.50	20.00
3-10: 7-Jet Dream begins	2.00	6.00	14.00
11-22: 21,22-Reprints	1.70	5.00	12.00

MAN FROM U.N.C.L.E., THE
1987 - Present ($1.50/$1.75, B&W)
Entertainment Comics

1-10	.25	.75	1.50

MAN FROM WELLS FARGO (TV)
No. 1287, Feb-Apr, 1962 - May-July, 1962 (Photo-c)
Dell Publishing Co.

4-Color 1287, 01-495-207	3.50	10.50	24.00

MANHUNT! (Becomes Red Fox #15 on)
Oct, 1947 - No. 14, 1953
Magazine Enterprises

1-Red Fox by L. B. Cole, Undercover Girl by Whitney, Space Ace begin; negligee panels	19.00	57.00	132.00
2-Electrocution-c	14.00	42.00	100.00
3-6	12.00	36.00	84.00
7-9: 7-Space Ace ends. 8-Trail Colt begins	10.00	30.00	70.00
10-G. Ingels-a	10.00	30.00	70.00
11(8/48)-Frazetta-a, 7 pgs.; The Duke, Scotland Yard begin	19.00	57.00	132.00
12	7.00	21.00	50.00
13(A-1 63)-Frazetta, r-/Trail Colt #1, 7 pgs.	17.00	51.00	120.00
14(A-1 77)-Bondage/hypo-c; last L. B. Cole Red Fox; Ingels-a	11.00	32.00	75.00

NOTE: *Guardineer* a-1-5; c-8. *Whitney* a-2-14; c-1-6,10. Red Fox by *L. B. Cole*-

#1-14. #15 was advertised but came out as Red Fox #15. Bondage c-6.

MANHUNTER (See Detective Comics & First Issue Special)
May, 1984 (76 pgs; high quality paper)
DC Comics

	Good	Fine	N-Mint
1-Simonson c/a(r)/Detective	.45	1.25	2.50

MANHUNTER
July, 1988 - Present ($1.00, color)
DC Comics

1-9	.25	.75	1.50

MAN IN BLACK (See Thrill-O-Rama) (Also see All New Comics, Front Page, Strange Story & Tally-Ho Comics)
Sept, 1957 - No. 4, Mar, 1958
Harvey Publications

1-Bob Powell c/a	6.00	18.00	42.00
2-4: Powell c/a	5.00	15.00	35.00

MAN IN FLIGHT (See 4-Color #836)

MAN IN SPACE (See Dell Giant #27 & 4-Color #716,954)

MAN OF PEACE, POPE PIUS XII
1950 (See Pope Pius XII... & Topix V2#8)
Catechetical Guild

All Powell-a	5.35	16.00	32.00

MAN OF STEEL, THE
1986 (June) - No. 6, 1986 (mini-series)
DC Comics

1-Byrne story, c/art begins; origin	.35	1.00	2.00
1-Alternate-c for newsstand sales	.30	.90	1.80
1-Distr. to toy stores by So Much Fun			
2-6: 2-Intro. Lois Lane, Jimmy Olsen. 3-Intro/origin Magpie. 4-Intro. new Lex Luthor	.60	1.20	
...The Complete Saga-Contains #1-6, given away in contest	35	1.00	2.00
Limited Edition, softcover	5.85	17.50	35.00

MAN OF WAR (See Liberty Scouts & Liberty Guards)
Nov, 1941 - No. 2, Jan, 1942
Centaur Publications

1-The Fire-Man, Man of War, The Sentinel, Liberty Guards, & VapoMan begin; Gustavson-c/a; Flag-c	75.00	225.00	525.00
2-Intro The Ferret; Gustavson-c/a	60.00	180.00	420.00

MAN OF WAR
Aug, 1987 - No. 3, Feb, 1988 ($1.75, color, Baxter)
Eclipse Comics

1-3	.30	.90	1.80

MAN O' MARS
1953; 1964
Fiction House Magazines

1-Space Rangers	13.00	40.00	90.00
I.W. Reprint #1/Man O'Mars #1; Murphy Anderson-a	2.75	8.00	16.00

MANTECH ROBOT WARRIORS
Sept, 1984 - No. 4, April, 1985
Archie Enterprises, Inc.

1-4		.40	.80

MAN-THING (See Fear, Marvel Comics Presents, Marvel Fanfare, Monsters Unleashed & Savage Tales)
Jan, 1974 - No. 22, Oct, 1975; Nov, 1979 - V2No. 11, July, 1981
Marvel Comics Group

1-Howard the Duck cont./Fear 19.(2nd app.)	.85	2.50	5.00
2-4	.25	.70	1.40
5-11-Ploog-a		.50	1.00

247

	Good	Fine	N-Mint

MAN-THING (continued)
12-22: 19-1st app. Scavenger. 21-Origin Scavenger & Man-Thing.

		Good	Fine	N-Mint
22-Howard the Duck cameo			.30	.60
V2#1(1979)			.40	.80
2-11: 6-Golden-c			.25	.50
Giant Size 1(8/74)-Ploog c/a			.60	1.20
Giant Size 2,3			.50	1.00
Giant Size 4(5/75)-Howard the Duck by Brunner; Ditko-a(r)				
		.85	2.50	5.00
Giant Size 5(8/75)-Howard the Duck by Brunner (p)				
		.85	2.50	5.00

NOTE: Alcala a-14, Gnt Size 3. Brunner c-1, Gnt Size 4. J. Buscema a-12p, 13p, 16p, Gnt Size 2p, 5p; c-Gnt Size 1r, 3r, 4r. Gil Kane c-4p, 10p, 12-20p, 21, Gnt-Size 3p, 5p. Ditko a-Gnt Size 1r, 3r. Kirby a-Gnt Size 1-3r. Mooney a-17, 18, 19p, 20-22, V2#1-3p. Ploog Man-Thing-5p, 6p, 7, 8, 9-11p, Gnt Size 1p; c-5, 6, 8, 9, 11. Powell a-Gnt Size 2r. Sutton a-13i, Gnt-Size 3r, 5i.

MAN WITH THE X-RAY EYES, THE (See X,... under Movie Comics)

MANY GHOSTS OF DR. GRAVES, THE (Doctor Graves #73 on)
5/67 - No. 60, 12/76; No. 61, 9/77 - No. 62, 10/77; No. 63, 2/78 - No. 65, 4/78; No. 66, 6/81 - No. 72, 5/82
Charlton Comics

	Good	Fine	N-Mint
1	.50	1.50	3.00
2-10	.25	.75	1.50
11-20		.50	1.00
21-44,46,48,50-72		.40	.80
45-1st Newton comic book work, 8pgs.	.35	1.00	2.00
47,49-Newton-a		.40	.80
Modern Comics Reprint 12,25 ('78)		.20	.40

NOTE: Aparo a-66r, 69r; c-66, 67. Byrne c-54. Ditko a-1, 7, 9, 11-13, 15-18, 20-22, 24, 26, 35, 37, 38, 40-44, 47, 48, 51-54, 58, 60r-65r, 70, 72; c-11-13, 16-18, 22, 24, 26-35, 38, 40, 55, 58, 62-65. Howard c-48. Newton a-45, 47p, 49p; c-49, 52. Sutton c/a-42, 49.

MANY LOVES OF DOBIE GILLIS (TV)
May-June, 1960 - No. 26, Oct, 1964
National Periodical Publications

	Good	Fine	N-Mint
1	10.00	30.00	70.00
2-5	4.30	13.00	30.00
6-10	3.70	11.00	26.00
11-26	2.85	8.50	20.00

MARAUDER'S MOON (See 4-Color #848)

MARCH OF COMICS (Boys' and Girls'. . .#3-353)
1946 - No. 488, Apr, 1982 (#1-4: No #'s)
(K.K. Giveaway) (Founded by Sig Feuchtwanger)
K. K. Publications/Western Publishing Co.

Early issues were full size, 32 pages, and were printed with and without an extra cover of slick stock, just for the advertiser. The binding was stapled if the slick cover was added; otherwise, the pages were glued together at the spine. Most 1948 - 1951 issues were full size, 24 pages, pulp covers. Starting in 1952 they were half-size and 32 pages with slick covers. 1959 and later issues had only 16 pages plus covers. 1952 -1959 issues read oblong; 1960 and later issues read upright.

	Good	Fine	N-Mint
1(nn)(1946)-Goldilocks; Kelly back-c; 16pgs., stapled			
	24.00	72.00	170.00
2(nn)(1946)-How Santa Got His Red Suit; Kelly-a(11 pgs., r-/4-Color 61)('44); 16pgs., stapled			
	24.00	72.00	170.00
3(nn)(1947)-Our Gang (Walt Kelly)	40.00	110.00	235.00
4(nn)Donald Duck by Carl Barks, ''Maharajah Donald'', 28 pgs.; Kelly-c?	428.00	1285.00	3000.00
5-Andy Panda	13.00	40.00	90.00
6-Popular Fairy Tales; Kelly-c; Noonan-a(2)	17.00	50.00	120.00
7-Oswald the Rabbit	17.00	50.00	120.00
8-Mickey Mouse, 32 pgs.	50.00	150.00	330.00
9(nn)-The Story of the Gloomy Bunny	8.00	24.00	56.00
10-Out of Santa's Bag	6.75	20.00	47.00
11-Fun With Santa Claus	5.35	16.00	37.00
12-Santa's Toys	5.35	16.00	37.00
13-Santa's Surprise	5.35	16.00	37.00
14-Santa's Candy Kitchen	5.35	16.00	37.00

	Good	Fine	N-Mint
15-Hip-It-Ty Hop & the Big Bass Viol	5.35	16.00	37.00
16-Woody Woodpecker (1947)	8.50	25.00	60.00
17-Roy Rogers (1948)	20.00	60.00	140.00
18-Popular Fairy Tales	10.00	30.00	70.00
19-Uncle Wiggily	7.50	22.50	52.00
20-Donald Duck by Carl Barks, ''Darkest Africa,'' 22 pgs.; Kelly-c			
	257.00	770.00	1800.00
21-Tom and Jerry	7.50	22.50	52.00
22-Andy Panda	7.50	22.50	52.00
23-Raggedy Ann; Kerr-a	12.00	35.00	84.00
24-Felix the Cat, 1932 daily strip reprints by Otto Messmer			
	20.00	60.00	140.00
25-Gene Autry	20.00	60.00	140.00
26-Our Gang; Walt Kelly	20.00	60.00	140.00
27-Mickey Mouse; r/in M. Mouse #240	34.00	100.00	238.00
28-Gene Autry	20.00	60.00	140.00
29-Easter Bonnet Shop	4.00	12.00	28.00
30-Here Comes Santa	3.35	10.00	22.00
31-Santa's Busy Corner	3.35	10.00	22.00
32-No book produced			
33-A Christmas Carol	3.35	10.00	22.00
34-Woody Woodpecker	5.85	17.50	40.00
35-Roy Rogers (1948)	19.00	57.00	135.00
36-Felix the Cat(1949)-by Messmer; '34 daily strip-r			
	15.00	45.00	105.00
37-Popeye	12.50	37.50	87.00
38-Oswald the Rabbit	5.85	17.50	40.00
39-Gene Autry	19.00	57.00	135.00
40-Andy and Woody	5.85	17.50	40.00
41-Donald Duck by Carl Barks, ''Race to the South Seas,'' 22 pgs.; Kelly-c; on Disney's reprint band list	200.00	600.00	1400.00
42-Porky Pig	5.85	17.50	40.00
43-Henry	3.75	11.00	26.00
44-Bugs Bunny	5.85	17.50	40.00
45-Mickey Mouse	27.00	80.00	190.00
46-Tom and Jerry	5.85	17.50	40.00
47-Roy Rogers	17.00	51.00	120.00
48-Greetings from Santa	2.75	8.00	19.00
49-Santa Is Here	2.75	8.00	19.00
50-Santa Claus' Workshop (1949)	2.75	8.00	19.00
51-Felix the Cat (1950) by Messmer	13.00	40.00	90.00
52-Popeye	10.00	30.00	70.00
53-Oswald the Rabbit	5.85	17.50	40.00
54-Gene Autry	16.00	48.00	110.00
55-Andy and Woody	5.00	15.00	35.00
56-Donald Duck-not by Barks; Barks art on back-c			
	22.00	65.00	140.00
57-Porky Pig	5.00	15.00	35.00
58-Henry	3.00	9.00	21.00
59-Bugs Bunny	5.00	15.00	35.00
60-Mickey Mouse	18.00	55.00	125.00
61-Tom and Jerry	4.35	13.00	30.00
62-Roy Rogers	16.00	48.00	110.00
63-Welcome Santa; ½-size, oblong	2.75	8.00	19.00
64(nn)-Santa's Helpers; ½-size, oblong	2.75	8.00	19.00
65(nn)-Jingle Bells (1950)-½-size, oblong	2.75	8.00	19.00
66-Popeye (1951)	9.00	27.00	62.00
67-Oswald the Rabbit	4.00	12.00	28.00
68-Roy Rogers	14.00	42.00	100.00
69-Donald Duck; Barks-a on back-c	19.00	57.00	125.00
70-Tom and Jerry	4.00	12.00	28.00
71-Porky Pig	4.00	12.00	28.00
72-Krazy Kat	6.00	18.00	42.00
73-Roy Rogers	12.00	36.00	84.00
74-Mickey Mouse (1951)	14.00	42.50	96.00
75-Bugs Bunny	4.00	12.00	28.00

Giant-Size Man-Thing #5, © MEG

The Many Ghosts Of Dr. Graves #45, © CC

March Of Comics #41, © WDC

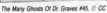

March Of Comics #82, © ERB

March Of Comics #142, © KING

March Of Comics #205, © M.G.M.

MARCH OF COMICS (continued)	Good	Fine	N-Mint
76-Andy and Woody	4.00	12.00	28.00
77-Roy Rogers	13.00	40.00	80.00
78-Gene Autry(1951)-Last regular size issue	13.00	40.00	80.00
79-Andy Panda (1952)-5x7'' size	2.75	8.00	19.00
80-Popeye	8.00	24.00	56.00
81-Oswald the Rabbit	3.00	9.00	21.00
82-Tarzan	14.00	42.00	100.00
83-Bugs Bunny	3.00	9.00	21.00
84-Henry	2.35	7.00	16.00
85-Woody Woodpecker	2.35	7.00	16.00
86-Roy Rogers	10.00	30.00	70.00
87-Krazy Kat	4.75	14.00	33.00
88-Tom and Jerry	2.35	7.00	16.00
89-Porky Pig	2.35	7.00	16.00
90-Gene Autry	10.00	30.00	70.00
91-Roy Rogers & Santa	10.00	30.00	70.00
92-Christmas with Santa	2.00	6.00	14.00
93-Woody Woodpecker (1953)	2.35	7.00	16.00
94-Indian Chief	5.50	16.50	40.00
95-Oswald the Rabbit	2.35	7.00	16.00
96-Popeye	7.00	20.00	50.00
97-Bugs Bunny	2.35	7.00	16.00
98-Tarzan-Lex Barker photo-c	14.00	42.00	100.00
99-Porky Pig	2.35	7.00	16.00
100-Roy Rogers	8.00	24.00	56.00
101-Henry	2.00	6.00	14.00
102-Tom Corbett (TV)-Painted-c	11.50	34.00	80.00
103-Tom and Jerry	2.00	6.00	14.00
104-Gene Autry	8.00	24.00	56.00
105-Roy Rogers	8.00	24.00	56.00
106-Santa's Helpers	2.00	6.00	14.00
107-Santa's Christmas Book - not published			
108-Fun with Santa (1953)	2.00	6.00	14.00
109-Woody Woodpecker (1954)	2.00	6.00	14.00
110-Indian Chief	3.50	10.50	24.00
111-Oswald the Rabbit	2.00	6.00	14.00
112-Henry	1.70	5.00	12.00
113-Porky Pig	2.00	6.00	14.00
114-Tarzan (Russ Manning)	14.00	42.00	100.00
115-Bugs Bunny	2.00	6.00	14.00
116-Roy Rogers	8.00	24.00	56.00
117-Popeye	7.00	20.00	50.00
118-Flash Gordon-Painted-c	10.00	30.00	70.00
119-Tom and Jerry	2.00	6.00	14.00
120-Gene Autry	8.00	24.00	56.00
121-Roy Rogers	8.00	24.00	56.00
122-Santa's Surprise (1954)	1.50	4.50	10.00
123-Santa's Christmas Book	1.50	4.50	10.00
124-Woody Woodpecker (1955)	1.70	5.00	12.00
125-Tarzan-Lex Barker photo-c	13.00	40.00	90.00
126-Oswald the Rabbit	1.70	5.00	12.00
127-Indian Chief	3.00	9.00	21.00
128-Tom and Jerry	1.70	5.00	12.00
129-Henry	1.50	4.50	10.00
130-Porky Pig	1.70	5.00	12.00
131-Roy Rogers	8.00	24.00	56.00
132-Bugs Bunny	1.70	5.00	12.00
133-Flash Gordon-Painted-c	8.50	25.50	60.00
134-Popeye	4.00	12.00	28.00
135-Gene Autry	7.00	21.00	50.00
136-Roy Rogers	7.00	21.00	50.00
137-Gifts from Santa	1.35	4.00	9.00
138-Fun at Christmas (1955)	1.35	4.00	9.00
139-Woody Woodpecker (1956)	1.70	5.00	12.00
140-Indian Chief	3.00	9.00	21.00
141-Oswald the Rabbit	1.70	5.00	12.00

	Good	Fine	N-Mint
142-Flash Gordon	8.50	25.50	60.00
143-Porky Pig	1.70	5.00	12.00
144-Tarzan (Russ Manning)-Painted-c	12.00	36.00	84.00
145-Tom and Jerry	1.70	5.00	12.00
146-Roy Rogers-Photo-c	8.00	24.00	56.00
147-Henry	1.35	4.00	9.00
148-Popeye	4.00	12.00	28.00
149-Bugs Bunny	1.70	5.00	12.00
150-Gene Autry	7.00	21.00	50.00
151-Roy Rogers	7.00	21.00	50.00
152-The Night Before Christmas	1.35	4.00	9.00
153-Merry Christmas (1956)	1.35	4.00	9.00
154-Tom and Jerry (1957)	1.70	5.00	12.00
155-Tarzan-Photo-c	12.00	36.00	84.00
156-Oswald the Rabbit	1.70	5.00	12.00
157-Popeye	3.00	9.00	21.00
158-Woody Woodpecker	1.70	5.00	12.00
159-Indian Chief	3.00	9.00	21.00
160-Bugs Bunny	1.70	5.00	12.00
161-Roy Rogers	5.70	17.00	40.00
162-Henry	1.35	4.00	9.00
163-Rin Tin Tin (TV)	3.00	9.00	21.00
164-Porky Pig	1.70	5.00	12.00
165-The Lone Ranger	6.50	19.50	45.00
166-Santa and His Reindeer	1.35	4.00	9.00
167-Roy Rogers and Santa	5.70	17.00	40.00
168-Santa Claus' Workshop (1957)	1.35	4.00	9.00
169-Popeye (1958)	3.00	9.00	21.00
170-Indian Chief	3.00	9.00	21.00
171-Oswald the Rabbit	1.50	4.50	10.00
172-Tarzan	10.00	30.00	70.00
173-Tom and Jerry	1.50	4.50	10.00
174-The Lone Ranger	6.50	19.50	45.00
175-Porky Pig	1.50	4.50	10.00
176-Roy Rogers	5.50	16.50	38.00
177-Woody Woodpecker	1.50	4.50	10.00
178-Henry	1.35	4.00	9.00
179-Bugs Bunny	1.50	4.50	10.00
180-Rin Tin Tin (TV)	3.00	9.00	21.00
181-Happy Holiday	1.20	3.50	8.00
182-Happi Tim	1.50	4.50	10.00
183-Welcome Santa (1958)	1.20	3.50	8.00
184-Woody Woodpecker (1959)	1.50	4.50	10.00
185-Tarzan-Photo-c	10.00	30.00	70.00
186-Oswald the Rabbit	1.50	4.50	10.00
187-Indian Chief	3.00	9.00	21.00
188-Bugs Bunny	1.50	4.50	10.00
189-Henry	1.20	3.50	8.00
190-Tom and Jerry	1.50	4.50	10.00
191-Roy Rogers	5.50	16.50	38.00
192-Porky Pig	1.50	4.50	10.00
193-The Lone Ranger	6.50	19.50	45.00
194-Popeye	3.00	9.00	21.00
195-Rin Tin Tin (TV)	3.00	9.00	21.00
196-Sears Special - not published			
197-Santa Is Coming	1.20	3.50	8.00
198-Santa's Helpers (1959)	1.20	3.50	8.00
199-Huckleberry Hound (TV)(1960)	2.15	6.50	15.00
200-Fury (TV)	3.50	10.50	24.00
201-Bugs Bunny	1.35	4.00	9.00
202-Space Explorer	4.60	14.00	32.00
203-Woody Woodpecker	1.35	4.00	9.00
204-Tarzan	7.00	21.00	50.00
205-Mighty Mouse	2.50	7.50	17.50
206-Roy Rogers-Photo-c	5.50	16.50	38.00
207-Tom and Jerry	1.35	4.00	9.00

MARCH OF COMICS (continued)	Good	Fine	N-Mint
208-The Lone Ranger-Clayton Moore photo-c	8.00	24.00	56.00
209-Porky Pig	1.35	4.00	9.00
210-Lassie (TV)	3.00	9.00	21.00
211-Sears Special - not published			
212-Christmas Eve	1.20	3.50	8.00
213-Here Comes Santa (1960)	1.20	3.50	8.00
214-Huckleberry Hound (TV)(1961)	2.00	6.00	14.00
215-Hi Yo Silver	4.00	12.00	28.00
216-Rocky & His Friends (TV)	4.30	13.00	30.00
217-Lassie (TV)	2.35	7.00	16.00
218-Porky Pig	1.35	4.00	9.00
219-Journey to the Sun	3.00	9.00	21.00
220-Bugs Bunny	1.35	4.00	9.00
221-Roy and Dale-Photo-c	5.00	15.00	35.00
222-Woody Woodpecker	1.35	4.00	9.00
223-Tarzan	7.00	21.00	50.00
224-Tom and Jerry	1.35	4.00	9.00
225-The Lone Ranger	5.00	15.00	35.00
226-Christmas Treasury (1961)	1.20	3.50	8.00
227-Sears Special - not published?			
228-Letters to Santa (1961)	1.20	3.50	8.00
229-The Flintstones (TV)(1962)	4.30	13.00	30.00
230-Lassie (TV)	2.35	7.00	16.00
231-Bugs Bunny	1.20	3.50	8.00
232-The Three Stooges	5.70	17.00	40.00
233-Bullwinkle (TV)	5.00	15.00	35.00
234-Smokey the Bear	1.35	4.00	9.00
235-Huckleberry Hound (TV)	2.00	6.00	14.00
236-Roy and Dale	3.65	11.00	25.00
237-Mighty Mouse	2.00	6.00	14.00
238-The Lone Ranger	5.00	15.00	35.00
239-Woody Woodpecker	1.35	4.00	9.00
240-Tarzan	5.70	17.00	40.00
241-Santa Claus Around the World	1.20	3.50	8.00
242-Santa's Toyland (1962)	1.20	3.50	8.00
243-The Flintstones (TV)(1963)	4.00	12.00	28.00
244-Mister Ed (TV)-Photo-c	2.65	8.00	18.00
245-Bugs Bunny	1.35	4.00	9.00
246-Popeye	2.50	7.50	17.50
247-Mighty Mouse	2.00	6.00	14.00
248-The Three Stooges	5.70	17.00	40.00
249-Woody Woodpecker	1.35	4.00	9.00
250-Roy and Dale	3.65	11.00	25.00
251-Little Lulu & Witch Hazel	13.50	41.00	95.00
252-Tarzan-Painted-c	5.50	16.50	40.00
253-Yogi Bear (TV)	2.65	8.00	18.00
254-Lassie (TV)	2.35	7.00	16.00
255-Santa's Christmas List	1.20	3.50	8.00
256-Christmas Party (1963)	1.20	3.50	8.00
257-Mighty Mouse	2.00	6.00	14.00
258-The Sword in the Stone (Disney)	5.70	17.00	40.00
259-Bugs Bunny	1.35	4.00	9.00
260-Mister Ed (TV)	2.00	6.00	14.00
261-Woody Woodpecker	1.35	4.00	9.00
262-Tarzan	5.50	16.50	40.00
263-Donald Duck-not Barks	6.00	18.00	36.00
264-Popeye	2.50	7.50	17.50
265-Yogi Bear (TV)	2.00	6.00	14.00
266-Lassie (TV)	2.00	6.00	14.00
267-Little Lulu; Irving Tripp-a	11.00	32.00	75.00
268-The Three Stooges	5.00	15.00	35.00
269-A Jolly Christmas	1.20	3.50	8.00
270-Santa's Little Helpers	1.20	3.50	8.00
271-The Flintstones (TV)(1965)	4.00	12.00	28.00
272-Tarzan	5.50	16.50	40.00
273-Bugs Bunny	1.35	4.00	9.00

	Good	Fine	N-Mint
274-Popeye	2.50	7.50	17.50
275-Little Lulu-Irving Tripp-a	9.00	27.00	62.00
276-The Jetsons (TV)	5.70	17.00	40.00
277-Daffy Duck	1.35	4.00	9.00
278-Lassie (TV)	2.00	6.00	14.00
279-Yogi Bear (TV)	2.00	6.00	14.00
280-The Three Stooges-Photo-c	5.00	15.00	35.00
281-Tom and Jerry	1.00	3.00	7.00
282-Mister Ed (TV)	2.00	6.00	14.00
283-Santa's Visit	1.20	3.50	8.00
284-Christmas Parade (1965)	1.20	3.50	8.00
285-Astro Boy (TV)	20.00	60.00	140.00
286-Tarzan	5.00	15.00	35.00
287-Bugs Bunny	1.00	3.00	7.00
288-Daffy Duck	1.00	3.00	7.00
289-The Flintstones (TV)	3.00	9.00	21.00
290-Mister Ed (TV)-Photo-c	1.70	5.00	12.00
291-Yogi Bear (TV)	1.70	5.00	12.00
292-The Three Stooges-Photo-c	5.00	15.00	35.00
293-Little Lulu; Irving Tripp-a	7.00	21.00	50.00
294-Popeye	.85	2.50	6.00
295-Tom and Jerry	1.00	3.00	7.00
296-Lassie (TV)-Photo-c	1.70	5.00	12.00
297-Christmas Bells	1.20	3.50	8.00
298-Santa's Sleigh (1966)	1.20	3.50	8.00
299-The Flintstones (TV)(1967)	3.00	9.00	21.00
300-Tarzan	5.00	15.00	35.00
301-Bugs Bunny	.85	2.50	6.00
302-Laurel and Hardy (TV)-Photo-c	3.50	10.50	24.00
303-Daffy Duck	.70	2.00	5.00
304-The Three Stooges-Photo-c	4.30	13.00	30.00
305-Tom and Jerry	.70	2.00	5.00
306-Daniel Boone (TV)-Photo-c	3.00	9.00	21.00
307-Little Lulu; Irving Tripp-a	5.70	17.00	40.00
308-Lassie (TV)-Photo-c	1.50	4.50	10.00
309-Yogi Bear (TV)	1.00	3.00	7.00
310-The Lone Ranger-Clayton Moore photo-c	5.70	17.00	40.00
311-Santa's Show	1.00	3.00	7.00
312-Christmas Album (1967)	1.00	3.00	7.00
313-Daffy Duck (1968)	.70	2.00	5.00
314-Laurel and Hardy (TV)	3.00	9.00	21.00
315-Bugs Bunny	.85	2.50	6.00
316-The Three Stooges	4.00	12.00	28.00
317-The Flintstones (TV)	2.65	8.00	18.00
318-Tarzan	4.65	13.00	32.00
319-Yogi Bear (TV)	1.50	4.50	10.00
320-Space Family Robinson (TV); Spiegle-a	6.50	19.50	45.00
321-Tom and Jerry	.70	2.00	5.00
322-The Lone Ranger	4.35	13.00	30.00
323-Little Lulu-not Stanley	3.50	10.50	24.00
324-Lassie (TV)-Photo-c	1.50	4.50	10.00
325-Fun with Santa	1.00	3.00	7.00
326-Christmas Story (1968)	1.00	3.00	7.00
327-The Flintstones (TV)(1969)	2.65	8.00	18.00
328-Space Family Robinson (TV); Spiegle-a	6.50	19.50	45.00
329-Bugs Bunny	.85	2.50	6.00
330-The Jetsons (TV)	4.30	13.00	30.00
331-Daffy Duck	.70	2.00	5.00
332-Tarzan	3.65	11.00	25.00
333-Tom and Jerry	.70	2.00	5.00
334-Lassie (TV)	1.15	3.50	8.00
335-Little Lulu	3.50	10.50	24.00
336-The Three Stooges	4.00	12.00	28.00
337-Yogi Bear (TV)	1.50	4.50	10.00
338-The Lone Ranger	4.35	13.00	30.00
339-(Did not come out)			

March Of Comics #245, © Warner Bros.

March Of Comics #290, © The Mister Ed Co.

March Of Comics #302, © Larry Harmon

March Of Comics #364, © Hanna-Barbera

March Of Comics #406, © WEST

March Of Comics #453, © KING

MARCH OF COMICS (continued)

	Good	Fine	N-Mint
340-Here Comes Santa (1969)	1.00	3.00	7.00
341-The Flintstones (TV)	2.65	8.00	18.00
342-Tarzan	3.65	11.00	25.00
343-Bugs Bunny	.70	2.00	5.00
344-Yogi Bear (TV)	1.15	3.50	8.00
345-Tom and Jerry	.70	2.00	5.00
346-Lassie (TV)	1.15	3.50	8.00
347-Daffy Duck	.70	2.00	5.00
348-The Jetsons (TV)	3.50	10.50	24.00
349-Little Lulu-not Stanley	3.00	9.00	21.00
350-The Lone Ranger	3.65	11.00	25.00
351-Beep-Beep, the Road Runner	1.35	4.00	9.00
352-Space Family Robinson (TV)-Spiegle-a	6.50	19.50	45.00
353-Beep-Beep, the Road Runner (1971)	1.35	4.00	9.00
354-Tarzan (1971)	3.00	9.00	21.00
355-Little Lulu-not Stanley	3.00	9.00	21.00
356-Scooby Doo, Where Are You? (TV)	2.00	6.00	14.00
357-Daffy Duck & Porky Pig	.70	2.00	5.00
358-Lassie (TV)	1.15	3.50	8.00
359-Baby Snoots	1.35	4.00	9.00
360-H. R. Pufnstuf (TV)-Photo-c	1.30	4.00	9.00
361-Tom and Jerry	.70	2.00	5.00
362-Smokey the Bear (TV)	.70	2.00	5.00
363-Bugs Bunny & Yosemite Sam	.70	2.00	5.00
364-The Banana Splits (TV)-Photo-c	.85	2.50	6.00
365-Tom and Jerry (1972)	.70	2.00	5.00
366-Tarzan	3.00	9.00	21.00
367-Bugs Bunny & Porky Pig	.70	2.00	5.00
368-Scooby Doo (TV)(4/72)	1.50	4.50	12.00
369-Little Lulu-not Stanley	2.30	7.00	16.00
370-Lassie (TV)-Photo-c	1.15	3.50	8.00
371-Baby Snoots	1.00	3.00	7.00
372-Smokey the Bear (TV)	.70	2.00	5.00
373-The Three Stooges	3.50	10.50	24.00
374-Wacky Witch	.70	2.00	5.00
375-Beep-Beep & Daffy Duck	.70	2.00	5.00
376-The Pink Panther (1972)	1.35	4.00	9.00
377-Baby Snoots (1973)	1.00	3.00	7.00
378-Turok, Son of Stone	6.50	19.50	45.00
379-Heckle & Jeckle New Terrytoons	.50	1.50	3.00
380-Bugs Bunny & Yosemite Sam	.50	1.50	3.00
381-Lassie (TV)	.85	2.50	6.00
382-Scooby Doo, Where Are You? (TV)	1.50	4.50	10.00
383-Smokey the Bear (TV)	.50	1.50	3.00
384-Pink Panther	1.00	3.00	7.00
385-Little Lulu	2.00	6.00	14.00
386-Wacky Witch	.50	1.50	3.00
387-Beep-Beep & Daffy Duck	.50	1.50	3.00
388-Tom and Jerry (1973)	.50	1.50	3.00
389-Little Lulu-not Stanley	2.00	6.00	14.00
390-Pink Panther	.70	2.00	5.00
391-Scooby Doo (TV)	1.30	4.00	9.00
392-Bugs Bunny & Yosemite Sam	.50	1.50	3.00
393-New Terrytoons (Heckle & Jeckle)	.50	1.50	3.00
394-Lassie (TV)	.70	2.00	5.00
395-Woodsy Owl	.50	1.50	3.00
396-Baby Snoots	.70	2.00	5.00
397-Beep-Beep & Daffy Duck	.50	1.50	3.00
398-Wacky Witch	.50	1.50	3.00
399-Turok, Son of Stone	5.70	17.00	40.00
400-Tom and Jerry	.50	1.50	3.00
401-Baby Snoots (1975) (r-/No. 371)	.70	2.00	5.00
402-Daffy Duck (r-/No. 313)	.50	1.50	3.00
403-Bugs Bunny (r-/No. 343)	.50	1.50	3.00
404-Space Family Robinson (TV)(r-/No. 328)	5.00	15.00	35.00
405-Cracky	.50	1.50	3.00

	Good	Fine	N-Mint
406-Little Lulu (r-/No. 355)	1.70	5.00	12.00
407-Smokey the Bear (TV)(r-/No. 362)	.50	1.50	3.00
408-Turok, Son of Stone	5.00	15.00	35.00
409-Pink Panther	.50	1.50	3.00
410-Wacky Witch	.35	1.00	2.00
411-Lassie (TV)(r-/No. 324)	.70	2.00	5.00
412-New Terrytoons (1975)	.35	1.00	2.00
413-Daffy Duck (1976)(r-/No. 331)	.35	1.00	2.00
414-Space Family Robinson (r-/No. 328)	3.50	10.50	24.00
415-Bugs Bunny (r-/No. 329)	.35	1.00	2.00
416-Beep-Beep, the Road Runner (r-/No. 353)	.35	1.00	2.00
417-Little Lulu (r-/No. 323)	1.70	5.00	12.00
418-Pink Panther (r-/No. 384)	.35	1.00	2.00
419-Baby Snoots (r-/No. 377)	.50	1.50	3.00
420-Woody Woodpecker	.35	1.00	2.00
421-Tweety & Sylvester	.35	1.00	2.00
422-Wacky Witch (r-/No. 386)	.35	1.00	2.00
423-Little Monsters	.50	1.50	3.00
424-Cracky (12/76)	.35	1.00	2.00
425-Daffy Duck	.35	1.00	2.00
426-Underdog (TV)	1.15	3.50	8.00
427-Little Lulu (r/No. 335)	1.15	3.50	8.00
428-Bugs Bunny	.35	1.00	2.00
429-The Pink Panther	.35	1.00	2.00
430-Beep-Beep, the Road Runner	.35	1.00	2.00
431-Baby Snoots	.50	1.50	3.00
432-Lassie (TV)	.50	1.50	3.00
433-Tweety & Sylvester	.35	1.00	2.00
434-Wacky Witch	.35	1.00	2.00
435-New Terrytoons	.35	1.00	2.00
436-Wacky Advs. of Cracky	.35	1.00	2.00
437-Daffy Duck	.35	1.00	2.00
438-Underdog (TV)	1.15	3.50	8.00
439-Little Lulu (r/#349)	1.15	3.50	8.00
440-Bugs Bunny	.35	1.00	2.00
441-The Pink Panther	.35	1.00	2.00
442-Beep-Beep, the Road Runner	.35	1.00	2.00
443-Baby Snoots	.50	1.50	3.00
444-Tom and Jerry	.35	1.00	2.00
445-Tweety and Sylvester	.35	1.00	2.00
446-Wacky Witch	.35	1.00	2.00
447-Mighty Mouse	.50	1.50	3.00
448-Cracky	.35	1.00	2.00
449-Pink Panther	.35	1.00	2.00
450-Baby Snoots	.35	1.00	2.00
451-Tom and Jerry	.35	1.00	2.00
452-Bugs Bunny	.35	1.00	2.00
453-Popeye	.35	1.00	2.00
454-Woody Woodpecker	.35	1.00	2.00
455-Beep-Beep, the Road Runner	.35	1.00	2.00
456-Little Lulu (r/#369)	.85	2.50	6.00
457-Tweety & Sylvester	.35	1.00	2.00
458-Wacky Witch	.35	1.00	2.00
459-Mighty Mouse	.35	1.00	2.00
460-Daffy Duck	.50	1.50	3.00
461-The Pink Panther	.35	1.00	2.00
462-Baby Snoots	.35	1.00	2.00
463-Tom and Jerry	.35	1.00	2.00
464-Bugs Bunny	.35	1.00	2.00
465-Popeye	.35	1.00	2.00
466-Woody Woodpecker	.35	1.00	2.00
467-Underdog (TV)	.85	2.50	6.00
468-Little Lulu (r/#385)	.70	2.00	4.00
469-Tweety & Sylvester	.35	1.00	2.00
470-Wacky Witch	.35	1.00	2.00
471-Mighty Mouse	.50	1.50	3.00

MARCH OF COMICS (continued)	Good	Fine	N-Mint
472-Heckle & Jeckle(12/80)	.35	1.00	2.00
473-Pink Panther(1/81)	.35	1.00	2.00
474-Baby Snoots	.35	1.00	2.00
475-Little Lulu (r/#323)	.50	1.50	3.00
476-Bugs Bunny	.35	1.00	2.00
477-Popeye	.35	1.00	2.00
478-Woody Woodpecker	.35	1.00	2.00
479-Underdog (TV)	.85	2.50	6.00
480-Tom and Jerry	.35	1.00	2.00
481-Tweety and Sylvester	.35	1.00	2.00
482-Wacky Witch	.35	1.00	2.00
483-Mighty Mouse	.50	1.50	3.00
484-Heckle & Jeckle	.35	1.00	2.00
485-Baby Snoots	.35	1.00	2.00
486-The Pink Panther	.35	1.00	2.00
487-Bugs Bunny	.35	1.00	2.00
488-Little Lulu (r/#335)	.50	1.50	3.00

MARCH OF CRIME (My Love Affair #1-6) (See Fox Giants)
No. 7, 7/50 - No. 2, 9/50; No. 3, 9/51
Fox Features Syndicate

	Good	Fine	N-Mint
7(#1)(7/50)-Wood-a	13.00	40.00	90.00
2(9/50)-Wood-a (exceptional)	11.50	34.00	80.00
3(9/51)	4.35	13.00	30.00

MARCO POLO
1962 (Movie classic)
Charlton Comics Group

	Good	Fine	N-Mint
nn (Scarce)-Glanzman-c/a, 25pgs.	8.50	25.50	60.00

MARGARET O'BRIEN (See The Adventures of. . .)

MARGE'S LITTLE LULU (Little Lulu #207 on)
No. 74, 6/45 - No. 164, 7-9/62; No. 165, 10/62 - No. 206, 8/72
Dell Publishing Co./Gold Key #165-206

Marjorie Henderson Buell, born in Philadelphia, Pa., in 1904, created *Little Lulu*, a cartoon character that appeared weekly in the *Saturday Evening Post* from Feb. 23, 1935 through Dec. 30, 1944. She was not responsible for any of the comic books. **John Stanley** did pencils only on all *Little Lulu* comics through at least #135 (1959). He did pencils and inks on *Four Color* #74 & 97. **Irving Tripp** began inking stories from #1 on, and remained the comic's illustrator throughout its entire run. **Stanley** did storyboards (layouts), pencils, and scripts in all cases and inking only on covers. His word balloons were written in cursive. **Tripp** and occasionally other artists at Western Publ. in Poughkeepsie, N.Y. blew up the pencilled pages, inked the blowups, and lettered them. **Arnold Drake** did storyboards, pencils and scripts starting with #197 (1970), amidst reprinted issues. **Buell** sold her rights exclusively to Western Publ. in Dec., 1971. The earlier issues had to be approved by **Buell** prior to publication.

	Good	Fine	N-Mint
4-Color 74('45)-Intro Lulu, Tubby & Alvin	90.00	270.00	630.00
4-Color 97(2/46)	47.00	140.00	330.00

(Above two books are all John Stanley - cover, pencils, and inks.)

	Good	Fine	N-Mint
4-Color 110('46)-1st Alvin Story Telling Time; 1st app. Willy			
	33.00	100.00	230.00
4-Color 115-1st app. Boys' Clubhouse	33.00	100.00	230.00
4-Color 120, 131: 120-1st app. Eddie	30.00	90.00	210.00
4-Color 139('47),146,158	27.00	81.00	190.00
4-Color 165 (10/47)-Smokes doll hair & has wild hallucinations. 1st Tubby detective story	27.00	81.00	190.00
1(1-2/48)-Lulu's Diary feat. begins	56.00	168.00	390.00
2-1st app. Gloria; 1st Tubby story in a L.L. comic; 1st app. Miss Feeny	29.00	87.00	200.00
3-5	25.00	75.00	175.00
6-10: 7-1st app. Annie; Xmas-c	18.00	54.00	125.00
11-20: 19-1st app. Wilbur. 20-1st app. Mr. McNabbem			
	15.00	45.00	105.00
21-30: 26-r/F.C. 110. 30-Xmas-c	11.50	34.00	80.00
31-38,40: 35-1st Mumday story	10.00	30.00	70.00
39-Intro. Witch Hazel in "That Awful Witch Hazel"			
	11.00	32.00	76.00
41-60: 42-Xmas-c. 45-2nd Witch Hazel app. 49-Gives Stanley &			

	Good	Fine	N-Mint
others credit	8.50	25.50	60.00
61-80: 63-1st app. Chubby (Tubby's cousin). 68-1st app. Prof. Cleff. 78-Xmas-c. 80-Intro. Little Itch (2/55)	6.50	19.50	45.00
81-99: 90-Xmas-c	4.00	12.00	30.00
100	4.60	14.00	35.00
101-130: 123-1st app. Fifi	3.50	10.50	24.00
131-164: 135-Last Stanley-p	2.65	8.00	20.00
165-Giant; . . . In Paris ('62)	4.00	12.00	32.00
166-Giant; . . . Christmas Diary ('62-'63)	4.00	12.00	32.00
167-169	2.15	6.50	15.00
170,172,175,176,178-196,198-200-Stanley-r. 182-1st app. Little Scarecrow Boy	1.30	4.00	9.00
171,173,174,177,197	.85	2.50	6.00
201,203,206-Last issue to carry Marge's name	.55	1.65	4.00
202,204,205-Stanley-r	1.00	3.00	7.00
. . .& Tubby in Japan (12 cents)(5-7/62) 01476-207			
	5.70	17.00	40.00
. . .Summer Camp 1(8/67-G.K.-Giant) '57-58-r	4.65	14.00	32.00
. . .Trick 'N' Treat 1(12–)(12/62-Gold Key)	5.00	15.00	35.00

NOTE: *See Dell Giant Comics #23, 29, 36, 42, 50, & Dell Giants for annuals. All Giants not by Stanley from L.L. on Vacation (7/54) on. Irving Tripp a-#1 on. Christmas c-7, 18, 30, 42, 78, 90, 126, 250. Summer Camp issues #173, 177, 181, 189, 197, 201, 206.*

MARGE'S LITTLE LULU (See Golden Comics Digest #19, 23, 27, 29, 33, 36, 40, 43, 46 & March of Comics #251, 267, 275, 293, 307, 323, 335, 349, 355, 369, 385, 406, 417, 427, 439, 456, 468, 475, 488)

MARGE'S TUBBY (Little Lulu)(See Dell Giants)
No. 381, Aug, 1952 - No. 49, Dec-Feb, 1961-62
Dell Publishing Co./Gold Key

	Good	Fine	N-Mint
4-Color 381-Stanley script; Irving Tripp-a	12.00	36.00	84.00
4-Color 430,444-Stanley-a	7.00	21.00	50.00
4-Color 461 (4/53)-1st Tubby & Men From Mars story; Stanley-a			
	6.50	19.50	45.00
5 (7-9/53)-Stanley-a	5.00	15.00	35.00
6-10	3.50	10.50	24.00
11-20	2.85	8.50	20.00
21-30	2.35	7.00	16.00
31-49	2.00	6.00	14.00
. . .& the Little Men From Mars No. 30020-410(10/64-G.K.)-25 cents; 68 pgs.	5.00	15.00	40.00

NOTE: *John Stanley did all storyboards & scripts through at least #35 (1959). Lloyd White did all art except F.C. 381, 430, 444, 461 & #5.*

MARGIE (See My Little. . .)

MARGIE (TV)
No. 1307, Mar-May, 1962 - No. 2, July-Sept, 1962 (Photo-c)
Dell Publishing Co.

	Good	Fine	N-Mint
4-Color 1307, 2	2.30	7.00	16.00

MARGIE COMICS (Formerly Comedy) (Reno Browne #50 on) (Also see Cindy & Teen Comics)
No. 35, Winter, 1946-47 - No. 49, Dec, 1949
Marvel Comics (ACI)

	Good	Fine	N-Mint
35	3.70	11.00	26.00
36-38,42,45,47-49	2.00	6.00	12.00
39,41,43(2),44,46-Kurtzman's "Hey Look"	2.65	8.00	18.00
40-Three "Hey Looks," three "Giggles & Grins" by Kurtzman			
	3.75	11.25	26.00

MARINES (See Tell It to the . . .)

MARINES ATTACK
Aug, 1964 - No. 9, Feb-Mar, 1966
Charlton Comics

1	.60	1.20
2-9	.50	1.00

Marco Polo, © CC

Marge's Little Lulu Trick 'N' Treat #1, © WEST

Margie Comics #49, © MEG

Marines In Battle #1, © MEG

Marmaduke Mouse #10, © QUA

Martin Kane #4 (#1), © FOX

MARINES AT WAR (Tales of the Marines #4)
No. 5, April, 1957 - No. 7, Aug, 1957
Atlas Comics (OPI)

	Good	Fine	N-Mint
5-7	.60	1.80	4.00

NOTE: *Colan a-5. Drucker a-5. Everett a-5. Maneely a-5. Orlando a-7. Severin c-5.*

MARINES IN ACTION
June, 1955 - No. 14, Sept, 1957
Atlas News Co.

1-Rock Murdock, Boot Camp Brady begin	1.70	5.00	12.00
2-14	.85	2.50	6.00

NOTE: *Berg a-2, 8, 9, 11, 14. Heath c-2, 9. Maneely c-1. Severin a-4; c-7-11, 14.*

MARINES IN BATTLE
Aug, 1954 - No. 25, Sept, 1958
Atlas Comics (ACI No. 1-12/WPI No. 13-25)

1-Heath-c; Iron Mike McGraw by Heath; history of U.S. Marine Corps. begins	3.00	9.00	21.00
2	1.50	4.50	10.00
3-6,8-10: 4-Last precode (2/55)	1.30	4.00	9.00
7-Six pg. Kubert/Moskowitz-a	2.00	6.00	14.00
11-16,18-22,24	.85	2.50	6.00
17-Williamson-a, 3 pgs.	3.00	9.00	21.00
23-Crandall-a; Mark Murdock app.	1.70	5.00	12.00
25-Torres-a	1.70	5.00	12.00

NOTE: *Berg a-22. Drucker a-6. Everett a-4, 15; c-21. Heath c-1. Maneely c-24. Orlando a-6. Pakula a-6. Powell a-16. Severin c-12.*

MARINE WAR HEROES (Charlton Premiere #19)
Jan, 1964 - No. 18, Mar, 1967
Charlton Comics

1		.60	1.20
2-18		.50	1.00

NOTE: *Montes/Bache a-1,14,18; c-1.*

MARK, THE
Sept, 1987 - Present ($1.75, $1.95, color)
Dark Horse Comics

1-4	.30	.85	1.70

MARK HAZZARD: MERC
Nov, 1986 - No. 12, Oct, 1987
Marvel Comics Group

1-Morrow-a begins		.60	1.20
2-12		.50	1.00
Annual 1(11/87)		.60	1.20

MARK OF ZORRO (See 4-Color #228)

MARKSMAN, THE (Also see Champions)
Jan., 1988 - Present ($1.95, color)
Hero Comics

1-7: 1-Origin The Marksman, Rose begins	.35	1.00	1.95

MARK STEEL
1967, 1968, 1972 (24 pgs.) (Color)
American Iron & Steel Institute (Giveaway)

1967,1968-"Journey of Discovery with..."; Neal Adams art		2.35	7.00	16.00
1972-"...Fights Pollution;" Adams-a	1.35	4.00	8.00

MARK TRAIL
Oct, 1955 - No. 5, Summer, 1959
Standard Magazines (Hall Syndicate)/Fawcett Publ. No. 5

1-Sunday strip-r	4.00	12.00	28.00
2-5	2.00	6.00	14.00
...Adventure Book of Nature 1(Summer, 1958; Pines)-100 pg. Giant; contains 78 Sunday strip-r	5.00	15.00	35.00

MARMADUKE MONK
No date; 1963 (10 cents)

I. W. Enterprises/Super Comics

	Good	Fine	N-Mint
1-I.W. Reprint, 14-(Super Reprint)('63)	.35	1.00	2.00

MARMADUKE MOUSE
Spring, 1946 - No. 65, Dec, 1956
Quality Comics Group (Arnold Publ.)

1	5.00	15.00	35.00
2	2.65	8.00	18.00
3-10	2.00	6.00	14.00
11-30	1.50	4.50	10.00
31-65	1.00	3.00	7.00
Super Reprint #14(1963)	.35	1.00	2.00

MARS
Jan, 1984 - No. 12, Jan, 1985 (Mando paper)
First Comics

1-12: 2-The Black Flame begins. 10-Dynamo Joe begins		.50	1.00

MARS
Oct, 1987 ($1.95, color)
Epic Comics (Marvel)

1-Exist?	.35	1.00	2.00

MARS & BEYOND (See 4-Color #866)

MARSHAL LAW
Oct, 1987 - Present ($1.95, Adults)
Epic Comics (Marvel)

1	.85	2.50	5.00
2	.50	1.50	3.00
3-6	.35	1.00	2.00

M.A.R.S. PATROL TOTAL WAR (Total War #1,2)
No. 3, Sept, 1966 - No. 10, Aug, 1969 (All-Painted-c)
Gold Key

3-Wood-a	1.70	5.00	12.00
4-10	.85	2.50	6.00

MARTHA WAYNE (See The Story of . . .)

MARTIAN MANHUNTER
May, 1988 - No. 4, Aug., 1988 ($1.25, color, limited series)
DC Comics

1-4: 2-Batman cameo		.65	1.30

MARTIN KANE (Formerly My Secret Affair) (Radio-TV)(Private Eye)
No. 4, June, 1950 - No. 2, Aug, 1950
Fox Features Syndicate (Hero Books)

4(#1)-Wood-c/a(2); used in SOTI, pg. 160; photo back cvr.		14.00	42.00	100.00
2-Orlando-a, 5pgs; Wood-a(2)	10.00	30.00	70.00

MARTY MOUSE
No date (1958?) (10 cents)
I. W. Enterprises

1-Reprint	.35	1.00	2.00

MARVEL ACTION UNIVERSE (TV)
Jan, 1989 ($1.00, color, one-shot)
Marvel Comics

1-R/Spider-Man And His Amazing Friends		.50	1.00

MARVEL ADVENTURES (. . .Adventure #4 on)
Dec, 1975 - No. 6, Oct, 1976
Marvel Comics Group

1-#1-6 r-/Daredevil 22-27		.25	.50
2-6		.20	.40

MARVEL AND DC PRESENT (Featuring the Uncanny X-Men and the New Teen titans)
Nov, 1982 (One Shot, 68pgs, $2.00 cover, printed on Baxter paper)

MARVEL AND DC PRESENT (continued)
Marvel Comics Group/DC Comics

	Good	Fine	N-Mint
1-Simonson/Austin c/a; Perez-a(p)	1.15	3.50	7.00

MARVEL BOY (Astonishing #3 on; see Marvel Super Action #4)
Dec, 1950 - No. 2, Feb, 1951
Marvel Comics (MPC)

1-Origin Marvel Boy by Russ Heath	27.00	81.00	190.00
2-Everett-a	24.00	72.00	168.00

MARVEL CHILLERS
Oct, 1975 - No. 7, Oct, 1976
Marvel Comics Group

1-Intro. Modred the Mystic; Kane-c(p)		.30	.60
2-5,7: 3-Tigra, the Were-Woman begins (origin), ends #7. Chaykin/ Wrightson-c. 7-Kirby-c, Tuska-p		.25	.50
6-Byrne-a(p); Buckler-c(p)		.50	1.00

MARVEL CLASSICS COMICS SERIES FEATURING . . . (Also see
Pendulum Ill. Class.)
1976 - No. 36, Dec, 1978 (52 pgs., no ads)
Marvel Comics Group

1-Dr. Jekyll and Mr. Hyde	.25	.75	1.50

2-27,29-36: 2-Time Machine, 3-Hunchback of Notre Dame, 4-20,000
Leagues Under the Sea, 5-Black Beauty, 6-Gulliver's Travels, 7-Tom
Sawyer, 8-Moby Dick, 9-Dracula, 10-Red Badge of Courage,
11-Mysterious Island, 12-The Three Musketeers, 13-Last of the
Mohicans, 14-War of the Worlds, 15-Treasure Island, 16-Ivanhoe,
17-The Count of Monte Cristo, 18-The Odyssey, 19-Robinson Crusoe,
20-Frankenstein, 21-Master of the World, 22-Food of the Gods,
23-The Moonstone, 24-She, 25-The Invisible Man, 26-The Illiad,
27-Kidnapped, 29-Prisoner of Zenda, 30-Arabian Nights, 31-First Man
in the Moon, 32-White Fang, 33-The Prince and the Pauper,
34-Robin Hood, 35-Alice in Wonderland, 36-A Christmas Carol

each....		.50	1.00
28-First M. Golden-a; The Pit and the Pendulum	.85	2.50	5.00

NOTE: **Adkins** c-1i, 4i, 12i. **Alcala** a-34i; c-34. **Bolle** a-35. **Buscema** c-17p, 19p, 26p.
Golden a-28. **Gil Kane** c-1-16p, 21p, 22p, 24p, 32p. **Nebres** a-5; c-24i. **Nino** a-2, 8, 12.
Redondo a-1, 9. No. 1-12 were reprinted from Pendulum Ill. Classics.

MARVEL COLLECTORS ITEM CLASSICS
Feb, 1965 - No. 22, Aug, 1969 (Marvel's Greatest #23 on)(68 pgs.)
Marvel Comics Group(ATF)

1-Fantastic Four, Spider-Man, Thor, Hulk, Iron Man-r begin	1.50	4.50	9.00
2 (4/66) - 4	.85	2.50	5.00
5-22	.40	1.25	2.50

NOTE: All reprints; Ditko, Kirby art in all.

MARVEL COMICS (Marvel Mystery #2 on)
October, November, 1939
Timely Comics (Funnies, Inc.)

NOTE: The first issue was originally dated October 1939. Most copies have a black circle
stamped over the date (on cover and inside) with "November" printed over it. However,
some copies do not have the November overprint and could have a higher value. Most
No. 1's have printing defects, i.e., tilted pages which caused trimming into the panels usually
on right side and bottom. Covers exist with and without gloss finish.

1-Origin Sub-Mariner by Bill Everett(1st newsstand app.); 1st 8 pgs. was
produced for **Motion Picture Funnies Weekly** #1 which was probably
not distributed outside of advance copies; Human Torch by Carl Burgos,
Kazar the Great, & Jungle Terror (only app.); intro. The Angel by Gustavson, the Masked Raider (ends #12); cover by sci/fi pulp illustrator Frank
R. Paul

	Good	Fine	VF-NM
	4200.00	12,600.00	27,000.00

(Only one known copy exists in Mint condition which traded twice in 1986
for $69,000 & later for $82,000, once in 1987 for $82,000. Two other copies
are known in NM-M condition & their value would vary beyond the VF-
NM price)

MARVEL COMICS PRESENTS
Sept, 1988 - Present (Bi-weekly, color, $1.25)
Marvel Comics

	Good	Fine	N-Mint
1-Wolverine by Buscema in #1-10	.35	1.00	2.00
2-18: 10-Colossus begins; 17-Cyclops begins	.60		1.25

MARVEL COMICS SUPER SPECIAL (Marvel Super Special #5 on)
September, 1977 - No. 41(?), Nov., 1986 (nn 7) (Magazine; $1.50)
Marvel Comics Group

	Good	Fine	N-Mint
1-Kiss, 40 pgs. comics plus photos & features; Simonson-a(p); also see Howard the Duck #12	3.00	9.00	21.00
2-Conan (3/78)	.50	1.50	3.00
3-Close Encounters of the Third Kind (6/78); Simonson-a	.35	1.00	2.00
4-The Beatles Story (8/78)-Perez/Janson-a	1.00	3.00	6.00
5-Kiss (12/78)	2.65	8.00	18.00
6-Jaws II (12/78)	.25	.75	1.50
8-Battlestar Galactica-tabloid size	.35	1.00	2.00
8-Battlestar Galactica publ. in reg. magazine format; low distribu- tion ($1.50)8½x11''	.85	2.50	5.00
9-Conan	.35	1.00	2.00
10-Star Lord	.35	1.00	2.00

11-13-Weirdworld begins #11; 25 copy special press run of each
with gold seal and signed by artists (Proof quality), Spring-June,
1979

	10.00	30.00	60.00
11-Weirdworld (regular issue)	.70	2.00	4.00
12-Weirdworld (regular issue)	.40	1.25	2.50
13-Weirdworld (regular issue)	.30	.90	1.80
14-Adapts movie 'Meteor'		.60	1.20
15-Star Trek with photos & pin-ups($1.50)		.60	1.20
15-with $2.00 price(scarce); the price was changed at tail end of a 200,000 press run	.70	2.00	4.00

16-20: 16-'Empire Strikes Back'-Williamson-a, 17-Xanadu, 18-Raid-
ers of the Lost Ark, 19-For Your Eyes Only (James Bond), 20-
Dragonslayer

each...	.30	.90	1.80

21-40 (Movie adaptations): 21-Conan, 22-Bladerunner; Williamson-a;
Steranko-c, 23-Annie, 24-The Dark Crystal, 25-Rock and Rule-
w/photos, 26-Octopussy (James Bond), 27-Return of the Jedi,
28-Krull, 29-Tarzan of the Apes (Greystoke movie), 30-Indiana Jones
and the Temple of Doom, 31-The Last Star Fighter, 32-The Muppets
Take Manhattan, 33-Buckaroo Bonzai, 34-Sheena, 35-Conan The
Destroyer, 36-Dune, 37-2010, 38-Red Sonja-movie adapt. 39-Santa
Claus: The Movie. 40-Labyrinth

each....	.35	1.00	2.00
41-Howard The Duck-movie adapt.(11/86)	.45	1.25	2.50

NOTE: **J. Buscema** a-1, 2, 9, 11-13, 18p, 21, 35, 40; c-11(part), 12. **Chaykin** a-9, 19p;
c-18, 19. **Colan** a(p)-6, 10, 14. **Spiegle** a-29. **Stevens** a-27. **Williamson** a-27.

MARVEL DOUBLE FEATURE
Dec, 1973 - No. 21, Mar, 1977
Marvel Comics Group

1-Captain America & Iron Man-r begin	.30		.60
2-21: 17-r/Iron Man & Sub-Mariner No. 1	.25		.50

NOTE: Colan a-1-19p(r). Gil Kane a-15p(r). Kirby a-1r, 2-8p(r), 17p(r); c-17-20.

MARVEL FAMILY (Also see Captain Marvel No. 18)
Dec, 1945 - No. 89, Jan, 1954
Fawcett Publications

1-Origin Captain Marvel, Captain Marvel Jr., Mary Marvel, & Uncle
Marvel retold; Black Adam origin & 1st app.

	60.00	180.00	420.00
2	32.00	95.00	225.00
3	23.00	70.00	160.00
4,5	18.00	54.00	125.00
6-10: 7-Shazam app.	14.00	42.00	100.00
11-20	10.00	30.00	70.00
21-30	8.00	24.00	56.00

Marvel And DC Present #1, © Marvel/DC

Marvel Collector's Item Classics #4, © MEG

Marvel Comics Super Special #4, © MEG

Marvel Family #41, © FAW

Marvel Fanfare #3, © MEG

Marvel Mystery Comics #2, © MEG

MARVEL FAMILY (continued)	Good	Fine	N-Mint
31-40	6.50	19.50	45.00
41-46,48-50	5.00	15.00	35.00
47-Flying Saucer c/stry	6.00	18.00	42.00
51-76,79,80,82-89	4.30	13.00	30.00
77-Communist Threat-c	6.50	19.50	45.00
78,81-Used in POP, pgs. 92,93	4.60	14.00	32.00

MARVEL FANFARE
March, 1982 - Present ($1.25-$1.95, slick paper) (Direct Sale only)
Marvel Comics Group

	Good	Fine	N-Mint
1-Spider-Man/Angel team-up; 1st Paul Smith story	1.35	4.00	8.00
2-Spider-Man, Ka-Zar, The Angel. F.F. origin retold	1.50	4.50	9.00
3-X-Men & Ka-Zar	.85	2.50	5.00
4-X-Men & Ka-Zar	1.00	3.00	6.00
5-Dr. Strange, Capt. America	.50	1.50	3.00
6-15: 6-Spider-Man, Scarlet Witch. 7-Incredible Hulk. 8-Dr. Strange; Wolf Boy begins. 9-Man-Thing. 10-13-Black Widow. 14-The Vision. 15-The Thing by Barry Smith, c/a	.35	1.10	2.20
16-43: 16,17-Skywolf. 18-Capt. America. 19-Cloak and Dagger. 20,21-The Thing/Incr. Hulk. 22,23-Iron Man vs. Dr. Octopus. 24-26-Weirdworld. 27-45: 27-Daredevil/Spider-Man. 28-Alpha Flight. 29-Hulk. 30-Moon Knight. 31,32-Capt. America. 33-X-Men. 34-37-Warriors Three. 38-Moon Knight/Dazzler. 39-Moon Knight/Hawkeye. 40-Angel/Rogue & Storm. 41-Doc. Strange. 42-Spider-Man. 43-Sub-Mariner/Human Torch	.35	1.10	2.20

NOTE: **Art Adams** c-13. **Austin** a-1i, 4i, 33i, 38i; c-8i, 33i. **Byrne** a-1p, 29; c-29. **Golden** a-1, 2, 4p; c-1, 2. **Infantino** c/a(p)-8. **Gil Kane** a-8-11p. **Miller** a-18; c-1(Back-c), 18. **Perez** a-10, 11p, 12, 13p; c-10p-13p. **Rogers** a-5p; c-5p. **Russell** a-5i, 6i, 8-11i, 43i; c-5i, 6. **Paul Smith** a-1p, 32, 4p; c-4p. **Williamson** a-30i.

MARVEL FEATURE (See Marvel Two-In-One)
Dec, 1971 - No. 12, Nov, 1973 (No. 1,2: 25 cents)
Marvel Comics Group

1-Origin The Defenders; Sub-Mariner, The Hulk & Dr. Strange; G.A. Sub-Mariner-r, Adams-c	1.35	4.00	8.00
2-G.A. 1950s Sub-Mariner-r	.70	2.00	4.00
3-Defender series ends	.70	2.00	4.00
4-7: 4-Begin Ant-Man series; brief origin		.50	1.00
8-Origin Antman & The Wasp		.50	1.00
9,10-Last Ant-Man. 9-Iron Man app.		.50	1.00
11,12-Thing team-ups. 11-Origin Fantastic-4 retold		.50	1.00

NOTE: **Bolle** a-9i. **Everett** a-1i, 3i. **Kane** c-3p, 7p. **Russell** a-7-10p. **Starlin** a-8, 11, 12; c-8.

MARVEL FEATURE (Also see Red Sonja)
Nov, 1975 - No. 7, Nov, 1976
Marvel Comics Group

1-Red Sonja begins; Adams r/Savage Sword of Conan #1	.25	.75	1.50
2-7	.25	.75	1.50

NOTE: **Thorne** c/a-2-7.

MARVEL FUMETTI BOOK
April, 1984 (One shot) ($1.00 cover price)
Marvel Comics Group

1-Art Adams-a		.40	.80

MARVEL GRAPHIC NOVEL
1982 - Present ($5.95-$6.95)
Marvel Comics Group (Epic Comics)

1 (First Printing)-Death of Captain Marvel	2.50	7.50	15.00
1 (2nd & 3rd Printing)	1.00	3.00	6.00
2-Elric: The Dreaming City	1.35	4.00	8.00
3-Dreadstar; Starlin-a, 48pgs.	1.20	3.50	7.00
4-The New Mutants-Origin	1.70	5.00	10.00

	Good	Fine	N-Mint
4-2nd Print	1.00	3.00	5.95
5-X-Men; book-length story	1.85	5.50	11.00
5-2nd Print	1.00	3.00	5.95
6-The Star Slammers, 7-Killraven, 8-Super Boxers, 9-The Futurians			
10-Heartburst, 11-Void Indigo, 12-The Dazzler, 13-Starstruck, 14-The Swords Of The Swashbucklers, 15-The Raven Banner (Asgard),			
16-The Aladdin Effect, 17-Revenge Of The Living Monolith,			
18-She Hulk	1.00	3.00	6.00
19-The Witch Queen of Acheron (Conan)	1.20	3.50	7.00
20-Greenberg the Vampire	1.70	5.00	10.00
21-Marada The She-Wolf	1.20	3.50	7.00
22-Amaz. Spider-Man in Hooky by Wrightson	1.70	5.00	10.00
23-Dr. Strange. 24-Love And War (Daredevil) by Miller. 25-Alien Legion. 26-Dracula. 27-Avengers. 28-Conan The Reaver. 29-The Big Chance (Thing vs. Hulk). 30-A Sailor's Story. 31-Wolfpack. 33-Thor. 34-Predator & Prey (Cloak & Dagger). 36-Willow (movie adapt.). 37-Hercules	1.20	3.50	7.00
32-Death Of Groo ($5.95)	1.35	4.00	8.00
35-Hitler's Astrologer (The Shadow, $12.95)	3.00	9.00	18.00
38-Silver Surfer ($14.95)	3.00	9.00	17.50

NOTE: **Aragones** a-27, 32. **Byrne** c/a-18. **Kaluta** a-13, 35p; c-13. **Miller** a-24p. **Simonson** a-6; c-6. **Starlin** c/a-1,3. **Williamson** a-34. **Wrightson** c-29i.

MARVEL MASTERWORKS
Nov., 1987 - Present ($29.95, color-r)
Marvel Comics

1-Spiderman, r-AF 15 & AS 1-10	5.00	15.00	29.95
2-Fantastic-4 r-1-10	5.00	15.00	29.95
3-X-Men, r-1-10	5.00	15.00	29.95

MARVEL MINI-BOOKS
1966 (50 pgs., B&W; 5/8''x7/8'') (6 different issues)
Marvel Comics Group (Smallest comics ever published)

Captain America, Spider-Man, Sgt. Fury, Hulk, Thor

	.35	1.00	2.00
Millie the Model		.50	1.00

NOTE: Each came in six different color covers, usually one color: Pink, yellow, green, etc.

MARVEL MOVIE PREMIERE (Magazine)
Sept, 1975 (One Shot) (Black & White)
Marvel Comics Group

1-Burroughs ''The Land That Time Forgot'' adaptation			
	.35	1.00	2.00

MARVEL MOVIE SHOWCASE
Nov, 1982 - No. 2, Dec, 1982 (68 pgs.)
Marvel Comics Group

1,2-Star Wars movie adaptation r/Star Wars #1-6			
		.60	1.20

MARVEL MOVIE SPOTLIGHT
Nov, 1982 (68 pgs.)
Marvel Comics Group

1-Edited r/Raiders of the Lost Ark #1-3; Buscema-c/a(p)			
		.40	.80

MARVEL MYSTERY COMICS (Formerly Marvel Comics) (Marvel Tales No. 93 on)
No. 2, Dec, 1939 - No. 92, June, 1949
Timely /Marvel Comics (TP 2-17/TCI 18-54/MCI 55-92)

2-American Ace begins, ends #3; Human Torch (blue costume) by Burgos, Sub-Mariner by Everett continues; 2pg. origin recap Human Torch	630.00	1890.00	4400.00
3-New logo from Marvel pulp begins	360.00	1080.00	2520.00
4-Intro. Electro, the Marvel of the Age (ends #19), The Ferret, Mystery Detective (ends #9)	290.00	870.00	2030.00
5 (Scarce)	455.00	1365.00	3185.00

MARVEL MYSTERY COMICS (continued)	Good	Fine	N-Mint
6,7	180.00	540.00	1260.00
8-Human Torch & Sub-Mariner battle	235.00	700.00	1645.00
9-(Scarce)-Human Torch & Sub-Mariner battle			
	288.00	865.00	2015.00
10-Human Torch & Sub-Mariner battle, conclusion; Terry Vance, the			
Schoolboy Sleuth begins, ends #57	155.00	465.00	1085.00
11	115.00	345.00	800.00
12-Classic Kirby-c	115.00	345.00	800.00
13-Intro. & 1st app. The Vision by S&K; Sub-Mariner dons new			
costume, ends #15	130.00	390.00	910.00
14-16	80.00	240.00	560.00
17-Human Torch/Sub-Mariner team-up by Everett/Burgos; pin-up on			
back-c	92.00	275.00	645.00
18	74.00	220.00	520.00
19-Origin Toro in text	78.00	235.00	545.00
20-Origin The Angel in text	74.00	220.00	520.00
21-Intro. & 1st app. The Patriot; not in #46-48; pin-up on back-c			
	67.00	200.00	470.00
22-25: 23-Last Gustavson Angel; origin The Vision in text. 24-Injury-to-eye story	59.00	178.00	415.00
26-30: 27-Ka-Zar ends; last S&K Vision who battles Satan. 28-Jimmy Jupiter in the Land of Nowhere begins, ends #48; Sub-Mariner vs. The Flying Dutchman	52.00	156.00	365.00
31-Sub-Mariner by Everett ends, begins again #84			
	51.00	154.00	360.00
32-1st app. The Boboes	51.00	154.00	360.00
33,35-40: 40-Zeppelin-c	51.00	154.00	360.00
34-Everett, Burgos, Martin Goodman, Funnies, Inc. office appear in story & battles Hitler; last Burgos Human Torch	59.00	178.00	415.00
41,43,45-48-Last Vision & Flag-c	46.00	138.00	320.00
44-Classic Super Plane-c	46.00	138.00	320.00
49-Origin Miss America	59.00	178.00	415.00
50-Mary becomes Miss Patriot (origin)	45.00	135.00	315.00
51-60: 53-Bondage-c	41.00	122.00	285.00
61,62,64-Last German War-c	37.00	110.00	260.00
63-Classic Hitler War-c; The Villainess Cat-Woman only app.			
	37.00	110.00	260.00
65,66-Last Japanese War-c	37.00	110.00	260.00
67-75: 74-Last Patriot. 75-Young Allies begin	35.00	105.00	245.00
76-78: 76-10 Chapter Miss America serial begins, ends #85.			
	35.00	105.00	245.00
79-New cover format; Super Villains begin on cover; last Angel			
	31.50	95.00	220.00
80-1st app. Capt. America in Marvel Comics	35.00	105.00	245.00
81-Captain America app.	31.50	95.00	220.00
82-Origin Namora; 1st Sub-Mariner/Namora team-up; Captain America app.	53.00	160.00	370.00
83,85: 83-Last Young Allies. 85-Last Miss America; Blonde Phantom app.	31.50	95.00	220.00
84-Blonde Phantom, Sub-Mariner by Everett; Captain America app.	36.00	108.00	250.00
86-Blonde Phantom i.d. revealed; Captain America app.; last Bucky app.	36.00	108.00	250.00
87-1st Capt. America/Golden Girl team-up	40.00	120.00	280.00
88-Golden Girl, Namora, & Sun Girl (1st in Marvel Comics) x-over; Captain America, Blonde Phantom app.; last Toro	36.00	108.00	250.00
89-1st Human Torch/Sun Girl team-up; 1st Captain America solo; Blonde Phantom app.	38.00	115.00	265.00
90-Blonde Phantom un-masked; Captain America app.			
	34.00	102.00	240.00
91-Capt. America app.; intro Venus; Blonde Phantom & Sub-Mariner end	34.00	102.00	240.00
92-Feature story on the birth of the Human Torch and the death of Professor Horton (his creator); 1st app. The Witness in Marvel			

	Good	Fine	N-Mint
Comics; Captain America app.	63.00	190.00	440.00
(Very rare) 132 Pg. issue, B&W, 25 cents (1943-44)-printed in N. Y.; square binding, blank inside covers; has Marvel No. 33-c in color; contains 2 Capt. America & 2 Marvel Mystery Comics-r			
(Two known copies)	250.00	750.00	1750.00

NOTE: *Crandall* a-26i. *Everett* c-7-9, 27, 84. *Schomburg* c-3-11, 13-15, 18, 19, 22-29, 33, 35, 36, 39-48, 50-57, 59, 63-66. Bondage covers-3, 4, 7, 12, 28, 29, 49, 50, 52, 56, 57, 58, 59, 65. Remember Pearl Harbor issues-#30, 31.

MARVEL NO-PRIZE BOOK, THE
Jan, 1983 (One Shot, Direct Sale only)
Marvel Comics Group

1-Golden-c		.50	1.00

MARVEL PREMIERE
April, 1972 - No. 61, Aug, 1981
Marvel Comics Group

1-Origin Warlock by Gil Kane/Adkins; origin Counter-Earth			
	1.00	3.00	6.00
2-Warlock ends; Kirby Yellow Claw-r	.85	2.50	5.00
3-Dr. Strange series begins, Smith-a(p)	1.25	3.75	7.50
4-Smith/Brunner-a	.70	2.00	4.00
5-10: 10-Death of the Ancient One	.35	1.00	2.00
11-14: 11-Origin-r by Ditko. 14-Intro. God; last Dr. Strange			
	.30	.80	1.60
15-Iron Fist begins (origin), ends #25	.85	2.50	5.00
16-20	.35	1.00	2.00
21-24,26-28: 26-Hercules. 27-Satana. 28-Legion of Monsters			
	.25	.80	1.60
25-Byrne's 1st Iron Fist	.85	2.50	5.00
29-56: 35-Origin/1st app. 3-D Man. 47-Origin new Ant-Man			
		.40	.80
57-Dr. Who (1st U.S. app.)	.35	1.00	2.00
58-60-Dr. Who	.25	.75	1.50
61-Star Lord		.50	1.00

NOTE: *Austin* a-50i, 56i; c-46i, 50i, 56i, 58. *Brunner* a-4i, 6p, 9-14p; c-9-14. *Byrne* a-47p, 48p. *Giffen* a-31p, 44p; c-44. *Gil Kane* a-1p, 2p, 15p; c-1p, 22-24p, 27p, 36p, 37p. *Kirby* c-26, 29-31, 35. *Layton* a-47i, 48i; c-47. *McWilliams* a-25i. *Miller* c-49p, 53p, 58p. *Nebres* a-44i; c-38i. *Nino* a-38i. *Perez* c/a-38p, 45p, 46p. *Ploog* a-38; c-5-7. *Russell* a-7p. *Simonson* a-60; c-57. *Starlin* a-8p; c-8. *Sutton* a-41, 43, 50p, 61; c-50p, 61. #57-60 were published with two different prices on cover.

MARVEL PRESENTS
October, 1975 - No. 12, Aug, 1977
Marvel Comics Group

1-Bloodstone app.		.40	.80
2-Origin Bloodstone; Kirby-c		.30	.60
3-Guardians of the Galaxy		.50	1.00
4-7,9,11,12-Guardians of the Galaxy		.40	.80
8-Reprints Silver Surfer #2		.40	.80
10-Starlin-a(p)		.40	.80

NOTE: *Austin* a-6i. *Kane* c-1p.

MARVEL PREVIEW (Magazine) (Bizarre Advs. #25 on)
Feb, 1975 - No. 24, Winter, 1980 (B&W) ($1.00)
Marvel Comics Group

1-Man Gods From Beyond the Stars; Adams-a(i) & cover; Nino-a			
	.35	1.00	2.00
2-Origin The Punisher (see Amaz. Spider-Man 129); 1st app. Dominic Fortune; Morrow-c	5.70	17.00	40.00
3-Blade the Vampire Slayer	.35	1.00	2.00
4-Star-Lord & Sword in the Star (origins & 1st app.)			
	1.20	3.50	7.00
5,6-Sherlock Holmes	.35	1.00	2.00
7-9: 7-Satana, Sword in the Star app., 8-Legion of Monsters, 9-Man-God; origin Star Hawk, ends #20	.35	1.00	2.00
10-Thor the Mighty; Starlin-a	.35	1.00	2.00
11-Star-Lord; Byrne-a	.35	1.00	2.00

Marvel Mystery Comics #49, © MEG

Marvel Premiere #3, © MEG

Marvel Preview #1, © MEG

Marvel Spotlight #5, © MEG

Marvel Super-Hero Contest Of Champions #3, © MEG

Marvel Super-Heroes #18, © MEG

	Good	Fine	N-Mint
MARVEL PREVIEW (continued)			
12-20: 12-Haunt of Horror, 15-Star-Lord, 16-Detectives, 17-Black Mark by G. Kane, 18-Star-Lord, 19-Kull, 20-Bizarre Advs.			
	.35	1.00	2.00
21,22,24: 21-Moon Knight; Ditko-a, 22-King Arthur. 24-Debut Paradox	.35	1.00	2.00
23-Miller-a; Bizarre Advs.	.35	1.00	2.00

NOTE: *Adams* a-20i(r). *Buscema* a-22, 23. *Byrne* a-11. *Colan* a-16p, 18p, 23p; c-16p. *Giffen* a-7. *Infantino* a-14. *Kaluta* a-12; c-15. *Miller* a-23. *Morrow* a-8i; c-2-4. *Perez* a-20p. *Ploog* a-8. *Starlin* c-13, 14.

MARVEL SAGA, THE
Dec, 1985 - Present
Marvel Comics Group

1	.40	1.25	2.50
2-25		.60	1.20

NOTE: *Williamson* a-9i, 10i; c-10-12i, 14i, 16i.

MARVEL'S GREATEST COMICS (Marvel Coll. Item Classics #1-22)
No. 23, Oct, 1969 - No. 96, Jan, 1981
Marvel Comics Group

23-30	.25	.75	1.50
31-34,38-96		.50	1.00
35-37-Silver Surfer-r/Fantastic Four #48-50		.50	1.00

NOTE: *Dr. Strange, Fantastic-4, Iron Man, Watcher-#23,24. Capt. America, Dr. Strange, Iron Man, Fantastic-4-#25-28. Fantastic Four-#38-96. Buscema a-85-92r; c-87-92r. Ditko a-23-28r. Kirby a(r)-1-82; c-75, 77p, 80p.*

MARVELS OF SCIENCE
March, 1946 - No. 4, June, 1946
Charlton Comics

1-(1st Charlton comic)-A-Bomb sty	6.50	19.50	45.00
2-4	3.50	10.50	24.00

MARVEL SPECIAL EDITION (Also see Special Collectors' Edition)
1975 - 1978 (84 pgs.) (Oversized)
Marvel Comics Group

1-Spider-Man(r); Ditko-a(r)	.25	.75	1.50
1-Star Wars ('77); r-Star Wars #1-3	.25	.75	1.50
2-Star Wars ('78); r-Star Wars #4-6		.50	1.00
3-Star Wars ('78, 116 pgs.); r-Star Wars #1-6		.50	1.00
3-Close Encounters ('78, 56 pgs., movie)		.50	1.00
V2#2(Spr. '80, $2.00, oversized)-"Star Wars: The Empire Strikes Back;" r-/Marvel Comics S. Special 16		.50	1.00

NOTE: *Chaykin* c/a-1(1977), 2, 3. *Stevens* a-2i(r), 3i(r).

MARVEL SPECTACULAR
Aug, 1973 - No. 19, Nov, 1975
Marvel Comics Group

1-Thor-r begin by Kirby		.30	.60
2-19		.25	.50

MARVEL SPOTLIGHT
11/71 - No. 33, 4/77; 7/79 - V2No. 11, 3/81
Marvel Comics Group

1-Origin Red Wolf; Wood inks, Adams-c	.50	1.50	3.00
2-(Giant, 52pgs.)-Venus-r by Everett; origin Werewolf by Ploog; Adams-c	.30	.90	1.80
3,4-Werewolf ends #4		.60	1.20
5-Origin/1st app. Ghost Rider	1.35	4.00	8.00
6-8-Last Ploog issue	.50	1.50	3.00
9-11-Last Ghost Rider	.25	.75	1.50
12-20: 12-The Son of Satan begins (Origin)		.40	.80
21-27: 25-Sinbad. 26-Scarecrow. 27-Sub-Mariner		.30	.60
28,29-Moon Knight	.50	1.50	3.00
30-The Warriors Three, 31-Nick Fury		.30	.60
32-Intro/partial origin Spider-Woman		.50	1.00
33-Deathlok		.40	.80
V2#1-7,9-11: Capt. Marvel #1-4. 5-Dragon Lord. 6,7-StarLord; origin			

	Good	Fine	N-Mint
#6. 9-11-Capt. Universe app.		.30	.60
8-Capt. Marvel; Miller a(p)	.35	1.00	2.00

NOTE: *Austin* c-V2#2i, 8. *J. Buscema* c/a-30p. *Ditko* a-V2#4, 5, 9-11; c-V2#4, 9-11. *Kane* c-21p, 32p. *Kirby* c-29. *McWilliams* a-20i. *Miller* a-V2#8p; c-V2#2, 5p, 7p, 8p. *Mooney* a-8i, 10i, 14-17p, 24p, 27, 32i. *Nasser* a-33p. *Ploog* a-2-5, 6-8p; c-3-9. *Sutton* a-9-11p, V2#6, 7. #29-25 cent & 30 cent issues exist.

MARVEL SUPER ACTION (Magazine)
January, 1976 (One Shot) (76 pgs.; black & white)
Marvel Comics Group

1-Origin & 2nd app. Dominic Fortune; The Punisher app., Weird World & The Huntress; Evans & Ploog-a	4.30	13.00	30.00

MARVEL SUPER-ACTION
May, 1977 - No. 37, Nov, 1981
Marvel Comics Group

1-Capt. America-r by Kirby begin		.30	.60
2-5: 4-Marvel Boy-r(origin)/M. Boy #1		.25	.50
6-37: 11-C.A. Origin-r. 14-37-Avengers-r		.25	.50

NOTE: *Buscema* a(r)-14p, 15p; c-18-20, 22, 35r-37. *Evans* a-1. *Everett* a-4. *Heath* a-4. *Ploog* a-1. *Smith* a-27r, 28r. *Steranko* a(r)-12p, 13p; c-12, 13.

MARVEL SUPER-HERO CONTEST OF CHAMPIONS
June, 1982 - No. 3, Aug, 1982 (Mini-Series)
Marvel Comics Group

1-Features nearly all Marvel characters currently appearing in comics	.85	2.50	5.00
2,3	.85	2.50	5.00

MARVEL SUPER HEROES
October, 1966 (68 pgs.) (1st Marvel One-shot)
Marvel Comics Group

1-r-origin Daredevil; Avengers-r; G.A. Sub-Mariner & H. Torch-r/M. Mystery No. 8	1.35	4.00	8.00

MARVEL SUPER-HEROES (Fantasy Masterpieces #1-11)
(Also see Giant Size Super Heroes) (#1-20 68 pgs.)
No. 12, 12/67 - No. 31, 11/71; No. 32, 9/72 - No. 105, 1/82
Marvel Comics Group

12-Origin & 1st app. Capt. Marvel of the Kree; G.A. H. Torch, Destroyer, Capt. America, Black Knight, Sub-Mariner-r	.85	2.50	5.00
13-G.A. Black Knight, Torch, Vision, Capt. America, Sub-Mariner-r; Capt. Marvel app.	.35	1.00	2.00
14-G.A. Sub-Mariner, Torch, Mercury, Black Knight, Capt. America reprints; Spider-Man app.	.35	1.00	2.00
15-Black Bolt cameo in Medusa; G.A. Black Knight, Sub-Mariner, Black Marvel, Capt. America-r	.35	1.00	2.00
16-Origin & 1st app. Phantom Eagle; G.A. Torch, Capt. America, Black Knight, Patriot, Sub-Mariner-r	.35	1.00	2.00
17-Origin Black Knight; G.A. Torch, Sub-Mariner, All-Winners Squad reprints	.35	1.00	2.00
18-Origin Guardians of the Galaxy; G.A. Sub-Mariner, All-Winners Squad-r	.35	1.00	2.00
19-G.A. Torch, Marvel Boy, Black Knight, Sub-Mariner-r; Smith-c(p)	.35	1.00	2.00
20-Reprints Young Men #24 w/-c	.35	1.00	2.00
21-105: All-r ish. 31-Last Giant ish.		.50	1.00

NOTE: *Austin* a-104. *Colan* a-12p, 13p, 15p, 18p; c-12, 13, 15, 18. *Everett* a-14i, 15i(r), 18r, 19r, 33r; c-85(r). New *Kirby* c-22, 27. *Maneely* a-15r, 19r. *Severin* a-83-85i(r), 100-02r; c-100-02r. *Starlin* c-47. *Tuska* a-19p.

MARVEL SUPER-HEROES SECRET WARS (See Secret Wars II)
May, 1984 - No. 12, Apr, 1985 (Limited series)
Marvel Comics Group

1	.60	1.75	3.50
2-4	.35	1.00	2.00
5-7: 6-The Wasp dies. 7-Intro. new Spider-Woman			
	.35	1.00	2.00

MARVEL SUPER-HEROES (continued)	Good	Fine	N-Mint
8-Spider-Man's new costume explained	.35	1.00	2.00
9-12	.35	1.00	2.00

MARVEL SUPER SPECIAL (See Marvel Comics Super. . .)

MARVEL TAILS STARRING PETER PORKER THE SPECTACULAR SPIDER-HAM
Nov, 1983 (One Shot)
Marvel Comics Group

	Good	Fine	N-Mint
1-Peter Porker, the Spectacular Spider-Ham, Captain Americat, Goose Rider, Hulk Bunny app.	.50		1.00

MARVEL TALES (Marvel Mystery #1-92)
No. 93, Aug, 1949 - No. 159, Aug, 1957
Marvel/Atlas Comics (MCI)

	Good	Fine	N-Mint
93	30.00	90.00	210.00
94-Everett-a	25.00	75.00	175.00
95,96,99,101,103,105	13.00	40.00	90.00
97-Sun Girl, 2 pgs; Kirbyish; one story used in N.Y. State Legislative document	18.00	54.00	125.00
98-Krigstein-a	14.00	42.00	100.00
100	14.00	42.00	100.00
102-Wolverton-a "The End of the World," 6 pgs.	27.00	81.00	190.00
104-Wolverton-a "Gateway to Horror," 6 pgs; Heath-c	25.00	75.00	175.00
106,107-Krigstein-a. 106-Decapitation story	12.00	36.00	84.00
108-120: 118-Hypo-c/panels in End of World story. 120-Jack Katz-a	7.00	21.00	50.00
121,123-131: 128-Flying Saucer-c. 131-Last precode (2/55)	5.70	17.00	40.00
122-Kubert-a	6.50	19.50	45.00
132,133,135-141,143,145	3.50	10.50	24.00
134-Krigstein, Kubert-a; flying saucer-c	5.00	15.00	35.00
142-Krigstein-a	4.65	14.00	32.00
144-Williamson/Krenkel-a, 3 pgs.	5.00	15.00	35.00
146,148-151,154,155,158	2.30	7.00	16.00
147-Ditko-a	3.70	11.00	26.00
152-Wood, Morrow-a	4.00	12.00	28.00
153-Everett End of World c/story	3.70	11.00	26.00
156-Torres-a	3.50	10.50	24.00
157,159-Krigstein-a	4.65	14.00	32.00

NOTE: *Andru* a-103. *Briefer* a-118. *Check* a-147. *Colan* a-105, 107, 118, 120, 121, 127, 131. *Drucker* a-127, 135, 141, 146, 150. *Everett* a-98, 104, 106(2), 108(2), 131, 148, 151, 153, 155; c-109, 111, 114, 117, 127, 143, 147-151, 153, 155, 156. *Forte* a-125, 130. *Heath* a-113, 118, 119; c-104-106, 130. *Gil Kane* a-117. *Lawrence* a-130. *Maneely* a-111, 126, 129; c-108, 116, 120, 129, 152. *Mooney* a-154. *Morrow* a-150, 152, 156. *Orlando* a-149, 151, 157. *Pakula* a-121, 144, 150, 152, 156. *Powell* a-136, 137, 150, 154. *Ravielli* a-117. *Rico* a-97, 99. *Romita* a-108. *Sekowsky* a-96-98. *Sinnott* a-105. *Tuska* a-114 *Whitney* a-107. *Wildey* a-126, 138.

MARVEL TALES (. . . Annual #1,2: . . . Starring Spider-Man #123 on)
1964 - Present (No. 1-32, 72 pgs.)
Marvel Comics Group

	Good	Fine	N-Mint
1-Origin Spider-Man, Hulk, Ant/Giant Man, Iron Man, Thor, & Sgt. Fury; all-r	8.50	25.50	60.00
2 ('65)-r-X-Men #1(origin), Avengers #1(origin) & origin Dr. Strange/ Str. Tales #115	3.60	11.00	25.00
3 (7/66)-Spider-Man-r begin	1.35	4.00	8.00
4,5	.85	2.50	5.00
6-10	.70	2.00	4.00
11-15: 13-Origin Marvel Boy-r/M. Boy #1	.35	1.00	2.00
16-30: 30-New Angel story	.25	.75	1.50
31-74,76,80-97		.50	1.00
75-Origin Spider-Man-r		.50	1.00
77-79-Drug issues-r/Spider-Man No. 96-98		.50	1.00
98-Death of Gwen Stacy-r/A. Spider-Man #121		.50	1.00
99-Death Green Goblin-r/A. Spider-Man #122		.50	1.00

	Good	Fine	N-Mint
100-(52 pgs.)-New Hawkeye/Two Gun Kid sty		.50	1.00
101-105-All Spider-Man-r		.50	1.00
106-1st Punisher-r/A. Spider-Man #129	.70	2.00	4.00
107-133-All Spider-Man-r		.40	.80
134-136-Dr. Strange-r begin; SpM stories continue. 134-Dr. Strange r/Strange Tales 110		.40	.80
137-Origin-r Dr. Strange; shows original unprinted-c & origin Spider-Man/Amazing Fantasy 15	.35	1.00	2.00
137-Nabisco giveaway		.50	1.00
138-Reprints all Amazing Spider-Man #1	.35	1.00	2.00
139-144: r-/Amazing Spider-Man #2-7 with original covers		.40	.80
145-190: Spider-Man-r		.40	.80
191 (68 pgs.)-r/Spider-Man 96-98		.40	.80
192 (52 pgs., $1.25)-r-Spider-Man 121,122		.40	.80
193-199		.40	.80
200-Double size ($1.25)-Miller c/a(p)	.65		1.30
201-208,210-222		.40	.80
209-Reprints 1st app. The Punisher/Amazing Spider-Man #129	.35	1.00	2.00

NOTE: *All are reprints with some new art. Austin* a-100i. *Byrne* a-193p-198p, 201p-208p. *Ditko* a-1-30, 83, 100, 137-55. *G. Kane* a-71, 81, 98-101p; c-125-127p, 130p, 137-55. *Mooney* a-63, 95-97i, 103(i). *Nasser* a-100p.

MARVEL TEAM-UP (See Marvel Treas. Ed. #18 & Official Marvel Index To. . .)
March, 1972 - No. 150, Feb, 1985
Marvel Comics Group

NOTE: *Spider-Man team-ups in all but Nos. 18,23,26,29,32,35,97,104,105,137.*

	Good	Fine	N-Mint
1-H-T	2.50	7.50	15.00
2,3-H-T	1.35	4.00	8.00
4-X-Men	1.50	4.50	9.00
5-10: 5-Vision. 6-Thing. 7-Thor. 8-The Cat. 9-Iron Man. 10-H-T	.70	2.00	4.00
11-20: 11-Inhumans. 12-Werewolf. 13-Capt. America. 14-Sub-Mariner 15-Ghost Rider (new). 16-Capt. Marvel. 17-Mr. Fantastic. 18-H-T/ Hulk. 19-Ka-Zar. 20-Black Panther	.50		1.50
21-30: 21-Dr. Strange. 22-Hawkeye. 23-H-T/Iceman. 24-Brother Voodoo. 25-Daredevil. 26-H-T/Thor. 27-Hulk. 28-Hercules. 29-H-T/Iron Man. 30-Falcon	.25	.75	1.50
31-40: 31-Iron Fist. 32-H-T/Son of Satan. 33-Nighthawk. 34-Valkyrie. 35-H-T/Dr. Strange. 36-Frankenstein. 37-Man-Wolf. 38-Beast. 39-H-T. 40-Sons of the Tiger/H-T	.25	.75	1.50
41-50: 41-Scarlet Witch. 42-The Vision. 43-Dr. Doom; retells origin. 44-Moondragon. 45-Killraven. 46-Deathlok. 47-Thing. 48-Iron Man. 49,50-Dr. Strange/Iron Man	.25	.75	1.50
51,52,56-58: 51-Dr. Strange/Iron Man. 52-Capt. America. 56-Daredevil. 57-Black Widow. 58-Ghost Rider		.50	1.00
53-Woodgod/Hulk; new X-Men, 1st by Byrne	1.00	3.00	6.00
54-Hulk/Woodgod; Byrne-a(p)	.60	1.75	3.50
55,59,60: 55-Warlock. 59-Yellowjacket/The Wasp. 60-The Wasp-All Byrne-a	.60	1.75	3.50
61-70: 61-H-T. 62-Ms. Marvel. 63-Iron Fist. 64-Daughters of the Dragon. 65-Capt. Britain (1st U.S. app.). 66-Capt. Britain; 1st app. Arcade. 67-Tigra. 68-Man-Thing. 69-Havock. 70-Thor-All Bryne-a	.25	.75	1.50
71,72,76: 71-Falcon. 72-Iron Man. 76-Dr. Strange. Byrne-c	.25	.75	1.50
73,77,78,80: 73-Daredevil. 77-Ms. Marvel. 78-Wonder Man. 80-Dr. Strange/Clea	.25	.75	1.50
74-Not Ready for Prime Time Players (Belushi)	.25	.75	1.50
75,79: 75-Power Man. 79-Mary Jane Watson as Red Sonja. Both Byrne-a(p)	.40	1.25	2.50
81-88,90: 81-Satana. 82-Black Widow. 83-Nick Fury. 84-Shang-Chi. 85-Shang-Chi/Black Widow/Nick Fury. 86-Guardians of the Galaxy. 87-Black Panther. 88-The Invisible Girl. 90-Beast			

Marvel Team-Up Annual #1, © MEG   Marvel Treasury Edition #7, © MEG   Marvin Mouse #1, © MEG

MARVEL TEAM-UP (continued)	Good	Fine	N-Mint
		.40	.80
89-Nightcrawler	.25	.75	1.50

91-99: 91-Ghost Rider. 92-Hawkeye. 93-Werewolf by Night. 94-SpM vs. The Shroud. 95-Nick Fury/Shield; intro. Mockingbird. 96-Howard The Duck. 97-Spider-Woman/Hulk. 98-Black Widow. 99-Machine Man
.40 .80

100-Fantastic-4(Double size); origin/1st app. Karma, one of the New Mutants; origin Storm; X-Men x-over; Miller-a/c(p); Byrne-a
1.00 3.00 6.00

101-116: 101-Nighthawk(Ditko-a). 102-Doc Samson. 103-Ant-Man. 104-Hulk/Ka-Zar. 105-Hulk/Powerman/Iron Fist. 106-Capt. America. 107-She-Hulk. 108-Paladin; Dazzler cameo. 109-Paladin/Dazzler. 110-Iron Man. 111-Devil-Slayer. 112-King Kull. 113-Quasar. 114-Falcon. 115-Thor. 116-Valkyrie
.40 .80

| 117-Wolverine | .50 | 1.50 | 3.00 |
| 118-Professor X | .25 | .75 | 1.50 |

119-149: 118-Professor X. 119-Gargoyle. 120-Dominic Fortune. 121-Human Torch. 122-Man-Thing. 123-Daredevil. 124-The Beast. 125-Tigra. 126-Hulk & Powerman/Son of Satan. 127-The Watcher. 128-Capt. America. 129-The Vision. 130-Scarlet Witch. 131-Frogman. 132-Mr. Fantastic. 133-Fantastic-4. 134-Jack of Hearts. 135-Kitty Pryde; X-Men cameo. 136-Wonder Man. 137-Aunt May/Franklin Richards. 138-Sandman. 139-Nick Fury, 140-Black Widow. 141-Daredevil; new SpM/Black Widow app. 142-Captain Marvel. 143-Starfox. 144-Moon Knight. 145-Iron Man. 146-Nomad. 147-Human Torch; SpM old costume. 148-Thor. 149-Cannonball
.40 .80

150-X-Men ($1.00); B. Smith-c	.50	1.50	3.00
Annual 1(1976)-New X-Men app.	1.35	4.00	8.00
Annual 2(12/79)-SpM/Hulk	.25	.75	1.50
Annual 3(11/80)-Hulk/Power Man/Machine Man/Iron Fist; Miller-c(p)	.25	.75	1.50
Annual 4(10/81)-SpM/Daredevil/Moon Knight/Power Man/Iron Fist; brief origins of each; Miller-c(p)/a	.25	.75	1.50
Annual 5(1982)-SpM/The Thing/Scarlet Witch/Dr. Strange/Quasar	.25	.75	1.50
Annual 6(10/83)-New Mutants, Cloak & Dagger app.	.25	.75	1.50
Annual 7(10/84)-Alpha Flight; Byrne-c(i)	.25	.75	1.50

NOTE: Art Adams c-141p. Austin a-79i; c-76i, 79i, 96i, 101i, 112i, 130i. Bolle a-9i. Byrne a(p)-53-55, 59-70, 75, 79, 100; c-68p, 72p, 75, 76p, 79p, 129i, 133i. Colan a-87p. Ditko a-101. Kane a(p)-4-6, 13, 14, 16-19, 23; c(p)-4, 13, 14, 17-19, 23, 25, 26, 32-35, 37, 41, 44, 45, 47, 53, 54. Miller c-95p, 99p, 102p, 106. Mooney a-2i, 7i, 8, 10p, 11p, 16i, 24p, 29p, 72, 93i, Annual 5i. Nasser a-89p; c-101p. Simonson c-99i, 148. Paul Smith c-131, 132. Starlin c-27. Sutton a-93p. "H-T" means Human Torch; "SpM" means Spider-Man; "S-M" means Sub-Mariner.

MARVEL TREASURY EDITION ($1.50-$2.50)
Sept, 1974 - No. 28, 1981 (100 pgs.; oversized, reprints)
Marvel Comics Group

1-Spider-Man	.35	1.00	2.00
2-Fantastic Four, Silver Surfer	.50	1.00
3-The Mighty Thor	.50	1.00
4-Conan; Smith-c/a	.25	.75	1.50

5-14,16,17: 5-The Hulk (origin), 6-Doctor Strange, 7-Avengers, 8-Christmas stories; Spider-Man, Hulk, Nick Fury, 9-Giant; Superhero Team-up, 10-Thor, 11-Fantastic Four, 12-Howard the Duck, 13-Giant Super-hero Holiday Grab-Bag, 14-Spider-Man, 16-Super-hero Team-up; The Defenders (origin) & Valkyrie, 17-The Hulk
.50 1.00

| 15-Conan; Smith, Adams-i | .35 | 1.00 | 2.00 |

18-Marvel Team-up; Spider-Man's 1st team-ups with the X-Men
.25 .75 1.50

19-28: 19-Conan the Barbarian, 20-Hulk, 21-Fantastic Four, 22-Spider-Man, 23-Conan, 24-Rampaging Hulk, 25-Spider-Man vs. The Hulk, 26-The Hulk; Wolverine app., 27-Spider-Man, 28-Spider-Man/Superman; (origin of each)
.50 1.00

NOTE: Reprints-2,3,5,7-9,13,14,16,17. Adams a-6(i), 15. Brunner a-6, 12; c-6. Buscema a-15, 19, 28; c-28. Colan c-12p. Ditko a-1, 6. Kirby a-2, 10, 11; c-7. Smith c/a-4.

MARVEL TREASURY OF OZ (See MGM's Marvelous. . .)
1975 (oversized) ($1.50)
Marvel Comics Group

	Good	Fine	N-Mint
1-The Marvelous Land of Oz; Buscema-a	.60	1.20

MARVEL TREASURY SPECIAL (Also see 2001: A Space Odyssey)
1974; 1976 (84 pgs.; oversized) ($1.50)
Marvel Comics Group

Vol. 1-Spider-Man, Torch, Sub-Mariner, Avengers "Giant Superhero Holiday Grab-Bag"
.50 1.00

Vol. 1-Capt. America's Bicentennial Battles (6/76)-Kirby-a; Smith inks, 11 pgs.
.50 1.00

MARVEL TRIPLE ACTION
2/72 - No. 24, 3/75; No. 25, 8/75 - No. 47, 4/79
Marvel Comics Group

1-Giant (52 pgs.)		.40	.80
2-4		.40	.80
5-47: 7-Starlin-c. 45,46-X-Men-r		.40	.80
Giant-Size 1(5/75), 2(7/75)		.50	1.00

NOTE: Fantastic Four reprints-#1-4; Avengers reprints-#5 on. Buscema a(r)-35p, 36p, 38p, 39p, 41, 42, 43p, 44p, 46p, 47p. Ditko a-2r; c-47. Kirby a(r)-1-4p. Tuska a(r)-40p, 43i, 46i, 47i.

MARVEL TWO-IN-ONE (See The Thing)
January, 1974 - No. 100, June, 1983
Marvel Comics Group

1-Thing team-ups begin	1.15	3.50	7.00
2-4: 3-Daredevil app.	.60	1.75	3.50
5-Guardians of the Galaxy	.70	2.00	4.00
6-10	.50	1.50	3.00
11-20	.35	1.10	2.20
21-40: 29-2nd app. Spider-Woman	.25	.70	1.40
41,42,44-49		.50	1.00
43,50,53-55-Byrne-a. 54-Death of Deathlok	.40	1.25	2.50
51-Miller-a(p)	.50	1.50	3.00
52-Moon Knight app.	.35	1.00	2.00
56-82: 60-Intro. Impossible Woman. 61-63-Warlock app.		.40	.80
83,84-Alpha Flight app.	.50	1.50	3.00
85-99: 93-Jocasta dies. 96-X-Men cameo		.30	.60
100-Double size, Byrne scripts	.25	.75	1.50
Annual 1(6/76)-Liberty Legion x-over	.25	.80	1.60
Annual 2(2/77)-Starlin c/a; Thanos dies	1.25	3.75	7.50
Annual 3(7/78), 4(9/79)		.50	1.00
Annual 5(9/80), 6(10/81)		.40	.80
Annual 7(10/82)-The Champion/Champion; Sasquatch, Colossus app.		.50	1.00

NOTE: Austin c-42i, 54i, 56i, 58i, 61i, 63i, 66i. John Buscema a-30p, 45; c-30p. Byrne a-43p, 50p, 53-55p; c-43, 53p, 56p, 98i, 99i. Gil Kane a-1p, 2p; c(p)-1-3, 9, 11, 14, 28. Kirby c-10, 12, 19p, 20, 25, 27. Mooney a-18i, 38i, 90i. Nasser a-70p. Perez a-56-58p, 60p, 64p, 65p; c-32p, 33p, 42p, 50-52p, 54p, 55p, 57p, 58p, 61-66p, 70p. Roussos a-Annual 1i. Simonson c-43i; Annual 6i. Starlin c-6, Annual 1. Tuska a-6p.

MARVEL UNIVERSE (See Official Handbook. . .)

MARVIN MOUSE
September, 1957
Atlas Comics (BPC)

| 1-Everett c/a; Maneely-a | 2.65 | 8.00 | 18.00 |

MARY JANE & SNIFFLES (See 4-Color #402,474)

MARY MARVEL COMICS (Monte Hale #29 on) (Also see Captain Marvel #18, Marvel Family, Shazam, & Wow)
Dec, 1945 - No. 28, Sept, 1948
Fawcett Publications

1-Captain Marvel intro. Mary on-c; intro/origin Georgia Sivana

MARY MARVEL COMICS (continued)	Good	Fine	N-Mint
	55.00	165.00	385.00
2	26.00	78.00	182.00
3	19.00	57.00	132.00
4	15.00	45.00	105.00
5-8: 8-Bulletgirl x-over in Mary Marvel	13.00	40.00	90.00
9,10	10.00	30.00	70.00
11-20	7.50	22.00	52.00
21-28	6.50	19.50	45.00

MARY POPPINS (See Walt Disney Showcase No. 17 & Movie Comics)

MARY'S GREATEST APOSTLE (St. Louis Grignion de Montfort)
No date (16 pages; paper cover)
Catechetical Guild (Topix) (Giveaway)

	2.35	7.00	16.00

MARY WORTH (See Love Stories of . . . & Harvey Comic Hits #55)
March, 1956
Argo

| 1 | 3.50 | 10.50 | 24.00 |

MASK
Dec, 1985 - No. 4, Mar, 1986 (mini-series)
DC Comics

| 1-(Sat. morning TV show) | .35 | 1.00 | 2.00 |
| 2-4 | .25 | .70 | 1.40 |

MASK
Feb, 1987 - No. 9, Oct, 1987
DC Comics

| 1 | | .60 | 1.20 |
| 2-9 | | .45 | .90 |

MASK COMICS
Feb-Mar, 1945 - No. 2, Apr-May, 1945; No. 2, Fall, 1945
Rural Home Publications

1-Classic L. B. Cole Satan-c/a; Palais-a	72.00	215.00	500.00
2-(Scarce)Classic L. B. Cole Satan-c; Black Rider, The Boy Magician, & The Collector app.	36.00	108.00	250.00
2(Fall, 1945)-No publ.-same as regular #2; L. B. Cole-c	26.00	78.00	180.00

MASKED BANDIT, THE
1952
Avon Periodicals

| nn-Kinstler-a | 8.50 | 25.50 | 60.00 |

MASKED MAN, THE
12/84 - No. 10, 4/86; No. 11, 10/87 - Present ($1.75-$2.00; Baxter)
Eclipse Comics

1-Origin retold	.35	1.00	2.00
2-8: 3-Origin Aphid-Man	.30	.90	1.80
9-12 ($2.00; B&W)	.30	.90	1.80

MASKED MARVEL (See Keen Det. Funnies)
Sept, 1940 - No. 3, Dec, 1940
Centaur Publications

| 1-The Masked Marvel begins | 78.00 | 235.00 | 550.00 |
| 2,3: 2-Gustavson, Tarpe Mills-a | 50.00 | 150.00 | 350.00 |

MASKED RAIDER, THE (Billy The Kid #9 on; Frontier Scout, Daniel Boone #10-13; also see Blue Bird)
6/55 - No. 8, 7/57; No. 14, 8/58 - No. 30, 6/61
Charlton Comics

1-Painted-c	3.70	11.00	26.00
2	2.00	6.00	14.00
3-8: 8-Billy The Kid app.	1.60	4.80	11.00
14,16-30: 22-Rocky Lane app.	1.15	3.50	8.00
15-Williamson-a, 7 pgs.	2.35	7.00	16.00

MASKED RANGER
April, 1954 - No. 9, Aug, 1955
Premier Magazines

	Good	Fine	N-Mint
1-The M. Ranger, his horse Streak, & The Crimson Avenger (origin) begin, end #9; Woodbridge/Frazetta-a; Check-a	14.00	42.00	100.00
2,3	3.70	11.00	26.00
4-8-All Woodbridge-a. 5-Jesse James by Woodbridge. 6-Billy The Kid by Woodbridge. 7-Wild Bill Hickok by Woodbridge. 8-Jim Bowie's Life Story	5.00	15.00	35.00
9-Torres-a; Wyatt Earp by Woodbridge	5.50	16.50	38.00

NOTE: *Woodbridge c/a-1,4-9.*

MASK OF DR. FU MANCHU, THE (See Dr. Fu Manchu)
1951
Avon Periodicals

| 1-Sax Rohmer adapt.; Wood c/a, 26 pgs., Hollingsworth-a | 70.00 | 210.00 | 490.00 |

MASQUE OF THE RED DEATH (See Movie Classics)

MASTER COMICS
Mar, 1940 - No. 133, Apr, 1953 (No. 1-6: oversized issues)
(#1-3, 15 cents, 52pgs.; #4-6, 10 cents, 36pgs.)
Fawcett Publications

1-Origin Master Man; The Devil's Dagger, El Carim, Master of Magic, Rick O'Say, Morton Murch, White Rajah, Shipwreck Roberts, Frontier Marshal, Streak Sloan, Mr. Clue begin (all features end #6)	160.00	480.00	1120.00
2	75.00	225.00	525.00
3-5	50.00	150.00	350.00
6-Last Master Man	55.00	165.00	385.00

NOTE: *#1-6 rarely found in near mint to mint condition due to large-size format.*

7-(10/40)-Bulletman, Zoro, the Mystery Man (ends #22), Lee Granger, Jungle King, & Buck Jones begin; only app. The War Bird & Mark Swift & the Time Retarder	95.00	285.00	665.00
8-The Red Gaucho (ends #13), Captain Venture (ends #22) & The Planet Princess begin	45.00	135.00	315.00
9,10: 10-Lee Granger ends	40.00	120.00	280.00
11-Origin Minute-Man	75.00	225.00	525.00
12	50.00	150.00	350.00
13-Origin Bulletgirl	70.00	210.00	490.00
14-16: 14-Companions Three begins, ends #31	40.00	120.00	280.00
17-20: 17-Raboy-a on Bulletman begins. 20-Captain Marvel cameo app. in Bulletman	45.00	135.00	315.00
21-(Scarce)-Captain Marvel x-over in Bulletman; Capt. Nazi origin	171.00	515.00	1200.00
22-Captain Marvel Jr. x-over in Bulletman; Capt. Nazi app; bondage-c	142.00	425.00	1000.00
23-Capt. Marvel Jr. begins, vs. Capt. Nazi	115.00	345.00	800.00
24,25,29	42.00	125.00	295.00
26-28,30-Captain Marvel Jr. vs. Capt. Nazi. 30-Flag-c	42.00	125.00	295.00
31,32: 32-Last El Carim & Buck Jones; Balbo, the Boy Magician intro. in El Carim	29.00	87.00	205.00
33-Balbo, the Boy Magician (ends #47), Hopalong Cassidy (ends #49) begins	29.00	87.00	205.00
34-Capt. Marvel Jr. vs. Capt. Nazi	29.00	87.00	205.00
35	29.00	87.00	205.00
36-40: 40-Flag-c	27.00	81.00	190.00
41-Bulletman, Capt. Marvel Jr. & Bulletgirl x-over in Minute-Man; only app. Crime Crusaders Club (Capt. Marvel Jr., Minute-Man, Bulletman & Bulletgirl)-only team in Fawcett Comics	69.00	205.00	205.00
42-47,49: 47-Hitler becomes Corpl. Hitler Jr. 49-Last Minute-Man	17.00	51.00	120.00

Mary Marvel Comics #18, © FAW

Mask Comics #1, © RH

Master Comics #5, © FAW

Master Comics #48, © FAW   The Masterworks Series Of Great... #1, © Seagate/DC   Maverick Marshal #1, © CC

	Good	Fine	N-Mint
MASTER COMICS (continued)			
48-Intro. Bulletboy; Capt. Marvel cameo in Minute-Man			
	18.00	54.00	125.00
50-Radar, Nyoka the Jungle Girl begin; Capt. Marvel x-over in			
Radar; origin Radar	12.00	36.00	84.00
51-58	8.00	24.00	56.00
59-62: Nyoka serial ''Terrible Tiara'' in all; 61-Capt. Marvel Jr.			
1st meets Uncle Marvel	9.50	28.50	65.00
63-80	6.00	18.00	42.00
81-92,94-99: 88-Hopalong Cassidy begins (ends #94). 95-Tom			
Mix begins (ends #133)	5.50	16.50	38.00
93-Krigstein-a	5.70	17.00	40.00
100	6.00	18.00	42.00
101-106-Last Bulletman	4.00	12.00	28.00
107-131	3.50	10.50	24.00
132-B&W and color illos in POP	4.85	14.50	34.00
133-Bill Battle app.	5.70	17.00	40.00
NOTE: *Mac Raboy* a-15-39, 40 in part, 42, 58; c-21-49, 51, 52, 54, 56, 58, 59.			
MASTER DETECTIVE			
1964 (Reprint)			
Super Comics			
10,17,18: 17-Young King Cole; McWilliams-a	.40	1.20	2.40
MASTER OF KUNG FU (Formerly Special Marvel Edition; see Marvel			
Comics Presents)			
No. 17, April, 1974 - No. 125, June, 1983			
Marvel Comics Group			
17-Starlin-a; intro Black Jack Tarr	.40	1.20	2.40
18-20: 19-Man-Thing app.	.35	1.00	2.00
21-23,25-30		.60	1.20
24-Starlin, Simonson-a	.25	.75	1.50
31-40: 33-1st Leiko Wu		.40	.80
41-99		.30	.60
100-(Double size)		.60	1.20
101-117,119-124: 104-Cerebus cameo		.30	.60
118,125-(Double size)		.50	1.00
Giant Size 1(9/74)-Russell-a; Yellow Claw-r	.25	.75	1.50
Giant Size 2-r/Yellow Claw #1		.60	1.20
Giant Size 3,4(6/75)-r/Yellow Claw		.60	1.20
Annual 1(4/76)-Iron Fist		.60	1.20
NOTE: *Austin* c-63i, 74i. *Buscema* c-44p. *Gulacy* a(p)-18-20, 22, 25, 29-31, 33-35, 38, 39, 40(p&i), 42-50. Giant Size #1, 2; c-51, 55, 64, 67. *Gil Kane* c(p)-20, 38, 39, 42, 45, 59, 63. *Nebres* c-73i. *Starlin* a-17p; c-54. *Sutton* a-42i.			
MASTER OF THE WORLD (See 4-Color #1157)			
MASTERS OF TERROR (Magazine)			
July, 1975 - No. 2, Sept, 1975 (Black & White) (All Reprints)			
Marvel Comics Group			
1-Brunner, Smith-a; Morrow-c; Adams-a(i)(r); Starlin-a(p)			
Gil Kane-a	.30	.90	1.80
2-Reese, Kane, Mayerik-a; Steranko-c		.60	1.20
MASTERS OF THE UNIVERSE			
Dec, 1982 - No. 3, Feb, 1983 (mini-series)			
DC Comics			
1		.60	1.20
2,3: 2-Origin He-Man & Ceril		.50	1.00
NOTE: *Alcala* a-1i, 2i. *Tuska* a-1-3p; c-1-3p. #2 has 75 & 95 cent cover price.			
MASTERS OF THE UNIVERSE (Comic Album)			
1984 (8½x11''; $2.95; 64 pgs.)			
Western Publishing Co.			
11362-Based on Mattel toy & cartoon	.50	1.50	2.95
MASTERS OF THE UNIVERSE (TV)			
May, 1986 - No. 12, March, 1988			
Star Comics/Marvel #? on			
1		.55	1.10

	Good	Fine	N-Mint
2-7		.40	.80
8-12 ($1.00)		.50	1.00
...The Motion Picture (11/87, $2.00)-Tuska-p	.35	1.00	2.00
MASTERWORKS SERIES OF GREAT COMIC BOOK ARTISTS, THE			
May, 1983 - No. 3, Dec, 1983 (Baxter paper)			
Sea Gate Distributors/DC Comics			
1,2-Shining Knight by Frazetta r-/Adventure. 2-Tomahawk by			
Frazetta-r	.25	.75	1.50
3-Wrightson-c/a(r)	.25	.75	1.50
MATT SLADE GUNFIGHTER (Stories of Romance & Kid Slade Gun-			
fighter #5 on?; See Western Gunfighters)			
May, 1956 - No. 4, Nov, 1956			
Atlas Comics (SPI)			
1-Williamson/Torres-a; Maneely-c/a	6.50	19.50	45.00
2-Williamson-a	4.65	14.00	32.00
3,4: 4-Maneely-a	2.30	7.00	16.00
MAUD			
1906 (32 pgs. in color; 10x15½'') (cardboard covers)			
Frederick A. Stokes Co.			
By Fred Opper	14.00	42.00	100.00
MAVERICK (TV)			
No. 892, 4/58 - No. 19, 4-6/62 (All have photo-c)			
Dell Publishing Co.			
4-Color 892 (#1): James Garner/Jack Kelly photo-c begin			
	5.70	17.00	40.00
4-Color 930,945,962,980,1005 (6-8/59)	5.00	15.00	35.00
7 (10-12/59) - 14: Last Garner/Kelly-c	4.00	12.00	28.00
15-18: Jack Kelly/Roger Moore photo-c	4.00	12.00	28.00
19-Jack Kelly-c	4.00	12.00	28.00
MAVERICK MARSHAL			
Nov, 1958 - No. 7, May, 1960			
Charlton Comics			
1	1.50	4.50	10.00
2-7	.85	2.50	6.00
MAX BRAND (See Silvertip)			
MAYA (See Movie Classics)			
March, 1968			
Gold Key			
1 (10218-803)(TV)	1.15	3.50	8.00
MAZE AGENCY, THE			
Dec, 1988 - Present ($1.75, color)			
Comico			
1,2	.30	.90	1.75
MAZIE (...& Her Friends) (See Mortie, Stevie & Tastee-Freez)			
1953 - No. 12, 1954; No. 13, 12/54 - No. 22, 9/56; No. 23, 9/57 -			
No. 28, 8/58			
Mazie Comics(Magazine Publ.)/Harvey Publ. No. 13-on			
1-(Teen-age)-Stevie's girl friend	1.50	4.50	10.00
2	.70	2.00	5.00
3-10	.60	1.80	4.00
11-28	.35	1.00	2.00
MAZIE			
1950 - 1951 (5 cents) (5x7¼''-miniature)(52 pgs.)			
Nation Wide Publishers			
1-Teen-age	1.30	4.00	9.00
2-7	.70	2.00	5.00
MAZINGER (See First Comics Graphic Novel)			
'MAZING MAN			
Jan, 1986 - No. 12, Dec, 1986			

'MAZING MAN (continued)			
DC Comics	Good	Fine	N-Mint
1		.50	1.00
2-11: 7,8-Hembeck-a		.40	.80
12-Dark Knight part-c by Miller		.40	.80
Special 1('87), 2(4/88) (both $2.00)	.30	.90	1.80

McCRORY'S CHRISTMAS BOOK
1955 (36 pgs.; slick cover)
Western Printing Co. (McCrory Stores Corp. giveaway)

nn-Painted-c	1.35	4.00	8.00

McCRORY'S TOYLAND BRINGS YOU SANTA'S PRIVATE EYES
1956 (16 pgs.)
Promotional Publ. Co. (Giveaway)
Has 9 pg. story plus 7 pg. toy ads

	1.00	3.00	6.00

McCRORY'S WONDERFUL CHRISTMAS
1954 (20 pgs.; slick cover)
Promotional Publ. Co. (Giveaway)

	1.35	4.00	8.00

McHALE'S NAVY (TV) (See Movie Classics)
May-July, 1963 - No. 3, Nov-Jan, 1963-64 (Photo-c)
Dell Publishing Co.

1	1.70	5.00	12.00
2,3	1.50	4.50	10.00

McKEEVER & THE COLONEL (TV)
Feb-Apr, 1963 - No. 3, Aug-Oct, 1963
Dell Publishing Co.

1-Photo-c	2.30	7.00	16.00
2,3	1.70	5.00	12.00

McLINTOCK (See Movie Comics)

MD
Apr-May, 1955 - No. 5, Dec-Jan, 1955-56
E. C. Comics

1-Not approved by code	5.75	17.50	40.00
2-5	4.35	13.00	30.00

NOTE: *Crandall, Evans, Ingels, Orlando* art in all issues; *Craig c-1-5.*

MECHA
June, 1987 - Present ($1.75-$1.95, color)
Dark Horse Comics

1-4	.30	.90	1.80

MECHANICS
Oct, 1985 - No. 3, Dec, 1985 ($2.00 cover; adults only)
Fantagraphics Books

1-Love & Rockets in all	.60	1.75	3.50
2,3	.35	1.00	2.00

MEDAL FOR BOWZER, A
No date (1948-50?)
Will Eisner Giveaway

Eisner-c/script	15.00	45.00	105.00

MEDAL OF HONOR COMICS
Spring, 1946
A. S. Curtis

1	4.65	14.00	32.00

MEET ANGEL (Formerly Angel & the Ape)
No. 7, Nov-Dec, 1969
National Periodical Publications

7-Wood-a(i)	.50	1.50	3.00

MEET CORLISS ARCHER (My Life #4 on)(Radio/Movie)
March, 1948 - No. 3, July, 1948

Fox Features Syndicate

	Good	Fine	N-Mint
1-(Teen-age)-Feldstein c/a	27.00	81.00	190.00
2-Feldstein-c only	20.00	60.00	140.00
3-Part Feldstein-c only	14.00	42.00	100.00

NOTE: *No. 1-3 used in Seduction of the Innocent, pg. 39.*

MEET HERCULES (See Three Stooges)

MEET HIYA A FRIEND OF SANTA CLAUS
1949 (18 pgs.?) (paper cover)
Julian J. Proskauer/Sundial Shoe Stores, etc. (Giveaway)

	3.00	9.00	18.00

MEET MERTON
Dec, 1953 - No. 4, June, 1954
Toby Press

1-(Teen-age)-Dave Berg-a	2.30	7.00	16.00
2-Dave Berg-a	1.30	4.00	9.00
3,4-Dave Berg-a	.85	2.50	6.00
I.W. Reprint #9		.60	1.20
Super Reprint #11('63), 18		.60	1.20

MEET MISS BLISS
May, 1955 - No. 4, Nov., 1955
Atlas Comics (LMC)

1-Al Hartley-a	3.70	11.00	26.00
2-4	2.00	6.00	14.00

MEET MISS PEPPER (Formerly Lucy...)
No. 5, April, 1954 - No. 6, June, 1954
St. John Publishing Co.

5-Kubert/Maurer-a	11.50	34.00	80.00
6-Kubert/Maurer-a; Kubert-c	9.00	27.00	62.00

MEET THE NEW POST GAZETTE SUNDAY FUNNIES
3/12/49 (16 pgs.; paper covers) (7¼x10¼'')
Commercial Comics (insert in newspaper)
Pittsburgh Post Gazette

Dick Tracy by Gould, Gasoline Alley, Terry & the Pirates, Brenda Starr, Buck Rogers by Yager, The Gumps, Peter Rabbit by Fago, Superman, Funnyman by Siegel & Shuster, The Saint, Archie, & others done especially for this book. A fine copy sold at auction in 1985 for $276.00.

Estimated value....			$150—$300

MEGALITH (Also see The Revengers & Zero Patrol)
Mar, 1985 - Present
Continuity Comics

1,2-Neal Adams-a	.35	1.00	2.00

MEGATON
11/83; No. 2, 10/85 - Present (B&W)
Megaton Publ.

1,2 ($2.00, 68 pgs.)	.35	1.00	2.00
3-8 ($1.50) (#3, 44 pgs.; #4, 52 pgs.)	.25	.75	1.50
V2#1-3 ($1.50, color)	.25	.75	1.50
Special 1 ($2.00, '87)	.35	1.00	2.00
X-Mas 2 ('87)	.35	1.00	2.00

MEGATON MAN (Also see The Return Of...)
Dec, 1984 - No. 10, 1986 ($2.00; Baxter paper)
Kitchen Sink Enterprises

1-Silver-Age heroes parody	1.35	4.00	8.00
2	.50	1.50	3.00
3-10: 6-Border Worlds begins	.40	1.25	2.50

MEL ALLEN SPORTS COMICS
No. 5, Nov, 1949 - No. 6, Jan, 1950?
Standard Comics

5(#1 on inside)-Tuska-a	5.70	17.00	40.00
6	3.50	10.50	24.00

MD #3, © WMG   Meet Corliss Archer #2, © FOX   Meet Miss Pepper #5, © STJ

Menace #7, © MEG

Men's Adventures #27, © MEG

Merry Christmas From Mickey Mouse, © WDC

MELVIN MONSTER
Apr-June, 1965 - No. 10, Oct, 1969
Dell Publishing Co.

	Good	Fine	N-Mint
1-By John Stanley	7.00	21.00	50.00
2-10-All by Stanley. #10 r-/#1	4.65	14.00	32.00

MELVIN THE MONSTER (Dexter The Demon #7)
July, 1956 - No. 6, July, 1957
Atlas Comics (HPC)

1-Maneely-c/a	3.00	9.00	21.00
2-6: 4-Maneely c/a	1.70	5.00	12.00

MENACE
March, 1953 - No. 11, May, 1954
Atlas Comics (HPC)

1-Everett-a	10.00	30.00	70.00
2-Post-atom bomb disaster by Everett; anti-Communist propaganda/torture scenes	6.50	19.50	45.00
3,4,6-Everett-a	5.00	15.00	35.00
5-Origin & 1st app. The Zombie by Everett (reprinted in Tales of the Zombie #1)(7/53)	8.50	25.50	60.00
7,10,11: 7-Frankenstein story. 10-H-Bomb panels	4.30	13.00	30.00
8-End of world story	4.30	13.00	30.00
9-Everett-a r-in Vampire Tales #1	5.00	15.00	35.00

NOTE: *Colan a-6. Everett a-1-6, 9; c-1-6. Heath a-1-8; c-10. Katz a-11. Maneely a-3. Powell a-11. Romita a-3, 6, 11. Shelly a-10. Sinnott a-2. Tuska a-1, 2, 5.*

MEN AGAINST CRIME (Formerly Mr. Risk)
No. 3, Feb, 1951 - No. 7, Oct, 1951 (Hand of Fate #8 on)
Ace Magazines

3-Mr. Risk app.	3.50	10.50	24.00
4-7: 4-Colan-a; entire book reprinted as Trapped! #4	1.85	5.50	13.00

MEN, GUNS, & CATTLE (See Classics Special)

MEN IN ACTION (Battle Brady #10 on)
April, 1952 - No. 9, Dec, 1952
Atlas Comics (IPS)

1	3.00	9.00	21.00
2	1.20	3.50	8.00
3-6,8,9: 3-Heath c/a	1.00	3.00	7.00
7-Krigstein-a	2.75	8.00	18.00

MEN IN ACTION
April, 1957 - No. 9, 1958
Ajax/Farrell Publications

1	2.00	6.00	14.00
2	1.00	3.00	7.00
3-9	.85	2.50	6.00

MEN INTO SPACE (See 4-Color No. 1083)

MEN OF BATTLE (See New...)

MEN OF COURAGE
1949
Catechetical Guild
Contains bound Topix comics-V7#2,4,6,8,10,16,18,20

	3.00	9.00	21.00

MEN OF WAR
August, 1977 - No. 26, March, 1980
DC Comics, Inc.

1-Origin Gravedigger, cont'd. in #2		.30	.60
2-26		.25	.50

NOTE: *Chaykin a-9, 10, 12-14, 19, 20. Evans c-25. Kubert c-2-23, 24p, 26.*

MEN'S ADVENTURES (Formerly True Adventures)
No. 4, Aug, 1950 - No. 28, July, 1954

Marvel/Atlas Comics (CCC)

	Good	Fine	N-Mint
4(#1)(52 pgs.)	6.50	19.50	45.00
5-Flying Saucer story	3.50	10.50	24.00
6-8: 8-Sci/fic story	2.65	8.00	18.00
9-20: All war format	1.50	4.50	10.00
21,22,24-26: All horror format	1.70	5.00	12.00
23-Crandall-a; Fox-a(i)	3.50	10.50	24.00
27,28-Captain America, Human Torch, & Sub-Mariner app. in each	19.00	57.00	132.00

NOTE: *Berg a-16. Burgos c-27. Everett a-10, 14, 22, 25, 28; c-14, 21-23. Heath a-8, 24. Lawrence a-23. Mac Pakula a-25. Post a-23. Powell a-27. Reinman a-12. Robinson c-19. Romita a-22. Sinnott a-21. Adventure-#4-8; War-#9-20; Horror-#21-26.*

MEN WHO MOVE THE NATION
(Giveaway) (Black & White)
Publisher unknown

Neal Adams-a	2.65	8.00	16.00

MEPHISTO VERSUS FOUR HEROES (See Silver Surfer #3)
Apr, 1987 - No. 4, July, 1987 ($1.50, mini-series)
Marvel Comics Group

1	.35	1.00	2.00
2-4	.30	.80	1.60

MERC (See Mark Hazzard: Merc)

MERCHANTS OF DEATH
July, 1988 - Present ($3.50, B&W/16pgs. color, 44pg. magazine)
Acme Press (Eclipse)

1-5: 4,5-Toth-c	.60	1.75	3.50

MERLIN JONES AS THE MONKEY'S UNCLE (See Movie Comics and The Misadventures of... under Movie Comics)

MERLINREALM 3-D (Blackthorne 3-D series #2)
Oct, 1985 ($2.25)
Blackthorne Publ., Inc.

1-1st printing	.35	1.15	2.30

MERRILL'S MARAUDERS (See Movie Classics)

MERRY CHRISTMAS (See A Christmas Adv., Donald Duck..., Dell Giant #39, & March of Comics #153)

MERRY CHRISTMAS, A
1948 (nn) (Giveaway)
K. K. Publications (Child Life Shoes)

	2.75	8.00	16.00

MERRY CHRISTMAS
1956 (7¼x5¼")
K. K. Publications (Blue Bird Shoes Giveaway)

	1.00	3.00	6.00

MERRY CHRISTMAS FROM MICKEY MOUSE
1939 (16 pgs.) (Color & B&W)
K. K. Publications (Shoe store giveaway)

Donald Duck & Pluto app.; text with art (Rare); c-reprint/Mickey Mouse Mag. V3/3 (12/37)	70.00	200.00	400.00

MERRY CHRISTMAS FROM SEARS TOYLAND
1939 (16 pgs.) (In color)
Sears Roebuck Giveaway

Dick Tracy, Little Orphan Annie, The Gumps, Terry & the Pirates	15.00	45.00	90.00

MERRY COMICS
December, 1945 (No cover price)
Carlton Publishing Co.

nn-Boogeyman app.	4.30	13.00	30.00

MERRY COMICS
1947
Four Star Publications

MERRY COMICS (continued)	Good	Fine	N-Mint
1	3.70	11.00	26.00

MERRY-GO-ROUND COMICS
1944 (132 pgs.; 25 cents); 1946; 9-10/47 - No. 2, 1948
LaSalle Publ. Co./Croyden Publ./Rotary Litho.

nn(1944)(LaSalle)	7.00	21.00	50.00
21	2.00	6.00	14.00
1(1946)(Croyden)	3.50	10.50	24.00
V1#1,2('47-'48; 52 pgs.)(Rotary Litho. Co. Ltd., Canada);			
Ken Hultgren-a	2.30	7.00	16.00

MERRY MAILMAN (See Funny Animals)

MERRY MOUSE (Also see Space Comics)
June, 1953 - No. 4, Jan-Feb, 1954
Avon Periodicals

1	3.50	10.50	24.00
2-4	2.00	6.00	12.00

METAL MEN (See Brave & the Bold, DC Comics Presents, and Showcase)
4-5/63 - No. 41, 12-1/69-70; No. 42, 2-3/73 - No. 44, 7-8/73;
No. 45, 4-5/76 - No. 56, 2-3/78
National Periodical Publications/DC Comics

1	7.00	21.00	50.00
2	3.50	10.50	24.00
3-5	2.30	7.00	16.00
6-10	1.70	5.00	12.00
11-20	1.15	3.50	8.00
21-30: 27-Origin Metal Men	.85	2.50	5.00
31-41(1968-70)	.70	2.00	4.00
42-44(1973)-Reprints	.50	1.50	3.00
45('76)-49-Simonson-a in all	.50	1.50	3.00
50-56: 50-Part-r. 54,55-Green Lantern x-over	.50	1.50	3.00

NOTE: Aparo c-53-56. Giordano c-45, 46. Kane a-30, 31p; c-31. Simonson a-45-49; c-47-52. Staton a-50-56.

METAMORPHO (See Action, Brave & the Bold, First Issue Special, & World's Finest)
July-Aug, 1965 - No. 17, Mar-Apr, 1968
National Periodical Publications

1	2.65	8.00	18.00
2-5	1.15	3.50	8.00
6-9	1.00	3.00	6.00
10-Origin & 1st app. Element Girl (1-2/67)	1.00	3.00	6.00
11-17	.50	1.50	3.00

NOTE: Ramona Fraden a-1-4. Orlando a-5, 6; c-5-9, 11. Sal Trapani a-7-16.

METEOR COMICS
November, 1945
L. L. Baird (Croyden)

1-Captain Wizard, Impossible Man, Race Wilkins app.; origin Baldy			
Bean, Capt. Wizard's sidekick; Bare-breasted mermaids story	11.50	34.00	80.00

MGM'S MARVELOUS WIZARD OF OZ
November, 1975 (84 pgs.; oversize) ($1.50)
Marvel Comics Group/National Periodical Publications

1-Adaptation of MGM's movie (See Marvel Treasury of . . .)	.70	2.00	4.00

M.G.M.'S MOUSE MUSKETEERS (Formerly M.G.M.'s The Two Mouseketeers)
No. 670, Jan, 1956 - No. 1290, Mar-May, 1962
Dell Publishing Co.

4-Color 670	1.00	3.00	7.00
4-Color 711,728,764	.85	2.50	6.00
8 (4-6/57) - 21 (3-5/60)	.75	2.25	5.00
4-Color 1135,1175,1290	.85	2.50	6.00

M.G.M.'S SPIKE AND TYKE
No. 499, Sept, 1953 - No. 1266, Dec-Feb, 1961-62
Dell Publishing Co.

	Good	Fine	N-Mint
4-Color 499	1.30	4.00	9.00
4-Color 577,638	1.00	3.00	7.00
4(12-2/55-56)-10	.85	2.50	6.00
11-24(12-2/60-61)	.75	2.25	5.00
4-Color 1266	.85	2.50	6.00

M.G.M.'S THE TWO MOUSKETEERS (See 4-Color 475,603,642)

MICHAELANGELO, TEENAGE MUTANT NINJA TURTLE
1986 (One shot) ($1.50)
Mirage Studios

1	1.00	3.00	6.00

MICKEY AND DONALD (Walt Disney's . . . #3 on)
Mar, 1988 - Present (95 cents, color)
Gladstone Publishing

1-Don Rosa-a; r-/1949 Firestone giv.	.85	2.50	5.00
2	.40	1.25	2.50
3	.35	1.00	2.00
4-10: Barks-r	.60	1.20	

MICKEY AND DONALD IN VACATIONLAND (See Dell Giant No. 47)

MICKEY & THE BEANSTALK (See Story Hour Series)

MICKEY & THE SLEUTH (See Walt Disney Showcase #38,39,42)

MICKEY FINN (Also see Feature Funnies)
Nov?, 1942 - V3No. 2, May, 1952
Eastern Color 1-4/McNaught Synd. No. 5 on (Columbia)/Headline V3No.2

1	14.00	42.00	100.00
2	7.00	21.00	50.00
3-Charlie Chan app.	5.00	15.00	35.00
4	3.50	10.50	24.00
5-10	2.30	7.00	16.00
11-15(1949): 12-Sparky Watts app.	1.70	5.00	12.00
V3#1,2(1952)	1.15	3.50	8.00

MICKEY MOUSE
1931 - 1934 (52 pgs.; 10x9¾''; cardboard covers)
David McKay Publications

1(1931)	80.00	240.00	500.00
2(1932)	60.00	180.00	400.00
3(1933)-All color Sunday reprints; page #'s 5-17, 32-48 reissued			
in Whitman #948	120.00	350.00	700.00
4(1934)	50.00	150.00	350.00

NOTE: Each book reprints strips from previous year - dailies in black and white in #1,2,4; Sundays in color in No. 3. Later reprints exist; i.e., #2 (1934).

MICKEY MOUSE
1933 (Copyright date, printing date unknown)
(30 pages; 10x8¾''; cardboard covers)
Whitman Publishing Co.

948-(1932 Sunday strips in color)	80.00	240.00	500.00

NOTE: Some copies were bound with a second front cover upside-down instead of the regular back cover; both covers have the same art, but different right and left margins. The above book is an exact, but abbreviated reissue of David McKay No. 3 but with ½-inch of border trimmed from the top and bottom.

MICKEY MOUSE (See The Best of Walt Disney Comics, Cheerios giveaways, Dynabrite Comics, 40 Big Pages . . ., Gladstone Comic Album, Merry Christmas From . . ., Walt Disney's C&S & Wheaties)

MICKEY MOUSE (. . . Secret Agent #107-109; Walt Disney's . . . #148-205?) (See Dell Giants for annuals)
No. 16, 1941 - No. 84, 7-9/62; No. 85, 11/62 - No. 218, 7/84;
No. 219, 10/86 - Present
Dell Publ. Co./Gold Key No. 85-204/Whitman No. 205-218/
Gladstone No. 219 on

Metal Men #10, © DC

Mickey And Donald #1, © WDC

Mickey Finn #1, © McNaught Synd.

Mickey Mouse Four Color #16, © WDC

Mickey Mouse #244, © WDC

Mickey Mouse Book, 1930, © WDC

MICKEY MOUSE (continued) — Good / Fine / VF-NM

4-Color 16(1941)-1st M.M. comic book-"vs. the Phantom Blot" by Gottfredson — 270.00 / 810.00 / 1890.00
(Prices vary widely on this book)

	Good	Fine	N-Mint
4-Color 27(1943)-"7 Colored Terror"	48.00	145.00	335.00
4-Color 79(1945)-By Carl Barks (1 story)	60.00	180.00	420.00
4-Color 116(1946)	16.00	48.00	110.00
4-Color 141,157(1947)	14.00	42.00	100.00
4-Color 170,181,194('48)	12.00	36.00	84.00
4-Color 214('49),231,248,261	9.50	28.50	65.00
4-Color 268-Reprints/WDC&S #22-24 by Gottfredson ("Surprise Visitor")	9.50	28.50	65.00
4-Color 279,286,296	8.00	24.00	56.00
4-Color 304,313(#1),325(#2),334	5.70	17.00	40.00
4-Color 343,352,362,371,387	4.30	13.00	30.00
4-Color 401,411,427(10-11/52)	3.50	10.50	24.00
4-Color 819-M.M. in Magicland	2.00	6.00	14.00
4-Color 1057,1151,1246(1959-61)-Album	1.70	5.00	12.00
28(12-1/52-53)-32,34	1.70	5.00	12.00
33-(Exists with 2 dates, 10-11/53 & 12-1/54)	1.70	5.00	12.00
35-50	1.15	3.50	8.00
51-73,75-80	.85	2.50	6.00
74-Story swipe-'The Rare Stamp Search'/4-Color 422-'The Gilded Man'	1.15	3.50	8.00
81-99: 93,95-titled "Mickey Mouse Club Album"	.85	2.50	6.00
100-105: Reprints 4-Color 427,194,279,170,343,214 in that order	1.00	3.00	7.00
106-120	.75	2.25	5.00
121-130	.70	2.00	4.00
131-146	.50	1.50	3.00
147-Reprints "The Phantom Fires" from WDC&S 200-202	.85	2.50	5.00
148-Reprints "The Mystery of Lonely Valley" from WDC&S 208-210	.85	3.50	5.00
149-158	.35	1.00	2.00
159-Reprints "The Sunken City" from WDC&S 205-207	.70	2.00	4.00
160-170: 162-170-r	.35	1.00	2.00
171-178,180-199		.50	1.00
179-(52 pgs.)		.40	.80
200-r-Four Color 371		.40	.80
201-218		.40	.80
219-1st Gladstone issue; The Seven Ghosts serial-r begins by Gottfredson	.70	2.00	4.00
220,221	.50	1.50	3.00
222-225: 222-Editor-in Grief strip-r	.40	1.25	2.50
226-230	.25	.75	1.50
231-243: 240-r/March of Comics #27		.50	1.00
244 (100 pgs., $2.95)-60th anniversary	.50	1.50	2.95

NOTE: *Reprints #195-97, 198(⅔), 199(⅓), 200-208, 211(½), 212, 213, 215(⅓), 216-218.*

	Good	Fine	N-Mint
Album 01-518-210(Dell), 1(10082-309)(9/63-Gold Key)	.85	2.50	6.00
...& Goofy "Bicep Bungle"(1952, 16 pgs., 3¼x7") Fritos giveaway, soft-c (also see D. Duck & Ludwig Von Drake)	2.35	7.00	14.00
...& Goofy Explore Business(1978)		.40	.80
...& Goofy Explore Energy(1976-1978) 36 pgs.; Exxon giveaway in color; regular size		.40	.80
...& Goofy Explore Energy Conservation(1976-1978)-Exxon		.40	.80
...& Goofy Explore The Universe of Energy(1985) 20pgs.; Exxon giveaway in color; regular size		.40	.80
Club 1(1/64-G.K.)(TV)	1.75	5.25	12.00
Mini Comic 1(1976)(3¼x6½")-Reprints 158			.15
New Mickey Mouse Club Fun Book 11190 (Golden Press, $1.95; 224pgs, 1977)	.40	1.20	2.40
Surprise Party 1(30037-901, G.K.)(1/69)-40th Anniversary (see Walt Disney Showcase #47)	2.35	7.00	16.00
Surprise Party 1(1979)-r-/'69 ish	.35	1.00	2.00

MICKEY MOUSE BOOK
1930 (4 printings, 20pgs., magazine size, paperbound)
Bibo & Lang

nn-Very first Disney book with games, cartoons & songs; only Disney book to offer the origin of Mickey (based on a story originated by 11 yr. old Bobette Bibo). First app. Mickey & Minnie Mouse. Clarabelle Cow & Horace Horsecollar app. on back cover. Walt Disney, so the story goes, named him 'Mickey Mouse' after the green color of Ireland because he ate old green cheese. The book was printed in black & green to reinforce the Irish theme.

NOTE: The first printing has a daily Win Smith M. Mouse strip at bottom of back cover; the reprints are blank in this area. Most copies are missing pages 9 & 10 which contain a puzzle to be cut out. Ub Iwerks-c

	Good	Fine	VF-NM
First Printing (complete)	170.00	510.00	1190.00
First Printing (Pgs. 9&10 missing)	80.00	320.00	560.00
2nd-4th Printings (complete)	120.00	360.00	840.00
2nd-4th Printings (pgs. 9&10 missing)	60.00	180.00	420.00

MICKEY MOUSE CLUB MAGAZINE (See Walt Disney...)

MICKEY MOUSE CLUB SPECIAL (See The New Mickey Mouse...)

MICKEY MOUSE COMICS DIGEST
1986 - No. 6, 1987 (96 pgs.)
Gladstone Publishing

	Good	Fine	N-Mint
1-3 ($1.25)		.60	1.25
4-6 ($1.50)	.25	.75	1.50

MICKEY MOUSE MAGAZINE
V1No.1, Jan, 1933 - V1No.9, Sept, 1933 (5¼x7¼")
No. 1-3 published by Kamen-Blair (Kay Kamen, Inc.)
Walt Disney Productions

(Scarce)-Distributed by dairies and leading stores through their local theatres. First few issues had 5 cents listed on cover, later ones had no price.

	Good	Fine	VF-NM
V1#1	130.00	380.00	910.00
2-9	65.00	195.00	455.00

MICKEY MOUSE MAGAZINE
V1No.1, Nov, 1933 - V2No.12, Oct, 1935
Mills giveaways issued by different dairies
Walt Disney Productions

	Good	Fine	N-Mint
V1#1	35.00	105.00	245.00
2-12: 2-X-Mas ish.	17.00	51.00	120.00
V2#1-12: 2-X-Mas ish.. 4-St. Valentine-c	12.00	36.00	84.00

MICKEY MOUSE MAGAZINE (Becomes Walt Disney's Comics & Stories) (No V3/1, V4/6)
Summer, 1935 (June-Aug, indicia) - V5/12, Sept, 1940
V1/1-5, V3/11,12, V4/1-3 are 44 pgs; V2/3-100 pgs; V5/12-68 pgs; rest are 36 pgs.
K. K. Publications/Western Publishing Co.

	Good	Fine	VF-NM
V1#1 (Large size, 13¼x10¼"; 25 cents)-Contains puzzles, games, cels, stories and comics of Disney characters. Promotional magazine for Disney cartoon movies and paraphernalia	140.00	420.00	980.00

Note: *Some copies were autographed by the editors & given away with all early one year subscriptions.*

	Good	Fine	VF-NM
2 (Size change, 11½x8½"; 10/35; 10 cents)-High quality paper begins; Messmer-a	85.00	255.00	595.00

MICKEY MOUSE MAGAZINE (continued)

	Good	Fine	VF-NM
3,4: 3-Messmer-a	50.00	150.00	350.00
5-1st Donald Duck solo-c; last 44pg. & high quality paper issue	50.00	150.00	350.00
6-9: 6-36 pg. issues begin; Donald becomes editor. 8-2nd Donald solo-c. 9-1st Mickey/Minnie-c	40.00	120.00	280.00
10-12, V2#1,2: 11-1st Pluto/Mickey-c; Donald fires himself and appoints Mickey as editor	35.00	105.00	245.00
V2#3-Special 100 pg. Christmas issue (25 cents); Messmer-a; Donald becomes editor of Wise Quacks	70.00	200.00	490.00
4-Mickey Mouse Comics & Roy Ranger (adventure strip) begin; both end V2#9; Messmer-a	30.00	90.00	210.00

	Good	Fine	N-Mint
5-Ted True (adventure strip, ends V2#9) & Silly Symphony Comics (ends V3#3) begin	25.00	75.00	175.00
6-9: 6-1st solo Minnie-c. 6-9-Mickey Mouse Movies cut-out in each	25.00	75.00	175.00
10-1st full color issue; Mickey Mouse (by Gottfredson) ends V3#12) & Silly Symphony (ends V3/3) full color Sunday-r, Peter The Farm Detective (ends V5#8) & Ole Of The North (ends V3#3) begins	35.00	105.00	245.00
11-13: 12-Hiawatha-c & feat. sty	25.00	75.00	175.00
V3#2-Big Bad Wolf Halloween-c	25.00	75.00	175.00
3 (12/37)-1st app. Snow White & The Seven Dwarfs (before release of movie)(possibly 1st in print); Mickey Christmas-c	35.00	105.00	245.00
4 (1/38)-Snow White & The Seven Dwarfs serial begins (on stands before release of movie); Ducky Symphony (ends V3#11) begins	28.00	84.00	195.00
5-1st Snow White & Seven Dwarfs-c (St. Valentine's Day)	28.00	84.00	195.00
6-Snow White serial ends; Lonesome Ghosts app. (2 pp.)	25.00	75.00	175.00
7-Seven Dwarfs Easter-c	23.00	70.00	160.00
8-10: 9-Dopey-c. 10-1st solo Goofy-c	21.50	65.00	150.00
11,12 (44 pgs; 8 more pages color added). 11-Mickey The Sheriff serial (ends V4#3) & Donald Duck strip-r (ends V3#12) begin. Color feature on Snow White's Forest Friends	25.00	75.00	175.00
V4#1 (10/38; 44 pgs.)-Brave Little Tailor-c/feature story, nominated for Academy Award; Bobby & Chip by Otto Messmer (ends V4#2) & The Practical Pig (ends V4#2) begin	25.00	75.00	175.00
2 (44 pgs.)-1st Huey, Dewey & Louie-c	23.00	70.00	160.00
3 (12/38, 44 pgs.)-Ferdinand The Bull-c/feature story, Academy Award winner; Mickey Mouse & The Whalers serial begins, ends V4#12	25.00	75.00	175.00
4-Spotty, Mother Pluto strip-r begin, end V4#8	21.00	62.00	145.00
5-St. Valentine's day-c. 1st Pluto solo-c	23.00	75.00	175.00
7 (3/39)-The Ugly Duckling-c/feature story, Academy Award winner	23.00	75.00	175.00
7 (4/39)-Goofy & Wilbur The Grasshopper classic-c/feature story from 1st Goofy cartoon movie; Timid Elmer begins, ends V5#5	23.00	75.00	175.00
8-Big Bad Wolf-c from Practical Pig movie poster; Practical Pig feature story	23.00	75.00	175.00
9-Donald Duck & Mickey Mouse Sunday-r begin; The Pointer feature story, nominated for Academy Award	23.00	75.00	175.00
10-Classic July 4th drum & fife-c; last Donald Sunday-r	28.00	84.00	195.00
11-1st slick-c; last over-sized ish	21.00	65.00	150.00
12 (9/39; format change, 10¼x8¼'')-1st full color, cover to cover issue. Donald's Penguin-c/feature	27.00	81.00	190.00
V5#1-Black Pete-c; Officer Duck-c/feature story; Autograph Hound feature story; Robinson Crusoe serial begins			

	Good	Fine	N-Mint
2-Goofy-c; 1st app. Pinocchio (cameo)	27.00	81.00	190.00
3 (12/39)-Pinocchio Christmas-c (Before movie release). Pinocchio serial begins; 1st app. Jiminy Crickett	35.00	105.00	245.00
4,5: 5-Jiminy Crickett-c; Pinocchio serial ends; Donald's Dog Laundry feature story	28.00	84.00	195.00
6-Tugboat Mickey feature story; Rip Van Winkle feature begins, ends V5#8	26.00	78.00	182.00
7-2nd Huey, Dewey & Louie-c	26.00	78.00	182.00
8-Last magazine size issue; 2nd solo Pluto-c; Figaro & Cleo feature story	26.00	78.00	182.00
9 (6/40; change to comic book size)-Jiminy Crickett feature story; Donald-c & Sunday-r begin	35.00	100.00	245.00
10-Special Independence Day issue	35.00	100.00	245.00
11-Hawaiian Holiday & Mickey's Trailer feature stories; last 36 pg. issue	35.00	100.00	245.00
12 (Format change)-The transition issue (68 pgs.) becoming a comic book. With only a title change to follow, becomes Walt Disney's Comics & Stories #1 with the next issue	130.00	390.00	910.00
V4#1 (Giveaway)	20.00	60.00	140.00

NOTE: **Otto Messmer**-a is in many issues of the first two-three years. The following story titles and issues have gags created by **Carl Barks**: V4#3(12/38)-'Donald's Better Self' & 'Donald's Golf Game;' V4#4(1/39)-'Donald's Lucky Day;' V4#7(3/39)-'Hockey Champ;' V4#7(4/39)-'Donald's Cousin Gus;' V4#9(6/39)-'Sea Scouts;' V4#12(9/39)-'Donald's Penguin;' V5#9(6/40)-'Donald's Vacation;' V5#10(7/40)-'Bone Trouble;' V5#12(9/40)-'Window Cleaners.'

MICKEY MOUSE MARCH OF COMICS:
1947 - 1951 (Giveaway)
K. K. Publications

	Good	Fine	N-Mint
8(1947)-32 pgs.	50.00	150.00	330.00
27(1948)	34.00	100.00	238.00
45(1949)	27.00	80.00	190.00
60(1950)	18.00	55.00	125.00
74(1951)	14.00	42.50	96.00

MICKEY MOUSE SUMMER FUN (See Dell Giants)

MICKEY MOUSE'S SUMMER VACATION (See Story Hour Series)

MICROBOTS, THE
December, 1971 (One Shot)
Gold Key

	Good	Fine	N-Mint
1 (10271-112)	.85	2.50	5.00

MICRONAUTS
Jan, 1979 - No. 59, Aug, 1984 (Mando paper #53 on)
Marvel Comics Group

	Good	Fine	N-Mint
1-Intro/1st app. Baron Karza	.40	1.25	2.50
2-5		.60	1.20
6-10: 7-Man-Thing app. 8-1st app. Capt. Universe. 9-1st app. Cilicia	.45		.90
11-20: 13-1st app. Jasmine. 15-Death of Microtron. 15-17-Fantastic-4 app. 17-Death of Jasmine. 20 Ant-Man app.	.45		.90
21-30: 21-Microverse series begins. 25-Origin Baron Karza. 25-29-Nick Fury app. 27-Death of Biotron	.45		.90
31-34: Dr. Strange app. #34,35	.45		.90
35-Double size; origin Microverse; intro Death Squad	.45		.90
36-Giffen-a(p)	.45		.90
37-New X-Men app.; Giffen-a(p)	.35	1.00	2.00
38-First direct sale	.25	.80	1.60
39,40: 40-Fantastic-4 app.	.45		.90
41-59: 57-Double size	.45		.90
nn-Reprints #1-3; blank UPC; diamond on top	.20		.40
Annual 1(12/79)-Ditko c/a	.30	.90	1.80
Annual 2(10/80)-Ditko c/a	.50		1.00

Mickey Mouse Magazine V1#5, © WDC

Mickey Mouse Magazine V4#2, © WDC

Micronauts #1 (1/79), © MEG

Midnight Mystery #2, © ACG   The Mighty Atom And The Pixies #6 (1949), © ME   The Mighty Crusaders #7, © AP

MICRONAUTS (continued)
NOTE: #38-on distributed only through comic shops. *Adams* c-7i. *Chaykin* a-13-18p. *Ditko* a-39p. *Giffen* a-36p, 37p. *Golden* a-1-12p; c-2-6p, 7-23, 24p, 38, 39. *Guice* a-48-58p; c-49-58. *Gil Kane* a-38, 40p-45p; c-40-45. *Layton* c-33-37. *Miller* c-31.

MICRONAUTS
Oct, 1984 - No. 20, May, 1986
Marvel Comics Group

	Good	Fine	N-Mint
V2#1-20		.35	.70

NOTE: *Golden* a-1; c-1, 6. *Guice* a-4p; c-2p.

MICRONAUTS SPECIAL EDITION
Dec, 1983 - No. 5, Apr, 1984 ($2.00; mini-series; Baxter paper)
Marvel Comics Group

		Good	Fine	N-Mint
1: 1-5 r/original series 1-12			.70	1.40
2-5: Guice-c(p)-all			.70	1.40

MIDGET COMICS (Fighting Indian Stories)
Feb, 1950 - No. 2, Apr, 1950 (5-3/8"x7-3/8")
St. John Publishng Co.

1-Matt Baker-c	4.65	14.00	32.00
2-Tex West, Cowboy Marshal	2.35	7.00	16.00

MIDNIGHT
April, 1957 - No. 6, June, 1958
Ajax/Farrell Publ. (Four Star Comic Corp.)

1-Reprints from Voodoo & Strange Fantasy with some changes			
	3.70	11.00	26.00
2-5	1.70	5.00	12.00
6-Baker-r/Phantom Lady	3.50	10.50	24.00

MIDNIGHT MYSTERY
Jan-Feb, 1961 - No. 7, Oct, 1961
American Comics Group

1-Sci/Fic story	2.65	8.00	18.00
2-7: 7-Reinman-a	1.50	4.50	10.00

NOTE: *Reinman* a-1, 3. *Whitman* a-1, 4-6; c-1, 3, 5, 7.

MIDNIGHT TALES
Dec, 1972 - No. 18, May, 1976
Charlton Press

V1#1		.60	1.20
2-10,15-18		.40	.80
11-14-Newton-a		.40	.80
12,17(Modern Comics reprint, 1977)		.15	.30

NOTE: *Adkins* a-12i, 13i. *Ditko* a-12. *Howard* (Wood imitator) a-1-15, 17, 18; c-1-18. *Staton* a-1, 3-11, 13. *Sutton* a-3-5, 7-10.

MIGHTY ATOM, THE (. . .& the Pixies #6)
(Formerly The Pixies No. 1-5)
No. 6, 1949; 11/57 - No. 6, 8-9/58
Magazine Enterprises

6(1949-M.E.)-no month (1st Series)	2.30	7.00	16.00
1-6(2nd Series)-Pixies-r	1.00	3.00	7.00
I.W. Reprint #1(nd)	.30	.90	1.80
Giveaway(1959, '63, Whitman)-Evans-a	1.35	4.00	8.00
Giveaway ('65r, '67r, '68r, '73r, '76r)		.50	1.00

MIGHTY BEAR (Formerly Fun Comics, Mighty Ghost #4)
No. 13, Jan, 1954 - No. 14, Mar, 1954; 9/57 - No. 3, 2/58
Star Publ. No. 13,14/Ajax-Farrell (Four Star)

13,14-L. B. Cole-c	3.00	9.00	21.00
1-3('57-'58)Four Star (Ajax)	1.00	3.00	7.00

MIGHTY COMICS (. . .Presents) (Formerly Flyman)
No. 40, Nov, 1966 - No. 50, Oct, 1967
Radio Comics (Archie)

40-Web	1.00	3.00	6.00
41-Shield, Black Hood	.85	2.50	5.00
42-Black Hood	.85	2.50	5.00

	Good	Fine	N-Mint
43-Shield, Web & Black Hood	.85	2.50	5.00
44-Black Hood, Steel Sterling & The Shield	.85	2.50	5.00
45-Shield & Hangman; origin Web retold	.85	2.50	5.00
46-Steel Sterling, Web & Black Hood	.85	2.50	5.00
47-Shield Hood & Mr. Justice	.85	2.50	5.00
48-Shield & Hangman; Wizard x-over in Shield	.85	2.50	5.00
49-Steel Sterling & Fox; Black Hood x-over in Steel Sterling			
	.85	2.50	5.00
50-Black Hood & Web; Inferno x-over in Web	.85	2.50	5.00

NOTE: *Paul Reinman* a-40-50.

MIGHTY CRUSADERS, THE (Also see Fly Man, Advs. of the Fly)
Nov, 1965 - No. 7, Oct, 1966
Mighty Comics Group (Radio Comics)

1-Origin The Shield	1.50	4.50	10.00
2-Origin Comet	1.00	3.00	7.00
3-Origin Fly-Man	1.00	3.00	7.00
4-Fireball, Inferno, Firefly, Web, Fox, Bob Phantom, Blackjack, Hangman, Zambini, Kardak, Steel Sterling, Mr. Justice, Wizard, Capt. Flag, Jaguar x-over	1.00	3.00	6.00
5-Intro. Ultra-Men (Fox, Web, Capt. Flag) & Terrific Three (Jaguar, Mr. Justice, Steel Sterling)	.85	2.50	5.00
6,7: 7-Steel Sterling feature; origin Fly-Girl	.85	2.50	5.00

NOTE: *Reinman* a-6.

MIGHTY CRUSADERS, THE (All New Advs. of. . .#2)
3/83 - No. 13, 9/85 ($1.00, 36 pgs, Mando paper)
Red Circle Prod./Archie Ent. No. 6 on

1-Origin Black Hood, The Fly, Fly Girl, The Shield, The Wizard, The Jaguar, Pvt. Strong & The Web	.45	.90
2-13: 2-Mister Midnight begins. 4-Darkling replaces Shield. 5-Origin Jaguar, Shield begins. 7-Untold origin Jaguar		
	.45	.90

NOTE: *Buckler* a-1-3, 4i, 5p, 7p, 8i, 9i; c-1-10p.

MIGHTY GHOST (Formerly Mighty Bear)
No. 4, June, 1958
Ajax/Farrell Publ.

4	1.00	3.00	7.00

MIGHTY HERCULES, THE (TV)
July, 1963 - No. 2, Nov, 1963
Gold Key

1,2(10072-307,311)	3.00	9.00	21.00

MIGHTY HEROES, THE (TV) (Funny)
Mar, 1967 - No. 4, July, 1967
Dell Publishing Co.

1-1957 Heckle & Jeckle-r	.85	2.50	6.00
2,3	.60	1.80	4.00
4-Two 1958 Mighty Mouse-r	.60	1.80	4.00

MIGHTY MARVEL WESTERN, THE
10/68 - No. 46, 9/76 (#1-14: 68 pgs.; #15,16: 52 pgs.)
Marvel Comics Group

1-Begin Kid Colt, Rawhide Kid, Two-Gun Kid-r	.40	.80
2-10	.30	.60
11-20	.30	.60
21-30: 24-Kid Colt-r end. 25-Matt Slade-r begin	.30	.60
31,33-36,38,46: 31-Baker-r	.30	.60
32-Origin-r/Ringo Kid #23; Williamson-r/Kid Slade #7		
	.30	.60
37-Williamson, Kirby-r/Two-Gun Kid 51	.30	.60

NOTE: *Jack Davis* a(r)-21-24. *Kirby* a(r)-1-3, 6, 9, 12, 14, 16, 29, 32, 36, 41, 43, 44; c-29. *Maneely* a(r)-22. No Matt Slade-r#43.

MIGHTY MIDGET COMICS, THE (Miniature)
No date; circa 1942-1943 (36 pages) (Approx. 5x4")

267

THE MIGHTY MIDGET COMICS (continued)
(Black & White & Red) (Sold 2 for 5 cents)
Samuel E. Lowe & Co.

	Good	Fine	N-Mint
Bulletman #11(1943)-R-/cover/Bulletman #3	3.00	9.00	21.00
Captain Marvel #11	3.00	9.00	21.00
Captain Marvel #11 (Same as above except for full color ad on back cover; this issue was glued to cover of Captain Marvel #20 and is not found in fine-mint condition)	3.00	9.00	21.00
Captain Marvel Jr. #11	3.00	9.00	21.00
Captain Marvel Jr. #11 (Same as above except for full color ad on back-c; this issue was glued to cover of Captain Marvel #21 and is not found in fine-mint condition)	3.00	9.00	21.00
Golden Arrow #11	2.00	6.00	14.00
Ibis the Invincible #11(1942)-Origin; r-/cover/Ibis #1	3.00	9.00	21.00
Spy Smasher #11(1942)	3.00	9.00	21.00

NOTE: The above books came in a box called "box full of books" and was distributed with other Samuel Lowe puzzles, paper dolls, coloring books, etc. They are not titled Mighty Midget Comics. All have a war bond seal on back cover which is otherwise blank. These books came in a "Mighty Midget" flat cardboard counter display rack.

	Good	Fine	N-Mint
Balbo, the Boy Magician #12	1.50	4.50	10.00
Bulletman #12	3.00	9.00	21.00
Commando Yank #12	2.00	6.00	14.00
Dr. Voltz the Human Generator	1.50	4.50	10.00
Lance O'Casey #12	1.50	4.50	10.00
Leatherneck the Marine	1.50	4.50	10.00
Minute Man #12	3.00	9.00	21.00
Mister Q	1.50	4.50	10.00
Mr. Scarlet & Pinky #12	3.00	9.00	21.00
Pat Wilton & His Flying Fortress	1.50	4.50	10.00
The Phantom Eagle #12	2.00	6.00	14.00
State Trooper Stops Crime	1.50	4.50	10.00
Tornado Tom; r-/from Cyclone #1-3; origin	2.00	6.00	12.00

MIGHTY MOUSE (See Adventures of . . ., Dell Giant #43, Giant Comics Edition, March of Comics #205, 237, 247, 257, 459, 471, 483, Oxydol-Dreft, Paul Terry's, & Terry-Toons Comics)

MIGHTY MOUSE (1st Series)
Fall, 1946 - No. 4, Summer, 1947
Timely/Marvel Comics (20th Century Fox)

1	45.00	135.00	315.00
2	22.00	65.00	154.00
3,4	16.00	48.00	110.00

MIGHTY MOUSE (2nd Series) (Paul Terry's . . . #62-71)
Aug, 1947 - No. 67, 11/55; No. 68, 3/56 - No. 83, 6/59
St. John Publishing Co./Pines No. 68 (3/56)

5(#1)	16.00	48.00	110.00
6-10	7.00	21.00	50.00
11-19	4.30	13.00	30.00
20 (11/50) - 25-(52 pgs.)	3.70	11.00	26.00
20-25-(36 pg. editions)	3.50	10.50	24.00
26-37: 35-Flying saucer-c	2.65	8.00	18.00
38-45-(100 pgs.)	6.00	18.00	42.00
46-83: 62,64,67-Painted-c. 82-Infinity-c	1.70	5.00	12.00
Album 1(10/52)-100 pgs.	12.00	36.00	84.00
Album 2(11/52-St. John) - 3(12/52) (100 pgs.)	10.00	30.00	70.00
Fun Club Magazine 1(Fall, 1957-Pines, 100 pgs.) (TV-Tom Terrific)	6.50	19.50	45.00
Fun Club Magazine 2-6(Winter, 1958-Pines)	3.70	11.00	26.00
3-D 1-(1st printing-9/53)(St. John)-stiff covers	18.00	54.00	125.00
3-D 1-(2nd printing-10/53)-slick, glossy covers, slightly smaller	15.00	45.00	105.00
3-D 2(11/53), 3(12/53)-(St. John)	13.00	40.00	90.00

MIGHTY MOUSE (TV)(3rd Series)(Formerly Advs. of Mighty Mouse)
No. 161, Oct, 1964 - No. 172, Oct, 1968
Gold Key/Dell Publishing Co. No. 166-on

	Good	Fine	N-Mint
161(10/64)-165(9/65)-(Becomes Advs. of . . . No. 166 on)	1.50	4.50	10.00
166(3/66), 167(6/66)-172	1.15	3.50	8.00

MIGHTY MOUSE (TV)
1987 - No. 2, 1987 ($1.50, color)
Spotlight Comics

1,2: New stories	.25	.75	1.50
. . .And Friends Holiday Special (11/87, $1.75)	.30	.90	1.75

MIGHTY MOUSE ADVENTURES (Advs. of . . . #2 on)
November, 1951
St. John Publishing Co.

1	14.00	42.00	100.00

MIGHTY MOUSE ADVENTURE STORIES
1953 (384 pgs.) (50 Cents)
St. John Publishing Co.

Rebound issues	25.00	75.00	175.00

MIGHTY SAMSON (Also see Gold Key Champion)
7/64 - No.20, 11/69?; No.21, 8/72; No.22, 12/73 - No.31, 3/76; No. 32, 8/82 (Painted-c #1-31)
Gold Key

1-Origin; Thorne-a begins	1.15	3.50	8.00
2-5	.75	2.25	5.00
6-10: 7-Tom Morrow begins, ends #20	.50	1.50	3.00
11-20	.35	1.00	2.00
21-32: 21,22,32-r		.50	1.00

MIGHTY THOR (See Thor)

MIKE BARNETT, MAN AGAINST CRIME (TV)
Dec, 1951 - No. 6, 1952
Fawcett Publications

1	5.00	15.00	35.00
2	3.00	9.00	21.00
3,4,6	2.15	6.50	15.00
5-"Market for Morphine" cover/story	3.75	11.25	26.00

MIKE SHAYNE PRIVATE EYE
Nov-Jan, 1962 - No. 3, Sept-Nov, 1962
Dell Publishing Co.

1	1.50	4.50	10.00
2,3	1.15	3.50	8.00

MILITARY COMICS (Becomes Modern #44 on)
Aug, 1941 - No. 43, Oct, 1945
Quality Comics Group

1-Origin Blackhawk by C. Cuidera, Miss America, The Death Patrol by Jack Cole (also #2-7,27-30), & The Blue Tracer by Guardineer; X of the Underground, The Yankee Eagle, Q-Boat & Shot & Shell, Archie Atkins, Loops & Banks by Bud Ernest (Bob Powell) (ends #13) begin	235.00	705.00	1645.00
2-Secret War News begins (by McWilliams #2-16); Cole-a	115.00	345.00	800.00
3-Origin/1st app. Chop Chop	85.00	255.00	600.00
4	77.00	230.00	540.00
5-The Sniper begins; Miss America in costume #4-7	62.00	185.00	435.00
6-9: 8-X of the Underground begins (ends #13). 9-The Phantom Clipper begins (ends #16)	50.00	150.00	350.00
10-Classic Eisner-c	55.00	165.00	385.00
11-Flag-c	40.00	120.00	280.00
12-Blackhawk by Crandall begins, ends #22	55.00	165.00	385.00
13-15: 14-Private Dogtag begins (ends #83)	37.00	110.00	260.00
16-20: 16-Blue Tracer ends. 17-P.T. Boat begins	30.00	90.00	210.00

The Mighty Midget Comics #11, © FAW

Mighty Mouse Fun Club Magazine #1, © Terry Toons

Military Comics #14, © QUA

Millennium #1, © DC

Millie The Model #11, © MEG

Miracleman #11, © Eclipse Comics

	Good	Fine	N-Mint
MILITARY COMICS (continued)			
21-31: 22-Last Crandall Blackhawk. 27-Death Patrol revived			
	27.00	81.00	190.00
32-43	24.00	72.00	168.00

NOTE: *Berg* a-6. *J. Cole* a-1-3, 27-32. *Crandall* a-12-22; c-13-22. *Eisner* c-1, 9, 10. *McWilliams* a-2-16. *Powell* a-1-13. *Ward* Blackhawk-30, 31(15 pgs. each); c-29, 30.

MILITARY WILLY
1907 (14 pgs.; ½ in color (every other page))
(regular comic book format)(7x9½'')(stapled)
J. I. Austen Co.

By F. R. Morgan	12.00	36.00	84.00

MILLENIUM
Jan, 1988 - No. 8, Feb, 1988 (nd) (Weekly mini-series)
DC Comics

1-Staton c/a(p) begins	.35	1.00	2.00
2-4	.25	.75	1.50
5-8	.25	.75	1.50

MILLENNIUM INDEX
Mar., 1988 ($2.00)
Independent Comics Group

1,2	.35	1.00	2.00

MILLIE, THE LOVABLE MONSTER
Sept-Nov, 1962 - No. 6, Jan, 1973
Dell Publishing Co.

12-523,211, 2(8-10/63)	1.00	3.00	7.00
3(8-10/64)	.85	2.50	6.00
4(7/72), 5(10/72), 6(1/73)	.70	2.00	4.00

NOTE: *Woggon* a-3-6; c-3-6. 4 reprints 1; 5 reprints 2; 6 reprints 3.

MILLIE THE MODEL (See Comedy Comics, A Date With..., Gay Comics, Life With... & Modeling With...)
1945 - No. 207, December, 1973
Marvel/Atlas/Marvel Comics (SPI/Male/VPI)

1	20.00	60.00	140.00
2 (10/46)-Millie becomes The Blonde Phantom to sell Blonde Phantom perfume; a pre-Blonde Phantom app. (see All-Select #11, Fall, '46)	12.00	36.00	84.00
3-7: 5- Willie app. 7-Willie smokes extra strong tobacco	5.70	17.00	40.00
8,10-Kurtzman's ''Hey Look''	5.70	17.00	40.00
9-Powerhouse Pepper by Wolverton, 4 pgs.	9.50	28.50	65.00
11-Kurtzman-a, 'Giggles 'n Grins	4.65	14.00	32.00
12,15,17-20	2.65	8.00	18.00
13,14,16-Kurtzman's ''Hey Look''	3.50	10.50	24.00
21-30	2.00	6.00	14.00
31-60	1.30	4.00	9.00
61-99	.70	2.00	5.00
100	1.00	3.00	7.00
101-106,108-207: 154-New Millie begins (10/67). 192-(52 pgs.)	.35	1.00	2.00
107-Jack Kirby app. in story	.35	1.00	2.00
Annual 1(1962)	3.00	9.00	21.00
Annual 2-10(1963-11/71)	1.50	4.50	10.00
Queen-Size 11(9/74), 12(1975)	.70	2.00	4.00

MILLION DOLLAR DIGEST
11/86 - No. 7, 11/87; No. 8, 4/88 - Present ($1.25-$1.75, digest size)
Harvey Publications

1-8		.60	1.25
9-14	.30	.90	1.75

MILT GROSS FUNNIES
Aug, 1947 - No. 2, Sept, 1947
Milt Gross, Inc. (ACG?)

1,2	4.00	12.00	28.00

MILTON THE MONSTER & FEARLESS FLY (TV)
May, 1966
Gold Key

	Good	Fine	N-Mint
1 (10175-605)	3.00	9.00	21.00

MINUTE MAN (See Master & Mighty Midget Comics)
Summer, 1941 - No. 3, Spring, 1942
Fawcett Publications

1	65.00	195.00	455.00
2,3	50.00	150.00	350.00

MINUTE MAN
No date (B&W; 16 pgs.; paper cover blue & red)
Sovereign Service Station giveaway

American history	1.00	3.00	6.00

MINUTE MAN ANSWERS THE CALL, THE
1942 (4 pages)
By M. C. Gaines (War Bonds giveaway)

Sheldon Moldoff-a	6.00	18.00	42.00

MIRACLE COMICS
Feb, 1940 - No. 4, March, 1941
Hillman Periodicals

1-Sky Wizard, Master of Space, Dash Dixon, Man of Might, Dusty Doyle, Pinkie Parker, The Kid Cop, K-7, Secret Agent, The Scorpion, & Blandu, Jungle Queen begin; Masked Angel only app.	50.00	150.00	350.00
2	30.00	90.00	210.00
3,4: 3-Bill Colt, the Ghost Rider begins. 4-The Veiled Prophet & Bullet Bob app.	27.00	81.00	190.00

MIRACLEMAN
Aug, 1985 - Present (Mando paper, 7-10)
Eclipse Comics

1-r-/of British Marvelman series; Alan Moore scripts in all	.50	1.50	3.00
1-Gold edition	2.50	7.50	15.00
1-Silver edition	.70	2.00	4.00
2-12: 9,10-Origin Miracleman. 9-Shows graphic scenes of childbirth		.60	1.25
13-15	.30	.90	1.75
3-D 1 (12/85)	.40	1.25	2.50
2-D 1 (B&W, 100 copy limited signed & numbered edition)	.40	1.25	2.50

MIRACLEMAN FAMILY
May, 1988 - No. 2, Sept, 1988 ($1.95, color, mini-series)
Eclipse Comics

1,2	.35	1.00	1.95

MIRACLE OF THE WHITE STALLIONS, THE (See Movie Comics)

MIRACLE SQUAD, THE
Aug, 1986 - No. 4, 1987 ($2.00, color, mini-series)
Upshot Graphics (Fantagraphics Books)

1-4	.35	1.00	2.00

MISADVENTURES OF MERLIN JONES, THE (See Movie Comics & Merlin Jones as the Monkey's Uncle under Movie Comics)

MISCHIEVOUS MONKS OF CROCODILE ISLE, THE
1908 (8½x11½''; 4 pgs. in color; 12 pgs.)
J. I. Austen Co., Chicago

By F. R. Morgan; reads longwise	7.00	21.00	50.00

MISS AMERICA COMICS (Miss America Mag. #2 on)
1944 (One Shot)
Marvel Comics (20CC)

1-2 pgs. pin-ups	48.00	145.00	335.00

MISS AMERICA MAGAZINE (Formerly Miss America) (Miss America #51 on)
V1#2, Nov, 1944 - No. 93, Nov, 1958   **Good**   **Fine**   **N-Mint**
Miss America Publ. Corp./Marvel/Atlas (MAP)

	Good	Fine	N-Mint
V1#2: Photo-c of teenage girl in Miss America costume; Miss America, Patsy Walker (intro.) comic stories plus movie reviews & stories; intro. Buzz Baxter & Hedy Wolfe	43.00	130.00	300.00
3,5-Miss America & Patsy Walker stories	16.00	48.00	110.00
4-Betty Page photo-c (See Cupid #2, My Love #4); Miss America & Patsy Walker story	20.00	60.00	140.00
6-Patsy Walker only	4.00	12.00	28.00
V2#1(4/45)-6(9/45)-Patsy Walker continues	2.00	6.00	14.00
V3#1(10/45)-6(4/46)	2.00	6.00	14.00
V4#1(5/46)-3(7/46)	1.60	4.70	11.00
V4#4 (8/46; 68pgs.)	1.60	4.70	11.00
V4#5 (9/46)-Liz Taylor photo-c	3.50	10.50	24.00
V4#6 (10/46; 92pgs.)	1.60	4.70	11.00
V5#1(11/46)-6(4/47), V6#1(5/47)-3(7/47)	1.60	4.70	11.00
V7#1(8/47)-14,16-23(6/49)	1.30	4.00	9.00
V7#15-All comics	1.60	4.70	11.00
V7#24(7/49)-Kamen-a	1.50	4.50	10.00
V7#25(8/49), 27-44(3/52), VII,nn(5/52)	1.30	4.00	9.00
V7#26(9/49)-All comics	1.60	4.70	11.00
V1,nn(7/52)-V1,nn(1/53)(#46-49)	1.30	4.00	9.00
V7#50(Spring '53), V1#51-V7?#54(7/53)	1.15	3.50	8.00
55-93	1.15	3.50	8.00

NOTE: Photo-c #1, V2#4, 5, V3#5, V4#4,6, V7#15, 16, 24, 26, 34, 37, 38.. Powell a-V7#31.

MISS BEVERLY HILLS OF HOLLYWOOD
Mar-Apr, 1949 - No. 9, July-Aug, 1950 (52 pgs.)
National Periodical Publications

	Good	Fine	N-Mint
1 (Meets Alan Ladd)	19.00	57.00	132.00
2-William Holden photo-c	14.00	42.00	100.00
3-5: 3,4-Part photo-c	11.50	34.00	80.00
6,7,9	10.00	30.00	70.00
8-Reagan photo on-c	14.00	42.00	100.00

MISS CAIRO JONES
1945
Croyden Publishers

1-Bob Oksner daily newspaper-r (1st strip story); lingerie panels	11.50	34.00	80.00

MISS FURY COMICS (Newspaper strip reprints)
Winter, 1942-43 - No. 8, Winter, 1946
Timely Comics (NPI 1/CmPI 2/MPC 3-8)

1-Origin Miss Fury by Tarpe' Mills (68 pgs.) in costume w/pin-ups	135.00	405.00	945.00
2-(60 pgs.)-In costume w/pin-ups	60.00	180.00	420.00
3-(60 pgs.)-In costume w/pin-ups	50.00	150.00	350.00
4-(52 pgs.)-Costume, 2 pgs. w/pin-ups	42.00	125.00	295.00
5-(52 pgs.)-In costume w/pin-ups	37.00	110.00	260.00
6-(52 pgs.)-Not in costume in inside stories, w/pin-ups	33.00	100.00	230.00
7,8-(36 pgs.)-In costume 1 pg. each, no pin-ups	33.00	100.00	230.00

MISSION IMPOSSIBLE (TV)
5/67 - No. 4, 10/68; No. 5, 10/69 (No. 1-5 have photo-c)
Dell Publishing Co.

1	4.00	12.00	28.00
2-5: #5-r #1's-c	3.00	9.00	21.00

MISS LIBERTY (Becomes Liberty)
1945 (MLJ reprints)
Burten Publishing Co.

1-The Shield & Dusty, The Wizard, & Roy, the Super Boy app.;

	Good	Fine	N-Mint
r-/Shield-Wizard #13	13.00	40.00	90.00

MISS MELODY LANE OF BROADWAY
Feb-Mar, 1950 - No. 3, June-July, 1950 (52 pgs.)
National Periodical Publications

1	19.00	57.00	132.00
2,3	14.00	42.00	100.00

MISS PEACH
Oct-Dec, 1963; 1969
Dell Publishing Co.

1-Jack Mendelsohn-a/script	5.00	15.00	35.00
...Tells You How to Grow(1969; 25 cents)-Mell Lazarus-a; also given away (36 pgs.)	3.00	9.00	21.00

MISS PEPPER (See Meet Miss Pepper)

MISS SUNBEAM (See Little Miss...)

MISS VICTORY (See Holyoke One-Shot #3, Veri Best Sure Fire & Veri Best Sure Shot Comics)

MR. & MRS.
1922 (52 pgs.) (9x9½'', cardboard-c)
Whitman Publishing Co.

By Briggs (B&W, 52pgs.)	7.00	21.00	50.00
28 pgs.-(9x9½'')-Sunday strips-r in color	13.00	42.00	90.00

MR. & MRS. BEANS (See Single Series #11)

MR. & MRS. J. EVIL SCIENTIST (TV)(See The Flintstones)
Nov, 1963 - No. 4, Sept, 1966 (Hanna-Barbera)
Gold Key

1-From The Flintstones	1.70	5.00	12.00
2-4	1.15	3.50	8.00

MR. ANTHONY'S LOVE CLINIC
Nov, 1949 - No. 5, Apr-May, 1950 (52 pgs.)
Hillman Periodicals

1-Photo-c	4.00	12.00	28.00
2	2.30	7.00	16.00
3-5: 5-Photo-c	2.00	6.00	14.00

MR. BUG GOES TO TOWN (See Cinema Comics Herald)

MR. DISTRICT ATTORNEY (Radio/TV)
Jan-Feb, 1948 - No. 67, Jan-Feb, 1959 (52 pgs. 1-23)
National Periodical Publications

1	21.50	64.00	150.00
2	10.00	30.00	70.00
3-5	8.00	24.00	56.00
6-10	6.50	19.50	45.00
11-20	5.00	15.00	35.00
21-43: 43-Last pre-code (1-2/55)	3.70	11.00	26.00
44-67	2.65	8.00	18.00

MR. DISTRICT ATTORNEY (See 4-Color #13 & The Funnies #35)

MISTER ED, THE TALKING HORSE (TV)
Mar-May, 1962 - No. 6, Feb, 1964 (All photo-c; photo back-c, 1-6)
Dell Publishing Co./Gold Key

4-Color 1295	4.00	12.00	28.00
1(11/62)-6 (Gold Key)-Photo-c	2.00	6.00	14.00
(See March of Comics #244,260,282,290)			

MR. MAGOO (TV) (The Nearsighted..., ...& Gerald McBoing Boing 1954 issues; formerly Gerald...)
No. 6, Nov-Jan, 1953-54; 1963 - 1965
Dell Publishing Co.

6	5.00	15.00	35.00
4-Color 561(5/54),602(11/54)	5.00	15.00	35.00
4-Color 1235,1305('61)	4.00	12.00	28.00

Miss America Magazine V1#2, © MEG

Miss Beverly Hills Of Hollywood #1, © DC

Mr. District Attorney #5, © DC

Mr. Monster's Hi-Voltage Super Science #1, © Eclipse   Mister Mystery #7, © Stanmore   Mister X #5, © Vortex Publ.

	Good	Fine	N-Mint
MR. MAGOO (continued)			
3(9-11/63) - 5	3.50	10.50	24.00
4-Color 1235(12-536-505)(3-5/65)-2nd Printing	2.35	7.00	16.00

MISTER MIRACLE (See Brave & the Bold & Canc. Comic Caval.)
3-4/71 - No. 18, 2-3/74; No. 19, 9/77 - No. 25, 8-9/78; 1987
National Periodical Publications/DC Comics (#7,8-52 pgs.)

1	.35	1.00	2.00
2	.25	.75	1.50
3-10: 4-Boy Commando-r begin. 9-Origin Mr. Miracle			
		.60	1.20
11-17: 15-Intro/1st app. Shilo Norman	.40	.80	
18-Barda & Scott Free wed; New Gods app.	.40	.80	
19-22-Rogers-a(p)	.40	.80	
23-25-Golden-a(p)	.25	.50	
Special 1(1987, 52 pgs., $1.25)	.65	1.30	

NOTE: **Austin** a-19i. **Ditko** a-6r. **Golden** c-25p. **Heath** a-24i, 25i; c-25i. **Kirby** a(p)/c-1-18. **Nasser** a-19i. **Rogers** c-19, 20p, 21p, 22-24. **Wolverton** a-6r. 4-8 contain **Simon & Kirby** Boy Commando reprints from Detective 82,76, Boy Commandos 1,3, Detective 64 in that order.

MISTER MIRACLE
Jan, 1989 - Present (1.00, color)
DC Comics

1,2-Spin-off from Justice League International		.50	1.00

MR. MIRACLE (See Holyoke One-Shot #4 & Super Duck #3)

MR. MONSTER (See Airboy-Mr. Monster Special, Dark Horse Presents, Super Duper Comics & Vanguard Ill. #7)
Jan, 1985 - No. 10, June, 1987 ($1.75, color, Baxter paper)
Eclipse Comics

1	1.70	5.00	10.00
2-Dave Stevens-c	.70	2.00	4.00
3-9: 8-Alan Moore scripts	.50	1.50	3.00
10-6-D issue	.30	.90	1.80
. . .In 3-D	.35	1.00	2.00

MR. MONSTER
Feb., 1988 - Present ($1.75, B&W)
Dark Horse Comics

1-4: 1,2-Origin	.30	.95	1.90

MR. MONSTER'S. . .
May, 1986 - Present ($1.75, color)
Eclipse Comics

1 (5/86)-Mr. Monster's Three Dimensional High Octane Horror #1; Kubert/Powell-r	.40	1.25	2.50
1. . .in 2-D: 100 copies signed & #'d (B&W)	1.00	3.00	6.00
2 (8/86). . .High Octane Horror #1; Grandenetti, Wolverton, Evans-r			
	.30	.90	1.80
3 (9/86). . .True Crime #1; Cole-r	.30	.90	1.80
4 (11/86). . .True Crime #2	.30	.90	1.80
5 (1/87). . .Hi-Voltage Super Science #1; r-/Vic Torry & His Flying Saucer #1 by Powell	.30	.90	1.80
6 (3/87). . .High Shock Schlock #1	.30	.90	1.80
7 (5/87). . .High Shock Schlock #2; Wolverton-r			
	.30	.90	1.80
8 (7/87). . .Weird Tales of the Future #1; Wolverton-r			
	.30	.90	1.80

MR. MUSCLES (Formerly Blue Beetle #18-21)
No. 22, Mar, 1956 - No. 23, Aug, 1956
Charlton Comics

22,23	2.00	6.00	14.00

MISTER MYSTERY
Sept, 1951 - No. 19, Oct, 1954
Mr. Publ. (Media Publ.) No. 1-3/SPM Publ./Stanmore (Aragon)

1-Kurtzmanesque horror story	17.00	51.00	120.00

	Good	Fine	N-Mint
2,3-Kurtzmanesque story	12.00	36.00	84.00
4,6: Bondage-c; 6-Torture	12.00	36.00	84.00
5,8,10	10.00	30.00	70.00
7-"The Brain Bats of Venus" by Wolverton; partially re-used in Weird Tales of the Future #7	38.00	115.00	265.00
9-Nostrand-a	11.00	32.00	75.00
11-Wolverton "Robot Woman" story/Weird Mysteries #2, cut up, rewritten & partially redrawn	20.00	60.00	140.00
12-Classic injury to eye-c	27.00	81.00	190.00
13,14,17,19	7.00	21.00	50.00
15-"Living Dead" junkie story	10.00	30.00	70.00
16-Bondage-c	10.00	30.00	70.00
18-"Robot Woman" by Wolverton reprinted from Weird Mysteries #2; decapitation, bondage-c	17.00	51.00	120.00

NOTE: **Andru** c/a-1, 2p. **Bailey** c-10-19(most). Bondage-c 7. Some issues have graphic dismemberment scenes.

MISTER Q (See Mighty Midget Comics)

MR. RISK (Formerly All Romances; Men Against Crime #3 on)
No. 7, Oct, 1950 - No. 2, Dec, 1950
Ace Magazines

7,2	2.30	7.00	16.00

MR. SCARLET & PINKY (See Mighty Midget Comics)

MISTER UNIVERSE (Professional wrestler)
July, 1951 - No. 2, Oct, 1951 - No. 5, April, 1952
Mr. Publications Media Publ. (Stanmor, Aragon)

1	7.00	21.00	50.00
2-'Jungle That Time Forgot', 24pg. story	5.00	15.00	35.00
3-Marijuana story	5.00	15.00	35.00
4,5-"Goes to War"	2.65	8.00	18.00

MR. X
June, 1984 - Present ($1.50-$2.25; direct sales; Baxter paper; color)
Mr. Publications/Vortex Comics

1	1.15	3.50	7.00
2	.75	2.25	4.50
3-5	.60	1.75	3.50
6-10	.40	1.25	2.50
11-14: 13-Kaluta-c; 14-on are 2.25	.35	1.10	2.25
Graphic Novel ($11.95)	2.00	6.00	12.00
Hardcover limited edition	5.85	17.50	35.00

MISTY
Dec, 1985 - No. 6, May, 1986 (mini-series)
Star Comics (Marvel)

1-Millie The Model's niece		.35	.70
2-6		.40	.80

MITZI COMICS (. . .Boy Friend #2 on)(See All Teen)
Spring, 1948 (One Shot)
Timely Comics

1-Kurtzman's "Hey Look" plus 3 pgs. "Giggles 'n' Grins"			
	5.70	17.00	40.00

MITZI'S BOY FRIEND (Formerly Mitzi; becomes Mitzi's Romances)
No. 2, June, 1948 - No. 7, April, 1949
Marvel Comics

2	2.65	8.00	18.00
3-7	1.70	5.00	12.00

MITZI'S ROMANCES (Formerly Mitzi's Boy Friend)
No. 8, June, 1949 - No. 10, Dec, 1949
Timely/Marvel Comics

8	2.65	8.00	18.00
9,10: 10-Painted-c	1.70	5.00	12.00

MOBY DICK (See 4-Color #717, Feature Presentations #6, and King Classics)

MOBY DUCK (See W. D. Showcase #2,11, Donald Duck #112)
10/67 - No. 11, 10/70; No. 12, 1/74 - No. 30, 2/78
Gold Key (Disney)

	Good	Fine	N-Mint
1	.85	2.50	6.00
2-5	.70	2.00	4.00
6-11	.35	1.00	2.00
12-30: 21,30-r		.60	1.20

MODEL FUN (With Bobby Benson)
No. 3, Winter, 1954-55 - No. 5, July, 1955
Harle Publications

3-Bobby Benson	2.65	8.00	18.00
4,5-Bobby Benson	1.60	4.80	11.00

MODELING WITH MILLIE (Formerly Life With Millie)
No. 21, Feb, 1963 - No. 54, June, 1967
Atlas/Marvel Comics Group (Male Publ.)

21	1.00	3.00	7.00
22-30	.70	2.00	5.00
31-54	.50	1.50	3.00

MODERN COMICS (Formerly Military Comics #1-43)
No. 44, Nov, 1945 - No. 102, Oct, 1950
Quality Comics Group

44	23.00	70.00	160.00
45-52: 49-1st app. Fear, Lady Adventuress	14.00	42.00	100.00
53-Torchy by Ward begins (9/46)	20.00	60.00	140.00
54-60: 55-J. Cole-a	13.00	40.00	90.00
61-77,79,80: 73-J. Cole-a	12.00	36.00	84.00
78-1st app. Madame Butterfly	13.00	40.00	90.00
81-99,101: 82,83-One pg. J. Cole-a	12.00	36.00	84.00
100	12.00	36.00	84.00
102-(Scarce)-J. Cole-a; some issues have Spirit by Eisner	16.00	48.00	110.00

NOTE: *Crandall* Blackhawk-#46-51, 54, 56, 58-60, 64, 67-70, 73, 82, 83. *Jack Cole* a-73. *Gustavson* a-47. *Ward* Blackhawk-#52, 53, 55 (15 pgs. each). Torchy in #53-102; by *Ward* only in #53-89(9/49); by *Gil Fox* #93, 102.

MODERN LOVE
June-July, 1949 - No. 8, Aug-Sept, 1950
E. C. Comics

1	40.00	120.00	280.00
2-Craig/Feldstein-c	31.00	92.00	220.00
3-Spanking panels	26.00	78.00	180.00
4-6 (Scarce): 4-Bra/panties panels	37.00	110.00	260.00
7,8	28.00	84.00	195.00

NOTE: *Feldstein* a-in most issues; c-1, 3-8. *Ingels* a-1, 2, 4-7. *Wood* a-7. (Canadian reprints known; see Table of Contents.)

MOD LOVE
1967 (36 pages) (50 cents)
Western Publishing Co.

1	1.50	4.50	10.00

MODNIKS, THE
Aug, 1967 - No. 2, Aug, 1970
Gold Key

10206-708(#1), 2	.75	2.25	5.00

MOD SQUAD (TV)
Jan, 1969 - No. 3, Oct, 1969 - No. 8, April, 1971
Dell Publishing Co.

1	1.50	4.50	10.00
2-8: 8 reprints #2. 3-Photo-c	1.00	3.00	7.00

MOD WHEELS
March, 1971 - No. 19, Jan, 1976
Gold Key

1	1.00	3.00	6.00
2-19: 11,15-Extra 16pgs. ads	.50	1.50	3.00

MOE & SHMOE COMICS
Spring, 1948 - No. 2, Summer, 1948
O. S. Publ. Co.

	Good	Fine	N-Mint
1	3.50	10.50	24.00
2	2.30	7.00	16.00

MOEBIUS
Oct, 1987 - Present ($9.95, $12.95, graphic novel, adults)
Epic Comics (Marvel)

1,2,4-6	1.70	5.00	9.95
3 ($12.95)	2.15	6.50	12.95

MOLLY MANTON'S ROMANCES (My Love #3)
Sept, 1949 - No. 2, Dec, 1949 (52 pgs.)
Marvel Comics (SePI)

1-Photo-c	3.70	11.00	26.00
2-Titled 'Romances of . . .'; photo-c	2.65	8.00	18.00

MOLLY O'DAY (Super Sleuth)
February, 1945 (1st Avon comic)
Avon Periodicals

1-Molly O'Day, The Enchanted Dagger by Tuska (r-/Yankee #1), Capt'n Courage, Corporal Grant app.	30.00	90.00	210.00

MONKEES, THE (TV)(Also see Circus Boy, Not Brand Echh #3, Teen-Age Talk, Teen Beam & Teen Beat)
March, 1967 - No. 17, Oct, 1969 (#1-4,6,7,10 have photo-c)
Dell Publishing Co.

1	4.30	13.00	30.00
2-17: 17 reprints #1	2.15	6.50	15.00

MONKEY & THE BEAR, THE
Sept, 1953 - No. 3, Jan, 1954
Atlas Comics (ZPC)

1-Howie Post-a	2.00	6.00	14.00
2,3	1.15	3.50	8.00

MONKEYSHINES COMICS (Ernie #24? on)
Summer, 1944 - No. 26, May, 1949
Ace Periodicals/Publishers Specialists/Current Books/Unity Publ.

1	3.70	11.00	26.00
2	2.00	6.00	14.00
3-10	1.50	4.50	10.00
11-26: 23,24-Fago c/a	1.15	3.50	8.00

MONKEY SHINES OF MARSELEEN
1909 (11½x17") (28 pages in two colors)
Cupples & Leon Co.

By Norman E. Jennett	10.00	30.00	70.00

MONKEY'S UNCLE, THE (See Merlin Jones As . . . under Movie Comics)

MONROES, THE (TV)
April, 1967
Dell Publishing Co.

1-Photo-c	1.75	5.25	12.00

MONSTER
1953
Fiction House Magazines

1-Dr. Drew by Grandenetti; reprint from Rangers Comics	16.00	48.00	110.00
2	13.00	40.00	90.00

MONSTER CRIME COMICS (Also see Crime Must Stop)
October, 1952 (52 pgs., 15 cents)
Hillman Periodicals

1 (Scarce)	35.00	105.00	245.00

MONSTER HOWLS (Magazine)
December, 1966 (Satire) (35 cents) (68 pgs.)

Modern Comics #100, © QUA

Modern Love #3, © WMG

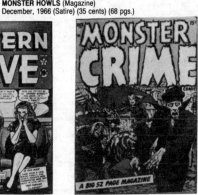

Monster Crime Comics #1, © HILL

Monte Hale Western #33, © FAW

Moon Girl And The Prince #7, © WMG

Moon Knight #1 (11/80), © MEG

MONSTER HOWLS (continued)
Humor-Vision

	Good	Fine	N-Mint
1	.85	2.50	5.00

MONSTER HUNTERS
8/75 - No. 9, 1/77; No. 10, 10/77 - No. 18, 2/79
Charlton Comics

1-Howard-a, Newton-c		.40	.80
2-Ditko-a		.40	.80
3-11		.30	.60
12,13,15-18-All reprints		.25	.50
14-Special all-Ditko issue		.50	1.00
1,2(Modern Comics reprints, 1977)		.15	.30

NOTE: *Ditko a-6, 8, 10, 13-15r, 18r; c-13-15, 18. Howard r-13. Morisi a-1. Staton a-1,13. Sutton a-2, 4; c-2, 4.*

MONSTER OF FRANKENSTEIN (See Frankenstein)

MONSTERS ON THE PROWL (Chamber of Darkness #1-8)
No. 9, 2/71 - No. 27, 11/73; No. 28, 6/74 - No. 30, 10/74
Marvel Comics Group (No. 13,14: 52 pgs.)

9-Smith inks		.50	1.00
10-30		.30	.60

NOTE: *Ditko a-9r, 14r, 16r. Kirby r-10-17, 21, 23, 25, 27, 28, 30; c-9, 25. Kirby/Ditko r-14, 17-20, 22, 24, 26, 29. Marie/John Severin a-16(Kull). 9-13, 15-contain one new story. Woodish art by Reese-11.*

MONSTERS UNLEASHED (Magazine)
July, 1973 - No. 11, April, 1975; Summer, 1975 (B&W)
Marvel Comics Group

1	.35	1.00	2.00
2-The Frankenstein Monster begins	.60	1.20	
3-Adams-c; The Man-Thing begins (origin-r)-Adams-a			
	.25	.75	1.50
4-Intro. Satana, the Devil's daughter; Krigstein-r			
	.25	.75	1.50
5-7: 7-Williamson-a(r)	.60	1.20	
8,10,11: 8-Adams-r. 10-Origin Tigra		.50	1.00
9-Wendigo app.	.40	1.25	2.50
Annual 1(Summer,'75)-Kane-a		.50	1.00

NOTE: *Boris c-2, 6. Brunner a-2; c-11. J. Buscema a-2p, 4p, 5p. Colan a-1, 4r. Davis a-3r. Everett a-2r. G. Kane a-3. Morrow a-3; c-1. Perez a-8. Reese a-1, 2. Tuska a-3p. Wildey a-1r.*

MONTANA KID, THE (See Kid Montana)

MONTE HALE WESTERN (Movie star; Formerly Mary Marvel #1-28;
also see Picture News #8, Real Western Hero, Six-Gun Heroes,
Western Hero & X-Mas Comics)
No. 29, Oct, 1948 - No. 88, Jan, 1956
Fawcett Publications/Charlton No. 83 on

29-(#1, 52pgs.)-Photo-c begin, end #82; Monte Hale & his horse			
Pardner begin	20.00	60.00	140.00
30-(52 pgs.)-Big Bow and Little Arrow begin, end #34; Captain			
Tootsie by Beck	11.50	34.00	80.00
31-36,38-40-(52 pgs.): 34-Gabby Hayes begins, ends #80.			
39-Captain Tootsie by Beck	10.00	30.00	70.00
37,41,45,49-(36 pgs.)	6.00	18.00	42.00
42-44,46-48,50-(52 pgs.): 47-Big Bow & Little Arrow app.			
	6.50	19.50	45.00
51,52,54-56,58,59-(52 pgs.)	5.00	15.00	35.00
53,57-(36 pgs.): 53-Slim Pickens app.	4.00	12.00	28.00
60-81: 36pgs. #60-on. 80-Gabby Hayes ends	4.00	12.00	28.00
82-Last Fawcett issue (6/53)	5.00	15.00	35.00
83-1st Charlton issue (2/55); B&W photo back-c begin. Gabby			
Hayes returns, ends #86	5.00	15.00	35.00
84 (4/55)	4.00	12.00	28.00
85-86	3.65	11.00	25.00
87-Wolverton-r, ½pg.	4.00	12.00	28.00
88-Last issue	4.00	12.00	28.00

NOTE: *Gil Kane a-33?, 34? Rocky Lane ½-1 pg. (Carnation ad)-38, 40, 41, 43, 44, 46, 55.*

MONTY HALL OF THE U.S. MARINES (See With the Marines...)
Aug, 1951 - No. 11, 1953
Toby Press

	Good	Fine	N-Mint
1	3.65	11.00	25.00
2	2.85	8.50	20.00
3-5	2.50	7.50	17.00
6-11	1.85	5.50	13.00

NOTE: *3-5 full page pin-ups (Pin-Up Pete) by Jack Sparling in all.*

MOON, A GIRL...ROMANCE, A (Becomes Weird Fantasy #13 on;
formerly Moon Girl #1-8)
No. 9, Sept-Oct, 1949 - No. 12, Mar-Apr, 1950
E. C. Comics

9-Moon Girl cameo; spanking panels	52.00	156.00	365.00
10,11	40.00	120.00	280.00
12-(Scarce)	55.00	165.00	385.00

NOTE: *Feldstein, Ingels art in all. Canadian reprints known; see Table of Contents.*

MOON GIRL AND THE PRINCE (#1) (Moon Girl #2-6; Moon Girl
Fights Crime #7,8; becomes A Moon, A Girl, Romance #9 on)
Fall, 1947 - No. 8, Summer, 1949
E. C. Comics (Also see Happy Houlihans)

1-Origin Moon Girl	60.00	180.00	420.00
2	35.00	105.00	245.00
3,4: 4-Moon Girl vs. a vampire	30.00	90.00	210.00
5-E.C.'s 1st horror story, "Zombie Terror"	62.00	185.00	435.00
6-8-(Scarce): 7-Origin Star (Moongirl's sidekick)			
	34.00	102.00	240.00

NOTE: *#2 & #3 are 52 pgs., #4 on, 36 pgs. Canadian reprints known; (see Table of Contents.)*

MOON KNIGHT (Also see The Hulk, Marvel Preview #21, Marvel
Spotlight & Werewolf by Night #32)
November, 1980 - No. 38, July, 1984 (Mando paper No. 33 on)
Marvel Comics Group

1-Origin resumed in #4	.30	.90	1.80
2-34,36-38: 4-Intro Midnight Man. 25-Double size			
		.50	1.00
35-(52 pgs., $1.00)-X-men app.	.25	.75	1.50

NOTE: *Austin c-27i, 31i. Kaluta c-36-38. Miller c-9, 12p, 13p, 15p, 27p.*

MOON KNIGHT
June, 1985 - No. 6, Dec, 1985
Marvel Comics Group

1(V2#1)-Double size; new costume		.50	1.00
2-6		.50	1.00

MOON KNIGHT SPECIAL EDITION
Nov, 1983 - No. 3, Jan, 1984 (mini-series) (Baxter paper, $2.00)
Marvel Comics Group

1-3: 1-Hulk-r	.25	.75	1.50

MOON MULLINS
1927 - 1933 (52 pgs.) (daily B&W strip reprints)
Cupples & Leon Co.

Series 1('27)-By Willard	12.00	36.00	84.00
Series 2('28), Series 3('29), Series 4('30)	9.00	27.00	62.00
Series 5('31), 6('32), 7('33)	7.00	21.00	50.00
Big Book 1('30)-B&W	15.00	45.00	105.00

MOON MULLINS (See Popular, Superbook #3 & Super Comics)
1941 - 1945
Dell Publishing Co.

4-Color 14(1941)	19.00	57.00	132.00
Large Feature Comic 29(1941)	13.00	40.00	90.00
4-Color 31(1943)	11.50	34.00	80.00
4-Color 81(1945)	6.00	18.00	42.00

MOON MULLINS
Dec-Jan, 1947-48 - No. 8, 1949 (52 pgs.)
Michel Publ. (American Comics Group)

	Good	Fine	N-Mint
1-Alternating Sunday & daily strip-r	8.00	24.00	56.00
2	4.30	13.00	30.00
3-8	3.50	10.50	24.00

NOTE: Milt Gross a-2, 4-6, 8. Willard r-all.

MOON PILOT (See 4-Color #1313)

MOONSHADOW
5/85 - No. 12, 2/87 ($1.50-$1.75)(Adults only)
Epic Comics (Marvel)

1-Origin	.50	1.50	3.00
2-12: 11-Origin	.35	1.00	2.00

MOON-SPINNERS, THE (See Movie Comics)

MOPSY (See TV Teens & Pageant of Comics)
Feb, 1948 - No. 19, Sept, 1953
St. John Publ. Co.

1-Part-r; r-/"Some Punkins" by Neher	10.00	30.00	70.00
2	5.00	15.00	35.00
3-10(1953): 8-Lingerie panels	4.00	12.00	28.00
11-19: 19-Lingerie-c	3.50	10.50	24.00

NOTE: #1, 4-6, 8, 13, 19 have paper dolls.

MORE FUN COMICS (Formerly New Fun #1-6)
No. 7, Jan, 1936 - No. 127, Nov-Dec, 1947 (No. 7,9-11 paper-c)
National Periodical Publications

	Good	Fine	VF-NM
7(1/36)-Oversized, paper-c; 1 pg. Kelly-a	230.00	690.00	1610.00
8(2/36)-Oversized (10x12"), slick-c; 1 pg. Kelly-a	200.00	600.00	1400.00
9(3-4/36)(Very Rare)-Last Henri Duval by Siegel & Shuster	200.00	600.00	1400.00
10,11(7/36): 11-1st 'Calling All Cars' by Siegel & Shuster	130.00	390.00	910.00
12(8/36)-Slick-c begin	115.00	345.00	805.00
V2#1(9/36, #13)	115.00	345.00	805.00
2(10/36, #14)-Dr. Occult in costume (Superman prototype) begins, ends #17; see The Comics Magazine	130.00	390.00	910.00
V2#11(11/36, #15), 16(V2#4), 17(V2#5)-Cover numbering begins #16.			
16-Xmas-c	85.00	255.00	595.00
18-20(V2#8, 5/37)	65.00	195.00	455.00

	Good	Fine	N-Mint
21(V2#9)-24(V2#12, 9/37)	45.00	135.00	315.00
25(V3#1, 10/37)-27(V3#3, 12/37): 27-Xmas-c	45.00	135.00	315.00
28-30: 30-1st non-funny cover	45.00	135.00	315.00
31-35: 32-Last Dr. Occult	38.00	115.00	265.00
36-40: 36-The Masked Ranger begins, ends #41. 39-Xmas-c	36.00	108.00	250.00
41-50	32.00	95.00	225.00
51-1st app. The Spectre (in costume) in one panel ad at end of Buccaneer story	80.00	240.00	560.00
52-Origin The Spectre (out of costume), Part 1 by Bernard Baily; last Wing Brady (Rare)	1285.00	3855.00	9000.00
53-Origin The Spectre (out of costume), Part 2; Capt. Desmo (Scarce)	828.00	2485.00	5800.00
(Prices vary widely on above two books)			
54-The Spectre in costume; last King Carter	315.00	945.00	2200.00
55-(Scarce)-Dr. Fate begins (Intro & 1st app.); last Bulldog Martin	300.00	900.00	2100.00
56-60: 56-Congo Bill begins	145.00	435.00	1015.00
61-66: 63-Last St. Bob Neal. 64-Lance Larkin begins	100.00	300.00	700.00
67-(Scarce)-Origin Dr. Fate; last Congo Bill & Biff Bronson	150.00	450.00	1050.00

	Good	Fine	N-Mint
68-70: 68-Clip Carson begins. 70-Last Lance Larkin	90.00	270.00	630.00
71-(Scarce)-Origin & 1st app. Johnny Quick by Mort Wysinger	145.00	435.00	1015.00
72-Dr. Fate's new helmet; last Sgt. Carey, Sgt. O'Malley & Captain Desmo	80.00	240.00	560.00
73-(Rare)-Origin & 1st app. Aquaman; intro. Green Arrow & Speedy	215.00	645.00	1500.00
74-2nd Aquaman	86.00	258.00	600.00
75-80: 76-Last Clip Carson; Johnny Quick by Meskin begins, ends #97. 80-1st small logo	77.00	230.00	540.00
81-88: 87-Last Radio Squad	57.00	170.00	400.00
89-Origin Green Arrow & Speedy Team-up	65.00	195.00	455.00
90-99: 93-Dover & Clover begin. 97-Kubert-a. 98-Last Dr. Fate	36.00	108.00	250.00
100	50.00	150.00	350.00
101-Origin & 1st app. Superboy (not by Siegel & Shuster); last Spectre issue	245.00	735.00	1715.00
102-2nd Superboy	63.00	190.00	440.00
103-3rd Superboy	46.00	138.00	320.00
104-107: 104-1st Superboy-c. 105-Superboy-c. 107-Last J. Quick & Superboy; Superboy-c	38.00	115.00	265.00
108-120: 108-Genius Jones begins	6.00	18.00	42.00
121-124,126: 121-123,126-Post-c	5.00	15.00	35.00
125-Superman on cover	27.00	81.00	190.00
127-(Scarce)-Post c/a	13.00	40.00	90.00

NOTE: Cover features: The Spectre-#52-55, 57-60, 62-67. Dr. Fate-#55, 56, 61, 68-76. The Green Arrow & Speedy-#77-85, 99, 101; w/Dover & Clover-#98. Johnny Quick-#86, 87, 100. Genius Jones-#108-127. Baily a-45, 52-on; c-52-55,57-60,62-67. Al Capp a-45(signed Koppy). Guardineer c-47. Kiefer a-20. Moldoff c-51.

MORE SEYMOUR (See Seymour My Son)
October, 1963
Archie Publications

1	1.35	4.00	8.00

MORE TRASH FROM MAD (Annual)
1958 - No. 12, 1969
E. C. Comics

nn(1958)-8 pgs. color Mad reprint from #20	9.00	27.00	62.00
2(1959)-Market Product Labels	6.00	18.00	42.00
3(1960)-Text book covers	5.00	15.00	35.00
4(1961)-Sing Along with Mad booklet	5.00	15.00	35.00
5(1962)-Window Stickers; r-/from Mad #39	3.00	9.00	21.00
6(1963)-TV Guise booklet	3.50	10.50	24.00
7(1964)-Alfred E. Neuman commemorative stamps	2.00	6.00	14.00
8(1965)-Life size poster-A. E. Neuman	2.00	6.00	14.00
9,10(1966-67)-Mischief Sticker	1.50	4.50	10.00
11(1968)-Campaign poster & bumper sticker	1.50	4.50	10.00
12(1969)-Pocket medals	1.50	4.50	10.00

NOTE: Kelly Freas c-1, 2, 4. Mingo c-3, 5-9, 12.

MORGAN THE PIRATE (See 4-Color #1227)

MORLOCK 2001
Feb, 1975 - No. 3, July, 1975
Atlas/Seaboard Publ.

1-Origin & 1st app.		.50	1.00
2		.30	.60
3-Ditko/Wrightson-a; origin The Midnight Man & The Midnight Men		.60	1.20

MORTIE (Mazie's Friend)
Dec, 1952 - No. 4, June, 1953?
Magazine Publishers

1	2.65	8.00	18.00
2	1.50	4.50	10.00

Moon Mullins #2, © N.Y. News Synd.

More Fun Comics #54, © DC

More Fun Comics #125, © DC

Motion Picture Comics #107, © Republic Pictures   Movie Classics (Circus World), © DELL   Movie Classics (Masque Of the Red Death), © Alta-Vista

	Good	Fine	N-Mint
MORTIE (continued)			
3,4	1.00	3.00	7.00

MORTY MEEKLE (See 4-Color #793)

MOSES & THE TEN COMMANDMENTS (See Dell Giants)

MOTHER GOOSE (See Christmas With Mother Goose & 4-Color #41,59,68,862)

MOTHER OF US ALL
1950? (32 pgs.)
Catechetical Guild Giveaway

	2.00	6.00	12.00

MOTHER TERESA OF CALCUTTA
1984
Marvel Comics Group

1		.60	1.25

MOTION PICTURE COMICS (See Fawcett Movie Comics)
1950 - No. 114, Jan, 1953 (All-photo-c)
Fawcett Publications

	Good	Fine	N-Mint
101-"Vanishing Westerner"-Monte Hale	22.00	65.00	154.00
102-"Code of the Silver Sage"-Rocky Lane (1/51)			
	20.00	60.00	140.00
103-"Covered Wagon Raid"-Rocky Lane (3/51)			
	20.00	60.00	140.00
104-"Vigilante Hideout"-Rocky Lane (5/51)-book length Powell-a			
	20.00	60.00	140.00
105-"Red Badge of Courage"-Audie Murphy; Bob Powell-a (7/51)			
	26.00	78.00	180.00
106-"The Texas Rangers"-George Montgomery (9/51)			
	21.00	64.00	150.00
107-"Frisco Tornado"-Rocky Lane (11/51)	19.00	57.00	132.00
108-"Mask of the Avenger"-John Derek	13.00	40.00	90.00
109-"Rough Rider of Durango"-Rocky Lane	19.00	57.00	132.00
110-"When Worlds Collide"-George Evans-a (1951); Williamson & Evans drew themselves in story; (Also see Famous Funnies No. 72-88)			
	68.00	205.00	475.00
111-"The Vanishing Outpost"-Lash LaRue	22.00	65.00	154.00
112-"Brave Warrior"-Jon Hall & Jay Silverheels			
	12.00	36.00	84.00
113-"Walk East on Beacon"-George Murphy; Shaffenberger-a			
	8.50	25.50	60.00
114-"Cripple Creek"-George Montgomery (1/53)			
	10.00	30.00	70.00

MOTION PICTURE FUNNIES WEEKLY (Amazing Man #5 on?)
1939 (36 pgs.)(Giveaway)(Black & White)
No month given; last panel in Sub-Mariner story dated 4/39
(Also see Colossus, Green Giant & Invaders No. 20)
First Funnies, Inc.

1-Origin & 1st printed app. Sub-Mariner by Bill Everett (8 pgs.); Fred Schwab-c; reprinted in Marvel Mystery #1 with color added over the craft tint which was used to shade the black & white version; Spy Ring, American Ace (reprinted in Marvel Mystery No. 3) app. (Rare)-only seven (7) known copies, all with brown pages.	2500.00	5000.00	—
Covers only to #2-4 (set)			600.00

NOTE: The only seven known copies (with an eighth suspected) were discovered in 1974 in the estate of the deceased publisher. Covers only to issues No. 2-4 were also found which evidently were printed in advance along with #1. #1 was to be distributed only through motion picture movie houses. However, it is believed that only advanced copies were sent out and the motion picture houses not going for the idea. Possible distribution at local theaters in Boston suspected. The last panel of Sub-Mariner contains a rectangular box with "Continued Next Week" printed in it. When reprinted in Marvel Mystery, the box was left in with lettering omitted.

MOUNTAIN MEN (See Ben Bowie)

MOUSE MUSKETEERS (See M.G.M.'s . . .)

MOUSE ON THE MOON, THE (See Movie Classics)

MOVIE CLASSICS
Jan, 1953 - Dec, 1969
Dell Publishing Co.

	Good	Fine	N-Mint
(Before 1962, most movie adapt. were part of the 4-Color Series)			
Around the World Under the Sea 12-030-612 (12/66)			
	1.30	4.00	9.00
Bambi 3(4/56)-Disney; r-/4-Color 186	1.30	4.00	9.00
Battle of the Bulge 12-056-606 (6/66)	1.30	4.00	9.00
Beach Blanket Bingo 12-058-509	4.00	12.00	28.00
Bon Voyage 01-068-212 (12/62)-Disney; photo-c			
	1.30	4.00	9.00
Castilian, The 12-110-401	2.00	6.00	14.00
Cat, The 12-109-612 (12/66)	1.15	3.50	8.00
Cheyenne Autumn 12-112-506 (4-6/65)	3.50	10.50	24.00
Circus World, Samuel Bronston's 12-115-411; John Wayne app.			
John Wayne photo-c	5.50	16.50	38.00
Countdown 12-150-710 (10/67); James Caan photo-c			
	1.30	4.00	9.00
Creature, The 1 (12-142-302) (12-2/62-63)	2.30	7.00	16.00
Creature, The 12-142-410 (10/64)	1.30	4.00	9.00
David Ladd's Life Story 12-173-212 (10-12/62)-Photo-c			
	5.70	17.00	40.00
Die, Monster, Die 12-175-603 (3/66)-Photo-c	1.75	5.25	12.00
Dirty Dozen 12-180-710 (10/67)	2.65	8.00	18.00
Dr. Who & the Daleks 12-190-612 (12/66)-Photo-c			
	11.00	33.00	75.00
Dracula 12-231-212 (10-12/62)	1.70	5.00	12.00
El Dorado 12-240-710 (10/67)-John Wayne; photo-c			
	8.00	24.00	56.00
Ensign Pulver 12-257-410 (8-10/64)	1.50	4.50	10.00
Frankenstein 12-283-305 (3-5/63)	1.75	5.25	12.00
Great Race, The 12-299-603 (3/66)-Natallie Wood, Tony Curtis photo-c	2.30	7.00	16.00
Hallelujah Trail, The 12-307-602 (2/66) (Shows 1/66 inside); Burt Lancaster, Lee Remick photo-c	3.50	10.50	24.00
Hatari 12-340-301 (1/63)-John Wayne	5.00	15.00	35.00
Horizontal Lieutenant, The 01-348-210 (10/62)	1.30	4.00	9.00
Incredible Mr. Limpet, The 12-370-408; Don Knotts photo-c			
	1.70	5.00	12.00
Jack the Giant Killer 12-374-301 (1/63)	4.65	14.00	32.00
Jason & the Argonauts 12-376-310 (8-10/63)-Photo-c			
	5.00	15.00	35.00
Lancelot & Guinevere 12-416-310 (10/63)	4.65	14.00	32.00
Lawrence 12-426-308 (8/63)-Story of Lawrence of Arabia; movie ad on back-c; not exactly like movie	3.50	10.50	24.00
Lion of Sparta 12-439-301 (1/63)	1.50	4.50	10.00
Mad Monster Party 12-460-801 (9/67)	4.35	13.00	30.00
Magic Sword, The 01-496-209 (9/62)	3.00	9.00	21.00
Masque of the Red Death 12-490-410 (8-10/64)-Vincent Price photo-c	2.30	7.00	16.00
Maya 12-495-612 (12/66)-Part photo-c	2.30	7.00	16.00
McHale's Navy 12-500-412 (10-12/64)	1.70	5.00	12.00
Merrill's Marauders 12-510-301 (1/63)-Photo-c	1.50	4.50	10.00
Mouse on the Moon, The 12-530-312 (10/12/63)-Photo-c			
	1.70	5.00	12.00
Mummy, The 12-537-211 (9-11/62) 2 different back-c issues			
	2.00	6.00	14.00
Music Man, The 12-538-301 (1/63)	1.50	4.50	10.00
Naked Prey, The 12-545-612 (12/66)-Photo-c	3.50	10.50	24.00
Night of the Grizzly, The 12-558-612 (12/66)-Photo-c			
	2.00	6.00	14.00
None But the Brave 12-565-506 (4-6/65)	3.00	9.00	21.00
Operation Bikini 12-597-310 (10/63)-Photo-c	2.00	6.00	14.00
Operation Crossbow 12-590-512 (10-12/65)	2.00	6.00	14.00
Prince & the Pauper, The 01-654-207 (5-7/62)-Disney			
	2.00	6.00	14.00

MOVIE CLASSICS (continued)   **Good Fine N-Mint**
Raven, The 12-680-309 (9/63)-Vincent Price photo-c
    2.30   7.00   16.00
Ring of Bright Water 01-701-910 (10/69) (inside shows
  No. 12-701-909)   2.30   7.00   16.00
Runaway, The 12-707-412 (10-12/64) 1.15   3.50   8.00
Santa Claus Conquers the Martians 12-725-603 (3/60)-Regular issue
  with number & price; photo-c 5.00 15.00 35.00
  Another version given away with a Golden Record, SLP 170, nn,
  no price (3/66) Complete with record 10.00 30.00 70.00
Six Black Horses 12-750-301 (1/63)-Photo-c 1.75   5.25 12.00
Ski Party 12-743-511 (9-11/65)-Frankie Avalon photo-c
    3.35 10.00 23.00
Smoky 12-746-702 (2/67) 1.15   3.50   8.00
Sons of Katie Elder 12-748-511 (9-11/65); John Wayne app., Photo-c
    9.50 28.50 65.00
Tales of Terror 12-793-302 (2/63)-Evans-a 1.15   3.50   8.00
Three Stooges Meet Hercules 01-828-208 (8/62)-Photo-c
    4.00 12.00 28.00
Tomb of Ligeia 12-830-506 (4-6/65) 1.30   4.00   9.00
Treasure Island 01-845-211 (7-9/62)-Disney; r-/4-Color 624
    1.00   3.00   7.00
Twice Told Tales (Nathaniel Hawthorne) 12-840-401 (11-1/63-64);
  Vincent Price photo-c 1.75   5.25 12.00
Two on a Guillotine 12-850-506 (4-6/65) 1.30   4.00   9.00
Valley of Gwangi 01-880-912 (12/69) 4.65 14.00 32.00
War Gods of the Deep 12-900-509 (7-9/65) 1.30   4.00   9.00
War Wagon, The 12-533-709 (9/67); John Wayne app.
    7.00 21.00 50.00
Who's Minding the Mint? 12-924-708 (8/67)-Photo-c
    1.30   4.00   9.00
Wolfman, The 12-922-308 (6-8/63) 1.30   4.00   9.00
Wolfman, The 1(12-922-410)(8-10/64)-2nd printing; 4-/#12-922-308
    1.30   4.00   9.00
Zulu 12-950-410 (8-10/64)-Photo-c 3.35 10.00 35.00

MOVIE COMICS (See Fawcett Movie Comics & Cinema Comics Herald)

MOVIE COMICS
April, 1939 - No. 6, Sept, 1939 (Most all photo-c)
National Periodical Publications/Picture Comics

1-"Gunga Din,""Son of Frankenstein,""The Great Man Votes,"
  "Fisherman's Wharf,"&"Scouts to the Rescue part 1; Wheelan
  "Minute Movies" begin 150.00 450.00 1050.00
2-"Stagecoach,""The Saint Strikes Back,""King of the Turf,"
  "Scouts to the Rescue" part 2, "Arizona Legion"
    90.00 270.00 630.00
3-"East Side of Heaven,""Mystery in the White Room,""Four
  Feathers,""Mexican Rose" with Gene Autry, "Spirit of Culver,"
  "Many Secrets,""The Mikado" 75.00 225.00 525.00
4-"Captain Fury," Gene Autry in "Blue Montana Skies,""Streets
  of N.Y." with Jackie Cooper, "Oregon Trail" part 1 with Johnny
  Mack Brown, "Big Town Czar" with Barton MacLane, & "Star
  Reporter" with Warren Hull 67.00 200.00 470.00
5-"Man in the Iron Mask,""Five Came Back,""Wolf Call,""The
  Girl & the Gambler,""The House of Fear,""The Family Next
  Door,""Oregon Trail" part 2 67.00 200.00 470.00
6-"The Phantom Creeps,""Chumps at Oxford,"&"The Oregon
  Trail" part 3 90.00 270.00 630.00
NOTE: Above books contain many original movie stills with dialogue from movie scripts.

MOVIE COMICS
Dec, 1946 - No. 4, 1947
Fiction House Magazines

1-Big Town & Johnny Danger begin; Celardo-a
    25.00 75.00 175.00
2-"White Tie & Tails" with William Bendix; Mitzi of the Movies be-

gins by Matt Baker, ends #4 17.00 51.00 120.00
3-Andy Hardy 17.00 51.00 120.00
4-Mitzi In Hollywood by Matt Baker 21.00 62.00 146.00

MOVIE COMICS
Oct, 1962 - March, 1972
Gold Key/Whitman

Alice in Wonderland 10144-503 (3/65)-Disney; partial reprint of
  4-Color 331 1.75   5.25 12.00
Aristocats, The 1 (30045-103)(3/71)-Disney; with pull-out
  poster (25 cents) 4.30 13.00 30.00
Bambi 1 (10087-309)(9/63)-Disney; reprints 4-Color 186
    2.00   6.00 14.00
Bambi 2 (10087-607)(7/66)-Disney; reprints 4-Color 186
    1.70   5.00 12.00
Beneath the Planet of the Apes 30044-012 (12/70)-with
  pull-out poster; photo-c 3.50 10.50 24.00
Big Red 10026-211 (11/62)-Disney-Photo-c 1.15   3.50   8.00
Big Red 10026-503 (3/65)-Disney; reprints 10026-211-Photo-c
    1.15   3.50   8.00
Blackbeard's Ghost 10222-806 (6/68)-Disney 1.50   4.50 10.00
Buck Rogers Giant Movie Ed. 11296 (Whitman), 02489 (Marvel)-2
  formats; 1979; tabloid size; $1.50; adaptation of movie; Bolle,
  McWilliams-a .35   1.00   2.00
Bullwhip Griffin 10181-706 (6/67)-Disney; Manning-a; photo-c
    2.35   7.00 16.00
Captain Sindbad 10077-309 (9/63)-Manning-a; photo-c
    3.50 10.50 24.00
Chitty Chitty Bang Bang 1 (30038-902)(2/69)-with pull-out poster;
  Disney; photo-c 3.50 10.50 24.00
Cinderella 10152-508 (8/65)-Disney; reprints 4-Color 786
    1.50   4.50 10.00
Darby O'Gill & the Little People 10251-001(1/70)-Disney; reprints
  4-Color 1024 (Toth-a)-Photo-c 3.00   9.00 21.00
Dumbo 1 (10090-310)(10/63)-Disney; reprints 4-Color 668
    1.50   4.50 10.00
Emil & the Detectives 10120-502 (2/65)-Disney; photo-c
    2.35   7.00 16.00
Escapade in Florence 1 (10043-301)(1/63)-Disney; starring
  Annette Funicello 4.65 14.00 32.00
Fall of the Roman Empire 10118-407 (7/64); Sophia Loren photo-c
    2.00   6.00 14.00
Fantastic Voyage 10178-702 (2/67)-Wood/Adkins-a; photo-c
    2.65   8.00 18.00
55 Days at Peking 10081-309 (9/63)-Photo-c 2.30   7.00 16.00
Fighting Prince of Donegal, The 10193-701 (1/67)-Disney
    1.70   5.00 12.00
First Men in the Moon 10132-503 (3/65)-Fred Fredericks-a; photo-c
    2.30   7.00 16.00
Gay Purr-ee 30017-301(1/63, 84pgs.) 3.50 10.50 24.00
Gnome Mobile, The 10207-710 (10/67)-Disney 2.30   7.00 16.00
Goodbye, Mr. Chips 10246-006 (6/70)-Peter O'Toole photo-c
    2.00   6.00 14.00
Happiest Millionaire, The 10221-804 (4/68)-Disney
    1.30   4.00   9.00
Hey There, It's Yogi Bear 10122-409 (9/64)-Hanna-Barbera
    2.30   7.00 16.00
Horse Without a Head, The 10109-401 (1/64)-Disney
    1.50   4.50 10.00
How the West Was Won 10074-307 (7/63)-Tufts-a
    3.50 10.50 24.00
In Search of the Castaways 10048-303 (3/63)-Disney; Haley Mills-
  photo-c 4.00 12.00 28.00
Jungle Book, The 1 (6022-801)(1/68-Whitman)-Disney; large
  size (10x13½"); 59 cents 2.00   6.00 14.00
Jungle Book, The 1 (30033-803)(3/68, 68 pgs.)-Disney; same cont-

Movie Classics (Santa Claus Conquers...), © DELL   *Movie Classics (Three Stooges...), © Normandy Prod.*   *Movie Comics #1 (4/39), © DC*

Movie Comics (Old Yeller), © WDC   Movie Comics (A Tiger Walks), © WDC   Movie Love #10, © FF

MOVIE COMICS (continued)	Good	Fine	N-Mint
ents as Whitman #1	1.30	4.00	9.00
Jungle Book, The 1 (6/78, $1.00 tabloid)	.60	1.20	
Jungle Book ('84)-r-/Giant	.40	.80	
Kidnapped 10080-306 (6/63)-Disney; reprints 4-Color 1101;			
photo-c	1.15	3.50	8.00
King Kong 30036-809(9/68-68 pgs.)-painted-c	2.35	7.00	16.00
King Kong nn-Whitman Treasury($1.00,68pgs.,1968), same cover as			
Gold Key issue	.70	2.00	4.00
King Kong 11299(#1-786, 10x13¼'', 68pgs., 1978)			
	.50	1.00	
Lady and the Tramp 10042-301 (1/63)-Disney; r-4-Color 629			
	1.50	4.50	10.00
Lady and the Tramp 1 (1967-Giant; 25 cents)-Disney; r-part of Dell			
#1	2.50	7.50	20.00
Lady and the Tramp 2 (10042-203)(3/72)-Disney; r-4-Color 629			
	1.15	3.50	8.00
Legend of Lobo, The 1 (10059-303)(3/63)-Disney; photo-c			
	1.15	3.50	8.00
Lt. Robin Crusoe, U.S.N. 10191-610 (10/66)-Disney; Dick Van Dyke			
photo-c	1.50	4.50	10.00
Lion, The 10035-301 (1/63)-Photo-c	1.15	3.50	8.00
Lord Jim 10156-509 (9/65)-Photo-c	1.75	5.25	12.00
Love Bug, The 10237-906 (6/69)-Disney-Buddy Hackett photo-c			
	1.50	4.50	10.00
Mary Poppins 10136-501 (1/65)-Disney; photo-c			
	3.00	9.00	21.00
Mary Poppins 30023-501 (1/65-68 pgs.)-Disney; photo-c			
	4.00	12.00	28.00
McLintock 10110-403 (3/64); John Wayne app.; photo-c			
	8.50	25.50	60.00
Merlin Jones as the Monkey's Uncle 10115-510 (10/65)-Disney;			
Annette Funicello front/back photo-c	2.30	7.00	16.00
Miracle of the White Stallions, The 10065-306 (6/63)-Disney			
	1.75	5.25	12.00
Misadventures of Merlin Jones, The 10115-405 (5/64)-Disney			
Annette Funicello photo front/back-c	2.65	8.00	18.00
Moon-Spinners, The 10124-410 (10/64)-Disney; Haley Mills photo-c			
	4.00	12.00	28.00
Mutiny on the Bounty 1 (10040-302)(2/63)-Marlon Brando photo-c			
	2.00	6.00	14.00
Nikki, Wild Dog of the North 10141-412 (12/64)-Disney;			
reprints 4-Color 1226	1.15	3.50	8.00
Old Yeller 10168-601 (1/66)-Disney; reprints 4-Color 869; photo-c			
	1.15	3.50	8.00
One Hundred & One Dalmations 1 (10247-002) (2/70)-Disney;			
reprints 4-Color 1183	1.50	4.50	10.00
Peter Pan 1 (10086-309)(9/63)-Disney; reprints 4-Color 442			
	2.00	6.00	12.00
Peter Pan 2 (10086-909)(9/69)-Disney; reprints 4-Color 442			
	1.15	3.50	8.00
Peter Pan 1 ('83)-r/4-Color 442	.40	.80	
P.T. 109 10123-409 (9/64)-John F. Kennedy	3.00	9.00	21.00
Rio Conchos 10143-503(3/65)	3.00	9.00	21.00
Robin Hood 10163-506 (6/65)-Disney; reprints 4-Color 413			
	1.50	4.50	10.00
Shaggy Dog & the Absent-Minded Professor 30032-708 (8/67-Giant,			
68 pgs.)-Disney; reprints 4-Color 985,1199	3.50	10.50	24.00
Sleeping Beauty 1 (30042-009)(9/70)-Disney; reprints 4-Color 973;			
with pull-out poster	3.00	9.00	21.00
Snow White & the Seven Dwarfs 1 (10091-310)(10/63)-Disney;			
reprints 4-Color 382	1.75	5.25	12.00
Snow White & the Seven Dwarfs 10091-709 (9/67)-Disney;			
reprints 4-Color 382	1.50	4.50	10.00
Snow White & the Seven Dwarfs nn(2/84)-r-/4-Color 382			
	.40	.80	
Son of Flubber 1 (10057-304)(4/63)-Disney; sequel to "The			

	Good	Fine	N-Mint
Absent-Minded Professor''	1.75	5.25	12.00
Summer Magic 10076-309 (9/63)-Disney; Haley Mills; Manning-a			
	4.65	14.00	32.00
Swiss Family Robinson 10236-904 (4/69)-Disney; reprints			
4-Color 1156; photo-c	1.75	5.25	12.00
Sword in the Stone, The 30019-402 (2/64-Giant, 84 pgs.)-Disney			
	3.50	10.50	24.00
That Darn Cat 10171-602 (2/66)-Disney; Haley Mills photo-c			
	4.00	12.00	28.00
Those Magnificent Men in Their Flying Machines 10162-510 (10/65);			
photo-c	1.75	5.25	12.00
Three Stooges in Orbit 30016-211 (11/62-Giant, 32 pgs.)-All photos			
from movie; stiff-photo-c	5.70	17.00	40.00
Tiger Walks, A 10117-406 (6/64)-Disney; Torres, Tufts-a; photo-c			
	2.35	7.00	16.00
Toby Tyler 10142-502 (2/65)-Disney; reprints 4-Color 1092; photo-c			
	1.50	4.50	10.00
Treasure Island 1 (10200-703)(3/67)-Disney; reprints 4-Color 624;			
photo-c	1.15	3.50	8.00
20,000 Leagues Under the Sea 1 (10095-312)(12/63)-Disney;			
reprints 4-Color 614	1.15	3.50	8.00
Wonderful Adventures of Pinocchio, The 1 (10089-310)(10/63)-			
Disney; reprints 4-Color 545	1.15	3.50	8.00
Wonderful Adventures of Pinocchio, The 10089-109 (9/71)-Disney;			
reprints 4-Color 545	1.15	3.50	8.00
Wonderful World of the Brothers Grimm 1 (10008-210)(10/62)			
	2.65	8.00	18.00
X, the Man with the X-Ray Eyes 10083-309 (9/63)-Ray Milland			
photo on-c	3.50	10.50	24.00
Yellow Submarine 35000-902 (2/69-Giant, 68 pgs.)-with pull-out			
poster; The Beatles cartoon movie	6.00	18.00	42.00

MOVIE LOVE (See Personal Love)
Feb, 1950 - No. 22, Aug, 1953
Famous Funnies

	Good	Fine	N-Mint
1-Dick Powell photo-c	5.00	15.00	35.00
2	2.65	8.00	18.00
3-7,9	2.35	7.00	16.00
8-Williamson/Frazetta-a, 6 pgs.	26.00	78.00	180.00
10-Frazetta-a, 6 pgs.	32.00	95.00	225.00
11,12,14-16	2.15	6.50	15.00
13-Ronald Reagan photo-c with 1 pg. bio.	10.00	30.00	70.00
17-One pg. Frazetta ad	3.15	9.50	22.00
18-22	1.85	5.50	13.00

NOTE: *Each issue has a full-length movie adaptation with photo covers.*

MOVIE THRILLERS
1949 (Movie adaptation; photo-c)
Magazine Enterprises

1-"Rope of Sand" with Burt Lancaster	18.00	54.00	125.00

MOVIE TOWN ANIMAL ANTICS (Formerly Animal Antics; Raccoon Kids #52 on)
No. 24, Jan-Feb, 1950 - No. 51, July-Aug, 1954
National Periodical Publications

24-Raccoon Kids continue	4.30	13.00	30.00
25-51	3.15	10.00	22.00

NOTE: **Sheldon Mayer** *a-26-33, 35, 37-41, 43, 44, 47, 49-51.*

MOVIE TUNES COMICS (Formerly Animated . . .; Frankie No. 4 on)
No. 3, Fall, 1946
Marvel Comics (MgPC)

3-Super Rabbit, Krazy Krow, Silly Seal & Ziggy Pig			
	4.00	12.00	28.00

MOWGLI JUNGLE BOOK (See 4-Color #487,582,620)

MR. (See Mister)

277

MS. MARVEL
Jan, 1977 - No. 23, Apr, 1979
Marvel Comics Group

	Good	Fine	N-Mint
1-Buscema-a		.50	1.00
2-Origin		.30	.60
3-23: 5-Vision app. 20-New costume		.25	.50

NOTE: *Austin c-14i, 16i, 17i, 22i. Buscema a-1-3p; c(p)-2, 4, 6, 7, 15. Infantino a-14p, 19p. Gil Kane c-8. Mooney a-4-8p, 13p, 15-18p. Starlin c-12.*

MS. MYSTIC (Also see Captain Victory...)
10/82; No. 2, 2/84 (Color, $1.00)
Pacific Comics

1-Origin; intro Erth, Ayre, Fyre & Watr; Adams script/a/c			
	.35	1.00	2.00
2 ($1.50)-Adams c/a & script	.25	.75	1.50

MS. MYSTIC
1987 - Present? ($2.00, color, Baxter paper)
Continuity Comics

1-3: Adams-c/a; #1,2-r/Pacific #1,2	.35	1.00	2.00

MS. TREE'S THRILLING DETECTIVE ADVENTURES (Ms. Tree #4 on) (Baxter paper #4-9)
2/83 - No. 9, 7/84 - No. 10, 8/84 - No. 18, 5/85; No. 19, 6/85 -Present
Eclipse Comics/Aardvark-Vanaheim 10-18/Renegade Press 19 on

1	.70	2.00	4.00
2-8: 2-Scythe begins	.35	1.00	2.00
9-Last Eclipse & last color issue	.30	.90	1.80
10,11 (Aardvark-Vanaheim) 2-tone	.30	.90	1.80
12-49,51 ($1.70; $2.00 #34 on).	.35	1.00	2.00
50-Contains flexi-disc; 52 pgs.	.70	2.00	3.95
Summer Special 1(8/86)	.50	1.50	3.00
...1950s 3-D Crime (7/87, no glasses)-Johnny Dynamite in 3-D			
	.40	1.25	2.50

NOTE: *Miller pin-up-1-4,6. Johnny Dynamite-r begin #36 by Morisi.*

MS. TREE/MIKE MIST IN 3-D
Aug, 1985 (One Shot)
Renegade Press

1-With glasses	.50	1.50	3.00

MS. VICTORY SPECIAL (Also see Capt. Paragon & Femforce)
Jan, 1985 (nd)
Americomics

1	.30	.85	1.70

MUGGSY MOUSE (Also see Tick Tock Tales)
1951 - 1953; 1963
Magazine Enterprises

1(A-1 33)	2.00	6.00	14.00
2(A-1 36)-Racist-c	4.00	12.00	28.00
3(A-1 39), 4(A-1 95), 5(A-1 99)	1.00	3.00	7.00
Super Reprint #14(1963)	.30	.80	1.60
I.W. Reprint #1,2 (nd)	.30	.80	1.60

MUGGY-DOO, BOY CAT
July, 1953 - No. 4, Jan, 1954
Stanhall Publ.

1-Irving Spector-a	2.30	7.00	16.00
2-4	1.30	4.00	9.00
Super Reprint #12('63), 16('64)		.60	1.20

MUMMY, THE (See Movie Classics)

MUNDEN'S BAR ANNUAL
April, 1988 (52pgs.; $2.95; color)
First Comics

1-r/from Grimjack; Fish Police story	.50	1.50	3.00

MUNSTERS, THE (TV)
Jan, 1965 - No. 16, Jan, 1968

Gold Key	Good	Fine	N-Mint
1 (10134-501)-Photo-c	7.00	21.00	50.00
2	4.30	13.00	30.00
3-5: 4-Photo-c	3.60	11.00	25.00
6-16	2.85	8.50	20.00

MUPPET BABIES, THE (TV)(See Star Comics Mag.)
Aug, 1985 - Present (Children's book)
Star Comics/Marvel #18 on

1-13		.45	.90
14-26 ($1.00)		.45	.90

MUPPETS TAKE MANHATTAN, THE
Nov, 1984 - No. 3, Jan, 1985
Star Comics (Marvel)

1-3-Movie adapt. r-/Marvel Super Special		.30	.60

MURDER, INCORPORATED (My Private Life #16 on)
1/48 - No. 15, 12/49; (2 No.9's); 6/50 - No. 3, 8/51
Fox Feature Syndicate

1 (1st Series)	14.00	42.00	100.00
2-Transvestism, electrocution story; #1,2 have 'For Adults Only' on-c	11.50	34.00	80.00
3-7,9(4/49),10(5/49),11-15	5.00	15.00	35.00
8-Used in **SOTI**, pg. 160	10.00	30.00	70.00
9(3/49)-Possible use in **SOTI**, pg. 145; r-Blue Beetle #56('48)			
	9.00	27.00	63.00
5(6/50)(2nd Series)-Formerly My Desire	4.00	12.00	28.00
2(8/50)-Morisi-a	3.00	9.00	21.00
3(8/51)-Used in **POP**, pg. 81; Rico-a; lingerie-c/panels			
	6.00	18.00	42.00

MURDEROUS GANGSTERS
July, 1951; No. 2, Dec, 1951 - No. 4, June, 1952
Avon Periodicals/Realistic No. 3 on

1-Pretty Boy Floyd, Leggs Diamond; 1 pg. Wood			
	18.00	54.00	125.00
2-Baby-Face Nelson; 1 pg. Wood	11.00	32.00	76.00
3-Painted-c	9.50	28.00	65.00
4-''Murder by Needle'' drug story; Mort Lawrence-a; Kinstler-c			
	11.00	32.00	76.00

MURDER TALES (Magazine)
V1No.10, Nov, 1970 - V1No.11, Jan, 1971 (52 pages)
World Famous Publications

V1#10-One pg. Frazetta ad	.70	2.00	4.00
11-Guardineer-r; bondage-c	.35	1.00	2.00

MUSHMOUSE AND PUNKIN PUSS (TV)
September, 1965 (Hanna-Barbera)
Gold Key

1 (10153-509)	3.00	9.00	21.00

MUSIC MAN, THE (See Movie Classics)

MUTANT MISADVENTURES OF CLOAK AND DAGGER
Oct., 1988 - Present (#1: $1.25; #2-on: $1.50, color)
Marvel Comics

1-X-Factor app.	.25	.75	1.50
2-4: 2-Russell-i. 4-Austin-c(i)		.60	1.25

MUTANTS & MISFITS
1987 - Present ($1.95, color)
Silverline Comics (Solson)

1-3	.35	1.00	2.00

MUTINY (Stormy Tales of Seven Seas)
Oct, 1954 - No. 3, Feb, 1955
Aragon Magazines

1	5.70	17.00	40.00

Ms. Tree's 1950's 3-D Crime #1, © Renegade Press

Muggsy Mouse #1, © ME

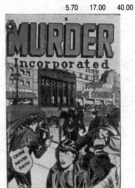
Murder, Incorporated #2 (2nd series), © FOX

Mutt And Jeff #30, © Ball Syndicate

My Date Comics #1, © HILL

My Favorite Martian #1, © Jack Cherton TV

MUTINY (continued)

	Good	Fine	N-Mint
2,3: 2-Capt. Mutiny. 3-Bondage-c	3.00	9.00	21.00

MUTINY ON THE BOUNTY (See Classics III. 100 & Movie Comics)

MUTT & JEFF (. . .Cartoon, The)
1910 - 1916 (5¾x15½'') (Hardcover-B&W)
Ball Publications

	Good	Fine	V. Fine
1(1910)(68 pgs., 50 cents)	27.00	81.00	190.00
2(1911), 3(1912)(68 pgs.)	27.00	81.00	190.00
4(1915)(68 pgs., 50 cents) (Rare)	33.00	100.00	230.00
5(1916)(84 pages, 60 cents) (Rare)	37.00	110.00	260.00

NOTE: Cover variations exist showing Mutt & Jeff reading various newspapers; i.e., The Oregon Journal, The American, and The Detroit News. Reprinting of each issue began soon after publication. No. 5 may not have been reprinted. Values listed include the reprints.

MUTT & JEFF
1916 - 1933? (B&W dailies) (9½x9½''; stiff cover; 52 pgs.)
Cupples & Leon Co.

	Good	Fine	V. Fine
6-22-By Bud Fisher	15.00	45.00	105.00

NOTE: Later issues are somewhat rarer.

nn(1920)-(Advs. of . . .) 16x11''; 20 pgs.; reprints 1919 Sunday strips	27.00	81.00	190.00
Big Book nn(1926, 144pgs., hardcovers)	22.00	65.00	154.00
w/dust jacket. . . .	32.00	95.00	225.00
Big Book 1(1928)-Thick book (hardcovers)	22.00	65.00	154.00
w/dust jacket. . . .	32.00	95.00	225.00
Big Book 2(1929)-Thick book (hardcovers)	22.00	65.00	154.00
w/dust jacket. . . .	32.00	95.00	225.00

NOTE: The Big Books contain three previous issues rebound.

MUTT & JEFF
1921 (9x15'')
Embee Publ. Co.

Sunday strips in color (Rare)	50.00	150.00	350.00

MUTT AND JEFF (See All-American, Popular & Xmas Comics)
Summer, 1939 (nd) - No. 148, Nov, 1965
All American/National 1-103(6/58)/Dell 104(10/58)-115
(10-12/59)/Harvey 116(2/60)-148

	Good	Fine	N-Mint
1(nn)-Lost Wheels	72.00	215.00	505.00
2(nn)-Charging Bull (Summer 1940, nd; on sale 6/20/40)	40.00	120.00	280.00
3(nn)-Bucking Broncos (Summer 1941, nd)	27.00	81.00	190.00
4(Winter, '41), 5(Summer,'42)	20.00	60.00	140.00
6-10	11.50	34.00	80.00
11-20	7.00	21.00	50.00
21-30	5.50	16.50	38.00
31-50	3.50	10.50	24.00
51-75-Last Fisher issue. 53-Last 52pgs.	2.15	6.50	15.00
76-99,101-103: 76-Last precode (1/55)	1.50	4.50	10.00
100	1.75	5.25	12.00
104-148: 117,118,120-131-Richie Rich app.	.85	2.50	6.00
. . .Jokes 1-3(8/60-61, Harvey)-84 pgs.; Richie Rich in all; Little Dot in #2,3	1.50	4.50	10.00
. . .New Jokes 1-4(10/63-11/65, Harvey)-68 pgs.; Richie Rich in #1-3; Stumbo in #1	.75	2.25	5.00

NOTE: Issues 1-74 by Bud Fisher. 86 on by Al Smith. Issues from 1963 on have Fisher reprints. Clarification: early issues signed by Fisher are mostly drawn by Smith.

MY BROTHERS' KEEPER
1973 (36 pages) (35-49 cents)
Spire Christian Comics (Fleming H. Revell Co.)

nn		.50	1.00

MY CONFESSIONS (My Confession #7&8; formerly Western True Crime; A Spectacular Feature Magazine #11)
No. 7, Aug, 1949 - No. 10, Jan-Feb, 1950

Fox Feature Syndicate

	Good	Fine	N-Mint
7-Wood-a, 10 pgs.	10.00	30.00	70.00
8-Wood-a, 18 pgs.	8.00	24.00	56.00
9,10	3.50	10.50	24.00

MY DATE COMICS
July, 1947 - V1No.4, Jan, 1948 (1st Romance comic)
Hillman Periodicals

1-S&K-c/a	10.00	30.00	70.00
2-4-S&K, Dan Barry-a	6.00	18.00	42.00

MY DESIRE (Formerly Jo-Jo) (Murder, Inc. #5 on)
No. 30, Aug, 1949 - No. 4, April, 1950
Fox Feature Syndicate

30(#1)	4.35	13.00	30.00
31 (#2), 3,4	2.85	8.50	20.00
31 (Canadian edition)	1.50	4.50	10.00
32(12/49)-Wood-a	8.00	24.00	56.00

MY DIARY
Dec, 1949 - No. 2, Mar, 1950
Marvel Comics (A Lovers Mag.)

1,2: 1-Photo-c	3.50	10.50	24.00

MY DOG TIGE (Buster Brown's Dog)
1957 (Giveaway)
Buster Brown Shoes

	1.70	5.00	10.00

MY EXPERIENCE (Formerly All Top; Judy Canova #23 on)
No. 19, Sept, 1949 - No. 22, Mar, 1950
Fox Feature Syndicate

19-Wood-a	10.00	30.00	70.00
20	2.85	8.50	20.00
21-Wood-a(2)	11.00	33.00	76.00
22-Wood-a, 9 pgs.	8.00	24.00	56.00

MY FAVORITE MARTIAN (TV)
1/64; No.2, 7/64 - No. 9, 10/66 (No. 1,3-9 have photo-c)
Gold Key

1-Russ Manning-a	4.00	12.00	28.00
2	2.30	7.00	16.00
3-9	2.00	6.00	14.00

MY FRIEND IRMA (Radio/TV) (Formerly Western Life Romances)
No. 3, June, 1950 - No. 47, Dec, 1954; No. 48, Feb, 1955
Marvel/Atlas Comics (BFP)

3-52 pgs.	5.00	15.00	35.00
4-Kurtzman-a, 10 pgs.	6.00	18.00	42.00
5-"Egghead Doodle" by Kurtzman, 4 pgs.	4.35	13.00	30.00
6,8,10: 9-paper dolls, 1pg.; Millie app.	2.30	7.00	16.00
7-One pg. Kurtzman	2.85	8.50	20.00
11-22	1.60	4.80	11.00
23-One pg. Frazetta	1.60	4.80	11.00
24-48	1.15	3.50	8.00

MY GIRL PEARL
4/55 - #4, 10/55; #5, 7/57 - #6, 9/57; #7, 8/60 - #11, ?/61
Atlas Comics

1	3.50	10.50	24.00
2	1.70	5.00	12.00
3-6	1.15	3.50	8.00
7-11	.70	2.00	5.00

MY GREATEST ADVENTURE (Doom Patrol #86 on)
Jan-Feb, 1955 - No. 85, Feb, 1964
National Periodical Publications

1-Before CCA	36.00	108.00	250.00
2	16.00	48.00	110.00

MY GREATEST ADVENTURE (continued)	Good	Fine	N-Mint
3-5	12.00	36.00	84.00
6-10	6.50	19.50	45.00
11-15,19	4.00	12.00	28.00
16-18,20,21,28-Kirby-a; 18-Kirby-c	4.30	13.00	28.00
22-27,29,30	2.65	8.00	18.00
31-40	1.70	5.00	12.00
41-57,59	1.15	3.50	8.00
58,60,61-Toth-a; Last 10 cent ish.	1.70	5.00	12.00
62-76,78,79	.85	2.50	5.00
77-Toth-a	1.00	3.00	7.00
80-(6/63)-Intro/origin Doom Patrol; origin Robotman, Negative Man,			
& Elasti-Girl	11.00	32.00	75.00
81,85-Toth-a	5.00	15.00	35.00
82-84	2.65	8.00	18.00

NOTE: *Anderson* a-42. *Colan* a-77. *Meskin* a-25, 26, 32, 39, 45, 50, 56, 57, 61, 64, 70, 73, 74, 76, 79; c-76. *Moreira* a-11, 17, 20, 23, 25, 27, 37, 40-43, 46, 48, 55-57, 59, 60, 62-65, 67, 69, 70. *Roussos* c/a-71-73.

MY GREATEST THRILLS IN BASEBALL
Date? (16 pg. Giveaway)
Mission of California

	Good	Fine	N-Mint
By Mickey Mantle	22.00	65.00	154.00

MY GREAT LOVE
Oct, 1949 - No. 4, Apr, 1950
Fox Feature Syndicate

1	5.00	15.00	35.00
2-4	2.85	8.50	20.00

MY INTIMATE AFFAIR (Inside Crime #3)
Mar, 1950 - No. 2, May, 1950
Fox Feature Syndicate

1	5.00	15.00	35.00
2	2.85	8.50	20.00

MY LIFE (Formerly Meet Corliss Archer)
No. 4, Sept, 1948 - No. 15, July, 1950
Fox Feature Syndicate

4-Used in SOTI, pg. 39; Kamen/Feldstein-a	16.00	48.00	110.00
5-Kamen-a	8.00	24.00	56.00
6-Kamen/Feldstein-a	8.00	24.00	56.00
7-Wash cover	4.65	14.00	32.00
8,9,11-15	2.85	8.50	20.00
10-Wood-a	8.00	24.00	56.00

MY LITTLE MARGIE (TV)
July, 1954 - No. 54, Nov, 1964
Charlton Comics

1-Photo-c	7.00	21.00	50.00
2-Photo-c	3.50	10.50	24.00
3-7,10	2.00	6.00	14.00
8,9-Infinity-c	2.30	7.00	16.00
11-13: part-photo-c (#13, 8/56)	1.60	4.80	11.00
14-19	1.30	4.00	9.00
20-(100 page ish)	3.00	9.00	21.00
21-35-Last 10 cent ish?	.85	2.50	6.00
36-53	.45	1.35	3.00
54-Beatles on cover; lead story spoofs the Beatle haircut craze of			
the 1960's	4.65	14.00	32.00

NOTE: *Doll cut-outs in 32,33,40,45,50.*

MY LITTLE MARGIE'S BOY FRIENDS (TV) (Freddy V2#12 on)
Aug, 1955 - No. 11, Apr?, 1958
Charlton Comics

1-Has several Archie swipes	3.70	11.00	26.00
2	2.00	6.00	14.00
3-11	1.15	3.50	8.00

MY LITTLE MARGIE'S FASHIONS (TV)
Feb, 1959 - No. 5, Nov, 1959
Charlton Comics

	Good	Fine	N-Mint
1	2.85	8.50	20.00
2-5	1.50	4.50	10.00

MY LOVE
July, 1949 - No. 4, Apr, 1950 (All photo-c)
Marvel Comics (CLDS)

1-Photo-c	2.85	8.50	20.00
2,3	1.50	4.50	10.00
4-Betty Page photo-c (See Cupid #2, Miss. Amer. #4)			
	6.00	18.00	42.00

MY LOVE
Sept, 1969 - No. 39, Mar, 1976
Marvel Comics Group

1-9		.30	.60
10-Williamson-r/My Own Romance #71; Kirby-a		.60	1.20
11-20: 14-Morrow-c/a		.20	.40
21,22,24-39: 38,39-Reprints		.20	.40
23-Steranko-r/Our Love Story #5	.35	1.00	2.00
Special(12/71)		.30	.60

MY LOVE AFFAIR (March of Crime #7 on)
July, 1949 - No. 6, May, 1950
Fox Feature Syndicate

1	5.50	16.50	38.00
2	3.00	9.00	21.00
3-6-Wood-a	8.00	24.00	56.00

MY LOVE LIFE (Formerly Zegra)
No. 6, June, 1949 - No. 13, Aug, 1950; No. 13, Sept, 1951
Fox Feature Syndicate

6-Kamenish-a	6.50	19.50	45.00
7-13	3.00	9.00	21.00
13 (9/51)	2.30	7.00	16.00

MY LOVE MEMOIRS (Formerly Women Outlaws; Hunted #13 on)
No. 9, Nov, 1949 - No. 12, May, 1950
Fox Feature Syndicate

9,11,12-Wood-a	8.00	24.00	56.00
10	2.85	8.50	20.00

MY LOVE SECRET (Formerly Phantom Lady) (Animal Crackers #31)
No. 24, June, 1949 - No. 30, June, 1950; 1954
Fox Feature Syndicate/M. S. Distr.

24-Kamen/Feldstein-a	7.00	21.00	50.00
25-Possible caricature of Wood on-c?	3.50	10.50	24.00
26,28-Wood-a	8.00	24.00	56.00
27,29,30: 30-photo-c	2.65	8.00	18.00
53-(Reprint, M.S. Distr.) 1954? nd given; formerly Western Thrillers			
(Crimes by Women #54). Photo-c	1.70	5.00	11.50

MY LOVE STORY (Hoot Gibson Western #5 on)
Sept, 1949 - No. 4, Mar, 1950
Fox Feature Syndicate

1	5.50	16.50	38.00
2	3.00	9.00	21.00
3,4-Wood-a	8.00	24.00	56.00

MY LOVE STORY
April, 1956 - No. 9, Aug, 1957
Atlas Comics (GPS)

1	2.30	7.00	16.00
2	1.15	3.50	8.00
3-Matt Baker-a	2.15	6.50	15.00
4-6,8,9	.85	2.50	6.00

My Life #4, © FOX

My Little Margie's Fashions #1, © CC

My Love Memoirs #9, © FOX

My Secret #2, © SUPR

My Secret Life #26, © FOX

Mysteries #1, © SUPR

	Good	Fine	N-Mint
MY LOVE STORY (continued)			
7-Matt Baker, Toth-a	2.15	6.50	15.00
NOTE: *Colletta* a 1(2), 4(2), 5.			
MY ONLY LOVE			
July, 1975 - No. 9, Nov, 1976			
Charlton Comics			
1,2,4-9		.20	.40
3-Toth-a	.35	1.00	2.00
MY OWN ROMANCE (Formerly My Romance; Teen-Age			
Romance #77 on)			
No. 4, Mar, 1949 - No. 76, July, 1960			
Marvel/Atlas (MjPC/RCM No. 4-59/ZPC No. 60-76)			
4-Photo-c	3.50	10.50	24.00
5-10: 9,10-Photo-c	1.70	5.00	12.00
11-20: 14-Powell-a	1.30	4.00	9.00
21-42: 42-Last precode (2/55)	1.00	3.00	7.00
43-54,56-60	.75	2.25	5.00
55-Toth-a	2.30	7.00	16.00
61-70,72-76	.55	1.65	4.00
71-Williamson-a	3.75	11.25	26.00
NOTE: *Colletta* a-45(2), 48, 50, 55; c-58i, 61. *Everett* a-25; c-58p. *Morisi* a-18. *Romita* a-36. *Tuska* a-10.			
MY PAL DIZZY (See Comic Books, Series I)			
MY PAST (. . .Confessions) (Formerly Western Thrillers)			
No. 7, Aug, 1949 - No. 11, April, 1950 (Crimes Inc. #12)			
Fox Feature Syndicate			
7	4.35	13.00	30.00
8-10	3.00	9.00	21.00
11-Wood-a	8.00	24.00	56.00
MY PERSONAL PROBLEM			
11/55; No. 2, 2/56; No. 3, 9/56 - No. 4, 11/56; 10/57 - No. 3, 5/58			
Ajax/Farrell/Steinway Comic			
1	2.65	8.00	18.00
2-4	1.50	4.50	10.00
1('57-'58)-Steinway	1.15	3.50	8.00
MY PRIVATE LIFE (Formerly Murder, Inc.)			
No. 16, Feb, 1950 - No. 17, April, 1950			
Fox Feature Syndicate			
16,17	3.50	10.50	24.00
MYRA NORTH (See The Comics, Crackajack Funnies, 4-Color #3 & Red Ryder)			
MY REAL LOVE			
No. 5, June, 1952			
Standard Comics			
5-Toth-a, 3 pgs.; Tuska, Cardy, Vern Greene-a; photo-c			
	4.35	13.00	30.00
MY ROMANCE (My Own Romance #4 on)			
Sept, 1948 - No. 3, Jan, 1949			
Marvel Comics (RCM)			
1	3.50	10.50	24.00
2,3: 2-Anti-Wertham editorial (11/48)	1.70	5.00	12.00
MY ROMANTIC ADVENTURES (Formerly Romantic Adventures)			
No. 68, 8/56 - No. 115, 12/60; No. 116, 7/61 - No. 138, 3/64			
American Comics Group			
68	1.85	5.50	13.00
69-85	1.00	3.00	7.00
86-Three pg. Williamson-a (2/58)	2.85	8.50	20.00
87-100	.50	1.50	3.50
101-138	.35	1.00	2.00
NOTE: *Whitney* art in most.			
MY SECRET (Our Secret #4 on)			
Aug, 1949 - No. 3, Oct, 1949			

	Good	Fine	N-Mint
Superior Comics, Ltd.			
1	3.70	11.00	26.00
2,3	2.65	8.00	18.00
MY SECRET AFFAIR (Martin Kane #4)			
Dec, 1949 - No. 3, April, 1950			
Hero Book (Fox Feature Syndicate)			
1-Harrison/Wood-a, 10 pgs.	9.50	28.50	65.00
2-Wood-a (poor)	5.50	16.50	38.00
3-Wood-a	8.00	24.00	56.00
MY SECRET CONFESSION			
September, 1955			
Sterling Comics			
1-Sekowsky-a	2.00	6.00	14.00
MY SECRET LIFE (Formerly West. Outlaws; Romeo Tubbs #26 on)			
No. 22, July, 1949 - No. 27, May, 1950			
Fox Feature Syndicate			
22	3.70	11.00	26.00
23,26-Wood-a, 6 pgs.	8.00	24.00	56.00
24,25,27	2.30	7.00	16.00
NOTE: The title was changed to Romeo Tubbs after #25 even though #26 & 27 did come out.			
MY SECRET LIFE (Formerly Young Lovers; Sue & Sally Smith #48 on)			
No. 19, Aug, 1957 - No. 47, Sept, 1962			
Charlton Comics			
19	.80	2.40	5.50
20-35	.40	1.25	2.50
36-47: 44-Last 10 cent ish.		.50	1.00
MY SECRET MARRIAGE			
May, 1953 - No. 24, July, 1956			
Superior Comics, Ltd.			
1	3.50	10.50	24.00
2	1.70	5.00	12.00
3-24	1.30	4.00	9.00
I.W. Reprint #9	.30	.90	1.80
NOTE: Many issues contain Kamenish art.			
MY SECRET ROMANCE (A Star Presentation #3)			
Jan, 1950 - No. 2, March, 1950			
Hero Book (Fox Feature Syndicate)			
1-Wood-a	9.00	27.00	62.00
2-Wood-a	8.00	24.00	56.00
MY SECRET STORY (Formerly Captain Kidd #25; Sabu #30 on)			
No. 26, Oct, 1949 - No. 29, April, 1950			
Fox Feature Syndicate			
26	4.00	12.00	28.00
27-29	3.00	9.00	21.00
MYSTERIES (. . .Weird & Strange)			
May, 1953 - No. 11, Jan, 1955			
Superior/Dynamic Publ. (Randall Publ. Ltd.)			
1	8.50	25.50	60.00
2-A-Bomb blast story	4.35	13.00	30.00
3-9,11	3.00	9.00	21.00
10-Kamenish c/a r-/Strange Mysteries #2; cover from a panel in			
S.M. #2	3.70	11.00	26.00
MYSTERIES OF SCOTLAND YARD (See A-1 Comics #121)			
MYSTERIES OF UNEXPLORED WORLDS (See Blue Bird) (Son of Vulcan V2#49 on)			
Aug, 1956 - No. 48, Sept, 1965			
Charlton Comics			
1	10.00	30.00	70.00

MYSTERIES OF UNEXPLORED WORLDS (continued)

	Good	Fine	N-Mint
2-No Ditko	2.85	8.50	20.00
3,4,6,8,9-Ditko-a	6.50	19.50	45.00
5-Ditko c/a (all)	7.00	21.00	50.00
7-(68 pg. ish, 2/58); Ditko-a	8.00	24.00	56.00
10-Ditko-c/a(4)	7.00	21.00	50.00
11-Ditko-c/a(3)-signed J. Kotdi	7.00	21.00	50.00
12,19,21-24,26-Ditko-a	5.00	15.00	35.00
13-18,20	1.50	4.50	10.00
25,27-30	1.00	3.00	7.00
31-45	.45	1.35	3.00
46(5/65)-Son of Vulcan begins (origin)	.70	2.00	4.00
47,48	.50	1.50	3.00

NOTE: *Ditko c-3-6, 10, 11, 19, 21-24.*

MYSTERIOUS ADVENTURES
March, 1951 - No. 24, Mar, 1955; No. 25, Aug, 1955
Story Comics

	Good	Fine	N-Mint
1	13.00	40.00	90.00
2	6.50	19.50	45.00
3,4,6,10	4.65	14.00	32.00
5-Bondage-c; torture	5.70	17.00	40.00
7-Daggar in eye panel; dismemberment	10.00	30.00	70.00
8-Eyeball story	8.00	24.00	55.00
9-Extreme violence, gore, ax murder	5.70	17.00	40.00
11(12/52)-Used in **SOTI**, pg. 84.	10.00	30.00	70.00
12-Dismemberment, eyes ripped out	11.00	32.00	75.00
13-Dismemberment	10.00	30.00	70.00
14-E.C. Old Witch swipe; extreme violence, decapitation, etc.	5.70	17.00	40.00
15-Violence; beheading, acid in face, face carved with knife	11.00	32.00	75.00
16-Violence, dismemberment, injury to eye	11.00	32.00	75.00
17-Violence, dismemberment	11.00	32.00	75.00
18-Used in Senate Investigative report, pgs. 5,6; E.C. swipe/ T.F.T.C. 35; extreme violence, dismemberment, severed heads, etc.	11.00	32.00	75.00
20-Violence, head split open, fried body organs-used by Wertham in the Senate hearings	11.00	32.00	75.00
21-Blood drainage story, hanging panels, intestines pulled out; bondage/beheading-c	11.00	32.00	75.00
22-'Cinderella' parody	5.00	15.00	35.00
23-Disbrow-a	5.70	17.00	40.00
24,25	4.35	13.00	30.00

NOTE: *Tothish art by Ross Andru-#22, 23. Bache a-8. Cameron a-5-7. Harrison a-12. Hollingsworth a-3-8, 12. Schaffenberger a-24, 25. Wildey a-15, 17.*

MYSTERIOUS ISLAND (See 4-Color #1213)

MYSTERIOUS ISLE
Nov-Jan, 1963/64 (Jules Verne)
Dell Publishing Co.

	Good	Fine	N-Mint
1	1.00	3.00	7.00

MYSTERIOUS STORIES (Horror From the Tomb #1)
Dec-Jan, 1954-1955 - No. 7, Dec, 1955
Premier Magazines

	Good	Fine	N-Mint
2-Woodbridge-c	8.00	24.00	56.00
3-Woodbridge c/a	6.00	18.00	42.00
4-7: 5-Cinderella parody. 6-Woodbridge-c	5.00	15.00	35.00

NOTE: *Hollingsworth a-2,4.*

MYSTERIOUS SUSPENSE
October, 1968
Charlton Comics

	Good	Fine	N-Mint
1-The Question app. by Ditko-c/a	2.00	6.00	14.00

MYSTERIOUS TRAVELER (See Tales of the . . .)

MYSTERIOUS TRAVELER COMICS (Radio)
Nov, 1948 - No. 4, 1949
Trans-World Publications

	Good	Fine	N-Mint
1-Powell-c/a(2); Poe adaptation, 'Tell Tale Heart'	19.00	57.00	132.00
2-4	12.00	36.00	84.00

MYSTERY COMICS
1944 - No. 4, 1944 (No month given)
William H. Wise & Co.

	Good	Fine	N-Mint
1-The Magnet, The Silver Knight, Brad Spencer, Wonderman, Dick Devins, King of Futuria, & Zudo the Jungle Boy begin	28.00	85.00	200.00
2-Bondage-c	19.00	55.00	130.00
3-Lance Lewis, Space Detective begins	17.00	51.00	120.00
4(V2No.1 inside)	17.00	51.00	120.00

NOTE: *Schomburg c-1-4.*

MYSTERY COMICS DIGEST
March, 1972 - No. 26, Oct, 1975
Gold Key

	Good	Fine	N-Mint
1-Ripley's; reprint of Ripley's #1 origin Ra-Ka-Tep the Mummy; Wood-a	.85	2.50	5.00
2-Boris Karloff; Wood-a; 1st app. Werewolf Count Wulfstein	.40	1.25	2.50
3-Twilight Zone (TV); Crandall, Toth & George Evans-a; 1st app. Tragg & Simbar the Lion Lord; 2 Crandall/Frazetta-a r-Twilight Zone #1	.40	1.25	2.50
4-Ripley's Believe It or Not; 1st app. Baron Tibor, the Vampire	.35	1.00	2.00
5-Boris Karloff Tales of Mystery; 1st app. Dr. Spektor	.35	1.00	2.00
6-Twilight Zone (TV); 1st app. U.S. Marshal Reid & Sir Duane	.35	1.00	2.00
7-Ripley's Believe It or Not; origin The Lurker in the Swamp; 1st app. Duroc	.60	1.20	
8-Boris Karloff Tales of Mystery	.60	1.20	
9-Twilight Zone (TV); Williamson, Crandall, McWilliams-a; 2nd Tragg app.	.40	1.25	2.50
10,13-Ripley's Believe It or Not	.50	1.00	
11,14-Boris Karloff Tales of Mystery. 14-1st app. Xorkon	.40	.80	
12,15-Twilight Zone (TV)	.40	.80	
16,19,22,25-Ripley's Believe It or Not	.40	.80	
17-Boris Karloff Tales of Mystery; Williamson-r	.25	.75	1.50
18,21,24-Twilight Zone (TV)	.40	.80	
20,23,26-Boris Karloff Tales of Mystery	.40	.80	

NOTE: *Dr. Spektor app.-#5,10-12,21. Durak app.-#15. Duroc app.-#14 (later called Durak). King George 1st app.-#8.*

MYSTERY IN SPACE
Apr-May, 1951 - No. 110, Sept, 1966; (#1-3: 52 pgs.)
No. 111, Sept, 1980 - No. 117, March, 1981
National Periodical Publications

	Good	Fine	N-Mint
1-Frazetta-a, 8 pgs.; Knights of the Galaxy begins, ends #8	120.00	360.00	840.00
2	50.00	150.00	350.00
3	40.00	120.00	280.00
4,5	27.00	81.00	190.00
6-10: 7-Toth-a	21.50	64.00	150.00
11-15: 13-Toth-a	16.00	48.00	110.00
16-18,20-25: Interplanetary Insurance feature by Infantino in all. 24-Last precode issue	14.00	42.00	100.00
19-Virgil Finlay-a	16.00	48.00	110.00
26-34,36-40: 26-Space Cabbie begins	8.50	25.50	60.00
35-Kubert-a	9.50	28.50	65.00
41-52: 47-Space Cabbie feature ends	5.70	17.00	40.00

Mysterious Adventures #2, © Story Comics

Mysterious Stories #7, © PG

Mystery Comics #4, © WHW

Mystery Men #3, © FOX

Mystery Tales #12, © MEG

Mystic #5, © MEG

MYSTERY IN SPACE (continued)

	Good	Fine	N-Mint
53-Adam Strange begins (1st app. in Showcase)			
	37.00	110.00	260.00
54	15.00	45.00	105.00
55	11.00	32.00	75.00
56-60	8.00	24.00	56.00
61-71: 61-1st app. Adam Strange foe Ulthoon. 62-1st app. A.S. foe			
Mortan. 63-Origin Vandor. 66-Star Rovers begin. 68-Dust Devils			
app. 71-Last 10 cent ish.	4.65	14.00	32.00
72-80: 75-JLA x-over in Adam Strange	3.50	10.50	24.00
81-86	2.00	6.00	14.00
87-90-Hawkman in all	1.15	3.50	8.00
91-102: 91-End Infantino art on Adam Strange. 92-Space Ranger			
begins. 94,98-Adam Strange/Space Ranger team-up. 102-Adam			
Strange ends	.75	2.25	4.50
103-Origin Ultra, the Multi-Alien; Space Ranger ends			
	.75	2.25	4.50
104-110(9/66)	.35	1.10	2.20
111(9/80)-117		.60	1.20

NOTE: **Anderson** a-2, 4, 8-10, 12-17, 19, 45-48, 51, 57, 61-64, 70, 76, 87-98; c-9, 10, 15-25, 87, 89, 105-108, 110. **Aparo** a-111. **Austin** a-112i. **Craig** a-114, 116. **Ditko** a-111, 114-116. **Drucker** a-13, 14. **Golden** a-113p. **Sid Greene** a-78, 91. **Infantino** a-1-8, 11, 14-25, 27-46, 48, 49, 51, 53-91, 103, 117; c-60-86, 88, 90, 91, 105, 107. **Gil Kane** a-18, 100-102; c-52, 101. **Kubert** a-113; c-111-15. **Newton** a-117p. **Rogers** a-111. **Sekowsky** a-52. **Simon & Kirby** a-4(2 pgs.). **Spiegle** a-111, 114. **Starlin** c-116. **Sutton** a-112. **Tuska** a-115p; 117p.

MYSTERY MEN COMICS
Aug, 1939 - No. 31, Feb, 1942
Fox Features Syndicate

	Good	Fine	N-Mint
1-Intro. & 1st app. The Blue Beetle, The Green Mask, Rex Dexter			
of Mars by Briefer, Zanzibar by Tuska, Lt. Drake, D-13-Secret			
Agent by Powell, Chen Chang, Wing Turner, & Captain Denny			
Scott	128.00	385.00	895.00
2	60.00	180.00	420.00
3 (10/39)	50.00	150.00	350.00
4-Capt. Savage begins	45.00	135.00	315.00
5	35.00	105.00	245.00
6-8	30.00	90.00	210.00
9-The Moth begins	26.00	78.00	180.00
10-Wing Turner by Kirby	26.00	78.00	180.00
11-Intro. Domino	20.00	60.00	140.00
12,14-18	18.00	54.00	125.00
13-Intro. Lynx & sidekick Blackie	20.00	60.00	140.00
19-Intro. & 1st app. Miss X (ends #21)	20.00	60.00	140.00
20-25,27-31	16.50	50.00	115.00
26-The Wraith begins	16.50	50.00	115.00

NOTE: **Briefer** a-1-15, 20, 24; c-9. **Cuidera** a-22. **Lou Fine** c-1-8. **Powell** a-1-15, 24. **Simon** c-10-12. **Tuska** a-1-15, 22, 24, 27. Bondage-c 1, 3, 7, 8, 25, 27-29, 31.

MYSTERY TALES
March, 1952 - No. 54, Aug, 1957
Atlas Comics (20CC)

	Good	Fine	N-Mint
1	14.00	42.00	100.00
2-Krigstein-a	8.00	24.00	56.00
3-9: 6-A-Bomb panel	5.00	15.00	35.00
10-Story similar to 'The Assassin' from Shock SuspenStories			
	5.70	17.00	40.00
11,13-17,19,20: 20-Electric chair ish.	3.00	9.00	21.00
12-Matt Fox-a	4.30	13.00	30.00
18-Williamson-a	5.70	17.00	40.00
21-Matt Fox-a; decapitation story	4.30	13.00	30.00
22-Forte/Matt Fox c; a(i)	5.70	17.00	40.00
23-26 (2/55)-Last precode issue	2.85	8.50	20.00
27,29-32,34,35,37,38,41-43,49,49	1.70	5.00	12.00
28-Jack Katz-a	3.00	9.00	21.00
33-Crandall-a	3.65	11.00	26.00
36,39-Krigstein-a	3.65	11.00	26.00

	Good	Fine	N-Mint
40,45-Ditko-a	3.65	11.00	26.00
44,51-Williamson/Mayo-a	4.65	14.00	32.00
46-Williamson/Krenkel-a	4.65	14.00	32.00
47-Crandall, Ditko, Powell-a	4.00	12.00	28.00
50-Torres, Morrow-a	3.35	10.00	23.00
52,53	1.70	5.00	12.00
54-Crandall, Check-a	3.00	9.00	21.00

NOTE: **Ayers** a-52. **Berg** a-17, 51. **Colan** a-1, 3, 18, 35, 43. **Everett** a-2, 29, 33, 35, 41, 43; c-8-11, 14, 38, 39, 41, 43, 44, 46, 48-51, 53. **Fass** a-16. **Forte** a-21, 22. **Matt Fox** a-12?, 21, 22; c-22. **Heath** a-3; c-3, 15, 17, 26. **Heck** a-25. **Kinstler** a-15. **Mort Lawrence** a-26, 32, 34. **Maneely** a-1, 9, 14, 22; c-12, 23, 24, 27. **Mooney** a-3, 40. **Morisi** a-43, 49, 52. **Morrow** a-50. **Pakula** a-16. **Powell** a-21, 29, 37, 38, 47. **Robinson** a-7p, 42. **Roussos** a-44. **Severin** c-52. **Tuska** a-10, 12, 14. **Whitney** a-2.

MYSTERY TALES
1964
Super Comics

	Good	Fine	N-Mint
Super Reprint #16,17('64)	.50	1.50	3.00
Super Reprint #18-Kubert art/Strange Terrors #4			
	.50	1.50	3.00

MYSTIC (3rd Series)
March, 1951 - No. 61, Aug, 1957
Marvel/Atlas Comics (CLDS 1/CSI 2-21/OMC 22-35/CSI 35-61)

	Good	Fine	N-Mint
1-Atom bomb panels	16.00	48.00	110.00
2	8.50	25.50	60.00
3-Eyes torn out	5.70	17.00	40.00
4-''The Devil Birds'' by Wolverton, 6 pgs.	20.00	60.00	140.00
5,7-10	4.65	14.00	32.00
6-''The Eye of Doom'' by Wolverton, 7 pgs.	20.00	60.00	140.00
11-20: 16-Bondage/torture c/story	4.30	13.00	30.00
21-25,27-30,32-36-Last precode (3/55). 25-E.C. swipe			
	3.50	10.50	24.00
26-Atomic War, severed head stories	4.00	12.00	28.00
31-Sid Check-a	3.50	10.50	24.00
37-51,53-57,61	2.00	6.00	14.00
52-Wood, Crandall-a	5.00	15.00	35.00
58,59-Krigstein-a	3.50	10.50	24.00
60-Williamson/Mayo-a, 4 pgs.	3.85	11.50	27.00

NOTE: **Andru** a-23, 25. **Ayers** a-53; c-8. **Cameron** a-51. **Check** a-60. **Colan** a-3, 7, 12, 21, 37. **Drucker** a-46, 52, 56. **Everett** a-8, 9, 17, 40, 44, 57; c-18, 21, 42, 47, 49, 51-55, 58, 59, 61. **Forte** a-52. **Fox** a-24i. **Heath** a-1; c-10, 22, 23, 25, 30. **Infantino** a-12. **Kane** a-8, 24p. **Jack Katz** a-31, 33. **Mort Lawrence** a-19, 37. **Maneely** a-22, 24, 58; c-15, 28, 29, 31. **Moldoff** a-29. **Morisi** a-52. **Morrow** a-51. **Orlando** a-57, 61. **Pakula** a-52. **Powell** a-52, 55, 56. **Robinson** a-5. **Romita** a-11, 15. **Sale** a-53. **Sekowsky** a-1, 2, 4, 5. **Severin** c-56. **Tuska** a-15. **Whitney** a-33. **Wildey** a-28, 30. Canadian reprints known-title 'Startling'.

MYSTICAL TALES
June, 1956 - No. 8, Aug, 1957
Atlas Comics (TPI 1-5/TCI 8-10)

	Good	Fine	N-Mint
1-Everett c/a	9.50	28.50	65.00
2,4: 2-Berg-a	4.30	13.00	30.00
3-Crandall-a	5.00	15.00	35.00
5-Williamson-a, 4 pgs.	5.50	16.50	38.00
6-Torres, Krigstein-a	4.60	14.00	32.00
7-Torres, Orlando, Crandall, Everett-a	4.00	12.00	28.00
8-Krigstein, Check-a	4.60	14.00	32.00

NOTE: **Everett** a-1, 7; c-1-4, 6, 7. **Orlando** a-1, 2. **Powell** a-1, 4.

MYSTIC COMICS (1st Series)
March, 1940 - No. 10, Aug, 1942
Timely Comics

	Good	Fine	N-Mint
1-Origin The Blue Blaze, The Dynamic Man, & Flexo the Rubber			
Man; Zephyr Jones, 3X's & Deep Sea Demon app.; The Magician			
begins;c-from Spider pulp V18#1, 6/39	360.00	1080.00	2520.00
2-The Invisible Man & Master Mind Excello begin; Space Rangers,			
Zara of the Jungle, Taxi Taylor app	145.00	435.00	1015.00
3-Origin Hercules, who last appears in #4	115.00	345.00	805.00

MYSTIC COMICS (continued)

	Good	Fine	N-Mint
4-Origin The Thin Man & The Black Widow; Merzak the Mystic app.; last Flexo, Dynamic Man, Invisible Man & Blue Blaze. (Some issues have date sticker on cover; others have July w/August overprint in silver color); Roosevelt assassination-c	135.00	405.00	945.00
5-Origin The Black Marvel, The Blazing Skull, The Sub-Earth Man, Super Slave & The Terror; The Moon Man & Black Widow app.	130.00	390.00	910.00
6-Origin The Challenger & The Destroyer	110.00	330.00	770.00
7-The Witness begins (origin); origin Davey & the Demon; last Black Widow; Simon & Kirby-c	90.00	270.00	630.00
8	77.00	230.00	540.00
9-Gary Gaunt app.; last Black Marvel, Mystic & Blazing Skull	77.00	230.00	530.00
10-Father Time, World of Wonder, & Red Skeleton app.; last Challenger & Terror	77.00	230.00	530.00

NOTE: *Schomburg* a-1-4. *Bondage c-1,2,9.*

MYSTIC COMICS (2nd Series)
Oct, 1944 - No. 4, Winter, 1944-45
Timely Comics (ANC)

	Good	Fine	N-Mint
1-The Angel, The Destroyer, The Human Torch, Terry Vance the Schoolboy Sleuth, & Tommy Tyme begin	64.00	192.00	450.00
2-Last Human Torch & Terry Vance; bondage-hypo-c	40.00	120.00	280.00
3-Last Angel (two stories) & Tommy Tyme	37.00	110.00	260.00
4-The Young Allies app.	32.00	95.00	225.00

MY STORY (. . . True Romances in Pictures #5,6) (Formerly Zago)
No. 5, May, 1949 - No. 12, Aug, 1950
Hero Books (Fox Features Syndicate)

	Good	Fine	N-Mint
5-Kamen/Feldstein-a	7.00	21.00	50.00
6-8,11,12: 12-Photo-c	3.00	9.00	21.00
9,10-Wood-a	8.00	24.00	56.00

MYTHADVENTURES
Mar, 1984 - #12, 1986 (B&W)
WaRP Graphics/Apple Comics #11, 12

	Good	Fine	N-Mint
1-4: Early issues mag. size	.30	.90	1.80
5-12: 12 ($1.75)	.25	.75	1.50

MYTH CONCEPTIONS
Nov., 1987 - Present ($1.75/$1.95, B&W)
Apple Comics

	Good	Fine	N-Mint
1-7		.30	.90	1.80

MY TRUE LOVE (Formerly Western Killers #64; Frank Buck #70 on)
No. 65, July, 1949 - No. 69, March, 1950
Fox Features Syndicate

	Good	Fine	N-Mint
65	4.35	13.00	30.00
66-69: 69-Morisi-a	3.00	9.00	21.00

NAKED PREY, THE (See Movie Classics)

'NAM, THE (See Savage Tales #1, 2nd series)
Dec, 1986 - Present
Marvel Comics Group

	Good	Fine	N-Mint
1-Golden a(p)/c begins, ends #13	2.85	8.50	17.00
1 (2nd printing)	.70	2.00	4.00
2	2.00	6.00	12.00
3,4	1.15	3.50	7.00
5-7	.85	2.50	5.00
8-10	.50	1.50	3.00
11-20	.35	1.00	2.00
21-28: 25-begin $1.50-c	.25	.75	1.50

'NAM MAGAZINE, THE
August, 1988 - Present ($2.00, B&W, 52pgs)
Marvel Comics

	Good	Fine	N-Mint
1-10: Each issue reprints two of the comic	.35	1.00	2.00

NAMORA (See Marvel Mystery & Sub-Mariner)
Fall, 1948 - No. 3, Dec, 1948
Marvel Comics (PrPI)

	Good	Fine	N-Mint
1-Sub-Mariner x-over in Namora; Everett-a	60.00	180.00	420.00
2-The Blonde Phantom & Sub-Mariner story; Everett-a	50.00	150.00	350.00
3-(Scarce)-Sub-Mariner app.; Everett-a	44.00	132.00	310.00

NANCY AND SLUGGO (See Comics On Parade & Sparkle Comics)
No. 16, 1949 - No. 23, 1954
United Features Syndicate

	Good	Fine	N-Mint
16(#1)	3.50	10.50	24.00
17-23	2.00	6.00	14.00

NANCY & SLUGGO (Nancy #146-173; formerly Sparkler Comics)
No. 121, Apr, 1955 - No. 192, Oct, 1963
St. John/Dell No. 146-187/Gold Key No. 188 on

	Good	Fine	N-Mint
121(4/55)(St. John)	3.00	9.00	21.00
122-145(7/57)(St. John)	2.00	6.00	14.00
146(9/57)-Peanuts begins, ends #192 (Dell)	1.70	5.00	12.00
147-161 (Dell)	1.50	4.50	10.00
162-165,177-180-John Stanley-a	3.50	10.50	24.00
166-176-Oona & Her Haunted House series; Stanley-a	3.70	11.00	26.00
181-187(3-5/62)(Dell)	1.30	4.00	9.00
188(10/62)-192 (G.Key)	1.30	4.00	9.00
4-Color 1034(9-11/59)-Summer Camp	1.70	5.00	12.00

(See Dell Giant #34,45 & Dell Giants)

NANNY AND THE PROFESSOR (TV)
Aug, 1970 - No. 2, Oct, 1970 (Photo-c)
Dell Publishing Co.

	Good	Fine	N-Mint
1(01-546-008), 2	2.00	6.00	14.00

NAPOLEON (See 4-Color No. 526)

NAPOLEON & SAMANTHA (See Walt Disney Showcase No. 10)

NAPOLEON & UNCLE ELBY (See Clifford McBride's . . .)
July, 1942 (68 pages) (One Shot)
Eastern Color Printing Co.

	Good	Fine	N-Mint
1	13.00	40.00	90.00
1945-American Book-Strafford Press (128 pgs.) (8x10½''-B&W reprints; hardcover)	6.50	19.50	45.00

NATHANIEL DUSK
Feb, 1984 - No. 4, May, 1984 (mini-series; Baxter paper)
DC Comics (Direct Sale only)

	Good	Fine	N-Mint
1-Intro/origin		.60	1.20
2-4 ($1.25): Colan c/a		.60	1.20

NATHANIEL DUSK II
Oct, 1985 - No. 4, Jan, 1986 (mini-series; Baxter paper)
DC Comics

	Good	Fine	N-Mint
1 ($2.00 cover); Colan c/a	.30	.90	1.80
2-4		.55	1.10

NATIONAL COMICS
July, 1940 - No. 75, Nov, 1949
Quality Comics Group

	Good	Fine	N-Mint
1-Uncle Sam begins; Origin sidekick Buddy by Eisner; origin Wonder Boy & Kid Dixon; Merlin the Magician (ends #45); Cyclone, Kid Patrol, Sally O'Neil Policewoman, Pen Miller (ends #22), Prop Powers (ends #26), & Paul Bunyan (ends #22) begin	160.00	480.00	1120.00
2	75.00	225.00	525.00
3-Last Eisner Uncle Sam	60.00	180.00	420.00

Mystic Comics #5 (1st series), © MEG

Myth Conceptions #1, Apple Comics

The 'Nam #1, © MEG

National Comics #1, © QUA   Nature Boy #4, © CC   Navy Combat #1, © MEG

NATIONAL COMICS (continued)	Good	Fine	N-Mint
4-Last Cyclone	43.00	130.00	300.00
5-(11/40)-Quicksilver begins (3rd w/lightning speed?); origin Uncle Sam	55.00	165.00	385.00
6-11: 8-Jack & Jill begins (ends #22). 9-Flag-c	40.00	120.00	280.00
12	30.00	90.00	210.00
13-16-Lou Fine-a	37.00	110.00	260.00
17,19-22	27.00	81.00	190.00
18-(12/41)-Shows orientals attacking Pearl Harbor; on stands one month before actual event	33.00	100.00	230.00
23-The Unknown & Destroyer 171 begin	30.00	90.00	210.00
24-26,28,30: 26-Wonder Boy ends	21.00	63.00	145.00
27-G-2 the Unknown begins (ends #46)	21.00	63.00	145.00
29-Origin The Unknown	21.00	63.00	145.00
31-33: 33-Chic Carter begins (ends #47)	18.00	54.00	125.00
34-40: 35-Last Kid Patrol. 39-Hitler-c	11.00	32.00	76.00
41-47,49,50: 42-The Barker begins	8.50	25.50	60.00
48-Origin The Whistler	8.50	25.50	60.00
51-Sally O'Neil by Ward, 8 pgs. (12/45)	11.50	34.50	80.00
52-60	6.50	19.50	45.00
61-67: 67-Format change; Quicksilver app.	4.65	14.00	32.00
68-75: The Barker ends	2.85	8.50	20.00

NOTE: Cole Quicksilver-13; Barker-43; c-43, 46, 47, 49. Crandall Uncle Sam-11-13 (with Fine), 25, 26; c-24-26, 30-33, 43. Crandall Paul Bunyan-10-13. Fine Uncle Sam-13 (w/Crandall), 17, 18; c-1-14, 16, 18, 21. Guardineer Quicksilver-27. Gustavson Quicksilver-14-26. McWilliams a-23-28, 55, 57. Uncle Sam-c #1-41. Bondage c-5.

NATIONAL CRUMB, THE (Magazine-Size)
August, 1975 (52 pages) (Satire)
Mayfair Publications

1	.70	2.00	4.00

NATIONAL VELVET (TV)
May-July, 1961 - March, 1963 (All photo-c)
Dell Publishing Co./Gold Key

4-Color 1195	2.30	7.00	16.00
4-Color 1312	2.00	6.00	14.00
01-556-207,12-556-210	1.70	5.00	12.00
1(12/62), 2(3/63)-Gold Key	1.70	5.00	12.00

NATURE BOY (Formerly Danny Blaze; Li'l Rascal Twins #6 on)
No. 3, March, 1956 - No. 5, Feb, 1957
Charlton Comics

3-Origin; Blue Beetle story; Buscema-a	11.50	34.00	80.00
4,5	8.00	24.00	56.00

NOTE: Buscema a-3, 4p, 5; c-3. Powell a-4.

NATURE OF THINGS (See 4-Color No. 727,842)

NAVY ACTION (Sailor Sweeney #12-14)
Aug, 1954 - No. 11, Apr, 1956; No. 15, 1/57 - No. 18, 8/57
Atlas Comics (CDS)

1-Powell-a	3.50	10.50	24.00
2	1.70	5.00	12.00
3-11: 4-Last precode (2/55)	1.20	3.50	8.00
15-18	.85	2.50	6.00

NOTE: Berg a-9. Colan a-8. Drucker a-7, 17. Everett a-3, 7, 16; c-16, 17. Heath c-6. Maneely a-8, 18; c-1. Pakula a-3. Reinman a-17.

NAVY COMBAT
June, 1955 - No. 20, Oct, 1958
Atlas Comics (MPI)

1-Torpedo Taylor begins by D. Heck	3.50	10.50	24.00
2	1.70	5.00	12.00
3-10	1.15	3.50	8.00
11,13,15,16,18-20	1.00	3.00	7.00
12-Crandall-a	2.00	6.00	14.00
14-Torres-a	2.00	6.00	14.00
17-Williamson-a, 4 pgs.	2.75	8.00	18.00

NOTE: Berg a-10,11. Drucker a-7, 11. Everett a-3, 20; c-8 & 9 w/Tuska, 10, 13-16. Pakula a-7. Powell a-20.

NAVY HEROES
1945
Almanac Publishing Co.

	Good	Fine	N-Mint
1-Heavy in propaganda	3.70	11.00	26.00

NAVY: HISTORY & TRADITION
1958 - 1961 (nn) (Giveaway)
Stokes Walesby Co./Dept. of Navy

1772-1778, 1778-1782, 1782-1817, 1817-1865, 1865-1936, 1940-1945	2.00	6.00	14.00
1861: Naval Actions of the Civil War: 1865	2.00	6.00	14.00

NAVY PATROL
May, 1955 - No. 4, Nov, 1955
Key Publications

1	2.00	6.00	14.00
2-4	1.00	3.00	7.00

NAVY TALES
Jan, 1957 - No. 4, July, 1957
Atlas Comics (CDS)

1-Everett-c; Berg, Powell-a	3.00	9.00	21.00
2-Williamson/Mayo-a, 5 pgs; Crandall-a	3.50	10.50	24.00
3,4-Krigstein-a; Severin-c. 4-Crandall-a	2.30	7.00	16.00

NAVY TASK FORCE
Feb, 1954 - No. 8, April, 1956
Stanmor Publications/Aragon Mag. No. 4-8

1	2.00	6.00	14.00
2	1.00	3.00	7.00
3-8	.85	2.50	6.00

NAVY WAR HEROES
Jan, 1964 - No. 7, Mar-Apr, 1965
Charlton Comics

1		.60	1.20
2-7		.50	1.00

NAZA (Stone Age Warrior)
Nov-Jan, 1963/64 - No. 9, March, 1966
Dell Publishing Co.

1 (12-555-401)-Painted-c	.85	2.50	6.00
2-9: 2-4-Painted-c	.55	1.65	4.00

NEAT STUFF
July, 1985 - Present ($1.95/$2.25/$2.50, adults)
Fantagraphics Books

1	.35	1.00	2.00
2-10	.30	.90	1.80
11,12 ($2.50)	.40	1.25	2.50

NEBBS, THE
1928 (Daily B&W strip reprints; 52 pages)
Cupples & Leon Co.

By Sol Hess; Carlson-a	6.00	18.00	42.00

NEBBS, THE (Also see Crackajack Funnies)
1941 - 1945
Dell Publishing Co./Croydon Publishing Co.

Large Feat. Comic 23(1941)	8.00	24.00	56.00
1(1945, 36 pgs.)-Reprints	4.65	14.00	32.00

NEGRO (See All-Negro)

NEGRO HEROES (True, Real Heroes, & Calling All Girls-r)
Spring, 1947 - No. 2, Summer, 1948
Parents' Magazine Institute

1	27.00	81.00	190.00

NEGRO HEROES (continued)

	Good	Fine	N-Mint
2-Jackie Robinson story	30.00	90.00	210.00

NEGRO ROMANCE (Negro Romances #4?)
June, 1950 - No. 3, Oct, 1950 (All photo-c)
Fawcett Publications

1-Evans-a	65.00	195.00	455.00
2,3	50.00	150.00	350.00

NEGRO ROMANCES (Formerly Negro Romance?)
No. 4, May, 1955   (Romantic Secrets #5 on?)
Charlton Comics

4-Reprints Fawcett #2	35.00	105.00	245.00

NEIL THE HORSE (See Charlton Bullseye #2)
2/83 - No. 10, 12/84; No. 11, 4/85 - Present (B&W)
Aardvark-Vanaheim #1-10/Renegade Press #11 on

1 ($1.40)	.70	2.00	4.00
1-2nd print	.30	.85	1.70
2	.40	1.25	2.50
3-13: 13-Dbl size. 11,13-w/paperdolls	.35	1.00	2.00
14,15-Double size ($3.00)	.50	1.50	3.00

NELLIE THE NURSE (Also see Gay Comics)
1945 - No. 36, Oct, 1952; 1957
Marvel/Atlas Comics (SPI/LMC)

1	10.00	30.00	70.00
2	4.30	13.00	30.00
3,4	3.70	11.00	26.00
5-Kurtzman's "Hey Look"	4.30	13.00	30.00
6-8,10: 7,8-Georgie app. 10-Millie app.	2.65	8.00	18.00
9-Wolverton-a, 1 pg.	2.85	8.50	20.00
11,14-16,18-Kurtzman's "Hey Look"	3.70	11.00	26.00
12-"Giggles 'n' Grins" by Kurtzman	2.85	8.50	20.00
13,17,19,20: 17-Annie Oakley app.	2.30	7.00	16.00
21-27,29,30	2.00	6.00	14.00
28-Kurtzman's Rusty reprint	2.30	7.00	16.00
31-36: 36-Post-c	1.50	4.50	10.00
1('57)-Leading Mag. (Atlas)-Everett-a,20p.	1.30	4.00	9.00

NELLIE THE NURSE (See 4-Color No. 1304)

NEMESIS THE WARLOCK (Also see Spellbinders)
Sept, 1984 - No. 7, Mar, 1985 (Limited series; 36 pgs.)
Eagle Comics (Baxter paper)

1-7: 2000 A.D. reprints	.25	.75	1.50

NEUTRO
January, 1967
Dell Publishing Co.

1-Jack Sparling c/a	.75	2.25	5.00

NEVADA (See Zane Grey's Stories of the West #1)

NEVER AGAIN (War stories; becomes Soldier & Marine V2#9)
Aug, 1955 - No. 2, Oct?, 1955; No. 8, July, 1956 (no No. 3-7)
Charlton Comics

1	3.00	9.00	21.00
2 (Becomes Fightin' Air Force #3), 8(Formerly Foxhole?)	1.60	4.70	11.00

NEW ADVENTURE COMICS (Formerly New Comics; becomes
Adventure Comics #32 on)
V1No.12, Jan, 1937 - No. 31, Oct, 1938
National Periodical Publications

	Good	Fine	VF-NM
V1#12-Federal Men by Siegel & Shuster continues; Jor-L mentioned	100.00	300.00	700.00
V2#1(2/37, #13), V2#2 (#14)	72.00	215.00	505.00

	Good	Fine	N-Mint
15(V2#3)-20(V2#8): 15-1st Adventure logo. 16-1st Shuster-c; 1st non-funny cover. 17-Nadir, Master of Magic begins, ends #30			

	Good	Fine	N-Mint
	72.00	215.00	505.00
21(V2#9),22(V2#10, 2/37)	60.00	180.00	420.00
23-31	50.00	150.00	350.00

NEW ADVENTURE OF WALT DISNEY'S SNOW WHITE AND THE SEVEN DWARFS, A (See Snow White Bendix Giveaway)

NEW ADVENTURES OF CHARLIE CHAN, THE (TV)
May-June, 1958 - No. 6, Mar-Apr, 1959
National Periodical Publications

1 (Scarce)	20.00	60.00	140.00
2 (Scarce)	11.00	32.00	75.00
3-6 (Scarce)	9.50	28.50	65.00

NOTE: *Sid Greene a-1-6i. Gil Kane a-1-6p.*

NEW ADVENTURES OF HUCK FINN, THE (TV)
December, 1968 (Hanna-Barbera)
Gold Key

1-"The Curse of Thut"; part photo-c	1.30	4.00	9.00

NEW ADVENTURES OF PETER PAN (Disney)
1953 (36 pgs.; 5x7¼") (Admiral giveaway)
Western Publishing Co.

	4.65	14.00	32.00

NEW ADVENTURES OF PINOCCHIO (TV)
Oct-Dec, 1962 - No. 3, Sept-Nov, 1963
Dell Publishing Co.

12-562-212	5.00	15.00	35.00
2,3	4.00	12.00	28.00

NEW ADVENTURES OF ROBIN HOOD (See Robin Hood)

NEW ADVENTURES OF SHERLOCK HOLMES (See 4-Color #1169, 1245)

NEW ADVENTURES OF SUPERBOY, THE
Jan, 1980 - No. 54, June, 1984
DC Comics

1		.60	1.20
2-5		.50	1.00
6-10		.40	.80
11-47: 11-Superboy gets new power. 15-Superboy gets new parents. 28-Dial "H" For Hero begins, ends #49. 45-47-1st app. Sunburst		.30	.60
48,49,51-54 (75 cent-c)		.40	.80
50 ($1.25, 52 pgs.)		.60	1.25

NOTE: *Buckler a-9p; c-36p. Giffen a-50; c-50. 40i. Gil Kane c-32p, 33p, 35, 39, 41-49. Miller c-51. Starlin a-7.*

NEW ADVS. OF THE PHANTOM BLOT, THE (See Phantom Blot, The)

NEW AMERICA
Nov, 1987 - No. 4, Feb, 1986 (Color, $1.75, Baxter)
Eclipse Comics

1-4-Scout mini-series	.30	.90	1.80

NEW ARCHIES, THE
Oct, 1987 - Present
Archie Comic Publ.

1-12: 3-Xmas ish.		.40	.75

NEW ARCHIES DIGEST
1988 - Present ($1.35, digest size)
Archie Comics

1-5	.25	.70	1.35

NEW BOOK OF COMICS (Also see Big Book Of Fun)
1937; Spring, 1938 (100 pgs. each) (Reprints)
National Periodical Publications

1(Rare)-1st regular size comic annual; 2nd DC annual; contains r-/New Comics #1-4 & More Fun #9; r-Federal Men (8pgs.), Henri Duval (1pg.), & Dr. Occult in costume (1pg.) by Siegel & Shuster;

Negro Romance #2, © FAW

The New Adventures Of Charlie Chan #6, © DC

New America #1, © Eclipse Comics

New Fun Comics #6, © DC   New Funnies #90, © DELL   The New Guardians #1, © DC

	Good	Fine	N-Mint
NEW BOOK OF COMICS (continued)			
Moldoff, Sheldon Mayer (15pgs.)-a	300.00	900.00	2100.00
2-Contains r-/More Fun #15 & 16; r-/Dr. Occult in costume (a Superman proto-type), & Calling All Cars (4pgs.) by Siegel & Shuster	180.00	540.00	1260.00

NEW COMICS (New Adventure #12 on)
12/35 - No. 11, 12/36 (No. 1-6, paper cover) (No. 1-5, 84 pgs.)
National Periodical Publications

	Good	Fine	N-Mint
V1#1-Billy the Kid, Sagebrush 'n' Cactus, Jibby Jones, Needles, The Vikings, Sir Loin of Beef, Now-When I Was a Boy, & other 1-2 pg. strips; 2 pgs. Kelly art(1st)-(Gulliver's Travels); Sheldon Mayer-a(1st)	375.00	1125.00	2625.00
2-Federal Men by Siegel & Shuster begins (Also see The Comics Magazine #2); Sheldon Mayer, Kelly-a. (Rare)	200.00	600.00	1400.00
3-6: 3,4-Sheldon Mayer-a which continues in The Comics Magazine #1; 5-Kiefer-a	115.00	345.00	805.00
7-11L 11-Christmas-c	90.00	270.00	630.00

NOTE: #1-6 rarely occur in mint condition.

NEW DEFENDERS (See Defenders)

NEW DNAGENTS, THE (Formerly DNAgents)
Oct., 1985 - No. 17, Mar, 1987 (Mando paper)
Eclipse Comics

V2#1-Origin recap		.50	1.00
2-6		.40	.80
7-12: (95 cent-c). 9,10-Airboy app.		.50	1.00
13-17 ($1.25-c)		.60	1.20
3-D 1 (1/86)	.40	1.15	2.30
2-D 1 (1/86)-Limited ed. (100 copies)	.85	2.50	5.00

NEW FUN COMICS (More Fun #7 on)
Feb, 1935 - No. 6, Oct, 1935 (10x15'', No. 1-4,6-slick covers)
(No. 1-5, 36 pgs; 68 pgs. No. 6-on)
National Periodical Publications

	Good	Fine	V. Fine
V1#1 (1st DC comic); 1st app. Oswald The Rabbit. Jack Woods (cowboy) begins	860.00	2585.00	5600.00
2(3/35)-(Very Rare)	645.00	1940.00	4200.00
3-5(8/35): 5-Soft-c	290.00	870.00	1890.00
6(10/35)-1st Dr. Occult (Superman proto-type) by Siegel & Shuster (Leger & Reughts); last ''New Fun'' title. ''New Comics #1 begins in Dec. which is reason for title change to More Fun; Henri Duval (ends #9) by Siegel & Shuster begins; paper-c	355.00	1065.00	2310.00

NEW FUNNIES (The Funnies #1-64; Walter Lantz...#109 on; #259,260,272,273-New TV...; #261-271-TV Funnies)
No. 65, July, 1942 - No. 288, Mar-Apr, 1962
Dell Publishing Co.

	Good	Fine	N-Mint
65(#1)-Andy Panda in a world of real people, Raggedy Ann & Andy, Oswald the Rabbit (with Woody Woodpecker x-overs), Li'l Eight Ball & Peter Rabbit begin	87.00	261.00	260.00
66-70: 67-Billy & Bonnie Bee by Frank Thomas & Felix The Cat begin. 69-2pg. Kelly-a; The Brownies begin (not by Kelly)	17.00	51.00	120.00
71-75: 72-Kelly illos. 75-Brownies by Kelly?	11.00	32.00	75.00
76-Andy Panda (Carl Barks & Pabian-a); Woody Woodpecker x-over in Oswald ends	57.00	171.00	400.00
77,78: 78-Andy Panda in a world with real people ends	11.00	32.00	75.00
79-81	8.00	24.00	56.00
82-Brownies by Kelly begins; Homer Pigeon begins	9.50	28.50	65.00
83-85-Brownies by Kelly in ea. 83-X-mas-c. 85-Woody Woodpecker, 1pg. strip begins	9.50	28.50	65.00
86-90: 87-Woody Woodpecker stories begin	4.30	13.00	30.00
91-99	2.85	8.50	20.00

	Good	Fine	N-Mint
100 (6/45)	3.50	10.50	24.00
101-110	2.15	6.50	15.00
111-120: 119-X-mas-c	1.60	4.80	11.00
121-150: 143-X-mas-c	1.15	3.50	8.00
151-200: 155-X-mas-c. 168-X-mas-c, 182-Origin & 1st app. Knothead & Splinter. 191-X-mas-c	.85	2.50	6.00
201-240	.70	2.00	5.00
241-288: 270-Walter Lantz c-app. 281-1st story swipe/WDC&S #100	.60	1.80	4.00

NOTE: Early issues written by John Stanley.

NEW GODS, THE (New Gods #12 on)(See Adventure, First Issue Spec. & Super-Team Family)
2-3/71 - No. 11, 10-11/72; No. 12, 7/77 - No. 19, 7-8/78
National Periodical Publications/DC Comics

1-Intro/1st app. Orion	.70	2.00	4.00
2	.40	1.25	2.50
3-19: 4-Origin Manhunter-r. 5,7,8-Young Gods feature. 7-Origin Orion. 9-1st app. Bug	.60	1.20	

NOTE: #4-9(52 pgs.) contain Manhunter-r by Simon & Kirby from Adventure #73, 74, 75, 76, 77, 78 with covers in that order. Adkins i-12-14, 17-19. Kirby c/a-1-11p. Newton c-p12-14, 16-19. Starlin c-17. Staton c-19p.

NEW GODS, THE
5/84 - No. 6, 11/84 ($2.00; direct sale; Baxter paper)
DC Comics

1-New Kirby-c begin; r-/New Gods 1&2	.35	1.00	2.00
2-6: 6-Original art by Kirby	.35	1.00	2.00

NEW GUARDIANS, THE
Sept., 1988 - Present ($1.25, color)
DC Comics

1-Double size ($2.00)-Staton-c/a begins	.35	1.00	2.00
2-6		.60	1.25

NEW HEROIC (See Heroic)

NEW HUMANS, THE
Dec., 1987 - Present ($1.95, B&W)
Eternity Comics

1-8: 1-Origin	.30	.90	1.80

NEWLYWEDS
1907 - 1917 (cardboard covers)
Saalfield Publ. Co.

...& Their Baby' by McManus; Saaalfield, 1907, 13x10,'' 52pgs.			
daily strips in full color	26.00	78.00	182.00
...& Their Baby's Comic Pictures, The, by McManus, Saalfield, 1917, 14x10,'' 22pgs, oblong, cardboard-c, reprints 'Newlyweds' (Baby Snookums stips) mainly from 1916; blue cover; says for painting & crayoning, but some pages in color. (Scarce)	20.00	60.00	140.00

NEW MEN OF BATTLE, THE
1949 (nn) (Carboard covers)
Catechetical Guild

nn(V8#1-V8#6)-192pgs.; contains 6 issues of Topix rebound	2.00	6.00	14.00
nn(V8#7-V8#11)-160pgs.; contains 5 issues of Topix	2.00	6.00	14.00

NEW MUTANTS, THE (Also see Marvel Graphic Novel)
March, 1983 - Present
Marvel Comics Group

1	1.35	4.00	8.00
2,3	.70	2.00	4.00
4-10: 10-1st app. Magma	.60	1.75	3.50
11-20: 18-Intro. Warlock	.40	1.25	2.50
21-Double size; new Warlock origin	.50	1.50	3.00

	Good	Fine	N-Mint
THE NEW MUTANTS (continued)			
22-30: 23-25-Cloak & Dagger app.	.40	1.25	2.50
31-40	.35	1.00	2.00
41-49	.25	.75	1.50
50-Double size	.35	1.00	2.00
51-58 ($1.25)	.35	1.00	2.00
59-Fall of The Mutants begins, ends #61	.35	1.00	2.00
60-Double size	.25	.75	1.50
61-Fall of The Mutants ends	.25	.75	1.50
62-72: 68-Intro Spyder		.50	1.00
Annual 1 (1984)	.40	1.25	2.50
Annual 2 (10/86; $1.25)	.35	1.00	2.00
Annual 3(9/87, $1.25)	.25	.75	1.50
Annual 4('88, $1.75)	.50	1.50	3.00
Special 1-Special Edition ('85; 64 pgs.)-ties in with X-Men Alpha			
Flight mini-series; A. Adams/Austin-a	.85	2.50	5.00

NOTE: *Art Adams* c-38, 39. *Austin* c-57i. *Sienkiewicz* c/a-18-25. *Simonson* c-11p. *B. Smith* c-46. *W. Smith* c-43. *Williamson* a-7i.

NEW PEOPLE, THE (TV)
Jan, 1970 - No. 2, May, 1970
Dell Publishing Co.

1,2	1.15	3.50	8.00

NEW ROMANCES
No. 5, May, 1951 - No. 21, Apr?, 1954
Standard Comics

5	3.50	10.50	24.00
6-9: 6-Barbara Bel Geddes, Richard Basehart "Fourteen Hours";			
	1.70	5.00	12.00
10,14,16,17-Toth-a	4.00	12.00	28.00
11-Toth-a; Liz Taylor, Montgomery Clift photo-c			
	5.00	15.00	35.00
12,13,15,18-21	1.15	3.50	8.00

NOTE: *Celardo* a-9. *Moreira* a-6. *Tuska* a-7, 20. Photo c-6-16.

NEW TALENT SHOWCASE (Talent Showcase No. 16 on)
Jan, 1984 - No. 19, Oct, 1985 (Direct sales only)
DC Comics

1-10: Features new strips & artists		.35	.70
11-19 ($1.25): 18-Williamson c(i)		.35	.70

NEW TEEN TITANS, THE (See DC Comics Presents 26, Marvel and DC Present & Teen Titans; Tales of the Teen Titans #41 on)
November, 1980 - No. 40, March, 1984
DC Comics

1-Robin, Kid Flash, Wonder Girl, The Changeling, Starfire, The			
Raven, Cyborg begin; partial origin	2.50	7.50	15.00
2	1.35	4.00	8.00
3-Origin Starfire; Intro The Fearsome 5	1.00	3.00	6.00
4-Origin continues; J.L.A. app.	1.00	3.00	6.00
5-10: 6-Origin Raven. 7-Cyborg origin. 8-Origin Kid Flash retold.			
10-Origin Changeling retold	.70	2.00	4.00
11,12	.50	1.50	3.00
13-15: 13-Return of Madame Rouge & Capt. Zahl; Robotman revived.			
14-Return of Mento; origin Doom Patrol. 15-Death of Madame			
Rouge & Capt. Zahl; intro. new Brotherhood of Evil			
	.35	1.00	2.00
16-20: 16-1st app. Capt. Carrot (free 16 pg. preview). 18-Return of			
Starfire. 19-Hawkman teams-up	.25	.75	1.50
21-30: 21-Intro Night Force in free 16 pg. insert; intro Brother Blood.			
23-1st app. Vigilante (not in costume), & Blackfire. 24-Omega Men			
app. 25-Omega Men cameo. 26-1st Terra. 29-The New Brother-			
hood of Evil & Speedy app. 30-Terra joins the Titans			
	.35	1.00	2.00
31-40: 38-Origin Wonder Girl. 39-Kid Flash quits			
		.50	1.00
Annual 1(11/82)-Omega Men app.	.25	.75	1.50

	Good	Fine	N-Mint
Annual 2(9/83)-1st app. Vigilante in costume		.50	1.00
Annual 3(1984)-Death of Terra		.50	1.00
nn(11/83-Keebler Co. Giveaway)-In cooperation with "The Presi-			
dent's Drug Awareness Campaign."		.60	1.20
nn-(re-issue of above on Mando paper for direct sales market);			
America Soft Drink Ind. version; I.B.M. Corp. version			
		.50	1.00

NOTE: *Perez* a-1-4p, 6-40p, Annual 1p, 2p; c-1-12, 13-17p, 18-21, 22p, 23p, 24-37, 38,39(painted), 40, Annual 1, 2.

NEW TEEN TITANS, THE (The New Titans #50 on)
Aug, 1984 - No. 49, Nov, 1988 ($1.25-$1.75; deluxe format)
DC Comics

1-New storyline; Perez c/a	1.00	3.00	6.00
2,3	.60	1.75	3.50
4-10: 5-Death of Trigon. 7-9-Origin Lilith. 8-Intro Kole.			
10-Kole joins	.35	1.10	2.20
11-39: 13,14-Crisis x-over. 20-Original T. Titans return. (#37 on, $1.75).			
	.25	.80	1.60
40-49: 47-Origin all Titans	.25	.75	1.50
Annual 1 (9/85)-Intro. Vanguard	.35	1.10	2.20
Annual 2 (8/86; $2.50): Byrne c/a(p); origin Brother Blood; intro			
new Dr. Light	.50	1.50	3.00
Annual 3 (11/87)-Intro. Danny Chase	.35	1.10	2.30
Annual 4 ('88, $2.50)-Perez-c	.40	1.25	2.50

NOTE: *Orlando* c-33p. *Perez* c/a 1-6; c-20, 22, 23. *Perez* a-1-6; c-1-6, 19-23, 43. *Steacy* c-47.

NEW TERRYTOONS (TV)
6-8/60 - No. 8, 3-5/62; 10/62 - No. 54, 1/79
Dell Publishing Co./Gold Key

1('60-Dell)-Deputy Dawg, Dinky Duck & Hashimoto San begin			
	1.70	5.00	12.00
2-8('62)	1.00	3.00	7.00
1(30010-210)(10/62-G.Key, 84 pgs.)-Heckle & Jeckle begins			
	3.00	9.00	24.00
2(30010-301)-84 pgs.	2.50	7.50	20.00
3-10	.85	2.50	6.00
11-20	.60	1.75	3.50
21-30	.25	.75	1.50
31-54		.40	.80

NOTE: Reprints: #4-12, 38, 40, 47. (See March of Comics #393, 412, 435)

NEW TESTAMENT STORIES VISUALIZED
1946 - 1947
Standard Publishing Co.

"New Testament Heroes—Acts of Apostles Visualized, Book I"
"New Testament Heroes—Acts of Apostles Visualized, Book II"
"Parables Jesus Told"   Set 10.00   30.00   60.00
NOTE: *All three are contained in a cardboard case, illustrated on front and info about the set.*

NEW TITANS, THE (Formerly The New Teen Titans)
No. 50, Dec, 1988 - Present ($1.75, color)
DC Comics

50-54: Perez-c/a; 50-painted-c	.30	.85	1.75

NEW TV FUNNIES (See New Funnies)

NEW WAVE, THE
6/10/86 - No. 13, 3/87 (#1-8, bi-weekly, 20 pgs.; #9-13, monthly)
Eclipse Comics

1-Origin		.30	.60
2-8: 6-Origin Megabyte		.30	.60
9-13 ($1.50)	.25	.75	1.50
. . .Versus the Volunteers 3-D 1,2(4/87)	.40	1.25	2.50

NEW WORLD (See Comic Books, Series I)

NEW YORK GIANTS (See Thrilling True Story of the Baseball Giants)

New Romances #7, © STD

New Terrytoons #1 (1960), © DELL

The New Titans #50, © DC

The Next Nexus #1, © First Comics   Nickel Comics #6, © FAW   Nick Fury, Agent Of Shield #5, © MEG

NEW YORK STATE JOINT LEGISLATIVE COMMITTEE TO STUDY THE PUBLICATION OF COMICS, THE
1951, 1955
N.Y. State Legislative Document

This document was referenced by Wertham for **Seduction of the Innocent**. Contains numerous repros from comics showing violence, sadism, torture, and sex.
1955 version (196p, No. 37, 2/23/55)-Sold for $180 in 1986.

NEW YORK WORLD'S FAIR
1939, 1940 (100pgs.; cardboard covers) (DC's 4th & 5th annuals)
National Periodical Publications

	Good	Fine	N-Mint
1939-Scoop Scanlon, Superman (blonde haired Superman on-c), Sandman, Zatara, Slam Bradley, Ginger Snap by Bob Kane begin	265.00	795.00	1855.00
1940-Batman, Hourman, Johnny Thunderbolt app.	155.00	465.00	1085.00

NOTE: The 1939 edition was published at 25 cents. Since all other comics were 10 cents, it didn't sell. Remaining copies were repriced with 15 cents stickers placed over the 25 cents price. Four variations on the 15 cents stickers known. It was advertised in other DC comics at 25 cents. Everyone who sent a quarter through the mail for it received a free Superman #1 or#2 to make up the dime difference. The 1940 edition was priced at 15 cents.

NEXT MAN
Mar, 1985 - No. 5, Oct, 1985 ($1.50 cover; Baxter paper)
Comico

1	.50	1.50	3.00
2-5	.30	.90	1.80

NEXT NEXUS, THE
Jan, 1989 - No. 4, April, 1989 ($1.95, mini-series, color, Baxter)
First Comics

1-4: By Baron & Rude	.35	1.00	1.95

NEXUS (Also see First Comics Graphic Novel & The Next Nexus)
6/81 - No. 6, 3/84; No. 7, 4/85 - Present
(Direct sale only, 36 pgs.; V2/1('83)-printed on Baxter paper
Capital Comics/First Comics No. 7 on

1-B&W version; magazine size	6.00	18.00	36.00
1-B&W 1981 limited edition; 500 copies printed and signed; same as above except this version has a 2-pg. poster & a pencil sketch on paperboard by Rude	8.00	24.00	48.00
2-B&W, magazine size	2.65	8.00	16.00
3-B&W, magazine size; contains 33⅓ rpm record ($2.95 price)	1.10	3.30	6.60
V2#1-Color version	.70	2.00	4.00
2-8: 8-Nexus' origin begins	.50	1.50	3.00
9-49,51-53	.30	1.00	2.00
50 ($3.50, 52 pgs.)	.60	1.75	3.50

NOTE: **Bissette** c-29. **Rude** c-3(B&W), V2#1-22, 24-27, 33-36, 39-42, 45-48, 50; a-1-3, V2#1-7, 8p-16p, 18p-22p, 24p-27p, 33p-36p, 39p-42p, 45p-48p, 50. **Paul Smith** a-37, 38, 43, 44, 51-53p; c-37, 38, 43, 44, 51-53.

NICKEL COMICS
1938 (Pocket size - 7½x5½")(132 pgs.)
Dell Publishing Co.

1-"Bobby & Chip" by Otto Messmer, Felix the Cat artist. Contains some English reprints	22.00	65.00	154.00

NICKEL COMICS
May, 1940 - No. 8, Aug, 1940 (36 pgs.; Bi-Weekly; 5 cents)
Fawcett Publications

1-Origin/1st app. Bulletman	90.00	270.00	630.00
2	43.00	130.00	300.00
3	38.00	115.00	265.00
4-The Red Gaucho begins	32.00	95.00	225.00
5-7	27.00	81.00	190.00
8-World's Fair-c; Bulletman moved to Master Comics #7 in Oct.	27.00	81.00	190.00

NOTE: **Beck** c-5-8. **Jack Binder** c-1-4. Bondage c-5.

NICK FURY, AGENT OF SHIELD (See Shield & Marv. Spotlight #31)
6/68 - No. 15, 11/69; No. 16, 11/70 - No. 18, 3/71
Marvel Comics Group

	Good	Fine	N-Mint
1	2.00	6.00	12.00
2,3	1.35	4.00	8.00
4-Origin retold	1.15	3.50	7.00
5-Classic-c	1.35	4.00	8.00
6,7	1.00	3.00	6.00
8-11: 9-Hate Monger begins (ends #11). 11-Smith-c	.40	1.25	2.50
12-Smith c/a	.45	1.40	2.80
13-18: 16-18, all-r	.25	.75	1.50

NOTE: **Adkins** a-3i. **Craig** a-10i. **Sid Greene** a-12i. **Kirby** a-16-18r. **Springer** a-4, 6, 7, 8p, 9, 10p, 11; c-8, 9. **Steranko** a(p)-1-3, 5; c-1-7.

NICK FURY, AGENT OF SHIELD
Dec, 1983 - No. 2, Jan, 1984 ($2.00; 52 pgs.; Baxter paper)
Marvel Comics Group

1,2-Nick Fury-r; Steranko-c/a	.25	.75	1.50

NICK FURY VS. SHIELD
June, 1988 - No. 6, Dec., 1988 ($3.50, 52pgs, color, deluxe format)
Marvel Comics

1-Steranko-c	2.50	7.50	15.00
2	3.35	10.00	20.00
3	1.15	3.50	7.00
4-6	.70	2.00	4.00

NICK HALIDAY
May, 1956
Argo

1-Daily & Sunday strip-r by Petree	3.70	11.00	26.00

NIGHT AND THE ENEMY (Graphic Novel)
1988 (8½x11") (color; 80pgs.; $11.95)
Comico

1-Harlan Ellison scripts/Ken Steacy-c/a; r/Epic Ill. & new-a	2.00	6.00	11.95
1-2nd print	2.00	6.00	11.95
1-Limited edition ($39.95)	7.00	20.00	39.95

NIGHT BEFORE CHRISTMAS, THE (See March of Comics No. 152)

NIGHTCRAWLER
Nov, 1985 - No. 4, Feb, 1986 (mini-series; from X-Men)
Marvel Comics Group

1-Cockrum c/a	.40	1.25	2.50
2-4	.25	.75	1.50

NIGHT FORCE, THE
Aug, 1982, No. 14, Sept, 1983
DC Comics

1		.40	.80
2-14: 13-Origin The Baron. 14-Nudity panels		.30	.60

NOTE: **Colan** c/a-1-14p. **Giordano** c-1i, 2i, 4i, 5i, 7i, 12i.

NIGHTINGALE, THE
1948 (14 pgs., 7¼x10¼", ½B&W) (10 cents)
Henry H. Stansbury Once-A-Time Press, Inc.

(Very Rare)-Low distribution; distributed to Westchester County & Bronx, N.Y. only; used in **Seduction of the Innocent**, pf. 312,313 as the 1st and only "good" comic book ever published. Ill. by Doug kingman; 1,500 words of text, printed on high quality paper & no word balloons. Copyright registered 10/22/48, distributed week of 12/5/48. (By Hans Christian Andersen)   Estimated value $125

NIGHTMARE
Summer, 1952 - No. 2, Fall, 1952; No. 3,4 1953 (Painted-c)
Ziff-Davis (Approved Comics)/St. John No. 3,4

1-1pg. Kinstler-a; Tuska-a(2)	14.00	42.00	100.00
2-Kinstler-a-Poe's "Pit & the Pendulum"	11.50	34.00	80.00

NIGHTMARE (continued)	Good	Fine	N-Mint
3-Kinstler-a	9.50	28.50	65.00
4	7.00	21.00	50.00

NIGHTMARE (Formerly Weird Horrors #1-9) (Amazing Ghost Stories #14 on)
No. 10, Dec, 1953 - No. 13, Aug, 1954
St. John Publishing Co.

10-Reprints Ziff-Davis Weird Thrillers #2 with new Kubert-c plus 2 pgs. Kinstler, & Toth-a	18.00	54.00	125.00
11-Krigstein-a; Poe adapt., "Hop Frog"	12.00	36.00	84.00
12-Kubert bondage-c; adaptation of Poe's 'The Black Cat;' Cannibalism story	10.00	30.00	70.00
13-Reprints Z-D Weird Thrillers 3 with new cover; Powell-a(2), Tuska-a; Baker-c	6.00	18.00	42.00

NOTE: *Anderson* a-10. *Colan* a-10.

NIGHTMARE (Magazine)
Dec, 1970 - No. 23, Feb, 1975 (B&W) (68 pages)
Skywald Publishing Corp.

1-Everett-a	1.00	3.00	6.00
2-5: 4-Decapitation story	.70	2.00	4.00
6-Kaluta-a	.70	2.00	4.00
7,9,10	.50	1.50	3.00
8-Features E. C. movie "Tales From the Crypt;" reprints some E.C. comics panels	1.30	4.00	9.00
11-20: 12-Excessive gore, severed heads. 20-Severed head-c	.35	1.00	2.00
21-(1974 Summer Special)-Kaluta-a	.35	1.00	2.00
22-Tomb of Horror issue	.35	1.00	2.00
23-(1975 Winter Special)	.35	1.00	2.00
Annual 1(1972)-B.Jones-a	.50	1.50	3.00
Winter Special 1(1973)	.50	1.50	3.00
Yearbook-nn(1974)	.50	1.50	3.00

NOTE: *Adkins* a-5. *Boris* c-2, 3, 5 (#4 is not by Boris). *Byrne* a-20p. *Everett* a-4, 5. *Jones* a-6, 21; c-6. *Katz* a-5. *Reese* a-4, 5. *Wildey* a-5, 6, 21, '74 Yearbook. *Wrightson* a-9.

NIGHTMARE & CASPER (See Harvey Hits #71) (Casper & Nightmare #6 on)(See Casper The Friendly Ghost)
Aug, 1963 - No. 5, Aug, 1964 (25 cents)
Harvey Publications

1	5.35	16.00	32.00
2-5	2.35	7.00	14.00

NIGHTMARES (See Do You Believe in...)

NIGHTMARES
May, 1985 - No. 2, May, 1985 (Baxter paper)
Eclipse Comics

1,2	.30	.90	1.80

NIGHTMASK
Nov, 1986 - No. 12, Oct, 1987
Marvel Comics Group

1		.45	.90
2-12		.40	.80

NIGHT MUSIC (See Eclipse Graphic Album Series)
Dec, 1984 - No. 7, Feb, 1988 ($1.75, Baxter paper)
Eclipse Comics

1-3: 3-Russell's Jungle Book adapt.	.35	1.10	2.20
4,5-Pelleas And Melisande (dbl. titled)	.35	1.00	2.00
6-Salome' (dbl. titled)	.35	1.00	2.00
7-Red Dog #1	.35	1.00	2.00
Graphic Novel	1.35	4.00	8.00

NIGHT NURSE
Nov, 1972 - No. 4, May, 1973
Marvel Comics Group

	Good	Fine	N-Mint
1-4		.40	.80

NIGHT OF MYSTERY
1953 (no month) (One Shot)
Avon Periodicals

nn-1pg. Kinstler-a, Hollingsworth-c	12.00	36.00	84.00

NIGHT OF THE GRIZZLY, THE (See Movie Classics)

NIGHT RIDER
Oct, 1974 - No. 6, Aug, 1975
Marvel Comics Group

1-#1-6 reprints Ghost Rider #1-6		.50	1.00
2-6		.30	.60

NIGHTVEIL (See Femforce)
Nov, 1984 - No. 6, 1985 ($1.75, color)
Americomics/AC Comics

1	.50	1.50	3.00
2-6	.35	1.00	2.00
Special 1 ('88, $1.95)	.35	1.00	2.00

NIGHTWINGS (See DC Science Fic. Graphic Novel)

NIKKI, WILD DOG OF THE NORTH (See 4-Color 1226 & Movie Comics)

1984 (Magazine) (1994 #11 on)
June, 1978 - No. 10, Jan, 1980 ($1.50)
Warren Publishing Co.

1	.50	1.50	3.00
2-10	.30	.90	1.80

NOTE: *Alcala* a-1-3. 5i. *Corben* a-1-8; c-1,2. *Nino* a-1-10, 20(2). *Thorne* a-7-10. *Wood* a-1, 2, 5i.

1994 (Formerly 1984) (Magazine)
No. 11, Feb, 1980 - No. 29, Feb, 1983
Warren Publishing Co.

11-29: 27-The Warhawks return	.35	1.00	2.00

NOTE: *Corben* c-26. *Nino* a-11-21, 25, 26, 28; c-21. *Redondo* c-20. *Thorne* a-11-14, 17-21, 25, 26, 28, 29.

NINJA
Oct., 1986 - Present ($1.80/$1.95, B&W)
Eternity Comics

1-13	.25	.80	1.60
Ninja Special 1 ('87, $1.95)	.30	.95	1.90
Graphic Novel 1 (B&W, $6.95)	1.15	3.50	6.95
Graphic Novel 2 (B&W, $6.95)	1.15	3.50	6.95

NINJA ELITE
1987 - Present ($1.50/$1.95, B&W)
Adventure Publications

1	.50	1.50	3.00
2-7	.25	.75	1.50

NINJA HIGH SCHOOL
1987 - No. 3, 8/87; No. 4, 1/88 - Present ($1.50/$1.95, B&W)
Antarctic Press/Eternity Comics

1-8	.25	.80	1.60
Special 1-3 ($2.25; B&W)	.35	1.10	2.25
Graphic Novel 1 ('88, $6.95, B&W)	1.15	3.50	6.95

NIPPY'S POP
1917 (Sunday strip reprints-B&W) (10½x13½'')
The Saalfield Publishing Co.

32 pages	6.00	18.00	42.00

NOAH'S ARK
1973 (35-49 Cents)
Spire Christian Comics/Fleming H. Revell Co.

By Al Hartley		.40	.80

Nightmare #10, © STJ

Night Music #2, © Eclipse Comics

Ninja High School #1, © Antarctic Press

Normalman 3-D Annual #1, © Renegade Press

Northwest Mounties #1, © STJ

Nuts! #4, © PG

NOMAN (See Thunder Agents)
Nov, 1966 - No. 2, March, 1967 (68 pgs.)
Tower Comics

	Good	Fine	N-Mint
1-Wood/Williamson-c; Lightning begins; Dynamo cameo; Kane-a(p)			
	2.00	6.00	14.00
2-Wood-c only; Dynamo x-over; Whitney-a-#1,2			
	1.15	3.50	8.00

NONE BUT THE BRAVE (See Movie Classics)

NOODNIK COMICS (See Pinky the Egghead)
1953; No. 2, Feb, 1954 - No. 5, Aug, 1954
Comic Media/Mystery/Biltmore

3-D(1953-Comic Media)(#1)	20.00	60.00	140.00
2-5	2.15	6.50	15.00

NORMALMAN
Jan, 1984 - No. 12, Dec, 1985
Aardvark-Vanaheim/Renegade Press

1-5	.35	1.10	2.20
6-12	.35	1.20	2.40
Annual 1(3-D, '86, $2.25)	.40	1.25	2.50
The Novel (Publ. by Slave Labor Graphics)($12.95)-R/all issues			
	2.15	6.50	12.95

NORTH AVENUE IRREGULARS (See Walt Disney Showcase #49)

NORTH TO ALASKA (See 4-Color No. 1155)

NORTHWEST MOUNTIES (Also see Approved Comics)
Oct, 1948 - No. 4, July, 1949
Jubilee Publishers/St. John

1-Rose of the Yukon by Matt Baker; Walter Johnson-a; Lubbers-c			
	16.50	50.00	115.00
2-Baker-a; Lubbers-c. Ventrilo app.	12.00	36.00	84.00
3-Bondage-c, Baker-a; Sky Chief, K-9 app.	13.00	40.00	90.00
4-Baker-c, 2 pgs.; Blue Monk app.	13.00	40.00	90.00

NO SLEEP 'TIL DAWN (See 4-Color #831)

NOT BRAND ECHH (Brand Echh #1-4)
Aug, 1967 - No. 13, May, 1969 (No. 9-13: 68 pages)
Marvel Comics Group

1	1.35	4.00	8.00
2-4: 3-Origin Thor, Hulk & Capt. America; Monkees, Alfred E. Neuman cameo. 4-X-Men app.	.75	2.25	4.50
5-8: 5-Origin/intro. Forbush Man. 7-Origin Fantastical-4 & Stuporman. 8-Beatles cameo; X-Men satire	.75	2.25	4.50
9-13-All Giants. 9-Beatles cameo. 10-All-r; The Old Witch, Crypt Keeper & Vault Keeper cameos. 12,13-Beatles cameo, Avengers satire #12	.75	2.25	4.50

NOTE: Colan a-4p, 5p, 8p. Everett a-1i. Kirby a(p)-1,3,5-7,10; c-1. Severin a-1; c-3, 7, 8. Sutton a-4, 5i, 7i, 8; c-5. Archie satire-No. 9.

NO TIME FOR SERGEANTS (TV)
No. 914, July, 1958 - No. 3, Aug-Oct, 1965
Dell Publishing Co.

4-Color 914 (Movie)-Toth-a	6.00	18.00	42.00
1(2-4/65)-3 (TV): Photo-c	2.30	7.00	16.00

NOVA (The Man Called . . . No. 22-25)
Sept, 1976 - No. 25, May, 1979
Marvel Comics Group

1-Origin	.35	1.00	2.00
2-25		.50	1.00

NOTE: Austin c-21i, 23i. John Buscema a(p)-1, 2, 3p, 8p, 21; c-1p, 2, 15. Infantino a(p)-15-20, 22-25; c-17-20, 21p, 23p, 24p. Kirby c-4p, 5, 7. Nebres c-25i. Simonson a-23i.

NOW AGE ILLUSTRATED (See Pendulum Ill. Classics)

NUCLEUS (Also see Cerebus)
May, 1979 ($1.50, B&W, adult fanzine)

Heiro-Graphic Publications

	Good	Fine	N-Mint
1-Contains "Demonhorn" by Dave Sim, 1st app. of Cerebus The Aardvark, 4 pg. story	11.00	32.00	75.00

NUKLA
Oct-Dec, 1965 - No. 4, Sept, 1966
Dell Publishing Co.

1-Origin Nukla	1.15	3.50	8.00
2,3	.75	2.25	5.00
4-Ditko-a, c(p)	.85	2.50	6.00

NURSE BETSY CRANE (Formerly Teen Secret Diary)
Aug, 1961 - No. 27, Mar, 1964 (See Soap Opera Romances)
Charlton Comics

V2#12-27	.25	.75	1.50

NURSE HELEN GRANT (See The Romances of . . .)

NURSE LINDA LARK (See Linda Lark)

NURSERY RHYMES
1950 - No. 10, July-Aug, 1951 (Painted-c)
Ziff-Davis Publ. Co. (Approved Comics)

2	5.50	16.50	38.00
3-10: 10-Howie Post-a	3.50	10.50	24.00

NURSES, THE (TV)
April, 1963 - No. 3, Oct, 1963 (Photo-c: #1,2)
Gold Key

1	1.50	4.50	10.00
2,3	.85	2.50	6.00

NUTS! (Satire)
March, 1954 - No. 5, Nov, 1954
Premiere Comics Group

1-Hollingsworth-a	6.50	19.50	45.00
2,4,5: 5-Capt. Marvel parody	4.30	13.00	30.00
3-Drug "reefers" mentioned	5.00	15.00	35.00

NUTS (Magazine) (Satire)
Feb, 1958 - No. 2, April, 1958
Health Knowledge

1	2.85	8.50	20.00
2	2.00	6.00	14.00

NUTS & JOLTS (See Large Feat. Comic #22)

NUTSY SQUIRREL (Formerly Hollywood Funny Folks)
(Also see Comic Cavalcade)
No. 61, 9-10/54 - No. 69, 1-2/56; No. 70, 8-9/56 - No. 71, 10-11/56; No. 72, 11/57
National Periodical Publications

61-Mayer-a; Grossman-a in all	3.00	9.00	21.00
62-72: Mayer a-62,65,67-72	1.70	5.00	12.00

NUTTY COMICS (Funny animal)
Winter, 1946
Fawcett Publications

1-Capt. Kidd story; 1pg. Wolverton-a	6.50	19.50	45.00

NUTTY COMICS
1945 - No. 8, June-July, 1947
Home Comics (Harvey Publications)

nn-Helpful Hank, Bozo Bear & others	3.00	9.00	21.00
2-4	2.00	6.00	14.00
5-8: 5-Rags Rabbit begins (1st app.); infinity-c			
	1.50	4.50	10.00

NUTTY LIFE
No. 2, Summer, 1946
Fox Features Syndicate

NUTTY LIFE (continued)

	Good	Fine	N-Mint
2		3.50	10.50	24.00

NYOKA, THE JUNGLE GIRL (Formerly Jungle Girl; see Master Comics #50 & XMas Comics)
No. 2, Winter, 1945 - No. 77, June, 1953 (Movie serial)
Fawcett Publications

	Good	Fine	N-Mint
2	32.00	95.00	225.00
3	18.00	54.00	125.00
4,5	15.00	45.00	105.00
6-10	11.00	32.00	75.00
11,13,14,16-18-Krigstein-a	11.00	32.00	75.00
12,15,19,20	8.50	25.50	60.00
21-30	5.50	16.50	38.00
31-40	4.00	12.00	28.00
41-50	3.00	9.00	21.00
51-60	2.30	7.00	16.00
61-77	1.70	5.00	12.00

NOTE: Photo-c from movies 25,27,28,30-70. Bondage c-4, 5, 7, 8, 14, 24.

NYOKA, THE JUNGLE GIRL (Formerly Zoo Funnies; Space Adventures #23 on)
No. 14, Nov, 1955 - No. 22, Nov, 1957
Charlton Comics

14	2.85	8.50	20.00
15-22	2.00	6.00	14.00

OAKY DOAKS
July, 1942 (One Shot)
Eastern Color Printing Co.

1	13.00	40.00	90.00

OAKLAND PRESS FUNNYBOOK, THE
9/17/78 - 4/13/80 (16 pgs.) (Weekly)
Full color in comic book form; changes to tabloid size 4/20/80-on
The Oakland Press

Contains Tarzan by Manning, Marmaduke, Bugs Bunny, etc. (low distribution); 9/23/79 - 4/13/80 contain Buck Rogers by Gray Morrow & Jim Lawrence

	.30	.80	1.60

OBIE
1953 (6 cents)
Store Comics

1	.70	2.00	4.00

OBNOXIO THE CLOWN
April, 1983 (One Shot) (From Crazy Magazine)
Marvel Comics Group

1-Vs. the X-Men		.30	.60

OCCULT FILES OF DR. SPEKTOR, THE
4/73 - No. 24, 2/77; No. 25, 5/82 (Painted-c #1-24)
Gold Key/Whitman No. 25

1-1st app. Lakota; Baron Tibor begins	.70	2.00	4.00
2-5	.35	1.00	2.00
6-10	.25	.75	1.50
11-13: 11-1st app. Spektor as Werewolf		.50	1.00
14-Dr. Solar app.		.50	1.00
15-25: 25-Reprints		.50	1.00
9(Modern Comics reprint, 1977)		.15	.30

NOTE: Also see Dan Curtis, Golden Comics Digest 33, Gold Key Spotlight, Mystery Comics Digest 5, & Spine Tingling Tales.

ODELL'S ADVENTURES IN 3-D (See Adventures in . . .)

OFFICIAL CRISIS ON INFINITE EARTHS INDEX, THE
March, 1986
Independent Comics Group (Eclipse)

1	.50	1.50	3.00

OFFICIAL CRISIS ON INFINITE EARTHS CROSSOVER INDEX, THE
July, 1986
Independent Comics Group (Eclipse)

	Good	Fine	N-Mint
1	.50	1.50	3.00

OFFICIAL DOOM PATROL INDEX, THE
Feb, 1986 - No. 2, Mar, 1986 (2 part series)
Independent Comics Group (Eclipse)

1,2	.35	1.00	2.00

OFFICIAL HANDBOOK OF THE CONAN UNIVERSE
June, 1985 (One Shot)
Marvel Comics

1	.65		1.30

OFFICIAL HANDBOOK OF THE MARVEL UNIVERSE, THE
Jan, 1983 - No. 15, May, 1984
Marvel Comics Group

1-Lists Marvel heroes & villains (letter A)	1.00	3.00	6.00
2 (B-C)	.85	2.50	5.00
3-5: 3-(C-D). 4-(D-G). 5-(H-J)	.70	2.00	4.00
6-9: 6-(K-L). 7-(M). 8-(N-P). 9-(O-S)	.50	1.50	3.00
10-12: 10-(S). 11-(S-U). 12-(U-Z)	.40	1.25	2.50
13-15: 13,14-Book of the Dead. 15-Weaponry catalogue			
	.40	1.25	2.50

NOTE: Byrne c/a(p)-1-14; c-15p. Grell a-9. Layton a-2, 5, 7. Miller a-2, 3. Nebres a-3, 4, 8. Simonson a-11. Paul Smith a-1-3, 6, 7, 9, 10, 12. Starlin a-7. Steranko a-8p.

OFFICIAL HANDBOOK OF THE MARVEL UNIVERSE, THE
Dec, 1985 - Present ($1.50 cover; maxi-series)
Marvel Comics Group

1(V2/1)	.70	2.00	4.00
2-5	.50	1.50	3.00
6-10	.40	1.25	2.50
11-20	.35	1.00	2.00
Trade paperback Vol. 1-9	1.15	3.50	7.00

OFFICIAL HAWKMAN INDEX, THE
Nov, 1986 - No. 2, Dec, 1986 ($2.00)
Independent Comics Group

1,2	.35	1.00	2.00

OFFICIAL JUSTICE LEAGUE OF AMERICA INDEX, THE
April, 1986 - No. 8, Mar, 1987 ($2.00, Baxter)
Independent Comics Group (Eclipse)

1-8	.35	1.10	2.20

OFFICIAL LEGION OF SUPER-HEROES INDEX, THE
Dec, 1986 - Present ($2.00)
Independent Comics Group

1-5	.35	1.00	2.00

OFFICIAL MARVEL INDEX TO MARVEL TEAM-UP
Jan, 1986 - Present
Marvel Comics Group

1-6	.65		1.30

OFFICIAL MARVEL INDEX TO THE AMAZING SPIDER-MAN
Apr, 1985 - No. 9, Dec, 1985
Marvel Comics Group

1	.35	1.00	2.00
2-9	.25	.75	1.50

OFFICIAL MARVEL INDEX TO THE AVENGERS
June, 1987 - No. 8, Oct, 1988 ($2.95)
Marvel Comics Group

1-8	.50	1.50	3.00

OFFICIAL MARVEL INDEX TO THE FANTASTIC FOUR
Dec, 1985 - Present

Nyoka, The Jungle Girl #16, © FAW

Official Handbook Of The Marvel Univ. #7 (1983), © MEG

The Official Justice League Of America Index #1, © ICG

Official True Crime Cases #24, © MEG   *O.G. Whiz #4, © GK*   *The Omega Men Annual #1, © DC*

	Good	Fine	N-Mint
OFFICIAL MARVEL INDEX TO THE FANTASTIC FOUR (continued)			
Marvel Comics Group			
1-5		.65	1.30
OFFICIAL MARVEL INDEX TO THE X-MEN, THE			
Mar, 1987 - Present ($2.95)			
Marvel Comics Group			
1-8		.50	1.50	3.00
OFFICIAL SOUPY SALES COMIC (See Soupy Sales)			
OFFICIAL TEEN TITANS INDEX, THE			
Aug, 1985 - No. 5, 1986 ($1.50 cover)			
Independent Comics Group (Eclipse)			
1-5	.25	.75	1.50
OFFICIAL TRUE CRIME CASES (Formerly Sub-Mariner #23; All-True			
Crime Cases #26 on)			
No. 24, Fall, 1947 - No. 25, Winter, 1947-48			
Marvel Comics (OCI)			
24(#1)-Burgos-a	5.70	17.00	40.00
25-Kurtzman's "Hey Look"	4.65	14.00	32.00
OF SUCH IS THE KINGDOM			
1955 (36 pgs., 15-)			
George A. Pflaum			
nn-R-/1951 Treasure Chest	1.15	3.50	8.00
O.G. WHIZ (See Gold Key Spotlight #10)			
2/71 - No. 6, 5/72; No. 7, 5/78 - No. 11, 1/79 (No. 7-52 pgs.)			
Gold Key			
1,2-John Stanley scripts	5.00	15.00	35.00
3-6(1972)	2.00	6.00	14.00
7-11('78-'79)-Part-r: 9-Tubby app.	.60	1.75	3.50
OH, BROTHER! (Teen Comedy)			
Jan, 1953 - No. 5, Oct, 1953			
Stanhall Publ.			
1-By Bill Williams	2.00	6.00	14.00
2-5	1.15	3.50	8.00
OH SKIN-NAY!			
1913			
P.F. Volland & Co.			
nn-The Days Of Real Sport by Briggs	9.00	27.00	62.00
OH SUSANNA (See 4-Color #1105)			
OKAY COMICS			
July, 1940			
United Features Syndicate			
1-Captain & the Kids & Hawkshaw the Detective reprints			
	17.00	51.00	120.00
OK COMICS			
July, 1940 - No. 2, Oct, 1940			
United Features Syndicate			
1-Little Giant, Phantom Knight, Sunset Smith, & The Teller Twins			
begin	27.00	81.00	190.00
2 (Rare)-Origin Mister Mist	27.00	81.00	190.00
OKLAHOMA KID			
June, 1957 - No. 4, 1958			
Ajax/Farrell Publ.			
1	3.00	9.00	21.00
2-4	1.50	4.50	10.00
OKLAHOMAN, THE (See 4-Color #820)			
OLD GLORY COMICS			
1944 (Giveaway)			
Chesapeake & Ohio Railway			

	Good	Fine	N-Mint
Capt. Fearless reprint	2.35	7.00	16.00
OLD IRONSIDES (See 4-Color #874)			
OLD YELLER (See 4-Color #869, Movie Comics, and Walt Disney Showcase #25)			
OMAC (One Man Army, . . .Corps. #4 on)			
Sept-Oct, 1974 - No. 8, Nov-Dec, 1975			
National Periodical Publications			
1-Origin		.40	.80
2-8: 8-2pg. Adams ad		.25	.50
NOTE: *Kirby a-1-8p; c-1-7p.* **Kubert** *c-8. See Kamandi No. 59 & Cancelled Comic Cavalcade.*			
OMAHA THE CAT DANCER			
1987 - Present (B&W, adults)			
Steeldragon/Kitchen Sink #3 on			
1-Preview	2.00	6.00	12.00
1	1.35	4.00	8.00
1-2nd print	.35	1.00	2.00
2	.85	2.50	5.00
3-9	.35	1.00	2.00
O'MALLEY AND THE ALLEY CATS			
April, 1971 - No. 9, Jan, 1974 (Disney)			
Gold Key			
1	1.30	4.00	9.00
2-9	.70	2.00	5.00
OMEGA ELITE			
1987 ($1.25, color)			
Blackthorne Publishing			
1-Starlin-c		.60	1.25
OMEGA MEN, THE (See Green Lantern #141)			
Dec, 1982 - No. 38, May, 1986 ($1.00-$1.50; Baxter paper)			
DC Comics			
1	.25	.75	1.50
2-Origin Broot		.50	1.00
3-30: 7-Origin The Citadel. 26,27-Alan Moore scripts. 30-Intro			
new Primus		.50	1.00
31-38: 31-Crisis x-over. 34,35-Teen Titans x-over		.50	1.00
Annual 1(11/84, 52 pgs.), 2(11/85)	.25	.75	1.50
NOTE: **Giffen** *c/a-1-6p.* **Morrow** *a-24r.* **Nino** *a-16, 21; c-16, 21.*			
OMEGA THE UNKNOWN			
March, 1976 - No. 10, Oct, 1977			
Marvel Comics Group			
1		.40	.80
2-10: 2-Hulk app. 3-Electro app.		.30	.60
NOTE: **Kane** *c(p)-3, 5, 8, 9.* **Mooney** *a-1-3, 4p, 5, 6p, 7, 8i, 9, 10.*			
OMNI MEN			
1987 - No. 3, 1987? ($1.25, color)			
Blackthorne Publishing			
1-3		.60	1.25
ONE, THE			
July, 1985 - No. 6, Feb, 1986 (mini-series; adults only)			
Epic Comics (Marvel)			
1-Post nuclear holocaust super-hero	.25	.75	1.50
2-6: 2-Intro. The Other	.25	.75	1.50
ONE-ARM SWORDSMAN, THE			
1987 ($2.75, color)			
Lueng's Publ./Victory			
1-3	.45	1.40	2.75
ONE HUNDRED AND ONE DALMATIANS (See 4-Color #1183, Movie Comics, and Walt Disney Showcase #9,51)			

293

100 PAGES OF COMICS
1937 (Stiff covers; square binding)
Dell Publishing Co.

	Good	Fine	N-Mint
101(Found on back cover)-Alley Oop, Wash Tubbs, Capt. Easy, Og			
Son of Fire, Apple Mary, Tom Mix, Dan Dunn, Tailspin Tommy,			
Doctor Doom	50.00	150.00	350.00

100-PAGE SUPER SPECTACULAR (See DC...)

$1,000,000 DUCK (See Walt Disney Showcase #5)

ONE MILLION YEARS AGO (Tor #2 on)
September, 1953
St. John Publishing Co.

1-Origin; Kubert-c/a	15.00	45.00	105.00

ONE SHOT (See 4-Color...)

1001 HOURS OF FUN (See Large Feature Comic #13)

ON STAGE (See 4-Color #1336)

ON THE AIR
1947 (Giveaway) (paper cover)
NBC Network Comic

(Rare)	10.00	30.00	70.00

ON THE DOUBLE (See 4-Color #1232)

ON THE LINKS
December, 1926 (48 pages) (9x10'')
Associated Feature Service

Daily strip-r	7.00	21.00	50.00

ON THE ROAD WITH ANDRAE CROUCH
1973, 1977 (39 cents)
Spire Christian Comics (Fleming H. Revell)

nn		.50	1.00

ON THE SPOT (Pretty Boy Floyd...)
Fall, 1948
Fawcett Publications

nn-Bondage-c	12.00	36.00	84.00

OPERATION BIKINI (See Movie Classics)

OPERATION BUCHAREST (See The Crusaders)

OPERATION CROSSBOW (See Movie Classics)

OPERATION PERIL
Oct-Nov, 1950 - No. 16, Apr-May, 1953 (52 pgs.: #1-5)
American Comics Group (Michel Publ.)

1-Time Travelers, Danny Danger (by Leonard Starr) & Typhoon			
Tyler (by Ogden Whitney) begin	9.50	28.50	65.00
2	5.70	17.00	40.00
3-5: 3-Horror story. 5-Sci/fi story	5.00	15.00	35.00
6-12-Last Time Travelers	4.65	14.00	32.00
13-16: All war format	1.70	5.00	12.00

NOTE: *Starr a-2. Whitney a-1,2,6-10,12; c-1,3,5,8,9.*

ORAL ROBERTS' TRUE STORIES (Junior Partners #120 on)
1956 (no month) - No. 119, 7/59 (15 cents)(No #102: 25 cents)
TelePix Publ. (Oral Roberts' Evangelistic Assoc./Healing Waters)

V1No.1(1956)-(Not code approved)-''The Miracle Touch''			
	6.00	18.00	42.00
102-(only issue approved by code)(10/56)	3.00	9.00	21.00
103-119: 115-(114 on inside)	2.00	6.00	14.00

NOTE: *Also see Happiness & Healing For You.*

ORANGE BIRD, THE
No date (1980) (36 pgs.; in color; slick cover)
Walt Disney Educational Media Co.

Included with educational kit on foods		.30	.60

ORIENTAL HEROES
Aug., 1988 - Present ($1.50, color)
Jademan Comics

	Good	Fine	N-Mint
1-4	.25	.75	1.50

ORIGINAL ASTRO BOY, THE (See Astro Boy)
Sept, 1987 - Present ($1.50 - $1.75, color)
Now Comics

1-Ken Steacy painted-c/a begin	.70	2.00	4.00
2	.45	1.40	2.80
3	.40	1.20	2.40
4-10	.35	1.00	2.00
11-17	.30	.90	1.80

ORIGINAL BLACK CAT, THE
Oct. 6, 1988 ($2.00, color)
Recollections

1-Elias-r; bondage-c	.35	1.00	2.00

ORIGINAL E-MAN AND MICHAEL MAUSER, THE
Oct, 1985 - No. 7, April, 1986 ($1.75 cover; Baxter paper)
First Comics

1-Has r-/Charlton's E-Man & Vengeance Squad			
	.35	1.00	2.00
2-6	.30	.90	1.80
7 ($2.00; 44 pgs.)-Staton-a	.35	1.00	2.00

ORIGINAL SHIELD, THE
April, 1984 - No. 4, Oct, 1984
Archie Enterprises, Inc.

1-Origin Shield		.35	.70
2-4		.35	.70

ORIGINAL SWAMP THING SAGA, THE (See DC Spec. Series #2,14,17,20)

OSCAR COMICS (Formerly Funny Tunes; Awful...#11 & 12)
(Also see Cindy Comics)
No. 24, Spring, 1947 - No. 10, Apr, 1949; No. 13, Oct, 1949
Marvel Comics

24(1947)	3.70	11.00	26.00
25(Sum, '47)-Wolverton-a plus Kurtzman's ''Hey Look''			
	6.00	18.00	42.00
3-9,13: 8-Margie app.	2.65	8.00	18.00
10-Kurtzman's ''Hey Look''	3.50	10.50	24.00

OSWALD THE RABBIT (Also see New Fun Comics #1)
No. 21, 1943 - No. 1268, 12-2/61-62 (Walter Lantz)
Dell Publishing Co.

4-Color 21(1943)	20.00	60.00	140.00
4-Color 39(1943)	14.00	42.00	100.00
4-Color 67(1944)	10.00	30.00	70.00
4-Color 102(1946)-Kelly-a, 1 pg.	9.50	28.50	65.00
4-Color 143,183	3.70	11.00	26.00
4-Color 225,273	2.30	7.00	16.00
4-Color 315,388	1.50	4.50	10.00
4-Color 458,507,549,593	1.00	3.00	7.00
4-Color 623,697,792,894,979,1268	.85	2.50	6.00

OSWALD THE RABBIT (See March of Comics #7, 38, 53, 67, 81, 95, 111, 126, 141, 156, 171, 186, The Funnies, New Funnies & Super Book #8, 20)

OUR ARMY AT WAR (Sgt. Rock #302 on)
Aug., 1952 - No. 301, Feb, 1977
National Periodical Publications

1	32.00	95.00	225.00
2	15.00	45.00	105.00
3	14.00	42.00	100.00
4-Krigstein-a	14.00	42.00	100.00
5-7	7.00	21.00	50.00
8-11,14-Krigstein-a	8.00	24.00	56.00

On The Spot, © FAW

The Original Astro Boy #2, © NBC

Oscar Comics #8, © MEG

Our Army At War #13, © DC

Our Flag Comics #2, © ACE

Our Gang Comics #4, © M.G.M.

OUR ARMY AT WAR (continued)	Good	Fine	N-Mint
12,15-20	5.70	17.00	40.00
13-Krigstein c/a; flag-c	8.00	24.00	56.00
21-31: Last precode (2/55)	4.00	12.00	28.00
32-40	3.00	9.00	21.00
41-60	2.50	7.50	18.00
61-70	1.70	5.00	12.00
71-80	1.30	4.00	9.00
81-1st Sgt. Rock app. by Andru & Esposito in Easy Co. story			
	15.00	45.00	105.00
82-Sgt. Rock cameo in Easy Co. story (6 panels)			
	5.70	17.00	40.00
83-1st Kubert Sgt. Rock	8.00	24.00	55.00
84,86-90	3.50	10.50	24.00
85-1st app. & origin Ice Cream Soldier	4.30	13.00	30.00
91-All Sgt. Rock issue	4.65	14.00	32.00
92-100: 92-1st app. Bulldozer. 95-1st app. Zack 1.35		4.00	9.00
101-120: 101-1st app. Buster. 111-1st app. Wee Willie & Sunny.			
113-1st app. Jackie Johnson. 118-Sunny dies. 120-1st app.			
Wildman	1.00	3.00	6.00
121-127,129-150: 126-1st app. Canary. 139-1st app. Little Sure Shot			
	.85	2.50	5.00
128-Training & origin Sgt. Rock	1.15	3.50	7.00
151-Intro. Enemy Ace by Kubert	1.15	3.50	7.00
152-157,159-163,165-170: 153,155-Enemy Ace stories. 157-Two pg. pin-			
up. 162,163-Viking Prince x-over in Sgt. Rock			
	.75	2.25	4.50
158-1st app. & origin Iron Major(1965), formerly Iron Captain			
	.90	2.75	5.50
164-Giant G-19	.90	2.75	5.50
171-176,178-181	.35	1.00	2.00
177-(80 pg. Giant G-32)	.40	1.25	2.50
182,183,186-Adams-a; 186-Origin retold	.70	2.00	4.00
184,185,187-189,191-199: 184-Wee Willie dies. 189-Intro. The Teen-			
age Underground Fighters of Unit 3	.25	.75	1.50
190-(80 pg. Giant G-44)	.35	1.00	2.00
200-12 pg. Rock story told in verse; Evans-a	.25	.75	1.50
201-Krigstein-r/No. 14	.25	.75	1.50
202,206-215		.50	1.00
203-(80 pg. Giant G-56)-All-r, no Sgt. Rock	.25	.75	1.50
204,205-All-r, no Sgt. Rock		.50	1.00
216,229-(80 pg. Giants G-68 and G-80)	.25	.75	1.50
217-228,230-239,241		.50	1.00
240-Adams-a		.60	1.20
242-(50 cent ish. DC-9)-Kubert-c		.50	1.00
243-301: 249-Wood-a		.50	1.00

NOTE: **Alcala** a-251. **Drucker** a-27, 67, 68, 79, 82, 83, 96, 164, 177, 203, 212, 243r, 244, 269r, 275r, 280r. **Evans** a-165-175, 200, 266, 269, 270, 274, 276, 278, 280. **Glanzman** a-218, 220, 222, 223, 225, 227, 230-32, 238, 240, 241, 244, 247, 248, 256-59, 261, 265-67, 271, 282, 283, 298. **Grell** a-287. **Heath** a-50, & most 176-271. **Kubert** a-38,59, 67, 68 & most issues from 83-165. **Maurer** a-233, 237, 239, 240, 280, 284, 288, 290, 291, 295. **Severin** a-252, 265, 267, 269r, 272. **Toth** a-235, 241, 254. **Wildey** a-283-85, 287p.

OUR FIGHTING FORCES
Oct-Nov, 1954 - No. 181, Sept-Oct, 1978
National Periodical Publications/DC Comics

1-Grandenetti c/a	24.00	72.00	168.00
2	11.50	34.00	80.00
3-Kubert-c; last precode (3/55)	9.50	28.50	65.00
4,5	7.00	21.00	50.00
6-9	5.70	17.00	40.00
10-Wood-a	8.00	24.00	56.00
11-20	3.50	10.50	24.00
21-30	2.65	8.00	18.00
31-40	2.00	6.00	14.00
41-44: 41-Unknown Soldier tryout	1.50	4.50	10.00
45-Gunner & Sarge begin (ends #94)	5.15	15.50	36.00

	Good	Fine	N-Mint
46-50	1.00	3.00	7.00
51-64: 64-Last 10 cent issue	.85	2.50	5.00
65-90	.60	1.75	3.50
91-100: 95-Devil-Dog begins, ends 98. 99-Capt. Hunter begins,			
ends #106	.40	1.25	2.50
101-122: 106-Hunters Hellcats begin. 116-Mlle. Marie app. 121-			
Intro. Heller	.25	.75	1.50
123-Losers (Capt. Storm, Gunner/Sarge, Johnny Cloud) begin			
	.25	.75	1.50
124-181: 134,146-Toth-a	.25	.75	1.50

NOTE: **Adams** c-147. **Drucker** a-28, 37, 39, 42-44, 49, 53, 133r. **Evans** a-149, 164-74, 177-81. **Glanzman** a-125-28, 132, 134, 138-41, 143, 144. **Heath** a-2, 16, 18, 28, 41, 44, 49, 114, 135r-138r. **Kirby** a-151-162p; c-152-159. **Kubert** c/a in many issues. **Maurer** a-135. **Redondo** a-166. **Severin** a-123-30, 131, 132-50.

OUR FIGHTING MEN IN ACTION (See Men In Action)

OUR FLAG COMICS
Aug, 1941 - No. 5, April, 1942
Ace Magazines

1-Captain Victory, The Unknown Soldier & The Three Cheers begin			
	90.00	270.00	630.00
2-Origin The Flag	45.00	135.00	315.00
3-5: 5-Intro & 1st app. Mr. Risk	37.00	110.00	260.00

NOTE: **Anderson** a-1, 4. **Mooney** a-1; c-2.

OUR GANG COMICS (With Tom & Jerry #39-59; becomes Tom & Jerry #60 on; based on film characters)
Sept-Oct, 1942 - No. 59, June, 1949
Dell Publishing Co.

1-Our Gang & Barney Bear by Kelly, Tom & Jerry, Pete Smith, Flip			
& Dip, The Milky Way begin	60.00	180.00	420.00
2	27.00	81.00	190.00
3-5: 3-Benny Burro begins	18.00	54.00	125.00
6-Bumbazine & Albert only app. by Kelly	31.00	92.00	220.00
7-No Kelly story	14.00	42.00	100.00
8-Benny Burro begins by Barks	31.00	92.00	215.00
9-Barks-a(2): Benny Burro & Happy Hound; no Kelly story			
	25.00	75.00	175.00
10-Benny Burro by Barks	20.00	60.00	140.00
11-1st Barney Bear & Benny Burro by Barks; Happy Hound by Barks			
	20.00	60.00	140.00
12-20	12.00	36.00	84.00
21-30	9.00	27.00	63.00
31-36-Last Barks issue	6.50	19.50	45.00
37-40	2.65	8.00	18.00
41-50	2.00	6.00	14.00
51-57	1.75	5.25	12.00
58,59-No Kelly art or Our Gang story	1.50	4.50	12.00

NOTE: **Barks** art in part only. **Barks** did not write Barney Bear stories #30-34. (See March of Comics #3,26). Early issues have photo back-c.

OUR LADY OF FATIMA
3/11/55 (15 cents) (36 pages)
Catechetical Guild Educational Society

395	3.00	9.00	21.00

OUR LOVE (Romantic Affairs #3)
Sept, 1949 - No. 2, Jan, 1950
Marvel Comics (SPC)

1	3.50	10.50	24.00
2-Photo-c	1.70	5.00	12.00

OUR LOVE STORY
Oct, 1969 - No. 38, Feb, 1976
Marvel Comics Group

1	.55	1.65	4.00
2-4,6-13: 9-J. Buscema-a	.35	1.00	2.00

OUR LOVE STORY (continued)	Good	Fine	N-Mint
5-Steranko-a	1.30	4.00	9.00
14-New story by Gary Fredrich & Tarpe' Mills	.55	1.65	4.00
15-38		.40	.80

OUR MISS BROOKS (See 4-Color #751)

OUR SECRET (Formerly My Secret)
No. 4, Dec, 1949 - No. 8, Jun, 1950
Superior Comics Ltd.

	Good	Fine	N-Mint
4-Kamen-a; spanking scene	4.00	12.00	28.00
5,6,8	2.65	8.00	18.00
7-Contains 9 pg. story intended for unpublished Ellery Queen #5			
	3.00	9.00	21.00

OUTBURSTS OF EVERETT TRUE
1921 (32 pages) (B&W)
Saalfield Publ. Co.

	Good	Fine	N-Mint
1907 (2-panel strips reprint)	8.00	24.00	56.00

OUTCASTS
Oct, 1987 - No. 12, Sept, 1988 ($1.75, mini-series, color)
DC Comics

	Good	Fine	N-Mint
1	.35	1.00	2.00
2-12	.30	.90	1.80

OUTER LIMITS, THE (TV)
Jan-Mar, 1964 - No. 18, Oct, 1969 (All painted-c)
Dell Publishing Co.

	Good	Fine	N-Mint
1	2.65	8.00	18.00
2	1.30	4.00	9.00
3-10	.85	2.50	6.00
11-18: 17 reprints #1; 18-r-#2	.55	1.65	4.00

OUTER SPACE (Formerly This Mag. Is Haunted, 2nd Series)
May, 1958 - No. 25, Dec, 1959; Nov, 1968
Charlton Comics

	Good	Fine	N-Mint
17-Williamson/Wood style art; not by them (Sid Check?)			
	4.00	12.00	28.00
18-20-Ditko-a	5.70	17.00	40.00
21-25: 21-Ditko-c	2.85	8.50	20.00
V2#1(11/68)-Ditko-a, Boyette-c	1.00	3.00	7.00

OUTLAW (See Return of the...)

OUTLAW FIGHTERS
Aug, 1954 - No. 5, April, 1955
Atlas Comics (IPC)

	Good	Fine	N-Mint
1-Tuska-a	4.00	12.00	28.00
2-5: 5-Heath-c/a, 7pgs.	2.15	6.50	15.00
NOTE: *Heath a-5; c-5. Maneely c-2. Pakula a-2. Reinman a-2. Tuska a-1, 2.*

OUTLAW KID, THE (1st Series; see Wild Western)
Sept, 1954 - No. 19, Sept, 1957
Atlas Comics (CCC No. 1-11/EPI No. 12-29)

	Good	Fine	N-Mint
1-Origin; The Outlaw Kid & his horse Thunder begin; Black Rider app.	7.00	21.00	50.00
2-Black Rider app.	3.60	11.00	25.00
3-Woodbridge/Williamson-a	2.65	8.00	18.00
4-7,9	2.00	6.00	14.00
8-Williamson/Woodbridge-a, 4 pgs.	4.00	12.00	28.00
10-Williamson-a	4.00	12.00	28.00
11-17,19	1.70	5.00	12.00
18-Williamson-a	3.70	11.00	26.00
NOTE: *Berg a-4, 7, 13. Maneely c-1-3, 5-8, 11, 12, 18. Pakula a-3. Severin c-10. Shores a-1. Wildey a-1(3), 2-8, 10-18; c-4.*

OUTLAW KID, THE (2nd Series)
Aug, 1970 - No. 30, Oct, 1975
Marvel Comics Group

1,2-Reprints; Wildey-a		.60	1.20

	Good	Fine	N-Mint
3,9-Williamson-a(r)		.50	1.00
4-8		.40	.80
10-Origin; new material begins, ends #16		.25	.50
11-30: 27-Origin r-/No. 10		.25	.50
NOTE: *Berg a-7. Gil Kane c-10, 11, 15, 28. Roussos a-10i, 27i(r). Severin c-1. Wildey a-1r, 3r, 6r, 7r, 9, 19, 21, 22, 26. Williamson a-28r. Woodbridge a(p)-9r.*

OUTLAWS
Feb-Mar, 1948 - No. 9, June-July, 1949
D. S. Publishing Co.

	Good	Fine	N-Mint
1	11.00	32.00	75.00
2-Ingels-a	11.00	32.00	75.00
3,5,6: 3-Not Frazetta	4.30	13.00	30.00
4-Orlando-a	5.70	17.00	40.00
7,8-Ingels-a in each	8.00	24.00	56.00
9-(Scarce)-Frazetta-a, 7 pgs.	27.00	81.00	190.00
NOTE: *Another No. 3 was printed in Canada with Frazetta art "Prairie Jinx", 7 pgs. McWilliams a-6.*

OUTLAWS, THE (Formerly Western Crime Cases?)
No. 10, May, 1952 - No. 13, Sept, 1953; No. 14, April, 1954
Star Publishing Co.

	Good	Fine	N-Mint
10-L. B. Cole-c	3.50	10.50	24.00
11-14-L. B. Cole-c. 14-Kamen, Feldstein-a	2.35	7.00	16.00

OUTLAWS OF THE WEST (Formerly Cody of the Pony Express #10)
No. 11, 7/57 - No. 81, 5/70; No. 82, 7/79 - No. 88, 4/80
Charlton Comics

	Good	Fine	N-Mint
11	3.00	9.00	21.00
12,13,15-17,19,20	1.50	4.50	10.00
14-(68 pgs., 2/58)	1.70	5.00	12.00
18-Ditko-a	4.00	12.00	28.00
21-30	.75	2.25	5.00
31-50	.45	1.35	3.00
51-70: 54-Kid Montana app. 64-Captain Doom begins (1st app.)		.50	1.00
71-81: 73-Origin & 1st app. The Sharp Shooter, last app. #74. 75-Last Capt. Doom. 80,81-Ditko-a		.40	.80
82-88		.30	.60
64,79(Modern Comics-r, 1977, '78)		.15	.30

OUTLAWS OF THE WILD WEST
1952 (132 pages) (25 cents)
Avon Periodicals

	Good	Fine	N-Mint
1-Wood back-c; Kubert-a (3 Jesse James-r)	15.00	45.00	105.00

OUT OF SANTA'S BAG (March of Comics #10)

OUT OF THE NIGHT (The Hooded Horseman #18 on)
Feb-Mar, 1952 - No. 17, Oct-Nov, 1954
American Comics Group (Creston/Scope)

	Good	Fine	N-Mint
1-Williamson/LeDoux-a, 9 pgs	19.00	57.00	132.00
2-Williamson-a, 5 pgs.	15.00	45.00	105.00
3,5-10: 9-Sci/Fic sty	5.00	15.00	35.00
4-Williamson-a, 7 pgs.	15.00	45.00	105.00
11,12,14-16	3.50	10.50	24.00
13-Nostrand-a	4.35	13.00	30.00
17-E.C. Wood swipe; lingerie panels	4.00	12.00	28.00
NOTE: *Landau a-14, 16, 17. Shelly a-12.*

OUT OF THE PAST A CLUE TO THE FUTURE
1946? (16 pages) (paper cover)
E. C. Comics (Public Affairs Comm.)

	Good	Fine	N-Mint
Based on public affairs pamphlet-"What Foreign Trade Means to You"	11.50	34.00	80.00

OUT OF THE SHADOWS
No. 5, July, 1952 - No. 14, Aug, 1954
Standard Comics/Visual Editions

The Outer Limits #1, © United Artists   *Outlaws Of The West #14, © CC*   *Out Of The Night #4, © ACG*

Out Of the Shadows #10, © STD

Pacific Presents #1, © Pacific Comics

Pancho Villa, © AVON

OUT OF THE SHADOWS (continued)	Good	Fine	N-Mint
5-Toth-p; Moreira, Tuska-a	8.50	25.50	60.00
6-Toth/Celardo-a	7.00	21.00	50.00
7-Jack Katz-a(2)	4.65	14.00	32.00
8,10	3.50	10.50	24.00
9-Crandall-a(2)	5.00	15.00	35.00
11-Toth-a, 2 pgs.	4.00	12.00	28.00
12-Toth/Peppe-a(2)	8.00	24.00	56.00
13-Cannabalism story	5.00	15.00	35.00
14-Toth-a	5.00	15.00	35.00

NOTE: *Katz a-6(2), 7(2), 11, 12. Sekowsky a-10, 13.*

OUT OF THIS WORLD
June, 1950 (One Shot)
Avon Periodicals

1-Kubert-a(2) (one reprint/Eerie #1-'47) plus Crom the Barbarian by Giunta (origin); Fawcette-c	35.00	105.00	245.00

OUT OF THIS WORLD
Aug, 1956 - No. 16, Dec, 1959
Charlton Comics

1	5.70	17.00	40.00
2	2.65	8.00	18.00
3-6-Ditko-a(4) each	9.50	28.50	65.00
7-(68 pgs., 2/58; 15 cents)-Ditko-c/a(4)	9.50	28.50	65.00
8-(68 pgs., 5/58)-Ditko-a(2)	7.00	21.00	50.00
9-12,16-Ditko-a	5.70	17.00	40.00
13-15	1.50	4.50	10.00

NOTE: *Ditko c-3-7,11,12,16. Reinman a-10.*

OUT OUR WAY WITH WORRY WART (See 4-Color No. 680)

OUTPOSTS
June, 1987 - Present? ($1.25, color)
Blackthorne Publishing

1-4		.60	1.20

OUTSIDERS, THE (Also see Batman & the...)
Nov, 1985 - No. 28, Feb, 1988
DC Comics

1	.30	.90	1.80
2-28: 21-Intro. Strike Force Kobra. 22-E.C. parody; Orlando-a. 25-Atomic Knight app.	.25	.75	1.50
Annual 1 (12/86; $2.50)	.40	1.25	2.50
Special 1 (7/87, $1.50)	.25	.75	1.50

OUTSTANDING AMERICAN WAR HEROES
1944 (16 pgs.) (paper cover)
The Parents' Institute

nn-Reprints from True Comics	2.30	7.00	16.00

OVERSEAS COMICS (Also see G.I. & Jeep Comics)
1944 (7¼x10¼''; 16 pgs. in color)
Giveaway (Distributed to U.S. armed forces)

23-65-Bringing Up Father, Popeye, Joe Palooka, Dick Tracy, Superman, Gasoline Alley, Buz Sawyer, Li'l Abner, Blondie, Terry & the Pirates, Out Our Way	3.00	9.00	21.00

OWL, THE
April, 1967; No. 2, April, 1968
Gold Key

1,2-Written by Jerry Siegel	1.00	3.00	7.00

OXYDOL-DREFT
1950 (Set of 6 pocket-size giveaways; distributed through the mail as a set) (Scarce)
Oxydol-Dreft

1-Li'l Abner, 2-Daisy Mae, 3-Shmoo	7.00	21.00	50.00
4-John Wayne; Williamson/Frazetta-c from John Wayne #3	9.00	28.00	62.00

	Good	Fine	N-Mint
5-Archie	6.00	18.00	42.00
6-Terrytoons Mighty Mouse	4.00	12.00	28.00

NOTE: *Set is worth more with original envelope.*

OZ (See MGM's Marvelous..., Marvel Treasury... & First Comics Graphic Novel)

OZARK IKE
Feb, 1948; Nov, 1948 - No. 24, Dec, 1951; No. 25, Sept, 1952
Dell Publishing Co./Standard Comics

4-Color 180(1948-Dell)	5.75	17.25	40.00
B11, B12, 13-15	4.35	13.00	30.00
16-25	3.50	10.50	24.00

OZ-WONDERLAND WARS, THE
Jan, 1986 - No. 3, March, 1986 (mini-series)
DC Comics

1-3	.35	1.00	2.00

OZZIE & BABS (TV Teens #14 on)
1947 - No. 13, Fall, 1949
Fawcett Publications

1-Teen-age	4.00	12.00	28.00
2	2.00	6.00	14.00
3-13	1.50	4.50	10.00

OZZIE & HARRIET (See The Adventures of...)

PACIFIC COMICS GRAPHIC NOVEL
Sept, 1984
Pacific Comics

1-The Seven Samuroid; Brunner-a	1.00	3.00	6.00

PACIFIC PRESENTS
10/82 - No. 2, 4/83; No. 3, 3/84 - No. 4, 6/84
Pacific Comics

1-The Rocketeer app.; Stevens-c/a	.70	2.00	4.00
2-The Rocketeer app.; nudity; Stevens-c/a	.50	1.50	3.00
3,4: 3-1st Vanity	.35	1.00	2.00

NOTE: *Conrad a-3, 4; c-3. Ditko a-1-3. Stevens c/a-1, 2.*

PADRE OF THE POOR
nd (Giveaway) (16 pgs.; paper cover)
Catechetical Guild

	2.35	7.00	14.00

PAGEANT OF COMICS (See Jane Arden & Mopsy)
Sept, 1947 - No. 2, Oct, 1947
Archer St. John

1-Mopsy strip-r	5.00	15.00	35.00
2-Jane Arden strip-r	5.00	15.00	35.00

PANCHO VILLA
1950
Avon Periodicals

nn-Kinstler-c	12.00	36.00	84.00

PANDA KHAN (Also see Chronicles Of...)
No. 3, 1988 - No. 4? ($2.00, B&W)
Abacus Press

3,4	.35	1.00	2.00

PANHANDLE PETE AND JENNIFER (TV)
July, 1951 - No. 3, Nov, 1951
J. Charles Laue Publishing Co.

1	3.50	10.50	24.00
2,3	2.30	7.00	16.00

PANIC (Companion to Mad)
Feb-Mar, 1954 - No. 12, Dec-Jan, 1955-56
E. C. Comics (Tiny Tot Comics)

1-Used in Senate Investigation hearings; Elder draws entire E. C.

PANIC (continued)	Good	Fine	N-Mint
staff	7.00	21.00	50.00
2	5.50	16.50	38.00
3-Senate Subcommittee parody; Davis draws Gaines, Feldstein & Kelly, 1 pg.; Old King Cole smokes marijuana			
	3.70	11.00	26.00
4-Infinity-c	3.70	11.00	26.00
5-11	3.50	10.50	24.00
12 (Low distribution; many thousands were destroyed)			
	4.60	14.00	32.00

NOTE: *Davis a-1-12; c-12. Elder a-1-12. Feldstein c-1-3,5. Kamen a-1. Orlando a-1-9. Wolverton c-4, panel-3. Wood a-2-9, 11, 12.*

PANIC (Magazine) (Satire)
7/58 - No. 6, 7/59; V2No.10, 12/65 - V2No.12, 1966
Panic Publications

1	2.00	6.00	14.00
2-6	1.15	3.50	8.00
V2#10-12: Reprints earlier issues	.70	2.00	4.00

NOTE: *Davis a-3(2 pgs.), 4, 5, 10; c-10. Elder a-5. Powell a-V2#10. Torres a-1-5.*

PARADAX (Also see Strange Days)
1986 (One shot)
Eclipse Comics

1	.35	1.00	2.00

PARADAX
April, 1987 - No. 2, August, 1987 ($1.75, color, mature readers)
Vortex Comics

1,2-nudity, adult language	.35	1.15	2.30

PARADE (See Hanna-Barbera...)

PARADE COMICS (Frisky Animals on Parade #2 on)
Sept, 1957
Ajax/Farrell Publ. (World Famous Publ.)

1	1.50	4.50	10.00

NOTE: *Cover title: Frisky Animals on Parade.*

PARADE OF PLEASURE
1954 (192 pgs.) (Hardback book)
Derric Verschoyle Ltd., London, England

By Geoffrey Wagner. Contains section devoted to the censorship of American comic books with illustrations in color and black and white. (Also see **Seduction of the Innocent**). Distributed in USA by Library Publishers, N. Y.

	30.00	90.00	210.00
with dust jacket....	55.00	165.00	385.00

PARAMOUNT ANIMATED COMICS (See Harvey Comics Hits #60,62)
Feb, 1953 - No. 22, July, 1956
Harvey Publications

1-Baby Huey, Herman & Katnip, Buzzy the Crow begin			
	10.00	30.00	70.00
2	6.00	18.00	42.00
3-6	5.00	15.00	35.00
7-Baby Huey becomes permanent cover feature; cover title becomes Baby Huey with #9	10.00	30.00	70.00
8-10: 9-Infinity-c	4.00	12.00	28.00
11-22	2.65	8.50	18.00

PARENT TRAP, THE (See 4-Color #1210)

PAROLE BREAKERS
Dec, 1951 - No. 3, July, 1952
Avon Periodicals/Realistic #2 on

1(#2 on inside)-c-/Avon paperback 283	15.00	45.00	105.00
2-Kubert-a; c-/Avon paperback 114	12.00	36.00	84.00
3-Kinstler-c	10.00	30.00	70.00

PARTRIDGE FAMILY, THE (TV)
March, 1971 - No. 21, Dec, 1973

Charlton Comics	Good	Fine	N-Mint
1	1.15	3.50	8.00
2-4,6-21	.70	2.00	4.00
5-Partridge Family Summer Special (52 pgs.); The Shadow, Lone Ranger, Charlie McCarthy, Flash Gordon, Hopalong Cassidy, Gene Autry & others app.	1.50	4.50	10.00

PASSION, THE
1955
Catechetical Guild

394	3.35	10.00	20.00

PAT BOONE (TV)(Also see Superman's Girlfriend Lois Lane #9)
Sept-Oct, 1959 - No. 5, May-Jun, 1960
National Periodical Publications

1-Photo-c	15.00	45.00	105.00
2-5: 4-Previews 'Journey To The Center Of The Earth'. 2,5-Photo-c	11.00	32.00	75.00

PATCHES
Mar-Apr, 1945 - No. 11, Nov, 1947
Rural Home/Patches Publ. (Orbit)

1-L. B. Cole-c	9.00	27.00	62.00
2	4.35	13.00	30.00
3-8,10,11: 5-L.B. Cole-c	3.70	11.00	26.00
9-Leav/Krigstein-a, 16 pgs.	4.35	13.00	30.00

PATHWAYS TO FANTASY
July, 1984
Pacific Comics

1-Barry Smith-c/a; J. Jones-a	.25	.75	1.50

PATORUZU (See Adventures of...)

PATSY & HEDY
Feb, 1952 - No. 110, Feb, 1967
Atlas Comics/Marvel (GPI/Male)

1	5.00	15.00	35.00
2	2.65	8.00	18.00
3-10	2.00	6.00	14.00
11-20	1.30	4.00	9.00
21-40	1.00	3.00	7.00
41-60	.55	1.65	4.00
61-110: 88-Lingerie panel	.30	.80	1.60
Annual 1('63)	1.70	5.00	12.00

PATSY & HER PALS
May, 1953 - No. 29, Aug, 1957
Atlas Comics (PPI)

1	4.35	13.00	30.00
2	2.15	6.50	15.00
3-10	1.70	5.00	12.00
11-29: 24-Everett-c	1.15	3.50	8.00

PATSY WALKER (Also see All Teen, A Date With Patsy, Girls' Life, Miss America Magazine & Teen Comics)
1945 (no month) - No. 124, Dec, 1965
Marvel/Atlas Comics (BPC)

1	16.00	48.00	110.00
2	8.00	24.00	56.00
3-10: 5-Injury-to-eye-c	5.00	15.00	35.00
11,12,15,16,18	2.85	8.50	20.00
13,14,17,19-22-Kurtzman's "Hey Look"	4.00	12.00	28.00
23,24	2.30	7.00	16.00
25-Rusty by Kurtzman; painted-c	4.00	12.00	28.00
26-29,31: 26-31: 52 pgs.	2.00	6.00	14.00
30-Egghead Doodle by Kurtzman, 1pg. (52 pgs.)			
	3.50	10.50	24.00
32-57: Last precode (3/55)	1.30	4.00	9.00

Panic #11, © WMG

Pat Boone #2, © DC

Patsy And Her Pals #10, © MEG

Paul Terry's Comics #89, © M.G.M.

Peacemaker #1 (1/88), © DC

Peanuts #4, © Charles Schulz

PATSY WALKER (continued)	Good	Fine	N-Mint
58-80	.80	2.40	5.50
81-99: 92,98-Millie x-over	.45	1.35	3.00
100	.55	1.60	4.00
101-124	.25	.75	1.50
Fashion Parade 1('66)-68 pgs.	1.70	5.00	12.00

NOTE: Painted c-25-28. 21-Anti-Wertham editorial. *Al Jaffee* c-57, 58.

PAT THE BRAT (Adventures of Pipsqueak #34 on)
June, 1953; Summer, 1955 - No. 33, July, 1959
Archie Publications (Radio)

nn(6/53)	6.00	18.00	42.00
1(Summer, 1955)	4.00	12.00	28.00
2-4-(5/56) (#5-14 not published)	2.00	6.00	14.00
15-(7/56)-33	1.15	3.50	8.00

PAT THE BRAT COMICS DIGEST MAGAZINE
October, 1980
Archie Publications

1		.50	1.00

PATTY POWERS (Formerly Della Vision #3)
No. 4, Oct, 1955 - No. 7, Oct, 1956
Atlas Comics

4	2.35	7.00	16.00
5-7	1.30	4.00	9.00

PAT WILTON (See Mighty Midget Comics)

PAUL
1978 (49 cents)
Spire Christian Comics (Fleming H. Revell Co.)

		.40	.80

PAULINE PERIL (See The Close Shaves of . . .)

PAUL REVERE'S RIDE (See 4-Color #822 & Walt Disney Showcase #34)

PAUL TERRY'S ADVENTURES OF MIGHTY MOUSE (See Adventures of . . .)

PAUL TERRY'S COMICS (Formerly Terry-Toons Comics; becomes Adventures of Mighty Mouse No. 126 on)
No. 85, Mar, 1951 - No. 125, May, 1955
St. John Publishing Co.

85,86-Same as Terry-Toons #85, & 86 with only a title change			
	3.70	11.00	26.00
87-99: 89-Mighty Mouse begins, ends #125	2.30	7.00	16.00
100	2.85	8.50	20.00
101-104,107-125: 121-Painted-c	2.00	6.00	14.00
105,106-Giant Comics Edition, 100pgs. (9/53, ?)			
	6.50	19.50	45.00

PAUL TERRY'S HOW TO DRAW FUNNY CARTOONS
1940's (14 pages) (Black & White)
Terrytoons, Inc. (Giveaway)

Heckle & Jeckle, Mighty Mouse, etc.	5.50	16.50	38.00

PAUL TERRY'S MIGHTY MOUSE (See Mighty Mouse)

PAUL TERRY'S MIGHTY MOUSE ADVENTURE STORIES
1953 (384 pgs.) (50 cents) (cardboard covers)
St. John Publishing Co.

nn	32.00	95.00	225.00

PAWNEE BILL
Feb, 1951 - No. 3, July, 1951
Story Comics

1-Bat Masterson, Wyatt Earp app.	4.65	14.00	32.00
2,3: 3-Origin Golden Warrior; Cameron-a	2.30	7.00	15.00

PAY-OFF (This Is the . . . , . . . Crime, . . . Detective Stories)
July-Aug, 1948 - No. 5, Mar-Apr, 1949 (52 pages)

D. S. Publishing Co.	Good	Fine	N-Mint
1	5.00	15.00	35.00
2	3.50	10.50	24.00
3-5	2.65	8.00	18.00

PEACEMAKER, THE (Also see Fightin' 5)
Mar, 1967 - No. 5, Nov, 1967
Charlton Comics

1-Fightin' Five begins	.35	1.00	2.00
2,3,5	.25	.75	1.50
4-Origin The Peacemaker	.30	.90	1.80
1,2(Modern Comics reprint, 1978)		.15	.30

PEACEMAKER
Jan, 1988 - No. 4, April, 1988 ($1.25, mini-series)
DC Comics

1-4		.65	1.30

PEANUTS (Charlie Brown) (See Fritzi Ritz, Nancy & Sluggo, Tip Top, Tip Topper & United Comics)
No. 878, 2/58 - No. 13, 5-7/62; 5/63 - No. 4, 2/64
Dell Publishing Co./Gold Key

4-Color 878(#1)	5.00	15.00	35.00
4-Color 969,1015('59)	4.00	12.00	28.00
4(2-4/60)	3.00	9.00	21.00
5-13	2.00	6.00	14.00
1(G.Key)	2.65	8.00	18.00
2-4	1.70	5.00	12.00
1(1953-54)-Reprints United Features' Strange As It Seems, Willie, Fernand	4.65	14.00	32.00

PEBBLES & BAMM BAMM (TV)
Jan, 1972 - No. 36, Dec, 1976 (Hanna-Barbera)
Charlton Comics

1	1.50	4.50	10.00
2-10	.85	2.50	5.00
11-36	.70	2.00	4.00

PEBBLES FLINTSTONE (TV)
Sept, 1963 (Hanna-Barbera)
Gold Key

1 (10088-309)	3.00	9.00	21.00

PECKS BAD BOY
1906 - 1908 (Strip reprints) (11¼x15¾'')
Thompson of Chicago (by Walt McDougal)

. . .& Cousin Cynthia(1907)-In color	17.00	51.00	120.00
. . .& His Chums(1908)-Hardcover; in full color; 16 pgs.			
	17.00	51.00	120.00
Advs. of. . .And His Country Cousins (1906)-In color, 18 pgs., oblong	17.00	51.00	120.00
Advs. of. . .in Pictures(1908)-In color; Stanton & Van V. Liet Co.			
	17.00	51.00	120.00

PEDRO (Also see Romeo Tubbs)
No. 18, June, 1950 - No. 2, Aug, 1950?
Fox Features Syndicate

18(#1)-Wood c/a(p)	11.00	32.00	75.00
2-Wood-a?	8.50	25.50	60.00

PEE-WEE PIXIES (See The Pixies)

PELLEAS AND MELISANDE (See Night Music #4,5)

PENALTY (See Crime Must Pay the . . .)

PENDULUM ILLUSTRATED BIOGRAPHIES
1979 (B&W)
Pendulum Press

19-355x-George Washington/Thomas Jefferson, 19-3495-Charles Lindbergh/Amelia

PENDULUM ILLUSTRATED BIOGRAPHIES (continued)
Earhart, 19-3509-Harry Houdini/Walt Disney, 19-3517-Davy Crockett/Daniel Boone-Redondo-a, 19-3525-Elvis Presley/Beatles, 19-3533-Benjamin Franklin/Martin Luther King Jr, 19-3541-Abraham Lincoln/Franklin D. Roosevelt, 19-3568-Marie Curie/Albert Einstein-Redondo-a, 19-3576-Thomas Edison/Alexander Graham Bell-Redondo-a, 19-3584-Vince Lombardi/Pele, 19-3592-Babe Ruth/Jackie Robinson, 19-3606-Jim Thorpe/Althea Gibson

Softback	1.50
Hardback	4.50

NOTE: *Above books still available from publisher.*

PENDULUM ILLUSTRATED CLASSICS (Now Age Illustrated)
1973 - 1978 (62pp, B&W, 5-3/8x8") (Also see Marvel Classics)
Pendulum Press

64-100x(1973)-Dracula-Redondo art, 64-131x-The Invisible Man-Nino art, 64-0968-Dr Jekyll and Mr Hyde-Redondo art, 64-1005-Black Beauty, 64-1010-Call of the Wild, 64-1020-Frankenstein, 64-1025-Hucklebury Finn, 64-1030-Moby Dick-Nino-a, 64-1040-Red Badge of Courage, 64-1045-The Time Machine-Nino-a, 64-1050-Tom Sawyer, 64-1055-Twenty Thousand Leagues Under the Sea, 64-1069-Treasure Island, 64-1326(1974)-Kidnapped, 64-1336-Three Musketeers-Nino art, 64-1344-A Tale of Two Cities, 64-1352-Journey to the Center of the Earth, 64-1360-The War of the Worlds-Nino-a, 64-1379-The Greatest Advs of Sherlock Holmes-Redondo art, 64-1387-Mysterious Island, 64-1395-Hunchback of Notre Dame, 64-1409-Helen Keller-story of my life, 64-1417-Scarlet Letter, 64-1425-Gulliver's Travels, 64-2618(1977)-Around the World in Eighty Days, 64-2626-Captains Courageous, 64-2634-Connecticut Yankee, 64-2642-The Hound of the Baskervilles, 64-2650-The House of Seven Gables, 64-2669-Jane Eyre, 64-2677-The Last of the Mohicans, 64-2685-The Best of O'Henry, 64-2693-The Best of Poe-Redondo-a, 64-2707-Two Years Before the Mast, 64-2715-White Fang, 64-2723-Wuthering Heights, 64-3126(1978)-Ben Hur-Redondo art, 64-3134-A Christmas Carol, 64-3142-The Food of the Gods, 64-3150-Ivanhoe, 64-3169-The Man in the Iron Mask, 64-3177-The Prince and the Pauper, 64-3185-The Prisoner of Zenda, 64-3193-The Return of the Native, 64-3207-Robinson Crusoe, 64-3215-The Scarlet Pimpernel, 64-3223-The Sea Wolf, 64-3231-The Swiss Family Robinson, 64-3851-Billy Budd, 64-386/x-Crime and Punishment, 64-3878-Don Quixote, 64-3886-Great Expectations, 64-3894-Heidi, 64-3908-The Iliad, 64-3916-Lord Jim, 64-3924-The Mutiny on Board H.M.S. Bounty, 64-3932-The Odyssey, 64-3940-Oliver Twist, 64-3959-Pride and Prejudice, 64-3967-The Turn of the Screw

Softback	1.45
Hardback	4.50

NOTE: All of the above books can be ordered from the publisher; some were reprinted as Marvel Classic Comics #1-12. In 1972 there was another brief series of 12 titles which contained Classics III. artwork. They were entitled *Now Age Books Il-lustrated*, but can be easily distinguished from later series by the small Classics Il-lustrated logo at the top of the front cover. The format is the same as the later series. The 48 pg. C.I. art was stretched out to make 62 pgs. After Twin Circle Publ. ter-minated the Classics III. series in 1971, they made a one year contract with Pendulum Press to print these twelve titles of C.I. art. Pendulum was unhappy with the contract, and at the end of 1972 began their own art series, utilizing the talents of the Filipino artist group. One detail which makes this rather confusing is that when they redid the art in 1973, they gave it the same identifying no. as the 1972 series. All 12 of the 1972 C.I. editions have new covers, taken from internal art panels. In spite of their recent age, all of the 1972 C.I. editions are very rare. Mint copies would fetch at least $50. Here is a list of the 1972 series, with C.I. title no. counterpart:

64-1005 (CI#60-A2)   64-1010 (CI#91)   64-1015 (CI-Jr #503)   64-1020 (CI#26)
64-1025 (CI#19-A2)   64-1030 (CI#5-A2)   64-1035 (CI#169)   64-1040 (CI#98)
64-1045 (CI#133)   64-1050 (CI#50-A2)   64-1055 (CI#47)   64-1060 (CI-Jr#535)

PENDULUM ILLUSTRATED ORIGINALS
1979 (in color)
Pendulum Press

	Good	Fine	N-Mint
94-4254-Solarman: The Beginning	.30	.80	1.60

PENNY
1947 - No. 6, 9-10/49 (Newspaper reprints)
Avon Comics

1-Photo & biography of creator	5.00	15.00	35.00
2-5	2.65	8.00	18.00
6-Perry Como photo on-c	3.00	9.00	21.00

PEP COMICS (See Archie Giant Series Mag. #576,589)
Jan, 1940 - No. 411?, 1987
MLJ Magazines/Archie Publications No. 56 (3/46) on

1-Intro. The Shield by Irving Novick (1st patriotic hero); origin The Comet by Jack Cole, The Queen of Diamonds & Kayo Ward; The

---

Rocket, The Press Guardian (The Falcon #1 only), Sergeant Boyle, Fu Chang, & Bentley of Scotland Yard

	Good	Fine	N-Mint
	165.00	495.00	1155.00
2-Origin The Rocket	70.00	210.00	490.00
3	55.00	165.00	385.00
4-Wizard cameo	47.00	140.00	330.00
5-Wizard cameo in Shield story	47.00	140.00	330.00
6-10: 6-Transvestite story in Sgt. Boyle. 8-Last Cole Comet, no Cole art in #6,7	35.00	105.00	245.00
11-Dusty, Shield's sidekick begins; last Press Guardian, Fu Chang	35.00	105.00	245.00
12-Origin Fireball; last Rocket & Queen of Diamonds	47.00	140.00	330.00
13-15	32.00	95.00	225.00
16-Origin Madam Satan; blood drainage-c	47.00	140.00	330.00
17-Origin The Hangman; death of The Comet	95.00	285.00	665.00
18-20-Last Fireball	30.00	90.00	210.00
21-Last Madam Satan	30.00	90.00	210.00
22-Intro. & 1st app. Archie, Betty, & Jughead(12/41); (also see Jack-pot)	210.00	630.00	1470.00

(Prices vary widely on this book.)

	Good	Fine	N-Mint
23	57.00	170.00	400.00
24,25	49.00	147.00	342.00
26-1st app. Veronica Lodge	55.00	165.00	385.00
27-30: 30-Capt. Commando begins	39.00	117.00	273.00
31-35: 34-Bondage/Hypo-c	28.00	84.00	195.00
36-1st Archie-c	47.00	140.00	330.00
37-40	25.00	66.00	154.00
41-50: 41-Archie-c begin. 47-Last Hangman issue; infinity-c. 48-Black Hood begins (5/44); ends #51,59,60	16.00	48.00	110.00
51-60: 52-Suzie begins. 56-Last Capt. Commando. 59-Black Hood not in costume; spanking & lingerie panels; Archie dresses as his aunt; Suzie ends. 60-Katy Keene begins, ends #154	11.50	34.00	80.00
61-65-Last Shield. 62-1st app. Li'l Jinx	8.50	25.50	60.00
66-80: 66-G-Man Club becomes Archie Club (2/48)	6.50	19.50	45.00
81-99	4.35	13.00	30.00
100	5.00	15.00	35.00
101-130	2.00	6.00	14.00
131-149	1.00	3.00	7.00
150,152,157,159-Jaguar stories in all	.65	2.00	4.50
151,154,160-The Fly stories in all	.65	2.00	4.50
153,155,156,158-Flygirl stories in all	.65	2.00	4.50
161-167,169-200	.35	1.00	2.50
168-Jaguar app.	.55	1.65	4.00
201-260		.50	1.00
261-411: 383-Marvelous Maureen begins (Sci/fi). 393-Thunderbunny begins	.35		.70

NOTE: *Biro a-2, 4, 5. Jack Cole a-1-5, 8. Fuje a-39, 45, 47. Meskin a-5, 11(2). Novick c-1-10, 20, 22, 23, 25. Schomburg c-38. Bob Wood a-2, 4-6, 11. Katy Keene by Bill Woggon in many later issues. Bondage c-7, 12, 13, 15, 18, 21, 31, 32.*

PEPE (See 4-Color #1194)

PERCY & FERDIE
1921 (52 pages) (B&W dailies, 10x10", cardboard-c)
Cupples & Leon Co.

By H. A. MacGill	7.00	21.00	50.00

PERFECT CRIME, THE
Oct, 1949 - No. 33, Feb?, 1953 (#2-12, 52 pgs.)
Cross Publications

1-Powell-a(2)	6.50	19.50	45.00
2 (4/50)	4.00	12.00	28.00
3-7,9,10: 7-Steve Duncan begins, ends #30	3.50	10.50	24.00

Penny #1, © AVON

Pep Comics #17, © AP

Pep Comics #30, © AP

The Perfect Crime #18, © Cross Publ.   Personal Love #32, © FF   Peter Porkchops #4, © DC

THE PERFECT CRIME (continued)	Good	Fine	N-Mint
8-Heroin drug story	5.50	16.50	38.00
11-Used in SOTI, pg. 159	6.00	18.00	42.00
12-14	2.15	6.50	15.00
15-"The Most Terrible Menace"-2 pg. drug editorial	3.85	11.50	27.00
16,17,19-25,27-29,31-33	1.70	5.00	12.00
18-Drug cover, heroin drug propaganda story, plus 2 pg. drug editorial	8.50	25.50	60.00
26-Drug-c with hypodermic; drug propaganda story	10.00	30.00	70.00
30-Strangulation cover	7.00	21.00	50.00

NOTE: Powell a-No. 1,2,4. Wildey a-1,5. Bondage c-11.

PERFECT LOVE
No. 10, 8-9/51 (cover date; 5-6/51 indicia date); No. 2, 10-11/51 -No. 10, 12/53
Ziff-Davis(Approved Comics)/St. John No. 9 on

10(#1)(8-9/51)	5.00	15.00	35.00
2(10-11/51)	3.00	9.00	21.00
3,6,7: 3-Painted-c	2.30	7.00	16.00
4,8 (Fall, '52)-Kinstler-a; last Z-D issue	2.65	8.00	18.00
5-Woodbridge-a? Photo-c	2.30	7.00	16.00
9,10 (10/53, 12/53, St. John): 9-Kinstler painted-c. 10-Photo-c	2.30	7.00	16.00

PERRI (See 4-Color #847)

PERRY MASON (See Feature Books #49,50 (McKay))

PERRY MASON MYSTERY MAGAZINE (TV)
June-Aug, 1964 - No. 2, Oct-Dec, 1964
Dell Publishing Co.

1,2: 2-Raymond Burr photo-c	1.30	4.00	9.00

PERSONAL LOVE (Also see Movie Love)
Jan, 1950 - No. 33, June, 1955
Famous Funnies

1	5.70	17.00	40.00
2	3.50	10.50	24.00
3-7,10	3.00	9.00	21.00
8,9-Kinstler-a	3.50	10.50	24.00
11-Toth-a	5.50	16.50	38.00
12,16,17-One pg. Frazetta	3.50	10.50	24.00
13-15,18-23	2.30	7.00	16.00
24,25,27,28-Frazetta-a in all-8,7&6 pgs.	26.00	78.00	180.00
26,29-31,33: 31-Last pre-code (2/55)	1.70	5.00	12.00
32-Classic Frazetta-a, 8 pgs.	45.00	135.00	315.00

NOTE: All have photo-c. Everett a-5, 9, 10, 24. Kirk Douglas photo c-32.

PERSONAL LOVE (Going Steady V3#3 on)
V1No.1, Sept, 1957 - V3No.2, Nov-Dec, 1959
Prize Publ. (Headline)

V1#1	2.00	6.00	14.00
2	1.15	3.50	8.00
3-6(7-8/58)	.85	2.50	6.00
V2#1(9-10/58)-V2#6(7-8/59)	.75	2.25	5.00
V3#1-Wood/Orlando-a	1.50	4.50	10.00
2	.55	1.65	4.00

NOTE: Photo covers on most issues.

PETER COTTONTAIL
Jan, 1954; Feb, 1954 - No. 2, Mar, 1954
Key Publications

1(1/54)-Not 3-D	3.70	11.00	26.00
1(2/54)-(3-D); written by Bruce Hamilton	14.00	42.00	100.00
2-Reprints 3-D #1 but not in 3-D	2.65	8.00	18.00

PETER GUNN (See 4-Color #1087)

PETER PAN (See New Adventures of . . ., 4-Color #442,446,926, Movie Classics &

Comics & Walt Disney Showcase #36)

PETER PANDA
Aug-Sept, 1953 - No. 31, Aug-Sept, 1958
National Periodical Publications

	Good	Fine	N-Mint
1-Grossman-c/a in all	13.00	40.00	90.00
2	6.00	18.00	42.00
3-10	5.00	15.00	35.00
11-31	2.30	7.00	16.00

PETER PAN TREASURE CHEST (See Dell Giants)

PETER PARKER (See The Spectacular Spider-Man)

PETER PAT (See Single Series #8)

PETER PAUL'S 4 IN 1 JUMBO COMIC BOOK
No date (1953)
Capitol Stories

1-Contains 4 comics bound; Space Adventures, Space Western, Crime & Justice, Racket Squad in Action	17.00	51.00	120.00

PETER PENNY AND HIS MAGIC DOLLAR
1947 (16 pgs.; paper cover; regular size)
American Bankers Association, N. Y. (Giveaway)

nn-(Scarce)-Used in SOTI, pg. 310, 311	7.00	21.00	50.00
Another version (7¼x11'')-redrawn, 16 pgs., paper-c	5.00	15.00	35.00

PETER PIG
No. 5, May, 1953 - No. 6, Aug, 1953
Standard Comics

5,6	1.50	4.50	10.00

PETER PORKCHOPS (See Leading Comics #23)
11-12/49 - #61, 9-11/59; #62, 10-12/60 (52 pgs.: #1-5)
National Periodical Publications

1	14.00	42.00	100.00
2	7.00	21.00	50.00
3-10	5.00	15.00	35.00
11-30	3.50	10.50	24.00
31-62	2.00	6.00	14.00

NOTE: Otto Feur a-all. Sheldon Mayer a-30-38, 40-44, 46-52, 61.

PETER PORKER, THE SPECTACULAR SPIDER-HAM
May, 1985 - No. 15, Sept, 1987
Star Comics (Marvel)

1	.35	1.00	2.00
2-15: 13-Halloween ish.		.50	1.00

PETER POTAMUS (TV)
January, 1965 (Hanna-Barbera)
Gold Key

1	2.30	7.00	16.00

PETER RABBIT (See Large Feature Comic #1, New Funnies #65 & Space Comics)

PETER RABBIT
1922 - 1923 (9¼x6¼'') (paper cover)
John H. Eggers Co. The House of Little Books Publishers

B1-B4-(Rare)-(Set of 4 books which came in a cardboard box)-Each book reprints ½ of a Sunday page per page and contains 8 B&W and 2 color pages; by Harrison Cady each. . . .	18.00	54.00	125.00

PETER RABBIT (Adventures of . . .; New Advs. of . . .later issues)
1947 - No. 34, Aug-Sept, 1956
Avon Periodicals

1(1947)-Reprints 1943-44 Sunday strips; contains a biography & drawing of Cady	23.00	70.00	160.00
2 (4/48)	18.00	54.00	125.00

PETER RABBIT (continued)	Good	Fine	N-Mint
3 ('48) - 6(7/49)-Last Cady issue	16.50	50.00	115.00
7-10(1950-8/51)	3.00	9.00	21.00
11(11/51)-34('56)-Avon's character	1.85	5.50	13.00
. . .Easter Parade (132 pgs.; 1952)	10.00	30.00	70.00
. . .Jumbo Book(1954-Giant Size, 25 cents)-6 pgs. Jesse James by Kinstler	15.00	45.00	105.00

PETER RABBIT
1958
Fago Magazine Co.

1	2.65	8.00	18.00

PETER, THE LITTLE PEST (#4 titled Petey)
Nov, 1969 - No. 4, May, 1970
Marvel Comics Group

1	.50	1.50	3.00
2-4-Reprints Dexter the Demon & Melvin the Monster	.35	1.00	2.00

PETER WHEAT (The Adventures of . . .)
1948 - 1956? (16 pgs. in color) (paper covers)
Bakers Associates Giveaway

nn(No.1)-States on last page, end of 1st Adventure of . . .; Kelly-a	22.00	65.00	140.00
nn(4 issues)-Kelly-a	17.00	50.00	100.00
6-10-All Kelly-a	12.00	36.00	72.00
11-20-All Kelly-a	10.00	30.00	60.00
21-35-All Kelly-a	8.00	24.00	48.00
36-66	5.00	15.00	30.00
. . .Artist's Workbook ('54, digest size)	4.50	13.50	27.00
. . .Four-In-One Fun Pack (Vol. 2, '54), oblong, comics w/puzzles	5.00	15.00	30.00
. . .Fun Book ('52, 32pgs., paper-c, B&W & color, 8¼"x10¾"), contains cut-outs, puzzles, games, magic & pages to color	7.00	21.00	50.00

NOTE: *Al Hubbard art #36 on; written by Del Connell.*

PETER WHEAT NEWS
1948 - No. 30, 1950 (4 pgs. in color)
Bakers Associates

Vol. 1-All have 2 pgs. Peter Wheat by Kelly	20.00	60.00	140.00
2-10	13.00	40.00	80.00
11-20	6.75	20.00	40.00
21-30	4.00	12.00	24.00

NOTE: *Early issues have no date & Kelly art.*

PETE'S DRAGON (See Walt Disney Showcase #43)

PETE THE PANIC
November, 1955? (mid 1950s)
Stanmor Publications

nn	1.30	4.00	9.00

PETEY (See Peter, the Little Pest)

PETTICOAT JUNCTION (TV)
Oct-Dec, 1964 - No. 5, Oct-Dec, 1965 (Photo-c)
Dell Publishing Co.

1	3.70	11.00	26.00
2-5	2.00	6.00	14.00

PETUNIA (See 4-Color #463)

PHANTASMO (See Large Feat. Comic #18)

PHANTOM, THE
1939 - 1949
David McKay Publishing Co.

Feature Books 20	40.00	120.00	280.00
Feature Books 22	34.00	100.00	237.00
Feature Books 39	24.00	72.00	168.00

	Good	Fine	N-Mint
Feature Books 53,56,57	19.00	57.00	132.00

PHANTOM, THE (See Ace Comics, Defenders Of The Earth, Eat Right to Work . . ., Future Comics, Harvey Comics Hits #51,56, Harvey Hits #1, 6, 12, 15, 26, 36, 44, 48 & King Comics)

PHANTOM, THE (nn 29-Published overseas only) (Also see Comics Reading Library)
Nov, 1962 - No. 17, July, 1966; No. 18, Sept, 1966 - No. 28, Dec, 1967; No. 30, Feb, 1969 - No. 74, Jan, 1977
Gold Key (No.1-17)/King (No.18-28)/Charlton (No.30 on)

1-Manning-a	4.30	13.00	30.00
2-King, Queen & Jack begins, ends #11	1.70	5.00	12.00
3-10	1.30	4.00	9.00
11-17: 12-Track Hunter begins	.85	2.50	6.00
18-Flash Gordon begins; Wood-a	1.15	3.50	8.00
19,20-Flash Gordon ends	.85	2.50	6.00
21-24,26,27: 21-Mandrake begins. 20,24-Girl Phantom app. 26-Brick Bradford app.	.70	2.00	5.00
25-Jeff Jones-a; 1 pg. Williamson ad	1.00	3.00	7.00
28(nn)-Brick Bradford app.	.70	2.00	5.00
30-40: 36,39-Ditko-a	.55	1.65	4.00
41-66: 46-Intro. The Piranha. 62-Bolle-c	.50	1.50	3.00
67-71,73-Newton c/a; 67-Origin retold	.50	1.50	3.00
72	.35	1.00	2.00
74-Newton Flag-c; Newton-a	.50	1.50	3.00

NOTE: *Aparo a-36-38; c-35-38, 60, 61. Painted-c No. 1-17.*

PHANTOM, THE
May, 1988 - No. 4, Aug., 1988 ($1.25, color, mini-series)
DC Comics

1-4: Orlando-c/a	.25	.75	1.50

PHANTOM BLOT, THE (#1 titled New Adventures of . . .)
Oct, 1964 - No. 7, Nov, 1966 (Disney)
Gold Key

1 (Meets The Beagle Boys)	2.00	6.00	14.00
2-1st Super Goof	1.50	4.50	10.00
3-7	1.15	3.50	8.00

PHANTOM EAGLE (See Mighty Midget Comics & Marvel Super Heroes #16)

PHANTOM LADY (1st Series) (My Love Secret #24 on) (Also see All Top, Daring Adventures, Jungle Thrills, and Wonder Boy)
Aug, 1947 - No. 23 April, 1949
Fox Features Syndicate

13(#1)-Phantom Lady by Matt Baker begins; The Blue Beetle app.	110.00	330.00	770.00
14(#2)	68.00	205.00	475.00
15-P.L. injected with experimental drug	58.00	175.00	405.00
16-Negligee-c, panels	58.00	175.00	405.00
17-Classic bondage cover; used in **SOTI**, illo-"Sexual stimulation by combining 'headlights' with the sadist's dream of tying up a woman"	145.00	435.00	1015.00
18,19	52.00	155.00	365.00
20-23: 23-Bondage-c	44.00	132.00	310.00

NOTE: *Matt Baker a-in all; c-13, 15-21. Kamen a-22, 23.*

PHANTOM LADY (2nd Series) (See Terrific Comics) (Formerly Linda)
Dec-Jan, 1954/1955 - No. 4, June, 1955
Ajax/Farrell Publ.

V1#5(#1)-by Matt Baker	27.00	81.00	190.00
V1#2-Last pre-code	22.00	65.00	154.00
3,4-Red Rocket	18.00	54.00	125.00

PHANTOM PLANET, THE (See 4-Color No. 1234)

PHANTOM STRANGER, THE (1st Series)
Aug-Sept, 1952 - No. 6, June-July, 1953
National Periodical Publications

Peter Rabbit #5, © AVON

The Phantom #1 (5/88), © KING

Phantom Lady #17, © FOX

302

THE PHANTOM STRANGER (continued)	Good	Fine	N-Mint
1 (Scarce)	50.00	150.00	350.00
2 (Scarce)	37.00	110.00	260.00
3-6 (Scarce)	30.00	90.00	210.00

PHANTOM STRANGER, THE (2nd Series) (See Showcase)
May-June, 1969 - No. 41, Feb-Mar, 1976
National Periodical Publications

1	1.15	3.50	7.00
2,3,5-10	.50	1.50	3.00
4-Adams-a	1.00	3.00	6.00

11-41: 22-Dark Circle begins. 23-Spawn of Frankenstein begins by
Kaluta; series ends #30. 31-The Black Orchid begins. 39-41-
Deadman app.   .25   .75   1.50

NOTE: *Adams* a-4; c-3-19. *Aparo* a-7-26; c-20-24, 33-41. *B. Bailey* a-27-30. *Dezuniga*
a-14-16, 19-22, 31, 34. *Grell* a-33. *Kaluta* a-23-25; c-26. *Meskin* r-15, 16, 18. *Redondo*
a-32, 35, 36. *Sparling* a-20. *Starr* a-17r. *Toth* a-15r. Black Orchid by *Carrilo*-38-41. Dr.
13 solo in-13, 18, 20. Frankenstein by *Kaluta*-23-25; by *Baily*-27-30. No Black
Orchid-33, 34, 37.

PHANTOM STRANGER
Oct, 1987 - No. 4, Jan, 1988 (mini-series, 75 cents, color)
DC Comics

1	.25	.75	1.50
2-4		.50	1.00

PHANTOM WITCH DOCTOR
1952 (Also see Eerie No. 8)
Avon Periodicals

1-Kinstler-c, 7 pgs.	20.00	60.00	140.00

PHANTOM ZONE, THE
January, 1982 - No. 4, April, 1982
DC Comics

1-Superman app. in all		.40	.80
2-4: Batman, Gr. Lantern app.		.30	.60

NOTE: *Colan* a-1-4p; c-1-4p. *Giordano* c-1-4i.

PHAZE
Apr., 1988 - Present ($2.25, color)
Eclipse Comics

1-3: 2-Gulacy painted-c	.35	1.10	2.25

PHIL RIZZUTO (Baseball Hero)
1951 (New York Yankees)
Fawcett Publications

nn-Photo-c	20.00	60.00	140.00

PHOENIX
Jan, 1975 - No. 4, Oct, 1975
Atlas/Seaboard Publ.

1-Origin		.30	.60
2,3: 3-Origin & only app. The Dark Avenger		.25	.50
4-New origin/costume The Protector (formerly Phoenix)			
		.25	.50

NOTE: *Infantino* appears in #1,2. *Austin* a-3i. *Thorne* c-3.

PHOENIX (. . .The Untold Story)
April, 1984 (One shot; $2.00)
Marvel Comics Group

1-Byrne/Austin-r/X-Men 137 with original unpublished ending			
	1.00	3.00	6.00

PICNIC PARTY (See Dell Giants)

PICTORIAL CONFESSIONS (Pictorial Romances #4 on)
Sept, 1949 - No. 3, Dec, 1949
St. John Publishing Co.

1-Baker-c/a(3)	12.00	36.00	84.00
2-Baker-a; photo-c	6.00	18.00	42.00
3-Kubert, Baker-a; part Kubert-c	8.50	25.50	60.00

PICTORIAL LOVE STORIES (Formerly Tim McCoy)
No. 22, Oct, 1949 - No. 26, July, 1950
Charlton Comics

	Good	Fine	N-Mint
22-26-"Me-Dan Cupid" in all	5.00	15.00	35.00

PICTORIAL LOVE STORIES
October, 1952
St. John Publishing Co.

1-Baker c/a	10.00	30.00	70.00

PICTORIAL ROMANCES (Formerly Pictorial Confessions)
No. 4, Jan, 1950; No. 5, Jan, 1951 - No. 24, Mar, 1954
St. John Publishing Co.

4-All Baker	9.50	28.50	65.00
5,10-All Matt Baker issues	7.00	21.00	50.00
6-9,12,13,15,16-Baker-c, 2-3 stories	5.00	15.00	35.00
11-Baker c/a(3); Kubert-a	6.00	18.00	42.00
14,21-24-Baker-c/a each	3.70	11.00	26.00
17-20(7/53)-100 pgs. each; Baker-c/a	10.00	30.00	70.00

NOTE: *Matt Baker* art in most issues. *Estrada* a-19(2).

PICTURE NEWS
Jan, 1946 - No. 10, Jan-Feb, 1947
Lafayette Street Corp.

1-Milt Gross begins, ends No. 6; 4 pg. Kirby-a; A-Bomb-c/story			
	11.00	32.00	75.00
2-Atomic explosion panels; Frank Sinatra, Perry Como stories			
	5.00	15.00	35.00
3-Atomic explosion panels; Frank Sinatra, June Allyson stories			
	4.00	12.00	28.00
4-Atomic explosion panels; "Caesar and Cleopatra" movie adaptation; Jackie Robinson story	4.65	14.00	32.00
5-7: 5-Hank Greenberg story. 6-Joe Louis c/story			
	2.65	8.00	18.00
8-Monte Hale story(9-10/46; 1st?)	4.65	14.00	32.00
9-A-Bomb story; "Crooked Mile" movie adaptation; Joe DiMaggio story	4.65	14.00	32.00
10-A-Bomb story; Krigstein, Gross-a	4.35	13.00	30.00

PICTURE PARADE (Picture Progress #5 on)
Sept, 1953 - V1/4, Dec, 1953 (28 pages)
Gilberton Company (Also see A Christmas Adventure)

V1#1-Andy's Atomic Adventures-A-bomb blast-c; (Teachers version distr. to schools exists)	5.70	17.00	40.00
2-Around the World with the United Nations			
	5.00	15.00	35.00
3-Adventures of the Lost One(The Amer. Indian), 4-A Christmas Adventure (r-under same title in '69)	5.00	15.00	35.00

PICTURE PROGRESS (Formerly Picture Parade)
V1No.5, Jan, 1954 - V3No.2, Oct, 1955 (28-36 pgs.)
Gilberton Corp.

V1#5-News in Review 1953, 6-The Birth of America, 7-The Four Seasons, 8-Paul Revere's Ride, 9-The Hawaiian Islands(5/54),			
V2#1-The Story of Flight(9/54), 2-Vote for Crazy River(The Meaning of Elections), 3-Louis Pasteur, 4-The Star Spangled Banner, 5-News in Review 1954, 6-Alaska: The Great Land, 7-Life in the Circus, 8-The Time of the Cave Man, 9-Summer Fun(5/55)			
each....	2.30	7.00	16.00
V3#1-The Man Who Discovered America, 2-The Lewis & Clark Expedition each....	2.30	7.00	16.00

PICTURE SCOPE JUNGLE ADVENTURES (See Jungle Thrills)

PICTURE STORIES FROM AMERICAN HISTORY
1945 - 1947 (#1,2-56 pgs.; #3-52pgs.)
National/All-American/E. C. Comics

1	6.00	18.00	42.00
2-4	4.00	12.00	28.00

PICTURE STORIES FROM SCIENCE
Spring, 1947 - No. 2, Fall, 1947
E.C. Comics

	Good	Fine	N-Mint
1,2	7.00	21.00	50.00

PICTURE STORIES FROM THE BIBLE
Fall, 1942-3 & 1944-46
National/All-American/E.C. Comics

	Good	Fine	N-Mint
1-4('42-Fall,'43)-Old Testament (DC)	7.00	21.00	50.00
Complete Old Testament Edition, 232pgs.(1943-DC); contains #1-4	10.00	30.00	70.00
Complete Old Testament Edition (1945-publ. by Bible Pictures Ltd.)-232 pgs., hardbound, in color with dust jacket	10.00	30.00	70.00

NOTE: *Both Old and New Testaments published in England by Bible Pictures Ltd. in hardback, 1943, in color, 376 pages, and were also published by Scarf Press in 1979 (Old Test., $9.95) and in 1980 (New Test., $7.95)*

	Good	Fine	N-Mint
1-3(New Test.; 1944-46, DC)-52pgs. ea.	6.00	18.00	42.00
The Complete Life of Christ Edition (1945)-96pgs.; contains #1&2 of the New Testament Edition	8.00	24.00	56.00
1,2(Old Testament-r in comic book form)(E.C., 1946; 52pgs.)	6.00	18.00	42.00
1-3(New Testament-r in comic book form)(E.C., 1946; 52pgs.)	6.00	18.00	42.00
Complete New Testament Edition (1946-E.C.)-144 pgs.; contains #1-3	8.50	25.50	60.00

NOTE: *Another British series entitled* **The Bible Illustrated** *from 1947 has recently been discovered, with the same internal artwork. This eight edition series (5-OT, 3-NT) is of particular interest to Classics III. collectors because it exactly copied the C.I. logo format. The British publisher was Thorpe & Porter, who in 1951 began publishing the British Classics III. series. All editions of The Bible III. have new British painted covers. While this market is still new, and not all editions have as yet been found, current market value is about the same as the first U.S. editions of Picture Stories From The Bible.*

PICTURE STORIES FROM WORLD HISTORY
Spring, 1947 - No. 2, Summer, 1947 (52,48 pgs.)
E.C. Comics

	Good	Fine	N-Mint
1,2	6.00	18.00	42.00

PINHEAD & FOODINI (TV)(Also see Foodini)
July, 1951 - No. 4, Jan, 1952
Fawcett Publications

	Good	Fine	N-Mint
1-Photo-c; 52 pgs.	6.50	19.50	45.00
2-Photo-c	4.65	14.00	32.00
3,4: 3-Photo-c	3.00	9.00	21.00

PINK LAFFIN
1922 (9x12")(strip-r)
Whitman Publishing Co.

...the Lighter Side of Life,...He Tells 'Em,...and His Family,
...Knockouts; Ray Gleason-a (All rare)

	Good	Fine	N-Mint
each...	8.00	24.00	56.00

PINK PANTHER, THE (TV)
April, 1971 - No. 87, 1984
Gold Key

	Good	Fine	N-Mint
1-The Inspector begins	1.20	3.50	8.00
2-10	.70	2.00	4.00
11-30: Warren Tufts-a #16-on	.40	1.20	2.50
31-60	.25	.75	1.50
61-87		.50	1.00
Kite Fun Book(1972)-16pgs.	.70	2.00	4.00
Mini-comic No. 1(1976)(3¼x6½")		.50	1.00

NOTE: *Pink Panther began as a movie cartoon. (See Golden Comics Digest #38, 45 and March of Comics #376, 384, 390, 409, 418, 429, 441, 449, 461, 473, 486); #37, 72, 80-85 contain reprints.*

PINKY LEE (See Adventures of...)

PINKY THE EGGHEAD
1963 (Reprints from Noodnik)
I.W./Super Comics

	Good	Fine	N-Mint
I.W. Reprint #1,2(nd)		.60	1.20
Super Reprint #14		.60	1.20

PINOCCHIO (See 4-Color #92,252,545,1203, Movie Comics under Wonderful Advs. of..., Mickey Mouse Mag. V5#3, Thrilling Comics #2, Wonderful Advs. of...,World's Greatest Stories #2 & New Advs. of...)

PINOCCHIO
1940 (10 pages; linen-like paper)
Montgomery Ward Co. (Giveaway)

	Good	Fine	N-Mint
	12.00	36.00	84.00

PINOCCHIO AND THE EMPEROR OF THE NIGHT
Mar., 1988 (52 pgs., $1.25)
Marvel Comics

	Good	Fine	N-Mint
1-Adapts film		.60	1.25

PINOCCHIO LEARNS ABOUT KITES (Also see Donald Duck & Brer Rabbit) (Disney)
1954 (8 pages) (Premium)
Pacific Gas & Electric Co./Florida Power & Light

	Good	Fine	N-Mint
	20.00	60.00	130.00

PIN-UP PETE (Also see Monty Hall...& Great Lover Romances)
1952
Toby Press

	Good	Fine	N-Mint
1-Jack Sparling pin-ups	9.00	27.00	62.00

PIONEER MARSHAL (See Fawcett Movie Comics)

PIONEER PICTURE STORIES
Dec, 1941 - No. 9, Dec, 1943
Street & Smith Publications

	Good	Fine	N-Mint
1	10.00	30.00	70.00
2	5.70	17.00	40.00
3-9	4.65	14.00	32.00

PIONEER WEST ROMANCES (Firehair #1,2,7-11)
No. 3, Spring, 1949 - No. 6, Winter, 1949-50
Fiction House Magazines

	Good	Fine	N-Mint
3-(52 pgs.)-Firehair continues	8.00	24.00	55.00
4-6	6.00	18.00	42.00

PIPSQUEAK (See The Adventures of...)

PIRACY
Oct-Nov, 1954 - No. 7, Oct-Nov, 1955
E. C. Comics

	Good	Fine	N-Mint
1-Williamson/Torres-a	12.00	36.00	85.00
2-Williamson/Torres-a	9.00	27.00	62.00
3-7	7.00	21.00	50.00

NOTE: *Crandall a-in all; c-2-4. Davis a-1, 2, 6. Evans a-3-7; c-7. Ingels a-3-7. Krigstein a-3-5, 7; c-5, 6. Wood a-1, 2; c-1.*

PIRANA (See Thrill-O-Rama #2,3)

PIRATE CORPS, THE
1987 - No. 5, 1988 ($1.95, color #3 on)
Eternity Comics

	Good	Fine	N-Mint
1-5	.30	.95	1.90

PIRATE OF THE GULF, THE (See Superior Stories #2)

PIRATES COMICS
Feb-Mar, 1950 - No. 4, Aug-Sept, 1950 (All 52 pgs.)
Hillman Periodicals

	Good	Fine	N-Mint
1	7.00	21.00	50.00
2-Berg-a	4.00	12.00	28.00
3,4-Berg-a	3.00	9.00	21.00

Picture Stories From Science #1, © WMG

Pioneer West Romances #6, © FH

Pirates Comics #3, © HILL

Planet Comics #13, © FH

Plastic Man #4, © QUA

Plastic Man #3 (4/67), © DC

P.I.'S: MICHAEL MAUSER AND MS. TREE, THE
Jan., 1985 - No. 3, May, 1985 (mini-series)
First Comics

	Good	Fine	N-Mint
1-3: Staton c/a(p)		.65	1.30

PITT, THE (Also see The Draft)
Mar., 1988 (one shot, $3.25, 52 pgs.)
Marvel Comics

1-Ties into Starbrand, D.P. 7	.70	2.00	4.00

PIUS XII MAN OF PEACE
No date (12 pgs.; 5½x8½'') (B&W)
Catechetical Guild Giveaway

	4.00	12.00	28.00

PIXIE & DIXIE & MR. JINKS (TV)(See Jinks, Pixie, And Dixie & Whitman Comic Books)
July-Sept, 1960 - Feb, 1963 (Hanna-Barbera)
Dell Publishing Co./Gold Key

4-Color 1112	3.00	9.00	21.00
4-Color 1196,1264	2.30	7.00	16.00
01-631-207 (Dell)	2.00	6.00	14.00
1(2/63-G.K.)	2.00	6.00	14.00

PIXIE PUZZLE ROCKET TO ADVENTURELAND
November, 1952
Avon Periodicals

1	5.00	15.00	35.00

PIXIES, THE (Advs. of . . .) (Mighty Atom #6 on)
Winter, 1946 - No. 4, Fall?, 1947; No. 5, 1948
Magazine Enterprises

1-Mighty Atom	3.50	10.50	24.00
2-5-Mighty Atom	1.70	5.00	12.00
I.W. Reprint #1(1958), 8-(Pee-Wee Pixies), 10-I.W. on cover, Super on inside	.50	1.50	3.00

PLANET COMICS
Jan, 1940 - No. 73, Winter, 1953
Fiction House Magazines

1-Origin Auro, Lord of Jupiter; Flint Baker & The Red Comet begin; Eisner-Fine-c	330.00	990.00	2300.00
2-(Scarce)	160.00	480.00	1120.00
3-Eisner-a	135.00	405.00	945.00
4-Gale Allen and the Girl Squadron begins	115.00	345.00	805.00
5,6-(Scarce)	105.00	315.00	735.00
7-11	88.00	265.00	615.00
12-The Star Pirate begins	88.00	265.00	615.00
13-15: 13-Reff Ryan begins. 15-Mars, God of War begins	65.00	195.00	455.00
16-20,22	60.00	180.00	420.00
21-The Lost World & Hunt Bowman begin	66.00	200.00	460.00
23-26: 26-The Space Rangers begin	60.00	180.00	420.00
27-30	47.00	141.00	330.00
31-35: 33-Origin Star Pirates Wonder Boots, reprinted in #52. 35-Mysta of the Moon begins	40.00	120.00	280.00
36-45: 41-New origin of ''Auro, Lord of Jupiter.'' 42-Last Gale Allen. 43-Futura begins	35.00	105.00	245.00
46-52,54-60	26.00	78.00	180.00
53-Used in SOTI, pg. 32; bondage-c	28.00	84.00	195.00
61-64	18.00	54.00	125.00
65-68,70: 65-70-All partial-r of earlier issues	17.00	51.00	120.00
69-Used in POP, pgs. 101,102	18.00	54.00	125.00
71-73-No series stories	14.00	42.00	100.00
I.W. Reprint #1(nd)-r-/#70; c-from Attack on Planet Mars			
	2.85	8.50	20.00
I.W. Reprint #8 (r-/#72), 9-r-/#73	2.85	8.50	20.00

NOTE: **Anderson** a-33-38, 40-51 (Star Pirate). **Matt Baker** a-53-59 (Mysta of the

Moon). **Celardo** c-12. **Evans** a-50-64 (Lost World). **Fine** c-2, 5. **Ingels** a-24-31, 56-61 (Auro, Lord of Jupiter). **Renee** c-33, 35, 39. **Tuska** a-30 (Star Pirate). **M. Whitman** a-51, 52 (Mysta of the Moon), 54-56 (Star Pirate). **Starr** a-59.

PLANET COMICS
1988 - Present (2.00, color)
Blackthorne Publishing

	Good	Fine	N-Mint
1,2-Dave Stevens-c; new stories	.35	1.00	2.00

PLANET OF THE APES (Magazine) (Also see Advs. on the . . .)
Aug., 1974 - No. 29, Feb, 1977 (B&W) (Based on movies)
Marvel Comics Group

1-Ploog-a	.40	1.25	2.50
2-Ploog-a	.35	1.00	2.00
3-10	.25	.70	1.40
11-20		.50	1.00
21-29		.40	.80

NOTE: **Alcala** a-7-11, 17-22, 24. **Ploog** a-1-8, 11, 13, 14, 19. **Sutton** a-11, 12, 15, 17, 19, 20, 23, 24, 29.

PLANET OF VAMPIRES
Feb, 1975 - No. 3, July, 1975
Seaboard Publications (Atlas)

1-Adams-c(i); 1st Broderick c/a(p)	.40	.80
2-Adams-c, 3-Heath-c/a	.30	.60

PLANET TERRY
April, 1985 - No. 12, March, 1986 (children's comic)
Star Comics/Marvel

1-12		.35	.70

PLASTIC MAN (Also see Police & Smash #17)
Sum, 1943 - No. 64, Nov, 1956
Vital Publ. No. 1,2/Quality Comics No. 3 on

nn(#1)-'In The Game of Death;' Jack Cole-c/a begins; ends-#64?			
	115.00	345.00	805.00
2(nn, 2/44)-'The Gay Nineties Nightmare'	72.00	215.00	500.00
3 (Spr, '46)	48.00	145.00	335.00
4 (Sum, '46)	42.00	125.00	295.00
5 (Aut, '46)	35.00	105.00	245.00
6-10	25.00	75.00	175.00
11-20	22.00	65.00	154.00
21-30: 26-Last non-r issue?	17.00	51.00	120.00
31-39	13.00	40.00	90.00
40-Used in POP, pg. 91	14.00	42.00	100.00
41-64: 53-Last precode issue	10.00	30.00	70.00
Super Reprint 11('63, r-/#16), 16 (r-#21, Cole-a), 18('64-Spirit app. by Eisner/Police 95)	2.00	6.00	14.00

NOTE: **Cole** r-44,49,56,58,59 at least.

PLASTIC MAN (See Brave & the Bold and DC Special #15)
11-12/66 - No. 10, 5-6/68; No. 11, 2-3/76 - No. 20, 10-11/77
National Periodical Publications/DC Comics

1	1.00	3.00	6.00
2-5: 4-Infantino-c	.60	1.75	3.50
6-10('68)	.40	1.25	2.50
11('76)-20: 17-Origin retold	.25	.75	1.50

NOTE: **Gil Kane** c/a-1. **Mortimer** a-4. **Sparling** a-10.

PLASTIC MAN
Nov., 1988 - No. 4, Feb, 1989 ($1.00, mini-series)
DC Comics

1-4: 1-Origin; Woozy Winks app	.50	1.00

PLAYFUL LITTLE AUDREY (TV)(Also see Little Audrey #25)
6/57 - No. 110, 11/73; No. 111, 8/74 - No. 121, 4/76
Harvey Publications

1	11.50	34.50	80.00
2	5.70	17.00	40.00
3-5	5.00	15.00	35.00

305

PLAYFUL LITTLE AUDREY (continued)	Good	Fine	N-Mint
6-10	3.35	10.00	23.00
11-20	1.70	5.00	12.00
21-40	1.35	4.00	9.00
41-60	.85	2.50	5.00
61-80	.50	1.50	3.00
81-99	.40	1.25	2.50
100: 52 pg. Giant	.70	2.00	4.00
101-103: 52 pg. Giants	.50	1.50	3.00
104-121	.35	1.00	2.00

PLOP!
Sept-Oct, 1973 - No. 24, Nov-Dec, 1976
National Periodical Publications

	Good	Fine	N-Mint
1,5-Wrightson-a		.40	.80
2-4,6-10		.30	.60
11-24: 21-24-Giant size, 52 pgs.		.25	.50

NOTE: Alcala a-1-3. Anderson a-5. Aragones a-1-22, 24. Ditko a-16p. Evans a-1.
Orlando a-21, 22; c-21. Sekowsky a-5, 6p. Toth a-11. Wolverton a-4, 22, 23(1 pg.);
c-1-12, 14, 17, 18. Wood a-14, 16i, 18-24; c-13, 15, 16, 19.

PLUTO (See Cheerios Premiums, Four Color #537, Mickey Mouse
Magazine, Walt Disney Showcase #4,7,13,20,23,33 & Wheaties)
No. 7, 1942; No. 429, 10/52 - No. 1248, 11-1/61-62 (Walt Disney)
Dell Publishing Co.

	Good	Fine	N-Mint
Large Feature Comic 7(1942)	60.00	180.00	420.00
4-Color 429,509	2.65	8.00	18.00
4-Color 595,654	2.00	6.00	14.00
4-Color 736,853,941,1039,1143,1248	1.50	4.50	10.00

POCAHONTAS
1941 - No. 2, 1942
Pocahontas Fuel Company

	Good	Fine	N-Mint
nn(#1), 2	4.35	13.00	30.00

POCKET COMICS
Aug, 1941 - No. 4, Jan, 1942 (Pocket size; 100 pgs.)
Harvey Publications (1st Harvey comic)

	Good	Fine	N-Mint
1-Origin The Black Cat, Cadet Blakey the Spirit of '76, The Red Blazer, The Phantom, Sphinx, & The Zebra; Phantom Ranger, British Agent #99, Spin Hawkins, Satan, Lord of Evil begin	38.00	115.00	265.00
2	25.00	75.00	175.00
3,4	19.00	57.00	132.00

POGO PARADE (See Dell Giants)

POGO POSSUM (Also see Animal Comics & Special Delivery)
April, 1946 - No. 16, April-June, 1954
Dell Publishing Co.

	Good	Fine	N-Mint
4-Color 105(1946)-Kelly-c/a	57.00	171.00	400.00
4-Color 148-Kelly-c/a	47.00	141.00	330.00
1-(10-12/49)-Kelly c/a in all	42.00	125.00	295.00
2	21.00	62.00	147.00
3-5	16.00	48.00	110.00
6-10: 10-Infinity-c	13.00	40.00	90.00
11-16: 11-X-mas-c	11.50	34.00	80.00

NOTE: #1-4,9-13: 52 pgs.; #5-8,14-16: 36 pgs.

POLICE ACTION
Jan, 1954 - No. 7, Nov, 1954
Atlas News Co.

	Good	Fine	N-Mint
1-Violent-a by Robert Q. Sale	4.65	14.00	32.00
2	2.30	7.00	16.00
3-7: 7-Powell-a	2.00	6.00	14.00

NOTE: Ayers a-4, 5. Colan a-1. Forte a-1, 2. Mort Lawrence a-5. Maneely a-3; c-1, 5. Reinman a-6.

POLICE ACTION
Feb, 1975 - No. 3, June, 1975

Atlas/Seaboard Publ.

	Good	Fine	N-Mint
1-Lomax, N.Y.P.D., Luke Malone begin; McWilliams-a; bondage-c		.40	.80
2,3: 2-Origin Luke Malone, Manhunter		.30	.60

NOTE: Ploog art in all. Sekowsky/McWilliams a-1-3. Thorne c-3.

POLICE AGAINST CRIME
April, 1954 - No. 9, Aug, 1955
Premiere Magazines

	Good	Fine	N-Mint
1-Disbrow-a; extreme violence - man's face slashed with knife; Hollingsworth-a	5.70	17.00	40.00
2-Hollingsworth-a	3.00	9.00	21.00
3-9	2.00	6.00	14.00

POLICE BADGE #479 (Spy Thrillers #1-4)
No. 5, Sept, 1955
Atlas Comics (PrPI)

	Good	Fine	N-Mint
5-Maneely-c	2.00	6.00	14.00

POLICE CASE BOOK (See Giant Comics Editions)

POLICE CASES (See Authentic... & Record Book of...)

POLICE COMICS
Aug, 1941 - No. 127, Oct, 1953
Quality Comics Group (Comic Magazines)

	Good	Fine	N-Mint
1-Origin Plastic Man by Jack Cole, The Human Bomb by Gustavson, & No. 711; intro. Chic Carter by Eisner, The Firebrand by R. Crandall, The Mouthpiece, Phantom Lady, & The Sword	255.00	765.00	1785.00
2-Plastic Man smuggles opium	130.00	390.00	910.00
3	105.00	315.00	735.00
4	90.00	270.00	630.00
5-Plastic Man forced to smoke marijuana	90.00	270.00	630.00
6,7	80.00	240.00	560.00
8-Manhunter begins (origin)	95.00	285.00	665.00
9,10	75.00	225.00	525.00
11-The Spirit strip-r begin by Eisner(Origin-strip #1)	125.00	375.00	875.00
12-Intro. Ebony	80.00	240.00	560.00
13-Intro. Woozy Winks; last Firebrand	80.00	240.00	560.00
14-19: 15-Last No. 711; Destiny begins	52.00	155.00	365.00
20-The Raven x-over in Phantom Lady; features Jack Cole himself	52.00	155.00	365.00
21,22-Raven & Spider Widow x-over in Phantom Lady #21; cameo in Phantom Lady #22	37.00	110.00	260.00
23-30: 23-Last Phantom Lady. 24-Chic Carter becomes The Sword, only issue. 24-26-Flatfoot Burns by Kurtzman in all	32.00	95.00	225.00
31-41-Last Spirit-r by Eisner	23.00	70.00	160.00
42,43-Spirit-r by Eisner/Fine	20.00	60.00	140.00
44-Fine Spirit-r begin, end #88,90,92	17.00	51.00	120.00
45-50:(#50 on-c, #49 on inside)(1/46)	17.00	51.00	120.00
51-60: 58-Last Human Bomb	13.00	40.00	90.00
61,62,64-88	11.50	34.00	80.00
63-(Some issues have #65 printed on cover, but #63 on inside) Kurtzman-a, 6pgs.	11.50	34.00	80.00
89,91,93-No Spirit	11.00	32.00	75.00
90,92-Spirit by Fine	11.50	34.00	80.00
94-99,101,102: Spirit by Eisner in all; 101-Last Manhunter. 102-Last Spirit & Plastic Man by Jack Cole	15.00	45.00	105.00
100	17.00	51.00	120.00
103-Content change to crime - Ken Shannon begins (1st app.)	8.00	24.00	56.00
104-111,114-127-Crandall-a most issues	5.50	16.50	38.00
112-Crandall-a	5.50	16.50	38.00
113-Crandall-c/a(2), 9 pgs. each	5.70	17.00	40.00

NOTE: Most Spirit stories signed by Eisner are not by him; all are reprints. Cole c-17, 19-21, 24-26, 28-31, 36-38, 40-42, 45-48, 65-68, 69, 73, 75. Crandall Firebrand-1-8.

Pocket Comics #1, © HARV

Police Against Crime #2, © PG

Police Comics #11, © QUA

Police Line-Up #3, © AVON   Polly Pigtails #22, © PMI   Popeye #67, © KING

POLICE COMICS (continued)
Spirit by Eisner 1-41, 94-102; by Eisner/Fine-42, 43; by Fine-44-88, 90, 92. 103, 109, Bondage c-103, 109, 125.

POLICE LINE-UP
Aug, 1951 - No. 4, July, 1952 (Painted-c)
Realistic Comics/Avon Periodicals

	Good	Fine	N-Mint
1-Wood-a, 1 pg. plus part-r; spanking panel-r/Saint #5			
	15.00	45.00	105.00
2-Classic story "The Religious Murder Cult," drugs, perversion			
r-/Saint #5; c-/Avon paperback 329	13.00	40.00	90.00
3-Kubert-a(r)/part-c, Kinstler-a	8.00	24.00	56.00
4-Kinstler-a	8.00	24.00	56.00

POLICE THRILLS
1954
Ajax/Farrell Publications

1	3.00	9.00	21.00

POLICE TRAP (Public Defender In Action #7 on)
8-9/54 - No. 4, 2-3/55; No. 5, 7/55 - No. 6, 9/55
Mainline No. 1-4/Charlton No. 5,6

1-S&K covers-all issues	5.70	17.00	40.00
2-4	2.85	8.50	20.00
5,6-S&K-c/a	5.00	15.00	35.00

POLICE TRAP
No. 11, 1963; No. 16-18, 1964
Super Comics

Reprint #11,16-18	.50	1.50	3.00

POLL PARROT
Poll Parrot Shoe Store/International Shoe
1950 - 1951; 1959 - 1962
K. K. Publications (Giveaway)

1 ('50)-Howdy Doody; small size	2.65	8.00	18.00
2-4('50)-Howdy Doody	1.70	5.00	12.00
2('59)-16('61): 2- The Secret of Crumbley Castle. 5-Bandit Busters.			

7-The Make-Believe Mummy. 8-Mixed Up Mission('60). 10-The Frightful Flight. 11-Showdown at Sunup. 13- . . .and the Runaway Genie. 14-Bully for You. 16- . . .& the Rajah's Ruby('62)

	.50	1.50	3.00

POLLY & HER PALS (See Comic Monthly #1)

POLLYANNA (See 4-Color #1129)

POLLY PIGTAILS (Girls' Fun & Fashion Mag. #44 on)
Jan, 1946 - V4No.43, Oct-Nov, 1949
Parents' Magazine Institute/Polly Pigtails

1-Infinity-c; photo-c	5.00	15.00	35.00
2	2.30	7.00	16.00
3-5	1.75	5.25	12.00
6-10: 7-Photo-c	1.35	4.00	9.00
11-30: 22-Photo-c	1.15	3.50	8.00
31-43	1.00	3.00	7.00

PONY EXPRESS (See Four Color #942)

PONYTAIL
7-9/62 - No. 12, 10-12/65; No. 13, 11/69 - No. 20, 1/71
Dell Publishing Co./Charlton No. 13 on

12-641-209(#1)	.75	2.25	5.00
2-12	.50	1.50	3.00
13-20	.35	1.00	2.00

POP COMICS (7 cents)
1955 (36 pgs.; 5x7''; in color)
Modern Store Publ.

1-Funny animal	.50	1.50	3.00

POPEYE (See Comic Album #7,11,15, Comics Reading Libraries, Eat Right to

Work . . ., Giant Comic Album, King Comics, Magic Comics, March of Comics #37, 52, 66, 80, 96, 117, 134, 148, 157, 169, 194, 246, 264, 274, 294, 453, 465, 477 & Wow Comics, 1st series)

POPEYE (See Thimble Theatre)
1935 (25 cents; 52 pgs.; B&W) (By Segar)
David McKay Publications

	Good	Fine	N-Mint
1-Daily strip serial reprints-"The Gold Mine Thieves"			
	45.00	135.00	315.00
2-Daily strip-r	36.00	107.00	250.00

NOTE: *Popeye first entered Thimble Theatre in 1929.*

POPEYE
1937 - 1939 (All by Segar)
David McKay Publications

Feature Books nn (100 pgs.) (Very Rare)	385.00	1155.00	2700.00
Feature Books 2 (52 pgs.)	50.00	150.00	350.00
Feature Books 3 (100 pgs.)-r-/nn issue with a new-c			
	42.00	125.00	295.00
Feature Books 5,10 (76 pgs.)	34.00	100.00	237.00
Feature Books 14 (76 pgs.) (Scarce)	48.00	145.00	335.00

POPEYE (Strip reprints through 4-Color #70)
1941 - 1947; #1, 2-4/48 - #65, 7-9/62; #66, 10/62 - #80, 5/66; #81, 8/66 - #92, 12/67; #94, 2/69 - #138, 1/77; #139, 5/78 - #171, 7/84 (no #93,160,161)
Dell #1-65/Gold Key #66-80/King #81-92/Charlton #94-138/Gold Key #139-155/Whitman #156 on

Large Feat. Comic 24('41)-½ by Segar	34.00	100.00	237.00
4-Color 25('41)-by Segar	37.00	110.00	260.00
Large Feature Comic 10('43)	28.00	84.00	195.00
4-Color 17('43)-by Segar	30.00	90.00	210.00
4-Color 26('43)-by Segar	28.00	84.00	195.00
4-Color 43('44)	19.00	57.00	132.00
4-Color 70('45)-Title: . . .& Wimpy	16.00	48.00	110.00
4-Color 113('46-original strips begin),127,145('47),168			
	8.50	25.50	60.00
1(2-4/48)(Dell)	20.00	60.00	140.00
2	10.00	30.00	70.00
3-10	8.50	25.50	60.00
11-20	6.50	19.50	45.00
21-40	4.35	13.00	30.00
41-45,47-50	3.50	10.50	24.00
46-Origin Swee' Pee	5.00	15.00	35.00
51-60	2.30	7.00	16.00
61-65 (Last Dell issue)	2.00	6.00	14.00
66,67-both 84 pgs. (G. Key)	3.50	10.50	28.00
68-80	1.70	5.00	12.00
81-92,94-100	.85	2.50	6.00
101-130	.70	2.00	5.00
131-143,145-159,162-171	.55	1.65	4.00
144-50th Anniversary issue	.55	1.65	4.00

NOTE: *Reprints-#145, 147, 149, 151, 153, 155, 157, 163-68(½), 170.*

Bold Detergent giveaway (Same as regular issue #94)			
	.35	1.00	2.00
. . .Kite Fun Book ('77, 5x7¼'', 16p., soft-c)	1.00	3.00	6.00

POPEYE
1972 - 1974 (36 pgs. in color)
Charlton (King Features) (Giveaway)

E-1 to E-15 (Educational comics)	.25	.75	1.50
nn-Popeye Gettin' Better Grades-4 pgs. used as intro. to above			
giveaways (in color)	.25	.75	1.50

POPEYE CARTOON BOOK
1934 (40 pgs. plus cover)(8½x13'')(cardboard covers)
The Saalfield Publ. Co.

2095-(Rare)-1933 strip reprints in color by Segar; each page contains a vertical half of a Sunday strip, so the continuity reads row

POPEYE CARTOON BOOK (continued)   **Good**   **Fine**   **N-Mint**
by row completely across each double page spread. If each page is
read by itself, the continuity makes no sense. Each double page
spread reprints one complete Sunday page (from 1933).

	Good	Fine	N-Mint
	80.00	240.00	560.00
12 Page Version	44.00	132.00	308.00

POPEYE SPECIAL
Summer, 1987 - No. 2, Sept, 1988 ($1.75-$2.00, color)
Ocean Comics

	Good	Fine	N-Mint
1-Origin	.50	1.50	3.00
2 ($2.00)	.50	1.50	3.00

POPPLES (TV, Movie)
Dec, 1986 - No. 5, Aug, 1987
Star Comics (Marvel)

		Fine	N-Mint
1-3-Based on toys		.35	.70
4,5 ($1.00)		.45	.90

POPPO OF THE POPCORN THEATRE
10/29/55 - 1956 (published weekly)
Fuller Publishing Co. (Publishers Weekly)

	Good	Fine	N-Mint
1	2.35	7.00	16.00
2-13	1.15	3.50	8.00

NOTE: *By* **Charles Biro**. *10 cent cover, given away by supermarkets such as IGA.*

POP-POP COMICS
No date (Circa 1945) (52 pgs.)
R. B. Leffingwell Co.

	Good	Fine	N-Mint
1-Funny animal	4.00	12.00	28.00

POPSICLE PETE FUN BOOK (See All-American #6)
1947, 1948
Joe Lowe Corp.

nn-36 pgs. in color; Sammy 'n' Claras, The King Who Couldn't
Sleep & Popsicle Pete stories, games, cut-outs

	Good	Fine	N-Mint
	4.60	14.00	32.00
Adventure Book ('48)	3.70	11.00	26.00

POPULAR COMICS
Feb, 1936 - No. 145, July-Sept, 1948
Dell Publishing Co.

	Good	Fine	N-Mint
1-Dick Tracy, Little Orphan Annie, Terry & the Pirates, Gasoline Alley, Don Winslow, Harold Teen, Little Joe, Skippy, Moon Mullins, Mutt & Jeff, Tailspin Tommy, Smitty, Smokey Stover, Winnie Winkle & The Gumps begin (all strip-r)	130.00	390.00	910.00
2	65.00	195.00	455.00
3	50.00	150.00	350.00
4,5: 5-Tom Mix begins	40.00	120.00	280.00
6-10: 8,9-Scribbly, Reglar Fellers app.	30.00	90.00	210.00
11-20: 12-Xmas-c	25.00	75.00	175.00
21-27-Last Terry & the Pirates, Little Orphan Annie, & Dick Tracy	18.00	54.00	125.00
28-37: 28-Gene Autry app. 31,32-Tim McCoy app. 35-Christmas-c; Tex Ritter app.	15.00	45.00	105.00
38-43-Tarzan in text only. 38-Gang Busters (radio) & Zane Grey's Tex Thorne begins?	17.00	51.00	120.00
44,45: 45-Tarzan-c	11.50	34.00	80.00
46-Origin Martan, the Marvel Man	16.00	48.00	110.00
47-50	11.50	34.00	80.00
51-Origin The Voice (The Invisible Detective) strip begins	12.00	36.00	84.00
52-59: 55-End of World sty	10.00	30.00	70.00
60-Origin Professor Supermind and Son	11.00	32.00	75.00
61-71: 63-Smilin' Jack begins	9.00	27.00	62.00
72-The Owl & Terry the Pirates begin; Smokey Stover reprints begin	13.00	40.00	90.00
73-75	10.00	30.00	70.00
76-78-Capt. Midnight in all	11.50	34.00	80.00

	Good	Fine	N-Mint
79-85-Last Owl	9.50	25.50	65.00
86-99: 98-Felix the Cat, Smokey Stover-r begin	7.00	21.00	50.00
100	8.50	25.50	60.00
101-130: 115-Last Dick Tracy-r	4.65	14.00	32.00
131-145: 142-Last Terry & the Pirates	4.00	12.00	28.00

POPULAR FAIRY TALES (See March of Comics #6,18)

POPULAR ROMANCE
No. 5, Dec, 1949 - No. 29, 1954
Better-Standard Publications

	Good	Fine	N-Mint
5	3.50	10.50	24.00
6-9	2.15	6.50	15.00
10-Wood-a, 2 pgs.	3.65	11.00	25.00
11,12,14-21,28,29	1.70	5.00	12.00
13-Severin/Elder-a, 3 pgs.	2.00	6.00	14.00
22-27-Toth-a	4.60	14.00	32.00

NOTE: *All have photo-c.* **Tuska** *art in most issues.*

POPULAR TEEN-AGERS (Secrets of Love) (Formerly School Day Romances)
Sept, 1950 - No. 23, Nov, 1954
Star Publications

	Good	Fine	N-Mint
5-Toni Gay, Honey Bunn, etc.; L. B. Cole-c	10.00	30.00	70.00
6-8 (7/51)-Toni Gay, Honey Bunn, etc.; all have L. B. Cole-c; 6-Negligee panels	9.00	27.00	62.00
9-(. . .Romances; 1st romance issue, 10/51)	3.50	10.50	24.00
10-(. . .Secrets of Love)	3.50	10.50	24.00
11,16,18,19,22,23	2.85	8.50	20.00
12,13,17,20,21-Disbrow-a	3.50	10.50	24.00
14-Harrison/Wood-a; 2 spanking scenes	11.50	34.50	80.00
15-Wood?, Disbrow-a	8.00	24.00	55.00
Accepted Reprint 5,6 (nd); L.B. Cole-c	2.00	6.00	14.00

NOTE: *All have* **L. B. Cole** *covers.*

PORE LI'L MOSE
1902 (30 pgs.; 10½x15''; in full color)
New York Herald Publ. by Grand Union Tea
Cupples & Leon Co.

By R. F. Outcault; 1 pg. strips about early Negroes

	Good	Fine	N-Mint
	35.00	105.00	245.00

PORKY PIG (. .& Bugs Bunny #40-69)
No. 16, 1942 - No. 109, July, 1984
Dell Publishing Co./Gold Key No. 1-93/Whitman No. 94 on

	Good	Fine	N-Mint
4-Color 16(1942)	35.00	105.00	245.00
4-Color 48(1944)-Carl Barks-a	70.00	210.00	490.00
4-Color 78(1945)	13.00	40.00	90.00
4-Color 112(7/46)	8.00	24.00	56.00
4-Color 156,182,191('49)	5.70	17.00	40.00
4-Color 226,241('49),260,271,277,284,295	4.00	12.00	28.00
4-Color 303,311,322,330	2.65	8.00	18.00
4-Color 342,351,360,370,385,399,410,426	2.00	6.00	14.00
25 (11-12/52)-30	1.15	3.50	8.00
31-50	.55	1.65	4.00
51-81(3-4/62)	.45	1.35	3.00
1(1/65-G.K.)(2nd Series)	.75	2.25	5.00
2,4,5-Reprints 4-Color 226,284 & 271 in that order	.45	1.35	3.00
3,6-10	.35	1.00	2.00
11-50		.50	1.00
51-109		.30	.60
Kite Fun Book (1960, 16pgs., 5x7¼'', soft-c)	2.00	6.00	12.00

NOTE: *Reprints-#1-8, 9-35(½); 36-46,58,67,69-74,76,78,102-109(½-½).*

PORKY PIG (See Bugs Bunny &. . ., March of Comics #42, 57, 71, 89, 99, 113, 130, 143, 164, 175, 192, 209, 218, 367, and Super Book #6, 18, 30)

Popsicle Pete Fun Book, © Joe Lowe Corp.

Popular Comics #48, © DELL

Popular Teen-Agers #14, © STAR

Power Comics #1 (1st print), © Power Comics

Powerhouse Pepper #4, © MEG

Primer #1, © Comico

PORKY'S BOOK OF TRICKS
1942 (48 pages) (8½x5½")
K. K. Publications (Giveaway)

	Good	Fine	N-Mint
7 pg. comic story, text stories, plus games & puzzles	25.00	75.00	175.00

POST GAZETTE (See Meet the New...)

POWDER RIVER RUSTLERS (See Fawcett Movie Comics)

POWER COMICS
1944 - 1945
Holyoke Publ. Co./Narrative Publ.

	Good	Fine	N-Mint
1-L. B. Cole-c	15.00	45.00	105.00
2-4: 2-Dr. Mephisto begins. 3,4-L. B. Cole-c; Miss Espionage app. each	13.00	40.00	90.00

POWER COMICS
1977 - No. 5, Dec., 1977 (B&W)
Power Comics Co.

	Good	Fine	N-Mint
1-A Boy And His Aardvark app. by Dave Sims; first Dave Sims aardvark	5.00	15.00	30.00
1-Reprint (3/77, black-c)	1.35	4.00	8.00
2-Cobalt Blue app.	2.00	6.00	12.00
3-Nightwitch app.	.35	1.00	2.00
4,5: 4-Northern Light. 5-Bluebird app.	.35	1.00	2.00

POWER FACTOR
1987 - No. 3, 1987? ($1.95, color)
Wonder Color Comics

	Good	Fine	N-Mint
1-3	.35	1.10	2.25

POWER GIRL (See Infinity, Inc. & Showcase #97-99)
June, 1988 - No. 4, Sept., 1988 ($1.00, mini-series)
DC Comics

	Good	Fine	N-Mint
1-4		.50	1.00

POWERHOUSE PEPPER COMICS (See Gay & Joker Comics)
No. 1, 1943; No. 2, May, 1948 - No. 5, Nov, 1948
Marvel Comics (20CC)

	Good	Fine	N-Mint
1-(60 pgs.)-Wolverton-c/a in all	55.00	165.00	385.00
2	33.00	100.00	230.00
3,4	32.00	95.00	225.00
5-(Scarce)	38.00	115.00	265.00

POWER LINE
May, 1988 - Present ($1.25-$1.50, color)
Epic Comics (Marvel)

	Good	Fine	N-Mint
1-3: 2-Williamson-i; 3-Austin-i, Dr. Zero app.		.60	1.25
4,5-Morrow-a	.25	.75	1.50

POWER LORDS
Dec, 1983 - No. 3, Feb, 1984 (mini-series; Mando paper)
DC Comics

	Good	Fine	N-Mint
1-3-Based on Revell toys		.40	.80

POWER MAN (Formerly Hero for Hire; ..& Iron Fist #68 on)
No. 17, Feb, 1974 - No. 125, Sept, 1986
Marvel Comics Group

	Good	Fine	N-Mint
17-20: 17-Iron Man app.	.40	1.20	2.40
21-31: 31-Part Adams-i		.60	1.20
32-47: 36-Reprint. 45-Starlin-c		.50	1.00
48-Byrne-a; Powerman/Iron Fist 1st meet	.50	1.50	3.00
49,50-Byrne-a(p); 50-Iron Fist joins Cage	.50	1.50	3.00
51-56,58-60: 58-Intro El Aguila		.40	.80
57-New X-Men app.	.85	2.50	5.00
61-125: 75-Double size. 87-Moon Knight app. 90-Unus app. 109-The Reaper app. 100-Double size; origin K'un L'un. 125-Double size		.40	.80
Giant-Size 1('75)	.25	.80	1.60

	Good	Fine	N-Mint
Annual 1(11/76)		.50	1.00

NOTE: *Austin* c-102i. *Byrne* a-48-50; c-102, 104, 106, 107. *Kane* c(p)-24, 25, 28, 48. *Miller* a-68; c-66-68, 70-74, 80i. *Mooney* a-53i, 55i. *Nebres* a-76p. *Nino* a-42i, 43i. *Perez* a-27. *Tuska* a-17p, 20p, 24p.

POWERMOWERMAN AND POWER MOWER SAFETY
1966 (16 pgs.) (Giveaway)
Frank Burgmeier Co. (Outdoor Power Equipment Inst.)

	Good	Fine	N-Mint
nn-Vaughn Bode'-a	22.00	65.00	130.00

POWER OF THE ATOM (See Secret Origins #29)
Aug., 1988 - Present ($1.00, color)
DC Comics

	Good	Fine	N-Mint
1-7: 6-Byrne-p		.50	1.00

POWER PACK
Aug, 1984 - Present
Marvel Comics Group

	Good	Fine	N-Mint
1-($1.00)	.75	2.25	4.50
2-5	.50	1.50	3.00
6-8-Cloak & Dagger app.	.35	1.00	2.00
9-18	.25	.75	1.50
19-Dbl. size; Cloak & Dagger, Wolverine app.	.60	1.75	3.50
20-24		.60	1.25
25-Double size	.30	.90	1.80
26-Direct sale; Cloak & Dagger app.		.60	1.25
27-Mutant massacre, Wolverine app.	.60	1.75	3.50
28-43: 42-1st Inferno tie-in		.50	1.00

POW MAGAZINE (Bob Sproul's) (Satire Magazine)
Aug, 1966 - No. 3, Feb, 1967 (30 cents)
Humor-Vision

	Good	Fine	N-Mint
1-3: 2-Jones-a. 3-Wrightson-a	1.00	3.00	7.00

PREHISTORIC WORLD (See Classics Illusstrated Special Issue)

PREMIERE (See Charlton Premiere)

PRESTO KID, THE (See Red Mask)

PRETTY BOY FLOYD (See On the Spot)

PREZ (See Cancelled Comic Cavalcade & Supergirl #10)
Aug-Sept, 1973 - No. 4, Feb-Mar, 1974
National Periodical Publications

	Good	Fine	N-Mint
1-Origin		.30	.60
2-4		.25	.50

PRICE, THE (See Eclipse Graphic Album Series)

PRIDE AND THE PASSION, THE (See 4-Color #824)

PRIDE OF THE YANKEES, THE
1949 (The Life of Lou Gehrig)
Magazine Enterprises

	Good	Fine	N-Mint
nn-Photo-c; Ogden Whitney-a	25.00	75.00	175.00

PRIMAL MAN (See The Crusaders)

PRIMER (Comico...)
Oct, 1982 - No. 6, Feb, 1984 (B&W)
Comico

	Good	Fine	N-Mint
1 (52 pgs.)	1.00	3.00	6.00
2-1st app. Grendel & Argent by Wagner	7.50	22.50	45.00
3-5	.70	2.00	4.00
6-Intro & 1st app. Evangeline	2.50	7.50	15.00

PRIMUS (TV)
Feb, 1972 - No. 7, Oct, 1972
Charlton Comics

	Good	Fine	N-Mint
1-5,7-Staton-a in all	.35	1.00	2.00
6-Drug propaganda story	.35	1.00	2.00

PRINCE & THE PAUPER, THE (See Movie Classics)

PRINCE NAMOR, THE SUB-MARINER
Sept, 1984 - No. 4, Dec, 1984 (mini-series)
Marvel Comics Group

	Good	Fine	N-Mint
1	.25	.75	1.50
2-4		.50	1.00

PRINCE NIGHTMARE
1987 ($2.95, color, 68 pgs.)
Aaaargh! Associated Artists

Book 1	.50	1.50	3.00

PRINCE VALIANT (See Comics Reading Libraries, Feature Books #26, McKay, and 4-Color #567, 650, 699, 719, 788, 849, 900)

PRISCILLA'S POP (See 4-Color #569,630,704,799)

PRISON BARS (See Behind . . .)

PRISON BREAK!
1951 (Sept) - No. 5, Sept, 1952
Avon Periodicals/Realistic No. 3 on

	Good	Fine	N-Mint
1-Wood-c & 1 pg.; has r-/Saint #7 retitled Michael Strong Private Eye	17.00	51.00	120.00
2-Wood-c/Kubert-a plus 2 pgs. Wood-a	12.00	36.00	84.00
3-Orlando, Check-a; c-/Avon paperback 179	10.00	30.00	70.00
4,5: Kinstler-c. 5-Infantino-a	9.00	27.00	62.00

PRISONER, THE (TV)
1988 - No. 4, Jan, 1989 ($3.50, mini-series, squarebound)
DC Comics

1-Book A	.75	2.25	4.50
2-4	.60	1.75	3.50

PRISON RIOT
1952
Avon Periodicals

1-Marijuana Murders-1 pg. text; Kinstler-c	13.00	40.00	90.00

PRISON TO PRAISE
1974 (35 cents)
Logos International

True Story of Merlin R. Carothers		.30	.60

PRIVATE BUCK (See Large Feature Comic #12 & 21)

PRIVATEERS
Aug., 1987 - No. 2, 1987 ($1.50, color)
Vanguard Graphics

1,2	.25	.75	1.50

PRIVATE EYE (Rocky Jordan . . . #6-8)
Jan, 1951 - No. 8, March, 1952
Atlas Comics (MCI)

1	5.00	15.00	35.00
2,3-Tuska c/a(3)	3.50	10.50	24.00
4-8	2.65	8.00	18.00

NOTE: *Henkel a-6(3), 7; c-7. Sinnott a-6.*

PRIVATE EYE (See Mike Shayne . . .)

PRIVATE SECRETARY
Dec-Feb, 1962-63 - No. 2, Mar-May, 1963
Dell Publishing Co.

1,2	1.00	3.00	7.00

PRIVATE STRONG (See The Double Life of . . .)

PRIZE COMICS (. . .Western #69 on) (Also see Treasure Comics)
March, 1940 - No. 68, Feb-Mar, 1948
Prize Publications

1-Origin Power Nelson, The Futureman & Jupiter, Master Magician; Ted O'Neil, Secret Agent M-11, Jaxon of the Jungle, Bucky

	Good	Fine	N-Mint
Brady & Storm Curtis begin	72.00	215.00	505.00
2-The Black Owl begins	35.00	105.00	245.00
3,4	27.00	81.00	190.00
5,6: Dr. Dekkar, Master of Monsters app. in each	25.00	75.00	175.00
7-Black Owl by S&K; origin/1st app. Dr. Frost & Frankenstein; The Green Lama, Capt. Gallant, The Great Voodini & Twist Turner begin; Kirby-c	55.00	165.00	385.00
8,9-Black Owl & Ted O'Neil by S&K	30.00	90.00	210.00
10-12,14-20: 11-Origin Bulldog Denny. 16-Spike Mason begins	25.00	75.00	175.00
13-Yank & Doodle begin (origin)	30.00	90.00	210.00
21-24	14.00	42.00	100.00
25-30	11.00	32.00	75.00
31-33	8.00	24.00	56.00
34-Origin Airmale, & Yank & Doodle; The Black Owl joins army, Yank & Doodle's father assumes Black Owl's role	9.00	27.00	62.00
35-40: 35-Flying Fist & Bingo begin. 37-Intro. Stampy, Airmale's sidekick; Hitler-c	7.00	21.00	50.00
41-50: 45-Yank & Doodle learn Black Owl's I.D. (their father). 48-Prince Ra begins	5.00	15.00	35.00
51-62,64-68: 53-Transvestism sty. 55-No Frankenstein. 64-Black Owl retires	4.65	14.00	32.00
63-Simon & Kirby c/a	6.50	19.50	45.00

NOTE: *Briefer a 7-on; c-65, 66. J. Binder a-16; c-22, 26, 29.*

PRIZE COMICS WESTERN (Prize Comics #1-68)
No. 69(V7No.2), Apr-May, 1948 - No. 119, Nov-Dec, 1956
Prize Publications (Feature) (No. 69-84, 52 pgs.)

	Good	Fine	N-Mint
69(V7#2)	6.50	19.50	45.00
70-75	4.65	14.00	32.00
76-Randolph Scott photo-c; ''Canadian Pacific'' movie adapt.	6.50	19.50	45.00
77-Photo-c; Severin, Mart Bailey-a; 'Streets of Laredo' movie adapt.	5.00	15.00	35.00
78-Photo-c; Kurtzman-a, 10 pgs.; Severin, Mart Bailey-a; 'Bullet Code,' & 'Roughshod' movie adapt.	8.00	24.00	56.00
79-Photo-c; Kurtzman-a, 8 pgs.; Severin & Elder, Severin, Mart Bailey-a; 'Stage To Chino' movie adapt.	8.00	24.00	56.00
80,81-Photo-c; Severin/Elder-a(2)	5.00	15.00	35.00
82-Photo-c; 1st app. The Preacher by Mart Bailey; Severin/Elder-a(3)	5.00	15.00	35.00
83,84	4.00	12.00	28.00
85-American Eagle by John Severin begins (1-2/50)	11.00	32.00	75.00
86,92,95,101-105	4.65	14.00	32.00
87-91,93,94,96-99,110,111-Severin/Elder a(2-3) each	5.00	15.00	35.00
100	7.00	21.00	50.00
106-108,112	3.50	10.50	24.00
109-Severin/Williamson-a	6.00	18.00	42.00
113-Williamson/Severin-a(2)	6.50	19.50	45.00
114-119: Drifter series in all; by Mort Meskin 114-118	2.65	8.00	18.00

NOTE: *Fass a-81. Severin & Elder c-88, 92, 94-96, 98. Severin a-72, 75, 77-79, 83-86, 96, 97, 100-105; c-most 85-109. Simon & Kirby c-75, 83.*

PRIZE MYSTERY
May, 1955 - No. 3, Sept, 1955
Key Publications

	Good	Fine	N-Mint
1	3.00	9.00	21.00
2,3	2.00	6.00	14.00

PROFESSIONAL FOOTBALL (See Charlton Sport Library)

The Prisoner #1, © ITC Entertainment

Prize Comics #63, © PRIZE

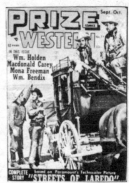

Prize Comics Western #77, © PRIZE

Psychoanalysis #1, © WMG

Public Defender In Action #12, © CC

Punch Comics #1, © CHES

PROFESSOR COFFIN
No. 19, Oct, 1985 - No. 21, Feb, 1986
Charlton Comics

	Good	Fine	N-Mint
19-21: Wayne Howard-a(r)		.40	.80

PROJECT: HERO
Aug, 1987 ($1.50, color)
Vanguard Graphics (Canadian)

1	.25	.75	1.50

PROWLER (Also see Revenge of The Prowler)
July, 1987 - No. 4, Oct, 1987 ($1.75, color)
Eclipse Comics

1-4	.30	.85	1.70

PROWLER IN "WHITE ZOMBIE", THE
Oct, 1988 ($2.00, B&W, Baxter paper)
Eclipse Comics

1-Adapts Bela Lugosi movie White Zombie	.35	1.00	2.00

PSI FORCE
Nov, 1986 - No. 32, Feb, 1989 (.75-$1.25)
Marvel Comics Group

1-32	.25	.75	1.50
Annual 1 (10/87)		.65	1.30

PSYCHO (Magazine)
Jan, 1971 - No. 24, Mar, 1975 (68 pgs.; B&W) (no No.22?)
Skywald Publishing Corp.

1-All reprints	.85	2.50	5.00
2-Origin & 1st app. The Heap, & Frankenstein series by Adkins	.50	1.50	3.00
3-10	.35	1.00	2.00
11-21,23: 13-Cannabalism. 18-Injury to eye-c. 20-Severed Head-c	.35	1.00	2.00
24-1975 Winter Special	.35	1.00	2.00
Annual 1('72)	.50	1.50	3.00
Fall Special('74)	.35	1.00	2.00
Yearbook(1974-nn)	.35	1.00	2.00

NOTE: *Boris* c-3, 5. *Buckler* a-4 ,5. *Everett* a-3-6. *J. Jones* a-6, 7, 9; c-12. *Kaluta* a-13. *Katz/Buckler* a-3. *Morrow* a-1. *Reese* a-5. *Sutton* a-3. *Wildey* a-5.

PSYCHOANALYSIS
Mar-Apr, 1955 - No. 4, Sept-Oct, 1955
E. C. Comics

1-All Kamen c/a; not approved by code	6.00	18.00	42.00
2-4-Kamen-c/a in all	4.60	14.00	32.00

PSYCHOBLAST
Nov,1987 - No. 9, July, 1988 ($1.75, color)
First Comics

1-9	.30	.90	1.80

P.T. 109 (See Movie Comics)

PUBLIC DEFENDER IN ACTION (Formerly Police Trap)
No. 7, Mar, 1956 - No. 12, Oct, 1957
Charlton Comics

7	3.00	9.00	21.00
8-12	1.70	5.00	12.00

PUBLIC ENEMIES
1948 - No. 9, June-July, 1949
D. S. Publishing Co.

1	5.70	17.00	40.00
2-Used in SOTI, pg. 95	8.00	24.00	56.00
3-5: 5-Arrival date of 10/1/48	3.50	10.50	24.00
6,8,9	3.00	9.00	21.00
7-McWilliams-a; injury to eye panel	4.60	14.00	32.00

PUDGY PIG
Sept, 1958 - No. 2, Nov, 1958
Charlton Comics

	Good	Fine	N-Mint
1,2	1.00	3.00	7.00

PUMA BLUES
1986 - Present ($1.70, B&W)
Aardvark One International

1	.75	2.25	4.50
1-2nd print	.30	.85	1.70
2	.35	1.00	2.00
3-21	.30	.85	1.70
Trade Paperback (12/88)	2.50	7.50	14.95

PUNCH & JUDY COMICS
1944; No. 2, Fall, 1948 - V3No.9, Dec, 1951
Hillman Periodicals

V1#1-(1944, 60 pgs.)	5.70	17.00	40.00
2 (Fall, '48)	3.00	9.00	21.00
3-12(7/46)	2.00	6.00	14.00
V2#1,3-9	1.50	4.50	10.00
V2#2,10-12, V3#1-Kirby-a(2) each	7.00	21.00	50.00
V3#2-Kirby-a	6.00	18.00	42.00
3-9	1.30	4.00	9.00

PUNCH COMICS
Dec, 1941 - No. 26, Dec, 1947
Harry 'A' Chesler

1-Mr. E, The Sky Chief, Hale the Magician, Kitty Kelly begin	40.00	120.00	280.00
2-Captain Glory app.	20.00	60.00	140.00
3	17.00	51.00	120.00
4	15.00	45.00	105.00
5	11.50	34.00	80.00
6-8	10.00	30.00	70.00
9-Rocketman & Rocket Girl & The Master Key begin	12.00	36.00	84.00
10-Sky Chief app.; J. Cole-a; Master Key r-/Scoop 3	10.00	30.00	70.00
11-Origin Master Key-r/Scoop 1; Sky Chief, Little Nemo app.; Jack Cole-a; Fineish art by Sultan	11.00	32.00	75.00
12-Rocket Boy & Capt. Glory app; Skull-c	9.50	28.50	65.00
13-17,19: 13-Cover has list of 4 Chesler artists' names on tombstone	8.50	25.50	60.00
18-Bondage-c; hypodermic panels	11.00	32.00	75.00
20-Unique cover with bare-breasted women	17.00	51.00	120.00
21-Hypo needle story	9.50	28.50	65.00
22-26: 22,23-Little Nemo-not by McCay	8.00	24.00	56.00

PUNCHY AND THE BLACK CROW
No. 10, Oct, 1985 - No. 12, Feb, 1986
Charlton Comics

10-12: Al Fago funny animal-r		.40	.80

PUNISHER (Also see Amaz. Spider-Man, Captain America #241, Daredevil #182-184, 257, Marvel Preview #2, Marvel Super Action, Marvel Tales, Spect. Spider-Man #81-83 & new Strange Tales #13,14)
Jan, 1986 - No. 5, May, 1986 (mini-series)
Marvel Comics Group

1-Double size	2.85	9.00	20.00
2	2.00	6.00	12.00
3	1.35	4.00	8.00
4,5	1.15	3.50	7.00
Trade Paperback-r/1-5, 1988	1.35	4.00	8.00

PUNISHER
July, 1987 - Present
Marvel Comics Group

PUNISHER (continued)	Good	Fine	N-Mint
V2#1	1.00	3.00	6.00
2	.60	1.75	3.50
3-5	.40	1.25	2.50
6-10	.25	.75	1.50
11-16		.60	1.20
Annual 1(8/88)-Evolutionary War app.	.70	2.00	4.00

PUNISHER WAR JOURNAL
Nov., 1988 - Present ($1.50, color)
Marvel Comics

1-Origin The Punisher; Matt Murdock cameo	.40	1.25	2.50
2-4: 2,3-Daredevil x-over	.30	.90	1.80

PUPPET COMICS
Spring, 1946 - No. 2, Summer, 1946
George W. Dougherty Co.

1,2-Funny animal	3.50	10.50	24.00

PUPPETOONS (See George Pal's. . .)

PURE OIL COMICS (Also see Salerno Carnival of Comics, 24 Pages of Comics, & Vicks Comics)
Late 1930's (24 pgs.; regular size) (paper cover)
Pure Oil Giveaway

nn-Contains 1-2 pg. strips; i.e., Hairbreadth Harry, Skyroads, Buck Rogers by Calkins & Yager, Olly of the Movies, Napoleon, S'Matter Pop, etc.	25.00	75.00	175.00
Also a 16 pg. 1938 giveaway with Buck Rogers	20.00	60.00	140.00

PURPLE CLAW, THE (Also see Tales of Horror)
Jan., 1953 - No. 3, May, 1953
Minoan Publishing Co./Toby Press

1-Origin	10.00	30.00	70.00
2,3: 1-3 r-in Tales of Horror #9-11	5.70	17.00	40.00
I.W. Reprint #8-Reprints #1	.80	2.40	4.80

PUSSYCAT (Magazine)
Oct, 1968 (B&W reprints from Men's magazines)
Marvel Comics Group

1-(Scarce)-Ward, Everett, Wood-a; Everett-c	13.00	40.00	90.00

PUZZLE FUN COMICS (Also see Jingle Jangle)
Spring, 1946 - No. 2, Summer, 1946 (52 pgs.)
George W. Dougherty Co.

1(1946)-Gustavson-a	8.00	24.00	56.00
2	6.00	18.00	42.00

NOTE: #1,2('46) each contain a **George Carlson** cover plus a 6 pg. story "Alec in Fumbleland;" also many puzzles in each.

QUADRANT
1983 - No. 7, 1986 (B&W, nudity, adult)
Quadrant Publications

1-Peter Hsu-c/a in all	8.50	25.50	60.00
2	3.35	10.00	20.00
3	1.70	5.00	10.00
4	1.15	3.50	7.00
5	.85	2.50	5.00
6,7	.50	1.50	3.00

QUAKER OATS (Also see Cap'n Crunch)
1965 (Giveaway) (2½x5½") (16 pages)
Quaker Oats Co.

"Plenty of Glutton," "Lava Come-Back," "Kite Tale," "A Witch in Time"		.50	1.00

QUEEN OF THE WEST, DALE EVANS (TV)(See Western Roundup under Dell Giants)
No. 479, 7/53 - No. 22, 1-3/59 (All photo-c; photo back c-4-8, 15)
Dell Publishing Co.

	Good	Fine	N-Mint
4-Color 479('53)	7.00	21.00	50.00
4-Color 528('54)	5.00	15.00	35.00
3(4-6/54)-Toth-a	5.70	17.00	40.00
4-Toth, Manning-a	5.70	17.00	40.00
5-10-Manning-a. 5-Marsh-a?	4.00	12.00	28.00
11,19,21-No Manning 21-Tufts-a	3.00	9.00	21.00
12-18,20,22-Manning-a	3.50	10.50	24.00

QUENTIN DURWARD (See 4-Color #672)

QUESTAR ILLUSTRATED SCIENCE FICTION CLASSICS
1977 (224 pgs.) ($1.95)
Golden Press

11197-Stories by Asimov, Sturgeon, Silverberg & Niven; Star stream-r	.50	1.50	3.00

QUESTION, THE (See Charlton Bullseye & Mysterious Suspense)

QUESTION, THE
Feb, 1987 - Present (Mature readers)
DC Comics

1-Sienkiewicz painted-c begin	.70	2.00	4.00
2	.50	1.50	3.00
3-5	.40	1.25	2.50
6-15: 8-Intro. The Mikado	.35	1.00	2.00
16-24 (Mint)	.30	.90	1.75
Annual 1 (9/88)	.40	1.25	2.50

QUESTPROBE
8/84; No. 2, 1/85; No. 3, 11/85 (limited series)
Marvel Comics Group

1		.40	.80
2,3		.40	.80

QUICK-DRAW McGRAW (TV) (Hanna-Barbera)
No. 1040, 12-2/59-60 - No. 11, 7-9/62; No. 12, 11/62; No. 13, 2/63; No. 14, 4/63; No. 15, 6/69
Dell Publishing Co./Gold Key No. 12 on

4-Color 1040	3.70	11.00	26.00
2(4-6/60)-6	2.65	8.00	18.00
7-11	1.70	5.00	12.00
12,13-Title change to . . .Fun-Type Roundup (84 pgs.)	3.50	10.50	28.00
14,15	1.50	4.50	10.00

(See Whitman Comic Books)

QUICK-DRAW McGRAW (TV)(See Spotlight #2)
Nov, 1970 - No. 8, Jan, 1972 (Hanna-Barbera)
Charlton Comics

1	1.00	3.00	7.00
2-8	.70	2.00	4.00

QUICK-TRIGGER WESTERN (. . .Action #12; formerly Cowboy Action)
No. 12, May, 1956 - No. 19, Sept, 1957
Atlas Comics (ACI No. 12/WPI No. 13-19)

12-Baker-a	4.00	12.00	28.00
13-Williamson-a, 5 pgs.	4.65	14.00	32.00
14-Everett, Crandall, Torres-a; Heath-c	4.00	12.00	28.00
15-Torres, Crandall-a	3.00	9.00	21.00
16-Orlando, Kirby-a	2.65	8.00	18.00
17-Crandall-a	2.30	7.00	16.00
18-Baker-a	2.30	7.00	16.00
19	1.50	4.50	10.00

NOTE: **Colan** a-16. **Maneely** a-15, 17; c-15, 18. **Morrow** a-18. **Powell** a-14. **Severin** c-13,16,17,19. **Shores** a-16. **Tuska** a-17.

QUINCY (See Comics Reading Libraries)

RACCOON KIDS, THE (Formerly Movietown Animal Antics)
No. 52, Sept-Oct, 1954 - No. 64, Nov, 1957

Queen Of The West, Dale Evans #20, © Roy Rogers   The Question #1, © DC   Quick Draw McGraw #4 (Dell), © Hanna-Barbera

Racket Squad In Action #13, © CC   Raggedy Ann And Andy #12, © DELL   Ralph Snart Adventures V2#1, © NOW Comics

	Good	Fine	N-Mint
THE RACCOON KIDS (continued)			
National Periodical Publications (Arleigh No. 63,64)			
52-Doodles Duck by Mayer	3.70	11.00	26.00
53-64: 53-62-Doodles Duck by Mayer	2.30	7.00	16.00
RACE FOR THE MOON			
March, 1958 - No. 3, Nov, 1958			
Harvey Publications			
1-Powell-a(5); ½-pg. S&K-a; c-redrawn from Galaxy Science Fiction			
pulp (5/53)	5.70	17.00	40.00
2-Kirby/Williamson c(r)/a(3)	13.50	40.50	95.00
3-Kirby/Williamson c/a(4)	14.50	43.50	100.00
RACER-X			
Aug., 1988 - Present (color)			
Now Comics			
0-Deluxe ($3.50)	.60	1.75	3.50
1 (9/88)	.30	.90	1.80
2-4	.30	.90	1.75
RACKET SQUAD IN ACTION			
May-June, 1952 - No. 29, March, 1958			
Capitol Stories/Charlton Comics			
1	7.00	21.00	50.00
2-4	3.00	9.00	21.00
5-Dr. Neff, Ghost Breaker app; headlights-c	4.30	13.00	30.00
6-Dr. Neff, Ghost Breaker app.	3.00	9.00	21.00
7-10: 10-Explosion-c	2.65	8.00	18.00
11-Ditko c/a	8.50	25.50	60.00
12-Ditko explosion-c (classic); Shuster-a(2)	17.00	51.00	120.00
13-Shuster (c/p)/a; acid in woman's face	2.65	8.00	18.00
14-"Shakedown"-marijuana story	5.00	15.00	35.00
15-28	2.00	6.00	14.00
29-(68 pgs.)(15 cents)	2.65	8.00	18.00
RADIANT LOVE (Formerly Daring Love #1)			
No. 2, Dec, 1953 - No. 6, Aug, 1954			
Gilmor Magazines			
2	2.65	8.00	18.00
3-6	1.70	5.00	12.00
RAGAMUFFINS			
Jan, 1985 (One Shot)			
Eclipse Comics			
1-Eclipse Magazine-r, w/color	.30	.90	1.80

RAGGEDY ANN AND ANDY (See Dell Giants, March of Comics #23 & New Funnies)
No. 5, 1942 - No. 533, 2/54; 10-12/64 - No. 4, 3/66
Dell Publishing Co.

	Good	Fine	N-Mint
4-Color 5(1942)	30.00	90.00	210.00
4-Color 23(1943)	22.00	65.00	154.00
4-Color 45(1943)	17.00	51.00	120.00
4-Color 72(1945)	15.00	45.00	105.00
1(6/46)-Billy & Bonnie Bee by Frank Thomas	15.00	45.00	105.00
2,3: 3-Egbert Elephant by Dan Noonan begins	7.00	21.00	50.00
4-Kelly-a, 16 pgs.	8.00	24.00	56.00
5-10: 7-Little Black Sambo, Black Mumbo & Black Jumbo only app; Christmas-c	6.00	18.00	42.00
11-20	4.65	14.00	32.00
21-Alice In Wonderland cover/story	4.65	14.00	32.00
22-27,29-39(8/49), 4-Color 262(1/50)	3.50	10.50	24.00
28-Kelly-c	4.00	12.00	28.00
4-Color 306,354,380,452,533	3.00	9.00	21.00
1(10-12/64-Dell)	1.15	3.50	8.00
2,3(10-12/65), 4(3/66)	.75	2.25	5.00

NOTE: Kelly art ("Animal Mother Goose")-#1-34, 36, 37; c-28. Peterkin Pottle by John Stanley in 32-38.

RAGGEDY ANN AND ANDY
Dec, 1971 - No. 6, Sept, 1973
Gold Key

	Good	Fine	N-Mint
1	.70	2.00	4.00
2-6	.35	1.00	2.00

RAGGEDY ANN & THE CAMEL WITH THE WRINKLED KNEES (See Dell Jr. Treasury #8)

RAGMAN (See Batman Family #20, Brave & The Bold #196 & Cancelled Comic Cavalcade)
Aug-Sept, 1976 - No. 5, June-July, 1977
National Periodical Publications/DC Comics No. 5

1-Origin		.40	.80
2-Origin concludes; Kubert-c		.30	.60
3-5: 4-Drug use story		.25	.50

NOTE: Kubert a-4 ,5; c-1-5. Redondo studios a-1-4.

RAGS RABBIT (See Harvey Hits #2, Harvey Wiseguys & Tastee Freez)
No. 11, June, 1951 - No. 18, March, 1954
Harvey Publications

	Good	Fine	N-Mint
11(See Nutty Comics #5 for 1st app.)	1.15	3.50	8.00
12-18	1.00	3.00	7.00

RAIDERS OF THE LOST ARK
Sept, 1981 - No. 3, Nov, 1981 (Movie adaptation)
Marvel Comics Group

1: 1-3 r/Marvel Comics Super Special #18		.40	.80
2,3		.30	.60

NOTE: Buscema a(p)-1-3; c(p)-1. Simonson a-2i, 3i.

RAINBOW BRITE AND THE STAR STEALER
1985
DC Comics

nn-Movie adapt.		.40	.80

RALPH KINER, HOME RUN KING
1950 (Pittsburgh Pirates)
Fawcett Publications

	Good	Fine	N-Mint
nn-Photo-c	20.00	60.00	140.00

RALPH SNART ADVENTURES
June, 1986 - V2#9, 1987; V3#1 - Present ($1.25, B&W)
Now Comics

1	.70	2.00	4.00
2,3	.50	1.50	3.00
V2#1 (11/86)-Origin Rodent Ralph	.40	1.25	2.50
V2#2-9	.25	.75	1.50
V3#1 (9/88, $1.75, color)	.35	1.00	2.00
V3#2-4	.30	.90	1.80
Book 1	1.35	4.00	8.00

RAMAR OF THE JUNGLE (TV)
1954 (no month); No. 2, 9/55 - No. 5, 9/56
Toby Press No. 1/Charlton No. 2 on

	Good	Fine	N-Mint
1-Jon Hall photo-c	6.00	18.00	42.00
2-5	4.65	14.00	32.00

RAMPAGING HULK, THE (Magazine) (The Hulk #10 on; see Marvel Treas. Ed.)
Jan, 1977 - No. 9, June, 1978
Marvel Comics Group

1-Bloodstone featured	.50	1.50	3.00
2-Old X-Men app; origin old & new X-Men in text	.50	1.50	3.00
3-9	.35	.75	1.50

NOTE: Alcala a-1-3i, 5i, 8i. Buscema a-1. Giffen a-4. Nino a-4i. Simonson a-1-3p. Starlin a-4(w/Nino), 7; c-4, 5, 7.

RANGE BUSTERS
Sept, 1950 - No. 8, 1951
Fox Features Syndicate

	Good	Fine	N-Mint
1	6.50	19.50	45.00
2	3.50	10.50	24.00
3-8	2.85	8.50	20.00

RANGE BUSTERS (Formerly Cowboy Love?; Wyatt Earp, Frontier
Marshall #11 on)
No. 8, May, 1955 - No. 10, Sept, 1955
Charlton Comics

8	3.00	9.00	21.00
9,10	1.50	4.50	10.00

RANGELAND LOVE
Dec, 1949 - No. 2, Mar, 1950
Atlas Comics (CDS)

1,2	4.00	12.00	28.00

RANGER, THE (See 4-Color #255)

RANGE RIDER (See Flying A's . . .)

RANGE RIDER, THE (See 4-Color #404)

RANGE ROMANCES
Dec, 1949 - No. 5, Aug, 1950 (#5-52 pgs.)
Comic Magazines (Quality Comics)

1-Gustavson-c/a	11.50	34.00	80.00
2-Crandall-c/a; "spanking" scene	16.00	48.00	110.00
3-Crandall, Gustavson-a; photo-c	9.00	27.00	62.00
4-Crandall-a; photo-c	7.00	21.00	50.00
5-Gustavson-a; Crandall-a(p); photo-c	8.00	24.00	56.00

RANGERS COMICS (. . .of Freedom #1-7)
Oct, 1941 - No. 69, Winter, 1952-53
Fiction House Magazines (Flying stories)

1-Intro. Ranger Girl & The Rangers of Freedom; ends #7, cover app. only-#5	72.00	215.00	505.00
2	33.00	100.00	230.00
3	27.00	81.00	190.00
4,5	24.00	72.00	167.00
6-10: 8-U.S. Rangers begin	20.00	60.00	140.00
11,12-Commando Rangers app.	18.00	54.00	125.00
13-Commando Ranger begins-not same as Comm. Rangers	18.00	54.00	125.00
14-20	13.00	40.00	90.00
21-Intro/origin Firehair (begins)	17.00	51.00	120.00
22-30: 23-Kazanda begins, ends #28. 28-Tiger Man begins (origin). 30-Crusoe Island begins, ends #40	12.00	36.00	84.00
31-40: 33-Hypodermic panels	11.00	32.00	75.00
41-46	8.50	25.50	60.00
47-56-"Eisnerish" Dr. Drew by Grandenetti	9.50	28.50	65.00
57-60-Straight Dr. Drew by Grandenetti	6.50	19.50	45.00
61,62,64-66: 64-Suicide Smith begins	5.50	16.50	38.00
63-Used in POP, pgs. 85, 99	5.70	17.00	40.00
67-69: 67-Space Rangers begin, end #69	5.50	16.50	38.00

NOTE: *Bondage, discipline covers, lingerie panels are common.* **Baker** *a-36-38.* **John Celardo** *a-36-39.* **Lee Elias** *a-21-28.* **Evans** *a-19, 38-45, 47, 52.* **Ingels** *a-13-16.* **Larsen** *a-34.* **Bob Lubbers** *a-30-38, 40, 42, 44; c-42, 44.* **Moreira** *a-44, 45.* **Tuska** *a-16, 17, 19, 22.*

RANGO (TV)
August, 1967
Dell Publishing Co.

1-Tim Conway photo-c	1.75	5.25	12.00

RAPHAEL (See Teenage Mutant Ninja Turtles)
1985 (One shot, $1.50, B&W)
Mirage Studios

1	.90	2.75	5.50

	Good	Fine	N-Mint
1-2nd print. (11/87)-New-c & 8pgs.-a	.50	1.50	3.00

RATFINK (See Frantic & Zany)
October, 1964
Canrom, Inc.

1-Woodbridge-a	2.35	7.00	14.00

RAT PATROL, THE (TV)
March, 1967 - No. 5, Nov, 1967; No. 6, Oct, 1969
Dell Publishing Co.

1-Christopher George photo-c	3.50	10.50	24.00
2	2.30	7.00	16.00
3-6: 3-6-Photo-c	1.70	5.00	12.00

RAVEN, THE (See Movie Classics)

RAVENS AND RAINBOWS
Dec, 1983 (Baxter paper)
Pacific Comics

1-Jeff Jones-c/a(r); nudity scenes	.25	.75	1.50

RAWHIDE (TV)
Sept-Nov, 1959 - June-Aug, 1962; July, 1963 - No. 2, Jan, 1964
Dell Publishing Co./Gold Key

4-Color 1028	10.00	30.00	70.00
4-Color 1097,1160,1202,1261,1269	8.00	24.00	56.00
01-684-208(8/62-Dell)	7.00	21.00	50.00
1(10071-307, G.K.), 2	5.70	17.00	40.00

NOTE: *All have Clint Eastwood photo-c.* **Tufts** *a-1028.*

RAWHIDE KID
3/55 - No. 16, 9/57; No. 17, 8/60 - No. 151, 5/79
Atlas/Marvel Comics (CnPC No. 1-16/AMI No. 17-30)

1-Rawhide Kid, his horse Apache & sidekick Randy begin; Wyatt Earp app.	16.00	48.00	110.00
2	8.00	24.00	56.00
3-5	4.30	13.00	30.00
6,8-10	3.50	10.50	24.00
7-Williamson-a, 4 pgs.	4.30	13.00	30.00
11-15	2.15	6.50	15.00
16-Torres-a	2.65	8.00	18.00
17-Origin by J. Kirby	4.00	12.00	28.00
18-22,24-30	1.50	4.50	10.00
23-Origin by J. Kirby	3.50	10.50	24.00
31,32,36-44: 40-Two-Gun Kid x-over. 42-1st Larry Lieber issue	1.15	3.50	8.00
33-35-Davis-a. 35-Intro & death of The Raven	1.70	5.00	12.00
45-Origin retold	1.70	5.00	12.00
46-Toth-a	1.70	5.00	12.00
47-70: 50-Kid Colt x-over. 64-Kid Colt story. 66-Two-Gun Kid story. 67-Kid Colt story	.70	2.00	5.00
71-85: 79-Williamson-a(r)	.50	1.50	3.00
86-Origin-r; Williamson-a r-/Ringo Kid #13, 4 pgs.	.40	1.25	2.50
87-99,101-115: Last new story	.25	.75	1.50
100-Origin retold & expanded	.30	.90	1.80
116-151	.25	.75	1.50
Special 1(9/71)-Reprints	.25	.75	1.50

NOTE: *Ayers a-13, 14, 16.* **Colan** *a-145p, 148p.* **Davis** *a-125r.* **Everett** *a-54r, 65, 66, 88, 96i, 148i(r).* **Gulacy** *c-147.* **Heath** *c-4.* **G. Kane** *a-101, 144.* **Keller** *a-5.* **Kirby** *a-17-32, 34, 42, 43, 84, 86, 92, 109r, 112r, 137r; Spec. 1; c-17-35, 40, 41, 43-47, 137.* **Maneely** *c-1, 2, 5, 14.* **McWilliams** *a-41.* **Morisi** *a-13.* **Severin** *a-16; c-8, 13.* **Torres** *a-99r.* **Tuska** *a-14.* **Williamson** *a-95r, 111r.*

RAWHIDE KID
Aug, 1985 - No. 4, Nov, 1985 (mini-series)
Marvel Comics Group

1-4		.50	1.00

Range Romances #5, © QUA

Raphael #1 (2nd print), © Mirage Studios

Rawhide #01-684-208, © CBS

Real Clue Crime Stories V5#9, © HILL

Real Fact Comics #5, © DC

Real Life Comics #7, © STD

REAGAN'S RAIDERS
Aug., 1986 - No. 3 ($1.95, B&W)
Solson Publications

	Good	Fine	N-Mint
1-Ayers-a	.70	2.00	4.00
2	.40	1.25	2.50
3	.35	1.00	2.00

REAL ADVENTURE COMICS (Action Adventure #2 on)
April, 1955
Gillmor Magazines

1	1.50	4.50	10.00

REAL CLUE CRIME STORIES (Formerly Clue)
June, 1947 - V8No.3, May, 1953
Hillman Periodicals

V2#4(#1)-S&K c/a(3); Dan Barry-a	11.50	34.00	80.00
5-7-S&K c/a(3-4); 7-Iron Lady app.	10.00	30.00	70.00
8-12	2.00	6.00	14.00
V3#1-8,10-12, V4#1-8,11,12	1.70	5.00	12.00
9-Used in SOTI, pg. 102	5.00	15.00	35.00
V4#9,10-Krigstein-a	3.50	10.50	24.00
V5#1-5,7,8,10,12	1.30	4.00	9.00
6,9,11-Krigstein-a	2.65	8.00	18.00
V6#1-5,8,9,11	1.15	3.50	8.00
6,7,10,12-Krigstein-a. 10-Bondage-c	2.30	7.00	16.00
V7#1-3,5,7-11, V8#1-3	1.15	3.50	8.00
4,12-Krigstein-a	2.30	7.00	16.00
6-1 pg. Frazetta ad	1.30	4.00	9.00

NOTE: *Barry* a-9, 10; c-V2#8. *Briefer* a-V6#6. *Fuje* a- V2#11. *Infantino* a-V2#8; c-V2#11. *Lawrence* a-V5#7. *Powell* a-V4#11, 12. V5#4,5,7 are 68 pgs.

REAL EXPERIENCES (Formerly Tiny Tessie)
No. 25, January, 1950
Atlas Comics (20CC)

25	1.70	5.00	12.00

REAL FACT COMICS
Mar-Apr, 1946 - No. 21, July-Aug, 1949
National Periodical Publications

1-S&K-a; Harry Houdini sty; Just Imagine begins (not by Finlay)			
	19.00	57.00	132.00
2-S&K-a; Rin-Tin-Tin sty	11.50	34.00	80.00
3-H.G. Wells, Lon Chaney sty	5.70	17.00	40.00
4-Virgil Finlay-a on 'Just Imagine' begins, ends #12 (2 pgs. ea.);			
Jimmy Stewart sty	11.50	34.00	80.00
5-Batman/Robin-c; 5pg. story about creation of Batman & Robin;			
Tom Mix story	35.00	105.00	245.00
6-Origin & 1st app. Tommy Tomorrow by Finlay; Flag-c; 1st writing			
by Harlan Ellison (letter column, non-professional)			
	40.00	120.00	280.00
7-(No. 6 on inside)-Roussos-a	5.00	15.00	35.00
8-2nd app. Tommy Tomorrow by Finlay	22.00	65.00	154.00
9-S&K-a; Glenn Miller story	8.50	25.50	60.00
10-Vigilante by Meskin	8.50	25.50	60.00
11,12: 11-Kinstler-a	5.00	15.00	35.00
13-Dale Evans and Tommy Tomorrow cover/stories			
	19.00	57.00	132.00
14,17,18: 14-Will Rogers story	4.65	14.00	32.00
15-Nuclear Explosion part-c	5.00	15.00	35.00
16-Tommy Tomorrow app.; 1st Planeteers?	19.00	57.00	132.00
19-Sir Arthur Conan Doyle story	4.65	14.00	32.00
20-Kubert-a, 4 pgs; Daniel Boone story	8.50	25.50	60.00
21-Kubert-a, 2 pgs; Kit Carson story	4.65	14.00	32.00

NOTE: *Roussos* a-1-4.

REAL FUN OF DRIVING!!, THE
1965, 1967 (Regular size)
Chrysler Corp.

Shaffenberger-a, 12pgs.

	Good	Fine	N-Mint
Shaffenberger-a, 12pgs.	.85	2.50	5.00

REAL FUNNIES
Jan, 1943 - No. 3, June, 1943
Nedor Publishing Co.

1-Funny animal, humor; Black Terrier app. (clone of The Black			
Terror)	10.00	30.00	70.00
2,3	5.00	15.00	35.00

REAL GHOSTBUSTERS, THE
Aug., 1988 - Present ($1.75, color)
Now Comics

1-Based on movie	.50	1.50	3.00
2-4	.35	1.00	2.00

REAL HEROES COMICS
Sept., 1941 - No. 16, Oct, 1946
Parents' Magazine Institute

1-Roosevelt c/story	10.00	30.00	70.00
2	4.00	12.00	28.00
3-5,7-10	3.00	9.00	21.00
6-Lou Gehrig c/sty	3.50	10.50	24.00
11-16: 13-Kiefer-a	2.00	6.00	14.00

REAL HIT
1944 (Savings Bond premium)
Fox Features Publications

1-Blue Beetle-r	8.50	25.50	60.00

NOTE: *Two versions exist, with and without covers. The coverless version has the title, No. 1 and price printed at top of splash page.*

REALISTIC ROMANCES
July-Aug, 1951 - No. 17, Aug-Sept, 1954 (no No. 9-14)
Realistic Comics/Avon Periodicals

1-Kinstler-a; c/Avon paperback 211	8.50	25.50	60.00
2	4.00	12.00	28.00
3,4	3.35	10.00	23.00
5,8-Kinstler-a	3.65	11.00	25.00
6-c/Diversey Prize Novels 6; Kinstler-a	4.00	12.00	28.00
7-Evans-a?; c/Avon paperback 360	4.00	12.00	28.00
15,17	2.65	8.00	18.00
16-Kinstler marijuana story-r/Romantic Love #6			
	5.00	15.00	35.00
I.W. Reprint #1,8,9	.45	.90	1.80

NOTE: *Astarita* a-2-4,7,8.

REAL LIFE COMICS
Sept., 1941 - No. 59, Sept, 1952
Nedor/Better/Standard Publ./Pictorial Magazine No. 13

1-Uncle Sam c/story	12.00	36.00	84.00
2	5.70	17.00	40.00
3-Hitler cover	8.50	25.50	60.00
4,5: 4-Story of American flag "Old Glory"	3.70	11.00	26.00
6-10	2.85	8.50	20.00
11-20: 17-Albert Einstein sty.	2.15	6.50	15.00
21-23,25,26,28-30: 29-A-Bomb sty	1.65	5.00	11.50
24-Story of Baseball	3.00	9.00	21.00
27-Schomburg A-Bomb-c; sty. of A-Bomb	4.00	12.00	28.00
31-33,35,36,42-44,48,49	1.30	4.00	9.00
34,37-41,45-47: 34-Jimmy Stewart sty. 37-Sty. of motion pictures;			
Bing Crosby sty. 38-Jane Froman sty. 39-"1,000,000 A.D." sty.			
40-Bob Feller sty. 41-Jimmie Foxx sty.; "Home Run" Baker sty.			
45-Sty. of Olympic games; Burl Ives sty. 46-Douglas Fairbanks			
Jr. & Sr. sty. 47-George Gershwin sty.	1.70	5.00	12.00
50-Frazetta, 5 pgs.	11.50	34.00	80.00
51-Jules Verne "Journey to the Moon" by Evans			
	5.00	15.00	35.00

REAL LIFE COMICS (continued)

	Good	Fine	N-Mint
52-Frazetta-a, 4 pgs.; Severin/Elder-a(2); Evans-a			
	12.00	36.00	84.00
53-57-Severin/Elder-a	3.00	9.00	21.00
58-Severin/Elder-a(2)	3.50	10.50	24.00
59-1pg. Frazetta; Severin/Elder-a	3.50	10.50	24.00

NOTE: *Some issues had two titles.* **Guardineer** *a-40(2), 44.* **Schomburg** *c-1, 2, 4, 5, 7, 11, 13-21, 23, 24, 26, 28, 30-32, 34-40, 42, 44-47. Photo-c 5,6.*

REAL LIFE SECRETS (Real Secrets #2 on)
Sept, 1949 (One shot)
Ace Periodicals

1-Painted-c	3.00	9.00	21.00

REAL LIFE STORY OF FESS PARKER (Magazine)
1955
Dell Publishing Co.

1	5.00	15.00	35.00

REAL LIFE TALES OF SUSPENSE (See Suspense)

REAL LOVE (Formerly Hap Hazard)
No. 25, April, 1949 - No. 76, Nov, 1956
Ace Periodicals (A. A. Wyn)

25	3.50	10.50	24.00
26	1.70	5.00	12.00
27-L. B. Cole-a	3.00	9.00	21.00
28-35	1.15	3.50	8.00
36-66: 66-Last pre-code (2/55)	1.00	3.00	7.00
67-76	.75	2.25	5.00

NOTE: *Photo-c No. 50-76. Painted-c No. 46.*

REALM, THE
Feb., 1986 - Present ($1.50, B&W)
Arrow Comics/WeeBee Comics #13 on

1	1.35	4.00	8.00
2	.50	1.50	3.00
3-14: ($1.95, #13 on)	.25	.75	1.50
Book 1	.85	2.50	4.95

REAL McCOYS, THE (TV)
No. 1071, 1-3/60 - 5-7/1962 (Photo-c)
Dell Publishing Co.

4-Color 1071-Toth-a	6.00	18.00	42.00
4-Color 1134-Toth-a	6.00	18.00	42.00
4-Color 1193,1265	5.00	15.00	35.00
01-689-207 (5-7/62)	4.30	13.00	30.00

REAL SCREEN COMICS (#1 titled Real Screen Funnies; TV Screen
Cartoons #129-138)
Spring, 1945 - No. 128, May-June, 1959 (#1-40, 52 pgs.)
National Periodical Publications

1-The Fox & the Crow, Flippity & Flop, Tito & His Burro begin			
	50.00	150.00	350.00
2	24.00	72.00	170.00
3-5	13.00	40.00	90.00
6-10 (2-3/47)	9.50	28.50	65.00
11-20 (10-11/48): 13-Crow x-over in Flippity & Flop			
	7.00	21.00	50.00
21-30 (6-7/50)	5.00	15.00	35.00
31-50	3.70	11.00	26.00
51-99	2.65	8.00	18.00
100	3.50	10.50	24.00
101-128	2.00	6.00	14.00

REAL SECRETS (Formerly Real Life Secrets)
No. 2, Nov, 1950 - No. 5, May, 1950
Ace Periodicals

2	3.00	9.00	21.00
3-5: 3-Photo-c	1.60	4.70	11.00

REAL SPORTS COMICS (All Sports Comics #2 on)
Oct-Nov, 1948 (52 pgs.)
Hillman Periodicals

	Good	Fine	N-Mint
1-12 pg. Powell-a	12.00	36.00	84.00

REAL WAR STORIES
July, 1987 (52 pgs., $2.00, color)
Eclipse Comics

1-Bolland, Bissette, Totleben-a	.35	1.00	2.00
1-2nd print (2/88)	.35	1.00	2.00

REAL WESTERN HERO (Formerly Wow #1-69; becomes Western
Hero #76 on)
No. 70, Sept, 1948 - No. 75, Feb, 1949 (All 52 pgs.)
Fawcett Publications

70(#1)-Tom Mix, Monte Hale, Hopalong Cassidy, Young Falcon			
begin	17.00	51.00	120.00
71-Gabby Hayes begins; Captain Tootsie by Beck			
	11.50	34.00	80.00
72-75: 72-Captain Tootsie by Beck. 75-Big Bow and Little Arrow			
app.	8.50	25.50	60.00

NOTE: *Painted/photo c-70-73; painted c-74,75.*

REAL WEST ROMANCES
4-5/49 - V1#6, 3/50; V2/1, Apr-May, 1950 (All 52 pgs. & photo-c)
Crestwood Publishing Co./Prize Publ.

V1#1-S&K-a(p)	7.00	21.00	50.00
2-Spanking panel	7.00	21.00	50.00
3-Kirby-a(p) only	3.00	9.00	21.00
4-S&K-a; Whip Wilson, Reno Browne photo-c			
	4.60	14.00	32.00
5-Audie Murphy, Gale Storm photo-c; S&K-a			
	3.70	11.00	26.00
6-S&K-a	3.70	11.00	26.00
V2#1-Kirby-a(p)	3.00	9.00	21.00

NOTE: **Meskin** *a-V1#5.* **Severin & Elder** *a-V1#3-6, V2#1.* **Leonard Starr** *a-1-3. Photo-c V1#1-5, V2#1.*

REAP THE WILD WIND (See Cinema Comics Herald)

REBEL, THE (See 4-Color #1076,1138,1207,1262)

RECORD BOOK OF FAMOUS POLICE CASES
1949 (132 pages) (25 cents)
St. John Publishing Co.

nn-Kubert-a(3) r-/Son of Sinbad; Baker-c	18.00	54.00	125.00

RED ARROW
May-June, 1951 - No. 3, Oct, 1951
P. L. Publishing Co.

1	3.50	10.50	24.00
2,3	2.00	6.00	14.00

RED BALL COMIC BOOK
1947 (Red Ball Shoes giveaway)
Parents' Magazine Institute

Reprints from True Comics	1.50	4.50	10.00

RED BAND COMICS
Feb, 1945 - No. 4, May, 1945
Enwil Associates

1	10.00	30.00	70.00
2-Origin Bogeyman & Santanas	8.50	25.50	60.00
3,4-Captain Wizard app. in both; each has identical contents/c			
	7.00	21.00	50.00

RED CIRCLE COMICS
Jan, 1945 - No. 4, April, 1945
Rural Home Publications (Enwil)

1-The Prankster & Red Riot begin	10.00	30.00	70.00

Real Screen Comics #15, © DC

Real West Romances #1, © PRIZE

Red Band Comics #2, © Enwil Associates

Red Circle Comics #3, © RH   Red Mask #44, © ME   Red Mountain Featuring Quantrell's Raiders, © AVON

	Good	Fine	N-Mint
RED CIRCLE COMICS (continued)			
2-Starr-a; The Judge (costumed hero) app.	7.00	21.00	50.00
3,4-Starr-c/a. 3-The Prankster not in costume	5.00	15.00	35.00
4-(dated 4/45)-Leftover covers to #4 were later restapled over early 1950s coverless comics. Variations in the coverless comics used are endless; Woman Outlaws, Dorothy Lamour, Crime Does Not Not Pay, Sabu, Diary Loves, Love Confessions & Young Love			
V3/3 known	4.65	14.00	32.00

RED CIRCLE SORCERY (Chilling Advs. in Sorcery #1-5)
No. 6, Apr, 1974 - No. 11, Feb, 1975
Red Circle Productions (Archie)

6-11: 8-Only app. The Cobra	.40		.80

NOTE: *Chaykin a-6, 10. B. Jones a-7(w/Wrightson, Kaluta, J. Jones). McWilliams a-10. Morrow a-6, 8, 11; c-6-11. Thorne a-8, 10. Toth a-8, 9. Wood a-10.*

RED DOG (See Night Music #7)

RED DRAGON COMICS (1st Series) (Formerly Trail Blazers; see
Super Magician V5#7, 8)
No. 5, Jan, 1943 - No. 9, Jan, 1944
Street & Smith Publications

	Good	Fine	N-Mint
5-Origin Red Rover, the Crimson Crimebuster; Rex King, Man of Adventure, Captain Jack Commando, & The Minute Man begin; text origin Red Dragon; Binder-c	30.00	90.00	210.00
6-Origin The Black Crusader & Red Dragon (3/43)	22.00	65.00	154.00
7	17.00	51.00	120.00
8-The Red Knight app.	17.00	51.00	120.00
9-Origin Chuck Magnon, Immortal Man	17.00	51.00	120.00

RED DRAGON COMICS (2nd Series)
Nov, 1947 - No. 6, Jan, 1949; No. 7, July, 1949
Street & Smith Publications

1-Red Dragon begins; Elliman, Nigel app.; Ed Cartier-c/a	28.50	85.00	200.00
2-Cartier-c	23.00	70.00	160.00
3-1st app. Dr. Neff by Powell; Elliman, Nigel app.	18.00	54.00	125.00
4-Cartier c/a	20.00	60.00	140.00
5-7	14.00	42.00	100.00

NOTE: *Maneely a-5,7. Powell a-2-7; c-3,5,7.*

REDDY GOOSE
No. 2, Jan, 1959 - No. 16, July, 1962 (Giveaway)
International Shoe Co. (Western Printing)

nn,2-16	.50	1.50	3.00

REDDY KILOWATT (5 cents) (Also see Story of Edison)
1946 - No. 2, 1947; 1956 - 1960 (no month) (16 pgs.; paper cover)
Educational Comics (E. C.)

nn-Reddy Made Magic	12.00	35.00	70.00
nn-Reddy Made Magic (1958)	5.35	16.00	32.00
2-Edison, the Man Who Changed the World (¾" smaller than #1)	12.00	35.00	70.00
...Comic Book 2 (1954)-"Light's Diamond Jubilee"	6.75	20.00	40.00
...Comic Book 2 (1958)-"Wizard of Light," 16 pgs.	5.35	16.00	32.00
...Comic Book 3 (1956)-"The Space Kite," 8 pgs.; Orlando story; regular size	5.35	16.00	32.00
...Comic Book 3 (1960)-"The Space Kite," 8 pgs.; Orlando story; regular size	4.75	14.00	28.00

NOTE: *Several copies surfaced in 1979.*

REDDY MADE MAGIC
1956, 1958 (16 pages) (paper cover)
Educational Comics (E. C.)

1-Reddy Kilowatt-r (splash panel changed)	8.00	24.00	48.00

	Good	Fine	N-Mint
1 (1958 edition)	5.00	15.00	30.00

RED EAGLE (See Feature Books #16, McKay)

REDEYE (See Comics Reading Libraries)

RED FOX (Manhunt #1-14)
1954
Magazine Enterprises

15(A-1 108)-Undercover Girl app.; L.B. Cole c/a (Red Fox); r-from Manhunt; Powell-a	8.00	24.00	56.00

REDFOX
Jan., 1986 - Present ($1.75, B&W)
Harrier Comics/Valkyrie Press #11 on

1	1.50	4.50	9.00
1-2nd print	.35	1.00	2.00
2	.85	2.50	5.00
3	.60	1.75	3.50
4	.50	1.50	3.00
5-19	.35	1.00	2.00

RED GOOSE COMIC SELECTIONS (See Comic Selections)

RED HAWK (See A-1 Comics #90 & Straight Arrow #2)

RED HEAT
July, 1988 ($2.00, B&W)
Blackthorne Publishing

1	.35	1.00	2.00
...In 3-D (7/88, $2.50)	.40	1.25	2.50

RED ICEBERG, THE
1960 (10 cents) (16 pgs.) (Communist propaganda)
Impact Publ. (Catechetical Guild)

(Rare)-'We The People'-back-c	37.00	110.00	240.00
2nd version-'Impact Press'-back-c	43.00	130.00	280.00

NOTE: *This book was the Guild's last anti-communist propaganda book and had very limited circulation. 3 - 4 copies surfaced in 1979 from the defunct publisher's files. Other copies do turn up.*

RED MASK (Formerly Tim Holt)
No. 42, 6-7/1954 - No. 53, 5/56; No. 54, 9/57
Magazine Enterprises No. 42-53/Sussex No. 54

42-Ghost Rider by Ayers continues, ends #50; Black Phantom continues; 3-D effect c/stories begin	12.00	36.00	84.00
43-3-D effect-c/stories	10.00	30.00	70.00
44-50-3-D effect stories only. 50-Last Ghost Rider	9.50	28.50	65.00
51-The Presto Kid begins by Ayers (1st app.); Presto Kid-c begins, ends #54; last 3-D effect story	9.50	28.50	65.00
52-Origin The Presto Kid	9.50	28.50	65.00
53,54-Last Black Phantom	6.00	18.00	42.00
I.W. Reprint #1 (r-/#52), 2,3 (r-/#51), 8 (nd; Kinstler-c)	.80	2.40	4.80

NOTE: *Ayers art on Ghost Rider & Presto Kid. Bolle art in all (Red Mask); c-43, 44, 49. Guardineer a-52. Black Phantom in #42-44, 47-50, 53, 54.*

RED MOUNTAIN FEATURING QUANTRELL'S RAIDERS
1952 (Movie) (Also see Jesse James #28)
Avon Periodicals

Alan Ladd; Kinstler c/a	14.00	42.00	100.00

"RED" RABBIT COMICS
Jan., 1947 - No. 22, Aug-Sept, 1951
Dearfield Comic/J. Charles Laue Publ. Co.

1	4.65	14.00	32.00
2	2.30	7.00	16.00
3-10	1.70	5.00	12.00
11-22: 18-Flying Saucer-c (1/51)	1.50	4.50	9.00

RED RAVEN COMICS (Human Torch #2 on)
August, 1940   (Also see Sub-Mariner #26, 2nd series)
Timely Comics

	Good	Fine	N-Mint
1-Origin Red Raven; Comet Pierce & Mercury by Kirby, The Human Top & The Eternal Brain; intro. Magar, the Mystic & only app.; Kirby-c	430.00	1290.00	3010.00

(Prices vary widely on this book)

RED RYDER COMICS (Hi Spot #2)(Movies, radio)
(Also see Crackajack Funnies)
9/40; No. 3, 8/41 - No. 5, 12/41; No. 6, 4/42 - No. 151, 4-6/57
Hawley Publ. No. 1-5/Dell Publishing Co.(K.K.) No. 6 on

	Good	Fine	N-Mint
1-Red Ryder, his horse Thunder, Little Beaver & his horse Papoose strip reprints begin by Fred Harman; 1st meeting of Red & Little Beaver; Harman line-drawn-c #1-85	80.00	240.00	560.00
3-(Scarce)-Alley Oop, King of the Royal Mtd., Capt. Easy, Freckles & His Friends, Myra North & Dan Dunn strip-r begin	50.00	150.00	350.00
4,5	27.00	81.00	190.00
6-1st Dell issue	27.00	81.00	190.00
7-10	20.00	60.00	140.00
11-20	14.00	42.00	100.00
21-32-Last Alley Oop, Dan Dunn, Capt. Easy, Freckles	8.50	25.50	60.00
33-40 (52 pgs.)	6.00	18.00	42.00
41 (52 pgs.)-Rocky Lane photo back-c; photo back-c begin, end #57	6.50	19.50	45.00
42-46 (52 pgs.). 46-Last Red Ryder strip-r	5.00	15.00	35.00
47-53 (52 pgs.). 47-New stories on Red Ryder begin	4.00	12.00	28.00
54-57 (36 pgs.)	3.50	10.50	24.00
58-73 (36 pgs.). 73-Last King of the Royal Mtd. strip-r by Jim Gary	3.00	9.00	21.00
74-85,93 (52 pgs.)-Harman line-drawn-c	3.50	10.50	24.00
86-92 (52 pgs.)-Harman painted-c	3.50	10.50	24.00
94-96 (36 pgs.)-Harman painted-c	2.15	6.50	15.00
97,98,107,108 (36 pgs.)-Harman line-drawn-c	2.15	6.50	15.00
99,101-106 (36 pgs.)-Jim Bannon Photo-c	2.15	6.50	15.00
100 (36 pgs.)-Bannon photo-c	2.65	8.00	18.00
109-118 (52 pgs.)-Harman line-drawn-c	1.85	5.50	13.00
119-129 (52 pgs.). 119-Painted-c begin, not by Harman, end #151	1.60	4.70	11.00
130-144 (36 pgs., #130-on)	1.50	4.50	10.00
145-148: 145-Title change to Red Ryder Ranch Magazine with photos	1.30	4.00	9.00
149-151: 149-Title changed to Red Ryder Ranch Comics	1.30	4.00	9.00
4-Color 916 (7/58)	1.60	4.70	11.00
Buster Brown Shoes Giveaway (1941, 32pgs., color, soft-c)	19.00	57.00	132.00
Red Ryder Super Book Of Comics 10 (1944; paper-c; 32 pgs.; blank back-c)-Magic Morro app.	19.00	57.00	132.00
Red Ryder Victory Patrol-nn(1944, 32 pgs.)-r-/#43,44; comic has a paper-c & is stapled inside a triple cardboard fold-out-c; contains membership card, decoder, map of R.R. home range, etc. Herky app. (Langendorf Bread giveaway; sub-titled 'Super Book of Comics')	35.00	105.00	245.00
Wells Lamont Corp. giveaway (1950)-16 pgs. in color; regular size; paper-c; 1941-r	17.00	52.00	120.00

NOTE: **Fred Harman** a-1-99; c-1-98, 107-118. Don Red Barry, Allan Rocky Lane, Wild Bill Elliott & Jim Bannon starred as Red Ryder in the movies. Robert Blake starred as Little Beaver.

RED RYDER PAINT BOOK
1941   (148 pages) (8½x11½'')
Whitman Publishing Co.

	Good	Fine	N-Mint
Reprints 1940 daily strips	14.00	42.00	100.00

RED SEAL COMICS
10/45 - No. 18, 10/46; No. 19, 6/47 - No. 22, 12/47
Harry 'A' Chesler/Superior Publ. No. 19 on

	Good	Fine	N-Mint
14-The Black Dwarf begins; Little Nemo app; bondage/hypo-c; Tuska-a	18.00	54.00	125.00
15-Torture story	14.00	42.00	100.00
16-Used in **SOTI**, pg. 181, illo-''Outside the forbidden pages of de Sade, you find draining a girl's blood only in children's comics;'' drug club story r-later in Crime Reporter #1; Veiled Avenger & Barry Kuda app; Tuska-a	22.00	65.00	154.00
17-Lady Satan, Yankee Girl & Sky Chief app; Tuska-a	11.50	34.00	80.00
18,20-Lady Satan & Sky Chief app.	11.50	34.00	80.00
19-No Black Dwarf-on cover only; Zor, El Tigre app.	9.50	28.50	65.00
21-Lady Satan & Black Dwarf app.	9.50	28.50	65.00
22-Zor, Rocketman app. (68 pgs.)	9.50	28.50	65.00

REDSKIN (Famous Western Badmen #13 on)
Sept, 1950 - No. 12, Oct, 1952
Youthful Magazines

	Good	Fine	N-Mint
1	4.00	12.00	28.00
2	2.30	7.00	16.00
3-12: 6,12-Bondage-c	2.00	6.00	14.00

RED SONJA (Also see Conan #23, Kull & The Barbarians, Marvel Feature & Savage Sword Of Conan #1)
1/77 - No. 15, 5/79; V1/1, 2/83 - V2/2, 3/83;
V3/1, 8/83 - V3/4, 2/84; V3/5, 1/85 - V3/13, 1986
Marvel Comics Group

	Good	Fine	N-Mint
1	.40	1.25	2.50
2-5	.35	1.00	2.00
6-15, V1#1,V2#2		.50	1.00
V3#1,2 ($1.00)		.60	1.20
V3#3-13 (65-75 cents)		.50	1.00

NOTE: **Brunner** c-12-14. **J. Buscema** a(p)-12, 13, 15; c-V1No.1. **Nebres** a-V3/3i. **N. Redondo** a-8i, V3/2i, 3i. **Simonson** a-V3No.1. **Thorne** a-1-11; c-1-11.

RED SONJA: THE MOVIE
Nov, 1985 - No. 2, Dec, 1985 (limited-series)
Marvel Comics Group

	Good	Fine	N-Mint
1,2-Movie adapt-r		.40	.80

RED TORNADO
July, 1985 - No. 4, Oct, 1985 (mini-series)
DC Comics

	Good	Fine	N-Mint
1-4		.50	1.00

RED WARRIOR
Jan, 1951 - No. 6, Dec, 1951
Marvel/Atlas Comics (TCI)

	Good	Fine	N-Mint
1-Tuska-a	5.00	15.00	35.00
2	2.85	8.50	20.00
3-6: 4-Origin White Wing, his horse	2.30	7.00	16.00

RED WOLF (See Avengers #80 & Marvel Spotlight #1)
May, 1972 - No. 9, Sept, 1973
Marvel Comics Group

	Good	Fine	N-Mint
1-Kane/Severin-c		.30	.60
2-9: 9-Origin sidekick, Lobo (wolf)		.25	.50

NOTE: **G. Kane** c-1p, 2.

REESE'S PIECES
Oct, 1985 - No. 2, Oct, 1985
Eclipse Comics

	Good	Fine	N-Mint
1,2-B&W-r in color	.35	1.00	2.00

REFORM SCHOOL GIRL!
1951

Red Raven Comics #1, © MEG

Red Ryder Comics #102, © DELL

Redskin #2, © YM

Reform School Girl!, © REAL   Reid Fleming, World's Toughest Milkman V2#1, © Eclipse   Reno Browne, Hollywood's Greatest Cowgirl #51, © MEG

REFORM SCHOOL GIRL! (continued)
Realistic Comics

	Good	Fine	N-Mint
nn-Used in **SOTI**, pg. 358, & cover ill. with caption "Comic books are supposed to be like fairy tales"	100.00	300.00	700.00
(Prices vary widely on this book)			

NOTE: The cover and title originated from a digest-sized book published by Diversey Publishing Co. of Chicago in 1948. The original book "House of Fury," Doubleday, came out in 1941. The girl's real name which appears on the cover of the digest and comic is Marty Collins, Canadian model and ice skating star who posed for this special color photograph for the Diversey novel.

REGENTS ILLUSTRATED CLASSICS
1981 (Plus more recent reprintings)
(48 pgs., b&w-a with 14 pages of teaching helps)
Prentice Hall Regents, Englewood Cliffs, NJ 07632

NOTE: This series contains Classics Ill. art, and was produced from the same illegal source as **Cassette Books**. But when Twin Circle sued to stop the sale of the Cassette Books, they decided to permit this series to continue. This series was produced as a teaching aid. The 20 title series is divided into four levels based upon number of basic words used therein. There is also a teacher's manual for each level. All of the titles are still available from the publisher for about $5 each retail. The reason to call for mail order purchases is (201)767-5937. Almost all of the issues have new covers taken from some interior art panel. Here is a list of the series by Regents ident. no. and the Classics Ill. counterpart.

16770(CI#24-A2) 18333(CI#3-A2) 21668(CI#13-A2) 32224(CI#21) 33051(CI#26)
35788(CI#84) 37153(CI#16) 44460(CI#19-A2) 44808(CI#18-A2) 52395(CI#4-A2)
58627(CI#5-A2) 60067(CI#30) 68405(CI#23-A1) 70302(CI#29) 78192(CI#7-A2)
78193(CI#10-A2) 79679(CI#85) 92046(CI#1-A2) 93062(CI#64) 93512(CI#24)

REGGIE (Formerly Archie's Rival . . . ; Reggie & Me #19 on)
No. 15, Sept, 1963 - No. 18, Nov, 1965
Archie Publications

15(9/63), 16(10/64)	4.50	13.50	32.00
17(8/65), 18(11/65)	4.50	13.50	32.00

NOTE: Cover title No. 15,16 is Archie's Rival . . .

REGGIE AND ME (Formerly Reggie)
No. 19, 8/66 - No. 126, 9/80 (No. 50-68: 52 pgs.)
Archie Publications

19-Evilheart app.	2.00	6.00	12.00
20-23-Evilheart app.; with Pureheart #22	1.00	3.00	6.00
24-40	.35	1.00	2.00
41-60		.40	.80
61-126		.25	.50

REGGIE'S JOKES (See Reggie's Wise Guy Jokes)

REGGIE'S WISE GUY JOKES
Aug, 1968 - No. 60, Jan, 1982 (#5 on are Giants)
Archie Publications

1	1.70	5.00	12.00
2-4	.70	2.00	5.00
5-10	.35	1.00	2.00
11-28		.40	.80
29-60		.25	.50

REGISTERED NURSE
Summer, 1963
Charlton Comics

1-Reprints Nurse Betsy Crane & Cynthia Doyle			
	.35	1.00	2.00

REG'LAR FELLERS (See All-American Comics, Popular Comics & Treasure Box of . . .)
1921 - 1929
Cupples & Leon Co./MS Publishng Co.

	Good	Fine	N-Mint
1(1921)-52 pgs. B&W dailies (Cupples & Leon, 10x10'')	9.00	27.00	62.00
1925, 48 pgs. B&W dailies (MS Publ.)	9.00	27.00	62.00
Softcover (1929, nn, 36 pgs.)	9.00	27.00	62.00
Hardcover (1929)-B&W reprints, 96 pgs.	10.00	30.00	70.00

REG'LAR FELLERS
No. 5, Nov, 1947 - No. 6, Mar, 1948
Visual Editions (Standard)

	Good	Fine	N-Mint
5,6	3.50	10.50	24.00

REG'LAR FELLERS HEROIC (See Heroic)

REID FLEMING, WORLD'S TOUGHEST MILKMAN
Aug., 1986 ($2.50, B&W); Dec., 1986 - Present
Eclipse Comics

1 (3rd print, large size, 8/86)	.85	2.50	5.00
V2#1 (12/86, reg. size, $2.00 B&W)	.50	1.50	3.00
1-2nd print	.40	1.25	2.50
2,3 ($2.00)	.40	1.25	2.50
V2#2-2nd print	.35	1.00	2.00

RELUCTANT DRAGON, THE (See 4-Color #13)

REMEMBER PEARL HARBOR
1942 (68 pages)
Street & Smith Publications

nn-Uncle Sam-c	19.00	57.00	132.00

RENO BROWNE, HOLLYWOOD'S GREATEST COWGIRL (Formerly Margie; Apache Kid #53 on)
No. 50, April, 1950 - No. 52, Sept, 1950 (52 pgs.)
Marvel Comics (MPC)

50-Photo-c	10.00	30.00	70.00
51,52: 51-Photo-c	8.50	25.50	60.00

REPTILICUS (Reptisaurus #3 on)
Aug, 1961 - No. 2, Oct, 1961
Charlton Comics

1 (Movie)	4.65	14.00	32.00
2	3.00	9.00	21.00

REPTISAURUS (Reptilicus #1,2)
Jan, 1962 - No. 8, Dec, 1962; Summer, 1963
Charlton Comics

V2#3-8: 8-Montes/Bache c/a	1.70	5.00	12.00
Special Edition 1 (1963)	1.70	5.00	12.00

RESCUERS, THE (See Walt Disney Showcase #40)

RESTLESS GUN (See 4-Color #934,986,1045,1089,1146)

RETIEF (Keith Laumer's)
April, 1987 - No. 8, 1988 ($1.75, B&W)
Mad Dog Graphics

1-6	.30	.85	1.70

RETIEF OF THE C.D.T.
1988 ($2.00, B&W)
Mad Dog Graphics

1	.35	1.00	2.00

RETURN FROM WITCH MOUNTAIN (See Wald Disney Showcase #44)

RETURN OF GORGO, THE (Formerly Gorgo's Revenge)
No. 2, Aug, 1963 - No. 3, Fall, 1964
Charlton Comics

2,3-Ditko-a, c-#3; based on M.G.M. movie	3.00	9.00	21.00

RETURN OF KONGA, THE (Konga's Revenge #2 on)
1962
Charlton Comics

nn	2.65	8.00	18.00

RETURN OF MEGATON MAN
July, 1988 - No. 3 ($2.00, color)
Kitchen Sink

1-3	.35	1.00	2.00

RETURN OF THE OUTLAW
Feb, 1953 - No. 11, 1955
Toby Press (Minoan)

	Good	Fine	N-Mint
1-Billy the Kid	3.50	10.50	24.00
2	1.70	5.00	12.00
3-11	1.30	4.00	9.00

REVEALING LOVE STORIES (See Fox Giants)

REVEALING ROMANCES
Sept, 1949 - No. 6, Aug, 1950
Ace Magazines

1	3.00	9.00	21.00
2	1.50	4.50	10.00
3-6	1.15	3.50	8.00

REVENGE OF THE PROWLER
Feb., 1988 - No. 4, June, 1988 ($1.75/$1.95, color)
Eclipse Comics

1-4: 2-($2.50) Contains flexidisc	.30	.90	1.75

REVENGERS, THE (Featuring Armor And Silverstreak)
Sept, 1985 - No. 6, 1987 - Present
Continuity Comics

1-Origin; Adams c/a	.35	1.00	2.00
1-Newsstand, 1987, $2.00	.35	1.00	2.00
2-6	.35	1.00	2.00

REVENGERS STARRING MEGALITH
Sept, 1985
Continuity Comics

1-Adams c/a, scripts	.35	1.00	2.00

REX ALLEN COMICS (Movie star)(Also see 4-Color #877 & Western Roundup under Dell Giants)
No. 316, Feb, 1951 - No. 31, Dec-Feb, 1958-59 (All-photo-c)
Dell Publishing Co.

4-Color 316(#1)(52 pgs.)-Rex Allen & his horse Koko begin; Marsh-a	11.00	32.00	75.00
2 (9-11/51, 36 pgs.)	5.70	17.00	40.00
3-10	4.65	14.00	32.00
11-20	3.70	11.00	26.00
21-23,25-31	3.50	10.50	24.00
24-Toth-a	4.30	13.00	30.00

NOTE: *Manning* a-20,27-30. Photo back-c 316,2-12,20,21.

REX DEXTER OF MARS (See Mystery Men Comics)
Fall, 1940
Fox Features Syndicate

1-Rex Dexter, Patty O'Day, & Zanzibar (Tuska-a) app.; Briefer-c/a	70.00	210.00	490.00

REX HART (Formerly Blaze Carson; Whip Wilson #9 on)
No. 6, Aug, 1949 - No. 8, Feb, 1950 (All photo-c)
Timely/Marvel Comics (USA)

6-Rex Hart & his horse Warrior begin; Black Rider app; Captain Tootsie by Beck	8.00	24.00	56.00
7,8: 18pg. Thriller in each. 8-Blaze the Wonder Collie app. in text	6.00	18.00	42.00

REX MORGAN, M.D. (Also see Harvey Comics Library)
Dec, 1955 - No. 3, 1956
Argo Publ.

1-Reprints Rex Morgan daily newspaper strips & daily panel-r of "These Women" by D'Alessio & "Timeout" by Jeff Keate	5.00	15.00	35.00
2,3	3.00	9.00	21.00

REX THE WONDER DOG (See The Adventures of...)
RHUBARB, THE MILLIONAIRE CAT (See 4-Color #423,466,563)

RIBTICKLER (Also see Fox Giants)
1945 - No. 9, Aug, 1947; 1957 - 1959
Fox Feature Synd./Green Publ. (1957)/Norlen (1959)

	Good	Fine	N-Mint
1	4.00	12.00	28.00
2	2.00	6.00	14.00
3-9: 3,7-Cosmo Cat app.	1.50	4.50	10.00
3,7,8 (Green Publ.-1957)	.85	2.50	6.00
3,7,8 (Norlen Mag.-1959)	.85	2.50	6.00

RICHARD DRAGON, KUNG-FU FIGHTER (See Brave & the Bold)
Apr-May, 1975 - No. 18, Nov-Dec, 1977
National Periodical Publications/DC Comics

1,2: 2-Starlin-a(p). 3-Kirby-c; a(p).		.45	.90
3-18: 4-8-Wood inks		.30	.60

RICHARD THE LION-HEARTED (See Ideal a Classic...)

RICHIE RICH (See Harvey Collectors Comics, Harvey Hits, Little Dot, Little Lotta, Little Sad Sack, Million Dollar Digest, Mutt & Jeff, Super Richie, and 3-D Dolly)

RICHIE RICH (...the Poor Little Rich Boy) (See Harvey Hits #3,9)
11/60 - No. 218, 10/82; No. 219, 10/86 - Present
Harvey Publications

1-(See Little Dot for 1st app.)	90.00	250.00	440.00
2	40.00	100.00	180.00
3-5	20.00	60.00	120.00
6-10: 8-Christmas-c	12.50	37.50	75.00
11-20	5.35	16.00	32.00
21-40	3.00	9.00	18.00
41-60	2.00	6.00	12.00
61-80: 65-1st app. Dollar the Dog	1.20	3.50	7.00
81-100	.70	2.00	4.00
101-111,117-120	.50	1.50	3.00
112-116: All 52 pg. Giants	.60	1.80	3.60
121-140	.40	1.25	2.50
141-160: 145-Infinity-c	.35	1.00	2.00
161-180	.25	.75	1.50
181-238		.50	1.00

RICHIE RICH AND...
Oct., 1987 - Present
Harvey Comics

1 (75 cents)		.40	.75
2-6 ($1.00)		.50	1.00

RICHIE RICH AND BILLY BELLHOPS
October, 1977 (One Shot) (52pgs.)
Harvey Publications

1	.50	1.50	3.00

RICHIE RICH AND CADBURY
10/77; No. 2, 9/78 - No. 23, 7/82 (#1-10, 52pgs.)
Harvey Publications

1	.70	2.00	4.00
2-5	.35	1.00	2.00
6-10		.50	1.00
11-23		.40	.80

RICHIE RICH AND CASPER
Aug, 1974 - No. 45, Sept, 1982
Harvey Publications

1	1.15	3.50	7.00
2-5	.50	1.50	3.00
6-10: 10-Xmas-c	.35	1.00	2.00
11-20		.50	1.00
21-40: 22-Xmas-c		.40	.80
41-45		.30	.60

RICHIE RICH AND CASPER IN 3-D
Dec., 1987 ($2.50)

Rex Allen Comics #5, © DELL

Rex Hart #6, © MEG

Richie Rich #1, © HARV

Richie Rich Dollars & Cents #11, © HARV   *Richie Rich Millions #45, © HARV*   *Richie Rich Success Stories #17, © HARV*

RICHIE RICH AND CASPER IN 3-D (continued)
Blackthorne Publ.

	Good	Fine	N-Mint
1	.40	1.25	2.50

RICHIE RICH AND DOLLAR THE DOG (See Richie Rich #65)
9/77 - No. 24, 8/82 (#1-10, 52pgs.)
Harvey Publications

1	.70	2.00	4.00
2-10	.35	1.00	2.00
11-24		.50	1.00

RICHIE RICH AND DOT
October, 1974 (One Shot)
Harvey Publications

1	1.00	3.00	6.00

RICHIE RICH AND GLORIA
Sept, 1977 - No. 25, Sept, 1982 (#1-11, 52pgs.)
Harvey Publications

1	.70	2.00	4.00
2-5	.35	1.00	2.00
6-25		.40	.80

RICHIE RICH AND HIS GIRLFRIENDS
April, 1979 - No. 16, Dec, 1982
Harvey Publications

1: 52 pg. Giant	.50	1.50	3.00
2: 52 pg. Giant	.40	1.20	2.40
3-10	.35	1.00	2.00
11-16		.40	.80

RICHIE RICH AND HIS MEAN COUSIN REGGIE
April, 1979 - No. 3, 1980 (50 cents) (#1,2-52pgs.)
Harvey Publications

1	.35	1.00	2.00
2-3: (#4 was advertised, but never released)	.25	.75	1.50

RICHIE RICH AND JACKIE JOKERS
Nov, 1973 - No. 48, Dec, 1982
Harvey Publications

1: 52 pg. Giant	1.70	5.00	10.00
2,3: 52 pg. Giants	1.00	3.00	6.00
4,5	.85	2.50	5.00
6-10	.50	1.50	3.00
11-20	.35	1.00	2.00
21-40		.50	1.00
41-48		.40	.80

RICHIE RICH AND TIMMY TIME
Sept, 1977 (50 Cents) (One Shot) (52 pages)
Harvey Publications

1	.50	1.50	3.00

RICHIE RICH BANK BOOKS
Oct, 1972 - No. 59, Sept, 1982
Harvey Publications

1	2.65	8.00	16.00
2-5	1.00	3.00	6.00
6-10	.70	2.00	4.00
11-20	.50	1.50	3.00
21-30	.35	1.00	2.00
31-40		.50	1.00
41-59		.40	.80

RICHIE RICH BEST OF THE YEARS
Oct, 1977 - No. 6, June, 1980 (Digest) (128 pages)
Harvey Publications

1(10/77)-Reprints, #2(10/78)-Reprints, #3(6/79-75 cents)

	.35	1.00	2.00

	Good	Fine	N-Mint
4-6(11/79-6/80-95 cents)		.50	1.00

RICHIE RICH BILLIONS
10/74 - No. 48, 10/82 (#1-33, 52pgs.)
Harvey Publications

1	1.70	5.00	10.00
2-5	.85	2.50	5.00
6-10	.70	2.00	4.00
11-20	.35	1.00	2.00
21-33 (Last 52 pgs.)		.50	1.00
34-48		.40	.80

RICHIE RICH CASH
Sept, 1974 - No. 47, Aug, 1982
Harvey Publications

1	1.70	5.00	10.00
2-5	.85	2.50	5.00
6-10	.50	1.50	3.00
11-20	.35	1.00	2.00
21-30		.50	1.00
31-47		.40	.80

RICHIE RICH, CASPER & WENDY NATIONAL LEAGUE
June, 1976 (52 pages)
Harvey Publications

1	.70	2.00	3.00

RICHIE RICH COLLECTORS COMICS (See Harvey Coll. Comics)

RICHIE RICH DIAMONDS
8/72 - No. 59, 8/82 (#1, 23-45: 52pgs.)
Harvey Publications

1: 52 pg. Giant	2.65	8.00	16.00
2-5	1.00	3.00	6.00
6-10	.70	2.00	4.00
11-22	.50	1.50	3.00
23-30	.35	1.00	2.00
31-45: 39-Origin Little Dot		.50	1.00
46-50		.40	.80
51-59		.30	.60

RICHIE RICH DIGEST
Oct, 1986 - Present ($1.25-$1.75, digest-size)
Harvey Publications

1-16		.60	1.25

RICHIE RICH DIGEST STORIES (. . . Magazine #?-on)
10/77 - No. 17, 10/82 (Digest) (132 pages) (75-95 cents)
Harvey Publications

1-Reprints	.30	.80	1.60
2-17: 4-Infinity-c		.40	.80

RICHIE RICH DIGEST WINNERS
12/77 - No. 16, 9/82 (Digest) (132 pages) (75-95 Cents)
Harvey Publications

1	.30	.80	1.60
2-16		.40	.80

RICHIE RICH DOLLARS & CENTS
8/63 - No. 109, 8/82 (#1-43: 68 pgs.; 44-60, 71-94: 52pgs.)
Harvey Publications

1: (#1-64 are all reprint issues)	8.00	24.00	56.00
2	4.00	12.00	24.00
3-5: 3-r/1st app. R.R./Little Dot #1	2.35	7.00	14.00
6-10	1.70	5.00	10.00
11-20	1.35	4.00	8.00
21-30	.85	2.50	5.00
31-43: Last 68 pg. issue	.50	1.50	3.00
44-60: All 52 pgs.	.40	1.20	2.40

RICHIE RICH DOLLARS & CENTS (cont'd)	Good	Fine	N-Mint
61-70	.35	1.00	2.00
71-94: All 52 pgs.		.50	1.00
95-109: 100-Anniversary issue		.40	.80

RICHIE RICH FORTUNES
Sept, 1971 - No. 63, July, 1982 (#1-15: 52pgs.)
Harvey Publications

1	2.35	7.00	16.00
2-5	1.15	3.50	7.00
6-10	.85	2.50	5.00
11-15: Last 52 pg. Giant	.70	2.00	4.00
16-30	.35	1.00	2.00
31-40		.50	1.00
41-63		.40	.80

RICHIE RICH GEMS
Sept, 1974 - No. 43, Sept, 1982
Harvey Publications

1	1.70	5.00	10.00
2-5	.85	2.50	5.00
6-10	.50	1.50	3.00
11-20	.35	1.00	2.00
21-30		.50	1.00
31-43		.40	.80

RICHIE RICH GOLD AND SILVER
Sept, 1975 - No. 42, Oct, 1982 (#1-27: 52pgs.)
Harvey Publications

1	1.35	4.00	8.00
2-5	.70	2.00	4.00
6-10	.35	1.00	2.00
11-27		.50	1.00
28-42		.40	.80

RICHIE RICH HOLIDAY DIGEST MAGAZINE (. . .Digest #4)
1/80 - No. 3, 1/82; No. 4, 3/88 - Present (Published annually)
Harvey Publications

1-3: All X-Mas-c		.50	1.00
4-(3/88, $1.25), 5-(2/89, $1.75)		.60	1.25

RICHIE RICH INVENTIONS
Oct, 1977 - No. 26, Oct, 1982 (#1-11, 52pgs.)
Harvey Publications

1	.70	2.00	4.00
2-5	.35	1.00	2.00
6-11		.50	1.00
12-26		.40	.80

RICHIE RICH JACKPOTS
Oct, 1972 - No. 58, Aug, 1982 (#41-43, 52pgs.)
Harvey Publications

1	2.65	8.00	16.00
2-5	1.00	3.00	6.00
6-10	.70	2.00	4.00
11-20	.35	1.00	2.00
21-30	.25	.75	1.50
31-50		.50	1.00
51-58		.40	.80

RICHIE RICH MILLION DOLLAR DIGEST (. . .Magazine #?-on)(Also see Million Dollar Digest)
October, 1980 - No. 10, Oct, 1982
Harvey Publications

1-10		.50	1.00

RICHIE RICH MILLIONS
9/61; No. 2, 9/62 - No. 113, 10/82 (#1-48: 68 pgs.; 49-64, 85-97: 52 pgs.)
Harvey Publications

1: (#1-5 are all reprint issues)	10.00	30.00	70.00
2	5.00	15.00	35.00
3-10: (All other giants are new & reprints)	3.35	10.00	23.00
11-20	1.70	5.00	12.00
21-30	1.00	3.00	6.00
31-48: Last 68 pg. Giant	.80	2.30	4.60
49-64: 52 pg. Giants	.50	1.50	3.00
65-74	.35	1.00	2.00
75-94: 52 pg. Giants	.40	1.20	2.40
95-100		.50	1.00
101-113		.40	.80

RICHIE RICH MONEY WORLD
Sept, 1972 - No. 59, Sept, 1982
Harvey Publications

1: 52 pg. Giant	2.65	8.00	16.00
2-5	1.00	3.00	6.00
6-10: 9,10-R. Rich mistakenly named Little Lotta on covers			
		.50	1.50	3.00
11-20	.35	1.10	2.20
21-30	.25	.75	1.50
31-50		.50	1.00
51-59		.40	.80

RICHIE RICH PROFITS
Oct, 1974 - No. 47, Sept, 1982

	Good	Fine	N-Mint
1	2.00	6.00	12.00
2-5	1.00	3.00	6.00
6-10	.50	1.50	3.00
11-20	.35	1.00	2.00
21-30		.50	1.00
31-47		.40	.80

RICHIE RICH RELICS
Jan, 1988 - Present (All reprints, .75-$1.00)
Harvey Comics

1-4		.50	1..00

RICHIE RICH RICHES
7/72 - No. 59, 8/82 (#1, 2, 41-45: 52pgs.)
Harvey Publications

1: 52 pg. Giant	2.00	6.00	12.00
2: 52 pg. Giant	1.15	3.50	7.00
3-5	1.00	3.00	6.00
6-10	.50	1.50	3.00
11-20	.35	1.00	2.00
21-40		.50	1.00
41-45: 52 pg. Giants		.60	1.20
46-59		.40	.80

RICHIE RICH SUCCESS STORIES
11/64 - No. 105, 9/82 (#1-38: 68 pgs., 39-55, 67-90: 52pgs.)
Harvey Publications

1	8.00	24.00	56.00
2-5	3.00	9.00	21.00
6-10	2.00	6.00	12.00
11-30: 27-1st Penny Van Dough (8/69)	1.00	3.00	6.00
31-38: Last 68 pg. Giant	.85	2.50	5.00
39-55: 52 pgs.	.50	1.50	3.00
56-66	.35	1.00	2.00
67-90: 52 pgs. (Early issues are reprints)		.60	1.20
91-105		.40	.80

RICHIE RICH TREASURE CHEST DIGEST (. . .Mag. #3)
4/82 - No. 3, 8/82 (95 Cents, Digest Magazine)
Harvey Publications

1-3		.50	1.00

RICHIE RICH VACATIONS DIGEST
11/77; No. 2, 10/78 - No. 7, 10/81; No. 8, 8/82 (Digest, 132 pgs.)
Harvey Publications

1-Reprints	.25	.80	1.60
2-8		.50	1.00

RICHIE RICH VAULTS OF MYSTERY
Nov, 1974 - No. 47, Sept, 1982
Harvey Publications

1	1.50	4.50	9.00
2-10	.70	2.00	4.00
11-20	.35	1.00	2.00
21-30	.25	.75	1.50
31-47		.40	.80

RICHIE RICH ZILLIONZ
10/76 - No. 33, 9/82 (#1-4: 68pgs.; #5-18: 52pgs.)
Harvey Publications

1	1.35	4.00	8.00
2-4: Last 68 pg. Giant	.70	2.00	4.00
5-10	.35	1.00	2.00
11-18: Last 52 pg. Giant		.50	1.00
19-33		.40	.80

RICKY
September, 1953
Standard Comics (Visual Editions)

5	1.30	4.00	9.00

RICKY NELSON (TV)(See Sweethearts V2#42)
No. 956, 12/58 - No. 1192, 6/61 (All photo-c)
Dell Publishing Co.

4-Color 956,998	10.00	30.00	70.00
4-Color 1115,1192-Manning-a	10.00	30.00	70.00

RIDER, THE (Frontier Trail #6)
March, 1957 - No. 5, 1958
Ajax/Farrell Publ. (Four Star Comic Corp.)

1-Swift Arrow, Lone Rider begin	3.00	9.00	21.00
2-5	1.50	4.50	10.00

RIFLEMAN, THE (TV)
No. 1009, 7-9/59 - No. 12, 7-9/62; No. 13, 11/62 - No. 20, 10/64
Dell Publ. Co./Gold Key No. 13 on

4-Color 1009	7.00	21.00	50.00
2 (1-3/60)	5.70	17.00	40.00
3-Toth-a, 4 pgs.	6.50	19.50	45.00
4,5,7-10	4.30	13.00	30.00

The Rifleman #6, © Four Star   The Ringo Kid Western #5, © MEG   Rip Hunter Time Master #1, © DC

	Good	Fine	N-Mint
THE RIFLEMAN (continued)			
6-Toth-a, 4pgs.	5.00	15.00	35.00
11-20	4.00	12.00	28.00

NOTE: *Warren Tufts a-2-9. All have Chuck Connors photo-c. Photo back-c, #13-15.*

RIMA, THE JUNGLE GIRL
Apr-May, 1974 - No. 7, Apr-May, 1975
National Periodical Publications

1-Origin, part 1		.60	1.20
2-4-Origin, part 2,3,&4		.40	.80
5-7: 7-Origin & only app. Space Marshal		.30	.60

NOTE: *Kubert c-1-7. Nino a-1-5. Redondo a-1-6.*

RING OF BRIGHT WATER (See Movie Classics)

RINGO KID, THE (2nd Series)
1/70 - No. 23, 11/73; No. 24, 11/75 - No. 30, 11/76
Marvel Comics Group

1(1970)-Williamson-a r-from #10, 1956		.40	.80
2-30: 20-Williamson-r/#1		.25	.50

NOTE: *Wildey a-13r.*

RINGO KID WESTERN, THE (1st Series)(See Wild Western)
Aug, 1954 - No. 21, Sept, 1957
Atlas Comics (HPC)/Marvel Comics

1-Origin; The Ringo Kid & his horse Arab begin			
	7.00	21.00	50.00
2-Black Rider app.; origin Arab	4.00	12.00	28.00
3-5	2.65	8.00	18.00
6-8-Severin-a(3) each	3.50	10.50	24.00
9,11,14-21	1.70	5.00	12.00
10,13-Williamson-a, 4 pgs.	3.70	11.00	26.00
12-Orlando-a, 4 pgs.	2.00	6.00	14.00

NOTE: *Berg a-8. Maneely a-1-5, 15, 18, 20, 21; c-1-6, 8, 13, 15, 16, 18, 20. J. Severin c-10, 11. Sinnott a-1. Wildey a-16-18.*

RIN TIN TIN (See March of Comics #163,180,195)

RIN TIN TIN (TV) (. . .& Rusty #21 on; see Western Roundup)
Nov, 1952 - No. 38, May-July, 1961; 1963 (All Photo-c)
Dell Publishing Co./Gold Key

4-Color 434 (#1)	4.65	14.00	32.00
4-Color 476,523	3.50	10.50	24.00
4(3-5/54)-10	3.00	9.00	21.00
11-20	2.30	7.00	16.00
21-38	2.00	6.00	14.00
1(11/63-G.K.) . . .& Rusty	2.00	6.00	14.00

RIO
June, 1987 (64 pgs., $8.95, color)
Comico

1-Wildey-c/a	1.50	4.50	8.95

RIO BRAVO (See 4-Color #1018)

RIO CONCHOS (See Movie Comics)

RIOT (Satire)
Apr, 1954 - No. 3, Aug, 1954; No. 4, Feb, 1956 - No. 6, June, 1956
Atlas Comics (ACI No. 1-5/WPI No. 6)

1-Russ Heath-a	5.70	17.00	40.00
2-Li'l Abner satire by Post	4.30	13.00	30.00
3-Last precode (8/54)	3.50	10.50	24.00
4-Infinity-c; Marilyn Monroe '7 Year Itch' movie satire; Mad Rip-off ads	5.00	15.00	35.00
5-Marilyn Monroe, John Wayne parody; part photo-c			
	5.70	17.00	40.00
6-Lorna of the Jungle satire by Everett; Dennis the Menace satire cover/story			
	3.50	10.50	24.00

NOTE: *Berg a-3. Burgos c-1, 2. Colan a-1. Everett a-1, 4, 6. Heath a-1. Maneely a-1, 2, 4-6; c-3, 4, 6. Post a-1-4. Reinman a-2. Severin a-4-6.*

RIPCORD (See 4-Color #1294)

RIP HUNTER TIME MASTER (See Showcase)
Mar-Apr, 1961 - No. 29, Nov-Dec, 1965
National Periodical Publications

	Good	Fine	N-Mint
1	10.00	30.00	70.00
2	5.70	17.00	40.00
3-5: 5-Last 10 cent issue	3.60	11.00	25.00
6,7-Toth-a in each	3.00	9.00	21.00
8-15	2.15	6.50	15.00
16-29: 29-G. Kane-c	1.50	4.50	10.00

RIP IN TIME
Aug., 1986 - No. 5, 1987 ($1.50, B&W)
Fantagor Press

1-Corben-c/a	.50	1.50	3.00
2-5	.25	.75	1.50

RIP KIRBY (See Feat. Books #51,54, Harvey Comics Hits #57, & Street Comix)

RIPLEY'S BELIEVE IT OR NOT!
Sept, 1953 - No. 4, March, 1954
Harvey Publications

1-Powell-a	5.70	17.00	40.00
2-4	3.00	9.00	21.00
J. C. Penney giveaway (1948)	4.00	12.00	28.00

RIPLEY'S BELIEVE IT OR NOT! (Formerly . . .True War Stories)
No. 4, April, 1967 - No. 94, Feb, 1980
Gold Key

4-McWilliams-a	1.50	4.50	10.00
5-Subtitled ''True War Stories;'' Evans-a	.85	2.50	6.00
6-9: 6-McWilliams-a. 8-Orlando-a	.85	2.50	6.00
10-Evans-a(2)	.85	2.50	6.00
11-14,16-20	.55	1.65	4.00
15-Evans-a	.55	1.65	4.00
21-30	.50	1.50	3.00
31-38,40-60	.35	1.00	2.00
39-Crandall-a	.40	1.25	2.50
61-94: 74,77-83 (52 pgs.)	.25	.75	1.50
Story Digest Mag. 1(6/70)-4¾x6½''	.50	1.50	3.00

NOTE: *Evanish art by Luiz Dominguez #22-25, 27, 30, 31, 40. McWilliams a-65, 70, 89. Sparling c-68. Reprints-#74,77-84,87 (part); 91,93 (all). Williamson, Wood-a-80r/#1.*

RIPLEY'S BELIEVE IT OR NOT! (See Ace Comics, All-American Comics, Mystery Comics Digest #1, 4, 7, 10, 13, 16, 19, 22, 25)

RIPLEY'S BELIEVE IT OR NOT TRUE GHOST STORIES (Becomes . . .True War Stories) (See Dan Curtis)
June, 1965 - No. 2, Oct, 1966
Gold Key

1-Williamson, Wood & Evans-a; photo-c	2.30	7.00	16.00
2-Orlando, McWilliams-a	1.30	4.00	9.00
Mini-Comic 1(1976-3¼x6½'')		.30	.60
11186(1977)-Golden Press; 224 pgs. ($1.95)-Reprints			
	.50	1.50	3.00
11401(3/79)-Golden Press; 96 pgs. ($1.00)-Reprints			
		.60	1.20

RIPLEY'S BELIEVE IT OR NOT TRUE WAR STORIES (Formerly . . .True Ghost Stories; becomes Ripley's Believe It or Not #4 on)
Nov, 1966
Gold Key

1(#3)-Williamson-a	1.70	5.00	12.00

RIPLEY'S BELIEVE IT OR NOT! TRUE WEIRD
June, 1966 - No. 2, Aug, 1966 (B&W Magazine)
Ripley Enterprises

1,2-Comic stories & text	.40	1.20	2.40

RIVETS (See 4-Color #518)

RIVETS (A dog)
Jan, 1956 - No. 3, May, 1956
Argo Publ.

	Good	Fine	N-Mint
1-Reprints Sunday & daily newspaper strips	2.65	8.00	18.00
2,3	1.50	4.50	10.00

ROAD RUNNER, THE (See Beep Beep...)

ROBERT E. HOWARD'S CONAN THE BARBARIAN
1983 (No month) ($2.50, printed on Baxter paper)
Marvel Comics Group

	Good	Fine	N-Mint
1-r-/Savage Tales No. 2,3 by Smith; c-r/Conan No. 21 by Smith	.45	1.25	2.50

ROBIN (See Aurora)

ROBIN HOOD (See 4-Color #413,669, King Classics, Movie Comics, & The Advs. of...)

ROBIN HOOD (...& His Merry Men, The Illustrated Story of...) (See Classic Comics #7 & Classics Giveaways, 12/44)

ROBIN HOOD (New Adventures of...)
1952 (36 pages) (5x7¼")
Walt Disney Productions (Flour giveaways)

	Good	Fine	N-Mint
"New Adventures of Robin Hood," "Ghosts of Waylea Castle," & "The Miller's Ransom" each....	1.70	5.00	12.00

ROBIN HOOD (Adventures of... #7, 8)
No. 52, Nov, 1955 - No. 6, June, 1957
Magazine Enterprises (Sussex Publ. Co.)

	Good	Fine	N-Mint
52-Origin Robin Hood & Sir Gallant of the Round Table	4.00	12.00	28.00
53, 3-6	2.65	8.00	18.00
I.W. Reprint #1,2 (r-#4), 9 (r-#52)(1963)	.50	1.50	3.00
Super Reprint #10 (r-#53?), 11,15 (r-#5), 17('64)	.50	1.50	3.00

NOTE: *Bolle* a-in all; c-52. *Powell* a-6.

ROBIN HOOD (Not Disney)
May-July, 1963 (One shot)
Dell Publishing Co.

	Good	Fine	N-Mint
1	1.00	3.00	7.00

ROBIN HOOD ($1.50)
1973 (Disney) (8½x11''; cardboard covers) (52 pages)
Western Publishing Co.

	Good	Fine	N-Mint
96151-"Robin Hood," based on movie, 96152-"The Mystery of Sherwood Forest," 96153-"In King Richard's Service," 96154-"The Wizard's Ring" each....	.70	2.00	4.00

ROBIN HOOD AND HIS MERRY MEN (Formerly Danger & Adv.)
No. 28, April, 1956 - No. 38, Aug, 1958
Charlton Comics

	Good	Fine	N-Mint
28	2.30	7.00	16.00
29-37	1.30	4.00	9.00
38-Ditko-a, 5 pgs.	4.00	12.00	28.00

ROBIN HOOD'S FRONTIER DAYS (...Western Tales)
No date (Circa 1955) 20 pages, slick-c (Seven issues?)
Shoe Store Giveaway (Robin Hood Stores)

	Good	Fine	N-Mint
nn	2.30	7.00	16.00
nn-Issues with Crandall-a	3.50	10.50	24.00

ROBIN HOOD TALES (National Periodical #7 on)
Feb, 1956 - No. 6, Nov-Dec, 1956
Quality Comics Group (Comic Magazines)

	Good	Fine	N-Mint
1	4.00	12.00	28.00
2-5-Matt Baker-a	4.65	14.00	32.00
6	2.00	6.00	14.00
Frontier Days giveaway (1956)	1.70	5.00	12.00

ROBIN HOOD TALES (Continued from Quality)
No. 7, Jan-Feb, 1957 - No. 14, Mar-Apr, 1958
National Periodical Publications

	Good	Fine	N-Mint
7	8.50	25.50	60.00
8-14	7.00	21.00	50.00

ROBINSON CRUSOE (Also see King Classics)
Nov-Jan, 1963-64
Dell Publishing Co.

	Good	Fine	N-Mint
1	1.00	3.00	7.00

ROBO-HUNTER (Also see Sam Slade...)
April, 1984 - No. 6, 1984
Eagle Comics

	Good	Fine	N-Mint
1-6-2000 A.D.-r		.50	1.00

ROBOT COMICS
June, 1987 (One shot, D.F. #2, $2.00, B&W)
Renegade Press

	Good	Fine	N-Mint
0-Bob Burden story/art	.40	1.25	2.50

ROBOTECH DEFENDERS
Mar, 1985 - No. 2, Apr, 1985 (mini-series)
DC Comics

	Good	Fine	N-Mint
1,2	.40	1.20	2.40

ROBOTECH IN 3-D
Aug, 1987 ($2.50)
Comico

	Good	Fine	N-Mint
1-Adapts TV show; Steacy-c	.40	1.25	2.50

ROBOTECH MASTERS (TV)
July, 1985 - No. 23, Apr, 1988
Comico

	Good	Fine	N-Mint
1	.50	1.50	3.00
2,3	.35	1.00	2.00
4-23 (#23, $1.75)	.25	.75	1.50

ROBOTECH SPECIAL
May, 1988 (One shot, $2.50, color, 44pgs)
Comico

	Good	Fine	N-Mint
1-Ken Steacy wraparound-c; part photo-c	.40	1.25	2.50

ROBOTECH THE GRAPHIC NOVEL
Aug, 1986 ($5.95, 8½x11'', 52 pgs.)
Comico

	Good	Fine	N-Mint
1-Origin SDF-1; intro T.R. Edwards; Ken Steacy c/a	1.00	3.00	6.00
1-2nd printing	1.00	3.00	6.00

ROBOTECH: THE MACROSS SAGA (Formerly Macross)(TV)
No. 2, Feb, 1985 - Present
Comico

	Good	Fine	N-Mint
2	1.35	4.00	8.00
3-5	.50	1.50	3.00
6,7	.40	1.25	2.50
8-25	.25	.75	1.50
26-32 ($1.75)	.30	.90	1.75

ROBOTECH: THE NEW GENERATION (TV)
July, 1985 - No. 25, July, 1988
Comico

	Good	Fine	N-Mint
1	.50	1.50	3.00
2-4	.35	1.00	2.00
5-21	.25	.75	1.50
22-25	.30	.90	1.75

ROBOTIX
Feb, 1986 (One Shot)
Marvel Comics Group

Robin Hood And His Merry Men #31, © CC

Robotech Masters #2, © Comico

Robotech Special #1, © Comico

The Rocketeer Adventure Magazine #1, © Comico   Rocket Kelly #1, © FOX   Rocky Lane Western #1, © FAW

	Good	Fine	N-Mint
ROBOTIX (continued)			
1-Based on toy		.50	1.00
ROBOTMEN OF THE LOST PLANET (Also see Space Thrillers)			
1952			
Avon Periodicals			
1-3pg. Kinstler-a	56.00	170.00	390.00
ROB ROY (See 4-Color #544)			
ROCK AND ROLLO (Formerly T.V. Teens)			
V2No.14, Oct, 1957 - No. 19, Sept, 1958			
Charlton Comics			
14-19	1.00	3.00	7.00
ROCKET COMICS			
Mar, 1940 - No. 3, May, 1940			
Hillman Periodicals			
1-Rocket Riley, Red Roberts the Electro Man(Origin), The Phantom Ranger, The Steel Shark, The Defender, Buzzard Barnes, Lefty Larson, & Man With a Thousand Faces begin			
	65.00	195.00	455.00
2,3	40.00	120.00	280.00
ROCKETEER, THE (See Eclipse Graphic Album Series, Pacific Presents & Starslayer #2)			
ROCKETEER ADVENTURE MAGAZINE, THE			
July, 1988 - Present ($2.00, color)			
Comico			
1-Dave Stevens-c/a in all; Kaluta back-up-a	.60	1.75	3.50
2,3	.40	1.25	2.50
ROCKETEER SPECIAL EDITION, THE			
Nov, 1984 ($1.50; Baxter paper)			
Eclipse Comics			
1-Dave Stevens-c/a	.90	2.75	5.50
ROCKET KELLY (See The Bouncer & Green Mask #10)			
1944; Fall, 1945 - No. 5, 10-11/46			
Fox Feature Syndicate			
nn (1944)	8.50	25.50	60.00
1	8.50	25.50	60.00
2-The Puppeteer app. (costumed hero)	5.70	17.00	40.00
3-5: 5-(#5 on cover, #4 inside)	5.00	15.00	35.00
ROCKETMAN (See Hello Pal & Scoop Comics)			
June, 1952			
Ajax/Farrell Publications			
1-Rocketman & Cosmo	12.00	36.00	84.00
ROCKET RACCOON			
May, 1985 - No. 4, Aug, 1985 (mini-series)			
Marvel Comics Group			
1-4	.25	.75	1.50
ROCKETS AND RANGE RIDERS			
May, 1957 (16 pages, soft-c) (Giveaway)			
Richfield Oil Corp.			
Toth-a	10.50	30.00	70.00
ROCKET SHIP X			
September, 1951; 1952			
Fox Features Syndicate			
1	35.00	105.00	245.00
1952 (nn, nd, no publ.)-Edited '51-c	22.00	65.00	154.00
ROCKET TO ADVENTURE LAND (See Pixie Puzzle...)			
ROCKET TO THE MOON			
1951			
Avon Periodicals			

	Good	Fine	N-Mint
nn-Orlando c/a; adapts Otis Aldebert Kline's "Maza of the Moon"			
	55.00	165.00	385.00
ROCK HAPPENING (Harvey Pop Comics:)(See Bunny)			
Sept, 1969 - No. 2, Nov, 1969			
Harvey Publications			
1,2: Featuring Bunny	1.15	3.50	8.00
ROCKY AND HIS FIENDISH FRIENDS (TV)(Bullinkle)			
Oct, 1962 - No. 5, Sept, 1963 (Jay Ward)			
Gold Key			
1 (84 pgs.)	7.50	22.50	60.00
2,3 (84 pgs.)	5.00	15.00	40.00
4,5 (Regular size)	4.00	12.00	28.00
Kite Fun Book ('63, 16p, soft-c, 5x7¼")	5.00	15.00	35.00
Kite Fun Book ('70, 16p, soft-c, 5x7¼")	3.50	10.50	24.00
ROCKY AND HIS FRIENDS (See 4-Color #1128, 1152, 1166, 1208, 1275, 1311 and March of Comics No. 216)			
ROCKY JONES SPACE RANGER (See Space Adventures #15-18)			
ROCKY JORDAN PRIVATE EYE (See Private Eye)			
ROCKY LANE WESTERN (Rocky Allan Lane starred in Republic movies (for a short time as Red Ryder) & TV)(See Black Jack & Six Gun Heroes)			
May, 1949 - No. 87, Nov, 1959			
Fawcett Publications/Charlton No. 56 on			
1 (36 pgs.)-Rocky, his stallion Black Jack, & Slim Pickens begin; photo-c begin, end #57; photo back-c	40.00	120.00	280.00
2 (36 pgs.)-Last photo back-c	14.00	42.00	100.00
3-5 (52 pgs.). 4-Captain Tootsie by Beck	11.50	34.00	80.00
6,10 (36 pgs.)	9.00	27.00	62.00
7-9 (52 pgs.)	10.00	30.00	70.00
11-13,15-17 (52 pgs.): 15-Black Jack's Hitching Post begins, ends #25	7.00	21.00	50.00
14,18 (36 pgs.)	6.50	19.50	45.00
19-21,23,24 (52 pgs.): 20-Last Slim Pickens. 21-Dee Dickens begins, ends #55,57,65-68	6.50	19.50	45.00
22,25-28,30 (36 pgs. begin)	5.70	17.00	40.00
29-Classic complete novel "The Land of Missing Men,"-hidden land of ancient temple ruins (r-in #65)	7.00	21.00	50.00
31-40	5.50	16.50	38.00
41-54	4.65	14.00	32.00
55-Last Fawcett issue (1/54)	5.50	16.50	38.00
56-1st Charlton issue (2/54)-Photo-c	5.50	16.50	38.00
57,60-Photo-c	3.70	11.00	26.00
58,59,61-64: 59-61-Young Falcon app. 64-Slim Pickens app.	3.50	10.50	24.00
65-R-/#29, "The Land of Missing Men"	3.70	11.00	26.00
66-68: Reprints #30,31,32	2.65	8.00	18.00
69-78,80-86	2.65	8.00	18.00
79-Giant Edition, 68 pgs.	3.70	11.00	26.00
87-Last issue	3.50	10.50	24.00
NOTE: *Complete novels in #10, 14, 18, 22, 25, 30-32, 36, 38, 39, 49. Captain Tootsie in #4, 12, 20. Big Bow and Little Arrow in #11, 28, 63. Black Jack's Hitching Post in #15-25, 64, 73.*			
ROD CAMERON WESTERN (Movie star)			
Feb, 1950 - No. 20, April, 1953			
Fawcett Publications			
1-Rod Cameron, his horse War Paint, & Sam The Sheriff begin; photo front/back-c begin	25.00	75.00	175.00
2	13.00	40.00	90.00
3-Novel length story "The Mystery of the Seven Cities of Cibola"	10.00	30.00	70.00
4-10: 9-Last photo back-c	8.50	25.50	60.00
11-19	7.00	21.00	50.00

ROD CAMERON WESTERN (continued)	Good	Fine	N-Mint
20-Last issue & photo-c	8.00	24.00	56.00

NOTE: *Novel length stories in No. 1-8,12-14.*

RODEO RYAN (See A-1 Comics #8)

ROGER BEAN, R. G. (Regular Guy)
1915 - 1917 (34 pgs.; B&W; 4¾x16''; cardboard covers)
(No. 1 & 4 bound on side, No. 3 bound at top)
The Indiana News Co.

	Good	Fine	N-Mint
1-By Chic Jackson (48 pgs.)	7.00	21.00	50.00
2-4	5.00	15.00	35.00

ROGER DODGER (Also in Exciting #57 on)
No. 5, Aug, 1952
Standard Comics

5-Teen-age	1.15	3.50	8.00

ROG 2000
June, 1982 ($2.95)
Pacific Comics

nn-Byrne c/a-r	.70	2.00	4.00

ROG 2000
1987 - No. 2, 1987 ($2.00, mini-series, color)
Fantagraphics Books

1,2-Byrne-r	.35	1.00	2.00

ROGUE TROOPER
Oct, 1986 - Present (color, $1.25-$1.50)
Quality Comics

1-19: 6-Dbl. size		.50	1.00
20,21/22	.25	.75	1.50

ROLY POLY COMIC BOOK
1945 - 1946 (MLJ reprints)
Green Publishing Co.

1-Red Rube & Steel Sterling begin	11.00	32.00	75.00
6-The Blue Circle & The Steel Fist app.	5.50	16.50	38.00
10-Origin Red Rube retold; Steel Sterling story (Zip #41)			
	6.00	18.00	42.00
11,12,14: 11,14-The Black Hood app.	6.00	18.00	42.00
15-The Blue Circle & The Steel Fist app.; cover exact swipe from Fox Blue Beetle #1	14.00	42.00	105.00

ROM
December, 1979 - No. 75, Feb, 1986
Marvel Comics Group

1-Based on a Parker Bros. toy-origin	.40	1.25	2.50
2-5	.25	.75	1.50
6-16: 13-Saga of the Space Knights begins		.60	1.20
17,18-X-Men app.	.40	1.25	2.50
19-24,26-30: 19-X-Men cameo		.45	.90
25-Double size		.60	1.20
31-49: 32-X-Men cameo		.40	.80
50-Double size		.50	1.00
51-56		.40	.80
57-Alpha Flight app.	.25	.75	1.50
58-75: 65-X-Men & Beta Ray Bill app.		.40	.80
Annual 1(11/82)		.60	1.20
Annual 2(11/83), 3(1984)		.50	1.00
Annual 4(1985)		.60	1.20

NOTE: *Austin* c-3i, 18i, 61i. *Byrne* a-74i; c-56, 57, 74. *Ditko* a-59-64p. *Golden* c-7-12, 19. *Guice* a-61i; c-55, 58, 60p. *Layton* a-59i; c-15, 59i. *Miller* c-3p, 17p, 18p. *Russell* a(i)-64, 65, 67, 69; c-64, 65i, 66. *P. Smith* c-59p. *Starlin* c-67.

ROMANCE (See True Stories of . . .)

ROMANCE AND CONFESSION STORIES (See Giant Comics Ed.)
No date (1949) (100pgs.)
St. John Publishing Co.

	Good	Fine	N-Mint
1-Baker c/a; remaindered St. John love comics			
	20.00	60.00	140.00

ROMANCE DIARY
December, 1949 - No. 2, March, 1950
Marvel Comics (CDS)(CLDS)

1,2	3.50	10.50	24.00

ROMANCE OF FLYING, THE (See Feature Books #33)

ROMANCES OF MOLLY MANTON (See Molly Manton)

ROMANCES OF NURSE HELEN GRANT, THE
August, 1957
Atlas Comics (VPI)

1	1.50	4.50	10.00

ROMANCES OF THE WEST
Nov, 1949 - No. 2, Mar, 1950 (52 pgs.)
Marvel Comics (SPC)

1-Movie photo of Calamity Jane/Sam Bass	6.00	18.00	42.00
2	4.00	12.00	28.00

ROMANCE STORIES OF TRUE LOVE (Formerly Love Problems & Advice)
No. 45, 5/57 - No. 50, 3/58; No. 51, 9/58 - No. 52, 11/58
Harvey Publications

45-51	1.00	3.00	7.00
52-Matt Baker-a	2.35	7.00	16.00

NOTE: *Powell* a-45,46,48-50.

ROMANCE TALES
No. 7, Oct, 1949 - No. 9, March, 1950 (No. 7,8-photo-c)
Marvel Comics (CDS)

7	2.65	8.00	18.00
8,9: 8-Everett-a	1.70	5.00	12.00

ROMANCE TRAIL
July-Aug, 1949 - No. 6, May-June, 1950
National Periodical Publications

1-Kinstler, Toth-a; Jimmy Wakely photo-c	14.00	42.00	100.00
2-Kinstler-a; photo-c	7.00	21.00	50.00
3-Photo-c; Kinstler, Toth-a	7.00	21.00	50.00
4-Photo-c; Toth-a	6.50	19.50	45.00
5,6: 5-Photo-c	5.50	16.50	38.00

ROMAN HOLIDAYS, THE (TV)
Feb, 1973 - No. 4, Nov, 1973 (Hanna-Barbera)
Gold Key

1	1.35	4.00	8.00
2-4	1.00	3.00	6.00

ROMANTIC ADVENTURES (My. . . #49-67, covers only)
Mar-Apr, 1949 - No. 67, July, 1956 (My. . . No. 68 on)
American Comics Group (B&I Publ. Co.)

1	3.50	10.50	24.00
2	1.70	5.00	12.00
3-10	1.15	3.50	8.00
11-20 (4/52)	.85	2.50	6.00
21-46,48-52: 52-Last Pre-code (2/55)	.65	2.00	4.50
47-3-D effect	1.50	4.50	10.00
53-67	.50	1.50	3.50

NOTE: *#1-23, 52 pgs.* *Shelly* a-40. *Whitney* c/art in many issues.

ROMANTIC AFFAIRS (Formerly Our Love?)
No. 3, March, 1950
Marvel Comics (Select Publications)

3-Photo-c; from Romances of Molly Manton #2			
	1.70	5.00	12.00

Rogue Trooper #11, © Quality Comics

Romance Trail #1, © DC

Romantic Adventures #50, © ACG

Romantic Love #6, © REAL   Romantic Secrets #1, © FAW   Ronin #4, © DC

ROMANTIC CONFESSIONS
Oct, 1949 - V3No.1, April-May, 1953
Hillman Periodicals

	Good	Fine	N-Mint
V1#1-McWilliams-a	4.00	12.00	28.00
2-Briefer-a; negligee panels	2.15	6.50	15.00
3-12	1.50	4.50	10.00
V2#1,2,4-8,10-12	1.15	3.50	8.00
3-Krigstein-a	2.65	8.00	18.00
9-One pg. Frazetta ad	1.50	4.50	10.00
V3#1	1.00	3.00	7.00

NOTE: *McWilliams a-V2#2.*

ROMANTIC HEARTS
Mar, 1951 - No. 9, Aug, 1952; July, 1953 - No. 12, July, 1955
Story Comics/Master/Merit Pubs.

1(3/51) (1st Series)	3.50	10.50	24.00
2	1.70	5.00	12.00
3-9	1.50	4.50	10.00
1(7/53) (2nd Series)	2.00	6.00	14.00
2	1.30	4.00	9.00
3-12	1.00	3.00	7.00

ROMANTIC LOVE
No. 4, June, 1950
Quality Comics Group

4 (6/50)(Exist?)	1.70	5.00	12.00
I.W. Reprint #2,3,8		.60	1.20

ROMANTIC LOVE
9-10/49 - No. 3, 1-2/50; No. 4, 2-3/51 - No. 13, 10/52; No. 20, 3-4/54 -
No. 23, 9-10/54 (no #14-19)
Avon Periodicals/Realistic

1-c-/Avon paperback 252	10.00	30.00	70.00
2	5.00	15.00	35.00
3-c-/paperback Novel Library 12	5.00	15.00	35.00
4-c-/paperback Diversey Prize Novel 5	5.00	15.00	35.00
5-c-/paperback Novel Library 34	5.00	15.00	35.00
6-"Thrill Crazy"-marijuana story; c-/Avon paperback 207;			
Kinstler-a	7.00	21.00	50.00
7,8; 8-Astarita-a(2)	4.35	13.00	30.00
9-c-/paperback/Novel Library 41; Kinstler-a	5.00	15.00	35.00
10-c-/Avon paperback 212	5.00	15.00	35.00
11-c-/paperback Novel Library 17; Kinstler-a	5.00	15.00	35.00
12-c-/paperback Novel Library 13	5.00	15.00	35.00
13,21,22: 22-Kinstler-c	4.35	13.00	30.00
20-Kinstler-c/a	4.35	13.00	30.00
23-Kinstler-c	3.65	11.00	25.00
nn(1-3/53)(Realistic-r)	2.85	8.50	20.00

NOTE: *Astarita a-7,10,11,21. Painted c-7, 9, 10, 11.*

ROMANTIC MARRIAGE (Cinderella Love #25 on)
No. 1-3 (1950, no month); No. 4, 5-6/51 - No. 17, 9/52; No. 18,
9/53 - No. 24, Sept, 1954 (#1-8, 52 pgs.)
Ziff-Davis/St. John No. 18 on

1-Photo-c	5.50	16.50	38.00
2-Painted-c	3.00	9.00	21.00
3-9: 3,8,9-Painted-c; 5-7-Photo-c	2.30	7.00	16.00
10-Unusual format; front-c is a painted-c; back-c is a photo-c complete with logo, price, etc.	4.00	12.00	28.00
11-17 (9/52; last Z-D ish.): 13-Photo-c	2.00	6.00	14.00
18-22,24: 20-Photo-c	2.00	6.00	14.00
23-Baker-c	2.30	7.00	16.00

ROMANTIC PICTURE NOVELETTES
1946
Magazine Enterprises

1-Mary Worth-r	7.00	21.00	50.00

ROMANTIC SECRETS (Becomes Time For Love)
Sept, 1949 - No. 39, 4/53; No. 5, 10/55 - No. 52, 11/64 (#1-5, photo-c)
Fawcett/Charlton Comics No. 5 (10/55) on

	Good	Fine	N-Mint
1	3.50	10.50	24.00
2,3	1.65	5.00	12.00
4,9-Evans-a	2.65	8.00	18.00
5-8,10	1.50	4.50	10.00
11-23	1.15	3.50	8.00
24-Evans-a	2.30	7.00	16.00
25-39	.85	2.50	6.00
5 (Charlton)(10/55, formerly Negro Romances #4?)			
	1.85	5.50	13.00
6-10	1.00	3.00	7.00
11-20	.45	1.35	3.00
21-35: Last 10 cent ish?	.35	1.00	2.50
36-52('64)		.40	.80

NOTE: *Bailey a-20. Powell a(1st series)-5,7,10,12,16,17,20,26,29,33,34,36,37. Photo c(1st series)-1-5, 25, 27, 33. Sekowsky a-26.*

ROMANTIC STORY (Cowboy Love #28 on)
11/49 - No. 22, Sum, 1953; No. 23, 5/54 - No. 27, 12/54; No. 28, 8/55
- No. 130, 11/73
Fawcett/Charlton Comics No. 23 on

1-Photo-c begin, end #22,24	4.35	13.00	30.00
2	2.15	6.50	15.00
3-5	1.65	5.00	12.00
6-14	1.50	4.50	10.00
15-Evans-a	2.30	7.00	16.00
16-22(Sum, '53; last Fawcett ish.). 21-Toth-a?	1.15	3.50	8.00
23-39,41-50: 26,29-Wood swipes	1.15	3.50	8.00
40-(100 pgs.)	3.15	9.50	22.00
51-56,58-80	.45	1.35	3.00
57-Hypo needle story	.70	2.00	4.00
81-130		.40	.80

NOTE: *Powell a-7,8,16,20,30.*

ROMANTIC THRILLS (See Fox Giants)

ROMANTIC WESTERN
Winter, 1949 - No. 3, June, 1950 (Photo-c all)
Fawcett Publications

1	5.50	16.50	38.00
2-Williamson, McWilliams-a	8.00	24.00	56.00
3	3.50	10.50	23.00

ROMEO TUBBS (Formerly My Secret Life)
No. 26, 5/50 - No. 28, 7/50; No. 1, 1950; No. 27, 12/52
Fox Feature Syndicate/Green Publ. Co. No. 27

26-Teen-age	5.00	15.00	35.00
27-Contains Pedro on inside; Wood-a	7.00	21.00	50.00
28, 1	3.70	11.00	26.00

RONALD McDONALD (TV)
Sept, 1970 - No. 4, March, 1971
Charlton Press (King Features Synd.)

1		.50	1.00
2-4		.25	.50

RONIN
July, 1983 - No. 6, Apr, 1984 (mini-series) (52 pgs., $2.50)
DC Comics

1-Miller script, c/a in all	1.00	3.00	6.00
2	.85	2.50	5.00
3-5	.70	2.00	4.00
6	1.35	4.00	8.00
Trade paperback	2.50	7.50	15.00

ROOK (See Eerie Mag. & Warren Presents: The Rook)
November, 1979 - No. 14, April, 1982

ROOK (continued)
Warren Publications

	Good	Fine	N-Mint
1-Nino-a		.40	.80
2-14: 3,4-Toth-a		.30	.60

ROOKIE COP (Formerly Crime and Justice?)
Nov, 1955 - No. 33, Aug, 1957
Charlton Comics

27	2.65	8.00	18.00
28-33	1.50	4.50	10.00

ROOM 222 (TV)
Jan, 1970; No. 2, May, 1970 - No. 4, Jan, 1971
Dell Publishing Co.

1,2,4: 2,4-Photo-c. 4 r-/#1	1.75	5.25	12.00
3-Marijuana story	1.50	4.50	10.00

ROOTIE KAZOOTIE (TV)(See 3-D-ell)
No. 415, Aug, 1952 - No. 6, Oct-Dec, 1954
Dell Publishing Co.

4-Color 415	3.50	10.50	24.00
4-Color 459,502	3.00	9.00	21.00
4(4-6/54)-6	2.65	8.00	18.00

ROOTS OF THE SWAMPTHING
July, 1986 - No. 5, Nov, 1986 ($2.00, Baxter)
DC Comics

1-5: All Wrightson-r	.35	1.00	2.00

ROUND THE WORLD GIFT
No date (mid 1940's) (4 pages)
National War Fund (Giveaway)

	10.00	30.00	70.00

ROUNDUP (Western Crime)
July-Aug, 1948 - No. 5, Mar-Apr, 1949 (52 pgs.)
D. S. Publishing Co.

1-1pg. Frazetta on 'Mystery of the Hunting Lodge'?; Ingels-a?	6.50	19.50	45.00
2-Marijuana drug mention story	5.00	15.00	35.00
3-5	3.50	10.50	24.00

ROYAL ROY
May, 1985 - No. 6, Mar, 1986 (Children's book)
Star Comics (Marvel)

1-6		.35	.70

ROY CAMPANELLA, BASEBALL HERO
1950
Fawcett Publications

nn-Photo-c	20.00	60.00	140.00

ROY ROGERS (See March of Comics #17, 35, 47, 62, 68, 73, 77, 86, 91, 100, 105, 116, 121, 131, 136, 146, 151, 161, 167, 176, 191, 206, 221, 236, 250)

ROY ROGERS AND TRIGGER
April, 1967
Gold Key

1-Photo-c; reprints	2.00	6.00	14.00

ROY ROGERS COMICS (See Western Roundup under Dell Giants)
No. 38, 4/44 - No. 177, 12/47 (52 pgs.-#38-166)
Dell Publishing Co.

4-Color 38 (1944)-49pg. story; photo front/back-c on all 4-Color ish.	45.00	135.00	315.00
4-Color 63 (1945)-Color photos inside-c	30.00	90.00	210.00
4-Color 86,95 (1945)	23.00	70.00	160.00
4-Color 109 (1946)	18.00	54.00	125.00
4-Color 117,124,137,144	13.00	40.00	90.00
4-Color 153,160,166: 166-48pg. story	10.00	30.00	70.00
4-Color 177 (36 pgs.)-32pg. story	10.00	30.00	70.00

ROY ROGERS COMICS (. . .& Trigger #92(8/55)-on)(Roy starred in Republic movies, radio & TV) (Singing cowboy) (Also see Dale Evans, Queen of the West . . ., It Really Happened #8 & Roy Roger's Trigger)
Jan, 1948 - No. 145, Sept-Oct, 1961 (36pgs.#1-19)
Dell Publishing Co.

	Good	Fine	N-Mint
1-Roy, his horse Trigger, & Chuck Wagon Charley's Tales begin; photo-c begin, end #145	36.00	108.00	250.00
2	17.00	51.00	120.00
3-5	14.00	42.00	100.00
6-10	10.00	30.00	70.00
11-19: 19- . . .Charley's Tales ends	7.00	21.00	50.00
20 (52 pgs.)-Trigger feature begins, ends #46	7.00	21.00	50.00
21-30 (52 pgs.)	6.00	18.00	42.00
31-46 (52 pgs.): 37-X-mas-c	5.00	15.00	35.00
47-56 (36 pgs.): 47-Chuck Wagon Charley's Tales returns, ends #133			
49-X-mas-c. 55-Last photo back-c	4.00	12.00	28.00
57 (52 pgs.)-Heroin drug propaganda story	4.60	14.00	32.00
58-70 (52 pgs.): 61-X-mas-c	3.50	10.50	24.00
71-80 (52 pgs.): 73-X-mas-c	2.85	8.50	20.00
81-91 (36 pgs. #81-on): 85-X-mas-c	2.65	8.00	18.00
92-Title changed to Roy Rogers and Trigger (8/55)			
	2.65	8.00	18.00
93-99,101-110,112-118	2.65	8.00	18.00
100-Trigger feature returns, ends #133?	4.00	12.00	28.00
111,119-124-Toth-a	4.35	13.00	30.00
125-131	3.00	9.00	21.00
132-144-Manning-a. 144-Dale Evans feat.	3.50	10.50	24.00
145-Last issue	4.00	12.00	28.00
. . .& the Man From Dodge City (Dodge giveaway, 16 pgs., 1954)-Frontier, Inc. (5x7¼")	10.00	30.00	70.00
Official R.R. Riders Club Comics (1952; 16 pgs., reg. size, paper-c)	11.00	32.00	75.00

NOTE: Buscema a-2 each-74-108. Manning a-123, 124, 132-144. Marsh a-110. Photo back-c No. 1-9, 11-35, 38-55.

ROY ROGERS' TRIGGER (TV)
No. 329, May, 1951 - No. 17, June-Aug, 1955
Dell Publishing Co.

4-Color 329-Painted-c	5.70	17.00	40.00
2 (9-11/51)-Photo-c	3.50	10.50	24.00
3-5: Painted-c #3-on	1.70	5.00	12.00
6-17	1.15	3.50	8.00

RUDOLPH, THE RED NOSED REINDEER (See Limited Collectors Edition #20,24,33,42,50)

RUDOLPH, THE RED NOSED REINDEER
1939 (2,400,000 copies printed); Dec, 1951
Montgomery Ward (Giveaway)

Paper cover - 1st app. in print; written by Robert May; ill. by Denver Gillen	8.35	25.00	50.00
Hardcover version	10.00	30.00	70.00
1951 version (Has 1939 date)-36 pgs., illos in three colors; red-c	3.00	9.00	21.00

RUDOLPH, THE RED-NOSED REINDEER
1950 - No. 13?, Winter, 1962-63
(Issues are not numbered) (15 different issues known)
National Periodical Publications

1950 issue; Grossman-c/a begins	4.65	14.00	32.00
1951-54 issues (4 total)	3.00	9.00	21.00
1955-62 issues (8 total)	1.60	4.70	11.00

NOTE: The 1962-63 issue is 84 pages. 13 total issues published.

RUFF & REDDY (TV)
No. 937, 9/58 - No. 12, 1-3/62 (Hanna-Barbera)
Dell Publishing Co./Gold Key

4-Color 937(1st Hanna-Barbera book)	3.00	9.00	21.00

Rookie Cop #27, © CC

Roots Of The Swampthing #1, © DC

Roy Rogers Comics #3, © Roy Rogers

Rulah Jungle Goddess #24, © FOX　　*Rust #4, © NOW Comics*　　*Sable #1, © First Comics*

	Good	Fine	N-Mint
RUFF & REDDY (continued)			
4-Color 981,1038	2.00	6.00	14.00
4(1-3/60)-12	1.50	4.50	10.00

RUGGED ACTION (Strange Stories of Suspense #5 on)
Dec, 1954 - No. 4, June, 1955
Atlas Comics (CSI)

1	3.50	10.50	24.00
2-4: 2-Last precode (2/55)	1.70	5.00	12.00

NOTE: *Ayers a-2, 3. Maneely c-2, 3. Severin a-2.*

RULAH JUNGLE GODDESS (Formerly Zoot; I Loved #28 on) (Also
see All Top Comics & Terrors of the Jungle)
No. 17, Aug, 1948 - No. 27, June, 1949
Fox Features Syndicate

17	27.00	81.00	190.00
18-Classic girl-fight interior splash	24.00	72.00	170.00
19,20	22.00	65.00	154.00
21-Used in **SOTI**, pg. 388,389	24.00	72.00	170.00
22-Used in **SOTI**, pg. 22,23	22.00	65.00	154.00
23-27	16.00	48.00	110.00

NOTE: *Kamen c-17-19,21,22.*

RUNAWAY, THE (See Movie Classics)

RUN BABY RUN
1974 (39 cents)
Logos International

By Tony Tallarico from Nicky Cruz's book		.30	.60

RUN, BUDDY, RUN (TV)
June, 1967 (Photo-c)
Gold Key

1 (10204-706)	1.50	4.50	10.00

RUST
July, 1987 - No. 15, 1988; V2#1 - Present ($1.50-$1.75, color)
Now Comics

1-15, V2#1	.30	.90	1.75

RUSTY, BOY DETECTIVE
Mar-April, 1955 - No. 5, Nov, 1955
Good Comics/Lev Gleason

1-Bob Wood, Carl Hubbell-a begins	2.85	8.50	20.00
2-5	1.70	5.00	12.00

RUSTY COMICS (Formerly Kid Movie Comics; Rusty and Her Family
#21, 22; The Kelleys #23 on; see Millie The Model)
No. 12, Apr, 1947 - No. 22, Sept, 1949
Marvel Comics (HPC)

12-Mitzi app.	6.00	18.00	42.00
13	3.00	9.00	21.00
14-Wolverton's Powerhouse Pepper (4 pgs.) plus Kurtzman's "Hey Look"	6.00	18.00	42.00
15-17-Kurtzman's "Hey Look"	5.00	15.00	35.00
18,19	2.00	6.00	14.00
20-Kurtzman, 5 pgs.	5.00	15.00	35.00
21,22-Kurtzman, 17 & 22 pgs.	8.00	24.00	56.00

RUSTY DUGAN (See Holyoke One-Shot #2)

RUSTY RILEY (See 4-Color #418,451,486,554)

SAARI (The Jungle Goddess)
November, 1951
P. L. Publishing Co.

1	17.00	51.00	120.00

SABLE (Formerly Jon Sable, Freelance)
Mar, 1988 - Present ($1.75-$1.95, color)
First Comics

1-12 ($1.95 #10 on)	.35	1.00	2.00

SABOTAGE (See The Crusaders)

SABRE (See Eclipse Graphic Album Series)
10/78; 1/79; 8/82 - No. 14, 8/85; (Baxter paper #4 on)
Eclipse Comics

	Good	Fine	N-Mint
1-($1.00)-Sabre & Morrigan Tales begin	.25	.75	1.50
2-14: 4-6-Origin Incredible Seven		.50	1.00

NOTE: *Colan c-11p. Gulacy c/a-1, 2.*

SABRINA'S CHRISTMAS MAGIC (See Archie Giant Series Mag. #196, 207, 220, 231, 243, 455, 467, 479, 491, 503, 515)

SABRINA, THE TEEN-AGE WITCH (TV) (See Archie's TV Laugh-Out,
...Madhouse, Archie Giant Series #544 & Chilling Advs. In Sorcery)
April, 1971 - No. 77, Jan, 1983 (Giants No. 1-17)
Archie Publications

1	2.15	6.50	15.00
2	1.00	3.00	7.00
3-5: 3,4-Archie's Group x-over	.50	1.50	3.00
6-10	.35	1.00	2.00
11-20		.60	1.20
21-77		.30	.60

SABU, "ELEPHANT BOY" (Movie; formerly My Secret Story)
No. 30, June, 1950 - No. 2, Aug, 1950
Fox Features Syndicate

30(#1)-Wood-a; photo-c	10.00	30.00	70.00
2-Photo-c; Kamen-a	6.00	18.00	45.00

SACRAMENTS, THE
October, 1955 (25 cents)
Catechetical Guild Educational Society

304	2.00	6.00	12.00

SACRED AND THE PROFANE, THE (See Eclipse Graphic Album Series)

SAD CASE OF WAITING ROOM WILLIE, THE
1950? (nd) (14 pgs. in color; paper covers; regular size)
American Visuals Corp. (For Baltimore Medical Society)

By Will Eisner (Rare)	27.00	81.00	190.00

SADDLE JUSTICE (Happy Houlihans #1,2; becomes Saddle
Romances #9 on)
No. 3, Spring, 1948 - No. 8, Sept-Oct, 1949
E. C. Comics

3-The first E. C. by Bill Gaines to break away from M. C. Gaines' old Educational Comics format. Craig, Feldstein, H. C. Kiefer, & Stan Asch-a. Mentioned in **Love and Death**	25.00	75.00	175.00
4-1st Graham Ingels E. C.-a	25.00	75.00	175.00
5-8-Ingels-a in all	23.00	70.00	160.00

NOTE: *Craig and Feldstein art in most issues. Canadian reprints known; see Table of Contents. Craig c-3, 4. Ingels c-5-8.*

SADDLE ROMANCES (Saddle Justice #3-8; continued as Weird
Science #12 on)
No. 9, Nov-Dec, 1949 - No. 11, Mar-Apr, 1950
E. C. Comics

9-Ingels-c/a	30.00	90.00	210.00
10-Wood's 1st work at E. C.; Ingels-a	32.00	95.00	225.00
11-Ingels-a	30.00	90.00	210.00

NOTE: *Canadian reprints known; see Table of Contents. Feldstein c-10.*

SADIE SACK (See Harvey Hits #93)

SAD SACK AND THE SARGE
Sept, 1957 - No. 155, June, 1982
Harvey Publications

1	5.00	15.00	35.00
2	2.00	6.00	14.00
3-10	1.70	5.00	12.00
11-20	1.00	3.00	6.00

SAD SACK AND THE SARGE (continued)	Good	Fine	N-Mint
21-50	.40	1.20	2.40
51-90,97-100		.50	1.00
91-96: All 52 pg. Giants		.60	1.20
101-155		.25	.50

SAD SACK COMICS (See Harvey Collector's Comics #16, Little Sad Sack, Tastee Freez Comics #4 & True Comics #55)
Sept, 1949 - No. 287, Oct, 1982
Harvey Publications

	Good	Fine	N-Mint
1-Infinity-c; Little Dot begins (1st app.); civilian issues begin, end			
#21	20.00	60.00	140.00
2-Flying Fool by Powell	9.50	28.50	65.00
3	5.70	17.00	40.00
4-10	3.50	10.50	24.00
11-21	2.35	7.00	16.00
22-("Back In the Army Again" on covers #22-36). "The Specialist" story about Sad Sack's return to Army	1.35	4.00	8.00
23-50	.85	2.50	5.00
51-100	.50	1.50	3.00
101-150	.25		1.50
151-222		.40	.80
223-228 (25 cent Giants, 52 pgs.)	.25	.75	1.50
229-287: 286,287 had limited distribution		.40	.80
3-D 1 (1/54-titled "Harvey 3-D Hits")	10.00	30.00	70.00
Armed Forces Complimentary copies, HD #1-40 ('57-'62)	.50	1.50	3.00

NOTE: The Sad Sack Comics comic book was a spin-off from a Sunday Newspaper strip launched through John Wheeler's Bell Syndicate. The previous Sunday page and the first 21 comics depicted the Sad Sack in civvies. Unpopularity caused the Sunday page to be discontinued in the early '50s. Meanwhile Sad Sack returned to the Army, by popular demand, in issue No. 22, remaining there ever since. Incidentally, relatively few of the first 21 issues were ever collected and remain scarce due to this.

SAD SACK FUN AROUND THE WORLD
1974 (no month)
Harvey Publications

	Good	Fine	N-Mint
1-About Great Britain		.40	.80

SAD SACK GOES HOME
1951 (16 pgs. in color)
Harvey Publications

	Good	Fine	N-Mint
nn-by George Baker	3.50	10.50	24.00

SAD SACK LAUGH SPECIAL
Winter, 1958-59 - No. 93, Feb, 1977 (#1-60: 68 pgs.; #61-76: 52 pgs.)
Harvey Publications

	Good	Fine	N-Mint
1	3.00	9.00	21.00
2	1.50	4.50	10.00
3-10	1.35	4.00	8.00
11-30	.70	2.00	4.00
31-60: Last 68 pg. Giant	.40	1.20	2.40
61-76: 52 pg. issues	.35	1.00	2.00
77-93		.50	1.00

SAD SACK NAVY, GOBS 'N' GALS
Aug, 1972 - No. 8, Oct, 1973
Harvey Publications

	Good	Fine	N-Mint
1: 52 pg. Giant		.50	1.00
2-8		.30	.60

SAD SACK'S ARMY LIFE (See Harvey Hits #8, 17, 22, 28, 32, 39, 43, 47, 51, 55, 58, 61, 64, 67, 70)

SAD SACK'S ARMY LIFE (...Parade #1-57, ...Today #58 on)
Oct, 1963 - No. 60, Nov, 1975; No. 61, May, 1976
Harvey Publications

	Good	Fine	N-Mint
1: 68 pg. issues begin	2.00	6.00	14.00
2-10	1.00	3.00	6.00
11-20	.40	1.20	2.40

	Good	Fine	N-Mint
21-34: Last 68 pg. issue	.35	1.00	2.00
35-51: All 52 pgs.		.50	1.00
52-61		.30	.60

SAD SACK'S FUNNY FRIENDS (See Harvey Hits #75)
Dec, 1955 - No. 75, Oct, 1969
Harvey Publications

	Good	Fine	N-Mint
1	3.50	10.50	24.00
2-10	1.70	5.00	10.00
11-20	.85	2.50	5.00
21-30	.40	1.20	2.40
31-50		.50	1.00
51-75		.30	.60

SAD SACK'S MUTTSY (See Harvey Hits #74, 77, 80, 82, 84, 87, 89, 92, 96, 99, 102, 105, 108, 111, 113, 115, 117, 119, 121)

SAD SACK USA (...Vacation #8)
Nov, 1972 - No. 7, Nov, 1973; No. 8, Oct, 1974
Harvey Publications

	Good	Fine	N-Mint
1		.50	1.00
2-8		.25	.50

SAD SACK WITH SARGE & SADIE
Sept, 1972 - No. 8, Nov, 1973
Harvey Publications

	Good	Fine	N-Mint
1: 52 pg. Giant		.50	1.00
2-8		.25	.50

SAD SAD SACK WORLD
Oct, 1964 - No. 46, Dec, 1973 (#1-31: 68 pgs.; #32-38: 52 pgs.)
Harvey Publications

	Good	Fine	N-Mint
1	.85	2.50	6.00
2-10	.40	1.20	2.40
11-31: Last 68 pg. issue	.35	1.00	2.00
32-38: All 52 pgs.	.25	.75	1.50
39-46		.50	1.00

SAGA OF BIG RED, THE
Sept, 1976 ($1.25) (In color)
Omaha World-Herald

	Good	Fine	N-Mint
nn-by Win Mumma; story of the Nebraska Cornhuskers (sports)			
	.30	.80	1.60

SAGA OF CRYSTAR, CRYSTAL WARRIOR, THE
May, 1983 - No. 11, Feb, 1985
Marvel Comics Group

	Good	Fine	N-Mint
1-($2.00; Baxter paper)	.35	1.00	2.00
2-5		.30	.60
6-Golden-c	.25	.75	1.50
7-11: Golden c-7-9,11; 10,11($1.00); 11-Alpha Flight app.			
		.30	.60

SAGA OF RA'S AL GHUL, THE
Jan, 1988 - No. 4, Apr, 1988 (mini-series, $2.50, color)
DC Comics

	Good	Fine	N-Mint
1-4: Batman reprints; Neal Adams-c/a (r)	.40	1.25	2.50

SAGA OF SWAMP THING, THE (Swamp Thing #39-41,46 on)
May, 1982 - Present (Later issues for mature readers)
DC Comics

	Good	Fine	N-Mint
1-Origin retold; Phantom Stranger series begins; ends #13; movie adapt.	.25	.75	1.50
2-15: 2-Photo-c from movie		.50	1.00
16-19: Bissette-a	.35	1.00	2.00
20-1st Alan Moore issue	3.60	11.00	25.00
21-New origin	3.60	11.00	25.00
22-25: 24-JLA x-over	1.50	4.50	10.00
26-30	1.00	3.00	6.00

Sad Sack Laugh Special #1, © HARV

The Saga Of Ra's Al Ghul #1, © DC

The Saga Of Swamp Thing #1, © DC

The Saint #8, © AVON

Samson #14, © AJAX

Samurai V3#1, © Aircel Publ.

	Good	Fine	N-Mint
THE SAGA OF SWAMP THING (continued)			
31-35	.50	1.50	3.00
36-40	.35	1.00	2.00
41-45	.25	.75	1.50
46-52: 46-Crisis x-over		.60	1.20
53-Double size ($1.25)	.25	.75	1.50
54-60		.45	.90
61-66: Direct only. 64-Last Moore ish.		.50	1.00
67-82 ($1.25): 79-Superman-c/story		.65	1.30
Annual 1(11/82)-Movie Adaptation		.50	1.00
Annual 2(1/85)	.50	1.50	3.00
Annual 3(10/87, $2.00), 4(10/88)	.35	1.00	2.00
Saga of the Swamp Thing ($10.95, '87)-reprints #20-26			
	1.85	5.50	10.95

NOTE: *Bissette* a(p)-16-19, 21-27, 29, 30, 34-36, 39-42, 44, 46, 50, 64p; c-17i, 24p-32p, 35p-37p, 40p, 44p, 46p-50p, 51-56, 57i, 58, 61, 62, 63p. *Kaluta* c-74. *Spiegle* a-1-3, 6. *Totleben* a(i)-10, 16-27, 29, 31, 34-40, 42, 44, 46, 48, 50, 53, 55i; c-25-32i, 33, 35-40i, 42i, 44i, 46-50i, 53, 55i, 59p, 64, 65, 68, 73, 76, 80, Annual 4. *Wrightson* a-18i(r), 33r; c-57p.

SAGA OF THE SUB-MARINER, THE
Nov., 1988 - No. 12, 1989 ($1.25-$1.50, color, limited series)
Marvel Comics

1-4: Buckler-c/a in all		.60	1.25
5,6 ($1.50)	.25	.75	1.50

SAILOR ON THE SEA OF FATE (See First Comics Graphic Novel)

SAILOR SWEENEY (Navy Action #1-11, 15 on)
No. 12, July, 1956 - No. 14, Nov, 1956
Atlas Comics (CDS)

12-14: 12-Shores-a. 13-Severin-c	2.00	6.00	14.00

SAINT, THE (Also see Movie Comics(DC) #2 & Silver Streak #18)
Aug, 1947 - No. 12, Mar, 1952
Avon Periodicals

1-Kamen bondage c/a	28.00	84.00	195.00
2	15.00	45.00	105.00
3,4: 4-Lingerie panels	12.00	36.00	84.00
5-Spanking panel	18.00	54.00	125.00
6-Miss Fury app., 14 pgs.	20.00	60.00	140.00
7-c-/Avon paperback 118	11.00	32.00	76.00
8,9(12/50): Saint strip-r in #8-12; 9-Kinstler-c	9.00	27.00	62.00
10-Wood-a, 1 pg; c-/Avon paperback 289	9.00	27.00	62.00
11	6.50	19.50	45.00
12-c-/Avon paperback 123	8.50	25.50	60.00

NOTE: *Lucky Dale, Girl Detective* in #1,2,4,6. *Hollingsworth* a-4, 6. *Painted-c* 8,10,11.

ST. GEORGE
1988 - Present ($1.25-$1.50, color)
Epic Comics (Marvel)

1,2: 1-Sienkiewicz-c		.60	1.25
3-5 ($1.50)	.25	.75	1.50

SALERNO CARNIVAL OF COMICS (Also see Pure Oil Comics, 24 Pages of Comics, & Vicks Comics)
Late 1930s (16 pgs.) (paper cover) (Giveaway)
Salerno Cookie Co.

nn-Color reprints of Calkins' Buck Rogers & Skyroads, plus other strips from Famous Funnies	25.00	75.00	175.00

SALIMBA (3-D)
1986 - No. 2, Sept, 1986
Blackthorne Publ.

1,2-Jungle girl stories	.35	1.10	2.25

SALOME' (See Night Music #6)

SAM HILL PRIVATE EYE
1950 - No. 7, 1951
Close-Up

	Good	Fine	N-Mint
1-Negligee panel	5.00	15.00	35.00
2	3.00	9.00	21.00
3-7	2.30	7.00	16.00

SAM SLADE ROBOHUNTER
Oct, 1986 - Present ($1.25-$1.50, color)
Quality Comics

1-19		.50	1.00
20,21/22	.25	.75	1.50

SAMSON (1st Series) (Capt. Aero #7 on; see Big 3 Comics)
Fall, 1940 - No. 6, Sept, 1941 (See Fantastic Comics)
Fox Features Syndicate

1-Powell-a, signed 'Rensie;' Wing Turner by Tuska app; Fine-c?			
	55.00	165.00	385.00
2-Dr. Fung by Powell; Fine-c?	26.00	78.00	180.00
3-Navy Jones app.; Simon-c	21.00	62.00	147.00
4-Yarko the Great, Master Magician by Eisner begins; Fine-c?			
	17.00	51.00	120.00
5,6: 6-Origin The Topper	17.00	51.00	120.00

SAMSON (2nd Series)
No. 12, April, 1955 - No. 14, Aug, 1955
Ajax/Farrell Publications (Four Star)

12-Wonder Boy	8.00	24.00	56.00
13,14: 13-Wonder Boy, Rocket Man	5.70	17.00	40.00

SAMSON (See Mighty Samson)

SAMSON & DELILAH (See A Spectacular Feature Magazine)

SAMUEL BRONSTON'S CIRCUS WORLD (See Circus World under Movie Comics)

SAMURAI (Also see Eclipse Graphic Album Series #14)
1985 - No. 23, 1987 ($1.70, B&W); V2#1, '88 - No. 3, '88 (color); V3#1, '88 - Present ($1.95, B&W)
Aircel Publ.

1	2.00	6.00	12.00
1-2nd print (1/86)	.50	1.50	3.00
1-3rd print	.30	.85	1.70
2	.70	2.00	4.00
2-2nd print	.30	.85	1.70
3-23	.35	1.00	2.00
V2#1-3 (Color, $2.00, 1988)	.35	1.00	2.00
V3#1-4 (B&W, $1.95)	.35	1.00	1.95

SAMURAI PENGUIN
1986 - Present ($1.50, B&W/color #6 on)
Slave Labor Graphics

1	.50	1.50	3.00
2-5	.35	1.00	2.00
6,7	.30	.90	1.75

SAMUREE
May, 1987 - Present ($2.00, color)
Continuity Comics

1-5	.35	1.00	2.00

SANDMAN, THE (See Adventure Comics #40)
Winter, 1974; No. 2, Apr-May, 1975 - No. 6, Dec-Jan, 1975-76
National Periodical Publications

1-Kirby-a		.30	.60
2-6: 6-Kirby/Wood c/a		.25	.50

NOTE: *Kirby* a-1p, 4-6p; c-1-5.

SANDMAN
Jan, 1989 - Present ($2.00, mature readers)
DC Comics

1,2	.35	1.00	2.00

331

SANDS OF THE SOUTH PACIFIC
January, 1953
Toby Press

	Good	Fine	N-Mint
1	9.50	28.50	65.00

SANTA AND HIS REINDEER (See March of Comics #166)

SANTA AND POLLYANNA PLAY THE GLAD GAME
Aug, 1960 (16 pages) (Disney giveaway)
Sales Promotion

	Good	Fine	N-Mint
	1.00	3.00	6.00

SANTA AND THE ANGEL (See 4-Color #259 & Dell Jr. Treasury #7)

SANTA & THE BUCCANEERS
1959
Promotional Publ. Co. (Giveaway)

	Good	Fine	N-Mint
Reprints 1952 Santa & the Pirates	.50	1.50	3.00

SANTA & THE CHRISTMAS CHICKADEE
1974 (20 pgs.)
Murphy's (Giveaway)

	Good	Fine	N-Mint
		.50	1.00

SANTA & THE PIRATES
1952
Promotional Publ. Co. (Giveaway)

	Good	Fine	N-Mint
Marv Levy c/a	.85	2.50	5.00

SANTA AT THE ZOO (See 4-Color #259)

SANTA CLAUS AROUND THE WORLD (See March of Comics #241)

SANTA CLAUS CONQUERS THE MARTIANS (See Movie Classics)

SANTA CLAUS FUNNIES
No date (1940s) (Color & B&W; 8x10''; 12pgs., heavy paper)
W. T. Grant Co. (Giveaway)

	Good	Fine	N-Mint
March Of Comics-r?	6.75	20.00	40.00

SANTA CLAUS FUNNIES (Also see Dell Giants)
Dec?, 1942 - No. 1274, Dec, 1961
Dell Publishing Co.

	Good	Fine	N-Mint
nn(#1)(1942)-Kelly-a	30.00	90.00	210.00
2(12/43)-Kelly-a	20.00	60.00	140.00
4-Color 61(1944)-Kelly-a	20.00	60.00	140.00
4-Color 91(1945)-Kelly-a	14.00	42.00	100.00
4-Color 128('46),175('47)-Kelly-a	12.00	36.00	84.00
4-Color 205,254-Kelly-a	11.00	32.00	76.00
4-Color 302,361	2.30	7.00	16.00
4-Color 525,607,666,756,867	1.70	5.00	12.00
4-Color 958,1063,1154,1274	1.50	4.50	10.00

NOTE: *Most issues contain only one Kelly story.*

SANTA CLAUS PARADE
1951; 1952; 1955 (25 cents)
Ziff-Davis (Approved Comics)/St. John Publishing Co.

	Good	Fine	N-Mint
nn(1951-Ziff-Davis)-116 pgs. (Xmas Special)	6.50	19.50	45.00
2(12/52-Ziff-Davis)-100 pgs.; Dave Berg-a	5.70	17.00	40.00
V1#3(1/55-St. John)-100 pgs.	5.00	15.00	35.00

SANTA CLAUS' WORKSHOP (See March of Comics #50,168)

SANTA IS COMING (See March of Comics #197)

SANTA IS HERE (See March of Comics #49)

SANTA ON THE JOLLY ROGER
1965
Promotional Publ. Co. (Giveaway)

	Good	Fine	N-Mint
Marv Levy c/a	.50	1.50	3.00

SANTA! SANTA!
1974 (20 pgs.)
R. Jackson (Montgomery Ward giveaway)

	Good	Fine	N-Mint
nn	.50	1.00	

SANTA'S BUSY CORNER (See March of Comics #31)

SANTA'S CANDY KITCHEN (See March of Comics #14)

SANTA'S CHRISTMAS BOOK (See March of Comics #123)

SANTA'S CHRISTMAS COMICS
December, 1952 (100 pages)
Standard Comics (Best Books)

	Good	Fine	N-Mint
nn-Supermouse, Dizzy Duck, Happy Rabbit, etc.	5.00	15.00	35.00

SANTA'S CHRISTMAS COMIC VARIETY SHOW
1943 (24 pages)
Sears Roebuck & Co.

Contains puzzles & new comics of Dick Tracy, Little Orphan Annie, Moon Mullins, Terry & the Pirates, etc.

	Good	Fine	N-Mint
	8.50	25.50	60.00

SANTA'S CHRISTMAS LIST (See March of Comics #255)

SANTA'S CHRISTMAS TIME STORIES
nd (late 1940s) (16 pgs.; paper cover)
Premium Sales, Inc. (Giveaway)

	Good	Fine	N-Mint
	2.00	6.00	12.00

SANTA'S CIRCUS
1964 (half-size)
Promotional Publ. Co. (Giveaway)

	Good	Fine	N-Mint
Marv Levy c/a	.50	1.50	3.00

SANTA'S FUN BOOK
1951, 1952 (regular size, 16 pages, paper-c)
Promotional Publ. Co. (Murphy's giveaway)

	Good	Fine	N-Mint
	1.70	5.00	10.00

SANTA'S GIFT BOOK
No date (16 pgs.)
No Publisher

	Good	Fine	N-Mint
Puzzles, games only	1.00	3.00	6.00

SANTA'S HELPERS (See March of Comics #64,106,198)

SANTA'S LITTLE HELPERS (See March of Comics #270)

SANTA'S NEW STORY BOOK
1949 (16 pgs.; paper cover)
Wallace Hamilton Campbell (Giveaway)

	Good	Fine	N-Mint
	3.00	9.00	18.00

SANTA'S REAL STORY BOOK
1948, 1952 (16 pgs.)
Wallace Hamilton Campbell/W. W. Orris (Giveaway)

	Good	Fine	N-Mint
	2.35	7.00	14.00

SANTA'S RIDE
1959
W. T. Grant Co. (Giveaway)

	Good	Fine	N-Mint
	1.35	4.00	8.00

SANTA'S RODEO
1964 (half-size)
Promotional Publ. Co. (Giveaway)

	Good	Fine	N-Mint
Marv Levy-a	.70	2.00	4.00

SANTA'S SECRETS
1951, 1952? (16 pgs.; paper cover)
Sam B. Anson Christmas giveaway

	Good	Fine	N-Mint
	2.00	6.00	12.00

SANTA'S SHOW (See March of Comics #311)

SANTA'S SLEIGH (See March of Comics #298)

Sands Of The South Pacific #1, © TOBY

Santa Claus Funnies (1940s), © W. T. Grant

Santa's New Story Book, © W. H. Campbell

Sarge Steel #7, © CC

The Savage She-Hulk #1, © MEG

Savage Tales #2 (10/73), © MEG

SANTA'S STORIES
1953 (regular size; paper cover)
K. K. Publications (Klines Dept. Store)

	Good	Fine	N-Mint
Kelly-a	12.00	36.00	84.00

SANTA'S SURPRISE (See March of Comics #13)

SANTA'S SURPRISE
1947 (36 pgs.; slick cover)
K. K. Publications (Giveaway)

	2.75	8.00	16.00

SANTA'S TINKER TOTS
1958
Charlton Comics

1-Based on "The Tinker Tots Keep Christmas"			
	1.30	4.00	8.00

SANTA'S TOYLAND (See March of Comics #242)

SANTA'S TOYS (See March of Comics #12)

SANTA'S TOYTOWN FUN BOOK
1952, 1953?
Promotional Publ. Co. (Giveaway)

Marv Levy-c	1.00	3.00	6.00

SANTA'S VISIT (See March of Comics #283)

SANTIAGO (See 4-Color #723)

SARGE SNORKEL (Beetle Bailey)
Oct., 1973 - No. 17, Dec, 1976
Charlton Comics

1		.50	1.00
2-17		.30	.60

SARGE STEEL (Becomes Secret Agent #9 on; see Judomaster)
Dec, 1964 - No. 8, Mar-Apr, 1966
Charlton Comics

1-Origin	.35	1.00	2.00
2-8: 6-Judo Master app.	.25	.75	1.50

SAVAGE COMBAT TALES
Feb, 1975 - No. 3, July, 1975
Atlas/Seaboard Publ.

1-3: 1-Sgt. Stryker's Death Squad begins (origin). 2-Only app. Warhawk		.30	.60

NOTE: *McWilliams a-1-3; c-1. Sparling a-1, 3. Toth a-2.*

SAVAGE HENRY
Jan., 1987 - Present ($1.75, B&W)
Vortex Comics

1-6		.30	.85	1.70

SAVAGE RAIDS OF GERONIMO (See Geronimo #4)

SAVAGE RANGE (See 4-Color #807)

SAVAGE SHE-HULK, THE (Also see She-Hulk)
Feb, 1980 - No. 25, Feb, 1982
Marvel Comics Group

1-Origin & 1st app.	.25	.75	1.50
2-25: 25-52 pgs.	.25	.75	1.50

NOTE: *Austin a-25i; c-23i-25i. J. Buscema a-1p; c-1, 2p. Golden c-8-11.*

SAVAGE SWORD OF CONAN, THE (Magazine)
Aug, 1974 - Present (B&W)(Mature readers)
Marvel Comics Group

1-Smith-r; Buscema/Adams/Krenkel-a; origin Blackmark by Gil Kane(part 1) & Red Sonja (3rd app.)	2.85	9.00	20.00
2-Adams-c; Chaykin/Adams-a	1.50	4.50	9.00
3-Severin/Smith-a; Adams-a	1.15	3.50	7.00
4-Adams/Kane-a(r)	1.00	3.00	6.00

	Good	Fine	N-Mint
5-10	.85	2.50	5.00
11-20	.70	2.00	4.00
21-50	.50	1.50	3.00
51-158: 70-Article on movie. 83-Red Sonja-r by Adams from #1	.25	.75	1.50
Annual 1('75)-B&W, Smith-r (Conan #10,13)	.50	1.50	3.00

NOTE: *Adams a-14p, 60, 83p(r). Alcala a-2 ,4, 7, 12, 15-20, 23, 24, 28, 59, 67, 69, 75, 76i, 80i, 82i, 83i, 89. Austin a-78i. Boris c-1, 4, 5, 7, 9, 10, 12, 15. Brunner a-30; c-8, 30. Buscema a-1-5, 7, 10-12, 15-24, 26-28, 31, 32, 36-43, 45, 47-58p, 60-67p, 70, 71-74p, 76-81p, 87-96p, 98, 99p-101p; c-40. Corbin a-4, 16, 29. Finlay a-16. Golden a-98, 101; c-150. Kaluta a-11, 18; c-3, 91, 93. Gil Kane a-2, 3, 8, 13r, 29, 47, 64, 65, 67, 85p, 86p. Krenkel a-9, 11, 14, 16, 24. Morrow a-7. Nebres a-93i, 101i, 107, 114. Newton a-6. Nino a/c-6. Redondo c-48, 50, 52, 56, 57, 85i, 90, 96i. Simonson a-7, 8, 12, 15-17. Smith a-7, 16, 24, 82r. Starlin c-26. No. 8 & 10 contain a Robert E. Howard Conan adaptation.*

SAVAGE TALES (Magazine) (B&W)
May, 1971; No. 2, 10/73; No. 3, 2/74 - No. 12, Summer, 1975
Marvel Comics Group

1-Origin & 1st app. The Man-Thing by Morrow; Conan the Barbarian by Barry Smith, Femizons by Romita begin; Ka-Zar app.	7.00	20.00	40.00
2-Smith, Brunner, Morrow, Williamson, Wrightson-a (reprint/Creatures on the Loose #10); King Kull app.	2.50	7.50	15.00
3-Smith, Brunner, Steranko, Williamson-a	1.70	5.00	10.00
4,5-Adams-c; last Conan (Smith-r/#4) plus Kane/Adams-a.			
5-Brak the Barbarian begins, ends #8	1.00	3.00	6.00
6-Ka-Zar begins; Williamson-r; Adams-c	.50	1.50	3.00
7-Adams-i	.50	1.50	3.00
8-Shanna, the She-Devil begins, ends #10; Williamson-r	.50	1.50	3.00
9,11	.40	1.20	2.40
10-Adams-a(i), Williamson-r	.50	1.50	3.00
Annual 1(Summer'75)(#12 on inside)-Ka-Zar origin by G. Kane; B&W; Smith-r/Astonishing Tales	.40	1.20	2.40

NOTE: *Boris c-7,10. Buscema a-5r, 6p, 8p; c-2. Fabian c-8. Heath a-10p, 11p. Kaluta c-9. Maneely a-2r. Starlin a-5. Robert E. Howard adaptations-1-4.*

SAVAGE TALES (Magazine size)
Nov., 1985 - No. 9?, Mar, 1987 (B&W) ($1.50) (Mature readers)
Marvel Comics Group

1-1st app. The Nam; Golden-a	1.50	4.50	10.00
2-9: Golden-a	.25	.75	1.50

SCAMP (Walt Disney)(See Walt Disney's C&S #204)
No. 703, 5/56 - No. 1204, 8-10/61; 11/67 - No. 45, 1/79
Dell Publishing Co./Gold Key

4-Color 703(No. 1)	1.70	5.00	12.00
4-Color 777,806('57),833	1.15	3.50	8.00
5(3-5/58)-10(6-8/59)	.85	2.50	6.00
11-16(12-2/60-61)	.70	2.00	5.00
4-Color 1204(1961)	.85	2.50	6.00
1(12/67-G.K.)-Reprints begin	.55	1.65	4.00
2(3/69)-10	.35	1.00	2.00
11-20	.25	.75	1.50
21-45		.40	.80

NOTE: *New stories-#20(in part), 22-25, 27, 29-31, 34, 36-40, 42-45. New covers-#11, 12, 14, 15, 17-25, 27, 29-31, 34, 36-38.*

SCAR FACE (See The Crusaders)

SCARECROW OF ROMNEY MARSH, THE (See W.D. Showcase #53)
April, 1964 - No. 3, Oct, 1965 (Disney TV Show)
Gold Key

10112-404 (#1)	2.65	8.00	18.00
2,3	1.70	5.00	12.00

SCARLET IN GASLIGHT
Nov., 1987 - #4, 1988 ($1.95, B&W)
Eternity Comics

SCARLET IN GASLIGHT (continued)

	Good	Fine	N-Mint
1-4	.35	1.00	2.00
Graphic Novel 1 (r/#1-4)	1.35	4.00	7.95

SCARLET O'NEIL (See Harvey Comics Hits #59 & Invisible...)

SCARY TALES
8/75 - No. 9, 1/77; No. 10, 9/77 - No. 20, 6/79; No. 21,
8/80 - No. 46, 10/84
Charlton Comics

	Good	Fine	N-Mint
1-Origin & 1st app. Countess Von Bludd, not in No. 2	.40	.80
2-11	.30	.60
12-36,39,46-All reprints	.30	.60
37,38,40-45-New-a. 38-Mr. Jigsaw app.	.30	.60
1(Modern Comics reprint, 1977)	.15	.30

NOTE: *Adkins a-31i; c-31i. Ditko a-3, 5, 7, 8(2), 11, 12, 14-16r, 18(3)r, 19r, 21r, 30r, 32, 39r; c-5, 11, 14, 18, 30, 32. Newton a-31p; c-31p. Powell a-18r. Staton a-1(2 pgs.), 4, 20r; c-1, 20. Sutton a-9; c-4, 9.*

SCAVENGERS
Feb., 1988 - Present ($1.25-$1.50, color)
Quality Comics

	Good	Fine	N-Mint
1-7		.60	1.25
8-10: 9,10-Guice-c	.25	.75	1.50

SCHOOL DAY ROMANCES (...of Teen-Agers #4) (Popular Teen-Agers #5 on)
Nov-Dec, 1949 - No. 4, May-June, 1950
Star Publications

	Good	Fine	N-Mint
1-Tony Gayle (later Gay), Gingersnapp	7.00	21.00	50.00
2,3	4.00	12.00	28.00
4-Ronald Reagan photo-c	12.00	36.00	84.00

NOTE: All have *L. B. Cole* covers.

SCHWINN BICYCLE BOOK (...Bike Thrills, 1959)
1949; 1952; 1959 (10 cents)
Schwinn Bicycle Co.

	Good	Fine	N-Mint
1949	2.30	7.00	16.00
1952-Believe It or Not type facts; comic format; 36 pgs.	1.35	4.00	8.00
1959	1.00	3.00	6.00

SCIENCE COMICS (1st Series)
Feb, 1940 - No. 8, Sept, 1940
Fox Features Syndicate

	Good	Fine	N-Mint
1-Origin Dynamo (called Electro in #1), The Eagle, & Navy Jones; Marga, The Panther Woman, Cosmic Carson & Perisphere Payne, Dr. Doom begin; bondage/hypo-c	115.00	345.00	800.00
2	60.00	180.00	420.00
3,4: 4-Kirby-a	50.00	150.00	350.00
5-8	35.00	105.00	245.00

NOTE: *Cosmic Carson by Tuska-#1-3; by Kirby-#4. Lou Fine c-1-3 only.*

SCIENCE COMICS (2nd Series)
January, 1946 - No. 5, 1946
Humor Publications (Ace Magazines?)

	Good	Fine	N-Mint
1-Palais c/a in No. 1-3; A-Bomb-c	4.00	12.00	28.00
2	2.30	7.00	16.00
3-Feldstein-a, 6 pgs.	5.50	16.50	38.00
4,5	2.00	6.00	14.00

SCIENCE COMICS
May, 1947 (8 pgs. in color)
Ziff-Davis Publ. Co.

	Good	Fine	N-Mint
nn-Could be ordered by mail for 10 cents; like the nn Amazing Advs. (1950)-used to test the market	22.00	65.00	154.00

SCIENCE COMICS
March, 1951
Export Publication Ent., Toronto, Canada

Distr. in U.S. by Kable News Co.

	Good	Fine	N-Mint
1-Science Adventure stories plus some true science features	2.00	6.00	14.00

SCIENCE FICTION SPACE ADVENTURES (See Space Adventures)

SCOOBY DOO (...Where are you? #1-16,26; ...Mystery Comics #17-25,27 on) (TV) (See March Of Comics #356,368,382,391)
March, 1970 - No. 30, Feb, 1975
Gold Key

	Good	Fine	N-Mint
1	2.65	8.00	18.00
2-5	1.30	4.00	9.00
6-10	.85	2.50	6.00
11-20: 11-Tufts-a	.70	2.00	4.00
21-30	.40	1.25	2.50

SCOOBY DOO (TV)
April, 1975 - No. 11, Dec, 1976 (Hanna Barbera)
Charlton Comics

	Good	Fine	N-Mint
1	1.00	3.00	7.00
2-5	.60	1.75	3.50
6-11	.40	1.25	2.50

SCOOBY-DOO (TV)
Oct, 1977 - No. 9, Feb, 1979
Marvel Comics Group

	Good	Fine	N-Mint
1-Dyno-Mutt begins	.40	1.25	2.50
2-9		.50	1.00

SCOOP COMICS
November, 1941 - No. 8, 1946
Harry 'A' Chesler (Holyoke)

	Good	Fine	N-Mint
1-Intro. Rocketman & Rocketgirl; origin The Master Key; Dan Hastings begins; Charles Sultan c/a	35.00	105.00	245.00
2-Rocket Boy app; Injury to eye story (Same as Spotlight #3)	20.00	60.00	140.00
3-Injury to eye story-r from #2	15.00	45.00	105.00
4-8	11.50	34.00	80.00

SCOOTER (See Swing with...)

SCOOTER COMICS
April, 1946
Rucker Publ. Ltd. (Canadian)

	Good	Fine	N-Mint
1-Teen-age/funny animal	2.65	8.00	18.00

SCORPION
Feb, 1975 - No. 3, July, 1975
Atlas/Seaboard Publ.

	Good	Fine	N-Mint
1-Intro.; bondage-c by Chaykin		.40	.80
2-Wrightson, Kaluta, Simonson-a(i)		.30	.60
3-Mooney-a(i)		.25	.50

NOTE: *Chaykin a-1,2.*

SCORPIO ROSE
Jan, 1983; No. 2, Oct, 1983 (Baxter paper)
Eclipse Comics

	Good	Fine	N-Mint
1-Dr. Orient back-up story begins	.35	1.00	2.00
2-Origin	.35	1.00	2.00

NOTE: *Rogers c/a 1,2.*

SCOTLAND YARD (Inspector Farnsworth of...) (Texas Rangers in Action #5 on?)
June, 1955 - No. 4, March, 1956
Charlton Comics Group

	Good	Fine	N-Mint
1-Tothish-a	5.00	15.00	35.00
2-4: 2-Tothish-a	3.00	9.00	21.00

SCOUT (See Eclipse Graphic Album #16, New America & Swords of Texas)(Becomes Scout: War Shaman)
12/85 - No. 24, 10/87 ($1.75 - $1.25)

Scavengers #1, © Quality Comics

Science Comics #3 (1st series), © FOX

Scoop Comics #3, © CHES

Scout: War Shaman #1, © Eclipse Comics

Sea Devils #11, © DC

Sea Hunt #5, © United Artists

SCOUT (continued)
Eclipse Comics

	Good	Fine	N-Mint
1	1.25	3.75	7.50
2-8,11,12: 11-Monday: The Eliminator begins	.40	1.25	2.50
9,10: 9-Airboy app. 10-Bissette-a	.35	1.00	2.00
13-15,17,18,20-24 ($1.75)	.35	1.00	2.00
16-Scout 3-D Special ($2.50)	.40	1.25	2.50
16-Scout 2-D	.40	1.25	2.50
19-Contains Flexidisk ($2.50)	.50	1.50	3.00
. . .Handbook 1 (1987, $1.75, B&W)	.30	.90	1.75

SCOUT: WAR SHAMAN (Formerly Scout)
March, 1988 - Present ($1.95, color)
Eclipse Comics

1-7	.35	1.00	2.00

SCREAM (. . .Comics) (Andy Comics #20 on)
Fall, 1944 - No. 19, April, 1948
Humor Publications/Current Books(Ace Magazines)

1	5.00	15.00	35.00
2	2.65	8.00	18.00
3-15: 11-Racist humor (Indians)	2.00	6.00	14.00
16-Intro. Lily-Belle	2.00	6.00	14.00
17,19	1.70	5.00	12.00
18-Transvestism, hypo needle story	3.70	11.00	26.00

SCREAM (Magazine)
Aug, 1973 - No. 11, Feb, 1975 (68 pgs.) (B&W)
Skywald Publishing Corp.

1	.50	1.50	3.00
2-5: 2-Origin Lady Satan. 3 (12/73)-#3 found on pg. 22	.30	.80	1.60
6-11: 6-Origin The Victims. 9-Severed head-c	.50	1.00

SCRIBBLY (See All-American, Buzzy, The Funnies & Popular Comics)
8-9/48 - No. 13, 8-9/50; No. 14, 10-11/51 - No. 15, 12-1/51-52
National Periodical Publications

1-Sheldon Mayer-a in all; 52pgs. begin	43.00	130.00	300.00
2	24.00	72.00	170.00
3-5	21.50	64.00	150.00
6-10	14.00	42.00	100.00
11-15: 13-Last 52 pgs.	11.50	34.00	80.00

SEA DEVILS (See DC Special #10,19, DC Super-Stars #14,17, Limited Collectors Ed. #39,45, & Showcase)
Sept-Oct, 1961 - No. 35, May-June, 1967
National Periodical Publications

1	9.50	28.00	65.00
2-Last 10 cent issue	4.65	14.00	32.00
3-5	2.30	7.00	16.00
6-10	1.70	5.00	12.00
11,12,14-20	1.00	3.00	7.00
13-Kubert, Colan-a	1.10	3.30	7.50
21,23-35	.80	2.40	5.50
22-Intro. International Sea Devils; origin & 1st app. Capt. X & Man Fish	.80	2.40	5.50

NOTE: *Heath a-1-10; c-1-10,14-16.*

SEADRAGON (Also see The Epsilon Wave)
May, 1986 - No. 8, 1987 ($1.75, color)
Elite Comics

1-8	.30	.90	1.80
1 (2nd printing)	.30	.85	1.70

SEA HOUND, THE (Capt. Silver's Log Of The. . .)
1945 (no month) - No. 4, Jan-Feb, 1946
Avon Periodicals

nn	5.00	15.00	35.00

	Good	Fine	N-Mint
2-4 (#2, 9-10/45)	3.50	10.50	24.00

SEA HOUND, THE (Radio)
No. 3, July, 1949 - No. 4, Sept, 1949
Capt. Silver Syndicate

3,4	3.00	9.00	21.00

SEA HUNT (TV)
No. 928, 8/58; No. 994, 10-12/59; No. 4, 1-3/60 - No. 13, 4-6/62
Dell Publishing Co. (All have Lloyd Bridges photo-c)

4-Color 928	5.00	15.00	35.00
4-Color 994, 4-13: Manning-a #4-6,8-11,13	4.00	12.00	28.00
4-Color 1041-Toth-a	5.70	17.00	40.00

SEARCH FOR LOVE
Feb-Mar, 1950 - No. 2, Apr-May, 1950 (52 pgs.)
American Comics Group

1	3.50	10.50	24.00
2	1.85	5.50	13.00

SEARCHERS (See 4-Color #709)

SEARS (See Merry Christmas From. . .)

SEASON'S GREETINGS
1935 (6¼x5¼'') (32 pgs. in color)
Hallmark (King Features)

Cover features Mickey Mouse, Popeye, Jiggs & Skippy. ''The Night Before Christmas'' told one panel per page, each panel by a famous artist featuring their character. Art by Alex Raymond, Gottfredson, Swinnerton, Segar, Chic Young, Milt Gross, Sullivan (Messmer), Herriman, McManus, Percy Crosby & others (22 artists in all)

Estimated value. . . .		$200.00 — $400.00	

SECRET AGENT (Formerly Sarge Steel)
Oct, 1966 - V2No.10, Oct, 1967
Charlton Comics

V2#9-Sarge Steel part-r begins	.35	1.00	2.00
10-Tiffany Sinn, CIA app. (from Career Girl Romances #39); Aparo-a		.50	1.00

SECRET AGENT (TV)
Nov, 1966 - No. 2, Jan, 1968
Gold Key

1,2-Photo-c	2.00	6.00	14.00

SECRET AGENT X-9
1934 (Book 1: 84 pgs.; Book 2: 124 pgs.) (8x7½'')
David McKay Publications

Book 1-Contains reprints of the first 13 weeks of the strip by Alex Raymond; complete except for 2 dailies 36.00 108.00 250.00
Book 2-Contains reprints immediately following contents of Book 1, for 20 weeks by Alex Raymond; complete except for two dailies.
Note: Raymond mis-dated the last five strips from 6/34, and while the dating sequence is confusing, the continuity is correct. 30.00 90.00 210.00

SECRET AGENT X-9 (See Feature Books #8, McKay & Magic Comics)

SECRET AGENT Z-2 (See Holyoke One-Shot No. 7)

SECRET DIARY OF EERIE ADVENTURES
1953 (One Shot) (Giant-100 pgs.)
Avon Periodicals

(Rare) Kubert-a; Hollingsworth-c; Check back-c
82.00 246.00 575.00

SECRET HEARTS
9-10/49 - No. 6, 7-8/50; No. 7, 12-1/51-52 - No. 153, 7/71
(No. 1-6, photo-c; all 52 pgs.)
National Periodical Publications (Beverly)(Arleigh No. 50-113)

335

SECRET HEARTS (continued)	Good	Fine	N-Mint
1	18.00	40.00	90.00
2-Toth-a	6.50	19.50	45.00
3,6 (1950)	5.00	15.00	35.00
4,5-Toth-a	6.50	19.50	45.00
7(12-1/51-52) (Rare)	6.50	19.50	45.00
8-10 (1952)	3.50	10.50	24.00
11-20	2.65	8.00	18.00
21-26: 26-Last precode (2-3/55)	2.00	6.00	14.00
27-40	1.70	5.00	12.00
41-50	1.00	3.00	7.00
51-60	.70	2.00	5.00
61-75: Last 10 cent ish	.50	1.50	3.00
76-109	.35	1.00	2.00
110-"Reach for Happiness" serial begins, ends #138		.60	1.20
111-119,121-133,135-138		.50	1.00
120,134-Adams-c	.35	1.00	2.00
139,140		.50	1.00
141,142-"20 Miles to Heartbreak," Chapter 2 & 3 (See Young Love for Chapter 1 & 4); Toth, Colletta-a		.40	.80
143-148,150-153: 144-Morrow-a. 153-Kirby-i		.25	.50
149-Toth-a		.50	1.00

SECRET ISLAND OF OZ, THE (See First Comics Graphic Novel)

SECRET LOVE (See Fox Giants)

SECRET LOVE
12/55 - No. 3, 8/56; 4/57 - No. 5, 2/58; No. 6, 6/58
Ajax-Farrell/Four Star Comic Corp. No. 2 on

	Good	Fine	N-Mint
1(12/55-Ajax)	2.30	7.00	16.00
2,3	1.30	4.00	9.00
1(4/57-Ajax)	1.85	5.50	13.00
2-6: 5-Bakerish-a	1.15	3.50	8.00

SECRET LOVE (See Sinister House of...)

SECRET LOVES
Nov, 1949 - No. 6, Sept, 1950 (#5, photo-c)
Comic Magazines/Quality Comics Group

	Good	Fine	N-Mint
1-Ward-c	9.00	27.00	62.00
2-Ward-c	8.50	25.50	60.00
3-Crandall-a	5.50	16.50	38.00
4,6	2.85	8.50	20.00
5-Suggestive art-"Boom Town Babe"	4.35	13.00	30.00

SECRET LOVE STORIES (See Fox Giants)

SECRET MISSIONS
February, 1950
St. John Publishing Co.

	Good	Fine	N-Mint
1-Kubert-a	8.00	24.00	56.00

SECRET MYSTERIES (Formerly Crime Mysteries & Crime Smashers)
No. 16, Nov, 1954 - No. 19, July, 1955
Ribage/Merit Publications No. 17 on

	Good	Fine	N-Mint
16-Horror, Palais-a	5.00	15.00	35.00
17-19-Horror; #17-mis-dated 3/54?	3.50	10.50	24.00

SECRET ORIGINS (See 80 Page Giant #8)
Aug-Oct, 1961 (Annual) (Reprints)
National Periodical Publications

	Good	Fine	N-Mint
1('61)-Origin Adam Strange (Showcase #17), Green Lantern (G.L. #1), Challs (partial/Showcase #6, 6 pgs. Kirby-a). J'onn J'onzz (Det. #225), New Flash (Showcase #4). Green Arrow (1pg. text). Superman-Batman team (W. Finest #94). Wonder Woman (W. Woman #105)	13.00	40.00	90.00

SECRET ORIGINS
Feb-Mar, 1973 - No. 6, Jan-Feb, 1974; No. 7, Oct-Nov, 1974
National Periodical Publications (All reprints)

	Good	Fine	N-Mint
1-Origin Superman, Batman, The Ghost, The Flash (Showcase #4); Infantino & Kubert-a	.25	.75	1.50
2-Origin new Green Lantern, the new Atom, & Supergirl; Kane-a		.50	1.00
3-Origin Wonder Woman, Wildcat		.50	1.00
4-Origin Vigilante by Meskin, Kid Eternity		.50	1.00
5-Origin The Spectre; Colan-c(p)		.45	.90
6-Origin Blackhawk & Legion of Super Heroes		.45	.90
7-Origin Robin, Aquaman		.45	.90

SECRET ORIGINS
April, 1986 - Present (All origins)(52 pgs. #6 on)
DC Comics

	Good	Fine	N-Mint
1-Origin Superman	.50	1.50	3.00
2-Blue Beetle	.35	1.10	2.25
3-5: 3-Capt. Marvel. 4-Firestorm, 5-Crimson Avenger, Shadow Lass, Dollman	.35	1.00	2.00
6-10: 6-G.A. Batman. 7-Green Lantern, G.A. Sandman, 8-Doll Man, 9-G.A. Flash, Skyman, 10-Phantom Stranger.	.30	.90	1.75
11-20: 11-G.A. Hawkman, Power Girl, 12-Challs of Unknown, G.A. Fury, 13-Nightwing, Johnny Thunder, 14-Suicide Squad, 15-Spectre, Deadman, 16-G.A. Hourman, Warlord, 17-Adam Strange, Dr. Occult, 18-G.A. Gr. Lantern, The Creeper, 19-Uncle Sam, The Guardian, 20-Batgirl, G.A. Dr. Mid-Nite	.25	.75	1.50
21-37: 21-Jonah Hex, Black Candor. 22-Manhunters. 23-Floronic Man/ Guardians of the Universe. 24-Blue Devil/Dr. Fate. 25-L.S.H./Atom. 26-Bl. Lightning/Miss America. 27-Zatara/Zatanna. 28-Midnight/ Nightshade. 29-Power-Atom/Mr. America. 30-Plastic Man/Elongated Man. 31-J.S.A. 32-J.L.A. 33-35-Justice League International. 36-Green Lantern/Poison Ivy. 37-Legion Of Substitute Heroes/ Doctor Light	.25	.75	1.50
Annual 1 (8/87)-Doom Patrol by Byrne c/a	.35	1.00	2.00
Annual 2 ('88, $2.00)-Origin Flash	.35	1.00	2.00

NOTE: *Art Adams* a-33i. *Bolland* c-7. *Giffen* a-18p. *Gil Kane* a-2, 28; c-2p. *Morrow* a-21. *Orlando* a-10. *Steacy* a-35. *Tuska* a-9p.

SECRET ORIGINS OF SUPER-HEROES (See DC Special Series #10,19)

SECRET ROMANCE
10/68 - No. 41, 11/76; No. 42, 3/79 - No. 48, 2/80
Charlton Comics

	Good	Fine	N-Mint
1	.25	.75	1.50
2-10: 9-Reese-a		.50	1.00
11-48		.30	.60

NOTE: *Beyond the Stars app.-No. 9,11,12,14.*

SECRET ROMANCES
April 1951 - No. 27, July, 1955
Superior Publications Ltd.

	Good	Fine	N-Mint
1	4.60	14.00	32.00
2	2.65	8.00	18.00
3-10	2.35	7.00	16.00
11-13,15-18,20-27	1.65	5.00	11.50
14,19-Lingerie panels	2.65	8.00	18.00

SECRET SERVICE (See Kent Blake of the...)

SECRET SIX (See Action Comics Weekly)
Apr-May, 1968 - No. 7, Apr-May, 1969
National Periodical Publications

	Good	Fine	N-Mint
1-Origin	.85	2.50	5.00
2-7	.60	1.75	3.50

SECRET SOCIETY OF SUPER-VILLAINS
May-June, 1976 - No. 15, June-July, 1978
National Periodical Publications/DC Comics

	Good	Fine	N-Mint
1-Origin; JLA cameo		.65	1.30
2-5: 2-Re-intro/origin Capt. Comet; Gr. Lantern x-over		.30	.60

Secret Loves #5, © QUA

Secret Missions #1, © STJ

Secret Origins #1 (1961), © DC

Secrets Of The Legion Of Super-Heroes #3, © DC   Seduction Of The Innocent #1, © Eclipse Comics   Select Detective #1, © DS

SECRET SOCIETY OF SUPER-VILLAINS (continued)

	Good	Fine	N-Mint
6-15: 9,10-Creeper x-over. 15-G.A. Atom, Dr. Midnite, & JSA app.			
		.25	.50

NOTE: *Jones a-'77 Special. Orlando a-11i.*

SECRET SOCIETY OF SUPER-VILLAINS SPECIAL (See DC Special Series #6)

SECRETS OF HAUNTED HOUSE
4-5/75 - No. 5, 12-1/75-76; No. 6, 6-7/77 - No. 14, 10-11/78;
No. 15, 8/79 - No. 46, 3/82
National Periodical Publications/DC Comics

1		.50	1.00
2-46: 31-Mr. E series begins, ends #41		.25	.50

NOTE: *Buckler c-32-40p. Ditko a-9, 12, 41, 45. Golden a-10. Howard a-13i. Kaluta c-8, 10, 11, 14, 16, 29. Kubert c-41, 42. Sheldon Mayer a-43p. McWilliams a-35. Newton a-30p. Nino a-1, 13, 19. Orlando c-13, 30, 43, 45i. Redondo a-4, 29. Rogers c-26. Spiegle a-31-41. Wrightson c-5, 44.*

SECRETS OF HAUNTED HOUSE SPECIAL (See DC Spec. Ser. #12)

SECRETS OF LIFE (See 4-Color #749)

SECRETS OF LOVE (See Popular Teen-Agers . . .)

SECRETS OF LOVE AND MARRIAGE
Aug, 1956 - V2No.25, June, 1961
Charlton Comics

V2#1	1.30	4.00	9.00
V2#2-6	.55	1.65	4.00
V2#7-9(All 68 pgs.)	.45	1.35	3.00
10-25	.35	1.00	2.00

SECRETS OF MAGIC (See Wisco)

SECRETS OF SINISTER HOUSE (S.H. of Secret Love #1-4)
No. 5, June-July, 1972 - No. 18, June-July, 1974
National Periodical Publications

5-9: 7-Redondo-a		.30	.60
10-Adams-a(i)	.50	1.50	3.00
11-18: 17-Toth-r?		.25	.50

NOTE: *Alcala a-6, 13, 14. Kaluta c-6, 7, 11. Nino a-8, 11-13. c-6. Ambrose Bierce adaptation-#14.*

SECRETS OF THE LEGION OF SUPER-HEROES
Jan, 1981 - No. 3, March, 1981 (mini-series)
DC Comics

1-Origin of the Legion		.50	1.00
2-Retells origins of Braniac 5, Shrinking Violet, Sun-Boy, Bouncing Boy, Ultra-Boy, Matter-Eater Lad, Mon-El, Karate Kid, & Dream Girl		.40	.80
3		.40	.80

SECRETS OF TRUE LOVE
February, 1958
St. John Publishing Co.

1	1.50	4.50	10.00

SECRETS OF YOUNG BRIDES
No. 5, 9/57 - No. 44, 10/64; 7/75 - No. 9, 11/76
Charlton Comics

5	1.30	4.00	9.00
6-10: 8-Negligee panel	.55	1.65	4.00
11-20	.45	1.35	3.00
21-30: Last 10 cent ish?	.35	1.00	2.00
31-44		.50	1.00
1-9		.25	.50

SECRET SQUIRREL (TV)
October, 1966 (Hanna-Barbera)
Gold Key

1	2.65	8.00	18.00

	Good	Fine	N-Mint
Kite Fun Book (1966, 16p, 5x7¼'', soft-c)	2.30	7.00	16.00

SECRET STORY ROMANCES (Becomes True Tales of Love?)
Nov, 1953 - No. 21, Mar, 1956
Atlas Comics (TCI)

1-Everett-a	3.00	9.00	21.00
2	1.50	4.50	10.00
3-11: 11-Last pre-code (2/55)	1.15	3.50	8.00
12-21	1.00	3.00	7.00

NOTE: *Colletta a-10,14,15,17,21; c-10,14,17.*

SECRET VOICE, THE (See Great American Comics)

SECRET WARS II (Also see Marvel Super Heroes . . .)
July, 1985 - No. 9, Mar, 1986 (maxi-series)
Marvel Comics Group

1-Byrne/Austin-c	.35	1.00	2.00
2-9: 9-Double sized (75 cents)	.25	.75	1.50

SECTAURS
June, 1985 - No. 10?, 1986
Marvel Comics Group

1-Based on Coleco Toys		.50	1.00
1-Coleco giveaway; diff-c		.50	1.00
2-10		.50	1.00

SEDUCTION OF THE INNOCENT (Also see N. Y. State Joint Legis. Committee to Study . . .)
1953, 1954 (399 pages) (Hardback)
Rinehart & Co., Inc., N. Y. (Also printed in Canada by Clarke, Irwin & Co. Ltd., Toronto)

Written by Dr. Fredric Wertham

(1st Version)-with bibliographical note intact (several copies got out before the comic publishers forced the removal of this page)

		70.00	150.00
with dust jacket		150.00	300.00
(2nd Version)-		42.00	90.00
with dust jacket		65.00	140.00
(3rd Version)-Published in England by Kennikat Press, 1954, 399pp. has bibliographical page		30.00	60.00
1972 r-/of 3rd version; 400pgs w/bibliography page; Kennikat Press		12.00	24.00

NOTE: *Material from this book appeared in the November, 1953(Vol.70, pp50-53,214) issue of the **Ladies' Home Journal** under the title "What Parents Don't Know About Comic Books." With the release of this book, Dr. Wertham reveals seven years of research attempting to link juvenile delinquency to comic books. Many illustrations showing excessive violence, sex, sadism, and torture are shown. This book was used at the Kefauver Senate hearings which led to the Comics Code Authority. Because of the influence this book had on the comic industry and the collector's interest in it, we feel this listing is justified. Also see **Parade of Pleasure**.*

SEDUCTION OF THE INNOCENT!
Nov, 1985 - Present ($1.75 cover)
Eclipse Comics

1-10: Double listed under cover title	.35	1.00	2.00
. . .3-D 1(10/85; $2.25 cover)-Contains unpub. Advs. Into Darkness			
#15 (pre-code) (36 pgs.); Dave Stevens-c	.40	1.15	2.30
2-D 1 (100 copy limited signed & numbered edition)(B&W)			
	.85	2.50	5.00
. . .3-D 2 (4/86)-Baker, Toth-a	.40	1.25	2.50
2-D 2 (100 copy limited signed & numbered edition)(B&W)			
	.85	2.50	5.00

SELECT DETECTIVE
Aug-Sept, 1948 - No. 3, Dec-Jan, 1948-49
D. S. Publishing Co.

1-Matt Baker-a	7.00	21.00	50.00
2-Baker, McWilliams-a	5.00	15.00	35.00
3	4.30	13.00	30.00

SEMPER FI (Tales of the Marine Corps)
Dec., 1988 - Present (75 cents, color)
Marvel Comics

	Good	Fine	N-Mint
1-5: Severin-c/a, Glanzman back-up-a in all	.60		1.25

SENSATIONAL POLICE CASES (Becomes Captain Steve Savage, 2nd series)
1952; 1954
Avon Periodicals

	Good	Fine	N-Mint
nn-100 pg. issue (1952, 25 cents)-Kubert & Kinstler-a	17.00	51.00	120.00
1 (1954)	5.70	17.00	40.00
2,3: 2-Kirbyish-a	4.35	13.00	30.00
4-Reprint/Saint #5	4.35	13.00	30.00

SENSATIONAL POLICE CASES
No date (1963?)
I. W. Enterprises

	Good	Fine	N-Mint
Reprint #5-Reprints Prison Break #5(1952-Avon); Infantino-a	1.00	3.00	7.00

SENSATION COMICS (. . . Mystery #110 on)
Jan, 1942 - No. 109, May-June, 1952
National Periodical Publ./All-American

	Good	Fine	N-Mint
1-Origin Mr. Terrific, Wildcat, The Gay Ghost, & Little Boy Blue; Wonder Woman(cont'd from All Star #8), The Black Pirate begin; intro. Justice & Fair Play Club	285.00	855.00	2000.00

1-Reprint, Oversize 13½''x10''. **WARNING:** This comic is an exact duplicate reprint of the original except for its size. DC published it in 1974 with a second cover titling it as a Famous First Edition. There have been many reported cases of the outer cover being removed and the interior sold as the original edition. The reprint with the new outer cover removed is practically worthless.

	Good	Fine	N-Mint
2	130.00	390.00	910.00
3-W. Woman gets secretary's job	76.00	228.00	530.00
4-1st app. Stretch Skinner in Wildcat	67.00	200.00	470.00
5-Intro. Justin, Black Pirate's son	50.00	150.00	350.00
6-Origin/1st app. Wonder Woman's magic lasso	42.00	125.00	295.00
7-10	40.00	120.00	280.00
11-20: 13-Hitler, Tojo, Mussolini-c	35.00	105.00	245.00
21-30	24.00	72.00	170.00
31-33	19.00	57.00	132.00
34-Sargon, the Sorcerer begins, ends #36; begins again #52	19.00	57.00	132.00
35-40: 38-Xmas-c	16.00	48.00	110.00
41-50: 43-The Whip app.	14.00	42.00	100.00
51-60: 51-Last Black Pirate. 56,57-Sargon by Kubert	13.00	40.00	90.00
61-80: 63-Last Mr. Terrific. 65,66-Wildcat by Kubert. 68-Origin Huntress	12.00	36.00	84.00
81-Used in SOTI, pg. 33,34; Krigstein-a	15.00	45.00	105.00
82-90: 83-Last Sargon. 86-The Atom app. 90-Last Wildcat	10.00	30.00	70.00
91-Streak begins by Alex Toth	10.00	30.00	70.00
92,93: 92-Toth-a, 2 pgs.	9.50	28.50	65.00
94-1st all girl issue	11.50	34.00	80.00
95-99,101-106: Wonder Woman ends. 99-1st app. Astra, Girl of the Future, ends 106. 105-Last 52 pgs.	11.50	34.00	80.00
100	14.00	42.00	100.00
107-(Scarce)-1st mystery issue; Toth-a	19.00	57.00	132.00
108-(Scarce)-J. Peril by Toth(p)	14.00	42.00	100.00
109-(Scarce)-J. Peril by Toth(p)	19.00	57.00	132.00

NOTE: **Krigstein** a-(Wildcat)-81, 83, 84. **Moldoff** Black Pirate-1-25; Black Pirate not in 34-36, 43-48. Wonder Woman by H. G. Peter, all issues except #8, 17-19, 21.

SENSATION MYSTERY (Sensation #1-109)
No. 110, July-Aug, 1952 - No. 116, July-Aug, 1953
National Periodical Publications

	Good	Fine	N-Mint
110-Johnny Peril	11.50	34.00	80.00
111-116-Johnny Peril in all	10.00	30.00	70.00

NOTE: **Colan** a-114p. **Giunta** a-112. **G. Kane** c-112, 113, 115.

SENTINELS OF JUSTICE, THE (See Captain Paragon & . . .)

SERGEANT BARNEY BARKER (G. I. Tales #4 on)
Aug, 1956 - No. 3, Dec, 1956
Atlas Comics (MCI)

	Good	Fine	N-Mint
1-Severin-a(4)	6.00	18.00	42.00
2,3-Severin-a(4)	3.50	10.50	24.00

SERGEANT BILKO (Phil Silvers) (TV)
May-June, 1957 - No. 18, Mar-Apr, 1960
National Periodical Publications

	Good	Fine	N-Mint
1	14.00	42.00	100.00
2	10.00	30.00	70.00
3-5	8.50	25.50	60.00
6-18: 11,12,15-Photo-c	6.50	19.50	45.00

SGT. BILKO'S PVT. DOBERMAN (TV)
June-July, 1958 - No. 11, Feb-Mar, 1960
National Periodical Publications

	Good	Fine	N-Mint
1	11.50	34.00	80.00
2	8.00	24.00	56.00
3-5: 5-Photo-c	5.70	17.00	40.00
6-11: 6,9-Photo-c	4.65	14.00	32.00

SGT. DICK CARTER OF THE U.S. BORDER PATROL (See Holyoke One-Shot)

SGT. FURY (& His Howling Commandos)(See Spec. Marv. Ed.)
May, 1963 - No. 167, Dec, 1981
Marvel Comics Group

	Good	Fine	N-Mint
1-1st app. Sgt. Fury; Kirby/Ayers c/a	20.00	60.00	140.00
2-Kirby-a	6.50	19.50	45.00
3-5: 3-Reed Richards x-over. 4-Death of Junior Juniper. 5-1st Baron Strucker app.; Kirby-a	2.85	9.00	20.00
6-10: 8-Baron Zemo, 1st Percival Pinkerton app. 10-1st app. Capt. Savage (the Skipper)	1.50	4.50	10.00
11,12,14-20: 14-1st Blitz Squad. 18-Death of Pamela Hawley	1.00	3.00	6.00
13-Captain America app.; Kirby-a	1.50	4.50	10.00
21-50: 25-Red Skull app. 27-1st Eric Koenig app., origin Fury's eye patch. 34-Origin Howling Commandos. 35-Eric Koeing joins Howlers 43-Bob Hope, Glen Miller app. 44-Flashback-Howlers 1st mission.	.70	2.00	4.00
51-167: 64-Capt. Savage & Raiders x-over. 76-Fury's Father app. in WWI story. 98-Deadly Dozen x-over. 100-Captain America, Fantastic Four cameos; Stan Lee, Martin Goodman & others app.			
101-Origin retold. 167-r/#1	.35	1.00	2.00
Annual 1('65, 72 pgs.)	1.35	4.00	8.00
Special 2-7('66-11/71)	.35	1.00	2.00

NOTE: **Ditko** a-15i. **Gil Kane** c-37, 96. **Kirby** a-1-8, 13p, 167p. Special 5; c-1-20, 25, 167p. **Severin** a-44-46, 48, 162, 164; inks-49-79; c-44, 46, 110, 149i, 155i, 162-166. **Sutton** a-57p. Reprints in #80, 82, 85, 87, 89, 91, 93, 95, 99, 101, 103, 105, 107, 109, 111, 145.

SGT. FURY AND HIS HOWLING DEFENDERS (See The Defenders)

SERGEANT PRESTON OF THE YUKON (TV)
No. 344, Aug, 1951 - No. 29, Nov-Jan, 1958-59
Dell Publishing Co.

	Good	Fine	N-Mint
4-Color 344(#1)-Sergeant Preston & his dog Yukon King begin; painted-c begin, end #18	5.00	15.00	35.00
4-Color 373,397,419('52)	3.50	10.50	24.00
5(11-1/52-53)-10(2-4/54)	3.00	9.00	21.00
11,12,14-17	2.30	7.00	16.00
13-Origin S. Preston	3.00	9.00	21.00

Sensation Comics #2, © DC

Sgt. Fury #13, © MEG

Sergeant Preston Of the Yukon #10, © Sgt. Preston

77 Sunset Strip #1, © Warner Bros.

The Shadow #2 (1/74), © Conde Nast Publ.

Shadow Comics V2#4, © Conde Nast Publ.

	Good	Fine	N-Mint
SGT. PRESTON OF THE YUKON (continued)			
18-Origin Yukon King; last painted-c	3.00	9.00	21.00
19-29: All photo-c	3.00	9.00	21.00

SERGEANT PRESTON OF THE YUKON
1956 (4 comic booklets) (Soft-c, 16p, 7x2½" & 5x2½")
Giveaways with Quaker Cereals

"How He Found Yukon King, The Case That Made Him A Sergeant, How Yukon King Saved Him From The Wolves, How He Became A Mountie" each . . .   4.00   12.00   28.00

SGT. ROCK (Formerly Our Army at War)
No. 302, March, 1977 - No. 422, July, 1988
National Periodical Publications/DC Comics

302-350: 318-Reprints		.60	1.25
351-422		.50	1.00
Annual 2(9/82), 3(8/83), 4(8/84)		.50	1.00
Special #1 (10/88, $2.00)-Kubert, Adams-r	.35	1.00	2.00
Special #2 (1988, $2.00)-Kubert-c/a, Toth-r/B&B	.35	1.00	2.00

NOTE: *Estrada* a-322, 327, 331, 336, 337, 341, 342i. *Glanzman* a-384, 421. *Kubert* a-302, 303, 305r, 306, 328, 356, 368, 373; c-317, 318r, 319-323, 325-333-on, Annual 2, 3. *Spiegle* a-382, Annual 2, 3. *Thorne* a-384. *Toth* a-385r.

SGT. ROCK SPECIAL (See DC Special Series #3)

SGT. ROCK SPECTACULAR (See DC Special Series #13)

SGT. ROCK'S PRIZE BATTLE TALES (See DC Spec. Series #18)
Winter, 1964 (One Shot) (Giant - 80 pgs.)
National Periodical Publications

1-Kubert, Heath-r; new Kubert-c	1.00	3.00	6.00

SGT. STRYKER'S DEATH SQUAD (See Savage Combat Tales)

SERGIO ARAGONES' GROO THE WANDERER (See Groo. . .)

SEVEN DEAD MEN (See Complete Mystery #1)

SEVEN DWARFS (See 4-Color #227,382)

SEVEN SEAS COMICS
Apr, 1946 - No. 6, 1947 (no month)
Universal Phoenix Features/Leader No. 6

1-South Sea Girl by Matt Baker, Capt. Cutlass begin; Tugboat Tessie by Baker app.	27.00	81.00	190.00
2	23.00	70.00	160.00
3-6: 3-Six pg. Feldstein-a	21.50	65.00	150.00

NOTE: *Baker* a-1-6; c-3-6.

1776 (See Charlton Classic Library)

7TH VOYAGE OF SINBAD, THE (See 4-Color #944)

77 SUNSET STRIP (TV)
No. 1066, 1-3/60 - No. 2, 2/63 (All photo-c)
Dell Publ. Co./Gold Key

4-Color 1066-Toth-a	5.70	17.00	40.00
4-Color 1106,1159-Toth-a	5.00	15.00	35.00
4-Color 1211,1263,1291, 01-742-209(7-9/62)-Manning-a in all	4.00	12.00	28.00
1(11/62-G.K.), 2-Manning-a in each	3.50	10.50	24.00

77TH BENGAL LANCERS, THE (See 4-Color #791)

SEYMOUR, MY SON (See More Seymour)
September, 1963
Archie Publications (Radio Comics)

1	2.65	8.00	18.00

SHADE, THE CHANGING MAN (See Cancelled Comic Cavalcade)
June-July, 1977 - No. 8, Aug-Sept, 1978
National Periodical Publications/DC Comics

1-Ditko c/a in all		.40	.80
2-8		.30	.60

SHADOW, THE
Aug, 1964 - No. 8, Sept, 1965
Archie Comics (Radio Comics)

	Good	Fine	N-Mint
1	1.30	4.00	9.00
2-8-The Fly app. in some issues	.85	2.50	6.00

SHADOW, THE
Oct-Nov, 1973 - No. 12, Aug-Sept, 1975
National Periodical Publications

1-Kaluta-a begins	.70	2.00	4.00
2	.40	1.25	2.50
3-Kaluta/Wrightson-a	.50	1.50	3.00
4,6-Kaluta-a ends	.35	1.00	2.00
5,7-12: 11-The Avenger (pulp character) x-over	.25	.75	1.50

NOTE: *Craig* a-10. *Cruz* a-10-12. *Kaluta* a-1, 2, 3p, 4, 6; c-1-4, 6, 10-12. *Kubert* c-9. *Robbins* a-5, 7-9; c-5, 7.

SHADOW, THE
May, 1986 - No. 4, Aug, 1986 (mini-series) (mature readers)
DC Comics

1	1.15	3.50	7.00
2-4	.75	2.25	4.50

SHADOW, THE (Also see Marvel Graphic Novel #35)
Aug, 1987 - Present ($1.50, mature readers)
DC Comics

1	.50	1.50	3.00
2-20: 13-Death of The Shadow	.35	1.00	2.00
Annual 1 (12/87, $2.25)-Orlando-a	.40	1.25	2.50
Annual 2 (12/88, $2.50)	.40	1.25	2.50
. . .Blood & Judgement ($12.95)-r-Shadow #1-4 (1986)	2.20	6.50	12.95

SHADOW COMICS (Pulp, radio)
March, 1940 - V9No.5, Aug, 1949
Street & Smith Publications

NOTE: *The Shadow first appeared in Fame & Fortune Magazine, 1929, began on radio the same year, and was featured in pulps beginning in 1931. The early covers of this series were reprinted from the pulp covers.*

V1#1-Shadow, Doc Savage, Bill Barnes, Nick Carter, Frank Merriwell, Iron Munro, the Astonishing Man begin	120.00	360.00	840.00
2-The Avenger begins, ends #6; Capt. Fury only app.	50.00	150.00	350.00
3(nn-5/40)-Norgil the Magician app. (also #9)	40.00	120.00	280.00
4,5: 4-The Three Musketeers begins, ends #8. 5-Doc Savage ends	33.00	100.00	230.00
6,8,9	28.00	84.00	195.00
7-Origin & 1st app. Hooded Wasp & Wasplet; series ends V3#8	25.00	75.00	175.00
10-Origin The Iron Ghost, ends #11; The Dead End Kids begins, ends #14	25.00	75.00	175.00
11-Origin The Hooded Wasp & Wasplet retold	25.00	75.00	175.00
12-Dead End Kids app.	21.50	65.00	150.00
V2#1,2(11/41): 2-Dead End Kid story	20.00	60.00	140.00
3-Origin & 1st app. Supersnipe; series begins; Little Nemo story	25.00	75.00	175.00
4,5: 4-Little Nemo story	15.00	45.00	105.00
6-9: 6-Blackstone the Magician app.	14.00	42.00	100.00
10-Supersnipe app.	14.00	42.00	100.00
11,12	14.00	42.00	100.00
V3#1-12: 10-Doc Savage begins, not in V5#5, V6#10-12, V8#4	12.00	36.00	84.00
V4#1-12	11.00	32.00	75.00
V5#1-12	9.50	28.50	65.00
V6#1-11: 9-Intro. Shadow, Jr.	8.00	24.00	56.00
12-Powell-c/a; atom bomb panels	13.00	40.00	90.00

SHADOW COMICS (continued)

	Good	Fine	N-Mint
V7#1,2,5,7-9,12: 2,5-Shadow, Jr. app.; Powell-a	13.00	40.00	90.00
3,6,11-Powell c/a	14.00	42.00	100.00
4-Powell c/a; Atom bomb panels	16.00	48.00	110.00
10(1/48)-Flying Saucer issue; Powell c/a (2nd of this theme; see The Spirit 9/28/47)	18.00	54.00	125.00
V8#1-12-Powell-a	14.00	42.00	100.00
V9#1,5-Powell-a	13.00	40.00	90.00
2-4-Powell c/a	14.00	42.00	100.00

NOTE: *Powell art in most issues beginning V6#12.*

SHADOW OF THE BATMAN
Dec, 1985 - No. 5, Apr, 1986 ($1.75 cover; mini-series)
DC Comics

1	.60	1.75	3.50
2-5: Detective-r	.45	1.40	2.80

NOTE: *Austin a-2-4. Rogers c/a 1-5.*

SHADOW PLAY
June, 1982
Whitman Publications

1		.30	.60

SHADOWS FROM BEYOND (Formerly Unusual Tales)
October, 1966
Charlton Comics

V2#50-Ditko-c	.50	1.50	3.00

SHADOW WAR OF HAWKMAN
May, 1985 - No. 4, Aug, 1985 (mini-series)
DC Comics

1-Alcala inks		.50	1.00
2-4		.50	1.00

SHAGGY DOG & THE ABSENT-MINDED PROFESSOR (See 4-Color
#985, Movie Comics & Walt Disney Showcase #46)

SHANNA, THE SHE-DEVIL (See Savage Tales #8)
Dec, 1972 - No. 5, Aug, 1973
Marvel Comics Group

1-Steranko-a		.40	.80
2-5: 2-Steranko-c		.30	.60

SHARK FIGHTERS, THE (See 4-Color No. 762)

SHARP COMICS (Slightly large size)
Winter, 1945-46 - V1No.2, Spring, 1946 (52 pgs.)
H. C. Blackerby

V1#1-Origin Dick Royce Planetarian	13.00	40.00	90.00
2-Origin The Pioneer; Michael Morgan, Dick Royce, Sir Gallagher, Planetarian, Steve Hagen, Weeny and Pop app.	10.00	30.00	70.00

SHARPY FOX (See Comic Capers & Funny Frolics)
1958; 1963
I. W. Enterprises/Super Comics

1,2-I.W. Reprint (1958)	.35	1.00	2.00
14-Super Reprint (1963)	.35	1.00	2.00

SHATTER
June, 1985 (One Shot; Baxter paper, color)
First Comics

1-1st computer-generated artwork in a comic book	.60	1.80	3.60
1-2nd printing	.35	1.00	2.00

NOTE: *1st printings have the number "1" included in the row of numbers at the bottom of the indicia.*

SHATTER
Dec, 1985 - No. 14, April, 1988 ($1.75 cover; deluxe paper)
First Comics

	Good	Fine	N-Mint
1-Computer-generated art and lettering	.50	1.50	3.00
2-14	.35	1.00	2.00

SHAZAM (See Giant Comics to Color & Limited Collector's Edition)

SHAZAM! (TV)(See World's Finest)
Feb, 1973 - No. 35, May-June, 1978
National Periodical Publications/DC Comics

1-1st revival of original Captain Marvel(origin retold), by Beck; Captain Marvel Jr. & Mary Marvel x-over		.60	1.25
2-7,9,10: 2-Infinity-c; re-intro Mr. Mind & Tawney. 4-Origin retold. 10-Last Beck ish.		.50	1.00
8-100 pgs.; reprints Capt. Marvel Jr. by Raboy; origin/C.M. #80; origin Mary Marvel/C.M. #:8		.60	1.20
11-Shaffenberger-a begins		.50	1.00
12-17-All 100 pgs.; 15-Lex Luthor x-over		.60	1.20
18-35: 25-1st app. Isis. 34-Origin Capt. Nazi & Capt. Marvel Jr. retold		.50	1.00

NOTE: *Reprints in #1-8,10,12-17,21-24. Beck a-1-10, 12-17r, 21-24r; c-1, 3-9. Nasser c-35p. Newton a-35p. Raboy a-5r, 8r, 17r. Shaffenberger a-11, 14-20, 25, 26, 27p, 28, 29-31p, 33i, 35r; c-20, 22, 23, 25, 26i, 27i, 28-33.*

SHAZAM: THE NEW BEGINNING
Apr, 1987 - No. 4, July, 1987 (mini-series)
DC Comics

1-New origin Capt. Marvel	.25	.75	1.50
2-4		.60	1.20

SHEA THEATRE COMICS
No date (1940's) (32 pgs.)
Shea Theatre

Contains Rocket Comics; MLJ cover in mono color

	10.00	20.00	30.00

SHEENA
Dec, 1984 - No. 2, Feb, 1985 (Limited series)
Marvel Comics Group

1,2-r/Marvel Super Special; movie adaption		.40	.80

SHEENA, QUEEN OF THE JUNGLE (See Jumbo Comics, Jerry Iger's Classic. . ., & 3-D. . .)
Spring, 1942 - No. 18, Winter, 1952-53 (#1,2, 68 pgs.)
Fiction House Magazines

1-Sheena begins	100.00	300.00	700.00
2 (Winter, 1942/43)	50.00	150.00	350.00
3 (Spring, 1943)	35.00	105.00	245.00
4, 5 (Fall, 1948 - Sum., '49)	20.00	60.00	140.00
6,7 (Spring, '50 - '50, 52 pgs.)	18.00	54.00	125.00
8-10('50, 36 pgs.)	16.00	48.00	110.00
11-17	13.00	40.00	90.00
18-Used in POP, pg. 98	13.50	42.00	95.00
I.W. Reprint #9-Reprints #17	2.50	7.50	15.00

SHEENA 3-D (. . .Special, Blackthorne)
Jan, 1985; May, 1985 ($2.00)
Eclipse Comics/Blackthorne Publishing

1-(Eclipse) Dave Stevens-c	.45	1.40	2.80
1-r/1953 3-D Sheena; Dave Stevens-c	.35	1.00	2.00

SHE-HULK (Also see The Savage She-Hulk)
May, 1989 - Present
Marvel Comics

1-By John Byrne	.25	.75	1.50

SHERIFF BOB DIXON'S CHUCK WAGON (TV)
November, 1950 (See Wild Bill Hickok #22)
Avon Periodicals

1-Kinstler c/a(3)	7.00	21.00	50.00

Shadow Of The Batman #1, © DC

Sheena, Queen Of The Jungle #13, © FH

Sheriff Bob Dixon's Chuck Wagon #1, © AVON

Shield Wizard Comics #5, © AP

Shocking Mystery Cases #50, © STAR

Shock SuspenStories #7, © WMG

SHERIFF OF COCHISE, THE
1957 (16 pages) (TV Show)
Mobil Giveaway

	Good	Fine	N-Mint
Shaffenberger-a	1.00	3.00	7.00

SHERIFF OF TOMBSTONE
Nov, 1958 - No. 17, Sept, 1961
Charlton Comics

V1#1-Williamson/Severin-c	3.50	10.50	24.00
2	1.60	4.80	11.00
3-17	1.00	3.00	7.00

SHERLOCK HOLMES (See 4-Color #1169,1245, Marvel Prev. & Spect. Stories)

SHERLOCK HOLMES (All New Baffling Advs. of) (Young Eagle No. 3 on?)
Oct, 1955 - No. 2, Mar, 1956
Charlton Comics

1-Dr. Neff, Ghost Breaker app.	20.00	60.00	140.00
2	17.00	51.00	120.00

SHERLOCK HOLMES (Also see The Joker)
Sept-Oct, 1975
National Periodical Publications

1-Cruz-a; Simonson-a	.50		1.00

SHERRY THE SHOWGIRL (Showgirls #4)
7/56 - No. 3, 12/56; No. 5, 4/57 - No. 7, 8/57
Atlas Comics

1	3.50	10.50	24.00
2	2.00	6.00	14.00
3,5-7	1.50	4.50	10.00

SHIELD (Nick Fury & His Agents of . . .) (See Nick Fury)
Feb, 1973 - No. 5, Oct, 1973
Marvel Comics Group

1-Steranko-c	.35	1.00	2.00
2-Steranko flag-c	.35	1.00	2.00
3-5: 1-5 all contain-r from Strange Tales #146-155.			
3-5-Cover-r	.35	1.00	2.00

NOTE: *Buscema* a-3p(r). *Kirby* layouts 1-5; c-3 (w/Steranko). *Steranko* a-4r.

SHIELD, THE (Becomes Shield-Steel Sterling #3; #1 titled 'Lancelot Strong;' also see Advs. of the Fly, Double Life of Private Strong, Fly Man, Mighty Comics, & The Mighty Crusaders)
June, 1983 - No. 2, Aug, 1983
Archie Enterprises, Inc.

1,2: Steel Sterling app.		.45	.90

SHIELD-STEEL STERLING (Formerly The Shield)
No. 3, Dec, 1983 (Becomes Steel Sterling No. 4)
Archie Enterprises, Inc.

3-Nino-a		.45	.90

SHIELD WIZARD COMICS (Also see Pep & Top-Notch Comics)
Summer, 1940 - No. 13, Spring, 1944
MLJ Magazines

1-(V1#5 on inside)-Origin The Shield by Irving Novick & The Wizard by Ed Ashe, Jr; Flag-c	115.00	345.00	800.00
2-Origin The Shield retold; intro. Wizard's sidekick, Roy	52.00	156.00	365.00
3,4	35.00	105.00	245.00
5-Dusty, the Boy Detective begins	30.00	90.00	210.00
6-8: 6-Roy the Super Boy begins	26.00	78.00	180.00
9,10	23.00	70.00	160.00
11-13: 13-Bondage-c	21.50	65.00	150.00

SHIP AHOY
November, 1944 (52 pgs.)
Spotlight Publishers

	Good	Fine	N-Mint
1-L. B. Cole-c	5.50	16.50	38.00

SHMOO (See Al Capp's . . . & Washable Jones & . . .)

SHOCK (Magazine)
(Reprints from horror comics) (Black & White)
May, 1969 - V3No.4, Sept, 1971
Stanley Publications

V1#1-Cover-r/Weird Tales of the Future #7 by Bernard Baily	1.00	3.00	6.00
2-Wolverton-r/Weird Mysteries 5; r-Weird Mysteries 7 used in SOTI; cover r-/Weird Chills #1	1.00	3.00	6.00
3,5,6	.50	1.50	3.00
4-Harrison/Williamson-r/Forbidden Worlds #6	.85	2.50	5.00
V2#2, V1#8, V2#4-6, V3#1-4	.50	1.50	3.00

NOTE: *Disbrow* r-V2#4; bondage c-V1#4, V2#6, V3#1.

SHOCK DETECTIVE CASES (Formerly Crime Fighting Detective)
(Becomes Spook Detective Cases No. 22)
No. 20, Sept, 1952 - No. 21, Nov, 1952
Star Publications

20,21-L.B. Cole-c	4.00	12.00	28.00

NOTE: *Palais* a-20. No. 21-Fox-r.

SHOCK ILLUSTRATED (Magazine format)
Sept-Oct, 1955 - No. 3, Spring, 1956
E. C. Comics

1-All by Kamen; drugs, prostitution, wife swapping	3.50	10.50	24.00
2-Williamson-a redrawn from Crime SuspenStories #13 plus Ingels, Crandall, & Evans	4.00	12.00	28.00
3-Only 100 known copies bound & given away at E.C. office; Crandall, Evans-a	100.00	300.00	700.00
(Prices vary widely on this book)			

SHOCKING MYSTERY CASES (Formerly Thrilling Crime Cases)
No. 50, Sept, 1952 - No. 60, Oct, 1954
Star Publications

50-Disbrow ''Frankenstein'' story	10.00	30.00	70.00
51-Disbrow-a	4.75	14.00	33.00
52-55,57-60	4.00	12.00	28.00
56-Drug use story	4.75	14.00	33.00

NOTE: *L. B. Cole* covers on all; a-60(2 pgs.). *Hollingsworth* a-52. *Morisi* a-55.

SHOCKING TALES DIGEST MAGAZINE
Oct, 1981 (95 cents)
Harvey Publications

1-1957-58-r; Powell, Kirby, Nostrand-a		.50	1.00

SHOCK SUSPENSTORIES
Feb-Mar, 1952 - No. 18, Dec-Jan, 1954-55
E. C. Comics

1-Classic Feldstein electrocution-c. Bradbury adaptation	43.00	130.00	300.00
2	26.00	78.00	180.00
3	17.00	51.00	120.00
4-Used in SOTI, pg. 387,388	19.00	58.00	130.00
5-Hanging-c	17.00	51.00	115.00
6,7: 6-Classic bondage-c. 7-Classic face melting-c	20.00	60.00	140.00
8-Williamson-a	18.00	55.00	120.00
9-11: 10-Junkie story	13.00	40.00	90.00
12-''The Monkey''-classic junkie cover/story; drug propaganda ish.	18.00	54.00	125.00
13-Frazetta's only solo story for E.C., 7 pgs.	23.00	70.00	160.00
14-Used in Senate Investigation hearings	10.00	30.00	70.00
15-Used in 1954 Reader's Digest article, ''For the Kiddies to Read''			

SHOCK SUSPENSTORIES (continued)

	Good	Fine	N-Mint
	10.00	30.00	70.00
16-"Red Dupe" editorial; rape story	10.00	30.00	70.00
17,18	10.00	30.00	70.00

NOTE: *Craig a-11; c-11. Crandall a-9-13, 15-18. Davis a-1-5. Evans a-7, 8, 14-18; c-16-18. Feldstein c-1, 7-9, 12. Ingels a-1, 2, 6. Kamen a-in all; c-10. Krigstein a-14, 18. Orlando a-1, 3-7, 9, 10, 12, 16, 17. Wood a-2-15; c-2-6, 14.*

SHOGUN WARRIORS
Feb, 1979 - No. 20, Sept, 1980
Marvel Comics Group

1-Raydeen, Combatra, & Dangard Ace begin		.40	.80
2-20		.25	.50

SHOOK UP (Magazine) (Satire)
November, 1958
Dodsworth Publ. Co.

V1#1	1.00	3.00	6.00

SHORT RIBS (See 4-Color #1333)

SHORT STORY COMICS (See Hello Pal,...)

SHORTY SHINER
June, 1956 - No. 3, Oct, 1956
Dandy Magazine (Charles Biro)

1	2.00	6.00	14.00
2,3	1.30	4.00	9.00

SHOTGUN SLADE (See 4-Color #1111)

SHOWCASE (See Cancelled Comic Cavalcade & New Talent...)
3-4/56 - No. 93, 9/70; No. 94, 8-9/77 - No. 104, 9/78
National Periodical Publications/DC Comics

	Good	Fine	N-Mint
1-Fire Fighters	64.00	193.00	450.00
2-King of the Wild; Kubert-a	24.00	70.00	165.00
3-The Frogmen	20.00	60.00	140.00
4-Origin The Flash (1st Silver Age app.) & The Turtle; Kubert-a	229.00	685.00	1600.00
5-Manhunters	19.00	56.00	130.00
6-Origin Challengers by Kirby, partly r-/in Secret Origins #1 & Challengers of the Unknown #64,65	54.00	161.00	375.00
7-Challengers by Kirby r-in/Challengers of the Unknown #75	32.00	95.00	225.00
8-The Flash; intro/origin Capt. Cold	86.00	257.00	600.00
9,10-Lois Lane	29.00	86.00	200.00
11,12-Challengers by Kirby	26.00	80.00	185.00
13-The Flash; origin Mr. Element	61.00	182.00	425.00
14-The Flash; origin Dr. Alchemy, former Mr. Element	61.00	182.00	425.00
15,16-Space Ranger	14.00	42.00	100.00
17-Adam Strange-Origin & 1st app.	37.00	112.00	260.00
18,19-Adam Strange	22.00	65.00	155.00
20-1st app/origin Rip Hunter; Moriera-a	8.50	25.50	60.00
21-Rip Hunter; Sekowsky-a	8.00	24.00	55.00
22-Origin & 1st app. Silver Age Green Lantern by Gil Kane	82.00	246.00	575.00
23,24-Green Lantern. 23-Nuclear explosion-c	30.00	90.00	210.00
25,26-Rip Hunter by Kubert	4.30	13.00	30.00
27-29-Sea Devils by Heath, c/a	5.70	17.00	40.00
30-Origin & 1st app. Silver Age Aquaman	8.00	24.00	55.00
31-33-Aquaman	3.60	11.00	25.00
34-Origin & 1st app. Silver Age Atom by Kane & Anderson	11.00	32.00	75.00
35-The Atom by Gil Kane; last 10 cent ish.	5.00	15.00	35.00
36-The Atom by Gil Kane	5.00	15.00	35.00
37-1st app. Metal Men	8.00	24.00	55.00
38-40-Metal Men	3.00	9.00	21.00
41,42-Tommy Tomorrow	1.35	4.00	9.00

43-Dr. No (James Bond); Nodel-a; originally published as British

	Good	Fine	N-Mint
Classics III. #158A, and as #6 in a European Detective series, all with a diff. painted-c. This Showcase #43 version is actually censored, deleting all racial skin color, and dialogue thought to be racially demeaning	18.00	54.00	125.00
44-Tommy Tomorrow	1.00	3.00	7.00
45-Sgt. Rock; origin retold; Heath-c	1.85	5.50	13.00
46,47-Tommy Tomorrow	.90	2.75	5.50
48,49-Cave Carson	.90	2.75	5.50
50,51-I Spy (Danger Trail-r by Infantino), King Farady story (not reprint-#50)	.90	2.75	5.50
52-Cave Carson	.90	2.75	5.50
53,54-G.I. Joe; Heath-a	.90	2.75	5.50
55,56-Dr. Fate & Hourman	.90	2.75	5.50
57,58-Enemy Ace by Kubert	.90	2.75	5.50
59-Teen Titans	3.00	9.00	21.00
60-The Spectre by Anderson	.90	2.75	5.50
61,64-The Spectre by Anderson	.75	2.25	4.50
62-Origin/1st app. Inferior Five	.50	1.50	3.00
63,65-Inferior Five	.35	1.00	2.00
66,67-B'wana Beast		.50	1.00
68,69,71-Maniaks		.50	1.00
70-Binky		.50	1.00
72-Top Gun (Johnny Thunder-r)-Toth-a		.60	1.20
73-Creeper; Ditko c/a	.85	2.50	5.00
74-Anthro; Post c/a	.25	.80	1.60
75-1st app/origin Hawk & the Dove; Ditko c/a	.70	2.00	4.00
76-Bat Lash	.40	1.20	2.40
77-Angel & Ape		.60	1.20
78-Jonny Double		.60	1.20
79-Dolphin; Aqualad origin-r	.30	.90	1.80
80-Phantom Stranger-r; Adams-c	.50	1.50	3.00
81-Windy & Willy	.30	.90	1.80
82-Nightmaster by Grandenetti & Giordano; Kubert-c	.30	.90	1.80
83,84-Nightmaster by Wrightson/Jones/Kaluta in each; Kubert-c. 84-Origin retold	1.35	4.00	8.00
85-87-Firehair; Kubert-a	.50	1.50	3.00
88-90-Jason's Quest: 90-Manhunter 2070 app.		.50	1.00
91-93-Manhunter 2070; origin-92		.50	1.00
94-Intro/origin new Doom Patrol & Robotman	.25	.80	1.60
95,96-The Doom Patrol. 95-Origin Celsius		.50	1.00
97-99-Power Girl; origin-97,98; JSA cameos		.50	1.00
100-(52 pgs.)-Features most Showcase characters		.50	1.00
101-103-Hawkman; Adam Strange x-over		.50	1.00
104-(52 pgs.)-O.S.S. Spies at War		.50	1.00

NOTE: *Anderson a-22-24i, 34-36i, 55, 56, 60, 61, 64, 101-03i; c-50i, 51i, 55, 56, 60, 61, 64. Aparo c-94-96. Estrada a-104. Infantino a/c-4, 8, 13, 14; c-50p, 51p. Gil Kane a-22-24p, 34-36p; c-17-19, 22-24, 31, 34-36. Kirby c-6, 7, 11, 12. Kubert a-2, 4i, 25, 26, 45, 53, 54, 72; c-25, 26, 53, 54, 57, 58, 82-87, 101-04. Orlando a-62p, 63p, 97i; c-62, 63, 97i. Sekowsky a-65p. Sparling a-78. Staton a-94, 95-99p, 100; c-97-100p.*

SHOWGIRLS (Formerly Sherry the Showgirl #3)
No. 4, 1-2/57?; June, 1957 - No. 2, Aug, 1957
Atlas Comics (MPC No. 2)

	Good	Fine	N-Mint
4	2.00	6.00	14.00
1-Millie, Sherry, Chili, Pearl & Hazel begin	3.70	11.00	26.00
2	2.00	6.00	14.00

SHROUD OF MYSTERY
June, 1952
Whitman Publications

1		.30	.60

SHURIKEN (Also see Blade Of...)
Summer, 1985 - No. 7, May, 1987 ($1.50, B&W)
Victory Productions

1	1.35	4.00	8.00

Showcase #4, © DC

Showcase #34, © DC

Showcase #74, © DC

The Silent Invasion #2, © Renegade Press

Silly Tunes #1, © MEG

Silver Streak Comics #8, © LEV

	Good	Fine	N-Mint
SHURIKEN (continued)			
1-Reprint (Wint./86)	.25	.75	1.50
2 (Fall/85)	.35	1.00	2.00
3-7	.25	.75	1.50
Graphic Novel ($7.95, Blackthorne Publ.)	1.35	4.00	8.00

SICK (Magazine) (Satire)
Aug, 1960 - No. 140?, 1980?
Feature Publ./Headline Publ./Crestwood Publ. Co./Hewfred Publ./
Pyramid Comm./Charlton Publ. No. 109 (4/76) on

V1#1-Torres-a	5.70	17.00	40.00
2-5-Torres-a in all	3.00	9.00	21.00
6	1.50	4.50	10.00
V2#1-8(#7-14)	1.15	3.50	8.00
V3#1-8(#15-22)	1.00	3.00	7.00
V4#1-5(#23-27)	1.00	3.00	6.00
28-40	.70	2.00	4.00
41-140: 45 has #44 on-c & #45 on inside	.50	1.50	3.00
Annual 1969, 1970, 1971	1.00	3.00	6.00
Annual 2-4('80)	.60	1.75	3.50
Special 2 ('78)	.35	1.00	2.00

NOTE: **Davis** c/a in most issues of #16-27, 30-32, 34, 35. **Simon** a-1-3. **Torres** a-V2#7, V4#2, V6#1-3. Civil War Blackouts-23, 24.

SIDESHOW
1949 (One Shot)
Avon Periodicals

1-(Rare)-Similar to Bachelor's Diary	16.00	48.00	110.00

SIEGEL AND SHUSTER: DATELINE 1930s
11/84 - No. 2, 9/85 (Baxter paper #1; $1.50-$1.75)
Eclipse Comics

1-Unpubbed samples of strips from 1935; includes 'Interplanetary			
Police;' Shuster-c	.25	.75	1.50
2 (B&W)-Unpubbed strips	.25	.75	1.50

SILENT INVASION, THE
April, 1986 - No. 12, March, 1988 ($1.70/$2.00, B&W)
Renegade Press

1-UFO sightings of '50s	.70	2.00	4.00
2	.60	1.75	3.50
3-12	.40	1.25	2.50
Book 1	1.35	4.00	7.95

SILK HAT HARRY'S DIVORCE SUIT
1912 (5¾x15½") (B&W)
M. A. Donoghue & Co.

Newspaper reprints by Tad (Thomas Dorgan)	8.00	24.00	56.00

SILLY PILLY (See Frank Luther's . . .)

SILLY SYMPHONIES (See Dell Giants)

SILLY TUNES
Fall, 1945 - No. 7, June, 1947
Timely Comics

1-Silly Seal, Ziggy Pig begin	5.70	17.00	40.00
2	3.00	9.00	21.00
3-7	2.30	7.00	16.00

SILVER (See Lone Ranger's Famous Horse . . .)

SILVERBLADE
Sept, 1987 - No. 12, Sept, 1988
DC Comics

1-Colan c/a(p) in all	.25	.75	1.50
2-12	.25	.75	1.50

SILVERHAWKS
Aug, 1987 - No. 6, June, 1988 ($1.00)
Star Comics/Marvel #6

	Good	Fine	N-Mint
1-6		.50	1.00

SILVERHEELS (See Eclipse Graphic Album #12)
Dec, 1983 - No. 3, May, 1984
Pacific Comics

1-3	.35	1.00	2.00

SILVER KID WESTERN
Oct, 1954 - No. 5, 1955
Key/Stanmor Publications

1	3.50	10.50	24.00
2	1.70	5.00	12.00
3-5	1.30	4.00	9.00
I.W. Reprint #1,2	.50	1.50	3.00

SILVER STAR
Feb, 1983 - No. 6, Jan, 1984 (Color)
Pacific Comics

1-6		.50	1.00

NOTE: **Kirby** a-1-5p; c-1-5p.

SILVER STREAK COMICS (Crime Does Not Pay #22 on)
Dec, 1939 - May, 1942; 1946 (Silver logo-#1-5)
Your Guide Publs. No. 1-7/New Friday Publs. No. 8-17/Comic House
Publ./Newsbook Publ.

1-Intro. The Claw by Cole (r-/in Daredevil #21), Red Reeves, Boy Magician; & Captain Fearless; The Wasp, Mister Midnight begin; Spirit Man app. Silver metallic-c begin, end #5 (Scarce)	310.00	930.00	2170.00
2-The Claw by Cole; Simon c/a	135.00	405.00	945.00
3-1st app. & origin Silver Streak (2nd with lightning speed); Dickie Dean the Boy Inventor, Lance Hale, Ace Powers, Bill Wayne, & The Planet Patrol begin	120.00	360.00	840.00
4-Sky Wolf begins; Silver Streak by Jack Cole (new costume); intro. Jackie, Lance Hale's sidekick	65.00	195.00	455.00
5-Jack Cole c/a(2)	75.00	225.00	525.00
6-(Scarce)-Origin & 1st app. Daredevil (blue & yellow costume) by Jack Binder; The Claw returns; classic Jack Cole Claw-c	260.00	780.00	1820.00
(Prices vary widely on this book)			
7-Claw vs. Daredevil (new costume-blue & red) by Jack Cole & 3 other Cole stories (38 pgs.)	160.00	480.00	1120.00
8-Claw vs. Daredevil by Cole; last Silver Streak	100.00	300.00	700.00
9-Claw vs. Daredevil by Cole	71.00	215.00	500.00
10-Origin Captain Battle; Claw vs. Daredevil by Cole	68.00	205.00	475.00
11-Intro. Mercury by Bob Wood, Silver Streak's sidekick; conclusion Claw vs. Daredevil by Rico; in 'Presto Martin,' 2nd pg., news paper says 'Roussos does it again.'	46.00	138.00	325.00
12-14: 13-Origin Thun-Dohr	38.00	115.00	265.00
15-17-Last Daredevil issue	35.00	105.00	245.00
18-The Saint begins; by Leslie Charteris (See Movie Comics 2, DC)	28.00	84.00	195.00
19-21(1942): 20,21 have Wolverton's Scoop Scuttle	18.00	54.00	125.00
22,24(1946)-Reprints	13.00	40.00	90.00
23-Reprints?; bondage-c	13.00	40.00	90.00
nn(11/46)(Newsbook Publ.)-R-/S.S. story from #4-7 plus 2 Captain Fearless stories, all in color; bondage/torture-c	24.00	70.00	170.00

NOTE: **Binder** c-3, 4, 13-15, 17. **Jack Cole** a-(Daredevil)-#6-10, (Dickie Dean)-#3-10, (Pirate Prince)-#7, (Silver Streak)-#4-8, nn; c-5 (Silver Streak), 6-8 (Daredevil). **Everett** Red Reed begins #20. **Guardineer** a-#8-13. **Don Rico** a-11-17 (Daredevil); c-11, 12, 16. **Simon** a-3 (Silver Streak). **Bob Wood** a-9 (Silver Streak); c-9, 10. Claw c-#1, 2, 6-8.

SILVER SURFER (See Fantastic Four, Fantasy Masterpieces V2/1, Marvel Comics Presents, Marvel Graphic Novel, Marvel Presents #8, Marvel's Greatest Comics &

SILVER SURFER (continued)
Tales To Astonish)

SILVER SURFER, THE
Aug, 1968 - No. 18, Sept, 1970; June, 1982 (No. 1-7: 68 pgs.)
Marvel Comics Group

	Good	Fine	N-Mint
1-Origin by John Buscema (p); Watcher begins (origin), ends #7			
	9.30	28.00	65.00
2	3.60	11.00	25.00
3-1st app. Mephisto	3.15	10.00	22.00
4-Low distribution; Thor app.	6.50	19.50	45.00
5-7-Last giant size. 5-The Stranger app. 6-Brunner inks. 7-			
Brunner-c	2.00	6.00	14.00
8-10	1.50	4.50	10.00
11-18: 14-Spider-Man x-over. 18-Kirby c/a	1.00	3.00	7.00
V2#1 (6/82, 52 pgs.)-Byrne-c/a	.85	2.50	5.00

NOTE: *Adkins a-8-15i. Brunner a-6i. J. Buscema a-1-17p. Colan a-1-3p. Reinman a-1-4i.*

SILVER SURFER, THE (See Marvel Graphic Novel #38)
July, 1987 - Present
Marvel Comics Group

1-Double size ($1.25)	.70	2.00	4.00
2	.40	1.25	2.50
3-10	.30	.90	1.80
11-20: 19-Rogers-a		.60	1.20
Annual 1 (8/88, $1.75)-Evolutionary War app.	.40	1.25	2.50

SILVER SURFER, THE
Dec, 1988 - No. 2, Jan, 1989 ($1.00, limited series)
Epic Comics (Marvel)

1,2; By Stan Lee & Moebius	.25	.75	1.50

SILVERTIP (Max Brand)
No. 491, Aug, 1953 - No. 898, May, 1958
Dell Publishing Co.

4-Color 491	4.00	12.00	24.00
4-Color 572,608,637,667,731,789,898-Kinstler-a; all painted-c			
	3.00	9.00	21.00
4-Color 835	2.30	7.00	16.00

SINBAD, JR (TV Cartoon)
Sept-Nov, 1965 - No. 3, May, 1966
Dell Publishing Co.

1	1.70	5.00	12.00
2,3	1.00	3.00	7.00

SINBAD (See Movie Comics: Capt. Sinbad, and Fantastic Voyages of Sindbad)

SINGING GUNS (See Fawcett Movie Comics)

SINGLE SERIES (Comics on Parade #30 on)(Also see John Hix . . .)
1938 - No. 28, 1942 (All 68 pgs.)
United Features Syndicate

1-Captain and the Kids (#1)	35.00	105.00	245.00
2-Broncho Bill (1939) (#1)	22.00	65.00	154.00
3-Ella Cinders (1939)	20.00	60.00	140.00
4-Li'l Abner (1939) (#1)	32.00	95.00	225.00
5-Fritzi Ritz (1939)	13.00	40.00	90.00
6-Jim Hardy by Dick Moores (#1)	18.00	54.00	125.00
7-Frankie Doodle	13.00	40.00	90.00
8-Peter Pat (On sale 7/14/39)	13.00	40.00	90.00
9-Strange As It Seems	13.00	40.00	90.00
10-Little Mary Mixup	13.00	40.00	90.00
11-Mr. and Mrs. Beans	13.00	40.00	90.00
12-Joe Jinks	12.00	36.00	84.00
13-Looy Dot Dope	11.50	34.00	80.00
14-Billy Make Believe	11.50	34.00	80.00
15-How It Began (1939)	13.00	40.00	90.00
16-Illustrated Gags (1940)-Has ad for Captain and the Kids #1 reprint			

	Good	Fine	N-Mint
listed below	7.00	21.00	50.00
17-Danny Dingle	10.00	30.00	70.00
18-Li'l Abner (#2 on-c)	25.00	75.00	175.00
19-Broncho Bill (#2 on-c)	18.00	54.00	125.00
20-Tarzan by Hal Foster	70.00	210.00	490.00
21-Ella Cinders (#2 on-c; on sale 3/19/4Q)	16.00	48.00	110.00
22-Iron Vic	13.00	40.00	90.00
23-Tailspin Tommy by Hal Forrest (#1)	15.00	45.00	105.00
24-Alice in Wonderland (#1)	19.00	57.00	132.00
25-Abbie and Slats	17.00	51.00	120.00
26-Little Mary Mixup (#2 on-c, 1940)	13.00	40.00	90.00
27-Jim Hardy by Dick Moores (1942)	13.00	40.00	90.00
28-Ella Cinders and Abbie and Slats (1942)	16.00	48.00	110.00
1-Captain and the Kids (1939 reprint)-2nd Edition			
	20.00	60.00	140.00
1-Fritzi Ritz (1939 reprint)-2nd edition	11.50	34.00	80.00

NOTE: *Some issues given away at the 1939-40 New York World's Fair (#6).*

SINISTER HOUSE OF SECRET LOVE, THE (Secrets of Sinister House No. 5 on)
Oct-Nov, 1971 - No. 4, Apr-May, 1972
National Periodical Publications

1		.50	1.00
2-4: 3-Toth-a, 36 pgs.		.35	.70

SIR LANCELOT (See 4-Color #606,775)

SIR WALTER RALEIGH (See 4-Color #644)

SISTERHOOD OF STEEL (See Eclipse Graphic Album #13)
12/84 - No. 8, 2/86 ($1.50; Baxter paper) (Adults only)
Epic Comics (Marvel)

1-(Women mercenaries)	.35	1.10	2.20
2-8	.30	.90	1.80

6 BLACK HORSES (See Movie Classics)

SIX FROM SIRIUS
July, 1984 - No. 4, Oct, 1984 (mini-series; $1.50)
Epic Comics (Marvel)

1-Gulacy c/a in all	.35	1.00	2.00
2-4	.30	.90	1.80

SIX FROM SIRIUS II
Feb, 1986 - No. 4, May, 1986 (Adults only)
Epic Comics (Marvel)

1-4	.25	.75	1.50

SIX-GUN HEROES
March, 1950 - No. 23, Nov, 1953 (Photo-c #1-23)
Fawcett Publications

1-Rocky Lane, Hopalong Cassidy, Smiley Burnette begin			
	22.00	65.00	154.00
2	13.00	40.00	90.00
3-5	10.00	30.00	70.00
6-15: 6-Lash LaRue begins	7.00	21.00	50.00
16-22: 17-Last Smiley Burnette. 18-Monte Hale begins			
	6.50	19.50	45.00
23-Last Fawcett issue	7.00	21.00	50.00

SIX-GUN HEROES (Cont'd from Fawcett; Gunmasters #84 on)
No. 24, Jan, 1954 - No. 83, Mar-Apr, 1965 (All Vol. 4)
Charlton Comics

24-Tom Mix, Lash Larue	5.70	17.00	40.00
25	3.50	10.50	24.00
26-30	2.85	8.50	20.00
31-40-Tom Mix, Lash Larue, Rocky Lane, Tex Ritter			
	2.00	6.00	14.00
41-46,48,50	1.70	5.00	12.00
47-Williamson-a, 2 pgs; Torres-a	2.85	8.50	20.00

The Silver Surfer #14 (3/70), © MEG

Single Series #19, © UFS

Six-Gun Heroes #22, © FAW

Skyman #2, © CCG

Sky Wolf #1, © Eclipse Comics

Slam Bang Comics #3, © FAW

	Good	Fine	N-Mint
SIX-GUN HEROES (continued)			
49-Williamson-a, 5 pgs.	2.85	8.50	20.00
51-60: 58-Gunmaster app.	1.15	3.50	8.00
61,63-70	.85	2.50	6.00
62-Origin, Gunmaster	1.00	3.00	7.00
71-83: 76-Gunmaster begins	.60	1.80	4.00
1962 Shoe Store giveaway	.35	1.00	2.00

SIXGUN RANCH (See 4-Color #580)

SIX-GUN WESTERN
Jan, 1957 - No. 4, July, 1957
Atlas Comics (CDS)

	Good	Fine	N-Mint
1-Crandall-a; two Williamson text illos	5.50	16.50	38.00
2,3-Williamson-a in both	5.00	15.00	35.00
4-Woodbridge-a	2.00	6.00	14.00

NOTE: *Ayers a-2, 3. Maneely c-2, 3. Orlando a-2. Pakula 3-2. Powell a-3. Romita a-1, 4. Severin c-1, 4. Shores a-2.*

SIX MILLION DOLLAR MAN (TV)(Magazine)
June, 1976 - No. 7, Nov, 1977 (B&W)
Charlton Comics

	Good	Fine	N-Mint
1-Adams c/a	.50	1.50	3.00
2-Adams-c	.30	.80	1.60
3-7: 3-Adams part inks	.60		1.20

SIX MILLION DOLLAR MAN (TV)
6/76 - No. 4, 1/77; No. 5, 10/77; No. 6, 2/78 - No. 9, 6/78
Charlton Comics

	Good	Fine	N-Mint
1-Staton c/a	.30	.80	1.60
2-Adams-c; Staton-a		.50	1.00
3-9		.30	.60

SKATEMAN
Nov, 1983 (One Shot) (Baxter paper)
Pacific Comics

	Good	Fine	N-Mint
1-Adams c/a	.25	.75	1.50

SKATING SKILLS
1957 (36 & 12 pages; 5x7", two versions) (10 cents)
Custom Comics, Inc.
Chicago Roller Skates

	Good	Fine	N-Mint
Resembles old ACG cover plus interior art	.50	1.50	3.00

SKEEZIX
1925 - 1928 (Strip reprints) (soft covers) (pictures & text)
Reilly & Lee Co.

	Good	Fine	N-Mint
...and Uncle Walt (1924)-Origin	8.50	25.50	60.00
...and Pal (1925)	6.00	18.00	42.00
...at the Circus (1926)	6.00	18.00	42.00
...& Uncle Walt (1927)	6.00	18.00	42.00
...Out West (1928)	6.00	18.00	42.00
Hardback Editions...	9.00	27.00	62.00

SKELETON HAND (...In Secrets of the Supernatural)
Sept-Oct, 1952 - No. 6, July-Aug, 1953
American Comics Group (B&M Dist. Co.)

	Good	Fine	N-Mint
1	10.00	30.00	70.00
2	6.50	19.50	45.00
3-6	5.00	15.00	35.00

SKI PARTY (See Movie Classics)

SKIPPY'S OWN BOOK OF COMICS (See Popular Comics)
1934 (52 pages) (Giveaway)
No publisher listed

	Good	Fine	N-Mint
nn-(Rare)-Strip-r by Percy Crosby	220.00	660.00	1540.00

Published by Max C. Gaines for Phillip's Dental Magnesia to be advertised on the Skippy Radio Show and given away with the purchase of a tube of Phillip's Tooth Paste. This is the first four-color comic book of reprints about one character.

SKULL, THE SLAYER
August, 1975 - No. 8, Nov, 1976
Marvel Comics Group

	Good	Fine	N-Mint
1-Origin; Gil Kane-c		.40	.80
2-8: 2-Gil Kane-c. 8-Kirby-c		.30	.60

SKY BLAZERS (Radio)
Sept, 1940 - No. 2, Nov, 1940
Hawley Publications

	Good	Fine	N-Mint
1-Sky Pirates, Ace Archer, Flying Aces begin	17.00	51.00	120.00
2	13.00	40.00	90.00

SKY KING "RUNAWAY TRAIN" (TV)
1964 (16 pages) (regular size)
National Biscuit Co.

	Good	Fine	N-Mint
	1.30	4.00	9.00

SKYMAN (See Big Shot & Sparky Watts)
Fall?, 1941 - No. 2, 1941; No. 3, 1948 - No. 4, 1948
Columbia Comics Group

	Good	Fine	N-Mint
1-Origin Skyman, The Face, Sparky Watts app.; Whitney-a; 3rd story r-/Big Shot #1	30.00	90.00	210.00
2 (1941)-Yankee Doodle	17.00	51.00	120.00
3,4 (1948)	10.00	30.00	70.00

SKY PILOT
No. 10, 1950(nd) - No. 11, Apr-May, 1951 (Saunders painted-c)
Ziff-Davis Publ. Co.

	Good	Fine	N-Mint
10,11-Frank Borth-a	4.00	12.00	28.00

SKY RANGER (See Johnny Law...)

SKYROCKET
1944
Harry 'A' Chesler

	Good	Fine	N-Mint
nn-Alias the Dragon, Dr. Vampire, Skyrocket app.	8.00	24.00	56.00

SKY SHERIFF (Breeze Lawson...) (Also see Exposed)
Summer, 1948
D. S. Publishing Co.

	Good	Fine	N-Mint
1-Edmond Good-a	5.00	15.00	35.00

SKY WOLF (Also see Airboy)
Mar., 1988 - No. 3, May?, 1988 ($1.75, color, limited series)
Eclipse Comics

	Good	Fine	N-Mint
1-3	.30	.90	1.80

SLAINE, THE BERSERKER
July, 1987 - Present ($1.25-$1.50, color)
Quality Comics

	Good	Fine	N-Mint
1-13,16	.25	.75	1.50
14/15-two issue #s in one	.25	.75	1.50

SLAM BANG COMICS (Western Desperado #8)
March, 1940 - No. 7, Sept, 1940
Fawcett Publications

	Good	Fine	N-Mint
1-Diamond Jack, Mark Swift & The Time Retarder, Lee Granger, Jungle King begin	50.00	150.00	350.00
2	24.00	72.00	170.00
3	21.00	62.00	146.00
4-7: 7-Bondage-c	18.00	54.00	125.00

SLAM BANG COMICS
nd
Post Cereal Giveaway

	Good	Fine	N-Mint
9-Dynamic Man, Echo, Mr. E, Yankee Boy app.	1.70	5.00	12.00

SLAPSTICK COMICS
nd (1946?) (36 pages)

SLAPSTICK COMICS (continued)

Comic Magazines Distributors	Good	Fine	N-Mint
nn-Firetop feature; Post-a(2)	5.70	17.00	40.00

SLASH-D DOUBLECROSS
1950 (132 pgs.) (pocket size)
St. John Publishing Co.

Western comics	6.50	19.50	45.00

SLASH MARAUD
Nov., 1987 - No. 6, April, 1988 ($1.75, mini-series)
DC Comics

1-6	.35	1.00	2.00

SLAUGHTERMAN (See Primer #1 for 1st app.)
Feb., 1983 - No. 2, 1983 (B&W)
Comico

1	.40	1.25	2.50
2	.60	1.75	3.50

SLAVE GIRL COMICS (See Malu. . . & White Princess of/Jungle #2)
Feb., 1949 - No. 2, Apr, 1949 (52 pgs.)
Avon Periodicals

1-Larsen c/a	50.00	150.00	350.00
2-Larsen-a	35.00	105.00	245.00

SLEDGE HAMMER (TV)
Feb., 1988 - No. 2, Mar., 1988 ($1.00, color)
Marvel Comics

1,2		.50	1.00

SLEEPING BEAUTY (See Dell Giants, 4-Color #973,984, Movie Comics)

SLICK CHICK COMICS
1947(nd) - No. 3, 1947(nd)
Leader Enterprises

1	5.00	15.00	35.00
2,3	3.50	10.50	24.00

SLIM MORGAN (See Wisco)

SLUGGER (of the Little Wise Guys)
April, 1956
Lev Gleason Publications

1-Biro-c	1.70	5.00	12.00

SMASH COMICS (Lady Luck #86 on)
Aug, 1939 - No. 85, Oct, 1949
Quality Comics Group

1-Origin Hugh Hazard & His Iron Man, Bozo the Robot, Espionage, Starring Black X by Eisner, & Invisible Justice; Chic Carter & Wings Wendall begin	65.00	195.00	455.00
2-The Lone Star Rider app; Invisible Hood gains power of invisibility	30.00	90.00	210.00
3-Captain Cook & John Law begin	21.00	62.00	146.00
4,5: 4-Flash Fulton begins	19.00	57.00	132.00
6-12: 12-One pg. Fine-a	15.00	45.00	105.00
13-Magno begins; last Eisner issue; The Ray app. in full page ad; The Purple Trio begins	15.00	45.00	105.00
14-Intro. The Ray by Lou Fine & others	110.00	330.00	770.00
15,16	55.00	165.00	385.00
17-Wun Cloo becomes plastic super-hero by Jack Cole (9-months before Plastic Man)	55.00	165.00	385.00
18-Midnight by Jack Cole begins (origin)	65.00	195.00	455.00
19-22: Last Fine Ray; The Jester begins-#22	36.00	108.00	250.00
23,24: 24-The Sword app.; last Chic Carter; Wings Wendall dons new costume #24,25	28.00	84.00	195.00
25-Origin Wildfire	33.00	100.00	230.00

	Good	Fine	N-Mint
26-30: 28-Midnight-c begin	24.00	72.00	170.00
31,32,34: Ray by Rudy Palais; also #33	19.00	57.00	132.00
33-Origin The Marksman	23.00	70.00	160.00
35-37	19.00	57.00	132.00
38-The Yankee Eagle begins; last Midnight by Jack Cole			
	19.00	57.00	132.00
39,40-Last Ray issue	14.50	43.50	100.00
41,43-50	6.65	20.00	46.00
42-Lady Luck begins by Klaus Nordling	9.50	28.50	65.00
51-60	6.00	18.00	42.00
61-70	5.00	15.00	35.00
71-85	4.65	14.00	32.00

NOTE: *Cole* a-17-38, 68, 69, 72, 73, 78, 80, 83, 85; c-38, 60-62, 69, 75, 80. *Crandall* a-(Ray)-23-29, 35-38; c-36, 39, 40, 43, 44, 46. *Fine* a(Ray)-14, 15, 16(w/Tuska). 17-22. *Fuje* Ray-30. *Gil Fox* a-6-7, 9, 11-13. *Guardineer* a-(The Marksman)-39-7, 49, 52. *Gustavson* a-4-7, 9, 11-13 (The Jester)-22-46; (Magno)-13-21; (Midnight)-39(*Cole* inks), 49, 52, 63-65. *Kotzky* a-(Espionage)-33-38; c-45, 47. *Nordling* a-49, 52, 63-65. *Powell* a-11,12, (Abdul the Arab)-13-24.

SMASH HIT SPORTS COMICS
Jan, 1949
Essankay Publications

V2#1-L.B. Cole c/a	5.50	16.50	38.00

S'MATTER POP?
1917 (44 pgs.; B&W; 10x14''; cardboard covers)
Saalfield Publ. Co.

By Charlie Payne; ½ in full color; pages printed on one side	7.00	21.00	50.00

SMILE COMICS (Also see Gay Comics, Tickle, & Whee)
1955 (52 pages; 5x7¼'') (7 cents)
Modern Store Publ.

1	.50	1.50	3.00

SMILEY BURNETTE WESTERN (See Six Gun Heroes)
March, 1950 - No. 4, Oct, 1950 (All photo-c)
Fawcett Publications

1	14.00	42.00	100.00
2-4	10.00	30.00	70.00

SMILIN' JACK (See Popular Comics, Super Book #1,2,7,19 & Super)
No. 5, 1940 - No. 8, Oct-Dec, 1949
Dell Publishing Co.

4-Color 5	38.00	115.00	265.00
4-Color 10 (1940)	35.00	105.00	245.00
Large Feature Comic 12,14,25 (1941)	25.00	75.00	175.00
4-Color 4 (1942)	28.00	84.00	195.00
4-Color 14 (1943)	23.00	70.00	160.00
4-Color 36,58 (1943-44)	13.00	40.00	90.00
4-Color 80 (1945)	11.00	32.00	76.00
4-Color 149 (1947)	8.00	24.00	56.00
1 (1-3/48)	8.00	24.00	56.00
2	4.65	14.00	32.00
3-8 (10-12/49)	3.50	10.50	24.00
Popped Wheat Giveaway(1947)-1938 reprints; 16 pgs. in full color			
	.80	2.40	4.80
Shoe Store Giveaway-1938 reprints; 16 pgs.	2.65	8.00	18.00
Sparked Wheat Giveaway(1942)-16 pgs. in full color			
	2.30	7.00	16.00

SMILING SPOOK SPUNKY (See Spunky)

SMITTY (See Treasure Box of Famous Comics)
1928 - 1933 (B&W newspaper strip reprints)
(cardboard covers; 9½x9½'', 52 pgs.; 7x8¼'', 36 pgs.)
Cupples & Leon Co.

Slave Girl Comics #1, © AVON

Smash Comics #8, © QUA

Smilin' Jack #8, © N.Y. News Synd.

Smitty #3 (8-10/48), © N.Y. News Synd.   Snappy Comics #1, © PRIZE   Snooper And Blabber Detectives #3, © Hanna-Barbera

	Good	Fine	N-Mint
SMITTY (continued)			
1928-(96pgs. 7x8¾")	10.00	30.00	70.00
1928-(Softcover, 36pgs., nn)	11.50	34.00	80.00
1929-At the Ball Game, 1930-The Flying Office Boy, 1931-The Jockey,			
1932-In the North Woods....each....	8.00	24.00	56.00
1933-At Military School	8.00	24.00	56.00
Mid-1930s issue (reprint of 1928 Treasure Box issue)-36 pgs.;			
7x8¾"	6.50	19.50	45.00
Hardback Editions (100 pgs., 7x8¼") with dust jacket			
each....	13.00	40.00	90.00

SMITTY (See Popular Comics, Super Book #2,4 & Super Comics)
No. 11, 1940 - No. 7, Aug-Oct, 1949; Apr, 1958
Dell Publishing Co.

	Good	Fine	N-Mint
4-Color 11 (1940)	21.50	65.00	150.00
Large Feature Comic 26 (1941)	14.00	42.00	100.00
4-Color 6 (1942)	12.00	36.00	84.00
4-Color 32 (1943)	10.00	30.00	70.00
4-Color 65 (1945)	8.00	24.00	56.00
4-Color 99 (1946)	6.50	19.50	45.00
4-Color 138 (1947)	5.70	17.00	40.00
1 (11-1/47-48)	5.70	17.00	40.00
2	3.00	9.00	21.00
3,4 (1949)	2.00	6.00	14.00
5-7	1.50	4.50	10.00
4-Color 909	1.50	4.50	10.00

SMOKEY BEAR (TV) (See March Of Comics #362,372,383,407)
Feb, 1970 - No. 13, Mar, 1973
Gold Key

1	.70	2.00	4.00
2-13	.45	1.25	2.50

SMOKEY STOVER (See Popular Comics, Super Book #5,17,29 & Super Comics)

SMOKEY STOVER
No. 7, 1942 - No. 827, Aug, 1957
Dell Publishing Co.

4-Color 7 (1942)-Reprints	20.00	60.00	140.00
4-Color 35 (1943)	11.00	32.00	75.00
4-Color 64 (1944)	8.00	24.00	56.00
4-Color 229 (1949)	2.65	8.00	18.00
4-Color 730,827	1.70	5.00	12.00
General Motors giveaway (1953)	3.00	9.00	21.00
National Fire Protection giveaway('53 & '54)-16 pgs., paper-c			
	3.00	9.00	21.00

SMOKEY THE BEAR (See Forest Fire for 1st app.)
No. 653, 10/55 - No. 1214, 8/61 (See March of Comics #234)
Dell Publishing Co.

4-Color 653	2.65	8.00	18.00
4-Color 708,754,818,932	2.00	6.00	14.00
4-Color 1016,1119,1214	1.50	4.50	10.00
True Story of..., The('59)-U.S. Forest Service giveaway-Publ. by			
Western Printing Co. (reprinted in '64 & '69)-Reprints 1st 16 pgs.			
of 4-Color 932	.85	2.50	6.00

SMOKY (See Movie Classics)

SMURFS (TV)
Dec, 1982 (No month given) - No. 3, Feb, 1983
Marvel Comics Group

1-3		.30	.60
...Treasury Edition 1(64pgs.)-r/#1-3	.40	1.25	2.50

SNAFU (Magazine)
Nov, 1955 - V2#2, Mar, 1956 (B&W)
Atlas Comics (RCM)

V1#1-Heath/Severin-a	4.65	14.00	32.00
V2#1,2-Severin-a	3.00	9.00	21.00

SNAGGLEPUSS (TV)(See Spotlight #4)
Oct, 1962 - No. 4, Sept, 1963 (Hanna-Barbera)
Gold Key

	Good	Fine	N-Mint
1	2.30	7.00	16.00
2-4	1.50	4.50	10.00

SNAP (Jest #10?)
1944
Harry 'A' Chesler

9-Manhunter, The Voice	5.00	15.00	35.00

SNAPPY COMICS
1945
Cima Publ. Co. (Prize Publ.)

1-Airmale app.	3.50	10.50	24.00

SNARKY PARKER (See Life with...)

SNIFFY THE PUP
No. 5, Nov, 1949 - No. 18, Sept, 1953
Standard Publications (Animated Cartoons)

5-Two Frazetta text illos	3.50	10.50	24.00
6-10	1.00	3.00	7.00
11-18	.55	1.65	4.00

SNOOPER AND BLABBER DETECTIVES (TV) (See Whitman Comic Books)
Nov, 1962 - No. 3, May, 1963 (Hanna-Barbera)
Gold Key

1	2.30	7.00	16.00
2,3	1.70	5.00	12.00

SNOW FOR CHRISTMAS
1957 (16 pages) (Giveaway)
W. T. Grant Co.

	1.20	3.50	7.00

SNOW WHITE (See Christmas With..., 4-Color #49,227,382, Mickey Mouse Mag., & Movie Comics)

SNOW WHITE AND THE SEVEN DWARFS
1952 (32 pgs.; 5x7¼", soft-c) (Disney)
Bendix Washing Machines

	5.00	15.00	35.00

SNOW WHITE AND THE SEVEN DWARFS
April, 1982 (60 cent cover price)
Whitman Publications

nn-r/4-Color #49		.30	.60

SNOW WHITE AND THE 7 DWARFS IN "MILKY WAY"
1955 (16 pgs., 5x7¼", soft-c) (Disney premium)
American Dairy Association

	5.00	15.00	35.00

SNOW WHITE AND THE SEVEN DWARFS
1957 (small size)
Promotional Publ. Co.

	2.75	8.00	19.00

SNOW WHITE AND THE SEVEN DWARFS
1958 (16 pgs, 5x7¼", soft-c) (Disney premium)
Western Printing Co.

"Mystery of the Missing Magic"	3.50	10.50	24.00

SOAP OPERA LOVE
Feb, 1983 - No. 3, June, 1983
Charlton Comics

1-3		.25	.50

SOAP OPERA ROMANCES
July, 1982 - No. 5, March, 1983

SOAP OPERA ROMANCES (continued)
Charlton Comics   **Good Fine N-Mint**
1-5-Nurse Betsy Crane-r   .25   .50

SOJOURN ($1.50)
9/77 - No. 2, 1978 (Full tabloid size) (Color & B&W)
White Cliffs Publ. Co.

1-Tor by Kubert, Eagle by Severin, E. V. Race, Private Investigator
 by Doug Wildey, T. C. Mars by S. Aragones begin plus other
 strips   .30   .80   1.60
2   .30   .80   1.60

SOLARMAN
Jan, 1989 - Present ($1.00, color)
Marvel Comics
1   .50   1.00

SOLDIER & MARINE COMICS (Fightin' Army #16 on)
No. 11, 12/54 - No. 15, 8/55; V2No.9, V2No.11
Charlton Comics (Toby Press of Conn. V1No.11)
V1#11 (12/54)   1.00   3.00   7.00
V1#12(2/55)-15   .50   1.50   3.50
V2#9(Formerly Never Again; Jerry Drummer V2#10 on)
                                              .50   1.50   3.50
NOTE: *Bob Powell a-11.*

SOLDIER COMICS
Jan, 1952 - No. 11, Sept, 1953
Fawcett Publications
1   3.00   9.00   21.00
2   1.50   4.50   10.00
3-5   1.35   4.00   9.00
6,7,9-11   .85   2.50   6.00
8-Illo. in POP   2.00   6.00   14.00

SOLDIERS OF FORTUNE
Feb-Mar, 1951 - No. 13, Feb-Mar, 1953
American Comics Group (Creston Publ. Corp.)
1-Capt. Crossbones by Shelly, Ace Carter, Lance Larson begin
                                             7.00   21.00   50.00
2   4.65   14.00   32.00
3-10: 6-Bondage-c   3.50   10.50   24.00
11-13 (War format)   1.00   3.00   7.00
NOTE: *Shelly a-1-3, 5. Whitney a-6, 8-11, 13; c-1-3, 5, 6. Most issues are 52 pages.*

SOLDIERS OF FREEDOM
1987 - Present? ($1.75, color)
Americomics
1   .30   .90   1.80

SOLO AVENGERS
Dec, 1987 - Present
Marvel Comics
1   .35   1.10   2.20
2-5   .25   .70   1.40
6-15: 11-Intro Bobcat   .50   1.00

SOLO EX-MUTANTS
Jan., 1988 - Present ($1.95, B&W)
Eternity Comics
1-5   .35   1.00   2.00

SOLOMON AND SHEBA (See 4-Color #1070)

SOLOMON KANE
Sept, 1985 - No. 6, Mar, 1986 (mini-series)
Marvel Comics Group
1   .50   1.00
2-6: 3,4-Williamson-a   .45   .90

SOMERSET HOLMES (See Eclipse Graphic Album Series)
9/83 - No. 4, 4/84; No. 5, 11/84 - No. 6, 12/84 ($1.50; Baxter)
Pacific Comics/Eclipse Comics No. 5, 6   **Good Fine N-Mint**
1-B. Anderson c/a; Cliff Hanger by Williamson begins, ends #6
                                              .40   1.25   2.50
2-6   .35   1.00   2.00

SONG OF THE SOUTH (See 4-Color #693 & Brer Rabbit)

SONIC DISRUPTORS
12/87 - No. 7, 7/88 ($1.75, limited series; mature readers)
DC Comics
1-7   .30   .90   1.80

SON OF AMBUSH BUG (Also see Ambush Bug)
July, 1986 - No. 6, Dec, 1986
DC Comics
1-Giffen c/a(p) in all   .50   1.00
2-6   .40   .80

SON OF BLACK BEAUTY (See 4-Color #510,566)

SON OF FLUBBER (See Movie Comics)

SON OF SATAN (Also see Marvel Spotlight #12)
Dec, 1975 - No. 8, Feb, 1977
Marvel Comics Group
1-Mooney-a   .40   .80
2-Origin The Possessor   .25   .50
3-8: 4,5-Russell-a(p). 8-Heath-a   .20   .40

SON OF SINBAD (Also see Daring Adventures, Abbott & Costello)
February, 1950
St. John Publishing Co.
1-Kubert c/a   26.00   78.00 180.00

SON OF TOMAHAWK (See Tomahawk)

SON OF VULCAN (Mysteries of Unexplored Worlds #1-48; Thunderbolt, V3#51 on)
Nov, 1965 - V2No.50, Jan, 1966
Charlton Comics
49,50   .50   1.50   3.00

SONS OF KATIE ELDER (See Movie Classics)

SORCERY (See Chilling Adventures in... & Red Circle...)

SORORITY SECRETS
July, 1954
Toby Press
1   2.30   7.00   16.00

SOUPY SALES COMIC BOOK (TV)(The Official...)
1965
Archie Publications
1   5.00   15.00   35.00

SOUTHERN KNIGHTS, THE (Formerly Crusaders No. 1)
No. 2, 1983 - No. 7, 9/84; No. 8, 1984 - Present ($1.75, B&W)
Guild Publ./Fictioneer Books(Comics Interview) No. 8 on
2-Magazine size   1.70   5.00   10.00
3   .85   2.50   5.00
4,5   .70   2.00   4.00
6-10   .50   1.50   3.00
11-15   .40   1.25   2.50
16-20   .35   1.00   2.00
21-30   .30   .90   1.80
Graphic Novels #1-4   .85   2.50   5.00

SPACE ACE
1952
Magazine Enterprises

Soldier Comics #8, © FAW   *Son Of Sinbad #1, © STJ*   *The Southern Knights #10, © Fictioneer Books*

Space Busters #1, © Z-D   Space Family Robinson #5, © GK   Space Man #8, © DELL

	Good	Fine	N-Mint
SPACE ACE (continued)			
5(A-1 61)-Guardineer-a	15.00	45.00	105.00
SPACE ACTION			
June, 1952 - No. 3, Oct, 1952			
Ace Magazines (Junior Books)			
1	23.00	70.00	160.00
2,3	19.00	57.00	132.00
SPACE ADVENTURES (War At Sea #22 on)			
7/52 - No. 21, 5/56; No. 23, 5/58 - No. 59, 11/64; V3/60,			
10/67; V1/2, 7/68 - V1No.8, 7/69; No. 9, 5/78 - No. 13, 3/79			
Capitol Stories/Charlton Comics			
1	12.00	36.00	84.00
2	6.00	18.00	42.00
3-5	5.00	15.00	35.00
6,8,9	4.30	13.00	30.00
7-Transvestism story	6.00	18.00	42.00
10-Ditko c/a	17.00	51.00	120.00
11-Ditko c/a(2)	17.00	51.00	120.00
12-Ditko-c (Classic)	20.00	60.00	140.00
13-(Fox-r, 10-11/54); Blue Beetle story	5.70	17.00	40.00
14-Blue Beetle story (Fox-r, 12-1/54-55)	4.65	14.00	32.00
15,17-19: 15-18-Rocky Jones app.(TV)	4.00	12.00	28.00
16-Krigstein	9.50	28.50	65.00
20-Reprints Fawcett's ''Destination Moon''	11.00	32.00	76.00
21-(8/56) (no #22)	5.00	15.00	35.00
23-(5/58; formerly Nyoka, The Jungle Girl)-Reprints Fawcett's			
''Destination Moon''	9.50	28.50	65.00
24,25,31,32-Ditko-a	6.50	19.50	45.00
26,27-Ditko-a(4) each	8.00	24.00	56.00
28-30	2.00	6.00	14.00
33-1st app./origin Captain Atom by Ditko (3/60)			
	13.00	40.00	90.00
34-40,42-All Captain Atom by Ditko	6.50	19.50	45.00
41,43,46-59	.70	2.00	4.00
44,45-Mercury Man in each	.70	2.00	4.00
V3#60(10/67)-Origin Paul Mann & The Saucers From the Future			
	.35	1.00	2.00
2-8('68-'69)-All Ditko-a; Aparo-a #2	.60	1.20	
9-13('78-'79)-Capt. Atom-r/Space Advs. by Ditko; 9-Origin-r			
	.40	.80	
NOTE: Aparo a-V3#60. Ditko c-12, 31-42. Shuster a-11.			
SPACE BUSTERS			
Spring/52 - No. 3, Fall/52 (Painted covers by Norman Saunders)			
Ziff-Davis Publ. Co.			
1-Krigstein-a	30.00	90.00	210.00
2,3: 2-Kinstler-a(2pgs.); Krigstein-a(3)	24.00	72.00	170.00
NOTE: Anderson a-2. Bondage c-2.			
SPACE CADET (See Tom Corbett,...)			
SPACE COMICS			
No. 4, Mar-Apr, 1954 - No. 5, May-June, 1954			
Avon Periodicals			
4,5-Space Mouse, Peter Rabbit, Super Pup, & Merry Mouse app.			
	2.30	7.00	16.00
I.W. Reprint #8 (nd)-Space Mouse-r	.50	1.50	3.00
SPACE DETECTIVE			
July, 1951 - No. 4, July, 1952			
Avon Periodicals			
1-Rod Hathway, Space Det. begins, ends #4; Wood c/a(3)-23 pgs.;			
''Opium Smugglers of Venus'' drug story; Lucky Dale-r/Saint #4			
	62.00	185.00	435.00
2-Tales from the Shadow Squad story; Wood/Orlando-c; Wood			
inside layouts	30.00	90.00	210.00
3-Kinstler-c	19.00	57.00	132.00

	Good	Fine	N-Mint
4-Kinstler-a	19.00	57.00	132.00
I.W. Reprint #1(Reprints #2), 8(Reprints cover #1 & part Famous			
Funnies #191)	1.35	4.00	8.00
I.W. Reprint #9	1.35	4.00	8.00
SPACE EXPLORER (See March of Comics #202)			
SPACE FAMILY ROBINSON (TV)(...Lost in Space #15 on)(Lost in			
Space #37 on)			
Dec, 1962 - No. 36, Oct, 1969 (All painted covers)			
Gold Key			
1-(low distr.); Spiegle-a in all	7.00	21.00	50.00
2(3/63)-Became Lost in Space	3.70	11.00	26.00
3-10: 6-Captain Venture begins	2.00	6.00	14.00
11-20	1.15	3.50	8.00
21-36	.70	2.00	5.00
SPACE FAMILY ROBINSON (See March of Comics #320,328,352,404,414)			
SPACE GHOST (TV) (Also see Golden Comics Digest #2 & Hanna			
Barbera Super TV Heroes)			
March, 1967 (Hanna-Barbera) (TV debut was 9/10/66)			
Gold Key			
1 (10199-703)-Spiegle-a	8.00	24.00	55.00
SPACE GHOST (TV) (Graphic Novel)			
12/87 (One Shot) (52pgs.; deluxe format; $3.50)			
Comico			
1-(Hanna-Barbera)-Rude c/a(p)	.85	2.50	5.00
SPACE GIANTS, THE			
1979 (One shot, $1.00, B&W, TV)			
FBN Publications			
1-Based on Japanese TV series	3.15	9.50	22.00
SPACE KAT-ETS (in 3-D)			
Dec, 1953 (25 cents)			
Power Publishing Co.			
1	18.00	54.00	125.00
SPACEMAN (Speed Carter...)			
Sept, 1953 - No. 6, July, 1954			
Atlas Comics (CnPC)			
1	16.00	48.00	110.00
2	11.00	32.00	75.00
3-6	8.50	25.50	60.00
NOTE: Everett c-1, 3. Maneely a-1-6?; c-6. Tuska a-5(3).			
SPACE MAN			
No. 1253, 1-3/62 - No. 8, 3-5/64; No. 9, 7/72 - No. 10, 10/72			
Dell Publishing Co.			
4-Color 1253 (1-3/62)	3.00	9.00	21.00
2,3	1.50	4.50	10.00
4-8	.85	2.50	6.00
9-Reprints #1253	.40	1.25	2.80
10-Reprints #2	.35	1.00	2.00
SPACE MOUSE (Also see Space Comics)			
April, 1953 - No. 5, Apr-May, 1954			
Avon Periodicals			
1	3.70	11.00	26.00
2	2.15	6.50	15.00
3-5	1.50	4.50	10.00
SPACE MOUSE (Walter Lantz... #1; see Comic Album #17)			
No. 1132, 8-10/60 - No. 5, 11/63 (Walter Lantz)			
Dell Publishing Co./Gold Key			
4-Color 1132,1244	1.15	3.50	8.00
1(11/62)(G.K.)	1.15	3.50	8.00
2-5	.85	2.50	6.00

SPACE MYSTERIES
1964 (Reprints)
I.W. Enterprises

	Good	Fine	N-Mint
1-r-/Journey Into Unknown Worlds #4 w/new-c	.50	1.50	3.00
8,9	.50	1.50	3.00

SPACE: 1999 (TV)
Nov, 1975 - No. 7, Nov, 1976
Charlton Comics

	Good	Fine	N-Mint
1-Staton-c/a; origin Moonbase Alpha		.60	1.20
2-Staton-a		.50	1.00
3-6: All byrne-a; c-5	.50	1.50	3.00
7		.50	1.00

SPACE: 1999 (TV)(Magazine)
Nov, 1975 - No. 8, Nov, 1976 (B&W)
Charlton Comics

1-Origin Moonbase Alpha; Morrow c/a	.50	1.50	3.00
2,3-Morrow c/a	.30	.90	1.80
4-8 (#7 shows #6 on inside)	.30	.80	1.60

SPACE PATROL (TV)
Summer/52 - No. 2, Oct-Nov/52 (Painted-c by Norman Saunders)
Ziff-Davis Publishing Co. (Approved Comics)

1-Krigstein-a	35.00	105.00	245.00
2-Krigstein-a	30.00	90.00	210.00
. . .'s Special Mission (8 pgs., B&W, Giveaway)	50.00	150.00	300.00

SPACE PIRATES (See Archie Giant Series #533)

SPACE SQUADRON (Space Worlds #6)
June, 1951 - No. 5, Feb, 1952
Marvel/Atlas Comics (ACI)

1	18.00	54.00	125.00
2	14.00	42.00	104.00
3-5	11.50	34.00	80.00

SPACE THRILLERS
1954 (Giant) (25 cents)
Avon Periodicals

nn-(Scarce)-Robotmen of the Lost Planet; contains 3 rebound
  comics of The Saint & Strange Worlds. Contents could vary

	68.00	205.00	475.00

SPACE TRIP TO THE MOON (See Space Adventures #23)

SPACE WAR (Fightin' Five #28 on)
Oct, 1959 - No. 27, Mar, 1964; No. 28, Mar, 1978 - No. 34, 3/79
Charlton Comics

V1#1	5.00	15.00	35.00
2,3	2.15	6.50	15.00
4,5,8,10-Ditko c/a	7.00	21.00	50.00
6-Ditko a-c	5.70	17.00	40.00
7,9,11-15: Last 10 cent ish?	1.50	4.50	10.00
16-27	1.00	3.00	7.00
28,29,33,34-Ditko c/a(r)	2.65	8.00	18.00
30-Ditko c/a(r); Staton, Sutton/Wood-a	3.00	9.00	21.00
31-Ditko c/a; atom-blast-c	3.00	9.00	21.00
32-r-/Charlton Premiere V2#2	.30	.90	1.80

NOTE: *Sutton a-30, 33.*

SPACE WESTERN (Formerly Cowboy Western Comics; becomes
Cowboy Western Comics #46 on)
No. 40, Oct, 1952 - No. 45, Aug, 1953
Charlton Comics (Capitol Stories)

40-Intro Spurs Jackson & His Space Vigilantes			
	22.00	65.00	154.00
41,43-45	16.00	48.00	110.00
42-Atom bomb explosion-c	18.00	54.00	125.00

SPACE WORLDS (Space Squadron #1-5)
No. 6, April, 1952
Atlas Comics (Male)

	Good	Fine	N-Mint
6	9.00	27.00	62.00

SPANKY & ALFALFA & THE LITTLE RASCALS (See The Little Rascals)

SPANNER'S GALAXY
Dec, 1984 - No. 6, May, 1985 (mini-series)
DC Comics

1-Mandrake c/a begins		.50	1.00
2-6: 2-Intro sidekick Gadg		.40	.80

SPARKIE, RADIO PIXIE (Big John & Sparkie #4)
Winter, 1951 - No. 3, 1952 (Painted-c)
Ziff-Davis Publ. Co.

1	7.00	21.00	50.00
2,3	5.70	17.00	40.00

SPARKLE COMICS
Oct-Nov, 1948 - No. 33, Dec-Jan, 1953-54
United Features Syndicate

1-Li'l Abner, Nancy, Captain & the Kids	6.00	18.00	42.00
2	3.00	9.00	21.00
3-10	2.15	6.50	15.00
11-20	1.50	4.50	10.00
21-33	1.15	3.50	8.00

SPARKLE PLENTY (See 4-Color #215 & Harvey Com. Libr. #2)

SPARKLER COMICS (1st Series)
July, 1940 - No. 2, 1940
United Feature Comic Group

1-Jim Hardy	17.00	51.00	120.00
2-Frankie Doodle	12.00	36.00	84.00

SPARKLER COMICS (2nd Series)(Nancy & Sluggo #121 on)
July, 1941 - No. 120, Jan, 1955
United Features Syndicate

1-Origin Sparkman; Tarzan (by Hogarth in all issues), Captain &			
the Kids, Ella Cinders, Danny Dingle, Dynamite Dunn, Nancy,			
Abbie & Slats, Frankie Doodle, Broncho Bill begin; Sparkman			
c-#1-12	65.00	195.00	455.00
2	30.00	90.00	210.00
3,4	25.00	75.00	175.00
5-10: 9-Sparkman's new costume	20.00	60.00	140.00
11-13,15-20: 12-Sparkman new costume-color change. 19-1st Race			
Riley	17.00	51.00	120.00
14-Hogarth Tarzan-c	20.00	60.00	140.00
21-24,26,27,29,30: 22-Race Riley & the Commandos strips begin,			
ends #44	13.00	40.00	90.00
25,28,31,34,37,39-Tarzan-c by Hogarth	17.00	51.00	120.00
32,33,35,36,38,40	8.00	24.00	56.00
41,43,45,46,48,49	5.70	17.00	40.00
42,44,47,50-Tarzan-c	10.00	30.00	70.00
51,52,54-70: 57-Li'l Abner begins (not in #58); Fearless Fosdick			
app.-#58	4.00	12.00	28.00
53-Tarzan-c by Hogarth	8.50	25.50	60.00
71-80	3.50	10.50	24.00
81,82,84-90: 85-Li'l Abner ends. 86-Lingerie panels			
	2.65	8.00	18.00
83-Tarzan-c	4.65	14.00	32.00
91-96,98-99	2.30	7.00	16.00
97-Origin Casey Ruggles by Warren Tufts	4.65	14.00	32.00
100	2.85	8.50	20.00
101-107,109-112,114-120	1.70	5.00	12.00
108,113-Toth-a	5.00	15.00	35.00

SPARKLING LOVE
June, 1950; 1953

Space: 1999 #1 (comic version), © CC

Space Thrillers, © AVON

Sparkler Comics #2 (8/41), © UFS

Sparky Watts #1, © CCG

Special Marvel Edition #11, © MEG

Spectacular Features Magazine #3, © FOX

SPARKLING LOVE (continued)
Avon Periodicals/Realistic (1953)

	Good	Fine	N-Mint
1(Avon)-Kubert-a; photo-c	11.50	34.00	80.00
nn(1953)-Reprint; Kubert-a	5.00	15.00	35.00

SPARKLING STARS
June, 1944 - No. 33, March, 1948
Holyoke Publishing Co.

1-Hell's Angels, FBI, Boxie Weaver & Ali Baba begin			
	6.50	19.50	45.00
2	3.70	11.00	26.00
3-Actual FBI case photos & war photos	2.65	8.00	18.00
4-10: 7-X-mas-c	2.00	6.00	14.00
11-19: 13-Origin/1st app. Jungo The Man-Beast	1.70	5.00	12.00
20-Intro Fangs the Wolf Boy	2.00	6.00	14.00
21-29,32,33: 29-Bondage-c	1.70	5.00	12.00
31-Spanking panel; Sid Greene-a	2.00	6.00	14.00

SPARK MAN (See Sparkler Comics)
1945 (One Shot) (36 pages)
Frances M. McQueeny

1-Origin Spark Man; female torture story; cover redrawn from Sparkler No. 1	11.50	34.00	80.00

SPARKY WATTS (Also see Columbia Comics)
Nov?, 1942 - No. 10, 1949
Columbia Comic Corp.

1(1942)-Skyman & The Face app; Hitler-c	13.00	40.00	90.00
2(1943)	6.50	19.50	45.00
3(1944)	5.70	17.00	40.00
4(1944)-Origin	5.00	15.00	35.00
5(1947)-Skyman app.	4.00	12.00	28.00
6('47),7,8('48),9,10('49)	2.65	8.00	18.00

SPARTACUS (See 4-Color #1139)

SPECIAL AGENT (Steve Saunders...)
Dec, 1947 - No. 8, Sept, 1949
Parents' Magazine Institute (Commended Comics No. 2)

1-J. Edgar Hoover photo-c	4.00	12.00	28.00
2	2.00	6.00	14.00
3-8	1.50	4.50	10.00

SPECIAL COLLECTORS' EDITION
Dec, 1975 (No month given) (10¼x13½")
Marvel Comics Group

1-Kung Fu, Iron Fist & Sons of the Tiger	.30	.90	1.80

SPECIAL COMICS (Hangman #2 on)
Winter, 1941-42
MLJ Magazines

1-Origin The Boy Buddies (Shield & Wizard x-over); death of The Comet; origin The Hangman retold	90.00	270.00	630.00

SPECIAL DELIVERY
1951 (32 pgs.; B&W)
Post Hall Synd. (Giveaway)

Origin of Pogo, Swamp, etc.; 2 pg. biog. on Walt Kelly
(One copy sold in 1980 for $150.00)

SPECIAL EDITION (See Gorgo, Reptisaurus)

SPECIAL EDITION (U. S. Navy Giveaways)
1944 - 1945 (Regular comic format with wording simplified, 52pgs.)
National Periodical Publications

1-Action (1944)-reprints Action 80	70.00	210.00	490.00
2-Action (1944)-reprints Action 81	70.00	210.00	490.00
3-Superman (1944)-reprints Superman 33	70.00	210.00	490.00
4-Detective (1944)-reprints Det. 97	75.00	225.00	525.00
5-Superman (1945)-reprints Superman 34	70.00	210.00	490.00

	Good	Fine	N-Mint
6-Action (1945)-reprints Action 84	70.00	210.00	490.00

SPECIAL EDITION COMICS
1940 (Aug.) (One Shot, 68pgs.)
Fawcett Publications

1-1st book devoted entirely to Captain Marvel; C.C. Beck c/a; only app. of C. Marvel with belt buckle; C. Marvel appears with button-down flap, 1st story (came out before Captain Marvel #1)			
	260.00	780.00	1820.00

NOTE: Prices vary widely on this book. Since this book is all Captain Marvel stories, it
is actually a pre-Captain Marvel #1. There is speculation that this book almost
became **Captain Marvel** #1. After **Special Edition** was published, there was an editor
change at Fawcett. The new editor commissioned Kirby to do a nn **Captain Marvel**
book early in 1941. This book was followed by a 2nd book several months later. This
2nd book was advertised as a #3 (making Special Edition the #1, & the nn issue the
#2). However, the 2nd book did come out as a #2.

SPECIAL EDITION X-MEN
Feb, 1983 (One Shot) (Baxter paper, $2.00)
Marvel Comics Group

1-r-/Giant-Size X-Men plus one new story	1.00	3.00	6.00

SPECIAL MARVEL EDITION (Master of Kung Fu #17 on)
Jan, 1971 - No. 16, Feb, 1974
Marvel Comics Group

1-Thor begins (r)		.35	.70
2-4-Last Thor (r); all Giants		.30	.60
5-14: Sgt. Fury-r; 11 r/Sgt. Fury #13 (Captain America)			
		.30	.60
15-Master of Kung Fu begins; Starlin-a; origin & 1st app. Nayland Smith & Dr. Petric		.60	1.20
16-1st app. Midnight; Starlin-a		.60	1.20

SPECIAL MISSIONS (See G.I. Joe...)

SPECIAL WAR SERIES (Attack V4#3 on?)
Aug, 1965 - No. 4, Nov, 1965
Charlton Comics

V4No.1-D-Day (See D-Day listing)	.35	1.00	2.00
2-Attack!	.25	.75	1.50
3-War & Attack	.25	.75	1.50
4-Judomaster	1.00	3.00	6.00

SPECTACULAR ADVENTURES (See Adventures)

SPECTACULAR FEATURE MAGAZINE, A (Formerly My Confessions)
(Spectacular Features Magazine #12)
No. 11, April, 1950
Fox Feature Syndicate

11-Samson & Delilah	12.00	36.00	84.00

SPECTACULAR FEATURES MAGAZINE (Formerly A Spectacular Feature Magazine)
No. 12, June, 1950 - No. 3, Aug, 1950
Fox Feature Syndicate

12-Iwo Jima; photo flag-c	12.00	36.00	84.00
3-Drugs/prostitution story	8.50	25.50	60.00

SPECTACULAR SPIDER-MAN, THE (See Marvel Treasury Edition and Marvel Special Edition)

SPECTACULAR SPIDER-MAN, THE (Magazine)
July, 1968 - No. 2, Nov, 1968 (35 cents)
Marvel Comics Group

1-(Black & White)	1.20	3.50	7.00
2-(Color)-Green Goblin app.	1.00	3.00	6.00

SPECTACULAR SPIDER-MAN, THE (Peter Parker. .#54-132,134)
Dec, 1976 - Present
Marvel Comics Group

1	1.35	4.00	8.00

THE SPECTACULAR SPIDER-MAN (cont'd)	Good	Fine	N-Mint
2-5	.70	2.00	4.00
6-10	.60	1.75	3.50
11-20	.50	1.50	3.00
21,24-26	.40	1.25	2.50
22,23-Moon Knight app.	.45	1.40	2.80
27-Miller's 1st Daredevil	1.70	5.00	10.00
28-Miller Daredevil (p)	1.35	4.00	8.00
29-57,59: 33-Origin Iguana	.35	1.00	2.00
58-Byrne a(p)	.50	1.50	3.00
60-Double size; origin retold with new facts revealed			
	.35	1.05	2.10
61-63,65-68,71-74	.25	.75	1.50
64-1st Cloak & Dagger app.	1.50	4.50	9.00
69,70-Cloak & Dagger app.	.75	2.25	4.50
75-Double size	.35	1.00	2.00
76-80	.25	.75	1.50
81,82-Punisher app.	1.00	3.00	6.00
83-Origin Punisher retold	1.15	3.50	7.00
84-93,97-99: 98-Intro The Spot	.25	.75	1.50
94-96-Cloak & Dagger app.	.25	.75	1.50
100-Double size	.35	1.00	2.00
101-130: 107-Death of Jean DeWolf. 111-Secret Wars II tie-in. 128-Black Cat new costume	.50	1.00	
131-Six part Kraven tie-in	.50	1.50	3.00
132-139: 139-Origin Tombstone	.25	.75	1.50
140-Punisher cameo app.	.25	.75	1.50
141-Punisher app.	.35	1.00	2.00
142-146: 143-Punisher app.	.50	1.00	
Annual 1 (12/79)	.25	.75	1.50
Annual 2 (8/80)-1st app. & origin Rapier	.25	.75	1.50
Annual 3 (11/81)-Last Manwolf	.25	.75	1.50
Annual 4 (11/84), 5 (10/85)	.25	.75	1.50
Annual 6 ('85), 7 (11/87)	.25	.75	1.50
Annual 8 ('88, $1.75)-Evolutionary War app.	.40	1.25	2.50

NOTE: **Austin** c-21. **Byrne** c(p)-17, 43, 58, 101, 102. **Giffen** a-120p. **Miller** c-46p, 48p, 50, 51p, 52p, 54p, 55, 56p, 57, 60. **Mooney** a-7i, 11i, 21p, 23p, 25p, 26p, 29-34p, 36p, 37p, 39i, 41, 42i, 49p, 50i, 51i, 53p, 54-57i, 59-66i, 68i, 71i, 73-79i, 81-83i, 85i, 87-99i, 102i, 125p, Annual 1i, 2p. **Nasser** c-37p. **Perez** c-10. **Simonson** c-54i.

SPECTACULAR STORIES MAGAZINE (Formerly A Star Presentation)
No. 4, July, 1950 - No. 3, Sept, 1950
Fox Feature Sydicate (Hero Books)

4-Sherlock Holmes	18.00	54.00	125.00
3-The St. Valentine's Day Massacre	11.00	32.00	75.00

SPECTRE, THE (See Adventure, More Fun, Showcase & Wrath Of . . .)
Nov-Dec, 1967 - No. 10, May-June, 1969
National Periodical Publications

1-Anderson c/a	1.85	5.50	11.00
2-5-Adams c/a; 3-Wildcat x-over	1.25	3.75	7.50
6-8,10: 7-Hourman app.	.75	2.25	4.50
9-Wrightson-a	.90	2.75	5.50

NOTE: **Anderson** inks-#6-8.

SPECTRE, THE
Apr, 1987 - Present ($1.00, new format)
DC Comics

1-Colan-a(p) begins; Kaluta-c	.35	1.10	2.25
2-10: 3-Kaluta-c. 10-Morrow-a	.25	.75	1.50
11-23		.60	1.25
Annual 1 ('88, $2.00)	.35	1.00	2.00

NOTE: **Art Adams** c-Annual #1. **Colan** a-1-6p. **Morrow** a-9-15.

SPEEDBALL (See Amazing Spider-Man Annual #12)
Oct., 1988 - Present (75 cents, color)
Marvel Comics

	Good	Fine	N-Mint
1-7: Ditko/Guice a-1-4; Ditko c-5	.40		.80

SPEED BUGGY (TV)(Also see Fun-In #12,15)
July, 1975 - No. 9, Nov, 1976 (Hanna-Barbera)
Charlton Comics

1-9		.25	.50

SPEED CARTER SPACEMAN (See Spaceman)

SPEED COMICS (New Speed)
Oct, 1939 - No. 44, 1-2/47 (No.14-16: pocket size, 100 pgs.)
Brookwood Publ./Speed Publ./Harvey Publications No. 14 on

1-Origin Shock Gibson; Ted Parrish, the Man with 1000 Faces begins; Powell-a	72.00	215.00	500.00
2-Powell-a	35.00	105.00	245.00
3	22.00	65.00	154.00
4-Powell-a	19.00	57.00	132.00
5	18.00	54.00	125.00
6-11: 7-Mars Mason begins, ends #11	15.00	45.00	105.00
12 (3/41; shows #11 in indicia)-The Wasp begins; Major Colt app. (Capt. Colt #12)	18.00	54.00	125.00
13-Intro. Captain Freedom & Young Defenders; Girl Commandos, Pat Parker, War Nurse begins; Major Colt app.	22.00	65.00	154.00
14-16 (100 pg. pocket size, 1941): 14-2nd Harvey comic (See Pocket). 15-Pat Parker dons costume, last in costume #23; no Girl Commandos	17.00	51.00	120.00
17-Black Cat begins (origin), r-/Pocket #1; not in #40,41	27.00	81.00	190.00
18-20	15.00	45.00	105.00
21,22,25-30: 26-Flag-c	13.00	40.00	90.00
23-Origin Girl Commandos	19.00	57.00	132.00
24-Pat Parker team-up with Girl Commandos	13.00	40.00	90.00
31-44: 38-Flag-c	10.00	30.00	70.00

NOTE: **Briefer** a-6, 7. **Kubert** a-7-11(Mars Mason), 37, 38, 42-44. **Powell** a-1, 2, 4-7, 28, 31, 44. **Schomburg** c-31, 32, 34-36. **Tuska** a-3, 6, 7. Bondage c-18, 35.

SPEED DEMONS (Formerly Frank Merriwell at Yale?; Submarine Attack #11 on)
No. 5, Feb, 1957 - No. 10, 1958
Charlton Comics

5-10	.50	1.50	3.00

SPEED RACER (See Racer-X)
July, 1987 - Present (#1-3: $1.50, 4 on: $1.75; color)
Now Comics

1	.60	1.75	3.50
1-2nd printing	.25	.75	1.50
2-10	.35	1.00	2.00
11-15	.30	.90	1.75
Special 1 (3/88, $2.00)-Origin Mach 5	.35	1.00	2.00
Special 2 ('88, $3.50)	.60	1.75	3.50

NOTE: **Steacy** c-3,4,11-14, Special #1.

SPEED SMITH THE HOT ROD KING
Spring, 1952
Ziff-Davis Publishing Co.

1-Saunders painted-c	7.00	21.00	50.00

SPEEDY GONZALES (See 4-Color #1084)

SPEEDY RABBIT
nd (1953); 1963
Realistic/I. W. Enterprises/Super Comics

nn (1953)	.85	2.50	6.00
I.W. Reprint #1 (2 versions w/diff. c/stories exist)	.30	.80	1.60
Super Reprint #14(1963)	.30	.80	1.60

The Spectacular Spider-Man #82, © MEG

The Spectre #1 (1967), © DC

Speed Comics #2, © HARV

Spellbinders #8, © Quality Comics

Spellbound #33, © MEG

Spider-Woman #1, © MEG

SPELLBINDERS
Dec, 1986 - No. 12, Jan, 1988 (52 pgs.)
Quality Comics

	Good	Fine	N-Mint
1-12: Nemesis The Warlock, Amadeus Wolf		.65	1.30

SPELLBOUND (See The Crusaders)

SPELLBOUND (Tales to Hold You... #1, Stories...)
3/52 - No. 23, 6/54; No. 24, 10/55 - No. 34, 6/57
Atlas Comics (ACI 1-15/Male 16-23/BPC 24-34)

1	14.00	42.00	100.00
2-Edgar A. Poe app.	8.00	24.00	56.00
3-5: 3-Cannibalism story	6.00	18.00	42.00
6-Krigstein-a	6.00	18.00	42.00
7-10	4.30	13.00	30.00
11-16,18-20	3.50	11.00	25.00
17-Krigstein-a	4.65	14.00	32.00
21-23-Last precode (6/54)	3.00	9.00	21.00
24,26-28,30,31,34	2.00	6.00	14.00
25-Orlando-a	2.00	6.00	14.00
29-Ditko-a	3.00	9.00	21.00
32,33-Torres-a	4.00	12.00	28.00

NOTE: *Colan* a-17. *Everett* a-2, 5, 7, 10, 16, 28, 31; c-2, 8, 9, 14, 17-19, 28, 30. *Forte/Fox* a-16. *Heath* a-2, 4, 8-10, 12, 14, 16; c-3, 4, 12, 16, 20, 21. *Infantino* a-15. *Maneely* a-7, 14, 27; c-10, 24, 31. *Mooney* a-5, 13, 18. *Mac Pakula* a-22, 32. *Post* a-8. *Powell* a-19, 20, 32. *Robinson* a-1. *Romita* a-24, 26, 27. *Severin* c-29. *Sinnott* a-8, 16.

SPELLBOUND
Jan, 1988 - No. 6, Apr, 1988 ($1.50, bi-weekly; Baxter)
Marvel Comics

1-5	.25	.75	1.50
6 (52 pgs., $2.25)	.35	1.10	2.25

SPENCER SPOOK (Formerly Giggle; see Advs. of...)
No. 100, Mar-Apr, 1955 - No. 101, May-June, 1955
American Comics Group

100,101	1.30	4.00	9.00

SPIDER-MAN (See Amazing..., Marvel Tales, Marvel Team-Up, Spidey Super Stories, Spectacular... & Web Of...)

SPIDER-MAN AND DAREDEVIL
March, 1984 (One-Shot; $2.00; deluxe paper)
Marvel Comics Group

1-r-/Spectacular Spider-Man #'s 26-28 by Frank Miller			
	.35	1.10	2.25

SPIDER-MAN AND HIS AMAZING FRIENDS
Dec, 1981 (One shot) (See Marvel Action Universe)
Marvel Comics Group

1-Adapted from TV cartoon show; Green Goblin app.; Spiegle-a(p)			
	.25	.75	1.50

SPIDER-MAN COMICS MAGAZINE
Jan, 1987 - No. 13, 1988 ($1.50, Digest-size)
Marvel Comics Group

1-13-Reprints	.25	.75	1.50

SPIDER-MAN GRAPHIC NOVEL
Summer, 1987 ($5.95)
Marvel Comics

1-Kingpin app.	1.00	3.00	5.95

SPIDER-MAN VS. WOLVERINE
Feb, 1987 (One-shot, 68 pgs.)
Marvel Comics Group

1-Williamson-i; intro Charlemagne	.90	2.75	5.50

SPIDER-WOMAN (Also see Marvel Spotlight #32)
April, 1978 - No. 50, June, 1983 (See Marvel Two-In-One)
Marvel Comics Group

	Good	Fine	N-Mint
1-New origin & mask added		.60	1.25
2-20: 20-Spider-Man app.		.60	1.25
21-36,39-49: 37-Photo-c; 47-New look		.60	1.25
37,38-New X-Men x-over; 37-1st Siryn; origin retold			
	.35	1.10	2.20
50-Double size; photo-c; Death of S-W		.60	1.25

NOTE: *Austin* a-37i. *Byrne* c-26p. *Layton* c-19. *Miller* c-32p.

SPIDEY SUPER STORIES (Spider-Man)
Oct, 1974 - No. 57, Mar, 1982 (35 cents) (no ads)
Marvel/Children's TV Workshop

1-(Stories simplified)		.30	.60
2-57		.25	.50

SPIKE AND TYKE (See M.G.M.'s...)

SPIN & MARTY (TV) (Walt Disney's)(See W. Disney Showcase #32)
No. 714, June, 1956 - No. 1082, Mar-May, 1960 (All photo-c)
Dell Publishing Co. (Mickey Mouse Club)

4-Color 714	3.70	11.00	26.00
4-Color 767,808	3.50	10.50	24.00
4-Color 826-Annette Funicello photo-c	7.00	21.00	50.00
5(3-5/58) - 9(6-8/59)	3.00	9.00	21.00
4-Color 1026,1082	3.00	9.00	21.00

SPINE-TINGLING TALES (Doctor Spektor Presents...)
May, 1975 - No. 4, Jan, 1976
Gold Key

1-1st Tragg r-/Mystery Comics Digest #3		.40	.80
2-Origin Ra-Ka-Tep r-/Mystery Comics Digest #1; Dr. Spektor #12			
		.40	.80
3-All Durak issue; (r)		.40	.80
4-Baron Tibor's 1st app. r-/Mystery Comics Digest #4			
		.40	.80

SPIRAL PATH, THE
7/86 - No. 2, 7/86 ($1.75, Baxter, color, mini-series)
Eclipse Comics

1,2	.35	1.00	2.00

SPIRAL ZONE
2/88 - No. 4, 5/88 ($1.00, mini-series)
DC Comics

1-4-Based on Tonka toys		.50	1.00

SPIRIT, THE (Weekly Comic Book)
6/2/40 - 10/5/52 (16 pgs.; 8 pgs.) (no cover) (in color)
(Distributed through various newspapers and other sources)
Will Eisner

NOTE: *Eisner* script, pencils/inks for the most part from 6/2/40-4/26/42; a few stories assisted by Jack Cole, Fine, Powell and Kotsky.

6/2/40(#1)-Origin; reprinted in Police #11; Lady Luck (Brenda Banks) by Chuck Mazoujian & Mr. Mystic by S. R. (Bob) Powell begin			
	60.00	180.00	420.00
6/9/40(#2)	26.00	78.00	180.00
6/16/40(#3)-Black Queen app. in Spirit	17.00	51.00	110.00
6/23/40(#4)-Mr. Mystic receives magical necklace			
	13.00	40.00	90.00
6/30/40(#5)	13.00	40.00	90.00
7/7/40(#6)-Black Queen app. in Spirit	13.00	40.00	90.00
7/14/40(#7)-8/4/40(#10)	10.00	30.50	70.00
8/11/40-9/22/40	9.00	27.00	62.00
9/29/40-Ellen drops engagement with Homer Creep			
	8.00	24.00	56.00
10/6/40-11/3/40	8.00	24.00	56.00
11/10/40-The Black Queen app.	8.00	24.00	56.00
11/17/40, 11/24/40	8.00	24.00	56.00
12/1/40-Ellen spanking by Spirit on cover & inside; Eisner-1st 3			

THE SPIRIT (continued)	Good	Fine	N-Mint
pgs., J. Cole rest	11.50	34.00	80.00
12/8/40-3/9/41	5.70	17.00	40.00
3/16/41-Intro. & 1st app. Silk Satin	10.00	30.00	70.00
3/23/41-6/1/41: 5/11/41-Last Lady Luck by Mazoujian; 5/18/41-Lady Luck by Nick Viscardi begins, ends 2/22/42			
	5.70	17.00	40.00
6/8/41-2nd app. Satin; Spirit learns Satin is also a British agent			
	8.50	25.50	60.00
6/15/41-1st app. Twilight	7.00	21.00	50.00
6/22/41-Hitler app. in Spirit	5.00	15.00	35.00
6/29/41-1/25/42,2/8/42	5.00	15.00	35.00
2/1/42-1st app. Duchess	7.00	21.00	50.00
2/15/42-4/26/42-Lady Luck by Klaus Nordling begins 3/1/42			
	5.00	15.00	35.00
5/3/42-8/16/42-Eisner/Fine/Quality staff assists on Spirit			
	4.00	12.00	24.00
8/23/42-Satin cover splash; Spirit by Eisner/Fine although signed by Fine	8.00	24.00	56.00
8/30/42,9/27/42-10/11/42,10/25/42-11/8/42-Eisner/Fine/Quality staff assists on Spirit	4.00	12.00	24.00
9/6/42-9/20/42,10/18/42-Fine/Belfi art on Spirit; scripts by Manly Wade Wellman	2.75	8.00	16.00
11/15/42-12/6/42,12/20/42,12/27/42,1/17/43-4/18/43,5/9/43-8/8/43-Wellman/Woolfolk scripts, Fine pencils, Quality staff inks			
	2.75	8.00	16.00
12/13/42,1/3/43,1/10/43,4/25/43,5/2/43-Eisner scripts/layouts; Fine pencils, Quality staff inks	3.35	10.00	20.00
8/15/43-Eisner script/layout; pencils/inks by Quality staff; Jack Cole-a	2.00	6.00	12.00
8/22/43-12/12/43-Wellman/Woolfolk scripts, Fine pencils, Quality staff inks; Mr. Mystic by Guardineer-10/10/43-10/24/43			
	2.00	6.00	12.00
12/19/43-8/13/44-Wellman/Woolfolk/Jack Cole scripts; Cole, Fine & Robin King-a; Last Mr. Mystic-5/14/44	1.70	5.00	10.00
8/22/44-12/16/45-Wellman/Woolfolk scripts; Fine art with unknown staff assists	1.70	5.00	10.00

NOTE: Scripts/layouts by Eisner, or Eisner/Nordling, Eisner/Mercer or Spranger/Eisner; inks by Eisner or Eisner/Spranger in issues 12/23/45-2/2/47.

	Good	Fine	N-Mint
12/23/45-1/6/46	4.00	12.00	28.00
1/13/46-Origin Spirit retold	6.00	18.00	42.00
1/20/46-1st postwar Satin app.	5.70	17.00	40.00
1/27/46-3/10/46: 3/3/46-Last Lady Luck by Nordling			
	4.00	12.00	28.00
3/17/46-Intro. & 1st app. Nylon	5.70	17.00	40.00
3/24/46,3/31/46,4/14/46	4.00	12.00	28.00
4/7/46-2nd app. Nylon	5.00	15.00	35.00
4/21/46-Intro. & 1st app. Mr. Carrion & His Buzzard Pet Julia			
	6.50	19.50	45.00
4/28/46-5/12/46,5/26/46-6/30/46: Lady Luck by Fred Schwab in issues 5/5/46-11/3/46	4.00	12.00	28.00
5/19/46-2nd app. Mr. Carrion	5.00	15.00	35.00
7/7/46-Intro. & 1st app. Dulcet Tone & Skinny	6.00	18.00	42.00
7/14/46-9/29/46	4.00	12.00	28.00
10/6/46-Intro. & 1st app. P'Gell	7.00	21.00	50.00
10/13/46-11/3/46,11/16/46-11/24/46	4.00	12.00	28.00
11/10/46-2nd app. P'Gell	5.00	15.00	35.00
12/1/46-3rd app. P'Gell	4.65	14.00	32.00
12/8/46-2/2/47	3.70	11.00	26.00

NOTE: Scripts, pencils/inks by Eisner except where noted in issues 2/9/47-12/19/48.

	Good	Fine	N-Mint
2/9/47-7/6/47: 6/8/47-Eisner self satire	3.70	11.00	26.00
7/13/47-"Hansel & Gretel" fairy tales	5.70	17.00	40.00
7/20/47-Li'L Abner, Daddy Warbucks, Dick Tracy, Fearless Fosdick parody; A-Bomb blast-c	5.70	17.00	40.00
7/27/47-9/14/47	3.70	11.00	26.00
9/21/47-Pearl Harbor flashback	3.70	11.00	26.00

	Good	Fine	N-Mint
9/28/47-1st mention of Flying Saucers in comics-3 months after 1st sighting in Idaho on 6/25/47	8.00	24.00	56.00
10/5/47-"Cinderella" fairy tales	5.70	17.00	40.00
10/12/47-11/30/47	3.70	11.00	26.00
12/7/47-Intro. & 1st app. Powder Pouf	6.00	18.00	42.00
12/14/47-12/28/47	3.70	11.00	26.00
1/4/48-2nd app. Powder Pouf	5.00	15.00	35.00
1/11/48-1st app. Sparrow Fallon; Powder Pouf app.			
	5.00	15.00	35.00
1/18/48-He-Man ad cover; satire issue	5.00	15.00	35.00
1/25/48-Intro. & 1st app. Castanet	5.70	17.00	40.00
2/1/48-2nd app. Castanet	4.00	12.00	28.00
2/8/48-3/7/48	3.70	11.00	26.00
3/14/48-Only app. Kretchma	4.00	12.00	28.00
3/21/48,3/28/48,4/11/48-4/25/48	3.70	11.00	26.00
4/4/48-Only app. Wild Rice	4.00	12.00	28.00
5/2/48-2nd app. Sparrow	3.70	11.00	26.00
5/9/48-6/27/48,7/11/48,7/18/48: 6/13/48-Television issue			
	3.70	11.00	26.00
7/4/48-Spirit by Andre Le Blanc	2.75	8.00	16.00
7/25/48-Ambrose Bierce's "The Thing" adaptation classic by Eisner/Grandenetti	8.00	24.00	56.00
8/1/48-8/15/48,8/29/48-9/12/48	3.70	11.00	26.00
8/22/48-Poe's "Fall of the House of Usher" classic by Eisner/Grandenetti	8.00	24.00	56.00
9/19/48-Only app. Lorelei	4.30	13.00	30.00
9/26/48-10/31/48	3.70	11.00	26.00
11/7/48-Only app. Plaster of Paris	5.00	15.00	35.00
11/14/48-12/19/48	3.70	11.00	26.00

NOTE: Scripts by Eisner or Feiffer or Eisner/Feiffer or Nordling. Art by Eisner with backgrounds by Eisner, Grandenetti, Le Blanc, Stallman, Nordling, Dixon and/or others in issues 12/26/48-4/1/51 except where noted.

	Good	Fine	N-Mint
12/26/48-Reprints some covers of 1948 with flashbacks			
	3.70	11.00	26.00
1/2/49-1/16/49	3.70	11.00	26.00
1/23/49,1/30/49-1st & 2nd app. Thorne	6.75	20.00	35.00
2/6/49-8/14/49	3.70	11.00	26.00
8/21/49,8/28/49-1st & 2nd app. Monica Veto	6.75	20.00	35.00
9/4/49,9/11/49	3.70	11.00	26.00
9/18/49-Love comic cover; has gag love comic ads on inside			
	7.35	22.00	38.00
9/25/49-Only app. Ice	4.65	14.00	32.00
10/2/49,10/9/49-Autumn News appears & dies in 10/9 ish.			
	4.65	14.00	32.00
10/16/49-11/27/49,12/18/49,12/25/49	3.70	11.00	26.00
12/4/49,12/11/49-1st & 2nd app. Flaxen	4.30	13.00	30.00
1/1/50-Flashbacks to all of the Spirit girls-Thorne, Ellen, Satin, & Monica	6.50	19.50	45.00
1/8/50-Intro. & 1st app. Sand Saref	9.00	27.00	62.00
1/15/50-2nd app. Saref	6.50	19.50	45.00
1/22/50-2/5/50	3.70	11.00	26.00
2/12/50-Roller Derby ish.	4.00	12.00	28.00
2/19/50-Half Dead Mr. Lox - Classic horror	4.65	14.00	32.00
2/26/50-4/23/50,5/14/50,5/28/50,7/23/50-9/3/50	3.70	11.00	26.00
4/30/50-Script/art by Le Blanc with Eisner framing			
	1.70	5.00	10.00
5/7/50,6/4/50-7/16/50-Abe Kanegson-a	1.70	5.00	10.00
5/21/50-Script by Feiffer/Eisner, art by Blaisdell, Eisner framing			
	1.70	5.00	10.00
9/10/50-P'Gell returns	5.00	15.00	35.00
9/17/50-1/7/51	3.70	11.00	26.00
1/14/51-Life Magazine cover; brief biography of Comm. Dolan, Sand Saref, Silk Satin, P'Gell, Sammy & Willum, Darling O'Shea, & Mr. Carrion & His Pet Buzzard Julia, with pin-ups by Eisner	4.65	14.00	32.00

The Spirit, 3/16/41, © Will Eisner

The Spirit, 7/7/46, © Will Eisner

The Spirit, 9/18/49, © Will Eisner

The Spirit, 7/27/52, © Will Eisner

The Spirit #18 (Quality), © Will Eisner

The Spirit #3 (Fiction House), © Will Eisner

	Good	Fine	N-Mint
THE SPIRIT (continued)			
1/21/51,2/4/51-4/1/51	3.70	11.00	26.00
1/28/51-"The Meanest Man in the World" classic by Eisner			
	4.65	14.00	32.00
4/8/51-7/29/51,8/12/51-Last Eisner issue	3.70	11.00	26.00
8/5/51,8/19/51-7/20/52-Not Eisner	1.70	5.00	10.00
7/27/52-(Rare)-Denny Colt in Outer Space by Wally Wood; 7 pg.			
S/F story of E.C. vintage	40.00	120.00	280.00
8/3/52-(Rare)-"Mission...The Moon" by Wood			
	40.00	120.00	280.00
8/10/52-(Rare)-"A DP On The Moon" by Wood			
	40.00	120.00	280.00
8/17/52-(Rare)-"Heart" by Wood/Eisner	42.00	125.00	240.00
8/24/52-(Rare)-"Rescue" by Wood	40.00	120.00	280.00
8/31/52-(Rare)-"The Last Man" by Wood	40.00	120.00	280.00
9/7/52-(Rare)-"The Man in The Moon" by Wood			
	40.00	120.00	280.00
9/14/52-(Rare)-Eisner/Wenzel-a	8.00	24.00	56.00
9/21/52-(Rare)-"Denny Colt, Alias The Spirit/Space Report" by			
Eisner/Wenzel	14.00	42.00	100.00
9/28/52-(Rare)-"Return From The Moon" by Wood			
	40.00	120.00	280.00
10/5/52-(Rare)-"The Last Story" by Eisner	14.00	42.00	100.00
Large Tabloid pages from 1946 on (Eisner) - Price 30 percent over			
listed prices.			

NOTE: Spirit sections came out in both large and small format. Some newspapers went to the 8-pg. format months before others. Some printed the pages so they cannot be folded into a small comic book section; these are worth less. (Also see Three Comics & Spiritman).

SPIRIT, THE (Section)
January 9, 1966
N. Y. Sunday Herald Tribune

	Good	Fine	N-Mint
New 5-pg. Spirit story by Eisner; 2 pg. article on super-heroes; 2			
pgs. color strips (BC, Miss Peach, Peanuts, Wizard of Id)			
	13.00	40.00	80.00

SPIRIT, THE (1st Series)
1944 - No. 22, Aug, 1950
Quality Comics Group (Vital)

nn(#1)-"Wanted Dead or Alive"	38.00	115.00	265.00
nn(#2)-"Crime Doesn't Pay"	24.00	72.00	170.00
nn(#3)-"Murder Runs Wild"	18.00	54.00	125.00
4,5	13.50	40.00	95.00
6-10	12.00	36.00	84.00
11	11.00	32.00	76.00
12-17-Eisner-c	19.00	57.00	132.00
18-21-Strip-r by Eisner; Eisner-c	27.00	81.00	190.00
22-Used by N.Y. Legis. Comm; Classic Eisner-c			
	42.00	125.00	295.00
Super Reprint #11-r/Quality Spirit #19 by Eisner			
	1.35	4.00	8.00
Super Reprint #12-r/Quality Spirit #17 by Fine			
	1.00	3.00	6.00

SPIRIT, THE (2nd Series)
Spring, 1952 - 1954
Fiction House Magazines

1-Not Eisner	17.00	51.00	120.00
2-Eisner c/a(2)	20.00	60.00	140.00
3-Eisner/Grandenetti-c	13.00	40.00	90.00
4-Eisner/Grandenetti-c; Eisner-a	16.00	48.00	110.00
5-Eisner c/a(4)	20.00	60.00	140.00

SPIRIT, THE
Oct, 1966 - No. 2, Mar, 1967 (Giant Size, 68 pgs.)
Harvey Publications

1-Eisner-r plus 9 new pgs.(Origin Denny Colt, Take 3, plus 2

	Good	Fine	N-Mint
filler pages)	4.00	12.00	24.00
2-Eisner-r plus 9 new pgs.(Origin of the Octopus)			
	4.00	12.00	24.00

SPIRIT, THE (Underground)
Jan, 1973 - No. 2, Sept, 1973 (Black & White)
Kitchen Sink Enterprises (Krupp Comics)

1-New Eisner-c, 4 pgs. new Eisner-a plus-r (titled Crime			
Convention)	1.00	3.00	6.00
2-New Eisner-c, 4 pgs. new Eisner-a plus-r(titled Meets P'Gell)			
	1.35	4.00	8.00

SPIRIT, THE (Magazine)
4/74 - No. 16, 10/76; No. 17, Winter, 1977 - No. 41, 6/83
Warren Publ. Co./Krupp Comic Works No. 17 on

1-Eisner-r begin	.80	2.40	4.80
2-5	.50	1.50	3.00
6-9,11-16: 7-All Ebony ish. 8-Female Foes ish. 12-X-Mas ish.			
	.40	1.20	2.40
10-Origin	.50	1.40	2.80
17,18(8/78)		.60	1.20
19-21-New Eisner-a plus Wood #20,21		.60	1.20
22,23-Wood-r		.60	1.20
24-35: 28-r-last story (10/5/52)		.60	1.20
36-Begin Spirit Section-r; r-1st story (6/2/40) in color; new			
Eisner c/a (18 pgs.)($2.95)	.50	1.50	3.00
37-r-2nd story in color plus 18 pgs. new Eisner-a			
	.50	1.50	3.00
38-41: r-3rd-6th story in color	.50	1.50	3.00
Special 1('75)-All Eisner-a	.30	.90	1.80

NOTE: Covers pencilled/inked by Eisner only #1-9,12-16; painted by Eisner & Ken Kelly #10 & 11; painted by Eisner #17-up; one color story reprinted in #1-10. Austin a-30i. Byrne a-30p. Miller a-30p.

SPIRIT, THE
Oct, 1983 - Present (Baxter paper) ($2.00)
Kitchen Sink Enterprises

1-Origin; r/12/23/45 Spirit Section	.70	2.00	4.00
2-r/sections 1/20/46-2/10/46	.70	2.00	4.00
3-r/sections 2/17/46-3/10/46	.70	2.00	4.00
4-r/sections 3/17/46-4/7/46	.70	2.00	4.00
5-11 ($2.95 cover)	.50	1.50	3.00
12-48 ($1.95 cover, B&W)	.35	1.00	2.00
...In 3-D (11/85)-Eisner-r; new Eisner-c	.35	1.00	2.00

SPIRITMAN (Also see Three Comics)
No date (1944) (10 cents)
(Triangle Sales Co. ad on back cover)
No publisher listed

1-Three 16pg. Spirit sections bound together, (1944, 48 pgs.,			
10 cents)	12.00	35.00	84.00
2-Two Spirit sections (3/26/44, 4/2/44) bound together; by Lou			
Fine	9.20	27.50	64.00

SPIRIT WORLD (Magazine)
Fall, 1971 (Black & White)
National Periodical Publications

1-Kirby-a/Adams-c	.70	2.00	4.00

SPITFIRE
1944 (Aug) - 1945 (Female undercover agent)
Malverne Herald (Elliot)(J. R. Mahon)

132,133: Both have Classics Gift Box ads on b/c with checklist to			
#20	8.00	24.00	56.00

SPITFIRE AND THE TROUBLESHOOTERS
Oct, 1986 - No. 9, June, 1987 (Codename: Spitfire #10 on)
Marvel Comics Group

SPITFIRE AND THE TROUBLESHOOTERS (continued)

	Good	Fine	N-Mint
1-9		.50	1.00

SPITFIRE COMICS (Also see Double Up)
Aug, 1941 - No. 2, Oct, 1941 (Pocket size; 100 pgs.)
Harvey Publications?

	Good	Fine	N-Mint
1-Origin The Clown, The Fly-Man, The Spitfire & The Magician From Bagdad	24.00	72.00	170.00
2	19.00	57.00	132.00

SPOOF!
Oct, 1970; No. 2, Nov, 1972 - No. 5, May, 1973
Marvel Comics Group

	Good	Fine	N-Mint
1-Infinity-c		.30	.60
2-5		.25	.50

SPOOK (Formerly Shock Detective Cases)
No. 22, Jan, 1953 - No. 30, Oct, 1954
Star Publications

	Good	Fine	N-Mint
22-Sgt. Spook-r; acid in face story	7.00	21.00	50.00
23,25,27: 27-two Sgt. Spook-r	5.00	15.00	35.00
24-Used in SOTI, pg. 182,183-r/Inside Crime 2; Transvestism story	10.00	30.00	70.00
26-Disbrow-a	5.75	17.00	40.00
28,29-Rulah app.; Jo-Jo in #29	5.75	17.00	40.00
30-Disbrow c/a(2); only Star-c	5.75	17.00	40.00

NOTE: *L. B. Cole covers-all issues; a-28(1pg.). Disbrow a-26(2), 28, 29(2), 30(2); No. 30 r-/Blue Bolt Weird Tales #114.*

SPOOK COMICS
1946
Baily Publications/Star

	Good	Fine	N-Mint
1-Mr. Lucifer app.	9.00	27.00	62.00

SPOOKY (The Tuff Little Ghost; see Casper The Friendly Ghost)
11/55 - 139, 11/73; No. 140, 7/74 - No. 155, 3/77; No. 156, 12/77 -
No. 158, 4/78; No. 159, 9/78; No. 160, 10/79; No. 161, 9/80
Harvey Publications

	Good	Fine	N-Mint
1-Nightmare begins (See Casper #19)	13.00	40.00	90.00
2	6.00	18.00	42.00
3-10(1956-57)	3.00	9.00	21.00
11-20(1957-58)	1.50	4.50	10.00
21-40(1958-59)	.70	2.00	5.00
41-60	.50	1.50	3.00
61-80	.35	1.10	2.20
81-100	.30	.90	1.80
101-120	.25	.70	1.40
121-126,133-140		.60	1.20
127-132: All 52 pg. Giants	.25	.75	1.50
141-161		.40	.80

SPOOKY HAUNTED HOUSE
Oct, 1972 - No. 15, Feb, 1975
Harvey Publications

	Good	Fine	N-Mint
1	1.00	3.00	6.00
2-5	.50	1.50	3.00
6-10	.30	.80	1.60
11-15		.60	1.20

SPOOKY MYSTERIES
No date (1946) (10 cents)
Your Guide Publ. Co.

	Good	Fine	N-Mint
1-Mr. Spooky, Super Snooper, Pinky, Girl Detective app.	4.00	12.00	28.00

SPOOKY SPOOKTOWN
9/61; No. 2, 9/62 - No. 52, 12/73; No. 53, 10/74 - No. 66, Dec, 1976
Harvey Publications

	Good	Fine	N-Mint
1-Casper, Spooky; 68 pgs. begin	5.70	17.00	40.00
2	3.00	9.00	20.00
3-5	2.75	8.00	16.00
6-10	1.35	4.00	8.00
11-20	1.00	3.00	6.00
21-39: Last 68 pg. issue	.50	1.50	3.00
40-45: All 52 pgs.	.35	1.00	2.00
46-66	.30	.80	1.60

SPORT COMICS (True Sport Picture Stories #4 on?)
Oct, 1940(No mo.) - No. 4, Nov, 1941
Street & Smith Publications

	Good	Fine	N-Mint
1-Life story of Lou Gehrig	15.00	45.00	105.00
2	8.50	25.50	60.00
3,4	7.00	21.00	50.00

SPORT LIBRARY (See Charlton Sport . . .)

SPORTS ACTION (Formerly Sport Stars)
No. 2, Feb, 1950 - No. 14, Sept, 1952
Marvel/Atlas Comics (ACI No. 2,3/SAI No. 4-14)

	Good	Fine	N-Mint
2-Powell painted-c; George Gipp life story	6.50	19.50	45.00
3-Everett-c	5.00	15.00	35.00
4-11,14: Weiss-a. 9,10-Maneely-c	4.30	13.00	30.00
12-Everett-c	5.00	15.00	35.00
13-Krigstein-a	5.00	15.00	35.00

NOTE: *Title may have changed after No. 3, to Crime Must Lose No. 4 on, due to publisher change.*

SPORT STARS
2-3/46 - No. 4, 8-9/46 (½ comic, ½ photo magazine)
Parents' Magazine Institute (Sport Stars)

	Good	Fine	N-Mint
1-"How Tarzan Got That Way" story of Johnny Weissmuller	11.50	34.00	80.00
2-Baseball greats	8.00	24.00	56.00
3,4	5.70	17.00	40.00

SPORT STARS (Sports Action #2 on)
Nov, 1949 (52 pgs.)
Marvel Comics (ACI)

	Good	Fine	N-Mint
1-Knute Rockne; painted-c	11.00	32.00	75.00

SPORT THRILLS (Formerly Dick Cole)
No. 11, Nov, 1950 - No. 15, Nov, 1951
Star Publications

	Good	Fine	N-Mint
11-Dick Cole app; Ted Williams & Ty Cobb life stories	5.70	17.00	40.00
12-L. B. Cole c/a	4.00	12.00	28.00
13-15-All L. B. Cole-c; 13-Dick Cole app.	4.00	12.00	28.00
Accepted Reprint #11 (#15 on-c, nd); L.B. Cole-c	1.70	5.00	12.00
Accepted Reprint #12 (nd); L.B. Cole-c; Joe DiMaggio & Phil Rizzuto life stories	1.70	5.00	12.00

SPOTLIGHT (TV)
Sept, 1978 - No. 4, Mar, 1979 (Hanna-Barbera)
Marvel Comics Group

	Good	Fine	N-Mint
1-Huckleberry Hound, Yogi Bear, 2-Quick Draw McGraw, Augie Doggie, 3-The Jetsons, Yakky Doodle, 4-Magilla Gorilla, Snagglepuss		.25	.50

SPOTLIGHT COMICS
Nov, 1944 - No. 3, 1945
Harry 'A' Chesler (Our Army, Inc.)

	Good	Fine	N-Mint
1-The Black Dwarf, The Veiled Avenger, & Barry Kuda begin; Tuska-c	20.00	60.00	140.00
2	16.00	48.00	110.00
3-Injury to eye story(Same as Scoop #3)	18.00	54.00	125.00

Spook #24, © STAR

Sports Action #3, © MEG

Spotlight Comics #2, © CHES

Spy Cases #14, © MEG   Spy Smasher #5, © FAW   Squeeks #3, © LEV

SPOTTY THE PUP (Becomes Super Pup? or Space Comics?)			
No. 2, Oct-Nov?, 1953 - No. 3, Dec-Jan, 1953-54			
Avon Periodicals/Realistic Comics	Good	Fine	N-Mint
2,3	1.50	4.50	10.00
nn (1953, Realistic-r)	.85	2.50	6.00

SPUNKY (. . .Junior Cowboy)(. . .Comics #2 on)			
April, 1949 - No. 7, Nov, 1951			
Standard Comics			
1,2-Text illos by Frazetta	3.50	10.50	24.00
3-7	1.30	4.00	9.00

SPUNKY THE SMILING SPOOK			
Aug, 1957 - No. 4, May, 1958			
Ajax/Farrell (World Famous Comics/Four Star Comic Corp.)			
1-Reprints from Frisky Fables	2.00	6.00	14.00
2-4	1.15	3.50	8.00

SPY AND COUNTERSPY (Spy Hunters #3 on)			
Aug-Sept, 1949 - No. 2, Oct-Nov, 1949 (52 pgs.)			
American Comics Group			
1-Origin, 1st app. Jonathan Kent, Counterspy	5.70	17.00	40.00
2	4.00	12.00	28.00

SPY CASES (Formerly The Kellys)			
No. 26, Sept, 1950 - No. 19, Oct, 1953			
Marvel/Atlas Comics (Hercules Publ.)			
26	5.00	15.00	35.00
27,28(2/51): 27-Everett-a; bondage-c	3.50	10.50	24.00
4(4/51) - 7,9,10: 7-Tuska-a	2.00	6.00	14.00
8-A-Bomb-c/story	2.65	8.00	18.00
11-19: 11-14-War format	1.70	5.00	12.00

SPY FIGHTERS			
March, 1951 - No. 15, July, 1953			
Marvel/Atlas Comics (CSI)			
1	5.70	17.00	40.00
2-Tuska-a	2.65	8.00	18.00
3-13	2.00	6.00	14.00
14,15-Pakula-a(3), Ed Win-a	2.30	7.00	16.00

SPY-HUNTERS (Formerly Spy & Counterspy)			
No. 3, Dec-Jan, 1949-50 - No. 24, June-July, 1953 (#3-11, 52 pgs.)			
American Comics Group			
3-Jonathan Kent begins, ends #10	5.70	17.00	40.00
4-10: 4,8-Starr-a	3.50	10.50	24.00
11-15,17-22,24	2.00	6.00	14.00
16-Williamson-a (9 pgs.)	5.50	16.50	38.00
23-Graphic torture, injury to eye panel	6.00	18.00	42.00
NOTE: *Whitney* a-many issues; c-7, 8, 10-12, 16.			

SPYMAN (Top Secret Adventures on cover)			
Sept, 1966 - No. 3, Feb, 1967			
Harvey Publications			
1-Steranko-a(p)-1st pro work; 1pg. Adams ad; Tuska c/a,			
Crandall-a(i)	.50	1.50	3.00
2,3: Simon-c. 2-Steranko-a(p)	.35	1.00	2.00

SPY SMASHER (See Mighty Midget, Whiz & X-Mas Comics)			
Fall, 1941 - No. 11, Feb, 1943			
Fawcett Publications			
1-Spy Smasher begins; silver metallic-c	110.00	330.00	770.00
2-Raboy-c	55.00	165.00	385.00
3,4: 3-Bondage-c	45.00	135.00	315.00
5-7: Raboy-a; 6-Raboy c/a	40.00	120.00	280.00
8-11: 9,10-Hitler-c	35.00	105.00	245.00
Well Known Comics (1944, 12 pgs., 8½x10½'', paper-c, glued			
binding, printed in green; Bestmaid/Samuel Lowe giveaway			
	15.00	45.00	90.00

SPY THRILLERS (Police Badge No. 479 #5)			
Nov, 1954 - No. 4, May, 1955			
Atlas Comics (PrPI)	Good	Fine	N-Mint
1	4.30	13.00	30.00
2-Last precode (1/55)	2.65	8.00	18.00
3,4	1.70	5.00	12.00

SQUADRON SUPREME			
Sept, 1985 - No. 12, Aug, 1986 (maxi-series)			
Marvel Comics Group			
1	.30	.90	1.80
2-11		.50	1.00
12-Double size ($1.25)	.25	.75	1.50

SQUEEKS			
Oct, 1953 - No. 5, June, 1954			
Lev Gleason Publications			
1-Funny animal; Biro-c	3.00	9.00	21.00
2-Biro-c	1.50	4.50	10.00
3-5: 3-Biro-c	1.15	3.50	8.00

STAINLESS STEEL RAT			
Oct, 1985 - No. 6, Mar, 1986 (limited-series)			
Eagle Comics			
1 (52 pgs., $2.25 cover)	.35	1.10	2.20
2-6 (36 pgs.)	.25	.75	1.50

STALKER			
June-July, 1975 - No. 4, Dec-Jan, 1975-76			
National Periodical Publications			
1-Origin & 1st app; Ditko/Wood c/a		.40	.80
2-4-Ditko/Wood c/a		.30	.60

STAMP COMICS (Stamps. . . . on-c; Thrilling Advs. In . . #8)			
Oct, 1951 - No. 7, Oct, 1952 (No. 1: 15 cents)			
Youthful Magazines/Stamp Comics, Inc.			
1('Stamps' on indicia No. 1)	10.00	30.00	70.00
2	5.70	17.00	40.00
3-6: 3,4-Kiefer, Wildey-a	5.00	15.00	35.00
7-Roy Krenkel, 4 pgs.	8.50	25.50	60.00
NOTE: *Promotes stamp collecting; gives stories behind various commemorative stamps. No. 2, 10 cents printed over 15 cents c-price. Kiefer a-1-7. Kirkel a-1-6. Napoli a-2-7. Palais a-2-4, 7.*			

STANLEY & HIS MONSTER (Formerly The Fox & the Crow)			
No. 109, Apr-May, 1968 - No. 112, Oct-Nov, 1968			
National Periodical Publications			
109-112	.85	2.50	6.00

STAR BLAZERS			
Apr, 1987 - No. 4, July, 1987 (mini-series, color, $1.75)			
Comico			
1-4	.30	.95	1.90

STAR BRAND			
Oct, 1986 - No. 19, May, 1989			
Marvel Comics Group			
1-13: 3-Williamson-i		.60	1.20
14-19 ($1.25): 16-18-Byrne-c/a, scripts		.60	1.20
Annual 1 (10/87)		.65	1.30

STAR COMICS			
Feb, 1937 - V2No.7 (No. 23), Aug, 1939 (#1-6: large size)			
Ultem Publ. (Harry 'A' Chesler)/Centaur Publications			
V1#1-Dan Hastings (s/f) begins	65.00	195.00	455.00
2	32.00	95.00	225.00
3-6 (#6, 9/37): 5-Little Nemo	27.00	81.00	190.00
7-9: 8-Severed head centerspread; Impy & Little Nemo by Winsor McCay Jr, Popeye app. by Bob Wood; Mickey Mouse-c app.	25.00	75.00	175.00

STAR COMICS (continued)

	Good	Fine	N-Mint
10 (1st Centaur; 3/38)-Impy by Winsor McCay Jr; Don Marlow by Guardineer begins	40.00	120.00	280.00
11-1st Jack Cole comic-a, 1 pg. (4/38)	25.00	75.00	175.00
12-15: 12-Riders of the Golden West begins; Little Nemo app. 15-Speed Silvers by Gustavson & The Last Pirate by Burgos begins	25.00	75.00	175.00
16 (12/38)-The Phantom Rider begins, ends V2#6	25.00	75.00	175.00
V2#1(#17, 2/39)	25.00	75.00	175.00
2-7(#18-23): 2-Diana Deane by Tarpe Mills app. 3-Drama of Hollywood by Mills begins. 7-Jungle Queen app.	22.00	65.00	154.00

NOTE: *Biro c-9, 10. Burgos a-15, 16, V2#1-7. Ken Ernst a-10, 12, 14. Gill Fox c-V2#2. Guardineer a-6, 8-14. Gustavson a-13-16, V2#1-7. Tarpe Mills a-15, V2#1-7. Bob Wood a-10, 12, 13; c-8.*

STAR COMICS MAGAZINE
Dec, 1986 - No. 13, 1988 ($1.50, Digest-size)
Star Comics (Marvel)

1-13: Heathcliff, Muppet Babies, Ewoks, Carebears, Top Dog, Alf, Flintstone Kids app.	.25	.75	1.50

STAR FEATURE COMICS
1963
I. W. Enterprises

Reprint #9-Stunt-Man Stetson app.	.50	1.50	3.00

STARFIRE (See New Teen Titans & Teen Titans)
Aug-Sept, 1976 - No. 8, Oct-Nov, 1977
National Periodical Publications/DC Comics

1-Origin & 1st app; (CCA stamp fell off cover art; so it was approved by code)		.50	1.00
2-8		.30	.60

STAR HUNTERS (See DC Super Stars #16)
Oct-Nov, 1977 - No. 7, Oct-Nov, 1978
National Periodical Publications/DC Comics

1-Newton-a(p)		.30	.60
2-6		.25	.50
7-Giant		.30	.60

NOTE: *Buckler a-4p-7p; c-1p-7p. Layton a-1i-5i; c-1i-6i. Nasser a-3p. Sutton a-6i.*

STARK TERROR (Magazine)
Dec, 1970 - No. 5, Aug, 1971 (52 pages) (B&W)
Stanley Publications

1-Bondage, torture-c	.85	2.50	5.00
2-4 (Gillmor/Aragon-r)	.50	1.50	3.00
5 (ACG-r)	.50	1.50	3.00

STARLET O'HARA IN HOLLYWOOD (Teen-age)
Dec, 1948 - No. 4, Sept, 1949
Standard Comics

1-Owen Fitzgerald-a in all	7.00	21.00	50.00
2	5.00	15.00	35.00
3,4	4.00	12.00	28.00

STAR-LORD THE SPECIAL EDITION (Also see Marvel Comics Super Special #10, Marvel Premiere & Preview & Marvel Spotlight V2#6,7)
Feb, 1982 (One Shot) (Direct sale, 1st Baxter paper comic)
Marvel Comics Group

1-Byrne/Austin-a; Austin-c, Golden-a(p)	.50	1.50	3.00

STARMAN (See Adventure, First Issue Special, Justice League & Showcase)
Oct, 1988 - Present ($1.00, color)
DC Comics

1-Origin	.25	.75	1.50
2-5: 4-Intro The Power Elite		.50	1.00

STARMASTERS
Mar, 1984
Americomics

	Good	Fine	N-Mint
1-The Women of W.O.S.P. & Breed begin	.25	.75	1.50

STAR PRESENTATION, A (Formerly My Secret Romance #1,2; Spectacular Stories #4) (Also see This Is Suspense)
No. 3, May, 1950
Fox Features Syndicate (Hero Books)

3-Dr. Jekyll & Mr. Hyde by Wood & Harrison (reprinted in Startling Terror Tales #10); 'The Repulsing Dwarf' by Wood; Wood-c	40.00	120.00	280.00

STAR QUEST COMIX (Warren Presents . . . on cover)
October, 1978
Warren Publications

1		.50	1.00

STAR RAIDERS (See DC Graphic Novel #1)

STAR RANGER (Cowboy Comics #13 on)
Feb, 1937 - No. 12, May, 1938 (Large size: No. 1-6)
Ultem Publ./Centaur Publications

1-(1st Western comic)-Ace & Deuce, Air Plunder	70.00	210.00	490.00
2	35.00	105.00	245.00
3-6	30.00	90.00	210.00
7-9: 8-Christmas-c	25.00	75.00	175.00
V2#10 (1st Centaur; 3/38)	40.00	120.00	280.00
11,12	30.00	90.00	210.00

NOTE: *J. Cole a-10, 12; c-12. Ken Ernst a-11. Gill Fox a-8(illo), 9, 10. Guardineer a-3, 6, 7, 8(illos), 9, 10, 12. Gustavson a-8-10, 12. Bob Wood a-8-10.*

STAR RANGER FUNNIES (Formerly Cowboy Comics?)
V1No.15, Oct, 1938 - V2No.5, Oct, 1939
Centaur Publications

V1#15-Eisner, Gustavson-a	40.00	120.00	280.00
V2#1 (1/39)	30.00	90.00	210.00
2-5: 2-Night Hawk by Gustavson. 4-Kit Carson app.	25.00	75.00	175.00

NOTE: *Jack Cole a-V2#1,3; c-V2#1. Guardineer a-V2#3. Gustavson a-V2#2. Pinajian c/a-V2#5.*

STAR REACH CLASSICS
Mar, 1984 - No. 6, Aug, 1984 ($1.50; color; Baxter paper)
Eclipse Comics

1-Adams-r/Star Reach #1	.35	1.00	2.00
2-6	.25	.75	1.50

NOTE: *Brunner c/a-4r. Nino a-3r. Russell c/a-3r.*

STARR FLAGG, UNDERCOVER GIRL (See Undercover. . .)

STARRIORS
Aug, 1984 - No. 4, Feb, 1985 (limited-series)
Marvel Comics Group

1-Based on Tomy Toy robots	.60	1.20	
2-4	.50	1.00	

STARS AND STRIPES COMICS
May, 1941 - No. 6, Dec, 1941
Centaur Publications

2(#1)-The Shark, The Iron Skull, Aman, The Amazing Man, Mighty Man, Minimidget begin; The Voice & Dash Dartwell, the Human Meteor, Reef Kinkaid app.; Gustavson Flag-c	90.00	270.00	630.00
3-Origin Dr. Synthe; The Black Panther app.	65.00	195.00	455.00
4-Origin/1st app. The Stars and Stripes; injury to eye-c	55.00	165.00	385.00
5(#5 on cover & inside)	40.00	120.00	280.00

Star Comics V2#1, © CEN

Star Ranger #9, © CEN

Stars And Stripes Comics #3, © CEN

Star Spangled Comics #8, © DC   Star Spangled Comics #94, © DC   Startling Comics #1, © BP

STARS AND STRIPES COMICS (continued)	Good	Fine	N-Mint
5(#6)-(#5 on cover, #6 on inside)	40.00	120.00	280.00

NOTE: *Gustavson* c/a-3. *Myron Strauss* c-5.

STARSLAYER
9/81 - No. 6, 4/83; No. 7, 8/83 - No. 34, 11/85
Pacific Comics/First Comics No. 7 on

1-Origin; excessive blood & gore	.50	1.50	3.00
2-Intro & origin the Rocketeer by Dave Stevens			
	1.15	3.50	7.00
3-Rocketeer continues	.85	2.50	5.00
4	.35	1.00	2.00
5-2nd app. Groo the Wanderer by Aragones	1.25	3.75	7.50
6,7: 7-Grell-a ends	.35	1.00	2.00
8-34: 10-Intro Grimjack (ends #17). 19-Starslayer meets Grimjack; book length story. 20-The Black Flame begins, ends #33			
	.50	1.00	

NOTE: *Grell* a-1-7; c-1-8. *Sutton* a-17p, 20-22p.

STAR SPANGLED COMICS (. . .War Stories #131 on)
Oct., 1941 - No. 130, July, 1952
National Periodical Publications

1-Origin Tarantula; Captain X of the R.A.F., Star Spangled Kid(See Action #40) & Armstrong of the Army begin			
	123.00	370.00	860.00
2	55.00	165.00	385.00
3-5	37.00	110.00	260.00
6-Last Armstrong/Army	25.00	75.00	175.00
7-Origin/1st app. The Guardian by S&K, & Robotman by Paul Cassidy; The Newsboy Legion & TNT begin; last Captain X			
	150.00	450.00	1050.00
8-Origin TNT & Dan the Dyna-Mite	75.00	225.00	525.00
9,10	65.00	195.00	455.00
11-17	53.00	160.00	370.00
18-Origin Star Spangled Kid	65.00	195.00	455.00
19-Last Tarantula	53.00	160.00	370.00
20-Liberty Belle begins	53.00	160.00	370.00
21-29-Last S&K issue; 23-Last TNT. 25-Robotman by Jimmy Thompson begins	40.00	120.00	280.00
30-40	19.00	57.00	132.00
41-50	15.00	45.00	105.00
51-64: Last Newsboy Legion & The Guardian; 53 by S&K			
	14.00	42.00	100.00
65-Robin begins with cover app.	30.00	90.00	210.00
66-68,70-80	14.00	42.00	100.00
69-Origin Tomahawk	17.00	51.00	120.00
81-Origin Merry, Girl of 1000 Gimmicks	12.00	36.00	84.00
82,83,85,86: 83-Capt. Compass begins, ends #130			
	12.00	36.00	84.00
84,87 (Rare)	13.00	40.00	90.00
88-94: Batman-c/stories in all. 88-Last Star Spangled Kid. 91-Federal Men begin, end #93. 94-Manhunters Around the World begin, end #121	13.00	40.00	90.00
95-99	10.00	30.00	70.00
100	13.00	40.00	90.00
101-112,114,115,117-121: 114-Retells Robin's origin. 120-Last 52 pgs.			
	8.00	24.00	56.00
113-Frazetta-a, 10 pgs.	25.00	75.00	175.00
116-Flag-c	9.00	27.00	62.00
122-Ghost Breaker begins (origin), ends #130	8.00	24.00	56.00
123-129	6.50	19.50	45.00
130	8.00	24.00	56.00

NOTE: *Most all issues after #29 signed by Simon & Kirby are not by them.* **Batman** c/stories-88-94.

STAR SPANGLED WAR STORIES (Star Spangled Comics #1-130; The Unknown Soldier #205 on) (See Showcase)
No. 131, 8/52 - No. 133, 10/52; No. 3, 11/52 - No. 204, 2-3/77

National Periodical Publications	Good	Fine	N-Mint
131(#1)	22.00	65.00	154.00
132	14.00	42.00	100.00
133-Used in POP, Pg. 94	14.00	42.00	100.00
3-5: 4-Devil Dog Dugan app.	10.00	30.00	70.00
6-Evans-a	8.00	24.00	56.00
7-10	6.00	18.00	42.00
11-20	4.65	14.00	32.00
21-30: Last precode (2/55)	3.50	10.50	24.00
31-33,35-40	2.65	8.00	18.00
34-Krigstein-a	4.35	13.00	30.00
41-50	2.15	6.50	15.00
51-83: 67-Easy Co. story w/o Sgt. Rock	1.85	5.50	13.00
84-Origin Mlle. Marie	4.00	12.00	28.00
85-89-Mlle. Marie in all	2.30	7.00	16.00
90-1st Dinosaur issue	7.00	21.00	50.00
91-100	1.70	5.00	12.00
101-120	1.00	3.00	7.00
121-133,135-137-Last dinosaur story; Heath Birdman-#129,131			
	.70	2.00	4.00
134,144-Adams-a plus Kubert #144	.85	2.50	5.00
138-Enemy Ace begins by Joe Kubert	.70	2.00	4.00
139-143,145-148,152,153,155	.45	1.25	2.50
149,150-Viking Prince by Kubert	.50	1.50	3.00
151-1st Battle Album	.35	1.00	2.00
154-Origin Unknown Soldier	.35	1.00	2.00
156-1st Battle Album		.50	1.00
157-161-Last Enemy Ace		.50	1.00
162-204: 181-183-Enemy Ace vs. Balloon Buster serial app.			
	.40	.80	

NOTE: *Drucker* a-59, 61, 64, 66, 67, 73-84. *Estrada* a-149. *John Giunta* a-72. *Glanzman* a-167, 171, 172, 174. *Heath* c-67. *Kaluta* a-197; c-167. *Kubert* a-6-162(most later issues), 200. *Maurer* a-160. *Severin* a-65. *Simonson* a-170, 172, 174, 180. *Sutton* a-168. *Thorne* a-183. *Toth* a-164. *Wildey* a-161. *Suicide Squad* in 110, 116-18, 120, 121, 127.

STARSTREAM (Adventures in Science Fiction)
1976 (68 pgs.; cardboard covers) (79 cents)
Whitman/Western Publishing Co.

1-Bolle-a	.30	.80	1.60
2-4-McWilliams & Bolle-a	.60		1.20

STARSTRUCK
Mar., 1985 - No. 6, Feb, 1986 ($1.50; adults only)
Epic Comics (Marvel)

1-Nudity & strong language	.25	.75	1.50
2-6	.25	.75	1.50

NOTE: *Kaluta* a-1-6; c-1-6.

STAR STUDDED
1945 (25 cents; 132 pgs.); 1945 (196 pgs.)
Cambridge House/Superior Publishers

1-Captain Combat by Giunta, Ghost Woman, Commandette, & Red Rogue app.	11.50	34.00	80.00
nn-The Cadet, Edison Bell, Hoot Gibson, Jungle Lil (196 pgs.); copies vary - Blue Beetle in some	9.50	28.50	65.00

STAR TEAM
1977 (20 pgs.) (6½x5'')
Marvel Comics Group (Ideal Toy Giveaway)

nn		.15	.30

STARTLING COMICS
June, 1940 - No. 53, May, 1948
Better Publications (Nedor)

1-Origin Captain Future-Man Of Tomorrow, Mystico (By Eisner/Fine), The Wonder Man; The Masked Rider begins; drug use story			
	65.00	195.00	455.00

STARTLING COMICS (continued) | Good | Fine | N-Mint

	Good	Fine	N-Mint
2	27.00	81.00	190.00
3	21.00	62.00	146.00
4	15.00	45.00	105.00
5-9	12.00	36.00	84.00
10-The Fighting Yank begins (origin & 1st app.)			
	50.00	150.00	350.00
11-15: 12-Hitler, Hirohito, Mussolini-c	14.00	42.00	100.00
16-Origin The Four Comrades; not in #32,35	17.00	51.00	120.00
17-Last Masked Rider & Mystico	11.00	32.00	75.00
18-Pyroman begins (origin)	26.00	78.00	180.00
19	11.50	34.00	80.00
20-The Oracle begins; not in #26,28,33,34	11.50	34.00	80.00
21-Origin The Ape, Oracle's enemy	11.00	32.00	75.00
22-33	10.00	30.00	70.00
34-Origin The Scarab & only app.	11.00	32.00	75.00
35-Hypodermic syringe attacks Fighting Yank in drug story			
	11.00	32.00	75.00
36-43: 36-Last Four Comrades. 40-Last Capt. Future & Oracle. 41-Front Page Peggy begins. 43-Last Pyroman			
	10.00	30.00	70.00
44-Lance Lewis, Space Detective begins; Ingels-c			
	17.00	51.00	120.00
45-Tygra begins (Intro/origin)	15.00	45.00	105.00
46-Ingels c/a	15.00	45.00	105.00
47-53: 49-Last Fighting Yank. 50,51-Sea-Eagle app.			
	12.00	36.00	84.00

NOTE: *Ingels* c-44, 46(Wash). *Schomburg (Xela)* c-21-43; 47-53 (airbrush). *Tuska* c-45? Bondage c-16, 21, 37, 46-49.

STARTLING TERROR TALES
5/52 - No. 14, 2/53; No. 4, 4/53 - No. 11, 1954
Star Publications

	Good	Fine	N-Mint
10-(1st Series)-Wood/Harrison-a (r-A Star Presentation #3)			
Disbrow/Cole-c	20.00	60.00	140.00
11-L. B. Cole Spider-c; r-Fox's ''A Feat. Presentation #5''			
	10.00	30.00	70.00
12,14	3.65	11.00	25.00
13-Jo-Jo-r; Disbrow-a	4.00	12.00	28.00
4-7,9,11('53-54) (2nd Series)	3.00	9.00	21.00
8-Spanking scene; Palais-a(r)	5.00	15.00	35.00
10-Disbrow-a	4.00	12.00	28.00

NOTE: *L. B. Cole* covers-all issues. *Palais* a-V2#11r.

STAR TREK (TV) (See Dan Curtis)
7/67; No. 2, 6/68; No. 3, 12/68; No. 4, 6/69 - No. 61, 3/79
Gold Key

	Good	Fine	N-Mint
1	7.00	21.00	50.00
2-5	4.30	13.00	30.00
6-9: 1-9-Photo-c	2.85	8.50	20.00
10-20	1.70	5.00	12.00
21-30	1.15	3.50	8.00
31-40	.85	2.50	5.00
41-61: 52-Drug propaganda story	.60	1.75	3.50
. . .the Enterprise Logs nn(8/76)-Golden Press, 224 pgs. ($1.95)-Reprints No. 1-8 plus 7 pgs. by McWilliams (#11185)			
	1.00	3.00	7.00
. . .the Enterprise Logs Vol.2('76)-Reprints #9-17 (#11187)			
	.85	2.50	6.00
. . .the Enterprise Logs Vol.3('77)-Reprints #18-26 (#11188); McWilliams-a (4 pgs.)	.70	2.00	5.00
Star Trek Vol.4(Winter '77)-Reprints #27,28,30-36,38 (#11189) plus 3 pgs. new art	.70	2.00	5.00

NOTE: *McWilliams* a-38, 40-44, 46-61. #29 reprints #1; #35 reprints #4; #37 reprints #5; #45 reprints #7. The tabloids all have photo covers and blank inside covers. Painted covers #10-44, 46-59.

STAR TREK
April, 1980 - No. 18, Feb, 1982

Marvel Comics Group	Good	Fine	N-Mint
1-r/Marvel Super Special; movie adapt.	.30	.90	1.80
2-18		.60	1.20

NOTE: *Austin* c-18i. *Buscema* a-13. *Gil Kane* a-15. *Miller* c-5. *Nasser* c/a-7. *Simonson* c-17.

STAR TREK
Feb, 1984 - Present (Mando paper)
DC Comics

	Good	Fine	N-Mint
1-Sutton-a(p) begin	.90	2.75	5.50
2-5	.70	2.00	4.00
6-10 (75 cent cover)	.50	1.50	3.00
11-20	.35	1.00	2.00
21-32	.25	.75	1.50
33 ($1.25)	.35	1.00	2.00
34-49		.50	1.00
50 ($1.50, 52 pgs.)	.25	.75	1.50
51-58		.50	1.00
Annual 1 (10/85)	.35	1.00	2.00
Annual 2 (9/86), 3('88, $1.50)	.35	1.00	2.00

NOTE: *Morrow* a-28, 35, 36. *Orlando* c-8i. *Perez* c-1-3. *Spiegle* a-19. *Starlin* c-24, 25. *Sutton* a-1-6p, 8-18p, 20-27p, 29p, 31-34p, 39-52p, 55p; c-4-6p, 8-22p, 46p.

STAR TREK MOVIE SPECIAL
June, 1984 - No. 2, 1987 (68pgs; $1.50)
DC Comics

	Good	Fine	N-Mint
1-Adapts Star Trek III; Sutton-a(p)	.25	.75	1.50
2-Adapts Star Trek IV; Sutton-a	.35	1.00	2.00

STAR TREK: THE NEXT GENERATION (TV)
Feb, 1988 - No. 6, July, 1988 (Mini series)
DC Comics

	Good	Fine	N-Mint
1 (52 pgs.)-Based on TV show	.40	1.25	2.50
2-6 ($1.00)	.25	.75	1.50

STAR WARS (Movie) (See Contemporary Motivators, The Droids, The Ewoks, Marvel Movie Showcase & Marvel Special Edition)
July, 1977 - No. 107, Sept, 1986
Marvel Comics Group

	Good	Fine	N-Mint
1-(Regular 30 cent edition)-Price in square w/UPC code			
	1.35	4.00	8.00
1-(35 cent cover; limited distribution - 1500 copies?)- Price in square w/UPC code	26.00	80.00	185.00
2-4	.70	2.00	4.00
5-10	.50	1.50	3.00
11-20	.35	1.00	2.00
21-37	.25	.75	1.50
38-44: 39-The Empire Strikes Back r-begin, ends #44			
	.35	1.00	2.00
45-107: 100-Dbl. size		.50	1.00
1-9-Reprints; has ''reprint'' in upper lefthand corner of cover or on inside or price and number inside a diamond with no date or UPC on cover; 30 cents and 35 cents issues published			
		.25	.50
Annual 1 (12/79)	.35	1.00	2.00
Annual 2 (11/82), 3(12/83)		.60	1.20

NOTE: *Austin* c-11-15i, 21i, 38; c-12-15i, 21i. *Byrne* c-13p. *Chaykin* a-1-10p; c-1. *Golden* c/a-38. *Miller* c-47p. *Nebres* c/a-Annual 2. *Simonson* a-16p, 49p, 51-63p, 65p, 66p; c-16, 49-51, 52p, 53-62, Annual 1. *Williamson* a-39-44p, 50p; c-39, 40, 41-44p, 98.

STAR WARS IN 3-D
Nov., 1987 - Present ($2.50)
Blackthorne Publishing

	Good	Fine	N-Mint
1-4	.40	1.25	2.50

STAR WARS: RETURN OF THE JEDI
Oct, 1983 - No. 4, Jan, 1984 (Mini-series)
Marvel Comics Group

	Good	Fine	N-Mint
1-4-Williamson-a(p) in all		.50	1.00

Startling Comics #10, © BP

Star Trek #1 (DC), © Paramount

Star Trek: The Next Generation #1, © Paramount

Steve Canyon Comics #1, © Milton Caniff

Stig's Inferno #7, © Eclipse Comics

Stories By Famous Authors Illustrated #2, © Seaboard

	Good	Fine	N-Mint
STAR WARS: RETURN OF THE JEDI (cont.)			
Oversized issue ('83; 10¾x8¼''; 68 pgs.; cardboard-c)-Reprints above 4 issues	.50	1.50	2.95

STATIC (Also see Ditko's World)
No. 11, Oct., 1985 - No. 12, Dec., 1985
Charlton Comics

11,12: Ditko c/a		.40	.80

STEEL CLAW, THE
Dec, 1986 - No. 4, Mar, 1987 (mini-series)
Quality Comics

1-3		.45	.90
4 ($1.50)		.60	1.20

STEELGRIP STARKEY
July, 1986 - No. 6, June, 1987 (mini-series)($1.50, Baxter)
Epic Comics (Marvel)

1-6	.25	.75	1.50

STEEL STERLING (Formerly Shield-Steel Sterling; see Blue Ribbon, Mighty Comics, Mighty Crusaders & Zip Comics)
No. 4, Jan, 1984 - No. 7, July, 1984
Archie Enterprises, Inc.

4-7: 6-McWilliams-a		.40	.80

STEEL, THE INDESTRUCTIBLE MAN
March, 1978 - No. 5, Oct-Nov, 1978
DC Comics, Inc.

1		.30	.60
2-5: 5-Giant		.25	.50

STEVE CANYON (See 4-Color #519, 578, 641, 737, 804, 939, 1033, and Harvey Comics Hits #52)

STEVE CANYON
1959 (96 pgs.; no text; 6¾x9''; hardcover)(B&W inside)
Grosset & Dunlap

100100-Reprints 2 stories from strip (1953, 1957)	3.00	9.00	21.00
100100 (softcover edition)	2.50	7.50	17.00

STEVE CANYON COMICS
Feb, 1948 - No. 6, Dec, 1948 (Strip reprints) No. 4,5-52pgs.
Harvey Publications

1-Origin; has biog of Milton Caniff; Powell-a, 2pgs.; Caniff-a	13.50	40.50	95.00
2-Caniff, Powell-a	10.00	30.00	70.00
3-6: Caniff, Powell-a in all. 6-Intro Madame Lynx	8.50	25.50	60.00
Dept. Store giveaway #3(6/48, 36pp)	8.50	25.50	60.00
. . .'s Secret Mission (1951, 16 pgs., Armed Forces giveaway) -Caniff-a	8.00	24.00	56.00
Strictly for the Smart Birds-16 pgs., 1951; Information Comics Div. (Harvey) Premium	8.00	24.00	56.00

STEVE CANYON IN 3-D
June, 1986 (One shot, $2.25)
Kitchen Sink Press

1		.40	1.15	2.30

STEVE DONOVAN, WESTERN MARSHAL (TV)
No. 675, Feb, 1956 - No. 880, Feb, 1958 (All photo-c)
Dell Publishing Co.

4-Color 675-Kinstler-a	4.00	12.00	28.00
4-Color 768-Kinstler-a	3.50	10.50	24.00
4-Color 880	2.30	7.00	16.00

STEVE ROPER
April, 1948 - No. 5, Dec, 1948
Famous Funnies

	Good	Fine	N-Mint
1-Contains 1944 daily newspaper-r	4.65	14.00	32.00
2	2.30	7.00	16.00
3-5	2.00	6.00	14.00

STEVE SAUNDERS SPECIAL AGENT (See Special Agent)

STEVE SAVAGE (See Captain. . .)

STEVE ZODIAC & THE FIRE BALL XL-5 (TV)
January, 1964
Gold Key

1 (10108-401)	4.00	12.00	28.00

STEVIE (Also see Mazie & Mortie)
Nov, 1952 - No. 6, April, 1954
Mazie (Magazine Publ.)

1	1.30	4.00	9.00
2-6	.85	2.50	6.00

STEVIE MAZIE'S BOY FRIEND (See Harvey Hits #5)

STEWART THE RAT (See Eclipse Graphic Album Series)

ST. GEORGE (See Saint George)

STIGG'S INFERNO
1985 - No. 7, Mar., 1987 ($2.00, B&W)
Vortex Publs./Eclipse Comics #6 on

1	1.00	3.00	6.00
2-4	.50	1.50	3.00
5-7	.35	1.00	2.00
Graphic Album ($6.95, B&W, 100 pgs.)	1.15	3.50	7.00

STONEY BURKE (TV)
June-Aug, 1963 - No. 2, Sept-Nov, 1963
Dell Publishing Co.

1,2	1.15	3.50	8.00

STONY CRAIG
1946 (No #)
Pentagon Publishing Co.

Reprints Bell Syndicate's ''Sgt. Stony Craig'' newspaper strips	3.50	10.50	24.00

STORIES BY FAMOUS AUTHORS ILLUSTRATED (Fast Fiction #1-5)
No. 6, Aug, 1950 - No. 13, March, 1951
Seaboard Publ./Famous Authors Ill.

1-Scarlet Pimpernel-Baroness Orczy	15.00	45.00	105.00
2-Capt. Blood-Raphael Sabatini	15.00	45.00	105.00
3-She, by Haggard	17.00	51.00	120.00
4-The 39 Steps-John Buchan	10.00	30.00	70.00
5-Beau Geste-P. C. Wren	10.00	30.00	70.00

NOTE: The above five issues are exact reprints of Fast Fiction #1-5 except for the title change and new Kiefer covers on #1 and 2. The above 5 issues were released before Famous Authors #6.

6-Macbeth, by Shakespeare; Kiefer art (8/50); used in SOTI, pg. 22,143. Kiefer-c; 36p	12.00	36.00	84.00
7-The Window; Kiefer-c/a; 52p	10.00	30.00	70.00
8-Hamlet, by Shakespeare; Kiefer-c/a; 36p	12.00	36.00	84.00
9-Nicholas Nickleby, by Dickens; G. Schrotter-a; 52p	10.00	30.00	70.00
10-Romeo & Juliet, by Shakespeare; Kiefer-c/a; 36p	10.00	30.00	70.00
11-Ben-Hur; Schrotter-a; 52p	11.00	32.00	76.00
12-La Svengali; Schrotter-a; 36p	11.00	32.00	76.00
13-Scaramouche; Kiefer-c/a; 36p	11.00	32.00	76.00

NOTE: Artwork was prepared/advertised for #14, The Red Badge Of Courage. Gilberton bought out Famous Authors, Ltd. and used that story as C.I. #98. Famous Authors, Ltd. then published the Classics Junior series. The Famous Authors titles were published as part of the regular Classics Ill. Series in Brazil starting in 1952.

STORIES OF CHRISTMAS
1942 (32 pages; paper cover) (Giveaway)
K. K. Publications

	Good	Fine	N-Mint
Adaptation of "A Christmas Carol;" Kelly story-"The Fir Tree"			
Infinity-c	40.00	100.00	200.00

STORIES OF ROMANCE (Formerly Matt Slade Gunfighter?)
No. 5, Mar, 1956 - No. 13, Aug, 1957
Atlas Comics (LMC)

	Good	Fine	N-Mint
5-Baker-a?	2.15	6.50	15.00
6-13	1.15	3.50	8.00

NOTE: *Ann Brewster* a-13. *Colletta* a-9(2); c-5.

STORMY (See 4-Color #537)

STORY HOUR SERIES (Disney)
1948, 1949; 1951-1953 (36 pgs.) (4½x6¼")
Given away with subscription to Walt Disney's Comics & Stories
Whitman Publishing Co.

	Good	Fine	N-Mint
nn(1948)-Mickey Mouse and Boy Thursday	5.00	15.00	35.00
nn(1948)-Mickey Mouse Miracle Maker	5.00	15.00	35.00
nn(1948)-Minnie Mouse and Antique Chair	5.00	15.00	35.00
nn(1949)-The Three Orphan Kittens(B&W & color)			
	2.35	7.00	16.00
nn(1949)-Danny-The Little Black Lamb	2.35	7.00	16.00
800-Donald Duck in "Bringing Up the Boys"			
1948 Paper Cover	8.00	24.00	56.00
1953	4.00	12.00	28.00
801-Mickey Mouse's Summer Vacation			
1948 Paper Cover	4.00	12.00	28.00
1951, 1952 edition	2.00	6.00	14.00
802-Bugs Bunny's Adventures			
1948 Paper Cover	3.00	9.00	21.00
803-Bongo			
1948 Paper Cover	3.35	8.00	18.00
804-Mickey and the Beanstalk			
1948 Paper Cover	3.35	10.00	23.00
808-15(1949)-Johnny Appleseed	2.75	8.00	18.00
1948 Hard Cover Edition of each....$2.00 - $3.00 more			

STORY OF EDISON, THE
1956 (16 pgs.) (Reddy Killowatt)
Educational Comics

	Good	Fine	N-Mint
Reprint of Reddy Killowatt #2(1947)	4.75	14.00	30.00

STORY OF HARRY S. TRUMAN, THE
1948 (16 pgs.) (in color, regular size)(Soft-c)
Democratic National Committee (Giveaway)

	Good	Fine	N-Mint
Gives biography on career of Truman; used in SOTI, pg. 311			
	15.00	45.00	105.00

STORY OF JESUS (See Classics Special)

STORY OF MANKIND, THE (See 4-Color #851)

STORY OF MARTHA WAYNE, THE
April, 1956
Argo Publ.

	Good	Fine	N-Mint
1-Newspaper-r	1.60	4.70	11.00

STORY OF RUTH, THE (See 4-Color #1144)

STORY OF THE COMMANDOS, THE (Combined Operations)
1943 (68 pgs..; B&W) (15 cents)
Long Island Independent (Distr. by Gilberton)

	Good	Fine	N-Mint
nn-All text (no comics); photos & illustrations; ads for Classic			
Comics on back cover (Rare)	11.50	34.00	80.00

STORY OF THE GLOOMY BUNNY, THE (See March of Comics #9)

STRAIGHT ARROW (Radio)(See Best of the West, Great Western)
Feb-Mar, 1950 - No. 55, Mar, 1956 (all 36 pgs.)

Magazine Enterprises

	Good	Fine	N-Mint
1-Straight Arrow (alias Steve Adams) & his palomino Fury begin;			
1st mention of Sundown Valley & the Secret Cave; Whitney-a			
	19.30	58.00	135.00
2-Red Hawk begins by Powell (Origin), ends #55			
	9.50	28.50	65.00
3-Frazetta-c	18.50	55.00	130.00
4,5: 4-Secret Cave-c	5.70	17.00	40.00
6-10	4.65	14.00	32.00
11-Classic story "The Valley of Time," with an ancient civilization			
made of gold	5.00	15.00	35.00
12-19	3.50	10.50	24.00
20-Origin S. Arrow's Shield	5.00	15.00	35.00
21-Origin Fury	5.70	17.00	40.00
22-Frazetta-c	14.00	42.00	100.00
23,25-30: 25-Secret Cave-c. 28-Red Hawk meets The Vikings			
	3.00	9.00	21.00
24-Classic story "The Dragons of Doom!" with prehistoric			
pteradactyls	4.65	14.00	32.00
31-38	2.65	8.00	18.00
39-Classic story "The Canyon Beast," with a dinosaur egg hatching			
a Tyranosaurus Rex	3.50	10.50	24.00
40-Classic story "Secret of The Spanish Specters," with Con-			
quistadors' lost treasure	3.50	10.50	24.00
41,42,44-54: 45-Secret Cave-c	2.15	6.50	15.00
43-Intro & 1st app. Blaze, S. Arrow's Warrior dog			
	2.65	8.00	18.00
55-Last issue	3.00	9.00	21.00

NOTE: *Fred Meagher* a 1-55; c-1,2,4-21,23-55. *Powell* a 2-55. Many issues advertise the radio premiums associated with Straight Arrow.

STRAIGHT ARROW'S FURY (See A-1 Comics #119)

STRANGE
March, 1957 - No. 6, May, 1958
Ajax-Farrell Publ. (Four Star Comic Corp.)

	Good	Fine	N-Mint
1	4.65	14.00	32.00
2	2.30	7.00	16.00
3-6	2.00	6.00	14.00

STRANGE ADVENTURES
Aug-Sept, 1950 - No. 244, Oct-Nov, 1973 (No. 1-12: 52 pgs.)
National Periodical Publications

	Good	Fine	N-Mint
1-Adaptation of "Destination Moon;" Kris KL-99 & Darwin Jones			
begin; photo-c	95.00	285.00	665.00
2	45.00	135.00	315.00
3,4	28.00	84.00	195.00
5-8,10: 7-Origin Kris KL-99	26.00	78.00	180.00
9-Captain Comet begins (6/51, Intro/origin)	70.00	210.00	490.00
11,14,15	20.00	60.00	140.00
12,13,17-Toth-a	22.00	65.00	154.00
16,18-20	14.00	42.00	100.00
21-30	12.00	36.00	84.00
31,34-38	10.00	30.00	70.00
32,33-Krigstein-a	11.50	34.00	80.00
39-Ill. in SOTI-"Treating police contemptuously" (top right)			
	20.00	60.00	140.00
40-49-Last Capt. Comet; not in 45,47,48	9.00	27.00	62.00
50-53-Last precode issue (2/55)	6.50	19.50	45.00
54-70	4.00	12.00	28.00
71-99	2.85	8.50	20.00
100	4.00	12.00	28.00
101-110: 104-Space Museum begins by Sekowsky			
	2.00	6.00	14.00
111-116,118-120: 114-Star Hawkins begins, ends #185; Heath-a			
in Wood E.C. style	1.60	4.80	11.00
117-Origin Atomic Knights	8.00	24.00	55.00

The Story Of The Commandos, © L.I. Independent

Straight Arrow #22, © ME

Strange Adventures #9, © DC

Strange Confessions #1, © Z-D

Strange Journey #4, © AJAX

Strange Planets #11, © AVON

STRANGE ADVENTURES (continued)	Good	Fine	N-Mint
121-134: 124-Origin Faceless Creature. 134-Last 10 cent issue			
	1.15	3.50	7.50
135-145	.85	2.50	5.00
146-160: 159-Star Rovers app. 160-Last Atomic Knights			
	.50	1.50	3.00
161-179: 161-Last Space Museum. 163-Star Rovers app. 170-			
Infinity-c. 177-Origin Immortal Man	.35	1.00	2.00
180-Origin Animal Man	.35	1.00	2.00
181-186,188-204: 201-Last Animal Man	.50	1.00	
187-Origin The Enchantress	.50	1.00	
205-Intro & origin Deadman by Infantino	2.50	7.50	15.00
206-Adams-a begins	1.35	4.00	8.00
207-210	1.15	3.50	7.00
211-216-Last Deadman	1.00	3.00	6.00
217-244: 217-Adam Strange & Atomic Knights-r begin. 226-236(68-			
52 pgs.): 231-Last Atomic Knights-r	.25	.60	.50

NOTE: **Adams** a-206-216; c-207-216, 228, 235. **Anderson** a-8-52, 94, 96, 97, 99, 115, 117, 119-163, 217r, 218r, 222-25r, 222, 226, 242(r); c/r-157i, 190i, 217-224, 228-31, 233, 235-39, 241-43. **Ditko** a-188, 189. **Drucker** a-42, 43, 45. **Finlay** a-2, 3, 6, 7, 210r, 229r. **Infantino** a-10-101, 106-151, 154, 157-163, 180, 190, 223-25p(r), 242p(r); c/r-190p, 197, 199-211, 218-221, 223-244. **Kaluta** c-238, 240. **Gil Kane** a-8-116, 124, 125, 130, 138, 146-157, 173-186, 204r, 222r, 227-231r; c-154p, 157p. **Kubert** a-55(2 pgs.), 226; c-219, 220, 225-227, 232, 234. **Moriera** c-71. **Morrow** c-230. **Powell** a-4. **Mike Sekowsky** a-71p, 97-162p, 217p(r), 218p(r); c-206, 217-219r. **Simon & Kirby** a-2r (2 pg.) **Sparling** a-201. **Toth** a-8, 12, 13, 17-19. **Wood** a-154i. **Chris KL99** in 1-3, 5, 7, 9, 11, 15. **Capt. Comet** covers-9-14, 17-19, 24, 26, 27, 32-44.

STRANGE AS IT SEEMS (See Famous Funnies-A Carnival of Comics, Feature Funnies #1, The John Hix Scrap Book & Peanuts)

STRANGE AS IT SEEMS
1932 (64 pgs.; B&W; square binding)
Blue-Star Publishing Co.

1-Newspaper-r	13.00	40.00	90.00

NOTE: Published with and without No. 1 and price on cover.

Ex-Lax giveaway(1936,24pgs,5x7'',B&W)-McNaught Synd.			
	2.00	6.00	14.00

STRANGE AS IT SEEMS
1939
United Features Syndicate

Single Series 9, 1,2	13.00	40.00	90.00

STRANGE CONFESSIONS
Jan-Mar, 1952 - No. 4, Fall, 1952
Ziff-Davis Publ. Co. (Approved)

1(Scarce)-Photo-c; Kinstler-a	18.00	54.00	125.00
2(Scarce)	11.50	34.00	80.00
3(Scarce)-#3 on-c, #2 on inside; photo-c	11.00	32.00	76.00
4(Scarce)-Reformatory girl story	11.00	32.00	76.00

STRANGE DAYS
Oct, 1984 - No. 3, Apr, 1985 ($1.75; Baxter paper)
Eclipse Comics

1-3-Freakwave & Johnny Nemo & Paradax from Vanguard Ill.; nudi-			
ty, violence, strong language	.35	1.00	2.00

STRANGE FANTASY
Aug, 1952 - No. 14, Oct-Nov, 1954
Harvey Publ./Ajax-Farrell No. 2 on

2(8/52)-Jungle Princess story; no Black Cat; Kamenish-a; r-/Ellery			
Queen #1	8.00	24.00	56.00
2(10/52)-No Black Cat or Rulah; Bakerish, Kamenish-a; hypo/			
meat-hook-c	7.00	21.00	50.00
3-Rulah story, called Pulah	7.00	21.00	50.00
4-Rocket Man app.	5.70	17.00	40.00
5,6,8,10,12,14	4.30	13.00	30.00
7-Madam Satan/Slave story	5.00	15.00	35.00
9(w/Black Cat), 9(w/Boy's Ranch; S&K-a)	6.00	18.00	42.00
9-Regular app.	4.30	13.00	30.00

	Good	Fine	N-Mint
11-Jungle story	5.00	15.00	35.00
13-Bondage-c; Rulah (Kolah) story	7.00	21.00	50.00

STRANGE GALAXY (Magazine)
V1No.8, Feb, 1971 - No. 11, Aug, 1971 (B&W)
Eerie Publications

V1#8-Cover-r/from Fantastic V19#3 (2/70) (a pulp)			
	.70	2.00	4.00
9-11	.50	1.50	3.00

STRANGE JOURNEY
Sept, 1957 - No. 4, June, 1958 (Farrell reprints)
America's Best (Steinway Publ.) (Ajax/Farrell)

1	5.70	17.00	40.00
2-4	3.50	10.50	24.00

STRANGE LOVE (See Fox Giants)

STRANGE MYSTERIES
Sept, 1951 - No. 21, Jan, 1955
Superior/Dynamic Publications

1-Kamenish-a begins	15.00	45.00	105.00
2	8.00	24.00	56.00
3-5	5.70	17.00	40.00
6-8	5.00	15.00	35.00
9-Bondage 3-D effect-c	6.50	19.50	45.00
10-Used in **SOTI**, pg. 181	6.50	19.50	45.00
11-18	3.70	11.00	26.00
19-r-/Journey Into Fear #1; cover is a splash from one story;			
Baker-a(2)(r)	6.50	19.50	45.00
20,21-Reprints; 20-r-/#1 with new-c	3.00	9.00	21.00

STRANGE MYSTERIES
1963 - 1964
I. W. Enterprises/Super Comics

I.W. Reprint #9; Rulah-r	.60	1.80	3.60
Super Reprint #10-12,15-17('63-'64): #12-reprints Tales of Horror #5			
(3/53) less-c. #15,16-reprints The Dead Who Walk			
	.60	1.80	3.60
Super Reprint #18-R-/Witchcraft #1; Kubert-a	.60	1.80	3.60

STRANGE PLANETS
1958; 1963-64
I. W. Enterprises/Super Comics

I.W. Reprint #1(nd)-E. C. Incred. S/F #30 plus-c/Strange Worlds #3			
	5.00	15.00	35.00
I.W. Reprint #8	1.70	5.00	12.00
I.W. Reprint #9-Orlando/Wood-a (Strange Worlds #4); c-from			
Flying Saucers #1	6.00	18.00	42.00
Super Reprint #10-22 pg. Wood-a from Space Detective #1; c-/			
Attack on Planet Mars	6.00	18.00	42.00
Super Reprint #11-25 pg. Wood-a from An Earthman on Venus			
	9.20	27.50	64.00
Super Reprint #12-Orlando-a from Rocket to the Moon			
	5.85	17.50	40.00
Super Reprint #15-Reprints Atlas stories; Heath, Colan-a			
	1.35	4.00	9.00
Super Reprint #16-Avon's Strange Worlds #6; Kinstler, Check-a			
	2.00	6.00	14.00
Super Reprint #17	1.35	4.00	9.00
Super Reprint #18-Reprints Daring Adventures; Space Busters,			
Explorer Joe, The Son of Robin Hood; Krigstein-a			
	2.00	6.00	14.00

STRANGE SPORTS STORIES (See Brave & the Bold, DC Special, and DC Super Stars #10)
Sept-Oct, 1973 - No. 6, July-Aug, 1974
National Periodical Publications

STRANGE SPORTS STORIES (continued)	Good	Fine	N-Mint
1		.30	.60
2-6: 3-Swan/Anderson-a		.25	.50

STRANGE STORIES FROM ANOTHER WORLD
No. 2, Aug, 1952 - No. 5, Feb, 1953 (Unknown World #1)
Fawcett Publications

	Good	Fine	N-Mint
2-Saunders painted-c	12.00	36.00	84.00
3-5-Saunders painted-c	8.00	24.00	56.00

STRANGE STORIES OF SUSPENSE (Rugged Action #1-4)
No. 5, Oct, 1955 - No. 16, Aug, 1957
Atlas Comics (CSI)

	Good	Fine	N-Mint
5(#1)	7.00	21.00	50.00
6,9	4.00	12.00	28.00
7-E. C. swipe cover/Vault of Horror #32	4.65	14.00	32.00
8-Williamson/Mayo-a; Pakula-a	5.50	16.50	38.00
10-Crandall, Torres, Meskin-a	5.50	16.50	38.00
11	2.65	8.00	18.00
12-Torres, Pakula-a	3.00	9.00	21.00
13-E.C. art swipes	2.65	8.00	18.00
14-Williamson-a	4.00	12.00	28.00
15-Krigstein-a	3.50	10.50	24.00
16-Fox, Powell-a	4.00	12.00	28.00

NOTE: *Everett a-6, 7, 13; c-9, 11-14. Heath a-5. Maneely c-5. Morrow a-13. Powell a-8. Severin c-7. Wildey a-14.*

STRANGE STORY (Also see Front Page)
June-July, 1946 (52 pages)
Harvey Publications

	Good	Fine	N-Mint
1-The Man in Black Called Fate by Powell	9.00	27.00	62.00

STRANGE SUSPENSE STORIES (Lawbreakers Suspense Stories
#10-15; This Is Suspense #23-26; Captain Atom V1#78 on)
6/52 - No. 5, 2/53; No. 16, 1/54 - No. 22, 11/54; No. 27, 10/55 -
No. 77, 10/65; V3No. 1, 10/67 - V1No.9, 9/69
Fawcett Publications/Charlton Comics No. 16 on

	Good	Fine	N-Mint
1-(Fawcett)-Powell, Sekowsky-a	17.00	51.00	120.00
2-George Evans horror story	10.00	30.00	70.00
3-5 (2/53)-George Evans horror stories	8.50	25.50	60.00
16(1-2/54)	5.70	17.00	40.00
17,21	4.65	14.00	32.00
18-E.C. swipe/HOF 7; Ditko-a(2)	11.00	32.00	75.00
19-Ditko electric chair-c; Ditko-a	13.00	40.00	90.00
20-Ditko c/a(2)	11.00	32.00	75.00
22(11/54)-Ditko-c, Shuster-a; last pre-code issue; becomes This Is Suspense	8.50	25.50	60.00
27(10/55)-(Formerly This Is Suspense #26?)	2.00	6.00	14.00
28-30,38	1.70	5.00	12.00
31-33,35,37,40,51-Ditko c/a(2-3)	5.70	17.00	40.00
34-Story of ruthless business man-Wm. B. Gaines; Ditko-c/a	8.00	24.00	56.00
36-(68 pgs.); Ditko-a	7.00	21.00	50.00
39,41,52,53-Ditko-a	5.00	15.00	35.00
42-44,46,49,54-60	1.30	4.00	9.00
45,47,48,50-Ditko c/a	4.00	12.00	28.00
61-74	.50	1.50	3.00
75(6/65)-Origin Captain Atom by Ditko-r/Space Advs.	6.50	19.50	45.00
76,77-Ditko Captain Atom-r/Space Advs.	2.30	7.00	16.00
V3#1(10/67)-4	.35	1.00	2.00
V1#2-9: 2-Ditko-a, atom bomb-c		.60	1.20

NOTE: *Alascia a-19. Aparo a-V3/1. Bailey a-1-3; c-5. Evans c-4. Montes/Bache c-66. Powell a-4. Shuster a-19, 21.*

STRANGE TALES (Dr. Strange #169 on)
6/51 - No. 168, 5/68; No. 169, 9/73 - No. 188, 11/76
Atlas (CCPC No. 1-67/ZPC No. 68-79/VPI No. 80-85)/Marvel No.
86(7/61) on

	Good	Fine	N-Mint
1	65.00	195.00	455.00
2	30.00	90.00	210.00
3,5: 3-Atom bomb panels	22.00	65.00	154.00
4-''The Evil Eye,'' cosmic eyeball sty	24.00	72.00	170.00
6-9	16.50	50.00	115.00
10-Krigstein-a	17.00	51.00	120.00
11-14,16-20	8.00	24.00	56.00
15-Krigstein-a	8.50	25.50	60.00
21,23-27,29-32,34-Last precode ish(2/55): 27-Atom bomb panels	6.50	19.50	45.00
22-Krigstein, Forte/Fox-a	6.85	21.00	48.00
28-Jack Katz story used in Senate Investigation report, pgs. 7 & 169	6.85	21.00	48.00
33-Davis-a	6.50	19.50	45.00
35-41,43,44	4.00	12.00	28.00
42,45,59,61-Krigstein-a; #61 (2/58)	5.00	15.00	35.00
46-52,54,55,57,60: 60 (8/57)	3.00	9.00	21.00
53-Torres, Crandall-a	5.00	15.00	35.00
56-Crandall-a	4.30	13.00	30.00
58,64-Williamson-a in each, with Mayo-#58	4.65	14.00	32.00
62-Torres-a	3.50	10.50	24.00
63,65	3.00	9.00	21.00
66-Crandall-a	3.50	10.50	24.00
67-80-Ditko/Kirby-a. 79-Dr. Strange proto-type app.	3.00	9.00	21.00
81-92-Last 10 cent ish. Ditko/Kirby-a	2.65	8.00	18.00
93-100-Kirby-a	2.15	6.50	15.00
101-Human Torch begins by Kirby (10/62)	21.00	54.00	150.00
102	10.00	25.00	70.00
103-105	8.00	20.00	55.00
106,108,109	5.70	14.00	40.00
107-Human Torch/Sub-Mariner battle	6.50	16.00	45.00
110-Intro Dr. Strange, Ancient One & Wong by Ditko	18.50	47.00	130.00
111-2nd Dr. Strange	4.30	11.00	30.00
112,113	3.70	7.50	21.00
114-Acrobat disguised as Captain America, 1st app. since the G.A.; intro. & 1st app. Victoria Bentley	3.70	9.50	26.00
115-Origin Dr. Strange; Sandman (villain) app.	8.50	21.00	60.00
116-120: 116-Thing/Torch battle	1.70	5.00	12.00
121-129,131-133: Thing/Torch team-up in all; 126-Intro Clea	1.00	3.00	6.00
130-The Beatles cameo	1.15	3.00	8.00
134-Last Human Torch; Wood-a(i)	1.00	3.00	6.00
135-Origin Nick Fury, Agent of Shield by Kirby	1.50	4.50	10.00
136-147,149: 146-Last Ditko Dr. Strange who is in consecutive stories since No. 113	.70	2.00	4.00
148-Origin Ancient One	.85	2.50	5.00
150(11/66)-J. Buscema 1st work at Marvel	.70	2.00	4.00
151-1st Marvel work by Steranko (w/Kirby)	.85	2.50	5.00
152,153-Kirby/Steranko-a	.70	2.00	4.00
154-158-Steranko-a/script	.70	2.00	4.00
159-Origin Nick Fury; Intro Val; Captain America app; Steranko-a	.85	2.50	5.00
160-162-Steranko-a/scripts; Cap. America app.	.70	2.00	4.00
163-166,168-Steranko-a(p)	.70	2.00	4.00
167-Steranko pen/script; classic flag-c	.85	2.50	5.00
169,170-Brother Voodoo origin in each; series ends #173		.50	1.00
171-177: 174-Origin Golem. 177-Brunner-c		.50	1.00
178-Warlock by Starlin with covers; origin Warlock & Him	1.00	3.00	6.00
179-181-Warlock by Starlin with covers. 179-Intro/1st app. Pip the Troll. 180-Intro Gamora	.60	1.75	3.50
182-188		.25	.50
Annual 1(1962)-Reprints from Str. Tales #73,76,78, Tales of Sus-			

Strange Suspense Stories #19. © CC

Strange Tales #20. © MEG

Strange Tales #101, © MEG

Strange Terrors #3, © STJ

Strange Worlds #4, © AVON

Strange Worlds #4, © MEG

STRANGE TALES (continued)	Good	Fine	N-Mint
pense #7,9, Tales to Astonish #1,6,7, & Journey Into Mystery			
#53,55,59	10.00	30.00	70.00

Annual 2(1963)-r/from Str. Tales #67, Str. Worlds (Atlas) #1-3,
World of Fantasy #16, Human Torch vs. Spider-Man by Kirby/
Ditko; Kirby-c ... 8.50 19.50 50.00

NOTE: **Briefer** a-17. **Burgos** a-123p. **J. Buscema** a-174p. **Colan** a-11, 20, 53, 169-73p, 188p. **Davis** c-71. **Ditko** a-46, 50, 67-122, 123-25p, 126-146, 175r, 182-88r; c-33, 51, 93, 115, 121, 146. **Everett** a-4, 21, 40-42, 73, 147-52, 164i; c-8, 10, 11, 13, 24, 45, 49-54, 56, 58, 60, 61, 63, 148, 150, 152, 158i. **Forte** a-27, 43, 50, 53, 60. **Heath** c-20. **Kamen** a-45. **G. Kane** c-170-72-, 173, 182p. **Kirby** Human Torch-101-105, 108, 109, 114, 120; Nick Fury-135p, 141-43p; (Layouts)-135-153; other Kirby a-67-100p; c-68-70, 72-92, 94, 95, 101-114, 116-123, 125-130, 132-135, 136p, 138-145, 147, 149, 151p. **Lawrence** a-29. **Leiber/Fox** a-110, 111, 113. **Maneely** a-3, 42; c-33. **Moldoff** a-20. **Mooney** a-174i. **Morisi** a-53. **Orlando** a-41, 44, 46, 49, 52. **Powell** a-42, 44, 49, 54, 130-34p; c-131p. **Reinman** a-50, 74, 88, 91, 95, 104, 106, 113i; 124-127i. **Robinson** a-17. **Sekowski** a-3, 11. **Starlin** a-178, 179, 180p, 181p; c-178-80, 181p. **Steranko** a-151-61, 162-68p; c-151i, 153, 155, 157, 159, 161, 163, 165, 167. **Tuska** a-14, 169p. **Wildey** a-42. **Woodbridge** a-59. Fantastic Four cameo-101-134. Jack Katz app.-26.

STRANGE TALES
Apr, 1987 - No. 19, Oct, 1988
Marvel Comics Group

V2#1		.50	1.00
2-19: 10-Austin-a. 13,14-Punisher app.		.40	.80

NOTE: **Austin** c-10, 12i, 13i. **Williamson** a-3i.

STRANGE TALES OF THE UNUSUAL
Dec, 1955 - No. 11, Aug, 1957
Atlas Comics (ACI No. 1-4/WPI No. 5-11)

	Good	Fine	N-Mint
1-Powell-a	8.50	25.50	60.00
2	4.30	13.00	30.00
3-Williamson-a, 4 pgs.	5.50	16.50	38.00
4,6,8,11	2.15	6.50	15.00
5-Crandall, Ditko-a	4.65	14.00	32.00
7-Kirby, Orlando-a	3.50	10.50	24.00
9-Krigstein-a	3.50	10.50	24.00
10-Torres, Morrow-a	3.00	9.00	21.00

NOTE: **Baily** a-6. **Everett** a-2, 6; c-6, 9, 11. **Heck** a-1. **Maneely** c-1. **Orlando** a-7. **Pakula** a-10. **Romita** a-1.

STRANGE TERRORS
June, 1952 - No. 7, Mar, 1953
St. John Publishing Co.

1-Bondage-c; Zombies spelled Zoombies on-c; Finesque-a			
	11.50	34.00	80.00
2	5.70	17.00	40.00
3-Kubert-a; painted-c	9.00	27.00	62.00
4-Kubert-a(r-/in Mystery Tales #18); Ekgren-c; Fineesque-a;			
Jerry Iger caricature	16.50	50.00	115.00
5-Kubert-a; painted-c	9.00	27.00	62.00
6-Giant, 100 pgs.(1/53); bondage-c	13.00	40.00	90.00
7-Giant, 100 pgs.; Kubert-c	17.00	51.00	120.00

NOTE: **Cameron** a-6, 7. **Morisi** a-6.

STRANGE WORLD OF YOUR DREAMS
Aug, 1952 - No. 4, Jan-Feb, 1953
Prize Publications

1-Simon & Kirby-a	18.00	54.00	125.00
2,3-Simon & Kirby-a. 2-Meskin-a	13.00	40.00	90.00
4-S&K-c; Meskin-a	11.50	34.00	80.00

STRANGE WORLDS (#18 continued from Avon's Eerie #1-17)
Nov, 1950 - No. 22, Sept-Oct, 1955 (no No. 11-17)
Avon Periodicals

1-Kenton of the Star Patrol by Kubert (r-/Eerie #1-'47); Crom			
the Barbarian by John Giunta	38.00	115.00	265.00
2-Wood-a; Crom the Barbarian by Giunta; Dara of the Vikings app.;			
used in SOTI, pg. 112; injury to eye panel			
	33.00	100.00	230.00

	Good	Fine	N-Mint
3-Wood/Orlando-a(Kenton), Wood/Williamson/Frazetta/Krenkel/			
Orlando-a (7 pgs.); Malu Slave Girl Princess app.; Kinstler-c			
	77.00	230.00	540.00
4-Wood c/a (Kenton); Orlando-a; origin The Enchanted Daggar;			
Sultan-a	32.00	95.00	225.00
5-Orlando/Wood-a (Kenton); Wood-c	27.00	81.00	190.00
6-Kinstler-a(2); Orlando/Wood-c, Check-a	17.00	51.00	120.00
7-Kinstler, Fawcette & Becker/Alascia-a	13.00	40.00	90.00
8-Kubert, Kinstler, Hollingsworth & Lazarus-a; Lazarus-c			
	14.00	42.00	100.00
9-Kinstler, Fawcette, Alascia-a	13.00	40.00	90.00
10	12.00	36.00	84.00
18-Reprints "Attack on Planet Mars" by Kubert			
	13.50	40.00	95.00
19-Reprints Avon's Robotmen of the Lost Planet			
	13.50	40.00	95.00
20-War stories; Wood-c(r)/U.S. Paratroops #1	3.65	11.00	25.00
21,22-War stories	3.35	10.00	23.00
I.W. Reprint #5-Kinstler-a(r)/Avon's #9	1.35	4.00	8.00

STRANGE WORLDS
Dec, 1958 - No. 5, Aug, 1959
Marvel Comics (MPI No. 1,2/Male No. 3,5)

1-Kirby & Ditko-a; flying saucer issue	16.50	50.00	115.00
2-Ditko c/a	8.50	25.50	60.00
3-Kirby-a(2)	7.00	21.00	50.00
4-Williamson-a	9.30	28.00	65.00
5-Ditko-a	7.00	21.00	50.00

NOTE: **Buscema** a-3. **Ditko** a-1-5; c-2. **Kirby** a-1, 3; c-1, 3-5.

STRAWBERRY SHORTCAKE
June, 1985 - No. 7, April, 1986 (Children's comic)
Star Comics (Marvel)

1-7: Howie Post-a		.35	.70

STRAY TOASTERS
1988 - No. 4, April, 1989 (squarebound, $3.50, color, mini-series)
Epic Comics (Marvel)

1-4: Sienkiewicz story & art	.60	1.75	3.50

STREET COMIX (50 cents)
1973 (36 pgs.) B&W) (20,000 print run)
Street Enterprises/King Features

1-Rip Kirby		.40	.80
2-Flash Gordon		.60	1.20

STREETFIGHTER
8/86 - No. 4, Spr, 1987 ($1.75, color, mini-series)
Ocean Comics

1-4: 2-Origin begins	.30	.85	1.70

STRICTLY PRIVATE
July, 1942 (#1 on sale 6/15/42)
Eastern Color Printing Co.

1,2	10.00	30.00	70.00

STRIKE!
Aug, 1987 - No. 6, 1988 ($1.75, color)
Eclipse Comics

1-6	.35	1.00	2.00
...Vs. Sgt. Strike Special 1 (5/88, $1.95)	.30	1.00	2.00

STRIKEFORCE: MORITURI
Dec, 1986 - Present
Marvel Comics Group

1	.40	1.25	2.50
2-5	.30	.90	1.80
6-12,14		.60	1.20

STRIKEFORCE: MORITURI (continued)	Good	Fine	N-Mint
13-Double size	.25	.75	1.50
15-32 ($1.00)		.60	1.25
33-35 ($3.50 format)	.60	1.75	3.50

STRONG MAN (Also see Complimentary Comics)
Mar-Apr, 1955 - No. 4, Sept-Oct, 1955
Magazine Enterprises

	Good	Fine	N-Mint
1(A-1 130)-Powell-c/a	8.50	25.50	60.00
2(A-1 132), 3(A-1 134), 4(A-1 139)-Powell-a	7.00	21.00	50.00

STRONTIUM DOG
Dec, 1985 - No. 4, Mar, 1986 (mutie series; $1.25 cover)
Eagle Comics

		Fine	N-Mint
1-4		.65	1.30
Special 1 ('86)-Moore scripts	.25	.75	1.50

STRONTIUM DOG
July, 1987 - Present ($1.25-$1.50, color)
Quality Comics

	Good	Fine	N-Mint
1-13,16: 13-Guice-c	.25	.75	1.50
14/15-two issue #s in one	.25	.75	1.50

STUMBO THE GIANT (See Harvey Hits #49,54,57,60,63,66,69,72,78,88 & Hot Stuff #2)

STUMBO TINYTOWN
Oct, 1963 - No. 13, Nov, 1966
Harvey Publications

	Good	Fine	N-Mint
1	9.50	28.50	65.00
2	5.00	15.00	35.00
3-5	3.50	10.50	24.00
6-13	2.50	8.00	18.00

STUNTMAN COMICS (Also see Thrills Of Tomorrow)
Apr-May, 1946 - No. 2, June-July, 1946; No. 3, Oct-Nov, 1946
Harvey Publications

	Good	Fine	N-Mint
1-Origin Stuntman by S&K reprinted in Black Cat #9	50.00	150.00	350.00
2-S&K-a	33.00	100.00	230.00
3-Small size (5½x8½''); B&W; 32 pgs.; distributed to mail subscribers only; S&K-a; Kid Adonis by S&K reprinted in Green Hornet #37. Estimated value... $250.00-$400.00			

(Also see All-New #15, Boy Explorers #2, Flash Gordon #5 & Thrills of Tomorrow)

SUBMARINE ATTACK (Formerly Speed Demons)
No. 11, May, 1958 - No. 54, Feb-Mar, 1966
Charlton Comics

	Good	Fine	N-Mint
11	.70	2.00	5.00
12-20	.50	1.50	3.00
21-54	.25	.75	1.50

NOTE: *Glanzman* c/a-25. *Montes/Bache* a-38, 40, 41.

SUB-MARINER (See All-Select, All-Winners, Blonde Phantom, Daring, The Defenders, Human Torch, The Invaders, Iron Man, Men's Adventures, Marvel Mystery, Motion Picture Funnies Weekly, Namora, Prince Namor, The..., Saga Of The..., USA & Young Men)

SUB-MARINER, THE (2nd Series)(Sub-Mariner #31 on)(Also see Marvel Spotlight #27 & Tales To Astonish, 2nd series)
May, 1968 - No. 72, Sept, 1974 (No. 43: 52 pgs.)
Marvel Comics Group

	Good	Fine	N-Mint
1-Origin Sub-Mariner	2.15	6.50	15.00
2-Triton app.	.85	2.50	5.00
3-10: 5-1st Tiger Shark	.50	1.50	3.00
11-13,15-20: 19-1st Sting Ray	.25	.75	1.50
14-Sub-Mariner vs. G.A. Human Torch; death of Toro	.35	1.00	2.00

21-72: 37-Death of Lady Dorma. 35-Ties into 1st Defenders story; 38-Origin. 44,45-Sub-Mariner vs. H. Torch. 50-1st app. Nita, Namor's niece. 61-Last artwork by Everett; 1st 4 pgs. completed

	Good	Fine	N-Mint
by Mortimer; pgs. 5-20 by Mooney. 62-1st Tales of Atlantis, ends			
#66	.25	.75	1.50
Special 1(1/71)		.50	1.00
Special 2(1/72)-Everett-a		.50	1.00

NOTE: *Bolle* a-67i. *Buscema* a(p)-1-8, 20, 24. *Colan* a-10p, 11p, 40p, 43p, 46-49p, *Spec.* 1p, 2; c(p)-10, 11, 40. *Craig* a-17, 19-23i. *Everett* a-45r, 50-55, 57, 58, 59-61(plot), 63(plot); c-47, 48i, 55, 57-59i, 61, *Spec.* 2. *G. Kane* c(p)-42-52, 58, 66, 70, 71. *Mooney* a-24i, 25i, 32-35i, 39i, 42i, 44i, 45i, 60i, 61i, 65p, 66i, 68i. *Severin* c/a-38i. *Starlin* c-59p. *Tuska* a-41p, 42p, 69-71p. *Wrightson* a-36i.

SUB-MARINER COMICS (1st Series) (The Sub-Mariner #1,2 33-42) (Official True Crime Cases #24 on; Amazing Mysteries #32 on; Best Love #33 on)
Spring, 1941 - No. 23, Sum, '47; No. 24, Wint, '47 - No. 31, 4/49; No. 32, 7/49; No. 33, 4/54 - No. 42, 10/55
Timely/Marvel Comics (TCI 1-7/SePI 8/MPI 9-32/Atlas Comics (CCC 33-42))

	Good	Fine	N-Mint
1-The Sub-Mariner by Everett & The Angel begin	371.00	1100.00	2600.00
2-Everett-a	180.00	540.00	1260.00
3-Churchill assassination-c; 40 pg. S-M story	125.00	375.00	875.00
4-Everett-a, 40 pgs.; 1 pg. Wolverton-a	110.00	330.00	770.00
5	80.00	240.00	560.00
6-10: 9-Wolverton-a, 3 pgs.; flag-c	60.00	180.00	420.00
11-15	42.00	125.00	295.00
16-20	37.00	110.00	260.00
21-Last Angel; Everett-a	29.00	86.00	200.00
22-Young Allies app.	29.00	86.00	200.00
23-The Human Torch, Namora x-over	29.00	86.00	200.00
24-Namora x-over	29.00	86.00	200.00
25-The Blonde Phantom begins, ends No. 31; Kurtzman-a; Namora x-over	30.00	105.00	245.00
26,27	32.00	95.00	225.00
28-Namora cover; Everett-a	32.00	95.00	225.00
29-31 (4/49): 29-The Human Torch app. 31-Capt. America app.	32.00	95.00	225.00
32 (7/49, Scarce)-Origin Sub-Mariner	50.00	150.00	350.00
33 (4/54)-Origin Sub-Mariner; The Human Torch app.; Namora x-over in Sub-Mariner, #33-42	29.00	86.00	200.00
34,35-Human Torch in each	20.00	60.00	140.00
36,37,39-41: 36,39-41-Namora app.	20.00	60.00	140.00
38-Origin Sub-Mariner's wings; Namora app.	26.00	78.00	182.00
42-Last issue	23.00	70.00	160.00

NOTE: *Angel by Gustavson-*#1. *Everett* a-1-4, 22, 24, 26-42; c-32, 33, 40. *Maneely* a-38; c-37, 39-41. *Schomburg* c-1-4, 6, 8-14, 16-18, 20. *Shores* c-38. Bondage c-13, 22, 24, 25, 34.

SUBURBAN HIGH LIFE
June, 1987 - Present ($1.75, B&W)
Slave Labor Graphics

	Good	Fine	N-Mint
1-4	.25	.80	1.60

SUE & SALLY SMITH (Formerly My Secret Life)
No. 48, 11/62 - No. 54, 11/63 (Flying Nurses)
Charlton Comics

		Fine	N-Mint
V2#48-54		.50	1.00

SUGAR & SPIKE (Also see The Best of DC)
Apr-May, 1956 - No. 98, Oct-Nov, 1971
National Periodical Publications

	Good	Fine	N-Mint
1 (Scarce)	55.00	165.00	385.00
2	27.00	81.00	190.00
3-5	24.00	72.00	170.00
6-10	16.00	48.00	110.00
11-20	12.00	36.00	84.00
21-29,31,40: 26-Xmas-c	6.50	19.50	45.00
30-Scribbly x-over	8.00	24.00	56.00

The Sub-Mariner #4, © MEG

Sub-Mariner Comics #9, © MEG

Sugar & Spike #26, © DC

Sugar Bowl Comics #1, © FF

Sun Girl #1, © MEG

Sunset Carson #1, © CC

	Good	Fine	N-Mint
SUGAR & SPIKE (continued)			
41-60	3.00	9.00	21.00
61-80: 72-Origin & 1st app. Bernie the Brain	2.00	6.00	14.00
81-98: 85-68 pgs.; r-#72. #96-68 pgs. #97,98-52 pgs.			
	1.50	4.50	10.00

NOTE: *All written and drawn by Sheldon Mayer.*

SUGAR BEAR
No date (16 pages) (2½x4½")
Post Cereal Giveaway

"The Almost Take Over of the Post Office," "The Race Across the
   Atlantic," "The Zoo Goes Wild" each 40   .80

SUGAR BOWL COMICS (Teen-age)
May, 1948 - No. 5, Jan, 1949
Famous Funnies

	Good	Fine	N-Mint
1-Toth-c/a	7.00	21.00	50.00
2,4,5	2.30	7.00	16.00
3-Toth-a	5.00	15.00	35.00

SUGARFOOT (See 4-Color #907,992,1059,1098,1147,1209)

SUICIDE SQUAD (See Doom Patrol And . . . Special & Legends)
May, 1987 - Present
DC Comics

1	.30	.90	1.80
2	.25	.75	1.50
3-22: 16-Re-intro Shade The Changing Man		.50	1.00
Annual 1 ('88, $1.50)	.25	.75	1.50

SUMMER FUN (See Dell Giants)

SUMMER FUN (Formerly Li'l Genius; Holiday Surprise #55)
No. 54, Oct, 1966 (Giant)
Charlton Comics

54	.35	1.00	2.00

SUMMER LOVE (Formerly Brides in Love?)
V2#46, 10/65; V2#47, 10/66; V2#48, 11/68
Charlton Comics

V2#46-Beatle c/sty	2.65	8.00	18.00
47-Beatle story	2.65	8.00	18.00
48	.35	1.00	2.00

SUMMER MAGIC (See Movie Comics)

SUNDANCE (See 4-Color #1126)

SUNDANCE KID (Also see Blazing Six-Guns)
June, 1971 - No. 3, Sept, 1971 (52 pages)
Skywald Publications

1-Durango Kid; 2 Kirby Bullseye-r		.60	1.20
2-Swift Arrow, Durango Kid, Bullseye by S&K; Meskin plus 1 pg.			
origin		.40	.80
3-Durango Kid, Billy the Kid, Red Hawk-r		.30	.60

SUNDAY FUNNIES
1950
Harvey Publications

1	1.50	4.50	10.50

SUN DEVILS
July, 1984 - No. 12, June, 1985 (12-issue series; $1.25)
DC Comics

1-12: 6-Death of Sun Devil		.60	1.20

SUN FUN KOMIKS
1939 (15 cents; black, white & red)
Sun Publications

1-Satire on comics	13.00	40.00	90.00

SUN GIRL (See Marvel Mystery Comics #88)
Aug, 1948 - No. 3, Dec, 1948

	Good	Fine	N-Mint
Marvel Comics (CCC)			
1-Sun Girl begins; Miss America app.	50.00	150.00	350.00
2,3: 2-The Blonde Phantom begins	37.00	110.00	260.00

SUNNY, AMERICA'S SWEETHEART
No. 11, Dec, 1947 - No. 14, June, 1948
Fox Features Syndicate

11-Feldstein c/a	25.00	75.00	175.00
12-14-Feldstein c/a; 14-Lingerie panels	22.00	65.00	154.00
I.W. Reprint #8-Feldstein-a; r-Fox issue	4.00	12.00	28.00

SUN-RUNNERS (Also see Tales of the . . .)
2/84 - No. 3, 5/84; No. 4, 11/84 - No. 6, '86 (Baxter paper)
Pacific Comics/Eclipse Comics/Amazing Comics

1-6: P. Smith-a	.25	.80	1.60
Christmas Special 1	.30	.95	1.90

SUNSET CARSON (Also see Cowboy Western)
Feb, 1951 - No. 4, 1951
Charlton Comics

1-Photo/retouched-c. (Scarce, all issues)	54.00	162.00	380.00
2	37.00	110.00	260.00
3,4	26.00	77.00	180.00

SUPER ANIMALS PRESENTS PIDGY & THE MAGIC GLASSES
Dec, 1953
Star Publications

3-D 1-L. B. Cole-c	22.00	65.00	154.00

SUPER BOOK OF COMICS
nd (1943?) (32 pgs., soft-c) (Pan-Am/Gilmore Oil/Kelloggs premiums)
Western Publishing Co.

nn-Dick Tracy (Gilmore)-Magic Morro app.	30.00	90.00	210.00
1-Dick Tracy & The Smuggling Ring; Stratosphere Jim app. (Rare)			
(Pan-Am)	26.00	78.00	180.00
2-Smitty, Magic Morro	5.00	15.00	35.00
3-Moon Mullins?	4.00	12.00	28.00
4-Red Ryder, Magic Morro	4.00	12.00	28.00
5-Don Winslow, Magic Morro (Gilmore)	4.00	12.00	28.00
5-Don Winslow, Stratosphere Jim (Pan-Am)	4.00	12.00	28.00
6-Terry & the Pirates	9.00	27.00	62.00
6-Don Winslow, McWilliams-a	5.00	15.00	35.00
7-Little Orphan Annie	5.00	15.00	35.00
8-Dick Tracy?	10.00	30.00	70.00
9-Terry & the Pirates	8.00	24.00	56.00

SUPER-BOOK OF COMICS
(Omar Bread & Hancock Oil Co. giveaways)
1944 - No. 30, 1947 (Omar); 1947 - 1948 (Hancock) (16 pgs.)
Western Publishing Co.

Note: The Hancock issues are all exact reprints of the earlier Omar
issues. The issue numbers were removed in some of the reprints.

1-Dick Tracy (Omar, 1944)	16.00	48.00	110.00
1-Dick Tracy (Hancock, 1947)	12.00	36.00	84.00
2-Bugs Bunny (Omar, 1944)	3.50	10.50	24.00
2-Bugs Bunny (Hancock, 1947)	2.65	8.00	18.00
3-Terry & the Pirates (Omar, 1944)	8.00	24.00	56.00
3-Terry & the Pirates (Hancock, 1947)	6.00	18.00	42.00
4-Andy Panda (Omar, 1944)	3.50	10.50	24.00
4-Andy Panda (Hancock, 1947)	2.65	8.00	18.00
5-Smokey Stover (Omar, 1945)	2.65	8.00	18.00
5-Smokey Stover (Hancock, 1947)	1.70	5.00	12.00
6-Porky Pig (Omar, 1945)	3.50	10.50	24.00
6-Porky Pig (Hancock, 1947)	2.65	8.00	18.00
7-Smilin' Jack (Omar, 1945)	3.50	10.50	24.00
7-Smilin' Jack (Hancock, 1947)	2.65	8.00	18.00
8-Oswald the Rabbit (Omar, 1945)	2.65	8.00	18.00
8-Oswald the Rabbit (Hancock, 1947)	1.70	5.00	12.00

SUPER-BOOK OF COMICS (continued)	Good	Fine	N-Mint
9-Alley Oop (Omar, 1945)	8.50	25.50	60.00
9-Alley Oop (Hancock, 1947)	7.00	21.00	50.00
10-Elmer Fudd (Omar, 1945)	2.65	8.00	18.00
10-Elmer Fudd (Hancock, 1947)	1.70	5.00	12.00
11-Little Orphan Annie (Omar, 1945)	4.35	13.00	30.00
11-Little Orphan Annie (Hancock, 1947)	3.00	9.00	21.00
12-Woody Woodpecker (Omar, 1945)	2.65	8.00	18.00
12-Woody Woodpecker (Hancock, 1947)	1.70	5.00	12.00
13-Dick Tracy (Omar, 1945)	9.00	27.00	62.00
13-Dick Tracy (Hancock, 1947)	7.00	21.00	50.00
14-Bugs Bunny (Omar, 1945)	2.65	8.00	18.00
14-Bugs Bunny (Hancock, 1947)	1.70	5.00	12.00
15-Andy Panda (Omar, 1945)	2.30	7.00	16.00
15-Andy Panda (Hancock, 1947)	1.70	5.00	12.00
16-Terry & the Pirates (Omar, 1945)	7.00	21.00	50.00
16-Terry & the Pirates (Hancock, 1947)	5.00	15.00	35.00
17-Smokey Stover (Omar, 1946)	2.65	8.00	18.00
17-Smokey Stover (Hancock, 1948?)	1.70	5.00	12.00
18-Porky Pig (Omar, 1946)	2.30	7.00	16.00
18-Porky Pig (Hancock, 1948?)	1.70	5.00	12.00
19-Smilin' Jack (Omar, 1946)	2.65	8.00	18.00
nn-Smilin' Jack (Hancock, 1948)	1.70	5.00	12.00
20-Oswald the Rabbit (Omar, 1946)	2.30	7.00	16.00
nn-Oswald the Rabbit (Hancock, 1948)	1.70	5.00	12.00
21-Gasoline Alley (Omar, 1946)	4.00	12.00	28.00
nn-Gasoline Alley (Hancock, 1948)	3.00	9.00	21.00
22-Elmer Fudd (Omar, 1946)	2.30	7.00	16.00
nn-Elmer Fudd (Hancock, 1948)	1.70	5.00	12.00
23-Little Orphan Annie (Omar, 1946)	3.50	10.50	24.00
nn-Little Orphan Annie (Hancock, 1948)	2.65	8.00	18.00
24-Woody Woodpecker (Omar, 1946)	2.30	7.00	16.00
nn-Woody Woodpecker (Hancock, 1948)	1.70	5.00	12.00
25-Dick Tracy (Omar, 1946)	7.00	21.00	50.00
nn-Dick Tracy (Hancock, 1948)	5.00	15.00	35.00
26-Bugs Bunny (Omar, 1946)	2.30	7.00	16.00
nn-Bugs Bunny (Hancock, 1948)	1.70	5.00	12.00
27-Andy Panda (Omar, 1946)	2.30	7.00	16.00
27-Andy Panda (Hancock, 1948)	1.70	5.00	12.00
28-Terry & the Pirates (Omar, 1946)	7.00	21.00	50.00
28-Terry & the Pirates (Hancock, 1948)	5.00	15.00	35.00
29-Smokey Stover (Omar, 1947)	2.30	7.00	16.00
29-Smokey Stover (Hancock, 1948)	1.70	5.00	12.00
30-Porky Pig (Omar, 1947)	2.30	7.00	16.00
30-Porky Pig (Hancock, 1948)	1.70	5.00	12.00
nn-Bugs Bunny (Hancock, 1948)-Does not match any Omar ish.	1.70	5.00	12.00

SUPERBOY (See Adventure, Aurora, DC Comics Presents, DC Super Stars, 80 page Giant #10, More Fun, and The New Advs. of . . .)

SUPERBOY (. . .& the Legion of Super Heroes with #231)
(Becomes The Legion of Super Heroes No. 259 on)
Mar-Apr, 1949 - No. 258, Dec, 1979 (#1-16, 52 pgs.)
National Periodical Publications/DC Comics

	Good	Fine	N-Mint
1	230.00	690.00	1610.00
2-Used in SOTI, pg. 35-36,226	88.00	265.00	615.00
3	65.00	195.00	455.00
4,5: 5-Pre-Supergirl tryout	55.00	165.00	385.00
6-10: 8-1st Superbaby. 10-1st app. Lana Lang	38.00	115.00	265.00
11-15	30.00	90.00	210.00
16-20	21.00	62.00	145.00
21-26,28-30	16.00	48.00	110.00
27-Low distribution	17.00	51.00	120.00
31-38: 38-Last pre-code ish.	11.50	34.00	80.00
39-50 (7/56)	8.50	25.50	60.00
51-60: 55-Spanking-c	5.70	17.00	40.00

	Good	Fine	N-Mint
61-67	4.65	14.00	32.00
68-Origin/1st app. original Bizarro (10-11/58)	8.00	24.00	55.00
69-77,79: 75-Spanking-c. 76-1st Supermonkey. 77-Pre-Pete Ross tryout	3.50	10.50	24.00
78-Origin Mr. Mxyzptlk & Superboy's costume	5.15	15.50	36.00
80-1st meeting Superboy/Supergirl (4/60)	3.50	10.50	24.00
81-85,87,88: 82-1st Bizarro Krypto. 83-Origin & 1st app. Kryptonite Kid	2.85	8.50	20.00
86(1/61)-4th Legion app; Intro Pete Ross	8.00	24.00	55.00
89(6/61)-Mon-el 1st app.	6.50	19.50	45.00
90-92: 90-Pete Ross learns Superboy's I.D. 92-Last 10 cent issue	2.65	8.00	18.00
93(12/61)-10th Legion app; Chameleon Boy app.	3.15	9.50	22.00
94-97,99	1.50	4.50	10.00
98(7/62)-19th Legion app; Origin & intro. Ultra Boy; Pete Ross joins Legion	2.50	7.50	17.00
100-Ultra Boy app; 1st app. Phantom Zone villains, Dr. Xadu & Erndine. 2 pg. map of Krypton; origin Superboy retold; r-cover of Superman 1; Pete Ross joins Legion	5.70	17.00	40.00
101-120: 104-Origin Phantom Zone. 115-Atomic bomb-c. 117-Legion app.	1.00	3.00	6.00
121-128: 124(10/65)-1st app. Insect Queen (Lana Lang). 125-Legion cameo. 126-Origin Krypto the Super Dog retold with new facts	.50	1.50	3.00
129,138 (80-pg. Giant G-22,35)	.60	1.75	3.50
130-137,139,140: 131-Legion cameo (statues). 132-1st app. Supremo	.40	1.25	2.50
141-146,148-155,157-164,166-173,175,176: 145-Superboy's parents re-gain their youth. 172,173,176-Legion app.; 172-Origin Yango (Super Ape)	.35	1.00	2.00
147(6/68)-Giant G-47; origin Saturn Girl, Lightning Lad, & Cosmic Boy	.85	2.50	5.00
156,165,174 (Giants G-59,71,83)	.50	1.50	3.00
177-184,186,187 (All 52 pgs.): 184-Origin Dial H for Hero-r	.50	1.00	
185-100 pg. Super Spec. #12; Legion app.-c, story; Teen Titans, Kid Eternity, Star Spangled Kid-r	.25	.75	1.50
188-196: 188-Origin Karkan. 191-Origin Sunboy retold; Legion app. 193-Chameleon Boy & Shrinking Violet get new costumes. 195-1st app. Erg/Wildfire; Phantom Girl gets new costume. 196-Last Superboy solo story	.50	1.00	
197-Legion begins; Lightning Lad's new costume	.75	2.25	4.50
198,199: 198-Element Lad & Princess Projectra get new costumes	.35	1.00	2.00
200-Bouncing Boy & Duo Damsel marry; Jonn' Jonzz' cameo	.75	2.25	4.50
201,204,206,207,209: 201-Re-intro Erg as Wildfire. 204-Supergirl resigns from Legion. 206-Ferro Lad & Invisible Kid app. 209-Karate Kid new costume	.35	1.00	2.00
202,205-(100 pgs.): 202-Light Lass gets new costume	.45	1.25	2.50
203-Invisible Kid dies	.50	1.50	3.00
208-(68 pgs.)	.45	1.25	2.50
210-Origin Karate Kid	.45	1.25	2.50
211-220: 212-Matter-Eater Lad resigns. 216-1st app. Tyroc who joins Legion in #218	.30	.90	1.80
221-249: 226-Intro. Dawnstar. 228-Death of Chemical King. 240-origin Dawnstar	.60	1.20	
250-258: 253-Intro Blok	.50	1.00	
Annual 1(Sum/64, 84 pgs.)-Origin Krypto-r	3.00	9.00	21.00
. . .Spectacular 1(1980, Giant)-Distr. through comic stores; mostly-r	.50	1.00	

NOTE: **Adams** c-143, 145, 146, 148-155, 157-161, 163, 164, 166-168, 172, 173, 175, 176, 178. **Ditko** a-257p. **Grell** a-202i, 203-219, 220-24p, 235p; c-207-232, 235, 236p, 237,

Super-Book Of Comics #21, © WEST

Superboy #1, © DC

Superboy #126, © DC

Supercar #3, © GK   Super Comics #25, © DELL   Super Duper Comics #3, © F. E. Howard

SUPERBOY (continued)
239p, 240p, 243p, 246, 258. **Nasser** a(p)-222, 225, 226, 230, 231, 233, 236. **Simonson** a-237p. **Starlin** a(p)-239, 250, 251; c-238. **Staton** a-227p, 243-249p, 252-258p; c-247-51p. **Tuska** a-172, 173, 176, 235p. **Wood** inks-152-155, 157-161. Legion app.-172, 173, 176, 177, 183, 184, 188, 190, 191, 193, 195.

SUPER BRAT
January, 1954 - No. 4, July, 1954
Toby Press

	Good	Fine	N-Mint
1 (1954)	1.70	5.00	12.00
2-4: 4-Li'l Teevy by Mel Lazarus	.85	2.50	6.00
I.W. Reprint #1,2,3,7,8('58)		.40	.80
I.W. (Super) Reprint #10('63)		.40	.80

SUPERCAR (TV)
Nov, 1962 - No. 4, Aug, 1963 (All painted covers)
Gold Key

1	4.30	13.00	30.00
2-4	3.00	9.00	21.00

SUPER CAT (Also see Animal Crackers & Frisky Animals)
Sept, 1957 - No. 4, May, 1958
Ajax/Farrell Publ. (Four Star Comic Corp.)

1('57-Ajax)	1.70	5.00	12.00
2-4	1.00	3.00	7.00

SUPER CIRCUS (TV)
January, 1951 - No. 5, 1951 (Mary Hartline)
Cross Publishing Co.

1-Cast photos on-c	3.50	10.50	24.00
2	2.30	7.00	16.00
3-5	1.70	5.00	12.00

SUPER CIRCUS (TV)
No. 542, March, 1954 - No. 694, Mar, 1956 (Feat. Mary Hartline)
Dell Publishing Co.

4-Color 542,592,694: Mary Hartline photo-c	2.65	8.00	18.00

SUPER COMICS
May, 1938 - No. 121, Feb-Mar, 1949
Dell Publishing Co.

1-Terry & The Pirates, The Gumps, Dick Tracy, Little Orphan Annie, Gasoline Alley, Little Joe, Smilin' Jack, Smokey Stover, Smitty, Tiny Tim, Moon Mullins, Harold Teen, Winnie Winkle begin	80.00	240.00	560.00
2	40.00	120.00	280.00
3	35.00	105.00	245.00
4,5	27.00	81.00	190.00
6-10	22.00	65.00	154.00
11-20	18.00	54.00	125.00
21-29: 21-Magic Morro begins (Origin, 2/40)	15.00	45.00	105.00
30-"Sea Hawk" movie adaptation-c/story with Errol Flynn	15.00	45.00	105.00
31-40	11.50	34.00	80.00
41-50: 43-Terry & The Pirates ends	10.00	30.00	70.00
51-60	7.00	21.00	50.00
61-70: 67-X-mas-c	5.70	17.00	40.00
71-80	5.00	15.00	35.00
81-99	4.30	13.00	30.00
100	5.00	15.00	35.00
101-115-Last Dick Tracy (moves to own title)	3.50	10.50	24.00
116,118-All Smokey Stover	3.00	9.00	21.00
117-All Gasoline Alley	3.00	9.00	21.00
119-121: 119-121-Terry & The Pirates app.	3.00	9.00	21.00

SUPER COPS, THE
July, 1974 (One Shot)
Red Circle Productions (Archie)

1-Morrow-c/a		.30	.60

SUPER CRACKED (See Cracked)

SUPER DC GIANT (25 cents) (No #1-12)
No. 13, 9-10/70 - No. 26, 7-8/71; No. 27, Summer, 1976
National Periodical Publications

	Good	Fine	N-Mint
S-13-Binky	.35	1.00	2.00
S-14-Top Guns of the West; Kubert-c; Trigger Twins, Johnny Thunder, Wyoming Kid-r	.35	1.00	2.00
S-15-Western Comics; Kubert-c; Pow Wow Smith, Vigilante, Buffalo Bill-r	.35	1.00	2.00
S-16-Best of the Brave & the Bold; Kubert-a	.35	1.00	2.00
S-17-Love 1970	.25	.75	1.50
S-18-Three Mouseketeers; Dizzy Dog, Doodles Duck, Bo Bunny-r; Sheldon Mayer-a	.25	.75	1.50
S-19-Jerry Lewis; no Adams-a	.25	.75	1.50
S-20-House of Mystery; Adams-c; Kirby-a(3)(r)	.25	.75	1.50
S-21-Love 1971		.50	1.00
S-22-Top Guns of the West	.25	.75	1.50
S-23-The Unexpected		.50	1.00
S-24-Supergirl		.50	1.00
S-25-Challengers of the Unknown; all Kirby/Wood-r	.25	.75	1.50
S-26-Aquaman (1971)		.50	1.00
27-Strange Flying Saucers Adventures (Fall, '76)		.50	1.00

NOTE: *Sid Greene* a-27p(r). *Heath* a-27r. *G. Kane* a-14r, 15r, 27p(r).

SUPER-DOOPER COMICS
1946 (10 cents)(32 pages)(paper cover)
Able Manufacturing Co.

1-The Clock, Gangbuster app.	5.70	17.00	40.00
2	2.65	8.00	18.00
3,4,6	2.00	6.00	14.00
5,7-Capt. Freedom & Shock Gibson	3.50	10.50	24.00
8-Shock Gibson, Sam Hill	3.50	10.50	24.00

SUPER DUCK COMICS (The Cockeyed Wonder) (See Jolly Jingles)
Fall, 1944 - No. 94, Dec, 1960
MLJ Mag. No. 1-4(9/45)/Close-Up No. 5 on (Archie)

1-Origin	17.00	51.00	120.00
2	8.00	24.00	56.00
3-5: 3-1st Mr. Monster	6.00	18.00	42.00
6-10	4.30	13.00	30.00
11-20	2.65	8.00	18.00
21,23-40	2.00	6.00	14.00
22-Used in **SOTI**, pg. 35,307,308	3.50	10.50	24.00
41-60	1.30	4.00	9.00
61-94	1.00	3.00	7.00

SUPER DUPER
1941
Harvey Publications

5-Captain Freedom & Shock Gibson app.	11.00	32.00	75.00
8,11	5.70	17.00	40.00

SUPER DUPER COMICS (Formerly Latest Comics?)
May-June, 1947
F. E. Howard Publ.

3-Mr. Monster app.	3.50	10.50	24.00

SUPER FRIENDS (TV) (Also see Best of DC & Limited Coll. Ed.)
Nov, 1976 - No. 47, Aug, 1981
National Periodical Publications/DC Comics

1-Superman, Batman, Wonder Woman, Aquaman, Atom, Robin, Wendy, Marvin & Wonder Dog begin		.30	.60
2-10: 7-1st app. Wonder Twins, & The Seraph. 8-1st app. Jack O'Lantern. 9-1st app. Icemaiden		.25	.50
11-47: 13-1st app. Dr. Mist. 14-Origin Wonder Twins. 25-1st app. Green Fury. 31-Black Orchid app. 47-Origin Green Fury		.25	.50

SUPER FRIENDS (continued)
NOTE: *Estrada a-1p, 2p. Orlando a-1p. Staton a-43, 45.*

SUPER FRIENDS SPECIAL, THE
1981 (Giveaway) (no code or price) (no ads)
DC Comics

	Good	Fine	N-Mint
1		.30	.60

SUPER FUN
January, 1956 (By A.W. Nugent)
Gillmor Magazines

1-Comics, puzzles, cut-outs	1.30	4.00	9.00

SUPER FUNNIES (. . .Western Funnies #3,4)
Dec, 1953 - No. 4, June, 1954
Superior Comics Publishers Ltd. (Canada)

1-(3-D)-Dopey Duck; make your own 3-D glasses cut-out inside front-c; did not come w/glasses	23.00	70.00	160.00
2-Horror & crime satire	2.30	7.00	16.00
3-Geronimo, Billy The Kid app.	1.70	5.00	12.00
4-(Western-Phantom Ranger)	1.70	5.00	12.00

SUPERGEAR COMICS
1976 (4 pages in color) (slick paper)
Jacobs Corp. (Giveaway)

(Rare)-Superman, Lois Lane; Steve Lombard app.	1.00	3.00	6.00

NOTE: *500 copies printed, over half destroyed?*

SUPERGIRL (See Action, Adv., Brave & the Bold, Daring New Advs. of. . ., Super DC Giant, Superman Family, & Super-Team Family)
11/72 - No. 9, 12-1/73-74; No. 10, 9-10/74
National Periodical Publications

1-Zatanna begins; ends #5		.50	1.00
2-5: 5-Zatanna origin-r		.40	.80
6-10: 8-JLA x-over		.30	.60

NOTE: *Zatanna in #1-5,7(Guest); Prez-#10.*

SUPERGIRL (Formerly Daring New Advs. of. . .)
No. 14, Dec, 1983 - No. 23, Sept, 1984
DC Comics

14,15,17-23: 20-New Teen Titans app.		.40	.80
16-Ambush Bug app.		.60	1.20
Movie Special (1985)-Adapts movie		.60	1.20
Giveaway ('84, '86 Baxter, nn)(American Honda/U.S. Dept. Transportation)-Torres-a		.60	1.20

SUPER GOOF (Walt Disney) (See The Phantom Blot)
Oct, 1965 - No. 74, 1982
Gold Key No. 1-57/Whitman No. 58 on

1	1.15	3.50	8.00
2-10	.55	1.65	4.00
11-20	.45	1.35	3.00
21-30	.35	1.00	2.00
31-50		.50	1.00
51-74		.30	.60

NOTE: *Reprints in #16,24,28,29,37,38,43,45,46,54(1/2),56-58,65(1/2),72(r-#2).*

SUPER GREEN BERET (Tod Holton. . .)
April, 1967 - No. 2, June, 1967 (68 pages)
Lightning Comics (Milson Publ. Co.)

1,2	.70	2.00	5.00

SUPER HEROES (See Marvel. . . & Giant-Size. . .)

SUPER HEROES
Jan, 1967 - No. 4, June, 1967
Dell Publishing Co.

1-Origin & 1st app. Fab 4	1.15	3.50	8.00
2-4	.85	2.50	6.00

SUPER-HEROES BATTLE SUPER-GORILLAS (See DC Special #16)
Winter, 1976-77 (One Shot, 52 pgs.)
National Periodical Publications

	Good	Fine	N-Mint
1-Superman, Batman, Flash stories; Infantino-a(p); all-r		.30	.60

SUPER HEROES PUZZLES AND GAMES
1979 (32 pgs.) (regular size)
General Mills Giveaway (Marvel Comics Group)

Four 2-pg. origin stories of Spider-Man, Captain America, The Hulk, Spider-Woman	.50	1.50	3.00

SUPER-HEROES VERSUS SUPER-VILLAINS
July, 1966 (no month given)(68 pgs.)
Archie Publications

1-Flyman, Black Hood, The Web, Shield-r; Reinman-a	1.50	4.50	10.00

SUPERICHIE (Formerly Super Richie)
No. 5, Oct, 1976 - No. 18, Jan, 1979
Harvey Publications

5-18: All 52 pg. Giants		.25	.50

SUPERIOR STORIES
May-June, 1955 - No. 4, Nov-Dec, 1955
Nesbit Publishing Co.

1-Invisible Man app.	6.50	19.50	45.00
2-The Pirate of the Gulf by J.H. Ingrahams	3.50	10.50	24.00
3-Wreck of the Grosvenor	3.50	10.50	24.00
4-O'Henry's "The Texas Rangers"	4.00	12.00	28.00

NOTE: *Morisi c/a in all.*

SUPER MAGIC (Super Magician #2 on)
May, 1941
Street & Smith Publications

V1#1-Blackstone the Magician app.; origin & 1st app. Rex King (Black Fury); not Eisner-c	33.00	100.00	230.00

SUPER MAGICIAN COMICS (Super Magic #1)
No. 2, Sept, 1941 - V5No.8, Feb-Mar, 1947
Street & Smith Publications

V1#2-Rex King, Man of Adventure app.	13.00	40.00	90.00
3-Tao-Anwar, Boy Magician begins	8.00	24.00	56.00
4-Origin Transo	7.00	21.00	50.00
5-12: 8-Abbott & Costello sty. 11-Supersnipe app.	7.00	21.00	50.00
V2#1-The Shadow app.	7.00	21.00	50.00
2-12: 5-Origin Tigerman. 8-Red Dragon begins	4.00	12.00	28.00
V3#1-12: 5-Origin Mr. Twilight	4.00	12.00	28.00
V4#1-12: 11-Nigel Elliman begins	3.70	11.00	26.00
V5#1-6	3.70	11.00	26.00
7,8-Red Dragon by Cartier	11.50	34.00	80.00

SUPERMAN (See Action Comics, Advs. of. . ., All-New Coll. Ed., All-Star Comics, Best of DC, Brave & the Bold, DC Comics Presents, Heroes Against Hunger, Limited Coll. Ed., Man of Steel, Special Edition, Taylor's Christmas Tabloid, Three-Dimension Advs., World Of Krypton, World Of Smallville & World's Finest Comics)

SUPERMAN (Adventures Of. . . #424 on)
Summer, 1939 - No. 423, Sept, 1986
National Periodical Publications/DC Comics

1(nn)-1st four Action stories reprinted; origin Superman by Siegel & Shuster; has a new 2 pg. origin plus 4 pgs. omitted in Action story	3700.00	11,000.00	24,000.00

(No known copy exists beyond Vf-NM condition)

1-Reprint, Oversize 13½ "x10." **WARNING:** This comic is an exact duplicate reprint of the original except for its size. DC published it in 1978 with a second cover titling it as a Famous First Edition. There have been many reported cases of the outer cover being removed and the interior sold as the original edition. The reprint with the new outer cover

Super Funnies #1, © SUPR

Super Magic #1, © S & S

Superman #1, © DC

Superman #5, © DC

Superman #61, © DC

Superman #156, © DC

SUPERMAN (continued)
removed is practically worthless.

	Good	Fine	N-Mint
2-All daily strip-r	460.00	1380.00	3220.00
3-2nd story-r from Action #5; 3rd story-r from Action #6			
	330.00	990.00	2310.00
4-1st mention of Daily Planet	235.00	705.00	1645.00
5	190.00	570.00	1330.00
6,7: 7-1st Perry White?	142.00	425.00	1000.00
8-10: 10-1st bald Luthor	115.00	345.00	805.00
11-13,15: 13-Jimmy Olsen app.	86.00	260.00	600.00
14-Patriotic Shield-c by Fred Ray	100.00	300.00	700.00
16-20: 17-Hitler, Hirohito-c	73.00	220.00	510.00
21-23,25	57.00	170.00	400.00
24-Flag-c	67.00	200.00	470.00
26-29: 28-Lois Lane Girl Reporter series begins, ends #40,42			
	52.00	155.00	365.00
28-Overseas edition for Armed Forces; same as reg. #28			
	52.00	155.00	365.00
30-Origin & 1st app. Mr. Mxyztplk (pronounced "Mix-it-plk"); name later became Mxyzptlk ("Mix-yez-pit-l-ick"); the character was inspired by a combination of the name of Al Capp's Joe Blyfstyk (the little man with the black cloud over his head) & the devilish antics of Bugs Bunny	87.00	260.00	610.00
31,32,34-40	40.00	120.00	280.00
33-(3-4/45)-3rd story app. Mxyzptlk	45.00	135.00	315.00
41-50: 45-Lois Lane as Superwoman (see Action 60 for 1st app.)			
	32.00	95.00	225.00
51,52	27.00	81.00	190.00
53-Origin Superman retold	57.00	170.00	400.00
54,56-60	27.00	81.00	190.00
55-Used in **SOTI**, pg. 33	29.00	87.00	205.00
61-Origin Superman retold; origin Green Kryptonite (1st Kryptonite story)	48.00	145.00	335.00
62-65,67-70: 62-Orson Welles app. 65-1st Krypton Foes: Mala, K120, & U-Ban	27.00	81.00	190.00
66-2nd Superbaby story	28.00	84.00	195.00
71-75: 75-Some have #74 on-c	25.00	75.00	175.00
72-Giveaway(9-10/51)-(Rare)-Price blackened out; came with banner wrapped around book	33.00	100.00	230.00
76-Batman x-over; Superman & Batman learn each other's I.D.			
	57.00	170.00	400.00
77-80: 78-Last 52 pgs.	22.00	65.00	154.00
81-Used in **POP**, pg. 88	22.00	65.00	154.00
82-90	20.00	60.00	140.00
91-95: 95-Last precode issue	19.00	57.00	132.00
96-99	14.00	42.00	100.00
100 (9-10/55)	43.00	129.00	300.00
101-110	11.50	34.00	80.00
111-120	9.30	28.00	65.00
121-130: 123-Pre-Supergirl tryout. 127-Origin/1st app. Titano. 128-Red Kryptonite used (4/59). 129-Intro/origin Lori Lemaris, The Mermaid	7.50	22.00	52.00
131-139: 139-Lori Lemaris app.	5.70	17.00	40.00
140-1st Blue Kryptonite & Bizarro Supergirl; origin Bizarro Jr. #1			
	5.70	17.00	40.00
141-145,148: 142-2nd Batman x-over	3.50	10.50	24.00
146-Superman's life story	5.00	15.00	35.00
147(8/61)-7th Legion app; 1st app. Legion of Super-Villains; intro. Adult Legion	6.00	18.00	42.00
149(11/61)-9th Legion app.-cameo; last 10 cent issue			
	6.00	18.00	42.00
150-162: 158-1st app. Flamebird & Nightwing & Nor-Kan of Kandor. 152(4/62)-15th Legion app. 155(8/62)-20th Legion app; Lightning Man & Cosmic Man, & Adult Legion app. 156,162-Legion app. 157-Gold Kryptonite used (see Adv. 299); Mon-el app.; Lightning Lad cameo (11/62). 161-1st told death of Ma and Pa Kent			

	Good	Fine	N-Mint
	2.65	8.00	18.00
163-166,168-180: 169-Last Sally Selwyn. 172,173-Legion cameo			
	1.50	4.50	10.00
167-New origin Brainiac & Brainiac 5; intro Tixarla (Later Luthor's wife)	1.70	5.00	12.00
181,182,184-186,188-192,194-196,198-200: 181-1st 2965 story/series 189-Origin/destruction of Krypton II. 199-1st Superman/Flash race	1.00	3.00	7.00
183,187,193,197 (Gnts G-18,G-23,G-31,G-36)	1.15	3.50	8.00
201-203-206,208-211,213-216,218-221,223-226,228-231,234-238: 213-Brainiac-5 app.	.70	2.00	4.00
202,207,212,217,222,227,239 (Giants G-42,G-48,G-54,G-60,G-66, G-72,G-84). 207-Legion app.	.85	2.50	5.00
232(Giant, G-78)-All Krypton issue	.85	2.50	5.00
233-1st app. Morgan Edge, Clark Kent switch from newspaper reporter to TV newscaster	.70	2.00	4.00
240-Kaluta-a	.40	1.25	2.50
241-244 (52 pgs.). 243-G.A.-r/#38	.35	1.00	2.00
245-DC 100 pg. Super Spec. #7; Air Wave, Kid Eternity, Hawkman, Atom-r	.45	1.40	2.80
246-248,250,251,253 (All 52 pgs.): 246-G.A.-r/#40. 248-World of Krypton story. 251-G.A.-r/#45. 253-Finlay-a, 2pgs., G.A.-r/#13			
	.50		1.00
249,254-Adams-a. 249-(52 pgs.); origin & 1st app. Terra-Man by Adams (inks)	.85	2.50	5.00
252-DC 100 pg. Super Spec. #13; Ray, Black Condor, Starman, Dr. Fate, Hawkman, Spectre app.; Adams-c	.70	2.00	4.00
255-263: 263-Photo-c		.50	1.00
264-1st app. Steve Lombard	.25	.75	1.50
265-271,273-277,279-283,285-299: 292-Origin Lex Luthor retold			
		.50	1.00
272,278,284-All 100 pgs. G.A.-r in all	.25	.75	1.50
300-Retells origin	.50	1.50	3.00
301-399: 301,320-Solomon Grundy app. 323-Intro. Atomic Skull. 327-329(44 pgs.). 330-More facts revealed about I. D. 338-The bottled city of Kandor enlarged. 372-Superman 2021 app. 376-Free 16 pg. preview of Daring, New Advs. of Supergirl			
		.50	1.00
400 (10/84, $1.50, 68 pgs.)-Many top artists featured			
	.35	1.00	2.00
401-422: 415-Crisis x-over		.50	1.00
423		.50	1.50	3.00
Annual 1(10/60)-Reprints 1st Supergirl/Action #252; r-/Lois Lane #1			
	17.00	51.00	120.00
Annual 2(1960)-Brainiac, Titano, Metallo, Bizarro origin-r			
	12.00	36.00	84.00
Annual 3(1961)	8.50	25.50	60.00
Annual 4(1961)-11th Legion app; 1st Legion origins-text & pictures			
	7.00	21.00	50.00
Annual 5(Sum, '62)-All Krypton issue	5.00	15.00	35.00
Annual 6(Wint, '62-'63)-Legion-r/Adv. #247	3.50	11.00	25.00
Annual 7(Sum/'63)-Origin-r/Superman-Batman team/Adv. 275; r-1955 Superman dailies	3.00	9.00	21.00
Annual 8(Wint, '63-'64)	2.15	6.50	15.00
Annual 9(9/83)-Toth/Austin-a	.35	1.00	2.00
Annual 10(11/84; $1.25)	.35	1.00	2.00
Annual 11(9/85)-Moore scripts	.35	1.00	2.00
Annual 12 (8/86)	.35	1.00	2.00
Special 1(3/83)-G. Kane c/a; r-that appeared in Germany			
	.35	1.00	2.00
Special 2(3/84, 48pgs.)	.35	1.00	2.00
Special 3(4/85; $1.25)	.35	1.00	2.00
The Amazing World of Superman "Official Metropolis Edition" ($2.00; 1973, 14x10½")-Origin retold	1.35	4.00	8.00
Kelloggs Giveaway-(⅔ normal size, 1954)-r-two stories/Superman #55	30.00	90.00	200.00

	Good	Fine	N-Mint
...Meets the Quik Bunny ('87, Nestles Quik premium, 36 pgs.)		.50	1.00
...Movie Special-(9/83)-Adaptation of Superman III		.50	1.00
		.50	1.00
Pizza Hut Premium(12/77)-Exact-r of #97,113	.25	.75	1.50

Radio Shack Giveaway-36pgs. (7/80) 'The Computers That Saved Metropolis;' Starlin/Giordano-a; advertising insert in Action 509, New Advs. of Superboy 7, Legion of Super-Heroes 265, & House of Mystery 282. (All comics were 64 pgs.) Cover of inserts printed on newsprint. Giveaway contains 4 extra pgs. of Radio Shack advertising that inserts do not.

	.25	.75	1.50
Radio Shack Giveaway-(7/81) 'Victory by Computer'	.25	.75	1.50
Radio Shack Giveaway-(7/82) 'Computer Masters of Metropolis'		.50	1.00
11195(2/79,224pg,$1.95)-Golden Press	.40	1.20	2.40

NOTE: **Adams** a-249i, 254z; c-204-208, 210, 212-215, 219, 231, 233-237, 240-243, 249-252, 254, 263, 307, 308, 313, 314, 317. **Adkins** a-323i. **Austin** c-368i. **Wayne Boring** art-late 1940's to early 1960's. **Buckler** a-352p, 363p, 364p, 369p; c-324-327p, 356p, 363p, 368p, 369p, 373p, 376p, 378p. **Burnley** a-252r. **Fine** a-252r. **Gil Kane** a-272r, 367, 372, 375; c-374p, 375p, 377, 381, 382, 384-90, 392, Annual 9. **Kubert** c-216. **Morrow** a-238. **Perez** c-364p. **Starlin** c-355. **Staton** a-354i, 355i. **Williamson** a-408-410i, 412i, 416i; c-408i, 409i. **Wrightson** a-416.

SUPERMAN
Jan, 1987 - Present (Bi-weekly #19 on)
DC Comics

	Good	Fine	N-Mint
1-Byrne c/a begins; intro Metallo	.40	1.25	2.50
2-10: 7-Origin/1st app. Rampage		.60	1.20
11-28: 11-1st app. Mr. Mxyzptlk. 13,14-Millenium x-over. 20-Doom Patrol app., Supergirl revived in cameo		.50	1.00
Annual 1 (8/87)-No Byrne-a	.25	.75	1.50
Annual 2 ('88)-Byrne-a; Newsboy Legion	.25	.75	1.50

SUPERMAN & THE GREAT CLEVELAND FIRE (Giveaway)
1948 (4 pages, no cover)(Hospital Fund)
National Periodical Publications

	Good	Fine	N-Mint
in full color	43.00	130.00	300.00

SUPERMAN FAMILY, THE (Formerly Superman's Pal Jimmy Olsen)
No. 164, Apr-May, 1974 - No. 222, Sept, 1982
National Periodical Publications/DC Comics

164-Jimmy Olsen, Supergirl, Lois Lane begin	.60	1.20	
165-176 (100-68 pgs.)	.45	.90	
177-181 (52 pgs.)	.40	.80	
182-$1.00 ish. begin; Marshall Rogers-a; Krypto begins, ends #192	.25	.75	1.50
183-193,195-222: 183-Nightwing-Flamebird begins, ends #194. 189-Brainiac 5, Mon-el app. 191-Superboy begins, ends #198. 200-Book length story	.40	.80	
194-Rogers-a	.25	.75	1.50

NOTE: **Adams** c-182-185. **Anderson** a-186i. **Buckler** c-190p, 191p, 209p, 210p, 215p, 217p, 220p. **Jones** a-191-193. **Gil Kane** c-221p, 222p. **Mortimer** a-191-193p, 199p, 201-22p. **Orlando** a-186i, 187i. **Rogers** a-182, 194. **Staton** a-191-194, 196p. **Tuska** a-203p, 207-209p.

SUPERMAN (Miniature)
1942; 1955 - 1956 (3 issues; no #'s; 32 pgs.)
The pages are numbered in the 1st issue: 1-32; 2nd: 1A-32A, and 3rd: 1B-32B
National Periodical Publications

No date-Py-Co-Pay Tooth Powder giveaway (8 pgs.; circa 1942)	45.00	135.00	315.00
1-The Superman Time Capsule (Kellogg's Sugar Smacks)(1955)	22.00	65.00	154.00
1A-Duel in Space	17.00	51.00	120.00
1B-The Super Show of Metropolis (also #1-32, no B)	17.00	51.00	120.00

NOTE: *Numbering variations exist. Each title could have any combination-No. 1, 1A, or 1B.*

SUPERMAN IV MOVIE SPECIAL
Oct, 1987 (one shot, $2.00, color)
DC Comics

	Good	Fine	N-Mint
1	.35	1.00	2.00

SUPERMAN RECORD COMIC
1966 (Golden Records)
National Periodical Publications

(with record)-Record reads origin of Superman from comic; came with iron-on patch, decoder, membership card & button; comic

r-/Superman 125, 146	4.65	14.00	32.00
comic only	2.00	6.00	14.00

SUPERMAN'S BUDDY (Costume Comic)
1954 (4 pgs.) (One Shot) (Came in box w/costume; slick-paper/c)
National Periodical Publications

1-(Rare)-w/box & costume	65.00	195.00	455.00
Comic only	35.00	105.00	245.00

SUPERMAN'S CHRISTMAS ADVENTURE
1940, 1944 (16 pgs.) (Giveaway)
Distr. by Nehi drinks, Bailey Store, Ivey-Keith Co., Kennedy's Boys Shop, Macy's Store, Boston Store
National Periodical Publications

1(1940)-by Burnley	75.00	225.00	525.00
nn(1944)	60.00	180.00	420.00

SUPERMAN SCRAPBOOK (Has blank pages; contains no comics)

SUPERMAN'S GIRLFRIEND LOIS LANE (See 80 Pg. Giants #3,14, Showcase, & Superman Family)

SUPERMAN'S GIRLFRIEND LOIS LANE (Also see Lois Lane)
3-4/58 - No. 136, 1-2/74; No. 137, 9-10/74
National Periodical Publications

1	46.00	138.00	320.00
2	21.00	62.00	145.00
3	15.00	45.00	105.00
4,5	12.00	36.00	85.00
6-10: 9-Pat Boone app.	7.50	22.00	52.00
11-20: 14-Supergirl x-over	4.00	12.00	28.00
21-29: 23-1st app. Lena Thorul, Lex Luthor's sister. 29-Aquaman, Batman, Green Arrow cameo; last 10 cent issue	2.00	6.00	14.00
30-32,34-49: 47-Legion app.	1.00	3.00	7.00
33(5/62)-Mon-el app.	1.35	4.00	9.00
50-Triplicate Girl, Phantom Girl & Shrinking Violet app.	.70	2.00	4.00
51-55,57-67,69,70	.25	.75	1.50
56-Saturn Girl app.	.35	1.00	2.00
68-(Giant G-26)	.35	1.00	2.00
71-76,78: 74-1st Bizarro Flash		.50	1.00
77-(Giant G-39)		.60	1.20
79-Adams-c begin, end No. 95,108		.50	1.00
80-85,87-94: 89-Batman x-over; all Adams-c		.50	1.00
86-(Giant G-51)-Adams-c		.60	1.20
95-(Giant G-63)-Wonder Woman x-over; Adams-c		.60	1.20
96-103,105-111: 105-Origin/1st app. The Rose & the Thorn. 108-Adams-c		.50	1.00
104-(Giant G-75)		.50	1.00
108-Adams-c		.50	1.00
112,114-123 (52 pgs.): 111-Morrow-a. 122-G.A.-r/Superman #30. 123-G.A. Batman-r		.50	1.00
113-(Giant G-87)		.50	1.00
124-137: 130-Last Rose & the Thorn. 132-New Zatanna story. 136-Wonder Woman x-over		.50	1.00
Annual 1(Sum,'62)	3.60	11.00	25.00

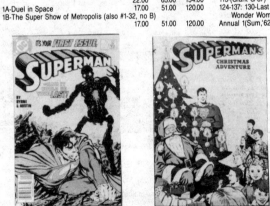

Superman #1 (1/87), © DC

Superman's Christmas Adventure #1, © DC

Superman's Girlfriend Lois Lane Annual #1, © DC

Superman's Pal Jimmy Olsen #44, © DC

Superman: The Earth Stealers #1, © DC

Super-Mystery Comics V1#4, © ACE

SUPERMAN'S GIRLFRIEND LOIS LANE (continued)

	Good	Fine	N-Mint
Annual 2(Sum,'63)	2.15	6.50	15.00

NOTE: **Buckler** a-117-121p. **Curt Swan** a-1-50(most).

SUPERMAN'S PAL JIMMY OLSEN (Superman Family #164 on)
(See 80 Page Giants)
Sept-Oct, 1954 - No. 163, Feb-Mar, 1974
National Periodical Publications

	Good	Fine	N-Mint
1	75.00	225.00	525.00
2	32.00	95.00	225.00
3-Last pre-code ish.	21.00	64.00	150.00
4,5	15.00	45.00	105.00
6-10	11.00	32.00	75.00
11-20	7.00	21.00	50.00
21-30: 29-1st app. Krypto in J.O.	3.60	11.00	25.00
31-40: 31-Origin Elastic Lad. 33-One pg. biography of Jack Larson			
(TV Jimmy Olsen). 36-Intro Lucy Lane	2.15	6.50	15.00
41-47,49,50: 41-1st J.O. Robot	1.50	4.50	10.00
48-Intro/origin Superman Emergency Squad	1.50	4.50	10.00
51-56: 56-Last 10 cent issue	1.00	3.00	6.00
57-61,64-69: 57-Olsen marries Supergirl	.55	1.60	3.20
62(7/62)-18th Legion app.; Mon-el, Elastic Lad app.			
	1.35	4.00	8.00
63(9/62)-Legion of Super-Villains app.	.60	1.80	3.60
70-Element Lad app.	.55	1.60	3.20
71,74,75,78,80-84,86,89,90: 86-J.O. Robot becomes Congorilla			
	.35	1.00	2.00
72(10/63)-Legion app; Elastic Lad (Olsen) joins	.50	1.50	3.00
73-Ultra Boy app.	.40	1.25	2.50
76,85-Legion app.	.50	1.50	3.00
77-Olsen with Colossal Boy's powers & costume; origin Titano retold			
	.40	1.25	2.50
79(9/64)-Titled The Red-headed Beatle of 1000 B.C.			
	.40	1.25	2.50
87-Legion of Super-Villains app.	.50	1.50	3.00
88-Star Boy app.	.35	1.00	2.00
91-94,96-98,101-103,105,107-110	.50	1.00	
95,104 (Giants G-25,G-38). 95-Transvestite story	.60	1.20	
99-Legion app; Olsen with powers/costumes of Lightning Lad, Sun			
Boy, & Star Boy	.30	1.00	2.00
100-Legion cameo app.	.30	1.00	2.00
106-Legion app.	.60	1.20	
111,112,114-121,123-130,132	.50	1.00	
113,122,131 (Giants G-50,G-62,G-74)	.50	1.00	
133-Newsboy Legion by Kirby begins	.30	1.00	2.00
134-140: 135-G.A. Guardian app. 136-Origin new Guardian. 140-			
(Giant G-86)	.50	1.00	
141-148: 141-Newsboy Legion reprints by S&K begin (52 pg. issues			
begin). 142-148-Newsboy Legion-r	.50	1.00	
149,150-G.A. Plastic Man reprint in both; last 52 pg. ish. 150-			
Newsboy Legion app.	.50	1.00	
151-163	.50	1.00	

NOTE: Issues #141-148 contain **Simon & Kirby** Newsboy Legion reprints from Star
Spangled #7, 8, 9, 10, 11, 12, 13, 14 in that order. **Adams** c-109-112, 115, 117, 118, 120,
121, 132, 134-136, 147, 148. **Kirby** a-133-139p, 141-148p; c-133, 139, 145p. **Kirby/Adams**
c-137, 138, 141-144, 146.

SUPERMAN SPECTACULAR (Also see DC Special Series #5)
1982 (Magazine size)(Square binding)
DC Comics

1	.35	1.00	2.00

SUPERMAN: THE EARTH STEALERS
1988 (one-shot, $2.95, 52pgs, prestige format)
DC Comics

1-Byrne scripts; painted-c	.60	1.75	3.50

SUPERMAN: THE SECRET YEARS
Feb, 1985 - No. 4, May, 1985 (mini-series)
DC Comics

	Good	Fine	N-Mint
1-Miller-c on all	.25	.75	1.50
2-4		.50	1.00

SUPERMAN 3-D (See Three-Dimension Adventures)

SUPERMAN-TIM (Becomes Tim)
1942 - May, 1950 (½-size) (B&W Giveaway)
Superman-Tim Stores/National Periodical Publications

	Good	Fine	N-Mint
8/42, 2/43, 3/43, 6/43, 8/43, 9/43, 3/44, 2/45, 11/49 issues-Two pg.			
Superman illos	8.50	25.50	60.00
10/43, 12/43, 2/44, 4/44-1/45, 3/45, 4/45, 4/46, 6/46, 8/46 issues-no			
Superman	6.50	19.50	45.00
9/46-1st stamp album issue (worth more if complete with Superman			
stamps)	7.00	21.00	50.00
10/46-1st Superman story	14.00	42.00	100.00
11/46, 12/46, 1/47, 2/47, 3/47, 4/47, 5/47-8/47 issues-Superman story			
	14.00	42.00	100.00
9/47-Stamp album issue & Superman sty	16.00	48.00	110.00
10/47, 11/47, 12/47-Superman stories	14.00	42.00	100.00
1/48, 2/48, 6/48, 8/48, 10/48, 11/48, 2/49-4/49, 12/49-5/50 issues-no			
Superman	5.50	16.50	40.00
9/48-Stamp album issue	6.50	19.50	45.00

NOTE: 16 pgs. through 9/47; 8 pgs. 10/47 on? The stamp album issues (3) may contain Superman stamps that were made to glue in these books. Books with the stamps
included would be worth more, and the value would depend upon completeness of the
album. There is no stamp album in the 9/49 issue.

SUPERMAN VS. THE AMAZING SPIDER-MAN
(Also see Marvel Treasury Edition No. 28)
April, 1976 (100 pgs.) ($2.00) (Over-sized)
National Periodical Publications/Marvel Comics Group

1	.50	1.50	3.00
1-2nd printing; 5000 numbered copies signed by Stan Lee & Car-			
mine Infantino on front cover & sold through mail			
	.85	2.50	5.00

SUPERMAN WORKBOOK
1945 (One Shot) (68 pgs; reprints) (B&W)
National Periodical Publ./Juvenile Group Foundation

c-r/Superman #14	65.00	195.00	455.00

SUPERMOUSE (...the Big Cheese; see Coo Coo Comics)
12/48 - No. 34, 9/55; No. 35, 4/56 - No. 45, Fall, 1958
Standard Comics/Pines No. 35 on (Literary Ent.)

1-Frazetta text illos (3)	14.00	42.00	100.00
2-Frazetta text illos	8.00	24.00	56.00
3,5,6-Text illos by Frazetta in all	6.00	18.00	42.00
4-Two pg. text illos by Frazetta	6.50	19.50	45.00
7-10	2.00	6.00	14.00
11-20: 13-Racist humor (Indians)	1.50	4.50	10.00
21-45	1.00	3.00	7.00
1-Summer Holiday issue (Summer,'56-Pines)-100 pgs.			
	3.50	10.50	24.00
2-Giant Summer issue (Summer,'58-Pines)-100 pgs.			
	3.00	9.00	21.00

SUPER-MYSTERY COMICS
July, 1940 - V8#6, July, 1949
Ace Magazines (Periodical House)

V1#1-Magno, the Magnetic Man & Vulcan begin			
	66.00	200.00	460.00
2	32.00	95.00	225.00
3-The Black Spider begins	25.00	75.00	175.00
4-Origin Davy	22.00	65.00	154.00
5-Intro. The Clown; begin series	22.00	65.00	154.00

SUPER-MYSTERY COMICS (continued)	Good	Fine	N-Mint
6(2/41)	19.00	57.00	132.00
V2#1(4/41)-Origin Buckskin	19.00	57.00	132.00
2-6(2/42)	17.00	51.00	120.00
V3#1(4/42),2: 1-Vulcan & Black Ace begin	15.00	45.00	105.00
3-Intro. The Lancer; Dr. Nemesis & The Sword begin; Kurtzman c/a(2) (Mr. Risk & Paul Revere Jr.)	21.00	62.00	146.00
4-Kurtzman-a	17.00	51.00	120.00
5-Kurtzman-a(2); L.B. Cole-a; Mr. Risk app.	18.00	54.00	125.00
6(10/43)-Mr. Risk app.; Kurtzman's Paul Revere Jr.; L.B. Cole-a	18.00	54.00	125.00
V4#1(1/44)-L.B. Cole-a	13.00	40.00	90.00
2-6(4/45): 2,5,6-Mr. Risk app.	11.00	32.00	75.00
V5#1(7/45)-6	8.50	25.50	60.00
V6#1-6: 3-Torture story. 4-Last Magno. Mr. Risk app. in #2,4-6	7.00	21.00	50.00
V7#1-6, V8#1-4,6	7.00	21.00	50.00
V8#5-Meskin, Tuska, Sid Greene-a	8.50	25.50	60.00

NOTE: *Sid Greene* a-V7#4. *Mooney* c-V1#5, 6. *V2#1*-6. *Palais* c/a-V5#3,4. Bondage c-V2#5, 6, V3#2, 5.

SUPERNATURAL THRILLERS
12/72 - No. 6, 11/73; No. 7, 7/74 - No. 15, 10/75
Marvel Comics Group

1-Itl-Sturgeon adaptation, 2-The Invisible Man, 3-The Valley of the Worm		.40	.80
4-Dr. Jekyll & Mr. Hyde, 5-The Living Mummy, 6-The Headless Horseman		.25	.50
7-15: 7-The Living Mummy begins		.25	.50

NOTE: *Brunner* c-11. *Buckler* a-5p. *Ditko* a-8r, 9r. *G. Kane* a-3p; c-3, 9p, 15p. *Mayerik* a-2p, 7, 8, 9p, 10p, 11. *McWilliams* a-14i. *Mortimer* a-4. *Steranko* c-1, 2. *Sutton* a-15. *Tuska* a-6p. *Robert E. Howard story-#3*.

SUPER POWERS
7/84 - No. 5, 11/84; 9/85 - No. 6, 2/86; 9/86 - No. 4, 12/86
DC Comics

1-Kirby-c		.60	1.20
2-5		.45	.90
1-('85)Kirby c/a in all; 1st app Samurai from Super Friends TV show; Capt. Marvel, Dr. Fate join		.50	1.00
2-6		.45	.90
1-4 ('86)		.40	.80

SUPER PUP (Formerly Spotty the Pup?) (See Space Comics)
No. 4, Mar-Apr, 1954 - No. 5, 1954
Avon Periodicals

4,5	1.50	4.50	10.00

SUPER RABBIT (See All Surprise, Animated Movie Tunes, Comedy Comics, Comic Capers, Ideal Comics, It's A Duck's Life, Movie Tunes & Wisco)
Fall, 1943 - No. 14, Nov, 1948
Timely Comics (CmPI)

1-Hitler-c	28.00	86.00	200.00
2	14.00	42.00	104.00
3-5	8.00	24.00	56.00
6-Origin	6.50	19.50	45.00
7-10; 9-Infinity-c	4.65	14.00	32.00
11-Kurtzman's "Hey Look"	5.70	17.00	40.00
12-14	3.70	11.00	26.00
I.W. Reprint #1,2('58),7,10('63)	.70	2.00	4.00

SUPER RICHIE (Superichie #5 on)
Sept, 1975 - No. 4, Mar, 1976 (All 52 pg. Giants)
Harvey Publications

1	.35	1.00	2.00
2-4		.50	1.00

SUPERSNIPE COMICS (Army & Navy #1-5)			
Oct, 1942 - V5No.1, Aug-Sept, 1949 (Also see Shadow Comics V2/3)			
Street & Smith Publications	Good	Fine	N-Mint
V1#6-Rex King Man of Adventure(costumed hero) by Jack Binder begins; Supersnipe by George Marcoux continues from Army & Navy #5; Bill Ward-a	28.00	86.00	200.00
7,8,10-12: 11-Little Nemo app.	17.00	51.00	120.00
9-Doc Savage x-over in Supersnipe; Hitler-c	20.00	60.00	140.00
V2#1-12: 1-Huck Finn by Clare Dwiggins begins, ends V3#5	12.00	36.00	84.00
V3#1-12: 8-Bobby Crusoe by Dwiggins begins, ends V3#12	9.00	27.00	62.00
V4#1-12, V5#1: V4#10-Xmas-c	6.50	19.50	45.00

NOTE: *Doc Savage in some issues.*

SUPERSPOOK (Formerly Frisky Animals on Parade)
No. 4, June, 1958
Ajax/Farrell Publications

4	1.50	4.50	10.00

SUPER SPY (See Wham)
Oct, 1940 - No. 2, Nov, 1940 (Reprints)
Centaur Publications

1-Origin The Sparkler	62.00	185.00	435.00
2-The Inner Circle, Dean Denton, Tim Blain, The Drew Ghost, The Night Hawk by Gustavson, & S.S. Swanson by Glanz app.	45.00	135.00	315.00

SUPER STAR HOLIDAY SPECIAL (See DC Special Series #21)

SUPER-TEAM FAMILY
10-11/75 - No. 15, 3-4/78 (#1-4: 68 pgs.; #5 on: 52 pgs.)
National Periodical Publications/DC Comics

1-Reprints; Adams, Kane/Wood		.40	.80
2-7: 4-7-Reprints		.25	.50
8-15-New stys; Chall. of the Unknown in #8-10		.25	.50

NOTE: *Adams* a-1r-3r. *Brunner* c-3. *Buckler* c-8p. *Estrada* a-2. *Tuska* a-7r. *Wood* a-1i(r), 3.

SUPER TV HEROES (See Hanna-Barbera . . .)

SUPER-VILLAIN CLASSICS
May, 1983 (One Shot)
Marvel Comics Group

1-"Galactus the Origin"		.50	1.00

SUPER-VILLAIN TEAM-UP
8/75 - No. 14, 10/77; No. 15, 11/78; No. 16, 5/79; No. 17, 6/80
Marvel Comics Group

1-Sub-Mariner app.	.25	.75	1.50
2-17: 5-1st Shroud. 7-Origin The Shroud		.50	1.00
Giant-Size 1(3/75, 68 pgs.)-Craig inks-r		.50	1.00
Giant-Size 2(6/75, 68 pgs.)-Dr. Doom, Sub-Mariner app.		.40	.80

NOTE: *Buckler* c-4p, 5p, 7p. *Buscema* c-1. *Byrne/Austin* c-14. *Ditko* a-Gnt-Size 2r. *Evans* a-1p, 3p. *Everett* a-1p. *Giffen* a-8p, 13p; c-13p. *Kane* c-2p, 9p. *Mooney* a-4i. *Sekowsky* a-Gnt-size 2p. *Starlin* c-6. *Tuska* a-1p, 15p(r). *Wood* a-15p(r).

SUPER WESTERN COMICS (Also see Buffalo Bill)
Aug, 1950 - No. 4, Mar, 1951
Youthful Magazines

1-Buffalo Bill begins; Calamity Jane app; Powell-c/a	3.70	11.00	26.00
2-4	2.00	6.00	14.00

SUPER WESTERN FUNNIES (See Super Funnies)

SUPERWORLD COMICS
April, 1940 - No. 3, Aug, 1940 (All have 68 pages)
Hugo Gernsback (Komos Publ.)

Supersnipe Comics V1#9, © S & S

Super Spy #1, © CEN

Super Western Comics #1, © YM

Superworld Comics #2, © Hugo Gernsback

Suspense Comics #11, © Continental Magazines

Swamp Thing #4, © DC

	Good	Fine	N-Mint
SUPERWORLD COMICS (continued)			

1-Origin Hip Knox, Super Hypnotist; Mitey Powers & Buzz Allen,
the Invisible Avenger, Little Nemo begin; cover by Frank R. Paul

	Good	Fine	N-Mint
1	100.00	300.00	700.00
2-Marvo 1,2 Go+, the Super Boy of the Year 2680	70.00	210.00	490.00
3	55.00	165.00	385.00

SURE-FIRE COMICS (Lightning Comics #4 on)
June, 1940 - No. 4, Oct, 1940 (Two No. 3's)
Ace Magazines

V1#1-Origin Flash Lightning; X-The Phantom Fed, Ace McCoy,
Buck Steele, Marvo the Magician, The Raven, Whiz Wilson

(Time Traveler) begin	55.00	165.00	385.00
2	35.00	105.00	245.00
3(9/40)	27.00	80.00	190.00
3(#4)(10/40)-nn on-c, #3 on inside	27.00	80.00	190.00

SURF 'N' WHEELS
Nov, 1969 - No. 6, Sept, 1970
Charlton Comics

1		.60	1.20
2-6		.50	1.00

SURGE
July, 1984 - No. 4, Jan, 1985 (mini-series) ($1.50; Baxter paper)
Eclipse Comics

1-4-Ties into DNAgents series	.30	.90	1.80

SURPRISE ADVENTURES (Formerly Tormented)
Mar, 1955 - No. 5, July, 1955
Sterling Comic Group

3-5: 3,5-Sekowsky-a	1.50	4.50	10.00

SUSIE Q. SMITH (See Four Color #323,377,453,553)

SUSPENSE (Radio/TV; Real Life Tales of... #1-4) (Amazing
Detective Cases #3 on?...change to horror)
Dec, 1949 - No. 29, Apr, 1953 (#1-8,17-23: 52 pgs.)
Marvel/Atlas Comics (CnPC No. 1-10/BFP No. 11-29)

1-Powell-a; Peter Lorre, Sidney Greenstreet photo-c from			
Hammett's 'The Maltese Falcon'	16.00	48.00	110.00
2-Crime stories; photo-c	8.00	24.00	55.00
3-Change to horror	8.00	24.00	55.00
4,7-10	5.00	15.00	35.00
5-Krigstein, Tuska, Everett-a	5.70	17.00	40.00
6-Tuska, Everett, Morisi-a	5.00	15.00	35.00
11-17,19,20: 14-Hypo-c; A-Bomb panels	4.65	14.00	32.00
18,22-Krigstein-a	5.00	15.00	35.00
21,23,26-29	3.50	10.50	24.00
24-Tuska-a	4.00	12.00	28.00
25-Electric chair c/a	7.00	21.00	50.00

NOTE: *Briefer a-5, 7, 27. Colan a-8(2), 9. Everett a-5, 6(2), 19, 23, 28; c-21-23, 26. Fu-je a-29. Heath a-5, 6, 8, 10, 12, 14; c-14, 19, 24. Maneely a-29; c-15, 19. Morisi a-6. Palais a-10. Rico a-7-9. Robinson a-29. Romita a-25. Sekowsky a-11, 13, 14. Sinnott a-23, 25. Tuska a-5, 6, 12; c-12. Whitney a-15, 16, 22.*

SUSPENSE COMICS
Dec, 1943 - No. 12, Dec?, 1946
Continental Magazines

1-The Grey Mask begins; bondage/torture-c; L. B. Cole-a, 7pgs.			
	35.00	105.00	245.00
2-Intro. The Mask; Rico, Giunta, L. B. Cole-a, 7pgs.			
	21.00	62.00	146.00
3-L.B. Cole-a; Schomburg-c	21.00	62.00	146.00
4-6: 5-Schomburg-c	19.00	57.00	132.00
7,9,10	18.00	54.00	125.00
8-Classic L. B. Cole spider-c	40.00	120.00	280.00
11-Classic Devil-c	27.00	81.00	190.00
12-r-#7-c	18.00	54.00	125.00

NOTE: *L. B. Cole c-6-12. Larsen a-11. Palais a-10,11. Bondage c-1, 3, 4.*

SUSPENSE DETECTIVE
June, 1952 - No. 5, Mar, 1953
Fawcett Publications

	Good	Fine	N-Mint
1-Evans-a, 11 pgs; Baily c/a	10.00	30.00	70.00
2-Evans-a, 10 pgs.	5.70	17.00	40.00
3,5	4.65	14.00	32.00
4-Bondage-c	5.70	17.00	40.00

NOTE: *Baily a-4, 5. Sekowsky a-2, 4, 5; c-5.*

SUSPENSE STORIES (See Strange Suspense Stories)

SUZIE COMICS (Formerly Laugh Comix; see Pep Comics & Top-
Notch Comics #28)
No. 49, Spring, 1945 - No. 100, Aug, 1954
Close-Up No. 49,50/MLJ Mag./Archie No. 51 on

49-Ginger begins	11.50	34.00	80.00
50-55: 54-Transvestism story	8.50	25.50	60.00
56-Katy Keene begins by Woggon	7.50	22.50	52.00
57-65	5.00	15.00	35.00
66-80	4.30	13.00	30.00
81-87,89-99	3.70	11.00	26.00
88-Used in POP, pg. 76,77; Bill Woggon draws himself in story			
	5.00	15.00	35.00
100-Last Katy Keene	4.30	13.00	30.00

NOTE: *Katy Keene in 53-82,85-100.*

SWAMP FOX, THE (See 4-Color #1179 & Walt Disney Presents #2)

SWAMP FOX, THE
1960 (14 pgs, small size) (Canada Dry Premiums)
Walt Disney Productions

Titles: (A)-Tory Masquerade, (B)-Rindau Rampage, (C)-Turnabout
Tactics; each came in paper sleeve, books 1,2 & 3;

Set with sleeves	3.50	10.50	24.00
Comic only	1.00	3.00	6.00

SWAMP THING (See Brave & Bold, DC Comics Presents 8&85, DC
Spec. Series 2, 14, 17, 20, House of Sec. 92, Roots of the..., & The
Saga of...)
Oct-Nov, 1972 - No. 24, Aug-Sept, 1976
National Periodical Publications/DC Comics

1-c/a by Wrightson begin	1.00	3.00	6.00
2	.50	1.50	3.00
3-Intro. Patchworkman	.40	1.25	2.50
4-10: 7-Batman app. 10-Last Wrightson issue	1.00	2.00	
11-24-Redondo-a; 23-Swamp Thing reverts back to Dr. Holland			
		.50	1.00

NOTE: *J. Jones a-9i. Kaluta a-9i. Redondo c-12-19, 21.*

SWAT MALONE
Sept, 1955
Swat Malone Enterprises

V1#1-Hy Fleishman-a	4.00	12.00	28.00

SWEENEY (Buz Sawyer's Pal, Roscoe...)
1949
Standard Comics

4,5-Crane-a #5	3.50	10.50	24.00

SWEE'PEA (See 4-Color #219)

SWEETHEART DIARY (Cynthia Doyle #66-on)
Wint, 1949; No. 2, Spr, 1950; No. 3, 6/50 - No. 5, 10/50; No. 6,
1951(nd); No. 7, 9/51 - No. 14, 1/53; No. 32, 10/55; No. 33, 4/56 - No.
65, 8/62 (No. 1-14, photo-c)
Fawcett Publications/Charlton Comics No. 33 on

1	5.50	16.50	38.00
2	3.00	9.00	21.00
3,4-Wood-a	8.00	24.00	56.00

SWEETHEART DIARY (continued)	Good	Fine	N-Mint
5-10: 8-Bailey-a	2.35	7.00	16.00
11-14-Last Fawcett issue	1.30	4.00	9.00
32 (10/55; 1st Charlton ish.)(Formerly Cowboy Love #31)			
	1.15	3.50	8.00
34-40	.85	2.50	6.00
41-60	.35	1.00	2.00
61-65		.40	.80

SWEETHEARTS (Formerly Captain Midnight)
No. 68, 10/48 - No. 121, 5/53; No. 122, 3/54; No. 23, 5/54 - No. 137, 12/73
Fawcett Publications/Charlton No. 122 on

	Good	Fine	N-Mint
68-Robert Mitchum photo-c	4.60	14.00	32.00
69-80: 72-Baker-a?	2.00	6.00	14.00
81-84,86-93,95-99	1.50	4.50	10.00
85,94,103,105,110,117-George Evans-a	2.35	7.00	16.00
100	1.85	5.50	13.00
101-Powell-a	1.65	5.00	11.50
102,104,106-109,112-116,118,121	1.15	3.50	8.00
111-1 pg. Ronald Reagan biog	3.50	10.50	24.00
119-Marilyn Monroe photo-c; also appears in story; part Wood-a			
	10.00	30.00	70.00
120-Atom Bomb story	3.50	10.50	24.00
122-(1st Charlton? 3/54)-Marijuana story	2.15	6.50	15.00
V2/23 (5/54)-28: Last precode ish (2/55)	.85	2.50	6.00
29-39,41,43-45,47-50	.60	1.80	4.00
40-Photo-c; Tommy Sands story	1.00	3.00	7.00
42-Ricky Nelson photo-c/sty	1.50	4.50	10.00
46-Jimmy Rodgers photo-c/sty	1.00	3.00	7.00
51-60	.55	1.65	4.00
61-80	.30	1.00	2.00
81-100		.50	1.00
101-137		.25	.50
NOTE: Photo c-68-121.

SWEETHEART SCANDALS (See Fox Giants)

SWEETIE PIE (See 4-Color #1185,1241)

SWEETIE PIE
Dec, 1955 - No. 15, Fall, 1957
Ajax-Farrell/Pines (Literary Ent.)

1-By Nadine Seltzer	2.35	7.00	16.00
2 (5/56; last Ajax?)	1.15	3.50	8.00
3-15 (#3-10, exist?)	.85	2.50	6.00

SWEET LOVE
Sept, 1949 - No. 5, May, 1950
Home Comics (Harvey)

1-Photo-c	2.00	6.00	14.00
2-Photo-c	1.50	4.50	10.00
3,4: 3-Powell-a; 4-Photo-c	1.35	4.00	9.00
5-Kamen, Powell-a; photo-c	2.75	8.00	18.00

SWEET ROMANCE
October, 1968
Charlton Comics

1		.40	.80

SWEET SIXTEEN
Aug-Sept, 1946 - No. 13, Jan, 1948
Parents' Magazine Institute

1-Van Johnson's life story; Dorothy Dare, Queen of Hollywood Stunt Artists begins (in all issues); part photo-c			
	5.00	15.00	35.00
2-Jane Powell, Roddy McDowall ''Holiday in Mexico'' photo-c			
	3.50	10.50	24.00
3-6,8-11: 6-Dick Haymes story	2.35	7.00	16.00
7-Ronald Reagan's life story	10.00	30.00	70.00

	Good	Fine	N-Mint
12-Bob Cummings, Vic Damone story	3.50	10.50	24.00
13-Robert Mitchum's life story	4.00	12.00	28.00

SWIFT ARROW (Also see Lone Rider & The Rider)
2-3/54 - No. 5, 10-11/54; 4/57 - No. 3, 9/57
Ajax/Farrell Publications

1(1954) (1st Series)	4.65	14.00	32.00
2	2.00	6.00	14.00
3-5: 5-Lone Rider sty	1.70	5.00	12.00
1 (2nd Series) (Swift Arrow's Gunfighters #4)	1.70	5.00	12.00
2,3: 2-Lone Rider begins	1.50	4.50	10.00

SWIFT ARROW'S GUNFIGHTERS (Formerly Swift Arrow)
No. 4, Nov, 1957
Ajax/Farrell Publ. (Four Star Comic Corp.)

4	1.70	5.00	12.00

SWING WITH SCOOTER
6-7/66 - No. 35, 8-9/71; No. 36, 10-11/72
National Periodical Publications

1	.75	2.50	6.00
2-10	.60	1.75	3.50
11-32,35,36	.35	1.00	2.00
33-Interview with David Cassidy	.35	1.00	2.00
34-Interview with Ron Ely (Doc Savage)	.35	1.00	2.00
NOTE: Orlando a-1-11; c-1-11, 13, #20, 33, 34: 68 pgs.; #35: 52 pgs.

SWISS FAMILY ROBINSON (See 4-Color #1156, King Classics, & Movie Comics)

SWORD & THE DRAGON, THE (See 4-Color #1118)

SWORD & THE ROSE, THE (See 4-Color #505,682)

SWORD IN THE STONE, THE (See March of Comics #258 & Movie Comics)

SWORD OF LANCELOT (See Movie Comics)

SWORD OF SORCERY
Feb-Mar, 1973 - No. 5, Nov-Dec, 1973
National Periodical Publications

1-Leiber Fafhrd & The Grey Mouser; Adams/Bunkers inks; also #2; Kaluta-c	.25	.75	1.50
2-Wrightson-c(i); Adams-a(i)	.25	.75	1.50
3-5: 5-Starlin-a; Conan cameo		.60	1.20
NOTE: Chaykin a-1p, 2-4; c-2p, 3-5. Kaluta a-3i. Simonson a-1i, 3p, 4, 5p; c-5. Starlin a-5p.

SWORD OF THE ATOM
Sept, 1983 - No. 4, Dec, 1983 (Mini-series)
DC Comics

1-Kane c/a begins		.50	1.00
2-4		.50	1.00
Special 1(7/84), 2(7/85): Kane c/a each		.65	1.30
Special 3(6/88, $1.50)		.65	1.30

SWORDS OF TEXAS
10/87 - No. 4, Jan, 1988 ($1.75, color, mini-series,Baxter)
Eclipse Comics

1-4: Scout app.	.30	.90	1.80

SWORDS OF THE SWASHBUCKLERS (See Marvel Graphic Novel)
5/85 - No. 12, 6/87 ($1.50; Mature readers)
Epic Comics (Marvel)

1-Butch Guice-c/a cont'd from Marvel Graphic Novel			
	.25	.80	1.60
2-12	.25	.80	1.60

SYPHONS
July, 1986 - No. 7, 1987 ($1.50, $1.75, color)
Now Comics

1-7	.25	.75	1.50

Sweethearts #106, © FAW

Swift Arrow #5, © AJAX

Syphons #3, © NOW Comics

Tales Calculated To Drive You Bats #7, © AP

Tales From The Crypt #20, © WMG

Tales Of Horror #1, © TOBY

TAFFY COMICS
Mar-Apr, 1945 - No. 12, 1948
Rural Home/Orbit Publ.

	Good	Fine	N-Mint
1-L.B. Cole-c; origin of Wiggles The Wonderworm plus 7 chapter WWII funny animal adv.	5.50	16.50	38.00
2-L.B. Cole-c	3.50	10.50	24.00
3,4,6-12: 6-Perry Como c/story. 7-Duke Ellington, 2pgs.	2.65	8.00	18.00
5-L.B. Cole-c; Van Johnson story	3.50	10.50	24.00

TAILGUNNER JO
Sept., 1988 - No. 6, Holiday, 1988-'89 ($1.25, color)
DC Comics

1-6		.60	1.25

TAILSPIN
November, 1944
Spotlight Publishers

nn-Firebird app.; L.B. Cole-c	5.50	16.50	38.00

TAILSPIN TOMMY STORY & PICTURE BOOK
1931? (nd) (Color stip reprints; 10½x10'')
McLoughlin Bros.

266-by Forrest	13.00	40.00	90.00

TAILSPIN TOMMY
1932 (100 pages)(hardcover)
Cupples & Leon Co.

(Rare)-B&W strip reprints from 1930 by Hal Forrest & Glenn Claffin	16.00	48.00	110.00

TAILSPIN TOMMY (Also see Popular Comics)
1940; 1946
United Features Syndicate/Service Publ. Co.

Single Series 23('40)	15.00	45.00	105.00
Best Seller (nd, '46)-Service Publ. Co.	8.00	24.00	55.00

TALENT SHOWCASE (See New Talent Showcase)

TALES CALCULATED TO DRIVE YOU BATS
Nov, 1961 - No. 7, Nov, 1962; 1966
Archie Publications

1	3.50	10.50	24.00
2	1.70	5.00	12.00
3-6	1.20	3.50	8.00
7-Storyline change	.70	2.00	5.00
1('66)-25 cents	.85	2.50	6.00

TALES FROM THE CRYPT (Formerly The Crypt Of Terror; see Three Dimensional . . .)
No. 20, Oct-Nov, 1950 - No. 46, Feb-Mar, 1955
E.C. Comics

20	42.00	125.00	295.00
21-Kurtzman-r/Haunt of Fear #15/1	35.00	105.00	245.00
22-Moon Girl costume at costume party, one panel	28.00	84.00	195.00
23-25	21.00	62.00	146.00
26-30	16.50	50.00	115.00
31-Williamson-a(1st at E.C.); B&W and color illos. in POP; Kamen draws himself, Gaines & Feldstein; Ingels, Craig & Davis draw themselves in his story	21.00	62.00	146.00
32,35-39	13.00	40.00	90.00
33-Origin The Crypt Keeper	21.00	62.00	146.00
34-Used in POP, pg. 83; lingerie panels	13.00	40.00	90.00
40-Used in Senate hearings & in Hartford Cournat anti-comics editorials-1954	13.00	40.00	90.00
41-45: 45-2pgs. showing E.C. staff	11.50	34.00	80.00
46-Low distribution; pre-advertised cover for unpublished 4th horror title 'Crypt of Terror' used on this book	13.00	40.00	90.00

NOTE: **Craig** a-20, 22-24; c-20. **Crandall** a-38, 44. **Davis** a-24-46; c-29-46. **Elder** a-37, 38. **Evans** a-32-34, 36, 40, 41, 43, 46. **Feldstein** a-20-23; c-21-25, 28. **Ingels** a-in all. **Kamen** a-20, 22, 25, 27-31, 33-36, 39, 41-45. **Krigstein** a-40, 42, 45. **Kurtzman** a-21. **Orlando** a-27-30, 35, 37, 39, 41-45. **Wood** a-21, 24, 25; c-26, 27. Canadian reprints known; see Table of Contents.

TALES FROM THE CRYPT (Magazine)
No. 10, July, 1968 (35 cents)(B&W)
Eerie Publications

	Good	Fine	N-Mint
10-Contains Farrell reprints from 1950s	.70	2.00	4.00

TALES FROM THE GREAT BOOK
Feb, 1955 - No. 4, Jan, 1956
Famous Funnies

1-Story of Samson	3.50	10.50	24.00
2-4-Lehti-a in all	1.70	5.00	12.00

TALES FROM THE TOMB
Oct, 1962 - No. 2, Dec, 1962
Dell Publishing Co.

1(02-810-210)(Giant)-All stories written by John Stanley	2.00	6.00	14.00
2	1.35	4.00	9.00

TALES FROM THE TOMB (Magazine)
V1#6, July, 1969 - V7#1, Feb, 1975 (52 pgs.)
Eerie Publications

V1#6-8	.85	2.50	6.00
V2#1-3,5,6: 6-Rulah-r	.50	1.50	3.00
4-LSD story-r/Weird V3#5	.85	2.50	6.00
V3#1-Rulah-r	.70	2.00	5.00
2-6('70),V4#1-5('72),V5#1-6('73),V6#1-6('74),V7#1('75)	.50	1.50	3.00

TALES OF ASGARD
Oct, 1968 (68 pages); Feb, 1984 ($1.25, 52 pgs.)
Marvel Comics Group

1-Thor r-/from Journey into Mystery #97-106; new Kirby-c	.35	1.00	2.00
V2#1 (2/84)-Thor-r; Simonson-c	.40		.80

TALES OF DEMON DICK & BUNKER BILL
1934 (78 pgs; 5x10½''; B&W)(hardcover)
Whitman Publishing Co.

793-by Dick Spencer	8.00	24.00	56.00

TALES OF EVIL
Feb, 1975 - No. 3, July, 1975
Atlas/Seaboard Publ.

1		.30	.60
2-Intro. The Bog Beast		.25	.50
3-Origin The Man-Monster		.25	.50

NOTE: Lieber c-1. Sekowsky a-1. Sutton a-2. Thorne c-2.

TALES OF GHOST CASTLE
May-June, 1975 - No. 3, Sept-Oct, 1975
National Periodical Publications

1-3: 1,3-Redondo-a. 2-Nino-a		.25	.50

TALES OF G.I. JOE
Jan, 1988 - Present (color)
Marvel Comics

1 ($2.25)	.40	1.15	2.30
2-14 ($1.50)(#1-4-r/G.I. Joe #1-4)	.25	.75	1.50

TALES OF HORROR
June, 1952 - No. 13, Oct, 1954
Toby Press/Minoan Publ. Corp.

1	8.50	25.50	60.00
2-Torture scenes	6.50	19.50	45.00

	Good	Fine	N-Mint

TALES OF HORROR (continued)

	Good	Fine	N-Mint
3-8,13	4.30	13.00	30.00
9-11-Reprints Purple Claw #1-3	4.65	14.00	32.00
12-Myron Fass c/a; torture scenes	5.00	15.00	35.00

NOTE: *Andru a-5. Bailey a-5. Myron Fass a-2, 3, 12; c-1-3, 12. Hollingsworth a-2. Sparling a-6, 9; c-9.*

TALES OF JUSTICE
No. 53, May, 1955 - No. 67, Aug, 1957
Atlas Comics(MjMC No. 53-66/Male No. 67)

53	4.00	12.00	28.00
54-57	2.65	8.00	18.00
58,59-Krigstein-a	3.50	10.50	24.00
60-63,65	1.50	4.50	10.00
64,67-Crandall-a	2.65	8.00	18.00
66-Torres, Orlando-a	2.65	8.00	18.00

NOTE: *Everett a-53, 60. Orlando a-65, 66. Powell a-54. Severin c-58, 65.*

TALES OF SUSPENSE (Captain America #100 on)
Jan, 1959 - No. 99, March, 1968
Atlas (WPI No. 1,2/Male No. 3-12/VPI No. 13-18)/Marvel No. 19 on

1-Williamson-a, 5 pgs.	36.00	108.00	250.00
2,3	14.00	42.00	100.00
4-Williamson-a, 4 pgs; Kirby/Everett c/a	16.00	48.00	110.00
5-10	9.50	28.50	65.00
11,13-20: 14-Intro. Colossus. 16-Intro Metallo (Pre-Iron Man prototype)	6.50	19.50	45.00
12-Crandall-a	7.00	21.00	50.00
21-25: 25-Last 10 cent ish.	4.00	12.00	28.00
26-38: 32-Sazzik The Sorcerer app. (Dr. Strange proto-type)	3.00	9.00	21.00
39 (3/63)-Origin & 1st app. Iron Man; 1st Iron Man story-Kirby layouts	75.00	188.00	525.00
40-Iron Man in new armor	29.00	72.00	200.00
41	14.00	35.00	100.00
42-45: 45-Intro. & 1st app. Happy & Pepper	7.00	18.00	50.00
46,47	3.50	9.00	25.00
48-New Iron Man armor	4.30	11.00	30.00
49-51: 49-X-Men x-over. 50-1st app. Mandarin	2.15	5.50	15.00
52-1st app. The Black Widow	3.00	7.50	21.00
53-Origin The Watcher (5/64; 2nd app.); Black Widow app.	2.15	5.50	15.00
54-56	1.50	4.50	10.00
57-1st app./Origin Hawkeye (9/64)	4.30	11.00	30.00
58-Captain America begins (10/64)	1.00	3.00	7.00
59-Iron Man plus Captain America features begin; intro Jarvis, Avenger's butler	1.00	3.00	7.00
60,61,64	.85	2.50	5.00
62-Origin Mandarin (2/65)	.85	2.50	5.00
63-Origin Captain America (3/65)	.85	2.50	5.00
65-1st Silver-Age Red Skull (6/65)	.85	2.50	5.00
66-Origin Red Skull	.85	2.50	5.00
67-94,96-99: 69-1st app. Titanium Man. 75-Intro/1st app. Agent 13 later named Sharon Carter. 76-Intro Batroc & Sharon Carter, Agent 13 of Shield. 79-Intro Cosmic Cube. 94-Intro Modok	.85	2.50	5.00
95-Capt. America's i.d. revealed	.85	2.50	5.00

NOTE: *Colan a-39, 73-99p; c(p)-73, 75, 77, 79, 81, 83, 85-87, 89, 91, 93, 95, 97, 99. Craig a-99i. Crandall a-12. Davis a-38. Ditko/Kirby art in most issues #1-15, 17-49. Everett a-8. Forte a-5, 9. Heath a-10. Gil Kane a-88p, 89-91; c-88, 89-91p. Kirby a(p)-40, 41, 43, 59-75, 77-86, 92-99; layouts-69-75, 77; c(p)-29-56, 58-72, 74, 76, 78, 80, 82, 84, 86, 92, 94, 96, 98. Leiber/Fox a-42, 43, 45, 51. Reinman a-26, 44i, 49i, 52i, 53i. Tuska a-58, 70-74. Wood c/a-71i.*

TALES OF SWORD & SORCERY (See Dagar)

TALES OF TERROR
1952 (no month)
Toby Press Publications

	Good	Fine	N-Mint
1-Fawcette-c; Ravielli-a	5.00	15.00	35.00

NOTE: *This title was cancelled due to similarity to the E.C. title.*

TALES OF TERROR (See Movie Classics)

TALES OF TERROR (Magazine)
Summer, 1964
Eerie Publications

1	1.30	4.00	9.00

TALES OF TERROR
July, 1985 - No. 13, July, 1987 ($2.00; Baxter paper; mature readers)
Eclipse Comics

1	.40	1.25	2.50
2-13: 3-Morrow-a. 7-Bissette, Bolton-a	.35	1.00	2.00

TALES OF TERROR ANNUAL
1951 - 1953 (25 cents) (132 pgs.)
E.C. Comics

nn(1951)(Scarce)-Feldstein infinity-c	200.00	600.00	1400.00
2(1952)-Feldstein-c	100.00	300.00	700.00
3(1953)	70.00	210.00	490.00

No. 1 contains three horror and one science fiction comic which came out in 1950. No. 2 contains a horror, crime, and science fiction book which generally had cover dates in 1951, and No. 3 had horror, crime, and shock books that generally appeared in 1952. All E.C. annuals contain four complete books that did not sell on the stands which were rebound in the annual format, minus the covers, and sold from the E.C. office and on the stands in key cities. The contents of each annual may vary in the same year.

TALES OF TERROR ILLUSTRATED (See Terror Ill.)

TALES OF TEXAS JOHN SLAUGHTER (See 4-Color #997)

TALES OF THE BEANWORLD
Feb., 1985 - No. 10, 1988 ($1.50/$2.00, B&W)
Beanworld Press/Eclipse Comics

1	.70	2.00	4.00
2-10	.35	1.00	2.00

TALES OF THE GREEN BERET
Jan, 1967 - No. 5, Oct, 1969
Dell Publishing Co.

1	1.00	3.00	7.00
2-5: 5 reprints #1	.75	2.25	5.00

NOTE: *Glanzman a 1-4.*

TALES OF THE GREEN LANTERN CORPS
May, 1981 - No. 3, July, 1981
DC Comics

1-Origin of G.L. & the Guardians; Staton-a(p)		.45	.90
2,3-Staton-a(p)		.30	.60
Annual 1 (1/85)-G. Kane c/a		.65	1.30

TALES OF THE INVISIBLE SCARLET O'NEIL (See Harv. Comics Hits #59)

TALES OF THE KILLERS (Magazine)
V1No.10, Dec, 1970 - V1No.11, Feb, 1971 (52pgs.)(B&W)
World Famous Periodicals

V1#10-One pg. Frazetta	1.15	3.50	8.00
11	.70	2.00	4.00

TALES OF THE LEGION (Formerly The Legion of Super-Heroes)
No. 314, Aug, 1984 - Present
DC Comics

314-320: 314-Origin The White Witch		.40	.80
321-354: r-/Legion S.H. (Baxter series)		.45	.90
Annual 4 ('86), 5 (10/87)		.60	1.20

TALES OF THE MARINES (Devil-Dog Dugan #3)
Feb, 1957 (Marines At War #5 on)
Atlas Comics (OPI)

Tales Of Suspense #1, © MEG

Tales Of Terror Annual #2, © WMG

(caption center: Tales Of Suspense #58, © MEG)

Tales Of The Mysterious Traveler #5, © CC   Tales Of The Teenage Mutant Ninja Turtles #2, © Mirage   Tales To Astonish #38, © MEG

	Good	Fine	N-Mint
TALES OF THE MARINES (continued)			
4-Powell-a	1.20	3.50	8.00

TALES OF THE MYSTERIOUS TRAVELER (See Mysterious...)
8/56 - No. 13, 6/59; V2/14, 10/85 - No. 15, 12/85
Charlton Comics

1-No Ditko-a	13.00	40.00	90.00
2-Ditko-a(1)	11.50	34.00	80.00
3-Ditko c/a(1)	10.00	30.00	70.00
4-6-Ditko c/a(3-4)	13.50	40.00	95.00
7-9-Ditko-a(1-2)	10.00	30.00	70.00
10,11-Ditko-c/a(3-4)	11.50	34.00	80.00
12,13	4.00	12.00	28.00
14,15 (1985)-Ditko c/a		.40	.80

TALES OF THE NEW TEEN TITANS
June, 1982 - No. 4, Sept, 1982 (mini-series)
DC Comics

1-Origin Cyborg-book length story	.35	1.00	2.00
2-4: 2-Origin Raven. 3-Origin Changeling. 4-Origin Starfire	.25	.75	1.50

NOTE: *Perez* a-1-4p; c-1-4.

TALES OF THE PONY EXPRESS (See 4-Color #829, 942)

TALES OF THE SUN RUNNERS
July, 1986 - No. 3 ($1.50, color)
Sirius Comics/Amazing Comics No. 3 on

V2#1	.25	.75	1.50
V2#2,3 ($1.95)	.35	1.00	2.00
Christmas Special 1(12/86)	.25	.75	1.50

TALES OF THE TEENAGE MUTANT NINJA TURTLES
May, 1987 - Present (B&W, $1.50)
Mirage Studios

1	.40	1.25	2.50
2-8	.30	.90	1.80

TALES OF THE TEEN TITANS (Formerly The New...)
No. 41, April, 1984 - No. 91, July, 1988
DC Comics

41-49,51-59: 44-1st app/origin Terminator; Jericho & Nightwing join. 46-Aqualad & Aquagirl join. 53-Intro Azreal. 56-Intro Jinx. 57-Neutron app. 59-r/DC Comics Presents 26
	.40	.80
50-Double size	.50	1.00
60-91: r/New Teen Titans Baxter series. 69-Origin Kole. #83-91, $1.00 cover	.40	.80
Annual 3('84; $1.25)-Death of Terra	.60	1.20
Annual 4(11/86)-r, 5('87)	.60	1.20

TALES OF THE TEXAS RANGERS (See Jace Pearson...)

TALES OF THE UNEXPECTED (The Unexpected #105 on)(See Super DC Giant)
Feb-Mar, 1956 - No. 104, Dec-Jan, 1967-68
National Periodical Publications

1	30.00	90.00	210.00
2	13.00	40.00	90.00
3-5	8.00	24.00	56.00
6-10	5.50	16.00	38.00
11,12,14	3.00	9.00	21.00
13,15-18,21-23: Kirby-a. 16-Character named 'Thor' with a magic hammer - not like later Thor	4.00	12.00	28.00
19,20,24-39: 24-Cameron-c/a	2.00	6.00	14.00
40-Space Ranger begins, ends #82	11.00	32.00	75.00
41-50	1.70	5.00	12.00
51-67: 67-Last 10 cent ish.	1.00	3.00	7.00
68-80	.85	2.50	5.00
81-100: 91-1st Automan (also in #94,97)	.50	1.50	3.00
101-104	.25	.75	1.50

NOTE: *Adams* c-104. *Anderson* a-50. *Brown* a-50-82(Space Ranger). *Heath* a-31, 49. *Bob Kane* a-24, 48. *Kirby* a-12, 24; c-22. *Meskin* a-15, 18, 26, 27, 35, 66. *Moreira* a-16, 39, 38, 44, 62; c-38.

TALES OF THE WEST (See 3-D...)

TALES OF THE WIZARD OF OZ (See 4-Color #1308)

TALES OF THE ZOMBIE (Magazine)
Aug, 1973 - No. 10, Mar, 1975 (75 cents)(B&W)
Marvel Comics Group

	Good	Fine	N-Mint
V1#1-Reprint/Menace #5; origin	1.00	3.00	6.00
2,3: 2-Everett biography & memorial	.70	2.00	4.00
V2#1(#4)-Photos,text of Bond movie 'Live & Let Die'	.70	2.00	4.00
5-10: 8-Kaluta-a	.70	2.00	4.00
Annual 1(Summer,'75)(#11)-B&W; Everett, Buscema-a	.70	2.00	4.00

NOTE: *Alcala* a-7-9. *Boris* c-1-4. *Colan* a-2r, 6. *Heath* a-5r. *Reese* a-2. *Tuska* a-2r.

TALES OF THUNDER
March, 1985
Deluxe Comics

1-Dynamo, Iron Maiden & Menthor app.; Giffen-a	.35	1.00	2.00

TALES OF VOODOO (Magazine)
V1No.11, Nov, 1968 - V7No.6, Nov, 1974
Eerie Publications

V1#11	1.00	3.00	7.00
V2#1(3/69)-V2#4(9/69)	.60	1.75	3.50
V3#1-6('70): 4-'Claws of the Cat' redrawn from Climax #1	.60	1.75	3.50
V4#1-6('71), V5#1-6('72), V6#1-6('73), V7#1-6('74)	.60	1.75	3.50
Annual 1	.70	2.00	4.00

NOTE: *Bondage-c-V1No.10, V2No.4, V3No.4.*

TALES OF WELLS FARGO (See 4-Color #876, 968, 1023,1075, 1113, 1167, 1215, & Western Roundup under Dell Giants)

TALES TO ASTONISH (Becomes The Incredible Hulk #102 on)
Jan, 1959 - No. 101, March, 1968
Atlas (MAP No. 1/ZPC No. 2-14/VPI No. 15-21/Marvel No. 22 on

1-Jack Davis-a	37.00	112.00	260.00
2-Ditko-c	17.00	51.00	120.00
3	14.00	42.00	100.00
4	10.00	30.00	70.00
5-Williamson-a, 4 pgs.	11.00	32.00	75.00
6-10	7.00	21.00	50.00
11-20	4.65	14.00	32.00
21-26	3.00	9.00	21.00
27-1st Antman app. (1/62); last 10 cent ish.	100.00	250.00	700.00
28-34	2.65	8.00	18.00
35-2nd Antman, 1st in costume; begin series	36.00	90.00	250.00
36	14.00	35.00	100.00
37-40	7.00	18.00	50.00
41-43	3.50	9.00	25.00
44-Origin & 1st app. The Wasp	4.30	11.00	30.00
45-48: 46-1st Crimson Dynamo	2.85	7.00	20.00
49-Antman becomes Giant Man	4.30	11.00	30.00
50-58: 50-Origin/1st app. Human Top. 52-Origin/1st app. Black Knight	1.70	5.00	12.00
59-Giant Man vs. Hulk feat. story	2.60	6.50	18.00
60-Giant Man/Hulk dbl. feat. begins	2.15	5.50	15.00
61-70: 62-1st app./origin The Leader; new Wasp costume. 65-New Giant Man costume. 68-New Human Top costume. 69-Last Giant Man. 70-Sub-Mariner & Incred. Hulk begins	1.15	3.50	8.00
71-80	.85	2.50	6.00
81-91: 90-1st app. The Abomination	.85	2.50	6.00

379

TALES TO ASTONISH (continued)

	Good	Fine	N-Mint
92,93-Silver Surfer app.	.85	2.50	6.00
94-99	.85	2.50	6.00
100,101: 100-Hulk battles Sub-Mariner	.85	2.50	6.00

NOTE: **Berg** a-1. **Burgos** a-62-64p. **Buscema** a-85-87p. **Colan** a(p)-70-76, 78-82, 84, 85, 101; c(p)-71-76, 78, 80, 82, 84, 86, 88, 90. **Ditko** a-most issues-1-48, 50i, 60-67. **Everett** a-78, 79i, 80-84, 85-90i, 94i, 95, 96; c(i)-79-81, 83, 86, 88. **Forte** a-6. **Kane** a-76, 88-91i; c-89, 91. **Kirby** a(p)-1-34(most), 35-40, 44, 49-51, 68-70, 82, 83; lay-outs-71-84; c(p)-1-48, 50-70, 72, 73, 75, 77, 78, 79, 81, 85, 90. **Leiber/Fox** a-47, 48, 50, 51. **Powell** a-65-69p, 73, 74. **Reinman** a-6, 36, 45, 46, 54i, 56-60i.

TALES TO ASTONISH (2nd Series)
Dec, 1979 - No. 14, Jan, 1981
Marvel Comics Group

	Good	Fine	N-Mint
V1#1-Buscema-r from Sub-Mariner #1	.30		.60
2-14: Reprints Sub-Mariner 2-14	.25		.50

TALES TO HOLD YOU SPELLBOUND (See Spellbound)

TALKING KOMICS
1957 (20 pages) (Slick covers)
Belda Record & Publ. Co.

Each comic contained a record that followed the story - much like the Golden Record sets. Known titles: Chirpy Cricket, Lonesome Octopus, Sleepy Santa, Grumpy Shark, Flying Turtle, Happy Grasshopper
with records...	.80	2.40	4.80

TALLY-HO COMICS
December, 1944
Swappers Quarterly (Baily Publ. Co.)

	Good	Fine	N-Mint
nn-Frazett's 1st work as Giunta's assistant; Man in Black horror story; violence; Giunta-c	20.00	60.00	140.00

TALOS OF THE WILDERNESS SEA
Aug, 1987 (One Shot, $2.00, color)
DC Comics

	Good	Fine	N-Mint
1	.35	1.00	2.00

TALULLAH (See Comic Series I)

TAMMY, TELL ME TRUE (See 4-Color #1233)

TARANTULA (See Weird Suspense)

TARAS BULBA (See Movie Classics)

TARGET: AIRBOY
Mar., 1988 ($1.95, color)
Eclipse Comics

	Good	Fine	N-Mint
1	.35	1.00	1.95

TARGET COMICS (...Western Romances #106 on)
Feb, 1940 - V10/3(#105), Aug, Sept, 1949
Funnies, Inc./Novelty Publications/Star Publications

	Good	Fine	N-Mint
V1#1-Origin & 1st app. Manowar, The White Streak by Burgos, & Bulls-Eye Bill by Everett; City Editor (ends #5), High Grass Twins by Jack Cole(ends #4), T-Men by Joe Simon(ends #9), Rip Rory (ends #4), Fantastic Feature Films by Tarpe Mills (ends #39, & Calling 2-R(ends #14) begin; Marijuana use story	160.00	480.00	1120.00
2	75.00	225.00	525.00
3,4	55.00	165.00	385.00
5-Origin The White Streak in text; Space Hawk by Wolverton begins (See Circus)	125.00	375.00	875.00
6-The Chameleon by Everett begins; White Streak origin cont'd. in text	70.00	210.00	490.00
7-Wolverton Spacehawk-c (Scarce)	165.00	495.00	1155.00
8,9,12	52.00	155.00	365.00
10-Intro. & 1st app. The Target; Kirby-c	70.00	210.00	490.00
11-Origin The Target & The Targeteers	65.00	195.00	455.00
V2#1,2: 1-Target by Bob Wood; flag-c	38.00	115.00	265.00
3-5: 4-Kit Carter, The Cadet begins	25.00	75.00	175.00
6-9:Red Seal with White Streak in 6-10	25.00	75.00	175.00

	Good	Fine	N-Mint
10-Classic-c	28.00	84.00	195.00
11,12	25.00	75.00	175.00
V3#1-10-Last Wolverton issue. 8-Flag-c. 10-Gulliver's Travels story	25.00	75.00	175.00
11,12	3.70	11.00	26.00
V4#1-5,7-12	2.15	6.50	15.00
6-Targetoons by Wolverton, 1 pg.	2.30	7.00	16.00
V5#1-8	1.85	5.50	13.00
V6#1-10, V7#1-12	1.50	4.50	10.00
V8#1,3-5,8,9,11,12	1.50	4.50	10.00
2,6,7-Krigstein-a	2.00	6.00	14.00
10-L.B. Cole-c	4.60	14.00	32.00
V9/1,3,6,8,10,12, V10/2-L.B. Cole-c	4.60	14.00	32.00
V9/2,4,5,7,9,11, 10/1,3	1.50	4.50	10.00

NOTE: **Jack Cole** a-1-8. **Everett** a-1-9. **Tarpe Mills** a-1-4, 6, 8, 11, V3#1. **Rico** a-V7#4, 10, V8#5, 6, V9#3. **Simon** a-1, 2.

TARGET: THE CORRUPTORS (TV)
No. 1306, Mar-May, 1962 - No. 3, Oct-Dec, 1962 (Photo-c)
Dell Publishing Co.

	Good	Fine	N-Mint
4-Color 1306, #2,3	2.30	7.00	16.00

TARGET WESTERN ROMANCES (Formerly Target)
No. 106, Oct-Nov, 1949 - No. 107, Dec-Jan, 1949-50
Star Publications

	Good	Fine	N-Mint
106-Silhouette nudity panel; L.B. Cole-c	10.00	30.00	70.00
107-L.B. Cole-c; lingerie panels	7.00	21.00	50.00

TARGITT
March, 1975 - No. 3, July, 1975
Atlas/Seaboard Publ.

	Good	Fine	N-Mint
1-Origin; Nostrand-a in all	.30		.60
2,3: 2-1st in costume	.25		.50

TARZAN
(See Aurora, Comics on Parade, Crackajack, DC 100-Page Super Spec., Famous Feat. Stories 1, Golden Comics Digest #4,9, Jeep Comics 1-29, Jungle Tales of..., Limited Coll. Edition, Popular, Sparkler, Sport Stars 1, Tip Top & Top Comics)

TARZAN
No. 5, 1939 - No. 161, Aug, 1947
Dell Publishing Co./United Features Syndicate

	Good	Fine	N-Mint
Large Feat. Comic 5('39)-(Scarce)-by Hal Foster; r-1st dailies from 1929	80.00	240.00	560.00
Single Series 20(:40)-by Hal Foster	70.00	210.00	490.00
4-Color 134(2/47)-Marsh-a	34.00	105.00	240.00
4-Color 161(8/47)-Marsh-a	30.00	90.00	210.00

TARZAN (...of the Apes #138 on)
1-2/48 - No. 131, 7-8/62; No. 132, 11/62 - No. 206, 2/72
Dell Publishing Co./Gold Key No. 132 on

	Good	Fine	N-Mint
1-Jesse Marsh-a begins	60.00	180.00	420.00
2	35.00	105.00	245.00
3-5	25.00	75.00	175.00
6-10: 6-1st Tantor the Elephant. 7-1st Valley of the Monsters	21.00	62.00	146.00
11-15: 11-Two Against the Jungle begins, ends #24. 13-Lex Barker photo-c begin	18.00	54.00	125.00
16-20	13.00	40.00	90.00
21-24,26-30	10.00	30.00	70.00
25-1st "Brothers of the Spear" episode; series ends #156,160,161, 196-206	12.00	36.00	84.00
31-40	6.00	18.00	42.00
41-54: Last Barker photo-c	4.65	14.00	32.00
55-60: 56-Eight pg. Boy story	3.70	11.00	26.00
61,62,64-70	2.65	8.00	18.00
63-Two Tarzan stories, 1 by Manning	3.00	9.00	21.00
71-79	2.30	7.00	16.00
80-99: 80-Gordon Scott photo-c begin	2.65	8.00	18.00

Tales To Astonish #101, © MEG

Target: Airboy #1, © Eclipse Comics

Target Comics V1#7, © STAR

Tarzan #100, © ERB

Tarzan #207, © ERB

Tastee-Freez Comics #1, © HARV

TARZAN (continued)	Good	Fine	N-Mint
100	3.00	9.00	21.00
101-109	2.00	6.00	14.00
110 (Scarce)-Last photo-c	2.30	7.00	16.00
111-120	1.50	4.50	10.00
121-131: Last Dell issue	1.15	3.50	8.00
132-154: Gold Key issues	.85	2.50	6.00
155-Origin Tarzan	1.00	3.00	7.00
156-161: 157-Banlu, Dog of the Arande begins, ends #159, 195.			
169-Leopard Girl app.	.70	2.00	5.00
162,165,168,171-Ron Ely photo-c	.85	2.50	6.00
163,164,166-167,169-170: 169-Leopard Girl app.	.55	1.65	4.00
172-199,201-206: 178-Tarzan origin r-/#155; Leopard Girl app, also			
in #179, 190-193	.50	1.50	3.00
200 (Scarce)	.75	2.25	5.00
Story Digest 1(6/70)-G.K.	.75	2.25	5.00

NOTE: #162, 165, 168, 171 are TV issues. #1-153 all have **Marsh** art on Tarzan. #154-161, 163, 164, 166, 167, 172-177 all have **Manning** art on Tarzan. #178, 202 have **Manning** Tarzan reprints. No "Brothers of the Spear" in #1-24, 157-159, 162-195. #39-126, 128-156 all have **Russ Manning** art on "Brothers of the Spear." #196-201, 203-205 all have **Manning** B.O.T.S. reprints; #25-38, 127 all have **Jesse Marsh** art on B.O.T.S. #206 has a **Marsh** B.O.T.S. reprint. **Doug Wildey** art-#179-187. Many issues have front and back photo covers.

TARZAN (Continuation of Gold Key series)
No. 207, April, 1972 - No. 258, Feb, 1977
Naional Periodical Publications

207-Origin Tarzan by Joe Kubert, part 1; John Carter begins (origin);			
52 pg. issues thru #209	.50	1.50	3.00
208-210: Origin, parts 2-4. 209-Last John Carter. 210-Kubert-a			
	.25	.75	1.50
211-Hogarth, Kubert-a		.50	1.00
212-214: Adaptations from "Jungle Tales of Tarzan." 213-Beyond			
the Farthest Star begins, ends #218		.50	1.00
215-218,224,225-All by Kubert. 215-part Foster-r		.50	1.00
219-223: Adapts "The Return of Tarzan" by Kubert		.50	1.00
226-229: 226-Manning-a		.50	1.00
230-100 pgs.; Kubert, Kaluta-a(p); Korak begins, ends #234; Carson			
of Venus app.	.25	.75	1.50
231-234: Adapts "Tarzan and the Lion Man;" all 100 pgs.; Rex, the			
Wonder Dog r-#232, 233		.50	1.00
235-Last Kubert issue; 100 pgs.		.50	1.00
236,237,239-258: 240-243 adapts "Tarzan & the Castaways."			
238-68 pgs.		.50	1.00
250-256 adapts "Tarzan the Untamed." 252,253-r/#213			
		.50	1.00
Comic Digest 1(Fall,'72)(DC)-50 cents; 160 pgs.; digest size;			
Kubert-c, Manning-a	.35	1.00	2.00

NOTE: **Anderson** a-207, 209, 217, 218. **Chaykin** a-216. **Finlay** a(r)-212. **Foster** strip-r #208, 209, 211, 221. **Heath** a-230i. **G. Kane** a-232p, 233p. **Kubert** a-207-25, 227-35, 257r, 258r; c-207-249, 253. **Lopez** a-250-550p; c-250p, 251, 252, 254. **Manning** strip-r 230-235, 238. **Morrow** a-208. **Nino** a-231-234. **Sparling** a-230. **Starr** a-233r.

TARZAN
June, 1977 - No. 29, Oct, 1979
Marvel Comics Group

1		.35	.70
2-29: 2-Origin by J. Buscema		.25	.50
Annual 1 (10/77)		.35	.70
Annual 2 (11/78), Annual 3 (10/79)		.25	.50

NOTE: **Adams** c-11i, 12i. **Alcala** a-9i, 10i; c-8i, 9i. **Buckler** c-25-27p, Annual 3p. **John Buscema** a-1, 4-18p; c-1-7, 8p, 9p, 10, 11p, 12p, 13, 14p-19p, 21p, 22, 23p, 24p, 28p. **Buscema** c/a-Annual 1. **Mooney** a-22i. **Nebres** a-22i. **Russell** a-29i.

TARZAN BOOK (The Illustrated . . .)
1929 (80 pages)(7x9'')
Grosset & Dunlap

1(Rare)-Contains 1st B&W Tarzan newspaper comics from 1929. Cloth reinforced spine & dust jacket (50 cents); Foster-c

	Good	Fine	N-Mint
with dust jacket . . .	50.00	150.00	350.00
without dust jacket . . .	22.00	65.00	154.00

2nd Printing(1934)-76 pgs.; 25 cents; 4 Foster pages dropped; paper spine, circle in lower right cover with 25 cents price. The 25 cents is barely visible on some copies   15.00   45.00   105.00
1967-House of Greystoke reprint-7x10'', using the complete 300 illustrations/text from the 1929 edition minus the original indicia, foreword, etc. Initial version bound in gold paper & sold for $5. Officially titled **Burroughs Biblophile #2**. A very few additional copies were bound in heavier blue paper

Gold binding . . .	2.65	8.00	18.00
Blue binding . . .	3.50	10.50	24.00

TARZAN FAMILY, THE (Formerly Korak)
No. 60, Nov-Dec, 1975 - No. 66, Nov-Dec, 1976
(No. 60-62: 68 pgs.; No. 63 on: 52 pgs.)
National Periodical Publications

60-Korak begins; Kaluta-r		.30	.60
61-66		.25	.50

NOTE: Carson of Venus-r 60-65. New John Carter-62-64, 65r, 66r. New Korak-60-65. Pellucidar feature-66. **Foster** Tarzan Sunday r-60('32)-63. **Kaluta** Carson of Venus-60-65. **Kubert** a-61, 64; c-60-64. **Manning** strip-r 60-62, 64. **Morrow** a-66r.

TARZAN KING OF THE JUNGLE (See Dell Giant #37,51)

TARZAN, LORD OF THE JUNGLE
Sept, 1965 (Giant)(soft paper cover)(25 cents)
Gold Key

1-Marsh-r	2.65	8.00	18.00

TARZAN MARCH OF COMICS (See March of Comics #82, 98, 114, 125, 144, 155, 172, 185, 204, 223, 240, 252, 262, 272, 286, 300, 332, 342, 354, 366)

TARZAN OF THE APES
July, 1984 - No. 2, Aug, 1984
Marvel Comics Group

1,2: Origin-r/Marvel Super Spec.		.30	.60

TARZAN OF THE APES TO COLOR
1933 (24 pages)(10¾x15¼'')(Coloring book)
Saalfield Publishing Co.

988-(Very Rare)-Contains 1929 daily-r with some new art by Hal Foster. Two panels blown up large on each page; 25 percent in color; believed to be the only time these panels ever appeared in color.
                                                                        75.00   225.00   525.00

TARZAN'S JUNGLE ANNUAL (See Dell Giants)

TARZAN'S JUNGLE WORLD (See Dell Giant #25)

TASMANIAN DEVIL & HIS TASTY FRIENDS
November, 1962
Gold Key

1-Bugs Bunny & Elmer Fudd x-over	4.00	12.00	28.00

TASTEE-FREEZ COMICS
1957 (36 pages)(10 cents)(6 different issues)
Harvey Comics

1-Little Dot, 3-Casper	3.35	10.00	23.00
2-Rags Rabbit, 5-Mazie	2.00	6.00	14.00
4-Sad Sack	2.00	6.00	14.00
6-Dick Tracy	4.00	12.00	28.00

TAYLOR'S CHRISTMAS TABLOID
Mid 1930s, Cleveland, Ohio
Dept. Store Giveaway (Tabloid size; in color)

nn-(Very Rare)-Among the earliest pro work of Siegel & Shuster; one full color page called "The Battle in the Stratosphere," with a pre-Superman look; Shuster art throughout. (Only 1 known copy)
             Estimated value . . . $900.00

TEAM AMERICA (See Capt. America 269)
June, 1982 - No. 12, May, 1983

Marvel Comics Group	Good	Fine	N-Mint
1-Origin; Ideal Toy motorcycle characters		.40	.80
2-12: 11-Ghost Rider app. 12-Double size		.30	.60

TEAM YANKEE
Jan, 1989 - No. 6, Feb, 1989 ($1.95, weekly limited series, color)
First Comics

1-6	.35	1.00	1.95

TEDDY ROOSEVELT & HIS ROUGH RIDERS
1950
Avon Periodicals

1-Kinstler-c; Palais-a; Flag-c	10.00	30.00	70.00

TEDDY ROOSEVELT ROUGH RIDER (See Classics Special)

TEE AND VEE CROSLEY IN TELEVISION LAND COMICS
(Also see Crosley's House of Fun)
1951 (52 pgs.; 8x11''; paper cover; in color)
Crosley Division, Avco Mfg. Corp. (Giveaway)

Many stories, puzzles, cut-outs, games, etc.	2.65	8.00	18.00

TEENA
No. 11, 1948 - No. 15, 1948; No. 20, 8/49 - No. 22, 10/50
Magazine Enterprises/Standard Comics

A-1 #11-Teen-age	2.30	7.00	16.00
A-1 #12, 15	1.70	5.00	12.00
20-22 (Standard)	1.15	3.50	8.00

TEEN-AGE BRIDES (True Bride's Experiences #8)
Aug, 1953 - No. 7, Aug, 1954
Harvey/Home Comics

1-Powell-a	2.00	6.00	14.00
2-Powell-a	1.50	4.50	10.00
3-7; 3,6-Powell-a	1.35	4.00	9.00

TEEN-AGE CONFESSIONS (See Teen Confessions)

TEEN-AGE CONFIDENTIAL CONFESSIONS
July, 1960 - No. 22, 1964
Charlton Comics

1	.55	1.65	4.00
2-10	.35	1.00	2.00
11-22		.50	1.00

TEEN-AGE DIARY SECRETS (Formerly Blue Ribbon Comics;
becomes Diary Secrets #10 on)
Sept, 1949 - No. 9, Aug, 1950
St. John Publishing Co.

nn(9/49)-oversized issue; Baker-a	9.50	28.50	65.00
6 (9/49) - 8-Photo-c; Baker-a(2-3) in each	6.50	19.50	45.00
9-Pocket size	8.00	24.00	56.00

TEEN-AGE DOPE SLAVES (See Harvey Comics Library #1)

TEENAGE HOTRODDERS (Top Eliminator #25 on)
April, 1963 - No. 24, July, 1967
Charlton Comics

1	.70	2.00	4.00
2-24	.35	1.00	2.00

TEEN-AGE LOVE (See Fox Giants)

TEEN-AGE LOVE (Formerly Intimate?)
V2No.4, July, 1958 - No. 96, Dec, 1973
Charlton Comics

V2#4	1.00	3.00	7.00
5-9	.60	1.75	3.50
10(9/59)-35		1.00	2.00
36-96: 61&62-Jonnie Love begins (origin)		.20	.40

TEENAGE MUTANT NINJA TURTLES (Also see Anything Goes,
Donatello, First Comics Graphic Novel, Grimjack #26, Leonardo,
Michaelangelo, Raphael & Tales Of The. . .)
1984 - Present ($1.50, B&W)

Mirage Studios	Good	Fine	N-Mint
1-1st printing	27.00	80.00	160.00
1-2nd printing	5.00	15.00	30.00
1-3rd printing	1.35	4.00	8.00
1-4th	.85	2.50	5.00
1-5th printing, new-c	.35	1.00	2.00
2-1st printing	7.00	20.00	40.00
2-2nd printing	1.35	4.00	8.00
2-3rd printing; new Corben-c/a (2/85)	.60	1.75	3.50
3	3.35	10.00	20.00
3-2nd printing	.50	1.50	3.00
3-Variant, 500 copies, given away in NYC. Has 'Laird's Photo' in white rather than light blue	6.15	18.50	37.00
4	1.60	4.75	9.50
4-2nd printing (5/87)	.35	1.05	2.10
5	1.15	3.50	7.00
5-2nd printing (11/87)	.35	1.00	2.00
6	.85	2.50	5.00
6-2nd printing	.35	1.00	2.00
7-4pg. Corben color insert; 1st color TMNT	.70	2.00	4.00
8-18: 8-Rion 2990 begins	.50	1.50	3.00
8-2nd printing	.25	.75	1.50
Book 1,2($1.50, B&W): 2-Corben-c	.25	.75	1.50

TEENAGE MUTANT NINJA TURTLES ADVENTURES (TV)
8/88 - No. 3, 12/88; 3/89 - Present ($1.00, color, mini-series)
Archie Comics

1-Adapts TV cartoon series	.35	1.00	2.00
2,3	.25	.75	1.50
1,2 (2nd series)		.50	1.00

TEEN-AGE ROMANCE (Formerly My Own Romance)
No. 77, Sept, 1960 - No. 86, March, 1962
Marvel Comics (ZPC)

77-86	.60	1.80	3.60

TEEN-AGE ROMANCES
Jan, 1949 - No. 45, Dec, 1955
St. John Publ. co. (Approved Comics)

1-Baker c/a(1)	13.00	40.00	90.00
2-Baker c/a	8.00	24.00	56.00
3-Baker c/a(3); spanking panel	8.50	25.50	60.00
4,5,7,8-Photo-c; Baker-a(2-3) each	5.70	17.00	40.00
6-Slightly large size; photo-c; part magazine; Baker-a (10/49)	5.70	17.00	40.00
9-Baker c/a; Kubert-a	8.50	25.50	60.00
10-12,20-Baker c/a(2-3) each	5.70	17.00	40.00
13-19,21,22-Complete issues by Baker	9.00	27.00	62.00
23-25-Baker c/a(2-3) each	4.85	14.50	34.00
26,27,33,34,36-42-Last Precode, 3/55; Baker-a. 38-Suggestive-a	3.50	10.50	24.00
28-30-No Baker-a	1.70	5.00	12.00
31-Baker-c	2.15	6.50	15.00
32-Baker c/a, 1pg.	2.15	6.50	15.00
35-Baker c/a, 16pgs.	3.65	11.00	25.00
43-45-Baker-a	2.50	7.50	17.00

TEEN-AGE TALK
1964
I.W. Enterprises

Reprint #1-Monkees photo-c	1.00	3.00	6.00
Reprint #5,8,9	.30	.80	1.60

Team Yankee #1, © First Comics   Teenage Mutant Ninja Turtles #13, © Mirage Studios

Teen-Age Romances #19, © STJ

Teen Comics #26, © MEG   Teen Titans #1, © DC   Tegra Jungle Empress #1, © FOX

TEEN-AGE TEMPTATIONS (Going Steady #10 on)(See True Love Pic)
Oct, 1952 - No. 9, Aug, 1954
St. John Publishing co.

	Good	Fine	N-Mint
1-Baker c/a; has story "Reform School Girl" by Estrada			
	15.00	45.00	105.00
2-Baker-c	5.00	15.00	35.00
3-7,9-Baker c/a	8.50	25.50	60.00
8-Teenagers smoke reefers; Baker c/a	9.00	27.00	62.00

NOTE: *Estrada a-1, 4, 5.*

TEEN BEAM (Teen Beat #1)
No. 2, Jan-Feb, 1968 (Monkees photo-c)
National Periodical Publications

	Good	Fine	N-Mint
2-Orlando, Drucker-a(r)	.85	2.50	6.00

TEEN BEAT (Teen Beam #2)
Nov-Dec, 1967
National Periodical Publications

1-Photos & text only; Monkees photo-c	1.15	3.50	8.00

TEEN COMICS (Formerly All Teen; Journey into Unknown Worlds #36 on)
No. 21, April, 1947 - No. 35, May, 1950
Marvel comics (WFP)

21-Kurtzman's "Hey Look"; Patsy Walker, Cindy, Georgie, Margie app.	4.00	12.00	28.00
22,23,25,27,29,31-35	2.30	7.00	16.00
24,26,28,30-Kurtzman's "Hey Look"	3.50	10.50	24.00

TEEN CONFESSIONS
Aug, 1959 - No. 97, Nov, 1976
Charlton Comics

1	3.00	9.00	21.00
2	1.30	4.00	9.00
3-10	.95	2.80	6.50
11-30	.40	1.20	2.80
31-Beatles-c	2.65	8.00	18.00
32-36,38-97: 89,90-Newton-c	.50		1.00
37 (1/66)-Beatles Fan Club story; Beatles-c	2.65	8.00	18.00

TEENIE WEENIES, THE
1950 - 1951 (Newspaper reprints)
Ziff-Davis Publishing Co.

10,11	5.00	15.00	35.00

TEEN-IN (Tippy Teen)
Summer, 1968 - No. 4, Fall, 1969
Tower Comics

nn(Summer,'68), nn(Spring,'69),3,4	.70	2.00	4.00

TEEN LIFE (Formerly Young Life)
No. 3, Winter, 1945 - No. 5, Fall, 1945
New Age/Quality Comics Group

3-June Allyson photo-c	3.00	9.00	21.00
4-Duke Ellington story	2.15	6.50	15.00
5-Van Johnson, Woody Herman & Jackie Robinson articles			
	3.00	9.00	21.00

TEEN ROMANCES
1964
Super Comics

10,11,15-17-Reprints		.30	.60

TEEN SECRET DIARY (Nurse Betsy Crane #12 on)
Oct, 1959 - No. 11, June, 1961; No. 1, 1972
Charlton Comics

1	1.30	4.00	9.00
2	.55	1.65	4.00
3-11	.35	1.00	2.50

	Good	Fine	N-Mint
1(1972)		.30	.60

TEEN TALK (See Teen)

TEEN TITANS (See Brave & the Bold, DC Super-Stars #1, Marvel & DC Present, New Teen Titans, Official. . .Index and Showcase)
1-2/66 - No. 43, 1-2/73; No. 44, 11/76 - No. 53, 2/78
National Periodical Publications/DC Comics

1-Titans join Peace Corps; Batman, Flash, Aquaman, Wonder Woman cameos	8.50	25.50	60.00
2	3.60	11.00	25.00
3-5: 4-Speedy app.	1.70	5.00	12.00
6-10: 6-Doom Patrol app.	1.15	3.50	8.00
11-18: 11-Speedy app. 18-1st app. Starfire	.85	2.50	6.00
19-Wood-i; Speedy begins as regular	.85	2.50	6.00
20-22: All Adams-a. 21-Hawk & Dove app. 22-Origin Wonder Girl			
	1.00	3.00	7.00
23-Wonder Girl dons new costume	.85	2.50	5.00
24	.85	2.50	5.00
25-Flash, Aquaman, Batman, Green Arrow, Green Lantern, Superman, & Hawk & Dove guests	.85	2.50	5.00
26-30: 29-Hawk & Dove & Ocean Master app. 30-Aquagirl app.			
	.85	2.50	5.00
31-43: 31-Hawk & Dove app. 36,37-Superboy-r. 38-Green Arrow/ Speedy-r; Aquaman/Aqualad story. 39-Hawk & Dove-r. (36-39, 52 pgs.)	.70	2.00	4.00
44-47,49-52: 44-Mal becomes the Guardian. 46-Joker's Daughter begins. 50-Intro. Teen Titans West; 1st revival original Bat-Girl	.50	1.50	3.00
48-Intro Bumblebee; Joker's daughter becomes Harlequin			
	.50	1.50	3.00
53-Origin retold	.50	1.50	3.00

NOTE: *Aparo a-36. Buckler c-46-53. Kane a(p)-19,22-24, 39r. Tuska a(p)-31,36,38,39.*

TEEN TITANS SPOTLIGHT
Aug, 1986 - Present
DC Comics

1	.25	.75	1.50
2,3		.50	1.00
4-10: 7-Guice's 1st work at DC		.40	.80
11-20		.35	.70
21-24 ($1.00)		.50	1.00

TEEPEE TIM (Formerly Ha Ha Comics)
No. 100, Feb-Mar, 1955 - No. 102, June-July, 1955
American Comics Group

100-102	.55	1.65	4.00

TEGRA JUNGLE EMPRESS (Zegra #2 on)
August, 1948
Fox Features Syndicate

1-Blue Beetle, Rocket Kelly app.; used in SOTI, pg. 31			
	19.00	57.00	132.00

TELEVISION (See TV)

TELEVISION COMICS
No. 5, Feb, 1950 - No. 8, Nov, 1950
Standard Comics (Animated Cartoons)

5-1st app. Willy Nilly	2.30	7.00	16.00
6-8: 6 has #2 on inside	1.50	4.50	10.00

TELEVISION PUPPET SHOW
1950 - No. 2, Nov, 1950
Avon Periodicals

1,2: Speedy Rabbit, Spotty The Pup	4.65	14.00	32.00

TELEVISION TEENS MOPSY (See TV Teens)

TELL IT TO THE MARINES
Mar, 1952 - No. 15, July, 1955
Toby Press Publications

	Good	Fine	N-Mint
1-Lover O'Leary and His Liberty Belles (with Pin-ups), ends #6			
	5.00	15.00	35.00
2-Madame Cobra app. c/story	3.50	10.50	24.00
3,5	2.65	8.00	18.00
4-Transvestism story	4.35	13.00	30.00
6-12,14,15: 7-9,14-Photo-c	1.50	4.50	10.00
13-John Wayne photo-c	2.00	6.00	14.00
I.W. Reprint #1,9	.30	.90	1.80
Super Reprint #16('64)	.30	.90	1.80

TEN COMMANDMENTS (See Moses & the... and Classics Special)

TENDER LOVE STORIES
Feb, 1971 - No. 4, July, 1971 (All 52pgs.)(25 cents)
Skywald Publ. Corp.

1-4	.30	.80	1.60

TENDER ROMANCE (Ideal Romance #3 on)
Dec., 1953 - No. 2, Feb, 1954
Key Publications (Gilmour Magazines)

1-Headlight & lingerie panels	5.50	16.50	38.00
2	2.65	8.00	18.00

TENNESSEE JED (Radio)
nd (1945) (16 pgs.; paper cover; regular size; giveaway)
Fox Syndicate? (Wm. C. Popper & Co.)

nn	7.00	21.00	50.00

TENNIS (For Speed, Stamina, Strength, Skill)
1956 (16 pgs.; soft cover; 10 cents)
Tennis Educational Foundation

Book 1-Endorsed by Gene Tunney, Ralph Kiner, etc. showing how tennis has helped them	1.70	5.00	12.00

TENSE SUSPENSE
Dec, 1958 - No. 2, Feb, 1959
Fago Publications

1,2	1.50	4.50	10.00

TEN STORY LOVE (Formerly a pulp magazine with same title)
V29/3, 6-7/51 - V36/5(#209), 9/56 (#3-6, 52 pgs.)
Ace Periodicals

V29#3(#177)-Part comic, part text	3.00	9.00	21.00
4-6(1/52)	1.50	4.50	10.00
V30#1(3/52)-6(1/53)	1.15	3.50	8.00
V31#1(2/53),V32#2(4/53)-6(12/53)	.85	2.50	6.00
V33#1(1/54)-3(5#54, #195), V34#4(7/54, #196)-6(10/54, #198)			
	.80	2.40	5.50
V35#1(12/54, #199)-3(4/55, #201)-Last precode	.75	2.25	5.00
V35#4-6(9/55, #201-204), V36#1(11/55, #205)-3, 5(9/56, #209)			
	.55	1.65	4.00
V36#4-L.B. Cole-a	1.15	3.50	8.00

TEN WHO DARED (See 4-Color #1178)

TERMINATOR, THE
Sept., 1988 - Present ($1.75, color, Baxter paper)
Now Comics

1-Based on movie	.85	2.50	5.00
2	.50	1.50	3.00
3,4	.35	1.00	2.00

TERRAFORMERS
April, 1987 - No. 2?, 1987 ($1.95, color)
Wonder Color Comics

1,2	.35	1.00	2.00

TERRANAUTS
Aug, 1986 - No. 2?, 1986 ($1.75, color)
Fantasy General Comics

	Good	Fine	N-Mint
1,2	.30	.85	1.70

TERRIFIC COMICS
Jan, 1944 - No. 6, Nov, 1944
Continental Magazines

1-Kid Terrific; opium story	27.00	81.00	190.00
2-The Boomerang by L.B. Cole & Ed Wheelan's "Comics" McCormick, called the world's No. 1 comic book fan begins; Schomburg-c	23.00	70.00	160.00
3,4: 3-Diana becomes Boomerang's costumed aide			
	21.00	62.00	148.00
5-The Reckoner begins; Boomerang & Diana by L.B. Cole; Schomburg bondage-c	23.00	70.00	160.00
6-L.B. Cole c/a	24.00	72.00	168.00

NOTE: *L.B. Cole a-1, 2(2), 3-6. Fuje a-5, 6. Rico a-2.*

TERRIFIC COMICS (Formerly Horrific, Wonder Boy #17 on)
No. 14, Dec, 1954 - No. 16, Mar, 1955
Mystery Publ.(Comic Media)/(Ajax/Farrell)

14-Art swipe/Advs. into Unknown 37; injury-to-eye-c; page-2, panel 5 swiped from Phantom Stranger #4; surrealistic Palais-a; Human Cross story	5.70	17.00	40.00
15,16-No Phantom Lady. 16-Wonder Boy app. (precode)			
	4.65	14.00	32.00

TERRIFYING TALES
No. 11, Jan, 1953 - No. 15, Apr, 1954
Star Publications

11-Used in POP, pgs. 99,100; all Jo-Jo-r	16.00	48.00	110.00
12-All Jo-Jo-r; L.B. Cole splash	12.00	36.00	84.00
13-All Rulah-r; classic devil-c	17.00	51.00	120.00
14-All Rulah reprints	12.00	36.00	84.00
15-Rulah, Zago-r; used in SOTI-r/Rulah #22	12.00	36.00	84.00

NOTE: *All issues have L.B. Cole covers; bondage covers-No. 12-14.*

TERROR ILLUSTRATED (Adult Tales of...)
Nov-Dec, 1955 - No. 2, Spring, 1956 (Magazine)
E.C. Comics

1	5.70	17.00	40.00
2	5.00	15.00	35.00

TERRORS OF THE JUNGLE (Formerly Jungle Thrills)
No. 17, May, 1952 - No. 10, Sept, 1954
Star Publications

17-Reprints Rulah #21, used in SOTI; L.B. Cole bondage-c			
	15.00	45.00	105.00
18-Jo-Jo-r	10.00	30.00	70.00
19,20(1952)-Jo-Jo-r; Disbrow-a	9.00	27.00	62.00
21-Jungle Jo, Tangi-r; used in POP, pg. 100 & color illos.			
	11.00	32.00	75.00
4,6,7-Disbrow-a	9.00	27.00	62.00
5,8,10: All Disbrow-a. 5-Jo-Jo-r. 8-Rulah, Jo-Jo-r. 10-Rulah-r			
	9.00	27.00	62.00
9-Jo-Jo-r; Disbrow-a; Tangi by Orlando	9.00	27.00	62.00

NOTE: *L.B. Cole c-all; bondage c-17, 19, 21, 5, 7.*

TERROR TALES (See Beware Terror Tales)

TERROR TALES (Magazine)
V1#7, 1969 - V6#6, 12/74; V7#1, 4/76 - V10, 1979?
(V1-V6, 52 pgs.; V7 on, 68 pgs.)
Eerie Publications

V1#7	.85	2.50	6.00
V1#8-11('69): 9-Bondage-c	.70	2.00	4.00
V2#1-6('70), V3#1-6('71), V4#1-7('72), V5#1-6('73), V6#1-6('74)			
	.60	1.75	3.50

Tell It To The Marines #5, © TOBY

Terrific Comics #4, © Continental Magazines

Terror Illustrated #1, © WMG

Terry-Toons Comics #3 (1st series), © Paul Terry

Tessie The Typist #17, © MEG

The Texan #1, © STJ

	Good	Fine	N-Mint
TERROR TALES (continued)			
V7#1,4(no V7#2), V8#1-3('77), V9, V10	.60	1.75	3.50
V7#3-LSD story-r/Weird V3#5	.60	1.75	3.50

TERRY AND THE PIRATES (See Merry Christmas. . ., Popular Comics, Super-book #3,5,9,16,28, & Super Comics)

TERRY AND THE PIRATES
1939 - 1953 (By Milton Caniff)
Dell Publishing Co.

	Good	Fine	N-Mint
Large Feat. Comic 2('39)	40.00	120.00	280.00
Large Feat. Comic 6('39)-1936 dailies	38.00	115.00	265.00
4-Color 9(1940)	40.00	120.00	280.00
Large Feature Comic 27('41), 6('42)	27.00	81.00	190.00
4-Color 44('43)	24.00	72.00	170.00
4-Color 101('45)	16.00	48.00	110.00
Buster Brown Shoes giveaway(1938)-32 pgs.; in color	20.00	60.00	140.00
Canada Dry Premiums-Books #1-3(1953-Harvey)-2x5''; 36 pgs.	5.00	15.00	35.00
Family Album(1942)	8.50	25.50	60.00
Gambles Giveaway ('38)-16 pgs.	4.35	13.00	26.00
Gillmore Giveaway('38)-24 pgs.	5.00	15.00	30.00
Popped Wheat Giveaway('38)-Reprints in full color; Caniff-a	.85	2.50	5.00
Shoe Store giveaway('38, 16pp, soft-c)(2-diff.)	3.00	9.00	18.00
Sparked Wheat Giveaway('42)-16 pgs. in full color	4.60	14.00	32.00

TERRY AND THE PIRATES
1941 (16 pgs.; regular size)
Libby's Radio Premium

	Good	Fine	N-Mint
''Adventure of the Ruby of Genghis Khan'' - Each pg. is a puzzle that must be completed to read the story	8.50	25.50	60.00

TERRY AND THE PIRATES (Formerly Boy Explorers; Long John Silver & the Pirates #30 on) (Daily strip-r) (Two #26's)
No. 3, 4/47 - No. 26, 4/51; No. 26, 6/55 - No. 28, 10/55
Harvey Publications/Charlton No. 26-28

	Good	Fine	N-Mint
3(#1)-Boy Explorers by S&K; Terry & the Pirates begin by Caniff	20.00	60.00	140.00
4-S&K Boy Explorers	13.00	40.00	90.00
5-10	7.00	21.00	50.00
11-Man in Black app. by Powell	7.00	21.00	50.00
12-20: 16-Girl threatened with red hot poker	5.35	16.00	37.00
21-26(4/51)-Last Caniff issue	4.75	14.00	33.00
26-28('55)(Formerly This Is Suspense)-Not by Caniff	3.70	11.00	26.00

NOTE: **Powell** a (Tommy Tween)-5-10,12,14; 15-17(½-2 pgs.).

TERRY BEARS COMICS (TerryToons, The. . . #4)
June, 1952 - No. 3, Oct, 1952
St. John Publishing Co.

	Good	Fine	N-Mint
1	1.70	5.00	12.00
2,3	1.60	4.70	11.00

TERRY-TOONS COMICS (1st Series) (Becomes Paul Terry's Comics #85 on; later issues titled ''Paul Terry's. . .'') (See Giant Comics Ed.)
Oct, 1942 - No. 86, Feb?, 1951 (Two #60s)
Timely/Marvel No. 1-60 (8/47)(Becomes Best Western No. 58 on?, Marvel)/St. John No. 60 (9/47) on

	Good	Fine	N-Mint
1 (Scarce)-feat. characters that 1st app. on movie screen; Gandy Goose begins	45.00	135.00	315.00
2	22.00	65.00	154.00
3-5	13.00	40.00	90.00
6-10	9.50	28.50	65.00
11-20	6.00	18.00	42.00
21-37	4.00	12.00	28.00
38-Mighty Mouse begins (1st app.)(11/45)	35.00	105.00	245.00

	Good	Fine	N-Mint
39-2nd Mighty Mouse app.	12.00	36.00	84.00
40-49: 43-Infinity-c	5.00	15.00	35.00
50-1st app. Heckle & Jeckle	11.50	34.00	80.00
51-60(8/47): 55-Infinity-c. 60(9/47)-Atomic explosion panel	3.70	11.00	26.00
61-84	2.30	7.00	16.00
85,86-Same book as Paul Terry's Comics #85,86 with only a title change	2.30	7.00	16.00

TERRY-TOONS COMICS (2nd Series)
June, 1952 - No. 9, Nov, 1953
St. John Publishing Co./Pines

	Good	Fine	N-Mint
1	4.00	12.00	28.00
2	2.65	8.00	18.00
3-9	2.00	6.00	14.00
Giant Summer Fun Book 101,102(Summer,'57-Summer,'58)(TV, Tom Terrific app.)	2.65	8.00	18.00

TERRYTOONS, THE TERRY BEARS (Formerly Terry Bears)
No. 4, Summer, 1958
Pines Comics

	Good	Fine	N-Mint
4	1.30	4.00	9.00

TESSIE THE TYPIST (Tiny Tessie #24; see Comedy Comics, Gay & Joker Comics)
Summer, 1944 - No. 23, Aug, 1949
Timely/Marvel Comics (20CC)

	Good	Fine	N-Mint
1-Doc Rockblock & others by Wolverton	20.00	60.00	140.00
2-Wolverton's Powerhouse Pepper	12.00	36.00	84.00
3-No Wolverton	3.70	11.00	26.00
4,5,7,8-Wolverton-a	7.00	21.00	50.00
6-Kurtzman's ''Hey Look,'' 2 pgs. Wolverton	8.00	24.00	56.00
9-Wolverton's Powerhouse Pepper (8 pgs.) & Kurtzman's ''Hey Look'' (1)	9.00	27.00	62.00
10-4 pgs. Wolverton's Powerhouse Pepper	8.00	24.00	56.00
11-8 pgs. Wolverton's Powerhouse Pepper	9.00	27.00	62.00
12-4 pgs. Wolverton's Powerhouse Pepper & 1 pg. Kurtzman's ''Hey Look''	8.00	24.00	56.00
13-4 pgs. Wolverton's Powerhouse Pepper	7.00	21.00	50.00
14-1 pg. Wolverton's Dr. Whackyhack, 1½ pgs. Kurtzman's ''Hey Look''	5.00	15.00	35.00
15-3 pgs. Kurtzman's ''Hey Look'' & 3 pgs. Giggles 'n' Grins	5.00	15.00	35.00
16-18-Kurtzman's ''Hey Look'' (?, 2 & 1)	3.50	10.50	24.00
19-Eight pg. Annie Oakley	2.30	7.00	16.00
20-23: 20-Anti-Wertham editorial (2/49)	1.85	5.50	13.00

NOTE: Lana app.-21. Millie The Model app.-13,15,17,21. Rusty app.-10,11,13,15,17.

TEXAN, THE (Fightin' Marines #15 on; Fightin' Texan #16 on)
Aug, 1948 - No. 15, Oct, 1951
St. John Publishing Co.

	Good	Fine	N-Mint
1-Buckskin Belle	6.50	19.50	45.00
2	3.50	10.50	24.00
3,5,10: 10-Over-sized issue	3.00	9.00	21.00
4,7,15-Baker c/a	5.70	17.00	40.00
6,9-Baker-c	3.50	10.50	24.00
8,11,13,14-Baker c/a(2-3) each	5.70	17.00	40.00
12-All Matt Baker; Peyote story	7.00	21.00	50.00

NOTE: Matt Baker c-6-15. Larsen a-6, 8. Tuska a-1, 2, 8.

TEXAN, THE (See 4-Color #1027,1096)

TEXAS JOHN SLAUGHTER (See 4-Color #997,1181 & W. Disney Presents #2)

TEXAS KID (See Two-Gun Western, Wild Western)
Jan, 1951 - No. 10, July, 1952
Marvel/Atlas Comics (LMC)

	Good	Fine	N-Mint
1-Origin; Texas Kid (alias Lance Temple) & his horse Thunder begin; Tuska-a	6.50	19.50	45.00

TEXAS KID (continued)

	Good	Fine	N-Mint
2	3.00	9.00	21.00
3-10	2.30	7.00	16.00

NOTE: *Maneely a-1-4 c-3, 5-10.*

TEXAS RANGERS, THE (See Superior Stories No. 4 and Jace Pearson of...)

TEXAS RANGERS IN ACTION (Formerly Captain Gallant or Scotland Yard?) (See Blue Bird Comics)
No. 5, July, 1956 - No. 79, Aug, 1970
Charlton Comics

	Good	Fine	N-Mint
5	2.30	7.00	16.00
6-10	1.15	3.50	8.00
11-Williamson-a(5,5,&8 pgs.); Torres-a	4.35	13.00	30.00
12,14-20	.70	2.00	5.00
13-Williamson-a, 5 pgs; Torres-a	3.35	10.00	23.00
21-30: 30-Last 10 cent ish?	.70	2.00	4.00
31-59	.35	1.00	2.00
60-Rileys Rangers begin		.60	1.20
61-70: 65-1st app. The Man Called Loco, origin-#67		.50	1.00
71-79		.40	.80
76(Modern Comics-r, 1977)		.15	.30

TEXAS SLIM (See A-1 Comics #2-8,10)

TEX DAWSON, GUN-SLINGER (Gunslinger #2 on)
January, 1973 (Also see Western Kid)
Marvel Comics Group

	Good	Fine	N-Mint
1-Steranko-c; Williamson-a(r); Tex Dawson-r	.30		.60

TEX FARNUM (See Wisco)

TEX FARRELL
Mar-Apr, 1948
D. S. Publishing Co.

	Good	Fine	N-Mint
1-Tex Farrell & his horse Lightning begin; Shelly-c	5.00	15.00	35.00

TEX GRANGER (Formerly Calling All Boys; see True Comics)
No. 18, June, 1948 - No. 24, Sept, 1949
Parents' Magazine Institute/Commended

	Good	Fine	N-Mint
18-Tex Granger & his horse Bullet begin	4.00	12.00	28.00
19	2.65	8.00	18.00
20-24: 22-Wild Bill Hickok story	2.00	6.00	14.00

TEX MORGAN (See Blaze Carson, Wild Western)
Aug, 1948 - No. 9, Feb, 1950
Marvel Comics (CCC)

	Good	Fine	N-Mint
1-Tex Morgan, his horse Lightning & sidekick Lobo begin	9.00	27.00	62.00
2	6.50	19.50	45.00
3-6: 4-Arizona Annie app.	4.65	14.00	32.00
7-9: All photo-c. 7-Captain Tootsie by Beck. 8-18pg. story "The Terror of Rimrock Valley;" Diablo app.	6.50	19.50	45.00

NOTE: *Tex Taylor app.-6,7,9.*

TEX RITTER WESTERN (Movie star; singing cowboy; see Six-Gun Heroes, Western Hero)
Oct, 1950 - No. 46, May, 1959 (Photo-c, 1-21)
Fawcett No. 1-20 (1/54)/Charlton No. 21 on

	Good	Fine	N-Mint
1-Tex Ritter, his stallion White Flash & dog Fury begin; photo front/back-c begin	25.00	75.00	175.00
2	14.00	42.00	100.00
3-5: 5-Last photo back-c	12.00	36.00	84.00
6-10	10.00	30.00	70.00
11-19	6.50	19.50	45.00
20-Last Fawcett issue (1/54)	7.00	21.00	50.00
21-1st Charlton issue; photo-c (3/54)	7.00	21.00	50.00
22	4.00	12.00	28.00
23-30: 23-25-Young Falcon app.	3.00	9.00	21.00

	Good	Fine	N-Mint
31-38,40-45	2.65	8.00	18.00
39-Williamson-c/a (1/58)	4.35	13.00	30.00
46-Last issue	3.00	9.00	21.00

NOTE: *B&W photo back-c #23-32.*

TEX TAYLOR (See Blaze Carson, Kid Colt, Tex Morgan, Wild West, Wild Western, & Wisco)
Sept, 1948 - No. 9, March, 1950
Marvel Comics (HPC)

	Good	Fine	N-Mint
1-Tex Taylor & his horse Fury begin	9.50	28.50	65.00
2	5.70	17.00	40.00
3	4.65	14.00	32.00
4-6: All photo-c. 4-Anti-Wertham editorial. 5,6-Blaze Carson app.	5.00	15.00	35.00
7-Photo-c; 18pg. Movie-Length Thriller "Trapped in Time's Lost Land!" with sabre toothed tigers, dinosaurs; Diablo app.	7.00	21.00	50.00
8-Photo-c; 18pg. Movie-Length Thriller "The Mystery of Devil-Tree Plateau!" with dwarf horses, dwarf people & a lost miniature Inca type village; Diablo app.	7.00	21.00	50.00
9-Photo-c; 18pg. Movie-Length Thriller "Guns Along the Border!" Captain Tootsie by Schreiber; Nimo The Mountain Lion app.	7.00	21.00	50.00

THANE OF BAGARTH
No. 24, Oct, 1985 - No. 25, Dec, 1985
Charlton Comics

	Good	Fine	N-Mint
24,25		.40	.80

THAT DARN CAT (See Movie Comics and Walt Disney Showcase #19)

THAT'S MY POP! GOES NUTS FOR FAIR
1939 (76 pages) (B&W)
Bystander Press

	Good	Fine	N-Mint
nn-by Milt Gross	7.00	21.00	50.00

THAT THE WORLD MAY BELIEVE
No date (16 pgs.) (Graymoor Friars distr.)
Catechetical Guild Giveaway

	Good	Fine	N-Mint
	1.70	5.00	10.00

THAT WILKIN BOY (Meet Bingo...)
Jan, 1969 - No. 52, Oct, 1982
Archie Publications

	Good	Fine	N-Mint
1	1.35	4.00	8.00
2-10	.70	2.00	4.00
11-26 (last Giant issue)	.35	1.00	2.00
27-52		.50	1.00

T.H.E. CAT (TV)
Mar, 1967 - No. 4, Oct, 1967 (All have photo-c)
Dell Publishing Co.

	Good	Fine	N-Mint
1	1.50	4.50	10.00
2-4	1.00	3.00	7.00

THERE'S A NEW WORLD COMING
1973 (35-49 Cents)
Spire Christian Comics/Fleming H. Revell Co.

	Good	Fine	N-Mint
		.50	1.00

THEY ALL KISSED THE BRIDE (See Cinema Comics Herald)

THEY RING THE BELL
1946
Fox Feature Syndicate

	Good	Fine	N-Mint
1	6.00	18.00	42.00

THIEF OF BAGHDAD (See 4-Color #1229)

THIMBLE THEATRE STARRING POPEYE
1931, 1932 (52 pgs.; 25 cents; B&W)

Tex Farrell #1, © DS

Tex Ritter Western #3, © CC

Tex Taylor #9, © MEG

The Thing! #12, © CC   This Is War #5, © STD   This Magazine Is Haunted #18 (1st series), © CC

THIMBLE THEATRE STARRING POPEYE (continued)
Sonnet Publishing Co.

	Good	Fine	N-Mint
1-Daily strip serial-r in both by Segar	50.00	150.00	350.00
2	45.00	135.00	315.00

NOTE: Probably the first Popeye reprint book. Popeye first entered Thimble Theatre in 1929.

THIMK (Magazine) (Satire)
May, 1958 - No. 6, May, 1959
Counterpart

1	2.30	7.00	16.00
2-6	1.30	4.00	9.00

THING!, THE (Blue Beetle #18 on)
Feb, 1952 - No. 17, Nov, 1954
Song Hits No. 1,2/Capitol Stories/Charlton

1	21.50	65.00	150.00
2,3	16.00	48.00	110.00
4-6,8,10	12.00	36.00	84.00
7-Injury to eye-c & inside panel. E.C. swipes from VOH #28			
	23.00	70.00	160.00
9-Used in **SOTI**, pg. 388 & illo-"Stomping on the face is a form of brutality which modern children learn early"			
	26.00	78.00	180.00
11-Necronomicon story; Hansel & Gretel parody; Injury-to-eye panel; Check-a	20.00	60.00	140.00
12-"Cinderella" parody; Ditko-c/a; lingerie panels			
	32.00	95.00	225.00
13,15-Ditko c/a(3 & 5); 13-Ditko E.C. swipe/HOF #15/1-"House of Horror"	32.00	95.00	225.00
14-Extreme violence/torture; Rumpelstiltskin story; Ditko c/a(4)			
	32.00	95.00	225.00
16-Injury to eye panel	17.00	51.00	120.00
17-Ditko-c; classic parody-"Through the Looking Glass;" Powell-a(r)			
	25.00	75.00	175.00

NOTE: Excessive violence, severed heads, injury to eye are common No. 5 on.

THING, THE (Also see Fantastic Four, Marvel Fanfare & Marvel Two-In-One)
July, 1983 - No. 36, June, 1986
Marvel Comics Group

1-Byrne scripts 1-13,18 on; life story of Ben Grimm			
		.60	1.20
2-36		.50	1.00

NOTE: Byrne a-2i, 7; c-1, 7.

THIRTEEN (. . . Going on 18)
11-1/61-62 - No. 25, 12/67; No. 26, 7/69 - No. 29, 1/71
Dell Publishing Co.

1	3.50	10.50	24.00
2-10	2.65	8.00	18.00
11-29; 26-29-r	2.00	6.00	14.00

NOTE: John Stanley script-No. 3-29; art?

THIRTY SECONDS OVER TOKYO (Also see Guadacanal Diary)
1943 (Movie) (Also see American Library)
David McKay Co.

nn(B&W, text & pictures)	16.00	48.00	110.00

THIS IS SUSPENSE! (Formerly Strange Suspense Stories; Strange Suspense Stories #27 on)
No. 23, Feb, 1955 - No. 26, Aug, 1955
Charlton Comics

23-Wood-a(r)/A Star Presentation #3-"Dr. Jekyll & Mr. Hyde"			
	11.00	32.00	75.00
24-Evans-a	4.00	12.00	28.00
25,26	2.30	7.00	16.00

THIS IS THE PAYOFF (See Pay-Off)

THIS IS WAR
No. 5, July, 1952 - No. 9, May, 1953
Standard Comics

	Good	Fine	N-Mint
5-Toth-a	5.50	16.50	38.00
6,9-Toth-a	4.30	13.00	30.00
7,8	1.20	3.50	8.00

THIS IS YOUR LIFE, DONALD DUCK (See 4-Color #1109)

THIS MAGAZINE IS CRAZY (Crazy V3#3 on)
V3#2, July, 1957 (68 pgs.) (25 cents) (Satire)
Charlton Publ. (Humor Magazines)

V3#2	1.00	3.00	6.00

THIS MAGAZINE IS HAUNTED (Danger and Adventure #22 on)
Oct, 1951 - No. 14, 12/53; No. 15, 2/54 - V3/21, Nov, 1954
Fawcett Publications/Charlton No. 15(2/54) on

1-Evans-a(i?)	15.00	45.00	105.00
2,5-Evans-a	11.00	32.00	75.00
3,4	5.70	17.00	40.00
6-9,11,12,14	4.65	14.00	32.00
10-Severed head-c	6.85	21.00	48.00
13-Severed head c/story	6.00	18.00	42.00
15,20	4.00	12.00	28.00
16,19-Ditko-c. 19-Injury-to-eye panel; story r-/#1			
	9.50	28.50	65.00
17-Ditko-c/a(3); blood drainage story	13.00	40.00	100.00
18-Ditko-c/a; E.C. swipe/Haunt of Fear 5; injury-to-eye panel			
	12.00	36.00	84.00
21-Ditko-c, Evans-a	9.50	28.50	65.00

NOTE: Bailey a-1, 3, 4, 21r/#1. Powell a-3-5, 11, 12, 17. Shuster a-18-20.

THIS MAGAZINE IS HAUNTED (2nd Series) (Formerly Zaza the Mystic; Outer Space #17 on)
V2No.12, July, 1957 - V2No.16, April, 1958
Charlton Comics

V2#12-14-Ditko c/a in all	10.00	30.00	70.00
15-No Ditko c/a	1.50	4.50	10.00
16-Ditko-a	7.00	21.00	50.00

THIS MAGAZINE IS WILD (See Wild)

THIS WAS YOUR LIFE (Religious)
1964 (3½x5½'') (40 pgs.) (Black, white & red)
Jack T. Chick Publ.

nn		.40	.80
Another version (5x2¾'', 26pgs.)		.60	1.20

THOR (Formerly Journey Into Mystery)(Also see Marvel Coll. Item Classics, Marvel Graphic Novel 33, Marvel Preview, Marvel Spec., Marvel Treas. Ed., Spec. Marv. Ed. & Tales of Asgard)
March, 1966 - Present
Marvel Comics Group

126	1.50	4.50	10.00
127-133,135-140	1.00	3.00	6.00
134-Intro High Evolutionary	1.35	4.00	8.00
141-145,150: 146-Inhumans begin, end #151	.85	2.50	5.00
146,147-Origin The Inhumans	.85	2.50	5.00
148,149-Origin Black Bolt in each; 149-Origin Medusa, Crystal, Maximus, Gorgon, Kornak	.85	2.50	5.00
151-157,159,160	.85	2.50	5.00
158-Origin-r/No. 83; origin Dr. Blake, concludes #159			
	1.00	3.00	6.00
161,163,164,167,170-179-Last Kirby issue	.70	2.00	4.00
162,168,169-Origin Galactus	.85	2.50	5.00
165,166-Warlock(Him) app.	.90	2.75	5.50
180,181-Adams-a	1.00	3.00	6.00
182-192,194-199	.40	1.25	2.50
193-(52 pgs.); Silver Surfer x-over	1.15	3.50	7.00

THOR (continued)	Good	Fine	N-Mint
200	.50	1.50	3.00
201-299: 225-Intro. Firelord. 294-Origin Asgard & Odin	.25	.75	1.50
300-End of Asgard; origin of Odin & The Destroyer	.35	1.00	2.00
301-336		.50	1.00
337-Simonson-a begins; Beta Ray Bill becomes new Thor	1.10	3.25	6.50
338	.50	1.50	3.00
339,340: 340-Donald Blake returns as Thor	.25	.75	1.50
341-373,375-381,383: 373-X-Factor tie-in		.50	1.00
374-Mutant massacre; X-Factor app.	.60	1.75	3.50
382-Anniversary issue ($1.25)	.25	.75	1.50
384-Intro. new Thor	.35	1.00	2.00
385-399: 395-Intro The Earth Force		.50	1.00
400 ($1.75, 68 pgs.)-Origin Loki	.30	.90	1.75
Giant-Size 1('75)		.50	1.00
Special 2(9/66), 3(1967)-See Journey Into Mystery for 1st annual	.70	2.00	4.00
Special 4('67-12/71)	.50	1.50	3.00
Annual 5(11/76)	.25	.75	1.50
Annual 6(10/77), 7(9/78), 8(11/79)	.25	.75	1.50
Annual 9(11/81), 10(11/82), 11(11/83)	.25	.75	1.50
Annual 12(11/84)	.25	.75	1.50
Annual 13(12/85)	.25	.75	1.50

NOTE: **Adams** c-179-181. **Austin** a-342i, 346i; c-312i. **Buscema** a(p)-178, 182-213, 215-226, 231-238, 241-253, 254r, 256-259, 272-278, 283-285, 370, Annual 6, 8; c(p)-175, 182-196, 198-200, 202-204, 206, 211, 212, 215, 219, 221, 226, 256, 259, 261, 262, 272-278, 283, 289, 370, Annual 6. **Everett** a(i)-143, 170-175; c(i)-171, 172, 174, 176, 241. **Gil Kane** a-318p; c(p)-201, 205, 207-10, 216, 220, 222, 223, 231, 233-40, 242, 243, 318. **Kirby** a(p)-126-177, 179, 194, 254r; c(p)-126-169, 171-174, 176, 177, 178, 249-253, 255, 257, 258, Annual 5, Special 1-4. **Mooney** a(i)-201, 204, 214-16, 218, 322i, 324i, 325i, 327i. **Simonson** a-260-71p, 337-54, 357-367, 380, Annual 7p; c-260, 263-71, 337-55, 357-369, 371, 373-382, Annual 7. **Starlin** c-213.

THOSE ANNOYING POST BROS.
Jan., 1985 - Present ($1.75, B&W)
Vortex Comics

	Good	Fine	N-Mint
1	.40	1.15	2.30
2-10	.35	1.00	2.00

THOSE MAGNIFICENT MEN IN THEIR FLYING MACHINES (See Movie Comics)

THREE CABALLEROS (See 4-Color #71)

THREE CHIPMUNKS, THE (See 4-Color #1042)

THREE COMICS (Also see Spiritman)
1944 (10 cents, 48pgs.) (2 different covers exist)
The Penny King Co.
1,3,4-Lady Luck, Mr. Mystic, The Spirit app. (3 Spirit sections bound together)-Lou Fine-a | 13.00 | 40.00 | 90.00
NOTE: No. 1 contains Spirit Sections 4/9/44 - 4/23/44, and No. 4 is also from 4/44.

3-D (NOTE: The prices of all the 3-D comics listed include glasses. Deduct 40-50 percent if glasses are missing, and reduce slightly if glasses are loose.)

3-D ACTION
Jan, 1954 (Oversized) (15 cents)(2 pairs glasses included)
Atlas Comics (ACI)
1-Battle Brady | 21.50 | 65.00 | 150.00

3-D ADVENTURE COMICS
Aug, 1986 (One shot)
Stats, Etc.
1-Promo material | .25 | .75 | 1.50

3-D ALIEN TERROR
June, 1986
Eclipse Comics
1-Morrow-a; Old Witch, Crypt-Keeper, Vault Keeper cameo

	Good	Fine	N-Mint
	.40	1.25	2.50
...in 2-D: 100 copies signed & numbered (B&W)	.70	2.00	4.00

3-D ANIMAL FUN (See Animal Fun)

3-D BATMAN
1953, Reprinted in 1966
National Periodical Publications
1953-Reprints Batman #42 & 48; Tommy Tomorrow app. | 52.00 | 156.00 | 365.00
1966-Tommy Tomorrow app. | 14.00 | 42.00 | 100.00

3-D CIRCUS
1953 (25 cents)
Fiction House Magazines
1 | 21.50 | 65.00 | 150.00

3-D COMICS (See Tor, 3-D, and Mighty Mouse)

3-D DOLLY
December, 1953 (2 pairs glasses included)
Harvey Publications
1-Richie Rich story redrawn from his 1st app. in Little Dot #1 | 12.00 | 36.00 | 84.00

3-D-ELL
1953 (3-D comics) (25 cents)
Dell Publishing Co.
1,2-Rootie Kazootie | 20.00 | 60.00 | 140.00
3-Flukey Luke | 19.00 | 57.00 | 132.00

3-D FEATURES PRESENT JET PUP
Oct-Dec, 1953
Dimensions Public
1-Irving Spector-a(2) | 21.00 | 62.00 | 146.00

3-D FUNNY MOVIES
1953 (25 cents)
Comic Media
1-Bugsey Bear & Paddy Pelican | 19.00 | 57.00 | 132.00

3-D HEROES (Blackthorne 3-D series #3)
Feb, 1986 ($2.25)
Blackthorne Publishing, Inc.
1 | .40 | 1.25 | 2.50

THREE-DIMENSION ADVENTURES (Superman)
1953 (Large size)
National Periodical Publications
Origin Superman (new art) | 60.00 | 180.00 | 420.00

THREE DIMENSIONAL ALIEN WORLDS (See Alien Worlds)
July, 1984 (One-Shot)
Pacific Comics
1-Bolton/Stevens, Art Adams-a | .85 | 2.50 | 5.00

THREE DIMENSIONAL DNAGENTS (See New DNAgents)

THREE DIMENSIONAL E. C. CLASSICS (Three Dimensional Tales From the Crypt No. 2)
Spring, 1954 (Prices include glasses; came with 2 pair)
E. C. Comics
1-Reprints: Wood (Mad #3), Krigstein (W.S. #7), Evans (F.C. #13), & Ingels (CSS #5); Kurtzman-c | 35.00 | 105.00 | 245.00
NOTE: Stories redrawn to 3-D format. Original stories not necessarily by artists listed. CSS: Crime SuspenStories; F.C.: Frontline Combat; W.S.: Weird Science.

THREE DIMENSIONAL TALES FROM THE CRYPT (Formerly Three Dimensional E. C. Classics)
Spring, 1954 (Prices include glasses; came with 2 pair)
E. C. Comics

Thor #338, © MEG

3-D Action #1, © MEG

3-D Dolly #1, © HARV

3-D Sheena, Jungle Queen #1, © FH   The 3-D Zone #9, © Ray Zone   Three Stooges #22, © Norman Maurer Prod.

THREE DIMENSIONAL TALES FROM THE CRYPT (continued)

	Good	Fine	N-Mint
2-Davis (TFTC #25), Elder (VOH #14), Craig (TFTC #24), & Orlando (TFTC #22) stories; Feldstein-c	37.00	110.00	260.00

NOTE: *Stories redrawn to 3-D format. Original stories not necessarily by artists listed. TFTC: Tales From the Crypt; VOH: Vault of Horror.*

3-D LOVE
December, 1953 (25 cents)
Steriographic Publ. (Mikeross Publ.)

1	21.50	65.00	150.00

3-D NOODNICK (See Noodnick)

3-D ROMANCE
January, 1954 (25 cents)
Steriographic Publ. (Mikeross Publ.)

1	21.50	65.00	150.00

3-D SHEENA, JUNGLE QUEEN (See Sheena 3-D Special)
1953
Fiction House Magazines

1	35.00	105.00	245.00

3-D TALES OF THE WEST
Jan, 1954 (Oversized) (15 cents)(2 pair glasses included)
Atlas Comics (CPS)

1 (3-D)	21.50	65.00	150.00

3-D THREE STOOGES (Also see Three Stooges)
Sept, 1986 - No. 3?? ($2.50)
Eclipse Comics

1-3 (10/87)-Maurer-r	.60	1.75	3.50
1-3 (2-D)	.60	1.75	3.50

3-D WHACK (See Whack)

3-D ZONE, THE
Feb, 1987 - Present ($2.50)
The 3-D Zone(Renegade Press)/Ray Zone

1-6: 1-r-/A Star Presentation, 2-Wolverton-r, 3-Picture Scope Jungle Advs., 4-Electric Fear, 5-Krazy Kat-r, 6-Ratfink	.40	1.25	2.50
7-10: 7-Hollywood 3-D; Jayne Mansfield photo-c, 8-High Seas 3-D, 9-Redmask-r, 10-Jet 3-D; Powell & Williamson-r	.40	1.25	2.50
11-16: 11-Danse Macabre; Matt Fox c/a(r). 12-3-D Presidents. 13-Flash 13-Gordon. 14-Tyranostar. 15-3-Dementia Comics; Kurtzman-c, Kubert, Maurer-a. 16-Space Vixens; Dave Stevens-c/a	.40	1.25	2.50

3 FUNMAKERS, THE
1908 (64 pgs.) (10x15'')
Stokes and Company

Maude, Katzenjammer Kids, Happy Hooligan (1904-06 Sunday strip reprints in color)	26.00	78.00	180.00

3 LITTLE PIGS (See 4-Color #218)

3 LITTLE PIGS, THE (See Walt Disney Showcase #15,21)
May, 1964 - No. 2, Sept, 1968 (Walt Disney)
Gold Key

1-Reprints 4-Color 218	1.00	3.00	7.00
2	.75	2.25	5.00

THREE MOUSEKETEERS, THE (1st Series)
3-4/56 - No. 24, 9-10/59; No. 25, 8-9/60 - No. 26, 10-12/60
National Periodical Publications

1	7.00	21.00	50.00
2	3.50	10.50	24.00
3-10	2.65	8.00	18.00
11-26	1.70	5.00	12.00

NOTE: *Rube Grossman a-1-26. Sheldon Mayer a-1-8; c-1,3,4,6,7.*

THREE MOUSEKETEERS, THE (2nd Series) (See Super DC Giant)
May-June, 1970 - No. 7, May-June, 1971
National Periodical Publications

	Good	Fine	N-Mint
1-Mayer-a	.25	.75	1.50
2-7-Mayer-a (68 pgs.) #5-7)		.30	.60

THREE NURSES (Formerly Confidential Diary; Career Girl Romances #24 on)
V3#18, May, 1963 - V3#23, Mar, 1964
Charlton Comics

V3#18-23		.60	1.20

THREE RASCALS
1958; 1963
I. W. Enterprises

I.W. Reprint #1 (Says Super Comics on inside)-(M.E.'s Clubhouse Rascals), #2('58)	.30	.80	1.60
10('63)-Reprints #1	.30	.80	1.60

THREE RING COMICS
March, 1945
Spotlight Publishers

1	3.00	9.00	21.00

THREE ROCKETEERS (See Blast-Off)

THREE STOOGES (See Comic Album #18, The Little Stooges, March of Comics #232, 248, 268, 280, 292, 304, 316, 336, 373, Movie Classics & Comics & 3-D Three Stooges)

THREE STOOGES
Feb, 1949 - No. 2, May, 1949; Sept, 1953 - No. 7, Oct, 1954
Jubilee No. 1,2/St. John No. 1 (9/53) on

1-(Scarce, 1949)-Kubert-a; infinity-c	45.00	135.00	315.00
2-(Scarce)-Kubert, Maurer-a	35.00	105.00	245.00
1(9/53)-Hollywood Stunt Girl by Kubert, 7 pgs.	30.00	90.00	210.00
2(3-D, 10/53)-Stunt Girl story by Kubert	22.00	65.00	154.00
3(3-D, 11/53)	20.00	60.00	140.00
4(3/54)-7(10/54)	12.00	36.00	84.00

NOTE: *All issues have Kubert-Maurer art. Maurer c-1,2('49), 1('53).*

THREE STOOGES
No. 1043, Oct-Dec, 1959 - No. 55, June, 1972
Dell Publishing Co./Gold Key No. 10 (10/62) on

4-Color 1043 (#1)	6.00	18.00	42.00
4-Color 1078,1127,1170,1187	4.30	13.00	30.00
6(9-11/61) - 10: 6-Professor Putter begins; ends #16	3.50	10.50	24.00
11-14,16-20: 17-The Little Monsters begin (5/64)(1st app.?)	3.00	9.00	21.00
15-Go Around the World in a Daze (movie scenes)	3.50	10.50	24.00
21,23-30	2.00	6.00	14.00
22-Movie scenes/'The Outlaws Is Coming'	3.50	10.50	24.00
31-55	1.70	5.00	12.00

NOTE: *All Four Colors, 6-50,52-55 have photo-c.*

3 WORLDS OF GULLIVER (See 4-Color #1158)

THRILL COMICS (See Flash Comics, Fawcett)

THRILLER
Nov, 1983 - No. 12, Nov, 1984 ($1.25; Baxter paper)
DC Comics

1-Intro Seven Seconds		.50	1.00
2-12: 2-Origin. 5,6-Elvis satire. 10($2.00)		.50	1.00

THRILLING ADVENTURES IN STAMPS COMICS
Jan, 1953 (25 cents) (100 pages) (Formerly Stamp Comics)
Stamp Comics, Inc. (Very Rare)

THRILLING ADVENTURES IN STAMPS COMICS (continued)

	Good	Fine	N-Mint
V1#8-Harrison, Wildey, Kiefer, Napoli-a	20.00	60.00	140.00

THRILLING ADVENTURE STORIES (See Tigerman)
Feb, 1975 - No. 2, July-Aug, 1975 (B&W) (68 pgs.)
Atlas/Seaboard Publ.

	Good	Fine	N-Mint
1-Tigerman, Kromag the Killer begin; Heath, Thorne-a	.40	1.20	2.40
2-Toth, Severin, Simonson-a; Adams-c	.40	1.20	2.40

THRILLING COMICS
Feb, 1940 - No. 80, April, 1951
Better Publ./Nedor/Standard Comics

	Good	Fine	N-Mint
1-Origin Doc Strange (37 pgs.); Nickie Norton of the Secret Service begins	58.00	175.00	405.00
2-The Rio Kid, The Woman in Red, Pinocchio begin	26.00	78.00	182.00
3-The Ghost & Lone Eagle begin	24.00	72.00	168.00
4-10	16.00	48.00	110.00
11-18,20	12.00	36.00	84.00
19-Origin The American Crusader, ends #39,41	17.00	51.00	120.00
21-30: 24-Intro. Mike, Doc Strange's sidekick. 29-Last Rio Kid	10.00	30.00	70.00
31-40: 36-Commando Cubs begin	8.00	24.00	56.00
41-52: 41-Hitler bondage-c. 44-Hitler-c. 52-The Ghost ends	6.50	19.50	45.00
53-The Phantom Detective begins; The Cavalier app.; no Commando Cubs	6.50	19.50	45.00
54-The Cavalier app.; no Commando Cubs	6.50	19.50	45.00
55-Lone Eagle ends	6.50	19.50	45.00
56-Princess Pantha begins	13.00	40.00	90.00
57-60	12.00	36.00	84.00
61-65: 61-Ingels-a; The Lone Eagle app. 65-Last Phantom Detective & Commando Cubs	12.00	36.00	84.00
66-Frazetta text illo	11.50	34.00	80.00
67,70-73: Frazetta-a(5-7 pgs.) in each. 72-Sea Eagle app.	18.00	54.00	125.00
68,69-Frazetta-a(2), 8 & 6 pgs.; 9 & 7 pgs.	19.00	57.00	132.00
74-Last Princess Pantha; Tara app. Buck Ranger, Cowboy Detective begins	6.00	18.00	42.00
75-78: 75-Western format begins	3.50	10.50	24.00
79-Krigstein-a	4.60	14.00	32.00
80-Severin & Elder, Celardo, Moreira-a	4.60	14.00	32.00

NOTE: Bondage c-5, 9, 13, 20, 22, 27-30, 38, 41, 52, 54, 70. Kinstler a-45, 48. Leo Morey a-7. Schomburg (Xela) c-11-18, 36-71; airbrush 62-71. Tuska a-63. Woman in Red not in #19, 23, 31-33, 39-45. No. 72 exists as a Canadian reprint with no Frazetta story.

THRILLING CRIME CASES (Shocking Mystery Cases #50 on)
No. 41, June-July, 1950 - No. 49, 1952
Star Publications

	Good	Fine	N-Mint
41	5.00	15.00	35.00
42-44-Chameleon story-Fox-r	4.35	13.00	30.00
45-48: 47-Used in POP, pg. 84	4.00	12.00	28.00
49-Classic L. B. Cole-c	11.00	32.00	76.00

NOTE: All have L. B. Cole-c; a-43p, 45p, 46p, 49(2pgs.). Disbrow a-48. Hollingsworth a-48.

THRILLING ROMANCES
No. 5, Dec, 1949 - No. 26, June, 1954
Standard Comics

	Good	Fine	N-Mint
5	3.50	10.50	24.00
6,8	1.70	5.00	12.00
7-Severin/Elder-a, 7 pgs.	3.00	9.00	21.00
9,10-Severin/Elder-a	2.35	7.00	16.00
11,14-21,26	1.15	3.50	8.00
12-Wood-a, 2 pgs.; photo-c	4.35	13.00	30.00

	Good	Fine	N-Mint
13-Severin-a	2.00	6.00	14.00
22-25-Toth-a	3.70	11.00	26.00

NOTE: All photo-c. Celardo a-9,16. Colletta a-23, 24(2). Tuska a-9.

THRILLING TRUE STORY OF THE BASEBALL GIANTS
1952 (2nd issue titled . . . Baseball Yankees)
Fawcett Publications

	Good	Fine	N-Mint
Each . . . .(photo-c)	23.00	70.00	160.00

THRILLOGY
Jan, 1984 (One-shot)
Pacific Comics

	Good	Fine	N-Mint
1-Conrad c/a		.50	1.00

THRILL-O-RAMA
Oct, 1965 - No. 3, Dec, 1966
Harvey Publications (Fun Films)

	Good	Fine	N-Mint
1-Fate (Man in Black) by Powell app.; Doug Wildey-a; Simon-c	.85	2.50	6.00
2-Pirana begins; Williamson 2 pgs.; Fate (Man in Black) app.; Tuska/Simon-c	.85	2.50	6.00
3-Fate (Man in Black) app.; Sparling-c	.50	1.50	3.00

THRILLS OF TOMORROW (Formerly Tomb of Terror)
No. 17, Oct, 1954 - No. 20, April, 1955
Harvey Publications

	Good	Fine	N-Mint
17-Powell-a (horror); r/Witches Tales #7	2.35	7.00	16.00
18-Powell-a (horror); r/Tomb of Terror #1	2.00	6.00	14.00
19,20-Stuntman by S&K (r/from Stuntman 1 & 2); 19 has origin & is last pre-code (2/55)	13.50	40.50	95.00

NOTE: Palais a-17.

THROBBING LOVE (See Fox Giants)

THROUGH GATES OF SPLENDOR
1973, 1974 (36 pages) (39-49 cents)
Spire Christian Comics (Fleming H. Revell Co.)

	Good	Fine	N-Mint
nn		.40	.80

THUMPER (See 4-Color #19 & 243)

THUN'DA (. . . King Of The Congo)
1952 - 1953
Magazine Enterprises

	Good	Fine	N-Mint
1(A-1 47)-Origin; Frazetta c/a; only comic done entirely by Frazetta; Cave Girl app.	97.00	290.00	680.00
2(A-1 56)	12.00	36.00	84.00
3(A-1 73), 4(A-1 78)	9.00	27.00	62.00
5(A-1 83), 6(A-1 86)	8.00	24.00	56.00

NOTE: Powell c/a-2-6.

THUN'DA TALES (See Frank Frazetta's . . .)

THUNDER AGENTS (See Tales Of Thunder)
11/65 - No. 17, 12/67; No. 18, 9/68, No. 19, 11/68, No. 20, 11/69 (No. 1-16: 68 pgs.; No. 17 on: 52 pgs.)
Tower Comics

	Good	Fine	N-Mint
1-Origin & 1st app. Dynamo, Noman, Menthor, & The Thunder Squad; 1st app. The Iron Maiden	5.00	15.00	35.00
2-Death of Egghead	2.65	8.00	18.00
3-5: 4-Guy Gilbert becomes Lightning who joins Thunder Squad; Iron Maiden app.	1.70	5.00	12.00
6-10: 7-Death of Menthor. 8-Origin & 1st app. The Raven	1.15	3.50	8.00
11-15: 13-Undersea Agent app.; no Raven sty	.85	2.50	6.00
16-19	.70	2.00	4.00
20-All reprints	.50	1.50	3.00

NOTE: Crandall a-1, 4p, 5p, 18, 20r; c-18. Ditko a-6, 7p, 12p, 13, 14p, 16, 18. Kane a-1, 5p, 6p, 14, 16p; c-14, 15. Tuska a-1p, 7, 8, 10, 13-17, 19. Whitney a-9p, 10, 13, 15. 17, 18; c-17. Wood a-1-11,iw/Ditko-12,18), (inks-#9, 13, 14, 16, 17), 19i, 20r; c-1-8, 9i, 10-13(#10 w/Williamson(p)), 16.

Thrilling Comics #70, © STD

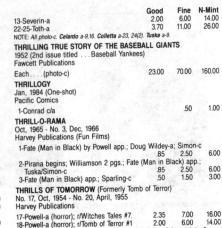

Thun'da #2, © ME

Thunder Agents #3, © TC

Thunderbolt #1, © CC   *Tick Tock Tales #23, © ME*   *Tillie The Toiler #7 (Cupples & Leon), © KING*

T.H.U.N.D.E.R. AGENTS (See Blue Ribbon Comics, Hall of Fame
Featuring the..., JCP Features & Wally Wood's...)
May, 1983 - No. 2, Jan, 1984
JC Comics (Archie Publications)

	Good	Fine	N-Mint
1,2-New material	.35	1.00	2.00

THUNDER BIRDS (See Cinema Comics Herald)

THUNDERBOLT (See The Atomic...)

THUNDERBOLT (Peter Cannon...)
Jan, 1966; No. 51, Mar-Apr, 1966 - No. 60, Nov, 1967
Charlton Comics

1-Origin	.70	2.00	4.00
51-(Formerly Son Of Vulcan #50)	.35	1.00	2.00
52-58: 54-Sentinels begin. 58-Last Thunderbolt & Sentinels			
	.25	.75	1.50
59,60: 60-Prankster app.	.60	1.20	
Modern Comics-r. 57,58('77)	.15	.30	

NOTE: *Aparo a-60. Morisi a-1, 51-56, 58; c-1, 51-56, 58, 59.*

THUNDERBUNNY (Also see Blue Ribbon Comics, Charlton Bullseye
& Pep #393)
Jan, 1984 (Direct sale only)
Red Circle Comics

1-Origin	.60	1.20	

THUNDERCATS (TV)
Dec, 1985 - No. 24, June, 1988
Star Comics/Marvel #22 on

1-Mooney c/a begins	.70	2.00	4.00
2-(65 & 75 cent cover exist)	.40	1.25	2.50
3-24: 12-Begin $1.00-c; 20-Williamson-i	.50	1.00	

THUNDERMACE
Mar, 1986 - Present ($1.50, B&W)
RAK Graphics

1-Two color-c	3.35	10.00	20.00
1-2nd print, multi-color-c	.35	1.00	2.00
2-5 ($1.75)	.25	.80	1.60
Graphic Novel 1 (B&W-r)	.85	2.50	5.00

THUNDER MOUNTAIN (See 4-Color #246)

TICK, THE
June, 1988 - Present ($1.75; B&W)
New England Comics Press

1	.70	2.00	4.00
2	.40	1.25	2.50

TICKLE COMICS (Also see Gay, Smile, & Whee Comics)
1955 (52 pages) (5x7¼'') (7 cents)
Modern Store Publ.

1	.40	1.20	2.40

TICK TOCK TALES
Jan, 1946 - No.34, 1951
Magazine Enterprises

1-Koko & Kola begin	4.65	14.00	32.00
2	2.30	7.00	16.00
3-10	1.70	5.00	12.00
11-34: 19-Flag-c. 23-Muggsy Mouse, The Pixies & Tom-Tom The			
Jungle Boy app.	1.15	3.50	8.00

TIGER (Also see Comics Reading Libraries)
March, 1970 - No. 6, Jan, 1971 (15 cents)
Charlton Press (King Features)

1	.30	.80	1.60
2-6		.50	1.00

TIGER BOY (See Unearthly Spectaculars)

TIGER GIRL
September, 1968
Gold Key

	Good	Fine	N-Mint
1 (10227-809)	1.75	5.25	12.00

NOTE: *Sparling c/a; written by Jerry Siegel.*

TIGERMAN (Also see Thrilling Adv. Stories)
April, 1975 - No. 3, Sept, 1975
Seaboard Periodicals (Atlas)

1		.40	.80
2,3-Ditko-p in each		.30	.60

TIGER WALKS, A (See Movie Comics)

TILLIE THE TOILER
1925 - 1933 (52 pgs.) (B&W daily strip reprints)
Cupples & Leon Co.

nn (#1)	9.00	27.00	62.00
2-8	6.00	18.00	42.00

NOTE: *First strip app. was January, 1921.*

TILLIE THE TOILER (See Comic Monthly)
No. 15, 1941 - No. 237, July, 1949
Dell Publishing Co.

4-Color 15(1941)	19.00	57.00	132.00
Large Feature Comic 30(1941)	11.50	34.00	80.00
4-Color 8(1942)	11.50	34.00	80.00
4-Color 22(1943)	9.50	28.50	65.00
4-Color 55(1944)	7.00	21.00	50.00
4-Color 89(1945)	6.00	18.00	42.00
4-Color 106('45),132('46)	5.00	15.00	35.00
4-Color 150,176,184	3.70	11.00	26.00
4-Color 195,213,237	3.50	10.50	24.00

TILLY AND TED-TINKERTOTLAND
1945 (Giveaway) (20 pgs.)
W. T. Grant Co.

nn-Christmas comic	2.00	6.00	14.00

TIM (Formerly Superman-Tim; becomes Gene Autry-Tim)
June, 1950 (Half-size, B&W)
Tim Stores

4 issues	2.50	7.50	15.00

TIME BANDITS
Feb, 1982 (One shot)
Marvel Comics Group

1-Movie adaptation		.50	1.00

TIME BEAVERS (See First Comics Graphic Novel)

TIME FOR LOVE (Formerly Romantic Secrets)
V2#53, Oct, 1966 - No. 47, May, 1976
Charlton Comics

V2#53(10/66), 1(10/67), 2(12/67)-20		.60	1.20
21-47		.15	.30

TIMELESS TOPIX (See Topix)

TIME MACHINE, THE (See 4-Color #1085)

TIMESPIRITS
Jan, 1985 - No. 8, Mar, 1986 ($1.50, Baxter paper; adults only)
Epic Comics (Marvel)

1	.30	.90	1.80
2-8: 4-Williamson-a	.25	.75	1.50

TIME TO RUN
1973 (39, 49 cents)
Spire Christian Comics (Fleming H. Revell Co.)

nn-by Al Hartley (from Billy Graham movie)		.40	.80

TIME TUNNEL, THE (TV)
Feb, 1967 - No. 2, July, 1967
Gold Key

	Good	Fine	N-Mint
1,2-Photo back-c	2.00	6.00	14.00

TIME TWISTERS
Sept, 1987 - Present ($1.25-$1.50, color)
Quality Comics

1-10: Alan Moore scripts in 1-4, 6-9		.60	1.25
11-15 ($1.50)	.25	.75	1.50

TIME 2: THE EPIPHANY (See First Comics Graphic Novel)

TIME WARP
Oct-Nov, 1979 - No. 5, June-July, 1980 ($1.00)
DC Comics, Inc.

1		.40	.80
2-5		.30	.60

NOTE: *Aparo* a-1. *Buckler* a-1p. *Chaykin* a-2. *Ditko* a-1-4. *Kaluta* c-1-5. *G. Kane* a-2. *Nasser* a-4. *Newton* a-1-5p. *Orlando* a-2. *Sutton* a-1-3.

TIME WARRIORS THE BEGINNING
1986 (Aug) - No. 2, 1986? (color, $1.50)
Fantasy General Comics

1-Alpha Track/Skellon Empire	.25	.75	1.50
2		.40	.75

TIM HOLT (Movie star) (Becomes Red Mask #42 on; also see Crack Western #72, & Great Western)
1948 - No. 41, April-May, 1954 (All 36 pgs.)
Magazine Enterprises

1(A-1 14)-Photo-c begin, end No. 18, 29; Tim Holt, His horse Lightning & sidekick Chito begin	32.00	95.00	225.00
2(A-1 17)(9-10/48)	20.00	60.00	140.00
3(A-1 19)-Photo back-c	13.50	40.00	95.00
4(1-2/49),5: 5-Photo back-c	11.00	32.00	76.00
6-1st app. The Calico Kid (alias Rex Fury), his horse Ebony & Sidekick Sing-Song (begin series); photo back-c	12.00	36.00	84.00
7-10: 7-Calico Kid by Ayers. 8-Calico Kid by Guardineer (r-/in Great Western 10). 9-Map of Tim's Home Range	9.00	27.00	62.00
11-The Calico Kid becomes The Ghost Rider (Origin & 1st app.) by Dick Ayers (r-/in Great Western 8); his horse Spectre & sidekick Sing-Song begin series	24.00	72.00	170.00
12-16,18-Last photo-c	6.50	19.50	45.00
17-Frazetta Ghost Rider-c	25.00	75.00	175.00
19,22,24: 19-Last Tim Holt-c; Bolle line-drawn-c begin	5.00	15.00	35.00
20-Tim Holt becomes Redmask (Origin); begin series; Redmask-c #20-on	9.50	28.50	65.00
21-Frazetta Ghost Rider/Redmask-c	21.50	65.00	150.00
23-Frazetta Redmask-c	19.00	57.00	132.00
25-1st app. Black Phantom	10.00	30.00	70.00
26-30: 28-Wild Bill Hickok, Bat Masterson team up with Redmask. 29-B&W photo-c	5.00	15.00	35.00
31-33-Ghost Rider ends	4.30	13.00	30.00
34-Tales of the Ghost Rider begins (horror)-Classic "The Flower Women" & "Hard Boiled Harry!"	5.00	15.00	35.00
35-Last Tales of the Ghost Rider	4.30	13.00	30.00
36-The Ghost Rider returns, ends No. 41; liquid hallucinogenic drug story	5.50	16.50	38.00
37-Ghost Rider classic "To Touch Is to Die!," about Inca treasure	5.50	16.50	38.00
38-The Black Phantom begins; classic Ghost Rider "The Phantom Guns of Feather Gap!"	5.50	16.50	38.00
39-41: All 3-D effect c/stories	12.00	36.00	84.00

NOTE: *Dick Ayers* a-7, 9-41. *Bolle* a-1-41; c-19,20,22,24-28,30-41.

TIM IN SPACE (Formerly Gene Autry Tim; becomes Tim Tomorrow)
1950 (½-size giveaway) (B&W)
Tim Stores

	Good	Fine	N-Mint
	1.70	5.00	10.00

TIM McCOY (Formerly Zoo Funnies; Pictorial Love Stories #22 on)
No. 16, Oct, 1948 - No. 21, Aug-Sept, 1949 (Western movie stories)
Charlton Comics

16-John Wayne, Montgomery Clift app. in 'Red River;' photo back-c	14.00	42.00	100.00
17-21: 17-Rod Cameron app.	11.50	34.00	80.00

TIM McCOY, POLICE CAR 17
1934 (32 pgs.) (11x14¾") (B&W) (Like Feature Books)
Whitman Publishing Co.

674-1933 movie ill.	11.50	34.00	80.00

TIMMY (See 4-Color #715,823,923,1022)

TIMMY THE TIMID GHOST (Formerly Win-A-Prize?; see Blue Bird)
No. 3, 2/56 - No. 44, 10/64; No. 45, 9/66; 10/67 - No. 23, 7/71; V4/24, 9/85 - No. 26, 1/86
Charlton Comics

3(1956) (1st Series)	2.30	7.00	16.00
4,5	1.15	3.50	8.00
6-10	.60	1.80	4.00
11,12(4/58,10/58)(100pgs.)	1.70	5.00	12.00
13-20	.60	1.75	3.50
21-45('66)	.25	.75	1.50
1(10/67)	.35	1.00	2.00
2-23		.50	1.00
24-26 (1985): Fago-r		.40	.80
Shoe Store Giveaway		.40	.80

TIM TOMORROW (Formerly Tim In Space)
8/51, 9/51, 10/51, Christmas, 1951 (5x7¾")
Tim Stores

Prof. Fumble & Captain Kit Comet in all	1.35	4.00	8.00

TIM TYLER (See Harvey Comics Hits #54)

TIM TYLER (Also see Comics Reading Libraries)
1942
Better Publications

1	6.00	18.00	42.00

TIM TYLER COWBOY
No. 11, Nov, 1948 - No. 18, 1950
Standard Comics (King Features Synd.)

11	4.00	12.00	28.00
12-18	2.65	8.00	18.00

TINKER BELL (See 4-Color #896,982, & Walt Disney Showcase #37)

TINY FOLKS FUNNIES (See 4-Color #60)

TINY TESSIE (Tessie #1-23; Real Experiences #25)
No. 24, Oct, 1949
Marvel Comics (20CC)

24	1.70	5.00	12.00

TINY TIM (Also see Super Comics)
No. 4, 1941 - No. 235, July, 1949
Dell Publishing Co.

Large Feature Comic 4('41)	18.00	54.00	125.00
4-Color 20(1941)	19.00	57.00	132.00
4-Color 42(1943)	11.00	32.00	75.00
4-Color 235	3.50	10.50	24.00

TINY TOT COMICS
Mar, 1946 - No. 10, Nov-Dec, 1947 (For younger readers)
E. C. Comics

Time Twisters #1, © Quality Comics

Tim Holt #21, © ME

Tim McCoy #16, © CC

Tip Top Comics #20, © UFS

T-Man #11, © QUA

TNT Comics #1, © Charles Publ.

	Good	Fine	N-Mint
TINY TOT COMICS (continued)			
1(nn) (52 pgs.)	13.00	40.00	90.00
2 (5/46, 52 pgs.)	10.00	30.00	70.00
3-10: 10-Christmas-c	8.50	25.50	60.00

TINY TOT FUNNIES (Formerly Family Funnies)
June, 1951 (Becomes Junior Funnies)
Harvey Publ. (King Features Synd.)

	Good	Fine	N-Mint
9-Flash Gordon, Mandrake	2.50	7.50	17.00

TINY TOTS COMICS
1943 (Not reprints)
Dell Publishing Co.

	Good	Fine	N-Mint
1-Kelly-a(2); fairy tales	30.00	90.00	210.00

TIPPY & CAP STUBBS (See 4-Color #210,242 & Popular Comics)

TIPPY'S FRIENDS GO-GO & ANIMAL
July, 1966 - No. 15, Oct, 1969 (25 cents)
Tower Comics

1	.85	2.50	6.00
2-7,9-15: 12-15 titled ''Tippy's Friend Go-Go''	.60	2.00	4.00
8-Beatles on front/back-c	2.30	7.00	16.00

TIPPY TEEN (See Vicki)
Nov, 1965 - No. 27, Feb, 1970 (25 cents)
Tower Comics

1	.70	2.00	5.00
2-27: 5-1pg. Beatle pin-up	.50	1.50	3.00
Special Collectors' Editions('69-nn)(25 cents)	.50	1.50	3.00

TIPPY TERRY
1963
Super/I. W. Enterprises

Super Reprint #14('63)-Little Grouchy reprints	.60		1.20
I.W. Reprint #1 (nd)	.60		1.20

TIP TOP COMICS
4/36 - No. 210, 1957; No. 211, 11-1/57-58 - No. 225, 5-7/61
United Features No. 1-187/St. John No. 188-210/Dell Publishing Co.
No. 211 on

	Good	Fine	N-Mint
1-Tarzan by Hal Foster, Li'l Abner, Broncho Bill, Fritzi Ritz, Ella Cinders, Capt. & The Kids begin; strip-r	140.00	420.00	980.00
2	65.00	195.00	455.00
3	50.00	150.00	350.00
4	38.00	115.00	265.00
5-10: 7-Photo & biography of Edgar Rice Burroughs. 8-Christmas-c	30.00	90.00	210.00
11-20: 20-Christmas-c	22.00	65.00	154.00
21-40: 36-Kurtzman panel (1st published comic work)	20.00	60.00	140.00
41-Has 1st Tarzan Sunday	20.00	60.00	140.00
42-50: 43-Mort Walker panel	17.00	51.00	120.00
51-53	14.00	42.00	100.00
54-Origin Mirror Man & Triple Terror, also featured on cover	19.00	57.00	132.00
55,56,58,60: Last Tarzan by Foster	13.00	40.00	90.00
57,59,61,62-Tarzan by Hogarth	17.00	51.00	120.00
63-80: 65,67-70,72-74,77,78-No Tarzan	9.00	27.00	62.00
81-90	8.00	24.00	56.00
91-99	5.70	17.00	40.00
100	6.50	19.50	45.00
101-140: 110-Gordo story. 111-Li'l Abner app. 118, 132-no Tarzan	3.70	11.00	26.00
141-170: 145,151-Gordo story. 157-Last Li'l Abner; lingerie panels	2.65	8.00	18.00
171-188-Tarzan reprints by B. Lubbers in all. #177?-Peanuts by Schulz begins; no Peanuts in #178,179,181-183	2.85	8.50	20.00

	Good	Fine	N-Mint
189-225	1.60	4.80	11.00
Bound Volumes (Very Rare) sold at 1939 World's Fair; bound by publ. in pictorial comic boards. (Also see Comics on Parade)			
Bound issues 1-12	160.00	480.00	1120.00
Bound issues 13-24	100.00	300.00	700.00
Bound issues 25-36	75.00	225.00	525.00

NOTE: *Tarzan covers-#3, 9, 11, 13, 16, 18, 21, 24, 27, 30, 32-34, 36, 37, 39, 41, 43, 45, 47, 50, 52 (all worth 10-20 percent more). Tarzan by Foster-#1-40, 44-50; by Rex Maxon-#41-43; by Byrne Hogarth-#57, 59, 62.*

TIP TOPPER COMICS
Oct-Nov, 1949 - No. 28, 1954
United Features Syndicate

	Good	Fine	N-Mint
1-Li'l Abner, Abbie & Slats	4.00	12.00	28.00
2	2.30	7.00	16.00
3-5	2.00	6.00	14.00
6-10	1.70	5.00	12.00
11-25: 17-22,24,26-Peanuts app. (2 pgs.)	1.50	4.50	10.00
26-28-Twin Earths	3.50	10.50	24.00

NOTE: *Many lingerie panels in Fritzi Ritz stories.*

T-MAN
Sept, 1951 - No. 38, Dec, 1956
Quality Comics Group

	Good	Fine	N-Mint
1-Jack Cole-a	11.00	32.00	75.00
2-Crandall-c	5.70	17.00	40.00
3,6-8: Crandall-c	4.65	14.00	32.00
4,5-Crandall c/a each; 5-Drug test	5.50	16.50	38.00
9-Crandall-c	4.00	12.00	28.00
10,12	2.65	8.00	18.00
11-Used in **POP**, pg. 95 & color illo.	5.70	17.00	40.00
13-19,21-24,26	2.30	7.00	16.00
20-H-Bomb explosion-c/story	5.50	16.50	38.00
25-All Crandall-a	4.65	14.00	32.00
27-38	1.85	5.50	13.00

NOTE: *Anti-communist stories are common. Bondage c-15.*

TNT COMICS
Feb, 1946 (36 pgs.)
Charles Publishing Co.

	Good	Fine	N-Mint
1-Yellowjacket app.	7.00	21.00	50.00

TOBY TYLER (See Movie Comics & 4-Color #1092)

TODAY'S BRIDES
11/55; No. 2, 2/56; No. 3, 9/56; No. 4, 11/56
Ajax/Farrell Publishing Co.

	Good	Fine	N-Mint
1	3.00	9.00	21.00
2-4	1.50	4.50	10.00

TODAY'S ROMANCE
No. 5, March, 1952 - No. 8, Sept, 1952
Standard Comics

	Good	Fine	N-Mint
5	2.65	8.00	18.00
6-Toth-a	3.50	10.50	24.00
7,8	1.30	4.00	9.00

TOKA (Jungle King)
Aug-Oct, 1964 - No. 10, Jan, 1967 (Painted-c)
Dell Publishing Co.

	Good	Fine	N-Mint
1	.50	1.50	3.00
2	.35	1.00	2.00
3-10	.25	.70	1.40

TOMAHAWK (Son of... #131-140 on-c; see Star Spangled Comics & World's Finest #65)
Sept-Oct, 1950 - No. 140, May-June, 1972
National Periodical Publications

TOMAHAWK (continued)	Good	Fine	N-Mint
1	40.00	120.00	280.00
2-Frazetta/Williamson-a, 4 pgs.	23.00	70.00	160.00
3-5	12.00	36.00	84.00
6-10: 7-Last 52 pgs.	8.50	25.50	60.00
11-20	5.70	17.00	40.00
21-27,30: Last precode (2/55)	4.00	12.00	28.00
28-1st app. Lord Shilling (arch-foe)	5.00	15.00	35.00
29-Frazetta-r/Jimmy Wakely #3, 3 pgs.	12.00	36.00	84.00
31-40	3.00	9.00	21.00
41-50	2.30	7.00	16.00
51-56,58-60	1.70	5.00	12.00
57-Frazetta-r/Jimmy Wakely #6, 3 pgs.	6.50	19.50	45.00
61-77: 77-Last 10 cent ish.	1.00	3.00	7.00
78-85: 81-1st app. Miss Liberty. 83-Origin Tomahawk's Rangers			
	.50	1.50	3.00
86-100: 96-Origin/1st app. The Hood, alias Lady Shilling			
	.25	.75	1.50
101-130,132-138,140: 107-Origin/1st app. Thunder-Man			
		.50	1.00
131-Frazetta-r/Jimmy Wakely #7, 3 pgs.; origin Firehair retold			
	.35	1.00	2.00
139-Frazetta-r/Star Spangled #113		.60	1.20

NOTE: *Adams* c-116-119, 121, 123-130. Firehair by *Kubert*-131-134, 136. *Maurer* a-138. *Severin* a-135.

TOM AND JERRY (See Comic Album #4, 8, 12, Dell Giant #21, Dell Giants, Golden Comics Digest #1, 5, 8, 13, 15, 18, 22, 25, 28, 35, & March of Comics #21, 46, 61, 70, 88, 103, 119, 128, 145, 154, 173, 190, 207, 224, 281, 295, 305, 321, 333, 345, 361, 365, 388, 400, 444, 451, 463, 480)

TOM AND JERRY (. .Comics, early issues) (M.G.M.)
(Formerly Our Gang No. 1-59) (See Dell Giants for annuals)
No. 193, 6/48; No. 60, 7/49 - No. 212, 7-9/62; No. 213, 11/62 -
No. 291, 2/75; No. 292, 3/77 - No. 342, 5/82 - No. 344, 1982?
Dell Publishing Co./Gold Key No. 213-327/Whitman No. 328 on

	Good	Fine	N-Mint
4-Color 193 (#1)	7.00	21.00	50.00
60	4.30	13.00	30.00
61	3.50	10.50	24.00
62-70: 66-X-mas-c	2.65	8.00	18.00
71-80: 77-X-mas-c	2.00	6.00	14.00
81-99: 90-X-mas-c	1.70	5.00	12.00
100	2.00	6.00	14.00
101-120	1.30	4.00	9.00
121-140: 126-X-mas-c	1.00	3.00	7.00
141-160	.75	2.25	5.00
161-200	.55	1.65	4.00
201-212(7-9/62)(Last Dell ish.)	.45	1.35	3.00
213,214-(84 pgs.)-titled ". . .Funhouse"	1.50	4.50	12.00
215-240: 215-titled ". . .Funhouse"	.45	1.35	3.00
241-270	.35	1.00	2.00
271-300: 286 "Tom & Jerry"	.25	.75	1.50
301-344		.40	.80
Mouse From T.R.A.P. 1(7/66)-Giant, G. K.	1.75	5.25	14.00
Summer Fun 1(7/67, 68pgs.)(Gold Key)-R-/Barks' Droopy/Summer			
Fun No. 1	1.75	5.25	14.00
. . .Kite Fun Book (1958, 5x7¼", 16pgs.)	1.50	4.50	12.00

NOTE: *#60-87, 98-121, 268, 277, 289, 302 are 52 pages. Reprints-#225, 241, 245, 247, 252, 254, 266, 268, 270, 292-327, 329-342, 344.*

TOMB OF DARKNESS (Formerly Beware)
No. 9, July, 1974 - No. 23, Nov, 1976
Marvel Comics Group

		Good	Fine	N-Mint
9-19: 17-Woodbridge-r/Astonishing #62			.25	.50
20-Everett Venus r-/Venus #19			.25	.50
21-23: 23-Everett-a(r)			.25	.50

NOTE: *Ditko* a-15r; 19r.

TOMB OF DRACULA (See Giant-Size Dracula & Dracula Lives)
April, 1972 - No. 70, Aug, 1979

Marvel Comics Group

	Good	Fine	N-Mint
1-Colan-p in all	.85	2.50	5.00
2-9: 3-Intro. Dr. Rachel Van Helsing & Inspector Chelm. 6-Adams-c			
	.30	.90	1.80
10-1st app. Blade the Vampire Slayer	.35	1.00	2.00
11,12,14-20: 12-Brunner-c(p)		.60	1.20
13-Origin Blade the Vampire Slayer	.25	.70	1.40
21-40		.45	.90
41-70: 43-Wrightson-c. 70-Double size	.35		.70

NOTE: *Colan* a-1-70p; c(p) 8, 38-42, 44-56, 58-70.

TOMB OF DRACULA (Magazine)
Nov, 1979 - No. 6, Sept, 1980 (B&W)
Marvel Comics Group

	Good	Fine	N-Mint
1		.60	1.20
2,4-6: 2-Ditko-a (36 pgs.)	.35	1.00	2.00
3-Miller-a	.35	1.00	2.00

NOTE: *Buscema* a-4p, 5p. *Chaykin* c-5, 6. *Colan* a(p)-1, 3-6. *Miller* a-3.

TOMB OF LIGEIA (See Movie Classics)

TOMB OF TERROR (Thrills of Tomorrow #17 on)
June, 1952 - No. 16, July, 1954
Harvey Publications

	Good	Fine	N-Mint
1	6.50	19.50	45.00
2	4.35	13.00	30.00
3-Bondage-c; atomic disaster story	5.00	15.00	35.00
4-7: 4-Heart ripped out	4.35	13.00	30.00
8-12-Nostrand-a	4.35	13.00	30.00
13-Special S/F ish	6.50	19.50	45.00
14-Check-a; special S/F ish	6.50	19.50	45.00
15-S/F ish.; c-shows head exploding; Nostrand-a(r)			
	8.50	25.50	60.00
16-Special S/F ish; Nostrand-a	6.00	18.00	42.00

NOTE: *Kremer* a-1, 7; c-1. *Palais* a-2, 3, 5-7. *Powell* a-1, 3, 5, 9-16. *Sparling* a-12, 13, 15.

TOMBSTONE TERRITORY (See 4-Color #1123)

TOM CAT (Formerly Bo, Atom The Cat #9 on)
No. 4, Apr, 1956 - No. 8, July, 1957
Charlton Comics

	Good	Fine	N-Mint
4-Al Fago c/a	1.50	4.50	10.00
5-8	.85	2.50	6.00

TOM CORBETT, SPACE CADET (TV)
No. 378, 1-2/52 - No. 11, 9-11/54 (All painted covers)
Dell Publishing Co.

	Good	Fine	N-Mint
4-Color 378-McWilliams-a	6.00	18.00	42.00
4-Color 400,421-McWilliams-a	5.00	15.00	35.00
4(11-1/53) - 11	3.00	9.00	21.00

TOM CORBETT SPACE CADET (See March of Comics #102)

TOM CORBETT SPACE CADET (TV)
May-June, 1955 - V2No.3, Sept-Oct, 1955
Prize Publications

	Good	Fine	N-Mint
V2#1	8.50	25.50	60.00
2,3: 3-Meskin-c	7.00	21.00	50.00

TOM, DICK & HARRIET (See Gold Key Spotlight)

TOM LANDRY AND THE DALLAS COWBOYS
1973 (35-49 cents)
Spire Christian Comics/Fleming H. Revell Co.

	Good	Fine	N-Mint
nn	.25	.75	1.50

TOM MIX (. . .Commandos Comics #10-12)
Sept, 1940 - No. 12, Nov, 1942 (36 pages); 1983 (One-shot)
Given away for two Ralston box-tops; in cereal box, 1983
Ralston-Purina Co.

	Good	Fine	N-Mint
1-Origin (life) Tom Mix; Fred Meagher-a	65.00	195.00	455.00

Tomahawk #1, © DC　　*Tom And Jerry #88, © M.G.M.*　　*Tomb Of Terror #16, © HARV*

Tom Mix #1 (Ralston), © FAW

Tom-Tom, The Jungle Boy #1 (1947), © ME

Top Cat #5 (Gold Key), © Hanna-Barbera

TOM MIX (continued)	Good	Fine	N-Mint
2	37.00	110.00	260.00
3-9	32.00	95.00	225.00
10-12: 10-Origin Tom Mix Commando Unit; Speed O'Dare begins.			
12-Sci/fi-c	24.00	72.00	170.00
1983-'Taking of Grizzly Grebb,' Toth-a; 16 pg. miniature			
	1.00	3.00	6.00

TOM MIX WESTERN (Movie, radio star) (Also see The Comics, Crackajack Funnies, Master Comics, 100 Pages Of Comics, Popular Comics, Real Western Hero, Six Gun Heroes, Western Hero & X-Mas Comics)
Jan, 1948 - No. 61, May, 1953 (52pgs., 1-17)
Fawcett Publications

	Good	Fine	N-Mint
1 (Photo-c, 52 pgs.)-Tom Mix & his horse Tony begin; Tumbleweed Jr begins, ends #52,54,55	38.00	115.00	265.00
2 (Photo-c)	22.00	65.00	154.00
3-5 (Painted/photo-c): 5-Billy the Kid & Oscar app.			
	18.00	54.00	125.00
6,7 (Painted/photo-c)	14.00	42.00	100.00
8-Kinstler tempera-c	14.00	42.00	100.00
9,10 (Painted/photo-c)-Used in SOTI, pgs. 323-325			
	14.00	42.00	100.00
11-Kinstler oil-c	12.00	36.00	84.00
12 (Painted/photo-c)	11.00	32.00	75.00
13-17 (Painted-c, 52 pgs.)	11.00	32.00	75.00
18,22 (Painted-c, 36 pgs.)	9.00	27.00	62.00
19 (Photo-c, 52 pgs.)	11.00	32.00	75.00
20,21,23 (Painted-c, 52 pgs.)	9.00	27.00	62.00
24,25,27-29 (52 pgs.): 24-Photo-c begin, end #61. 29-Slim Pickens app.	9.00	27.00	62.00
26,30 (36 pgs.)	8.00	24.00	56.00
31-33,35-37,39,40,42 (52 pgs.): 39-Red Eagle app.			
	6.85	21.00	48.00
34,38 (36 pgs. begin)	5.70	17.00	40.00
41,43-60	4.00	12.00	28.00
61-Last issue	5.00	15.00	35.00

NOTE: *Photo-c from 1930s Tom Mix movies (he died in 1940). Many issues contain ads for John Wayne, Rocky Lane, Space Patrol and other premiums. Captain Tootsie by C.C. Beck in No. 6-11, 20.*

TOMMY OF THE BIG TOP
No. 10, Sept, 1948 - No. 12, Mar, 1949
King Features Syndicate/Standard Comics

	Good	Fine	N-Mint
10-By John Lehti	3.00	9.00	21.00
11,12	1.70	5.00	12.00

TOM SAWYER (See Famous Stories & Advs. of . . .)

TOM SAWYER & HUCK FINN
1925 (52 pgs.) (10¾x10'') (stiff covers)
Stoll & Edwards Co.
By Dwiggins; reprints 1923, 1924 Sunday strips in color

	9.00	27.00	62.00

TOM SAWYER COMICS
1951? (paper cover)
Giveaway
Contains a coverless Hopalong Cassidy from 1951; other combinations possible. 1.00 3.00 6.00

TOM SKINNER-UP FROM HARLEM (See Up From Harlem)

TOM TERRIFIC! (TV)(See Mighty Mouse Fun Club Mag. #1)
Summer, 1957 - No. 6, Fall, 1958
Pines Comics (Paul Terry)

	Good	Fine	N-Mint
1	8.00	24.00	56.00
2-6	5.70	17.00	40.00

TOM THUMB (See 4-Color #972)

TOM-TOM, THE JUNGLE BOY (See Tick Tock Tales)
1947; Nov, 1957 - No. 3, Mar, 1958
Magazine Enterprises

	Good	Fine	N-Mint
1-Funny animal	3.50	10.50	24.00
2,3(1947)	2.00	6.00	14.00
1(1957)(& Itchi the Monk), 2,3('58)	1.00	3.00	7.00
I.W. Reprint No. 1,2,8,10		.40	.80

TONKA (See 4-Color #966)

TONTO (See The Lone Ranger's Companion . . .)

TONY TRENT (The Face #1,2)
1948 - 1949
Big Shot/Columbia Comics Group

	Good	Fine	N-Mint
3,4: 3-The Face app. by Mart Bailey	5.00	15.00	35.00

TOODLE TWINS, THE
1-2/51 - No. 10, 7-8/51; 1956 (Newspaper reprints)
Ziff-Davis (Approved Comics)/Argo

1	3.50	10.50	24.00
2	2.30	7.00	16.00
3-9	2.00	6.00	14.00
10-Painted-c, some newspaper-r	2.00	6.00	14.00
1(Argo, 3/56)	1.70	5.00	12.00

TOONERVILLE TROLLEY
1921 (Daily strip reprints) (B&W) (52 pgs.)
Cuppples & Leon Co.

1-By Fontaine Fox	13.00	40.00	90.00

TOOTS & CASPER (See Large Feature Comic #5)

TOP ADVENTURE COMICS
1964 (Reprints)
I. W. Enterprises

1-Reprints/Explorer Joe #2; Krigstein-a	.70	2.00	4.00
2-Black Dwarf	.80	2.40	4.80

TOP CAT (TV) (Hanna-Barbera)
12-2/61-62 - No. 3, 6-8/62; No. 4, 10/62 - No. 31, 9/70
Dell Publishing Co./Gold Key No. 4 on

1	2.65	8.00	18.00
2-5	1.70	5.00	12.00
6-10	1.30	4.00	9.00
11-20	.85	2.50	6.00
21-31: 21,24,25,29-Reprints	.60	1.80	4.00
Kite Fun Book (1963, 16pgs., 5x7¼'', soft-c)	1.15	3.50	8.00

TOP CAT (TV) (Hanna-Barbera)(See TV Stars #4)
Nov, 1970 - No. 20, Nov, 1973
Charlton Comics

1	1.00	3.00	6.00
2-10	.50	1.50	3.00
11-20	.25	.75	1.50

NOTE: *#8 (1/72) went on sale late in 1972 between #14 and #15 with the January 1973 issues.*

TOP COMICS
July, 1967 (All rebound issues)
K. K. Publications/Gold Key

nn-The Gnome-Mobile (Disney-movie)	.50	1.50	3.00

1-Beagle Boys (#7), Bugs Bunny, Chip 'n' Dale, Daffy Duck (#50), Flintstones, Flipper, Huckleberry Hound, Huey, Dewey & Louie, Junior Woodchucks, Lassie, The Little Monsters (#71), Moby Duck, Porky Pig (has Gold Key label - says Top Comics on inside), Scamp, Super Goof, Tarzan of the Apes (#169), Three Stooges (#35), Tom & Jerry, Top Cat (#21), Tweety & Sylvester (#7), Walt Disney C&S (#322), Woody Woodpecker, Yogi Bear, Zorro known; each character given own book
.30 .90 1.80

TOP COMICS (continued)	Good	Fine	N-Mint
1-Uncle Scrooge (#70)	1.00	3.00	6.00
1-Donald Duck (not Barks), Mickey Mouse	.70	2.00	4.00
1-The Jetsons	.85	2.50	6.00

2-Bugs Bunny, Daffy Duck, Donald Duck (not Barks), Mickey Mouse (#114), Porky Pig, Super Goof, Three Stooges, Tom & Jerry, Tweety & Sylvester, Uncle Scrooge (#71)-Barks-c, Walt Disney's C&S (r-/#325), Woody Woodpecker, Yogi Bear (#30), Zorro (r-#8; Toth-a)

	.30	.90	1.80
2-Snow White & 7 Dwarfs(6/67)(1944-r)	.80	2.40	4.80
3-Donald Duck	.50	1.50	3.00
3-Uncle Scrooge (#72)	1.00	3.00	6.00

3-The Flintstones, Mickey Mouse (r-/#115), Tom & Jerry, Woody Woodpecker, Yogi Bear

	.35	1.00	2.00

4-The Flintstones, Mickey Mouse, Woody Woodpecker

	.35	1.00	2.00

NOTE: Each book in this series is identical to its counterpart except for cover, and came out at same time. The number in parentheses is the original issue it contains.

TOP DETECTIVE COMICS
1964 (Reprints)
I. W. Enterprises

9-Young King Cole & Dr. Drew (not Grandenetti)			
	.40	1.20	2.40

TOP DOG (See Star Comics Mag.)
Apr, 1985 - No. 14, June, 1987 (Children's book)
Star Comics (Marvel)

1-13		.35	.70
14		.50	1.00

TOP ELIMINATOR (Formerly Teenage Hotrodders; Drag 'n' Wheels #30 on)
No. 25, Sept, 1967 - No. 29, July, 1968
Charlton Comics

25-29		.50	1.00

TOP FLIGHT COMICS
1947; July, 1949
Four Star Publications/St. John Publishing Co.

1	3.50	10.50	24.00
1(7/49)-Hector the Inspector	2.30	7.00	16.00

TOP GUN (See 4-Color #927)

TOP GUNS (See Super DC Giant & Showcase #72)

TOPIX (. . . Comics) (Timeless Topix-early issues) (Also see Men of Courage & Treasure Chest)(V1-V5#1,V7#1-20-paper-c)
11/42 - V10No.15, 1/28/52 (Weekly - later issues)
Catechetical Guild Educational Society

V1#1(8pgs.,8x11'')	6.00	18.00	36.00
2,3(8pgs.,8x11'')	3.35	10.00	20.00
4-8(16pgs.,8x11'')	2.50	7.50	15.00
V2#1-10(16pgs.,8x11''): V2#8-Pope Pius XII	2.50	7.50	15.00
V3#1-10(16pgs.,8x11'')	2.00	6.00	12.00
V4#1-10	2.00	6.00	12.00
V5#1(10/46,52pgs.)-9,12-15(12/47)-#13 shows V5#4			
	1.00	3.00	6.00
10,11-Life of Christ eds.	2.35	7.00	14.00
V6#1-14	.70	2.00	4.00
V7#1(9/1/48)-20(6/15/49), 32pgs.	.70	2.00	4.00
V8#1(9/19/49)-3,5-11,13-30(5/15/50)	.70	2.00	4.00
4-Dagwood Splits the Atom(10/10/49)-Magazine format			
	1.35	4.00	8.00
12-Ingels-a	2.75	8.00	16.00
V9#1(9/25/50)-11,13-30(5/14/51)	.50	1.50	3.00
12-Special 36pg. Xmas ish., text illos format			
	.85	2.50	5.00
V10#1(10/1/51)-15	.50	1.50	3.00

NOTE: Hollingsworth a-V10#14.

TOP JUNGLE COMICS
1964 (Reprint)
I. W. Enterprises

	Good	Fine	N-Mint
1(nd)-Reprints White Princess of the Jungle #3, minus cover			
	.80	2.40	4.80

TOP LOVE STORIES
No. 8, 11-12/49 - No. 3, 5/51 - No. 19, 3/54
Star Publications

8	3.85	11.50	27.00
9, 3-5,7-9	3.00	9.00	21.00
6-Wood-a	6.35	19.00	44.00
10-16,18,19-Disbrow-a	3.35	10.00	23.00
17-Wood art (Fox-r)	5.00	15.00	35.00

NOTE: All have L. B. Cole covers.

TOP-NOTCH COMICS (. . . Laugh #28-45; Laugh #46 on)
Dec, 1939 - No. 45, June, 1944
MLJ Magazines

1-Origin The Wizard; Kardak the Mystic Magician, Swift of the Secret Service (ends No. 3), Air Patrol, The Westpointer, Manhunters (by J. Cole), Mystic (ends #2) & Scott Rand (ends #3) begin

	90.00	270.00	630.00

2-Dick Storm (ends #8), Stacy Knight M.D. (ends #4) begin; Jack Cole-a

	45.00	135.00	315.00

3-Bob Phantom, Scott Rand on Mars begin; J. Cole-a

	35.00	105.00	245.00

4-Origin/1st app. Streak Chandler on Mars; Moore of the Mounted only app.; J. Cole-a

	30.00	90.00	210.00

5-Flag-c; origin/1st app. Galahad; Shanghai Sheridan begins (ends #8); Shield cameo

	25.00	75.00	175.00

6-The Shield app.	22.00	65.00	154.00

7-The Shield x-over in Wizard; The Wizard dons new costume

	32.00	95.00	225.00

8-Origin The Firefly & Roy, the Super Boy	37.00	110.00	260.00

9-Origin & 1st app. The Black Hood; Fran Frazier begins

	90.00	270.00	630.00
10	38.00	115.00	265.00
11-20	24.00	72.00	170.00

21-30: 23,24-No Wizard, Roy app. in each. 25-Last Bob Phantom, Roy app. 26-Roy app. 27-Last Firefly. 28-Suzie begins. 29-Last Kardak

	21.00	62.00	146.00

31-44: 33-Dotty & Ditto by Woggon begins. 44-Black Hood series ends

	11.00	32.00	75.00
45-Last issue	6.50	19.50	45.00

NOTE: J. Binder a-1-3. Meskin a-2,3, 15. Woggon a-33-40, 42. Bondage c-17, 19. Black Hood also appeared on radio in 1944.

TOPPER & NEIL (See 4-Color #859)

TOPPS COMICS
1947
Four Star Publications

1-L. B. Cole-c	4.30	13.00	30.00

TOPS
July, 1949 - No. 2, Sept, 1949 (68 pgs, 25 cents) (10¼x13¼'')
(Large size-magazine format; for the adult reader)
Tops Magazine, Inc. (Lev Gleason)

1 (Rare)-Story by Dashiell Hammett; Crandall/Lubbers, Tuska, Dan Barry, Fuje-a; Biro painted-c

	57.00	170.00	400.00

2 (Rare)-Crandall/Lubbers, Biro, Kida, Fuje, Guardineer-a

	50.00	150.00	350.00

TOPS COMICS (See Tops in Humor)
1944 (Small size, 32 pgs.) (7¼x5'')
Consolidated Book (Lev Gleason)

Top Jungle Comics #1, © AVON

Top Love Stories #6, © STAR

Top-Notch Comics #9, © AP

396

Tor #3 (5/54), © STJ   Torchy #4, © QUA   Tough Kid Squad Comics #1, © MEG

	Good	Fine	N-Mint		Good	Fine	N-Mint
TOPS COMICS (continued)				2-6: 2-Origin-r/St. John #1		.25	.50
2001-The Jack of Spades	9.50	28.50	65.00	NOTE: *Kubert a-1; 2-6r; c-1-6. Toth a(p)-3r.*			
2002-Rip Raider	4.65	14.00	32.00	**TOR (3-D)**			
2003-Red Birch (gag cartoons)	1.00	3.00	7.00	July, 1986 - No. 2, Aug, 1987			
TOPS COMICS				Eclipse Comics			
1944 (132 pages) (10 cents)				1-r-/One Million Years Ago	.40	1.25	2.50
Consolidated Book Publishers				2-D 1-Limited signed & numbered edition	.40	1.25	2.50
nn(Color-c, inside in red shade & some in full color)-Ace Kelly				2-r-/Tor 3-D #2	.40	1.25	2.50
by Rick Yager, Black Orchid, Don on the Farm, Dinky Dinkerton				2-D 2-Limited signed & numbered edition	.40	1.25	2.50
(Rare)	14.00	42.00	100.00	**TORCHY** (. . .Blonde Bombshell) (See Dollman, Military, & Modern)			
NOTE: *This book is printed in such a way that when the staple is removed, the strips on the left side of the book correspond with the same strips on the right side. Therefore, if strips are removed from the book, each strip can be folded into a complete comic section of its own.*				Nov, 1949 - No. 6, Sept, 1950			
				Quality Comics Group			
				1-Bill Ward-c, Gil Fox-a	75.00	225.00	525.00
TOP SECRET				2,3-Fox c/a	32.00	95.00	225.00
January, 1952				4-Fox c/a(3), Ward-a, 9pgs.	42.00	125.00	295.00
Hillman Publ.				5,6-Ward c/a, 9 pgs; Fox-a(3) each	52.00	155.00	365.00
1	7.00	21.00	50.00	Super Reprint #16('64)-R-/#4 with new-c	6.00	18.00	36.00
TOP SECRET ADVENTURES (See Spyman)				**TORMENTED, THE** (Surprise Adventure #3)			
TOP SECRETS (. . .of the F.B.I.)				July, 1954 - No. 2, Sept, 1954			
Nov, 1947 - No. 10, July-Aug, 1949				Sterling Comics			
Street & Smith Publications				1,2	5.00	15.00	35.00
1-Powell c/a	11.00	32.00	75.00	**TORNADO TOM** (See Mighty Midget Comics)			
2-Powell c/a	7.00	21.00	50.00	**TOTAL ECLIPSE**			
3-6,8-10-Powell-a	6.50	19.50	45.00	May, 1988 - No. 5, 1988 ($3.95, color, deluxe size, 52pgs)			
7-Used in SOTI, pg. 90 & illo.-"How to hurt people;" used by N.Y.				Eclipse Comics			
Legis. Comm.; Powell c/a	12.00	36.00	84.00	Book 1-5: 3-Intro/1st app. new Black Terror	.70	2.00	3.95
NOTE: *Powell c-1-3,5-10.*				**TOTAL ECLIPSE: THE SERAPHIM OBJECTIVE**			
TOPS IN ADVENTURE				Nov, 1988 ($1.95, color, one-shot, Baxter paper)			
Fall, 1952 (132 pages)				Eclipse Comics			
Ziff-Davis Publishing Co.				1-Airboy, Valkyrie, The Heap app.	.35	1.00	2.00
1-Crusader from Mars, The Hawk, Football Thrills, He-Man;				**TOTAL WAR** (M.A.R.S. Patrol #3 on)			
Powell-a; painted-c	20.00	60.00	140.00	July, 1965 - No. 2, Oct, 1965 (Painted covers)			
TOPS IN HUMOR (See Tops Comics?)				Gold Key			
1944 (Small size) (7¼x5")				1,2-Wood-a	1.70	5.00	12.00
Consolidated Book Publ. (Lev Gleason)				**TOUGH KID SQUAD COMICS**			
2001(#1)-Origin The Jack of Spades, Ace Kelly by Rick Yager,				March, 1942			
Black Orchid (female crime fighter) app.	10.00	30.00	70.00	Timely Comics (TCI)			
2	5.00	15.00	35.00	1-(Scarce)-Origin The Human Top & The Tough Kid Squad; The			
TOP SPOT COMICS				Flying Flame app.	250.00	750.00	1750.00
1945				**TOWER OF SHADOWS** (Creatures on the Loose #10 on)			
Top Spot Publ. Co.				Sept, 1969 - No. 9, Jan, 1971			
1-The Menace, Duke of Darkness app.	8.00	24.00	56.00	Marvel Comics Group			
TOPSY-TURVY				1-Steranko, Craig-a		.60	1.20
April, 1945				2-Neal Adams-a		.50	1.00
R. B. Leffingwell Publ.				3-Smith, Tuska-a		.50	1.00
1-1st app. Cookie	2.65	8.00	18.00	4-Kirby/Everett-c		.50	1.00
TOR (Formerly One Million Years Ago)				5,7-Smith(p), Wood-a (Wood draws himself-1st pg., 1st panel-#5)			
No. 2, Oct, 1953; No. 3, May, 1954 - No. 5, Oct, 1954					.25	.75	1.50
St. John Publishing Co.				6,8: Wood-a; 8-Wrightson-c		.50	1.00
3-D 2(10/53)-Kubert-a	10.00	30.00	70.00	9-Wrightson-c; Roy Thomas app.		.50	1.00
3-D 2(10/53)-Oversized, otherwise same contents				Special 1(12/71)-Adams-a		.50	1.00
	9.00	27.00	62.00	NOTE: *J. Buscema a-1p, 2p. Colan a-3p, 6p. J. Craig a-1. Ditko a-6, 9r, Special 1. Everett a-9(i)r; c-5i. Kirby a-9(p)r. Severin c-5p, 6. Steranko a-1. Wood a-5-8. Issues 1-9 contain new stories with some pre-Marvel age reprints in 6-9. H. P. Lovecraft adaptation-9.*			
3-D 2(11/53)-Kubert-a	9.00	27.00	62.00				
3-5-Kubert-a; 3-Danny Dreams by Toth	10.00	30.00	70.00				
NOTE: *The two October 3-D's have same contents and Powell art; the Nov. issue is titled 3-D Comics.*				**TOWN & COUNTRY**			
TOR (See Sojourn)				May, 1940			
May-June, 1975 - No. 6, Mar-Apr, 1976				Publisher?			
National Periodical Publications				Origin The Falcon	22.00	65.00	154.00
1-New origin by Kubert		.30	.60				

TOWN THAT FORGOT SANTA, THE			
1961 (24 pages) (Giveaway)			
W. T. Grant Co.	Good	Fine	N-Mint
nn	1.35	4.00	9.00

TOYBOY
Oct, 1986 - Present ($2.00, color, Baxter paper)
Continuity Comics

1-6: 1,2-Adams-c. 1-Adams-a	.30	.85	1.70

TOYLAND COMICS
Jan, 1947 - No. 4, July?, 1947
Fiction House Magazines

1	8.00	24.00	56.00
2-4: 3-Tuska-a	5.00	15.00	35.00
148 pg. issue	11.00	32.00	75.00
NOTE: All above contain strips by Al Walker.

TOY TOWN COMICS
1945 - No. 7, May, 1947
Toytown/Orbit Publ./B. Antin/Swapper Quarterly

1-Mertie Mouse; L. B. Cole-c/a	8.00	24.00	56.00
2-L. B. Cole-a	4.30	13.00	30.00
3-7-L. B. Cole-a	3.50	10.50	24.00

TRAGG AND THE SKY GODS (See Gold Key Spotlight, Mystery
Comics Digest #3,9 & Spine Tingling Tales) (Painted-c #3-8)
June, 1975 - No. 8, Feb, 1977; No. 9, May, 1982
Gold Key/Whitman No. 9

1-Origin		.60	1.20
2-9: 4-Sabre-Fang app. 8-Ostellon app.; 9-r #1		.40	.80
NOTE: Santos a-1,2,9r; c-3-7. Spiegel a-3-8.

TRAIL BLAZERS (Red Dragon #5 on)
1941 - 1942
Street & Smith Publications

1-True stories of American heroes	12.00	36.00	84.00
2	8.50	25.50	60.00
3,4	7.00	21.00	50.00

TRAIL COLT
1949
Magazine Enterprises

nn(A-1 24)-7 pg. Frazetta r-in Manhunt #13; Undercover Girl app.; The Red Fox by L. B. Cole; Ingels-c; (Scarce)	26.00	78.00	180.00
2(A-1 26)-Undercover Girl; Ingels-c; L. B. Cole-a, 6pgs.	20.00	60.00	140.00

TRANSFORMERS, THE (TV)
Sept, 1984 - Present (75 cents, $1.00)
Marvel Comics Group

1-Based on Hasbro toy	.60	1.75	3.50
2,3	.35	1.00	2.00
4-10	.25	.75	1.50
11-49: 21-Intro The Aerialbots		.50	1.00
NOTE: Second and third printings of all issues exist.

TRANSFORMERS COMICS MAGAZINE, THE
Oct, 1986 - No. 11, 1988 ($1.50, Digest-size)
Marvel Comics Group

1-11	.25	.75	1.50

TRANSFORMERS: HEADMASTERS
July, 1987 - No. 4, Jan, 1988 (mini-series)
Marvel Comics Group

1	.35	1.00	2.00
2-4	.25	.75	1.50

TRANSFORMERS IN 3-D
1987 - Present ($2.50)
Blackthorne Publishing

	Good	Fine	N-Mint
1-4	.40	1.25	2.50

TRANSFORMERS, THE MOVIE
Dec, 1986 - No. 3, Feb, 1987 (mini-series)
Marvel Comics Group

1-Adapts animated movie	.25	.75	1.50
2,3		.50	1.00

TRANSFORMERS UNIVERSE, THE
Dec, 1986 - No. 4, March, 1987 ($1.25, mini-series)
Marvel Comics Group

1-A guide to all characters	.35	1.00	2.00
2-4		.65	1.30

TRAPPED
1951 (Giveaway) (16 pages) (soft cover)
Harvey Publications (Columbia University Press)

Drug education comic (30,000 printed?) distributed to schools. Mentioned in SOTI, pgs. 256,350	2.00	6.00	12.00
NOTE: Many copies surfaced in 1979 causing a setback in price; beware of trimmed edges, because many copies have a brittle edge.

TRAPPED!
Oct, 1954 - No. 5, June?, 1955
Periodical House Magazines (Ace)

1 (All-r)	3.70	11.00	26.00
2-5: 4-r-entire Men Against Crime 4	2.00	6.00	14.00
NOTE: Colan a-1, 4. Sekowsky a-1.

TRAVELS OF HAPPY HOOLIGAN, THE
1906 (10¼"x15¾", 32 pgs., cardboard covers)
Frederick A. Stokes Co.

1905-r	20.00	60.00	140.00

TRAVELS OF JAIMIE McPHEETERS, THE (TV)
December, 1963
Gold Key

1-Kurt Russell	1.70	5.00	12.00

TREASURE BOX OF FAMOUS COMICS
Mid 1930's (36 pgs.) (6-7/8"x8½") (paper covers)
Cupples & Leon Co.

Box plus 5 titles: Reg'lar Fellers(1928), Little Orphan Annie(1926), Smitty(1928), Harold Teen(1931), How D. Tracy & D. Tracy Jr. Caught The Racketeers (1933) (These are abbreviated versions of hardcover editions) (Set)	70.00	200.00	450.00
NOTE: Dates shown are copyright dates; all books actually came out in 1934 or later.

TREASURE CHEST (Catholic Guild; also see Topix)
3/12/46 - V27#8, July, 1972 (Educational comics)
George A. Pflaum (not publ. during Summer)

V1#1	7.00	21.00	50.00
2-6 (5/21/46): 5-Dr. Styx app. by Baily	3.00	9.00	21.00
V2#1 (9/3/46) - 6	1.50	4.50	10.00
V3#1-5,7-20 (1st slick cover)	1.50	4.50	10.00
V3#6-Jules Verne's ''Voyage to the Moon''	3.35	10.00	22.00
V4#1-20 (9/9/48-5/31/49)	1.35	4.00	8.00
V5#1-20 (9/6/49-5/31/50)	1.00	3.00	6.00
V6#1-20 (9/14/50-5/31/51)	1.00	3.00	6.00
V7#1-20 (9/13/51-6/5/52)	.70	2.00	4.00
V8#1-20 (9/11/52-6/4/53)	.70	2.00	4.00
V9#1-20 ('53-'54)	.50	1.50	3.00
V10#1-20 ('54-'55)	.50	1.50	3.00
V11('55-'56), V12('56-'57)	.50	1.50	3.00
V13#1,3-5,7,9,10,12-V17#1 ('57-'63)	.35	1.00	2.00

Toyboy #1, © Continuity Comics

Toy Town Comics #2, © Toytown

Trapped (giveaway), © HARV

Treasury Of Comics #4 (9/47), © UFS

Triple Threat #1, © HOKE

Trollords #2, © Tru Studios

	Good	Fine	N-Mint
TREASURE CHEST (continued)			
V13#2,6,8,11-Ingels-a	2.00	6.00	14.00
V17#2-'This Godless Communism' series begins (Not in V17#3,7,11) Cover shows hammer & sickle over Statue of Liberty; 8pg. Crandall-a of family life under communism			
	9.00	27.00	62.00
V17#3-7,9,11,13-15,17,19	.30	.80	1.60
V17#8-Shows red octopus encompassing Earth, firing squad; 8pg. Crandall-a	6.50	19.50	45.00
V17#10-'This Godless Communism'-how Stalin came to power, part I; Crandall-a	6.00	18.00	42.00
V17#12-Stalin in WWII, forced labor, death by exhaustion; Crandall-a	6.00	18.00	42.00
V17#16-Kruschev takes over; de-Stalinization	6.00	18.00	42.00
V17#18-Kruschev's control; murder of revolters, brainwash, space race by Crandall	6.00	18.00	42.00
V17#20-End of series; Kruschev-people are puppets, firing squads hammer & sickle over Statue of Liberty, snake around communist manifesto by Crandall	6.00	18.00	42.00
V18,V19#5,11-20,V20('64-'65)	.40	.80	
V18#5-'What About Red China?'-describes how communists took over China	2.75	8.00	16.00
V19#1-4,6-10-'Red Victim' anti-communist series in all	2.75	8.00	16.00
V21-V25('65-'70)-(two V24#5's 11/7/68 & 11/21/68) (no V24#6)	.30	.60	
V26, V27#1-8 (V26,27-68 pgs.)	.30	.60	
Summer Edition V1#1-6('66), V2#1-6('67)	.20	.40	

NOTE: *Anderson* a-V18#13. *Borth* a-V7/10-19 (serial), V8/8-17 (serial), V9/1-10 (serial) V13/2, 6, 11, V15/2, V18/1, V19/4, 11, 19, V20/10, 15, 16, 18, V21/5, V22/7, 9, 14, V24/7, Summer Ed. V1/3, 5. *Crandall* a-V7/20, V16/7, 9, 12, 14, 17, 20; V17/1, 2, 4, 5, 14, 16-18, 20; V18/1, 7, 9, 10, 15, 17, 19; V19/4, 11, 13, 16, 19; V20/1, 2, 6, 9, 10, 12, 14-16, 18, 20; V21/1-3, 5, 8, 9, 11, 13, 16, 17; V22/2/3, 7, 9-11, 14, 16, 20; V23/3, 6, 9, 13, 16; V24/7, 8, 10; V25/16; V27/1, 3-5r, 6r, 8(2 pg.), Summer Ed. V1/3, 5; c-V16/7, V18/10, V19/4, V21/5, 9, V22/7, 11, V23/9, 16 at least. *Powell* a-V10/11. V19/11, 15, V10/13, V13/6, 8 all have wraparound covers. All the above Crandall issues should be priced by condition from $4-8.00 unless already priced.

	Good	Fine	N-Mint
TREASURE CHEST OF THE WORLD'S BEST COMICS			
1945 (500 pgs.) (hardcover)			
Superior, Toronto, Canada			
Contains Blue Beetle, Captain Combat, John Wayne, Dynamic Man, Nemo, Li'l Abner; contents can vary - represents random binding of extra books; Capt. America on-c	35.00	105.00	245.00
TREASURE COMICS			
No date (1943) (324 pgs.; cardboard covers) (50 cents)			
Prize Publications? (no publisher listed)			
1-(Rare)-Contains Prize Comics #7-11 from 1942 (blank inside-c)	130.00	390.00	910.00
TREASURE COMICS			
June-July, 1945 - No. 12, Fall, 1947			
Prize Publications (American Boys' Comics)			
1-Paul Bunyan & Marco Polo begin; Highwayman & Carrot Topp only app.; Kiefer-a	10.00	30.00	70.00
2-Arabian Knight, Gorilla King, Dr. Styx begin	5.00	15.00	35.00
3,4,9,12: 9-Kiefer-a	3.50	10.50	24.00
5-Marco Polo-c; Kirby a(p); Krigstein-a	6.85	21.00	48.00
6,11-Krigstein-a; c-#11	6.00	18.00	42.00
7,8-Frazetta, 5 pgs. each	22.00	65.00	154.00
10-Kirby c/a	8.50	25.50	60.00

TREASURE ISLAND (See 4-Color #624, King Classics & Movie Classics & Comics)

TREASURY OF COMICS
1947; No. 2, July, 1947 - No. 4, Sept, 1947; No. 5, Jan, 1948
St. John Publishing Co.

	Good	Fine	N-Mint
nn(#1)-Abbie 'n' Slats (nn on-c, #1 on inside)	8.00	24.00	56.00
2-Jim Hardy	6.00	18.00	42.00
3-Bill Bumlin	4.30	13.00	30.00
4-Abbie 'n' Slats	5.50	16.50	38.00
5-Jim Hardy Comics #1	5.50	16.50	38.00

TREASURY OF COMICS
Mar, 1948 - No. 5, 1948; 1948-1950-(Over 500 pgs., $1.00)
St. John Publishing Co.

	Good	Fine	N-Mint
1	11.00	32.00	75.00
2(#2 on-c, #1 on inside)	6.50	19.50	45.00
3-5	5.50	16.50	38.00
1-(1948, 500 pgs., hard-c)-Abbie & Slats, Abbott & Costello, Casper, Little Annie Rooney, Little Audrey, Jim Hardy, Ella Cinders (16 books bound together) (Rare)	90.00	270.00	630.00
1(1949, 500pgs.)-Same format as above	90.00	270.00	630.00
1(1950, 500pgs.)-Same format as above; different-c; (Also see Little Audrey Yearbook) (Rare)	90.00	270.00	630.00

TREASURY OF DOGS, A (See Dell Giants)

TREASURY OF HORSES, A (See Dell Giants)

TREKKER (See Dark Horse Presents)
May, 1987 - Present (B&W)
Dark Horse Comics

	Good	Fine	N-Mint
1-9	.25	.75	1.50
... Collection ($5.95, B&W)	1.00	3.00	5.95

TRIALS OF LULU AND LEANDER, THE
1906 (32 pgs. in color) (10x16'')
William A. Stokes Co.

	Good	Fine	N-Mint
By F. M. Howarth	14.00	42.00	100.00

TRIGGER (See Roy Rogers...)

TRIGGER TWINS
Mar-Apr, 1973 (One Shot)
National Periodical Publications

	Good	Fine	N-Mint
1-Trigger Twins & Pow Wow Smith-r; Infantino-a(p)		.40	.80

TRIPLE GIANT COMICS (See Archie All-Star Spec. under Archie Comics)

TRIPLE THREAT
Winter, 1945
Special Action/Holyoke/Gerona Publ.

	Good	Fine	N-Mint
1-Duke of Darkness, King O'Leary	6.00	18.00	42.00

TRIP WITH SANTA ON CHRISTMAS EVE, A
No date (early 50's) (16 pgs.; full color; paper cover)
Rockford Dry Goods Co. (Giveaway)

	Good	Fine	N-Mint
	2.00	6.00	12.00

TROLLORDS
2/86 - No. 15, 1988; V2#1, 11/88 - Present (1-15: $1.50, B&W)
Tru Studios/Comico

	Good	Fine	N-Mint
1	1.70	5.00	10.00
1-2nd print	.40	1.25	2.50
2	.60	1.75	3.50
3-15	.35	1.00	2.00
V2#1,2 ($1.75, color, Comico)	.30	.90	1.75
Special 1 ($1.75)	.35	1.00	2.00

TROUBLE SHOOTERS, THE (See 4-Color #1108)

TROUBLE WITH GIRLS, THE
Aug., 1987 - Present ($1.95. B&W)
Malibu Comics/Eternity Comics #7-14/Comico #15 on

	Good	Fine	N-Mint
1	.50	1.50	3.00
2-14	.35	1.00	1.95

THE TROUBLE WITH GIRLS (continued)	Good	Fine	N-Mint
Annual 1 ($2.95, '88)	.50	1.50	2.95
Graphic Novel 1 (7/88-r)	1.15	3.50	6.95

TRUE ADVENTURES (Formerly True Western)(Men's Advs. #4 on)
No. 3, May, 1950 (52 pgs.)
Marvel Comics (CCC)

3-Powell, Sekowsky-a	5.00	15.00	35.00

TRUE ANIMAL PICTURE STORIES
Winter, 1947 - No. 2, Spr-Summer, 1947
True Comics Press

1,2	3.00	9.00	21.00

TRUE AVIATION PICTURE STORIES (Aviation Adventures & Model Building #16)
1942 - No. 15, Sept-Oct, 1946
Parents' Magazine Institute

1-(#1 & 2 titled . . .Aviation Comics Digest)(not digest size)			
	7.00	21.00	50.00
2	3.70	11.00	26.00
3-14	3.00	9.00	21.00
15-(titled "True Aviation Advs. & Model Building")			
	2.65	8.00	18.00

TRUE BRIDE'S EXPERIENCES (Formerly Teen-Age Brides)
(True Bride-To-Be Romances No. 17 on)
No. 8, Oct, 1954 - No. 16, Feb, 1956
True Love (Harvey Publications)

8	1.70	5.00	12.00
9,10: 10-Last pre-code (2/55)	1.35	4.00	9.00
11-15	1.00	3.00	7.00
16-Spanking issue	5.00	15.00	35.00

NOTE: *Powell a-8-10, 12, 13.*

TRUE BRIDE-TO-BE ROMANCES (Formerly True Bride's Exp.)
No. 17, Apr, 1956 - No. 30, Nov, 1958
Home Comics/True Love (Harvey)

17-S&K-c, Powell-a	2.00	6.00	14.00
18-20,22,25-28,30	1.00	3.00	7.00
21,23,24-Powell-a	1.20	3.50	8.00
29-Powell, 1 pg. Baker-a	1.35	4.00	9.00

TRUE COMICS (Also see Outstanding American War Heroes)
April, 1941 - No. 84, Aug, 1950
True Comics/Parents' Magazine Press

1-Marathon run story	13.00	40.00	90.00
2-Everett-a	7.00	21.00	50.00
3-Baseball Hall of Fame story	6.50	19.50	45.00
4,5: 4-Sty. of American flag "Old Glory." 5-Life story of Joe Louis			
	5.70	17.00	40.00
6-Baseball World Series sty.	5.00	15.00	35.00
7-10	4.00	12.00	28.00
11-20: 13-Harry Houdini sty. 14-Charlie McCarthy sty. 15-Flag-c; Bob Feller sty. 17-Brooklyn Dodgers sty. 18-Story of America begins, ends #26	3.50	10.50	24.00
21-30	3.00	9.00	21.00
31-Red Grange story	2.65	8.00	18.00
32-45: 39-FDR story	2.00	6.00	14.00
46-George Gershwin sty.	2.00	6.00	14.00
47-Atomic bomb issue	4.00	12.00	28.00
48-67: 55(12/46)-1st app. Sad Sack by Baker, ½ pg. 58-Jim Jeffries (boxer) sty.; Harry Houdini sty. 59-Bob Hope sty. 66-Will Rogers story	1.50	4.50	10.00
68-1st oversized ish?; Steve Saunders, Special Agent begins			
	2.30	7.00	16.00
69-72,74-79: 69-Jack Benny sty. 71-Joe DiMaggio sty. 78-Stan Musial sty	1.30	4.00	9.00
73-Walt Disney's life story	2.35	7.00	16.00

	Good	Fine	N-Mint
80-84 (Scarce)-All distr. to subscribers through mail only; paper-c;			
81-Red Grange sty	18.00	54.00	125.00
(Prices vary widely on these books)			

NOTE: *Bob Kane a-7. Palais a-80. Powell c/a-80. #80-84 have soft covers and combined with Tex Granger, Jack Armstrong, and Calling All Kids. #68-78 featured true FBI adventures.*

TRUE COMICS AND ADVENTURE STORIES
1965 (Giant) (25 cents)
Parents' Magazine Institute

1,2-Fighting Hero of Viet Nam; LBJ on-c	.70	2.00	4.00

TRUE COMPLETE MYSTERY (Formerly Complete Mystery)
No. 5, April, 1949 - No. 8, Oct, 1949
Marvel Comics (PrPI)

5	7.00	21.00	50.00
6-8: 6,8-Photo-c	5.70	17.00	40.00

TRUE CONFESSIONS
1949
Fawcett Publications

1	5.00	15.00	35.00

TRUE CONFIDENCES
1949 (Fall) - No. 4, June, 1950 (All photo-c)
Fawcett Publications

1-Has ad for Fawcett Love Adventures #1 but publ. as Love Memoirs #1 as Marvel pub!. the title first	5.00	15.00	35.00
2-4: 4-Powell-a	2.30	7.00	16.00

TRUE CRIME CASES
1944; V1No.6, June-July 1949 - V2No.1, Aug-Oct, 1949
St. John Publishing Co.

1944-(100 pgs.)	19.00	57.00	132.00
V1#6, V2#1	4.30	13.00	30.00

TRUE CRIME COMICS (Also see Complete Book of. . .)
No. 2, May, 1947; No. 3, Jul-Aug, 1948 - No. 6, June-Jul, 1949; V2No.1, Aug-Sept, 1949 (52 pgs.)
Magazine Village

2-Jack Cole c/a; used in **SOTI**, pg. 81,82 plus illo.-"A sample of the injury-to-eye motif" & illo.-"Dragging living people to death;" used in **POP**, pg. 105; "Murder, Morphine and Me" classic drug propaganda story used by N.Y. Legis. Comm.			
	87.00	261.00	610.00
3-Classic Cole c/a; drug sty with hypo, opium den & withdrawing addict	56.00	168.00	390.00
4-Jack Cole-c/a; c-taken from a story panel in #3; r-(2) SOTI & POP stories/#2	50.00	150.00	350.00
5-Jack Cole-c; Marijuana racket story	25.00	75.00	175.00
6	10.00	30.00	70.00
V2#1-Used in **SOTI**, pgs. 81,82 & illo.-"Dragging living people to death;" Toth, Wood (3 pgs.), Roussos-a; Cole-r from #2			
	36.00	108.00	252.00

NOTE: *V2#1 was reprinted in Canada as V2#9 (12/49); same cover & contents minus Wood-a.*

TRUE GHOST STORIES (See Ripley's . . .)

TRUE LIFE ROMANCES (. . .Romance on cover)
Dec, 1955 - No. 3, Aug, 1956
Ajax/Farrell Publications

1	3.50	10.50	24.00
2	1.70	5.00	12.00
3-Disbrow-a	2.65	8.00	18.00

TRUE LIFE SECRETS
Mar-April, 1951 - No. 28, Sept, 1955; No. 29, Jan, 1956
Romantic Love Stories/Charlton

1	4.35	13.00	30.00

True Aviation Adventures & Model Building #15, © PMI

True Comics #14, © PMI

True Crime Comics #4, © Magazine Village

True Love Pictorial #3, © STJ   True 3-D #2, © HARV   True War Romances #1, © QUA

TRUE LIFE SECRETS (continued)	Good	Fine	N-Mint
2	2.65	8.00	18.00
3-12,15-19	2.00	6.00	14.00
13-Headlight-a	5.35	16.00	37.00
14-Drug mention story(marijuana)	3.15	9.50	22.00
20-22,24-29: 25-Last precode (3/55)	1.50	4.50	10.00
23-Suggestive-c	2.65	8.00	18.00

TRUE LIFE TALES
No. 8, Oct, 1949 - No. 2, Jan, 1950
Marvel Comics (CCC)

8(10/49), 2(1/50)-Photo-c	3.00	9.00	21.00

TRUE LOVE
Jan, 1986 - No. 2, Jan, 1986 ($2.00, Baxter paper)
Eclipse Comics

1,2-Love stories-r from pre-code Standard Comics; Toth-a			
	.35	1.00	2.00

TRUE LOVE CONFESSIONS
May, 1954 - No. 11, Jan, 1956
Premier Magazines

1-Marijuana story	4.00	12.00	28.00
2	1.70	5.00	12.00
3-11	1.30	4.00	9.00

TRUE LOVE PICTORIAL
1952 - No. 11, Aug, 1954
St. John Publishing Co.

1	5.50	16.50	38.00
2	2.65	8.00	18.00
3-5(All 100 pgs.): 5-Formerly Teen-Age Temptations (4/53);			
Kubert-a-#3,5; Baker-a-#3-5	15.00	45.00	105.00
6,7-Baker c/a	5.70	17.00	40.00
8,10,11-Baker c/a	5.00	15.00	35.00
9-Baker-a	3.70	11.00	26.00

TRUE MOVIE AND TELEVISION (Part magazine)
No. 1, Aug, 1950 - No. 3, Nov, 1950 (52 pgs.) (10 cents)
Toby Press

1-Liz Taylor photo-c; Gene Autry, Shirley Temple, Li'l			
Abner app.	19.00	57.00	132.00
2-Frazetta John Wayne illo	12.00	36.00	84.00
3-June Allyson-c; Montgomery Cliff, Esther Williams, Andrews			
Sisters app; Li'l Abner feat.	12.00	36.00	84.00
NOTE: 16 pages in color, rest movie material in black & white.

TRUE SECRETS (Formerly Love Dramas?)
No. 3, Mar, 1950; No. 4, Feb, 1951 - No. 40, Sept, 1956
Marvel (IPS)/Atlas Comics (MPI)

3 (52 pgs.)	3.50	10.50	24.00
4,5,7-10	1.70	5.00	12.00
6,22-Everett-a	2.30	7.00	16.00
11-20	1.30	4.00	9.00
21,23-28: 28-Last pre-code (2/55)	1.00	3.00	7.00
29-40	.85	2.50	6.00
NOTE: Colletta a-34, 36; c-24.

TRUE SPORT PICTURE STORIES (Formerly Sport Comics)
Feb, 1942? - V5/2, July-Aug, 1949
Street & Smith Publications

V1#5	10.00	30.00	70.00
6-12 (1942-43)	5.70	17.00	40.00
V2#1-12 (1944-45)	4.65	14.00	32.00
V3#1-12 (1946-47)	3.50	10.50	24.00
V4#1-12 (1948-49)	2.65	8.00	18.00
NOTE: Powell a-V3#10, V4#1-4, 6-8, 10-12; V5#1, 2; c-V4#5-7, 9, 10.

TRUE STORIES OF ROMANCE
Jan, 1950 - No. 3, May, 1950 (All photo-c)

Fawcett Publications	Good	Fine	N-Mint
1	4.35	13.00	30.00
2,3	2.65	8.00	18.00

TRUE STORY OF JESSE JAMES, THE (See 4-Color #757)

TRUE SWEETHEART SECRETS
5/50; No. 2, 7/50; No. 3, 1951(nd); No. 4, 9/51 - No. 11, 1/53
Fawcett Publications (All photo-c)

1-Photo-c; Debbie Reynolds?	4.35	13.00	30.00
2-Wood-a, 11 pgs.	8.00	24.00	56.00
3-11: 4,5-Powell-a	2.35	7.00	16.00

TRUE TALES OF LOVE (Formerly Secret Story Romances)
No. 22, April, 1956 - No. 31, Sept, 1957
Atlas Comics (TCI)

22	1.60	4.70	11.00
23-31-Colletta-a in most	.85	2.50	6.00

TRUE TALES OF ROMANCE
No. 4, June, 1950
Fawcett Publications

4	2.65	8.00	18.00

TRUE 3-D
Dec, 1953 - No. 2, Feb, 1954
Harvey Publications

1-Nostrand, Powell-a	5.70	17.00	40.00
2-Powell-a	10.00	30.00	70.00
NOTE: Many copies of #1 surfaced in 1984.

TRUE-TO-LIFE ROMANCES
No. 8, 11-12/49; No. 9, 1-2/50; No. 3, 4/50 - No. 5, 9/50; No. 6, 1/51 -
No. 23, 10/54
Star Publications

8('49)	5.00	15.00	35.00
9,3-10: 3-Janet Leigh/Glenn Ford photo on-c	4.35	13.00	30.00
11,22,23	4.00	12.00	28.00
12-14,17-21-Disbrow-a	6.00	16.00	37.00
15,16-Wood & Disbrow-a in each	8.35	25.00	58.00
NOTE: Kamen a-13. Kamen/Feldstein a-14. All have L.B. Cole covers.

TRUE WAR EXPERIENCES
Aug, 1952 - No. 4, Dec, 1952
Harvey Publications

1	2.35	7.00	16.00
2-4	1.35	4.00	9.00

TRUE WAR ROMANCES
Sept, 1952 - No. 21, June, 1955
Quality Comics Group

1-Photo-c	4.60	14.00	32.00
2	2.30	7.00	16.00
3-10: 9-Whitney-a	1.85	5.50	13.00
11-21: 20-Last precode (4/55). 14-Whitney-a	1.50	4.50	10.00

TRUE WAR STORIES (See Ripley's...)

TRUE WESTERN (True Adventures #3)
Dec, 1949 - No. 2, March, 1950
Marvel Comics (MMC)

1-Photo-c; Billy The Kid app.	5.70	17.00	40.00
2: Alan Ladd photo-c	6.50	19.50	45.00

TRUE WEST ROMANCE
1952
Quality Comics Group

21 (Exist?)	2.65	8.00	18.00

TRUMP (Magazine format)
Jan, 1957 - No. 2, Mar, 1957

TRUMP (continued)
HMH Publishing Co.

	Good	Fine	N-Mint
1-Harvey Kurtzman satire	8.50	25.50	60.00
2-Harvey Kurtzman satire	7.00	21.00	50.00

NOTE: *Davis, Elder, Heath, Jaffee* art-#1,2; *Wood*-#1. #2-article by Mel Brooks.

TRUMPETS WEST (See 4-Color #875)

TRUTH ABOUT CRIME (See Fox Giants)

TRUTH ABOUT MOTHER GOOSE (See 4-Color #862)

TRUTH BEHIND THE TRIAL OF CARDINAL MINDSZENTY, THE (See Cardinal...)

TRUTHFUL LOVE (Formerly Youthful Love)
No. 2, July, 1950
Youthful Magazines

	Good	Fine	N-Mint
2-Ingrid Bergman's true life story	2.30	7.00	16.00

TRY-OUT WINNER BOOK
Mar, 1988
Marvel Comics

	Good	Fine	N-Mint
1-Spider-Man vs. Doc. Octopus		.60	1.25

TUBBY (See Marge's...)

TUFF GHOSTS STARRING SPOOKY
7/62 - No. 39, 11/70; No. 40, 9/71 - No. 43, 10/72
Harvey Publications

	Good	Fine	N-Mint
1	4.00	12.00	24.00
2-5	2.00	6.00	12.00
6-10	1.35	4.00	8.00
11-20	.70	2.00	4.00
21-30	.50	1.50	3.00
31-39,43		.50	1.00
40-42: 52 pg. Giants		.60	1.20

TUFFY
1949 - 1950
Standard Comics

	Good	Fine	N-Mint
1-All by Sid Hoff	2.65	8.00	18.00
2	1.30	4.00	9.00
3-10	1.15	3.50	8.00

TUFFY TURTLE
No date
I. W. Enterprises

	Good	Fine	N-Mint
1-Reprint	.30	.80	1.60

TUROK, SON OF STONE (See Golden Comics Digest #31, March of Comics #378,399,408, and Dan Curtis)
No. 596, 12/54 - No. 29, 6-8/62; No. 30, 12/62 - No. 125, 1/80; No. 126, 3/81 - No. 130, 4/82
Dell Publ. Co. No. 1-29/Gold Key No. 30-125/Whitman No. 126 on

	Good	Fine	N-Mint
4-Color 596 (12/54)(#1)	21.50	65.00	150.00
4-Color 656 (10/55)	15.00	45.00	105.00
3(3-5/56)-5	11.00	32.00	75.00
6-10	7.00	21.00	50.00
11-20	3.70	11.00	26.00
21-30: 30-back-c pinups begin	2.00	6.00	14.00
31-50: 31-Drug use story	1.00	3.00	7.00
51-60	.70	2.00	4.00
61-83: 63-Only line drawn-c	.35	1.00	2.00
84-Origin & 1st app. Hutec	.35	1.00	2.00
85-130: 114-(52 pgs.)		.50	1.00
Giant 1(30031-611) (11/66)	4.00	12.00	32.00

NOTE: *Alberto Gioletti* painted-c No. 30-129. *Sparling* a-126-30. Reprints-#36, 54, 57, 75, 112, 118, 125, 127-130(½).

TURTLE SOUP
Sept, 1987 (one shot, B&W, $2.00, 76 pgs.)

Mirage Studios

	Good	Fine	N-Mint
1-Feat. Teenage Mutant Ninja Turtles	.50	1.50	3.00

TV CASPER & COMPANY
Aug, 1963 - No. 46, April, 1974 (25 cent Giants)
Harvey Publications

	Good	Fine	N-Mint
1: 68 pg. Giants begin	4.30	13.00	30.00
2-5	2.00	6.00	14.00
6-10	1.35	4.00	8.00
11-20	.70	2.00	4.00
21-31: Last 68 pg. issue	.50	1.50	3.00
32-46: All 52 pgs.		.50	1.00

TV FUNDAY FUNNIES (See Famous TV...)

TV FUNNIES (See New Funnies)

TV FUNTIME (See Little Audrey)

TV LAUGHOUT (See Archie's...)

TV SCREEN CARTOONS (Formerly Real Screen)
No. 129, July-Aug, 1959 - No. 138, Jan-Feb, 1961
National Periodical Publications

	Good	Fine	N-Mint
129-138 (Scarce)	2.00	6.00	14.00

TV STARS (TV)(Hanna-Barbera)
Aug, 1978 - No. 4, Feb, 1979
Marvel Comics Group

	Good	Fine	N-Mint
1-Great Grape Ape app.		.50	1.00
2,4: 4-Top Cat app.		.40	.80
3-Toth-c/a	.60	1.75	3.50

TV TEENS (Formerly Ozzie & Babs; Rock and Rollo #14 on)
Feb, 1954 - V2No.13, July, 1956
Charlton Comics

	Good	Fine	N-Mint
V1#14-Ozzie & Babs	3.50	10.50	24.00
15	1.85	5.50	13.00
V2#3(6/54) - 7-Don Winslow	2.15	6.50	15.00
8(7/55)-13-Mopsy	1.85	5.50	13.00

TWEETY AND SYLVESTER (1st Series)
No. 406, June, 1952 - No. 37, June-Aug, 1962
Dell Publishing Co.

	Good	Fine	N-Mint
4-Color 406	1.70	4.00	12.00
4-Color 489,524	1.00	3.00	7.00
4 (3-5/54) - 20	.85	2.50	6.00
21-37	.55	1.65	4.00

(See March of Comics #421,433,445,457,469,481)

TWEETY AND SYLVESTER (2nd Series)
Nov, 1963; No. 2, Nov, 1965 - No. 121, July, 1984
Gold Key No. 1-102/Whitman No. 103 on

	Good	Fine	N-Mint
1	.85	2.50	6.00
2-10	.45	1.35	3.00
11-30	.25	.75	1.50
31-70		.50	1.00
71-121: 99,119-r(⅓)		.30	.60
Kite Fun Book (1965, 16pgs., 5x7¼'', soft-c)	.50	1.50	3.00
Mini Comic No. 1(1976)-3¼x6½''		.30	.60

12 O'CLOCK HIGH (TV)
Jan-Mar, 1965 - No. 2, Apr-June, 1965 (Photo-c)
Dell Publishing Co.

	Good	Fine	N-Mint
1,2	2.30	7.00	16.00

24 PAGES OF COMICS (No title) (Also see Pure Oil Comics, Salerno Carnival of Comics, & Vicks Comics)
Late 1930s
Giveaway by various outlets including Sears
Contains strip reprints-Buck Rogers, Napoleon, Sky Roads, War on

Trump #1, © Harvey Kurtzman *Tuffy #8, © STD* *12 O'Clock High #1, © 20th Century-Fox*

The Twilight Zone #8, © Cayuga Prod.

Two-Fisted Tales #19, © WMG

Two-Gun Kid #13, © MEG

24 PAGES OF COMICS (continued)	Good	Fine	N-Mint
Crime	20.00	60.00	140.00

20,000 LEAGUES UNDER THE SEA (See 4-Color #614, King Classics, and Movie Comics)

TWICE TOLD TALES (See Movie Classics)

TWILIGHT AVENGER, THE
July, 1986 - No. 2, 1987 ($1.75, color, mini-series)
Elite Comics

1,2	.35	1.00	2.00

TWILIGHT ZONE, THE (TV) (See Dan Curtis)
No. 1173, 3-5/61 - No. 91, 4/79; No. 92, 5/82
Dell Publishing Co./Gold Key/Whitman No. 92

4-Color 1173-Crandall/Evans-c/a	5.00	15.00	35.00
4-Color 1288-Crandall/Evans c/a	4.00	12.00	28.00
01-860-207 (5-7/62-Dell)	3.50	10.50	24.00
12-860-210 on-c; 01-860-210 on inside(8-10/62-Dell)-Evans c/a; Crandall/Frazetta-a(2)	3.50	10.50	24.00
1(11/62-Gold Key)-Crandall,Evans-a	3.00	9.00	21.00
2	1.50	4.50	10.00
3,4,9-Toth-a, 11,10 & 15 pgs.	1.75	5.25	12.00
5-8,10,11	1.15	3.50	8.00
12-Williamson-a	1.65	5.00	10.00
13,15-Crandall-a	1.65	5.00	10.00
14-Williamson/Orlando/Crandall/Torres-a	2.00	6.00	12.00
16-20	.85	2.50	6.00
21-Crandall-a(r)	.70	2.00	4.00
22-24	.50	1.50	3.00
25-Evans/Crandall-a(r)	.50	1.50	3.00
26-Crandall, Evans-a(r)	.50	1.50	3.00
27-Evans-a(2)(r)	.50	1.50	3.00
28-32: 32-Evans-a(r)	.35	1.00	2.00
33-42,44-50,52-70	.25	.75	1.50
43-Crandall-a	.30	.90	1.80
51-Williamson-a	.30	.90	1.80
71-92: 71-Reprint. 83,84-(52 pgs.)		.50	1.00
Mini Comic #1(1976-3¼x6½'')		.30	.60

NOTE: *Bolle a-13(w/McWilliams), 50, 57, 59. McWilliams a-59. Orlando a-19, 20, 22, 23. Sekowsky a-3. (See Mystery Comics Digest 3, 6, 9, 12, 15, 18, 21, 24). Reprints-26(½), 71, 73, 79, 83, 84, 86, 92. Painted-c 1-91.*

TWINKLE COMICS
May, 1945
Spotlight Publishers

1	5.70	17.00	40.00

TWIST, THE
July-September, 1962
Dell Publishing Co.

01-864-209-painted-c	3.00	9.00	21.00

TWISTED TALES (See Eclipse Graphic . . . #15)
11/82 - No. 8, 5/84; No. 9, 11/84; No. 10, 12/84 (Baxter paper)
Pacific Comics/Independent Comics Group No. 9, 10/Blackthorne

1-Nudity/Violence in all	.60	1.75	3.50
2-10	.35	1.00	2.00
3-D 1-r/earlier issues in 3-D	.40	1.25	2.50

NOTE: *Alcala a-1. John Bolton painted c-4, 6, 7; a-7. Conrad a-1, 3, 5; c-1, 3, 5. Guice a-8. Morrow a-10. Ploog a-2. Wildey a-3. Wrightson a(Painted)-10; c-2.*

TWISTED TALES OF BRUCE JONES, THE
Feb, 1986 - No. 4, Mar, 1986 ($1.75, Baxter)
Eclipse Comics

1-4	.35	1.00	2.00

TWO BIT THE WACKY WOODPECKER (See Wacky . . .)
1951 - No. 3, May, 1953

Toby Press			
	Good	Fine	N-Mint
1	2.30	7.00	16.00
2,3	1.30	4.00	9.00

TWO FACES OF COMMUNISM (Also see Double Talk)
1961 (36 pgs.; paper cover) (Giveaway)
Christian Anti-Communism Crusade, Houston, Texas

	10.00	30.00	70.00

TWO-FISTED TALES (Formerly Haunt of Fear #15-17)
No. 18, Nov-Dec, 1950 - No. 41, Feb-Mar, 1955
E. C. Comics

18(#1)-Kurtzman-c	61.00	182.00	430.00
19-Kurtzman-c	45.00	135.00	315.00
20-Kurtzman-c	27.00	81.00	190.00
21,22-Kurtzman-c	21.00	62.00	145.00
23-25-Kurtzman-c	15.00	45.00	105.00
26-35: 33-"Atom Bomb" by Wood	12.00	36.00	80.00
36-41	7.35	22.00	50.00
Two-Fisted Annual, 1952	61.00	182.00	430.00
Two-Fisted Annual, 1953	45.00	135.00	315.00

NOTE: *Berg a-29. Craig a-18, 19, 32. Crandall a-35, 36. Davis a-20-36, 40; c-30, 34, 35, 41, Annual 2. Evans a-34, 40, 41; c-40. Feldstein a-18. Krigstein a-41. Kubert a-32, 33. Kurtzman a-18-25; c-18-29, 31, Annual 1. Severin a-26, 28, 29, 31, 34-41 (No.37-39 are all-Severin issues); c-36-39. Severin/Elder a-19-29, 31, 33, 36. Wood a-18-28, 30-35, 41; c-32, 33. Special issues: #26 (ChanJin Reservoir), 31 (Civil War), 35 (Civil War). Canadian reprints known; see Table of Contents.*

TWO-GUN KID (Also see All Western Winners, Best Western, Black Rider, Blaze Carson, Kid Colt, Western Winners, Wild West, & Wild Western)
3/48(No mo.) - No. 10, 11/49; No. 11, 12/53 - No. 59, 4/61; No. 60, 11/62 - No. 92, 3/68; No. 93, 7/70 - No. 136, 4/77
Marvel/Atlas (MCI) No. 1-10/HPC No. 11-59/Marvel No. 60 on)

1-Two-Gun Kid & his horse Cyclone begin; The Sheriff begins	30.00	90.00	210.00
2	13.00	40.00	90.00
3,4: 3-Annie Oakley app.	9.50	25.50	65.00
5-Pre-Black Rider app. (Wint. 48/49); Spanking panel. Anti-Wertham editorial (1st?)	11.50	34.00	80.00
6-10 (11/49)	7.00	21.00	50.00
11 (12/53)-Black Rider app.	5.70	17.00	40.00
12-Black Rider app.	5.70	17.00	40.00
13-20	4.65	14.00	32.00
21-24,26-29	3.50	10.50	24.00
25,30-Williamson-a in both, 5 & 4 pgs.	4.65	14.00	32.00
31-33,35,37-40	2.65	8.00	18.00
34-Crandall-a	3.00	9.00	21.00
36,41,42,48-Origin in all	2.85	8.50	20.00
43,44,47	1.70	5.00	12.00
45,46-Davis-a	2.65	8.00	18.00
49,50,52,55,57-Severin-a(3) in each	1.70	5.00	12.00
51-Williamson-a, 5pgs.	3.00	9.00	21.00
53,54,56	.85	2.50	6.00
58,60-New origin. 58-Last 10 cent ish.	.85	2.50	6.00
59,61-80: 64-Intro. Boom-Boom	.40	1.25	2.50
81-92: 92-Last new story; last 12 cent ish.		.60	1.20
93-100,102-136		.40	.80
101-Origin retold#58	.30		.60

NOTE: *Ayers a-26, 27. Davis c-45-47. Everett a-82, 91. Fuje a-13. Heath c-13, 21, 23. Keller a-16, 19, 28. Kirby a-54, 55, 57-62, 75-77, 90, 95, 101, 119, 120, 129; c-10, 52, 54-65, 67-72, 74-76, 116. Maneely a-20; c-16, 19, 20, 25-28, 49. Powell a-38, 102, 104. Severin a-29, 51. Tuska a-12. Whitney a-87, 89-91, 98-113, 124, 129; c-87, 89, 91, 113. Wildey a-21. Williamson a-110r. Kid Colt in #13, 14, 16-21.*

TWO GUN WESTERN (1st Series) (Formerly Casey Crime Photographer)
No. 5, Nov, 1950 - No. 14, June, 1952
Marvel/Atlas Comics (MPC)

TWO GUN WESTERN (continued)

	Good	Fine	N-Mint
5-The Apache Kid (Intro & origin) & his horse Nightwind begin by Buscema	7.00	21.00	50.00
6-10: 8-Kid Colt, The Texas Kid & his horse Thunder begin?	4.30	13.00	30.00
11-14: 13-Black Rider app.	3.50	10.50	24.00

NOTE: *Maneely a-6, 7, 9; c-6, 11-13. Romita a-8. Wildey a-8.*

2-GUN WESTERN (2nd Series) (Formerly Billy Buckskin; Two-Gun Western #5 on)
No. 4, May, 1956
Atlas Comics (MgPC)

	Good	Fine	N-Mint
4-Apache Kid; Ditko-a	5.70	17.00	40.00

TWO-GUN WESTERN (Formerly 2-Gun Western)
No. 5, July, 1956 - No. 12, Sept, 1957
Atlas Comics (MgPC)

	Good	Fine	N-Mint
5-Apache Kid, Kid Colt Outlaw, Doc Holiday begin; Black Rider app.	4.00	12.00	28.00
6,7,10	2.00	6.00	14.00
8,12-Crandall-a	3.50	10.50	24.00
9,11-Williamson-a in both, 5 pgs. each	4.00	12.00	28.00

NOTE: *Ayers a-9. Everett c-12. Kirby a-12. Maneely a-6, 8, 12; c-5, 6, 8. Morrow a-9, 10. Powell a-7, 11. Severin c-10.*

TWO MOUSEKETEERS, THE (See 4-Color #475,603,642 under M.G.M.'s . . .; becomes M.G.M.'s Mouse Musketeers)

TWO ON A GUILLOTINE (See Movie Classics)

2000 A.D. MONTHLY/PRESENTS (. . .Showcase #25 on)
4/85 - No. 6, 9/85; 4/86 - Present (Mando paper)
Eagle Comics/Quality Comics No. 5 on

1-5: #1-4-r/British series featuring Judge Dredd; Alan Moore scripts begin	.25	.75	1.50
6 ($1.25)	.25	.75	1.50
1-26		.65	1.30
27/28-two issue #s in one, Guice-c	.25	.75	1.50

2001: A SPACE ODYSSEY (Marvel Treasury Special)
Oct, 1976 (One Shot) (Over-sized)
Marvel Comics Group

1-Kirby, Giacoia-a	.35	1.00	2.00

2001, A SPACE ODYSSEY
Dec, 1976 - No. 10, Sept, 1977 (Regular size)
Marvel Comics Group

1-Kirby c/a in all		.30	.60
2-10: 8-Origin/1st app. Machine Man (called Mr. Machine)		.25	.50
Howard Johnson giveaway(1968, 8pp); 6pg. movie adaptation, 2pg. games, puzzles		.25	.50

2010
Apr, 1985 - No. 2, May, 1985
Marvel Comics Group

1,2-r/Marvel Super Special		.40	.80

UFO & ALIEN COMIX
Jan, 1978 (One Shot)
Warren Publishing Co.

Toth, Severin-a(r)	.30	.80	1.60

UFO & OUTER SPACE (Formerly UFO Flying Saucers)
No. 14, June, 1978 - No. 25, Feb, 1980 (all painted covers)
Gold Key

14-Reprints UFO Flying Saucers #3	.35	1.00	2.00
15,16-Reprints		.60	1.20
17-20-New material	.25	.75	1.50
21-25: 23-McWilliams-a. 24-3 pg.-r. 25-r-UFO Flying Saucers #2 w/cover		.50	1.00

UFO ENCOUNTERS
May, 1978 (228 pages) ($1.95)
Western Publishing Co.

	Good	Fine	N-Mint
11192-Reprints UFO Flying Saucers	.70	2.00	4.00
11404-Vol.1 (128 pgs.)-See UFO Mysteries for Vol.2	.35	1.00	2.00

UFO FLYING SAUCERS (UFO & Outer Space #14 on)
Oct, 1968 - No. 13, Jan, 1977 (No. 2 on, 36 pgs.)
Gold Key

1(30035-810) (68 pgs.)	1.15	3.50	8.00
2(11/70), 3(11/72), 4(11/74)	1.00	3.00	6.00
5(2/75)-13: Bolle-a No. 4 on	.70	2.00	4.00

UFO MYSTERIES
1978 (96 pages) ($1.00) (Reprints)
Western Publishing Co.

11400(96 pgs., $1.00)	.25	.75	1.50
11404(Vol.2)-Cont'd from UFO Encounters, pgs. 129-224	.25	.75	1.50

ULTRA KLUTZ
June, 1986 - Present ($1.50-$2.00, B&W)
Onward Comics

1	.70	2.00	4.00
2-26	.25	.75	1.50

UNBIRTHDAY PARTY WITH ALICE IN WONDERLAND (See 4-Color #341)

UNCANNY TALES
June, 1952 - No. 56, Sept, 1957
Atlas Comics (PrPI/PPI)

1-Heath-a	17.00	51.00	120.00
2	8.50	25.50	60.00
3-5	7.00	21.00	50.00
6-Wolvertonish-a by Matt Fox	7.00	21.00	50.00
7,8,10: 8-Tothish-a	6.50	19.50	45.00
9-Crandall-a	6.50	19.50	45.00
11-20: 17-Atom bomb panels; anti-communist story. 19-Krenkel-a	5.00	15.00	35.00
21-27: 25-Nostrand-a?	4.30	13.00	30.00
28-Last precode ish (1/55); Kubert-a; #1-28 contain 2-3 sci/fic stories each	5.70	17.00	40.00
29-41,43-49,52	2.00	6.00	14.00
42,54,56-Krigstein-a	3.00	9.00	21.00
50,53,55-Torres-a	3.00	9.00	21.00
51,57-Williamson-a (#57, exist?)	4.00	12.00	28.00

NOTE: *Bailey a-51. Briefer a-19, 20. Cameron a-47. Colan a-11, 16, 17. Drucker a-37, 42, 45. Everett a-2, 7, 12, 32, 36, 39, 47, 48; c-7, 11, 17, 39, 41, 50, 52, 53. Fass a-9. Forte a-27. Heath a-13, 14; c-10. Keller a-3. Lawrence a-14, 17, 19, 23, 27, 28, 35. Maneely a-4, 8, 10, 16, 29, 35; c-2, 22, 26, 33, 38. Moldoff a-23. Morrow a-46, 51. Orlando a-49, 50, 53. Powell a-12, 18, 38, 43, 50, 53, 56. Robinson a-3. 13. Roussos a-8. Sale a-47. Sekowsky a-25. Tothish-a by Andru-27. Wildey a-48.*

UNCANNY TALES
Dec, 1973 - No. 12, Oct, 1975
Marvel Comics Group

1-Crandall-a(r-'50s #9)		.30	.60
2-12		.25	.50

NOTE: *Ditko reprints-#4, 6-8, 10-12.*

UNCANNY X-MEN, THE (See X-Men)

UNCANNY X-MEN AND THE NEW TEEN TITANS (See Marvel and DC Present)

UNCANNY X-MEN AT THE STATE FAIR OF TEXAS, THE
1983 (36 pgs.)(One-Shot)
Marvel Comics Group

nn	1.10	3.25	6.50

Two Gun Western #5 (11/50), © MEG

Ultra Klutz #23, © Jeff Nicholson

Uncanny Tales #12, © MEG

Uncle Scrooge #219, © WDC

Uncle Scrooge Adventures #1, © WDC

Undercover Girl #7, © ME

UNCLE CHARLIE'S FABLES
Jan, 1952 - No. 5, Sept, 1952
Lev Gleason Publications

	Good	Fine	N-Mint
1-Norman Maurer-a; has Biro's picture	4.00	12.00	28.00
2-Fuje-a; Biro photo; Biro painted-c	3.00	9.00	21.00
3-5: 4-Biro-c	2.30	7.00	16.00

UNCLE DONALD & HIS NEPHEWS DUDE RANCH (See Dell Giant #52)

UNCLE DONALD & HIS NEPHEWS FAMILY FUN (See Dell Giant #38)

UNCLE JOE'S FUNNIES
1938 (B&W)
Centaur Publications

	Good	Fine	N-Mint
1-Games/puzzles, some interior art; Bill Everett-c	21.50	65.00	150.00

UNCLE MILTY (TV)
Dec, 1950 - No. 4, July, 1951 (52 pgs.)
Victoria Publications/True Cross

	Good	Fine	N-Mint
1-Milton Berle	17.00	51.00	120.00
2	8.50	25.50	60.00
3,4	7.00	21.00	50.00

UNCLE REMUS & HIS TALES OF BRER RABBIT (See 4-Color #129, 208, 693)

UNCLE SAM QUARTERLY (Blackhawk #9 on)
Autumn, 1941 - No. 8, Fall, 1943 (Also see National Comics)
Quality Comics Group

	Good	Fine	N-Mint
1-Origin Uncle Sam; Fine/Eisner-a, chapter headings, 2 pgs. by Eisner. (2 versions: dark cover, no price; light cover with price); Jack Cole-a	105.00	315.00	735.00
2-Cameos by The Ray, Black Condor, Quicksilver, The Red Bee, Alias the Spider, Hercules & Neon the Unknown; Eisner, Fine c/a	50.00	150.00	350.00
3-Tuska-c/a	35.00	105.00	245.00
4	30.00	90.00	210.00
5-8	25.00	75.00	175.00

NOTE: *Kotzky or Tuska a-4-8.*

UNCLE SAM'S CHRISTMAS STORY
1958
Promotional Publ. Co. (Giveaway)

	Good	Fine	N-Mint
Reprints 1956 Christmas USA	1.00	3.00	7.00

UNCLE SCROOGE (Disney)(See Dell Giants 33,55, Four Color #178, Gladstone Comic Album & WDC&S #98)
No. 386, 3/52 - No. 39, 8-10/62; No. 40, 12/62 - No. 209, 1984; No. 210, 10/86 - Present
Dell No. 1-39/Gold Key No. 40-173/Whitman No. 174-209/Gladstone No. 210-on

	Good	Fine	N-Mint
4-Color 386(#1)-in "Only a Poor Old Man" by Carl Barks; r-in Uncle Scrooge & Donald Duck #1('65) & The Best of Walt Disney Comics('74)	58.00	175.00	405.00
4-Color 456(#2)-in "Back to the Klondike" by Carl Barks; r-in Best of U.S. & D.D. #1('66)	27.00	81.00	190.00
4-Color 495(No.3)-r-in #105	24.00	72.00	170.00
4(12-2/53-54)	19.00	57.00	132.00
5-r-in W.D. Digest #1	15.00	45.00	105.00
6-r-in U.S. #106,165 & Best of U.S. & D.D. #1('66)	14.00	42.00	100.00
7-r-in Best of D.D. & U.S. #2('67)	11.00	32.00	75.00
8-10: 8-r-in #111. 9-r-in #104. 10-r-in #67	8.50	25.50	60.00
11-20	7.00	21.00	50.00
21-30	6.00	18.00	42.00
31-40	5.00	15.00	35.00
41-50	3.70	11.00	26.00
51-60	3.50	10.50	24.00
61-66,68-70: 70-Last Barks issue with original story			

	Good	Fine	N-Mint
	2.65	8.00	18.00
67,72,73-Barks-r	1.70	5.00	12.00
71-Written by Barks only	1.70	5.00	12.00
74-One pg. Barks-r	1.15	3.50	7.00
75-81,83-Not by Barks	1.15	3.50	7.00
82,84-Barks-r begin	1.15	3.50	7.00
85-100	1.00	3.00	6.00
101-110	.85	2.50	5.00
111-120	.70	2.00	4.00
121-141,143-152,154-157	.60	1.75	3.50
142-Reprints 4-Color 456 with-c	.70	2.00	4.00
153,158,162-164,166,168-170,178,180: No Barks		.50	1.00
159-160,165,167,172-176-Barks-a	.25	.75	1.50
161(r-#14), 171(r-#11), 177(r-#16), 179(r-#9), 183(r-#6)-Barks-r	.25	.75	1.50
181(r-4-Color 495), 195(r-4-Color 386)	.25	.70	1.40
182,186,191-194,197-202,204-206: No Barks		.40	.80
184,185,187,188-Barks-a		.50	1.00
189(r-#5), 190(r-#4), 196(r-#16), 203(r-#12), 207(r-#93,92), 208(r-U.S. #18), 209(r-U.S. #21)-Barks-r		.60	1.20
210-1st Gladstone issue	.85	2.50	5.00
211-218	.40	1.25	2.50
219-Son Of The Sun by Rosa	1.45	4.25	8.50
220-Don Rosa story	.50	1.50	3.00
221-230: 210(r-WDC&S 134, 1st Beagle Boys). 224-Rosa c/a. 227-Rosa-a	.25	.75	1.50
231-236		.50	1.00
Uncle Scrooge & Money(G.K.)-Barks-r/from WDC&S #130 (3/67)	4.00	12.00	24.00
Mini Comic #1(1976)(3¼x6½'')-R-/U.S. #115; Barks-c			.20

NOTE: *Barks c-4-Color 386, 456, 495, #4-37, 39, 40, 43-71.*

UNCLE SCROOGE ADVENTURES (Walt Disney's...#4 on)
Nov, 1987 - Present
Gladstone Publishing

	Good	Fine	N-Mint
1: Barks-r #1,2,4,6-8	.70	2.00	4.00
2-5: 5-Rosa c/a	.25	.75	1.50
6-12: 9-Rosa-a		.50	1.00

UNCLE SCROOGE & DONALD DUCK
June, 1965 (25 cents) (Paper cover)
Gold Key

	Good	Fine	N-Mint
1-Reprint of 4-Color #(#1) & lead story from 4-Color 29	8.35	25.00	50.00

UNCLE SCROOGE COMICS DIGEST
1986 - No. 6, 1987 ($1.25, Digest-size)
Gladstone Publishing

	Good	Fine	N-Mint
1-6		.60	1.25

UNCLE SCROOGE GOES TO DISNEYLAND (See Dell Giants)
Aug, 1985 ($2.50)
Gladstone Publishing Ltd.

	Good	Fine	N-Mint
1-r/Dell Giant w/new-c by Mel Crawford, based on old cover	.40	1.25	2.50
Comics Digest 1 ($1.50, digest size)	.25	.75	1.50

UNCLE WIGGILY (See 4-Color #179, 221, 276, 320, 349, 391, 428, 503, 543, & March of Comics #19)

UNDERCOVER GIRL (Starr Flagg)
1952 - 1954
Magazine Enterprises

	Good	Fine	N-Mint
5(#1)(A-1 62)	18.00	54.00	125.00
6(A-1 98), 7(A-1 118)-All have Starr Flagg	15.00	45.00	105.00

NOTE: *Powell c-6,7. Whitney a-5-7.*

UNDERDOG (TV) (See March of Comics 426,438,467,479)
July, 1970 - No. 10, Jan, 1972; Mar, 1975 - No. 23, Feb, 1979
Charlton Comics/Gold Key

	Good	Fine	N-Mint
1	2.00	6.00	14.00
2-10	.70	2.00	5.00
1 (G.K.)	1.50	4.50	10.00
2-10	.60	1.80	4.00
11-23: 13-1st app. Shack of Solitude	.50	1.50	3.00
Kite Fun Book('74)-5x7''; 16 pgs.	.70	2.00	4.00

UNDERDOG
1987 - No. 3?, 1987 ($1.50, color)
Spotlight Comics

1-3	.25	.75	1.50

UNDERDOG IN 3-D
1988 ($2.50)
Blackthorne Publishing

1	.40	1.25	2.50

UNDERSEA AGENT
Jan, 1966 - No. 6, Mar, 1967 (68 pages)
Tower Comics

1-Davy Jones, Undersea Agent begins	.70	2.00	5.00
2-6: 2-Jones gains magnetic powers. 5-Origin & 1st app. of Merman. 6-Kane?/Wood-c(r)	.60	1.80	4.00

NOTE: Gil Kane a-3-6; c-4, 5. Moldoff a-2i.

UNDERSEA FIGHTING COMMANDOS
May, 1952 - No. 5, Jan, 1953; 1964
Avon Periodicals

1-Ravielli-c	4.00	12.00	28.00
2	2.50	7.50	17.50
3-5	2.15	6.50	15.00
I.W. Reprint #1,2('64)	.85	2.00	4.00

UNDERWATER CITY, THE (See 4-Color #1328)

UNDERWORLD (True Crime Stories)
Feb-Mar, 1948 - No. 9, June-July, 1949 (52 pgs.)
D. S. Publishing Co.

1-Moldoff-c; excessive violence	13.50	41.00	95.00
2-Moldoff-c; Ma Barker story used in **SOTI**, pg. 95; female electrocution panel; lingerie art	14.00	42.00	100.00
3-McWilliams c/a; extreme violence, mutilation	11.00	32.00	75.00
4-Used in **Love and Death** by Legman; Ingels-a	8.50	25.50	60.00
5-Ingels-a	5.70	17.00	40.00
6-9: 8-Ravielli-a	4.65	14.00	32.00

UNDERWORLD
Dec, 1987 - No. 4, Mar, 1988 (mini-series, $1.00, adults)
DC Comics

1-4		.50	1.00

UNDERWORLD CRIME
June, 1952 - No. 9, Oct, 1953
Fawcett Publications

1	9.50	28.50	65.00
2	4.65	14.00	32.00
3-6,8,9 (8,9-exist?)	4.00	12.00	28.00
7-Bondage/torture-c	10.00	30.00	70.00

UNDERWORLD STORY, THE
1950 (Movie)
Avon Periodicals

nn-(Scarce)-Ravielli-c	13.00	40.00	90.00

UNEARTHLY SPECTACULARS
Oct, 1965 - No. 3, Mar, 1967
Harvey Publications

	Good	Fine	N-Mint
1-Tiger Boy; Simon-c	.50	1.50	3.00
2-Jack Q. Frost app.; Wood, Williamson, Kane art; r-1 story/ Thrill-O-Rama #2	1.70	5.00	10.00
3-Jack Q. Frost app.; Williamson/Crandall-a; r-from Alarming Advs. No. 1, 1962	1.70	5.00	10.00

NOTE: Crandall a-3r. G. Kane a-2. Orlando a-3. Simon, Sparling, Wood c-2. Simon/Kirby a-3r. Torres a-1. Wildey a-1(3). Williamson a-2, 3r. Wood a-2(2).

UNEXPECTED, THE (Formerly Tales of the . . .)
No. 105, Feb-Mar, 1968 - No. 222, May, 1982
National Periodical Publications/DC Comics

105-115,117,118,120,122-127		.60	1.20
116,119,121,128-Wrightson-a	.25	.75	1.50
129-156: 132-136-(52 pgs.)		.50	1.00
157-162-(All 100 pgs.)		.50	1.00
163-188		.30	.60
189,190,192-195 ($1.00 size)		.40	.80
191-Rogers-a(p) ($1.00 size)		.50	1.00
196-222: 205-213-Johnny Peril app. 210-Time Warp app.		.30	.60

NOTE: Adams c-110, 112-118, 121, 124. J. Craig a-195. Ditko a-189, 221p, 222p; c-222. Drucker a-107. Giffen a-219, 212. Kaluta c-203, 212. Kirby a-127, 162. Kubert c-204, 214-16, 219-21. Mayer a-217p, 220, 221p. Moldoff a-136r. Moreira a-133. Mortimer a-212p. Newton a-204p. Orlando a-202; c-191. Perez a-217p. Redondo a-155, 195. Reese a-145. Sparling a-107, 205-09p, 212p. Spiegle a-217. Starlin c-198. Toth a-126r, 127r. Tuska a-132, 136, 139, 152, 180, 200p. Wildey a-193. Wood a-122i, 133i, 137i, 138i. Wrightson a-161r(2 pgs.). Johnny Peril in #106-117.

UNEXPECTED ANNUAL, THE (See DC Spec. Series #4)

UNIDENTIFIED FLYING ODDBALL (See Walt Disney Showcase #52)

UNITED COMICS
Aug, 1940 - No. 26, Jan-Feb, 1953
United Features Syndicate

1-Fritzi Ritz & Phil Fumble	11.50	34.00	80.00
2-Fritzi Ritz, Abbie & Slats	6.00	18.00	42.00
3-9-Fritzi Ritz, Abbie & Slats	3.70	11.00	26.00
10-26: 25-Peanuts app.	2.00	6.00	14.00

NOTE: Abbie & Slats reprinted from Tip Top.

UNITED NATIONS, THE (See Classics Illustrated Special Ed.)

UNITED STATES AIR FORCE PRESENTS: THE HIDDEN CREW
1964 (36 pages) (full color)
U.S. Air Force

Shaffenberger-a	.50	1.50	3.00

UNITED STATES FIGHTING AIR FORCE
Sept, 1952 - No. 29, Oct, 1956
Superior Comics Ltd.

1	3.50	10.50	24.00
2	1.70	5.00	12.00
3-10	1.00	3.00	7.00
11-29	.85	2.50	6.00
I.W. Reprint #1,9(nd)	.40	1.10	2.20

UNITED STATES MARINES
1943 - No. 4, 1944; No. 5, 1952 - 1953
William H. Wise/Life's Romances Publ. Co./Magazine Enterprises
No. 5-8/Toby Press

nn-Mart Bailey-a	4.00	12.00	28.00
2-Bailey-a	3.00	9.00	21.00
3,4	2.65	8.00	18.00
5(A-1 55), 6(A-1 60), 7(A-1 68), 8(A-1 72)	2.35	7.00	16.00
7-11 (Toby)	1.00	3.00	7.00

NOTE: Powell a-5-7.

UNIVERSAL PRESENTS DRACULA (See Dell Giants)

Underdog #2 (1987), © Leonardo TV Prod.

Undersea Fighting Commandos #1, © AVON

United States Fighting Air Force #17, © SUPR

Unknown Worlds #1, © ACG

The Unseen #13, © STD

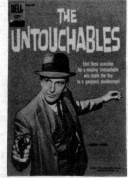
The Untouchables #12-879-210, © Desilu & Langford Prod.

UNKEPT PROMISE
1949 (24 pages)
Legion of Truth (Giveaway)

	Good	Fine	N-Mint
Anti-alcohol	6.00	18.00	42.00

UNKNOWN MAN, THE
1951 (Movie)
Avon Periodicals

nn-Kinstler-c	12.00	36.00	84.00

UNKNOWN SOLDIER (Formerly Star-Spangled War Stories) (See Brave & the Bold #146)
No. 205, Apr-May, 1977 - No. 268, Oct, 1982
National Periodical Publications/DC Comics

205-268: 251-Enemy Ace begins. 268-Death of Unknown Soldier. 248,249-Origin		.30	.60

NOTE: *Evans* a-265-67; c-235. *Kubert* c-Most. *Miller* a-219p. *Severin* a-251-53, 260, 261, 265-67. *Simonson* a-254-256. *Spiegle* a-258, 259, 262-64.

UNKNOWN SOLDIER, THE
Winter, 1988-'89 - No. 12, 1989 ($1.50, maxi-series, mature readers)
DC Comics

1,2	.25	.75	1.50

UNKNOWN WORLD (Strange Stories From Another World #2 on)
June, 1952
Fawcett Publications

1-Norman Saunders painted-c	12.00	36.00	84.00

UNKNOWN WORLDS (See Journey Into. . .)

UNKNOWN WORLDS
Aug, 1960 - No. 57, Aug, 1967
American Comics Group/Best Synd. Features

1	4.30	13.00	30.00
2-5	2.00	6.00	14.00
6-15: 15-Last 10 cent ish?	1.30	4.00	9.00
16-19	1.00	3.00	7.00
20-Herbie cameo	1.15	3.50	8.00
21-35	.70	2.00	5.00
36-''The People vs. Hendricks'' by Craig; most popular ACG story ever	.85	2.50	6.00
37-46	.50	1.50	3.00
47-Williamson-a r-from Adventures Into the Unknown #96, 3 pgs.; Craig-a	.70	2.00	5.00
48-57	.35	1.00	2.00

NOTE: *Ditko* a-49, 50p, 54. *Forte* a-3, 6, 11. *Landau* a-56(2). *Reinman* a-3, 9, 36. John Force, Magic Agent app.-No. 35, 36, 48, 50, 52, 54, 56.

UNKNOWN WORLDS OF FRANK BRUNNER
Aug, 1985 - No. 2, Aug, 1985 ($1.75 cover)
Eclipse Comics

1,2-B&W-r in color	.30	.90	1.80

UNKNOWN WORLDS OF SCIENCE FICTION
1/75 - No. 6, 11/75; 12/76 (B&W Magazine) ($1.00)
Marvel Comics Group

1-Williamson/Wood/Torres/Frazetta r-/Witzend #1, Adams r-/Phase 1; Brunner & Kaluta-r	.50	1.50	3.00
2	.40	1.20	2.40
3-6	.40	1.20	2.40
Special 1(12/76)-100 pgs.; Newton-c; Nino-a	.40	1.20	2.40

NOTE: *Brunner* a-2; c-4, 6. *Chaykin* a-5. *Colan* a(p)-1, 3, 5. *Corben* a-4. *Kaluta* a-2; c-2. *Morrow* a-3, 5. *Nino* a-3, 6. *Perez* a-2, 3.

UNSANE
June, 1954
Star Publications

15-Disbrow-a(2); L. B. Cole-c	11.50	34.00	80.00

UNSEEN, THE
1952 - No. 15, July, 1954
Visual Editions/Standard Comics

	Good	Fine	N-Mint
5-Toth-a	8.50	25.50	60.00
6,7,9,10-Jack Katz-a	5.70	17.00	40.00
8,11,13,14	4.00	12.00	28.00
12,15-Toth-a; Tuska-a, #12	7.00	21.00	50.00

NOTE: *Fawcette* a-13, 14. *Sekowsky* a-7, 8(2), 10, 13.

UNTAMED LOVE
Jan, 1950 - No. 5, Sept, 1950
Quality Comics Group (Comic Magazines)

1-Ward-c, Gustavson-a	11.00	32.00	76.00
2,4: 2-Photo-c	6.00	18.00	42.00
3,5-Gustavson-a	6.50	19.50	45.00

UNTAMED LOVE (Frank Frazetta's)
Nov., 1987 ($2.00, color)
Fantagraphics Books

1	.35	1.00	2.00

UNTOLD LEGEND OF THE BATMAN, THE
7/80 - No. 3, 9/80 (mini-series)
DC Comics

1-Origin		.45	.90
2,3		.30	.60

NOTE: *Aparo* a-1i, 2, 3. *Byrne* a-1p.

UNTOUCHABLES, THE (TV)
No. 1237, 10-12/61 - No. 4, 8-10/62 (Robert Stack photo-c)
Dell Publishing Co.

4-Color 1237,1286	4.00	12.00	28.00
01-879-207, 12-879-210(01879-210 on inside)	3.50	10.50	24.00
Topps Bubblegum premiums-2½x4½'', 8 pgs. (3 different issues) ''The Organization, Jamaica Ginger, The Otto Frick Story (drug), 3000 Suspects, The Antidote, Mexican Stakeout, Little Egypt, Purple Gang, Bugs Moran Story, & Lily Dallas Story''			
	1.70	5.00	12.00

UNUSUAL TALES (Blue Beetle & Shadow From Beyond #50 on)
Nov, 1955 - No. 49, Mar-Apr, 1965
Charlton Comics

1	6.50	19.50	45.00
2	2.65	8.00	18.00
3-5	2.00	6.00	14.00
6-8-Ditko c/a	7.00	21.00	50.00
9-Ditko c/a, 20 pgs.	8.50	25.50	60.00
10-Ditko c/a(4)	9.50	28.50	65.00
11-(68 pgs., 3/58); Ditko-a(4)	9.50	28.50	65.00
12,14-Ditko-a	5.00	15.00	35.00
13,16-20	1.30	4.00	9.00
15-Ditko c/a	5.70	17.00	40.00
21,24,28	.85	2.50	6.00
22,25-27,29-Ditko-a	3.00	9.00	21.00
23-Ditko-c	1.30	4.00	9.00
30-49	.60	1.80	4.00

NOTE: *Colan* a-11. *Ditko* c-22,23,25-27, 31(part).

UP FROM HARLEM (Tom Skinner. . .)
1973 (35-49 Cents)
Spire Christian Comics (Fleming H. Revell Co.)

		.50	1.00

UP-TO-DATE COMICS
No date (1938) (36 pgs.; B&W cover) (10 cents)
King Features Syndicate

nn-Popeye & Henry cover; The Phantom, Jungle Jim & Flash Gordon by Raymond, The Katzenjammer Kids, Curley Harper &

UP-TO-DATE COMICS (continued)

	Good	Fine	N-Mint
others	17.00	51.00	120.00

(Variations to above contents exist.)

UP YOUR NOSE AND OUT YOUR EAR (Magazine)
April, 1972 - No. 2, June, 1972 (52 pgs.) (Satire)
Klevart Enterprises

V1#1,2	.30	.90	1.80

USA COMICS
Aug, 1941 - No. 17, Fall, 1945
Timely Comics (USA)

	Good	Fine	N-Mint
1-Origin Major Liberty (called Mr. Liberty #1), Rockman by Wolverton, & The Whizzer by Avison; The Defender with sidekick Rusty & Jack Frost begin; The Young Avenger only app.; S&K-c plus 1 pg.	285.00	860.00	2000.00
2-Origin Captain Terror & The Vagabond; last Wolverton Rockman	145.00	435.00	1015.00
3-No Whizzer	112.00	335.00	785.00
4-Last Rockman, Major Liberty, Defender, Jack Frost, & Capt. Terror; Corporal Dix app.	94.00	280.00	660.00
5-Origin American Avenger & Roko the Amazing; The Blue Blade, The Black Widow & Victory Boys; Gypo the Gypsy Giant & Hills of Horror only app.; Sergeant Dix begins; no Whizzer. Hitler-c	80.00	240.00	560.00
6-Captain America, The Destroyer, Jap Buster Johnson, Jeep Jones begin; Terror Squad only app.	85.00	255.00	595.00
7-Captain Daring, Disk-Eyes the Detective by Wolverton app.; origin & only app. Marvel Boy; Secret Stamp begins; no Whizzer, Sergeant Dix	73.00	220.00	510.00
8-10: 9-Last Secret Stamp. 10-The Thunderbird only app.	53.00	160.00	370.00
11,12: 11-No Jeep Jones	43.00	130.00	300.00
13-17: 13-No Whizzer; Jeep Jones ends. 15-No Destroyer; Jap Buster Johnson ends	32.00	95.00	225.00

NOTE: *Schomburg c-6, 12. Shores c-11.*

U.S. AGENT (See Jeff Jordan. . .)

USAGI YOJIMBO (See Albedo)
July, 1987 - Present ($2.00, B&W)
Fantagraphics Books

1	.70	2.00	4.00
1-2nd print	.35	1.00	2.00
2-12	.35	1.00	2.00

USAGI YOJIMBO SUMMER SPECIAL
1986 ($2.75, One shot, B&W)
Fantagraphics Books

1-Reprints early Albedo issues	2.00	6.00	12.00

U.S. AIR FORCE COMICS (Army Attack #38 on)
Oct, 1958 - No. 37, Mar-Apr, 1965
Charlton Comics

1	1.15	3.50	8.00
2	.60	1.80	4.00
3-10	.50	1.50	3.00
11-20	.25	.75	1.50
21-37		.50	1.00

NOTE: *Glanzman c/a-9, 10, 12. Montes/Bache a-33.*

USA IS READY
1941 (68 pgs.) (One Shot)
Dell Publishing Co.

1-War propaganda	17.00	51.00	120.00

U.S. BORDER PATROL COMICS (Sgt. Dick Carter of the . . .) (See Holyoke One Shot)

U.S. FIGHTING MEN
1963 - 1964 (Reprints)

Super Comics

	Good	Fine	N-Mint
10-Avon's With the U.S. Paratroops	.50	1.50	3.00
11,12,15-18	.30	.80	1.60

U.S. JONES (Also see Wonderworld Comics #28)
Nov, 1941 - No. 2, Jan, 1942
Fox Features Syndicate

1-U.S. Jones & The Topper begin	50.00	150.00	350.00
2	35.00	105.00	245.00

U.S. MARINES
Fall, 1964 (One shot)
Charlton Comics

1	.30	.80	1.60

U.S. MARINES IN ACTION!
Aug, 1952 - No. 3, Dec, 1952
Avon Periodicals

1-Louis Ravielli c/a	3.35	10.00	23.00
2,3: 3-Kinstler-c	1.65	5.00	11.50

U.S. 1
May, 1983 - No. 12, Oct, 1984
Marvel Comics Group

1		.30	.60
2-12		.25	.50

NOTE: *Golden c-5-7, 9, 10, 12.*

U.S. PARATROOPS (See With the . . .)

U.S. PARATROOPS
1964?
I. W. Enterprises

1-Wood-c r/With the. . . #1	.50	1.50	3.00
8-Kinstler-c	.50	1.50	3.00

U.S. TANK COMMANDOS
June, 1952 - No. 4, March, 1953
Avon Periodicals

1-Kinstler-c	3.75	11.25	26.00
2-4: 2-Kinstler-c	2.15	6.50	15.00
I.W. Reprint #1,8	.40	1.10	2.20

NOTE: *Kinstler a-3, 4, I.W. #1; c-1-4, I.W. #1, 8.*

"V"
Feb, 1985 - No. 18, July, 1986
DC Comics

1-Based on TV movie & series	.25	.75	1.50
2-18		.45	.90

VACATION COMICS (See A-1 Comics #16)

VACATION DIGEST
Sept, 1987 ($1.25, digest size)
Harvey Comics

1		.60	1.25

VACATION IN DISNEYLAND (Also see Dell Giants)
Aug-Oct, 1959 - May, 1965 (Walt Disney)
Dell Publishing Co./Gold Key (1965)

4-Color 1025-Barks-a	6.00	18.00	42.00
1(30024-508)(G.K.)-Reprints Dell Giant #30 & cover to #1('58)	1.50	4.50	12.00

VACATION PARADE (See Dell Giants)

VALKYRIE (See Airboy)
May, 1987 - No. 3, July, 1987 ($1.75, mini-series)
Eclipse Comics

1	.50	1.50	3.00
2-Holly becomes new Black Angel	.50	1.50	3.00
3	.50	1.50	3.00

USA Comics #3, © MEG

U.S. Jones #1, © FOX

U.S. Tank Commandos #2, © AVON

Valor #2, © WMG   Vampirella #3, © WP   Vault Of Horror #14, © WMG

VALKYRIE!
July, 1988 - No. 3, Sept, 1988 ($1.75, color, mini-series)
Eclipse Comics

	Good	Fine	N-Mint
1-3	.30	.90	1.75

VALLEY OF THE DINOSAURS (TV) (Hanna-Barbera)
April, 1975 - No. 11, Dec, 1976
Charlton Comics

1-Howard inks		.40	.80
2-11: 2-Howard inks		.30	.60

VALLEY OF GWANGI (See Movie Classics)

VALOR
Mar-Apr, 1955 - No. 5, Nov-Dec, 1955
E. C. Comics

1-Williamson/Torres-a; Wood c/a	15.00	45.00	105.00
2-Williamson c/a; Wood-a	13.00	40.00	90.00
3-Williamson, Crandall-a	9.25	28.00	65.00
4-Wood-c	9.25	28.00	65.00
5-Wood c/a; Williamson/Evans-a	8.00	24.00	55.00

NOTE: *Crandall* a-3, 4. *Ingels* a-1, 2, 4, 5. *Krigstein* a-1-5. *Orlando* a-3, 4; c-3. *Wood* a-1, 2, 5; c-1, 4, 5.

VALOR THUNDERSTAR AND HIS FIREFLIES
Dec, 1986 - No. 3?, 1987 (mini-series, $1.50, color)
Now Comics

1	.25	.75	1.50

VAMPIRELLA (Magazine)(See Warren Presents)
Sept, 1969 - No. 112, Feb, 1983; No. 113, Jan, 1988?
Warren Publishing Co.

1-Intro. Vampirella	8.50	25.50	60.00
2-Amazonia series begins, ends #12	2.65	8.00	18.00
3 (Low distribution)	10.00	30.00	70.00
4-7	2.00	6.00	14.00
8-Vampi begins by Tom Sutton as serious strip (early issues-gag line)	1.35	4.00	9.00
9-Smith-a	2.00	6.00	14.00
10-No Vampi story	1.35	4.00	9.00
11-15: 11-Origin, 1st app. Pendragon. 12-Vampi by Gonzales begins	1.20	3.50	8.00
16-18,20-25: 17-Tomb of the Gods begins, ends #22	.85	2.50	6.00
19 (1973 Annual)	1.20	3.50	8.00
26,28-36,38-40: 30-Intro. Pantha. 31-Origin Luana, the Beast Girl. 33-Pantha ends	.70	2.00	5.00
27 (1974 Annual)	1.00	3.00	7.00
37 (1975 Annual)	.85	2.50	6.00
41-45	.40	1.25	2.50
46-Origin	.50	1.50	3.00
47-50: 50-Spirit cameo	.30	.90	1.80
51-99: 93-Cassandra St. Knight begins, ends #103; new Pantha series begins, ends 108	.25	.75	1.50
100 (96pg. r-special)-Origin retold	.30	.90	1.80
101-113: 108-Torpedo series by Toth begins	.25	.75	1.50
Annual 1('72)-New origin Vampirella by Gonzales; reprints by Adams(#1), Wood(#9)	8.50	25.00	50.00
Special 1 ('77; large-square bound)	.85	2.50	5.00

NOTE: *Adams* a-1, 10p, 19p. *Alcala* a-90, 93i. *Bode'/Todd* c-3. *Bode'/Jones* c-4. *Boris* c-9. *Brunner* a-10. *Corben* a-30, 31, 33, 54. *Crandall* a-1, 19. *Frazetta* c-1, 5, 7, 11, 31. *Jones* a-5, 9, 12, 27, 32, 33, 34, 50i. *Nino* a-59i, 61i, 67, 76, 85, 90. *Ploog* a-14. *Smith* a-9. *Sutton* a-11. *Toth* a-90i, 108, 110. *Wood* a-9, 10, 12, 19, 27; c-9. *Wrightson* a-33, 63. All reprint issues-37, 74, 83, 87, 91, 105, 107, 109, 111. Annuals from 1973 on are included in regular numbering. Later annuals are same format as regular issues.

VAMPIRE TALES (Magazine)
Aug, 1973 - No. 11, June, 1975 (B&W) (75 cents)
Marvel Comics Group

1-Morbius, the Living Vampire begins by Pablo Marcos

	Good	Fine	N-Mint
	.35	1.00	2.00
2-Intro. Satana; Steranko-r	.25	.75	1.50
3-11: 3-Satana app. 5-Origin Morbius. 6-1st Lilith app. 8-1st Blade app.		.60	1.20
Annual 1(10/75)	.25	.75	1.50

NOTE: *Alcala* a-6, 8, 9i. *Boris* c-4, 6. *Chaykin* a-7. *Everett* a-1r. *Gulacy* a-7p. *Heath* a-9. *Infantino* a-3r. *Gil Kane* a-4, 5r.

VANGUARD ILLUSTRATED
Nov, 1983 - No. 11, Oct., 1984
Pacific Comics

1-Nudity scenes	.25	.75	1.50
2-4 (Baxter paper)	.25	.75	1.50
5,6,8-11	.25	.75	1.50
7-1st app. Mr. Monster	1.15	3.50	7.00

NOTE: *Evans* a-7. *Kaluta* a-5, 7p. *Perez* a-6; c-6. *Rude* a-3-5; c-4.

VANITY (See Pacific Presents)
Jun, 1984 - No. 2, Aug, 1984 ($1.50)
Pacific Comics

1,2-Origin	.25	.75	1.50

VARIETY COMICS
1944 - 1945; 1946
Rural Home Publications/Croyden Publ. Co.

1-Origin Captain Valiant	7.00	21.00	50.00
2-Captain Valiant	4.00	12.00	28.00
3(1946-Croyden)-Captain Valiant	3.50	10.50	24.00
4,5	2.65	8.00	18.00

VARIETY COMICS (See Fox Giants)

VARSITY
1945
Parents' Magazine Institute

1	2.35	7.00	16.00

VAUDEVILLE AND OTHER THINGS
1900 (10½"x13") (in color) (18+ pgs.)
Isaac H. Blandiard Co.

By Bunny	19.00	57.00	132.00

VAULT OF EVIL
Feb, 1973 - No. 23, Nov, 1975
Marvel Comics Group

1 (Reprints begin)		.35	.70
2-23: 3,4-Brunner-c		.25	.50

NOTE: *Ditko* a-14r, 15r, 20-22r. *Drucker* a-10r(Mystic #52), 13r(Uncanny Tales #42). *Everett* a-11r(Menace #2), 13r(Menace #4); c-10. *Heath* a-5r. *Krigstein* a-20r(Uncanny Tales #54). *Tuska* a-6r.

VAULT OF HORROR (War Against Crime #1-11)
No. 12, Apr-May, 1950 - No. 40, Dec-Jan, 1954-55
E. C. Comics

12	107.00	320.00	750.00
13-Morphine story	50.00	150.00	350.00
14	43.00	130.00	300.00
15	36.00	108.00	250.00
16	28.00	84.00	195.00
17-19	21.00	62.00	146.00
20-22,24,25	16.00	48.00	110.00
23-Used in POP, pg. 84	16.50	50.00	115.00
26-B&W & color illos in POP	16.50	50.00	115.00
27-35	12.00	36.00	84.00
36-"Pipe Dream"-classic opium addict story by Krigstein; 'Twin Bill' cited in articles by T.E. Murphy & Wertham	12.00	36.00	84.00
37-Williamson-a	12.00	36.00	84.00
38-39: 39-Bondage-c	10.00	30.00	70.00

VAULT OF HORROR (continued)

	Good	Fine	N-Mint
40-Low distribution	11.00	32.00	76.00

NOTE: *Craig art in all but No. 13 & 33; c-12-40. Crandall a-33, 34, 39. Davis a-17-38. Evans a-27, 28, 30, 32, 33. Feldstein a-12-16. Ingels a-13-20, 22-40. Kamen a-15-22, 25, 29, 35. Krigstein a-36, 38-40. Kurtzman a-12, 13. Orlando a-24, 31, 40. Wood a-12-14.*

V. . .-COMICS (Morse code for "V" - 3 dots, 1 dash)
Jan, 1942 - No. 2, Mar-Apr, 1942
Fox Features Syndicate

1-Origin V-Man & the Boys; The Banshee & The Black Fury, The Queen of Evil, & V-Agents begin	50.00	150.00	350.00
2-Bondage/torture-c	40.00	120.00	280.00

VECTOR
1986 - No. 3, Nov, 1986 ($1.50, color)
Now Comics

1-3-Computer-generated art		.70	1.40

VENGEANCE SQUAD
July, 1975 - No. 6, May, 1976
Charlton Comics

1-Mike Mauser, Private eye begins by Staton		.40	.80
2-6: Morisi-a in all		.25	.50
5,6(Modern Comics-r, 1977)		.15	.30

VENTURE
Aug, 1986 - No. 2, 1986? ($1.75, color)
AC Comics (Americomics)

1,2	.35	1.00	2.00

VENUS (See Marvel Spotlight #2 & Weird Wonder Tales)
August, 1948 - No. 19, April, 1952
Marvel/Atlas Comics (CMC 1-9/LCC 10-19)

1-Venus & Hedy Devine begin; Kurtzman's "Hey Look"	40.00	120.00	280.00
2	23.00	70.00	160.00
3,5	20.00	60.00	140.00
4-Kurtzman's "Hey Look"	21.00	62.00	146.00
6-9: 6-Loki app. 7,8-Painted-c	19.00	57.00	132.00
10-S/F-horror ish. begin (7/50)	20.00	60.00	140.00
11-S/F end of the world(11/50)	24.00	72.00	168.00
12	18.00	54.00	125.00
13-19-Venus by Everett, 2-3 stories each; covers-#13,15-19	25.00	75.00	175.00

NOTE: *#3-5-content changes to teen-age. Bondage c-17. Colan a-12.*

VERI BEST SURE FIRE COMICS
No date (circa 1945) (Reprints Holyoke One-Shots)
Holyoke Publishing Co.

1-Captain Aero, Alias X, Miss Victory, Commandos of the Devil Dogs, Red Cross, Hammerhead Hawley, Capt. Aero's Sky Scouts, Flagman app.	12.00	36.00	84.00

VERI BEST SURE SHOT COMICS
No date (circa 1945) (Reprints Holyoke One-Shots)
Holyoke Publishing Co.

1-Capt. Aero, Miss Victory by Quinlan, Alias X, The Red Cross, Flagman, Commandos of the Devil Dogs, Hammerhead Hawley, Capt. Aero's Sky Scouts	12.00	36.00	84.00

VERY BEST OF DENNIS THE MENACE, THE
July, 1979 - No. 2, Apr, 1980 (132 pgs., Digest, 95 cents, $1.00)
Fawcett Publications

1,2-Reprints		.50	1.00

VERY BEST OF DENNIS THE MENACE, THE
April, 1982 - No. 3, Aug, 1982 (Digest Size) ($1.25)
Marvel Comics Group

1-3-Reprints		.65	1.25

NOTE: *Hank Ketcham c-all. A few thousand of #1 & 2 were printed with a DC emblem.*

V FOR VENDETTA
Sept., 1988 - No. 10, 1989 ($2.00, color, maxi-series, mature readers)
DC Comics

	Good	Fine	N-Mint
1-Alan Moore scripts in all	.75	2.25	4.50
2-5	.50	1.50	3.00
6-10	.40	1.25	2.50

VIC AND BLOOD
Oct., 1987 - No. 2, 1988 ($2.00, B&W)
Mad Dog Graphics

1,2-Harlan Ellison adapt., Corben-a	.35	1.00	2.00

VIC BRIDGES FAZERS SKETCHBOOK AND FACT FILE
Nov., 1986 ($1.75, color)
AC Comics

1	.30	.90	1.80

VIC FLINT (Crime Buster. . .)(See Authentic Police Cases)
August, 1948 - No.5, April, 1949 (Newspaper reprints; NEA Service)
St. John Publishing Co.

1	5.00	15.00	35.00
2	3.00	9.00	21.00
3-5	2.30	7.00	16.00

VIC FLINT
Feb, 1956 - No. 2, May, 1956 (Newspaper reprints)
Argo Publ.

1,2	2.65	8.00	18.00

VIC JORDAN
April, 1945
Civil Service Publ.

1-1944 daily newspaper-r	5.00	15.00	35.00

VICKI (Humor)
Feb, 1975 - No. 4, July, 1975 (No. 1,2: 68 pgs.)
Atlas/Seaboard Publ.

1-Reprints Tippy Teen	.50	1.50	3.00
2-4	.30	.80	1.60

VICKI VALENTINE (. . .SUMMER SPECIAL #1)
July, 1985 - No. 4, July, 1986 ($1.70 cover; B&W)
Renegade Press

1-4: Woggon, Rausch-a; all have paper dolls. 2-Christmas issue			
	.30	.85	1.70

VICKS COMICS (Also see Pure Oil Comics, Salerno Carnival of Comics, & 24 Pages of Comics)
nd (circa 1938) (68 pgs. in color) (Giveaway)
Eastern Color Printing Co. (Vicks Chemical Co.)

nn-Famous Funnies-r (before #40). Contains 5 pgs. Buck Rogers (4 pgs. from F.F. #15, & 1 pg. from #16) Joe Palooka, Napoleon, etc. app.	55.00	165.00	385.00
nn-16 loose, untrimmed page giveaway; paper-c; r/Famous Funnies #14; Buck Rogers, Joe Palooka app.	20.00	60.00	140.00

VICKY
Oct., 1948 - No. 5, June, 1949
Ace Magazine

nn(10/48)	2.65	8.00	18.00
4(12/48), nn(2/49), 4(4/49), 5(6/49)	2.00	6.00	14.00

VIC TORRY & HIS FLYING SAUCER (See Mr. Monster's Hi-Voltage Super Science)
1950 (One Shot)
Fawcett Publications

Book-length saucer story by Powell; photo/painted-c	25.00	75.00	175.00

Venus #11, © MEG

V For Vendetta #1, © DC

Vic Torry & His Flying Saucer, © FAW

Victory Comics #3, © HILL

Vietnam Journal #1 (1st print), © Apple Comics

Voodoo #2, © AJAX

VICTORY COMICS
Aug, 1941 - No. 4, Dec, 1941
Hillman Periodicals

	Good	Fine	N-Mint
1-The Conqueror by Bill Everett, The Crusader, & Bomber Burns begin; Conqueror's origin in text; Everett-c; #1 by Funnies, Inc.	82.00	245.00	575.00
2-Everett-c/a	45.00	135.00	315.00
3,4	32.00	95.00	225.00

VIC VERITY MAGAZINE
1945 - No. 7, Sept, 1946 (A comic book)
Vic Verity Publications

1-C. C. Beck-c/a	5.70	17.00	40.00
2	4.00	12.00	28.00
3-7: 6-Beck-a. 7-Beck-c	3.50	10.50	24.00

VIDEO JACK
Nov, 1987 - No. 6, Nov, 1988 ($1.25, color)
Epic Comics (Marvel)

1-6: 6-N. Adams, Wrightson, others-a	.65	1.30

VIETNAM JOURNAL
Nov., 1987 - Present ($1.75/$1.95, B&W)
Apple Comics

1-Don Lomax-c/a/scripts	.60	1.75	3.50
1-2nd print	.35	1.00	1.95
2	.40	1.25	2.50
3-8	.35	1.00	1.95

VIGILANTE, THE (Also see Action Comics #42)
Oct, 1983 - No. 50, Feb, 1988 ($1.25; Baxter paper)
DC Comics

1-Origin	.90	2.75	5.50
2	.60	1.75	3.50
3-10: 3-Cyborg app. 6,7-Origin	.40	1.25	2.50
11-50: 20,21-Nightwing app. 35-Origin Mad Bomber			
	.30	.90	1.75
Annual 1 (10/85)	.40	1.25	2.50
Annual 2 (11/86)	.35	1.10	2.25

NOTE: *Newton a-4p. Steacy c-50.*

VIGILANTES, THE (See 4-Color #839)

VIKINGS, THE (See 4-Color #910)

VILLAINS AND VIGILANTES
Dec, 1986 - No. 4, 1987 (mini-series, $1.50, color)
Eclipse Comics

1-4	.30	.90	1.75

VIRGINIAN, THE (TV)
June, 1963
Gold Key

1(10060-306)-Part photo-c	2.00	6.00	14.00

VISION AND THE SCARLET WITCH, THE (See Marvel Fanfare)
Nov, 1982 - No. 4, Feb, 1983 (mini-series)
Marvel Comics Group

1	.30	.90	1.75
2-4: 2-Nuklo & Future Man app.		.60	1.25

VISION AND THE SCARLET WITCH, THE (See The Avengers #150)
Oct, 1985 - No. 12, Sept, 1986 (maxi-series)
Marvel Comics Group

1 (V2/1)-Origin; 1st app. in Avengers #57	.30	.90	1.75
2-5: 2-West Coast Avengers x-over	.25	.75	1.50
6-12		.60	1.25

VISIONARIES
Nov, 1987 - No. 6, Sept, 1988
Star Comics/Marvel #3 on

	Good	Fine	N-Mint
1	.25	.75	1.50
2-6		.50	1.00

VISIONS
1979 - No. 5, 1983 (B&W, fanzine)
Vision Publications

1-Flaming Carrot begins	20.00	60.00	120.00
2	5.85	17.50	35.00
3	2.50	7.50	15.00
4-Flaming Carrot-c & info.	3.35	10.00	20.00
5-Flaming Carrot app. (1 pg.)	1.70	5.00	10.00

NOTE: *After #4, Visions became an annual publication of The Atlanta Fantasy Fair.*

VOID INDIGO (Also see Marvel Graphic Novel)
Nov, 1984 - No. 2, Mar, 1985 ($1.50, Baxter paper)
Epic Comics (Marvel)

1-Continues from Graphic Novel	.35	1.00	2.00
2-Sex, violence shown	.35	1.00	2.00

VOODA (Jungle Princess) (Formerly Voodoo)
No. 20, April, 1955 - No. 22, Aug, 1955
Ajax-Farrell (Four Star Publications)

20-Baker c/a	8.00	24.00	56.00
21,22-Baker-a plus Kamen/Baker story, Kimbo Boy of Jungle, & Baker-c (p) in all	7.00	21.00	50.00

NOTE: *#20-Baker r-r/Seven Seas #4.*

VOODOO (Vooda #20 on)
May, 1952 - No. 19, Jan-Feb, 1955
Ajax-Farrell (Four Star Publ.)

1-South Sea Girl-r by Baker	15.00	45.00	105.00
2-Rulah story-r plus South Sea Girl from Seven Seas #2 by Baker (name changed from Alani to El'nee)	12.00	36.00	84.00
3-Bakerish-a; man stabbed in face	9.50	28.50	65.00
4,8-Baker-r. 8-Severed head panels	9.50	28.50	65.00
5-7,9,10: 5-Nazi flaying alive. 6-Severed head panels			
	7.50	22.50	52.00
11-14,16-18: 14-Zombies take over America. 17-Electric chair panels	6.00	18.00	42.00
15-Opium drug story-r/Ellery Queen #3	7.00	21.00	50.00
19-Bondage-c; Baker-a(2)(r)	10.00	30.00	70.00
Annual 1(1952)(25 cents); Baker-a	26.00	78.00	180.00

VOODOO (See Tales of . . .)

VORTEX
Nov., 1982 - Present ($1.50, B&W)
Vortex Publs.

1-Peter Hsu-a, nudity	4.00	12.00	28.00
2-1st app. Mister X (on-c only)	1.35	4.00	8.00
3	1.00	3.00	6.00
4-8	.50	1.50	3.00
9-15	.35	1.00	2.00

VOYAGE TO THE BOTTOM OF THE SEA (TV)
No. 1230, 9-11/61 - No. 16, 4/70 (Painted covers)
Dell Publishing Co./Gold Key

4-Color 1230(Movie-1961)	3.50	10.50	24.00
10133-412(G.K.-12/64)	2.30	7.00	16.00
2(7/65) - 5: Photo back-c, 1-5	1.50	4.50	10.00
6-14	1.00	3.00	7.00
15,16-Reprints	.45	1.35	3.00

VOYAGE TO THE DEEP
Sept-Nov, 1962 - No. 4, Nov-Jan, 1964 (Painted-c)
Dell Publishing Co.

1	1.50	4.50	10.00
2-4	1.00	3.00	7.00

WACKY ADVENTURES OF CRACKY (Also see Gold Key Spotlight)
Dec, 1972 - No. 12, Sept, 1975
Gold Key

	Good	Fine	N-Mint
1	.70	2.00	4.00
2	.35	1.00	2.00
3-12		.50	1.00

(See March of Comics #405,424,436,448)

WACKY DUCK (Formerly Dopey Duck?; Justice #7 on)
No. 3, Fall, 1946 - No. 6, Summer, 1947; 8/48 - No. 2, 10/48
Marvel Comics (NPP)

	Good	Fine	N-Mint
3	5.50	16.50	38.00
4-Infinity-c	7.00	21.00	50.00
5,6('46-47)	4.65	14.00	32.00
1,2(1948)	3.50	10.50	24.00
I.W. Reprint #1,2,7('58)	.30	.90	1.80
Super Reprint #10(I.W. on-c, Super-inside)	.30	.90	1.80

WACKY QUACKY (See Wisco)

WACKY RACES (TV)
Aug, 1969 - No. 7, Apr, 1972 (Hanna-Barbera)
Gold Key

	Good	Fine	N-Mint
1	1.50	4.50	10.00
2-7	.85	2.50	6.00

WACKY SQUIRREL
Oct., 1987 - Present ($1.75, B&W)
Dark Horse Comics

	Good	Fine	N-Mint
1-4	.30	.90	1.75
Halloween Adventure Special	.30	.90	1.75
Summer Fun Special	.35	1.00	2.00

WACKY WITCH (Also see Gold Key Spotlight)
March, 1971 - No. 21, Dec, 1975
Gold Key

	Good	Fine	N-Mint
1	1.00	3.00	6.00
2	.60	1.75	3.50
3-21	.35	1.00	2.00

(See March of Comics #374,398,410,422,434,446,458,470,482)

WACKY WOODPECKER (See Two Bit . . .)
1958; 1963
I. W. Enterprises/Super Comics

	Good	Fine	N-Mint
I.W. Reprint #1,2,7(nd-r-/Two Bit . . .)	.30	.90	1.80
Super Reprint #10('63)	.30	.90	1.80

WAGON TRAIN (1st Series) (TV) (See Western Roundup)
No. 895, Mar, 1958 - No. 13, Apr-June, 1962 (All photo-c)
Dell Publishing Co.

	Good	Fine	N-Mint
4-Color 895 (#1)	5.00	15.00	35.00
4-Color 971,1019	3.50	10.50	24.00
4(1-3/60),6-13	3.00	9.00	21.00
5-Toth-a	3.50	10.50	24.00

WAGON TRAIN (2nd Series)(TV)
Jan, 1964 - No. 4, Oct, 1964 (All photo-c)
Gold Key

	Good	Fine	N-Mint
1	3.00	9.00	21.00
2-4: 3,4-Tufts-a	2.00	6.00	14.00

WAITING ROOM WILLIE (See Sad Case of . . .)

WALLY (Teen-age)
Dec, 1962 - No. 4, Sept, 1963
Gold Key

	Good	Fine	N-Mint
1	1.15	3.50	8.00
2-4	.75	2.25	5.00

WALLY THE WIZARD
Apr, 1985 - No. 12, Mar, 1986 (Children's comic)

Star Comics (Marvel)

	Good	Fine	N-Mint
1-12: Bob Bolling-c/a		.35	.70

WALLY WOOD'S T.H.U.N.D.E.R. AGENTS (See Thunder Agents)
Nov, 1984 - No. 5?, 1986? (52 pgs.; $2.00)
Deluxe Comics

	Good	Fine	N-Mint
1,2	.40	1.25	2.50
3-5	.35	1.00	2.00

NOTE: *Giffen* a-1p, 2p. *Perez* a-1p, 2.

WALT DISNEY CHRISTMAS PARADE (Also see Christmas Parade)
Winter, 1977 (224 pgs.) (cardboard covers, $1.95)
Whitman Publishing Co. (Golden Press)

	Good	Fine	N-Mint
11191-Barks-a r-/Christmas in Disneyland #1, Dell Christmas Parade #9, Dell Giant #53	.40	1.20	2.40

WALT DISNEY COMICS DIGEST
June, 1968 - No. 57, Feb, 1976 (50 cents) (Digest size)
Gold Key

	Good	Fine	N-Mint
1-Reprints Uncle Scrooge #5; 192 pgs.	3.00	9.00	21.00
2-4-Barks-r	1.70	5.00	12.00
5-Daisy Duck by Barks (8 pgs.); last published story by Barks (art only) plus 21 pg. Scrooge-r by Barks	2.00	6.00	14.00
6-13-All Barks-r	1.00	3.00	6.00
14,15	.70	2.00	4.00
16-Reprints Donald Duck #26 by Barks	1.35	4.00	8.00
17-20-Barks-r	.80	2.40	4.80
21-31,33,35-37-Barks-r; 24-Toth Zorro	.70	2.00	4.00
32	.50	1.50	3.00
34-Reprints 4-Color 318	1.35	4.00	8.00
38-Reprints Christmas in Disneyland #1	1.00	3.00	6.00
39-Two Barks-r/WDC&S #272, 4-Color 1073 plus Toth Zorro-r	.80	2.40	4.80
40-Mickey Mouse-r by Gottfredson	.50	1.50	3.00
41,45,47-49	.30	.90	1.80
42,43-Barks-r	.50	1.50	3.00
44-(Has Gold Key emblem, 50 cents)-Reprints 1st story of 4-Color 29,256,275,282	2.00	6.00	14.00
44-Republished in 1976 by Whitman; not identical to original; a bit smaller, blank back-c, 69 cent-c	1.00	3.00	6.00
46,50-Barks-r	.50	1.50	3.00
51-Reprints 4-Color 71	.80	2.40	4.80
52-Barks-r/WDC&S #161,132	.50	1.50	3.00
53-Reprint/Dell Giant #30	.30	.80	1.60
54-Reprint/Donald Duck Beach Party #2	.30	.80	1.60
55-Reprint/Dell Giant #49	.30	.80	1.60
56-Reprint/Uncle Scrooge #32 (Barks) plus another Barks story	.50	1.50	3.00
57-Reprint/Mickey Mouse Almanac('57) & two Barks stories	.50	1.50	3.00

NOTE: #1-10, 196 pgs.; #11-41, 164 pgs.; #42 on, 132 pgs. Old issues were being reprinted & distributed by Whitman in 1976.

WALT DISNEY PRESENTS (TV)
No. 997, June-Aug, 1959 - No. 6, Dec-Feb, 1960-61 (All photo-c)
Dell Publishing Co.

	Good	Fine	N-Mint
4-Color 997	3.00	9.00	21.00
2(12-2/60)-The Swamp Fox(origin), Elfego Baca, Texas John Slaughter (Disney TV Show) begin	2.00	6.00	14.00
3-6	2.00	6.00	14.00

WALT DISNEY'S COMICS AND STORIES (Cont. of Mickey Mouse Magazine) (#1-30 contain Donald Duck newspaper reprints) (Titled 'Comics And Stories' #264 on)
10/40 - No. 263, 8/62; No. 264, 10/62 - No. 510, 1984; No. 511, 10/86 - Present
Dell Publishing Co./Gold Key No. 264-473/Whitman No. 474-510/ Gladstone No. 511 on

Voyage To The Bottom Of The Sea #5, © 20th Century-Fox

Wagon Train #6 (1st series), © Revue Prod.

Walt Disney Presents #5, © WDC

Walt Disney's Comics And Stories #4 (Special), © WDC   Walt Disney's Comics And Stories #73, © WDC   Walt Disney's Comics And Stories #511, © WDC

WALT DISNEY'S COMICS AND STORIES (continued)
NOTE: The whole number can always be found at the bottom of the title page in the lower left-hand or right hand panel.

	Good	Fine	VF-NM
1(V1#1-c; V2#1-indicia)-Donald Duck strip-r by Al Taliaferro & Gottfredson's Mickey Mouse begin	350.00	1400.00	3500.00
(Prices vary widely on this book)			

	Good	Fine	N-Mint
2	220.00	660.00	1760.00
3	100.00	300.00	700.00
4-X-mas-c	75.00	225.00	525.00
4-Special promotional, complimentary issue; cover same except one corner was blanked out & boxed in to identify the giveaway (not a paste-over). This special pressing was probably sent out to former subscribers to Mickey Mouse Mag. whose subscriptions had expired. (Rare-five known copies)	115.00	345.00	800.00
5	60.00	180.00	420.00
6-10	47.00	140.00	330.00
11-14	40.00	120.00	280.00
15-17: 15-The 3 Little Kittens (17 pgs.). 16-The 3 Little Pigs (29 pgs.); X-mas-c. 17-The Ugly Duckling (4 pgs.)	34.00	100.00	240.00
18-21	28.00	84.00	195.00
22-30: 22-Flag-c	24.00	72.00	170.00
31-Donald Duck by Carl Barks begins; see Four Color #9 for first Barks D.D.	150.00	450.00	1050.00
32-Barks-a	90.00	270.00	630.00
33-Barks-a (infinity-c)	60.00	180.00	420.00
34-Gremlins by Walt Kelly begin, end #41; Barks-a	50.00	150.00	350.00
35,36-Barks-a	42.00	125.00	295.00
37-Donald Duck by Jack Hannah	20.00	60.00	140.00
38-40-Barks-a. 39-Christmas-c. 40-Gremlins by Kelly	29.00	86.00	200.00
41-50-Barks-a; 41-Gremlins by Kelly	24.00	72.00	168.00
51-60-Barks-a; 51-Christmas-c. 52-Li'l Bad Wolf begins, ends #203 (not in #55)	18.00	54.00	125.00
61-70: Barks-a. 61-Dumbo story. 63,64-Pinocchio stories. 63-c-swipe from New Funnies 94. 64-X-mas-c. 65-Pluto story. 66-Infinity-c.			
67,68-M. Mouse Sunday-r by Bill Wright	14.00	42.00	100.00
71-80: Barks-a. 75-77-Brer Rabbit stories, no Mickey Mouse. 76-X-Mas-c	11.00	32.00	75.00
81-87,89,90: Barks-a. 82-84-Bongo stories. 86-90-Goofy & Agnes app. 89-Chip 'n' Dale story	9.50	28.50	65.00
88-1st app. Gladstone Gander by Barks	11.50	34.00	80.00
91-97,99: Barks-a. 95-1st WDC&S Barks-c. 96-No Mickey Mouse; Little Toot begins, end #97. 99-X-Mas-c	7.50	22.50	52.00
98-1st Uncle Scrooge app. in WDC&S	14.00	42.00	100.00
100-Barks-a	8.50	25.50	60.00
101-106,108-110-Barks-a	6.50	19.50	45.00
107-Barks-a; Taliaferro-r. Donald acquires super powers	6.50	19.50	45.00
111,114,117-All Barks	5.00	15.00	35.00
112-Drug (ether) issue (Donald Duck)	5.50	16.50	38.00
113,115,116,118-123: Not by Barks. 116-Dumbo x-over. 121-Grandma Duck begins, ends #168; not in #135,142,146,155	2.15	6.50	15.00
124,126-130-All Barks. 124-X-Mas-c	4.35	13.00	30.00
125-Intro. & 1st app. Junior Woodchucks; Barks-a	6.50	19.50	45.00
131,133,135-139-All Barks	4.35	13.00	30.00
132-Barks-a(2) (D. Duck & Grandma Duck)	5.15	15.50	36.00
134-Intro. & 1st app. The Beagle Boys	8.00	24.00	56.00
140-1st app. Gyro Gearloose by Barks	8.00	24.00	56.00
141-150-All Barks. 143-Little Hiawatha begins, ends #151,159	2.65	8.00	18.00
151-170-All Barks	2.35	7.00	16.00

	Good	Fine	N-Mint
171-200-All Barks	2.00	6.00	14.00
201-240: All Barks. 204-Chip 'n' Dale & Scamp begin	1.70	5.00	12.00
241-283: Barks-a. 241-Dumbo x-over. 247-Gyro Gearloose begins, ends #274. 256-Ludwig Von Drake begins, ends #274	1.50	4.50	9.00
284,285,287,290,295,296,309-311-Not by Barks	.85	2.50	5.00
286,288,289,291-294,297,298,308-All Barks stories; 293-Grandma Duck's Farm Friends. 297-Gyro Gearloose. 298-Daisy Duck's Diary-r	1.35	4.00	8.00
299-307-All contain early Barks-r (#43-117). 305-Gyro Gearloose	1.50	4.50	9.00
312-Last Barks issue with original story	1.35	4.00	8.00
313-315,317-327,329-334,336-341	.70	2.00	4.00
316-Last issue published during life of Walt Disney	.70	2.00	4.00
328,335,342-350-Barks-r	.85	2.50	5.00
351-360-w/posters inside; Barks reprints (2 versions of each with & without posters)-without posters…	.75	2.25	4.50
351-360-With posters	1.15	3.50	8.00
361-400-Barks-r	.75	2.25	4.50
401-429-Barks-r	.50	1.50	3.00
430,433,437,438,441,444,445,466,506,509,510-No Barks		.35	.70
431,432,434-436,439,440,442,443-Barks-r	.25	.75	1.50
446-465,467-505,507,508-510: All Barks-r		.50	1.00
511-Wuzzles by Disney studio	.85	2.50	5.00
512	.50	1.50	3.00
513-520	.30	.90	1.80
521-540		.60	1.20

NOTE: (#1-38, 68 pgs.; #39-42, 60 pgs.; #43-57, 61-134, 163-168, 446, 447, 52 pgs.; #58-60, 135-142, 169-Present, 36 pgs.)

NOTE: **Barks** art in all issues #31 on, except where noted; c-95, 96, 104, 108, 109, 130-72, 174-78, 183, 198-200, 204, 206-09, 212-16, 218, 220, 226, 228-33, 235-38, 240-43, 247, 250, 253, 256, 260, 261, 276-83, 288-92, 295-98, 301, 303, 304, 306, 307, 309, 310, 313-16, 319, 321, 322, 324, 326, 328, 329, 331, 332, 334, 341, 342, 350, 351. Kelly covers(most)-34-94, 97-103, 105, 106, 110-123. Walt Disney's Comics & Stories featured Mickey Mouse serials which were in practically every issue from #1 through #394. The titles of the serials, along with the issues they are in, are listed in previous editions. Floyd Gottfredson Mickey Mouse serials in issues #1-61, 63-74, 77-92 plus ''Mickey Mouse in a Warplant'' (3 pgs.), and ''Pluto Catches a Nazi Spy'' (4 pgs.) in #62; ''Mystery Next Door,'' #93; ''Sunken Treasure,'' #94; ''Aunt Marissa,'' #95; ''Gangland,'' #98; ''Thanksgiving Dinner,'' #99; and ''The Talking Dog,'' #100. Mickey Mouse by Paul Murry #152 on except 155-57 (Dick Moore), 327-29 (Tony Strobl), 348-50 (Jack Manning). Don Rosa story-a-523, 524, 526, 528, 531. Al Taliaferro Silly Symphonies in #5-''Three Little Pigs;'' #13-''Birds of a Feather;'' #14-''The Boarding School Mystery;'' #15-''Cookieland'' and ''Three Little Kittens;'' #16-''Three Little Pigs;'' #17-''The Ugly Duckling'' and ''The Robber Kitten;'' #19-''Penguin Isle;'' and ''Bucky Bug'' in #20-23, 25, 26, 28 (one continuous story from 1932-34; first 2 pgs. not Taliaferro).

WALT DISNEY'S COMICS & STORIES
1943 (36 pgs.) (Dept. store Xmas giveaway)
Walt Disney Productions

	Good	Fine	N-Mint
nn	45.00	135.00	300.00

WALT DISNEY'S COMICS & STORIES
Mid 1940's ('45-48), 1952 (4 pgs. in color) (slick paper)
Dell Publishing Co.(Special Xmas offer)

1940's version - subscription form for WDC&S - (Reprints two different WDC&S covers with subscription forms printed on inside covers)	8.50	25.50	60.00
1952 version	5.00	15.00	35.00

WALT DISNEY'S COMICS DIGEST
1986 - No. 8, 1987
Gladstone Publishing

1-8		.60	1.25

WALT DISNEY SHOWCASE
Oct, 1970 - No. 54, Jan, 1980 (No. 44-48, 49-54, 52pp)
Gold Key

WALT DISNEY SHOWCASE (continued)	Good	Fine	N-Mint
1-Boatniks (Movie)-Photo-c	1.00	3.00	6.00
2-Moby Duck	.50	1.50	3.00
3-Bongo & Lumpjaw-r	.35	1.00	2.00
4-Pluto-r	.35	1.00	2.00
5-$1,000,000 Duck (Movie)-Photo-c	.70	2.00	4.00
6-Bedknobs & Broomsticks (Movie)	.70	2.00	4.00
7-Pluto-r	.35	1.00	2.00
8-Daisy & Donald	.35	1.00	2.00
9-101 Dalmatians (cartoon feature); r-4-Color 1183			
	.50	1.50	3.00
10-Napoleon & Samantha (Movie)-Photo-c	.70	2.00	4.00
11-Moby Duck-r	.25	.75	1.50
12-Dumbo-r/4-Color 668	.35	1.00	2.00
13-Pluto-r	.30	.90	1.80
14-World's Greatest Athlete (Movie)-Photo-c	.70	2.00	4.00
15-3 Little Pigs-r	.25	.75	1.50
16-Aristocats (cartoon feature); r-Aristocats #1	.70	2.00	4.00
17-Mary Poppins; r-M.P. #10136-501-Photo-c	.70	2.00	4.00
18-Gyro Gearloose; Barks-r/4-Color #1047,1184	.70	2.00	4.00
19-That Darn Cat; r-T.D.C. #10171-602-Haley Mills photo-c			
	.50	1.50	3.00
20-Pluto-r	.25	.75	1.50
21-Li'l Bad Wolf & The Three Little Pigs	.30	.90	1.80
22-Unbirthday Party with Alice in Wonderland; r-4-Color #341			
	.50	1.50	3.00
23-Pluto-r	.25	.75	1.50
24-Herbie Rides Again (Movie); sequel to "The Love Bug"-Photo-c			
	.35	1.00	2.00
25-Old Yeller (Movie); r-4-Color #869-Photo-c	.35	1.00	2.00
26-Lt. Robin Crusoe USN (Movie); r-Lt. Robin Crusoe USN			
#10191-601-Photo-c	.35	1.00	2.00
27-Island at the Top of the World (Movie)-Photo-c			
	.40	1.25	2.50
28-Brer Rabbit, Bucky Bug-r/WDC&S 58	.25	.75	1.50
29-Escape to Witch Mountain (Movie)-Photo-c	.50	1.50	3.00
30-Magica De Spell; Barks-r/Uncle Scrooge #36 & WDC&S #258			
	1.00	3.00	6.00
31-Bambi (cartoon feature); r-4-Color #186	.50	1.50	3.00
32-Spin & Marty-r/F.C. 1026; Mickey Mouse Club (TV)-Photo-c			
	.70	2.00	4.00
33-Pluto-r/F.C. 1143	.25	.75	1.50
34-Paul Revere's Ride with Johnny Tremain (TV); 4-Color #822-r			
	.25	.75	1.50
35-Goofy-r/F.C. 952	.25	.75	1.50
36-Peter Pan-r/F.C. 442	.25	.75	1.50
37-Tinker Bell & Jiminy Cricket-r/FC 982,989	.25	.75	1.50
38-Mickey & the Sleuth, Part 1	.25	.75	1.50
39-Mickey & the Sleuth, Part 2	.25	.75	1.50
40-The Rescuers (cartoon feature)	.40	.90	1.80
41-Herbie Goes to Monte Carlo (Movie); sequel to "Herbie Rides			
Again"-Photo-c	.35	1.00	2.00
42-Mickey & the Sleuth	.25	.75	1.50
43-Pete's Dragon (Movie)-Photo-c	.50	1.50	3.00
44-Return From Witch Mountain (new) & In Search of the Castaways			
-r(Movies)-Photo-c; 68 pg. giants begin	.50	1.50	3.00
45-The Jungle Book (Movie); r-#30033-803	.50	1.50	3.00
46-The Cat From Outer Space (Movie)(new), & The Shaggy Dog			
(Movie)-r/F.C. 985-Photo-c	.50	1.50	3.00
47-Mickey Mouse Surprise Party-r	.50	1.50	3.00
48-The Wonderful Advs. of Pinocchio-r/F.C. 1203; last 68 pg.			
issue	.50	1.50	3.00
49-North Avenue Irregulars (Movie); Zorro-r/Zorro 11; 52 pgs.			
begin; photo-c	.25	.75	1.50
50-Bedknobs & Broomsticks-r/#6; Mooncussers-r/World of Adv.			
#1-Photo-c	.25	.75	1.50
51-101 Dalmatians-r	.25	.75	1.50

	Good	Fine	N-Mint
52-Unidentified Flying Oddball (Movie); r-/Picnic Party 8-Photo-c			
	.25	.75	1.50
53-The Scarecrow-r (TV)	.25	.75	1.50
54-The Black Hole (Movie)-Photo-c	.25	.75	1.50

WALT DISNEY'S MAGAZINE (TV)(Formerly Walt Disney's Mickey Mouse Club Magazine) (50 cents) (Bi-monthly)
V2No.4, June, 1957 - V4No.6, Oct, 1959
Western Publishing Co.

	Good	Fine	N-Mint
V2#4-Stories & articles on the Mouseketeers, Zorro, & Goofy and			
other Disney characters & people	3.50	10.50	24.00
V2#5, V2#6(10/57)	3.50	10.50	24.00
V3#1(12/57), V3#3-6(10/58)	2.00	6.00	14.00
V3#2-Annette photo-c	4.65	14.00	32.00
V4#1(12/58) - V4#2-4,6(10/59)	2.00	6.00	14.00
V4#5-Annette photo-c	3.50	10.50	24.00

NOTE: V2#4-V3#6 were 11½x8½", 48 pgs.; V4#1 on were 10x8", 52 pgs. (Peak circulation of 400,000).

WALT DISNEY'S MERRY CHRISTMAS (See Dell Giant #39)

WALT DISNEY'S MICKEY MOUSE CLUB MAGAZINE (TV)(Becomes Walt Disney's Magazine) (Quarterly)
Winter, 1956 - V2#3, April, 1957 (11½x8½") (48 pgs.)
Western Publishing Co.

	Good	Fine	N-Mint
V1#1	10.00	30.00	70.00
2-4	5.00	15.00	35.00
V2#1-3	4.00	12.00	28.00
Annual(1956)-Two different issues; ($1.50-Whitman); 120 pgs., card-			
board covers, 11¾x8¾"; reprints	10.00	30.00	70.00
Annual(1957)-Same as above	7.00	21.00	50.00

WALT DISNEY'S WHEATIES PREMIUMS (See Wheaties)

WALTER LANTZ ANDY PANDA (Also see Andy Panda)
Aug, 1973 - No. 23, Jan, 1978 (Walter Lantz)
Gold Key

1-Reprints	.35	1.00	2.00
2-10-All reprints		.40	.80
11-23: 15,17-19,22-Reprints		.15	.30

WALT KELLY'S...
Dce, 1987 - Present ($1.75-$2.50, color, Baxter)
Eclipse Comics

...Christmas Classics 1 ('87, $1.75)-Kelly-r/Peter Wheat & Santa			
Claus Funnies	.30	.90	1.75
...Springtime Tales 1 (4/88, $2.50)	.40	1.25	2.50

WALT SCOTT'S CHRISTMAS STORIES (See 4-Color #959,1062)

WAMBI, JUNGLE BOY (See Jungle Comics)
Spring, 1942 - No. 3, Spring, 1943; No. 4, Fall, 1948 - No. 18, Winter, 1952-53 (#1-3, 68 pgs.)
Fiction House Magazines

	Good	Fine	N-Mint
1-Wambi, the Jungle Boy begins	27.00	81.00	190.00
2 (1942)-Kiefer-c	14.00	42.00	100.00
3 (1943)-Kiefer c/a	11.00	32.00	75.00
4 (1948)-Origin in text	6.50	19.50	45.00
5 (Fall, '49, 36pgs.)-Kiefer c/a	5.50	16.50	38.00
6-10: 7-52 pgs.	4.65	14.00	32.00
11-18	3.50	10.50	24.00
I.W. Reprint #8('64)-R-/#12 with new-c	1.00	3.00	6.00

WANDERERS (See Adventure Comics 375, 376)
June, 1988 - Present ($1.25, color)
DC Comics

1-9: 1-Steacy-c; 3-LSH app.		.65	1.30

WANTED COMICS
No. 9, Sept-Oct, 1947 - No. 53, April, 1953 (#9-33, 52 pgs.)
Toytown Publications/Patches/Orbit Publ.

Walt Kelly's Christmas Classics #1, © Eclipse Comics

Wambi, Jungle Boy #3, © FH

Wanderers #1, © DC

Wanted Comics #31, © Orbit Publ.   War Against Crime! #1, © WMG   War Comics #1 (12/50), © MEG

WANTED COMICS (continued)	Good	Fine	N-Mint
9	5.00	15.00	35.00
10,11: 10-Giunta-a; radio's Mr. D. A. app.	3.00	9.00	21.00
12-Used in **SOTI**, pg. 277	6.00	18.00	42.00
13-Heroin drug propaganda story	4.65	14.00	32.00
14-Marijuana drug mention story, 2 pgs.	2.65	8.00	18.00
15-17,19,20	2.00	6.00	14.00
18-Marijuana story, 'Satan's Cigarettes'; r-in #45 & retitled	10.00	30.00	70.00
21-Krigstein-a	2.65	8.00	18.00
22-Extreme violence	3.00	9.00	21.00
23,25-34,36-38,40-44,46-48,53	1.15	3.50	8.00
24-Krigstein-a; 'The Dope King,' marijuana mention story	4.65	14.00	32.00
35-Used in **SOTI**, pg. 160	4.65	14.00	32.00
39-Drug propaganda story "The Horror Weed"	5.50	16.50	38.00
45-Marijuana story from #18	5.50	16.50	38.00
49-Has unstable pink-c that fades easily; rare in mint condition	1.85	5.00	11.50
50-Surrealist-c; horror stys	5.00	15.00	35.00
51-"Holiday of Horror"-junkie story; drug-c	5.00	15.00	35.00
52-Classic "Cult of Killers" opium use story	5.00	15.00	35.00

NOTE: *Buscema c-50. Lawrence and Leav c/a most issues. Syd Shores c/a-48.*

WANTED: DEAD OR ALIVE (See 4-Color #1102,1164)

WANTED, THE WORLD'S MOST DANGEROUS VILLAINS
July-Aug, 1972 - No. 9, Aug-Sept, 1973 (All reprints)
National Periodical Publications (See DC Special)

	Good	Fine	N-Mint
1-Batman, Green Lantern, & Green Arrow		.60	1.20
2-4: 2-Batman & The Flash. 3-Dr. Fate, Hawkman, & Vigilante. 4-Green Lantern & Kid Eternity		.40	.80
5-9: 5-Dollman/Green Lantern. 6-Starman/Wildcat/Sargon. 7-Johnny Quick/Hawkman/Hourman. 8-Dr. Fate/Flash. 9-S&K Sandman/Superman		.30	.60

NOTE: *Kubert a-3i; 6, 7.*

WAR
7/75 - No. 9, 11/76; No. 10, 9/78 - No. 49?, 1984
Charlton Comics

		Fine	N-Mint
1		.15	.30
2-49: 47-r		.15	.30
7,9(Modern Comics-r, 1977)		.15	.30

WAR ACTION
April, 1952 - No. 14, June, 1953
Atlas Comics (CPS)

	Good	Fine	N-Mint
1	4.00	12.00	28.00
2	1.70	5.00	12.00
3-6,8-10,14	1.35	4.00	9.00
7-Pakula-a	1.35	4.00	9.00
11-13-Krigstein-a	2.75	8.00	18.00

NOTE: *Heath a-1; c-7, 14. Keller a-6. Maneely a-1.*

WAR ADVENTURES
Jan, 1952 - No. 13, Feb, 1953
Atlas Comics (HPC)

	Good	Fine	N-Mint
1-Tuska-a	3.50	10.50	24.00
2	1.50	4.50	10.00
3-7,9-13	1.35	4.00	9.00
8-Krigstein-a	2.75	8.00	18.00

NOTE: *Heath a-5; c-4, 5, 13. Pakula a-3. Robinson a-3; c-10.*

WAR ADVENTURES ON THE BATTLEFIELD (See Battlefield)

WAR AGAINST CRIME! (Vault of Horror #12 on)
Spring, 1948 - No. 11, Feb-Mar, 1950
E. C. Comics

	Good	Fine	N-Mint
1	37.00	110.00	260.00

	Good	Fine	N-Mint
2,3	21.00	62.00	146.00
4-9: 9-Morphine drug use story	20.00	60.00	140.00
10-1st Vault Keeper app.	53.00	160.00	370.00
11-2nd Vault Keeper app.	46.00	138.00	320.00

NOTE: *All have Craig covers. Feldstein a-4, 7-9. Ingels a-1, 2, 8.*

WAR AND ATTACK (Also see Special War Series #3)
Fall, 1964 - V2No.63, Dec, 1967
Charlton Comics

	Good	Fine	N-Mint
1-Wood-a	.85	2.50	5.00
V2#54(6/66)-#63 (Formerly Fightin' Air Force)		.50	1.00

NOTE: *Montes/Bache a-55, 56, 60, 63.*

WAR AT SEA (Formerly Space Adventures)
No. 22, Nov, 1957 - No. 42, June, 1961
Charlton Comics

	Good	Fine	N-Mint
22	1.00	3.00	7.00
23-30	.50	1.50	3.50
31-42	.35	1.00	2.00

WAR BATTLES
Feb, 1952 - No. 9, Dec, 1953
Harvey Publications

	Good	Fine	N-Mint
1	2.75	8.00	18.00
2	1.50	4.50	10.00
3-5,7-9	1.35	4.00	9.00
6-Nostrand-a	2.35	7.00	16.00

NOTE: *Powell a-1-3, 7.*

WAR BIRDS
1952
Fiction House Magazines

	Good	Fine	N-Mint
1	5.00	15.00	35.00
2	2.65	8.00	18.00
3-7 (4-7 exist?)	2.50	7.50	17.50

WAR COMBAT (Combat Casey #6 on)
March, 1952 - No. 5, Nov, 1952
Atlas Comics (LBI 1/SAI 2-5)

	Good	Fine	N-Mint
1	3.00	9.00	21.00
2	1.50	4.50	10.00
3-5	1.15	3.50	8.00

NOTE: *Berg a-2, 4, 5. Henkel a-5. Maneely a-1, 4.*

WAR COMICS (See Key Ring Comics)
May, 1940 (No mo. given) - No. 8, Feb-Apr, 1943
Dell Publishing Co.

	Good	Fine	N-Mint
1-Sikandur the Robot Master, Sky Hawk, Scoop Mason, War Correspondent begin	22.00	65.00	154.00
2-Origin Greg Gilday	11.00	32.00	75.00
3-Joan becomes Greg Gilday's aide	7.00	21.00	50.00
4-Origin Night Devils	8.50	25.50	60.00
5-8	5.00	15.00	35.00

WAR COMICS
Dec, 1950 - No. 49, Sept, 1957
Marvel/Atlas (USA No. 1-41/JPI No. 42-49)

	Good	Fine	N-Mint
1	5.00	15.00	35.00
2	2.65	8.00	18.00
3-10	2.00	6.00	14.00
11-20	1.50	3.50	8.00
21,23-32: Last precode (2/55). 26-Valley Forge story	1.00	3.00	7.00
22-Krigstein-a	3.00	9.00	21.00
33-37,39-42,44,45,47,48	.85	2.50	6.00
38-Kubert/Moskowitz-a	2.00	6.00	14.00
43,49-Torres-a. 43-Davis E.C. swipe	2.00	6.00	14.00
46-Crandall-a	2.00	6.00	14.00

WAR COMICS (continued)

NOTE: *Colan a-4, 48, 49. Drucker a-37, 43, 48. Everett a-17. Heath a-7-9, 19; c-11, 26, 29; 31. G. Kane a-19. Maneely c-37. Orlando a-42, 48. Pakula a-26. Reinman a-26. Robinson a-15; c-13. Severin a-26; c-48.*

WAR DOGS OF THE U.S. ARMY
1952
Avon Periodicals

	Good	Fine	N-Mint
1-Kinstler c/a	6.35	19.00	44.00

WARFRONT
9/51 - #35, 11/58; #36, 10/65; #37, 9/66 - #38, 12/66; #39, 2/67
Harvey Publications

1	3.50	10.50	24.00
2	1.70	5.00	12.00
3-10	1.35	4.00	9.00
11,12,14,16-20	.85	2.50	6.00
13,15,22-Nostrand-a	2.75	8.00	18.00
21,23-27,29,31-33,35	.70	2.00	5.00
28,30,34-Kirby-c	1.35	4.00	9.00
36-Dynamite Joe begins, ends #39; Williamson-a			
	1.35	4.00	9.00
37-Wood-a, 17pgs.	1.35	4.00	9.00
38,39-Wood-a, 2-3 pgs.; Lone Tiger app.	.85	2.50	6.00

NOTE: *Powell a-1-6, 9-11, 14, 17, 20, 23, 25-28, 30, 31, 34, 36. Powell/Nostrand a-12, 13, 15. Simon c-36?, 38.*

WAR FURY
Sept, 1952 - No. 4, March, 1953
Comic Media/Harwell (Allen Hardy Associates)

1-Heck c/a in all; Bullet hole in forehead-c	2.65	8.00	18.00
2-4: 4-Morisi-a	1.35	4.00	9.00

WAR GODS OF THE DEEP (See Movie Classics)

WAR HEROES (See Marine War Heroes)

WAR HEROES
July-Sept, 1942 (no month); No. 2, Oct-Dec, 1942 - No. 10, Oct-Dec, 1944; No. 11, Mar, 1945
Dell Publishing Co.

1	8.00	24.00	56.00
2	3.50	10.50	24.00
3,5: 3-Pro-Russian back-c	3.00	9.00	21.00
4-Disney's Gremlins app.	8.00	24.00	56.00
6-11: 6-Tothish-a by Discount	2.65	8.00	18.00

NOTE: *No. 1 was to be released in July, but was delayed. Cameron a-6.*

WAR HEROES
May, 1952 - No. 8, April, 1953
Ace Magazines

1	2.65	8.00	18.00
2	1.35	4.00	9.00
3-8	1.20	3.50	8.00

WAR HEROES
Feb, 1963 - No. 27, Nov, 1967
Charlton Comics

1	.50	1.50	3.00
2-10	.30	.80	1.60
11-27: 27-1st Devils Brigade by Glanzman		.30	.60

NOTE: *Montes/Bache a-3-7, 21, 25, 27; c-3-7.*

WAR IS HELL
Jan, 1973 - No. 15, Oct, 1975
Marvel Comics Group

1-Williamson-a(r), 3pgs.		.40	.80
2-9-All reprints		.30	.60
10-15		.15	.30

NOTE: *Bolle a-3r. Powell, Woodbridge a-1. Sgt. Fury reprints-7, 8.*

WARLOCK (The Power of . . .) (See Str. Tales & Marvel Premiere)
Aug, 1972 - No. 8, Oct, 1973; No. 9, Oct, 1975 - No. 15, Nov, 1976
Marvel Comics Group

	Good	Fine	N-Mint
1-Origin by Kane	.85	2.50	5.00
2,3	.40	1.20	2.40
4-8: 4-Death of Eddie Roberts	.35	1.00	2.00
9-15-Starlin-c/a in all. 10-Origin Thanos & Gamora. 14-Origin Star Thief	.35	1.00	2.00

NOTE: *Buscema a-2p; c-8p. G. Kane a-1p, 3-5p; c-1p, 2, 3, 4p, 5p, 7p. Starlin a-9-14p, 15; c-12p, 13-15. Sutton a-1-8i.*

WARLOCK
12/82 - No. 6, 5/83 ($2.00) (slick paper) (Direct Sales only)
Marvel Comics Group

1-Starlin Warlock r-/Str. Tales #178-180; Starlin-c			
	.35	1.00	2.00
2(1/83)-Starlin Warlock r-/Str. Tales #180,181 & Warlock #9; Starlin-c	.35	1.00	2.00
3-Starlin-a(r)/Warlock #10-12	.35	1.00	2.00
4-Starlin-a(r)/Warlock #12-15	.35	1.00	2.00
5-Starlin-a(r)/Warlock #15	.35	1.00	2.00
6	.35	1.00	2.00
Special Edition #1(12/83)	.35	1.00	2.00

NOTE: *Byrne a-5r. Starlin a-3-6r; c-1-4.*

WARLOCK 5
Nov., 1986 - Present ($1.70, B&W)
Aircel Publishing

1	1.15	3.50	7.00
2	.85	2.50	5.00
3	1.50	4.50	9.00
4-6	1.15	3.50	7.00
7-9	1.00	3.00	6.00
10,11	.60	1.75	3.50
12-18	.35	1.00	2.00
Compilation 1-r/#1-5 ($5.95)	1.00	3.00	5.95
Compilation 2-r/#6-9 ($5.95)	1.00	3.00	5.95

WARLORD (See First Issue Special)
1-2/76; No.2, 3-4/76; No.3, 10-11/76 - No. 133, Wint, 1988-89
National Periodical Publications/DC Comics #123 on

1-Story cont'd. from 1st Issue Special #8	2.50	7.50	15.00
2-Intro. Machiste	1.15	3.50	7.00
3-5	.85	2.50	5.00
6-10: 6-Intro Mariah. 7-Origin Machiste. 9-Dons new costume			
	.75	2.25	4.50
11-20: 11-Origin-r. 12-Intro Aton. 15-Tara returns; Warlord has son			
	.60	1.80	3.60
21-30: 27-New facts about origin. 28-1st app. Wizard World			
	.40	1.25	2.50
31-36,39,40: 32-Intro Shakira. 39-Omac ends. 40-Warlord gets new costume	.35	1.00	2.00
37,38-Origin Omac by Starlin. 38-Intro Jennifer Morgan, Warlord's daughter	.35	1.00	2.00
41-47,49-52: 42-47-Omac back-up series. 49-Claw The Unconquered app. 50-Death of Aton. 51-r-/No.1.	.25	.75	1.50
48-(52pgs.)-1st app. Arak; contains free 16pg. Arak Son of Thunder; Claw The Unconquered app.	.35	1.00	2.00
53-80: 55-Arion Lord of Atlantis begins, ends No. 62. 63-The Barren Earth begins; contains free 16pg. Masters of the Universe			
	.50	1.00	
81-99,101-128: 91-Origin w/new facts	.50	1.00	
100-Double size ($1.25)	.65	1.30	
123-132: 125-Death of Tara	.50	1.00	
133 ($1.50, 52 pgs.)	.25	.75	1.50
Remco Toy Giveaway (2¾x4'')	.50	1.00	
Annual 1(11/82)-Grell c, a(p)	.35	1.00	2.00

War Dogs Of The U.S. Army #1, © AVON

War Fury #1, © Comic Media

Warlock 5 #14, © Aircel Publ.

Wartime Romances #2, © STJ   Wasteland #1, © DC   Watchmen #3, © DC

	Good	Fine	N-Mint
WARLORD (continued)			
Annual 2(10/83)		.50	1.00
Annual 3(9/84), 4(8/85), 5(9/86), 6(10/87)		.65	1.30

NOTE: **Grell** a-1-15, 16-50p, 51r, 52p, 59p, Annual 1p; c-1-700, 100-104, 112, 116, 117, Annual 1, 5. **Wayne Howard** a-64i. **Starlin** a-37-39p.

WARLORDS (See DC Graphic Novel #2)

WARP
March, 1983 - No. 19, Feb, 1985 ($1.00-$1,25, Mando paper)
First Comics

1-Sargon-Mistress of War app.	.30	.90	1.80
2-5: 2-Faceless Ones begins	.65	1.30	
6-10: 10-New Warp advs., & Outrider begin	.50	1.00	
11-19		.45	.90
Special 1(7/83, 36 pgs.)-Origin Chaos-Prince of Madness; origin of Warp Universe begins, ends #3	.50	1.00	
Special 2(1/84)-Lord Cumulus vs. Sargon Mistress of War ($1.00)		.50	1.00
Special 3(6/84)-Chaos-Prince of Madness	.50	1.00	

NOTE: **Brunner** a-1-9p; c-1-9. **Chaykin** a(p)-Special 1; c-Special 1. **Ditko** a-2-4. **Staton** a-1i. No. 1-9 are adapted from the Warp plays.

WARPATH
Nov, 1954 - No. 3, April, 1955
Key Publications/Stanmor

1	3.50	10.50	24.00
2,3	2.00	6.00	14.00

WARP GRAPHICS ANNUAL
Dec, 1985; 1988 ($2.50 cover)
WaRP Graphics

1-Elfquest, Blood of the Innocent, Thunderbunny & Myth-adventures app.	.50	1.50	3.00
1 ('88)	.50	1.50	3.00

WARREN PRESENTS
Jan, 1979 - No. 14, Nov, 1981
Warren Publications

1-14-Eerie, Creepy, & Vampirella-r	.50	1.00	
...The Rook 1 (5/79)-r/Eerie #82-85	.50	1.00	

WAR REPORT
Sept, 1952 - No. 5, May, 1953
Ajax/Farrell Publications (Excellent Publ.)

1	2.65	8.00	18.00
2	1.35	4.00	9.00
3,5	1.20	3.50	8.00
4-Used in POP, pg. 94	2.00	6.00	14.00

WARRIOR COMICS
1945 (1930s DC reprints)
H.C. Blackerby

1-Wing Brady, The Iron Man, Mark Markon	4.60	14.00	32.00

WARRIORS
1987 - Present ($1.95, B&W)
Adventure Publications

1-Hsu painted-c	.60	1.75	3.50
2-7	.35	1.00	2.00

WAR ROMANCES (See True...)

WAR SHIPS
1942 (36 pgs.)(Similar to Large Feature Comics)
Dell Publishing Co.

Cover by McWilliams; contains photos & drawings of U.S. war ships

	6.00	18.00	42.00

WAR STORIES
1942 - No. 8, Feb-Apr, 1943
Dell Publishing Co.

	Good	Fine	N-Mint
1	8.00	24.00	56.00
2	4.35	13.00	30.00
3,4,6-8: 6-8-Night Devils	4.00	12.00	38.00
5-Origin The Whistler	5.50	16.50	38.00

WAR STORIES (Korea)
Sept, 1952 - No. 5, May, 1953
Ajax/Farrell Publications (Excellent Publ.)

1	2.65	8.00	18.00
2	1.35	4.00	9.00
3-5	1.20	3.50	8.00

WAR STORIES (See Star Spangled...)

WART AND THE WIZARD
Feb, 1964 (Walt Disney)
Gold Key

1 (10102-402)	1.75	5.25	12.00

WARTIME ROMANCES
July, 1951 - No. 18, Nov, 1953
St. John Publishing co.

1-All Baker-a	10.00	30.00	70.00
2-All Baker-a	6.00	18.00	42.00
3,4-All Baker-a	5.75	17.25	40.00
5-8-Baker c/a(2-3) each	5.15	15.50	36.00
9-12,16,18-Baker c/a each	3.75	11.25	26.00
13-15,17-Baker-c only	2.75	8.25	19.00

WAR VICTORY ADVENTURES (#1 titled War Victory Comics)
Summer, 1942 - No. 3, Winter, 1943-44 (5 cents)
U.S. Treasury Dept./War Victory/Harvey Publ.

1-(Promotion of Savings Bonds)-Featuring America's greatest comic art by top syndicated cartoonists; Blondie, Joe Palooka, Green Hornet, Dick Tracy, Superman, Gumps, etc.; (36 pgs.); All profits contributed to U.S.O.	18.00	54.00	125.00
2-Powell-a	9.50	28.50	65.00
3-Capt. Red Cross (cover & text only); Powell-a	7.00	21.00	50.00

WAR WAGON, THE (See Movie Classics)

WAR WINGS
October, 1968
Charlton Comics

1		.50	1.00

WASHABLE JONES & SHMOO
June, 1953
Harvey Publications

1	11.00	32.00	75.00

WASH TUBBS (See The Comics, Crackajack Funnies & 4-Color #11,28,53)

WASTELAND
Dec, 1987 - No. 18, 1989 ($1.75, color, adults)
DC Comics

1-5(4/88), 5(5/88), 6(5/88)-18: 13-Orlando-a	.30	.90	1.80

WATCHMEN
Sept, 1986 - No. 12, Oct, 1987 (12 issue maxi-series)
DC Comics

1-Alan Moore scripts in all	1.15	3.50	7.00
2,3	.85	2.50	5.00
4-12	.65	1.90	3.75
Trade paperback ('87, $14.95)	2.65	8.00	16.00
Hardcover (SF Book Club, $15)	4.15	12.50	25.00
Hardcover (Limited, Graphitti Designs, $50)	12.50	37.50	75.00
Hardcover (French #1-6, word balloons in French)	2.50	7.50	15.00

	Good	Fine	N-Mint
DC Portfolio (24 plate, $20)	4.15	12.50	25.00
Signed/Limited French Portfolio (2000 copies, $50)			
	25.00	75.00	150.00
Limited/Numbered Button set ($4.95)	2.50	7.50	15.00

WATCH OUT FOR BIG TALK
1950
Giveaway

	Good	Fine	N-Mint
Dan Barry-a (about crooked politicians)	2.35	7.00	16.00

WATER BIRDS AND THE OLYMPIC ELK (See 4-Color #700)

WEATHER-BIRD (See Comics From... & Free Comics to You...)
1958 - No. 16, July, 1962 (Giveaway)
International Shoe Co./Western Printing Co.

	Good	Fine	N-Mint
1	.70	2.00	4.00
2-16	.45	1.25	2.50

NOTE: The numbers are located in the lower bottom panel, pg. 1. All feature a character called Weather-Bird.

WEATHER BIRD COMICS (See Comics From Weather Bird)
1957 (Giveaway)
Weather Bird Shoes
nn-Contains a comic bound with new cover. Several combinations possible; contents determines price (40 - 60 percent of contents).

WEB OF EVIL
Nov, 1952 - No. 21, Dec, 1954
Comic Magazines/Quality Comics Group

	Good	Fine	N-Mint
1-Used in **SOTI**, pg. 388. Jack Cole-a; morphine use story			
	16.00	48.00	110.00
2,3-Jack Cole-a	8.50	25.50	60.00
4,6,7-Jack Cole c/a	9.50	28.50	65.00
5-Electrocution-c; Jack Cole-c/a	11.50	34.00	80.00
8-11-Jack Cole-a	5.70	17.00	40.00
12,13,15,16,19-21	3.50	10.50	24.00
14-Part Crandall-c; Old Witch swipe	4.65	14.00	32.00
17-Opium drug propaganda story	4.00	12.00	28.00
18-Acid-in-face story	4.65	14.00	32.00

NOTE: *Jack Cole a(2 each)-2, 6, 8, 9. Ravielli a-13.*

WEB OF HORROR (Magazine)
Dec, 1969 - No. 3, Apr, 1970
Major Magazines

	Good	Fine	N-Mint
1-Jones-c; Wrightson-a	3.00	9.00	18.00
2-Jones-c; Wrightson-a(2), Kaluta-a	2.00	6.00	12.00
3-Wrightson-c; Brunner, Kaluta, Bruce Jones, Wrightson-a			
	2.00	6.00	12.00

WEB OF MYSTERY
Feb, 1951 - No. 29, Sept, 1955
Ace Magazines (A. A. Wyn)

	Good	Fine	N-Mint
1	11.00	32.00	75.00
2-Bakerish-a	7.00	21.00	50.00
3-10	5.70	17.00	40.00
11-18,20-26: 13-Surrealistic-c. 20-r/The Beyond #1			
	4.65	14.00	32.00
19-r-Chall. of Unknown #6 used in N.Y. Legislative Committee			
	5.00	15.00	35.00
27-Bakerish-a(r-/The Beyond #2); last pre-code issue			
	4.00	12.00	28.00
28,29: 28-All-r	3.00	9.00	21.00

NOTE: This series was to appear as "Creepy Stories," but title was changed before publication. *Cameron a-6, 8, 12, 13, 17, 18-20, 22, 24, 25, 27; c-8, 13, 17. Colan a-4. Palais a-28r. Sekowsky a-1-3, 7, 8, 11, 14, 21, 29. Tothish a-by Bill Discount r-1. #29-all-r, 19-28-partial-r.*

WEB OF SPIDER-MAN, THE
Apr, 1985 - Present
Marvel Comics Group

	Good	Fine	N-Mint
1	1.15	3.50	7.00
2,3	.70	2.00	4.00
4-8	.50	1.50	3.00
9-13	.40	1.25	2.50
14-28,30: 19-Intro Humbug & Solo	.35	1.00	2.00
29-Wolverine app.	.60	1.75	3.50
31-Six part Kraven storyline	.70	2.00	4.00
32-Kraven storyline cont.	.50	1.50	3.00
33,34		.60	1.25
35-48: 38 ($1.00)		.50	1.00
Annual 1 (9/85)	.35	1.10	2.20
Annual 2 (9/86)-New Mutants; Art Adams-a	.70	2.00	4.00
Annual 3 (10/87)	.30	.90	1.80
Annual 4 (10/88, $1.75)-Evolutionary War app.	.35	1.10	2.20

WEDDING BELLS
Feb, 1954 - No. 19, Nov, 1956
Quality Comics Group

	Good	Fine	N-Mint
1-Whitney-a	5.50	16.50	38.00
2	2.65	8.00	18.00
3-9: 8-Last precode (4/55)	1.70	5.00	12.00
10-Ward-a, 9 pgs.	6.85	20.50	48.00
11-14,17	1.30	4.00	9.00
15-Baker-a	2.00	6.00	14.00
16-Baker-c/a	3.15	9.50	22.00
18,19-Baker-a each	2.65	8.00	18.00

WEEKENDER, THE
1945 - 1946 (52 pages)
Rucker Publ. Co.

	Good	Fine	N-Mint
V1#4(1945)	8.50	25.50	60.00
V2#1-36 pgs. comics, 16 in newspaper format with photos; partial Dynamic Comics reprints; 4 pgs. of cels from the Disney film Pinocchio; Little Nemo story by Winsor McCay, Jr.; Jack Cole-a			
	11.50	34.00	80.00

WEEKLY COMIC MAGAZINE
May 12, 1940 (16 pgs.) (Full Color)
Fox Publications

(1st Version)-8 pg. Blue Beetle story, 7 pg. Patty O'Day story; two copies known to exist. Estimated value....	$500.00
(2nd Version)-7 two-pg. adventures of Blue Beetle, Patty O'Day, Yarko, Dr. Fung, Green Mask, Spark Stevens, & Rex Dexter; one copy known to exist Estimated value....	$400.00

Discovered with business papers, letters and exploitation material promoting **Weekly Comic Magazine** for use by newspapers in the same manner of **The Spirit** weeklies. Interesting note: these are dated three weeks before the first **Spirit** comic. Letters indicate that samples may have been sent to a few newspapers. These sections were actually 15½x22" pages which will fold down to an approximate 8x10" comic booklet. Other various comic sections were found with the above, but were more like the Sunday comic sections in format.

WEIRD (Magazine)
1/66 - V8#6, 12/74; V9#1, 1/75 - V10#3, 1977
(V1-V8, 52 pgs.; V9 on, 68 pgs.)
Eerie Publications

	Good	Fine	N-Mint
V1#10(#1)-Intro. Morris the Caretaker of Weird (ends V2#10); Burgos-a	.70	2.50	6.00
11,12	.50	1.50	3.00
V2#1-4-10/67), V3#1(1/68), V2#6(4/68)-V2#7,9,10(12/68), V3#1(2/69)-V3#4	.50	1.50	3.00
V2#8-Reprints Ditko's 1st story/Fantastic Fears #5			
	.70	2.00	4.00
5(12/69)-Rulah reprint; "Rulah" changed to "Pulah;" LSD story-reprinted in Horror Tales V4#4, Tales From the Tomb V2#4, & Terror Tales V7#3	.50	1.50	3.00
V4#1-6('70), V5#1-6('71), V6#1-7('72), V7#1-7('73), V8#1-6('74), V9#1-4(1/75-'76)(no V9#1), V10#1-3('77)	.50	1.50	3.00

Web Of Evil #7, © QUA

Web Of Mystery #3, © ACE

The Web Of Spider-Man #29, © MEG

The Weird #1, © DC

Weird Fantasy #14 (#2), © WMG

Weird Horrors #7, © STJ

WEIRD, THE
Apr., 1988 - No. 4, July, 1988 ($1.50, color, mini-series)
DC Comics

	Good	Fine	N-Mint
1-Wrightson c/a in all	.40	1.25	2.50
2-4	.35	1.00	2.00

WEIRD ADVENTURES
May-June, 1951 - No. 3, Sept-Oct, 1951
P. L. Publishing Co. (Canada)

1-"The She-Wolf Killer" by Matt Baker, 6 pgs.			
	12.00	36.00	84.00
2-Bondage/hypodermic panel; opium den text story			
	8.50	25.50	60.00
3-Male bondage/torture-c; severed head story			
	7.00	21.00	50.00

WEIRD ADVENTURES
No. 10, July-Aug, 1951
Ziff-Davis Publishing Co.

10-Painted-c	8.00	24.00	56.00

WEIRD CHILLS
July, 1954 - No. 3, Nov, 1954
Key Publications

1-Wolverton-a r-/Weird Mysteries No. 4; blood transfusion-c			
	19.00	57.00	132.00
2-Injury to eye-c	20.00	60.00	140.00
3-Bondage E.C. swipe-c	9.50	28.50	65.00
NOTE: Baily c-1.			

WEIRD COMICS
April, 1940 - No. 20, Jan, 1942
Fox Features Syndicate

1-The Birdman, Thor, God of Thunder (ends #5), The Sorceress of Zoom, Blast Bennett, Typhon, Voodoo Man, & Dr. Mortal begin; Fine bondage-c	100.00	300.00	700.00
2-Lou Fine-c	50.00	150.00	350.00
3,4: 3-Simon-c. 4-Torture-c	33.00	100.00	230.00
5-Intro. Dart & sidekick Ace (ends #20); bondage/hypo-c			
	36.00	108.00	250.00
6,7-Dynamite Thor app. in each	33.00	100.00	230.00
8-Dynamo, the Eagle & sidekick Buddy & Marga, the Panther Woman begin	33.00	100.00	230.00
9	25.00	75.00	175.00
10-Navy Jones app.	25.00	75.00	175.00
11-16: 16-Flag-c	22.00	65.00	154.00
17-Origin The Black Rider	22.00	65.00	154.00
18-20: 20-Origin The Rapier; Swoop Curtis app; Churchill, Hitler-c			
	22.00	65.00	154.00

WEIRD FANTASY (Formerly A Moon, A Girl, Romance; becomes Weird Science-Fantasy #23 on)
No. 13, May-June, 1950 - No. 22, Nov-Dec, 1953
E. C. Comics

13(#1) (1950)	80.00	240.00	560.00
14-Necronomicon story; atomic explosion-c	45.00	130.00	300.00
15,16: 16-Used in SOTI, pg. 144	35.00	105.00	245.00
17 (1951)	28.00	85.00	195.00
6-10	21.50	65.00	150.00
11-13 (1952)	16.00	48.00	110.00
14-Frazetta/Williamson(1st team-up at E.C.)/Krenkel-a, 7 pgs.; Orlando draws E.C. staff	30.00	90.00	210.00
15-Williamson/Evans-a(3), 4,3,&7 pgs.	18.00	54.00	125.00
16-19-Williamson/Krenkel-a in all. 18-Williamson/Feldstein-c			
	16.00	48.00	110.00
20-Frazetta/Williamson-a, 7 pgs.	18.00	54.00	125.00
21-Frazetta/Williamson-c & Williamson/Krenkel-a			
	30.00	90.00	210.00

	Good	Fine	N-Mint
22-Bradbury adaptation	12.50	37.50	85.00

NOTE: Crandall a-22. Elder a-17. Feldstein a-13(#1)-8; c-13(#1)-18 (#18 w/Williamson), 20. Kamen a-13(#1)-16, 18-22. Krigstein a-22. Kurtzman a-13(#1)-17(#5), 6. Orlando a-9-22 (2 stories in #16); c-19, 22. Severin/Elder a-18-21. Wood a-13(#1)-14, 17(2 stories ea. in #10-13). Canadian reprints exist; see Table of Contents.

WEIRD HORRORS (Nightmare #10 on)
June, 1952 - No. 9, Oct, 1953
St. John Publishing Co.

1-Tuska-a	13.00	40.00	90.00
2	6.50	19.50	45.00
3-Hashish story	7.00	21.00	50.00
4,5	5.70	17.00	40.00
6-Ekgren-c	12.00	36.00	84.00
7-Ekgren-c; Kubert, Cameron-a	13.00	40.00	90.00
8,9-Kubert c/a	9.50	28.50	65.00

NOTE: Cameron a-7, 9. Finesque a-1-5. Morisi a-3. Bondage c-8.

WEIRD MYSTERIES
Oct, 1952 - No. 14, Jan, 1955
Gillmore Publications

1-Partial Wolverton-c swiped from splash page "Flight to the Future" in Weird Tales of the Future #2; "Eternity" has an Ingels swipe	18.00	54.00	125.00
2-"Robot Woman" by Wolverton; Bernard Baily-c-reprinted in Mister Mystery #18; acid in face panel	36.00	108.00	250.00
3,6: Both have decapitation-c.	11.50	34.00	80.00
4-"The Man Who Never Smiled" (3 pgs.) by Wolverton; B. Baily skull-c	28.00	84.00	195.00
5-Wolverton story "Swamp Monster," 6 pgs.	32.00	95.00	225.00
7-Used in SOTI, illo-"Indeed" & illo-"Sex and blood"			
	21.50	65.00	150.00
8-Wolverton-c panel reprint/No. 5; used in a 1954 Readers Digest anti-comics article by T. E. Murphy entitled "For the Kiddies to Read"	11.00	32.00	75.00
9-Excessive violence, gore & torture	9.50	28.50	65.00
10-Silhouetted nudity panel	8.50	25.50	60.00
11-14 (#13,14-Exist?)	6.50	19.50	45.00

NOTE: Baily c-2-8, 10-12.

WEIRD MYSTERIES (Magazine)
Mar-Apr, 1959 (68 pages) (35 cents) (B&W)
Pastime Publications

1-Torres-a; E. C. swipe from TFTC No. 46 by Tuska-"The Ragman"	2.00	6.00	14.00

WEIRD MYSTERY TALES (See DC 100 Page Super Spectacular)

WEIRD MYSTERY TALES (See Cancelled Comic Cavalcade)
Jul-Aug, 1972 - No. 24, Nov, 1975
National Periodical Publications

1-Kirby-a		.50	1.00
2-24		.20	.40

NOTE: Alcala a-5, 10, 13, 14. Aparo c-4. Bolle a-8. Howard a-4. Kaluta a-24; c-1. G. Kane a-10. Kirby a-1, 2p, 3p. Nino a-5, 6, 9, 13, 16, 21. Redondo a-9. Starlin a-2-4. Wood a-23. Wrightson c-21.

WEIRD SCIENCE (Formerly Saddle Romances) (Becomes Weird Science-Fantasy #23 on)
No. 12, May-June, 1950 - No. 22, Nov-Dec, 1953
E. C. Comics

12(#1) (1950)	82.00	245.00	575.00
13	45.00	135.00	315.00
14,15 (1950)	41.00	123.00	285.00
5-10: 5-Atomic explosion-c	25.00	75.00	175.00
11-14 (1952)	16.00	48.00	110.00
15-18-Williamson/Krenkel-a in each; 15-Williamson-a. 17-Used in POP, pgs. 81,82	19.00	57.00	130.00
19,20-Williamson/Frazetta-a, 7 pgs each. 19-Used in SOTI, illo-"A			

419

WEIRD SCIENCE (continued)   **Good**   **Fine** **N-Mint**

young girl on her wedding night stabs her sleeping husband to
death with a hatpin. . ."   25.00   75.00 175.00
21-Williamson/Frazetta-a, 6 pgs.; Wood draws E.C. staff; Gaines
& Feldstein app. in story   25.00   75.00 175.00
22-Williamson/Frazetta/Krenkel-a, 8 pgs.; Wood draws himself
in his story - last pg. & panel 25.00   75.00 175.00
NOTE: *Elder a-14, 19. Evans a-22. Feldstein a-12(#1)-8; c-12(#1)-8, 11. Ingels a-15.*
Kamen a-12(#1)-13, 15-18, 20, 21. Kurtzman a-12(#1)-7. Orlando a-10-22. Wood
a-12(#1), 13(#2), 5-22 (#9, 10, 12, 13 all have 2 Wood stories); c-9, 10, 12-22. Canadian
reprints exist; see Table of Contents.

WEIRD SCIENCE-FANTASY (Formerly Weird Science & Weird Fant-
asy) (Becomes Incredible Science Fiction #30)
No. 23 Mar, 1954 - No. 29, May-June, 1955
E. C. Comics

23-Williamson & Wood-a   18.00   55.00 125.00
24-Williamson & Wood-a; Harlan Ellison's 1st professional story,
'Upheaval,' later adapted into a short story as 'Mealtime,' and
then into a TV episode of Voyage to the Bottom of the Sea as
'The Price of Doom'   18.00   55.00 125.00
25-Williamson-c; Williamson/Torres/Krenkel-a plus Wood-a
        22.00   65.00 154.00
26-Flying Saucer Report; Wood, Crandall, Orlando-a
        17.00   51.00 120.00
27   18.00   55.00 125.00
28-Williamson/Krenkel/Torres-a; Wood-a 22.00   65.00 154.00
29-Frazetta-c; Williamson/Krenkel & Wood-a 42.00 125.00 295.00
NOTE: *Crandall a-26, 27, 29. Evans a-26. Feldstein c-24, 26, 28. Kamen a-27, 28.*
Krigstein a-23-25. Orlando a-in all. Wood a-in all; c-23, 27.

WEIRD SCIENCE-FANTASY ANNUAL
1952, 1953 (Sold thru the E. C. office & on the stands in some major
cities; 25 cents, 132 pgs.)
E. C. Comics

1952-Feldstein-c   104.00 312.00 725.00
1953   66.00 200.00 460.00
NOTE: *The 1952 annual contains books cover-dated in 1951 & 1952, and the 1953 an-*
nual from 1952 & 1953. Contents of each annual may vary in same year.

WEIRD SUSPENSE
Feb, 1975 - No. 3, July, 1975
Atlas/Seaboard Publ.

1-Tarantula begins   .30   .60
2,3: 3-Buckler-c   .25   .50

WEIRD SUSPENSE STORIES (Canadian reprint of Crime SuspenStories #1-3;
see Table of Contents)

WEIRD TALES OF THE FUTURE
March, 1952 - No. 8, July, 1953
S.P.M. Publ. No. 1-4/Aragon Publ. No. 5-8

1-Andru-a(2)   24.00   72.00 170.00
2,3-Wolverton-c/a(3) each. 2-"Jumpin Jupiter" satire by Wolverton
begins, ends #5   48.00 145.00 335.00
4-"Jumpin Jupiter" satire by Wolverton; partial Wolverton-c
        23.00   70.00 160.00
5-Wolverton-c/a(2)   48.00 145.00 335.00
6-Bernard Baily-c   12.00   36.00 84.00
7-"The Mind Movers" from the art to Wolverton's "Brain Bats of
Venus" from Mr. Mystery #7 which was cut apart, pasted up,
partially redrawn, and rewritten by Harry Kantor, the editor;
Bernard Baily-c   24.00   72.00 170.00
8-Reprints Weird Mysteries #1(10/52) minus cover; gory cover
showing heart ripped out 11.00   32.00 75.00

WEIRD TALES OF THE MACABRE (Magazine)
Jan, 1975 - No. 2, Mar, 1975 (B&W) (75 cents)
Atlas/Seaboard Publ.

1-Jones-c   .35   1.00 2.00

        Good   **Fine** **N-Mint**
2-Boris Vallejo-c, Severin-a   .30   .80 1.60

WEIRD TERROR (Also see Horrific)
Sept, 1952 - No. 13, Sept, 1954
Allen Hardy Associates (Comic Media)

1-"Portrait of Death," adapted from Lovecraft's "Pickman's
Model;" lingerie panels, Hitler story 11.50   28.50 80.00
2-Text on Marquis DeSade, Torture, Demonology, & St. Elmo's Fire
        5.70   17.00 40.00
3-Extreme violence, whipping, torture; article on sin eating, dowsing
        5.00   15.00 35.00
4-Dismemberment, decapitation, article on human flesh for sale,
Devil, whipping   8.50   25.50 60.00
5-Article on body snatching, mutilation; cannibalism story
        5.00   15.00 35.00
6-Dismemberment, decapitation, man hit by lightning
        8.50   25.50 60.00
7,9,10   5.00   15.00 35.00
8-Decapitation story; Ambrose Bierce adapt. 7.00   21.00 50.00
11-End of the world story with atomic blast panels; Tothish-a by Bill
Discount   7.00   21.00 50.00
12-Discount-a   4.65   14.00 32.00
13-Severed head panels   5.00   15.00 35.00
NOTE: *Don Heck a/c-most issues. Landau a-6. Morisi a-2-5, 7, 9, 12. Palais a-1, 5, 6,*
8(2), 10, 12. Powell a-10. Ravielli a-11, 20.

WEIRD THRILLERS
Sept-Oct, 1951 - No. 5, Oct-Nov, 1952 (#2-4, painted-c)
Ziff-Davis Publ. Co. (Approved Comics)

1-Ron Hatton photo-c   14.00   42.00 100.00
2-Toth, Anderson, Colan-a   11.50   34.00 80.00
3-Two Powell, Tuska-a   8.50   25.50 60.00
4-Kubert, Tuska-a   10.00   30.00 70.00
5-Powell-a   8.50   25.50 60.00
NOTE: *Anderson a-2. Roussos a-4. #2, 3 reprinted in Nightmare #10 & 13; #4,5 r-/in*
Amazing Ghost Stories #16 & #15.

WEIRD WAR TALES
Sept-Oct, 1971 - No. 124, June, 1983
National Periodical Publications/DC Comics

1   .25   .75 1.50
2-7,9,10: 5,6,10-Toth-a. 7-Krigstein-a   .30 .60
8-Adams c/a(i)   .30   .90 1.80
11-50: 36-Crandall, Kubert r-/No.2   .25 .50
51-63,65-67,69-124: 69-Sci-Fic ish. 93-Origin Creature Commandos.
101-Origin G.I. Robot   .20 .40
64,68-Miller-a   .40 .80
NOTE: *Austin a-51i, 52i. Bailey a-21, 33. Crandall a-2r, 36r. Ditko a-46p, 49p, 95, 99,*
104-106. Drucker a-2, 3. Evans a-17, 22, 35, 46, 74, 82; c-73, 74, 82, 83, 85. Giffen
a-124p. Grell a-67. Heath a-3, 59. Howard a-53i. Kaluta c-12. Gil Kane c-115, 116, 118.
Kubert a-1-4, 7, 36, 68, 69; c-51, 6G, 62-69, 72, 75-81, 84, 86-88, 90-96, 100, 103, 104,
106, 107, 123, 124. Lopez a-108. Maurer a-5. Meskin a-4r. Morrow c-54. Newton
a-82p, 122p. Nino a-9. Redondo a-10, 13, 30, 38, 42, 52. Rogers a-51p, 52p.
Sekowsky a-75p. Simonson a-10, 72. Sparling a-86p. Spiegle a-96, 97, 107, 109-112.
Starlin c-89. Staton c-108p. Sutton a-66, 87, 91, 92, 103. Tuska a-103p, 122p.

WEIRD WESTERN TALES (Formerly All-Star Western)
No. 12, June-July, 1972 - No. 70, Aug, 1980 (No. 12: 52 pgs.)
National Periodical Publications/DC Comics

12-Bat Lash, Pow Wow Smith reprints; El Diablo by Adams/
Wrightson   .25   .75 1.50
13,15-Adams-a; c-#15   .25   .75 1.50
14-Toth-a   .40 .80
16-28,30-70: 39-Origin/1st app. Scalphunter   .20 .40
29-Origin Jonah Hex   .40 .80
NOTE: *Ditko a-99. Evans inks-39-48; c-39i, 40, 47. G. Kane a-15. Kubert c-12, 33.*
Starlin c-44, 45. Wildey a-26.

Weird Science-Fantasy #24, © WMG

Weird Tales Of The Future #7, © Aragon Publ.

Weird Thrillers #1, © Z-D

Weird Worlds #8, © DC

Wendy, The Good Little Witch #1, © HARV

Werewolf By Night #7, © MEG

WEIRD WONDER TALES
Dec, 1973 - No. 22, May, 1977
Marvel Comics Group

	Good	Fine	N-Mint
1-Wolverton-a r-from Mystic #6		.40	.80
2-22: 16-18-Venus r-by Everett/Venus #19,18 & 17. 19-22-Dr. Druid (Droom)-r		.25	.50

NOTE: All Reprints: Check a-1. Colan a-17r. Ditko a-4, 5, 10-13, 19-21. Drucker a-12, 20. Everett a-3(Spellbound #16), 6(Astonishing #10), 9(Adv. Into Mystery #5). Kirby a-6, 11, 13, 16-22; c-17, 19, 20. Krigstein a-19. Kubert a-22. Maneely a-8. Mooney a-7p. Powell a-3r; 7. Torres a-7. Wildey a-2.

WEIRD WORLDS (See Adventures Into...)

WEIRD WORLDS (Magazine)
V1#10(12/70), V2#1(2/71) - No. 4, Aug, 1971 (52 pgs.)
Eerie Publications

V1#10	.50	1.50	3.00
V2#1-4	.35	1.00	2.00

WEIRD WORLDS
Aug-Sept, 1972 - No. 9, Jan-Feb, 1974; No. 10, Oct-Nov, 1974
National Periodical Publications

1-Edgar Rice Burrough's John Carter of Mars & David Innes begin; Kubert-c		.50	1.00
2-7: 7-Last John Carter		.40	.80
8-10: 8-Iron Wolf begins by Chaykin		.30	.60

NOTE: Adams a-2i, 3i. John Carter by Anderson-No. 1-3. Chaykin c-7, 8. Kaluta a-4; c-5, 6, 10. Orlando a-4i; c-2-4. Wrightson a-2i.

WELCOME BACK, KOTTER (TV) (See Limited Collectors Ed. #57)
Nov, 1976 - No. 10, Mar-Apr, 1978
National Periodical Publications/DC Comics

1-Sparling a(p)		.40	.80
2-10: 3-Estrada-a		.30	.60

WELCOME SANTA (See March of Comics #63,183)

WELLS FARGO (See Tales of...)

WENDY PARKER COMICS
July, 1953 - No. 8, July, 1954
Atlas Comics (OMC)

1	3.50	10.50	24.00
2	1.70	5.00	12.00
3-8	1.30	4.00	9.00

WENDY, THE GOOD LITTLE WITCH (TV)
8/60 - No. 82, 11/73; No. 83, 8/74 - No. 93, 4/76
Harvey Publications

1	8.35	25.00	50.00
2	4.00	12.00	24.00
3-5	3.35	10.00	20.00
6-10	2.50	7.50	15.00
11-20	1.70	5.00	10.00
21-30	.85	2.50	5.00
31-50	.50	1.50	3.00
51-69	.40	1.20	2.40
70-74: All 52 pg. Giants	.50	1.50	3.00
75-93	.25	.75	1.50

NOTE: (See Casper the Friendly Ghost & Harvey Hits #7,16,21,23,27,30,33)

WENDY WITCH WORLD
10/61; No. 2, 9/62 - No. 52, 12/73; No. 53, 9/74
Harvey Publications

1: 68 pg. Giants begin	5.35	16.00	32.00
2-5	2.75	8.00	16.00
6-10	1.70	5.00	10.00
11-20	1.00	3.00	6.00
21-30	.50	1.50	3.00
31-39: Last 68 pg. issue	.35	1.00	2.00
40-45: 52 pg. issues	.25	.75	1.50

	Good	Fine	N-Mint
46-53		.60	1.20

WEREWOLF (Super Hero)
Dec, 1966 - No. 3, April, 1967
Dell Publishing Co.

1	.35	1.00	2.00
2,3		.50	1.00

WEREWOLF BY NIGHT (See Marvel Spotlight)
Sept, 1972 - No. 43, Mar, 1977
Marvel Comics Group

1-Ploog-a-cont'd./Marvel Spotlight #4	.35	1.00	2.00
2-31: 15-New origin Werewolf		.25	.50
32-Origin & 1st app. Moon Knight	1.50	4.50	9.00
33-Moon Knight app.	.85	2.50	5.00
34-36,38-43: 35-Starlin/Wrightson-c		.25	.50
37-Moon Knight app; part Wrightson-c	.40	1.25	2.50
Giant Size 2(10/74, 68 pgs.)(Formerly G-S Creatures)-Frankenstein app; Ditko-a(r).		.30	.60
Giant Size 3-5(7/75, 68 pgs.); 4-Morbius the Living Vampire app.		.30	.60

NOTE: Bolle a-6i. Ditko a-Gnt. Size 2r. G. Kane a-11p, 12p; c-21, 22, 24-30, 34p, Gnt. Size 3-5. Mooney a-7i. Ploog 1-4p, 5, 6p, 7p, 13-16p; c-5-8, 13-16. Reinman a-8i. Sutton a(i)-9, 11, 16, 35.

WEREWOLVES & VAMPIRES (Magazine)
1962 (One Shot)
Charlton Comics

1	3.00	9.00	21.00

WEST COAST AVENGERS
Sept, 1984 - No. 4, Dec, 1984 (mini-series; Mando paper)
Marvel Comics Group

1-Hawkeye, Iron Man, Mockingbird, Tigra	1.15	3.50	7.00
2-4	.75	2.25	4.50

WEST COAST AVENGERS
Oct, 1985 - Present (regular series)
Marvel Comics Group

1 (V2/1)	.85	2.50	5.00
2,3	.60	1.75	3.50
4-6	.45	1.40	2.75
7-10	.35	1.10	2.25
11-20	.35	1.00	2.00
21-30		.60	1.25
31-44: 42-Byrne a(p) begins		.50	1.00
Annual 1 (10/86)	.35	1.00	2.00
Annual 2 (9/87)	.30	.90	1.75
Annual 3 (10/88, $1.75)-Evolutionary War app.	.35	1.00	2.00

WESTERN ACTION
1964
I. W. Enterprises

7-Reprint	.30	.90	1.80

WESTERN ACTION
February, 1975
Atlas/Seaboard Publ.

1-Kid Cody by Wildey & The Comanche Kid stories; intro. The Renegade		.30	.60

WESTERN ACTION THRILLERS
April, 1937 (100 pages)(Square binding)
Dell Publishers

1-Buffalo Bill, The Texas Kid, Laramie Joe, Two-Gun Thompson, & Wild West Bill app.	35.00	105.00	245.00

WESTERN ADVENTURES COMICS (Western Love Trails #7 on)
Oct, 1948 - No. 6, Aug, 1949

WESTERN ADVENTURES COMICS (continued)
Ace Magazines

	Good	Fine	N-Mint
nn(#1)-Sheriff Sal, The Cross-Draw Kid, Sam Bass begin			
	10.00	30.00	70.00
nn(#2)(12/48)	5.00	15.00	35.00
nn(#3)(2/49)-Used in SOTI, pgs.30,31	5.70	17.00	40.00
4-6	4.00	12.00	28.00

WESTERN BANDITS
1952 (Painted-c)
Avon Periodicals

1-Butch Cassidy, The Daltons by Larsen; Kinstler-a; c-part			
r-/paperback Avon Western Novel 1	8.00	24.00	56.00

WESTERN BANDIT TRAILS (See Approved Comics)
Jan, 1949 - No. 3, July, 1949
St. John Publishing Co.

1-Tuska-a; Baker-c; Blue Monk, Ventrilo app.	9.00	27.00	62.00
2-Baker-c	6.00	18.00	42.00
3-Baker c/a, Tuska-a	7.00	21.00	50.00

WESTERN COMICS (See Super DC Giant)
Jan-Feb, 1948 - No. 85, Jan-Feb, 1961 (52pgs., 1-27)
National Periodical Publications

1-The Wyoming Kid & his horse Racer, The Vigilante (Meskin-a),			
The Cowboy Marshal, & Rodeo Rick begin			
	25.00	75.00	175.00
2	13.50	41.00	95.00
3,4-Last Vigilante	11.50	34.00	80.00
5-Nighthawk & his horse Nightwind begin (not in #6); Captain			
Tootsie by Beck	10.00	30.00	70.00
6,7,9,10	8.00	24.00	56.00
8-Origin Wyoming Kid; 2pg. pin-ups of rodeo queens			
	10.00	30.00	70.00
11-20	5.50	16.50	38.00
21-40: 27-Last 52 pgs.	4.65	14.00	32.00
41-49: Last precode (2/55). 43-Pow Wow Smith begins, ends #85			
	3.50	10.50	24.00
50-60	3.50	10.50	24.00
61-85-Last Wyoming Kid. 77-Origin Matt Savage Trail Boss. 82-1st			
app. Fleetfoot, Pow Wow's girlfriend	2.00	6.00	14.00

NOTE: *Gil Kane, Infantino art in most. Meskin a-1-4. Moreira a-35, 37, 39. Post a-3-5.*

WESTERN CRIME BUSTERS
Sept, 1950 - No. 10, Mar-Apr, 1952
Trojan Magazines

1-Six-Gun Smith, Wilma West, K-Bar-Kate, & Fighting Bob Dale			
begin; headlight-a	11.00	32.00	75.00
2	6.50	19.50	45.00
3-5: 3-Myron Fass-c	6.00	18.00	42.00
6-Wood-a	17.00	51.00	120.00
7-Six-Gun Smith by Wood	17.00	51.00	120.00
8	5.50	16.50	38.00
9-Tex Gordon & Wilma West by Wood; Lariat Lucy app.			
	17.00	51.00	120.00
10-Wood-a	15.00	45.00	105.00

WESTERN CRIME CASES (The Outlaws #10 on?)
No. 9, Dec, 1951
Star Publications

9-White Rider & Super Horse; L. B. Cole-c	2.65	8.00	18.00

WESTERN DESPERADO COMICS (Formerly Slam Bang)
1940 (Oct.?)
Fawcett Publications

8-(Rare)	27.00	81.00	190.00

WESTERNER, THE (Wild Bill Pecos)
No. 14, June, 1948 - No. 41, Dec, 1951 (#14-31, 52 pgs.)

"Wanted" Comic Group/Toytown/Patches

	Good	Fine	N-Mint
14	4.00	12.00	28.00
15-17,19-21: 19-Meskin-a	2.00	6.00	14.00
18,22-25-Krigstein-a	3.70	11.00	26.00
26(4/50)-Origin & 1st app. Calamity Kate, series ends #32;			
Krigstein-a	4.65	14.00	32.00
27-Krigstein-a(2)	5.50	16.50	38.00
28-41: 33-Quest app. 37-Lobo, the Wolf Boy begins			
	1.70	5.00	12.00

NOTE: *Mort Lawrence c-19, 27. Syd Shores c-35, 40.*

WESTERNER, THE
1964
Super Comics

Super Reprint #15,16(Crack West. #65), 17	.25	.75	1.50

WESTERN FIGHTERS
Apr-May, 1948 - V4No.7, Mar-Apr, 1953 (#1-V3#2, 52 pgs.)
Hillman Periodicals/Star Publ.

V1#1-Simon & Kirby-c	11.00	32.00	75.00
2-Kirby-a(p)?	4.30	13.00	30.00
3-Fuje-c	3.50	10.50	24.00
4-Krigstein, Ingels, Fuje-a	4.30	13.00	30.00
5,6,8,9,12	2.65	8.00	18.00
7,10-Krigstein-a	4.30	13.00	30.00
11-Williamson/Frazetta-a	16.00	48.00	110.00
V2#1-Krigstein-a	4.30	13.00	30.00
2-12: 4-Berg-a	1.50	4.50	10.00
V3#1-11	1.30	4.00	9.00
12-Krigstein-a	4.00	12.00	28.00
V4#1,4-7	1.30	4.00	9.00
2,3-Krigstein-a	3.50	10.50	24.00
3-D 1(12/53, Star Publ.)-L. B. Cole-c	16.00	48.00	110.00

NOTE: *Kinstlerish a-V2#6, 8, 9, 12; V3#2, 5-7, 11, 12; V4#1(plus cover). McWilliams a-11. Powell a-V2#2. Reinman a-1-11. Rowich c-6i.*

WESTERN FRONTIER
Apr-May, 1951 - No. 7, 1952
P. L. Publishers

1	3.70	11.00	26.00
2	2.00	6.00	14.00
3-7	1.50	4.50	10.00

WESTERN GUNFIGHTERS (1st Series) (Apache Kid #11-19)
No. 20, June, 1956 - No. 27, Aug, 1957
Atlas Comics (CPS)

20	3.50	10.50	24.00
21,25-27	2.00	6.00	14.00
22-Wood & Powell-a	7.00	21.00	50.00
23-Williamson-a	5.00	15.00	35.00
24-Toth-a	4.00	12.00	28.00

NOTE: *Colan a-27. Heath a-25. Maneely a-25; c-22, 23, 25. Pakula a-23. Severin c-27. Woodbridge a-27.*

WESTERN GUNFIGHTERS (2nd Series)
Aug, 1970 - No. 33, Nov, 1975 (#1-6: 68 pgs.; #7: 52 pgs.)
Marvel Comics Group

1-Ghost Rider, Fort Rango, Renegades & Gunhawk app.			
		.50	1.00
2-33: 2-Origin Nightwind (Apache Kid's horse). 7-Origin Ghost			
Rider retold. 10-Origin Black Rider. 12-Origin Matt Slade			
		.25	.50

NOTE: *Baker a-2r. Everett a-6i. G. Kane c-29, 31. Kirby a-1p(r), 10, 11. Kubert a-2r. Maneely a-2, 10r. Morrow a-29r. Severin c-10. Smith a-4. Steranko c-14. Sutton a-1, 2i, 3, 4. Torres a-26('57). Wildey a-8r, 9r. Williamson a-2r, 18r. Woodbridge a-27('57). Renegades in #4, 5; Ghost Rider-#1-7.*

WESTERN HEARTS
Dec, 1949 - No. 10, Mar, 1952

Western Bandit Trails #1, © STJ

The Westerner #27, © Toytown

Western Gunfighters #20 (6/56), © MEG

Western Kid #4 (6/55), © MEG

Western Love #2, © PRIZE

Western Outlaws #19, © FOX

WESTERN HEARTS (continued)
Standard Comics

	Good	Fine	N-Mint
1-Severin-a; Whip Wilson & Reno Browne photo-c			
	6.50	19.50	45.00
2-Williamson/Frazetta-a, 2 pgs; photo-c	11.50	34.00	80.00
3	2.30	7.00	16.00
4-7,10-Severin & Elder, Al Carreno-a. 5,6-Photo-c			
	2.65	8.00	18.00
8-Randolph Scott/Janis Carter photo-c/"Santa Fe;" Severin & Elder-a	3.50	10.50	24.00
9-Whip Wilson & Reno Browne photo-c; Severin & Elder-a			
	4.00	12.00	28.00

WESTERN HERO (Wow #1-69; Real Western Hero #70-75)
No. 76, Mar, 1949 - No. 112, Mar, 1952
Fawcett Publications

	Good	Fine	N-Mint
76(#1, 52 pgs.)-Tom Mix, Hopalong Cassidy, Monte Hale, Gabby Hayes, Young Falcon (ends #78,80), & Big Bow and Little Arrow (ends #102,105) begin; painted-c begin	13.00	40.00	90.00
77 (52 pgs.)	8.50	25.50	60.00
78,80-82 (52 pgs.): 81-Capt. Tootsie by Beck	8.50	25.50	60.00
79,83 (36 pgs.): 83-Last painted-c	6.50	19.50	45.00
84-86,88-90 (52 pgs.): 84-Photo-c begin, end #112. 86-Last Hopalong Cassidy	7.00	21.00	50.00
87,91,95,99 (36 pgs.): 87-Bill Boyd begins, ends #95			
	5.70	17.00	40.00
92-94,96-98,101 (52 pgs.): 96-Tex Ritter begins. 101-Red Eagle app.			
	6.50	19.50	45.00
100 (52 pgs.)	7.00	21.00	50.00
102-111 (36pgs. begin)	5.70	17.00	40.00
112-Last issue	6.50	19.50	45.00

NOTE: ½-1 pg. Rocky Lane (Carnation) in 80-83,86,88,97.

WESTERN KID (1st Series)
Dec, 1954 - No. 17, Aug, 1957
Atlas Comics (CPC)

	Good	Fine	N-Mint
1-Origin; The Western Kid (Tex Dawson), his stallion Whirlwind & dog Lightning begin	6.00	18.00	42.00
2	3.00	9.00	21.00
3-8	2.30	7.00	16.00
9,10-Williamson-a in both, 4 pgs. each	4.00	12.00	28.00
11-17	1.70	5.00	12.00

NOTE: Ayers a-6, 7. Maneely c-2-7, 10, 14. Romita a-1-17; c-1, 12. Severin c-17.

WESTERN KID, THE (2nd Series)
Dec, 1971 - No. 5, Aug, 1972
Marvel Comics Group

1-Reprints; Romita-c		.25	.50
2,4,5: 2-Severin-c. 4-Everett-r		.20	.40
3-Williamson-r		.25	.50

WESTERN KILLERS
1948 - No. 64, May, 1949; No. 6, July, 1949
Fox Features Syndicate

	Good	Fine	N-Mint
nn(nd, F&J Trading Co.)-Range Busters	5.00	15.00	35.00
60 (9/48)-Extreme violence; lingerie panel	7.00	21.00	50.00
61-64, 6: 61-J. Cole-a	4.30	13.00	30.00

WESTERN LIFE ROMANCES (My Friend Irma #3?)
Dec, 1949 - No. 2, Mar, 1950 (52 pgs.)
Marvel Comics (IPP)

	Good	Fine	N-Mint
1-Whip Wilson & Reno Browne photo-c	4.00	12.00	28.00
2-Spanking scene	6.50	19.50	45.00

WESTERN LOVE
July-Aug, 1949 - No. 5, Mar-Apr, 1950 (All photo-c & 52 pgs.)
Prize Publications

1-S&K-a; Randolph Scott "Canadian Pacific" photo-c (see Prize

	Good	Fine	N-Mint
#76)	7.00	21.00	50.00
2,5-S&K-a: 2-Whip Wilson & Reno Browne photo-c			
	5.70	17.00	40.00
3,4	4.00	12.00	28.00

NOTE: Meskin & Severin/Elder a-2-5.

WESTERN LOVE TRAILS (Formerly Western Adventures)
No. 7, Nov, 1949 - No. 9, Mar, 1950
Ace Magazines (A. A. Wyn)

	Good	Fine	N-Mint
7	4.65	14.00	32.00
8,9	3.00	9.00	21.00

WESTERN MARSHAL (See Steve Donovan . . . & Ernest Haycox's 4-Color 534, 591, 613, 640 [based on Haycox's "Trailtown"])

WESTERN OUTLAWS (My Secret Life #22 on)
No. 17, Sept, 1948 - No. 21, May, 1949
Fox Features Syndicate

	Good	Fine	N-Mint
17-Kamen-a; Iger shop-a in all; 1 pg. 'Death and the Devil Pills' r-in Ghostly Weird 122	9.50	28.50	65.00
18-21	5.00	15.00	35.00

WESTERN OUTLAWS
Feb, 1954 - No. 21, Aug, 1957
Atlas Comics (ACI No. 1-14/WPI No. 15-21)

	Good	Fine	N-Mint
1-Heath, Powell-a	5.70	17.00	40.00
2	2.65	8.00	18.00
3-10: 7-Violent-a by R.Q. Sale	2.00	6.00	14.00
11,14-Williamson-a in both, 6 pgs. each	4.00	12.00	28.00
12,18,20,21	1.50	4.50	10.00
13-Baker-a	2.30	7.00	16.00
15-Torres-a	2.65	8.00	18.00
16-Williamson text illo	1.65	5.00	12.00
17-Crandall-a, Williamson text illo	3.00	9.00	21.00
19-Crandall-a	2.30	7.00	16.00

NOTE: Ayers a-7, 10, 18, 20. Bolle a-21. Colan a-5, 17. Everett a-9, 10. Heath a-1; c-3, 4, 8, 16. Kubert a-9p. Maneely a-13, 16, 17; c-5, 7, 9, 10, 12, 13. Morisi a-18. Powell a-3, 15, 16. Romita a-7, 13. Severin a-8, 16; c-17, 18, 20. Tuska a-6.

WESTERN OUTLAWS & SHERIFFS (Formerly Best Western)
No. 60, Dec, 1949 - No. 73, June, 1952
Marvel/Atlas Comics (IPC)

	Good	Fine	N-Mint
60 (52 pgs.)	5.50	16.50	38.00
61-65: 61-Photo-c	3.70	11.00	26.00
66,68-73	2.65	8.00	18.00
67-Cannibalism story	4.00	12.00	28.00

NOTE: Maneely a-62,67; c-62,69,70,73. Robinson a-68. Tuska a-69.

WESTERN PICTURE STORIES (1st Western Comic)
Feb, 1937 - No. 4, June, 1937
Comics Magazine Company

	Good	Fine	N-Mint
1-Will Eisner-a	80.00	240.00	560.00
2-Will Eisner-a	50.00	150.00	350.00
3,4: 3-Eisner-a	40.00	120.00	280.00

WESTERN PICTURE STORIES (See Giant Comics Editions #6,11)

WESTERN ROMANCES (See Target . . .)

WESTERN ROUGH RIDERS
Nov, 1954 - No. 4, May, 1955
Gillmor Magazines No. 1,4 (Stanmor Publications)

	Good	Fine	N-Mint
1	2.65	8.00	18.00
2-4	1.50	4.50	10.00

WESTERN ROUNDUP (See Dell Giants & Fox Giants)

WESTERN TALES (Formerly Witches . . .)
No. 31, Oct, 1955 - No. 33, July-Sept, 1956
Harvey Publications

	Good	Fine	N-Mint
31,32-All S&K-a; Davy Crockett app. in ea.	5.70	17.00	40.00

WESTERN TALES (continued)

	Good	Fine	N-Mint
33-S&K-a; Jim Bowie app.	5.70	17.00	40.00

NOTE: #32 & 33 have Boy's Ranch reprints.

WESTERN TALES OF BLACK RIDER (Formerly Black Rider; Gunsmoke Western #32 on)
No. 28, May, 1955 - No. 31, Nov, 1955
Atlas Comics (CPS)

28 (#1): The Spider dies	5.00	15.00	35.00
29-31	3.70	11.00	26.00

NOTE: Lawrence a-30. Maneely c-28-30. Severin a-28. Shores c-31.

WESTERN TEAM-UP
November, 1973
Marvel Comics Group

1-Origin & 1st app. The Dakota Kid; Rawhide Kid-r; Gunsmoke Kid-r by Jack Davis		.25	.50

WESTERN THRILLERS (My Past Confessions #7 on)
Aug, 1948 - No. 6, June, 1949
Fox Features Syndicate

1-''Velvet Rose''-Kamenish-a; ''Two-Gun Sal,'' ''Striker Sisters'' (all women outlaws issue)	17.00	51.00	120.00
2	5.70	17.00	40.00
3,6: 3-Tuska-a, Heath-c	4.65	14.00	32.00
4,5-Bakerish-a; Butch Cassidy app. #5	6.50	19.50	45.00
52-(Reprint, M.S. Dist.)-1954? No date given (Becomes My Love Secret #53)	2.00	6.00	14.00

WESTERN THRILLERS (Cowboy Action #5 on)
Nov, 1954 - No. 4, Feb, 1955 (All-r/ Western Outlaws & Sheriffs)
Atlas Comics (ACI)

1-Ringo Kid. Severin-c?	5.00	15.00	35.00
2-4	2.65	8.00	18.00

NOTE: Heath c-3. Maneely a-1; c-2. Powell a-4. Robinson a-4. Romita c-4. Tuska a-2.

WESTERN TRAILS
May, 1957 - No. 2, July, 1957
Atlas Comics (SAI)

1-Ringo Kid app.; Severin-c	3.00	9.00	21.00
2-Severin-c	2.00	6.00	14.00

NOTE: Bolle a-1,2. Maneely a-1,2. Severin c-1,2.

WESTERN TRUE CRIME (Becomes My Confessions)
No. 15, Aug, 1948 - No. 6, June, 1949
Fox Features Syndicate

15-Kamenish-a	9.50	28.50	65.00
16-Kamenish-a	5.00	15.00	35.00
3,5,6	3.00	9.00	21.00
4-Johnny Craig-a	8.50	25.50	60.00

WESTERN WINNERS (Formerly All-West. Winners; Black Rider #8)
No. 5, June, 1949 - No. 7, Dec, 1949
Marvel Comics (CDS)

5-Two-Gun Kid, Kid Colt, Black Rider	11.00	32.00	75.00
6-Two-Gun Kid, Black Rider, Heath Kid Colt story; Captain Tootsie By Beck	8.50	25.50	60.00
7-Randolph Scott Photo-c w/true stories about the West	8.50	25.50	60.00

WEST OF THE PECOS (See 4-Color #222)

WESTWARD HO, THE WAGONS (See 4-Color #738)

WHACK (Satire)
Oct, 1953 - No. 3, May, 1954
St. John Publishing Co.

1-(3-D)-Kubert-a; Maurer-c	17.00	51.00	120.00
2,3,Kubert-a in each; 3-Maurer-c	6.50	19.50	45.00

WHACKY (See Wacky)

WHAM COMICS (See Super Spy)
Nov, 1940 - No. 2, Dec, 1940
Centaur Publications

	Good	Fine	N-Mint
1-The Sparkler, The Phantom Rider, Craig Carter and the Magic Ring Detector, Copper Slug, Speed Silvers by Gustavson, Speed Centaur & Jon Linton (s/f) begin	65.00	195.00	455.00
2-Origin Blue Fire & Solarman; The Buzzard app.	50.00	150.00	350.00

WHAM-O GIANT COMICS (98 cents)
1967 (Newspaper size) (One Shot) (Full Color)
Wham-O Mfg. Co.

1-Radian & Goody Bumpkin by Wally Wood; 1 pg. Stanley-a; Lou Fine, Tufts-a; wraparound-c	1.70	5.00	12.00

WHAT DO YOU KNOW ABOUT THIS COMICS SEAL OF APPROVAL?
nd (1955) (4pgs.; color; slick paper-c)
No publisher listed (DC Comics Giveaway)

(Rare)	45.00	135.00	315.00

WHAT IF. . .?
Feb, 1977 - No. 47, Oct, 1985; June, 1988 (All 52 pgs.)
Marvel Comics Group

1-Brief origin Spider-Man, Fantastic-4	1.15	3.50	7.00
2-Origin The Hulk retold	.75	2.25	4.50
3-5	.65	1.90	3.80
6-10: 9-Origins Venus, Marvel Boy, Human Robot, 3-D Man	.45	1.30	2.60
11,12	.40	1.25	2.50
13-Conan app.	.70	2.00	4.00
14-26: 22-Origin Dr. Doom retold	.30	.90	1.80
27-X-Men app.; Miller-c	.90	2.75	5.50
28-Daredevil by Miller	1.10	3.30	6.60
29-Golden-c	.25	.75	1.50
30-Wolverine app.	.85	2.50	5.00
31-X-Men app.; death of Hulk, Wolverine & Magneto	.50	1.50	3.00
32,36-Byrne-a	.25	.75	1.50
33,34: 34-Marvel crew each draw themselves	.25	.75	1.50
35-What if Elektra had lived?; Miller/Austin-a	.25	.75	1.50
37-47: 37-Old X-Men app.	.25	.75	1.50
Special 1 ($1.50, 6/88)-Iron Man, F.F., Thor app.	.25	.75	1.50

NOTE: Austin a-27p, 32i, 34, 35i; c-35i, 36i. J. Buscema a-13p, 15p; c-10, 13p, 23p. Byrne a-32i, 36; c-36p. Colan a-21p; c-17p, 18p, 21p. Ditko a-35, Special 1. Golden c-40, 42. Guice a-40p. Gil Kane a-3p, 24p; c-2-4p, 7p, 8p. Kirby a-11p; c-9p, 11p. Layton a-32i, 33i; c-30, 32p, 33i, 34. Miller a-28p, 32i, 35p; c-27, 28p. Mooney a-8i, 30i. Perez a-15p. Simonson a-15p, 32i. Starlin a-32i. Stevens a-16i. Sutton a-2i, 18p, 28. Tuska a-5p.

WHAT'S BEHIND THESE HEADLINES
1948 (16 pgs.)
William C. Popper Co.

Comic insert-''The Plot to Steal the World''	1.35	4.00	8.00

WHAT THE-?!
Aug., 1988 - No. 4, Nov., 1988 ($1.25, color)
Marvel Comics

1-4	.25	.75	1.50

WHEATIES (Premiums) (32 titles)
1950 & 1951 (32 pages) (pocket size)
Walt Disney Productions

(Set A-1 to A-8, 1950)
A-1 Mickey Mouse & the Disappearing Island, A-2 Grandma Duck, Homespun Detective, A-3 Donald Duck & the Haunted Jewels, A-4 Donald Duck & the Giant Ape, A-5 Mickey Mouse, Roving Reporter, A-6 Li'l Bad Wolf, Forest Ranger, A-7 Goofy, Tightrope Acrobat, A-8 Pluto & the Bogus

Money each....	2.00	6.00	12.00

Western Tales Of Black Rider #31, © MEG

Western Trails #1, © MEG

Wham Comics #1, © CEN

Whip Wilson #10, © MEG

White Princess Of The Jungle #2, © AVON

White Rider And Super Horse #5, © STAR

WHEATIES (continued)

	Good	Fine	N-Mint
(Set B-1 to B-8, 1950)			

B-1 Mickey Mouse & the Pharoah's Curse, B-2 Pluto, Canine Cowpoke, B-3 Donald Duck & the Buccaneers, B-4 Mickey Mouse & the Mystery Sea Monster, B-5 Li'l Bad Wolf in the Hollow Tree Hideout, B-6 Donald Duck, Trail Blazer, B-7 Goofy & the Gangsters, B-8 Donald Duck, Klondike Kid

each....	1.70	5.00	10.00
(Set C-1 to C-8, 1951)			

C-1 Donald Duck & the Inca Idol, C-2 Mickey Mouse & the Magic Mountain, C-3 Li'l Bad Wolf, Fire Fighter, C-4 Gus & Jaq Save the Ship, C-5 Donald Duck in the Lost Lakes, C-6 Mickey Mouse & the Stagecoach Bandits, C-7 Goofy, Big Game Hunter, C-8 Donald Duck Deep-Sea Diver

each....	1.70	5.00	10.00
(Set D-1 to D-8, 1951)			

D-1 Donald Duck in Indian Country, D-2 Mickey Mouse and the Abandoned Mine, D-3 Pluto & the Mysterious Package, D-4 Bre'r Rabbit's Sunken Treasure, D-5 Donald Duck, Mighty Mystic, D-6 Mickey Mouse & the Medicine Man, D-7 Li'l Bad Wolf and the Secret of the Woods, D-8 Minnie Mouse, Girl Explorer

each....	1.70	5.00	10.00

NOTE: *Some copies lack the Wheaties ad.*

WHEE COMICS (Also see Tickle, Gay, & Smile Comics)
1955 (52 pgs.) (5x7¼") (7 cents)
Modern Store Publications

1-Funny animal	.40	1.20	2.40

WHEELIE AND THE CHOPPER BUNCH (TV)
July, 1975 - No. 7, July, 1976 (Hanna-Barbera)
Charlton Comics

1,2-Byrne-a (1st work)	.85	2.50	5.00
3-7-Staton-a	.40	1.25	2.50

WHEN KNIGHTHOOD WAS IN FLOWER (See 4-Color #505, 682)

WHEN SCHOOL IS OUT (See Wisco)

WHERE CREATURES ROAM
July, 1970 - No. 8, Sept, 1971
Marvel Comics Group

1-Kirby/Ayers-r	.25	.50	
2-8-Kirby-r	.20	.40	

NOTE: *Ditko r-1, 2, 4, 6, 7.*

WHERE MONSTERS DWELL
Jan, 1970 - No. 38, Oct, 1975
Marvel Comics Group

1-Kirby/Ditko-a(r)	.40	.80	
2-10: 4-Crandall-a(r)	.30	.60	
11,13-37	.20	.40	
12-Giant issue	.30	.60	
38-Williamson-r/World of Suspense #3	.30	.60	

NOTE: *Ditko a(r)-4, 8, 10, 12, 17-19, 23-25, 37. Reinman a-4r. Severin c-15.*

WHERE'S HUDDLES? (TV) (See Fun-In #9)
Jan, 1971 - No. 3, Dec, 1971 (Hanna-Barbera)
Gold Key

1	.85	2.50	5.00
2,3: 3 r-most #1	.50	1.50	3.00

WHIP WILSON (Movie star) (Formerly Rex Hart; Gunhawk #12 on; see Western Hearts, Western Life Romances, Western Love)
No. 9, April, 1950 - No. 11, Sept, 1950 (52pgs., 9,10; 36pgs., 11)
Marvel Comics

9-Photo-c; Whip Wilson & his horse Bullet begin; origin Bullet; issue #23 listed on splash page; cover changed to #9			
	15.00	45.00	105.00
10,11-Photo-c	12.00	36.00	84.00
I.W. Reprint #1('64)-Kinstler-c; r-Marvel #11	1.00	3.00	7.00

WHIRLWIND COMICS
June, 1940 - No. 3, Sept, 1940
Nita Publication

	Good	Fine	N-Mint
1-Cyclone begins (origin)	40.00	120.00	280.00
2,3	25.00	75.00	175.00

WHIRLYBIRDS (See 4-Color #1124,1216)

WHISPER (Female Ninja)
Dec, 1983 - No. 2, 1984 ($1.50; Baxter paper)
Capital Comics

1-Origin; Golden-c	1.25	3.75	7.50
2	.60	1.80	3.60

WHISPER
June, 1986 - Present
First Comics

V2#1-9		.65	1.30
10-21 ($1.75)	.30	.90	1.80
Special 1 (11/85, First Comics)	.40	1.25	2.50

WHITE CHIEF OF THE PAWNEE INDIANS
1951
Avon Periodicals

nn-Kit West app.; Kinstler-c	7.00	21.00	50.00

WHITE EAGLE INDIAN CHIEF (See Indian Chief)

WHITE INDIAN
July, 1953 - 1954
Magazine Enterprises

11(A-1 94), 12(A-1 101), 13(A-1 104)-Frazetta-r(Dan Brand) in all from Durango Kid	18.00	54.00	126.00
14(A-1 117), 15(A-1 135)-Check-a; Torres-a/#15			
	6.50	19.50	45.00

NOTE: *#11 reprints from Durango Kid #1-4; #12 from #5, 9, 10, 11; #13 from #7, 12, 13, 16.*

WHITE PRINCESS OF THE JUNGLE (Also see Top Jungle & Jungle Adventures)
July, 1951 - No. 5, Nov, 1952
Avon Periodicals

1-Origin of White Princess (Taanda) & Capt'n Courage (r); Kinstler-c	23.00	70.00	160.00
2-Reprints origin of Malu, Slave Girl Princess from Avon's Slave Girl Comics #1 w/Malu changed to Zora; Kinstler c/a(2)			
	17.00	51.00	120.00
3-Origin Blue Gorilla; Kinstler c/a	13.00	40.00	90.00
4-Jack Barnum, White Hunter app.; r-/Sheena #9			
	11.00	32.00	75.00
5-Blue Gorilla by Kinstler	11.00	32.00	75.00

WHITE RIDER AND SUPER HORSE (Indian Warriors #7 on; also see Blue Bolt #1, Four Most & Western Crime Cases)
Dec, 1950 - No. 6, Mar, 1951
Novelty-Star Publications/Accepted Publ.

1	4.35	13.00	30.00
2,3	2.75	8.00	18.00
4-6-Adapt. "The Last of the Mohicans"	3.00	9.00	21.00
Accepted Reprint #5,6 (nd); L.B. Cole-c	1.70	5.00	14.00

NOTE: *All have L. B. Cole covers.*

WHITE WILDERNESS (See 4-Color #943)

WHITMAN COMIC BOOKS
1962 (136 pgs.; 7¾x5¾"; hardcover) (B&W)
Whitman Publishing Co.

1-Yogi Bear, 2-Huckleberry Hound, 3-Mr. Jinks and Pixie & Dixie, 4-The Flintstones, 5-Augie Doggie & Loopy de Loop, 6-Snooper & Blabber Fearless Detectives/Quick Draw McGraw of the Wild West 7-Bugs Bunny-(r)-/from #47,51,53,54 & 55

WHITMAN COMIC BOOKS (continued)

	Good	Fine	N-Mint
each	.50	1.50	3.00

8-Donald Duck-reprints most of WDC&S #209-213. Includes 5 Barks stories, 1 complete Mickey Mouse serial & 1 Mickey Mouse serial missing the 1st episode

	7.75	22.00	44.00

NOTE: Hanna-Barbera #1-6(TV), original stories. Dell reprints-#7, 8.

WHIZ COMICS (Formerly Flash & Thrill Comics #1)
No. 2, Feb, 1940 - No. 155, June, 1953
Fawcett Publications

1-(nn on cover, #2 inside)-Origin & 1st newsstand app. Captain Marvel (formerly Captain Thunder) by C. C. Beck (created by Bill Parker), Spy Smasher, Golden Arrow, Ibis the Invincible, Dan Dare, Scoop Smith, Sivana, & Lance O'Casey begin

	Good	Fine	VF-NM
	2800.00	8400.00	18,200.00

(Only one known copy exists in Mint condition which has not sold)

1-Reprint, oversize 13½"x10". **WARNING:** This comic is an exact duplicate reprint of the original except for its size. DC published in in 1974 with a second cover titling it as a Famous First Edition. There have been many reported cases of the outer cover being removed and the interior sold as the original edition. The reprint with the new outer cover removed is practically worthless.

	Good	Fine	N-Mint
2-(nn on cover, #3 inside); cover to Flash #1 redrawn, pg. 12, panel 4; Spy Smasher reveals I.D. to Eve	315.00	945.00	2200.00
3-(#3 on cover, #4 inside)-1st app. Beautia	200.00	600.00	1400.00
4-(#4 on cover, #5 inside)	161.00	483.00	1125.00
5-Captain Marvel wears button-down flap on splash page only	120.00	360.00	840.00
6-10: 7-Dr. Voodoo begins (by Raboy-#9-22)	90.00	270.00	630.00
11-14	58.00	175.00	405.00
15-Origin Sivana; Dr. Voodoo by Raboy	75.00	225.00	525.00
16-18-Spy Smasher battles Captain Marvel	75.00	225.00	525.00
19,20	40.00	120.00	280.00
21-Origin & 1st app. Lt. Marvels	43.00	130.00	300.00
22-24: 23-Only Dr. Voodoo by Tuska	33.00	100.00	235.00
25-Origin/1st app. Captain Marvel Jr., x-over in Capt. Marvel; Capt. Nazi app; origin Old Shazam in text	100.00	300.00	700.00
26-30	26.00	78.00	180.00
31,32: 31-1st app. The Trolls	20.00	60.00	140.00
33-Spy Smasher, Captain Marvel x-over on cover and inside	25.00	75.00	175.00
34,36-40-The Trolls in #37	18.00	54.00	125.00
35-Captain Marvel & Spy Smasher-c	20.00	60.00	140.00
41-50: 43-Spy Smasher, Ibis, Golden Arrow x-over in Capt. Marvel. 44-Flag-c. 47-Origin recap (1pg.)	11.50	34.00	80.00
51-60: 52-Capt. Marvel x-over in Ibis. 57-Spy Smasher, Golden Arrow, Ibis cameo	8.50	25.50	60.00
61-70	7.00	21.00	50.00
71,77-80	5.50	16.50	38.00
72-76-Two Captain Marvel stories in each; 76-Spy Smasher becomes Crime Smasher	6.00	18.00	42.00
81-99: 86-Captain Marvel battles Sivana Family. 91-Infinity-c	5.50	16.50	38.00
100	7.00	21.00	50.00
101,103-105	4.30	13.00	30.00
102-Commando Yank app.	4.30	13.00	30.00
106-Bulletman app.	4.30	13.00	30.00
107-141,143-152: 107-White House photo-c. 108-Brooklyn Bridge photo-c. 112 (photo-c),139-Infinity-c	3.70	11.00	26.00
142-Used in POP, pg. 89	4.35	13.00	30.00
153-155-(Scarce)	8.50	25.50	60.00

Wheaties Giveaway(1946, Miniature)-6½x8¼'', 32 pgs.; all copies were taped at each corner to a box of Wheaties and are never found in fine or mint condition; ''Capt. Marvel & the Water Thieves,'' Golden Arrow, Ibis stories

	13.00	40.00	80.00

NOTE: Krigstein Golden Arrow-No. 75, 78, 91, 95, 96, 98-100. Wolverton ½ pg. ''Culture Corner''-No. 65-68, 70-85, 87-96, 98-100, 102-109, 112-121, 123, 125, 126, 128-131, 133, 134, 136, 142, 143, 146.

WHODUNIT
Aug-Sept, 1948 - No. 3, Dec-Jan, 1948-49 (#1, 52 pgs.)
D.S. Publishing Co.

	Good	Fine	N-Mint
1-Baker-a, 7pgs.	6.00	18.00	42.00
2-Morphine story	3.50	10.50	24.00
3	2.65	8.00	18.00

WHODUNNIT?
June, 1986 - No. 3, April, 1987 (Color, $2.00)
Eclipse Comics

1-3	.30	.90	1.80

WHO IS NEXT?
January, 1953
Standard Comics

5-Toth, Sekowsky, Andru-a	8.00	24.00	56.00

WHO'S MINDING THE MINT? (See Movie Classics)

WHO'S WHO IN STAR TREK
March, 1987 - No. 2, April, 1987
DC Comics

1,2-Chaykin-c	.85	2.50	5.00

WHO'S WHO IN THE LEGION OF SUPER-HEROES
Apr., 1987 - No. 7, Nov., 1988 ($1.25, color index)
DC Comics

1-7		.65	1.30

WHO'S WHO: THE DEFINITIVE DIRECTORY OF THE DC UNIV.
3/85 - No. 26, 4/87 (26 issue maxi-series, no ads)
DC Comics

1-DC heroes from A-Z	.25	.75	1.50
2-26		.60	1.20

NOTE: Kane a-1,3, Kirby a-3. Perez c-1, 2, 3-5p, 13, 14p, 15, 16p, 17, 18p.

WHO'S WHO UPDATE '87
Aug., 1987 - No. 5, Dec, 1987 ($1.25, color)
DC Comics

1-5	.25	.75	1.50

WHO'S WHO UPDATE '88
Aug., 1988 - No. 4, Nov., 1988 ($1.25)
DC Comics

1-4		.60	1.25

WILBUR COMICS (Also see Zip Comics)(Teen-age)
Sum', No. 87, 11/59; No. 88, 9/63; No. 89, 10/64; No. 90, 10/65 (No. 1-46: 52 pgs.)
MLJ Magazines/Archie Publ. No. 8, Spr.'46 on

	Good	Fine	N-Mint
1	23.00	70.00	160.00
2(Fall,'44)	11.50	34.00	80.00
3,4(Wint,'44-'45; Spr,'45)	10.00	30.00	70.00
5-1st app. Katy Keene-begin series; Wilbur story same as Archie story in Archie #1 except that Wilbur replaces Archie	37.00	110.00	260.00
6-10(Fall,'46): 7-Transvestism issue	9.50	28.50	65.00
11-20	5.00	15.00	35.00
21-30(1949)	4.00	12.00	28.00
31-50	2.00	6.00	14.00
51-69: 59-Last 10 cent ish?	1.15	3.50	8.00
70-90	.85	2.50	5.00

NOTE: Katy Keene in No. 5-56, 58-69.

WILD
Feb, 1954 - No. 5, Aug, 1954
Atlas Comics (IPC)

1	6.00	18.00	42.00
2	3.50	10.50	24.00

Whiz Comics #1, © FAW

Whiz Comics #51, © FAW

Who Is Next? #5, © STD

Wild Bill Hickok #14, © AVON   Wild Boy Of The Congo #10 (#1), © Z-D   Wild Western #5, © MEG

WILD (continued)

	Good	Fine	N-Mint
3-5	3.00	9.00	21.00

NOTE: *Berg* a-5; c-4. *Burgos* c-3. *Colan* a-4. *Everett* a-1-3. *Heath* a-2, 3, 5. *Maneely* a-1-3, 5; c-1, 5. *Post* a-2, 5. *Ed Win* a-1, 3.

WILD (This Magazine Is . . .) (Magazine)
Jan., 1968 - No. 3, 1968 (52 pgs.) (Satire)
Dell Publishing Co.

1-3	.85	2.50	5.00

WILD ANIMALS
Dec, 1982 (One-Shot)
Pacific Comics

1-Funny animal; Sergio Aragones-a		.50	1.00

WILD BILL ELLIOTT (Also see Western Roundup)
No. 278, 5/50 - No. 643, 7/55 (No #11,12) (All photo-c)
Dell Publishing Co.

4-Color 278(#1, 52pgs.)-Titled "Bill Elliott;" Bill & his horse
Stormy begin; photo front/back-c begin	8.50	25.50	60.00
2 (11/50), 3 (52 pgs.)	4.30	13.00	30.00
4-10(10-12/52)	3.70	11.00	26.00
4-Color 472(6/53),520(12/53)-Last photo back-c	3.70	11.00	26.00
13(4-6/54) - 17(4-6/55)	3.50	10.50	24.00
4-Color 643	3.50	10.50	24.00

WILD BILL HICKOK (Also see Blazing Sixguns)
Sept-Oct, 1949 - No. 28, May-June, 1956
Avon Periodicals

1-Ingels-c	11.50	34.00	80.00
2-Painted-c; Kit West app.	5.70	17.00	40.00
3,5-Painted-c	3.00	9.00	21.00
4-Painted-c by Howard Winfield	3.00	9.00	21.00
6-10,12: 8-10-Painted-c; 9-Ingels-a?	3.00	9.00	21.00
11,14-Kinstler c/a	3.65	11.00	25.00
13,15,17,18,20,23	2.15	6.50	15.00
16-Kamen-a; r-3 stories/King of the Badmen of Deadwood	3.00	9.00	21.00
19-Meskin-a	2.15	6.50	15.00
21-Reprints 2 stories/Chief Crazy Horse	2.15	6.50	15.00
22-Kinstler-a; r-/Sheriff Bob Dixon's . . .	2.15	6.50	15.00
24-27-Kinstler-c/a(r)	2.85	8.50	20.00
28-Kinstler-c/a (new); r-/Last of the Comanches			
	2.85	8.50	20.00
I.W. Reprint #1-Kinstler-c	.50	1.50	3.00
Super Reprint #10-12	.50	1.50	3.00

NOTE: *#23, 25 contain numerous editing deletions in both art and script due to code. Kinstler c-6, 7, 11-14, 17, 18, 20-22, 24-28. Howard Larsen a-1, 2(3), 4(4), 5(3), 7(3),.. 9(3), 11(4), 12(4), 17, 18, 21(2), 22, 24(3), 26. Meskin a-7. Reinman a-17.*

WILD BILL HICKOK & JINGLES (TV)(Formerly Cowboy Western)
March, 1958 - 1960 (Also see Blue Bird)
Charlton Comics

68,69-Williamson-a	3.70	11.00	26.00
70-Two pgs. Williamson-a	2.00	6.00	14.00
71-76 (#75,76, exist?)	1.15	3.50	8.00

WILD BILL PECOS (See The Westerner)

WILD BOY OF THE CONGO (Also see Approved Comics)
No. 10, Feb-Mar, 1951 - No. 15, June, 1955
Ziff-Davis No. 10-12,4-6/St. John No. 7? on

10(2-3/51)-Origin; bondage-c by Saunders; used in SOTI, pg. 189
	7.00	21.00	50.00
11(4-5/51),12(8-9/51)-Norman Saunders-c	4.00	12.00	28.00
4(10-11/51)-Saunders bondage-c	4.00	12.00	28.00
5(Winter,'51)-Saunders-c	3.50	10.50	24.00
6,8,9(10/53), 10: 6-Saunders-c	3.00	9.00	21.00
7(8-9/52)-Baker-c; Kinstler-a	3.70	11.00	26.00
11-13-Baker-c(St. John)	3.70	11.00	26.00

	Good	Fine	N-Mint
14(4/55)-Baker-c; r-#12('51)	3.70	11.00	26.00
15(6/55)	2.30	7.00	16.00

WILD DOG
Sept, 1987 - No. 4, Dec, 1987 (Mini-series)
DC Comics

1-4		.40	.80

WILD FRONTIER (Cheyenne Kid #8 on)
Oct, 1955 - No. 7, April, 1957
Charlton Comics

1-Davy Crockett	2.65	8.00	18.00
2-6-Davy Crockett in all	1.30	4.00	9.00
7-Origin Cheyenne Kid	1.30	4.00	9.00

WILD KINGDOM (TV)
1965 (Giveaway) (regular size) (16 pgs., slick-c)
Western Printing Co.

Mutual of Omaha's. . .	1.00	3.00	7.00

WILD WEST (Wild Western #3 on)
Spring, 1948 - No. 2, July, 1948
Marvel Comics (WFP)

1-Two-Gun Kid, Arizona Annie, & Tex Taylor begin
	8.50	25.50	60.00
2-Captain Tootsie by Beck	7.00	21.00	50.00

WILD WEST (Black Fury #1-57)
No. 58, November, 1966
Charlton Comics

V2#58		.60	1.20

WILD WESTERN (Wild West #1,2)
No. 3, 9/48 - No. 57, 9/57 (52pgs, 3-11; 36pgs, 12-on)
Marvel/Atlas Comics (WFP)

3(#1)-Two-Gun Kid, Tex Morgan, Tex Taylor, & Arizona Annie begin
	8.50	25.50	60.00
4-Last Arizona Annie; Captain Tootsie by Beck; Kid Colt app.			
	6.50	19.50	45.00
5-2nd app. Black Rider (1/49); Blaze Carson, Captain Tootsie by Beck app.	7.00	21.00	50.00
6-8: 6-Blaze Carson app; Anti-Wertham editorial			
	5.00	15.00	35.00
9-Photo-c; Black Rider begins, ends #19	5.70	17.00	40.00
10-Charles Starrett photo-c	7.00	21.00	50.00
11-(Last 52 pg. issue)	4.30	13.00	30.00
12-14,16-19: All Black Rider-c/stories. 12-14-The Prairie Kid & his horse Fury app.	3.50	10.50	24.00
15-Red Larabee, Gunhawk (Origin), his horse Blaze, & Apache Kid begin, end #22; Black Rider c/story	4.65	14.00	32.00
20-29: 20-Kid Colt-c begin	3.00	9.00	21.00
30-Katz-a	3.50	10.50	24.00
31-37,39,40	2.00	6.00	14.00
38-War issue; Kubert-a	2.00	6.00	14.00
41-47,49-51,53,57	1.50	4.50	10.00
48-Williamson/Torres-a, 4 pgs; Drucker-a	4.00	12.00	28.00
52-Crandall-a	3.00	9.00	21.00
54,55-Williamson-a in both, 5 & 4 pgs., #54 with Mayo plus 2 text illos.	3.50	10.50	24.00
56-Baker-a?	2.00	6.00	14.00

NOTE: *Annie Oakley in #46, 47. Apache Kid in #15-22, 39. Arizona Kid in #21, 23. Arrowhead in #34-39. Black Rider in #5, 9-19, 33-44. Fighting Texan in #17. Kid Colt in #4-6, 9-11, 20-47, 52, 54-56. Outlaw Kid in #43. Red Hawkins in #13, 14. Ringo Kid in #26, 39, 41, 43, 44, 46, 47, 50, 52-56. Tex Morgan in #3, 4, 6, 9, 11. Tex Taylor in #3-6, 9, 11. Texas Kid in #23-25. Two-Gun Kid in #3-6, 9, 11, 12, 33-39, 41. Wyatt Earp in #47. Ayers a-41. Berg a-26; c-24. Colan a-49. Forte a-28, 30. Heath a-4, 5, 8; c-34, 44. Keller a-24, 26, 29-40, 44-46, 52. Maneely a-10, 12, 15, 16, 28, 35, 38, 40, 41, 43-45; c-18-22, 33, 35, 36, 38, 39, 41, 45. Morisi a-23, 52. Pakula a-52. Powell a-51. Severin a-46, 47. Shores a-3, 5, 30, 31, 33, 35, 36, 38, 41; c-4, 5. Sinnott a-34-39.*

427

WILD WESTERN (continued)
Wildey a-43. Bondage c-19.

WILD WESTERN ACTION (Also see The Bravados)
March, 1971 - No. 3, June, 1971 (52 pgs.)
Skywald Publishing Corp. (Reprints)

	Good	Fine	N-Mint
1-Durango Kid, Straight Arrow; with all references to "Straight" in the story relettered to "Swift;" Bravados begin			
	.50	1.00	
2-Billy Nevada, Durango Kid	.30	.60	
3-Red Mask, Durango Kid	.30	.60	

WILD WESTERN ROUNDUP
Oct, 1957; 1964
Red Top/Decker Publications/I. W. Enterprises

1(1957)-Kid Cowboy-r	1.00	3.00	7.00
I.W. Reprint #1('60-61)	.25	.75	1.50

WILD WEST RODEO
1953 (15 cents)
Star Publications

1-A comic book coloring book with regular full color cover & B&W inside	2.30	7.00	16.00

WILD WILD WEST, THE (TV)
June, 1966 - No. 7, Oct, 1969
Gold Key

1,2-McWilliams-a	3.50	10.50	24.00
3-7	2.65	8.00	18.00

WILKIN BOY (See That. . .)

WILLIE COMICS (Formerly Ideal #1-4; Crime Cases #24 on; Li'l Willie #20 & 21) (See Gay, Millie The Model & Wisco)
#5, Fall, 1946 - #19, 4/49; #22, 1/50 - #23, 5/50 (No #20 & 21)
Marvel Comics (MgPC)

5(#1)-Nellie The Nurse, Margie begin	4.30	13.00	30.00
6,8,9	2.00	6.00	14.00
7(1),10,11-Kurtzman's "Hey Look"	3.50	10.50	24.00
12,14-18,22,23	1.70	5.00	12.00
13,19-Kurtzman's "Hey Look"	2.65	8.00	18.00

NOTE: *Cindy app.-17. Jeanie app.-17. Little Lizzie app.-22.*

WILLIE MAYS (See The Amazing. . .)

WILLIE THE PENGUIN
April, 1951 - No. 6, April, 1952
Standard Comics

1	1.30	4.00	9.00
2-6	.85	2.50	5.00

WILLIE THE WISE-GUY (Also see Cartoon Kids)
Sept, 1957
Atlas Comics (NPP)

1: Kida, Maneely-a	1.15	3.50	9.00

WILLIE WESTINGHOUSE EDISON SMITH THE BOY INVENTOR
1906 (36 pgs. in color) (10x16")
William A. Stokes Co.

By Frank Crane	17.00	51.00	120.00

WILLOW
Aug., 1988 - No. 3, Oct, 1988 ($1.00, color)
Marvel Comics

1-3-R/Marvel Graphic Novel 36 (movie adapt.)	.50	1.00

WILL ROGERS WESTERN (See Blazing & True Comics #66)
No. 5, June, 1950 - No. 2, Aug, 1950
Fox Features Syndicate

5,2: Photo-c	8.50	25.50	60.00

WILL-YUM (See 4-Color #676,765,902)

WIN A PRIZE COMICS (Timmy The Timid Ghost #3 on?)
Feb, 1955 - No. 2, Apr, 1955
Charlton Comics

	Good	Fine	N-Mint
V1#1-S&K-a; Poe adapt; E.C. War swipe	19.00	57.00	132.00
2-S&K-a	13.50	41.00	95.00

WIND RAGE
1987 ($1.25, color)
Blackthorne Publishing

1	.60	1.25

WINDY & WILLY
May-June, 1969 - No. 4, Nov-Dec, 1969
National Periodical Publications

1-4: r/Dobie Gillis with some art changes	.25	.75	1.50

WINGS COMICS
Sept, 1940 - No. 124, 1954
Fiction House Magazines

1-Skull Squad, Clipper Kirk, Suicide Smith, Jane Martin, War Nurse, Phantom Falcons, Greasemonkey Griffin, Parachute Patrol & Powder Burns begin	65.00	195.00	455.00
2	32.00	95.00	225.00
3-5	24.00	72.00	170.00
6-10	20.00	60.00	140.00
11-15	17.00	51.00	120.00
16-Origin Captain Wings	18.00	54.00	125.00
17-20	13.00	40.00	90.00
21-30	12.00	36.00	84.00
31-40	11.00	32.00	75.00
41-50	8.00	24.00	56.00
51-60: 60-Last Skull Squad	7.00	21.00	50.00
61-67: 66-Ghost Patrol begins (becomes Ghost Squadron #71)	7.00	21.00	50.00
68,69: 68-Clipper Kirk becomes The Phantom Falcon-origin, Part 1; Part 2-#69	7.00	21.00	50.00
70-72: 70-1st app. The Phantom Falcon in costume, origin-Part 3; Capt. Wings battles Col. Kamikaze in all	5.50	16.50	38.00
73-99	5.50	16.50	38.00
100	6.50	19.50	45.00
101-114,116-124: 111-Last Jane Martin. 112-Flying Saucer c/story	4.00	12.00	28.00
115-Used in POP, pg. 89	4.60	14.00	32.00

NOTE: *Bondage covers are common. Captain Wings battles Sky Hag-#75, 76; . . . Mr. Atlantis-#85-92; . . . Mr. Pupin(Red Agent)-#98-103. Capt. Wings by Elias-#52-64; by Lubbers-#29-32,70-103; by Renee-#33-46. Evans a-85-103, 108(Jane Martin). Larsen a-52, 59, 64, 73-77. Jane Martin by Fran Hopper-#68-84; Suicide Smith by John Celardo-#76-103; by Hollingsworth-#105-109; Ghost Patrol by Maurice Whitman-#83-103; Skull Squad by M. Baker-#52-60; Clipper Kirk by Baker-#60, 61; Ghost Squadron by Whitman-#72-77, 104-110. Elias c-61-69. Fawcette c-6, 7, 10, 11, 17, 24-27, 30, 32. Lubbers c-75-100. Tuska a-5.*

WINGS OF THE EAGLES, THE (See 4-Color #790)

WINKY DINK (Adventures of. . .)
No. 75, March, 1957 (One Shot)
Pines Comics

75-Marv Levy c/a	1.50	4.50	10.00

WINKY DINK (See 4-Color #663)

WINNIE-THE-POOH
January, 1977 - No. 33, 1984 (Walt Disney)
(Winnie-The-Pooh began as Edward Bear in 1926 by Milne)
Gold Key No. 1-17/Whitman No. 18 on

1-New art	.25	.75	1.50
2-4,6-11		.40	.80
5,12-33-New material		.35	.70

WINNIE WINKLE
1930 - 1933 (52 pgs.) (B&W daily strip reprints)

Willie The Wise-Guy #1, © MEG

Wings Comics #31, © FH

Wings Comics #112, © FH

Winter World #1, © Eclipse Comics

Witchcraft #3, © AVON

Witches Tales #21, © HARV

	Good	Fine	N-Mint

WINNIE WINKLE (continued)
Cupples & Leon Co.

	Good	Fine	N-Mint
1	8.00	24.00	56.00
2-4	5.70	17.00	40.00

WINNIE WINKLE (See Popular & Super Comics)
1941 - No. 7, Sept-Nov, 1949
Dell Publishing Co.

Large Feature Comic 2('41)	10.00	30.00	70.00
4-Color 94('45)	8.00	24.00	56.00
4-Color 174	4.65	14.00	32.00
1(3-5/48)-Contains daily & Sunday newspaper-r from 1939-1941			
	3.70	11.00	26.00
2 (6-8/48)	2.30	7.00	16.00
3-7	1.60	4.80	11.00

WINTERWORLD
Sept, 1987 - No. 3, Mar, 1988 (mini-series, $1.75, color)
Eclipse Comics

1-3	.30	.90	1.80

WISCO/KLARER COMIC BOOK (Miniature)
1948 - 1964 (24 pgs.) (3½x6¾")
Given away by Wisco "99" Service Stations, Carnation Malted Milk, Klarer Health Wieners, Fleers Dubble Bubble Gum, Rodeo All-Meat Wieners, Perfect Potato Chips, & others; see ad in Tom Mix #21
Marvel Comics/Vital Publications/Fawcett Publications

Blackstone & the Gold Medal Mystery(1948)	2.65	8.00	16.00
Blackstone "Solves the Sealed Vault Mystery"(1950)			
	2.65	8.00	16.00
Blaze Carson in "The Sheriff Shoots It Out"(1950)			
	2.65	8.00	16.00
Captain Marvel & Billy's Big Game (r-/Capt. Marvel Adv. #76)			
	24.00	70.00	155.00
(Prices vary widely on this book)			
China Boy in "A Trip to the Zoo" #10	.85	2.50	5.00
Indoors-Outdoors Game Book	.85	2.50	5.00
Jim Solar Space Sheriff in "Battle for Mars," "Between Two Worlds," "Conquers Outer Space," "The Creatures on the Comet," "Defeats the Moon Missile Men," "Encounter Creatures on Comet," "Meet the Jupiter Jumpers," "Meets the Man From Mars," "On Traffic Duty," "Outlaws of the Spaceways," "Pirates of the Planet X," "Protects Space Lanes," "Raiders From the Sun," "Ring Around Saturn," "Robots of Rhea," "The Sky Ruby," "Spacetts of the Sky," "Spidermen of Venus," "Trouble on Mercury"	2.35	7.00	14.00
Johnny Starboard & the Underseas Pirates('48)	.70	2.00	4.00
Kid Colt in "He Lived by His Guns" ('50)	3.00	9.00	18.00
Little Aspirin as "Crook Catcher" #2('50)	.60	1.80	3.60
Little Aspirin in "Naughty But Nice" #6(1950)	.60	1.80	3.60
Return of the Black Phantom (not M.E. character)(Roy Dare)			
	1.00	3.00	6.00
Secrets of Magic	1.00	3.00	6.00
Slim Morgan "Brings Justice to Mesa City" #3			
	1.30	4.00	8.00
Super Rabbit(1950)-Cuts Red Tape, Stops Crime Wave!			
	1.20	3.50	7.00
Tex Farnum, Frontiersman(1948)	1.50	4.50	9.00
Tex Taylor in "Draw or Die, Cowpoke!"('50)	2.65	8.00	16.00
Tex Taylor in "An Exciting Adventure at the Gold Mine"('50)			
	2.35	7.00	14.00
Wacky Quacky in "All-Aboard"	.50	1.50	3.00
When School Is Out	.50	1.50	3.00
Willie in a "Comic-Comic Book Fall" #1	.50	1.50	3.00
Wonder Duck "An Adventure at the Rodeo of the Fearless Quacker!" (1950)	.50	1.50	3.00
Rare uncut version of three; includes Capt. Marvel, Tex Farnum,			

	Good	Fine	N-Mint
Black Phantom	Estimated value. . . .		$300.00

WISE GUYS (See Harvey...)

WISE LITTLE HEN, THE
1934 (48 pgs.); 1935; 1937 (Story book)
David McKay Publ./Whitman

2nd book app. Donald Duck; Donald app. on cover with Wise Little Hen & Practical Pig; painted cover; same artist as the B&W's from Silly Symphony Cartoon, The Wise Little Hen (1934)(McKay)

	27.00	81.00	190.00
1935 Edition with dust jacket; 44 pgs. with color, 8¾x9¾" (Whitman)	22.00	65.00	154.00
888(1937)-9½x13", 12 pgs. (Whitman) Donald Duck app.			
	15.00	45.00	105.00

WITCHCRAFT (See Strange Mysteries, Super Reprint #18)
Mar-Apr, 1952 - No. 6, Mar, 1953
Avon Periodicals

1-Kubert-a; 1pg. Check-a	25.00	75.00	175.00
2-Kubert & Check-a	15.00	45.00	105.00
3,6: 3-Kinstler, Lawrence-a	11.00	32.00	75.00
4-People cooked alive c/s	11.50	34.00	80.00
5-Kelly Freas-c	16.00	48.00	110.00

NOTE: *Hollingsworth* a-4-6; c-4, 6.

WITCHES TALES (Witches Western Tales #29,30)
Jan, 1951 - No. 28, Dec, 1954 (date misprinted as 4/55)
Witches Tales/Harvey Publications

1-1pg. Powell-a	11.50	34.50	80.00
2-Eye injury panel	4.00	12.00	28.00
3-7,9,10	3.35	10.00	23.00
8-Eye injury panels	3.85	11.50	27.00
11-13,15,16: 12-Acid in face story	3.00	9.00	21.00
14,17-Powell/Nostrand-a. 17-Atomic disaster story			
	5.00	15.00	35.00
18-Nostrand-a; E.C. swipe/Shock S.S.	5.00	15.00	35.00
19-Nostrand-a; E.C. swipe/"Glutton"	5.00	15.00	35.00
20-24-Nostrand-a. 21-E.C. swipe; rape story. 23-Wood E.C. swipes/ Two-Fisted Tales #34.	5.00	15.00	35.00
25-Nostrand-a; E.C. swipe/Mad Barber	5.00	15.00	35.00
26-28: 27-r-/#6 with diff.-c. 28-r-/#8 with diff.-c			
	2.50	7.50	17.00

NOTE: *Check* a-24. *Kremer* a-18; c-25. *Nostrand* a-17-25; 14, 17(w/Powell). *Palais* a-1, 2, 4(2), 5(2), 7-9, 12, 14, 15, 17. *Powell* a-3-7, 10, 11, 19-27. Bondage-c 1, 3, 5, 6, 8, 9.

WITCHES TALES (Magazine)
V1No.7, July, 1969 - V7No.1, Feb, 1975 (52 pgs.) (B&W)
Eerie Publications

V1#7(7/69) - 9(11/69)	.70	2.00	4.00
V2#1-6('70), V3#1-6('71)	.50	1.50	3.00
V4#1-6('72), V5#1-6('73), V6#1-6('74), V7#1	.50	1.50	3.00

NOTE: *Ajax/Farrell* reprints in early issues.

WITCHES' WESTERN TALES (Formerly Witches Tales) (Western Tales #31 on)
No. 29, Feb, 1955 - No. 30, April, 1955
Harvey Publications

29,30-S&K-r/from Boys' Ranch including-c	7.00	21.00	50.00

WITCHING HOUR, THE
Feb-Mar, 1969 - No. 85, Oct, 1978
National Periodical Publications/DC Comics

1-Toth plus Adams, 3 pgs.	.45	1.30	2.60
2,6		.50	1.00
3,5-Wrightson-a; Toth-a(p)	.25	.75	1.50
4,7,9-12: Toth-a in all		.50	1.00
8-Adams-a	.35	1.00	2.00

THE WITCHING HOUR (continued)	Good	Fine	N-Mint
13-Adams c/a, 2pgs.	.25	.75	1.50
14-Williamson/Garzon, Jones-a; Adams-c	.25	.75	1.50
15-85: 38-(100 pgs.)		.25	.50

NOTE: Combined with The Unexpected with No. 189. Adams c-7-11, 13, 14. Alcala a-24, 27, 33, 41, 43. Anderson a-9, 38. Cardy c-4, 5. Kaluta a-7. Kane a-12p. Morrow a-10, 13, 15, 16. Nino a-31, 40, 45, 47. Redondo a-20, 23, 24, 34, 65. Reese a-23. Toth a-38r. Tuska a-12. Wood a-12i, 15.

WITH THE MARINES ON THE BATTLEFRONTS OF THE WORLD
1953 (no month) - No. 2, March, 1954 (photo covers)
Toby Press

	Good	Fine	N-Mint
1-John Wayne story	11.50	34.00	80.00
2-Monty Hall in #1,2	2.00	6.00	14.00

WITH THE U.S. PARATROOPS BEHIND ENEMY LINES (Also see U.S. Paratroops..; #2-5 titled U.S. Paratroops..)
1951 - No. 6, Dec, 1952
Avon Periodicals

	Good	Fine	N-Mint
1-Wood-c & inside-c	8.00	24.00	56.00
2	4.35	13.00	30.00
3-6	3.65	11.00	25.00

NOTE: Kinstler a-2, 5, 6; c-2, 4, 5.

WITNESS, THE (Also see Amazing Mysteries, Captain America 71, Ideal 4, Marvel Mystery 92 & Mystic #7)
Sept, 1948
Marvel Comics (MjMe)

	Good	Fine	N-Mint
1(Scarce)-No Everett-c	40.00	120.00	280.00

WITTY COMICS
1945
Irwin H. Rubin Publ./Chicago Nite Life News No. 2

	Good	Fine	N-Mint
1-The Pioneer, Junior Patrol	4.65	14.00	32.00
2-The Pioneer, Junior Patrol	2.65	8.00	18.00
3-7-Skyhawk	2.00	6.00	14.00

WIZARD OF OZ (See Classics Ill. Jr. 535, Dell Jr. Treasury No. 5, First Comics Graphic Novel, 4-Color No. 1308, Marvelous..., & Marvel Treasury of Oz)

WOLF GAL (See Al Capp's...)

WOLFMAN, THE (See Book & Record Set & Movie Classics)

WOLFPACK
2/88 ($7.95); 8/88 - No. 12, 1989 (limited series)
Marvel Comics

	Good	Fine	N-Mint
1-1st app./origin (Marvel Graphic Novel #31)	1.35	4.00	7.95
1-12		.40	.75

WOLVERINE (See Alpha Flight, Havok & ..., Incred. Hulk #180, Incred. Hulk &..., Kitty Pryde And..., Marvel Comics Presents, Spider-Man vs..., & The X-Men #94)
Sept, 1982 - No. 4, Dec, 1982 (mini-series)
Marvel Comics Group

	Good	Fine	N-Mint
1-Frank Miller-c/a(p)	2.00	6.00	12.00
2,3-Miller-c/a(p)	1.50	4.50	9.00
4-Miller-c/a(p)	1.70	5.00	10.00

WOLVERINE
Nov, 1988 - Present ($1.50, color, Baxter paper)
Marvel Comics

	Good	Fine	N-Mint
1: Buscema-p in 1-5; Williamson-i in 1,4,5	.50	1.50	3.00
2-5	.25	.75	1.50

WOMAN OF THE PROMISE, THE
1950 (General Distr.) (32 pgs.) (paper cover)
Catechetical Guild

	Good	Fine	N-Mint
nn	5.00	15.00	30.00

WOMEN IN LOVE (A Feature Presentation #5)
Aug, 1949 - No. 4, Feb, 1950
Fox Features Synd./Hero Books

	Good	Fine	N-Mint
1	11.00	32.00	76.00
2-Kamen/Feldstein-c	8.50	25.50	60.00
3	5.70	17.00	40.00
4-Wood-a	8.00	24.00	56.00

WOMEN IN LOVE
Winter, 1952 (100 pgs.)
Ziff-Davis Publishing Co.

	Good	Fine	N-Mint
nn-Kinstler-a (Scarce)	20.00	60.00	140.00

WOMEN OUTLAWS (My Love Memories #9 on)
July, 1948 - No. 8, Sept, 1949 (Also see Red Circle)
Fox Features Syndicate

	Good	Fine	N-Mint
1-Used in SOTI, illo-''Giving children an image of American womanhood''; negligee panels	27.00	81.00	190.00
2-Spanking panel	23.00	70.00	160.00
3-Kamen-a	20.00	60.00	140.00
4-8	14.00	42.00	100.00
nn(nd)-Contains Cody of the Pony Express; same cover as #7	11.00	32.00	75.00

WOMEN TO LOVE
No date (1953)
Realistic

	Good	Fine	N-Mint
nn-(Scarce)-Reprint/Complete Romance No. 1; c-/Avon paperback 165	20.00	60.00	140.00

WONDER BOY (Formerly Terrific Comics) (See Bomber Comics)
No. 17, May, 1955 - No. 18, July, 1955
Ajax/Farrell Publ.

	Good	Fine	N-Mint
17-Phantom Lady app. Bakerish a/c	10.00	30.00	70.00
18-Phantom Lady app.	9.50	28.50	65.00

NOTE: Phantom Lady not by Matt Baker.

WONDER COMICS (Wonderworld #3 on)
May, 1939 - No. 2, June, 1939
Fox Features Syndicate

	Good	Fine	N-Mint
1-(Scarce)-Wonder Man only app. by Will Eisner; Dr. Fung (by Powell), K-51 begins; Bob Kane-a; Eisner-c	295.00	885.00	2065.00
2-(Scarce)-Yarko the Great, Master Magician by Eisner begins; 'Spark' Stevens by Bob Kane, Patty O'Day, Tex Mason app. Lou Fine's 1st-c; a(2pgs.)	160.00	480.00	1120.00

WONDER COMICS
May, 1944 - No. 20, Oct, 1948
Great/Nedor/Better Publications

	Good	Fine	N-Mint
1-The Grim Reaper & Spectro, the Mind Reader begin; Hitler/ Hirohito bondage-c	30.00	90.00	210.00
2-Origin The Grim Reaper; Super Sleuths begin, end #8,17	18.00	54.00	125.00
3-5	16.00	48.00	110.00
6-10: 6-Flag-c. 8-Last Spectro. 9-Wonderman begins	13.00	40.00	90.00
11-14-Dick Devens, King of Futuria begins #11, ends #14	16.00	48.00	110.00
15-Tara begins (origin), ends #20	17.00	51.00	120.00
16,18: 16-Spectro app.; last Grim Reaper. 18-The Silver Knight begins	15.00	45.00	105.00
17-Wonderman with Frazetta panels; Jill Trent with all Frazetta inks	18.00	54.00	125.00
19-Frazetta panels	17.00	51.00	120.00
20-Most of Silver Knight by Frazetta	21.50	65.00	150.00

NOTE: Ingels c-11, 12. Schomburg (Xela) c-1-10; (airbrush)-13-20. Bondage-c 12, 13, 15.

WONDER DUCK (See Wisco)
Sept, 1949 - No. 3, Mar, 1950

Wolverine #1 (11/88), © MEG   *Wonder Boy #17, © AJAX*   *Wonder Comics #10, © BP*

Wonder Woman #6 (Fall/43), © DC

Wonder Woman #1 (2/87), © DC

Wonderworld Comics #19, © FOX

WONDER DUCK (continued)
Marvel Comics (CDS)

	Good	Fine	N-Mint
1	3.70	11.00	26.00
2,3	2.65	8.00	18.00

WONDERFUL ADVENTURES OF PINOCCHIO, THE (See Movie Comics & Walt Disney Showcase #48)
April, 1982 (Walt Disney)
Whitman Publishing Co.

3-(Cont. of Movie Comics?); r-/FC #92		.30	.60

WONDERFUL WORLD OF DUCKS (See Golden Picture Story Book)
1975
Colgate Palmolive Co.

1-Mostly-r		.30	.60

WONDERFUL WORLD OF THE BROTHERS GRIMM (See Movie Comics)

WONDERLAND COMICS
Summer, 1945 - No. 9, Feb-Mar, 1947
Feature Publications/Prize

1	3.50	10.50	24.00
2-Howard Post-c	1.70	5.00	12.00
3-9: 4-Post-c	1.30	4.00	9.00

WONDER MAN
Mar, 1986 (One-Shot, 52 pgs.)
Marvel Comics Group

1	.25	.75	1.50

WONDERS OF ALADDIN, THE (See 4-Color #1255)

WONDER WOMAN (See Adventure, All-Star Comics, Brave & the Bold, DC Comics Presents, Legend of . . . , Sensation Comics, and World's Finest)

WONDER WOMAN
Summer, 1942 - No. 329, Feb, 1986
National Periodical Publications/All-American Publ./DC Comics

	Good	Fine	N-Mint
1-Origin Wonder Woman retold (see All-Star #8); r-/Famous 1st Editions; H. G. Peter-a begins	285.00	855.00	2000.00
2-Origin & 1st app. Mars; Duke of Deception app.	95.00	285.00	665.00
3	70.00	210.00	490.00
4,5: 5-1st Dr. Psycho app.	52.00	155.00	365.00
6-10: 6-1st Cheetah app.	40.00	120.00	280.00
11-20	30.00	90.00	210.00
21-30	22.00	65.00	154.00
31-40	16.00	48.00	110.00
41-44,46-48	13.00	40.00	90.00
45-Origin retold	22.00	65.00	154.00
49-Used in SOTI, pgs. 234,236. Last 52 pg. ish	13.00	40.00	90.00
50-(44 pgs.)-Used in POP, pg. 97	10.00	30.00	70.00
51-60	9.50	28.50	65.00
61-72: 62-Origin of W.W. i.d. 64-Story about 3-D movies. 70-1st Angle Man app. 72-Last pre-code	8.00	24.00	56.00
73-90: 80-Origin The Invisible Plane	6.00	18.00	42.00
91-94,96-99: 97-Last H. G. Peter-a. 99-Origin W.W. i.d. with new facts	4.00	12.00	28.00
95-A-Bomb-c	4.65	14.00	32.00
100	5.00	15.00	35.00
101-104,106-110: 107-1st advs. of Wonder Girl; 1st Merboy; tells how W.W. won her costume	3.15	9.50	22.00
105-(Scarce)-Wonder Woman's secret origin; W. Woman appears as a girl (not Wonder Girl)	6.50	19.50	45.00
111-120	1.85	5.50	13.00
121-126: 122-1st app. Wonder Tot. 124-1st app. Won. Wom. Family. 126-Last 10 cent ish.	1.10	3.30	7.50
127-130: 128-Origin The Invisible Plane retold	1.00	3.00	7.00
131-150	.85	2.50	5.00

	Good	Fine	N-Mint
151-158,160-170	.70	2.00	4.00
159-Origin retold	.85	2.50	5.00
171-178	.50	1.50	3.00
179-195: 179-Wears no costume to issue #203. 180-Death of Steve Trevor. 195-Wood inks?	.45	1.25	2.50
196 (52 pgs.)-Origin r-/All-Star 8	.50	1.50	3.00
197,198 (52 pgs.)-r	.50	1.50	3.00
199,200-Jones-c; 52 pgs.	.85	2.50	5.00
201-210: 204-Return to old costume; death of I Ching. 202-Fafhrd & The Grey Mouser debut		.60	1.20
211-217: 211,214(100 pgs.), 217 (68 pgs.)		.50	1.00
218-230: 220-Adams assist. 223-Steve Trevor revived as Steve Howard & learns W.W.'s I.D. 228-Both W. Women team up & new World War II stories begin, end #243		.50	1.00
231-240: 237-Origin retold		.50	1.00
241-260: 241-Intro Bouncer. 248-Steve Trevor Howard dies. 250-Intro/ origin Orana, the new W. Woman. 251-Orana dies		.50	1.00
261-286: 269-Last Wood a(i) for DC? (7/80). 271-Huntress & 3rd Life of Steve Trevor begin		.50	1.00
287-New Teen Titans x-over	.25	.75	1.50
288-299: 288-New costume, logo. 291-93-Three part epic with Super-Heroines		.50	1.00
300-Double-sized, 76 pg. anniversary issue; Giffen-a; New Teen Titans, JLA app.	.25	.75	1.50
301-309: 308-Huntress begins		.50	1.00
310-328 (75 cent cover)		.50	1.00
329-Double size		.65	1.30
Pizza Hut Giveaways (12/77)-Reprints #60,62		.40	.80

NOTE: Colan a-288-305p; c-288-90p. Giffen a-300p. Grell c-217. Kaluta c-297. Gil Kane c-294p, 303-05, 307, 312, 314. Miller c-298p. Morrow c-233. Nasser a-232p; c-231p, 232p. Perez c-283p, 284p. Spiegle a-312. Staton a-241p, 271-287p, 289p, 290p, 294-99p; c-241p, 245p, 246p.

WONDER WOMAN
Feb, 1987 - Present
DC Comics

	Good	Fine	N-Mint
1-New origin; Perez c/a begins	.50	1.50	3.00
2-5	.25	.75	1.50
6-10		.65	1.30
11-20: 18-Free 16pg sty		.55	1.10
21-28		.50	1.00
Annual 1 ('88, $1.50)-Art Adams-a	.25	.75	1.50

WONDER WOMAN SPECTACULAR (See DC Special Series #9)

WONDER WORKER OF PERU
No date (16 pgs.) (B&W) (5x7")
Catechetical Guild (Giveaway)

	1.70	5.00	10.00

WONDERWORLD COMICS (Formerly Wonder Comics)
No. 3, July, 1939 - No. 33, Jan, 1942
Fox Features Syndicate

	Good	Fine	N-Mint
3-Intro The Flame by Fine; Dr. Fung (Powell-a), K-51 (Powell-a?), & Yarko the Great, Master Magician (Eisner-a) continues; Eisner/Fine-c	100.00	300.00	700.00
4	52.00	155.00	365.00
5-10	48.00	145.00	335.00
11-Origin The Flame	55.00	165.00	385.00
12-20: 13-Dr. Fung ends	28.00	84.00	195.00
21-Origin The Black Lion & Cub	25.00	75.00	175.00
22-27: 22,25-Dr. Fung app.	20.00	60.00	140.00
28-1st app/origin U.S. Jones; Lu-Nar, the Moon Man begins	24.00	72.00	168.00
29,31-33: 32-Hitler-c	15.00	45.00	105.00
30-Origin Flame Girl	27.00	81.00	190.00

431

WONDERWORLD COMICS (continued)
NOTE: *Yarko by Eisner-No. 3-11. Eisner text illos-3. Lou Fine c/a-3-11; c-12, 13, 15; text illos-4. Nordling a-4-14. Powell a-3-12. Tuska a-5-9. Bondage-c 14, 15, 28, 31, 32.*

WOODSY OWL (See March of Comics #395)
Nov, 1973 - No. 10, Feb, 1976
Gold Key

	Good	Fine	N-Mint
1	.25	.75	1.50
2-10		.50	1.00

WOODY WOODPECKER (Walter Lantz... #73 on?)(See Dell Giants for annuals, The Funnies, New Funnies & Jolly Jingles)
No. 169, 10/47 - No. 72, 5-7/62; No. 73, 10/62 - No. 201, 4/84 (nn 192)
Dell Publishing Co./Gold Key No. 73-187/Whitman No. 188 on

	Good	Fine	N-Mint
4-Color 169-Drug turns Woody into a Mr. Hyde	7.00	21.00	50.00
4-Color 188	5.00	15.00	35.00
4-Color 202,232,249,264,288	3.00	9.00	21.00
4-Color 305,336,350	2.00	6.00	14.00
4-Color 364,374,390,405,416,431('52)	1.70	5.00	12.00
16 (12-1/52-53) - 30('55)	1.15	3.50	8.00
31-50	.75	2.25	5.00
51-72 (Last Dell)	.55	1.65	4.00
73-75 (Giants, 84 pgs., Gold Key)	1.75	5.25	14.00
76-80	.50	1.50	3.00
81-100	.35	1.00	2.00
101-120		.60	1.20
121-191,193-201		.40	.80
Christmas Parade 1(11/68-Giant)(G.K.)	1.70	5.00	12.00
Clover Stamp-Newspaper Boy Contest('56)-9 pg. story-(Giveaway)	.85	2.50	6.00
In Chevrolet Wonderland(1954-Giveaway)(Western Publ.)-20 pgs., full story line; Chilly Willy app.	3.00	9.00	21.00
Kite Fun Book (1956, 5x7¼", 16p, soft-c)	4.00	12.00	28.00
Meets Scotty McTape(1953-Scotch Tape giveaway)-16 pgs., full size	2.30	7.00	16.00
Summer Fun 1(6/66-G.K.)(84 pgs.)	2.25	6.75	18.00

NOTE: *15 cent editions exist. Reprints-No. 92, 102, 103, 105, 106, 124, 125, 152, 153, 157, 162, 165, 194(½)-200(½).*

WOODY WOODPECKER (See Comic Album #5,9,13, Dell Giant #24, 40, 54, Dell Giants, The Funnies, Golden Comics Digest #1, 3, 5, 8, 15, 16, 20, 24, 32, 37, 44, March of Comics #16, 34, 85, 93, 109, 124, 139, 158, 177, 184, 203, 222, 239, 249, 261, 420, 454, 466, 478, New Funnies & Super Book #12, 24)

WOOLWORTH'S CHRISTMAS STORY BOOK
1952 - 1954 (16 pgs., paper-c) (See Jolly Christmas Book)
Promotional Publ. Co.(Western Printing Co.)

nn	2.00	6.00	14.00

NOTE: *1952 issue-Marv Levy c/a.*

WOOLWORTH'S HAPPY TIME CHRISTMAS BOOK
1952 (Christmas giveaway, 36 pgs.)
F. W. Woolworth Co.(Whitman Publ. Co.)

nn	2.00	6.00	14.00

WORLD AROUND US, THE (Ill. Story of...)
Sept, 1958 - No. 36, Oct, 1961 (25 cents)
Gilberton Publishers (Classics Illustrated)

	Good	Fine	N-Mint
1-Dogs	2.00	6.00	14.00
2-Indians-Crandall-a	1.70	5.00	12.00
3-Horses; L. B. Cole-c	1.70	5.00	12.00
4-Railroads	1.70	5.00	12.00
5-Space; Ingels-a	3.00	9.00	21.00
6-The F.B.I.; Disbrow, Evans, Ingels-a	2.30	7.00	16.00
7-Pirates; Disbrow, Ingels-a	3.00	9.00	21.00
8-Flight; Evans, Ingels, Crandall-a	2.65	8.00	18.00
9-Army; Disbrow, Ingels, Orlando-a	2.65	8.00	18.00
10-Navy; Disbrow, Kinstler-a	1.70	5.00	12.00
11-Marine Corps.	1.70	5.00	12.00
12-Coast Guard	1.30	4.00	9.00

	Good	Fine	N-Mint
13-Air Force; L.B. Cole-c	1.70	5.00	12.00
14-French Revolution; Crandall, Evans-a	3.50	10.50	24.00
15-Prehistoric Animals; Al Williamson-a, 6 & 10 pgs. plus Morrow-a	3.70	11.00	26.00
16-Crusades	2.65	8.00	18.00
17-Festivals-Evans, Crandall-a	2.65	8.00	18.00
18-Great Scientists; Crandall, Evans, Torres, Williamson, Morrow-a	3.00	9.00	21.00
19-Jungle; Crandall, Williamson, Morrow-a	4.000	12.00	28.00
20-Communications; Crandall, Evans-a	3.70	11.00	26.00
21-American Presidents	2.65	8.00	18.00
22-Boating; Morrow-a	1.70	5.00	12.00
23-Great Explorers; Crandall, Evans-a	1.70	5.00	12.00
24-Ghosts; Morrow, Evans-a	2.30	7.00	16.00
25-Magic; Evans, Morrow-a	2.65	8.00	18.00
26-The Civil War	3.00	9.00	21.00
27-Mountains (High Advs.); Crandall/Evans, Morrow, Torres-a	2.30	7.00	16.00
28-Whaling; Crandall, Evans, Morrow-a; L.B. Cole-c	2.00	6.00	14.00
29-Vikings; Crandall, Evans, Torres, Morrow-a	2.65	8.00	18.00
30-Undersea Adventure; Crandall/Evans, Kirby-a	3.70	11.00	26.00
31-Hunting; Crandall/Evans, Ingels, Kinstler, Kirby-a	3.00	9.00	21.00
32-For Gold & Glory; Morrow, Kirby, Crandall, Evans-a	2.65	8.00	18.00
33-Famous Teens; Torres, Crandall, Evans-a	2.30	7.00	16.00
34-Fishing; Crandall/Evans, Ingels-a	2.00	6.00	14.00
35-Spies; Kirby, Evans, Morrow-a	2.00	6.00	14.00
36-Fight for Life (Medicine); Kirby-a	2.00	6.00	14.00

NOTE: *See Classics Ill. Special Edition. Another World Around Us issue entitled The Sea had been prepared in 1962 but was never published in the U.S. It was published in the British/European World Around Us series. Those series then continued with seven additional WAU titles not in the U.S. series.*

WORLD FAMOUS HEROES MAGAZINE
Oct, 1941 - No. 4, Apr, 1942 (a comic book)
Comic Corp. of America (Centaur)

	Good	Fine	N-Mint
1-Gustavson-c; Lubbers, Glanzman-a; Davy Crockett story; Flag-c	35.00	105.00	245.00
2-Lou Gehrig life story; Lubbers-a	18.00	54.00	125.00
3,4-Lubbers-a; 4-Wild Bill Hickok app.	16.00	48.00	110.00

WORLD FAMOUS STORIES
1945
Croyden Publishers

1-Ali Baba, Hansel & Gretel, Rip Van Winkle, Mid-Summer Night's Dream	5.00	15.00	35.00

WORLD IS HIS PARISH, THE
1953 (15 cents)
George A. Pflaum

The story of Pope Pius XII	3.50	10.50	22.00

WORLD OF ADVENTURE (Walt Disney's...)(TV)
April, 1963 - No. 3, Oct, 1963
Gold Key

1-3-Disney TV characters; Savage Sam, Johnny Shiloh, Capt. Nemo, The Mooncussers	.75	2.25	5.00

WORLD OF ARCHIE, THE (See Archie Giant Series Mag. #148, 151, 156, 160, 165, 171, 177, 182, 188, 193, 200, 208, 213, 225, 232, 237, 244, 249, 456, 461, 468, 473, 480, 485, 492, 497, 504, 509, 516, 521, 532, 543, 554, 565, 574, 587)

WORLD OF FANTASY
May, 1956 - No. 19, Aug, 1959
Atlas Comics (CPC No. 1-15/ZPC No. 16-19)

1	8.50	25.50	60.00

The World Around Us #35, © GIL

World Famous Heroes Magazine #4, © CEN

World Of Adventure #1, © WDC

World Of Fantasy #16, © MEG

World Of Smallville #1, © DC

World's Finest Comics #9, © DC

	Good	Fine	N-Mint
WORLD OF FANTASY (continued)			
2-Williamson-a, 4 pgs.	6.00	18.00	42.00
3-Sid Check, Roussos-a	3.50	10.50	24.00
4-7	2.65	8.00	18.00
8-Matt Fox, Orlando, Berg-a	4.30	13.00	30.00
9-Krigstein-a	3.50	10.50	24.00
10,13-15	2.00	6.00	14.00
11-Torres-a	3.50	10.50	24.00
12-Everett-c	2.00	6.00	14.00
16-Williamson-a, 4 pgs.; Ditko, Kirby-a	4.75	14.25	33.00
17-19-Ditko, Kirby-a	4.00	12.00	28.00

NOTE: Ayers a-3. Berg a-5, 6, 8. Check a-3. Ditko a-17, 19. Everett c-4, 5-7, 9, 13. Kirby c-15, 17-19. Krigstein a-9. Maneely c-14. Morrow a-7,8,14. Orlando a-8,13,14. Powell a-4, 6. Sale a-3.

WORLD OF GIANT COMICS, THE (See Archie All-Star Specials under Archie Comics)

WORLD OF JUGHEAD, THE (See Archie Giant Series Mag. #9, 14, 19, 24, 30, 136, 143, 149, 152, 157, 161, 166, 172, 178, 183, 189, 194, 202, 209, 215, 227, 233, 239, 245, 251, 457, 463, 469, 475, 481, 487, 493, 499, 505, 511, 517, 523, 531, 542, 553, 564, 576, 590)

WORLD OF KRYPTON, THE (World of . . . #3)
7/79 - No. 3, 9/79; 12/87 - No. 4, 3/88 (Both mini-series)
DC Comics, Inc.

1 ('79)-Jor-El marries Lara	.40	.80
2,3: 3-Baby Superman sent to Earth; Krypton explodes; Mon-el app.	.30	.60
1-4 (2nd series)-Byrne scripts; Byrne/Simonson-c	.40	.80

WORLD OF METROPOLIS, THE
Aug., 1988 - No. 4, July, 1988 (Mini-series)
DC Comics

1-4: Byrne scripts	.50	1.00

WORLD OF MYSTERY
June, 1956 - No. 7, July, 1957
Atlas Comics (GPI)

1-Torres, Orlando-a	7.00	21.00	50.00
2-Woodish-a	2.35	7.00	16.00
3-Torres, Davis, Ditko-a	4.35	13.00	30.00
4-Davis, Pakula, Powell-a; Ditko-c	4.35	13.00	30.00
5,7: 5-Orlando-a	2.35	7.00	16.00
6-Williamson/Mayo-a, 4 pgs.; Ditko-a; Crandall text illo	4.60	14.00	32.00

NOTE: Colan a-7. Everett c-1-3. Romita a-2. Severin c/a-7.

WORLD OF SMALLVILLE
Apr., 1988 - No. 4, July, 1988 ($1.75, color, mini-series)
DC Comics

1-4: Byrne scripts	.60	1.20

WORLD OF SUSPENSE
April, 1956 - No. 8, July, 1957
Atlas News Co.

1-Orlando-a	7.00	21.00	50.00
2-Ditko-a	4.00	12.00	28.00
3,7-Williamson-a in both, 4 pgs. each; #7-with Mayo	4.35	13.00	30.00
4-6,8	2.35	7.00	16.00

NOTE: Berg a-6. Ditko a-2. Everett a-1, 5; c-6. Heck a-5. Orlando a-5. Powell a-6. Reinman a-4. Roussos a-6.

WORLD OF WHEELS (Formerly Dragstrip Hotrodders)
Oct., 1967 - No. 32, June, 1970
Charlton Comics

17-20-Features Ken King	.60	1.20
21-32-Features Ken King	.50	1.00
Modern Comics Reprint 23('78)	.15	.30

WORLD OF WOOD
1986 - No. 4 (mini-series, $1.75, color)
Eclipse Comics

	Good	Fine	N-Mint
1-4	.30	.90	1.80

WORLD'S BEST COMICS (. . .Finest #2 on)
Spring, 1941 (Cardboard-c)(DC's 6th annual format comic)
National Periodical Publications (100 pgs.)

1-The Batman, Superman, Crimson Avenger, Johnny Thunder, The King, Young Dr. Davis, Zatara, Lando, Man of Magic, & Red, White & Blue begin (inside-c blank)	315.00	945.00	2200.00

WORLDS BEYOND (Worlds of Fear #2 on)
Nov, 1951
Fawcett Publications

1-Powell, Bailey-a	10.00	30.00	70.00

WORLD'S FAIR COMICS (See N. Y. . . .)

WORLD'S FINEST COMICS (World's Best #1)
No. 2, Sum, 1941 - No. 323, Jan, 1986 (early issues-100 pgs.)
National Periodical Publ./DC Comics (No.1-17 cardboard covers)

2 (100 pgs.)	145.00	435.00	1015.00
3-The Sandman begins; last Johnny Thunder; origin & 1st app. The Scarecrow	125.00	375.00	875.00
4-Hop Harrigan app.; last Young Dr. Davis	90.00	270.00	630.00
5-Intro. TNT & Dan the Dyna-Mite; last King & Crimson Avenger	90.00	270.00	630.00
6-Star Spangled Kid begins; Aquaman app.; S&K Sandman with Sandy in new costume begins, ends #7	70.00	210.00	490.00
7-Green Arrow begins; last Lando, King, & Red, White & Blue; S&K art	70.00	210.00	490.00
8-Boy Commandos begin	62.00	185.00	435.00
9-Batman cameo in Star Spangled Kid; S&K-a; last 100pg. ish. Hitler, Mussolini, Tojo-c	57.00	170.00	400.00
10-S&K-a	57.00	170.00	400.00
11-17-Last cardboard cover issue	50.00	150.00	350.00
18-20: 18-Paper covers begin; last Star Spangled Kid	46.00	138.00	320.00
21-30: 30-Johnny Peril app.	33.00	100.00	230.00
31-40: 33-35-Tomahawk app.	28.00	84.00	195.00
41-50: 41-Boy Commandos end. 42-Wyoming Kid begins, ends #63. 43-Full Steam Foley begins, ends #48. 48-Last square binding.	25.00	75.00	175.00
49-Tom Sparks, Boy Inventor begins	22.00	65.00	154.00
51-60: 52-Zatara ends. 59-Manhunters Around the World begins, ends #62	22.00	65.00	154.00
61-64: 63-Capt. Compass app.	19.00	57.00	132.00
65-Origin Superman; Tomahawk begins, ends #101	23.00	70.00	160.00
66-70-(15 cent issues)(Scarce)-Last 68pg. issue	21.50	65.00	150.00
71-(10 cent issue)(Scarce)-Superman & Batman begin as team	27.00	81.00	190.00
72,73-(10 cent issues)(Scarce)	20.00	60.00	140.00
74-80: 74-Last pre-code ish.	10.00	30.00	70.00
81-90: 88-1st Joker/Luthor team-up. 90-Batwoman's 1st app. in World's Finest	6.50	19.50	45.00
91-93,95-99: 96-99-Kirby Green Arrow	4.35	13.00	30.00
94-Origin Superman/Batman team retold	10.00	30.00	70.00
100	8.50	25.50	60.00
101-121: 102-Tommy Tomorrow begins, ends. #124. 113-Intro. Miss Arrowette in Green Arrow; 1st Batmite/ Mxyzptlk team-up.			
121-Last 10 cent issue	2.85	8.50	20.00
122-141: 125-Aquaman begins, ends #139. 140-Last Green Arrow	1.50	4.50	10.00
142-Origin The Composite Superman(Villain); Legion app.	1.50	4.50	10.00

433

WORLD'S FINEST COMICS (continued)	Good	Fine	N-Mint
143-150: 143-1st Mailbag	1.00	3.00	7.00
151-160: 156-1st Bizarro Batman	.85	2.50	5.00
161,170 (80-Pg. Giant G-28,G-40)	.70	2.00	4.00
162-169,171-174: 168,172-Adult Legion app.	.50	1.50	3.00
175,176-Adams-a; both r-J'onzz J'onzz origin/Det. 225,226			
	.70	2.00	4.00

177,178,180-187,189-196,198-204: 182-Silent Knight-r/Brave & Bold #6. 186-Johnny Quick-r. 187-Green Arrow origin-r/Adv. #256. 190-93-Robin-r. 198,199-3rd Superman/Flash race

	.25	.75	1.50
179,188,197 (80-Pg. Giant G-52,G-64,G-76)	.35	1.00	2.00

205-6 pgs. Shining Knight by Frazetta/Adv. #153; 52 pgs.; Teen Titans x-over

	.25	.75	1.50
206 (80-Pg. Giant G-88)	.25	.75	1.50
207-212 (52 pgs.)		.50	1.00

213-222: 215-Intro. Batman Jr. & Superman Jr. 217-Metamorpho begins, ends #220; Batman/Superman team-up begins

		.50	1.00

223,226-Adams-a(r); 100 pgs.; 223-Deadman origin; 226-S&K, Toth-r; Manhunter part origin-r/Det. 225,226

		.50	1.00
224,225,227,228-(100 pgs.)		.50	1.00
229-243: 229-r-origin Superman-Batman team		.50	1.00

244-248: 244-Green Arrow, Black Canary, Wonder Woman, Vigilante begin; $1.00 size begins. 246-Death of Stuff in Vigilante; origin Vigilante retold. 248-Last Vigilante

		.50	1.00
249-The Creeper begins by Ditko, ends #255	.25	.75	1.50
250-The Creeper origin retold by Ditko		.50	1.00

251-262: 253-Captain Marvel begins. 255-Last Creeper. 256-Hawkman begins. 257-Black Lightning begins

		.50	1.00

263-282 ($1.00): 268-Capt. Marvel Jr origin retold. 274-Zatanna begins. 279,280-Capt. Marvel Jr. & Kid Eternity learn they are brothers. 271-Origin Superman/Batman team retold

		.50	1.00
283-297 (36 pgs.)		.50	1.00
284-Legion app.		.50	1.00
298,299 (75 cent issues begin)		.50	1.00
300-(52pgs., $1.25)-New Teen Titans app. by Perez			
	.25	.75	1.50
301-323: 304-Origin Null and Void		.50	1.00

Giveaway (c. 1944-45, 8 pgs., in color, paper-c)-Johnny Everyman-r/W. Finest

	11.50	34.00	80.00

NOTE: **Adams** a-230r; c-174-176, 178-180, 182, 183, 185, 186, 199-205, 208-211, 244-246, 258. **Austin** a-244-246i. **Burnley** a-8, 10; c-7-9, 12. **Colan** a-274p. **Ditko** a-249-255. **Giffen** c-284p. **G. Kane** a-38, 174r, 282, 283; c-281, 282, 289. **Kirby** a-187. **Kubert** Zatara-40-44. **Miller** c-285p. **Morrow** a-245-248. **Nasser** a(p)-244-246, 259, 260. **Newton** a-253-281p. **Orlando** a-224r. **Perez** a-300; c-271, 276, 277p, 278p. **Robinson** a-2, 9, 13-15; c-2-4, 6. **Rogers** a-259p. **Roussos** a-212r. **Simonson** c-291. **Spiegle** a-275-78, 284. **Staton** a-252p, 273p. **Toth** a-228r. **Tuska** a-230r, 250p, 252p, 254p, 257p, 283p, 284p, 308p.

(Also see 80 Pg. Giant #15.)

WORLD'S FINEST COMICS DIGEST (See DC Special Series #23)

WORLD'S GREATEST ATHLETE (See Walt Disney Showcase #14)

WORLD'S GREATEST SONGS
Sept, 1954
Atlas Comics (Male)

1-(Scarce) Heath & Harry Anderson-a; Eddie Fisher life story			
	13.00	40.00	90.00

WORLD'S GREATEST STORIES
Jan, 1949 - No. 2, May, 1949
Jubilee Publications

1-Alice in Wonderland	9.00	27.00	62.00
2-Pinocchio	7.00	21.00	50.00

WORLD'S GREATEST SUPER HEROES
1977 (3¾x3¾'') (24 pgs. in color) (Giveaway)
DC Comics (Nutra Comics) (Child Vitamins, Inc.)

Batman & Robin app.; health tips	.25	.75	1.50

WORLDS OF FEAR (Worlds Beyond #1)
V1No.2, Jan, 1952 - V2No.10, June, 1953
Fawcett Publications

V1#2	8.50	25.50	60.00
3-Evans-a	7.00	21.00	50.00
4-6(9/52)	6.50	19.50	45.00
V2#7-9	5.00	15.00	35.00
10-Saunders Painted-c; man with no eyes surrounded by eyeballs-c	11.00	32.00	75.00

NOTE: **Powell** a-2, 4, 5. **Sekowsky** a-4, 5.

WORLDS UNKNOWN
May, 1973 - No. 8, Aug, 1974
Marvel Comics Group

1-R-/from Astonishing #54; Torres, Reese-a		.30	.60
2-8		.20	.40

NOTE: **Adkins/Mooney** a-5. **Buscema** a/c-4p. **W. Howard** c/a-3i. **Kane** a(p)-1,2; c(p)-5, 6, 8. **Sutton** a-2. **Tuska** a(p)-7, 8; c-7p. No. 7, 8 has Golden Voyage of Sinbad movie adaptation.

WORLD WAR STORIES
Apr-June, 1965 - No. 3, Dec, 1965
Dell Publishing Co.

1	1.00	3.00	7.00
2,3: 1-3-Glanzman-a	.70	2.00	4.00

WORLD WAR II (See Classics Special Ed.)

WORLD WAR III
Mar, 1953 - No. 2, May, 1953
Ace Periodicals

1-(Scarce)-Atomic bomb-c	35.00	105.00	245.00
2-Used in POP, pg. 78 and B&W & color illos.			
	26.00	78.00	182.00

WORST FROM MAD, THE (Annual)
1958 - No. 12, 1969 (Each annual cover is reprinted from the cover of the Mad issues being reprinted)
E. C. Comics

nn(1958)-Bonus; record labels & travel stickers; 1st Mad annual; r-/Mad #29-34	11.00	32.00	75.00
2(1959)-Bonus is small 33⅓ rpm record entitled ''Meet the Staff of Mad;'' r-/Mad #35-40	15.00	45.00	105.00
3(1960)-20''x30''campaign poster ''Alfred E. Neuman for President;'' r-/Mad #41-46	8.00	24.00	56.00
4(1961)-Sunday comics section; r-/Mad #47-54	8.00	24.00	56.00
5(1962)-Has 33⅓ record; r-/Mad #55-62	12.00	36.00	85.00
6(1963)-Has 33⅓ record; r-/Mad #63-70	13.00	40.00	90.00
7(1964)-Mad protest signs; r-/Mad #71-76	5.00	15.00	35.00
8(1965)-Build a Mad Zeppelin	6.00	18.00	42.00
9(1966)-33⅓ rpm record	9.50	28.50	65.00
10(1967)-Mad bumper sticker	3.00	9.00	21.00
11(1968)-Mad cover window stickers	3.00	9.00	21.00
12(1969)-Mad picture postcards; Orlando-a	3.00	9.00	21.00

NOTE: Covers: **Bob Clarke**-#8. **Mingo**-#7, 9-12.

WOTALIFE COMICS
No. 3, Aug-Sept, 1946 - No. 12, July, 1947; 1959
Fox Features Syndicate/Norlen Mag.

3-Cosmo Cat	3.00	9.00	21.00
4-12-Cosmo Cat	1.70	5.00	12.00
1('59-Norlen)-Atomic Rabbit, Atomic Mouse	1.30	4.00	9.00

WOTALIFE COMICS
1957 - No. 5, 1957
Green Publications

World's Finest Comics #271, © DC

Worlds Of Fear #5, © FAW

Wotalife Comics #11, © FOX

Wow Comics #5, © FAW

The Wrath Of The Spectre #1, © DC

Wyatt Earp #4, © MEG

WOTALIFE COMICS (continued)	Good	Fine	N-Mint
1	1.30	4.00	9.00
2-5	.85	2.50	6.00

WOW COMICS
July, 1936 - No. 4, Nov, 1936 (52 pgs., magazine size)
Henle Publishing Co.

	Good	Fine	N-Mint
1-Fu Manchu; Eisner-a	125.00	375.00	875.00
2-Ken Maynard, Fu Manchu, Popeye by Segar; Eisner-a	85.00	255.00	595.00
3-Eisner-c/a(3); Popeye by Segar, Fu Manchu, Hiram Hick by Bob Kane, Space Limited app.	85.00	255.00	595.00
4-Flash Gordon by Raymond, Mandrake, Popeye by Segar, Tillie The Toiler, Fu Manchu, Hiram Hick by Bob Kane; Eisner-a(3), Briefer-c	110.00	330.00	770.00

WOW COMICS (Real Western Hero #70 on)(See XMas Comics)
Wint, 1940-41; No. 2, Summer, 1941 - No. 69, Fall, 1948
Fawcett Publications

	Good	Fine	N-Mint
nn(#1)-Origin Mr. Scarlet by S&K; Atom Blake, Boy Wizard, Jim Dolan, & Rick O'Shay begin; Diamond Jack, The White Rajah, & Shipwreck Roberts, only app.; the cover was printed on unstable paper stock and is rarely found in fine or mint condition; blank inside-c; bondage-c by Beck (Rare)	625.00	1875.00	5000.00
(Prices vary widely on this book)			
2-The Hunchback begins	60.00	180.00	420.00
3	37.00	110.00	260.00
4-Origin Pinky	43.00	130.00	300.00
5	30.00	90.00	210.00
6-Origin The Phantom Eagle; Commando Yank begins	24.00	72.00	170.00
7,8,10	23.00	70.00	160.00
9 (1/6/43)-Capt. Marvel, Capt. Marvel Jr., Shazam app.; Scarlet & Pinky x-over; Mary Marvel c/stories begins (cameo #9)	32.00	95.00	225.00
11-17,19,20: 15-Flag-c	14.00	42.00	100.00
18-1st app. Uncle Marvel (10/43); infinity-c	16.00	48.00	110.00
21-30: 28-Pinky x-over in Mary Marvel	8.50	25.50	60.00
31-40	5.70	17.00	40.00
41-50	4.35	13.00	30.00
51-58: Last Mary Marvel	3.65	11.00	25.00
59-69: 59-Ozzie begins. 65-69-Tom Mix app.	3.00	9.00	21.00

WRATH OF THE SPECTRE, THE
May, 1988 - No. 4, Aug., 1988 ($2.50, color, mini-series)
DC Comics

	Good	Fine	N-Mint
1-4	.40	1.25	2.50

WRECK OF GROSVENOR (See Superior Stories #3)

WRINGLE WRANGLE (See 4-Color #821)

WULF THE BARBARIAN
Feb, 1975 - No. 4, Sept, 1975
Atlas/Seaboard Publ.

		Fine	N-Mint
1-Origin		.40	.80
2-Intro. Berithe the Swordswoman; Adams, Wood, Reese-a		.30	.60
3,4		.25	.50

WYATT EARP (Hugh O'Brian Famous Marshal)
No. 860, 11/57 - No. 13, 12-2/1960-61 (Photo-c)
Dell Publishing Co.

	Good	Fine	N-Mint
4-Color 860 (#1)-Manning-a	6.00	18.00	42.00
4-Color 890,921(6/58)-All Manning-a	3.70	11.00	26.00
4 (9-11/58) - 12-Manning-a	3.50	10.50	24.00
13-Toth-a	4.30	13.00	30.00

WYATT EARP
11/55 - No. 29, 6/60; No. 30, 10/72 - No. 34, 6/73

Atlas Comics/Marvel No. 23 on (IPC)	Good	Fine	N-Mint
1	6.00	18.00	42.00
2-Williamson-a, 4 pgs.	4.35	13.00	30.00
3-6,8-11: 3-Black Bart app. 8-Wild Bill Hickok app.	2.00	6.00	14.00
7,12-Williamson-a, 4pgs. ea.; #12 May Mayo	3.50	10.50	24.00
13-19: 17-1st app. Wyatt's deputy, Grizzly Grant	1.70	5.00	12.00
20-Torres-a	2.00	6.00	14.00
21-Davis-c	1.70	5.00	12.00
22-24,26-29: 22-Ringo Kid app. 23-Kid From Texas app. 29-Last 10 cent issue	.85	2.50	6.00
25-Davis-a	1.50	4.50	10.00
30-Williamson-r ('72)		.40	.80
31,33,34-Reprints		.25	.50
32-Torres-a(r)		.30	.60

NOTE: Ayers a-8, 17. Everett c-6. Kirby c-25, 29. Maneely a-1; c-1, 3, 4, 8, 12, 17, 20. Maurer a-3(4), 4(4), 8(4). Severin a-4, 10; c-10, 14. Wildey a-5, 17, 24, 28.

WYATT EARP FRONTIER MARSHAL (Formerly Range Busters)
No. 12, Jan, 1956 - No. 72, Dec, 1967 (Also see Blue Bird)
Charlton Comics

	Good	Fine	N-Mint
12	2.00	6.00	14.00
13-19	1.00	3.00	7.00
20-Williamson-a(4), 8,5,5,& 7 pgs.; 68 pgs.	5.50	16.50	38.00
21-30	.55	1.65	4.00
31-72: 31-Crandall-r		.60	1.20

XENON
Dec, 1987 - No. 23, Nov 1, 1988 ($1.50, Bi-weekly, B&W)
Eclipse Comics

		Fine	N-Mint
1		.40	1.25	2.50
2-23		.25	.75	1.50

X-FACTOR
Feb, 1986 - Present
Marvel Comics Group

	Good	Fine	N-Mint
1-Double size; Layton/Guice-a	1.35	4.00	8.00
2,3	.85	2.50	5.00
4,5	.75	2.25	4.50
6-10	.50	1.50	3.00
11-20	.40	1.25	2.50
21-23	.30	.90	1.80
24-26: Fall Of The Mutants. 26-New outfits	.40	1.25	2.50
27-30		.70	1.40
31-38: 35-Origin Cyclops		.50	1.00
Annual 1 (10/86), 2 (10/87)	.40	1.25	2.50
Annual 3 ('88, $1.75)-Evolutionary War app.	.50	1.50	3.00

XMAS COMICS
12?/1941 - No. 2, 12?/1942 (324 pgs.) (50 cents)
No. 3, 12?/1943 - No. 7, 12?/1947 (132 pgs.)
Fawcett Publications

	Good	Fine	N-Mint
1-Contains Whiz #21, Capt. Marvel #3, Bulletman #2, Wow #3, & Master #18; Raboy back-c. Not rebound, remaindered comics printed at same time as originals	125.00	375.00	875.00
2-Capt. Marvel, Bulletman, Spy Smasher	65.00	195.00	455.00
3-7-Funny animals	15.00	45.00	105.00

XMAS COMICS
No. 4, Dec, 1949 - No. 7, Dec, 1952 (196 pgs.)
Fawcett Publications

	Good	Fine	N-Mint
4-Contains Whiz, Master, Tom Mix, Captain Marvel, Nyoka, Capt. Video, Bob Colt, Monte Hale, Hot Rod Comics, & Battle Stories. Not rebound, remaindered comics—printed at the same time as originals	26.00	78.00	180.00
5-7-Same as above	23.00	70.00	160.00

XMAS FUNNIES
No date (paper cover) (36 pgs.?)
Kinney Shoes (Giveaway)

	Good	Fine	N-Mint
Contains 1933 color strip-r; Mutt & Jeff, etc.	10.00	30.00	70.00

X-MEN, THE (See Amazing Adventures, Capt. America #172, Classic X-Men, Heroes For Hope. . . , Kitty Pryde & . . . , Marvel & DC Present, Marvel Fanfare, Marvel Graphic Novel, Marvel Team-up, Marvel Triple Action, Nightcrawler, Official Marvel Index To . . . , Special Edition . . . , The Uncanny . . . , & X-Terminators)

X-MEN, THE (The Uncanny. . .#142)
Sept, 1963 - Present
Marvel Comics Group

	Good	Fine	N-Mint
1-Origin X-Men; 1st app. Magneto	107.00	321.00	750.00
2-1st app. The Vanisher	47.00	141.00	330.00
3-1st app. The Blob	23.00	70.00	160.00
4-1st Quick Silver & Scarlet Witch & Brotherhood of the Evil Mutants	19.00	56.00	130.00
5	15.00	45.00	105.00
6-10: 8-1st Unus the Untouchable. 9-Avengers app. 10-1st Silver-Age app. Ka-Zar	11.50	34.00	80.00
11-15: 11-1st app. The Stranger. 12-Origin Prof. X. 14-1st app. Sentinels. 15-Origin Beast	8.00	24.00	55.00
16-20: 19-1st app. The Mimic	5.00	15.00	35.00
21-27,29,30	4.00	12.00	28.00
28-1st app. The Banshee	4.65	14.00	32.00
31-37	2.85	8.50	20.00
38-Origin The X-Men feat. begins, ends #57	3.15	9.50	22.00
39,40: 39-New costumes	2.65	8.00	18.00
41-49: 42-Death of Prof. X (Changeling disguised as). 44-Red Raven app. (G.A.). 49-Steranko-c; 1st Polaris	2.00	6.00	14.00
50,51-Steranko c/a	2.85	8.50	20.00
52	1.70	5.00	12.00
53-Smith c/a; 1st Smith comic book work	3.00	9.00	21.00
54,55-Smith-c	2.40	7.50	17.00
56-63,65-Adams-a. 56-Intro Havoc without costume. 65-Return of Prof. X. 58-1st app. Havoil	3.15	9.50	22.00
64-1st Sunfire app.	2.30	7.00	16.00
66	1.50	4.50	10.00
67-80: 67-All-r. 67-70,72-(52 pgs.)	1.50	4.50	10.00
81-93-r-#39-45 with-c	1.50	4.50	10.00
94(8/75)-New X-Men begin; Colossus, Nightcrawler, Thunderbird, Storm, Wolverine, & Banshee join; Angel, Marvel Girl, & Iceman resign	16.00	48.00	110.00
95-Death Thunderbird	6.50	19.50	45.00
96-99	4.30	13.00	30.00
98,99 (30 cent cover)	5.00	15.00	35.00
100-Old vs. New X-Men; part origin Phoenix	5.00	15.00	35.00
101-Phoenix origin concludes	4.40	13.00	31.00
102-107: 102-Origin Storm. 104-Intro. Star Jammers. 106-Old vs. New X-Men	2.70	8.00	19.00
108-1st Byrne X-Men	4.65	14.00	32.00
109-1st Vindicator	4.00	12.00	28.00
110,111: 110-Phoenix joins	2.40	7.50	17.00
112-119: 117-Origin Prof. X	2.15	6.50	15.00
120-1st app. Alpha Flight (cameo), story line begins	4.00	12.00	28.00
121-1st Alpha Flight (full story)	4.30	13.00	30.00
122-128: 124-Colossus becomes Proletarian	2.00	6.00	12.00
129-Intro Kitty Pryde	2.50	7.50	15.00
130-1st app. The Dazzler by Byrne	2.30	7.00	14.00
131-135: 131-Dazzler app. 134-Phoenix becomes Dark Phoenix	1.70	5.00	10.00
136,138: 138-Dazzler app.	1.45	4.25	8.50
137-Giant; death of Phoenix	1.85	5.50	11.00
139-Alpha Flight app.; Kitty Pryde joins	2.15	6.50	13.00

	Good	Fine	N-Mint
140-Alpha Flight app.	2.40	7.50	17.00
141-Intro Future X-Men & The New Brotherhood of Evil Mutants; death of Frank Richards	1.70	5.00	10.00
142,143: 142-Deaths of Wolverine, Storm & Colossus. 143-Last Byrne issue	1.00	3.00	6.00
144-150: 145-Old X-Men app. 148-Spider-Woman, Dazzler app. 150-Double size	.85	2.50	5.00
151-157,159-164: 161-Origin Magneto. 162-Wolverine app. 163-Origin Binary. 164-1st app. Binary as Carol Danvers	.60	1.75	3.50
158-1st app. Rogue in X-Men	.70	2.00	4.00
165-Paul Smith-a begins	.85	2.50	5.00
166-Double size; Paul Smith-a	.70	2.00	4.00
167-170: 167-New Mutants x-over. 168-1st app. Madelyne Pryor	.50	1.50	3.00
171-1st app. Rogue	.85	2.50	5.00
172-174: 174-Phoenix cameo	.50	1.50	3.00
175-Double size; anniversary issue; Phoenix returns? Paul Smith c/a	.60	1.75	3.50
176-185: 181-Sunfire app.	.40	1.25	2.50
186-Double-size; Barry Smith/Austin-a	.50	1.50	3.00
187-192,194-199	.35	1.00	2.00
193-Double size	.50	1.50	3.00
200-Double size	.50	1.50	3.00
201-209	.35	1.00	2.00
210-213-Mutant Massacre	.50	1.50	3.00
214-224	.25	.75	1.50
225-227: Fall Of The Mutants. 226-Double size	.50	1.50	3.00
228-241,243: 229-$1.00 app.	.25	.75	1.50
242-Double size, X-Factor app.	.25	.75	1.50
Annual 3(2/80)	1.25	3.75	7.50
Annual 4(11/80)	1.00	3.00	6.00
Annual 5(10/81)	.70	2.10	4.25
Annual 6(11/82)	.50	1.50	3.00
Annual 7(1/84), 8(12/84)	.40	1.25	2.50
Annual 9(1985)-New Mutants; Art Adams-a	1.00	3.00	6.00
Annual 10(1/87)-Art Adams-a	1.00	3.00	6.00
Annual 11(11/87)	.35	1.00	2.00
Annual 12('88, $1.75)-Evolutionary War app.	.40	1.25	2.50
Giant-Size 1(Summer,'75, 50 cents)-1st app. new X-Men; Intro Nightcrawler, Storm, Colossus & Thunderbird; Wolverine app.	13.50	34.00	95.00
Giant-Size 2(11/75)-51 pgs. Adams-a(r)	2.85	9.00	20.00
Special 1(12/70)-Kirby-c/a; origin The Stranger	2.85	9.00	20.00
Special 2(11/71)	2.85	9.00	20.00

NOTE: **Art Adams** a-Annual 9, 10, 12p. **Neal Adams** c-56-63. **Adkins** c-34. **Austin** a-108i, 109i, 111-17i, 119-43i, 196i, 204i, 228i, Annual 3i, 7i, 9i; c-109-111i, 114-22i, 123i, 124-41i, 142, 143, 228i, Annual 3i. **Buscema** c-42, 43p, 45p. **Byrne** a-108p, 109p, 111-43p; c-113-16p, 127p, 129p, 131-41p. Ditko a-90i. **Everett** c-73. **Golden** a-Annual 7p. **G. Kane** c(p)-33, 74-76, 79, 80, 94, 95. **Kirby** a(p)-1-17 (#12-17, 24, 27-29, 32, 67i-layouts); c(p)-1-22, 25, 26, 30, 31, 35. **Layton** a-105i; c-112i, 113i. **Miller** c-Annual 3. **Perez** c/a-Annual 3p; c-112p, 128p, Annual 3p. **Roussos** a-84i. **Simonson** a-171p; c-171. **B. Smith** a-198, 205, 214; c-186, 198. **Paul Smith** a-165-70p, 172-75p; c-165-70, 172-75. **Sparling** a-78p. **Steranko** a-50p, 51p; c-49-51. **Sutton** a-106i. **Toth** a-12p, 67p(r). **Tuska** a-40-42i, 44-46p, 88i(r); c-39-41, 77p, 78p. **Williamson** a-202i, 203i, 211i; c-202i, 203i, 206i. **Wood** c-14i. 25 cent & 30 cent issues of #98 & 99 exist.

X-MEN/ALPHA FLIGHT
Jan, 1986 - No. 2, Jan, 1986 ($1.50 cover; mini-series)
Marvel Comics Group

	Good	Fine	N-Mint
1,2: 1-Intro The Berserkers; Paul Smith-a	.60	1.75	3.50

X-MEN AND THE MICRONAUTS, THE
Jan, 1984 - No. 4, April, 1984 (mini-series)
Marvel Comics Group

	Good	Fine	N-Mint
1-Guice-c/a(p) in all	.25	.75	1.50
2-4	.25	.75	1.50

The X-Men #2, © MEG

The X-Men #95, © MEG

The X-Men And The Micronauts #2, © MEG

Yanks In Battle #1, © QUA

Yellow Claw #2, © MEG

Yellowjacket Comics #8, © Frank Comunale

X-MEN CLASSICS
Dec, 1983 - No. 3, Feb, 1984 ($2.00; Baxter paper)
Marvel Comics Group

	Good	Fine	N-Mint
1-3: Adams-r/X-Men	.50	1.50	3.00

X-MEN VS. THE AVENGERS
Apr, 1987 - No. 4, July, 1987 (Mini-series)(Baxter paper)
Marvel Comics Group

1	.60	1.75	3.50
2-4	.40	1.25	2.50

X-TERMINATORS
Oct., 1988 - No. 4, Jan., 1989 ($1.00, color, mini-series)
Marvel Comics

1-X-Men/X-Factor tie-in; Williamson-i	.40	1.25	2.50
2	.25	.75	1.50
3,4		.50	1.00

X, THE MAN WITH THE X-RAY EYES (See Movie Comics)

X-VENTURE
July, 1947 - No. 2 Nov, 1947 (Super heroes)
Victory Magazines Corp.

1-Atom Wizard, Mystery Shadow, Lester Trumble	24.00	72.00	168.00
2	15.00	45.00	105.00

XYR (See Eclipse Graphic Album series #21)

YAK YAK (See 4-Color #1186,1348)

YAKKY DOODLE & CHOPPER (TV) (Also see Spotlight #3)
Dec, 1962 (Hanna-Barbera)
Gold Key

1	2.35	7.00	16.00

YALTA TO KOREA
1952 (8 pgs.) (Giveaway) (paper cover)
M. Phillip Corp. (Republican National Committee)

Anti-communist propaganda book	15.00	45.00	90.00

YANG (See House of Yang)
11/73 - No. 13, 5/76; V14/14, 9/85 - No. 17, 1/86
Charlton Comics

1-Origin		.50	1.00
2-5		.30	.60
6-13(1976)		.20	.40
14-17(1986)		.40	.80
3,10,11(Modern Comics-r, 1977)		.15	.30

YANKEE COMICS
Sept, 1941 - No. 4, Mar, 1942
Harry 'A' Chesler

1-Origin The Echo, The Enchanted Dagger, Yankee Doodle Jones, The Firebrand, & The Scarlet Sentry; Black Satan app.	38.00	115.00	265.00
2-Origin Johnny Rebel; Major Victory app.; Barry Kuda begins	23.00	70.00	160.00
3,4	19.00	57.00	132.00
4 (nd, '40s; 7¼x5'', 68pgs, distr. to the service)-Foxy Grandpa, Tom, Dick & Harry, Impy, Ace & Deuce, Dot & Dash, Ima Slooth by Jack Cole (Remington Morse publ.)	1.70	5.00	12.00

YANKS IN BATTLE
Sept, 1956 - No. 4, Dec, 1956
Quality Comics Group

1	2.50	7.50	17.00
2-4	1.20	3.50	8.00

YANKS IN BATTLE
1963
I. W. Enterprises

	Good	Fine	N-Mint
Reprint #3	.25	.75	1.50

YARDBIRDS, THE (G. I. Joe's Sidekicks)
Summer, 1952
Ziff-Davis Publishing Co.

1-By Bob Oskner	3.50	10.50	24.00

YARNS OF YELLOWSTONE
1972 (36 pages) (50 cents)
World Color Press

Illustrated by Bill Chapman	.50	1.50	3.00

YELLOW CLAW
Oct, 1956 - No. 4, April, 1957
Atlas Comics (MjMC)

1-Origin by Joe Maneely	22.00	65.00	154.00
2-Kirby-a	18.00	54.00	125.00
3,4-Kirby-a; 4-Kirby/Severin-a	16.00	48.00	110.00

NOTE: *Everett* c-3. *Maneely* c-1. *Reinman* a-2i, 3. *Severin* c-2, 4.

YELLOWJACKET COMICS (Jack in the Box #11 on; see TNT)
Sept, 1944 - No. 10, June, 1946
E. Levy/Frank Comunale

1-Origin Yellowjacket; Diana, the Huntress begins	16.00	48.00	110.00
2	9.00	27.00	62.00
3,5	8.00	24.00	56.00
4-Poe's 'Fall Of The House Of Usher' adaptation	9.00	27.00	62.00
6-10: 7,8-Has stories narrated by old witch in 'Tales of Terror'	7.00	21.00	50.00

YELLOWSTONE KELLY (See 4-Color #1056)

YELLOW SUBMARINE (See Movie Comics)

YOGI BEAR (TV) (Hanna-Barbera)
No. 1067, 12-2/59-60 - No. 9, 7-9/62; No. 10, 10/62 - No. 42, 10/70
Dell Publishing Co./Gold Key No. 10 on

4-Color 1067 (#1)	3.50	10.50	24.00
4-Color 1104,1162 (5-7/61)	2.65	8.00	18.00
4(8-9/61) - 6(12-1/61-62)	2.00	6.00	14.00
4-Color 1271(11/61), 1349(1/62)	2.00	6.00	14.00
7(2-3/62) - 9(7-9/62)-Last Dell	1.70	5.00	12.00
10(10/62-G.K.), 11(1/63)-titled ''Y.B. Jellystone Jollies''-80 pgs.; 11-Xmas-c	2.25	6.75	18.00
12(4/63), 14-20	1.50	4.50	10.00
13(7/63)-Surprise Party, 68 pgs.	2.25	6.75	18.00
21-30	1.00	3.00	7.00
31-42	.60	1.80	4.00
...Kite Fun Book('62, 16 pgs., soft-c)	1.50	3.50	8.00

YOGI BEAR (See Dell Giant #41, March of Comics #253, 265, 279, 291, 309, 319, 337, 344, Whitman Comic Books & Movie Comics under ''Hey There It's. . .'')

YOGI BEAR (TV)
Nov, 1970 - No. 35, Jan, 1976 (Hanna-Barbera)
Charlton Comics

1	.70	2.00	4.00
2-6,8-35: 28-31-partial-r	.35	1.00	2.00
7-Summer Fun (Giant); 52 pgs.	.35	1.00	2.00

YOGI BEAR (TV)(See The Flintstones, 3rd series & Spotlight #1)
Nov, 1977 - No. 9, Mar, 1979
Marvel Comics Group

1-Flintstones begin		.40	.80
2-9		.20	.40

YOGI BEAR'S EASTER PARADE (See The Funtastic World of Hanna-Barbera #2)

YOGI BERRA (Baseball hero)			
1951 (Yankee catcher)			
Fawcett Publications	Good	Fine	N-Mint
nn-Photo-c	23.00	70.00	160.00

YOSEMITE SAM (. . .& Bugs Bunny)
Dec, 1970 - No. 81, Feb, 1984
Gold Key/Whitman

1	.70	2.00	4.00
2-10	.40	1.25	2.50
11-30		.60	1.20
31-81: 81-r(⅓)		.30	.60

(See March of Comics #363,380,392)

YOUNG ALLIES COMICS (All-Winners #21; see Kid Komics)
Summer, 1941 - No. 20, Oct, 1946
Timely Comics (USA 1-7/NPI 8,9/YAI 10-20)

1-Origin The Young Allies; 1st meeting of Capt. America & Human Torch; Red Skull app.; S&K c/splash	205.00	615.00	1435.00
2-Captain America & Human Torch app.; Simon & Kirby-c	90.00	270.00	630.00
3-Fathertime, Captain America & Human Torch app.	73.00	220.00	510.00
4-The Vagabond & Red Skull, Capt. America, Human Torch app.	57.00	170.00	400.00
5-Captain America & Human Torch app.	42.00	125.00	295.00
6-10: 10-Origin Tommy Tyme & Clock of Ages; ends #19	32.00	95.00	225.00
11-20: 12-Classic decapitation story; Schomburg-c	25.00	75.00	175.00

YOUNG ALL-STARS
June, 1987 - Present ($1.00, deluxe format, color)
DC Comics

1-1st app. Iron Munro & The Flying Fox	.70	2.00	4.00
2,3	.35	1.00	2.00
4-22: 7-on ($1.25)	.25	.75	1.50
Annual 1 ('88, $2.00)	.35	1.00	2.00

YOUNG BRIDES
Sept-Oct, 1952 - No. 29, Jul-Aug, 1956 (Photo-c #1-3)
Feature/Prize Publications

V1#1-Simon & Kirby-a	5.70	17.00	40.00
2-S&K-a	3.00	9.00	21.00
3-6-S&K-a	2.65	8.00	18.00
V2#1,3-7,10-12 (#7-18)-S&K-a	2.15	6.50	15.00
2,8,9-No S&K-a	1.00	3.00	7.00
V3#1-3(#19-21)-Last precode (3-4/55)	.85	2.50	6.00
4,6(#22,24), V4#1,3(#25,27)	.75	2.25	5.00
V3#5(#23)-Meskin-c	1.15	3.50	8.00
V4#2(#26-All S&K ish	2.00	6.00	14.00
V4#4(#28)-S&K-a, V4#5(#29)	1.15	3.50	8.00

YOUNG DR. MASTERS (See Advs. of Young Dr. Masters)

YOUNG DOCTORS, THE
January, 1963 - No. 6, Nov, 1963
Charlton Comics

V1#1	.25	.75	1.50
2-6		.60	1.20

YOUNG EAGLE
12/50 - No. 10, 6/52; No. 3, 7/56 - No. 5, 4/57 (Photo-c, 1-10)
Fawcett Publications/Charlton

1	7.00	21.00	50.00
2	4.00	12.00	28.00
3-9	3.00	9.00	21.00
10-Origin Thunder, Young Eagle's Horse	2.35	7.00	16.00
3-5(Charlton)-Formerly Sherlock Holmes?	1.15	3.50	8.00

YOUNG HEARTS
Nov, 1949 - No. 2, Feb, 1950
Marvel Comics (SPC)

	Good	Fine	N-Mint
1-Photo-c	3.00	9.00	21.00
2	1.60	4.70	11.00

YOUNG HEARTS IN LOVE
1964
Super Comics

17,18-17-r/Young Love V5#6, 4-5/62	.25	.75	1.50

YOUNG HEROES (Formerly Forbidden Worlds #34)
No. 35, Feb-Mar, 1955 - No. 37, June-July, 1955
American Comics Group (Titan)

35-37-Frontier Scout	1.70	5.00	12.00

YOUNG KING COLE (Becomes Criminals on the Run)
Fall, 1945 - V3/12, July, 1948
Premium Group/Novelty Press

V1#1-Toni Gayle begins	6.00	18.00	42.00
2	4.00	12.00	28.00
3-6	3.50	10.50	24.00
V2#1-7(7/47)	2.65	8.00	18.00
V3#1,3-6,12	2.00	6.00	14.00
2-L.B. Cole-a	2.65	8.00	18.00
7-L.B. Cole-c/a	4.00	12.00	28.00
8-11-L.B. Cole-c	3.35	10.00	23.00

YOUNG LAWYERS, THE (TV)
Jan, 1971 - No. 2, April, 1971
Dell Publishing co.

1,2	1.15	3.50	8.00

YOUNG LIFE (Teen Life #3 on)
Spring, 1945 - No. 2, Summer, 1945
New Age Publ./Quality Comics Group

1-Skip Homeier, Louis Prima stories	3.70	11.00	26.00
2-Frank Sinatra c/story	3.00	9.00	21.00

YOUNG LOVE
2-3/49 - No. 73, 12-1/56-57; V3#5, 2-3/60 - V7#1, 6-7/63
Prize(Feature)Publ.(Crestwood)

V1#1-S&K c/a(2)	10.00	30.00	70.00
2-Photo-c begin; S&K-a	4.35	13.00	30.00
3-S&K-a	3.00	9.00	21.00
4-5-Minor S&K-a	2.15	6.50	15.00
V2#1(#7)-S&K-a	3.00	9.00	21.00
2-5(#8-11)-Minor S&K-a	1.70	5.00	12.00
6,8(#12,14)-S&K-c only	2.15	6.50	15.00
7,9-12(#13,15-18)-S&K c/a	3.00	9.00	21.00
V3#1-4(#19-22)-S&K c/a	2.15	6.50	15.00
5-7,9-12(#23-25,27-30)-Photo-c resume; S&K-a	1.70	5.00	12.00
8(#26)-No S&K	1.30	4.00	9.00
V4#1,6(#31,36)-S&K-a	1.70	5.00	12.00
2-5,7-12(#32-35,37-42)-Minor S&K-a	1.50	4.50	10.00
V5#1-12(#43-54), V6#1-9(#55-63)-Last precode; S&K-a-some	1.15	3.50	8.00
V6#10-12(#64-66)	1.00	3.00	7.00
V7#1-7(#67-73)	.55	1.65	4.00
V3#5(2-3/60),6(4-5/60)(Formerly All For Love)	.45	1.35	3.00
V4#1(6-7/60)-6(4-5/61)	.45	1.35	3.00
V5#1(6-7/61)-6(4-5/62)	.45	1.35	3.00
V6#1(6-7/62)-6(4-5/63), V7#1	.35	1.00	2.00

NOTE: *Severin/Elder* a-V1#3. **S&K** art not in #53, 57, 58, 61, 63-65. **Meskin** a-27. Photo c-V3#5-V5#11.

YOUNG LOVE
#39, 9-10/63 - #120, Wint./75-76; #121, 10/76 - #126, 7/77

Yogi Berra, © FAW

Young Allies Comics #3, © MEG

Young Eagle #3, © FAW

Young Men #4, © MEG

Youthful Romances #2, © Pix-Parade

Zago, Jungle Prince #4, © FOX

	Good	Fine	N-Mint
YOUNG LOVE (continued)			
National Periodical Publ.(Arleigh Publ. Corp #49-60)/DC Comics			
39-50	.50	1.50	3.00
51-70: 64-Simon & Kirby-a	.35	1.00	2.00
71,72,74-77,80		.60	1.20
73,78,79-Toth-a	.25	.75	1.50
81-126: 107-114 (100 pgs.). 122-Toth-a		.30	.60
YOUNG LOVER ROMANCES (Formerly & becomes Great Lover. .?)			
No. 4, June, 1952 - No. 5, Aug, 1952			
Toby Press			
4,5-Photo-c	1.30	4.00	9.00
YOUNG LOVERS (My Secret Life #19 on)			
No. 16, 7/56 - No. 18, 5/57 (Formerly Brenda Starr?)			
Charlton Comics			
16,17('56)	1.30	4.00	9.00
18-Elvis Presley picture-c, text story (biography)			
	23.00	70.00	160.00
YOUNG MARRIAGE			
June, 1950			
Fawcett Publications			
1-Powell-a; photo-c	4.00	12.00	28.00
YOUNG MASTER			
Nov., 1987 - Present ($1.75, B&W)			
New Comics Group			
1-6	.35	1.00	2.00
YOUNG MEN (Formerly Cowboy Romances)(. . .on the Battlefield			
#12-20(4/53); . . .In Action #21)			
No. 4, 6/50 - No. 11, 10/51; NO.12, 12/51 - No. 28, 6/54			
Marvel/Atlas Comics (IPC)			
4-52 pgs.	4.00	12.00	28.00
5-11	2.30	7.00	16.00
12-23	2.00	6.00	14.00
24-Origin Captain America, Human Torch, & Sub-Mariner which are			
revived thru #28. Red Skull app.	30.00	90.00	210.00
25-28	22.00	65.00	154.00
NOTE: *Berg* a-7, 17, 20; c-17. *Colan* a-15. Sub-Mariner by *Everett* #24-28. *Everett* a-18-20. *Heath* a-13, 14. *Maneely* c-12, 15.			
YOUNG REBELS, THE (TV)			
January, 1971			
Dell Publishing Co.			
1-Photo-c	1.00	3.00	6.00
YOUNG ROMANCE COMICS (The 1st romance comic)			
Sept-Oct, 1947 - V16#4, June-July, 1963 (#1-33, 52 pgs.)			
Prize/Headline (Feature Publ.)			
V1#1-S&K c/a(2)	11.50	34.00	80.00
2-S&K c/a(2-3)	6.50	19.50	45.00
3-6-S&K c/a(2-3) each	5.00	15.00	35.00
V2#1-6(#7-12)-S&K c/a(2-3) each	4.35	13.00	30.00
V3#1-3(#13-15)-Last line drawn-c; S&K c/a	2.15	6.50	15.00
4-12(#16-24)-Photo-c; S&K c/a	2.15	6.50	15.00
V4#1-11(#25-35)-S&K-a	1.70	5.00	12.00
12(#36)-S&K, Toth-a	4.00	12.00	28.00
V5#1-12(#37-48), V6#4-12(#52-60)-S&K-a	1.70	5.00	12.00
V6#1-3(#49-51)-No S&K-a	1.50	4.50	10.00
V7#1-11(#61-71)-S&K-a in most	1.70	5.00	12.00
V7#12(#72), V8#1-3(#73-75)-Last precode (12-1/54-55)-No S&K-a			
	1.00	3.00	7.00
V8#4(#76, 4-5/55), 5(#77)-No S&K	.85	2.50	6.00
V8#6-8(#78-80, 12-1/55-56)-S&K-a	1.30	4.00	9.00
V9#3,5,6(#81, 2-3/56, 83,84)-S&K-a	1.15	3.50	8.00
4, V10#1(#82,85)-All S&K-a	1.50	4.50	10.00
V10#2-6(#86-90, 10-11/57)-S&K-a	1.15	3.50	8.00

	Good	Fine	N-Mint
V11#1,2,5,6(#91,92,95,96)-S&K-a	1.15	3.50	8.00
3,4,(#93,94), V12#2,4,5(#98,100,101)-No S&K	.85	2.50	6.00
V12#1,3,6(#97,99,102)-S&K-a	1.15	3.50	8.00
V13#1(#103)-S&K, Powell-a	1.30	4.00	9.00
2-6(#104-108)	.45	1.35	3.00
V14#1-6, V15#1-6, V16#1-4(#109-124)	.35	1.00	2.00
NOTE: *Meskin* a-16, 24(2), 47. *Robinson/Meskin* a-6. *Leonard Starr* a-11. Photo c-16-32,34-65.			
YOUNG ROMANCE COMICS			
No. 125, Aug-Sept, 1963 - No. 208, Nov-Dec, 1975			
National Periodical Publ.(Arleigh Publ. Corp. No. 127)			
125-153,155-162	.40	1.20	2.40
154-Adams-c	.50	1.50	3.00
163,164-Toth-a		.50	1.00
165-196: 170-Michell from Young Love ends; Lily Martin, the			
Swinger begins		.40	.80
197 (100 pgs.)-208	.25		.50
YOUR DREAMS (See Strange World of. . .)			
YOUR TRIP TO NEWSPAPERLAND			
June, 1955 (12 pgs.; 14x11½")			
Philadelphia Evening Bulletin (Printed by Harvey Press)			
Joe Palooka takes kids on tour through newspaper			
	2.65	8.00	18.00
YOUR UNITED STATES			
1946			
Lloyd Jacquet Studios			
Used in **SOTI**, pg. 309,310; Sid Greene-a	11.50	34.00	80.00
YOUTHFUL HEARTS (Daring Confessions #4 on)			
May, 1952 - No. 3, 1952			
Youthful Magazines			
1-''Monkey on Her Back'' swipes E.C. drug story from Shock			
SuspenStories #12	10.00	30.00	70.00
2,3	4.60	14.00	32.00
NOTE: *Doug Wildey* art in all.			
YOUTHFUL LOVE (Truthful Love #2)			
May, 1950			
Youthful Magazines			
1	3.00	9.00	21.00
YOUTHFUL ROMANCES			
8-9/49 - No. 14, 10/52; No. 15, 1/53 - No. 18, 7/53; No. 5, 9/53 - No. 8, 5/54			
Pix-Parade #-14/Ribage			
1-(1st ser.)-Titled Youthful Love-Romances	7.00	21.00	50.00
2	4.00	12.00	28.00
3-5	3.50	10.50	24.00
6,7,9-14(10/52, Pix-Parade; becomes Daring Love #15); 7-Tony			
Martin photo on-c	2.30	7.00	16.00
8-Wood-c	8.50	25.50	60.00
15-18 (Ribage)	2.35	7.00	16.00
5(9/53, Ribage)	1.85	5.50	13.00
6,7(#7, 2/54)	1.50	4.50	10.00
8(5/54)	1.50	4.50	10.00
ZAGO, JUNGLE PRINCE (My Story #5 on)			
Sept, 1948 - No. 4, March, 1949			
Fox Features Syndicate			
1-Blue Beetle app.-partial r-/Atomic #4 (Toni Luck)			
	16.00	48.00	110.00
2,3-Kamen-a	12.00	36.00	84.00
4-Baker-c	11.00	32.00	75.00

ZANE GREY'S STORIES OF THE WEST
No. 197, 9/48 - 11/64 (All painted-c)
Dell Publishing Co./Gold Key 11/64

	Good	Fine	N-Mint
4-Color 197(9/48)	6.00	18.00	42.00
4-Color 222,230,236('49)	4.65	14.00	32.00
4-Color 246,255,270,301,314,333,346	3.50	10.50	24.00
4-Color 357,372,395,412,433,449,467,484	2.65	8.00	18.00
4-Color 511-Kinstler-a	3.00	9.00	21.00
4-Color 532,555,583,604,616,632(5/55)	2.65	8.00	18.00
27(9-11/55) - 39(9-11/58)	2.30	7.00	16.00
4-Color 996(5-7/59)	2.30	7.00	16.00
10131-411-(11/64-G.K.)-Nevada; r-4-Color #996	1.30	4.00	9.00

ZANY (Magazine)(Satire)(See Ratfink & Frantic)
Sept, 1958 - No. 4, May, 1959
Candor Publ. Co.

	Good	Fine	N-Mint
1-Bill Everett-c	3.00	9.00	21.00
2-4	1.70	5.00	12.00

ZATANNA SPECIAL (See Adventure Comics #413)
1987 (One shot, $2.00)
DC Comics

	Good	Fine	N-Mint
1	.35	1.00	2.00

ZAZA, THE MYSTIC (Formerly Charlie Chan; This Magazine Is Haunted V2#12 on)
April, 1956 - No. 11, Sept, 1956
Charlton Comics

	Good	Fine	N-Mint
10,11	3.00	9.00	21.00

ZEGRA JUNGLE EMPRESS (Formerly Tegra)(My Love Life #6 on)
No. 2, Oct, 1948 - No. 5, April, 1949
Fox Features Syndicate

	Good	Fine	N-Mint
2	18.00	54.00	125.00
3-5	13.00	40.00	90.00

ZERO PATROL, THE
Nov, 1984 - No. 3? 1987? ($2.00, color)
Continuity Comics

	Good	Fine	N-Mint
1-3: Adams c/a; Megalith begins	.25	.75	1.50
1,2 (reprints, 1987)	.25	.75	1.50

ZIGGY PIG-SILLY SEAL COMICS (See Animated Movie-Tunes, Comic Capers, Krazy Komics & Silly Tunes)
Fall, 1944 - No. 6, Fall, 1946
Timely Comics (CmPL)

	Good	Fine	N-Mint
1-Vs. the Japs	7.00	21.00	50.00
2	3.50	10.50	24.00
3-5	3.00	9.00	21.00
6-Infinity-c	5.50	16.50	38.00
I.W. Reprint #1('58)-r/Krazy Komics	.50	1.50	3.00
I.W. Reprint #2,7,8	.25	.75	1.50

ZIP COMICS
Feb, 1940 - No. 47, Summer, 1944
MLJ Magazines

	Good	Fine	N-Mint
1-Origin Kalathar the Giant Man, The Scarlet Avenger, & Steel Sterling; Mr. Satan, Nevada Jones & Zambini, the Miracle Man, War Eagle, Captain Valor begins	95.00	285.00	665.00
2	46.00	138.00	320.00
3	36.00	108.00	250.00
4,5	30.00	90.00	210.00
6-9: 9-Last Kalathar & Mr. Satan	26.00	78.00	180.00
10-Inferno, the Flame Breather begins, ends #13	24.00	72.00	168.00
11,12: 11-Inferno without costume	22.00	65.00	154.00
13-17,19: 17-Last Scarlet Avenger	22.00	65.00	154.00
18-Wilbur begins (1st app.)	25.00	75.00	175.00
20-Origin Black Jack (1st app.)	33.00	100.00	230.00

	Good	Fine	N-Mint
21-26: 25-Last Nevada Jones. 26-Black Witch begins; last Captain Valor	21.00	62.00	147.00
27-Intro. Web	32.00	95.00	225.00
28-Origin Web	32.00	95.00	225.00
29,30	18.00	54.00	125.00
31-38: 34-1st Applejack app. 35-Last Zambini, Black Jack. 38-Last Web issue	13.00	40.00	90.00
39-Red Rube begins (origin, 8/43)	13.00	40.00	90.00
40-47: 45-Wilbur ends	8.50	25.50	60.00

NOTE: *Biro* a-5, 9, 17; c-4-7, 9, 11, 12, 14, 17. *Meskin* a-1-3, 5-7, 9, 10, 12, 13, 15, 16 at least. *Novick* c-19, 20, 24, 25, 31. Bondage c-8, 9, 33, 34.

ZIP-JET (Hero)
Feb, 1953 - No. 2, Apr-May, 1953
St. John Publishing Co.

	Good	Fine	N-Mint
1,2-Rocketman-r/Punch Comics; #1-c from splash in Punch #10	14.00	42.00	100.00

ZIPPY THE CHIMP (CBS TV Presents. . .)
No. 50, March, 1957 - No. 51, Aug, 1957
Pines (Literary Ent.)

	Good	Fine	N-Mint
50,51	1.30	4.00	9.00

ZODY, THE MOD ROB
July, 1970
Gold Key

	Good	Fine	N-Mint
1	.70	2.00	4.00

ZOO ANIMALS
No. 8, 1954 (36 pages; 15 cents)
Star Publications

	Good	Fine	N-Mint
8-(B&W for coloring)	1.30	4.00	9.00

ZOO FUNNIES (Tim McCoy #16 on)
Nov, 1945 - No. 15, 1947
Charlton Comics/Children Comics Publ.

	Good	Fine	N-Mint
101(#1)(1945)-Al Fago-c	5.00	15.00	35.00
2(9/45)	2.30	7.00	16.00
3-5	2.00	6.00	14.00
6-15: 8-Diana the Huntress app.	1.50	4.50	10.00

ZOO FUNNIES (Becomes Nyoka, The Jungle Girl #14 on?)
July, 1953 - No. 13, Sept, 1955; Dec, 1984
Capitol Stories/Charlton Comics

	Good	Fine	N-Mint
1-1st app.? Timothy The Ghost; Fago-c/a	3.50	10.50	24.00
2	1.70	5.00	12.00
3-7 (8/46)	1.30	4.00	9.00
8-13-Nyoka app.	3.50	10.50	24.00
1('84)		.40	.80

ZOONIVERSE
8/86 - No. 6, 6/87 ($1.25, color, mini-series; Mando paper)
Eclipse Comics

	Good	Fine	N-Mint
1-4		.65	1.30
5,6 ($1.70)	.25	.75	1.50

ZOO PARADE (See 4-Color #662)

ZOOM COMICS
December, 1945 (One Shot)
Carlton Publishing Co.

	Good	Fine	N-Mint
nn-Dr. Mercy, Satannas, from Red Band Comics; Capt. Milksop origin retold	14.00	42.00	100.00

ZOOT (Rulah #17 on)
nd (1946) - No. 16, July, 1948 (Two #13s & 14s)
Fox Features Syndicate

	Good	Fine	N-Mint
nn-Funny animal only	8.00	24.00	56.00
2-The Jaguar app.	6.50	19.50	45.00

Ziggy Pig-Silly Seal Comics #2, © MEG

Zip Comics #4, © AP

Zoo Funnies #2 (9/45), © CC

Zoot #14 (3/48), © FOX

Zorro #12 (Dell), © WDC

Zot! #11, © Eclipse Comics

ZOOT (continued)	Good	Fine	N-Mint
3(Fall,'46) - 6-Funny animals & teen-age	3.70	11.00	26.00
7-Rulah, Jungle Goddess begins (6/47); origin & 1st app.			
	30.00	90.00	210.00
8-10	22.00	65.00	154.00
11-Kamen bondage-c	24.00	72.00	168.00
12-Injury-to-eye panels	14.00	42.00	100.00
13(2/48)	14.00	42.00	100.00

14(3/48)-Used in **SOTI**, pg. 104, ''One picture showing a girl nailed by her wrists to trees with blood flowing from the wounds, might be taken straight from an ill. ed. of the Marquis deSade''

	Good	Fine	N-Mint
	17.00	50.00	120.00
13(4/48), 14(5/48)	14.00	42.00	100.00
15,16	14.00	42.00	100.00

ZORRO (Walt Disney with #882)(TV)(See Eclipse Graphic Album)
May, 1949 - No. 15, Sept-Nov, 1961 (Photo-c 882 on)
Dell Publishing Co.

	Good	Fine	N-Mint
4-Color 228	14.00	42.00	100.00
4-Color 425,497	7.00	21.00	50.00
4-Color 538-Kinstler-a	8.00	24.00	56.00
4-Color 574,617,732	7.00	21.00	50.00
4-Color 882-Photo-c begin; Toth-a	5.70	17.00	40.00
4-Color 920,933,960,976-Toth-a in all	5.70	17.00	40.00
4-Color 1003('59)	4.65	14.00	32.00

	Good	Fine	N-Mint
4-Color 1037-Annette Funicello photo-c	7.00	21.00	50.00
8(12-2/59-60)	3.50	10.50	24.00
9,12-Toth-a	3.70	11.00	26.00
10,11,13-15-Last photo-c	2.65	8.00	18.00

NOTE: **Warren Tufts** a-4-Color 1037, 8, 9, 13.

ZORRO (Walt Disney)(TV)
Jan, 1966 - No. 9, March, 1968 (All photo-c)
Gold Key

	Good	Fine	N-Mint
1-Toth-a	2.65	8.00	18.00
2,4,5,7-9-Toth-a	2.00	6.00	14.00
3,6-Tufts-a	1.70	5.00	12.00

NOTE: #1-9 are reprinted from Dell issues. **Tufts** a-3,4. #3-r/#12-c & #8 inside; #4-r/#9-c & insides; #6-r/#11(all); #7a-r/#14-c.

ZOT! (See Advs. of . . .)
4/84 - No. 10, 7/85; No. 11, 1/87 - Present ($1.50, Baxter paper)
Eclipse Comics

	Good	Fine	N-Mint
1	1.15	3.50	7.00
2,3	.65	1.90	3.75
4-10: 4-Origin. 10-Last color ish.	.35	1.00	2.00
11-21 (B&W)	.35	1.00	2.00

Z-2 COMICS (Secret Agent . . .)(See Holyoke One-Shot #7)

ZULU (See Movie Classics)

443

FIRST IN SERVICE...

DIAMOND IS NOW #1

Call us and find out why we have quietly grown to be the largest and finest comic distributor.

- **REORDERS**—We order plenty of extra copies to have important books on hand for your reorders. If sold out, we search all 17 Diamond warehouses and, if we can't fill your order, then we go directly to the publisher. It's important to us to fill your needs...promptly.

- **WIDEST PRODUCT SELECTION**—Our new comics and books selection is second to none. We also carry Donruss and other baseball cards, a full gaming line, plus T-shirts, posters, toys, videos, specialty magazines, and occasional exclusive items.

- **SUPPLIES**—We keep available your high profit steady sellers: Boxes, bags, mylar, dividers, backing boards, and baseball card supplies.

- **SEVENTEEN LOCATIONS**—From New York to

Los Angeles are ready to serve both U.S. and International Customers. Direct delivery by our trucks in many areas. Direct shipment via UPS and air freight from our Sparta, Illinois warehouse. Let us show you the best and fastest way to get your books.

- **QUALIFIED DIAMOND WAREHOUSE MANAGERS AND EMPLOYEES** who are fast, careful, and helpful. Just starting up? Ready to expand? We can help you with product selection, ordering tips, and far more.

- **INFORMATION**—We have the answers to your questions. We're here to serve you.

DIAMOND PREVIEWS describes and illustrates Coming Items each month, and the bi-monthly COMPLETE CATALOG describes and pictures all important specialty items still available for your reorders.

EXPERIENCED PEOPLE READY TO SERVE YOU.
DIAMOND COMIC DISTRIBUTORS

FOR INFORMATION Call (301) 298-2981 and ask for either of our account representatives, Bill Neuhaus or Mindy Moran.

1718-G Belmont Ave., Baltimore, MD 21207

FACES...

...ONLY A FAN COULD LOVE
FROM
DARK HORSE
COMICS

SHE-HULK

Doctors Discover: Vegetarian Diet Turns Women Buxom and Green

Future Ninja Warrior May Be a Dream Hoax!

S.H.I.E.L.D.

Super-Spy Finds Fountain of Youth

IT'S TRUE!! MARVEL'S NEW SERIES PREMIERE MEANS SIX NEW MONTHLY TITLES ARE COMING YOUR WAY!!

QUASAR — Ships 6/13

WHAT IF — Ships 3/21

N TH MAN THE ULTIMATE NINJA — Ships 4/11

THE SENSATIONAL SHE-HULK — Ships 1/3

Marc Spector MOON KNIGHT — Ships 2/20

SHIELD — Ships 5/16

REQUIRING FANS WANT TO KNOW...

I Love Lucy #535(#1), 1954. © Lucille Ball & Desi Arnaz

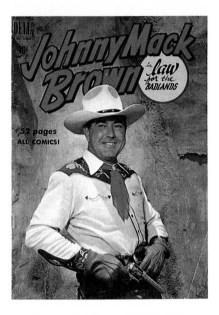

Johnny Mack Brown #269(#1), 1950. © Johnny M. Brown

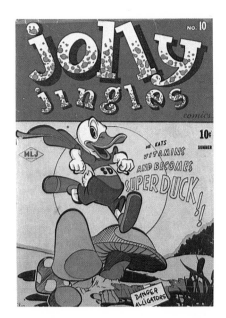

Jolly Jingles #10, 1943. First Super Duck. © MLJ

King Comics #16, 1937. © KING

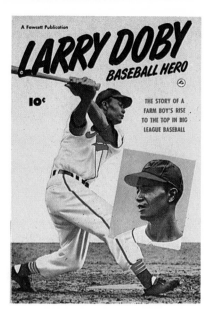

Larry Doby #1, 1950. © FAW

Lars Of Mars #11, 1951. © Z-D

Leave It To Beaver #1191, 1961. © Gomalco Prod.

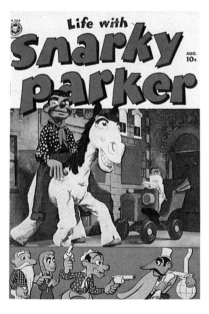

Life With Snarky Parker #1, 1950. © FOX

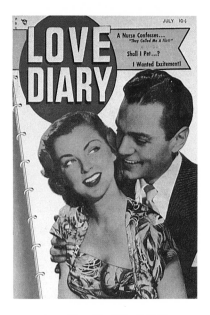

Love Diary #1, 1949. © OUR

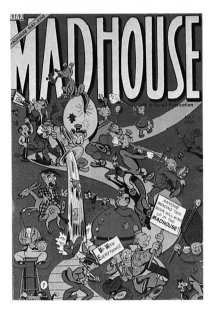

Madhouse #2, 1954. © AJAX

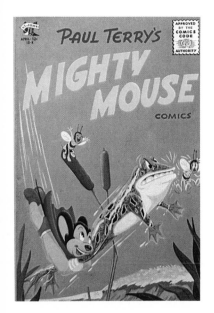

Mighty Mouse #62, 1955. © M.G.M.

Millie The Model Comics #11, 1948. © MCG

Modern Comics #44(#1), 1945. © QUA

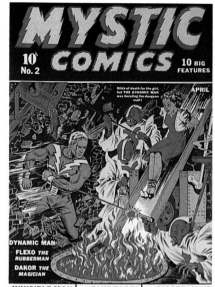

Mystic Comics #2, 1940. © MCG

New Adventure Comics #18, 1937. © DC

Peter Paul's 4 In 1 Jumbo Comic Book #1, 1953. © CC

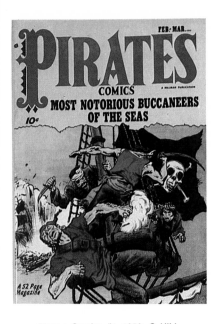

Pirates Comics #1, 1950. © HILL

Planet Comics #5, 1940. © FH

Rangers Comics #4, 1942. © FH

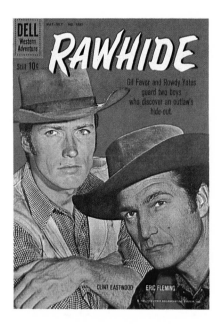

Rawhide #1097, 1960. © CBS

Rex Dexter Of Mars #1, 1940. © FOX

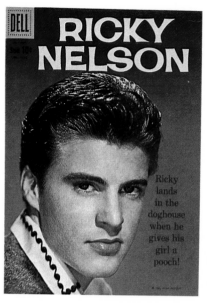

Ricky Nelson # 1115, 1960. © Ozzie Nelson

Sands Of The South Pacific #1, 1953.
© TOBY

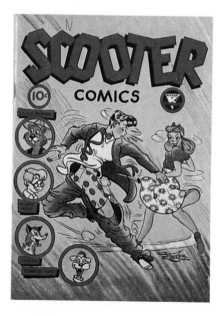

Scooter Comics #1, 1946. © Rucker

Single Series #15, 1939. © UFS

Skeleton Hand #1, 1952. © ACG

Space Ghost #1, 1966. © Hanna-Barbera

Star Spangled Comics #65, 1947. © DC

Strange Adventures #6, 1951. © DC

Superworld Comics #1, 1940. © Komos Publ.

Television Puppet Show #1, 1950. © AVON

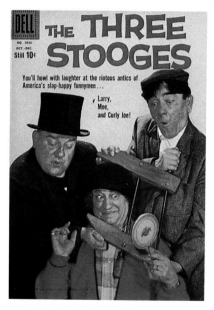

The Three Stooges #1043, 1959. © Norman Maurer Prod.

Tim McCoy #16(#1), 1948. © CC

USA Comics #4, 1941. © MCG

Vacation Parade #3, 1952. © WDC

Walt Disney's Comics & Stories #8, 1941.
© WDC

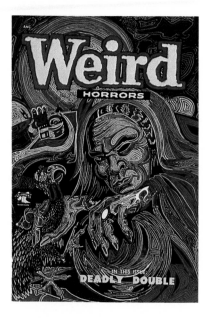

Weird Horrors #7, 1953. Ekgren cover art.
© STJ

Wings Comics #1, 1940. © FH

Wonderworld Comics #3, 1939. © FOX

World's Best Comics #1, 1941. © DC

JOIN THE PARADE TO...

458

461

The HOUSE OF COLLECTIBLES Series

☐ Please send me the following price guides—
☐ I would like the most current edition of the books listed below.

THE OFFICIAL PRICE GUIDES TO:

☐ 753-3	American Folk Art (ID) 1st Ed.	$14.95
☐ 199-3	American Silver & Silver Plate 5th Ed.	11.95
☐ 513-1	Antique Clocks 3rd Ed.	10.95
☐ 283-3	Antique & Modern Dolls 3rd Ed.	10.95
☐ 287-6	Antique & Modern Firearms 6th Ed.	11.95
☐ 755-X	Antiques & Collectibles 9th Ed.	11.95
☐ 289-2	Antique Jewelry 5th Ed.	11.95
☐ 362-7	Art Deco (ID) 1st Ed.	14.95
☐ 447-X	Arts and Crafts: American Decorative Arts, 1894–1923 (ID) 1st Ed.	12.95
☐ 539-5	Beer Cans & Collectibles 4th Ed.	7.95
☐ 521-2	Bottles Old & New 10th Ed.	10.95
☐ 532-8	Carnival Glass 2nd Ed.	10.95
☐ 295-7	Collectible Cameras 2nd Ed.	10.95
☐ 548-4	Collectibles of the '50s & '60s 1st Ed.	9.95
☐ 740-1	Collectible Toys 4th Ed.	10.95
☐ 531-X	Collector Cars 7th Ed.	12.95
☐ 538-7	Collector Handguns 4th Ed.	14.95
☐ 748-7	Collector Knives 9th Ed.	12.95
☐ 361-9	Collector Plates 5th Ed.	11.95
☐ 296-5	Collector Prints 7th Ed.	12.95
☐ 001-6	Depression Glass 2nd Ed.	9.95
☐ 589-1	Fine Art 1st Ed.	19.95
☐ 311-2	Glassware 3rd Ed.	10.95
☐ 243-4	Hummel Figurines & Plates 6th Ed.	10.95
☐ 523-9	Kitchen Collectibles 2nd Ed.	10.95
☐ 080-6	Memorabilia of Elvis Presley and The Beatles 1st Ed.	10.95
☐ 291-4	Military Collectibles 5th Ed.	11.95
☐ 525-5	Music Collectibles 6th Ed.	11.95
☐ 313-9	Old Books & Autographs 7th Ed.	11.95
☐ 298-1	Oriental Collectibles 3rd Ed.	11.95
☐ 761-4	Overstreet Comic Book 18th Ed.	12.95
☐ 522-0	Paperbacks & Magazines 1st Ed.	10.95
☐ 297-3	Paper Collectibles 5th Ed.	10.95
☐ 744-4	Political Memorabilia 1st Ed.	10.95
☐ 529-8	Pottery & Porcelain 6th Ed.	11.95
☐ 524-7	Radio, TV & Movie Memorabilia 3rd Ed.	11.95
☐ 081-4	Records 8th Ed.	16.95
☐ 763-0	Royal Doulton 6th Ed.	12.95
☐ 280-9	Science Fiction & Fantasy Collectibles 2nd Ed.	10.95
☐ 747-9	Sewing Collectibles 1st Ed.	8.95
☐ 358-9	Star Trek/Star Wars Collectibles 2nd Ed.	8.95
☐ 086-5	Watches 8th Ed.	12.95
☐ 248-5	Wicker 3rd Ed.	10.95

THE OFFICIAL:

☐ 760-6	Directory to U.S. Flea Markets 2nd Ed.	5.95
☐ 365-1	Encyclopedia of Antiques 1st Ed.	9.95
☐ 369-4	Guide to Buying and Selling Antiques 1st Ed.	9.95
☐ 414-3	Identification Guide to Early American Furniture 1st Ed.	9.95
☐ 413-5	Identification Guide to Glassware 1st Ed.	9.95
☐ 412-7	Identification Guide to Pottery & Porcelain 1st Ed.	$9.95
☐ 415-1	Identification Guide to Victorian Furniture 1st Ed.	9.95

THE OFFICIAL (SMALL SIZE) PRICE GUIDES TO:

☐ 309-0	Antiques & Flea Markets 4th Ed.	4.95
☐ 269-8	Antique Jewelry 3rd Ed.	4.95
☐ 085-7	Baseball Cards 8th Ed.	4.95
☐ 647-2	Bottles 3rd Ed.	4.95
☐ 544-1	Cars & Trucks 3rd Ed.	5.95
☐ 519-0	Collectible Americana 2nd Ed.	4.95
☐ 294-9	Collectible Records 3rd Ed.	4.95
☐ 306-6	Dolls 4th Ed.	4.95
☐ 762-2	Football Cards 8th Ed.	4.95
☐ 540-9	Glassware 3rd Ed.	4.95
☐ 526-3	Hummels 4th Ed.	4.95
☐ 279-5	Military Collectibles 3rd Ed.	4.95
☐ 764-9	Overstreet Comic Book Companion 2nd Ed.	4.95
☐ 278-7	Pocket Knives 3rd Ed.	4.95
☐ 527-1	Scouting Collectibles 4th Ed.	4.95
☐ 494-1	Star Trek/Star Wars Collectibles 3rd Ed.	3.95
☐ 088-1	Toys 5th Ed.	4.95

THE OFFICIAL BLACKBOOK PRICE GUIDES OF:

☐ 092-X	U.S. Coins 27th Ed.	4.95
☐ 095-4	U.S. Paper Money 21st Ed.	4.95
☐ 098-9	U.S. Postage Stamps 11th Ed.	4.95

THE OFFICIAL INVESTORS GUIDE TO BUYING & SELLING:

☐ 534-4	Gold, Silver & Diamonds 2nd Ed.	12.95
☐ 535-2	Gold Coins 2nd Ed.	12.95
☐ 536-0	Silver Coins 2nd Ed.	12.95
☐ 537-9	Silver Dollars 2nd Ed.	12.95

THE OFFICIAL NUMISMATIC GUIDE SERIES:

☐ 254-X	The Official Guide to Detecting Counterfeit Money 2nd Ed.	7.95
☐ 257-4	The Official Guide to Mint Errors 4th Ed.	7.95

SPECIAL INTEREST SERIES:

☐ 506-9	From Hearth to Cookstove 3rd Ed.	17.95
☐ 504-2	On Method Acting 8th Printing	6.95

TOTAL		

SEE REVERSE SIDE FOR ORDERING INSTRUCTIONS

464

469

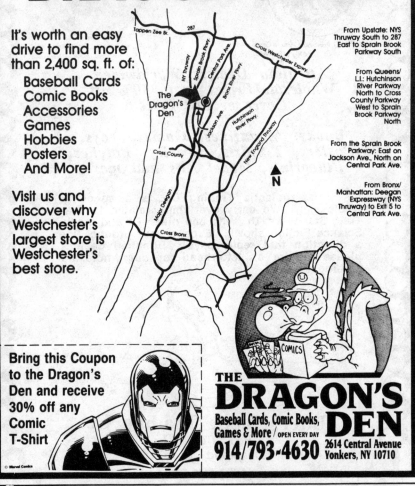

ALL ROADS LEAD
TO THE
DRAGON'S DEN

It's worth an easy drive to find more than 2,400 sq. ft. of:

Baseball Cards
Comic Books
Accessories
Games
Hobbies
Posters
And More!

Visit us and discover why Westchester's largest store is Westchester's best store.

From Upstate: NYS Thruway South to 287 East to Sprain Brook Parkway South

From Queens/L.I.: Hutchinson River Parkway North to Cross County Parkway West to Sprain Brook Parkway North

From the Sprain Brook Parkway: East on Jackson Ave., North on Central Park Ave.

From Bronx/Manhattan: Deegan Expressway (NYS Thruway) to Exit 5 to Central Park Ave.

THE DRAGON'S DEN

Baseball Cards, Comic Books, Games & More / OPEN EVERY DAY

914/793-4630 2614 Central Avenue Yonkers, NY 10710

474

© DC

© MCG

© FH

WANTED
OLD COMICS!!
$CASH REWARD$

FOR THESE AND MANY OTHER ELUSIVE COMIC BOOKS FROM THE GOLDEN AGE. SEEKING WHITE PAGE COLLECTIBLE COPIES IN VG OR BETTER CONDITION. ALSO GOLDEN AGE **BOUND VOLUMES WANTED.**

© DC

© DC

© DC

479

SECOND GENESIS
3 WEST COAST WAREHOUSES FOR RETAILER SERVICE

Complete line of comic book publishers: Marvel, DC, Gladstone, First, Eclipse, Comico, Dark Horse and all the independent publishers.

Specialty products: Trade Paperbacks, T-Shirts, Games, Calendars, Graphic Novels, and more.

Supplies: Long and short comic boxes, magazine boxes, dividers, 9 different sizes of polypropylene bags, baseball sheets, backing boards and mylar products.

Call one of our warehouses for our thick monthly catalog. **Providing wholesale services to retailers since 1976.**

NEW PUBLISHERS: Solicitation material or new product information should go to our Portland Warehouse.

SEATTLE WAREHOUSE
Manager: Al Clover
223 1/2 Ninth Ave. North
Seattle, WA 98109
(206) 624-6210

PORTLAND WAREHOUSE
Main Office
Manager: Kathy Moullet
Catalog Editor: Tim Androes
Controller: Lance Casebeer
5860 NE Going Street
Portland, OR 97218
(503) 281-1821

LOS ANGELES WAREHOUSE
Manager: Glen Quasny
6223 Randolph Street
Commerce, CA 90040
(213) 888-0466

SO FUNNY HE'LL KILL YOU!

THE MISADVENTURES OF THE BUMBLING BARBARIAN ARE AVAILABLE AT:

1971 WANTAGH AVE.
WANTAGH, NY 11793
(516) 783-8700

Collector's Comics
Laurie & Jim Wanser

167 DEER PARK AVE.
BABYLON, NY 11702
(516) 321-4347

- ROLE PLAYING GAMES
- SUBSCRIPTION SERVICE

- MINIATURES
- UNDERGROUNDS

GROO TM & © 1988 Sergio Aragones. Marvel Comics is a registered trademark of the Marvel Entertainment Group, Inc.

1,000,000 COMIX INC.

THE LEADING INTERNATIONAL FRANCHISOR OF COMIC BOOK STORES OFFERS YOU A UNIQUE OPPORTUNITY.

Comic collecting is the fastest growing recession resistant hobby today. We offer a unique, highly successful, proven formula. An initial 15-40K investment puts successful candidates into a highly grossing, upscale "turnkey" store, stocked in depth, that provides immediate upper level income and **SOLID** long term growth. **YOUR GROWTH!**

Equipped with a huge 10,000 back issue opening stock (provided at store opening – no extra cost) including many high priced books, and with continual training, support, and nationwide advertising in the *comic books* themselves franchisees revel in success. W. Strike (Toronto, Mississauga franchise) "Our store in one month alone topped $20,000 in sales".

Join the team that has changed comic book retailing. Master franchises are still available for many areas, on a limited basis. If you like comics, kids, and upper level income you owe it to yourself to become your own boss. *Be in business for yourself, but not by yourself.*
$25.00 APPLICATION FEE. You'll receive a video cassette demonstrating our store concept. Include your name, address and a financial curriculum vitae along with your $25.00.

Send to: **1,000,000 COMIX INC.**
             c/o The President
             Franchise Department
             P.O. Box 4953
             St. Laurent (Montreal) Quebec
             Canada H4L-4Z6
             Franchise Hotline!
             (514) 630-4518

Already own a store? Become a 1,000,000 Comix affiliate. Get **great** back issue discounts on all store packages, catalogs, and more!

Already existing franchises

Canada

Montreal, Quebec
Corporate Headquarters
1539 Van Horne
(514) 277-5788
6290 Somerled
(514) 486-1175
(Check for new Montreal
stores opening soon)
1260 Dollard
(514) 366-1233
Halifax, Nova Scotia
6251 Quinpool Rd.
(902) 425-5594
Moncton, New Brunswick
345 Mountain Rd.
(506) 855-0056
Ontario
2400 Guelph Line, (Burlington)
(416) 332-5600
2150 Burnhamthorpe Rd.
South Common Mall, (Mississauga)
(416) 828-8208

US Stores

New Jersey
875 Mantua Pike
Southwood
Shopping Centre
Woodbury Heights
(609) 384-8844

Affiliates
Comix Plus
1475 McDonald St.
St. Laurent, Que.
Canada
(514) 334-0732

CUSTOMIZED START-UP PACKAGES
FOR RETAILERS, COLLECTORS, INVESTORS.

These packages are available to retailers as well as collectors. We are able to offer the lowest priced, best quality store or start-up packages in existence! Our warehouse has bulked up even more with an estimated purchase of 1.2 million comics from Glenwood Distribution Inc. (we bought out the majority of their comic stock). Although all store packages are available, it is advised that you phone first, as to assess postage costs to your area. **Coming to Montreal? We'll be glad to help you personally select your stock** (by appointment only). Our complete GIANT CATALOG of Golden Age, Silver Age and Marvel comics is available for $1.00 (free with any purchase).

OUR MOST POPULAR PACKAGES

Package A: 10 key Marvel titles (ASM, Cap. America, Spiderman, Daredevil, Conan, Hulk, Thor, Fantastic Four, Avengers, Peter Parker, Iron Man). Each title includes 30% minimum, (i.e. 25-40 early 12¢ issues or more) of earlier sought after issues per title. 850 comics (or 80-90/title, avg. 85) **Most fine or better**, max. 4 per number, except early issues (VG or better). These packages always includes high-priced books such as Conans between 1-10; Spidermans between 10-20, Daredevils between 3-20, etc. These titles are the most consistent movers in the majority of comic book stores. Suggestions appreciated. Early issues vary with our stock but you can be assured that there will be a healthy chunk of early Marvels in every package. Cost $1,475.00 U.S. plus postage. Take half of this package for $845.00 plus postage. Note, many of these Marvels will retail for between $4.00-$10.00; and Marvels are steadily increasing in value all the time, just take a look at this year's Spiderman prices between #20-100. This package boasts many happy customers "I want to thank you and your staff personally for the great job you did in helping us out and setting up our store" *Michael Halbleib, Marvel-us Comics, Great Falls, Montana.*

Package B: Includes Package A plus 50 X-Men between #94-150. Also includes 300 other Marvels (Marvel Team up, 2 in 1, Presents, and others) avg., near fine or better. Sum: 13 titles avg., 80 comics per title and 50 X-Men between #94-150. Total 1,090 key comic books for $1,995.00 U.S. plus postage. Note, X-Men are a consistent seller and these are the most in demand numbers.

Package C: X-Men #1-200 plus all annuals (avg., fine or better) $3,000.00 plus postage. (Guide value equals $4,116.10 in mint). OR, X-Men #1-200 (#1-10 avg., VG; #20-93 avg., fine or better; #94 up avg., very fine or better) $1,995.00 plus postage OR #1-20 avg., G/VG; #21-93 avg., VG or better; #94-200 avg., near fine or better $1,450.00 U.S. plus postage. This is a truly great investment lot.

Mini X-Men package: #13-200 avg., N/F or better $2,400.00 U.S. plus postage. OR #13-100 avg., VG or better, #101-120 avg., F— or better, #121 up avg., F for better $1,390.00 U.S. plus postage.

Package D: X-Men #94-150 avg., very fine or better $850.00;   Avg., fine or better $650.00;   Avg., VG or better $430.00 plus postage.

Package E: Convention Special 2,000 Marvel, D.C. and independents. (Max 5 of a number. Most fine or better. Nobody can beat the price of $675.00 plus postage).

Package F: Start-up Special 100 Marvel comics, max 5 of a number, many 5-10 years old, most VF or better $25.00 plus postage.

Package G: Archie Avalanche. Great store stock. Most $0.65 cover and up; multiples; 300 Archies $49.00 plus postage (order in multiples of 300. Call for larger order discounts).

Package H: Cheapie Special. 900 comics; anything and everything. Many with cover prices of $2.00 or more. Multiples. Cost $150.00 plus postage.

Package I: Magazine Massacre. 100 mags (many sci-fi, comics, war, etc.) 100 mags at $25.00; some multiples, plus postage.

Package J: Amazing, Amazing Spiderman Lot. Instant Spidy collection #1-250 plus annuals avg., F+ or better $3,800.00. ($4,317.00 at mint guide. OR #1-20 avg., fine, #21-100 avg., F/VF; #100-250 avg. VF or better (90% plus annuals avg., fine or better – $2,500.00 **OR** #1-20 avg., G/VG, #21-100 avg., VG/F; #100 up avg., fine or better – $1,999.00 **OR** #1-250 avg., G/VG or better – $1,300.00 (restorers delight!).

Package J1: Mini Spidey Set A) #7-250 plus annuals, most fine or better, a steal at $1,999.00 plus postage. B) #7-250 (#7-30 avg., VG/VG+; #31-100 avg., VG; #101 up avg., NF or better) take it for $1,500.00 OR #7-250 (#7-30 avg., G/VG; #31-70 avg., VG—; #71-150 avg., VG/VG+; #150 up avg., VG/F or better) $1,300.00 plus postage.

Package K: Fantabulous Fantastic Four Lot. #1-300 plus annuals avg., F/VF or better – $4,900.00 ($5,919.00 by guide in mint) **OR** #1-300 plus annuals (#1-20 avg., near fine; #21-100 avg., F/VF or better; #100 up avg., VF or better – $3,500.00 **OR** #1-20 avg., G/VG; #21-100 avg., VG; #100 up avg., fine or better $2,500.00) **OR** #1-150 avg., good or better, #151 up avg., VG or better, most fine. $1,850.00 plus postage.

Package K1: Mini FF A) #14-250 plus annuals. (#14-250 avg., NF or better) $2,320.00 plus postage. OR B) #14-250 (#14-30 avg., VG/F or better, #30-250 avg., NF or better) $1,885.00 plus postage. OR C) #14-250 (#14-40 avg., G/VG, #41-70 avg., VG—, #71-100 avg., VG, #101-250 avg., VG/F or better) $999.00 plus postage.

Package L: Instant Conan #1-200 all high grade (near VF or better) $600.00 plus postage.

Package M: Super Special Groo #1 (Pacific scarce) $9.00 (guide equals $11.00) 5 or more $7.50 each.

Package N: Peter Hsu's Scarcest Work – Quadrant. Scarce print runs makes this a truly good investment. #1 (scarce) $100.00 (low quantities) #2 $40.00 (3 or more at $29.00 each) #3 $20.00 (3 or more $16.00 each) #4 (rare) $15.00 (3 or more $10.00 each)

Package O: (Cheap) Quality Special. 100 issues composed of 25 issues each of the following titles between #100-250. Amazing Spiderman, Daredevil, Fantastic Four, Conan; avg., VG/F or better. Cost (believe it or not!) $100.00 plus postage.

Package P: Small Quality Special. 50 Marvel comics, mainly 15¢ cover price and higher, all super heros most fine or better $22.00 plus postage.

Package Q: Quick Steal! 50 different 12¢ cover priced Marvel comics VG or better, super special; (most super hero) $45.00 plus postage.

Package R: Ridiculous and Racy! 50 different comics with a $1.25 or greater cover price for only $15.00 plus postage.

Package S: 80% Off Cover Price Special! Includes mainly independents. Lots of good sellable, collectable material (ex. Johnny Quest, Elflord, Samurai, Jon Sable, American Flagg, Lone Wolf) all at 80% off cover, our choice, multiples, order in $50.00 increments. i.e. $50.00 gives you $250.00 (by cover price) of material $100.00 order gives you $500.00 (by cover price) of great merchandise. Make your customers happy.

Package T: The Titanic Complete Marvel collection of key books – Amazing Spiderman, Fantastic Four, Daredevil, Conan, X-Men, and Avengers. #1-200 (except Conan #1-200) avg., N/fine or better, includes all annuals. Guides at around $20,000.00. Your cost $14,000.00 plus postage. **OR** same package, avg., VG $8,700.00 **OR** same package, avg., G/VG $5,825.00. The Mini-Mother; Amazing Spiderman #10-200, Fantastic Four #10-200, Daredevil #3-200, Conan #1-200, X-Men #10-200, and Avengers #8-200; A) avg. fine or better $7,120.00 B) avg., VG or better $4,999.00 C) avg., G/VG $3,425.00 plus postage.

489

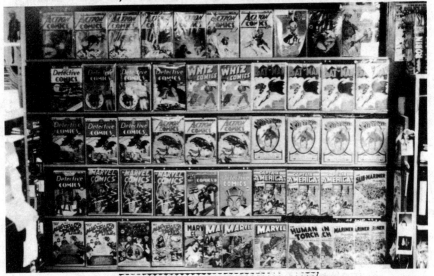

FANTAZIA

2 South Central Ave., Hartsdale, N.Y. 10530

(914) 946-3306   (914) 946-1236

We are paying the following prices for the titles and numbers listed. Please call if you have the books to sell. Payment will be immediate upon receiving your materials. Remember, we're the only dealer in the world who can say "UNLIMITED FUNDS" available, and mean it. Just ask around. This list was compiled Jan 1, 1989 and represents **permanent** wants in any quantity. Our pay prices are upscaled weekly, just call for a current price quote on your material.

WANTED

COMIC TITLE	#	GOOD	VG	FN	VF	NM	MINT
Action	583	N/W	N/W	N/W	N/W	$5	$8
Adventure	247	$160	$300	$500	$750	$1200	$1750
Adventure	40	$240	$480	$800	$1400	$2000	$2500
Adventure	48	$225	$450	$750	$1250	$1825	$2200
All American	16	$850	$1650	$2800	$4250	$6000	$8000
All American	61	$95	$185	$275	$425	$650	$875
Amazing Fantasy	15	$200	$400	$700	$1200	$1750	$2750
Avengers	1	N/W	N/W	$200	$375	$550	$800
Batman	1	$1600	$3000	$4500	$7000	$10,500	$17,500
Batman	47	$100	$190	$300	$475	$650	$850
Brave & Bold	28	N/W	$150	$275	$500	$750	$1000
Brave & Bold	54	N/W	N/W	$20	$35	$50	$75
Capt. America	100	N/W	N/W	N/W	$15	$25	$35
Daredevil	1	N/W	$75	$110	$200	$275	$350
Detective	168	$100	$225	$350	$475	$600	$1000
Detective	225	N/W	$125	$250	$500	$750	$1000
Detective	27	$3,500	$7,000	$11,000	$16,250	$22,500	$50,000
Detective	31	$300	$750	$1200	$1750	$2500	$3500
Detective	33	$600	$1250	$2000	$2800	$4000	$6000
Detective	38	$600	$1250	$2000	$2750	$3800	$5500
Detective	40	$150	$300	$450	$675	$900	$1200
FF	1	$150	$350	$575	$1000	$1875	$3200
FF	25,26	N/W	N/W	$20	$30	$42	$60
Flash	105	N/W	N/W	$200	$400	$650	$950
G.L. (40's)	1	$300	$600	$1050	$1450	$2200	$3200
G.L. (60's)	1	N/W	N/W	$175	$275	$525	$850
Hulk	181	N/W	N/W	$25	$50	$75	$100
Iron Man	1	N/W	N/W	$30	$50	$75	$100
JLA	1	$100	$200	$300	$500	$800	$1150
Journey Into Mys.	83	N/W	N/W	$200	$400	$650	$950
Metal Men	1	N/W	N/W	$22	$35	$65	$100
More Fun	55	$300	$600	$900	$1200	$1650	$2400
Mystery In Space	53	N/W	N/W	$125	$175	$250	$375
Showcase	13,14	N/W	N/W	$200	$300	$450	$675
Showcase	22	N/W	N/W	$200	$400	$675	$1200
Showcase	34	N/W	N/W	$30	$60	$85	$125
Showcase	37	N/W	N/W	$20	$35	$55	$75
Showcase	4	$200	$450	$800	$1500	$2500	$5000
Showcase	8	N/W	N/W	$300	$500	$700	$1000
Silver Surfer	1	N/W	N/W	$22	$35	$50	$70
Spiderman	1	N/W	$250	$500	$900	$1400	$2000
Spiderman	129	N/W	N/W	$22	$45	$75	$110
Superman	100	N/W	N/W	$135	$200	$300	$425
Superman	87	N/W	N/W	N/W	$175	$275	$400
Tales Of Suspense	39	N/W	$125	$250	$375	$550	$825
Tales To Astonish	27	N/W	$125	$225	$350	$500	$750
X-Men	1	$100	$200	$300	$525	$800	$1250

We also need the following general ranges of books not listed above and will pay substantial prices for their acquisition: Avengers 2-14; Batman 2-150; Capt. America 1-78, Detective 1-275; FF 2-20, 48-50; Flash 1, 86, 92, 105-140; JLA 2-22, 29, 30; MGA 1, 81-86; Myst. In Space 53-75; Spiderman 2-15; Superman 2-150; Tales Of Suspense 40-53; X-Men 1, 94, GS 1, etc. If it's quality stuff, we want it!

493

DO YOU THINK NEW COMICS COST TOO MUCH?
THEN DO SOMETHING ABOUT IT.

M & M CORDIALLY INVITES YOU TO STATE OF THE ART COMIC BOOK BUYING.

FEATURING:
—Fully computerized order and invoicing system.
—Monthly credits for late and resolicited books.
—Detailed monthly order form.
—Free promo material with every shipment.
—5 years experience in comic mail order, and mail order is all we do.
—Discounts up to 52%.
—No minimum order.
—Weekly news items on every invoice.
—Expertly packed boxes to ensure your books arrive in great condition.
—Yet get what you order, because we order it for you and only you.
—Customer Satisfaction — we have **never** had a complaint written to any publication we advertise in.

And this is just the tip of the iceberg. WE ARE WITHOUT A DOUBT THE BEST COMIC SERVICE OUT THERE.

If you're not ordering from us, you're probably paying too much and you're not getting everything you ordered.

FIND OUT WHAT YOU'RE MISSING
Call of write now for our FREE order form.

M & M
P.O. Box 6
9325 Bradford Lane
Orland Park, IL 60462
312-349-2486
Visa & Mastercard Accepted

494

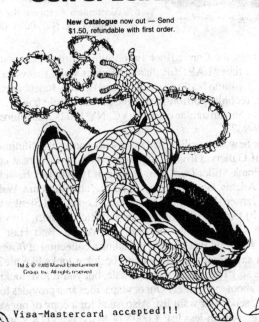
496

501

HUGH O'KENNON

2204 HAVILAND DRIVE
RICHMOND, VA. 23229

Tel (804) 270-2465

Buying - Selling - Collector's Comic Books

I Offer The Following To ALL Customers:

- ACCURATE GRADING
- SATISFACTION GUARANTEED
- PROMPT DEPENDABLE SERVICE
- REASONABLE PRICING
- EXPERIENCE

Selling – A list of all Comics for sale is available. Please forward 50 cents for a copy (refundable with first order).

Buying – Write for MY offer before you sell your comic books.

ED KALB

P.O. Box 4111, Mesa, AZ 85211-4111, 1-602-832-5176 (anytime 9-9 MDT)

"SERVING COLLECTORS WORLDWIDE SINCE 1967"

BUYING LIST #12

The following is a listing of comics we are buying and the prices we pay per issue.

Simply send your comics for our immediate payment. Any individual (dealer or collector) reading this ad may send single copies of any comic listed.

Please contact us for go ahead word, before sending shipments that exceed $500. Otherwise simply send comics for payment.

All offers listed will be honored thru March 1990

GOOD OR BETTER WANTED

These prices will be paid for comics in GOOD OR BETTER CONDITION.

ABBOTT AND COSTELLO (St. John)
- any issues 2.50

ACE COMICS
- any issues 2.50

ACES HIGH
- any issues 4.00

ACTION COMICS
- 31-52 .... 25.00
- 53-90 .... 17.00
- 91-120 .... 15.00
- 121-161 .... 14.00
- 162-201 .... 9.00
- 202-220 .... 6.00
- 221-240 .... 4.00
- 241-251,253-255 .... 3.00
- 252 .... 35.00
- 256-266,268-300 .... 2.00
- 267 .... 15.00

ADVENTURE COMICS
- 42-80 .... 30.00
- 81-91 .... 25.00
- 92-120 .... 19.00
- 121-169 .... 12.00
- 170-209 .... 10.00
- 210 .... 35.00
- 211-246 .... 6.00
- 248-260 .... 4.00
- 261-266,268-271 .... 3.00
- 267 .... 25.00
- 272-299,301-310 .... 2.00
- 300 .... 14.00
- 311-329 .... 1.00

ADVS INTO TERROR
- any issues 2.00

ADVS INTO WEIRD WORLDS
- any issues 2.00

AIRBOY COMICS (Hillman)
- any issues 2.00

ALAN LADD
- any issues 7.00

ALL AMERICAN COMICS
- 3-15 .... 22.00
- 28-70 .... 19.00
- 71-102 .... 15.00

ALL AMERICAN WESTERN
- 102-126 .... 2.00

ALLEY OOP
- any issues 3.00

ALL FLASH
- 3-10 .... 25.00
- 11-32 .... 17.00

ALL-NEW COMICS
- any issues 8.00

ALL SELECT COMICS
- any issues 24.00

ALL STAR (1940-1951)
- any issues 25.00

ALL STAR WESTERN
- 58-119 .... 2.00

ALL WINNERS
- any issues 25.00

AMAZ. ADULT FANTASY
- 7-14 .... 4.00

AMAZING FANTASY
- 15 .... 120.00

AMAZING- MAN COMICS
- any issues 16.00

AMAZ. MYSTERY FUNNIES
- any issues 15.00

AMAZING SPIDER-MAN
- 1 .... 110.00
- 2 .... 36.00
- 3 .... 25.00
- 4 .... 18.00
- 5,6 .... 15.00
- 7-10 .... 10.00
- 11-15 .... 8.00
- 16-20 .... 6.00
- 21-30 .... 2.00
- 31-40 .... 1.00

AMERICA'S BEST
- any issues 5.00

AMERICA'S GREATEST
- any issues 10.00

ANDY DEVINE
- any issues 3.00

ANNIE OAKLEY
- any issues 2.00

APACHE KID
- any issues 1.50

AQUAMAN (1962)
- 1 .... 12.00
- 2-10 .... 1.50

ASTONISHING (Atlas)
- any issues 2.00

ATLAS/MARVEL Horror titles, pre 1963
- any issues 1.50

ATLAS/MARVEL Western titles, pre 1960
- any issues 1.00

ATLAS/MARVEL War titles, pre 1960
- any issues 1.00

ATLAS/MARVEL Crime, Spy titles, pre 1960
- any issues 1.00

ATOM (1962)
- 1 .... 14.00
- 2-14 .... 1.50

AVENGERS (Marvel)
- 1 .... 55.00
- 2 .... 17.00
- 3 .... 12.00
- 4 .... 20.00
- 5 .... 7.00
- 6-10 .... 5.00
- 11-22 .... 2.00

BATMAN
- 17-30 .... 30.00
- 31-50 .... 19.00
- 51-89 .... 12.00
- 90-100 .... 8.00
- 101-110 .... 5.00
- 111-130 .... 4.00
- 131-143 .... 2.50
- 144-169 .... 1.50
- Annual 1-7 .... 1.50

BAT MASTERSON
- any issues 2.50

BATTLE (Atlas)
- any issues 1.00

BATTLE ACTION
- any issues 1.00

BATTLEFRONT
- any issues 1.00

BATTLE GROUND
- any issues 1.00

BEANY AND CECIL
- any issues 1.50

BEN BOWIE
- any issues 1.50

BEST OF THE WEST
- any issues 2.50

BIG SHOT
- any issues 1.50

BILL BOYD WESTERN
- any issues 5.00

BILLY THE KID (Toby)
- any issues 1.50

BLACK CAT COMICS
- 1-30 .... 5.00

BLACKHAWK
- 9-20 .... 14.00
- 21-40 .... 10.00
- 41-62 .... 6.00
- 63-86 .... 4.00
- 87-108 .... 3.00
- 109-118 .... 1.50
- 119-169 .... .75

BLACK HOOD (1944-1946)
- any issues 9.00

BLACK RIDER
- 8-27 .... 1.50

BLACK TERROR
- any issues 6.00

BLONDE PHANTOM
- 12-22 .... 14.00

BLUE BEETLE (1939-1950)
- any issues 4.00

BLUE BOLT
- any issues 1.50

BLUE RIBBON (1939-1942)
- any issues 12.00

BOB COLT
- any issues 5.00

BOB HOPE (1950-1959)
- any issues 1.00

BOB STEELE WESTERN
- any issues 5.00

BOY COMICS
- any issues 1.50

BOY COMMANDOS ('42-49)
- any issues 4.00

BOZO THE CLOWN (Dell)
- any issues 1.00

BRAVE AND THE BOLD
- 1-24 .... 8.00
- 25-27,31-33 .... 2.00
- 28 .... 40.00
- 29,30 .... 17.00
- 34-50 .... 1.00

BUCK JONES
- any issues 2.00

BUFFALO BILL JR.
- any issues 1.50

BULLETMAN
- 1-16 .... 17.00

BUSTER CRABBE
- any issues 3.00

CAPTAIN AERO
- any issues 3.00

CAPTAIN AMERICA ('41-54)
- any issues 25.00

CAPTAIN & THE KIDS
- any issues 1.00

CAPTAIN EASY
- any issues 2.00

CAPTAIN MARVEL ADVS.
- 5-10 .... 20.00
- 11-25 .... 12.00
- 26-46 .... 6.00
- 47-150 .... 4.00

CAPTAIN MARVEL JR.
- any issues 4.00

CAPTAIN MIDNIGHT
- any issues 4.00

CAPTAIN SCIENCE
- any issues 10.00

CATMAN
- any issues 5.00

CHAMP/CHAMPION COMICS (1939-1944)
- any issues 12.00

CHEYENNE
- any issues 2.00

CISCO KID
- any issues 2.00

CLUE COMICS
- any issues 3.00

COLT .45
- any issues 2.00

COMBAT CASEY
- any issues 1.00

COMBAT KELLY (Atlas)
- any issues 1.00

COMIC CAVALCADE
- 1-29 .... 16.00

COWGIRL ROMANCES
- any issues 2.00

CRACKAJACK FUNNIES
- any issues 6.00

CRACK COMICS
- any issues 4.00

CRACK WESTERN
- any issues 2.00

CRIME SMASHERS
- any issues 3.00

CRIME SUSPENSTORIES
- any issues 10.00

DALE EVANS (DC)
- any issues 4.00

DALE EVANS (Dell)
- any issues 2.00

DAREDEVIL (Marvel)
- 1 .... 40.00
- 2 .... 15.00
- 3 .... 7.00
- 4,5 .... 5.00
- 6-10 .... 2.00

DAREDEVIL (old)
- 1941-1944 any 5.00
- 1945-1949 any 2.00
- 1950-1956 any 1.50

DC COMICS, with photo covers, 1950-1959, any titles/issues 1.00

DEAN MARTIN & JERRY LEWIS, any issues 2.00

DELL COMICS, with photo covers, 1950-1959, any titles/issues 1.00

DETECTIVE COMICS
- 50-90 .... 25.00
- 91-176 .... 17.00
- 177-216 .... 12.00
- 217-240 .... 6.00
- 241-260 .... 5.00
- 261-300 .... 2.00
- 301-310 .... 1.50

DICK TRACY (Dell/Harvey)
- any issues 4.00

DOBIE GILLIS
- any issues 2.00

DOLLMAN (1941-1953)
- any issues 5.00

DONALD DUCK (Dell)
- any issues 1.00

DURANGO KID
- any issues 3.00

DYNAMIC COMICS ('41-'48)
- any issues 6.00

EERIE (Avon)
- any issues 4.00

EXCITING COMICS
- any issues 6.00

FAIRY TALE PARADE
- any issues 5.00

FAMOUS FUNNIES (pre-'56)
- any issues 1.50

FAMOUS MONSTERS OF FILMLAND (magazine)
- 1 .... 40.00
- 2-6 .... 20.00
- 7-10 .... 10.00
- 11-26 .... 5.00
- 27-32 .... 3.00

FANTASTIC COMICS
- any issues 12.00

FANTASTIC FOUR
- 1 .... 110.00
- 2 .... 50.00
- 3 .... 37.00
- 4 .... 35.00
- 5 .... 22.00
- 6-12 .... 15.00
- 13-20 .... 8.00
- 21-33,48 .... 3.00
- 34-39 .... 1.50

FAWCETT MOVIE COMIC
- any issues 5.00

FEATURE COMICS
- any issues 3.00

FEATURE FUNNIES
- any issues 4.00

FELIX THE CAT (1943-1965)
- any issues 1.00

FIGHT COMICS
- any issues 4.00

FIGHTING YANK
- any issues 7.00

FIREHAIR COMICS ('48-'51)
- any issues 4.00

THE FLAME
- any issues 6.00

FLASH COMICS
- 11-30 .... 25.00
- 31-50 .... 18.00
- 51-104 .... 16.00

THE FLASH
- 105 .... 40.00
- 106 .... 20.00
- 107-110 .... 7.00
- 111-133 .... 2.00

FLASH GORDON (Dell/Harvey)
- any issues 4.00

FLYING A'S RANGE RIDERS
- any issues 2.00

FRANKENSTEIN COMICS
- any issues 4.00

FRONTLINE COMBAT
- any issues 8.00

THE FUNNIES
- any issues 5.00

GABBY HAYES WESTERN
- 1-51,53,55 .... 3.00

GENE AUTRY COMICS
- any issues 2.00

GHOST (1951-1954)
- any issues 5.00

GHOST RIDER (1950-1954)
- any issues 6.00

G. I. JOE (1950-1957)
- any issues 2.00

GREEN HORNET ('40-1949)
- any issues 9.00

GREEN LANTERN ('41-1949)
- any issues 22.00

GREEN LANTERN
- 1 .... 40.00
- 2 .... 15.00
- 3-5 .... 6.00
- 6-10 .... 3.00
- 11-19 .... 2.00

GREEN MASK
- any issues 5.00

GUNSMOKE (Dell)
- any issues 1.50

HANGMAN COMICS
- any issues 20.00

HAUNT OF FEAR
- any issues 12.00

HAVE GUN, WILL TRAVEL
- any issues 2.50

HECKLE AND JECKLE (1951-1956)
- any issues 1.00

HERBIE
- any issues 1.00

HIT COMICS
- any issues 4.00

HOPALONG CASSIDY (Fawcett)-any issues 3.00

HOPALONG CASSIDY (DC)-any issues 2.00

Ed Kalb, page 2, Buying List #10

HOUSE OF MYSTERY (1951-1959)-any issues . 1.00

HOUSE OF SECRETS (1956-1959)-any issues . 1.00

HOWDY DOODY
- any issues 1.00

HUMAN TORCH (1940-1954)
- any issues 22.00

I LOVE LUCY
- any issues 3.00

IMPACT
- any issues 4.00

INCREDIBLE HULK
- 1 .... 90.00
- 2 .... 25.00
- 3-6 .... 16.00

INCREDIBLE SCIENCE-FIC.
- 30-33 .... 16.00

INDIAN CHIEF
- any issues 1.00

INDIANS
- any issues 1.50

JACE PEARSON
- any issues 2.00

JACKIE GLEASON
- any issues 9.00

JIMMY OLSEN
- 1954-1959, any 2.00
- 1960-1964, any .... .50

JIMMY WAKELY
- any issues 4.00

JOE PALOOKA
- any issues 1.50

JOHNNY MACK BROWN
- any issues 2.00

JOHN WAYNE ADVENTURE COMICS, any issues ... 9.00

JO-JO COMICS (1947-1949)
- any issues 5.00

JOKER COMICS
- any issues 2.00

JOURNEY INTO MYSTERY
- 1952-1962, any 2.00
- 83 .... 55.00
- 84 .... 12.00
- 85-89 .... 7.00
- 90-95 .... 4.00
- 96-112 .... 2.50

JOURNEY INTO UNKNOWN WORLDS, any issues .. 2.00

JUMBO COMICS
- any issues 4.00

JUNGLE COMICS
- any issues 4.00

JUNGLE JIM (1949-1959)
- any issues 1.50

JUSTICE LEAGUE OF AMERICA
- 1 .... 50.00
- 2,3 .... 12.00
- 4-10 .... 5.00
- 11-20 .... 3.00
- 21,22 .... 5.00
- 23-39 .... 1.00

KAANGA COMICS ('49-'54)
- any issues 3.00

KATZENJAMMER KIDS
- any issues 1.50

KEEN DETECTIVE FUNNIES
- any issues 12.00

KEN MAYNARD WESTERN
- 1-8 .... 8.00

KID COLT OUTLAW
- 1948-1959, any 1.00

KID ETERNITY
- any issues 4.00

KING COMICS
- any issues 2.50

KING OF THE ROYAL MOUNTED, any issues . 2.00

KRAZY KAT
- any issues 2.00

LAND OF THE LOST
- any issues 5.00

LASH LARUE WESTERN
- 1-47 .... 4.00

LAUREL AND HARDY (St. John), any issues 5.00

LAWMAN
- any issues 2.00

LIL ABNER
- any issues 2.50

LITTLE LULU (Dell)
- any issues 1.50

LOIS LANE
- 1958-1959, any 3.00
- 1960-1964, any .... .50

LONE RANGER (Dell)
- with photo covers 2.50
- without photo covers ... 1.50

LORNA THE JUNGLE GIRL
- any issues 2.00

MAD COMICS/Magazine
- 1 .... 60.00
- 2-5 .... 15.00
- 6-23 .... 10.00
- 24 .... 15.00
- 25 .... 8.00
- 26-30 .... 6.00
- 31-39 .... 4.00
- 40-49 .... 2.00
- 50-69 .... 1.00

MAGIC COMICS
- any issues 1.50

MARVEL FAMILY
- any issues 4.00

MARVEL MYSTERY COMICS, any issues .. 25.00

MARVEL TALES (1949-1957), any issues 2.00

MARY MARVEL
- any issues 5.00

MASTER COMICS
- any issues 4.00

MAVERICK
- any issues 2.00

MELVIN MONSTER
- any issues 1.00

MILITARY COMICS
- any issues 14.00

MISTER MYSTERY
- any issues 4.00

MODERN COMICS
- any issues 6.00

MONTE HALE WESTERN
- any issues 4.00

MORE FUN
- 18-107 .... 22.00
- 108-127 .... 4.00

MOTION PICTURE COMICS
- 101-114 .... 5.00

MY GREATEST ADV.
- 1955-1959, any 1.00

MYSTERY IN SPACE
- 1951-1961, any 3.00
- 1962-1964, any 1.00

MYSTERY MEN COMICS
- any issues 9.00

MYSTERY TALES (Atlas)
- any issues 2.00

MYSTIC
- any issues 2.00

MYSTICAL TALES
- any issues 2.00

NATIONAL COMICS
- any issues 3.00

NYOKA THE JUNGLE GIRL
- any issues 2.00

OUR ARMY AT WAR
- 1952-1959, any .... .75

OUR FIGHTING FORCES
- 1954-1959, any .... .75

OUTLAW KID (Atlas)
- any issues 1.00

PANIC (1954-1956)
- any issues 3.00

PEP COMICS
- 1940-1943, any 12.00
- 1944-1948, any 3.00

PHANTOM LADY
- any issues 12.00

PIRACY
- any issues 7.00

PLANET COMICS
- 31-60 .... 15.00
- 61-73 .... 10.00

PLASTIC MAN (1943-1956)
- any issues 6.00

POGO POSSUM
- any issues 4.00

POLICE COMICS
- 1941-1946, any 9.00
- 1947-1953, any 4.00

POPEYE (Dell)
- any issues 1.00

POPULAR COMICS
- any issues 3.00

PRIZE COMICS
- any issues 3.00

PRIZE COMICS WESTERN
- any issues 2.50

PUNCH COMICS
- any issues 4.00

RANGERS COMICS
- any issues 4.00

RAWHIDE
- any issues 3.00

REAL FACT COMICS
- any issues 3.00

REAL MCCOYS
- any issues 2.00

REBEL
- any issues 2.00

RED DRAGON
- any issues 8.00

RED RYDER
- any issues 2.00

REX ALLEN
- any issues 2.00

RIFLEMAN
- any issues 2.00

RINGO KID WESTERN (Atlas), any issues 1.50

RIN TIN TIN
- any issues 1.50

ROCKY LANE
- 1949-1953, any 4.00
- 1954-1959, any 1.50

ROD CAMERON WESTERN
- any issues 4.00

ROY ROGERS (Dell)
- any issues 2.00

RULAH JUNGLE GODDESS
- any issues 10.00

THE SAINT
- ANY ISSUES 6.00

SCIENCE COMICS (1940)
- any issues 20.00

SEA HUNT
- any issues 2.00

SENSATION COMICS
- 5-20 .... 20.00
- 21-34 .... 12.00
- 35-81 .... 8.00
- 82-109 .... 7.00

SERGEANT BILKO
- any issues 2.50

SGT. FURY
- 1 .... 15.00
- 2-5 .... 2.00
- 6-13 .... 1.00

SGT. PRESTON OF THE YUKON, any issues 2.00

77 SUNSET STRIP
- any issues 2.50

SHADOW COMICS
- 1940-1949, any 6.00

SHEENA, QUEEN OF THE JUNGLE (1942-1953)
- any issues 6.00

SHIELD WIZARD
- any issues 14.00

SHOCK SUSPENSTORIES
- any issues 10.00

SHOWCASE
- 1-24 .... please write
- 25-40 .... 2.00

SILLY SYMPHONIES
- any issues 1.50

SILVER STREAK
- 1939-1942, any 14.00

SIX GUN HEROES (Fawcett)
- any issues 5.00

SMASH COMICS
- any issues 4.00

SPARKLER COMICS
- any issues 1.50

SPEED COMICS
- any issues 7.00

SPELLBOUND (Atlas)
- any issues 2.00

SPIN AND MARTY
- any issues 1.50

THE SPIRIT (Quality, Fiction House), any issues 7.00

SPY SMASHER (1941-1943)
- any issues 20.00

STAR COMICS
- any issues 10.00

STAR SPANGLED COMICS
- 11-29 .... 22.00
- 30-65 .... 9.00
- 66-100 .... 7.00
- 101-130 .... 4.00

STAR SPANGLED WAR STORIES (1952-1959)
- any issues .... .75

STARTLING COMICS
- any issues 6.00

STRAIGHT ARROW
- any issues 2.00

STRANGE ADVENTURES
- 1950-1959, any 1.00

STRANGE TALES
- 1951-1962, any 2.00
- 101 .... 12.00
- 102-105 .... 4.00
- 106-109 .... 3.00
- 110 .... 8.00
- 111-127 .... 1.00

SUB-MARINER COMICS
- 1941-1955, any 22.00

SUGAR & SPIKE
- 1956-1959, any 1.50

SUGARFOOT
- any issues 2.00

SUPERBOY
- 4-10 .... 22.00
- 11-20 .... 12.00
- 21-38 .... 7.00
- 39-50 .... 4.00
- 51-68 .... 3.00
- 69-100 .... 1.50

SUPER COMICS
- any issues 2.00

SUPERMAN
- 26-40 .... 25.00
- 41-50 .... 20.00
- 51-76 .... 17.00
- 77-95 .... 12.00
- 96-120 .... 6.00
- 121-130 .... 3.00
- 131-149 .... 2.00
- 150-169 .... 1.50
- Annual 1960-1964, any . 2.00

SUPER MYSTERY COMICS
- any issues 3.00

SUPERSNIPE COMICS
- any issues 3.00

SUSPENSE (1943-1953)
- any issues 2.00

TALES FROM THE CRYPT
- 1950-1955, any 12.00

TALES OF SUSPENSE
- 1959-1962, any 2.00
- 39 .... 55.00
- 40 .... 14.00
- 41 .... 8.00
- 42-45 .... 4.00
- 46-50 .... 3.00
- 51-60 .... 1.50

TALES OF THE UNEXPECTED, 1956-1959, any ... 1.00

TALES TO ASTONISH
- 1959-1962, any 2.00
- 27 .... 45.00
- 28-34 .... 2.00
- 35 .... 15.00
- 36 .... 7.00
- 37-40 .... 4.00
- 41-50 .... 2.50
- 51-62 .... 1.50

TARZAN (Dell)
- any issues 1.00

TARZAN'S JUNGLE ANNUAL, any issues ... 1.50

TERRORS OF THE JUNGLE
- any issues 5.00

TEX MORGAN
- any issues 2.00

TEX RITTER
- 1-21 .... 4.00

TEX TAYLOR
- any issues 2.00

THE THING! (1952-1954)
- any issues 6.00

THREE STOOGES
- 1949-1962, any 2.00
- Gold Key, any 1.00

THRILLING COMICS
- any issues 4.00

TIM HOLT
- any issues 3.00

T-MAN
- any issues 1.00

TOMAHAWK
- 1950-1955, any 1.50
- 1956-1959, any 1.00

TOM CORBETT, SPACE CADET, any issues 2.00

TOM MIX WESTERN
- any issues 4.00

TONTO
- any issues 1.50

TOP NOTCH/LAUGH
- any issues 5.00

TORCHY (1949-1950)
- any issues 20.00

TUROK (1954-1961)
- any issues 2.00

TV COMICS, any TV show comic with a photo cover 1950-1965 .... 1.00

TWO FISTED TALES
- any issues 9.00

TWO GUN KID
- 1948-1959, any 1.00

UNCANNY TALES (Atlas)
- any issues 2.00

UNCLE SCROOGE (Dell)
- any issues 3.00

USA COMICS
- any issues 22.00

VALOR
- any issues 7.00

VAULT OF HORROR
- any issues 10.00

VENUS
- any issuessssssssssss. 10.00

VOODOO/VOODA
- 1952-1955, any 3.00

WAGON TRAIN
- any issues 2.00

WALT DISNEY'S COMICS & STORIES (Dell), any ... 1.00

WAMBI, THE JUNGLE BOY
- any issues 2.00

WAR AGAINST CRIME!
- any issues 8.00

WAR COMICS (Atlas)
- any issues 1.00

WEIRD COMICS
- any issues 14.00

WEIRD FANTASY
- any issues 14.00

WEIRD SCIENCE
- any issues 14.00

WEIRD SCIENCE FANTASY
- any issues 14.00

WESTERN COMICS (DC)
- any issues 1.50

WESTERN HERO
- any issues 4.00

WESTERN ROUNDUP
- any issues 2.50

WHIZ COMICS
- any issues 4.00

WILD BILL ELLIOTT
- any issues 2.00

WILD BOY OF THE CONGO
- any issues 2.00

WILD WESTERN (Atlas)
- any issues 1.00

WINGS COMICS
- any issues 3.50

WITCHES TALES
- 1951-1955, any 2.00

WOMEN OUTLAWS
- any issues 5.00

WONDER COMICS
- any issues 9.00

WONDER WOMAN
- 4-10 .... 25.00
- 11-20 .... 18.00
- 21-40 .... 10.00
- 41-60 .... 7.00
- 61-90 .... 5.00
- 91-110 .... 2.50
- 111-139 .... 1.50

WONDERWORLD COMICS
- any issues 11.00

WORLD OF FANTASY
- any issues 2.00

WORLD'S FINEST COMICS
- 9-20 .... 30.00
- 21-30 .... 20.00
- 31-73 .... 14.00
- 74-90 .... 4.50
- 91-100 .... 3.00
- 101-139 .... 1.50

WOW COMICS
- 1940-1943, any 6.00
- 1944-1948, any 3.00

WYATT EARP (Dell)
- any issues 2.00

WYATT EARP (Atlas)
- any issues 1.00

X-MEN
- 1 .... 70.00
- 2 .... 25.00
- 3,4 .... 12.00
- 5 .... 9.00
- 6-10 .... 6.00
- 11-20 .... 2.50
- 21-66 .... 1.00

YELLOW JACKET COMICS
- any issues 5.00

YOUNG ALLIES COMICS
- any issues 22.00

YOUNG MEN
- any issues 1.00

ZANE GREY'S STORIES OF THE WEST, any issues . 1.00

ZIP COMICS
- any issues 6.00

ZORRO (Dell)
- any issues 2.00

SALES CATALOG AVAILABLE 50 Cents

507

509

#1

ACTION COMICS No. 1
AMAZING FANTASY No. 15
(1st SPIDERMAN)
BATMAN No. 1
FANTASTIC FOUR No. 1
SPIDERMAN No. 1
SUPERMAN No. 1

Sleuthing done dirt cheap!
Can't find that number one (or origin issue)? Then why not try me?
Yes, I have **all** of the No. 1 issues shown above & other **hard-to-find** comics especially
those much sought after **early Marvels** (there are always available in stock a near complete
set of all Marvel titles).

And besides this I also have the following:

(A) WALT DISNEY COMICS - all titles: Mickey Mouse, Donald Duck, Uncle Scrooge,
and Disney Collectibles.

(B) DC COMICS (Golden Age, Silver Age up to the present-old Flash, Green Lantern,
Superman, Batman, and other Super-Heros.

(C) GOLDEN AGE & SILVER AGE) comics. These include Quality, Timely, Fox,
Avon, Fiction House, Fawcett, Motion Picture Comics, Dell, Westerns, Funny Animal Comics,
Classics, etc.

(D) MAD comics - Panic, Humbug, Trump, Help & Horror, Crime & **EC** comics.

(E) BIG LITTLE BOOKS - all major and minor titles. Also available - the **original**
Cupples & Leon comic "books".

(F) Rare **PULPS** - science fiction & pulp hero titles.

(G) ORIGINAL ART - including fine classic as well as modern artists.

(H) SUNDAY COMIC PAGES - Just about every major & minor comic strip character
from the early **1900's** to the **1950's.** Strips include; **Little Nemo, Krazy Kat, Mickey
Mouse, Donald Duck, Popeye, Tarzan, Flash Gordon, Prince Valiant, Terry & The
Pirates, Dick Tracy, Superman** & many, many more too numerous to list here.

I also **BUY & TRADE,** so let me know what you have. For my latest **GIANT** 1989 catalog
"Number One Plus", write to the address below enclosing $1.00 in cash (or stamps).
Hurry now or you could miss out on getting that issue you've been looking for!

SPECIAL — SPECIAL: MOVIE SALE

A ONCE IN A LIFE-TIME OFFER! Huge Catalog listing hundreds and hundreds
of rare (and **ORIGINAL**) movie posters, lobby cards, autographed photos from the
1930's to the 1980's. You'll find your favorite movie stars as: Bogart, Gable, Garbo,
Garland, Laurel & Hardy, Presley, Disney Titles & many, many more. Wide selection
from B-Westerns, Horror, Science-Fiction, Comedy, Musicals, Etc. Act **NOW** to
receive my "1989 **MOVIE CATALOG**".

(NOTE: Those wishing to receive **ONLY** the Movie Catalog **MUST** enclose
50 cents & a self-addressed stamped envleope. Want lists also welcomed. If you
wish to receive **BOTH** the Comic & the Movie catalog, send $1.50).

Write: **HAL VERB
P.O. BOX 1815
SAN FRANCISCO, CA 94101**

Holy Special Collector's Edition Batman Fans!

In Celebration of the Caped Crusader's fiftieth Anniversary, **Bob Kane** announces the publication of his autobiography . . . . *Batman and Me.*

Read the inside story of Kane's creation of Batman and Robin, his collaboration with writer Bill Finger on the Golden Age Batman stories, and the origins of comics' greatest villains. This book is rich with anecdotes about the pioneering days of the comics industry, Kane's relationship to celebrities like Marilyn Monroe, the inspiration for Batman's girlfriend Vicki Vale, and his first-hand account of the production and filming of the new Batman movie. It will be lavishly illustrated with material from Kane's private files much of which has never been published or reprinted before. Included in the illustrations are pre-Batman art, the first drawings of Batman, the photos which inspired the Joker and the Catwoman, film clips and posters from the 1940s Batman movie serials, reproductions of Kane's fine art Batman lithographs, and other rare Batman memorabilia. Topping it off are reprints in full color of a number of never before reprinted Golden Age Batman stories, written by Bill Finger and drawn by Bob Kane, and the first Batman daily and Sunday comic strips from 1943.

WRITE FOR INFORMATION NOW!!

For information about specific contents and prices of editions, please write to: **Batman and Me**, c/o Tom Andrae, 2605 Virginia St., Berkeley, Calif. 94709. Please **mail no money**; you will be notified when the book is available. This book will be published in two editions--**The Special Deluxe Collector's Edition**, individually numbered and limited to 2500 copies and **autographed by Bob Kane** and the regular trade edition. Copies of the limited edition ordered by mail will be **personally inscribed to the buyer**. This book is certain to become one of the most sought after of all Batman collectibles--a must not only for the Batman enthusiast but anyone interested in the history of the comic book industry.

WRITE FOR DETAILS NOW!!

CLASSIFIED ADVERTISING

517

Classified Advertising (continued)

  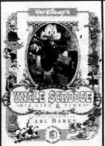